Footprint **Indonesia** Handbook

The travel guide

Joshua Eliot, Liz Capaldi, Jane Bickersteth
with David Woodley and Jasmine Saville

We have left you,
The calm lagoon without a ripple,
Sheltered by a leafy mountain
From wind and storm.
For once we have woken up from a pleasant
dream.

Soetan Takdir Alisjahbana,
'To Sea, The New Generation'

Indonesia Handbook
Third edition
© Footprint Handbooks Ltd 2001

Published by Footprint Handbooks
6 Riverside Court
Lower Bristol Road
Bath BA2 3DZ. England
T +44 (0)1225 469141
F +44 (0)1225 469461
Email discover@footprintbooks.com
Web www.footprintbooks.com

ISBN 1 900949 51 2
CIP DATA: A catalogue record for this book is available from the British Library

In USA, published by
NTC/Contemporary Publishing Group
4255 West Touhy Avenue, Lincolnwood
(Chicago), Illinois 60712-1975, USA
T 847 679 5500 F 847 679 2494
Email NTCPUB2@AOL.COM

ISBN 0-658-00654-1
Library of Congress Catalog Card
Number 00-132880

® Footprint Handbooks and the Footprint mark are a registered trademark of Footprint Handbooks Ltd.

All rights reserved. No part of this publication may be reproduced, stored in a retrieval system, or transmitted, in any form or by any means, electronic, mechanical, photocopying, recording, or otherwise, without the prior permission of Footprint Handbooks Ltd.

Neither the black and white nor coloured maps are intended to have any political significance.

Credits

Series editors
Patrick Dawson and Rachel Fielding

Editorial
Editor: Sarah Thorowgood
Maps: Sarah Sorensen

Production
Typesetting: Emma Bryers, Leona Bailey and Angus Dawson
Maps: Robert Lunn and Claire Benison
Colour maps: Kevin Feeney

Cover: Camilla Ford

Design
Mytton Williams

Photography
Front cover: Impact Photos
Back cover: Axiom
Inside colour section: Art Directors and Trip, Graham Cox, James Davis Worldwide, Eye Ubiquitous, Ffotograff, getty one Stone, Robert Harding Picture Library, Impact Photos, Duncan MacArthur, Pictures Colour Library and John Wright.

Print
Manufactured in Italy by LEGOPRINT

Every effort has been made to ensure that the facts in this Handbook are accurate. However, travellers should still obtain advice from consulates, airlines etc about current travel and visa requirements before travelling. The authors and publishers cannot accept responsibility for any loss, injury or inconvenience however caused.

Contents

1

7	**A foot in the door**
10	Culture
11	Wildlife
12	Ancient worship
13	High life, low life
14	Water worlds
15	A day in the life

2

17	**Essentials**
19	**Planning your trip**
19	Where to go
19	Transport and travelling
20	Highlights
25	When to go
25	Tours and tour operators
28	Language
29	**Before you travel**
29	Entry requirements
30	What to take
30	Customs
31	**Money**
32	**Getting there**
32	Air
34	Boat
34	Road
34	**Touching down**
34	Airport information
36	Tourist information
37	Rules, customs and etiquette
38	Safety
39	Where to stay
41	**Getting around**
41	Air
42	Train
42	Bus
44	Bicycling
45	Car hire
45	Other local transport
47	Sea
47	**Keeping in touch**
47	Communications
48	Media
49	**Food and drink**
49	Food
51	Drink
51	**Shopping**
52	**Holidays and festivals**
52	National holidays and other festivals
53	Islamic holidays
54	**Health**
54	Before you go
56	On the road
60	When you return home
60	Further information
61	**Further reading**
61	Magazines
61	Books on Southeast Asia
62	Books on Indonesia
68	The internet
70	Short wave radio (KHz)
70	**Tourism: counting the costs**

3

75	**Java**
78	**Jakarta**
105	**West Java**
106	The far west
109	The west coast
117	Bogor
122	West Central Highlands & South Coast
131	Bandung
153	The north coast plain
159	**Central Java & Yogyakarta**
159	South Central Java
163	Yogyakarta
185	Borobudur
200	Solo (Surakarta)
219	Central Java's north coast
222	Semarang
238	**East Java**
239	The rump of East Java
246	Malang
255	Surabaya
267	Madura Island
273	The Far East
298	**Background**

4

307	**Bali**
322	Denpasar
326	**South Bali**
350	Nusa Penida and Nusa Lembongan

Left: Java, with well over 100 million people, is one of the most intensively cultivated islands in the world. Hillsides have been cut into sequences of terraces and in many areas three crops of rice are grown each year. *Page 16*: Prambanan on the Prambanan Plain in Central Java, (see page 12).

353	The Bukit Peninsula and Nusa Dua	533	West Sumatra	653	The Northwest Coast
365	**North and east from Denpasar**	535	Bukittingi	654	Kapuas River
		554	Padang	656	Background
366	Ubud	563	Mentawi Islands		
379	North of Ubud	570	Riau		**7**
380	Gianyar to Mount Batur via Bangli	591	South Sumatra	675	**Sulawesi**
		591	Jambi	678	**Makassar (Ujung Pandang)**
387	Pura Besakih and Mount Agung	594	Palembang		
		602	Bengkulu	689	**South of Makassar**
390	East Bali and Regency of Karangasem	607	Bandar Lumpung	689	Bira
		610	Background	692	Makassar to Toraja via Pare Pare
408	North from Denpasar to Lake Bratan		**6**		
				692	Pare Pare
413	**North Coast, Buleleng Regency**	613	**Kalimantan**	694	Watampone (Bone)
		616	**South Kalimantan (Kalsel)**	695	Sengkang
416	Singaraja			698	Toraja
418	West of Singaraja	617	Banjarmasin	708	Rantepao
430	**The West**	626	**Central Kalimantan (Kalteng)**	717	**The Mamasa Valley**
435	**Background**			719	Mamasa Town
	5	626	Palangkaraya	723	**Southeast Sulawesi**
		627	Pangkalanbun	723	Kendari
453	**Sumatra**	627	Tanjung Puting National Park & Orang Utan Rehabilitation Centre	725	Buton & Muna Islands
456	Ins and outs			727	**Pendolo to Palu**
459	North Sumatra			727	Pendolo
459	Medan	628	**East Kalimantan (Kaltim)**	728	Kolonodale
473	Bukit Lawang			731	Tentena
484	Lake Toba	629	Balikpapan	735	Palu
503	Sibolga	634	Samarinda	738	Poso
508	Nias Island	639	Tenggarong	740	Togian Islands & Tomini Bay
513	Aceh	639	Mahakam River		
514	Banda Aceh	644	The Apo Kayan	743	**Poso to Manado**
526	Gunung Leuser National Park	646	**West Kalimantan (Kalbar)**	743	Toli Toli
				743	Gorontalo
		647	Pontianak	746	Manado

757	Bunaken National Marine Park				926	Merauke
760	Background				927	Wasur National Park
					929	Timika, Kuala Kencana and Tembagapura
					929	Background

8

765	**West Nusa Tenggara**	815	**East Nusa Tenggara**	
768	**Lombok**	818	Ins and outs	
768	Ins and outs	819	Komodo	
771	Ampenan – Mataram – Cakranegara	824	**Flores**	
777	Lombok's west coast	825	Labuanbajo to Ende	
782	The Gilis	839	Ende to Larantuka	
789	Northwest coast and Mount Rinjani	848	Lembata	
792	Central Lombok and the West	851	Alor	
795	East Lombok	854	**Sumba**	
795	South Lombok and the south coast	868	**West Timor**	
800	Background	876	Roti (Rote)	
803	**Sumbawa**	878	Savu (Sabu, Sawu)	

12

935	**Background**
937	History
944	Modern Indonesia
959	Culture
964	Land and environment

13

973	**Footnotes**
975	Fares and timetables
992	Glossary
996	Indonesian food glossary
997	Index
1007	Shorts
1008	Advertisers
1009	Map Index
1011	Colour maps

804	Alas
804	Taliwang
805	Maluk
805	Sumbawa Besar
808	Moyo Island
809	Mount Tambora
810	Sumbawa Besar to Bima-Raba
810	Dompu
810	Hu'u
811	Bima-Raba
813	Sape

879	**Maluku**
882	Ambon
891	Lease Islands
891	Saparua
893	Seram
895	Banda Islands
904	Ternate & Tidore
908	Halmahera
910	Southeast Maluku
912	**Background**

Inside front cover
Hotel and restaurant price guide
Dialling codes
Lost credit cards

Inside back cover
Map symbols
Weights and measures

915	**Irian Jaya**
918	Ins and outs
919	Biak
920	Jayabura and Sentani
922	The Baliem Valley
924	Wamena

Right: Jakarta – Indonesia's 10 million-strong capital. Political and economic heart of the sprawling archipelago. **Below**: A house with a view, Lombok. Houses raised on stilts have many advantages: they are cooler, protected from flooding, and keep pests and animals at arm's length. **Bottom left**: Stalls and vendors provide an important service, selling cooked food, goods and amenities to all classes of Indonesian. This mobile cart, or kaki lima, is in Solo. **Overleaf**: Mobile homes. Pedicabs, known as becaks (pronounced, 'bejaks'), are the main form of transport in many towns, though they are banned from Jakarta. Becak drivers, many from the countryside, often live in their machines.

A foot in the door

It's been said a thousand times: Indonesia is an unlikely country. If the lure of cloves and nutmeg hadn't enticed the Dutch to follow the Portuguese and the Spanish and venture eastwards; if colonial pretensions of power hadn't induced the Dutch to transform a trading presence into a territorial project; if the British hadn't ultimately failed in their attempts to take a slice of the action; if local kingdoms and sultanates had managed to assuage the demands of the Dutch and keep them at bay…then Indonesia would not exist. Instead the Dutch, alternatively pushed, pulled and caressed by the ebb and flow of history found that, by the early years of the 20th century, they had constructed an empire in the East more by accident than by design.   **Accidental empire**

Such are the quirks of history. The result, today, is that of all the countries of Asia, Indonesia is the hardest to corral. There is no point in looking for a shared history prior to the colonial period, or a shared culture, or even a certain uniformity of environment. Divided between over 13,000 islands, hundreds of languages and cultures, several time zones, and spread over an expanse of sea linking Asia with Australasia, it is truly a kaleidoscopic place. Significantly, the one aspect of life that would seem to link eight out of 10 Indonesians, their adherence to Islam, was intentionally overlooked by the country's first two presidents, who believed it would divide rather than unite. As a result, though Indonesia may have the world's largest Muslim population it is not an Islamic state.

For the average tourist this is probably all beside the point. But it does help explain why a 600-word introduction to Indonesia cannot do justice to such a country and why it is so difficult to write in generic terms about a place that is so self-evidently varied.

So what impressions are visitors likely to take away with them? The pungent smell of clove cigarettes as they queued, tired and hot, to have their passport stamped at immigration control in Jakarta or Denpasar. That first bus or *ojek* journey when the expression 'life is cheap' became terrifyingly meaningful. A long evening spent watching a bewitching dance drama in the hills of Bali. Or the bemusement of being faced with a McDonald's menu including 'McSatay'. That initial glimpse of Mount Bromo's crater as the sun rose over the Tengger Highlands of East Java. Or the horror at the sheer level of butchery that marks the funeral ceremonies of the Toraja peoples of Sulawesi, when it becomes brutally apparent that meat is not always packaged in plastic. People will tuck, as we always do, their own personal set of memories in their mental knapsack. Some may be just those things that guidebooks rattle on about: coral reefs, ancient monuments, fascinating cultures, pristine beaches, luxuriant forests… But many more are not covered in any guide. These are the everyday circumstance, the commonplace activity, the unscripted encounter, and the generally run-of-the-mill. For many, Indonesia, at root, will be memorable simply because it is so very different from Berkhamstead, Biloxi or Bruges.   **Cloves, nutmeg and McSatays**

This short introduction began by highlighting the improbable way that Indonesia was pieced together by the Dutch. It was then held in place by the country's first two presidents, Sukarno and Suharto. With Suharto's forced and violent resignation in 1998 so the possibility that the country might unravel, if only at the edges, has become a reality. East Timor has already departed the Indonesian fold and the provinces of Aceh in Sumatra and Irian Jaya in New Guinea are also agitating for independence. Instability has wracked other areas of the country over the last 12 months, particularly Maluku but also parts of Sulawesi, West Timor and Lombok. The result of all this internationally publicised violence is that the bottom has fallen out of the tourist industry. Even Bali – which has been largely untouched by problems elsewhere in the archipelago – has had to struggle to keep numbers from plummeting. For other regions, such as Maluku, there has been a tourism meltdown. But while Indonesia is facing serious domestic challenges, large areas of the country are still very much open and safe for tourists.   **Brave new world?**

Culture

Right: Shadow puppet plays, or *wayang kulit*, are one of Indonesia's (or Java's) defining art forms. The puppet master spices up tales from the epics with references to current events. **Below**: Indonesia's 200 million-plus population is 80% Muslim, giving it by far the largest Muslim population in the world. But it is not an officially Islamic state.

Right: A fruity temple offering in Hindu Bali. **Above**: Cremation marked with spectacular celebration on Nusa Lembongan, off Bali's south coast.

Wildlife

Left: Indonesia's 'living dinosaur', the Komodo dragon, is the world's largest lizard.
Below: Orang utans are found in Sumatra and Kalimantan. They have been threatened by rampant deforestation and devastating forest fires. 'Rehabilitation' centres reintroduce captured animals back into the wild and provide places where tourists can come face-to-face with the apes.

Left: Indonesia's flora, like this orchid on Bali, is almost as remarkable – and generally more colourful – than its fauna. **Above**: The Bali tiger is extinct; the Java tiger is probably extinct – although reports of sightings occasionally occur. The Sumatran tiger, much smaller than its Indian, Chinese and Russian brethren, is hanging on by the skin of its teeth in the island's protected areas.

Ancient worship

Right: Originally reserved as a place of worship for the royal families of Bali, Pura Besakih, 22 puras scattered over the slopes of sacred Mount Agung, is Bali's holiest temple.
Below: Borobudur on Java, a UNESCO World Heritage Site, is the largest single Buddhist structure in the world. Built over a period of 75 years, it is constructed from 1.6 million blocks of stone and decorated with 5 kilometres of reliefs and 500 statues of the Buddha.
Bottom: Moss-covered carvings near the upland village of Ubud on Bali.

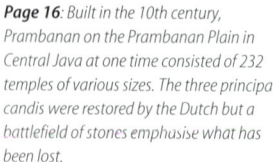

Page 16: Built in the 10th century, Prambanan on the Prambanan Plain in Central Java at one time consisted of 232 temples of various sizes. The three principal candis were restored by the Dutch but a battlefield of stones emphasise what has been lost.

High life, low life

Indonesia has its highs and lows: you can trek in the Tengger Highlands of East Java and climb to the crater of Mount Bromo, or you can wade through Irian Jaya's swamplands...or just lie low on a beach.

Top left: *Gunung Semeru and Gunung Bromo are just two of Java's 121 volcanoes which run like a spine through the island.* **Top right**: *Lombok beach scene – a picture postcard image of the tropical idyll.* **Above**: *Hindu horsemen of East Java's Tengger Highlands take tourists to Gunung Bromo's caldera to see the sun rise.* **Left**: *Irian Jaya, with its expanses of forest and swamp, devoid of road or settlement, is one of Indonesia's – indeed one of the world's – great unexplored regions.*

Water worlds

Right: The owners of this modest house on Sumbawa's coast keep in touch with the world – as people do across the archipelago – through ostentatious 'parabolas', satellite dishes. **Below**: Multicoloured stars and stripes. The Bunaken National Marine Park in north Sulawesi has some of the finest diving and snorkelling in Southeast Asia.

Right: With more than 13,000 islands, boats have always been an important form of communication in Indonesia. From simple outrigger canoes like this one to grand *pinisi* schooners, they still carry passengers and ply trade. **Above**: Dolphin watching at Lovina, on Bali's north coast. A more relaxed place than better-known resorts, like Kuta, to the south.

A day in the life

Left: The whale hunters of Lamalera, on the island of Lembata in Nusa Tenggara harpoon whales – mainly sperm whales – from rowing boats. The harpooner leaps from the bow to plunge the blade deep into the quarry.
Below: The informal economy is alive and well in Indonesia. People sell everything from beach balls to salak from a myriad of carts, trolleys and tables. Without their input Indonesia would quickly grind to a halt.

Left: Indonesia's markets, like this one on Lombok, are colourful and ubiquitous. Unlike most other Muslim societies, women in Indonesia handle money and play a full part in commerce and trade – indeed they dominate it in many areas. **Above**: While Indonesia may be urbanising and industrialising, the main livelihood for many people remains agriculture, and rice is the pre-eminent crop. Here a farm labourer uproots rice seedlings for transplanting.

Essentials

Essentials

19	**Planning your trip**	45	Car hire
19	Where to go	45	Other local transport
19	Transport and travelling	47	Sea
20	Highlights		
25	When to go	47	**Keeping in touch**
25	Tours and tour operators	47	Communications
28	Language	48	Media
29	**Before you travel**	49	**Food and drink**
29	Entry requirements	49	Food
30	What to take	51	Drink
30	Customs		
		51	**Shopping**
31	**Money**		
		52	**Holidays and festivals**
32	**Getting there**	52	National holidays and other festivals
32	Air		
34	Boat	53	Islamic holidays
34	Road		
		54	**Health**
34	**Touching down**	54	Before you go
34	Airport information	56	On the road
36	Tourist information	60	When you return home
37	Rules, customs and etiquette	60	Further information
38	Safety		
		61	**Further reading**
39	**Where to stay**	61	Magazines
		61	Books on Southeast Asia
41	**Getting around**	62	Books on Indonesia
41	Air	68	The internet
42	Train	70	Short wave radio (KHz)
42	Bus		
44	Bicycling	70	**Tourism: counting the costs**

Planning your trip

Where to go

For most people, seeing 'Indonesia' – *in toto* – is an impossibility. The country is simply too large. In addition, overland travel in some areas of the country is slow and exhausting and travelling from Aceh in the north of Sumatra to Jayapura, the capital of Irian Jaya as the crow flies (and it is rarely possible to fly like a crow in Indonesia!), involves a journey of around 5,000 km – the equivalent of travelling from Athens to Delhi or Vancouver to Mexico City. Many people are happy to explore Bali alone – an island, albeit a special one, which accounts for less than half a percent of Indonesia's total land area.

The sheer size of Indonesia, coupled with poor roads in some areas, and the special problems of skipping through an archipelago of over 13,000 islands, means that an itinerary has to be carefully planned. Those with two months to spare (the length of a standard visa) can work their way from Sumatra to Timor, or vice versa, but even with the luxury of eight weeks, they will be forced not just to miss the odd town but entire regions – Sulawesi, Kalimantan or Maluku, for example.

Transport and travelling

Compared with roads in the west, those in Indonesia are poor. Even in Java, Indonesia's heartland and the centre of economic activity, there are just a handful of stretches of road that could even remotely be labelled 'highways'. Over much of the rest of the country all-weather roads only link the most important centres. In the wet season even these may be periodically impassable due to flooding, subsidence and land slips. Large areas of Sumatra, Kalimantan and Irian Jaya are, to all intents and purposes, inaccessible to even the most determined traveller.

Below is only a selection of places of interest & is not by any means exhaustive. It is designed to assist in planning a trip to the region

That, so to speak, is the bad news (or the good news, depending on one's viewpoint). The good news is that many of the horror stories of the past, when bus passengers were regularly stranded for days in towns that they would now wish to forget are, to a large extent, history. It is possible – though perhaps not enjoyable – to catch a bus through the entire length of Sumatra or Sulawesi, for example.

A second factor to bear in mind is the challenge of travelling between the smaller islands. This is particularly pertinent in Nusa Tenggara and Maluku where there may be just one ferry a day between some islands, sometimes just one a week. Flying, though in theory a much faster alternative, has its own problems. It is often impossible to book flights between the more out of the way spots, and even a booked seat may magically disappear if a VIP (and there are an awful lot of VIPs in Indonesia) should suddenly decide to make the journey.

Java and Bali Java and Bali have slow but abundant year-round public transport, including train on Java as well as bus. The comparatively short distances involved means that even travelling from one end of Java to the other is possible in a day. The concentration of people and economic enterprise means that there are many bus services, from the luxury a/c 'Vip' buses to slow and cramped 'Ekonomi' vehicles. There are also tour buses geared to foreigners on many routes. Jakarta and Denpasar, Bali's capital, are also serviced by more international airlines than any other cities in the country. Note that Jakarta suffers from serious road congestion.

Sumatra Sumatra's size – it is the fourth largest island in the world – makes travelling an ordeal. Most visitors take a well defined route from Medan (where there are sea links with Malaysia) through to Brastagi, Toba, Bukittinggi and Padang. Transport between these towns is fairly well provided for with tour and a/c buses. Beyond these towns, though, bus transport is less well developed, although provincial centres will always have some a/c and Vip services. There is a limited rail service in the south of the island and domestic airlines serve the main provincial centres. There are also international air links with Medan from Singapore, Penang and Kuala Lumpur; and with Padang via Pekanbaru from Singapore. Regular ferries link the southern tip of Sumatra with Java.

Kalimantan Kalimantan's size and geography – it has vast swamps – makes overland travel difficult. The major towns have coastal locations and there are reasonable road links between Banjarmasin, Balikpapan and Samarinda, and from Pontianak to the East Malaysian state of Sarawak. However, it is not possible to travel overland across Kalimantan, even following the coast. To travel inland – or 'upriver' – it is often necessary to fly or go by boat. There are international connections with Singapore from Banjarmasin, Pontianak, Tarakan and Palangkaraya, and it is also possible to enter Kalimantan overland from Sarawak.

Sulawesi Sulawesi's strange spidery shape means that nowhere is far from the sea, and ships work their way around the coasts. With the completion of the (almost) all-weather trans-Sulawesi highway, it is also possible to bus it all the way from Ujung Pandang in the south (now renamed Makassar) to Manado in the north. But beyond this main 'highway' roads are poor and bus services may be limited. Ujung Pandang has good air and sea links with other parts of the country and Manado in the north is also well served. There are international air connections between Makassar and Singapore and between Manado and Singapore and Davao (Philippines), and domestic airlines serve the main provincial towns.

Lombok and East Nusa Tenggara Transport on Lombok is comparatively good and roads are reasonable. Travelling east from here, road conditions tend to deteriorate, although the main highway rarely – except after torrential storms or an earthquake! – descends into impassability. Ferries link the main islands, usually daily, although smaller islands off the main east-west route may be served less frequently. There are air services to most islands, but these are often over-booked, unbooked and multi-booked without apparently any consideration to the number of seats on the aircraft. There are international air connections between Kupang in West Timor and Darwin in Australia.

Maluku Maluku consists of a multitude of islands spread over a vast area of sea. There are air links between many of the larger and more important islands but, as in Nusa Tenggara, there is a tendency for booked seats to disappear. Passenger ships serve many ports in Maluku but they may call infrequently. On the larger, but often sparsely populated and thickly jungled islands like Seram, Buru and Halmahera, bus services are usually slow and intermittent, and in some cases non-existent.

Irian Jaya Indonesian New Guinea remains one of the great unknown corners of the world. Large areas are inaccessible except to those with months on their hands, a pocket full of anti-malarials, and very stout walking boots. The main towns are linked by air and sometimes by sea with other parts of the country, and there are also international air connections between Biak and the US. A road between Jayapura and Wamena is under construction, although some people believe (and hope) that it will be washed away just as soon as the tarmac is dry. The government requires visitors to obtain a *surat jalan*, or travel letter, before venturing beyond the main towns.

Timetabling a visit Indonesia is so vast that even two months – the length of a visitor's visa – is not nearly enough time to see the country; it is long enough to whizz through the archipelago, see the key sights and lie on the main beaches, but little more. This is why many people consider that visitors should restrict themselves to exploring one or two areas rather than just scratching the surface of many places. Two weeks is a good length of time to discover Bali, a month to experience Java or Sulawesi. Those intending to go to the more out of the way spots in Maluku or Nusa Tenggara might find they need a full two months for those regions alone.

Highlights

Wildlife **Java** Visit **Ujung Kulon** at the far west of Java for the very slim chance of seeing one of the rarest large mammals in the world (the Javan Rhinoceros); and **Sukamade** at the far east of the island for turtle egg-laying.
Sumatra Go to **Bukit Lawang** to visit the Orang Utan Rehabilitation Centre; **Gunung Leuser National Park** for possibly the richest fauna on the island.

Kalimantan The **Tanjung Puting National Park** and Orang Utan Rehabilitation Centre is the most visited park in Kalimantan.
Sulawesi Visit **Bantimurung Falls** with its diminishing butterflies that astounded Alfred Russel Wallace when he visited in 1856; or the **Tangkoko Batu Angus National Park** for its unique fauna.
East Nusa Tenggara Komodo's famous 'dragons'.
Irian Jaya Has a unique flora and fauna, vast uncharted areas, great potential, but it is poorly developed, except in the **Wasur National Park**.

Java Bogor, Indonesia's most venerable hill station, is within easy reach of Jakarta; Cisarua, Cibodas and Cipanas, are three hill resorts in a stunning position, but marred by ugly architecture; there are also five more hill resorts: Tawangmangu; Sarangan; Tretes; Batu, and Selekta, in Central and East Java.   *Hill stations*
Bali Ubud is the most sophisticated and foreigner-centric hill resort in Indonesia.
Sumatra Brastagi is Sumatra's original colonial hill retreat, a good location for trekking in the surrounding hills; Bukittinggi in the Minang area of West Sumatra is now more popular and more attractive.
Sulawesi Malino is 70 km outside Ujung Pandang at over 1,000 m and **Kakas Kasen** is close to Manado and near the active Mount Lokon.

Java Ujung Kulon, possibly Java's best-run national park, is also the last home of the Javan rhino in Indonesia; the Botanical Gardens at **Bogor**, established in 1817; the upland **Cibodas** Botanical Gardens created in 1899 for high altitude and temperate plants and the adjoining **Gede-Pangrango** National Park; **Bromo-Tengger-Semeru** National Park encompassing a series of imposing volcanoes.   *National Parks & Botanical Gardens*
Sumatra The well run **Gunung Leuser** National Park and the important but less developed **Kerinci-Seblat** National Park; the **Way Kambas** National Park with its herd of elephants.
Kalimantan The **Tanjung Puting** and **Kutai** National Parks both have a reasonable level of amenities for visitors.
Sulawesi The **Morowali** National Park is possibly the finest on Sulawesi but has a low level of facilities; the **Lore Lindu** National Park has good trekking and interesting megaliths; **Tangkoko Batu Angus** National Park has good facilities and a unique fauna.
East Nusa Tenggara Visit **Komodo** National Park for its dragons and good amenities.
Maluku Manusela National Park on Seram – rarely visited and lacking in facilities but a natural wonderland.
Irian Jaya The **Wasur** National Park outside Merauke is the most accessible park in Irian Jaya with the best facilities.

Java The **Gede-Pangrango** National Park, east of Bogor, and **Mount Merapi** and **Kaliurang**, near Yogyakarta, for mountain treks; the **Bromo-Tengger-Semeru** National Park for trekking from volcanic cone to cone; **Mount Ijen** in the far east of Java for more adventurous trekking.   *Trekking*
Sumatra Bukit Lawang and the **Gunung Leuser** Reserve for good trails and a convenient base; **Brastagi** and **Mount Sibayak** for upland walks; **Lake Toba** for walks in an incomparable location within the world's largest volcanic crater; challenging treks on **Nias** and the **Mentawi** islands; walks in the hills around **Bukittinggi** including stiff mountain climbs.
Kalimantan Trekking in the **Meratus Dayak** area around Loksado and in the **Kutai** and **Tanjung Puting** National Parks; exploring the Dayak areas of the **Mahakam** and **Kapuas** rivers and the **Apo Kayan**.
Sulawesi Excellent trekking in the uplands of **Toraja**; good hikes in the **Lore Lindu** National Park with its megaliths; walks in the volcanic hills to the south of Manado.
Lombok and Sumbawa Climbing **Mount Rinjani** is one of the most rewarding and spectacular climbs in the country; **Mount Tambora** on Sumbawa is less commonly climbed – and very hot!
East Nusa Tenggara Climbing **Mount Kelimutu** for the sunrise is popular.
Irian Jaya Excellent trekking around Wamena in the **Baliem Valley**.

Natural features

Java **Krakatau** offers a fascinating glimpse of the makings of the world; the **Puncak Pass** is perhaps Java's most spectacular stretch of road; the **Tangkuban Prahu Crater** outside Bandung provides an easily reached view into a steaming volcanic crater; **Dieng** is a mystical volcanic upland plateau, cold and often shrouded in cloying mists; **Mount Bromo** is Indonesia's most famous volcano; **Mount Ijen** a less visited alternative.

Bali The volcanoes of **Mount Batur** and **Mount Agung**, upland **Lake Bratan**, and the iridescent terraced **paddy fields** of the south and east – all well trodden by countless tourists.

Sumatra **Takengon** for its upland lake in the Gayo Highlands; **Lake Toba** and the stupendous crater which it occupies; **Lake Maninjau** and **Lake Singkarak** not far from Bukittingi for their peaceful and remarkable locations.

Sulawesi The caves at **Taman Purbakala Leang Leang** outside Ujung Pandang; **Lake Tempe** with **Sengkang** nearby; **Lake Poso**, an upland lake with a rich and unique fauna; active **Mount Lokon** south of Manado; **Lake Tondano** and its hot water springs.

Lombok and Sumbawa **Mount Rinjani** for its views (when clear), crater and crater lake; **Mount Tambora** for a hot but rewarding climb to the summit of a volcano that changed the world's climate.

East Nusa Tenggara **Mount Kelimutu** on Flores and its three-coloured crater lakes.

Beaches & coastal idylls

Java **Pulau Seribu** for island resorts within easy reach of Jakarta; **Labuan** and **Carita** beaches are popular weekend getaways for frazzled Jakartans, but scarcely remarkable save for their proximity to Krakatau; **Pelabuhanratu**, **Pangandaran** and **Parangtritis** are three south coast beach resorts that all offer poor water, a stiff pronunciation challenge and at times dangerous currents; **Pacitan** is probably the most attractive of the south coast's resorts; **Pasir Putih** on the north coast is a distinctively Indonesian-style beach resort with family planning posters and demure swim-wear.

Bali The island has a succession of beach resorts: frenetic **Kuta**, ersatz **Nusa Dua**, more refined **Sanur**, emerging **Candi Dasa** and **Lovina** Beach, plus other quieter places such as **Amed** and **Tulamben** on the east coast and **Pemuteran** on the northwest coast.

Sumatra **Sabang** and **Weh** Island off Sumatra's northern tip for an alternative place to catch a tan; **Lagundi Bay** on **Nias** Island, best known for its surfing; the **Riau Islands** (Batam and Bintan) for sophisticated but rather generic resorts, geared to Singapore's beach-starved population.

Sulawesi The **Togian Islands** for a place close to paradise; **Donggala** outside Palu for somewhere closer at hand; the **Bunaken** National Marine Park, best known as a dive site.

Lombok and Sumbawa **Senggigi**, Lombok's most developed beach resort; the **Gilis** (islands) for a more traveller-oriented destination; while **Kuta** is Lombok's emerging beach area.

East Nusa Tenggara Modest beaches and islands near **Kupang** in West Timor.

Maluku Poorish beaches near **Ambon**, excellent on **Saparua**, surprisingly poor on **Banda**, superb on lesser visited islands but expect almost no amenities.

Irian Jaya Good beaches near **Biak**; modest beaches around **Jayapura**.

Diving

Java **Pulau Seribu** and **Carita** and **Labuan** beaches for accessible but only modest diving.

Bali Lots of dive outfits and some reasonable dive sites, but better for beginners than for the cognoscenti.

Sumatra **Sabang** and **Weh** Island off Sumatra's northern tip for good diving.

Sulawesi The **Togian Islands** for excellent snorkelling; the **Bunaken** National Marine Park for superb diving with good dive companies and a wide range of amenities.

Lombok and Sumbawa Reasonable diving and dive companies at **Senggigi** and on the **Gilis** in Lombok; good snorkelling on **Moyo** Island off Sumbawa.

East Nusa Tenggara Diving near **Maumere** in Flores, now much recovered from the earthquake of December 1992.

Maluku Modest diving at **Ambon**, excellent on **Banda**.

Irian Jaya Good snorkelling off the islands around **Biak**.

Surfing & rafting

Java **Grajagan Bay** on the south coast of East Java for a fine left break.

Bali The most popular surfing in Indonesia with some good breaks, but a tendency to become over-crowded at peak times of year; rafting on the Ayung River.

Sumatra Rafting on the **Alas** River through the **Gunung Leuser** National Park; surfing at **Lagundi Bay** on **Nias** Island.
Kalimantan Rafting on the **Amandit**.
Sulawesi White-water rafting on the **Sadang** River.
Lombok and Sumbawa Surfing is not as good as Bali but both **Gili Air** and **Desert Point** off Bangko Bangko can be excellent. The south coast is more reliable: **Kuta** and **Tanjung Aan**, or further west, **Selong Blanak** and **Blongas**; going east, **Awang Bay** and **Gumbang Bay**. Modest surfing at **Taliwang** and **Maluk** on Sumbawa, better at **Hu'u**.

Java Cirebon, Yogyakarta and Surakarta (Solo) have the finest **kratons** (palaces) in the country; Imogiri, outside Yogyakarta, is the site of the **tombs of the Mataram rulers**, Borobudur and the candis of the Prambanan Plain are the two most spectacular collections of **historical monuments** in the country; enigmatic Candi Ceto and Candi Sukuh are beautifully positioned at 1,000 m; the candis of the Dieng Plateau and Bandungan, though plain and small, also enjoy wonderful upland locations; Sangiran is the site where **'Java Man'** was unearthed; the mausoleum of Indonesia's first President Sukarno is situated in Blitar, while 14th century Candi Panataran lies outside the town; the elegant east Javanese candis all lie within easy reach of Malang; Trowulan, the formerly grand capital of the Majapahit Empire, is also accessible from Malang as well as Surabaya.
Bali Bali's most notable **temples** are Besakih, Uluwatu and Tanah Lot; other historical sites include the **caves** of Goa Gajah and ancient **stone carvings** of Yeh Pulu, the **burial chambers** of Gunung Kawi; and the **royal bathing pools** of Tirtagangga.
Sumatra The **Batak tombs**, **houses** and **megaliths** of Lake Toba; Padang Lawas, a rarely visited collection of around 25 temples spread over a large area; the megaliths near Pagaralam.
Sulawesi Old Gowa outside Sulawesi was the heart of the Sultanate of Gowa; the **megaliths** of the Bada and Banua valleys in the Lore Lindu National Park; the **megalithic sarcophagi** at Sawangan near Manado.
Lombok and Sumbawa Though not comparable with similar places on Bali, the **Mayura Water Palace and Gardens** and **Pura Mayura** in Mataram-Cakranegara on Lombok are worthwhile, and so too is the **Taman Narmada** and the **Waktu Telu Temple** and the modest **Sultan's Palace** on Sumbawa.
East Nusa Tenggara Megaliths, tombs, traditional houses, festivals and weaving villages of **Sumba**.
Maluku Remnants of the **Portuguese and Dutch presence** in the Spice Islands, evident on Ambon, Saparua, Tidore and Ternate, but particularly Banda.

Historical sites: temples & palaces

Java Kota or Old Batavia in Jakarta offers a glimpse of the **old Dutch East Indies**, while Banten, a day's outing from Jakarta, has the ruins of a once great **pre-colonial trading sultanate**; Bandung is one of Indonesia's **architectural gems**, with possibly the finest collection of 'tropical' Art Deco architecture in the world; Tegal, Kudus and Tuban were formerly important sultanates on Java's north coast, with three of Java's oldest and most revered **mosques**; Surabaya's Kalimas Harbour for its **penisi schooners**.
Bali Tenganan, the village home of Bali's 'original' inhabitants.
Sumatra The **traditional houses and villages** of the Batak and Minangkabau of West and North Sumatra, and of Nias Island; Bengkulu is arguably the most charming **modern town** in Sumatra.
Kalimantan Banjarmasin's **floating market**.
Sulawesi Ujung Pandang's Paotere Harbour usually has a number of elegant **penisi schooners** docked; the villages around Rantepao for traditional **soaring-roofed houses**; Gorontalo retains more of its colonial architectural heritage than most Indonesian towns.

Historical sites: towns

Java Madura Island, cut off from the Java 'mainland', has a distinctive culture most evident in the enthusiastic annual bull races.
Bali For the greatest concentration of things 'cultural' in Indonesia, from dances to funeral ceremonies and traditional villages.
Sumatra Banda Aceh is one of Indonesia's most staunchly Muslim areas; the Batak area

Culture

Indonesia's climate

Region	Season		Rainfall
	Dry	Wet	
Java	January-August	December-February	West 2,360 mm
			Central 2,400 mm
			East 1,660 mm
Bali	May-October	November-April	Average 2,150 mm
Sumatra	June-July	October-April	West coast 4-6,000 mm
			Other areas 3,000 mm
Kalimantan	July-September	–	Average 3,810 mm
Sulawesi	August-September	December-February	Manado 3,352 mm
			Ujung Pandang 3,188 mm
			Palu 533 mm
Nusa Tenggara	April-October	–	East Flores &
			Sumba 8-900 mm
North Maluku	–	May-October	Ambon 3,450 mm
Southeast Maluku	December-March	–	Ceram 1,400 mm
Irian Jaya	–	–	North coast 2,500 mm
			Interior 5-8,000 mm
			Merauke 1,500 mm

NB *The distinction between the wet and dry seasons is least pronounced in Sumatra, Sulawesi, North Maluku and Irian Jaya; and most pronounced in Nusa Tenggara and Southeast Maluku.*

encompassing Lake Toba and Brastagi is worth exploring; equally distinctive in their culture are the Minangkabau of West Sumatra (Bukittinggi) with their high-roofed houses; the cultures of the Nias and Mentawi islands is often paraded as 'stone age', with Nias offering particularly fine traditional villages.

Kalimantan The Dayak culture of Kalimantan is less well preserved than that of the neighbouring East Malaysian states, but the Mahakam and Kapuas rivers and the Apo Kayan are all worth exploring.

Sulawesi The incomparable culture of the Toraja.

East Nusa Tenggara Central and west Flores for its **traditional villages**; Larantuka in east Flores for its unique **Christian cultural tradition**; **whaling** in Lamalera.

Irian Jaya Much of Irian Jaya offers interesting cultural possibilities, but they are best developed and most accessible in the Baliem Valley where the **Dani** live.

Museums **Java** The **National** Museum in Jakarta is Indonesia's best and largest collection; the Museum **Prabu Geusan Ulun** in Sumedang and the **Ambarawa Railway** Museum both have charming, and slightly wacky, collections; the **kraton** (palace) museums in Cirebon, Yogyakarta and Solo are worthwhile; while Kudus has a wonderfully politically incorrect **kretek** (cigarette) museum.

Bali The Museum **Bali** in Denpasar has one of the best – and best presented – provincial collections.

Sumatra Medan's **North Sumatra** Museum contains a motley collection; the **Ethnological Museum of Simanindo** on Lake Toba's Samosir Island recreates Batak culture in a traditional village; Palembang's **South Sumatra** Museum contains some fine pieces.

Kalimantan Musium **Negeri** in Pontianak has provincial exhibits.

Sulawesi The **Ujung Pandang** State Museum, and for a reasonable provincial collection the Museum of **Central Sulawesi** in Palu.

East Nusa Tenggara The **Blikan Blewut** Museum outside Maumere; Kupang's good Museum of **East Nusa Tenggara**.

Indonesian Tourist Promotion offices overseas

Australia Level 10,5 Elizabeth Street, Sydney NSW 2000, Australia. T61-02-2333630, F61-02-233629, 3573478.
Japan 2nd Floor Sankaido Building, 1-9-13 Akasaka, Minatoku, Tokyo 10, Japan. T03-358553588, 35869736, F03-35821397. Asean 10, Collyer Quay, 15-07 Ocean Building, Singapore 0104. T65-02-5342837, F65-02-5334287.
Taiwan 5th Floor, 66 Sung Chiang Road, Taipei, Taiwan ROC. T02-5377620, F02-5376621.
Europe Wiessenhuttenstrasse 17, D-6000 Frankfurt/Main, Germany. T69-233677/78, F69-230840.
United Kingdom 3-4 Hanover Street, London W1 9HH, England. T44-71-4930030, 4930334, F44-71-4931747.
North America 3457 Wilshire Boulevard, Los Angeles, CA 90010, USA. T1-213-3872078, F1-213-3804876.

Java Taman Mini for Indonesia in miniature and **Taman Impian Jaya Ancol** for Indonesia's stab at Disneyland, both in Jakarta.	Entertainment parks
Java Jakarta for most things; Yogyakarta for handicrafts and especially **batik** and silver **jewellery**; Solo for batik and **'antiques'**; Pekalongan for its distinctive batiks; Jepara for its **woodwork** and **furniture**. **Bali** Has an array of products including **paintings**, **jewellery**, **woodcarving**, **batik** and **garments**, often skilfully designed for Western tastes. **Sumatra** Traditional **woodcarvings** from Nias Island. **Kalimantan** 'Tribal' **handicrafts** and some **textiles**. **Sulawesi** Rantepao for **Torajan handicrafts**, **textiles** and **'antiques'**. **Lombok and Sumbawa** Lombok for **pottery** and **textiles**. **East Nusa Tenggara** Flores, Sumba and Timor for their varied traditional **textiles**. **Irian Jaya** Tribal **handicrafts**, the best coming from the Asmat people of the southeast, but more commonly made in the Wamena area of the Baliem Valley.	Shopping & Handicrafts

When to go

Indonesia is a vast country and although the whole area is 'tropical' – in other words it is hot (at sea level) – it encompasses several rainfall zones. This means that there is no particular 'best time to visit' – it just depends on where you are going. The chart above gives a broad idea of the seasons across the archipelago and the levels of rainfall in different parts of the country at different times of year. Bear in mind that some areas have annual rainfall of just 500 mm, while others receive a drenching 6,000 mm.

Travelling overland in the wet season in some areas can present problems, especially if intending to venture off the main highways. Parts of Sumatra, Sulawesi, Kalimantan, Nusa Tenggara and Irian Jaya can all be cut off after severe storms. However, the main highways that the government has now largely built through the major islands – like the Trans-Sumatran highway – are usually open all year round. Travelling during the wet season can also have advantages. Hotel prices are generally negotiable and resorts that may be excessively crowded at peak times of year can be wonderfully quiet.

Tours and tour operators

Arc Journeys, small group or bespoke tours to Southeast Asia and elsewhere, arc@travelarc.com, www.travelarc.com **Asian Journeys**, a range of tours by a well established company, mail@asianjourneys.com, www.asianjourneys.com **Dragoman**, adventure and cultural tours and expeditions to Southeast Asia and beyond, wl@dragoman.co.uk, www.dragoman.co.uk **Exodus**, small group walking and trekking holidays, adventure tours and more, sales@exodustravels.co.uk, www.exodus.co.uk	*Local tour operators are listed in individual town entries & in the practical introductions to each major island or island group*

Embassies and consulates overseas

Note not all Indonesian embassies are listed below. For a full listing of embassies of the world, including Indonesia, see: http://www.embassyworld.com/embassy/indonesia1.htm
Argentina, Chile, Uruguay and Paraguay, Mariskal Ramon Castila 2901, 1425 Buenos Aires, Argentina. T0054-11-8016622, 8016655, 8017142, F8024448, Tx18704 INDON AR. Cable: INDONESIA BUENOS AIRES.
Australia: Embassy, in Australia, 8 Darwin Avenue, Yarralumla, Canberra - ACT 2600. T0061-2-2508600, F2508666. Cable: PERWAKILAN.
Consulate, 236-238 Maroubra Road, Maroubra, NSW – 2035. T3449933, 297741 (Commercial Office).
Consulate, 72 Queen's Road, Melbourne VIC-3004. T5252755, F5251588, TxAA35223 KRIMEL.
Consulate, 134 Adelaide Tce, East Perth, WA-6004. T2215858, F2215688.
Consulate, 18 Harry Chan Avenue, Darwin, NT 0800. T410048, F412709. Postal Address: PO Box 1953, Darwin NT. 0801.
Austria, A-1180 Wien, Gustav, Tschermakg 5-7, AUSTRIA.
Brazil, Bolivia and Peru, Setor Embaixada Sul Avenida, Das Nacoes Yuadra, 805, Lote 20 Caixa Postal 08934, Brasilia. T055-61-2430102, 2430233, 2444904, F2431713, Tx612541 EDIB BR 611079 EDIB BR, Cable: INDONESIA BRASIL.

Canada: Embassy, 287 MacLaren Street, Ottawa, Ontario, Canada K2P 0L9. T001-613-2367403, F5632858.
Consulate, Toronto 129 Jarvis Street, Toronto, Ontario, M5C 2H6, Canada. T001-416-3604020, F3604295.
Consulate, Vancouver 1455 West Georgia Street, 2nd Floor, Vancouver, B.C. V6G 2T3. T001-604-6828855, F6628396.
Representative on the ICAO Council, 1000 Sherbrooke Street West # 986, Montreal, Quebec, H3A 3G4. T001-514-2858276.
People's Republic of China, Sanlitun Diplomatic Office Building B, Beijing, 100600 China. T0086-10-5325484-9, F5325366. Tx221035 KBRIB CN. Cable: INDONESIA BEIJING.
Finland, Kuusisaarentie 3, 00340 Helsinki, Finland. T00358-9-458 2100, F4582882. www.iit.edu/~syafsya/finland/helsinki1.html
Germany, Bernkasteler Str. 2, D-53175, Bonn. T0049-228-382990.
Japan: Embassy, Higashi Gotanda 5-2-9, Shinagawa-ku, Tokyo, Japan. T0081-3-34414201, 3441-4209, F34471697, TxINDONJ-22920. Cable: INDONESIA TOKYO.
Consulate, Kato Building 3rd Floor, Kyomachi 76-1, Chuo-ku, Kobe 605, Japan. T0081-78-3211656, F3920792, Tx5624166, INDKOBJ. Cable: PERWAKIN KOBE.
Consulate, Hokkaido Island 883-3 Chome 4-Jo, Miyayanomori, Chuo-ku, Sapporo, Japan. T0081-11-2516002 (day), 6434531 (night).

Explore Worldwide, small group adventure tours across the world, including Southeast Asia, www.explore.co.uk
Footprint Adventures, trekking and wildlife trips to Southeast Asia and wider, sales@footprint-adventures.co.uk, www.footprint-adventures.co.uk
Gecko, small group adventure tours to Southeast Asia, geckotravel@cs.com, www.geckotravel.co.uk
Guerba, adventure and discovery holidays, www.guerba.co.uk
Silk Steps, specialized itineraries ranging from trekking, diving, cultural and wildlife trips to several destinations in Asia, info@silksteps.co.uk, www.silksteps.co.uk
STA Travel, Priory House, 6 Wright's Lane, London W8 6TA, T0870-1606070, www.statravel.co.uk
Symbiosis, small group expeditions to Southeast Asia, info@symbiosis-travel.co.uk, www.symbiosis-travel.co.uk
Teaching and Projects Abroad, offers work and experiences while you travel, info@teaching-abroad.co.uk, www.teaching-abroad.co.uk
The Imaginative Traveller, adventure tours to the world, including Southeast Asia, info@imaginative-traveller.com
Worldwide Adventures Abroad, adventure tours organized for/in small groups, abroad@globalnet.co.uk, www.adventures-abroad.com

Consulate, Kyushu Island Kyuden Bldg.1-82, Watanabe-Dori, Chuo-ku, Fukuoka, Japan. T0011-92-7613031.
Kenya, Utalli Hous 3rd Floor, Uhuru Highway/Loita Street, PO Box 48868, Nairobi, Kenya. T00254-2-215874/5, 215848, F340721, Tx23171 INDO KE.
Cable: INDONESIA NAIROBI.
Democratic People's Republic of Korea, 5 Foreigner's Building Moon So Dong, Taedongkang, District Pyong Yang, Democratic People's Republic of Korea, PO Box 178. T00850-2-817425, Tx35030 INDON KP.
Cable: INDONESIA PYONG YANG.
Laos, Route Phone Keng, Boite Postale 277, Vientiane R.D.P.L, Laos. T00856-2373.2370, Tx4333 INDVTELS, Cable: INDONESIA VIENTIANE.
Myanmar and Nepal, 100, Pyidaungsu Yeiktha Road, PO Box 1401 Yangon, Myanmar. T0095-1-81174, 81358, Tx21355 TINDON BM.
Cable: PERWAKIN YANGON.
Netherlands, T. Asserlaan 8, 2517 KC The Hague. T0031-70-3108151.
New Zealand, 70 Glen Road, Kelburn, Wellington, New Zealand. T0064-4-4758697/8/9, F4759374, Tx3892 (INDON NZ).
Sri Lanka & Malvides, No. 1, Police Park Terrace-Colombo-5, Sri Lanka. T0094-1-580113, 580194, Tx21223 KBRI CE.
Cable: INDONESIA COLOMBO.

Turkey, Abdullah Cevdet Sok No. 10, PK.C 42 Cankaya-06680 Ankara, Turkey. T0090-312-4382190/91/92, 4388712, F4382193, Tx067-43250 INDO TR.
Cable: INDONESIA ANKARA.
United States of America: Embassy, 2020 Massachussetts Ave, N.W. Washington, DC 20036. T001-202-7755200.
Consulate, Two Illinois Center, 233 North Michigan Avenue Suite, 1422 Chicago, Illinois 60601, USA. T001-312-9380101, F9383148, Tx210222 INAC UR.
Cable: INDONESIA CHICAGO.
Consulate, 1111 Columbus Avenue, San Francisco, CA 94133. T001-415-4749571, F4414320.
Consulate, Texas c/o Thomas E. Jamail, Jr. (Bidang Penerangan), 10900 Richmond Avenue, Houston, TX 77042. T001-713-7851691, F7809644, kjrihous@accesscomm.net
Consulate, 5 East 68th Street, New York, NY 10017. T001-212-8790600.
Consulate, Los Angeles, kjri@kjri-la.com, www.kjri.com
Vietnam, 50 Ngo Quyen Street, Hanoi, Vietnam. T0084-4-256316, 253353, 253324, 252788, F259274, Tx411434 INDOHA VT.
Cable: INDONESIA HANOI.
Zimbabwe, 3 Duthie Avenue, Belgravia, PO Box 8296, Causeway, Harare, Zimbabwe. T00263-732561, 737447, F737479, Tx22451 INDONHR ZW.

Cambodia
Central Asia
China
Ethiopia
India
Indonesia
Laos
Myanmar
Philippines
South Korea
Thailand
Vietnam

Silk Steps

Experience & Explore

Tel: 0117 9402800 Fax: 0117 9406900
Email: info@silksteps.co.uk Web: www.silksteps.co.uk
Silk Steps Ltd, 83 Quakers Rd, Downend
Bristol, BS16 6NH, England

Language

The national language is **Bahasa Indonesia**, which is written in Roman script (see page 989). There are 250 regional languages and dialects, of which Sundanese (the language of West Java and Jakarta) is the most widespread. The Bataks of North Sumatra have a number of mutually intelligible languages which are, in essence, forms of primitive *Bahasa*. In Padang and elsewhere in West Sumatra, the population speak *Minang* – which is also similar to 'Bahasa'. Despite the bewildering array of regional languages, most of the younger generation will be able to speak Bahasa – about 70% of the population. English is the most common foreign language, although there are Dutch speakers amongst the older generation and some Portuguese is still spoken in East Timor.

Bahasa Indonesia is a relatively easy language to learn, and visitors may have a small but functional vocabulary after just a few weeks. Unlike Thai, it is not tonal and is grammatically very straightforward. However, this does not mean it is an easy language to speak well. A small number of useful words and phrases are listed in the box below. There are many cheap, pocket-sized Indonesian-English dictionaries available in Indonesia. They are fine for the odd request for a towel or a slightly cleaner room, but anyone wishing to learn more will find them disappointing. The best dictionary is John Echols and Hassan Shadily's twin volume edition (best bought in Jakarta), but it is hardly handy in terms of size and weight and is mostly used by scholars of Indonesia. For visitors interested in studying Bahasa Indonesia in more depth, the Cornell course, though expensive, is recommended. Cassettes are available from Southeast Asia Publications Office, East Hill Plaza, Ithaca, New York 14853, USA, T607-2553827.

Language courses in Indonesia The best way to learn Indonesian is to study it intensively in Indonesia. In **Jakarta**, courses are available through: *The Indonesian/American Cultural Centre*, Jl Pramuka Kav 30, T021-8583241; *The Australian Cultural Centre* (the Indonesian Australia Language Foundation), Jl Rasuna Said (at the Embassy), T021-5213350; *The French Cultural Centre*, T021-3908585; *The Goethe Institute*, T021-8581139. In **Yogyakarta**, another centre where overseas students study Indonesian, courses are run by: *The Realia Language School*, T0274-564969, which is recommended; it is cheaper if a group learns together. **In Bali**, courses are run by the *Bali Language and Cultural Centre*, Jl Tukad Pakerisan 80, Denpasar, T0361-239331.

Study South-East Asia — **THE UNIVERSITY OF HULL**

Burma Brunei Cambodia Malaysia Indonesia Thailand Laos Philippines Vietnam

Undergraduate and postgraduate degree programmes taught in a specialist department by experts in the South-East Asia region

Further information
web www.hull.ac.uk/seas — tel/fax +44 (0)1482 465758

Before you travel

Entry requirements

All visitors to Indonesia must possess passports valid for at least six months from their date of arrival in Indonesia and, in theory, they should have proof of onward travel. Many visitors find that immigration officials are happy with some indication that sufficient funds (for example Travellers' cheques) are available to purchase a return flight.

Passports

Visas are **not** required for nationals of ASEAN countries (Brunei, Laos, Malaysia, Myanmar, Philippines, Singapore, Thailand and Vietnam), Argentina, Australia, Austria, Belgium, Brazil, Canada, Chile, Denmark, Egypt, Finland, France, Germany, Greece, Iceland, Ireland, Italy, Japan, Kuwait, Liechtenstein, Luxembourg, Malta, Mexico, Morocco, the Netherlands, New Zealand, Norway, Saudi Arabia, South Korea, Spain, Sweden, Switzerland, Taiwan, Turkey, UAE, UK, USA and Venezuela. Tourists may stay for a maximum of two months (non-extendable). Entry or exit must be through one of the so-called 'Gateway' cities. These are Ambon, Bali, Balikpapan, Bandung, Batam (Riau), Biak, Jakarta, Kupang, Manado, Mataram, Medan, Padang, Pekanbaru, Pontianak and Surabaya airports; the seaports of Ambon, Batam (Riau), Belawan (Medan), Benoa (Bali), Dumai, Jakarta, Manado, Padangbai (Bali), Semarang, Surabaya and Tanjung Pinang (Riau); and the single visa-free land crossing at Entikong in Kalimantan. If entering **or leaving** the country through any other city, a visa is required. These can be obtained from any Indonesian embassy or consulate, are only valid for one month, but can be extended (apply at an immigration office).

Visas

For nationals of countries other than those listed above, visas can be obtained from any Indonesian embassy or consulate, but are valid for one month only (extension possible). Two passport photographs and a small fee are required, plus a confirmed onward flight.

Business visas People intending to work in Indonesia need to take their passport, two photos and a covering letter from their company to an Indonesian embassy or consulate. The application takes 24 hours to process, maximum stay five weeks.

Visa extension Jl Teuku Umar I, Jakarta, T349811. Note that extensions are not possible on the standard 60 day tourist pass. It is necessary to leave the country, and then re-enter. Financial penalties for over-staying are steep. If you are unavoidably delayed and unable to leave the country, immigration officers may allow a couple of days' leeway, but only in exceptional circumstances.

None required unless visitors have been in a cholera, yellow fever or smallpox infected area six days prior to arrival.

Vaccinations
See also 'Health' page 54

Other health problems Malaria tablets and mosquito repellent are essential. **Warning**: do

Cambodia
Indonesia
Laos
Malaysia
Papua New Guinea
Philippines
Thailand
Vietnam

The Specialists in environmentally & culturally sensitive travel to South East Asia. Consultancy, tailor-made holidays and scheduled small group adventures.

Tel.: +44 (0)20 7924 5906
Fax: +44 (0)20 7924 5907

info@symbiosis-travel.co.uk • www.symbiosis-travel.co.uk

not go diving if you are taking Larium (Mefloquine). Some local residents swear by *Minyak Gosok Tawan* (lemon balm oil) or *Minyak Kayu Putih* (camphor oil) to keep mosquitoes at bay. Tiger Balm is also good for itchy bites. **NB** There are no strong mosquito repellents available outside Jakarta. The locally produced *Autan* is not terribly effective. See Jakarta shopping for details of repellent available. An American company has designed a tailored mosquito net which covers the wearer in fine mesh and offers protection as you move around; contact Ben's Bug Armor, Long Rd, T00-1-510-540 4763.

What to take

Travellers usually tend to take too much. Almost everything is available in Indonesia's main towns and cities – and often at a lower price than in the West. Remoter areas, inevitably, are less well supplied.

Suitcases are not appropriate if you are intending to travel overland by bus. A backpack, or even better a travelpack (where the straps can be zipped out of sight), is recommended. Travelpacks have the advantage of being hybrid backpacks-suitcases; they can be carried on the back for easy porterage, but they can also be taken into hotels without the owner being labelled a 'hippy'. **NB** For serious hikers, a backpack with an internal frame is still by far the better option for longer treks.

In terms of **clothing**, dress in Indonesia is relatively casual – even at formal functions. Suits are not necessary except in a few of the most expensive restaurants. However, though formal attire may be the exception, dressing tidily is the norm. Women particularly should note that in many areas of Indonesia, they should avoid offending Muslim sensibilities and dress 'demurely' (ie keep shoulders covered and wear below-knee skirts or trousers). This is particularly true in Aceh in North Sumatra and West Sumatra, in parts of Java, and in Sumbawa. Note that this does not generally apply in beach resorts. It is usually warm (except in highland areas), so only one thin sweater or sweatshirt is usually necessary. Cotton clothes are most appropriate: they are light, dry quickly, and are cool. A sarong is useful when bathing in public or lounging in the evening – but it is best to buy one after arrival.

There is a tendency, rather than to take inappropriate articles of clothing, to take too many of the same article. Laundry services are cheap, and the turn-around rapid. It is also worth remembering that clothes are cheap should something fall apart or get lost.

Checklist Bumbag; Earplugs; First aid kit (See also 'Health' section); Insect repellent and/or electric mosquito mats, coils; International driving licence; Passport (valid for at least six months); Photocopies of essential documents; Short wave radio; Spare passport photographs; Sun protection; Sunglasses; Swiss Army knife; Torch; Umbrella; Wet wipes; Zip-lock bags. Those intending to stay in **budget accommodation** might also include: Cotton sheet sleeping bag; Money belt; Padlock (for hotel room and pack); Sarong (or buy on arrival); Soap; Student card; Toilet paper; Towel; Travel wash. For **women travellers**: a supply of tampons (although these are available in most towns); a wedding ring for single female travellers who might want to help ward off the attentions of amorous admirers.

Customs

Duty free allowance Two litres of alcohol, 200 cigarettes or 50 cigars or 100 grammes of tobacco, along with a reasonable amount of perfume.

Currency regulations A limit of 50,000Rp can be carried in or out of the country. There are no restrictions on the import or export of foreign currency, either cash or Travellers' cheques.

Prohibited items Narcotics, arms and ammunition, TV sets, radio/cassette recorders, pornographic objects or printed matter, printed matter in Chinese characters and Chinese medicines. In theory, approval should also be sought for carrying transceivers, movie film and video cassettes. Photographic equipment, computers, typewriters and tape recorders should also be declared on arrival, although for tourists this is not assiduously enforced.

Money

Providing US$ estimates of costs of living in Indonesia has been tricky over the last few years. In 1997, US$1 would buy you 2,500Rp. By mid-1998 this had spiralled down (or up, if you were a tourist, that is) to more than 13,000Rp. And the exchange rate as this book went to press was 9,500Rp (December 2000). In other words, visitors to Indonesia over the last few years have found their Dollars, Francs, Pounds, Yen and Guilders have gone an awful lot further – notwithstanding some periods of rapid inflation.

Cost of living

Visitors staying in first class hotels and eating in hotel restaurants will probably spend 300,000Rp a day and upwards. Tourists staying in cheaper a/c accommodation, and eating in local restaurants, will probably spend about 150,000Rp a day. A backpacker, staying in fan-cooled guesthouses and eating cheaply, might expect to be able to live on 30,000Rp a day. A meal in a simple warung should cost 5-10,000Rp, in a local restaurant about 10-20,000Rp, and in a swish hotel coffee shop 20,000Rp+. Of course it is best not to calculate your budget simply by multiplying the number of days you intend to stay by the figures given above. A long bus journey, a trip by air, a couple of days' diving, or the need to hire a guide on a trek, for example, would throw such careful calculations right out. Examples of domestic air, road, rail and sea fares are given on pages 975 to 989. Finally, a word of caution. Because of the volatility of the domestic currency, coupled with rapid inflation, prices have been highly unstable. Or rather they have escalated – at least in rupiah terms. There is every chance that you will find that the bus and other prices quoted here may have increased, sometimes markedly. But just remember, it is still a lot cheaper than a couple of years back!

Major credit cards are accepted in larger hotels, airline offices, department stores and some restaurants, although this method of payment is often subject to a 3% surcharge. Visa and MasterCard are the most widely accepted. It is not so easy to use credit cards to get cash advances, although major banks in the main cities may do it – especially in Java and Bali. Banks in larger towns and tourist centres across the archipelago have ATMs (Automatic Teller Machines) which provide credit card advances. Again, Visa and MasterCard are most widely taken and the cirrus system is also offered by many banks. If you are visiting very remote areas for a long period, it can make sense to obtain Indonesian Post Office Travellers' cheques in one of the big cities. These are then easily changed into rupiahs in any post office in the country. For **lost credit cards** call the following toll free numbers or visit the websites:
Visa: T001-803-1-933-6294 or www.visa.com
American Express cards and TCs: T001-803-61005 or www.americanexpress.com
Master card: T001-803-1-887 0623, www.mastercard.com
Western Union: www.westernunion.com

Credit cards

Banks, credit card cash withdrawals
Bank Bali	MasterCard, Cirrus
Bank Internasional Indonesia (BII)	MasterCard, Visa, Cirrus
Bank Central Asia (BCA)	MasterCard, Visa, Cirrus
Lippo Bank	MasterCard, Cirrus
BNI	MasterCard, Cirrus

The unit of currency in Indonesia is the **rupiah** (Rp). 1Rp equals 100 sen. Denominations are 100Rp, 500Rp, 1,000Rp, 5,000Rp, 10,000Rp, 20,000Rp and 50,000Rp. Coins are minted in 25Rp, 50Rp, 100Rp and 500Rp denominations. **NB** When taking US$ in cash, make sure that the bills are new and crisp, as banks in Indonesia can be fussy about which bills they accept (Flores and Sulawesi are particularly bad). Larger denomination US$ bills also tend to command a premium exchange rate. Note, finally, that during the recent period of extreme exchange rate volatility, places outside main centres tended to give poor rates. Shop around: there can be great variations between exchange rates offered by different banks and money changers. Current rates of exchange for rupiah from the *Bank of Indonesia* are available on http://www.bü.co.id/english/headline/ex_rates.htm#TODAY; alternatively, check http://www.oanda.com/converter/classic

Currency

Travellers' cheques
It is not possible to buy TCs using credit cards in Indonesia, the only exception being American Express

In more out of the way places it is worth making sure that you have a stock of smaller notes and coins – it can be hard to break larger bills.

Travellers' cheques (TCs) can usually be changed in larger towns and tourist destinations. In smaller towns and more out of the way spots it may not be possible to change TCs. The US$ is the most readily acceptable currency, both for TCs and cash, and it is best to carry US$ denominated TCs if travelling outside the major tourist centres. If staying in tourist centres TCs denominated in any major currency will do, but note that rates for US$ tend to be better simply because most transactions are in US$. Occasionally money changers charge a commission – check beforehand. If changing cash, note that banks like bills in pristine condition, and a better rate is often given for larger denomination notes – eg US$50 or US$100.

American Express TCs denominated in US$ are probably the easiest to change. We have had reports that Thomas Cook Cheques are not always accepted by banks in provincial towns (Standard Chartered Bank will accept Thomas Cook Visa TCs, and Hong Kong Bank will accept Thomas Cook Mastercard TCs), although this seems to be only true out of the main tourist centres. Money changers often give better rates than banks. Hotels will sometimes change TCs (usually in popular tourist destinations), but rates vary a great deal from competitive to appalling, so it is worth checking.

Banks Two of the better banks, at least for most visitors' needs, are **BNI** (Bank Negara Indonesia) and **BCA** (Bank Central Asia). *BNI* is reliable and efficient and most of their branches will change US$ TCs. They also give one of the best rates and have offices across the archipelago. *BCA* is also very efficient and they are usually likely to change TCs denominated in 'unusual' (from the Indonesian perspective) currencies. But *BCA* does not have such a wide distribution of branches. Another bank which deals with foreign currencies efficiently is **Bank Ekspor Impor**.

Bali As an international tourist destination, it is easier to change money – either cash or TCs in all major currencies – in Bali than any other spot in Indonesia. All the tourist centres offer money changing facilities at competitive rates. Cash advances can be obtained on Visa cards from *BCA* in Denpasar. However, the airport rates are not as competitive as in-town rates. The very best rates in Indonesia are from the money changers in Kuta; the larger denomination notes get a better rate (in other words, the rate for a $100 bill is significantly better than that for a $10 bill). Always check the amount you receive very, very carefully, as scams are in abundance.

Credit card representatives *Amex*: Bali Beach Hotel, Sanur, T288449; Galleria Nusa Dua, Shop A5, T773334, F773306. *Diners Club*: Jl Veteran 5, Denpasar, T227138. **Visa & Mastercharge**: Bank Duta, Jl Hayam Wuruk 165, Denpasar, T226578.

Getting there
Air

For information on connections with Bali see page 312, & for Medan see page 473. For getting to other areas of Indonesia, see the relevant chapter's Ins & outs sections

The three main gateways into Indonesia are Jakarta, Bali and Medan (Sumatra). Batam is also becoming increasingly popular, although arrivals are mostly by sea, from Singapore (see page 579). *Garuda*, the national flag carrier, flies between Jakarta and Europe, the US, other Asian cities, and Australia and New Zealand. Most of the major European carriers have reduced the number of flights to Jakarta; *British Airways* stopped flying to Indonesia altogether in 1999 and their flights have yet to return to pre-crisis levels of frequency. The following carriers operate from Europe to Jakarta: *Air France*, *KLM* and *Lufthansa*. There are direct flights from Amsterdam, Frankfurt, London (three times a week from Gatwick), Paris and Rome. Many visitors fly to Jakarta via Singapore. There are flights approximately every two hours between Singapore and Jakarta, and three flights a day between Singapore and Denpasar (Bali). *British Airways*, *Singapore Airlines* and *Qantas* all fly from London to Singapore. There are also flights via Bangkok, Kuala Lumpur and Hong Kong. *Garuda* and *Singapore Airlines* operate many flights from Singapore.

STA TRAVEL

FOR STUDENTS AND YOUNG TRAVELLERS

250 BRANCHES WORLDWIDE

LOW COST FLIGHTS → ADVENTURE TOURS → TRAVEL PASSES

SKI → ISIC/YOUTH CARDS → ACCOMMODATION → INSURANCE

CAR HIRE → EXPERT ADVICE FROM WELL TRAVELLED STAFF

For Bookings and Enquiries:
0870 160 6070

Find fares, check availability, enter competitions, book online or find your local branch @

 www.statravel.co.uk

STA TRAVEL LTD

The political and economic crisis led to a sharp fall in both the number of Indonesians travelling abroad and of foreign tourists entering Indonesia. As a result, many carriers cut the frequency of flights to Indonesia. However, on 1 January 2001, the government is lifting the US$105 outbound tax currently levied on Indonesian nationals and permanent residents (an effort to raise revenue during the depths of economic crisis). Some commentators are forecasting a 40% rise in flights to Indonesia by Asian and European carriers to meet the expected increase in demand.

From Australasia From Auckland with *Garuda*; from Sydney with *Qantas*, *Garuda* and *Ansett*; from Melbourne with *Garuda*; from Perth flights with *Garuda*, *Qantas* and *Singapore Airlines*. There are also flights between Kupang (West Timor) and Darwin, Australia.

From Europe There are direct flights from London (*Garuda*), Amsterdam (*KLM* and *Garuda*), Frankfurt (*Lufthansa* and *Garuda*), Zurich (*Garuda*), Paris (*Air France* and *Garuda*), Rome (*Garuda*), Vienna (*Lauda Air*) and Moscow (*Aeroflot*).

From the Far East *Japan Airlines* and *Garuda* have flights from Tokyo; *Garuda* and *Japan Asia Airlines* fly from Osaka. From Hong Kong, *Cathay Pacific*, *Garuda* and *China Airlines*. From Seoul flights with *Garuda* and *Korean Airlines*. From Taipei flights with *Garuda*, *Eva*, *China Airlines* and *Sempati*. From Beijing with *Air China* and *Garuda*. From Ho Chi Minh City with *Garuda*.

From South Asia There are many direct flights from Singapore, Bangkok or Kuala Lumpur; also from Manila with *Garuda* and *Philippine Airlines*.

From the USA & Canada From Los Angeles fly direct with *Garuda*.

Boat

Visitors can enter Indonesia by sea without a visa, at the gateway ports of Ambon, Batam (Riau), Belawan (Medan), Benoa (Bali), Dumai, Jakarta, Manado, Padangbai (Bali), Semarang, Surabaya and Tanjung Pinang (Riau). There are regular ferries from Singapore to Batam (see page 579), and from Penang, Lumut and Port Kelang (all in Malaysia) to Medan's Belawan Port (see page 474). The Penang-Belawan route is by far the most popular. There is also a ferry service from Melaka to the city of Dumai (Sumatra). Otherwise visitors will have to take a freighter or some other form of irregular sea transport.

For those interested in booking a passage on a cargo ship travelling to Indonesia, contact the *Strand Cruise Centre*, Charing Cross Shopping Concourse, The Strand, London WC2N 4HZ, T020-78366363, F0202-74970078. Another company booking berths on freighters is *Wagner Frachtschiffreissen*, Stadlerstrasse 48, CH-8404 Winterthur, Switzerland, T052-2421442, F052-2421487.

Road

The only gateway overland crossing is at Entikong, which links the East Malaysian city of Kuching in Sarawak with the capital of West Kalimantan, Pontianak.

Touching down

Airport information

Jakarta's **Soekarno-Hatta International Airport** lies 30 km northwest of the city. It is Indonesia's main international gateway and has two separate terminal complexes 5 km apart: one for domestic connections (terminals A to D) and the other for international flights (E to H). The only exception is the national flag carrier, *Garuda*, which operates out of the international terminal.

Touching down

Hours of business Hours of business are highly variable; there are not even standard opening hours for government offices. The listing below is a rule of thumb:
Banks: foreign banks 0800-1200 Mon-Fri and 0800-1100 Sat; local banks 0800-1300, 1330-1600 Mon-Sat. Banks in hotels may stay open longer.
Businesses: most businesses open 0800/0900-1200, 1300-1600/1700 Mon-Fri.
Government offices: 0800-1500 Mon-Thu, 0800-1130 Fri and 0800-1400 Sat.
Museums: 0830 or 0900-1400 Tue-Thu, 0900-1100 Fri, 0900-1300 Sat and 0900-1500 Sun, closed Mon.
Shops: 0900-2000 Mon-Fri, 0900-1300 Sat, sometimes on Sun. In smaller towns, shops may close for a siesta between 1300 and 1700.
Official time All the islands included in this book come under Central Indonesia time, GMT+8 (which, for the record, includes South and East Kalimantan and Sulawesi, as well as Bali and Nusa Tenggara).
Voltage 220 volts, 50 cycles in the big cities; 110 volts in some areas. Plugs are usually rounded and two pin; sometimes sockets are recessed. It is easy enough to find adaptors in local electrical shops. More expensive hotels often have three-pin plugs. Power surges are not common and well protected electrical equipment such as lap-top computers can be used.
Weights and measures Metric, although local units are still in use in some areas.

Airport facilities
Facilities at the airport include car rental (*Avis*, *Bluebird Limo* and *Hertz*), currency exchange booths, ATMs (cash machines), left luggage facilities (outside the arrivals hall), hotel booking counter (about which we have received complaints concerning the sending of visitors to sub-standard hotels for which the reservation office staff receive a commission), a taxi desk, tourist information desk (with maps), the *Transit Hotel* (see below), the *Transit Restaurant*, Dunkin Donuts, McDonald's, a Post Office for 24 hours, long-distance calls, fax, telex and postal facilities. The faint aroma of Kretek (clove) cigarettes as one steps off the plane clearly tells passengers that they have arrived in Indonesia.

Airport hotels
If in transit, it may not be worthwhile travelling into the city. **A-A+** *Sheratan Bandara*, situated about 3 km from the airport, T5597777, F5597700. Very comfortable and generic hotel offering good level of service. **A** *Quality Hotel Aspac*, Terminal 2/E, T559008, F5590018, for short or longer stays, basic but adequate. **B** *Cengkareng Transit*, Jl Jurumudi, T611964, 10 minutes from the airport, neither very pleasant nor very good value, but may be necessary to stay here if in transit or catching an early flight. Free shuttle bus from and to the airport.

Transport to town
The drive in from the airport is moderately interesting for first-timers. Not only does the city sprawl out here in a disjointed and apparently random fashion, but there are also shrimp ponds and some mangrove replanting – the latter a modest stab at environmental correctness. The shrimp ponds – for those who might be thinking of heading off for some *udang paggang* (grilled prawns) to celebrate their arrival – are fed with human waste. Metered taxis to the city centre cost about 40-50,000Rp. The fare on the meter has a surcharge of 2,300Rp added on plus toll fees of 6,000Rp (for the airport and city toll roads). A/c Damri buses run every 30 minutes (operating between 0300 and 1900) from the airport to five points in the city centre, including Gambir train station, Kemayoran and Blok M (all 4,000Rp). See page 78 for more details on transport from the airport. It is a 10 minute walk from Gambir to Jl Jaksa where most of the budget accommodation is to be found.

Other international airports
Denpasar's (Bali) Ngurah Rai Airport has direct flights from Singapore, Kuala Lumpur, Hong Kong, Japan and Amsterdam (see page 312 for details). **Medan's Polonia Airport** has direct flights from Singapore, Penang and Kuala Lumpur on *Garuda*, *Singapore Airlines* and *MAS* (see page 473 for details). **Kupang's El Tari Airport** has flights from Darwin, Australia (see page 840), while there are flights from Los Angeles, via Honolulu, to **Biak**, Irian Jaya (see page 826). **Pontianak's Supadio Airport** has connections with Kuching (East Malaysia) and Singapore (see page 826), as does **Balikpapan's Sepinggang Airport** (see page 634). From

Pekanbaru's Simpangtiga Airport, there are flights to Melaka and Kuala Lumpur (Malaysia) and to Singapore (see page 575).

Airport tax This is 30,000Rp on international flights. Anywhere between 5,500 and 11,000Rp on domestic flights, depending on the airport. (Airports/provincial governments are allowed some leeway in setting their own taxes.) Domestic tax is usually included in the cost of the ticket – and it should be indicated on the ticket.

Tourist information

Tourist offices
For other offices, see relevant town entry

The Directorate General of Tourism is to be found in Jakarta. Administratively, it is under the Department of Tourism, Post and Telecommunications, which has offices throughout the country. These offices are known as Kanwil Depparpostel. Each of Indonesia's provinces also has its own tourist office, known as *Deparda* or *Dinas Pariwisata*. **Indonesia Government Tourist Offices** *Department Of Tourism*, Post And Telecommunication, Jl Merdeka Barat No. 16-19, Jakarta 10110. T062-021-3838412, 3838417, Tx: INTOUR IA, F02-021-3848245. *Directorate General Of Tourism* (DGT) Jl Merdeka Barat No. 16-19, Jakarta 10110, T062-021-3838217, 3838220, Telex: INTOUR IA, Cable: INTO JAKARTA, F062-021-3867589, 3860828.

Disabled travellers As a poor country, Indonesia has almost no infrastructure to enable disabled people to travel easily. Pavements are frequently very high, nine inches or so, uneven and ridden with holes and missing slabs. Buildings, including shops and museums, are frequently reached via steps with no ramps for wheelchair access. Public transport is frequently cramped and overcrowded. Some of the Western-owned hotels at the top end of the market do go out of their way to provide wheelchair access and facilities for disabled visitors. For travel to this area, it would be best to contact a specialist travel agent or organization dealing with travellers with special needs. In the UK, contact *RADAR* (The Royal Association for Disability and Rehabilitation), 12 City Forum, 250 City Road, London, EC1V 8AF, T020-72503222, T020-72504119. In North America, *Society for the Advancement of Travel for the Handicapped* (SATH), Suite 610, 347 5th Avenue, New York, NY 10016, T212-4477284.

Gay & lesbian travellers Indonesia is surprisingly tolerant of homosexuality given that it goes against the tenets of both Muslim and traditional Balinese religions. Homosexuality is not illegal; the age of consent is 16 years for men and women. Indonesian men are generally more affectionate in public, which allows foreign gay men to blend in more easily. Bali is the only island with an established gay area centred on Kuta, with certain bars, restaurants and areas which are patronized by, but not exclusive to, gay people. Few Indonesian men make a living as 'rent boys'; however, as a supposedly wealthy foreigner you will be expected to pay for meals, transport and accommodation. For more information contact: *Yayasan Yusada Bhakti*, Jl Belimbing Gang Y4, Denpasar.

Student travellers Anyone in full-time education is entitled to an **International Student Identity Card** (ISIC). These are issued by student travel offices and travel agencies across the world, and offer special rates on all forms of transport and other concessions and services. The ISIC head office is: *ISIC Association*, 479 Herengracht, 10-17-BS, Amsterdam, T31-204421280.

Women travellers Women travelling alone face greater difficulties than men or couples. Young southeast Asian women rarely travel without a partner, so it is believed to be strange for a western woman to do so. Western women are often believed to be of easy virtue – a view perpetuated by Hollywood and in local films, for example. To minimize the pestering that will occur, dress modestly – particularly in staunchly Muslim areas such as Aceh and West Sumatra, and in more out-of-the-way spots where locals may be unfamiliar with tourists. Comments, sometimes derogatory, will be made however carefully you dress and act; simply ignore them. Toiletries such as tampons are available in Indonesia's main cities, but may not be in more out of the way places.

Working in the country

A tourist visa does not give you the right to work. In a country on the brink of financial chaos, with high unemployment, job opportunities are extremely limited. Teaching English is the best option, often for room and board rather than cash. If you have a specialist skill such as diving instructor, you might find work in that field.

Rules, customs and etiquette

Conduct

As a rule, Indonesians are courteous and understanding. Visitors should be the same. As foreigners, visitors are often given the benefit of the doubt when norms are transgressed. However, it is best to have a grasp of at least the basics of accepted behaviour. In tourist areas and large cities, westerners and their habits are better understood; but in remote areas you should be more aware of local sensibilities. There are also some areas – such as Aceh in North Sumatra – that are more fervently Muslim than other parts of the country. With such a diverse array of cultures and religions, accepted conduct varies. Specific cultural notes are given in the appropriate introductory sections. Generally, the more popular an area is (as a tourist destination) the more understanding local people are likely to be of tourist habits. But this is not to imply that anything goes. It is also true that familiarity can breed contempt, so even in places like Bali it is important to be sensitive to the essentials of local culture.

Drugs

Penalties are harsh – expect a lengthy jail term at least – for trafficking even modest quantities.
 Prisoners Abroad is a charity dedicated to supporting UK nationals in prison abroad. As the charity writes: "Arrest, trial and imprisonment are devastating in a familiar environment, supported by family and friends. Abroad it is much worse". Young men and women caught with drugs may find themselves facing sentences of 10 years or more, often in appalling conditions. Volunteers can help *Prisoners Abroad*, and similar organizations, by becoming a pen pal, donating a magazine subscription, or sending books, for example. If you or a friend find yourself in the unfortunate position of being in jail, or facing a jail term, then contact the charity at: *Prisoners Abroad*, Freepost 82, Roseberry Avenue, London EC1B 1XB, UK, T020-78333467, F020-78333460 (if telephoning or faxing from abroad then the code is +44171). Further information on the charity and its work can also be obtained from the above address.

Calmness

Like other countries of southeast Asia, a calm attitude is highly admired, especially if things are going wrong. Keep calm and cool when bargaining, or waiting for a delayed bus or appointment.

Dress

Indonesia is largely a Muslim country and women should be particularly careful not to offend. Dress modestly and avoid shorts, short skirts and sleeveless dresses or shirts (except at the beach). Public nudity and topless bathing are not acceptable.

Clothing

Light clothing is suitable all the year round, except at night in the mountains. Shorts, miniskirts and singlets should be limited to beachwear only. Proper decorum should be observed when visiting places of worship; shorts are not permitted in mosques, shoulders and arms should be covered, and women must cover their heads. Formal dress for men normally consists of a batik shirt and trousers; suits are rarely worn. Local dress is *batik* for men and *kebaya* for women.

Face

People should not be forced to lose face in public; especially in front of colleagues. Putting someone in a position of *malu* or social shame should be avoided.

Gifts

If you are invited to somebody's home, it is customary to take a gift. This is not opened until after the visitor has left. Most small general stores have a range of pre-wrapped and boxed gifts, appropriate for a variety of occasions including weddings. These are usually items of china or glasses.

Heads, hands & feet	The head is considered sacred and should never be touched (especially those of children). Handshaking is common among both men and women, but the use of the left hand to give or receive is taboo. When eating with fingers, use the right hand only. Pointing with your finger is considered impolite; use your thumb to point, beckon buses (or any person) with a flapping motion of your right hand down by your side. When sitting with others, do not cross your legs; it is considered disrespectful. In addition, do not point with your feet and keep them off tables. Shoes are often not worn in the house and should be removed on entering.
Punctuality	**Jam karet** or 'rubber time' is a peculiarly Indonesian phenomenon. Patience and a cool head are very important; appointments are rarely at the time arranged.
Open affection	Public displays of affection between men and women is considered objectionable. However, Indonesians of the same sex tend to be more affectionate – holding hands, for example – than in the West.
Religion	Indonesia is the largest Muslim country in the world. In Java, **Islam** is a synthesis of Islam, Buddhism, Hinduism and animism – although the extent to which it is 'syncretic' is vigorously debated (see page 305). Orthodox Islam is strongest in northern Sumatra (Aceh), but is also present in parts of Sulawesi, Kalimantan and West Java. For a brief background to Islam, see page 960. **Mosques** are sacred houses of prayer; non-Muslims can enter a mosque, so long as they observe the appropriate customs: remove shoes before entering, dress appropriately (neatly and fully covered, avoiding singlets, shorts or short skirts), do not disturb the peace, and do not walk too close to or in front of somebody who is praying. During the fasting month of Ramadan, do not eat, drink or smoke in the presence of Muslims during daylight hours. Bali has remained a **Hindu** island (see page 445), and remnants of Hinduism are also evident in parts of central and East Java. To enter a temple or *pura* on Bali, it is often necessary to wear a sash around the waist (at some temples a sarong is also required); these are available for hire at the more popular temples, or can be bought for about 1,200Rp (7,000Rp for a sarong). Modest and tidy dress is also required when visiting Hindu temples; women should not enter wearing short dresses or with bare shoulders. Do not use flash-guns during ceremonies. Women menstruating are requested not to enter temples. **Christianity** is a growing religion in Sulawesi (see page 701) and in East Nusa Tenggara (page 817). Although not a religion, **Pancasila** is – or was – the Indonesian state ideology. However, now that Suharto has gone and the New Order has become an Old Order, pancasila does not have the resonance it once did. Even so, most people were brought up believing that it was the glue holding this disparate group of countries together (see page 944). For a more comprehensive background to do's and don'ts in Indonesia see: Draine, Cathy and Hall, Barbara, *Culture Shock! Indonesia* (Times Books: Singapore, 1986).
Tipping	Tipping is not usual in Indonesia. A 10% service charge is added to bills at more expensive hotels (in addition to tax of 11%). Porters expect to be tipped about 500Rp a bag. In more expensive restaurants, where no service is charged, a tip of 5-10% is sometimes appropriate. Taxi drivers (in larger towns) appreciate a small tip (200-300Rp). *Parkirs* always expect payment for 'watching' your car – 500Rp.

Safety

Despite the recent media coverage of riots and other disturbances in Indonesia, it remains a safe country and violence against foreigners is rare (but see below for a check list of places that have seen civil disturbances in recent months). However, there have been numerous reports of an increase in thefts and robberies during the economic crisis, as people struggle to survive in extremely difficult times. Inevitably, tourists – by definition, wealthy – have been especially targeted. Some visitors have taken to private transport (hire cars, taxis and the like) and flying to avoid overnight buses and trains, where the majority of thefts take place. Those who cannot afford the costs of private transport and air travel should take particular care on buses and trains, especially on the more popular tourist routes. 'Shuttle buses', which specialize in carrying travellers on Bali and Lombok, and tourist minibuses on the more popular routes on Sumatra, Java and Sulawesi, are usually safer than public buses when it comes to petty theft. Thefts are also common in shopping centres and other places where tourists congregate.

Theft and deception were a problem even before the economic crisis. It is advisable for travellers to carry all valuables in a moneybelt. Avoid carrying large amounts of cash; Travellers' cheques can be changed in most major towns. Pickpockets frequent the public transport systems. Reports of robbery on the overnight trains through Java are common. Take great care of your belongings on these longer journeys on public transport. Keep a close watch on your bags going through security checkpoints at airports; some travellers have reported that their bags were stolen before they could retrieve them after having passed through the X-ray machine. Do not leave valuables in hotel rooms; most of the more expensive hotels will have safety deposit boxes. Many guesthouses have 'open air' bathrooms, ie with only a partial roof. A favoured means of entering rooms is over the bathroom wall and through the bathroom door, therefore it is essential to lock bathroom doors in this type of accommodation. Petty theft is a growing problem in all places frequented by travellers. In Jakarta it is also recommended that passengers in taxis keep their doors locked: thefts while stuck in traffic jams are becoming more common.

Single women should take particular care – it is unusual for women to travel alone and those who do will find Indonesians concerned for their safety. There is a notion held by too many Indonesians that western women, by definition, are loose, so pestering males may be a problem. Be firm, but be polite. Older women travelling alone will not be faced with such problems and will be treated with great respect.

Beware of the confidence tricksters who are widespread in tourist areas. Sudden reports of unbeatable bargains or closing down sales are usual ploys.

The following areas of Indonesia saw disturbances during 1998, 1999 and 2000. Note, however, that these were localized, usually short-term, and almost never affected foreign visitors (bar journalists, that is): Jakarta and areas of East Java; West Kalimantan; Aceh in north Sumatra; Ambon, Tidore and Halmahera in Maluku (the Spice Islands); Ujung Pandang (Makassar) and Poso in Sulawesi; Mataram on Lombok; and East Timor and some areas of neighbouring West Timor. Bali also experienced some violence, but it was quickly contained. For latest information of conditions in Indonesia, see the **British Foreign & Commonwealth Office**'s travel advisory website (http://www.fco.gov.uk/travel/), and/or the **US State Department**'s equivalent site (http://travel.state.gov/travel_warnings.html). Note, however, that these tend to be written by diplomats based in capital or other major cities and tend to be rather generic in their advice.

Where to stay

Tourist and business centres usually have a good range of accommodation for all budgets. Bali, for example, has some of the finest hotels in the world – at a corresponding price – along with excellent middle and lower-range accommodation. However, visitors venturing off the beaten track may find hotels restricted to dingy 'Chinese' establishments and over-priced places catering for local businessmen and officials. The best run and most competitively priced budget accommodation is found in popular tourist spots – like Bali and Yogya. It is almost always worth bargaining in Chinese hotels, and in middle and upper grade establishments. This is particularly true for hotels in tourist destinations which attract a fair amount of local weekend business: the weekday room rate may be as much as 50% of the weekend rate. Cheaper places may not give discounts, although as a general rule it is worth negotiating. All hotels are required to display their room rates (for every category of room) on a *daftar harga*, or price list. This is invariably either in public view in the reception area or will be produced when you ask about room rates. Note that Indonesians prefer to be on the ground floor, so rooms on higher floors are usually cheaper.

Terminology can be confusing: a *losmen* is a lower price range hotel; in parts of Sumatra

See individual towns' 'Sleeping' sections Hotels are marked on maps with a symbol: ■

Hotel price guide

L over US$100. Luxury: hotels in this bracket number a handful and are to be found only in Jakarta and Bali. All facilities, combined with sumptuous rooms and excellent service.
AL US$50-100. International class: only to be found in a few cities and tourist destinations. They should provide the entire range of business services (fax, translation, seminar rooms etc), sports facilities (gym, swimming pool etc), Asian and Western restaurants, bars, and discotheques.
A US$25-50. First class: will usually offer good business, sports and recreational facilities, with a range of restaurants and bars.
B 75,000-150,000Rp. Tourist class: in tourist destinations, these will probably have a swimming pool and all rooms will have air-conditioning and an attached bathroom. Other services include one or more restaurants and 24-hours coffee shop/room service. Most will have televisions in the rooms.
C 50,000-75,000Rp. Economy: rooms should be air-conditioned and have attached bathrooms with hot water. A restaurant and room service will probably be available, but little else.
D 30,000-50,000Rp. Budget: rooms are unlikely to be air-conditioned, although they should have an attached bathroom or mandi. Toilets may be either Western-style or of the 'squat' Asian variety, depending on whether the town is on the tourist route. Toilet paper may not be provided. Many in this price range, out of tourist areas, are 'Chinese' hotels. Bed linen and towels are usually provided, and there may be a restaurant.
E 15,000-30,000Rp. Guesthouse: fan-cooled rooms, often with shared mandi and Asian 'squat' toilet. Toilet paper and towels are unlikely to be provided, although bed linen will be. Guesthouses on the tourist route have better facilities and are sometimes excellent sources of information, offering cheap tours and services such as bicycle and motorcycle hire. Places in this category vary a great deal, and can change very rapidly. Other travellers are the best source of up-to-the-minute reviews.
F under 15,000Rp. Guesthouse: fan-cooled rooms, shared mandi and 'squat' toilet. Rooms can be tiny, dark and dingy, with wafer-thin walls. There are also some real bargains in this bracket. Standards change very fast and other travellers are the best source of information. Homestays are usually also in our **E-F** categories. The difference between a guesthouse (or losmen) and a homestay is that in the latter guests live within the family house, while in the former they sleep separately.
NB More expensive hotels often quote their room rates in US$. Depending on the exchange rate, there may be a currency overlap between hotel categories L, AL and A (all quoted here in US$) and B and below (quoted in rupiah).

and in some other areas, losmen are known as *penginapan*; a *wisma* is a guesthouse, but these can range in price from cheap to moderately expensive; finally, a *hotel* is a hotel, but can range from the cheap and squalid up to a Hilton. **NB** The government has introduced a ruling requiring all tourist accommodation to have Indonesian names rather than use Western words. Thus the *City Guesthouse* might be renamed *Wisma Kota*; the *Samudra Beach* would become the *Pantai Samudra*. It seems that this edict is not being assiduously enforced and many hotels are ignoring it – or at least adopting it in a rather half-baked way. Nonetheless, be prepared for hotel name changes and also some variation on name use.

There is a 'star' system in use in Indonesia and it can give a rough guide to the price of the establishment (although it is a rating of facilities not of quality). The '*melati*' (flower) system is for cheaper hotels; while the '*bintang*' (star) system is for higher rated, and therefore more expensive, hotels. As in most countries, five star (luxury) is top of the range.

Hotels Hotels are listed under eight categories, according to the *average* price of a double/twin room for one night. It should be noted that many hotels will have a range of rooms, some with air conditioning (a/c) and attached bathroom facilities, others with just a fan and shared facilities. Prices can therefore vary a great deal. The best rooms in any hotel are usually termed 'vip'. If a hotel entry lists 'some a/c', then these rooms are likely to be in the upper part of the range, perhaps even in the next category. Hotels in the middle and lower price categories often provide breakfast in the room rate. In the more out-of-the-way places or in hotels geared to

Indonesians, this is usually fried rice or something similar. White bread, margarine and chocolate vermicelli is also strangely popular as a breakfast pick-me-up. In the more expensive hotels, service charge (10%) and government tax (11%) are added onto the bill; they are usually excluded from the quoted room rate. More expensive hotels tend to quote their prices in US$. (This was not much of an issue when the rupiah/US$ exchange rate was stable, but in mid-1997 the rupiah weakened dramatically. While hotels that priced their rooms in rupiahs became significantly 'cheaper' for many foreign visitors, those that quoted their rates in US$ did not.) **NB** During the off-season, hotels in tourist destinations may halve their room rates, so it is always worthwhile bargaining or asking whether there is a 'special' price.

Peculiarities of Indonesian hotels include the tendency to build rooms without windows and, more appealingly, to design middle and lower range hotels around a courtyard.

Baths and showers are not a feature of many cheaper losmen. Instead a **mandi** – a water tank and ladle – is used to wash. The tub is not climbed into; water is ladled from the tub and splashed over the head. Some bathrooms will also have a shower attachment, occasionally with hot water although more often not. The traditional Asian toilet is of the squat variety. (Toilets are euphemistically called *kamar kecil* – the universal 'small room' – or *way say*, as in the initials 'WC'.) These can take some time to become accustomed to and many visitors never become entirely happy with the system, swaying precariously over the hole as their thigh muscles strain. Water scooped from a mandi, or a large water jar, is used to 'flush' the bowl. In popular tourist destinations, and also in larger more cosmopolitan towns (even if they are not favoured tourist destinations), western toilets are beginning to replace the Asian variety. They are seen, in some quarters, as a sign of progress. Toilet paper is not traditionally used; the faithful left hand and water suffice. Some travellers take their own supply of toilet paper – although be aware that not all systems can deal with toilet paper. The division between 'western' and 'Asian' is not clear cut, and it is not uncommon to find bathrooms which mix 'n' match according to whim: a hot water shower, cold water mandi and Asian loo, for example. In cheaper accommodation you are expected to bring your own towels, soap and toilet paper, and the bed may consist only of a bottom sheet and pillow with no top sheet (so it is useful to bring your own if you want to keep the mosquitoes at bay).

Bathing & toilets

Camping is not common in Indonesia and even in national parks camping facilities are poor and limited. Indonesians find it strange that anyone should want to camp out when it is possible to stay in a hotel.

Camping

Getting around

Air

This is the most convenient and comfortable way to travel around Indonesia. **Garuda** and **Merpati**, now sister-companies, service all the main provincial cities. *Merpati* tends to operate the short-hop services to smaller towns and cities, particularly in Eastern Indonesia.

The other main domestic airlines are **Bouraq**, **Mandala** and **Sempati**. Note that the *Sempati* was declared bankrupt in 1999, but its routes are likely to be taken over by a new airline, **Indonesian Airlines**). *Bouraq's* network is concentrated in Kalimantan and Eastern Indonesia (Maluku, Sulawesi and Nusa Tenggara); *Sempati's* (or rather, its possible successor) in Kalimantan, Sumatra, Java and Sulawesi; while *Mandala* has the most restricted network, serving only a handful of cities in Java, Sumatra, Sulawesi and Maluku. Smallest of all are **DAS**, **SMAC** and **Deraya**, which tend to service smaller towns in the Outer Islands, especially Kalimantan and Sumatra. On some routes, *Bouraq*, *Mandala* and *Sempati* offer fares that are marginally cheaper than *Garuda/Merpati*, but there is very little in it. There are also non-commercial air services such as the **Missionary Aviation Fellowship** (MAF) and **Associated Missions Aviation** (AMA), which offer non-scheduled flights in Irian Jaya, Kalimantan and Sulawesi, to more out of the way spots. **NB** These are not commercial airlines and can refuse passage. See page 975 for a listing of air fares.

The economic crisis threw Indonesia's airline industry into turmoil. Many routes were cut or the frequency of flights was reduced as economic hardship reduced the numbers of people flying. *Sempati*, with massive debts that it was unable to service, was bankrupted. However, a number of new airlines were on the verge of beginning operations as Indonesia's increasingly deregulated industry (another product of the economic crisis) enticed new investors into the fray. During 2000, **Mentari Airlines** began operations in Eastern Indonesia (Nusa Tenggara and Maluku); **Indonesian Airlines** is due to take over many of *Sempati's* routes (concentrated in Kalimantan, Sumatra, Java and Sulawesi), while **Pelita Airlines**, which has been operating charter services for some years (it is owned by *Petamina*, the national oil company), is also due to begin commercial, scheduled operations.

Safety & maintenance standards are reasonable, although Indonesian airlines do have their share of accidents

By international standards, flights in Indonesia are cheap (see page 975 for a table of fares). It is also considerably cheaper buying tickets in Indonesia than it is purchasing them abroad. Offices in larger towns will usually accept credit card payment, although smaller branch offices in out-of-the-way places will often only take cash payment. Some airlines give student reductions; others don't. It is worth carrying an international student card (ISIC) and producing it when booking a ticket. Note that there can be difficulties booking seats on some legs (particularly in Nusa Tenggara and Maluku). During holiday periods (for example, the Islamic festival Lebaran when the entire nation seems to be on the move, and the traditional holiday period of August), flights are booked up some time ahead. That said, 'no shows' are many and it is always worth going to the airport even if the plane is said to be 'full'. It is essential to reconfirm tickets.

Garuda/Merpati offers a **Visit Indonesia Decade Pass**. The basic pass is for three 'stretches' (legs) and costs US$300 (plus 10% VAT). Each additional stretch costs a further US$100, up to a maximum of seven. The pass is valid for 60 days, with a minimum stay of five days, and can be used on all *Garuda/Merpati* routes except 'pioneer' services (perintis). These passes are obtainable by non-Indonesian citizens outside Indonesia in Japan, Hong Kong, Australia, New Zealand, Europe and the US and, are non-refundable. They are also available in Indonesia, but whether you are purchasing in or out of the country, you must possess an incoming *Garuda International* or *British Airways* ticket. Note that conditions on air passes periodically change and should be checked carefully before booking.

Train

See page 977 for a train timetable & a basic fare listing

Passenger train services are limited to Java and certain areas of Sumatra, including a route in Lampung and South Sumatra, and in North Sumatra. Trains are usually slow and often delayed. Single track connects many major cities. First class is a/c with a dining car. There are two main trunk routes on Java: Jakarta-Cirebon-Semarang-Surabaya and Jakarta-Bandung-Yogyakarta-Surakarta (Solo)-Surabaya. The principal services are identified by name, for example, the **Bima** is the a/c night-express from Jakarta via Yogya and Solo, to Surabaya (16 hours); the **Mutiara Utara** is the northern route train to Surabaya via Semarang; the **Senja Utama Solo** is the express train to Yogya and Solo; while the **Senja Utama Semarang** is the express train to Cirebon and Semarang. There are three classes of train: **Executive** is first class, which has a/c coaches, reclining seats and breakfast included in the fare. **Business** (*bisnis*) has fan-cooled coaches and pillows provided; and **Economy**, with rather run down, well-used coaches, broken fans and windows which may or may not open – this class is subject to overcrowding. All three classes of seats can be booked. Reservations should be made well in advance; it is often easier through a travel agent in the town where you are staying.

Bus

For details on road transport & conditions in a specific area, see the relevant regional introduction

Road transport in Indonesia has improved greatly in recent years, and main roads on most of the islands are generally in reasonably good condition. The single major exception is Irian Jaya, and to a lesser extent Kalimantan, where air transport is the only sensible way to get around. It should be noted that in many areas in Indonesia during the rainy season and after severe storms, even main roads may be impassable.

For selected official bus prices see page 980

Most Indonesians, as well as many visitors, get around by bus. The network is vast – there are buses from Bali to Banda Aceh, a distance of almost 4,300 km – and although it is not always quick or comfortable, buses are the cheapest way to travel. Buses – and particularly non-a/c buses – are often overfilled and seats are designed for Indonesian, rather than western bodies. A/c buses are generally less cramped. 'VIP' (pronounced as it is spelt – 'vip') buses are more comfortable still. There are also *bis pariwisata* – tourist buses – which have more space and may stop-off at *objek wisata* (tourist sights) en route. There are a range of bus alternatives:

bis ekonomi – speaks for itself really; the bottom rung of the bus ladder. Slow, uncomfortable, often full, but dirt cheap. A great way to meet Indonesians and to interface with farm animals, but probably not recommended for long journeys.

bis patas – express buses, non-a/c. Marginally more comfortable than *ekonomi*, and also faster.

bis malam – (over)night buses. Usually a/c (and cold), probably the fastest buses, tend to arrive at their destinations very early in the morning.

bis pariwisata – tourist buses. More leg room, priced slightly cheaper than VIP buses but not as comfortable. Often minibuses rather than large coaches. Some stop off at tourist sights en route.

bis VIP – 'luxury' buses; a/c, more leg room, better service, usually driven with a little more care and attention.

The seats at the front of buses are the most comfortable, but also the most dangerous (crash-wise). In May 1993, it was reported that the police had asked bus drivers to pray before setting off. Some people recommend booking two seats for comfort, although on non-a/c buses it is difficult to lounge over two seats free from guilt when the vehicle is packed. Roads are often windy and rough, and buses are badly sprung (or totally un-sprung). Despite harrowingly fast speeds at times, do not expect to average much more than 40 km per hour (particularly on Flores and Sulawesi) except on the best highways. Overnight buses (*bis malam*) are usually faster and recommended for longer journeys. However, a/c *bis malam* can be very cold and a sarong or blanket is useful. Their other disadvantages are that the scenery passes in the darkness and they invariably arrive at anti-social, inconvenient times of day (or night). **NB** Watch out for pickpockets.

The key word when travelling by bus is 'patience'. On non-a/c buses, be prepared for a tedious 'trawl' around town (for up to an hour) collecting passengers, until the bus is full to overflowing. Buses stop regularly for refreshments at dubious looking roadside restaurants, hawkers cram the aisle, selling hot sate, fruit, sweets, sunglasses, magazines, even pornographic playing cards. Loud music and violent videos keep the passengers either in heaven or purgatory. As most Indonesians have still to be convinced that smoking is bad for your health ("that's only true with western cigarettes, *kreteks* [Indonesian clove cigarettes] are good for you") or that some people might find it distasteful, buses – and especially a/c buses – are also often fogged with cigarette smoke. The buses themselves are usually plastered with perplexing names such as 'No Problem – Banana on the Road', 'Sweet Memory', 'No Time for Love', 'Pash Boy's' and 'Khasoggi'. But, despite the drawbacks, buses are not only the cheapest and often the only way to get about, they are also one of the best ways to see the scenery and to meet Indonesians.

In many towns, bus companies have their offices at the bus terminal. However, this is not always true, and some long-distance buses may depart directly from a bus company's office located in another part of town to the terminal. Larger towns may also have several bus terminals, serving different points of the compass. These are often out of town, with regular bemos linking the various terminals with one another and with the town centre. In smaller towns, buses will sometimes pick up passengers from outside their losmen or hotel (although occasionally passengers may be asked for a surcharge). They may also drop passengers outside a losmen at the other end of the journey.

Tickets can be obtained from bus company offices or through travel agents; shop around for the best fare – bargaining is possible. It is sensible to book a day or so ahead for longer journeys. During Ramadan and at Lebaran, all forms of public transport are packed. Estimated journey times are often wildly inaccurate. Although it is possible to book 'through' tickets, involving a change of vehicle in some town en route to your destination, this is not always the quickest, and almost certainly not the cheapest way to get from A to B. It can involve a long wait for a connecting bus and because the ticket ties you to one company (or its associated company), it is not possible to switch between firms. Connecting tickets, strangely, also tend to work out more expensive than buying two single tickets.

NB Bus fares vary a great deal depending on level of service (a/c, reclining seats, express etc), the size of the vehicle (coach or minibus), the number of seats, the time of departure, the age of the vehicle, and between bus companies (which is related to their reputation for safety and timeliness).

In the main tourist areas on Java, Bali and Lombok, look out for **shuttle buses**. These operate almost exclusively for the benefit of foreigners connecting the most popular destinations, with a fixed daily timetable. They will pick up and drop off passengers at their hotels and take a very great deal of the hassle out of ground travel, though you miss much of the local colour.

Bicycling

We have had a number of letters from people who have bicycled through various parts of Indonesia. The advice below is collated from their comments, and is meant to provide a general guideline for those intending to travel by bicycle. There may be areas, however, where the advice does not hold true. (Some of the letters we have received even disagree on some points.)

Bike type Touring, hybrid or mountain bikes are fine for most roads and tracks in Indonesia – take an ordinary machine; nothing fancy.

Spares Readily available for most machines, and even small towns have bicycle repair shops where it is often possible to borrow larger tools such as vices. Mountain bikes have made a big impact in the country, so accessories for these are also widely available – although their quality might not be up to much. What is less common are components made of unusual materials – titanium and composites, for example. It is best to use common accessories. It may also be worthwhile forging a good relationship with a bike shop back home, just in case a spare is not available – and then it can be couriered out. It is better to have a 'free' rear wheel, as opposed to a free hub and cassette, as the latter are generally not available, while free rear wheels are widely sold.

Attitudes to bicyclists The view seems to be that it depends on the area. In Nusa Tenggara people are generally very welcoming and warm. In Bali bicyclists tend to be ignored. Officials, though, may view independent cyclists with some suspicion. Cars and buses often travel on the hard shoulder, and few expect to give way to a bicycle. Be very wary, especially on main roads.

Road conditions The maps in this guide are not sufficiently detailed for bicycling, and a good colour map is useful in determining contours and altitude, as well as showing minor roads.

Taking bikes on buses, ferries and taxis Expect to pay a surcharge of about a third to a half of the cost of the ticket for buses and ferries. They are used to taking bicycles (although the more expensive a/c tour buses may prove reluctant). Most taxi drivers are not so keen on carrying bicycles – be ready to throw it in the boot and have bungee cords close at hand.

Bicycles on airlines Many international airlines take bicycles free-of-charge, provided they are not boxed. Take the peddles off and deflate the tyres. Domestic airlines sometimes charge, although there does not seem to be a hard-and-fast rule.

In general Avoid major roads, avoid major towns, avoid Java. (Such is the traffic on Java that even on small roads it can be worryingly lethal. The island is also very mountainous.)

Useful equipment Pollution mask if travelling to large cities; basic toolkit – although there always seems to be help near at hand, and local workshops seem to be able to improvise a solution to just about any problem – including a puncture repair kit, spare tubes, spare tyre, pump; good map of the area; bungee cords; first aid kit; water filter.

Driving in Indonesia

Renting a self-drive car in Indonesia has several advantages: it is a flexible, relatively quick, convenient and comfortable means of travel, and is a good way of experiencing the countryside and getting to out-of-the-way spots. But there are several dangers worth highlighting. As in many other Southeast Asian countries, 'might is right' – smaller vehicles give way to larger ones. A driver flashing his headlights normally means 'don't mess with me'. Although Indonesians are a very courteous people, this does not apply when in a car. Traffic does not always remain in the allotted lanes – it is best to adopt a strategy of follow-the-leader and go with the flow. Cutting in is an accepted way of changing lanes. After driving in Indonesia, many people leave firmly believing that the guiding principle adhered to by most road users is that 'Time is money and lives are cheap'.

If involved in an accident, it is best to go to the nearest police station to report the incident, rather than waiting at the scene. Signposting is generally poor, so be sure to get a good map. Often the best way to find the names of roads is to look at signs on shops, mosques, schools, hospitals, and so on. Many towns have complicated one-way systems, which take a bit of negotiating. Every town has its army of semi-official traffic wardens – often dressed in orange jumpsuits – waiting with whistle poised to usher motorists into a parking spot. All 'parkir' must be paid for. Petrol is cheap and Pertamina stations are found on all main highways.

Unnecessary equipment A tent is generally not needed. Every small town will have a guesthouse of some description. Nor is it worth taking a stove, cooking utensils, sleeping bag, food ... it is almost always possible to get food and a place to sleep – and cheaply, too. The equipment is simply a burden. The exceptions to this are the really back-of-beyond areas of Indonesia. In addition, Kalimantan seems to be well provided with camping grounds, as are Sabah, Sarawak and Peninsular Malaysia. A 'D' lock is not really necessary – they are hefty and a simple cable lock will suffice. Many bicyclists take their machines into their rooms at night.

Car hire

Cars can be hired for self-drive (see box) or with a driver. Chauffeur-driven vehicles are available by the hour or by the day, and cost about 15,000Rp per hour for use within a city, rather more if travelling out of town. For an out-of-town trip expect to pay about 200,000Rp (you would also be expected to buy the driver his lunch, drinks and such like). A cheaper alternative is to simply charter a bemo for the day.

See individual town transport sections for listings

Generally, self-drive cars are only available at the more popular tourist destinations (for example, Bali and Lombok) and in the bigger cities (for example, Jakarta, Medan, Yogya and Surabaya); expect to pay about US$40-50 per day depending on the company, and the condition and type of vehicle. In Bali and Lombok, there are numerous small operations that offer cars and jeeps for hire, and prices in Bali and Lombok are probably the lowest of all. For car rental offices, see the appropriate town entry. International groups like *Avis* and *Hertz* operate in many of the large towns.

Other local transport

Small three-wheeled motor scooters similar to the Thai *tuk-tuk*. They are probably the cheapest form of 'taxi' after the becak, but are only available in big cities – in Jakarta, they are orange and usually rather scruffy.

Bajaj

Becaks or bicycle rickshaws are one of the cheapest, and most important, forms of short-distance transport in Indonesia. Literally hundreds of thousands of poor people make a living driving becaks. However, they are now illegal in central Jakarta and often officially barred from main thoroughfares in other large cities. They are a good – and sedate – way to explore the backstreets and alleys of a city, and can be chartered by the hour or for a particular journey. Bargain hard and agree a fare before boarding.

Becaks

Bemos These are small buses or adapted pick-ups which operate fixed routes. The name originates from 'motorized becak' (*becak motor*). They carry four to six passengers and are found in Jakarta, Bandung, Semarang, Surabaya and Surakarta (Solo). The bemo is gradually being replaced by the larger oplet (see below). They usually run fixed routes for fixed fares (it varies between towns, but around 500Rp), but can also be chartered by the hour or day.

Bis kayu Trucks converted into buses with bench seats down each side. They are now only in use on minor roads on some islands in Nusa Tenggara, such as Flores. Slow and uncomfortable, they often ply unsealed roads.

Horsecarts These come in various shapes and sizes. *Dokars* are two-wheeled pony carts carrying two to three passengers, found, for example, in Padang, West Sumatra. In Lombok dokars are known as *cidomos*, while in Bima-Raba (Sumbawa) they are proudly named *Ben Hurs*. *Andongs* are larger four-wheeled horse-drawn wagons, carrying up to six people. These are found mainly in Yogya, Surakarta and a different version in Bogor. Horse-drawn transport is still very common in the countryside, and 'stands' of carts can be seen arrayed at most markets.

Inter-city taxis/share taxis Share taxis make particular sense for a party of four or five. Inter-city 'share taxis' are more expensive than buses, but are usually a quicker and cheaper alternative to going by air or private taxi. They are not available in all towns and only tend to run the busier routes, like Jakarta to Bandung. They depart when all five seats are taken.

Motorbike hire Available at many beach resorts and increasingly in other towns. Rates per day vary according to size and condition of the machine, but range from 25,000Rp to 50,000Rp. It is illegal to ride without a helmet, although this can just be a construction worker's hard hat. Many machines are poorly maintained: check brakes and lights before paying. See the pointers on driving in Indonesia in the car hire section above, and in the box. The most likely place to find bikes for hire is from guesthouses and losmen geared to foreign tourists.

Ojeks These are motorcycle taxis – a form of transport which is becoming increasingly popular. Ojek riders, often wearing coloured jackets, congregate at junctions, taking passengers pillion to their destination. Agree a price before boarding and bargain hard.

Oplets Larger versions of bemos carrying 10-12 passengers. They have a bewildering number of other names – *Daihatsu* in Semarang, *Angkuta* in Solo, *Microlets* in Malang and Jakarta, while in rural areas they tend to be called *Colts*. In larger cities, bemos/colts often follow fixed routes. They are sometimes colour coded, sometimes numbered, sometimes have their destinations marked on the front – and sometimes all three. For intra-city trips there is usually a fixed fare – it varies between towns, but around 500Rp – although it is worth asking one of your fellow passengers what the *harga biasa* (normal price) is, or watch what is being handed to the driver or his sidekick by fellow passengers. In the countryside, routes can vary and so do fares; be prepared to bargain. Oplets can also be chartered by the hour or day (bargain hard).

Taxis Taxis are metered in the major cities. Unmetered taxis can be shared for longer journeys. **NB** Drivers cannot usually change large bills. All registered taxis, minibuses and rental cars have yellow number plates; black number plates are for private vehicles, and red are for government-owned vehicles. Pirate taxis (with black number plates) tend to operate at airports, supermarkets and in city centres.

Bicycles In some of the more popular tourist destinations, guesthouses and some tour companies hire out bicycles. These vary a great deal in quality – check the breaks before you set off! See above for some general pointers of bicycling in Indonesia. Expect to pay about 20,000Rp per day for a locally or Chinese-built mountain bike.

Sea

The national shipping company is **PELNI**, standing for Pelayaran Nasional Indonesia. Its head office is at Jl Gajah Mada 14, Jakarta, T6334342, F3854130. For ticket offices, see relevant town entries. Note that many travel agents also sell *Pelni* tickets and, although they levy a small surcharge, may be far more convenient. *Pelni* operates an expanding fleet of modern passenger ships which ply fortnightly circuits throughout the archipelago (see timetables). The ships are well run and well maintained, have an excellent safety record, and are a comfortable and leisurely way to travel. Each accommodates 500-2,250 passengers in five classes, has central a/c, a bar, restaurant and cafetería. In 1999 there were 21 ships in the Pelni fleet, with one more vessel due to join in 2000.

First class cabins have attached bathrooms and TV sets. Classes I-IV are single sex – unless a group takes the whole cabin. Class II has four bunks per cabin, Class III six bunks, and Class IV eight bunks. Fares include all meals (no matter what class), and classes I-IV are cabin classes, while class V is 'deck' class (in fact, in a large a/c room where mattresses can be rented for 2,500Rp). Note that even first class cabins are 'inside', ie they have no portholes. All classes tend to be chilly so don't get caught with nothing more than a pair of shorts and a T-shirt. It may be possible to leave bags at the ship's information desk. Booking ahead (maximum seven days) is advisable, although in smaller ports of call it may only be possible to make reservations four days in advance. Get hold of an up-to-date *Pelni* timetable when you arrive. Even with this to hand, it is advisable, when planning a trip, to check in a big *Pelni* office that departure dates are the same as given on the timetable. Often the smaller agents only work on the basis of the timetable, which may not necessarily be accurate. When queueing for tickets, it is sometimes worth following the locals' example and pushing your way to the front, or at least actively defending your position in the queue; this may ensure that you actually get a berth and a mattress. Having said that, it sometimes can seem like a free-for-all once you are on board and you will need to grab the first cabin you can find.

In addition to these ships, *Pelni* also operates a so-called 'pioneer' service – *Pelayaran Perintis* – serving smaller, more out-of-the-way ports. *Perintis* vessels are important means of travel in Maluku, for example. These ships have no cabins but take passengers 'deck' class. Like their more illustrious sister vessels, they are generally well run and safe, if not always comfortable. Finally, there are the mixed cargo boats and ships which go just about everywhere. Passage can be secured just by visiting the port and asking around. **NB** Safety equipment may not be up to standard, and level of comfort is minimal.

Boat
See map & table for Pelni ports & timetables, pages 982 & 987

Keeping in touch

Communications

Email has caught on fast in Indonesia, and any town of any size has its cyber café. This is especially true of tourist destinations. To remain in email contact with people back home while travelling, sign up for a free account with one of the email service providers such as:
Hotmail: http://www.hotmail.com
Yahoo: http://mail.yahoo.com
Rocketmail: http://www.rocketmail.com
NetAddress: http://www.netaddress.usa.net

You'll be asked for a name and password. As you travel you can download your emails at any of the growing number of cyber cafés.

Email & internet access
See individual town directories for local listings

The postal service is relatively reliable; though important mail should be registered. Every town and tourist centre has either a *kantor pos* (post office) or postal agent, where you can buy stamps, post letters and parcels; in many cases they also provide poste restante services. For poste restante, have your letters addressed using your surname first, underlined and in capitals if possible. (Otherwise you may find your letters filed under your Christian name.)

Postal services

Kantor pos keep official government hours : 0800-1400 Monday-Saturday. Postal agents open much longer hours, often until 2200 daily.

Faxes and telexes can be sent from major hotels and *Perumtel*, *Telekom* and *Wartel* offices, found in most major towns. These are often open 24 hours. Post and telex/fax offices are listed under 'Communications' in each town entry.

Telephone services Indonesia has a comprehensive telecommunications network, which links the islands throughout the country and boasts its own satellite (Indosat). Every town has its communication centres (*Warpostel*), where you can make local, interlocal (between other areas within Indonesia) and international calls and faxes. Most *Warpostels* open early in the morning and operate until around midnight. Interlocal calls are cheaper after 2100, so centres tend to be very busy then. International calls have a cheap rate between midnight and 0800, and all Saturday and Sunday. Calls are expensive. There is a wide network of card phones and coin phones (taking 50Rp and 100Rp coins) throughout Jakarta and other main towns and cities, in hotels, shopping centres and street corners. Telephone cards (*Kartu telepon*) are sold in *Warpostels*, supermarkets and a wide range of shops. Sold according to number of units at the rate of 82.5Rp per unit, so that a 100 unit card costs 8,250Rp. Cards come in the following units: 60, 100, 140, 280, 400 and 680.

International calls can be made from card phones and from *Perumtel*, *Telekom* and *Wartel* offices, which are often open 24 hours. Indosat is located at Jakarta Theatre, Jl Thamrin, Jakarta, just opposite McDonalds, 10 minutes' walk from Jl Jaksa (open 24 hours). Direct international dialling and collect calls can be made from here. **International enquiries**: 102. **Operator**: 101. **Local enquiries**: 108. **Long distance enquiries**: 106. **International country code**: 62. Local telephone codes are given in each entry under the heading 'Post and telecommunications'. All telephone numbers marked in the text with a prefix 'J' mean that they are Jakarta numbers.

Media

Newspapers English language newspapers are the *Indonesia Times*, *Jakarta Post* (which carries international news from Reuters reports and English football league reports, and is also published on Bali) and *Indonesia Observer/Sunday Observer*. With Indonesia's halting progress towards democratization, one of the outcomes is the emergence of a much more independent and combative press. Of the international newspapers available in Indonesia, the *Asian Wall Street Journal* and the *International Herald Tribune* can be purchased in Jakarta and some other major cities and tourist destinations; so too can the Singapore *Straits Times*. Among English language magazines, the most widely available are the *Economist*, *Time*, *Newsweek* and the Hong Kong-based *Far Eastern Economic Review*. The latter provides the most comprehensive regional coverage and is well-informed.

Radio *Radio Republik Indonesia* (RRI) broadcasts throughout the country. News and commentary in English is broadcast for about an hour a day. Shortwave radios will pick up Voice of America, the BBC World Service and Australian Broadcasting. See page 70 for BBC and VoA frequencies.

Television Indonesia has put satellites into geostationary orbit so that television pictures can be received anywhere in the archipelago. The vast 'parabolas' outside many houses, including shacks which may not even have piped water, testifies to the power of television and the priorities of many Indonesian households. Televisi Republik Indonesia (TVRI) is the government-run channel. There are also four private stations – although these rigorously toe the government line when it comes to reporting news. Hotels also usually receive satellite TV and if they have a significant foreign clientele they may well tune into English language channels. CNN, BBC, Star, Television Australia, Malaysian, Philippine and Thai television can all be received in Indonesia.

Food and drink

Food

Although Indonesia is made up of a bewildering array of ethnic groups dispersed over 5,000,000 sq km of land and sea, the main staple across the archipelago is rice. Today, alternatives such as corn, sweet potatoes and sago, which are grown primarily in the dry islands of the East, are regarded as 'poor man's food', and rice is the preferred staple.

Indonesians will eat rice – or *nasi* (milled, cooked rice) – at least three times a day. Breakfast often consists of left-over rice, stir-fried and served up as *nasi goreng*. Mid-morning snacks are often sticky rice cakes or *pisang goreng* (fried bananas). Rice is the staple for lunch, served up with two or three meat and vegetable dishes and followed by fresh fruit. The main meal is supper, which is served quite early and again consists of rice, this time accompanied by as many as five or six other dishes. *Sate/satay* (grilled skewers of meat), *soto* (a nourishing soup) or *bakmi* (noodles, a dish of Chinese origin) may be served first.

In many towns (particularly in Java), sate, soto or bakmi vendors roam the streets with carts containing charcoal braziers, ringing a bell or hitting a block (the noise will signify what he or she is selling), looking for customers in the early evenings. These carts are known as *kaki lima* – literally 'five legs'. There are two schools of thought as to the origins of the term. Most people maintain that they are named after the three 'legs' of the cart plus the two of the vendor. But *pedagang* (vendor) *kaki lima* (abbreviated to PK5 in newspaper reports) also refers to hawkers who peddle their wares from stalls and from baskets hung from shoulder poles. The second interpretation of the term maintains that *kaki lima* in fact refers to the pavement, which formerly used to have a width of 5 ft. This is a less obvious, and rather more attractive interpretation.

Larger foodstalls, where there is too much to cart around, tend to set up in the same place every evening in a central position in town. These *warungs*, as they are known, may be temporary structures or more permanent buildings, with simple tables and benches. In the larger cities, there may be an area of warungs, all under one roof. Often a particular street will become known as the best place to find particular dishes like *martabak* (savoury meat pancakes) or *gado gado* (vegetable salad served with peanut sauce). It is common to see some warungs being labelled *wartegs*. These are stalls selling dishes from Tegal, a town on Java's north coast – Warung Tegal = warteg. More formalized restaurants are known simply as *rumah makan*, literally 'eating houses', often shortened to just 'RM'. Another term for cheaper restaurants is 'Depot', which is often rather appropriate. A good place to look for cheap stall food is in and around the market or *pasar* (from the Arabic *bazaar*); night markets or *pasar malam* are usually better for eating than day markets.

Feast days, such as Lebaran marking the end of Ramadan, are a cause for great celebration and traditional dishes are served. *Lontong* or *ketupat* are made at this time (they are both versions of boiled rice – simmered in a small container or bag, so that as it cooks, the rice is compressed to make a solid block). This may be accompanied by *sambal goreng daging* (fried beef in a coconut sauce) in Java or *rendang* (curried beef) in Sumatra. *Nasi kuning* (yellow rice) is traditionally served at a *selamatan* (a Javanese celebration marking a birth, the collection of the rice harvest or the completion of a new house).

In addition to rice, there are a number of other common ingredients used across the country. Coconut milk, ginger, chilli peppers and peanuts are used nationwide, while dried salted fish and soybeans are important sources of protein. In coastal areas, fish and seafood tend to be more important than meat. As Indonesia is over 80% Muslim, pork is not widely eaten, although Chinese restaurants usually serve it, and in some areas, such as Bali, Christian Flores, around Lake Toba in Sumatra and the Toraja area of Sulawesi, it is much more in evidence.

Restaurant price guide

Expensive 50,000Rp+.
Hotel restaurants and exclusive restaurants.

Mid-range 20,000-50,000Rp. Restaurants in tourist class hotels and more expensive local restaurants.

Cheap 10,000-20,000Rp.
Coffee shops and basic restaurants.

Very cheap under 10,000Rp.
Generally a warung or roadside stall.

Popular Indonesian dishes

Bubur – rice porridge. Bubur hitam is black glutinous rice boiled with sugar, garnished with coconut milk and served warm.
Cap cai – mixed, stir-fried vegetables, with various additions – such as pork and squid – and served with rice (Chinese).
Gado-gado – steamed vegetable salad, hard-boiled egg, krupuk and tempe, served with a peanut sauce and sometimes rice.
Ketupat – compressed, boiled rice; usually served with satay.
Lumpia – spring rolls; fried egg pancake stuffed with chicken, shrimps and vegetables (Chinese).
Martabak – pancake, either sweet or savoury, the latter usually in Java when it is stuffed with mutton, eggs and onions; served crispy with a curry sauce.
Mie goreng – the same as nasi goreng, but the rice is replaced by noodles.
Nasi campur – a rice platter, similar to nasi rames; often cold, usually consisting of bean curd, chicken, beans and rice; campur means 'to mix'.
Nasi goreng – fried rice, served with shrimps, small pieces of meat, onion, garlic and cucumber.
Nasi gudeg – rice, chicken and jackfruit, cooked in coconut milk (Javanese).
Nasi kuning – yellow rice, usually a festival dish, cooked with turmeric and coconut milk; sometimes served with beef.
Nasi lemak – rice cooked with coconut milk and garnished with ikan bilis (fried anchovies), egg and cucumber.
Nasi liwet – rice and chicken cooked in coconut milk (Javanese).
Nasi rames – rice with meat and vegetables on top, accompanied by serundeng and krupuk (Padang).
Nasi uduk – rice cooked in coconut milk with spices.
Opor ayam – chicken cooked in a mild creamy coconut sauce.
Pisang goreng – banana fritters; coated in batter and deep fried.
Rendang – hot, dry beef curry (Padang) cooked in coriander, laos powder and tumeric; a W Sumatra speciality.
Rijstaffel – literally, 'rice table', rice served with as many as 16 other dishes (Dutch-Indonesian).
Sate – perhaps the Malay world's most famous dish: slivers of skewered meat, marinated, cooked over a charcoal fire and served with a peanut sauce and lontong (compressed rice).
Sayur lodeh – mixed vegetables in coconut milk (Javanese).
Serabi – scotch pancakes, made from rice flour, santen (coconut milk) and sugar (Javanese-Cirebon).
Soto – a soup of clear chicken stock, flavoured with lemon grass, to which is added glass noodles, hard-boiled eggs, chopped shallots, beansprouts, sambal and/or shredded chicken.

Regional cuisines

Although Indonesia is becoming more homogeneous as Javanese culture spreads to the Outer Islands, there are still distinctive regional cuisines. The food of **Java** itself embraces a number of regional forms, of which the most distinctive is **Sundanese**. *Lalap*, a Sundanese dish, consists of raw vegetables and is said to be the only Indonesian dish where vegetables are eaten uncooked. Characteristic ingredients of Javanese dishes are soybeans, beef, chicken and vegetables; characteristic flavours are an interplay of sweetness and spiciness. Probably the most famous regional cuisine, however, is **Padang** or **Minang** food, which has its origins in West Sumatra province. Padang food has 'colonized' the rest of the country and there are Padang restaurants in every town, no matter how small. Dishes tend to be hot and spicy (see page 536), using quantities of chilli and turmeric, and include *rendang* (dry beef curry), *kalo ayam* (creamy chicken curry) and *dendeng balado* (fried seasoned sun-dried meat with a spicy coating). In **Eastern Indonesia**, seafood and fish are important elements in the diet, and fish grilled over an open brazier (*ikan panggang* or *ikan bakar*) and served with spices and rice is a delicious, common dish. The **Toraja** of Sulawesi eat large amounts of pork, and specialities include black rice (*nasi hitam*) and fish or chicken cooked in bamboo (*piong*). There are large numbers of Chinese people scattered across the archipelago and, like other countries of the region, **Chinese** restaurants are widespread.

Drink

Water must be boiled before it is safe to drink. If boiling it yourself be aware that some organisms (such as the one which causes amoebic dysentry) can survive up to five minutes of boiling, so anything less could be dangerous. Hotels and most restaurants, as a matter of course, should boil the water they offer customers. Ask for *air minum*, literally 'drinking water', *air putih* or *air mendidih* (boiled water). You may have to try both *air putih* and *air mendidih* to get what you want; in some places, if you ask for *air mendidih* you will get boiling hot water rather than the previously boiled water. On Bali, *air putih* usually means cold but previously boiled water. Many restaurants provide a big jug of boiled water on each table. But in cheaper establishments it is probably best to play safe and ask for bottled water.

Over the last few years, '**mineral water**' – of which the most famous is *Aqua* ('aqua' has become the generic word for mineral water) – has become increasingly popular. It is now available from Aceh to Irian Jaya, in all but the smallest and most remote towns. There have been some reports of empty mineral water bottles being refilled with tap water: check the seal before accepting a bottle. Bottled water is cheap: in 1999 a small bottle cost around 1,200Rp.

Western **bottled and canned drinks** like *Sprite*, *Coca-Cola*, *7-Up* and *Fanta* are widely available in Indonesia and are comparatively cheap. Alternatively, most restaurants will serve *air jeruk* – citrus **fruit juices** – with or without ice (*es*). The **milk of a fresh coconut** is a good thirst quencher and a good source of potassium and glucose. Fresh fruit juices vary greatly in quality; some are little more than water, sugar and ice. Ice in many places is fine, but in cheaper restaurants and away from tourist areas many people recommend taking drinks without ice. Javanese, Sumatran, Sulawesi or Timorese **coffee** (*kopi*), fresh and strong, is an excellent morning pick-you-up. It is usually served sweet (*kopi manis*) and black; if you want to have it without sugar, ask for it *tidak pakai gula*. The same goes for other drinks habitually served with mountains of sugar (like fruit juices). **Milk** (*susu*) is available in tourist areas and large towns, but it may be sweetened condensed milk. **Tea** (*teh*), usually weak, is obtainable almost everywhere. Hot ginger tea is a refreshing alternative.

Although Indonesia is a predominantly Muslim country, alcoholic drinks are widely available. The two most popular **beers** – light lagers – are the locally brewed *Anker* and *Bintang* brands. Imported **spirits** like whisky and gin are usually only sold in the more expensive restaurants and hotels. They are comparatively expensive – about 8-10,000Rp for a large bottle in a restaurant. There are, however, a number of local brews including *brem* (rice wine), *arak* (rice whisky) and *tuak* (palm wine).

Tipping & tax in restaurants

Expect to pay a 21% tax and service charge in the more expensive restaurants, particularly in tourist areas of Bali and Lombok. Even the cheaper restaurants serving foreigners may add 10% to the bill.

Shopping

Indonesia offers a wealth of distinctive handicrafts and other products. Best buys include textiles (batik and ikat), silverwork, woodcarving, puppets, paintings and ceramics. Bali has the greatest choice of handicrafts. It is not necessarily the case that you will find the best buys in the area where a particular product is made; the larger cities, especially Jakarta, sell a wide range of handicrafts and antiques from across the archipelago at competitive prices.

Tips on buying

Early morning sales may well be cheaper, as salespeople often believe the first sale augers well for the rest of the day. **Bargaining**: except in the larger fixed price stores, bargaining (with good humour) is expected; start bargaining at 50-60% lower than the asking price. Do not expect to achieve instant results; if you walk away from the shop, you will almost certainly be followed, with a lower offer. If the salesperson agrees to your price, you should really feel obliged to purchase – it is considered very ill mannered to agree on a price and then not buy the article.

Antiques There are some good antique shops in Jakarta and a handful of other regional centres, but bargains usually need to be 'rooted out' by visiting little out-of-the-way shops. Antiques include Dutch memorabilia and Chinese ceramics (Indonesia was on the trade route between China and India), as well as local products like Javanese carvings and Sulawesi metalwork. **NB** There are also a huge number of fakes on the market – you only have to walk down Jl Surabaya (Jakarta's most popular flea market) to see men openly 'distressing' work, then to be sold as 150-year-old heirlooms.

Batik Centres of batik-making are focused on Java. Yogyakarta and Solo (Surakarta) probably offer the widest choice, although Cirebon and Pekalongan (both on the north coast) offer their own distinctive styles. There is also a good range of batik on sale in Jakarta. The traditional hand-drawn batiks (*batik tulis*) are naturally more expensive than the modern printed batiks. For more information on batik, see page 307.

Clothing Very reasonably priced western-style clothes can be found in most of the bigger cities. Large department stores and markets are the best places to browse. Children's clothes are also very good value (although dyes may run). Bali offers the best fashion clothing.

Ikat This dyed and woven cloth is found on the islands of Bali, Lombok and Nusa Tenggara (Sumba, Flores, Timor), although it is not cheap and is sometimes of rather dubious quality. For more information, see page 443.

Jewellery Gems mined in Indonesia include diamonds and black opals from Kalimantan and pearls from Maluku. Contemporary-style jewellery is made in Bali (although some is of poor quality). There are several good jewellery shops in Jakarta, mostly found in five-star hotels. West Sumatra and Aceh are both known for their silverwork.

Metalwork The traditional Malay sword, the *kris* is the most popular buy. Both antique and modern examples are available. For more information, see page 90.

Painting Yogyakarta is a centre of painting, with several workshops of artists who have achieved worldwide acclaim. Work includes oil and batik painting. Ubud (Bali) has, since the 1930s, been a centre for local artists and is a good place to buy tropical-style paintings (see page 443).

Wayang puppets Wayang is a Javanese and Balinese art form and puppets are most widely available on these two islands, particularly in Yogyakarta and Jakarta. For more information, see page 306.

Weaving Baskets of all shapes and sizes are made for practical, everyday use, out of rattan, bamboo, sisal, and nipah and lontar palm. The intricate baskets of Lombok are particularly attractive.

Woodcarving This ranges from the clearly ersatz and tourist oriented (Bali), to fine classical pieces (Java), to 'primitive' (Irian Jaya). The greatest concentration of woodcarvers work in Bali, producing skilful modern designs as well as more traditional pieces.

Holidays and festivals

National holidays and other festivals

See below for a separate listing of Muslim holidays and festivals. **NB** These holidays are subject to change.

January **Tahun Baru**, New Year's Day (1st: public holiday). **New Year's Eve** is celebrated with street carnivals, shows, fireworks and all-night festivities. In Christian areas, festivities are more exuberant, with people visiting each other on New Year's Day and attending church services.

Imlek, Chinese New Year (movable, 24-25 January 2001, 12-14 February 2002). It is not an official holiday, but many Chinese shops and businesses close for at least two days. Within the Chinese community, younger people visit their relatives, children are given *hong bao* (lucky money), new clothes are bought and any unfinished business is cleared up before the New Year. — **January/February**

Wafat Isa Al-Masih, Good Friday (movable: public holiday, 13 April 2001, 29 March 2002). **Nyepi** (movable: public holiday, 26 March 2001). **Balinese Saka New Year** (1995 = 1917). **Kartini Day** (21 April). A ceremony held by women to mark the birthday of Raden Ajeng Kartini, born in 1879 and proclaimed as a pioneer of women's emancipation. The festival is rather like mother's day, in that women are supposed to be pampered by their husbands and children, although it is women's organizations like the Dharma Wanita who get most excited. Women dress in national dress. — **March/April**

Waisak Day (movable: public holiday). Marks the birth and death of the historic Buddha; at Candi Mendut outside Yogyakarta, a procession of monks carrying flowers, candles, holy fire and images of the Buddha walk to Borobudur. **Kenaikan Isa Al-Masih** or Ascension Day (movable: public holiday). — **May**

Independence Day (17th: public holiday). This is the most important national holiday, celebrated with processions, dancing and other merry-making. Although it is officially on the 17th, festivities continue for a whole month, towns are decorated with bunting and parades cause delays to bus travel, there seems to be no way of knowing when each town will hold its parades. — **August**

Hari Pancasila (1st). This commemorates the Five Basic Principles of Pancasila (see page 944). **Armed Forces Day** (5th). The anniversary of the founding of the Indonesian Armed Forces, with military parades and demonstrations. — **October**

Christmas Day (25th: public holiday). Celebrated by Christians – the Bataks of Sumatra, the Toraja and Minahasans of Sulawesi and in some of the islands of Nusa Tenggara, and Irian Jaya. — **December**

Islamic holidays

NB Muslim festivals are lunar and move forward 10 or 11 days each year. Dates for the year 2001 are given here and those for 2002 noted at the end of this entry.

See website www.holidayfestival.com

Idhul Adha (movable, 6th: public holiday). Celebrated by Muslims to mark the 10th day of Zulhijgah, the 12th month of the Islamic calendar when pilgrims celebrate their return from the Haj to Mecca. In the morning, prayers are offered and, later, families hold 'open house'. This is the 'festival of the sacrifice' and is the time when burial graves are cleaned, and an animal (a cow or goat) is sacrificed by those who can afford it to be distributed to the poor. This commemorates the willingness of Abraham to sacrifice his son. Indonesian men who have made the pilgrimage to Mecca (the Haj) wear a white skull-hat. The Haj is one of the five keystones of Islam. — **March**

Muharram (movable, 26th: public holiday), Muslim New Year. Marks the first day of the Muslim calendar, and celebrating the Prophet Muhammad's journey from Mecca to Medina on the lunar equivalent of 16 July 622 AD. Religious discussions and lectures commemorate the day. — **March**

Garebeg Maulud (or Maulud Nabi Muhammed, birthday of the Prophet Mohammed) (movable, 4th: public holiday), to commemorate Prophet Muhammad's birthday in 571 AD. Processions and Koran recitals in most big towns. Celebrations begin a week before the actual day and last a month, with *selamatans* in homes, mosques and schools. — **June**

Al Miraj (or Isra Miraj Nabi Muhammed) (movable, 15th). The ascension of the Prophet Mohammad when he is led through the seven heavens by the archangel. He speaks with God and returns to earth the same night, with instructions which include the five daily prayers. — **October**

54 HOLIDAYS & FESTIVALS

November — **Awal Ramadan** (movable, 17th-18th). The first day of Ramadan, a month of fasting for all Muslims. During this month, Muslims abstain from all food and drink (as well as smoking) from sunrise to sundown – if they are very strict, Muslims do not even swallow their own saliva during daylight hours. It is strictly adhered to in more conservative areas like Aceh and West Sumatra, and many restaurants remain closed during daylight hours – making life rather tiresome for non-Muslims. Every evening for 30 days before breaking of fast, stalls are set up which sell traditional Malay cakes and delicacies. The only people exempt from fasting are the elderly, those who are travelling, and women who are pregnant or are menstruating.

December — **Idul Fitri** (Aidil Fitri) or **Lebaran** (movable, 16th-17th: public holiday) is a two day celebration which marks the end of the Muslim fasting month of Ramadan, and is a period of prayer and celebration. In order for Hari Raya to be declared, the new moon of Syawal has to be sighted; if it is not, fasting continues for another day. It is the most important time of the year for Muslim families to get together; Indonesians living in towns and cities return home to their village, where it is 'open house' for relatives and friends, and special delicacies are served. Mass prayers are held in mosques and squares. This is not a good time to travel. Trains, planes and buses are booked up weeks in advance and hotels are also often full.

Islamic festivals for 2002 — Idul Fitri, 6 December; Idhul Adha, 23 February; Muharram, 15 March; Garebeg Maulad, 25 May; Al Miraj, 5 October; Awal Ramadan, 6 November.

Health

The traveller to Indonesia is inevitably exposed to health risks not encountered in North America, Western Europe or Australasia. All of the countries have a tropical climate; nevertheless, the acquisition of true tropical disease by the visitor is probably conditioned as much by the rural nature and standard of hygiene of the countries concerned than by the climate. There is an obvious difference in health risks between the business traveller who tends to stay in international class hotels in large cities and the backpacker trekking through rural areas. There are no hard and fast rules to follow; you will often have to make your own judgements on the healthiness or otherwise of your surroundings.

Medical care — Medical care is very variable; medical culture is quite different from the other neighbouring countries, although there are some good hospitals in Jakarta and other main cities. The likelihood of finding a doctor who speaks English and a good standard of care diminishes very rapidly as you move away from the big cities. In the rural areas there are systems and traditions of medicine wholly different from the western model, and you may be confronted with less orthodox forms of treatment such as herbal medicine and acupuncture. At least you can be sure that local practitioners have a lot of experience with the particular diseases of their region. If you are in a city it may be worthwhile calling on your embassy to provide a list of recommended doctors.

Before you go

Basic supplies — You may find the following items useful to take with you from home: suntan cream, insect repellent, flea powder, mosquito net, coils or tablets, tampons, condoms, contraceptives, water sterilizing tablets, anti-malaria tablets, anti-infective ointment, dusting powder for feet, travel sickness pills, anti-acid tablets, anti-diarrhoea tablets, sachets of rehydration salts, a first aid kit and disposable needles.

Take out **medical insurance**. You should also have a dental check-up, obtain a spare glasses prescription and, if you have a long-standing condition such as diabetes, high blood pressure, heart/lung disease or a nervous disorder, arrange for a check-up with your doctor who can at the same time provide you with a letter explaining details of your medical condition. Check the current practice for malaria prophylaxis (prevention) for the countries you intend to visit.

If you are a long way away from medical help, a certain amount of self-administered medication may be necessary and you will find many of the drugs available have familiar names. However, always check the date stamping (sell-by date) and buy from reputable pharmacists because the shelf life of some items, especially vaccines and antibiotics, is markedly reduced in hot conditions. Unfortunately, many locally produced drugs are not subjected to quality control procedures and so can be unreliable. There have, in addition, been cases of substitution of inert materials for active drugs. With the following precautions and advice you should keep as healthy as usual. Make local enquiries about health risks if you are apprehensive and take the general advice of European, Australian or North American families who have lived or are living in the area.

Medicines

Smallpox vaccination is no longer required. Neither is cholera vaccination, despite the fact that the disease occurs – but not at present in epidemic form – in some of these countries. Yellow fever vaccination is not required either, although you may be asked for a certificate if you have been in a country affected by yellow fever immediately before travelling to Indonesia.

Vaccination

Typhoid (monovalent) One dose followed by a booster one month later. Immunity from this course lasts 2-3 years. An oral preparation is also available.

The following vaccinations are recommended

Poliomyelitis This is a live vaccine generally given orally, but a full course consists of three doses with a booster in tropical regions every 3-5 years.

Tetanus One dose should be given, with a booster at six weeks and another at six months. Ten yearly boosters thereafter are recommended.

Meningitis and Japanese B encephalitis (JVE) There is an extremely small risk of these rather serious diseases; both are seasonal and vary according to region. Meningitis can occur in epidemic form; JVE is a viral disease transmitted from pigs to man by mosquitoes. For details of the vaccinations, consult a travel clinic.

Infectious hepatitis (jaundice) This is common throughout Indonesia and, more widely, in Southeast Asia. It seems to be frequently caught by travellers. The main symptoms are stomach pains, lack of appetite, nausea, lassitude and yellowness of the eyes and skin. Medically speaking, there are two types: the less serious but more common is hepatitis A for which the best protection is careful preparation of food, the avoidance of contaminated drinking water and scrupulous attention to toilet hygiene. Human normal immunoglobulin (gammaglobulin) confers considerable protection against the disease and is particularly useful in epidemics. It should be obtained from a reputable source and is certainly recommended for travellers who intend to travel and live rough. The injection should be given as close as possible to your departure and as the dose depends on the likely time you are to spend in potentially infected areas, the manufacturers' instructions should be followed. A vaccination against hepatitis A has recently become generally available and is safe and effective. Three shots are given over six months and confer excellent protection against the disease for up to 10 years. Eventually this vaccine is likely to supersede the use of gammaglobulin.

The other, more serious, version is **hepatitis B**, which is acquired as a sexually transmitted disease, from a blood transfusion or an injection with an unclean needle, or possibly by insect bites. The symptoms are the same as hepatitis A but the incubation period is much longer.

You may have had jaundice before or you may have had hepatitis of either type before without becoming jaundiced, in which case it is possible that you could be immune to either hepatitis A or B (or C or a number of other letters). This immunity can be tested for before you travel. If you are not immune to hepatitis B already, a vaccine is available (three shots over six months), and if you are not immune to hepatitis A already, then you should consider having gammaglobulin or a vaccination.

Children should, in addition to the above, be properly protected against **diphtheria**, **whooping cough**, **mumps** and **measles**. Teenage girls, if they have not had the disease, should be given a **rubella** (German measles) vaccination. Consult your doctor for advice on **BCG** inoculation against tuberculosis: the disease is still common in the region.

On the road

AIDS AIDS is increasingly prevalent in Indonesia and in many of the other countries of Southeast Asia. Thus, it is not wholly confined to the well known high risk sections of the population, ie homosexual men, intravenous drug abusers, prostitutes and the children of infected mothers. Heterosexual transmission is probably now the dominant mode of infection and so the main risk to travellers is from casual sex. The same precautions should be taken as when encountering any sexually transmitted disease. In some Southeast Asian countries – Thailand is an example – almost the entire population of female prostitutes is HIV positive, and in other parts intravenous drug abuse is common. Indonesia, although it does not seem to have so serious an AIDS problem on its hand as Thailand and places like Cambodia and Myanmar, does have the potential for considerable growth in HIV infection rates. The AIDS virus (HIV) can be passed via unsterile needles which have been previously used to inject an HIV positive patient, but the risk of this is very small indeed. It would, however, be sensible to check that needles have been properly sterilized or disposable needles used. The chance of picking up hepatitis B in this way is much more of a danger. Be wary of carrying disposable needles. Customs officials may find them suspicious. The risk of receiving a blood transfusion with blood infected with the HIV virus is greater than from dirty needles because of the amount of fluid exchanged. Supplies of blood for transfusion are supposed to be screened for HIV in all reputable hospitals so the risk should be small. Catching the virus which causes AIDS does not necessarily produce an illness in itself; the only way to be sure if you feel you have been put at risk is to have a blood test for HIV antibodies on your return to a place where there are reliable laboratory facilities. However, the test does not become positive for many weeks.

Malaria Malaria is prevalent in Indonesia. Malaria remains a serious disease, and you are advised to protect yourself against mosquito bites as above and to take prophylactic (preventative) drugs. Start taking the tablets a few days before exposure and continue to take them six weeks after leaving the malarial zone. Remember to give the drugs to babies and children, pregnant women also.

The subject of malaria prevention is becoming more complex as the malaria parasite becomes immune to some of the older drugs. In particular, there has been an increase in the proportion of cases of falciparum malaria which are resistant to the normally used drugs. It would not be an exaggeration to say that we are near to the situation where some cases of malaria will be untreatable with presently available drugs.

Before you travel you must check with a reputable agency the likelihood and type of malaria in the countries which you intend to visit. Take their advice on prophylaxis, but be prepared to receive conflicting advice. Because of the rapidly changing situation in the Southeast Asian region, the names and dosage of the drugs have not been included. But Chloroquine and Proguanil may still be recommended for the areas where malaria is still fully sensitive. At least one informed source considers Indonesia to fall in this category; ie you should be adequately protected by taking Chloroquine and Proguanil. Doxycycline, Mefloquine and Quinghaosu are presently being used in resistant areas. Halofantrine Quinine and tetracycline drugs remain the mainstays of treatment. The mainstay of malaria prevention is to avoid being bitten! Cover yourself with an insect repellent, particularly during the hours between dusk and dawn; those containing DET are most effective (see below). Citronella, an essential oil, used in a base of moisturizer, or in candles, is highly effective as a deterrent to mosquitoes. Also B12 tablets (found in high concentrations in beer and garlic) may help to prevent bites, although this has not been clinically proven. The bonus with this approach is that there are no long- or short-term side effects.

It is still possible to catch malaria even when taking prophylactic drugs, although this is unlikely. If you do develop symptoms (high fever, shivering, severe headache and sometimes diarrhoea) seek medical advice immediately. The risk of the disease is obviously greater the further you move from the cities into rural areas, with primitive facilities and standing water.

Heat & cold Full acclimatization to tropical temperatures takes about two weeks and during this period it is normal to feel relatively apathetic, especially if the humidity is high. Drink plenty of water (up to 15 litres a day are required when working physically hard in the tropics). Use salt on

A miracle of nature: the devil's powder

Quinine has saved more lives than any other medicine used for the treatment of infectious diseases. It comes from the bark of the Cinchona tree, native to Peru, where the Indians used the ground bark to treat fever. In 1632, an Augustinian monk living in Peru wrote describing how effective this treatment was in curing fever. Word spread, and by 1640 Jesuits', or Peruvian bark as it was then called, had reached Europe where malaria was widespread.

At that time many Protestants said they would rather die than take the Jesuits cure. Cromwell called it the 'devil's powder' and though dying of malaria, refused to use it. Without the bark of the Cinchona tree and its alkaloids, European colonial expansion in Southeast Asia would not have been possible. Indeed, the 'Chemical News' of 1867 states that without quinine many countries would have been uninhabitable to Europeans, the Panama Canal would not have been built, and the outcome of the American War of Independence may have been influenced by Washington's purchase of the drug to supply his troops.

By the early 19th century the bark was becoming increasingly scarce and expensive, such was the demand for the miracle drug. The Peruvian authorities were naturally anxious to maintain their monopoly on the Cinchona tree. However, in 1836, under the auspices of the Director of Kew Gardens in London, two Britons, a naturalist and a clerk with the East India Company, set off on a perilous journey into the high Andes, intent on procuring Cinchona seeds and saplings. Their mission was a success and plantations were established in India. In 1820, the pure chemical derivative, quinine, was isolated from the bark; this made dosing easier - 0.5 gm of pure quinine rather than 30 gm of bark - and prevented charlatans from selling the adulterated bark.

At this time another Englishman, Charles Ledger, whilst travelling in the Andes in search of alpaca wool, discovered that a particular species of the tree, Cinchona Ledgeriana, had the highest levels of quinine in its bark. Having failed in his attempt to interest British botanists in his find, he sold the seeds of Ledgeriana to the Dutch, who set up plantations in Java and soon held the monopoly in production of quinine. As production increased, the price dropped from US$100 per kilo in 1880 to US$7 per kilo in 1893. Synthetic anti-malarial drugs were developed following the Japanese invasion of Java during the Second World War.

The Cinchona plantations in the East are still a major source of quinine. The trees are harvested after eight to 12 years and stripped of their bark; about 5,000 tons of bark are processed each year. The Cinchona belongs to the same family, Rubiacea, as coffee and gardenia.

---

your food and avoid extreme exertion. Tepid showers are more cooling than hot or cold ones. Large hats do not cool you down but do prevent sunburn. Remember that, especially in highland areas, there can be a large and sudden drop in temperature between sun and shade and between night and day, so dress accordingly. Loose-fitting cotton clothes are best for hot weather. Warm jackets and woollens are often necessary after dark at high altitude.

Insects

These can be a great nuisance. Some, of course, are carriers of serious diseases such as malaria, dengue fever or filariasis and various worm infections. The best way of keeping mosquitoes away at night is to sleep off the ground with a mosquito net and to burn mosquito coils containing Pyrethrum. Aerosol sprays or a 'flit gun' may be effective, as are insecticidal tablets which are heated on a mat that is plugged into the wall socket (if taking your own, check the voltage of the area you are visiting so that you can take an appliance that will work; similarly, check that your electrical adaptor is suitable for the repellent plug; note that they are widely available in the region).

You can, in addition, use personal insect repellent, of which the best contain a high concentration of diethyltoluamide (**DET**). Liquid is best for arms and face (take care around eyes and make sure you do not dissolve the plastic of your spectacles). Aerosol spray on clothes and ankles deter mites and ticks. Liquid DET suspended in water can be used to impregnate cotton clothes and mosquito nets. The latter are now available in wide mesh form which are lighter to carry and less claustrophobic to sleep under.

If you are bitten, itching may be relieved by cool baths and antihistamine tablets (take care with alcohol or when driving), corticosteroid creams (great care – never use if any hint of septic poisoning) or by judicious scratching. Calamine lotion and cream have limited effectiveness, and antihistamine creams have a tendency to cause skin allergies and are therefore not generally recommended. Bites which become infected (a common problem in the tropics) should be treated with a local antiseptic or antibiotic cream such as Cetrimide, as should infected scratches. Skin infestations with body lice, crabs and scabies are unfortunately easy to pick up. Use gamma benzene hexachloride for lice and benzyl benzoate for scabies. Crotamiton cream alleviates itching and also kills a number of skin parasites. Malathion lotion is good for lice, but avoid the highly toxic full strength Malathion which is used as an agricultural insecticide.

Intestinal upsets Practically nobody escapes intestinal infections, so be prepared for them. Most of the time they are due to the insanitary preparation of food. Do not eat uncooked fish, vegetables or meat (especially pork), fruit without the skin (always peel fruit yourself), or food that is exposed to flies (particularly salads). Tap water may be unsafe, especially in the monsoon seasons, and the same goes for stream water or well water. Filtered or bottled water is usually available and safe, but you cannot always rely on it. If your hotel has a central hot water supply, this is safe to drink after cooling. Ice should be made from boiled water but rarely is, so stand your glass on the ice cubes instead of putting them in the drink. Dirty water should first be strained through a filter bag (available from camping shops) and then boiled or treated. Bringing the water to a rolling boil at sea level is sufficient. In the highlands, you have to boil the water a bit longer to ensure that all the microbes are killed (because water boils at a lower temperature at altitude). Various sterilizing methods can be used and there are proprietary preparations containing chlorine or iodine compounds. Pasteurized or heat-treated milk is now fairly widely available, as is ice cream and yoghurt produced by the same methods. Unpasteurized milk products, including cheese, are sources of tuberculosis, brucellosis, listeria and food poisoning germs. You can render fresh milk safe by heating it to 62°C for 30 minutes, followed by rapid cooling or by boiling. Matured or processed cheeses are safer than fresh varieties.

Fish and shellfish are popular foods throughout Indonesia but can be the source of health problems. Shellfish which are eaten raw will transmit food poisoning or hepatitis if they have been living in contaminated water. Certain fish accumulate toxins in their bodies at certain times of the year, which give rise to illness when they are eaten. The phenomenon known as 'red tide' can also affect fish and shellfish that eat large quantities of tiny sea creatures and thereby become poisonous. The only way to guard against this is to keep as well informed as possible about fish and shellfish quality in the area you are visiting. Most countries impose a ban on fishing in periods when red tide is prevalent, although this is often flouted.

Diarrhoea Diarrhoea is usually the result of food poisoning, but can occasionally result from contaminated water. There are various causes – viruses, bacteria, protozoa (like amoeba), salmonella and cholera organisms. It may take one of several forms, coming on suddenly or rather slowly. It may be accompanied by vomiting or severe abdominal pain, and the passage of blood or mucus (when it is called dysentery).

All kinds of diarrhoea, whether or not accompanied by vomiting, respond favourably to the replacement of water and salts taken as frequent small sips of some kind of rehydration solution. There are proprietary preparations consisting of sachets of oral rehydration electrolyte powder which are dissolved in water, or make up your own by adding half a teaspoonful of salt (3.5 grams) and four tablespoons of sugar (40 grams) to a litre of boiled water. If it is possible to time the onset of diarrhoea to the minute, then it is probably viral or bacterial and/or the onset of dysentery. The treatment in addition to rehydration is Ciprofloxacin (500 mgs every 12 hours). The drug is now widely available as are various similar ones. Ciprofloxacin can be taken as a one-off dose or more commonly as a course of three, five or seven days. It is an antibiotic, so it is important to complete the course.

If the diarrhoea has come on slowly or intermittently, then it is more likely to be protozoal, ie caused by amoeba or giardia, and antibiotics will have no effect. These cases are best treated by a doctor, as should any diarrhoea continuing for more than three days. If there are severe stomach cramps, the following drugs may help: Loperamide (Imodium, Arret) and Diphenoxylate with Atropine (Lomotil). The drug usually used for giardia or amoeba is Metronidazole (Flagyl) or Tinidazole (Fasigyu).

The lynchpins of treatment for diarrhoea are rest, fluid and salt replacement, antibiotics such as Ciprofloxacin for the bacterial types, and special diagnostic tests and medical treatment for amoeba and giardia infections. Salmonella infections and cholera can be devastating diseases and it would be wise to get to a hospital as soon as possible if these were suspected. Fasting, peculiar diets and the consumption of large quantities of yoghurt have not been found useful in calming travellers' diarrhoea or in rehabilitating inflamed bowels. Oral rehydration has, especially in children, been a lifesaving technique, and as there is some evidence that alcohol and milk might prolong diarrhoea, they should probably be avoided during, and immediately after, an attack. There are ways of preventing travellers' diarrhoea for short periods of time when visiting these countries by taking antibiotics, but these are ineffective against viruses and, to some extent, against protozoa. This technique should not be used other than in exceptional circumstances. Some preventatives such as Enterovioform can have serious side effects if taken for long periods.

Sunburn & heat stroke

The burning power of the tropical sun is phenomenal, especially in highland areas. Always wear a wide-brimmed hat, and use some form of sun cream or lotion on untanned skin. Normal temperate zone suntan lotions (protection factors up to 7) are not much good. You need to use the types designed specifically for the tropics or for mountaineers or skiers, with a protection factor between 7 and 15 or higher. Glare from the sun can cause conjunctivitis so wear sunglasses, particularly on beaches.

There are several varieties of heat stroke. The most common cause is severe dehydration. Avoid this by drinking lots of non-alcoholic fluid, and adding salt to your food. Heatstroke results when the body's cooling system breaks down. Symptoms include a very high body temperature, flushed red skin, an erratic pulse, reduced perspiration; this is a serious condition that in extreme cases can result in death. Immediate treatment is to lower the patient's body temperature to 102°F by wrapping in towels or sheets soaked in cold water, with use of a fan if available, or having a tepid bath; hospital treatment may be needed. Spending too long, unprotected, under the hot sun can also result in heatstroke.

Snake & other bites & stings

If you are unlucky enough to be bitten by a venomous snake, spider, scorpion, centipede or sea creature, try (within limits) to catch or kill the animal for identification. Reactions to be expected are shock, swelling, pain and bruising around the bite, soreness of the regional lymph glands, nausea, vomiting and fever. If, in addition, any of the following symptoms should follow closely, get the victim to a doctor without delay: numbness, tingling of the face, muscular spasms, convulsions, shortness of breath or haemorrhage. Commercial snake-bite or scorpion-sting kits may be available, but these are only useful against the specific type of snake or scorpion for which they are designed. The serum has to be given intravenously so is not much good unless you have had some practise in making injections into veins. If the bite is on a limb, immobilize it and apply a tight bandage between the bite and the body, releasing it for 90 seconds every 15 minutes. Reassurance of the victim is very important because death from snake bite is very rare. Do not slash the bite area and try to suck out the poison because this sort of heroism does more harm than good. Hospitals usually hold stocks of snake-bite serum. The best precaution is not to walk in long grass with bare feet, sandals or in shorts.

When swimming in an area where there are poisonous fish, such as stone or scorpion fish (also called by a variety of local names) or sea urchins on rocky coasts, tread carefully or wear plimsolls/trainers. The sting of such fish is intensely painful. This can be relieved by immersing the injured part of the body in water as hot as you can bear for as long as it remains painful. This is not always very practical and you must take care not to scald yourself, but it does work. Avoid spiders and scorpions by keeping your bed away from the wall, look under lavatory seats and inside your shoes in the morning. In the rare event of being bitten, consult a doctor.

Rabies

Remember that rabies is endemic in many Southeast Asian countries. If you are bitten by a domestic or wild animal, do not leave things to chance. Scrub the wound with soap and water and/or disinfectant, try to have the animal captured (within limits) or at least determine its ownership where possible, and seek medical assistance at once. The course of treatment depends on whether you have already been satisfactorily vaccinated against rabies. If you have (and this is worthwhile if you are spending lengths of time in developing countries), then some further doses of vaccine are all that is required. Human diploid cell vaccine is the best, but expensive: other, older kinds of vaccine such as that derived from duck embryos may be the only types available. These are effective, much cheaper and interchangeable generally with the human derived types. If not already vaccinated, then anti-rabies serum (immunoglobulin) may be required in addition. It is wise to finish the course of treatment whether the animal survives or not.

Dengue fever

Dengue fever is present in Indonesia. It is a viral disease transmitted by mosquitoes and causes severe headaches and body pains. Complicated types of dengue known as haemorrhagic fevers occur throughout Asia, but usually in persons who have caught the disease a second time. Thus, although it is a very serious type it is rarely caught by visitors. There is no treatment, you must just avoid mosquito bites.

Other common problems

Intestinal worms are common and the more serious ones, such as hook worm, can be contracted by walking barefoot on infested earth or beaches.

Influenza and **respiratory diseases** are common, perhaps made worse by polluted cities and rapid temperature and climatic changes – accentuated by air-conditioning.

Prickly heat is a very common itchy rash, best avoided by frequent washing and by wearing loose clothing. It can be helped by the use of talcum powder, allowing the skin to dry thoroughly after washing.

Athlete's foot and other fungal infections are best treated by sunshine and a proprietary preparation such as Tolnaftate.

When you return home

On returning home, remember to take anti-malarial tablets for six weeks. If you have had attacks of diarrhoea, it is worth having a stool specimen tested in case you have picked up amoebic dysentery. If you have been living rough, a blood test may also be worthwhile to detect worms and other parasites.

Further information

Information regarding country-by-country malaria risk can be obtained from the World Health Organization (WHO) or in Britain from the Ross Institute, London School of Hygiene and Tropical Medicine, Keppel Street, London WCIE 7HT, which also publishes a highly recommended book: *The Preservation of Personal Health in Warm Climates*. The Centres for Disease Control (CDC) in Atlanta, Georgia, USA will provide equivalent information, T404 639 3311. The organization MASTA (Medical Advisory Service for Travellers Abroad), based at the London School of Hygiene and Tropical Medicine (T0171-631 4408), will provide up-to-date country-by-country information on health risks. Further information on medical problems overseas can be obtained from *Travellers Health, how to stay healthy abroad*, edited by Richard Dawood (Oxford University Press, 1992). This is highly recommended, especially to the intrepid traveller. A more general publication, with hints on health and much more besides, is John Hatt's new edition of *The Tropical Traveller* (Penguin, 1993).

Health websites: *MASTA*, http://www.masta.org/home.html (UK). Provides up-to-date country-by-country information on health risks. If you want more information on malaria, try the *Malaria Foundation International* website http://www.malaria.org This site is a mine of information on every aspect of malaria. Two other tropical health oriented sites are www.uclh.org/htd, the site for the **Hospital for Tropical Diseases in London**, and www.tropicalscreening.com The **CDC** (see above) also have a useful website at http://www.cdc.gov/cdc.html The **British FCO** (Foreign and Commonwealth Office) have a travellers advice site at http://www.fco.gov.uk, which also includes some health related information, as does www.nhsdirect.nhs.uk For a website with a child health focus check out www.medicineplanet.com **E-med**, T020-73502079, www.e-med.co.uk, is a new company that can provide medical advice to travellers whilst they are abroad. Having subscribed, send them an email to doctor@e-med.co.uk, describe your symptoms and you will receive advice from a GP within two hours.

Further reading

Magazines

Asiaweek (weekly). A lightweight *Far Eastern Economic Review*; rather like a regional *Time* magazine in style.
The Far Eastern Economic Review (weekly). Authoritative Hong Kong-based regional magazine (they have correspondents based in Jakarta). Their correspondents provide knowledgeable, in-depth analysis, particularly on economics and politics.
Inside Indonesia, published quarterly by the Indonesia Resources and Information Programme (IRIP) in Australia. Generally outspoken and radical (ie anti-government) in tone; excellent for background information on issues usually not covered in the press. For information on subscribing write to Inside Indonesia, PO Box 190, Northcote 3070, Australia.

Books on Southeast Asia

Cambridge History of Southeast Asia (1992, Cambridge University Press: Cambridge). Two volume edited study, long and expensive, with contributions from most of the leading historians of the region. A thematic and regional approach is taken, not a country one, although the history is fairly conventional.
Caufield, C *In the Rainforest* (1985, Heinemann: London). This readable and well-researched analysis of rainforest ecology and the pressures on tropical forests is part-based in the region.
Clad, James *Behind the Myth: Business, Money and Power in Southeast Asia* (1989, Unwin Hyman: London). Clad, formerly a journalist with the Far Eastern Economic Review, distilled his experiences in this book; as it turned out, rather disappointingly – it is a hotch-potch of journalistic snippets.
Conrad, Joseph *Lord Jim* (1900, Penguin: London). The tale of Jim, who abandons his ship and seeks refuge from his guilt in Malaya, earning the sobriquet Lord.
Conrad, Joseph *Victory: An Island Tale* (1915, Penguin: London). Arguably Conrad's finest novel, based in the Malay Archipelago.
Conrad, Joseph *The Rescue* (1920, Penguin: London). Set in the Malay Archipelago in the 1860s; the hero, Captain Lingard, is forced to choose between his Southeast Asian friend and his countrymen.
Dingwall, Alastair *Traveller's Literary Companion to South-east Asia* (1994, In Print: Brighton). Experts on Southeast Asian language and literature select extracts from novels and other books by western and regional writers. The extracts are annoyingly brief, but it gives a good overview of what is available.
Dumarçay, Jacques *The Palaces of South-East Asia: Architecture and Customs* (1991, OUP: Singapore). A broad summary of palace art and architecture in both mainland and island Southeast Asia.
Fraser-Lu, Sylvia *Handwoven textiles of South-East Asia* (1988, OUP: Singapore). Well-illustrated, large-format book with informative text.
Higham, Charles *The archaeology of mainland Southeast Asia from 10,000 BC to the fall of Angkor* (1989, Cambridge University Press: Cambridge). Best summary of changing views of the archaeology of the mainland.

King, Ben F and Dickinson, EC *A Field Guide to the Birds of South-East Asia* (1975, Collins: London). Best regional guide to the birds of the region.

Miettinen, Jukko O *Classical Dance and Theatre in South-East Asia* (1992, OUP, Singapore). Expensive, but accessible survey of dance and theatre, mostly focusing on Indonesia, Thailand and Burma.

Osborne, Milton *Southeast Asia: an introductory history* (1979, Allen & Unwin: Sydney). Good introductory history, clearly written, published in a portable paperback edition.

Rawson, Philip *The art of Southeast Asia* (1967, Thames & Hudson: London). Portable general art history of Cambodia, Vietnam, Thailand, Laos, Burma, Java and Bali; by necessity, rather superficial.

Reid, Anthony *Southeast Asia in the Age of Commerce 1450-1680* (1988, Yale University Press: New Haven). Perhaps the best history of everyday life in Southeast Asia, looking at such themes as physical well-being, material culture and social organization.

Reid, Anthony *Southeast Asia in the Age of Commerce 1450-1680: Expansion and Crisis* (1993, Yale University Press: New Haven). Volume 2 in this excellent history of the region.

Rigg, Jonathan *Southeast Asia: A Region in Transition* (1991, Unwin Hyman: London). A thematic geography of the ASEAN region, providing an insight into some of the major issues affecting the region today.

Rigg, Jonathan *Southeast Asia: the Human Landscape of Modernization and Development* (1997, Routledge: London). An examination of the human implications of rapid economic growth and reform across the Southeast Asian region.

SarDesai, DR *Southeast Asia: Past and Present* (1989, Macmillan: London). Skilful but at times frustratingly thin history of the region from the first century to the withdrawal of US forces from Vietnam.

Savage, Victor R *Western Impressions of Nature and Landscape in Southeast Asia* (1984, Singapore University Press: Singapore). Based on a geography PhD thesis, the book is a mine of quotations and observations from western travellers.

Sesser, Stan *The Lands of Charm and Cruelty: Travels in Southeast Asia* (1993, Picador: Basingstoke). A series of collected narratives first published in the New Yorker, including essays on Singapore, Laos, Cambodia, Burma and Borneo. Finely observed and thoughtful, the book is an excellent travel companion.

Steinberg, DJ et al *In search of Southeast Asia: A Modern History* (1987, University of Hawaii Press: Honolulu). The best standard history of the region; it skilfully examines and assesses general processes of change and their impacts from the arrival of the Europeans in the region.

Vatikiotis, Michael *Political Change in Southeast Asia: Trimming the Banyan Tree* (1996, London: Routledge). This Far Eastern Economic Review correspondent argues that political change in Southeast Asia must be viewed through a Southeast Asian lens and not as a mirror of Western processes.

Wallace, Alfred Russel *The Malay Archipelago: The Land of the Orang-utan and the Bird of Paradise; a Narrative of Travel with Studies of Man and Nature* (1869, MacMillan: London). A classic of natural history writing, recounting Wallace's eight years in the archipelago and now reprinted.

Waterson, Roxana *The living house: an anthropology of architecture in South-East Asia* (1990, OUP: Singapore). Illustrated, academic book on Southeast Asian architecture, fascinating material for those interested in such things.

Young, Gavin *In Search of Conrad* (1991, Hutchinson: London). This well-known travel writer retraces the steps of Conrad; part travel-book, part fantasy, it is worth reading but not up to the standard of his other books.

Books on Indonesia

Western novels & biography

Conrad, Joseph Perhaps the finest novelist of the Malay archipelago, books include *Lord Jim* and *Victory*, both widely available in paperback editions from most bookshops.

Couperus, Louis *The Hidden Force* (1994, Quartet Books: London). A translation of this Dutch novel originally written in 1900, Couperus was a dandy, who liked to shock. His book deals with the culture clash of locals and colonials and the underlying corruption and decedence of the colonial way of life. All a little dated now, but caused a stir at the time of writing.

Deane, S Ambon *Isle of Spices* (1979, Murray). An amusing and informative account of her two years spent teaching there in the 1970s. The second half is particularly interesting, with accounts of the customs and rituals of the islands and the continuing influence of Adat traditions and beliefs. Out of print, but found in public libraries.
Forster, Harold *Flowering Lotus: a View of Java in the 1950s* (1989, OUP: Singapore). Forster recounts his life as an English lecturer at Gajah Mada University in Yogya in the 1950s; closely observed and informative of the period just after independence.
Koch, CJ *The Year of Living Dangerously* (1978). Average novel transformed into a well-received film; romance based in Java during the 1965 attempted coup.
Van der Post, Laurens *The Seed and the Sower* (1963, Penguin: London). The semi-autobiographical account of Laurens van der Post's internment in a Japanese prisoner of war camp outside Bandung. Was made into a film starring David Bowie: *Merry Christmas Mr Lawrence*.
Van der Post, Laurens *The Night of the New Moon* (1970, Penguin: London). Like his better-known *The Seed and the Sower*, this is based on his internment in a Japanese prisoner of war camp; it is rather more introspective and philosophical, though.

Indonesian literature available in English

Lubis, Mochtar *Twilight in Djakarta* (1957). One of the finest works of modern Indonesian fiction; tells of the poverty and destitution in 1950s Jakarta; journalist Lubis was imprisoned for his writings.
Lubis, Mochtar *A Road with No End* (1968, Hutchinson). Originally published in Indonesian in 1952, and regarded as one of the classic of Indonesian literature, it draws heavily on French existentialist philosophy. The novel tells the story of Isa, a teacher in Java, and the turmoil of the early years of independence.
Lubis, Mochtar *Tiger!* (1991, Select Books: Singapore). A novel based in Sumatra, first published in Indonesian in 1975.
Toer, Pramoedya Ananta *This Earth of Mankind* (1979, Penguin: Ringwood, Australia). Along with the other three books in this series – *Child of all Nations*, *Footsteps*, and *Glass House* – this represents some of the finest of modern Indonesian writing. It tells the story of the writer Minke caught between the Dutch and modernity, and his own people and tradition. Toer was imprisoned on Buru Island between 1965 and 1979 and his books remain banned in Indonesia.

Travel

Barley, Nigel *Not a Hazardous Sport* (1988, Penguin: London). A humorous and entertaining book in which anthropologist Barley heads off to Toraja, and convinces a team of builders to travel to London to construct a traditional house for the Museum of Mankind.
Bickmore, Albert S *Travels in the East Indian archipelago* (1869, OUP: Singapore). Published at the same time as Wallane's much more famous tome, this is not nearly as important a text but, written by an American, it does provide a very different gloss. Republished in 1991 by OUP, Singapore.
Bird, Isabella *The Golden Chersonese* (1883 and reprinted 1983, Murray, reprinted by Century Paperback: London). The account of a late 19th century female visitor to the region who shows her gumption, facing everything from natives to crocs.
Lewis, Norman *An Empire of the East* (1994, Jonathan Cape: London). Norman Lewis' latest travel book in which he explores three politically sensitive areas: East Timor, Irian Jaya and Aceh, North Sumatra. Given the regions to which he selected to travel, beneath the languid surface it is, inevitably, a highly critical book; well written and seemingly innocently provocative.
Mjoberg, Eric *Forest Life and Adventures in the Malay Archipelago* (OUP: Singapore).
Naipaul, VS *Among the believers* (1981). A rather self-indulgent account of Naipaul's visit to Indonesia.
Wallace, Alfred Russel *The Malay Archipelago* (1869). See the comments under Natural history, below.
Wilcox, Harry *Six Moons over Sulawesi* (1989, OUP: Singapore). First published in 1949 as *White Stranger: Six Months in Celebes*, it recounts the six months sojourn of Harry Wilcox in Toraja, who went there to recover from the horrors of the war.

History

Abeyasekere, S *Jakarta: A History* (1989, OUP: Jakarta). A skilful and comprehensive history of Jakarta; the best available.

Anderson, B *Java in a time of revolution: occupation and resistance 1944-1946* (1972). The best study of the period by one of the world's leading political scientists.

Loeb, Edwin M *Sumatra: its History and People* (1972 – first published 1935, OUP: Kuala Lumpur). Despite being over 50 years old this book is still worthwhile reading, and the best of its type.

Marsden, William *The History of Sumatra* (1783, 1811, OUP: Singapore). Like Raffles' study of Java, a book by a polymath who believed history was also geography, anthropology and natural history; now available as an expensive reprint.

Raffles, Thomas *The History of Java* (1817, OUP: Singapore). The first history of Java, fascinating for Raffles' observations, sections have still yet to be bettered; available as a reprint, but large, cumbersome and expensive.

Ricklefs, MC *A History of Modern Indonesia, c1300 to the Present* (1981, Macmillan: London). Dense but informative, and probably the best modern history of Indonesia. A new edition has recently been published.

Smithies, Michael *Yogyakarta, cultural heart of Indonesia* (1986, OUP: Singapore). Good background to the city and its culture.

Times Travel Library *Jakarta* (1987, Times Editions: Singapore). Photographic guide to Jakarta with reasonable background text.

Van der Post, Laurens *The Admiral's Baby* (1997, London: John Murray). Sir Laurens van der Post's last book – the story of the role that the British played in Indonesia in the immediate aftermath of the Second World War and in which he played a central role. Much of the book concentrates on the attempts to restrain Indonesians from militancy in their desire to secure independence, while emphasizing to the Dutch that the past cannot be recreated.

Natural history

Cranbrook, Earl of *Riches of the Wild: Land Mammals of South-East Asia* (1987, OUP).

Flannery, Tim *Throwim Way Leg, adventures in the jungles of New Guinea* (1998, London: Weidenfeld & Nicholson). Vivid and memorable account of the author's adventures as a field biologist in the jungles and mountains of New Guinea, one of the earth's last frontiers. Here he chronicles his hilarious and sometimes dangerous encounters as he searches for new species of wildlife, and discovers animals previously known only as ice-age fossils. 'Throwim Way Leg' is New Guinea pidgin meaning 'to go on a journey', and describes the thrusting first step of what may become a very long trek.

Holmes, Derek and Nash, Stephen *The Birds of Java and Bali* (1989, OUP: Singapore). Manageable, lightweight book with good colour illustrations.

Wallace, Alfred Russel *The Malay Archipelago: the Land of the Orang-utan and the Bird of Paradise; a Narrative of Travel with Studies of Man and Nature* (1869). A classic of Victorian travel writing by one of the finest naturalists of the period. Wallace travelled through all of the islands of Southeast Asia over a period of eight years. The original is now re-printed.

Whitten, Tony and Whitten, Jane *Wild Indonesia* (1992, New Holland: London). Illustrated large format coffee-table book but with good text, written by specialists on Indonesia's natural history. Provides background to the country's major national parks and characteristic species and forest formations. Wonderfully illustrated.

The *Ecology of Indonesia* (listed below) series has expanded so that it now consists of seven volumes, amounting to a total of around 6,000 pages. Heavy stuff and expensive (at around £50 each), but definitive.

Whitten, Anthony et al *The Ecology of Sumatra* (1984, Gajah Mada University Press: Yogya). Like its sister book on Sulawesi, a dense but informative and authoritative account of the island's ecology.

Whitten, Anthony et al *The Ecology of Sulawesi* (1988, Gajah Mada University Press: Yogyakarta). Dense, comprehensive study of Sulawesi ecology.

Whitten, Anthony and Whitten, Jane (Eds.) *Indonesian Heritage: Wildlife* and *Indonesian Heritage: Plants* (1996, Singapore: Editions Didier Millet). Two volumes in the encyclopaedia of Indonesian heritage series. Large format, full of colour illustrations and specially commissioned artwork, written in an accessible style by experts in the field.

Whitten, Anthony et al *The Ecology of Java and Bali* (1997). Nearly 1,000 pages of information.

Whitten, Kathy et al *The Ecology of Kalimantan* (1997). Another monster tome in this series, running to over 800 pages with 40+ colour illustrations.
Monk, Kathryn A et al *The Ecology of Nusa Tenggara and Maluku* (1997). Almost 1,000 pages long.
Tomascik, Tomas and Mah, Anmarie Janice (1997) *The Ecology of the Indonesian Seas*. Two volumes.

Geography, anthropology, politics & development

Anti-Slavery Society *West Papua: Plunder in Paradise* (1990, Anti-Slavery Society: London). Records the people of Irian Jaya's fight for independence – the title speaks for itself.
Barnes, RH *Sea Hunters of Indonesia: Fishers and Weavers of Lamalera*, (1996, Oxford: Clarendon Press). Oxford anthropologist Bob Barnes has been working among the people of Lamalera for many years and this is the culmination of his studies. In many ways it is an old fashioned work in terms of approach: a meticulous documentation of the lives and livelihoods of these people of East Nusa Tenggara. Extensive information on whaling.
Budiardjo, Carmel *Surviving Indonesia's Gulags* (1996, London: Cassell). The author of this book is a Jewish Londoner who married an Indonesian, moved to Jakarta and worked as a civil servant and university lecturer during Sukarno's presidency. She was imprisoned in 1967 and the book recounts her horrific time in gaol. She now lives in London again and continues to campaign enthusiastically for human rights in Indonesia, despite her age of over 70. She was awarded the Right Livelihood Award – a sort of alternative Nobel Peace Prize – in December 1995.
Carle, Rainer (Ed.) *Cultures and Societies of North Sumatra* (1981, Dietrich Rimmer Verlag: Berlin).
Donner, Wolf *Land Use and Environment in Indonesia* (1987, Hurst: London). Rather laboured but detailed summary of Indonesia's environmental problems and prospects.
Geertz, Clifford *Agricultural Involution: the Process of Ecological Change in Indonesia* (1963, University of California Press: Berkeley). Classic book by perhaps the foremost anthropologist of Indonesia; looks at rice and shifting cultivation and conditions in 19th and 20th century Java; some of his views have been vigorously attacked in recent years. Hard to get hold of.
Kis-Jovak, J et al *Banua Toraja: Changing Patterns in Architecture and Symbolism among the Sa'dan Toraja* (1988, Sulawesi, Royal Tropical Institute: Amsterdam). Wonderful black and white photo-essay with informative text.
Loeb, Edwin M *Sumatra: its History and People* (1972, first published 1935, OUP: Kuala Lumpur). Despite being over 50 years old this book is still worthwhile reading, and the best of its type.
Nooy-Palm, Netty *The Sa'dan Toraja: A Study of their Social Life and Religion – Rituals of the East and West* (1986, Foris: Dordrecht). Dense but very informative anthropological work.
Petocz, Ronald G *Conservation and Development in Irian Jaya* (1989, EJ Brill: Leiden).
Rigg, Jonathan (Ed.) *Indonesian Heritage: The Human Environment* (1996, Singapore: Editions Didier Millet). A volume in the encyclopaedia of Indonesian heritage series. Large format, full of colour illustrations and specially commissioned artwork, written in an accessible style by experts in the field.
Schwarz, Adam *A Nation in Waiting: Indonesia in the 1990s* (1994, Boulder: Westview Press). An excellent, readable and well informed account of Indonesia's contemporary economy and politics. Adam Schwarz was the *Far Eastern Economic Review*'s correspondent in Jakarta.
Stuart Fox, David *Once a Century: Pura Besakih and the Eka Dasa Rudra Festival* (1982, Penerbit Citra Indonesia: Jakarta).
Volkman, Toby A *Feasts of Honour: Ritual and Change in the Toraja Highlands* (1985, University of Illinois Press: Urbana). Readable account – part academic, part personal – of an anthropologist's stay in Toraja.
Vatikiotis, Michael *Indonesian Politics under Suharto* (1993, London: Routledge). When this book was written, Vatikiotis was Jakarta bureau chief of the *Far Eastern Economic Review*, and the book demonstrates an intimate knowledge of Indonesian politics and politicians. It is said he had to move posts because he simply became too close to influential Indonesians.
Waterson, Roxana *The Living House: An Anthropology of Architecture in South-East Asia* (1990, Singapore: OUP). Although this is an academic anthropological work, it is written in a style and presented in a format that makes it comparatively accessible. The colour and black and white illustrations combine with an excellent text, to make it an invaluable companion (although it is rather heavy) for anyone interested in traditional houses.

Arts **Beek, Aart van** *Life in the Javanese Kraton* (1990, OUP: Singapore). Useful and interesting short history to the kraton or palace.
Djelantik, AAM *Balinese Paintings* (1990, OUP: Singapore). Concise history of Balinese painting, also covering the major contemporary schools of art.
Dumarçay, Jacques *Borobudur* (1978, OUP: Singapore). Concise account of Borobudur's construction and meaning. A good, lightweight introduction to take along.
Dumarçay, Jacques *The Temples of Java* (1986, OUP: Singapore). Short art history of Java's main temples; rather dry and, for the really interested, rather thin.
Heuken, Adolf *Historical Sites of Jakarta* (1982, Cipta Loka Caraka: Jakarta). Probably the best background text available.
Jessup, Helen I *Court Arts of Indonesia* (1990, Asia Society Galleries: New York). Lavishly illustrated book produced for the Festival of Indonesia exhibition; good background on the pieces displayed.
Miksic, John *Borobudur: Golden Tales of the Buddha, Bamboo and Periplus* (1990, London and Singapore). Well illustrated book written by an academic in the history department at the National University of Singapore, and therefore with a better text than most coffee table books.
Saunders, Kim Jane *Contemporary tie and dye textiles of Indonesia* (1997, Kuala Lumpur: Oxford University Press).
Schneebaum, Tobias *Embodied Spirits: Ritual Carvings of the Asmat* (1990, Peabody Museum: Salem, Mass).
Smithies, Michael *Yogyakarta, Cultural Heart of Indonesia* (1986, OUP: Singapore). Good background to the city and its culture.
Warming, Wanda and Gaworski, Michael *The world of Indonesian textiles* (1981, Serindia Publications: London). Summarizes all the processes of production and provides an outline of the major regional styles; illustrated.

Encyclopaedias An illustrated 15 volume encyclopaedia of Indonesia has been published by Editions Didier Millet in Singapore. The large format books, covering history, natural history, economy, society and ritual, languages and literature, and art and architecture, will run to over 1,000,000 words, with 8,500 images including maps, photographs and specially produced artwork. By the beginning of 1997 the first five volumes had been published – with 187 scholars contributing to their production (Ancient history, Early modern history, Human environment, Plants and Animals).

Books on Indonesian Borneo (Kalimantan) **NB** Some of the books below refer to events largely, even entirely, in Malaysian Borneo (ie Sarawak and Sabah) or Brunei. They are nonetheless recommended as highly descriptive of jungle and tribal life.

Bock, Carl *The headhunters of Borneo* (1985, first published 1881, OUP: Singapore). Bock was a Norwegian naturalist and explorer and was commissioned by the Dutch to make a scientific survey of southeastern Borneo. His account, though, makes much of the dangers and adventures that he faced, and some of his 'scientific' observations are, in retrospect, clearly highly faulty. Nonetheless, this is an entertaining account.
Chapman, F Spencer *The Jungle is Neutral*. An account of a British guerrilla force fighting the Japanese in Borneo – not as enthralling as Tom Harrisson's book, but still worth reading.
Hanbury-Tenison, Robin *Mulu, the Rain Forest* (1980, Arrow/Weidenfeld). This is the product of an Royal Geographical Society trip to Mulu in the late 1970s; semi-scholarly and useful.
Harrisson, Tom *World Within* (1959, Hutchinson: London). During World War Two, explorer, naturalist and ethnologist Tom Harrisson was parachuted into Borneo to help organize Dayak resistance against the occupying Japanese forces. This is his extraordinary account.
Hose, Charles *The Field Book of a Jungle Wallah* (1985, first published 1929, OUP: Singapore). Hose was an official in Sarawak and became an acknowledged expert on the material and non-material culture of the tribes of Sarawak. He was one of that band of highly informed, perceptive and generally benevolent colonial administrators.
Keith, Agnes *Land Below the Wind* (1969, Ulverscroft: Leicester). Perhaps the best-known English language book on Sabah.

King, Victor T (Ed.) *The Best of Borneo Travel* (1992, Oxford University Press: Oxford). A compilation of travel accounts from the early 19th century through to the late 20th. An excellent companion to take while exploring the island. Published in portable paperback.
O'Hanlon, Redmond *Into the Heart of Borneo* (1984, Salamander Press: Edinburgh). One of the best recent travel books on Borneo. This highly amusing and perceptive romp through Borneo, in the company of poet and foreign correspondent James Fenton, includes an ascent of the Rejang River and does much to counter the more romanticized images of Bornean life.
Payne, Robert *The White Rajahs of Sarawak*. Readable account of the extraordinary history of this East Malaysian state.
Payne, Junaidi et al *Pocket Puide to Birds of Borneo* (World Wildlife Fund/Sabah Society).
Payne, Junaidi et al *A Field Guide to the Mammals of Borneo*, (World Wildlife Fund/Sabah Society). Good illustrations, reasonable text, but very dry.

Books on Bali

Belo, Jane (Ed.) *Traditional Balinese Culture* (1970, Columbia University Press: New York). Collection of academic papers mostly focusing upon dance, music and drama.
Covarrubias, Miguel *Island of Bali* (1937, Cassell: London; reprinted, OUP: Singapore, 1987). The original, full treatment of Bali's culture; despite being over 50 years old, it is still an excellent background to the island and is highly entertaining.
Djelantik, AAM *Balinese Paintings* (1990, OUP: Singapore). Concise history of Balinese painting, also covering the major contemporary schools of art.
Eiseman, Fred and Margaret *Woodcarvings of Bali* (1988, Periplus: Berkeley).
Eiseman, Fred *Bali: Sekala and Niskala*. Volume 1 *Essays on Religion, Ritual and Art*, and volume 2 *Essays on Society, Tradition and Craft* (1989 and 1990, Periplus: Berkeley). Considered by many to be the most informative books on the Balinese way of life. Sekala is what you see: a colourful world of ceremony, ritual, dance and drama. Niskala is what you don't see: the all pervading forces of the occult – gods, demons, magic – which are every bit as real to the Balinese. Highly recommended.
Lansing, J Stephen *Priests and Programmers: Technologies of Power in the Engineered Landscape of Bali* (1991, Princeton University Press: Princeton). An anthropological account of Bali's irrigation system; interesting for rice fans.
Stuart Fox, David *Once a Century: Pura Besakih and the Eka Dasa Rudra Festival* (1982, Penerbit Citra Indonesia: Jakarta).

Books on Maluku

Deane, S *Ambon: Island of Spices* (1979, London: Murray). For details, see the entry under Biography, above.
Hanna, Willard A *Indonesian Banda: colonialism and its aftermath in the nutmeg islands* (1991, Banda Neira, Indonesia: Yayasan Warisan dan Budaya).
Milton, Giles *Nathaniel's nutmeg: or the true and incredible adventures of the spice trader who changed the course of history* (1999, London: Hodder & Stoughton). See the summary under Books on Maluku, below. Fascinating account of 17th century exploration and the history of the European search for spices, culminating in the exchange of the tiny island of Run by the British for present day Manhattan held by the Dutch. Despite perilous journeys, fortunes were made at a time when 10 pounds of nutmeg cost less than an English penny to buy, but could be sold for more than £2.10s in London. Highly readable and well-researched, full of extraordinary anecdotes and an enthralling evocation of the life of a sailor and adventurer in these times.

Films about or based on Indonesia

Merry Christmas Mr Lawrence. A film starring David Bowie based on Laurens van der Post's novel *The Seed and the Sower*, a semi-autobiographical account of his internment in a Japanese prisoner of war camp outside Bandung.
The Year of Living Dangerously. Well received film based on the romantic novel by C J Koch, based in Java during the 1965 attempted coup.

Maps of islands of Southeast Asia

A decent map is an indispensable aid to travelling. Although maps are usually available locally, it is sometimes useful to buy a map prior to departure to plan routes & itineraries

Nelles publish a good series of maps of the major islands and island groups: Java, Bali, Sumatra, Kalimantan, Sulawesi, Maluku, Irian Jaya and Nusa Tenggara.

Periplus Travel Maps: recent series of maps to the major islands including some to individual provinces – like Bali, East Java and West Java. Good on tourist site information and often with good insert city maps.

Travel Treasure Maps, Knaus Publications: arty map series concentrating on the major tourist destinations – Bali, Lake Toba, Toraja etc. Sometimes with inset city plans and hiking trails.

Regional maps Bartholomew *Southeast Asia* (1:5,800,000); Nelles *Southeast Asia* (1:4,000,000).

Country maps Nelles *Indonesia* (1:4,000,000); Nelles *Java and Bali* (1:650,000); Nelles *Java* (1:1,500,000); Nelles *Sulawesi* (1:1,500,000); Nelles *Sumatra* (1:1,500,000); Nelles *Irian Jaya and Maluku* (1:1,500,000); Nelles *Kalimantan* (1:1,500,000); Nelles *Java and Nusa Tenggara* (1:1,500,000); Nelles *Bali*. Gescenter International *Indonesia and Malaysia* (1:2,000,000); Periplus *Bali*; Periplus *Lombok*; Periplus *Central Java and Yogyakarta*; Periplus *East Java and Surabaya*; Periplus *West Java and Bandung*; Periplus *North Sulawesi and Manado*; Periplus *South Sulawesi and Ujung Pandang*; Periplus *North Sumatra and Medan*; Periplus *West Sumatra and Padang*; Periplus *Riau and Batam*; Travel Treasure Map *Sumatra: Lake Toba and the Minang Highlands*.

City maps Nelles *Jakarta*.

Other maps Tactical *Pilotage Charts* (TPC, US Airforce) (1:500,000); *Operational Navigational Charts* (ONC, US Airforce) (1:500,000). Both of these are particularly good at showing relief features (useful for planning treks); less good on roads, towns and facilities.

Locally available maps Maps are not always available beyond Jakarta and a few larger cities, and often the quality of information is poor.

Map shops In London, the best selection is available from *Stanfords*, 12-14 Long Acre, Covent Garden, London WC2E 9LP, T020-78361321, F020-78360189.

The internet

General tourism-related sites

http://www.visit-indonesia.com The official web site of the Indonesian tourism promotion board.

http://www.accessindo.com/travel/body_index.html Information on hotels, tours, guidebooks, travel forums, tips and more.

http://www.travelmole.com A useful site for general travel information; also provide a free electronic newsletter. Good links.

www.pata.org The Pacific Asia Travel Association, better known simply as PATA, with a useful news section arranged by country, links to airlines and cruise lines, and some information on educational, environmental and other initiatives.

www.yahoo.com/Regional Countries/[name of country] Insert name of country to access practical information, including material from other travel guides.

World Travel starts at Stanfords
Maps and Guides for all corners of the world
visit our website:
www.stanfords.co.uk
or our flagship store at:
12 - 14 Long Acre, Covent Garden, London, WC2
Telephone 020 7836 1321 / Fax 020 7836 0189

Maps

www.lib.utexas.edu/Libs/PCL/Map_collection/asia/htm Up-to-date maps of Asia showing relief, political boundaries and major towns.
http://plasma.nationalgeographic.com/mapmachine National Geographic's cartographic division, which takes maps from their current Atlas of the World.
www.expediamaps.com US biased but still pretty comprehensive. Key in a town and wait for it to magically appear.

Weather & geographical information

www.rainorshine.com A simple but effective weather site with five-day forecasts for 800 cities worldwide.
http://www.volcanoes.usgs.gov General site on volcanoes with lots of background information.

Travel advisories

www.travel.state.gov/travel_warnings.html The US State Department's continually updated travel advisories on its Travel Warnings & Consular Information Sheets page.
www.fco.gov.uk/travel The UK Foreign and Commonwealth Office's travel warning section.

Travel & health

www.cdc.gov/travel Managed by the Center for Disease Control and Prevention (CDC) in Atlanta, this is one of the best health sites providing detailed and authoritative information, including special sections on such diseases, ailments and concerns as malaria, dengue fever, HIV/AIDS, rabies and Japanese encephalitis.
www.tripprep.com Shoreland's Travel Health Online provides health advice by country.

Hotel sites

www.citynet.com/asia/asia Hotel booking information for Asia.
www3.sympatico.ca/donna.mcsherry/asia.htm The Budget Traveller's Guide to Sleeping in Airports.

Cyber cafés

www.netcafeguide.com/ Around 2,000 cyber cafés in 113 countries are listed here, and it also provides discussion forums for travellers and a language section.

Newspapers, news & the media

http://www.indopubs.com/archives An alternative news service for Indonesia reporting all those things you won't read about in the Jakarta Post.
http://www.iit.edu/~syafsya An Indonesian super-site with excellent links to Indonesian language newspapers.
www.isop.ucla.edu/eas/web/asia-web.htm For information on Asian radio and television broadcasts. Access includes free downloadable software.

Currencies

www.oanda.com/converter/classic Select your two currencies by clicking on a list, and wham – the exchange rate is provided.

Business-related websites

www.stern.nyu.edu/globalmacro Home page of a professor of economics – Roubini – who has collated all the information on the Asian financial and economic crisis, and there's a lot.

Miscellaneous

http://www.halcyon.com/FWDP/help.html Site of the Centre for World Indigenous Studies; focus tends to be rather America-centric, but still a good place to start for those interested in Fourth World (tribal) issues.
http://www.ics.bc.ca/ica/membert.html Site of the Indonesia-Canada Alliance NGO Partnerships; focus is on indigenous peoples in Indonesia and Canada.
http://www.pip.dknet.dk/~pip1917/publicat.html Site of the International Work Group for Indigenous Affairs (IWGIA); good links with related sites and a good source of articles.
http://www.dra.nl/~broeke/ Dutch website on India and Indonesia. Good links to other Indonesian sites and also on Indonesians in Holland.
http://www.pactok.net/docs/inside/index.htm The home page of Australian-based campaigning magazine *Inside Indonesia*, including some articles and index.
http://www.nla.gov.au/1/asian/indo/ Indonesia home page of the National Library of Australia – excellent.

http://www.mawar.inn.bppt.go.id/ Indonesia home page based in Jakarta, but good place to start a search of websites for Indonesia.
http://www.umanitoba.ca/indonesian/homepage.html Another home page with good links to other servers and broad range of information.
http://www.ndio.co.id Indonesia's National Development Information Office; good for stats and other ephemera.
http://www.iias.leidenuniv.nl This site links with the International Institute of Asian Studies in the Netherlands; material tends to be more academic and research associated.
http://www.mdx.ac.uk/www/hap/brc.html Contents of the Borneo Research Bulletin and list of members of the Borneo Research Council.
http://pears.lib.ohio-state.edu/AsianStudies/AsianStudies.html Huge range of links with information on topics from sports and travel to economics and engineering.
http://coombs.anu.edu.au/WWWVL-AsianStudies.html Assortment of material from across Asian region.
http://coombs.anu.edu.au/asia-www-monitor.html Produced by ANU's Research School of Pacific and Asian Studies, this site provides evaluations and summaries of Asian sites.
http://www.nbr.org Centre for papers on Asia covering strategic, economic and political issues.
www.library.wisc.edu/guides/SEAsia 'Gateway to Southeast Asia' from University of Wisconsin, numerous links.

Short wave radio (KHz)

British Broadcasting Corporation (BBC, London) **Southeast Asian service** 3915, 6195, 9570, 9740, 11750, 11955, 15360; **Singapore service** 88.9MHz; **East Asian service** 5995, 6195, 7180, 9740, 11715, 11750, 11945, 11955, 15140, 15280, 15360, 17830, 21715.
Voice of America (VoA, Washington) **Southeast Asian service** 1143, 1575, 7120, 9760, 9770, 15185, 15425; **Indonesian service** 6110, 11760, 15425.
Radio Beijing Southeast Asian service (English) 11600, 11660.
Radio Japan (Tokyo) Southeast Asian service (English) 11815, 17810, 21610.

Tourism: counting the costs

"Tourism is like fire. It can either cook your food or burn your house down." This sums up the ambivalent attitude that many people have regarding the effects of tourism. It is one of Indonesia's largest foreign exchange earners, and the world's largest single industry; yet many people in receiving countries would rather tourists go home. Tourism is seen to be the cause of polluted beaches, rising prices, loose morals, consumerism, and much else besides.

The word 'tourist' is derived from 'travail', meaning work or torment. Travail, in turn, has its roots in the Latin word *tripalium*, which was a three-pronged instrument of torture. For many people struggling through interior Borneo, this etymology should strike a chord. And yet, as *The Economist* pointed out in a survey of the industry in 1991:

"The curse of the tourist industry is that it peddles dreams: dreams of holidays where the sun always shines, the children are always occupied, and where every evening ends in the best sex you have ever had." (Economist, 1991.)

Most international tourists come from a handful of wealthy countries – half from just five countries (the USA, Germany, the UK, Japan and France) and 80% of the rest from 20 countries. This is why many see tourism as the new 'imperialism', imposing alien cultures and ideals on sensitive and unmodernized peoples. The problem, however, is that discussions of the effects of tourism tend to degenerate into simplifications – culminating in the drawing up of a checklist of 'positive' and 'negative' effects. Although such tables may be useful in highlighting problem areas, they also do a disservice by reducing a complex issue to a simple set of rather one-dimensional 'costs' and 'benefits'. Different destinations will be affected in different ways; these effects are likely to vary over time; and different groups living in a particular destination will feel the effects of tourism in different ways and to varying degrees.

Tourism development guidelines

Tourism should capitalize on local features (cultural and natural), so as to promote the use of local resources.

Attention should be given to the type of tourist attracted. A mix of mass and individual will lead to greater local participation and better balance.

Tourist development should be integrated with other sectors. Co-ordination between agencies is crucial.

Facilities created should be made available to locals, at subsidized rates if necessary.

Resources such as beaches and parks must remain in the public domain.

Different tourists and tourist markets should be exploited so as to minimize seasonal variations in arrivals and employment.

A tourist threshold should be identified and adhered to.

Environmental impact assessments and other surveys must be carried out.

Provision of services to tourists must be allied with improvements in facilities for locals.

Development should be focused in areas where land use conflicts will be kept to a minimum.

Supplies, where possible, should be sourced locally.

Assistance and support should be given to small-scale, local entrepreneurs.

At no time or place can tourism (or any other influence) be categorized as uniformly 'good' or 'bad'. Tourism can take a young Australian backpacker on US$5 a day to a losmen on one of the islands off Lombok, an American tourist to a luxury hotel on Bali where a room can cost over US$200 a night, or an elderly couple on a cruise through the islands of Nusa Tenggara.

Searching for culture

Indonesia is one of the richest cultural areas in the world, and many tourists are attracted to the country because of its exotic peoples from the Dayaks of Borneo, to the Dani of Irian Jaya and the Minangkabau and Bataks of Sumatra. When cultural erosion is identified, the tendency is to blame this on tourists and tourism. Turner and Ash have written that tourists are the "suntanned destroyers of culture", while Bugnicourt argues that tourism "... encourages the imitation of foreigners and the downgrading of local inhabitants in relation to foreign tourists; it incites the pillage of art work and other historical artefacts; it leads to the degeneration of classical and popular dancing, the profanation and vulgarization of places of worship, and the perversion of religious ceremonies; it creates a sense of inferiority and a cultural demoralization which 'fans the flames of anti-development' through the acquisition of undesirable cultural traits" (1977).

The problem with views like this is that they assume that change is bad, and that indigenous cultures are unchanging. It sees local peoples as victims of change, rather than masters of their own destinies. It also assumes that tourism is an external influence, when in fact it quickly becomes part of the local landscape. Cultural change is inevitable and on-going, and 'new' and 'traditional' are only judgements, not absolutes. Thus, new cultural forms can quickly become key markers of tradition. Tourists searching for an 'authentic' experience are assuming that tradition is tangible, easily identifiable and unchanging.

'Tribal' people wearing American baseball caps are assumed to have succumbed to western culture. But such changes really say next to nothing about an individual's strength of identity. There are also problems with identifying cultural erosion, let alone linking it specifically with tourism, rather than with the wider processes of 'modernization'. This is exemplified in the case of Bali, where tourism is paraded by some as the saviour of Balinese culture and by others as its destroyer.

Yet the authorities on Bali are clearly at a loss as to how to balance their conflicting views: "... the view of tourism held by the Balinese authorities is blatantly ambivalent, the driving force of a modernization process which they welcome as ardently as they fear. Tourism in their eyes appears at once the most promising source of economic development and as the most subversive agent for the spread of foreign cultural influences in Bali". (Michel Picard, 'Cultural tourism in Bali', 1992.)

Tourist art: fine art, degraded art

Tourist art, both material (for example sculpture) and non-material (like dances), is another issue where views sharply diverge. The mass of inferior 'airport' art on sale to tourists demonstrates, to some, the corrosive effects of tourism. It leads craftsmen and women to mass-produce second rate pieces for a market that appreciates neither their cultural or symbolic worth, nor their aesthetic value. Yet tourism can also give value to craft industries that would otherwise be undermined by cheap industrial goods. Some people argue that the craft traditions of Indonesia should be allied with tourism to create vibrant new rural industries. The corrosive effects of tourism on arts and crafts also assumes that artists and craftsmen are unable to distinguish between fine pieces and pot-boilers. Many produce inferior pieces for the tourist market while continuing to produce for local demand, the former effectively subsidizing the latter.

Some researchers have also shown how there is a tendency for culture to be 'invented' for tourists, and for this to then become part of 'tradition'. Michel Picard has shown in the case of Bali how dances developed for tourists are now paraded as paragons of national cultural heritage. The same is true of art, where the anthropologist Lewis Hill of the Centre for South-East Asian Studies at the University of Hull has demonstrated how objects made for the tourist market in one period are later enthusiastically embraced by the host community.

Environment & tourism

The environmental deterioration that is linked to tourism is due to a destination area exceeding its 'carrying capacity', as a result of overcrowding. But carrying capacity is notoriously difficult to pin down in any exact manner. A second dilemma facing those trying to encourage greater environmental consciousness is the so-called 'tragedy of the commons', better described in terms of Chinese restaurants. When a group of people go to a Chinese restaurant with the intention of sharing the bill, each customer will tend to order a more expensive dish than he or she would normally do – on the logic that everyone will be doing the same, and the bill will be split. In tourism terms, it means that hotel owners will always build those few more bungalows or that extra wing, to maximize their profits, reassured in the knowledge that the environmental costs will be shared among all hotel owners. So, despite most operators appreciating that over-development may 'kill the goose that lays the golden eggs', they do so anyway. In short, tourism contains the seeds of its own destruction.

But many developing countries have few other development opportunities. Those in Southeast Asia are blessed with beautiful landscapes and exotic cultures, and tourism is a cheap development option. Other possibilities cost more to develop and take longer to take-off. It is also true that 'development', however it is achieved, has cultural and environmental implications. For many, tourism is the least environmentally corrosive of the various options open to poor countries struggling to achieve rapid economic growth.

The 'post-tourist' & the traveller

In the last few years a new tourist has appeared; or at least a new type of tourist has been identified – the 'post-tourist'. The post-tourist is part of the post-modern world. He or she is aware that nothing is authentic; that every tourist experience is new and different; that tourism begins at home, in front of the television. The whole globe is a stage on and in which the post-tourist can revel; the crass and crude is just as interesting and delightful as the traditional and authentic to the post-tourist. He – or she – is abundantly aware that he is a tourist, not a brave and inquisitive searcher for culture and truth; just another sunburnt, probably overweight, almost certainly ignorant, foreigner, spending money to have a holiday (not a travel 'experience') in a foreign country. Paradoxically, this lack of apparent discernment is what is seen to identify the post-tourist as truly discerning. Feifer, in 1985, stated that the post-tourist is well aware he is "not a time-traveller when he goes somewhere historic; not an instant noble savage when he stays on a tropical beach; not an invisible observer when he visits a native compound. Resolutely 'realistic', he cannot evade his condition of outsider". Of course, all this could be discounted as the meaningless meanderings of a group of academics with little better to do than play with words and ideas. But there is something akin to the post-tourist of the academic world beginning to inhabit the real world of tourism. These people might have once been described as just cynics, marvelling in the shear ironies of life. They are tourists for whom tourism is a game to be taken lightly; people who recognize that they are just another 'guest', another consumer of the tourist experience. No-one, and nothing, special.

The 'traveller', in contrast to the post-tourist, finds it hard even to think of him or herself as a tourist at all. This, of course, is hubris, built upon the notion that the traveller is an 'independent' explorer somehow beyond the bounds of the industry. Anna Borzello, in an article entitled 'The myth of the traveller' in the journal *Tourism in Focus* (no. 19, 1994), writes that "Independent travellers cannot acknowledge – without shattering their self-image – that to many local people they are simply a good source of income. ...[not] inheritors of Livingstone, [but] bearers of urgently needed money". Although she does, in writing this, grossly underestimate the ability of travellers to see beyond their thongs and friendship bracelets, she does have a more pertinent point when she argues that it is important for travellers realistically to appraise their role as tourists, because: "Not only are independent travellers often frustrated by the gap between the way they see themselves and the way they are treated, but unless they acknowledge that they are part of the tourist industry they will not take responsibility for the damaging effects of their tourism."

Guide books & tourism

Guide books themselves have been identified by some analysts as being part of the problem. They are selective in two senses. First, they tend to pick selectively destination areas, towns and regions. This is understandable: one book cannot cover all the possibilities in a country. Then, and second, they selectively pick sights, hotels and restaurants within those places. Given that many travellers use guide books to map out their journey, this creates a situation where books determine the spatial pattern of tourist flows. As John McCarthy writes in *Are Sweet Dreams Made of This? Tourism in Bali and Eastern Indonesia* (1994, IRIP: Victoria, Australia): "Such is the power of guide books that, unless they are carefully written, one writer's point of view can determine the commercial success or failure of a hotel or restaurant for years after. Even when the enterprise changes, the loathing or love of a travel writer who passed through a village 3 years ago remains too potent a testimony".

There are no easy answers to this. If guide books were more diverse; if travellers really were more independent; and if guide books were not so opinionated and subjective, then this would all help in spreading the tourism phenomenon. But none of these is likely: guide books exist to 'guide'; humans are by nature subjective; and the notion of the free spirit 'traveller' has always, in the most part, been a mirage brought on by a romantic collective sense of what tourism *should* be. One answer is for books to become more specialist, and certainly one identifiable trend is towards guide books covering sub-national regions – Jakarta, Bali and Sumatra, for example. It seems that people are now more willing to spend an extended period of time exploring one area, rather than notching up a large number of 'must do's'. Although even such specialist books also tend to suffer from the dangers of selectivity noted above, those people who do spend a longer period of time in an area are in a position to be more selective themselves, and to rely more on their own experiences rather than those of a guide book writer who may have visited a town in a bad mood three years previously.

In the opening page to his *Illustrated Guide to the Federated Malay States*, Cuthbert Woodville Harrison wrote: "It has become nowadays so easy and so common a venture to cross the world that the simple circumnavigation of the globe 'merely for wantonness' is very rapidly ceasing to be in fashion. But as the rough places of the earth become smooth to the travellers, and they no longer fear 'that the gulfs will wash us down', there is growing amongst them a disposition to dwell awhile in those lands whose climate and inhabitants most differ from ours. The more completely such places are strange to us the more do they attract us, and the more isolated they have lived hitherto, the more do we feel called upon to visit them now." Cuthbert Woodville Harrison's book was published in 1923.

Suggested reading & tourism pressure groups

In the UK, ***Tourism Concern*** aims to "promote greater understanding of the impacts of tourism on host communities and environments", "to raise awareness of the forms of tourism that respect the rights and interests of [local] people", and to "work for change in current tourism practice". Annual membership is £15.00, which includes subscription to their magazine *In Focus*. Tourism Concern, Froebel College, Roehampton Lane, London SW15 5PU, T020-88789053.

Java

3

Java

78	**Jakarta**	219	Central Java's north coast
105	**West Java**	222	Semarang
106	The far west	238	**East Java**
109	The west coast	239	The rump of East Java
117	Bogor	246	Malang
122	West Central Highlands & South Coast	255	Surabaya
131	Bandung	267	Madura Island
153	The north coast plain	273	The Far East
159	**Central Java & Yogyakarta**	298	**Background**
159	South Central Java	298	History
163	Yogyakarta	300	Geography
185	Borobudur	301	Culture
200	Solo (Surakarta)		

Java is Indonesia's political, economic and cultural heartland. With 60% of the country's population, the capital Jakarta, and the great bulk of Indonesia's industrial muscle, Java is the critical piece in the Indonesian jigsaw. It was here that many of the early, pre-colonial empires and kingdoms were based – reflected in monuments like Borobudur and Prambanan, and in many smaller temples. Cities like Yogyakarta and Solo remain vibrant artistic and cultural centres, while Bogor and Bandung show more clearly the hand of the relatively short-lived Dutch presence. The latter, particularly, is renowned for its Art-Deco architecture. Jakarta, as Indonesia's capital, has the most restaurants, the largest museums, and the widest array of shopping, but it is not a particularly enticing city.

The hand of humans has always had to contend with the forces of nature and nowhere is this clearer than in the battle against Java's volcanoes. From Krakatoa off the west coast of Java to Mount Bromo in East Java, a spine of active volcanoes runs through the island. While these volcanoes periodically bring destruction, they also provide the geographical basis for a string of hill resorts and towns including Cibodas and Cipanas in the west, the Dieng Plateau in Central Java, and Tretes, Seleka and Batu in the east.

And finally, Java may not have coral reefs to rival those of Sulawesi, Maluku and Nusa Tenggara but it does have a number of beach resorts from Pangandaran and Pacitan, both popular with budget travellers, through to Anyer and Carita Beach, popular as weekend get-aways for hassled Jakartans.

Jakarta

Phone code: 021
Colour map 3, grid A1
Population: 11,500,000

Jakarta is Indonesia's centre of commerce and communications, of manufacturing activity and consumption, of research and publishing. It has the highest per capita income and the greatest concentration of rupiah billionaires. Until the economic and political troubles of the recent past, Jakarta was a city on the fast track to sophistication – or that, at least, is what it seemed given the first-class hotels, glass and steel shopping-malls, European restaurants and throbbing nightclubs. But the economic crisis has put paid to all that, for the time being. Jakarta is not often rated very highly as a tourist attraction, but if visitors can tolerate the traffic, then it is possible to spend an enjoyable few days visiting the excellent museums, admiring the architectural heritage of the Dutch era, strolling through the old harbour or discovering some of the many antique, arts and crafts shops.

Ins and outs

Getting there
See also Essentials chapter, page 32 & 'Transport', page 101

Jakarta's **Soekarno-Hatta Airport**, where most visitors will be arriving from, lies 25 km northwest of the city, and connects Jakarta with all other major cities and towns in the country, as well as regional and global destinations. State-owned *Garuda* and *Merpati Airlines* operate out of Terminal A, all other international airlines from Terminal B (for airport facilities, see page 34). Terminal C is used by domestic airlines other than *Garuda* and *Merpati*, including *Bouraq* and *Mandala*. Shuttle buses link the international and domestic terminals, but they stop early evening. **Transport to town**: there is a city 'air terminal' on the street floor level of the Plaza Indonesia (taxi drivers know it better as Sogo), Jl MH Thamrin 28-30. For US$25 they will organize reconfirmation of flights, airport transfer and baggage check-in – although this fee is pretty extortionate considering the buses only leave twice a day! Limousine service, 80,000Rp, metered taxis, about 40-50,000Rp (plus toll fees of 6,000Rp and surcharge of 2,300Rp). The unofficial taxi drivers who solicit for fares from unsuspecting tourists are usually a more expensive option than metered taxis – and also more risky. A good tip is to go up to the 2nd floor where there are less hasslers and many empty taxis. The airport authorities now hand out complaints cards for visitors to complete, setting out the toll charges and surcharges applicable. Allow at least an hour to reach the airport from the centre of town, more at peak times. Damri a/c bus connections from Terminal 2 F/E with the Gambir railway station every 30 mins from 0300-1900 (60 mins, 4,000Rp). A problem with this way of getting into town – at least for some people – is that few taxi drivers at Gambir want to take fares down-town – consequently they overcharge. But it is convenient for Jl Jaksa (the centre for budget accommodation) which is just a 10 min walk away from Gambir. A/c Damri buses also run to Blok M, Jl Bulungan, and Kemayoran (former domestic airport). Many of the 1st class hotels lay on transport. In addition, if travelling on *Merpati*, it is possible to check in at Gambir and then take advantage of their free airport shuttle. If you are travelling straight to Bogor, there is a frequent direct bus service from Terminal 2, recommended if you can't face Jakarta on Day 1.

Getting around
See also 'Transport', page 101

Tourist offices *Directorate General of Tourism*, Jl Kramat Raya 81, T3103117, F3101146, has handouts on all regions of the country, but many of limited use for those travelling independently. The *Jakarta Tourist Office* is in the Jakarta Theatre Building, Jl MH Thamrin 81, T332067. They supply maps and information on sights in the city and are the most helpful and friendly to be found in Jakarta, open: Mon-Sat 0900-1630. See also 'Shopping' below for recommended maps.

24 hours in Jakarta

The best area to spend a half or full day exploring is **Kota** and **Sunda Kelapa**. Kota is the old Dutch quarter while Sunda Kelapa was the original port. Both are attractive and are also compact enough to walk around with museums, some Dutch-era buildings, markets, and bars and cafés. The **National Museum**, on the west side of Medan Merdeka is excellent and certainly worth visiting if you have a penchant for dusty relics. To gain an insight into the construction of 'Indonesia' head out to **Taman Mini-Indonesia Indah** where the country's cultures have been conveniently packaged into 27 ersatz houses. For shopping, the **Jalan Surabaya** flea market is probably the most entertaining place to go, although expect fantastic ancient artefacts to be cunningly forged. For more run-of-the-mill articles head for one of Jakarta's large, air-conditioned shopping malls like **Blok M** in Kebayoran Baru, south of the city centre.

Gastronomically Jakarta, as one would expect, offers most things. **Jalan Jaksa**, where much of the cheaper accommodation is concentrated, has an array of restaurants serving standard Indonesian dishes and travellers' food. **Jalan Tamrin** has more up-market restaurants while a good place to sample the range of Indonesian food is at one of the city's food courts – like that in Plaza Indonesia. Clubs and discos tend to open late – around 2200 or even 2300. The longest-running and most popular is **Tanamur** on Jalan Abang Tanah Timur. Most of the larger hotels have their own, usually more sedate, clubs and discos.

History

Evidence suggests that there was a Hindu settlement on the site of modern-day Jakarta as early as the 5th century. By the 12th century, Sunda Kelapa, the old harbour of Jakarta, was flourishing as a port serving the Sundanese Kingdom of Pajajaran, south of Bogor. In 1513, the first Portuguese mariners arrived from Melaka (in Malaysia) in search of spices. No trading-post was established during this first visit, but a few years later they returned bearing gifts for the King of Sunda. In 1522 a Treaty of Friendship was concluded, and the Portuguese were given permission to erect a godown.

From trading-post to Queen of the east, 16th-18th century

By the end of the 16th century, the Dutch had superseded the Portuguese in their race to dominate the lucrative trade in spices, centred on the East Indonesian islands of the Moluccas or Maluku (see page 912). Appreciating the commercial attractions of the large harbour at Sunda Kelapa, the Dutch began to shift their operations from Banten (see page 107), and in 1610 they were given permission by Prince Fatahillah to build a godown on the east bank of the Ciliwung River. By 1618 they had abused their agreement by converting the godown into a fort. At the same time, the English were also busy jostling for position and Prince Fatahillah gave them permission to build a lodge, in the hope of keeping the increasingly powerful Dutch at bay. In spite of limited English support, it was all to no avail. In 1619, a Dutch, fleet arrived led by Jan Pieterszoon Coen, who led an attack on the town, and razed it to the ground. A new town renamed **Batavia**, was built and became the property of the Dutch East India Company (or VOC – Vereenigde Oost-Indische Compagnie), with Coen as its first governor-general. Under Dutch rule, Batavia became a thriving centre for trade and the most powerful city in the archipelago.

The Javanese kingdoms of Banten and Mataram (based near Yogyakarta and Surakarta) did try to dislodge the Dutch – unsuccessfully. But it would be wrong to think of the Dutch 'ruling' Java during these early decades. The VOC was initially only interested in Batavia as a port and base from which to manage the spice trade. By 1757, however, Banten and the sultans of Mataram were vassals of the VOC based at Batavia, a city which had become known by then in Europe as the 'Queen of the East'.

During the 18th century, Batavia developed a reputation as the unhealthiest town in the East – a White Man's graveyard. When designing the city, the Dutch had made the mistake of attempting to recreate Holland, digging canals and ditches in an

From 18th-20th century

The Chinese of Java and Jakarta

From as early as the 17th century, the Chinese formed an indispensable element of Jakarta's population. But it was not until the middle of the 18th century that large numbers of Chinese began to arrive in the city, driven out of South China by famine and economic hardship, and attracted by the lure of employment.

Unfortunately, many of the immigrants failed to secure work and were seen as a nuisance by the VOC. The Dutch attempted to control the situation by deporting unemployed Chinese to Ceylon, but rumours spread that deportees were being dumped in the Java Sea. The Chinese formed gangs and attacked Dutch outposts, resulting in a government search for arms in all Chinese homes in 1740. When the search began, shots were heard, a fire broke out and bedlam ensued. Chinese were attacked, robbed and killed by Dutch citizens, soldiers and sailors. 500 who were being held prisoner in the City Hall were slaughtered after the bailiff gave the order for them all to be killed. It is estimated that in all, between 5,000 and 10,000 Chinese were massacred. During the riot, much of the old city was destroyed. Batavia never really recovered from this incident, not so much because the fabric of the city had been destroyed, but because the economic heart – the Chinese – had been decimated.

This incident did not prevent the Chinese population of Jakarta achieving great economic power – although it did presage an even more horrific massacre of Chinese in 1965 (see box, page 951). By the 19th century, there were already the beginnings of a deep-seated antipathy towards the Chinese on the part of the indigenous Javanese population. But even then, the numbers of Chinese were hardly large: in 1870, Chinese in the Indies numbered only 250,000. These were known as peranakan – literally 'half-caste' – Chinese men inter-married and, to a large degree, assimilated into Javanese society. Many lost their ability to read, write, or even speak Chinese. Their position in society was often as middlemen, marketing rice, selling fertilizers, and providing credit to farmers. However, this gradual process of assimilation was not to last. The increasing nationalism of mainland China broke upon the shores of the Indonesian archipelago, making the peranakan conscious of their roots.

Peranakan families began to enrol their children into Chinese language schools, and to verse them in the culture and ideals of their homeland. But far more important than this change of heart was the influx of large numbers of Chinese totok, attracted to the Indies by the economic opportunities to be found there. Importantly, the men were also accompanied by large numbers of totok women, so that pure Chinese families could be formed. Peranakan Chinese found themselves alienated from Dutch, Javanese and Chinese society. As was said of one Peranakan, Kapitein Cina Tan Jin Sing of Yogya in 1813: Cina wurung, Londa durung, Jawa Tanggung – "No longer a Chinese, not yet a Dutchman, a half-baked Javanese". In the 1930s the Partai Tionghoa Indonesia (Chinese Indonesian Party) was formed to represent the interests of the Chinese in the country, who by that time numbered about 1,250,000, or 2% of the total population of Indonesia.

Since independence, the Chinese have found themselves facing government-sanctioned discrimination – at least until very recently. The Chinese language was outlawed in the 1960s, the use of Chinese characters in public made illegal at the same time (the ban was only lifted in August 1994), and the position of Chinese businessmen sometimes made very difficult.

---

already swampy area surrounded by marshland and jungle. The effect was to create – to use a word popular at the time – a noxious 'miasma'. The canals were often stagnant and quickly became open sewers – there was scarcely a toilet in the city – choked with rotting carcasses, human 'ordure', slime and filth: perfect conditions for the spread of disease, notably cholera and malaria.

The mortality rate was stunningly high; in 1806 the English traveller Sir John Barrows concluded, from studying a register of deaths, that *every* soldier sent out to Batavia had "perished there"; a posting to the city was, in effect, a death sentence. The geographer Victor Savage, in his book *Western impressions of nature and landscape in Southeast Asia*, writes that Batavia was "in the western sphere, the most notoriously insalubrious place in Southeast Asia, and possibly the world".

At the beginning of the 19th century, under the leadership of Governor-General Daendels (1808-10), a clean-up operation was undertaken. Canals were filled in, rivers were cleared and became free-flowing, and swamps were drained and brought under cultivation. Paddy fields close to the city were abandoned, and a new Batavia was built on a higher elevation, 4 km from the old city.

When the Napoleonic Wars in Europe resulted in the annexation of Holland by the French, the British, led by Thomas Stamford Raffles, invaded Java in 1811 and took control of the island (see page 300). Raffles' administration only lasted until 1816, when he was forced to hand control back to the Dutch. He left Java to establish Singapore, which eventually eclipsed Batavia as the most important regional trading centre. From 1820 through to the early part of the 20th century, Batavia flourished and once again earned itself another glowing title – this time the 'Pearl of the Orient'.

At the end of 1941, the Japanese began their whirlwind invasion of Southeast Asia, taking Batavia on 5 March 1942. They renamed the city **Jakarta**, a shortened version of Jayakarta. With the imminent defeat of the Japanese, Indonesia proclaimed its independence on 17 August 1945, under the leadership of Sukarno and Mohammad Hatta. However, the Dutch were not prepared to give up sovereignty so easily and, in 1946, Jakarta again became the capital of a decidedly shaky colony. Over the next three years, nationalist groups throughout the country gained in influence and the Dutch came to realize that their colonial ambitions had reached the end of the road. In 1949, Sukarno returned to the capital in a blaze of glory to become the first President of the new Republic of Indonesia (see page 942).

Modern Jakarta

Today, Jakarta is a sprawling, cosmopolitan city, the centre of government, commerce and industry, with a population of 11,500,000 in 1995 – making it much the largest city in Indonesia. Growth has been extremely rapid. Jakarta, like Bangkok, is perceived by the poorer rural Indonesians as a city paved with gold, and they have flocked to the capital in their thousands. A survey in 1985 revealed that 40% of Jakarta's population had been born outside the city.

The central area is dominated by large office blocks, international hotels and wide, tree-lined roads. Off the main thoroughfares, the streets become smaller and more intimate, almost village-like. These are the densely inhabited *kampungs* where immigrants have tended to live – one-storey, tile-roofed houses crammed together and linked by a maze of narrow paths. Initially, kampungs developed their own identity, with people from particular language and ethnic groups, even from particular towns, congregating in the same place and maintaining their individual identities. Today those distinctions are less obvious, but the names of the kampungs are a reminder of their origins: Kampung Bali, Kampung Aceh (North Sumatra) and Kampung Makassar (Ujung Pandang), for example.

The traditional inhabitants of Jakarta are the **Betawi**, who today reside predominantly in southern Jakarta. Perhaps the most distinctive feature of their material culture are ondel-ondel, large human effigies that lead Betawi parades accompanied by traditional Betawi music. Ondel-ondel are made in pairs. The male (with a red face) is meant to represent a bodyguard of the Betawi of the past. Their moustaches, made from palm fibre, represent strength and bravery. The white faced female ondel-ondel is meant to represent politeness and purity. They tower 2.5m high and span 0.8m in diameter. Together, the male and female ondel-ondel welcome guests of honour or act as escorts during parades.

Population

During the last half century its population has grown spectacularly. In 1942 the city had 563,000 inhabitants; in the next 10 years this more than doubled and by the census of 1971 had reached 4,579,000. The figure today is close to 11,000,000 as the city grows at a rate of over 200,000 a year.

Sights

Kota or Old Batavia
To get to Kota or the Old City from the centre of town, take bus P16 or P17 to Terminal Bis Kota, or microlet M08 or M12 (among others), or a taxi

The city of Jakarta developed from the small area known as **Kota**, which stretches from the Pasar Ikan, or Fish Market, to Jalan Jembatan Batu, just south of Kota train station. The area is about 8 km north of both Monas and many of the city's hotels and guesthouses, so a bus or taxi ride is needed to get here (see the end of this section for details on transport). North of Pasar Ikan was the old harbour town of **Sunda Kelapa**, which thrived from the 12th century to 1527. *Sunda* refers to the region of West Java and *Kelapa* means coconut, and the port is still worth a visit today. Impressive Bugis or Makassar schooners dock here on their inter-island voyages and can be seen moored along the wharf (see page 683). Gradually, they are being supplanted by modern freighters, but for the time being at least it is possible to see these graceful ships being loaded and unloaded by wiry barefooted men, who cross precariously between the wharf and the boats along narrow planks. It is also sometimes possible to arrange a passage on one of the boats to Kalimantan and elsewhere in the archipelago – ask around. ■ *Admission to harbour area 250Rp. Open 0800-1800 Mon-Sun.*

On the southern edge of Sunda Kelapa and close to the Lookout Tower (see below) is the original, and still functioning, **Pasar Ikan** (Fish Market). The market is an odd mixture of ship chandlers, tourist stalls and food outlets. Amongst the merchandise on sale are sea shells, toy *kijangs*, carvings and unfortunate stuffed animals. Close by at Jalan Pasar Ikan 1 is the **Bahari** (or Maritime) **Museum**, which was one of the original Dutch warehouses used for storing spices, coffee and tea. Today, it is home to a generally rather unimpressive maritime collection. However, upstairs is an interesting display of photographs dating from the late 19th and earlier 20th centuries, recording life on board the steamships that linked Batavia with Holland. The museum is worth a visit for the building rather than its contents. ■ *Admission 1000Rp (extra for cameras). Open 0900-1500 Tue-Thu and Sun, 0900-1430 Fri and 0900-1230 Sat.* Other warehouses behind this museum were built between 1663 and 1669. The area around the Pasar Ikan is due to be developed further as a tourist attraction (this has been on the cards for some years now and has yet to manifest itself), recreating the atmosphere of the Dutch period by renovating and reconstructing the original buildings.

Overlooking the fetid **Kali Besar** (Big Canal), choked with rubbish and biologically dead, is the **Lookout Tower** (or *Uitkijk*), built in 1839 on the walls of the Dutch fortress Bastion Culemborg (itself constructed in 1645). The tower was initially used to spy on (and signal to) incoming ships, and later as a meteorological post – a role it continued to fill until this century. From the top of the tower there are views north over the port of Sunda Kelapa and south to the city, over an area of poor housing and urban desolation. It is under reconstruction at present and is not open to the public.

Less than 1 km from the Bahari Museum and Sunda Kelapa, south along either Jalan Cangkeh or Jalan Kapak, is one of the last **Dutch-era drawbridges** across the Kali Besar. It was built over two centuries ago and is known as the Chicken Market Bridge, but it has been allowed to fall into disrepair. Continuing south for another 200m or so, walking past old Dutch warehouses, godowns and other commercial buildings, is **Fatahillah Square**, or **Taman Fatahillah**. This was the heart of the old Dutch city and the site of public executions and punishments – hangings, death by impalement and public floggings. It was also a bustling market place. In the middle of the square is a small, domed building (rebuilt in 1972), the site of the old drinking fountain. The Dutch were unaware that the water from this fountain was infested, and it contributed to the city's high incidence of cholera and consequently high death-rate (see page 80). On the south side of the square is the **Fatahillah Museum**, on the site of the first City Hall built in 1620. A second hall was constructed in 1627 and today's building was completed in 1710. A fine example of Dutch architecture (reminiscent of the old city hall of Amsterdam), it became a military headquarters after independence and finally the **Museum of the History of Jakarta** in 1974. It is a lovely building but, like so many Indonesian museums, the collection is poorly laid out. It contains Dutch

JAKARTA: SIGHTS **83**

Jakarta general

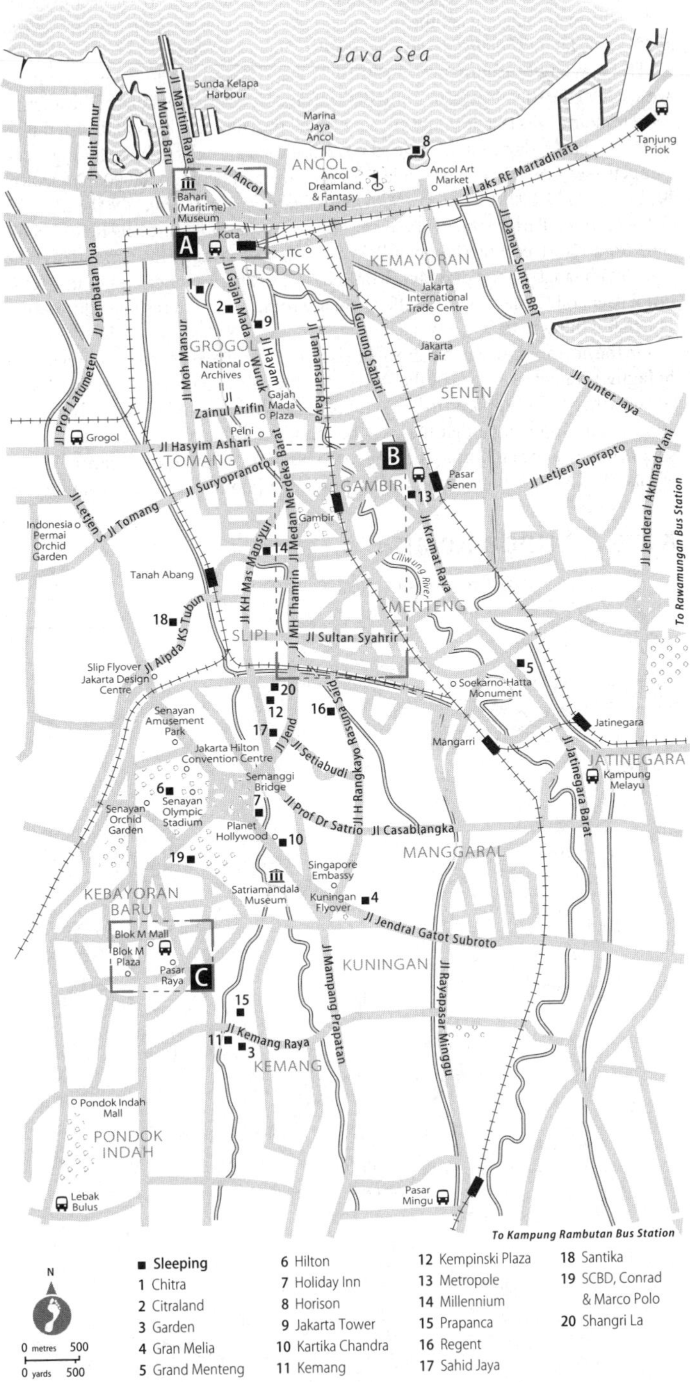

■ **Sleeping**	6 Hilton	12 Kempinski Plaza	18 Santika	
1 Chitra	7 Holiday Inn	13 Metropole	19 SCBD, Conrad	
2 Citraland	8 Horison	14 Millennium	& Marco Polo	
3 Garden	9 Jakarta Tower	15 Prapanca	20 Shangri La	
4 Gran Melia	10 Kartika Chandra	16 Regent		
5 Grand Menteng	11 Kemang	17 Sahid Jaya		

Related maps:
A *Kota and Sunda Kelapa, page 84*
B *Jakarta centre, page 87*
C *Blok M & Pasar Raya, page 100*

furniture and VOC memorabilia. In the courtyard behind the museum, two *ondel-ondel* figures stand outside another room of rather down-at-heel exhibits. Below the main building are the prison cells. ■ *Admission 5,000Rp. Open Tue-Thu 0900-1500, Fri and Sun 0900-1400, Sat 0900-1230, closed Mon.*

The **Wayang Museum**, previously called the Museum of Old Batavia, is on the west side of the square at Jalan Pintu Besar Utara 27. All that remains of the original 1912 building is its façade. Until 1974 it housed the collection now in the Fatahillah Museum, and today contains a good collection of wayang kulit and wayang golek puppets (see page 305). Well made examples are sold here for 50,000-100,000Rp. ■ *Admission 1,000Rp. Open 0900-1500 Tue-Thu and Sun, 0900-1430 Fri, 0900-1230 Sat.* Performances of wayang kulit or wayang golek are held here on Sundays from 1000 (see 'Entertainment'). West from the Wayang Museum and over the Kali Besar (canal) is the **Toko Merah** or Red House. This was once the home of Governor-General Gustaaf van Imhoff. There are some other interesting 18th century Dutch buildings in the vicinity.

On the north side of Fatahillah Square is an old Portuguese bronze cannon called **Si Jagur**, brought to Batavia by the Dutch after the fall of Melaka in 1641. The design of a clenched fist is supposed to be a symbol of cohabitation and it is visited by childless women in the hope that they will be rendered fertile. On the east side of the square is the **Balai Seni Rupa** (the Fine Arts Museum), formerly the Palace of Justice at Jalan Pos Kota 2. Built in the 1860s, it houses a poor exhibition of paintings by

Kota & Sunda Kelapa

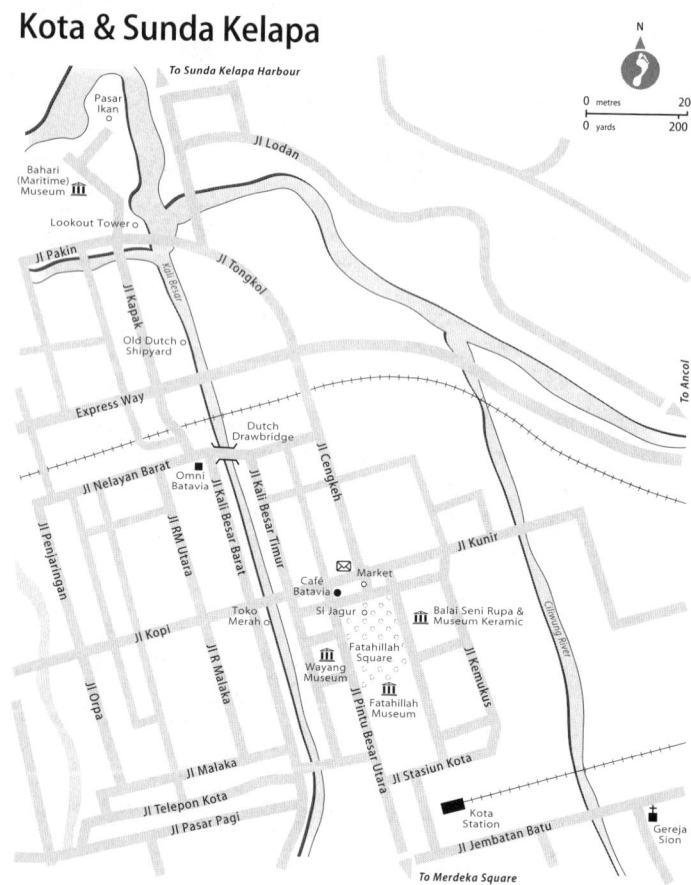

Indonesian artists. The building is shared with the **Museum Keramik**, a collection of badly displayed ceramics. ■ *Admission 1,000Rp. Open 0900-1430 Tue-Sat.* The most stylish place to eat and drink on the square is at the *Café Batavia* – itself something of an architectural gem in Indonesian terms. It was built in stages between 1805 and 1850 and is the second oldest building on the square (after the City Hall). Particularly fine is the renovated Grand Salon upstairs, made of Java teak. The café was opened at the end of 1993 and is frequented by foreigners and the Indonesian wealthy (see 'Eating' below). There is a **tourist information office** next to the café and, next to this, a **clothes market** which functions every day except Sunday.

East of Kota railway station on the corner of Jalan Jembatan Batu and Jalan Pangeran is the oldest church in Jakarta, **Gereja Sion**, also known as the 'old Portuguese Church' or 'Gereja Portugis'. It was built for the so-called 'Black Portuguese', Eurasian slaves brought to Batavia by the Dutch from Portuguese settlements in India and Ceylon. These slaves were promised freedom, provided that they converted to the Dutch Reformed Church. The freed men and women became a social group known as *Mardijkers* or 'Liberated Ones'. The church was built in 1693 and is a fine example of the Baroque style, with a handsome carved wooden pulpit and an elaborately carved organ. The four chandeliers are of yellow copper. ■ *Admission by donation in the adjacent church office.*

South of Fatahillah Square is **Glodok**, or **Chinatown**. This lay outside the original city walls and was the area where the Chinese settled after the massacre of 1740 (see page 80). Despite a national ban on the public display of Chinese characters which was only rescinded in August 1994, Glodok's warren of back streets still feels like a Chinatown: with shophouses, enterprise and activity, and temples tucked behind shop fronts. Midway between Fatahillah Square and Merdeka Square is the **National Archives** or **Arsip Nasional**. This building (which no longer holds the National Archives) was erected in 1760 as a country house for Reiner de Klerk, a wealthy resident who subsequently became governor-general. Since 1925, it has been owned by the state and now houses an interesting collection of Dutch furniture.

Central Jakarta

The enormous **Medan Merdeka**, or Liberty Square, dominates the centre of Jakarta. It measures 1sq km and is one of the largest city squares in the world. In the centre of Medan Merdeka is the **National Monument (Monas)**, a 137m-high pinnacle meant to represent a *lingga* and thus symbolize fertility and national independence. This massive obelisk was commissioned by President Sukarno in 1961 to celebrate Indonesia's independence from the Dutch. Construction entailed the bulldozing of a large squatter community to make way for the former President's monumental ambitions. It is known among residents of the city, rather irreverently, as Sukarno's Last Erection. Covered in Italian marble, it is topped by a bronze flame (representing the spirit of the revolutionaries), coated in 35kg of gold leaf. Take the lift to the observation platform for magnificent views over the city. In the basement below the monument is a **museum**, housing dioramas depicting the history of Indonesia's independence. The entrance to the museum is north of the road immediately in front of the monument (access is through an underground tunnel), where there is a **statue of Diponegoro** (a Javanese hero, see page 170) on horseback. He was held prisoner by the Dutch at the Batavia town hall, before being exiled to Manado in North Sulawesi. ■ *Admission 500Rp for museum, 4,000Rp to take the lift to the top (price includes museum entrance), 500Rp for camera, 500Rp for video, 2,500Rp for booklet with English description of the dioramas. Open 0800-1730 Mon-Fri, Sat and Sun 0800-1900.*

On the west side of the square is the neo-classical **National Museum**. Established in 1860 by the Batavian Fine Arts Society, it is an excellent museum and well worth a visit. Set around a courtyard, the collection consists of some fine stone sculpture (mostly of Hindu gods), a textile collection (recently skilfully reorganized), and a collection of mainly Chinese ceramics found in Indonesia. Next to the ceramics is a display of bronzeware, including some magnificent Dongson drums and krisses

Jakarta's heroic monuments

A particular feature of the city is the monumental heroic sculpture which dominates many busy intersections. Commissioned by Sukarno, these sculptures were conceived as one element in his remodelling of Jakarta as a great modern city. In the same vein as Communist heroic art, they also romanticize Indonesia's struggle for independence. Examples include the two waving figures of the **Welcome Monument**, on the traffic circle between the Hotel Indonesia and the Mandarin Hotel. The so-called **Farmers' Monument** or Patung Tani depicts a couple bidding farewell, as the husband leaves to join the revolution. Sculpted by two Russians and with Communist overtones, it has not been the favourite monument of Jakartans in recent years; a group even lobbied for its removal. Other monuments include the muscular **Irian Jaya Freedom Monument** (also known as the Incredible Hulk) in the centre of Lapangan Banteng, which shows a man symbolically breaking free from his chains; and the distinctly uninspired **Youth Monument**, to the south on Jalan Jend Sudirman, known as Hot Plate Harry or The Pizza Man. Indonesians call this last monument Adu, Panas ('Ow, Hot') or Pertamina – a reference to the national oil company and the volatility of its product. Finally, there is the **Dirgantara Monument** (or Pancoran), which can be seen from the highway to Bogor. It has various names: the Dutch in Jakarta call it Ard Schenk because the figure's arms are like those of a skater in motion; some Indonesians call it **Truper** (a corruption of Trooper), because the ragged clothes look like the remains of a parachute; while many English-speaking residents refer to it as the **7-Up Man** because of the statue's pedestal. The latest addition to Jakarta's monuments is the figure of Arjuna Wijaya (Arjuna driving a chariot of galloping horses), near the National Museum on the corner of Jalan Thamrin, which looks as though it has been sculpted out of white chocolate.

(see box page 90). The pre-history room is well laid out. Its collection includes the skull cap and thigh bone of Java Man, a rare example of *Homo erectus* (see page 205). The ethnographic collection has been reorganized recently and includes an excellent range of masks, puppets, household articles, musical instruments and some models of traditional buildings representing cultures from several of the main islands in the archipelago. ■ *Admission (350Rp) and camera charge. Open 0830-1430 Tue-Thu and Sun, 0830-1130 Fri, 0830-1330 Sat. Good volunteer guides available: English (Tue, Wed, Thu), German (Thu), French (Wed), Dutch and Japanese (Tue) language tours are available, usually between 0900 and 1000. See the Jakarta Post for details as times and days vary, or call the Indonesian Heritage Society on T360551, ext 22. There is a handicraft shop and a telecommunications centre here (visitors can make faxes, telexes and long distance phone calls), set up by a museum co-operative.*

To the west of the National Museum, down Jalan Tanah Abang 1, is the rarely visited **Museum Taman Prasasti** or the **Ancient Inscription Museum**. This open-air museum occupies part of a former Christian cemetery, the Kebon Jahe Kober, where high-ranking Dutch officials were buried from the late 18th century onwards, including Mrs Olivia Marianne Raffles (Stamford Raffles' first wife). The curators have also felt the site appropriate for the display of traditional gravestones from Indonesia's 27 provinces. ■ *Admission 250Rp. Open (in theory – do not be surprised to find it closed): 0900-1500 Tue-Thu, 0900-1300 Fri, 0900-1400 Sat.*

On the north side of the square is the neo-classical Presidential Palace or **Istana Merdeka**, built in 1861 and set in immaculate gardens. Originally named **Koningsplein Paleis**. President Sukarno resided at the Istana Merdeka, but President Suharto moved to a more modest residence and the building is now only used for state occasions. Behind the palace is the older **State Palace** (Istana Negara), next to the Bina Graha (the presidential office building). This palace was built for a Dutchman at the end of the 18th century and was the official residence of Dutch Governors-General, before the Koningsplein Palace was built. To get to the State Palace, walk down Jalan Veteran 3 and turn west on Jalan Veteran.

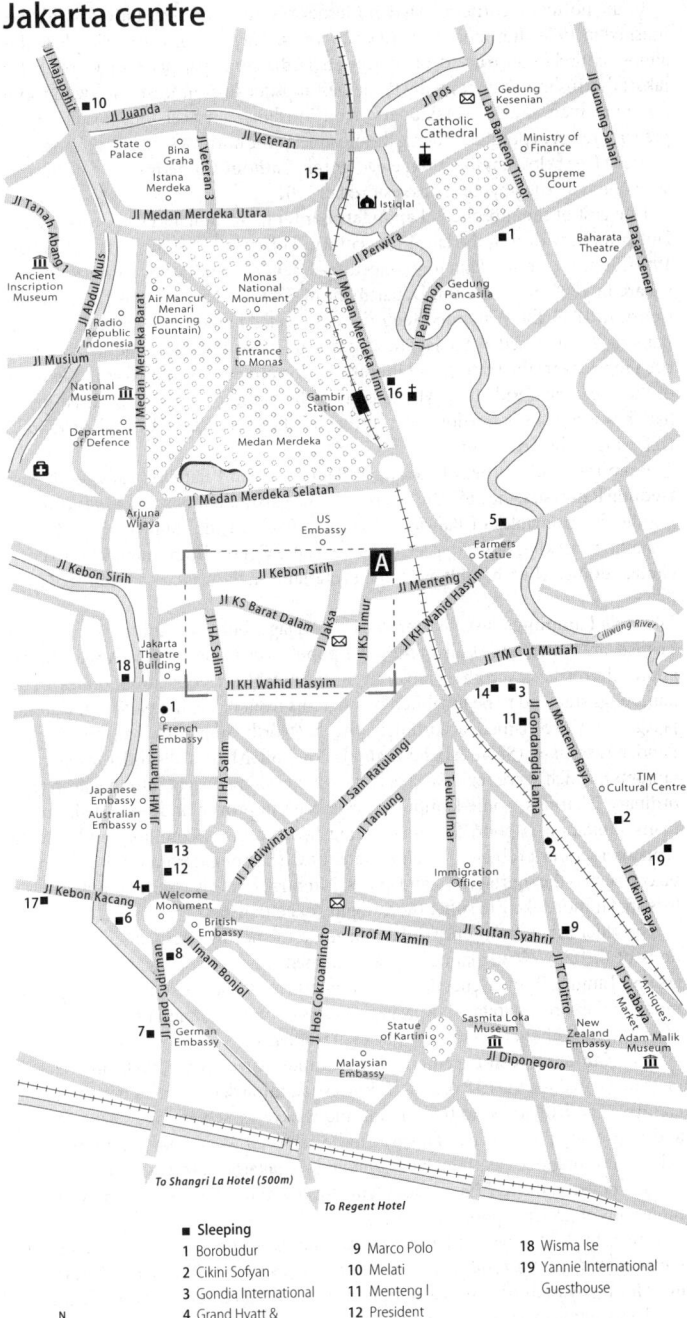

In the northeast corner of Medan Merdeka is the impressive **Istiqlal Mosque**, finished in 1978 after more than 10 years' work. The interior is very simple and is almost entirely constructed of marble. It is the principal place of worship for Jakarta's Muslims and reputedly the largest mosque in Southeast Asia, with room for more than 10,000 worshippers. Non-Muslims can visit the mosque when prayers are not in progress. Facing the mosque, in the northwest corner of Lapangan Banteng (see below), is the strange neo-gothic **Catholic Cathedral**; its date of construction is unknown, but it was restored in 1901.

Due east of the mosque is **Lapangan Banteng**, or 'Buffalo Field', used by the Dutch military during the late 18th century. This area has some of Jakarta's best 19th-century colonial Dutch architecture. Daendels built a huge palace on this square in 1809; it is now the Department of Finance. Next door is the Supreme Court. In 1828, the Waterloo Memorial was erected in the centre of the Lapangan Banteng. Demolished by the Japanese during their wartime occupation, it has since been replaced by the **Irian Jaya Liberation Monument**. Positioned as it is in front of the Treasury, residents wryly joked that the figure's stance, with raised, open hands, was not one of freedom but represented the exclamation '*kosong*', or 'empty' (referring to the Treasury).

From the south corner of Lapangan Banteng, Jalan Pejambon runs south past **Gedung Pancasila**, the building where Sukarno gave his famous *proklamasi*, outlining the five principles of Pancasila (see page 944). At the southern end of Jalan Pejambon, backing onto Merdeka Square, is the **Gereja Immanuel**, an attractive circular domed church, built by Dutch Protestants in the classical style in 1835.

Other sights Jakarta's **kampungs**, usually translated as 'village' but really untranslatable into English, are home to the bulk of the city's population. (They are clearly seen on the approach to Jakarta airport – look out for the patchworks of ochre rooftiles.) The kampungs still tend to be inhabited by migrants from particular parts of the archipelago, and are named accordingly: Aceh (North Sumatra), Bali and Ujung Pandang Makassar (Sulawesi), for example. They often have stalls and *warungs* (restaurants), which serve regional specialities and offer an insight into the lifestyle of ordinary Jakartans. Some kampungs have been improved and upgraded, but in many sanitation is poor, flooding during heavy rains is common, and disease remains a serious problem. Drinking water has to be bought from vendors in some places, such is the shortage of stand-pipes. Although crime is a minor problem, visitors are far more likely to suffer the indignity of getting lost.

The older urban kampungs of Jakarta are in the northwestern and eastern portions of the city. Newer kampungs are situated more peripherally, for example, around Tanjung Priok. Generally, the newer settlements have less of a sense of 'community'; they are inhabited by large numbers of transient migrants who have less of an affinity with their temporary places of residence.

The **Kampung Improvement Programme** dates from 1969, and is still on-going – making the KIP one of the longest-running development projects in the country. The KIP aimed to build roads and walkways, schools and health clinics, and to provide piped water. This was to be achieved while retaining most of the existing housing stock. Although the *kampungs* of Jakarta represent high concentrations of poverty, the KIP has undoubtedly helped to improve conditions for many thousands of Jakarta's poor.

One of the best books on Jakarta's kampungs is Alison Murray's *No Money, no honey: a study of street traders and prostitutes in Jakarta* (1992, OUP: Jakarta). She lived for many months within a kampung and recounts the lives of the inhabitants first hand and with great sensitivity.

West of the city centre The **Textile Museum**, near the Tanah Abang Market (and railway station), Jalan Satsuit Tuban 4, T5606613, is housed in an airy Dutch colonial house set back from the road. It contains a good range of Indonesian textiles, both batik and ikat.

■ *Admission 500Rp. Open Tue-Thu 0900-1600, Fri 0900-1130, Sat 0900-1300, closed Mon. Getting there: Bus P16.*

The **Adam Malik Museum**, housing a unique private collection, is on the north side of Jalan Diponegoro at number 29, west from the junction with Jalan Surabaya. His widow still lives in the house. The quirky collection includes cameras, radios, walking sticks and watches, as well as Chinese ceramics, woodcarving from Irian Jaya, stone carvings from Java, rather ostentatious furniture, guns, krisses and some interesting Russian icons. The problem with this museum is its lack of discrimination. The interesting and the commonplace, the skilled and the inept, are massed together. ■ *Admission 2,500Rp. Open 0100-1500 Tue-Sat, 0930-1600 Sun. Get there by bus or taxi.*

South of the city centre

The **Satriamandala Museum**, or Armed Forces Museum, lies to the south of the city on Jalan Gatot Subroto, opposite the *Kastika Chandra Hotel*. It was formerly the home of Dewi Sukarno, wife of the late President. Today it houses a display of armaments and a series of dioramas, showing steps towards Indonesia's independence. ■ *Open 0900-1530 Tue-Sun.*

A night-time drive, or perhaps even a walk down **Jalan Latuharhary** in Menteng, reveals a seedier – or at least an alternative – side of life in Jakarta. Transvestites, dressed up to the nines, and known as *banci* (meaning hermaphrodite or homosexual) or *waria*, hawk their wares. Foreign visitors may be astonished not only by the beauty of these 'imitation ladies', but also by the fact that this is countenanced in an otherwise relatively strict Muslim society. Transvestites have, in fact, a long and honourable tradition not just in Indonesia but throughout Southeast Asia.

The large, wholesale, **Pasar Cikini**, in the district of Menteng, is worth a visit to see the range of fruit, vegetables, fish and other fresh products trucked in from the surrounding countryside and the coast for sale in Jakarta. The second floor houses a gold market.

Excursions

Taman Mini-Indonesia is a 120-ha 'cultural park', 10 km southeast of Jakarta (but closer to 20 km from the centre). Completed in 1975, there are 27 houses, each representing one of Indonesia's provinces and built in the traditional style of that region, although the building materials used are modern substitutes. Frustratingly, no translation of the descriptions is offered. All the houses are set around a lake with boats for hire. It is possible to drive around the park on weekdays or, alternatively, walk, take the mini train, cable car or horse and cart (small charges for these). The cable car takes passengers over the lake, upon which there is a replica of the whole archipelago. The **Keong Mas Theatre** (so-called because its shape resembles a golden snail) presents a superb not-to-be-missed film on Indonesia, projected on the world's largest imax screen (check in *Jakarta Post* for viewing times). ■ *Admission 3,000Rp.* The **Museum Indonesia**, a Balinese-style building, houses a good collection of arts and crafts and costumes from across the archipelago. ■ *Open 0900-1500.* The **Museum Komodo** is, as the name suggests, built in the form of the *Varanus komodiensis*, better known as the Komodo dragon (see page 822). It houses dioramas of Indonesian fauna and flora. ■ *Open 0800-1500.* There's also an aquarium, an insectarium, an orchid garden, aviaries and a swimming pool. ■ *Admission to the park 2,500Rp (1,000Rp for children) plus additional charges for major attractions. Open 0800-1700 Mon-Sun. Getting there: 18 km and a rather arduous journey by public transport from the city centre – take a bus to Kampung Rambutan terminal and from there a bemo to the park (1-1½ hrs), or a taxi from town for about 15,000Rp.* **Sleeping D** *Desa Wisata*, near Museum Komodo, popular with families and student groups.

Taman Mini-Indonesia

Taman Impian Jaya Ancol lies 10 km north of Merdeka Square, on the waterfront east of Sunda Kelapa. Built on reclaimed land, it is Southeast Asia's largest recreation park. The greatest attraction here is *Fantasyland*, a Disneyland copy, with plenty of

Taman Impian Jaya Ancol

> ### The kris: martial and mystic masterpiece of the Malay world

The kris occupies an important place in Malay warfare, art and philosophy. It is a short sword – the Malay word keris means dagger – and the blade may be either straight or sinuous (there are over 100 blade shapes), sharpened on both edges. Such was the high reputation of these weapons that they were exported as far afield as India. Krisses are often attributed with peculiar powers – one was reputed to have rattled violently before a family feud. Another, kept at the museum in Taiping, has a particularly bloodthirsty reputation. It would sneak away after dark, kill someone, and then wipe itself clean before miraculously returning to its display cabinet. Because each kris has a power and spirit of its own, they must be compatible with their owners. Nor should they be purchased – a kris should be given or inherited.

The fact that so few kris blades have been unearthed has led some people to assume that the various Malay kingdoms were peaceful and adverse to war. The more likely explanation is that pre-Muslim Malays attributed such magical power to sword blades that they were only very rarely buried. The art historian Jan Fontein writes that "the process of forging the sword from clumps of iron ore and meteorite into a sharp blade of patterned steel is often seen as a parallel to the process of purification to which the soul is subjected after death by the gods".

The earliest confirmed date for a kris is the 14th century – they are depicted in the reliefs of Candi Panataran and possibly also at Candi Sukuh, both on Java. However, in all likelihood they were introduced considerably earlier – possibly during the 10th century. A European visitor to Java in 1515 commented: "Every man in Java, rich or poor, must have a kris in his house ... no man between the ages of 12 or 80 may go out of doors without a kris in his belt". Even women sometimes wore krisses.

---

rides and very popular with children. But there is also a drive-in cinema, sporting facilities (including a golf course) and the *Pasar Seni* art market, as well as an *oceanarium* (10,000Rp) and a *swimming pool complex/Waterworld* (7,000Rp weekdays, 11,000Rp weekdays and holidays). Accommodation, restaurants and foodstalls are all available. The park can become very crowded at weekends.
■ *Admission to park at main gate 2,500Rp on weekdays, 3,000Rp at the weekends. There are additional charges for most of the attractions. Fantasyland: 13,000Rp pays for use of all the rides, 15,000Rp includes 'Waterworld', or buy an all-inclusive ticket for 21,000Rp weekdays, 23,000Rp Sat, 25,000Rp Sun. The park is open 24 hrs a day, but most attractions are open from 1000-2200. Getting there: by bus number 64 or 65 from Kota station, or by minibus M15, or bus 60 or 22 from Senen.* **NB** *Taxis are hard to find at the end of the day; avoid venturing onto the main road after dark – both locals and foreigners have been robbed.*

Lubang Buaya Heroes Monument Also known as 'Crocodile Hole' Heroes Monument, this is a memorial park that lies 15 km southeast of town. It is dedicated to the six army generals and one officer slain in the abortive Communist-inspired coup d'état in 1965 (see page 942). ■ *Getting there: by bus from the Kampung Rambutan terminal, south of the city.*

Ragunan Zoo Ragunan Zoo is in Ragunan, 15 km south of the city centre; see the famous Komodo dragon (see page 822) and other regional animals. Not a particularly edifying spectacle, with empty cages, rubbish and few signs – so it is all too easy to get lost in the 185 ha. The numerous uniformed staff scoot about on motorbikes. ■ *Admission 1,500Rp, 750Rp for children. Open 0700-1700 Mon-Sun. Getting there: not an easy place to get to, but a P19 bus goes from Jalan Thamrin in the centre of town.*

Pulau Seribu Pulau Seribu or the 'Thousand Islands' are situated just off the coast, northwest of Jakarta (see page 106). The closest thing to a tropical island paradise within easy reach of the capital. ■ *Getting there: by ferry, hydrofoil, helicopter or speedboat from Ancol Marina.*

Krisses are forged by beating nickel or nickeliferous meteoritic material into iron in a complex series of laminations (iron from meteors is particularly prized because of its celestial origin). After forging, ceremonies are performed and offerings made before the blade is tempered. The *empu*, or swordsmith, was a respected member of society, who was felt to be imbued with mystical powers. After forging the blade, it is then patinated using a mixture of lime juice and arsenicum. Each part of the sword, even each curve of the blade, has a name and the best krisses are elaborately decorated. Inlaid with gold, the cross-pieces carved into floral patterns and animal motifs, grips made of ivory and studded with jewels, they are works of art.

But they were also tools of combat. In the Malay world, a central element of any battle was the amok. Taken from the Malay verb *mengamok*, the amok was a furious charge by men armed with krisses, designed to spread confusion within the enemy ranks (hence the English expression 'to run amok'). Amok warriors would be committed to dying in the charge and often dressed in white to indicate self-sacrifice. They were often drugged with opium or cannabis. It was also an honourable way for a man to commit suicide. Alfred Russel Wallace in *The Malay Archipelago* (1869) writes: "He grasps his kris-handle, and the next moment draws out the weapon and stabs a man to the heart. He runs on, with the bloody kris in his hand, stabbing at everyone he meets. 'Amok! Amok!' then resounds through the streets. Spears, krisses, knives and guns are brought out against him. He rushes madly forward, kills all he can – men, women and children – and dies overwhelmed by numbers...."

Recommended reading: Frey, Edward (1986) *The Kris: mystic weapon of the Malay world*, OUP: Singapore.

Banten Banten is a historic town 100 km west of Jakarta on Java's north coast (see page 107). ■ *Getting there: Banten can be visited in a day from the capital, provided you hire a car or taxi.*

Bogor Bogor is a hill resort 60 km south of Jakarta and famous for its *Botanical Gardens* (see page 118). Nearby is the *Safari Park* at Cisarua (see page 120) and the *Puncak Pass* (see page 128). ■ *Getting there: by bus from the Kampung Rambutan terminal (1½ hrs); by train from Gambir station (1-1½ hrs).*

Bandung Bandung is one of Indonesia's largest cities, almost 200 km from Jakarta (see page 131). ■ *Getting there: by bus from the Kampung Rambutan terminal 5 hrs; by train from the Gambir station 3 hrs, or by minibus with Media, Jalan Johar 15, T343643.*

Tours The tours outlined below can be organized by any of the travel agents or tour operators found in the major hotel complexes. City tours can include a visit to the National Museum, Old Batavia, Pasar Ikan and Sunda Kelapa, Taman Mini and a batik factory or the flea market on Jalan Surabaya. Evening tours can be arranged to Ancol Amusement Park and the Pasar Seni (an arts and crafts market within Ancol), with dinner included. Out-of-town tours can be arranged to Bogor and the Puncak Pass, the Safari Park at Cisarua, Bandung and the Tangkuban Perahu crater. One-day tours by hovercraft to Pulau Seribu are organized on Sunday and holidays, 0700-1700, 1 hour 20 minutes ride, T325608 for more information. There are also day tours to the west, to visit the historic site of Banten and the beach at Anyer, on the west coast.

Cruise holidays starting from Tanjung Priok, Jakarta's port, are available with the *Island Explorer*, a luxury 18 cabin ship. From December to March it travels from Jakarta to Krakatau, the Ujung Kulon National Park and to Sumatra to see an elephant training centre. The rest of the year it cruises between Bali and Kupang (Timor) (see page 313), Jalan Let Jen S Parman 78, Slipi, Jakarta Barat, T593401, F593403.

Essentials

Sleeping
■ on maps pages 83, 87 & 94
Price codes: see inside front cover

Around Merdeka Square **L** *Regent*, Jl HR Rasuna Said, T2523456, F2524480. Situated in the city's Golden Triangle, popular with businessmen, comfortable rooms, good service, pool, tennis, health club. **L** *Borobudur*, Jl Lapangan Banteng Selatan, T3805555, F3809595, welcome@hotelborobudur.com Recently renovated. **AL** *Hyatt Aryaduta*, Jl Prapatan 44-46, T3861234, F380990. A/c, restaurant, pool, recently renovated. **AL** *Sari Pan Pacific*, Jl MH Thamrin 6, T323707, F3904815, saripan@panpac.co.id A/c, several restaurants, pool, large tower block (over 500 rooms) in central position, with good facilities including health and business centres. **A** *Millennium*, Jl Fachrudin 3, T2303636, F2300880, www.millenniumjkt.com, msj@cbn.net.id An excellent hotel for its price, maintains international standards with good facilities and comfortable rooms, excellent breakfasts. Recommended. **B** *Sriwijaya*, Jl Veteran 1, T3440409, F3446543. A/c, European restaurant, 5 mins from Gambir train station, good location. **B** *Transaera*, Jl Merdeka Timur 16, T3451373. Old colonial hotel.

Menteng and Cikini **L** *Grand Hyatt*, 4th Flr, *Plaza Indonesia*, Jl Jend MH Thamrin, PO Box 4546, T3901234, F3906426. A/c, restaurant, pool, very smart new block in central location next to Plaza Indonesia – an extensive shopping mall. 5th floor facilities include landscaped garden with pool, tennis, squash courts and fitness centre. The 450 rooms are plush and very sophisticated, an excellent hotel with prices to match. **L** *Shangri La*, Jl Jend Sudirman, T5707440, F5703531. A/c, restaurant, bars, pool, fitness centre, very plush, very sophisticated, newest and glitziest of the luxury hotels. **AL** *Indonesia*, Jl MH Thamrin, T3906262, F3141508. A/c, restaurant, pool, Jakarta's original premier hotel, built in 1962 for the Asian Games, reputedly with war reparations from the Japanese. Recently refurbished and still popular, although there is no way of getting rid of its ugly exterior, the 586 rooms are only average at this price and the whole hotel still feels rather dated. **AL** *Mandarin Oriental*, Jl MH Thamrin, PO Box 3392, T3141307, F3148680. A/c, several restaurants, pool, sandwiched in between Jl Thamrin and Jl Imam Bonjol, this hotel is immaculately maintained, with superb service and large rooms. **AL** *President*, Jl MH Thamrin 59, T2301122, F3143631. Japanese owned and frequented almost entirely by Japanese businessmen and tourists, 315 Japanese minimalist rooms, not much of Indonesia evident here. **AL** *Sahid Jaya*, Jl Jend Sudirman 86, T5704400, F5700602. A/c, restaurant, pool, recently renovated, popular with tour groups and Indonesian businessmen but still rather lacking in ambience. **A** *Grand Menteng*, Jl Matraman Raya 21, T882153, F882398. A/c, restaurant, pool, fitness centre, central. **A** *Kartika Plaza*, Jl MH Thamrin 10, T3141008, F3905301. A/c, restaurants, good pool, recently renovated, with central position in city and popular with businessmen, gym. **A** *Menteng 1*, Jl Gondangdia Lama 28, T2304832, F3144151. A/c, restaurant, pool, snooker parlour, rather a tacky hotel with no style whatsoever. **A** *Paragon*, Jl Wahid Hasyim 29, T3917070 F3160715, www.paragon.co.id paragon@ub.net.id Not much known about this hotel, except that it does good low season offers on rooms, worth a phone call. **A-B** *Cikini Sofyan*, Jl Cikini Raya 79, T3100304, F3100432. A/c, restaurant, 115 well-appointed rooms, health centre, a small(ish) hotel which makes a good alternative to the larger mid-range places. **A-B** *Marco Polo*, Jl Cik Ditiro 19, T2301777, F3107138. A/c, restaurant (with cheap, excellent buffet dinners and breakfasts), pool. A rather unprepossessing hotel with 181 featureless rooms and lobby, but recently renovated. Clean, and good facilities including satellite TV and fridge in each room, computer facility, just like rooms in any other city hotel on the planet but quite good value. **B** *Gondia International Guesthouse*, Jl Gondia Kecil 22, off Jl RP Soeroso, T3909211. A/c, quiet location, comfortable rooms set around a courtyard, price includes breakfast, friendly atmosphere. **B** *Yannie International Guesthouse*, Jl Raden Saleh Raya 35, T3140012. A/c, hot water, price includes breakfast, good value, clean bedding but rooms could do with a revamp, popular.

Other parts of the city **L-AL** *Gran Melia Jakarta*, Jl HR Rasuna Said Kav X-0, T5268080, F5268181, granmel@indo.net.id, www.solmelia.com Restaurants, pool, fitness and business centres, tennis, elegant hotel with 400 plus rooms and landscaped gardens at the southern edge of the city centre, executive floor and meticulous service. **AL** *Ambhara*, Jl Iskandarsyah

Raya I, T2710800, F7220582. A/c, pool, 250-room hotel located near Blok M in the southern part of town and therefore away from many of the sights, comfortable enough but rather clinical. **AL** *Citraland*, Jl S Parman, T5660640, F5681616. North of town, towards Glodok, a/c, restaurant, pool, set above a shopping plaza and run by the Swiss Belhotel group. **AL** *Equatorial*, Jl Fachrudin 3, T2303636, F2300880. West of city in Tanah Abang area, another addition to the more upmarket range of hotels – no details yet from people who have stayed here. **AL** *Hilton*, Jl Jend Gatot Subroto, T5703600, F5733089. A/c, several restaurants, large pool, considered by many to be the best hotel in town, it includes a penthouse with its own swimming pool, set in lovely gardens, with good sports and business facilities. **AL-A** *Horison*, Jl Pantai Indah, Jaya Ancol, T6406000, F6406123, www.horison.co.id hhj@indo.net.id Billed an 'international resort hotel', restaurant, pool, fitness centre, tennis courts, health spa, rather out of town, within the Ancol entertainment park on the beach, good for children and for sport. **AL** *Kempinski Plaza*, Jl Jend Sudirman Kav 10, T2510888, F2511777, midplaza@indosat.net.id, www.kempinskijakarta.com Located within the CBD, this new hotel has an air of elegance, with 360 rooms and the usual amenities. **AL** *Omni Batavia*, Jl Kali Besar Barat 44-46, Kota, T6904118, F6904092. A/c, restaurants, pool, out of the centre in a rather inconvenient position for exploring the centre of the city by foot, 400-odd rooms in this grand newish hotel. **AL** *Santika*, Jl AIPDA KS Tuban 7, T5361777, F5483457. Almost 300 rooms in this hotel block, restaurants, pool, tennis court, ballroom, business centre, uninspired but efficient. **A** *Jayakarta Tower*, Jl Hayam Wuruk 126, T6294408, F6295000. A/c, restaurant, pool, not a very convenient location. **A** *Kartika Chandra*, Jl Jend Gatot Subroto, T5251008, F5204238. A/c, restaurant, pool, uninspired, plain decor but good sized rooms. **A** *Kemang*, Jl Kemang Raya, T7993208, a/c, restaurant, pool, inconvenient location south of the city. **A** *Setiabudi Palace*, Jl Setiabudi Raya 24, T5254640, F5254651. A/c, restaurant, pool, a first rate hotel with very competitive rooms rates, large rooms and friendly, professional management, good pool. Recommended. **B** *Chitra*, Jl Toko Tiga 23 Glodok, T6596283, F6291125. A/c, friendly, good service but command of English is poor. Big Indonesian breakfast included, clean rooms but a rather run down building, looking a bit shabby, seems to be frequented mainly by Chinese, long way to city centre, area around hotel is dirty but very interesting (markets etc). **B** *Fabiola*, Jl Gajah Mada 27, T6394008. **B** *Melati*, Jl Hayam Waruk 1, T3841943, F360526. **B** *Prapanca*, Jl Prapanca Raya 30, T712630, F7395030. South of the city, good value.

Jalan Jaksa and nearby streets The area around Jl Jaksa has quite a number of budget guesthouses, as well as some new tourist hotels. Most guesthouses do not include breakfast in their room rate. There are also a number of travel agents on this road as well as a post office, laundry services and several travellers' eating houses, cyber cafés and second-hand bookshops.

To get to Jl Jaksa from Pulo Gadung bus terminal, take Bus No 507. To get to Tanjung Priok (for Pelni boats), catch Bus No P14 on Jl Kebon Sirih Raya

A *Cemara*, Jl Cemara 1, T3149985, F324668. A/c, restaurant, excellent mid-range hotel, small, central position, enthusiastic service. Recommended. **A** *Cipta*, Jl KH Wahid Hasyim 53, T3904701. 48 plain rooms with TV and fridge, overpriced. From the street it looks somewhat like a Tuscan pagoda, good central location. **A** *Sabang Metropolitan*, Jl Agus Salim 11, T3857621, F372642. A/c, restaurant, pool, jazz club, good central location but rooms and hotel give off an aura of the mid-1970s. **A-B** *Ibis Tamarin*, Jl KH Wahid Hasyim 77, T3912323, F3157707, ibistam@vision.net.id A/c, restaurant, small pool, fitness centres, satellite TV, well-equipped mid-range place with 130 rooms in central location. Free security boxes and helpful staff. **A-B** *Arcadia*, Jl KH Wahid Hasyim 114, T2300050, F2300995, arcadia@indosat.net.id Modern Art-Deco in style, the 96 rooms are small but decorated with more panache than usual – lots of chrome and deep colours. Excellent showers, huge pillows and green or blue light-infused aquarium-esque lifts. Small, with personal service. Recommended. **B** *Karya*, Jl Jaksa 32-34, T314084, F3142789, www.ihra.co.id/new_karya, ht.karya@rad.net.id This place has been recently renovated and has, in the process, lost some of its charm. It is comfortable enough, with a/c, hot water, satellite TV and the like, but it is overpriced and rather characterless. The top storey restaurant has good views (steaks are a speciality) but mediocre food. **B** *Margot*, Jl Jaksa 15C, T3913830, F324641. A/c, restaurant, en suite bathroom, satellite TV, new upmarket (for Jl Jaksa) hotel, good value but rooms are dark and small, 'business centre', car rental, restaurant in basement, pub, live music. **B-C** *Indra International*, Jl Wahid Hasyim 63, T3152858 F323465, indrahtl@indosat.net.id Renovation in 1995 has vastly improved this hotel. Some a/c, rooms with hot water showers and cable TV, relaxed and comfortable. **B-D** *Djody*, Jl Jaksa 33-35, T3151404, F3142368. Some a/c, attractive quiet courtyard set back off the road, reasonable rooms but some rather small. More expensive rooms with a/c and attached mandi, but no hot water, good, fast laundry service. Recommended. **C** *Norbek*, Jl Jaksa 14, T330392. Some a/c, restaurant (limited menu, but good value). Range of rooms, a couple with a/c, some with attached showers. Rather dark and the communal facilities could be better maintained. Remains popular but there are more salubrious places to stay at this price. Arrange taxis to airport. **C-E** *Nick's Corner*, Jl Jaksa 16-18, T3141988, F3107814. A/c, dormitory rooms as well as hospital-clean rooms with attached bathroom, suffers from unfriendly management and lack of natural light. **C-E** *Tator*, Jl Jaksa 37, T323940, F325124. Some a/c, plain but very clean rooms and bathrooms, more expensive rooms with a/c and attached shower rooms, no hot water, friendly management. Tea, coffee and (unusually) breakfast included in the price. Recommended. **D-E** *Borneo*, Jl Kebon Sirih Barat Dalam 35, T3140095. Café, small rooms, some with attached mandi, popular but recent visitors report rather surly management (**F** for dorm beds). **E** *Yusmen*, Jl Jaksa. Laundry service and tea available. **D-F** *Jusran*, Jl Kebon Sirih Barat 616 (off Jl Jaksa), T3140373. Simple and clean rooms with shared mandi, quiet and friendly, down a quiet alley.

Jalan Jaksa

- **Sleeping**
- 1 Arcadia *C2*
- 2 Ary & Naomij *A2*
- 3 Bintang Kejora *B2*
- 4 Bloem Steen *A3*
- 5 Borneo *B2*
- 6 Cemara *C3*
- 7 Cipta *C2*
- 8 Djody *B2*
- 9 Djody Hostel *A2*
- 10 Hostel 36 *B2*
- 12 Indra International *C2*
- 13 Jusran *A2*
- 14 Karya *B2*
- 15 Kresna *A3*
- 16 Lia *B1*
- 17 Margot *A2*
- 18 Nick's Corner *A2*
- 19 Norbek *A2*
- 20 Paragon *C3*
- 21 Pondok Wisata Jaya *A1*
- 22 Rifa *B1*
- 24 Tator *B2*
- 25 Wisma Delima *A2*

- **Eating**
- 1 Angie's Café *A2*
- 2 Jnsa Bundo *A2*
- 3 Memories Café *A2*
- 4 Pappa
- 5 Romanu *B2*
- 6 Sizzlers *B1*
- 7 Tony Roma's

E *Ari and Naomy Hostel*, Jl Kebon Sirih Barat V11 3, T3190434. Opened in 1998. Simple, clean rooms in a well-run guesthouse down a quiet gang. Clean communal showers and toilets. **E** *Bintang Kejora Hostel*, Jl Kebon Sirih Barat Dalam 52 (off Jl Jaksa, south end), T323878. Rooms are (relatively) large with fans, shared showers and toilets, its popularity should not excuse the poor quality of the rooms but the management are friendly – note that downstairs rooms are particularly noisy. **E** *Bloem Steen*, Jl Kebon Sirih Timur 1, T323002. A small and popular guesthouse down a quiet alley off Jl Jaksa. Rooms upstairs are better, with small balconies – all have shared showers and toilets. **E** *Djody Hostel*, Jl Jaksa 27, T3151404, F3142368. Old style bungalow converted into a guesthouse. Reasonable rooms and shared mandi, but for a more upmarket place try the *Djody Hotel* just up the road at No 35. **E** *Lia Hostel*, Jl Kebon Sirih Barat 1 gg8. Quiet little place down a narrow long gangway and behind a high wall in a largely residential area. Very peaceful, reasonable rooms. **E** *Kresna*, Jl Kebon Sirih Timur 1 175, T325403. Clean, some rooms with attached bathroom, rooms can be rather dark, but friendly and set back off the road down a quiet alley. A shade superior to the *Bloem Steen* immediately next door. Recommended. **E** *Wisma Ise*, Jl KHW Hasyim 168, just west of Jl MH Thamrin, T333463. Some a/c, some private bathrooms, friendly owners, central location, good value. **E-F** *Hotel Rifa*, Jl Kebon Sirih Barat Dalam 36A (off Jl Jaksa, southern end), small rooms, some with attached bathrooms, rather hot and cramped, grubby and run down. **E-F** *Pondok Wisata Jaya*, Jl Kebon Sirih Barat Dalam 10 (off Jl Jaksa, southern end), T3104126. Quiet, larger and more airy than most, with small garden and clean rooms, recommended.

Soekarno-Hatta Airport **AL** *Quality Hotel AsPAC*, Terminal 2/E, T5590008, F5590018, airport@vision.net.id Short stays available (6 hrs) from 0800-1800 for US$60. **AL** *Sheraton Bandara*, 5 mins from airport, T5597777, excellent hotel with a good swimming pool. **B** *Huswah Transit* Jl Husein Sastra Negara, 5-10 mins drive from the airport, T5555885. A hotel bus will pick up and collect .

Eating
Jakarta is a good place to eat out, with a wide choice of Indonesian, other Asian & international cuisines

Indonesian Expensive: *Oasis*, Jl Raden Saleh Raya 47, T3150646. Also serves International food. Dutch governor's house built in 1928, the walls are adorned with Indonesian arts and crafts, famous for its Rijstaffel served by a dozen waitresses, all carrying a different dish, one of the best restaurants in town, local music performances, reservations necessary. **Mid-range**: *Bengawan Solo*, Sahid Jaya Hotel, Jl Jend Sudirman 86, central Javanese cuisine. *Café Bintang*, 2nd basement, Blok M Mall. A new café, open from 11am until 2am. Indonesian food and live Dangdut music. *Jimbani Café*, Jl Kemang Raya 85, T7994472. A Balinese style café, very trendy and a favourite spot for stars. *Padi-Padi*, Jl Kemang Selatan Raya 101B, also has a small selection of international food. Beautifully designed restaurant in Javanese colonial style. There are small padi fields, lotus ponds, live traditional music and a very relaxed atmosphere. Highly recommended. **Cheap**: *Handayani*, Jl Matraman Raya 45. Recommended. *Tinoor Asli Manado*, Jl Gondangolama 33A, simple but tasty Sulawesi (north) dishes served in dusty canteen-esque restaurant catering almost entirely to locals. **Very cheap**: *Bami Gajah Mada*, Jl Gajah Mada 92, and Studio 21 cinema, Jl MH Thamrin. Cheap noodle house. Recommended. *Saté House Senayan*, Jl Kebon Sirih 31A, saté and gado gado. Recommended.

There are also **cheap** restaurants in the **Jl Jaksa** area for both **Indonesian** and **international** dishes, including the *Jasa Bundo*, which serves the best Padang food on the street. For Padang food (from West Sumatra), there is a concentration of excellent restaurants along Jl Tanah Abang 1 (running off Jl Abdul Muis, not far from the National Museum). All are in our **cheap** and **very cheap** categories; try *Sepakat* or *Surya*. The *Natrabu* and *Restoran Sederhana* on Jl Agus Salim (between Jl Wahid Hasyim and Jl Sirih) are considered the best Padang restaurants in town. In the **mid-range** category are: *Tan Goei*, Jl Besuki 14, a good Sundanese restaurant (fish, saté) and *Raden Kuring*, Jl Raden Saleh 62, purveyor of the best Sundanese cuisine in the capital, served in a relaxing ambience of traditional music and bamboo décor.

Other Asian cuisine Expensive: *Nippon-Kan*, Hilton Hotel, Jl Gatot Subroto, expensive but good value Japanese. *Arirang*, Jl Makaham 1/28, Korean barbecue. Recommended. *Chikuyo-Tei*, Summit Mas Tower, Jl Jend Sudirman, Japanese. Recommended. *Keyaki*, Sari

Pacific Hotel, Jl MH Thamrin 6, Japanese. Recommended. ***Lanna Thai***, Jl Kusuma Atmaja 85, excellent Thai cuisine, but the portions are rather small. Elegantly decorated with antiques. A bar upstairs. ***Shima***, Aryaduta Hotel, Jl Prapatan 44, reputedly serves the best Japanese food in town. ***Suan Thai***, Jl Jend Sudirman Kav. 11 (closes at 2200). Best Thai and seafood restaurant in Jakarta. ***Xin Hwa (Chinese)*** and *Tokio Joe* (Japanese) at the Mandarin Oriental Hotel, Jl MH Thamrin, have been recommended. **Mid-range**: *Hazara*, Jl KH Wahid Hasyim 11 (next to the Arcadia Hotel), good North Indian food including fine tandoori dishes, succulent goat curry and oddities like curried crab. A popular bar upstairs. ***Queen's Tandoor***, Jl Veteran 1/6 (near mosque Istiqlal), is the canteen of the Indian community. On the same street (1/17) is the slightly more elegant *Maharani*. North and South Indian food is served as well as Chinese and seafood dishes. ***Summer Palace***, Tedja Buana Building, 8th Flr, Jl Menteng Raya 29, Sezchuan. Large but reliable restaurant. Recommended. ***wwwok!***, Jl Kemang Raya 9. A noodle bar and cyber café serving a variety of noodle and rice dishes from all over Asia. Downstairs for a quick lunch or log on, upstairs for lounge-cats. One of the coolest places to hang out in town. **Cheap**: *Kikugawa*, Jl Cikini IV 13, Japanese, central location, good value. *Sahara*, Jl Veteran 1. Possibly better and definitely cheaper Indian food than Hazara. ***Gang Gang Sulai***, Jl Cideng Timur 65. ***Phinisi floating restaurant***, Ancol, also serves seafood.

International Expensive: *Ambiente*, Aryaduta Hotel, Jl Prapatan, best Northern Italian in town, but nonetheless overpriced for Jakarta. ***Café Batavia***, Fatahillah Square, T6915531, open 24 hrs, stylish and sophisticated bar and bistro serving Indonesian and international dishes in superbly renovated early 19th-century building, good food in great surroundings but very expensive for Indonesia. Recommended. ***Le Bistro***, Jl Wahid Hasyim 75, Jakarta's 1st French restaurant, established 15 years ago, classic French favourites such as bouillabaisse and Lamb Provençale. ***Bruschetta***, Borobudur Intercontinental Hotel, Jl Lapangan Banteng, Italian, expensive but excellent. ***Empire Grill***, 35th Flr, Menara Imperium Building, Jl Rasuna Said. A revolving restaurant with stunning views of Jakarta. Good, but expensive international cuisine. *Maxis*, Plaza Indonesia, Jl MH Thamrin, small Italian café, classic Italian dishes, average quality. ***Melati Café***, Sari Pacific Hotel, Jl MH Thamrin. ***Kafe Pisa***, Jl Gereja Theresia 1, Italian restaurant, inside and outside dining, delicious pasta and a great ice-cream selection. ***Taman Sari***, Hilton Hotel, Jl Gatot Subroto. Recommended. *Zigolini*, *Mandarin Oriental Hotel*, Jl MH Thamrin, superb Italian cuisine, popular restaurant among journalists. **Mid-range**: *Art and Curio*, Jl Cikini IV, 8, is a long standing Jakarta institution serving good Dutch and European food. (Rp20,000 for a main dish). ***Chillis***, Jl Thamrin, right next door to Hard Rock Café, up an escalator above Sarinah Department Store. Steaks, burgers, fries; a cheaper version of its neighbour. Happy Hours. ***Fashion Café***, BNI Building, Jl Sudirman Kav 1, T5744488, a place for young posers. ***Galeri TC***, Jl Kemang Raya 24A. Well designed restaurant with some Indonesian specialities as well as international, has a bar, art gallery, book shop and internet access. A popular meeting place. ***Hard Rock Café***, Jl Thamrin (1st Flr of Sarinah block), T3903513, burgers and fries, lively atmosphere and live music after 2300. ***Komodo Airways***, Atlet Century Hotel, Jl Pintu Satu, Senayan, T5712041, café in Komodo dragon style, pizzas. ***Pete's Tavern***, Bank Jaya Building, basement, Jl Thamrin, Mongolian barbecue (all you can eat for set price of US$3). They also have a pool table and band. ***Pizzaria***, Hilton Hotel, Jl Gatot Subroto, outdoor, set in Balinese garden, over-loud live music. ***Planet Hollywood***, Jl Gatot Subroto 16 (beside Kartika Chandra Hotel), T5267827, overpriced, limited menu but the young and trendy still go there, live entertainment Thur-Sat from 2200. Open 7 days a week from 1130 to 0130. *Sizzlers*, Jl HA Salim, good steaks, buffet salad bar. ***Tony Roma's***, Jl KH Wahid Hasyim (close to the intersection with Jl Jaksa), part of the US chain – rib specialities and other American-style dishes. **Cheap**: *Amigos*, Arthaloka Building, Jl Jend Sudirman; Jl Kemang Selatan Raya; Jakarta Theatre Building, Jl Thamrin; Lippo Building, Jl Gatot Subroto. A chain of Mexican food restaurants, live country and western music after 1800. ***Jaya Pub***, Jl MH Thamrin, pub food. ***Mel's Diner***, Jl Agus Salim 21A (commonly known as Jl Sabang), is the best place for breakfast in town, short of 5 star hotels. Open 0700-midnight, closes on Sun (Rp10,000 a dish).

Seafood Mid-range: *Kuningan*, Jl HOS Cokroaminoto 122. ***Seafood Senayan***, Jl Pakubuwono V1/6 and Jl HOS Cokroaminoto 78, fresh, Chinese style. ***Seafood Terrace***, Grand Hyatt Hotel, Jl

Thamrin. Recommended. *Yun Nyan*, Jl Batuceper 69 (off Jl Hayam Wuruk), closed Mon. Recommended. **Cheap**: *Nelayan*, Manggala Wanabakti Building, Jl Gatot Subroto, T5700248, also serves Chinese, large, very popular, reservations necessary, recommended.

Travellers' food Jl Jaksa has the greatest concentration, and of these, the most popular are: *Memories* at Jl Jaksa 17 which serves waffles, shakes, steaks, fries and some Indonesian dishes; *Angie's* at No 15, serving much the same; and the *Pappa Restoran*, which, seemingly, serves just about everything from Indian dishes like biryani through to steaks and burgers, classic Indonesian and Chinese dishes – even breakfast.

Foodstalls Cheap: *Hotel Indonesia*, Jl MH Thamrin, buffet of different Indonesian cuisines, a good place to survey the variety. *Jl HA Salim* has a great number of cheap regional restaurants, western, Padang, Sundanese etc. *Jalan Mangga Besar* has night-time warungs. *Jalan Pecenongan* (also known as Jalan Used Cars) – warungs at night, used car workshops by day, particularly good seafood, recommended (BYOB). *Sarinah's Department Store* on Jl MH Thamrin (at the intersection with Jl KH Wahid Hasyim) has a *Foodcourt* in the basement, good range of cheapish Indonesian dishes (cheap) served in pristine a/c restaurant, with English language menu explaining what each dish consists of. Recommended. The basement of *Pasar Raya*, Blok M, has a variety of reliably good 'stalls' (not just Indonesian). The top floor of *Sogo*, in the Plaza Indonesia, has similar stalls. *Café Tenda Semanggi*, in the middle of the Central Business District, near Bengkel Night Park (taxi drivers know it), is an open air area which has been used for a cluster (around 60) of upmarket food stalls, mainly Indonesian cuisine. The food stalls were first opened by local film stars and singers as a form of income when work was scarce during the economic crisis. A really happening place with great atmosphere. Consequently, one of the nicest places to eat in Jakarta. Open from 1800-0100. In *Jl Kendal*, Menteng, there are a street full of good Indonesian foodstalls.

Bakeries Popular (and good) in Jakarta. There are a number down Jl Hayam Wuruk and in some hotels, eg *Hilton*, *Sari Pacific*, *Hyatt* and *Mandarin*. *Sakura Anpan* on Jl HA Salim has been recommended.

Cyber cafés *Click Cyber House*, Jl Jaksa 29. Open from 0900 until 1700. *wwwok!*, Jl Kemang Raya 9, the most relaxed and comfortable cyber café in Jakarta, also a noodle and drinks bar. Open from 1130 until 2330. *P.T. Amanda Bali International*, Jl Wahid Hasyim 110 (next to Hazara), open 24 hrs. *Internet Corner*, 1st Flr, Plaza Indonesia, Jl Thamrin (next to the *Grand Hyatt hotel*), open from 1000 until 2130. *Twilite Café*, Jl Kemang Raya 24A, Kemang.

Bars & clubs

Amigos, Jakarta Theatre Building, Jl MH Thamrin 9, Country and Western band. *Café Batavia*, Fatahillah Square, very stylish bar and restaurant in renovated 19th-century building, great atmosphere, sky-high prices for Indonesia, every cocktail from *Sex on the Beach* to an *Orgasm*. Live jazz at night. Open 24 hrs. *B.A.T.S.*, Shangri La Hotel, Jl Jend Sudirman, T5705440 ext 6400. Popular with expats, New York style bar and restaurant. *B.B's*, Jl Cokroaminoto (in a small road next to Menteng Plaza), is the current ex-pat hot spot (mainly journalists). *C.J's*, Hotel Mulia, Jl Asia Afrika, a popular place for young trendy Indonesians, well known Indonesians musicians hang out here. A very relaxed but vibrant atmosphere. *D'Bar*, Jl Kemang Raya, turns into a lively club later in the evenings and on weekends. Lovely outside area in the back, with a small pool where conversations can be had when the club gets going. *Hard Rock Café*, Jl MH Thamrin (1st Flr Sarinah block), expensive drinks, occasional live music, bit of a pick-up joint, open 1100 until 0200. *Jamz*, Jl Garnsun Dalam 8, a fashionable place to listen to jazz, also full of musicians. Three rooms, bars and a restaurant. *Jaya Pub*, behind the Jaya Building, Jl MH Thamrin 12, an expat hangout, can get lively, live music. *Kudus Bar*, Jakarta Hilton, Jl Gatot Subroto. *Lava Lounge*, Mandarin Oriental Hotel, Jl Thamrin, plays top 40 music and classic disco. *Morgans*, Dai Ichi Hotel, Senen, décor based around this make of British convertible sports car. *O'Reilly's*, Grand Hyatt, Plaza Indonesia, upmarket Irish pub with style, live music and bar food, expensive. *Tavern*, Aryaduta Hotel, Jl Prapatan 44/48. *Prego*, Jl Iskandarsyah Raya Blok A 4-5, the place where the Indonesian 'beautiful people' go. A refreshing addition to Blok M's night life. **Pendopo Bar**, *Borobudur Hotel*, Jl Lap Banteng Selatan, open 1100-0100, Mon-Fri. **Sportsman's Bar**, Jl Pelatehan I, No 6-8 (Blok M), Kebayoran Baru, popular expat haunt for sports fanatics, TV shows live sport and pre-recorded from around the world, bar meals. **Top Gun Bar**, opposite Sportsman's Bar, Blok M. **Karaoke** bars abound.

Nightclubs Most places start up around 2300. *D'Bar*, Jl Kemang Selatan, small but stylish club with a nice outside seating area for when you want to talk. *De Leila*, Patra Jasa Building, Jl Gatot Subroto, is a superb Dangdut club, with live dangdut bands as well as pop music from the Middle East, India and Africa. *Hailai*, in the former Jailai Sports Arena, is to be found along from Ancol Bay; Sydney 2000, Gelodok Raya, Jl Hayam Wuruk, Flr 8 and Bengkel, off Semanggi flyover, Lot 13 CBD. *Jalan-Jalan*, Jl Rasuna Said, trendy, well designed club, gay nights on Sun. *J.J's* is the club next door to *Tanamur*, more of a chill out place compared to Tanamur, but there is a small dance floor. *Mata Bar*, Wisma Metropolitan II, Flr 16, Jl Sudirman Kav 29-31, popular with Indonesians but not a very attractive design. *Musro*, Borobudur Hotel, popular with locals, good dance floor. Jl Palatehan in Blok M provides the seedier side to Jakarta life. For the large-scale nightclub scene, try Stadium, Jl Mangga Besar. *Pasar Putih*, Jl Bangka 11, 1, popular Indonesian hangout, live music, good atmosphere. *Salsa*, Jl Kemang Raya 10A, generally good Salsa music and one of the hot spots in town at the moment. *Tanamur*, Jl Tanah Abang Timur 14, one of the oldest discos, popular with expats, tourists and every variety of Jakarta night life – definitely an experience, packed at weekends. *Zanzibar*, Victoria Lintas Building, Flr 2, Jl Sultan Hasanudin 47-51, popular place but quite a small dance floor.

Entertainment

For a schedule of events, look in the 'Where to Go' section of the Jakarta Post. A new monthly magazine, Djakarta!, is rumoured to be appearing at any time, & will be the most comprehensive guide to events in the city

Cinemas Jakarta is a city for cinema-goers; there are many complexes in the shopping malls, showing the latest American films. Little censorship of violence, but no sex or anti-religious action allowed. The Indonesian way is to provide subtitles rather than to dub, so soundtracks are generally in English.

Cultural shows *Ganesha*, a volunteer group interested in Indonesian culture, organize a Tue evening lecture series at the Erasmus Huis, Jl HR Rasuna Said, next door to the Netherlands Embassy (T 5252321). Check the Jakarta Post and hotels for details; *Gedung Kesenian*, Jl Gedung Kesenian 1, organizes wayang orang performances, piano recitals, theatre and other cultural events, a modern art gallery is attached to the theatre, hotels should provide information on their programme or phone, T3808283. *Pasar Raya Theatre*, 2000-2100 Fri. *Taman Ismail Marzuki* (or TIM) just off Jl Cikini Raya, T322606, is the focal point of cultural activities in the city with performances almost every night, the centre contains exhibition halls, two art galleries, theatres, cinema complex and a planetarium, their monthly calendar of events is usually available at hotel-counters or from Jakarta Tourist Office, or call T322606 for information. Theatre Utan Kayu (or TUK) on Jl Utan Kayu 68, T8567622, is the most happening contemporary cultural hub in the city. As well as regular dance and theatre events, there is a gallery and an excellent bookshop. *The Indonesian/American Cultural Centre*, on Jl Pramuka Kav 30, T8583241, has exhibits, films and lectures on Indonesia. *French Cultural Centre*, Jl Salemba Raya 25, T3908585, organizes screenings of French films and has a library.

Foreign cultural centres Many of the embassies have a cultural institute attached, with a regular programme of cultural events including film screenings, talks and exhibitions. The *British Council*, Wijoyo Centre, Jl Jend Sudirman 56; the Indonesian/American Cultural Centre; the *Australian Cultural Centre* (at the Embassy), Jl Rasuna Said Kav C 15-16, T021 5227111; the *French Cultural Centre*; Erasmus Huis (the Dutch cultural centre), Jl Rasuna Said Kav 5-3, T021 5252321; the *Goethe Institute*, Jl Mataram Raya 23, T021 8509719; the *Indonesian Heritage Society* at the National Museum; the *Italian Cultural Centre* at the Italian Embassy.

Gamelan *Miss Tjitjih's Theatre*, Jl Kabel Pendek, Sundanese folk drama, 1900 and 2100 Mon-Sun. *National Museum*, 0930-1030 Sun; *Taman Mini*, Sun.

Jakarta Fair Annual event from 15 Jun-13 Jul, now at a new site, the old Kemayoran Airport northeast of the city centre, entertainment, art market etc. Admission charge. Open 1700-2300.

Traditional dance *Bharata Theatre*, Jl Pasar Senen 15, has nightly performances of wayang orang and Ketoprak from 2015-2400 (except Sat). *Taman Mini*, Sun and hols 1000-1400.

Wayang *Wayang Museum* has alternate wayang kulit and wayang golek performances 1000-1400 Sun (200Rp). Alternate wayang kulit and wayang golek shows at the *National Museum*, 2000 Sun (entrance included in museum entry ticket). *Bharata Theatre*, Jl Kalilio 15, Pasar Senen puts on Wayang Orang performances, T4214937 for more information; as do *Teater Populer*, Jl Kebun Pala I (in Tanah Abang), T3143041 for details.

Festivals

Ramadan Visitors should note that there is an exodus from Jakarta during this time and services may be reduced. The upside is that there is no traffic. **April** *Anniversary of Taman Mini* (20th), performances of traditional music and dance. **May** *Jakarta International Cultural Performance*, a festival of music and dance from around Indonesia and also from other areas of Southeast Asia. **June** *Anniversary of Jakarta* (22nd), commemorates the founding of Jakarta. Followed by the *Jakarta Fair* which lasts 1 month. **August** *Jalan Jaksa Street Fair*, 7 days of entertainment, including dance and music.

Sports

Bowling At Ancol, Monas and Kebayoran Bowling Centres. **Fitness centres** Many of the big hotels have these. **Golf** There are several courses around town. *Jakarta Golf Club*, Jl Rawamungan Muka Raya, T4754736. *Kebayoran Golf Course*, Jl Asia Afrika Senayan, T582508. *Padang Golf Jaya Ancol*, Jl Lodan Timur Ancol, T682122. *Klub Golf Cengkareng*, beside the airport on the toll road, T55911111. *Golf Links Indonesia* is a central organization which will provide listings of courses around Indonesia, T75816154, golflink@indosat.net.id **Spectator sports** Jai alai (similar to pelota) – said to be the fastest ball game in the world – can be seen at Ancol, 2100 Mon-Sun. **Swimming** All the major hotels have pools; some will allow non-residents to use their pools for a small charge, eg *Kartika Plaza*, Jl MH Thamrin (5,000Rp) – pleasant and not overcrowded, with poolside service. *Hotel Indonesia*, Jl MH Thamrin (10,000Rp). Other pools are at *Ancol Waterworld* and *Taman Mini Ancol Waterworld*, 7,000Rp. **Waterskiing** At Ancol.

Shopping
Fixed priced stores are becoming more common in Jakarta, but bargaining is still the norm wherever there is no marked price. When buying antiques & handicrafts, bargain down to 30%-40% of the original asking price, especially on Jl Surabaya

Antiques *Jalan Kebon Sirih Timur Dalam* supports a row of antique shops said to be among the best in town – the goods on sale here are more likely to be genuine that anywhere else. The street is only 200m or so long and it is worth wandering along it to check out the shops. It is particularly good for ceramics. Among the best (from north to south) are: *Guci* at No 39. *Mitra Budaya* at No 21 and *Djody* at 20/22. Jl Palatehan 1 (near Blok M), south of town in Kebayoran, has several shops selling antiques and Indonesian handicrafts. The mass of stalls which line the famous *Jalan Surabaya* is a great place to browse for smaller objects – anything from Golek puppets, wood carvings to brass ship's chandlery. There is little genuine for sale here – men sit by the side of the road openly 'distressing' newly-made objects. The quality of the 'antiquing' is quite high and it's easy to be fooled into believing they are antiques. Bargain hard (offer third or quarter of price). *Jalan Majapahit*, northwest of Merdeka Square, houses a number of shops with genuine antiques. *Jalan Ciputat Raya* is quite a distance south of town, with better quality antiques and good furniture.

Bangka tin Locally mined pewter from *Pigura*, Palatehan 1/41; also at Pasar Raya, *Sarinah* and hotel boutiques.

Batik *Ardiyanto*, Pasar Raya (3rd Flr), Jl Iskandarsyah 11/2. *Batik Keris*, Danar Hadi, Jl Raden Saleh 1A; *Batik Semar*, Jl Tomang Raya 54. *Government Batik Cooperative (GKBI)*, Jl Jend Sudirman 28. *Iwan Tirta*, Jl Panarukan 25 or Hotel Borobudur; 1 floor of Pasar Raya (Blok M), is devoted to batik. *Pasar Tanar Abang*, a market west of Merdeka Square, has good modern textiles, batik and ikat by the metre. *Srikandi*, Jl Melawai VI/6A. A batik factory at Jl Bendungan Hilir 2, in Senayan, is open to visitors.

Bookshops *Gunung Agung Bookstore* on Jl Kwitang 6 (east of Jl Jaksa) for English books. *Gramedia*, Jl Gajah Mada 109 and Jl Melawai IV/13 in Blok M. Maruzen bookshop in Pasar Raya, Blok M department store. The Plaza Indonesia on Jl Thamrin has a couple of bookshops including the Singapore chain *Times Bookshop* and the Japanese owned Kinokunya bookshop, both stock a good range of English books and travel guides; as do many of the major hotels. Jl Jaksa is a good place to buy second-hand books – both novels and travel guides – in most European languages. *Book Exchange*: there are 2 book exchanges on Jl Jaksa.

Maps The *Discover Jakarta City Map* is adequate (and free from the Jakarta Tourist office). *Nelles* produces a good street map and for the most detail the *Jakarta Street Atlas* (published by Falk) is invaluable. **Newspapers** *Jakarta Post* is an English language paper with some information on events around town, it also has very good news coverage. *The Indonesian Observer* is the struggling competitor.

Clothes Children's clothes are good value at *Pasar Raya* (Blok M). Adult fashions are improving and are also good value. *Sarinah Department Store* for international designs at reasonable prices and rack upon rack of ethnic clothing (such as batik shirts, dresses and jackets). Some of the large chain batik shops now supply ready-made batik, hand-painted silk and ikat in modern designs.

Department stores *Borobudur*, Jl HA Salim 32-B, Menteng, or Block M; Jl Melawai III. *Cahaya*, Jl Pasar Baru, Block M. *Keris*, Jl HOS Cokrominoto 87-89, Menteng. *Matahari*, Jl Pasar Baru 522-56, Jl Melawai III. *Mega Pasaraya*, Jl Sultan Iskandarsyah II/2; Block M. *Sarinah Jaya*, Sarinah Building, Jl MH Thamrin II. *Seibu*, Jl Iskandarsyah II, Block M. *Sogo*, Plaza Indonesia, Jl MH Thamrin.

Electronic goods For the best bargains, try *Mangga Dua*, in the northern part of the city. This is where the Chinese-Indonesians relocated after their electrical shops in Glodok were ransacked in the May 1998 riots.

Fine Art Several galleries in Kemang, South Jakarta. *Edwin's Gallery*, Jl Kemang Raya 21; *Duta Fine Arts*, Jl Kemang Utara 1/55A, set in classical villa, well established place.

Furniture Jakarta is a good place to buy Indonesian specialities such as Palembang chests, painted Madura chests, Javanese chairs, planter's chairs, cupboards and boxes. Jl Kemang Raya and Jl Ciputat Raya (the latter is rather out of town, southwest) both contain a number of furniture shops and are good places to start.

Gold Gold market on the 2nd floor of *Pasar Cikini*, off Jl Pegangasaan Timur (an extension of Jl Cikini Raya), Menteng. Other suppliers can be found in *Blok M*.

Handicrafts Found at *Pasar Raya* and the *Sarinah Department Store*, in *Blok M* and Jl Palatehan 1 (Pigura at 41, Djenta at 37). *Indonesian Bazaar*, Hilton Hotel; *Pasar Seni* in Ancol. Jl Pasar Baru for Balinese woodcarving, silver workshops etc. Another *Sarinah Department Store* with 2 floors of handicrafts and batik from across Indonesia is on Jl MH Thamrin (at the Intersection with Jl KH Wahid Hasyim).

Jewellery *Pasar Raya*, Blok M. *Sogo* (Plaza Indonesia), Jl Kemang Raya. For precious stones, try the *Indonesian Bazaar*, Hilton Hotel or *Pasar Uler*, north-east of town in Tanjung Priok. For 'cheap' jewellery, the prices are higher than in Yogya or Bali.

Blok M & Pasar Raya

Paintings *Duta Fine Arts Foundation*, Jl Bangka 1/55A. *Hadiprana Galleries*, Jl Palatehan 1/38. *Harris Art Gallery*, Jl Cipete 41. *Oet's Gallery*, Jl Palatehan 1/33. *Pasar Seni* (art market) at Ancol.

Shopping centres There is now a glut of these ultra-modern, ultra-expensive malls in town; full of imported goods beyond the pocket of the average resident. Avoid malls at the weekend, especially Suns, when Jakartans take their families to go 'cuci mata' (window shopping). The showcase is *Plaza Indonesia*, Grand Hyatt Hotel, Jl MH Thamrin, the most exclusive mall, where Sogo Department Store can be found. Plaza Senayan, Jl Asia Afrika 8, is the most recently built and has the most designer shops, there are also a few nice cafés tucked away in the corners. *Blok M*, south of town in Kebayoran Baru, is still the largest, it includes *Matahari*, *Melawai Plaza* and *Pasar Raya*, for Indonesian arts and crafts. Blok M is well served by buses and is easily accessible but a fair way from the centre of town, it is both a smart new Plaza and across the road a cheaper alternative of shops and stalls. *Sarinah* Jl Thamrin, 2 floors of Indonesian arts and crafts. *Pondok Indah Mall*, south of town in Pondok Indah, one of the trendier malls. *Glodok Plaza* is north of town on Jl Hayam Wuruk and is another large shopping complex; *Pasar Baru* is north of Merdeka Square.

Supermarkets For all westerners' deli cravings, visit *Kemchicks*, Jl Kemang Raya 3, south of town. *Hero's* and *Continent* supermarkets are two chains which have stores across the city. *Sogo Department Store* (basement), part of Plaza Indonesia, Jl MH Thamrin, good selection of imported food, expensive. *Sarinah* (basement), Jl Thamrin, expensive.

Tour operators Most larger hotels have travel agents. This list is not comprehensive but includes many of the larger outfits. Most will arrange city tours, out-of-town day tours & also longer tours throughout Indonesia

For agents and companies geared to the needs of those on a lower budget, Jl Jaksa is probably the best bet. Bus and train tickets are booked for destinations across the archipelago and other services provided. Of the larger companies are: *Atlantictour*, B-15, Harmoni Plaza Building, Jl Suryopranoto 2, T2310011, F376760. *Colors of Asia Travel*, Niaga Tower, 16th Flr, Jl Jend Sudirman, T2505370, F2505371, run tours to all parts of the archipelago, professional and well-run. *Continental*, Komplek Duta Merlin Blok A/22, Jl Gajah Mada 3-5, T3803442. *Kalpataru Adventure*, Jl Galur Sari II/54, T882150. Organize wildlife tours to Krakatau and Ujung Kulon as well as further afield to Komodo, Kalimantan and Flores. *Kaltim Adventure Tour*, Jl Tanah Abang 11/23, T361950, F3802678, specializes in trekking tours to East Kalimantan. *Musi Holiday Travel Agency*, Jl Wahid Hasyim 12C, T3800727. *Natrabu*, Jl Agus Salim 29A, T331728. *Pacto*, Jl Taman Kemeng II Blok D2, T7975874, F7975881. *Pantravel*, Kartika Plaza, Jl MH Thamrin 10, T320908. *Puri Tour*, Duta Merlin Complex Blok C 56-57, Jl Gajah Mada 3-5, T3844646. *Rakata Adventure*, Jl Matraman 102, T8582436, specialists in adventure destinations around Indonesia, reliable. *Robertur Kencana*, Jl Jaksa 20B, T332926, can organize visa extension or cheap trips to Singapore to renew visa. *RTQ*, Jl Jaksa 25C, T3904501. Efficient service, Mr Baginda speaks good English and is used to dealing with foreign visitors. Recommended for cheap flights and bus travel around Indonesia, photocopying, telephone calls, maps. *Satriavi*, Jl Prapatan 32, T3803944, F3806556. *Seabreeze*, Jl Jaksa 38, T3902996. *Setia Tour*, Glodok Plaza, Jl Pinangsia Raya, T336183. *Sona Topas*, Panin Bank Building, Jl Jend Sudirman 1, T710636, Borobudur Hotel, 3rd Flr, T361738, and Hotel Indonesia, T3107567. *Tomaco*, Jakarta Theatre Building, Jl MH Thamrin 9, T317435. *Universal Tour*, Jl Pintu Besar Selatan 82C, T6901669; *Vayatour*, President Hotel, Jl Thamrin, T3100720.

Transport

Local **Bajaj** (orange motorized 3-wheelers, Indian made, pronounced bajai): sometimes known as 'panzer' bajaj because of their tank-like behaviour. There have been rumours that the government would like to do away with bajajs, as they have been deemed 'anti-humane'. They are already barred from Jakarta's main thoroughfares. Nonetheless, they remain the cheapest way to get around other than by bus or on foot. Negotiate price furiously before boarding and expect to pay a minimum of 2,000Rp for a short journey. **Bus**: most fares 500Rp around town. Crowded, especially during rush hour, and beware of pickpockets. **Express buses** (marked 'P' for Patas) are smaller and less crowded, 800Rp. Patas a/c express buses, 2,300Rp. **Car hire**: most international companies strongly recommend a driver and local expats believe it is pure madness to attempt tackling the streets of Jakarta oneself, visitors do, though, and survive. Cars with driver can be hired by the day for about US$50. *Avis*, Jl Diponegoro 25, T3142900, F331845, also desks at Soekarno-Hatta Airport and the Borobudur Intercontinental Hotel. *Bluebird*, Jl Hos,

Cokroaminoto 107, T332064, F332175. **National**, Kartika Plaza Hotel, Jl MH Thamrin 10, T333423/3143423. **Toyota Rentacar**, Jl Gaya Motor 111/3, Sunter 11, T6506565, F6512621. Considered to be the best in town, with new cars at a very competitive rate. **Helicak**: strange looking motorized bubbles, now rather rare. **Microlet**: similar to colts; blue vans with set routes, 400-600Rp. **Ojek**: motorcycle taxis; the fastest way to get from A to B during the rush hour (or at just about any other time) but not for the faint hearted. **Taxi**: the most comfortable and convenient way to get around the city. There are numerous companies in Jakarta, some more reliable than others. The company with the most cars is **Prestasi Taxis** (blue cabs – deceptively, the same colour as Blue Bird Taxis). Avoid Prestasi taxis as there has been reports of muggings in these taxis recently. The most reliable is **Blue Bird** (T7941234 to book), most drivers speak English and 'care for the customer' is evident, because they are regulated the prices are the cheapest too. **Dian Taksi** (T5807070) and **Express taxis** (T7340455) are recommended. Avoid taxi drivers who refuse to use their meters (*Argos*) and make a point of locking the doors (especially after dark). Theft while stuck in traffic is becoming more common – most thieves are after just watches and money. Tipping is not usual, but round up the fare on the meter to the nearest 1,000Rp. Remember to have sufficient small bills to pay the fare. 2,000Rp flagfall and 900Rp for each additional km.

Train Jakarta has 4 railway stations. The advantage of travelling by train, rather than taking a bus, is that it saves on a tiresome journey to one of the out of town bus terminals – the railway stations are far more central. The main station is **Gambir**, on the east side of Merdeka Square (Jl Merdeka Timur). Regular connections with Bogor 1 hr 20 mins (3rd class only), or non-stop, 50 mins on business class, and Bandung 3 hrs. Connections with Yogya 10 hrs, Solo and Surabaya 14½ hrs. Left luggage locker facility here in upstairs restaurant, open 0300-2200, 15,000Rp for 24 hrs. **Kota** station, in the old town also services Bandung and Yogya, and Surabaya (via Semarang and Cirebon). Night trains tend to depart from Kota. **Tanah Abang** station connects towns in West Java with Jakarta, including the port of Merak, 5 hrs – the ferry departure point to Sumatra. The train leaves at 0749 and costs 2,000Rp economy (the only class available). **Pasar Senen** connects the north coast towns of Cirebon, Semarang and Surabaya (see timetable on page 977). Note that trains departing from Gambir often also stop at the Kota station.

Road Bus: there are 3 city bus terminals, all some distance from the city centre. **Kalideres Terminal**, T592274, on the west edge of the city, 15 km from the centre, serves the west coast, including Merak with a handful of connections on to Sumatra (most Sumatra buses depart from the Pulo Gadung terminal). Damri buses Nos 20, 26, 46A, 204, 913, 208, P02, P03, P6A, P7A and P18 all serve Kalideres terminal. **Kampung Rambutan**, about 15 km south of the city, is a relatively new terminal primarily serving Bogor, Bandung and other towns and cities in West Java. Buses to Sumatra and some other major long haul destinations including Surabaya and Yogya also leave from Kampung Rambutan. Bus No 502 from Jl Kebon Sirih, at the north end of Jl Jaksa, goes to Kampung Rambutan. **Pulo Gadung Terminal**, T881763, 12 km east of the centre at the junction of Jl Bekasi Timur Raya and Jl Perintis Kemerdekaan, serves Central and East Java including the towns of Cirebon 5 hrs, Yogya 12 hrs, Surabaya 15 hrs and Malang 18 hrs. Pulo Gadung is also the main bus terminal for Sumatra, with buses going to all the major towns – even as far as Banda Aceh, some 3,000 km north. Bali is served from Pulo Gadung, often via cities in East Java, and this terminal is by far the busiest of the three. Bus Nos 42, 44, 50, 51, 52, 55, 56, 57, 58, 59, 77, 501, 502, 504, 507, 508, 509, 907, P4, P5, P7, P7A, P9 and P13A all serve Pulo Gadung terminal. **Booking bus tickets**: private bus companies have their offices at these terminals. Alternatively, purchase tickets from a travel agent. The largest concentration of agents who book bus tickets is to be found on Jl Jaksa.

Sea Boat: Jakarta's port is Tanjung Priok, 15 km from the city centre. The state-owned shipping company *Pelni* has its head office at Jl Gajah Mada 14, T343307. Its ticket office is at Jl Angkasa 20, T4217406. A counter on the 2nd floor of the building is much less crowded for ticket purchase (entrance on right of building). Two photocopies of passport are required (photocopying shop on left of building, as you face it). The Pelni ships Kerinci, Kambuna, Umsini, Lawit, Sirimau, Ciremai, Dobonsolo, Bukitraya, Bukit Singuntang, Lambelo and Simabung dock here. There are also many more Pelni agents in town, which though they levy a small surcharge are often far more convenient. The Jakarta Tourist Board, Jakarta Theatre Building, has information on sailing schedules, although these must be viewed as guidelines only (see page 988). **Getting to Tanjung Priok**: Bus No 60 from Jl Pos or Bus No P14 from Jl Kebon Sirih, off Jl Jaksa. Or take a taxi. Allow at least an hour. It is less than 1 km from the bus station at Tanjung Priok to the Pelni dock.

Airline offices International airline offices: *Air France*, Summitmas I, 9th Flr, Jl Jend Sudirman Kav 29-32, T5202262. *Air India*, Wisma Dharma Niaga, Jl Abdul Muis 6-8-10, T3858846. *British Airways*, Menara BDN, 11th Flr, Jl. Thamrin 5, T2300277. *Cathay Pacific*, T5151747, Borobudur Hotel, Jl Lap Banteng, Selatan, T3806660. *China Airlines*, Jl Jend Sudirman 32, T2510789. *Emirates*, Sahid Jaya Hotel, 2nd Flr, Jl Jend Sudirman, T5742440. *Japan Airlines*, Mid Plaza, Ground Floor, Jl Jend Sudirman Kav 10-11, T5723211. *KLM*, Summitmas II, 17th Flr, Jl Jend Sudirman Kav 61-62, T2526730. *Korean Air*, Wisma Bank Dharmala, 1st Flr, Jl Jend Sudirman, T5212180. *Lufthansa*, Panin Centre Building, 2nd Flr, Jl Jend Sudirman 1, T5702005. *Malaysian Airlines System*, World Trade Centre, Ground 1st, Jl Jend Sudirman Kav 29-31, T5229682, F5229790. *Myanmar Airways*, Lippo Life Building, 7th Flr, Jl HR Rasuna Said Kav 10, T5200202. *Philippine Airlines*, 11th Flr, Suite 1105 Mashill Tower, Jl Jend Sudirman Kav 25, T5267780, F5267789. *Qantas*, BDN Building, Jl MH Thamrin 5, T2300277. *Royal Brunei Airlines*, World Trade Centre, 11th Flr, Jl Jend Sudirman Kav 29-31, T5211842. *Royal Jordanian*, 3rd Flr, Borobudur Intercontinental Hotel, Jl Lapangan Banteng Selatan, T3441915. *Scandinavian Airlines System*, S Wijoyo Building, Jl Jend Sudirman 71, T2524081. *Saudi Arabian Airlines*, Bumiputera Building, 7th Flr, Jl Jend Sudirman Kav 75, T5710615. *Silk Air*, Chase Building, Jl Jend Sudirman Kav 21, T5206899. *Singapore Airlines*, Chase Building, Jl Jend Sudirman Kav 21, T5704422. *Swissair*, Borobudur Hotel, Jl Lap Banteng, T373608. *Thai International*, BDN Building, Jl MH Thamrin 5, T3140607. **Domestic airline offices**: *Bouraq*, Jl Angkasa 1-3, T6548888. *Garuda*, BDN Building, Jl Thamrin 5, T2311801, Jl Merdeka Selatan 13, T5710510, also ticket sales offices at Hotel Indonesia, T3100568, Borobudur Hotel, T360048 and in the Jakarta International Trade Centre, T2600244. *Mandala*, Jl Veteran I No 34, T4246100 and Hotel Kartika Chandra, Jl Gatot Subroto. *Merpati*, Jl Angkasa 2, T6544444.

Banks Most of the larger hotels will have money changing facilities, and banks and money changers can be found throughout the city centre; particularly, for example, in shopping centres. Jl Jaksa now also has many money changers, with competition keeping the rate good. Many banks give cash on credit cards. Bank Bali and Lippobank ATMs give cash advances on Mastercard. Note that on Sun it can be difficult to change TCs. Below is a list of the head offices of the main local banks, and international banks only. **Local banks**: Bali, Jl Sudirman, cashpoint BNI with numerous branches around town, charges no commission on TCs (Mastercard, Access). *Bumi Daya*, Jl Imam Bonjol 61. *Central Asia*, Jl Sudirman Kav. 22-23; *Dagang Negara*, Jl MH Thamrin 5. *Indonesia*, Jl MH Thamrin 2. *Negara Indonesia*, Jl Jend Sudirman 1. Lippo, Jl Jend Gatot Subroto. **Foreign banks**: *American Express*, Jl Rasuna Said BIX-1. *Bank of America*, Wisma Antara, Jl Merdeka Selatan 17. *Bangkok Bank*, Jl MH Thamrin 3. *Banque Nationale de Paris*, Skyline Building, Jl MH Thamrin 9. *Barclays Bank*, Wisma Metropolitan 1, Jl Jend Sudirman Kav-29. *Standard Chartered Bank*, Atria Square Building, Jl Sudirman 33A. *Chase Manhattan*, Jl Merdeka Barat 6. *Citibank*, Jl MH Thamrin 55. *City Bank*, Jl Sudirman, cashpoint (Visa, Mastercard, Access). *Deutsche Bank*, Gedung Eurasbank, Jl Imam Bonjol 80. *Hongkong & Shanghai Bank*, Jl Hayam Wuruk 8 and 1st Flr, World Trade Centre, Jl Sudirman 29-31, cashpoint (Visa, Global). *Westpac*, Summitmas Tower Building, Jl Jend Sudirman.

Communications General Post Office and Internet: Jl Pos Utara 2, Pasar Baru (or access from Jl Lapangan Banteng). Internet access now available in most of the larger post offices, prices around 10,000Rp per hr. Poste Restante open Mon-Fri 0800-1600, Sat 0800-1300. **Internet**: Internet cafes are appearing at a rapid pace in Jakarta, there is a good one along Jl Jaksa which provides free drinks for its users and travel services too. Just round the corner is P.T. Amanda Bali International on Jl Wahid Hasyim 110 (next to Hazara restaurant and bar), open 24 hrs. There are 2 Internet cafes in Pasar Raya, Blok M on the 7th and 8th Flrs. See also 'Cyber cafés' above. **Post Offices**: on Jl Gajah Mada, Jl Fatahillah 3 (Kota); Jl Sumenep 9 (Menteng); Jl Cikini Raya. **Telegraph office**: Jl Merdeka Selatan 12. **Telephone office**: Telkom, Jakarta Theatre Building, Jl M H Thamrin 81. (Open every day, 24 hrs. IDD and fax service available). There are numerous Warpostel and other telephone offices dotted around the city.

Embassies & consulates *Australia*, Jl HR Rasuna Said Kav C 15-16, T5227111, F5227101; *Austria*, Jl Diponegoro 44, T338090, F3904927. *Belgium*, Jl Wisma BCA, 5th Flr, Jl Jend Sudirman Kav 22-23, T5710510, F5700676. Brunei, Wisma BCA, 8th Flr, Jl Jend Sudirman, T5782180. *Burma* (Myanmar), Jl H Agus Salim 109, T3140440, F327204. *Canada*, Wisma Metropolitan I, 15th Flr, Jl Jend Sudirman Kav 29,

T5250709, F5712251. **Czechoslovakia**, Jl Gereja Theresia 20, T3904075, F336282. **Denmark**, Bina Mulia Building, 4th Flr, Jl HR Rasuna Said Kav 10, T5204350, F5209162. **Finland**, Bina Mulia Building I, 10th Flr, Jl HR Rasuna Said Kav 10, T5207408. **France**, Jl MH Thamrin 20, T3142807. **Germany**, Jl Raden Saleh 54-56, T323908, F3144984. **Greece**, Jl Kebon Sirih 16, T347016. **Hungary**, Jl HR Rasuna Said Kav X, T5203459, F5203461. **India**, Jl HR Rasuna Said Kav S-1, Kuningan, T5204150. **Italy**, Jl Diponegoro 45, T337445, F3107860. **Laos**, Jl Kintamani Raya C-15 33, T5202673, F5229601. **Malaysia**, Jl HR Rasuna Said Kav X, 6, T5224947. **Netherlands**, Jl HR Rasuna Said Kav S-3, T5251515. **New Zealand**, Jl Diponegoro 41, T330680, F3153686. **Norway**, Bina Mulia Building, 4th Flr, Jl HR Rasuna Said Kav 10, T5251990, F5207365. **Philippines**, Jl Imam Bonjol 6-8, T3100302. **Singapore**, Jl HR Rasuna Said Block X, Kav 2, T5201489. **Spain**, Jl H Agus Salim 61, T335937, F325996. **Sweden**, Bina Mulia Building I, 7th Flr, Jl HR Rasuna Said Kav 10, T5201551, F5252652. **Switzerland**, Jl HR Rasuna Said Block X, 3/2, T5256061, F5202289. **Thailand**, Jl Imam Bonjol 74, T3905052 **UK**, Jl MH Thamrin 75, T330904, F3141824. **USA**, Jl Medan Merdeka Selatan 5, T3442211. **Vietnam**, Jl Teuku Umar 25, T3100358, F3149615.

Libraries *British Council Library*, T2524115, Wijoyo Centre, Jl Jend Sudirman 56, open 0900-1300 (visitors must join to use the library). *Australian Cultural Centre*, Jl Rasuna Said (at the Embassy), library open Mon-Fri 1030-1530.

Medical facilities 24 hr emergency ambulance service: T334030. **Hospitals:** Cipto Mangunkusumo, Jl Diponegoro 71, T332029. Metropolitan Medical Centre, Jl HR Rasuna Said Kav C21, Kuningan, T5203435, F5203417, recommended by Swiss Embassy, reasonable facilities, doctors speak English, service is good. Pondok Indah, Jl Metro Duta 1, T767525. St Carolus, Jl Salemba Raya 41, T8580091. **Pharmacy:** *Guardian Pharmacy*, Plaza Indonesia, Pondok Indah Mall or Blok M Plaza, only place supplying a strong mosquito repellent – Mijex. **Private clinics with English speaking doctors:** Medical Scheme, Setia Budi Building, Kuningan; SOS Medika, Jl Puri Sakti 10/10, T7393014. **Red Cross:** Jl Kramat Raya 47.

Places of worship Anglican: All Saints, Jl Prapatan, opposite Hyatt Aryaduta Hotel; St Patrick's Cathedral (see *Jakarta Post* for times of services). **Catholic:** St Canisiut, Jl Menteng Raya. **Methodist:** Jemaat Anugerah, Jl Daan Mogot 100, every Sun, 0800.

West Java

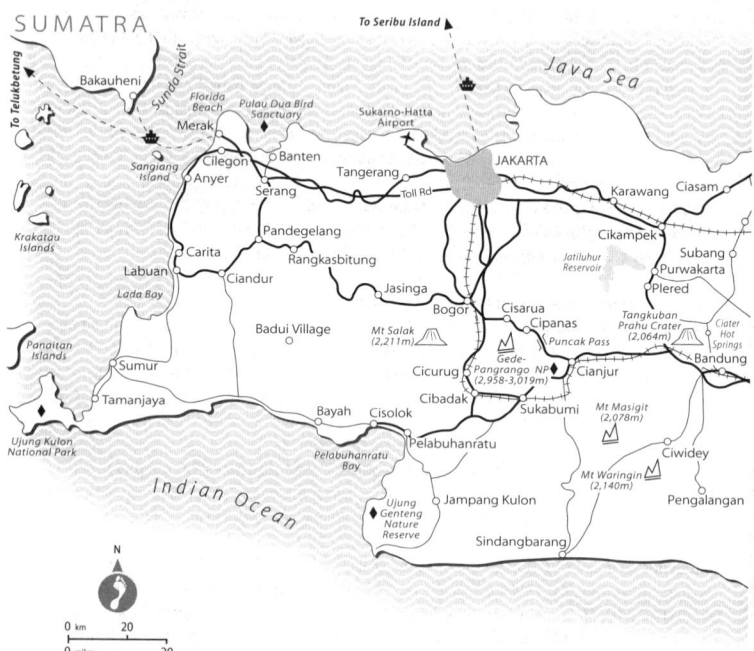

Useful addresses American Express: Jl. Rasuna Said BIX-1, T5703310. **British Council:** Wijoyo Centre, Jl Jend Sudirman 71, T587411, F586181 (visitors must join to use the facilities). **Immigration:** Jl Warung Buncit Raya 207, T7996340, or Jl Tengku Umar 1, T3909744, or Jl Batutulis Raya 1, T3845459, or at the airport, T5501764. **Police:** Jl Jend Sudirman 45, T587771. **The PHPA office:** Gedung Manggala Wanabakti Building, Jl Jend Gatot Subroto, Senayan, Block 1, 8th Flr.

West Java

The Province of West Java accounts for much of the west third of the island of Java, bar the Special Territory of Greater Jakarta which is a province in its own right. Long regarded as the most prosperous of the provinces of Java (excepting Jakarta), West Java supports the greatest concentration of people and the most prestigious universities in Indonesia, as well as important industrial enterprises. The province covers 46,300 sq km and has a population of around 40,000,000. The capital of West Java is the hill city of Bandung with a population of close to 3,000,000.

West Java consists of three distinct geographical regions: the south and west coasts, the central highlands, and the northern coastal plain. A lack of good agricultural land, poor natural harbours and the difficulties of overland communication makes the south and west coast region the poorest area in West Java. The **south coast** has the beach resorts of **Pangandaran** and **Pelabuhanratu**, while the west coast has **Carita** and **Anyer**, as well as the famous **Ujung Kulon National Park**.

The **Central Highlands** is an area of spectacular scenery, dominated by a series of impressive volcanoes. During the colonial era, the highlands were developed as an area of plantation agriculture, with stands of coffee, tea, cinchona (the bark of which was used to produce quinine) and other crops. The two hill towns of **Bogor** and **Bandung** expanded on the back of the plantation economy. With the gradual decline of the plantation sector Bogor lost out to more dynamic Javanese cities, although Bandung has managed to make the transition and is now a centre of manufacturing and higher education. In place of plantation crops, farmers now grow so-called palawija (non-rice food) crops – cassava, maize, groundnuts, sweet potatoes and various beans. It is this region which holds the greatest attractions for the visitor: the cool, hill resorts of Bogor and those in the vicinity of the **Puncak Pass**; the university city of Bandung, and hiking in the highlands around towns such as **Garut**.

The third region, the **Northern Coastal Plain**, is an area of intensive rice production. At the very northwest corner of this region, an industrial centre has developed around the town of **Cilegon**, exploiting the improved communications which link Jakarta with Sumatra via the port of Merak. Other than Jakarta, the largest town on the north coast is **Cirebon**, at the east edge of the province and famous for its distinctive style of batik.

The far west

Pulau Seribu

Colour map 3, grid A1   Pulau Seribu, or 'Thousand Islands', clearly named by the mathematically challenged, actually consists of just 112 small islands. Just to the west of Jakarta, off Java's north coast, they are becoming increasingly popular as a tourist destination. The Dutch VOC had a presence on the islands from the 17th century, building forts, churches and shipyards.

Pulau Onrust is one of the closest islands to the mainland. It was used by the Dutch from the early 17th century and became an important ship repair centre; by 1775 as many as 2,000 people were living on the island. But in the 1800s the British sacked and burnt the small settlement, so that today only ruins remain. **Pulau Bidadari** also has ruins of a fort and leper hospital built by the VOC. It lies 15 km from Ancol (45 mins by speedboat). **Pulau Laki** is one of the inner islands situated 3 km offshore from Tanjung Kait west of Jakarta.

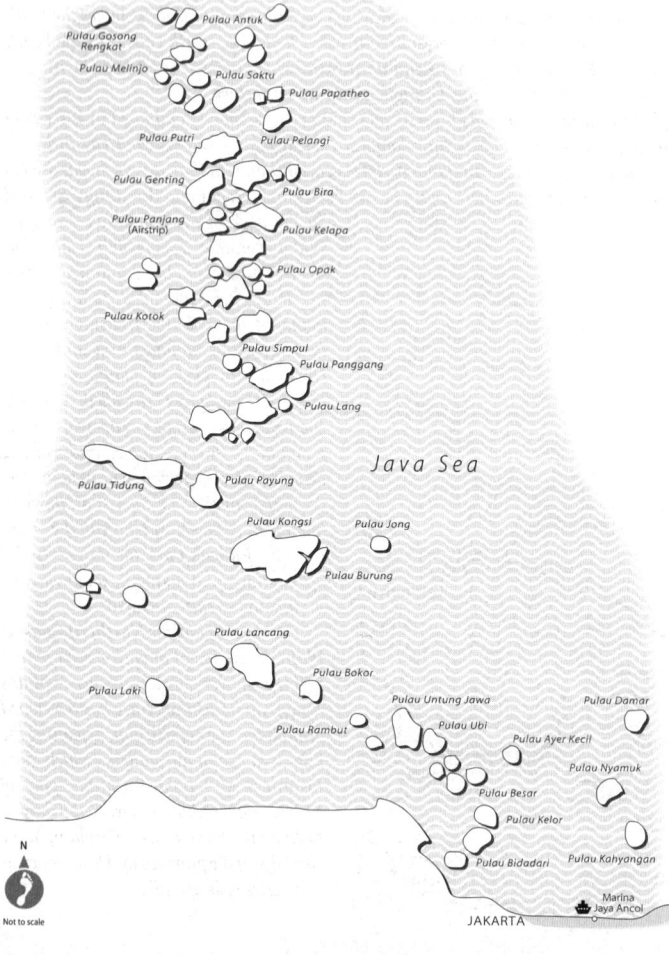

Pulau Seribu

Venturing further north into the Java Sea, there are a succession of privately-owned resorts including **Pulau Ayer**, **Pulau Putri**, **Pulau Pelangi**, **Pulau Kotok** and **Pulau Panjang**, in that order. They have beautiful beaches and offer snorkelling, scuba diving, jet skiing and windsurfing.

Pulau Bidadari A-B Cottage accommodation (both land and floating) and restaurant, managed by *Marina Ancol*, Taman Impian Jaya Ancol, T680048. **Pulau Ayer A** *Pulau Ayer Resort Hotel*, contact *Sarotama Prima Perkasa*, Jl Ir H Juanda 111/6, T3850274. Cottages available, some built over the sea, pool, tennis, jetski, fishing, snorkelling and diving facilities. **Pulau Putri and Pulau Pelangi AL-A** These 2 island resorts, to the north of the atoll, are both managed by *Pulau Seribu Paradise*, Jl Wahid Hasyim 69, T7975157/58. Both places are very well managed, Pelangi offers a/c, fridge and outdoor shower, Putri has Balinese thatched cottages. **Pulau Kotok A** Contact *Kotok Island Resort*, Jl Saraswati 48, T7209625, F7256302. Simple wooden bungalow accommodation (a/c and non a/c) and restaurant, together with a full range of watersports facilities including diving. **Pulau Laki A** *Pulau Laki Resort*, contact Ancol Marina at T6401142. Cottages with pool, tennis, jet-ski, windsurfing, scuba, fishing etc. **Pulau Macan Besar L-AL** *Matahari Island Resort*, contact *PT Jakarta International Hotels Management*, suite 103, *Hotel Borobudur*, Jl Lapangan Banteng Selatan, T/F453678. Cottage accommodation on 6 ha island with bathrooms and TV, swimming pool, price includes all meals and transfer from Ancol Marina. **Pulau Antuk Barat** and **Pulau Antuk Timur** are amongst the most northern islands and are managed by the same company. These are the most exclusive places to stay: **AL** Antuk Barat has 34 cottages, Japanese restaurant, swimming pool and dive shop. *Antuk Timur*, contact Pulau Seribu Marine Resort, Jl Pangaran Jayakarta 115 Blok B 13/14, 6262629, F6262627. 56 cottages, restaurant, tennis courts and marine sports rental shop.

B *Pulau Papa Theo*, PT Batemuri Tours, *Wisata International Hotel*, Jl Thamrin, T320807. The most basic of all accommodation within these isles – thatched cottages on the beach. **Pulau Sepa** is generally promoted by travel agents and is next to **Pelangi Island**. Boats leave daily at 0800 from Pier 19 and return from Sepa at 1500 (2 hr journey). An overnight stay is good value as all meals are buffet style. Also provided with good facilities – jet-skiing, diving, snorkelling, glass bottom boat tours. Contact T6928828/6901658.

Sleeping
Many of the travel agents in Jakarta offer package tours to the islands. The price usually includes the boat trip to the island of choice & back to Jakarta, accommodation & food

Air There is an airstrip on Pulau Panjang. The trip takes 25 mins from Jakarta. Boat transfers to other islands.

Transport

Sea Boat: a regular ferry service goes to **Onrust** and **Bidadari**, leaving Marina Jaya at Ancol at 0700 and returning from the islands at 1430. The journey takes 30 mins-1 hr. If you do not want to take the package option offered by the resorts, then go to either Onrust or Bidadari and find a fisherman to take you out on his boat for the day to explore the outer islands. It should cost around 100,000Rp. Most of the resorts have their own boats, which will pick up from Ancol in the mornings. People going on day trips can also take these boats.

Banten

West of Jakarta and 10 km north of Serang and the Jakarta-Merak toll road lies a rather scruffy but quite charming little port; all that remains of the once-powerful sultanate of Banten (or Bantam). The town is very crowded on Sundays, with hoardes of day-trippers from Jakarta, but on other days it is a picture of serene tranquility.

Colour map 3, grid A1
Population: 30,000

Banten was the centre of an Islamic Empire from the 12th to 15th centuries which managed to retain its independence from neighbouring Mataram. It derived its wealth from controlling the lucrative trade in pepper and other spices. Situated on the strategic Sunda Strait, the kingdom conquered Lampung in South Sumatra and Pajajaran in West Java.

History

The sultanate reached the height of its power during the reign of Sultan Agung (1651-83), ironically just at the time that the Dutch and English were intensifying their presence in the area around Batavia (Jakarta). It is likely that Banten was the largest city in Java (possibly Indonesia) until as late as the 19th century; Raffles in his *History of Java* thought the sultanate had a total population of 232,000. Even so, contemporary accounts record that people living on the outskirts of the city still had to contend with the threat of tigers.

Sultan Agung, suspicious of Dutch and, to a lesser extent, English intentions, made frequent attacks on Batavia, finally declaring war in 1680. But the Sultanate had nothing to match Dutch military technology and by 1684 Agung, after his forces had suffered great losses, was defeated. With Agung vanquished, Banten became a vassal state of Batavia. However, it was not until 1832 that the last vestiges of the Sultans' power were eliminated by the Dutch when they finally formally annexed the territory and abolished the sultanate. By that time, the harbour had silted up and the focus of Javanese trade had shifted to other locations. Today, 30,000 people live here – but visiting the place, you would think the population was only several hundred.

Banten is reputedly famous for its *debus* dancing, where men, who have learned to control fear and pain, go into a trance and have themselves burned and beaten, eat glass, roll around on barbed wire and emerge at the end of their ordeal uninjured, save for minor scratches. However, it is now rare to see this ordeal enacted.

Sights The site of the historic city of Banten lies outside 'New' Banten, at **Banten Lama** (Old Banten). The make-up from Serang crosses a bridge and the minaret of the mosque can be seen in the distance. To the right of the path to the mosque is the **Museum Situs Kerpurbakalaan**, with a modest display of archaeological artefacts unearthed in the surrounding area. ■ *Open 0900-1600 Tue-Sat. Admission by donation.* Close by is the **Mesjid Agung**, an example of Hindu-Islamic architecture, built in 1556 by Sultan Maulana Jusuf, son of Hasanuddin, and still very much in use. The mosque's minaret is 30m tall and can be climbed, but the staircase is one of the narrowest in the world, and gets narrower the higher you get. Larger people are advised not to attempt it. The views from the top are magnificent, weather permitting. The minaret was designed by a Dutch Muslim (some sources maintain it was built by a Chinese Muslim) at about the same time as the mosque. ■ *Admission by donation.* Near and just to the south of the mosque are some ruined walls and excavated foundations – all that remains of the **Surosowan Palace**, built by Sultan Hasanuddin, destroyed during the reign of Sultan Agung, rebuilt, and then finally levelled by the Dutch Governor-General Daendels in 1832. ■ *Admission by donation.*

Northwest of the mosque are the ruins of **Spellwijck Fortress**, built by the Dutch in 1682 (and subsequently extended), in an attempt to keep Sultan Agung at bay. Near the fort are tombs of the Dutch soldiers who died in the battle for Banten. West of the fort is a large 200-year-old renovated Chinese temple, **Klenteng**, which is still in use today. Just outside the town, back on the road to Serang and just before the bridge over the river, are the ruins of the **Istana Kaibon**, the palace of Queen Aisyah, mother of Banten's last sultan. It was destroyed by the Dutch in 1832, at the same time that Banten lost its final struggle with Batavia for even a small morsel of independence. The Dutch, symbolically, used the bricks to construct their own buildings.

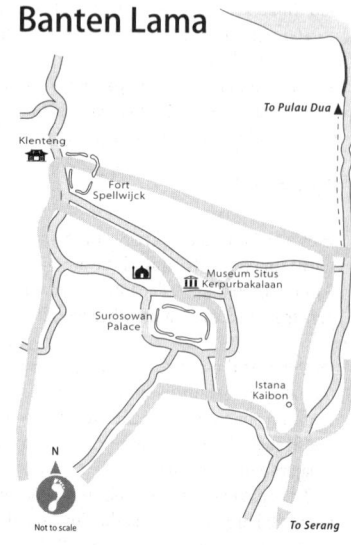

Banten Lama

Pulau Dua is a low-lying 8 ha island, 3 miles off the coast from Banten and, being Indonesia's (and one of the world's) major **bird sanctuaries**, an ornithologist's dream. There are good, though sometimes poorly maintained, observation towers for viewing nesting sites. The island has no accommodation, but guides are available to point out birdlife. **NB** Companies in Banten offer tours to Pulau Dua for 100,000Rp, but it is much cheaper to go to Karanghantu and organize it all for yourself there. ■ *Getting there: from Karanghantu Harbour, 1 km from Banten. The boat ride takes 30 mins and a 2-hr tour costs about 50,000Rp. The island can also be reached by land, along a recently made causeway, but locals advise against making this crossing alone.*

Pulau Dua
The island is best visited between Mar & Jul when at least 50 migratory birds arrive on the island to breed

There is no accommodation in Banten. The nearest town with a (very limited) range of accommodation is **Serang**, 10 km south of Banten where there is **E** *Abati*, Jl Jend Sudirman 36, not far from bus station, T81641. Clean and quiet, despite being opposite the football ground. Good night market in town for food.

Sleeping

Foodstalls surround the car-park by the mesjid.

Eating

Debus performances at Jl Kebonjati 34 on Sat nights (5,000Rp). Debus players are Islamic ascetics who have practised self-mutilation for generations. They are said to suffer no ill effects, as they meditate whilst undertaking the mutilation.

Entertainment

There are at least 2 English-speaking tour guides (including *Jellys*, who is often found in and around the Surosowan Palace) who make their living from guiding tourists round Banten. They know their material and are well worth seeking out for those who want to know more about Banten's glorious past.

Tour operators

There are several ways to get to, and around Banten. Possibly the most pleasant is to hire (pedal) bikes in Jakarta and take them on the train to Karanghantu – 2 hrs from Tanah Abang station, 5,000Rp (and then pedal around the whole area (which is flat)). **Road Bus**: from Jakarta's Kalideres station to Serang, 2 hrs. From Serang, Pakupatan Bus Terminal, catch an angkutan to Banten from the minibus station at Pasar Lama – 30 mins (1,000Rp – don't be forced to pay more). They drop off by the mosque. **Taxi**: from Jakarta, 2-3 hrs (100,000Rp). **Private car**: take the toll road to the Banten turnoff, head to Kramatwatu, and then turn right down a narrow lane at the big white mosque in the town centre to get to Banten. **Train** Slow local trains run from Tanah Abang Station in Jakarta to Serang and Karanghantu.

Transport
10 km from Serang, 100 km from Jakarta

The west coast

In the early 1990s the far west coast was an idyllic, undisturbed retreat, with few condominiums and even fewer hotels. Now that has all changed. From Merak on the northwest tip, where the ferry leaves for Sumatra, down to Labuan, 50 km south along the coast, practically every square centimetre of beach which is not an industrial complex has been developed or is about to be developed.

South of the country's biggest steel complex at Cilegon, there used to be several distinct villages – **Anyer**, **Pasauran**, **Karang Bolang**, **Carita** and **Labuan**. Now it is practically impossible to see where one ends and the next begins. And on the other side of the road, condominiums are springing up. These are mainly weekend homes for Jakarta's burgeoning middle class. Most are what Indonesians would describe as 'very, very, very simple houses', with a floor space of less than 35 sq m. There are few planning controls and money talks very loudly here, resulting in ghastly edifices masquerading as grandiose hotels scattered between a few more attractively designed guesthouses and bungalow complexes. Unfortunately, the infrastructure, in particular road construction, is not keeping pace with the level of housing construction.

From Sunday night to Saturday morning the area is a ghost town. Many hotels are empty for days on end, the beaches are deserted, and you can more or less set your own prices.

Ins and outs

Getting there Buses go from the Kalideres bus station in West Jakarta to Anyer and Labuan. It costs about 5,000Rp on the cheapest buses to go all the way to Labuan, but you can jump off at any point along the way. There are also local minibuses that ply up and down the road. If you want a seat on the journey back to Jakarta, it is advisable to get one of these buses to either Anyer or Labuan (whichever is closer to where you are) and get on the bus at the terminal. It is possible to flag down Jakarta-bound buses but they might already be full (unlikely). It takes 2½ hrs by bus from Carita to Jakarta by bus, and at weekends an hour or 2 longer. Or, alternatively, take a bus to Serang and then change to one of the more comfortable trains from there. The trains have the added advantage of delivering their passengers right to the heart of Jakarta.

Getting around For a stress-free visit, avoid the area at weekends. On Sat mornings the stream of escapees from Jakarta that began as a trickle the night before turns into a flood, with nose-to-tail traffic from the toll road exit at Cilegon to Carita. There is a big market in Anyer at the weekend to catch the passing trade, which makes the road even more congested.

Sleeping There are well over 50 places to stay along the coast, none of them cheap as owners are cashing in on the soaring demand. Many places have cottages as well as rooms. These may contain up to 4 bedrooms but can accommodate many more people than the number of beds imply – most are not concerned about how many people sleep in each bedroom.

Eating There are few restaurants outside the centres of the villages and those that do exist offer little more than basic fare. There are many fresh seafood sellers, although look closely to see how fresh the fish is and also many sellers' 1kg weights do not weigh 1kg!

Merak

Phone code: 0254
Colour map 3, grid A1

Merak is the point of departure and arrival for **Sumatra** and is one of the dirtiest and noisiest towns in Java.

Excursions The massive **Krakatau Steelworks** are 14 km outside Merak on the road to Jakarta, near the town of Cilegon. PT Krakatau Steel is one of the two largest state enterprises in the country (the other being PT Nusantara at Bandung). Built by the state oil company Pertamina during the period of booming oil prices between 1973 and 1982, it received investments totalling nearly US$4 billion. It is said that the construction of the plant involved corruption on a scale unheard of even in Indonesia. ■ *There are no longer tours of the plant but it is possible to talk your way in, provided you are wearing a little more than shorts and a T-shirt.*

Florida Beach is a few kilometres north of Merak and has good sand, but is too close to Merak to be attractive to most visitors.

Sleeping
The accommodation in Merak is over-priced; only people waiting for a ferry stay here

The hotels are situated along the main road to the ferry. Within recent years a number of new upmarket hotels have opened which has helped matters. **A-B** *Hotel Feri Merak*, Jl Raya Pelabuhan 30, T572081/2, F571530. This 3 star hotel comes fully equipped with all the facilities of a hotel in this range. The Japanese restaurant serves excellent food. A major bonus over the other hotels is the excellent pool. **A-B** *Hotel Merpati*, Jl Raya Merak, T570234, F571678. The most recent place to open during our last visit in mid-1999. It is very colourful with appealing modern architecture. Some rooms have a seaview. There is little to separate this from *Hotel Feri Merak*, only to say the rooms are finished to a slightly higher standard and that it does not have a pool. **A-B** *Merak Beach*, Jl Raya Merak, T71015, F71450. A/c, beach frontage, restaurant, comfortable but cannot compete with the newer and better equipped hotels in this range. **C-D** *Hotel Anda*, Jl Florida 4, T572522. Some a/c, close to the ferry, rooms are serviceable but nothing to jump up and down about – avoid those closest to the road. **D** *Hotel Robinson*, Jl Florida 7, T571960. Close to the ferry and almost next door to the *Hotel Anda*. Rather smelly and grubby, its only plus being the short walk to the ferry. **E** *Sulawesi I and sister Sulawesi II*, both at Jl Pelabuhan 8, little to recommend but the cheapest in town.

Eating

Foodstalls line Jl Raya Merak; the choice is over to you.

Transport

140 km from Jakarta

The fast toll road is complete all the way from Jakarta to Merak. The old road, used by many lorries and buses, is slow and busy. **Road Bus**: the station is close to the ferry dock. Regular connections with Jakarta's Kalideres station, 2½ hrs. (Buses also run from Jakarta's Pulo Gadung and Kampung Rambutan terminals, but not as frequently.) Buses are also available from Merak to major regional centres in Java including Bandung, Yogya, Bogor, Solo and Cirebon, but these leave less frequently. For Anyer Carita and Labuan buses leave from the Cilegon terminal (catch a local minibus there, 1,000Rp). **Train** The station is close to the ferry. Connections with Jakarta's Tanah Abang station early morning and early afternoon 3½-4 hrs (2,000Rp). **Sea Boat**: regular car ferries link Merak with Bakauheni on the south tip of Sumatra. Times of departure vary through the year, but normally there are about 15 crossings per day, 1½ hrs, 2,300Rp, 1,000Rp extra for a/c class. There is a 'Superjet' service which takes just 30 mins but is more than twice as expensive. This service operates every hour or so between 0600 and 1400.

Directory

Useful addresses Police: located next to the ferry terminal entrance, T571002.

Anyer

Phone code: 0254
Colour map 3, grid A1

South of Cilegon and Merak is the small town of Anyer, once an important Dutch port. Much of the town was destroyed by the tidal wave which followed the eruption of Krakatau in 1883. The most notable feature of the town is the elegant white iron **lighthouse**, built by Queen Wilhelmina of the Netherlands in 1885-86, following the Krakatau disaster. Also worth a visit is the fish market held in the mornings.

There are three **tourist information centres** close together at Km 9 on the road north of Carita, which can organize trips and guides at far more reasonable prices than the hotels. The other two centres are the *Blue Marlin* (T83302) and *Rakata Tourism* (T81124, 82400). Various tours arranged including surfing on Pilau Panaitan (US$50 for five people). Boing, the manager, speaks good English and comes recommended. All three also have restaurants either attached or close by.

Excursions

Pulau Sangiang is a jungle-clothed island in the Sunda Strait. The waters around the island offer good diving and snorkelling (both coral and Second World War wrecks). It is now no longer possible to land on Sangiang; the navy has sold bits off to developers who have guards, sirens and dogs to keep out the nosey. Don't let anyone in Anyer or Carita convince you otherwise. There is no accommodation on the island. ■ *Getting there: chartered traditional wooden boats take about 1½ hrs from Anyer Kidul, a speedboat takes about half the time.*

Krakatau (see page 116) and **Ujung Kulon** (see page 114) can both be reached from Anyer.

Most hotels can arrange **boat trips** and other excursions for you, but they are invariably more expensive than if you do it yourself. A good boat hire centre in Anyer is contactable on T601603, opposite the *Mata Air rumah makan*. It charges 250,000 Rp for a boat that can easily fit 12 people and a crew for pottering around the coast or going out to Sangiang Island. (**NB** hold on to your provisions, as alcohol may go walk-about.)

Sleeping

Weekday rates are often sharply discounted (up to 50% in some cases) from the weekend rate

Accommodation is strung out along the coast, and caters mostly to Jakarta's middle and upper classes. It makes it difficult to check out the competition if you are travelling by public transport.

L *Patra Jasa (Anyer Beach Hotel)*, Jl Raya Karang Bolong, T602700, F601872, J 510503. A/C, large airy and comfortable rooms. A recent addition is their 'floating café' situated right by the sea. This place gets very popular especially with regular parties, catering for over 500 guests. **L-AL** *Sol Elite Marbella*, T602345, F602346. Huge but surprisingly attractive 5-star hotel, comes with usual features for this price range, and also with a particularly good range of watersports. **AL** *Hotel Jayakarta*, Jl Raya Karang Bolong Km 17/135, PO Box 12, Anyer, T601781, F601783. Prices based on 4 sharing (and 30% cheaper during weekdays), loads of sports facilities, includes breakfast, tours arranged, restaurant, in need of renovation, there are better hotels in this category. **AL** *Mambruk Beach Resort*, Jl Raya Karang Bolong, T601602, F601723, Jakarta T716318, mambruk@indosat.net.id Set in attractive gardens, a/c, restaurant, pool, tennis courts, diving, sailing and fishing, the coast is rocky so the only swimming is in the hotel pool. Looks flash, but flatters to deceive. **AL** *Sol Nuasa Bali*, Jl Raya Karong Bolong, T602236, reservations T8580130 F8583966, ktitan@idola.net.id Prices for 4 people sharing and varies depending on view. Bungalow accommodation, catering more for families and those intending to stay longer than 1 night. The receptionist Iking is a very knowledgeable chap with much information about the area. **AL** *Tambang Ayam*, T601284. The room rates here seem expensive on first glance but the price quoted is for 4 people. Accommodation is in cottages – watch out for the low verandah roofs – that could do with some refurbishment and an injection of money. For a weekend visit, booking is essential. **A** *Ancott*, Jl Raya Anyer Km 21, T601556, Jakarta T7994809. A/c, pool, some bungalows self-catering, located on a quiet strip of beach, popular and good value for the area. **A** *Anyer Beach Hometel & Resort*, Jl Raya Karang Bolong Km 17/153, T629224, F6295000. A/c, pool, large, clean bungalows. **A** *Anyer Seaside Cottages (Ancott)*, Jl Raya Karang Bolong Km 21, T601556/9, F601558. Welcoming rooms, finished with traditional materials, beach frontage.

Transport *Jakarta: 119 km, Labuan: 41 km*
Road Bus: regular connections with **Jakarta's** Kalideres station, **Merak** (26 km) and **Cilegon** (12 km). **NB** It may be necessary to change buses in Cilegon.

Labuan/Carita Beach

Phone code: 0253
Colour map 3, grid A1

Labuan is the main point of departure for the Ujung Kulon National Park (see page 114) and for Krakatau (page 116). There is a 3 km-long sandy beach here with reasonable surf (best in the afternoon), but it's dirty from the creeks which run down into the sea. The only decent stretch of beach is the one adjacent to the condominiums, where the staff sweep the beach every morning and then burn the debris (so you must put up with the smell if you are downwind).

Sleeping Before the collapse of the rupiah, prices of resorts here had soared, pushing most places out of the reach of budget travellers. While conditions are very different today, there is no budget accommodation as such before the *Losmen Sunset View*. There is a selection of **C-D** grade places near the National Park Office, all quite similar.

All prices are weekend prices (knock 50% off on weekdays)
Carita Beach Many of the places to stay here are noisy because of their proximity to the main coastal road. **AL** *La Gundi Carita Cottages*, Jl Raya Carita Km 9, Jakarta, T7224382, F72101859. Prices are for 4 people sharing, no hot water, or a/c, beach fronted bungalows, range of watersports, 30% discounts available during the week. **L-AL** *Krakatau Surf Carita*, Jl Raya Pantai Carita Km 163, T83849, F83851. Attractive new hotel with modern, well equipped rooms set right on the beach. **AL** *Puri Retno*, T0254-650191/2/3. Balinese-style cottage accommodation, price quoted is for a cottage for 4 people, this is one of the better places to stay along this coast line. For a weekend stay, booking in advance is essential. **A** *Carita Beach Resort*, T202222, 5720361, F5720360. Next door to *Mutiara Carita Cottages* and owned by the same group, a/c, restaurant, pool, rooms in main block (grand but not particularly refined) and some cottages, tennis court, good for families. **A** *Mutiara Carita Cottages*, T5720361, F5720360. Pool, wooden cottages with attached kitchens, beach is only average here. **A** *Pelangi Kasih Cottages*, T81686. The more expensive rooms built around the restaurant are not as good value as the nearby economy rooms. **A-C** *Desiana*, T201010, F593316. A/c, restaurant, boat trips, the beach here is poor and rather dirty, although the

The Javan rhinoceros (Rhinoceros Sondaicus): the rarest mammal on Earth?

The Javan (also known as the lesser, or Javan one-horned) rhinoceros was once distributed from Upper Burma south to Java, but is now thought to be restricted to a small population in the Ujung Kulon National Park, West Java and a second, even smaller group, in Vietnam. When Europeans first arrived in Southeast Asia, the Javan rhinoceros was still to be found in Sumatra, Malaya, Thailand, Burma and Vietnam. Their disappearance was due to over-hunting. The Belgian big game hunter, Baron Robert de Charcourt, killed 300 rhinoceros in his lifetime (mostly in Africa). He met his end in Sumatra when, appropriately, he was killed by one of the wounded beasts that he had been terrorizing for so many years. A British newspaper, recording his fate, reported: "Shortly before he died, de Charcourt opened his eyes once more and said with a loud, clear voice to his head boy: 'Mark him down, Latiki. He is number 300...'". As one A Hoogerwerf notes "it is only to be regretted that such 'heroes' lived so long".

In 1930, various estimates of the numbers of sondaicus left ranged from five to 100. By 1970 there was thought to be only a single herd of 28 animals, giving it the dubious honour of being the rarest large mammal in the world. However, with the protection against poaching now given by the guards of the Ujung Kulon National Park, the numbers have increased to approximately 60 animals. In 1990, Vietnamese naturalists discovered to their – and the world's – amazement, another small herd in Vietnam.

The Javan rhinoceros' distinctive 'armour plated' appearance is due to the folds of skin which delineate the neck and legs from the body. With an average shoulder height of 1.6m, they carry a single horn, and inhabit dense lowland forest. They particularly enjoy wallowing in mud and are rarely found far from water. Their small stature (for a rhino) and tendency to inhabit thick forest, rather than the open savannas and grasslands like their African cousins, makes them difficult to spot.

As with other rhinos, the value of the powdered horn as a universal medicine for the Chinese led to widespread hunting and its extermination throughout Southeast Asia bar these two small, relict populations. The female only gives birth once every three to four years, so rebuilding the population will be a long, perhaps a fruitless, process. The supposed effectiveness of rhino horn as a cure-all was noted by George Rumphius in his *Amboinese rariteitenkamer*, written during his long stay in the East Indies from 1654 to 1702 as a VOC official. He claimed it cured snakebite, could indicate the presence of poison in drink (the drink was said to foam if drunk from a horn cup) and, of course, was an aphrodisiac. But it is not just the horn (say kak) that is prized. Hooves (sie kok sze), 'salt' from the hide (say goe phwee), 'two blunt teeth lying between the canine teeth', and even the undigested contents of the stomach, are believed to have medicinal powers. Gee (1964) notes that the horn placed under the bed of pregnant mothers would alleviate the pain of birth: "Persons owning a horn would rent it out to expectant mothers for the equivalent of 30 pounds each time!". He goes on: "Yet another absurd belief was that a rhino horn left to soak in a filled bucket turned the water into a sort of elixir of life, of which members of a family would sip a spoonful every day!". The outcome of these unfounded beliefs was not a happy one for the Javan, as well as other rhinoceros.

hotel is homely and friendly but overpriced. **C** *Rakata Hotel and Restaurant*, Jl Raya Pantai Cartia Km 9, T81171, F82400. Some small, fan rooms with bathrooms attached, and some newer rooms with TV and a/c. Avoid the rooms near the street, as the noise level is bad. This is the best mid-range hotel. They will store luggage for you here if you go off trekking.

Labuan Town and Carita Village **C** *Losmen Sunset View*, Carita Village, past the Lippo Condos, T81075. 10 km north of Labuan, good budget place, friendly and well maintained. **C** *Pulu Sari*, Jl Raya Lubian, T81738. About 2 km beyond village. Appealing, with natural finishes and open layout, rooms very basic yet comfortable, no en suite facilities, no shower. **D** *Caringin* Jl Caringin 20 (Carita side of Labuan town), set around a poor courtyard and with grimy mandis. **D** *Ramayana*, near National Park office, T81386. No a/c but the best of the cheapies, well set back from the road, fan rooms.

Transport
Jakarta: 158 km,
Anyer: 41 km,
Merak: 67 km

Local Bemos: bemos from Labuan to Carita cost 500Rp (despite claims to the contrary by the becak drivers who congregate around visiting *orang putih* at the bus station). **Road Bus**: regular connections with **Jakarta's** Kalideres station (2½-3 hrs) and with **Merak** and **Cilegon**. To reach **Carita Beach** there are bemos during the day, but in the evenings it is necessary to take a becak. If travelling to **Bogor**, it is possible to avoid Jakarta by taking a bus via **Rangkaskitung**; the service is infrequent and the road from Rangkaskitung onwards is poor, 5½ hrs.

Directory

Useful addresses PHPA office: Jl Perintis Kemerdekaan 43 (Labuan-Carita road, 2 km from Labuan towards Carita), T81217. **Police**: in Carita, T81032, in Labuan, T81110.

Ujung Kulon National Park

Best time to visit:
Apr-Nov
Colour map 3, grid A1

This peaceful wilderness occupies 162,000 ha of land and sea on the southwest tip of Java, and contains some of the last stands of tropical lowland rainforest on densely populated Java. It is a little-visited haven for people wishing to escape the crowds and enjoy some walking on the cool trails through the forest. The park comprises a chunk of the 'mainland', along with several islands (including Panaitan, Peucang and Handeuleum) and the surrounding sea. The eruption of Krakatau in 1883, and the subsequent tidal wave, destroyed some of the lowland tropical rainforest here and trees fossilized by volcanic dust bear witness to the event. It has recently been given World Heritage status – one of only two natural World Heritage sites in Indonesia (the other being Komodo Island).

Ujung Kulon National Park

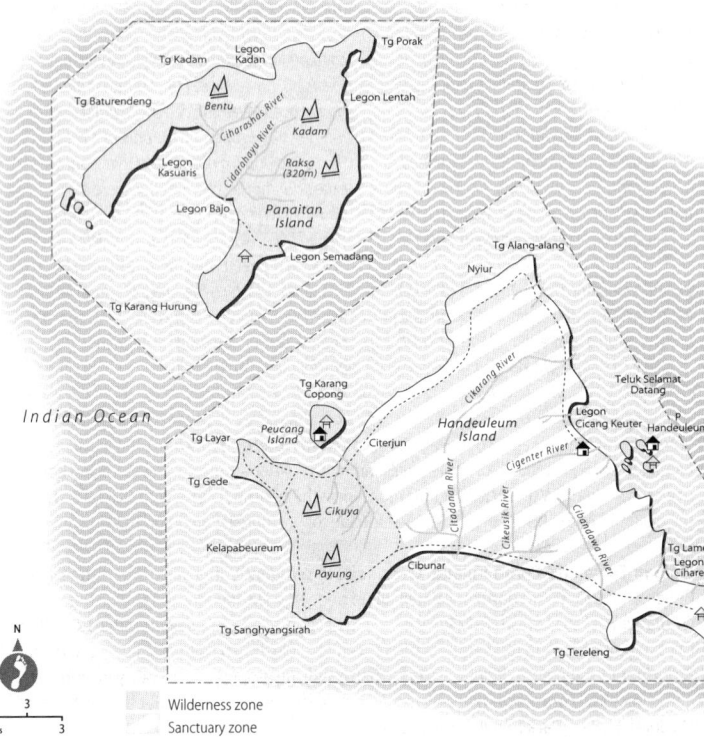

The Park's main claim to fame is its small population of **Javan Rhinoceros** (see box, page 113) – although these are very rarely seen by visitors to the park. There are some 30 species of mammal in the park, including wild pig, barking deer (*muntjak*), wild buffalo (*banteng*), leopard, the rare leaf-eating monkey, crab-eating macaques and civets. Nine of the mammals to be found at Ujung Kulon are on the Red List of threatened mammals, and there are over 50 species of rare plants. The park also supports a diverse community of birdlife – about half of the known species of bird (around 270 species) to be found on Java are present in the park, including hornbills. Other wildlife includes 21 species of snake. There are a number of established trails through the park's forests, the most popular being the three-day hike from Tamanjaya to Peucang Island. Marine life is abundant around Peucang Island and off the northern coast, with an estimated 75 types of coral and 181 species of fish. In contrast to the calm waters of the North coast, the South is rugged and wave-swept and in consequence is becoming increasingly popular with surfers. **Peucang Island** is a good place to go to see small animals – deer, pig, monkey (keep windows closed at night), bats and monitor lizards.

Handeuleum Island's attractions include an area where banteng (wild buffalo) can be seen grazing, canoe trips up the Cigenter River, a two hour walk to the Curung Waterfall through an area frequented by rhino, and motorboat trips up the Cikabeumbeum River through mangrove forest. Best time to visit: during the dry season, April-October.

Sights
One guide informed us that you would need to go 3 weeks without washing if you wanted to catch a glimpse of a rhino

The PHPA office (park office) recommends that visitors hiking through the park employ a guide (20,000-30,000Rp per day plus his keep), porters and cooks are also available. Enquire at the PHPA office in Labuan (address above). ■ *Admission: a permit must be obtained only if you intend to undertake scientific research or are a professional photographer; entrance tickets are available from the PHPA office in Labuan at Jl Perintis Kemerdekaan 43, T81217. 2,000Rp per person, plus 2,500Rp per person insurance (for search and rescue), for a period of 7 days. Office hours 0730-1400 Mon-Thu, 0730-1100 Fri and Sat.*

Permits & guides

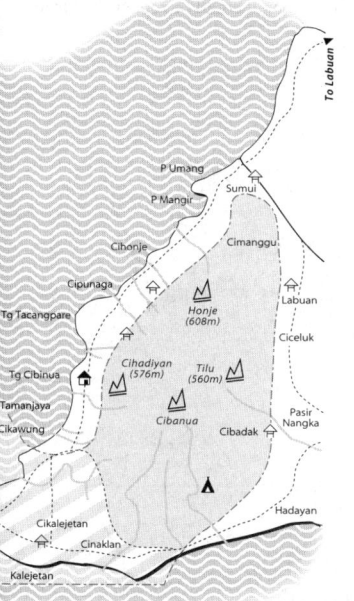

Peucang Island A *Peucang Lodges* 16 double bedrooms, a/c, restaurant, hot water, TV, all meals provided. **B** *Peucang Guesthouse* (the original guesthouse in the park) holds a maximum of 12 people in 5 double/triple rooms, with attached bathrooms for 3 rooms, price includes breakfast. Simple restaurant on the island.

Handeuleum Island C Attractive Swiss-style cottages, with 4 bedrooms, sleeping a maximum of 10 people, shared bathroom.

Tamanjaya (mainland village) **C** *Wanawisata Lodges*, 2 lodges, each with 3 bedrooms and shared bathroom.

Camping Sites are available throughout the park, but no facilities are provided.

Sleeping
Ranger's huts are primitive & could do with some attention

Eating Take your own food and water. There are restaurants at the accommodation site on Peucang Island. For campers, take all your food and drink with you.

Tour operators It is best to organize trips to Ujung Kulon from Jakarta or from the Carita/Labuan area. The tourism centres can arrange 4-5 day trips (it is not really worth going for less than 4 days) and charge about $200 per person (minimum 4). Hotels also offer trips but none are as cheap. If you have time on your hands it is also possible to arrange a park permit through the PHPA office in Labuan (see above) and make you own way to the park, picking up a guide at the entrance. *Wanawisata Tours and Travel*, Gedung Manggala, Wanabhakti Blok 4, PO BOX 63, T5700238, F5701141. Organize 2-4 day tours to the park, Krakatau, the Baduy Tribe and Pilau Dua.

Hard bargaining skills are required

Transport **Road Bus**: regular connections with **Jakarta's** Kalideres station to Labuan (10,000Rp). From there, take a bus to Sumur, and then an *ojek* to Tamanjaya. Four-wheel drive vehicles can also negotiate the road to Tamanjaya. Alternatively, go by boat from Labuan (see below).

Sea Boat: to hire a boat which holds 15-20 people costs 1,000,000Rp. Another way to reach the islands is to take a tour (4 days with tents provided for $150-175).

Krakatoa

Colour map 3, grid A1 Krakatoa is the site of the largest volcanic eruption ever recorded. The explosion occurred on the morning of the 27 August 1883, had a force equivalent to 2,000 Hiroshima bombs, and resulted in the death of 36,000 people. Tidal waves (*tsunami*) 40m high, radiating outwards at speeds, reportedly, of over 500 km per hour, destroyed coastal towns and villages. The explosion was heard from Sri Lanka to Perth (Australia) and the resulting waves led to a noticeable surge in the English Channel. The explosion was such that the 400m-high cone was replaced by a marine trench 300m deep.

Rupert Furneau writes in his book *Krakatoa* (1965): "At 10 o'clock plus two minutes, three-quarters of Krakatoa Island, 11 square miles of its surface, an area not much less than Manhattan, a mass of rock and earth one and one-eighth cubic miles in extent, collapsed into a chasm beneath. Nineteen hours of continuous eruption had drained the magma from the chamber faster than it could be replenished from

Krakatoa

below. Their support removed, thousands of tons of roof rock crashed into the void below. Krakatoa's three cones caved in. The sea bed reared and opened in upheaval. The sea rushed into the gaping hole. From the raging cauldron of seething rocks, frothing magma and hissing sea, spewed an immense quantity of water ... From the volcano roared a mighty blast, Krakatoa's death cry, the greatest volume of sound recorded in human history".

In 1927, further volcanic activity caused a new island to rise above the sea – Anak Krakatoa (child of Krakatau). Today this island stands 200m above sea-level and visitors may walk from the east side of the island upon the warm, devastated landscape through deep ash, to the main crater. It remains desolate and uninhabited, though the other surrounding islands have been extensively recolonized (a process carefully recorded by naturalists; the first visitor after the 1883 explosion noted a spider vainly spinning a web). Check that the volcano is safe to visit and take thick-soled walking shoes (Krakatoa is still avowedly active: between 1927 and 1992 it erupted no less than 73 times). There is good snorkelling and diving in the water around the cliffs; the undersea thermal springs cause abundant marine plant growth and this in turn attracts a wealth of sea creatures, big and small. *Best time to visit*: the sea crossing is calmest and the weather best April-June and September-October. Between November and March there are strong currents and often rough seas.

NB At present, tourists are prohibited from setting foot on Anak Krakatau but some boatmen are willing to break the rules. It is very dangerous: the volcano is unpredictable and liable to start spewing rocks, dust and other debris without warning. In 1993, travellers died getting too close to the active cone.

Tours Day trips to the volcano used to be priced at between $250 and $400 with a guide and depending on the size of boat and engine, but this was before the crash of rupiah; in US$ terms the cost should be lower.

Transport **Sea Boat**: it may be possible to charter boats from Anyer, Carita and Labuan. Locals have gained a reputation for overcharging and then providing unseaworthy boats. (It is said that two Californian women spent 3 weeks drifting in the Sunda Strait, living on sea-water and toothpaste, before being washed ashore near Bengkulu in West Sumatra.)

Bogor

Phone code: 0251
Colour map 3, grid A1

Bogor is centred on the lush botanical gardens, with views over red-tiled roofs stacked one on top of the other and toppling down to the Ciliwung River which runs through the middle of the town and gardens. The Ciliwung, which has cut a deep gorge, has also become a convenient place to discard rubbish, marring some of the views in the process. The town has a large community of Christians, and a surprising number of Western fast food outlets and department stores. These serve the population of wealthy Indonesians who live here and commute into Jakarta. A scattering of old colonial buildings is still to be found around town – for instance, set back from the road on Jalan Suryakencana.

The town lies 290m above sea-level in an upland valley, surrounded by mounts Salak, Pangrango and Gede. Average temperatures are a pleasant 26°C, significantly cooler than Jakarta, but rainfall is the highest in Java at 3,000-4,000mm per year. The Dutch, quite literally sick to death of the heat, humidity and the swampy conditions of Jakarta, developed Bogor as a hill retreat.

Ins and outs

Getting there
See also 'Transport', page 122

Bogor is just 60 km south of Jakarta and with a fast toll road is easily reached on a day trip from the capital. However, it is worth staying here for longer than just a handful of hours. Recent improvements in the Bogor-Jakarta link has made Bogor a thriving commuter town, and, increasingly, the first stop from the airport for tourists who only want to see Jakarta on day trips from Bogor (rather than the other way around). The bus station is south of the famous Botanical Gardens, a longish walk of short bemo ride from the town centre, and there are frequent connections with Jakarta's Kampung Rambutan terminal and with Jakarta's Soekarno-Hatta International Airport. There are also buses onto Bandung via the Puncak Pass (3 hrs) and further afield to Yogya, Solo and Bali. The train station is close to the town centre and there are regular connections with Jakarta's Gambir station.

Getting around Bogor is a small town and because it is much cooler here than Jakarta, walking is a pleasant option. But there are becaks, bajajs, taxis, colts and delmans (horse-drawn carts) too. Bogor's **tourist office** seems to move on a yearly basis, just to keep visitors and guide book writers on their toes; it is now back in a building to the right of the city hall, Juanda 10, T338052, F326530. Otong Soekander, who runs the office, speaks good English and is very knowledgeable. Maps and pamphlets are available. Open 0700-1400 Mon-Thu, 0800-1100 Fri, 0700-1300 Sat.

History

Bogor is perhaps best known as the site of one of the finest Botanical Gardens in Southeast Asia. In 1745, Governor-General Imhoff built a palace here which he named 'Buitenzorg' ('Without a Care'), modelling it on Blenheim Palace in Oxfordshire, England. The palace later burnt down, but was rebuilt and became the official residence of successive governor-generals from 1870 to 1942, including Stamford Raffles, governor-general of Java during the Napoleonic Wars. A memorial to Raffles' first wife, who died while he was governor-general of the Dutch East Indies, stands in the Botanical Gardens.

Sights

Botanical Gardens
There are said to be 2,735 plant species

The superb Botanical Gardens (Kebun Raya) dominate the centre of the city, covering an immense 87 ha. The gardens are thought to have been established under the instructions of Sir Stamford Raffles. Certainly, Raffles was a keen botanist; however, it was the Dutch Governor-General Van der Capellen who commissioned the transformation of the gardens into arguably the finest in Asia. The botanist Professor Reinhardt, from Kew Gardens in England, undertook the major portion of the work in 1817. The gardens became world renowned for their research into the cash crops of the region (tea, rubber, coffee, tobacco and chinchona – from the bark of which quinine is derived). The giant water lily, as well as a variety of orchids, palms and bamboos, can be seen here today. It used to be possible to see the giant Rafflesia flower as well, but the specimen has now died. ■ *Admission 2,500Rp, Mon-Sat, 1,000Rp Sun and holidays, guides available sometimes for 20,000Rp per hour, (more chance in the mornings). Open 0800-1600 Mon-Sun.*

Presidential Palace
Deer graze in front of the imposing Presidential Palace or Istana Bogor, which lies within the Gardens, directly north of the main gates (there is also an entrance on Jalan Ir H Juanda). The Palace was a particular favourite of President Sukarno and contains a large collection of his paintings, sculpture and ceramics (he had a passion for the female nude). Sukarno lived here under 'house arrest' from 1967 until his death in 1970. Today, it is used as a guesthouse for important visitors and for high-level meetings. ■ *Those planning to visit the Istana Bogor must think ahead. Only groups of 10 or more are admitted after permission has been secured through the Istana or the tourist office (see below), at least a week ahead of the planned visit. Guests must be formally dressed and children under 10 are not admitted because of the value and fragility of the objects. If visitors can meet all these requirements they deserve a prize.*

Museums The **Zoological Museum** is on the left of the entrance to the Botanical Gardens and was founded in 1894. It contains an extensive collection of stuffed, dried and otherwise preserved fauna (over 15,000 species), of which only a small proportion is on show at any one time. The museum also has a library. ■ *Admission 1,000Rp. Open 0800-1630 Mon-Sun, except Fri when it is closed between 1100 and 1330.* There is also a **Herbarium** associated with the Botanical Gardens, on Jalan Ir H Juanda, across the road from the west gate to the Gardens. It is said to have a collection of 2,000,000 specimens, which seems suspiciously inflated. ■ *Admission 500Rp. Open 0800-1330 Mon-Thu and 0800-1000 Fri.* A second museum, probably even less interesting to the average visitor, is the **Bogor Army Museum** on Jalan Merdeka which mainly charts Indonesia's struggle for independence. Well worth a visit. ■ *Admission 500Rp. Open Mon-Thu 0900-1400.*

Jalan Otista (also known as Otto Iskandardinata) is a road running along the south edge of the Botanical Gardens. The street is lined with stalls selling fruit, rabbits (not to eat), some batik, children's clothes and unneccessary plastic objects. The main **market area** is along Jalan Dewi Sartika, where stalls, hawkers, shoppers, colts and becaks struggle for space. A fascinating area to walk and watch, absorbing the atmosphere.

Jalan Otista

The **gong foundry** at Jalan Pancasan 17, near the river and southeast of the Gardens, is one of the few foundries left in Indonesia – on one side of the street is the foundry, and on the other the gong stands are carved from wood. Visitors can watch metalsmiths making gongs in the traditional manner – a process which takes between one and three days per gong. The factory is about a 35 minute walk southeast from the town centre. Walk south down Jalan Empang and then turn right onto Jalan Pahlawan (see map). Next door to the foundry, in addition to selling gongs, **traditional puppets** of high quality are on offer – and at far lower prices than in

Gong foundry
A fast film is advisable if you want to take photographs

Bogor

■ **Sleeping**
1 Abu Pensione
2 Bogor Inn
3 Elsana Transit
4 Firman Pensione
5 New Mirah
6 Pajajarum Mall
7 Pakuan Homestay
8 Pakuan Palace
9 Pangrango
10 Pangrango 2
11 Puri Bali
12 Ramayana Rest-U
13 Salak
14 Wisma Gumang Gede
15 Wisma Permata

● **Eating**
1 Bogor Permai Coffeeshop & Bakery
2 Kentucky Fried Chicken
3 Singapore Bakery

Jakarta. About 200m on from the gong foundry is a small **tofu factory**, a fascinating insight into the simple process of tofu making. Fresh tofu is sold to local villages. A wayang maker has his home and factory along Lebak Kantin Rt.02, well worth a visit (T383758). Claims to be the 'original puppet maker'.

Jalan Batutulis A **batutulis** (meaning 'inscribed stone'), dating from the 16th century and erected by one of the sons of a Pajajaran king, is housed in a small shrine 3 km south of town on Jalan Batutulis (which runs off Jalan Bondongon). ■ *Admission by donation. Open 0800-1600 Mon-Sun. Getting there: take an Angkutan (Green Colt) No 02.*

Excursions

Taman Safari Just before Cisarua, 2½ km off the main road, is an open-air safari park. It also houses a mini zoo and offers amusement rides, elephant and horse riding, various animal shows throughout the day, a waterfall, swimming pool, restaurant and camping facilities. ■ *Admission: 10,000Rp (7,500Rp for children). Open 0900-1700 Mon-Fri, 0800-1700 Sat, Sun and holidays. Getting there: take a bus heading for Cisarua and ask to be let off at the turning to the park. Motorbike taxis ply the route from the main road to the park gates.*

Sleeping B-C *Safari Garden Hotel* is on the main road, Jalan Raya Puncak 601, T4747, F4111, J7695482, restaurant, pool and sports facilities, 170-odd rooms, some bungalows.

Essentials

Sleeping **A-B** *Pangrango 2*, Jl Pajajaran 32 (back side of old *Pangrango*, see below for details), 50m from the northeast end of the gardens, T321482, F377750. A/c, own bathroom, pool (and children's pool), TV, very comfortable and clean. **A-B** *Salak*, Jl Ir H Juanda 8, T350400, F350800, salak@bogor.wasantara.net.id Newly renovated, smart hotel with sweeping marble entrance, originally built in 1906. Full a/c, telephone, TV, good business facilities, central position for palace and botanical gardens.

B *Bogor Inn*, Jl Kumbang 12A, T328134. Most a/c, hot water, Imelda Marcos could have been commissioned to do the interior decorating for this hotel, charming owner called Mary, with good English. Recommended. **B** *Pakuan Palace*, Jl Pakuan 5, T311207, F311207/323062. A/c, good range of business facilities for a hotel in this bracket, near new Pajajarum Mall, catch an Angkutan from the centre of Bogor. Clean, comfortable, pool, popular with families. **B** *Pangrango I*, Jl Pangrango 23, T328670, F314060. A/c, pool, price includes breakfast, a good hotel with 73 large rooms set in a courtyard around the pool. Those rooms with pool 'views' somewhat public and more expensive, very clean with numerous enthusiastic staff. Recommended. **B** *Wisma Mirah II*, Jl Mandalawangi 3, T312385. Some a/c, price includes breakfast, peaceful and welcoming. **B** *Wisma Srigunking*, Jl Pakuan 12, T319430. Comfortable and elegant rooms in homely yet palatial surroundings with dining room and fully equipped kitchen, clean, good value.

C *Abu Pensione*, Jl Mayor Oking 15, T322893. 100m from the train station and probably the best place to stay in Bogor for most people on most budgets. Renovations have provided rooms with private bathrooms, some a/c, excellent condition. Well-run by Selfi and mother. Selfi speaks good English and organizes walking tours, worth a visit even if not staying. A good source of information, breakfast not included but good value with a limitless supply of toast available. **C** *Elsana Transit*, Jl Sawojajar 36, T322522. Rooms set around an attractive courtyard, but the courtyard is better than the rooms which are rather shabby, especially the bathrooms, no hot water, price includes breakfast. **C** *KWIK* (International Youth Hostel), Desa Tonjong Km 36, T31523. Pool, new, not really a hostel, with tennis and conference facilities, outside Bogor at Km 36. **C** *Hotel Mirah*, Jl Pangrango 9A, T348044, F329423. A large villa set above the town centre in a quiet, leafy area of Bogor, the rooms are set around numerous courtyards, most with hot water, TV, telephone, decent pool with café, clean and professionally managed, popular with Indonesians but rarely frequented by overseas visitors. **C** *Pakuan Homestay*, Jl Pakuan 12, T319430. Small pension on the outskirts of town on the road to Cisarua run by a Dutch woman. Only 19 large and very clean rooms, small garden at the back, attached bathrooms, attractive views of tiled roofs, well-managed and well-located for new shopping centre and shuttle bus to Jakarta airport. 10 min walk to Botanical Gardens. To get to the homestay take Angkutan 06. **C** *Permata*, Jl Raya Pajajaran 35, T318007, F311082. A/c, hot water, price includes breakfast. This used to be an immaculate little hotel – it has gone downhill and is now rather shabby and lacklustre, an extension further disfigures a hotel which has all too rapidly gone to seed. **C-D** *Wisma Gunung Gede*, Jl Raya Pajajaran 36, T324148. Nestling in the shadow of Pangrango 2, this excellent hostel has 10 large, clean rooms, all offering a/c, TV and minibar. Friendly management, highly recommended and well priced.

D *Firman Pensione*, Jl Paledang 48, T323246. Small rooms (some very small), some bathrooms, price includes breakfast, amongst the cheapest places to stay. Friendly and popular, the manageress and her daughter speak good English, views over fields and rooftops from its hilltop position. **D** *Puri Bali*, Jl Pledang 30, 10 big rooms with friendly service, large garden, but running to seed, price includes breakfast, restaurant, family atmosphere, discount for longer stay. **D** *Ramayana Rest-U*, Jl Ir H Juanda 54, T320364. Old colonial building with basic but clean rooms, price includes basic breakfast, tea and coffee all day. **D** *Wisma Mirah I*, Jl RE Martadinata 17, T323520. Out of town. Some a/c, price includes breakfast, more expensive rooms with a/c and hot water, cheapest with shared mandi and cold water, rooms are darkish, small garden and low rise, not very attractive.

Indonesian Bogor, like many towns, has a profusion of Padang restaurants, but in this case they are almost all owned by one man and the food is virtually the same, so there is nothing to choose between them gastronomically. All are in our 'cheap' price category.

Dewi Sri, Jl Raya Pajajaran. Near bus station, simple Indonesian food. *Kabayan*, Jl Bina Marga 2, T311849. Renowned even in Jakarta for its local Sundanese food. Recommended. *Sahabat*, Jl Jend Surdirman 12, T325195. Excellent for noodles. *Ponyo*, Jl Raya Pajajaran, specializes in Sundanese food. *Ramayana*, Jl Dewi Sartika 34, also serves Chinese and International. *Simpang Raya*, Jl Pajajaran 7, near the bus station, Padang food. *Trio*, Jl Ir H Juanda 38, Jl Pajajaran, near the bus station. For a quiet and beautiful setting, the cafeteria in the botanical garden (at the north-eastern end) is set in the open air (but is roofed), it serves simple Indonesian dishes and drinks and ice-cream and has a small 'library', so you can read while you eat.

Western *Kentucky Fried Chicken*, Jl Raya Pajajaran, near the bus station. *Lautan*, Jl Jend Sudirman 15, also serves Chinese food. *McDonald's*, in the Pajajaram Mall, opposite the bus station. *Pizza Hut*, Jl Pajajaran, 200m south of the bus station. Other fast food restaurants are to be found on the top floor of shopping centres: *Bogor Plaza* and *Internusa*.

Foodstalls On Jl Dewi Sartika (during the evening) and Pasar Bogor (during the day and evening) and along Jl Suryakencana. *Taman Jajar* 'food court' on Jl Mayor Oking.

Bakeries *Bogor Permai*, Jl Jend Sudirman 23A, good coffee in modern a/c restaurant attached to small supermarket, cakes are rather sickly but a good place for a break. *Jumbo Modern Bakery*, Jl Raya Pajajaran 3F. *Singapore*, Jl Suryakencana.

Cinema *Ramayana Cinema*, Jl Dewi Sartika. **Sundanese dance, gamelan and Wayang golek** Mekah Galuh Pakuan, Jl Layung Sari Rt 6/XIV, south of town, just off Jl Pahlawan, performances once a month on 4th Sat.

Batik *Batik Semar*, Jl Capten Muslihat 7. **Books** *Gunung Agung*, Jl Raya Pajajaran (Internusa Shopping Centre), *Toko Buku Bookstore*, Jl Otto Iskandarinata 80 (near

Eating
Two local specialities are 'asinan Bogor', sliced fruit in sweet water, & 'tuge gorehg', fried beansprouts served with a spicy chilli sauce

Entertainment

Shopping

intersection with Jl Raya Pajajaran). **Handicrafts** *Kenari Indah*, Jl Pahlawan. *Pasar Bogor* on Jl Suryakencana. **Market** *Kebon Kembang* on Jl Dewi Sartika. **Shopping centres** *Dewi Sartika Plaza*, Jl Dewi Sartika. *Internusa Building*, Jl Raya Pajajaran, severely damaged by a fire in 1995, but still quite a number of shops are open, entrance is on a side street left of the burnt out front. *Ramayana Department Store*, Jl Dewi Sartika. *Bogor Plaza*, almost opposite the main entrance to the Botanic Gardens. **Wayang golek** Lebak Kantin Rt 2/VI.

Sports **Golf** Jl Dr Semeru, T322891. Clubs are available for hire. To get to the course take angkutan No 03 from the bus station. **Swimming pool** *Villa Duta Real Estate*, Jl Pakuan.

Tour operators *Arcana Safariyah Tours*, Jl Jend Sudirman 23A, T328629. *Budhy Persada*, Jl Siliwangi 37H, T328788. *Finisa Jasa Lestari*, Jl Jend Sudirman 14A, T328914. *Mulia Rahayu*, Jl Mayor Oking 1-2 (opposite *Pensione Abu*), T324150. Recommended. *Panorama*, T313348, Jl Suryakencana 214, T321847. *Tropical Wind*, Jl Sempur 30, T320272.

Transport **Local** There are **becaks**, **bajajs** and **taxis**. **Colts** (Angkutan or angkots): omnipresent green machines; seem to be more of them than there are passengers. Fixed fare of 500Rp around town, destinations marked on the front. Blue angkots run to out of town destinations. **Delman** (horse-drawn carts): from outside the bus station or the entrance to the Botanical Gardens. **Taxis**: Omega Motor, Jl Pajajaran 217, T311242. Tropical Wind, Jl Sempur 30, T320272. **Car hire**: car and driver are available for charter from **Abu Pensione**, Jl Mayor Oking 15.

60 km south of Jakarta. A fast toll road makes the trip to Bogor rapid, though scenically unexciting

Road Bus: the station is just off Jl Raya Pajajaran, south from the Botanical Gardens and opposite the intersection with the toll road from Jakarta. Frequent connections with Jakarta's **Kampung Rambutan**. Green bemos from here to the centre of town cost 300Rp. Regular connections with Bandung, via the Puncak Pass, 3 hrs. For a/c buses to Yogya, Solo and Bali, it is best to go to one of the tour companies which run bus services. *Budhy Persada*, *Arcana*, *Safariyah*, *Panorama* and *Mulia Tahayu* all operate such services. See 'Tour operators' above for addresses. Also connections with Merak, Labuan and Pelabuhanratu. A very fast, efficient service runs from Jakarta airport to Bogor bus station. Every 30 mins, 8,000Rp.

Train The station (a colonial building) is northwest of the Botanical Gardens on Jl Rajapermas, also known as Jl Stasiun. Regular connections every 30 mins or so with Jakarta's **Gambir** station, 50 mins-1 hr 20 mins (2,500-6,500Rp). Trains leave from Jakarta's **Kota** station, but also stop at Gambir on their way through the capital, then stopping en route to Bogor. Note that there are no trains on to **Bandung**.

Directory **Banks** A number on Jl Ir H Juanda and Jl Capten Muslihat, eg *BNI 46*, Jl Ir H Juanda 42 and *Central Asia*, Jl Ir H Juanda 24. *Pembangunan Daeran*, Jl Capten Muslihat 13. There is a money changer at Jl Siliwangi 62, but it does not accept TCs nor is it open on Sun or public holidays. **Communications** Internet: 10,000Rp per hr, Mon-Fri 0730-1900, Sat 0730-1800. Post office: Jl Ir H Juanda 3, almost opposite Tourist Information Centre. Telephone exchange: Jl Pengadilan 8 for international calls, fax, telex. 50% discount between 2100 and 0600. **Medical facilities** Chemist: Jl Raya Pajajaran, near bus station. Doctor: Jl Ir H Juanda 40. Hospital: Jl Pajajaran 80, T24080. **Useful addresses** Immigration: Jl Jend A Yani 65, T22870. Police: Jl Capten Muslihat 16. PHPA: Jl Ir H Juanda 9 (for permits to visit National Parks).

West Central Highlands and South Coast

Sukabumi and Selabintana

Phone code: 0266
Colour map 3, grid A1

Sukabumi is a small city with a population of around 100,000, southeast of Bogor. Most people travelling on to Bandung take the road through the Puncak Pass and so by-pass Sukabumi. It is easy enough to navigate the town either by foot or *angkot*, and because there is little of interest for the casual visitor this shouldn't take long. There are, rather refreshingly, no tours or activities and no tourist information centre.

But though Sukabumi may have no obvious charms or enticements, that is not true of the surrounding towns and countryside. Most of the area's tourist industry appears to be situated 7 km north towards Mount Gede, at the hill resort of Selabintana.

Selabintana is a very small town, much more peaceful than Sukabumi, situated on the mountain slopes towards Mount Gede National Park. It is surrounded by a golf course and tea plantations and is very popular with Indonesian holidaymakers, making it busy at weekends and school holidays but relatively quiet during the week. Because few foreign tourists stay here it has a very different atmosphere from better known hill towns. This is a place for middle and upper class Indonesians from Jakarta and Bandung to spend the weekend. It is also extensively used for conferences. A great place to see how Indonesians like to enjoy themselves.

Sukabumi **A** *Hotel and Restoran Tamansari*, Jl Surya Kencana 112, T225008, F229253. Price includes breakfast and a welcome drink. Rooms are attractively furnished, TV, western loo and shower, large pool, restaurant, nice atmosphere, landscaped grounds, very friendly and helpful staff, good standard of English spoken. **B** *Hotel Daun Hijau*, Jl RE Martadinata 55, T221352. Rooms have TV, western-style loo and shower head but no hot water, central location so it's noisy, basic but clean, restaurant with Indonesian food only, simple snacks and essential goods available in reception area.

Sleeping

Selabintana **A-B** *Selabintana*, Jl Selabintana Km 7, T221501, F223383. Booking necessary, located at the top of the hill, dark overpriced rooms, TV, western loo, bath and showerhead with hot water, clean, sparsely decorated, nothing special for the price. Choice of rooms, bungalows with 1 bedroom but no cooking facilities and maisonettes are on 2 floors. Extensive grounds including 2 swimming pools, golf course, tennis courts, market stall, numerous koi carp ponds. The hotel is very popular with Jakarta weekenders and for business conferences, which means it tends to get overcrowded, noisy and dirty (and is fully booked). This is the 'in place', but other hotels in the area are better value. **A-C** *Pangrango*, Jl Selabintana Km 7, T211532, F221520. Impressive reception with chandelier, very smartly dressed staff with good English, nearly as many facilities as *Hotel Selabintana* though on a smaller scale, pool, disco, restaurant, tennis courts. Most of the rooms are part of maisonettes with more than 1 bedroom and, like all hotels in the area, they cater for middle/upper class Indonesians and are slightly surprised to be confronted with Western tourists. **A-C** *Sukabumi Indah*, Jl Selabintana Km 6, 5 Sukabumi, T224818. Lovely pool, quiet setting, tennis court, gardens and restaurant (Indonesian food only), often fully booked at weekends. Cheaper rooms have squat loo and mandi, more expensive cottages have bath, hot water and western loo, best hotel in Selabintana. Recommended. **B-C** *Melinda*, Jl Selabintana Km 6, T224444. Very ugly concrete block with clean rooms and hot water in the more expensive ones. Also has bar/restaurant/disco. **C** *Café Pondok Mandiri*, Jl Selabintana Km 6, 25. Similar calibre as *Hotel Intan* but perhaps cleaner, only has 7 rooms. **D** *Intan*, Jl Selabintana Km 6, T223091. Cheapest hotel, squat loos, mandi, no hot water and noisy (from the mosque).

Sukabumi centre

■ Sleeping
1 Daun Hijau
2 Perwata Hijau
3 Rengauis
4 Sinar Reseui
5 Tamansari

The legend of Nyi Loro Kidul, the Queen of the South Seas

Nyi Loro Kidul, the Queen of the South Seas, is mentioned in the ancient history of Java, the Babad Tanah Jawi, as well as a number of other manuscripts. She was born a princess in the ancient West Javanese kingdom of Pajajaran, but her thirst for power forced her father to place a curse upon her head. He said that she would, indeed, have greater power than he but, that she would wield it only over the Southern Seas. Re-incarnated as the extraordinarily beautiful Nyi Loro Kidul – more powerful than all the spirits – the goddess has been closely associated with kingship. Even during the coronation of Hamengkubuwono X of Yogyakarta in 1989, some of the participants said that she was present, wearing a transparent green kabaya.

One of the nine walis (Muslim saints), Sunan Senopati, is said to have found her sleeping – naked, fat and snoring, with huge breasts. Nonetheless, in the Babad Tanah Jawi, Senopati is recorded as having asked, with about as much subtlety as a latterday Casanova: "Dear, I would like to see how your bedroom is arranged". He was whisked off to her watery palace where he became her lover. After three days of bliss he was allowed to return home. Sultan Hamengkubuwono IX of Yogyakarta also claimed he was visited by the temptress on many occasions, and that she gave him strength in times of difficulty.

Throughout Java there are places linked with the legend of Nyi Loro Kidul – Mount Merapi, Mount Lawu, Parangtritis, the Kraton in Yogya, Solo and Tawangmangu. Even today, male swimmers in the sea off Java's south coast are advised not to wear green. If they do, they too are at risk of being taken by the goddess to her abode beneath the sea.

Camping Located 6 km further up the hillside from Jl Selabintana. Take a bemo to Taman Nasional (Mount Gede National Park). Tents for hire. Popular with guitar-strumming Indonesians. Entry to park: 100Rp from here.

Transport **Local** To get to Selabintana from Sukabumi, catch an **angkot** (No 10, most are marked 'Selabintana') from Sukabumi (500Rp to the main area of hotels). **Bemos** also transport people between Sukabumi and Selabintana and to local sights.

Road Bus: regular bus connections between Sukabumi and major towns including **Bogor** and **Bandung**.

Selabintana

Pelabuhanratu

Phone code: 0268
Colour map 3, grid A1

Pelabuhanratu is a lively fishing town, more popular with Jakartans than with foreign visitors, with kilometre after kilometre of rather dirty-coloured sand beaches. The surf is generally moderate, although Cimaja (see 'Excursions') has a reputation of sorts as a surfing beach. Local folklore has it that the waters off Pelabuhanratu are home to a mythical goddess, **Nyi Loro Kidul**, the Queen of the South Seas. In the large *Samudra Beach Hotel*, room 18 is kept permanently empty for her. The room is decorated with blue silk and watery paintings by a Balinese artist said to be possessed by the spirit of the goddess. President Sukarno is said to have spent the night in room 18, sharing the night with Loro Kidul. Admirers also come here and leave gifts – perfume, brushes, combs and the like. The goddess is said to claim anyone who ventures into the sea wearing green, especially men, whisking them away to her watery lair.

The town itself is small and easy to get around. In the centre is the very colourful **harbour** and **Pasar Ikan** or fish market, with a good array of denizens of the deep, and a smell which permeates the whole town. Fish auctions are held at 1000 and 1800. Opposite the fish market is the **main market**, equally vibrant, selling yet more fish, as well as the usual wide selection of fruit, vegetables, spices and clothes – including some sarongs. Just off shore are many *pagangs* – spider-like bamboo fishing riggers. The fishermen live on these riggers, inside small tents.

Pantai Citepus is the most popular beach, about 3 km from town on the road to Cisolok. The beach is lined with official stalls, restaurants and tank traps (presumably put there by the Japanese to thwart an American landing – there are very few places along Java's inhospitable south coast where it is possible to mount a landing). The beach is wide and sandy and paddy fields descend from the hills to within yards of the beach. It's an attractive spot. ■ *Getting there: take any colt heading for Cisolok.*

Excursions
Currents here can be vicious & swimming dangerous – possibly explaining the legend of Nyi Loro Kidul

Bat Cave lies 3 km from the harbour in Pelabuhanratu. Best time to visit is at dusk when the bats awaken and swarm out of the cave. ■ *Getting there: take an angkot down the small road between the fish market and the BCA Bank.*

Cimaja beach, a small pebble beach, is about 9 km west of town and 100m walk off the road (down a path through padi fields between *Mirasa Restaurant* and a surf shop). It is popular with surfers and can get quite crowded. See map next page.
■ *Getting there: take any colt heading for Cisolok.*

Other surfing beaches lie further west, between **Cisolok** and **Bayah**. The breaks here are less crowded, particularly during the wet season. Other good surfing places include **Batu Karas** (see page 148) and **Ombad Tujuh** in Ujung Genteng National Park (good breaks and can be reached by boat from losmen in Cimaja). Boats can take tourists out to **Ujung Genteng**, where there is good fishing and great surf but not any places to stay.

Karanghawu 'cliff' beach is west of Cimaja and 12 km from town. The beach is popular, but the 'cliff' is really just a finger of rock jutting into the sea. ■ *Getting there: take any colt heading for Cisolok.*

Cisolok Hot Springs can be found 16 km from Pelabuhanratu and about a 20-30 minute walk from Cisolok. The springs are set in a verdant valley. **Sleeping C** *Wisma Tenang*; **B-C** *Pantai Mutiara*, a/c, swimming pool. Both these places are near Cisolok, close to the beach. ■*Getting there: take a bemo from Pelabuhanratu to Cisolok and walk.*

There are a number of small guesthouses and more upmarket hotels in town, but the area of **Cimaja**, to the northwest of town, provides a more relaxing atmosphere. To get there, take any *angkot* or motorbike heading out of Pelabuhanratu up the hill towards Cimaja.

Sleeping
Room rates can double during holiday periods

Pelabuhanratu town B *Pondok Dewata*, Jl Kidang Kencana 22, T41022, F41532. A/c, lovely furnishings, beautiful stone bathroom, shower, hot water, western loo, TV and own veranda. Very pretty gardens, great but small pool in centre of cottages with disco/bar/restaurant. Bit close to centre of town and therefore noisy. Fronts onto quiet black sand beach. Views of the harbour and picturesque cane fishing platforms – especially interesting at night when their onboard fires are burning. **D** *Wisma Karang Naya*, Jl Siliwangi 82. Best of the rather poor selection of cheaper places to stay in town, the opulence of the lobby is not reflected in the rooms, some with attached bathrooms. **E** *Penginapan Laut Kidaul*, Jl Siliwangi 148, T41041. Rather run down but friendly management and the rooms are kept clean despite the decrepitude. **E** *Wisma Putra*, Jl Siliwangi 86. Rooms are rather dark, some with mandi.

Hotels on the coast AL *Ocean Queen*, just before Utari Village, T021-7660359/ 0266-432567. Run by an Englishman the hotel consists of 4 and 3-roomed bungalows, beautiful pool and clean, private beach. It comes recommended by a recent visitor. Weekday rates are reduced. **AL** *Samudra Beach*, Jl Cisolok (6 km from town), T41200, F41203. A/c, shower, hot water, phone, TV, large pool. Nine-storey international-style hotel right on the beach with furnishings looking a bit dated, several restaurants (pricey), pool tables, tennis, shops, balcony with magnificent views of the ocean, special deals on weekdays. **A** *Padi Padi*, Jl Citepus Raya, T42124, F42125. 2.5 km west of town. Laser disc TV, en suite stone-walled bathrooms, hot showers. Rooms beautifully decorated with antique furnishings, views over padi fields to the sea or onto garden. Open-air café with relaxed atmosphere – hammocks, cushions and chess overlooking the beach, good restaurant (see below). A (well-heeled) surfer's hang-out with a wide range of sports facilities. **AL-C** *Pondok Kencana*, Jl Cisolok Km 8, Cimaja, T41465, F41466. Run by an ageing Australian surfer. Standard rooms consist of villas on stilts with fully equipped kitchen, western loo, shower, hot water, fridge, some also with lounge and dining room. Cheaper rooms have shared kitchen and bathroom which is used by long-staying surfers. Great sea views, friendly staff with good English, possible to rent surfboards and arrange fishing trips from here. Tennis court, barbecue, cocktail bar and surf shop on site. **B** *Bayu Amrta*, Jl Cisolok, T41031, F41344. A/c, hot water, western loo, great sea view, above beach with views back to the town, fishing trips arranged. **B** *Bukit Indah*, Jl Cisolok, T41331, F41233. Set up on a hill to the west of town – great views. A/c, clean but dark rooms, hot water, TV. Restaurant (specializes in Japanese and Korean food). **B** *Utari Village*, Jl Raya Cibangban, out of town in Cibareno (contact address in Jakarta: Utari Umarjadi Puri Blok a-10, Jl Wijaya II Kebayoran Baru Jakarta Selatan, T7206773, F7210145). Must book up at least 1 week in advance either at the Jakarta address/tel or at *Losmen Daun-Daun* in Cimaja (see 'Excursions', above), spectacular villa situated about 20 km further along the coast road, heading west from Cimaja near to Cibangban beach. The house is located in an elevated position with excellent coastline views. Stunning place to relax and get away from the crowds. Good value for money, western loo, shower, hot water.

Cimaja

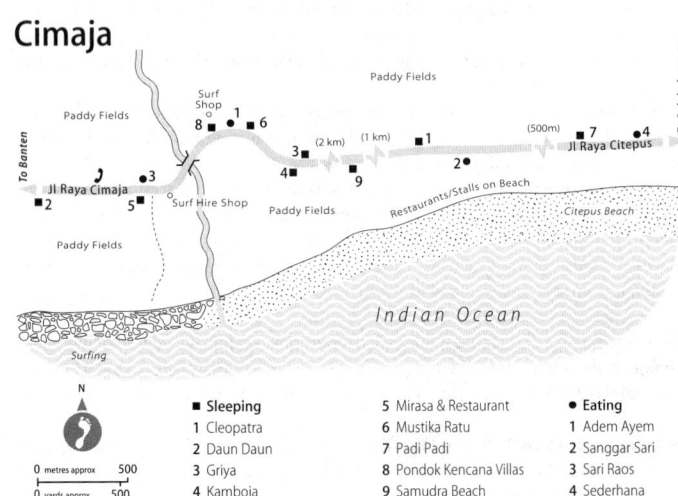

■ Sleeping
1 Cleopatra
2 Daun Daun
3 Griya
4 Kamboja
5 Mirasa & Restaurant
6 Mustika Ratu
7 Padi Padi
8 Pondok Kencana Villas
9 Samudra Beach

● Eating
1 Adem Ayem
2 Sanggar Sari
3 Sari Raos
4 Sederhana

C *Cleopatra*, Jl Raya Citepus 114, T41185. Some a/c, small pool, friendly and clean.
C *Kamboja*, Jl Raya Cimaja Km 8. Room holds 2 double beds, clean but expensive for what it is – only worth it if 4 share together. **D** *Daun Daun*, Jl Raya Cisolok 39, Km 9, T41501. Brand new losmen, brightly decorated to appeal to young surfers, a kind of Bali meets Pelabuhanratu. Immaculately clean rooms with fans, shared bathroom with hot shower, extremely good value. **D** *Mirasa Losmen*, Jl Raya Cimaja 12, T4506. Very basic, not particularly clean losmen, popular because of price, cheerful staff, restaurant (see below). **D** *Mustika Ratu*, Jl Raya Cisolok I, Cimaja, T41233. Price includes breakfast, clean, very good for price, playground.

Eating There is plenty of reasonably priced seafood to be found in Pelabuhanratu, especially towards the northern end of the main street. Many seafood and Chinese restaurants of similar basic standard and price can be found along the coast road between Pelabuhanratu and Cimaja.

Seafood Expensive: *Padi Padi*, Jl Citepus Raya, excellent seafood (choose your own lobster/crab from tanks kept below the restaurant). Indonesian cuisine, beautifully presented, antique surroundings, hammocks overlooking the sea and rice fields, billiard tables, chess and backgammon. Most relaxing restaurant in Pelabuhanratu. *Wantilan*, Jl Kidang Kencana 22, T41022, F41532. Cisolok road 1 km from town just past *Pondok Dewata*, large international menu, with good seafood, lovely veranda with tables outside, bar, cocktails. Small portions and a bit overpriced. **Mid-range**: *Daun Daun*, Jl Raya Cisolok 39, Km 9, Cimaja, T41501. Sandwiches as well as Indonesian food, brightly coloured with surf theme. **Cheap**: *Mirasa*, Jl Raya Cimaja 12, T4506. Basic Australian snacks plus usual Indonesian meals, popular with travellers and very friendly staff.

Festivals **April** *Pesta Nelayan* (movable), a thanksgiving to Nyi Loro Kidul, the Queen of the South Seas. Flowers are scattered on the sea from a decorated boat and a buffalo is sacrificed. Various events – competitions and cultural shows – are held on the previous evening.

Sports **Deep sea fishing**: boats can be chartered with *Padi Padi*. **Diving**: there are some mediocre dive sites off Pelabuhanratu, particularly to the south of town. A day's diving costs around US$80. *Moray Diving*, T41686. **Massage**: at *Padi Padi*. **Surfing**: surfboards can be hired from a number of places including *Padi Padi*. **Watersports**: jet skis, snorkelling equipment, fishing tackle (and deep sea fishing equipment) can all be hired from *Padi Padi*. Jet skis available from *Pondok Dewata*. **White water rafting**: along the Cimandiri River starting from Cibadak with *Cherokeendo Benua Wisata*, Jl Benda III 15, Jakarta, T62 217231745, cherr@pacific.net.id (organized through *Padi Padi*).

Transport *90 km from Bogor*

Local Becaks, **horse-drawn carts**, **colts**: regular colts run from near the bus terminal in town to Cisolok, passing all the hotels and beaches en route. **Bikes**: mountain bikes with or without helmets from *Padi Padi*.

Road Bus: a planned toll road from Jakarta to Sukabumi has been a long time in coming, but is expected to increase the popularity of the area. The station is near the centre of town, just inland from the fish market. Regular connections with **Bogor**, 2½ hrs, and **Bandung** via **Sukabumi**. There are no direct buses from Jakarta – catch a bus to Bogor and get a connection onward, or a bus to Sukabumi, 2 hrs from there.

Train From Bogor to Cibadak, and then take a colt.

Directory **Banks** *Bank Central Asia*, Jl Siliwangi 109 – only bank in town where TCs can be cashed (open 1000-1400). There are several places where US$ cash can be exchanged in town (including *Toko Apollo*). **Communications Telephone centre**: Jl Kidang Kencana, for international calls. Only local calls from Kiosk in Cimaja.

Bogor to Bandung via the Puncak Pass

The journey from Bogor to Bandung via the Puncak Pass includes one of the most spectacular stretches of road in Indonesia. From Bogor, Route 2 climbs from 300m to the Puncak Pass at 2,900m, passing rice terraces and tea plantations, and with magnificent views (on a clear day) over the surrounding landscape. The invigorating climate led to the creation of a number of hill resorts in the vicinity of the pass, including Cisarua and Cipanas. The Gede-Pangrango National Park offers fine hiking. From the Puncak Pass, the road descends to the town of Cianjur, and from there runs 68 km to the capital of West Java, the university city of Bandung. **NB** Avoid this road in both directions on a Friday and Sunday, if you don't want to sit in a traffic jam.

Puncak Pass & Cisarua
Phone code: 0251
Colour map 3, grid A1

After Cisarua the journey begins to become more attractive; the views open up, the developments disappear and the road begins to wind through immaculately kept tea plantations, rice terraces and bamboo forest, climbing steadily in the process to the **Puncak Pass** at 2,900m.

On the road up to the pass, **Cisarua** nestles in the foothills; a potentially attractive place to stop for walks but now disfigured by uncontrolled development. Just after Cisarua is the **Taman Safari**, an open air safari and amusement park with accommodation (see page 120 for details). While just after Cisarua, travelling up to the Puncak Pass is the **Gunung Mas Tea Factory and Estate**. The plantation is open to visitors who are shown the tea factory and can walk in the plantation, watching pickers pluck off the young leaves. ■ *Admission 1,500Rp to see the factory, 500Rp to simply walk around. Open Tue-Sun. To get to the plantation, take one of the bemos that continually ply up and down the road. Ask for Pabrik Teh Gunung Mas.*

After the Tea Plantation the road spirals its way up the last few kilometres to the Puncak Pass itself, where daytime temperatures are 20°C or less and the night distinctly cold. There is only one place to stay up here – the *Puncak Pass Hotel* (see below), which is also an excellent food/coffee stop. The hills are often shrouded in mist but on clear days it is possible to see all the way to Jakarta.

Cilember Waterfall is only a 30 minute walk from the *Kopo Hostel*. Excellent as a short break, you are likely to meet other walkers along the route, good for picnics and swimming.

Sleeping
Hotel rates escalate during weekends & holidays when rooms are in demand by domestic tourists. Even on weekdays the room rates are inflated when compared with most other areas of Java

There are a surprising number of places to stay (and eat) along this road, catering largely to Indonesian tourists attempting to escape from the heat of the plain. **A-B** *Puncak Pass Hotel*, Jl Raya Puncak, T512503, F512180. Restaurant, pool, tennis, just over the pass itself, in a spectacular position, dating from the colonial period, it is still the best hotel in the area, bungalows have wonderful views (sometimes) and some have log fires at night. **B** *Cisarua Indah Mountain Resort*, Jl Raya Puncak, Km 82, Cisarua, T253064, F254005, cira@indo.net.id Positioned just outside Cisarua going up to the Puncak Pass, new hotel with accommodation either side of the main road, many rooms with excellent views, large pool. **B** *Parama*, Jl Raya Puncak, Km 32, Cisarua, T252626, F253436. Bungalows built in 'Balinese' style set in a fantasy grotto of concrete, rooms are clean and well kept, children's play area and pool are a bonus. **B** *Permai International Hotel*, Jl Raya Puncak, Km 82, Cisarua, T258667. Located opposite the entrance to the Safari Park, the restaurant has good views down the valley but the rooms are poor, no hot water and badly maintained with squat loos, often dirty. **C-E** *Kopo Hostel and Bungalows*, Jl Raya Puncak 557 (next to the petrol station in Cisarua), T254296. Private rooms and dormitory accommodation, the best of the cheaper places to stay in Cisarua, good variety of budget tours with helpful English-speaking guides.

Eating
Rindu Alam, almost at the Pass, surprisingly good food for such a large, ugly restaurant, and a wonderful position. *Puncak Pass Hotel*, Jl Raya Puncak. The food here is reasonable but the position makes a stop almost essential. On the terrace it is possible to sip fresh Javanese coffee and eat Hollandsche Poffertjes (deep fried batter balls dusted with sugar) and Puncak Pannekoek (pancakes), while looking down (sometimes) to the plain below.

Shopping

Cisarua specializes in the production and sale of brass and glass lamps which are sold from numerous shops along the main road. Basketry and rattan and bamboo work is also widely sold.

Sports

Horse riding Small ponies, scarcely strong enough – one would have thought – to take the weight of the average *orang putih*, can be hired. 'Riders' are then led around in a rather desultory fashion.

Transport

20 km from Cisarua to Bogor, 98 km from Cisarua to Bandung, 9 km from Cisarua to Puncak Pass. **Road Bus**: regular connections from **Jakarta's** Kampung Rambutan terminal to **Cianjur** or **Bandung** via the Puncak Pass; ask to be let off, the buses don't officially stop here. Also regular bus connections with **Bogor**. **Bemos** continually run up and down the pass linking Cisarua with Puncak and beyond (1,500Rp).

Cibodas and Cipanas

Phone code: 0263
Colour map 3, grid A2

Cibodas and Cipanas are two hill resorts that, with recent rapid ribbon growth along the road, now effectively merge with one another. Like Cisarua, an apparent lack of any planning controls has almost ruined an area with a massive natural selling point: its position. The two towns are garish and noisy, the hotels almost without exception unsightly, and only occasionally does the truly stupendous location shine through. Nonetheless these two resort towns are a place to stop before descending to Bandung – indeed, there is nowhere else – and some of the hotels are decent enough.

Sights

There is a turning to the right, 10 km beyond Puncak Pass and 1½ km before Cipanas town (easily missed – look out for a green sign 'Taman National Park', or 'Vila Pesong Anggrek'; if coming from Bandung, look for the sign 'Hotel Vila Yasmin'), leading to the **Cibodas Botanical Gardens** which cover 60 ha. The 3½ km drive or walk up to the gardens from the turn-off is through a spectacular array of flowering shrubs and other plants; 'nurseries' line the route. The beautifully maintained Gardens were created in 1889 and are an extension of the Gardens in Bogor, but for temperate and high altitude species. They remain an important research centre and get very crowded during the holidays. ■ *Admission 1,600Rp on Sun, 2,000Rp Mon-Sat.*

The Gardens are also the starting point for climbs up Mount Gede (2,958m) and Mount Pangrango (3,019m), through the **Gede-Pangrango National Park**. The Park was established in 1862, covers 150sq km and is the oldest in Indonesia. It is largely the sheer age and accessibility of the Park which explains why it has so many plant species found here but nowhere else: botanists have had well over a century to root them out. The most famous botanical sight is a field of Javanese Edelweiss (*Anaphalis javonica*) – the so-called *alun-alun* – found to the north of Mount Gede. The climb to the summit of either of the two peaks takes a full day – 6-8 hours. It is possible to camp on the slopes, but warm clothing and sleeping bags are essential. There are also other, shorter, hikes for the less ambitious. Permits must be obtained from the PHPA office (just before the entrance to the gardens); it is vital that you have a good photocopy of your passport to secure a pass, but still permission is not always granted. ■ *PHPA office open: 0700-1430 Mon-Thu, 0700-1100 Fri, 0700-1330 Sat. Getting*

The best time of year for climbing is from May to Oct & guides are recommended for those who have not climbed the routes before

Cisarua

to the gardens: catch a colt from Cipanas to Ranahan, or charter one.

See also page 146

The spa town of **Cipanas** is 1½ km on down the road towards Bandung, from the turn-off for the Cibodas Gardens. Here hot sulphur baths are fed by springs that issue from the slopes of Mount Guntur which last erupted in 1889. These public baths are crowded and rather unpleasant. The mountain resort is centred on the **Istana Cipanas** – Sukarno's elegant summer retreat, set in attractive gardens but not open to the public. Like Cisarua, this is primarily an Indonesian resort town, although it makes a good stopping place on the road to Bandung.

Bird conservation Cipanas is an important centre in Java for bird conservation. The executive director is Adam Supriatna who is willing and keen to talk about the area and its birdlife. The office is just on the left before you enter the park gates. T521462, kpbciba@cianjur.wasantara.net.id

Puncak Pass to Bandung After descending from the Puncak Pass and reaching the large market town of Cianjur, the road passes through the comparatively rich and fertile agricultural lands of the **Bandung Plain**. The route crosses the **Tarum River**, which at this point in its course has cut a deep, spectacular gorge. The **Saguling Dam**, which helps to irrigate the rice lands of the area, is 15 km south. A speciality of the area is *tapai*; dried, peeled, white cassava which is sold from numerous stalls along the road. Also sold are painted pottery animals, and over-sized carved wooden fruit. About 20 km west of Bandung is the brick and tile-making town of **Pandalarang**. The town is coated in a thin layer of dust, and kilns rise up between the houses, providing work and a livelihood – and probably pulmonary illnesses too – to many of the people living in the area.

Sleeping

There is a profusion of hotels & holiday homes in the area between Cipodas & Cipanas. Note that room rates increase at the weekends & holidays

A-B *Indo Alam*, Jl Raya Cipanas, west of Cipanas centre, T512701, F512703. Restaurant, pool, a sprawling series of bungalows, some designed for large families somewhat featureless and like a 1950s holiday camp, tennis court. **A** *Novus Panghehar*, Jl Sindanglaya Raya 180, Cipanas, T511335, F512785, www.soneva-pavilion.com A well-designed hotel with an excellent position on a spur, geared mostly to the conference market, the rooms are very comfortable, fitness centre, shops and good pool. Recommended. **B-C** *New Puri Meru*, Jl Singdanglaya 184, Cipanas, T512415, F518857. The hotel was recently extended and the rooms in the new wing are the most luxurious, but even the older rooms are surprisingly well maintained compared with the stairwells and corridors, with clean bathrooms, hot water and satellite TV, good restaurant and good value stay. **C** *Hotel Bukit Raya Permai*, Raya Cipanas 219, T512505 F512995. Clean large rooms with TV and telephone, decent sized pool and feeling of space, good for large groups. **C** *Hotel Sentosa*, Jl Raya Cipanas 87, Cipanas, T512612. An older hotel with some new rooms, consists of bungalows with sitting areas and bathrooms, all with hot water, plain and rather dark, even new rooms could now do with a lick of paint and are going to seed. **C-D** *Maras Motel*, Jl Raya Cipanas, T512602. 25 basic rooms, clean and practical, geared for families, popular with Indonesian holidaymakers. **C-D** *Pondok Pemuda Cibodas*, near PHPA office, T512807. Attractive position and usually empty during the week, rooms rather pricey though and lack of English makes for little information about the surrounding area, dorm beds available. **D** *Botanical Gardens Guesthouse*, T512233. In the Gardens, restaurant, large rooms, recommended for its position and atmosphere, bookings can be made at the Bogor Botanical Gardens, don't depend on availability as are often booked up with groups, ring first. **D** *Villa Cipanas Indah*, Jl Tengah 8, T512513. A 10 min walk west of Istana at the centre of the town, some rooms with hot water, slightly shabby but the manageress is very helpful, guides available. **E** *Freddy's Homestay*, Jl Kebun Raya, T515473. Bright, clean rooms with shared mandi are cheap, dorms even better value with breakfast included. An excellent place to stay, and Freddy and his son speak very good English and Dutch and provide endless information about the botanical gardens. The local bird conservation centre is based here. Recommended.

Transport 32 km from Cipanas to Bogor, 86 km from Cipanas to Bandung, 12 km from Cipanas to Puncak Pass. **Road Bus**: regular connections from **Jakarta's** Kampung Rambutan terminal to **Cianjur**

or **Bandung** via the **Puncak Pass**; ask to be let off, the buses don't officially stop here. Also regular bus connections with **Bogor**. **Bemos**: these constantly run up to the **Puncak Pass** and from there to **Cisarua**, as well as down to **Cianjur**. They can be hailed with no trouble.

Communications Post Office & telephone office: near the centre of Cipanas at Jl Raya, Cipanas 109 (after the main market and before the Istana Cipanas). **Directory**

Bandung

Set in a huge volcanic basin, at an altitude of 700m and surrounded by mountains, Bandung has one of the most pleasant climates in Java, where the daytime temperature averages 22°C. The town centre is modern, unattractive and overcrowded, and some patience is needed in seeking out the town's main attraction: namely, its fine collection of Art Deco architecture, built between 1920 and 1940 when Bandung was the sophisticated European town of the Dutch East Indies.

Phone code: 022
Colour map 3, grid A2

The third largest city in Indonesia, Bandung is also the capital of the province of West Java. The city has a population of over 2,000,000, with a further 3,000,000 living in the surrounding area, making this one of the most densely populated regions of Java. Such has been the growth of the city that in 1989 its administrative boundaries were extended, doubling the area of the city overnight.

Ins and outs

Bandung is the province of West Java's largest city and offers a good range of transport options. The airport is 4 km from town. But many more people arrive here by train or bus. The train station is in the centre of town and there are services travelling west to Jakarta and east to Surabaya. Less conveniently located are Bandung's 2 long-distance bus terminals. The Leuwi Panjang terminal is 5 km south of town and serves destinations to the west, including Jakarta and places in Sumatra. The Cicaheum terminal is on the edge of town to the east, and buses from here run to Yogya, Solo, Surabaya and Bali and to towns on Java's north coast like Cirebon and Semarang. Both bus terminals are linked to the centre of town by bemo.

Getting there
See also 'Transport', page 142

This can be quite a struggle. Roads are often jammed and a rather complicated 1 way system can be confusing to the uninitiated. However, because Bandung is 700m above sea level, the climate is far cooler than lowland cities like Jakarta and Surabaya and walking is an option. Colts and town buses provide the main means of local transport. Taxis and car hire companies are also to be found here.

Getting around
See also 'Transport', page 142

In their office at the northeast corner of the city square on Jl Asia Afrika, the staff of the **Bandung Visitor Information Centre**, T4206644, can tell you anything you want to know about Bandung and the surrounding area, open 0900-1700 Mon-Sat (in theory). The office organizes 'designer' tours, custom made to suit each visitor's interests; eg, an architectural tour of the town, a pre-historic tour, a trip to the volcanoes, or a tour to Sundanese tribes and a Dragon village. They also organize transport on to Yogya, Pangandaran. Very helpful, particularly the English speaking Ajid Suryana. There is also an office at the railway station. **West Javan Regional Tourist Office** is at Jl Cipaganti 153, T81490, F87976, on the north edge of the city, open 0700-1900 Mon-Sun.

History

The first reference to Bandung dates from 1488, and in 1614 Juliaen de Silva wrote of "a city called Bandung comprising 25 to 30 houses". Known as Kota Kembang (the flower city), Bandung was developed by the Dutch in the late 19th century as a cool retreat from the sweltering plains of Jakarta, and it became the country's first resort town. In 1811, Governor-General Daendels encouraged the regent, Dalem Wiranatajusumah II, to move his capital 10 km to the north, so that the town would link up with the new 1,000 km-long Great Post Make-up which was under construction. In the 1880s a railway was

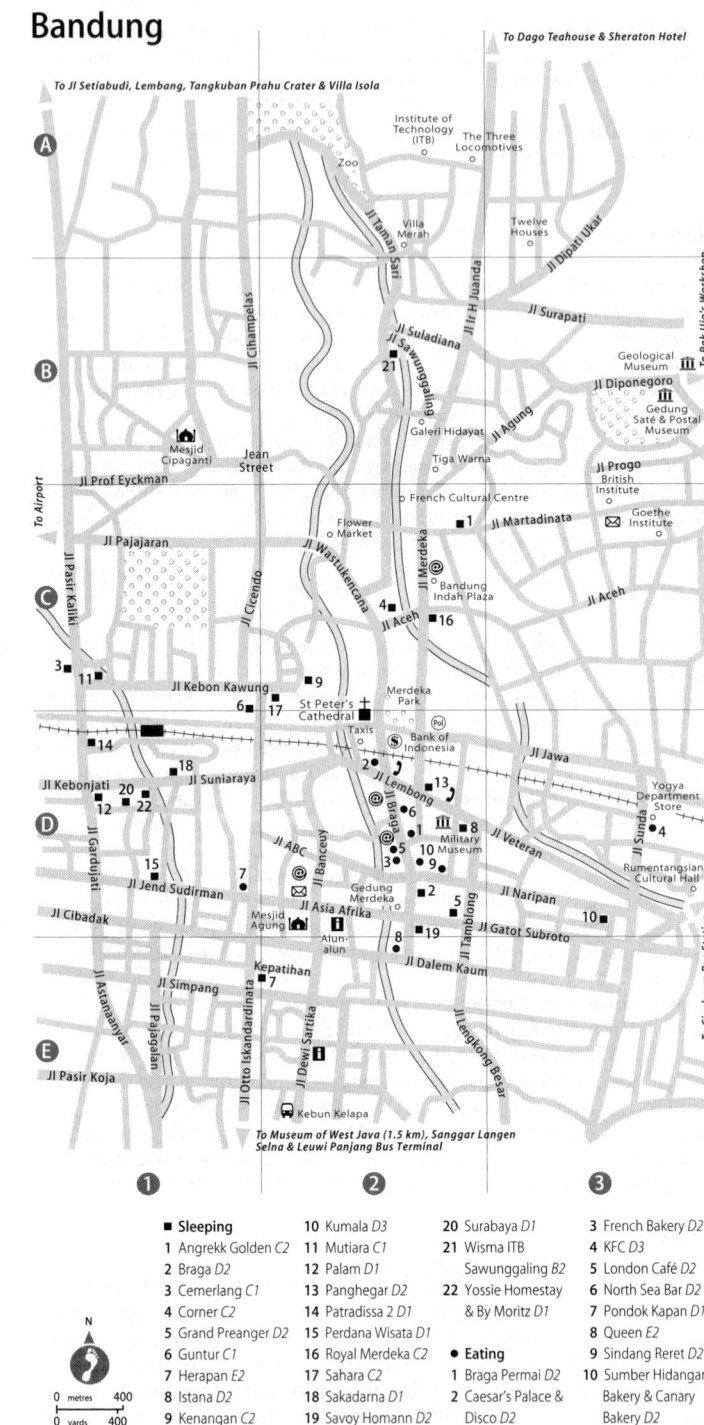

Bandung's Art Deco heritage

★ **The Three Locomotives**: three identical houses in streamline modern Art Deco style, Jalan Ir H Juanda 113, 115 and 117 (architect: AF Aalbers).

★ **Twelve Houses**: 1939, in Prairie style Art Deco, Jalan Pagar Gunung (architect: AF Aalbers).

★ **Tiga Warna**: 1938, Curvilinear Functionalism Art Deco, Jalan Dr Haji Juanda and Jalan Sultan Agung (architect: AF Aalbers).

★ **Dinas Rendapatan Daerah**: 1930-35, Early Functionalism, Jalan Juanda 37 (architect: AF Aalbers).

★ **Villa Merah**: 1922, Jalan Tamansari 78 (architect: Wolff Schoemacher).

★ **Boekkit Tinggi**: 1925, Jalan Taman Sari (architect: Wolff Schoemacher).

★ **Mesjid Cipaganti**: 1933, the only mosque designed by Schoemacher, Jalan Cipaganti 85 (architect: Wolff Schoemacher).

★ **St Peter's Cathedral**: 1932, Jalan Merdeka 10 (architect: Wolff Schoemacher).

★ **Villa Ang Eng Kan**: 1930, Geometric Art Deco building of great beauty (architect: FW Brinkman).

If you are interested in learning more about Bandung's architectural heritage, a visit to the **Bandung Society for Heritage Conservation** (Bandung Paguyuban Pelestarian Budaya), Hotel Savoy Homann, Jl Asia Afrika 112, is worthwhile, they welcome interested travellers as well as professional researchers. Their offices are open Monday-Saturday 0900-1700. The hotel also hosts talks on the history of its architecture, Monday and Friday 1030 and 1430.

completed linking the city with Batavia (Jakarta) and Bandung's future was assured. By the end of the century, the town had become the headquarters for the Dutch army and the centre of the plantation industry centred on the Priangan Highlands. There were even plans tabled to move the capital from Batavia to Bandung – plans that were interrupted by the Japanese invasion in 1942.

Bandung is regarded as the intellectual heart of Java, with over 50 universities and colleges situated in and around the city. It is no accident that former Minister for Science and Technology, Dr Habibie (who took over from Suharto as President in 1998), decided to establish Indonesia's first aircraft industry – IPTN or Industri Pesawat Terbang Nusantara – just outside the city in 1976. The factory assembles helicopters and aeroplanes under licence from CASA of Spain, Messerschmitt of Germany, Bell of the USA and Aerospatiale of France; it also makes parts for Boeing. In 1995, an Indonesian-built commuter aircraft, the N-250, was wheeled out of a hangar here for its maiden flight – on the 50th anniversary of Indonesia's independence.

In the early part of the century, Bandung was a centre of the fledgling independence movement. It was here in 1928 that the historic 'Youth Pledge' committed students to serve only one Indonesia and speak one language – Bahasa Indonesia. A remarkable pledge considering that at the time the Dutch still had complete control over the country, and the islands were divided into sultanates and a heterogenous patchwork of ethnic, cultural, religious and linguistic groups. Rather later, Bandung was the site of the inaugural meeting of the Non-Aligned Movement in 1955. The conference was attended by 29 countries, which showed Sukarno and Indonesia leading the developing world for the first time. Jalan Asia-Afrika, one of the city's main thoroughfares, is named after the event. In 1992, Indonesia hosted the NAM conference for a second time; on this occasion though, Indonesia was very much less revolutionary, its leaders radiating moderation and pragmatism.

The Institut Pasteur (now called the Bio Farma) became famous as a centre for research and production of the smallpox vaccine, as well as a serum against rabies. Before the war, Bandung produced 90% of the world's quinine (from the bark of the cinchona tree). The Bandung Institute of Technology, arguably Indonesia's most prestigious university, was founded in 1920 by the Dutch. Sukarno, Indonesia's first president, studied here. In the realm of culture, Bandung is also the centre for wayang golek (see page 304) and the angklung orchestra.

Sights

Colonial Art Deco
If you want to photograph these buildings, bear in mind that several are occupied by the military, & sensitivities are acute

Bandung is recognized as one of three cities in the world with '**tropical Art Deco**' architecture (the others being Miami, Florida and Napier, New Zealand). The Bandung Society for Heritage Conservation has a register of well-over 600 category I and II monuments in Bandung (see box). Of all the Art Deco architects the one most closely associated with Bandung was Wolff Schoemacher. He graduated with Ed Cuypers from the Delft Technical University in the Netherlands, and then moved to Bandung where he designed hundreds of buildings. In theory, any building over 50 years old is protected and the Mayor of Bandung is said to be appreciative of the need to preserve this heritage. But with the cowboy atmosphere that pervades many other towns and cities, the preservationists will need to be ever watchful.

The most impressive Art Deco building, lying in the centre of town, is the **Savoy Homann Hotel** on Jalan Asia Afrika, built in 1938 by AF Aalbers and still retaining period furniture and fittings. It has been meticulously renovated at a cost of US$2m so that visitors can savour a hotel that numbers Charlie Chaplin, Ho Chi Minh and Zhou En-lai among its guests. From the exterior it has been likened to a radio; the interior to an ocean liner. Aalbers is said to have wanted to remind Dutch guests of the ships that brought them to the country. Opposite is the **Preanger Hotel**, built in 1889 but substantially redesigned by Wolff Schoemacher in 1928. The remaining Art Deco wing faces Jalan Asia Afrika. West on Jalan Asia Afrika is the **Gedung Merdeka** (also known as the Asia Afrika building). Originally built in 1895, it was completely renovated in 1926 by Wolff Schoemacher, Aalbers and Van Gallen Last, and today houses an exhibition of photographs of the first Non-Aligned Movement conference held here in 1955 (hence the name of the street). ■ *Open 0800-1800 Mon-Fri.*

Jalan Braga is often said to be Bandung's colonial heart. Sadly though, most of the original façades have been disfigured or entirely replaced. North of the railway line, also on Jalan Braga, is the **Bank of Indonesia** designed by Ed Cuypers in the 1920s. Either side are church buildings designed by Schoemacher. Additional notable Art Deco buildings in Bandung are listed in the box on page 133.

North of the centre

The north suburbs of Bandung are the most attractive part of the city, leafy and green – this is University Land. **Gedung Sate** on Jalan Diponegoro was built in the 1920s and is one of Bandung's more imposing public buildings, with strong geometric lines and a formal garden. Within the building, but rather hidden away, is the **Museum Post and Philately**, at Jalan Cilaki 37. Almost opposite is the **Geological Museum** at No 57 (reputed to be the largest in Southeast Asia). It houses skeletons of prehistoric elephants, rhinos, fossilized trees and a meteor weighing 156 kg which fell on Java in 1884. But most notably, it is home to the skull of 'Java Man' (see page 937). Unfortunately, there's no information in English. ■ *Open 0900-1500 Mon-Thu, 0900-1100 Fri and Sat, shut Sun.* Also north of the city centre on Jalan Taman Sari, the **Bandung Institute of Technology** or **ITB** was built by Maclaine Pont in 1918 and represents another good example of the architecture of the Art Deco era. Off Jalan Taman Sari, just before the ITB travelling north, is the **Kebun Binatang**, Bandung's **zoo** housing Komodo dragons among other beasts. It is set in beautiful surroundings and is well worth a visit. Very crowded on Sunday and holidays. ■ *Admission 2,500Rp (5,000Rp on Sun and holidays). Open 0800-1600 Mon-Sun.* Not far south of the zoo is the rather bizarre '**Jean Street**' on Jalan Cihampelas. Shopkeepers vie for the most elaborate shopfront in an attempt to lure trade. It is a most surreal experience to wander amongst this collection of larger-than-life plaster Rambos, sausages, helicopters, James Bonds and other figures and images, and worth a visit even if you are not intending to shop. There are not just jeans for sale here: all types of clothes, tapes and merchandise for Bandung's large population of students and trendies. The streets are also lined with stalls selling fresh coconuts and durian ice cream – which emits the usual overwhelming smell. To get to the street, take an Angkutan kota running up Jalan Pasir Kaliki and then walk through Jalan Prof Eyckman (Jean Street itself is

Bandung – factory visits

The excellent and innovative Bandung City Council are encouraging visitors to see more of 'real' city life. One element of this is to encourage people to seek out the small factories that are the life blood of Bandung.

Lilian Candle Factory (Jalan Aksan 18, T612200): run by the Chinese Tan family, this factory is a home industry producing candles from paraffin that range in size from a few centimetres to over 2m in height. Most are produced for Chinese temples – of which the most complex take two years to complete – but Christmas candles and others can be made to order. Prices range from 400Rp to 20,000Rp. Open 0800-1800 Mon-Sat. Getting there: best by taxi, 3 km from town.

Yun Sen Tofu Factory (Jalan Jend Sudirman): tofu or tempe is made from soybean paste, coagulated with acetic acid or a fungal spore and then pressed to remove excess water. The Yun Sen factory welcomes visitors Mon-Fri 0900-1600, close to town square.

Chinese Paper Houses (Jalan Cibadak-Gang Ibu Aisah): Bandung's large Chinese population, despite attempts at assimilation, retain many of their Taoist and Confucianist rites and rituals. Paper houses with all the paraphernalia of a real home are made for the deceased, to furnish them in their life after death. And not just beds and kitchens; modernity demands that bamboo and paper swimming pools, cars and satellite dishes are also painstakingly produced. Every element must be made of flammable material so that the dead receive the gifts in heaven. The best place to see paper houses and their accoutrements being made is on Jalan Cibadak, near the Vihara Leng An in Gang [Lane] Ibu Aisah. Vihara Leng An is open 1000-1600 Mon-Sat.

Kerupuk Factory (Jalan Kopo-Gang Pak Sahdi 27): kerupuk or krupuk, deep-fried spiced tapioca (cassava) crackers, are produced in their zillions in Bandung. One survey (how it was done, goodness knows) estimated that 2,200,000 were consumed every day; nearly a billion a year. Bandung's first krupuk factory was established in 1925 by Haji Sukarna and his descendants continue to run four enterprises in the same street – just off Jalan Kopo. The crackers are moulded out of tapioca flour and then dried in the sun, before being deep-fried just before selling. Dried (but un-fried) krupuk can be stored long-term. Getting there: Jalan Kopo-Gang [Lane] Pak Sahdi is opposite the Immanuel Hospital. Open: working hours.

Wayang Golek Factory (Jalan Pangarang Bawah IV No 78/17B): wayang golek puppets are produced by numerous workshops in Bandung (see page 304 for details on wayang theatre). Some of the finest are made by Pak Ruchiyat, in whose factory they are carved from lightweight albasia wood and then painted and decorated by his wife, Ibu Ruchiyat and her assistants. See 'Shopping', below, for details on buying puppets. Open 0800-1600 Mon-Sat. There are also Wayang Golek factories on Jl Kebon Kawung, Jl Cipacing and Jl Padiasuka 118.

---

one-way running south). **Jalan Pasar Selatan** is a more recent imitation of the original, lined with stores selling denim.

South of the centre

South of town, the **Museum of West Java** (Negeri Propinsi Jawa Barat) is on the corner of Jalan Otto Iskandardinata and the ring road. It houses artefacts tracing the development and history of West Java. ■ *Admission 300Rp. Open Tue - Sun 0900-1400, shut Mon.*

Markets

Like many Indonesian cities, Bandung has a number of markets. **Pasar Kota Kembang** runs along a narrow lane linking Jalan Asia-Afrika and Jalan Dalem Kaum, and specializes in clothes, shoes and accessories. **Pasar Baru** is in Chinatown and is a good place to buy textiles, including batik; the basement houses a vegetable market. **Jalan Pasar Utara** is a food market selling snacks and many West Javanese culinary specialities. Not far from the Ciroyom Terminal is the **Pasar Jatayu** on Jalan Arjuna, which houses a few antique and junk shops among the second-hand motorcycle outlets; there are also some places selling military memorabilia nearby.

Bandung's largest **flower market**, supplied from the many upland nurseries around the city, is on Jalan Wastukencana.

Further north still (7 km) is the **Dago Teahouse**, to be found behind the Pajajaran University housing complex at the end of Jalan Ir H Juanda. It was renovated in 1991, and provides a cultural hall and open-air theatre for evening Sundanese dance performances. There are good views of the city from here and an excellent restaurant. ■ *Entrance 300Rp. Getting there: catch a Dago colt up Jalan Ir H Juanda (the colts terminate at Terminal Dago, not far from the Tea House).*

Walks The Bandung tourist office has identified a number of walks in the city through the Central Business District (CBD), Chinatown and elsewhere. For maps and further information contact the tourist office – good background information on buildings and the city's history is available.

Tours The tourist office on Jalan Asia Afrika will organize tours in and around town, as will many of the travel agents (depending on season and demand). Typical tours visit the Tangkuban Prahu crater and Ciater hotsprings (five hours, 125,000Rp per person), architecturally interesting buildings around town (3 hrs, 50,000Rp per person) and an angklung music performance, plus traditional Sundanese dancing (three hours, 24,000Rp per person). Many places organize day trips to Mount Papandayan, with a guide leading visitors all over the mountain and a bath in a sulphur spring. For those who want to hire a car and driver to visit the surrounding area, men hang around the tourist information office on the town square (*alun-alun*). Expect to pay up to 200,000Rp for a day.

Excursions

Most visitors who venture out of the city travel north into the volcanic **Priangan Highlands** that surround Bandung, to see neat tea plantations, colossal craters and natural hotsprings.

Villa Isola lies on the route north of Jalan Setiabudi, 6 km from the city centre, and is yet another fine Art Deco building, set on a hill overlooking the city. ■ *Getting there: regular minibuses and colts ply this route out of Bandung. Either travel direct from the train station or via Terminal Ledeng at the northern edge of the city.*

Lembang Lembang, 16 km north of Bandung, is a popular resort town on an upland plateau with restaurants, hotels and pony-drawn carts. It is famous for its pleasant climate and abundance of fresh flowers and fruit. The town can be used as a base to explore the uplands and visit such places as the Tangkuban Prahu Crater and the Ciater Hot Springs (see below). Garden nurseries line the road into Lembang and the town also supports the internationally respected **Bosscha Observatory** (visits must be prearranged). ■ *Getting there: regular minibuses connect Lembang with Bandung's Terminal Ledeng, on Jalan Dr Setiabudi on the northern edge of the city. To get to Terminal Ledeng, take a colt going up Jalan Pasir Kaliki. There are also colts running direct to Lembang from the train station in the centre of town.*

Sleeping B (for new wing), **C** (in old building) *Grand Hotel*, Jl Raya Lembang 272, T2786829, F2786829. Is the best place to stay in Lembang, an old hotel with an unimpressive restaurant, a swimming pool and tennis courts renovated by Aalbers of *Savoy Homann* fame, now with an additional wing, large garden compound, hot water in all rooms, the older wing is cheaper and remains the more stylish. **B** *Sangria Hotel*, Jl Hortikultura, T2788777, F2787045. We have not managed to see this hotel but it has been recommended by a recent traveller as a comfortable place to stay. **B/C** *Hotel Panorama Lembang*, Jl Raya Tangkuban Perahu 29, T2786030, F2786780. Great views with small, comfortable rooms and reasonable restaurant, pricey. **C** *Sindang Reret II*, Jl Raya Cikole, Km 22, T2786129, F286119. A large resort above Lembang with a profusion of bamboo and concrete, a stagnant pool holds massive carp which children feed crisps and other nutritious snacks, but the rooms are OK and the water is hot.

Tangkuban Prahu Crater Tangkuban Prahu Crater (the capsized boat crater) is one of the most popular tourist sights in the vicinity of Bandung and possibly the most accessible volcanic crater in Indonesia. The route up to the volcano from Lembang passes through rich agricultural land, with terraces of market garden crops clawing their way up the hillsides, chincona trees (the bark is used to produce quinine), teak and wild ginger. The entrance to the 'park' is 9 km from Lembang. The drive from the gate snakes through a forest of giant pines reminiscent of a set from *Jurassic Park*. 3km from the gate is the lower car park (with restaurant and tourist stalls). From here the road continues upwards for another 1 km to the rim of the impressive **Ratu Crater**. Alternatively, there is a footpath from the lower car park to the Ratu Crater (1.5 km), and another from there to the smaller **Domas Crater** (1 km). Another path links the Domas and Ratu Craters (1.2 km). It is also possible to walk all the way round the Ratu Crater. Though visited by numerous tour buses and inhabited by large numbers of souvenir sellers, the natural splendour of the volcano makes the trip worthwhile. Ratu rises to an altitude of 1,830m, and the crater drops precipitously from the rim. Bursts of steam and the smell of sulphur bear witness to the volcanic activity latent beneath the surface.

The curious shape of the summit of Tangkuban Prahu has given rise to the Sundanese *Legend of Prince Sangkuriang*, who unknowingly fell in love with his mother, Dayang Sumbi. She tried to prevent their marriage, insisting that her betrothed create a lake and canoe before sun-rise on their wedding day. Sangkuriang seemed to be endowed with magical powers and he nearly achieved

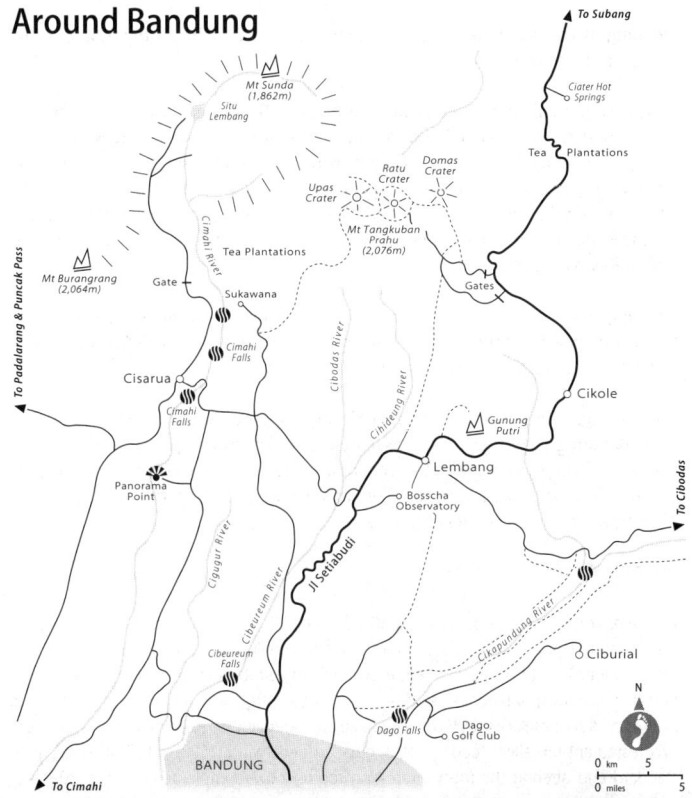

this impossible task when Dayang Sumbi called upon the gods to hasten the sun to rise, in order to prevent their forbidden union. Sangkuriang was so angry that he kicked his nearly finished canoe, which landed upside down on the horizon, thus creating this silhouette. The wildlife in the surrounding forest includes a small population of native gibbons. At the summit, hawkers sell anklungs to bemused tourists while tapping out *Auld Lang Syne* or *Happy Birthday To You*. They also vigorously proffer assorted lurid clothes, synthetic fur hats, bags and rucksacks, as well as wooden carvings, animals made of small seashells and herbal remedies such as *kayu naga*. This resembles green, hairy twiglets, and is reputedly good for rheumatism and backache. The twiglets are boiled in water and the resultant malodorous brew is drunk. ■ *Admission 1,250Rp, 400Rp for car. Guides are available for off-path treks (inadvisable without a guide because of the emissions of sulphurous gases), but unnecessary for the well defined path to the Domas Crater. Getting there: bus or colt heading for Subang from either the Kebun Kelapa terminal or from the minibus stop opposite the train station – and ask to be dropped off at the entrance to the crater (about 25 km from the city). Hitch or walk (3½ km) from here. At the weekend there are colts which go all the way up to the summit.*

Ciater Hot Springs Ciater Hot Springs are 6½ km on from Tangkuban Prahu, the road following the mountain side and winding through tea plantations. There are brilliantly clear hot water pools and waterfalls here situated on the side of a hill; unfortunately, the complex is rather seedy and run down, a sign of tourist overload. ■ *Admission 3,000Rp, car 5,000Rp, and another 2,000Rp to bathe. Getting there: take a colt or bus towards Subang, asking to be let off at Air Panas Ciater; the hotel and springs are 150m off the main road.*

Sleeping **B** *Sari Ater Hotel*, on site, T200319, F200772. **D** *Pondok Gunungsari*, Jl Raya Ciater. Small, clean homestay.

Ciwidey Ciwidey is a small town about 14 km southwest of Bandung; it is much less touristy and more rural than Ciater – and well worth the effort of getting there. Continuing along the road, up the Ciwidey valley, the route climbs up past Cimanggu (at the 42 km marker) where there is a small park and hot pools fed from Mount Patuha (2,400m). The hill sides here are planted with tea bushes. Among the largest estates are the Rancabali and Malabar estates. ■ *Getting there: regular connections from the Kebon Kelapa terminal, 1½ hrs.*

Sleeping There are several places to stay in Ciwidey, or close by, including the **E-F** *Penginapan Sederhana* in town, and the rather more salubrious **B-C** *Sindang Reret Hotel*, T237602, out of town, with hot water.

Candi Cangkuang Candi Cangkuang is an eighth-century Hindu monument and can be visited in a day from Bandung (see page 145). The temple is 48 km from the city on the road to Garut. ■ *Getting there: catch a bus from Bandung's Cicaheum terminal on Jalan Jend A Yani, travelling east towards Tasikmalaya and Banjar; get off 2 km after Kadungura, in the village of Leles.*

Essentials

Sleeping
■ *on map page 132*

AL *Chedi Hotel*, Jl Ranca Bentang 56-58, T230333, F230633, chedibdg@ghmhotels.com A/c, restaurant, pool, 49 rooms in this modernist, minimalist hotel, lots of style, situated several kilometres north of the city centre overlooking countryside to the north, so not well placed for that spontaneous, spur-of-the-moment stroll around the sights. **A** *Grand Preanger*, Jl Asia Afrika 81, T431631, F430034, preanger@indo.net.id, www.aerowisata.com A/c, restaurant (excellent food), pool, original art deco wing (1928), refurbished to a high standard and offering the most interesting rooms, now 'complemented' by a 10-storey modern addition, central location, fitness centre, good facilities and well-run. **A** *Kumala*, Jl Asia Afrika 140, T445141, F438852. A/c, restaurant, pool, a rather featureless hotel, but comfortable enough, Sundanese dance and music every Wed and Sat evening. **A** *Panghegar*, Jl Merdeka 2, T432286, F431583, www.panghegar-online.com panhegar@idola.net.id A/c, restaurant, pool, health club, 200 rooms and most facilities, but now rather dated compared with the competition, and cannot even claim heritage status to make up for it. **A** *Savoy Homann*, Jl Asia Afrika 112, T432244, F436187. A/c, restaurant (see places to eat), bars, pool, superb art deco building, renovated but retaining original furnishings. Central mature garden with caged birds, good location – the best and most interesting place to stay in town, prices and atmosphere indicate this hotel has fallen on hard times, recommended for a visit, even for a drink. **A** *Sheraton*, 3 km north at Jl Ir H Juanda 390, T2500303, F2500301, www.sheraton.com/bandung Recently expanded, a/c, restaurant, pool, international standard hotel with good facilities (fitness centre etc). **A** *Sri Manganti*, Jl Sumatera 52-54, T4203009, F439601. Trying to compete with the top international hotels, this does not fall far short, excellent facilities available and rooms are spacious and clean, but prices are reasonable. **A-B** *Hotel Royal Merdeka*, Jl Merdeka 34, T4200555, F438210. Many rooms in this clean, comfortable hotel, good value and recommended. **A-B** *Trio*, Jl Gardujati 55-61, T631055, F431126. A/c, courtyard style hotel, rooms rather dated but spacious, clean and light. Good positioning for main sights, good value.

B *Angrekk Golden Hotel*, Jl R.E.Martadinata 15, T4205537, F431565. Fairly basic but comfortable, good position opposite central department store, rooms are suprisingly quiet. **B** *Cemerlang Hotel*, Jl Pasirkaliki 45, T671383, F631675. Close to the train station, new hotel with 77 rooms, overlooking central courtyard, large open rooms with excellent showers, good restaurant. **B** *Guntur*, Jl Otto Iskandarinata 20 (on the main road), T4203763. 1960s hotel apparently stuck in a time warp, bathrooms with hot water, low rise, central courtyard "where you can get rid of your fatigue". **B** *Istana*, Jl Lembong 44, T433025, F432757. A/c, good restaurant, pool, 51 comfortable rooms, most facilities but rather lacklustre and colourless. A place to stay for those who are looking for function rather than style. **B** *Mutiara*, Jl Kebon Kawung 60-62, T4200333, F4204961. A/c, close to the train station, 3-storey motel-style hotel, rooms are large and slightly shabby but quiet and well equipped, secure car parking. **B** *Perdana Wisata*, Jl Jend Sudirman 66-68, T438238, F432818. A/c, Japanese restaurant, modern hotel, central courtyard with pool. **B** *Wisma ITB Sawunggaling*, Jl Sawunggaling 13, T4218254, F4218253, www.sawunggaling.Elga.net.id, sawunggaling@elga.net.id Stylish, arty hotel with very high standard of cleanliness and service, good value coffee shop and cocktail bar with good food. Recommended.

D *Patradissa 2*, Jl Pasirkaliki Blk No 12, T4202645. Small, clean rooms with own bathroom and hot water, good buffet breakfast included in price, good value.

Budget hotels can be found around the railway station on Jl Kebonjati and Jl Pasir Kaliki. **C** *Kenangan Hotel*, Jl Kebon Sirih 4, T435284, F4213243. Well located off the main road, quiet rooms, helpful staff, good restaurant and coffee shop, recommended for those who want to venture off the backpackers beaten track. **D** *Corner*, Jl Wastukencana 8, T436871. Dark rooms with a surfeit of mosquitoes and a deficit of sheets, friendly enough but only worth staying here if pushed, rooms have attached showers with hot water, breakfast included. **D** *Hotel Palam* Jl Belakang Pasar 119, T/F43260. Popular hotel, all rooms with hot water and a/c, good sized rooms and parking available. **D** *Sahara*, Jl Oltoiskandarinata 3, T4204684. Villa in large garden, cheaper rooms with shared mandi, metal frame beds in bare shabby rooms, 300m from the railway station. **D** *Surabaya*, Jl Kebonjati 71, T436791. Victorian railway hotel, one of the few cheaper hotels with some style, a rambling place with wooden floors and large rooms, bit of a reputation as somewhere which can be rented by the hour, dirty. **D-F** *Yossie Homestay & Yossie Homestay II*, Jl Kebonjati 53, T4205453, F441224. Food made to order, communal mandi, tours to local sights, run by friendly young people, some German spoken, noisy (close to road), rooms are basic and dirty, no breakfast.

E *Sakadarna*, Jl Kebonjati 78, T439897. Restaurant (basic), much nicer than the other *Sakadarna* at No 50 and closer to the railway station, small rooms. **E-F** *Welcome By Moritz*, Jl Kebonjati 41 (Kompleks Luxor Permai 35), T4205788, F4207495. Very popular with backpackers, run by young, English-speaking Indonesians, western toilets, evenings lively with local guitar players congregating downstairs, well managed and a good source of information, dorm beds available (**F**), make sure you check out on time, any time after midday will be charged for. Recommended.

Eating Local dishes including *gorengan*, a form of vegetable-based tempura, *bandrek* and *bajigur*, both drinks made of ginger and sweetened coconut milk respectively, *pecel lele* (fried eels with a piquant sauce) and *comro* made from cassava and tempe. There are also a remarkable number of bakeries in Bandung, the best selection concentrated on Jl Braga.

Indonesian Expensive: *Savoy Homann Hotel*, Jl Asia Afrika 112, traditional Rijsttafel dinner served nightly. **Mid-range**: *Handayani*, Jl Sukajadi 153, best Javanese restaurant in Bandung. **Cheap**: *Saté Ponorogo*, Jl Jend Gatot Subroto 38, very good value open-air saté restaurant. *Sindang Deret*, Jl Naripang, T4203440. Excellent fish, cheap and a good place to try lots of different dishes.

Chinese Mid-range: *Queen*, Jl Dalem Laum 79, large and very popular place serving excellent Cantonese food.

Japanese Expensive: *Dai Shogun*, Jl Cihampelas 125, serves probably the best, but also the most expensive Japanese food in town. **Mid-range**: *Paregu*, Jl Martadinata 91, cheaper Japanese restaurant with good value buffet lunch.

Sundanese Cheap: *Babakan Siliwangi*, Jl Siliwangi 7, near the zoo. Open-air restaurant with large menu. Recommended. *Pondok Kapau*, Jl Asia Afrika 43, excellent Padang food, with seafood specialities, try the whole spicy octopus. *Ponyo*, Jl Malabar 60. Recommended by locals for its Sundanese specialities, popular.

International Mid-range: *Amsterdam Café*, Jl Braga. Burgers and steaks at inflated prices. **Cheap**: *Tizi's*, Jl Kidang Pananjung 3 (off Jl Juanda). Fabulous home-baked breads, pastries and – surprisingly – sausages. Also serves pizzas, steaks and ice-cream. A good place to go if you are homesick for European food. **Very cheap**: *Eliza Garden*, Jl Kepatihan 21. Attractive courtyard, simple food. *Victoria Café*, western café come restaurant with good prices, at the back of Bandung Plaza. *London Café*, Jl Braga (next to French Bakery). English papers, excellent choice of well-priced food and pastries. Club sandwiches particularly recommended (5,000Rp) for a hungry traveller.

Foodstalls Probably the best are arrayed down a tiny alley off Jl Bungsu, near the Puri Nas Bakery (open 1730 on). Stalls are also to be found on Jl Merdeka, Jl Martadinata, Jl Diponegoro (near the RRI building), Jl Cikapundung Barat and Jl Dalem Kaum, west of the *alun alun*. Most are night stalls only. Of all the stalls, the one with the greatest local reputation is Pak Aceng's *Es compur* (mixed ice) cart which he sets up on Jl Kapatihan near the Damai shop. He has been selling here for over 25 years. 300m west of the railway station is an excellent *martabak* stall (cheese, chocolate, banana).

Another way of trying Bandung's range of food is by going to the *Food Centre* at the **Matahari Department store** on Jl Cikapundung Barat, good, cheap dishes and it is possible to see what you are getting.

Bakeries *Braga Permai*, Jl Braga 58, large bakery-cum-restaurant with tables outside, very clean but the cakes are rather sickly. *French Bakery*, Jl Braga, the best bakery in town, authentic French cakes, pastries and bread for the westerner looking for a fix. *Sumber Hidangan*, Jl Braga. *The Canary Bakery* and restaurant (near intersection with Jl Naripan), Jl Braga. *Victoria Bakery* junction of Jl Pagar and Jl Gunung, housed in a noteable Art Deco building.

Bandung has a great array of bars, pubs and clubs, with good bands and atmosphere. *Laga* **Bars & clubs**
Pub, Jl Junjunan 164, T215164, excellent bands, great atmosphere and very popular with
Indonesians and Westerners alike. ***Fame Station***, Wisma Lippo Lantai II, Jl Gatot Subroto 2,
T307858, F307868. Bar with cover bands positioned at top of bank skyscraper. Great night
view of city, popular. ***North Sea Bar***, Jl Braga, most popular expat bar with typical pub fare,
western beers and wine, pool table. ***O'Hara's Tavern***, Lobby Level, *Hotel Perdana Wisata*, Jl
Jend Sudirman 66-68, T438238, another recommended bar due to its atmosphere and popularity – good bands.

Discos *La Dream Palace*, Jl Asia Afrika, Plaza Lt 2, open 2100-0200. ***Lipstick Discoskate***,
Gedung Palaguna Lt IV (1200-2100 for disco-skating, 2130-0200 for standard disco). ***Studio
East***, 2nd Flr, Premier Building, Jl Cihampelas 129. Open 2100-0200, very popular student
place, large dance floor. ***Polo***, Menara Bri Tower, Jl Asia Afrika 57-59, T4205325. Open
2300-0200, expensive. Music house.

Nightclubs There are a number on Jl Jend Sudirman, eg ***Panama*** at No 72, ***Oriental*** at No
134 and ***Paramount*** at No 291 (all 2000-0200). But the nightclub housed in the most beautiful building and interior décor of 1960s must be ***Caesar's Palace and Disco*** on Jl Braga, near
the intersection with Jl Lembang, the ubiquitous karaoke is deafening. Open 0800-late.

Adu Domba (ram fights) T236970, most Suns at *Ranca Buni*, near Ledeng, north of town **Entertainment**
on Jl Setiabudi. Get there by Lembung bus to Ledung terminal. Walk down Jl Sersan Bejuri
then turn left; many helpful locals around, if you get lost.
Angklung (hand-held bamboo chimes) Performances at *Pak Udjo's workshop*, Jl
Padasuka 118 (8 km northeast of the town centre), when there are 20 or more people,
T71714, beginning 1530. Getting there by taking a Cicaheum colt and getting off at the intersection with Jl Padasuka, near the Cicaheum bus station. Pak Udjo's workshop is a 7 min walk,
on the right-hand side of the street. ***ASTI, Institute of Fine Arts***, Jl Buah Batu 212, T304532 for
angkung and other performances; information on performance schedule from the tourist
information office.
Art galleries Bandung is a centre of modern art, possibly because of ITB's excellent fine art
faculty. Galleries including ***Bandung***, Jl Siliwangi 16, north of town, predominantly Bandung
artists are shown here, some ceramics and specialist art books, changing exhibitions by
international artists. ***Braga***, Jl Braga 68, displays well known Indonesian artists, both living
and dead. ***Hidayat***, Jl Sulanjana 36, paintings, graphics and ceramics. ***Rainbow Gallery***, Jl
Sukajadi, open everyday 0900-1600, works of young aspiring Indonesian artists, some innovative work, well worth a visit. See 'Shopping', below, for telephone details.
Cinemas Opposite *Hotel Braga* on Jl Braga. ***Sartika 21***, near intersection of Jl Aceh and Jl
Merdeka; ***Vanda***, Jl Merdeka, near Jl Jawa and the City Hall.
Cultural shows Martial arts, dances etc every Sun morning at the *zoo*, 0900-1300. Admission is the entrance fee to zoo. *Museum of West Java* on Jl Otto stages a cultural performance
every Sun.
Jaipongan dance Another traditional Sundanese dance form – which is now popular in
parts of Kalimantan and Sumatra – performances at *Museum of West Java*, Jl Otto
Iskandarinata, Weds 1400.
Ketuk Tilu dance A traditional social dance accompanied by gamelan music at the
Sanggar Langen Selna, Jl Otto Iskandarinata 541A. Professional dancers encourage you to
join them in a dance (for which you pay). Nightly from 2100, 8,000Rp, now more like a nightclub later on in the evening.
Sundanese dance & gamelan recitals At *Hotel Panghegar* on Jl Merdeka on Wed and Sat
at 1930, no charge but the audience is expected to eat or drink.
Wayang golek Performances at *Sindangreret restaurant*, Jl Nirapan 7-9 (near Jl Braga), on
Sat from 0700-2300 or an epic 8 hr performance every 2nd Sat of the month at the
Rumentangsiang Cultural Hall (an Art Deco building), near the Kosambi market on Jl Jend
A Yani.

142 BANDUNG: ESSENTIALS

Shopping **Angklung instruments** Jl Madurasa.
Antiques *Tasin Art*, Jl Braga 28.
Art galleries Bandung is viewed as a centre for Indonesian arts and there are a number of galleries in town exhibiting work by promising young Indonesians. Centrally located are the *Braga Art Gallery*, Jl Braga 68, T438058, open 0900-2100, Mon-Sun; and the *Elegance Art Gallery*, Jl Banceuy 8, T437061, open 0930-1900 Mon-Sat. North of the town centre are 2 more galleries: *Bandung Gallery*, Jl Siliwangi 16, T81199, open 0900-1700, Mon-Sat; and *Hidayat Gallery*, Jl Sulanjana 36, T436038, open 1000-1700, Mon-Sat.
Bookshops All over town, but especially north of the centre around the university.
Ceramics There is a *Ceramics Research Institute* on Jl Jend A Yani near the Pasar Cicadas; examples can be purchased from *Bandung Gallery*, Jl Siliwangi 16, *Kundhika*, Jl Gunung Batu 178 and *Uun Kusnadi*, Jl Kenangan 9A.
Handicrafts Next to *Sarinah department store* on Jl Braga. Opposite is the *Indonesian National Crafts Council* (No 15). Cheapest batiks and clothes at Pasar Baru in Chinatown.
Jeans Jl Pasar Celatan, off Jl Otto Iskandarinata, for whacky shop fronts and cheap jeans, also Jl Cihampelas for more weird shop fronts and bargain clothing.
Jewellery *Runa*, a husband and wife team, produce perhaps the best modern jewellery in Bandung. It is on sale at many of the major hotels, eg *Preanger*, *Savoy Homann* and the *Sheraton*.
Leather Jl Braga 113, Jl A Yani 618.
Rubber stamp production An area of stalls and shops carving out stamps, Jl Cikapundung Barat and Jl Asia Afrika – have your name carved in rubber for 5,000Rp.
Shoes Good buy here, Jl Cibaduyut (south of town on Jl Kopo) for a wide variety.
Shopping centres An abundance, eg *Bandung Indah Plaza* (the biggest and best), Jl Merdeka 56; *Matahari Shopping Centre*, Town Square (Alun-alun); *Sarinah Dept Store*, Jl Braga 10.
Night Market Jl Sudirman, cheap clothes and fruit, paraffin lamps add a mysterious romantic touch.
Wayang Golek *Pa Aming*, Jl M Ramdhan 4 and *Pa Ruchiyat*, Jl Pangarang Bawah IV No 78/17B (behind No 20 in the alleyway). Both are workshops where you can also buy and the latter is reputed to sell perhaps the finest worked examples. Pak Ruchiyat has over 35 year's experience; note that prices – which range from 20,000Rp to 60,000Rp for most puppets – are fixed. Shops along Jl Braga sell puppets.

Sports **Golf** *Dago Golf Course*, top end of Jl Ir H Juanda, T2502587.

Tour operators There are about 25 travel agents in town; most are branches of Jakarta-based companies. *Interlink*, Jl Wastukencana 5. *Natrabu*, Braga Hotel, Jl Braga 8 (be careful – they overcharge for reconfirmation of flights); *Nitour*, Jl Tamblong 2. *Pacto Tours and Travel*, Jl Asia Afrika 112 (in the *Savoy Homann Hotel*). *Satriavi*, *Grand Preanger Hotel*, Jl Asia Afrika 81, T50677, or at *Hotel Panghegar*, Jl Merdeka 2, T440192.

Transport **Local** Most roads in the centre of town are 1-way. This, coupled with the dense traffic,
187 km southeast makes it quite a struggle getting around town. Bandung must have more orange-suited traf-
of Jakarta, 400 km fic wardens than any other town on Java, ready to direct traffic dangerously (and collect their
west of Yogya 300Rp *parkir*). **Bus**: city buses go north-south or east-west; west on Jl Asia Afrika, east on Jl Kebonjati (beware that Nos 9 and 11 stop at 2100) south on Jl Otto Iskandarinata, north on Jl Astanaanyar, 250Rp. **Becaks** (very colourfully painted). **Car rental**: *Avis*, Grand Hotel Preanger, Jl Asia Afrika 81, T431631, and *Sheraton Inn Bandung*, Jl Ir H Juanda 390, T2500303; *National Car Rental* at *Istana Hotel*, Jl Lembong 21. **Colts** (Angkutan kota): 500Rp around town, up to 1,000Rp for longer journeys. Station on Jl Kebonjati. **Delmans**: small, 2-wheeled carriages are available for hire. **Taxi**: 3 or 4 companies run metered taxi services. Taxis can also be chartered by the hour.

Air Bandung's **airport** is 4 km from the city, T614100. Transport to town by taxi, 15,000Rp. Regular connections on *Garuda/Merpati*, *Sempati* and *Bouraq* with other destinations in Java, Sumatra, Kalimantan, Sulawesi, Bali, Lombok, Nusa Tenggara, Maluku and Irian Jaya.

Train The station is in the centre of town behind the bemo station, on Jl Stasion Barat. Regular connections with **Jakarta's** Kota and Gambir stations, although the best service is the hourly *Parahyangan* express from Gambir. Journey time 3-4 hrs (Bisnis 65,000Rp). There are 2 trains daily to **Surabaya**, 13 hrs, and 8 hrs to **Yogya** (prices vary, average bisnis 35,000Rp, economy 7,000Rp). To get from the railway station to the Cicaheum Bus Station take a Big Bus No 1.

Road 18 km east of Bandung the road divides, turning northeast along the **Great Post Make-up**, constructed under the direction of Governor-General Daendels between 1808 and 1810 for the defence of the island against the English. An engineering feat which required unprecedented numbers of *corvée* labourers, stretches of the road are carved through steep gorges and along narrow river valleys, and cost many lives. The route ends at the coastal city of **Cirebon**, a total of 130 km from Bandung. **Bus**: Bandung has 2 long-distance bus terminals: The new terminal for destinations to the west is the **Leuwi Panjang** terminal, 5 km south of the city centre on Jl Soekarno-Hatta. (This has replaced the old Kebun Kelapa terminal). The Leuwi Panjang terminal handles a/c and non-a/c buses to the west, including **Jakarta** (Kampung Rambutan terminal), **Bogor** and destinations in **Sumatra**. Terminal **Cicaheum** on Jl Jend A Yani serves destinations to the east and north, including **Yogya**, **Solo**, **Surabaya**, **Garut**, **Tasikmalaya**, **Cirebon** and **Semarang**. There are also occasional direct buses to **Pangandaran**. Tickets for a/c night buses can be bought on Jl Kebonjati, near the *Hotel Surabaya*. Regular connections with Jakarta's Kampung Rambutan terminal, 2½-3 hrs on an a/c bus (with *P.T. Pakar Utama*, Jl Pramuka, East Jakarta), Bogor 3½ hrs (6,000Rp, non a/c), Pelabuhanratu 4 hrs, Cirebon 3½ hrs, Yogya 12 hrs. The old Kebun Kelapa terminal on Jl Dewi Sartika now just handles local services and buses to **Lembang**, **Subang** and **Ciwidey**, and other destinations in the vicinity of Bandung depart from here. **Minibus**: 2 companies from **Jakarta** – *4848*, Jl Kramet Raya 23, T357656, and *Media*, Jl Johar 15, T343643 – run minibuses to Bandung (4 hrs). You can book minibuses away from Bandung from the tourist office on Jl Asia Africa, eg. To Pangandaran for 20,000Rp door to door. **Taxi**: share taxis for 6 cost about the same as the train.

Directory

Airline offices *Bouraq*, Jl Cihampelas 27, T438795. *Garuda/Merpati*, Jl Asia Afrika 73-75, T441226, F4204497, opposite *Hotel Savoy Homann*. *Mandala*, Jl Halimun 15, T303868. *Sempati*, at *Hotel Panghegar*, Jl Merdeka 2, T430477. **Banks & money changers** *American Express*, T51983. *Arta Mulia*, Jl Jend Sudirman 51. *BPD*, Jl Braga. *Djasa Arta*, corner of Jl Suniaraja and Jl Otto Iskandarinata. *Dwipa Mulia*, Jl Asia Afrika 148. *Golden Money Changer*, Jl Otto Iskandarinata 127. *Interstate Investment*, Jl Naripan 28. *Metro Jasa*, Jl Jend Gatot Subroto 21. *Sejahtera Bagian Utama*, Jl Suniaraja 55. **Communications** Post Office and internet: Jl Asia Afrika 49, corner of Jl Asia Afrika and Jl Banceuy, Poste Restante available. Internet available daily 0800-2100, 10,000Rp per hr, be prepared for slow service. Also internet cafés on Jl Braga and in the Bandung Indah Plaza. Also Jl Pahlawan 87. **Telephone and fax**: *Wartel*, Jl Asia Afrika (opposite *Savoy Homann Hotel*), for international calls and fax. **Embassies & consulates** Austria, Jl Prabu Dimuntur 2A, T439505, F430505. France, Jl Purnawarman 32, T445864. Netherlands, Jl Diponegoro 25, T431419. **Medical facilities** Chemist: *Dewi Sartika*, Jl R Dewi Sartika 89 (24 hrs). Hospital: *Adventist Hospital*, Jl Cihampelas 161, T82091. **Useful addresses** *British Council*, Jl Lembong, near *Hotel Panghegar*. Immigration (local office), Jl Surapati 82, T72081. *PHPA*, Jl Jend A Yani 276.

Sumedang

Phone code: 0261
Colour map 3, grid A2

Sumedang is a medium-sized town rarely visited by tourists, but it makes for a pleasant enough stopping off point between Bandung and Cirebon, especially if taking the back roads from Bandung via Tangkuban Prahu Crater and Ciater (see 'Excursions', below). The town's most notable point of interest is a good provincial museum (see below).

Sights

The **Museum Prabu Geusan Ulun** (at Jalan Prabu Geusan Ulun 40) is situated in the grounds of the District Office, on the southeast side of the town square, about 2 km from Sumedang's commercial heart on the road to Bandung. The museum is housed in four colonial buildings and among the more interesting pieces on display are VOC cannon, a good selection of krisses, the uniforms of the Bupati's (Regent's) bodyguards, fine songket cloth woven with gold thread, a bed for the prince to recuperate in following the circumcision ceremony, and old hand-written korans. The museum also houses a considerable library of historic books and manuscripts. But the museum's finest pieces are the crown and associated regalia (*pusaka*) of the princes of Sumedang, which are locked away in a strong room. To be certain of seeing these 'crown jewels', it is necessary to arrange a viewing beforehand. The curator can sometimes open the strong room without prior notice, but do not count on it. In addition to the regalia, there is a good collection of gamelan orchestral instruments – the largest suspended on wooden frames made in Bangkok and dating from the late 19th century. The largest gong went missing in Europe while the orchestra was touring, only to be returned to Indonesia by the Dutch ambassador in 1989. ■ *There are gamelan performances held at the museum each Sun and Tue, 0800-1200 (with singing on Tue). Admission 1,000Rp (with guided tour by the curator in English, Dutch or Indonesian). Open 0800-1200 Mon-Thu, 0800-1100 Fri, 0800-1200 Sun.*

Excursions The trip between Sumedang and Bandung, via **Ciater** and **Tangkuban Prahu Crater**, is worthwhile in itself – a beautiful journey through terraced rice fields and small villages. Java at its bucolic finest. For details, see page 137.

Sleeping **B-C** *Hanjuang Hegar*, Jl Mayor Abdul Rachman 165, T201820, F201829. Some a/c, new hotel looking rather like a wedding cake on the Cirebon side of town about 500m from the centre, hot water, rooms are clean and comfortable but stylish in only the kitschest sense. **C-D** *Kencana Hotel*, Jl Pangeran Kornel 216, T201642. Some a/c, a villa hotel on the Bandung side of town about 2 km from the centre. Clean rooms with TVs and attached bathrooms but no hot water, the rooms at the back are quieter (the hotel is on the main road), an excellent and well-run place for such a small town. **D-E** *Wisma Gumer*, Jl Grabu Geusan Ulun, simple room with shared basic facilities, on the Bandung side of town.

Eating Most restaurants and stalls in Sumedang specialize, unsurprisingly, in West Javanese cuisine, including hot, spicy potato with liver, deep fried slivers of spicy tahu or bean curd (*tahu Sumedang*), and assorted offal. **Rumah Makan Bandung**, Jl Prabu Geusan Ulun 93 (1 km from town centre towards Bandung), has a limited choice of Sundanese dishes. There is a small **night food market** selling Sundanese snacks on Jl Palisari, which runs off the main Bandung-Cirebon road, 1 km from the town centre towards Bandung.

Entertainment **Cinema** *Diana Cinema* in town centre, with a/c and showing English language films. **Gamelan performances** At the Museum Prabu Geusan Ulun, Jl Prabu Geusan Ulun 40, 0800-1200 Sun and Tue (with singing on Tue). See 'Sights', above, for further details.

Transport **Road Bus**: the terminal is on the Cirebon side of town 2 km from the centre and colts constantly ply the route between the two. Regular connections with Bandung and Cirebon along the Great Post Rd. **Minibus**: there are also minibuses linking Sumedang with Bandung via Ciater and Tangkuban Prahu Crater (see Excursions, above).

40 km from Bandung, 90 km from Cirebon

Directory **Post Office**: Jl Prabu Geusan Ulun (1 km out of town on the road to Bandung).

Garut

Phone code: 0262
Colour map 3, grid B2

Few foreign tourists stop in this sleepy town 65 km southeast of Bandung, which was once a Dutch hill station and is magnificently set amidst towering volcanoes at an altitude of over 700m. **Gunung Guntur** is a source of some concern and has been the object of interest by vulcanologists since 1985 when local villagers noticed that spring water was rising in temperature. The volcano last erupted in 1847, but the long period of dormancy since then worries the experts who fear a cataclysmic event. The rocks in the surrounding area show evidence of pyroclastic lava flows – a superheated mixture of molten rock and gas – spreading 40 km outwards from the volcano. Such flows can travel at 100 km per hour, so if the worst occurs remember to check out quickly.

The area is also renowned for its **orchards** and **tobacco**, and in the 1920s was a popular hill resort for wealthy residents of Batavia. It is a good point from which to visit Candi Cangkuang, volcanoes (eg Mount Papandayan), hot springs and lakes (see below). The surrounding area is also known for its **batik**. Running off Jl Jend A Yani is a colourful **fruit and general market**. Garut **tourist office**, Jl Pamuka 5, like other small tourist offices, is enthusiastic but has little of substance to offer. It is hidden away, up a flight of stairs, at the back of a government building.

Candi Cangkuang is a small eighth-century temple set on an island in the middle of a peaceful, water lily-covered lake. The **Candi** was first listed in a report of the Dutch Archaeological Service in 1914. It was then 'rediscovered' in 1966, and restored in 1976. The temple is simple in design, square, only 8.5m high and built of andesite. It is one of the only Hindu temples to have been found in West Java and is thought, because of the absence of architectural ornamentation and the primitive building techniques, to predate Borobudur and the candis of the Dieng Plateau. It is believed to date from the 8th century, although some authorities consider it to be even older. Within the candi there is a statue of Siva riding upon his vehicle, the bull Nandi. Compared with other monuments in Java it is quite plain, although the position could hardly be more beautiful. At the foot of the temple is the **Tomb of Arief Mohammad**, a 17th-century warrior who is said to have been a very holy man who resisted the Dutch in Batavia. Surprisingly, when the tomb was excavated, no human remains were found. His descendants live in a hamlet 150m west of the temple, where one of the traditional houses has been restored. There are several taboos connected with this strange village: the houses cannot be altered, pilgrims are not permitted to pay homage at the tomb on Wednesday, four-legged animals cannot be kept within the village compound, and musical instruments are forbidden during festivals. It is almost as if the inhabitants made up the prohibitions on an evening when there was nothing better to do. There is a small **museum** 50m northwest of the candi. ■ *To get there, take a regular bus or colt travelling out of town on the Bandung road and ask to be let off at the turning for the lake and candi. This narrow road off to the right is easy to miss – there is only a small sign. The turning is 13 km north of Garut in the village of Leles (also known as Cangkuang). Travelling from Bandung, the turning is 2 km south of Kadungura (48 km from Bandung). Horse-drawn carts wait at the turning to transport visitors the 3 km from the main highway, through beautiful countryside, to Lake Cangkuang. To reach the candi, take one of the (modified for tourists) bamboo rafts across the lake to the island. It is also possible to walk the 2 km around the edge of the lake.*

The turning for the **Cipanas hot springs** is at the Km 4 mark, travelling north from Garut towards Bandung, see page 146. ■ *Regular bemos from the Guntur Terminal to Tarogong. A bemo from Tarogong to Cipanas takes only a few minutes.*

Mount Papandayan is an active volcano (2,622m) with remarkable bubbling sulphur pools, 36 km southwest of town. The journey here is spectacular with Garut-Cisurapan road rising through terraced rice fields. ■ *Catch a bus to Arjuna and hike, 2-3 hrs, or take a minibus from Garut to Cisurapan, then an ojek to the crater.*

Excursions

Sleeping
There are better places to stay in Cipanas (see following entry), a short bemo ride away

C-E *Paseban*, Jl Otto Iskandardinata 260, T81127. Restaurant, some rooms with hot water, average, bungalows set amongst gardens, older rooms a little shabby, newer ones better, with hot water, price includes breakfast. **D** *Hotel Familie Ayu*, Jl Ranggalawe 66, T231508. Just off the main road and not far from the alun-alun, rooms are dark. **D** *Kondang Sari*, Jl Raya Bayongbong, T234125. On outskirts, not great. **D** *Wisma PKPN-Ri*, Jl Ciledug 79, T231508. Best of a very bad bunch with clean, spacious rooms and situated near to the town centre. **E** *Penginapan & Pemandian Cipta Rasa 2*, Jl Raya Cipanas 101. Large private mandi with non-stop running hot water from the springs. **E-F** *Penginapan Kota*, Jl Ciledug 241. Basic rooms.

146 GARUT

Entertainment **Cinemas** *Sumbersari*, Jl Jend A Yani 162, not very modern, but the best there is.

Shopping **Department stores** *Asia Department Store*, Jl Jend A Yani 142, has a supermarket; *Matahari Department Store*, Jl Jend A Yani; *Nusantara Department Store*, Jl Siliwangi, has a supermarket.

Transport *65 km from Bandung* **Local** The bemo station is near the intersection of Jl Jend A Yani and Jl Cikuray; bemos from here to local towns.

Road Bus: Garut's Guntur terminal is on the north edge of town. Regular connections with **Bandung**, **Tasikmalaya**, **Yogya** and **Banjar**. **Bemo**: connections with **Cipanas** via **Tarogong**. **Train** The railway station is a Dutch-period building a few hundred metres from the town square, off Jl Jend A Yani – but no passenger trains stop here.

Directory **Banks** *Bank Central Asia*, Jl Ciledug 156. *BNI 1946*, Jl Jend A Yani 56. **Communications** Post Office: Jl Jend A Yani 40.

Cipanas and Cipanas Hot Springs

Phone code: 0262
Colour map 3, grid A2

Cipanas is just 6 km from Garut, and the hot springs a further 2 km on. The turning for Cipanas is at the Km 4 mark, travelling north from Garut towards Bandung. The road from here to Cipanas is 2 km long and passes from Tarogong (a few kilometres before Garut), through terraced fish farms lined with coconut groves. The springs are 2 km above Cipanas town, an easy and attractive walk. The waters are supposed to have healing properties, but female bathers may find that they attract more attention than they might desire. All hotels and losmen have 'sunken' mandis almost like baths, with warm water and steps into them which is a pleasant change to normal ice cold morning mandis. As Cipanas is located in the mountains, air conditioning or fans are not necessary.

Tours The *Tirtagangga Hotel* runs one-day tours to Papandayan volcano, the Cisaruni Tea Estate, Kamojang Crater and Candi Cangkuang.

Sleeping
As mentioned above, all hotels & losmen have sunken mandis, almost like baths, with warm water

B *Sumber Alam*, T21027. Range of rooms, attractive and relaxing place, discounts available on weekdays, western loo, TV, more expensive pretty thatched bungalows on stilts over hot water ponds, narrow paths over ponds, pool, restaurant with large choice and reasonable prices. Hotel shop sells souvenirs including slightly tasteless ties made entirely out of butterfly wings. **B** *Tirtagangga*, Jl Raya Cipanas 130,

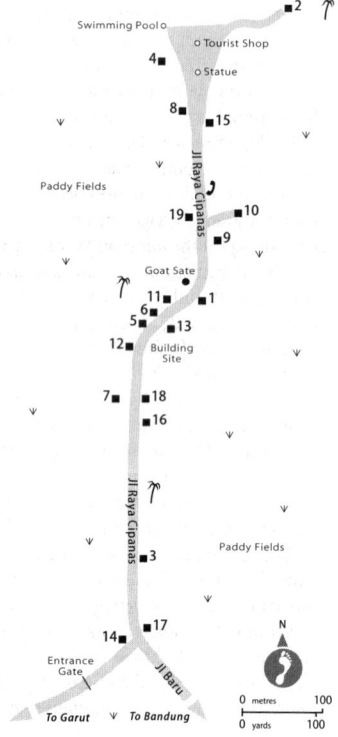

Cipanas

- **Sleeping**
1 Adi Tuta Marta
2 Antralina
3 Banyu Arta
4 Cipanas Indah & Restaurant
5 Cipta Rasa
6 Kurnia Artha
7 Nugraha
8 Penginapan Cipta Bela
9 Pondok Asri
10 Pondok Bayu Kencana
11 Pondok Melati
12 Rahayu
13 Sumber Alam & Restaurant
14 Surya Alam
15 Tirtagangga
16 Tirta Merta
17 Tirta Merta 2
18 Tirta Sari
19 Wulandari

T231811. High rise hotel, well furnished rooms with showers and baths, TV and mini bar. Hot water pool, tennis court and western restaurant. By far the best place to stay in Cipanas. The porters wear traditional dress. **B-C** *Cipanas Indah*, Jl Cipanas 113, T233736. Clean bungalows, pool and gardens. Pricey on weekends and holidays but good value during the week. **C** *Cipta Bela*, Jl Cipanas, T231494. Overpriced but each room with 2 double beds. **C** *Tirta Merta*, Jl Cipanas, T231085. Rooms are comfortably furnished with 2 double beds, TV and carpet, restaurant and shop. **D** *Nugraha*, Jl Cipanas 96, T234829. Excellent value accommodation for price. Large, clean rooms with TV and a balcony at the front, and views over bubbling ponds and rice fields at the back. Recommended. **D** *Pondok Wulandari*, Jl Cipanas 99, T234675. Clean rooms with fan and TV, well priced. **D** *Rahayu*, Jl Cipanas, large beds with view over bubbling ponds, only few rooms. **D** *Tirta Merta 2*, Jl Cipanas, T231422. Two double beds in each room, restaurant. **E** *Melati*, Jl Cipanas, nice rooms for price, noisy as close to road.

Road Bemos: regular connections (No 04) from Garut's Terminal Guntur to Tarogong. A bemo from Tarogong costs 500Rp and takes only a few minutes to Cipanas. **Transport**

Tasik Malaya

Tasik, as it is known, is a thriving – but rarely visited – town and, frankly, there is not a great deal to do or see here. Mount Galunggung, an active volcano, lies 20 km northwest of Tasik. It most recently erupted in 1982 after a 63-year-long period of dormancy.

Phone code: 0262
Colour map 3, grid B2

On Boxing Day 1996 the town gained its 15 minutes of notoriety when a demonstration escalated into a sectarian riot of considerable violence and destruction. Four people were killed in the mayhem and much of the town centre was destroyed as churches, schools, factories and banks were razed. The cause of this moment of madness was the alleged beating of a Muslim teacher and two Islamic students in a police cell. As so often appears to be the case in recent years in Indonesia, this relatively localized grievance spread into a serious outbreak of anti-Christian and anti-Chinese violence.

At the top end of Jalan Pancasila is a good **bird market**. The **alun-alun** has some attractive gardens in its centre, while the **Mesjid Agung** facing onto the Alun-alun is unremarkable. One of Tasik's saving graces, though, is that it is an important **handicraft centre**. In particular, intricate rattan and pandan leaf products are made in the surrounding villages and a distinctive form of batik is also produced here. For details on buying handicrafts in town, see 'Shopping', below. The **tourist office**, *Dinas Pariwisata*, is on Jl Otto Iskandardinata 2. **Sights**

A-C *Crown Hotel*, Jl RE Martadinata 45, T332282, F333967. A/c, pool, slightly out of town on the road to Bandung, 60-odd modern rooms with good facilities, all rather plasticky – like an oversized *Pizza Hut*, popular with tour groups. **B-C** *Yudanegara Hotel*, Jl Yudanegara 19, T331922. A/c, in central location, Indonesian kitsch in style, rooms are fine though, and good value. **B-E** *Pencuk Widuri*, Jl RE Martadinata 51, T334342. Some a/c, out of town on the road to Bandung, converted villa with gardens, quiet rooms with sitting areas, a trifle dark. **C-D** *Wisma Galunggung*, Jl Yudanegara 32-34, T333296. Some a/c, the best place to stay in Tasik, old Dutch villa in central location, spotless rooms and bathrooms, attractive veranda, good rates and friendly service. Highly recommended. **D-E** *Kencana Hotel*, Jl Yudanegara 17, range of rooms, very central, no a/c but more expensive rooms are graced with TVs. **E-F** *Hotel Timur*, Jl Gang Kaum (just off Jl Yudanegara, in the centre of town near the Alun-alun) 5, T30928. Grubby, narrow, uncomfortable beds, basic. **Sleeping**

Cheap *RM Arum Sari*, Jl RE Martadinata 185, excellent grilled, spicy chicken and fish for which this restaurant has a reputation. *Ramona Bakery*, Jl Sutisana Sanjaya 51, for the best pastries in town. **Eating**

Shopping **Handicrafts** Numerous art and handicraft shops in town selling rattan products and the area's distinctive batik cloth. Try the shops along Jl Dr Sukarjo, which runs off the Alun-alun.

Transport 57 km from Garut, 121 km from Bandung, 116 km from Cirebon, 101 km from Pangandaran. **Train** The station is on Jl Cinulu, near the centre of town. **Road Bus**: the bus terminal is just off Jl Ir H Juanda (or Jl By-pass), which is to the southwest of town, several kilometres from the centre. Regular connections with **Bandung**, **Cirebon**, **Garut**, **Pangandaran** and other centres.

Directory **Banks** Bank Bali, Jl Dr Sukarjo. *Bank Bumi Daya*, Alun-alun (town square). **Communications** Post Office: Jl Otto Iskandardinata 6. **Telephone & fax**: *Wartel*, Simpang Lima (Jl Martadinata).

Pangandaran

Phone code: 0265
Colour map 3, grid B2
Admission to the isthmus: 2,000Rp

Pangandaran is situated on the neck of a narrow isthmus and offers the best beaches on the south coast of Java – which is not saying a great deal. Originally a fishing village, many of the local people now derive their livelihoods from tourism. At weekends, during peak season, the town is crowded with Indonesian tourists; out of season, on weekdays, it is like a ghost town and hotel and losmen prices can be bargained down accordingly. The high season runs between June and September, the low season from October to March.

PHPA **tourist office** is on the borders of the park at the south end of the isthmus, near the East Beach. Lia Natalia is an excellent English speaking representative and a good source of information. Private tour companies and travel agents also often bill themselves as 'tourist information centres' to help attract business.

Beaches The best beach is on the west side of the isthmus and is named **West Beach** (*Pantai Barat*). Swimming is not recommended here as currents are vicious. Souvenir shops line the beach front and it is here that most accommodation is concentrated. The east side of the isthmus (**East Beach** or *Pantai Timur*) is less developed; the water is often rough and swimming is poor, sometimes dangerous. Fishermen cast their nets from this shore and land their catches along the beach. Their colourful boats lining the shore are a lovely sight. The fish market is worth a visit in the mornings if you can stand the smell!

The promontory of the isthmus is a park – the **Penanjung National Park**. On both the east and west sides of the promontory are white sand beaches. It is possible to walk the 10 km around the shoreline of the peninsula, or hike through the jungle which is said to support small populations of buffalo, deer, tapirs, civet cats, porcupines and hornbills, although how they tolerate the herds of tourists is a mystery. The Rafflesia flower can, it is claimed, be seen here in season. The park also has some limestone caves. ■ *Admission to the park 1,750Rp, guides 20,000Rp for a tour lasting 4 hrs and worth the money. Open 0700-1730.*

Excursions **Batu Karas** is becomingly increasingly popular with Australian surfers. **Sleeping** 1 km from the beach **D** *Alana's Bungalows*, **D** *Teratai Cottage*, both have basic facilities, but *Teratai* has the added attraction of a pool. ■ *Get there by hired motorbike or take a bemo to Cijulang, then charter a motorbike the last 10 km to the beach from the main road.*

Green Canyon is a very popular day trip. Boat hire is regulated and costs 30,000Rp per *prahu* (which seat up to eight people). Travelling upriver, the foliage becomes denser and the rocks close in, until you find yourself entering a canyon. After 15-20 minutes, the boat's path is blocked by rocks. There is a large plunge pool here, swimming and rubber rings for hire. Best time to visit is during the week, as it gets crowded at weekends and holidays; a recommended trip. **Sleeping** Green Canyon has become so popular that there are now hostels for those who want to stay away from the activity of Pangandaran. Accommodation is cheap and basic but worth it. *Alana's Bungalow, Pemda Bungalows* and *Teretar Cottages* are all good options. ■ *Take a minibus from Pangandaran to Cijulang, and then an ojek from there. Most hotels run tours to the canyon, which will also*

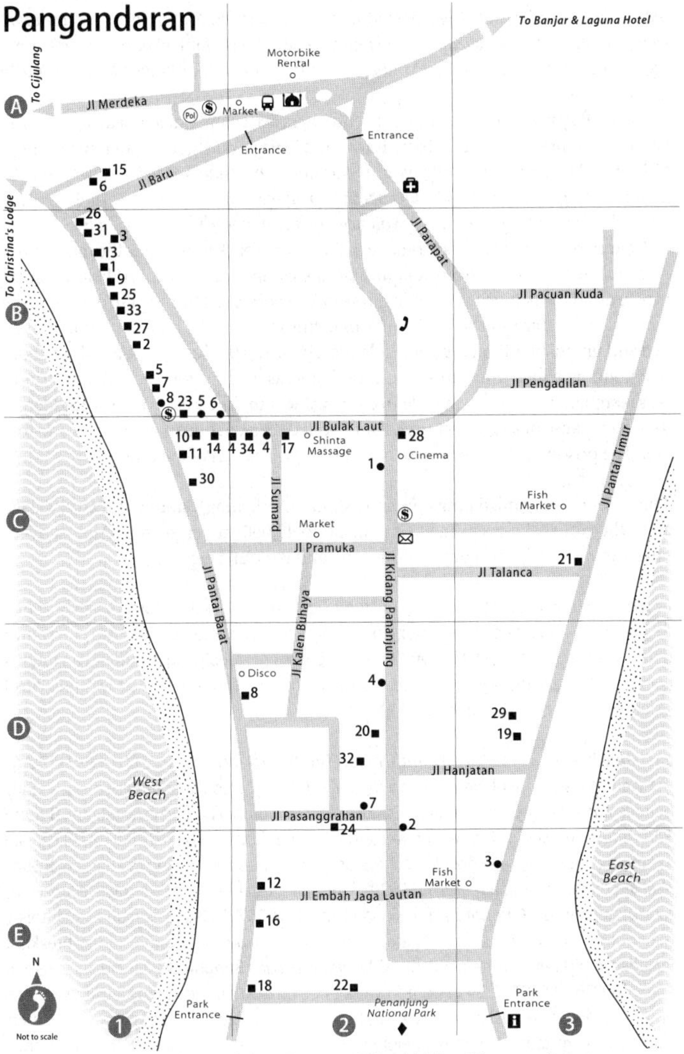

Pangandaran

■ Sleeping
1 Adam's Homestay *B1*
2 Argaloka *B1*
3 Bamboo House *B1*
4 Bima Sakti *C2*
5 Bintang Jelita *B1*
6 Bougenville *A1*
7 Bulak Laut *B1*
8 Bumi Nusantara *D2*
9 Duta *B1*
10 Holiday Inn *C1*
11 Karang Sari *C1*
12 Mangkubumi *E2*
13 Mini Tiga *B1*
14 Mutiara Selatan *C1*
15 Nelayan Beach *A1*
16 Niyur Indah *E2*
17 Nyiur Indah Beach II *C2*
18 Pangandaran Beach *E2*
19 Panorama *D3*
20 Pantai Indah Barat *D2*
21 Pantai Indah Timur *C3*
22 Pondok Moris *E2*
23 Pondok Pantai Sari *B1*
24 Pondok Pelang *D2*
25 Pondok Putri Duyung *B1*
26 Pondok Tirta *B1*
27 Sandaan *B1*
28 Socka *C2*
29 Sunrise *D3*
30 Sunset *C1*
31 Surya Pesona *B1*
32 Susan's *D2*
33 Uni Beach *B1*
34 Widuri *C2*

● Eating
1 Bamboe *C2*
2 Chez Mama Cilacap *D2*
3 Gatul's *E3*
4 Number One Café(s) *C2, D2*
5 Relax *B1*
6 RM Wahayu *B1*
7 Sari Harum *D2*
8 Scandinavian *B1*

include half a day's visit to local farming and craft industries. Alternatively visit the tourist information office for cheaper, good tours. Some agency tours can be overpriced, starting at 50,000Rp per person. Hire your own motorbike for the day or bicycle for 10,000Rp as an alternative.

Parigi Bay is west of Pangandaran, and offers better and quieter beaches than the isthmus, namely Batu Hiu, Batu Karas and Parigi, and good water for surfing.

■ *Regular buses run from Pangandaran bus station on Jalan Merdeka, ask specifically for a beach, eg Batu Karas. The bus doesn't go all the way – only to the bridge over the Green River (2,000Rp); from here you need to hire a motorbike or hitch a lift.*

Boat trip A worthwhile alternative to the bus trip back to Banjar is the much more enjoyable ferry journey from Kalipucang to Cilacap (see 'Transport' below). Local trips around the peninsula, stopping to swim or snorkel can be bargained for with the local fishermen (around 50,000Rp). Trips to tiny white sand islands (infrequently visited and uninhabited) off the peninsula cost about 100,000Rp for a boat ride of about one hour, and then you can stay on the island as long as you wish. A new trip to Nusakambangon is now available from Pangandaran. The island, once forbidden to tourists because of a high security prison located there, has unspoilt beaches and forests. The prison is no longer in use but worth a visit as part of the tour.

Tours Tour agencies organize jungle, boat (fishing, snorkelling), home industry, village and other tours. Prices range from 20,000 to 40,000Rp per person. Almost every hotel organizes trips to Yogya, Wonosobo and Bandung etc.
See 'Travel agents' below

Sleeping Accommodation is concentrated on the west side of the isthmus; in total there are something like 100 hotels and losmen, so below is only a selection. Rates can be bargained down during the low season (Oct-Mar). At Christmas, prices rise steeply, when Indonesian tourists flock here. Many of the hotels and guesthouses rent out family rooms – usually consisting of 2 double rooms and a living area.

East Beach (*Pantai Timur*) **A-B** *Pantai Indah Timur*, Jl Talanca 153, T639004, F639327. A/c, hot water, clean, rather bare but good room facilities, large pool and tennis courts, slightly better standard than its sister hotel on the west beach, outdoor barbecue restaurant. **B** *Bumi Pananjung*, a/c, simple rooms with western toilet and shower. A bit dark but lots of character and the rooms on the upper levels have pretty balconies overlooking the garden. **B** *Sunrise*, Jl Kidang Pananjung 175, T639220. Some a/c, restaurant, pool, attractive, spacious rooms, good value. **C** *Panorama*, Jl Kidang Pananjung 197, T639218. Fan and squat toilet, many of the attractive bamboo/thatch rooms are right on the seafront, good breakfast included, good value for Pangandaran. **C-D** *Laguna Beach Bungalows*, 1 Pengadilan Kebon Carik, T639761, F639762. 2 km from town but free pick-up service, run by a Dutch woman and her Indonesian husband. Very friendly staff, price includes breakfast, tea and coffee. Good, cheap, restaurant, with big helpings. Particularly good tiger prawns fresh from their prawn farm. Free bicycles and surfboard available, dorms (**F**). Recommended.

West Beach (*Pantai Barat*) **A-B** *Pantai Indah Barat*, Jl Kidang Pananjung 151, T639004, F639327. A/c, restaurant, pool, tennis courts, well furnished rooms with all mod cons. **B** *Adam's Homestay*, T/F639164. A/c, western toilet and shower, fridge, beautifully furnished rooms, balcony overlooking peaceful garden with hammocks and giant chess set, excellent and unusual spot, hotel also offers telephone service, tours and good bookshop. **B** *Bima Sakti*, Jl Bulak Laut 12, T639194, F639640. A/c, TV, hot water, well furnished rooms, pool in centre of courtyard, pleasant atmosphere. **B** *Bumi Nusantara*, central section, T639032, F639031. Some a/c, very clean, well designed and efficiently run, friendly, small elevated swimming pool overlooks the beach, good restaurant, range of rooms. Recommended. **B** *Niyur Indah I*, southern end, T639053, F639304. A/c, TV and hot water, restaurant with pretty gardens, overpriced, and now slightly seedy. **B** *Nyiur Indah Beach II*, T639349, F639642. New hotel in pleasant surroundings, well decorated, clean rooms but quite pricey for this bracket. **B** *Pondok Putri Duyung*, northern end, T639183, F639209. A/c, attractively built, 2 double rooms, living area, hot water, TV, not as clean as it could be, economy rooms better value than deluxe. **B** *Surya Pesona*, Jl Pamugaran Bulak Laut, T639428, F639289. Large pool, immaculate a/c rooms with bath, hot water shower, TV, excellent value economy rooms with western bathrooms, imposing yet attractive international-style resort, landscaped gardens, mini golf, children's play area, one of the best Pangandaran has to offer. Recommended. **B** *Uni Beach*, Jl Pamugaran Bulak Laut, T639224, F639536. A/c, TV, large rooms all with 2 double beds, good value. Recommended. **C** *Duta*, Jl Pamugaran, Bulak Laut, T630066. A/c, hot water, TV and western toilet, a bit delapidated. **C** *Pangandaran Beach*, Jl Pantai Pananjung 95, T639062. Southern end, some a/c, clean, large rooms, great position facing safe swimming part of beach, well kept gardens. Recommended. **C** *Sandaan*, Jl Pamugaran Bulak Laut, T639165, F630017. A/c, hot water, pool and pretty gardens, some rooms darker than others but clean, recommended for this price range. **C** *Susan's*, Jl Kalen Buhaya 20, inland from the beach, T639290. Some a/c, restaurant, pool, large bungalows with 10 rooms, kitchen facilities, ideal for long stay. Recommended. **C** *Pondok Tirta* T639235, Jl Pamugaran 140. Spotlessly clean and peaceful rooms furnished in pine, good value. **C** *Widuri*, Jl Bulak Laut 14, T630284. Western bathroom, TV, brand new hotel so very clean, cool atmosphere with blue interiors. **D** *Bamboo House*, northern end and not on beach, T639419, popular with backpackers, large, clean rooms in bungalows, excellent for the price. Recommended. **D** *Bintang Jelita*, T639297. Northern end, clean, with living area and 2 double bedrooms, well-run and popular. Recommended. **D** *Christina's Delta Gecko Lodge*, 4 km west of Pangandaran, on our last visit, some uncertainty hung around the future of this place – so it may have closed by the time this book hits the shelves. It lies a bejak drive from bus station – too far to walk. Attractive estate with 2-storey bungalows with a bathroom, to sleep 3-5 people, gardens, youth hostel atmosphere and a good place to meet other travellers, tours organized, free bicycles available and games room. Run by a friendly Australian women, fish barbecue on Wed night and accompanying cultural show, close to a river, where it's possible to swim. Recommended. **D** *Pondok Moris*, southern end of peninsular, near the park, T639490. Discreet little homestay, well-managed by family, set in delightful garden. **D** *Nelayan Beach* Jl Pamugaran, T639702. Down side alley at north end of beach, brand new hotel with 7 rooms backing onto a coconut plantation. Large, airy and clean rooms, excellent value and recommended. **D** *Pantai Sari*, Jl Bulak Laut, T639175. Inland from beach, northern end, some a/c, restaurant, attached bathrooms, a/c, rooms are good value. **E** *Bougenville Resort*, Jl Bulak Laut 133, T6793/0. Out of town and 3 km from the safe swimming beach but surprisingly popular, price decreases after 1 night here. Breakfast included, efficient laundry service, squat loos, very basic. **E** *Bulak Laut*, T639171. Northern end, chalet style with sitting-room and unusual bathrooms, discounts available and room rate includes breakfast – good value. **E** *Holiday Inn*, Jl Bulak Laut 50, T639285. Inland from beach at the northern end, popular place with squat loos and shabby bamboo rooms, but friendly staff and budget price. **E** *Mutiara Selatan*, T639416. Inland from beach at the northern end, clean basic rooms with western loos. Recommended for those on budget. **E** *Pondok Pelang*, Jl Pasanggrahan 7-13, T639023. Good clean rooms, simple but good value in a quiet location.

Eating

With something like 100 places to stay, there are also innumerable places to eat. Many are geared to western tastes. Not surprisingly, seafood is the best bet. *Amsterdam Café*, Jl Bulak Laut, western fare, pizzas and cocktails. *Bagus*, north of telephone exchange, very good value, healthy food and friendly owner. *Bamboe*, Jl Kidang Pananjung, just south of *Luta Travel Agent*, friendly management and good food. *Chez Mama Cilacap*, Jl Kidang Pananjung 197, T639098, a travellers' haven, western breakfasts, Indonesian food and seafood. *Gatul's*, East Beach, near the fish market, excellent seafood. *Hilmans*, close to the bus station, attached to a fish factory. Excellent, good value food in great atmosphere. *Mumbo's*, West Beach, next to *Mangkubumi*, seafood, Chinese, Indonesian. *Number One Café(s)*, Jl Bulak Laut 26, T630383, there are 3 restaurants with a variation of this name – confusingly, *No 1 Café No 1, No 1 Café No 2, No 1 Café No 3*. All are simple cafés with cheap juices, salads and pizzas (and cornflakes!), and fun décor. *Pantai Timur*, Jl E Jaga Lautan, East Beach, seafood, Chinese, Indonesian and International. *Relax Café*, Jl Bulak Laut 74, European-run 'classy' establishment, serving delicious milkshakes, open sandwiches and muesli in huge portions – it has its own bakery too. More pricey than most. **Rumah Makan Wahayu**, Jl Bulak Laut, the only pub in Pangandarang, newly built by a Dutch man, not yet popular. *Sari Harum*, Jl Pasanggrahan 2, Sundanese. *Scandinavian*, West Beach, just north of *Karang Sari Hotel*.

Entertainment **Cinemas** *Nanjung Cinema*, Jl Kidang Pananjung, north of post office. **Massage** *House of Shinta*, Jl Bulak Laut 11, T639970; 1 hr of massage/reflexology, 20,000Rp, not an especially relaxing atmosphere though.

Shopping Stalls on the beach and some shops on the central isthmus road, Jl Kidang Pananjung (for instance Luta at 107) – shell jewellery, shells, clothing, knick-knacks.

Sports **Swimming** The *Socka Hotel* on Jl Kidang Pananjung, north of the cinema, *Pantai Indah Timor* and *Panorama*, Jl Kidang Pananjung 197, all open their pools to non-residents. **Surf and boogie boards** For hire along the West Beach (10,000Rp).

Tour operators *Luta*, Jl Kidang Pananjang 107, T39294, organizes local tours and transport to and from Pangandaran; *Mumbo's*, West Beach (next to *Mangkubumi Hotel*), will organize buses to Jakarta, Yogya and Bandung. They also arrange the backwater boat trip from Kalipucang to Cilacap, with connecting minibus to Yogya (13,500Rp). *Delta Gecko*, organize a Green Canyon tour – much cheaper than the others and well worth it.

Transport **Local Becaks & bicycle hire**: along the beach and from guesthouses, approximately 20,000Rp per day. **Motorbike hire**: *Luta*, Jl Kidang Pananjung 107. **Car hire**: *Luta*, Jl Kidang Pananjung 107.

400 km from Jakarta, 129 km from Bandung, 66 km from Banjar & 312 km from Yogya

Train There are no direct trains linking Pangandaran with Jakarta, Yogya, Bandung or Solo. It is necessary to change in **Banjar**, a small town on the Bandung-Yogya road, and 66 km from Pangandaran. There are a number of cheap losmen over the railway bridge from the rail and bus stations in Banjar, for those who arrive too late to make a connection. The train and bus stations are 500m apart; becaks wait to take travellers between the two. Regular connections with **Jakarta** (10 hrs), **Bandung** (5 hrs), **Yogya** (6-8 hrs) and **Surabaya** to Banjar. Regular buses link Banjar with Pangandaran.

Road Bus: there are 2 stations on Jl Merdeka, north of the hotels and guesthouses (outside the main gates). Local bus connections tend to leave from the station at the eastern end of Jl Merdeka, not far from the main intersection before the gate, while express buses leave from the company terminal further west along Jl Merdeka. Regular buses link Pangandaran with **Banjar**, from where there are frequent buses onward to **Jakarta** (7-10 hrs), **Bogor** (via Ciawi), **Bandung** (6 hrs), **Yogya** and **Solo**, and less frequent buses to **Wonogiri** and **Madiun**. Jakarta-Banjar buses leave Jakarta's Cililitan station every hour. There are also some direct connections with **Jakarta** (8 hrs) and **Bandung**. More regular connections with **Ciamis** (2½ hrs), **Kalipucang** and **Tasik Malaya** (3 hrs). Travel agents in town sell tickets on the more popular routes.

Sea Boat: an alternative to the bus or train is to take the boat between Kalipucang (Pangandaran's 'port') and **Cilacap** through the Anakan Lagoon, an 'inland' sea. A recommended 4 hr journey and a gentle form of transport, the boat sails down the mangrove-clothed Tanduy River, stopping-off in various fishing villages on the way, before crossing the Anakan Lagoon. The Tanduy River marks the border between West Java and Central Java; in West Java the local language is Sundanese; in Central Java, Javanese. The last village before the ferry turns into the lagoon – **Majingklak** – is the easternmost village in West Java. The large island bordering the south of the Lagoon, and protecting it from the Indian Ocean, is **Kampangan Island**. In 1912, the Dutch depopulated the island, resettling 3 fishing villages, with the intention of making it a prison. The lagoon is one of Indonesia's largest areas of wetland and has a varied water bird population. For keen birdwatchers it is possible to jump ship at one of the fishing villages, sleep in a homestay, and then charter a boat to explore the lagoon early the next morning, before continuing the journey to Cilacap (or vice versa). Approaching Cilacap is LP Nusa Kembangan, Indonesia's top security prison. The boat docks at **Sleko**, outside Cilacap (see page 162). **Kalipucang** is 15 km from Pangandaran; take a local bus there. **NB** To catch a bus connection in Cilacap get either the 0600, 0700 or 0800 from Kalipucang, 4 hrs (there are also 2 afternoon departures at 1200 and 1300). From Cilacap the boats leave from Sleko harbour, 4 departures a day (0700, 0800, 1100 and 1300).

Directory

Banks & money changers *Bank Rakyat Indonesia*, Jl Kidang Pananjung 133 (near the intersection with Jl Talanca). Will change most currencies and TCs but rates here are poor. *Lotus Tour & Travel*, Jl Bulak Laut. **Communications** Post Office: Jl Kidang Pananjung 111 (Poste restante available here). **Telephone office**: Jl Kidang Pananjung (northern end). **International Phone Service**: *Adam's Homestay*, West Beach.

The north coast plain

Cirebon

Phone code: 0231
Colour map 3, grid A2

At the end of the 15th century, the kingdom of Cirebon reached its golden age under Sunan Gunung Jati, an ardent Muslim and one of the first *wali* – Muslim missionaries, now regarded as saints – to bring Islam to Java. He built the Pakungwati Kraton here in 1529. In 1677, the court was split into the Kasepuhan (elder) and Kanoman (younger) kratons. Unlike the kratons of Yogya and Solo, the kratons at Cirebon were not centres for the arts. Work was produced in nearby villages by guild-like organizations.

Today, Cirebon is a busy port and one of the north coast's industrial centres, with a population of 250,000. The city itself is open and breezy and feels coastal, despite the fact that the sea is usually out of sight. The city is famous for its distinctive batik, heavily influenced by Chinese designs (see box, page 154). Chinese began to settle in Cirebon about three centuries ago and today the ethnic Chinese population numbers about 25,000, 10 percent of the total. As in so many cities in Java, there is a simmering brew of anti-Chinese discontent and the authorities are constantly on the alert for sectarian violence. The area around Cirebon is a centre of chilli, mung bean and sugar cultivation.

Sights

Cirebon's **tourist information** office (*Dinas Pariwisata Daerah*) is on Jl Cipto 1 (at the intersection with Jl Kartini). It's not particularly helpful, indeed the office seems entirely empty. A brochure may be offered but the map is jealously guarded. ■ *Open 0800-1400 Mon-Thu, 0800-1100 Fri, 0800-1300 Sat*. Another office is sited 5 km out of town on the new bypass road, near Gua Sunyaragi. It has few brochures in English and the staff are less than helpful; for information and maps it is better to ask at one of the larger hotels.

Cirebon's main attractions are its **kratons**, of which there are four, all still inhabited by their powerless sultans. The most interesting is the large **Kraton Kasepuhan**, which was built on the site of the earlier Hindu Pakungwati Kraton of 1529 (the home of Sunan Gunung Jati's queen, Pakungwati). It is the oldest palace, built in 1677 – although since much remodelled (the last extensive renovation was in 1928). It is set on the south side of a square, and is approached along Jalan Kasepuhan through red brick split gates (*candi bentar*) – similar to Balinese temple gates (some of the newer hotels in Cirebon have imitated the same design element). In front of the kraton is the *Siti Inggil* – a very attractive brick enclosure,

The Singa Barong Carriage

Cirebon rock and cloud designs

The distinctive rock and cloud formations found not only on the batik of Cirebon but also in carvings on the carriages at the kratons, in the gates of the Kasepuhan kraton and in decoration at the strange water garden Sunyaragi, are known as megamendung and wadasan.

They are assumed to be derived from Chinese designs, probably adopted by local artisans after seeing ceramics and paintings brought by Chinese traders to the port. Each of the four courts developed their own particular styles, but all the designs featured clouds, rocks, gardens and heraldic animals.

with split gates and small wooden, tiled pendopos. Plates, brought here by Chinese traders, are set into the brick – it is regarded as the finest Siti Inggil in Java.

In the first of the kraton's white washed walled courtyards is a rather down-at-heel museum, with a badly displayed collection of gamelan sets, rice harvesting knives (*ani ani*), European glass, Indian chests and Portuguese armour. Towards the back of the compound, through some weathered wooden doors, are the Palace's three main rooms. They are wonderfully cool and airy, painted in soft greens, with Delft tiles and Chinese plates set into the walls. The painted ceiling of the first room is original (although the rattan roof is new), as is the second pillared room. The beautiful pendopo *Langgar Alit*, with its unusual four-branched central pillar, was part of the earlier Hindu Pakungwati Kraton and was used for private worship by the Sultan's family.

Back in the main courtyard, visitors should not leave the kraton without asking to see the main attraction: the *Singa Barong Carriage*. It is housed in a stable opposite the museum and is an extraordinary amalgam of Hindu, Buddhist and Islamic elements. Made in 1548 in the shape of a fantastic animal, the carriage would have been yoked to four white buffalo. It has the body and trunk of an elephant, the head of a naga, and the wings of a garuda, and when the carriage moved, the wings flapped. In its trunk the beast holds a three-pronged spear (symbolizing the three religions). On the back of the carriage is the distinctive Cirebon cloud and rock design carved in wood. It was used by former sultans on ceremonial occasions, although it is said that the carriage has not left the stable since it was installed there in the 1940s. Behind the carriage are three palanquins; the central one, constructed in 1777, was used for circumcision ceremonies and has a garuda head and fish tail. The one on the left was for carrying the sultan's children, the one on the right for his wife. ■ *Admission 2,000Rp (with an extra charge for cameras and video). Open 0800-1600 Mon-Sun.*

Next to the kraton, facing the square, is the **Mesjid Agung** on Jalan Jagasatru. Built in 1480 it is one of the oldest (and most revered) mosques in Indonesia, with the characteristic two-tiered roof found along the north coast of Java. Like other mosques in Demak and Kudus, the design shows links with pre-Islamic Hindu-Buddhist structures. The city's main mosque is the modern **Mesjid Raya Al-Taque** at the intersection of Jalan Kartini and Jalan Siliwangi, which imitates traditional Javanese style.

Kraton Kanoman is reached by walking from Jalan Kanoman through the **Pasar Kanoman** and across a rough piece of ground grazed by sheep. The market sells meat, fish, vegetables and cooked foods, along with dry goods of various kinds. Less attractive than Kasepuhan and less well cared for, the walls of the Kraton Kanoman at the

Chinese bird motif from a Cirebon batik.
Adapted from: Gillow, John (1992), Traditional Indonesian Textiles, Thames & Hudson: London

entrance are of red plaster, again with Chinese plates set into them. It was probably built in the 17th century, but has been substantially remodelled since then. Ask to see the 'museum' on the left-hand side of the compound, with an even more motley collection than the Kasepuhan Museum. Noteworthy are two more carriages, dating from the period of the 16th-century Pakungwati Kraton. The *Jempana Setia* may have been a litter used to carry the senior wife, or it may have been used to transport princes to the circumcision ceremony. It is of ornately carved wood in the Cirebon *megamendung-wadasan* style. The *Paksinagaliman* carriage is in the shape of a fantastic animal (an inferior version of the carriage at the Kraton Kasepuhan, see above) – a garuda, elephant and naga rolled into one ungainly beast. ■ *Admission 1,000Rp. Open 0800-1600 Mon-Sun.* Not too far from the Kraton Kanoman is the **Kraton Kacirebonan** – not really a palace at all but a house. It is an early 19th century off-shoot of the Kanoman and is the least interesting of the three. It is not open to the public.

Sunyaragi is a rather ugly 'grotto', built as a large pleasure garden (connected to the Kasepuhan Kraton) between 1720 and 1741. It was constructed on two levels, the upper area being an ornamental lake, with a small island only accessible by boat. Since then, it has been extensively altered, many would say ruined, and is now a maze of concrete caves. Locals promenade and picnic here on weekends and holidays. ■ *Admission 500Rp. Open 0700-1800 Mon-Sun. Sunyaragi is 3 km southwest of town; take an angkutan 'G2' down Jalan Kesambi (or 'G4', '0IB' and 'BX' which also pass the Cave) and get off at the intersection with Jalan Bypass (also known as Jalan Jend A Yani); the grotto is 500m north (right) on Jalan Bypass. Ask for 'Gua (cave) Sunyaragi'.*

Exploring the town on foot can be rewarding, as there are some attractive old buildings and a number of Chinese temples. The **Balai Kota** (town hall) was built in the 1920s and is a good example of Art Deco design. At the time, Cirebon was known as Kota Udang (City of Shrimps), and to celebrate this title the hall has moulds of shrimps climbing up the towers. Another notable building is the colonial offices of the **Bank Indonesia**, at the intersection of Jalan Kartini and Jalan Tuparev. Cirebon supports a number of markets: among the most accessible is the **Pasar Kanoman** on Jalan Kanoman; the 'morning' market or **Pasar Pagi** on Jalan Siliwangi is also worth a wander.

The Tomb of Sunan Gunung Jati, one of Java's nine 'Walis', is 5 km north of town, 100m off the road to Karangampel and Indramayu (it is signposted *Makam* [grave] *Gunung Jati*). This 15th-century mosque and cemetery is a popular pilgrimage site for devout Muslims. The whitewashed walls, like those of Cirebon's kratons, are inlaid with Chinese and Dutch plates and tiles. Gunung Jati's tomb is through wooden doors and is not open to visitors (the doors are sometimes opened on special occasions); the tomb in the open pavilion is that of Sultan Sulaeman. Also buried here is the Wali's Chinese wife Ong Tien, who fell in love with Sunan Jati while he was on a mission to China and implored her father to allow her to follow him to Java. She converted to Islam, but died three years after arriving in Cirebon. ■ *Admission free, officially, but donations include parking a car, entering the cemetery, leaving shoes, and entering the tomb site. To get there take an angkutan 'GG' or '06' which runs down Jalan Siliwangi/Raya Klayan, and ask to be let off at Makam Gunung Jati.*

Excursions

Trusmi is a village 6 km west of town, and is the best known of the various *batik villages* in the vicinity of Cirebon. Linked to the courts of the Sultans for many years, the small workshops produce high quality batik tulis (hand drawn designs), as well as stamped cloth (see page 306). Prices start at 15,000Rp and go as high as 165,000Rp for the very best quality cloth. One of the largest and best known workshops is the *Masina Batik Factory*. ■ *Get there by blue angkutan 'GP' or '04', which runs from Jalan Gunungsari, down Jalan Tuparev to Plered. In the village of Plered (really a suburb of Cirebon), turn right and walk down a becak-choked lane to Trusmi and its workshops (signposted).*

Sleeping

Most hotels are to be found along Jl Siliwangi

A *Apita Green*, Jl Tuparev 323, T200748, F200728. A/c restaurant, pool, new high-tech hotel 2 km out of town on road to Bandung, large attractive 'river' pool. Rooms are rather bland and somewhat pricey, but the management is friendly and enthusiastic. **A** *Bentani*, Jl Siliwangi 69, T203246, F207527, bentani@cirebon.wasantara.net.id Rooms are small and feminine, bathrooms a little too basic for the price, but generally a good standard, 2 restaurants, pool and pub, lower rooms quite dark. **A** *Puri Santika*, Jl Dr Wahidin 32, T200570, F200482, santika@cirebon.wasantara.net.id Stylish architecture and friendly individuality sets this hotel apart from all others in Cirebon. International standard with fitness centre, large pool, tennis court, restaurant (runs BBQs on Thur and Sat), business centre with internet access. **A-B** *Kharisma*, Jl RA Kartini 60, T202062, F202458. A/c, restaurant, disco, karaoke, gym, tennis court, pool, recently expanded, 99 rooms, built around pool and sunken bar, rather dated rooms, on edge of town centre, pretensions of provincial grandeur but it works well enough, discounts available. **A-B** *Patra Jasa*, Jl Tuparev 11 (2 km out of town on the road to Bandung), T29402, F27696. A/c, pool, tennis, good facilities. **A-B** *Hotel Prima Cirebon* (formerly the *Park Cirebon*), Jl Siliwangi 107, T205411, F205407. A/c restaurant, pool, karaoke bar, was once the flashiest place in town. Ignore the stained carpets as the rooms are still of a good standard, incorporating Islamic and Indonesian architectural elements. But in terms of value, this place is not what it used to be.

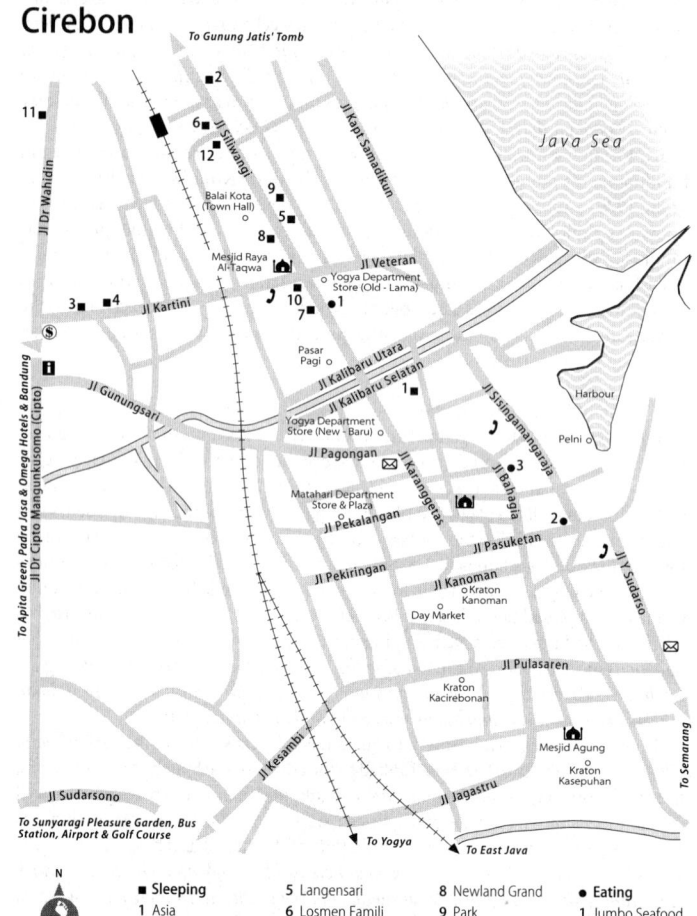

Cirebon

	Sleeping	5 Langensari	8 Newland Grand	• Eating
	1 Asia	6 Losmen Famili	9 Park	1 Jumbo Seafood
	2 Bentani	7 Losmen Semarang,	10 Priangan	2 KFC & Pizza Hut
	3 Cirebon Plaza	Mandala Cinema &	11 Puri Santika	at Hero Plaza
	4 Kharisma	Pasar Malam	12 Sidodadi	3 Maxim's Seafood

B *Cirebon Plaza*, Jl RA Kartini 64, T202062, F202458. A/c, restaurant, 34 rooms with satellite TV and minibar, modern hotel, the brochure maintains that: "The interior and furnishing manifest a fantastic conglomeration of Sundanese, Javanese, Islamic, Chinese and Dutch civilizations"; this, though, is scarcely evident, the *Plaza* is just another modern, albeit comfortable, Indonesian hotel. **C** *New Land Grand*, Siliwangi 98, T208623, F200369. Spacious, pink and tasteless rooms with poor electrics and generally shabby. The adjacent disco may be noisy but 2 free tickets are included if you can't sleep through it. Impressive colonial and colonnaded exterior. **C** *Omega Hotel*, Jl Tuparev 20, T204291. A/c, modern Indonesian kitsch with surfeit of plastic and velvet, inconvenient location nearly 2 km from centre of town on road to Bandung. **C** *Priangan*, Jl Siliwangi 108, T200862. Impressive marble entrance, a/c, good mid-range hotel, hot water, TV, central, clean and well-run with rooms on courtyard. Recommended. **C** *Hotel Sidodadi*, Jl Siliwangi 72, T202305, F204820. Good location for the station, round courtyard with shading mature trees, clean blue rooms with pleasant seating area. Recommended.

D-E *Langensari*, Jl Siliwangi 127, T201818. Some a/c, some with own bathrooms (rather poor with squat loos), basic, plain rooms, convenient for railway station. **D-E** *Nooraini*, Jl Jend A Yani 55, T201352. Good proximity to the bus station but far from the town centre, rooms are dark and basic, 3 beds to a room, squat loos and no shower but breakfast included. **E** *Asia*, Jl Kalibaru 15-17, T202183. Old building, popular and clean with courtyard, on quiet street, the rooms are well maintained and the owner, Bontot Komar, is very switched-on, a good central place to stay, good breakfasts. Recommended. **E** *Famili*, Jl Siliwangi 66, T207935, clean, plain rooms on a courtyard, shared mandi, clean simple rooms with very narrow beds, good location for railway station. **E** *Islam*, Jl Siliwangi 116, T203403. **E** *Losmen Semarang*, Jl Siliwangi 124. Clean but basic rooms, old building, good management, central, although rather noisy location in the middle of town.

Local specialities include *nasi jamblang* (rice served in dried teak leaves), *mie kocok*, *sate kalong* and *nasi tengko*. Cirebon has a reputation for producing some of the best seafood in Java. Try the spicy *udang mantegna* (prawns with tomato and cucumber) and the excellent squid (*cuci*).

Eating

Indonesian Mid-range to cheap: *Jumbo Seafood Restaurant*, Jl Siliwangi 185 (opposite the Mandala Cinema). Locals recommend it as one of the best seafood restaurants in the city, fish and seafood are displayed and cooked to Sundanese and Chinese recipes. Recommended. *Maxim's*, Jl Syarif Abdurachman 45-47. Also serves Chinese and seafood, large, popular with locals. Recommended. *Yogya Department Store*, Jl Karanggetas, food market on the ground floor selling good range of Indonesian dishes, excellent place to browse and try a range of dishes. *Baraya*, Jl Yos Sudarso 45.

Foodstalls *Pasar Kasepuhan*, on the square near Kraton Kasepuhan. *Pasar Malam*, a good place to try Cirebon's seafood is the night market by the Mandala Cinema on Jl Siliwangi.

Bakeries *La Palma Bakery*, Jl Siliwangi (near the Balai Kota). *Orchid German Bakery*, Jl Karanggetas 122.

Amusement parks Ade Irma Suryana Nasution Taman Rekreasi. **Cinemas** There are a number in town, with a/c, showing English soundtrack films. *Mandala*, Jl Siliwangi; *Matahari Dept Store*, Jl Pekiringan, showing up to 10 films a day. **Dance** *Topeng* (masked dance), at the Kraton Kasepuhan, 0800-1000 Sun. **Disco & karaoke** Big in Cirebon; try the *Aquarius* at the *Park Hotel*; the *Blue Diamond* at Jl Yos Sudarso 1 is open 1900-0200/0300, or the *Grand Disco* at the *Grand Hotel*. **Theatre** Open air theatre at Sunyaragi.

Entertainment

July: Kraton festival, a new festival (first staged in 1997) with an emphasis on Cirebon's palaces and royal links.

Festivals

Shopping

Best buys here are batik, rattan, topeng masks, wayang kulit & wayang golek puppets

Batik The Cirebon area produces its own style of very distinctive batik (see box above). The town contains many batik shops; a good number can be found on the ground floor of the *Matahari Plaza*, on Jl Pekiringan; other good shops including **Batik Keris**, Jl Pasuketan 81; **Batik Permana**, Jl Karanggetas 16; and **Batik Semar**, Jl Bahagia 36B.

Department stores *Matahari*, Jl Pekiringan; *Yogya Department Store* (Baru), Jl Karanggetas; *Yogya Department Store* (Lama), Jl Siliwangi 173.

Sports

Golf *Ciperna Golf Course*, owned by the state oil company Pertamina, is 6 km southwest of town and open to visitors. Angkutan 'GC' runs there.

Tour operators

Leo Star, Jl Karanggetas 227, T28395. *Mitra Tour*, Jl Siliwangi 69, T27726. *Nenggala Tour*, Jl Pasuketan 41, T26421.

Transport

248 km from Jakarta, 317 km from Yogya, 237 km from Semarang

Local Blue angkutans (**colts**) criss-cross town in their hundreds (500Rp), and there are also multitudes of becaks. A few meter taxis make up Cirebon's public transport system.

Air Lapangan Airport is 5 km southwest of the city, T27085; angkutan 'GC' and 'GG05' go past the airport (500Rp). Daily connections by *Garuda/Merpati* with **Jakarta**, **Bengkulu**, **Bandar Lampung**, **Balikpapan** and **Banjarmasin**.

Train The station, a rather attractive colonial-period structure, is at the north end of Jl Siliwangi, set back from the make-up on Jl Stasiun Kereta Api. Angkutans 'G6' and 'G5' run past the station. Cirebon connects with the southern line, which arrives at Gambir station in **Jakarta** (3¼-4 hrs) and links up with **Yogyakarta** (6¾ hrs). There are also services on the northern coastal line, which departs from the Kota station in Jakarta and links up with **Semarang** and **Surabaya** (see page 977 for timetable). Train tickets are best booked in advance – they are often sold out, especially at weekends and public holidays, so check availability. Large hotels do reserve tickets but charge a hefty commission.

Road Bus: the station is 2 km south of town, on Jl Bypass, also known as Jl Jend A Yani. Numerous Angkutans (colts) ply the route into town almost continually. All long distance buses leave from here and express and a/c companies have their offices at the station. Regular connections with **Jakarta** (5 hrs), **Semarang** (5 hrs), **Yogya** (7 hrs), **Bandung** (3½ hrs) and other major urban centres. **Minibus**: minibus connections with **Bandung**, **Yogyakarta** and **Semarang**. The minibus office is at Jl Karanggetas 7.

Sea Boat: few people reach Cirebon by sea, but the *Pelni* vessel *Lawit* does call here on its fortnightly circuit between Java and Kalimantan. The *Pelni* office is at the harbour (see timetables on page 988).

Directory

Banks *Bank Central Asia*, Jl Siliwangi (near Mandala Cinema). *Bank International Indonesia*, Jl Siliwangi 49. *Bumi Daya*, Jl Siliwangi 127. *Djasa Valasmas Artha*, Jl Yos Sudarso 56. *Valuta Sejati*, Jl Bahagia 53. **Communications** General Post Office and Internet: Jl Yos Sudarso 7, For internet access the rate is 8,000Rp per hr, open 24 hr. **Telephone & fax**: *Warpostel*, Jl Kartini 7 (opposite the mosque). **Useful addresses** Immigration: Jl Sisinga Mangaraja 33, T202955.

Central Java and Yogyakarta

The central portion of Java comprises the province of Central Java and the Special Territory of Yogyakarta – the latter being one of only two such regions in Indonesia (the other is Aceh at the north tip of Sumatra). Although this part of Java contains some of the most magnificent monuments in the world, it is at the same time one of the poorest areas of Indonesia. Part of the explanation lies in the incredibly high population densities: combined, Central Java and Yogyakarta had a population of nearly 32,000,000 in 1990, and in places farmers are crammed on to the land at a density of 2,000 per sq km.

In the 1960s, commentators were generally pessimistic about the ability of the region to escape the effects of what seemed to be such an intolerable burden of people. They highlighted the high incidence of malnutrition, the depths of poverty that existed, and could see little that might off-set a forthcoming 'Malthusian' catastrophe. Although conditions are still poor, the crisis has not materialized. Industrial growth – mostly small-scale cottage industries – has been encouraging, while agriculture with the aid of the technology of the 'Green Revolution' has managed, in the main, to keep production growing faster than population.

This central portion of Java lacks a city on the scale of Bandung in West Java or Surabaya in East Java. The largest towns are the historic **Yogyakarta** *and* **Surakarta (Solo)**. *Central Java was the focus of the magnificent Buddhist Sailendra and Hindu Sanjaya dynasties which built, respectively,* **Borobudur** *and the temples on the* **Prambanan Plain**. *It was also the focus of the later Mataram Kingdom, and the sultanates of Yogyakarta and Surakarta. It is to visit these archaeological and historical sites, and to stay in what has become one of the most popular tourist towns in Indonesia – namely Yogyakarta – that visitors make their way here in droves. A general introduction to the art and history of Central Java can be found, beginning on page 298.*

South Central Java

Cilacap

This coastal town has little to offer the tourist, but it is associated with the 'port' (really just a jetty) of Sleko, where the ferry from the beach resort of Pangandaran (see page 148) docks four times daily. Because the bus journey to Pangandaran is a circuitous 163 km from Cilacap, it makes sense to take the far more relaxing four hour ferry journey. There are numerous hotels in Cilacap for visitors who arrive too late to catch the ferry to Pangandaran or a bus on to Yogya, and it can also be used as a base for visits to the Jatijajar Caves (see 'Excursions').

Phone code: 0282
Colour map 3, grid B3

Sir Francis Drake, in his circumnavigation of the globe, anchored at Cilacap on 9 March 1580. The town offers one of the very few good anchorages on the wave-lashed south coast. Drake was favourably impressed by the locals, writing that they were a "loving, a very true and just dealing people". Today Cilacap is a (comparatively) important industrial/trading area, with a large Pertamina complex nearby. The whiff of fish in the air also hints that the town's fishing roots remain vibrant. There is a **tourist office** *Dinas Pariwisata*, on Jalan Jend A Yani 8 (opposite *Wijaya Kusuma Hotel*), T22481. Little English spoken and handouts are all (so far) in Indonesian, but you can get a map which is marginally useful.

Sights For those with time on their hands, there are one or two places of interest in Cilacap. At the southern end of town the Cilacap River flows into the sea, and along its course through the town can be seen a string of brightly coloured fishing boats. The main port, in fact quite an important one as there are very few good anchorages along Java's south coast, is the **Pelabuhan Cilacap** at the end of Jl Martadinata. (**NB** This is not the Sleko jetty – for Pangandaran – which is on the west side of town, at the end of Jl Jend Sudirman.) Also marketed as a 'sight' is **Teluk Penyu** or **Turtle Bay**. This lies to the east of the town, a 10 to 15-minute walk from the centre. It illustrates vividly the fact that in some places at least 'environmentalism' is no more than a slogan: numerous stuffed turtles, pangolins, civets, snakes and other animals, along with shells and gruesome souvenirs, are on sale at this dirty beach. The animals are not even well stuffed. Also here is the **Pasar Ikan** or fish market, where women sell fish, crabs and prawns on the beach. The beach may be interesting, but it is neither attractive or pleasant. Walking south along the beach road, past the Pertamina oil storage tanks, is the **Benteng Pendem** or **Pendem Fort** (about 1 or 2 km from the centre of town, near the small lighthouse). The fort was built by the Dutch between 1861 and 1879 and is now an 'objek wisata' (tourist sight) – it is a warren of caves, tunnels, storage rooms and barracks, and boys with torches offer to illuminate the fort for foreign visitors at exorbitant rates.

A good market to browse around is the **morning market** (mostly fish and fruit) at the eastern end of Jl Sutoyo, near the intersection with Jl Dr Wahidin. There is also a **Chinese temple** in the centre of Cilacap, at the intersection of Jl Martadinata and Jl Jend A Yani.

Excursions **Jatijajar caves** consist of gardens, pools and concrete figures, arranged within and around a cave complex (see page 173). ■ *Getting there: take a bus north to Route 2 and then another one east towards Kebumen and Yogya.*

Nusa Kambangan is a narrow island and nature reserve just off the coast, and is worth a visit if you have time to kill in Cilacap. ■ *Getting there: regular car and passenger ferries from Sleko pier.*

Central Java

Sleeping

A-B *Wijaya Kusuma*, Jl Jend A Yani 12A, T34871, F31150. A/c, restaurant, pool, attractive hotel in large garden compound in centre of town. **B-D** *Grand*, Jl Dr Wahidin 5-15, T21381, F22964. Some a/c, pool, great sprawling hotel with 94 rooms from cheap to expensive, check rooms as some are a mess, good pool and relatively central but could do with a management shake-up and a good clean – surface ostentation masks sloppy upkeep. **C** *Cilacap Inn*, Jl Jend Sudirman 1, T21543. Some a/c, hot water in better rooms, 1960s building washed in pink-red, rooms are fine and has a central location. **D-E** *Harnita Agung*, Jl Gatot Subroto 88, T21876. Some a/c, more of a truckers stop than a place for travellers from abroad. As buses go straight from the Sleko Pier, for most there will be no need to take advantage of this place's one plus point – its position close to the bus terminal. **D-E** *Teluk Penyu*, Jl Dr Wahidin 42-57, T21488. Some a/c, this hotel is split between 2 sides of the road and offers a range of rooms; fan rooms are clean with attached cold water mandis, the most expensive a/c rooms are large and well-decorated with hot water bathrooms and TVs (for some reason set into the wall between the beds), very good value compared with the established 'starred' hotels in town, the manager is keen and seems to be investing in improving his small hotel. **E** *Anggrek*, Jl Anggrek 16, T21835. The best of the cheaper places, rooms are clean with bright, white sheets, airy, set down quiet street not far from centre of town and the Sleko Pier. **E** *Losmen Sultana Adhi*, Jl Kol Sugiono 102, T22750. Large rooms and small mandis, walking distance from the centre of town, a little the worse for wear, quiet and reasonably friendly. **E-F** *Losmen Tiga*, Jl Mayor Sutoyo 61, good central locations, bare and basic rooms with shared bath but clean and welcoming, relaxing garden at rear.

Eating

Cheap *Perapatan*, Jl Jend A Yani (near intersection with Jl Martadinata), best Chinese food in town, moderate prices. **Bakeries** *Top Bakery*, Jl Jend A Yani (near Rita Supermarket).

Shopping

Supermarket Rita, Jl Jend A Yani (in centre of town).

Sports

Golf There is an 18-hole course north of town, said to be one of the best on Java. Ask at your hotel for further information regarding green fees.

Tour operators *MIC Holidays*, Jl DI Panjaitan 42 (at Sleko Jetty).

Transport
216 km west of Yogya, 50 km south of Purwokerto

Air Cilacap's small airport is 15 km north of town. Just 1 connection a day with Jakarta on Merpati.

Road Bus: minibuses leave for **Yogya** from the Sleko pier, and for **Wonosobo** and **Dieng** (5 hrs). The town's main bus terminal, though, is several kilometres north of the town centre at Jl Gatot Subroto 127, from where you can catch buses to major regional centres. Private a/c minibus companies also run services to Yogya and Jakarta. *Rahayu*, Jl Martadinata, operate buses to **Yogya**, and *Erny Travel*, Jl Sutoyo 54, to **Bogor** and **Jakarta**.

Sea Boat: the ferry to/from Kalipucang, **Pangandaran's** 'port', docks at Sleko Jetty on the western edge of town, at the end of Jl Jend Sudirman (where it becomes Jl DI Panjaitan). Departures at 0700, 0800, 1100 and 1300. It is possible to walk to the centre of town and hotels or losmen from here – about 15 mins, or take a bemo (see page 152 for details on the journey). The ferry leaves for Pangandaran at 0700, 0800, 1200 and 1300 and takes 4 hrs. To catch a bus onwards from Pangandaran, take a morning ferry from Cilacap, and then catch a becak and bemo to the bus station on the edge of town.

Directory Banks *Bank Central Asia*, Jl Jend A Yani 118. *Bank Danamon*, Jl Jend Sudirman. *Lippo Bank*, Jl Jend A Yani. **Communications Post Office**: Jl Jend A Yani 32.

Purwokerto

Phone code: 0281
Colour map 3, grid B3

This small city consists of little more than a central square, an impressive mosque and several long, straight streets, connecting the bus terminal at one end of the town to the railway station at the other. Nearby is **Baturden Mountain Resort**, which is at the foot of Gunung Slamet, about 10 minutes by bemo from the city (for 'Sleeping', see below). Around 20 minutes east of Purwokerto, at Kaliori, is **Goa Maria**, a recognized religious site where Catholics pay homage to a statue of Mary inside the cave. It was blessed by Pope John Paul II in 1989.

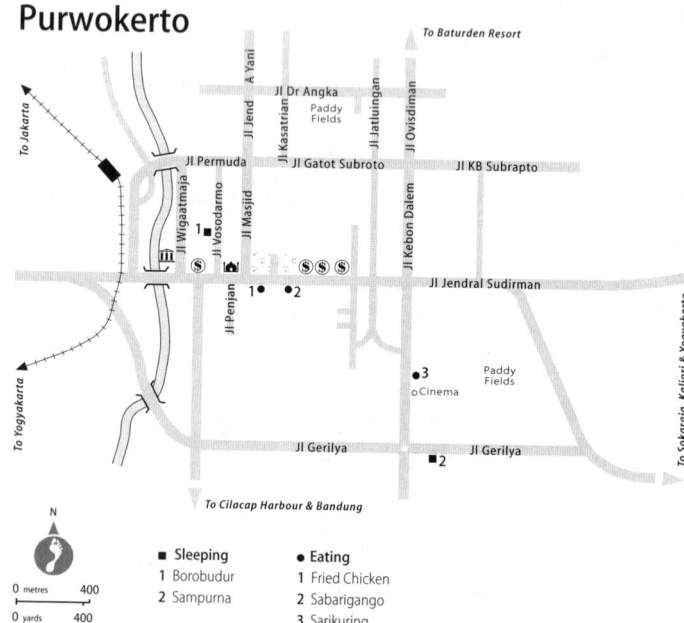

Purwokerto

■ Sleeping
1 Borobudur
2 Sampurna

● Eating
1 Fried Chicken
2 Sabarigango
3 Sarikuring

B *Borobudur*, Jl Yosodarmo 32, T35341, F31003. Massive step down in quality from *Dynasty*, quiet but quite plain rooms with western loo, TV, hot water, closer to centre of town. **Sleeping**
B *Dynasty*, Jl Dr Angka 71, T34321, F31328. New international-style hotel and seems somewhat out of place in Purwokerto, a/c, hot water, TV, coffee shop, comfortable bar with bands on some nights, restaurant with international menu, disco, karaoke, large pool, sauna and health centre, popular and often full at weekends. The following losmen are of similar (basic) standard; they are not geared-up for foreigners: **D** *Losmen Palapa*, Jl Situmpur. **D** *Losmen Pandawa*, Jl Jend Gatot Subroto 8, T41092. **D** *Losmen Remaja*, Jl Adhyaksa, T21346. **D** *Losmen Santosa*, Jl Jend Sudirman 391. Around the bus terminal and the railway station are a collection of even cheaper losmen. **D** *Losmen Sultana*, Jl Perintis Kemerdekaan 85, T41481. **D** *Losmen Widodo Asli*, Jl Kom Bb Soeprapto 33, T41634. Near to the bus terminal is **E** *Sampurna*, Jl Gerilya 47, the most pleasant hotel in this area of town.

Baturden Mountain Resort B *Hotel Rosenda*, Jl Parawisata, T32570, F32571. Swimming pool, hot water, tennis court, restaurant, bar and coffee shop. Best in town, and popular with tour groups.

Besides the usual rumah makan, there is also a fastfood fried chicken restaurant at Jl Jend Sudirman 500. **Eating**

Train It is possible to catch the train from Purwokerto to **Yoyga**, **Surabaya** or **Jakarta**. However, as most of the trains begin the trip elsewhere, it is not possible to book a seat and it is likely you will end up having to stand. Trains to each city leave 2 or 3 times daily. **Transport**

Road Bus: the bus terminal is at the far southern end of town, about 2 km from the centre. Connections with **Yogya**, **Cilacap**, **Wonosobo**, **Jakarta** and most other large centres.

Yogyakarta

Yogyakarta – usually shortened to Yogya and pronounced 'Jogja' – is probably the most popular tourist destination in Java. It is a convenient base from which to visit the greatest Buddhist monument in the world – Borobudur – and the equally impressive Hindu temples on the Prambanan Plain. The town itself also has a number of worthwhile attractions: the large walled area of the kraton, with the Sultan's palace, the ruined water gardens or 'Taman Sari', and a colourful bird market. Yogya is arguably the cultural capital of Java, and certainly its many private colleges and university attest to its being the island's educational heart, which also accounts for the younger, relatively affluent individuals you will see in the city. For the tourist, it is also one of the best centres for shopping and offers a good range of tourist services, from excellent middle range accommodation to well run tour companies.

Phone code: 0274
Colour map 3, grid B3

Yogya is situated at the foot of the volcano Mount Merapi, which rises to a height of 2,911m, to the north of the city. This peak is viewed as life-giving, and is set in opposition to the sea which is life-taking and situated to the south. The importance of orientation vis à vis Mount Merapi and the ocean is seen most clearly in the structure of the kraton, or Sultan's palace (see below).

Ins and outs

Yogyakarta may not be in the top league of Javanese towns by population, but because it is such an important destination for tourists it is well connected. Adisucipto domestic airport is 8 km east of town, and there are flights from here to destinations in Java and further afield. The train station is centrally situated on Jl Pasar Kembang, and there are regular services to Jakarta's Gambir station and east to Surabaya. (The night train is notorious for its nimble-fingered thieves). The Umbunharjo long distance bus terminal is 4 km southeast of the city centre, at the intersection of Jl Veteran and Jl Kemerdekaan. Buses of all types from *ekonomi* to

Getting there
See also 'Transport', page 182

super VIP depart for most towns in Java. Agents for tourist buses and minibuses can be found throughout the hotel and losmen areas of town and particularly on Jl Sosrowijayan.

Getting around While Yogya is not a small town by any means, exploring the city on foot, or a combination of foot and becak, is not beyond the realms of possibility. Becaks can be chartered by the hour or by the trip. It is more attractive, perhaps, but also considerably more expensive, to take an *andong* (horse-drawn carriage). Town buses (pick up a route map from the tourist office) and bemos and colts offer cheaper local transport options. Note that becak and bemo drivers have an unerring tendency to take their passengers on extended tours of shops and art galleries. Self-drive car and motorbike hire is also easy to come by in Yogya; this gives much greater flexibility when it comes to out of town excursions. Bicycles are also available, and taxis for hire by the trip or charter by the hour, half-day or day.

Tourist Information office, Jl Malioboro 14, T562811 ext 218. Free maps of the town and environs, information on cultural events, bus routes etc. One of the most helpful tourist offices in Indonesia. Open 0800-2000 Sun-Thu, 0800-1800 Fri, 0800-1900 Sat. There is also a tourist office counter at the railway station and a second at the airport.

History

The name Yogyakarta, or Yogya, is derived from the Sanskrit 'Ayodya' – the capital city of Rama in the Hindu epic, the Ramayana. The city was officially founded in 1755, although there were a succession of earlier settlements near the site, most notably the capital of the great Mataram Kingdom in the early 17th century (see page 300).

In the 1670s, the Mataram Kingdom based near Yogyakarta, under Amangkurat I, began to decline. At the same time, the Dutch East India Company (VOC) based at Batavia – present-day Jakarta – was growing in military might and commercial influence. By the mid-18th century, the VOC, whose leaders up until then had been loath to expand territorially, were forced to make their move. Worried that the power vacuum left by the crumbling Mataram Kingdom might be filled by competing colonial powers, the VOC sent a force to Mataram. In 1755, the Treaty of Giyanti partitioned the kingdom into three sultanates: the two senior houses of Pakubuwono (meaning 'Nail of the Universe') of Surakarta, and Hamengkubuwono (meaning 'He who holds the World on his Lap') of Yogyakarta, and the junior house of Mangkunegara, also of Surakarta. These three sultanates retained considerable independence, but ultimate power from that point rested with the Dutch. Pangeran Mangkubumi, the brother of Susuhunan Pakubuwono II of Surakarta became Sultan of Yogyakarta, and was known as Hamengkubuwono I. He reigned until his death in 1792 at the age of 80, during which time he had built up a powerful and prosperous state, which his son and successor Hamengkubuwono II was unable to maintain. Hamengkubuwono II was contemptuous of the Dutch, who were creating ill-feeling with their oppressive policies. Tension between the new French-backed Governor-General Daendels and the Javanese resulted in a rebellion led by Raden Ronggo. Daendels sent a force to Yogya in 1810, which succeeded in killing Ronggo and forcing the Sultan to step down in favour of his son, Hamengkubuwono III.

During the Napoleonic Wars, Daendels' successor Janssens surrendered to the British in Batavia in 1811. Taking advantage of this colonial upheaval, Hamengkubuwono II regained the throne from his son. The British Lieutenant-General in Batavia, Thomas Stamford Raffles, subsequently became aware of an alliance between the Sultan of Yogya and the Susuhunan of Solo, and mounted a force to attack the city in 1812. Hamengkubuwono II, never a great success in military matters, was again defeated and deposed. He was sent into exile on the island of Penang (Malaysia), and his pro-British son returned to the throne once more. At the same time as the Hamengkubuwono family were at war with one another, a certain Prince Notokusomo took advantage of the confusion by establishing a second

The Hamengkubuwono Sultans of Yogyakarta (1749 to the present day)

Hamengkubuwono I or Mangkubumi (1749-92)
Established the Sultanate and the City of Yogyakarta after fighting the Dutch for almost a decade. Built the Kraton and the water gardens.

Hamengkubuwono II (1792-1810, 1811-12, 1826-28)
Not a man to match his father in stature, his undiplomatic behaviour made him unpopular with the Dutch. He was deposed three times by the Dutch and English, had two queens, 31 concubines and 80 children.

Hamengkubuwono III (1810-11, 1812-14)
Popular with the colonial powers and, as a result, unpopular with the Javanese aristocracy. It was during his reign, and that of his father, that the Sultanate lost all effective power.

Hamengkubuwono IV (1814-22)
Ascended to the throne at the age of 13, and died under mysterious circumstances eight years later.

Hamengkubuwono V (1822-26, 1828-55)
Ascended to the throne at the age of three, under the tutelage of a Dutch-appointed committee. It was at this time that Prince Diponegoro (Hamenkubuwono V's uncle) stirred up rebellion and led the Java War from 1825 to 1830.

Hamengkubuwono VI

Hamengkubuwono VII

Hamengkubuwono VIII (1921-39)
His great love was wayang theatre, and his reign saw a revival of this and other Javanese arts.

Hamengkubuwono IX (1940-88)
Reigned through the difficult periods of the Japanese Occupation and then the formation of the Republic. He gave support to the fledgling independence movement, and allowed the kraton to become a focus of resistance. Died in 1989, highly respected and loved by his people.

Hamengkubuwono X (1989-)
Said to be both an astute politician and businessman.

---

kraton in the city, naming himself Pangeran Pakualam I in 1813. For the next 16 years there were four princes in the two cities of Yogya and Solo.

Daendels and Raffles were both committed to ruling Java, not just controlling the island, and they introduced numerous administrative reforms that effectively emasculated the sultans of Yogyakarta. Yet this period saw a flowering of Javanese culture, and one of the centres was the city of Yogya. As the historian John Smail writes, "a large new court literature grew up. The art of *batik* achieved its classical form and colours (indigo blue and rust brown), the repertoire of the *wayang kulit* was enlarged and its music refined and developed, and a new dance drama, *wayang orang*, grew out of the *wayang kulit* tradition". Smail goes on to note how "the Javanese language was polished into an instrument of superb social precision, so that Javanese came to speak what were almost different dialects, according to whether they were addressing social superiors, inferiors or equals". It is as if the sultans and *priyayi* or aristocracy of Yogyakarta and elsewhere, denied power, had redirected their energies into the arts and into the perfection of social custom.

The **Second World War** effectively ended the Dutch colonial period in Indonesia, and a focus of the conflict between the independence movement and the colonial authorities was Yogyakarta. Sukarno and Hatta, who had both publicly supported the Japanese, announced the independence of Indonesia on 17 August 1945 in Jakarta, just two days after the Japanese had surrendered to the Allies. The Dutch, with British support, managed to retake Jakarta, and Sukarno and Hatta were forced to flee into the Javanese interior. The kraton of Yogyakarta, the residence of the Sultan, became the centre of rebellion and the city itself the informal capital of the Republic of Indonesia. The first university of the new nation – Gajah Mada – was established within the kraton's walls.

166 YOGYAKARTA: HISTORY

Yogyakarta

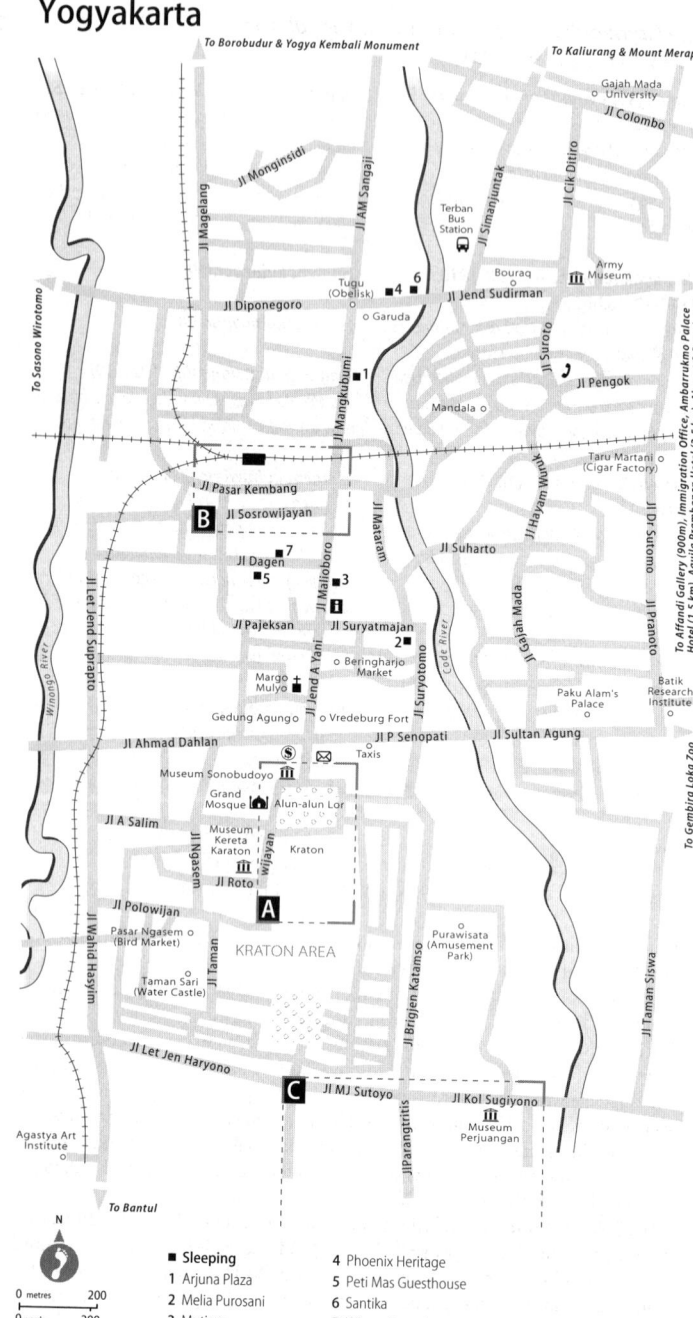

Related maps:
A Yogya Kraton, page 168
B Jalan Prawrotaman, page 176

■ Sleeping
1 Arjuna Plaza
2 Melia Purosani
3 Mutiara
4 Phoenix Heritage
5 Peti Mas Guesthouse
6 Santika
7 Wisma Persada

In December 1948, the Dutch launched their **second Police Action** and Yogya was taken without a struggle. The leaders of the independence movement made the mistake of believing that world opinion would be on their side and prevent the Dutch from taking any precipitous action. Sukarno and Hatta were captured, and dispatched into exile. The rump of the independence army managed to flee into the countryside, from where they conducted a guerrilla war against the Dutch, capturing Yogya once again in 1949. One year later, Indonesia was to become truly independent and the focus of politics moved back to Jakarta.

Sights

Yogya's main street is Jl Malioboro, which runs from north to south. At its south end, the street becomes Jl Jend A Yani and then Jl Trikora, which leads into the kraton and the grassed square known as the Alun-alun Lor. This square was the site of major events such as tiger and buffalo fights, which were staged here from 1769. A raised stand afforded the sultan and any visiting Dutch dignitaries a good view of the spectacle. The tiger was deemed to represent the foreigner and the buffalo, the Indonesian. Invariably, the buffalo would win the contest – often with some help – but the symbolism was lost on the Dutch. Nonetheless, the unperceptive Dutch still succeeded in dominating Yogya and Indonesia. There are two sacred *waringin* trees (*Ficus benjamina*) in the centre of the square. The *waringin* represents the sky and the square fence or *waringin kurung* surrounding the trees, the earth with its four quarters. At the same time, the tree is said to symbolize chaotic nature, and the fence human order.

Alun-alun Lor

At the northwest edge of the Alun-alun Lor is the **Museum Sonobudoyo**. It was established in 1935 as a centre for Javanese culture, and the collection is housed, appropriately, within a traditional Javanese building. It contains a good selection of Indonesian art, largely Javanese, including a collection of wayang puppets, but also some Balinese woodcarvings. ■ *Admission 1,000Rp. Open 0900-1300 Mon-Sat 0800-1230 Sun (see 'Entertainment', page 180)*. On the southwest side of the Alun-alun Lor is the **Grand Mosque**, built in Javanese style, with a wooden frame and a tiled roof.

The **Kraton**, or *Keraton* (see page 303), of Yogyakarta was one of three such palaces that came into existence when the kingdom of Mataram was partitioned after the Treaty of Giyanti was signed with the VOC in 1755. It has been described as a city within a city; it not only houses the Sultan's Palace, but also a maze of shops, markets and private homes supporting many thousands of people. This section only deals with the inner palace; the kraton actually extends far further, 'beginning' 1 km north at the far end of Jl Malioboro.

The Kraton of Yogyakarta
Numbers in brackets relate to key of plan on next page

The Kraton was started in 1756 by the first Sultan, Mangkubumi (who became Hamengkubuwono I in 1749), and finished almost 40 years later near the end of his reign. The teak wood used to construct the palace came from the sacred forest of Karangkasem on Mount Kidul. It is largely made up of *pendopo* or open pavilions, enclosed within interconnecting rectangular courtyards. The entire complex is surrounded by high white washed walls. John Crawfurd, who was an assistant to Raffles and later to make his mark in both Siam and Burma, wrote of the Kraton in 1811:

"The actual palace occupies the centre and is surrounded by the dwellings of the princes, and those of attendants and retainers. The principal approach is from the north, and through a square called the *Alun-alun* it is here that the prince shows himself to his subjects ..."

Facing the Alun-alun Lor is the **Pageleran** (1), a large open *pendopo*, originally employed as a waiting place for government officials. Today, this pendopo is used for traditional dance and theatrical performances. There are a number of further pendopo surrounding this one, containing mediocre displays of regal clothing. The very first classes of the newly-created Gajah Mada University were held under these shaded pavilions. To the south of the Pageleran, up some steps, is the **Siti Inggil** (**2**), meaning 'high ground'. This is the spot where new sultans are crowned. Behind the Siti Inggil is the **Bronjonolo Gate** (**3**), which is kept closed. ■ *Admission to this area of the Kraton is free. Open 0800-1300 Mon-Sun, 0800-1100 Fri.*

The entrance to the main body of the Palace is further south, down Jl Rotowijayan – on the west side of the Pageleran complex. The first courtyard is the shaded **Kemangdungan** or **Keben** (**4**), with two small pendopo, where the *abdi dalem* or palace servants gather. The 'black' sand that covers most of the ground around the pendopo and other buildings in the kraton is from the beaches of the south coast. In this way, it is ensured that the Queen of the South Seas, Nyi Loro Kidul (see page 124), with whom the Sultan is believed to have intimate relations, is present throughout the palace.

The **Srimanganti** (meaning 'to wait for the king') **Gate** (**5**) leads into a second, rather more impressive, courtyard with two pendopos facing each other; the **Srimanganti** (**6**) to the right and the **Trajumas** (**7**) to the left. The former was used to receive important guests, while the latter probably served as a court of law. The Srimanganti now contains gongs and other instruments that make up a *gamelan* orchestra. The Trajumas houses palanquins, litters and chairs, as well as a cage in which the Sultan's children played. It is said that the children were placed in here, aged eight months, and given a selection of objects – pens, money, books – to play with; whichever took their interest indicated their future careers.

The **Donapratopo Gate** (**8**), flanked by two *gupala* or *raksasa* statues to protect the palace from evil, leads into the heart of the palace where the Sultan and his family had their private quarters. Notice the way that gateways never give direct access to courtyards; they were designed in this way to confuse spirits attempting to make their way into the complex.

Yogya Kraton

1 Pageleran
2 Siti Inggil
3 Bronjonolo Gate
4 Kemangdungan
5 Srimangati Gate
6 Srimangati Pendopo
7 Trajumas Pendopo
8 Donapratopo Gate
9 Purwaretna building
10 Gedung Kuning
11 Bangsal Kencono (Golden Pavilion)
12 Bangsal Proboyekso & Gedung Keputrian
13 Bangsal Manis
14 Kesatrian

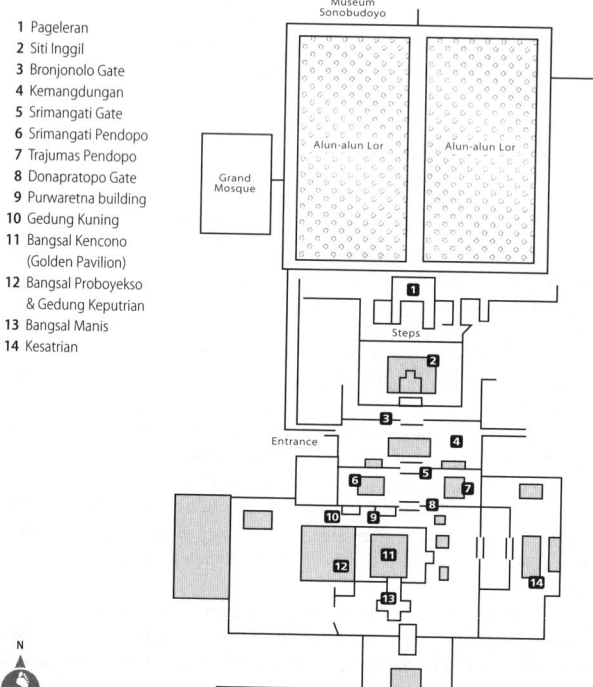

Inside this gate, immediately on the right, is the Sultan's office, the **Purwaretna** (9). Beyond it is the **Gedung Kuning** (10), an impressive yellow building which continues to be the Sultan's private residence. Both are roped-off from the public.

The central and most impressive pavilion in the complex is the **Bangsal Kencono** (11) or Golden Pavilion. The four teak pillars in the centre represent the four elements. On each is symbolized the three religions of Java: Hinduism (a red motif on the top of the columns), Buddhism (a golden design based on the lotus leaf) and Islam (black and gold letters of the Koran). Unfortunately, because the pavilion is roped-off, it is difficult to see the pillars clearly. Behind the Golden Pavilion to the west is the **Bangsal Proboyekso** (12) (which contains the armoury) and the **Gedung Keputrian** (12), the residence of the Sultan's wives and children, both closed to the public. Immediately to the south of the Golden Pavilion is the **Bangsal Manis** (13), the dining room. **Kemakanan**, a pendopo to the south reached through a set of gates, is used for wayang performances at the end of Ramadan. To the east, through another gate (to the side of which is a large drum made from the wood of the jackfruit tree) there is another courtyard, the **Kesatrian** (14). The Sultan's sons lived here. In the central pendopo of this courtyard there is another gamelan orchestra on display. Performances are held every Monday and Wednesday, 1030-1200 (the performance is included in the price of the entrance). At the east side of this courtyard is a collection of paintings, the best being by Raden Saleh, a 19th-century court painter who gained a reputation of sorts (and whose grave can be found in Bogor). The photographs of the sultans and their wives are more interesting. North of the Kesatrian is the **Gedung Kopo**, originally the hospital and now a museum housing gifts to the sultans. There are also a pair of rooms given over to memorabilia of Hamengkubuwono IX, who died in 1988. ■ *Admission to complex 3,000Rp, camera is 500Rp extra. Open 0900-1400 Sat-Thu, 0900-1300 Sun. NB the palace can be partially closed on official ceremonial days.*

Close to the Palace, on Jl Rotowijayan, is the **Museum Kereta Karaton**, which houses the royal carriages. ■ *Admission 500Rp. Open 0900-1600 Tue-Sun.*

From the Palace it is a 5-10 minute walk to the Taman Sari. Walk south along Jl Rotowijayan and turn left at the Dewi Srikandi Art Gallery. A number of batik painting galleries are down this road, which leads into Jl Ngasem and then onto the **Pasar Ngasem** or bird market, an interesting place to wander. Song birds, and particularly turtle doves (Genus *Streptopelia*), are highly-prized by the Javanese. It is sometimes said that wives take second place to a man's song bird and that they can cost as much as US$15,000, although this seems hard to believe. Popular are the spotted-necked dove (*Streptopelia chinensis*), the Javan turtle dove (*Streptopelia bitorquata*) and the zebra dove (*Geopelia striata*). Hand-made, split bamboo bird-cages are a good buy.

By picking your way through the Pasar Ngasem it is possible to reach the **Taman Sari**, which was known to the Dutch as the waterkasteel or 'Water Castle', as it is still called. This is a maze of underground passageways, ruins and pools, built as a pleasure garden by the first Sultan, Mangkubumi, in 1765, at the same time as the Kraton. The *Babad Mangkubumi* gives a slightly later date – 1683 according to the Javanese calendar or AD 1757-58. Surrounded by high walls, it was the sultan's hideaway. He constructed three bathing pools – for his children, his *putri* (girls) and himself. A tower allowed the Sultan to watch his 'girls' bathing and to summon them to his company. In addition, there were a series of underwater corridors and even a partly underwater mosque. It is these labyrinths which have led some historians to speculate that it was also built as a retreat in times of war. By climbing the stairs over the entrance gate it is possible to look over the surrounding kampung: this was originally an artificial lake, with a large colonnaded pavilion in the middle. Unfortunately, the gardens were damaged during the British attack on Yogya in 1812 and restoration programmes have been rather unsympathetic. It is difficult to imagine the gardens as they were – as a place of contemplation. Most visitors enter the water gardens from Jl Taman, through the east gate, which leads into the bathing pool area

Diponegoro: Prince and early freedom fighter

Prince Diponegoro (1785-1855) was the son of Sultan Hamengkubuwono III. He was both a learned and a devout man, dedicating much of his life to the study of the Islamic scriptures and to prayer. But he was also a man with a mission. He fervently hoped to return Java to its religious roots – by which he meant Islam, not Hinduism or Buddhism – and to cast off the infidel European yoke. Yet, even though he was a devout Muslim, he also believed in the power of the Southern Ocean Goddess, Nyi Loro Kidul (see page 124), and he visited the ancient sites of the Mataram Kingdom, hoping that their past power might somehow invigorate him. Prince Diponegoro still remains a symbol of the nationalist movement in Indonesia, and virtually every town in the country has a road named after him.

In 1825, Prince Diponegoro led a rebellion against the colonial powers based in Batavia (Jakarta). This heralded five years of war – the Java Wars – during which time half the population of Yogya either fled the sultanate, were killed, or died of starvation. With the defeat of Diponegoro and his supporters in 1830, the Dutch were in a position to exercise yet firmer control. From that moment on, the Javanese courts never regained their authority in the country and became merely centres of the arts and of etiquette. Power in Yogya was from then on in the hands of the Dutch resident.

or Umbul Binangun. This small section is the most complete area of the gardens, having been reconstructed in 1971. The gardens fell into disrepair following the death of Hamengkubuwono III, a process which was accelerated by a devastating earthquake in 1865. Much of the garden has no water in it now, which is disappointing. ■ *Admission 1,000Rp. Open 0900-1500 daily.*

To the southeast of the Kraton and Taman Sari on Jl Kol Sugiyono is the small **Museum Perjuangan**, or the Struggle for Independence Museum. As the name suggests, this commemorates Indonesia's Declaration of Independence on 17 August 1945 and has a less than inspiring collection of historical artefacts relating to the episode. ■ *Admission 1,000Rp. Open daily 0900-1330 except Mon.*

Vredeburg Fort & around The Vredeburg Fort lies to the north of the Kraton on the east side of Jl Jend A Yani, near the intersection with Jl P Senopati. It was built in 1765 by the Dutch as a military barracks. Restored in the late 1980s, the fort has lost what character it may have had, and today looks rather like an American shopping arcade (piped music adds to the effect). Now a museum, the fortress houses a series of dioramas depicting the history of Yogyakarta. ■ *Admission 1,000Rp. Open 0900-1300 Tue-Thu, 0900-1100 Fri, 0830-1400 Sat and Sun.* Close by is the **March 1st Monument**, which commemorates the taking of Yogya from the Dutch in 1949 by a band of guerrillas led by (then) Colonel Suharto. The **Beringharjo Market** is set back from Jl Jend A Yani on the same side of the street and just north of the Vredeburg Fort. A dimly-lit mixed market, it is an interesting and colourful place to wander with fruit, vegetables, fish and meat, batik and household goods – all jumbled together and seemingly fighting for air. Locals warn that numerous pickpockets operate here. On the other side of Jl Jend A Yani is **Margo Mulyo Church**, which dates from 1830.

Across the road from the fort is the **Gedung Agung**, built initially in 1823 and then rebuilt in 1869 after the devastating earthquake of 1865. It was the former home of the Dutch Resident in Yogya and is now a state guesthouse. Queen Elizabeth II of Great Britain, former Prime Minister Nehru of India and Queen Sirikit of Thailand have all stayed here. Between 1946 and 1949, President Sukarno lived in the Gedung Agung, while Yogya was the capital of an emerging independent Indonesia. South of the fort, on Jl P Senopati, are three impressive **colonial buildings**, the General Post Office (1910), Bank Indonesia and the Bank Negara Indonesia (1923).

Jl Malioboro & Mangkubumi North from the Vredeburg Fort, Jl Jend A Yani becomes Jl Malioboro; this is the tourist heart of Yogya, with shops, restaurants and a smattering of hotels. The town has the largest student population in Indonesia, and in the evenings they congregate along Jl Malioboro – no doubt for intellectual discussions, as well as eating and music – and stay there till 4 or 5 o'clock in the morning; this has become known as the 'Malioboro culture'. At its north extension, Jl Malioboro becomes Jl Mangkubumi.

To the west of Jl Mangkubumi in Tegalrejo is **Sasono Wirotomo**, or the **Diponegoro Museum**, a house built on the site of Prince Diponegoro's residence, which was levelled by the Dutch in 1825. The museum contains the prince's memorabilia, including a collection of weapons. ■ *Open 0800-1600 Mon-Sun.* At the end of Jl Malioboro is an **obelisk** or *tugu* which marks the north limit of the kraton. The original tugu was erected in 1755, but collapsed; the present structure dates from 1889. Aart van Beek, in his book *Life in the Javanese Kraton*, explains that this was "the focal point for the Sultan who would sit at an elevated place near the entrance of the palace and meditate by aligning his eyes with the *tugu* and the 3,000m high Merapi volcano behind, in the distance".

East of the centre

To the east of the town centre, on Jl Sultan Agung, is **Paku Alam's Palace**. A small part of the palace in the East Wing is a museum. ■ *Open 0900-1230 Tue-Sun.* Further east still, on Jl Kusumanegara, is the **Gembira Loka Zoo and Amusement Park**. It contains a reasonable range of Indonesian animals, including the Komodo dragon, orang utan, tiger and rhinoceros. ■ *Admission 3,000Rp. Open 0700-1800 Mon-Sun.*

Kota Gede, also known as Sar Gede, lies 5 km to the southeast of Yogya and was the capital of the 16th-century Mataram Kingdom. Nothing remains except for the **tombs** of the rulers of Mataram; in particular, Panembahan Senopati, the founder of the kingdom and his son Krapyak (the father of the famous Sultan Agung). Senopati's son-in-law, Ki Ageng Mangir, is also buried here, his tomb protruding into common ground as he was Senopati's foe. About 100m from the cemetery is the Watu Gilang, a stone on which Senopati killed Ki Ageng Mangir by smashing his head against it. Walled gardens and ponds with fish and a yellow turtle, with claimed magical powers ('several hundred years old'), add to the atmosphere. Like the tombs of Imogiri (see 'Excursions', below), visitors must wear traditional Javanese dress which can be hired at the entrance (500Rp). Kota Gede is better known for its **silver workshops** which date back to the 17th-century rule of Sultan Agung. Both traditional silver and black (oxydized) silverwork can be purchased. ■ *Admission by voluntary contribution. Open 1300-1600 Fri for the actual cemetery, but the other areas are open daily. Get to the tombs and workshops by taxi or by town bus (bis kota) No 4 or 8 from Jl Jend Sudirman, No 11 from Umbunharjo terminal and No 14 from Jl Prawirotaman.*

Taru Martani is a cigar factory on Jl Kompil B Suprapto, on the east side of town, which visitors can visit to watch the process of cigar manufacture. ■ *Open 0730-1500 Mon-Fri. There are English, Dutch and German speaking guides.*

Education capital

The **ISI (Indonesian Art Institute)** is based in Yagyakarta, with faculties of Fine Art, Dance and Music, which partly explains why so much vibrant art can be found around town. (The town is the best place to see wayang performances and traditional dance – see page 179.) In recent years it has become a popular town for Indonesian artists to base themselves. On the northern edge of the city is Indonesia's oldest, and one of its most prestigious, universities: **Gadjah Mada University** or UGM. It was 'founded' in December 1949, when Sultan Hamengkubuwono IX allowed students and their teachers to use the Siti Inggil within the precincts of the Kraton.

Excursions

Hindu and Buddhist monuments, including the largest Buddhist monument in the world, Borobudur (see page 185), the magnificent Hindu temples at Prambanan (see page 194) and the small Hindu temples on the Dieng Plateau (see page 214), can also all be visited on day trips from Yogya.

Mount Merapi Mount Merapi lies 30 km north of Yogya and on its slopes is the hill resort of **Kaliurang**. Both are accessible on a day excursion, although staying overnight is recommended (see page 184). ■ *Getting there: see the transport details in the Mount Merapi and Kaliurang entry.*

Tombs of the Mataram sultans **Imogiri**, 17 km to the south of Yogya, is the site of the tombs of the Mataram sultans, as well as the rulers of the Surakarta Kingdom. Perhaps the greatest Mataram king, Sultan Agung (reigned 1613-46), is buried here. He built the cemetery in 1645, preparing a suitably magnificent site for his grave, on a hillside to the south of his court at Kartasura. It is said that he chose this site so that he had a view of the Queen of the South (the sea goddess Nyi Loro Kidul). To reach his tomb (directly in front at the top of the stairway), and those of 23 other royal personages (Surakarta susuhunans to the left, Yogya sultans to the right), the visitor must stagger up 345 steps. Walk behind the tombs to the top of the hill for fine views of the surrounding countryside. Javanese dress, which can be hired at the site, is required to enter the mausoleums. The Yogyakartan equivalent of Chelsea Pensioners, with turbans and krisses, make sure correct behaviour is observed at all times. A **traditional ceremony** to thank God for water involving the filling of four bronze water containers – known as *enceh* – is held in the Javanese month of Suro; the first month of the year (June). The containers are placed at the gates of the cemetery and are an expression of gratitude to God for the provision of water. ■ *Admission by donation. Open: Agung's tomb is only open 1000-1300 Mon, 1330-1630 Fri and 1000-1330 Sun, although it is possible to climb up to the site at any time. Get there by bus or colt (buses continue on to Parangtritis from here – see below) (350Rp); it is a 1 km walk east to the foot of the stairs from Imogiri town (ask for the makam or cemetery). The bus journey is lovely, along a peaceful country road past paddy fields.*

Parangtritis Parangtritis is a small seaside resort 28 km south of Yogya (see page 183). It is accessible on a day excursion, although there are a number of places to stay. ■ *Getting there: regular connections with Yogya's Umbunharjo bus terminal, either via Kretek*

Yogya surroundings

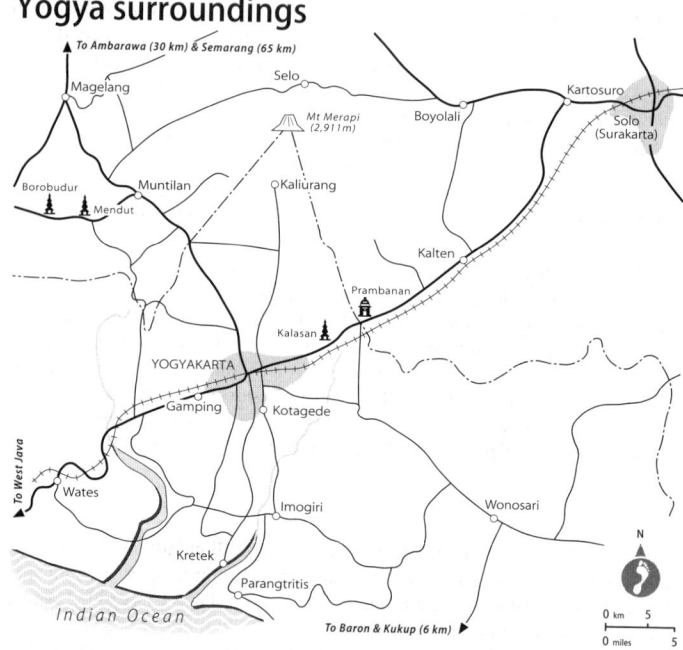

Courtship Javanese-style – the Lamaran

Many elements of traditional Javanese life are disappearing in the wake of western-style commercialization. **Lamaran** – the formal request by the parents of the groom to the bride's parents – is one such traditional ceremony. Like the Javanese language, it is laden with hidden meanings and metaphors.

Initially, the groom's family visits the bride's to broach the subject of marriage. But this must be done according to elaborate rules, and there should be no direct reference to the purpose of the visit. The father of the prospective groom might explain, opaquely, that "frost in the morning means rain in the evening", implying that he has come to discuss a 'cool' matter, which should not stir up strong emotions. The bride's father might reply by exclaiming that his daughter is a 'good for nothing', a spoilt girl and not yet an adult.

Two or three visits later, the matter is finally settled and a meeting is arranged at the prospective bride's house. This occasion is known as the nontoni (the 'looking over'). Again governed by tradition and formality, the girl serves her husband-to-be a cup of tea, avoiding any eye-contact. In the past, this would have been the young man's – or probably a boy's – first opportunity of stealing a sideways glance at his bride. The marriage itself is called the panggihan and is held at the bride's home.

---

along the main road and over the Opak River, or via Imogiri and Celuk (see above). The longer, rougher, trip via Imogiri passes through beautiful rural scenery.

Jatijajar Caves Jatijajar Caves are to be found in the side of a strange ridge of jagged hills, southwest of the small town of Gombong and 157 km west from Yogya. Outside the entrance is a large concrete dinosaur which acts as a spout for the underground spring (bathing pools here). Inside, there are stalactites and stalagmites, springs and theatrical statues of human beings and animals which apparently recount the history of the kingdom of Pahaharan. ■ *Admission 450Rp. Getting there: 7 km west of Gombong, turn left; the caves are 13 km off the main road. There are minibuses from Kebumen (50 km) and from Gombong. Gombong is accessible from Yogya, Cilacap and Semarang, among other towns.*

Karang Bolong Beach, near to the Jatijajar Caves, is known as a site for collecting bird's nests for the soup of the same name.

Tours For visitors without their own transport, one way to see the sights around Yogya is to join a tour. Although it is comparatively easy to get around by public transport, it can mean waiting around for the appropriate bus or bemo. Yogya has more than its fair share of companies offering tours to the sights in and around the city, mainly centred on Jl Prawirotaman. Listed below are a selection on offer; visit the tourist office for the latest information.

City tours to the Kraton, Taman Sari, batik factories, wayang performances and Kota Gede silver workshops. **Out of town tours** to Prambanan (25,000Rp), Borobudur (25,000Rp), the Dieng Plateau (50,000Rp), Kaliurang, Parangtritis, Solo and Candi Sukuh, Gedung Songo, Mount Bromo and Mount Merapi. The least expensive companies charge around 30,000Rp per day, depending on the distance to be driven, but make sure that you get a seat to yourself rather than being forced to share it. Taxis can also be commissioned for those who want to run their own schedule. Prices starting at 100,000Rp for a full day. Check various companies to select the vehicle and time of departure to suit your budget and needs (tours on non-a/c buses are considerably cheaper, for example). For more unusual tours, eg cycle tours, hidden temples, and tours with a strong bias on local culture, try the *Via Via Café* on Jl Prawirotaman, T386557, which is highly recommended. Generally watch out for hidden entrance charges either for yourself or, if you are hiring a car, for the parking of it.

Essentials

Sleeping
■ on maps page 166 & below

Yogya's different categories of accommodation tend to be grouped in particular areas of town. Most of the more expensive (our categories **L-A**), international-style hotels are to be found either on Jl Malioboro, in the centre of town, or on the road east to the airport (Jl Jend Sudirman). The former are in a convenient position if visitors wish to explore the city on foot from their hotels. Many of the middle-priced guesthouses (our categories **B-D**) are concentrated on Jl Prawirotaman, to the south of the Kraton, about 2 km from the city centre (a becak ride away). These are smallish private villas converted into hotels, some with just a handful of rooms. A number also have small swimming pools. On Jl Prawirotaman, a gaggle of restaurants, shops and tour companies have grown up to service the needs of those staying here. Finally, there is the budget accommodation (our categories **D-F**), which is concentrated on and around Jl Pasar Kembang and Jl Sosrowijayan, close to the train station. Again, there is a concentration of tour companies, travel agents, restaurants, car and motorcycle hire outfits, bus booking companies, and currency exchange offices here. Note, of course, that there are also hotels and losmen outside the above areas.

Jl Malioboro, off Jl Malioboro and Jl Mangkubumi **AL** *Melia Purosani Yogyakarta*, Jl Suryotomo 31, T589521, F588073, meliapur@idola.net.id, www.solmelia.com A/c, restaurant, pool, opened in 1994. 300 rooms in grand marble-filled hotel, facilities include huge pool, gym, extensive garden, shopping arcade, satellite TV, with a great central location – unlike many others in this price category. **A-B** *Natour Garuda*, Jl Malioboro 60, T566322, F563074, nahoga@yogya.wasantara.net.id A/c, restaurant, pool, large hotel block, with new addition that rather swamps the original hotel, but good facilities, international standard rooms and a central location. **B** *Arjuna Plaza*, Jl P Mangkubumi 44, T561862. A/c, comfortable rooms with dark teak panelling, pool and children's pool. Good value but far from the main sights. **B** *Mutiara* (new wing), Jl Malioboro 18, T563814, F561201. A/c, overpriced restaurant, pool, rooms and food rather expensive, but central position with good nightclub in the basement.

Jl Sosrowijayan and Jl Pasar Kembang **B** *Hotel Istana Batik*, Jl Pasar Kembang 29, T589853. A/c, small pool, price includes breakfast, attached mandi, attractive courtyard, elaborate in decoration, reasonable mid-range value. **B** *Mendut*, Jl Pasar Kembang 49,

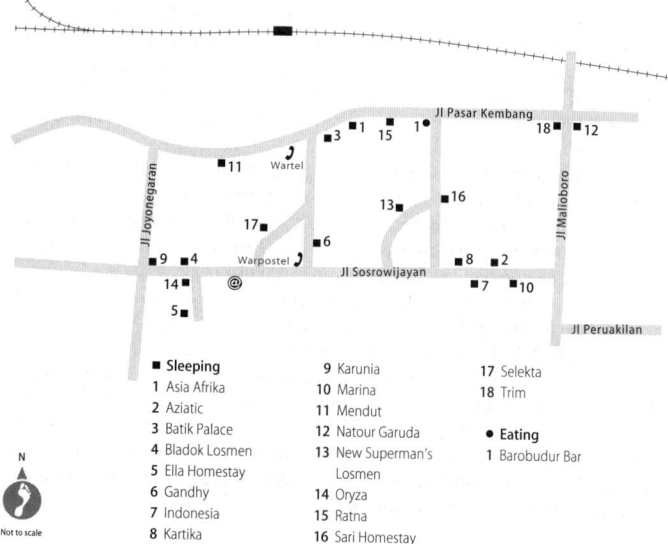

Jalan Sosrowijayan area

■ Sleeping
1 Asia Afrika
2 Aziatic
3 Batik Palace
4 Bladok Losmen
5 Ella Homestay
6 Gandhy
7 Indonesia
8 Kartika
9 Karunia
10 Marina
11 Mendut
12 Natour Garuda
13 New Superman's Losmen
14 Oryza
15 Ratna
16 Sari Homestay
17 Selekta
18 Trim

● Eating
1 Barobudur Bar

Not to scale

T563435, F564753, mendutia@yogya.wasantara.net.id A/c, restaurant, pool, hotel is squeezed on to a small area, rooms are good for the price, if very pedestrian in terms of style, central position. **B-C** *Peti Mas*, Jl Dagen 39, T561938, F580188. Some a/c, restaurant (slow service), nice pool, central cramped rooms and rather over-priced, but breakfast and afternoon cakes are included.

C *Hotel Asia Afrika*, Jl Pasar Kembang 21, T514489, F560139. Some a/c, cold water in standard rooms, restaurant, pool, small rooms set around an attractive peaceful courtyard, price includes breakfast, set back from road so not too noisy, popular with tour groups. **C** *Hotel Trim*, Jl Pasar Kembang 2, T514113, F560045. Some a/c, cool marble tiled rooms with clean showers and hot water, a good mid-range place to stay. **C-D** *Bladok Losmen*, Jl Sosrowijayan 76, T/F523832. About 30 very clean rooms, some a/c, some hot water showers, pool, good restaurant, enthusiastic and friendly staff, a well kept place in a central location, breakfast included. Recommended. **D** *Marina Hotel*, Jl Sosrowijayan 3, T514087. Formally named the *Marina Palace Hotel*, rooms are small and bright, good central location. **D** *Oryza*, Jl Sosrowijayan 49, dark rooms with fan, very clean and comfortable. Quiet considering its central location, includes breakfast. **D** *Sari Homestay*, Jl Sosrowijayan Gang I, bright but basic rooms built around a pretty courtyard, all rooms are with mandi, informative, friendly management. **D** *Hotel Selekta*, Jl Sosrowijayan, small alley off Gang II, popular and friendly with rooms that are surprisingly spacious and light, breakfast included. **D-E** *New Superman's Losmen*, Jl Sosrowijayan, despite its name, rooms are not that super. They are, however, large with interesting rock mandi's and an excellent breakfast included in the price.

E *Gandhy*, Jl Sosrowijayan Wetan Gang II/75, although they, incredibly, market themselves as "we're not the best, we're better" (who are they kidding?). This is, in fact, better than most with slightly lighter and cleaner rooms, geared for travellers. **E** *Kartika*, Jl Sosrowijayan 10, T562016. Get what you pay for, rather shabby rooms but basic and cheap. **E** *Karunia*, Jl Sosrowijayan 78, T/F565057. Some a/c, clean and well managed small hotel with good information, attractive roof terrace and small restaurant. **E** *Monica*, Jl Sosrowijayan, T580598, small, very clean hotel, with friendly and helpful staff. Quiet place, some rooms with balcony, price includes breakfast.

E-F *Ella Homestay*, Jl Sosrodipuran Gang I/487 (signposted off Jl Sosrowijayan), good food, quiet location away from the mass of losmen, rooms are a cut above the average, clean, good source of information and ISIC cards offer a reduction. Recommended. **E-F** *Indonesia*, Jl Sosrowijayan 9, T587659. Average rooms, some with attached mandi, mosquito net is essential. **F** *Aziatic*, Jl Sosrowijayan 6, price includes breakfast, all rooms off a central hallway but no fans, so tend to be hot as well as rather noisy; however, the management are very friendly, it is immaculate, secure and good value, tours arranged. Recommended.

Jl Prawirotaman A good selection of middle range accommodation is to be found on Jl Prawirotaman, south of the Kraton. The hotels are the best of their kind in Yogya. The area's single obvious disadvantage is that it is not very central, but the street provides numerous restaurants, shops, travel agents and cultural shows. *See map next page*

B-C *Airlangga*, Jl Prawirotaman 6-8, T378044, F371427. A/c, restaurant, pool, hot water within certain hours, the largest hotel on Jl Prawirotaman, professional management, live music in the evenings, some rooms rather dark with narrow beds, the atmosphere is more that of a hotel than guesthouse, price includes breakfast, good value. **B-C** *Metro*, Jl Prawirotaman 71, T/F37200. Large homestay with clean pool, rooms are bright, clean and attractive, safety deposit boxes and daily tours are available, good English-speaking management.

C *Kirana*, Jl Prawirotaman 30/38, T376600, F372262. Characterful old house with wildlife-packed central courtyard. A/c, hot water, elegantly furnished, rooms are clean and large. Some rooms set around the courtyard can be dull; choose those close to the pool, breakfast included. **C** *Rose*, Jl Prawirotaman 22, T577991. A/c, big pool (for the area), hot water, set around a large but rather jaded courtyard, good service and remains exceptionally popular, free pick-up from airport, tours arranged, friendly management, price includes breakfast. **C** *Sumaryo*, Jl Prawirotaman 22, T377522, F373507. Pool, price includes breakfast and afternoon tea, large rooms in spacious 1950s house with a fair amount of 1950s furniture, clean and friendly, a peaceful and quiet place to stay, attached mandi, there is also a cheaper annex – guests staying here have access to the pool too. Recommended. **C** *Hotel Bougainville*, Jl Parangtritis 67, T370279, F377431. Slow service but with a smile, rooms at the front are noisy but clean, hot water, TV, well priced. **C** *Wisma Gajah Guesthouse*, Jl Prawirotaman 4, T375659, F372037. Some a/c, small but attractive rooms, dated but spacious rooms, popular with tour groups. **C-D** *Wisma Gajah Guesthouse Annexe*, Jl Prawirotaman 111/595, T370846, F372037. A delightful back-end add-on to the *Wisma Gajah Guesthouse*, built in the fashion of a Chinese court, with reception in the left wing, a lovely little restaurant (with just 6 tables) in the middle and a row of only 5 rooms in the right wing. Fan and hot water. Recommended. **C** *Gallunggung*, Jl Prawirotaman 11, T380694. A/c, hot water, pool. Despite first appearances the rooms here are large and clean. Lovely shared balcony, overlooking the pool that catches the setting sun. **B-C** *Duta*, Jl Prawirotaman 20/26, T/F372064. Some a/c, small pool with waterfall flowing into it, homely atmosphere, friendly girls on front desk, pleasant garden and sitting area, the indoor garden is Japanese in flavour and is filled with songbirds, price includes a good breakfast. Having said all this, the owners have signed a contract with a tour company which has rather changed the atmosphere, but still recommended. **B-C** *Prambanan*, Jl Prawirotaman 14, T376167. Some a/c, small pool, some rooms with hot showers, good rooms, enthusiastic staff and attractive surroundings, the fan rooms are particularly good value for money, price includes a good American breakfast and tea and coffee available through the day. Recommended. **C** *Sriwijay*, Jl Prawirotaman 7, T571870. Non a/c, breakfast included, old house with attractive, small swimming pool, set around courtyard, fairly clean and ordered, rather curt staff, cold water showers and western toilets.

Jalan Prawirotaman

- **Sleeping**
1 Agung
2 Airlangga
3 Bougainville
4 Cepuri
5 Duta
6 Gallunggung
7 Hanoman's
8 Indra Prastha Homestay
9 Kirana
10 Mas Gun Guesthouse
11 Metro
12 Perwita Sari
13 Prambanan
14 Prayogo
15 Puspita
16 Rose
17 Sastika
18 Sriwijay
19 Sumaryu
20 Via Via
21 Wisma Borobudur
22 Wisma Gajah
23 Wisma Indah

- **Eating**
1 Baleanda & Gallery
2 Going Bananas
3 Hanoman
4 Proteck 8 Internet Café
5 Tante L'es

D *Wisma Borobudur*, Jl Prawirotaman 5, T576891, F573507. In an old house set around a central courtyard, small, friendly hostel, clean and well maintained, no a/c but with mandi, breakfast included, Beethoven busts for sale at reception. **D** *Perwita Sari*, Jl Prawirotaman 31, T577592. Some a/c, good pool. **E** *Mas Gun Guesthouse*, Jl Prawirotaman II, T379804. Excellent airy budget rooms, all with fans, good value. **D-E** *Wisma Indah*, Jl Prawirotaman 4. Clean, friendly family, breakfast at any time to fit in with departures and arrivals from excursions.

C *Hotel Cepuri*, Jl Prawirotaman II 597A, T378092, F372064. Fan rooms set around the swimming pool, shared or private bathrooms and western toilets, price includes breakfast. **D-E** *Indra Prastha Homestay*, Jl Prawirotaman, T374087. Non a/c, behind main street, a small quiet guesthouse set around a green brick road. Young, enthusiastic staff, rooms are simple but spotless with cold shower, showers en suite, peaceful garden, very good value in a medium priced area.

E *Agung*, Jl Parangtritis 42/30, T375512. Some a/c and hot water, shabby rooms but with restaurant, and one of the few places at this price with a pool. **D-E** *Puspita Guesthouse*, Jl Mayjend Sutoyo 64, T571065. Price includes good breakfast, helpful staff, good value for those on a budget.

Jl Jend Sudirman and Jl Adisucipto **L** *Sheriton Mustila*, Jl Laksda Adisucipto, Km 8.7, T511588, F511589, hsmyogya@indosat.net.id Beautiful and ornate, all modern amenities in this new hotel, 3 restaurants, pool and children's facilities. Excellent value if it is within your price range. **L** *Hotel Sahid Yogya*, Jl Babarsari, off Jl Adisucipto, T564596, F563183, sahidyg@idola.net.id www.sahid.com All the usual amenities featured in an international hotel. The rooms are on the small side for this category, but otherwise a comfortable place to stay. **AL** *Ambarrukmo Palace*, Jl Adisucipto, T566488, F563283. A/c, several restaurants, large pool, large, ugly block, one of the first international hotels to be built in Yogya in the 1960s and it shows, despite some attempt at modernization, inconvenient location out of town on the road to Borobudur. **AL** *Phoenix Heritage*, Jl Jend Sudirman 9-11, T566845, F566856. A/c, restaurant, pool, central hotel, with friendly efficient staff. **AL** *Santika*, Jl Jend Sudirman 19, T563036, F563669, stkyk@wasantara.net.id A/c, restaurant, good pool, plush with reasonable rates, business centre. **AL-A** *Yogya Palace*, Jl Adisucipto, Km 8, T566244, F566415. A/c, restaurant, pool, large hotel some way out of town on road to Surakarta, free shuttle service into town, but still rather inconvenient. For quality of the rooms, the rates are good if you can bear travelling for 20 mins to get just about anywhere. **A** *Aquila Prambanan*, Jl Adisucipto 48, T565005, F565009. A/c, restaurant, pool, new hotel rather sacrilegiously modelled on Prambanan itself, with inconvenient location near the airport (beyond the *Ambarrukmo Palace*), 200 rooms and atmosphere to match.

B *Hotel Batik Yogyakarta*, Jl P Mangkubumi 46, T562510. A/c, restaurant, small pool, simple comfort and simple rooms, peaceful atmosphere. **B** *Hotel Yogya Plassa*, Jl Tribrata 1, T580833, F520529. A/c, restaurant, loud disco and karaoke, but well priced for the standard, airport pick up.

Eating

Central Javanese cooking uses a lot of sugar, tapped from the *aren* palm which produces 'red' sugar. Typical dishes include *tape* (a sweet dish made from fermented cassava) and *ketan* (sticky rice). Yogya specialities include *ayam goreng* (fried chicken) and *gudeg* (rice, jackfruit, chicken and an egg cooked in a spicy coconut sauce).

Indonesian Cheap and very cheap: *Griya Bujana*, Jl Prawirotaman, range of Indonesian, Chinese and international food, overpriced but remains popular. *Palma*, Jl Prawirotaman, excellent food and service, reasonably priced. Recommended. *Hanoman's Forest Garden Restaurant*, Jl Tirtodipura, recently moved from Jl Prawirotaman, excellent local dishes, quiet and relaxed. *Tante Lies*, corner of Jl Prawirotaman and Jl Parangtritis, cheap Indonesian food and popular meeting place for travellers (mostly Dutch), cheap tours organized from here; however, its reputation belies the quality and range of food. *Bu Citro*, Jl Adisucipto Km 9, opposite the entrance to the airport, serves an excellent *gudeg*, the Yogya speciality.

Bird's nest soup

Indonesia produces around 60% of the world's production of edible bird's nests, and most of this comes from Java. One of the historical centres of production is the caves around Kabumen on Java's south coast, which have been harvested since the 18th century.

The tiny nests of the edible nest swiftlet are collected for bird's nest soup, a Chinese delicacy, across Southeast Asia. The semi-oval nests are made of silk-like strands of saliva secreted by the birds which, when cooked in broth, softens and becomes a little like noodles. Like so many Chinese delicacies, the nests are believed to have aphrodisiac qualities, and the soup has even been suggested as a cure for AIDS. The Vietnamese emperor Minh Mang (1820-40) is said to have owed his extraordinary vitality to his ordinate consumption.

The red nests are the most highly valued by the Chinese community – usually the nests of the edible nest swiftlet are white. Popularly, this colour is said to be the result of over-enthusiastic harvesting: the saliva turns red when the poor little creatures have to overwork their salivary glands. A more likely, if less colourful, explanation is that the red colour is linked to the chemical composition of the cave wall. The most common nests are those produced by the black-nest swiftlet, which also uses feathers to construct their valuable homes. The need to painstakingly remove the feathers makes these nests less valuable.

Most nests are destined for East Asia, but the Middle East is also becoming a significant new market. In Hong Kong a kilo of good quality nests may sell for US$2,000 and, not surprisingly therefore, nest concessions are vigorously policed. Concessions are sold by local governments for large sums and individual families have controlled some cave concessions for generations. Collecting the nests by scaling tens of metres up rickety bamboo ladders and scaffolds to the cave roof is a dangerous business – but the returns evidently make the risks worthwhile.

Sosro Café, Sosrowijayan Gang 11, generous portions of good food, Indonesian and Western. **Nusa Dua**, Jl Prawirotaman, happy hour 1700-1900, western, Indonesian, Chinese, 'Jappanesse' food, good, extensive menu worth investigating for itself alone – 'grilled fish served with aluminium foil'. **Simco**, Jl Prawirotaman 29, a medium sized, bamboo dominated restaurant, with usual mix of travellers' and Indonesia/Chinese food. **Suharti**, Jl Adisucipto 208, excellent *ayam goreng*.

Other Asian *Sintawang*, Jl Magelang 9, excellent Chinese and seafood. Recommended. *Oshin Yakiniku*, Jl Malioboro 33, Japanese and some European. *Yashinoki*, Jl Adisucipto 6, Japanese and some Indonesian.

International Cheap: *Kedai Kebun*, Jl Tirtodipura 3, T76114, garden, restaurant and art gallery serving good, well prepared Indonesian and western dishes in relaxing and beautiful surroundings, moderate prices and managed by Angelika, a European who has successfully blended Indonesian and European culinary tastes, good range of alcoholic drinks at reasonable prices. Recommended. *Legian*, Jl Perwakilan 9, roof-top restaurant overlooking Jl Malioboro, slow service but worth waiting for, good-value food (plus cocktails). *Palm House*, Jl Prawirotaman 12, range of Indonesian, Chinese and International food, excellent food at a good price, attractive ambience, popular, the chef worked on the French ship Mermoz. Recommended. *Going Bananas*, Jl Prawirotaman 48 (east end of street), snacks and light meals outside the shop. *Prambanan*, Jl Prawirotaman, Indonesian, Chinese, European – good. *Via Via Café*, Jl Prawirotaman, T386557, viavia@yogya.wasantara.net.id Friendly service, good food, excellent fresh salad and pasta dishes and good Indonesian food too, Belgian-owned. Also organize cooking courses for local dishes and provide lots of information on onward travel and tours around Yogya. They organize tours too, focusing on meeting local people. Recommended.

Fast food *McDonald's*, large branch at the south end of Jl Malioboro. *Pizza Hut*, Jl Jend Sudirman 3. *Kentucky Fried Chicken*, Jl Adisucipto 167 and Jl Malioboro 133.

Foodstalls On the east side of Jl Mangkubumi, along Jl Malioboro (best after 0900) and outside Pasar Beringharjo (excellent *martabak*), also along northeast corner of the Alun-alun.

Travellers' food Very cheap: Most travellers' food is catered for on Jl Prawirotaman. *Ana's*, Jl Sosrowijayan Gang 2, good pancakes, yoghurts etc, popular and usually a good source of information. *Capuccino*, Jl Pasar Kembang 17, restaurant and bar. *Foodstall* at the north end of Gang 1. Recommended. *Mamas*, Jl Pasar Kembang 71, long-established and still popular. *No Name Café* – southern end of Gang I, Jl Sosriwijayan, very good value, basic food in characterful atmosphere.

Borobudur, Jl Pasar Kembang, good atmosphere and live music every night from 2100.

Bars

Batik art galleries Three batik painters from Yogya have achieved an international reputation – Affandi, Amri Yahya and Sapto Hudoyo. The *Affandi Gallery* is at Jl Adisucipto 167 (town bus 8) on the banks of the Gajah Wong River. It lies next to the home of the Indonesian expressionist painter Affandi (1907-90). The gallery displays work by Affandi and his daughter Kartika. Open 0900-1600 Mon-Sun. The *Amri Gallery* is at Jl Gampingan 67 and *Sapto Hudoyo* has a studio on Jl Adisucipto, opposite the airport.

Entertainment
Up to date information on shows can be obtained from the tourist office, travel agents or from hotels. There is a wide choice of performances & venues, with something happening somewhere every night

Batik lessons At the *Batik Research Centre*, Jl Kusumanegara 2, plus a good exhibition; *Gapura Batik*, Jl Taman KP 3/177, T377835 (phone to book), 3 or 5 day courses (near main entrance to Taman Sari); *Lucy Batik*, Jl Sosrowijayan Gang 1. *Via Via*, Jl Prawirotaman, run day courses 0900-1500 for 35,000Rp.
Cinemas *Empire 21* and *Regent*, Jl Urip Sumoharjo (next to one another); *Indra*, Jl Jend A Yani 13A; *Ratih*, Jl P Mangkubumi 26. *Yogya Theatre*, Jl P Senapati 3.
Classical dance *Rehearsals*, Kraton, 1030-1200 Sun.
Gamelan Performances at the Kraton, 1030-1200 Mon and Wed; *Ambarrukmo Palace Hotel*, lobby, check performance times.
Indonesian language courses *Sanata Dharma Research Centre*, Jl Gejayan Mrican Baru Tromolpos 29. The centre runs a 4 week (120 hrs) intensive course, with lodging and meals. *Realia Language School* has been recommended, it's a reasonable price if several people wish to learn together. *School of Indo Puri Bahasa*, Jl Bausasras 59, T588192. 36/50 hrs at US$5 per hour per person. Also offer other activities. *Djoglo Art & Culture Centre*, Jl Timor-Timur, T880959, www.djiglo.or.id Teaches Indonesian and the 'motions of dancing'. *Via Via*, Jl Prawirotaman, T386557, gives a morning introduction to the Indonesian language at 20,000Rp per person.
Ketoprak Traditional Javanese drama at the auditorium of RRI Studio Nusantara 2, Jl Gejayan 2030, twice a month (see Tourist Board for details).
Massage *Anna Restaurant and Homestay*, Jl Sosrowijayan Gang II/127.
Modern art gallery *Cemeti*, Jl Ngadisuryan 7A (near the Taman Sari), has changing exhibits of good contemporary Indonesian and western artists. Open 0900-1500 Tues-Sun.
Modern Javanese dance *Hanoman's Restaurant*, Jl Tirtodipura, T372528, 1900-2100 Tue-Sat, table charge 7,500Rp, reservations should be made during the peak seasons. Gamelan performance and wayang performance. Gamelan audience participation possible after the show. Behind scenes viewing encouraged (and recommended).
Ramayana At the Kraton on Sun. *Ambarrukmo Palace Hotel*, Jl Adisucipto, 2000 Mon, Wed and Sat (either Pool Terrace or *Borobudur Restaurant*); *Arjuna Plaza Hotel*, Jl Mangkubumi, 1900-2100 Thur. Open-air performances at *Prambanan*, held on 'moonlight nights' between May and Oct, starting at 1930 and year-round at the *Trimurti Covered Theatre*, 1930-2130 Tues, Wed and Thur (Jan-Apr, Nov-Dec only). There are also regular performances at *Dalem Pujokusuman*, Jl Katamso, 2000-2200 Mon, Wed and Fri (6,000Rp); and at the *Purawisata Open Theatre* (THR), Jl Katamso, 2000-2200 Mon-Sun. Admission: 50,000Rp (it's worth it). Good buffet dinner served before the performance (75,000Rp for the ticket and the meal).
Samba music *Slomoth*, Jl Parangtritis 109 (leather puppet show), consult the tourist information office for the correct current times.
Wayang kulit Performances held at the *Agastya Art Institute*, Jl Gedongkiwo, T373513, 1500-1700 Sun-Fri; *Ambarbudaya* (Yogya's Craft Centre), Jl Adisucipto, across from

Ambarrukmo Palace Hotel 2030-2230, Mon, Wed and Sat; **Ambarrukmo Palace Hotel**, Jl Adisucipto, 2000-2100 Thur (*Gadri Bar*); **Auditorium Radio Republic Indonesia**, Jl Gejayan, every second Sat of the month, 2100-0530; **French Grill**, *Arjuna Plaza Hotel*, Jl Mangkubumi 48, 1900-2100 Tues; **Hanoman's Restaurant**, Jl Tirtodipura, 1900 Wed, Fri and Sun, 15,000Rp; **Museum Sonobudoyo**, Jl Trikora, 2000-2200 Mon-Sun; **Sasana Hinggil** (South Palace Square-Alun-alun Selaton), every second Sat of the month, 2100-0430; **Gubug Wayang-44**, Kadipaten Kulon, Kp 1/44, is a wayang kulit puppet workshop run by Olot Pardjono, who makes puppets for the Museum Sonobudoyo. Ask at the museum for information on when his workshop is open and how to get there (see page 167).

Wayang gedhog (Classical masked dance) Performances at the *Purawisata Open Theatre*, Jl Katamso, every Sun, 1300-1400.

Wayang golek Performances held at the **Agastya Art Institute**, Jl Gedongkiwo, 1500-1700 Sat (Menak story), 1100-1300 Mon-Sat (Ramayana story); **Hanoman's Restaurant**, Jl Prawirotoman, 1900 Mon and Thur, 7,500Rp; **Nitour**, Jl Ahmad Dahlan 71, 1100-1300 Mon-Sat; and at the Kraton on Sat.

Wayang orang At the Kraton every Sun, 1030-1200, nightly performances at the THR (the People's Amusement Park), Jl Brig Jen. Katamso; *Ambarrukmo Palace Hotel*, Jl Adisucipto, 2000-2100 Tues, Fri and Sun (at the *Borobudur Restaurant* 48, *Hanoman's Restaurant*, Jl Prawirotoman 9, 1900-2100 Tues and Sat, 7,500Rp).

Festivals

Being an ancient kingdom & a sultanate, Yogya is host to a number of colourful festivals

Grebeg Syawal (movable – **end of Ramadan**). A celebration by Moslems, thanking Allah for the end of this month of fasting. The day before is *Lebaran Day*, when the festivities begin with children parading through the streets. The next day, the military do likewise around the town and then a tall tower of groceries is carried through the streets, the provisions being distributed to the waiting people.

April/May **Labuhan** (movable – 26th day of 4th Javanese month Bakdomulud) (also held in Feb and Jul). Offerings made to the South Sea Goddess Nyi Loro Kidul. Especially colourful ceremony at Parangtritis, where offerings are floated on a bamboo palanquin and floated on the sea. Similar rituals are held on Mount Merapi and Mount Lawu.

June **Tamplak Wajik** (movable), ritual preparing of 'gunungan' or rice mounds in the Kraton, to the accompaniment of rhythmic gamelan and chanting to ward off evil spirits. **Grebeg Besar** (movable), a ceremony to celebrate the Muslim offering feast of Idul Adha. At 8 o'clock in the evening, the 'gunungan' mound of decorated rice is processed from the inner court of the Kraton to the Grand Mosque, where it is blessed and then distributed to the people.

July **Siraman Pusaka** (movable – 1st month of the Javanese year), ritual cleansing ceremony, when the sultan's heirlooms are cleaned. The water used is said to have magical powers. **Anniversary of Bantul** (20th), celebrated with a procession of sacred heirlooms in Paseban Square, Bantul, South Yogyakarta.

August **Kraton Festival** (movable), range of events including ancient ritual ceremonies, cultural shows, craft stalls. **Turtle dove singing contest** (second week), a national contest for the Hamengkubuwono X trophy, held in the south Alun-alun from 0700. **Saparan Gamping** (movable), held in Ambarketawang Gamping village, 5 km west of Yogya. This ancient festival is held to ensure the safety of the village. Sacrifices are made of life-sized statues of a bride and groom, made of glutinous rice and filled with brown sugar syrup, symbolizing human blood.

September **Rebo Wekawan** (2nd), held at the crossing of the Opak and the Gajah Wong rivers, where Sultan Agung is alleged to have met the Goddess Nyi Loro Kidul. **Sekaten** (movable – the 5th day of the Javanese month Mulud), a week long festival honouring the Prophet Mohammad's birthday. The festival starts with a midnight procession of the royal servants (*abdi dalem*), carrying 2 sets of gamelan instruments from the Kraton to the Grand Mosque. Here they are placed in opposite ends of the building, and played simultaneously. A fair is held before and during Sekatan in the Alun-alun Lor. **Tamplak Wajik** (5th day of Sekaten). Ritual preparation of 'gunungan' or mounds of rice, decorated with vegetables, eggs and cakes at the palace, to the accompaniment of a gamelan orchestra and chanting to ward off evil spirits. **Grebeg Mulud**, religious festival celebrating the birthday of Mohammad, and the climax of Sekatan. It is held on the last day of the festival (12th day of Mulud) and features a parade of the palace guard in the early morning, from the Kemandungan (in the kraton) to the Alun-alun Lor.

Shopping

Yogya offers an enormous variety of Indonesian handicrafts, usually cheaper than can be found in Jakarta. Avoid using a guide or becak driver to take you to a shop, as you will be charged more – their cut. There are hustlers everywhere in Yogya; do not be coerced into visiting an 'exhibition' – you will be led down alleyways and forced to purchase something you probably don't want. It is important to bargain hard. The main shopping street, Jl Malioboro, also attracts more than its fair share of 'tricksters', who maintain, for example, that their exhibition of batik paintings is from Jakarta and is in its last day, so prices are good – don't believe a word of it. The west side of Jl Malioboro is lined with stalls selling batik, wayang, topeng, woven bags. Best buys are modern batik designs, sarongs and leather goods. **NB** The quality of some of the merchandise can be very poor – eg the batik shirts – something that may be difficult to see at night.

Antiques Mainly found along Jl Tirtodipuran and Jl Prawirotaman (south of the Kraton) and Jl Malioboro, sell a range of curios. *Kasumba*, Jl Tirtodipuran 50. Upmarket antiques and handicraft shop selling furniture and curios. There is also a smaller outlet in the *Melia Purosani Hotel*.

Bamboo Split bamboo bird cages are a cheap and unusual buy; available from the Pasar Ngasem or bird market (see page 169).

Batik Yogya is a centre for both batik *tulis* and batik *cap* (see page 306), and it is widely available in lengths (which can be made up into garments) or as ready-made clothes. Many of the shops call themselves co-operatives and have a fixed price list, but it may still be possible to bargain. There are a number of shops along Jl Malioboro. Contemporary 'European' fashions can be found in a couple of shops on Jl Sosrowijayan Gang 1. Batik factories are to be found on Jl Tirtodipuran, south of the Kraton, where visitors can watch the cloth being produced. Batik paintings are on sale everywhere, with some of the cheapest available within the Kraton walls. There are some more shops down Jl Prawirotaman and off Jl Malioboro. But perhaps the best known outlet is the **Ardiyanto Studio**, Jl Magelang Km 5.8, T562777, F563280. The cloth may be expensive, but it is top quality. The Emperor of Japan and Hilary Clinton are reputed to be among the owner's clients. To get there, take any bus running towards Borobudur/Dieng, which pass the shop some 6 km out of the city. There is also an outlet shop, complete with prize photos of visiting signatories, in the mall of the Melia Purosani, Jl Suryotomo 31. Another shop which has been recommended is *Oasis* (address, unfortunately, unknown), beautiful batik clothes and materials.

Bookshops *Kakadu*, Jl Prawitotaman 41, for second-hand volumes; *Prawirotaman International bookstore*, Jl Prawirotaman 30; *Sari Ilmu*, Jl Malioboro 117-119, for maps and guidebooks. **Book exchange**: 2 on Jl Sosrowijayan, 1 opposite Gang 2. Numerous exchanges on Jl Prawirotaman.

Handicrafts Government crafts centre, *Desa Kerajinan*, on Jl Adisucipto (Jl Solo), and some shops along Jl Prawirotaman, as well as the stalls lining Jl Malioboro.

Ikat *Jadin Workshop*, Jl Modang 70B.

Leatherware Bags, suitcases, sandals and belts. All made from buffalo, cow or goat. Jl Malioboro has a selection of roadside stalls, as well as several shops specializing in leather goods. Jl Bugisan also has many small good value outlets.

Pottery Earthenware is produced in a number of specialist villages around Yogya. Best known is Kasongan, 7 km south of the city, which produces pots, vases and assorted kitchen utensils. Get there by bus towards Bantul; the village is 700m off the main road.

Silverware In Kota Gede, to the southeast of the city (most shops are to be found along Jl Kemesan), 2 major workshops – *MD Silver* and *Tom's Silver*. Numerous shops on Jl Prawirotaman. Try making your own ring with Via Via Tours, Jl Prawirotaman, 40,000Rp with instruction, and take home your finished article.

Topeng masks Widely available from stalls along Jl Malioboro and near Taman Sari.

Wayang kulit & wayang golek Widely available from roadside stalls along Jl Malioboro. They come in varying qualities of craftsmanship, so ask to see the best and the cheapest. Hard bargaining recommended.

Sport

Golf *Adisucipto Golf Course* (9 holes), 9 km out of town on Prambanan road. *Merapi Golf Course*, near the *Hyatt Hotel*.

Panahan Traditional archery, performed to celebrate the birth of Sultan Hamengkubuwono X.

Swimming Many hotels allow non-guests to use their pools, including **Ambarrukmo Palace**, Jl Adisucipto; **Colombo**, Jl Gejayan; **New Batik Palace**, Jl Mangkubumi; **Sri Wedari**, Jl Adisucipto.

Tour operators *Colors of Asia Travel*, Holiday Inn, Jl Adisucipto. **Kasatriyan Travel**, Jl Brigjen Katamso. **Intan Pelangi**, Jl Malioboro 18, T562895. **Jaya**, Jl Sosrowijayan 23. **Natrabu**, Ambarrukmo Palace Hotel, Jl Adisucipto, T588488. **Nitour**, Jl KHA Dahlan 71, T375165. **Pacto**, Ambarrukmo Palace, Jl Adisucipto, T566488. **Sahid**, Hotel Sahid Garden, Jl Babarsari, T587078. **Satriavi**, Ambarrukmo Palace Hotel, Jl Adisucipto, T566488. **Setia**, Natour Garuda Hotel, Jl Malioboro 72, T566353. **Via Via**, Jl Prawirotaman, offers excellent tours. **Yogya Rental**, Jl Pasar Kembang 85-88, T587648. **Vista Express**, Natour Garuda Hotel, Jl Malioboro, T563074. There are a number of companies around Jl Sosrowijayan and Jl Pasar Kembang, as well as Jl Prawirotaman, who will organize onward travel by *bis malam* and train. Many of the hotels offer similar services.

One person has been recommended to us by several of our readers. His name is **Lukas**, and you can ask for him at the airport information desk (T566666, F496679), or contact him privately – Subandi Lukasmoro, Jl Gambiran UH.V/318, T372782. He is reportedly professional, knowledgeable, reliable and flexible. He is said to undercut the commercial tour companies and provides a better service.

Transport
565 km from Jakarta, 327 km from Surabaya

Local Andong (horse-drawn carriage): traditional carriages with 4 wheels, the 2 in front being smaller, drawn by either 1 or 2 horses. They wait outside the railway station, the Kraton and next to the Bird Market. **Becak**: probably the best way to get around. Agree a price before boarding: approximately 500Rp per kilometre – or charter one for the day, approximately 2,000Rp per hour (a low price will probably mean numerous unwanted visits to batik factories and so on). **Bemos & colts**: colts around town (400Rp). Beware of the drivers who seem to offer a very good price; they will almost certainly take you to batik or silverware shops. **Bicycle hire**: along Jl Pasar Kembang or Gang 1 or 2, approximately 2,000Rp per day. **Bus**: Yogya town buses (*bis kota*) travel 17 routes criss-crossing the town; the tourist office sometimes has bus maps available (400Rp). Minibuses leave from the Terban station on Jl C Simanjuntak, northeast of the train station. **Car hire**: self-drive from *Avis*, at *Nitour*, Jl KH Ahmad Dahlan 71, T75165; *Bali Car Rental*, by the airport, 70,000-90,000Rp per day, a driver will cost an extra 20,000Rp per day and it usually means the hire is for 12 hrs rather than a full 24 hrs; *Fortuna*, Jl Jlagran 20-21 and on Jl Pasar Kembang; *National Car Rental* from *Sahid Garden Hotel*. **Motorbike hire**: along Jl Pasar Kembang and at *Fortuna*, Jl Jlagran 20-21, approximately 10,000-15,000Rp per day depending on size and condition of the machine. Check brakes, lights and horn before agreeing; bikes are sometimes poorly maintained. **Taxi**: the great majority of taxis in the city are now metered. Flagfall and 1st kilometre, 1,500Rp; 450Rp from each subsequent kilometres. Taxis/cars can be chartered for the day (from Jl Pasar Kembang 85, or from Jl Senopati, near the Post Office) for trips around town (10,000Rp per hour), or for longer trips to Borobudur, Prambanan etc (100,000Rp per day). Taxis can be ordered, call 885494/376107, Jl Prawirotaman, or *Central Taxi*, Jl Diponegoro 64.

Air Adisucipto Airport is 8 km east of town, along Jl Adisucipto (aka Jl Solo). Transport to town: minibuses from the Terban station on Jl Simanjuntak, travelling to Prambanan, pass the airport (1,000Rp), a taxi costs 15,000Rp. (Taxi desk in Arrivals Hall.) Regular connections on Garuda/Merpati, Sempati and Bouraq, with other destinations in Java, Sumatra, Kalimantan, Sulawesi, Bali, Lombok, Nusa Tenggara, Maluku and Irian Jaya.

Thieves are notorious on the overnight train between Jakarta & Surabaya via Yogya

Train The railway station is on Jl Pasar Kembang. Regular connections with **Jakarta's** Gambir station (12 hrs – the night train leaves at 1930 and arrives at 0630), **Bandung** (9 hrs), **Solo** (1 hr), and with **Surabaya** (8 hrs), see page 977 for timetable. **NB** The night train (*Utama Solo*) is hot, smoky and slow, with hourly awakenings by hawkers. There is a hotel reservation desk at the railway station.

Road Bus: Yogya is a transport hub and bus services are available to most places. Because it is such a popular tourist destination, there are also a/c tourist buses and minibuses in profusion. Agents are concentrated in the hotel/losmen areas. The Umbunharjo bus station is 4 km southeast of the city centre, at the intersection of Jl Veteran and Jl Kemerdekaan. Fastest services are at night (*bis malam*). Check times at the bus station or at the tourist office on Jl Malioboro. Regular connections with **Jakarta** (9 hrs) and **Bandung** (6 hrs), as well as many other cities and towns. To get to **Solo** (1½-2 hrs), or north to **Semarang** (3½ hrs), it is better to take a local bus, which can be hailed on the main roads. A/c buses from various agents along Jl Sosrowijayan (board bus here too) or from Jl Mangkubumi to, for example, **Jakarta**, **Bandung**, **Surabaya**, **Malang**, **Mataram**, **Probolinggo**, **Pangandaran** and **Denpasar**. **Colt**: private company colt offices are on Jl Diponegoro, to the west of the Tugu Monument. Seats are bookable and pick-up from hotels can be arranged. Regular connections with **Solo** and **Semarang**.

Directory

Airline offices *Bouraq*, Jl Menteri Supene 58, T562664, F383418. *Garuda*, Jl P Mangkubumi 56, T51440, F514400. *Mandala*, Melia Purosani Hotel, Jl Suryotomo 31, T/F589527. *Merpati*, Jl Panglima Sudirman 63, T514272, F566889. *Sempati*, Yogya International Hotel, Jl Marsda Adisucipto 38, T560706, F566200. **Banks** There are many banks in Yogya and because of the competition and the number of tourists who come here rates are good and most currencies and makes of TC are entertained. Good rates are especially found along Jl Prawirotaman. *Artamas Buana Jati*, Jl P Mangkubumi 4. *BNI*, near General Post Office, on Jl Senopati. *Bumi Daya*, Jl Sudirman 42. *CV Intan Biru Laut*, Jl Malioboro 18. *Dagang Negara*, Jl Sudirman 67. *Intrabilex*, Adisucipto Airport. *Niaga*, Jl Jend Sudirman 13. *Summa*, Jl Laksda Adisucipto 63. Money changer next to the *Hotel Asia Afrika*, Jl Pasar Kembang 17. Two money changers on Jl Prawirotaman. **Communications** General Post Office: Jl Senopati 2. Post Office: Jl Pasar Kembang 37 (for international phone calls and faxes). Telephone office: Jl Yos Sudarso 9. Open Mon-Sun, 24 hrs. IDD international calls. **Embassies & consulates** France, Jl Sagan 1, T566520. **Medical facilities** Hospitals: *Bethesda*, Jl Sudirman 70, T566300. *PKU Muhammadiyah*, Jl KHKA Dahlan 14, T566529. *Ludira Husada Tama Hospital*, Jl Wiratama 4, T620091. 24 hr clinic. Mobile number 082-2742896. *Ludira Husada Tansa Hospital*, Jl Wiratama 4, T3651. **Useful addresses** Immigration Office: Jl Adisucipto Km 10, T514948 (out of town on the road to the airport, close to Ambarrukmo Palace Hotel). Police: Jl Utara, on city ring road, T885494. Tourist police: Tourist Information, Jl Malioboro, T562811 for reporting robberies and seeking general information.

Parangtritis

Parangtritis is a small seaside resort, 28 km south of Yogya and 20 km from Imogiri. It caters largely to Indonesian weekend day-trippers – and they tend to come on Sundays only; the beach is best avoided on this day if you are looking for a peaceful time. Warungs line the black sand beach and the bay is enclosed at its eastern end by cliffs. Horse-drawn carts take tourists on trips along the beach, and the resort has a wonderfully dated and innocent air. An attractive avenue houses warungs and most of the losmen. The beach is a centre for the worship of the South Sea Goddess Nyi Loro Kidul; offerings to her from the Sultan (consisting of food, clothes, the Sultan's hair and cuttings from his nails) are made at the annual *Labuhan* ceremony (see page 180).

Phone code: 0274
Colour map 3, grid B3

The currents & undertow at the resort are vicious, & swimmers should exercise extreme caution; signs state that swimming is prohibited

Excursions

Inland from Parangtritis are **fresh water swimming pools** fed by natural springs, and to the west are the **Parang Wedang hot springs** (*air panas*), said to cure skin infections (which might keep people from even considering swimming there). Caves can be found to the east of town, most notably **Langse Cave** which is at sea-level and can only be reached along rickety bamboo ladders. The cave is a meditation spot.

There are some less frequented **beaches** to the east of Parangtritis – **Baron**, **Kukup** and **Krakal**, not far from the town of Kemadang. Snorkelling is reported to be reasonable at Krakal, a white sand beach stretching for 5 km. Kukup is a white sand beach with strong currents. **Sleeping** D-E cottages and rooms with mandi and squat toilet, restaurant with good seafood. ■ *To get there, take a bus from Yogya to Wonosari, then from Wonosari, as there is no public transport, hire a motorbike or charter a colt.*

Swimming is relatively safe at Baron it is protected from the sea & currents by coral ridges

A *Queen of the South*, T367196, F367197. The only 1st class hotel on the beach, on a cliff above the beach, elegant thatched bungalows, cliff-edge pool and bar, satellite TV, great views from the more expensive rooms, the Sultan of Yogya has stayed here several times, while making offerings during the Labuhan Ceremony; all the other hotels are located on the

Sleeping
Rates on Fri & Sat tend to be higher

broad avenue leading to the beach, with prices ranging from **D-E**, with a mandi and squat toilet. **D** *Rang Do*, 300m on from main avenue, popular. **E** *Agung Gardens*, mandi and fan, popular, reasonable source of information and average rooms, on main avenue. **E** *Budi*, small, with mandi, friendly, on main avenue. **E** *Yenny Homestay*, on main avenue. **F** *Widodo*, with mandi and fan, on main avenue. Both *Yennys* and *Agung Gardens* have restaurants selling travellers' food. The latter rents out motorbikes.

Sport The *Queen of the South* may be able to organize **hang-gliding** from the cliffs around the hotel. Courses start with training on the beach.

Transport **Road Bus**: regular connections with **Yogya's** Umbunharjo bus terminal, either via **Kretek** along the main road and over the Opak River (1 hr), or via **Imogiri** and **Celuk** (see page 172). The longer, rougher, trip via Imogiri passes through beautiful rural scenery.

Mount Merapi

Colour map 3, grid B3

Mount Merapi, whose name means 'giving fire', lies 30 km north of Yogya and is possibly the best known of all Java's many volcanoes. It rises to a height of nearly 3,000m and can be seen from the city. Because Merapi is still very active, it is closely watched by Indonesia's Directorate of Vulcanology who have an observatory here. Its first recorded eruption was in 1006 AD, when it killed the Hindu king Darmawangsa. It has been closed since November 1994, when there was an eruption.

It is imperative to take warm clothing – temperatures near the summit can reach zero – & energizing food. Tour operators often fail to stress the need for this kit

However, assuming that it might be possible to climb Merapi some time in the future, here is how it used to be done. Most people start from the village of **Selo** (on the north slope), from where it is a four hour trek up and 2½-3½ hours down. The trail is easy to follow but is steep and narrow in places (especially towards the top, where parts are quite gruelling); robust walking shoes are strongly advised – this is not suitable for the casual stroller. The spectacular views from the summit are best in the morning (0600-0800), which means a very early start, but it's well worth the effort. To see dramatic fireholes, take the path off to the left, about 25m from the summit. The route passes a ravine before reaching the fireholes – a 10-minute walk. Guides at Selo charge about 5,000Rp and will offer their houses for overnight stays. Tours are not recommended, as the guides urge the group to walk fast, and walking in a group in volcanic cinder can be dusty.

A more challenging climb can be made from **Kinahrejo**, on the southern slope. The village, which has no accommodation, is an hour's walk from Kaliurang (see next entry), and is 9 km from the summit (a 10 hour walk).

Transport **Road Bus**: it is tricky getting to Selo on public transport. Take a bus from Yogya to Kartosuro and then another bus to Boyolali, finally by minibus to Selo; leave Yogya in the morning, as afternoon buses are scarce. To get to Kinahrejo from Kaliurang, see below. Guides available.

Kaliurang

Phone code: 0293
Colour map 3, grid B3

The mountain resort of **Kaliurang** is 28 km north of Yogya, on the southern slopes of Merapi at just under 1,000m. It is the only point from which you can climb part way up Mount Merapi, good views of the lava avalanches. There are facilities here for tennis and swimming, and a waterfall near the bus station (admission 450Rp). Good walks include a short 2.5 km trek to

Plawangan Seismological Station, with views of the smoking giant (best in the morning, until about 0900-1000). The 'base stations' filled with warungs has an additional entrance charge of 500Rp per person. The Seismological Station and the road leading to it are periodically closed. If this route is closed, there is an alternative 2 km walk from the bus station to a belvedere, which overlooks the lava flow resulting from Mount Merapi's 1994 eruption. There are good views of the volcano on clear days.

Sleeping

D-E *Wisma Sejahter*, Jl Saiga, T95246. A converted school, clean rooms which interconnect but are generally large and well maintained. Quite pricey. **D-E** *Vogel's Homestay*, Jl Astomulyo 76, T895208. The most popular place to stay here, excellent source of information, well run, range of rooms available including dorm rooms. Christian, the owner, organizes early morning treks up Mount Merapi. **E** *Hotel Nguntaragati*, Jl Tiogo Tutri, clean and basic rooms with friendly family, large breakfast. **E** *Hotel Si Cantats*, Jl Tiago Tutri, good basic rooms, very cheap. **E** *Villa Sri Candi*, Jl Tiago Tutri, decent rooms in beautiful surrounds. **E** *Hotel Wijaya*, Jl Astomulyo, T895269. Hotel running to seed, rooms are clean but the beds sag, squat loos, use as a last resort. **F** *Wisma Gadda Mada II*, Jl Wretisa 447, very cheap military-style rooms, set off the main road, so it is quieter. **Camping**: pitch tents some distance from the trail, or you are liable to be woken by guided groups (from 0300), and theft is common.

Transport

Road Regular connections by **colt** with **Yogya's** Terban station. There are also **buses** from Yogya's Umbunharjo bus terminal.

Borobudur

Phone code: 0293
Colour map 3, grid B3

The travel business is only too ready to attach a superlative to the most mundane of sights. However, even travellers of a less jaundiced and world-weary age had little doubt, after they set their eyes on this feast of stone, that they were witnessing one of the wonders of the world. The German traveller Johan Scheltema, in his 1912 book Monumental Java, wrote, in truly monumental prose, that he felt the "fructifying touch of heaven; when tranquil love descends in waves of contentment, unspeakable satisfaction".

Ins and outs

Best time to visit
Early morning before the coaches arrive, although even by 0600 there can be many people here. Some visitors suggest sunset is the best time to be there as the view is not affected by mist (as it commonly is in the morning). Consider staying the night in Borobudur, to see the sun rise over the monument.

Opening times & admission to complex
Normally 10,000Rp, but the price has a tendancy to escalate to 20,000Rp at peak periods. Entrance to the museum is an extra 500Rp, but the use of video/camera is free. Discounts for parties of over 20 people. Price does not include a guide, and although guides vary, some visitors have reported them to be useful and knowledgeable. The 15,000Rp fee for a guide is money well spent. In theory, visitors should wait for a group to accumulate and then be shown round by a guide. However, many people simply explore the candi on their own. Open 0600-1700 (ticket office closes at 1630) Mon-Sun.

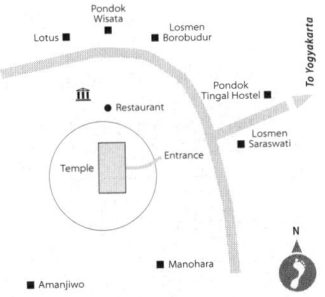

Borobudur: what's in a name?

The origin and meaning of the name Borobudur has been a source of dispute for many years. Some experts have maintained that it is derived from the Sanskrit words Vihara Buddha Uhr, meaning 'Buddhist Monastery on the Hill', and it is certainly situated on a slight rise above the surrounding plain. Other authorities reject this explanation, believing that boro is derived from the word biara, which means vihara or monastery, while budur is a place name, giving the monument the title 'Monastery of Budur'. De Casparis meanwhile, who uncovered a stone dated to the year 842 with the inscription Bhumisambharabhudara carved upon it, plumps for yet another explanation. The inscription means the 'Mountain of Virtues of the Ten Stages of the Bodhisattva', and he believes that the name is taken from the last part, Bharabhudara.

The site

History Borobudur was built when the Sailendra Dynasty of Central Java was at the height of its military and artistic powers. Construction of the monument is said to have taken about 75 years, spanning four or five periods from the end of the eighth century to the middle of the ninth century. Consisting of a nine-tiered 'mountain' rising to 34.5m, Borobudur is decorated with 5 km of superbly executed reliefs – some 1,500 in all – ornamented with 500 statues of the Buddha, and constructed of 1,600,000 andesite stones.

The choice of site on the densely populated and fertile valleys of the Progo and Elo rivers seems to have been partially dictated by the need for a massive labour force. Every farmer owed the kings of Sailendra a certain number of days labour each year – a labour tax – in return for the physical and spiritual protection of the ruler. Inscriptions from the ninth and tenth centuries indicate that there were several hundred villages in the vicinity of Borobudur. So, after the rice harvest, a massive labour force of farmers, slaves and others could be assembled to work on the monument. It is unlikely that they would have been resistant to working on the edifice – by so doing they would be accumulating merit and accelerating their progress towards nirvana.

Art historians have also made the point that the location of Borobudur, at the confluence of the Elo and Progo rivers, was probably meant to evoke, as Dumarçay says, "the most sacred confluence of all, that of the Ganga (Ganges) and the Yumna (Jumna)", in India. Finally, the monument is also close to a hill, just north of

Detail of Borobudur reliefs
Adapted from John Miksic, *Borobudur: golden tales of the Buddha*, Bemboo & Periplus, London & Singapore (1990)

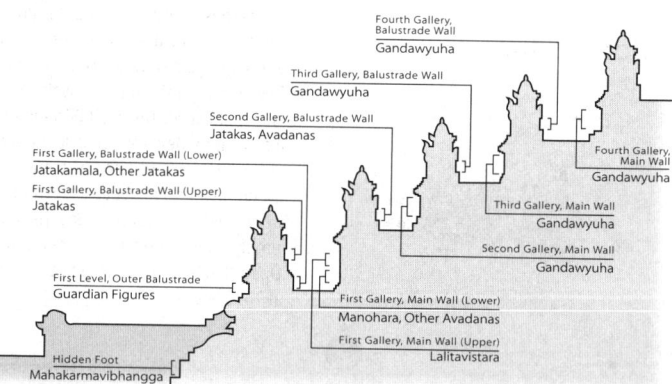

Magelang, called Tidar. Although hardly on the scale of the volcanoes that ring the Kedu Plain, this hill – known as the 'Nail of Java' – lies at the geographic centre of Java and has legendary significance. It is said that it was only after Java, which was floating on the sea, had been nailed to the centre of the earth that it became inhabitable.

The design

The temple is made of grey andesite – a volcanic rock – which was not quarried but 'mined' from river beds. Huge boulders are washed down volcano slopes during flood surges, and these were cut to size and transported to the building site. The blocks were linked by double dovetail clamps – no mortar was used in construction. It is thought that the sculpture was done *in situ*, after the building work had been completed. The stone was then covered in stucco and probably painted.

The large base platform was added at a later date and remains something of an enigma. It actually hides a panel of reliefs, known as the 'hidden foot'. Some authorities believe that this series of reliefs was always meant to be hidden, because they depict earthly desires (this was true of a similar series of panels at Angkor Wat in Cambodia). Other art historians maintain that this is simply too elaborate an explanation and that the base was added as a buttress. Inherent design faults meant that even during initial construction, subsidence was probably already setting in. In 1885 these subterranean panels were uncovered by Yzerman to be photographed, and then covered up again to ensure the stability of the monument.

Aspects of Borobudur's design were brilliant: the removal of rainwater, for example, was achieved by the use of gargoyles placed on the diagonals of the monument, transferring water down each level to the base, where it was collected in a gutter before being soaked up by the earth. Despite annual rainfall of 1800mm per year, this system would have coped admirably. Unfortunately, the latent instability of the overall structure led to subsidence, which in turn caused cracks to appear between the closely-laid stones, and this permitted water to seep into the heart of the man-made mountain, beginning a process of gradual deterioration.

The monument was planned so that the pilgrim would approach it from the east, along a path which started at Candi Mendut (see below). Architecturally, it is horizontal in conception, and in this sense contrasts with the strong verticality of Prambanan. However, architectural values were of less importance than the sculpture, and in a sense the monument was just an easel for the reliefs. Consideration had to be made for the movement of people, and the width of the galleries was dictated by the size of the panel, which had to be seen at a glance. It is evident that some of the reliefs were conceived as narrative 'padding', ensuring that continuity of story line was achieved. To 'read' the panels, start from the east stairway, keeping the monument on your right. This clockwise circumambulation is known as *pradaksina*. It means that while the balustrade or outer reliefs are read from left to right, those on the main, inner wall are viewed from right to left. The reliefs were carved in such a way that they are visually more effective when observed in this way.

The symbolism of Borobudur

Symbolically, Borobudur is an embodiment of three concepts: it is, at the same time, a *stupa*, a replica of the cosmic mountain *Mount Meru*, and a *mandala* (an instrument to assist meditation). Archaeologists, intent on interpreting the meaning of the monument, have had to contend with the fact that the structure was built over a number of periods spanning three-quarters of a century. As a result, new ideas were superimposed on older ones. In other words, it meant different things, to different people, at different periods.

Nonetheless, it is agreed that Borobudur represents the Buddhist transition from reality, through 10 psychological states, towards the ultimate condition of *nirvana* – spiritual enlightenment. Ascending the stupa, the pilgrim passes through these states by ascending through 10 levels. The lowest levels (including the hidden layer, of which a portion is visible at the southeast corner) depict the Sphere of Desire (*Kamadhatu*), describing the cause and effect of good and evil. Above this, the five lower quadrangular galleries, with their multitude of reliefs (put end to end they would measure 2.5 km), represent the Sphere of Form (*Rupadhatu*). These are in stark contrast to the bare upper circular terraces with their half-hidden Buddhas within perforated stupas, representing the Sphere of Formlessness (*Arupadhatu*) – nothingness or nirvana.

The reliefs & the statues of the Buddha

The inner (or retaining) wall of the first gallery is 3½m high and contains two series of reliefs, one above the other, each of 120 panels. The upper panels relate events in the historic Buddha's life – the *Lalitavistara* – from his birth to the sermon at Benares, while the lower depict his former lives, as told in the *Jataka* tales. The upper and lower reliefs on the balustrades (or outer wall) also relate Jataka stories as well as *Avadanas* – another Buddhist text, relating previous lives of the Bodhisattvas – in the northeast corner. After viewing this first series of reliefs, climb the east stairway – which was only used for ascending – to the next level. The retaining wall of the second gallery holds 128 panels in a single row 3m high. This, along with the panels on the retaining walls and (some of the) balustrades of the third gallery, tells the story of Sudhana in search of the Highest Wisdom – one of the most important Buddhist texts, otherwise known as *Gandawyuha*. Finally, the retaining wall of the fourth terrace has 72 panels depicting the *Bhadratjari* – a drawn out conclusion to the story of Sudhana, during which he vows to follow in the footsteps of Bodhisattva Samantabhadra. In total there are a bewildering 2,700 panels – a prodigious artistic feat, not only in terms of numbers, but also the consistently high quality of the carvings and their composition.

From these enclosed galleries, the monument suddenly opens out onto a series of bare, unadorned, circular terraces. On each are a number of small stupas, diminishing in size upwards from the first to third terrace, and pierced with lozenge-shaped openings. In total there are 72 such stupas, each containing a statue of the Buddha.

Including the Buddhas to be found in the niches opening outwards from the balustrades of the square terraces, there are a staggering 504 Buddha images. All are sculpted out of single blocks of stone. They are not representations of earthly beings who have reached nirvana, but transcendental saviours. The figures are strikingly simple, with a line delineating the edge of the robe, tightly-curled locks of hair, a top knot or *usnisa*, and an *urna* – the dot on the forehead. These last two features are distinctive bodily marks of the Buddha. On the square terraces, the symbolic gesture or mudra of the Buddha is different at each of the four compass points: the east-facing Buddhas are 'calling the earth to witness' or

Ship of the 9th century AD, carved on the temple of Borobodur, Central Java. The panel is on the eastern side of the monument, first gallery, main wall (lower), see below

bhumisparcamudra (with right hand pointing down towards the earth); to the west, they are in an attitude of meditation or *dhyanamudra* (hands together in the lap, with palms facing upwards), to the south, they express charity or *varamudra* (right hand resting on the knee); and to the north, the Buddhas express dispelling fear or *abhayamudra* (with the right hand raised). On the upper circular terraces, all the Buddhas are in the same mudra. Each Buddha is slightly different, yet all retain a remarkable serenity.

The main central stupa on the summit contains two chambers which are empty. There has been some dispute as to whether they ever contained representations of the Buddha. Those who believe that they did not, argue that because this uppermost level denotes nirvana – nothingness – it would have been symbolically correct to have left them empty. For the pilgrim, these spacious top levels were also designed to afford a chance to rest, before beginning the descent to the world of men. Any of the stairways, except the east one, could be used to descend.

The decline, fall & restoration of Borobudur

With the shift in power from Central to East Java in the 10th century (see page 301), Borobudur was abandoned and its ruin hastened by earthquakes. In 1814, Thomas Stamford Raffles appointed HC Cornelis to undertake investigations into the condition of the monument. Minor restoration was carried out intermittently over the next 80 years, but it was not until 1907 that a major reconstruction programme commenced. This was placed under the leadership of Theo Van Erp, and under his guidance much of the top of the monument was dismantled and then rebuilt. Unfortunately, within 15 years the monument was deteriorating once again, and the combined effects of the world depression in the 1930s, the Japanese occupation in the Second World War and then the trauma of independence, meant that it was not until the early 1970s that a team of international archaeologists were able to investigate the state of Borobudur once more. To their horror, they discovered that the condition of the foundations had deteriorated so much that the entire monument was in danger of caving in. In response, UNESCO began a 10-year restoration programme. This comprised dismantling all the square terraces – involving the removal of approximately 1,000,000 pieces of stone. These were then cleaned, while a new concrete foundation was built, incorporating new water channels. The work was finally completed in 1983 and the monument reopened by President Suharto.

Museum

There is a museum close to the monument which houses an exhibition showing the restoration process undertaken by UNESCO, and some pieces found on site during the excavation and restoration process. ■ *Admission 500Rp (students, 150Rp with ISIC card; note that the 10,000Rp ticket to see the monument includes entrance to the museum). Open 0600-1800 Mon-Sun.*

Candis around Borobudur

Candi Pawon was probably built at the same time as Borobudur and is laid out with the same east-west orientation. It may have acted as an ante-room to Borobudur, catering to the worldly interests of pilgrims. Another theory is that it acted as a crematorium. Candi Pawon is also known as 'Candi Dapur', and both words mean kitchen. The unusually small windows may have been this size because they were designed as smoke outlets. The shrine was dedicated to Kuvera, the God of Fortune. The temple sits on a square base and contains an empty chamber. The exterior has some fine reliefs of female figures within pillared frames – reminiscent of Indian carvings – while the roof bears tiers of stupas. Among the reliefs are *kalpataru* or wish-granting trees, their branches dripping with jewels, and surrounded by pots of money. Bearded dwarfs over the entrance pour out jewels from sacks. Insensitive and poorly informed restoration of Candi Pawon at the beginning of the 20th century has made architectural interpretation rather difficult.

Bhumisparcamudra – calling the earth goddess to witness. Sukhothai period, 13th-14th century.

Dhyanamudra – meditation. Sukhothai period, 13th-14th century.

Vitarkamudra – preaching, "spinning the Wheel of Law". Dvaravati Buddha, 7th-8th century, seated in the "European" manner.

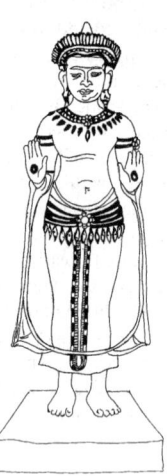
Abhayamudra – dispelling fear or giving protection. Lopburi Buddha, Khmer style 12th century.

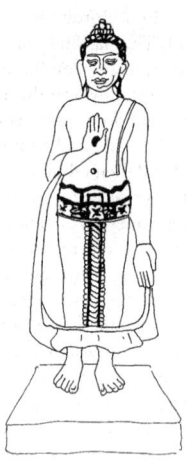
Abhayamudra – dispelling fear or giving protection; subduing Mara position. Lopburi Buddha, Khmer style 13th century.

Candi Mendut lies further east still and 3 km from Borobudur. It was built by King Indra in 800. It is believed the candi was linked to Borobudur by a paved walkway; pilgrims may have congregated at Mendut, rested or meditated at Pawon, and then proceeded to Borobudur. The building was rediscovered in 1836, when the site was being cleared for a coffee plantation. The main body of the building was restored by Van Erp at the beginning of this century, but the roof was left incomplete (it was probably a large stupa). The temple is raised on a high rectangular plinth and consists of a square cella containing three statues. The shrine is approached up a staircase, its balustrade decorated with reliefs depicting scenes from the jataka stories. The exterior is elaborately carved with a series of large relief panels of Bodhisattvas. One wall shows the **four-armed Tara** or **Cunda**, flanked by devotees, while another depicts **Hariti**, once a child-eating demon but here shown after her conversion to Buddhism, with children all around her. **Atavaka**, a flesh-eating ogre, is shown in this panel holding a child's hand and sitting on pots of gold. The standing male figure may be the **Bodhisattva Avalokitesvara**, whose consort is Cunda. There are also illustrations of classical Indian morality tales –

Mudras and the Buddha image

An artist producing an image of the Buddha does not try to create an original piece of art; he is trying to be faithful to a tradition which can be traced back over centuries. The Buddha can be represented either sitting, lying (indicating paranirvana), or standing, and (in Thailand) occasionally walking. Each image will be represented in a particular mudra or 'attitude', of which there are 40. The most common are:

Abhayamudra – dispelling fear or giving protection; right hand (sometimes both hands) raised, palm outwards, usually with the Buddha in a standing position.

Varamudra – giving blessing or charity; the right hand pointing downwards, the palm facing outwards, with the Buddha either seated or standing.

Vitarkamudra – preaching mudra; the ends of the thumb and index finger of the right hand touch to form a circle, symbolizing the Wheel of Law. The Buddha can either be seated or standing.

Dharmacakramudra – 'spinning the Wheel of Law'; a preaching mudra symbolizing the teaching of the first sermon. The hands are held in front of the chest, thumbs and index fingers of both joined, one facing inwards and one outwards.

Bhumisparcamudra – 'calling the earth goddess to witness' or 'touching the earth'; the right hand rests on the right knee with the tips of the fingers 'touching ground', thus calling the earth goddess Dharani/Thoranee to witness his enlightenment and victory over Mara, the king of demons. The Buddha is always seated.

Dhyanamudra – meditation; both hands resting open, palms upwards, in the lap, right over left.

Other points of note:

Vajrasana – yogic posture of meditation; cross-legged, both soles of the feet visible.

Virasana – yogic posture of meditation; cross-legged, but with the right leg on top of the left, covering the left foot (also known as paryankasana).

Buddha under Naga – a common image in Khmer art; the Buddha is shown seated in an attitude of meditation, with a cobra rearing up over his head. This refers to an episode in the Buddha's life when he was meditating; a rainstorm broke, and Nagaraja, the king of the nagas (snakes), curled up under the Buddha (seven coils) and then used his seven-headed hood to protect the Holy One from the falling rain.

Buddha calling for rain – a common image in Laos; the Buddha is depicted standing, both arms held stiffly at the side of the body, fingers pointing downwards.

---

look out for the fable of the tortoise and the two ducks on the left-hand side – and scenes from Buddhist literature. The interior is very impressive. There were originally seven huge stone icons in the niches; three remain. These three were carved from single blocks of stone which may explain why they have survived. The central Buddha is seated in the unusual European fashion and is flanked by his two reincarnations (Avalokitesvara and Vajrapani). Notice how the feet of both the attendant statues are black from constant touching by devotees. The images are seated on elaborate thrones backed against the walls but conceived in the round (similar in style to cave-paintings found in western Deccan, India). ■ *Admission 500Rp. Open 0600-1715 Sun-Mon.*

There are no architectural remains of another, Sivaite, monument called **Candi Banon**, which was once situated near Candi Pawon. Five large sculptures, all fine examples of the Central Javanese Period, recovered from the site can be seen in the National Museum in Jakarta.

Essentials

Sleeping
■ on map page 185

Most people visit Borobudur as a day trip from Yogya. However, accommodation is expanding here, and a new Aman Group hotel – the first on Java – means there is now a top of the range place to stay here. Although large international hotels are attracted to the area, many budget hostels are in demand and, as a result, the standard is generally poor.

L *Amanjiwo*, 10 mins drive and 30 mins walk from Borobudur, T88333, F88355, info-@amanresorts.com A fairly new resort and part of the Aman group. The hotel directly faces Borobudur and they arrange early morning trips to the temple to see the sun rise – magical. 34 suites set in semi-circular formation around the reception, each suite has its own little terraced area, with a shaded day bed and private swimming pool. Facilities include restaurant, bar, library, swimming pool and tennis centre. Exceptional quality of service and a truly magnificent hotel. **A** *Manohara Hotel* (formerly known as the *Taman Borobudur Hotel*, Borobudur Complex, T88131. Rather smart hotel, fantastic position, a/c, peaceful location and good value, but note that even by staying here – within the Borobudur complex – guests do not get access to Borobudur before the gates open at 0600, although there are stunning views of the sunrise and sunset over the temple. **D** *Pondok Tingal Hostel*, Jl Balaputradewa 32 (about 2 km from the temple towards Yogya), T88145, F88166. Traditional-style wooden building set around courtyard, clean smart rooms with bathroom and character, dorm beds (**E**) also available, room rate includes breakfast. **D** *Losmen Saraswati*, intersection of Jl Pramudawardani and Jl Balaputradewa, T88283. The building is currently being renovated, and should open early 2000. **E** *Losmen Borobudur*, Jl Pramudawardani 1, T88258. Very small rooms with mandi. **E** *Losmen Citra Rasa*, Jl Syailendra Raya (opposite the bus stop and market), rooms are OK, mandis are tiny, the more expensive rooms have small balconies, although on the main road the rooms are set back so not noisy, central position. **E** *Lotus Guesthouse*, Jl Medang Kamulan 2, T88281. Rather varying reports on this place, but generally favourable, looks onto Candi Borobudur itself, and is near the entrance to the bus park about 1 km from the main entrance, set near rice fields, rooms are clean and comparatively spacious, airy eating area. Recommended.

Eating

There are 2 restaurants within the complex, and a number around the stall and car park area, and in Borobudur Village. The *Saraswati* has a reasonable restaurant.

Festivals

May Waicak (movable, usually during full moon), celebrates the birth and death of the historic Buddha. The procession starts at Candi Mendut and converges on Borobudur at about 0400, all the monks and nuns carry candles – an impressive sight.

Transport
42 km northwest of Yogya, 90 km southwest of Semarang, 17 km south of Magelang

Local Bicycles: can be hired from some losmen/guesthouses (eg *Lotus Guesthouse*). An excellent way to visit candis Pawon and Mendut.

Road Bus: regular connections from Yogya's Umbunharjo terminal on Jl Kemerdekaan or from the street (ask at your hotel/guesthouse to find out where the bus stops). For those staying on Jl Prawirotaman, the best place is the corner of Jl Parangtritis and Jl May Jend Sutoyo. The buses run along Jl Sugiyono, Jl Sutoyo and Jl Haryono (1½-2 hrs). Note that the last bus back to Yogya leaves at 1800. Leave at 0500 to arrive early and avoid crowds. From the bus station in Borobudur, it is a 500m-walk to the monument. *Bis malam* (night) and *bis cepat* (express) tickets can be booked from the office opposite the market in the village. Buses to **Yogya**, **Jakarta**, **Bogor** and **Merak**. **Hire car or motorcycle**: travel north on the road to Magelang. After 32 km, turn left shortly after the town of Muntilan; 5½ km down this road is Candi Mendut, and after another 3 km, Borobudur. It is well signposted. Borobudur itself is behind the market. **Taxi**: this may be the best option for 3-4 people travelling together – cheaper than a hotel tour and without time restrictions. **Tour bus**: most visitors reach Borobudur on a tour from Yogya; it is the easiest way to reach the monument – although it is quite possible to visit Prambanan and Borobudur in a day on public transport – and prices start at about 25,000Rp (see page 173 for list of tour companies).

Banks *Bank Rakyat Indonesia*, near the entrance gate to Borobudur temple, inside the complex. **Communications** *Wartel* office (phone & telegram), Jl Pramudyawardani (opposite market). **Post Office**: Jl Pramudyawardani 10.

Directory

Magelang

Magelang, although a sizeable town with a population of 123,000, is really only used by tourists as a base from which to visit Borobudur, which lies 17 km to the south. It is also within reach of the **Dieng Plateau** (see page 214), which lies 90 km to the northwest. On the town square there are a number of colonial era buildings: including the offices of the former Dutch resident, built in 1810. The **Prince Diponegoro Museum** dates from 1920 and lies just to the west of the Alun-alun (town square), on Jl Diponegoro. At the western edge of town is the **Taman Kyai Langgeng**, a zoo-cum-activity park-cum-fantasy land with large pool, walking tracks and concrete animals set within colourful gardens. ■ *Admission 1,500Rp.* There is also a rather more interesting **Chinese Temple** on the Alun-alun (town square) near the Post Office. The town also has rather more than its fair share of appalling heroic sculptures. The **tourist information centre** is at the entrance to the Taman Kyai.

Phone code: 0293
Colour map 3, grid B3

B *Borobudur Indah*, Jl Jend A Yani 246, T64502, F63186. This featureless motel is situated on the main road, the rooms are set back and nothing special but adequate, with TV, a/c and hot water. Interesting model of Borobudur in the courtyard. **B** *Puri Asri*, Jl Cempaka 9, T64115, F64400, hotel@megelang.wasantara.net.id A real 'getaway' from surrounding cities, this hotel provides a variety of rooms, each with sweeping volcanic views, there is attention to detail and a homely feel. Facilities include fitness centre, children's playground, lovely pool and white water rafting. **B** *Wisata*, Jl Jend Sudirman 367 (at the south of town), T64089. Some a/c, keenly priced rooms, clean but lacking any distinguishing features, large, mostly geared to local businessmen, surprisingly tacky furniture for Indonesia, some rooms with lovely views. **B-D** *Trio Hotel*, Jl Jend Sudirman 68, T65095, F65098. Some a/c, restaurant, good pool, tennis, good, well-run hotel some distance from town centre, some rooms almost seem to be hewn from the living rock, such is the degree of concrete rock encrustation, now somewhat dated. **C** *Hotel Sriti*, Jl Daha 23, T63347. A gem of a hotel, centrally placed yet remarkably quiet, rooms are modern with the bathroom capturing the morning sun, very clean and busy hotel. **D** *Bayeman*, Jl Tentara Pelajar 45, T62050. Set around a beautiful courtyard, the rooms here are clean, high ceilinged but dark. Good bathrooms with a rarely found large bath. **D-E** *Pondok Wisata*, Jl Pramudha Wardani 44, T88362. Small hostel with equally small rooms, but the management are exceptionally friendly and very happy to make you feel at home. **E** *Loka Sari*, Jl Brig Jena Katamso 15, T62316. Centred around a car park, rooms are nicer than first impressions, with large comfortable beds and friendly management.

Sleeping
Most of the town's hotels are along Jl Jend A Yani

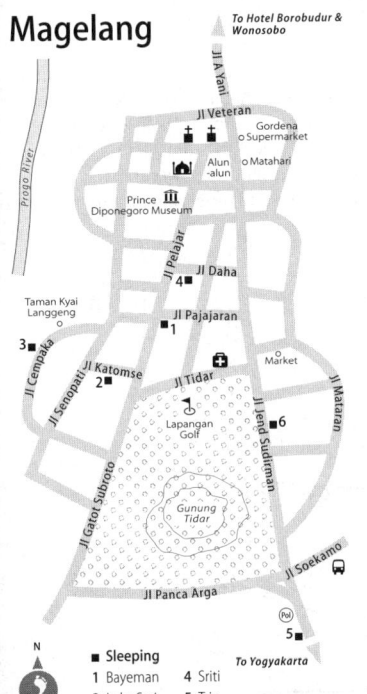

Magelang

Sleeping
1 Bayeman
2 Loka Sari
3 Puri Asri
4 Sriti
5 Trio
6 Wisata

Cheap *Matahari Food Baazar*, Jl Jend Yani 4; *Citrus Café*, Jl Pramudha Wardani,

Eating

western and Indonesian food, fast service and friendly, good for a filling meal. *California Fried Chicken*, Jl Jend Yani 10; *Pringondoni Restaurant* within the *Puri Asir Hotel*, surrounded by a lake, this restaurant serves Indonesian and international cuisine; *Sari Rosa*, Jl Jend Jani 432, mainly Indonesian and Chinese food.

Bakeries *Probitas Bakery*, Jl Pajang.

Entertainment **Cinemas** *Magelang Tidar*, Alun-alun (town square), modern a/c cinema showing English soundtrack films.

Shopping **Plazas/supermarkets** *Garden Pasar Raya*, Alun-alun (town square); *Matahari*, Jl Jend A Yani (town square).

Sports **White Water Rafting** Run by *Puri Asri Hotel*, T65115. 9 km of grade 2-3 rafting along the Progo River, finishing with a buffet.

Transport *43 km north of Yogya, 86 km south of Dieng, 18 km north of Borobudur*

Local Bemos: run across town and out to the bus terminal. The bemo terminal is at the south of town on Jl Jend Sudirman.

Road Bus: the terminal is out of town to the east on Jl Sukarno-Hatta; bemos link the terminal with the town centre. Regular connections with **Yogya** and other regional centres.

Directory **Banks** *Bank Central Asia*, Alun-alun (town square); *Bank Rakyat Indonesia*, Jl Jend Sudirman. **Communications** **Post Office**: Jl Jend A Yani 2 (town square).

Prambanan

Colour map 3, grid B3

The Prambanan Plain was the centre of the powerful 10th century Mataram Kingdom which vanquished the Sailendra Dynasty – the builders of Borobudur. At the height of its influence, Mataram encompassed both Central and East Java, together with Bali, Lombok, Southwest Borneo and South Sulawesi (see page 300 for more history). The magnificent temples that lie scattered over the Prambanan Plain – second only to Borobudur in size and artistic accomplishment – bear testament to the past glories of the kingdom. The village of Prambanan is little more than a way station, with a handful of warungs, a market and a bus stop. There are also a number of losmen and hotels here for those few

Prambanan Group

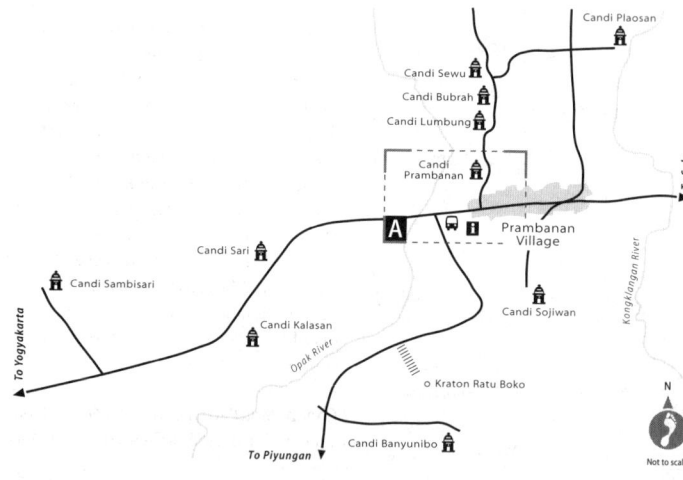

Related map: A Prambanan detail, page 198

people who might wish to stay overnight. There is a private **tourist information office** just east (towards Solo) of the bus stop. ■ *Admission to complex, 10,000Rp. Open 0600-1800 Mon-Sun. Guidebook, with descriptions of reliefs available from tourist information, 15,000Rp. Guides will show you around the complex, pointing out the various stories on the reliefs, for 7,500Rp. Audio visual show runs for 30 mins, most languages available, 2,000Rp. Museum entry 500Rp.*

Sights

After Borobudur, Candi Prambanan is probably the best-known archaeological sight in Indonesia. But, in addition to Prambanan, there are another six major candis on the Prambanan Plain, each with its own artistic character, and all well worth visiting. The account below describes the temples from east to west, travelling from Prambanan village towards Yogya (see map). From Yogya, the monuments are approached in reverse order. The Prambanan temple group have recently been restored by the Indonesian Archaeological Service (1991-94), and now stand in a neat, landscaped and well planned historical park.

Candi Prambanan or **Candi Lara Jonggrang** – Slender Maiden – as it is also known, stands on open ground and can be clearly seen from the road in Prambanan village. This is the principal temple on the Prambanan Plain, and the greatest Hindu monument in Java. In scale, it is similar to Borobudur, the central tower rising, almost vertically, over 45m. Built between 900 and 930 AD, Prambanan was the last great monument of the Central Javanese Period and – again like Borobudur – the architects were attempting to symbolically recreate the cosmic Mount Meru.

Originally, there were 232 temples at this site. The plan was focused on a square court, with four gates and eight principal temples. The three largest candis are dedicated to Brahma (to the south), to Vishnu (to the north) and, the central and tallest

Prambanan sanctuary complex

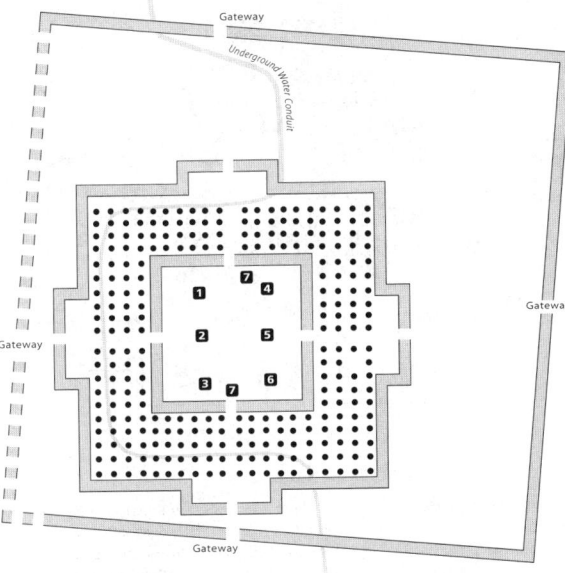

Not to scale

1 Candi Vishnu
2 Candi Siva
3 Candi Brahma
4 Candi 'B' or Candi Garuda
5 Candi Nandi
6 Candi 'A' or Candi Hamsa
7 Candi Apit

tower, to Siva. They are sometimes known as Candi Siva, Candi Brahma and Candi Vishnu. Facing each is a smaller shrine, dedicated to each of these gods' 'mounts'.

Candi Siva was restored by the Dutch, after an earthquake in the 16th century had left much of the temple in ruins. Like other Central Javanese candis, it was conceived as a square cell, with portico projections on each face, the porticos being an integral part of the structure. The tower was constructed as six diminishing storeys, each ringed with small stupas, and the whole surmounted by a larger stupa. The tower stands on a plinth with four approach stairways, the largest to the east, each with gate-towers imitating the main shrine and edged with similar shaped stupas. At the first level is an open gallery, with fine reliefs on the inside wall depicting the Javanese interpretation of the Hindu epic, the Ramayana (see box page 963). The story begins to the left of the east stairway and is read by walking clockwise – known as *pradaksina*. Look out for the *kalpataru*, or wishing trees, with parrots above them and guardians in the shape of rabbits, monkeys and geese or *kinaras*. The story continues on the balustrade of Candi Brahma. Each stairway at Candi Siva leads up into four separate rooms. In the east room is a statue of Siva, to the south is the sage Agastya, behind him – to the west – is his son Ganesh, and to the north is his wife Durga. Durga is also sometimes known as Lara Jonggrang, or Slender Maiden, and hence the alternative name for the Prambanan complex – Candi Lara Jonggrang.

The name of this monument is linked to the legend of King Boko and his son Bandung Bondowoso. Bandung loved a princess, Lara Jonggrang, who rejected his

Siva Temple

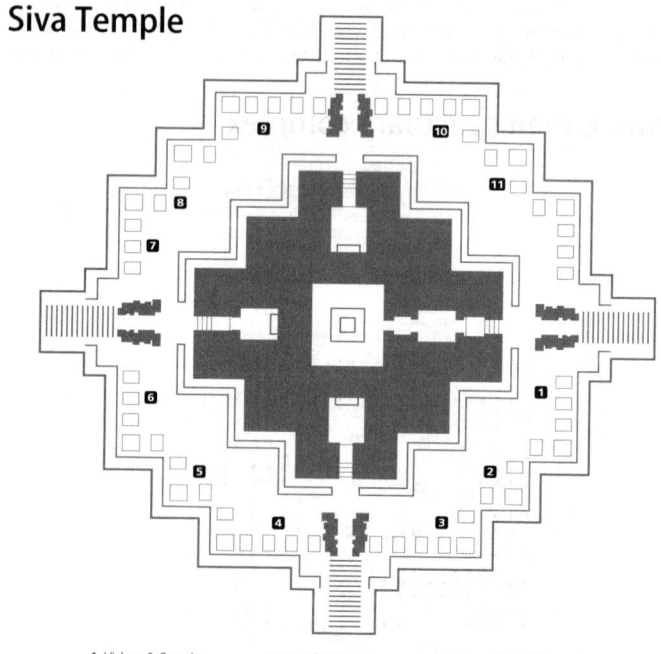

N
Not to scale

1 Vishnu & Garuda (Panel 1)
2 Rama & Laksmana fighting demons (Panel 4)
3 Rama winning hand of Sita (Panel 5)
4 Rama, Laksmana & Sita flee to forest (Panel 7)
5 Rama fighting demons (Panel 10)
6 Laksmana rejects Curpankha; Rama chases deer (Panel 12)
7 Rawana abducts Sita (Panel 13)
8 Rama meets Hanuman (Panel 15)
9 Rama fights Valin with Surgriva (Panel 18)
10 Hanuman spots Sita in Rawana's Palace (Panel 20)
11 Hanuman imprisoned; then escapes (Panel 21)

advances until her father was defeated in battle by King Boko. To save her father's life, Princess Lara agreed to marry Prince Bandung, but only after he had built 1,000 temples in a single night. Summoning an army of subterranean genies, Bandung was well on the way to meeting the target when Lara Jonggrang ordered her maids to begin pounding the day's rice. Thinking it was morning, the cocks crowed and the genies retreated back to their underground lair, leaving Bandung one short of his 1,000 temples. In an understandable fit of pique he turned her to stone – and became the statue of Durga. For those leaving Yogya by air, there is a mural depicting the legend at Adisucipto Airport.

The two neighbouring candis dedicated to Vishnu and Brahma are smaller. They have only one room each and one staircase on the east side, but have equally fine reliefs running round the galleries. On **Candi Vishnu**, the reliefs tell the stories of Krishna, while those on the balustrade of **Candi Brahma** are a continuation of the Ramayana epic which begins on Candi Siva. On the exterior walls of all three shrines can be seen voluptuous *apsaris*. These heavenly nymphs try to seduce gods, ascetics and mortal men; they encourage ascetics to break their vows of chastity and are skilled in the arts – poetry, dancing and painting.

Opposite these three shrines are the ruins of **three smaller temples**, recently renovated. Each is dedicated to the mount of a Hindu god: facing Candi Siva is Nandi the bull – Siva's mount; facing Candi Vishnu is (probably) Garuda, the mythical bird; and facing Candi Brahma (probably), Hamsa the goose. The magnificent statue of Nandi is the only mount which still survives.

This inner court is contained within a gated outer court. Between the walls are 224 smaller shrines – all miniature and simplified versions of the large central shrine – further enclosed by a courtyard.

From Candi Prambanan, it is possible to walk north to the ruined **Candi Lumbung**, currently under restoration, as well as **Candi Bubrah**. Together with **Candi Sewu** (see below), they form a loose complex of three temples.

Other candis near Candi Prambanan

Candi Sewu – meaning 'a thousand temples' – lies 1 km to the north of Candi Prambanan and was constructed over three periods spanning the years 778-810. To begin with, the building was probably a simple square cella, surrounded by four smaller temples, unconnected to the main shrine. Later, they were incorporated into the current cruciform plan, and the surrounding four rows of 240 smaller shrines were also built. These smaller shrines are all square in plan, with a portico in front. The central temple probably contained a bronze statue of the Buddha. The candi has been recently renovated. The complex is guarded by *raksasa* guardians brandishing clubs, placed here to protect the temple from evil spirits.

2 km to the northeast of Candi Prambanan is **Candi Plaosan**, built, probably, about 835, to celebrate the marriage of a princess of the Buddhist Sailendra Dynasty to a member of the court of the Hindu Sanjaya Dynasty. Candi Plaosan consists of two central sanctuaries surrounded by 116 stupas and 58 smaller shrines – presently ruined. Like Candi Sari, the two central shrines were built on two levels with six cellas. Each of the lower cellas may have housed a central bronze Buddha image, flanked by two stone Bodhisattvas (similar to Candi Mendut, page 190). Again, the shrines are guarded by raksasa. The monument is currently undergoing restoration.

The ruins of the late ninth-century **Kraton Ratu Boko** occupy a superb position on a plateau, 200m above the Prambanan Plain, and cover an area of over 15 ha. They are quite clearly signposted off the main road (south), 2 km. Because this was probably a palace (hence the use of the word kraton in its name), it is thought that the site was chosen for its strong natural defensive position. The hill may also have been spiritually important. Little is known of the 'palace'; it may have been a religious or a secular royal site – or perhaps both. Some authorities have even suggested it was merely a R&R centre for pilgrims visiting nearby Prambanan. Inscriptions found in the area celebrate the victory of a ruler, and may be related to the supremacy of the (Hindu) Sanjaya Dynasty over the Buddhist Sailendras.

For the visitor, it is difficult to make sense of the ruins – it is a large site, spread out over the hillside and needs some exploring. From the car park area, walk up some steps and then for about 1 km through rice fields. The dominant restored triple ceremonial porch on two levels gives an idea of how impressive the palace must have been. To the north of the porch are the foundations of two buildings, one of which may have been a temple – possibly a cremation temple. Turn south and then east to reach the major part of the site. Many of the ruins here were probably Hindu shrines, and the stone bases held wooden pillars which supported large pendopo, or open-sided pavilions. Beyond the palace was a series of pools and above the whole complex a series of caves. To get to Kraton Ratu Boko: take the road south before crossing the Opak River, towards Piyungan, for about 5 km. On the road, just over a bridge on the left-hand side, are steep stone stairs which climb 100m to the summit of the plateau and to the Kraton. Alternatively, it is possible to drive to the top; further on along the main road, a turning to the left leads to **Candi Banyunibo**, a small, attractive, restored Buddhist shrine dating from the ninth century. It is set in a well kept garden and surrounded by cultivated land. Just before the candi, a narrow winding road, negotiable by car and motorbike, leads up to the plateau and Ratu Boko.

2 km to the south of Prambanan village is **Candi Sojiwan**, another Buddhist temple, undergoing restoration.

Candis on the road west to Yogya About 3 km west of Candi Prambanan and Prambanan village, on the north side of the main road towards Yogya, is **Candi Sari**. This square temple, built around 825, is one of the most unusual in the area, consisting of two storeys and with the appearance of a third. With three cellas on each of the two levels and porticos almost like 'windows', it strongly resembles a house. Interestingly, reliefs at both Borobudur and Prambanan depict buildings – probably built of wood rather than stone – of similar design. Some art historians think that the inspiration for the design is derived from engravings on bronze Dongson drums. These were introduced into Indonesia from North Vietnam and date from between the second and fifth century BC. There is an example of just such a drum in the National Museum in Jakarta. It is thought that both the lower and the upper level cellas of the candi were used for worship, the latter being reached by a wooden stairway. The exterior is decorated with particularly accomplished carvings of goddesses, Bodhisattvas playing musical instruments, the female Buddhist deity Tara, and male naga-kings. Like Candi Kalasan, the stupas on the roof bear some resemblance to those at Borobudur. Inside, there are three shrines, which would originally have housed Buddha images. Nothing remains of the outer buildings or surrounding walls, but it would have been of similar design to Candi Plaosan. The candi was restored by the Dutch in 1929 and, like Candi Kalasan, is surrounded by trees and houses.

A short distance further west, and on the opposite side of the road from Candi Sari, is **Candi Kalasan** – situated just off the road in the midst of rice fields. The temple dates from 778, making it one of the oldest candis on Java. It is a Buddhist temple dedicated to the Goddess Tara and is thought to have been built either to honour the marriage of a princess of the Sailendra Dynasty, or as the sepulchre for a Sailendra prince's consort. The monument is strongly vertical and built in the form of a Greek cross – contrasting sharply with the squat and square Candi Sambisari. In fact, the plan of the temple was probably altered 12 years after

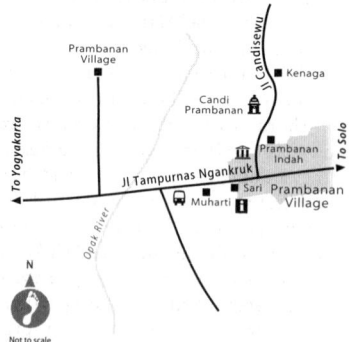

Prambanan detail

Prambanan as a holy water sanctuary

Water is a central element in the lives of many Southeast Asian societies. The Hindu myth of the Churning of the Oceans is reflected in the architecture of Angkor Wat in Cambodia and in the Khmer monuments of Thailand. The archaeologist Roy Jordaan believes that amerta – holy water – was also central to the symbolism and functioning of Prambanan. He writes: "On the basis of this myth [of the churning of the Oceans], the temple complex was built in such a way that the central temple area could be flooded with water on certain religious feast days, and function as a pool or a reservoir for the holy water that the priests made in a special temple ritual" (Jordaan, IIAS Newsletter, No 6, Autumn 1995). In searching out support for this theory of Prambanan as a swimming pool, Jordaan discovered reference to an underground water conduit in JW Ijzerman's Beschrijving der Oudheden Nabij de Grens der Residenties Soerakarta en Djogdjakarta, published in 1891. He hypothesizes that this was used to channel water into the temple precinct, transforming it into a holy water sanctuary. It also explains why Prambanan has drainage problems today: it was not because of some architectural slip, but because the temple was intended to be periodically flooded.

construction. Of the elaborately carved kalamakaras on the porticos projecting from each face, only the south example remains intact. They would have originally been carved roughly in stone and then coated with two layers of stucco, the second of which remained pliable just long enough for artists to carve the intricate designs. The four largest of the external niches are empty. The style of the reliefs is similar to Southeast Indian work of the same period. The roof was originally surmounted by a high circular stupa, mounted on an octagonal drum. Above the porticos are smaller stupas, rather similar in design to those at Borobudur. The only remaining Buddha images are to be found in niches towards the top of the structure. The building contains a mixture of Buddhist and Hindu cosmology – once again evidence of Java's religious syncretism. The main cella almost certainly contained a large bronze figure, as the pedestal has been found to have traces of metallic oxide. The side shrines would also have had statues in them, probably figures of the Buddha.

Another 5 km southwest from Candi Kalasan, towards Yogya, is the turn-off for **Candi Sambisari** – the temple is 2 km north of the main road. If travelling from Yogya, turn left at the Km 12.5 marker – about 9.5 km out of town. Candi Sambisari, named after the village nearby, sits 6.5m below ground level, surrounded by a 2m-high volcanic tuff wall. It has only recently been excavated from under layers of volcanic ash, having been discovered by a farmer in the mid-1960s. It is believed to have been buried by an eruption of Mount Merapi during the 14th century and, as a result, is well preserved. The candi was probably built in the early ninth century, and if this is so, then it was one of the last temples to be built during the Mataram period. A central, rather squat, square shrine still contains its original linga, indicating that this was a Hindu temple dedicated to Siva. There are also smaller boundary lingams surrounding the temple. On the raised gallery, in niches, there are fine carvings of Durga (north), Ganesh (east) and Agastya (south). Pillar-bases on the terrace indicate that the entire candi was once covered by a wooden pavilion. In front (and to the west) of the main temple are three smaller shrines, in rather poorer condition.

A *Prambanan Village*, Taman Martani, T496435, F496354. Very quiet setting offering lovely views of sunset and rise over Prambanan, separate cottages with fully equipped rooms and al fresco mandi. Pool, upstairs open restaurant with views. Recommended. **C-E** *Hotel Prambanan Indah*, Jl Candi Sewi 8, T497353. Simple hotel with a variety of rooms, ranging from 'hotel' type to dormitory beds, all share the same facilities including a pool. **E** *Hotel Kanaga*, some a/c, dark but clean rooms. **E** *Hotel Muharti*, Jl Tampurnas Ngangkruk 2, T496103. Cleaner rooms than the *Sari* but still dated with squat toilet. **E** *Hotel Sari*, opposite bus parking entrance to Prambanan, noisy rooms next to road, shabby but cheap.

Sleeping
There are a number of losmen in Prambanan village. Few people stay here because the candis are so easily accessible from either Solo or Yogya, but it may be worth doing so, to enjoy the sunrise & sunset

Entertainment **Ramayana ballet** (see page 305) At the open-air theatre at Candi Prambanan, 1900-2100, for 4 days every month over the full moon from May to Oct. Tickets available from tourist information at Candi Prambanan or from travel agents in Yogya. There are also performances year-round at the Trimurti Covered Theatre in Yogya (see page 179), 1930-2130.

Transport
17 km east of Yogya,
46 km west of Solo

Local In order to see the outlying candis, it is best to have some form of transport. If on a tour, enquire which candis are to be visited, or hire a taxi, minibus or motorbike from Yogya. Horse-drawn carts and minibuses wait at the bus station; they can be persuaded to drive visitors around. For the main temple group, a road 'train' now takes visitors around the candis, although it is also possible to walk – it is hot and tiring in the middle of the day. Alternatively, take a bus to Prambanan and work back, west or work east, ending at Prambanan.

Road Bus: regular connections with **Yogya**'s Umbulharjo bus station, or by minibus from the main roads in Yogya (30 mins). Connections with **Solo** (1½ hrs).

Solo (Surakarta)

Phone code: 0271
Colour map 3, grid B4

Situated between three of Java's highest volcanoes - Mount Merapi (2,911m) and Mount Merbabu (3,142m) to the west, and Mount Lawu (3,265m) to the east - Surakarta, better known simply as 'Solo', is Central Java's second royal city. The kraton, or palace, of the great ancient kingdom of Mataram was moved to Surakarta in the 1670s and the town remained the negara or capital of the kingdom until 1755, when

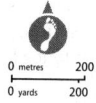

Related maps:
A Solo detail,
page 207

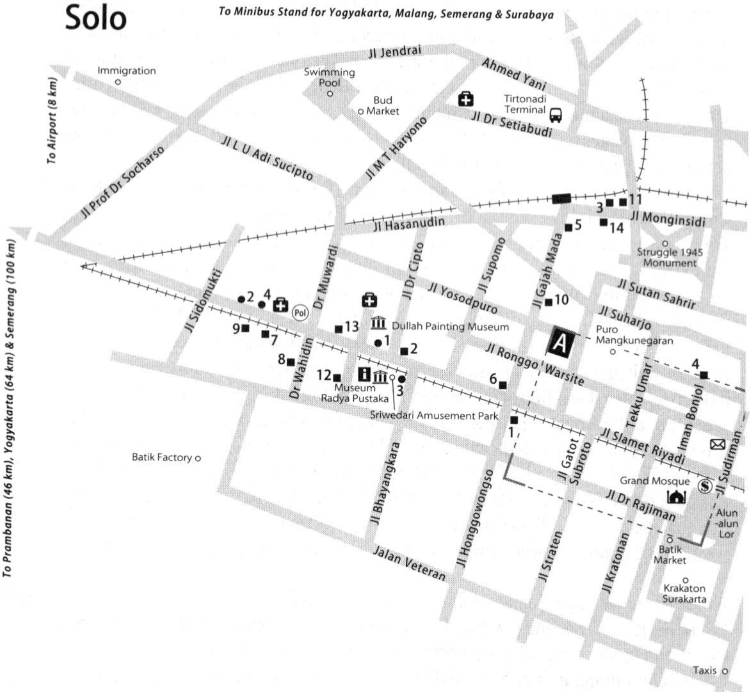

■ **Sleeping**
1 Cakra
2 Dana
3 Jayakarte
4 Kusuma Sahid
5 Mawar Indria
6 Novotel Solo
7 Putri Ayu
8 Ramayana
9 Riyadhi Palace
10 Sahid Raya Solo
11 San Francisco & Sinar Dhady
12 Sanashtri
13 Solo
14 Trihadhi

the VOC divided Mataram into three sultanates – two in Solo and one in Yogya. Although foreigners usually regard Yogya as Java's cultural heart, the Javanese often attach the sobriquet to Surakarta. Solo's motto is 'Berseri' - an acronym for Bersih, Sehat, Rapi, Indah (clean, healthy, neat, beautiful) - and the city has won several awards for being the cleanest in Indonesia.

Solo is quieter, smaller and more relaxed than Yogya – even though its population is more than 500,000 – and has pleasant, wide, clean and tree-lined streets. It is also less touristy than Yogya. Solo is one of the few towns in Indonesia which has bicycle lanes (on the main east-west road – Jl Slamet Riyadi) and they are almost as busy as the main roads. Reflecting the bicycle-friendly character of Solo, many tour companies run cycling tours of the city's places of interest. The city has gained a reputation as a good place to shop; not only is it a centre for the sale of batik – with a large market specializing in nothing else – but there is also an 'antiques' market which is worth visiting.

Ins and outs

Solo's **Adisumarmo Airport** is 10 km northwest of the city and there are connections with Singapore, as well as various destinations in Java and the Outer Islands. The **Balapan railway station**, just north of the city centre, provides connections with Jakarta, Surabaya and points along the way including Yogya. The **Tirtonadi bus station** is 2 km north of the city centre from where there are departures for many Javanese towns, as well as destinations in Bali, Lombok and Sumatra. It is easy to book night and express bus tickets through hotels, losmen and at tour and travel agencies. Local buses regularly leave Yogya for Solo (2 hrs).

Getting there
See also 'Transport', page 210

Bicycling is the best way to explore Solo – the city is more bicycle-friendly than just about any other Javanese town. **Angkutans** and town **buses** run along set routes. **Becaks** are useful for short local trips or for charter (it is also worth taking a becak to explore the streets to find some of the interesting colonial houses) and there are also **horse-drawn carts**. **Taxis** are available for charter for out-of-town trips.

Solo's **tourist office** is on Jl Slamet Riyadi 275 (next to, and behind, the Museum Radya Pustaka), T711435. It can supply town maps and some information on cultural events. Very helpful and good English spoken. Open 0800-1700 Mon-Sat. There are also tourist information centres at the bus station (very poor), the railway station and at the airport.

Getting around

Sights

The **Kraton Surakarta Hadiningrat**, better known as the **Kasunanan Palace**, is the senior of the city's two kratons (see page 303) and the more impressive. It lies south of the main east-west road, Jl Slamet Riyadi. Like the kraton in Yogya, the Kasunanan Palace faces north onto a square – the Alun-alun Lor – and follows the same basic design, consisting of a series of courtyards containing open-sided pavilions or pendopos.

Kraton Surakarta Hadiningrat

- Eating
1 Adem Ayam, KFC & Swensen's Ice Cream
2 Matahari
3 Oriental
4 Pizza Hut
5 Pringgon Dani

■ *Open most days 0830-1400, Sun 0830-1500, closed Fri.* On the west side of the Alun-alun is the **Grand Mosque**, built by Pangkubuwono III in 1750, though substantially embellished since then.

Entering the Kasunanan Palace, the first pendopo – the **Pagelaran** – is original, dating from 1745, and is used for public ceremonies. This is where visiting government officials would wait for an audience with the Susuhunan. From here, stairs lead up to the **Siti Inggil** or High Place, the area traditionally used for enthronements. Like Borobudur and Prambanan, the Siti Inggil represents the cosmic mountain Meru, but on a micro-scale. On the Siti Inggil is a large pendopo. The fore section of this pavilion was rebuilt in 1915, but the square section towards the rear (known as the **Bangsal Witana**), with its umbrella-shaped roof, is 250 years old.

Visitors are not permitted to enter the main palace compound through the large **Kemandungan Gates**. They must walk back out of the first compound, over a road, past the private entrance to the prince's quarters and an area used to store the royal carriages, through a second gate, to an entrance at the east of the main compound. Near the second gate is a school; this was originally a private school for the royal children but was opened to children of commoners at the time of independence. Walk through one courtyard to reach the large central courtyard, known as the *Plataran*. This shaded area, with its floor of black sand from the south coast, contains the main palace buildings. Much of the prince's private residence was destroyed in a disastrous fire in 1985, but has subsequently been restored. An electrical fault was the alleged cause of the fire, although local people believe that the Susuhunan neglected his duties and provoked the anger of the Goddess Nyi Loro Kidul (see page 124). Restoration was followed by extensive ceremonies to appease the Goddess.

The three **pendopo** on the left are original, and are used for gamelan performances. Behind them, along the walls of the courtyard, are palanquins which were once used for transporting princesses around the city. An octagonal tower, the **Panggung Songgobuwono**, survived the fire and was supposedly used by the Susuhunan to communicate with the Goddess Nyi Loro Kidul. Songgobuwono means 'Support of the Universe'.

The main pendopo, the **Sasana Sewaka**, is not original – it was restored in 1987 – although the Dutch iron pillars which support it, are. Strictly speaking, if members of the public are to have an audience with the Sultan, they have to walk upon their knees across the pendopo; look out for the cleaners, who crouch to sweep the floor. It is used for four ceremonies a year and sacred dances are held here once a year. Behind this pendopo is the private residence of the prince, with the **kasatrian** (the sons' quarters) to the right and the **keputren** (the daughters' quarters) to the left. A concrete area to the left was the site of the Dining Hall, which also burnt to the ground in the fire of 1985, and which is awaiting restoration once funds allow.

The guide leads visitors back to the first courtyard, where two sides of the square are a museum, containing an interesting collection of enthronement chairs, small bronze Hindu sculptures and three fine Dutch carriages which are 200-350 years old. ■ *Admission 1,000Rp, 1,000Rp for camera. Open 0830-1400 Mon-Thu, 0830-1500 Sun. All visitors are asked to wear a* samir *– a gold and red ribbon – as a mark of respect. Guide obligatory (they are the* abdi dalem *or palace servants).*

Pura Mangkunegaran The less impressive kraton, Pura Mangkunegaran at the north end of Jl Diponegoro, is still lived in by the princely family who built it. In 1757, the rebel prince Mas Said established a new royal house here, crowning himself Mangkunegoro I. But his power was never as great as the Susuhunan, and Mangkunegoro's deference to him is evident in the design of his palace, which faces south, towards the Susuhunan's Kraton. Much of the original structure has been restored. Built in traditional style, the layout is like other kratons, centred around a pendopo.

This central pendopo is the **Pendopo Agung**, (■ *open 0900-1400 daily, 0900-1300 Sun*), built in 1810 and one of the largest and most majestic in Java. Note how the ceiling is painted with cosmic symbols. Behind the central pendopo is a large room – the **Paringgitan** – which houses, amongst other things, a good collection of antique jewellery and coins of the Majapahit and Mataram periods. In a corridor behind this room are a large number of topeng masks. Voyeurs can peer through the windows into the private rooms of the present prince. Beautiful cool gardens and verandas give his quarters the air of a Victorian hunting lodge. Next to the ticket office are three fine carriages from London and Holland. ■ *Admission 2,500Rp. Open 0900-1400 Mon-Sat, 0900-1300 Sun. Guide obligatory (about 1 hr). Gamelan performances are held here (see 'Entertainment').*

The small **Museum Radya Pustaka** is housed in an attractive building on the main road, Jl Slamet Riyadi, next door to the Tourist Office. It contains a collection of wayang kulit, topeng, gamelan instruments, royal barge figureheads and some Hindu sculpture. ■ *Admission 500Rp. Open 0800-1300 Sat-Thu, 0800-1100 Fri, shut Mon.*
    Next door to the museum is **Sriwedari**, an amusement park. It is also the home of one of the most famous Javanese classical dancing troupes, specializing in wayang orang. ■ *Open 0800-2200 Mon-Sun. Park entrance on a Sat is 500Rp. Wayan orang performances from 2000 to 2300 Mon-Sat.*

Around Jalan Slamet Riyadi

There are several markets in Solo worth visiting. The antiques market, **Pasar Triwindu**, is situated off Jl Diponegoro, on the right-hand side, walking towards the Pura Mangkunegaran. This is the only authentic flea market in Central Java and is a wonderful place to browse through the piles of goods. There are some antiques to be found, but time is needed to search them out. Bargaining is essential. **Pasar Klewer**, situated just beyond the west gate of the Alun-alun Lor near the Kraton, is a batik-lover's paradise. It is filled with cloth, mostly locally produced batik – a dazzling array of both *cap* and *tulis* (see page 306). Prices are cheaper than the chain stores, but the market is very busy and first time visitors may be bemused into paying more than they should. It's best to go in the mornings, as it starts to wind down after lunch. Again, bargain hard. At the east side of the Alun-alun are a small number of shops and stalls selling fossils, carvings, krisses, puppets and masks. Don't expect to find anything of real quality, though.

Markets

Tour companies, losmen and hotels, as well as independent guides, all run cycling tours of Solo, trips to the Kraton, batik and gamelan factories, arak distillers, Prambanan, Sangiran, Candi Sukuh and Candi, or to surrounding villages to see rural life and crafts such as batik making, gamelan production, gold-smithing and leather-working. Prices vary considerably, but for city tours expect to pay around 20,000 to 25,000Rp, and for out-of-town tours anywhere from 40,000 to 75,000Rp, depending on the distance covered. Recommended are So'ud at the *Paradise Homestay* and Daniel K at *Westerners* or *Relax Homestay*. Most tours are 0900-1500. Some losmen and homestays will run two-day **batik classes**, for example the *Relax Homestay*.

Tours
See also 'Tour operators', page 210

Excursions

Candi Prambanan is easily accessible on public transport from Solo (see page 195). ■*Getting there: catch a bus from the Tirtonadi terminal, or a bus travelling west along Jl Slamet Riyadi. The other temples on the Yogya-Solo route are also just as easily accessible from Solo as Yogya (see page 197).*
    Kartasura is the abandoned site of a royal palace, the Kraton Kartasura, built in 1680 and abandoned 60 years later in 1742. Today, all that remains are the beautiful moss-encrusted brick walls and, within the walls, a peaceful graveyard dotted with fragrant frangipani trees. Buried here are some minor members of the Solo royal family. Admission by donation. ■*Open 0430-2300 Mon-Sun. Getting there: catch a bus from Solo towards Yogya and get off at the small town of Kartasura, by the*

West of Solo towards Yogyakarta

Candi Sukuh

Kartasura Market (Pasar Kartasura). From here walk due south for about 300m, and cross the main(ish) road; continue south for another 100m or so to reach the weathered walls. Ask for the Kraton Kartasura along the way.

Candi Sukuh and Candi Ceto, two of the most unusual and stunningly positioned temples in Indonesia, lie to the east of Solo, on the west slopes of Mount Lawu. Candi Sukuh stands at 910m above sea-level, and was probably built between 1434 and 1449 by the last king of the Majapahit Kingdom, Suhita. This enigmatic candi is situated in an area which had long been sacred and dedicated to ancestor-worship. The style is unlike any other temple in Java and has a close resemblance to South American Maya pyramid temples (which led archaeologists to believe, wrongly, that it was of an earlier date). It is built of laterite on three terraces, facing west. A path, between narrow stone gates, leads up from one terrace to the next, and steep stairs through the body of the main 'pyramid' to a flat summit. Good views over terraced fields down to the plain below.

The first terrace is approached through a gate from the west, which would have been guarded by *dvarapalas*, or temple guardians. The relief carvings on the gate are *candra sangkala* – the elements that make up the picture signify numbers which, in this instance, represent a date ('1359' is equivalent to 1437 AD). On the path of the first terrace is a relief of a phallus and vulva: it is said that if a woman's clothes tear on passing this relief, it signifies excessive promiscuity and she must purify herself. The gate to the second terrace is guarded by two more dvarapalas. On the terrace are a number of carved stones, including a depiction of two blacksmiths, one standing – probably Ganesh – the other squatting, in front of which is a selection of the weapons they have forged. The third, and most sacred, terrace is approached through a third gate. There are a number of relief carvings scattered over the terrace. The figures of many are carved in wayang form with long arms, and the principal relief depicts the Sudamala story. This story is performed in places where bodies are cremated, in order to ward off curses or to expel evil spirits. Also on the third terrace are standing winged figures (Garuda), giant turtles representing the underworld (strangely similar to the turtle stelae of pagodas in North Vietnam), and carvings of Bima and Kalantaka. It is thought Bima was the most important god worshipped here. A cult of Bima became popular among the Javanese élite in the 15th century: it was believed that Bima could bring the dead back to life.

The 'topless' pyramid itself has little decoration on it. It is thought that originally it must have been topped-off with a wooden structure. A carved phallus was found at the summit; it is now in the National Museum, Jakarta. Although Candi Sukuh is often called Java's 'erotic' temple, the erotic elements are not very prominent; a couple of oversized penises, little else. ■ *Small admission charge. Open 0615-1715 Mon-Sun. Getting there: take a bus from Solo's Tirtonadi station on Jl Jend A Yani to Karangpandan (41 km). Or pick up a bus on Jl Ir Sutami travelling east to Karangpandan. From Karangpandan, it is 12 km to Candi Sukuh. Most minibuses travel as far as Ngolrok, from where there are motorbike taxis up on the steep road to the top. From Candi Sukuh there is a well-worn stone path to the mountain resort of Tawangmangu (see below), an easy 1½-2 hrs' hike.*

Candi Ceto

For best views, visit the candi in the early morning; clouds roll in from mid-morning

At 1500m, Candi Ceto is considerably higher than Sukuh and lies 7 km to the north. Being harder to get to, fewer people go here. It is possible to walk between the two candis (it takes about four hours and there is no obvious trail, but it's worth the effort). It was built in 1470 and is the last temple to have been constructed during the Majapahit era. Candi Ceto shows close architectural affinities with the pura of Bali, where the Hindu traditions of Majapahit escaped the intrusion of Islam. Getting to the temple is an adventure in itself (although tours do run from Solo and Tawangmangu); the road passes tea estates, incredibly steeply terraced fields, and towards the end of the journey climbs seemingly almost vertically up the mountainside – the road ends at the temple.

Out of Java: Homo erectus

Most of the recent developments in our knowledge of human evolution have come from discoveries in Africa, but at the beginning of 1994, Sangiran and Mojokerto in Java emerged as a star location to rival the likes of the Olduvai Gorge.

Until these discoveries, it was assumed that Homo erectus *evolved in Africa and from there dispersed to Asia, including Java. The remains of three humans from Sangiran and Mojokerto had been thought to be less than 1,000,000 years old, making them the oldest hominids outside Africa, but not nearly as old as those unearthed in Africa. Now work by Garniss Curtis and Carl Swisher at the Institute of Human Origins in Berkeley, California, using new radiometric dating techniques, has revealed that they are probably nearer 1,800,000 years old. But doubts remain over the association of the dated crystals with the fossils: one of the problems are worries about the exact locations of the fossils (the Mojokerto fossil was found 60 years ago) and the complex geology of Java. Certainly, Curtis and Swisher have gone to great lengths to verify their early dates (for example, by including fossil remains from two locations and including the discoverer of the Sangiran examples in the work), appreciating that because of their enormous implications there would also be intense scrutiny.*

If the dates are verified, the work indicates that **H erectus** *spread from Africa almost immediately, rather than hanging around for 800,000 years before venturing into Eurasia, as previously believed. Anthropologists were always hard pressed to think of a reason why there was this 800,000 year delay. As Alan Walker at Johns Hopkins University remarks, they didn't "pack red-spotted handkerchiefs and set out for territories new", but gradually spread as the population grew, perhaps by 10 km per generation – reaching Java in a relatively speedy 25,000 years. The even more revolutionary notion that H erectus evolved in Asia and then spread to Africa is yet to gain many adherents, even though the dates for the Javanese and African fossils are almost the same. The reason is that there are no known antecedents to H erectus from Asia, while there are many from Africa. The belief that modern humans evolved in Africa has not been challenged by the new work, and in fact the multi-regional hypothesis (that humans evolved in numerous places and not just in Africa) has, it seems, been dealt a serious blow.*

Candi Ceto is one of the most stunningly positioned temples in Southeast Asia. It has recently been restored and is set on 12 levels. Nine would originally have had narrow open gateways (like those at Sukuh), but only seven of these remain. Pairs of reconstructed wooden pavilions, on stone platforms, lie to each side of the pathway on the final series of terraces. There is some sculpture (occasionally phallic) and strange stone decorations are set into the ground – again, very reminiscent of Mayan reliefs. ■ *Admission by donation. Open access. Getting there: from Karangpandan (see instructions on how to get to Candi Sukuh, above, for details on transport to Karangpandan) via Ngolrok, there are minibuses to the village of Kadipekso; from Kadipekso it may be possible to hitch, or catch a motorcycle taxi, the final 2½ km to the site. Alternatively walk, which is exhausting at this altitude. There are, however, now reportedly some direct bemos from Sukuh to Ceto, making this journey – until very recently an adventure in itself – much easier. The easiest way to reach Ceto, though, is to take a tour, see below.*

Tawangmangu is a hill resort town set at 1,200m, 12 km south of Kawangpandan and a total of 43 km from Solo (see page 211). *Getting there: buses leave regularly from Solo's Tirtonadi station, 2½ hrs, or pick up a bus on Jl Ir Sutami travelling east.*

Tawangmangu

Sangiran, 18 km north from Solo, is one of Java's most important archaeological sites. In 1891, Eugene Dubois found the skullcap and upper jaw molar of what he took to be an ape. But 11 months later, in August 1892, Dubois unearthed a femur which indicated that the 'ape' walked erect – he named this early hominid

Sangiran & Miri

Pithecantropus erectus – popularly known as 'Java Man'. This 'ape-man' was far more advanced than Dubois presumed and is now classified as a subspecies of *Homo erectus* – namely *Homo erectus erectus*. Since then, excavations at Sangiran have revealed a wealth of fossil hominid remains, along with a hoard of other fossils. Until very recently it was assumed that *Homo erectus* evolved in Africa and migrated to Java, for while the African fossils were dated to 1,800,000 BP, the examples from Java were thought to be only 700,000 years old (see box). The small Trinil Museum (opened 1989), in the nearby village of Krikilan, has a display including stegadon tusks, buffalo skulls, assorted fossils and, of course, examples of Java Man (craniums). Visitors are assaulted by locals selling fossils. Some (for example, the fish) are clearly of late 20th century origin, and recent important discoveries in the area have made the fossil sellers even more frantic and outrageous. ■ *Museum open 0900-1600, Mon-Sat. Small admission charge. Getting there: take a tour or catch a bus from Solo's Tirtonadi station towards Purwodadi; just beyond the 14km mark (in the village of Kalijambe), there is a road to the right signposted to Sangiran. The museum is 4 km along the road; take an ojek (1,500Rp), hitch or walk.*

Miri is further north from Sangiran, on the road to Purwodadi. This archaeological site and associated museum is less well known and not as well displayed as Sangiran. ■ *Getting there: turn left past the 21 km marker; the museum is some 2 km off the main road. Take a bus towards Purwodadi from Solo's Tirtonadi station and walk.*

Selo The hill village of Selo is accessible from Solo (buses from Tirtonadi station) and from here **Mount Merapi** can be climbed (see page 184).

Pacitan Pacitan is a small seaside resort 119 km south of Solo (see page 239). ■ *Getting there: there are a few direct buses from Solo's Tirtonadi station; alternatively, get a bus to Wonogiri, from where there are regular connections to Pacitan.*

Essentials

Sleeping
■ *on maps, pages 200 & 207*

Solo has a good range of excellent places to stay at all price levels, ranging from attractive, stylish colonial period hotels and villas, to clean, quiet and well-priced losmen and guesthouses. Newer hotels, for some unexplained reason, have a penchant for gross ostentation in terms of their interior decoration. The economic-cum-political crisis of 1998-99 saw many places suffer. But at least 1 lucky losman, though, acquired a new stereo TV, pawned from a large hotel which was unable to pay its wages.

A *Novotel Solo*, Jl Slamet Riyadi 272, T724555, F724666, nov.solo@slo.mega.net.id Opened mid-1997, a/c, restaurants, pool, business and fitness centres, jogging track, internet room, 142 rooms of a very high standard. **A-B** *Cakra*, Jl Brigjen Slamet Riyadi 201, T715847, F718334. A/c, restaurant, pool, garden, range of rooms available, but for many the Indonesian Louis XIV style of interior decoration may be simply too much to handle, gold, pillars and mirrors galore, the entrance is palatial, but there is a feeling of wear and tear the further into the hotel you go. **A-B** *Kusuma Sahid Prince*, Jl Sugiyopranoto 20, T746356, F744788, www.sahid.com, hskusuma@indo.net.id Housed in a beautiful old colonial building, this hotel offers excellent quality rooms and services once enjoyed by the Queen of Holland. Excellent value for money, large pool, restaurant, live music, remains the best hotel in Solo. **A-B** *Sahid Raya Solo*, Jl Gajah Mada 82, T744144, F744133, www.sahidraya.co.id, sahid_raya@slo.mega.net.id A/c, restaurant, worth a look if only for the uniforms of the staff, international standard rooms with great showers, sweeping views over Solo but also onto the shanty town below, pool and fitness centre, very helpful and professionally run. **A-B** *Solo Inn*, Jl Slamet Riyadi 366, T716075, F716076. A/c, restaurant, varied rooms but rather overpriced, it looks as though Gracelands has come to Solo, with or without Elvis, Greek columns and neon signs vie uncomfortably with one another. Regardless of the décor, white leather sofas included, rooms are comfortable and modern. **B** *Dana*, Jl Slamet Riyadi 286, T711976, F713880. Some a/c, some private bathrooms, colonial building with charm and a lovely garden, pleasant rooms, a reasonable comfortable spot but nothing fancy. **B** *Riyadhi Palace*, Jl Slamet Riyadi 335, T717181, F711552. Rather pretentious lobby but otherwise a good hotel, a little out of the centre but rooms are bright and modern.

C-D *Putri Ayu*, Jl Slamet Riyadi 293, T711812, F711812. Some a/c, set around a green-painted garden courtyard (giving the feeling of being inside a swimming pool), rooms can be rather small, cold water mandis but still good value, price includes breakfast, directly opposite *Pizza Hut*, slightly out of town. **C-D** *Sanashtri*, Jl Sutowijoyo 45, T/F715807. Short becak ride from town, warm toned and comfortable rooms, clean smelling with good bathrooms, quiet and friendly management. **D** *Cendana Homestay*, Gang Empu Panulah III 4, T752821. One of the cheaper places to stay in Solo, with friendly staff, but rooms are small and bathrooms doorless. **D** *Istana Griya*, Jl KHA Dahlan 22, T/F632667. This new hostel offers excellent value for money and many white, spotless rooms, adorned with colourful batiks. Some rooms have hot water, a/c and attached mandi, good source of information, and they also organize tours. Recommended. **D** *Mawar Melati*, Imam Bonjol Street 54, T636434. Fan, TV, average rooms, good for a stopover if catching an early train. **D** *Ny Hartini Guesthouse*, Jl Gatot Subroto, Gang Empu Baradah 85, T42152. Some a/c, quiet private house down an alley in a central position, rooms are small and rather dark, but very clean, some of the cheapest a/c rooms available in Solo here. **D** *Sekor Kadaton*, Jl Almad Dahlan 7, T661884. A/c, hot water, large rooms with beautiful wooden furniture adding to a colonial feel, huge bathrooms with shower, cool atmosphere. **D-F** *Kota*, Jl Slamet Riyadi 125, T632841. Around courtyard, clean but spartan, dormitory-like rooms, some with attached mandi, rooms to the front are noisy but good value. **E** *Jayakarta*, Jl Monginsidi, T746013. On the left-hand side of the station exit, rooms are simple with attached loo and tap, clean and good for position. **E** *Pension Lucie*, Jl Ambon 12, adjacent to Jl Ronggo Warsite, can be difficult to find down a small alley, very close to the Mangkunegaran Kraton, T53375. Six rooms with fans and shared mandis, bikes for hire, well managed by Topik, a friendly and easy going person with good English. Good sized, clean rooms, attractively decorated on the first floor, with a beautiful, simply decorated communal area, balcony with views over the rooftops, breakfast included. Recommended. **E** *Mama's Homestay*, off Jl Yos Sudarso, T52248. Some rooms adjacent to TV area, few twin beds but rooms are clean and large, shared bathrooms.

E *Paradise Homestay*, Jl Gatot Subroto, Gang Kidul 1/3, T754111. A beautifully converted old house down a quiet gangway in the heart of Solo. Works of art add character, rooms are not very large and not particularly clean either. **E** *Ramayana*, Jl Dr Wahidin 22, T712814. Some a/c, attractive 1-storey private villas set around garden courtyard, rooms are immaculate, cool and large, works of art and 1950s furniture meet Indonesian style with surprising effectiveness, the talking birds add charm, lovely atmosphere. Recommended. **E** *San Francisco*, down alley off Jl Monginsidi (near train station), T742232. Basic and worn but cheap. **E** *Hotel Trihadhi*, Jl Monginsidi 97, T637557. Best budget rooms in this area and some more pricey options, spacious rooms and bathrooms with only tap and loo, popular with Indonesians. Worth considering, but don't expect lots of travellers' information. **E-F** *Westerners* (*Pak Mawardi's Homestay*), Kampung Kemlayan Kidul 11 (right off Jl Yos Sudarso, from Jl Slamet Riyadi), T633106. Set in the old part of the city, this popular

Solo detail

■ **Sleeping**
1 Cerdana
2 Istana Griya
3 Kota
4 Mama's Homestay
5 Mawar Melati
6 Nirwana
7 Paradise
8 Pension Lucie
9 Sekar Kadaton
10 Westerners
11 Wisata Indah

● **Eating**
1 Cafe Atria & Internet
2 Café Bemo
3 Kasuma Sari
4 Monggo Pinarak Café & Internet
5 Warung Baru

guesthouse is difficult to find but worth the effort, rooms are clean, relaxed, quiet homely atmosphere, good source of information. **F** *Sinar Dhady*, down alley off Jl Monginsidi, (near train station). Shabby, dark and seemingly run by the Solo mafia, only for the desperate.

Eating Solo is renowned as a good place to eat and there is certainly no shortage of restaurants and warungs to choose from. Solo specialities include *nasi gudeg* (egg, beans, rice, vegetables and coconut sauce), *nasi liwet* (rice cooked in coconut milk and served with a vegetable) and *timlo* (embellished chicken broth). The Yogyanese speciality *gudeg* is also popular here. The only disappointment is that most places close between 2100 and 2130.

Indonesian Cheap: *Adem Ayam*, Jl Slamet Riyadi 342, specializes in *ayam goreng* (fried chicken), which is done to perfection, large and relatively cheap. *Pondok Bambu*, Jl Adisucipto 183 (out of town on way to airport), open restaurant with fish specialities. *Café Gamelan*, Jl Ahmad Dahlan 28. A little further up and on the other side of the road to *Warung Baru*. Excellent local cuisine. A tranquil place to eat good food and enjoy first class service. Try the avocado juice. *Pondok Segaran*, Sriwedari amusement park, good Javanese food. *Pringgon Dani*, Jl Sutan Syahrir, good food and a pleasant atmosphere. *Sari*, Jl Slamet Riyadi 421, excellent Javanese food. *Timlo Sastro*, Jl Balong 28, locals maintain this serves the best *timlo* in town, open till after lunch. *Tio Ciu*, north side of Jl Slamet Riyadi, near the shopping plaza, fresh seafood.

Very cheap: *Bakso Triwindu*, Jl Diponegoro, good vegetarian food. *Bu Mari's*, Jl Jend Gatot Subroto, recommends *gudeg*, open late. *Malioboro*, north end of Jl Diponegoro, for excellent *ayam bakar* (barbecued chicken). *Warung Baru*, Jl Ahmad Dahlan 8, excellent travellers' food and more. The charming manageress is an excellent source of information and the restaurant is also a rendezvous for Solo's community of foreigners, ask to see one of the numerous log books for travellers tips, the bicycle tours that run from here are highly praised. Recommended.

Other Asian cuisine Cheap: *Nikkoo*, Jl Slamet Riyadi, best Japanese restaurant in town, but also, by Indonesian standards, very expensive. *Centrum*, Jl RE Martinidata, a/c, good Chinese. *Orient*, Jl Slamet Riyadi, a/c, good Chinese, good seafood. *Oriental*, Jl Slamet Riyadi (next to the Radya Pustaka Museum), open for lunch and dinner extensive menu including pigeon, seafood, frog and pork, mostly Chinese dishes. Watch 2 skilled cooks produce all the food on just 2 woks – Mossimann might even learn something here about economy of pans.

International There is little to offer the westerner who does not have the stomach for Indonesian or Javanese food. Listed under Indonesian are a couple of places serving travellers' food. The better hotels will serve a limited number of western dishes. *Kentucky Fried Chicken*, Jl Slamet Riyadi. *Kasuma Sari*, Jl Slamet Riyadi 111, ice creams. *La Tansa*, Jl Imam Bonjol 31, bakery with good range of well priced Indonesian sweet breads and western-style baked goodies. *New Holland*, Jl Slamet Riyadi, recommended by many locals as the best bakery in the city. *Svensen's*, Jl Slamet Riyadi, ice creams. *American Modern Bakery*, Jl Briggand 90, wide range of sweet and savoury snacks. *American Donut*, Jl Slamet Riyadi 90, also recommended as a tasty bakery. *Monggo Piriarak Café*, Jl Dahlan 24, good western food.

Foodstalls There are many *warungs* and food carts to be found around Solo, which vary enormously in quality; 3rd floor of *Matahari* deptartment store at *Singosaren Plaza* offers a variety of Indonesian food; those who are fans of *bakso* should try the excellent street stall *Mas Tris*, Jl Honggowongso (just south from the intersection with Jl Slamet Riyadi); night market at Pujasari (Sriwedari Park), next to the Radya Pustaka Museum on Jl Slamet Riyadi, most Indonesian favourites like *saté* and *nasi ranies* can be bought, along with Chinese dishes and seafood like grilled fish and squid; carts set-up along the north side of Jl Slamet Riyadi in the afternoon and evening and sell delicious snacks (*jajan* in Javanese). On the south side of town, near Nonongan, saté stalls set-up in the evenings; stalls near the train station on Jl Monginsidi.

Entertainment

Cinemas Multi-screen, the *Solo 21*, in Sriwedari Park on Jl Slamet Riyadi (5,000Rp).
Cultural centres As the courts of Solo were denied administrative powers during the 2 centuries of colonial rule from 1757, the sultans (or 'Sunans', as they are known) devoted much of their energy to the promotion of Javanese arts and culture. This is reflected today in the presence in Solo of a **cultural centre** (*Pusat Kebudayaan*), an **academy of music** (*Konservatori Karawitan*) and an **academy of art** (*STSI*), with departments for dance, music, handicrafts and 'dalang' (the narrator of wayang kulit performances). The **RRI** (National Radio Station) Auditorium at Jl Marconi 51 (opposite the railway station) organizes cultural performances.
Dance practices Javanese classical dance at **Pura Mangkunegaran**, which is the oldest in Java, every Wed 1000-1200. Also at the **Kraton Surakarta Hadiningrat**, Sun 0900-1100, 1500-1600, entrance is free.
Gamelan At the **Pura Mangkunegaran** on Sat 1000-1200 and accompanied by dance on Wed at 0900. Admission – entrance fee to palace. Also at **Kusuma Sahid Prince Hotel**, 1800 Mon-Sun and *Aski*, 0900-1400 Mon-Thu, Sat.
Ketoprak Traditional folk drama performances at the RRI every 4th Tue of the month, 2000-2400.
Wayang Kulit RRI, every 3rd Tue and 3rd Sat of the month, from 0900 to 0500 the next morning.
Wayang Orang At the *Sriwedari Amusement Park* on Jl Slamet Riyadi, 2000-2300 Mon-Sat, and at the RRI every 2nd Tues of the month, 2000-2400.

Festivals

March/April Two-week long fair held in the **Sriwedari Amusement Park**. On the 1st day a procession parades from the King's Palace to Sriwedari, with stalls selling handicrafts.
June/July Kirab Pusaka Kraton (movable), a traditional ceremony held by the 2 kratons to celebrate the Javanese New Year. A procession of heirlooms, led by a sacred albino buffalo (the Kyai Slamet), starts at the Pura Mangkunegaran at 1900 and ends at the Kasunanan Palace at 2400. The ceremony dates back 250 years, from the time of Sultan Agung.
September Sekaten or Gunungan (movable), a 2-week long festival prior to Mohammad's birthday. The celebrations begin at midnight, with the procession of 2 sets of ancient and sacred gamelan instruments from the Kraton to the Grand Mosque. A performance is given on these instruments and at the end of the 2 weeks they are processed back to the Kraton. A fair is held on the alun-alun in front of the mosque. The closing ceremony is known as *Grebeg Maulud*, when a rice mountain (*gunungan*) is cut up and distributed to the crowds. The people believe that a small amount of 'gunungan' will bring prosperity and happiness.

Shopping
Solo has much to offer the shopper, particularly batik & 'antique' curios

Antique bric-à-brac *Pasar Triwindu*, off Jl Diponegoro (see sights). Much of the merchandise is poor quality, 'antique' bric-à-brac, but the odd genuine bargain also turns up. Bargaining is essential. There is also a good jumble of an antique shop on Jl Urip Sumoharjo, south of Jl Pantisari – some good things to be had here for those with the time to search through the dust, includes batik stamps, old masks, bells, carvings, Buddhas etc.
Batik Classical and modern designs, both *tulis* and *cap*, can be found at the Pasar Klewer, situated just beyond the west gate of the Alun-alun Lor, near the Kraton (see sights). Prices are cheaper than the chain stores, but the market is very busy and bargaining is essential. It is best to go in the mornings, as the market starts to wind down after lunch. **Batik Danar Hadi**, Jl Dr Rajiman 164; **Ce Pe**, Jl Ahmad Dahlan 4; **Batik Keris**, Jl Yos Sudarso 62, the best place to go for good quality and range. **Batik Semar**, Jl RM Said 148. It is also possible to see the batik-making process at Batik Semar.
Books *Toko Sekawan*, Jl Kartini, not much in English.
Ceramics *PKK Artshops*, Jl Alun-alun.
Department store *Matahari*, intersection of Jl Jend Gatot Subroto and Jl Dr Rajiman. 1998 saw the burning of 3 Matahari's in Solo, but it should have re-opened by the end of 1999. The biggest Matahari, recently opened, is at the western end of Jl Brigjen Slamet Riyadi.
Handicrafts (including masks, wayang costumes and leather puppets) **Bedoyo Srimpi**, Jl Dr Soepomo (opposite *Batik Srimpi*); **Pengrajin Wayang Kulit Saimono**, Sogaten RT/02/RW

XV, Pajang Laweyan Surakarta; *Sriwedari Amusement Park*, Jl Slamet Riyadi; *Usaha Pelajar*, Jl Majapahit 6-10; *Solo Art*, made-to-order tables, chairs, picture frames and even doorstops, good prices, details in Warung Baru Restaurant.

A fine example will cost thousands of dollars

Krisses These traditional knives (see page 90) can be bought at **Keris Fauzan**, Kampung Yosoroto RT 28/RW 82, Badran (Bpk Fauzan specializes in Keris production and sale), and also from the stalls at the eastern side of the Alun-alun Utara.

Markets *Pasar Besar* is on Jl Urip Sumoharjo and is the main market in Solo, excellent for fresh fruit and vegetables.

Music tapes Concentration of shops on Jl Gatot Subroto (at end near Jl Slamet Riyadi).

Supermarkets Several, including *Galael's* on Jl Slamet Riyadi (near the *Solo Inn*).

Sports **Golf** *Panasan Course*, northwest of town, near airport, T742245. **Swimming** At Kusuma Sahid Prince Hotel, entrance 7,000Rp.

Tour operators Mandira Tours, Jl Gadah Mada 77, T54558. *Natratour*, Jl Gadah Mada 86. *Nusantara*, Jl Urip Sumoharjo 65. *Rosalia 121 Solo Indah Tour*, Jl Slamet Riyadi 380, T741916. *Sahid Tours*, Jl Slamet Riyadi 318, T741916, F742012. *Sahid Tours and Travel*, Jl Slamet Riyadi 332, T742105. *Warung Baru*, Jl Ahmad Dahlan 8, really a restaurant, but this warung also runs highly recommended bicycle tours. *GPS Tours and Travel*, Jl KH Ahmad Dahlan 7.

Transport

585 km from Jakarta, 63 km northeast of Yogya, 262 km from Surabaya

Local Angkutan: ply fixed routes around town. The station is close to the intercity bus terminal at Gilingan. **Becaks**: for short trips around town, bargain hard. **Bicycles**: Solo is more bicycle-friendly than just about any other city on Java; bicycling is an excellent way to get around town. For hire from *Bamboo Homestay*, Jl Setyaki (behind Sriwedari); *Ramayana*, Jl Dr Wahidin 22; *Relax Homestay*, Jl Kemlayan; *Warung Baru*, Jl KH Ahmad Dahlan; and *Westerners*, Gang Kidul 11. About 5,000Rp for a good mountain bike. **Bus**: double-decker town bus (300Rp). **Carts**: horse-drawn carts. **Taxis**: metered ones in town.

Air Solo's **Adisumarmo Airport** is 10 km northwest of the city. Transport to town: taxis are available for the trip into town (15,000Rp); there is no easy public transport. Regular connections on *Garuda/Merpati* and *Sempati* with other destinations in **Java**, **Sumatra**, **Kalimantan**, **Sulawesi**, **Bali**, **Lombok**, **Nusa Tenggara**, **Muluku** and **Irian Jaya**. International connections: connections with **Singapore** on *Silk Air*.

Train Balapan station is on Jl Monginsidi (T632228). A/c connection with **Jakarta** (8-12 hrs, 9 trains daily), and on to **Surabaya** (7 hrs). Crowded local train daily from **Yogya** (1 hr 20 mins), see page 977 timetable.

Road Bus: the **Tirtonadi station** (T635097) is on Jl Jend A Yani, 2 km north of the city centre. Most bus companies have their offices on Jl Sutan Syahrir or Jl Urip Sumoharjo. Regular connections with most cities, including **Jakarta** (45,000Rp), **Bogor** (40,000Rp), **Bandung** (40,000Rp, 12 hrs), **Malang** (9 hrs), **Surabaya** (6 hrs), **Semarang** (5,000Rp, 2½ hrs), **Denpasar** (48,000Rp, 14 hrs). Night buses and express buses can be booked through most tour companies and many hotels and losmen. They run to most places in Java, and also to **Lovina Beach**, **Lombok/Mataram** and, in Sumatra, to **Padang**, **Medan** and **Bukittinggi**. Companies including *Java Baru*, Jl Dr Setiabudi 20, T52967. **Minibus**: the minibus terminal is near to the main Tirtonadi bus terminal; regular a/c connections with **Yogya**, 2 hrs, **Semarang**, **Surabaya** and **Malang**. **Taxi**: connections with **Yogya**.

Directory **Airline offices** *Bouraq*, Jl Gajah Mada 86, T634376. *Garuda Merpati*, Lippo Bank Bldg, Jl Slamet Riyadi 328, T744955. *Sempati Air*, Solo Inn, Jl Slamet Riyadi 366, T746240. *Silk Air*, Bank Central Asia (BCA), 3rd Flr, Jl Slamet Riyadi 7, T/F711355. **Banks** *Bank BCA*, Jl Slamet Riyadi 7 (takes VISA). *Bank Rakyat Indonesia*, Jl Slamet Riyadi. *Bumi Daya*, Jl Slamet Riyadi 16. *Central Asia*, Jl Slamet Riyadi 7. *Pan Indonesia*, Jl Major Kusmanto 7. *PT Grakarta* (money changer), Jl Slamet Riyadi 85. **Communications** Post Office: Jl Jend Sudirman 8, Jl Ronggo Warsite. Internet: *BB-Net* in Beteng Plaza, at eastern end of Jl Slamet Riyadi, northeast of Alun-alun Utara, 8,000Rp per hr.

Logikom Internet, Jl Ronggo Warsite, 7,000Rp per hr. *Monggo Pinarak Café*, Jl Dahlan 24, Internet 15,000Rp per hr. **Telephone office**: Jl Mayor Kusmanto 1 (24 hrs). *Wartel* (telephone & fax): Jl Slamet Riyadi 275A (at intersection with Jl Prof Dr Sutomo) and Jl Slamet Riyadi 175 (at *Hotel Kota*) (0530-2300). *Telkom*: Jl Mayor Kusmanto (near Post Office). **Medical facilities** *Hospital Kasih Ibu*, Jl Slamet Riyadi 404, T744422, most doctors here speak English. **Useful addresses** Immigration Office: Jl Adisucipto (out of town on way to airport), T748479. Police Station: Jl Adisucipto, T634500.

Tawangmangu

Tawangmangu is a hill resort at 1,200m, set on the west slopes of Mount Sewu (which rises another 2,000m to 3,265m). Good walks, fresh air and pony 'trekking'. A short walk away is **Grojogan Sewu Waterfall** (■ *open 0730-1630*) and up towards the top of town is the **Balekambang swimming pool** for cold dips. At the bottom of town, opposite the bus station, is a quaintly squalid **market**.

Phone code: 0271
Colour map 3, grid B4

Candi Sukuh (see page 204) can be reached on foot; it is a 1½-2 hour hike along the mountainside. Alternatively, catch a bus down the mountain to Karangpandan. **Candi Ceto** can be reached from Sukuh or via Karangpandan (see page 204).
    Sarangan is another hill resort 14 km to the east of Tawangmangu, and just into the neighbouring province of East Java (see the next entry for details). ■ *Getting there: by colt from Tawangmangu.*

Excursions
Tours to Candi Sukuh & Ceto are arranged by Komajaya Komaratih Hotel

A good range of hotels and losmen; the better hotels are cheaper than Solo for the same standard of accommodation, making it a good 'alternative' hill resort.

Sleeping
Over the weekend the resort is crowded with people from the plains, prices are therefore higher & the good places are often full

A-C *Komajaya Komaratih*, Jl Lawu Kav 150-151, T97125, F97205. Restaurant, pool, tennis, 'best' in town, good rooms, hot water, price includes breakfast, although it is a shame that more is not made of the views – the dining room, incredibly, has no windows bar those looking on to the parkway lot, **A** for a family room for 4. **B** *Pondok Garuda*, Jl Raya Tawangmangu, T97239, F97294. The best in town, attached bathrooms, and breakfast included. **C** *Pondok Sari*, Jl Timur Balekambang (to left of main Jl going up), pool, clean, hot water, good value, price includes breakfast. **D** *Muncul Sari*, Jl Lawu 87, T97101. Popular and the manager is friendly, rooms are darkish but clean with sitting areas to, in theory, admire the view (if there was one – which there isn't), attached cold water mandis, also rather dark and forbidding. **D** *Pondok Sari I*, Jl Utara Balekambang (100m from Pondok Sari), hot water and separate sitting-room. **E** *Losmen Mekar Indah*, Jl Lawu Tawangmangu, T97107. Reasonable rooms with own mandi. **E** *Losmen Ngesti Sariro*, Jl Lawu Tawangmangu, reasonable. **E** *Losmen Tejo Moyo*, Jl Lawu, T97149. Attached cold water mandis, rather fusty, but cheaper than most places up here. **E-F** *Balaistirahat Dana*, Jl Lawa 47, at the bottom of the hill. Probably the cheapest option around. Pretty basic. **E** *Pak Amat*, Jl Raya Tawangmangu (50m from bus station up hill), good cheap food in the restaurant. Bungalows set around garden, rooms a little musty and bathrooms rather grotty.

Pak Amat, Jl Lawu Kav, for cheap burgers, Wienerschnitzel and Indonesian dishes. *Sapto Argo*, Jl Lawu Tawangmangu.

Eating

Local Horses: are available for rent for about 10-15,000Rp per hour.

Transport
43 km from Solo

Road Bus: regular connections with **Solo's** Tirtonadi station (2½ hrs). **Minibuses** also run on, over the pass, and down to **Magelang**, where there are buses to **Kediri** and on. The station is at the lower end of the village, opposite the market. **Chartered minibus**: from the Balapan railway station in **Solo**. **Taxi**: from Solo (1 hr, about 50,000Rp per day).

Communications *Wartel*, Jl Raya Lawu 120A.

Directory

Sarangan

Phone code: 0351
Colour map 3, grid B4

Sarangan is a hill resort on the east slopes of Mount Lawu (3,265m). It can be approached either from the east, from Madiun, or from the west, from Solo via Tawangmangu. The town is centred around a lake (where there are facilities for fishing and rowing) and there are some beautiful views, but the resort itself is ugly. However, you can go riding, visit the waterfalls or go for walks in the cool mountain air. It is also a good base for climbing Mount Lawu. There is a **tourist office**, *Dinas Pariwisata*, and a post office, on the main road in town.

Excursions **Cemora Sewu** is the highest village hereabouts, almost at the pass. There are good walks amidst the mist and pines. There is a **camping** ground at Cemora Sewu – only for those with warm sleeping bags. ■ *Getting there: minibuses travelling between Sarangan and Tawangmangu pass through Cemora Sewu.*

Sleeping Hotels in Sarangan are over-priced. Even so, it is often booked-out over the weekend, although considerable discounts can be negotiated during the week. **C** *Hotel Mulia*, T98059. **C** *Rahayu*, T98019. **B-C** *Hotel Sarangan*, T98022. *Losmen Sri Maya*; *Wisma Dewi*.

Transport **Road** **Minibus**: Sarangan can be approached from either east or west. From the west, there are minibuses from Tawangmangu (another hill town), and from there regular connections with Solo. From the east, there are minibuses from Magetan, and regular bus connections between Magetan and Madiun.

Wonosobo

Phone code: 0286
Colour map 3, grid B3

A small mountain town with a cool climate, Wonosobo is the best base from which to visit the Dieng Plateau and its temples (see below). The town is built on a hillside and runs from the bus terminal at the bottom (unfortunately), to the town square at the top, a total distance of about 2 km. There is a **market** running between Jl Jend A Yani (the main road) and Jl Resimen, at the north end of town. The **tourist office** is on Jl Kartini 3, T21194. Useful pamphlet on Wonosobo, including maps. The staff speak excellent English. ■ *Open 0700-1400 Mon-Sat.*

Excursions **Dieng Plateau**, see below. ■ *Getting there: regular connections by bus from the minibus station near the market, in the centre of town (1 hr).*

Tours Angkutans can be chartered for tours to Dieng, from Jl Angkutan 45, T21880 (30,000-35,000Rp).

Sleeping **A-B** *Kresna Hotel*, Jl Pasukan Ronggolawe 30, T24111, F24112, kresna-htl@ magelang.wasantara.net.id First international hotel, with all the modern amenities, satellite TV, restaurant and café, large pool. Rooms are beautifully furnished. Tours to the Dieng Plateau are available with a good English-speaking guide. Recommended. **B** *Surya Asri*, Jl Jend A Yani 137, T22992, F23598. Poor restaurant, hot water, satellite TV, big breakfast included, very comfortable. **D** *Sri Kencono*, Jl Jend A Yani 81, T21551. Some a/c, hot water, central position, rooms are far better than immediate impressions of the hotel might indicate, spotlessly clean, light and airy. **D** *Nirwana*, Jl Resimen 18/36, T21066. Hot water, bath, clean and large rooms for the price, quiet, central for buses to Dieng, price includes breakfast. **D-E** *Perama*, Jl Jend A Yani 96, T21789. Hot water, bath, clean and airy rooms with some attempt at making a garden atmosphere, although the darkened glass makes the courtyard rooms rather dark, situated towards the bottom end of town, good value although cheaper rooms have cold water. **E** *Famili*, Jl Sumbing 6, T21396. Nice building, average rooms with outside mandi, a little overpriced. **E-F** *Citra Homestay*, Jl Angkutan 45, T21880. Clean and bright rooms price includes basic breakfast and tea and coffee through the day, central location 5 mins walk east from Dieng bus stop. **E-F** *Sindoro*, Jl Sumbing 5, T21179. Clean and central, near the Plaza, a good, cheap place to stay. **F** *Pondok Duta*, Jl Rumah Sakit 3, T21674. Situated 500m west of the town centre, good travellers' information, clean rooms, price includes breakfast, popular. **F** *Surya*, Jl Jend A Yani 4, T21272. Central position in town.

Eating

Mid-range and cheap *Dieng*, Jl Angkatan 29, Indonesian as well as international food served here, good meeting place, and the owner is also an excellent source of advice and information. *Cendawan Mas*, Jl Bismo, excellent Indonesian food with huge portions.

Cheap and very cheap *Asia*, Jl Angkatan 47, good Indonesian/Chinese dishes and some western food (including steaks). Beware the charges for drinks, which are twice what they should be. *Banyumas*, Jl Sumbing (near intersection with Jl Jend A Yani).

Shopping

Batik *Busaka Dewi*, Jl Jend A Yani, plus a number of shops around the market.

Transport

107 km northwest of Yogya, 134 km southeast of Pekalongan, 119 km southwest of Semarang

Local Bus: local bus including those for Dieng, leave from Jl Resimen near the market, just up the road from the colt station, 1,500Rp. **Carts**: horse carts or **dokar** are 2,000Rp for a tour of the town (1hr). Colt: the station is in the market on Jl Resimen.

Road Bus: the long-distance bus terminal is at the south end of Jl Jend A Yani, 1 km up hill from the town centre. Regular connections with Magelang 2 hrs (every 5 mins) (2,600Rp)

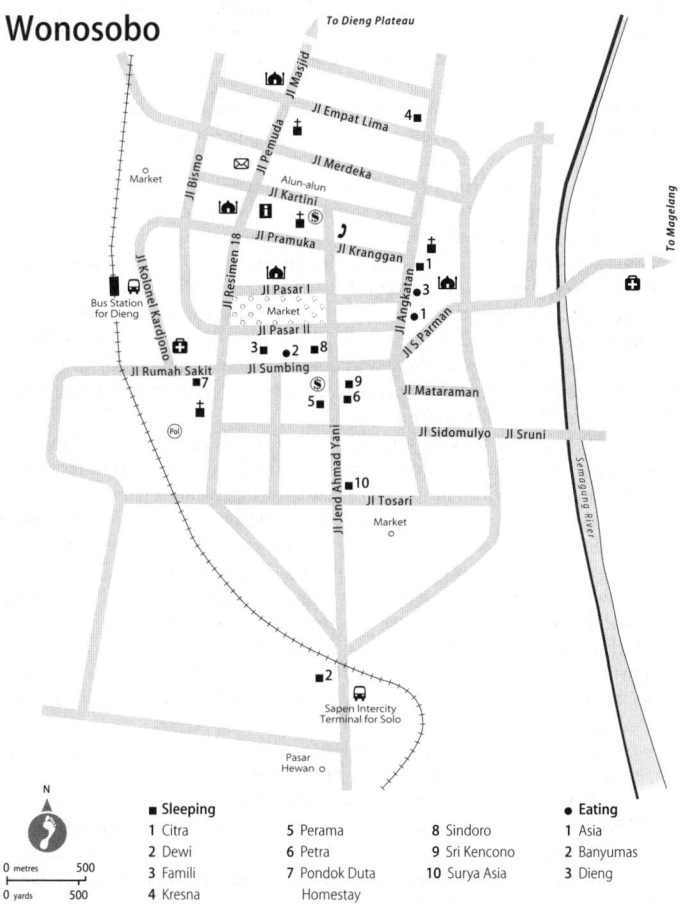

Wonosobo

Sleeping
1 Citra
2 Dewi
3 Famili
4 Kresna
5 Perama
6 Petra
7 Pondok Duta Homestay
8 Sindoro
9 Sri Kencono
10 Surya Asia

Eating
1 Asia
2 Banyumas
3 Dieng

and on to Yogya 40 mins (2,000Rp), Cilacap (via Purwokerto), and Semarang (via Ambarawa) 4 hrs (3,500Rp), Solo every 2 hrs. A/c minibuses operated by Rahayu Travel, Jl Jend A Yani 111, also run direct to Yogya and Cilacap 6 hrs.

Directory **Banks** *Bank Bri*, Jl Jend A Yani, top end, on corner of Jl Kartini near the tourist information office. **Medical facilities** Hospitals: *RSVP*, Jl RSVP, T21091/23878. **Communications** Area code: 0286. Post Office: Jl Pemuda, top of town on main square. *Warpostel* (fax & telephone), Jl Jend A Yani.

Reaching the Dieng Plateau From Wonosobo, the road climbs steeply north through spectacular scenery. Every square inch of land is cultivated, almost to the top of some of the mountains, and often on precipitous slopes. On a clear morning, there are stunning views back down to the valley. Eventually, at 1,800m and after 26 km, the road reaches the Dieng Plateau.

Dieng Plateau

Colour map 3, grid A/B3

The Dieng Plateau presents an extraordinary landscape; a rich volcanic basin of sulphur springs, lakes and the oldest Hindu temples on Java. Visitors sometimes report great disappointment on arriving at Dieng, having heard in advance of the stunning journey up to the 2,000m-high plateau. This is often because most people do not get here until after midday, when it can be misty and grey. It is undoubtedly best to travel to Dieng and explore the plateau in the clear highland mornings – this can only be achieved by staying in Wonosobo (26 km south) or in Dieng itself. Dieng tourist information is on Jl Raya (near the bus stop).

Sights The Dieng Plateau (Dieng comes from the Sanskrit word *Di-hyang*, meaning the 'Abode of the Gods') was occupied from the end of the seventh century to the 13th century. Eight temples remain, out of a possible 200, all of which were on a small scale and dedicated to Siva, the Hindu god of destruction. Little is known of the history of these temples, but the volatile volcanic landscape probably had something to do with the construction of so many candis here – the area was almost certainly considered an ideal place to communicate with the ancestors. Beginning at the end of the seventh century and ending in the late eighth or possibly early ninth centuries, these candis are some of the oldest on Java. Their construction was probably linked to the Central Javanese Sanjaya Dynasty. The names that the various candi have been given are not original, and give no indication of their dedication. Built on swampy ground, evidence remains of a vast, intricate underground drainage system, some of which still functions today.

At some point, and for some unknown reason, the Dieng Plateau was abandoned by the people who built the candis. Over the decades the natural swamp forest regenerated, and when the first Europeans reached the plateau at the beginning of the 19th century, the temples were hidden from view. As the forest was cleared for firewood so the ruins were rediscovered, only to be slowly dismantled as the finely hewn stone blocks were transported away by stone robbers to be used for building. This explains why only a handful of candis remain. As Jacques Dumarçay and John Miksic point out, the climate on the plateau was too cold to grow any tropical crops, and it is unlikely that there was ever any large resident population – bar "a few priests shivering in the cold air". The most recent inscription from Dieng is dated 1210, some time after which the plateau and its enigmatic temples were left to the swirling mists and bubbling sulphur pools.

Archaeologists believe that there were two building periods at Dieng. Candi Arjuna, Semar, Srikandi and Gatokaca all date from between the late seventh century to about 730, while Candi Puntadewa, Sembadra, Bima and Dvaravati were built between 730 and 780. The latter group were more elaborate. Nonetheless, the style of all the Dieng candis is box-like, with height and width of similar proportions, and little ornamentation. Outlined below is a circular route from Dieng village, which takes about three hours to walk. It takes in most of the shrines, a couple of sulphur springs and a sulphur lake.

On arrival from Wonosobo, the major group of shrines can be seen, looking rather small, in the middle of the plateau. From the minibus/taxi stand next to the *Losmen Budjono*, walk along the main road (towards Pekalongan) for 300m. There is a small track on the right that leads up to **Candi Dvaravati**, which dates from the middle of the eighth century. Returning to the main road, and walking 100m back towards the bus stop, is a road on the right leading to the main group of shrines.

Five small shrines remain amidst the foundations of a much larger group of buildings. They lack the ornamentation of candis on the lowlands, but their proportions are pleasing. The first temple to be reached by the footpath is **Candi Arjuna**. This and Candi Semar, which lies opposite, were probably the first temples to be built on Dieng. Arjuna originally housed a linga, which would have been ritually bathed each day. This necessitated the construction of a gutter through the north wall, which ends in an impressive gargoyle in the shape of a makara head. **Candi Semar** is squat and rectangular in shape, and would originally have housed a statue of Nandi the bull – Siva's vehicle. It and Candi Arjuna were built as a unit, dedicated to the cult of Siva. The roofless **Candi Srikandi** is the squarest and possibly the most beautiful of the candis on Dieng. It retains some fine carving on its exterior walls, with Vishnu on the north, Siva on the east and Brahma on the south wall – an unusual placement of these Hindu gods. Dumarçay postulates that at the early date these shrines were built, the placement conventions evident in later temples were not yet established. **Candi Puntadewa** is the tallest and most elegant in this group, resting on a large plinth, with a stairway leading up to the shrine. It has the characteristic door frame ornamentation of the monster kala vomiting out foliage. **Candi Sembadra** is the smallest shrine here, with narrow niches and a kala motif above the entrance. ■ *Open 0615-1715.*

From this group of candis, walk over the grazing land to **Candi Gatukaca**, set apart from the main group. It is believed that the base of this candi was extended in the middle of the ninth century in order to house another shrine. In so doing, the foundations were weakened and its ruin hastened. Close by on the other side of the

Dieng Plateau

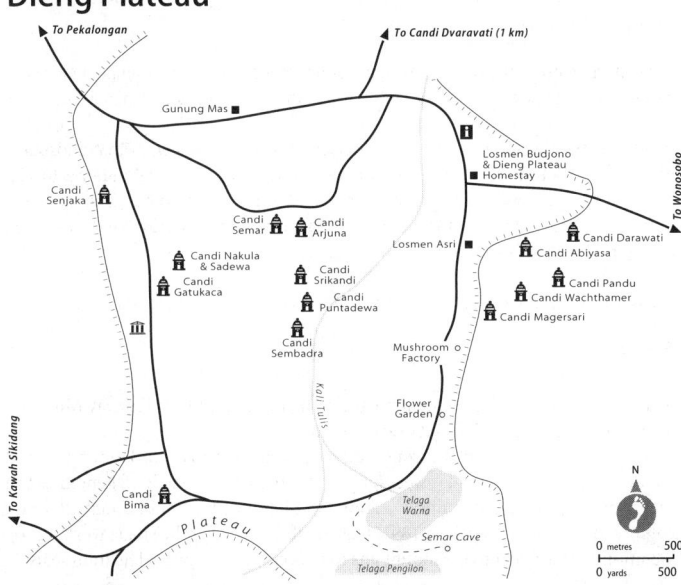

road is a rather unimpressive museum; more like a storehouse for sculptures of Hindu gods and lingam found on the plateau.

A 1 km walk south along this road leads to **Candi Bima**, built in a very different style, and unique in Java. The tower is a tall pyramid, with small heads in some of the niches on each layer. It shows strong stylistic links with the Orissan temples of East central India. It is thought that the architects must have had a plan of the Indian prototype, which they followed. The scale is very different, however, presumably because the builders had no way of knowing the proportions of the original. It has been vandalized with graffiti, but remains one of the most impressive monuments on the plateau, being considerably more elaborate than the others.

From Candi Bima turn west, and after another 1½-2 km the path arrives at **Kawah Sikidang**, bubbling mud pools, sulphurous odours and a scarred landscape. The **thermal springs** here are used to produce power, the geothermal station being just a short distance on from the springs. From Kawah Sikidang, walk back past Candi Bima, and turn left at the 'T' junction, 50m on from the temple. Less than a kilometre along this road is **Telaga Warna**, an emerald green **sulphur lake**. From here there is a path skirting the lake and leading to further sulphur lakes and the **Semar Cave** (ask for *Gua Semar*), among others. Close to Telaga Warna is a terraced flower garden, with such temperate plants as pansies, roses, marigolds and hydrangea. The garden is private. On past the mushroom factory, the road leads back to *Losmen Budjono*.

Excursions Ask a guide to accompany you on a 2 hour walk to the highest village on Java. If you leave at 0430, you will see spectacular views. A guide will cost you 5,000Rp.

Sleeping **D** *Gunung Mas*, Jl Raya, T92417. Opposite the road to the main temples, more expensive rooms with attached mandis and hot water, beautiful furniture – but otherwise much like the other places. **E-F** *Dieng Plateau Homestay*, definitely the best place to stay, rooms are clean and comfortable. Han the manager is very friendly and informative and speaks excellent English. Tours to the plateau are run from here. Recommended. **E-F** *Losmen Asri*, left from T-junction into the village from Wonosobo, rooms are adequate, but because this place is not so popular among backpackers it isn't such a mine of information as *Bu Jono* and the *Dieng Plateau Homestay*. **E-F** *Losmen Bu Jono*, Jl Raya, T22755. Restaurant, basic facilities with small rooms but friendly management and, like the *Dieng Plateau Homestay*, a good source of information.

If intending to stay overnight on the plateau, be sure to have some warm clothing as it gets very cold. One visitor reported that the losmen here have the coldest mandi water in Indonesia

Eating *Losmen Bu Jono*, Jl Raya, at intersection to Wonosobo road, cheap, simple Indonesian dishes, friendly atmosphere. *Dieng*, buffet style, with local dishes. Recommended.

Transport **Road Bus**: the bus stop is near the *Losmen Bu Jono*. Regular connections with **Wonosobo** 1 hr, **Yogya** and **Borobudur** (3 buses a day). It is also possible to reach **Pekalongan**, with difficulty, from Dieng – a trip of 105 km and 6 hrs. The Wonosobo-Dieng bus continues on to **Batur**. From there, there are **minibuses** to **Kalibening**, where it is possible to pick up an open topped van to **Pekalongan**.

26 km from Wonosobo

Directory **Banks** *Bank Rakyat Indonesia*, Jl Raya (next to Hotel Gunung Mas), will change US$ cash.

Ambarawa

Ambarawa would probably be on no one's itinerary, save for its Railway Museum. Even with the museum, it is not exactly popular.

The **Railway Museum** is through the town, past the road to Bandungan, and about 1 km off Jl Pemuda (it is well signposted). It is a charming, well kept museum set around the old Dutch railway station, and has a collection of about 12 steam engines, the oldest dating from 1891. It is possible to charter the single working cog locomotive and ride into the mountains to Bedono, 18 km away. The train seats 80 people and lunch is provided on the day-long outing. One day's notice required (write to: PJKA Wilayah Usaha Jawa, Jl MH Thamrin 3, Semarang, Jawa Tengah, Indonesia, or contact one of the main railway stations). ■ *Admission 500Rp. Open 0700-1630 Mon-Sun. It is a 1½ km walk from the centre of town to the museum.*

Few western or even domestic tourists find the need to spend the night in this small town, which is reflected in the fact it only contains 2 losmen, both within walking distance of the bus terminal. **F** *Hotel Aman*, Jl Pemuda 13, T0298-91791, basic, dark and decrepit, but even so this has to be pronounced the better choice. **F** *Melati Sederhana*, Jl Pemuda 37, very small dark rooms which can fit little more than a bed in them, and very shy staff who ran away when they saw the westerners coming.

Sleeping

Road Bus: to get to Ambarawa from Semarang, catch one of the direct 'medium' sized buses or catch a Semarang/Yogya bus, which pass through Ambarawa (45 mins from Semarang). Both leave from the Terboyo terminal. The road from Semarang to Ambarawa is notable for a row of trees just outside Semarang, which are home to thousands of white ibis. From Bandungan, just 6 km away, there are regular minibus connections.

Transport
32 km from Semarang, 6 km from Bandungan

Bandungan

Bandungan – yet another Javanese hill resort with a selection of wisma, losmen and one good hotel – is 1,000m above sea-level, on the slopes of the 2,050m-high Mount Ungaran. It is the most convenient place to stay when visiting the temples at Gedung Songo (see below) and is a good alternative base to Ambarawa, which is just 4 km, or a 500Rp bemo ride away.

*Phone code: 0298
Colour map 3, grid B3*

The Hindu temples of Gedung Songo are 7 km west of Bandungan, close to the village of **Duran**. The road to the site passes through an area of highland agriculture, with a great diversity of crops being cultivated – including such strange tropical sights as roses intercropped with cabbages. Set on the south slopes of Mount Ungaran at 1,200-1,300m, the temples of Gedung Songo – meaning 'nine buildings' in Javanese – are all Hindu and were probably built between 730 and 780.

Gedung Songo

The area has a number of volcanic vents which would have made it a revered site and probably explains the presence of these small candi, scattered over an area of several square kilometre. At weekends, the continuing magical and ritual importance of Gedung Songo becomes clear. Javanese come to the site to take the curative waters and to walk from complex to complex, carrying picnics to eat under the shady conifers. In the village of Duran, loudspeakers relay stories of the epics, drawing people under the spell of this magical place. The candis occupy one of the most spectacular positions of any group of temples in Java. The temperature is wonderfully cool after the plains, with mist characteristically hanging over the mountains behind.

Gedung Songo

The shrines are numbered 1-6, starting from the bottom. Temples 1, 2 and 3 lie on the east side of the deep ravine, through which runs a fast-flowing stream fed by a hot spring; 4, 5 and 6 lie on the western slopes. The main shrine in each group was dedicated to Siva. These temples became the prototype for subsequent Javanese Hindu temples. The sixth group is an excellent example; a square base is cut through by a stairway leading up to a portico on the west side of the building, which opens into a small square cella. The other three sides of the building are decorated by pilasters and a central niche which housed a statue. Three false storeys rise up above the central cella, decreasing in size and thus giving a deceptive impression of verticality. Group 3, though, is probably in the best state of preservation. The main Siva sanctuary shows the distinctive Javanese orientation of the Hindu gods: Durga, slaying the buffalo demon, on the northern face; elephant-headed Ganesh on the western wall (Ganesh is one of Siva's sons); and Agastya, a Saivite sage, on the southern wall. None of the shrines is particularly elaborate, although some display carvings of kala-makara heads and nagas. ■ *Admission 350Rp. Open 0700-1700 Mon-Sun. It is possible to walk around all the temples in 2-3 hrs, but it is exhausting at this altitude. An easier way of getting around is on horseback, 1½ hrs. Expect to pay about 2,500-3,000Rp for these old animals. To get there: catch a minibus towards Sumowono and get off after 3½ km at the junction, where a minor road runs steeply up the mountainside (it is signposted). The entrance is 2½ km up this road and ojeks wait at the bottom. If coming from Ambarawa, catch a minibus to Bandungan or through Bandungan to Sumowono.*

Sleeping Bandungan tends to be frequented by Indonesian tourists and there are many places to stay, including numerous cheap losmen. **A-B** *Rawa Pening Patrama*, Jl Pandanaran 33, west of Bandungan, T0298-711134. Restaurant (western cuisine), good pool, tennis courts. Large, cool rooms, with wonderful views and extensive gardens. Recommended. **D-E** *Trisukamaju*, Jl Widosari, very basic rooms. **D** *Girimulyo*, Jl Gitungan 79a, T0298-711175. Rather inaccessible, up a steep hill at the top end of town, but the rooms are OK once you've made it.

Eating Warungs and a few rumah makan.

Transport **Road** **Minibus**: regular connections with Ambarawa; from Semarang or Yogya, catch a bus
4 km from Ambarawa, or minibus to Ambarawa, then change.
35 km from Semarang

Salatiga

Phone code: 0298 Salatiga is a relatively small town by Indonesian standards, with a population of about
Colour map 3, grid B3 80,000. It is situated halfway between Semarang and Solo in the foothills of Mount Merabu, 600m above sea level. For a taste of unspoilt Java, this is an excellent place to visit. The locals are enormously friendly and welcoming, and the numerous churches and **mosques** in town make wandering the streets a rewarding experience. A large **market** stretching along Jl Jend Sudirman sells goods from good quality T-shirts to foodstuffs – although recent visitors have warned been to be wary of pickpockets. Salatiga supports a **university** – the Satya Wacana Christian University (SWCU) – with its campus situated on Jl Diponegoro. The SWCU runs a one month intensive Indonesian language and culture course, which is very popular with Australians. Its hostel, or Asrama, on Jl Kartini is an excellent gathering place to meet people and make friends.

The July-August dry season is the **best time to visit**, climatically speaking. However, this is also the period when the Satya Wacana Christian University holds its one month intensive Indonesian language and culture course, and 100-120 visitors (most from Australia) book up the town's hotels.

Sleeping **B-C** *Beringin*, Jl Jend Sudirman 160 (in the heart of town), T81129/61082. A/c, restaurant, TV and shower, breakfast included in rate, large and very clean rooms, staff are helpful and friendly and some English is spoken at the front desk. **C** *Maya*, Jl Kartini 15A (10 mins from town centre), T23179/23429. Restaurant, price includes breakfast, no baths or mosquito nets but clean, and staff are very helpful, very little English spoken though.

There are numerous Chinese and Indonesian rumah makan and warung in town. **Eating**
Mid-range to cheap *Kentucky Fried Chicken*, Jl Diponegoro. *Café Maya*, at the Maya
Hotel, Jl Kartini 15A, a good selection of Salatigan food, particularly good bakmi and nasi goreng, fresh juices and bintang available. *Pak Por*, Jl Kartini (near Café Maya), specializes in
chicken dishes from excellent *ayam bakar* (burnt chicken) to *ayam goreng* (fried chicken).

Local Dokars: charge about 4,000Rp for a 5-min ride. **Angkutans**: run along fixed routes **Transport**
(destination displayed on the roof) and can be flagged down. **Taxis** and **minibuses** can be *41 km north of Solo, 46*
booked at the front desks of the 2 hotels listed above. *km south of Semarang*

Long distance Bus: regular connection with **Semarang** and **Solo**. **Taxi**: connections
with **Semarang**.

Banks *Panin Bank*, Jl Diponegoro (opposite the Satya Wacana Christian University [SWCU] campus). **Directory**
The bank accepts Thomas Cook TCs in US and Australian dollars. **Communications Telephone:**
Wartel, Jl Diponegoro (next to the university campus) and Hotel Beringin both offer international calls.

Central Java's north coast

Tegal

Tegal is a north coast town with a history that belies its small size. Manageable, with *Phone code: 0283*
good and reasonable accommodation and a breezy, coastal air, it is an attractive *Colour map 3, grid A3*
alternative stopping-off point on the north coast route. 'Sights', at least in the formalized sense of the word, are pretty thin on the ground in Tegal. The **Mesjid
Agung Tegal**, on Jl Jend A Yani, exhibits classic Javanese lines. More interesting for
many though is likely to be the
Pelabuhan Tegal – Tegal Harbour at
the end of Jl Veteran – where traditional
perahu moor to load and unload their
cargoes of dry goods.

Tegal

A *Bahari Inn*, Jl Kolonel Soegiono 172, **Sleeping**
T52222, F58909. A/c, restaurant, pool, a
modern hotel 3 km west of the town centre,
with 80 modern and comfortable rooms, an
excellent pool and geared mainly to the convention market, usually empty. **D-E** *Hotel
Semeru*, Jl Jend A Yani 168, T61226. Simple
hotel in the centre of town, some attached
bathrooms, no hot water, basic.

Road Bus: regular connections with **Transport**
Cirebon and **Bandung** to the west, and *52 km from Cirebon,*
with **Surabaya** via **Pekalongan** and *57 km from*
Semarang to the east. *Pekalongan*

Banks *Bank Bumi Daya*, intersection of Jl **Directory**
Jend Sutoyo and Jl Diponegoro.
Communications Post Office: Jl Pemuda
(near the port).

Pekalongan

Phone code: 0285
Colour map 3, grid A3

Pekalongan is best known for the distinctive **batik** that is produced here and is known by the sobriquet 'Kota Batik'. Pastel shades, fine designs and floral and animal motifs are all characteristic of the area's work. There is a **Batik Museum** at Jl Majapahit 10, with a small display of characteristic designs from various areas of Java, along with a few tools. The museum is on the outskirts of town to the southwest of the centre, tucked away along with government offices and not far from the Balai Kota. Get there by becak and ask for **museum batik** near the *Balai Kota*. If the building is closed, ask the caretaker to unlock it. ■ *Open (in theory) 0900-1400 Mon-Sat.* Most of the best batik produced in Pekalongan and hereabouts is sold to outlets in Jakarta and elsewhere. There is surprisingly little good quality cloth available. The **Banjarsari market** on Jl Sultan Agung, for example, sells mostly low quality stuff, but is worth exploring. The smaller boutiques do have better cloth, and it can also be bought from the batik-making villages around town (see Excursions). Indeed, there is little reason to come to Pekalongan except to see, and perhaps to buy, batik – although the town does make a good stopping-off point on the north coast route.

The **town square** is off the main road, a short distance along Jl HM Wahid Hasim, where there is a **tourist office**, *Dinas Pariwisata*. ■ *Open 0700-1330, Mon-Sat*. The local mosque – a strange amalgam of lighthouse (the minaret), castle (the crenellated gateway) and Javanese (the tiered roof) – is situated on the west side of the square. There are also some **notable buildings** on the large roundabout to the north of town. The residence of the former Dutch resident of Pekalongan at Jl Diponegoro 1 is now the governor's office. The Post Office, also on Jl Diponegoro and close by, is housed in another impressive colonial structure. Pekalongan is also said to have the biggest **fish auction** in Java. Few tourists venture here, but because it is on the main north route between Surabaya and Jakarta, it has a good selection of losmen and restaurants.

North of town is **Pekalongan Port** and **Pasir Kencana**. The latter is marketed as a coastal resort, but the water here is usually too dirty to swim without fear of infection.

Excursions **Kedungwuni**, a town 9 km to the south of town, is a centre of *batik* production and sale where the production process can be observed. ■ *There are regular colts from town*. Another batik village, less well-known and rather harder to get to, is **Pekajangan**, 7 km south of town and off the road to Kedungwuni. Again, all the processes of batik making can be observed and fine cloth purchased. ■ *Getting there: no bemos run to Pekajangan, but it can be reached by a long (and expensive) becak ride or by walking from the road.*

Sleeping **B** *Nirwana*, Jl Dr Wahidin 11 (east side of town), T41691, F61841. Some a/c, restaurant, large pool, most luxurious place in town looking rather like a 1970s-style hotel, rooms are a little worn but very good for a small place like Pekalongan, professionally run, price includes breakfast. Recommended. **B-C** *Istana*, Jl Gajah Mada 23-25, T23581, F21252. Some a/c, popular with Indonesian business travellers but inconvenient location 2 km west of town centre, characterless small rooms, with high grand beds. Modern hotel with hot water and attached bathrooms, little to recommend it other than providing a clean room and bed. **C** *Jayadipa Hotel*, Jl Raya Boros 29, T/F24938. Some a/c, new hotel, good value with large clean rooms pleasantly furnished, but inconvenient location out of town towards Semarang. **C-D** *Hayam Wuruk*, Jl Hayam Wuruk 152-154, T41823. Some a/c, clean rooms with cool tiled floors and elaborate heavy furniture, the best rooms are outside rather than in the main block, central location, good value, no hot water but well-run and friendly. Recommended. **D-E** *Losmen Sari Dewi*, Jl Hayam Wuruk 1, T21248. Some a/c, large rooms with lovely furniture, excellent value, friendly. Recommended. **E** *Asia Losmen*, Jl KH Wahid Hasyim 49, T22125. Well sign-posted, rooms are rather poor but this is compensated for by the friendly management. **E-F** *Pekalongan*, Jl Hayam Wuruk 158, T21021. Old building with some character, next to the *Hayam Wuruk Hotel*, reasonable rooms with numerous beds in each room, good budget accommodation. **E-F** *Hotel Damai*, Jl Gajah Mada 7, T22968, located opposite the train station, most rooms are clean, bright and cheerful, excellent for this price.

Cheap *Maduroso*, Jl Merdeka, Indonesian. *Purimas Bakery*, intersection of Jl Hayam Wuruk and Jl KH Wahid Hasim, for the usual range of bright-coloured sticky cakes, cold drinks and coffee. *Remaja*, Jl Dr Cipto 17, serves Indonesian, international and Chinese (Chinese food recommended). *Nirwana Restaurant*, pricey but excellent.

Eating

Cinemas *Gajah Mada Theatre*, Jl Gajah Mada, a/c cinema showing films with English language soundtracks in centre of town.

Entertainment

Batik Pekalongan is famous as a centre of batik production and sale. The style is very different from that of Solo and Yogya; designs are fine, with intricate representations of flowers and birds. Colours tend to be softer, using pastel shades. There are many shops along the main road, Jl Hayam Wuruk, such as *Batik Puspa*, *Queen Batik* and *Batik Aneka*. *BL Batik*, at Jl KHM Mansyer 87, sells good quality made-up garments and lengths of cloth. *Jacky Batik*, Jl Surabaya 5A/1, is also a shop selling mostly high quality made up garments and is rather expensive. For cheap, low quality batik the best place to look around is the Pasar Banjarsari on Jl Sultan Agung, in the centre of town. Salesmen also hawk batik direct to hotel residents: again, most of the batik is poor, low quality cloth. To see the various stages of the batik-making process, it is best to visit one of the batik villages outside town (see 'Excursions'). **Shopping centres** *Pasar Raya Sri Ratu*, Jl Gajah Mada.

Shopping

Swimming Non-residents can swim at the *Nirwana Hotel*, Jl Dr Wahidin 11, admission is 8,000Rp for a full day.

Sports

Pekalongan

Tour operators *Amatama*, Jl Mansyer 25, T81121.

Transport **Local** Orange bemos (Angkutan kotas) are the main form of local transport. Plethora of becaks.

384 km from Jakarta, 101 km from Semarang, 409 km from Surabaya

Train The train station is just to the west of the centre of town at Jl Gajah Mada 10. Regular connections with **Jakarta** and **Surabaya** on slow daytime trains, but note that is is difficult to get a seat, so standing is usually the only option.

Road Bus: the intercity bus terminal is 2 km to the southeast of the town centre, near the intersection of Jl Dr Wahidin and Jl Dr Sutomo. Bemos constantly link the terminal with the town centre (500Rp). Connections with **Semarang** 2 hrs, **Bandung**, **Cirebon** 4 hrs (change at Tegal if necessary), **Solo**, **Dieng**, **Kudus**, **Demak**, **Sumedang**, **Tasik Malaya**, **Jakarta** and other major centres. **Minibus**: offices are concentrated on the main town square and they offer services to most major centres, including **Jakarta**, **Semarang**, **Bandung** and **Yogyakarta**.

Directory **Banks** Bank Central Asia, Jl Diponegoro. *Bank Danamon*, Jl Hayam Wuruk. *Exspor Inspor Indonesia*, Jl Hayam Wuruk 5. *Lippo Bank*, Jl Hayam Wuruk. **Communications** General Post Office: Jl Cendrawasih 1. **Internet**: Post Office on Jl Cendrawasih 1 charges 5,000Rp for 1 hr, but a slow server is almost guaranteed.

Semarang

Phone code: 024
Colour map 3, grid A3

Semarang is one of the oldest cities in Indonesia, and was the seat of the Dutch Governor of the northeast Provinces. It is situated between the shore and a small ridge of mountains and, consequently, is very hot. The town is divided into two parts: the coastal lowland, where most of businesses and industrial activities are to be found; and an inland, hilly, residential area. As one of colonial Java's more important trading centres, it has a reasonable collection of Dutch-era buildings, as well as Chinese shophouses and one or two impressive European-style structures. It is twinned with the Australian city of Brisbane.

Ins and outs

Getting there Compared with towns like Yogya and Solo, Semarang is comparatively rarely visited by tourists. But it is a more important commercial centre and is well connected. **Ahmad Yani domestic airport** is 5 km west of town, and there are flights to destinations in Java and further afield in the Indonesian archipelago. **Tawang train station**, just north of the city centre, is the main railway terminal, and there are connections along the north coast line with Jakarta and Surabaya. The **Terboyo bus terminal** is 3½ km from the city centre to the east and there are departures to most destinations in Java. Tickets can be booked at bus offices in town. Semarang is also an important port and *Pelni* vessels dock at Tanjung Emas, 2 km north of the city centre.

Getting around While it is possible to walk around the commercial heart of Semarang, many of the places of interest require a journey. Buses and colts ply fixed routes and there are also becaks – although these are banned from the main thoroughfares. Metered taxis are also available, which can be chartered by the hour, half day or day.

The **Central Java Tourist Office**, *Dinas Pariwisata*, Jl Imam Bonjol 209, T510924, is contained in a grand old building on the square with Tugu Muda and the staff are very helpful. Open 0700-1400 Mon-Thur, 0700-1100 Fri, 0700-1230 Sat. **Semarang Municipal Tourist Office**, *Dinas Pariwisata Kodia Semarang*, Jl Srivijaya 29, T311620, is at the old site of the zoo; colts drive down Jl Sriwijaya.

History

The city was ceded to the Dutch VOC in 1677 by the Mataram king Amangkurat I, in lieu of debts. A base was established along the coast at Jepara (which was already a trading centre), with additional trading-posts at Semarang, as well as at Surabaya, Rembang, Demak and Tegal. However, it was not until 1705 that the VOC finally brought Semarang firmly under its control. Only then did the Dutch move their headquarters here, and the town gradually grew in commercial influence.

Semarang's usefulness as a port waned with the gradual silting up of the harbour, and by the 19th century, the city had been eclipsed as Java's premier port by Surabaya. Even so, Semarang remains the largest city in Central Java. It is an important commercial centre with a population of over a million, a third of whom are thought to be of Chinese extraction. In 1741, the Chinese of Semarang responded to the murder of their kinsmen in Batavia (see page 80) by, in their turn, attacking the Dutch of Semarang. This turned out to be a misjudgement. The VOC, with the help of Cakraningrat IV of Madura, defeated the Chinese and slaughtered all those they could lay their hands on.

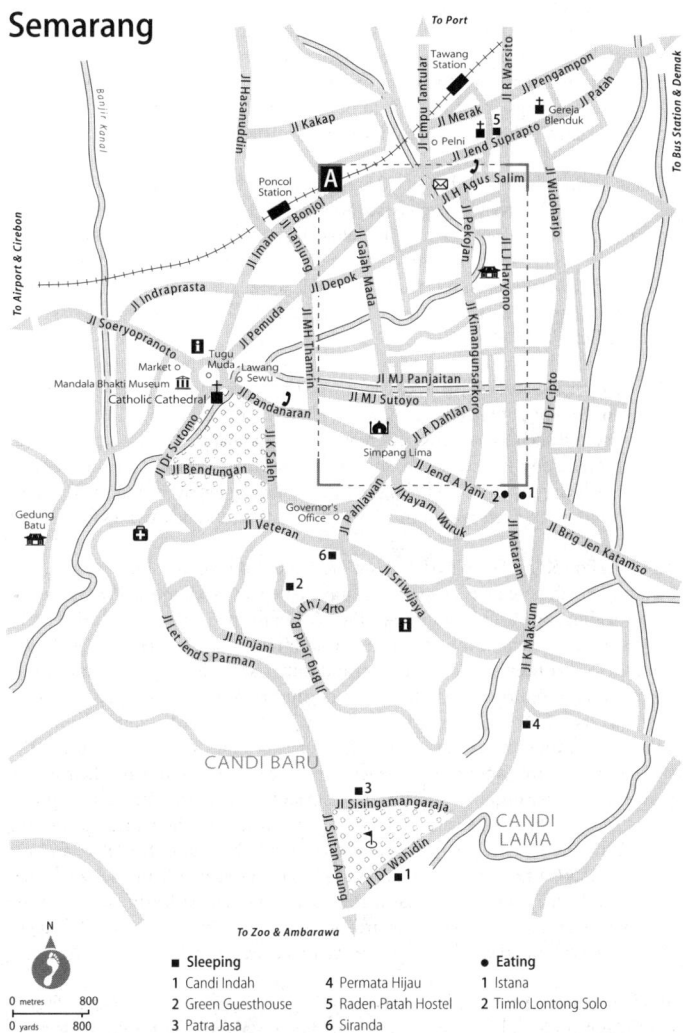

Semarang

- **Sleeping**
  1 Candi Indah
  2 Green Guesthouse
  3 Patra Jasa
  4 Permata Hijau
  5 Raden Patah Hostel
  6 Siranda

- **Eating**
  1 Istana
  2 Timlo Lontong Solo

Related Map:
Semarang Centre, *page 227*

Sights

Architecture Even though Semarang seems to be taking the shopping plaza route to urban development, Islamic, Chinese and European influences are still in evidence and there are numerous beautiful buildings dotted among the streets. Indeed, in parts at least, it is one of Java's most attractive cities. The best area to explore is that north and east from the Post Office on Jl Pemuda (itself a notable building). Roads with interesting buildings include Jl Jend Suprapto, Jl Kepodang, Jl Garuda, Jl Suari and Jl Merak, and the maze of streets cutting across and between these roads. **Gereja Blenduk** (*gereja* meaning church, *blenduk* meaning domed) – the Immanuel Protestant Church – on Jl Jend Suprapto 32 is the oldest church in Central Java, and the second oldest on the whole island. Built in 1753, and rather Wren-like in appearance, it is in the shape of a Greek cross fronted by four pillars. It has a handsome classical portico, a faded copper dome and, inside, a Baroque organ and pulpit. Opposite is a fine 1920s-style commercial building, the offices of Jiwasraya Assurance. Unfortunately, many of the buildings in this area have been abandoned, and most are in a state of deterioration. Before long, they may disappear entirely. For architectural enthusiasts, other buildings of interest are to be found in the hills to the south, an area known as **Candi**, where there are some wonderful decaying villas.

Tanjung Emas About 2 km north of the old town is Tanjung Emas – the port area. This is great fun. Elegant and impressively large *pinisi* schooners from Kalimantan, Sulawesi and elsewhere in the archipelago dock here, to unload their cargoes and re-provision. Wood is unloaded while goods like cars and cement are taken on board for the journey back to the Outer Islands. It is usually possible to walk through the port gates and around the quaysides. It is easiest to get up here by becak – ask for 'pelabuhan Tanjung Emas'.

Markets There are several attractive markets in town. The biggest market area is the **Pasar Johar**, to the south of Jl Agus Salim, where clothes, fruit, vegetables, kitchen equipment, rice and such like are sold. More interesting perhaps is the area of street-side stalls further along Jl Agus Salim and to the north, and especially along Jl MPU Tantular which runs north from Jl Agus Salim, following the river (well, open sewer). Traders and stall holders lay out small collections of clothes and carvings for sale.

Sam Poo Kong Temple *The area around the temple is low-lying and in 1992 there was a 2m-high storm surge, which caught many people asleep in their rickety shacks: 100 died*

The Sam Poo Kong Temple dates from 1772 and is one of the oldest on Java. The blending of Chinese and Javanese cultural elements is seen in the *dvarapala*, the club-wielding, pot-bellied bouncers either side of the main entrance. Buried in the temple is an assistant of the great Chinese admiral and adventurer Cheng Ho. He was said to have been so taken with Java and with Islam that he opted to stay behind when the ships returned to China. His very Muslim coffin lies shielded from view within a very Chinese pavilion (a high relief image of him, bearded and with junks on either side, fronts the coffin). Take off your shoes and walk behind the coffin through the narrow doorway to the left – people come here to have their wishes granted, a creative fusion of Taoism, animism and Islam. Hence the temple's popular name, the Chinese-Muslim Temple. A third name for the temple is **Gedung Batu**. This refers to the cave-cum-sanctuary built in honour of Sam Poo, an early Ming dynasty Chinese envoy who died in 1435. He travelled to Siam, Melaka, Sumatra and Sri Lanka – and twice to Java. The 'cave' is a small, dark artificial grotto (no shoes), with an alter of no particular artistic significance. ■ *Getting there: take a yellow minibus to Banjir Kanal (400Rp) and then either walk or take a becak (2,000Rp).*

Simpang Lima Simpang Lima (junction of five roads) is the huge main square in the centre of town. On the northwest side of the square is the modern **Mesjid Baiturahan**. On most other corners seem to be the greatest concentration of shopping plazas in central Java (see 'Shopping', below). In the evenings, boys and young men play football on the large expanse of grass in the centre. The **Tugu Muda** monument marks the centre of another square, about 1½ km northwest from Simpang Lima. The monument commemorates the five-day battle of Indonesian republican youth against Japanese troops at the end of the war. The square is surrounded by grand government buildings built by the Dutch (they planned more), the largest being the **Lawang Sewu** – the building of a thousand doors with its distinctive domed twin towers. A second Dutch era building contains the unremarkable **Mandala Bhakti Museum** (aka Museum Perjuangan) on Jl Sugiyopranoto. This used to be the Raad Van Yustitue, but now recounts an episode in Indonesia's struggle for independence with a motley collection of photographs, weapons and other memorabilia. ■ *Open 0800-1400 Tue-Thu, 0800-1130 Fri, 0800-1230 Sat, 0800-1300 Sun*. Another museum, rather farther out of town close to the airport on Jl Supratman, is the **Pronggo Warsito Museum**. It displays historical, cultural and archaeological pieces.

South of Jl H Agus Salim, off Jl Pekojan, Chinatown also contains some interesting buildings, notably those bordering the canal. There are a number of Chinese temples tucked away here, including the Confucian **Thay Kak Sie Pagoda**, along Gang Lombok. The main temple was built in 1772. Not far away and also on Jl H Agus Salim, opposite the *Metro Grand Park Hotel*, is the **Pasar Johar**, a good place to wander during the day and in the evening. The **zoo** (with botanical garden and recreation park) can be found south of town in Tinjomoyo, off Jl Teuku Umar. ■ *Getting there: charter a colt (3,000-5,000Rp) or take town bus (Bus Damri) No 04 (400Rp).*

Chinatown

Excursions

Demak is a historic town on the road to Kudus and Surabaya, 25 km from Semarang. Raden Patah established the Sultanate of Demak in 1500, when it became the first Islamic Kingdom on Java. Islam was introduced via India by Muslim traders and Demak, as one of Java's most important ports, was rapidly converted to the new religion. The town gained a reputation for the community of scholars or *pesantren* who established themselves here, and pilgrims would travel from all over Java and beyond to be taught by these holy men. Demak remained powerful until the end of the 16th century, when power shifted south to Mataram, near Yogyakarta. The oldest mosque in Central Java can be found in the town square, on the Semarang side of the centre. Founded by the nine *walis* (the first Muslim evangelists in Java) in 1478, the **Agung Demak Mosque** has the characteristic three-tiered roof of North Java. In the north part of the mosque is a graveyard of the family of Sultan Demak and the **tomb** of one of the nine walis is to be found here: Sunan Kalijaga. The mosque is an important pilgrimage spot and souvenir stalls line the outside walls, where posters of the nine walis can be bought. The main street leading from the square north towards Kudus, **Jl Sultan Patah**, is lined by houses with graceful, sweeping tiled roofs. These are the distinctive, traditional houses of the Kudus area – *rumah adat Kudus*. The **market** is also on this street marked by the presence of an over-sized starfruit.
■ *Getting there: by bus from Semarang's Terboyo station on Jl Patah (get there by town bus – Bus Damri – or bemo); the Demak station is on the Semarang side of town, a walk of less than 500m to the main square.*

Demak

Kudus, 19 km on from Demak and 50 km in total from Semarang, is another historically interesting town (see page 231). Another 30 km northwest from Kudus is the **woodcarving port of Jepara** (see page 233), where it is possible to catch boats to the **Karimunjawa Islands** (see page 235).

North of Semarang

Ambarawa town and its **Railway Museum** (*kereta api*) are 32 km from Semarang and 4 km off the main Semarang-Solo road. See page 216 for details. ■ *Getting there: catch one of the 'medium' sized buses, or catch a Semarang/Yogya bus, which pass through Ambarawa (45 mins from Semarang). Both leave from the Terboyo terminal.*

South of Semarang

The Hindu temples of **Gedung Songo** (see page 217) lie 13 km from Ambarawa, past the hill resort of **Bandungan**. ■*Getting there: by bus from Semarang to Ambarawa, 45 mins, and then one of the regular minibuses that climb up to Bandungan.*

Tours Tour companies in Semarang run day tours around the sights of the city, as well as to Borobudur, the Dieng Plateau, Kudus and Demak, Gedung Songo, Solo and cultural tours to, for example, Jepara (a woodcarving town). 'Teak plantation tours' to Cepu, 160 km east of Semarang: travelling in a steam locomotive, the tourist visits teak plantations in different stages of development. Contact Perum Perhutani, Jl Pehlawan 151, Semarang, T311611.

Essentials

Sleeping
■ on maps page 223 & opposite

AL *Graha Santika*, Jl Pandanaran 116-120, T413115, F413113. A/c, restaurant, pool, multi-storey hotel with central location overlooking Simpang Lima, facilities including a fitness centre. Efficient and reasonably luxurious place. **AL** *Ciputra*, Simpang Lima, T449888, F447888, www.hotelciputra.com, mailsmg@hotelciputra.com A/c, restaurants, pool. New hotel facing onto Simpang Lima. Facilities include a rooftop pool, business and fitness centres. Luxurious. Discounts and special deals available. **AL** *Patrajasa*, Jl Sisingamangaraja, PO Box 8, T314441, F314448. A/c, restaurant, pool, good views, good facilities, sophisticated, if now rather dated, not very convenient for city centre, odd nagas flank the main entrance looking rather like Basil Brush. **A** *Santika*, Jl A Yani 189, T412491, F414083, santika@idola.net.id Part of the same chain as *Graha Santika* – so it is efficient but featureless.

A-B *Metro*, Jl H Agus Salim 2-4, T547371, F510863. A/c, restaurant, fitness and business centres. A square, brown lump of a hotel with no redeeming architectural features. Since our last visit they have smartened the place up a bit, but the word 'characterful' still isn't the first to spring to mind. However, it has a good central location and the rooms are OK. Worth considering. **A-B** *Siranda*, Jl Diponegoro 1, T/F313271. A/c, early 1970s-style hotel, built on the hill overlooking Semarang with 60 time-warp rooms, but well maintained considering its age, and the rooms have good views (as the blurb puts it 'the hotel with view') and are reasonable value, price includes breakfast. **B** *Permata Hijau*, Jl Dr Wahidin 14-66, T315671. A/c, new development in Candi Baru, rather like a housing estate, rooms are large and cool, geared mainly to people with own transport, offering discounts to entice custom, very comfortable.

B-C *Dibya Puri*, Jl Pemuda 11, T547821, F544934. A/c, large restaurant. Colonial hotel which, if it doesn't get a facelift soon, will crumble to nothingness. As a result, rather scruffy, with odd mixture of modern and old, but central location and competitive rates. The best rooms are those at the back around a leafy courtyard with small sitting areas, price includes breakfast. **B-C** *Green Guesthouse*, Jl Kesambi 7, Candi Baru, T312642. Some a/c, attractive old-style hotel with large rooms (check the a/c though) and fine views looking south from Semarang, especially from the main terrace, efficiently run, out of town along quiet residential street in Candi Baru, price includes breakfast. Recommended. **B-C** *Quirin Hotel*, Jl Gajah Mada 44-52, T547063. A/c, restaurant. (This place used to be called the *Queen Hotel*, but the government forced the management to indigenize the name and they came up with *Quirin* as an alternative.) It's a great little hotel and one of the best places in this price category. The 40-odd rooms are set back from the road on 2 levels around a courtyard. They are spacious, clean, with good bathrooms (hot water), TV and minibar. Even the economy rooms, which aren't as light and airy, are good. The room rate includes a good buffet breakfast in the attached restaurant. Recommended. **B-D** *Hotel Djelita*, Jl MT Haryono, T543891, F545818. A small modern hotel close to a busy intersection. The better rooms come with a/c, TV, minibar and the rate includes breakfast. With cheaper rooms you only get tea/coffee. Hardly charming or characterful, but the rooms are OK. **B-D** *Candi Baru*, Jl Rinjani 21, T315272. A/c, old and attractive hotel which could do with some love and care, but with much more character than modern places. **B-D** *Telomoyo*, Jl Gajah Mada 138, T545436, F547037. Some a/c, modern, clean and comfortable, rooms are large and airy, tree-filled courtyard, friendly, efficient service.

Semarang centre

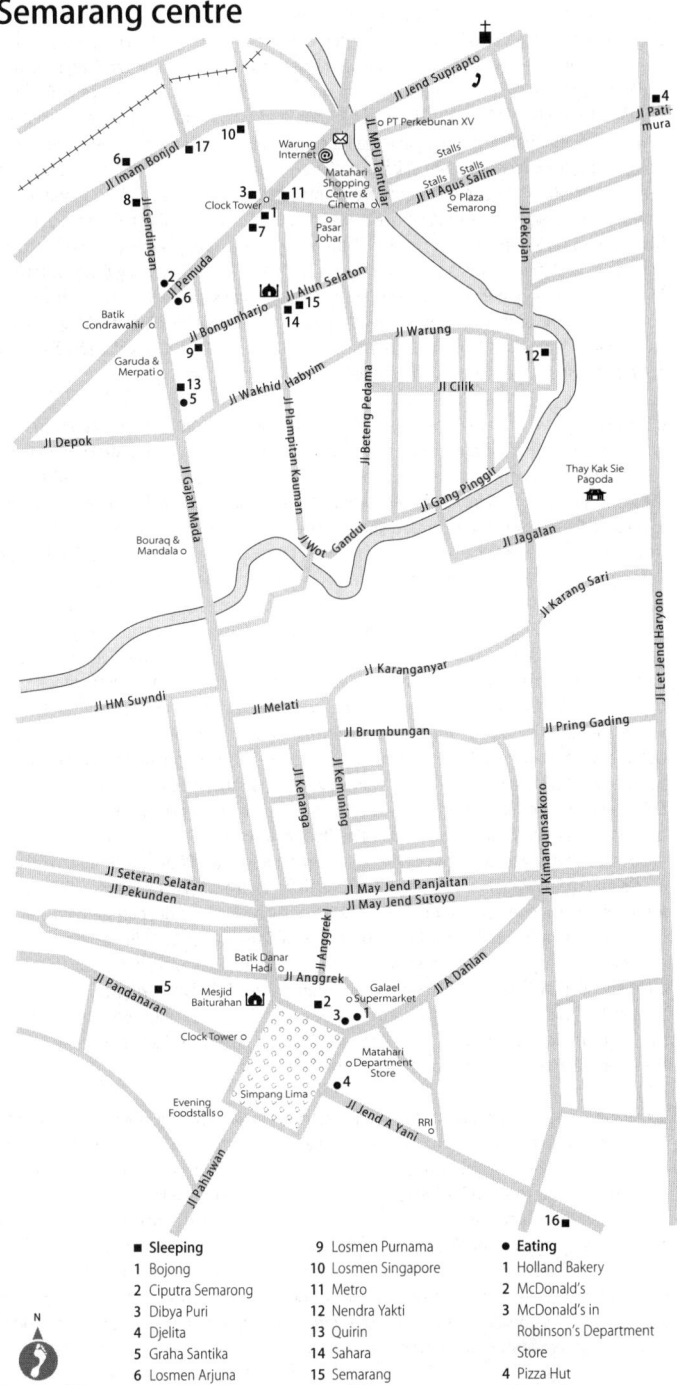

■ Sleeping	9 Losmen Purnama	● Eating
1 Bojong	10 Losmen Singapore	1 Holland Bakery
2 Ciputra Semarong	11 Metro	2 McDonald's
3 Dibya Puri	12 Nendra Yakti	3 McDonald's in
4 Djelita	13 Quirin	Robinson's Department
5 Graha Santika	14 Sahara	Store
6 Losmen Arjuna	15 Semarang	4 Pizza Hut
7 Losmen Bahagia	16 Sontika	5 Sarimanis
8 Losmen Martanova	17 Surya	6 Toko Oen

C *Bali*, Jl Imam Bonjol 146, T511761. Some a/c, not a very convenient location, rooms are clean, no hot water, no toilet seats, but acceptable for a night or two, Balinese split gates frame the entrance way and a leafy courtyard helps to add some character. **C** *Bukit Asri*, Jl Setiabudi 5, T475743. A/c, 4 km from town on road to Ambarawa, clean rooms. **C** *Candi Indah*, Jl Dr Wahidin 112, T312912, F312515. Some a/c, old house on a hill in Candi Baru, rooms are a little dark but the hotel is well run and maintained, located several kilometres from city centre. **C** *Nendra Yakti*, Jl Pekojan, Gang Pinggir 68, T544202, F550593. Some a/c, central location in Chinatown, rooms are comparatively airy and also clean, good value, although the block seems to have been designed by a prison architect. **C** *Surya*, Jl Imam Bonjol 28, T544250. Some a/c. A small modern hotel. Rooms have attached showers with no hot water, well maintained and the a/c rooms are good value. Tendency towards Imelda Marcos-eque interior decor as you work your way up towards the VIP rooms. Fun if you like your pillows pink and lacey. **C-E** *Hotel Rahayu*, Jl Imam Bonjol 35-37, T542532. All rooms have attached mandi and the more expensive include a/c and TV. This is a place for sleeping, not for enjoying – the rooms are functional and reasonably clean.

E *Losmen Arjuna*, Jl Imam Bonjol 51, T544186. Old style house with shutters and tiled roof. Rooms are noisy at the front, but clean enough and popular with locals. Attached mandis, convenient location for train station, good value, atmospheric and well maintained. One of the better places at this price. **E** *Hotel Bahagia*, Jl Pemuda 16-18, small losmen in centre of town used largely by Indonesian travelling salesmen. Shared mandis, scruffy with dirty mattresses – and not even a bargain. There are much better places to stay at this price. **E** *Hotel Bojong*, Jl Pemuda 8. There is little to recommend this place other than a central location. It is squeezed between a main intersection and a mosque. Rooms are small, dark and generally dirty. **E** *Losmen Singapore*, Jl Imam Bonjol 12, T543757. Rooms set attractively around a courtyard, atmospheric. Unfortunately the rooms themselves are rather grubby, shared bathroom. **E** *Losmen Tanjung*, Jl Tanjung 9-11, old Dutch era house, friendly management but away from town centre near an industrial complex (which operates at night). Cheaper rooms are rather fly-blown. **E-F** *Losmen Martanova*, Jl Gendingan 11. Small losmen in a Dutch-era, single-storeyed, tile-roofed villa. Rooms are, as usual, arranged around the back, but they are dark and none too clean, with shared mandis that could do with a good scrub. **E-F** *Losmen Purnama*, Jl Bangunharjo 96. This is the best of the cheap places near the centre of town. It is situated 50m down a small lane (too narrow for cars) which runs off Jl Pemuda (look for Bank Niaga on Jl Pemuda – the lane is almost opposite). Rooms, with shared mandi, are OK and the management are friendlier than most, with a family atmosphere. **E-F** *Raden Patah Hotel*, Jl Let Jen Suprapto 48, T511328. A small hotel in the old part of town, not far from the Gereja Blenduk. The building itself is a Dutch-era villa with a veranda and over-hanging eaves. The rooms, some with attached mandi, are plain but clean, the management friendly and it is well priced. Recommended. **E-F** *Hotel Sahara*, Jl Alun-alun Selatan 14. Small, cheap and rather grubby little hotel, close to the mosque in the centre of town. **F** *Hotel Semarang*, Jl Alun-alun Selatan 12A. Right next to the *Sahara Hotel*, and much the same: dark rooms, rather grubby, close to the mosque.

Eating

The Semarang speciality is 'bandeng' – a smoked fish which can be seen displayed on many a restaurant sign

Semarang has, seemingly, more restaurants per square inch than any other town in Java. Jl Gajah Mada and Jl HM Thamrin, which run parallel to one another north-south, have restaurants serving virtually every variety of Asian food (particularly Chinese). In the evenings, the best place to eat is at one of the many **foodstalls** which set up along the south end of Jl Gajah Mada and the north end of Jl Pahlawan, both leading into the large square (Simpang Lima) dominated by the massive Matahari shopping complex. These roadside restaurants, protected by awnings, specialize in particular types of cuisine and food: seafood, Javanese food, Minang food, saté and so on. The awnings are clearly labelled with the specialities of the house and the food is usually cheap, fresh and excellent. Another possibility is to try the *Pasar Johor Yaik* opposite the *Metro Hotel*, at the northeast end of Jl Pemuda, where excellent foodstall food is also available.

Indonesian Cheap and very cheap: *Rumah Makan Gajah Mada*, Jl Gajah Mada (near intersection with Jl Wahid Hasyim), excellent Chinese food in a/c splendour. *Tan Goei*, Jl

Tanjung 25, also serves Chinese food and ice-creams, popular. **Toko Oen**, Jl Pemuda 52 (north from intersection with Jl Gajah Mada), reasonable Indonesian food, good variety of ice-creams, some European food, all served in moth-eaten colonial splendour with rather incongruous polystyrene palms. The menu includes fried frogs, lamb chops, tournedos grillé and rather dry Dutch pastries (the best of the latter are those filled with nut paste). **Nglaras Roso**, Jl Haryono 701. Recommended. **Timlo Lontong Solo**, Jl Jend A Yani 182, Javanese.

Other Asian cuisine Cheap: *Miyako*, Jl Semeru VI/16, T475805, claimed by locals to be the best Japanese restaurant in Semarang, *Sabu-Sab* especially recommended. **Istana**, Jl Haryono 836, Chinese and international food. **Pringgading**, Jl Pringgading 54 off Jl LJ Haryono, excellent Chinese seafood. **Seoul Palace**, Jl Gajah Mada 99B.

International Cheap: *Sukarasa*, Jl Ungaran, French food.

Fast food The greatest concentration of fast food joints is around Simpang Lima, including *McDonald's* next to Robinson's; *KFC* in the Mal Ciputra; and *Pizza Hut* next to the Matahari Department Store. There is another *McDonald's* in the centre of town to the north, at the intersection of Jl Gajah Mada and Jl Pemuda.

Foodstalls *Simpang Raya*, Jl Imam Bonjol 40, reasonable Padang food. *Pasar Johar*, Jl HA Salim. **Bakeries** *Toko Oen*, Jl Pemuda 52, small bakery attached to this colonial-era restaurant (see above). Modest collection of cakes and pastries. *Sarimanis*, Jl Gajah Mada 56, a traditional Indonesian bakery with a few tables and a good selection of squidgy bread and fluorescent cakes. Right next to the *Quirin/Queen Hotel*. **Danish Bakery**, Jl Pandanaran. **Wijaya Bakery**, Jl Pemuda 38. **Holland Bakery**, Jl A Dahlan (close to Simpang Lima, behind Robinson's), usual range of Indonesian plastic cakes, along with savouries including burgers.

Bars

Karaoke: Jl KH Wahid Hasyim 121.

Entertainment

Cinemas *Gajah Mada*, Simpang Lima; *Manggala*, Jl Gajah Mada 119; *Studio 21*, *Citra Land Shopping Centre*, Simpang Lima.
Disco *Xanadu*, *Metro Hotel*, Jl HA Salim.
Ketoprak & wayang orang The Ngesti Pandowo, Jl Pemuda 116, Mon and Thur 2015.
Wayang kulit The RRI (Radio station), on Jl Jend A Yani, organize performances on the 1st Sat of every month.

Festivals

Dugderan Festival (movable), marks the start of the month-long Muslim fast, held in front of Grand Mosque.
July Jaran Sam Po, Chinese ceremony, procession to Thay Kak Sie Pagoda.
August Semarang Fair, month-long festivities every evening.
October Pertempuran Lima Hari (14th), held around the Tugu Muda to commemorate the 5 day battle of Indonesian youth against the Japanese in 1945.

Shopping

Batik *Batik Keris*, Mal Ciputra (on Simpang Lima); *Batik Pekalongan*, Jl Pemuda 66; *GKBI*, Jl Pemuda 48; *Kerta Niaga*, Jl Stadion 1A and Jl Gajah Mada; *Batik Cendrawasih*, corner of Jl Pemuda and Jl Gajah Mada; *Batik Danar Hadi*, Jl Gajah Mada (close to Simpang Lima).
Books *Gramedia*, Jl Panadanaran (next to the *Graha Santika Hotel*). Largest bookshop in Semarang.
Handicrafts *Toko Panjang*, Jl Widoharjo 31; *Wijaya*, Jl Gajah Mada 2.
Night market *Pasar Johar*, Jl A Salim, good place to wander, vast range of goods on sale.
Shopping plazas There are a number of shopping plazas and department stores around the Simpang Lima, where Jl Gajah Mada, Jl H Dahlan, Jl Jend A Yani, Jl Pahlawan and Jl Pandanaran all meet: *Citra Land*, *Matahari*, *Robinson's* and *Simpang Lima*, for example. In the city centre to the north, there are 2 on Jl H Agus Salim: the *Semarang Plaza* and *Matahari*.
Supermarkets Several on Simpang Lima, including *Galael's* in *Robinson's*.
Woodcarving *Kerta Niaga*, see above.

Sports **Bowling** 10-pin bowling at the *Patrajasa Hotel*, Jl Sisingamangaraja.
Golf *Semarang Golf Club*, Jl Sisingamangaraja 14, T312582, close to the *Patrajasa Hotel*, 9 holes.
Swimming *Patrajasa Hotel* has a pool open to the public.

Tour operators *Chiara*, Jl Seroja Selatan; *Electra Duta Wisata*, Jl Gajah Mada 1, T288444; *Media Tour*, Jl Pandanaran 116-120 (*Hotel Graha Santika*), T411729, F415176; *Nitour*, Jl Indraprasta 97; *Nusantara*, *Simpang Lima Shopping Centre*, Blok C6; *Satura*, *Simpang Lima Shopping Centre*, Blok I, II, III; *Tedjo Express*, Jl Haryono 786.

Transport
120 km north of Yogya, 485 km east of Jakarta, 308 km west of Surabaya

Local Bus: fixed price city buses (400Rp). **Colts & becaks**: ply the streets, although becaks are outlawed on the main streets. Becaks come colour coded in Semarang: blue ones are permitted to operate during the day, until about 1700, whereupon yellow machines take over the streets. **Taxi**: metered taxis, or rent them by the hour or the day.

Air Ahmad Yani airport is 5 km west of town off Jl Siliwangi. Transport to town: taxis charge a fixed fee to town. No 2 town bus goes from Jl Pemuda as far as the roundabout (as too do bemos running along the Rejomulyo – Mangkang route), but it is a 1 km walk down Jl Kalibanteng to the airport itself. Take a becak from here or, easier still, a taxi from town. Regular connections on Garuda/Merpati, Sempati, Mandala and Bouraq, with other destinations in Java, Sumatra, Kalimantan, Sulawesi, Bali, Lombok, Nusa Tenggara, Maluku and Irian Jaya.

Train There are 2 railway stations; Poncol is on Jl Imam Bonjol but is only for freight and some short trip passenger trains; the majority of passenger trains run from Tawang station on Jl Merak. Regular connections with **Jakarta** on the Mutiara Utara night express (7 hrs), which continues on to **Surabaya**. The Senja Utama from Jakarta is non a/c night train (8-10 hrs), connections with **Pekalongan** (4 hrs) (see page 977 for timetable).

Road Bus: Terminal Terboyo is on the east side of town, about 3½ km from the city centre, 200m north of the road towards Demak. Town buses travelling along Jl Pemuda travel out to the terminal, as do bemos. To buy tickets for onward journeys, plenty of bus companies have their offices here, although a/c bis malam (night bus) and VIP bus companies are concentrated along Jl Haryono. There is a taxi rank for journeys into town. Regular connections with **Kudus** (1 hr), **Yogya** (3½ hrs), **Solo** (2½ hrs), **Wonosobo** (4 hrs), **Surabaya** (9 hrs, night bus 20,000Rp), **Cirebon** (6 hrs), **Pekalongan** (3 hrs) and **Jakarta** (9 hrs). **Minibus**: minibuses leave from the corner of Jl HA Salim and Jl MT Haryono, with offices strung out south from this intersection. Regular connections with **Solo**, **Yogya**, **Cirebon** and **Jakarta**.

Sea Boat: Semarang's port is called Tanjung Emas and lies about 2 km north of the city centre. The *Pelni* ships *Lawit*, *Sirimau*, *Ciremai*, *Leuser*, *Binaiya* and *Pangrango* dock here en route for **Kalimantan**, **Sulawesi** and **Sumatra**. See schedules on page 988. The *Pelni* office is at Jl Tantular 25, T555156.

Directory **Airline offices** *Bouraq*, Jl Gajah Mada 16C, T515921. *Garuda/Merpati*, Jl Gajah Mada 11, T517137. *Mandala*, Bangkong Plaza B-7, Jl MT Haryono, T444736, F414116. *Sempati*, *Graha Santika Hotel*, Jl Pandanaran, T414086. **Banks** *Bank Central Asia*, Jl Pemuda. *BNI*, Jl LMT Haryono 16. *Bumi Daya*, Jl Kepodeng 34; *Ekspor Impor*, Jl M Tantular 19. *Supit Money Changer*, Jl Pemuda. **Communications** General Post Office: Jl Pemuda 4. *Internet cafés*: *Warung Internet Cyber Café*, Jl Pemuda 4 (right next to the GPO). Open: 0800-2200 Mon-Sat, 0800-2000 Sun. **Telecommunication office**: Jl Jend Suprapto 7 for fax and telephone services. **Wartel**, Jl Pandanaran. **Medical facilites** Hospitals: *William Booth*, Jl Letjen S Parman 5.

Kudus

Founded by the Muslim saint Sunan Kudus, Ja'far Shodik, Kudus developed as an important Islamic holy city and is still a pilgrimage centre today. Sunan Kudus is reputed to have been the fifth *imam* of the mosque at Demak – at that time the most powerful of the north coast *pasisir* states. The name Kudus is taken from the Arabic *al-Quds*, which means 'holy' or 'Jerusalem', and it is the only town in Java which has retained an Arabic name. Kudus and the surrounding countryside is still one of the most orthodox Muslim areas on Java. It is also relatively prosperous, enjoying the fruits of being a major kretek-producing town (see box). The **tourist office** is on Jl Jend A Yani 60, T24000.

Phone code: 0291
Colour map 3, grid A4

Less than 1 km off the main road into town from Semarang is a **kretek museum** on Jl Jetas Pejaten – only Indonesia could have a museum in praise of the cigarette. Models, machinery, dioramas, photo portraits and a collection of kretek packets make up the display. A traditional Kudus house (*rumah adat Kudus*) stands next to the museum (see below). ■ *Admission by donation. Open 0900-1400 Mon-Thu, 0900-1300 Sat, 0800-1400 Sun.*

Sights

Down an alleyway off Jl Sunan Kudus, the main road to Jepara, is the **Al-Manar** or **Al-Aqsa Mosque** (on Jl Menara). Built in 1549 by Sunan Kudus (the year AH [Anno Hijrae, the Islamic era] 956, equivalent to AD 1549, is inscribed over the *mihrab* which indicates the direction of Mecca) on the site of a Hindu-Javanese temple, its name is the same as the mosque at Jerusalem. It is an important place of pilgrimage for Muslims and interesting for non-Muslims, with its attractive red brick **Kudus Menara** or **Clock Tower**. The tower was built in 1685, and shows clear architectural links with the Hindu Majapahit Kingdom and with similar towers in Bali, notably the Kulkul towers found in temple compounds. It is possible that it was built as a pre-Islamic temple. Today, the drum at the top of the tower is used to call the faithful to prayer and the porcelain plates set into the walls – similar to decoration found on other mosques and

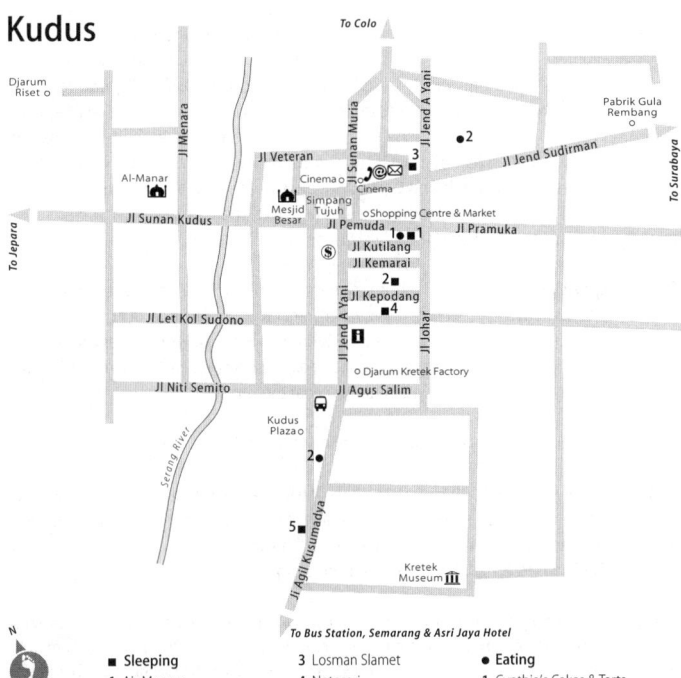

Kudus

■ **Sleeping**
1 Air Mancur
2 Losman Repodang Asri
3 Losman Slamet
4 Notosari
5 Prima Graha

● **Eating**
1 Cynthia's Cakes & Tarts
2 Hijau Mas

kratons – are thought to imitate Islamic tiles. It is possible to climb the steep stairs and then a wooden ladder to the top, where there are magnificent views of the town over a sea of tiled roofs. Behind the mosque, to the left of the main entrance, are a series of charming brick courtyards separated by weathered wooden doors. Each courtyard contains gravestones leading, eventually, to the revered **tomb of Sunan Kudus**. His mausoleum of finely carved stone is draped with a curtain of lace.

In town, on Jl Jend A Yani, is the large **Djarum kretek factory**, Kudus' major employer. ■ *Free tours of the factory are run on work days from 0800 (closed Fri).* Not far south from the factory, and facing onto the large new *Kudus Plaza* shopping centre, is a **Chinese Pagoda**.

Kudus is also famous for its **traditional houses** or *rumah adat Kudus*. It was here, and at the nearby port of Jepara, that woodcarving was developed to its highest degree of refinement and houses were decorated with elaborately carved internal and external screens. Abdul Syukur owns a traditional Kudus teak house on Jl Veteran, with just such intricately carved woodwork. ■ *To visit the house, contact the tourist office in Kudus and they will accompany you there.*

Excursions **Rembang** lies 60 km east of Kudus, on the north coast (see page 236). ■ *Getting there: regular connections with Kudus bus terminal.*

The historic town of **Demak** is 19 km south of Kudus (see page 231). ■ *Getting there: regular connections by colt and bus.*

Sleeping **B-C** *Asri Jaya*, Jl Agil Kusumadya, T38449/38629, F31897. This pricey holiday camp-style hotel is 4 km from the centre of the town but close to the bus station, a/c, restaurant, pool and hot water. Economy rooms are grubby but 2nd floor VIP rooms are good, corridors dark, dirty and grim, a lick of paint would do wonders. **C-D** *Air Mancur*, Jl Pemuda 70, T32514. Big hotel with even bigger courtyard, large range of rooms but all are fairly basic, none with shower. **D** *Notosari*, Jl Kepodang 12, T37227/37245, F35295. Central location but down quiet side street. Some a/c, restaurant, pool, VIP rooms have sitting area which makes the bedrooms rather dark. 'Utama' are better and cheaper (especially those on the upper floor which are lighter), some rooms with hot water, good position in town and a good standard make this the best place from which to explore Kudus on foot. **E** *Losmen Kepodang Asri*, Jl Kepodang 15, T337595. Down quiet side street near centre of town, rooms are well kept and the losmen is very popular with Indonesians, best of the cheaper places in town. **E** *Losmen Slamet*, Jl Jend Sudirman 63, T37579. Old, run-down building with charm, rooms are large and basic, but very cheap. **E-F** *Prima Graha*, Jl R Agil Kusumadya 8, T31620. Some a/c, small hotel down quiet lane about 2 km from centre of Kudus, rooms are clean and well-maintained, some with attached mandis, but exceptionally surly management.

Eating **Cheap** *Hijau Mas*, Jl Jend A Yani 1, good Indonesian food at good prices, closed Fri. *Pondok Gizi*, Jl Agil Kusumadya 59 (road into town from Semarang). *Sederhana*, Jl Agil Kusumadya 59B, excellent Indonesia, seafood specialities. Recommended. *Cynthia's Cakes and Tarts*, Jl Pemuda 90, good selection of cakes and brightly coloured pastries. *Soto Ayam Pak Denuh*, Jl Agil Kusumadya. Night stalls at Pasar Bitingan near the bus station.

Sports **Swimming** *The Asri Jaya Hotel* has a pool open to the public.

Transport **Road** **Bus**: the station is on the Semarang side of town, 4 km from the centre, on the main
51 km from Semarang Kudus – Semarang road. Colts take passengers into town. Regular connections with Semarang (1 hr), **Solo** (2 hrs) and **Kudus** (3½ hrs). **Colt**: the station is on Jl Jend A Yani, opposite the *Kudus Plaza*, connections with **Rembang** and **Jepara**.

Directory **Banks** *Bank Central Asia*, Jl Jend A Yani 91. *Bank Rakyat Indonesia*, Jl Jend Sudirman (near intersection with Jl Johar). **Communications** *Internet*: at the main post office on Jl Jend Sudirman 43, 0800-2100 Mon-Sat, 1000-1700 Sun. 8,000Rp per hr with exceptionally friendly staff. **Telephone office**: Jl Jend Sudirman (about 1 km from town centre). Open 0800-2100 Mon-Sat, 1000-1700 Sun.

Jepara

Jepara was once one of Java's largest and most powerful trading cities. By the end of the 16th century, it was surrounded by an impressive protective city wall and the kings and queens of Jepara sent fleets to attack Portuguese Melaka, one of which was said to be 100 vessels strong. The city state reached the height of its powers under the rule of the renowned Queen Kali-nyamat. Even at that time, Jepara was already well-known for the quality of its wood carving, a reputation which it has maintained through to the present day. When the Dutch first arrived here, they recorded that Jepara was supplying rice, palm sugar and cattle to other parts of Southeast Asia, and Van Goens in 1656 estimated the population of Jepara at 100,000. That the tide of history has turned against Jepara is clear: today, it is a small provincial town with a flourishing furniture industry – an industry which owes much to the boat building skills of former years.

Phone code: 0295
Colour map 3, grid A4

Sights

Once out of the suburbs of Kudus, the road to Jepara emerges onto a wide coastal agricultural plain where rice, sugar cane and beans are grown. About 20 km from Kudus, the first wood carving and furniture making workshops appear. For the next 5 km, all the way into the centre of Jepara, the road is lined with enterprises ranging in size from one man on a stool with a hammer and chisel, to large warehouse-sized operations. Piles of rough-hewn logs are stored at lumber yards, waiting to be transformed into furniture or carvings. Much is rather over-elaborate for western tastes, but there is also some elegant furniture of simpler design. Items such as garden benches, folding chairs and tables are widely available. Many workshops also arrange packing and shipping, so getting the pieces home need not be a problem.

Jepara itself is an attractive, clean, well planned and airy town. It is a pleasant place to pass a few days away. A walk can be taken along the fish quay – particularly rewarding

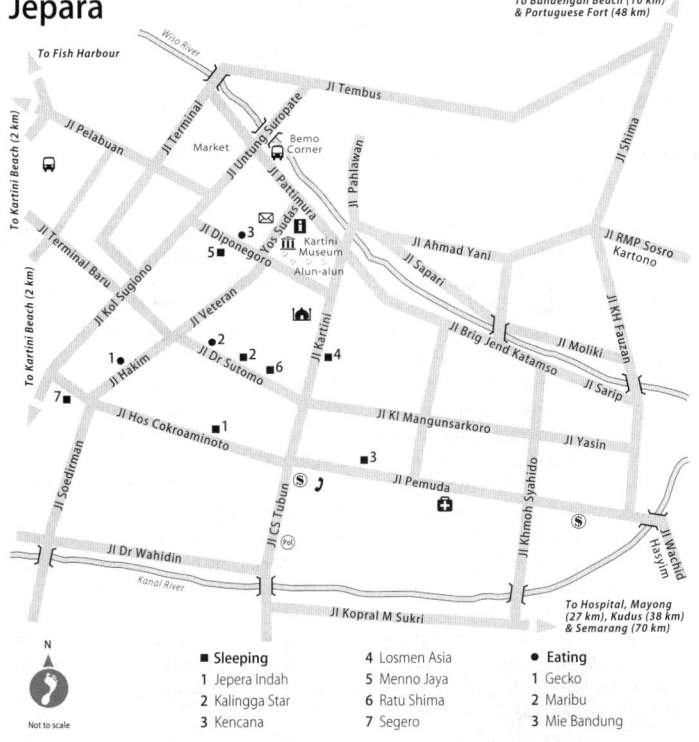

Jepara

■ Sleeping
1 Jepara Indah
2 Kalingga Star
3 Kencana
4 Losmen Asia
5 Menno Jaya
6 Ratu Shima
7 Segero

● Eating
1 Gecko
2 Maribu
3 Mie Bandung

Raden Kartini

Raden Ajeng Kartini was born in 1880, daughter of the Regent or *bupati* of Jepara. She was fortunate in having a father who did not entirely disagree with the idea of female education, and he sent her to the European lower school in Jepara. Here, the distinctly revolutionary belief that women should be educated and emancipated took hold. At the very end of the 19th century, the East Indies, like Europe, was caught up in the idea that, with the dawn of the 20th century, a new era would begin, one of enlightenment. Kartini was thrilled to be part of this change. She wrote to a friend on 12 January 1900: "Oh, it is splendid just to live in this age; the transition of the old into the new!".

Unfortunately, her dreams were not allowed time to unfold. She died at the tragically young age of 24 on 17 September 1904, while giving birth to her first child. Nonetheless, in her short life Kartini established a reputation for herself as a budding suffragette: she founded a school for the daughters of Javanese officials and promoted the rights of Javanese women. For her role, Kartini is immortalized on a banknote. However, there are rumours of dissent emanating from some quarters. The fact that Kartini was so European in outlook, and apparently pro-Dutch in a number of respects, means that her nationalist credentials are slightly sullied. Her burial place, and that of her sons' (at Desa Bulu, 20 km south of Rembang), has become a pilgrimage spot for Indonesian women nonetheless, and crowds travel here - particularly on 21 April, known as Kartini Day.

when the fishermen are unloading their catch. The **Kartini Museum** on Jl Alun-alun Jepara commemorates the local heroine RA Kartini, who's statue can be seen waving as you reach the town. It contains an assortment of her possessions including photographs, paintings and furniture, as well as detailing her struggle for greater female emancipation (see box). ■ *Admission 1,000Rp. Open 0800-1700 Mon-Sat, 0900-1700 Sun.* Also on the Alun-alun is the town's central mosque – the **Mesjid Baitul Ma'mur** – which is very well proportioned and one of the better modern mosques.

On a small hill on the north side of town are the ruins of a **Portuguese fort**. The hill-top position affords a good view of the port and surrounding *tambak* fisheries (see box, page 265). A worthwhile and pleasant late afternoon sortie. The **tourist office**, *Dinas Pariwisata Tingkat II Pati*, is on Jl Dr Wahidin 3, T81422.

Excursions **Bandengan Beach** lies 5 km east of Jepara. It is pleasant enough and safe for swimming. There is a camping ground nearby.

Sleeping **B** *Jepara Indah*, Jl HOS Cokroaminoto 12, T93548, jepara.inn@hotmail.com Imposing building, somewhat out of place amid the paddy fields, new hotel with a/c, large pool and good restaurant. Rooms are average even though this is the best in the area. Non-residents can use the pool for 5,000Rp a day. **C** *Kalingga Star*, Jl Dr Sutomo 16, T91054, F91443. Good hotel with wide range of rooms, best with attached bathrooms, a/c and hot water, excellent laundry service, surprisingly sophisticated for such a small place. **D** *Ratu Shima*, Jl Dr Sutomo 13-15, T/F91406. Popular, with friendly management. Good range of rooms with a/c and TV, all are clean and comfortable but with poor mandi, good restaurant and value, an excellent place to stay. **D-E** *Kencana*, Jl Pemuda 14-16, T92336. Some a/c, lower budget rooms are next to the main road and may be noisy, rooms are clean but quite a poor standard. **D-E** *Segoro*, Jl Ringin Jaya 2, T91982. Large marine coloured hotel with bright and cheerful air. Rooms are pleasant but bathrooms are without showers. Popular for longer stay furniture buyers. **E** *Losmen Asia*, Jl Kartini 32, best feature is its central position, dark, basic rooms in old, colonial villa, shared mandi, cheap. **E** *Menno Jaya*, Jl Diponegoro 40, T91143. Easy to miss off the main high street, rooms have small narrow beds but stunning furniture. Exceptionally friendly manager, the best of the lower range crop of hotels.

Eating **Cheap** *Maribu*, Jl Dr Soetomo, excellent fresh fish at reasonable prices, fruit juices recommended. *Mie Bandung*, Jl Diponegoro, good selection of cheap food, friendly management. *Gecko*, Jl Hakim, Dutch owner, panelled walls add to the lavish atmosphere, great European food but rather pricey.

Cinemas *Mutiara*, Alun-alun Jepara.

Entertainment

Textiles The area around Jepara town, and especially the village of Troso, is an important centre for the production of weft ikat, similar in design to that made at Gresik. The textiles are known as *tenunor lurik Troso* and their designs draw upon Gujarati (Indian) *patola* cloths.

Shopping

Road Bus: the terminal is off Jl Kol Sugiono on the northwest side of town, but still a relatively easy walk from the centre. Regular connections with **Kudus** and **Semarang**. Change at Semarang for buses to **Pekalongan** and destinations to **Jakarta**.

Transport
30 km from Kudus, 81 km from Semarang

Banks *Bank Dagang Negara*, Jl Pemuda; *Bank Negara Indonesia*, Jl Pemuda 46. **Communications Post Office:** Jl Pangl Sudirman (opposite the *Pati Hotel*). **Telephone & fax office:** Jl Pangl Sudirman 61 (opposite the *Pati Hotel*).

Directory

Karimunjawa Islands

The 27 Karimunjawa Islands lie around 90 km off-shore from Jepara and have been gazetted as a Marine National Park. Among the endangered flora and fauna are red coral, eagles and an array of forest plants. The population of the islands – four of the 27 are inhabited – are staunchly Muslim and few tourists make it out here. Nonetheless, there are a handful of losmen and homestays, and some good beaches and snorkelling (no diving facilities). The joy of Karimunjawa is the fact that this is a beach without the resort – although how long it will remain so is in the balance. Come with a stack of good books, expect simple food, and relax.

Colour map 3, grid A3

The biggest of the 27 islands in this small archipelago is **Pulau Karimunjawa** and most boats from the mainland dock on the island. Karimunjawa village has some homestay accommodation and the grave of Sunan Nyamplung is an hour's walk from the village. Karimunjawa is fringed with mangroves and has no good beaches, nor accessible coral for that matter. **Pulau Menjangan Kecil** is the place to go for the good beaches, but no accommodation. It is possible to base yourself at Karimunjawa village and then charter local boats to explore the other islands in the group.

Strictly speaking, to visit the national park it is necessary to obtain permission from the *Office of Nature Conservation* (KSDA), Jl Menteri Supeno 1/2, T(024) 414750, Semarang, or from the tourist office in Jepara at Jl Alun-alun Jepara 1 (on the main town square), T118. Both can provide further information on the islands (although their English is limited).

Karimunjawa village (Pulau Karimunjawa) A handful of homestays are available in the village; all fall in our **E** category. Ask at the dock on arrival.

Sleeping

Sambangan Island C beach chalets. These can be booked through *PT Pusakaraya Tours* in Kudus, or turn up and hope that they have rooms available.

Tengah Island C beach chalets on a not particularly attractive island, east of Karimunjawa. There is talk of a casino being developed on this island. These can be booked through *PT Satura Tours*, Jl Cendrawasih 4, Semarang, T0297-555555, or turn up and hope that rooms are available.

Wisma Wisata of Jepara Regency Government C VIP rooms are good value and price includes 3 Indonesian meals per day.

A few warung near the pieron Karimunjawa. Sporadic opening times. **Post Office**: Karimunjawa village. **Telkom**: Karimunjawa village. **Bank**: there are no money changing facilities here; bring sufficient for your stay.

Eating

Transport
90 km northwest of Jepara

Local Erratic **bemo** service. Inter-island fishing **boats** for hire.

Air There is a small airfield on Karimunjawa. Twice weekly flights from Semarang.

Sea Boat: 2 boats provide ferry connections from Jepara Port on Jl Patiunus on the northwest side of Jepara town, 4-7 hrs (the *KMP Muria 2* is much faster and departs twice weekly, whilst the *Kota Ukir* is slow and departs weekly). The Pelni ship *Pangrango* docks here on its fortnightly circuit. Chartering a boat to the islands is possible, as is simply to pay your passage on one of the fishing boats that make the journey, but they seem flimsy affairs upon which to be making this 90 km journey.

Pati

Phone code: 0295
Colour map 3, grid A4

Pati is a small and rather neat market town in an area of rice and sugar production, with a good hotel for such a place. It can be used as a stopping-off point on the north coast route. The town authorities appear to have invested heavily in grandiose statuary and elaborate street lamps. The **tourist office**, *Dinas Pariwisata Tingkat II Pati*, is on Jl Dr Wahidin 3, T81422.

Sleeping **C** *Pati Hotel*, Jl Pangl Sudirman 60, T81313. Some a/c, pool, old villa in large compound near the centre of town, range of rooms some with hot water, well-run, characterful and very acceptable for a small, out-of-the-way place like Pati. Recommended. **C-E** *Merdeka Hotel*, Jl Diponegoro 69 (north side of town), T81106. Some a/c, 44 rooms, quiet, set back from the road around a courtyard.

Transport
24 km from Kudus, 35 km from Rembang

Road Bus: the terminal is to the southeast of town, off the road to Surabaya, not far from the centre. Regular connections with **Kudus** and on to **Semarang**, and east to **Rembang**, **Tuban** and **Surabaya**.

Directory **Communications** Post Office: Jl Pangl Sudirman (opposite the *Pati Hotel*). Telephone & fax office: Jl Pangl Sudirman 61 (opposite the *Pati Hotel*).

Rembang

Phone code: 0295
Colour map 3, grid A4

Rembang is another small, north coast town with a distinct coastal feel: bright light, white-washed walls and – usually – a brisk sea breeze. Also, like some other towns on the north coast, it has languished into obscurity having once been a significant trading centre. Today it is best known for its associated with RA Kartini, the 'mother' of women's education and emancipation in Indonesia (see box, page 234). A statue of Kartini clutching a book stands on the traffic island on the coast road, Jl Diponegoro, by the tourist office. Rembang also has a fair collection of traditional **Kudus houses** and a large Christian community – evidenced in the number of churches.

The **railway station** has been closed for some years, but it is an attractive building with caged birds hanging from the rafters of the silent platform. **Rembang market** is on Jl Pemuda, the road to Blora.

Excursions **Lasem** is a charming batik-making town, 9 km east of Rembang. It was once one of the most important ship-building centres in Java, owing to the presence nearby of some of the finest stands of teak wood on the island. As ship-building fell into decline so, for a short time, Lasem became a thriving centre for *cap* and *tulis* batik-making, the business controlled by Chinese families. The houses here are Chinese-Portuguese colonial in style, and their weathered and rather ramshackle appearance makes Lasem an attractive place to spend a lazy few hours. Indeed, in its rather sub-provincial way, it is one of the most endearing towns on Java. The batik-making of old has withered and almost died, although there are still a handful

of *tulis* batik factories in town. The cloth is distinctive for its deep red blood colour – not found anywhere else in Indonesia. There is a fine Chinese temple here and although its former wealth has now almost entirely trickled away, Lasem still exudes cultured sophistication rarely found elsewhere on Java. **Sleeping** Available in basic rooms at the run down **E-F** *Gadjah Losmen*, on the main Tuban-Rembang road.
■ *Getting there: by regular bus from Rembang.*

Bonang is a small fishing village 5 km north of Lasem and 14 km from Rembang. The village is well known for its dried fish which are sold from numerous stalls lining the road. Bonang is also famous, in Indonesian terms, as the home of one of Java's nine walis – Sunan Bonang. A memorial to Sunan Bonang can be found at the top of a small hill, just off the main road, on the Tuban edge of the village. Sunan Bonang died here, but he is buried in Tuban (although this was not the intention – see the Tuban entry, below). Swimming at Bonang is not good; the shore is rocky, the water murky, and the currents can be strong. **Sleeping** is surprisingly good in Bonang at the **C-E** *Binangun Indah*, some a/c, set on a hill overlooking the sea on the Tuban edge of town, usually enjoying a cooling breeze, the rooms (some with attached bathrooms) here are clean and well maintained, a real alternative place to stay and take things extremely slowly. Recommended. ■ *Getting there: regular buses from Rembang (and Tuban), the town is on the main north coast route.*

C-E *Hotel Restu*, Jl P Sudirman 38, T91408. Some a/c, a small hotel on the coast road, better rooms with attached mandis, mostly frequented by travelling salesmen, but this shouldn't put people off – the rooms are OK. **E-F** *Losmen Perdana*, Jl P Sudirman 76, T381. Clean and very well priced basic rooms in a small villa, some with attached mandis.

Sleeping

Road Bus: the terminal is not far from the centre of town, just off Jl Diponegoro, the seafront road. Regular connections with **Semarang** via **Pati** and **Kudus**, and east to **Tuban** and **Surabaya**. There are also buses to **Bandung**.

Transport
59 km from Kudus, 97 km from Tuban

Banks *Bank Rakyat Indonesia*, Jl Diponegoro (the coast road). **Communications** Post Office: Jl Diponegoro. **Tourist offices** *Dinas Pariwisata* (Rembang Regency office), Jl Diponegoro 77 (near the centre of town), T91403. They only have a short, rather uninformative pamphlet to hand out to the few visitors who venture here.

Directory

East Java

East Java covers an area of 47,922 sq km and includes not only the east portion of Java, but also the island of Madura. The province is drained by two principal rivers – the Brantas and Bengawan Solo. Two-thirds of East Java is mountainous, its highest peak, Mount Semeru, reaching 3,676m. The population of over 35,000,000 is made up largely of Javanese, Madurese and Tenggerese. The ayam bekisar, *a cross-breed between a chicken and a green woodcock (and visible in most hotel lobbies), is one of East Java's symbols, and so too is the* sedap malam, *a white flower. For the visitor, the principal attractions of East Java are likely to lie in the magnificent volcanic scenery, the elegant candis and other architectural remains, and in the persistence – despite rapid economic change – of many facets of traditional life. Traditional forms of dress are still much in evidence in rural areas, as are buffalo-drawn wagons, horse-pulled carts and carriages and bicycles, and women tend to carry loads on their heads, rather than tied with a sarong on their backs as in Central and West Java.*

Like Central Java, East Java is rich in archaeological sites. The East Javanese Period of art and architecture began in 929 when King Sindok was forced to move his court to the rich Brantas River area, following the eruption of Mount Merapi in 928 (see page 301). The East Javanese Period spanned six centuries and included the kingdoms of Kediri (929-1222), Singasari (1222-92) and Majapahit (1292-1527). Among the various monuments, Candi Panataran is the greatest, although the elegant Candi Kidal and Candi Singasari, as well as Candi Jawi, are also significant.

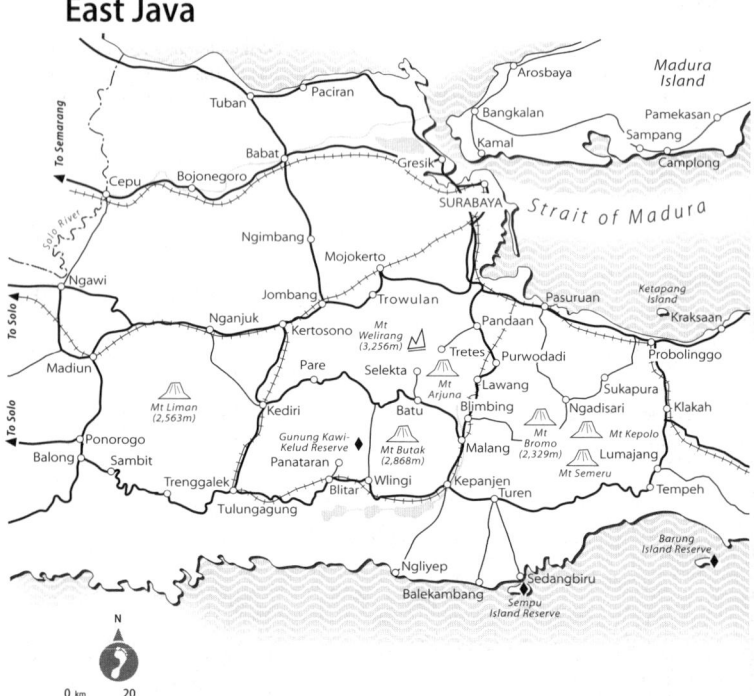

East Java

Not only is East Java one of the country's most densely populated provinces, it is also one of the richest. An industrial 'golden triangle' (in fact a diamond) is centred on the port of Surabaya, Indonesia's second largest city, and also includes the towns of Malang, Jombang and Pasuruan. More people are engaged in industrial activities and live in urban areas in East Java than in any other province in the country, except Jakarta. These industries are dominated by kretek (clove cigarette) manufacturing, sugar milling and weaving.

But this picture of East Java as a vibrant, modern province obscures great inequalities and continuing poverty in some of the more remote areas. In particular, Madura and the southwest districts such as Pacitan have not benefited from East Java's recent economic growth. Although it has been the province's expanding industries which have generated much of the economic growth in recent years, East Java still has a larger area under plantations – sugar cane, coffee, cloves and tobacco – than any other province except North Sumatra.

The rump of East Java

Pacitan

Pacitan is a small seaside resort 119 km south of Solo, enclosed within a sweeping crescent-shaped bay. The beach is usually almost deserted and the swimming is generally good. The surrounding countryside and villages provide many lovely walks; a good place for a taste of 'real' Javanese life, with a beach to boot.

Phone code: 0357
Colour map 3, grid B4

Gua Tabuhan, or the Musical Caves, are 15 km from Pacitan. They consist of several large caverns filled with stalagmites and stalactites, which (for a fee) locals will 'play' to make eerie sounds swell the interior. Boys tap the limestone stalactites while a man drums in the background. Quartz souvenirs are also on sale. ■ *Getting there: the caves are on the road to Wonogiri, 4 km after the small town of Punung. From here it is either a 4 km walk or an ojek ride.*

Excursions

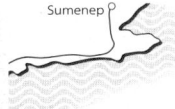

Pacitan has only recently developed as a tourist destination and accommodation is generally simple, although a few more up-market places are beginning to open.

Sleeping

C *Rumah Makan Srikandi*, Jl A Yani 67A, T81252. New place undergoing step-by-step expansion. Rooms are spotless and tastefully decorated, some with a/c, some with own shower and TV, excellent restaurant (see below). **D** *Happy Bay Beach Bungalows* (well signposted from the main road, if coming from Solo, get off the bus as it approaches Pacitan), T81474. Restaurant. Run by an Australian – Eric – and his Javanese wife, there are around 15 immaculate bungalows with attached showers and western toilets set in attractive gardens, deserted beach with good swimming,

Pacitan

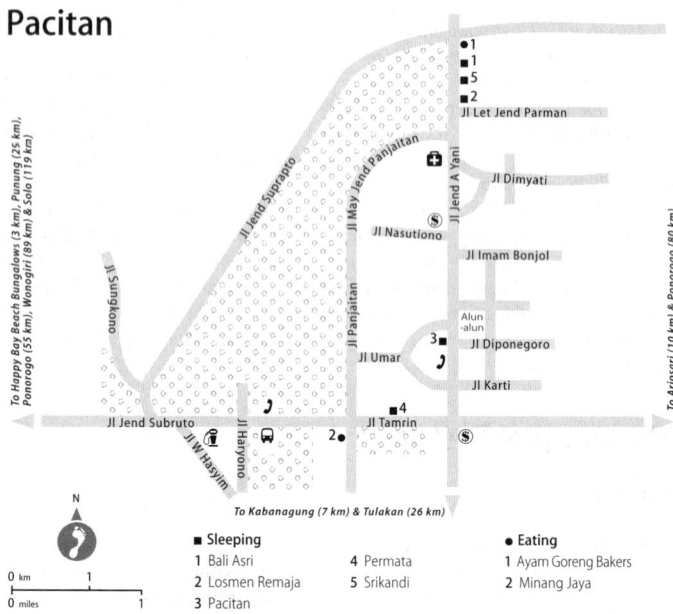

Sleeping
1 Bali Asri
2 Losmen Remaja
3 Pacitan
4 Permata
5 Srikandi

Eating
1 Ayam Goreng Bakers
2 Minang Jaya

games room, motorbikes for hire. Eric visits Yogya once a week and will give guests free lifts, a favourite retreat for foreigners living in Yogya; **D** *Hotel Pacitan*, Jl Jend A Yani 37 (on the Alun-alun), T81244. Large, rather dark a/c rooms with old furnishings, the cheaper fan rooms are better value. **D** *Permata*, Jl Gatot Subroto 26, T/F81240. The best hotel in the town centre, modern and attractive, with balconies overlooking a garden. Recommended. **D-E** *Bali Asri*, Jl A Yani 69, T81170. Fans and mandi, more expensive rooms have western toilet and TV. **D-F** *Losmen Remaja*, Jl Jend A Yani 67, T81088. Some a/c, cheap and unappealing.

Eating *Rumah Makan Srikandi*, good selection of seafood, sandwiches and juices (ice seaweed). At the front there is a well stocked shop.

Transport *119 km from Solo*

Local: motorbikes for hire from the *Happy Bay Beach Bungalows*. **Bus**: the bus terminal is on the Solo side of town, a short walk from the centre. There are a handful of direct buses from **Solo's** Tirtonadi terminal; alternatively, catch a bus to **Wonogiri** where there are frequent connections to Pacitan.

Directory **Banks** *Bank Rakyat Indonesia*, will change US$ TCs. **Communications Telephone**: there is a *Wartel* office on Jl Jend A Yani.

Madiun

Phone code: 0351
Colour map 3, grid B4

Madiun is the largest town in the western part of East Java (its population is around 200,000) and an important centre for the processing of sugar cane, which is grown in the surrounding area – as it has been since colonial days. Entering or leaving by the northeast (from Caruban), the road passes the **Rejo Agung sugar mill** - built in 1894 - and still in operation. There is also evidence of a vital past in the elegant villas that line roads such as Jl Yos Sudarso, and in the splendid governor's mansion on Jl Pahlawan. Madiun also remains an important centre for rolling stock production – again a role that it has inherited from the colonial period. The INKA works still occupy the same location they did under the Dutch.

The life-blood of the Indonesian male: the clove or 'kretek' cigarette

One of the most important upland crops in East Java is *cengkeh* or cloves. These are grown for a single purpose: to supply the massive *kretek* or clove cigarette industry. It is difficult to go anywhere in Indonesia where there is not the lingering scent of the spice. The centre of the industry is East Java, where it employs about 100,000 workers. The giant Gudang Garam factory at Kediri alone has over 40,000 employees, while Bentoel in Malang employs another 20,000. In Central Java, the centre of kretek production is the Djarum factory in Kudus. Over the course of the 1980s and 1990s, the traditional hand-made kretek has been displaced by the machine-made variety. At the same time, the kretek has been eating into the market share of so-called 'white' cigarettes.

In late 1990, former president Suharto's youngest son, Hutomo 'Tommy' Mandala Putra, used his impeccable contacts to set up a clove monopoly, known as BPCC. He managed to convince his father that the best way to help 500,000 poor clove farmers was to create such a monopoly, enabling him to buy the spice from farmers at 7,000Rp per kg – double the prevailing market price – and then sell it on to the captive kretek manufacturers for 12,700-15,000Rp per kg. The powerful manufacturers resisted the move by paying less to tobacco farmers. Tommy, in turn, secured US$325 mn in subsidized credits from the central Bank Indonesia and began to buy huge quantities of cloves, but mostly from powerful Chinese traders rather than from farmers. The monopoly seemed to be flying in the face of the government's attempts to de-regulate industry. By the beginning of 1992, BPCC was effectively bankrupt: it had no funds left to buy cloves, had built up a two year stock of the spice, and Tommy suggested – amidst much recrimination – that farmers burn half their crop to restore demand. BPCC became a semi-public monopoly, with farmers receiving only 4,000Rp per kg for their crop, while kretek manufacturers were still required to buy their stocks from BPCC. In mid-1993, Tommy admitted that his company was no longer able to service its loan from Bank Indonesia, and suggested that he borrow money from a commercial – but state-owned – bank to repay the central bank.

Surprisingly, during Indonesia's calamatous economic down-turn, Java's kretek factories found that demand was so buyant that they were actually hiring additional workers – even poaching skilled rollers from competitor factories. Why this was so, when most Indonesians were finding it hard even to buy rice and cooking oil, concentrated minds. Some people pointed to the large tax element in each packet of kretek, meaning that while most essentials were increasing rapidly in cost, the price of cigarettes was reletively stable. Or it could just be that a quick puff was one of the few ways that the average Indonesian could escape from his troubles. Significantly, cigarette consumption went up in the US during the Great Depression.

Excursions **Sarangan**, a hill resort, lies about 40 km west of Madiun (see page 212). ■ *Getting there:* take a bemo to Magetan via Maospati; from Magetan, catch a minibus up to Sarangan.

Sleeping **A-B** *Merdeka Hotel*, Jl Pahlawan 42, T2547, F2572. Pool, 120 a/c rooms with hot water in a hotel that dates back, in parts at least, to 1904, when it was named *The Grand*; the Japanese renamed it the *Yamato* in 1942 during their occupation of the East Indies, and it finally became the *Merdeka Hotel* in 1945; sadly there is little evidence of all this history, the rooms may be comfortable enough, but potential guests should not arrive with the impression that they will see a hotel dripping in colonial elegance. **B** *Kartika Hotel*, Jl Pahlawan 54, T51847, F51847. A/c, restaurant, this hotel opened a few years back and is still in reasonable nick. Rather bare and clinical rooms and lobby, comfortable and good value, discounts available. **D-E** *Hotel Madiun*, Jl Pahlawan 75, old villa, rather grubby but some character.

Eating Madiun is known locally for its *nasi pecel* – steamed rice with vegetables, peanut sauce and chicken. Another local delicacy is *brem*, a snack made from glutinous (sticky) rice.

The Madiun affair

Historically, Madiun is best remembered for an abortive Communist revolt in 1948, which proved to be one of the key turning points in the Revolution. That year was one of turmoil in Indonesia. The Dutch were attempting to regain control through their police action, while the independence movement was split between the left – headed by the Communist PKI – and the fledgling Republican government. Ousted from government during a purge, the PKI attempted to regain control by encouraging a wave of strikes and demonstrations by peasants and workers. By the middle of 1948, effective warfare had broken out between pro-PKI and pro-government soldiers. Those supporting the PKI were driven out of Solo and retreated to Madiun. Here, between 10,000 and 25,000 were out-numbered by government forces who backed Sukarno and his associates. When it became clear that ordinary soldiers had to choose between one side and the other, most sided with the Republican leaders. From that point, the insurrection was doomed. In all, it is thought, about 8,000 people were killed in and around Madiun. As Ricklefs writes in his History of Modern Indonesia, the Madiun affair caused the left "to be tainted forever with treachery against the revolution".

Entertainment **Cinemas**: *Lawu Indah*, Jl Pahlawan (near the *Merdeka Hotel*).

Transport **Train** Although very few people travel here by train, Madiun is on the main line between Jakarta, **Yogya** and **Solo** to the west, and **Surabaya** to the northeast. **NB** Not all the express trains stop here (the Bima express does).

83 km from Kediri,
89 km from Solo

Road Bus: regular connections east to **Surabaya**, **Bali** and **Malang**, and west to **Solo**, **Yogya** and **Jakarta**.

Directory **Banks** *Bank Rakyat Indonesia*, Jl Pahlawan. **Communications** Post Office: Jl Pahlawan 24.

Kediri

Phone code: 0354
Colour map 3, grid B4

In theory, Kediri should be an attractive town. It has a glorious past: it was the centre of an important pre-Islamic Kingdom between the 11th and 13th centuries and its location - nestling between two volcanoes, Mount Liman (2,563m) to the west and Mount Kawi (2,551m) to the east - appears, cartographically, also to augur well. In reality though, Kediri is an ugly town of 235,000 people (1990), with little to show for past glories.

Today, Kediri is not so much a one horse town as a one industry town: the massive **Gudang Garam** *kretek* cigarette factory, employing over 40,000 people, is based here, the largest single industrial concern (in terms of numbers employed) in all of Indonesia (see box). There are few sights either in town or roundabouts. At the end of Jl Pattimura, there is the **Tri Dharma** (or **Tjoe Hwie Kiong**) **Buddhist monastery**.

Excursions **Surowono** is a temple in the village of **Canggu**. It is currently undergoing renovation, but it exhibits some accomplished relief carving. ■ *Getting there: no public transport, and rather hard to find tucked away among the back roads. It is located about 5 km off the main Kediri-Pare road; turn right at a major intersection just outside Pare, where a concrete policeman stands guard in front of the local police station. Ask for directions along the way ('dimana Candi Surowono?') – and then get wonderfully lost.*

Tegurwangi is a little-visited candi about 8 km from the small town of Pare, northeast of Kediri. **Gua Selomangleng** is a meditation 'cave', hewn out of the rock and reminiscent of a pill box. The rooms are decorated with episodes from the Jataka tales (the previous lives of the historic Buddha), and inscriptions indicate that the cave was created between the 12th and early 15th centuries. The cave is a few kilometres due south of the small town of Tulungagung, itself south of Kediri. ■ *Getting there: it is easiest to take an ojek (motorcycle); otherwise, a Microlet 'A', along Jl Mastrip, runs in the right direction, although a change is necessary.*

Sri Aji Joyoboyo's tomb, a 13th-century king of Kediri, can be found in the village of Menang, near Pagu, 8 km from Kediri. ■ *The best time to visit the tomb is on Thu and Fri evenings, when there is a market and celebrations. Getting there: by bemo to Pagu.*

Sleeping

Kediri is not well-endowed with decent hotels, either at the top or bottom ends of the scale; there are no decent budget places to stay, and no classy joints.

B-C *Hotel Penataran*, Jl Dhoho 190, T84626, F41799. A/c, best hotel in town, which is not saying a great deal, clean rooms and central location. **C-D** *Safari Indah II*, Jl Panglima Sudirman 43, T82466. Some a/c, a rather scruffy, uninspired block of a hotel, although the rooms are just about OK, those at the front can be noisy, rather expensive for what you get. **D-E** *Hotel Pelapa*, Jl Brawijaya (near intersection with Jl Basuki Rachmat). Old and rather attractive villa, but the rooms are poor. **E** *Mustika*, Jl Panglima Sudirman 25. Basic losmen in the centre of town.

Eating

Two local food specialities are *getuk pisang* and *tahu* (bean curd), which are sold by numerous shops along Jl Pattimura. **Cheap** *Mirmar*, Jl Hayam Wuruk 12, Chinese restaurant serving tasty Chinese and Indonesian dishes in clean surroundings. *Zangrandl*, Jl Dhoho 10, ice creams in modern a/c comfort, hang out with the local high school drop outs.

Entertainment

Cinemas *Golden*, Jl Hayam Wuruk, new and very comfortable.

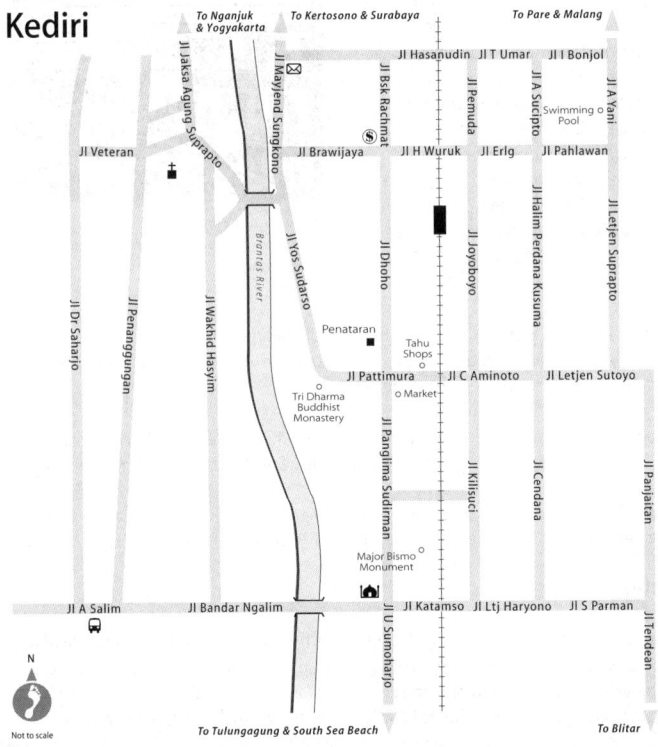

Kediri

The magic saus of Gudang Garam

The 'Big Four' kretek cigarette manufacturers are all found in East Java: Gudang Garam, Bentoel, Djarum and Sampurna. However, the Gudang Garam kretek cigarette factory in Kediri is by far the largest, and is in fact the largest single industrial enterprise in Indonesia, employing over 45,000 workers. Until the 1970s, kretek cigarette smoking was largely a lower class affair: the sophisticates of Jakarta spurned the kretek in favour of so-called 'white' (ie Virginia) cigarettes. Since then, though, a remarkable change in habits has occurred as kretek smoking has made in-roads into the middle classes and intelligentsia, to the extent that it has become very de rigeur, and a mark of Indonesian-ness.

It seems that the practice of mixing cloves and tobacco originated in Java during the late 18th century. But it was not until the late 19th century that the industry really took off, and like most such activities, the industry was dominated by Chinese businessmen. Gudang Garam was founded in Kediri in the late 1950s by Surya Wonowijojo (or Tjoa Ing Hwie – his Chinese name), where production has always been concentrated. Ing Hwie was born in Fujian, southern China, in 1926. From modest beginnings (all such things have 'modest beginnings'), Gudang Garam grew to stupendous proportions: by the late 1980s, the firm was producing over 40 billion cigarettes a year – in the late 1960s it was scarcely one billion. The secret of the success of Ing Hwie's company lay in the clove saus (sauce) that he divined. When this was allied to the famous 'yellow pack' in 1962, the fortunes of his company began to change. It is said that the logo of the company – a salt warehouse or gudang garam – came to Ing Hwie in a dream, and for good luck since then he has had an image of a gudang garam emblazoned on every pack. His competitors, jealous at the success of Gudang Garam, put it about that his saus contained not only cloves, but also cannabis. Ing Hwie died in 1985 of heart disease, probably brought on by his smoking. Doctors in New Zealand advised that he give up smoking; all he managed was to 'cut down' to one pack a day.

Although Gudang Garam does not dominate the market as it did in its heyday during the early 1980s, it is still the largest single employer in Indonesia. Kediri is, to all effects, Gudang Garam.

This account is based on Kenneth Young's 'Kediri and Gudang Garam: an industrial enclave in a rural setting", in: **Balanced development: East Java in the New Order** (edited by Howard Dick, James J Fox and Jamie Mackie), Oxford University Press: Singapore, 1993.

The famous logo of the Gudang Garam Kretek cigarette manufacturer. It depicts the salt warehouses, or gudang garam, after which the company is named

Transport *100 km from Malang, 83 km from Madiun*

Train The station is on Jl Stasiun, which runs off Jl Dhoho, in the centre of town. Kediri is on the main line between **Jakarta**, **Yogya** and **Solo** to the west, and **Surabaya** to the north-east. **NB** Not all the express trains stop here.

Road Bus: the terminal is on the outskirts of town on Jl Supratman. Regular connections with other major centres, including **Madiun**, **Solo**, **Yogya**, **Surabaya**, **Bali**, **Malang** and **Jakarta**.

Directory **Banks** Bank Central Asia, Jl Brawijaya (near the intersection with Jl Basuki Rachmat). **Communications Post Office**: Jl May Jend Sungkono. **Telephone & fax**: *Wartel*, Jl Hayam Wuruk 30.

Blitar

Phone code: 0342
Colour map 3, grid B5

Blitar, with a population of over 125,000, has two claims to fame: it is the site of former President Sukarno's mausoleum and is also the closest town to Candi Panataran. Today, despite the presence of Sukarno's grave, the town is a quiet backwater in comparison with other East Javanese towns such as Malang or Solo.

The main road, Jl Merdeka, runs east-west. At its west end, close to the intersection with Jl Mawar, is a small **Chinese temple – Tri Dharma Poo An Kiong**. Just a short distance further west still, along the street that leads to the bus station, is an enjoyable **market** selling spices, dried fish and other local products. There is an **archaeological museum** on Jl Sodancho Supriyadi.

Sights

Sukarno's mausoleum is on the outskirts of Blitar, about 2 km northeast of the town centre on Jl Slamet Riyadi, the road to Panataran. Against his wishes – former President Sukarno was buried here in Blitar, next to his mother. No doubt this backwater of Java was chosen to ensure that his grave did not become a focus of pilgrimage and dissent. In 1978 the grave was spruced-up; there is now an impressive open gateway, leading to a glass-enclosed pavilion which contains the engraved boulder marking the site of his burial. The number of stalls that line the road to the grave, and the abundance of becak drivers who wait hopefully around the entrance, demonstrate that Sukarno has not been entirely forgotten. Pilgrims prostrate themselves and flowers are scattered in front of the pavilion. ■ *Get to the grave by becak (ask for 'makam Bung Karno'), or walk.*

The **Museum Sukarno**, on Jl Sultan Agung 59, is the house where the ex-president lived as a child and photographs and other memorabilia are displayed. ■ *The museum is a little over 1 km from the town centre.*

Candi Panataran is 10 km north of Blitar and was built from 1345 to 1375 during the Majapahit Period, although work may have started during the Singasari era (1222-92). It is the largest and most important candi of the East Javanese Period and anticipates the design of later Balinese temples. Asymmetrical in layout, it consists of three stepped courtyards surrounded by a wall. The visitor approaches the temple from the lowest level to the west, past a pair of *raksasa* or *dvarapala*. The first courtyard originally contained two wooden buildings which would have been used as assembly rooms. All that remains is the base of a *terrace*, with fine bas-reliefs encircling it. These relate tales of the *kidungs*, with figures carved in the wayang-like stylization which is characteristic of East Javanese reliefs: flat, with no illusion of depth and with faces portrayed in profile. The north face of the terrace is the least weathered. Also in this courtyard is a small square building of vertical design, the so-called '*Date of the year temple*', built in 1369 (since restored) and a good example of East Javanese candi architecture (it is similar in appearance to Candi Kidal, see page 249).

The second court contains the larger *Naga Temple*, which has lost its top section (originally of wood and similar to a Balinese *meru*), but what remains is of very fine workmanship. It is identifiable by the four naga which wind around the top of the temple, supported by nine beautiful figures in royal attire. *Dvarapala* guard the entrance to the shrine, but the kala head above the door is now missing – although *tumpal* motifs can be seen at the front of each flight of steps. The building was used as a repository for sacred possessions.

Excursions

Panataran Complex

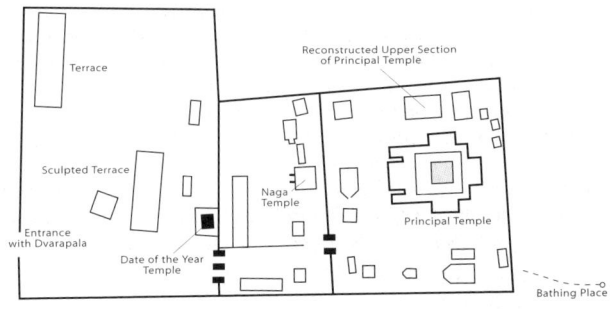
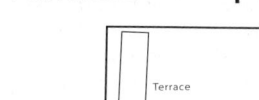

Not to scale

The highest and most east court contains the *principal shrine*, which was originally surrounded by four smaller structures, remnants of which remain. The main shrine stands to the rear of the complex, nearest to the mountains, enabling the gods to descend into the temple. The base is decorated with relief carvings representing the Ramayana, interspersed with carved animal motif medallions. Four guardian figures patrol the steps upwards, rather disturbingly standing on bands of skulls (behind one of them the artist has carved a lizard, perhaps his signature). The steps lead up to a second level where there are carved winged creatures. To the left of the temple is its reconstructed upper section.

Down some stairs, behind and to the right of the principal shrine, is a clear pool, lined with stone and carved with animals. The pool, which would have been the king's 'mandi', is filled with fish. ■ *Admission: by donation. Open: 0700-1700 Mon-Sun. Getting there: take a colt direct to Panataran or go by ojek.*

Candi Sawentar lies a few kilometres southeast of Blitar, near the village of the same name. This temple was built at the beginning of the 13th century and is similar in style to Candi Kidal. For some reason, it was never completed and when the candi was discovered, it was almost completely covered in volcanic debris. ■ *Getting there: by colt to Sawentar.*

Sleeping There are a number of hotels and losmen close to Sukarno's mausoleum, catering mainly to Indonesian 'pilgrims'.

B-E *Sri Lestari*, Jl Merdeka 173, T81766, F81763. Some a/c, restaurant, good rooms, attractive main colonial building, well-run range of accommodation, in old and new wings. Highly recommended. **C-E** *Sri Rejeki*, Jl TGP 13 (4 blocks on from main square, walking away from the bus station, take a right turn and it's on your left), T81770, good range of rooms. **E** *Losmen Damar Wulan*, Jl Anjasmoro 78, T81884. **E-F** *Hotel Santosa*, Jl Manur 2, central position near the bus terminal, simple rooms with attached mandi.

Eating **Cheap** *Sri Lestari*, Jl Merdeka, Indonesian including Rijstaffel and European. Recommended.

Transport **Local Colts**: the station is adjacent to the inter-city bus station on Jl Kerantil. **Dokars**: assemble near the bus and rail stations. **Motorcycle taxis** (ojeks): available for trips out of town. **Train** Station set back on Jl Wijaya Kusuma, to the south of Jl Merdeka. Connections with **Surabaya** via **Malang** (5 hrs) (see timetable, page 977). **Road** **Bus**: the station is on Jl Kerantil, the west continuation of Jl Merdeka. Connections with **Solo** (6 hrs), **Malang** (3 hrs), **Surabaya** (4 hrs) and **Jakarta**.

225 km from Solo, 77 km from Malang

Directory **Banks** *BNI*, Jl Kananga 9. **Communications** Post Office: Jl Wijaya Kusuma 1 (close to train station).

Malang

Phone code: 0341
Colour map 3, grid B5

Surrounded by volcanoes – Mount Butak (2,868m) to the west, Mount Arjuna (3,339m) to the north, and Mounts Kepolo (3,035m) and Bromo (2,329m) to the east – Malang is one of the most beautifully situated cities in Java. Lying at 450m, it is arguably Indonesia's largest hill resort, with a population of 650,000. During the colonial period, Malang was a small, quaint town where Dutch planters and civil servants could escape the heat of the lowlands. The elegant villas are still in evidence – for example, along the wide, tree-lined Jl Besar Ijen. Malang is a friendly town, with a cooler, pleasant climate, free from mass tourism and, although it is not noted for its sights, there are a number of places of interest within easy reach of the city, making it a good base or stopping-off point between Mount Bromo and Bali. The largest single industry in Malang is Bentoel's kretek factory, which employs over 20,000 people (see box, page 241).

Ins and outs

Malang has no airport. The nearest is at Surabaya, 90 km away. The main, central train station is close to the city centre and there are departures for Jakarta via Surabaya. Another, less frequently used station is Kota Lama, to the south of the city. Trains leave here for Jakarta via Blitar (slower). Confusingly, there are 3 bus terminals in Malang. The main Arjosari terminal lies to the north and serves most destinations. The Gadang terminal lies to the south and has departures for Blitar and Lumajang. The Landungsari terminal to the northeast serves Kediri, Batu and Selekta. Colts link the 3 terminals and the city centre. Simpler to book a ticket through one of the many tour companies.

Getting there
See also 'Transport', page 252

Malang is a hill town, and a leafy one at that, so walking is relatively pleasant. Becaks, colts and microlets provide the main modes of public transport. Metered taxis are available. In 2000 the two old tourist offices in Jl Kawi 41 and Jl Semeru 2 closed. A new Dinas Pariwisata (tourist office) has opened at Jl Jend A Yani 53, run by the provincial government.

Getting around

Sights

The city is divided into two by the Brantas River, which flows within a deep cutting. Tiled houses, some of colonial vintage, picturesquely – at least from a distance – tumble down the steep banks. In the east half of the city is Jl Tugu, with the uninspired **independence monument** as its centrepiece, facing which is the old Dutch town hall, renovated and renamed the **Balai Kota Malang**.

On the west bank of the Brantas, at the intersection of Jl Gatot Subroto/Laks Martadinata and Jl Zainal Zacse, is the large **Eng An Kiong Chinese Pagoda**. Nearby is the **Pasar Besar**, on Jl Pasar Besar and Jl Gatot Subroto, a large and very colourful market selling everything from fruit, to live animals, to batik. Other markets include the flower market, **Pasar Bunga**, and the nearby **Pasar Senggol**, a night market on Jl Brawijaya. The military **Museum Brawijaya** is at Jl Besar Ijen 25A, housed in a rather stylish 1940s or 1950s building with military equipment arranged out the front.

Around Malang

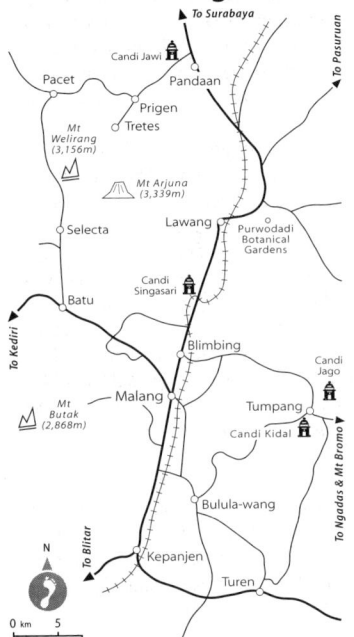

Excursions

The plain Candi Badut is thought to be the oldest surviving Hindu (Sivaite) temple in East Java, probably dating from 760 and built in honour of King Gajayana of the Kanjuruhan Kingdom (the earliest recorded kingdom in East Java). The word *badut* is derived from a Sanskrit word meaning 'joker', or 'a man who is fond of making jokes'. The candi is similar in design to the temples of Gedung Songo, but on a larger scale. It seems that the building was altered in the 13th century, which caused it to become unstable and so hastened its ruin. The niches are framed by kalamakaras and some still contain Hindu gods. The central cella would originally have held a linga. The temple was discovered in 1923 and has subsequently been renovated up to the lower

Candi Badut

section of the roof. It is located in an area of scrubland, on the outskirts of Malang, about 4 km to the northwest of the city centre and past the university. The route here winds through narrow suburban lanes and quite suddenly passes into rice fields. ■ *Getting there: take one of the 'Jalur M-K' microlets, which travel between Madyupuro and Karang Besuki. The candi is 100m on from the end of the route.*

Candi Singasari

Candi Singasari, the Purwodadi Gardens & Candi Jawi are all on or just off the main road, between Surabaya & Malang. It is easy to visit them en route between the two towns; simply hop off one bus (there are many) & onto another

Candi Singasari lies 9 km north of Malang, just off the main road running towards Surabaya. The candi is East Javanese in style, with its heavy pyramidal roofs, and was built around 1300 as one of the funerary sanctuaries for Kertanagara, the last king of the Singasari Dynasty. Its design varies from other candis of the period in that the square base is much larger than normal. The cellas are – unusually – set within this base, rather than in the body of the candi. The body contains narrow niches, crowned by *banaspati* heads. Its shape implies that it was either a symbol of the *linga* or that it was meant as a replica of Mount Meru. A flight of stairs leads up to the first terrace where there are five chambers. About 150m on from the candi are two enclosures on either side of the street, each containing an enormous, corpulent and demonic *dvarapala* statue with skull headbands and earrings, large staring eyes, sharp canine teeth and clasping a club. Traditionally, these giant figures were placed at the gateway to ward off evil spirits. ■ *Admission free. Open 0800-1700 daily. Getting there: take a bus or green microlet (LA) towards Surabaya or Lawang from Malang's Arjosari station (500Rp). The candi is 600m to the left (west), off the main road in Singasari town.*

Kebun Raya Purwodadi

The well kept and attractive Kebun Raya Purwodadi – the **Purwodadi Botanical Gardens** – lie 12 km north of Singasari (21 km from Malang), at the north edge of Purwodadi town. ■ *Admission 2500Rp. Open 0730-1600 Mon-Sun. Getting there: take a bus or microlet (No LA) towards Surabaya or Lawang from Malang's Arjosari station.* **Sleeping near Purwodadi** D *Niagara*, in Lawang, a few kilometres south of Purwodadi; on the main road, stylish but run-down.

Candi Jawi

Candi Jawi is a 13th century candi, 49 km north of Malang, just off the road running to Surabaya. The monument was built as a commemorative shrine to the last king of the Singasari Dynasty, King Kertanagara (1268-92). It is one of the most complete candis in East Java, and still shows the remains of the surrounding double enclosure as well as a brick-lined moat. Jawi is also perhaps the most graceful of all East Javanese shrines, with its tall, tapering tower rising to 17m.

The architecture of the monument shows elements of both Sivaism, in its foundations, and Buddhism, in its stupa-like finial. It also originally housed both a statue of Siva and the Buddha Aksobhya, so revealing the King's belief in the unity of Sivaism and Buddhism. Weathered reliefs of stories as yet undeciphered decorate the base. The upper door frame holds kala heads and there are a pair of makaras at the end of the stairs. Up these stairs is a small chamber containing a stone block. The candi was redesigned in the 14th century, and restored in 1938 and again in 1970. Close to Candi Jawi is the open air theatre Taman Chandra Wilwatika (see below). ■ *Getting there: the candi lies 49 km north of Malang, off the road to Surabaya. In the roadside town of Pandaan there is a turn-off for the hill resort of Tretes (see page 253), and 2 km up this road is Candi Jawi. Take a bus from Malang towards Surabaya and ask to be let off at Pandaan; walk the final 2 km or take a minibus heading for Tretes.*

Taman Chandra Wilwatika

This open air theatre, only 1 km from Candi Jawi and 48 km from Malang, stages performances of classical ballet on the second and fourth Saturday nights of each month, from June to November, 1930-2300. ■ *Getting there: the theatre lies 1 km downhill (and closer to the main road) from Candi Jawi (see above). Take a bus from Malang towards Surabaya and ask to be let off at Pandaan, walk the final kilometre or take a minibus heading for Tretes.*

Candi Jago

Also named Jajaghu, this candi can be found down a side street (and before the minibus station) off the main road in the town of Tumpang, 22 km east of Malang. The candi feels rather enclosed, as it is squashed into a small space and surrounded by houses. This Buddhist shrine was probably built around 1270-80, as a funerary monument to King Vishnuvardhana of the Singasari Dynasty. Today, the upper part of the cell and the tower are missing – it is thought that they were made of wood and palm, in the multi-tiered design characteristic of the Balinese meru. The candi is unusual in that the cella was placed at the back edge of a three-tiered base and is approached up a steep stairway. The finely carved friezes on all three levels of the base are important, as they appear to establish the existence of buildings with tiered roofs in the 13th century. The meaning of the friezes has not been firmly ascertained, although they seem to recount Hindu, Buddhist and local legends. However, on the basis of the reliefs, some commentators have argued that the temple dates from the later Majapahit Period. The four statues that were originally in the now ruined upper chamber are to be found in the National Museum, Jakarta (King Vishnuvardhana was portrayed in the form of a Buddhist god). ■ *Getting there: catch a minibus or white microlet from Malang's Arjosari station to Tumpang (750Rp) and walk the short distance from the minibus station.*

Candi Kidal

Candi Kidal is 7 km further on from Tumpang travelling southwest, and was built in the mid-13th century as a memorial shrine to King Anusapati, who died in 1248. Built of andesite, the shrine consists of a square cell with projecting porticos, set within low walls on a large plinth. The tower – now in ruins – would originally have been about 15m high and made up of three false storeys of diminishing height. However, its elegant proportions made it susceptible to earthquake damage and the structure has not survived the 750 years since it was built. Facing west, the stairway leads up to a chamber above which is a fearsome kala head. The icon within the inner chamber may have been the Siva statue, which is in the collection of a museum in Amsterdam, or it may have been a post-mortem image of King Anusapati, or both – often shrines of this kind housed an image of a god whom the departed king was believed to have represented on earth. Around the base are some fine carvings of garuda, depicting the story of garuda liberating his mother Winata from the tyranny of the dragon Kadru. ■ *Admission by donation. Getting there: catch a minibus from Malang's Arjosari station to Tumpang (750Rp), and then a colt or ojek from Tumpang station (another 500Rp). The route to the site passes through Tumpang for 1 km, before coming to a 'T' junction; turn right, the temple is on the left another 6 km along the road. It is set back from the street, so is easily missed.*

Selekta & Batu
Colour map 3, grid B5

Selekta and Batu are two hill resorts, 23 km from Malang (see page 254). ■ *Getting there: go from the Lendingsari bus station, change at Batu for Seleka, each journey 750Rp.*

Mount Bromo & Ngadas

Mount Bromo and Ngadas lie to the east of Malang. Most people visit Mount Bromo from Probolinggo (see page 274), although it is possible to climb the mountain from the village of Ngadas, on Bromo's south face. From Ngadas there are two trekking trails; one leads to the village of Ranupani, the highest community in Java, the other to Bromo's summit (12.5 km). The trekking here is more demanding than from Probolinggo, although the route is well worn and a guide is not required. It is possible to trek from Ngadas to Cemoro Lawang, from where minibuses run down to Probolinggo (see page 274). Villagers may offer their homes as guesthouses. ■ *Getting to Ngadas: catch a minibus from Malang's Arjosari station to Tumpang (22 km); from Tumpang catch a minibus to Gubuk Klakah, and from there a four-wheel drive vehicle (or hitch) up to Ngadas (another 22 km from Tumpang).*

Ngliyep & Balekambang

Ngliyep and Balekambang are two beach resorts, 67 km and 57 km south of Malang respectively. Bus from Gadang bus station. Both have accommodation. Ngliyep, with its rocky outcrops, has stunning scenery, but it is not safe to swim here. En route for the beach is the town of Kepanjen, where there is a hotel (**E** *Penginapan Panca Karya*, Jl Sawanggaling 18, next to the mosque, big clean rooms, no fans or mandis en suite). Both Ngliyep and Balekambang also provide basic losmen facilities. ■ *Getting there: by bus from Malang's Gadang station. For Balekambang, take a bus to Turen and then change (2 hrs on from here). For Ngliyep, take a bus to Kepanjen and change, or take a colt to Bantur and change.*

Pulau Sempu Pulau Sempu is an 877 ha nature park off Java's south coast, with excellent snorkelling and forest trails (see page 254). It is necessary to stay in the mainland village of Sedangbiru. ■ *Getting there: to get to Sedangbiru, take a bus from Malang's Gadang bus terminal to Turen, 30 mins (650Rp), then change to a blue minibus to Sedangbiru, 2 hrs (2,500Rp). From Sedangbiru, the short boat crossing should cost 5,000Rp.*

Essentials

Sleeping
■ *on map opposite*
Although Malang has a good selection of hotels, rooms get booked up quickly; so it is best to arrive early to secure a room in one of the better hotels

AL-A *Hotel Tugu Malang*, Jl Tugu 3, T363891, F362765, www.tuguhotels.com malang@tuguhotels.com Priceless hotel in terms of style and individuality, no 2 rooms are the same. The owner collects antiques which fill the 'regional' rooms, real attention to detail, beautiful bathrooms, some with hand-beaten aluminium baths. Good value by international standards and best in Malang. Recommended. **A** *Regent's Park*, Jl Jaksa Agung Suprapto 12-16, T363388, F355888, regent@indo.net.id A/c, poor restaurant, pool, western-style 'luxury' hotel with good range of facilities. But while the rooms may be of a good standard, they are uninspiring - and the colour of the décor leaves a lot to be desired. Location on the edge of the city centre. There is little to distinguish it from a host of other such hotels. **A-B** *Kartika Prince*, Jl Jaksa Agung Suprapto 17, T361900, F361911. A/c, restaurant, pool, 'Chinese' style luxury hotel, on the main road. The large greenhouse windows are effective but a clean would do wonders. Rooms lack care and attention, a revamp is called for as this hotel was obviously once lovely. **B** *Montana*, Jl Kahuripan 9, T362751, F361633. Adobe-style lobby not maintained throughout the hotel, average rooms but somewhat dated, efficient service, good buffet breakfast included, central. **B** *Hotel Tosari*, Jl KH Ahmad Dahlan 31, T326945, F367098. Variety of rooms off clean white corridors. The economy rooms could not be any smaller and some are noisy. Standard rooms are spotless, as are the surrounding mish-mash of patterned tiles; good value accommodation.

C *Kartika Kusuma*, Jl Kahuripan 12, T352266. Some rooms with a/c, TV and hot water, centrally located with lovely gardens. A comfortable, moderate nights stay. Recommended. **C** *Splendid Inn*, Jl Majapahit 4, PO Box 142, T366086, F363618. Most a/c, pool, TV, characterful but slightly jaded hotel with 1950s decor, next to Balai Kota, quiet with large rooms, each with comfy seating area but rather fusty, for those who prefer old Java to new western style, popular with foreign visitors and therefore often full. Recommended. **C** *Margosuko*, Jl Achmad Dahlan 40, T356789, F365750. Lovely entrance but elegance stretches no further, rooms scruffy and noisy, hot water, breakfast. **C** *Santosa*, Jl KH Agus Salim 24, T366889, F367098. Some a/c, good central position, rooms are moderate, some with sitting areas outside, hot water showers, economy rooms are a little small and dark and the ones downstairs near the entrance lobby are very noisy, particularly in early morning. **D** *Hotel Pelangi*, Jl Merdeka Selatan 3, T365156, F365466. Some a/c, good central location and attractive old high-ceilinged dining room (the hotel was built in 1915 when it was known as the *Palace Hotel*) decorated with old Dutch tiles, rooms are fine though the cheapest are pokey and next to noisy water boiler, it has lost some of the jaded charm of hotels like the *Splendid Inn* during its rather over-enthusiastic renovation. **D** *Malinda*, Jl KH Zainul Ariffin 39, T364402. Large rooms with 1960s furniture, good central position but tucked away so quiet, large white crisp rooms, poor bathrooms with cold water showers, some style and good value. Recommended. **C-D** *Menara*, Jl Pejajaran 5 (walking distance from railway station), T362871, F365750. Large comfy rooms if not a little dark, economy rooms of a poor standard and rather characterless, price includes breakfast. **C-D** *Willy's Indah* (near the railway station), new hotel, rooms with a/c and hot water attached bathrooms, breakfast included.

D *Aloha*, Jl Gajah Mada 7, T326950. Wacky Hawaian-style hotel like a seedy fair ground show, dark entrance rooms surround water feature but are poor, with many bare bricks. **D-E** *Helios*, Jl Pattimura 37 (walking distance from railway station), T362741. Set around courtyard, the rooms in the new wing are immaculate and more expensive, the old, cheaper economy rooms are excellent, homely, rather ramshackle feel, popular and good source of information. Recommended. **D-E** *Hotel Riche*, Jl Basuki Rachmat 1, T325460. Very unattractive looking hotel, but excellent central location and friendly management, they are working with a poor product, bar has the quaint 1950s feel, cinema style lobby, this is a warren of generally poor and rather grubby rooms, check carefully before booking in. **D-E** *Zabena Hotel*, Jl Jagung Suprapto 60A, T361772, F324560. North of town on the way to the Arjosari bus terminal. 16 clean rooms with attached showers in a renovated villa. Visitors have commented favourably on the friendliness of the place. Discounts for long stay visitors and tours arranged.

Malang

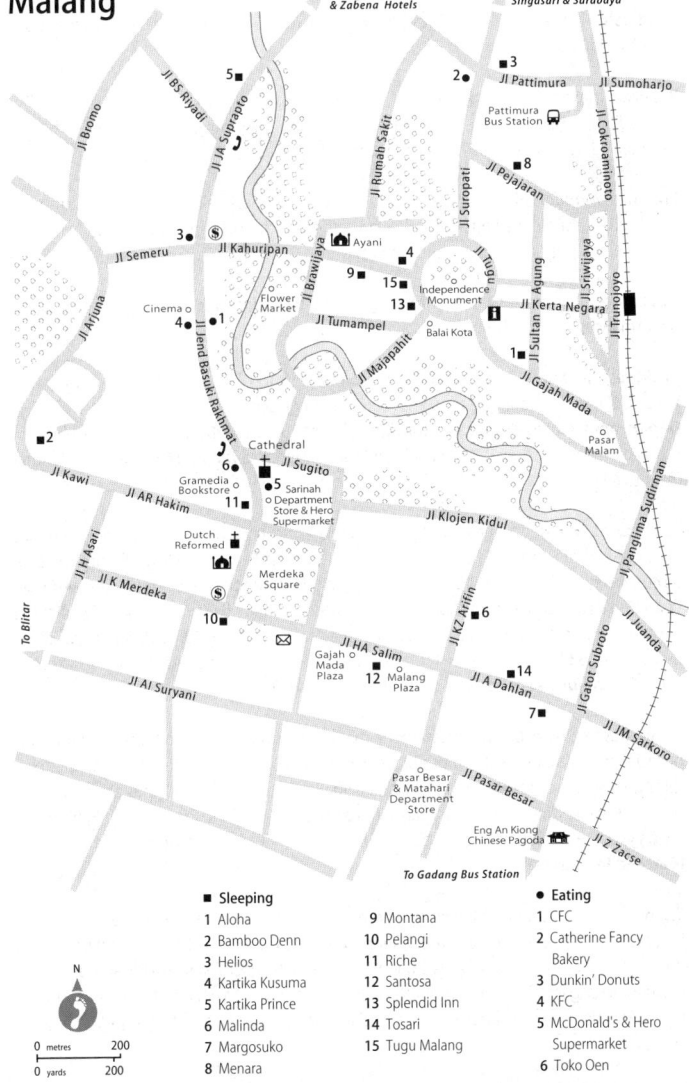

Sleeping
1 Aloha
2 Bamboo Denn
3 Helios
4 Kartika Kusuma
5 Kartika Prince
6 Malinda
7 Margosuko
8 Menara
9 Montana
10 Pelangi
11 Riche
12 Santosa
13 Splendid Inn
14 Tosari
15 Tugu Malang

Eating
1 CFC
2 Catherine Fancy Bakery
3 Dunkin' Donuts
4 KFC
5 McDonald's & Hero Supermarket
6 Toko Oen

Eating	**Cheap** *Melati Pavilion* (part of *Tugu Park Hotel*), Jl Tugu 3, this must be the best restaurant in town for the quality of food, service, décor and atmosphere, band and pianist. Recommended. *New Hong Kong*, Jl AR Hakim, best Chinese in town. *Minang Jaya*, Jl Jend Basuki Rakhmat 111, good Padang food. *Toko Oen*, Jl Basuki Rakhmat 5, younger sister of Semerang branch, hangar-like fossilized restaurant, serving an enormous array of Indonesian and European foods, also 26 varieties of ice cream, juices, sandwiches, Dutch breads and toast crackers. The restaurant has recently changed hands though and remains popular only due to its name – food is pricey but bland and the snacks have degenerated to match. *Dirga Surya*, Jl Jend Gatot Subroto 81, good Chinese.
	Fast food *Dunkin' Donuts*, Jl Semeru (next to East Java Information Office). *Kentucky Fried Chicken*, Jl Basuki Rachmat (near the BNI Bank). *McDonald's*, Jl Basuki Rachmat (next to *Sarinah's Dept Store* and opposite *Toko Oen's*).
	Foodstalls In the *Gajah Mada Plaza*, Jl H Agus Salimor, or at the night market at the south end of Jl Majapahit.
	Bakeries Next door to *Tugu Park Hotel* is an excellent bakery, with the best cakes in Java. Try the traditional Malang tempe cookies for a savoury travelling snack. *Catherine Bakery*, Jl Patimura 22, specializes in extravagantly decorated cakes.
Entertainment	**Cinemas** *Mandala*, Jl Agus Salim; Radio Republic Indonesia (RRI), first Sat of the month, 2100; Senaputra Amusement Park, last Wed of the month, 2000; *Studio Cinema*, Jl Merdeka Utara (central position on the main square).
Festivals	**November** Anniversary of Malang *Regency* (28th), commemorated with traditional art performances and other shows.
Shopping	**Antiques** *Art Shop Abu*, Jl May Jend Haryono 150 (on left-hand side of road on way towards Batu), small antique shop with some good pieces. **Department stores & plazas** *Matahari*, Jl Pasar Besar; *Metro Dept Store*, Jl Merdeka Utara (on the main square); *Sarinah Dept Store* and *Hero Supermarket*, Jl Basuki Rachmat (next to *McDonald's*).
Tour operators	Tours can be arranged to most sights around Malang, including the Hindu-Buddhist temples of Jago, Kidal, Singasari and Badut, and the hill resorts of Batu and Selekta. Return tours for Bromo leave at 0200 (90,000Rp). Prices are much the same between companies, although *Toko Oen's Tour and Information Service*, Jl Basuki Rachmat 5, T364052, F369497, offer the best and most imaginative deals. *Jack*, Jl A Yani 20i, T471061, F471062. *Mujur Surya*, 33A Jl Bromo, T322333, specializes in tours to Bromo. *Penghela Swedesi*, Jl Basuki Rakhmat, T362564. *Tanjung Permai*, Jl Basuki Rakhmat 41, T366924.
Transport *882 km from Jakarta,* *89 km from Surabaya*	**Local** Becaks, colts & microlets: are the main form of public transport (there are no town buses). The bus stops display route plans. Buses and colts run between the 3 bus stations, through the centre of town, fixed price fare of 500Rp. Letters on the front indicate the route – A-D is Arjosari to Dinoyo, A-G is Arjosari to Gadang, and D-G is Dinoyo to Gadang. Rather confusingly, Gadang to Dinoyo is D, Gadang to Arjosari is E, F or G, and Dinoyo to Arjosari is F. **Metered taxis** available.
	Train The central station, a building of perhaps 1930s vintage, is at the east end of Jl Kerta Negara. Trains leave here for Jakarta via Surabaya; the fastest service. There is another station to the south of the city, the Kota Lama Station. Trains leave here for Jakarta via **Blitar**. Trains coming in to Malang from the south continue on to the more convenient new central station. Regular connections with **Surabaya** (3 hrs) and **Jakarta** (12½ hrs) (see timetable, page 977).

Road Bus: Malang has 3 bus stations. The largest is Arjosari on Jl R Intan, to the north of town, which serves **Jakarta**, **Surabaya** (2½ hrs), **Probolinggo**, **Bandung**, **Denpasar** (Bali) and **Bogor**. For **Yogya** and **Solo**, change in Surabaya. The Gadang station on Jl Kol Sugiono, to the south of the city centre, serves **Blitar** (from where there are connections by the south route for Solo and Yogya), **Dampit** and **Lumajang**. The newish Landungsari station (formerly the Dinoyo station), on Jl M Haryono to the northeast, serves **Kediri**, **Batu**, **Selekta** and **Jombang**. Colts: link the 3 terminals with each other through the centre of the city. For those wishing to book *bis malam* to Jakarta, Yogya, Mataram (Lombok), Bali and elsewhere, there are offices across town. The Tourist Information Service at *Toko Oen's*, Jl Basuki Rakhmat 5, has good information on the range of choice. Tickets can also be bought from most other tour companies and from the 'Post Office' on Jl Suropati (near the *Helios Hotel*).

Directory

Airline offices Merpati (*Kartika Prince Hotel*), Jl Jaksa Agung Suprapto 17, T27962. *Sempati*, *Regent's Park Hotel*, Jl Jacksa Agung Suprapto 12-16. **Banks** A number in the town centre, of which the most efficient are: *Bank Bumi Daya*, Jl Merdeka Barat. *Bank Central Asia* (only changes money after 1200), corner Jl Basuki Rachmat and Jl Kahuripan. *BNI*, Jl Basuki Rachmat 75-77. *Lippobank*, Jl Merdeka Timur (on the main square). **Communications** General Post Office and Internet: Jl Merdeka Selatan, internet 7,000Rp per hr, open 24 hrs. **Telephone office:** Telekom, Jl Basuki Rachmat; Wartel, Jl Agus Salim (close to *Hotel Sentosa*). **Useful addresses** Immigration Office: Jl Raden Panji Suroso 4, T4039. PHPA office: Jl Raden Intan 6, T365100.

Tretes

Phone code: 0342
Colour map 3, grid B5

Tretes is a hill resort, set at 700m above sea-level on the northeast slopes of the twin peaks of Mount Arjuna (at 3,339m, one of the highest volcanoes on Java) and Mount Welirang (3,156m). The town is an attractive little place, cool at night, and with good views to the plain below and mountains above. Perhaps because it is a weekend retreat for wealthy Surabayans, accommodation is over-priced compared with Java's other hill resorts.

The **Kakek Bodo Waterfall** is a short walk south from town; walking uphill, take the road to the right before the river. The path begins before the *Dirga Hayu Hotel* and leads to the waterfall. There are numerous other **hiking trails** from Tretes; ask at hotels for information. The area around Tretes is said to produce some of the best fruit in Indonesia – particularly durians. There is a **fruit market** towards the bottom of town, near the intersection of Jl Ke Trawas and Jl Palembon.

Excursions

Candi Jawi is about 5 km down the mountain from Tretes (see page 248).

The **Botanical Gardens at Purwodadi** are 22 km from Tretes (see page 248). ■ *Getting there: catch a minibus to Pandaan, and from there, one of the many south-bound buses which run between Surabaya and Malang. The gardens are about 15 km south of Pandaan.*

Trowulan, the former capital of the Majapahit Kingdom, can be reached from Tretes. A beautiful mountain road winds for about an hour round the lower slopes of Mount Arjuna, past holiday homes for the Surabaya rich, to the site of the city (see page 263). ■ *Getting there: no regular colts or buses take this route; hire a car and driver for the journey.*

Sleeping

NB There is additional accommodation a few kilometres down the mountain at Prigen. Like so many other mountain get-away resorts on Java, accommodation can seem expensive – especially at weekends when prices inflate.

A *Natour*, Jl Pesanggrahan 2, T81776, F81101. Restaurant, pool, tennis, particularly good position on the edge of a gully, but rather spartan rooms and generally overpriced. **A** *Surya*, Jl Taman Wisata, T81991, F81058. Pool, tennis, most luxurious hotel in town, lacking in hill resort character, recently extended. **B** *Tanjung Plaza*, Jl Wilis 7, T81102. Rather scruffy. **C** *Wisma Semeru Indah*, Jl Semeru 7, T81701. Good views and reasonable rooms. **D** *Sri Katon*, Jl Taman Wisata. **Camping**: there is a camping ground at the Kakek Bodo Waterfall.

Sports	**Horse riding**: in the hills around. Men wait outside hotels with their somewhat mangy looking animals, in the hope of luring some custom.
Transport 55 km from Malang, 60 km from Surabaya	**Road Bus**: buses between Surabaya and Malang will drop passengers off at **Pandaan**. From here, minibuses travel up the mountain to Tretes.
Directory	**Banks** There are no banks in Tretes, although hotels will change money.

Selekta and Batu

Phone code: 0341
Colour map 3, grid B5

Selekta and Batu are 2 hill resorts, 4 km apart on the south face of Mount Arjuna and Mount Welirang, 23 km from Malang. Batu is marketed as Java's 'apple town' (the 1st tree was planted in 1908), although the apples are 2nd rate. **Candi Songgoriti**, dated to 732, can be reached from either resort. The turn-off for the candi is just out of Batu on the road towards Pare. (From Malang, take a bus from the Landungsari terminal and change at Batu for Songgoriti, 500Rp.) There are hot springs and pools, waterfalls and hiking trails around this beautiful scenery, sometimes referred to as Java's 'little Switzerland'. Batu and Selekta are popular with Malang residents and hotel rates rise considerably over the weekend, when hotels are often full.

Sleeping There are numerous places to stay in both towns, including the luxurious **A-B** *Kusuma Agro Wisata*, Jl Abdul Gani Atas, T593333, F593196. In Batu (with restaurant, swimming pool, tennis and various caged animals, set on hill above Batu, rather clinical, almost like a massive showhouse, but very comfortable nonetheless). Of the cheaper places – and most are pricey – the best are **E** *Losmen Kawi*, Jl Gajah Mada 19 (in Batu), T591139. Clean and friendly with attached mandi. **C-D** *Hotel Perdana*, Jl Gajah Mada 101, T591104. Hot water bathrooms, decent, clean and reasonably priced place, with some cheaper (older) rooms and also a more recent rear extension.

Transport **Road Bus**: buses leave from Malang's Landungsari station on Jl M Haryono, change at Batu for Seleka, each journey 750Rp.

Pulau Sempu and Sedangbiru

Colour map 3, grid B5

Pulau Sempu is an 877 ha nature reserve, clothed by dense forest and home to hundreds of colourful birds, large monitor lizards and snakes, as well as, reputedly, shy and retiring black leopards.

Located on the southeast of the island is a spectacular **salt water lagoon**. The tranquil turquoise water and pure white sand contrast with the surf which crashes in from the ocean at one side of the natural pool. Great views out to sea from the surrounding cliffs. The lagoon is rarely visited and is safe for swimming. It can be reached by a 3-4 hour walk along trails – boats cannot get here because the seaward side of the lagoon is protected by vicious rocks.

Also on the island is a **large freshwater fishing lake** – two hour's walk from the drop off point. **Pasir Putih** (a white sand beach on the north coast) is good for snorkelling – a 20 minute walk from the drop off point.

Only day trips are possible to Pulau Sempu, so it is necessary for visitors to stay in the beautiful fishing village of **Sedangbiru**, on the mainland. Just 100m of fast flowing channel separates Sedangbiru from the island reserve. During the summer months the village is a hive of activity, as workers from Jember and Banyuwangi visit for the fishing season. The harbour, filled with numerous *prahus*, dominates the village.

Sleeping **B-C** *Wisata Sedangbiru*, Jl Raya Sedangbiru. Immaculate beach bungalow with 3 double rooms and western bathrooms. Larger more expensive rooms have a/c and TV. Located just off the beach, facing out to the island – a very peaceful setting. **E-F** There are a couple of family homestays in the village, ask around.

Eating

Basic warungs.

Transport

Road and **Sea** To get to Sedangbiru, take a bus from Malang's Gadang bus terminal to Turen, 30 mins, then change to a blue minibus to Sedangbiru, 2 hrs. From Sedangbiru to Pulau Sempu, the short boat crossing should cost 5,000Rp. To enter the reserve, pay 5,000Rp at the PHPA office near the harbour. Hiring a guide is necessary (20,000Rp), as the island is a maze of tracks; official PHPA rangers are the cheaper option, although some locals know the island.

Surabaya

Phone code: 031
Colour map 3, grid B5

Surabaya has been an important port since the 16th century, and is now Indonesia's second largest city with a population of over 3,000,000 – 10 times the figure for 1940. It was developed by the VOC into Java's premier port in the mid-18th century and by 1900 it was the largest town in the Dutch East Indies, exceeding even Batavia in the size of its population. Surabaya remains an important manufacturing centre, and the city lies at the heart of one of the fastest growing industrial regions in Indonesia.

Surabaya is not a popular tourist destination. It has no sights to compare with those around Yogyakarta, and lies to the north of the overland route between Bali, Yogya and Jakarta. However, it is an important port for vessels sailing to Sulawesi, Maluku, Kalimantan and Nusa Tenggara, and is a frequent destination for local and foreign businessmen.

Ins and outs

Getting there

Surabaya is Java's second largest city, after Jakarta, and although it is not on many visitors' itineraries, it is a very important commercial centre. **Juanda International Airport** is 18 km south of the city, and there are flights to destinations in Java and the Outer Islands. Of the city's 3 train stations, the most convenient is the centrally located **Gubeng** terminal. There are trains from here to Jakarta, Solo, Yogya, Blitar, Malang and Banyuwangi. The **Pasarturi** station also serves Jakarta, but along the north coast route via Semarang. The massive **Bungurasih** bus terminal is 8 km south of the city centre and there are buses of all complexions to destinations in Java, as well as Sumatra, Bali, Lombok and Sumbawa. Town buses and bemos run out here from the city centre. The smaller **Oso Wilangan** terminal is 8 km west of town and serves destinations on Java's north coast, including Semarang. Minibus offices are concentrated on Jl Basuki Rachmat. After Jakarta, Surabaya's port of Tanjung Perak is Java's most important. A number of *Pelni* ships call here. The ferry for Madura leaves from **Kalimas Harbour**.

Getting around

Traffic in Surabaya is nightmarish, small becaks have been banned from the city centre and bemos and town buses, which follow fixed routes, provide the main means of public transport. Metered taxis are available and self-drive cars can also be hired.

There are various **tourist offices**: *East Java Tourism Office* near the zoo, range of pamphlets, maps and other information on East Java but weak on specifics; *Surabaya Municipal Tourist Development Board*, Jl Gayung Kebonsari 56C, T832029, only moderately helpful, some maps, open 0700-1500 Mon-Sat; *Tourist Information Centre*, Jl Pemuda 118, T524499, and Juanda International Airport.

Sights

Around Jalan Pemuda

The centre of Surabaya is marked by Jl Pemuda. Most of the city's better hotels and shopping centres are found within walking distance of this road. The immaculately maintained **Grahadi**, towards the west end of Jl Pemuda, was the residence of the Dutch colonial governor of East Java; today it is still the official residence of the

Surabaya

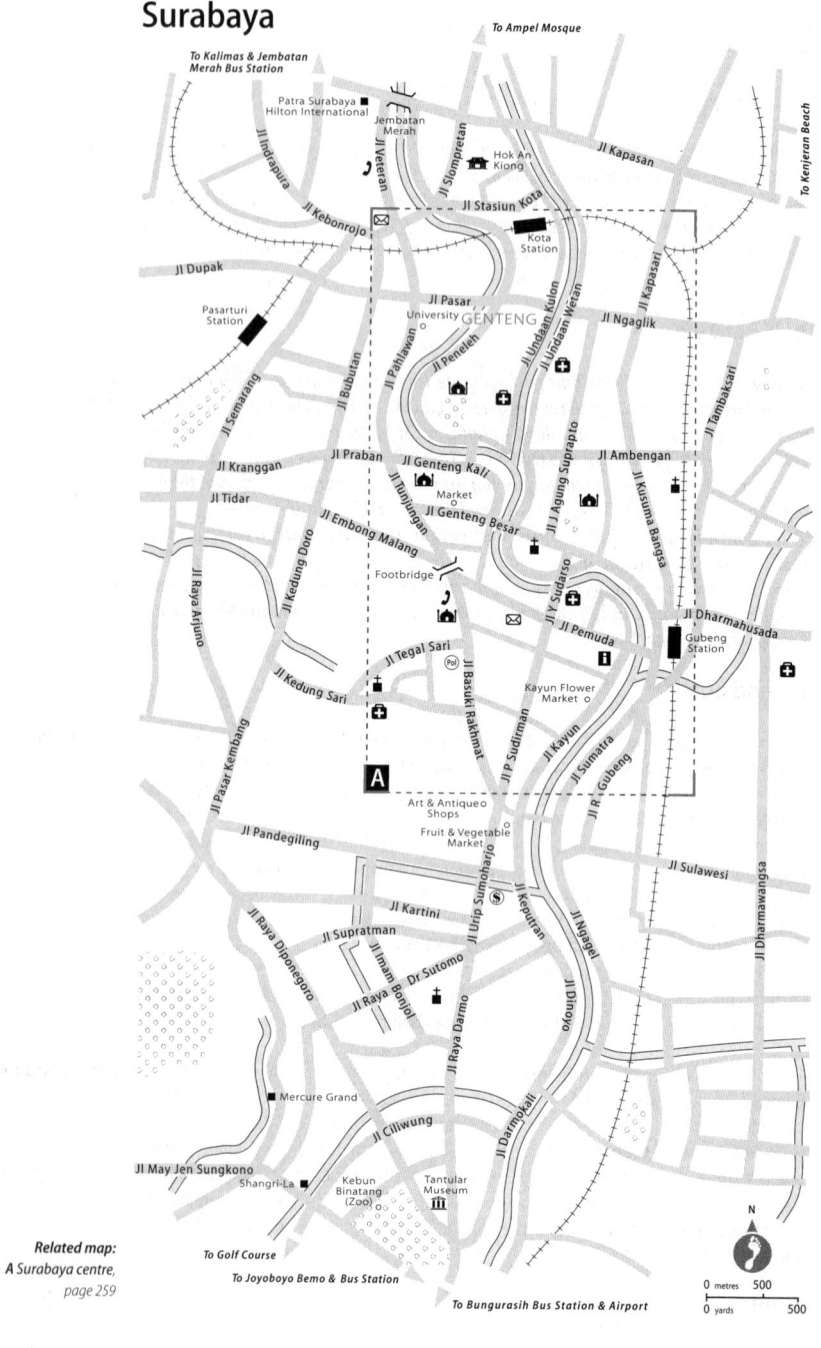

Related map:
A Surabaya centre,
page 259

Governor of East Java. Opposite is the stone statue known as **Joko Dolog** (guardian of the young teak forest). This was carved in 1326 as a memorial to the last king of the Singasari Dynasty, and was transferred here from Mojokerto by the Dutch.

At the north edge of the city is Kali Mas or River of Gold, a wharf at which traditional *perahu* moor. Most vessels here are Bugis *pinisi*, better known in the West as **Makassar schooners** (see page 683). It is claimed that these elegant boats are made without a single nail – they are pegged together. Pinisi link the islands of the archipelago, carrying mixed cargoes of lumber, barbed wire, glass, tinned goods, house tiles, just about anything that is relatively water resistant. Although modern cargo vessels are becoming more common, the versatility of the pinisi mean that they remain popular and profitable, and indeed represent one of the largest sailing fleets still operating in the world today. The wharf is on Jl Kalimas Baru, on the eastern side of the Tanjung Perak Port area. Strictly-speaking, photographs can only be taken with permission from the harbour master. Ask at the police post. The wharf is best visited in the morning; boats tend to leave by mid-morning.

Kali Mas

South of the port, to the east of the Surabaya River, is Kampung Arab or the Kasbah Quarter (it lies off Jl Kyai Mas Mansur). This is the heart of the old city, with narrow streets and a bazaar atmosphere. (The Indonesian word for market – *pasar* – is derived from the Arabic *bazaar*.) Among its buildings, the architecturally and historically most important is the **Ampel Mosque**, the oldest mosque in East Java, originally built by Sunan Ampel, one of the nine *walis*, in the 15th century. Sunan Ampel died in Surabaya in 1481 and his grave lies within the mosque compound. The site is a popular pilgrimage spot for Indonesians.

Kampung Arab

South of the Arab quarter is the **Jembatan Merah** or Red Bridge, a strategic site in the Battle of Surabaya waged during November 1945 (see box). Close to the bridge, on Jl Slompretan, is the Chinese temple **Hok An Kiong**, while just to the north of the bridge is Surabaya's Chinatown. The Hok An Kiong temple is three centuries old and traditional Chinese puppet shows are said to be held here in the middle and end of every month (every full and half moon). South of here is the **Tugu Pahlawan** or Heroes Monument, which stands in the centre of the rather unexciting main city square, opposite the Governor's office on Jl Pahlawan. It commemorates the thousands of young Muslims who poured into the city and died fighting against British forces during the Battle of Surabaya.

Jembatan Merah

The **Kayun Flower Market** is situated on Jl Kayun, while the **People's Amusement Park** (known as THR) is east of the river on Jl Kusuma Bangsa. This area is newly renovated and now includes a large shopping centre, cinema, open stage and children's amusement park. ■ *Open 1800-2300 Mon-Sun.*

Other sights

The **Kebun Binatang** (or **Zoo**) is within walking distance of the Joyoboyo bemo station on Jl Setail, but about 3 km from the centre of the city. It is one of the best zoos in Southeast Asia, with a good collection of local and regional animals. Most bemos run to Joyoboyo. ■ *Admission 1,500Rp (additional 400Rp for aquarium). Open 0900-1730 Mon-Sun.* Opposite the zoo on Jl Raya Diponegoro is the **Tantular Museum**, an ethnographic and archaeological museum with what might be termed an eclectic collection, including a steam-powered Daimler motorcycle and neolithic artefacts. ■ *Open: 0700-1400 Tue-Thu, 0700-1100 Fri, 0700-1230 Sat. Admission: 400Rp.*

Excursions

Trowulan lies 52 km southwest of Surabaya on the Surabaya-Solo road, not far from Mojokerto, see page 263. ■ *Getting there: take a bus from Surabaya's Bungurasih terminal travelling towards Jombang (there are many) and ask to be let off in Trowulan.*

Mount Bromo lies 145 km southeast of Surabaya (see page 276).

South & east of Surabaya

Kenjeran is a rather unexciting beach east of Surabaya. ■ *Getting there:* take a bemo, either line (lyn) 'S' (from Joyoboyo) or 'R1' (from Jembatan Merah).

North of Surabaya **Madura** can be visited as a day excursion – best during the **bull racing** season from August to October (see page 268).

Gresik lies 14 km north of Surabaya and is an ugly industrial satellite town, with one saving grace: it is the site of the grave of Sunan Giri, one of the nine imam (or walis) who are credited with having first brought Islam to Java. A staircase leads up past graves of other holy men to the imam's resting place, which is housed inside an attractive double chamber of heavily carved wood. To the left of the imam's grave are the graves of his children. The **festival** *Khol Sunan Giri* (30 September) commemorates the death of Sunan Giri. ■ *Getting there: microlets travel from Surabaya to Gresik, through an unattractive industrial landscape. Get off at a marked turning to the left, on Jl Sunan Giri (ask for 'makam Sunan Giri'); horse-drawn carts and ojeks wait at the end of the road to transport visitors and pilgrims the 1½ km to the tomb.*

Paciran lies on Java's north coast, 60 km northwest of Surabaya. Near here, on a hill top, is the intricately carved gateway of **Sendang Duwur**, named after the Muslim saint Sunan Sendang who was buried here in 1585. It is interesting for its combination of styles – the carving includes Arabic calligraphy alongside Hindu designs.
■ *Getting there: from the Bungurasih bus terminal, south of town.*

Tuban lies 100 km northwest of Surabaya on Java's north coast, see page 265.
■ *Getting there: buses from Bungurasih terminal, south of town.*

Tours
See also 'Tour operators', page 262

Local travel agents offer city tours, day trips to Mount Bromo, Trowulan and the ancient sites of the Majapahit Kingdom, as well as to Malang, Madura, Selecta and Batu. *PT Wisata Bahari Mas Permai*, Jl Tanjung Priok 11, T25268, F25559, provide 'traditional' day-long cruises on their *perahu* (schooner). The *East Java Regional Tourism Office*, in association with the provincial agricultural department (Jl Gayung Kebonsari 173, Wonocolo (south of centre), T811879), are pushing 'agrotourism': they organize tours of coffee estates, tobacco farms, coconut plantations, sugar cane mills and other similar 'sights'. There are also trips to a teak plantation, 150 km west of Surabaya (see page 226).

Essentials

Sleeping
Reflecting the status of the city as a business centre, not a tourist destination, there are a good number of mid & upper range hotels, but woefully few decent losmen & homestays

L *Majapahit Mandarin Oriental*, Jl Tunjungan 65, T5454333, F5454111. Built in 1910, it is stylish yet more personal than other international hotels. Rooms are extravagantly furnished, set around a courtyard and lovely pool. Highly recommended. **L-AL** *Radisson*, Jl Pemuda 31-37, T5316833, F5316393, www.radisson.com radsub@indosat.net.id Pool, located opposite the World Trade Centre, behind the Surabaya Plaza. A cool, relaxed atmosphere, excellent rooms, quiet and with extra added touches. Recommended. **L-AL** *Sheraton*, Jl Embong Malang 25-31, T5468000, F5468182 (next door to Tunjungan Plaza). Pool, jacuzzi, 2 floodlit tennis courts, fitness centre, jogging track, also has separate 'tower block' apartments. **AL** *Hyatt Regency*, Jl Basuki Rakhmat 106-108, T5311234, F5321508, hrssubloc@indosat.net.id A/c, restaurant, pool, all facilities. The best place to stay in Surabaya for atmosphere and décor. **AL** *Patra Surabaya Hilton*, Jl Gunungsari, T5682703, F5682081. Within minutes of the Yoni golf course, international hotel with all usual amenities, geared for the avid golfer, quite a distance from the town. **AL** *Shangri-La Hotel*, Jl May. Jend. Sungkono 120, T5661550, F5661570, www.shangri-la.com, sales@shangri-la.hotel_surabaya.co.id Large, international hotel with good facilities, lovely rooms, good restaurant, excellent (if you have your own transport) position near golf course, but far from the main city. **AL-A** *Novotel Surabaya*, Jl Ngagel 173-175, T568230, F5676317. A/c, restaurant, pool, tennis and squash courts, business and fitness centres, attractive low rise hotel with 138 spacious rooms and landscaped gardens, situated south of town, east of the zoo. **A** *Altea*, Jl Raya Darmo 68-76, T69501, F69204. A/c, restaurant. **A** *Mercure Grand Hotel*, Jl Raya Kupang Indah 37-39, T7328738, F7328731. International hotel with Mediterranean restaurant, deli and ice cream

SURABAYA: ESSENTIALS 259

Surabaya centre

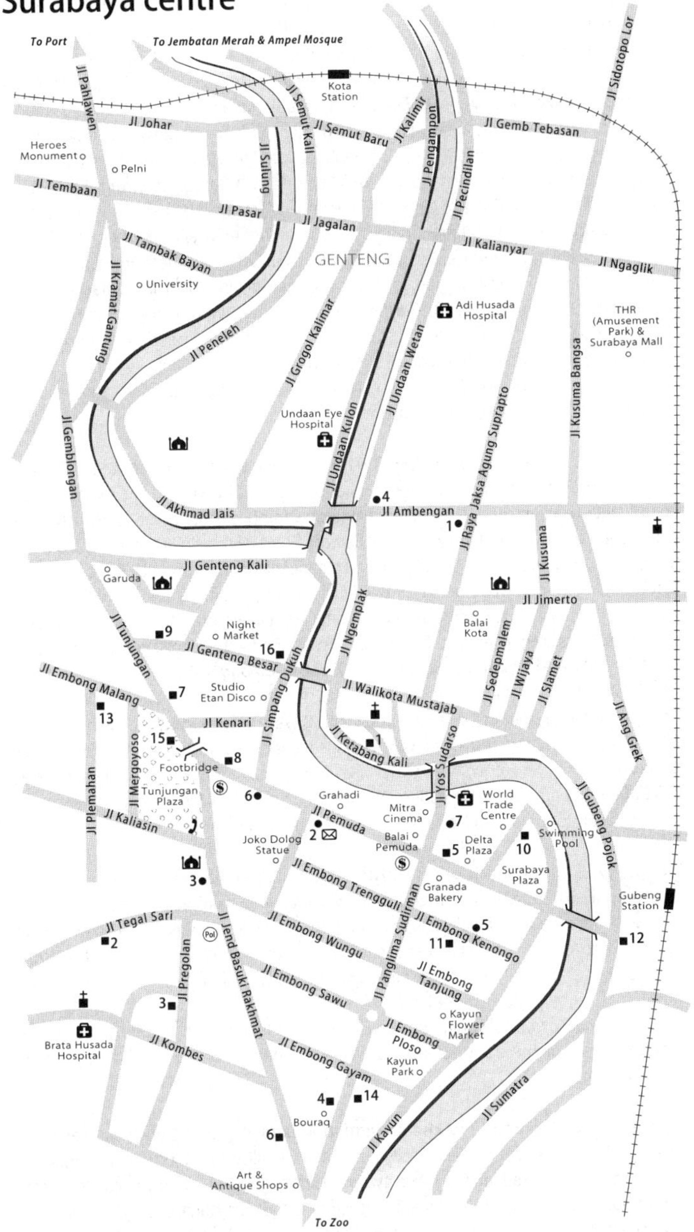

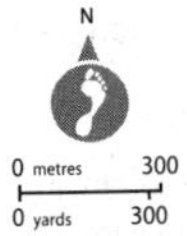

■ **Sleeping**
1 Bamboe Denn
2 Bisanta
3 Cendana
4 Elmi
5 Garden Palace & Garden
6 Hyatt Regency
7 Majapahit Mandarin Oriental
8 Natour Simpang
9 Paviljoen
10 Radisson
11 Remaja
12 Sahid Surabaya & Gubeng
13 Sheraton
14 Tanjung
15 Tunjung
16 Weta International

● **Eating**
1 Café Venezia
2 Iaman Sari Indah
3 KFC, Ice Cream Parlour & Galael Supermarket
4 Soto Ambengan
5 Turin
6 Wendy's Burger
7 Zangrandi Ice Cream Palace

shop, popular with Indonesian businessmen, good service. **A-B** *Bisanta*, Jl Tegalsari 85, T5457007, F5318928. Room rate includes 2 meals, coffee shop, a/c, TV, an imposing building with small rooms but well-presented. **A-B** *Cendana*, Jl KBP M Duryat, T5455667, F5314367, cendana@indo.net.id Comfortable rooms with minibar, TV and shower, for this price the rooms could do with a revamp. **A-B** *Elmi*, Jl Panglima Sudirman 42-44, T5322571, F5315615, elmihtl@indosat.id A/c, restaurant, large pool, modern and characterless, dark but sophisticated rooms, tastefully furnished with a telephone fitted above the loo for the ultimate in luxury. Fitness centre and sauna, pub with live music. **A-B** *Natour Simpang*, Jl Gubernur Surjo 1-3, T5342151, F5310157. Opposite Tungungan Plaza and the main thoroughfare, so rooms are noisy but comfortable. Could do with a spot of renovation to keep up with the competition. **B** *Garden Palace*, Jl Yos Sudarso 11, T5321001. Cantonese and Japanese restaurants, coffee shop, beauty salon, rooftop pool, price includes breakfast. Attached to the *Garden Palace* is the cheaper (**B**) *Garden Hotel*. Definitely worth considering: rooms are good, large and tastefully decorated, basic fitness centre and pool, good standard considering the price. **B-C** *Hotel Tunjungan*, Jl Tunjungan 102-104, T5466666, F5455514 (next to Plaza). High rise international hotel, with breakfast, a/c, cinema, excellent location, satellite TV, pool and fitness centre, runs good promotional packages.

B *Grand Park*, Jl Samundra, T331515, F333194. **B** *Paviljoen*, Jl Genteng Besar 94-98, T5343449. Some a/c, this is an old Dutch-era hotel that has been recently upgraded, the rooms are very good if a little basic, and it has a little more charm and atmosphere than other places in this price range, cheap and efficient laundry service. **B** *Remaja Hotel*, Jl Embong Kenongo 12, T5341359. Reception flustered to receive western guests, but friendly staff in this small but comfortable hotel, large rooms pricey but should fall. **B** *Sahid Surabaya*, Jl Sumatra 1, T5032711 F5036292, www.sahid.com, sahidsub@indosat.net.id Comfortable international standard rooms at Indonesian prices, fitness centre, restaurant and good views from the top floors, free airport transfer. **B** *Satelit*, Jl Mayjend Sungkono, T5615876, F5660404. **B** *Tanjung*, Jl Panglima Sudirman 43-45, T5316862, F5312291. Despite its grubby reception and stairwell, rooms are suprisingly good, large and tasteful (if pink is still in fashion), restaurant. **B** *Weta International*, Jl Genteng Kali 3-11, T5319494, F5345512. A/c, restaurant with loud piped music, badly lit corridors lead to light pine furnitured rooms, with good views over the river. Simple comfort in excellent position. **C-D** *Gubeng*, Jl Sumatera 18 (in front of the *Sahid Surabaya*), T5341603. A dirty rather squalid place with little to recommend it, bar its location close to the railway station.

D *Ganesha*, Jl Prapen Indah 41B, T818705. Price includes breakfast. **E** *Bamboe Denn*, Jl Ketabang Kali 6A, T5340333. Dorms (**F**), clean with narrow bunkbeds and individual lockers, double rooms adequate, the place to meet travellers, avoid lesson time if you don't want to be forced into teaching at the language school, basic food available, very friendly. **E** *Stasiun*, Jl Stasiun Kota 1, T20630. Next to the Surabaya Kota railway station.

Eating The *Tunjungan Plaza*, on Jl Tunjungan, houses a large selection of restaurants, serving Chinese, Javanese, Japanese and seafood, particularly good selection on the 5th floor and in the basement.

Indonesian Cheap and very cheap: *Rumah Makan Ria*, Jl M Duryat 7 (near *Hyatt Regency*). Sundanese specialities locally acclaimed, small restaurant, friendly. *Antika*, Jl Raya Darmo 1. Good Padang food. *Mie Ayam*, Jl Genteng Kali 119. Good, cheap food. *Mie Tunjungan*, Jl Genteng Kali 127 (near intersection with Jl Tunjungan). Good, cheap food. *Puri Garden*, Jl Pemuda 33-37 (in the *Delta Plaza*). Huge Indonesian menu. *Soto Ambengan*, Jl Ambengan 3. Locally renowned for its excellent soto. Recommended. *Coffee House*, Jl Praban 2 (near intersection with Jl Tunjungan). *Dewi Sri*, Jl Tunjungan 96-98. *Taman Sari Indah Restaurant*, Jl Pemuda (opposite Governors House), good East Javenese at reasonable prices.

Chinese *Phoenix*, Jl Mayjen. Sungkono. *Mahkota Restaurant*, Jl TAIS Nasution 23. Not just one restaurant but a veritable confection of them, on Floor 1 a Chinese restaurant, Floor 2 a

Karaoke and steak place, Floor 3 an Indonesian and international restaurant, and on Floor 4 a private room for goodness knows what. **Oriental**, Jl Taman AIS Nasutron 37, T5344651. Local reputation is that this place serves the best Chinese food in Surabaya and it's cheap too. **Japanese** *Hana*, *Altea Hotel*, Jl Raya Darmo 68-76, karaoke.

International Limited choice of restaurants, although the big hotels serve international food. **Cheap** *News Café*, Jl Panglima Sudirman 47-49. This bar-cum-restaurant (hosting live bands) has a small international menu of generally good dishes. *Café Venezia*, Jl Ambengan 16. Old-style villa with lovely grounds, international food and some Japanese and Korean dishes. *Granada Bakery*, intersection of Jl Pemuda and Jl Panglima Sudirman. *Pizza Hut*, *Delta Plaza* and *Tunjungan Plaza*. *Texas Fried Chicken*, Jl Basuki Rakhmat 16. *KFCs*, on every corner. *Wendy's Fast Food Hamburger Restaurant*, Jl Pemuda. *Arby's*, Jl Raya Gubeng 33; cafés in Surabaya Plaza are excellent, try the *Café Exelcior* for iced coffee.

Foodstalls *Kayun Park*, along Jl Kedung Doro, and a mass of warungs around Jl Genteng Besar.

Ice cream parlours *Mon Cheri*, 4th Flr, Tunjungan Plaza. *Zangrandi Ice Cream Palace*, Jl Yos Sudarso 15, stylish but noisy. *Turin*, Jl Embong Kenongo, serves excellent home-made ice cream and is run by an English teacher.

Bars There is a good selection of bars in Surabaya, which are becoming more sophisticated as the city's yuppies grow in number and in wealth. See 'Rock Music' in the Entertainment section below for bars with live music. The most popular and therefore the most expensive bar is *Club Deluxe* on Jl Tungungan, but this is where Surabaya's best live bands perform. Drinks in all the pubs are around 8,000Rp for draught beer and about 12,000Rp for spirits with a mixer. A variety of bands play in each bar. Depending on which night you visit, there might be country/blues or popular/current tunes. *Colors*, Jl Sumatra, is a gloomy den in a colonial period building. *Tequila Willies*, Jl Kayon 62, is slicker and less rough round the edges than *Colors* with, as the name suggests, pretensions to Mexican roots. *News Café*, Jl Panglima Sudirman 47-49 (open 1100-0100), is a bar-cum-restaurant with a media theme, local bands occasionally play here; other recommended bars are located in the large hotels: *Bongo's* (*Sheraton Hotel*) has vibrant Mexican and African decor. *Desperado's* (*Shangri-La Hotel*) is also a tex-mex restaurant, open 1700-0200 daily. *Gaslight Pub* (*Hotel Equator*), Jl Pakis Argosari 47, an Indonesian slant on the traditional British local. *Treasure Island* (*Hotel Garden Palace*), Jl Yos Sudarso 11, live music and nautical decor.

Entertainment

Cinemas *Mitra*, Jl Pemuda 15; *Studio 1-4*, Tunjungan Plaza, Jl Basuki Rakhmat (north end). **Classical Javanese dance performances & music** *French Culture Centre*, Jl Darmokali 10-12, T68639; *Goethe Institute*, Jl Taman Ade Irma Suryani, T40368; *Taman Budaya*, Jl Genteng Kali 85, lessons in these arts are also available here; *The People's Amusement Park* or *THR*, east of the river on Jl Kusuma Bangsa, stages performances of wayang, ketoprak, and other dances and drama (open 1800-2300 Mon-Sun).

Discos: Surabaya's largest disco is Studio Etan, on Jl Simpang Dukuh 38, open 2100-0200. It has a 2 level dance floor, adjoining pub and karaoke room. It's packed on Sat nights with teenage Indonesian 'clubbers'.

For any visitors wanting to tap into Surabaya's jumping club scene, it is worth getting hold of a copy of 'Surabaya Now!', a free monthly magazine geared to tourists & expat residents which lists all the clubs & the bands playing

Rock music *Colors*, Jl Sumatra, bar and music venue in colonial era building, hosts mostly local heavy metal bands, best from 2300 but open 1800-0200; *Laga*, Jl May Jend Sungkono 107, opposite the Shangri-La Hotel, rather lighter than *Colors*, local bands play cover songs after 2200, open 2000-0200, English pub atmosphere, free entrance; *Tequila Willies*, Jl Kayon 62, live music and occasional live shows, open 1800-0500 Mon-Sun. Local bands also play live at the *News Café*, Jl Panglima Sudirman 47-49 (open 1100-0100); and *Tavern* (*Hyatt Regency*), Jl Jend Basuki Rachmat (open 1700-0200).

Wayang kulit Performances staged every Sat at the Radio Republic Indonesia station, Jl Pemuda 82-90, studio 2, commencing 2000.

262 SURABAYA: ESSENTIALS

Festivals **May** *Anniversary of THR* (Peoples' Amusement Park) (19th), cultural performances and stalls at THR Surabaya Hall. Anniversary of founding of the city (3rd) held at Taman Surya, cultural performances and other ceremonies.
November *Heroes Day* (10th), centred around the Heroes Monument, commemorates those who died in the Battle of Surabaya in November 1945. Parades and various festivities.

Shopping **Antiques & handicrafts** Jl Basuki Rakhmat; *Sarinah Craft and Batik Centre*, Jl Tunjungan 7.
Batik *Batik Danar Hadi*, Jl Diponegoro 184; *Batik Keris*, Jl Tunjungan 12.
Books *Toko Buku Nasional*, Tunjungan Plaza, Jl Basuki Rakhmat.
Shopping malls Surabaya has an abundance of these. The *Delta Plaza* on Jl Pemuda is said to be the biggest in Southeast Asia; the *Plaza Surabaya*, Jl Pemuda 31-37, must come close; *Apollo Plaza*; *Indo Plaza*; *Surabaya Mall* on Jl Kusuma Bangsa, just south of the THR; *Tunjungan Plaza*, north end of Jl Basuki Rakhmat, the biggest mall in Surabaya, with outlets of Escada, Versace, Lacoste, Espirit, Bennetton, Sisley, McDonalds, KFC, nightclub and a cinema.

Sports **Bowling** *Wijaya Bowling Centre*, Jl Bubutan 1-7 (3rd floor).
Golf *Yani Golf Club*, Jl Gunungsari (next to *Patra Jasa Motel*, 5 km from city), T40834.
Swimming A number of the hotels allow visitors to use their pools, eg *Garden Palace*, Jl Yos Sudarso. The *Delta Plaza* on Jl Pemuda (at the back) has a large, usually empty, pool for serious swimmers (no shade available). The *Margorejo Indah Sports Centre*, Jl Margorejo (south of town), has a water world.

Tour operators *Haryono*, Jl Pang Sudirman 93, T41006; *Natrabu*, Jl Dinoyo 40, T68513; *Orient Express*, Jl Basuki Rakhmat 78, T43315; *Pacto*, Altea Miramar Hotel, Jl Raya Darmo 68-76, T69501; *Prima Vijaya Indah Tours*, Delta Plaza, Jl Pemuda 31, T514399; *Suman Tours*, Jl Yos Sudarso 17, T510417; *Wiedas Karya Gemilang*, Jl Pucang Rinenggo 1, T60110.

Transport
793 km from Jakarta,
327 km from Yogya,
89 km from Malang

Local Traffic in Surabaya is rightly infamous. To aid the pedestrian in their seemingly impossible quest to get to the other side, hand held stop signs have been introduced. The idea is that you pick up a sign on one side of the road and wave it hopefully in front of you as you cross. If successful, you can pass the stop sign on to another waiting pedestrian nervously contemplating his or her luck. **Becak**: banned from much of the city centre. **Bemo**: there are innumerable bemo routes, again some maps mark their routes. There is a flat rate fare of 350Rp. **Bus**: some town maps mark bus routes, 500Rp for regular buses, 2,000Rp for patas (express) buses. **Taxi**: metered, with flagfall at 1,300Rp, 900Rp for every subsequent kilometre. *Taksi Zebra*, T515555/512233. **Car hire**: self drive or with driver from *Avis*, Patra Surabaya Hilton International, Jl Gunung Sari, T582703.

Air Juanda International Airport is 18 km south of Surabaya. *Transport to town*: irregular town buses into town (1,000Rp); taxis cost about 30,000Rp, depending on destination. There is a fixed rate schedule; pay at the transport desk outside the arrivals hall. Regular connections on *Garuda/Merpati*, *Sempati* and *Bouraq*, with other destinations in Java, Sumatra, Kalimantan, Sulawesi, Bali, Lombok, Nusa Tenggara, Muluku and Irian Jaya. Tourist information desk.

Train Surabaya has 3 main railway stations. Gubeng, at the end of Jl Pemuda on Jl Gubeng Masjid, serves Jakarta, Solo, Yogya, Blitar, Malang and Banyuwangi. Some of these trains also stop at Kota station. Gubeng is the most convenient place to arrive by train in Surabaya (it is the most central station). Pasarturi station on Jl Semarang serves Jakarta via Semarang and other towns on the north route (see timetable, page 977). It is possible to buy a 'combination' ticket – train, ferry, bus – through to **Denpasar**, Bali (15 hrs). Regular connections with **Banyuwangi** (7 hrs), **Malang** (2 hrs), **Blitar** (5 hrs), **Semarang** (6½ hrs), **Solo** (4½ hrs), **Bandung** (14 hrs) and **Jakarta** (15 hrs).

Road Bus: the new Bungurasih station – the largest, so it is said, in Indonesia – was opened 8 km to the south of the city in 1991. It is at the intersection of Jl Jend A Yani and Jl Let Jen Sutoyo, and both town buses (bus P1 runs to Jl Tunjungan and Jl Pemuda) and bemos (often via Joyoboyo bus station) link it with the city centre. Regular connections with most destinations in Java; also buses to **Denpasar** (Bali), **Mataram** (Lombok), and **Sumbawa Besar** and **Bima** (Sumbawa). Night bus companies can be found at the Bungurasih Station or at offices on Jl Basuki Rachmat, Jl Arjuno and Jl Tidar. The Oso Wilangan terminal is 8 km west of the city centre and serves destinations on Java's north coast, including **Semarang**, **Kudus** and **Tuban**. **Minibus:** An attractive alternative to trekking out to 1 of the 2 bus terminals is to book a seat on a minibus which usually pick up from hotels. Minibus offices are concentrated on Jl Basuki Rachmat; it is also often possible to book seats through hotels.

Sea Boat: Surabaya is an important port of call for *Pelni* ships sailing to towns in Sulawesi, Kalimantan, and the islands of Maluku and Nusa Tenggara. In all, 13 *Pelni* ships dock here on their various fortnightly circuits. (See page 988 for map and schedules.) The Pelni ticket office is on Jl Pahlawan 20, opposite Tugu Pahlawan, T21041, helpful clerk with good English. There are also numerous unscheduled local cargo vessels sailing to destinations throughout the archipelago – ask the harbour master or simply wander around the Tanjung Perak port for the latest departures. To get to Tanjung Perak take town bus P1 or C. The ferry to **Kamal** on Madura leaves from Kalimas harbour every 20 mins, 500Rp per person, and takes 30 mins-1 hr to make the crossing. To get to Kalimas Harbour take bus P from outside Tungungan Plaza, 500Rp.

Directory

Airline Offices *Bouraq*, Jl Jend Sudirman 70-72, T5452918. *British Airways*, Jl Panglima Sudirman 70-72, T526383. *Cathay Pacific*, Jl Basuki Rakhmat 124-128, T517543. *Garuda*, Jl Tunjungan 29, T5457347. *KLM*, Jl Yos Sudarso 11, T520247. *Mandala*, Jl Raya Diponegoro 73, T587157, F587158. *Merpati*, Jl Urip Sumoharjo 68, T588111. *Sempati*, Hotel Hyatt Regency, Jl Basuki Rachmat 124-128, T5321612. *Thai*, Jl Panglima Sudirman 72, T40681. The following have offices or agency offices in town. Check in the yellow pages for telephone numbers: *Air France*; *Japan Airlines (JAL)*; *Lufthansa*; *Malaysian Airlines*; *Northwest*; *Qantas*; *Saudia*; *Singapore Airlines*; *United*. **Banks** There are numerous banks and money changers in town and most currencies and TCs are accepted. Among the best are BNI, Jl Pemuda and Bank Central Asia. Many banks are concentrated on Jl Tunjungan. ATM machines and banks are also found in Tunjunan Plaza, normal opening times 0900-1600. **Communications** Post Office: Jl Kebonrojo (poste restante here and internet access, 24 hr) and Jl Taman Apsari (off Jl Pemuda, near Joko Dolog). Telephone and fax: *Wartel*, Tunjungan Plaza (north end of Jl Basuki Rakhmat), open 24 hrs, Surabaya Plaza, 2nd floor. Internet: internet cafés are springing up at a remarkable pace in Surabaya. Try *Café Fresh* in the Tanjungan Plaza, on the 5th floor, for fast access, 3,000Rp for 15 mins, worth the extra money for time saved. **Embassies & consulates** Australia, Jl Pemuda 27-31, T5319123 (World Trade Centre). Belgium, Jl Raya Kupang Indah III/24, T716423. CIS, Jl Sumatra 116, T5342091. Denmark, Jl Sambas 7, T5675047. France, Jl Darmokali 10, T5678639. Germany, Taman AIS Nasution 15, T5343735. India, Jl Pahlawan 17-19, T5341565. Japan, Jl Sumatra 93, T5344677. Netherlands, Jl Sumatra 54, T5311612. UK, Jl Jemur Sari (south of town), PO Box 310, T5316663. USA, Jl Raya Dr Sutomo 33, T5676880. **Medical facilities** General Hospital, Jl Dharmahusada 6-8, T40061. St Vincentius Hospital, Jl Raya Diponegoro 51, T575446. **Useful addresses** Immigration Office: Jl Jend S Parman 58A, T818070.

Trowulan

Trowulan was the site of the capital of the powerful Majahapit Kingdom, which reached its zenith in the 14th century. The remains of temples, bathing pools and an artificial lake can be found spread over a wide area, and only the major buildings are described below. (The whole archaeological site covers some 100 sq km.) The ruins, most of which have undergone restoration, are built of red brick, making them quite distinctive from other Javanese temple complexes. Because this is an archaeological site, and not a town, there is no accommodation. The nearest town is **Mojokerto**, 8 km to the north, where there are some very mediocre places to stay, along with other facilities.

Phone code (Mojokerto): 0343
Colour map 3, grid B5

A good place to start is the excellent **museum**, which lies 1 km off the main road to the left, through a red-brick split gate. It houses a wealth of archaeological finds from the area, the majority dating from the Majapahit Period. Fine metalwork and sculpture, well displayed and labelled, give an indication of the sophistication of the

Sights

society. ■ *Admission 200Rp. Open 0700-1600 Tue-Sun.* Opposite the museum is the restored **Kolam Segaran**, a large artificial lake, measuring 375m x 175m. Contemporary accounts record that the lake was used as a banquet spot for the entertainment of foreign envoys. At the end of a repast, the precious plates and other tableware would be tossed nonchalantly into the lake to indicate the wealth that the kingdom had at its disposal.

From the lake and museum, continue south for 500m to a crossroads; turn left, and a further 2 km along this road is **Candi Bajang Ratu**, a tall slender gateway, with a pyramidal roof. It was built at the beginning of the 14th century and is believed to have been the entrance to a sacred building which has now disappeared. There is some ornamentation on the stepped upper levels. By the Majapahit Period, the entrance doorway had become the most important feature of the shrine – a feature which is duplicated in the pura of Bali. Bajang Ratu is the most complete of these gateways, although one of the smaller ones.

A further 1 km on is the unornamented **Candi Tikus**, situated on the left-hand side of the road. The shrine lies below ground level, and is believed to have been a ritual bathing place. The small pavilion set in the middle of the pool represented Mount Penanggungan (the East Javanese equivalent of Mount Meru), while the surrounding water evoked the sea. The candi was only discovered in 1914 when a plague of rats were found to be nesting in a mound. Upon excavation of the mound, the locals were surprised to discover a temple buried beneath the earth, along with the rats; this may be why it became known as Candi Tikus, 'tikus' meaning rat.

Leading off the main road is a narrow lane which runs to **Candi Brahu**, a rectangular temple with cellas projecting from each of its four sides. No decoration remains, and it is at present undergoing restoration. Returning to the main road, and 1.2 km back towards Mojokerto, is a turning on the right to **Candi Wringin Lawang** (so called because a banyan tree – 'wringin' – was found near the gate – 'lawang'). The site is about 200m off the main road and is also known as Candi Bentar because it resembles a temple cut in two, vertically.

Sleeping **For Trowulan in Mojokerto** Mojokerto, 8 km north of Trowulan, is the nearest large town to the site, and accommodation is available although none is particularly recommended. But if visitors wish to see the candi at their leisure, it may be necessary to be based here. **B-C** *Padepokan Cahaya Putra*, Trawas, T81759; **Swiss Indohotel**, Pacet-Cangar, T29328. Cheaper places to stay include: **C** *Hotel Sriwijaya*, Jl Raya Pacet I, some a/c; **E** *Hotel Tenera*, Jl Cokroaminoto 1, T22904.

Trowulan

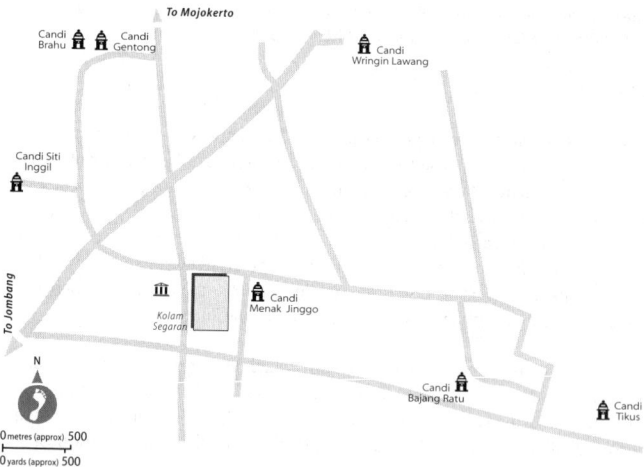

Tambak fisheries and the perils of over-production

All along the north coast of Java can be seen distinctive tambak or fish ponds. Although such ponds are also found on Bali, Southwest Sulawesi and in Northeast Java, the north coast of Java is the centre of tambak fisheries.

Traditionally, these fish ponds were dug on the leeward side of protective mangroves and then used to farm, especially prawns and milkfish. Salt water, rich with nutrients, is channelled into the ponds along specially dug ditches which, when mixed with river water and rain, produces the brackish conditions in which these fish and prawns thrive. Where production has kept to low-intensity traditional methods, the ponds have remained sustainably productive. But in the early 1980s, with prawn prices rising rapidly, farmers turned to the intensive production of tiger prawns. They installed water pumps and used purchased feed to increase production. The protective mangroves, so important as spawning grounds for fish, were removed, and fresh water contaminated with fertilizers and pesticides was channelled from paddy fields into the tambak. The high density of prawns led to devastating outbreaks of viral disease, and many farmers who had borrowed money to invest in new technology were bankrupted. The government, to protect the remaining mangroves along the north coast, has now banned the digging of any more ponds. Nonetheless, the tambak debacle represents a lesson in the dangers of over-enthusiastic expansion.

Local Becak: some of the sights can be reached on foot, although hiring a becak for a couple of hours is much easier; becak drivers wait for custom on the main road. **Road Bus**: Mojokerto is the nearest large town to Trowulan and buses run here from other main East Java towns, including **Surabaya**, **Jombang**, **Malang** and **Kediri**. If travelling from Surabaya though, it is not necessary to travel via Mojokerto. Take a bus from Surabaya's Bungurasih terminal travelling towards Jombang (there are many) and ask to be let off in Trowulan.

Transport
52 km from Surabaya,
8 km from Mojokerto

Tuban

Tuban is a coastal town, with wide airy streets and a Mediterranean feel. From the west, *tambak* (fish ponds) line the route into this sleepy fishing town and administrative centre (see page 265). Established in the 12th century, by the 16th century Tuban had become an important trading centre with a large Chinese population of merchants servicing the spice trade. The former wealth of this town is reflected in the fine Chinese ceramics which have been found in the vicinity, and in the pageantry of the jousts that were held on the alun-alun (or square) which are recorded in European accounts of the period. The Chinese presence is also reflected in the presence of what is reputed to be the largest Chinese temple in East Java – the **Klenteng Kwan Sing Bio**. This single-storeyed *klenteng*, with rampant dragons over the main entrance, lies to the west of the main square, on the coast, not far from the town centre.

The fine and beautiful **Mesjid Agung Tuban** (Jami'q Mosque), on the grand Alun-alun or main town square, honours Sunan Bonang, one of the nine Walis (saints) who introduced Islam to Java. The mosque was built in 1894 by the 35th regent of Tuban, Raden Toemenggoeng Koesoemodigdo, and was designed by the Dutch architect Toxopeus. It was renovated most recently in 1986. The **grave of Sunan Bonang**, who is thought to have died in 1525, is situated behind the mosque and has become an important pilgrimage spot. Old porcelain plates are set into the white-washed walls that surround the tomb, and to the right of the entrance way is a trough which, so it is said, was used to water elephants, the preferred mode of transport among the elite of the time. Stalls set up just to the south of the mosque. There is an afternoon and evening market down by the port and jetty near the centre of town, which offers delicious food at low market prices, and a daily market off Jl Gadjah Mada, on the inland side of town.

Phone code: 0356
Colour map 3, grid A4

Excursions **Kerek**, not much more than a village about 16 km west of Tuban, is one of the last areas where rural households still produce simple batik for home use and local sale. Home production of this type used to be the norm over much of Java: women would make cloth during the agricultural slack season, and then sell a few lengths in local markets. As Michael Hitchcock notes in his book *Indonesian Textiles* (British Museum Press: London, 1991), "in the late 1980s, traditional textiles, coloured using natural dyes and hand-spun cotton, were still being woven here; blue-black using indigo, yellow with *Cudrania*, bright red with Morinda and *Symplocos fasciculata*, and dark red with *Bruguiera*". ■ *Getting there: catch a bemo to the market town of Merakurak about 6 km west of Tuban; from here bemos run on to Kerek, about another 10 km west. Alternatively, charter a bemo or ojek.*

Sleeping **A-B** *Mustika*, Jl Teuku Umar 3, T22444, F21598. Some a/c, restaurant, a large, new and rather grandiose hotel on the west edge of town, wide range of bungalow rooms, some with baths and hot water, others with squat loos and cold water mandis, all are clean, but ask to see the full range of suites, with 2 bedrooms and 2 bathrooms and a sitting area, which are good value for groups. A planned expansion is to include tennis courts and pool, which is scheduled for completion in 2000. **A-B** *Tuba Tropis*, Jl Basuki Rachmad 3, T325800, F325888. This stylish hotel opened in 1997 and provides the best standard accommodation in Tuban. Tastefully decorated with extensive marble fittings, the hotel offers comfort and peace. Pool, fitness centre, Chinese restaurant, BBQ bar and café. Recommended. **B-D** *Purnama*, Jl Semarang 1, T21550. Some a/c, restaurant, attractive hotel on a large plot of land overlooking the sea, at the west edge of town on the road towards Rembang. Rooms are clean and sitting outside in the garden with a brisk sea breeze is a very enjoyable way to spend a hot and lazy afternoon, mosquito net is a necessity. **E** *Losmen Jawa Timur*, Jl Veteran 25, T22312. Rooms in an old villa, centrally located, friendly, some with attached bathrooms, all rooms are gaily painted to match the general theme of the town. Overall, this is a very atmospheric and pleasant place to stay at the price. **E-F** *Hotel Selamet*, Jl Panglima Sudirman 90, T21568. Old colonial-style station building, rooms have high ceilings and the floors are beautifully tiled, but the rooms are poorly looked after. Basic and cheap.

Eating *Cryslat Restaurant*, found within the **Tuban Topis Hotel**, Jl Basuki Rachmat 3. Excellent Chinese restaurant with chef imported from the 'mainland'. Good range of meat and fish dishes, but the music is loud and diners have a tendency to go karaoke when they've had a Bintang too many. *Permata Donuts*, Jl Veteran, somewhat out of place, this little café sells homemade brightly coloured pastries and donuts, as well as burgers, omelettes and excellent cheap fruit juices.

Foodstalls The best selection is at the afternoon and evening market, down by the port and jetty.

Madura Island

Local **Becas** are needed to get around town – it is spread out and hot.

Road **Bus**: the terminal is on the corner of Jl Sudirman and Jl Teuku Umar, at the northwest edge of town. Regular connections with **Surabaya** and **Semarang**, via **Rembang** and **Kudus**.

Banks *BNI*, Jl Bazuki Rachmat 115. *Bank Rakyat Indonesia*, Jl Veteran. **Communications** Post Office: Jl Sunan Bonang 8 (on town square next to the mosque). **Telephone office**: Jl Sudirman.

Transport
97 km from Rembang, 99 km from Surabaya

Directory

Madura Island

Separated from the mainland by a 3 km-wide strait, Madura is a world apart from Java. The island – 160 km long and 30 km wide – lies off the northwest coast and, although it is administered as part of the province of East Java, its people regard themselves as Madurese rather than Javanese. Ardent Muslims, and proud of a history of forceful independence, they speak a distinct language and have been partially insulated from the commercialization so evident in Java. The towns are slow-moving and low-key, the landscape is dry, and the people poor by Javanese standards. However, Madura is transformed during the kerapan sapi – or **bull racing** *season (see box) – when large numbers of tourists are drawn to this backwater of East Java.*

Colour map 3, grid A5

Madura is predominantly flat, with a ridge of hills running along the north coast. Most of its 3,000,000 population secure their livelihoods through farming (including growing tobacco), cattle breeding and fishing. Historically, there was little of economic value to interest the Dutch. Madura became regarded as a source of fine soldiers and also from the late 19th century as a source of salt, in which the colonial authorities maintained a lucrative monopoly. But more than anything else, Madura is famous for its bulls – and certainly they appear healthier-looking than in any other part of Java. Out of the racing season they are put to good use on the land, toning-up their muscles for the big event.

There are three principal towns on Madura: Bangkalan on the west coast and closest to Kamal (the port for Surabaya); Pamekasan, the island's capital in the south-central portion; and Sumenep to the east, which offers the greatest concentration of historical sights. The road between the three towns follows the south coast and is relatively quiet and well maintained, passing through small fishing villages notable for their colourful traditional boats moored along the shore.

Ins and outs

Car ferries leave every 20 mins, 24 hrs a day from north of Surabaya on Jl Kalimas Baru (see Surabaya map, city buses 'PI' and 'C' travel to the ferry dock), docking at Kamal, on the southwest coast of Madura, 30 mins-1 hr later. Minibuses wait at the Kamal dockside to transport passengers to Bangkalan and onward. There are direct buses from Surabaya's Bungurasih terminal through to Sumenep. Twice daily, ferries leave Kalianget (10 km southeast of Sumenep) at 0800 and 1300 for Jangkar (120 km northwest of Banyuwangi), 5½ hrs. **NB** There is no service on Wed or Sun.

Getting there

Two principal roads traverse the island. The main road begins in Bangkalan, runs southeast to Sampang (61 km), and then follows the coast to Pamekasan (another 29 km) and Sumenep, a total distance of 154 km. The

Getting around

Kerapan Sapi (bull racing)

Most tourists come to Madura to see the Kerapan Sapi (bull races) which are staged between August and October. Bull racing is said to have originated as a simple ploughing contest which, through time, has become institutionalized as an annual festival. The fastest bulls go to stud, on the theory that fast bulls also plough fast.

Like most rural festivals in Southeast Asia, Madura's bull racing occurs after the rice harvest, when farmers – free from the rigours of cultivation – have time to celebrate. However, the demands of tourism mean that today races are staged throughout the year. Associated with the races are parades, dancing and the music of the gamelan orchestra. The bulls are harnessed in pairs and race down a 120m course – taking about 10 seconds to cover the distance. The winner is the bull whose legs cross the line first.

Villages and districts compete against one another in knock-out competitions, culminating in the major contest – the Kerapan Besar or Grand Island Championship – which is held in Pamekasan in September and preceded by a week of celebrations and ceremonies. Leading up to the big race, bulls are fed up to 50 eggs a day and are dosed up with herbs and various potions of doubtful provenance. It is said they are even given massages and are sung to sleep.

There are bull racing stadiums in Bangkalan, Pamekasan and Sumenep. Panorama, the East Java tourist newspaper (April 1991), describes the Kerapan Sapi in these terms:

"A folk and home grown enthusiasm which came to existence long ago though lacking the rattle and scarf crew of English soccer or the baton-twirling beauties of college football as far as the crowd is concerned, its races, district against district, regency against regency, even village against village are superbly colorful."

---

longer, less well maintained, north route follows the north coast from Bangkalan, and after 11 km reaches the village of Arosbaya. Minibuses run regularly between the larger towns.

History

Before the 17th century, Madura was a Java in miniature. A number of royal courts or *dalem* controlled the local economy, and these were at the same time the spiritual, cultural and artistic focus of the island. Although today Madura is regarded as being one of the more ardent Muslim areas of Indonesia, the people of the island were not converted to Islam until the 16th century.

Madura was incorporated into the empire of the great Mataram king Sultan Agung during the siege of Surabaya, from 1620 to 1625. By all accounts, the campaign for Madura was long and arduous and Agung's army suffered considerable losses. He was forced to devastate the ricelands of the island and also to fight the island's women, who joined their menfolk to wage war against the invading army. On finally vanquishing the local forces in 1624, he set about unifying the island, placing it under the control of a single prince with a capital at Sampang. In less than 50 years, however, the empire that Sultan Agung had created – and of which Madura was a part – began to fragment.

In 1670, Prince Trunojoyo, buoyed-up by a prophesy that maintained he would be a great hero and that Mataram would fall, travelled to Madura to prepare for revolution. He defeated the local prince and his Javanese soldiers, and established a base at Pamekasan on the south coast. By 1671, he had control over the whole island and assembled an impressive army, exploiting the dislike that the local population felt over domination from Java. In 1675, Prince Trunojoyo sailed with his army to the mainland and took Surabaya. By 1677, the rebellion against Mataram was at its height and much of East Java was under rebel control. But with the support of the European troops of the VOC, who sided against Prince Trunojoyo, the rebellion ultimately failed in 1677. Three years later the island was divided into two – West and East Madura – and placed under the control of two royal lineages. Later, Mataram ceded East Madura (in 1705) and then West Madura (in 1743) to the Dutch.

But the defeat of Prince Trunojoyo was not to mean that Madura had been pacified. Over the next seven decades, Madurese lords would periodically mount campaigns and attack Java. It is this history which has given the Madurese a reputation of being a brave and warlike people. Indeed, many of the troops in the Dutch colonial army came from Madura. The Dutch divided the administration of Madura between three royal houses – based at Bangkalan, Pamekasan and Sumenep. These local lords maintained considerable power until the administrative reforms of 1816. By 1887, their influence had been eroded further still until they were reduced to the same status as *bupatis* in Java – mere aristocratic regency figureheads.

Bangkalan

Bangkalan is focused on a large central square or *Alun-alun*. It's a pleasant town with wide roads and little traffic. However, apart from seeing the *kerapan sapi*, there is little other reason to visit the town. There is a **small museum** near the square, with characteristic Madurese architecture housing ethnographic and historical artefacts, including agricultural tools and palm-leaf manuscripts. The bull racing stadium, the centre of activity during **kerapan sapi**, is 1 km out of town on the road south to Kamal. As well as the stadium out of town, races are often held in the central alun-alun during the bull racing season.

Excursions **Arosbaya** is a small village, 11 km northeast of town. Nearby, at Air Mata, is the royal cemetery of the Cakraningrat family, the lords of Sumenep, who dominated the island during the 17th and 18th centuries. Though the site is historically important, most visitors find the graves are a little disappointing – children use the cemetery as their playground. ■ *Getting there: 15 mins by colt from near the Alun-alun (500Rp). To get to Air Mata, stop just before you reach the town, at the road where the sign 'Welcome to Arosbaya' is located. The cemetery is along this road, so take another bemo (500Rp) or a horse cart (2,000Rp).*

Bangkalan

Sleeping **C** *Ningrat*, Jl H Moh Kholil 113, T3095388. On the edge of town. Cheapest rooms have shared mandis, more expensive have western loo and a/c, quiet and very clean. Traditionally decorated restaurant with limited menu of good Indonesian meals, a pleasant place to relax, a becak to the centre of town costs 1,000Rp. Recommended. **D-E** *Wisma Permuda*, Jl Veteran, huge multi-bedrooms, making this much cheaper if travelling with 5 or 6 others, basic, shared mandi, no a/c or shower, central position on the Alun-alun. **E** *Melati*, Jl Mayjen Sungkono 48, set back from the road, so easily missed, friendly staff; however, this does not make up for the overpriced and cramped rooms.

Eating Bangkalan is not a town to visit for gastronomic variety. *Cipta Rasa*, Jl Mayjen Sungkono, serves good Indonesian dishes in individual burners, keeping food heated while you eat, pleasant open front onto quiet road. *Mirasa*, Jl Tronojoyo, similar to the *Cipta Rasa* but with larger choice.

Sederhana, Jl Hasyimashari, similar menu to both the *Cipta Rasa* and the *Sederhana*, but slightly cheaper prices.

Festivals **August-October** **Kerapan Sapi**, traditional bull racing festival (see box, page 268).

Transport **Road Minibus**: the station is on the town square. Regular connections with **Kamal**, **Pamekasan** and **Sumenep**.

Directory **Communications** Post Office: Jl Trunojoyo 2.

Camplong

Phone code: 0234 Camplong is a beach resort, 29 km west of Pamekasan. It offers visitors a mini amusement park, swimming pool, as well as a beach – of sorts. The beach is black sand but, and more to the point, the water is filthy with raw sewage and not safe for swimming. On our last visit, there was also an oil tanker moored just offshore and oil storage canisters next door to the only hotel. Putting, delicately, the excreta to one side, there are traditional boats picturesquely moored along the shore, and there is also an excellent place to stay.

Sleeping **C** *Camplong Cottage*, Jl Raya Camplong, T21569. Recently built, consisting of 15 beach huts close to the sea, price includes breakfast, the cheapest have showers but cold water, more expensive have a/c and western loos. Good, but cheap, restaurant serving Indonesian food, though the karaoke is not likely to be to everyone's taste. The staff speak very good English. Spacious and good value for money – probably the best accommodation on Madura and certainly the most picturesque.

Transport **Minibus**: minibus connection with **Bangkalan** and **Pamekasan**.

Pamekasan

Phone code: 0234 Pamekasan is the capital of Madura island, but is still a low key, sleepy town of single-storeyed houses, with yellow shutters and attractive white-washed walled alleys.

Excursions **Sampang** is a small town not far from Camplong, on the main Bangkalan-Sumenep road. **Sleeping** *Setia*, Jl Imam Bonjol 100, T21063, near the centre of town, a/c, pool, no western toilets; *PKPN*, Jl Rajawali 9, T21166. A/c and balconies, not as good as *Setia*. ■ *Getting there: by minibus.*

Sleeping **C** *Madura Indah*, Jl Jokotole 40, T81775. A/c, western loos, very well maintained, best run hotel in town, popular. **D** *PKPN Hotel*, Jl Kemuning 2, T22353. No a/c or western loo, crowded, dirty and the furthest away from town. **D** *Trunojoyo*, Jl Trunojoyo 28, T81181. Rooms are reasonably clean, well run, western loo but no a/c or hot water, spacious. **D-F** *Purnama*, Jl Bonorogo 10A, T81375. Basic rooms with fan and own mandi, some rooms with a/c and TV, quite far from town and difficult to find. **D-F** *Ramayana*, Jl Niaga 55-57, T22406. With western toilet fan and shower, very clean with large number of rooms and small garden area. **E-F** *Garuda*, Jl Masigit 1, T22589. Good location right on the square, attractive old house in need of upkeep, basic and rather unpleasant rooms.

Eating *Rumah Makan Andini*, Jl Mesigit, next door to *Garuda Hotel*, T26219. Has tables outside, facing the Alun-alun, good juices. *Rumah Makan Telomoyo*, Jl Trunojoyo 19. Across the road from *Hotel Trunojoyo*, has a wide selection of Indonesian dishes.

Shopping **Batik** Jl Diponegoro 96.

Road Minibus: regular connections with Sumenep, Bangkalan and Kamal.

Banks *Bank Central Asia*, Jl Jokotole, will change TCs. **Communications** Post Office: Jl Masigit 3A.

Sumenep

Sumenep is the most frequently visited town on Madura, as it offers the most sights of historical interest. These are focused upon the large central square. On the north side of the square is the 18th century **Mesjid Jamik Mosque** with tiered roof, and fronted by a white and yellow washed Madurese gateway. On the opposite side of the square is the street leading to the kraton, Jl Dr Sutomo. On the right-hand side of this street is the badly maintained **Museum Daerah**, with a poorly displayed collection of mainly European pieces, including a carriage. Admission 300Rp. Open Monday-Sunday. Opposite is the 18th-century **kraton**, built by Panembahan Sumolo, where some of the rooms are open to the public and display a motley collection of

Transport
90 km from Bangkalan,
64 km from Sumenep

Directory

Phone code: 0328

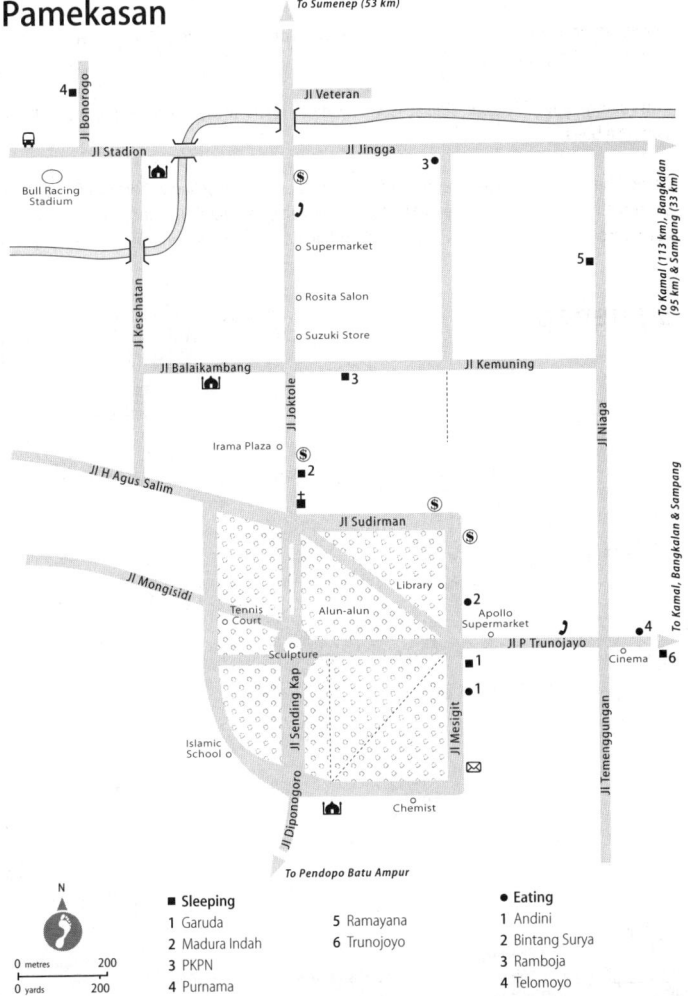

Pamekasan

■ Sleeping
1 Garuda
2 Madura Indah
3 PKPN
4 Purnama
5 Ramayana
6 Trunojoyo

● Eating
1 Andini
2 Bintang Surya
3 Ramboja
4 Telomoyo

Chinese ceramics, krisses, swords, topeng masks and wayang puppets. Next to the palace is a small water garden or **Taman Sari**. Enclosed by white-washed walls, it contains a clear bathing pool filled with fish. It is said that bathing in the pool will ensure eternal youth. Fields of tobacco intersperse the town, which is probably the easiest and most interesting to navigate of all the towns in Madura.

Excursions **Asta Tinggi** The graves of the sultan's family lie 1½ km west of the town.
Swimming is possible at the mediocre beach of **Pasongsongan**, northwest of Sumenep and home to traditional shipbuilders. **Sleeping** F *Coconut Rest House*, welcoming homestay. ■ *Getting there: by minibus.*

Sleeping D *Wijaya I*, Jl Trunojoyo, T62433. A/c and TV, western loo and veranda, efficiently run. **D-E** *Safari Jaya*, Jl Trunojoyo 90 (2 km south of town on road to Pamekasan), T62989. More expensive rooms have TV and a/c, good value but quite far out of town. **D-E** *Wijaya II*, Jl Trunojoyo 45-47, T21532. Some a/c, similar standard to sister losmen, *Wijaya I*; **D** *Wisma Sumekar*, Jl Gapura 3, T21713. Double bed with real mattress, a/c, western loo, TV. Better facilities than its rivals.

Eating **Cheap** *Bimba*, Jl Trunojoyo 41, Padang food. *Mawar*, Jl Diponegoro, Chinese. *Wijaya II*, Jl Trunojoyo 45-47, Indonesian.

Entertainment **Bull racing** Out of *kerapan sapi* season, ask the officials at the kraton or museum about staging a bull race.

Shopping **Batik** The Madurese have a distinctive form of batik, made up of flower patterns of red, purple and blue. Available from **Toko Mashur** (Koleksi Batik Madura), Jl Trunojoyo.
Furniture Several shops in Sumenep sell both antique and new furniture.

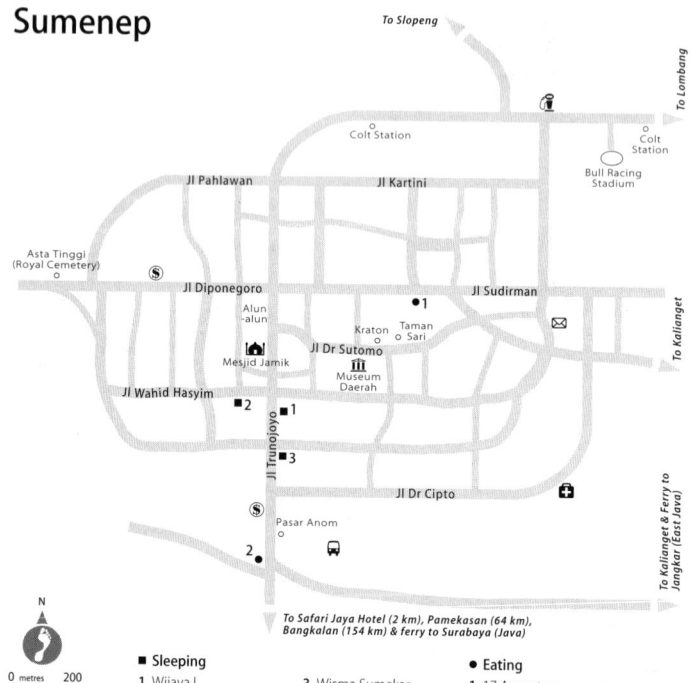

Road Minibus: the station is on Jl Trunojoyo, at the south side of town. Regular connections with **Bangkalan**, **Pamekasan** and **Kamal**. There are also some direct connections with Surabaya, Malang and Semarang.

Transport
64 km from Pamekasan, 154 km from Bangkalan

Sea Boat: see Madura, transport (page 267), and the Kalianget entry, below.

Banks *Bank Central Asia*, Jl Trunojoyo. **Communications Post Office**: east of the town centre, about 600m from the museum, 1 km from the Alun-alun and mosque. **Telekom office**: east of town past the Post Office.

Directory

Kalianget

Kalianget lies 10 km southeast of Sumenep and is the village from which ferries leave for the mainland. The area surrounding here is an important salt producing region.

E-F *Baitul Kamal*, Jl Gresik Putih 9. Opposite the entrance to the port and a convenient place to stay if you are intent on catching the 0800 ferry. Basic rooms with outside mandi, slightly more expensive have a fan, rather prison-like.

Sleeping

Boat: ferries leave at 0800 and 1300 for **Jangkar** on the mainland (120 km northwest of Banyuwangi, 5½ hrs, 5,500Rp); no service on Wed or Sun. Upon arrival in Jangkar, take a becak from the ferry to town (3 km). Excellent Chinese food at *Rumah Makan Bali* (**2**). There is no bus station in Jangkar; passengers wait by the side of the road.

Transport

The Far East

Pasuruan

Pasuruan was an independent principality that pre-dated the Dutch occupation of Java. Historical records show that it struggled to maintain its autonomy from more powerful East Java states, such as Demak, Surabaya and Mataram, during the 16th and 17th centuries – usually losing out in the process. Today, Pasuruan, with a population in 1990 of 134,000, is notable mainly for its impressive **architecture**. The Dutch developed the surrounding area as a centre of plantation crop production (mainly sugar), and the wealth generated is reflected in numerous grand and elegant **mansions** (eg on Jl Kusuma Bangsa, Jl Hassanudin and Jl Raya). Until the 1930s, Java – and especially East Java – was among the world's leading producers of sugar and, in fact, only Cuba exported more. The main square or Lampangan is dominated by an impressive and beautiful **Moorish-style mosque** on Jl Nusantara – one of the finest in East Java. It has been renovated in recent years.

Phone code: 0343
Colour map 3, grid B5

The **Pelabuhan (Port) Pasuruan** is at the end of Jl Pelabuhan, which runs off Jl Raya, a short walk from the centre of town. Pictureque vessels from all over the Indonesian archipelago dock here – the port is certainly worth exploring for those with some time on their hands.

There are no places to stay in Pasuruan geared to foreign budget travellers; there are, though, cheap rooms to be found in hotels meeting the needs of travelling Indonesian businessmen.

Sleeping

C *Pasuruan*, Jl Nusantara 46, T424494. Some a/c, set in a large compound set back from the road, central position, clean and spacious rooms with sitting areas outside, no hot water, but a professionally managed hotel with charming and enthusiastic staff and some style. Recommended. **C-E** *Wisma Karya*, Jl Raya 160, T426655. Some a/c, an extended old mansion in a central location which is mostly used by Indonesian businessmen and salesmen, the a/c rooms are acceptable although some are dirty – check before booking in.

Entertainment **Cinema** *Pasuruan 21*, Jl Raya Pasuruan Indah (behind the Bank Central Asia), modern a/c cinema showing English soundtrack films. *Himalaja*, Jl Nusantara (not far from the Lampangan – main square).

Snooker Play against the local wizards at the Duta Bhakti, Jl Raya Pasuruan Indah (behind the Bank Central Asia).

Transport
38 km from Probolinggo, 64 km from Surabaya

Local Bright blue **bemos**, **becaks**.

Train The railway station is an old colonial building in the centre of town on Jl Raya.

Road Bus: the bus terminal is just off Jl Anjas Moro (at the end of Jl Raya), at the east side of town, about 1.5 km from the centre. Becaks are available to ferry passengers into town. A/c and non-a/c buses to **Yogya**, **Semarang**, **Solo**, **Banyuwangi**, **Malang**, **Tretes**, **Surabaya**, **Sumenep** (Madura), **Probolinggo**, **Madiun**, **Jember** and other destinations in East Java.

Directory **Banks** *Bank Central Asia*, Jl Raya (not far from the railway station). *BNI*, Jl Jend A Yani 13. **Communications** *Post Office*: Jl KH Dahlan 1 (close to intersection with Jl Niaga, on the town square or Lampangan). **Telephone & fax:** *Wartel*, Jl Alun-alun Timur (on the town square or Lampangan).

Probolinggo

Phone code: 0335
Colour map 3, grid B5

Probolinggo is a commercial town of 150,000 inhabitants, which doubles up as a Javanese holiday resort. The inhabitants are a mixture of Javanese and Madurese, and most foreign visitors only stop off here en route to Mount Bromo. Probolinggo is noted for the grapes produced in the surrounding area, and in honour of the fruit the municipal authorities have created a giant bunch, out of concrete, on the main road into town from Pasaruan. It has earned Probolinggo a sobriquet *Kota Anggur* (Grape Town). More enjoyable still is the port, Pelabuhan Probolinggo, north from the town centre off Jl KH Mansyur – about a 1½ km walk. Brightly-coloured boats from all over Indonesia dock here, with their cargoes of mostly dry goods. The northern part of town, centred on Jl Suroyo and the Alun-alun, is the administrative heart of Probolinggo; the portion further east on Jl P Sudirman is the commercial heart, with the large **Pasar Barde** – a covered market. The '**tourist office**' faces the bus terminal. It is not a real tourist office, but an advice centre run by several tour companies here. We have received several complaints about the office and their business practices.

Excursions **Candi Jabung** lies 26 km east of Probolinggo, about 5 km on from the coastal town of Kraksaan, in the small village of Jabung. It was completed in 1354 and – unusually – is circular in plan (although the inner cella is square). It was a Buddhist shrine, built as a funerary temple for a Majapahit princess. The finial is now ruined but was probably in the form of a stupa. The candi is built of brick and was renovated in 1987 – as too was a smaller candi 20m to the west of the main structure. The candi is notable for its finely carved kala head. Visitors should sign the visitors' book. ■ *Getting there*: minibuses running east towards Sitabundo will stop at Candi Jabung. The village of Jabung is small and the candi rather poorly signposted (in 1994, the sign read 'C-nd-Jabung'). The candi is 500m off the main road, a pleasant walk through fruit groves.

The tiny island **Gili Ketapang** lies 8 km, or 45 minutes offshore, by boat from Probolinggo. No accommodation on the island yet. ■ *Getting there*: by boat from Probolinggo Port (see above), leaving through the day.

Sleeping **B-E** *Tampiarto Plaza*, Jl Suroyo 15, T42188, F422103. Some a/c, pool, wide range of rooms, from fan rooms with shared bathrooms to a/c suites with hot water baths, the best are very good, the cheapest are dark and rather grubby, as with most things you get what you pay for, but even those paying 24,000Rp get to use the pool and the place is quiet. **C** *Ratna*, Jl Raya Panglima Sudirman 16, T421597, F42226. Some a/c, a good value rather gruesome 3-storey structure, rooms in a wide range from non-a/c with shared mandi to a/c rooms with attached showers, clean and with central location, but staff are rather surly and uninterested. **D** *Bromo Permai II*, Jl Raya Panglima Sudirman 255, T/F23459. Some a/c, wide range of rooms with varied level of facilities, no hot water but a/c rooms are large, very clean and good value, as are the fan rooms with shared facilities, a 2-storey block around a courtyard with trees and a small pond, situated at the eastern edge of the commercial district, the same ownership as the *Bromo Permai I* on Mount Bromo, so they can book rooms easily – useful in the peak season. Recommended. **D** *Victoria*, Jl Suroyo 1-3 (near intersection with Jl Raya Panglima Sudirman), T421462, F421040. Some a/c, old hotel, more expensive rooms with hot water showers, varied in terms of upkeep and cleanliness, but generally all rooms are rather dark. Welcoming management and a reasonable place to spend a night or two. **E** *Tentrem Hotel*, Jl Raya Panglima Sudirman 61, T21049. Colonial villa converted into a low budget hotel, mostly frequented by Indonesians, rooms are cheap, generally dirty and not very cheerful.

Eating There are numerous warungs and other eating houses along Jl Raya Panglima Sudirman.

Entertainment **Cinemas** *Guntur*, Jl Dr Sutomo, a/c theatre showing English soundtrack films.

Tour operators **Warning** The travel agents in Probolinggo are notorious for charging inflated prices for bus tickets. It seems that people are charged for a return ticket to Bromo and then find that the return vehicle fails to materialize. The best way to avoid these problems is by only getting buses at the terminal and paying on the bus. The bus destinations are clearly signposted above the bus lanes on the roof. Queue here until the bus arrives or an official (they have name badges) points you in the correct direction. Ask for bags to be kept with you at the back of the bus, rather than in the luggage compartment. Normally, seating will be made for you so that you can watch over your own bag.

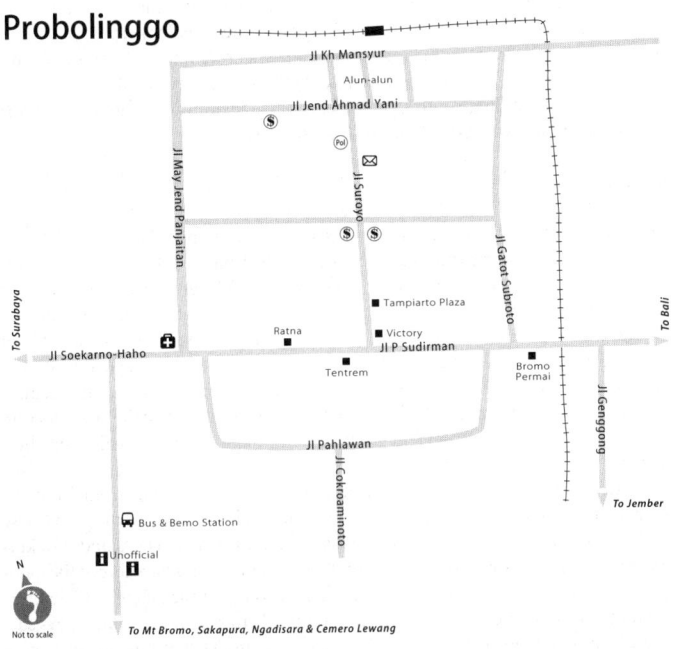

Transport
99 km from Surabaya, 190 km from Banyuwangi

Local Taxis: there are no taxi services, but it is possible to charter a bemo cheaply, haggle for it.

Train The train station is on the main square or Alun-alun, on Jl KH Mansyur, regular connections on the Mutiara Timur train with Surabaya and on to Yogyakarta, and Banyuwangi via Jember, 9 hrs.

Road Bus: all the bus destinations are written up clearly at the terminal and it is best to deal directly with the bus companies, rather than the tourist office. The bus Bayuangga terminal is on the west side of town, about 5 km from the centre, on the road up to Bromo. Bemos whisk bus passengers into town (500Rp). Regular connections with **Surabaya** 3 hrs, **Malang** 3 hrs and **Banyuwangi** 4 hrs. Night buses to **Denpasar**, Bali (8 hrs), leave at least twice a day at 1530 and 1930, if you miss one of these buses, economy buses are every hour. A/c buses to **Singaraja**, **Jakarta**, **Denpasar** and **Yogya** are available at regular times. **Minibus**: to Cemoro Lawang, 2 hrs (2,500Rp).

Directory Banks Bank Central Asia, Jl Suroyo. *Bank Rakyat Indonesia*, Jl Suroyo. **BNI**, Jl Suroyo. **Communications** Post Office: Jl Suroyo 33. **Telephone & fax:** *Wartel*, Jl Jend A Yani.

Probolinggo to Banyuwangi

34 km east from **Probolinggo** – to the east of **Paiton** – is a new, large, coal-fired power station, built by the Korean firm Hyundai with Japanese assistance. It dominates the coastline at this point and is fuelled with coal shipped in from Kalimantan. Also along this portion of coastline are large sugar estates, rice farms, prawn hatcheries and *tambak* fisheries (see page 265). Inland are the volcanoes which define the area. The uneven railways that run parallel to the road were laid when Dutch-controlled sugar estates covered much of the best land; today, they are still used to collect and transport the newly-cut cane. At the far northeast end of this 'Far East' of Java, the road skirts the **Baluran National Park**. The scenery changes quite suddenly from cultivated agricultural land to open savanna forest and teak plantations. For the next 20 km, there is scarcely any sign of human settlement. Periodic fires pass through this forest, producing, in some areas, a fire 'climax' vegetation, featuring trees species which are resistant to light burns. About 20 km north of **Banyuwangi**, travelling south, Bali appears, its golden beaches noticeably more inviting than those of much of the north coast of Java.

Mount Bromo

Phone code: 0335
Colour map 3, grid B5
Visit during the dry months from May to Nov. Avoid Mount Bromo on Indonesian public holidays

This active volcano stands at 2,329m and is one of the most popular natural sights on Java, lying within the **Bromo-Tengger-Semeru National Park**. The park consists of a range of volcanic mountains, the highest of which (and Java's highest) is at 3,676m. Mount Semeru is sometimes also called Mount Mahameru, the mountain abode of the Hindu gods. Wildlife in the park includes wild pig (*Sus scrofa*), Timor deer (*Cervus timorensis*), barking deer and leopard (*Pantera pardus*), as well as an abundance of flying squirrels. Perhaps the most distinctive tree is the cemara (*Casuarina junghuhniana*), which looks on first glance rather like the familiar conifer. It is, however, no relation and grows above 1,400m on the volcanic ash, where few other trees can establish themselves.

However, you are unlikely to see an abundance of wildlife in the Bromo-Tengger Park, unless you manage to get off the beaten track and away from all the human and vehicular traffic. As in other national parks on Java, leopards, civets and monkeys inhabit the forested areas. The recent problems with forest fires have forced the monkeys down out of the hills, occasionally raiding the villages in search of food. Rangers attempt to prevent the local people from shooting them, but they are not always successful. Some visitors have been partial to taking edelweiss, which is strictly prohibited. However, the rangers have been cultivating some of the plants to sell to tourists.

The local inhabitants of this area are the Tenggerese people, believed to be descended from the refugees of the Majapahit Kingdom, who fled their lands in 928 following the eruption of Mount Merapi. They embrace the Hindu religion and are the only group of Hindus left on Java today.

For many visitors to Indonesia, the trip to Bromo is their most memorable experience: seeing the sun bathe the crater in golden light, picking out the gulleys and ruts in the almost lunar landscape; sipping sweet *Kopi manis* after a 0330 start; and feeling the warmth of the sun on your face as the day begins. No wonder the Tenggerese view this area as holy, feeling a need to propitiate the gods. It is hard not to leave, feeling the divine hand has helped to mould this inspired landscape.

That's the good experience. But like most good things, there are those who are disappointed. In particular, you may find yourself surrounded by literally hundreds of other tourists (especially July-August), chattering and listening to their radios. It is hard to feel the divine hand in such circumstances. The viewpoint at Gunung Pananjakan is also suffering from the curse of over-popularity: it has become a popular stop for package tours from Surabaya. The buses even travel to the crater floor, making this area even more crowded at sunrise and entrenching further unsightly vehicle marks across the sea of sand.

Note that it is possible to visit the crater on a day trip from Probolinggo. The last minibus down the mountain from Cemoro Lawang leaves at 1600.

From Ngadisari via Probolinggo and Sukapura The easiest access to the park is from the north coast town of Probolinggo, via Sukapura and Ngadisari, and then to Cemoro Lawang on the edge of the caldera. The turning from Probolinggo is well signposted. The road starts in a dead straight line and begins to climb slowly through dense forested gulleys of dipherocarps. The road meanders, precariously at times, past fields of cabbage, onions and chillies. At some points a curious, almost coppiced weave of lurid small trees and chopped branches line the road and divide the fields like trellising. The route becomes steeper and steeper and only first gear seems feasible in the overladen minibuses. After Sukapura, the road becomes yet more precipitous. The National Park begins at the village of Ngadisari. The road narrows through here and continues up to Cemoro Lawang, where the tourist sellers appear. The throng of ponies let you know you have reached the top.

Reaching the crater

Mount Bromo crater & trails

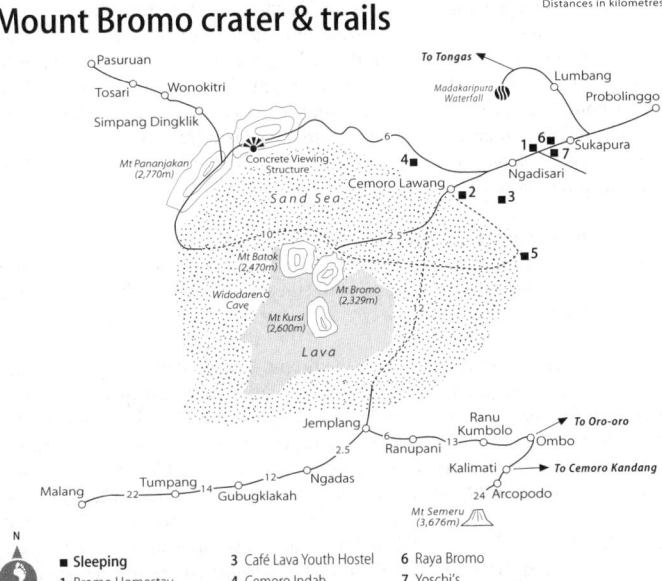

Not to scale

■ Sleeping
1 Bromo Homestay
2 Bromo Permai I
3 Café Lava Youth Hostel
4 Cemoro Indah
5 Lava View
6 Raya Bromo
7 Yoschi's

On arrival in Ngadisari, it is important to obtain a ticket (2,100Rp per person) from the 'tourist information' booth, in order to visit the crater's edge. This is the national park entrance fee and the money is used to protect and develop the area. The trip to the caldera is usually undertaken in the early morning, in order to watch the sun rise over the volcanoes. To reach the summit for dawn, an early start from Ngadisari is essential, leaving no later than 0330. It is easiest to travel to Cemoro Lawang (from Ngadisari) on one of the six-seater jeeps, organized by guesthouses in Ngadisari. It takes 20 minutes by road from Ngadisari to the outer crater at Cemoro Lawang, and is another 3 km walk from here to the edge of the crater. Either take a pony (it should cost about 10,000Rp per pony for a return trip) – a 30 minute ride – or walk for about one hour along a winding path marked by white boulders (sometimes indistinct in the early morning light), through a strange crater landscape of very fine grey sand, known as *Laut Pasir* or the Sand Sea. Vegetables and other crops are grown in the sand, and it is surprising that it doesn't just get blown or washed away. It is also possible to walk the entire way, about 5½ km, from Ngadisari (4-5 hours). The final ascent is up 250 concrete steps to a precarious metre-wide ledge, with a vertical drop down into the crater. Aim to reach the summit for sunrise at about 0530. As this is their business, Losmen-owners will wake visitors up in good time to make the crater edge by sunrise, and are also used to arranging transport.

From Tosari via Pasuruan It is also possible to approach the summit from Tosari, on the north slopes of the mountain. (The turn-off for Tosari is about 5 km out of Pasuruan, on the road to Probolinggo.) Take a minibus from Pasuruan to Tosari (31 km). From Tosari, take an ojek the 3 km to Wonokitri (sometimes minibuses continue on to here). Both mountain villages have basic accommodation available. There is a *PHPA* office at Wonokitri, where it is necessary to pay the park entrance fee of 2,100Rp per person. Jeeps and ojeks are available here to take visitors all the way to the summit of Gunung Panajakan. For those who want to walk, it is 5 km from Wonokitri to Simpang Dingklik and then another 4 km up to the summit of Gunung Panajakan. From the summit, a path leads to Cemoro Lawang. Leave before 0400 to see the sunrise over the crater.

From Ngadas via Malang and Tumpang Finally, visitors can reach Bromo's summit from the west, via Malang, Tumpang and Ngadas (see map). From Tumpang there are bemos to Gubugklakah, and from there it is a 12 km walk to Ngadas. From Ngadas it is a 2.5 km walk to the crater rim at Jemplang, and then another 12 km (three hours) across the crater floor to Bromo and Cemoro Lawang. At Jemplang it is also possible to branch off and climb Mount Semeru (see 'Excursions', below). This walk is much more of a trek and quite demanding – although easy enough for anyone with a reasonable level of fitness.

Equipment Take warm clothing as it can be very cold before sunrise. A scarf to act as a mask to protect against the sulphurous vapour, and a torch to light the way, can also be useful. Avoid opening cameras to change film at the summit; the thin dust can be harmful to the mechanism.

Trekking There are several worthwhile treks in the Bromo-Tengger-Semeru National Park. Ask at your hotel/losmen for information and (in most cases) a map. It is possible to trek from **Cemoro Lawang** to **Ngadas**, or vice versa; from Ngadas, minibuses run down to Tumpang and from there to Malang (see page 249). The trek takes about 4-6 hours; guides are available, but the route is well-marked. For the best view of Bromo, trek to **Mount Penanjakan**, 6 km from Cemoro Lawang. This trek is well worth it if you are staying up in Cemera Indah, as 6 km before sunrise is quite enough! The route is easy to follow but torches are a necessity, as is a degree of adventurous spirit. The trek takes about 1½ hours from Cemera, so it is best to leave before 0400 (ignore advice from hostels to leave by 0300, as that then entails a long, cold wait at the top). Take the road opposite the *Cemera Hostel* and follow the winding track which turns to gravel and rock. There are white posts leading the way up but these are difficult to spot in the dark. The track is direct until you reach some steps leading up to the right; these steps can be hard to find, but the track comes to a halt and turns back on itself about 25m after the steps up. At the top of the steps a large concrete shelter has been built, which somewhat blights the landscape but does provide a welcome seat. This is a great place to watch the sunrise as it is not at all busy, and only those who have made the effort to walk are up there.

Visitor's Centre at Cemoro Lawang: not far from *Café Lava*, range of photographs and maps, a good place to obtain information on Mount Semeru.

Mount Semeru, also known as Mount Mahameru ('seat of the Gods'), is Java's highest mountain and lies 13 km (as the crow flies) to the south of Mount Bromo. This route is only suitable for more experienced climbers/trekkers; a guide and appropriate equipment are also necessary.

Excursions

Climbing Mount Semeru Mount Semeru can be reached from Cemoro Lawang or, more easily, from Malang. If you also wish to visit Mount Bromo as well as climb Mount Semeru, then it is possible to trek four hours across the sea of sand (you may hire a horse to travel across the pasir laut from Cemoro Lawang – however, this is an unusual request and may cost around 80,000Rp).

For more information, enquire at the PHPA office in Malang, Jl Raden Intan 6, T65100, or at the information centre at Cemoro Lawang (see above)

The approach from **Malang** starts with a 22 km bemo ride to **Tumpang**, from which it is a further 26 km (1½ hours) bemo ride to **Ngadas**, where losmen accommodation is available. A further 2.5 km from Ngadas is **Jemplang** village, which is

Around Mount Bromo

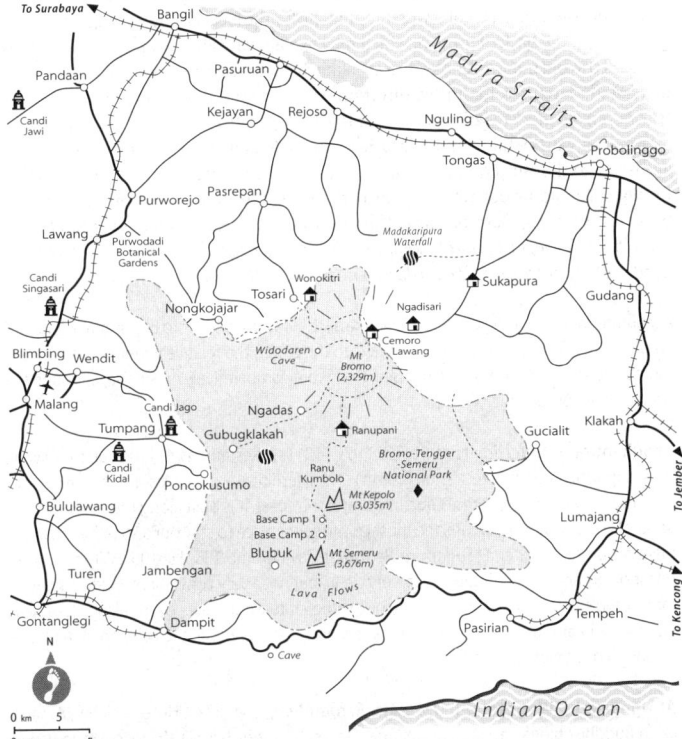

the arrival point for trekkers coming across the sea of sand from Cemoro Lawang. **Ranu Pani** is 6 km on, and this is where the PHPA post is located. For safety reasons, climbers must both check in and out at this post. It is possible to get a jeep as far as Ranu Pani, but any further and it's jalan jalan to the summit (another 37 km).

Climbers usually spend one night at Ranu Pani, either camping or in **F** *Pak Tasrip's Family Homestay*, T0334-84887, where there is a small restaurant, baggage storage and camping equipment for hire. From Ranopani, the next stop is **Ranu Kumbolo**. It takes 3-4 hours to walk the relatively flat 10 km trail. Climbers may replenish their water supplies at the beautiful freshwater lake here (2,400m above sea-level). At Ranu Kumbolo, there is a camping area and resthouse with cooking facilities (free).

From Ranu Kumbolo, the climb continues to **Kalimati** (4.5 km), passing through savanna – a great area for bird spotting. There is a campsite at Kalimati and a fresh water supply at **Sumbermani** (30 minutes, following the edge of the forest). The next stop is **Arcopodo**, one hour away. This is a popular camping stop for the second night on the mountain. (**NB** Some of the soil is unstable.) The climb to the summit of Semeru has to be carefully timed, as toxic gas from the **Jonggring Saloko** crater is dangerously blown around later in the day. It is unsafe to be on the mountain after midday. The heat from the sun also makes the volcanic sand more difficult to walk on. This last climb should therefore commence between 0200 and 0300. From the summit, climbers, on a clear day, have a fantastic view down into the crater, which emits clouds of steam every 10-15 minutes. Climbers are advised only to attempt Mount Semeru during the dry season, as sand avalanches and high winds can be a real danger during the wet season. The temperature at the summit ranges from 0°C to 4°C, so come prepared with warm clothing.

An interesting walk is to **Widodaren Cave**, halfway up **Mount Kursi**. It is rarely visited by tourists, but is a regular worshipping site for the local Hindu Tenggerese. There is a spring at the back of the *gua*, which may explain why local people view the site as sacred. To avoid hours of endlessly traversing the sand sea in search of the path leading up to Widodaren, ask for further directions from the park rangers in the visitor's centre or even get them to guide you. It is a 1½-hour walk from Cemoro Lawang.

Another worthwhile visit is to **Madakaripura Waterfall**. There are people on the approach to the 'air terju', who wait to lend visitors umbrellas to shield them from the water cascading down the narrow path through the hillside. Swimming is possible here. ■ *Getting there: the turn off for the waterfall is on the main road up to Bromo from Probolinggo, just before Sukapura. Hire an ojek or catch a bemo to Lumbang (1½ hrs drive). After which, it is a further 15 mins ride to the waterfall.*

Sleeping Accommodation is strung out from Sukapura all the way up to Cemoro Lawang, a distance of about 18 km. Generally, the closer one gets to the crater, the relatively more expensive the rooms become. At Cemoro Lawang itself, rooms are comparatively expensive, although the position is incomparable.

At Sukapura A *Hotel Raya Bromo*, T581103, F581142. Restaurant, tennis courts, easily the most sophisticated place to stay on Bromo with all facilities, and 1st class rooms with balconies and views down towards Probolinggo and the coast. It is built along the mountainside about 2 km up out of Sukapura, the most comfortable place to stay but also rather inconvenient for Bromo's crater. **D** *Sukapura Permai*, Jl Raya Bromo 135, T581067. All rooms with hot showers and attached squat loos, very clean, but not a very convenient location for visiting Bromo's crater. Not very convienient for the crater, but views overlooking the ravine nearby are beautiful. Few western visitors stay here, most preferring to carry on up higher to Ngadisari or Cemoro Lawang.

At Ngadisari & Wonotoro B *Dyah Ayu Rero Anteng*, T5478771. Hotel which feels more like a Buddhist hideaway, strange spiritual atmosphere which is satisfyingly overpowering.

Excellent place to 'get away'. Small bathrooms with large seating area, hot water and breakfast included. **C-E** *Bromo Permai I*, book at Bromo Permai in Probolinggo (Jl Sudirman 255, T432501, F541021). Large restaurant, the largest hostel in Cemoro Lawang with a wide range of rooms, the most expensive are the best available at the crater with good hot water showers, but the cheapest are rather dark. Rooms are overrated but you pay for the great position, check the range of rooms before deciding. **E-F** *Bromo Homestay*, Jl Wonokerto, T541022. Small, clean rooms, some with attached mandi (shared mandis can be very dirty), popular, with good information (but reports of surly management and often over-run with noisy tour groups). **D** *Losmen Pak Ida*, Wonotoro, clean rooms but very bare, no hot water and shared squat loos and mandi, little to recommend it beyond its cleanliness. **C-D** *Wisma Ucik*, Wonotoro. Clean, plain and colourless, but OK. Breakfast included. **C-D** *Yoschi's*, Jl Wonokerto 1, 2 km before Ngadisari, T23387. Restaurant and losmen run by a Dutch woman, married to a Javanese, who speaks good English, this is currently the best place to stay in Ngadisari, some rooms with hot water and attached showers, attractively furnished and designed with bamboo and ikat, the cottages are excellent value, restaurant serves good European and Indonesian dishes using local produce – onions, potatoes, tomatoes etc – and the losmen is a good source of information. Highly recommended.

At Cemoro Lawang (a good place to stay for early morning walks) **C-E** *Cemoro Indah*, T23457. Easily identified by the rearing horse outside the front, yards from the crater edge, some more expensive rooms are well decorated, with hot water and attached mandi, dirty and damp facilities, limited bedding provided, small breakfasts, restaurant, not particularly friendly, very cheap dorm rooms (**F**), not popular. Beware of leaving valuables, there have been reports of things going missing from here. In short, this is a hotel to avoid if you can. **B** *Bromo Permai I*, sister hotel to *Bromo Permai II* in Probolinggo, Jl P Sudirman 255, T/F23459. Located right opposite the Visitor's Centre, western toilet, hot water shower, American breakfast, good views of the crater from some rooms. Live band every night during peak season. **B-D** *Lava View*, T541069. Only a few metres from the ridge, good views, in a quieter position than most, and excellent food. Rooms offer large beds and good bathrooms, although the walls are a little thin. Tours are available. Price includes breakfast, excellent location and very friendly, hot water available. **D-F** *Café Lava Youth Hostel*, T/F541020. Offers the best range in budget accommodation, cheapest rooms at the caldera, most expensive with attached mandis but no hot water, rooms are all rather small and stuck out round the back, ramshackle but OK, no breakfast available. **Camping**: because the area is a national park, it is possible to camp. The camping site is just before the *Lava View Hostel*, a mere 20m from the lip of the crater. Ask at the National Park information booth, close to the *Bromo Permai I*, for more details.

All hotels can be full during peak season (Jul & Aug). All hostels have their own restaurants

At Tosari **A** *Bromo Cottages*, T031-515253, F511811. Restaurant, hot water, tennis courts, great views.

At Wonokiri **C** *Pendopo Agung*, hot water. **D** *Bromo Surya Indah Homestay*, T332411. Restaurant.

Cemoro Lawang All the hostels have their own restaurants, the best atmosphere is at *Café Lava*, where they do good banana porridge and mugs of tea. *Tengger Permai Café*, good value.

Eating

February Karo (movable, according to Tenggerese Calendar), held in Ngadisari and Wonokitri to commemorate the creation of Man by Sang Hyang Widi. Tenggerese men perform dances to celebrate the event.

Festivals

December Kasodo (movable, according to Tenggerese Calendar). This ceremony is linked to a legend which relates how a princess and her husband pleaded with the gods of the mountain to give them children. Their request was heeded on the condition that their youngest child should be sacrificed to the mountain. The couple then had 25 children, but were understandably reluctant to meet their side of the bargain. The mountain continued to erupt periodically to remind the couple of their vow. They finally conceded to the gods' wishes, and when the child was thrown into the abyss her voice could be heard chiding the parents for not offering her sooner and requesting that on the night of the full moon in the month of Kasado, offerings should be made to the mountain. The ceremony reaches a climax with a midnight pilgrimage to the crater, to make offerings to the gods. Ritual sacrifices of animals, and offerings of vegetables and fruit, are thrown into the crater to appease the gods.

Tour operators Travellers should be warned that the travel agents in Probolinggo are prone to selling a/c direct bus tickets for 2-3 times the normal going rate. Or they may sell a return ticket and fail to provide a vehicle for the return trip. To avoid this, take the bus from the terminal only and pay once on board.

Transport
2 hrs drive east of the city of Malang, 3 hrs south of Surabaya & 30 km southwest of Probolinggo. Avoid arriving too late in Probolinggo if you want to get up to Cemoro Lawang the same day; late in the day the only option is to charter a minibus

Road **Bus/minibus from Probolinggo**: the bus station is about 8 km from the railway station (in Probolinggo). So take a bemo to the bus station. Regular connections with Sukapura, Ngadisari and Cemoro Lawang, 1 hr to Ngadisari, 1½ hrs to Cemoro Lawang (2,500Rp to Ngadisari, 3,000Rp more from Ngadisari to Cemoro Lawang) (connections on to Surabaya or Malang). Jeeps at the railway station in Probolinggo go direct to Cemoro Lawang. The last minibus down the mountain from Cemoro Lawang leaves at 1600. Most losmen and guesthouses will arrange a/c bus connections to Jakarta, Denpasar, Yogyakarta and Lovina Beach (Bali). **Minibus charter from Probolinggo**: for about 60-70,000Rp, ask at any of the local hotels. **Minibus from Pasaruan** (1½ hrs from Malang and Surabaya): regular minibuses to Tosari. **Minibus from Malang**: take a bus to Tumpang and change onto a (rather irregular) minibus for the climb up to Ngadas (see page 249). **Bus from Surabaya**: it is even possible to get to Bromo from Surabaya without too much trouble. Take a bus from Surabaya's Bungurasih terminal to Probolinggo and then continue as above.

Directory **Banks** *Bank Rakyat Indonesia*, Sukapura; Guesthouses at Ngadisari and Cemoro Lawang (poor rates). **Communications** Post Office: Sukapura. **Tourist offices** National Park Information Booth, Cemoro Lawang (near *Bromo Permai I*), this is improving and is more frequently open. It has a range of photos and maps, and is a good place to gain some info before attempting Mount Semeru. **Information Offices**: opposite Probolinggo bus terminal (not offices as such, but tour companies willing to offer free information – with the hope they might also secure your business).

Pasir Putih

Phone code: 0332
Colour map 3, grid B5

Pasir Putih means 'white sand', but don't get too excited because the sand is, in fact, grey. This is not a very beautiful or a very wild beach resort. The hotels are rather over-priced, the scenery and the bay merely passable, and activities in the area, limited. Mostly frequented by Indonesians, it does not compare with resorts on Bali or elsewhere on Java. Snorkelling is possible, but the reef is degraded; boats are also available for hire.

Sleeping **B-D** *Sidho Muncul*, Jl Raya Pasir Putih, T91352. Some a/c, best on the beach with well-kept rooms and small verandas, located in the heart of the beach – may be the best here, but only the best of a poor bunch. **C-E** *Pasir Putih Inn*, T91522. Some a/c, hotel at west end of beach (Probolinggo end), rather overpriced for what you get – average rooms to go with an average beach resort – but the management have plans to expand and build new rooms and a pool, with apparently giant dinosaurs, what more can you say? **D** *Bayangkara*, Jl Raya Pasir Putih, T91083. Plain non-a/c rooms with cold water mandis, average from top to bottom. **D** *Hotel Mutiara*, Jl Raya Pasir Putih. Non-a/c rooms with cold water mandi, very plain and ordinary, with no attempt to introduce any character or atmosphere.

Festivals **November** Sapp sapp – traditional chicken race; chickens are released from boats on the water and they try to fly to the shore. The winner is the one that flies the furthest. Animal rights activists might have something to say about it.

Road Bus: buses travelling along the north coast all stop in Pasir Putih – regular connections with Banyuwangi and Probolinggo, as well as other centres on the main east-west route.

Transport
105 km from Banyuwangi, 82 km from Probolinggo

Comunications *Wartel* office (office & fax): *Pasir Putih Inn*.

Directory

Situbondo

Situbondo is an orderly, spread-out town of wide streets and low rise buildings. The **mosque** on the Alun-alun is impressive, although not historically or architecturally significant. Near the bus station is the new **Pasar Mimbaan Baru** – a market-cum-promenade walkway. The town's rather down-at-heel cinema is also here. In early October 1996, a serious anti-Christian riot led to the destruction of most of Situbondo's churches.

Phone code: 0338
Colour map 3, grid B5

C-E *Ramayana Hotel*, Jl Sepudi 11A, T61663. Some a/c, best place to stay in Situbondo, although hardly memorable, close to the bus terminal, the a/c rooms are clean with attached bathroom and are very reasonably priced. **E** *Hotel Karang Asem Indah*, Jl Raya Sudirman (on the main road entering town from Probolinggo), T81179. Attached bathrooms, cold water, rather run down and abandoned in appearance, rooms verging on the dirty.

Sleeping

93 km to Banyuwangi, 103 km to Probolinggo, 34 km to Bondowoso, 67 km to Jember. **Road Bus**: the terminal is in the centre of town on the corner of Jl Sepudi and Jl Jawa. Connections with Probolinggo, Surabaya, Jember via Bondowoso, Banyuwangi and Ketapang (for Bali).

Transport

Banks *Bank Rakyat Indonesia*, Jl Jend A Yani. **Communications Post Office**: Jl Jend A Yani 131 (on the main square). **Telephone & fax**: *Wartel*, Jl Sepudi 7 (near the bus terminal).

Directory

Bondowoso

Bondowoso is an attractive, and remarkably neat, little town, crammed onto the narrow plain of the Sampean River which flows northwards between Mount Raung (3,332m) to the east and Mount Argopuro (3,088m) to the west. The town is only 34 km inland from Situbondo, but because it is off the usual tourist route it receives comparatively few visitors. Nonetheless, it is a gem of a town; friendly, attractive and manageable. The area is also famous for its bull fights, best seen in the village of Tapen (see 'Excursions').

Phone code: 0332
Colour map 3, grid B5

Bull fights are held in the village of **Tapen**, 15 km northeast of Bondowoso on the road to Situbondo. The fights are held on Saturday and Sunday, throughout the year 0900-1700, 4,000Rp entrance. Best time to go is later in the day, to watch the winners of the preliminary rounds fighting it out. Bouts can last up to an hour. Fights rarely result in serious injury to the animal – the weaker bull simply runs away. The fights originally served the purpose of improving the breeding stock (see page 268), although the event has gradually evolved into a sport and now into a tourist attraction. ■ *Getting there: regular buses travel through Tapen, which is on the main Bondowoso-Situbondo road.*

Excursions

Ijen Crater is more easily accessible from Bondowoso than any other town (see page 285 for more details on the area and accommodation there). ■ *Getting there: regular minibuses as far as Sukosari. From Sukosari, there are no buses (unless chartered at inflated prices); most people take a truck to Sempol. From here, take an ojek to Paltuding; it is a 3-km walk to the crater itself. See the Ijen entry for more detail.*

D *Baru*, Jl Kartini 26, T21474. Indonesian breakfast included, basic but clean and good, tiled with wood furniture. **D-E** *Palm Hotel*, Jl Jend A Yani 32, T21505. Some a/c, restaurant, pool, the most sophisticated place to stay in town and don't be put off by the expensive looking exterior – it is very good value. The rooms are immaculately clean, some with shower and western loo, some overlooking the pool. All are spacious and airy. Cheap laundry service,

Sleeping
The hotels here are immaculately maintained & very good value

simple breakfast included in room rate, communal TV with satellite programmes at times, central location, less than 1 km from the Alun-alun, very good value, highly recommended. **E** *Kinanti Hotel*, Jl Santawi 583A, T41018. 2 km outside town centre, clean rooms at good rates, but it has a bad reputation locally, with thefts and even murders here. **E** *Anugerah*, Jl May Jend Sutoyo 12, T21870. Price includes breakfast, rooms with own mandi, clean and basic, some a/c, laundry service. At present the hotel front is a bit of a building site, friendly, good value. **E** *Slamet*, Jl PB Sudirman 45, T21516. Rooms with western loo and mandi, no restaurant, central location.

Eating **Cheap** *Santiago Fried Chicken Fast Food Restaurant*, Jl PB Sudirman 66-68, T21931. Also serves 'donuts' and burgers. *Sari Rasa Restoran*, Jl PB Sudirman 4. Clean and welcoming Indonesian restaurant, close to the Alun-alun at Jl Jaksa Agung Suprato 9. **Very cheap** *Depot Lezat*, Jl PB Sudirman 75. Cheap and local with no English. *Vita*, Jl Martanidata 39a. Also cheap and local.

Transport **Local** The *Palm Hotel* organizes **car rental** from the lobby, 90,000Rp for day's hire of an estate car.

34 km from Situbondo, 33 km from Jember, 100 km from Probolinggo, 113 km from Banyuwangi

Road Bus: regular connections with **Situbondo** and **Jember**, connections with **Probolinggo** (2½ hrs, 2,100Rp), **Surabaya** (4,100Rp) and **Banyuwangi**.

Train The station is about 500m from the bus terminal and easy to find. Economy passenger trains run to **Situbondo**, at 0655 and 1235, for 500Rp. Another train runs to **Banyuwangi** at 0618 and 1248, stopping at **Jember** (600Rp), **Tamanan** (300Rp), **Kalibaru** (1,300Rp) and **Banyuwangi** (1,800Rp).

Directory **Communications** Post Office: to 1 side of the Alun-alun at Jl Jaksa Agung Suprato 9. **Telephone office**: *Wartel*, Jl Dr Sutomo.

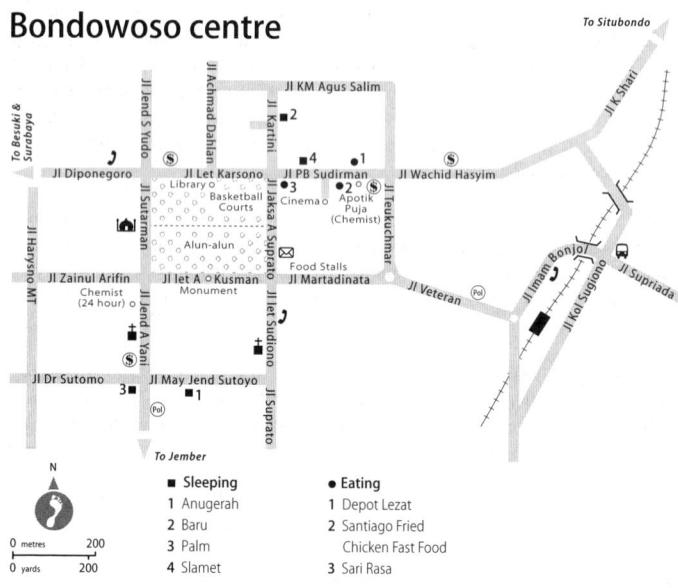

Bondowoso centre

● **Sleeping**
1 Anugerah
2 Baru
3 Palm
4 Slamet

● **Eating**
1 Depot Lezat
2 Santiago Fried Chicken Fast Food
3 Sari Rasa

Kopi luak – the best coffee in the world

The Indonesians are serious about their coffee. And in the average Indonesian's view, the best coffee – not just in Indonesia but in the world – is kopi luak. The luak is a small wild cat that inhabits this part of East Java. Possibly following an overdose of Nescafé advertisements, the luak has taken to eating coffee beans. But not just any old bean: these are carefully selected; only the very best and very ripest will do for the discerning luak. But not only is this nifty little creature quite a gastronome when it comes to coffee, but the beans are swallowed whole and pass through the animal undigested. That's where the coffee overs come into the equation. The droppings of the luak are methodically collected, the beans extracted from the rest of the excrement, cleaned (one hopes), roasted – and served. Sadly, kopi luak is almost never served, largely because the forests have gone. Without the forest there is nowhere for the luak to live, and without the luak there can be no luak excrement, and without the excrement, there simply cannot be any kopi kuak.

Mount Ijen

Mount Ijen forms the core of a reserve which spans the slopes and summits of three mountains – Mount Ijen, Mount Merapi (2,800m) and Mount Raung (3,332m). The crater lake at Ijen is a milky blue-green colour. The warm waters are rich in minerals and the dam that holds back the lake was built by the Dutch to protect crop land on the slopes of Mount Ijen. The crater is also mined for its sulphur, which solidifies into huge blocks near the springs that surround the crater lake, steam and volcanic gases hissing from fissures in the rock. About 200 heavily muscled men walk the 17 km up to the crater in the morning, load as much as 75 kg of sulphur into baskets, and then carry this heavy load, slung over their shoulders, back down the mountain. They are paid for the sulphur by weight at a factory outside Banyuwangi, and it is then used in the production of medicines and the processing of sugar. Despite the risks – and deaths are common from sulphur inhalation and minor eruptions – the miners are envied by others in their villages. They can earn as much as three times the wages of those who work in agriculture, and the families of the sulphur workers live comparatively well. It is thought that Ijen yields between 9 and 12 tonnes of sulphur a day.

Ijen is an excellent area to explore as there are a handful of mountain villages with homestays. It is possible to bus and trek from east to west, or *vice versa*, from Banyuwangi to Bondowoso. However, the easiest access point is from the west, from Bondowoso (see 'Excursions', Bondowoso). It is best to hire a guide (available at the homestays), though not essential, for the walk to the summit, which takes about six hours each way (34 km round trip) – or for the less eager, take a motorbike higher up the mountain. A third of the path is steep but cobbled; it was constructed by the Japanese during the Second World War, who needed sulphur for their munitions. Wildlife within the park includes leopard, pig, civet, peafowl and silver leaf-monkey. After a jungle walk, the landscape opens up and the climb is less steep to the crater's edge. The walk down the crater wall to the 175m deep sulphur lake is precipitous. The *Arabica Homestay* will provide a thermos of tea/coffee to take on your trek for 3,000Rp. They will also provide a local guide for the day for 30,000Rp.

Climbing Mount Ijen

Treks to the crater start from Pos Paltuding, where there is a national park post. From here it is a 3 km walk to the crater lip. From the crater lip it is possible to walk down into the crater itself, where workers mine sulphur from the volcanic outpourings, to the summit, or around the crater lip.

The **waterfall**, 500m down the valley from the *Catimore Homestay*, in Belawan, is worth a look. Along the way are bamboo shacks which look as though they are on the verge of collapse.

Excursions The *Arabica Homestay* arranges tours of the **coffee plantation** to see women picking and sorting the coffee beans, before they are dried in the sun outside the factory and then sorted again (a visit to the factory is 1,000Rp). ■ *Pick your own coffee from Jun to Aug for 3,000Rp, view the Lily gardens and waterfall for 2,500Rp (both need no less than 10 people in a group). A 2-km coffee walk costs 2,000Rp, 3 km horse ride costs 5,000Rp, a day's fishing with hire of equipment in water filled fields is 5,000Rp and a tour to Kawah Ijen costs 6,000Rp. Best time to visit: during the dry season, Apr-Oct.*

Sleeping Trucks drop visitors in Sempol, from where you must ask directions to your homestay.

The homestays have no telephones, but have a contact number in Surabaya, Jl Rajawali 44, T031-22360, F334389, & in Jember, Jl Gajah Mada 249, T0331-86861, F85550

Jampit/Kalisat B-D *Guest House Jampit*, Jampit is about 6 km to the south of Sempol, 14 km from Kawah Ijen, 20 mins by vehicle. Sister homestay to *Arabica*, swiss chalet set in lovely gardens. Variety of rooms, some with hot water. Recommended. **C-D** *Arabica Homestay* is far superior to the other homestays, and provides a (cheap) Indonesian lunch or dinner, tennis court 4,000Rp for 2 hrs with your own 2 ballboys, traditional dances for group tours (50,000Rp) and karaoke. *Homestay Kalisat*, hot water, restaurant, trekking and guides. **Sempol F** *Pesanggrahan*, ramshackle and not recommended, but the cheapest of the homestays. **Belawan** 4 km further along the road to Kawah Ijen, past the PHPA entrance post (pay 1,000Rp). **C** *Catimore Homestay*, has a pleasant garden front, space for 40 people, tiny dirty swimming pool and restaurant, western loo, shower and hot water, cheap restaurant, tennis court. Popular with European group tours. A nice enough place to stay if you want to make it to Kawah Ijen for sunrise. If not, it is overpriced and you would be better to stay in Bondowoso overnight. *Homestay Belawan*, hot water, restaurant. It is also possible to stay at the post where the trail starts (**E**), but there is no food available.

Transport **Local** **Jeep hire**: 50,000Rp for the day, seats 5 passengers; **truck hire**: 20 people, 50,000Rp, both from *Arabica Homestay*. **Bus**: there are 2 main routes up Ijen; 1 from the west and Bondowoso, and 1 from the east and Banyuwangi. If travelling by public transport, be prepared to be patient and keep your wits about you.

Travelling from the West, take an early morning bemo from Bondowoso terminal to Sukosari (500Rp), 20 mins. Bemos sometimes drop-off at Wonosari or Karduatak, rather than Sukosari; if this happens, just catch another one of the frequent mini-buses on to Sukosari. No bemos go from Sukosari to Sempol; you must go by truck. It is possible to charter a truck (20,000Rp 1 way) from here to Kawah Ijen, or a motorbike (5,000Rp). However, if you are willing to wait (no more than 30 mins in the morning), a passing crowded truck will take you to Sempol (1½ hrs), 1,000Rp. The road surface is very good but the road quite steep. It tends to get chilly quickly, so pack a sweater. From Sempol, there are ojeks the final 13 km to Pos Paltuding. **Travelling from the East and Banyuwangi** is the more popular route to Ijen. Take a bus from Banyuwangi towards Licin and get off in Jambu (this may entail a change of vehicles in Sasak Perot). Jambu is the turn-off for Kawah Ijen, and from here it is necessary to take an ojek as far as you can. It is 9 km to Sodong and it may be possible to travel a little further, but at some point the driver will leave you to walk the final stretch to Pos Paltuding. This is likely to be a 10 km or 2½ hrs trek. Chartered jeeps do go all the way, but expect to pay at least 50,000Rp.

Directory **Useful addresses** *PHPA* (Nature Conservancy) office, Sempol.

Kaliklatak

Kaliklatak is a plantation area, covering an area of about 1,000 ha on the slopes of Mount Merapi-Ijen, 20 km northwest of Banyuwangi. The principal crops grown here are coffee, cacao, cloves and rubber. Visitors can observe the entire process, from harvesting the crops through to their final packaging in the factory. Entrance to the plantation is through an elaborate stone gateway which leads to the 'white house'.

Sleeping B Wisata Irdjen, booking ahead (usually at least 30 days) essential, T0333-24896. During the rainy season, it may be possible to book a week prior to visiting. A difficult place to reach unless you plan well ahead. Many Dutch tour groups use the guesthouse, but it is seemingly unpopular with other nationalities. Modern cottages, tennis court, large restaurant, pool. Transport arranged after booking, or take a tour.

The Baluran Reserve is 40 km north of Banyuwangi, on the east coast, and abuts the larger Ijen-Merapi National Park. The reserve of 25,000 ha of wooded savanna supports small populations of monkeys, deer, wild buffalo, leopard, peafowl, green junglefowl and banteng (wild oxen). Naturalist Tony Whitten reports, however, that the reserve is threatened by domestic cattle encroaching on the park, the spread of the introduced tree species *Acacia nilotica* which is invading the grazing grasslands, and by the growth in the numbers of feral water buffalo which are not only competing with the wild banteng, but also risk introducing diseases to the wild ungulates. For the visitor, Baluran offers good walks, a pristine 15 km-long sandy beach facing the Bali Strait and good snorkelling.

Baluran Reserve
Colour map 3, grid B6
Permission to visit the park can be obtained either through the PHPA office in Banyuwangi, or at the Kantor Taman Wisata Baluran in Wonorejo, the entrance to the park. Visitors must pay an entrance fee of 2,000Rp.

Sleeping Guesthouses here can be booked through the PHPA in Banyuwangi, Jl Jend A Yani 108, T4118, or c/o *Taman Baluran*, T68453. There are 2 places to stay. **Bekol** is the best base for bird and animal watching. There is a guesthouse here (**F**), as well as the **E** *Wisma Tamu* which is rather more comfortable, and the *Pondok Peneliti* which is slightly more expensive but still in our **E** category. **Bama**, 3 km from Bekol, is on the coast and more suitable for swimming and snorkelling. **F** guesthouse here. **NB** Food and other supplies are not available in Bama, and there is only a limited range of supplies in Bekol. Supplies can be picked up in Galean, 2 km before Wonorejo; there are no shops to speak of in Wonorejo.

Transport Road Bus: take a bus from Banyuwangi or Ketapang heading along the coast, and ask to be dropped off at the park entrance in Wonorejo. Buses travelling along the coast road from the north, via **Probolinggo**, also run through **Wonorejo**. Ojeks and taxis wait there to take visitors to the coast (5,000Rp on an ojek, 15,000Rp by car).

Banyuwangi

Banyuwangi, on Java's east coast, is not noted either for its sights or its beauty. Formerly, many tourists were forced to pass through the town, as it is near the ferry port for Bali and trains stopped here. Now that a station has been built out at the ferry terminal, 9 km north at Ketapang (see Ketapang entry below), there is no need, and little incentive, to come to Banyuwangi. The **Mesjid Baiturrachman**, in the centre of town, is worth visiting if visitors have time to kill. There is a **Museum Daerah Blambangan** opposite the main square, which is not worth the effort. The market (**Pasar Banyuwangi**), Jl Susuit Tubon, near the centre of town, is located near to the Alun-alun, but is very dirty and the fruit and vegetables are of poor quality. Otherwise, Banyuwangi is a friendly, easy-going town, which is better than the usual transit towns travellers may find themselves stuck in. Head **tourist office** is at the dock, where ferries arrive from Bali. Branch office, Jl Diponegoro 2, T41282.

Phone code: 0333
Colour map 3, grid B6

B-D *Kumala*, Jl Jend A Yani 21B, T23287, F23533. Some rooms with hot water and a/c, an excellent place down a side street, quiet with airy garden, rooms are spacious and immaculate, friendly, professional service, central position. Price includes breakfast, welcome drink and evening snack. Recommended. **B-E** *Hotel Ikhtiar Surya*, Jl Gajah Mada 9, T21063. 1½ km out of the centre of town away from the bus station, but the best Banyuwangi has to offer, range of rooms. Recommended. **C-D** *Blambangan*, Jl Dr Wahidin 4, T21598. Located on 1 side of Alun-alun, some a/c, TV, breakfast, western loo, comfy chairs and table, most luxurious in town. Recommended. **C-D** *Hotel Pinang Sari*, Jl Basuki Rakhmat 116, T23266. Some a/c, hotel on the Ketapang (northern) edge of town, about 1 km from the bus terminal, excellent rooms, fairly priced with some style and panache, attractive verandas and garden, attentive service and professional management. Recommended. **C-E** *Baru*, Jl Pattimura 82-84, about 1½ km from the bus station (bemo for 500Rp), T21369. Own mandi, price

Sleeping

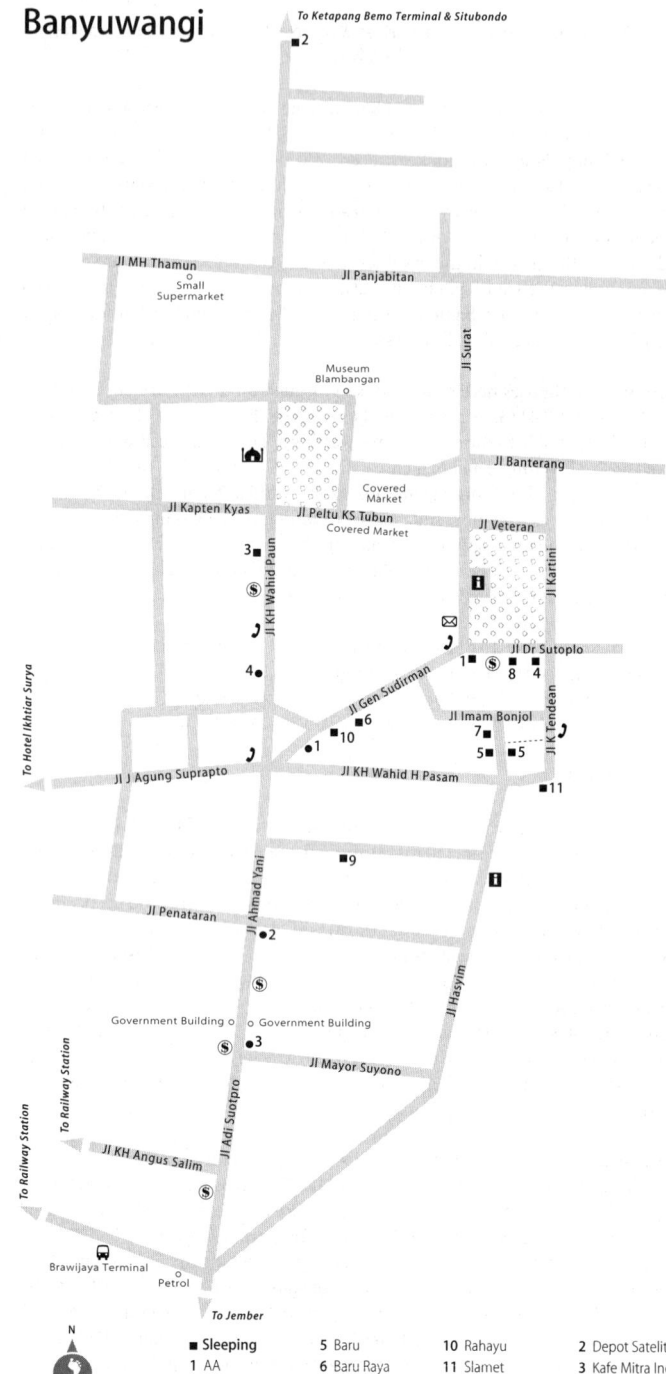

includes breakfast (if you can call it that), large clean rooms, friendly management, popular, helpful staff, Indonesian/Chinese restaurant with non-greasy edible dishes. Only drawback is proximity to mosque, so don't expect to sleep right through the night. Recommended. **D** *Slamet*, Jl Wahid Hasyim 96, T24675. Some a/c, own mandis, friendly enough. **D-F** *Hotel Barito*, Jl Dr Soetomo 41, T21574. Some a/c, strangely attractive, weathered, barrack-like hotel, most expensive rooms are small suites which must be the cheapest around, bathrooms could do with some serious scrubbing, but central location, a certain beach hut charm and value for money make this a possibility. **E** *Anda Losmen*, Jl Basuki Rakhmat 34, T23330. Closest losmen to Blambangan bus terminal and to centre of town, most convenient place to stay if you are trapped in Banyuwangi on your way to or coming back from Bali, rooms are large and clean, some with good attached mandis, hard to beat at the price, unfortunately noisy communal all-night TV. **E** *Gintangan Homestay*, Gintangan (30 km south of Banyuwangi). An alternative place to stay for those with time on their hands, friendly homestay with a lot to do in the area (on the eco-tourism/cultural tourism front), but hard to reach – from Blambangan terminal in Banyuwangi to Karang Ente terminal (500Rp); Karang Ente to Gladag (450Rp). Gladag to the homestay by becak (500Rp), about 3 km. **F** *Hotel Rahayu*, Jl Sutomo 30B, T21608. Next door to *Hotel Baru Raya* and of similar style, avoid if you can.

Cheap *Depot Asia*, Jl Dr Sutomo 12 (near intersection with Jl Jend Sudirman and Jend A Yani), wonderful Chinese-Indonesian food in a/c restaurant including excellent frog (try the *kodok goreng tempung* – deep fried frogs' legs) and pigeon, as well as superb fish and seafood, ice cold beers, highly recommended. *Rumak Makan Sulung*, by entrance to railway station – good value. *Samudra*, Jl Jend Sudirman 171. *Sariwangi Bakery*, Jl Jend Sudirman 162 (500m south of Blambangan bus terminal), excellent pastries and cakes. *Wina*, by Blambangan bus terminal. **2** *Kafe Mitra Indah*, Jl Ahmad Yani 93, the most westernized rumah makan in Banyuwangi, with a large choice of seafood, steaks, Indonesian and Chinese dishes. Serves fresh fruit juices, is spacious and has an adjoining bakery, with excellent cakes and sweetbreads. *Depot Satelit*, Jl A Yani 31, has usual Indonesian and Chinese choices, very popular.

Eating

Banyuwangi no longer serves as a necessary stopping-off point for people visiting Bali. Ketapang can be reached directly by train and bus. Regular bemos link Banyuwangi and Ketapang.

Transport
288 km from Surabaya, 194 km from Probolinggo

Local Bemos from the ferry terminal to town cost about 400Rp.

Road Bus: Banyuwangi has 2 bus terminals. The Blambangan terminal is at the north edge of town and serves Ketapang (for ferries to Bali), and stops along the north coast to Surabaya and Malang including Probolinggo. On the southern edge of town (4 km) is the Brawijaya terminal. To get here from the centre: take bemo (yellow) No 2 (300Rp). This terminal serves all towns southwest of Banyuwangi. Large buses go to **Jember** or **Kalibaru** and stop at all towns on route. Alight at **Jajag** for connections to the turtle beach at **Sukamade**, and at **Benculuk** for connections with **Grajagan** and the **Alas Purwo National Park**. **NB** There are no losmens in Benculuk and buses to Grajagan leave from here only in the morning and early afternoon, so don't get stuck here at night. Nor are there any losmen in nearby Jajag.

Train The main railway station is close to the ferry terminal at Ketapang (see Ketapang entry), but many trains also stop at Banyuwangi's 2 stations. Connections with **Probolinggo**, **Kalibaru**, **Jember**, **Bondowoso** and **Situbondo**.

Banks *Bank Rakyat Indonesia*, Jl Jacksa Agung; *BNI*, Jl Bantarang 46. *BCA*, Jl Banterang. **Communications Post Office**: Jl Diponegoro 1 (on main square). **Wartel (fax & telephone)**: Jl Bangka (at the Blambangan bus terminal). **Useful addresses** *PHPA office*, Jl Agus Salim 138, T24119.

Directory

South of Banyuwangi, settlements become more dispersed and forest and plantations more apparent. Rubber trees flank the route. The road then climbs up through a pass between **Mount Raung** (3,332m) to the north and the **Meru Betiri National Park** to the south. There are wonderful views over the plain below. Between **Jember**

Banyuwangi to Malang

and **Lumajang**, large rice fields, stands of teak and tobacco are the dominant land uses. Thatched barns used for the drying of tobacco leaf also line the road. Leaving Lumajang for **Malang**, the road passes through a second pass, with **Mount Bromo** to the north. Ahead is the imposing silhouette of **Mount Butak** (2,531 m).

Genteng
Phone code: 0333

This is a small unfriendly town, located on the road passing southwest out of Banyuwangi. It consists of little more than two roads which meet in the centre, close to the small bus/bemo station. Jajag and Kalibaru are larger and have more to offer, and Jajag is the stopping off point on the main road for further transportation to Sukamade (turtle beach). The town of Benculuk (further east from Genteng, on the same road from Banyuwangi) is the place to stop, before continuing en route to Grajagan or Plengkung and the Alas Purwo National Park.

Sleeping **D-E** *AJM or Agung Jaya Mahkota*, Jl Jember, on outskirts of town, about 1 km from bus station, T85346. The best place to stay, having an impressive mock 'white house' façade and the rooms are of a good standard; however, it is not very popular and the staff seemed a little confused to see guests turn up. Some rooms with a/c, hot water, sofa, TV and dressing table. Restaurant with Chinese and Indonesian food. **E** *Ramayana*, Jl Raya II, 500m from bus station heading away from traffic lights with a wartel next door, T5291. Next best hotel and good value for money. **E-F** *Agung Losmen*, Jl Diponegoro 9, closest losmen to the bus station, T5844. Cute, tiny dolls house front and miniature rooms, with just enough space to fit a minuscule double bed. Not recommended. **F** *Nusantara*, Jl Gambiran 350 (further down the road on the same side as *Agung*), T6964. Presently a building site; however, they have big plans to build a swimming pool soon, nothing special.

Transport **Road Bus**: regular connections with **Banywangi**.

Ketapang

Phone code: 0333
Colour map 3, grid B6

Ketapang is the ferry terminal for Bali and has developed into a thriving little centre that survives for no other reason. There are restaurants and warungs, a train station, large Pertamina distribution centre, tourist information office and one hotel a couple of kilometres to the south. The long line of lorries, their drivers patiently waiting for a space on the ferry, testifies to Ketapang's importance as a transport node.

The district **tourist office**, *Cabang Dinas Pariwista Daerah*, Jl Gatot Subroto, T41172, is not really geared-up for tourists and not much English spoken, but they do have information to give (100m up the road from the ferry terminal towards Banyuwangi, near car-ferry). *East Java Tourist Information Booth*, at the ferry terminal, can be very useful, or rather useless, depending on who is manning the booth.

Sleeping Only 1 place to stay at the **B-D** *Manyar Garden Hotel*, Jl Gatot Subroto, T24741, F24742. Some a/c, 2 km south of Ketapang, this place is pleasant enough but rather overpriced, it is the only hotel here so presumably feels able to push its rates up – try Banyuwangi if possible, places there are better value.

Transport
9 km north of Banyuwangi

Train The station is opposite the ferry terminal. Day and night connections with Surabaya's Kota terminal, 7 hrs. Combined bus-train tickets to **Denpasar** (Bali) available (see page 977).

Road Bus: there is a bus station just outside the ferry terminal. Connections with **Probolinggo** (for Mount Bromo), **Surabaya** and **Banyuwangi**.

Sea Boat: passenger and car ferries to and from **Gilimanuk**, on Bali dock at Ketapang. Boats depart every 30 mins, 24 hrs a day, 30 mins. The *Pelni* ship *Pangrango* docks here on its fortnightly circuit. **NB** If driving to Bali, note that it is not easy to obtain fuel between the ferry terminal at Gilimanuk and Denpasar, so fill up before leaving Java. To get to Ketapang, from

Banyuwangi catch a regular minibus from the Blambangan terminal on the north edge of town. *Pelni* boats dock here on their way to Nusa Tenggara.

Communications *Wartel* office (fax & telephone): at the ferry terminal.

Directory

Alas Purwo National Park

Alas Purwo (or 'ancient forest') National Park supports a collection of rare trees, as well as wildlife including leopard, banteng and wild boar. Relatively few people visit the park and the rangers are extremely keen to encourage more people to come.

Colour map 3, grid B6

Getting to Alas Purwo by public transport can be slightly confusing and tiresome, but is definitely worth the effort. Doubtless, the time it takes to get here partly explains the park's relative unpopularity, despite its many attractions. Take a minibus from the Brawijaya bus terminal in Banyuwangi to Kalipait, or a large bus to Benculuk and then a minibus to Kalipait (2,000Rp), 2 hrs. From Benculuk the road condition deteriorates; be prepared for a slow and bumpy ride. Unfortunately, public transport only goes as far as Kalipait, stopping just 2 km short of the PHPA post at Pasar Anyer. Though ojek riders offer their services for this final 2 km (2,000Rp), it is an easy enough walk. From the Pasar Anyer PHPA post, the rangers will take you by motorbike to Rowobendo (12 km or 45 mins), the entrance to the park (just a single hut and gate). From Rowobendo, it is a further 2 km to the beach at Trianggulasi where there is accommodation (see above). Total cost of transport from Pasar Anyer to Trianggulasi is 5,000Rp per motorbike.

Getting there
A permit is needed to enter the park, obtainable from the park office near Tegaldlimo or from the PHPA office in Banyuwangi

The park consists of a forest refuge on the remote **Blambangan Peninsula**, within which lies areas of untouched lowland tropical forest, alive with wildlife, which contrasts with its coastline of endless empty (off) white sand beaches, pounded by world-renowned surf. Alas Purwo is used for research, education and is an ideal haven in which to relax and escape from the usual hustle and bustle of Javanese life.

The park

The unspoilt beaches stretch for miles and are the breeding grounds for four species of turtle (*penyu*). Between April and October, egg-laying Green turtles and Olive Ridley turtles can be found near **Ngagelan**, where the rangers operate a turtle safe-hatching programme. There is also the rare chance of being able to see the huge 350kg leatherback turtles lumbering ashore. The best time to catch a glimpse of the turtles is very early morning, between 0200 and 0400. You may be fortunate enough to see turtles during the daylight hours too. If not, you can see the newly hatched turtles at the centre. The park rangers collect all the eggs they can find to protect them from poachers and predators. After being kept in cramped but protected conditions, the baby turtles are released back into the ocean – where most get consumed within hours of their release. Ngagelan is 6 km west of **Trianggulasi** and may be reached by foot or motorbike, along a well-marked jungle track or along the beach.

The shoreline of all the park is hazardous for swimming due to the huge surf and strong currents. Harmless reef sharks and whales are frequently sighted, which makes bathing even more exciting. From the beach at Trianggulasi, there are breathtaking views along the coast to the tip of the peninsula at Plengkung, and to the east and west to the sea cliffs of Grajagan.

The flora of the park ranges from dense tropical forest to lush coastal groves, the habitat for thousands of migrant birds. The dense forest is home to packs of wild dogs, civets and leopards, whereas playful, long-tailed leaf monkeys and macaques populate the coastal woodland. If you don't catch sight of an actual macaque, you will probably find evidence of their hunting. Clearly visible are trails in the sand, made as the monkeys drag the crabs they eat off the beach and into the safety of the forest. Unusual animals, they are also able to swim and have gained a semi-sacred status with some Hindus, especially in India. They are also said to be the monkeys on which is modelled the adage 'see no evil, hear no evil, speak no evil'.

Flora & fauna

Information & supplies There is a PHPA office in **Pasar Anyer**. Rangers show visitors around their 'Visitor's Centre', with various maps and photos of the park. There is a basic store here for necessities such as rice, noodles, corned beef, coffee etc and other dried foodstuffs – but it is worth bringing additional supplies from Banyuwangi or getting them at the market in Kalipait. **Park entrance permit**: 2,000Rp, payable at Rowobendo, the entrance to the park.

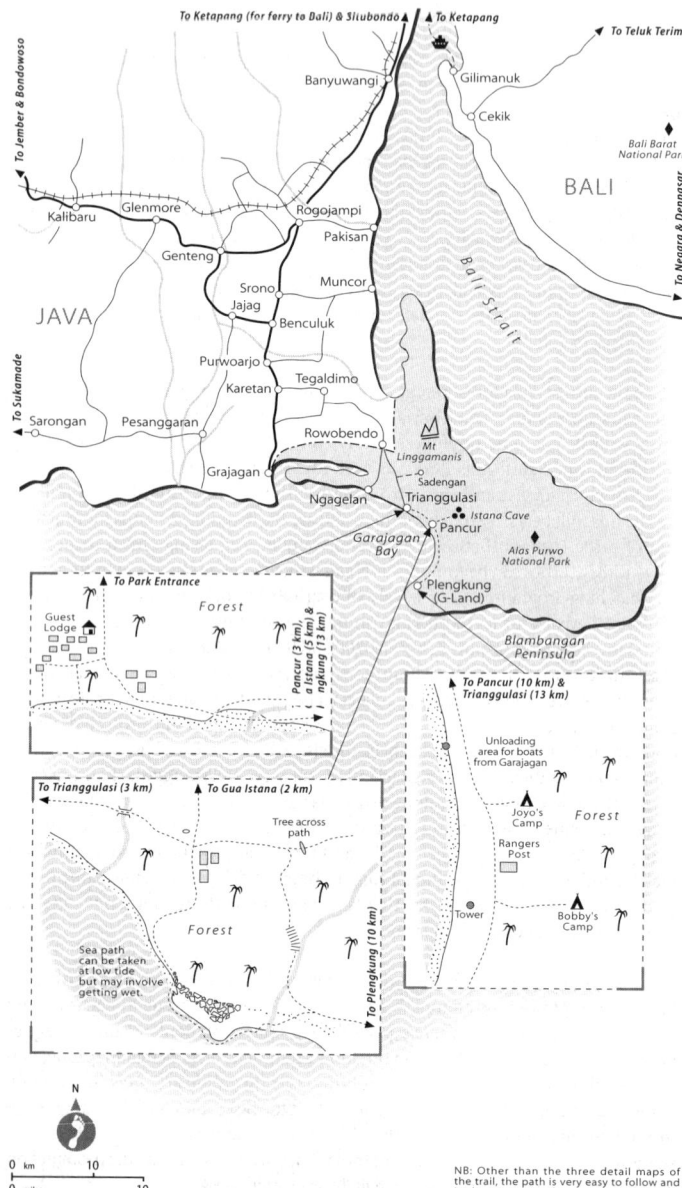

Alas Purwo National Park & surrounding areas

At **Trianggulasi**: **E** *Guesthouse*, 8 basic double bamboo huts on stilts, just 50m from the beach. No electricity, only gas lamps, 2 kitchens available for guests use, 2 outside mandis. **NB** Bring all your own supplies for the duration of your stay; there are no shops for several kilometres – the rangers tend to disapprove of visitors attempting to hunt wild peacock or banteng, to roast on their barbecue when their supplies run out. — **Sleeping**

The Hindu ceremony of **Pagerwesi** is held on the park's northern coast, every 210 days. Balinese, with banners and traditional dress, come to make offerings at the sea edge. — **Festivals**

Grajagan Bay and Plengkung ('G-Land')

Grajagan Bay is situated within the South Banyuwangi reserve, faces west and is renowned for its surfing. The beach is reputed to have one of the longest left breaks in the world, and is a pilgrimage spot for Australian surfers. — *Colour map 3, grid B6*

Road and **Sea**: most people get here on surfing tours from Bali, and they arrive by small boats from Grajagan. To get to Grajagan, take a bus from Banyuwangi to Benculuk, and from there a minibus to Grajagan. From Jember, catch a bus to Jajag, and then a connection to Grajagan. From Grajagan, boats leave every 3 days during tourist season (May-Sep), and to join the boat the cost is 100,000Rp per person. Alternatively, charter a fishing boat for the trip. There are no roads or motorcycle tracks leading to Plengkung, but it is possible to walk there from Trianggulasi, along an easy to follow forest path which never ventures more than a few metres from the beach. First follow the path to **Pancur** (3 km), before trekking the final 10 km to the peninsula. Accompanying guides (park rangers) can be hired for 15,000Rp, but are hardly needed. The walk takes 3-4 hrs. Take plenty of water. Although leopards do inhabit the forest (the Javan tiger is probably extinct), they are rarely sighted during the day and unlikely to be a danger. **NB** The camps are closed during the wet season (Dec-Apr), when storms and heavy rain make the area hazardous for surfing. — **Getting there**

Plengkung, colloquially known by the surfing fraternity as 'G-Land', is located at the tip of the park's peninsula and 14 km from the park entrance. Plengkung is home to the world's most awesome left-hand reef break, often reaching 4-5m. As waves usually break to the right, this adds an additional challenge to riding the wave. With its size and the proximity of the reef to the surface, it is not surprising how many surfers return to shore with broken boards, and worse. 'G-Land' should only be attempted by the very experienced. The biggest waves have even been given their own names: **Kongs** and **Money** trees are the most well-known places to surf, but **Speedies** is reputedly the best place to go to catch the line barrels. — **'G-Land'**

'G-Land' has gained an international profile since its inclusion in 1994 in the Quicksilver World Tour Circuit. The competition takes place during the first or second week of June every year (no set date), when the world's best 44 surfers battle it out, accompanied by a huge entourage of press and hangers-on, who take over all the accommodation available. Plengkung is therefore closed to the public (except on day trips) when the contest is in progress.

Tours to either of the jungle camps at 'G-Land' (see below) can be booked from *Tubes Surf Bar*, Poppies Lane 2, Kuta, Bali, T/F753510. The huge bulk of visitors to Plengkung come on organized tours straight from Bali, via boat from Grajagan. During the peak tourist season (May-Sep), these tours leave every three days from Kuta. A seven-night tour (including transport to and from Bali, all accommodation, food and drink) costs US$420 (US$370 for women) at *Bobby's* and US$325 at *Joyo's* (see below). — **Tours**

This consists of 2 'jungle camps': **B** *Joyo's*, run by *Pt Plengkung Indah Wisata*, Kuta, Bali, T031-5314752, F5313073, g-land.rad.net.id Slightly cheaper than *Bobby's*, keen to attract backpackers, price includes 5 beers a day. Buffet style meals (a mix of Western and Indonesian cuisine), there are also permanent tent structures (for 2 people), $30 each plus 5 cokes — **Sleeping**

daily. **B** *Bobby's*, run by *Pt Wanawisata Alamhayah*, Jl Pantai, Kuta, Bali, T0333-21485. Slightly better than *Joyo's*, with larger choice of western food, unlimited soft drinks and Carlsberg on tap. Price includes 3 meals and drinks.

Both the above surf camps consist of attractive, traditional-style bamboo huts, with outside (open air) shared bathrooms (with no roof, but western loo and shower, electricity). They also have recreation areas, with pool tables, table tennis, volleyball courts, a bar and evening showings of laser discs. Fishing tackle may be borrowed, and trips on one of the camp boats are available. **E** *PHPA post*, this is the cheaper alternative and is located between the 2 camps. Bring all your own food, only 2 rooms available at present, with no electricity.

Sukamade and Meru Betiri National Park

Colour map 3, grid B5   Sukamade is on East Java's south coast, within the Meru Betiri National Park. Since 1972, this 3 km long stretch of beach has been protected – to allow turtles to lay their eggs. The breeding season stretches from November to March and seven species lay their eggs on the beach. The most common are the green, hawksbill, snapping and giant leatherback. To see the turtles laying their eggs – between 80 and 180 in a nest – it is first necessary to obtain permission from the PHPA rangers. Loud noises, smoking, lights and flash cameras are not permitted – nor are the turtles allowed to be touched. The egg-laying season runs from April to October and the best time to be on the beach is from 2100 to 0200. **NB** No swimming allowed here. In early 1994, a tidal wave destroyed much of the beach and inundated several villages, drowning an estimated 200 people. The Sukamade Baru Estate was established in 1927 and now covers 1,200 ha, planted with coffee, coconut and rubber.

Getting there   Catch a bus from Banyuwangi to Pasanggaran, 2 hrs; from here there are minibuses to Sarongan, 97 km from Banyuwangi. From Sarongan there is 1 truck a day in the morning to Sukamade, returning at 0700. Alternatively, an ojek to Sukamade costs around 8-10,000Rp. It is also possible to reach Pasanggaran via the small market town of Jajag (see 'Sleeping', above) from Banyuwangi. **NB** Public transport to Sukamade is limited and unreliable. Chartering your own vehicle is another option, but a substantial truck or 4-wheeler will be needed to navigate the mountainous and pot-holed road, with several fords – one of which is virtually impassable in the wet season. The easily discouraged or less well funded traveller might be better advised to avoid this park and visit the slightly more accessible and equally tranquil Alas Purwo (see page 291), which is probably visited by just as many, if not more, turtles as Sukamade.

The park   **Meru Betiri National Park** covers 500 sq km and was declared a reserve in 1972. It represents the last significant area of lowland rain forest in Java. However, the park was really gazetted to protect the last specimens of the once common Javan tiger – a small sub-species of tiger. Although some claim that there may still be a handful of individuals left, most naturalists believe that the Javan tiger is extinct. The park is centred on Mount Betiri (1,223m) and supports leopard, banteng and rusa deer – the latter introduced to the area as prey for the leopards. Four species of turtle also come ashore to lay their eggs along this largely rocky coastline.

There are also some rare species of flowering plant. Meru Betiri is home to a species of Rafflesia, the *Rafflesia patma*. This is harvested by locals and sold to buyers near Solo, where it is processed and used in traditional medicines. *Balanophora fungosa*, which can also be found here, is another parasitic flower and contains waxy substances which can be processed to make candles. The lowland sandwiched between the park's two highest mountains, Gunung Betiri and Gunung Tajem, is an area of dense rainforest, and an ideal habitat for now rare flora and fauna. The park has its own observation platforms, where you can watch for animals like monkeys, kingfishers and giant hornbills.

Sleeping   **In Sukamade**   **D** *Wisma Sukamade*, space for up to 30 guests, enquiries at PHPA post in Banyuwangi or Ketapang, clean and spacious rooms with some western toilets and shower facilities. Price includes 2 meals. Helpful staff who will take you by jeep to visit the turtle nesting sites (or point you in the right direction for the 1 hr walk to the turtle beach).

In Jagjag C-D *Hotel Suriya*, Jl Yos Sudarso 2, T0333-94126. Some a/c, pool, very comfortable for such a small place. Cheaper accommodation includes the **D** *Hotel Baru Indah*, close to the bus terminal.

Jember

Jember is a dispersed, spread-out town, with wide, well-planned streets and an airy feel. It is surprisingly busy and sophisticated, and also one of the cleanest towns in Java. There are no sights or events and little to do but relax. A state-owned plantation company, called *Perkebunan XXVI*, have begun organizing tours (see 'Tours').

Phone code: 0331
Colour map 3, grid B5

Watu Ulo is a beautiful beach due south of Jember, about 10 km south of the small market town of Wuluhan. ■ *Getting there: by bemo to the Ambulu bus terminal, and from there a connection to Watu Ulo.*

Excursions

Perkebunan XXVI, Jl Gajah Mada 249, T21061, organize tours to coconut, rubber, cocoa and sugar cane plantations in the vicinity.

Tours

A-E *Bima*, Jl Gajah Mada 50, T86711, F81566. Large hotel situated in the centre of town, a/c, TV, western loo, bath, shower, more expensive rooms with hot water, coffee shop/restaurant serving Indonesian and Chinese dishes, as well as the occasional simple western dish such as sandwiches, soups and fruit juices (one of the few places in Jember these can be found), breakfast (Indonesian buffet style and toast) included. **B** *Bandung Permai*, Jl Hayam Wuruk 38, T84528. A/c, restaurant, pool, largest hotel in town – or rather on the outskirts of town as it is several kilometres from the centre – ugly 4-storey block, with mediocre but comfortable rooms. **B-C** *Safari Hotel*, Jl KH Dahlan 7, T81882, F81887. Some a/c, quiet garden compound, professionally managed with very clean rooms and bathrooms, modern but with more character than most such places, good location in town. Recommended.

Sleeping
■ *on map, page 296*

C-E *Lestari*, Jl Gajah Mada 347, T87920. Some a/c, rooms are good, but the hotel has a rather inconvenient location (for most) 3 km out of town on the road towards Lumajang and Surabaya, 3-storey building with what looks like strands of telephone wire hanging from the balconies, set down a narrow lane, hot water mandis. **C-F** *Mars*, Jl Diponegoro 43, T41573. Very close to town centre, this predominantly concrete building has a car park feel to it. Being on a junction of 2 main roads, it's noisy. Standard rooms have TV, fan, squat loo, with a basic breakfast included in the room rate. **D** *Seroja*, Jl PB Sudirman 2 (1 km from town centre on the way to the Arjoso bus terminal), T83905, F85580. Some a/c, quiet and clean, garden atmosphere and very helpful staff but noisy at times, breakfast, tea and coffee included.

D-E *Anugerah*, Jl Trunojoyo V/17, T87272. Clean, quite spacious, western loo, mandi and sink, each room has a lounge area. Breakfast of bread or noodles is included, very quiet and away from the main streets. **D-E** *Ratna*, Jl RA Kartini 45, T87490. A/c, spacious, with separate lounge area with TV, bathroom facilities are good, hot water, bath, western loo, nasi campur for breakfast. **D-E** *Merdeka*, Jl Raya Sultan Agung 136, T87625. 46 rooms, squat loo, clean, pleasant surroundings including small restaurant serving Indonesian food. Popular with Indonesians and is often fully booked. **E** *Anda*, Jl Kartini 40, T89475. Large, very clean rooms, each with fan, dressing table and large mirror, squat toilet, basic breakfast included, a number of helpful maps of the town and local area in reception. **E** *Kartika*, Jl Trunojoyo 91, T21057. Large and clean with very generous sized beds, a long mirror, wardrobe and sink that does not work, Indonesian style loo, lounge TV area. **E-F** *Nusantara*, Jl Wijiaya Kusuma 10, T87256. Fan, western loo, shower, fairly clean but nothing special; however, it is conveniently located close to the railway station. **F** *Kawi*, Jl Gatot Subroto 39, T426381. Rooms for 2 could easily fit 3 and they are happy for you to do this at no extra cost. Shared mandi, rather old rooms, nothing special but quite good value for money.

Eating *Cheap Californian Fried Chicken (CFC)*, Matahari Plaza, Jl Diponegoro 66. *Depo Anda*, Jl Gatot Subroto 31, T89476. Next to *Hotel Anda*, this small restaurant is very clean and well kept, a wide range of Indonesian foods. *Lestari*, Jl Kartini 16, T89162. This large, nicely decorated restaurant is airy and cool, with a wide selection of Indonesian food and excellent ice creams. *Taman Salero*, Jl Raya Sultan Agungi, T85177, serves masakan Padang. *Sari Utama*, Jl Gajah Mada 33, T87092/84233. Large TV screens where films are shown, stage used for karaoke, very large menu with English translations. All types of Indonesian and Chinese foods served, including sharks fin, pigeon, frog, cuttlefish, pork, beef, lobster and prawns.

Entertainment **Cinemas** *Johar 21 Cineplex*, Jl Diponegoro (in the *Matahari Centre*), modern a/c cinema complex.

Shopping **Batik** *Trisna Jaya Batik Shop*, Jl Trunojoyo 151, T85398, large selection of batik sarongs and clothes.
Books *Gramedia Bookshop*, *Matahari Shopping Centre*, Jl Diponegoro 66 and at Jl Trunjoyo. Sells maps, stationery, sports equipment and games, as well as books.
Chemist *Apotik Agung Parman*, Jl Raya Sultan Agung.
Shopping centres *Matahari Shopping Centre*, Jl Diponegoro 66, including *Gramedia Bookshop*, CFC, cinemas.

Jember

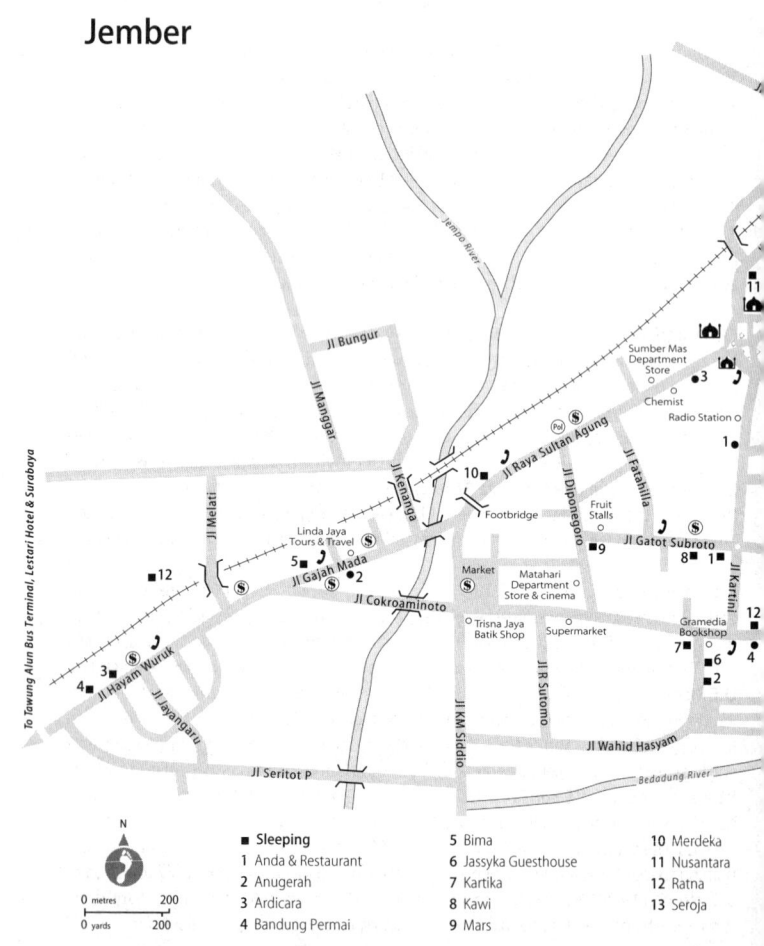

	Sleeping	5 Bima	10 Merdeka
	1 Anda & Restaurant	6 Jassyka Guesthouse	11 Nusantara
	2 Anugerah	7 Kartika	12 Ratna
	3 Ardicara	8 Kawi	13 Seroja
	4 Bandung Permai	9 Mars	

Local Becaks, town buses, bemos (300Rp).

Train The station is on the northern edge of town, Jl Wijaya Kusuma.

Road Bus: Jember has 4 bus terminals, all out of town. The Tawang Alun terminal is the largest, serving Banyuwangi, Surabaya and Probolinggo, and is 8 km from town on the road to Surabaya. The Ajung terminal serves Watu Ulo and is in Ambulu, 5 km from town. The Pakusari terminal serves Banyuwangi (although the Tawang Alun terminal has more buses running there) and is 5 km from town. Last, the Arjasa terminal serves Bondowoso (700Rp) and Situbondo, and is 6 km from town. Bemos link all the terminals (250Rp).

Banks *Bank Bali*, intersection of Jl Supratman and Jl. *Lippobank*, Jl Diponegoro. *Pertrokoan Trunojoyo Bank Central Asia*, Jl Gatot Subroto. **Communications** Post Office: Jl Sudirman (on the main square). **Telephone:** *Wartel* office, Jl Diponegoro 91.

Transport
33 km from Bondowoso, 67 km from Situbondo, 95 km from Banyuwangi, 70 km from Lumajang

Directory

Lumajang

Lumajang is a remarkably clean and tidy town, with an almost Mexican feel. The main market, the Pasar Baru, is at the intersection of Jl Kembar and Jl Jend A Yani. Most activity, commercial and otherwise, is concentrated along Jl Panglima Sudirman.

Phone code: 0334
Colour map 3, grid B5

● Eating
1 Lestari
2 Sari Utama
3 Taman Salero
4 Tokoroti-Kue & Donut

C-E *Gadjah Mada*, Jl Panglima Sudirman 42-58, T81174. Some a/c, quiet and peaceful, hot water baths in the more expensive rooms, fan rooms are the real bargain though, clean with large bathrooms, central location. Recommended. **C-E** *Hotel Lumajang*, Jl Jend A Yani, T81314, F83254. Some a/c, large compound with rooms built around a courtyard.

Cinemas: Jl Panglima Sudirman.

Swimming: public swimming pool, Jl Jend A Yani.

Local The main **bemo** terminal is in the centre of town at the intersection of Jl Kembar and Jl Tembus Terminal, close to the Pasar Baru.

Road Bus: the terminal has been relocated 6 km out of town (now imaginatively called the Terminal Baru) on Jl Jend A Yani, the road running north towards Probolinggo. Regular a/c and non-a/c connections with **Probolinggo**, **Malang**, **Jember**, **Banyuwangi** and **Ketapang** (for Bali).

Banks *Bank Bumi Daya*, Jl Panglima Sudirman; *Bank Central Asia*, Jl Panglima Sudirman 2. **Communications** Post Office: Jl Dr Sutomo. **Medical facilities** General Hospital, Jl Jend A Yani.

Sleeping

Entertainment

Sports

Transport
52 km from Probolinggo, 128 km from Malang, 70 km from Jember

Directory

Background

History

Java's epic and convoluted history encompasses an array of kingdoms, empires, sultanates and dynasties. Although the history portrayed below might give the impression that one kingdom neatly followed another in dominating the island, there were always a number of powers vying for influence at any one time. It was only a case of which dominated, when.

Sailendra (Central Java, mid-8th - 10th century) The Sailendra Dynasty of Central Java, which lasted for only two centuries, was the greatest of all the Javanese kingdoms, and produced architectural monuments of such grandeur and artistic brilliance that they are among the finest not just in Indonesia, but in the world. At the height of its power, Sailendra's sphere of influence stretched as far as Champa on the Vietnamese coast and Angkor in Cambodia. The kings of the Sailendra Dynasty derived their wealth and power from agriculture.

Of all the monuments erected by the Sailendras, none is more imposing than **Borobudur** – possibly the single most magnificent temple in Southeast Asia. This enormous edifice, built between 778 and 824, represented the cosmological and spiritual centre of the kingdom.

Sanjaya (Central & East Java, 8th-11th century) At about the same time as the Sailendra kings were building Borobudur, another Central Javanese Kingdom was also engaged in an extensive monument-building programme: Sanjaya (sometimes known as Mataram). In this instance, Hinduism, rather than Buddhism, was the dominant religion, but no less energy was expended. Foremost among this kingdom's temples was **Prambanan**, the finest Hindu shrine on Java. The Sanjaya Kingdom derived its wealth from controlling the spice trade between Maluku (the Moluccas), China and the sultanates of the Arab world. The control of port facilities focused on the strategic Strait of Melaka (Malacca). This led Sanjaya into open conflict with the more powerful kingdom of Srivijaya, based at Palembang, Sumatra. In 1006, Srivijaya defeated Sanjaya and sacked its capital, slaughtering many of its inhabitants. It was not until 1026 that Srivijaya's hold over the Strait of Melaka was relinquished, following an expedition headed by a prince from South India.

In 1020, a new figurehead emerged in the Sanjaya Kingdom – **Airlangga** – the son of a Balinese prince and a Sanjaya princess. His reign was peaceful and he restored relations with Srivijaya by marrying a Srivijayan princess. Religious syncretism was at its height during Airlangga's reign and he pragmatically recognized both Buddhism and Hinduism, hoping to appeal to supporters of both faiths. Following his death, the empire was divided into two kingdoms – Kediri and Janggala.

Kediri & Janggala (1050-1222) Kediri was centred in the Brantas River valley, near the site of the modern day city of the same name; while it is thought that Janggala was focused south of Surabaya, near Malang. Inscriptions indicate that Kediri became a locally powerful maritime kingdom, operating on the north coast of Java. It traded extensively in spices from Maluku with India, and was preferred as a port over Srivijaya because of its proximity to the source of those spices. Of Janggala, historians know almost nothing. However, in 1222, **Ken Angrok** of Kediri captured the lesser kingdom of Janggala, and then went on to kill the ruler of Kediri and establish his new kingdom at Singasari.

Between 1486 and 1512, the capital was moved from Majapahit, southwest to Kediri, perhaps to escape from the powerful Islamic incursion from the north coast. The move did nothing to prevent Demak from overpowering Kediri in 1527.

A summary of Javanese history 400-1870

400	First Hindu Kingdom of Tarumanegara is established		

Central Javanese Period 600-929
Sailendra Dynasty (mid-8th-10th century)
Sanjaya Dynasty (8th-11th century)

East Javanese Period 929-1527
King Sindok of Sanjaya (928-950)
1006 Srivijaya defeats Sanjaya Kingdom; King Airlangga of Sanjaya (1020-49)
1045 Partition of Sanjaya into Kediri & Janggala
Kediri Dynasty (929-1222)
Singasari Dynasty (1222-92)
King Ken Angrok (1222-27)
1222 King Ken Angrok conquers Janggala; King Kertanagara (1268-92)
Majapahit Dynasty (1292-1527)
Chief Minister Gajah Mada (1331-64)
1343 Javanese colony established on Bali
King Hayam Wuruk (1350-89)
1400 Decline of Majapahit

Islamic Period 1527-1757
1500 Sultanate of Demak
1527 Demak overpowers Kediri
Wali Dynasty in West Java; foundation of Jakarta
1575 Islamic Kingdom of Mataram
King Senopati (1575-1601)

Colonial Period 1513-1870
1513 Portuguese land at Sunda Kelapa; first European contact with Java
1522 Portuguese establish a godown at Sunda Kelapa
1602 VOC established
Sultan Agung of Mataram (1613-45)
1619 Batavia established by Jan Pieterszoon Coen
1628-29 Sultan Agung attacks Batavia, but fails to dislodge Dutch
1757 Dutch conquer Mataram and divide kingdom into 3 vassal sultanates;
Governor-General Daendels (1808-10)
British administration under Raffles (1811-16)
Java War (1825-30)
Culture System (1830-70)

The short-lived Singasari Kingdom was founded in East Java by Ken Angrok in 1222 after the defeat of Kediri and Janggala. The kingdom's greatest king was its last, **Kertanagara** (1268-1292). His aggressively expansionist policies took Singasari's influence beyond the confines of East Java and in 1290 he defeated the once powerful empire of Srivijaya.

Singasari (1222-92)

The Majapahit – or 'Bitter Gourd' – empire was the last and most powerful of the Javanese kingdoms, and at the height of its influence claimed suzerainty over parts of Sumatra, Malaya and Borneo. The capital of this far-flung empire was Trowulan, which at the time was one of the largest cities in Asia.

The flowering of the Majapahit Kingdom spanned the middle years of the 14th century and is associated with two brilliant men: **Gajah Mada** and **Hayam Wuruk**. Gajah Mada was a skilled general and consummate politician. During this time Java experienced what many regard as the island's golden years, and there was a flowering of the arts. Though ostensibly Buddhist, the king and his subjects also worshipped the Hindu gods Siva and Vishnu.

By 1402, Melaka (Malacca), on the Malay Peninsula, had been established as a trading-post and the importance of Java waned. At the same time the infiltration of Islam began to undermine the religious legitimacy of the kingdom. Majapahit finally fell to Demak, the Islamic state on Java's north coast, in 1478.

Majapahit (1292-1478)

Following the decline and subsequent fall of Majapahit at the beginning of the 15th century, Java entered a 200-year period of in-fighting between numerous small kingdoms and sultanates. Along the north coast, trading sultanates (so-called *pasisir* states) drew their religious inspiration from Islam and their wealth from controlling the spice trade between Maluku and Melaka. It was not until the early part of the 17th century that Java was once again to come under the influence of a single dominant power: Mataram.

Java in disarray: 1400-1600

Mataram (16th century-1757) The last of the great Javanese kingdoms, Mataram, was focused on Central Java, near Yogyakarta and Surakarta. The kingdom's finest leader was a devout Muslim, Sultan Agung (r. 1613- 45) . With the help of the Dutch, he vanquished the coastal trading states and promoted Islam in Java's interior. At its peak, his kingdom encompassed Surabaya in the east and Cirebon in the north. He had every intention of uniting the whole of Java, but was prevented from achieving this aim by the presence of the Dutch in Batavia (Jakarta).

In a number of respects, the Mataram Kingdom was weak. It generated 'income' by extracting the small agricultural surplus that a peasant family produced each year. By doing this many thousands of times, the king accumulated considerable wealth. But the basis of this wealth was wholly different from the coastal or *pasisir* kingdoms, whose economic power was founded on trade. Historians argue that Mataram managed to unite Java as a political whole, because there existed a common language and culture, and as historian John Smail says, "a political myth that was universally accepted because it rested on common religious beliefs". Such an explanation is only partially convincing, and the Mataram Empire was beginning to degenerate even as it reached the greatest extent of its power. Sultan Agung's son, Amangkurat I (r. 1645-77), faced a rebellion in 1672 after Mount Merapi erupted, and it was only with Dutch assistance and the crowning of a new king, Amangkurat II, that the kingdom was pieced back together. Ironically, the assistance afforded by the Dutch gave them a foothold and presaged their domination of Java by 1757.

Colonial expansion & control (1513-1870) Colonial contact with Java dates back to 1513, when a Portuguese expedition arrived off Sunda Kelapa (Jakarta). But the Portuguese were in no position to make their presence felt. Instead, it was the Dutch who were to extend their control over the archipelago. This was a gradual affair and for the first 150 years, Dutch influence was restricted to the town of Batavia (Jakarta) and its environs. The history of this period is recounted in the introduction to Jakarta (see page 79).

The Dutch, in the guise of the **Vereenigte Ooste-Indische Compagnie (VOC)** or Dutch East India Company, only began to expand their influence inland as the Mataram Kingdom went into decline.

Under the rule of the VOC, there was a modicum of expansion in commercial activity in Java. The arabica coffee bush had been found to grow well in the highlands of Priangan in the early 18th century and it quickly became one of Java's most valuable exports.

The **English East India Company** occupied the Dutch East Indies between 1811 and 1816. Just as the VOC had expanded into Java with some trepidation, so the English were equally reluctant to commit men and resources to an enterprise which appeared to offer little financial return.

Thomas Stamford Raffles became governor-general at the age of 30 in 1811. He introduced economic, political and social reforms, and improved the lives of the local population. Raffles was also a keen botanist and helped to establish the **gardens at Bogor** (see page 118), and commissioned the first archaeological survey of Borobudur.

From the final decades of the 19th century, the history of Java becomes intertwined with the history of Indonesia (see page 939).

Geography

Java stretches more than 1,000 km from east to west, but is only 81 km broad at its widest point, and covers an area of 132,187 sq km. The island lies over a volcanic arc that marks the boundary between two tectonic (continental) plates, making it one of the most volcanically active places on earth. There are 121 volcanoes on Java – more than any other country – of which between 27 and 35 are classified as active. This degree of vulcanicity has periodically led to catastrophe. Most famously, in 1883, the island of Krakatau, just off Java's west coast, exploded, killing 36,000 people (see page 116). Further back in history, in 928 or 929 AD, it is thought that Mount Merapi erupted, leading to the mass migration of the court and people of Central Java eastwards (see page 301). More recently, in 1982, Mount Galunggung in East Java erupted, causing 60,000 people to lose their homes and livelihoods.

Climate

The 'east monsoon' from June to August brings dry weather to Java, while the 'west monsoon' from December to February corresponds with the wet season. During the transitional months between these two seasons, rainfall can be even heavier than during the wet season. In general it becomes drier from west to east, and while the western two thirds of the island receives rain throughout the year, the eastern third of Java has a pronounced dry season. Average annual rainfall in West Java is 2,360mm, in Central Java, 2,400mm, and in East Java, only 1,660mm. Temperatures vary little through the year, averaging 26-27°C at sea-level.

Culture

Art and architecture

Of all the islands of Indonesia, none is more richly endowed with architectural monuments than Java. It is here that the former great empires of the country were centred, and their artistic achievements are still reflected in the temples and palaces that lie scattered across the mountains and plains of the central and east regions. West Java has far fewer remains, possibly because Buddhism never spread to the west.

The art and architecture of both the Central and East Javanese periods is known as '**Classical**', because it was influenced by the art and architecture of India. The question which still preoccupies scholars is whether the Indian or the Indonesian element should be stressed. During the 5th to 7th centuries, Indian culture arrived in Southeast Asia, along with Indian merchants (*vaisyas*) and religious men (*brahmanas*). The candi of Java appeared just at the time when Indian influence was strongest, and there are stylistic links between the earliest candi of the Dieng Plateau and Gedung Songo and some North and South Indian structures. In recent years, the tendency has been to stress the 'local genius' rather than the imported Indian traditions.

It is now argued that by the 8th and 9th centuries, Javanese artists had effectively created their own Javanese style of architecture and ornamentation.

Central Javanese period (730 AD-929 AD)

The **Central Javanese Period** embraces one of the most extraordinary periods of monument building, anywhere in the world. This was associated with the advent of the Sailendra Dynasty and the arrival of Buddhism. The building boom spanned two centuries from 730, during which Candi Kalasan, Candi Prambanan and Candi Borobudur were all built, along with numerous smaller temples. The temples were built of andesite, a porous volcanic stone found in abundance across Central Java. The period came to a spectacular end in 928 or 929, when Mount Merapi is thought to have erupted. Not only would such an eruption have affected agricultural production by coating the land in a deep layer of ash and lava, but it would doubtless have been taken as a sign that the gods were displeased, thus necessitating a move on religious grounds as well.

From the 10th century, the magnificent monuments of Central Java were left to be ravaged by earthquakes and storms, and consumed by the forest.

East Javanese Period (929 AD-1527 AD)

The East Javanese Period is associated with the dramatic move of the palace of King Sindok, along with his subjects, east in 929, to the fertile lands of East Java and the Brantas River. It seems that this massive migration followed the catastrophic eruption of Mount Merapi. The East Javanese Period spans just over six centuries and is dominated by the dynasties of Kediri (929-1222), Singasari (1222-92) and Majapahit (1293-1527).

Panataran is the greatest achievement of this age (see page 245), but many other monuments were built at this time, although none were on the scale or artistic magnificence of Borobudur or Prambanan.

The Islamic Period (1527-present)

The end of the Indianized period of monument building in Java, during the 15th and 16th centuries, coincided with the arrival of Islam from West India via Sumatra. Temple-building stopped, and mosque construction began. But this did not mean the rejection of local

The Javanese candi

The candis of Java – the word has been variously translated as 'sepulchral monument' and 'ancient shrine' – are the equivalent of the cathedrals of Europe. They were places of worship or homage, and dedicated either to deified kings or to gods and spirits. An important difference though is that, while cathedrals are designed to accommodate large numbers of the faithful, candis were exclusively the abodes of the gods. The gods descended to inhabit the monuments during special ceremonies, attended by only a handful of priests. Drawing heavily upon Indian cosmology, candis were representations of the universe in microcosm, with Mount Meru, the cosmic mountain and abode of the gods, at the centre, and surrounded by concentric circles of mountains, separated by oceans. The frequent presence of the lotus flower is linked to the belief that gods were born out of these flowers and then sat upon them.

A candi has three distinct elements: a square base, on which rests a single-celled, usually cuboid, shrine, and a stepped roof. This three-fold division mirrors the symbolic three-fold division of the universe into a lower Sphere of the Mortals (bhurloka) and an upper Sphere of the Gods (swarloka), between which is the Sphere of the Purified, where the objects of worship are placed (bhuwarloka). The base is larger than the shrine, so leaving room for the movement of people around the building. Under the shrine, a hole in the base contained the ashes of a dead king – perhaps explaining why they were called candis (= sepulchral monument).

The summit of the stepped roof is often surmounted with a stupa or linga shape. On the east side of the shrine, steps lead up to a portico which houses an icon. Numerous embellishments were added to this basic design: external niches, porticoes built out on all four walls, and steps added to the base to provide more wall space for decoration. Sculptural decoration also varied, but again there were common elements: for example, the kalamakara and kalanaga motifs above doorways (known as banaspati in East Java), which acted as door guardians, warding-off evil spirits.

The names given to most candis in Java – a notable exception being Borobudur – are not original. They date from the late 19th or early 20th century and rarely indicate the king or deity to which a particular shrine is dedicated. The names are often linked to nearby towns or villages, and other geographical features.

---

styles for imported ones. The early mosques had square floor plans like Javanese candis, and tiered roofs like the *pura* of Bali. They also had courtyards and split gates.

People of Java

Although it is common to hear people talk of the 'Javanese', Java supports a number of different cultural and linguistic groups of which the Javanese are only one, albeit the most numerous. The **Javanese** occupy the island's geographical and cultural heart, encompassing such royal cities as Surakarta and Yogyakarta, along with the important trading ports of the north coast. A broad distinction can be drawn between the courtly, refined and reserved *Kejawen* of the interior, and the more extrovert, 'coarse' and religiously orthodox inhabitants of the coastal *pasisir* areas. The Javanese are wet rice farmers *par excellence*, although population growth has meant that land holdings are growing smaller by the year – today they average 400 sq m per family (0.035 ha) – and many farmers have become landless agricultural labourers. The Javanese often have only one name, the upper classes choosing their own family name. This invariably ends in an 'o'.

The **Sundanese** are concentrated in the Priangan Highlands of West Java and share many of the same traditions as the Javanese. However, the great court culture of Central Java never made a great impact here. The land is less fertile, and villages tended to be more isolated and self-sufficient. The Sundanese are therefore less encumbered with complex rules of etiquette and behaviour. Like the Javanese of the north coast, they are orthodox Muslims. Sundanese family names commonly end in an 'a'.

The Javanese Kraton

While the candi is the characteristic building of the ancient kingdoms of Java, the kraton is of more recent times. The links between the two are clear in the importance of cosmology, or orientation. Aart van Beek, in his book Life in the Javanese Kraton, writes of the kraton of Yogya and Solo that:

"Both Kraton face north in the direction of the life-giving volcanoes ... these peaks represent the Kraton's sentinels. South is the ambivalent direction for the Javanese, for Ratu Loro Kidul, the Goddess of the Southern Ocean, lives there. It is an unsafe place, in a way a place of death ... The north and south sections of the palaces are in some ways mirror images of each other".

The word kraton, sometimes spelt keraton or karaton, is derived from ke-ratuan, which literally means the 'abode of the monarch'. This, in turn, links with the Sanskrit word negara, which means both kingdom and capital. The word kraton is usually translated into English as 'palace'. The king and his family, court officials, court entertainers and royal servants – the abdi dalem – lived within its walls. Traditional clothing of the abdi dalem *include a sarong, kris and iket (cloth head-covering).*

But the kraton was more than just a palace in both a physical and a spiritual sense. It included squares, mosques, streets and houses, and also served as the spiritual centre of the kingdom. Every part of the complex is symbolically important. Again, van Beek writes:

"As clouds are heavy with the promise of rain towards the rainy season, so is the Kraton pregnant with meaning. It is a magical world to the Javanese, full of rules and codes of proper conduct. A sacredness and cosmic energy is attributed not only to the Sultan or Susuhunan but also the buildings and the weapons within them."

Just as the kings of Mataram were conceived to radiate power, so too is a kraton's sultan. And to be close to the walls of the kraton is to be close to the protective, life-enhancing powers of the sultan.

The most distinctive building within the kraton is the open-sided pavilion or pendopo. The name is probably derived from the Sanskrit word mandapa, which means a pillared hall. The links between the pendopo and earlier candis are clear in the temples of the late East Javanese Period with their raised platforms and columns, such as those at Panataran. The pendopo is not just a feature of kraton architecture though; its essential elements can be seen repeated in the square pillared mosques of Indonesia, in the mosque pavilions or surambi of Sumatra and Kalimantan, and in the bale of Bali and Lombok.

Recommended reading: Aart van Beek (1990), Life in the Javanese Kraton, Oxford University Press: Singapore. Helen Ibbitson Jessup (1990), Court arts of Indonesia, Asia Society Galleries: New York.

Among Java's patchwork of peoples are the **Madurese**, inhabitants of the island of Madura. During the Dutch period, the Madurese made up a disproportionate share of the colonial army and have a reputation as fierce warriors. Also in East Java, the Hindu **Tenggerese** are thought to be descended from the Majapahit refugees who fled Central Java in the 10th century, following the eruption of Mount Merapi. Finally, the enigmatic **Badui** of West Java live in 35 isolated villages near Rangkasbitung. Outsiders are expressly excluded from the remote 'inner' Badui villages, although the 'outer' communities permit some limited contact.

Islam in Java

Java is a Muslim society: 90% of its population of over 100,000,000 are nominal Muslims. However, as Clifford Geertz pointed out in his brilliant book *The Religion of Java* (1960), less than half of this 90% can be viewed as Muslim in the sense that Islam is central and paramount to their beliefs. For the remainder, Islam is intertwined with pre-Islamic religions and beliefs. Peacock writes of the Javanese world that it is "composed of spiritual energies contained in forms and images, such as magically potent swords, sacred shrines, spirits, deities, teachers and rulers. The roots of this mixture can be traced back to the reign of the great Majapahit King Agung (1613-45), a devout Muslim".

The introduction of Islam to Java and the 9 Walis

One of the most significant processes in Indonesian history was the spread of Islam. When and how it occurred are not clear. Muslim traders had, presumably, been visiting Java and other islands in the archipelago from early in the 2nd millennium, and some had probably married local women and settled. But it was not until the 14th century that Islam appears to have spread from Trengganu on the Malay Peninsula, to Sumatra and from there to Java. It is assumed that Islam first made an impact on the north coast and then diffused to the interior, which was Hindu.

Dance, drama and music

The wayang: shadow puppet theatre

Wayang means 'shadow', and the art form is best translated as 'shadow theatre' or 'shadow play'. Some people believe that the wayang is Indian in origin, pointing to the fact that most of the characters are from Indian epic tales such as the Ramayana and Mahabharata. Others maintain that the art form stems from ancient Malayo-Polynesian culture. They say the puppets represented ancestral spirits, who were summoned to solve the problems of the living. It was only later that the medium was used to teach Indian spiritual values through such Hindu epic stories as the Ramayana and Mahabharata (see page 963).

There are various forms of wayang, and not all are 'shadow' theatre in the true sense. *Wayang purwa* or *wayang kulit* is the original shadow play and is performed using flat puppets, chiselled out of leather, and is associated with the Javanese and Balinese. *Wayang golek* uses three-dimensional cloth and wood puppets and is a Sundanese adaptation of wayang kulit. *Wayang berber* is enacted using painted paper or cloth scrolls, which are unrolled while the narrator chants the story. *Wayang topeng* is performed by masked, live actors, while *wayang wong* or *wayang orang* uses maskless live actors.

The commonest and oldest form of wayang is the *purwa* or *kulit*. These are finely carved and painted leather, two-dimensional puppets, jointed at the elbows and shoulders and manipulated using horn rods. In order to enact the entire repertoire of 179 plays, 200 puppets are needed. A single performance can last as long as nine hours. The plays have various origins. Some are animistic, featuring, for example, the Rice Goddess, Dewi Sri. Others are adapted from the epic literature; these are known as *pondok* or 'trunk' tales and include the Ramayana. Others have been developed over the years by influential puppet masters. They feature heroic deeds, romantic encounters, court intrigues, bloody battles and mystical observations, and are known as *carangan* or 'branch' tales.

The *gunungan*, or 'Tree of Life', is an important element of wayang theatre. It represents all aspects of life, and is always the same in design: shaped like a stupa, the tree has painted red flames on one side and a complex design on the other (this is the side which faces the audience). At the base of the tree are a pair of closed doors, flanked by two fierce demons or *yaksas*. Above the demons are two garudas and within the branches of the tree there are monkeys, snakes and two animals – usually an ox and a tiger. The gunungan is placed in the middle of the screen at the beginning and end of the performance – and sometimes between major scene changes. During the performance it stands at one side, and flutters across the screen to indicate minor scene changes.

Traditionally, performances were requested by individuals to celebrate particular occasions – for example, the seventh month of pregnancy (*tingkep*) – or to accompany village festivities. Admission was free, as the individual commissioning the performance would meet the costs. Of course, this has changed now and tourists invariably have to pay an entrance charge.

Javanese puppets are characteristically highly stylized, with long necks, very long arms and extended shoulders. To the wayang cognoscenti, every nuance of the puppet is significant. It tells, so to speak, a tale. There are 15 eye shapes, 11 mouths and 13 nose shapes, for example. Heroes are required to conform to the Javanese physical ideal. They must be slender, with long, elegant noses, down cast eyes (denoting humility and restraint) and balanced proportions. Major characters like Arjuna in the Mahabharata have numerous – more than 10 – puppet shapes, deployed according to the scene being enacted.

Traditionally, the shadows of the puppets were reflected onto a white cotton cloth, stretched across a wooden frame using the light from a bronze coconut oil lamp. Today, electric light is more common which has meant the unfortunate substitution of the flickering, mysterious shadows of the oil lamp, with the constant harsh light of the electric bulb. There are both day and night wayang performances.

The audience sits on both sides of the screen. Those sitting with the puppet master see a puppet play; those on the far side, out of view of the puppet master and the accompanying gamelan orchestra, see a shadow play. It is possible that in the past, the audience was segregated according to sex: men on the dalang's side of the screen, women on the shadow side.

The puppet master, or *dalang*, is a consecrated priest. The word is said to be derived from *galang*, meaning bright or clear, the implication being that the dalang makes the sacred texts understandable. He sits on a plinth, an arm's length away from the cloth screen. From this position he manipulates the puppets, while also narrating the story. Although any male can become a dalang, it is usual for sons to follow their fathers into the profession. The dalang is the key to a successful performance: he must be multi-skilled, have strength and stamina, be able to manipulate numerous puppets simultaneously, narrate the story, and give the lead to the accompanying gamelan orchestra. No wonder that an adept dalang is a man with considerable status.

Wayang topeng: masked dance

The masked dance either evolved from initiation rites in which a masked man indicated the ideal human state, or from the story of the Hindu god, Vishnu. In this story, Vishnu, on seeing the world to be an evil place, descended from the heavens to dance and try to change it by a release of spiritual energy. To preserve his anonymity, Vishnu danced disguised by a mask.

Wayang wong & the Ramayana

Wayang wong is the grandest form of dance drama performed on Java. Actors, often masked, play the characters, not puppets – although the movements of the actors often imitate puppets.

Wayang orang emerged as an attempt to popularize the dance-drama and bring it to a wider audience.

Music

The **gamelan orchestra** is the most important assemblage of musical instruments in Indonesia. It is essential to the performance of wayang plays, accompanies celebrations at the royal kratons, and is inextricably bound-up in ceremonies at Balinese temples. The gamelan is a Javanese and Balinese musical form, although there are important differences between the music of the two islands.

Gamelan orchestras vary according to the context in which they are being played. However, it is usual to have large hanging gongs or *gong*, medium-sized hanging gongs or *kempul*, inverted bronze bowls – either single (*ketuk*) or grouped in fives (*kenong*) – bronze xylophones constructed of heavy bars (*saron*) or lighter hanging bars (*gender*), a wooden xylophone or *gambang*, finger drums or *kendang*, a zither or *celempung*, and a two-stringed fiddle or *rebab*. Many of the instruments are made of bronze, and most are struck like percussion instruments. The only remaining workshops making these instruments are to be found in Bogor and Yogyakarta. (The **angklung** is a traditional and ancient Javanese instrument used to accompany story-telling and marching.

The most important members of a gamelan are the kendang drummer, who sets the tempo, and the lead gender player. The latter plays the *gender barung* and cues the other members of the orchestra.

Semar: the most sacred of all the puppets

Textiles

Batik Batik is the characteristic textile patterning technique of Java and Madura, and to a lesser degree, Bali, Lombok and Central Sulawesi. It is also prominent on the Malay Peninsula. Like *ikat* (see page 441), it is a method of **resist-dyeing**. But in this instance, the resist – beeswax – is applied to the woven cloth rather than to the yarn. The word batik may be derived from the Malay word *tik*, meaning to 'drip'. It is believed that batik may have replaced tattooing as a mark of status. In Eastern Indonesia, the common word for tattoo and batik is the same.

Traditionally, the **wax was painted onto the woven cloth** using a *canting* (pronounced 'janting'), a small copper cup with a spout, mounted on a bamboo handle. The cup is filled with melted wax, which flows from the spout like ink from a fountain pen – although the canting never touches the surface of the cloth. Cloth produced using a canting should be labelled *tulis* (literally, to write), and one sarong length can take from one to six months to complete. Reflecting the skill and artistry required to produce such batik, waxers used to be called *lukis* or painters. Drawing the design with a canting is a laborious process and has largely been replaced by stamping.

In the mid-19th century, **the 'modern' batik industry** was born with the invention of the *cap* (pronounced 'jap') – a copper, sometimes a wooden, stamp. This is dipped in wax, and then pressed onto the cloth. The cap revolutionized batik production. With the invention of the cap, so there evolved a parallel cap-making industry. Old copper stamps have become collectors' pieces, and now are only produced in large numbers in the towns of Solo, Pekalongan and, to a lesser extent, in Yogyakarta. Not only did the cap speed-up production, it also took the artistry out of waxing: waxers merely stamp the design onto the cloth. Some designs are produced using both the canting and the cap – such cloth is called *combinasi*.

Two types of wax are often used in the batik process. *Klowong* is a light and brittle wax that is used for the first stamping only, on both sides of the cloth. *Tembok* is darker and more durable, and needs to survive numerous washings, rewaxings and dyeings. If it cracks, then dye will reach the cloth. The marbled effect that is often viewed by visitors as characteristic of batik is due to this cracking of the tembok – Javanese regard such work as inferior.

Like weaving in many societies, the ability to produce finely-worked batik was expected of well-bred Javanese girls. Far fewer women make their own batik today, but they still appreciate and recognize well-made and well-designed cloth, and batiks worn at weddings and other functions are carefully, though surreptitiously, scrutinized by the guests.

Distinguishing hand-drawn from stamped batik It can be hard differentiating between drawn (*tulis*) and stamped (*cap*) batik, particularly in the case of the repetitious geometric designs of Central Java. Look for irregular lines and examine repetitive motifs like flowers carefully – stamped batik will show no variation. On poorly-executed stamped cloth, there may be a line at the point where two stamps have been imperfectly aligned. **NB** There is also machine-printed cloth with traditional batik designs: this can be identified by the clear design and colour on one side only; batik, whether drawn or printed, will have the design clearly revealed on both sides of the fabric.

Books on Textiles Hitchcock, Michael (1985), *Indonesian Textile Techniques*, Shire Ethnography: Aylesbury, UK. Hitchcock, Michael (1991), *Indonesian Textiles*, British Museum Press: London. Warming, Wanda and Gaworski, Michael (1981), *The World of Indonesian Textiles*, Serindia: London.

Kresna: a King & spiritual guide of Ajuna (a warrior & hero in the Pandawa cycle of plays).

Bali

4

Bali

322	Denpasar	408	North from Denpasar to Lake Bratan
326	**South Bali**	413	**North Coast, Buleleng Regency**
350	Nusa Penida and Nusa Lembongan	416	Singaraja
353	The Bukit Peninsula and Nusa Dua	418	West of Singaraja
365	**North and east from Denpasar**	430	**The West**
366	Ubud	435	**Background**
379	North of Ubud	435	History
380	Gianyar to Mount Batur via Bangli	437	Land and environment
387	Pura Besakih and Mount Agung	438	Art and architecture
390	East Bali and Regency of Karangasem	442	Culture

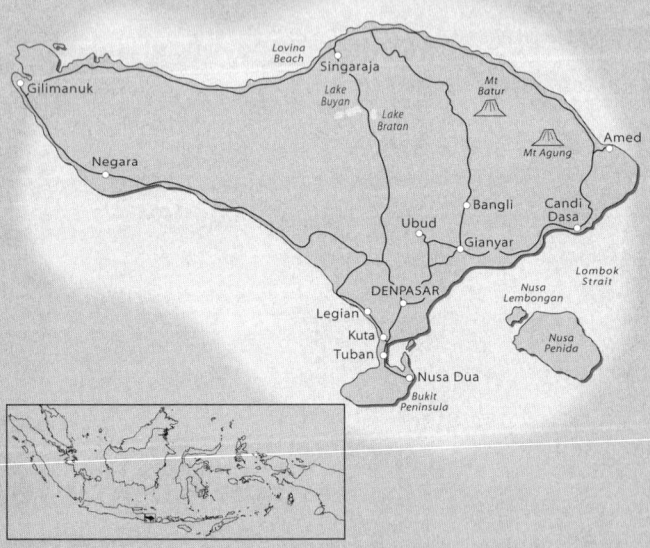

Bali is the original magical Isle. From the earliest years after its bloody incorporation within the expanding territories of the Dutch East Indies in the early 20th century, Westerners have been entranced by the heady combination of a fabulous landscape and a mesmerizing culture. Streams cascade down impossibly green mountainsides from sacred crater lakes, while dance dramas are performed to please the Gods. Artists and the artistically-inclined settled, worked and died amidst the rice fields and temples, reluctant to leave their Garden of Eden.

The advent of cheap air travel has brought increasing numbers of visitors, interested more in the attractions of the beach than of the temple and theatre. Today, hundreds of thousands of people visit Bali, many scarcely aware of the world beyond the sun lounger and the cocktail shaker. But while Bali may have changed – and the notion that Bali is on the verge of being 'ruined' is a constant motif in writings about the island from the 1930s – the singular magic of the place has not been erased.

Ins and outs

When to go

The best time to visit is the dry season between May and Oct, when it is slightly cooler and there is less chance of rain. The wet season runs from Nov to Apr when it is hot and humid, especially on the coast. At this time of year, Ubud can be cool and it is also wetter than the coast. Accommodation is priciest over Christmas and New Year and several weeks either side, which corresponds with the main holiday period in Australia. A second high season is during Jul and Aug, the northern hemisphere's holiday period. Out of these months, accommodation is often cheaper and the island is rather less crowded and frenetic.

Getting there

Air Denpasar's **Ngurah Rai International Airport** is at the south end of the island, just south of Kuta. It is one of Indonesia's 'gateway' cities, with international connections with Australia, Hong Kong, Europe, Singapore, Japan and North America; 24 hrs airport information, T227825/235169/222788/234606/234916. The office is outside the international departure area. A tourist office with a well-run hotel booking counter offers comprehensive details and prices of upmarket accommodation on Bali. Other facilities include money changers, bars, restaurant, shops and taxi counter. Left baggage is 3,300Rp per piece per day, with no limit on the time. The *Bali Satwika* is the airport restaurant, good value for such a place. There is a Garuda Reconfirmation office at the International arrivals hall. Open 0800-2100 Mon-Fri, 0900-2100 Sat and Sun.

Many international airlines have either cut their services altogether, or at least cut their frequency due to the down turn in Indonesia's tourist industry connected with the country's political difficulties

Shopping The *Plaza Bali*, at the end of the runway, includes craft shops, an art gallery, duty-free goods, a Chinese seafood restaurant and a theatre where cultural performances

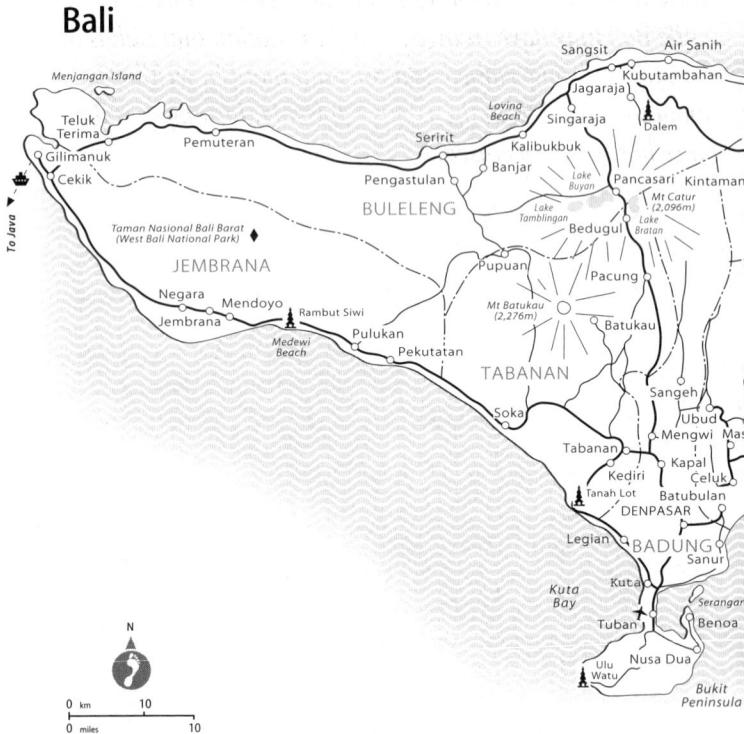

take place. **NB** Porters do not wait to ask whether you would like your baggage carried – they grab it and then demand 500Rp per piece – beware!

Sleeping 1 km from the airport (20 mins walk) **B-D** *Puri Nusantara Cottages Transit Hotel*, Jl Raya Tuban, Kuta, T0361-751649/752996. Spotless rooms with private bathroom, with fan or a/c, verandahs overlooking attractive gardens, free airport transfers, price including morning coffee, noisy but recommended. The airport accommodation service pretends not to know that this place exists in the hopes of steering visitors to more expensive hotels. If you arrive late at night or have an early morning flight, this place is ideal, though the airport transfer service finishes at about 1100, depending on when the driver decides to go home.

Transport to town There are fixed-price taxis from the airport, currently prices are: 11,000Rp to Kuta 1; 15,000Rp to Kuta 2 (in practice, anywhere past bemo corner is charged at the 2nd rate); 16,500Rp to Legian; 17,500Rp to Seminyak; 20,000Rp to north Seminyak (*Oberoi Hotel*); 20,000Rp to Denpasar; 25,000Rp to Sanur; 25,000Rp to Nusa Dua; 15,000Rp to Jimbaran; 27,000Rp to Tanjung Benoa; 60,000Rp to Ubud. Alternatively, walk out of the airport, past the toll gates, and catch a blue bemo running east to Kuta (1,000Rp), and from there to Denpasar for connections around the island (see Getting around, page 313). There are several car hire offices at the airport.

Airport tax is payable on departure – including children – which must be paid in local currency. 50,000Rp on international flights, 11,000Rp on domestic flights.

From Europe At the time of writing, the only direct flight from Europe to Bali is once a week with *Lauda Air*. There are easy connections from London via Vienna, and onward connections from Bali to Australia with *Ansett Airlines*. For details on getting to Jakarta, from where there are numerous daily connections with Bali, see page 32. *Garuda* operates a frequent service between Jakarta and Denpasar, though there has been a reduction in this service; flights may be cancelled at short notice and most flights depart fairly full, so you can no longer rely on getting a seat at the last minute. You can also fly from Europe to Singapore and change planes for an onward connection to Bali; there are flights approximately every 2 hrs between Singapore and Jakarta, and 3 flights a day between Singapore and Denpasar.

From USA There are direct flights from Los Angeles to Bali 5 times a week with *Garuda*.

From Asia Direct flights to Bali from most capital cities, including Hong Kong, Bangkok, Singapore, Taipei, Seoul, Tokyo, Osaka etc.

From Australia and New Zealand Direct flights to Bali from Darwin, Cairns, Brisbane, Sydney, Melbourne, Adelaide, Perth and Auckland. *Ansett Airlines* flies once a week on Wed, between Bali and Broome, Western Australia.

Departure tax On international flights that fly via Jakarta it is sometimes necessary to pay two departure taxes: at Bali the domestic tax of 11,000Rp and at Jakarta the international tax of 50,000Rp. Both must be paid for in Rupiah.

☞ Bali highlights

Temples The most important and impressively situated temple is **Besakih** on Mount Agung (page 387). **Uluwatu** is perched on a cliff-top on the Bukit Peninsula (page 359), while the coastal temple **Tanah Lot** (page 408) is the most photographed sight on Bali. Other notable temples include **Taman Ayun** at Mengwi (page 409) and **Kehen** at Bangli (page 381).

Other historical sights Within easy reach of Ubud are **Goa Gajah** or Elephant Cave (page 367), the ancient stone carvings at **Yeh Pulu** (page 367), the mysterious monumental burial chambers of **Mount Kawi** (page 379), and the holy springs at **Tirta Empul** (page 380). The royal bathing pools of **Tirtagangga** are in the east (page 402). The **Museum Bali** in Denpasar (page 322) has a good collection of ethnographic and archaeological exhibits.

Beaches The main beach resort areas are **Kuta** (page 327), **Sanur** (page 341) and **Nusa Dua** (see page 361); **Candi Dasa** (page 396), **Lovina Beach** (page 418), **Amed** (page 404) and **Tulamben** (page 405), are smaller and less developed.

Shopping Bali is a shopper's paradise; fashions in **Kuta** (page 330), craft villages north of **Sanur** (page 365), paintings and crafts in and around **Ubud** (page 366).

Natural sights Among the most notable is the extraordinary volcanic landscape of **Mount Batur** (page 384); the upland, almost alpine, area centred on **Lake Bratan** (page 410); the terraced rice fields of the south and east and the countryside around **Ubud** (page 366); and the **Bali Barat National Park** (page 431).

Sports Surfing (see page 15), **white water rafting** (page 370), **snorkelling, golf** (pages 364 and 412) and **diving** (page 22) are the most notable.

Culture & performance Balinese dancing around Ubud (page 377), and the **Bali Aga village** of Tenganan (page 396).

Train From Jakarta, take the train to Surabaya, a bus to Banyuwangi, and then the ferry to Bali. Alternatively, take the train all the way to Banyuwangi and catch a bus onwards from there. 'All in' train and bus tickets are available in Jakarta.

Road Most long distance bus companies have their offices on Jl Diponegoro and Jl Hasannudin in Denpasar. Regular overnight connections with most destinations in Java, for example to Surabaya, Malang, Yogyakarta, Bandung, Bogor and Jakarta. Examples of prices: a/c buses to Jakarta 30,800Rp; to Yogya 19,600Rp; to Surabaya 10,650Rp. If you are arriving from Java and wish to stay on the north coast, get off the bus at Gilimanuk (where the ferry docks) and take a bemo to Lovina beach (the price of the bemo is sometimes included in bus/ferry ticket).

Sea There are car ferries every 20 mins from Ketapang, just north of Banyuwangi on Java's East coast, to Gilimanuk on the west tip of Bali 30 mins (1,100Rp). Ferries run every 2 hrs each day from Lembar (Lombok) to Padangbai, near Candi Dasa, 4 hrs (4,500Rp or 6,700Rp; children half price). On arrival in Padangbai, touts besiege visitors to buy tickets on a bemo or shuttle bus to Kuta. There are cheaper public buses to Denpasar. There is a high-speed catamaran service between Benoa and Lembar (Lombok), the *Mabua Express* leaves Benoa twice a day for Lembar (Lombok). Travelling time is 2½ hrs and costs US$25 and US$30 depending on class (children 2-12 years half price), T721212, F732615 (on Lombok T0370-81195, F81124, for details; current departure timetable: leaves Benoa 0800, leaves Lembar 1730. A/c, aircraft seats. Buses to Padangbai leave from Denpasar's Batubulan terminal. Cruise liners dock at Benoa Port, T772521 on the Bukit Peninsula and occasionally at Padangbai. The *Pelni* ships *Dobonsolo*, *Binaiya* and *Tilongkabila* dock at Padangbai on its 2-week circuit (see schedule, page 988). The *Pelni* office is at Benoa, T228962. For Lombok, the ferry leaves from Padangbai.

Kencana Line run a daily, 117-seat, high-speed ferry service from Bali to Lombok, departing Benoa at 0730 hrs and Lembar at 1730, the journey takes 2½ hrs; 100,000Rp 1 way. There is also a daily Padangbai to Lembar service, departing Lembar at 1200 arriving in Padangbai at 1345, and departing Padangbai at 1500 arriving in Lembar at 1645; 50,000Rp one-way. For more information or bookings contact the Kencana Lines office at Benoa Harbour, T(0361)723601, F723604.

Getting around

The main form of the local transport is the bemo (a small van). Travelling by bemo, though cheap, does have its challenges. It sometimes requires a level of haggling which is extreme even by Indonesian standards. Also, travel by bemo often requires several changes, especially in the south, and most trips are routed through Denpasar where there are 5 different bemo terminals in different parts of town, serving different directions. Travel can, therefore, be frustrating and many visitors – except those with lots of time and little money – opt to charter a bemo, travel by taxi, or hire a self-drive vehicle of some variety. It is also worth noting that bemo services are less frequent in the afternoons, and out of the tourist centres are almost non-existent after nightfall. All the more popular resorts have outfits which rent out bicycles, motorbikes and cars. Finally, there are also metered taxis available in the more popular and populated parts of the island.

Air Regular domestic connections with Java, Sumatra, Maluku, Sulawesi, Lombok, Nusa Tenggara and Irian Jaya. Flights within Nusa Tenggara may require you to go via Bima with a change of plane (see route map). At the time of writing, due to the economic crisis, some routes have been suspended, particularly in East Nusa Tenggara, making it problematic to fly between, for example, east and west Flores. Hopefully the situation will improve in the coming months. A new carrier, Air Mark, T/F0361-757008, offers daily air services between Bali and Mataram on Lombok. Flight time is 20 mins and aircraft capacity is 20 passengers. Departure times are: from Lombok daily at 0730 and 1130; from Denpasar daily (except Thurs) 0930 and 1700. Flight connections include: Balikpapan (daily at 0640); Ende (daily, but you will have to go via Bima with a change of plane); Jakarta; Yogyakarta; Manado (daily at 0640); Mataram; Sumbawa Besar (Mon, Wed, Fri and Sun at 0930); Tana Toraja (Mon, Thu and Sat via Ujung Pandang, where you have to change planes); Makassar.

Boat **Cruises** *Bali Camar Yacht Charter*, T231591, *Wakalouka Cruises*, T0361-723629, 723659, F722077, and *Island Explorer Cruises*, T289856, organize cruises to Nusa Lembongan (see page 350); *Bali Hai*, T234331, luxurious catamaran day trips to Nusa Penida island for snorkelling and lunch, US$60, dinner cruise, US$30; *Golden Hawk*, Jl Sri Kesari 19, Sanur, T288860, old gaff-rigged ketch (tall ship) for day trips, fishing, snorkelling, lunch and alcoholic drinks, US$68; *Grand Komodo Tours*, Jl Bypass, Sanur, T287166, F287165, organize tours to Lombok, Komodo, Flores and Irian Jaya; *P&O Spice Island Cruises*, T0361-286283, F286284. Email toarie@spiceisland-cruises.com or visit *Spice Island Cruises* web page at www.spiceisland-cruises.com or www.indocom/cruises Jl Let Jen S Parmen 78, Slipi, Jakarta Barat, T5673401, F5673403. Organize luxury island-hopping cruises between Bali and Kupang (Timor), 2 week round-trip, calling at Komodo, Sumbawa, Flores and Sumba, one way trip about US$2,289, round trip US$4,180, they also organize a 7 day trip from Jakarta to Krakatau, up the east coast of Sumatra and south to the Ujung Kulon National Park, US$8,869; also 3 and 4 nights departing Bali every Mon and Fri with stops in Sumbawa.

Boats to Lombok leave from Benoa (see page 359) and Padangbai (see page 394)

Lombok and Komodo At the time of writing Spice Island cruises have cancelled their 3 and 4 day cruises from Bali to Komodo due to excesive new taxes imposed by the Indonesian Customs Department. The intention is to open a Darwin base and offer 8 and 15 day cruises between Darwin and Bali. If the Customs Department rescinds the new tax the original program of 3 and 4 day cruises between Bali and Komodo will be reinstated. For more information contact the above numbers or email.

Bounty Cruises offer two separate cruise options aboard a 500-passenger catamaran between Bali and Lombok. An 0800 departure from Benoa to Gili Meno returning to Bali at 1830 hrs costing US$95, or a 1030 departure from Senggigi on Lombok to the Gili islands returning to Senggigi at 1615 costing US$57; 50% discount for children 4-16 years. Bounty also offer one way trips between Bali and Lombok leaving Bali at 0800 hrs and Senggigi at

1615, the fare is US$35 and the journey takes 2½ hrs. Bounty Cruises T0361-753434, F752121. bounty@denpasar.wasantara.net.id

Bali Safari Cruises offers an extended overnight cruise called 'Day-Night-Day Sunset-Sailing' Nusa Lembongan, costing $US99 each. The sail boat cruise leaves Benoa at 1100 am and returns the following day at 1400. The cruise boat arrives late afternoon at Nusa Lembongan. Guests then take a glass-bottomed boat tour of the reef and a swim before returning to the cruise boat for a BBQ sunset dinner. The night is spent on the boat in a spacious cabin. Following breakfast the next morning the boat leaves for Benoa at about 1030. For more information visit Bali Safari Cruises' web site at www.balisafari.com/balisail.html or email to info@balisafari.com.

PT Motive Bali Tours and Travel, Jl Sekuta 11, Sanur, T289435, F289435, organize all the usual tours around the island and a 'Joy Flight' over Bali in a helicopter, 15-60 mins flight, US$85-195 with 4 passengers (more expensive if less); *Puri Tour*, Jl Padang Galak 7A, Sanur, T361-288788, F361-287269, organize 10-day pinisi boat cruises from Bali to Flores for US$150 per day, all inclusive.

Road **Bemo** Bali could be considered the Bemo Hell of Indonesia, with haggling reaching new levels. However, bemos are the cheapest way to get around the island. On top of the hassle factor, almost all journeys – especially in the south – require several changes, with an obligatory trip to Denpasar, the bemo 'node' for many destinations. So, to travel from, say, Kuta to Ubud means getting a bemo from Kuta to Denpasar's Tegal terminal, transferring to Kereneng and then, taking a cross-town trip to the Batubulan terminal, followed by another bemo from there to Ubud. This makes for slow and frustrating travelling and it can be almost as cheap and a lot quicker to charter a bemo (see below) or catch the tourist shuttle bus. It is also worth noting that bemo services are less frequent in the afternoons, and out of the tourist centres are almost non-existent after nightfall. In many areas bemos are 'colour coded', so that most, though not all, bemos running between particular destinations are the same colour. (Note also that Klungkung is often marked Semarapura, the old name for the town.) These days, in the countryside bemos are far more frequent and access is available to more villages than used to be the case and the situation is improving all the time. Services start very early in the morning, from 0500 or 0600 and tail off about 1700; there are more bemos in the morning than the afternoon. Approximate cost of travel is 1000Rp per kilometre, with a minimum charge of 1000Rp. However, in the main tourist centres bemo drivers are increasingly reluctant to take foreigners except at hugely inflated fares. **NB** Taxi/bemo drivers can be very pushy and find it hard to believe you may be happy to walk. Expect to be asked for double the correct fair, bemo drivers can sometimes be quite unpleasant in their attempts to over-charge you even when you know the correct fair, which you should ascertain in advance. Thefts on bemos are not as frequent as in past years but do still occur. Be wary of gangs pretending to run licenced bemos who pick up unsuspecting travellers, take them to a remote spot and steal their possessions and money. Always use registered bemos which have yellow and black licence plates.

The **different terminals** are as follows (**NB** Terminals serve other terminals as well as out of town destinations):

Ubung, north of town on Jl Cokroaminoto for trips to North and West Bali, including Gilimanuk and Singaraja, Mengwi, Tanah Lot, Bedugul, Negara and Java (see Transport to and from Bali).

Tegal, west of town, near the intersection of Jl Imam Bonjol and Jl G Wilis, for journeys to South Bali including Kuta, Legian, Sanur, Ngurah Rai Airport, Jimbaran, Nusa Dua and Uluwatu (in the morning).

Suci, near the intersection of Jl Diponegoro and Jl Hasanuddin for Benoa Port.

Batubulan, 6 km northeast of town just before the village of Batubulan on the road to Gianyar, for buses running east to Gianyar, Klungkung, Padangbai, Candi Dasa, Amlapura and Tirtagangga, and north to Ubud, Tampaksiring, Bangli, Penelokan and Kintamani.

Kereneng, at the east edge of town off Jl Kamboja (Jl Hayam Wuruk), has now been replaced as the station for central and East Bali by Batubulan; but bemos do still run from here to the other terminals.

Getting around Bali by bemo

Destination	Denpasar Terminal	Via	Destination	Denpasar Terminal	Via
Agung, Mount	Batubulan	Klungkung	Kuta	Tegal	-
Airport	Tegal	-	Lovina Beach	Ubung	Singaraja
Air Sanih	Ubung	Singaraja	Madewi Beach	Ubung	-
Amlapura	Batubulan	-	Mas	Batubulan	-
Bangli	-	Batubulan	Mengwi	Ubung	-
Banjar	Ubung	Singaraja	Negara	Ubung	-
Batubulan	Kereneng	-	Nusa Dua	Tegal	-
Batur, Mount	Batubulan	-	Padangbai Harbour		Batubulan - Gianyar
Bedugul	Ubung	-	Pejeng	Batubulan	Gianyar
Bedulu	Batubulan	Gianyar	Penelokan	Batubulan	Klungkung
Benoa Harbour	Suci	-	Penulisan	Batubulan	-
Benoa Village	Tegal	-	Sangeh	Wangaya	-
Besakih	Batubulan	Klungkung	Sanur	Kereneng	-
Candi Dasa	Batubulan	-	Singaraja	Ubung	-
Candi Kuning	Ubung	-	Sukawati	Batubulan	-
Celuk	Batubulan	-	Tabanan	Ubung	-
Gianyar	Batubulan	-	Tanah Lot	Ubung	Kediri
Gilimanuk	Ubung	-	Tampak Siring	Batubulan	Gianyar
Goa Gajah	Batubulan	Gianyar	Tenganan	Batubulan	-
Goa Lawah	Batubulan	-	Tirtagangga	Batubulan	Amlapura
Gunung Kawi	Batubulan	Gianyar	Ubud	Batubulan	-
Kehen Temple	Batubulan	Bangli	Uluwatu	Tegal	Pecatu
Klungkung	Batubulan	-			

Shuttle bus Several companies run shuttle bus services to popular destinations on Bali, with onward connections to Lombok and Sumbawa. These are geared to foreign travellers and offer the best value, hassle-free means of getting around. Most will pick you up from and drop you off at your hotel. They will also take you to the airport but are not allowed to pick up passengers from the airport.

One of the most reliable companies is **Perama**, Head Office, Jl Legian, Kuta, T751551, F751170. They have regular buses throughout the day to: Kuta, Denpasar Airport, Sanur, Ubud, Kintamani, Lovina, Bedugul, Padangbai, Candi Dasa, Tirtagangga, Tulamben, Air Sanih. *Perama* can take you to Nusa Lembongan via boat from Sanur. On Lombok they go to Mataram, Senggigi, Bangsal (for the Gili Islands), Kuta and Tetebatu. They also offer a service to Bima and Sape on Sumbawa Island, and boat service to Bima, Komodo and Flores (see page 827).

Hiring vehicles

Bicycles Can be hired for about 3,000Rp per day.

Cars For approximately 80,000Rp per day from local firms (though you might be able to hire for as little as 65,000Rp per day, or even less for weekly rentals if you are prepared to spend some time checking over vehicles), US$45 per day from international companies (eg *Avis*). **NB** Most hire cars cannot be taken off the island and an international driving licence is ABSOLUTELY essential these days. There are frequent road checks and if you don't have an international licence you will be fined on the spot, at least 35,000Rp. If you want to continue driving you will have to get a 1 month permit. This requires a trip into Denpasar where you will take a 2 page written test and provide a photograph and a thumb print; the cost is currently 60,000Rp. The written test is multiple choice and includes questions such as: 1) if you accidently run over and kill a person in a village and his family try to attack you, should you: a) try to convince them that you did not mean to do it, and could they call the police; and hope that the police arrive in time? Or b) Leave the scene quickly and go to the nearest police station? Another question centres on what to do if your silencer falls off. The questions are not as fanciful as they seem; in Shirley Deane's Ambon *Isle of Spices*, written, admittedly, in 1979, she tells of how the driver of the bus in which she was travelling, accidently hit a child and was almost stoned to death by angry villagers.

Look out for: the condition of the tyres (and the spare), the horn (absolutely essential), windscreen wipers, steering. In addition to worn tyres, the two most common failings are cars that pull violently to the left or right when you break suddenly (something you will do frequently on Bali), and dreadful steering with up to 15cm play, or more. Driving on Bali is challenging enough without having to cope with a hazardous vehicle. We rejected 8 before finding a road-worthy vehicle at a good price.

Motorbikes Hire costs from 25,000Rp per day. Strictly speaking, those without an international motorbike licence should obtain a temporary licence from the Police Station in Denpasar. Applicants need their passport, 3 photographs and their national driving licence; they will also need to undertake a short police driving test. (**NB** Few people bother with this.)

The present price of petrol is 1,000Rp per litre. When buying petrol, keep an eye on the pump and check your change. It seems that many petrol pump attendants will try to short change you one way or the other. They try to give you less petrol by switching quickly to the next customer and zeroing the meter before you can check how much has been put in your car. You should not have a problem finding petrol, the main roads are well supplied with petrol stations, usually on the outskirts of a big town, and quite a few are open 24 hrs.

Chartered bemo 'You want transport?' is a much used expression on Bali. Chartering a bemo is easy and often the best way to travel around the island. Expect to pay about 20,000Rp per hr, 100,000Rp for a full day. Drivers prefer to know your destination, rather than to be hired for half a day or day. **NB** Drivers may try to take you to a craft village as part of the deal.

Taxis There are now metered radio a/c taxis; T289090/289091/281919/759191, the Japanese cars are blue and yellow, with a taxi sign on the roof. Drivers often don't speak English, so insist that the meter is switched on; never agree a fixed price. Minimum fare is 3,000Rp. Trips within Kuta/Legian are around 5,000-10,000Rp. Kuta to Sanur costs 35,000Rp minimum. For chartering, it costs about 30,000-40,000Rp per hr by the meter. This is almost certainly a safer bet than bemos now.

Tours At the last count, the tourist office listed 136 tour companies, usually with little to choose between them. Most provide the same range of tours at competitive prices, although it is worth shopping around before booking. Check the numbers on the tour, whether the guide speaks good English, if entrance fees and meals are included, and whether the car/bus is air-conditioned. Most tour companies are concentrated in the principal tourist centres. Tours include: Lake Batur, volcano and Ubud, Denpasar City, Singaraja and Lake Bratan, Besakih Temple, Amlapura (Karangasem) and the East Coast, Uluwatu and Kuta Beach, Mengwi and Tanah Lot, Lovina and the North Coast; Dance evenings (kecak, legong, sanghyang, barong, Ramayana ballet, wayang); Nature Trek; Shopping Tour; Turtle Island and Snorkelling; Dolphin Tours.

There are also a number of 'specialist' tours, see tour entries in each resort

Where to stay

Sleeping Bali has the best range of accommodation in Indonesia. from luxury hotels of the highest standard to comfortable homestays. The degree of competition means that rooms are often very moderately priced, though recently rates have begun to rise as owners think in terms of western prices and take advantage of the confusion caused by the devaluation of the rupiah. Rates are usually reduced after the peak season; ask for a discount. Peak season is Christmas/New Year and Jul/Aug – hotels can get very full at these times. Accommodation is geared to foreign tastes with, for example, western toilets in most of the cheapest homestays. Except during high season you should have to pay no more than 50-60% of the listed price in hotels and guesthouses geared to the package tour trade. The rates offered by accommodation owners to tour companies are often very low, but these very low rates are seldom available to the independent traveller for fear of jeopardizing the hotels' relationship with the tour companies. In the aftermath of the economic crisis hotels were often quite desperate to fill rooms, and many luxury hotels in places like Nusa Dua offered their rooms to tour companies for as little as US$40 a night (one major hotel was alleged to have rates as low as US$28). The main beneficiaries have been Australian tour companies who usually pay half what the Japanese tour company pays for the same room. However, rates are beginning to rise again as tourist numbers increase.

A new type of hotel designated 'the boutique hotel' is appearing in tourist areas of Bali. These are smaller hotels, typically 60-100 rooms, without the extra facilities of the larger hotels, though the price is usually similar. They are rarely interested in the independent traveller, and gear their prices to the tour group market. Another feature of many hotels is the 'free-form' swimming pool; designed for people who want to wallow rather than exercise, it can be difficult to do any serious swimming unless the pool is pretty much empty.

When a well-known international hotel chain terminates its relationship with a local hotel, the reason is usually a failure on the part of the hotel owners (international chains only manage the hotels that bare their name, they rarely own the buildings) to make necessary renovations or improvements to bring the hotel up to international standards. Many Indonesian owned hotels do not meet international safety standards.

Long-stay rentals If you are interested in renting a house for a month or longer, the main areas favoured by ex-pats are: Seminyak, a beautiful seaside location in the ricefields north of Kuta; Sanur, particularly the Batu Jimbar area, Blanjong in the south of Sanur, and a village on the coast northeast of Sanur called Padanggalak; and the Ubud area. A number of self-catering options are also appearing along Jl By Pass Ngurah Rai, to the north of the Bukit Peninsula and near Benoa. Some are available on a nightly or weekly basis. See relevant sections or ask around.

Time-Share Several new time-share developments have been built recently in Jimbaran and Seminyak in the south, and at Manggis near Candi Dasa on the east coast. Some are perfectly respectable, operated by well-known companies such as RCI, others may not be. In particular, be warned that you may be approached by 'students' claiming to be doing a survey on behalf of the Bali Tourist Development Authority; you will be asked for your name, hotel and room number. This should ring alarm bells and you are strongly advised not to participate in the survey, which has nothing to do with tourism but is being operated by a timeshare company who will come to your hotel and try to 'hard-sell' you into buying their timeshare. You may also be approached by westerners working for the same company, who will feign enormous delight at discovering a fellow countryman and then attempt to lure you into their trap.

Private Villas Ltd, Suite 1102, Windsor House, 19-27 Wyndham St, Hong Kong, T852-5251336, F5377181, have recently started offering short-term rental of about 30 private villas in Bali. Most of these exclusive homes are owned by affluent foreigners who visit Bali for a short time each year. Rental starts at US$280 per day. Most villas have private pools and staff provided.

Retiring to Bali Good news for anyone hoping to retire to Bali. The government is finalizing a ruling (Menteri Kehakiman No. M.04-IZ.01.02 tahun 1998) that will permit the issuance of one year renewable visas for retirees 55 years of age or above. The visas, issued by overseas embassies, will be processed by nominated travel agents.

Residency In an effort to encourage investment, the government is introducing a new law which will allow individuals who invest a minimum of US$1mn to gain residency rights.

Warning Crime is inevitably on the increase given the present economic situation. While low by the standards of European cities, visitors should be wary and take precautions. There have been incidents of bag snatching, particularly by motorcyclists in Sanur, Kuta, Ubud and the Galeria shopping complex in Nusa Dua. Young children, particularly in the Kuta and Sanur areas, may swarm around you and try to distract your attention by offering an old newspaper or jewellery for sale, while hunting for your wallet or moneybelt.

Sports and special interest

Adventure *Bali Adventure Tours*, T721480, F721481, baliadventuretours@bali-paradise.com, www.bali-paradise.com/baliadventuretours White water rafting/river kayaking, US$59 for adults, US$40 for children including hotel transfers. Also do elephant safaris, jungle and rice paddy trekking, mountain cycling, US$52 for adults, US$35 for children, including hotel transfers and picnic lunch and tandem paragliding over the cliffs at Uluwatu, US$69 for adults, US$55 for children. *Bali Adventure Tours* was founded in 1989 by an Australian, Nigel Mason, who, with his Balinese wife Made Yanie, also owns *Yanies Restaurant* in Kuta. ***Sobek Expeditions***, T287059, F289448, sobek@denpasar.wasantara.net.it White water rafting, lake kayaking on Lake Tamblingan US$68, mountain cycling (Batur Trail, Batu Karu Trail) US$55, jungle trekking US$49.

Cricket *Bali International Cricket Club* plays every Sun at the *Grand Bali Beach Hotel*, Sanur. Visitors welcome, T0361-287431/754630.

Diving Diving around Bali is not the best in Indonesia, but the island does have the greatest concentration of dive shops and diving expertise. It is a good place to learn how to dive, but those who have experienced other spots in Southeast Asia or the Pacific may be disappointed. Bali's only decompression chamber is at Sanglah Public Hospital, Jl Sanglah, Denpasar, T227911. Dive spots include the **Menjangan Marine Park**, an island off the northwest tip of Bali, 30 mins by boat (depth 3-50m). Diving here is good, both on the inner and outer reef, although it is not recommended for beginners, as there is too much fragile coral which could be unintentionally damaged. **NB** Divers are contributing to the destruction of the coral in the park, as there are no buoys and the boatmen anchor on the coral. Morning is the best time to dive here. **Tulamben** is the submerged wreck of a US Liberty ship, sunk during the Second World War off the northeast coast, and is a haven for fish. The coral-covered wreck lies about 50m offshore, so it is a beach dive (10-30m), recommended by one keen diver; **Padangbai**, near Candi Dasa, for 3-20m dives; **Tepekong Island** (depth 15-30m), also Biaha and Mimpang Islands, all on the east coast, suitable for experienced divers only; **Lembongan** has sheltered coral reefs that provide excellent snorkelling; **Nusa Penida Islands**, 2 hrs by boat (depth 3-40m), diving here is good but be careful of the strong currents; **Amed**, off the northeast coast (depth 3-40m); and the reefs off Sanur and Nusa Dua beaches. With reputable companies expect to pay US$30 for 1 dive, US$80 for an introductory 1 day course, US$250 for a 4 day diving certificate. Most of the larger hotels have dive desks; see relevant sections for addresses of dive shops.

Baruna, T0361-753820, F753809, baruna@denpasar.wasantara.net.id, www.comcen.com.au/-baruna, and *Pro Dive*, T0361-286336, T/F288756, are 2 of the better dive companies, both PADI approved. *Pro Dive* is said to be the largest diving training organization in the world, with 28 centres throughout Australia and Indonesia. Typical prices are: Introductory 1 day course US$78; 4 day PADI Open Water Certificate US$298-350; dives at Sanur/Nusa Dua US$44; Tulamben/Amed US$58; Menjangan US$74, extra dive US$16.

Golf The *Handara Koseido Country Club*, one of the 50 best golf courses in the world, is in a beautiful position just north of Lake Bratan (see page 412) at Bedugul; green fee $100. *Bali Golf and Country Club* at Nusa Dua, T771791, F771797 for details. Tee-times from 0630 to 1600. Green fees, which include mandatory golf cart, US$142 for 18 holes, US$85 for 9 holes. Beautiful sea-side setting. Attractive clubhouse and pool. New Golf course at *Le Meridien Nirwana Bali Resort*, near Tanah Lot on the west coast (T815900, F815901). Nine-hole course at the *Bali Beach Hotel*, Green fee US$50 (50% discount for *Bali Beach Hotel* guests), 1 price for 9 holes, 18 holes or all day. Club hire: half set US$15.50, full set US$22.50, golf shoes US$4.50, caddy US$2.50.

Hash Runs on Bali Mon, Thu, Sat. Weekly Hash sheets can be found at *Borneo Restaurant* or Galael Supermarket in Sanur; *Lips* or *Glory Restaurant* in Kuta; *Beggar's Bush* in Ubud.

Horse riding An increasingly popular activity; several riding stables have opened in recent years and no doubt more will follow. One of the best places is **Umalas Stable**, Jl Lestari No 9x, Br Umalas, Kerobokan, just north of Seminyak, T0361-731402, F731403. Lessons for all abilities from beginners to advanced including dressage. 1-3 hr treks through the rice fields or along the beach at sunset. Tours include hotel pick-up and US$25,000 insurance. Prices from US$25 for an hour's group trek to US$70 for a 3-hr individual trek. Dressage/beginners lesson: 25/30 for group/individual. **Bali Horse Riding**, near Yeh Gangga, T0361-484437/413116, F487770. A variety of treks and an opportunity to swim with the horses. US$45 includes transport, meal and drinks.

Mountain biking Mountain biking is becoming increasingly popular, as a way of seeing the 'real' Bali, see 'Tours' page 331 and 'Sport' page 381.

Watersports Some of the dive companies, including **Baruna**, offer a varied programme of watersports: Fishing half-day US$50-75 per person, full day US$75-100 (including transport and lunch); parasailing US$10 a round; jet ski US$20 for 15 mins; windsurfing US$10 if experienced, US$15 beginners; canoe US$6 per hr; glass bottom boat US$15 per hr; water-skiing US$20 for 15 mins; banana boat US$10 per person.

Surfing Kuta Beach was the location upon which Bali's reputation as a surfer's paradise was based. Kuta is a beach break and these days the water is polluted with sewage: about 1 km out is a reef break, a left-hand barrel. However, there are other, better locations. Below is a very brief summary of conditions; far more information can be gleaned from surf shops and places where surfers hang out. Some of the best surfing in Bali is on the Bukit Peninsula. **Uluwatu**, about 2 km down a rough track, with a 'world famous' left break; the Peak is a high tide break, Race Track a mid-tide, and Outside Corner a low tide wave. If the current is too strong to reach the cave or onto the reef in front of the cave, make for the beach. Despite its reputation, waves can be few and far between: crowded and over-rated. **Padang Padang** is close to Uluwatu and can be reached along a track or by car/motorbike. The very hollow left is dangerous because of the cliff; very dangerous below mid-tide. Down from Padang Padang is **Bingin**; fast hollow left best at high to medium tides, at low tides it is dangerous and waves can 'suck dry' on the reef; often crowded. **Nyang Nyang**, accessible by track; both left and right. **Suluban**, not far from Jimbaran; the Annual Surf Championships are held here. Minibuses (C1) travel from Kuta to Uluwatu; tracks to the surfing beaches are reasonably well-marked along the road. Other surfing beaches include **Canggu**, near the village of Kerobokan, north on the Legian road (both left and right); and **Medewi**, about 75 km west of Denpasar, best above mid-tide. Boards can be hired for about 5,000-10,000Rp per day; repair and other services are also available – see relevant sections for surf shops.

Best time to surf: this is reasonable throughout the year, although the surf is definitely best between Jun and Aug. Between Oct and Apr there are good right-handers at **Nusa Dua** and **Sanur**, the latter only working for 20 days a year. *Tubes Bar*, Poppies Gang 2, Kuta, is a good source of surfing information.

Swimming At Tuban, just south of Kuta, there is **Waterbom Park**, Jl Kartika Plaza, T755676, F753517, waterbom@denpasar.wasantara.net.id Over 600m of water slides, water volleyball, spa offering traditional massage etc, gardens, restaurant, lockers and towels for hire (children under 12 must be accompanied by an adult). Most luxury hotels allow non-guests to use their facilities for a fee. Open daily 0900-1800. **Hard Rock Hotel**, Kuta, with one of the largest pools in Bali, charges 15,000Rp to non-guests.

Whitewater rafting All rivers on Bali are class II-III, but may rise in the wet season (Nov-Mar). Down the Ayung River near Ubud includes hotel pick-up, all equipment, insurance and lunch, organized by **Bali Adventure Tours** (see under Adventure) and **Sobek Expeditions**, T287059, F289448, sobek@denpasar.wasantara.net.it Adults US$68, children US$45. Established in 1989, committed to safety with professionally trained guides. Bali

Adventure Tours also organize mountain biking at Batur, sea kayaking and jungle trekking (see 'Tours', pages 331, 342 and 370, for details).

Wildlife parks *Bali Bird Walks*, T0361-975009. Led by Victor Mason, ornithologist and resident of Bali for over 20 years, in the Ubud area. *Bali Bird Park* (Taman Burung), Jl Serma Cok Ngurah Gambir, Singapadu, Balubulan, northeast of Denapasar, T0361-299352, 299612, F299614, balibirdpr@denpasar.wasantara.net.id   Around 250 species of birds including birds of paradise, the endangered Bali starling, and cassowaries. Rainforest walk-in aviary. Restaurant (Indonesian and western food), bar and souvenir shop. Open 0800-1800.

Bali Reptile Park (Rimpa Reptil), Jl Serma Cok Ngurah Gambir, Singapadu, Balubulan, north-east of Denapasar, T/F0361-299344, herpindo@denpasar.wasantara.net.id   Reptiles and dragons from Indonesia and the rest of the world, including Komodo dragons, king cobras, turtles and an 8m reticulated python. Information on the history of reptiles and conservation programmes. Open 0900-1800.

Camel Safaris, T773377 ext 210. *Hotel Nikko*, Nusa Dua. 1-hr camel rides through tropical bushland and along the beach, adults US$33, children (12 and under) US$17. **Elephant Safari Safari Park**, at Taro, 20 mins north of Ubud. An opportunity to feed, touch and watch the elephants in the landscaped grounds and lake. Elephant safaris from US$29 for adults, US$19 for children. These elephants even paint pictures! Information about the history and diversity of elephants, gift shop. Contact Bali Adventure Tours, T721480, F721481, baliadventuretours@bali-paradise.com, home page www.bali-paradise.com/baliadventuretours

Honeymoon Holidays   A growing number of tour companies feature special honeymoon packages to Bali. *Panorama Tours DMC*, T62-21-632 2156, F62-21-6385 8936, dmc@indosat.net.id   A variety of competitively priced tours.

Holidays and festivals

See page 444 for a fuller background to the main ceremonies

Bali is the festival capital of Southeast Asia; there is a festival every day of the year. With 20,000 temples, each celebrating its anniversary or *odalan* every 210 days (according to the Balinese *wuku* calendar), it is easy to see why.

The tourist office supplies a booklet cataloguing the year's festivals, while the *Bali News* (often found in hotel lobbies) lists current events. Both sources of information are extremely useful, as the Balinese calendar, in fact 2 calendars, is complex. The *wuku* calendar, which governs most, but not all, festivals, is lunar and runs, as noted above, over only 210 days. As a result, festival dates vary dramatically from year to year and a particular festival may be held twice in any 1 (365-day) year. Locals do not object to tourists being present at most of their ceremonies, but they do ask that visitors dress appropriately, with sarong and sash, and behave discreetly (see 'Rules, customs and etiquette', in the Essentials chapter, page 37).

Wuku Year Festivals (210-day calendar)

Day 1: *Galungan*, the most important holiday of the Balinese year. It is a 10-day festival marking the Balinese *wuku* 'New Year' (in fact, it comes mid-way through the year, but is usually translated as New Year). It also commemorates the creation of the world by the Supreme God and symbolizes the victory of good over evil. Women make *banten* (offerings of sweets, fruits and flowers), while men make *lawar* (a food made of vegetables and meat). Both are presented as thanksgiving offerings. *Penjors* (a variant of the *janur*, see page 445) are the long bamboo poles which can be seen on the right-hand side of every house entrance, with offerings such as fruit, cakes and flowers hanging from them as symbols of gratitude for the god's gift of life and prosperity. It is said that the offerings are hung on these tall poles – which it is a man's job to make – so that the gods can see them from their mountain abodes. *Barong* and other dances are traditionally held at this time.

Day 10: *Kuningan*, held 10 days after Galungan and marking the end of the holiday period. It is believed to be the day when the gods ascend back to Heaven, and is a time for honouring the souls of ancestors and saints who have lived their lives in accordance with the customs of their religion. Temple compounds are decorated with flowers and offerings are made.

Day 137: **Saraswati**, commemorates the Goddess of Learning and Knowledge, Batari Dewi Saraswati. All books are given to the Goddess to be blessed and no reading or writing is allowed.

Day 142: **Pangerwesi**, the word means 'iron fence', and the ceremony is dedicated to Shanghyang Pramesti Guru. It is particularly popular in the north.

Day 210: **Penampahan Galungan**, the day prior to Galungan when every Balinese prepares for the big day, slaughtering pigs and chickens and preparing offerings and food. It marks the end of the Wuku year.

Recurrent Wuku Festivals In addition to the above Wuku festivals, there are also a number of recurrent festival days which are regarded as propitious for making offerings. **Kadjeng-klion** is held every 15 days; **Tumpak**, every 35 days; **Budda-klion**, every 42 days; **Anggara-kasih**, every 35 days; and **Budda-wage**, every 35 days.

March: **Pengerupuk** (movable), the last day of the Balinese year. Purification sacrifices and offerings are made, while priests chant mantras to exorcize the demons of the old year. At night, gongs and cymbals are struck, and torchlit processions with *ogoh-ogoh* (large monsters) parade through the streets in order to exorcize the spirits. The spectacle is best in Denpasar, where thousands gather in Puputan Square before the start of the march.

Saka Year Festivals (354 to 356-day calendar)

Mar-Apr: **Nyepi** (movable) celebrates the *saka*, solar New Year, which is held at the Spring equinox. In the recent past it was a day of silence when everything closed down and no activity was allowed. It is hoped that the evil spirits roused by the previous night's activities will find Bali to be a barren land and will leave the island. People stayed indoors to meditate and pray; there were no fires, no work and no cooking. On the day before Nyepi long parades of traditionally dressed Balinese, carrying offerings and sacred objects, walk from their villages to nearby riverbanks and beaches to undertake ritual ablutions of purification and ask for their deity's blessing. As part of the *melasti* rites, the village gods in their *pratimas* (the small statue in which a god is invited to reside during a ceremony) are taken from the village temples and carried to the seashore for resanctification. Balinese believe that the sea will receive all evil and polluted elements, it is a place to cast off the evil words and deeds of the past year, and seek renewal and purification for the new Hindu year.

NB Visitors must stay within their hotel compounds from 0500 to 0500 the following day; the observance of Nyepi is very strict in this regard. **Warning** Independent travellers planning to visit Bali at this time might choose to avoid being on the island during *Nyepi*. Tourists are confined to their accommodation, which in a small guesthouse means you feel as if you have been placed under 'house arrest' – no swimming in the sea 10m from your bungalow, no strolls or other forms of exercise. While most of the taboos surrounding *Nyepi* have fallen by the wayside, the one prohibiting movement in the streets is strictly enforced by the 'religious police' in their green silk sarongs. You may well find yourself surrounded by Balinese having a wonderful time playing rock music, gambling, smoking, watching TV with a house full of guests, while you go crazy with boredom. Until recently, *Nyepi* was a day of silence and darkness (no electricity), but in the last 2 years the government has begun scheduling special '*Nyepi Day*' TV programmes. Many religious leaders believe the observation of Nyepi by foreigners has become too lax in recent years and sets a bad example. There are indications that some restrictions in hotels may be reinforced; for example, limitations on the use of sports facilities. Anyone arriving at Denpasar airport on the eve of Nyepi should be aware that most taxi drivers go home at 1700. The few who continue to offer a taxi service up to midnight ask exorbitant rates and may be unlicensed. Travellers would be well advised to arrange transport in advance with their accommodation. Temple Entrance Fee: Unless otherwise stated, 1,000Rp is the usual donation.

Denpasar

Phone code: 0361 Once the royal capital of the princely kingdom of Badung, there is little evidence now of Denpasar's past. Situated in the south of the island, about 5 km from the coast, Bali's capital has grown in the past 10-15 years from a sleepy village to a bustling city. Today, the town has a population of over 450,000 and is Bali's main trade and transport hub, with its central business area centred around Jalan Gajah Mada. Puputan Square pays homage to the tragic end of the Rajah and his court in 1906; it is named after the 'battle to the death' – or puputan – against a force of Dutch soldiers on the morning of 20 September (see page 436).

Ins and outs

Getting there Ngurah Rai airport is several kilometres south of Denpasar, beyond Kuta. There are good links from here with other destinations in Indonesia, and there are some international flights too. The Ubung bus terminal is 4 km or so north of the town centre. Buses leave here for major destinations in Java, including Jakarta, Yogyakarta and Surabaya. There are also buses eastwards to Mataram, on Lombok.

Getting around As Bali's capital, Denpasar is well connected with the rest of the island. No fewer than 5 terminals provide bemo services to various parts of the island and minibuses run between the different terminals. Metered taxis are also abundant in Denpasar. There are 2 **tourist offices**: *Denpasar Tourist Office*, on Jl Surapati 7, T223602 (open 0700-1400 Mon-Thu and Sat, 0700-1100 Fri) provides a free map, calendar of events and Bali brochure; and *Bali Government Tourism Office*, on Jl S Parman, T222387.

Sights

Museum Bali Denpasar is not a particularly attractive town and does not have much in the way of 'sights'. The major tourist attraction is easily found, in the centre of town, and is a focus for local hawkers. The Museum Bali was established in 1931 and is situated on the east side of Puputan Square. The entrance is on Jalan Mayor Wismu. The museum, built in 1910, mirrors the architecture of Balinese temples and palaces, and is contained within a series of attractive courtyards with well-kept gardens. The impressive collection of prehistoric artefacts, sculpture, masks, textiles, weaponry and contemporary arts and crafts was assembled with the help of Walter Spies, the German artist who made Bali his home. The artefacts on display are apparently only a small proportion of the museum's collection. Labelling could be better and there is no guide to the museum to help the inquisitive visitor. Nevertheless, it gives an impression of the breadth of the island's culture. ■ *T222680. 0800-1700 Tue-Thu, Sat and Sun, 0800-1530 Fri, closed Mon. Adult 500Rp, children 200Rp.*

Next door to the museum is the new **Pura Jaganatha**, a temple dedicated to the Supreme God *Sang Hyang Widi Wasa*. The statue of a turtle and two nagas signify the foundation of the world. The complex is dominated by the *Padma Sana* or lotus throne, upon which the gods sit. The central courtyard is surrounded by a moat filled with water-lilies and the most enormous carp.

Pura Masopahit From an archaeological perspective, Pura Masopahit is the most important temple in Denpasar. The main gateway to the pura faces the main street, but the entrance is down a side road off the west end of Jalan Tabanan. The temple is one of the oldest in Bali, probably dating from the introduction of Javanese civilization from Majapahit in the 15th century, after which it is named. It was badly damaged during the 1917 earthquake, but has since been partly restored. Note the fine, reconstructed, split gate, with its massive figures of a giant and a garuda.

The Taman Werdi Budaya Art Centre, on Jalan Nusa Indah, was established in 1973 to promote Balinese visual and performing arts. It contains an open-air auditorium, along with three art galleries. Arts and crafts are also sold here. Activity peaks during the annual Bali Festival of Art, held from mid-June for a month. ■ *0800-1700 Tue-Sun, closed on Mon. 250Rp.*

Taman Werdi Budaya Art Centre

Essentials

A *Natour's Bali*, Jl Veteran 3, T225681, F235347. 75 rooms, a/c, restaurant, pool, central location, built in the 1930s, it was the first hotel on Bali, rather frayed now but it does retain some charm. **B-C** *Chandra Garden*, Jl Diponegoro 114, T226425. 38 rooms, some a/c, popular with Indonesians, price includes breakfast. **B-C** *Pemecutan Palace*, Jl Thamrin 2, T223491. Some a/c, a reconstruction of a palace which was destroyed here by the Dutch in 1906, rooms are shabby. **C-D** *Pura Alit*, Jl Sutomo 26, T428831, F288766. Some a/c. **D** *Adi Yasa*, Jl Nakula 23, T222679. This place seems to have gone downhill. Recent visitors have reported that the rooms are dirty. Price includes breakfast. **D** *Dewi*, Jl Diponegoro 112, T226720. **D-E** *Dharmawisata*, Jl Imam Bonjol 89, T222186. Pool, clean rooms with own mandi.

Sleeping
Today, Denpasar is largely frequented by domestic tourists – foreign visitors either head for the beaches or inland to Ubud. Nonetheless, there is an adequate range of accommodation

Cheap *Hong Kong*, Jl Gajah Mada 89, a/c, a tour group stop, wide selection of Chinese dishes, empty fish tanks, some international dishes. *Atom Baru*, Jl Gajah Mada 106-108, Chinese, popular with the locals. *Kakman*, Jl Teuku Umar (half way to Kuta), excellent Indonesian.

Eating

Nusa Indah *Warung Wardani* for cheap, genuine Balinese food. Recommended. Several *warungs* are to be found within the Kumbasari market.

Cinemas *Wisata Complex*, Jl Thamrin 69, T423023.

Entertainment

Dance *SMKI* (untill recently called *KOKAR*), based in Batubulan, is a conservatory of dance. Students perform many different styles of traditional dance, accompanied by a gamelan orchestra. The *Werdi Budaya Art Centre* gives Kecak dance performances every day from 1830 to 1930.

Indonesian Language Courses *IALF, The Indonesian Australian Foundation*, JL Kapten Agung 17, T221782. Runs regular language courses in Denpasar, Sanur, Ubud and Legian.

Mid-June to mid-July The *Werdi Budaya Art Centre* presents an **Annual Arts Festival**, with demonstrations of local music, dance and performance. Hotels or the tourist office will supply a calendar of events.

Festivals

Department stores *Duta Plaza*, Jl Dewi Sartika; *Tiara Dewata* and *Matahari* both have a good range of goods, including reasonably priced children's clothes, English language books and some handicrafts. The former also has a public swimming pool. **Handicrafts** The *Sanggraha Kriya Asta*, T222942, 7 km east of the centre of town, is a government handicrafts shop, selling batik, jewellery, paintings and woodcarvings. The prices are set and quality is controlled. They will organize free transport to the shop from your hotel if telephoned. There are also a number of handicraft shops on Jl Thamrin, and on the 3rd floor of the Kumbasari Market (see 'Markets', below). **Markets** The biggest market in town (and the biggest on Bali) is the **Kumbasari Market**, off Jl Dr Wahidin, on the banks of the Badung River. It is a great place to browse, with a range of goods including textiles and handicrafts. **Textiles** A large selection of textiles is to be found in the shops along Jl Sulawesi.

Shopping

Arha Bali Rafting, Jl Muding Indah 11/4 Kerobakan, T427446, F427339, rafting on Klungkung River US$65-75, price including pick-up from your hotel and lunch. *Ayung River Rafting*, Jl Diponegoro 150B 29, T238759, F224236, rafting on Ayung River, US$63, including hotel pick-up and meal, also mountain cycling and trekking available. *Grand Komodo Tours*

Tour operators

324 DENPASAR: ESSENTIALS

& Travel, PO Box 3477, T287166, F287165, tours to Komodo and Lombok, from US$390 for 3 days to US$730 for 8 days, including full board but not air fares. **Bali Vacanza**, Jl Laksamana VI/1.4, T261576, F231652, 1 or 2 day trips to Yogyakarta and Lombok. **Waka Experience**, Jl Imam Bonjol No 335 X, T0361-723629, 723659, F722077. Members of the Cousteau Society. They organize *Wakalouka* luxury cruises on a catamaran to their upmarket resort on the island of Lombongan, taking 9 hrs (leaves Benoa harbour at 0900 for the 2 hr journey), which includes 5 hrs at their luxury reef club with swimming pool, watersports and games room; also included is a village tour, and the price of US$86 (children half price) includes transfers, gourmet Indonesian meal with wine and beer, sunset cocktails and all soft drinks. Also *Wakalouka Land Cruises* into the interior by Land Rover, taking in remote rice paddy, ancient quarries and hot springs, and a rustic restaurant in the heart of the rainforest, where food is cooked over traditional mud ovens and served on immaculate starched tablecloths, with Italian designer cutlery, US$83 per person covers the day-long trip and includes all the food

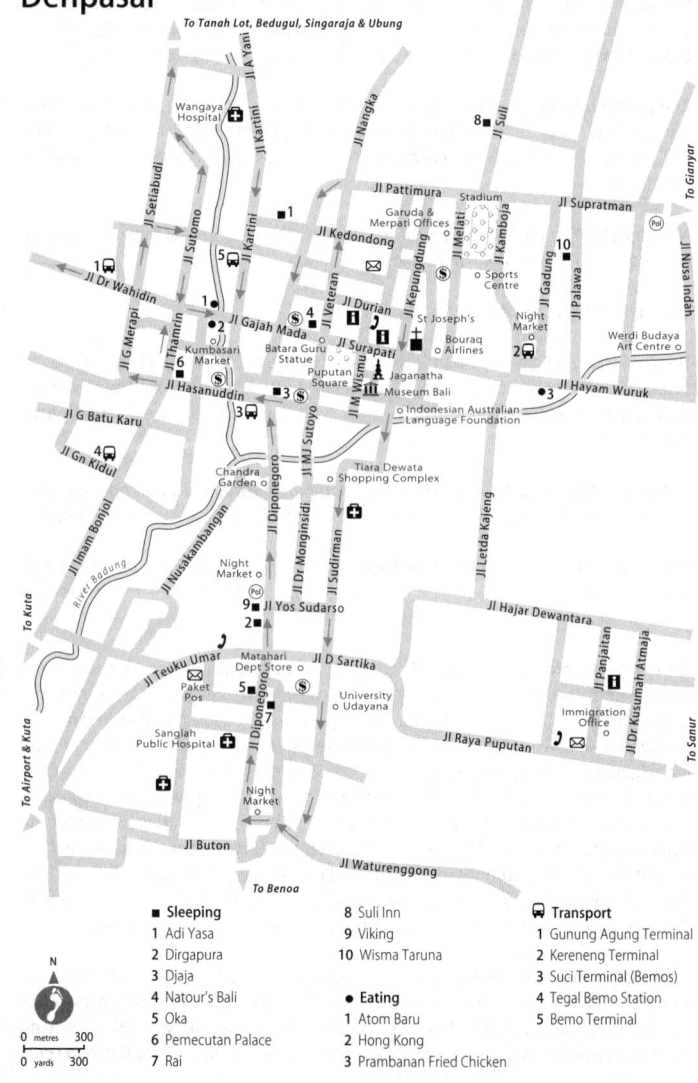

■ Sleeping	8 Suli Inn	🚌 Transport
1 Adi Yasa	9 Viking	1 Gunung Agung Terminal
2 Dirgapura	10 Wisma Taruna	2 Kereneng Terminal
3 Djaja		3 Suci Terminal (Bemos)
4 Natour's Bali	● Eating	4 Tegal Bemo Station
5 Oka	1 Atom Baru	5 Bemo Terminal
6 Pemecutan Palace	2 Hong Kong	
7 Rai	3 Prambanan Fried Chicken	

and drink you want, including refreshments from the capacious hampers carried on top of the Land Rover. Recommended. *Bali Safari Rafting*, Jl Hayam Wuruk 88a, T221315, F232268, organizes rafting on Telaga Waja River, US$65 including transfers, buffet lunch, refreshments, insurance.

Local Bemo: a few of the original, rickety and under-powered 3-wheeler bemos still travel between the main bemo terminals (1000Rp), criss-crossing town, although much more common these days are Japanese-built mini buses. It is also possible to charter these bemos for trips around town. From the terminals, of which there are several, bemos travel to all of Bali's main towns: the Ubung terminal, north of town on Jl Cokroaminoto, for trips to **West Bali**, **North Bali** and **Java**; Tegal, west of town, near the intersection of Jl Imam Bonjol and Jl G Wilis, for journeys to **South Bali**; Suci, near the intersection of Jl Diponegoro and Jl Hasanuddin, for **Benoa Port**; Kereneng, at the east edge of town off Jl Kamboja (Jl Hayam Wuruk), for destinations around town and for **Sanur**; while Batubulan, east of town just before the village of Batubulan on the road to Gianyar, for buses running east and to central Bali (see page 315 for more details). **Dokar**: pony-drawn carriages, now on the verge of extinction and/or asphyxiation. **Ojek**: motorcycle taxis, and the fastest way around town; ojek riders can be identified by their red jackets (1,000Rp minimum). **Taxi**: there are numerous un-metered cars that can be chartered by the hour or day, or which can be hired for specific journeys. Bargain hard. There are also some metered taxis. *Praja Bali Taxi*, pale blue taxis, all operate with meters and make no extra charge for call-out service, T701111.

Transport
As Denpasar is the transport hub of the island, it is easy to get to most of the main towns, beaches & sights from here

Air See page 313 for details. **Road Bemo**: these provide transportation from Denpasar's 5 terminals to most places on the island (see page 46 and above). Mini buses run between the various terminals (1000Rp). **Bus**: connections with **Java** from the Ubung terminal, just north of Denpasar on Jl Cokroaminoto. Express and night bus offices are concentrated near the intersection of Jl Diponegoro and Jl Hasanuddin; for example, *Chandra Ticketing*, Jl Diponegoro 114, T226425. Journey time and departure times for night and express buses are as follows: **Jakarta** 30 hrs (0630-0700), **Surabaya** 11 hrs (0700 and 1700-2000), **Malang** 10 hrs (1800-1930), **Yogyakarta/Solo** 16 hrs (1500-1600), **Semarang** 15 hrs (1600), **Bandung** 25 hrs (0700), **Bogor** 24 hrs (0700), **Blitar** 15 hrs (1900).

Airline offices *Bouraq*, Jl Sudirman 19A, T223564. *Garuda*, Jl Melati 61, T222788. *Mandala*, Jl Diponegoro 98 (Kerta Wijaya Plaza), T222751, F231659. *Merpati*, Jl Melati 57, T235358. *UTA*, Jl Bypass Ngurah Rai, T289225. **Banks** *Bank Bumi Daya*, Jl Veteran 2. *Bank Dagang Negara*, Jl Gajah Mada 2. *Bank Negara Indonesia*, Jl Gajah Mada 20. *Diners Club*, Jl Veteran 5, Denpasar, T227138. **Visa & Mastercharge**: *Bank Duta*, Jl Hayam Wuruk 165, Denpasar, T226578. **Communications** Post Office: Jl Raya Puputan, Renon. Open 0800-1400 Mon-Thu, 0800-1200 Fri, 0800-1300 Sat. *Poste Restante* available here. *Paket Pos* (packing service & parcel post): Jl Diponegoro 146. **Communications centre**: Jl Teuku Umar 6. **Embassies & consulates** Australia, Jl Mohammad Yamin 51, T235093. France, Jl Rayan Sesetan 46, T233555. Germany, Jl Pantai Karang 17, T288535, F288826. Japan, Jl Pemuda, Renon, T227628. Norway, Jl Jayagiri VII/10, T234834. **Medical services** Emergency dental clinic: Jl Pattimura 19, T222445. Hospitals: *Sanglah Public Hospital*, Jl Kesehatan Selatan 1, T227911. *Wangaya Hospital*, Jl Kartini, T222141; 24 hr on-call doctor and ambulance, Jl Cokroaminoto 28, T426393. This is the main hospital with the best emergency service. Some staff speak English. Bali's only decompression chamber for divers is located here. Bear in mind that medical facilities are not up to western standards. For any serious medical problem, Singapore is the best place to go. **Optician**: *International Optical*, Jl Gajah Mada 133, T226294. **Pharmacy**: *Apotik Kimia Farma*, Jl Diponegoro 123, T227812. **Places of worship** Catholic: *Church of St Joseph* on Jl Kepundung (1730 Sat, 0830, 1730 Sun). Evangelical Church: Jl Melati. Protestant Church: Jl Surapati. **Useful addresses** Emergencies: 24-hr helpline, T228996. Immigration office: Jl Panjaitan, off Jl Puputan Raya, T227828. Police: HQ, Jl Supratman, T110.

Directory

South Bali

Most visitors to Bali stay in one of the resorts at the south end of the island. Most famous is **Kuta**, *the original backpackers' haven, together with its north extension,* **Legian**; *both of these are fairly noisy, crowded, downmarket resorts. Much nicer is* **Seminyak**, *further north, which is still relatively rural. To the south of Kuta is a newly developed zone of hotels and restaurants named* **Tuban**. *Further south still is* **Jimbaran**, *a large village, as yet unspoilt, with some of Bali's top resorts nearby.* **Sanur** *is on Bali's east coast and offers largely middle range accommodation, though some newer budget places to stay have recently opened.* **Serangan**, *or Turtle Island, is a short distance offshore. Rather further off the east coast, in the Lombok Strait, are the two islands of* **Nusa Penida**, *with limited and very basic accommodation, and* **Nusa Lembongan**, *with a growing number of upmarket hotels; both are also accessible on a day trip.*

Kuta

Phone code: 0361

Kuta was the main port and arrival point for foreigners visiting south Bali for over 100 years, from early in the 18th century until first Benoa, and then the airport at Denpasar usurped its role. The town prospered as a hub of the slave trade in the 1830s, attracting an international cross-section of undesirables.

South Bali

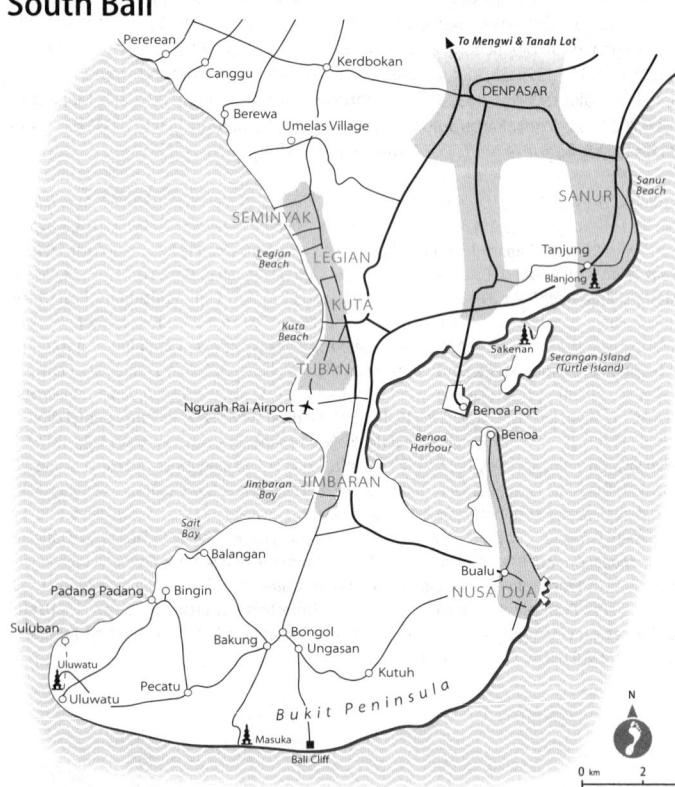

Miguel Covarrubias wrote in 1937 that Kuta and Sanur were "small settlements of fishermen who brave the malarial coasts". It was not until the 1960s that large numbers of Western travellers 'discovered' Kuta. Since then, it has grown into a highly developed beach resort with a mind-boggling array of hotels, restaurants and shops. While Sanur is no longer a backpackers' haven, there are still many cheap losmen in Kuta as well as a growing number of middle to high range accommodation.

Getting around Traffic in Kuta frequently comes to a standstill, despite the 1-way system. The main street, containing most of Kuta's shops, is Jl Legian, which runs north-south (traffic travels 1 way south). Jl Pantai meets Jl Legian at 'Bemo Corner' and is the main east-west road to the south end of the beach (with traffic going 1 way west). The beach road is northbound only. There is a government **Tourist Information Office**, on Jl Bakungsari, T756176, open daily 0800-1300, 1500-1800.

The town Many people dislike Kuta. Crowded beyond belief, with an infrastructure at breaking point as space runs out, accommodation owners have taken to building multi-storey concrete blocks of rooms to let, often in what were once pretty Balinese gardens. In the rainy season the drainage system is hopelessly inadequate, and some areas of Kuta become flooded and virtually impassable for several days at a time.

With the downturn in the economy, petty theft is becoming more of a problem. Locals accuse 'refugees' from eastern Java of being behind this increase in crime. Look out for groups of young children, both boys and girls, particularly in front of the *Hard Rock Hotel*, who will swarm over you, often waving an old newspaper or beaded jewellery to distract your attention while rifling through your pockets or money belt. If your hotel has a safe, it is worth leaving your money belt there – prominently displayed money belts, not surprisingly, seem to act as a magnet for thieves.

The beach Kuta Beach is a fine beach; a broad expanse of golden sand where local officials have taken fairly unsuccessful steps to limit the persistence of hawkers. It is because of its accessibility that it is popular with surfers, although better waves can be found elsewhere. It is an excellent spot for beginners and recreational surfers. Boards can be hired on the beach and there are usually locals who will offer their insider's knowledge of surf conditions. Strong and irregular currents can make swimming a little hazardous – look out for the warning notices and coloured flags that indicate which areas are safe for swimming on any particular day; the currents change from day to day. The sand is white to the south, but grey further north. The hordes of hawkers can be very aggressive, selling trinkets and offering hair-plaiting, manicure and massage services. The beach faces west, so is popular at sunset. There are allegations that levels of contamination in the sea at Kuta are above internationally accepted safety levels, though many people are happy to swim in the sea with no apparent ill effects.

Sleeping *It is advisable to book accommodation during the peak periods of Jul/Aug & at Christmas & New Year, as hotels are often full. There are countless places to stay in Kuta*

Taxi drivers are often reluctant to drive down Poppies Gangs I and II. Except when the area is flooded during the rainy season, Poppies Gang II is perfectly driveable, so it is worth trying to find a driver who will drop you by your chosen accommodation.

AL *Hard Rock Hotel*, Jl Pantai, Kuta, T761869, F761868, rock@ hardrockbeachclub.com Aimed at families and rock fans alike, it attracts people of all ages and nationalities, 418 rooms and suites situated around tropical gardens with sea or garden views. All rooms with a/c, fridge, safe, ceiling mounted TV, CD/cassette player, IDD, tea/coffee-making facilities, internet access (Nintendo games can be hired). Vast free-form swimming pool, million dollar audio-visual system in lobby featuring nightly live entertainment, karaoke rooms, rock information centre, internet centre, 7 restaurants and bars, all reasonably priced, serving excellent Indonesian, Mediterranean, Asian, American and Japanese food, including a New York-style deli and a sushi bar. Health club (free to guests) and spa with state of the art gym equipment.

A *Bali Anggrek Inn*, Jl Pantai, PO Box 435, T751265, F751766. A/c, restaurant, large pool, facing the beach, average rooms. **A** *Indah*, Poppies Gang II, T753267, F752787. Pool, central location for shopping, price including breakfast. **A** *Kulkul*, Jl Pantai, PO Box 97, T752520, F752519. A/c, restaurant, pool, on the beach road, well designed hotel with attractive rooms. Recommended. **A** *Poppies I*, Poppies Gang I, PO Box 378, T751059, F752364. A/c, pool, lovely garden, well-run hotel with cottage accommodation, very popular. **A** *Rama Palace*, Jl Pantai, PO Box 293, T752063, F753078. On the beach road, a/c, restaurant, pool, standard accommodation. **A** *Sahid Bali*, Jl Pantai, PO Box 1102, T753855, F752019. A/c, restaurant, pool, large hotel on the beachfront. **A** *Sol Inn*, 118 Jl Legian, T752167, F754372. New 1st-class hotel built in the centre of Kuta, 124 rooms, a/c, minibar, satellite TV, in-house movie, balcony, en suite bathroom, pool, Japanese restaurant, Indonesian restaurant, pub, 2 bars, simple but attractive pastel décor. **A-B** *Mutiara*, Poppies Gang I, T752091. Some a/c, attractive pool, nice garden, clean rooms.

B *Agung Cottages*, Jl Raya Legian, T751147. Some a/c, restaurant, good pool. Recommended. **B** *Aneka Beach*, Jl Pantai, T752067, F752892. A/c, pool, on the beach road, 3-storey hotel plus some thatched bungalows, attractive grounds. **B** *Bakungsari*, Jl Bakungsari, PO Box 1044, T755396, F752704. A/c, pool, built around a central swimming pool, clean rooms. **B** *Bali Bungalows*, PO Box 371, T755285, F751899. A/c, pool, near *Rama Palace* on the beach road, nice grounds. **B** *Bruna Beach*, PO Box 116, T751565, F753201. A/c, on beachfront road, average rooms, price including breakfast. **B** *Five One Cottages*, behind Poppies Gang I, a/c, small pool, hot water. **B** *Flora Beach*, Jl Bakungsari 13A, PO Box 1040, T751870, F751034. A/c, pool, new hotel with attractive pool and clean, well-designed rooms, one of the better

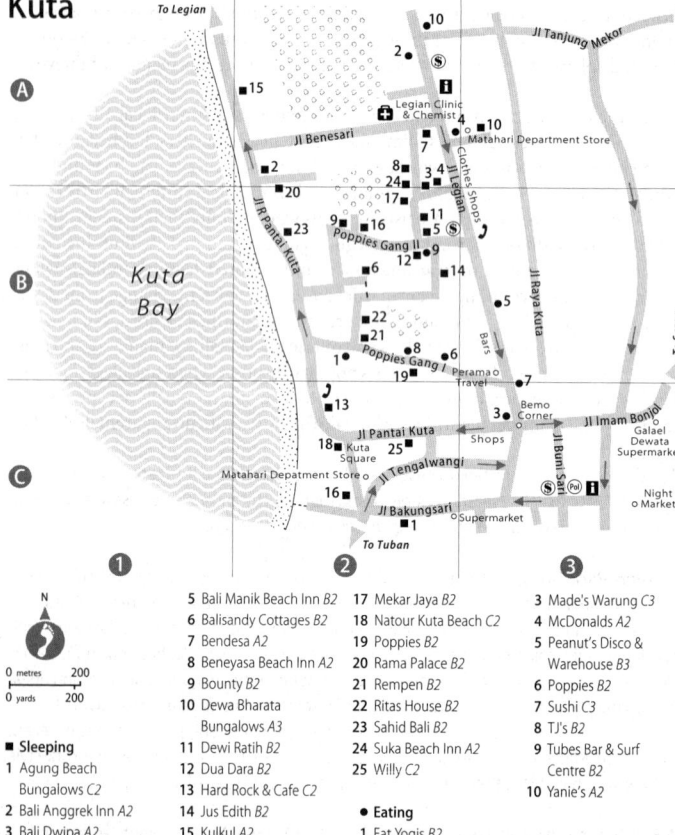

Kuta

■ **Sleeping**	5 Bali Manik Beach Inn *B2*	17 Mekar Jaya *B2*	3 Made's Warung *C3*
1 Agung Beach Bungalows *C2*	6 Balisandy Cottages *B2*	18 Natour Kuta Beach *C2*	4 McDonalds *A2*
2 Bali Anggrek Inn *A2*	7 Bendesa *A2*	19 Poppies *B2*	5 Peanut's Disco & Warehouse *B3*
3 Bali Dwipa *B2*	8 Beneyasa Beach Inn *A2*	20 Rama Palace *B2*	6 Poppies *B2*
4 Bali Indah Beach Inn *A2*	9 Bounty *B2*	21 Rempen *B2*	7 Sushi *C3*
	10 Dewa Bharata Bungalows *A3*	22 Ritas House *B2*	8 TJ's *B2*
	11 Dewi Ratih *B2*	23 Sahid Bali *B2*	9 Tubes Bar & Surf Centre *B2*
	12 Dua Dara *B2*	24 Suka Beach Inn *A2*	10 Yanie's *A2*
	13 Hard Rock & Cafe *C2*	25 Willy *C2*	
	14 Jus Edith *B2*	● **Eating**	
	15 Kulkul *A2*	1 Fat Yogis *B2*	
	16 Kuta Cottages *C2*	2 Il Pirata *A2*	

of the mid-range hotels. Recommended. **B** *Kuta Cottages*, Jl Bakungsari, PO Box 300, T751101. Pool, small hotel. **B** *Melasti*, Jl Kartika Plaza, PO Box 295, T751335, F751563. A/c, pool, on the beach, may be rather overpriced and living on its reputation, south end of Kuta. **B** *Satriya*, Poppies Gang II, T752741. Pool, hot water, clean rooms, price including breakfast. Recommended. **B** *Willy*, Jl Tengalwangi 18, T751281, F752641. Small, attractive pool, central location in Kuta, attractive rooms, built around a garden. Recommended. **B-C** *Agung Beach Bungalows*, Jl Bakungsari, T751263. Some a/c, pool, good location south of Jl Pantai. **B-C** *Dewa Bharata Bungalows*, Jl Legian, T/F751764. Clean rooms with a/c or fan, private bathroom all with hot water, shower and Western toilet, attractive gardens with good sized swimming pool, price includes meagre breakfast, not as well run as it used to be but still worth considering if you want a decent sized pool. *Dewa Bharata Bungalows* in Candi Dasa owned by same people. **C** *Jesen's Inn III*, Jl Bakungsari 19, T751561. Off the main road in a large palm-filled courtyard, rooms in the new wing are best. **B-C** *Dewi Ratih*, Poppies Gang II, T751694. Some a/c, small pool, hot water, price includes breakfast.

C *Barong Cottages*, Jl Legian, T751488, F751804. A/c, pool, 3-storey accommodation, nice garden, price including breakfast. **C** *Sorga Cottages*, off Poppies Gang II, some a/c, good pool, price including breakfast. **C-D** *Dharma Yudha*, Jl Bakungsari, T751685. Some a/c, friendly, but rooms are rather dark. **C-D** *Lasi Erawati*, Poppies Gang I, T751665. Fan, clean, nice garden. Recommended. **C-E** *Rita's House*, Poppies Gang I, T751760, F236021. 12 reasonably priced rooms with fan or a/c and private mandi with Western toilet, set around small garden, clean and relaxing.

D *Bali Manik Beach Inn*, Poppies Gang II, T752740. Own bathroom, clean, with a verandah in front of each room, price includes breakfast. Good value. **D** *Balisandy Cottages*, Poppies Gang II, T753344. 2-storey bungalows with private mandi, Western toilet, fan, set in spacious coconut grove away from the noise of Kuta, attractive décor, very clean and quiet. Good value and recommended. **D** *Bamboo Inn*, Gang Kresek 1, Jl Bakungsari, T751935. Friendly, clean, but not very close to the beach, price including breakfast. **D** *Kuta Suci*, just off Poppies Gang II, T752617. Small but clean rooms. **D** *Masa Inn*, Poppies Gang I, T752606. Fan, clean (motorbike hire). **D** *Rempen*, T753150. Just off Poppies Gang I. Perfectly adequate, fairly basic rooms in 3-storey block. Price includes simple breakfast. **D** *Sareg*, Jl Pantai Kuta, basic, Western toilets, clean. Recommended. **D-E** *Bendesa*, T751358. North of Poppies Gang II, just off Jl Legian. Set in large gardens, 35 rooms; the new rooms are bright and clean, older rooms are very basic and not particularly good value. All with private bathroom, Western toilet, shower. Price includes breakfast and tea all day. **D-E** *Dua Dara*, Jl Legian, Poppies Gang II, T754031. Well run, spotlessly clean simple rooms with fan, private bathrooms with shower and Western toilet, attractive small garden with family temple, price includes breakfast, safety deposit boxes available. Recommended.

E *Bali Dwipa I*, T751446/752247. Just north of Poppies Gang II, one of the nicer budget places in the area; 48 rooms in a 3-storey block with small garden and attractive atrium. Rooms are simple but clean, with private bathrooms, shower and Western toilets. Special longstay rates available, price including breakfast, friendly atmosphere and staff. Recommended. **E** *Bali Indah Beach Inn*, T752509. Just north of Poppies Gang II, basic but clean rooms, private bathrooms with shower and Western toilet (some without toilet seat), very friendly management, price including breakfast. **E** *Beneyasa Beach Inn*, just north of Poppies Gang II, T754180. 50 rooms set round gardens which sometimes flood in the wet season, providing nice breeding grounds for mosquitoes! Rooms are simple but clean, with private bathroom, Western toilet and shower. **E** *Jus Edith*, off Poppies Gang II to the south, basic but cheap and very popular. **E** *Komala Indah I*, opposite Poppies Cottages, Poppies Gang I, rooms with own bathroom. **E** *Mekar Jaya*, north of Poppies Gang II, basic but clean, rooms could do with redecoration. Private bathroom, shower, Western toilet (most without seats). **E** *Pension Arka Nini*, Jl Buni Sari 7. Very comfortable beds, toilet and mandi in room, price including good breakfast, friendly management, clean and quiet rooms, despite central location. **E** *Suka Beach Inn*, Just north of Poppies Gang II, T752793. One of the nicest of the budget places in this area; 54 rooms, some new, set around pretty gardens. Rooms are clean with private bathroom, shower and Western toilet. Very friendly management. Price includes breakfast. Motor bikes for hire. Popular. Recommended.

Eating *Most of the restaurants in Kuta offer a range of food, including Indonesian & international, so we have not split restaurants by cuisine categories*

Mid-range *Bebek Mas*, street-front of *Melasti Beach Bungalows*, Jl Kartika Plaza, T752750. Owned by Dutch chef Wim Hilgers. Seafood salad, crab and grapefruit salad, fettucini senora bianca, all recommended. Excellent Bebek Betutu (Balinese duck). Pasta night on Mon, Schnitzel night on Wed, Rifsttafel on Thu, Indonesian buffet on Sun. No a/c and the mosquitoes are bad. *Edelweiss*, on Jl By-Pass between Kuta and Nusa Dua. Run by Otto King, previously chef at *Nusa Dua Beach Hotel*. Austrian and international dishes, good steaks. *Hard Rock Hotel*, Jl Pantai. 7 restaurants and bars (see hotel entry), prices to suit every budget. *Hard Rock Café*, Jl Pantai, on 2 floors facing the sea. Serves American food, live bands each night.

Cheap *Aromas of Bali*, Jl Legian. Vegetarian food in a garden setting. *Indah Sari*, Jl Legian, near Bemo Corner. Indonesian grilled seafood. *Poppies*, Poppies Gang I. Attractive garden, good food (mostly international). Popular and recommended. *SC*, Jl Legian. Seafood, Chinese. *Sushi Restaurant*, Jl Legian, just up from Bemo Corner. Good, reasonably priced Japanese food. *TJ's*, Poppies Gang I. Good Mexican food and excellent margaritas. *Un's*, Poppies Gang I. Indonesian, travellers' food, seafood, both only average quality.

Very cheap *Bobbies*, towards Legian, to left of Jl Legian. Excellent value food, particularly the pizzas, and good breakfasts. Recommended. *Crown*, T754719. The fish on the menu here has been recommended. *Golden Palace International*, Poppies Gang II. Good lasagnes; opposite here is a small, popular and very cheap restaurant, with pizza, fried rice etc and cheap beer. *Made's Warung*, Jl Pantai. The oldest eating establishment on Kuta, serving Asian and travellers' food and still very popular. Recommended. *Murni's Warung*, Poppies II, halfway down Poppies II opposite *Kori Restaurant*. Incredibly cheap and tasty nasi campur, also fruit juices and coffee. This is where the locals eat. *Tree House*, Poppies Gang I. Travellers' food. *Yunna*, Poppies Gang II. Travellers' food, popular. *Burger King*, Jl Legian. *Il Pirata*, Jl Legian, 24-hr pizzeria. *Locanda Fat Yogi*, Poppies Gang I. Bakery and Italian restaurant with good pizzas. Recommended. *Mini's*, Jl Legian. Popular Chinese restaurant, with good seafood.

Bars *Kuta probably has the 'best' nightlife on Bali. Most of the bars are on Jl Legian*

Club Bruna, Jl Pantai (beach road, see 'Discos'). *Bali Rock*, Jl Melasti. *Lips Bar*, Jl Legian Raya – country and western music. *Sari Club*, Jl Legian. *The Bounty*, Jl Legian, popular Australian drinking-hole, with jugs of Margueritas and videos, happy hours 1800-1900, 2200-2300. Every Tues and Sat a pub crawl leaves *Peanuts*, on Jl Legian at 1830. Arrives at *Casablancas* (Jl Buni Sari – just south of Bemo Corner) at about 2200, where there is often live music. *Hard Rock Café*, Jl Pantai, expensive drinks, live (good) bands, big crowds, music starts about 2300 and goes on until 0200. *Tubes Bar*, a surfers hangout and excellent source of surfing information.

Entertainment **Balinese performing arts** Kecak, legong, Ramayana dance and Balinese music; performances take place at many of the major hotels. **Discos** *Peanut's*, Jl Legian (4,000Rp entry fee). *Warehouse* (next door to *Peanuts*), free entry. *Bruna Reggae Pub*, Jl Pantai, live local music starts at 2330 (8,000Rp entry fee). *Spotlights* and *Cheater's*, both on Jl Legian. Open-air discos at *Gado-Gado* (closed Mon and Thu) and *Double Six* (open Mon, Thu and Sat), both north of Legian, off Jl Dhyanapura and Jl Legian Cottage. Both these two are open from 0000 to 0400 (10,000Rp entry fee).

Shopping **Best buys** Kuta is one of the best places on Bali to shop for clothing; the quality is reasonable (sometimes good), and designs are close to the latest Western fashions, with a strong Australian bias for bright colours and bold designs. There is a good range of children's clothes shops. Silver jewellery is also a good buy (although some of it is of rather inferior quality). In addition, Kuta has a vast selection of 'tourist' trinkets and curios: leather goods, woodcarvings, mobiles, batik. Quality is poor-to-average. The boys hawking watches, at an asking price of up to 200,000Rp, buy them in Surabaya for 15,000Rp a kilo! Almost all the hawkers and stallholders are from Java. They are unskilled workers who live in cardboard boxes and often bring their troubles with them, which has led to a rise in petty crime, and has sorely tried the fabled tolerance of the Balinese. The new Kuta Square shopping centre has a variety of designer boutiques and a large *Matahari* department store (the cheapest place to stock up on food, drinking water and fruit). **Children's clothes shops** *Hop on Pop*, Jl Pantai 45. *Kuta Kidz*, Bemo Corner. *Outrageous*, Jl Legian Kaja 460. **Jewellery** Several shops on Jl Legian and Jl Pantai. *Shiraz Silver*, on Jl Bunisari, has some attractive silver jewellery. **Leather** Leather goods are generally poor quality but cheap and attractive – if you are buying a bag, check the handles are strong. *A-Sodig*, 3 Kuta Theatre St, sells made-to-measure leather jackets and trousers, and has good value boots and shoes. **Men's clothes** Shirts at *Aladdin's Cave*, Jl Legian, and in several shops around Bemo Corner. **Swimwear & sportswear** Jl Pantai, and from the surfing shops on Jl Legian and Jl Bakungsari. **T-shirts** A multitude of shops along Jl Legian; good designs from *Tony's* on Jl Bakungsari. **Women's clothes shops** Mostly along Jl Legian and Jl Pantai. Lots of lycra, available from *Coconut Tree*, Jl Legian. Outrageous sequined garments from *Dallas*, Jl Legian 496. Batik jump-suits and jackets from *Aladdin's Cave*, Jl Legian; *Bali Design*, good quality cotton fashions.

Bungy Jumping *Bali Bungy Co*, Jl Pura Puseh, Legian Kelod, T752658, open daily 0800-midnight, the first bungy jumping company in Bali – the unsightly 45m metal tower from which jumps are made is clearly seen from quite a long way away, free pick-up service is offered. **Diving** *Aquamarine Diving*, Jl Raya Seminyak 56, Kuta, T730107, F735368, 81-23944162 (mobile), www.aquamarinediving.com This company is owned and run by an Englishwoman, Annabel Thomas, a PADI instructor. It offers a personal service, uses Balinese divemasters who speak English (and Japanese) and has well-maintained equipment. PADI courses up to divemaster can be provided in English, German, Spanish, French and Japanese. **Massage** Numerous masseurs – with little professional training – roam the beach; more skilled masseurs can be found at hotels or specialist clinics around Kuta. **Surfing** Kuta is famous for its surfing, although the cognoscenti would now rather go elsewhere (see page 15). Surfboards are available for rent on the beach. Surf equipment is available from *The Surf Shop*, Jl Legian; *Amphibia Surf Shop*, Jl Legian; and *Ulu's Shop*, Jl Bakungsari. They will all provide information on currents, tides and latest surfing reports. **Swimming** Small pool and spa in historic building, centre of Kuta, opposite the Art Market, adult 3,000Rp, child 1,500Rp, towels and lockers for hire. Waterbom Park in Tuban is nearby (see Tuban entry).

Sports

Bali Adventure Tours, Jl Tunjung Mekar, T751292, F754334. An organized company owned by long-term Australian resident (the owner of *Yanies Restaurant* in Legian), they can help you with rafting or kayaking trips, mountain biking or trekking, US$40-56, including pick-up from hotel, lunch and insurance. *Gloria Tours & Travel Services*, Jl Raya Kerobokan 2, T730272, F730273. Bali sight-seeing tours, island tours, car rental. *Lila Tours Ltd*, Natour Kuta Beach Hotel, Jl Pantai Kuta 1, T761827, F761826, lilatur@indosat.net.id Locally owned and run tour company. *Perama*, Jl Legian 16, T751551. *Perama* organize shuttle buses all over the island and are one of the cheapest companies. Ask for a Member's Card and you will receive 10% discount on all journeys. Alternatively, keep your used Perama ticket and show it when buying your next ticket for a 10% discount.

Tour operators

Local Bemos: run from Bemo Corner up Jl Pantai to Legian (1,000Rp); and from just east of Bemo Corner, to Denpasar's Tegal terminal. Note that these days many bemo drivers are reluctant to pick up Westerners, except for a highly inflated fare. Bemos for charter also hang around Bemo Corner. **Bicycle hire**: 10,000Rp per day. **Car hire**: arrange through hotels, or one of the rental agencies in town, approximately 80,000Rp per day; there are also private cars (with drivers) that can be chartered by the hour or day, or for specific journeys. Bargain hard, expect to pay about 60,000Rp per day. Drivers can be found around Bemo Corner. **Motorbike hire**: arranged through travel agents, hotels or from operations on the street, from 20,000Rp per day.

Transport
11 km from Denpasar, 4 km from the airport

Road Bemo: to Tegal terminal in **Denpasar**, and from there, change to other terminals for next destination. **Shuttle bus**: to most tourist destinations on the island; shop around for best price. **Taxi**: 15,000Rp to the airport.

Directory **Airline offices** *Garuda, Natour Kuta Beach Hotel,* Jl Pantai, T751179. 0800-1700 Mon-Fri, 0900-1300 Sat and Sun. **Banks** Plenty of money changers on Jl Legian and its side streets. Very few, if any, are licensed, and most are masters of sleight of hand and deception: BE WARNED! You should take a calculator with you and count the money you receive very, very carefully. *Matahari* has a foreign exchange booth on the ground floor with reasonable rates. Also a handful of banks. Branches of **Lippo Bank** and **Danamon** in *Galael Plaza* (on road into Kuta from Denpasar). **Communications** Postal agent: Jl Legian; *poste restante* service. **Post Office**: Jl Raya Kuta, south of Jl Bakungsari. **Telecommunications centre**: Jl Legian, near Poppies Gang II. **Embassies & consulates** Netherlands, Jl Imam Bonjol 599, T751094, F752777. **Medical services** Clinic: Legian Clinic, Gang Benasari (off Jl Legian before Jl Melasti), T758503. Helpful staff who speak good English. The doctors do not charge, but any treatment starts at 75,000Rp plus the cost of medicines. Jl Raya Kuta 100, T753268, 24 hrs on call. *American CDC*, T(Atlanta)404-639-3311, web site: http://www.cdc.gov/cdc.html **Places of worship** Protestant service: 1000 Sun, Gang Menuh, Jl Legian.

Legian

Phone code: 0361 It is hard to say where Kuta ends and Legian begins, as the main shopping street, Jl Legian, dominates both places. Like Kuta, Legian is a shopping haven. North of Legian, you reach Seminyak which starts at Jl Double Six; the beach here is much less crowded, wide and sandy with a few mostly mid- to upmarket hotels dotted along it. Jalan Pura Bagus Taruna is also known as Rum Jungle Road. Jalan Dhyana Pura is also known as Jalan Abimanyu.

Sleeping **AL** *Bali Padma Hotel,* Jl Padma 1, T752111, F752140, padma@denspasar.wasantara.net.id On Legian beach, this large hotel has 400 rooms and cottages set in lush tropical gardens beside the sea. Usual facilities of a hotel in this class including pool, tennis courts and spa. **AL-A** *Legian Beach Hotel,* Jl Melasti, T751711. Large hotel popular with tour groups and families. **AL-A** *Hotel Puri Raja,* Jl Padma Utara, T754828, 755902, F754202. This has a good location beside the sea; 72 rooms with a/c, HW, fridge, TV, telephone. 2 large pools, gardens leading down to beach, 24-hr restaurant and room service. Good value, with off-season discount.

A *Bali Mandira,* Jl Padma, T751381, F752377. A/c, restaurant, large pool, close to sea, free airport pick-up. Recommended. **A** *Jayakarta Hotel* (formerly Kuta Palace), Jl Pura Bagus Teruna, PO Box 244, T751433, F752074. A/c, 5 restaurants, 2 pools, tennis, fitness centre, all facilities, facing the beach, large hotel with 2-storey blocks of accommodation and some family bungalows. A bustling tour group hotel. **A** *Legian Garden Cottages,* Jl Legian Cottage, T751876. A/c, pool, quiet except when the *Double Six Disco* is operating. **A** *Puri Tantra Beach Bungalows,* Jl Padma Utara 50 X, T/F753195. 6 attractive Balinese style bungalows with large bedroom/living room, storage room, kitchen (fridge but no cooker), HW and ceiling fan, verandah. Pretty tropical gardens, with Hindu temple in the grounds (you might be lucky and witness a traditional ceremony here), lead down to the beach. No pool. Safety deposit box and library. One of the most peaceful places to stay in Legian. Very helpful owner. Long stay discount available. Recommended. **A** *Rama Garden Cottages,* Jl Padma, T751971, F755909. 30 a/c rooms, artistic Balinese décor, minibar, private terrace, pool, restaurant. **A-B** *Adika Sari Bungalows,* Jl Padma Utara, north of Jl Padma, T751413, F755898; 23 clean, new rooms with a/c, HW. Set in cramped gardens with pool, 5 mins' walk from beach. Rates negotiable off-season. **A-B** *Puri Hijau Lestari* (formerly *Evergreen Puri*), access via beach road south of Jl Double Six, T730386. Looking rather neglected, 22 rooms with a/c or fan, cold water only. Garden but no pool. Its main attraction is that it is right on the beach. **A-B** *Puri Mangga Bungalows,* Jl Legian Cottages/Arjuna 23, T730447, F730307 (Att Indigo). 6 rather gloomy bungalows, with kitchen, living room, HW, fan etc. Long-term rates available, short-term rates are overpriced. Around 10-15 mins' walk to beach. **A-B** *Sinar Indah Beach Cottages,* Jl Padma Utara, T755905, 756008. 20 rooms plus 6, 2-storey bungalows. (US$320 monthly. Kitchen, living room, private small garden.) Attractive, new and very clean, fan, HW, garden, 3 mins' walk from beach. Use of *Hotel Balisani* swimming pool for 5,000Rp. Good value, price includes breakfast and tax. **A-B** *Sing Ken Ken,* Jl Double Six, T730980,

F780535. A short walk from the beach. Cramped grounds with average rooms. HW, a/c. Low season discount.

B *Garden View*, Jl Padma, T751559, F753265. A/c, pool, quiet location, a walk to the beach.
B *Laut Biru*, access via beach road South of Jl Double Six, T730289, F730590; 24 bungalows with kitchen, living room, 1 and 2 bedrooms etc. Price reflects the lack of luxury. Garden, beside sea, friendly staff. **B** *Legian Village*, Jl Padma, T751182. Some a/c, pool, popular.
B *Orchid Garden Cottage*, Jl Pura Bagus Taruna 525, PO Box 379, T751802. Small hotel, attractive gardens, clean. **B-C** *RJ's*, Jl Rum Jungle, T751922. Pool, good value, good food.
B-C *Three Brothers*, quiet hotel with cottages in a traditional Balinese garden courtyard, attractive and better value than its equivalent in Kuta.

C *Lumbung Sari*, Jl Three Brothers, T752009. Rather squashed in between other developments, cottage with kitchen, (**D**) no fan. **C-D** *Suri Wathi*, 12 Jl Menuh, T753162. Good value, simple rooms. Fairly quiet with nice pool. **D** *Legian Beach Bungalow*, Jl Padma, T751087. Good discount for longer stay. **D** *Oka*, Jl Padma, T751085. Small, clean, but hemmed in by other buildings. **D** *Puri Damai Cottage I*, Jl Padma, T751965. Popular. **D** *Sari Yasa Beach Inn I*, Jl Rum Jungle, T752836. Basic but OK rooms. **E** *Sri Beach Inn*, with bathroom, quiet.

Eating *Benny's*, Jl Pura Bagus Taruna, great range of coffee. *Do Drop Inn*, Jl Legian, steak-house, bar and restaurant. *Koko's Warung*, Jl Pura Bagus Taruna, Indian food. **Mid-range** *Poco Loco*, Jl Padma Utara, in the quieter northern end of Legian, popular, terraced Mexican restaurant, open evenings only. *Ryoshi Legian*, Jl Melasti, T761852. Popular Japanese restaurant serving a varied selection of favourites: Sushi, sashimi, noodles, tempura, yakitori, teriyaki, donburi and bento. Open 1100-midnight.

Bars *Bali@CyberCafé and restaurant*, Jl Pura Bagus, Taruna, T361761326, hchua@ idola.net.id, http://www.singnet.com.sg/~hchua/café.htm The first internet café on Bali, with 3 networked PCs, scanner, laser printer, colour printer etc. Also serves cheap food. An off-shoot of the Singapore café. *Do Drop Inn*, Jl Legian.

Shopping **Handicrafts** 'Antiques' and Indonesian fabrics at the north end of Jl Legian. **Swimwear and sportswear** Several good shops on Jl Legian and side streets.

Tour operators *Perama*, Jl Padma, for travel agent services. *Bali Jaran Jaran Kensana*, Logi Gardens Hotel, T975298, organize pony trekking around Tabanan, daily rate per person US$55, including hotel pick-up, tuition, buffet lunch, insurance.

Directory **Banks** Branch of *Lippo* bank and plenty of money changers along Jl Legian. **Embassies & consulates** Switzerland, c/o *Swiss Restaurant*, Jl Pura Bagus Taruna, T751735.

Tuban

Phone code: 0361 Although quieter and more up-market than Kuta, Tuban is still fairly built up. Lying just north of the airport and south of Kuta, the town is spread along busy Jl Kartika Plaza, and one of its main attractions is the convenience of its close proximity to the airport. At the lower end of the market, Tuban represents poor value compared to the Kuta/Legian area. There is a string of up-market hotels overlooking the bay beside a reasonable sandy beach, which cater mainly to tour groups. Tucked down side streets away from the beach are some budget places to stay, which would be convenient if you arrive late at night or have an early airport departure. There is limited access to the beach down a few public paths between the big hotels; the most useful path is on the extreme left, just inside the entrance to the *Bali Dynasty Hotel*. The large hotels have pools, sports and recreation facilities, and most also have organized cultural activities.

AL *Bali Dynasty Resort*, Jl Kartika Plaza, PO Box 2047, T752403, F752402; 225 rooms, all with usual facilities, free-form pool with kiddies section, poolside bar and restaurant, Chinese restaurant, tennis, promotion rates sometimes available, good value food, ideal for families. **AL** *Holiday Inn Bali Hai*, Jl Wana Segara 33, T753035, F754548 195 rooms, complimentary airport transfer, spacious rooms with a/c, fridge, tea and coffee-making facilities, some rooms with disabled facilities, pleasant shady pool with swim-up bar, kiddy pool, tennis, fitness centre, watersports facilities. **AL** *Ramada Bintang Bali*, Jl Kartika Plaza, T753292, F753288; 400 rooms, 5-star facilities, disabled facilities, fitness centre, pool, kids pool, bar, 5 restaurants including *Coconut Wharf* (recommended for Italian food), tennis, children's playground, all rooms a/c, minibar, balcony. **AL** *Santika Beach*, Jl Kartika Plaza, T751267, F751260, santika@denpasar.wasantara.net.id A/c, restaurants, 2 pools, tennis, rather featureless but pleasant enough. **AL-A** *Risata Bali Resor*, Jl Jenggala, T753340, F753354. Bustling with tour groups, despite being less attractive and less good value than some other nearby hotels. 146 rooms with the usual facilities: a/c, HW, IDD, TV, fridge, tropical gardens, pool, restaurant etc. Balinese stage for weekly cultural programme. Not beside the sea, 5 mins' walk to beach.

A *Bali Garden*, Jl Kartika Plaza, PO Box 1101, T752725, F753851. A/c, restaurant, pool, extensive facilities. **A** *Bali Rani*, Jl Kartika Plaza, PO Box 1034, T751369, F752673. One of the latest additions to the Tuban area, 104 rooms, each with a/c, satellite TV, in-house movie, minibar,

Sleeping
All rooms with private bathroom & Western toilet unless otherwise stated

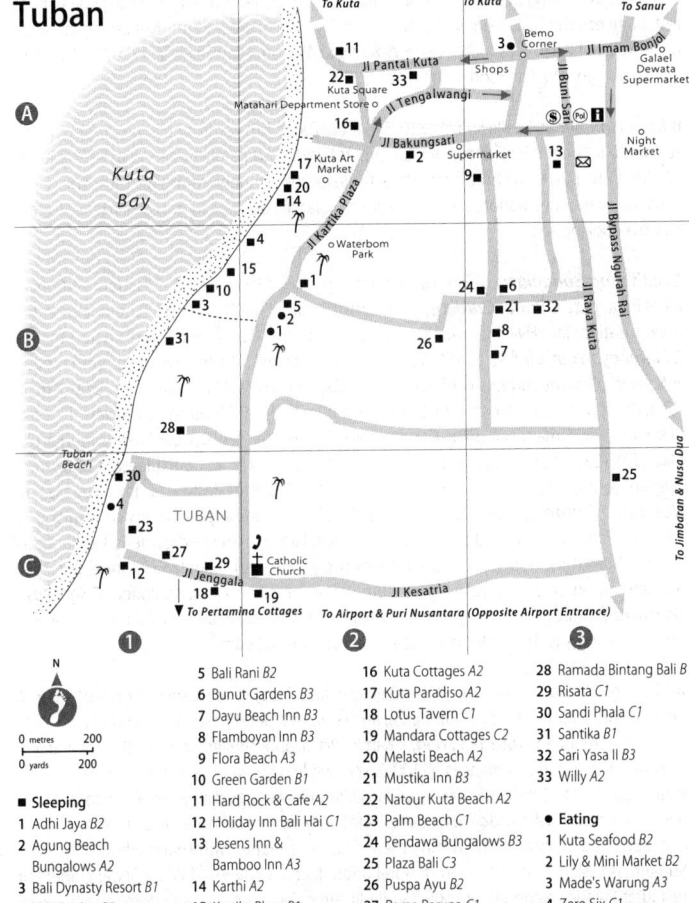

Tuban

❶
5 Bali Rani *B2*
6 Bunut Gardens *B3*
7 Dayu Beach Inn *B3*
8 Flamboyan Inn *B3*
9 Flora Beach *A3*
10 Green Garden *B1*
11 Hard Rock & Cafe *A2*
12 Holiday Inn Bali Hai *C1*
13 Jesens Inn & Bamboo Inn *A3*
14 Karthi *A2*
15 Kartika Plaza *B1*

❷
16 Kuta Cottages *A2*
17 Kuta Paradiso *A2*
18 Lotus Tavern *C1*
19 Mandara Cottages *C2*
20 Melasti Beach *A2*
21 Mustika Inn *B3*
22 Natour Kuta Beach *A2*
23 Palm Beach *C1*
24 Pendawa Bungalows *B3*
25 Plaza Bali *C3*
26 Puspa Ayu *B2*
27 Rama Baruna *C1*

❸
28 Ramada Bintang Bali *B1*
29 Risata *C1*
30 Sandi Phala *C1*
31 Santika *B1*
32 Sari Yasa II *B3*
33 Willy *A2*

● Eating
1 Kuta Seafood *B2*
2 Lily & Mini Market *B2*
3 Made's Warung *A3*
4 Zero Six *C1*

■ Sleeping
1 Adhi Jaya *B2*
2 Agung Beach Bungalows *A2*
3 Bali Dynasty Resort *B1*
4 Bali Garden *B2*

balcony, facilities include free-form pool and children's pool, Chinese restaurant, French bakery, pub. **A** *Dayu Beach Inn*, off Jl Kartika Plaza, T752263. 19 clean rooms with a/c or fan, HW, small pool, bar. **A** *Green Garden*, Jl Kartika Plaza 9, T754570; 25 comfortable, tiled rooms with wood furniture, a/c, fridge, TV, balcony overlooking small pool with waterfall, good Chinese seafood restaurant. **A** *Kartika Plaza*, Jl Kartika Plaza, PO Box 3084, T751067, F752475. A/c, 5 restaurants, large pool, part of the *Aerowisata* chain, facilities include squash courts, tennis, fitness centre, huge reception, some cottage-style accommodation. **A** *Kuta Paradiso Hotel*, formerly *Sol Paradiso* (no longer part of Sol Group), T761414, F756944, kutapar@denpasar.wasantara.net.id Primarily for tour groups. Usual facilities, pool, a/c, restaurant. **A** *Palm Beach Resor*, Jl Pantai Banjar Segara 1, T751661/2/752431, F752432; 99 bright rooms with pretty views and the usual facilities: a/c, HW, TV, fridge etc. Set in peaceful gardens with pool, 5 mins' walk from beach. Rate includes breakfast. **A** *Pendawa Bungalows*, off Jl Kartika Plaza, T752387, T/F757777. Down a lane leading away from the beach, just south of the Kartika Plaza, 38 clean rooms, the cheapest of which are a bit grim, all with private bathroom and Western toilet. A/c or fan, some cold water only. Set in pretty gardens with very small pool. Tax and breakfast extra. A bit overpriced these days. **A** *Putra Jasa*, Jl Kuta Beach, PO Box 3121, T751161. Formerly *Pertamina Cottages*, 5-star hotel, a/c, satellite TV, minibar, restaurants including the *Borsalino* for Italian food and *Yashi*, a Japanese restaurant, pool, children's pool, good sports facilities, rooms arranged in rather dated villas (4 rooms/villa), suites available. **A** *Hotel Rama Baruna*, Jl Jenggala (formerly Jl Wana Segara), T751557, F751768. One of the better hotels catering to the tour group market. Usual facilities: HW, a/c, tropical gardens, pool, restaurant etc. Open air Balinese theatre for weekly cultural programme. Not beside the sea, 4 mins' walk to beach. Reasonable value. **A-B** *Puspa Ayu*, off Jl Kartika Plaza, T756721. 15 rooms with a/c or fan, HW. Fan rooms a bit gloomy. Overpriced.

B *Karthi Inn*, Jl Kartika Plaza, T754810, F751708. Dated but comfortable, a/c, TV, pool with sunken bar, open-air Chinese restaurant. **B** *Sandi Phala*, off Jl Jenggala, T753708/9, F754889. The best value hotel with a beachside location, though rooms are rather plain and could do with redecoration, a/c, HW. Peaceful location, pool set in grassy gardens. Restaurant overlooking sea.

C *Alit's Kuta Bungalows*, Jl Puri Gerenceng, Tuban, T751968, F288766, 35 rooms. Convenient for airport. **C** *Bunut Gardens*, off Jl Kartika Plaza, T752971, 974732. 8 average rooms in quiet location; fan, HW, nice views from upstairs room. Also 4 rooms with shared mandi. **C** *Flamboyan Inn*, off Jl Kartika Plaza, T/F752610. 15 clean and attractive rooms with a/c and HW set in pleasant gardens with very small pool, 15 mins' walk to beach across busy main road. Overpriced on the rack rate, but price is negotiable. **C** *Mandara Cottages*, Jl Kartika Plaza, T751775. Small pool, open-air bathrooms. Recommended. **C** *Mustika Inn*, off Jl Kartika Plaza, T753298. The nicest of the budget places, 4 clean new rooms with pleasant views from upstairs rooms. No garden. Price includes continental breakfast, 10% tax extra. **C** *Puri Nusantara Cottages*, Jl Raya Tuban 56, T752996. Right by the airport, so very convenient, 35 spotless rooms, with fan and cold water only, set in large well-tended gardens. Left luggage facility. Prompt pick-up service to and from the airport, usually only up until about 2200 (depending on when the driver goes home). Price includes morning coffee. **C** *Sari Yasa Beach Inn II* (though some way from the beach!), off Jl Kartika Plaza, T752825. Basic, not very attractive rooms with private bathroom, 15 mins' walk to beach.

Eating **Mid-range** *Kaisar*, Jl Kartika Plaza, Balinese and Indonesian dishes. *Coconut Wharf*, *Bintang Bali*, Jl Kartika Plaza, poolside Italian restaurant, good pasta dishes, pizza and cocktails. Recommended. *Kuta Sea Food*, Jl Kartika Plaza, opposite *Bintang Bali*, theatre and restaurant, dancing performances (2100-2200) while you dine – mostly Chinese food, steamboat and seafood basket are popular, children's menu available, a definite tourist spot and a little grubby with it. *Bali Sea Food*, Jl Kartika Plaza, next door to *Kuta Sea Food*, similar in concept, but a bit cleaner, interesting menu features snapper with Thai sauce, Bali fish with Sumatra dressing, free pick-up from hotel offered. *Lotus Tavern*, Jl Wana Segara, open-air restaurant under alang-alang roof, candle-lit after dark, good salads, home-made pasta, wood-oven pizza, friendly atmosphere, pick-up from hotel offered. Recommended. *Metro Club*, Jl Kartika Plaza, more of a nightclub than restaurant, with happy hour from 1600 to 1900, wide range of dishes from Mexican tacos to Indonesian satay. *Zero Six*, T753196. Good location on beach in quiet area. Italian, Indonesian, Chinese and Western food, including pizza, fish and New Zealand steak.

Cheap *Croissants de France*, Jl Kartika Plaza, French bakery serves breakfast and snacks 0700-1100.

O'Brien's Fun Pub, *Holiday Inn Bali Hai*, a 'sporty' pub, open 1700-0100, happy hour 1800-1900.

Bars

Disco *BB Discotheque*, *Bintang Bali Hotel*, 1900-0200, fashion shows every Tue and Fri; *Waves Discotheque*, *Bali Dynasty Hotel*.

Entertainment

Kuta Square Relatively new shopping precinct on the boundary with Kuta, with a range of Western designer boutiques, internet cafés, restaurants, and a large Matahari department store and supermarket (this is the best place to get fresh fruit, no bargaining and prices are better than the market).

Shopping

Plaza Bali, department store, duty-free shop (selection of perfumes and cosmetics, clothing and pricy liquor), restaurant, venue for Balinese dancing.

Diving *Bali Dolphin Divers*, *Bali Garden Hotel*, Jl Kartika Plaza, T752725. They also provide fishing, parasailing, jet-skiing and water-skiing facilities. *OMI Dives*, Kompleks Ruko, Indah Permai Blok C5, Jl By Pass Ngurah Rai, T757484, F772982. Diving tours locally and on islands, US$65-95 for the day including 2 tanks, lunch box, instruction and insurance.

Sports
All the big hotels along Jl Kartika Plaza have watersports facilities, pools & tennis courts

Swimming *Waterbom Park*, Jl Kartika Plaza, T755676, F753517, waterbom@ denpasar.wasantara.net.id Within walking distance of Tuban hotels, open daily 0900-1800, over 600m of water slides, water volleyball, spa offering traditional massage etc, gardens, restaurant, lockers and towels for hire (children under 12 must be accompanied by an adult).

Surya Candra, Jl Wana Segara 25x, T754557, sightseeing around Bali, car rental.

Tour operators

Air Airline reservations: *Garuda* at *Natour Hotel*, on boundary with Kuta (see Kuta section).

Transport

Banks Bank opposite the *Bintang Bali*, money changers along Jl Kartika Plaza and Jl Wana Segara, most hotels change money too, but rates are not so good. **Places of worship** Sunday school for children every Sun 1100, *Kuta Retreat House*, Tuban. **Useful addresses Immigration**: south of town on the road to the airport, Jl Ngurah Rai, Tuban, T751038. **Police station**: Jl By-Pass, Tuban, T751598.

Directory

Seminyak

Phone code: 0361

This area to the north of Legian begins at Jl Double Six and runs northwards into unspoilt ricefields. With a fabulous coastline, spectacular sunsets and views of the mountains of North Bali on a clear day, it is still relatively quiet and unspoilt. However, month by month more development appears.

There is good surfing, but be warned: the sea here can be lethal. There are strong undercurrents and riptides – and no lifeguards.

Travelling north from Seminyak, you pass through **Petitenget** with its large temple made of white coral (covered in moss, so not looking white at all). Further north still, the village of **Batubelig** is in an undeveloped area, with a luxury hotel and a small guesthouse; again this is a surfing rather than swimming beach. Unless you are a keen walker, you will probably need to hire a car if staying in this area.

Sleeping

- Legian map, page 333. Accommodation in Seminyak often includes a kitchen & long-stay rates are frequently available

Long a favoured haunt of ex-pats, particularly those involved in the export of furniture, crafts and garments, some of the accommodation in Seminyak is in bungalows and houses available to rent monthly or long term. Look for signs along the streets, notices in the *Wartel* on Jl Dhyanapura or the small number of real estate agents. For shorter stays there are only a handful of budget accommodation options, with most properties in the mid to upper range. There are several real estate agencies that provide longstay and holiday rentals. *Intouch*, Jl Raya Seminyak 22, T731047/8, F730683, intouch@denpasar.wasantara.net.id They handle holiday rentals, sales and leasing. Also check out Rudy's Wartel in Jl Dhyanapura, which has a useful travellers' information board including accommodation, particularly long-stay bungalows in Seminyak area.

L *Puri Ratih*, Jl Puri Ratih, PO Box 1114, T751546, F751549, Seminyak. A/c, restaurant, pool, all suites, with own kitchen, living-room and garden, excellent facilities, owned by RCI, the timeshare group. **L** *The Legian*, Jl Lasmana, Seminyak, T730622, F730623, legian@gmhhotels.com Tall (far too tall), ugly building, a real blot on the coastal landscape of Seminyak. Built in 1997. Expensive, 70 large suites with well equipped kitchenette, elegant but rather dark and austere, all facing the sea. Pool, restaurant, bar, spa. Part of the Chedi group of hotels. **L-AL** *Bali Imperial*, Jl Dhyanapura, T754545, F751545. A/c, restaurant, pools, tennis, on a beachfront plot, with 121 luxurious rooms and one of the most inviting swimming pools in South Bali. **L-AL** *Bali Oberoi*, Jl Kayu Aya, PO Box 3351, T730361, F730791. North end of Legian on a peaceful stretch of sandy beach, surrounded by 5 ha of formal gardens. Built in 1972, the Oberoi was one of Bali's 1st luxury class hotels. The Luxury Lanai rooms are 4 independent rooms under 1 roof, with the expected facilities including a luxurious marble finished bathroom, complete with sunken bath, that opens onto a small, walled garden. Luxury villas are also available, some with private pools, resort facilities including pool (no paddling pool), health club, tennis, small amphitheatre for regular Balinese performances, 2 restaurants. Recommended.

AL *Villa Lumbung Hotel*, Jl Raya Petitenget 1000X, Petitenget, Batubelig, T730204, F731106. In a very peaceful location just north of Seminyak. 18 rooms in 2-storey *lumbung* style bungalows with thatched roofs, and 2 villas (with 3 bedrooms, living room and kitchen in private garden), scattered around pretty tropical gardens, built in 1997. Attractive décor; downstairs rooms have open-air bathrooms. A/c, HW, restaurant, bar, free-form swimming pool, 15 mins' walk to beach. **AL-A** *Ananda Bungalows*, Jl Kayu Aya, Basangkasa, north of Seminyak, T730526, F731563, aps@indo.net.id Newly built in Balinese village style, in peaceful setting on the northern edge of Seminyak, 1 and 2-storey bungalows with living room, kitchen, verandah and small private garden, a/c in bedroom only. Rooms are darkish and rather plain. Pretty gardens, smallish free-form pool. Nice views over ricefields from upstairs rooms which are brighter, 10 mins' walk to beach. Price negotiable, includes breakfast. **AL-A** *Bali Agung Village*, Jl Dhyanapura, T730367, F730469; 32 attractively decorated bungalows in beautiful tropical gardens with small pool. A/c, HW, fridge, IDD, restaurant, bar, cultural performances. Peaceful location on northern edge of Seminyak, 15 mins' walk to beach. Popular with specialist tour companies, therefore often full. **AL-A** *Ramah Village*, Gang Keraton, off Jl. Raya Legian, Seminyak, T/F731071/730793 (in Hamburg, Germany: T+49-40-221048, F221175), Balirama@jad.telkom.net.id In a quiet location beside a single remaining ricefield, down a small lane off Jl Legian. Beginning to show its age. 16 bungalows, some with 2 bedrooms, set in verdant gardens. Fan only, HW, kitchen, large verandah, fairly clean. Plunge pool. Long-stay rates available, 20 mins' walk to beach. Tax and breakfast extra. **AL-A** *Resor Seminyak*, formerly *Pesona Bali*, Jl Lasmana, Seminyak, T730814, F730815, pesonahti@indosat.net.id Built in 1988, peaceful location beside sea. Two-storey building set in extensive gardens, only the deluxe rooms have sea view. A/c, pool, 24 hr restaurant. Strong currents make swimming dangerous directly in front of the hotel. **AL-A** *Villa Kresna*, Jl Sarinade 19, off Jl Dhyanapura, T730317, F732847. Newly built, 2 rooms, 5 suites and 2 villas in a small, slightly cramped compound with small pool. A/c or fan, most with HW, unusual but pleasant hand-painted pastel décor. German owner, coffee shop serving German and international food, 3 mins' walk to beach. A little overpriced. **AL-A** *Villa Lalu*, off Jl Legian (opposite Alus Alum Supermarket), Seminyak, T731051, F731052, vilalalu@dps.mega.net.id 7 studios (5 without kitchens), very tastefully furnished, single-storey villas in very peaceful location, set around open gardens and good-sized pool. Large, bright rooms, well-equipped kitchen, a/c and fan, HW, IDD, TV, verandah, 24-hr childcare service, 20 mins' walk to beach. Recommended.

A *Century Saphir Bali Hotel*, Jl Abimanyu (also known as Jl Dhyanapura), Seminyak, T730573, F730518, saphir@dps.mega.net.id Clean, mid-range, typical tour group hotel, 127 rooms, 2 restaurants, pool, 24-hr room service, spa, tennis court, 10 mins' walk to beach. **A** *Dhyana Pura Hotel*, Jl Dhyanapura, T730442, F730463, dhyana-p@indosat.net.id 125 rooms, older rooms are a bit drab, a/c, HW, fridge, IDD. Pool, large gardens. Free airport transfers and shuttle to Kuta. Restaurant, bar, 24-hr room service. Conference facilities for up to 300 people, 10 mins' walk to beach. Nothing special. **A** *Peter's Place* (as yet unnamed, though may be called *Puri Manis*), next to *Oberoi Hotel*, T733255. 3 bungalows set in gardens with swimming pool, 3 mins' walk to beach. Fantastic value, but usually full with long-stay guests who pay up to 5,000,000Rp a month, or 1,000,000-1,500,000Rp a week (Peter doesn't take advance bookings). **A** *Raja Gardens*, Jl Camplung Tanduk off Jl Dhyanapura, T730494, F732805. 6 attractive, Balinese style rooms, set in lovely gardens with good-sized pool. Fan and cold water only. Not directly on beach, 3 mins' walk down path. Price does not include tax or breakfast. A bit overpriced. **A** *Sarinade Beach Inn*, Jl Sarinade 15, off Jl Dhyanapura, T730383/733604, F733605. 14 rather plain rooms, a/c or fan, HW, TV, minibar. Central, rather cramped courtyard, with pool but no garden. Restaurant, free airport transfers and shuttle to Kuta, 3 mins to beach. Price includes tax and breakfast. Overpriced, but may be negotiable down to 140,000Rp for a double. **A-B** *Bunga Seminyak Cottages*, Jl Camplung Tanduk off Jl Dhyanapura, T730239, F730905. 7 rooms and suites in good beachside location, set in pretty gardens with smallish pool. Rooms vary enormously, the suites are large and attractively decorated with marble bathrooms, whereas the rooms are rather small and drab. Cold water only, a/c. Price negotiable. Good value for the best rooms, price includes continental breakfast and tax. **A-B** *Hotel Puri Cendana*, Jl Dhyanapura, T730869, F730868. 6 cottages consisting of 24 rooms, 12 of which are 2-storey with living room downstairs and bedroom upstairs, all with a/c, mosquito net, HW. Set in tropical gardens with pool (only open between 1100 and 1900), restaurant, 4 mins' walk to beach. Breakfast and tax extra. **A-B** *Taman Ayu Cottage*, Jl Pantai Petitenget, Kerobokan, T730111/2, F730113. In quiet village location north of Seminyak, surrounded by ricefields (at the moment, but no doubt earmarked for future development). 41 rooms, clean but in need of some redecoration, a/c, HW, TV, balcony or verandah. Upstairs rooms have good views. Pool, restaurant, bar, 15 mins' walk to beach. Price negotiable.

B-C *Bali Reski Asih*, Jl Sari Dewi, T731045/6, F730342, 483359. In quiet location, 400m from tarmac road down rough track. 16 rooms with fan, some with HW or kitchens. Pretty gardens, pool. Price includes tax but not breakfast.

C *Kesuma Sari*, Jl Sarinade off Jl Dhyanapura, T233601, 730575. 6 rooms, not particularly attractive, in cramped grounds; rooms are clean and bright but in need of redecoration, 5 mins' walk to beach. **C** *Pandawa Bungalows*, Jl Raya Seminyak 36 B, T730359. 5 well-maintained, 2-storey bungalows, set in pretty gardens just off the main road. Upstairs bedroom, downstairs living room, bathroom, cold water only, fan. Good value, often full. **C-D** *Mesari Beach Inn*, Jl Camplung Tanduk off Jl Dhyanapura, T/F730401. This must be the best value in Seminyak. 10 rooms and bungalows right on the beach, set in large, well-tended gardens. No pool. Fairly basic, but a great location.

D *Ned's Hideaway*, Gang Bima 3 (off Jl Legian), T/F731270. Down a quiet lane off the main Legian/Seminyak road. Excellent value traveller's budget accommodation. 14 clean, simple rooms with HW, fan, bathroom, in a 2-storey block. Set in pretty garden with restaurant and bar, 20 mins' walk to beach. Price includes tax and breakfast.

Long stay (monthly rates only) *Sari Uma Cottages*, Jl Sarinade 3, Seminyak, T/F730916, 730496, Cell0811392808. 5 bungalows with 2 bedrooms, fully equipped kitchen, living room, 12 mins' walk to beach. Price includes gardener and maid service. Coffee shop on the premises, 5,000,000 Rp per month. **A** (per night) *Pondok Sarah* (sign just north of Jl Double Six), T732142, F732143. 14 very attractive, newly built bungalows with 1, 2 or 3 bedrooms, kitchen, living room, fan, hot water and small plunge pool. Peaceful location in north Legian. Italian owned. *Rudy's Wartel* on Jl Dhyanapura has a useful travellers' information board, with information on accommodation including long-stay bungalows.

Sleeping in Batubelig **AL** *Balisani Suites*, Jl Batubelig, Kerobokan, T730550, F730141, balisani@dps.mega.net.id 126 rooms and suites in peaceful seaside location. Built in Balinese village style, attractively decorated. Swimming pool, 4 restaurants and bars. Free shuttle to Kuta and airport transfers. **A** *Intan Bali Village*, PO Box 1089, Batubelig Beach, T752191, F752475. A/c, several restaurants, 2 pools, extensive sports facilities, large central block with some bungalow accommodation. Caters almost exclusively to tour groups, with little to attract the independent traveller. **B** *Batubelig Beach Bungalows*, Jl Batubelig 228, Kerobokan, T30078. 3 well-built and attractively furnished thatched roof bungalows, with kitchen, large bedroom and bathroom, HW, a/c, set in garden. Peaceful location 3 mins' walk to beach. Breakfast not included in rates. Longstay rates available. *Sastika Restaurant* on premises, very cheap and good value.

Eating **Mid-range** *Kafe Warisan*, Jl Raya Kerobokan (the continuation of Jl Legian north of Seminyak), T731175. Expensive restaurant set in an area of diminishing paddy fields, serving excellent French and Mediterranean food. Open for lunch, but more romantic for candlelit dinners. *Cin Cin*, Jl Dhyana Pura, friendly open-air restaurant on roadside, good salads, emphasis on German dishes, pool for use of clients. *La Lucciola*, Jl Kayu Aya, on the beach, most people go here for the fantastic setting, especially the sunset views. Primarily Italian food. Open until 2300. *Poco Loco*, Jl Padma Utara, terraced Mexican restaurant. *Ryoshi Seminyak*, Jl Raya Seminyak (the northern continuation of Jl Legian), T731152. Popular Japanese restaurant serving a varied selection of favourites: sushi, sashimi, noodles, tempura, yakitori, teriyaki, donburi and bento. Open 1100-midnight.

Cheap *Kin Khao Thai*, Jl Seminyak 37, authentic Thai food (with Thai chef), reasonably priced, modest portions. *Raja Laut*, Jl Dhyanapura. Good, primarily seafood restaurant, also serving Indonesian and Western dishes at reasonable prices. *Café BL*, Jl Dhyanapura. T732169, 732917. Good, reasonably priced food, artistically presented. Fish, Indonesian, European.

Directory **Communications** Several *Wartel* in the area, one of the best is *Rudy's* on Jl Dhyanapura.

Canggu

This area of coastline, only 20 minutes north of Legian, is slowly being developed and (at the moment) offers peace and rural tranquillity, traditional villages untouched by tourism, and frequent ceremonies and festivals at one of its many temples or on the beach.

Canggu district offers unspoilt, grey sand beaches, with the possibility of excellent surfing (easy 1-2m-high waves off left- and right-hand reef breaks), as well as swimming. The following beaches are all part of Canggu: Pererean, Banjartengah, Canggu, Tegal Gundul, Padang Linjong, Batu Bulong and Berewa. The villages from which the beaches draw their names are inland and most offer simple homestays, just ask around, local people are very friendly and helpful.

The drive to Canggu is very beautiful as you pass endless lush green paddy fields, coconut and banana palms, cows grazing, and only the occasional picturesque, small village full of temples and shrines.

Pererean Beach A completely undeveloped stretch of beach, with only **D** *Sunset Club Losmen*, 4 simple rooms with large, attached bathroom with Western toilet, breakfast and tax not included, upstairs restaurant (very cheap) with good views of coast, very peaceful and unspoilt. **Canggu Beach** A hotel will be open by the time this guide is published.

Sleeping

To reach Canggu you will need your own transport. Follow the main road north from Legian until you pick up signs for Canggu. The beach signposted 'Canggu Beach' is in fact Pererean Beach. To reach 'Canggu Beach' itself, turn left at the T-junction in Canggu village and keep going to the beach. If in doubt, ask for directions.

Transport

Berewa Beach

A very peaceful location (the drive from Kuta takes about 30-45 minutes; as yet there is no coast road) with an unspoilt beach backing onto ricefields, friendly local people and few tourists. There are a few unpretentious restaurants hoping to attract tourists from the local hotels; except during high season, these are usually only open for dinner. There are also a few small shops near the hotels. The main temple is 'Pura Dang Khayangan'; there has been a temple here since the 16th century.

Swimming in the sea here can be dangerous

These 3 hotels cater primarily for tour groups. With attractive and very peaceful locations beside the sea, they all offer the usual facilities: private bathrooms, a/c, TV, poolside bars etc. Prices should be negotiable off-season. Breakfast and tax extra. **AL** *Villa Ani Ani*, T/F65-755-2588, F755-3315, evilldes@singnet.com.sg 4 secluded villas in a private compound with swimming pool and open-air eating pavilion. Set in tropical gardens, each villa is well decorated in traditional Balinese style. 3 bedrooms, kitchen, bathroom a/c. Fully staffed including resident chef. **A-AL** *Dewata Beach Hotel*, Banjar Berewa, Desa Canggu 80361, PO Box 3271, Denpasar 80032, T0361-730263, F0361-730290, dewatabh@indo.net.id 168 rooms and suites. Facilities include swimming pool, tennis courts and children's playground, massage, reasonably priced restaurants, bars, theatre for Balinese dances. Free shuttle bus to Kuta. **A** *Bolare Beach Bungalows*, PO Box 3256 80, 032 Denpasar, T/F0361-730258. Probably the best value, rather ornate rooms with a/c, bathroom etc, could do with a little maintenance, facilities include restaurant, swimming pool etc. **A** *Legong Keraton Beach Cottages*, PO Box 617, Kuta, T0361-730280, F730285. Very ornate rooms, not to everyone's taste, restaurant, swimming pool, free airport transfer.

Sleeping

Horse riding at Umelas Village Horse riding is available at Umelas Stable north of Seminyak, in a rural area beside the sea. Jl Lestari No 9x, Br Umalas, Kerobokan, T0361-731402, F731403. Lessons for all abilities from beginners to advanced including dressage; 1-3 hr treks through the ricefields or along the beach at sunset. Tours include hotel pick-up and US$25,000 insurance. Prices from US$25 for an hour's group trek to US$70 for a 3-hr individual trek. Dressage/beginners lesson: US$25/30 for group/individual.

Sport

Sanur

The first of Bali's international resorts, Sanur falls midway between the elegant, upmarket Nusa Dua and the frenetic, youthful Kuta. Attracting a more sedate, middle-aged clientele, many on package tours, Sanur's attractions are its white sand beach, restaurants and shopping. This is also a centre for watersports with surfing, snorkelling by Serangan Island, and diving. Noticeably more expensive than Kuta, hotels tend to be mid-range to upmarket, though there are some pretty, more reasonably priced small guesthouses and an increasing number of cheaper homestays. Nightlife here does not compare to that of Kuta, although there are outstanding restaurants and several discos. The road parallel to the beach is lined with money changers, tourist shops (selling clothing and jewellery), tour companies, car rental outlets and shipping agents.

Phone code: 0361

Sights

Kite flying is a popular activity, especially in Aug, when strong trade winds are blowing & competitions take place. Teams gather with huge kites that require the united effort of several men to launch

The **Le Mayeur Museum** is just to the north of the *Bali Beach Hotel* and is named after the famous Belgian artist Adrien Yean Le Mayeur, who arrived in Bali in 1932. He was immediately captivated by the culture and beauty of the island, made Sanur his home and married a local beauty, Ni Polok, in 1935. He died in 1958. The museum contains his collection of local artefacts and some of Le Mayeur's work. The interior is dark and rather dilapidated, making the pieces difficult to view – a great shame because Le Mayeur's impressionistic works are full of tropical sunlight and colour. Le Mayeur's paintings were a great influence on a number of Balinese artists, including the highly regarded I Gusti Nyoman Nodya. ■ *Small admission charge. 0800-1400 Tue-Thu and Sun, 0800-1100 Fri, 0800-1200 Sat.*

Temples made of coral are dotted along Sanur beach. The presence of primitive, pyramid-shaped structures at many of these temples suggests their origin dates back to prehistoric times. At the southern, south-facing end of Sanur beach is the **Pura Mertasari**, a small temple under a canopy of trees which is considered to harbour exceptionally powerful forces of black magic. The *odalan* festival of this temple falls at the most favoured time in the Balinese calendar, two weeks after the Spring equinox. An unusual ritual trance dance, the *baris cina* (Chinese dance), is performed on the night of the festival. The dancers wear old Dutch army helmets and bayonets and the evening can end with a dramatically violent dance movement. A nearby village, **Singhi**, is home to the Black Barong, the most powerful Barong in Bali, made from the black feathers of a sacred, rare bird.

On a clear day there are fantastic views of several mountain ranges to the north, including Mount Agung and Mount Batur, especially beautiful at sunset and sunrise. There is a path running along the beach for the entire length of Sanur, though in places it is beginning to collapse. The beach varies in width along its length and disappears completely in some places; it is at its best in front of the *Grand Bali Beach Hotel*, *The Hyatt*, an area that includes the *Tanjung Sari* and adjacent hotels, and at the southern end. At Batu Jimbar, where the ex-pat crowd have built their beautiful seaside villas, the beach disappears completely. There are several roads and tracks leading down to the beach from Jl Danau Tamblingan along its length, including Jl Pantai Karang, where the German consul is situated, and Jl Segara Ayu.

Excursions

Serangan Island or Turtle Island is, as the name suggests, famous for its turtles which are caught in the surrounding sea, raised in pens, and then slaughtered for their meat – which explains why they are becoming rarer by the year. The formerly common green turtle is now said to be virtually extinct in the area. The beaches on the east coast of the island are best, with offshore coral providing good snorkelling. One of Bali's most important coastal temples is the **Pura Sakenan** in Sakenan village, at the north end of the island. Pura Sakenan's *odalan* or anniversary festival, held at Kuningan (the 210th day of the Balinese calendar), is thought by many to be one of the best on Bali. ■ *Getting there: boats can be chartered from Sanur or from Nusa Dua and Benoa. Usually visitors leave from a jetty just south of Kampung Mesigit and 2 km southwest of Sanur. From here there are regular public boats to Serangan Island; the problem is that tourists are often forced to charter a boat for far more; share if possible and bargain furiously. It is easier, and often just as cheap, to go on a tour. It is also possible to wade out to the island at low tide.*

Nusa Lembongan (see page 350) lies just off the coast. ■ *Boats leave every morning for the island from close to the Bali Beach Hotel, 1 hr (17,000Rp). Perama now run a boat service to the island, departing twice a day in high season at 1030 and 1630, in low season usually only the morning departure. The 27 km crossing takes about 40 mins. Departures from Nusa Lembongan are at 0900 and 1500 in high season. Perama office in Sanur is at Pino Restaurant, T287594.*

Tours

The major hotels on the beach all have tour companies which organize the usual range of tours: for example, to **Lake Bratan** (where water-skiing can be arranged); to

The plight of turtles on Bali and Lombok

Although the Muslims of Lombok do not eat turtle meat they do eat the eggs. On neighbouring Bali, turtle meat is considered a great delicacy; it is made into satay and lawar (a Balinese speciality consisting of ground meat, blood and spices) and is an important ingredient in the ceremonial feasts that accompany religious festivals. Up to 25,000 green turtles a year used to be killed for their meat. In 1990, following appeals by the Worldwide Fund for Nature and with the green turtle facing extinction, a law was passed banning fishermen from catching them, except for ceremonial use. However, with a market value over 250,000Rp there is a great temptation to catch them illegally. Hornbill turtles were caught for their shells but since 1992 trade in tortoiseshell has been banned by CITES.

Turtles cover vast distances; some from Southeast Asia have been sighted as far away as Greece, verifiable because of tagging. Turtles return to the beach where they were born to breed; the magnetism of that beach is imprinted in their brains and they know where to return to decades later. Having laid her eggs the mother turtle will dig a second dummy nest in order to deceive predators. Turtle hatchlings will not emerge if the sun is too hot; they wait for the cool air of night. Some research suggests that temperature influences gender with more females being born when the temperature of the nest is hotter. Turtle eggs are softer at one end to allow the hatchlings to break out easily without damaging neighbouring eggs. Even with man's help, when the hatchlings are released into the sea only as few as six out of 200 may survive.

Karangasem and **Tenganan**, to visit a traditional Aga village; to **Ubud**; white-water rafting on the **Agung River**; to the temples of **Tanah Lot** and **Mengwi**; to the **Bali Barat National Park**; to **Besakih Temple**; the *Golden Hawk* tall ship runs day trips to **Lembongan Island** (see page 350), as do *Island Explorer Cruises*, Ena Dive Center, Jl Tirta Ening 1, T287945, F287945, who also organize dolphin tours off Nusa Dua and provide watersports equipment, including PADI diving. *Sobek*, the 'adventure' tour company, are based in Sanur at Jl Tirta Ening 9, T287059. They can arrange bird watching and sporting activities (see 'Sports', page 348).

Sleeping
See map, page 344

Accommodation on Sanur is largely mid- to high-range, though recently a number of new and attractive budget guesthouses have opened along Jl Danau Tamblingan which offer excellent value for money. Much of the guesthouse accommodation is overpriced and disappointing, particularly compared to other parts of Indonesia but also to Bali. Fan rooms are hard to come by as most places have installed a/c in order to charge much higher prices. Prices are frequently geared to European tour groups who form the largest group of visitors; except during high season you should never have to pay more than 50% of the listed price, and even then many places still seem overpriced. Unless otherwise stated, all accommodation includes private bathroom and Western toilet.

L-AL *Tanjung Sari*, Jl Danau Tamblingan, PO Box 3025, Denpasar, T288441, F287930. A/c, restaurant, small pool, 29 bungalows with own sitting-room and outside pavilion, some tastefully decorated, others hideous. Very much in need of renovation and very overpriced. Gardens lead down to reasonable beach. **AL** *Bali Beach*, PO Box 275, Denpasar, T288511, F287917, J320107. North end of the beach, 523 rooms, a/c, restaurant, 3 large pools, 9-hole golf course, 10-pin bowling, tennis. Rooms in the high-rise block are a bit scruffy, though they have lovely sea views. The more recently built bungalows, to the south, are more attractive, though hot water is alleged to be a problem sometimes. Good facilities and fronting an excellent section of beach. Internet access in lobby (expensive). **AL** *Bali Hyatt*, Jl Danau Tamblingan , PO Box 392, T281234, F287693. A/c. This hotel has the best location in Sanur, peaceful, beside an excellent beach and surrounded by 36 acres of exquisite tropical gardens. Two lovely pools, 5 restaurants serving Asian and Western specialities. The hotel is decorated with many pieces of fine Balinese antique furniture and

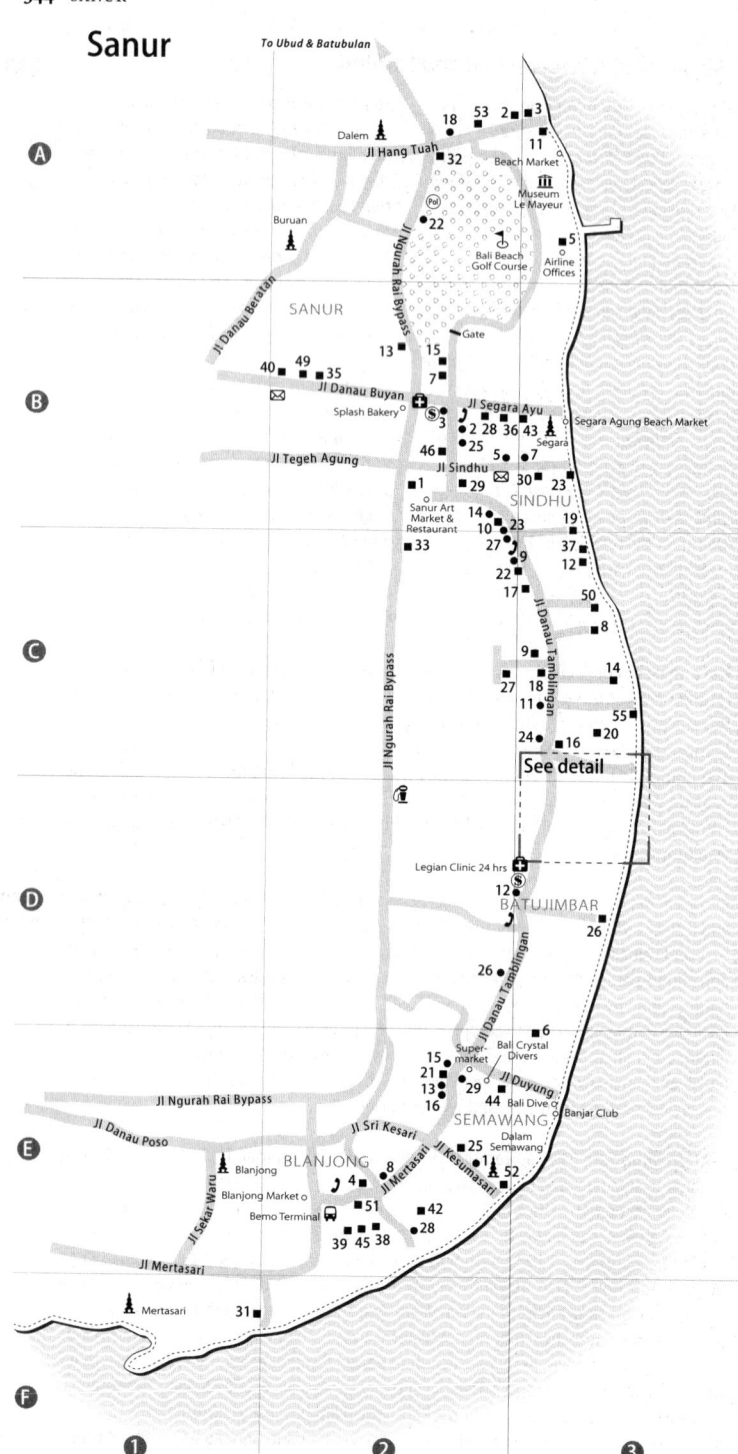

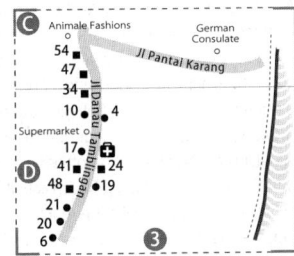

Not to scale

■ **Sleeping**
1 Abian Srama *B2*
2 Alit's Beach Bungalows *A2*
3 Ananda *A3*
4 Ari Putri *E2*
5 Bali Beach *A3*
6 Bali Hyatt *E3*
7 Bali Warma *B2*
8 Besakih Bungalows *C3*
9 Bumas *C3*
10 Coco, Luisa & Yulia Homestays *B2*
11 Diwangkara *A3*
12 Gazebo *C3*
13 Griya Ayu Inn *B2*
14 Griya Santrian Beach *C3*
15 House for rent *B2*
16 Julia Homestay *C3*
17 Kalpathara *C3*
18 Keke Homestay *C3*
19 La Taverna *B3*
20 Laghawa Beach Inn *C3*
21 Lestari Homestay *E2*
22 Made's Pub & Homestay *C3*
23 Natour Sindhu Beach *B3*
24 Orchid Villa *D3*
25 Palm Garden *E2*
26 Paneeda View *D3*
27 Pondok Wisata Prima *C2*
28 Puri Kelapa *B2*
29 Puri Mango Guesthouse *B2*
30 Queen Bali *B3*
31 Raddin *F1*
32 Radisson Bali Indonesia *A2*
33 Radisson Suites *C2*
34 Ramayana *D3*
35 Rani *B2*
36 Ratna *B2*
37 Respati Bali *C3*
38 Santrian *E2*
39 Sanur Beach *E2*
40 Sanur Indah *B2*
41 Sapanami Homestay *D3*
42 Sativa Sanur Cottages *E2*
43 Segara Village *B3*
44 Segara Agung *E2*
45 Semawang Beach *E2*
46 Sumi's Bungalows *B2*
47 Swastika *C3*
48 Taman Agung *D3*
49 Taman Sari *B2*
50 Tanjung Sari *C3*
51 Trophy Ayu & Pub *E2*
52 Villa Kesumasari *E2*
53 Watering Hole Guesthouse & Restaurant *A2*
54 Wirasana *C3*
55 Wisma Werdhapura *C3*

● **Eating**
1 Abian Boga *E2*
2 Bacu Warung *B2*
3 Bahagia's *B2*
4 Bali Indah *D3*
5 Borneo *B2*
6 Café Batu Jimbar *D3*
7 Carlo *B3*
8 Donald's Café *E2*
9 Jak's Kafe *C2*
10 Kaka Tua Warung *D3*
11 Kita *C3*
12 Kul Kul *D3*
13 Legong & Bar *E2*
14 Lotus Pond *B2*
15 Nelayan *E2*
16 Oka's *E2*
17 Penjor *D3*
18 Pino & Perama Bus *A2*
19 Rest & Eat *D3*
20 Ryoshi Sanu *D3*
21 Santai Internet *D3*
22 Several Warung *A2*
23 Swastika *B2*
24 Swastika Garden *C3*
25 Taman Istana *B2*
26 Telaga Naga *D2*
27 The Village *C2*
28 Trattoria da Marco *E2*
29 Warung Agung *E2*

paintings. The Spa has recently been voted one of the world's top 5 spas by *Cosmopolitan* magazine. A wide range of sports activities including tennis, badminton and watersports. A daily programme of cultural activities. *Camp Sanur* provides a full day of activities for children. Recommended. **AL** *Natour Sindhu Beach*, Jl Pantai Sindhu 14, PO Box 181, T288351, F289268, n.sindhu@denpasar.wasantara.net.id 60 darkish, bungalow-style rooms with verandah, large rather plain gardens leading down to beach. Pool, restaurant, a/c, minibar, telephone. **AL** *Puri Santrian and Griya Santrian*, Jl Danau Tamblingan 47 & 63, T288181, F288185, santrian@denpasar.wasantara.net.id 190 (60 newly built) rooms, a/c, fridge, 2 pools, several restaurants, watersports. Right on a good stretch of beach. **AL** *Raddin Hotel*, Jl Mertasari, T288833, F287303, 287772, radsanur@indosat.net.id Situated at the southern end of Sanur on a good white sand beach. 195 attractive rooms in 3-storey lumbung style bungalows (a separate room on each floor), with the usual facilities. 2 pools, tennis court, watersports. 3 reasonably priced restaurants and a bar. **AL** *Radisson Suites*, Jl Bypass Ngurah Rai 83, Sanur, T281481, F281482; 84, 1, 2 and 3 bedrooms, fully furnished apartments in a secure resort setting, ideal for families and self-catering. Set around attractive landscaped gardens and pool. Restaurant, poolside BBQ, fitness centre, laundry and self-service launderette, minimart, underground car park. Room service and grocery delivery. A/c, modern kitchen, satellite TV, IDD tel. Kids Club. Guests have full privileges at the *Radisson Hotel*. Free shuttle bus linking hotel, suites and beach. **AL** *Sanur Beach*, Jl Danau Tamblingan, PO Box 3276, T288011, F287566, sanurbch@indosat.net.id South end of beach, a/c, several restaurants (fish restaurant recommended), 2 lovely pools, sports facilities include fitness centre, 524 rooms, cheaper rooms small and functional, deluxe rooms more attractive, all rooms are in a 3-storey block. Primarily for tour groups. OK but not intimate. *Garuda* office is now located here. **AL-A** *Laghawa Villas*, see Laghawa Beach Inn, below, Jl Danak, Tamblingan, T288494, F289353. 3 villas with kitchen, living room etc. Long-stay rates available. **AL-A** *Radisson Bali Indonesia*, Jl Hang

Tuah 46, PO Box 3807, T281781, F281782, radbali@indosat.net.id This popular, luxury hotel offers excellent value for money; 329 nicely decorated rooms, a/c, fridge, tea and coffee making facilities. Landscaped pool area. Shuttle bus to Radisson managed beach which has showers and refreshments. Excellent programme of cultural activities. Sports including tennis and free introductory scuba diving lesson; the hotel is adjacent to a 9-hole golf course. Very helpful and friendly hotel staff. 5 restaurants and cafés including the Sanur Harum, with tasty, very reasonably priced Chinese food; excellent buffet breakfast. Spa offering a full range of Western and traditional Balinese treatments. Fitness centre. Kids club with activities to keep children occupied throughout the day. Convention centre with 9 conference rooms and capacity for up to 1,500 delegates. Throughout the year there are special offers which represent outstanding value, check their website at www.radisson.com

A *Ari Putri Hotel*, Sanur Beach Street, Banjar Semawang, T289188, F289190; 41 rooms with a/c, HW, minibar, balcony. Restaurant, bar, smallish pool. Popular with tour groups. **A** *Bumi Ayu*, Jl Bumi Ayu, PO Box 3511, T289101, F287517. Restaurant (excellent service), nice pool, attractive gardens; 58 bungalows with Balinese style décor, slightly claustrophobic, poorly lit rooms, a/c, verandah. Well run, but 15 mins' walk from the beach. Primarily tour groups. **A** *Bumas Hotel*, Jl Bumi Ayu 4, T286306/7, F288341; 74 large, clean but darkish rooms, with a/c, HW, verandah. Pretty gardens with 2 good pools. Primarily a tour group hotel. A bit overpriced, price includes tax and breakfast. **A** *Diwangkara*, Jl Hangtuah, T288577, F288894. 40 Balinese style rooms beside the sea, not much beach. Rooms are large and clean, but darkish with verandah, gardens and pool. A/c, HW. Lovely views from seaside restaurant. **A** *Hotel Bali Warma*, Jl Wira HBB 2, T285618, 285619, 285623, F285154. 20 rooms, bright new and clean. A/c, HW, fridge, small garden with pool. Quiet location, 12 mins' walk to beach. **A** *Hotel Kesumasari*, Jl Danau Tamblingan 22. Attractive rooms with a/c or fan, HW, some with fridge, verandah/balcony, nice views from upstairs rooms. Restaurant, pool, pretty gardens. Better value than many in Sanur and more spacious. **A** *Hotel Taman Agung Beach Inn*, Jl Danau Tamblingan 146, T288549, T/F289161; 27 fairly pleasant, clean rooms, 23 with a/c, 4 with fan, most with HW. Newer rooms have no verandah/balcony and no view. Attractive gardens, pool, 5 mins' walk to beach. **A** *La Taverna*, Jl Danau Tamblingan 29, PO Box 3040, T288497, F287126. Discounts available, restaurant (recommended), pool, 34 rooms are well decorated, attractive gardens leading down to sea and a not particularly good beach. More attractive than most Sanur hotels of this type. Popular with tour groups. **A** *Palm Garden* (*Taman Palem* in Indonesian), Jl Kesuma Sari 3, Semawang, T287041, F289571, plmgrd@indosat.net.id Towards southern end of Sanur. 19 pleasant rooms, fan or a/c, fridge, restaurant, small pool. Cramped grounds. Overpriced. **A** *Paneeda View Beach Hotel*, Jl Danau Tamblingan 89, T288425/289045, F286224/288300. Excellent location by sea, 44 pleasant cottages, a/c, HW, large pretty gardens running down to meagre beach. Lovely views from reasonably priced seaside restaurant. Good value for Sanur. **A** *Puri Kelapa Garden Cottages*, Jl Segara Ayu 1, T286135, F287417; 47 rooms, a/c, HW, fridge. Upstairs rooms are bright with views over garden, but downstairs rooms are darkish. Smallish pool. Overpriced. **A** *Queen Bali Hotel*, Jl Sindhu, T288054. An unprepossessing property, rooms are tatty and very dark. A/c, HW. **A** *Ratna Beach Hotel*, Jl Segara Ayu 10, T289109, F288413; 34 rather basic rooms. Cramped grounds, small pool, overpriced. **A** *Sativa Sanur Cottages*, Jl D Tamblingan 45, PO Box 3163, T/F287881. 50 rooms, a/c, crammed around smallish pool, accommodation is in fairly attractive, thatched cottages. No direct access to beach (15 mins' walk). Overpriced. **A** *Segara Desa* (*Segara Village*), Jl Segara Ayu, T288407; 2 mins' walk to sea. Clean, attractive rooms. Pleasant gardens, smallish pool, 2 restaurants, tennis court. **A** *Surya Beach*, Jl Mertasari, T288833, F287303, T021-5706421. South end of beach, a/c, restaurant, pool, sports facilities, large hotel with 2-storey cottage-style accommodation.

A-B *Laghawa Beach Inn*, Jl Danau Tamblingan, Sanur, T288494, F289353, laghawa@ indo.net.id 30 very clean rooms with fan or a/c, HW, set in pretty large gardens leading down to the beach. Pool, restaurant, bar. **A-B** *Gazebo Cottages*, Jl Danau Tamblingan 35, T288212, F288300; 76 pleasant rooms in a range of styles, 3 smallish pools, large, attractive Balinese-style gardens leading to beach. Peaceful, better value than many in Sanur. **A-B** *Hotel Segara Agung*, Jl Duyung 43, Semawang, T288446, 286804, F286113. 12 new, clean and attractive rooms in bungalows with a/c or fan, some with cold water only. Set in pretty gardens with smallish pool, restaurant and bar, 3 mins' walk to beach. Good value. Recommended. **A-B** *Pondok Wisata Prima* (*Prima Cottages*), Jl Bumi Ayu 15, T286369, F289153. 14 rooms, a/c or fan, HW. Rooms are clean and simple, darkish downstairs, nice views from upstairs balconies. Quiet location, small pool in pretty gardens, 20 mins' walk to beach. **A-B** *Respati Bali*, Jl Danau Tamblingan 33, T288427, F288046. A/c and fan rooms, 24 rooms, simply decorated, darkish. Small pool, pretty gardens running down to narrow beach. Overpriced. **A-B** *Swastika Bungalows*, Jl Danau Tamblingan 128, T288693, T287526; 81 attractive Balinese-style rooms, clean, open air bathrooms, a/c or fan, 2 pools, quiet location set back from road, 15 mins' walk from the beach, pleasant gardens, popular, central for shops and restaurants. **A-B** *Villa Kesumasari*, Jl Kesumasari 6, T287824, F288876. Small clean rooms with either a/c plus HW, TV and fridge; fan plus HW; or fan and cold water. Set around concrete courtyard, 1 min's walk from beach. Overpriced for the more expensive rooms. **A-C** *Made's Homestay and Pub*, Jl Danau Tamblingan 74, T/F288152. 15 pleasant rooms which would benefit from redecoration, 6 with a/c, 9 with fan, all with HW. Set in garden with small pool.

B *Alit's Beach Bungalows*, Jl Hang Tuah 41, T288560, F288766. North end of Sanur, 85 rather drab, but clean bungalows. Smallish pool, large Balinese-style gardens run down to sea, no beach. Restaurant, bar with pool table. **B** *Hotel Wirasana*, Jl Danau Tamblingan 138, T288632, F288561, wirasana@ indosat.net.id 18 spotless rooms with a/c or fan, HW. Set in large gardens. Guests can access the internet, and have use of the Hotel Swastika pool next door, 15 mins' walk to beach. Good value. **B** *Puri Mango Guest House*, Jl Danau Toba 15, Sindhu Sanur, T288411, 281293, F288598. 20 new, spotless rooms with a/c or fan, most with HW. Upstairs rooms have bright open outlook. Small pool, 5 mins' walk to sea. **B** *Ramayana*, Jl Danau Tamblingan 130, PO Box 3066, T288429. 20 small rooms, very clean with verandahs, a/c, nice garden. Small, family-run hotel, away from the beach (15 mins' walk), but you have use of the pools at *Swastika*, can be noisy. **B** *Sumi's Bungalows*, Jl Danau Tamblingan 14A. T285012. 5 bungalows and 8 small, but new and spotless rooms with fan and mosquito net. Set back from the road in small garden with pool. An attractive place and excellent value. Long-stay rates available. Recommended. **B** *Watering Hole*, Jl Hangtuah 37, T288289; 24 large, newly renovated rooms. Fan or a/c, fridge, balcony/verandah. Small garden. Front rooms could be noisy. Good value for Sanur, 3 mins' walk to sea. Good restaurant. **B** *Werdhapura Wisma*, behind Laghawa Beach Inn, Jl Danau Tamblingan, T288171, 286711. Fantastic value if you don't mind the lack of a pool, 60 attractive, clean rooms with a/c, HW, set in lovely large gardens beside the sea, with sea views from some of the verandahs. Restaurant with sea views. Very peaceful location. Government owned so it occasionally fills up with government employees. Recommended.

B-C *Griya Ayu Inn*, Jl Danau Buyan IV, no 24, T288313, F288654. Quiet place, more upmarket rooms have a/c, very clean, no hot water, friendly people. **B-C** *Penginapan Lestari Homestay*, Jl Danau Tamblingan 188, T288867. 10 clean but basic rooms, 3 a/c, 7 with fan, set in attractive gardens, 10 mins' walk to beach. Friendly staff, long-stay rates available. Good value. **C** *Yulia 2 Homestay*, Jl Danau Tamblingan 57, T287495. 6 clean rooms with fan. Excellent value. Recommended.

The following 3 budget places are in descending order of price and attractiveness, but all offer excellent value for money: **C** *Yulia 1 Homestay*, Jl Danau Tamblingan 38, T288089. 12 simple but clean rooms set in small, pretty gardens. **D** *Coco Homestay*, Jl Danau Tamblingan 42, T287391. 8 simple but attractive and spotless rooms set around small courtyard garden. Long-stay rates available. Recommended. **D** *Luisa Homestay*, Jl Danau Tamblingan 40, T289673. 11 new rooms, basic but clean. No garden. Friendly owner. About the cheapest place in Sanur.

D-E *Hotel Taman Sari*, Jl Danau Buyan, some a/c, good rooms for the price. **D-E** *Sapanami Homestay*, Gang Taman Agung 4, off Jl Danau Tamblingan. Possibly the cheapest place in Sanur. 8 rooms, 4 with own bathroom and shower, cold water only, fan, cheapest rooms have squat toilets. Use of kitchen.

Eating Many of the best restaurants in Sanur are concentrated at the south end of the beach, on Jl Danau Tamblingan. The 4 big hotels, namely the *Hyatt*, the *Radisson*, the *Bali Beach* and the *Sanur Beach*, all have several good restaurants, and many of the smaller hotels have good restaurants too with competitive prices. One reader has suggested that the turnover in all the restaurants on Jl Danau Tamblingan is low and, therefore, the food is not always fresh.

Expensive *Kita*, Jl Danau Tamblingan 104, average Japanese food.

Mid-range *Bali Moon*, Jl Danau Tamblingan 19. Italian, attractive setting in an open-air pavilion, good food. *Café Batu Jimbar*, Jl Danau Tamblingan 152, T287374. Pleasant open-air restaurant with a good choice of healthy dishes. Popular with local ex-pats. *Made's Bar and restaurant*, Jl Danau Tamblingan 51, seafood, Italian, Indonesian, generous portions, good food and atmosphere. Recommended. *Paon*, Jl Danau Tamblingan (not far from *Bali Hyatt*), seafood and steaks. *Tanjung Sari Hotel*, Jl Danau Tamblingan, excellent Indonesian and international food (French cook) served in elegant, peaceful surroundings, drinks at candlelit tables on the beach provide a romantic atmosphere. *Telaga Naga*, part of the *Hyatt Hotel* across the road, serves excellent, reasonably priced Chinese and Szechuan food in a romantic setting, surrounded by lotus ponds, pavilions and gardens. Open evenings only 1830-2300. *Ryoshi Sanur*, Jl Danau Tamblingan 150, T288473. Popular Japanese restaurant serving a varied selection of favourites: sushi, sashimi, noodles, tempura, yakitori, teriyaki, donburi and bento. Open 1100-midnight. *The Village Kampung*, Jl Danau Tamblingan 66, T/F285025. New, popular restaurant opened by Austrian chef. Western food, also occasional special 4 course dinners with live music. Open 0900-midnight. Recommended.

Cheap *Kalimantan*, Jl Pantai Sindhu 11, T289291, good atmosphere, good food (especially good breakfasts), good service and thousands of books waiting to be borrowed. *Mina Garden*, Jl Danau Tamblingan. Balinese, Indonesian, Italian and international, Balinese dance. Recommended. *Sanur Harum Chinese Restaurant at Radisson Bali Indonesia*, Jl Hang Tuah 46, very reasonably priced.

Very cheap *Jawa Barat*, south end of Jl Danau Tamblingan, Indonesian. *Mira*, opposite *Hotel Ramayana*, cheap and good value. *Terrazza Martini*, on the beach at the south end, small restaurant serving good Italian food. *Trattoria Da Marco*, on the beach at the south end, Italian. Recommended. *Watering Hole*, Jl Hangtuah 37, good Indonesian and Western food.

Entertainment **Dance** The *Sanur Beach Hotel* offers a buffet dinner with Legong (Mon), Ramayana Ballet (Wed), Genggong/frog dance (Sun), all at 1930. The *Tanjung Sari Hotel* has legong dance and gamelan performances on Sat nights. The *Penjor* restaurant (near the *Bali Hyatt Hotel*) stages legong dance performances on Tue, Thu and Sun 1930-2100, frog dance every Mon 2015, joged dance every Wed 2015 and janger dance every Fri 2015. **Disco** *Rumours*, Jl Sindhu, 2200-0400 (happy hours 2200-0100). **Jazz** *Gratan Bar*, Bali Hyatt Hotel, live music nightly, 2100-0100; *Olgas Lounge*, Surya Beach Hotel, 2000-1200. **Massage** On the beach, or at *Sehatku*, Jl D Tamblingan 23, T287880, 10,000Rp for a traditional massage. **Sauna/spa** *Sehatku*, Jl D Tamblingan 23, T287880, 40,000Rp. **Meditation** The *Bali Usada Meditation Center* in Sanur offers courses in meditation. Contact the *Bali Usada Meditation Center*, By Pass Ngurah Rai 23, Sanur, T0361 289209, F287726, usada@balimeditation.com, http://www.balimeditation.com

Sports **Diving** *Bali Marine Sports*, Jl Raja Bypass, Blanjong, T287872, F287872; *Baruna Watersports* at the *Bali Beach Hotel*, T288511, *Sanur Beach*, T288011, and *Bali Hyatt*, T288271, they are expensive but very professional, with well maintained equipment and very safe procedures; *Oceana Dive Centre*, Jl Bypass 78, T288652, F288652. **Golf** Nine-hole course at the *Bali Beach Hotel*, green fee US$50 (50% discount for *Bali Beach Hotel* guests), 1 price for 9 holes, 18 holes or all day. Club hire: half set US$15.50, full set US$22.50, golf shoes US$4.50, caddy US$2.50. **Jungle skirmish (aka Paintball)** *Bali Splat Mas*, T289073, 2 approximate 5-hr sessions a day, US$45 per session. **Mountain biking** *Sobek*, organize various trips around the interior, T287059. **Sea kayaking** *Sobek*, T287059. **Surfing** The reef here has one of the world's best right-hand breaks, but it is only on for about 28 days a year. Surfing in Sanur is best in the wet season Oct-Apr, and is possible with any tide depending on the size and direction of the swell. Beware of strong currents and riptides in high winds. To the north of Sanur, the right-hand break in front of the Grand Bali Beach Hotel is a fast 4-5m with some good barrels, but is best on a mid- or high-tide and needs a large swell. Opposite the *Tanjung Sari Hotel* at high tide, there is the possibility of a long, fast wall. For the biggest waves, hire a jukung to take you out to the channel opposite the *Bali Hyatt*, very good right handers on an incoming tide. **Ten-Pin Bowling** At the *Bali Beach Hotel*, 3,500Rp per person per game. **Watersports** Equipment available from the bigger hotels or on the beach. Typical prices per person: jet ski US$15 per 15 mins; parasailing US$10 per round; glass bottom boat US$15 (min 2); windsurfing US$8 per hr; water skiing US$15 per 15 mins; deep sea fishing US$240 inclusive (maximum 6 people for full day). **Whitewater rafting** *Sobek*, T287059.

Shopping

Batik *Popiler*, in Tohpati, 5 km north of Sanur beach, on the road to Batubulan. Recommended. **Clothing** *Animale*, on Jl Danau Tamblingan (see map), has the best selection of reasonably priced, good quality fashions. *Pisces*, Jl Sanur Beach (near the *Bali Hyatt*), has good designs. **Ikat** *Gego*, Jl Danau Toba 6, ikat and handwoven fabrics; *Nogo*, Jl Tamblingan 98, high quality ikat made in Gianyar and sold for 14,000Rp per metre for plain colours and 16,000Rp per metre for designs, plus ready-made clothing. They also sell batik. **Jewellery** *Bali Sun Sri*, Jl Bypass Ngurah Rai (out of town), has a wide selection of silver jewellery and good designs; *Pisces*, Jl Sanur Beach (near *Bali Hyatt*), sells a limited range of contemporary silver jewellery. **Leather and rattan bags** *The Hanging Tree*, Jl Tamblingan. **Supermarkets** *Galael Dewata*, on the By-Pass road, has closed down. The best supermarket these days is *Alas Arum* on Jl Danau Tamblingan at the northern end of Batu Jimbar, near Swastika Bungalows. This is a fairly large supermarket with a good selection of imported food, and is also the best place to buy fruit; prices are much better than the market where tourists are unlikely to get a bargain. **Tourist trinkets** T-shirts, bags, batik, at the north end of Jl Tanjung Sari.

Tour operators

Perama, Warung Pino, T287594. Shuttle bus service all over the island. *Barata Tours*, Cottage Arcade, The Grand Bali Beach, Sanur, Bali 80228, T285995, 282693, F285995.

Transport

6 km from Denpasar

Local Bemo: short hops within Sanur limits cost 1,000Rp. **Bicycle hire**: the *Bali Hyatt Hotel* has mountain bikes for hire. **Car hire**: larger national and international firms tend to be based at the bigger hotels; there are also many smaller outfits along the main road. Big companies charge about $45 per day, smaller ones about 80,000Rp per day. Note that cars cannot be taken off the island. *Avis*, *Bali Hyatt Hotel*, T288271 ext 85023; *Bali Car Rental*, Jl Ngurah Rai 17, T288550; *National*, *Bali Beach Hotel*, T288511 ext 1304.

BarataTours

Http://www.baratatours.bali.net
Mailto:barata@bali.net

Your Personal Ticket to Experience Bali and Beyond

Cottage Arcade, The Grand Bali Beach
Sanur, Bali 80228 - Indonesia
Phone: (62-361) 285995, 282693
Fax: (62-361) 285995

Road Bemo: regular connections on green bemos with **Denpasar's** Kreneng terminal and on blue bemos with Tegal terminal (both 2,000Rp); also regular connections with the Batubulan terminal, north of Sanur (2,000Rp). To airport, 25,000Rp. **Taxi**: most hotels will arrange airport transfer/pickup and will charge the same as, or often more than, taxis for the service (25,000Rp).

Directory **Airline offices** All of the following have offices in the Bali Beach Hotel: *Ansett Australia*, T289636/7; *Cathay Pacific*, T286001; *Japan Airlines*, T287576; *KLM*, T287577; *MAS*, T288511; *Qantas*, T751471; *Northwest Airlines*; *Lufthansa* open 0900-1700 Mon-Fri (closed for lunch 1200-1300), 0900-1130 Sat; *Continental Micronesia*; *Qantas*, Tel Toll Free 001 803 61 786; *Air France*, T287734. Open 0900-1700 Mon-Fri (closed for lunch 1230-1330), 0900-1230 Sat. *British Airways* (which no longer flies to Indonesia) are part of the Oneworld Alliance represented by Qantas on Bali, or can be contacted in Jakarta, T021 521 1500. *Garuda* have moved their office to the *Sanur Beach Hotel* at the southern end of Sanur, T288011. Opening hours are 0800-1700 Mon-Sat, 0800-1200 Sat. **Banks** There are several along the main street. **Communications** Perumtel telephone service: on the corner of Jl Tanjung Sari and Jl Sindu. **Post Office**: Jl Danau Buyan. **Postal agent**: Jl Tamblingan 66 (opposite *Taverna Bali Hotel*); including poste restante. **Wartel telephone service**: corner of Tanjung and Segara Ayu. Approximate rate to USA and Europe 5,000Rp per min. **Embassies & consulates** *Australia*, Jl Prof M Yamin 4, Renon (near Sanur), T235092, F231990; *France*, Jl Bypass Ngurah Rai 35X, Sanur, T285485; *Germany*, Jl Pantai Karang 17, T288535, F234834 (0800-1200 Mon-Fri); *Norway* and *Denmark*, Jl Jaya Giri VIII/10, Renon (near Sanur), T235098; *Japan*, Jl Raya Puputan, Renon (near Sanur), T227628, F231308; *Sweden & Finland*, Segara Village Hotel, Jl Segara Ayu, T288407/8, 288021. **Medical facilities** Dentist: Dr Alfiana Akinah, Jl Sri Kesari 17. Doctor: *Bali Beach Hotel* from 0800-1200 daily. Or ask at any major hotel such as *The Hyatt*, *Radisson* etc. Bali's first international standard hospital was planning to open in April 2000 in the Sanur area. Charges will range from 50,000Rp up to 400,000Rp per night for a VIP room. **Places of worship** Catholic: church service at *Bali Beach Hotel*, 1800 Sat, and *Bali Hyatt Hotel*, 1900 Sat (times may vary). Protestant: Bali Beach, 1800 Sun. **Useful addresses** Police: Jl By-Pass, T288597.

Nusa Penida and Nusa Lembongan

Phone code: 0361 These two islands, off Bali's southeast coast in the Lombok Strait, are relatively isolated from the 'mainland' and have not experienced the same degree of tourist development.

Nusa Lembongan Nusa Lembongan, the smaller of the two, is encircled by beautiful white sand beaches with stunning views of Mount Agung on Bali, especially at sunset. A favourite haunt of backpackers for years, Nusa Lembongan has now been discovered by mainstream tourism, and new upmarket places to stay are proliferating, along with a growing number of sporting and entertainment options. There is good surfing along the north shore, and the surrounding reefs with their clear waters and good visibility offer some of the best snorkelling and diving within easy reach of Bali. You may choose to arrange dives with an operator on Bali, although there is now a PADI dive operation based on the island, see below.

Measuring only 4 km by 2 km, the island is easily explored on foot. It is a pleasant place to stay for a few days and there are no cars, just motorbikes. The main village is **Desa Lembongan**, but most people stay in accommodation along the beach north of **Jungut Batu**. A tarmac road runs between the two villages, a distance of about 3 km. At low tide the seaweed beds are worth a visit. There is a track running right round the island which makes for a pleasant walk. For a cool, damp interlude, you can explore the underground house on the edge of Lembongan village, a network of caves, rooms and passages. Bring your own torch; the local kids will offer to act as guides. Boats for rent 5,000Rp per hour, 150,000Rp per day, motorbikes 12,000Rp per day.

The small island of **Nusa Ceningan** can be easily reached from Nusa Lembongan by hiring a boat. There is just one small village, no accommodation, but there are beaches with good surfing, snorkelling and diving; there are sharks in the waters here but they rarely attack.

Nusa Penida

The far larger sister island of Nusa Penida is rugged and barren, with steep cliffs along its south shore and sandy beaches to the north. It has a reputation among the Balinese as a cursed place, and criminals and outcasts used to be sent here to live out their days. Perhaps because of its reputation, Nusa Penida has not yet been caught up in the tourist mêlée and there is only basic losmen accommodation available in the main town **Sampalan**, and the village of **Toyapakeh** where boats from Bali arrive, although it might also be possible to persuade a local to take you in at other villages. Ask the *kepala desa* (headman). Most visitors come for the day only and visit the white sand beaches of the north coast. Very few make it to the sheer limestone cliffs of the south coast. The bat-filled cave at Karengsari may be a place of interest for some.

Tours

Bali Hai Cruises, Benoa Harbour, T720331, F720334, balihai@indosat.net.id, www.bali-paradise.com/balihai, run cruises from Benoa Harbour to Lembongan, prices US$40-90. Recommended.

Wakalouka Cruises, Benoa Harbour, T0361-723629, 723659, F722077. Programme of cruises from Benoa Harbour in luxury sailing catamaran to the *Wakanusa Resort* on Lembongan. Recommended.

Sea Rover, Jalan Segara Werdi 6, Harbour Beno is one of the numerous small companies operating day trips to Lembongan in simple motorboats, the tours cost under US$40, but the experience is downmarket.

The *Golden Hawk*, a tall ship over 100 years old, sails from Benoa Harbour to Lembongan for day trips, US$88 for all inclusive trip. *Golden Hawk Cruises* operate from Jalan Danau Poso 20A, Sanur, T/F28658.

Island Explorer Cruises, Jalan Sekar Waru 8, Sanur, T289856, F289837, organize day trips and an overnight package on sailing yacht and motorboats. Fishing, snorkelling, barbecue lunch provided (US$59-69).

Nusa Lembongan

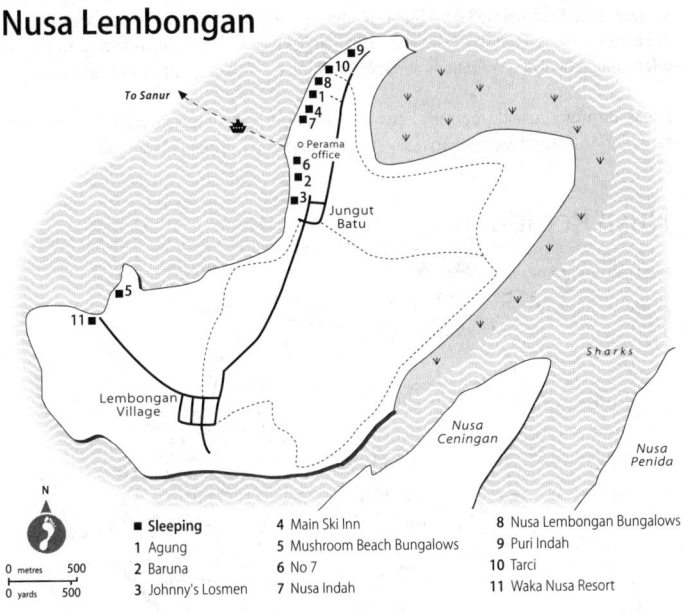

- **Sleeping**
- 1 Agung
- 2 Baruna
- 3 Johnny's Losmen
- 4 Main Ski Inn
- 5 Mushroom Beach Bungalows
- 6 No 7
- 7 Nusa Indah
- 8 Nusa Lembongan Bungalows
- 9 Puri Indah
- 10 Tarci
- 11 Waka Nusa Resort

Essentials

Sleeping: Nusa Lembongan
All the accommodation is beside the sea, with fabulous sunset views over Bali & Mt Agung

A *Coconuts Beach Resort*, newly opened with upmarket rustic bungalows and breathtaking sea views. **A** *Hai Tide Huts* run by Bali Hai Cruises, T720331, F720334, www.bali-paradise.com/balihai, balihai@indosat.net.id 6 large thatched roofed, 2-storey lumbung style rooms, with a/c. All overlooking the beach. Watersports, free-form swimming pool, bar and restaurant. **A** *Nusa Lembongan Resort*, T413375, F413376, sales@nusa-lembongan.com, www.nusa-lembongan.com Opened in mid-1999, boutique hotel set in gardens overlooking Sanghiang Bay. 12 villas, with a/c and the usual upmarket facilities, built in the traditional manner using natural materials. **A** *Waka Nusa Resort*, booking office Benoa Harbour, T723629/723659, F722077. Gated compound on the southwest coast of the island. 10 luxury bungalows contained in tiny private garden, simple but artistic décor, alang-alang roofs, polished woods, natural fabrics, pool, restaurant. Recommended. **B** *Pondok Baruna*, Jungutbatu, F288500. Recently renovated, 8 rooms with Western bathrooms, beachfront restaurant. **C-D** *Nusa Lembongan Bungalows* (booking office on Kuta at Jl Pantai Legian, T53071), attractive, clean and spacious rooms. **C-E** *Agung*, good restaurant, clean, thatched-roof bungalows, some with private mandi. **C-E** *Main Ski Inn*, 2-storey bungalows set in garden, upstairs rooms have balconies with sea views, can be noisy due to the restaurant serving good, cheap food overlooking the sea. **C-E** *Tarci*, 2-storey bungalows, some with private mandi, restaurant which also serves good and cheap food, beside the beach. **E** *Johnny's Losmen*, basic accommodation near the village.

Eating Most places to stay have their own restaurant; *Tarci* has a good reputation or try the fish at the *Main Ski Inn*.

Shopping **Textiles** Distinctive weft ikat cotton cloth is produced on Nusa Penida; usually in the form of a red *kamben*.

Sports **Scuba Diving** *World Diving Lembongan*, Pondok Baruna, Jungutbatu, F288500 (correspondence to Mark Micklefield, Jl Danau Maninjau, Gang 111 no 7, Sanur). Full range of PADI approved courses, English Divemaster. The islands of Nusa Lembongan and Nusa Penida offer a range of diving conditions and regular sightings of sharks, turtles and large rays.

Transport **Local Bemos**: run fairly regularly between Toyapakeh and Sampalan, with a more limited service to Suana and Klumpu. To really see the island you will need a motorbike.

Nusa Penida

Sea Boat: regular connections to Nusa Penida from either Padangbai or Kesamba, docking near Sampalan at (respectively) Buyuk or Toyapakeh (the boats from Kesamba are small junks), 1 hr. Locals pay 4,000Rp, but the boatmen demand 15,000Rp from foreigners. For Nusa Lembongan they leave every morning from near the *Bali Beach Hotel* (Sanur Beach) and dock at Jungut Batu. The public boats leave very early from 0500 depending on the tide. It is a 10 min walk from the accommodation north of Jungut Batu to the spot on the beach where the boats come in; no jetty, you wade over to the boat. There are also early morning boats between Nusa Penida and Nusa Lembongan. The best way to get to Nusa Lembongan is with *Perama*, who have 2 boats a day from Sanur. Schedules change so check for up-to-date times. Currently boats leave Sanur at 1030 and 1615, and leave Nusa Lembongan at 0900 and 1500. In the low season there may only be 1 boat a day, in the morning. The 27 km crossing takes about 40 mins, 17,500Rp. Departures from Sanur are 1030 and 1630 in high season. Perama office in Sanur is at Warung Pino, T287594 – *Perama's* shuttle bus service from the popular tourist destinations on Bali links up with the boats – pick up a copy of their timetable for full details. A faster way to reach the island is by catamaran which takes about 30 mins. There are also a growing number of cruise options from mainland Bali costing between US$50 and US$100, see page 313.

The Bukit Peninsula and Nusa Dua

The Bukit Peninsula starts 4 km south of Kuta, with just a narrow isthmus connecting it to the mainland, and extends over an area roughly 10 km from north to south and 18 km east to west. It is known locally as The Bukit or Bukit Badung. The area is of little use agriculturally and has been earmarked for tourist development.

Phone code: 0361

Ins and outs

Public transport only goes to the main population areas of Jimbaran, Nusa Dua and Benoa. Myriad tour companies offer trips to Uluwatu, but otherwise you will need your own transport to explore this area, much of which can more easily be reached by motorbike than car.

Getting around

The area

Most of the bukit (meaning hill in Indonesian) is dry rocky terrain with scrubby vegetation and little surface water. Popular with surfers since the early 1970s, it boasts some of the best surfing in Southeast Asia, and ranks in the top 10 of world surfing destinations. These days, thanks to the drilling of bore holes and a water treatment plant, the east coast has been developed into a verdant luxury resort fronted by clean sandy beaches. The peninsula is also the location of one of Bali's finest temples, **Uluwatu**, spectacularly located on a west-facing clifftop, especially enchanting at sunset. Good roads lead to Nusa Dua and Uluwatu, while rough roads and tracks lead to idyllic, isolated beaches, limestone caves and dramatic cliffs, rising up to 100m straight out of the sea. The remains of ancient temples can still be seen in remote coastal spots in the west and south.

On the west side of the isthmus is **Jimbaran Beach**, and on the east side, **Benoa**. The purpose-built luxury resort area of **Nusa Dua** also lies on the east side, to the south of Benoa. The Bukit Peninsula is a barren, arid, limestone tableland – the Dutch called it Tafelhoek – which once lay under the sea but now rises to 200m. Geologically, this barren landscape has more in common with Nusa Penida and provides a tremendous contrast with the lushness of the rest of south Bali.

The only 'sight' on the Bukit Peninsula is the **Uluwatu Temple** (see page 359) magnificently positioned on a clifftop overlooking the sea at the southwest extremity of the peninsula. Much of the west coast has remained relatively undeveloped because of the steep cliffs. But the excellent surf draws large numbers of surfers to the west coast. At the neck of the peninsula is the sandy Jimbaran Bay.

Jimbaran

About 15 minutes' drive south of Kuta, this is perhaps the nicest of the upmarket resorts in south Bali. The location is superb: a grand sweeping bay, a fine white sand beach (one of the best beaches on Bali), and spectacular sunsets. On a clear day you can see the hills of Tabanan in the distance.

Jimbaran Bay is a spiritual place of deep religious significance to local Balinese. For this reason, although it is sandwiched between the airport and Nusa Dua, the bay was passed by until recently. But over the last few years developers have moved in, despite local protestations, six hotels and a time-share property have already been built and more are planned.

Jimbaran is a large, relatively prosperous, tidy village, with a population of 3,500. Few foreigners venture into the village and the people seem rather more polite than in other tourist areas. This village is also renowned for the Barong dance, **Barong Ket**, staged by its residents, many of whom go into a trance during the performance. The dance season lasts for about six months of the year, during which time performances are held approximately every 15 days. Asked how they feel about going into trance most people say they find it very tiring, do not enjoy the experience and would like to stop; afterwards they are embarrassed at having made a public spectacle of themselves and for having lost control. The feeling is that they have been taken over by a negative force which they could not prevent.

In the middle of the village, set in its own large grounds, is the impressive **Ulun Siwi Temple**, dating from the 17th century. The 11-tiered meru indicates the temple's importance and the strength of religious feeling at the time it was built. During the rainy season the pavements on the outskirts of town can be very slippery.

Sleeping

This is very much an upmarket resort, with good luxury accommodation but very little for the budget traveller; the few cheap places seem overpriced for what they offer. There are also a few villas available to rent both long and short term

L *Four Seasons Resort*, T701010, F701020. Incorporating the best of Balinese pavilion design, this is a resort that is hard to beat. About 150 beautiful villas, each surrounded by a stone wall, are set on the slope above Jimbaran bay; each villa also has its own plunge-pool and sun-deck, the resort facilities feature beautifully landscaped gardens, 2 pools, tennis courts, spa with sauna, and 2, 1st-class restaurants including *PJ's* – a beachside place serving Mediterranean food. **L** *The Ritz-Carlton Hotel*, Jl Bukit Permai, T702222, F701555. Luxury hotel with the usual facilities, but suffers from its rather poor location.

L-AL *Bali Inter Continental Resort*, Jl Uluwatu 45, T701888, F701777, bali@ interconti.com, www.interconti.com/bali Set right on the bay, with a long stretch of beach frontage with 500m of spectacular sea views, this hotel has the best location in Jimbaran. A rather grand hotel designed in the style of an ancient Javanese water palace. Attractively furnished rooms with verandahs, set in extensive 35-ha landscaped gardens, 3 pools, sports centre, spa, 5 restaurants including a 1st-class Japanese teppanyaki bar. Conference facilities. Daily programme of cultural and sporting events. Recommended. **L-A** *Mimpi Jimbaran*, T701070, F701074. A small, exclusive development of 14 studios with kitchens, on a hillside overlooking Jimbaran Bay, with beautiful gardens, restaurant and poolside bar; the villas have their own private pools, monthly rates available, tennis, conference facilities.

AL *Keraton Bali*, Jl M. Rajapati, T701961, F701991, german@ denpasar.wasantara.net.id 99 cottages in typical Balinese style, rooms are only average, with a/c, fridge etc. Set in gardens leading down to the sea, 3 restaurants and bars, pool, sports facilities. Popular with tour groups. **AL** *Pansea Jimbaran*, T701605, F701320, panseabl@indosat.net.id 41 fairly attractive cottages with fan and a/c etc. 2 restaurants, pool, superb location overlooking Jimbaran bay. **AL-A** *Puri Kosala*, Jl Yoga Perkanti 2, T701673/702575, F702576. 6 beautifully furnished bungalows with marble floors, a/c and fan etc. Set in very pretty gardens with large pool, in a very peaceful location 3 mins' walk from the beach. **A** *Nelayan Jimbaran Bungalows and Homestay*, Jl Pantai Jimbaran 3, T/F702253. 10 rooms consisting of 6 bungalows and 4 homestay. Rooms are large, but fairly dark with a/c but cold water only, homestay rooms are more basic and smaller but brighter, all are set at the back of the restaurant and can be noisy. Tiny garden; 2 mins from beach.

About the closest Jimbaran gets to budget accommodation, but overpriced compared to other parts of Bali. **A** *Puri Bambu*, Jl Pengeracikan, Kedonganan, T701377, 701468/9, F701440. Down a side road, 6 mins' walk to the beach, this is one of the cheaper hotels in Jimbaran; 38 rooms, clean, fairly new and plain, with a/c, balcony/verandah etc. Pool in central courtyard, restaurant, bar, free shuttle bus to airport and Kuta, 50% discount off-season.

B *Pondok Kedai Dongan*, Jl Pantai Kedonganan 118X, T/F752667. Just across the road from the beach. 9 rooms with a/c and HW. Great views from upstairs restaurant. **B** *Puri Indra Prastha*, Jl Uluwatu 28A, T701552, 701544. One of the cheapest places to stay in Jimbaran, on the main road in town, 5 mins' walk to the beach. 11 rooms, clean but dark and fairly basic,

Jimbaran Bay

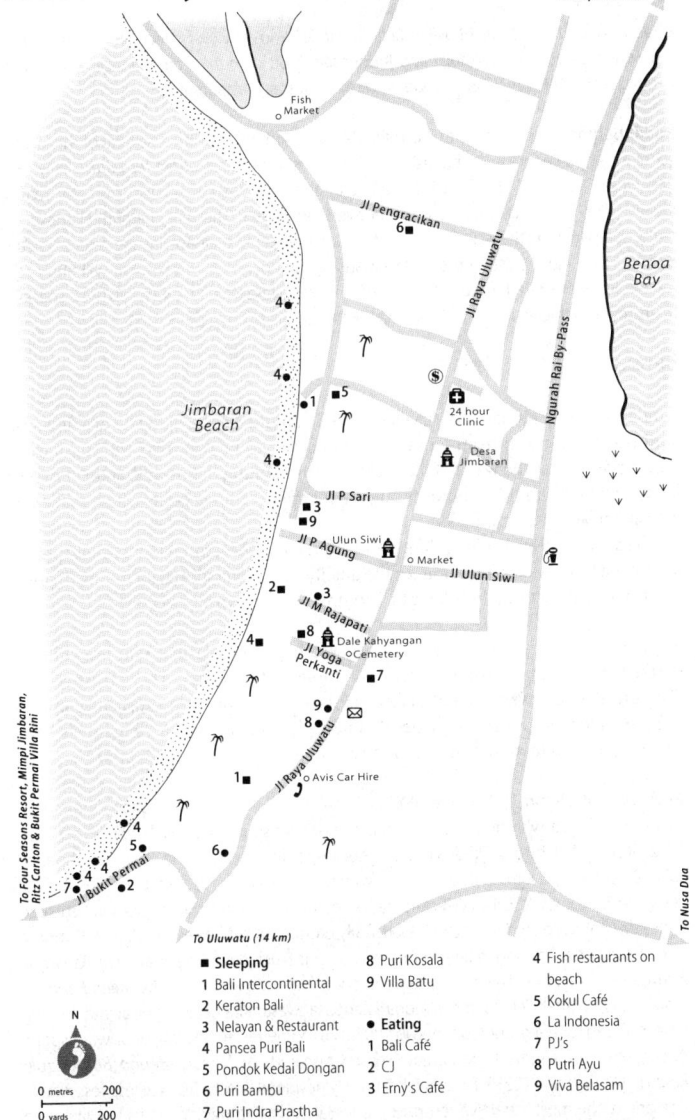

- **Sleeping**
  1 Bali Intercontinental
  2 Keraton Bali
  3 Nelayan & Restaurant
  4 Pansea Puri Bali
  5 Pondok Kedai Dongan
  6 Puri Bambu
  7 Puri Indra Prastha
  8 Puri Kosala
  9 Villa Batu

- **Eating**
  1 Bali Café
  2 CJ
  3 Erny's Café
  4 Fish restaurants on beach
  5 Kokul Café
  6 La Indonesia
  7 PJ's
  8 Putri Ayu
  9 Viva Belasam

with a/c or fan, and verandah, set around central courtyard overlooking pool. Restaurant, reasonable sized pool.

Eating Fish warungs right on the beach have sprung up in the last few years in 2 separate places: adjacent to the town and further south between the *The Four Seasons Resort* and *Intercontinental Hotel*. Open for lunch and dinner, but particularly popular in the evening. Diners choose their freshly caught fish, which is priced per kilo, and sit at tables outside on the beach or in tents while the fish is cooked, then served with salad, sauces and rice, followed by fruit salad, for an inclusive price. Of these, *Bali Café* in the 1st area is one of the better warungs and operates to high standard of cleanliness. At the southern end, just over the bridge, *Bagus Café* is popular with expats.

Mid-range *PJ's* (see *Four Seasons Resort* above), great views over Jimbaran bay.

Cheap *Nelayan Restaurant*, Jl Pantai Jimbaran 3. Good sea views from this upstairs restaurant which serves fish, Western and Indonesian food. *Pondok Kedai Dongan*, Jl Pantai Kedonganan 118X, T/F752667. Good views from upstairs restaurant.

Transport **Road** **Bemo**: connections with **Denpasar's** Tegal terminal. **Car hire**: several of the larger car hire companies are in Jimbaran on the Jl By Pass Nusa Dua. *Golden Bird Bali*, Jl Raya By Pass Nusa Dua 4, T701111, F701628, offers a range of transport services from car rental (Suzuki jeep, Toyota Kijang) to chauffeur driven cars (Volvo). They are one of the largest car rental companies on the island so they offer good break-down service, insurance etc. *Golden Bird* also manage the blue taxis on the island – amongst the few taxis you will find with meters. Recommended. *Toyota Rent a Car*, Jl By Pass Nusa Dua, T701747, F701741, specialize in Toyota vehicles, namely Kijang, Starlet and Corollas.

Benoa

Phone code: 0361 Benoa consists of a small fishing village called Tanjung Benoa, at the tip of a finger of land extending north from Nusa Dua, and is not to be confused with utilitarian Benoa port across the water. To travel between Tanjung Benoa and Benoa Port by land would take about an hour, though there are occasional boats which make the crossing in about 20 minutes.

The area between Tanjung Benoa and Nusa Dua is becoming increasingly popular. Benoa has a good reputation for the quality of its watersports, including diving - its principle attraction; the village of Tanjung Benoa is worth a visit.

Sights There is an interesting Chinese temple which you can visit if you are suitably dressed, as well as a mosque, a Hindu temple and a market. The tourist area of Tanjung Benoa covers four different banjars, which provide excellent gamelan orchestras for the cultural activities that take place regularly at the big hotels here. You might catch them rehearsing in the evenings.

Sleeping **AL** *Aston Bali Resort*, Jl Pratama 68X, T773577, F774954. New international hotel, 187 rooms, beside sea with pool, restaurant, bar and watersports. **AL** *Bali Tropik*, PO Box 41, T772130, F772131, btropik@indosat.net.id Located at the southern end of the Benoa peninsula, 103 attractive rooms in Balinese style, with good views from upstairs balconies. All with verandah/balcony, a/c, IDD, TV. 3 restaurants and bars, medium sized pool set in large gardens adjacent to an eroded area of beach. Daily programme of free events, free non-motorized watersports. Catering mainly to tour groups; price includes all meals and tax. **AL** *Grand Mirage*, T772147, F772148. A/c, restaurant, pools, new, big and brash. **AL** *Melia Benoa*, Jl Pratama, T771714, F771713, meliabenoa@denpasar.wasantara.net.id Typical international hotel catering to tour groups, opened in 1997, 128 rooms, restaurant, bar, pool, watersports, beside sea. Free shuttle to Kuta. Low season discount. **AL** *Novotel Benoa Bali* (*Coralia Resort*), Jl Pratama, T772239, F772237. Beautifully designed hotel with excellent resort facilities, one of the most attractive resort hotels in Bali - evoking tradition in its use of natural

All rooms with private bathroom & Western toilet unless otherwise stated. Jl Pratama is a busy road, without pavements, & at its narrower sections walking along it is not for the faint-hearted. Watersports are available at all the A & B category accommodations

Benoa

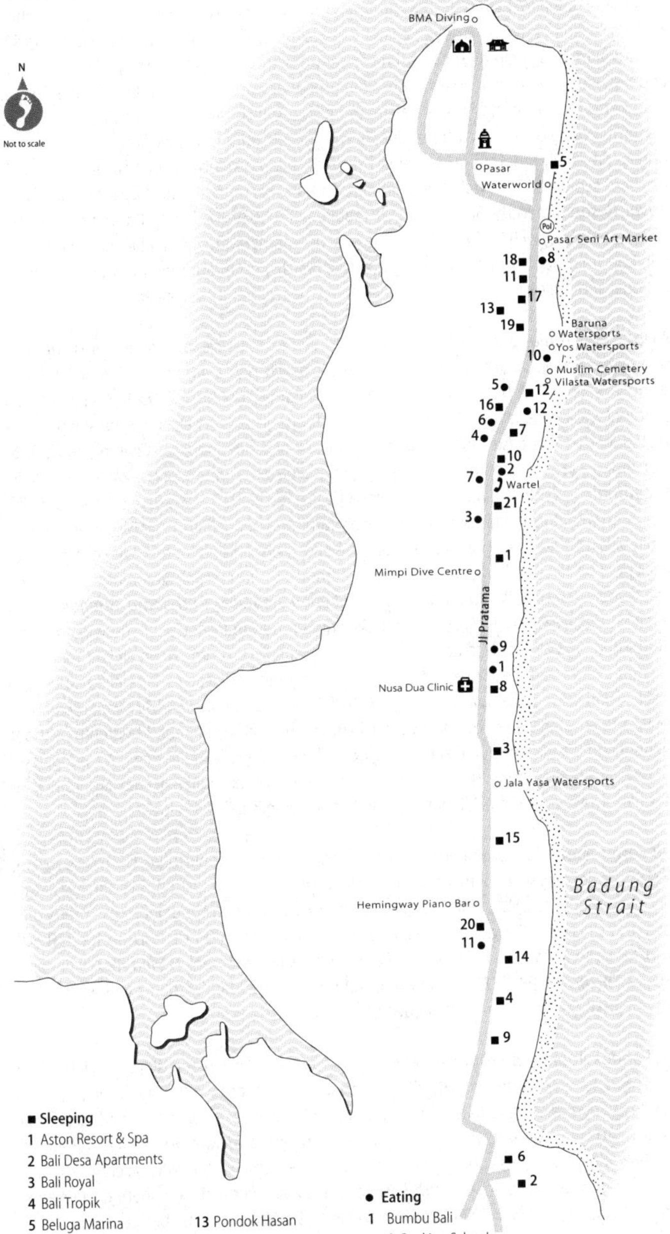

Not to scale

Badung Strait

- **Sleeping**
  1 Aston Resort & Spa
  2 Bali Desa Apartments
  3 Bali Royal
  4 Bali Tropik
  5 Beluga Marina
  6 Club Med
  7 Grand Mirage & Thaliasso Spa
  8 Matahari Terbit Bali
  9 Melia Benoa
  10 Mirage Resort
  11 Novotel Resort
  12 Pondok Agung
  13 Pondok Hasan
  14 Puri Benda
  15 Puri Tanjung
  16 Rasa Sayang Beach Inn
  17 Rasa Dua
  18 Sorga Nusa Dua
  19 Tanjung Mekar
  20 Villa Ayu
  21 Villa Bintang

- **Eating**
  1 Bumbu Bali & Cooking School
  2 Galang Bulan
  3 Jukung
  4 Kecak Bali
  5 Mini Restaurant & General Shop
  6 Noesa Garden, Bali Café & Tanjung Clinic
  7 Nyoman Bali
  8 Pantal Mina
  9 Sari Tanjung & Watersports
  10 Rai Seafood
  11 Taman
  12 Warung Ikan

materials, coconut wood, thatch and soft adobe patinas. Set in landscaped tropical gardens which lead down to the beach, 180 extremely attractive rooms, with a/c, minibar, tea/coffee making facilities, private garden or balcony. 12 luxurious beach cabanas beside the sea with private garden, 3 swimming pools, fitness centre with sauna and massage, floodlit tennis court, meeting rooms and an excellent programme of watersports. Outdoor theatre for cultural performances of traditional dance and music, which take place each evening; these performances are free to all hotel guests with no obligation to dine (unlike many resort hotels). Free daily programme of events. Excellent children's club providing a full day's activities, and separate kids' pool, 3 restaurants and bars. Recommended. **AL** *Suites Hotel Bali Royal Resort* (formerly *Bali Royal*), Jl Pratama. T771039, F771885. (In Vienna, Austria, T0043-1-9145851, F9113770). 13 Balinese style rooms with open plan bathroom, a/c, minibar. Small pool in gardens leading down to beach. Restaurant serving Indonesian, international and Austrian cuisine, room service. Very peaceful but overpriced.

A *Hotel Puri Tanjung*, Jl Pratama 62, T772121, F772424, 64 clean, simple rooms with a/c, verandah/balcony. Large gardens leading down to beach, pool area in need of some refurbishment. Restaurant. **A** *Hotel Villa Bintang*, Jl Pratama, T772010, F772009, vl_bintang@denpasar.wasantara.net.id 54 large rooms including 2 villas, a/c, balcony, 3 restaurants serving Indonesian, Japanese and Continental cuisine, 24-hr coffee shop, bar. Catering primarily to tour groups; attractive gardens beside sea with large pool. Watersports. Rates negotiable. **A** *Matahari Terbit Bali*, Jl Pratama, T771019, F772027, nyomanbali@denpasar.wasantara.net.id 20 new attractively furnished bungalows, a/c, HW, fridge, TV. Also family villa (US$225 per night) with 3 bedrooms and open air living room. Lovely gardens with small pool beside beach; marine sports. Beach front café, *Bumbu Bali Restaurant* (see below). Free airport transfer. Recommended. **A** *Puri Benoa* (formerly *Puri Joma Bungalows*), Jl Pratama 15B, T771634, F771635, pbenoa@denpasar.wasantara.net.id 10 new, completely refurbished bungalows, decorated in Balinese style with large rooms, open air bathroom; a/c, verandah. Restaurant beside sea. Smallish pool, set in pretty tropical gardens leading down to beach. Good value. **A** *Taman Damai*, T772514, F773589. Or Contact *Bali Air Marine Sport* near the village. Located 200m down track off main road; 5 bungalows for rent, 1 bedroom (without kitchen) and 2 bedrooms (with kitchen), large bathroom, fan, mosquito nets, HW. Bungalows are new, clean and simply furnished. Pretty gardens, small pool, parking. Free airport pick-up for stays of 1 week or more. Friendly caretaker speaks English. Good value.

A-B *Sorga Nusa Dua*, Jl Pratama (northern end of Benoa peninsula), T771604/772413, F77139. Under new management and undergoing complete renovation; 54 attractive, large, very clean rooms, a/c, HW, fridge, large verandah/balcony. Good sized pool set in pretty gardens, tennis courts. Restaurant serving Japanese, Indonesian and European food. **B** *Bali Resort Palace*, Jl Pratama, T772026, F772237. A/c, restaurant, pool. **B** *Villa Ayu*, Jl Pratama 61D, T772828/773703, F771242. 4 new, clean rooms, plus 2 family rooms with kitchen. All with a/c, HW. Small pool in small gardens.

B-C *Pondok Agung Homestay*, Jl Pratama 99, T/F771143. 7 clean newish rooms with a/c or fan, HW, use of kitchen, satellite TV, 2 upstairs verandahs overlooking pretty garden. **B-D** *Rasa Sayang*, Jl Pratama 88X, T771643. 11 rooms with a/c, 8 with fan, verandah, small gardens, 10 mins' walk to beach. Good value. **C** *Tanjung Mekar Homestay*, Jl Pratama, T772063. 4 new, spotless rooms, with spring beds, fan, cold water only, balcony, 10 mins' walk to beach. Good value. **D** *Pondok Hasam*, T772456. Perfectly adequate clean rooms. **D** *Rasa Dua*, Jl Pratama, T771571. Basic place, rooms with fan, private bathroom.

Eating **Mid-range** *Bumbu Bali*, excellent Balinese food. The owner, Heinz Von Holzen, owns 2 other good restaurants in Tanjung Benoa, the **Kecak** (cheap) and **The Nyoman** (very cheap), Jl Pratama, T772704. Open 0900-0000, Indonesian, Chinese and European food and seafood, free transport in Nusa Dua area (recommended); and a cooking school. For information about these: hvhfood@indosat.net.id

Cheap *Galang Bulan Bar and Restaurant*, Jl Pratama 70, T773708. Indonesian, Chinese, Japanese, European and seafood, free transport in Nusa Dua area. *Warung Ikan* (fish market restaurant), open 0600-2300. *Kecak*, see above. **Very cheap** *The Nyoman*, see above. *Taman Sari Restaurant*, Thai, Indonesian and European food. *Hemingway Piano Bar*, open 2000 onwards. There are a growing number of cafés and restaurants on the beachfront and along Jl Pratama, opposite the hotels.

Discos *Cool Bar*, Grand Mirage Hotel, open 2100-0000. **Cooking** Ex-pat Heinz Von Holzen has established an excellent cooking school at his *Bumbu Bali* restaurant. For more information, contact hvh@indosat.net.id **Entertainment**

A growing number of car hire outlets and shops selling tourist accessories and groceries are opening along Jl Pratama. **Shopping**

Marine activities and watersports The catamaran Quicksilver operates regular tours to Nusa Penida, leaving from the harbour at Tanjung Benoa. When choosing a dive centre it would be best to choose one with a PADI Certification. The following all have outlets in Benoa: *Baruna*, T753820, F753809; *Yos Diving*, T773774; *Vilasta*, T775122 ext 62; *Beluga Marine*; *Jala Yasa*. **Sports**

Tour Devco, T231592, organize trips on a tall ship to Nusa Lembongan; price includes lunch and watersports equipment. *The Bali International Yacht Club*, T288391, also organizes yacht and fishing trips to the islands. *Bali Hai Cruises* and *Wakalouka Cruises* specialize in trips to Lembongan Island from Benoa Port (see page 351). **Tour operators**

Road Bemo: connections with **Denpasar's** Suci terminal. **Sea Boat**: Benoa Port is the main port of call for cruise ships and yachts, as well as the place to come for anyone hoping to sign on as crew. Fast ferry service to eastern Indonesia on the 925 passenger ship *Barito*, leaves every Fri afternoon at 1800 on a 16 hr voyage to **Bima** (Sumbawa) and **Kupang** (Timor). Every Sun at midday the *Barito* makes a 7 hr hop to the port of **Surabaya** in eastern Java. For more information contact *Gama Dewata Bali Tours*, T0361-263568, T232704, F0361-263569. The *Pelni Line* ships, which visit Bali, dock here on their circuits around the Indonesian Archipelago and it is also the jumping off point for hydrofoils to Lombok. The *Mabua Express* leaves Benoa twice a day for **Lembar** (Lombok). Travelling time is 2½ hrs and costs US$25-30 depending on class (children 2-12 years half price), T721212, F732615 (on Lombok, T0370-81195, F81124) for details. Current departure timetable: leaves Benoa 0800, leaves Lembar 1730. A/c, aircraft type seats. The *Pelni* ships *Tatamailau*, *Awu*, *Dobonsolo* and *Tilongkabila* dock here. For Pelni information, T721377. **Transport**

Clinic: Tanjung Clinic, T773843, open 24 hrs; see map. Nusa Dua Clinic, 24 hrs, see map. **Directory**

Uluwatu Temple

Pura Uluwatu, also known as Pura Ulu Atu, is considered to be one of Bali's *sadkahyangan* – the six most important temples on the island. Its full name, *Pura Luhur Uluwatu*, literally means 'high headland', an apt name as the temple is spectacularly situated on the south tip of the Bukit Peninsula, perched on a cliff 70m above the sea. It is easily accessible but can be very crowded, and you may have to contend with an army of hawkers and unpleasant, but sacred, monkeys.

Pura Uluwatu may have been constructed during the 11th century, although it was substantially rebuilt in the 16th century – and as a result is rather difficult to date. The temple was owned by the Prince of Badung (today's Denpasar) and he alone was allowed to visit it. **History**

Uluwatu has several unusual features; it is built of hard grey coral, which means that the temple's decoration has survived the centuries of weathering remarkably well. Secondly, the *candi bentar* or split gate is shaped in the form of a stylized *garuda* (mythical bird) rather than with smooth sides, as is usual. Also unusually, two statues of Ganesh **The site** flank the inner gateway. It was at Uluwatu that the famous Hindu saint, Danghyang Nirartha, is reputed to have achieved *moksa*, or oneness, with the godhead. ■ *Entry by donation. Keep clear of the monkeys on the steps up to the entrance.*

Beaches

There are several good surfing beaches near Uluwatu, including **Bingin**, **Nyang Nyang** (on the south coast) and **Padang Padang** (just south of Jimbaran Bay) (see page 354). Most involve a walk of up to 2 km down stony tracks.

Sleeping

The popular surfing spots have warungs nearby, often at the clifftop from where steep steps lead down to a narrow beach & the surf. These offer standard Indonesian & Western food, & surfers often sleep in the very basic accommodation available at the warung

L-AL *Bali Cliff Resort*, Jl Pura Batu Pageh, Ungasan, T771992, F771993, info@ balicliff.com or bcr@indosat.net.id Stunning location perched on the edge of a cliff overlooking the Indian Ocean at the southern tip of Bali, a very romantic setting. Set in pretty gardens with ponds, walkways and an outdoor theatre for the occasional cultural performance. Accommodation is either in the main hotel or in private villas with pools. A travelator carries guests the 250ft down to sea level and a small white sand beach which disappears at high tide. Excellent and reasonably priced food in 5 restaurants, which offer fish, international, Indonesian, Italian and Japanese food and a pizzeria. One of the restaurants is situated at the bottom of the cliff in an ancient cave; here you can enjoy a buffet dinner and kecak dance every Sat night. 2 of the best pools in Bali; 1 superbly located at the cliff edge whose waters merge into the blue of the distant horizon, the other a full Olympic-size swimming pool which is never crowded. Fitness centre, children's playground. Free shuttle bus to airport, Kuta and Nusa Dua. Convention facilities for up to 600 people. Good surfing here. Recommended. **D** *Gobleg Inn*, off the track to the beach.

There are several places to stay inland near **Bongol**, on the road leading to the *Bali Cliff Resort* and Uluwatu Temple, 20 mins' drive from the airport:

A *Bukit Inn Villa Koyo*, T702927. Small, modern hotel with a/c. **A** *Jimbaran Resort Hills*. Modern hotel with Western facilities. **C** *Ugly Boys*, 3 kms, north of Ungasan. The cheapest accommodation in the area, popular with surfers, bar and café.

Eating

Bali Cliff Resort, Sunday brunch which includes the use of the resort's spectacular cliffside pool. See hotel entry for more information about the hotel's excellent restaurants.

Transport

20 km from Kuta

Road Minibus: minibuses (C1) leave from **Kuta** for Uluwatu; connections with **Denpasar's** Tegal terminal.

Uluwatu

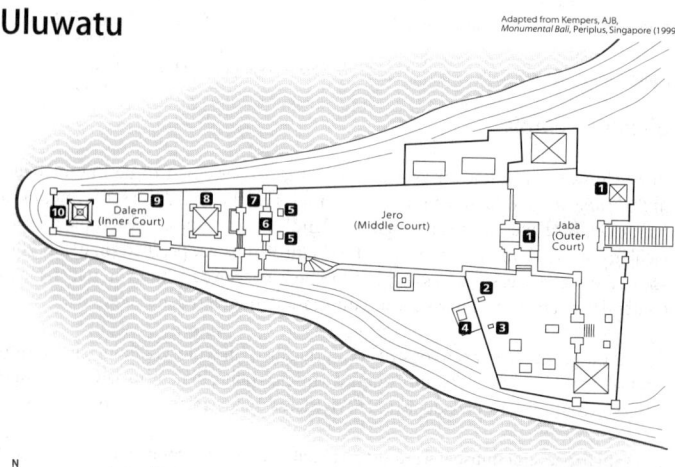

Adapted from Kempers, AJB, *Monumental Bali*, Periplus, Singapore (1999)

Not to scale

1 Candi bentar
2 Vishnu image
3 Brahma image
4 Dwijendra image
5 Ganesh doormen
6 Candi kurung
7 Aling-Aling
8 Bale Pemeyosan
9 Prasada
10 Triple-tiered meru dedicated to Dwijendra

Nusa Dua

Phone code: 0361

Nusa Dua is a 'planned resort' and the first hotels opened here in 1983. The barren landscape of the Bukit Peninsula has been transformed into a tropical haven: five-star hotels, beautiful gardens, tennis courts, horse riding and a golf course. The intention was to build a resort which would be isolated from the 'real' Bali and, in so doing, protect the locals from the excesses of international tourism.

There is none of the dirt and poverty associated with a Third World country. Overall, the effect may seem rather sterile and some visitors will find the ambience rather boring. Being on the east side of the island, you also miss out on the dramatic sunsets that are such a feature of many other resorts on Bali. Within the resort precinct, reached by roads running through the manicured lawns of the development, is the Galleria complex with travel agencies, airline offices, banks, a post office, restaurants, art shops, a supermarket, performing arts shows – in short, everything that a Western tourist could want. What Nusa Dua does not provide is any insight, indeed any sense, of what life in Bali is like. **Buala** village is just outside the entrance to Nusa Dua, a brief seven minutes' walk. It is a clean village with a range of small shops, stalls selling tourist goods, banks, a *Wartel*, restaurants and a Tragia supermarket that is better value than the one in the Galleria complex in Nusa Dua. You might even encounter a temple festival taking place in the village.

On the beach, the surf is gentle along the northern part of the shore, but the waves become bigger to the south. Both areas are popular with surfers. If you are not staying at one of the hotels, the beach is easily accessed east of the Galleria complex or further south at the end of the strip of luxury hotels, with parking lots at both places. That said, if you are not a surfer, there is nothing especially attractive about this beach, except for its cleanliness and the relative absence of hawkers.

Sleeping
The hotels below provide a wide variety of sports facilities – water-skiing, windsurfing, scuba diving, fishing, parasailing, horse riding & tennis

L *Amanusa*, PO Box 33, T772333, F772335. Set high above the Badung Straits, with sea views, 35 Balinese style bungalows, a/c, 4-poster bed, some suites with private pools, resort facilities including large swimming pool on Bali, Italian restaurant, local cuisine at terrace restaurant, tennis, mountain bikes, buggy service to beach or golf course. Recommended.

L-AL *Nusa Dua Beach*, PO Box 1028, T771210, F771229. A/c, 4 restaurants, pool, lush gardens and traditional Balinese buildings, good sports facilities, including a new spa centre, the new 'palace' extension is for the truly well-heeled.

L-AL *Sheraton Laguna*, PO Box 2044, T771327, F771326. Part of the Sheraton 'Luxury Collection'. One of the more luxurious hotels in Bali. The emphasis is on providing an intimate and relaxed atmosphere in surroundings of elegance and luxury, with personal service including 24 hr butler service. 269 fine rooms and 18 sumptuous suites. An outstanding spa and health club, 5 ha of swimmable freshwater lagoon with specially created beach, to which some of the rooms have their own private access; this is one of the largest pools in Bali. 3 bars and restaurants, including 'fine dining' at the Mayang Sari which features Balinese and International dishes, and is surrounded by lagoons and waterfalls. Wheelchair access. Recommended.

AL *Awani Bali Desa Apartments*, on the northern edge of Nusa Dua at the boundary with Tanjung Benoa, T772688, F772678, awaniss@indosat.net.id 28 very attractively decorated 2 and 3 bedroom villas with living room, marble floored dining room, well equipped kitchen, 2 bathrooms, hall, a/c, satellite TV, IDD, verandah, maid room, daily maid service. Some 2-storey villas with upstairs sea views. Pool, tennis court, garage, no direct beach access but use of *Club Med* beach, 3 mins' walk. Free airport transfers. Rates negotiable, long-stay rates available, good value for this area. **AL** *Bali Hilton International*, T771102, F771616, information@balihilton.com or blihil@indosat.net.id 538 rooms, some with great sea views. Designed to resemble a Balinese water palace with an imposing entrance and the grandest lobby in Bali. Set in 30 acres. Each evening there is a cultural performance in the Balinese theatre, with excellent buffet dinner. Special children's facilities. Weider fitness centre, spa and sauna. Daily programme of activities, covered tennis courts, squash, pool, full range of watersports, adjacent to 18-hole golf course. 6 restaurants and bars including Japanese, and pub with live music and dancing. Conference facilities for 700+600 people and business centre, 24 hr health clinic. Ayodya club offers 75 rooms and suites with upgraded facilities and private pool. Special rooms for disabled visitors. **AL** *Grand Hyatt*, PO Box 53, T771188, F771084. A/c, restaurant, 5 pools, opened Apr 1991, large and very plush, with extensive and elaborate grounds. **AL** *Hotel Nikko Royal Bali*, Jl Raya Nusa Dua Seletan, Nusa Dua Selatan, T773377, F773388, sales@nikkobali.com Dramatic location at the edge of a 40ft cliff, 395 well designed rooms and suites, 4 restaurants and 4 bars, health club, 4 inter-connected pools with 30m water slide, tennis, watersports, camel riding (contact Tel ext 210); 1 hr camel rides through tropical bushland and along the beach (adults US$33, children [12 and under] US$17), activities for children. **AL** *Jasmine Sekar Nusa Resort*, Jl Raya Nusa Dua Selatan, T773333, F775765, Jasmine@indosat.net.id One of the new boutique hotels. Each attractively decorated room is situated in a very small, enclosed courtyard, but absolutely no views and rather claustrophobic. Reasonably priced spa. The best feature of the hotel is its hilltop pool (one of 2 pools) and restaurant (mid-range), both with far-reaching views; 20 mins' walk to beach. Aimed at the tour group market, prices are very high for independent travellers. **AL** *Melia Bali Sol*, PO Box 1048, T771510, F771360. A/c, several restaurants (recommended), large and attractive pool, beautiful gardens, good sports facilities. **AL** *Putri Bali*, PO Box 1, T771020, F771139. A/c, restaurant, pool, set in attractive landscaped grounds, all facilities, and some cottage-style accommodation. **AL** *Sheraton Nusa Indah*, PO Box 36, T771906,

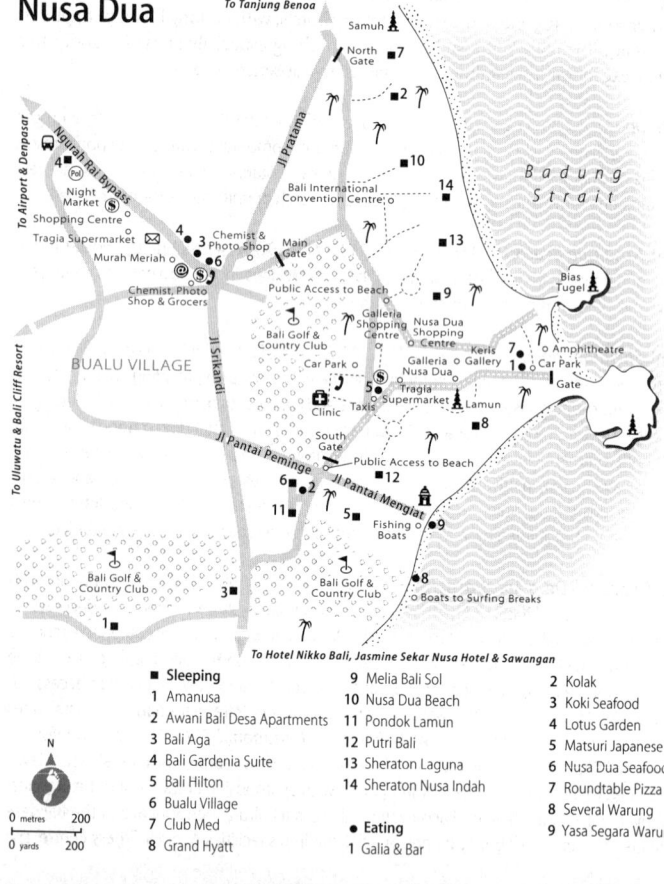

Nusa Dua

■ **Sleeping**
1 Amanusa
2 Awani Bali Desa Apartments
3 Bali Aga
4 Bali Gardenia Suite
5 Bali Hilton
6 Bualu Village
7 Club Med
8 Grand Hyatt
9 Melia Bali Sol
10 Nusa Dua Beach
11 Pondok Lamun
12 Putri Bali
13 Sheraton Laguna
14 Sheraton Nusa Indah

● **Eating**
1 Galia & Bar
2 Kolak
3 Koki Seafood
4 Lotus Garden
5 Matsuri Japanese
6 Nusa Dua Seafood
7 Roundtable Pizza
8 Several Warung
9 Yasa Segara Warung

F771908. Excellent, recently refurbished family resort. A/c, set in 25 acres of tropical gardens beside the sea with lagoons, a small aviary, iguana park and mini zoo. 369 very attractively decorated rooms, each with separate seating area and balcony, many rooms face the ocean. There are 12 family suites. An additional 23 suites have separate eating and pantry facilities. The 4 restaurants serve excellent, reasonably priced food, and include a Japanese and a fish restaurant. Large pool; fitness centre with cardiovascular equipment, sauna and massage; a full range of watersports. The hotel provides an outstanding programme of activities for children, the best of any hotel on the island; it includes a computer lab, 15 play stations, a/c 'class rooms' for lessons in Balinese music, dance and art, a supervised baby-sitting area for toddlers, swimming pool, playground and a mini-zoo. Wheelchair access. The largest conference centre on Bali, with capacity for 2,500 in the main hall, plus an additional 8 halls, with state of the art equipment, multilingual business centre, banqueting facilities. Guests can use the facilities of the *Sheraton Laguna* next door. **AL** *Bali Aga*, 8 Jl Nusa Dua Selatan, T776688, F773636, baliaga@indo.net.id Another new boutique hotel with no outstanding features, 15 mins' walk from the beach, 62 rooms.

A *Club Med*, PO Box 7, T771246, F771831. 2 restaurants, 3 pools, excellent sports facilities and cultural activities, and caters well for children. **A** *Hotel Bualu Village*, PO Box 6, T771310, F771313, htlbuala@indosat.net.id One of the cheaper hotels in Nusa Dua, smaller and more personal but not nearly as luxurious; neither is it on the beach (10 mins' walk or use the hotel shuttle bus which runs every 15-30 mins). Set in gardens, with 2 restaurants, bar, 2 pools, tennis, children's play area.

B *Lamun Guesthouse*, T771983, F771985; 24 fairly basic rooms in need of refurbishment, with a/c but only cold water; 12 mins' walk to beach. Easily the cheapest place in Nusa Dua, but you are not getting much for your money.

Eating All the hotels have a range of restaurants serving Indonesian, Balinese, other Asian cuisines and international food. The *Amanusa* has a 1st class Italian restaurant as well as local cuisine served in their terrace restaurant. Quality is generally good but prices are far higher than anywhere else in Bali – *Galleria Nusa Dua Shopping Complex* houses some restaurants at varying prices.

Mid-range *Matsuri Japanese Restaurant*, Galleria Nusa Dua Shopping Complex, T772267. Serves fairly expensive but often disappointing Japanese food. Open 1130-2300. *Sheraton Nusa Indah* has an elegant and very reasonably priced restaurant, *The Capsicum Café*, which serves excellent meals. In Buala village there is a growing number of restaurants that cater for clientele from the *Nusa Dua* hotels which are more reasonably priced, and there are cheap but clean local eateries near the Tragia supermarket. On the public beach south of the hotels, there are several cheaper warung selling fish dishes and the usual tourist fare (nasi goreng, sandwiches etc). **Cheap** *Prahu Yasa Segala Warung*, at the end of Jl Pantai Mengiat (between the Putri Bali Hotel and the Hilton).

Bars *Players Bar*, Nusa Dua Beach Hotel, happy hours 1900-2100, games room; *Lila Cita*, Grand Hyatt, open 1800-0200, happy hours 1800-2000, good cocktails.

Entertainment All the hotels have an outdoor theatre where nightly cultural performances take place, often in conjunction with dinner and for diners only. Some of the restaurants in the *Galleria Nusa Dua Shopping Complex* put on shows of Balinese dancing in the evening. A Barong procession winds its way through the shopping complex in the late afternoon during high season.

Festivals **Nusa Dua Annual Festival**, for 1 week spanning the end of Aug/beginning Sep. All events are free and open to hotel guests in the Nusa Dua area. The programme of mainly traditional Balinese cultural events includes a religious procession, demonstrations showing the preparations for traditional ceremonies and Balinese food, and exhibitions of art and handicrafts. Each evening performances of both traditional and modern Balinese dances and gamelan music take place at sunset in the Amphitheatre. Special children's programme of events.

Shopping   **Clothes**   The *Galleria Nusa Dua Shopping Complex* is the largest shopping complex on Bali and has smart clothing boutiques, jewellers, a duty-free store and supermarket. Several international designers have shops in the complex, including Dolce and Gabana, Armani, Versace, and Benetton. One of the best clothes shops is *Animale*, a current favourite with Westerners, and its prices are very reasonable. There is a large **Batik Keris** department store which sells clothes and handicrafts. As can be expected, prices are higher than elsewhere on the island, but the quality is good. The complex also boasts the best sports and golf shop in Bali – golf sets available for rent (US$20). There is a free shuttle bus running between the major hotels and the shopping complex on a fixed schedule. There is also a bus that runs every 40 mins and costs 2,000Rp per person.

Sports   **Diving**   *Bali Marine Sports*, Club Bualu, T771310; *Barrakuda Bali Dive*, *Bali Tropik Palace Hotel*, T772130, F772131; *Baruna Watersports* at the *Melia Bali Sol*, T771350, and Nusa Dua Beach, T771210. *Waterworld* at *Sheraton*, T777281, 774971, or visit their counter on the beach in front of the hotel. Prices are typically: US$298-375 for a PADI open water course, US$75 for an introductory dive at Nusa Dua, for certified divers US$65 at Nusa Dua Reef, US$125 for 2 dives at Nusa Penida, US$100 at Padangbai, Tulamben or Amed, US$125 at Menjangan Island.

Watersports   Most of the leading watersports companies are represented in Nusa Dua at the luxury hotels. Typical rates and sports on offer are: jet ski US$20-35 for 15 mins, price depends on how powerful the machine is; snorkelling US$25 per hr (minimum 2 people); yacht cruises US$1,000-1,800 for 3-6 hrs; fishing US$80 for 4 hrs; windsurfing US$15-25 per hr for hire of board, instruction available from US$60 for 3 hrs; sailing US$20 per hr; banana boat/parasailing US$15 a ride; glass bottom boat US$20 a ride; water-ski US$25 for 15 mins. You can get cheaper rates if you approach the company directly rather than go through your hotel.

Golf   18-hole *Bali Golf and Country Club* (opened 1991, designed by Nelson and Wright), T771791, F771797 for details. Tee-times from 0630-1600. Green fees, which include mandatory golf cart, US$142 for 18 holes, US$85 for 9 holes. Beautiful sea-side setting. Attractive clubhouse and pool.

Transport   *27 km from Denpasar, 9 km from airport*   **Local**   **Car hire**: *Avis*, *Nusa Dua Beach Hotel*, T771220 ext 739, and *Club Med*, T771521. **Taxi**: taxis and hotel cars will take guests into Kuta and elsewhere; prices are high.

Road   **Bemo**: from Jl Pantai in **Kuta** to Nusa Dua; and regular connections from **Denpasar's** Tegal terminal.

Directory   **Places of worship**   **Interdenominational** church service at the *Nusa Dua Beach Hotel*, 1730 Sun. **Catholic Mass**: Bali Sol, 1800 Sun.

North and east from Denpasar

Craft villages on the road from Denpasar to Ubud

A number of craft villages, each specializing in a different craft, from production of wood and stone carvings to gold and silver jewellery, line the busy main road north from Denpasar to Ubud. The concentration of workshops here is extraordinary – much of the products are exported around the world. The demands of the tourist industry have caused the mass production of second-rate pieces to become common. Nonetheless there are still some fine works to be found.

After 22 km climbing steadily through picturesque paddy fields & past steep-sided ravines, the road arrives at the hill resort & artists' colony of Ubud

Batubulan
Phone code: 0361

This ribbon-like village, stretched out for about 2 km along the road, is 8 km from Denpasar. It is renowned for its stone carving, although the production of carved wooden Balinese screens and doors is very much in evidence. In addition, there is a sizeable pottery industry here. **Barong**, **kecak** (fire dance) and **kris dances** are performed every day at the north end of the village. ■ *Times vary, 0900-1030, 1800-1930*. One of Bali's principal performing arts academies – KOKAR/SMKI – is based in Batubulan. Just outside Batubulan is the **Taman Burung Bali Bird Park**. ■ *T299352, 0900-1800*.

Celuk & Batuan
Phone code: 0361

Celuk, 4 km on from Batubulan and 12 km from Denpasar, supports large numbers of gold and silversmiths who sell their jewellery from countless shops and showrooms along the road. Much of the work is inferior, although there are some shops selling slightly better quality jewellery; for example, *Runa*, *Dede's*, Jl Grianyar 18 and *Banjar Telabah*. It is worth bargaining in these shops. Another 4 km north from Celuk is another woodcarving village, Batuan. A range of products are on sale, although the artists have a particular reputation for the quality of their carved wood panels.

Mas
Phone code: 0361

Finally, Mas, 20 km from Denpasar and 2 km south of Ubud, is a woodcarving village. In the mid-1980s this was the centre of woodcarving in Bali; now the industry is far more dispersed. Nevertheless, some of the finest (unpainted) works are still produced here and it is possible to watch the artists at work. Although there are numerous wood carvers based here, the workshop of *Ida Bagus Tilem* – the *Tilem Gallery*, T975099 - is recommended. His pieces are expensive, but Tilem's father was an accomplished artist, and his son's work is also highly regarded. The workshop of *Ketut Puja*, T975096, has also been recommended.

Kemenuh
Phone code: 0361

Kemenuh village, about 9 km southeast of Ubud, is another important wood carving centre, offering a range of pieces including huge mythical beasts, fine art and the usual Balinese objects at more competitive prices than Mas.

Sleeping B *Sua Bali Lodge*, Kemenuh village (Sua Bali is signposted from the Gianyar road, 7 km east of Ubud), T/F32141. 6 cottages in large grounds with private facilities. The lodge offers language tuition in both Balinese and Indonesian and is a unique opportunity to learn about the customs and culture of Bali. The founder set up the lodge with the aim of preserving the local environment and culture.

Ubud

Phone code: 0361

During the rainy season, Ubud gets much more rain than the coastal resorts & can be very wet & much cooler

Ubud is a rather dispersed community, spread over hills and valleys with deep forested ravines and terraced ricefields. For many tourists, Ubud has become the cultural heart of Bali, with its numerous artist's studios and galleries as well as a plentiful supply of shops selling clothes, jewellery and woodcarving. Unfortunately, the town has succumbed to tourism in the last few years, with a considerable amount of development.

Ins and outs

Getting there Public bemos stop at the central market, at the point where Jalan Wanasa Wana (Monkey Forest Road) meets Jl Raya, in the centre of Ubud. Peraman, T96316, which runs shuttle buses to the main tourist destinations, has a depot 15 mins' walk away from the centre of town on Jl Handman. They are increasingly reluctant to pick up or drop off at travellers' accommodations. *Nomad* also runs shuttle buses from their office, adjacent to *Nomad restaurant*, to the main tourist destinations, T975520. Their service is not as comprehensive as *Perama's* but they tend to be cheaper. Public bemos run from Ubud to Batubalan for connections south to Kuta, Sanur etc; Gianyur for connections east to Padangbai and Candi Dasa and north to Singaraga and Louina and Kintaman. *Perama* and *Nomad* run regular shuttle buses to the airport. There is often a surcharge for departures before 0900.

Bina Wisata **tourist office** is on Jl Raya Ubud (opposite the Puri Saren), open 1000-2000. Good for information on daily performances and walks in the Ubud area, but otherwise not very helpful.

History

Ubud was one of the more powerful of the principalities that controlled Bali, before the Dutch extended their control over the whole island at the beginning of this century. Though primarily an upland rice-growing area, it also gained an early reputation for the skill of its artists, particularly for the intricacy of their work. Perhaps it was the latent artistic temperament of the people of Ubud, coupled no doubt with the beauty of the place, that caused many of the entranced Western artists to base themselves here. The painter Walter Spies was invited to Bali by the Prince of Ubud, Raka Sukawati, and was so entranced with the place that he settled here – becoming the first of a series of bohemian Westerners to make Ubud their home (see page 440). In 1936, Spies, Bonnet (another artist) and the Prince established *Pita Maha*, the first artists' co-operative on the island. Since then Ubud has remained a centre of the arts in Bali, particularly painting, and many of the finest Balinese artists are based here or in the surrounding villages. Because of the influence of Spies, Bonnet and the artists' co-operative, there is a distinct style to much of the work. Paintings tend to be colourful and finely worked depictions of the natural world.

Sights

Much of the charm and beauty of Ubud lies in the natural landscape. There are few official 'sights' in the town itself – in contrast to the surrounding area (see 'Excursions' below). The **Museum Puri Lukisan**, in the centre of Ubud, contains examples of 20th century Balinese painting and carving (and that of Europeans who have lived here). ■ *500Rp, 0800-1600. See entertainment below for more information.*

Antonio Blanco, a Western artist who settled in Ubud, has turned his home into a gallery. The house is in a stunning position, perched on the side of a hill, but the collection is disappointing. Blanco – unlike Spies and Bonnet – has had no influence on the style of local artists. ■ *500Rp. To get there, walk west on the main road and over a ravine past Murnis Warung – the house is immediately on the left-hand side of the road at the end of the old suspension bridge.*

The **Museum Neka**, 1½ km from town, up the hill past Blanco's house; six Balinese-style buildings contain a good collection of traditional and contemporary Balinese and Javanese painting, as well as work by foreign artists who have lived in or visited Bali. There is a good art bookshop here and a good restaurant with views over the ravine. ■ *1,000Rp, 0900-1700 Mon-Sun.*

At the south end of Jl Monkey Forest is the forest itself, which is overrun with monkeys. An attractive walk through the forest leads to the **Pura Dalem Agung Padangtegal**, a Temple of the Dead. ■ *Admission to forest 1,000Rp.* Back in town on Jalan Raya Ubud, opposite Jalan Monkey Forest, is the **Puri Saren**, with richly carved gateways and courtyards. West of here behind the Lotus Café is the **Pura Saraswati**, with a pretty rectangular pond in front of it.

Do NOT enter the forest with food – these monkeys have been known to bite. You will only have 48 hrs to get to Jakarta for a rabies injection

Excursions

There are villages beyond Ubud which remain unspoilt and it is worth exploring the surrounding countryside, either on foot or by bicycle. Around Ubud, particularly to the north in the vicinity of Tampaksiring, and to the east near Pejeng and Gianyar, is perhaps the greatest concentration of temples in Bali. The most detailed and accurate guide to these pura is AJ Bernet Kempers's *Monumental Bali* (Periplus: Berkeley and Singapore, 1991). **Sangeh** and the **Pura Bukit Sari** are two temples about 25 km west of Ubud, but easier to reach via Mengwi (see page 409).

Craft villages line the route to Batubulan & Denpasar (see page 365)

Goa Gajah, or 'Elephant Cave', lies about 4 km east of Ubud, via Peliatan, on the right-hand side of the road and just before Bedulu. The caves are hard to miss as there is a large car park, with an imposing line of stallholders catering for the numerous coach trips. The complex is on the side of a hill overlooking the Petanu River, down a flight of steps.

Goa Gajah

Hewn out of the rock, the entrance to the cave has been carved to resemble the mouth of a demon and is surrounded by additional carvings of animals, plants, rocks and monsters. The name of the complex is thought to have been given by the first visitors who mistakenly thought that the demon was an elephant. The small, dimly lit, 'T'-shaped cave is man-made. It is reached by a narrow passage whose entrance is the demon's mouth. It contains 15 niches carved out of the rock. Those on the main passageway are long enough to lead archaeologists to speculate that they were sleeping chambers. At the end of one of the arms of the 'T' is a four-armed statue of Ganesh, and at the end of the other, a collection of lingams.

The **bathing pools** next to the caves are more interesting. These were only discovered in the mid-1950s by the Dutch archaeologist JC Krijgsman, who excavated the area in front of the cave on information provided by local people. He discovered stone steps and eventually uncovered two bathing pools (probably one for men and the other for women). Stone carvings of the legs of three figures were uncovered in each of the two pools. These seemed to have been cut from the rock at the same time that the pools were dug. Water spouts from the urns, held by the nymphs, into the two pools.

Stairs lead down from the cave and pool area to some meditation niches, with two small statues of the Buddha in an attitude of meditation. The remains of an enormous relief were also found in 1931, depicting several stupas. To get there, walk down from the cave and bathing pools, through fields, and over a bridge. The complex is thought to date from the 11th century. ■ *1,050Rp (500Rp extra for camera), children 300Rp. Dress – sarong. Getting there: a short ride by bemo from Ubud or from the Batubulan terminal outside Denpasar; alternatively, join a tour.*

Yeh Pulu is 2 km east of Goa Gajah, beautifully set amongst terraced ricefields, and a short walk along a paved path from the end of the road. This is a peaceful place, free from crowds and hawkers. It also happens to be the location of the local bath house. Yeh Pulu is one of the oldest holy places in Bali, dating from the 14th or 15th century. Cut into the rock are 20m of vigorous carvings depicting village life, intermingled with

Yeh Pulu

Hindu and Balinese gods: figures carrying poles, men on horseback, Krishna saluting, wild animals and vegetation. Originally these would have been plastered over – and perhaps painted – although almost all of the plaster has since weathered away. A small cell cut into the rock at the south end of the reliefs is thought to have been the abode of a hermit – who probably helped to maintain the carvings. Until 1937 when the site was renovated, water from the overhanging paddy fields washed over the carvings causing significant erosion. There is also a small bathing pool here. An old lady looks after the small shrine to Ganesh and ensures a donation is placed there.

Bernet Kempers, in his book *Monumental Bali*, interprets the sequence of carvings as follows, beginning at the top. There is an opening piece, followed by five 'scenes':

Opening: a standing man with his arm raised opens the yarn. This is probably Krishna, who as a young shepherd protected his friends from an irate Indra by using Mount Govardhana as an umbrella.

Around Ubud

■ Sleeping
1 Amandari
2 Cahaya Dewata
3 Kupu Kupu Barong
4 Taman Bebek

Scene I: a man carries two vessels (probably of palm wine) on a pole over his shoulders, and is led by a woman of high status towards a hut where an old woman waits at a pair of double doors.

Scene II: here, an old woman rests in a cave while a man, to her left, approaches with a hoe over his shoulder. Behind him sits an ascetic dwarf with a turban. On the far right is a demon with fangs and a large sacrificial ladle.

Scene III: surrounded by trees, a man on a horse gallops towards two figures, with weapons raised, who are attacking a bear (?), while a fourth man advances from behind. In the lower right corner, a frog with a sword fights for his life against a large snake.

Scene IV: two men, their hunting trip completed and successful, carry a pair of dead bears on a pole.

Scene V: a woman holds a horse's tail while two monkeys play on her back. She is either trying to restrain the horse and rider, or they are helping to pull her up a hill.

■ *550Rp. Dress – sarong and sash (for hire at site). It is probably possible to visit this site at any time, as there are no 'entrance gates'. Getting there: Yeh Pulu is 350m off the main Ubud-Gianyar road just south of the Tampaksiring turning, and is signposted to Bendung Bedaulu. Bemos from Ubud will drop passengers at the turning; it is an easy walk from there to the site.*

Sleeping and eating At the beginning of the path there is a restaurant, and close by is the **E** *Lantur Homestay*.

The road north from Bedulu

Gianyar Regency contains a number of important archaeological sites, the majority located near **Pejeng**, 4 km east of Ubud. This sacred area, inhabited since the Bronze age, contains over 40 temples as well as massive stone statues, carvings, sarcophagi, Buddhist sanctuaries, bathing sites and bronze artefacts. A number of artefacts have been removed to museums as far afield as Amsterdam, but many have remained *in situ*, beside rivers, in paddy fields or in nearby temples. Pejeng was once the centre of a great kingdom which flourished between the ninth and 14th centuries, before falling to the Majapahit. These days it is home to many Brahmin families.

An important archaeological discovery was made in early 1999. A sarcophagus, estimated to be 2,000 years old dating from the megalithic period, was found buried in a garden. The quality of carving of the images on the cover of the sarcophagus suggests a high level of artistic development on the island 2,000 years ago. This is perhaps a partial explanation for the high concentration of artisans still to be found in the Gianyar area.

The small, poorly labelled, **Purbakala Archaeological Museum**, consisting largely of a collection of sarcophagi, neolithic tools and Hindu relics, is 400m north of Bedulu. About 200m further north still is the **Pura Kebo Edan** or 'Mad Bull Temple', a rather ramshackle and ill-kept temple. Among the monumental weathered stone figures in the courtyard is a statue of Bima dancing on a corpse, its eyes open, protected under a wooden pavilion. The figure – sometimes known as the 'Pejeng Giant' – is renowned for its 'miraculous' penis, pierced with a peg or pin (used to stimulate women during intercourse, a feature of sexual relations across the region).

■ *Admission by donation. Dress: sarong.*

Pura Pusering Jagat (the 'Navel of the World' Temple) is 50m off the main road, a short distance north from Kebo Edan. **Pura Panataran Sasih** lies another 250m north in Pejeng and is thought to date from the ninth or 10th century. This temple was the original navel pura of the old Pejeng Kingdom. The entrance is flanked by a pair of fine stone elephants. Walk through impressive split gates to see the '**Moon of Pejeng**' (*sasih* means 'moon'). It is housed in a raised pavilion towards the back of the compound and is supposedly the largest bronze kettledrum in the world. In Balinese folklore, the drum is supposed to have been one of the wheels of the chariot that carries the moon across the night sky. The wheel fell to earth and was kept (still glowing with an inner fire) in the temple. It is said that one night a man climbed into the tower and urinated on the drum, extinguishing its inner fire, and paid for the desecration with his life. Visitors should on no account try to climb the tower for a better look at the drum. The drum is believed to date from the third century BC, although no-one is absolutely sure – certainly, it has been housed here for centuries. It may be a Dongson drum from Vietnam or it may be a later example produced elsewhere. The fine decoration on this incomparable piece of bronze work was first recorded – in a series of brilliantly accurate drawings – by the artist WOJ Nieuwenkamp in 1906 (although it was mentioned in a book by the blind chronicler GE Rumphius, published in 1705). A collection of 11th century stone carvings are also to be found here. ■ *Admission by donation. Dress – sarong. Getting there: by bemo from Ubud or from the Batubulan terminal outside Denpasar.*

Tours **Bird watching** walks around Ubud with *Bali Bird Walks* (possible sightings include Java Kingfisher, Bar-winged Prinia, Black-winged Starling, Java Sparrow, Scarlet-headed Flowerpecker), T975009, based at the Beggar's Bush pub, Tjampuhan, Ubud, US$30, including lunch and shared use of binoculars. Tours on Tuesday, Friday, Saturday and Sunday at 0900.

Day tours around the island can be booked from Jl Raya Ubud. Good choice of tours including temples, sunsets and volcano. From 30,000Rp to 45,000Rp full day. Beware of bus drivers taking you to a pre-arranged place for lunch, where the prices are high and the alternatives nil.

Mountain biking downhill all the way back from Mount Batur (90,000Rp) and Jungle Mountain trekking (85,000Rp), both with *Sobek Expeditions* (see below). Some places down Jl Monkey Forest do tandems. Expect to pay between 5,000Rp and 10,000Rp per day.

Whitewater rafting down the Ayung River with *Sobek Expeditions*, T287059, F289448, for a two hour trip with time to swim in the pools under the waterfalls while the raft waits, buffet lunch included; this is a well-organized, professionally run outfit, US$70 per person. Also *Bali Adventure Tours*, T751292, see page 331. *Bali Widya*, T976309, full day with meals, insurance and showers, US$65 - well recommended for a full day's entertainment. They also claim to go 'that bit further' than their competitors!

Essentials

Sleeping
■ *on maps, pages 368, 372 & 374*

Ubud has a wide choice of good value, clean and generally high quality accommodation, in often romantic and well-designed bungalows. Except in the more expensive hotels, breakfast is included in the rates. Remember to book ahead in peak seasons.

L *Amandari*, Kedewatan, 2 km northwest of town, T975333, F975335, amandari@indosat.net.id Restaurant, pool, magnificently positioned, set alone above the Ayung River among paddyfields, excellent service (personal staff for each of the 29 bungalows), beautiful rooms with private garden each protected by high walls. Recommended. **L** *Kupu Kupu Barong*, Kedewatan, T975478, F975079. Northwest of town, restaurant, pool, lovely position overlooking the Ayung River, superb service and rooms, no children under 12 years. **L-AL** *Pita Maha*, Jl Sanggingan, Campuhan, T974330, F974329, pitamaha@dps.mega.net.id 24 self-contained, traditional bales (villas). Stunning views over the Oos River valley and to Mount Agung. All villas are the ultimate in luxury,

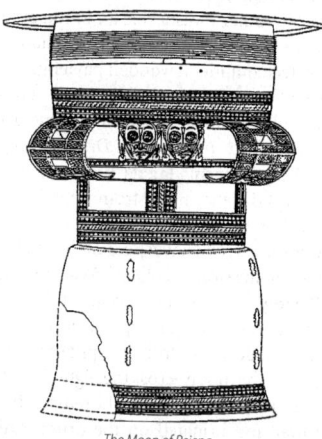

The Moon of Pejeng

very spacious, some rooms with private pools. Spectacular spring-water pool lapping over the edge of the ravine, open-air pavilion restaurant with ravine views. Recommended.
L-AL *The Chedi Ubud*, Desa Melinggih Kelod, Payangan, Gianyar, T975963, F975968. A/c, restaurant, pool, health spa, 65 rooms, quietly sophisticated, exquisite views, private garden and walkways, located north of Ubud village. **AL** *Kamandalu*, Jl Tegallalang, Banjar Nagi, 2 km from Ubud centre (complimentary shuttle service), T975825, F975851, kamandal@indo.net.id, www.kamandalu.com 58 luxurious, self-contained villas, built in traditional Balinese style, surrounded by ricefields overlooking the Petanu River valley, top of the range villas have private pools, large main pool, paddling pool attached, herbal spa, good restaurant, *Petulu*, Asian and international cuisine. Recommended. **AL** *Waka di Ume*, Jl Sueta, Desa Sambahan, T96178, F96179. A few kilometres above Ubud set amongst rice paddies, built in designer primitive style. Spacious rooms, fan only, luxurious marble bathroom. Rooftop restaurant serves genuine Balinese food, cascading swimming pool overlooking the rural valley, meditation chapel, sauna, steam baths, traditional massage, an oasis of tranquillity. Recommended.

A *Cahaya Dewata*, Kedewatan, in between the Amandari and Kupu Kupu Barong (out of town), T/F975495. Excellent restaurant, pool. Recommended. **A** *Champlung Sari*, Jl Monkey Forest 58. Smart hotel with 58 very comfortable rooms. Recommended. **A** *Dewi Sri*, Jl Hanoman, Padangtegal (near the intersection with Jl Monkey Forest), T975300, F975005. Pool, 2-storeyed thatched bungalows amid the ricefields, well-run. Recommended. **A** *Merpati Inn*, Jl Andong, T973083, F975862. This hotel is a little out of town. Very bright and clean, with a large pool, pricey. **A** *Padma Indah Cottages*, Campuan, T975719, F975091. A/c, restaurant, pool, cottages could sleep 4, attractive cottages but badly managed. **A** *Prada Guest House*, Jl Kajeng 1, T/F975122, pradaku@indola.net.id, www.angelfire.com/co/pradha/ Newly created guesthouse in traditional Balinese décor with Western influences, relaxed environment. Thoughtful touches add to the charm of the rooms, excellent service, well-priced. Highly recommended. **A** *Pringga Juwita*, off Jl Jawa Ubud, T/F975734. Small but secluded pool, fan, well designed bungalows set amongst flowing water gardens, rooms comfortable with obvious care taken. Recommended. **A** *Siti Bungalows*, Jl Kajeng 3, T975699, F975643. Eight sizeable rooms, with 4-poster beds, set around small lake, peaceful atmosphere, small pool. **A** *Taman Bebek Villas*, 2 km south of Amandari Hotel on Sayan-Ubud Rd, T/F975385. Eight, 1- or 2-bedroomed bungalows, with sitting areas and kitchenettes, a family-style homestay set in a beautiful garden above the Ayung River. Recommended. **A** *Tjampuhan*, Jl Raya Campuhan, PO Box 198, Gianyar, T975368, F975137. At west end of Jl Raya Ubud, over the river and up the hill, this hotel was originally the artist Walter Spies' home, restaurant, small spring-fed pool, stunning setting on the side of a ravine, watery gardens (complete with frogs), bungalows built up the ravine, romantic rooms, plans to revitalize its faded elegance, in the meantime the 'Raja' rooms are the best. **A** *Ubud Village Hotel*, Jl Monkey Forest, T975571, F975069. Lovely rooms set among beautiful gardens, large pool (open to non-residents), good restaurant. **A** *Ulun Ubud*, Sanggingan, T975762, F975524. Simple restaurant, pool, traditional Balinese style, attractive position on steep hillside facing the Campuan River, people work at the bottom of the gorge chipping out stones for carving, women carry the rocks on their heads up to the road. **A** *Villa Bukit Ubud*, by Neka Museum, Sanggingan, T975371, F975787. Restaurant with good views and good value food, good pool, pleasant a/c bungalows on edge of ravine, Balinese thatch roofs and surprising suburban comfort inside, a/c, hot water, good for families. Recommended. **A** *Villa Sanggingan*, just south of Neka Museum, Sanggingan, T974274, F974275. Lovely pool and breakfast room, good views, rooms away from the road are quieter.

A-B *Oka Kartini*, Jl Raya Ubud, T975193, F975759. Pool, small hotel with friendly staff, rooms are a little over-elaborate but thoughtfully designed, rooms with a/c in **A** price range, pleasant bar. Recommended.

B *Agung Cottages*, Jl Gautama 18, T975414. Separate bungalows set amidst beautiful gardens. Large rooms with front terraces. Recommended. **B** *Cendana Cottages*, Jl Monkey Forest, T973243. Large rooms overlook ricefields and give a feeling of space and tranquillity, open bathrooms with hot water, restaurant. **B** *Fibra Inn*, Jl Monkey Forest, T975451, F975125. Pool, good rooms and open-air bathrooms, hot water. Recommended. **B** *Grand Ubud Hotel*, Jl Monkey Forest, T974053, F975437. Lovely large rooms with good service, the pool is small. **B** *Gusti's Garden Bungalows*, Jl Monkey Forest, T973311. Good sized rooms with excellent views over fields and forest, hot water; pool in peaceful setting. **B** *Lokasari Guesthouse*, Jl Raya Andong, T/F975476. Slightly out of town on main road, good 2-storey family apartments with kitchen area and alfresco bathroom. Art gallery and café. **B** *Mumbul Inn*, T975995, F976478. Lovely views overlooking river. Peaceful and tastefully decorated rooms, with marble floors and baths, well priced. **B** *Nick's Pension*, off Jl Monkey Forest, this was once the popular place to stay in Ubud but has now gone to seed. Still in a fantastic position, hidden within the jungle, therefore peaceful and secluded. Overpriced and the rooms could do with redecoration. **B** *Pertiwi Bungalows*, Jl Monkey Forest, T975236, F975559. Restaurant, pool, lovely rooms, open-air bathroom. Recommended. **B** *Pringga Juwita Inn*, off Jl Raya Ubud and next to *Pringga Juwita Water Garden Cottages*, T/F975734. Bungalows in pleasant garden on edge of rice fields. **B** *Sehati*, Jl Jembawan 7, T975460. Lovely cool rooms

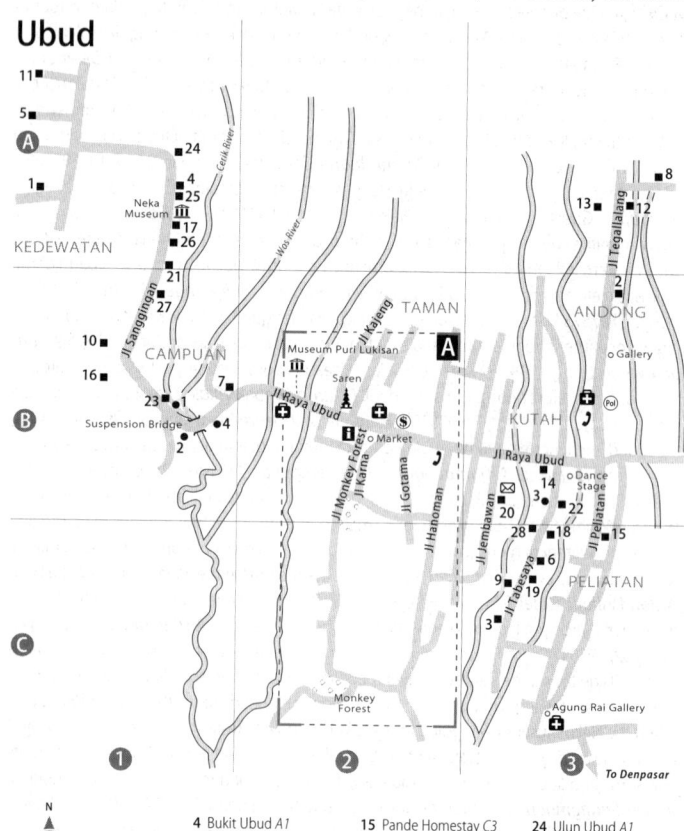

Ubud

4 Bukit Ubud *A1*	15 Pande Homestay *C3*	24 Ulun Ubud *A1*
5 Cahaya Dewata *A1*	16 Penestanan Bungalows *B1*	25 Villa Bukit Ubud *A1*
6 Family House *C3*	17 Pita Maha *A1*	26 Villa Sanggingan *A1*
7 Ibeh *B1*	18 Rona's *C3*	27 Wisata Cottages *B1*
8 Kamandalu *A3*	19 Sanjiwani *C3*	28 Yuliati House *C3*
9 Ketut Reri Homestay *C3*	20 Sehati & Matahari Cottages *B3*	
10 Kori Agung Cottages *B1*	21 Taman Indrakila *A1*	● Eating
11 Kupu Kupu Barong *A1*	22 Tangkas Homestay *B3*	1 Beggars Bush *B1*
12 Lokasari *A3*	23 Tjampuhan *B1*	2 Bridge *B1*
13 Merpati Inn *A3*		3 Jazz Café *B3*
14 Oka Kartini *B3*		4 Murnis Warung *B1*

■ Sleeping
1 Amandari *A1*
2 Banyan Tree Kamandalu *B3*
3 Biang's Homestay *C3*

Related map:
A Central Ubud,
page 374

overlooking a leafy ravine. Recommended. **B** *Sri Bungalows*, Jl Monkey Forest, T975394. Moderate sized rooms with hot water and pool, room walls a little grubby but overall a decent place to stay. **B** *Taman Indrakila* (was *Wisata Cottages*), Sanggigan, T/F975017, tikila@bali-paradise.com, www.bali-paradise.com/ tamanindrakila 15 well decorated rooms with lovely views and an 'away from it all' setting. Pool. Recommended. **B** *Ubud Inn Cottages*, Jl Monkey Forest, T975071, ubud_inn@indosat.net.id Well established cottages dotted around the large pool, variously priced rooms, simply furnished, some a/c; **B** *Villa Rasa Sayang*, Jl Monkey Forest, T975491. Large rooms overlooking pool (open to non-residents), peaceful atmosphere despite its central position. **B** *Yulia Village Inn*, Jl Monkey Forest, clean and well presented rooms, check for special prices, a little overpriced otherwise.

B *Villa Kerti Yasa*, Nyuh Kuning Village, T974377, F974377, reservations@villakertiyasa.com Small, friendly hotel in craft village of Nyuh kuning, around 5 min walk from the Monkey Forest and 10 mins' from Ubud itself. **B-C** *Artini*, hidden cottage, new, attractive rooms set amongst rice paddies off Jl Hanoman. **B-C** *Homestay Indraprastha*, 40 Jl Hanoman, T975549. Well-run homestay with clean rooms in beautiful, quiet garden bordering ricefields. Airport pick-up service available. **B-C** *Ibunda Inn*, Jl Monkey Forest, T97352. A travellers' Mecca. Basic clean rooms, good pool, popular with younger travellers. **B-E** *Matahari Cottages*, Jl Jembawan, T975459. More expensive rooms are well-designed and secluded, some hot water. Recommended.

C *Argaosoka Inn*, Jl Monkey Forest, T973221. Large rooms overlooking the forest. Outdoor breakfast room with fantastic views, friendly management. **C** *Bali Breeze*, Jl Hanoman. Accommodation is in thatched cottages. Lovely garden and views over paddy fields. Attached cold water shower. Recommended. **C** *Bali Ubud Cottages*, T975058, F286971. This place comes recommended by recent guests. **C** *Gria Jungutan*, Jl Monkey Forest, T975752. Very peaceful setting overlooking the forest. **C** *Kori Agung*, Penestanan-Campuan, T975166. A little out of town, off the main road, but lovely rooms with verandah, cold water showers only. Recommended. **C** *Kubu Ku*, Jl Monkey Forest, at the end of the road, set in the middle of paddy fields with lovely rooms. **C** *Lecuk Inn*, Jl Kajeng 15, T/F973445. Moderate rooms with balconies overlooking the river, outside bathrooms means showering with the mosquitoes and geckos. **C** *Mandia*, 30m off Jl Monkey Forest, T870571. Lovely garden atmosphere. Recommended. **C** *Monkey Forest Hideaway I & II*, Jl Monkey Forest. All rooms overlook the forest and rice terraces; some rooms in Monkey Forest Hideaway II with views overlooking Mount Agung. Recommended. **C** *Nari House*, Jl Monkey Forest, T975070. Small, personal hostel offering clean attractive rooms, all with hot water and an excellent breakfast. **C** *Nuriani Guesthouse*, just off Jl Hanoman, T975346. 12 clean, attractive rooms, small garden, upstairs rooms have views of rice paddies. **C** *Nusa Indah*, well built bungalows. **C** *Penestanan Bungalows*, Campuan, T975604, F975603. Small pool, a little out of town, set scenically on a hill overlooking paddy fields, good rooms, hot water. **C** *Puri Garden*, Jl Monkey Forest, T975395. Lovely water garden, good rooms, fan. Recommended. **C** *Puri Indah*, attractive accommodation, one of the better places. **C** *Puri Muwa*, Jl Monkey Forest, T975046. Well-decorated rooms in this pleasant, family run hostel. **C** *Pondok Impian*, Jl Hanoman, comes recommended by several visitors, the wok has an excellent reputation. **C** *Rumah Roda*, Jl Kajeng 24, T975487. Clean rooms with hot water and friendly management. Excellent breakfasts. **C** *Shanti Homestay*, Jl Kajeng 5. Spacious but basic rooms, friendly management who are keen to relay information about the surrounding area. **C** *Siddhartha's Shelter*, Penestanan Kaja (Campuan), T975748. West of town, set among paddy fields. **C** *Sonia's House*, Jl Karna 7, T975535. Variously priced bungalows, watch out for some stinking mattresses but overall a good place to stay. Pool, some a/c. **C** *Warsi Bungalows*, Jl Monkey Forest, T/F975311. Located opposite playing field, small hostel with hot water, fan and a recommended breakfast. **C** *Wisata Cottages*, Campuan, near Neka Museum, T/F950177. Pool, lovely position with views over paddy fields.

C-D *Family House*, Banjar Tebesaya 39, T974054. Expanding homestay with new rooms, each with elegant 4-poster beds, hot water, a cut above the rest for the price. **C-D** *Ketut Reri*

Central Ubud

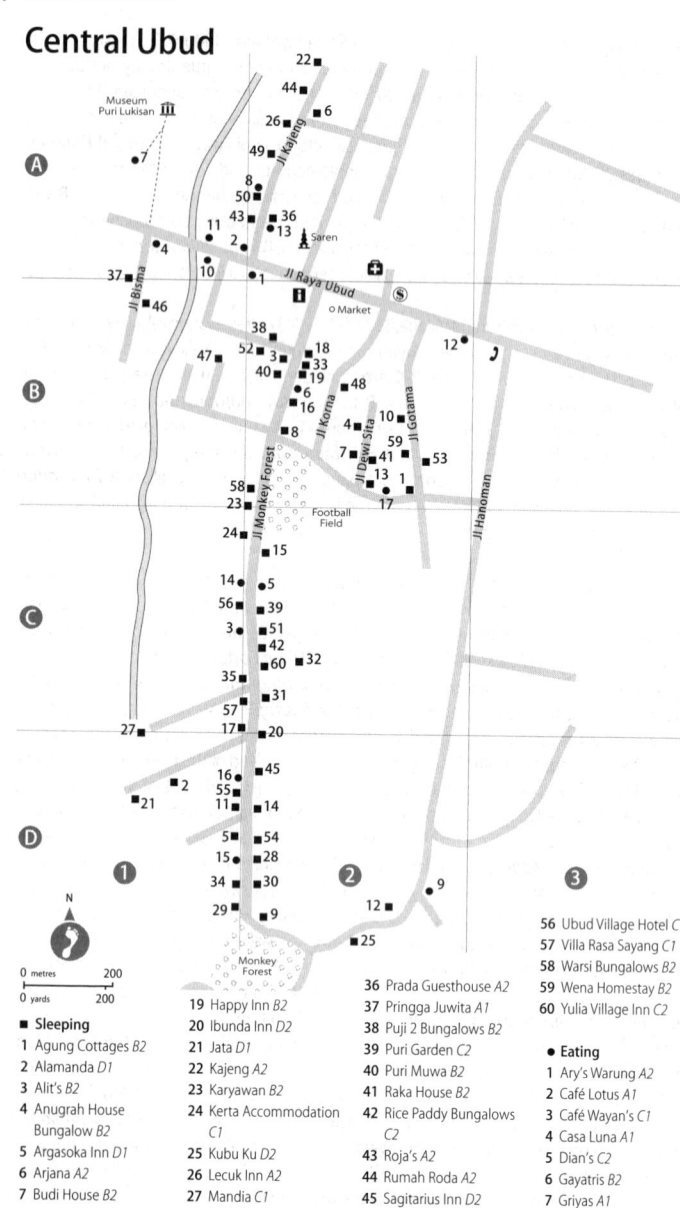

■ **Sleeping**
1 Agung Cottages *B2*
2 Alamanda *D1*
3 Alit's *B2*
4 Anugrah House Bungalow *B2*
5 Argasoka Inn *D1*
6 Arjana *A2*
7 Budi House *B2*
8 Candana Cottages *B2*
9 Champlung Sari *D2*
10 Darta Homestay *B2*
11 Dewi Ayu *D1*
12 Dewi Sri *D2*
13 Esty's House *B2*
14 Fibra Inn *D2*
15 Frog Pond *C2*
16 Gandra's House *B2*
17 Grand Ubud *C1*
18 Gusti's Garden Bungalows *B2*
19 Happy Inn *B2*
20 Ibunda Inn *D2*
21 Jata *D1*
22 Kajeng *A2*
23 Karyawan *B2*
24 Kerta Accommodation *C1*
25 Kubu Ku *D2*
26 Lecuk Inn *A2*
27 Mandia *C1*
28 Merthayasa Bungalows *D2*
29 Monkey Forest Hideaway *D1*
30 Monkey Forest Inn *D2*
31 Nari House *C2*
32 Paddy Fields Bungalows *C2*
33 Pandawa Homestay *B2*
34 Pande Permai Bungalows *D1*
35 Pertiwi Bungalows *C1*
36 Prada Guesthouse *A2*
37 Pringga Juwita *A1*
38 Puji 2 Bungalows *B2*
39 Puri Garden *C2*
40 Puri Muwa *B2*
41 Raka House *B2*
42 Rice Paddy Bungalows *C2*
43 Roja's *A2*
44 Rumah Roda *A2*
45 Sagitarius Inn *D2*
46 Sama's Cottages *B1*
47 Saras & Okawatis *B1*
48 Sonia's *B2*
49 Shanti & Arjanas Homestay *A2*
50 Siti Bungalows *A2*
51 Sri Bungalows *C2*
52 Suarsena House *B2*
53 Sudana Homestay *B2*
54 Ubud Inn Cottages *D2*
55 Ubud Terrace Bungalow *D1*
56 Ubud Village Hotel *C1*
57 Villa Rasa Sayang *C1*
58 Warsi Bungalows *B2*
59 Wena Homestay *B2*
60 Yulia Village Inn *C2*

● **Eating**
1 Ary's Warung *A2*
2 Café Lotus *A1*
3 Café Wayan's *C1*
4 Casa Luna *A1*
5 Dian's *C2*
6 Gayatris *B2*
7 Griyas *A1*
8 Han Snel's Garden *A2*
9 Kura Kura *D2*
10 Menera *A1*
11 Mumbuls *A1*
12 Nomad *B2*
13 Prada *A2*
14 Putra Bar *C1*
15 Swastis *D1*
16 Thai Food, Lotus Lane & Mendras Café *D1*
17 Tutmak *B2*

Homestay, Jl Tebesaya, T975591, small and friendly hostel with clean rooms, hot water. **C-D** *Rona's*, Jl Tebasaya 23, T973229. Short distance from town, popular, friendly family environment with lots of children around. Many guests there on long-stay basis – excellent rates negotiable, kitchen available, good grounds, restaurant. Recommended. **C-D** *Sama's Cottages*, Jl Birma, T973481. Clean comfortable rooms in a relaxed setting overlooking the rice fields, good value. **C-D** *Sanjiwari*, Jl Tebesaya 41, T/F973205, nithi@denpasar.wasantara.net.id Large, clean balcony rooms with cold water only, good views, kitchen available. **C-D** *Ubud Terrace Bungalows*, Jl Monkey Forest, T975690. Situated in a quiet grove, attractive décor, hot water, upstairs rooms have good sunset views.

D *Adinda Bungalows*, Jl Hanoman 64 (just off Hanoman in an alleyway). Attractive outlook over the ricefields, good beds, clean showers, balconies, giant breakfasts. Recommended. **D** *Agungs*, off Jl Raya Ubud (by *Nomad's restaurant*), friendly owner, but rooms are a little overpriced. **D** *Alamanda*, 50m off Jl Monkey Forest, T980571. Peaceful setting with exceptionally helpful staff. Rooms are spacious and cool, bathrooms very clean, use of kitchen and fridge, hot water. Recommended. **D** *Arganas*, Jl Kajeng. 8 rooms with alfresco mandi, clean but simple comfort, run by a friendly family, well priced. **D** *Baruna*, simple rooms, one of the cheaper places. **D** *Biang's Homestay*, Jl Tebsaya, T973207. 5 basic but cheap and clean rooms. Café specializing in vegetarian food. **D** *Dewangga*, off Jl Monkey Forest (by the football field). Attractive setting, nice garden, good rooms, open-air bathroom. Recommended. **D** *Dewi Ayu*, Jl Monkey Forest, T976119. Large airy rooms set within a colourful, well kept garden, fan, hot water. **D** *Frog Pond*, Jl Monkey Forest, next to playing field. Basic but clean rooms with outside mandi. **D** *Gandra's House*, Jl Monkey Forest, T976529. Set off road so quiet, decent colourful rooms with fan, some bathrooms with bath, breakfast (with brown bread), good value. **D** *Jata 3*, 25m from Alamanda, T973249. Small but quiet rooms, rural setting down a side road, hot water. **D** *Kajeng*, Jl Kajeng 29, T975018. Rooms with verandahs overlooking a ravine and duck pond, clean with attractive open-air mandis. **D** *Karyawan*, Jl Monkey Forest. Lovely gardens, clean. Recommended. **D** *Lecuk Inn*, Jl Kajeng 15. Open-air mandi, including breakfast, friendly people, big rooms with a terrace, attractive setting by river and lovely gardens. **D** *Merthayasa Bungalows*, Jl Monkey Forest (bottom of), standard rooms with hot water provide a comfortable stay. **D** *Monkey Forest Inn*, Jl Monkey Forest, good value clean rooms with fan, HW. Recommended. **D** *Mushroom Beach*, simple accommodation in excellent location. **D** *No 7*, attractive room, pretty garden. **D** *Paddy Fields*, off Jl Monkey Forest (opposite *Café Wayan*). Attractive position overlooking rice paddy, good breakfast, friendly owners. Recommended. **D** *Pramesti Cottages*, Jl Monkey Forest. 3 attractive 1- or 2-room cottages set in garden with pond, set back from the street in a rural setting – you hear the frogs at night – hot water. Recommended. **D** *Puri-Pusaka*, opposite Central Market, T975132. Good rooms. **D** *Rice Paddy Bungalows*, convenient central location in Jl Monkey Forest, modern rooms, clean, upstairs rooms have views over rice paddies. **D** *Sagitarius Inn*, Jl Monkey Forest. Set back from the road so very peaceful yet still central, rooms are newly painted, large and good value. **D** *Sama's*, off Jl Raya Ubud (by *Miro's restaurant*), wonderful position among paddy fields, 3 rooms, clean. Recommended. **D** *Sri*, Jl Monkey Forest, T975394. Very clean. Recommended. **D** *Wena Homestay*, Jl Godtama, T975416. Four good, homely rooms, a cut above the rest. Recommended.

D-E *Ibu Arsa*, Peliatan (east of town), older rooms are rather dark, the newer rooms are characterful with attractive open bathrooms, friendly. Recommended. **D-E** *Nyoman Astana's Bungalows*, Peliatan (next to *Siti Hotel*), attractive cosy rooms (the newer ones are more expensive) with attached bathrooms and hot water, beautiful quiet garden, price including a generous breakfast, excellent value for money. Recommended. **D-E** *Suarsena House*, Jl Arjuna, clean and central, more expensive rooms with large bathrooms.

E *Alit's*, Jl Monkey Forest, nice garden, clean rooms, friendly. **E** *Anom*, Jl Arjuna, central, only 3 rooms, but good. **E** *Anugrah House*, Jl Dewi Sita. Good, clean budget accommodation. **E** *Arjana*, Jl Kajeng 6, T978233. Quiet, clean rooms, good bathrooms. Recommended. **E** *Budi*, Jl Dewi Sita, off Jl Monkey Forest, T973307. 4 clean, large rooms set above the road, therefore quiet. Recommended for the price. **E** *Esty's House*, Jl Dewi Sita, T980571. 6 excellent rooms with fan in quiet area, bathrooms large and clean. Recommended. **E** *Pandawa Homestay*, Jl Monkey Forest, good value, big rooms. **E** *Pande Homestay*, Peliatan (east of town), friendly, clean. **E** *Puji 2*, Gunung Arjuna (off Jl Monkey Forest), large breakfast included, comfortable and the cheapest around. **E** *Puri Muwa*, Jl Monkey Forest, T975046. Well-decorated rooms. **E** *Raka House* (off Jl Meluti – near the football field), 3 or 4 rooms. Recommended. **E** *Roja's*, Jl Kajeng 1, attractive bungalows, well kept garden. Recommended. **E** *Sara's*, off Jl Monkey Forest (next to *Okawati's restaurant*), mandi, verandah and large breakfast, good value. Recommended. **E** *Sudana Homestay*, Jl Gotama, T976435. 3 light, pleasant rooms with fan, family run and welcoming environment, good budget accommodation. **E** *Sukerti*, Jl Bima, Banjar Kalah (near intersection with Jl Raya Ubud), clean and very friendly. **E** *Wayan Family Homestay*, Jl Hanoman, 5 rooms, hot shower, very clean, set in a pretty garden, very friendly owners. Recommended. **E** *Yuliati House*, Jl Tebsaya, T974044. Well-presented, clean budget rooms. Hostel lays on Balinese dancing in the evening, which is a good way to meet other travellers. Recommended.

Eating **Expensive** *Saffron*, Banyan Tree, Kamandalu, good quality spicy Asian food, interesting menu. Recommended. *Café Lotus*, Jl Raya Ubud, overlooks Puri Saraswati Palace, international (particularly Italian), pleasant situation and good atmosphere, but somewhat tarnished by the draining of the famous lotus ponds (closed Mon). *Café Wayan*, Jl Monkey Forest, international, some seafood, very popular, delicious desserts (if you can fit them in), Balinese buffet on Sun evenings, particularly recommended are the traditional Balinese ceremonial dishes for 2 to share (order 24 hrs in advance), tables arranged in a series of outdoor kiosks.

Food in Ubud is good, particularly international food. Most restaurants serve a mixture of Balinese, Indonesian & international dishes

Mid-range *Han Snel's Garden Restaurant*, Jl Kajeng, north of Jl Raya Ubud, very attractive setting and charming owners, generous, though pricey, servings (closed Sun). Recommended. *Thai restaurant*, Jl Monkey Forest, T977484. Recently opened, good food and ambience. Young Indonesian owner, Thai food cooked by a Thai chef. Excellent service and presentation. *Tjampuhan Hotel restaurant*, west end of Jl Raya Ubud, Indonesian and international, pleasant ravine-side setting. *Bridge Café*, near Antonio Blanco's House, positioned under suspension bridge offering good views, buffet at lunchtimes, large portions and excellent service. *Ryoshi Ubud*, Jl Raya Ubud, T976362. Popular Japanese restaurant serving a varied selection of favourites: sushi, sashimi, noodles, tempura, yakitori, teriyaki, donburi and bento. Open 1100-2400.

Cheap *Ary's Warung*, Jl Raya Ubud (opposite the temple complex), international and Indonesian food served in relaxed, occasionally bohemian atmosphere, with musical accompaniment, frequented by the Ubud cognoscenti, recommended for food but rather close to the main street. *Pradha Restaurant*, Jl Kajeng 1. Stylish Balinese décor in this small, intimate restaurant, with good food and service. Off the main tourist route. *Bumbu*, Suweta No 1, pleasant terrace off the main drag, good value food, excellent presentation, friendly service. Recommended. *Café Bali*, Jl Monkey Forest (bottom end of football field), international, attractive setting. Recommended. *Café Rona*, 23 Tebasaya, good tomato soup! *Casa Luna*, Jl Raya Ubud, opposite Museum Puri Lukisan, good range of International dishes, recommended (but small portions). *Dian's*, Jl Monkey Forest, well-cooked range of dishes, pleasant place for a drink. *Gayatri's*, Jl Monkey Forest, inexpensive and good for children. Recommended. *Ibu Rai*, Jl Monkey Forest (next to the football field), Balinese and international. Recommended. *Jaya Restaurant*, Jl Monkey Forest, good reasonably priced Indonesian and Western food. *Monkey Café*, Jl Monkey Forest, T96246. Small 2-storey café looking out onto paddy fields. Vegetarian menu with Indonesian and Western dishes. Highly recommended. *Mumbul's Garden Terrace*, Jl Raya Ubud, T975364. For excellent salads, international and Balinese food. Recommended. *Nomad*, Jl Raya Ubud, T975131. International and Balinese including Balinese duck and suckling pig, good guacamole. *Nuriani Restaurant*, Jl Hanoman, T975558. Excellent reasonably priced Indonesian and Western food, with pretty views over the paddy fields. Recommended. *Pondok Tjampuhan*, next to *Blanco's House*, pizza, Indonesian, Chinese, good position overlooking ravine. *Ubud Raya*, Jl Raya Ubud (east end), Javanese, Japanese and international. Recommended. *Bagus Café*, Jl Raya Ubud, Peliatan (southeast of the centre), Balinese specialities. *Griya's*, Jl Raya Ubud, barbecued chicken is recommended, but poor service. *Kura Kura*, Jl Monkey Forest (at the end, near Jl Padangtegal), Mexican. *Lilies*, Jl Monkey Forest. Recommended. *Miro's*, in garden set above Jl Raya Ubud, generous helpings, good food at very reasonable price, candle-lit at night, very atmospheric. Recommended. *Murni's Warung*, Indonesian and international (mostly American), an old-time favourite, good service (closed Wed). *Travellers' Café*, 16 Jl Hanoman, T977165. More than just another restaurant; a place where you can leave your pack whilst finding accommodation. Good 'travellers' book for latest tips from other travellers. International newspapers available. The manager, Mr Nyoman Wardana, is a good source of in-depth information about Balinese culture and current events. *Yudit Restaurant and Bakery*, Jl Monkey Forest, pizzas and good bread. Recommended. *Jazz Café*, Jl Sukma 2 Tebesaya, T976594. Good live music Tue and Fri. Good food and coffee. Run by Nina from England. Recommended.

Very cheap *Mai Bar*, Jl Hanoman 60, big restaurant with a beautiful garden near the paddy fields, music and fashion-shows, rice dishes, soups and coffee. Recommended. *Metri's*, Jl Hanoman, excellent bakery with brown bread and cakes, and good food. Recommended. *Tutmak Restaurant*, Jl Dewi Sita, small, friendly and inexpensive with good service and excellent food, large portions guaranteed, popular with travellers.

Bars *Putra Bar*, Jl Monkey Forest, well priced food (cheap to mid-range) and drink. Attracts travellers, great for evening entertainment such as live Reggae music or films on wide screen. *Jazz Café*, Jl Tebesaya, atmospheric surroundings make this a relaxed place for a drink or meal (cheap), with enticing menu and children's menu. Live music.

Beggar's Bush, near *Hotel Tjampuhan*, west of town on Jl Raya Ubud, English pub (some food). *Salzbar*, Jl Monkey Forest, live music on Tue and Thu. *Nomad*, Jl Raya Ubud, open late.

Entertainment

Artists' colonies Ubud has perhaps the greatest concentration of artists in Indonesia, exceeding even Yogya. Many will allow visitors to watch them at work in the hope that they will then buy their work. The *Pengosekan Community of Artists* is on Jl Bima. **Dance** There are numerous performances every day of the week; most begin at between 1900 and 2000 and cost 5,000Rp. A board at the *Bina Wisata Tourist Centre*, Jl Raya Ubud (opposite the palace), lists the various dances, with time (most performances start at 1930 or 2000), location and cost (almost entirely 7,000Rp). There are almost nightly performances at the *Puri Saren*, at the junction of Jl Raya Ubud and Jl Monkey Forest. Performances including legong, Mahabharata, barong, kecak, Ramayana ballet and wayang kulit (7,000Rp). At the Museum Puri Lukisan, there is a children-oriented troupe who perform gamelan and barong dances every Sun at 1030. Admission: 2,000Rp for museum entrance plus a donation. **Massage** *Mentari Massage Service Centre*, No 1 Anoman St, T97400. Professional massage, not a 'beach-rub', very popular, book in advance. *The Bodywork Centre*, Jl Hanoman 25, Padangtegal, T975720. This place offers everything from massage and milk bath to hair cuts and pedicures. **Videos** There is a very popular *Video Bar*, on the far side of the football field on Jl Monkey Forest. Two shows a night of Western films. Laser disc videos at *Menara Restaurant*, Jl Raya Ubud. Laser disc also at *Putra Bar*, Jl Monkey Forest.

Batik & ikat *Ibu Rai* travel agent, near *Lilies restaurant* on Jl Monkey Forest. *Kunang Kunang*, Jl Raya Ubud. *Lotus Studio*, Jl Raya Ubud. *Binal Art Studio*, Jl Tebesaya 48, lovely batiks made on site and to order.

Shopping
Ubud offers a good range of crafts for sale

Books *Ubud Bookshop*, Jl Raya Ubud (next to *Ary's Warung*), for a good range of English language books on the region; *Ubud Music*, Jl Raya Ubud, selection of English language books and local music; *Ganesha Bookshop*, Jl Raya Ubud, near Post Office. Owned and operated by a well-known writer/actor/musician, Ketut Yuliarsa, and his wife, Anita, the Ganesha Bookshop houses a vast collection of second-hand books including some antiquarian editions on Bali and Indonesia, in addition to its extensive collection of new books on Indonesian topics. Also CDs and tapes of Indonesian ethnic music and a collection of local instruments including gongs, cymbals, flutes and gamelan, which sometimes gives rise to a spontaneous Balinese 'jam' session; T976339, ganesha@bali-paradise.com, www.bali-paradise.com/ganesha **Book Exchange**, 3 on Jl Monkey Forest, 1 on Jl Gotama.

Clothing *Bali Rosa*, on Jl Raya Ubud, towards Campuan, for accessories (bags, belts, beaded pumps). Recommended. *Balika*, Jl Monkey Forest, for fashion clothing. *Hare Om*, Jl Monkey Forest, for well-designed but expensive hand-painted silk scarves and shirts. *Lotus Studio* for unusual designs and great hats; the market on the corner of Jl Raya Ubud and Jl Monkey Forest offers a range of 'travellers' clothes – T-shirts, batik etc. *Mutiara Art Company*, Jl Raya Ubud, good value batik shirts, mostly rayon but some cotton too, interesting designs. Recommended.

Jewellery There are a number of shops along Jl Raya Ubud. Good designs but the quality is not always very high – it looks better than it feels.

Paintings Ubud painters have a distinctive style, using bright colours and the depiction of natural and village scenes (see page 441). There is a large selection of paintings to be found in the town and galleries are concentrated along the east section of Jl Raya Ubud. It is possible to visit the artists in their homes; enquire at the galleries.

Pottery Near the post office, just off Jl Raya Ubud.

Shoes *Bali Rosa*, Jl Raya Ubud, for 'pumps'. *Hare Om* for a range of individually designed suede shoes. For handmade shoes, there is a place on Jl Mejuti, down the hill on the left. They also repair shoes here.

Wind chimes Shop specializing in wind chimes, at the end of Jl Monkey Forest, in the paddy fields – worth a visit.

Woodcarving Concentrated on the Peliatan road out of town. The so-called 'duck man' of Ubud (Ngurah Umum) is to be found on the road to Goa Gajah, with a selection of wooden fruits and birds. Recommended shop near the *Bamboo restaurant*, off Jl Monkey Forest, facing the football field.

Sports **Mountain biking** See 'Tours', page 370. **Swimming** Some hotel pools are open to non-residents, prices for a full day range between 5,000Rp and 20,000Rp. *Ubud Village*, Jl Monkey Forest, 20,000Rp (for the day; you can come and go as you like), *Gusti Garden* 10,000Rp; *Pande Permai* 10,000Rp; *Ubud Terrace Bungalows*, large pool, 5,000Rp; *Visa Rasa Sayong* 5,000Rp; *Puri Saraswati Bungalows* 10,000Rp. Also try the *Andong Inn*, Jl Andong 26A; *Champlong Sari Hotel* and *Okawatis Restaurant*, Jl Monkey Forest. **Whitewater rafting** See 'Tours', page 370.

Tour operators Double check airline tickets bought here; there have been complaints that despite assurances that flights are confirmed, on reaching the airport, visitors have found they are not. *Cahaya Sakti Utama*, Jl Raya Ubud, T975131, F975115; *Ibu Rai*, Jl Monkey Forest 72, T975066, recommended; *Kurnia*, Jl Raya Ubud, T975020 for buses to Lombok and around Bali, tours and car rental; *Nominasi*, Jl Monkey Forest 67-71, T975065.

Transport **Local Bicycle hire**: bicycles are the best way to get about (apart from walking); there are several hire places on Jl Monkey Forest, 3,000Rp per day. **Car hire**: hire shops on Jl Monkey Forest, 80,000Rp per day plus insurance for Suzuki 'jeep'; 100,000Rp per day for larger Toyota Kijang. **Motorbike hire**: several outfits on Jl Monkey Forest, from 30,000Rp per day.

Road Bemos: leave from the Pasar Ubud in the centre of town, at the junction of Jl Monkey Forest and Jl Raya Ubud; regular connections with **Denpasar's** Batubulan terminal (1,000Rp), airport (4,000Rp). **Bus**: there are 'shuttle' (in fact, not as regular as the name implies) buses to

Kuta, the **Ngurah Rai Airport** (10,000Rp), **Candi Dasa**, **Padangbai**, **Sanur**, **Denpasar**. Details are available at the travel or tour agents. Perama cut back their bus service in the wake of the economic crisis and currently run 11 buses a day to the airport, Kuta and Sanur; 7 buses a day to Ubud, 3 buses a day to **Lovina**; 3 buses a day to Padangbai, Candi Dasa, 1 a day to **Tirtagangga**, **Tulamben** and **Yeh Sanih**, and 2 buses a day to **Mataram** and **Senggigi**. Fares are 7,500Rp to the airport, 20,000Rp to Lovina, 15,000Rp to Padangbai and Candi Dasa, 35,000Rp to Mataram and Senggigi. Perama operates to the main tourist destinations on Bali and Lombok. They have an office on Jl Hanoman, T973316. **Taxi**: taxis congregate at the Pasar Ubud in the centre of town. **Boat** *Perama* has an office near the boat landing.

Directory

Banks Numerous money changers will change cash and TCs and offer rates similar to banks. **Communications Perumtel** (for fax, telex and international telephone): Jl Andong (close to intersection with Jl Raya Ubud) and Jl Raya Ubud (near *Nomad Bar and restaurant*), or on the road to Petulu, at the east end of Jl Raya Ubud. **Postal agents**: *Nominasi*, Jl Monkey Forest 67 and Jl Raya Ubud. **NB** they sometimes charge very high 'service charges'. **Post Office**: Jl Jembawan 1 (road running south off Jl Raya Ubud, opposite Neka Gallery); poste restante. **Useful addresses** **Medical**: Ubud Clinic, Jl Raya Campuhan (near Beggar's Bush), T974911, F975298, ubudclinic@usa.net.id, 24 hr medical service and dentist. **Police**: on the road to Petulu, east end of Jl Raya Ubud.

North of Ubud

Gunung Kawi

Gunung Kawi, literally the 'Mountain of the Poets', is one of the most impressive, and unusual, temples in Bali. A steep rock stairway, with high sides, leads down to the bottom of a humid, tree-filled, ravine. At the bottom lies the temple. The whole complex was literally hewn out of the rock during the 11th century, when it was thought to have been created as the burial temple for King Anak Wungsu and his wives, who probably threw themselves on his funeral pyre.

The site You descend 315 steps to a massive rock archway, and from there to the nine tombs which face each other on either side of the Pakerisan River. These two rows of candis, four on the south side and five on the north, were cut out of the rock. It is believed that the five on the north bank of the river were for the King and his four wives, whilst the four on the south bank may have been for four concubines. They resemble temples and are the earliest traces of a style of architecture which became popular in Java in the following centuries. As such they may represent the precursor to the Balinese *meru*.

East of the five candis, on the far side of the river, is a cloister of various courtyards and rooms, also carved out of the rock. They were created for the Buddhist priests who lived here (visitors are asked to remove their shoes before entering). Still farther away, on the other side of the river, is the so-called 'tenth tomb'. The local people call this tomb 'the priest's house'. The tenth tomb is, in all likelihood, a monastery and consists of a courtyard encircled by niches. To get to

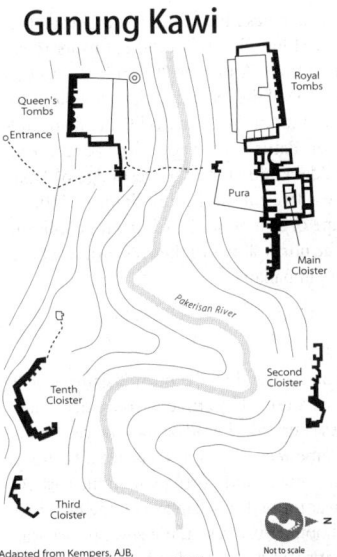

Adapted from Kempers, AJB, *Monumental Bali*, Periplus, Singapore (1991)

the tenth tomb take the path across the paddy fields, that runs from the rock-hewn gateway that leads down into the gorge; it is about a 1 km walk. ■ *1,000Rp. Dress – sash or sarong required.*

Sleeping There is accommodation close by in Tampaksiring, eg **Gusti Homestay**. Tampaksiring also has a number of good jewellery workshops.

Transport **Road Bemo**: connections with **Denpasar's** Batubulan terminal or from Ubud to Tampaksiring. It is about a 3 km walk from here, passing Tirta Empul (see below), although bemos also make the journey to the temple site.

Tirta Empul

Tirta Empul is 2 km north of Tampaksiring, 1 km on from Mount Kawi. The temple is one of the holiest sights on Bali and is a popular pilgrimage stop, evident by the maze of trinket stalls.

Tirta Empul is built on the site of a holy spring which is said to have magical healing powers. In the past, barong masks were bathed here to infuse them with supernatural powers during the dance. Originally constructed in 960, during the reign of Raja Candra Bayasingha, the temple is divided into three courtyards, and has been extensively restored with little of the original structure remaining – bar a few stone fragments. The outer courtyard contains two long pools fed by 30 or more water spouts, each of which has a particular function – for example, there is one for spiritual purification. The holy springs bubble up in the inner courtyard. During the *Galungan Festival*, sacred *barong* dance masks are brought here to be bathed in holy water. ■ *1,050Rp (500Rp extra for a camera).*

Transport **Road Bemo**: take a bemo from **Denpasar's** Batubulan terminal or Ubud towards Tampaksiring. The temple is 2 km north of the town centre; either walk or catch a bemo. From here it is a 1 km walk to Mount Kawi (see above).

Gianyar to Mount Batur via Bangli

Colour map 3, grid B6 East of Ubud is the royal town of Gianyar, which has little of interest to attract the tourist; 15km north of Gianyar, at the foot of Mount Batur, is another former royal capital, Bangli, with its impressive Kehen Temple. A further 20 km leads up the slopes of Mount Batur to the crater's edge – one of the most popular excursions in Bali. Along the rim of the caldera are the mountain towns of Penelokan and Kintamani, and the important temples of Batur and Tegen Koripan. From Penelokan, a road winds down into the caldera and along the west edge of Lake Batur. It is possible to trek from here up the active cone of Mount Batur (1,710m), which thrusts up through a barren landscape of lava flows. North from Penulisan, the road twists and turns for 36 km down the north slopes of the volcano, reaching the narrow coastal strip at the town of Kubutambahan.

Gianyar

Phone code: 0361 Gianyar is the former capital of the kingdom of Gianyar. In the centre of Gianyar, on Jl Ngurah Rai, is the **Agung Gianyar Palace**, surrounded by attractive red brick walls. This is the best example of a traditional Balinese Puri to be found on Bali and continues to be used by the royal family in much the same way as it always has been. Features include courtyards and pavilions with Dutch, Indian and Portuguese influences. At the turn of the century, the Regency of Gianyar formed an alliance with the Dutch in order to protect itself from its warring neighbours. As a result, the royal palace was spared the ravages and destruction, culminating in *puputan*, that befell other royal palaces in South Bali during the Dutch invasion. The rulers of Gianyar were allowed a far greater degree of autonomy than other rajas; this allowed them to consolidate their wealth and importance, resulting in the regency's current prosperity and the preservation of the royal palace. It is not normally open to the public, but the owner, Ide Anak Agung Gede Agung, a former politician and the rajah of Gianyar, does let visitors look around his house if you ask him. The bemo station is five minutes walk to the west of the palace, also on Jl Ngurah Rai. Traditionally regarded as Bali's weaving centre, there is only a limited amount of cloth on sale these days. Gianyar's other claim to fame is that it is said to have the best *babi guling* (roast suckling pig) on the island. Gianyar **tourist office** (*Dinas Pariwisata*) is on Jl Ngurah Rai 21, T93401. The office provides visitors with pamphlets on sights in the regency.

Sleeping

B *Agung Gianyar Palace Guesthouse*, within the Palace walls.

Entertainment

Dance At 1900, every Mon and Thu, a cultural show including dinner is staged at the *Agung Gianyar Palace*, T93943/51654.

Sports

Mountain biking Down into the volcano on the 'Batur Trail', organized by **Sobek Expeditions**, T287059 (US$45 including lunch), pickup from all the resorts.

Transport

27km from Denpasar. **Road Bemo**: regular connections with **Denpasar's** Batubulan terminal.

Bangli

Phone code: 0366

Bangli, the former capital of a mountain principality, is a peaceful, rather beautiful town, well maintained and spread out. Set in a rich farming area in the hills, there is much to enjoy about the surrounding scenery, especially the captivating views of the volcanic area to the north including Mount Agung and Mount Batur. Both the town itself and the countryside around afford many opportunities for pleasant walks. The area claims to have the best climate on Bali and the air is cooler than on the coast. Despite these attractions, Bangli is not on the main tourist routes and is all the more charming for that. There is a tourist offce, however - *Bangli Government Tourism Office*, on Jl Brigjen Ngurah Rai 24, T91537. ■*Open 0700-1400 Mon-Sat*. Very friendly and helpful, but little English is spoken and they are not really geared up for foreigners. Free booklet and map.

History

Balinese believe that Bangli is the haunt of *leyaks*, witches who practise black magic. In Bali, misfortune or illness is frequently attributed to leyaks, who often intervene on behalf of an enemy. In order to overcome this the Balinese visit a *balian*, a shaman or healer, who often has knowledge of the occult. As a result of the presence of leyak in the area, Bangli has a reputation for the quality of its *balian*, with supplicants arriving from all over the island, dressed in their ceremonial dress and bearing elaborate offerings. The people of Bangli are the butt of jokes throughout Bali, as Bangli is the site of the island's only mental hospital, built by the Dutch.

Sights

There is a **market** every three days in the centre of town. Locally grown crops include cloves, coffee, tobacco, vanilla, citrus fruit, rice, cabbages, corn and sweet potatoes; some of which are exported. Bangli lies close to the dividing line between wet-rice and dry-rice cultivation.

Most people come to Bangli to visit the **Pura Kehen**, one of Bali's more impressive temples and one of the most beautiful, set on a wooded hillside about 2 km to the north of the town centre. The Pura was probably founded in the 13th century. There is some dispute over the true origin of the temple, because inscriptions within the compound have been dated to the ninth century. It is the second largest on Bali and the state temple of Bangli regency. Elephants flank the imposing entrance, leading up to three terraced courtyards, through finely carved and ornamented gateways

decorated with myriad demons. The lower courtyard is dominated by a wonderful 400-year-old *waringin* tree (*Ficus benjamina*), with a monk's cell built high up in the branches. It is here that performances are held to honour the gods. The middle courtyard houses the offertory shrines, while the top-most courtyard contains an 11-tiered *meru* with a carved wood and stone base. The elaborate woodwork here is being beautifully restored and repainted by craftsmen. In the wall below, guides will point out the old Chinese plates cemented into it. Curiously, some of these depict rural England, with a watermill and mail coach drawn by four horses. Every three years in November (Rabu Kliwon Shinta in the Balinese calendar), at the time of the full moon (purnama), a major ceremony, Ngusabha, is held at the temple.
■ *1,000Rp per person plus 1,000Rp for a car. The temple is on the back road to Besakih and Penelokan. Outside there are stalls selling snacks and sarongs.*

The **Sasana Budaya Arts Centre** stages performances of traditional and modern drama, music and dance, as well as art and cultural exhibitions. It is one of the largest cultural centres on Bali, located about 100m from the Pura Kehen. Ask at the tourist office for information on performances. Bangli is particularly noted for its dance performances. Bangli also has one of the largest gamelan orchestras on Bali, captured from the ruler of Klungkung by the Dutch, who gave it to Bangli.

In the centre of town is the **royal palace** which houses eight branches of the former royal family. Built about 150 years ago and largely restored by the present descendants, the most important section is the Puri Denpasar where the last ruler of Bangli lived until his death almost 40 years ago. The temple of the royal ancestors is situated on the northwest side, diagonally opposite the *Artha Sastra Inn*; important ceremonies are still held here.

There is an impressive **Bale Kulkul** in the centre of town, three storeys high and supported on columns made of coconut palm wood; it is about 100 years old. There are in fact two kulkuls, *kulkul lanang* which is male, and *kulkul wadon* which is

North & east Bali

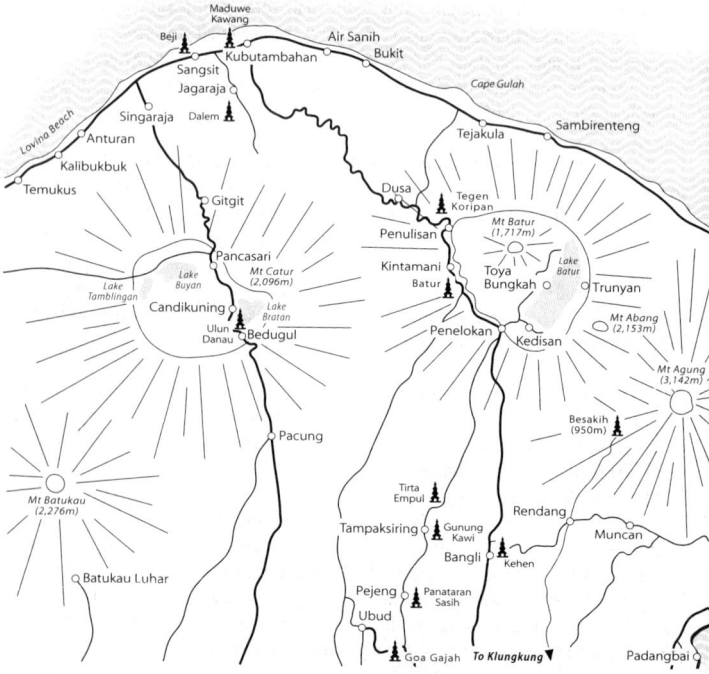

female. In times past the kulkul was sounded to summon the people, or act as an alarm warning of impending danger. The people of Bangli consider these kulkul to be sacred, and they are used during important temple festivals.

At the other end of town, the **Pura Dalem Penjungekan**, temple of the dead, is also worth a visit. The stone reliefs vividly depict the fate of sinners as they suffer in hell; hanging suspended with flames licking at their feet, being castrated, at the mercy of knife wielding demons, being impaled or having their heads split open. The carvings are based on the story of Bima on his journey to rescue the souls of his parents from hell. The destructive 'Rangda' features extensively. In the centre there is a new shrine depicting tales of Siwa, Durga and Ganesh. The temple is in a parkland setting with possibilities for walks.

Excursions

Bukit Demulih, at an altitude of about 300m, and the village of Demulih, lie to the south of the Tampaksiring road 3 km west of town (about one hour's walk). The small, pretty village has some well-carved temples, and a kulkul tower by the bale banjar. From here the villagers will show you the track up the hill, at the top of which is a small temple; en route you pass a sacred waterfall. If you walk along the ridge you will come to other temples and fine views over the whole of south Bali. ■ *Getting there: walk or take a bemo bound for Tampaksiring, get off after about 3 km, take the narrow, paved road south for 1 km to Demulih village.*

A pleasant walk east of Bangli leads to **Sibembunut**.

Bukit Jati, near Guliang about 2 km south of Bunutin, is another hill to climb for splendid views and scenic walks.

Sidan, just north of the main Gianyar to Klungkung road, 10 km south of Bangli, is notable for its **Pura Dalem**, which has some of the most vivid, spine-chilling depictions of the torture and punishment that awaits wrong-doers in hell. The carvings show people having their heads squashed, boiled or merely chopped off, and the wicked and evil widow Rangda dismembering and squashing babies. ■ *1,100Rp. There is a car park opposite the temple, and a stage where dance performances sometimes take place.*

Sleeping

C *Bangli Inn*, Jl Rambutan No 1, Bangli 80661, T/F91419. New hotel, 9 rooms which are clean and simple, with private bathroom, Western toilet. Friendly staff, but limited English. Price includes breakfast. **D-E** *Artha Sastra Inn*, Jl Merdeka 5, T91179; 14 rooms. Located in the inner court of the royal palace with plenty of atmosphere, although don't expect anything as grand as a European palace - Balinese palaces are not that grand. This is the place to stay in Bangli. The more expensive rooms are very clean, simple, with private bathroom and Western toilet; cheaper rooms have shared mandis with squat toilets. Restaurant (cheap). Recommended. **E** *Catur Aduyana Homestay*, Jl Lettu Lila 2, T91244; 7 rooms. Clean and pleasant homestay located 1 km to the south of the town centre. 3 rooms with private mandi, squat toilet, 4 rooms with shared mandi, squat toilet. Breakfast of tea/coffee and bread included. Friendly owner speaks no English. **E** *Losmen Dharma Putra*. Room rate including breakfast, a good, friendly, family-run losmen. **E-F** *Jaya Giri Homestay*, Jl Sri Wijaya 6, T92255. Pleasant, quiet location by the Pura Kehen, above Bangli town. Entrance is past the pay point for entry to the temple; just tell them you are going to the homestay and they will let you through for free. 6 rooms, though 4 were unavailable when we visited. Rooms are very dark and basic, 2 with private mandi, all squat toilet.

Eating There are warungs beside the bemo station in the centre of town, and a good night market opposite the *Artha Sastra Inn*, with the usual staple Indonesian/Balinese stall food including noodles, rice, nasi campur, satay etc. Near the *Catur Aduyana homestay*, opposite '*Yunika*', is a clean Rumah Makan. Foodstalls near the Pura Kehan sell simple snacks.

Transport **Road Bemo**: many, but not all, bemos are 'colour coded'. These days there are a plentiful supply of bemos running throughout the day, and most places are accessible by bemo if you are prepared to wait and do some walking. There are regular services between: **Denpasar's** Batubulan terminal, many connect through to **Singaraja**; the market in **Gianyar** (these bemos are usually blue); and **Klungkung**. Blue bemos wait at the Bangli intersection on the main road between Gianyar and Klungkung at Peteluan; so it's easy to change bemos here. The road climbs steadily up to Bangli with good views to the south. Generally, orange bemos run between Bangli and **Kintamani**; between Bangli and **Rendang**, bemos are generally black or brown and white; bemos also run between Bangli, **Besakih** and **Amlapura**, all fairly regularly from 0600 to 1700; fewer in the afternoon. The road from Bangli to Rendang is good but winding, with little traffic; it is also very pretty with deep ravines, streams and overhead viaducts made of bamboo and concrete.

Directory **Banks** Several banks including *Bank Rakyat Indonesia*, Jl Kusuma Yudha, T91019, in the centre of town by the Bale Kulkul, will change cash and TCs, open 0700-1600 Mon-Fri and 1000-1400 Sat. **Communications** Post office: Jl Kusuma Yudha 18, T91195. *Wartel*: just north of the tourist office, T91303, and on Jl Merdeka, T91001, open 24 hrs. **Medical services** General Hospital, Jl Kusuma Yudha 27, T91020. Chemists: *Apotik Kurnia Farma*, Jl Kusuma Yudha, and in Toko Obat Rhizoma, Jl Bridjen Ngurah Rai. **Useful services** Petrol Station: at the start of town on Jl Brigjen Ngurah Rai.

Mount Batur

See map, page 382 The spectacular landscape of Mount Batur is one of the most visited inland areas on Bali. Despite the hawkers, bustle and general commercialization, it still makes a worthwhile trip. The huge crater – 20 km in diameter – contains within it Lake Batur and the active Mount Batur (1,710m), with buckled lava flows on its slopes. The view at dawn from the summit is stunning. Although these days Mount Batur is less destructive than Mount Agung, it is the most active volcano on Bali having erupted 20 times during the past 200 years.

Lake Batur in the centre of the caldera is considered sacred.

Trekking A steep road winds down the crater side, and then through the lava boulders and along the west shore of Lake Batur. There are hot springs here and paths up the sides of Mount Batur, through the area's extraordinary landscape. Treks begin either from **Purajati** or **Toya Bungkah** (there are four, five or six hour treks), or around the lake (guides are available from the *Lake View Cottages* in Toya Bungkah). Aim to leave Toya Bungkah at about 0330. After reaching the summit it is possible to hike westwards along the caldera rim, though this hike is not for the faint-hearted as the ridge is extremely narrow in places with steep drops on both sides. The cinder track passes several of the currently most active craters, lava flows and fumaroles. In the north and east of the caldera the landscape is quite different. The rich volcanic soil, undisturbed by recent lava flows, supports productive agriculture. The vulcanology institute on the rim of the caldera monitors daily seismic activity.

Boats can be hired from the village of **Kedisan** on the south shore of Lake Batur – be prepared for the unpleasant, hard-line sales people here – or from Toya Bungkah, to visit the traditional Bali Aga village (see page 414) of Trunyan and its cemetery close by at Kuban, on the east side of the lake.

Trunyan
Numerous visitors have written to us saying how unfriendly the villages of this area are. They report a distinct lack of hospitality, an oppressive & unpleasant air – even palpable hostility

The Bali Aga are the original inhabitants of Bali, pre-dating the arrival of the Majapahit; records show that the area has been inhabited since at least the eighth century. Trunyan's customs are different from Tenganan (see page 396) – but these differences can only be noted during festival time, which tend to be rather closed affairs. Despite its beautiful setting beside Lake Batur with Mount Abang rising dramatically in the background, a visit can be disappointing. Most people come to visit the cemetery to view the traditional way of disposing of corpses. Like the Parsees of India, the corpses are left out to rot and be eaten by birds rather than being buried or cremated. It is claimed that the smell of rotting corpses is dissipated by the fragrance of the sacred banyan tree. The idea behind this custom is that the souls of the dead are carried up towards heaven by the birds; this flight to heaven propitiates the gods and results in improved prospects for the souls in their reincarnation in the next life. The corpses are laid out on enclosed bamboo rafts, but very likely all you will see is bones and skulls. The cemetery is only accessible by boat; make sure you pay at the end of your journey, otherwise the boatman may demand extra money for the return journey. The villagers are unfriendly and among the most aggressive on Bali; with a long tradition of begging for rice from other parts of the island as they were unable to grow their own, they now beg or demand money from tourists.

On the west rim of the crater are two villages, Kintamani and Penelokan. Large-scale restaurants here cater for the tour group hordes. The area is also overrun with hawkers selling batik and woodcarvings – some so vociferously as to scare the most hardened visitor. Penelokan is perched on the edge of the crater and its name means 'place to look'. About 5 km north of here, following the crater rim, is the rather drab town of Kintamani, which is a centre of orange and passionfruit cultivation. The town's superb position overlooking the crater makes up for its drabness. *Ged's trekking* is based here; they can advise on the best walks in the area and provide a guide for the more dangerous routes up to the crater rim.

Penelokan & Kintamani

Just south of Kintamani is Pura Batur, spectacularly positioned on the side of the crater. This is the new temple built as a replacement for the original Pura Batur, which was engulfed by lava in 1926. Although the temple is new and therefore not of great historical significance, it is in fact the second most important temple in Bali after Pura Besakih. As Stephen Lansing explains in his book *Priests and Programmers* (1991), the Goddess of the Crater Lake is honoured here and symbolically the temple controls water for all the island's irrigation systems. Ultimately, therefore, it controls the livelihoods of the majority of the population. A nine-tiered meru honours the Goddess and unlike other temples it is open 24 hours a day. A virgin priestess still selects 24 boys as priests, who remain tied as servants of the temple for the rest of their lives.

Pura Batur

Pura Tegeh Koripan is the last place on the crater rim, on the main road 200m north of Penulisan. Steep stairs (333 in all) lead up to the temple, which stands at a height of over 1,700m above sea level next to a broadcasting mast. The temple contains a number of highly weathered statues, thought to be portraits of royalty. They are dated between 1011 and 1335. Artistically they are surprising because they seem to anticipate later Majapahit works. The whole place is rather run down at the moment, though there are some signs that repairs are being attempted. ■ *1,000Rp, Mon-Sun. Getting there: catch a bemo running north and get off at Penulisan.*

Pura Tegeh Koripan

Toya Bungkah **C** *Lake View*, Gunawan. **C-D** *Under the Volcano*, good restaurant, clean rooms, friendly management. **D** *The Art Centre* (or *Balai Seni*), Toya Bungkah, quite old but

Sleeping

still a good place to stay. **F** *Nyoman Pangus Homestay*, the accommodation here is fine, but the food is poor value, with small portions, and the people rather unfriendly – like the village. **Penelokan B-D** *Lake View Homestay*, basic but good views over the lake. **C-D** *Gunawan Losmen*, clean, private bathroom, fantastic position. **Kintamani B** *Surya Homestay*, great position, new, more comfortable rooms now available. **D** *Segara Bungalow*. **C** *Puri Astina*, large clean rooms. *Losmen Sasaka*, stunning views over the crater and lake.

Eating *Segara*, in Kedisan, across road from boat jetty, clean, serves excellent lake fish, friendly staff.

Transport **Road Bemo**: from **Denpasar's** Batubulan terminal to **Bangli** and then another to **Penelokan**. Some bemos drive down into the crater to Kedisan and Toya Bungkah. **Bus**: regular coach services from **Denpasar** (2-3 hrs).

Alternative routes from Ubud to Mount Batur

If you have your own transport and are starting from Ubud, you can turn left at the end of Ubud's main street and take the back road heading north. This leads through an almost continuous ribbon of craft villages, mainly specializing in woodcarving, with pieces ranging in size from chains of monkeys to full size doors and 2m high *Garudas*. There are good bargains to be found in this area off the main tourist track. Follow the road through Petulu, Sapat and Tegalalong, and continue northwards.

The road, its surface not too good in places, climbs steadily through rice paddies and then more open countryside where cows and goats graze, before eventually arriving at the crater rim – 500m west of Penelokan.

The area around Mount Batur is considered very sacred and comprises numerous temples, small pretty villages and countryside consisting of rice fields littered with volcanic debris. There are several rugged backroutes from Ubud through this region. One of the most interesting villages is **Sebatu**, northeast of Ubud near Pura Mount Kawi, reached via a small road leading east from the northern end of **Pujung Kelod**. This village has a number of temples and is renowned for the refined quality of its dance troupe, its gamelan orchestra and its wood carving. The dance troupe has revived several unusual traditional dances including the telek dance and makes regular appearances overseas. **Pura Gunung Kawi** is a water temple with well maintained shrines and pavilions, a pool fed by an underground spring and open air public bathing.

From Mount Batur to the north coast

See map, page 382 From Penulisan, the main road runs down to the north coast which it joins at Kubutambahan. It is a long descent as the road twists down the steep hillsides, and there are many hairpin bends.

If exploring the northeast coast, a very pleasant alternative is to take the minor road which turns directly north, just short of a small village called Dusa. The turning is not well signed – ask to make sure you are on the right road.

This is a steep descent but the road is well made and quiet. The road follows ridges down from the crater of Mount Batur, with steep drops into ravines on either side. The route passes through clove plantations and small friendly villages, with stupendous views to the north over the sea. Behind, the tree-covered slopes lead back up to the crater.

The road eventually joins the coast road near Tegakula. Turn left, northwest, for Singaraja and Lovina, and right, southeast, for the road to Amlapura (see page 401).

Pura Besakih and Mount Agung

The holiest and most important temple on Bali is Pura Besakih, situated on the slopes of Bali's sacred Mount Agung. Twinned with Mount Batur to the northwest, Agung is the highest mountain on the island, rising to 3,140m. It is easiest to approach Besakih by taking the road north from Klungkung, a distance of 22 km. However, there are also two east-west roads, linking the Klungkung route to Besakih with Bangli in the west and Amlapura in the east. Although little public transport uses these routes, they are among the most beautiful drives in Bali, through verdant terraced rice paddies.

Besakih

Pura Besakih is not one temple, but a complex of 22 puras that lie scattered over the south slopes of Mount Agung, at an altitude of about 950m. Of these, the central, largest and most important is the Pura Penataran Agung, the Mother Temple of all Bali. It is here that every Balinese, whatever his or her clan or class, can come to worship – although in the past it was reserved for the royal families of Klungkung, Karangkasem and Bangli. The other 21 temples that sprawl across the slopes of Mount Agung surrounding the Mother Temple are linked to particular clans. **Mount Agung** is an active volcano and last erupted in 1963, killing 2,000 people. The area has been a sacred spot for several centuries.

See also map, page 382

The **Pura Penataran Agung**, which most visitors refer to as Pura Besakih, is dedicated to Siva and is of great antiquity.

Temple layout From the entrance gate, it is a 10 minute walk up to the temple, past a long row of souvenir stalls. Although it is possible to walk up and around the sides of the temple, the courtyards themselves are only open to worshippers. It is the spectacular position of this pura, rather than the quality of its workmanship, which makes it special: there are views over fields to the waters of the Lombok Strait.

Pura Besakih consists of three distinct sections (for general background to Balinese temple layout, see page 438). The entrance to the forecourt is through a *candi bentar* or split gate, immediately in front of which – unusually for Bali – is a *bale pegat*, which symbolizes the cutting of the material from the heavenly worlds. Also here is the *bale kulkul*, a pavilion for the wooden split gongs. At the far end of this first courtyard are two *bale mundar-mandir* or *bale ongkara*, their roofs supported by single pillars.

Entering the central courtyard, almost directly in front of the gateway, is the *bale pewerdayan*. This is the spot where the priests recite the sacred texts. On the left-hand wall is the *pegongan*, a pavilion where a gamelan orchestra plays during ceremonies. Along the opposite (right-hand) side of the courtyard is the large *bale agung*, where meetings of the Besakih village are held. The small *panggungan* or altar, in front and at the near end of the bale agung, is used to present offerings to the gods. The similar *bale pepelik* at the far end is the altar used to present offerings to the Hindu trinity – Vishnu, Brahma and Siva. These gods descend and assemble in the larger *sanggar agung*, which lies in front of the bale pepelik.

From the central courtyard, a steep stone stairway leads to the upper section, which is arranged into four terraces. The first of these terraces in the inner courtyard is split into an east (right) and west (left) half. To the right are two large *merus*; the meru with the seven-tiered roof is dedicated to the locally venerated god Ratu Geng, while the 11-tiered meru is dedicated to Ratu Mas. The three-tiered *kehen* meru is used to store the temple treasures. On the left-hand side is a row of four merus and two stone altars. The tallest meru, with seven tiers, is dedicated to Ida Batara Tulus Sadewa. Up some steps, on the second terrace, is another 11-tiered *meru*, this one dedicated to Ratu Sunar ing Jagat or Lord Light of the World. There are also a number of bale here; the bale in a separate enclosure to the left is dedicated to Sira Empu, the patron god of blacksmiths. Up some more stairs, to the third terrace, is yet a further 11-tiered meru, dedicated in this instance to Batara Wisesa. On the final terrace are two *gedongs* – covered buildings enclosed on all four sides – both dedicated to the god of Mount Agung.

At the back of the complex there is a path leading to three other major puras: **Gelap** (200m), **Pengubengan** (2.5km) and **Tirta** (2km). There are over 20 temples on these terraced slopes, dedicated to every Hindu god in the pantheon. ■ *0800 Mon-Sun, 3,000Rp for which you get a fistful of different tickets – an entry ticket, a camera ticket, a compulsory insurance ticket ... then, thinking it is safe to go back into the water... another ticket office on the climb up the hill where you have to sign in and are invited to make a further donation (ignore the vast sums that are claimed to have been donated). As the temple is an ill-kept shambles, one assumes that someone is creaming off a fair proportion. Guides available (about 2,000Rp). Best time to visit: early morning, before the tour groups.*

Tours   **Climbing Mount Agung** trips can be organized by the *Lake View Cottages* in Toya Bungkah, the price (100,000Rp up to US$25 or more) includes a guide, pick-up, transport to base camp, but no food.

Festivals   There are a total of 70 festivals held in and around Pura Besakih each year, with every shrine having its own festival. The 2 most important festivals are occasional ceremonies: The **Panca Wali Krama** is held every 10 years, while the **Eka Dasa Rudra** is held only once every 100 years and lasts for 2 months. In fact, 2 Eka Dasa Rudra festivals have been held this century.
January   New moon of 7th lunar month.
March/April   Nyepi (movable, full moon of 10th lunar month), the Balinese Saka new year, a month-long festival, which is attended by thousands of people from all over Bali, centring on the triple lotus throne.

Transport   **Road**   **Bemo/minibus**: regular minibuses from **Klungkung**; from **Denpasar** catch a bemo
22 km from Klungkung, 60 km from Denpasar   from the Batubulan terminal to Klungkung, and then get a connection on to Besakih (via **Rendang**). But bemos are irregular for this final leg of the journey and it makes more sense to charter a bemo for the entire trip, or rent a car or motorbike (chartering a bemo makes good sense in a group).

Mount Agung

Mount Agung is Bali's tallest and most sacred mountain, home of the Hindu gods and dwelling place of the ancestral spirits, it dominates the spiritual and physical life of the island. It is awe-inspiring, with its magnificent summit dominating the landscape over much of Bali. All directions on Bali are given in relation to this much revered mountain. Toward the mountain is called 'kaja', away from the mountain is 'kelod'. In a country where direction is of immense significance, this is the site of the most important of the nine directional temples (see page 438). Water from its sacred springs is the holiest and most sought after for temple rites. According to local legend, the god Pasupati created the mountain by dividing Mount Mahmeru, centre of the Hindu universe, in two - making Mount Agung and Mount Batur.

Standing 3,014m high, at its summit is a crater about 500m in width. In 1969, after lying dormant for more than 600 years, the volcano erupted causing massive destruction; over 1,600 people died in the eruption, a further 500 in the aftermath and 9,000 were made homeless. For a week the mountain spewed ash covering much of the island, and casting a cloud over East Java. Even today the scars left by the destruction are visible in the shape of lava flows and deep ravines. Much was read into the fact that the eruption took place at the time of Bali's greatest religious festival, Eka Dasa Rudra; this is a very superstitious community. One theory is that the mountain erupted because the priests were pressured into holding the ceremony before due time, to coincide with an important tourism convention that was taking place on Bali.

Climbing Mount Agung

Since this is a sacred mountain, access to Mount Agung is restricted during religious ceremonies, particularly in March and April. In any case the arduous climb should only be attempted during the dry season, May-Oct; even then conditions on the summit can be quite different from the coast. There are several routes up Mount Agung, but the two most popular depart from Besakih and Selat. The latter is shorter but you will not be able to reach the very highest point on the mountain, and views of part of the island are hidden behind the summit. You should be well prepared, the mountain is cold at night and you will need warm clothes, water, some food, a good torch and decent footwear. You will also need a guide, and should aim to reach the summit before 0700 to witness the spectacular sunrise; after 0800 the clouds may begin to build up, obscuring views.

From Besakih This route takes you to the summit, providing the best views in all directions. The longer of the two ascents, this climb takes about six hours, with another 4-5 hours for the demanding descent. You start out in forest, but once you reach the open mountain it becomes extremely steep. Guides can be hired at Besakih through the tourist office, who can also arrange nearby accommodation. Expect to pay about US$40 per person, this includes offerings at temples along the route.

From Selat By following this route you reach a point about 100m below the summit, which obscures all-round views. However, the climb only takes 3-4 hours; aim to start your climb by 0300 or 0400. From Selat, take the road to Pura Pasar Agung, then climb through forest before reaching the bare mountain. Guides can be arranged both in Muncan and Tirtagangga, as well as Selat. One recommended guide is I Ketut Uriada, a teacher who lives in Muncan; he can be contacted at his shop in that village. Costs start at about 40,000Rp, which includes temple contributions and registering with the local police. In Selat ask the local police about guides, they should be able to advise. In Tirtagangga ask at your accommodation; rates here tend to be higher, US$35 per person, which should include transport. There is good accommodation in Selat (see accommodation, page 408) or your guide may arrange cheaper accommodation at his home.

East Bali and Regency of Karangasem

Colour map 3, grid B6 The greatest of the former principalities of Bali is Klungkung, and its capital still has a number of sights which hint at its former glory. It is worth driving east of here into the Regency of Karangasem: to the ancient Bali Aga village of Tenganan, 3 km outside Candi Dasa, then inland and northeast to Amlapura (Karangkasem), with its royal palace (40 km from Klungkung), then 7 km north to the royal bathing pools of Tirtagangga. From here the road continues north, following the coast all the way to Singaraja (almost 100 km from Amlapura). The drive is very beautiful, passing black sand beaches and coconut groves, see page 428.

An area of great beauty dominated by Mount Agung (3,140m), Bali's highest and most sacred volcano, Karangasem is one of the most traditional parts of Bali and one of the most rewarding areas to explore. During the 17th and 18th centuries, Karangasem was the most powerful kingdom on Bali. Its sphere of influence extended to western Lombok, and the cross cultural exchanges which resulted endure to this day. During the 19th century, the regency co-operated with the Dutch, thus ensuring its continued prosperity.

Karangasem

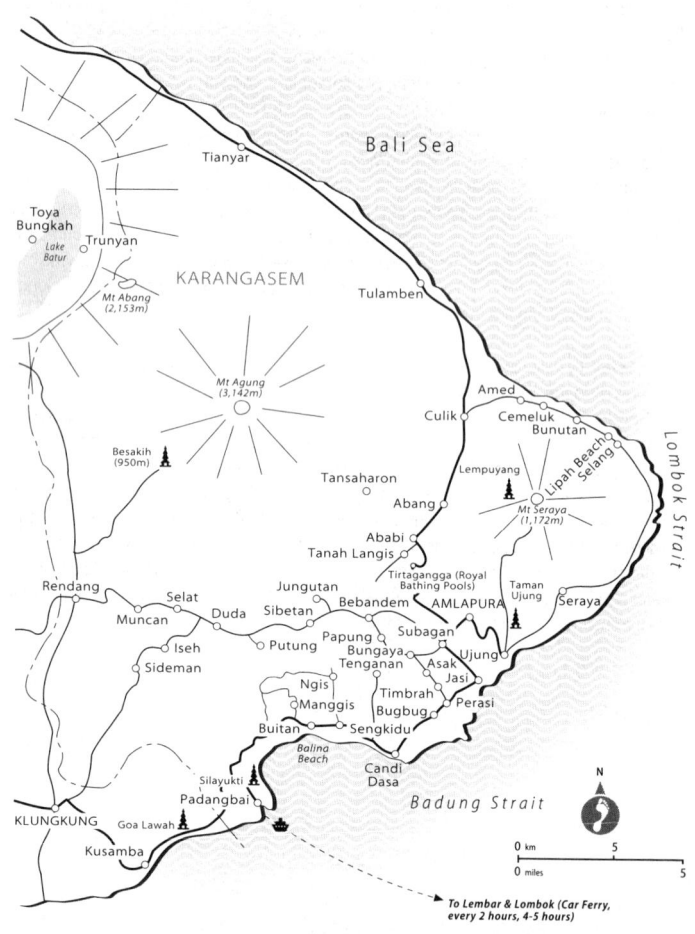

The massive eruption of Mount Agung in 1963 devastated much of the regency and traces of the lava flows can still be seen along the northeast coast, particularly north of Tulamben.

Ins and outs

Buses run most frequently in the morning starting early (from 0500 or 0600), and continue until about 1700 or later; on major routes. The frequency of buses is improving all the time. **From Denpasar (Batubulan terminal) to**: Gianyar 1 hr; Klungkung 1 hr 25 mins; Padangbai 1 hr 50 mins; Candi Dasa 2 hrs 10 mins; Amlapura 2½ hrs; Bangli 1 hr 20 mins; Singaraja (Sangket terminal) 4 hrs. **From Gianyar to**: Klungkung 25 mins; Padangbai 50 mins; Candi Dasa 1 hr 10 mins; Amlapura 1½ hrs; Ubud 25 mins; Bangli 20 mins; Singaraja (Sangket terminal) 3 hrs. **From Amlapura to**: Candi Dasa 20 mins; Tirtagangga 10 mins; Amed 30 mins; Tulemban 40 mins; Rendang 1 hr 20 mins; Besakih 1 hr 35 mins; Sideman 1¼ hrs; Singaraja (Penarukan terminal) 2 hrs 20 mins. **From Candi Dasa to**: Denpasar (Batubulan terminal) 2 hrs 10 mins; Padangbai 20 mins; Amlapura 20 mins; Tirtagangga 30 mins; Ubud 1 hr 35 mins; Besakih 2 hrs.

Several companies run tourist shuttle buses linking Padangbai, Candi Dasa, Tirtagangga and Tulemben with Ubud, Kuta, Sanur (and Nusa Lembongan by boat), Kintamani, Lovina, Bedugul and Air Sanih; Mataram, Bangsal, the Gili Islands, Kuta Lombok and Tetebatu on Lombok. One of the best is **Perama**, with offices in all the above places; allow 3 hrs to get to Denpasar airport from Candi Dasa.

By boat: from Padangbai: there is a round-the-clock (leaving every 2 hrs) ferry service to Lembar port on Lombok, taking 4-5 hrs. Small boats make the crossing to Nusa Penida very early every morning, taking about 1 hr 20 mins. From Kusumba: small boats leave early every morning for Nusa Penida and Nusa Lembongan, 1 hr 15 mins.

> **Getting there & away**
> *Bear in mind that all times are necessarily approximate & can vary enormously depending on traffic conditions from Denpasar, particularly on the main road from Klungkung to Denpasar*

While you can reach most of these villages by public bemo, it is better to hire a car. There are many scenic backroads which climb up into the hills, offering spectacular views when the weather is fine; be warned that some of these minor roads are in dreadful condition with numerous, huge potholes. The road leading up from Perasi through Timbrah and Bungaya to Bebandem is especially scenic and potholed. A much better road with outstanding views leads west from Amlapura to Rendang; *en route* you pass through an area famed for its salak fruit and in the vicinity of Muncan you will find beautiful rice terraces. From Rendang you can continue on up to Pura Besakih.

> **Getting around**

Klungkung

The **Puri Semarapura** was once the symbolic heart of the kingdom of Klungkung. All that remains of this palace on Jalan Untung Surapati are the gardens and two buildings; the rest was destroyed in 1908 by the Dutch during their advance on the capital and the ensuing *puputan*. The **Kherta Ghosa** or Hall of Justice, built in the 18th century by Ida Dewa Agung Jambe, was formerly the supreme court of the kingdom of Klungkung. It is famous for its ceiling murals painted in traditional, wayang style, with vivid illustrations of heaven (towards the top) and hell (on the lower panels). As a court, the paintings represent the punishment that awaits a criminal in the afterlife. The murals have been repainted several times this century. Miguel Covarrubias describes the nature of traditional justice in Bali in the following terms:

> *Phone code: 0366*
>
> **Sights**
> *Klungkung is also known by its former name Semarapura (particularly as the destination on buses)*

"A trial must be conducted with the greatest dignity and restraint. There are rules for the language employed, the behaviour of the participants, and the payment of trial expenses. It is interesting that the court procedure resembles that of cockfights in its rules and terminology. On the appointed day the plaintiff and the defendant must appear properly dressed, with their witnesses and their cases and declarations carefully written down. ... When the case has been thoroughly stated, the witnesses have testified and the evidence has been produced, the judges study the statements and go into deliberation among themselves until they reach a decision. Besides the witnesses and the material evidence, special attention is paid to the physical reaction of the participants during the trial, such as nervousness, change of colour in the face, or hard breathing."

The Kherta Ghosa was transformed into a Western court by the Dutch in 1908, when they added the carved seats, as they found sitting on mats too uncomfortable. It is said – although the story sounds rather dubious – that one of the Rajahs of Klungkung used the Kherta Ghosa as a watch tower. He would look over the town and when his eyes alighted on a particularly attractive woman going to the temple to make offerings, he would order his guards to fetch her and add the unsuspecting maid to his collection of wives.

Adjoining the Kherta Ghosa is the **Bale Kambangg** (or Floating Pavilion), originally built in the 18th century, but extensively restored since then. Like the Kherta Ghosa, the ceiling is painted with murals; these date from 1942.

Further along the same road, just past a school, is the attractive **Taman Gili**, also built in the 18th century. This consists of a series of open courtyards with finely carved stonework, in the centre of which is a floating pavilion surrounded by a lotus-filled moat. ■ *1,000Rp.*

To the east of the main crossroads in the centre of town – behind the shop fronts – is a bustling **market**, held here every three days and considered by many to be the best market on Bali, and also a large monument commemorating the *puputan*.

Excursions

Kamasan village, 4 km southeast of Klungkung, is an important arts centre where artists still practise the classical Wayang style of painting. Most of the artist families live in the banjar Sangging area of town. Artists from this village painted the original ceiling in the Kerta Gosa in Klungkung in the 18th century, as well as the recent restoration, using the muted natural colours (reds, blacks, blues, greens and ochres) typical of this school.

Goa Lawah, or 'bat cave', is one of the state temples of Klungkung. There are tunnels here which are reputed to lead as far as Pura Besakih. As the name suggests, the temple is overrun by bats and corresponding smells. *Getting there*: take a bemo heading for Padangbai or Candi Dasa.

Boats leave for **Nusa Penida** and **Nusa Lembongan** from the fishing village of Kusamba, 8 km southeast from Klungkung. On the beach are huts and shallow troughs used in salt production. The fishing fleet consists of hundreds of brightly painted outrigger craft with triangular sails, which operate in the Lombok Strait (similar to the *lis-alis* of Madura). They are fast and manoeuvrable, and can make way in even the lightest breezes. Boats leave Padangbai for Nusa Penida only.

Sleeping

E *Ramayana Palace*, Jl Diponegoro (east edge of the town on road to Candi Dasa), T21044.

Shopping

Textiles Although good examples are not easy to find, Klungkung is the centre of the production of royal *songket* cloth, traditionally made with silk but today more often from synthetics. The cloth is worn for ceremonial occasions and characteristically features abstracted floral designs, geometric patterns, wayang figures and animals. It takes 2 months to weave a good piece.

Transport

Road Bemo: regular connections with **Denpasar's** Batubulan terminal and points east – **Besakih**, **Amlapura**, **Candi Dasa**.

Boat Kusamba, from where there are boats to **Nusa Penida**.

Directory

Communications Post Office: to the west of the Kherta Ghosa.

Padangbai

Phone code: 0363

Padangbai has a beautiful setting, overlooking a crescent-shaped bay with golden sand beach, colourful *jukung* (fishing boats) and surrounded by verdant hills. This is the port for ferries to Lombok and boats to Nusa Penida (see page 350), and is a hive of excitement when ferries arrive and depart. When there are no ships calling, the town is quiet and relaxed. It is one of the best deep-water harbours in Bali, and many tankers ride at anchor in the approaches. There are beaches on either side of the town. Walking south from the pier and bus station, follow the road until you come to a tatty sign on the left indicating the rough, steep path that leads up and over the hill to **Pantai Cecil** (400m approximately, 15 minutes' walk). This is a beautiful, undeveloped white sand beach surrounded by grassy hills, the perfect setting for a quiet swim or evening stroll. There are two beachside warungs.

Sleeping

The most attractive rooms are in town. However, the best location is to the north along the bay, where rooms and bungalows are surrounded by gardens and coconut groves and are quieter; they are in need of refurbishment, though, and are overpriced for what they offer.

B-D *Puri Rai* (formerly *Rai Beach Inn*), 7 Jl Silayukti, T41385/6/7, F41386. Has attempted to go upmarket but rooms are very overpriced, rather spartan and unattractive, rooms and 2-storey bungalows (these have drab, plywood floors and easy access for mosquitoes), with fan or a/c, private mandi with Western toilets but not always toilet seats, restaurant (cheap). **D** *Pondok Serangan Inn*, Jl Segara, T41425. Clean, modern, 1st floor rooms with fan, private mandi, Western toilet, attractive, 1st floor balcony seating area with views of town and sea, pot plants and family shrine. Recommended. **D** *Topi*, east side of bay, restaurant, isolated position, clean and comfortable basic rooms, but creaky floors and thin walls makes for little privacy. **D-E** *Darma I Homestay*, Jl Silayukti Gang Tongkol No 6, T41394. In town, well run, very clean, modern rooms with private mandi and Western toilet, fan and mosquito nets, 1st floor balcony seating area with lovely sea views, good value. Recommended. **D-E** *Jati Wangi Inn*, Melanting 5 (owner at I Wayan Wista near market), clean, cool, friendly. **D-E** *Kerti Beach Inn*, Jl Silayukti, T41391. Outside town with garden, rooms are basic and need redecorating, private mandi with Western toilets, fan.

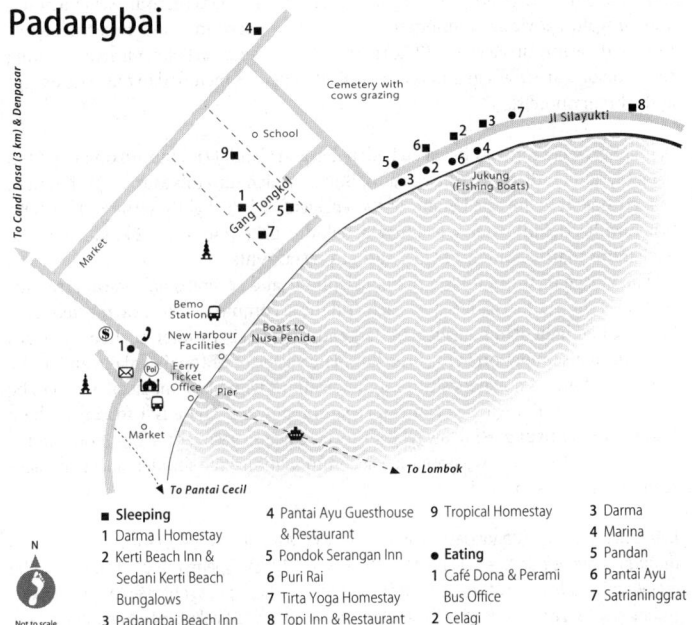

Padangbai

- ■ **Sleeping**
- 1 Darma I Homestay
- 2 Kerti Beach Inn & Sedani Kerti Beach Bungalows
- 3 Padangbai Beach Inn
- 4 Pantai Ayu Guesthouse & Restaurant
- 5 Pondok Serangan Inn
- 6 Puri Rai
- 7 Tirta Yoga Homestay
- 8 Topi Inn & Restaurant
- 9 Tropical Homestay

- ● **Eating**
- 1 Café Dona & Perami Bus Office
- 2 Celagi

- 3 Darma
- 4 Marina
- 5 Pandan
- 6 Pantai Ayu
- 7 Satrianinggrat

D-E *Padangbai Beach Inn*, Jl Silayukti, one of the best locations, outside town, set in large grounds, but rooms are fairly basic, the more expensive rooms with private mandi and Western toilet are OK, but the cheaper rooms are pretty grim with private squat toilet and shared shower. **D-E** *Pantai Ayu Guesthouse*, Jl Silayukti, T41396. Set on a hill overlooking Padangbai and the sea with fabulous views and flower-filled garden, well run, clean but rooms are a little older than some, private bathrooms, Western toilets, 3rd floor restaurant (cheap). Recommended. **D-E** *Satrianinggrat*, Jl Silayukti No 11, T41517. Outside town, in quiet garden location with pleasant view of coconut grove, behind restaurant, 4 new rooms with private mandi (no wash basin), Western toilet, fan, not particularly well built, somewhat overpriced. **D-E** *Sedani Kerti Beach Bungalows*, cottages and plain rooms on the beach front. **E** *Tirta Yoga Homestay* (opposite *Darma I Homestay*), Jl Silayukti Gang Tongkol, T41415. Set in pretty, small garden with shrine, clean rooms with fan, private mandi, Western toilet, new rooms are good value, older rooms smelt damp. **E** *Tropical Homestay*, Jl Silayukti 1A, T41398. Good (new) rooms, attractive courtyard, friendly staff, choice of breakfast, quite noisy, rooms with fan, private mandi, Western toilet.

Eating
All offer Indonesian & Western food

Mid-range *Pandan*, not by sea, but set in pretty gardens backing onto coconut grove. *Pantai Ayu*, Jl Silayukti, on the beach, also 3rd floor restaurant in guesthouse with fabulous views over Padangbai and sea - see sleeping - great seafood, money changer. *Topi Inn*, upstairs, with views. *Marina Restaurant* has lovely sea views, several small warungs along seafront.

Transport

Road Bemo: Padangbai is 2½ km off the main coastal road; connections with Denpasar's Batubulan terminal, Candi Dasa and Amlapura. **Bus**: from the bus station you can catch long distance buses, west to Java and east to Sumbawa and Lombok. **Sea Boat**: ferries for Lembar on Lombok leave daily, every 2 hrs, and take 4-5hrs , 4,800Rp, 9,300Rp in 1st class (children half price). The busiest departure is 0800, which is not a problem if one of the 2 large ultra-modern ferries is doing that sailing; otherwise try to get on as early as possible to secure a decent seat. Boats also depart for Nusa Penida (tourists pay 15,000Rp).

Padangbai to Candi Dasa

For many people Bali is at its best and most rewarding away from the tourist centres. Along the road leading from Padangbai to Candi Dasa there are several hotels and bungalow-style accommodation, which offer peace and quiet in secluded settings with beautiful sea views. (The rice paddies in these parts sprout an interesting selection of scarecrows in different styles!) Breakfast is included in the price except at the luxury hotels.

Manggis & Balina Beach
Phone code: 0363

Balina Beach lies midway between Padangbai and Candi Dasa (approximately 4 km from the latter) adjacent to the village of Buitan, which runs this tourist development as a co-operative for the benefit of the villagers. It is a slightly scruffy black sand beach with a definite tourist feel to it. Sengkidu village and beach 2 km further east have more charm. Sometimes there are strong currents.

The village of **Buitan** has a public telephone and several small warung/restaurants and shops; the road to the beach and the accommodation is signposted. Perhaps the highlight of this village is the large advertisement promoting the advantages of artificial insemination in pig breeding. The village of **Manggis**, inland and to the west of Buitan, is known locally for its associations with black magic; it is said to be the haunt of *leyaks*, witches with supernatural powers. There is a road from here leading up to **Putung**, 6 km away, with spectacular views over the Lombok Strait.

At present there are two upmarket accommodations; the simpler, cheaper places seem to have disappeared.

Sleeping **L** *Amankila* (outside Candi Dasa near the village of Manggis), T41333, F41555 (reservations through *Amanusa* at Nusa Dua, T0361-771267, F771266). Opened mid-1992, one of the renowned Aman group of hotels, in an outstanding location spread out over the hillside with stunning sea views. Designed with simple elegance to create a calming and peaceful milieu, and with only 35 guest pavilions and 3 vast swimming pools on different levels of the hill, it is easy to imagine you are the only guest in residence. **AL** *Serai*, Buitan, Manggis, Karangasem 80871, T41011, F41015. A luxury class hotel, set in a coconut grove beside the sea in total seclusion, 58 rooms (superior, deluxe and suites), a good location but the décor is rather functional, large swimming pool, restaurant, boutique, satellite TV, airport transfer. **A-B** *Balina Beach Bungalows (Pondok Pantai Balina)*, Balina Beach, Manggis, postal reservations: PT, Griyawisata Hotel Management, Wijaya Grand Centre Blok G No 20-21, Jl Darmawangsa Raya, Jakarta 12160, T021-41002/3/4/5, F41001; 42 Balinese style bungalows, set in large, tropical gardens with beautiful sea views, restaurant (cheap), bar and café overlooking the sea, small swimming pool. **A-B** *Puri Buitan*, Balina Beach, Manggis, postal reservations: PO Box 3444, Denpasar 80034, T/F0361-223718 (at hotel, T41021). 34 rooms in a featureless modern hotel, rooms are functional, lacking in character but clean, restaurant (cheap) overlooking the smallish pool, not particularly attractive or good value. **C-D** *Matahari Beach Bungalows* (formerly *Sunrise Beach Bungalows*), Buitan, Manggis, postal address: PO Box 287, Denpasar 80001, T41008/41009. Signposted from the main road, follow a steep path down the hill for about 50m, beautiful setting in a large coconut grove beside the sea, with a beach suitable for swimming though occasionally there is a current, and offering complete seclusion, 11 fairly attractive bungalows and rooms, very clean, some large family rooms, several of the cheapest rooms have a shared ceiling so your neighbours will probably hear your every movement; Ketut, the owner, speaks good English and is very helpful, he used to be in the tourist industry so is knowledgeable about Bali. **D-E** *Ampel Bungalows*, Manggis Beach, 6 km from Candi Dasa, just off the main road, T41209. A peaceful, rural setting overlooking rice paddies and the sea, 4 simple, very clean bungalows, with private mandi, signposted from the main road shortly after the *Amankila Hotel*.

Sengkidu Village

West of Candi Dasa (2km) is an authentic Balinese village as yet unravaged by tourism. The pretty backstreets lead down to the sea and beach. If arriving by bemo, ask the driver to let you off in the centre of the village by the temple and sign for *Candi Beach Cottage*. Follow the signpost to the right of the temple; the track leads to the beach and accommodation, 400m. Surrounded by coconut groves and tropical trees, Sengkidu offers an attractive alternative to Candi Dasa and is more pleasant and more interesting than Balina Beach. The village itself has a number of shops, fruit stalls and a temple where festivals are celebrated; foreigners are welcome to participate if they observe temple etiquette and wear the appropriate dress, otherwise they can watch.

Phone code: 0366

A *Candi Beach Cottage*, reservations: PO Box 3308, Denpasar 80033, T41234, F41111. Luxury hotel set in large, scenic tropical gardens, in a quiet location beside sea with access to beach, offering everything you would expect from a hotel in this class, popular with tour groups. **A-B** *Anom Beach Bungalows*, T/F0361-233998. 18 bungalows and rooms, attractively decorated with fan or a/c, airport transfer available, very overpriced, the grounds are not particularly attractive. **C-D** *Pondok Bananas (Pisang)*, T41065. Family-run, set in a large coconut grove beside the sea with access to beach, very peaceful and secluded, might suit an artist or writer looking for long term accommodation, 4 spotless rooms/bungalows. **D** *Puri Amarta* (*Amarta Beach Bungalows*), T41230. 10 bungalows set in large, attractive gardens beside the sea and beach, well-run and very popular, liable to be full even off-season, restaurant (cheap) beside sea. **D-E** *Dwi Utama*, T41053. 6 very clean rooms, with fan, private bathroom, beachside restaurant (cheap), access to good, small beach, well-tended, small garden, peaceful, good value. **D-E** *Nusa Indah Bungalows*, Sengkidu, signposted and reached via a separate track to the left of the temple, set in a peaceful location beside the sea, amidst coconut groves and rice paddies, 7 clean, simple bungalows with fan, access to small, rocky beach, beachside restaurant (cheap).

Sleeping

Cheap *Dwi Utama*. In addition to its beachside restaurant, it has a and shop which also acts as a Post Office. *Baliarsa Restaurant*. See also under accommodation.

Eating

Candi Dasa

Phone code: 0363 Candi Dasa is smaller, more intimate and offers better value for money than the main seaside resorts of Bali. It also provides an excellent base from which to explore the sights of East Bali.

The gold and black sand beach has been badly eroded. However, the lack of beach has saved Candi Dasa from overdevelopment. Even so, it is at its best off-season. There is no surf, so swimming is safe. **Candi Dasa temple** is on the opposite side of the road from the lagoon.

The village Candi Dasa gets its name from the temple on the hill overlooking the main road and the freshwater lagoon; the ancient relics in this temple indicate that there has been a village on this site since the 11th century.

Traditionally fishermen in these parts have gone out fishing each day from 0400 until 0800, and again in the afternoon from about 1430 until 1800. Although most people on Bali fear the sea as a place of evil spirits and a potential source of disaster, those who live near the sea and earn their living from it consider it a holy place and worship such sea gods as *Baruna*. The boats they use, **jukung**, are made from locally grown wood and bamboo, which is cut according to traditional ritual practice. The day chosen for cutting down the tree must be deemed favourable by the gods to whom prayers and offerings are then made, and a sapling is planted to replace it. Carved from a single tree trunk without using nails and with bamboo outriders to give it stability, the finished boat will be gaily coloured with the characteristic large eyes that enable it to see where the fish lurk. The design has not changed for thousands of years; it is very stable due to the low centre of gravity created by the way the sail is fastened. These days there are fewer fish to catch and many fishermen augment their living by taking tourists out snorkelling on the reef. *Jukung* cost about 850,000Rp.

In the rice field by the road to Tenganan are two ingenious **bird-scaring devices**, operated by a man sitting in a thatched hut. One is a metre-long bamboo pole with plastic bags and strips of bamboo; when the man pulls on the attached rope, the pole swings round, causing the bamboo strips to make a clacking noise and the plastic bags to flutter. The other consists of two four-metre-long bamboo poles which are hinged at one end, with flags and plastic bags attached; when the attached rope is pulled, the two poles swing round with flags and plastic bags waving.

Excursions The village of **Tenganan**, 3 km north of Candi Dasa, is reputed to be the oldest on Bali – and is a village of the Bali Aga, the island's original inhabitants before the Hindu invasion almost 1,000 years ago (see box, page 414). The walled community consists of a number of longhouses, rice barns, shrines, pavilions and a large village meeting hall, all arranged in accordance with traditional beliefs. Membership of the village is exclusive and until recently visitors were actively discouraged. The inhabitants have to have been born here and then to marry within the village; anyone who violates the rules is banished to a neighbouring community. Despite the studied maintenance of a traditional way of life, the inhabitants of Tenganan have taken the decision to embrace the tourist industry. It is in fact a very wealthy village, deriving income not only from tourism but also from a large area of communally owned and worked rice paddies and dryland fields.

Tenganan is one of the last villages to produce the unusual **double ikat** or *geringsing*, where both the warp and the weft are tie-dyed, and great skill is needed to align and then weave the two into the desired pattern (see box, page 441). The cloth is woven on body-tension (back-strap) looms with a continuous warp; colours used are dark rust, brown and purple, although newer pieces suffer from fading due to the use of inferior dyes. Motifs are floral and geometric, and designs are constrained to about 20 traditional forms. It is said that one piece of cloth takes about five years to complete and only six families still understand the process. Note that much of the cloth for sale in the village does not originate from Tenganan. ■ *Admission to village: by donation,* *vehicles prohibited. Getting there: it is possible to walk the 3 km to Tenganan; take the road heading north, 1 km to the west of Candi Dasa – it ends at the village. Alternatively, walk or catch a bemo heading west towards Klungkung, get off at the turning 1 km west of Candi Dasa and catch an ojek up to the village. Tours to Tenganan are also arranged by the bigger hotels and the tour agents on the main road. Bemos run past the turn-off for the village from Denpasar's Batubulan terminal.*

About 13 km southwest of Candi Dasa is the temple and cave of **Goa Lawah** (see page 392). ■ *Getting there: regular bemos run along the coast.*

Boats leave for **Nusa Penida** from Padangbai (see page 393).

The royal bathing pools of **Tirtagangga** (see page 402) and the town and palace of **Amlapura** (see page 401) are both within easy reach of Candi Dasa.

Three small islands with coral reefs are to be found: 30 minutes by boat from Candi Dasa. They make a good day trip for snorkelling or diving. Samuh village co-operative keeps goats on the largest of these islands, called **Nusa Kambing (goat island)**. Every six months the goats are transported back to the mainland by boat. Quite a sight if you are lucky enough to witness it. ■ *Getting there: most hotels and losmen will arrange a boat for the day.*

Sleeping There are many very reasonably priced places to stay. Most accommodation is sited adjacent to the beach on the seaward side of the main road. At the eastern end of Candi Dasa, where the main road bends to the left, a small road (Jl Banjar Samuh, there is no name sign but there are many signs indicating accommodations, including *Puri Bagus* and *Genggong*) leads off on the right, lined with accommodation on the seaward side. Known as Samuh village, this slightly rural area is perhaps the most attractive place to stay. Expect power cuts if you visit during the rainy season unless yours is one of the many places which have their own generators. Most include breakfast in their rates. Most hotels with swimming pools allow non-residents to use their pools for a charge of 6,000Rp per person.

AL *Puri Bagus* (east of lagoon), T51223, F52779. A/c, restaurant, pool, good rooms and attractive open-air bathrooms, shadeless pool area. **A** *Rama Ocean View*, T51864, F51866. A/c, restaurant, pool, on the road into Candi Dasa about 1 km from the town 'centre', tennis and fitness centre, good pool, overpriced catering mainly to tour groups, restaurant

Candi Dasa West

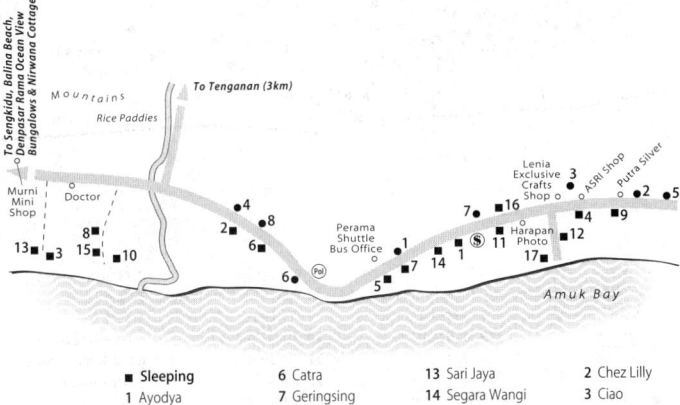

■ **Sleeping**
1 Ayodya
2 Bali Samudra
3 Bayu Paneeda
4 Candi Dasa Beach Bungalows II
5 Candidasa Sunrise
6 Catra
7 Geringsing
8 Flamboyant
9 Lilaberata
10 Pelangi
11 Puri Bali
12 Puri Pandan & Restaurant
13 Sari Jaya
14 Segara Wangi
15 Terrace
16 Water Garden
17 Wiratha's

● **Eating**
1 Candi Dasa
2 Chez Lilly
3 Ciao
4 Flamboyant
5 Hawaii
6 Lotus Seaview
7 TJ's
8 Topeng

(mid-range). **A-B** *Ida Beach Village*, Jl Banjar Samuh, postal address: PO Box 3270, Denpasar, T41118/9, F41041. Designed as a Balinese village, each bungalow is built in traditional style and set in its own small, private courtyard, very attractive rooms with a/c, some 2-storey bungalows with downstairs living room, swimming pool and access to beach, beachside restaurant (cheap). Recommended. **A-B** *Kubu Bali Bungalows*, T41532, 41256, F41531. These attractively furnished bungalows have a breathtaking location extending up the hill behind the *Kubu Bali* restaurant, with spectacular seaviews, a/c, set in extensive, beautiful, tropical water gardens with live gamelan music playing all day, there is a coffee shop and swimming pool set high on the hill, 4-star restaurant located on the high street, with the *Baliku Restaurant* beside the sea just across the main street, airport transfer available, highly recommended. **A-B** *Nirwana Cottages*, Candi Dasa Beach, Sengkidu, Amlapura 80871, T41136, 41903, F41543, nirwanacot@ denpasar.wasantara.net.id Situated outside Candi Dasa on the south side, 300m from the main road down a dirt track, 12 spotless bungalows built in the traditional Balinese style offering peace and tranquillity, set in a coconut grove beside a quiet beach with beautiful sea views. A/c, large pool with sunken bar, transport to/from airport available on request, *Seaside Restaurant* is highly recommended. **A-B** *Resor Prima Candidasa*, Jl Banjar Samuh, PO Box 01, Manggis 80871, T/F204440. A rather unattractive hotel catering mainly to tour groups, 28 rather dark rooms, a/c, pool, beach access. **A-B** *Water Garden*, PO Box 39, T35540. Restaurant, pool, individual cottages, set on the hillside in lovely gardens, each cottage has its own verandah overlooking a private lily pond, simple rooms with HW, very attractively laid out. Recommended.

B *Candi Dasa Beach Bungalows II*, Jl Raya Candi Dasa, T35536, F35537. A/c, 2 restaurants, pool, 2-storey blocks, set in beautiful garden, views from rooms vary, beach here is only so-so, food recommended. **B** *Samudra Indah*, T35542, F35542. A/c, pool, on the south edge of town, nice pool, comfortable but featureless rooms with hot water. **B-C** *Dewa Bharata Bungalows* (also has branch in Kuta, see Kuta section), T41090, 41091, F41091. Popular, located in the

Candi Dasa East

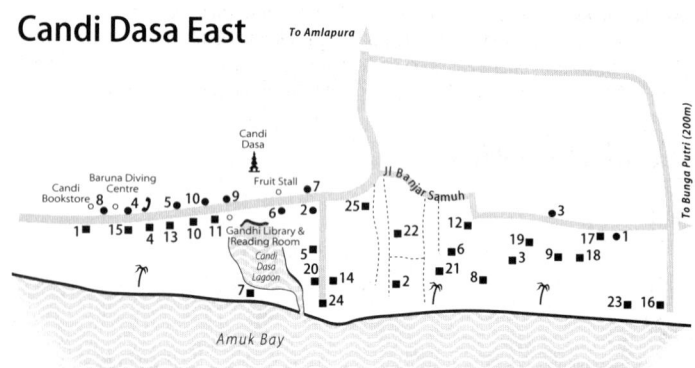

0 metres 100
0 yards 100

■ **Sleeping**
1 Agung Bungalows
2 Barong
3 Candi Dasa Park Resort
4 Dewa Bharata
5 Dewi
6 Dutha Cottages
7 Gandhi Ashram
8 Gengong Cottage
9 Ida Beach Village
10 Ida's
11 Kelapa Mas & Restaurant
12 Nani Beach Inn
13 Natia
14 Pandawa
15 Pondok Bamboo & Restaurant
16 Puri Bagus
17 Puri Pepaya
18 Puri Pudak Bungalows
19 Puri Oka
20 Rama Ocean View
21 Ramayana
22 Satria
23 Sekar Orchid Bungalows
24 Sindhu Brata
25 Srikandi

● **Eating**
1 Asoka
2 Astawa
3 Gloria
4 Kubu Bali
5 Legend Rock Café
6 Lila Arnawa Theatre & Restaurant
7 Raja's
8 Warung Nyoman
9 Rasmini Warung
10 Srijati

centre of town beside the sea, 24 attractive bungalows in well-tended tropical gardens, rooms with a/c or fan, swimming pool beside the sea, open air, reasonably priced, beachside restaurant offering Western, Indonesian and Chinese food. **B-C** *Puri Oka*, T41092, F41093. Small pool, simple but attractive rooms, restaurant overlooking the sea, the tiny beach here evaporates at high tide and there is no swimming, very overpriced. **B-D** *Puri Pudak* (east of lagoon), T41978. Well-designed, clean bungalows, with fan, attractive garden, beside sea but with no direct access which is a major drawback, a little overpriced. **B-D** *Sindhu Brata* (beside lagoon), T41825. Some a/c and hot water, clean with private bathroom, set in large attractive garden beside the sea with beach, restaurant (cheap) with sea views.

C *Pondok Bamboo*, T41534, F41818. In centre of town beside the sea, average rooms, new swimming pool and seaside restaurant. **C** *Pondok Impian Dasa*, T41897, F0361-96335. Bungalows and lumbungs (2-storey Balinese style buildings) set in rather plain gardens, with small sea frontage (no real beach) at the point where a slightly dirty village stream flows into the sea. Swimming pool. Seaside restaurant (cheap). **C-D** *Bayu Paneeda Beach Inn*, T41104. Peaceful location to west of town beside the sea with fabulous sea views, bungalows. A/c or fan, restaurant (cheap) with good sea views. **C-D** *Genggong Cottage*, Jl Banjar Samuh, T41105. 12 rooms set in large gardens with beach, rooms are clean but simple with fan, 2 rooms have hot water, rooms are overpriced but you are paying for the beach, a rare asset in Candi Dasa. **C-D** *Ida's*, T41096. Five bungalows set in a large coconut grove beside the sea with access to its own small beach, 2 large 2-storey bungalows and 3 smaller single storey bungalows, beautifully built in the traditional Balinese style with rattan floors, bamboo walls and screens, mosquito nets and private bathrooms. There is a local saying 'Coconuts have eyes', meaning that a falling coconut will not hit you!, manager/owner is Ida Ayu Srihati and her German husband, both of whom have lived in the USA for many years, and are an excellent source of local knowledge; Ida herself is related to the Klungkung royal family. Highly recommended, reservations advisable. **C-D** *Kelapa Mas*, PO Box 103, Amlapura 80801, T41047. Located on the eastern edge of town in a beautiful, traditional Balinese garden, beside the sea with its own small area of beach, spotless bungalows, some overlooking the sea, a/c or fan, second-hand book shop, (cheap) restaurant offering excellent food including seafood, Balinese specialities and performances of the Legong Dance on certain evenings. Excellent value. Recommended. **C-D** *Sekar Orchid Beach Bungalows*, Jl Banjar Samuh, PO Box 113, Candi Dasa, Bali 80851, T41086. 8 attractive rooms with private bathroom, some with hot water and bathtub, fan, set in large, pretty gardens beside the sea with a beach except at high tide, very well run and spotlessly clean, safety deposit box, Wendy the Javanese owner has lived in England and Germany and speaks both languages. Recommended. **C-E** *Barong*, Jl Banjar Samuh, T41127. Simple rooms with large comfortable bamboo beds, fan, and in the cheaper rooms minimal furniture and weatherbeaten, 'no maintenance' open air private bathrooms.

D *Agung Bungalows*, T235535. Good value for location in centre of town, situated beside the sea with access to beach, basic bungalows with private bathroom, set in large gardens with coconut palms. **D** *Bunga Putri* (east of lagoon), at the north end of the bay, restaurant, peaceful undeveloped setting, good rooms. Recommended. **D** *Puri Pandan*, PO Box 126, Amlapura 80801, T41541. Rooms average, bathrooms better than average with hot water. **D** *Srikandi* (east of lagoon), T53125. Clean rooms but rather close together, popular, new restaurant (cheap) beside sea serving Indonesian and Western food. **D-E** *Dutha Cottages*, Jl Banjar Samuh, T41143/5. 10 rooms beside the sea but with no direct access, fairly basic but clean, set in coconut grove with pretty gardens. **D-E** *Nani Beach Inn*, Jl Banjar Samuh, simple rooms set in coconut grove. **D-E** *Pandawa Homestay* (just east of lagoon), T41929. Closely spaced bungalows with fan and private bathroom, some with hot water, access to sea via tiny beach. **D-E** *Pepaya Bungalows*, Jl Banjar Samuh, T41567. Clean, simple rooms with fan and attractive private bathroom, set in large gardens but not beside the sea, attached to the *Asoka Restaurant*. **D-E** *Ramayana*, Jl Banjar Samuh, T/F41778. 3 simple but attractive bungalows with private mandi. **D-E** *Satria* (east of lagoon), attractive rooms, nice bathrooms, good value, but not on the beachside.

Gandhi Ashram, overlooking the lagoon at eastern end of town, this ashram is run according to Gandhian principles and guests follow strict codes of behaviour, by invitation to those who are genuinely interested in Gandhi's teachings, there are bungalows and more basic rooms, this was the first homestay to open in Candi Dasa, run by Ibu Gedong Oka.

Out of town D-E The following are all situated outside of town to the west, in a peaceful setting with access to the sea, well-sited for visits to Tenganan. Inland there are beautiful views of rice terraces and mountains, with possibilities for walks. These rice paddies are communal land owned by Tenganan village; you can watch the villagers rhythmically working the fields as if living in a different age, adjacent to but oblivious of the tourist world across the road. They all offer similar accommodation, consisting of basic bungalows with private bathrooms and Western toilets, fan, at similar prices, and in descending order of preference: *Terrace Beach Bungalows*, nice setting beside beach; *Taruna Homestay*, rooms could do with redecoration, good sea views, tea and coffee available all day; *Flamboyant Bungalows*, beside sea, rooms could do with redecoration, tea available all day; *Sari Jaya Sea Side Cottage*, T41149. Average rooms in attractive gardens beside the sea; *Pelangi Homestay*, T41270. Bungalows set in attractive gardens, not beside the sea but with easy access via adjacent accommodation.

Eating There are a variety of well-priced restaurants dotted along the main road with similar menus; seafood is the best bet. Most restaurants cater to perceived European tastes, which can be disappointing for anyone who likes Indonesian food. Many of the above accommodations have restaurants, often with sea views. The following are also recommended though quality and ingredients can vary enormously from day to day; you might have a delicious meal one day, order the exact same dish the next day and be very disappointed.

Several restaurants, including Kelapa Mas, Bali Tropical & Astawa, offer dance performances & gamelan recitals in the evenings

Mid-range Kubu Bali, good seafood and Chinese and Indonesian specialities. **Cheap** Astawa, popular, though you are paying for the décor. **Kelapa Mas**, good value and sometimes excellent food. **Legend Rock Café**, Western and Indonesian. **Pandan**, on the beach, daily Balinese buffet, reasonably priced international food. Recommended. **Raja's Restaurant and Cocktail Bar**. **TJ's Café**, Mexican, good food, friendly. Recommended. **Very cheap** Rasmini Warung, a genuine warung serving simple Indonesian food and the best Nasi Campur in town, though quality varies from day to day, excellent value.

Entertainment **Dance** Balinese dance performances staged nightly at 2100 at the *Pandan Harum* near the centre of town. Many restaurants offer performances of Balinese dance and gamelan music in the evenings; see under 'Eating'. The best performances are at the newly opened *Lila Arnaud* which has been designed as a theatre with a proper stage, prices include dinner. Several places have nightly shows of Western films on video; best of these is *Raja's*, whose Australian owner imports the latest films.

Shopping **Crafts** *Geringsing*, on the main road, sells double ikat cloth from Tenganan and other Balinese arts and crafts. *Lenia*, T41174, a good place to see *ata* baskets, these baskets are made from a locally grown vine which is much more durable than rattan, water resistant, it is claimed these baskets can last for up to 100 years, *Lenia* also has a small selection of Sumba blankets and other quality crafts. **Books** The best place for books is the **Candidasa Bookstore**, which has a reasonable selection of books on Bali and Indonesia as well as second-hand books, magazines and newspapers. The lady who runs it speaks excellent English and is very friendly and helpful. *Kelapa Mas* has a good selection of second-hand books. **Groceries** *Asri*, fixed price store for film, food and medicine. **Tailor** The Chinese lady who runs the Candi Dasa bookstore is also a tailor.

Sports **Diving** *Stingray Dive Centre*, Puri Bali Homestay. *Baruna Watersports*, Puri Bagus Hotel, T0361-753820/751223, F753809/752779, prices start from US$40 for 1 dive PADI course (4 days), US$300. Also available are fishing and watersports. **Snorkelling** Rent snorkels from hotels and charter a boat to go out to a reef.

Local Bicycle, motorbike and car hire from hotels, losmen and from shops along the main road.   **Transport**

Road Bemo: regular connections with **Denpasar's** Batubulan terminal, **Amlapura** and **Klungkung**. **Shuttle bus**: more expensive, but quicker, shuttle buses link Candi Dasa with **Denpasar**, **Ubud**, **Kuta**, **Lovina**, **Kintamani**, **Padangbai**, **Tirtagangga**, **Tulamben** and **Lombok** (7,500-20,000Rp). *Perama* is one of the best with an office in Candi Dasa, T41114/5.

Banks There are several money changers offering reasonable rates. **Communications** Postal   **Directory**
agent: opposite the *Candi Dasa Beach Bungalows*.

Amlapura (Karangasem)

At one time Amlapura, capital of the Regency of Karangasem, was the seat of one of   *Phone code: 0363*
the most powerful states in Bali. Today, this may be hard to believe – it is a quiet and
attractive town, with wonderful views of Mount Agung from its clean landscaped
streets. Little happens here. Earthquakes which accompanied the massive eruption
of Mount Agung in 1963 caused much damage, and in order to protect the town
from future devastation, the name of the capital was changed from Karangasem to
Amlapura to confuse the evil spirits who had wreaked this havoc. Several palaces are
to be found in Karangasem, the most accessible being the **Puri Agung**, or Puri
Kanginan, to the east of the main north-south road, Jalan Gajah Mada. The last king
of Karangasem was born at the Puri Agung. Entrance to the palace is through tall
gateways. To the south are a cluster of buildings, which would have been offices and
artist's workshops. Another gateway takes the visitor out of this first compound and
a door to the south leads into the major part of the palace. A pillared building faces
south onto a *bale Kembang* or floating pavilion. The buildings are all rather
run-down, and are rather architecturally eclectic, with European, Balinese and Chinese elements and motifs. There are interesting photographs from the early part of
this century and some rather tatty furniture. ■ *Small admission charge, 0800-1700
Mon-Sun.* There is a **market** to the south of the palace; the stallholders seem
strangely reluctant to bargain.

The ruined water palace of **Ujung** is very beautiful in its romantic decrepitude. It lies 8   **Excursions**
km south of town towards the coast and was built by the last King of Karangasem. The
hills of Lombok can be seen from the site, which is in a beautiful position at the edge of
the sea with the huge volcanic cone of Mount Agung inland. Most of the buildings
were destroyed during an earthquake in 1963. The palace must have been splendid in
its time. Now, you can wander among the large lotus ponds, still part full, and explore
the ruined pavilions. The bridges leading over the water to the old temple have all collapsed, and columns lean at crazy angles. Parts of the balustrades, their intricate carvings still intact, litter the ground. Although the rice terraces and steps up to the central
pavilion above the ponds are intact, the palace has the air of an ancient lost city. No
crowds or hawkers – eminently suitable for those with fertile imaginations. There are
plans to have the palace restored. On the nearby beach, the colourful fishing boats are
very picturesque, with children frolicking here every evening. ■ *Getting there: bemos
leave from the station near the market (south of the palace).*

Tirtagangga royal bathing pools are 7 km north of town (see next page).

Bebandem is the scene of an important cattle market held every three days, as is
usual with Balinese markets. On market day stalls are set up, selling everything from
medicines to sarongs. Ironsmiths take up their positions along the main road, producing cockfighting spurs, keris knives, farm tools etc. The animals start their journey to the village at dawn, often on foot, and the activity is over by 0900. ■ *Getting
there: by bemo from Amlapura.*

Abian Soan is a small peaceful village 4 km west of Amlapura with accommodation. E *Homestay Lila* is a genuine family homestay in a rural setting, beside the main
Amlapura to Bebandem road. The garden is full of fruit trees and wandering

chickens, geese and pigs. The five bungalows are characterful but a little primitive, with private mandis and squat toilets except for one seatless Western toilet. The garden extends down to a river with a small waterfall.

There are walks through the ricefields and a hill, **Bukit Kusambi**, a few kilometres away, with views of Mount Agung, Mount Seraya and Mount Rinjani in the distance, climb it at dawn to watch a spectacular sunrise. Surprisingly, the family speak very limited English. ■ *Getting there: take a bemo from the turn-off outside Amlapura bound for Rendang and get off after 3½ km. By car follow the road west to Rendang for 3.2 km, Homestay Lila is signposted on the main road. There is car parking in a neighbour's drive, though the gate is frequently shut.*

Sleeping E *Homestay Sidha Karya*, Jl Hasannudin. E *Lahar Mas Inn*, Jl Gatot Subroto 1. Small, friendly people. E *Losman Kembang Remaja*, 200m along the road to Bebandem outside of town, T21565. Fairly basic rooms with private mandi, squat toilet, few Westerners stay here.

Eating Cheap *RM Surabaya*, adjacent to the market, good Chinese and Indonesian dishes, popular with local expats, good value. *Pasar Malam*, near the main market, serves good local food. Restaurants close early at about 2100.

Transport **Road Bemo/minibus**: the bemo terminal is on Jl Kesatrian. Regular connections with **Denpasar's** Batubulan terminal and to **Manggis**, **Culik**, **Padangbai**, **Klungkung**, **Tirtagangga** and **Singaraja**. See map for bemo stops outside the main town for onward connections.

Directory Banks *Bank Rakyat Indonesia*, Jl Gajah Mada. Communications Post Office: Jl Gatot Subroto 25.

Tirtagangga

Phone code: 0363 Northwest of Amlapura by 7 km is the site of the royal bathing pools of Tirtagangga. The pools occupy a stunning position on the side of a hill, overlooking terraced ricefields. At harvest times the fields are full of people gathering the golden rice, and carrying it on poles back to the villages to dry. The complex consists of various pools (two of which visitors can swim in) fed by clear mountain streams, with water spouting from fountains and stone animals. It is popular with local people as well as visitors, and is a peaceful place to retreat to except at weekends and holidays when young Balinese arrive en masse on their motorbikes. ■ *500Rp, plus 2,000Rp to swim in the upper pool, 1,000Rp in the lower pool, children half price, Mon-Sun.*

Excursions There are many walks in the hills around Tirtagangga; the scenery is superb and there are several traditional villages worth visiting: **Abadi**; **Tanah Lingis**, with its interesting music group which sings in rhythms imitative of a gamelan orchestra, this musical form originated in Lombok and on Bali is found only in Karangasem; **Budakling**, with a Buddhist tradition that pre-dates the arrival of Hinduism on Bali, this village also produces good quality gold and silver pieces. There are spectacular walks up **Mount Agung**, one of which starts from the village of **Tanaharon**.

About 8 km northeast of Tirtagangga is temple **Pura Lempuyang** situated at an altitude of 1,060m, one of the more important temples on Bali. It is a steep climb, so make an early start to avoid the heat and enjoy the views before the clouds roll in. All these villages have traditional festivals during the year. Your accommodation can help you plan walks.

Sleeping B *Cabe Bali*, Temege, Tirtagangga, T/F22045, http://members.aol.com/cabebali Immaculate property run by a very friendly lady from Munich, Barbara Soetarto, this is one of the nicest places to stay in Karangasem. Set in glorious gardens with sea views, refreshing breezes, fruit trees and swimming pool. 3 beautifully decorated bungalows. Every room has views of both Mount Agung and the coast, with Nusa Penida in the distance. The café/restaurant (mid-range to cheap) is set in an open air pavilion surrounded by ponds. *Getting there by car/bemo*: coming from Amlapura, 5 km from town, turn left at the sign where the road bends sharply right, in Temege village, on the main road to Tirtagangga; follow a very rough track for 1 km. Airport pickup available, free if you stay a week. Highly recommended. 12 min walk from the centre of Titagangga along a narrow path beside the dykes. **B-C** *Puri Sawah* (formerly *Rice Terrace*), PO Box 110, Amlapura 80811, T21847, F21939. The 2-storey bungalow was built to a very high standard to accommodate friends and family visiting from the UK. The upstairs bungalow is decorated very tastefully in Balinese style, private bathroom with squat toilet. The attractive downstairs bungalow has a Western toilet. 4 additional rooms with private bathrooms, with cold water and Western toilets, the restaurant (mid-range to cheap) offers excellent Indonesian and Western food. Highly recommended.

C-D *Geria Gemalung*, Desa Ababi, Abang, Karangasem. No telephone, F21044. Situated just outside Tirtagangga: follow the main road heading north towards Amed for 1.4 km, turn left and follow this road for about 600m, turn left at the sign and follow the mud track for about 200m to this family owned accommodation. A very peaceful, verdant setting on the edge of a ravine overlooking Tirtagangga, with dramatic views to the coast. 6 clean, simple rooms with private bathrooms and verandahs, 4 with Western toilets, 2 older rooms with squat toilet. Restaurant (cheap) serving Balinese vegetarian food. A little overpriced.
C-D *Kusumajaya Inn*, T21250. Rooms in need of refurbishment (ants are a problem), no fans, all rooms with private bathroom, 1 with hot water, with grand views over the rice paddies to the distant sea, this view is shared by the functionally decorated, but cheap restaurant, trekking available, there are 99 rather gruelling steps up to the Inn from the road.
D *Prima Bamboo Homestay and Restaurant*, T21316, F21044. 7 rooms, well run, clean, set in immaculate gardens, terrific views of rice paddies and the coast, all rooms with fan, very peaceful, restaurant (cheap). Recommended. **D** *Tirta Ayu Homestay*, within the water garden itself, rather overpriced for 6 unexciting rooms but a great position. Rooms are clean with private bathrooms, set around lovely, very peaceful gardens, price includes access to the water gardens and swimming pools, restaurant (mid-range) overlooking water gardens with cool breezes (see below).

D-E *Dhangin Tamin Inn*, PO Box 132, Amlapura 80811, T22059. Rooms are attractive, very clean but rather dark, set around a pretty courtyard, fan, restaurant (very cheap).
D-E *Pondok Batur Indah*, Tanah Langis, 1 km past Geria Semalung, follow the rough mud track for about 300m, in same ownership as *Rijasa*, 500m from town centre by foot following a path through paddy fields (ask for directions at *Rijasa*), 1½ km by road, 4 basic rooms with private mandi, views. **D-E** *Rijasa Homestay and Restaurant*, T21873. Clean but drab and basic rooms with private mandi, set round simple gardens, owner can provide a map and information about local walks, restaurant (very cheap).

Eating

Cheap *Good Karma*, same ownership as *Good Karma Bungalows* at Amed, just outside the pools, friendly people, food recommended. *Tirta Ayu Restaurant*, T21697. An open-air restaurant within the water garden, with a fabulous position overlooking the pools and the terraced paddy fields beyond. **Very cheap** *Kusumajaya Inn and Prima*, on the hill with great views over the whole panorama down to the sea, good spot for lunch. *Nasi Campur* (see *Rijasa Homestay* above) has also been recommended.

Transport

Road Minibus/bemo: connections with **Amlapura**, **Culik**, **Kubu**, **Singaraja**. From Denpasar's Batubulan terminal catch a bemo to Amlapura, and get off at the intersection just before Amlapura to catch a connection up the hill to Tirtagangga. Tirtagangga is easily reached by public bemo as a day trip from **Candi Dasa** (where there is a much better choice of budget price accommodation), 30 mins door to door. Perama now operates to Tirtagangga, with connections to its route network on Bali and Lombok including Candi Dasa and Lovina. Perama stops in the central parking area. From Candi Dasa catch a bemo to Amlapura and ask to be let off at the turning for Tirtagangga (see map). There are many bemos here, you won't have to wait long for a connection to Tirtagangga.

Amed

Phone code: 0363

For peace and quiet, this area on the east coast, north of Tirtagangga, has much to offer. The drive from Culik via Amed to Lipah Beach is quite spectacular, especially on the return journey, with Mount Agung forming a magnificent backdrop to the coastal scenery. Numerous coves and headlands, with colourful fishing boats, complete the vista and offer endless possibilities for walks and picnics. The area became popular because of the good snorkelling and diving available here, the reef is just 10m from the beach with some good coral and a variety of fish. Amed is developing slowly with new guesthouses, hotels, restaurants and dive centres opening every year, some with spectacular hillside locations and stunning views of Mount Agung. At present much of the accommodation lies beyond Amed at Lipah Beach, reached along a dreadful, potholed road, part of which has been washed away. There is much talk of laying a new road in the near future! Own transport is recommended.

The area called Amed is in fact a 15 km stretch from Culik to Selang village, encompassing the villages of Amed, Cemeluk (also spelt Jemeluk), Bunutan and Selang. At present the first accommodation you come to is 5.7 km from Culik. If you go during the dry season you can watch the local men making salt; they also work year round as fishermen, setting off at 0500 and returning about 1000, and then going out again at 1500. It is possible to go out with them. As there is no irrigation system, farming is mainly done in the wet season when the men raise crops of peanuts, corn, pumpkin and beans, on the steeply sloping hillside inland from the road, to sell in the market at Amlapura. In dry spells, all the water needed for the crops is carried by the women up the steep slope, three times a day; a back-breaking chore. Most of the land is communally owned by the local Banjar.

Sleeping **AL-A** *Hotel Indra Udhyana*, Bunutan, T0361-241107, F234903. Luxury hotel, built in Balinese style, perched on the rock face right beside the sea. Set in landscaped gardens with views of Mount Agung, 35 bungalows each with a view and a private garden. Restaurant (mid-range) on 3 levels. Small conference hall. Medium sized swimming pool with sunken bar. The beach moves completely over the course of a year, appearing beside the hotel in Jul and Aug, then moving to the east about 100yds away. **A-B** *Coral View Villas* (in same ownership as *Hidden Paradise Cottages* next door, below, same address and T/F), 19 bungalows in attractive garden beside sea, new with attractive décor, private open-air bathrooms, fan or a/c, seaside bar and restaurant (mid-range to cheap), swimming pool, children's play area. Friendly staff, excellent food. **A-B** *Hidden Paradise Cottages*, Lipah Beach, PO Box 121, Amlapura, Bali, T0361-431273, F0361-423820 and 0363-21044. 16 bungalows in attractive gardens beside public beach, with fan or a/c, swimming pool, restaurant (mid-range to cheap). **B-C** *Wawa-Wewe II*, PO Box 124 Karangasem, 7 new attractive villas beside sea, fan, cold water only, mosquito nets, restaurant price includes excellent breakfast, good value. Recommended. **C** *Kusumajaya Beach Inn*, Jemeluk (also spelt Cemeluk) (same ownership as *Kusumajaya* at Tirtagangga), in unspoilt rural setting beside sea, more attractive location than Lipah Beach, Balinese-style bungalows in large, slightly unkempt gardens, fan, restaurant (cheap) overlooking the sea with beautiful views. Recommended, although staff can be less than helpful. **C-D** *Amed Beach Cottage* (Pantai Amed), Cemeluk, T/F0361-288192. Good location in large gardens running down to the sea. Large, simple, rooms. Rooms are rather dark. Owned by the *Mega Dive Centre*. Restaurant (mid-range to cheap) beside beach. **C-D** *Good Karma Beach Bungalows*, Lipah Beach, owner is planning to change name to *Pala Karma Beach Bungalows*, more expensive bungalows have attractive new décor, cold water, fan; cheaper bungalows are very close together and have squat toilets, restaurant (cheap) overlooking sea. **C-D** *Pondok Vienna Beach Bungalows*, Lipah Beach, 1 Wayan Utama, PO Box 112, Bali, bungalows in beachside garden setting with fan, private bathrooms and cold water, restaurant (cheap). **D** *Aiona Kebun Obat (Health Garden)*, Bunutan, Pos Keliling, Desa Bunutan, 80852 Abang, T0361-974865. 2 basic, bamboo bungalows with private mandi, squat toilet, in large overgrown gardens beside the sea. No electricity. Offers traditional Balinese healing, massage, meditation and sells locally made health products.

Vegetarian restaurant (mid-range to cheap). **D** *Amed Café Hostel (Pondok Kebun Wayan)*, 5-7 km from Culik, Amed. Perched on the hillside overlooking the sea, this accommodation offers good value for money. 11 simple, attractively furnished rooms with fan, mosquito net, most (9) with private bathrooms. Restaurant (cheap), excellent food. Live gamelan music is sometimes played. In high season they also have performances of local dances. Swimming from the beach just across the road. Ketut, the manager, is a mine of information. In high season (Jul and Aug) aim to arrive by 1100. Highly recommended. **D** *Wawa-Wewe*, Lipah. F22074, rodanet@denpasar.wasantara.net.id 4 very attractive bungalows. Set in pretty gardens with good snorkelling and swimming from the beach across the road. The owners, Deborah from England and her husband Made, are very friendly and knowledgeable about the local area and Balinese customs. (They also have a house available to rent nearby.) Small shop selling sarongs, jelly shoes (to protect your feet when you go swimming) and woodcarvings. Deborah is knowledgeable about Balinese crafts. Occasional performances of local dances and gamelan music. Book exchange. Restaurant (mid-range to cheap) serving excellent local and Western cuisine, with play area for children. The name *Wawa-Wewe* is a local Balinese saying which roughly translates as *comme ci comme ca*. Price includes breakfast and tax. Highly recommended. **F** *AOK and Eco Dive*, Cemeluk. Run by 'mad' Mike from England. Crash pads, basic, very cheap with shared facilities.

Eating Several new restaurants are opening to cater for the increased number of visitors. One of the best is *Wawa-Wewe* (see above). The restaurant at *Amed Café* also serves delicious food (see above).

Sports **Diving** *Mega Dive Center*, Cemeluk, T/F0361-288192. PADI courses, diving trips to all the main diving areas around Bali, US$30 for 1 dive.

Transport **Car** 45 mins to Amed from Candi Dasa. **Bemo** From **Amlapura** catch a bemo heading north to Culik and Singaraja. Change bemos at Culik; until noon there are a limited number of bright red bemos running along the coast east to Amed and Lipah, after 1200 you can catch an ojek or try and hitch a lift, otherwise it is a long walk. Perama stops at Culik. From here you can catch a bemo to Amed. There is a regular bemo service up to midday, but in the afternoon you may have to rely on ojek, motorcycle taxis.

Culik to Tulamben Returning to the main road at Culik, the drive north following the coast road affords stunning views of Mount Agung (you can easily understand why the mountain is worshipped by the Balinese) and enchanting seascapes. This eastern coast of Bali is drier than other parts of the island, the lush jungle vegetation giving way to scrub and open vistas. You can still see remnants of the lava flows from the eruption of Mount Agung in 1963 that caused widespread devastation in the regency of Karangasem.

Tulamben

Tulamben, an established dive centre, attracts divers because of the wreck of the American Liberty ship which sank just 40m from the shore; lying in shallow waters, it offers good snorkelling as well. The location is very scenic, with Mount Agung towering to the west of the deep blue sea, though the beach consists of grey/black pebbles with some litter. Tulamben lies about 9 km north of Amed. Like Amed, Tulamben is attracting a sprinkling of new hotels, guesthouses and dive centres each year.

Phone code: 0361

Sleeping **AL-B** *Mimpi Resort Tulamben* (reservations: Kawasan Bukit Permai, Jimbaran, Denpasar 80361, T701070, F701074). Sister resort to *Mimpi Jimbaran*, beautifully designed complex of cottages with private courtyards and cheaper rooms, set in glorious, landscaped gardens with fabulous views of Mount Agung. Well-equipped diving facilities offering PADI courses. Large swimming pool, restaurant (mid-range) with sea views. Recommended. **A** *Emerald Tulamben Beach Hotel*, T462673, F462347, tohpati@idola.net.id Spectacularly located, attractive rooms, some with sea views, with usual upmarket facilities including minibar, kettle, safe. The large, tropical gardens have a magnificent setting, with the sea on one side and Mount Agung rising majestically on the other. There is a 9-hole golf course and swimming pool with sunken bar. Restaurant (expensive to mid-range) with seaviews, international, Indonesian, Chinese and Japanese food, pizza. Activities include: scuba diving, snorkelling, fishing, sailing, aroma massage, horseback riding (the two horses roam the gardens) and off road motor bike. Helicopter pad. Recommended.

B-C *Bali Sorga Bungalows*, formerly Paradise Palm Beach Bungalows (reservations: *Friendship Shop*, Candi Dasa, T0363-41052). Good setting beside sea (pebble beach) with attractive gardens, but rather overpriced, 20 rooms with a/c or fan and hot water, diving arranged at sites off East and North Bali, prices from US$45 for 1 dive at Tulamben up to US$100 at Nusa Penida and Menjangan Island. **C** *Puri Aries*, across the road from the beach, one of the newer guesthouses here. **C** *Puri Madha*, close to the wreck of the Liberty ship, clean, functional rooms. **D** *Agung Cottages*, c/o of *Agung Cottages* at Candi Dasa, same ownership 0363-41535. From the south this is the first accommodation you come to before you reach Tulamben (see map). The only budget accommodation in the area. Simple bungalows with bright, clean rooms. The gardens stretch down to the sea and a shingle beach. Very peaceful with outstanding views of Mount Agung. **D** *Ganda Mayu Bungalows and Restaurant*, 8 bungalows ranging from rather basic to attractive depending on price, fan, situated beside the sea with beachside restaurant, diving can be arranged, one of the cheapest places to stay at Tulamben. **D** *Pondok Matahari*, rooms are a little basic.

West of Amlapura

See map, page 382

The road running west from Amlapura up into the foothills of Mount Agung is one of the most scenic on Bali, with stunning views of the sacred mountain, the coast to the south and spectacular terraced ricefields, especially near **Muncan**. The road deteriorates between Putung and Muncan, with a multitude of potholes, but is perfectly passable. West of Amlapura by 10km is Bebandem (see page 401). Turn right shortly after leaving Bebandem to reach the village of **Jungutan**; nearby is the **Tirta Telaga Tista**, one of three water palaces built by the rulers of Karangasem. Not exactly a palace, more a man-made lake fed by an underground spring, in a pretty and peaceful rural setting. Continuing along the main road you get to **Sibetan**, famed for the quality of its salak fruit. Salak can be identified by their brown skin which has the appearance of snakeskin, and is in season from December to March; inside, the fruit is crisp with a slightly medicinal flavour. The road here is lined with salak palms, growing about 3½m high with sharp prickles; further up the mountain slopes there are teak and clove plantations.

Transport Public bemos run regularly between Singaraja and Amlapura and Klungkung and Denpasar, passing through Tulamben, Perama stop in Tulamben en route between Padangbai, Candi Dassa, Air Sanin and Lovina.

Shortly after leaving Sibetan is **Putung** and a turning on the left for the *Pondok Bukit Putung*, perched on the edge of a cliff with magnificent views to the coast. In the evening the Burung Merpati bird makes a quite magical song by inflating its neck. There is now a road running from the village down to Manggis on the coast, a distance of about 8 km. Back on the main road you pass through the village of **Duda**, which holds an important ceremony at the time of the full moon in October.

Sideman & Iseh have some of the best views in Bali

Not long after leaving Duda is the turning for Iseh and Sideman on the left. This road travels south downhill, through glorious scenery with views to the coast, eventually reaching Klungkung. **Iseh** is home to some unique rituals. At the time of the harvest full moon, in the Pura Dalem, trance dances take place in which the dancers represent animals such as puppies, snakes and pigs, and even kitchen utensils such as pots and potlids, as well as evil spirits. After passing through Iseh you come to **Sideman**, 29 km from Amlapura, where there are now several places to stay (see

'Sleeping' below) and a good quality weaving factory, the *Pelangi Workshop*, where you can watch the process and buy *endek* from the weavers. Other workshops produce the expensive 'kain songket', using silk interwoven with gold and silver thread. (It has been alleged by a leading German magazine that dye from the weaving factories is poisoning the underground water supply which affects places as far away as Kuta.) Traditional varieties of rice are still grown here. There are endless possibilities for walks in an area where you feel you have stepped back 100 years in time; the local people seem gentle and very friendly as they go about their lives in a manner unchanged since their forebears, gathering firewood and farming in the time honoured way.

Situated in the hills 12 km north of Klungkung, this is one of the most beautiful areas of Bali. Not only are the ricefields some of the most breathtaking on the island, but Mount Agung rises in awesome majesty, dominating the landscape in an almost mystical way; while to the south there are views to the coast and the sea in the distance. The area was favoured by the artists Walter Spies and Theo Meyer who lived here in the 1930s, and the dramatic views from this area inspired some of their most outstanding Balinese landscapes. The house they lived in is available for long term rentals; enquire at *Patal Homestay* (see 'Sleeping', page 407). The writer Anna Mathews also stayed here for a year at the time of the 1963 eruption of Mount Agung. Her book '*Night of Purnama*' is an evocative account of life in the village prior to the eruption and the experience of living through that dramatic period.

Back on the main road you pass through **Selat**, 11 km from Rengdang and 21 km from Amlapura, a village that was badly destroyed by the 1963 eruption. This is the point of departure for the shorter of the two climbing routes up Mount Agung (see page 388), and there is good, reasonably priced accommodation here (see 'Sleeping', Putang). **Pura Pasar Agung**, one of Bali's nine directional temples, is located nearby, signposted from the main road. The road up to the temple climbs steeply past countryside scoured by lava flows. There is a car park just below the steps leading up to the temple, which has been completely rebuilt since its destruction in 1963.

The nearby village of **Padangaji** has a 'Gambuh' school; *gambuh* is a classical dance/drama with music that is slow and courtly. The road continues to **Muncan**, passing through some of the most breathtaking *sawah* landscapes on Bali, at their best just before the planting of the young rice seedlings when the fields are flooded. This is a peaceful area, with ravines, streams and the sounds of running water and birdsong. Just before Muncan you'll notice a sign: 'Antiques made to order'(!); and 5 km further on you reach Rendang and the road up to Besakih. From here you can cut across to Bangli or turn south to Klungkung; a steady stream of bemos connect Rendang with these two towns and with Amlapura.

Sleeping at Putung
Phone code: 0366

C-D *Pondok Bukit Putung*, Duda, Selat, Karangasem, T/F23039, reservations: *Balina Beach*, Manggis, Karangasem, T0363-41002-5, F41001; or direct as above. Perched on the edge of a cliff, with spectacular panoramic views of the ricefields below and the east coast of Bali. 5 rather basic bungalows. The whole complex is a bit rundown and badly in need of redecoration. Restaurant (cheap) with lovely views. Good walks in the cooler mountain air, 750m above sea level.

Transport 22 km by road west of Amlapura, 10 km west of Bebandem. The village can be reached via bemo from **Amlapura** to **Bebandem** (500Rp), change to a bemo heading for **Selat**, ask to be dropped at the turn off for Putung 1 km before **Duda** village, from here it is 1½ km to the bungalows and restaurant. Much easier by car.

Sleeping at Sideman
Phone code: 0366

All the properties in this area are owned by the local ruler, of the Satria caste, or his relatives. **A** *Patal Homestay*, 6 km from the main Amlapura-Rendang road, 1 km before Sideman village, T2001/23005, F23007. The outstanding place to stay in this area. Stunning views of Mount Agung to the north; to the south are panoramic views over the countryside to the coast. 2 huge, bright, older rooms with private bathrooms, cold water only. Family suite with 3 rooms,

2 en suite bathrooms with hot water. Beautiful, luxuriant gardens. Price includes full board. Very popular, many guests book in advance a month at a time. For Jul/Aug you need to book by Jan. Highly recommended. **A** *Sideman Homestay*, T23009, F23015. On right at the start of the village coming from the north, just before *Pelangi Weaving*; superb views to south coast. Rooms, however, are in need of renovation, very dark. Supremely overpriced. **A-B** *Subak Tabola Inn*, PO box 119, Klungkung, Bali 80701, T/F23015. Signposted from the main road 1½ km before the centre of Sideman, coming from the north. Follow a dreadful, rutted track for 1½ km, ignore the distances on their optimistic signs. Stunning location with views of both Mount Agung and the distant sea. 11 bungalows in what might be described as simple luxury, offering peace and seclusion. The large rooms are simply, but attractively decorated, cold water only, despite the cool evenings at this altitude, pool. Students at the 'Gambuh' school in nearby Padangaji provide performances and gamelan recitals. Restaurant (expensive to mid-range). Reservations essential in Jul/Aug. Choice of B&B, half or full board. Recommended.

Sleeping at Selat
Phone code: 0366

C-D *Pondok Wisata Puri Agung*, T23037, or c/o Jl Gili Biaha 3, Denpasar, T0361- 223663. On the main road through the village. Situated in the foothills of Mount Agung with fabulous views of the mountain, next to ricefields. 9 attractively furnished rooms. A good place to stay if you are planning to climb the mountain.

Transport Bemos: regular bemos, usually green, run from **Amlapura** via **Bebandem** and Selat to **Rendang**, and from **Klungkung** (also called by its old name Semarapura). From Rendang, connections to **Bangli** (black or brown and white bemos usually) and on to **Gianyar** (blue bemos) and **Denpasar**. Klungkung to Bebandem, green bemos run regularly throughout the day.

North from Denpasar to Lake Bratan

See maps, pages 368 & 382

Northwest of Denpasar by 15km is the town of Kapal. Shortly after Kapal, in the village of Bringkit, the road branches; west for Tanah Lot and Gilimanuk, and north for Lake Bratan, Singaraja and Lovina Beach. The coastal temple of Tanah Lot is 10 km off the main road and is a popular tourist attraction. The other arm of the fork runs north for 2 km to Mengwi (with its impressive temple complex). Continuing north, the road climbs through breathtaking terraced paddy fields to Lake Bratan, one of three crater lakes that fill part of a massive caldera. Mount Catur lies to the north of the lake and is the highest peak in the area at 2,096m.

Kapal

The meru and pottery-making town of Kapal is best-known for its red-brick **Pura Sada** which lies just south of the main road, past the bend near the market place (it is signposted). The pura is an important shrine of the former dynasty of the kingdom of Mengwi. Inside the enclosure is an unusual 10-m-high *prasada* or *prasat* (possibly explaining its name 'Pura Sada'), similar in style to Javanese candis, and dedicated to the king's ancestors.

Transport 15 km from Denpasar. **Bemo**: regular bemos from the Ubung terminal, just northwest of **Denpasar**.

Tanah Lot

Phone code: 0361
There are good coastline walks south from Tanah Lot

The coastal temple of Tanah Lot, perched on a rock at the edge of the shore-line and 30 km northwest of Denpasar, is probably the most photographed sight in Bali. The temple is one of the *sadkahyangan* – the six holiest shrines – and is said to have been built after the Hindu saint Danghyang Nirartha spent a night here and subsequently suggested that a temple be constructed on the spot.

The temple itself is small, and hardly remarkable artistically, with two-tiered merus and several other pavilions. What makes it special, and so popular, is its incomparable position. Built on a rock outcrop just off the coast, it can only be reached at low tide. The surrounding rocks are said to be inhabited by sea-snakes, but this does nothing to deter the hordes of visitors who clamber over the rocks and stroll along the beach. The profusion of trinket stalls, warungs and hawkers can be overpowering and detracts from the overall ambience of the location, but it is still well worth the visit, particularly in the late afternoon, when the sun sets behind the temple (and photographers line-up to catch the moment). ■ *1,500Rp. Facilities here include a money changer, restaurant and post office.*

A *Mutiara Tanah Lot Hotel and Restaurant*, T812939, F812935. Some a/c, bungalows are arranged out the back in a garden. They have attached bathrooms with hot water and the room rate includes breakfast. **A-B** *Dewi Sinta*, T812933, F813956. Some a/c, large restaurant with some villas out the back. The villas, with hot water, have an attractive position overlooking ricefields, close to the walkway to Tanah Lot and a pitching wedge from the new golf course. The hotel also has a small pool – which is open to non-residents – and a mini-library. There is a US$10 surcharge during the peak months from 22 Dec to 8 Jan. **B** *Bali Wisata Bungalows*, Yeh Gangga Beach, T261354. A/c, restaurant, saltwater pool, a dozen small bungalows close to rice paddies, the beach on one side and a pura on the other, 1 hr walk from Tanah Lot along the beach; to the cognoscenti: Bali as it used to be – quiet, relaxed, peaceful, only drawback is that the currents here are too strong for swimming in the sea. Recommended. **D** *Losmen Puri Lukisan Tanah Lot* (close to the public parking areas and tucked behind a painting gallery). Handful of rooms and the cheapest place to stay here.

Sleeping

The village of **Kediri** holds a big animal market at the Pasar Hewan, with cattle, goats, pot-bellied pigs, ducks and unhappy looking chickens bound together in bunches by their ankles; all in all, probably not a place for animal lovers.

Shopping

Road Bemo: connections with **Denpasar's** Ubung terminal, north of town to **Kediri** and then another from Kediri to Tanah Lot; be sure to leave Tanah Lot by 1400 in order to catch a connecting bemo from Kediri back to town. The turning for the temple is 20 km northwest of Denpasar on the road to Negara and Gilimanuk. From here it is a 10 km drive down a lovely road through paddy fields to the sea.

Transport

30 km from Denpasar. See section 'The West' for the route up the west coast from here, page 430

Mengwi

Mengwi, on the road north from Kapal towards Lake Bratan and Singaraja, is a market town which hosts an important cattle market every Wednesday and Sunday. Otherwise it is unremarkable, save for the **Pura Taman Ayun**. This impressive temple, with its classic design, lawns and ponds, is free from crowds and hawkers (especially before 1000), making it worth the visit. It was built for the founder of the Mengwi Kingdom in 1634. Surrounded by a moat, it consists, characteristically, of a series of three courtyards. The tallest gate leads into the back courtyard, where there are two rows of *palinggih-palinggih* or shrines for visiting deities on the north and east sides, each with ornate pillars and beautifully carved doors. On the west side are a number of *bales* or pavilions. The courtyard also contains a stone altar (*paibon*) with reasonable relief carvings. To the left of the main entrance there is a poor 'Museum of Complete Cremation' (admission by donation). There are two restaurants nearby, the Bali Green Restaurant and the Sari Royal Garden. ■ *Take the turning to the right opposite the colt station to get there.*

Phone code: 0361

Sangeh nutmeg forest is 15 km north of Mengwi (it is also known as 'monkey forest' because of the many monkeys found here) and is the sight of the **Pura Bukit Sari**. The temple was built at the beginning of the 17th century by the son of the King of Mengwi as a meditation temple. Today it is a *subak* (or irrigation) temple. ■ *Getting there: although the forest and temple are closest to Mengwi, it is difficult to get there on public transport except by returning to Denpasar's Ubung terminal and taking another*

Excursions

bemo north – which means a total journey of nearly 40 km. With private transport, it is easy to take the road east towards Kedampat.

Pura Luhur is an isolated mountain temple situated on the slopes of Mount Batukau (or 'shell' mountain), amidst tropical forest. ■ *Getting there: it is not easy to reach by public transport – it is best to charter a bemo from Denpasar or Mengwi, turning north at Tabanan. The final climb is steep.* On the way, visit the **hot springs** at **Penatahan, AL** *Yeh Panes*, Jl Batukaru, Desa Penatahan, T262356. These natural hot springs are part of a spa resort, with simple chalets, wooden floors and balconies, standing on a hillside overlooking swimming pool and spa area. The spa comprises a series of nine enclosed hot-spring rock pools with jacuzzi jets. Massage available. Towels and lockers for hire. Open air restaurant overlooking river. Tennis courts. Lunch and use of spa is US$48 per person. If you stay at the resort, use of the spa and breakfast is included in the room rate.

Pura Yeh Gangga is an attractive temple 15 km from Mengwi off the road north to Lake Bratan. Unusually, the base of the merus are constructed of stone, rather than wood, with porcelain set into the walls. A stone inscription discovered within the compound can be dated to 1334. ■ *Getting there: take a bemo running north towards Lake Bratan from Mengwi or Denpasar's Ubung terminal, and ask to be let off just after the village of Bereteh (and before Kukup). Take the turning to the left and walk through the village of Paang to Perean, where the pura can be found (a walk of about 1½ km).*

Transport
18 km from Denpasar

Road Bus: connections with **Denpasar's** Ubung terminal; buses turn off the main road to Gilimanuk at Bringkit, and fork north. Alternatively, big buses travel the main road from Denpasar to Gilimanuk from Denpasar's Ubung terminal; ask to be let off at the turning to Mengwi and Bedugul (in the village of Bringkit); bemos wait at this junction and run north.

Lake Bratan and Lake Buyan

Lake Bratan
Phone code: 0368

The beautiful, almost alpine, Lake Bratan is surrounded by the crater walls of the now extinct volcano, Mount Catur. This is a peaceful spot to visit, with cool evenings and away from the hassle of the beach resorts. Because of the altitude, it is much cooler here than at the coast. There are attractive walks around the lake and boats can be hired. On its west shore is the stunningly positioned and mystical **Pura Ulun Danau Bratan**, which seems to almost float on the water. The temple, set in well kept gardens, was built in 1633 by the King of Mengwi to honour the Goddess of the Lake who provides water for irrigation. Along with the temple at Lake Batur (see page 384), the Pura Ulun Danau Bratan is the most important of the various irrigation temples on Bali. Restaurant within the temple gardens for lunch and snacks. ■ *Admission charge and parking fee, 0800-1900 Mon-Sun. Toilets: 200Rp.* Outside the walls of this Hindu temple is a stupa with seated Buddha images in its niches, revealing Bali's Buddhist roots.

Bedugul

South of Candikuning, on the south lip of the crater, is the small town of **Bedugul**. There is a good permanent fruit, vegetable, flower and spice market here every day. There are many lovely walks in the hills round here. The wet season lasts longer than on the coast and this area can be very wet indeed; best months are May-October with daytime temperatures averaging 20°C, night time 16-18°C, maximum temperature is rarely above 24°C. The coldest, wettest month is January when temperatures average 16°C.

Near Bedugul, at an altitude of 1,240m, the road passes the **Bali Botanical Gardens**, Kebun Raya Eka Karya Bali. Opened in 1959 as a branch of the National Botanical Gardens in Bogor, the gardens cover nearly 130 ha on the slopes of Mount Pohon (*pohon* means tree in Indonesian). Over 650 species of tree and 450 varieties of orchid, some rare, grow here, though unfortunately few are labelled. It is a beautiful and very peaceful area especially on weekdays, and is also a good place for birdwatching. There are some temples in the grounds (see the map at the entrance),

the most interesting of which is Pura Teratai Bang; the sulphur in the earth here is believed to be beneficial for skin ailments which attracts some to the gardens.
■ *1000Rp plus 3,000Rp for cars. Weekdays 0700-1630, weekends 0800-1630. Getting there: 1½ hrs' drive from Lovina; a narrow road leads west from the corn-on-the-cob sculpture, just on the outskirts of Bedugul to the gardens.*

North from Lake Bratan, the road crosses the floor of the crater and as the road climbs up over its north walls, **Lake Buyan** comes into sight. This is another lake of great natural beauty and is the proposed site of a national park. Curious platforms about 50m from the shore are used by the locals for fishing. To get to the lake, stop the bemo by the entrance to *Lake Buyan Cottages* (there is a barrier on the left-hand side, travelling north), just before the road starts to climb out of the crater. There is a small surfaced road, passing a dilapidated temple on the right, to a car park where drinks are sold and fishing-rods are for hire. From here, it is possible to walk around the lake, if the water level is not too high. There are no watersports, so it is very peaceful. Coffee is grown on the hillsides around the lake.

Lake Buyan

Just 2 km north of Lake Bratan is the site of the **Handara Kosaido Country Club** and golf course, voted one of the world's 50 most beautiful courses (see below for details).

Air Terjun Gitgit lies about 15 km north of Lake Bratan, near the village of Gitgit. Well signposted from the main road, with a car park and rest area, a path leads the 500m to this waterfall, sometimes described as the most dramatic waterfall on Bali. Although not much more than 40m in height it is quite impressive, especially in the wet season, as it falls dramatically into a pool where the locals swim. According to local folklore, if you visit the falls with your boy/girlfriend the relationship will not endure. ■ *Admission on main road 500Rp, 15 mins' walk to the falls. Getting there: take a bemo heading for Singaraja; coming from Singaraja, take a bemo from the southern bus terminal, Sangket.*

Air Terjun Gitgit

Bedugul Tropical mountain climate with a temperature range of 18-24° C. Rainy season Nov-Apr. Accommodation here is often disappointing and somewhat overpriced. **A-AL** *Pacung Mountain Resort*, Jl Raya Pacung, Baturiti T21038/9, 0361-262461/2, F21043, Pacungmr@Denpasar.Wasantara.net.id 9 km south of Bedugul (60 mins' drive from Singaraja, 2 hrs from airport) on the main road with view over steep valley and terraced ricefields, beneath the peaks of Batukaru and Pohen mountains. 50 bungalows and small but comfortable rooms arranged on steep valley side, a/c, heated pool (a consideration at this altitude), health club, restaurant very popular with passing coach tours, good value buffet lunch. Recommended. **B** *Bedugul*, T0361-226593; 21197, F21198. Bland resort hotel beside lake, plain, rather drab rooms in need of renovation, clean bathrooms, most have view across the lake, noisy during the day, also some cottages. Canteen-like restaurant popular with tour groups. **B** *Bukit Permai*, T23663. On left of road at lip of crater before road descends into Bedugul, cottage-type accommodation, some rooms have fireplaces, but they smoke badly, compelling occupants to open windows and lose any benefit of the warmth, well-kept garden, excellent views towards Denpasar – awkward for lake visits without own transport.

Close to Bedugul market there are 3 cheaper places to stay, all within 10 mins' walk of lake, but no view of lake. **D** *Ibu Hadi*, T23497. Restaurant, new building, clean rooms, very steep staircase. Recommended. **D** *Mawar Indah*, T21190. Small, simple rooms, scrub garden (both the above are down the road with the Botanical Garden gateway). **D-E** *Sari Artha Inn*, T21011, just after market on left. Best rooms are on the hill away from the main road, clean with private mandi. Rooms by the road may be noisy. Reasonably priced.

Candikuning On reaching the lakeshore for the first time, there are 2 similar places to stay. Stop the bemo/bus here. **B-D** *Ashram Guesthouse*, T22439, F21101. Some a/c, restaurant (cheap and not recommended). A lovely lakeside setting with views of the lake temple from some verandahs, this is the best place to stay for views of lake. Rooms are spread out up the hill and are a little drab and soulless; the most expensive rooms have hot water with bath and

Sleeping near Lake Bratan
Phone code: 0368

It is important to be dropped off at your hotel, otherwise you may have quite a walk. Hotels listed are divided into 4 sections, with southernmost places listed first

Western toilet, cheapest rooms have shared mandi and squat toilet, most rooms have cold water only, making them a bit pricey considering that temperatures are coolish here in the mountains. Price depends on the views. Well kept gardens with tennis court, friendly staff, very relaxing. High season Jun/Aug and Dec/Jan, reservation necessary 1 month in advance, price includes breakfast and tax. **C-D** *Lila Graha*, restaurant, cottage type rooms, shady gardens, overlooks lake, above road.

Pancasari Bemo station here, approximately 2 km beyond temple. **L-AL** *Bali Danau Buyan* (formerly *Lake Buyan Cottages*), Jl Raya Bedugul, T0362-21351/23739, F21388. North of Lake Bratan by 5 km, 2 km from Handara Country Club. Nine luxurious individual cottages, each with 2 bedrooms, living room with fireplace, dining room with kitchen area and terrace, furnished to a high standard. 1 cottage with Japanese style rooms. Beautiful setting in immaculate gardens with views across Lake Buyan; tennis courts and putting greens. **A** *Handara Country Club*, entrance on right just before village, T28866/88944. Some bungalows, tennis, fitness centre, golf course, beautiful location, but rather overpriced. **A** *Pancasari Inn*, T53142. Just north of *Handara Country Club* on left-hand side, tennis, no lake views, last place to stay before road climbs out of the crater. **B** *Bukit Mungsu Indah* (before Bedugul, at Baturiti), price includes breakfast.

Air Terjun Gitgit C-D *Gitgit Hotel*. Fairly new and clean, situated amidst lush vegetation, rooms are fairly plain. All have private bathrooms, some with hot water. Restaurant (cheap).

Eating **In Bedugul close to market** *Ananda*, *Bogasari* and warungs.

Closer to the lake *Ashram Guesthouse*, *Lila Graha* or *Taliwang Bersaudara* (simple Lombok restaurant), good value, views across lake; *Perama Ulundanu*, in temple complex, lunch only, although they might be persuaded to open for dinner.

Sports **Golf** *Handara Country Club*, 18 holes, designed by the Australian golfer Peter Thomson; green fees 90,000Rp, clubs for hire, T28866. One of the 50 best golf courses in the world.

Watersports There are 3 locations to hire boats: **1)** temple complex (pedalo) 7,500Rp per 30 mins, circuit of lake in motorboat (15 mins), 4 people 14,000Rp, 5 people 17,500Rp; **2)** layby next to *Ashram Guesthouse*, rowboat 7,500Rp per 30 mins; **3)** *Bedugul Hotel* offers jet-skiing (US$10 per 15 mins), water-skiing (US$10), parasailing (US$10) and motorboats (US$15 per 30 mins).

Transport **Road Bemo**: to **Singaraja** from **Pancasari** – it should be possible to flag down passing
53 km from Denpasar, bemo rather than wait for them to fill up. Regular 'express' bemos leave from **Denpasar's**
35 km from Mengwi Ubung terminal for Singaraja (see below), passing through **Bedugul** and **Lake Bratan** en route, (1½ hrs). Perama stops here. The office is at the Sari Artha Inn, T21011, on the left just past the market heading north.

Lake **Tamblingan & Munduk** To the west of Lake Buyan lies Lake Tamblingan and a little further west still is the village of Munduk. This beautiful area lies 500m-1,500m above sea level and is part of a new scheme where visitors can stay in simple bungalows and can learn the ways of the Balinese people.

Sleeping *Puri Lumbung* (a *lumbung* is a Balinese rice barn and the houses have been built in a similar way). Visitors can learn anything from carving a wooden door frame to cooking a Balinese meal. Weaving, music playing (and the making of the instruments), learning about traditional medicines or repairing a fishing net are all part of the 'cultural experience'. For more information write to *Puri Lumbung*, Balai Pendidikan dan Latihan Pariwisata Bali (BPLP), Kotak Pos 2, Nusa Dua, Bali 80363. Recommended.

North Coast, Buleleng Regency

The north coast is a different world from the rest of Bali. Fewer rivers water this side of the island and there is less rainfall; as a result, the lushness of the south is replaced by savanna forest. The mountains to the south create a dramatic backdrop to the coastal scenery, providing an escape from the heat and opportunities for walks and drives while enjoying stunning views. Lying in the rain shadow of these mountains, the north is drier and less humid. Its primary attractions include its beaches, long stretches of black sand with safe swimming and some of the island's best snorkelling and diving, particularly off Pulau Menjangan. The sunsets can be spectacular, with Java's highest volcano, Mount Semeru, illuminated in the iridescent afterglow of the setting sun. Culturally, the north should not be underestimated either.

Colour map 3, grid B6

Ins and outs

Getting there & around

From the south by car Coming from the south over the mountains, the road from Lake Bratan is a long and twisting descent through clove and coffee groves. Singaraja, being the former Dutch capital of Bali and Nusa Tenggara, remains an important local town but has only a few attractions to entice the visitor. West from here is the resort of Lovina Beach (10km). The road continues west following the north coast, all the way to Gilimanuk (and the ferry for Java). The road east from Singaraja passes a number of important temples, built in distinctive North Balinese style (see section 'East of Singaraja'). The drive along the north coast eastwards and then south, passing by Tulemben and Amed, to Amlapura is very beautiful and peaceful, passing black sand beaches and coconut groves. The distance from Singaraja to Amlapura is almost 100 km. Beautiful walks can be taken in the hills behind Singaraja, with views over the coast to the sea.

Bus Bear in mind that all times are necessarily approximate and can vary enormously depending on traffic conditions. Buses run most frequently in the morning starting early (from 0500 or 0600), and continue until about 1700, continuing later on major routes. The frequency of buses is improving all the time.

From Singaraja *South*: (Sangket bus station) to **Denpasar** (Ubung Terminal) 3 hrs, Bedugul 1½ hrs, Gitgit 25 mins, Ubud 3 hrs. **West**: Banyuasri bus station, to **Gilimanuk** 2 hrs, to **Lovina** 20 mins, to **Pemuteran** 1½ hrs, to **Surabaya** 9 hrs. **East**: (Penarukan bus station) to **Denpasar** (Batubulan terminal) 3½ hrs, **Amlapura** 2¼ hrs, **Kintamani** 1 hr 40 mins, **Penelokan** 2 hrs, Sangsit 15 mins, **Air Sanih** 25 mins, **Sawan** 35 mins.

Shuttle bus *Perama* currently offers the best service. They have 2 offices in Lovina, in Kalibukbuk and Anturan, T41161/41104. From **Lovina** and **Air Sanih** there are connections with **Kuta**, **Sanur** (with a boat connection to Nusa Lembongan), **Ubud**, **Kintamani**, **Bedugul**, **Tulemben**, **Tirtagangga**, **Candi Dasa**, **Padangbai**, the **airport** and **Lombok**. They can also arrange tickets for Surabaya, Malang, Yogyakarta and Jakarta on Java, and Bima/Sape on Sumbawa.

History

Up until this century it was the north of Bali which had the greatest contact with the outside world. Prior to the building of Denpasar airport, Singaraja was the principal port and main entry point to the island. Lying on the main trading routes from Java eastwards, the area served as an entrepôt for Bugis, Arab and Chinese traders who

The Bali Aga: the original Balinese

In pre-history, Bali was populated by animists whose descendants today are represented by the Bali Aga, literally 'Original Balinese'. The Aga are now restricted to a few relic communities in North and East Bali, particularly in the regency of Karangkasem. Most have been extensively assimilated into the Hindu-Balinese mainstream. Miguel Covarrubias visited the Aga village of Tenganan in the 1930s, a village which even then was extraordinary in the extent to which it was resisting the pressures of change. He wrote:

"The people of Tenganan are tall, slender and aristocratic in a rather ghostly, decadent way, with light skins and refined manners.... They are proud and look down even on the Hindu-Balinese nobility, who respect them and leave them alone. They live in a strange communistic... system in which individual ownership of property is not recognized and in which even the plans and measurements of the houses are set and alike for everybody".

Even today, a distinction is still made between the Bali Aga and the Wong Majapahit. The latter arrived from Java following the fall of the Majapahit Kingdom at the end of the 15th century.

In former years, the Aga were probably cannibalistic. It has been said that Aga corpses used to be washed with water, which was allowed to drip onto a bundle of unhusked rice. This was then dried and threshed, cooked, moulded into the shape of a human being, and served to the relatives of the deceased. The eating of the rice figure is said to symbolize the ritual eating of the corpse, so imbibing its powers.

---

brought not only their products but also their religion and culture; many settled here, making the north coast their home. European influence also reached the north earlier than other parts of Bali and to this day parts of the north have a colonial feel, particularly Singaraja.

For most of its history the north has been geographically isolated from the south by the chain of volcanic mountains that run from east to west across the northern part of Bali. It was only as recently as the early part of the 20th century that roads were built through the mountains, which has allowed the region to develop a somewhat distinct culture.

The Dutch arrived in 1814, anxious to secure Bali in the face of an increasing British presence in the region. They established control after a bloody battle at Jagaraga in which the brave Balinese, armed only with kris' and spears, were unable to

North Bali (Buleleng Regency)

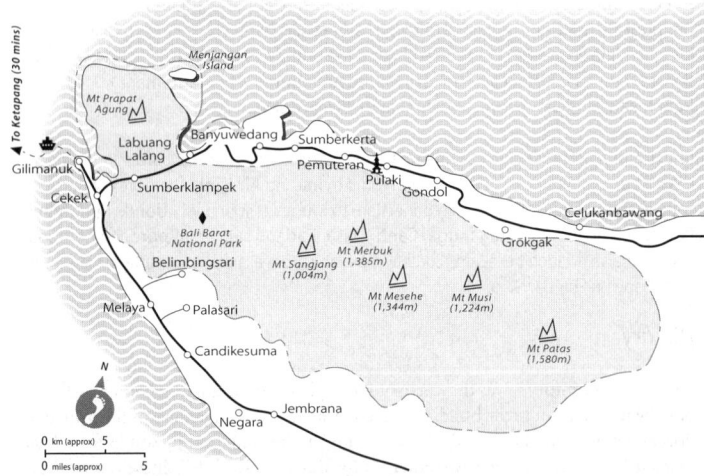

withstand the military superiority of the invaders; thousands of Balinese died as against about 30 Dutch soldiers. Notwithstanding their defeat, the Balinese continued to retaliate against Dutch rule over the next few decades.

In order to secure their authority and ensure the profitability of Bali, the Dutch set about improving the infrastructure. Roads were built, irrigation improved and cash crops such as coffee and spices were introduced. A member of the Buleleng royal family was appointed regent but under the authority of the Dutch. Singaraja became the seat of colonial administration, with jurisdiction ultimately over the whole of Bali and Lombok. The area thus came under Western influence more than half a century earlier than the south; it took the best part of 60 years before the south was subjugated, in 1909. Increasingly, European writers, traders and scholars began to visit and some settled. During the Second World War, the Japanese also made Singaraja their headquarters when they invaded the island. However, with the building of an airport near Denpasar, the Dutch moved their administrative capital to the more populous south. Benoa and Padangbai have now taken over as the main ports.

Village life in the north is not as rigidly defined; the family, rather than the banjar, is the focus of an individual's life to a greater extent than further south. This is partly because, with little wet rice cultivation, there is not the same need for mutual help and interdependence amongst the predominantly farming community. The class system is not as strong, either, partly as a result of the many outside social and religious influences the north has experienced, including the longer period of Dutch occupation. The Dutch in particular set out to control Balinese society, making changes where it suited them, often in total disregard of the class system; for example, in schools a high caste boy might be made to sit next to a lower caste girl, something that would never happen in traditional Balinese society. Women in Buleleng were the first on the island to cover their breasts, as the Dutch were concerned about the effect of bare breasts on their soldiers. But not all aspects of Dutch rule were bad. Buleleng's villagers were the first to be vaccinated against smallpox, and slavery was abolished here earlier than in other parts of the island. The slave trade had been Bali's economic mainstay throughout the 17th and 18th centuries.

The cosmopolitan nature of Buleleng's society, isolated from the south by the mountainous terrain, has also had an impact on culture and the arts, creating styles which are unique and distinctive. Many new forms of **dance**, **music** and **art** originated here. The frenzied gamalan style *gong kebyar*, now the predominant form on

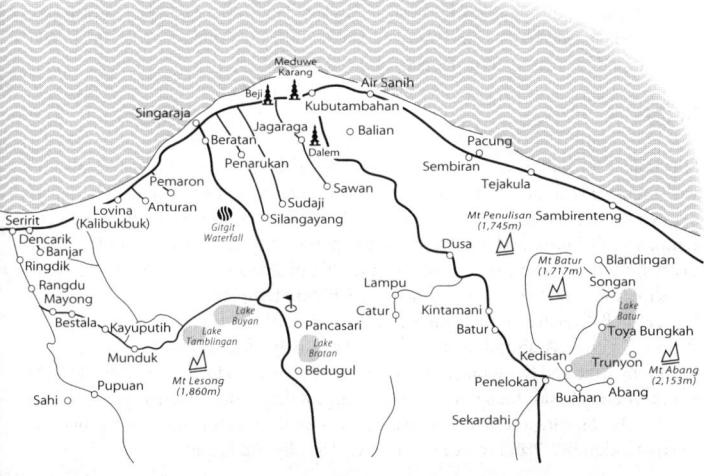

the island, originated in the north in 1915, influenced by Western musical forms including jazz. *Kebyar* replaced the slow, gentle, stately *gong gede*, and today there are only a handful of *gong gede* orchestras left on the island. Buleleng's dance troupes are held in high esteem and several new dance styles originated here, including a highly suggestive *Joged*. This erotic dance is even alleged to have ruined marriages at the height of its popularity, in the 1960s and 1970s, such was the erotic intensity of the movements performed by the young girl dancers. These days the dance is performed by a single dancer, wearing a headdress made of gilded leather and decorated with flowers. She dances erotically for a time, then with the fan she is holding, she taps one of the male members of the audience as an invitation for him to join her, and she presents him with a sash which must be tied around his waist. *Janger*, another dance, is performed by two rows of boys and girls facing each other and is very popular with Balinese youth; each sings in turn, usually about love, with much joking and use of slang. Crafts such as weaving, metalwork and pottery also show distinct regional variations; as do the flamboyant temple carvings.

There is less **rice** cultivation in the drier north, where the rich volcanic soils support crops of soybeans, peanuts, maize and tobacco as well as fruit. Some of the island's best grapes, mangoes and durian are grown here. Cattle are also a significant export. In season the growers sell mangoes from big baskets by the roadside; though if you are thinking of buying, be aware that if the fruit is too hard and unripe it will never become sweet.

Singaraja

Phone code: 0362 *Singaraja is the second largest city in Bali, with a population in excess of 100,000 and the capital of the regency of Buleleng. Since colonial times Singaraja has been an important educational and cultural centre, and with two universities in the town there is a sizeable student population. The name Singaraja means lion king, and the lion, symbol of bravery, courage and determination, is the emblem of Buleleng.*

Ins and outs

Getting there As Bali's 2nd city, Singaraja is well connected to other destinations on the island with buses leaving from 3 terminals serving different areas. The only out-of-island services are to Surabaya, on Java. Night buses leave from the Banyuasri terminal.

Getting around Bemos link Singaraja's 3 bus terminals. There are also horse-drawn dokars and ojeks providing trips around town. The **tourist office** is on Jl Veteran 23, T61141. The staff are very helpful and speak good English (ask for Nyoman Swela or Putu Tasraujiya). Maps of Buleleng, Lovina and Singaraja, as well as brochures detailing places of interest. Open 0800-1600 Mon-Thu and Sat, 0800-1100 on Fri, and 0800-1400 on Sun.

Sights

Singaraja is for the most part an attractive town with a lingering colonial feel, some well-preserved colonial architecture, and tiny winding backstreets in the southern part of town which make for pleasant wandering. In addition to its Dutch heritage there are remnants of Chinese and Muslim influence, particularly in the area behind the now decaying harbour where you can still see the old Chinese-style roofs behind the modern shopfronts. By the waterfront there is a **Chinese temple** (called *klenteng*), one of the few on Bali, with a Hindu temple nearby, and to the south a mosque. The descendants of Chinese, Arab and Bugis settlers still live in this area along streets nicknamed Kampong Arab and Kampong Bugis. On the western side of town there is an old **Chinese cemetery** beside the sea near Pantai Lingga at Bukit Suci, which means hallowed hill. In 1995 Singaraja won a nationwide award for the cleanest and best maintained town in Indonesia. People here are extremely friendly and helpful.

The centre of town lies at the intersection of Jl Gajah Made and Jl Jen A Yani; here you will find banks, post office, telephones, accommodation, restaurants and the **market**, which turns into a night market full of foodstalls in the evenings.

On Jl Veteran, next door to the tourist office, is the **Gedong Kirtya**, a manuscript library founded by the Dutch in 1928 when it was named the Kirtya Liefrinck van der Tuuk. It contains Bali's best collection of palm leaf illustrated books or *lontars*, which record local myths, magic formulas, literature and dances. Many were taken from the palace in Lombok during the Dutch campaign at the beginning of this century. Some of the Lombok manuscripts originated in Java, from where they were rescued during the disintegration of the Majapahit Empire. The palm leaves are cut into lengths of about 50cm and then incised with a sharp blade, the incisions filled with a mixture of soot and oil to accentuate the marks. They are then bound together using lengths of cord and protected between two wooden boards.

Excursions

In order to visit the sights of the north coast, most visitors base themselves in either Lovina Beach 10 km to the west of town, or Air Sanih 17 km to the east, both of which offer a choice of accommodation, restaurants and activities, and also provide a pleasant seaside location.

Singaraja

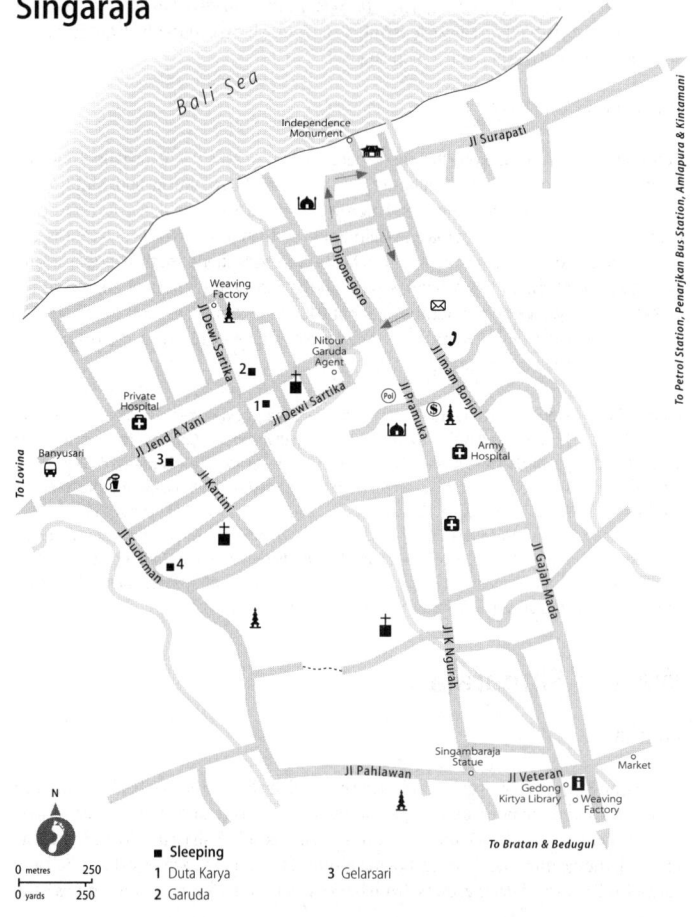

- **Sleeping**
1 Duta Karya
2 Garuda
3 Gelarsari

The temples of the north are interesting for their distinct north style of architecture; in general they are artistically 'busier', exhibiting much more elaborate and dense carving. For details on excursions, see pages 418 and 427 (headings for west, south and east of Singaraja).

Essentials

Sleeping Accommodation in Singaraja largely caters for Indonesian businessmen and tends to be in the centre of town; the main street running east-west, Jl Jend Yani, in particular has a number of these 'business' hotels. *Tresna homestay*, which used to be popular with travellers, has closed. **B-D** *Wijaya*, Jl Sudirman, T21915. A/c, range of good accommodation. **D-E** *Duta Karya*, Jl Jend A Yani, T21467. Some a/c, adequate. **E** *Garuda*, Jl Jend A Yani 76, T41191. Price includes breakfast. **E** *Gelarsari*, Jl Jend A Yani, T21495. **E** *Sakabindu*, Jl Jend A Yani, T21791.

Shopping **Textiles** Singaraja is known for its finely detailed ikats, both cotton and silk weft ikat; there are 2 weaving factories which are worth a visit to view the cloth they produce. At 42 Jl Dewi Sartika the *Berdikari weaving factory* (open 0800 to 1800 daily) produces exquisite reproductions of traditional Buleleng cloths, some made of silk. If you go in the morning you can see the process whereby the thread is spun and then woven into cloth. You can buy here as well; the high prices reflect the quality of the work. Towards the south of town just off Jl Veteran 22, behind the Gedong Kertya, is the *Puri Sidar Nadi Putra weaving factory* situated in the former royal palace, Puri Kawan (open 0800 to 1600), which produces high quality pieces of ikat from silk and cotton, with a shop attached.

Tour operators *Nitour*, Jl Jend A Yani, T22691.

Transport **Road** **Bus**: Singaraja has 3 bus stations, Penarukan on the east edge of town on Jl Surapati for destinations to the east. (**Amlapura** mostly yellow buses, **Kubu** and **Kintamani**.) Banyuasri on the west edge at the intersection of Jl Jend Sudirman and Jl Jend A Yani for destinations west of the town (**Lovina** and **Gilimanuk**) and Sangket (officially called Sukasada) on the south edge of town on Jl Mayor Metra for destinations south (**Denpasar** and **Bedugul**). **Night buses** (bis malam) leave from the Banyuasri terminal at approximately 1800 for Surabaya, arriving in **Surabaya** about 0400 (bus companies have their offices at *Taman Lila*, Jl Jend A Yani 2). **Bemos**: link the 3 terminals, fares within town are 400Rp. There are also some horse-drawn dokar.

78 km from Denpasar, 11 km from Lovina Beach

Directory **Airline offices** *Nitour*, Jl Jend A Yani 59, T22691, is the *Garuda* agent in Singaraja. **Banks** Several banks along Jl Ngurah Rai and Jl Jend A Yani, including *Bank Rakyat Indonesia*. **Communications** General Post Office: Jl Gajah Mada 158, Singaraja 81113; poste restante service. The **Telephone Office**: next to the post office, reasonable rates, overseas rates are displayed, and helpful staff. Open 24 hrs. **Medical services** Chemists: there are several chemists along Jl Ngurah Rai at nos 23, 27 and 28, also Singaraja Farma on Jl Jend A Yani. **Hospitals**: There are several hospitals in Singaraja. *General Hospital (Rumah Sakit Umum)*, Jl Ngurah Rai, T22046/22573. *Rumah Sakit Umum Angkatan Darat (RSAD)*, a military hospital which also treats members of the public, also on Jl Ngurah Rai, T22543. *Rumah Sakit Kerta Usada*, a private hospital with a dental section, Jl Jend A Yani 108, T22396.

West of Singaraja

Lovina

Phone code: 0362

Lovina, an 8 km stretch of grey sand, is the name given to an area that begins 7 km west of Singaraja and includes six villages and their associated beaches: from east to west they are Pemaron, Tukad Mungga, Anturan, Kalibukbuk, Kaliasem and Temukus, all of which merge into one another. Lovina is one of the larger beach resorts on Bali and caters to all ages and price groups, from backpackers and a few remnant hippies to an increasingly upmarket and package tour oriented clientele. Kalibukbuk is the heart of Lovina, the busiest, most developed part, with the greatest number of tourist facilities and nightlife. If you are looking for somewhere more peaceful try the area to the east which is currently less developed, more rural and peaceful.

The **tourist office** is next door to the police station. Open daily 0800-2000. They are very helpful, speak good English, supply maps, booklets and during high season can help you to find accommodation. Also offer tours and car hire at competitive prices; for example, a full day tour, 0900-1800, for two people, taking in the area around Lovina and up into the hills around Bedugul, costs 60,000Rp.

The beach The beach itself is quite narrow in places and the grey/black sand is not the prettiest, but the waters are calm, so swimming is very safe and there is reasonable snorkelling on the reef just off-shore. The beach is interspersed with streams running into the sea, where some villagers wash in the evening. Several areas are the preserve of the local fishermen whose dogs can be menacing if you are out for a walk, particularly in the evening. You can usually scare them off by bending down to pick up a few stones, only the most persistent wait for you to actually throw the stone at them. Hawkers are not as bad as they used to be but can still be a nuisance.

The most popular outing is an early morning boat trip to see the **dolphins** cavorting off the coast; there are two schools of dolphin which regularly swim off the coast. In the Kalibukbuk area the fishermen run a co-operative which fixes the number of people in each boat and the price, currently 10,000Rp; snorkelling is not included in the price. If you book through your hotel you will pay more for the convenience, but the price may include refreshments and the opportunity to go snorkelling afterwards. Boats set off at about 0600 and the tour usually lasts 1½ hrs. Bear in mind that there is no shade on the boats. People have mixed reactions to the experience. If yours is the first boat to reach the dolphin area then you may be rewarded with 12 dolphins leaping and playing, but as other boats arrive the dolphins may be chased away.

Bull races Bull races, *sapi gerumbungan*, take place on Independence Day, 17 August, and on some other national holidays such as Singaraja Day, 31 March, check exact dates at the tourist office. The Balinese name for the races is derived from the huge wooden bells *gerumbungan*, which the bulls (*sapi* in Indonesian) wear around their necks during the races. These bull races are unique to Buleleng and originated as a religious ceremony to propitiate the gods before planting the new rice crop. The specially trained bulls, decorated with colourful ornaments and silk banners, and with equally well dressed drivers, were originally raced over a flooded ricefield, usefully ploughing the field as they competed. Recently the event has been held on playing fields in the village of Kaliasem to the west of Kalibukbuk, primarily as a tourist attraction. However, in 1995 to commemorate the 50th anniversary of Indonesian Independence, the regional government decided to hold the event in its original form on a flooded ricefield in the village of Banjar, and they plan to make this an annual event. The winner is not necessarily the fastest; the appearance of the bull and driver are an important consideration when the judge decides the overall winner.

Excursions About 5 km to the west there are waterfalls at the village of **Labuhan Haji**, and a Buddhist monastery near the village of **Banjar Tegeha** with hot springs nearby. To the south there are cool highland areas with **lakes** and **botanical gardens** in the area surrounding Bedugul and Mount Batur; it can be very wet here except at the height of the dry season. To the east is **Singaraja**, the capital of the district, and beyond Singaraja there are interesting temples and other cultural sites, and the gamelan village of **Sawan**. (More information in the relevant sections.)

Sleeping

■ *on maps, pages 421 & 422*

Mosquitoes can be a problem, not all bungalows provide nets. During high season, Jul, Aug & the Christmas/New Year period, accommodation tends to be full with some people without reserved rooms being forced to spend their first night sleeping on the beaches

The central area of Kalibukbuk has the greatest concentration of accommodation, the widest choice of restaurants and nightlife, and most of the tourist facilities; however, it is becoming increasingly busy and built up. Some of the side roads to the east in the Anturan area offer more attractive and peaceful surroundings. To the west of Kalibukbuk towards Temukus, the road runs close to the beach, so accommodation here can be noisy; there are some new, attractive places here with beachfront locations, though prices seem a bit high.

AL *Hotel Damai*, new hotel in the hills overlooking Lovina. To reach it, turn south in Kalibukbuk by the *Khi Khi* restaurant at the sign for Kayuputih (see map), continue along a fairly narrow road climbing into the hills for about 10 mins, until you see the hotel on your right. Stunning location with spectacular views to the coast; temperatures a little cooler than sea level. The 8 bungalows have been built to the highest standards. Small pool, restaurant (expensive) providing gourmet food (at gourmet prices) with an extensive wine cellar; the chef trained with Paul Bocuse.

Pemaron (approximately 2 km west of Singaraja) **AL** *Puri Bagus Lovina*, PO Box 225, T21430, F22627. Sister hotel to the *Puri Bagus Candi Dasa* and of equally high quality, the best of the upmarket hotels in Lovina. Beautiful location beside sea, set in peaceful, secluded tropical gardens with fountains, gamelan music and large pool, thatched Balinese style bungalows provide attractive, bright rooms. 2 suites with private pool, kitchen and dining room; facilities are as expected in a hotel of this class, meeting room, restaurants and bar, watersports. 4 white ducks, the hotel's mascots, wander the grounds. **A-C** *Baruna Beach Cottages*, T41745, F41252. Beside the sea with good sea views, though the public beach is none too peaceful, smallish pool, rooms are overpriced and some would benefit from redecoration, cheapest rooms are dark and pokey, some a/c and hot water. **B-D** *Aldian Palace Hotel*, T25519. Very average hotel, not a good location, beside the road with no access to beach and no pool, 34 rooms, some with a/c, hot water, restaurant.

Tukad Mungga (approximately 7 km from Singaraja) **A-C** *Bali Taman Beach*, PO Box 149, T41126, F41840. A rather average upmarket hotel, disappointing for the price, beside the sea with smallish pool, tennis courts, 28 rooms, some a/c, hot water, rooms near road could be noisy. **B-D** *Puri Bedahulu*, T41731/23861. 11 rooms, set in tropical gardens beside the beach which can be noisy, rooms with fan, 2 with a/c and hot water, some rooms are small and rather dark. **C-E** *Yudha* (formerly *Simon Seaside Cottages*), PO Box 151, T41183, F411160. 20 rooms set in gardens beside sea, rooms have been attractively redecorated and include a new wing, all rooms have fans, upstairs rooms have balconies with beautiful sea views. **D-E** *Permai Beach Cottages*, T41471, F41224. 17 rooms set in gardens in a quiet location down a side road leading to the beach, a swimming pool is due to be built. Simple, clean rooms, fan, some with a/c, hot water and spring mattresses, good value and the cheapest a/c in Lovina, dive centre on premises. **E** *Suci Jati* (formerly *Jati Reef Bungalows*), same ownership as *Hotel Yudha*, PO Box 151, T41052, F41160. 16 rooms, set in large gardens next to beach.

Anturan (8½ km west of Singaraja) **A-B** *Hotel Celuk Agung*, PO Box 191, T41079, F41379; 28 rooms set in immaculate, large gardens, in very peaceful location surrounded by rice paddies, several mins' walk from the beach, clean and well-maintained, bath, hot water, some with a/c, restaurant (mid-range to cheap), large swimming pool, tennis courts, staff are very helpful and friendly. Recommended. **D-E** *Lila Cita*, superb location beside sea, but rooms are badly in need of renovation though they are clean. Fan, upstairs rooms with balconies and fine sea views. **D-E** *Perama Hotel*, T41161/41104. Small, basic rooms set around small Balinese style garden beside road, can be noisy as this is the location of the *Perama* shuttle bus operation, restaurant (cheap).

Banyualit (9 km west of Singaraja) **AL** *Hotel Mas Lovina Beach* (formerly *Las Brisas*, sister hotel *Bali Danau Buyan* near Bedugul), Jl Raya, F41236. Set in immaculate, completely secluded, tropical gardens with beautiful sea views, 10 spotless bungalows with full self-catering facilities, a/c, large beachside pool and restaurant. **A** *Hotel Aneka Lovina*, Jl

Raya Seririt, T41121/2, F41827. Catering largely for tour groups, set in lovely tropical gardens beside the sea, rooms are attractively furnished, facilities include restaurant and small pool. **A** *Sol Lovina* (formerly *Palma Beach Inn*), T41775, F41659. Part of the Sol Group offering typical package tour accommodation, beachside location with large pool, tennis courts. **B-C** *Banyualit Beach Inn*, PO Box 116, T41789, F41563. 20 rooms, seaside location with attractive pool, rooms are a bit overpriced, but clean, cheaper rooms are in semi-detached bungalows so you might hear your neighbours, fan or a/c, some with hot water.

Lovina Beach

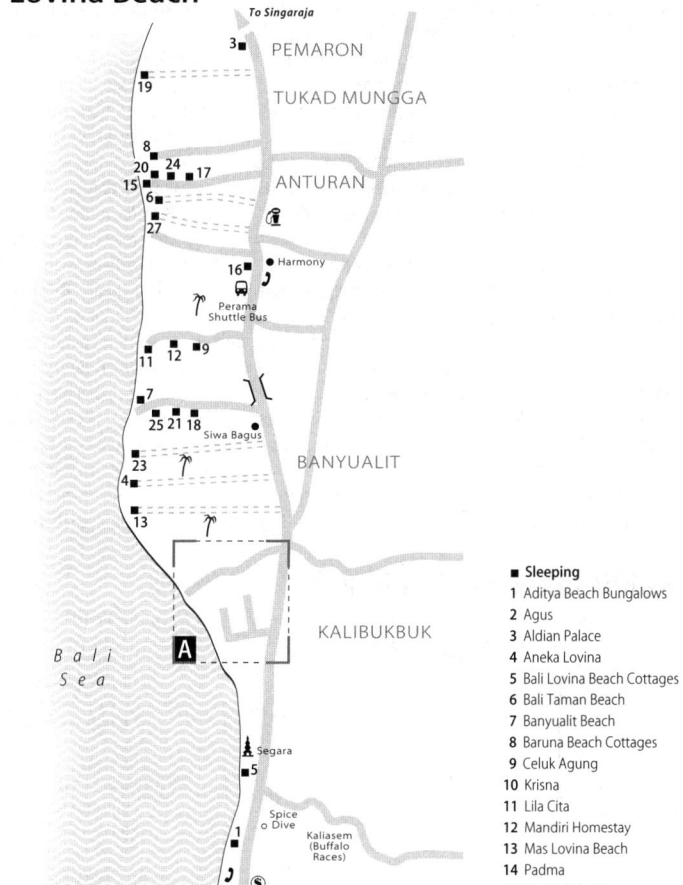

- **Sleeping**
- 1 Aditya Beach Bungalows
- 2 Agus
- 3 Aldian Palace
- 4 Aneka Lovina
- 5 Bali Lovina Beach Cottages
- 6 Bali Taman Beach
- 7 Banyualit Beach
- 8 Baruna Beach Cottages
- 9 Celuk Agung
- 10 Krisna
- 11 Lila Cita
- 12 Mandiri Homestay
- 13 Mas Lovina Beach
- 14 Padma
- 15 Pantai Bahagia
- 16 Perama
- 17 Permai Beach Cottages
- 18 Pringa
- 19 Puri Bagus
- 20 Puri Bedahulu
- 21 Ray Beach Inn 2
- 22 Samudra
- 23 Sol Lovina
- 24 Suci Jati
- 25 Suna
- 26 Toto
- 27 Yudha

Related map:
A Kalibukbuk,
page 422

C-D *Hotel Kalibukbuk*, T41701. Reasonably priced beside the sea though rooms are nothing special, the more expensive, upstairs rooms have pleasant sea views, fan or a/c. **D** *Ray Beach Inn 2*, T41088, set in small garden several mins' walk from beach, simple, clean, accommodation in 2-storey building with shared terrace/balcony and 1 detached bungalow, fan or a/c, restaurant (mid-range to cheap).

Kalibukbuk (10 km west of Singaraja) **A-B** *Bali Lovina Beach Cottages*, T22385/23478, F23478; 34 overpriced rooms adjacent to a good beach with pool, 6 bungalows have sea views, a/c, the remaining a/c rooms face each other and are clean but dark, 4 fan rooms are small and basic, restaurant (mid-range to cheap). **B-C** *Bayu Kartika Beach Bungalow*, T41055, F41219. Superb beachside location, 20 simple rooms with verandahs, mosquito nets. A/c rooms have open-air bathrooms, hot water and good sea views, fan rooms have cold water only and face sideways, overlooking the area the fishermen moor their boats, so may well be noisy early morning. Large gardens with plans to build a pool. Restaurant with sea views. Very friendly staff, manager plays gamelan. Long stay discount available. Recommended. **B-D** *Nirwana*, clean but no mosquito protection, nice rooms overlooking a garden, rather overpriced. **B-D** *Puri-Bali Bungalows*, T41485. 20 bungalows in garden setting with small pool, rooms are dark and simple, some with a/c, hot water. **B-D** *Rambutan Beach Cottages*, PO Box 195, T41388, F41057. Set in large, pretty gardens with small plunge pool, 18 simple but clean rooms with verandah, cold water in all but the most expensive rooms, fan, cheaper rooms face the car park, overpriced, restaurant (mid-range to cheap). **B-D** *Rini Hotel*, T41386. Set in tropical gardens, 20 spotlessly clean rooms, cheaper rooms are dark and basic, some with squat toilets, more expensive rooms are attractive but not particularly good value, all rooms, fan, some hot water, restaurant (mid-range to cheap). **B-E** *Angsoka Hotel*, T41841, F41023, angsoka@singaraja, wasantara.net.id 38 rooms, a popular place set in pretty tropical gardens with a small pool, there is a large range of rooms and prices, all with verandah, private bathroom, cheapest rooms have squat toilets, the most expensive rooms have baths, hot water and a/c, have a look at several rooms as price is not necessarily an indication of how attractive the room will be: the newer rooms are much nicer and much better value. Recommended. **C-E** *Puri Manik Sari*, T41089. Bright, new, clean accommodation set

Kalibukbuk, Lovina Beach

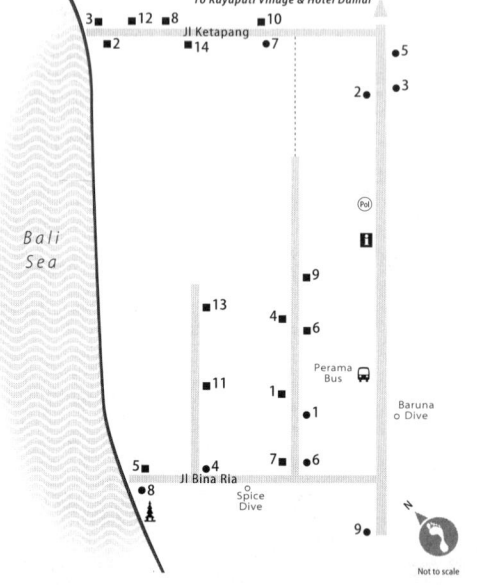

- **Sleeping**
1 Angsoka
2 Astina
3 Bayu Kartika Beach Bungalows
4 Harris Homestay
5 Nirwana
6 Padang
7 Pulestis Beach
8 Puri Bali Bungalows
9 Puri Manik Sari
10 Rambutan Beach Cottages
11 Ray Beach Inn I
12 Rini
13 Susila Beach Inn
14 Taman Lily

- **Eating**
1 Bali Apik
2 Chonos
3 Ciri Warung
4 Kakatua
5 Khi Khi
6 Nick's Warung
7 Sanary
8 Sea Breeze
9 Wina

in immaculate garden, 8 simple, reasonably priced rooms, fan, cheaper rooms near road may be noisy. Recommended. **D** *Pulestis Beach Hotel*, T41035. 14 rooms, set in gardens, rooms are rather dark and drab but reasonably priced. **D-E** *Astina*, very clean but no mosquito protection, some private mandis, dark rooms, but good value and run by friendly people. **D-E** *Harris Homestay*, T41152. A genuine homestay run by Betty from Germany who is very helpful and friendly, 5 attractively decorated, spotlessly clean rooms with private mandi, shower, squat toilet, mosquito nets, fan, good mattresses, price includes breakfast and tax. Recommended. **D-E** *Ray Beach Inn 1*, T41087 (same ownership as *Ray Beach Inn 2* in Banyualit). Basic accommodation in 2-storey block with shared verandahs/balconies; upstairs balconies have pleasant views and rooms are small but brighter and less claustrophobic than some of the cheaper places in this area, fan or a/c. **D-E** *Susila Beach Inn*, T61565. Price includes breakfast, friendly people but basic accommodation.

Temukus (11-13 km west of Singaraja) **A-C** *Aditya Beach Bungalows*, PO Box 134, T41059, F41342; 75 rooms, a large hotel set in attractive gardens beside the sea, the most expensive bungalows have good sea views from their verandahs, garden view rooms are a bit dark, cheaper rooms suffer from road noise and need renovation, all rooms have hot water, a/c or fan, attractive raised pool with sea views, restaurant (mid-range to cheap). **B-C** *Padma Hotel*, T/F41140, padma@ singaraja.wasantra. net.id   17 rooms, this new, clean hotel suffers from road noise and is overpriced, rooms are featureless with drab furnishings and tiny verandahs, a/c or fan, hot water, beside the sea with small pool, restaurant (mid-range to cheap). **C-D** *Agus*, T41202. 11 rooms, attractive beachside location but suffers from road noise, rooms are clean and bright, a/c or fan, restaurant (mid-range to cheap). **C-D** *Puri Tasik Madu*, towards Temukus, T21585. Restaurant, dark but characterful with 4-poster beds but nasty furniture, friendly owners. **D** *Villa Delima*, Villa Delima, Jl Seririt, T41141, delima@lovina.com   Refurbished in 1999, 8 en suite rooms, big, clean, good value, restaurant open until late. **D** *Samudra*, PO Box 15, some a/c, hot water. **E** *Toto*, 4 or 5 rooms, noisy bungalows near the road, better ones on the beach, good value.

Mid-range to cheap *Nick's Warung*, good fish. *Sea Breeze (Laut Angin)*, good Indonesian and European food but pricier than some places, English owner. *Bali Pub*, good fresh fish. Recommended. *Bali Apik*, specializes in pizzas and breakfasts as well as Indonesian and Chinese food. *Ciri Warung*, next to *Khi Khi Restaurant*, on non-beach side of the road, good Balinese food but meat can be tough (*nasi campur*). *Wina Restaurant*, excellent Chinese and Indonesian food. Recommended. *Puri Jaman Lorina*, excellent food, good value. *Sanary*, good Chinese food. *Susila*, fresh seafood (snapper, crab, squid) and Indian. Specialities including various thalis, lassi and chapaties.

Eating
Many of the restaurants at Lovina serve good, & reasonably priced, seafood

Live music At *Wina's* and *Malibu*. **Videos** Evening showings at *Malibu* and *Wina's*, both popular.

Entertainment

www.lovina.com/delima/
Tel:+62 (0)362 41141
E-mail: delima@lovina.com
Jalan Seririt, Temukus,
Lovina Beach, Bali, Indonesia.

• 8 spacious double/twin rooms with en-suite facilities and fans • patio or balconies for all rooms • shady courtyard with sun traps • spacious car/coach park

Villa Delima is a pretty hotel serving the budget traveller and is located just outside the hustle and bustle of Central Lovina on Bali's north coast. The hotel boasts good-sized, comfortable rooms, a pleasant bar-restaurant and is ideally situated for touring the peaceful northern part of Bali.

Sports	**Boat tours** Organized by the *Bali Lovina Beach Cottages*; other larger hotels and tour and dive companies. **Diving** Trips to **Menjangan Island** are easily organized from here (see page 427). *Spice Dive*, Kaliasem, US$45-60 for 2 dives, all including introductory training and 1 dive US$45; 5 day certification course US$230. *Spice Dive* also arrange offshore snorkelling trips (25,000Rp). Seems the best company on Lovina, with well maintained equipment and helpful, friendly staff, owner's wife is English. *Baruna*, Jl Seririt, Kalibukbuk, T41084, PADI Dive Centre Introductory (US$80) and 4-day open water certificate course US$300, 2 dives US$50, also offers fishing and watersports. **Lovina Marine Resort** and *Bali Lovina Beach Cottages* organize diving expeditions. **Fishing** Most hotels and losmen offer fishing trips (10,000Rp). **Golf** The only golf course in the north at present is the *Bali Handara Koseido Country Club*, at Pancasari near Bedugul. Approximately US$75 for a round of golf. **Sailing** Boats available for hire. **Snorkelling** Average snorkelling just off the beach. Snorkel hire 5,000Rp for 2 hrs; better marine life at Menjangan Island (25,000Rp for a day trip with *Spice Dive*). Equipment available from the *Bali Lovina Beach Cottages*, boat owners and dive shops, not all of equal quality. **Swimming** At the *Bali Lovina Beach Cottages*, 5,000Rp to non-residents. Most big hotels will let non-residents use the pool for between 5,000Rp and 10,000Rp if you look presentable.
Transport *11 km from Singaraja*	**Local** Car/motorbike/bicycle hire from several of the hotels; eg *Rambutan* have motorbikes for hire. *Perama* have reasonably priced car hire with insurance included. The tourist office also offers car hire. Be prepared for some hard bargaining; most hire companies quote in dollars. A 5/6 seat minibus with English speaking guide costs about US$20 a day (0830-2100), US$10 for half a day. **Road Bus**: from **Denpasar's** Ubung terminal, catch an express bus to Singaraja, 1½-2 hrs. The bus stops at **Singaraja's** Banyuasri terminal, from where there are regular buses to Lovina. There are also regular buses and minibuses from **Gilimanuk**, taking the north coast route, 1½ hrs (buses from Java will drop passengers off at Gilimanuk to catch a connection to Lovina – sometimes included in the cost of the ferry and bus ticket). **Shuttle bus**: 12,500Rp to Kuta, 7,500Rp to Ubud, 5,000Rp to Air Sanih, 20,000Rp to **Candi Dasa**, with *Perama*. *Perama* will pick you up from your hotel, but at Lovina they will only drop you off at one of their 2 offices in the Lovina area, or along the main road in between these.
Directory	**Banks** On the main road. **Communications** Postal agent on main road.

West of Lovina

Travelling west along the north coast	The road follows the flat, narrow coastal strip all the way to Gilimanuk, passing between the mountains and the sea. As you approach Pemuteran the scenery becomes more impressive, with the mountains rising dramatically just to the south of the road while the sea is close by to the north. After Banyuwedang the road passes through parts of the **West Bali National Park** (no charge for road vehicles entering this portion of the park). The village of **Labuhan Haji** is 5 km from the centre of Lovina; from here you will see signs for the **Singsing Air Terjun** (waterfall) a further 1 km away. Consisting of two falls with attendant pools where you can swim, Singsing is not as spectacular as some of the other waterfalls on Bali and is probably only worth visiting during the wet season. There is a car park with a warung nearby. The area provides pleasant walks along paths which pass other small waterfalls.
Brahma Vihara Asrama	About 10 km to the west of Kalibukbuk is the turning for the villages of **Dencarik** and **Banjar**, and a sign indicating the route to Bali's only Buddhist monastery, Brahma Vihara Asrama, which lies up a steep road just past the village of Banjar Tegeha. A Buddhist monastery was established here in the 1950s, but the present building dates back to 1971 and was built with financial help from both the Indonesian and Thai governments; the huge temple bell was donated by Thailand. The

building was damaged in an earthquake in 1976 but has been completely repaired. Architecturally, it combines traditional Buddhist elements, including stone reliefs showing scenes from Buddha's life, a stupa and a statue of Buddha decorated in gold leaf, with an overall Balinese feel. Naga guard the entrance, and there is a kulkul tower; overall, the temple is very colourful with bright orange roof tiles. Set in the hills with fine views to the sea, the monastery and grounds provide a peaceful and cool interlude from the heat and bustle below. Visitors are welcome, but they should be appropriately dressed and act with decorum. The monastery serves as a focus for Buddhist life on the island; Bali's Chinese community make frequent visits and the Dalai Lama visited in 1982. Education is an important aspect of monastery life; various courses, including meditation, are offered (check in advance when instruction in English is available). It is possible to stay overnight, but contact the monastery in advance of intended stay. A short walk west along a track from the monastery leads to Banjar Hot Springs.

These sacred hot springs are set in beautifully landscaped gardens and consist of three pools; eight naga spew the hot, sulphurous water from an underground spring into the first of the pools, from here the water overflows through the mouths of five more naga into a second pool. There are changing rooms, rather cramped and smelly, and a restaurant (cheap) which offers good food. The car park is about 400m from the holy springs. Very popular with the local population; if possible avoid Sundays and Tuesdays when groups come. ■ *Adult 1,000Rp, child 500Rp. Getting there: both the Banjar hot springs and the monastery, which are about 1 km apart, are easily reached from Lovina; take a bemo west to Dencarik, from where you can catch an ojek or make the steep climb on foot. From the village of Banjar it is a 1 km walk uphill; follow the signpost shortly after the village market. There is also a track which connects the monastery and springs, making a pleasant walk.*

Banjar Hot Springs
Phone code: 0362

Sleeping B *Pondok Wisata Grya Sari*, Air Panas Banjar, 200 m from the hot springs, signposted from the main road, 3 km. T92303, F92966. Set amidst lush vegetation in a peaceful location overlooking a ravine. Fourteen bungalows with attractive décor, spring mattresses, fan, clean bathrooms, large verandahs. Live gamelan music. Guests are entitled to free entry to the Banjar hot springs. There are plans to build a pool using water from a hot spring. Restaurant.

Seririt is 2 km further on. Turning south, the road starts climbing into the central mountains through spectacular terraces of rice paddies. There are many picturesque villages on this quiet road, and magnificent views. If you take the right fork at Pupuan, 25 km to the south, the road contours along the narrow mountain ridges, and eventually descends through villages and clove plantations to reach the main road along the south coast at Pekutatan, not far from the surfing beach at Medewi, on the main coast road from the south to Gilimanuk. The drive takes about two hours.

Seririt

At Pulaki, approximately 55 km west of Singaraja, there is a temple perched on a cliff with fine views out to sea. The temple itself is rather drab, a modern concrete construction. It is inhabited by bag-snatching grey macaques, considered 'holy' by the Balinese, which have a special penchant for raiding motorcycles. The site has an historical connection with the 16th century Javanese priest Nirartha. Legend recounts that a town of some 8,000 inhabitants lived on the site at the time of Nirartha's arrival. Their leader asked Nirartha that they be given supernatural powers which would allow them to become invisible. This was granted, and these invisible *gamang*, as they are called, exist to this day, living close by in Pura Melanting. Local Balinese keenly feel the presence of the 'gamang' and make offerings to appease them.

Pulaki

This small fishing village, 1 km west of Pulaki, lies on a sweeping bay with a backdrop of brooding, dormant volcanoes. These act as a rainbreak so the area receives slightly less rain, a consideration if you are travelling during the wet season. The

Pemuteran
Phone code: 0362

sunsets can be fantastic with views over Java and its stunning volcanic craters including Mount Semeru. The beach is public, with fishermen going about their business and mooring their boats, though the areas in front of hotels are kept clean and are relatively peaceful.

Offshore, there are reefs to swim to (five minutes by boat) which provide good snorkelling and diving; visibility is good (10-15m) with a slight current, there is a good variety of coral, reef fish, even the occasional 'manta', and impressive drop-offs. The area is beginning to see some development, with several upmarket hotels having appeared in the last two years. Reports suggest that wealthy property dealers from Java, including President Suharto's daughter, have bought up prime beachfront sites, and there are even rumours that a small airfield will be built at some time in the future to allow light aircraft to land. However, major development is probably a good way off, and at present the three hour drive from Denpasar acts as a deterrent.

Sleeping **L** *Puri Ganesha Villas*, Pemuteran, T93433, sales office T0361-261610/ 246712, F261611, www.puriganeshabali.com 4 very luxurious villas, each with its own private pool and dining pavilion. Owned by an English lady, cookery classes a feature. **L-AL** *Matahari Beach Resort*, PO Box 194, T92312, F92313. Set in glorious tropical gardens beside the sea, the 32 bungalows are beautifully decorated in Balinese style. Facilities include a magnificent pool, Padi diving courses (Open Water Course lasting 3-4 days 850,000Rp), dives at all the main sites around Bali (prices start at 80,000Rp for 1 dive; this is the only hotel on Bali with the right to provide direct access to Menjangan Island, Bali's best dive site), watersports, tennis. The hotel also offers classes in Balinese dance, stonecarving and drawing. Restaurant (expensive), outdoor raised performance area. Conference facilities for 80 people. **A-B** *Taman Sari Bali*, T92623/ T0361-288096 (travel agent), F0361-286297; 23 bungalows most attractively furnished in rustic style, set in spacious gardens beside the sea, fan or a/c, some rooms with hot water. A very peaceful setting though rooms are a bit pricey. Restaurant (mid-range) beside the sea, portions tend to be small. Offers meditation and yoga. Popular with specialist US tour groups. **A** *Taman Sari 2*, next door to *Taman Sari Bali* with just 5 bungalows. Reservations c/o *Taman Sari Bali*. **B-C** *Pondok Sari Beach Bungalows* and *Yos Dive Centre*, T/F92337. 20 modern, attractively decorated bungalows, fan or a/c, cold water. The more expensive bungalows face the sea. Set in large pretty gardens, running down to the beach with good swimming. Not as well managed as in the past. Restaurant (mid-range to cheap): the day we ate there the food was awful.

Diving Just to the east of *Pondok Sari Beach Bungalows* is *Reef Seen Aquatics Dive Centre*, T/F92339. Manager Chris Brown is Australian and a PADI instructor. Photographers are also catered for. There are safe dives off the beach as well as further afield, and he operates to high standards; not always the case in the Bali/Lombok area. Chris is very conservation minded and has launched the 'Turtle Project' to save the endangered local species. Prices range from US$30 for a single dive to US$70 for 2 people diving off Menjangan Island. The centre is easily reached by public bus from Singaraja (1½-2½ hrs, 60 km, 2,000Rp) and Gilimanuk/Cekik (1 hr, 30 km, 1,500Rp), buses run from 0500 to 1700.

Transport Take a bus from **Denpasar's** Ubung terminal to **Gilimanuk** (these are usually green) and then catch a connection on. From **Singaraja**, take a bemo from the Banyuasri terminal, running west towards Gilimanuk. Some buses also connect with **Amlapura** and **Klungkung**.

Labuan Lalang

About 15 km from Gilimanuk, Labuan Lalang is the most convenient base for visits to Menjangan Island (see 'Excursions' below). It will cost 2,000Rp to park your car (even if you just want to stroll down to the beach). There is a simple warung and a few basic losmen.

Pulau Menjangan (Deer Island) lies just off Bali's north coast and is part of the Bali Barat National Park (see also page 431). The island is uninhabited, fringed with mangroves, very beautiful and home to the rare Java deer and Bali white mynah. There are no losmen on the island and camping is not permitted. The island is surrounded by spectacular coral reefs and offers the best diving around Bali, with excellent visibility (25-35m) and a slight current. In addition to the good variety of coral there is also the wreck of a ship the 'Anker', and beyond 60m you might find the rare 'Genicanthus Bellus'. The snorkelling is excellent as well. Expect to pay close to 100,000Rp for four hours on the island; this includes 60,000Rp for the hire of the boat, and 15,000Rp for a guide. The guides will try to rent out snorkelling equipment. The nearest dive centres are at Pemuteran, about 15 km, 15 minutes' drive away; both 'Reef Seen Aquatics' (70,000Rp for a two-dive package with two people) and the *Matahari Beach Resort* (100,000Rp for two people) offer diving trips to Menjangan. All the dive centres on Bali offer trips to Menjangan, but it makes a long day if you are coming from the south or east of Bali. The trip by boat from Labuan Lalang takes 30 minutes.

Excursions

East from Singaraja

Pura Beji is situated just north of the main coastal road, 8 km east of Singaraja and nearly 20 km from Lovina Beach, near the village of **Sangsit**. The temple is dedicated to the rice goddess Dewi Sri and belongs to the local *subak* or irrigation society, which is served with the task of managing and allocating water resources among its members. The association of rice, water and religion reflects the dependence of rice cultivation upon an adequate and constant supply of water, and of people upon rice for their survival. This is a fine example of North Bali's exuberant style of temple architecture. The soft pink sandstone 'candi bentar' (split gate often found at the entrance) is a flamboyant mass of fanciful carvings of plants, animals, demons and nagas, certain to keep evil spirits at bay, while the walls of the temple itself are equally alive with carvings. Frangipani trees lend shade to the inner courtyard. Visitors are likely to be mobbed by the local children. The **Pura Dalem**, 500m northeast, is also worth a visit. The carved reliefs show scenes from the Mahabharatha, depicting Bima's journey to heaven and hell in search of his mother. On this journey he witnesses the rewards in heaven for those who have led a good life, and learns of the punishments in hell for those who have sinned. This story is one of the most popular subjects in wayang kulit. The carvings are both humorous and erotic; the erotica, enlarged genitalia, representations of coitus etc, are believed to frighten away evil spirits. ■ *Getting there: take a bemo to Singaraja and then another from Singaraja's Penarukan terminal.*

Sangsit & around
Phone code: 0362

Sleeping A-D *Berdikara Cottages*, T25195. Some rooms with a/c and hot water, private bathroom with Western toilets, attractive gardens with fruit trees, with open air theatre for dance performances, price includes breakfast, bar restaurant, long stay guests are offered lessons in Balinese dancing and hand weaving; they may also eat the fruit growing in the garden.

About 500m past Sangsit, 18 km from Lovina, is the turning for the villages of Jagaraga and Sawan. The first village, Jagaraga, 4 km inland from the main road, is famous for two reasons. In 1849 the Dutch wiped out virtually the entire settlement, in what has come to be known as the Puputan Jagaraga. The **Pura Dalem** – a Temple of the Dead – dedicated to Siwa the destroyer, is famous for its humorous depictions in stone relief of the Dutch invaders. Scenes show them arriving in boats which are attacked by sea monsters, in aircraft involved in aerial dogfights falling from the skies, being eaten by crocodiles and drinking beer. The most famous is the depiction of two rotund Dutchmen in a Model-T Ford being held up by armed bandits. Other reliefs show scenes from village life. Many of the images relate to the evil witch Rangda, related to Siwa's wife Durga, and a central character in the Barong dance.

Jagaraga & Sawan

There is also a statue of *Men Brayut* buried under a mound of offspring. Admission – suggested donation comparatively overpriced at 1,000Rp.

Sawan village, a further 4 km up the road, is the home of a well-known gamelan maker. Most days you can watch the gongs being cast and the frames and stands being intricately carved. Gamelan for sale here. ■ *Getting there: if travelling independently, turn right off the main coast road 500m beyond Sangsit, and then travel south for 4 km to the village of Jagaraga. To get there by public transport take a bemo from Singaraja's Penarukan terminal bound for Sawan. Alternatively, take a bemo going east and get off 500m past Sangsit at the turning for Jagaraga and Sawan; from there it is an 8 km walk uphill to Sawan (4 km to Jagaraga) or get a lift on an ojek.*

Pura Maduwe Karang

'The Temple of the Owner of the Land' is in the village of Kubutambahan, 12 km east of Singaraja, 23 km from Lovina Beach and on the main coast road near the turning to Kintamani. Like Pura Beji, the temple of Maduwe Karang is dedicated to ensuring a bountiful harvest, though not of irrigated rice, but of dry land crops. Many consider this to be the finest of North Bali's temples; though the carvings are not quite as exuberant as the Pura Beji, there is a certain realism and humanity to these whimsical creations which set them apart from those in North Bali's other temples. Outside the temple are 34 stone figures representing characters from the Ramayana, while inside floral themes and renditions of daily life abound, including a woman taking a bath and another making love. An interesting relief, found on the base of the inner temple wall, is the famous panel showing a Dutchman riding a bicycle with wheels made of flowers. Some people maintain that the cyclist is the artist WOJ Nieuwenkamp (1874-1950), who came to Bali in 1904 and decided to explore the island by bicycle. The temple is laid out on a grand scale; the grounds are well-tended with an abundance of fragrant Frangipani trees. Entrance by donation. ■ *Getting there: by bemo to Singaraja and then another from Singaraja's Penarukan Terminal on the eastern edge of town.*

Air Sanih
Phone code: 0362

Air Sanih lies 17 km east of Singaraja, on the coast. It has become quite a popular tourist spot because of its spring-fed pool. However, it has retained its local village atmosphere and is, as yet, unspoilt by mass tourism; the glistening black-sand beaches remain almost empty. The main season for visitors here seems to be July and August.

Sleeping **A** *Ciliks Beach Garden*, Air Sanih, Singaraja 81172, T/F26561. Two very large, very beautiful, luxury bungalows with marble floors, very tastefully decorated, mosquito nets, attractive bathrooms with hot water and squat toilets, beside the sea with verandah and garden, and separate pavilions for relaxing, offering complete privacy. Tasty Balinese cooking, and a traditional fishing boat available for hire. **A-E** *Puri Sanih Bungalows*, some a/c, restaurant, pool. The most expensive modern bungalows are right on the beach and have their own bathrooms, the cheapest atmospheric but decrepit (rooms on the 2nd floor have lovely views of the sea), immaculate gardens, tour groups catered for, largest place to stay on Air Sanih. **C** *Graha Ayu*, 2 attractive bungalows with fan, unfortunately on the wrong side of the road from the beach and with no immediate access to beach once you cross. **D** *Sunset Graha Beach*, on a hill above Air Sanih. The restaurant has a good view of the sea, but the bungalows are set behind, facing a rather neglected garden. Large, rather kitsch rooms, reasonably priced. **D** *Tara Beach Inn*, 4 bungalows with shower and Western toilet, 2 older thatched bungalows with squat toilet, all basic but with nice location beside sea, owners' dogs and children can be noisy, pub and restaurant. **D-E** *Puri Purtiwi*, on the main road 1 km east of Air Sanih; no telephone. Good beachside location; 9 rooms set in large, grassy, slightly unkempt gardens beside the sea. At the time of viewing the steps leading down to beach level were broken, leaving a 3m drop. Rooms are clean but a little dark. Restaurant (cheap).

Eating Mid-range: *Archipelago Restaurant*, on hill overlooking Air Sanih, is more upmarket. **Warungs**: there are several warungs opposite the *Puri Sanih Bungalows*, offering reasonably priced local and Western food, good cheap nasi campur and mie goreng at 1st small restaurant, in shop, as you enter Air Sanih from the west, on right side of road.

Transport Buses: pass through Air Sanih en route to **Gilimanuk** in the west and **Amlapura**, **Klungkung** and **Denpasar** in the east and south, starting from early morning about 0600 until 1700, or sometimes later these days. *Perama* now operates a shuttle bus to/from Air Sanih to all its destinations; eg 5,000Rp to **Lovina**, 10,000Rp to **Candi Dasa**, 20,000Rp to **Kuta**, 15,000Rp to **Ubud**. Perama buses run between Lovina and Padangbai, stopping in Air Sanih.

Cultural centres *Osho Abheeshu Meditation & Creative Centre*, F21108. Daily meditation programme creativity course, US$25 for 1 day.

Directory

Continuing east from Air Sanih, the road follows the coast, rounding Cape Sanih, with good views out to sea. After 7 km the road climbs to the site of **Pura Pondok Batu**, another splendidly situated temple associated with the eminent 16th century priest Nirartha. There is said to be a freshwater spring bubbling out of the sand, visible on the beach at low tide; people from neighbouring villages come here to get fresh water and bring their animals to drink.

East of Air Sanih

At the village of **Pacung**, 6 km beyong Pura Pondok Batu, there is a signposted turning to the 'Bali Aga' village of Sembiran, 3 km from the main road along a narrow road. Unlike **Tenganan** and Trunyan, two other villages associated with the original 'Bali Aga' inhabitants of the island, Sembiran has few reminders of its past other than the layout of the village which differs from traditional 'Hindu' villages. It is, however, believed to be the site of the oldest megalithic settlement on Bali and is known for its sacred *Baris* dance. The village of **Julah**, 1 km to the east, also dates back to ancient times and has the oldest temple in North Bali.

Sembiran

Three kilometres further along the main road brings the village of Tejakula, famous for its elaborate though decaying horse baths. These days horses are not washed here, though the public baths are still in use. The village also has a 'Banjar Pande', where silversmiths can be seen at work.

Tejakula

Eleven kilometres from Air Sanih, a minor road turns inland, climbing the steep ridges to Mount Batur's crater rim at Penulisan (see page 385 for this route).

There are not so many set piece sights along this coast; the beauty lies in the natural scenery. The road passes through small rural villages, the land is much drier here and there are none of the rice terraces, so prevalent elsewhere.

Sambirenteng is a village on the coast, with some accommodation. The **Les waterfall** is about 6 km from here and is worth a visit. **Sleeping B** *Alamanda*, bookable through a German travel agent – *Pike Travel*, Uwi Siegfriedsen, Ostersielzung 8, 25480, Friedrichstadt, T494881-930633, F494881-930699. Booking recommended. Prices are non-negotiable and the bill is payable in US$ only, restaurant, right on the edge of the sea, 12 back-to-nature bungalows on stilts, set amongst coconut palms. Lovely, clean rooms with Western bathrooms and friendly service. German owned, and also a dive centre, equipped with full sub-aqua gear. Snorkelling on the reef just off the beach. Diving offered at Tulamben, Ulami, Amed, Menjangan and Nusa Penida, as well as at Alamanda. Includes night dives, introductory dives available for 125,000Rp. Prices for two dives at each site, 95,000Rp-135,000Rp depending on site.

Sambirenteng & further south

A four hour hike from the main road up to **Trunyon** is signposted 1 km north of Tianyar; Tianyar is about 15 km southeast along the main road from Sambirenteng.

Further east, the land becomes more arid and the road skirts the lower slopes of Mount Batur and the ever imposing Mount Agung, punctuated by 20-30m wide dry water courses which have cut channels into the barren volcanic rock. Continuing southwards down the east coast you eventually come to **Tulamben**, a beachside village which has long been a Mecca for divers but which is now being developed for a broader market; several new hotels have been built in the last year (see page 405).

The West

Colour map 3, grid B6 The west of Bali, encompassing the regencies of Jembrana, Tabanan and Badung, is the least visited part of the island; most visitors merely pass through en route from the east of Bali to Java. There is a strong Muslim representation with settlers from Madura, Java and Sulawesi. At the west tip and 134 km from Denpasar is Gilimanuk, the ferry port for Java. Completely encompassing the port and much of the west is the Bali Barat National Park.

The west has some of Bali's most spectacular scenery. This is a largely rural area where most of the island's rice is grown, and there are spellbinding vistas of jade green rice terraces with misty mountains in the background. The coast has long stretches of superb, deserted beach strafed by rolling waves, good for surfing but swimming is dangerous due to strong currents and undertows. Some of Bali's prettiest and most traditional villages are also found here. With few visitors and with a paucity of accommodation, the area has preserved its Balinese feel and is one of the most rewarding to visit.

Ins and outs

Getting there & around Bear in mind that all times are necessarily approximate and can vary enormously. Coming from Denpasar, times will depend on traffic jams and the number of slow-moving, heavy lorries impeding progress. **Buses** run most frequently in the morning starting early (from 0500 or 0600), and continue until about 1800; on major routes buses usually continue later than this, and those connecting via Gilimanuk through to Java run virtually 24 hrs. The frequency of buses is improving all the time.

West Coast

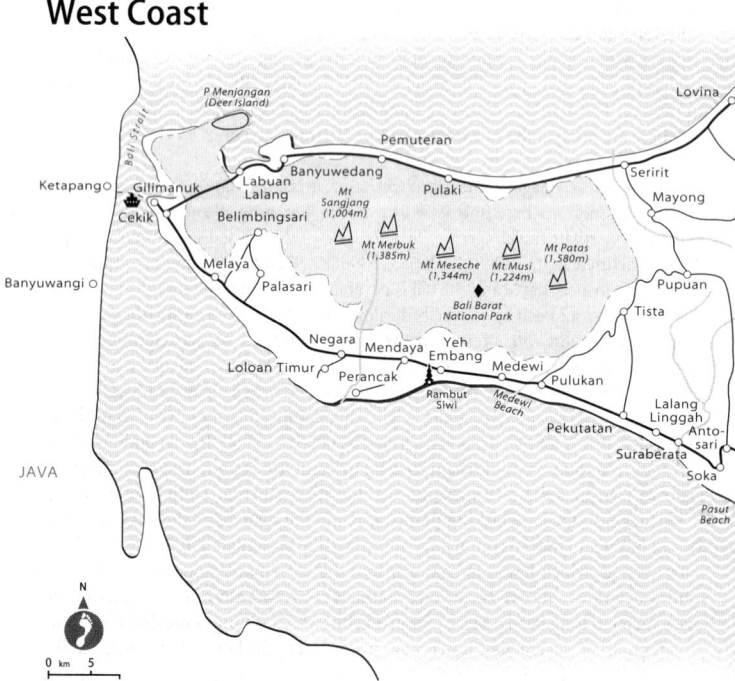

From Denpasar Buses run from the Ubung terminal: **Mengwi** 25 mins; **Tanah Lot** (via Kediri) 45 mins, **Tabanan** 30 mins; **Lalang Linggah** (for Balian Beach) 1 hr; **Medewi Beach** 90 mins; **Negara** 2 hrs; **Cekik** (entrance to Bali Barat National Park) 2 hrs 35 mins; **Gilimanuk** 2 hrs 45 mins; **Surabaya** on Java 11 hrs; **Yogyakarta/Solo** 16 hrs; **Jakarta** 30 hrs.

From Gilimanuk **Cekik** (for Bali Barat National Park) 12 mins; **Negara** 45 mins; **Medewi Beach** 1 hr 15 mins; **Labuan Linggah** (for Balian Beach) 1 hr 45 mins; **Tabanan** 2 hrs 15 mins; **Tanah Lot** (via Kediri) 2 hrs 20 mins; **Denpasar** 2¾ hrs; **Labuan Lalang** (for Pulau Menjangan) 20 mins; **Pemuteran** 30 mins; **Lovina** 1 hr 30 mins; **Singaraja** (Banyuasri Terminal) 2 hrs.

Gilimanuk and Cekik

Gilimanuk is the departure and arrival point for the ferry that runs between Bali and Java. There is no reason to stay here unless forced to; it is only a transit point. For archaeologists, however, Gilimanuk is important as the site of a bronze/iron age burial ground excavated in the 1960s and 1970s, thus providing evidence of prehistoric settlement on Bali. Cekik, the headquarters of the Bali Barat National Park, is 3 km south of Gilimanuk.

Phone code: 0365

The **Bali Barat** (or West Bali) **National Park** was established as recently as 1984, and covers over 75,000 ha straddling both the dry north coast and the forested, tropical south. The Bali white mynah or *jalak putih Bali* (*Leucopsar rothschildi*), better known by English speakers as the Bali starling, one of the rarest birds in the world, is found here, mostly confined to Menjangan Island. It is a small white bird, with black tips to its wings and tail, and a streak of blue around its eye (easily confused with the black-winged starling, which has wholly black wings and tail). The wild Javan buffalo (*Bos javanicus*) is also present in small numbers. Other less rare animals include monkeys, leopard, civets and the rusa, barking and mouse deers.

Excursions

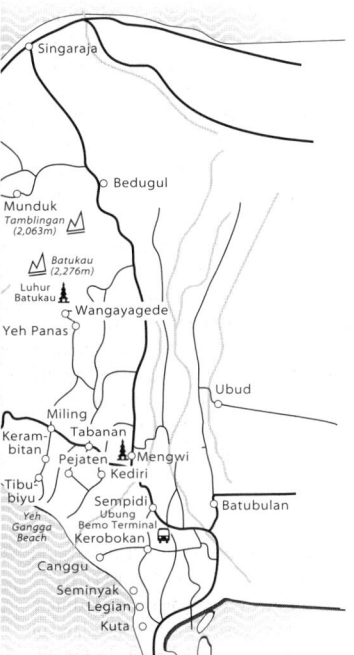

■ *The PHPA office for the Bali Barat National Park is in Cekik; there is also an office at Labuan Lalang, the jumping off point for boats to Pulau Menjangan (see page 427). Treks can be arranged from both offices, preferably a day in advance. The offices are open 0700-1600, most staff speak reasonable English and are helpful and friendly. Permits, costing 2,000Rp for 1 day, and information on trails can be obtained from the offices (permits are also available from the Forestry Department, Jl Suwung, Denpasar, and from Labuan Lalang). There is also a scale model of the park.* **NB** *Guides, costing from 20,000Rp depending on the length of the trek, are obligatory. Bring your own supplies when trekking as there no shops or warung at the park HQ.*

Gilimanuk There are several losmen along the main road through town to the ferry port, offering fairly basic accommodation. All in the **E** price range: *Nirwana*, *Nusantara 1 & 2* (the latter is off the main road, about 5 mins' walk along a side road going east of the ferry terminal and is therefore a bit quieter), *Kartika Candra*. Restaurant food is pretty average as well.

Sleeping

Cekik Camping is forbidden within the park but there is simple accommodation at the **D-F** *National Park Guest House*, beside the PHPA Office at Cekik, T40060 for reservations. You may also be able to **camp** in the grounds of the park HQ. For more luxurious accommodation, **Pemuteran** is the closest option, see page 426.

Transport
134 km from Denpasar, 88 km from Singaraja, 30 mins', driving time to Negara

Road Bus: regular connections with **Denpasar's** Ubung terminal. Connections with **Singaraja** via **Lovina Beach**. **Sea Ferry**: to **Ketapang** on Java: there is a brand new terminal. Fares are 1,000Rp for pedestrians and 11,000Rp for vehicles. Running 24 hrs a day, ferries leave every 20-30 mins during the day, less regularly at night. The 3 km crossing takes 30 mins. **NB** During Indonesian holidays and at weekends there may be a long wait for a boat.

Belimbingsari and Palasari

Phone code: 0365

These two Christian villages are well worth a visit. Easily reached from the main Gilimanuk to Negara road, there are several signposted turnings, including a turn to the left 17 km from Gilimanuk at signpost, or just past Melaya village. The drive climbs through picturesque scenery along quiet roads, with possibilities for rewarding walks, passing paddy fields and buffaloes with misty mountains in the background. You may pass Christan style *penjors*, smaller and less elaborate than their Hindu counterparts, with crosses as decoration. The air is a little cooler here. Villagers are friendly and will help with directions.

Belimbingsari, with a population of 700 Christians, is 6 km from the turnoff along a good road. The village is spotless and flower filled, and despite the Christian influence is very much culturally Balinese; the aim of these Christian communities has been to attain a religious rather than a cultural conversion. In both villages Balinese music and dance are taught, but using scenes and characters from the Bible rather than the great Hindu epics, the Ramayana and Mahabarata.

Each village boasts an attractive church: of the two, the **Protestant church** at Belimbingsari is perhaps the more interesting and attractive. Consecrated in 1981 and costing 100,000,000Rp to build, its appearance is Balinese although it was designed by an Australian architect. Entry is through a Balinese split gate decorated with Christian motifs, ascending a flight of steps with statues of guardian angels, through another Balinese-style gate into a beautiful tropical garden with a moat and ponds full of waterlilies. The church is circular, wooden and open to the air on all sides. The 30m high ceiling is divided into three 'levels' representing man's progress from earth to heaven. The priest speaks English and is very informative, but is frequently out visiting parishioners. In his absence you may be met by the church guardian, who has limited English but is very helpful and will willingly show you round (small donation in the box).

To reach **Palasari**, the name translates as 'garden of nutmeg trees', turn right out of Belimbingsari. After 2 km turn right again, 1 km later turn left, and after 800m turn right. Shortly after, you will catch sight of the imposing Catholic church, the largest in East Indonesia, on your left, with a picturesque backdrop of mountains.

In appearance it looks like a conventional European church with glass windows and wooden pews, despite the Balinese split entrance gate to keep out evil spirits, and the three thatched spires like *merus*. Made of pink sandstone and surrounded by immaculate gardens, it was completed in 1994. During church services or organ practice, music rings out through the village. From here it is 6.5 km back to the main road.

Negara

Phone code: 0365

Negara is the capital of the regency of Jembrana and quite a large town. It is clean and attractive, with wide, flower-filled avenues and some elegant horse-drawn carriages. The town is best known for the *mekepung* or **bullock races** which are held here between July and October. The sport was introduced by migrants from the island of Madura where the *kerapan sapi* (bull races) are the main form of entertainment.

Information on Negara's bull races can be obtained from the Bali Tourist Office on Jl S Parman in Denpasar. Races normally take place after the rice harvest.

Jembrana, home of the amazing Gamelan *Jegog*, is a further 3 km east of Negara.

Following the main road running along the coast southeast of Negara the first place of interest is Rambut Siwi Temple, about 8 km west of Medewi, 16 km east of Negara, off the main coast road, at the top of a cliff overlooking a black sand beach. This is another spectacularly located temple associated with the 16th century Hindu priest Danghyang Nirartha. Nirartha came to Bali in 1546 from his home on Java, with the aim of strengthening Balinese Hinduism so that it could withstand the onslaught of Islam. Leaving Java at a time when the rule of the Hindu Majapahit Kingdom was on the wane, ousted by the forces of Islam, he travelled throughout Bali teaching, building shrines and temples and gaining a reputation for his spiritual and supernatural powers. He is credited with being the founder of the most important branch of Balinese *pedandas* (high priests). Other temples associated with him include Tanah Lot and Uluwatu.

Rambut Siwi Temple
Large scale celebrations take place here every full moon. It is also a wonderful place to watch the sun blazing down across the Bali Strait over Java.

Sleeping

Negara E *Ana*, Jl Ngurah Rai 75, T65. **E** *Indraloka*, Jl Nakula 13.

Entertainment

Gamelan Jegog is a giant bamboo orchestra. These huge gamelan of 10 perform *Jegog Mebarung*, where several orchestras compete against each other in a frenzy of energy and sound; it is also a visually impressive event. Ask around for the time of a performance – there are no regular scheduled performances.

Transport

100 km from Denpasar, 34 km from Gilimanuk. **Road Bus**: regular connections with Gilimanuk and Denpasar's Ubung terminal.

Medewi Beach

Phone code: 0365

Medewi Beach is situated 22 km east of Negara, 70 km (1½ hours by car) west of Denpasar and about 4 km from the village of Pulukan. Medewi is a black sand beach and is good for surfing. The surrounding area has some fine scenery; the main road running southeast follows a beautiful rocky coastline, and mile after mile of empty beach with pounding surf, and the occasional coconut plantation. There is a choice of accommodation here and three restaurants, no other facilities. ■ *Getting there: take a bus running east towards Denpasar and ask to be let off at Pantai Medewi. If driving, there is a 24-hr petrol station 3 km southeast of Medewi.*

Sleeping

A-C *Medewi Beach Cottages*, Pantai Medewi, PO Box 126, T40029/40030, F41555/40034. Set in pleasant gardens beside the beach, with a nice pool (open to non-residents 5,000Rp), rooms are spotless but rather soulless. The more expensive rooms have a/c and hot water, refrigerator, cheaper rooms are dark and overlook the road, with fan; all have Western toilets. Price does not include breakfast. The best place to stay though rather overpriced. Restaurant (mid-range). **D-E** *Tin Jaya Bungalows*, Medewi Beach. 14 rooms, set in pretty gardens leading down to the sea. Rooms are on the whole disappointing, some are dark; there is a 2-storey *lumbung* (rice barn) style building with nice views, and some new, but tiny rooms with fan. All with private mandi, some Western toilets. Restaurant (mid-range).

Balian Beach

Phone code: 0361

Continuing down the main coast road you reach Balian Beach, about 25 km southeast of Medewi Beach (50 km west of Denpasar, 30 km west of Tabanan, 50 km from Negara), near the village of Lalang Linggah (10 km west of Antosari, 20 km east of Pulukan). This is one of the best surfing beaches on the west coast but swimming is dangerous; this is the Indian Ocean and there are rip-tides and undertows. There are many pleasant walks in the area through ricefields and plantations of cloves, vanilla,

434 BALIAN BEACH

coffee, coconut and cocoa, or following the river inland. To the east, past a fishing village, is a large tunnel running through the cliff-face and many caves and coves.

Sleeping **A** *Sacred River Retreat*, near the village of Suraberata, Tabanan. Postal address: No 1 Gang Keraton, Jl Raya Seminyak, T732165, F730904; Australia, T02-9999-3643. A pricey New Age Resort, Australian-owned, in a peaceful location overlooking a ravine, just to the west of *Balian Beach Bungalows*. 15 attractively decorated, thatched bungalows, small pool. Vegetarian restaurant (mid-range). Free airport pick-up. **B-E** *Balian Beach Bungalows*, Lalang Linggah Village, T/F813017. Set in a 6 acre coconut plantation overlooking the Balian River, within 300m of the beach. Rooms are being renovated. Some rooms have lovely views, most with private mandi, mosquito nets and squat or Western toilet. Also some cheaper dorm rooms with shared bathroom. Restaurant (mid-range to cheap) and bar. Information sheet with lots of useful local information, walking maps and travel details. A very attractive and peaceful place.

Transport From **Denpasar** (Ubung bus station), catch a bus bound for Negara or Gilimanuk and ask the driver to stop at **Lalang Linggah**. Coming from the northwest (**Java**, **Gilimanuk**, **Medewi**), get off the bus just after the bridge over the Balian River; all Java-Denpasar buses pass the entrance. From **Lovina** catch a bus west to **Seririt**, change to a bus going south through the mountains via **Pupuan**, and on to **Antosari** east of Lalang Linggah or **Pulukan** to the west; change again for a bus to Lalang Linggah, 1½ hrs from Legian by car.

Kerambitan
Phone code: 0361

Continuing southeast towards Tabanan, capital of the Tabanan Regency, you come to the turning for Kerambitan where you have the opportunity to stay at one of the larger royal palaces. This village is notable for a tradition of wayang-style painting, and unique music and dance forms. These include *tektekan*, a procession of men loudly playing wooden drums and cow bells, traditionally intended to frighten away evil spirits at times of drought or epidemic. Nearby are the temples **Tanah Lot** (see page 408) and **Pura Taman Ayun** at Mengwi (see page 409).

Sleeping **A** *Puri Anyar*, Kerambitan 82161, Tabanan, T237458/422298/812668, F263597. The palace spreads over 2 ha with numerous garden courtyards and family temples. It was built in 1667, renovated in 1935 and part of it opened as a hotel in 1987. These days 5 branches of the royal family related to the Tabanan royal family live here. One area has been set aside to provide 7 rooms with attached small garden and bathroom, with Western toilet and hot water. Rooms vary greatly with 1 rather grand formal bridal chamber; some, however, are small and dark and disappointing at the price. Cultural events, music, dance and theatre are sometimes staged in a raised performance area; these include *tektekan* (see above) and a trance drama *calonarang*. There is a small restaurant (no menu) and dinners can be arranged. Guests can also witness village life: making offerings, rice harvesting, games, dances etc. Across the road you can see the royal collection of musical instruments which are played at special ceremonies. *Getting there: from the main road 3 km northwest of Tabanan, turn south following signs for Kerambitan; about 6 km.*

Tibubiyu The small village of Tibubiyu, 10.4 km from main Tabanan road, about 1 km inland from the beach and 4 km south of Kerambitan, is a million miles away from tourist Bali. This village has only just made it to the 20th century; the rural community go about their daily lives and take part in the many religious ceremonies in a manner little changed from their forebears. The nearby, black sand beach, **Pasut beach**, is renowned for its therapeutic qualities. Swimming is inadvisable as there are strong offshore currents.

Yeh Gangga (Water of the Ganges) is another fine, black sand beach with strong currents and strange offshore rock formations. ■ *Getting there: turn southwest at the sign just over 1 km west of Tabanan, and follow a dreadful, potholed road for about 10 km.*

Sleeping C *BeeBees*, c/o Dewa Ayu Putu Barbara, Tibubiyu, Kerambitan 82161, Tabanan. Fax c/o Dr Dewa Made Suamba Negara, F0361-236021. 5 very simple, 2-storey thatched bungalows overlooking the ricefields. Situated just outside the village in a very peaceful setting, 10 mins' walk from the sea. Restaurant (mid-range). *Getting there: from Kerambitan: turn left at the end of the main street, then right at the Banyan tree. Soon you will reach Tibubiyu, BeeBees is signed.* **B-C** *Bali Wisata Bungalows*, Yeh Gangga, T261354. In peaceful location beside the sea. 6 large bungalows, some with cooking facilities, private bathroom with Western toilet. Small pool. Restaurant (mid-range).

Background

As far back as the 1930s, insightful commentators were predicting what lay in store for Bali. Miguel Covarrubias, for one, in his seminal book, *Island of Bali* (1937) wrote:

"Undoubtedly Bali will soon enough be 'spoiled' for those fastidious travellers who abhor all that which they bring with them. No longer will the curious Balinese of the remote mountain villages, still unaccustomed to the sight of whites, crowd around their cars to stare silently at the 'exotic' long-nosed, yellow-haired foreigners in their midst. But even when all the Balinese will have learned to wear shirts, to beg, lie, steal, and prostitute themselves to satisfy new needs, the tourists will continue to come to Bali to see the sights, snapping pictures frantically, dashing from temple to temple, back to hotel for meals, and on to watch rites and dances staged for them."

Certainly in recent years, Bali has suffered from the curse of being too popular, yet somehow the island has retained its beauty, if not always its charm, and the Balinese have traditionally believed that their island belongs to the gods and they are merely custodians entrusted to ensure its well-being.

History

Human settlement on Bali dates back to early prehistoric times. Archaeological finds unearthed at Cekik on the northwest tip of the island have been dated to about 1000 BC. The Bronze Age began before 300 BC, by which time a sophisticated megalithic culture had developed where both wet and dry rice cultivation were practised. The earliest written records, inscriptions on stone and metal dating back to the 9th century, show that both Hindu and Buddhist influences had already reached Bali from India.

The pattern of Javanese cultural influence over Bali was strengthened during the reign of Airlangga (1019-1042), one of the great Javanese rulers. As the son of a Balinese King, Udayana, and an East Javanese princess, Mahendradatta, he naturally forged strong links between Bali and Java.

The next event of significance was the invasion of Bali by the powerful Hindu Majapahit Kingdom of Central Java, in 1343 under the great minister and general Gajah Mada. Even today most of Bali's nobility trace their families back to the founding fathers of Majapahit. Those Balinese who refused to accept Majapahit influence escaped to remote locations on Bali and their ancestors are the Bali Aga who still live in villages such as Tenganan and Trunyan.

As Islam filtered into Java during the 15th century. Majapahit influence began to decline. In 1478 the last of the Majapahit princes accompanied by priests, artists and other courtesans fled to the Hindu haven of Bali. The prince declared himself King of Bali (his descendants are the rajas of Klungkung). This migration of the cream of Javanese artists and craftsmen laid the foundations for Bali's future pre-eminence in the arts.

One of Bali's most famous kings was Baturenggong who came to the throne in the middle of the 16th century and today enjoys almost mythical status. According to local chronicles, during his reign Bali was a haven of peace and prosperity and a centre for the arts. The influence of the kingdom extended west to include much of east Java and east to encompass Lombok and Sumbawa.

The Dutch first made contact with Bali in 1597, when a fleet landed on the island and enjoyed a long sojourn, falling in love with the people and the island. However, Bali offered little in the way of trade and was largely ignored by the European colonial powers until the 1830's when the Dutch, anxious to prevent Britain gaining a hold in the region, set out to gain sovereignty over the island. By this time relations between the Balinese, and what they perceived to be the arrogant, crude and ill-behaved Dutch, were already strained.

In 1849, at the third attempt, the Dutch finally conquered North Bali following their victory at Jagaraga, the capital of the North Balinese Kingdom of Buleleng. The Dutch, with their superior military technology, fought the brave Balinese, armed only with *kris'* and spears, losing only 30 men as opposed to the thousands of Balinese who died. Having conquered the North, the Dutch spent the next 40 years attempting to extend their influence over the rest of the island.

The Dutch attacked Lombok in 1894, which was under the control of the East Balinese Kingdom of Karangkasem (see page 443). When Lombok fell, so too did Karangkasem. In mid September 1906, as the Dutch closed in on Denpasar, the princes of Badung, rather than surrender, chose a more honourable course of action and announced that anyone who wished could accompany them in a *puputan* or 'fight to the end'. Most men, and many women as well, heeded their King's call. They dressed in their most splendid ceremonial clothes and wore their finest gold kris' to meet their death. In all, nearly 4000 Balinese chose death rather than surrender. The same sequence of events was to be repeated at other palaces across Bali, culminating in the *puputan* at the royal palace of Klungkung. For many Dutch soldiers, what was an overwhelming military victory had the sour taste of moral defeat. Bali was finally subdued. One reason the Balinese were so ready to commit mass suicide rather than surrender to the enemy was their belief that the spirit of a person who died in war would achieve Nirvana.

The problem now for the Dutch was how to make the island pay. One solution was to take control of the highly profitable opium trade operated by the Chinese and Buginese. From 1908 the use of opium was actively promoted, particularly among the royal families.

After the Dutch had gained full control of Bali, they set about reorganising the island in order to administer it more effectively. In the process some benefits accrued to the Balinese: roads were built, improvements were made in agriculture, health and education. Slavery was abolished; Kuta had long been an important port

The eight regencies of Bali

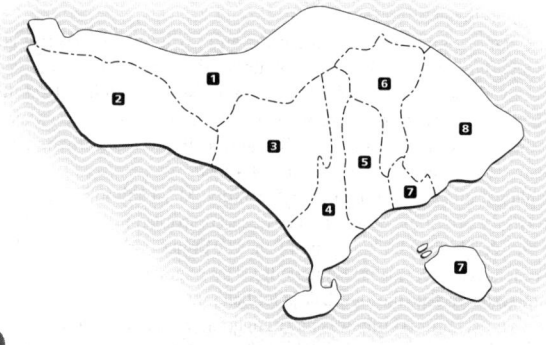

1 Buleleng 2 Jembrana 3 Tabanan 4 Badung 5 Gianyar 6 Bangli 7 Klungkung 8 Karangasem

Based on the former Balinese kingdoms. (A ninth regency, Mengwi, existed until the end of the 19th century)

in the slave trade. Suttee, the Hindu practice of wives leaping onto the funeral pyres of their dead husbands, was outlawed.

The main consequence of the Japanese occupation during World War Two was to show Indonesia that the Dutch were not invincible. This lead Sukarno to declare Independence on August 17th 1945. However, many Balinese were ambivalent towards rule by a Muslim majority. Despite this a Balinese resistance movement emerged and fought bravely against the Dutch and one hero to emerge at this time was Colonel I Gusti Ngurah Rai who fought a last ditch battle at Marga in Tabanan.

Following the departure of the Dutch Bali languished. Despite being half Balinese, Sukarno showed little interest in Bali, except to visit his palace at Tampaksiring. On these visits his entourage behaved badly; demanding, without payment, whatever took their fancy, and abducting women for sexual favours.

Many in Jakarta resented the favoured status Bali had enjoyed under Dutch administration. Bali was neglected resulting in increasing hardship for its peasant class who perhaps inevitably turned to the Indonesian Communist Party, the PKI. Thus during the late 1950s and early 1960s Bali became one of the strongholds of the PKI. Conflict ensued along class divides as the elite, made up of Sukarno supporters and Balinese capitalists, pursued their own interests at the expense of the population at large. A series of natural disasters culminating in the catastrophic eruption of Mount Agung, during Bali's most sacred ceremony *Eka Dasa Rudra*, increased public resentment towards the government.

With the failure of the attempted coup in Jakarta at the end of September 1965, a wave of violence erupted across the country. Nowhere was it more devastating than on Bali. The numbers killed in this orgy of violence will never be known. One estimate puts the figure at an astonishing 100,000. Rivers were reported to be choked with bodies and the graveyards overflowing with corpses. Today, few on the island will talk about this dark episode, and none with relish.

Land and environment

Geography

Bali is the westernmost island of the chain that makes up the Lesser Sundas, and is one of Indonesia's smallest provinces. It covers 5,561 sq km and has a population of 3,000,000. Like the other islands of the Lesser Sundas, it rises from the deep sea as a series of spectacular volcanic peaks, the highest of which – Mount Agung – exceeds 3,000m.

Separating Bali from Java is the narrow Bali Strait. It is 40-50m deep, and during the last Ice Age when sea-levels were considerably lower than today, Bali would have been connected to the mainland by a land bridge, allowing animals to move freely between the two. To the east, Bali is separated from the next of the Lesser Sunda Islands, Lombok, by the far deeper Lombok Strait. At its deepest, the water depth exceeds 1,300m – and even during the Pleistocene Ice Age the strait would have remained submerged. Wallace's Line, the division between the Asian and Australasian faunal realms, first identified by the great Victorian naturalist Alfred Russel Wallace, passes between the two islands (see page 801). Because of the depth of the water here, the strait is an important passage for nuclear submarines making the trip between the Indian and Pacific oceans.

One feature of life on an island that lies over the spot where two tectonic plates overlap, is great geological instability. One of the most serious earthquakes this century occurred in 1917. During January and February of that year, a series of tremors hit the east and south regions of the island, followed by the eruption of Mount Batur. When this activity came to an end on 20 February, a total of 2,431 temples had been badly damaged – including Pura Besakih on Mount Agung – 64,000 homes had been wrecked, and 1,500 people had died. The inference was clear to every Balinese: the gods were angry. It is partly for this reason that the Balinese have felt it necessary to build temples in great numbers to appease the spirits and therefore help prevent natural catastrophe.

Despite the devastating effects of periodic earthquakes and volcanic eruptions, Bali has also been blessed by nature in its rich and fertile soils and abundant rainfall. Farmers have exploited this natural wealth by creating terraces on the hillsides, cutting tunnels through the rock to carry irrigation water, and cultivating rice throughout the year.

Climate

Bali is hot and humid, but this is alleviated by ocean breezes and altitude. Annual rainfall averages 2,150mm, the driest months being August and September and the wettest, December and January. Temperatures at sea-level average 26°C (average maximum 32°C in March, average minimum 29°C in July) and vary only marginally through the year; in highland areas it is considerably cooler, about 20°C. In the wet season the humidity can be oppressive.

There are two seasons: the dry season from May to October; and the wet season from November to April. But this should not deter visitors. Rain tends to fall throughout the year, but it usually comes in short, sharp showers during the afternoon and early evening. If you do get caught in a period of low pressure, the sheer volume of rain can be very limiting and it may be worth considering a move to one of the (usually) drier islands to the east. (See page 25 for best time to visit.)

Art and architecture

The American anthropologist Margaret Mead, like many other observers of Balinese life, wrote that "everyone in Bali is an artist". This extends from painting and carving, through to the dramatic arts, and into ceremony and ritual. Most of Bali's art and architecture is linked to the 'Javanization' of the island that began in the 10th century with a marriage between two royal houses of Java and Bali. However, it was the fall of the Majapahit Empire in the 15th century and the escape of the remnants of the Majapahit court, together with many skilled artisans, that led to the greatest infusion of East Javanese art and architecture. While Java was undergoing a process of Islamization, Bali effectively preserved the Indo-Javanese cultural traditions, though adapting them to accord with existing Balinese traditions.

The Balinese pura

In Bali there are over 20,000 temples – or *pura* – and most villages should have at least three. The *pura puseh*, literally 'navel temple', is the village-origin temple where the village ancestors are worshipped. The *pura dalem* – or 'temple of the dead' – is usually found near the cremation ground. The *pura bale agung* is the temple of the great assembly hall and is used for meetings of the village. There are also irrigation temples, temples at particular geographical sites, and the six great temples or *sadkahyangan*.

As befits a country where direction is of immense significance, there are **nine directional temples**, *kayangan jagat*, found at notable geographical sites around the island, particularly high up on mountains, on imposing outcrops overlooking the sea and beside lakes. These are amongst the most sacred temples on Bali and their strategic locations have been chosen to ensure that they safeguard the entire island and its people. Besakih, high on the slopes of Bali's most sacred and highest mountain, Mount Agung, is the pre-eminent of these directional temples and corresponds to the ninth directional point, ie the centre. The others, of equal importance, guard the other eight directions. Starting from the southwest they are: Pura Luhur Uluwatu, Pura Luhur Batukau on Mount Batukau, Pura Ulun Danu Batur high on edge of the crater of Mount Batur (this temple used to be beside the lake, but eruptions in 1917 and 1926 caused so much destruction that it was moved to its present position with help from the Dutch colonial government), Pura Ulun Danu Bratan beside Lake Bratan, Pura Pasar Agung near Selat on the slopes of Mount Agung, Pura Lempuyang on Mount Lempuyang near Tirtagangga, Pura Goa Lawah near Padangbai, Pura Masceti near Lebih. Balinese visit the 'kayangan jagat' nearest their home village at the time of its odalan, anniversary festival, to seek protection and make offerings to the spirits. Finally, there is the mother temple, Pura Besakih.

Balinese pura are places where the gods rule supreme, and evil spirits are rendered harmless. But the gods must be appeased and courted if they are to protect people, so offerings are brought to the site. The buildings that constitute a temple are not as important as the ground, which is consecrated.

The temple complex consists of three courts (two in North Bali), each separated by walls: the front court, or *jaba*, the central court, or *jaba tengah*, and the inner court, or *jeroan*. The innermost court is the most sacred and is thought to represent heaven; the outermost, the underworld; and the central court, an intermediate place. The generalized description of the pura given below accords most closely with newer temples. Old temples, and particularly those on the north coast, tend to show differences in their configuration. **NB** Colonies of longtail macaques inhabit some temple sites; they should not be teased or fed, and certainly not purchased – as has been occurring. Macaques are social animals that suffer if removed from their family group.

Bali Pura

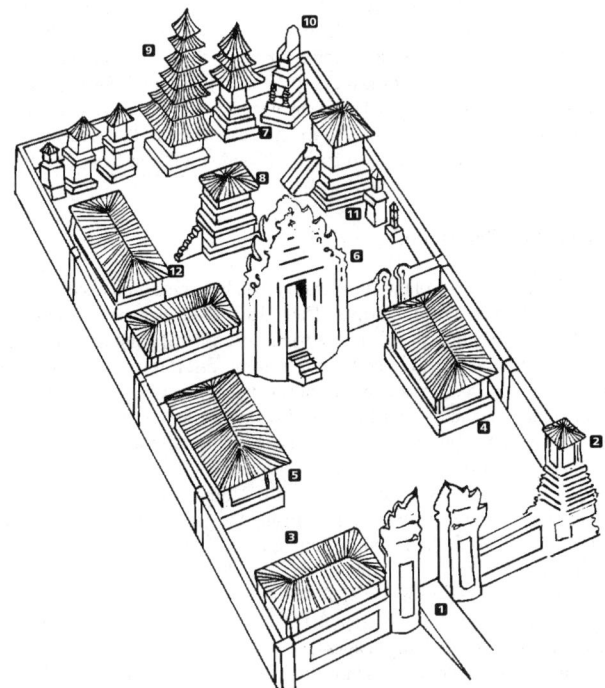

1 Candi Bentar (spilt gate)
2 Kulkul (drum tower)
3 Paon (kitchen)
4 Bale Gong
  (shed for gamelan orchestra)
5 Bale (resthouse for pilgrims)
6 Paduraksa
7 Jeroan (inner court)
8 Parungan or Pepelik
9 Meru (shrines of the gods)
10 Padmasana (stone throne for
   sun god Surya)
11 Sanggahs
   (secretaries of the gods)
12 Bale Piasan (sheds for offerings)

The outer court or jaba The entrance to the jaba is usually through a candi bentar, literally 'split temple' gate. The visual symbolism is clear – if the two halves of the gate are pushed together, closing the entranceway, they would form the shape of a complete candi.

Within the jaba are a number of structures. In one corner is the *bale kulkul* (*bale* = pavilion, *kulkul* = wooden gong), a pavilion in which hangs a large hollow, wooden, gong or drum. The kulkul is beaten during temple ceremonies and also in times of emergency or disaster – during an earthquake, for example. The bale and the kulkul are often decorated. Also within the jaba, it is not uncommon to find a *jineng* – a small barn used to store rice produced from the temple's own fields (*laba pura*).

The central court or jaba tengah The entrance leading to the central court is through the *candi kurung*. Like the split gate, and as the name implies, this is also in the form of a candi, but in this case a wooden doorway allows visitors to pass through. In a village pura, the centre of the jaba tengah will be dominated by an open pavilion with a roof of grass or reed. This is the *bale agung* or village conference hall. There is also often a *bale* for pilgrims who wish to stay overnight in the temple.

The inner court or jeroan The entrance to the inner court is through a second, larger, candi kurung called the *paduraksa*. The entrance way is usually guarded by a demon's head and rises up in the form of a pyramid. In larger temples, there may be three gateways, the central one of which is only opened during ceremonies. Along the back wall of the jeroan are the most sacred of the shrines. These may have multiple roofs – as many as 11. The greater the number of roofs, the more important the god. Also on the back wall, there is a stone pillar or *tugu*. It is at the tugu that offerings are left for the *taksu*, the god who's job it is to protect the temple and through whom the wishes of the gods are transmitted to the dancer during a trance dance. In the centre of the jeroan is the *parungan* or *pepelik* – the seat of all the gods, where they assemble during temple ceremonies. Finally, along the right-hand wall of the inner courtyard, are two *sanggahs* – *Ngurah Gde* and *Ngurah Alit*. These are the 'secretaries' of the gods; they ensure that temple offerings are properly prepared. (Condensed from: East Utrecht and B Hering (1986), *The temples of Bali*.)

Bali's artistic renaissance

During the early decades of the 20th century, Bali became famous as the haunt of a small community of Western artists. They 'discovered' Balinese art and laid the foundations for a significant artistic flowering. Up until that point, art had been produced for the pleasure of the gods and, in some cases, for aristocratic families. Among these early Western artists, the most famous were Walter Spies, the son of a German diplomat, and the Dutchman Rudolf Bonnet. Spies, who had first worked for the Sultan of Yogya, arrived in Bali on a short visit and was so taken with the island that he decided to stay. He was also a homosexual, and there seems little doubt that he found Bali less suffocating than Europe. Homosexual activity was accepted as a pursuit among unmarried young men, and the great anthropologist Margaret Mead defended him in these terms when he was tried for homosexuality in 1939. Over the years, Spies recorded Balinese music, collected its art, contributed to academic journals, and established the Bali Museum. He also painted a handful of rich paintings, recording in minute detail Bali's natural and cultural wealth. However, Spies was not keen to teach the Balinese.

In contrast, Rudolf Bonnet was more than happy to train and advise Balinese artists in Western techniques and to transmit the European aesthetic. In 1936, Bonnet and Spies established the first artists' co-operative – the *Pita Maha* (meaning Great or Noble Aspiration) at Ubud. Balinese artists would bring works to the co-operative and Bonnet and Spies would select those they felt were good enough for sale and exhibition. This naturally led to a trend towards Western tastes. Both Spies and Bonnet remained on Bali until the Japanese occupation from 1941 to 1945.

Cloth as art: Ikat in Southeast Asia

Ikat is a technique of patterning cloth characteristic of Southeast Asia and is produced from the hills of Burma to the islands of Eastern Indonesia. The word comes from the Malay word *mengikat* which means to bind or tie. Very simply, either the warp or the weft, and in one case both, are tied with material or fibre so that they resist the action of the dye. Hence the technique's name – resist dyeing. By dyeing, retieing and dyeing again through a number of cycles it is possible to build up complex patterns. Ikat is distinguishable by the bleeding of the dye which inevitably occurs no matter how carefully the threads are tied; this gives the finished cloth a blurred finish. The earliest ikats so far found date from the 14th-15th centuries.

To prepare the cloth for dyeing, the warp or weft is strung taut on a frame. Individual threads, or groups of threads are then tied tight with fibre and leaves. In some areas wax is then smeared on top to help in the resist process. The main colour is usually dyed first, secondary colours later. With complex patterns (which are done from memory, plans are only required for new designs) and using natural dyes, it may take up to 6 months to produce a piece of cloth. Prices are correspondingly high – in Eastern Indonesia for example, top grade cloths can easily exceed 1,000,000Rp ($500), and ritual cloths considerably more still. Today, the pressures of the market place mean that it is more likely that cloth is produced using chemical dyes (which need only one short soaking, not multiple long ones as with some natural dyes), and design motifs have generally become larger and less complex. Traditionally, warp ikat used cotton (rarely silk) and weft ikat, silk. Silk in many areas has given way to cotton, and cotton sometimes to synthetic yarns. Double ikat, where incredibly both the warp and the weft are tie-dyed, is produced in only one spot in Southeast Asia: the village of Tenganan in Eastern Bali.

Warp ikat:
Sumatra (Bataks)
Kalimantan (Dayaks)
Sulawesi (Toraja)
East Nusa Tenggara
(Savu, Flores, Sumba, Roti)
Double ikat:
East Bali

Weft ikat:
Sulawesi (Bugis)
Northeast Java
East Sumatra
Bali
Burma
(Shans) Thailand
Laos
Cambodia

Spies, Bonnet and other Western artists visiting Bali viewed the Balinese as innately talented and creative, but failed fully to appreciate – or at least to take note of – the traditional strictures under which most art was produced. Balinese craftsmen worked to strict formulas and there was little room for individual invention. Production was geared to copying existing works, not to creating new ones. As court art was in decline, Spies and Bonnet encouraged Bali's artists to produce for the emerging tourist market. This allowed the Balinese greater artistic freedom, and also led to a change in subject matter; from carving gods and mythical figures, they began to produce carvings and paintings of the natural world and everyday life. At the same time, there was a shift from realism to greater abstraction and expressionism, while the gaudy colours of traditional art were replaced with softer, more natural hues. The birth of Balinese modernism can be directly linked to the influence of this small group of Western artists.

Today, however, art in Bali is predominantly driven by the tourist market. That which sells to foreigners determines production: output is standardized, pieces are small and easily portable, designs are selected which sell well...in short, art is now an industry in Bali.

Balinese painting

Most of the paintings produced by artists in Ubud, Batuan and Penestanan are not 'traditional'. The artists use Western materials and methods, and work to an adapted Western aesthetic. Yet, Balinese works do have a quality which sets them apart and thus makes them distinctive.

In the past, Balinese painters worked in what has become known as the *wayang* style. Adapted from the wayang kulit or shadow play, figures were painted in profile or three-quarters view, with a strict use of colour. This style of painting was used for Balinese calendars, scrolls for temples and *langse*, and large rectangular works for palaces. Today, most of the few artists still working in the wayang style live near the southeast village of Kamasan.

In *Balinese Paintings*, the art historian AAM Djelantik divides Balinese painters into seven groups:

The **Traditionalists of Kamasan** mentioned above who continue to paint in the wayang style.

The **Traditional experimentalists of Kerambitan** (20 km southwest of Tabanan) who produce wayang-style paintings, but use additional colours (like blue and green) and a bolder, stronger style.

The **Pita Maha painters of Ubud** concentrate on realistically reproducing the natural world – fish, birds, frogs, tropical flora – in fresh and vibrant colours.

The **Pita Maha painters of Batuan** produce eclectic paintings; detailed scenes from Buddhist mythology, lively and innovative wayang-style images, and naive-style works – almost caricatures – that depict modern life with humour.

The **Young artists of Penestanan** make-up a group initially inspired by the Dutch painter Arie Smit who arrived in Bali in 1956; he took farm boys, and trained them, but also allowed their innate talent to emerge. The resulting works are bold and bright, naive in form, and depict everyday scenes.

The **Academicians** are artists who have received training at Western-style art schools in Java. Although the works sometimes employ Balinese or Javanese motifs and even techniques (for example, painting on batik), they are Western in inspiration and sometimes abstract.

The **Adventurers** are untrained Balinese artists who have broken away from Balinese tradition, experimenting with new styles and techniques. Their work is diverse and cannot be simply characterized.

Supporting the Balinese handicraft industry In 1993 a new NGO, *Yayasan Mitra Bali*, was established to support the small-scale handicraft producer in Bali, from initial production through to the final marketing of the object. The offices of *Yayasan Mitra Bali* are at Jalan Sulatri 2, Denpasar, T224397.

Culture

People

The original inhabitants of Bali are the Bali Aga, who still live in a handful of communities in the east of the island (see page 414). Since the intrusion of Javanese Hindu-Buddhist people and culture from the 10th century, the Bali Aga have been gradually relegated to a subordinate position. For most visitors today, the culture of Bali means that of the dominant Hindu population.

Despite population growth and considerable modernization, most Balinese still live in villages or *banjar* ranging in size from 200 to several thousand inhabitants. Family compounds or *kuren* are enclosed by high walls and are clustered around a central village courtyard. A kuren will support several families, all eating food from the same kitchen and worshipping at the same family altar. The family gods are paternal ancestors, and descent is patrilineal. The central courtyard is the place where villagers congregate for group activities; for wayang performances, village meetings, and periodic markets. In the past, each village would have been headed by a hereditary prince.

Balinese social structure is stratified in two ways. First, every individual belongs to a ranked descent group or *wangsa* ('peoples'). This system of ordering people is akin to the Indian caste system and was adopted after Javanese rule was established on the island. The nobility are divided into three castes – the *brahmanas* or priests, *satriyas* or ruling nobles, and *wesyas* or warriors. Members of these three castes are said to be the descendants of aristocrats from the Majapahit Kingdom who settled

The banjar

Every Balinese male is a member of a banjar, the basic unit of organization and local government. After marriage, a man is invited to join the banjar. This invitation is in reality a compulsion; if after the third summons, the man has not joined, he is declared 'dead' and loses most of his village rights – even the right to be cremated on the village cremation ground. The members of the banjar democratically elect one of their group to act as head (klian banjar). He enjoys the status and prestige of being head, and some other minor advantages such as additional rice during group festivities, but no cash payment for his work.

Members of the banjar are bound to assist one another in a variety of tasks. It is, in effect, a co-operative society. In any village there are likely to be a number of banjars, each drawing its members from a geographical neighbourhood. They sometimes own ricefields communally, the production going towards group festivities. Today, money owned through tourist activities – such as staging dances – also goes to the banjar, the society then redistributing it among its members. As Miguel Covarrubias wrote in 1937 (while ignoring the position of women): "Everyone enjoys absolute equality and all are compelled to help one another with labour and materials, often assisting a member to build his house, to prepare his son's wedding, or to cremate a relative."

---

here towards the end of the 15th century. But 90% of the population belong to the *sudras* or *jaba*; literally, the outsiders of the court. In addition to belonging to a caste, a Balinese will also belong to a far more egalitarian class structure based upon where a person lives. The *banjar* system of associations is the epitome of this (see page 443).

As dictated by Balinese tradition, a child is not placed on the floor until the 105th day of its life; he or she will be carried until able to stand and walk – never being allowed to crawl, as the Balinese believe this is animalistic. At 210 days (one Balinese year) the child is given its name. A ceremony occurs to celebrate puberty; first menstruation is followed by a tooth-filing ceremony (often occurring at the same time as the marriage ceremony). From the time of the tooth-filing ceremony, daughters are no longer the father's responsibility. Sons have their marriages financed for them by their fathers. Marriages are still sometimes pre-arranged among aristocratic families, although increasingly men want to choose their spouses (and vice versa) and mixed-caste relationships are occurring.

Language

The Balinese language uses three different forms to indicate the caste, status or social relationship that exists between the speaker and the person being spoken to. High Balinese is used when speaking to superiors who will reply using low Balinese. Low Balinese is also used between friends and equals. Middle Balinese is a form of polite speech used to address strangers and superiors.

Balinese names

Many Balinese names relate to the order of birth. For ordinary (Sudra) people Wayan is usually the firstborn, Made the second, Nyoman the third and Ketut fourth. For higher caste people, the firstborn is often called Raka, Putu or Kompiang, the secondborn Raj, the thirdborn Oka, and the fourthborn Alit. Names can also be indicative of caste; amongst Brahmans you find Ida Bagus for males and Ida Ayu for the females. Amongst the warrior caste, the Satria, Dewa and Anak Agung are common.

Religion

Except for small numbers of people in East Java, the Balinese are the only Indonesians who still embrace Hinduism – or at least a variant form of the Indian religion. While across Java and Sumatra, Islam replaced Hinduism, on Bali it managed to persist. Today, 95% of Balinese are still Hindu.

Known as *Hindu Dharma* or *Agama Hindu*, the Balinese religion is an unique blend of Buddhism, Hinduism and pre-Hindu animist beliefs. So, along with the worship of the Hindu trinity of Vishnu, Brahma and Siva, the Balinese also worship deified ancestors or *leluhur*, as well as deities of fertility, of the elements and of the natural world. The whole is suffused with a belief in a transcendental spiritual unity known as *Sang Hyang Widi*.

Reflecting the diverse roots of Balinese Hinduism, there is a corresponding variety of priests and other religious practitioners. There are high-ranking Brahmana priests of both Sivaite and Buddhist persuasions (Buddha is regarded as Siva's younger brother), lower order village priests or *jero mangku*, exorcists, herbal healers, and puppet masters or *dalang*.

The aim of Balinese Hinduism is to reach 'peace of spirit and harmony in the material life' by achieving a balance between philosophy, morals and ritual.

Festivals and ceremonies

The full moon occurs approximately every 29½ days. The Denpasar Municipality Tourist Office (Dinas Pariwisata Kotamadya Denpasar), Jalan Surapati 7, publishes an annual calendar of events listing, day by day, Bali's many festivals & their location

There can be few places of comparable size that have more ceremonies and festivals than Bali. The most common are temple anniversary celebrations, odalan. Every temple on the island holds an *odalan* usually once every 210 days, one complete cycle according to the Balinese *wuku*, also known as the *Pawukon* calendar; however, some temples schedule their odalans according to the lunar calendar, the Saka, with years consisting of 354-356 days. With more than 20,000 temples, every day is a festival day, somewhere.

The major ceremonies are those of marriage and cremation, both of which are traditionally costly affairs. Also important is tooth-filing. Along with these ceremonies, associated with a person's progression through his or her life-cycle, are a vast range of other rites, festivals and ceremonies.

Sesajen This is not a ceremony, so much as a ritual, but it is so commonplace that it is in some respects the most important religious activity on the island. Three times a day before meals, small woven coconut trays filled with glutinous rice, flowers and salt are sprinkled with holy water and are offered to the gods. They can be seen placed outside the front door of every house.

Eka Dasa Rudra This is the most important of Bali's festivals and is held, in theory, only once every 100 years at the 'Mother Temple' – Besakih – on Mount Agung. In 1963, the volcano erupted during the festival, killing 2,000 people. As a result, another had to be organized. It took place in 1979 and this time no catastrophe occurred (see page 387 for more details).

Panca Walikrama This festival is meant to take place once a decade at Besakih temple. However, in practice this has not happened, with only four festivals taking place this century, the last one in 1989.

Odalan The *odalan* festival celebrates the anniversary of a temple's consecration and is held over about three days, usually every 210 days according to the wuku, or pawukon calendar, but some temples follow the saka calendar with 354-356 days. Of the 66 main temple ceremonies, 40 are based on the wuku calendar and 26 on the saka. Wuku ceremonies occur at the time of the new moon, *tilem*, while saka ceremonies are usually held at the time of the full moon, *purnama*. The odalan at the nine directional temples are the grandest. This is the festival that visitors to Bali are most likely to see and it includes a great feast to which all the villagers are invited. The villagers prepare for odalan for many days beforehand by cleaning the temple, building altars and awnings, erecting flag poles, and preparing offerings. On the first day of the celebration, the ceremony starts with ritual cockfighting: the blood is a necessary offering to the gods as is the sacrifice of the most powerful fighting cock (see box, page 450). Women dress in their finest clothes – sarongs, sashes and head-dresses – and walk in procession to the temple. On their heads they carry their colourful offerings of fruit and rice cakes, arranged in beautiful and carefully balanced pyramids. The offerings remain at the

Penjor and janur

Visitors to Bali cannot fail to notice the tall, elegant bamboo poles called penjor which bend over the roads, signifying some celebration or festival. Hanging from the slender poles are decorations made out of the yellow leaf of the coconut, known as janur. Their design varies enormously, according to the festival and to the place where they are made. So many festivals take place on Bali that there are always penjor to be seen in varying states of decay. Travelling around Bali, visitors may notice arches of palms over the gateway to a house, with janur and banana leaves on either side; this usually signifies a wedding ceremony. Fruit and flowers are placed on (or within) the janur, as offerings to the gods. Any of the following may be seen dangling from the penjor: bananas, pineapples, plastic bags filled with pink liquid, coconuts, carrots, ears of corn and janur; all symbols of fertility. These penjor take about two hours to make and look very beautiful and delicate when first erected; their beauty fades a little as they dry out and turn brown after about two days. Janurs are not unique to Bali, and can also be found in parts of Java and North Sulawesi. Reliefs depicting janur on the ninth century Hindu temple of Prambanan, in Central Java, indicate that they have been made for many centuries.

temple for three days during which time they are sprinkled daily with holy water. At the end of this period, the food is taken home again and eaten.

During odalan, the men sit around the compound proudly wearing their krisses tucked into their sarongs. Over the three days the temple buzzes with activity; around the entrance locals set up stalls selling food and trinkets, medicine men market cure-alls, cockfights are staged, a gamelan orchestra plays, and in the evenings dance and wayang kulit performances take place. The inner courtyards are reserved for the sacred offerings and here the *pemangku* – or officiating priest – prays in front of the altars.

Marriage

In contrast with Western marriages, the traditional Balinese marriage is preceded by the honeymoon – or *ngrorod*. The prospective couple secretly prepare for their honeymoon and, on the day they select, arrange for the abduction of the bride with the complicity of a few close friends. The girl is expected to put up a good fight, but the event is staged. When the parents discover that their daughter has been kidnapped, they send a search party to look for her; again this is for show. During their time in hiding, the couple are expected to consummate their marriage before it happens – an event which is witnessed by the gods. The marriage itself is supposed to occur within 42 days of the abduction, but not before a substantial bride-price has been paid to the parents of the girl. From this point on, the girl becomes part of her future husband's family and relinquishes her own family affiliations. She adopts the groom's ancestral gods to symbolize this. Among aristocratic families marriages were usually pre-arranged (*mapadik*).

The marriage, or *masakapan*, is held on an auspicious day selected by the priest. Invitations are sent out asking guests to bring certain types and amounts of food. The bride and groom used to have their teeth filed during the ceremony if this had not already been done (see below). While the bride is being prepared for the marriage rite, men – arranged according to status – sit, eat and chew betel nut while being entertained by professional storytellers. The

Kidnapping (from a Baliness painting)
Source: Covarrubias, Miguel

rite varies from area to area, but usually the bride and groom offer food and drink to one another, and then eat together in public; an important symbolic act because in the past only married men and women were allowed to be seen eating food together. In the afternoon, the priest performs a ritual purification and blesses the couple.

Cremation   Cremation is the most important ceremony in the Balinese life-cycle. It is a time for celebration, not sorrow, and is wonderfully colourful. It is also an extremely costly affair, and people will begin to save for their cremation from middle age. Even the poorest family will need to spend about 1,000,000Rp, whilst wealthy families have been known to lavish hundreds of millions of rupiah. If there is not enough money saved, families may have to wait years – sometimes more than a decade – before they can hold the cremation of a loved one, thus releasing his or her soul. To avoid the wait, poorer people may be helped out by other members of the village, or they may share in a big ceremony when a number of bodies are cremated together. Another option is to be cremated with an aristocrat who needs a retinue to accompany him to the next life. Towards the end of 1992, the Rajah of Gianyar, 71-year-old Ide Anak Agung Gede Agung, staged an elaborate cremation for his former wife, two step-mothers and two of his late father's concubines: rumour had it that the total cost to the royal house – the richest on Bali – was as much as US$1,000,000.

Rich people may be cremated soon after they have died, in which case the corpse simply lies in state in the family compound. If there is going to be a considerable time period before cremation, then the body is either buried or mummified first. When enough money has been accumulated, an auspicious day is chosen by a priest for the cremation. The body is disinterred (if buried), the bones collected up, arranged in human form, and draped with a new white cloth. The corpse is carried back to the family compound and placed in a bamboo and paper tower, richly painted and decorated. Here it is adorned with jewellery and cloths decorated with magic symbols. Various rites are performed before the ceremony to awaken and satisfy the soul. An *adegan*, a dual effigy, is carved in palmleaf and sandalwood. On the day before the cremation the effigy is taken in a grand procession to a high priest, accompanied by the dead person's relatives dressed in their finest clothes.

For the cremation itself, a large bamboo tower is built; its size and shape is dictated by the caste of the dead person. A wooden life-size bull (for men) or cow (for women) is sometimes carved. On the morning of the cremation, friends and relatives are entertained by the family of the deceased and then the body is placed inside the bamboo tower. The village *kulkul* – or gong – is struck, and the construction is carried in a noisy procession (designed to confuse the soul of the departed so that it cannot return to the family home) to the cremation ground by other members of the dead person's *banjar*, or village association. The body is roughly handled as it is placed in the tower. At the cremation site, the wooden bull or cow and the corpse are set alight. After the incineration, the ashes are carried off in another raucous procession, to the nearest water, where they are thrown into the wind. The cremation is the most impressive of the Balinese ceremonies, but it is not one where any respect is shown for the corpse. The body is treated like an unclean container; it is the soul that is paramount. To illustrate the point, bodies are poked with sticks to help them burn, and are shown none of the respect evident in the funeral ceremonies of other religions.

Tooth-filing   The practice of tooth-filing was once common across island Southeast Asia. Savages, wild animals and demons have long, white teeth, so filing them down at puberty was necessary to ensure that at death a person would not be mistaken for a wild creature.

It is said that filing is necessary to control the six evil characteristics of the human condition, known as *sad ripu* – passion, greed, anger, confusion, jealousy and earthly intoxication. If someone dies without having had their teeth filed, the priest will often file the teeth of the corpse before cremation.

Dance, drama and music

Dance

Balinese dances, as with their music and theatre, were sacred, created as offerings to and enjoyment for the gods. It is only in recent times that troupes of 'professional' dancers performing for money have been formed. The Balinese are consummate dancers. Everyone dances, and dancing forms an essential element of private and public life accompanying every stage of a man's life. Of the various dances, those most often staged for tourists are the masked dance or *topeng*, the monkey dance or *kecak*, and the dance between the witch Rangda and the mythical lion, known as the *barong*. A brief description of the various dances is given below; tourists are normally provided with a printed sheet with information on the dance(s) when they attend a performance.

Kecak – or monkey dance – is in fact a relatively recent creation, invented by the German artist Walter Spies in the 1930s for a film. It was inspired by the chorus found in the sacred trance dance (or *sanghyang*), and the sound of the chattering crowd of men crouched watching a cockfight. A central person in a state of trance communicates with a god or ancestor, while the surrounding chorus of men rhythmically chant *kecak kecak kecak*, which encourages the state of trance and gives the dance its name. The dance itself is based on an episode from the Ramayana, and tells the story of when Sita is abducted by Ravana and subsequently rescued by an army of monkeys.

Barong – or kris dance – is also a trance dance, and while often described as the epitome of the battle between good and evil, its real purpose is to maintain harmony by balancing the forces of good and evil. Good, in the shape of the mythical *Barong*, a sacred animal, fights the evil witch *Rangda*. These dances, with their fantastic costumes, are among the most sacred and important of the Balinese dances. The Barong is the guardian of the village and the purpose of the dance is to exorcise the village of evil spirits at temple festivals and when disease or disaster strike. The origin of the Barong is unknown. Almost every village has a Barong which manifests itself in different forms, of which the *Barong ket* is the most common and sacred, looking somewhat like a Chinese lion with a magnificent bulgy eyed mask and a long shaggy coat. At the climax of the dance Barong confronts Rangda, and Barong's followers attack her with their kris. The witch's spell turns the kris of the Barong's accomplices against themselves. However, in their trance state they are protected by the powerful magic of the Barong, and the kris can do no harm. Inside the barong costume are two men who co-ordinate their movements with great agility and often humour. The masks themselves are believed to be infused with magic power, and are wrapped in sacred cloths and kept in the village temple. There is a special day to bless and celebrate the Barong when the streets of Bali are filled with processions of these colourful, mythological creatures. Rangda, the personification of evil, has bulging eyes and tusks and is linked to the Indian goddess Durga. She is also a source of great supernatural power and speaks in Kawi, the ancient Javanese tongue, using a whiney, sinister sounding voice. Like the barong (the word refers to both the dance and the mask), the mask of Rangda is also revered. The outcome of their confrontation is always a draw, a balance between good and evil, neither side wins and the battle goes on forever.

The evil witch Rangda, enemy of the mythical lion Barong, in the Barong dance from Balinese manuscript. Reproduced in Miguel Covvarrubia's Island of Bali (1937)

Sanghyang dedari – the Dance of the Holy Angels – is the best known and possibly the most beautiful of a type of trance dance known as *Sang* [Lord] *Hyong* [God]. Young girls perform this religious dance of exorcism, designed to rid a community of evil spirits, while a chorus of men and women provide accompaniment. The dancers are often relatives of temple servants and usually have no professional training. They are believed to be possessed by celestial nymphs, and at the end of the performance – traditionally – would walk on hot coals before being brought back to consciousness.

Legong – a Balinese dance for girls from eight to early teens (although today many tourist dances employ adult performers), which was created at the beginning of the 18th century. This is not a trance dance, but rigorous physical training is needed to perform the movements. Three dancers perform the most popular version, the *legong kraton*, a story taken from the East Javanese classic tale of Prince Panji. In this story, a bird warns the king of the futility of war, which he ignores, and is killed in battle. The dance is regarded as the finest, and most feminine, of Balinese dances, and the girls dress in fine silks and wear elaborate headdresses decorated with frangipani and other flowers. The dancers do not speak or sing – the lines of the story are recounted by singers accompanied by a gamelan orchestra. Because of the demands of the dance, girls must be taught – literally physically manipulated – from an early age, so that 'the dance enters their innermost being'.

Topeng – the wayang topeng is a masked dance which, in Bali, recounts stories of former kings and princes. In its purest form, it is performed in silence by a single actor who portrays a series of characters, changing his mask each time. Today, he is more likely to be accompanied by a narrator.

Jegog – a dance which originates from Jembrana. It is performed by young men and women accompanied by the music of the *jegog* – a bamboo xylophone not unlike the *angklung* of West Java.

Ramayana ballet – a portrayal of the great Hindu epic.

Wayang kulit – the famous shadow theatre of Java and Bali in which two-dimensional leather puppets are manipulated, their forms reflected onto a white cloth. In Bali, wayang kulit accords, it is thought, more closely with the original Majapahit form than does the Javanese equivalent. This can be seen in the puppets with their elaborate headdresses and costumes, and in the carving of the faces which is similar in style to the low relief carvings on Majapahit temples in East Java. Many of the themes of Wayang Kulit have an educational or moral lesson; for example, the story of Bima's search for holy water takes him to Heaven where he learns which actions merit rewards and which result in hideous punishment. As this is an effective and popular way for the public to absorb moral teachings, the government now uses Wayang Kulit to instil such secular duties as family planning, food hygiene and healthy living.

Gambuh – this is one of Bali's most ancient, and least known, dance dramas. Court tales are enacted in a highly stylized manner by actors dressed in rich costumes, and accompanied by a traditional orchestra. Revived from near cultural extinction, *gambuh* is occasionally performed at Pura Desa Batuan in Batuan village, south of Ubud. There is also a Gambuh School in Padangaji village near Selat in Karagasem, see page 407.

Legong costume.
Source: Cavarrubias, Miguel (1937)

Music Beryl de Zoete and Walter Spies, early foreign residents of Bali, wrote of its music in their paper of 1938, *Dance and drama in Bali*: "Music permeates their life to a degree which we can hardly imagine; a music of incomparable subtlety and intricacy, yet as simple as breathing. Like every other expression of Balinese life, it is easily accessible and at the same time inexhaustible in its interest and variety." It was Walter Spies, an American composer who was

Tourism and culture in Bali

One of the areas which has attracted attention among journalists, academics and many tourists who have been to Bali is the relationship between culture and tourism. Bali's tourist industry is unashamedly founded on culture. In a sense, it is the island's culture which is Bali's defining feature. In the 1970s the American anthropologist Philip McKean argued that far from destroying culture, tourism would support, nurture and reinforce culture. Indeed, partly as a result of his work, Bali became an exemplar of how tourism can be managed without undermining culture (see page 958 for a general discussion of the effects of tourism). Arts and crafts appeared to be revivified by the tourism experience, revenue earned was widely distributed through the banjar system of communal relations, and the Balinese appeared able to separate the sacred from the profane when it came to selling culture to tourists.

The tourism authorities in Bali embraced these views with alacrity. Cultural Tourism or *Pariwisata Budaya* was born in the 1970s. In 1986 the International Herald Tribune published an article with the title "Bali: paradise preserved". The article stated:

"If anything, tourism has pumped more life into the Balinese cultural Renaissance that began earlier this century. There are probably more superb artists and craftsmen in Bali today than at any time in its history."

Putting aside whether 'culture' can be reduced to just artists and craftsmen, this view is being challenged on a number of grounds. Most interesting perhaps is work which has tried to unravel what constitutes 'touristic culture', and what constitutes 'traditional culture' in Bali.

The sociologist Michel Picard wonders whether it is even possible to separate 'tourism' from 'culture' in the case of Bali. Many dances developed for tourists in the 1930s have, over time, become key markers of Balinese, and in some cases of Indonesian, culture. So making a distinction between what belongs to the world of 'tourism' and the world of 'tradition', is impossible. The two have merged. In short, 'cultural tourism' has become 'tourist culture'. As Adrian Vickers has written in his book Bali: a paradise created: "This 'culture', expressed in art and religion, is what is promoted in tourist literature, what tourists come to see, and what is eventually accepted by the Balinese themselves as a definition of what is important in their own society." Michel Picard then takes this perspective that tourism is defining culture for the Balinese themselves, one step further when he writes that the Balinese have become "self-conscious spectators of their own culture – taking the growing touristification cum Indonesianization of their culture as the very proof of its 'renaissance'".

---

captivated when he first heard a recording of Balinese music in the late 1920s in New York, who played a crucial role in detailing and preserving the music of the island. He acted as a patron, wrote a brilliant, seminal book entitled *Music in Bali* (1966), and spread the gospel around the capitals of the world. He even wrote an orchestral work – *Tabuh-Tabuhan* – based on Balinese musical formulas, for which he won a Pulitzer prize in 1936. Such was his love of Bali and its music, that what began as a short jaunt to the island turned into a life-long love affair.

Like Java, the basis of Balinese music is the gamelan orchestra. Sets of gamelan instruments – of which the gongs are regarded as the most important – are usually owned corporately, by the village or *banjar*. Making music is a tightly structured event; the notion of 'jamming' is simply not the Balinese way. Musicians learn their parts and the aim is for an orchestra to produce a perfect rendition of a composed piece. Reflecting this approach, the brilliance of Balinese music is in the whole, which is greater than its constituent parts. There are few superstars; it is the orchestra as a perfectly co-ordinated unit that determines success.

Most visitors to Bali hear Balinese music or see local dances in the context of their hotels. Although people often assume that such performances cannot be 'authentic', all gamelan and dance groups are regulated by LISTIBIYA, the government arts council. This means that the quality is invariably high, and although pieces are usually condensed to make them more 'acceptable' to tourist audiences, the quality of the

Experiencing Balinese music, dance & theatre

Cockfighting – Tajen

Cockfighting as entertainment was banned by the Indonesian government in 1981, but is still permitted as part of the ritual associated with all temple ceremonies including the odalan. The spilling of blood, *tabuh rah*, is necessary as purification, to appease the evil spirits *bhuta* and *kala*, and to ensure a good harvest. The building of a new guesthouse or restaurant may also occasion a cockfight and the requisite blood offering, but in this instance the cockfight is not legal.

Despite being illegal, cockfights still take place in secret throughout Bali purely as a betting medium, and may last for hours. They are usually staged in an arena or *wantilan* (the traditional village meeting hall, open sided and two-tiered), with space for up to 100 people. The Dutch banned the sport, to no avail, in the 1920s, because men would bet their life savings or even their wife. (For the record, the British government banned cockfighting in Great Britain in 1835.) It was the national pastime and almost every male owned a fighting cock.

Ritual fights usually take place outside the temple, and follow an ancient and complex ritual as set out in the sacred *lontar* manuscripts. The cocks are categorized according to size, markings and colour, and rules pertain as to the choice of an auspicious day for the ceremony. Each male member of the local *banjar* is expected to bring a cock, and a percentage of the prize money goes to the *banjar* and towards the cost of the ceremony. Specialists are hired to attach the razor sharp, 10-15cm long blades or *taji*, to the cocks' left leg; a system of handicapping is applied, whereby the blade can be set at different less efficient angles to ensure an even match if one cock is deemed superior to its opponent. These *taji* are considered to have magic powers; whilst being forged by the *pande* (blacksmith), special rituals and precautions must be followed.

There is a central bet decided by the *juru dalem*, a local village leader of unblemished character, in agreement with the owners of the two cocks who each put up half the money, often with the help of backers and friends. This can amount to as much as 1,000,000 and goes to the winning owner less 10-25% for the *banjar*. Following this, the spectators make their own bets, using a complex system of hand and facial signals. Nothing is written down, and while most bets are of small amounts, a village may put up a considerable sum on its chosen cock.

Most fights last only a few minutes. Any bird that runs out is disqualified. The defeated bird, if it survives, may become a family pet, but more likely it will die in battle and provide an especially tasty and auspicious meal.

Considerable prestige and financial gain may attach to the owner of a winning cock. Fighting cocks are prized by their owners, who pamper them, stroke, massage, wash them, give them names and train them. They are given special foods. They lead a celibate life in order to save all their energy and spirit for the fight.

The cocks are kept in *guwungan*, bell shaped baskets made of bamboo, which allow for a very limited amount of movement. The *guwungan* are placed along the roadside so that the cocks can watch the passers-by and not become bored, and also to get them used to the noise and frenzy they will experience as part of the eventual fight.

Cockfighting is very much an all-male event. Tourists of either sex are usually welcome, though this 'sport' is not for the fainthearted or for animal lovers.

---

performance is rarely affected. However, for a more authentic environment, it is necessary to visit a temple anniversary festival or *odalan* (see page 444). Performances usually begin in the late afternoon or early evening with a gamelan recital, and then continue after dark with dances and shadow plays. Note that visitors should dress and behave appropriately. The two main music academies are STSI (Werdi Budaya Art Centre) on Jalan Nusa Indah in Denpasar; and Kokar/SMKI in Batubulan. There is also an annual Bali Arts Festival held from mid-June to mid-July in Denpasar. See the table for a listing of where to see dances.

Many villages have a gamelan orchestra; these can often be heard practising in the evenings on the 'bale banjar', the platform used as a meeting place in the centre of the village.

Suggested reading Belo, Jane (edit) (1970) *Traditional Balinese culture*, Columbia University Press: New York. Collection of academic papers, most focusing upon dance, music and drama.

Cook, Vern (1996) *Bali behind the seen: recent fiction from Bali*, Darlington, Australia: Darma Printing. Short stories by Balinese and translated by Vern – hard to obtain outside Australia.

Covarrubias, Miguel (1937) *Island of Bali*, Cassell: London (reprinted, OUP: Singapore, 1987). The original treatment of Bali's culture and still considered by many to be the best study of Balinese society, despite being nearly 60 years old. It is an excellent background to the island and is highly entertaining.

Djelantik, AAM (1990) *Balinese paintings*, OUP: Singapore. Concise history of Balinese painting also covering the major contemporary schools of art.

Eiseman, Fred and Eiseman, Margaret (1988) *Woodcarvings of Bali*, Periplus: Berkeley.

Eiseman, Fred B (1989 and 1990) *Bali: Sekala and Niskala*, Vol I Essays on Religion, Ritual and Art. Vol II Essays on Society, Tradition and Craft, Periplus: Berkeley. Informative collection of essays giving an insight into the Balinese way of life.

Hobart, Angela (1987) *Dancing shadows of Bali: theatre and myth*, KPI: London. Academic book examining the wayang theatre in Bali.

Kempers, AJ Bernet (1991) *Monumental Bali: introduction to Balinese archaeology and guide to the monuments*, Periplus: Berkeley and Singapore. New edition of Kempers' 1977 book, with photos and additional 'guide' section; best available.

Lansing, J Stephen (1991) *Priests and Programmers: technologies of power in the engineered landscape of Bali*, Princeton University Press: Princeton. An anthropological account of Bali's irrigation system; interesting for rice enthusiasts.

McPhee, Colin (1986) *A House in Bali*, OUP: Singapore. An amusing and informed account of Balinese society and the role of music in society by the American composer who visited Bali in 1929.

Robinson, Geoffrey (1995) *The dark side of Paradise: political violence in Bali*, NY: Cornell University Press. This presents the Bali beneath the harmony and the beauty: an island with deep political and social divisions, where Dutch and then Indonesian administrations have manipulated people for their own ends. It offers a particularly detailed account of the 1965 massacre. Certainly an alternative book to take on holiday.

Stuart Fox, David (1982) *Once a century: Pura Besakih and the Eka Dasa Rudra Festival*, Penerbit Citra Indonesia: Jakarta.

Tenzer, Michael (1991) *Balinese music*, Periplus: Berkeley and Singapore. Illustrated summary of Balinese music, drawing heavily on Spies' work, best introduction available.

Utrecht, E and Hering, B (1987) 'The temples of Bali', *Kabar Seberang Sulating Maphilindo* 18: 161-74.

Vickers, Adrian (1989) *Bali: a paradise created*, Periplus: Berkeley and Singapore. Excellent account of the evolution of Bali as a tourist paradise; good historical and cultural background, informed without being turgid.

5

Sumatra

Sumatra

- **456** Ins and outs
- **459** North Sumatra
- **513** Aceh
- **533** West Sumatra
- **570** Riau
- **591** South Sumatra
- **610** Background

Although Sumatra does not have Java's historical and archaeological sights, it does offer magnificent natural landscapes. Perhaps most spectacular of all is the upland crater lake of Lake Toba. The forests, mountains, rivers and coasts all provide great trekking and rafting opportunities, some of the finest national parks in the country and pristine beaches.

There are also over a dozen ethnic groups on the island, who speak some 20 different dialects, including the peripatetic Minangkabau of West Sumatra, the Christian Bataks of North Sumatra, the Ferrant Muslims of Aceh and the tribal peoples of the islands of Nias and Mentawi.

As the world's forth largest island (nearly 475,000 sq km), Sumatra also acts as a 'safety valve' for Java's 'excess' population. About 60% of Indonesia's transmigrants – 4 million people – have been resettled on Sumatra, mostly in the south. Population densities here are less than one tenth those on neighbouring Java, although some areas – such as Lampung province – are beginning to suffer the effects of overcrowding.

Sumatra is also crucial to the Indonesian economy. It was in North Sumatra that Indonesia's first commercial oil well was sunk in 1871, and over 60% of the country's total petroleum and gas production comes from the island and the seas that surround it.

Ins and outs

When to go

Sumatra's climate varies considerably across the island. North of the equator the rainy season extends from October to April, and south of the equator from October to January. Road travel during the dry season is quicker and easier, but overland travel in the wet season is fine on the (largely) all-weather Trans-Sumatran Highway. The most comfortable time to travel is during the onset of the rains (September-October), when temperatures have cooled but showers have not become torrential. Most tourists visit between June and October, so travelling out of those months is relatively quiet and hotel rates can often be bargained down.

Getting there

Air Most visitors arrive at Medan, in the north, near the west coast of Sumatra, which offers international connections with Kuala Lumpur, Penang, Ipoh and Johor Bahru in Malaysia, and with Singapore. There are also flights from Singapore to Pekanbaru and Padang, the latter via Medan. There are domestic connections with Jakarta from all Sumatran provincial capitals.

Boat There is a twice weekly 'international' ferry linking Penang (Malaysia) with Belawan (Medan's port), 14 hours. Hydrofoils and high-speed catamarans also make the crossing daily, 4-5 hours. In addition to the popular Belawan-Penang route, there are also ferry connections from Belawan with Port Klang (Kuala Lumpur's port) and, via Penang, with Langkawi. For more details, see page 472. An alternative route into or out of Indonesia is to catch a regular high speed ferry from Singapore's World Trade Centre or Tanah Merah piers to Batam or Bintan islands in the Riau archipelago, 40 minutes. From there it is possible to catch a boat – fast or very slow – to Pekanbaru, up the Siak River on the Sumatran 'mainland' (see pages 585 and 577 for more details). There are also ferry connections between Melaka and Dumai, although this is not a very popular entry/exit point. The most important domestic seaborne entry/exit point is Bakauheni on Sumatra's south tip; hourly ferries link Bakauheni with Merak, West Java. The Pelni ship Rinjani docks at ports on Sumatra's east coast every fortnight, while the Kerinci does the same on the west coast.

Getting around

Where to go Travelling in Sumatra can be a time consuming business. Some key destinations – notably Lake Toba – have no airport and others – like Nias Island – have only intermittent air connections. Furthermore, distances can be great and with average road speeds of around 50 km per hour, even on the trans-Sumatran 'highway', it can take a while to get from A to B. This means that anyone intending to sample Sumatra in anything more than the most cursory of ways will need to allocate at least 10 days. The classic 'route' is to travel between Medan and Padang (which both have airports with daily flights), via Brastagi, Lake Toba and Bukittinggi. This really requires a minimum of 10 days and preferably two weeks. However, there are opportunities for shorter stays, and people living in the region regularly come to Sumatra for a week or less. Residents of Singapore in their thousands, for example, take weekend breaks in the Riau islands. It would also be quite feasible to fly into Medan and make for Lake Toba for five days or to Padang and take the bus up to Bukittinggi for a similar length of time. But long-haul visitors, with jet lag to deal with and perhaps a new climate too, would probably find such a short visit exhausting and ultimately less than satisfying.

Air This is the most convenient and comfortable way to travel around Sumatra. *Garuda* and *Merpati*, now sister-companies, service all the main provincial cities. Merpati tends to operate the short-hop services to smaller towns and cities. The other main domestic airlines on Sumatra are *Mandala* and *Indonesian Airlines*. Smallest of all are *DAS*, *SMAC* and *Deraya*, which tend to service smaller towns.

Sumatra highlights

Wildlife Bukit Lawang and the Orang Utan Rehabilitation Centre is the most popular wildlife 'experience' on Sumatra (page 473). The Gunung Leuser National Park is far richer in terms of fauna, but the animals tend to be rather more retiring (page 526).

Hill stations Brastagi is Sumatra's original colonial hill retreat, and a good location for trekking (page 477). Bukittinggi in the Minang area of West Sumatra is now both more popular and more attractive (page 535).

National parks The well-run Gunung Leuser National Park (page 526) and the important but less developed Kerinci-Seblat National Park (page 568) are the finest protected areas on Sumatra. In the far south of the island, the Way Kambas National Park is known for its herd of elephants (page 608).

Trekking Bukit Lawang and the Gunung Leuser Reserve both have good trails and a well developed tourist infrastructure. Brastagi and Mount Sibayak (page 479) offer upland walks. Lake Toba also has well developed walks and treks (page 484). There are longer and more challenging treks on Nias and Mentawi islands (page 508). Easy walks are on offer in the hills around Bukittinggi, as well as some stiff mountain climbs.

Natural features The little-visited town of Takengon (page 532) is based around an upland lake in the Gayo Highlands. Lake Toba is justifiably popular, a massive lake lodged in the centre of a stupendous crater. Lake Maninjau and Lake Singkarak (page 538), both not far from the hill town of Bukittingi, are small, relaxed and peaceful.

Beaches and islands Sabang and Weh Island off Sumatra's northern tip are the most popular beach destinations for backpackers (page 519). The west coast of Aceh is also dotted with small beach-side guesthouses. Thicker-walletted visitors tend to make for the Riau islands (page 570). Among surfers, Nias has almost legendary status (page 508).

Diving Sabang and Weh Island off Sumatra's northern tip offers excellent diving.

The Banyak Islands off the west coast are less-visited but developing as a dive site (page 525). There is also diving available from the Riau islands.

Surfing and rafting The most popular rafting river is the Alas, which flows through the Gunung Leuser National Park. Rafting expeditions are also organized down the Wampu, from Bohorok; the Asahan, from Lake Toba; and the Batang Anai and Ombilan, from Bukittinggi. Lagundi Bay on Nias Island is a Mecca for surfers.

Temples and palaces The Batak tombs, houses and megaliths of Lake Toba complement its natural beauty. Banda Aceh has one of Sumatra's finest mosques, as well as the tombs and palace of the sultans (page 514). Padang Lawas is a rarely visited collection of around 25 temples spread over a large area 70 km east of Padangsidempuan (page 506). The megaliths near Pagaralam, inland from Bengkulu, are also interesting (page 601).

Traditional architecture and modern towns The traditional houses and villages of the Batak and Karo areas of North Sumatra and the Minangkabau area of West Sumatra are memorable. So too are the traditional settlements of the Nias and Mentawi islands. Medan has the grandest architecture in Sumatra, while half-forgotten Bengkulu is arguably the most charming modern town on the island.

Culture Banda Aceh is one of Indonesia's most staunchly Muslim areas. The Batak area encompassing Lake Toba and Brastagi is also culturally significant. Equally distinctive is the culture of the matrilineal but also Muslim Minangkabau of West Sumatra (Bukittinggi). The cultures of the Nias and Mentawi islands are often paraded as 'stone age'.

Museums Medan's North Sumatra Museum (page 464) is probably the best museum on the island, but even this collection couldn't be described as much more than motley. Palembang's South Sumatra Museum, contains a few interesting pieces.

Train There is a limited rail network in South Sumatra, although some routes are only for freight. The only regular passenger service used by travellers is that linking Bandar Lampung, Palembang and Lubuklinggau.

Bus Buses are the main mode of long-distance travel. Steady improvements to the 2,500 km Trans-Sumatran 'Highway' (a misnomer – over large sections it is more like a village road, one and a half lanes wide), which runs down the entire island from Banda Aceh in the north to Bakauheni in the south, is making road travel much faster and more comfortable. It used to take 20 hours from Prapat to Bukittinggi, now it takes 10-14 hours depending on the vehicle. Roads off the Trans-Sumatran Highway are still generally poor, and in the rainy season delays of two days are not unknown while floodwaters subside. Travelling through the Bukit Barisan, or along the west coast, is still quite slow, with average speeds of 40-50 km/hour, as the road follows every turn of the mountain. 'Coach travel stories' are becoming a thing of the past and there are 'full' a/c, VIP or express buses plying all the major routes. The most highly regarded private bus companies are *ALS* and *ANS*.

Because tourists tend to have a lower pain threshold than locals – and a lower tolerance threshold to delayed departures – tourist buses now ply the more popular routes. In particular, the route from Padang, through Brastagi, Lake Toba and Sibolga, to Bukittinggi. These *bis parawisata* – tourist buses – are often eight-seat minibuses that leave at a set hour (roughly) and tend to arrive more quickly than the bis biasa – ordinary bus – alternatives. These tourist buses have some other advantages. They are safer; they often pick up and drop off at hotels in towns rather than at bus terminals on their ourtskirts; and they may also include stops at designated tourist sights en route (the dreaded objek wisata). The main disadvantage (other than cost) is that they reduce contact between locals and tourists and thereby cut out a rich area of social and cultural interaction.

Rules, customs and etiquette

Selected air fares

Banda Aceh to Jakarta	1,577,000
Batam to Jakarta	814,000
Batam to Ujung Pandang	1,600,000
Medan to Banda Aceh	397,500
Medan to Jakarta	1,156,000
Medan to Batam	633,400
Medan to Padang	681,100
Medan to Denpasar	1,777,000
Medan to Yogyakarta	1,444,900
Medan to Ujung Pandang	2,280,000
Padang to Jakarta	869,000
Palembang to Jakarta	456,000
Pekanbaru to Jakarta	880,000

Note: *fares are one-way, economy, quoted in rupiah, and were collected in mid-1999.*

Selected bus fares (Rp)

	Ekonomi	A/c
Medan to:		
Prapat	6,000	
Bandar Lumpung	85,000	
Bukittinggi	45,000	
Prapat to:		
Padang	35,000	50,000
Bukittinggi	30,000	42,000
Pekanbaru	32,000	
Jambi	42,000	
Palembang		65,000
Bengkulu	53,000	
Bandung (Java)	88,000	130,000
Bandar Lampung to:		
Palembang	17,500	
Padang	55,000	85,000
Bukittinggi to:		
Sibolga	20,000	
Bengkulu		35,000
Jakarta	45-55,000	80-110,000

Sumatra is home to a number of ethnic, religious and cultural groups. In the north, the province of Aceh is one of the most strictly Islamic in Indonesia and the same is also true of the Minang area of West Sumatra. Particular care should be taken to dress conservatively. In West Sumatra, there are also some additional rules of conduct that should be observed (see page 535).

Dress Most people in Sumatra are Muslim and women should be particularly careful not to offend. Dress modestly and avoid shorts, short skirts and sleeveless dresses or shirts (except at the beach). When visiting places of worship, shorts are not permitted in mosques, shoulders and arms should be covered, and women must cover their heads.

Safety

During 1998, 1999 and into 2000, there were civil disturbances and mass demonstrations in Aceh. The police and army came under attack on numerous occasions from pro-independence activists and they responded in kind. The army's activities in Aceh were being investigated as this book went to press.

Civil disturbances

Shopping

Local and regional handicrafts, textiles, jewellery and other works of art are the best and most distinctive buys in Sumatra.

Antiques There are some good antique shops in Medan, but bargains usually need to be 'rooted out' by visiting little out-of-the-way shops. Antiques include Dutch memorabilia and Chinese ceramics (Indonesia was on the trade route between China and India), as well as local products. There are a huge number of fakes on the market.
Clothing Very reasonably priced western-style clothes can be found in most of the bigger cities. Large department stores and markets are the best places to browse. Children's clothes are also very good value (although dyes may run).
Jewellery Gems mined in Indonesia include diamonds and black opals from Kalimantan and pearls from Maluku. West Sumatra and Aceh are both known for their silverwork.
Metalwork The traditional Malay sword, the *kris*, is the most popular buy. Both antique and modern examples are available.
Weaving Baskets of all shapes and sizes are made for practical, everyday use, out of rattan, bamboo, sisal and nipah.
Woodcarving This ranges from the clearly ersatz and tourist oriented to 'primitive'.

Sport and special interest travel

Sumatra offers considerable, although so far largely underdeveloped, scope for adventure travel. This includes **hiking**, **climbing**, **rafting** and **diving**. The Alas, Wampu, Asahan, Batang Anai and Ombilin rivers are all being used by rafting companies, and this number is likely to increase as the industry develops. Hiking is concentrated in the island's national parks, and especially in the Gunung Leuser and Kerinci-Seblat reserves. The mountains of the Bukit Barisan offer numerous opportunities for strenuous hikes, sometimes verging on climbs. More serious rock climbing is most developed in West Sumatra, particularly around Padang. Although not renowned for its diving, Weh Island is a good dive site. Pulau Banyak is being pushed as a dive site and companies also venture out from Padang. Cultural tours focus on Sumatra's diverse ethnic groups. These include the Batak of North Sumatra and the Minangkabau of West Sumatra. However, the more adventurous head for Nias Island off Sumatra's west coast to see the Niha and the more adventurous still for Mentawai, south of Nias.

North Sumatra

Medan

Medan is big, hot, noisy, congested and dirty, with only a few havens of greenery – for example, Merdeka Square – and no obvious 'sights' to enthrall the visitor. However, while the architecture is not notable by international standards it is significant in the Indonesian context, and Medan does provide a vivid and vivacious introduction to Asia for those who are new to the region. In addition, and perhaps because foreign tourists are less in evidence, the local people are generally warm and welcoming.

Phone code: 061
Population: 2,000,000
Colour map 2, grid A1

Ins and outs

Getting there
See Transport section, page 471, for further details

Medan is an international gateway and an easy, 1 hr hop by air from Singapore. There are also air connections with several Malaysian cities and all Indonesia's main centres. The airport is in the centre of town, so getting to your hotel is no great trauma. Medan's port of Belawan provides ferry services to Penang in Malaysia and is also visited by several Pelni vessels which run fortnightly circuits through the Indonesian archipelago. Medan has 2 bus terminals. The Amplas terminal, 8½ km south of the city centre, serves all destinations to the south. The Pinang Baris terminal, about 9 km to the northwest, serves destinations north of Medan. The train system is defunct.

Getting around

Medan is a nightmare to get around, many of the main access roads are choked with traffic. The 1-way system only seems to add to the frustration. However, becak drivers and taxis have become adept at chicken footing down side lanes and avoiding the main arteries. Going by rickshaw will provide your stomach with a nifty lead lining. Medan's **tourist office** (Kanwil Pariwisata) is on Jl Benteng Huruba (Alfalah) 22, T7862220, F7867992. Rather unhelpful and out of town. *North Sumatran Tourist Office* (Dinas Pariwisata), Jl Jend A Yani 107, T4538101, provides basic maps and, if you are lucky, a brochure, but it's not really much help. Open 0730-1430 Mon-Thu, 0730-1200 Fri, 0730-1330 Sat. *Dinas Pariwisata*, Jl Brig Jend Katamso 43, is another tourist office and this one is less helpful still. Some material available but little English spoken. It seems to be a bureaucrat's sinecure – and is often closed. There is also a tourist information booth at the airport, but it's not always open and the information available is very limited. Those who are interested in Medan's architectural heritage should try and get hold of *Tours through historical Medan and its surroundings*, by Dirk A Buiskool (1995). The pamphlet is sold in some hotel gift shops and is also available in the Dutch original.

Tours
See Essentials section, page 471, for further details

Tour companies have offices in most of the larger hotels and organize half day city tours, and day tours to Brastagi and to the orang utans at Bukit Lawang. Longer overnight tours to Lake Toba and to the Nias Islands are also offered by most tour agents. *Pacto Tours* run raft adventures down the Alas River from Medan. *Edelweiss* also organize rafting and trekking tours.

Background

During the period of Dutch rule, economic development was more marked in North Sumatra than in any other region outside Java. The volcanic soils of the area are rich and the land was rapidly cleared for plantation agriculture, particularly from the late 19th century on. Medan, North Sumatra's capital and the largest city in Sumatra, developed from little more than a village into the administrative hub of an agriculturally-based export economy. Large quantities of tea, rubber, coffee and tobacco were funnelled through Belawan – Medan's port – to the Melaka Strait and from there to Europe. To fuel this economic growth, the Dutch used immigrant Chinese labourers, and today Medan still has one of the largest Chinese populations in Indonesia. It remains the most important commercial centre in Sumatra. A visit to Medan quickly impresses on visitors the inequalities and inequities of Indonesia's development as darkened-windowed Mercedes purr past straining *becak* drivers.

Sights

Colonial buildings

The greatest concentration of colonial buildings is to be found along Jalan Balai Kota and its continuation, Jalan Jend A Yani, and around Merdeka Square. Few still perform their original functions as the headquarters of plantation companies, European clubs, and stately hotels. As Dirk A Buiskool explains in his pamphlet *Tours through historical Medan and its surroundings* (1995), from which much of the information below is taken, Medan underwent a building explosion during the first decade of the 20th century. The city's wealth and economic importance demanded many new buildings, and as these had to be constructed quickly there was a tendency towards standardization of design – producing what became known as 'normal architecture'.

Walking south from the northwest corner of the 'Esplanade', now – inevitably – renamed **Merdeka Square** (Independence Square), the first building of note is the **Central Post Office** at Jalan Bukit Barisan 1. It was begun in 1909 and completed in 1911 and is refreshingly unchanged. Inside, the main circular hall beneath the domed roof still contains its original post office counters. On the other side of the road was Medan's most stately hotel, the *Dharma Deli*. Today, a new block so dominates the site that the original hostelry is all but invisible. The *Dharma Deli* was formerly the *Hotel De Boer* and began life in 1898 as a modest place with just seven rooms. However, as Medan's economic influence grew, so the *Hotel De Boer* also expanded and by 1930 it had 120 rooms. Among the innovations introduced at the hotel was the so-called 'mosquito-less room': rooms where the windows were entirely enclosed in wire gauze, allowing people to sleep without mosquito nets. Perhaps the most famous person to have stayed at the hotel was the 'Oriental' dancer Mata Hari, a Dutchwoman who reinvented herself as a seductive Javanese princess and charmed Europe. She worked as a spy during the First World War and was tried and convicted by the French for collaborating with the Germans – on flimsy-evidence – and executed in 1917.

The **Padang** itself is notable for its huge, epiphyte-filled trees that skirt the square and provide relief from the sun. On the west side of the square are two more elegant buildings, side by side: the appropriately stolid Bank of Indonesia and the refined Balai Kota. The **Bank of Indonesia**, formerly the De Javasche Bank, was designed by Ed Cuypers in 1910 in Classical style. The **Balai Kota** was probably erected in 1908 and then modernized in 1923. The clock in the elegant tower was donated by Medan's most influential Chinese businessman – Tjong A Fie (see below). The new Balai Kota, or more fully the Kantor Wali Kotyamadya, is just over the river on Jalan Raden Saleh. The architect of this building has drawn on the original Balai Kota for inspiration, most obviously in the domed tower which imitates the original, barring the blank space where the clock should be.

The strip of buildings running the length of Jalan Jend A Yani from Merdeka Square south to Jalan Pemuda are very different to the buildings on the Padang; the latter is representative of the colonial government and the economic interests that sustained and supported it. These, however, were largely owned by Medan's Chinese business community – they are small **Sino-Dutch shophouses** where families would at the same time run their businesses and live, sleep and eat. Although many are marred by modern façades, they are nonetheless notable for their use of both Dutch and Chinese architectural flourishes and for their variety. Most notable of all is the run-down and romantically decrepit **Tjong A Fie Mansion** at Jalan Jend A Yani 105. This quasi-colonial/ quasi-Chinese house, with its green and beige paint scheme and peacock-topped entrance arch, was built by a wealthy Chinese businessman, after which it is named. Like other Chinese who found their fortunes in Southeast Asia, Tjong A Fie arrived in Medan from Guangdong (Canton) in 1875 almost penniless – he reputedly had a few pieces of silver sewn behind his belt. In Medan he gained the trust of the Dutch authorities and the Sultan, and became the supplier for many of the area's plantations. Before long he was a millionaire and Medan's 'Major' – the highest ranking member of the Chinese community. He was a great philanthropist, giving generously to good causes – a founder, for example, of the Colonial Institute (now the Tropical Institute) in Amsterdam. Opposite the mansion is the side street Jalan Jend A Yani I, which has a little reminder of the early days of independence in the spelling of the road name: Djl Djenderal A Yani. Walking north towards Merdeka Square a short distance is the **Tip Top Restaurant**, which began serving food and drinks in 1934 and continues to do so in a style which is redolent of the colonial period (see page 469). Just across the railway line at the end of Jalan Jend A Yani V is the **Vihara Kong Ti Niong** – Medan's oldest Chinese pagoda – although the building here is comparatively recent.

The Chinese community

Medan

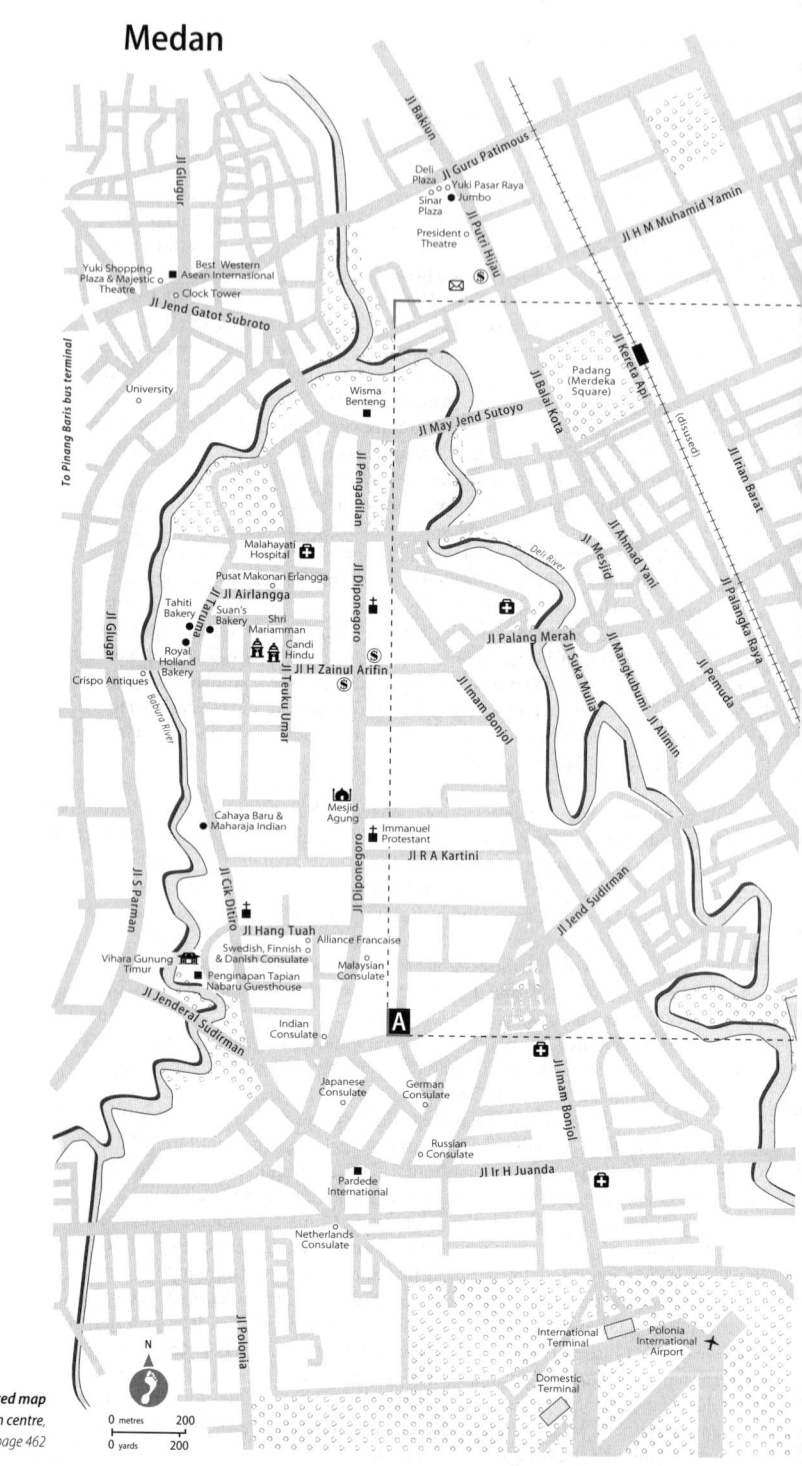

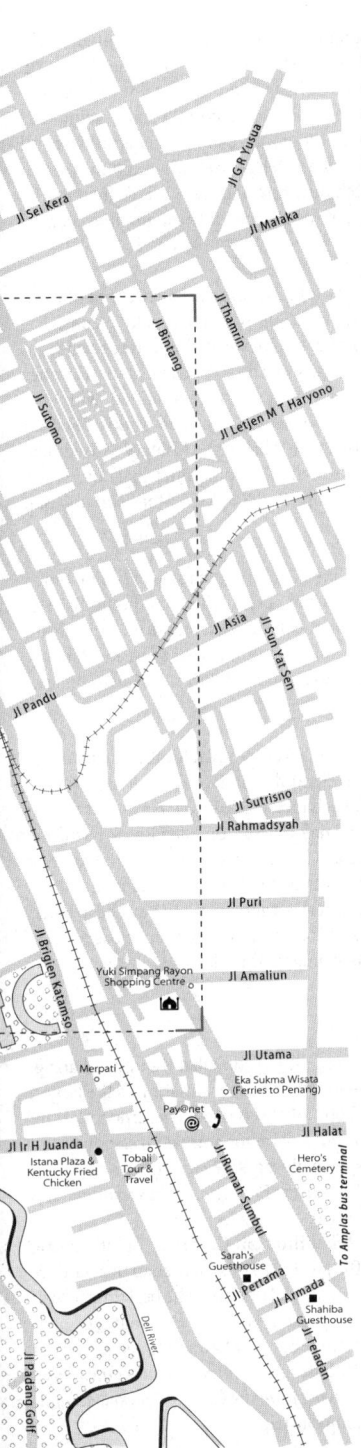

Temples, pogodas & mosques

Another road with historical buildings is the garden-like Jalan Jend Sudirman (Polonia quarter), southwest of the town square. At the southwest edge of the city is the **Vihara Gunung Timur**, at Jalan Hang Tuah 16, just west of Jalan Cik Ditiro. This building, erected in the late 1970s, is the largest Chinese pagoda in Medan. Set in a peaceful area, the main entrance to the temple is flanked by guardian lions. Filled with lanterns, incense and demons, the temple is a rewarding retreat from the bustle of the city. The highly decorated roof is probably its most notable feature. **NB** Photography is not allowed in the pagoda and remove shoes before entering the inner sanctuary. Locally known as **Candi Hindu** (Hindu temple), the Shri Mariamman is at Jalan H Zainul Arifin 130. The complex serves Medan's large South Asian community and the brightly painted figures of gods and animals stand out a mile. The temple welcomes visitors. This part of town, reasonably enough, is the Indian quarter and the temple has been recently renovated and expanded. However, there has been a Hindu temple on the site from 1884. The **Immanuel Protestant Church**, built in 1921 in Art-Deco style, can be found back towards the town centre at Jalan Diponegoro 25. Almost facing it on the other side of the road is the **Mesjid Agung**, with a towering new minaret.

The attractive **Mesjid Raya** or **Grand Mosque**, with its fine black domes and turquoise tiles, can be found at the corner of Jalan Sisingamangaraja and Jalan Mesjid Raya. The mosque was built in 1906 in 'Moroccan' style by Sultan Makmun Al-Rasyid, and designed by the Dutch architect Dingemans. The marble came from Italy, the chandelier from Amsterdam, and the stained-glass from China. In the grounds is a small enclosed plot containing the tombs of the sultans of the Istana Maimun Palace (see below), and a fairy-tale style minaret. It is just a shame that the mosque is on such a busy and ugly road – which detracts from its beauty. ■ *Admission by donation.*

To the west of the mosque, set back from the road on Jalan Brig Jen. Katamso, is the **Istana Maimun** – also known as the **Istana Sultan Deli**. This impressive building was designed by Captain Th van Erp, a Dutch architect working for the Royal Dutch Indies Army. It was constructed in 1888 as one element in a complex that included the Grand Mosque. The predominant colour is yellow – the colour of the royal house of Deli. It is eclectic architecturally, embracing Italian, Arab and Oriental styles. Inside are photographs of the various sultans and their wives, and a poor oil painting of the Sultan Deli himself who built the palace. The interior includes a few pieces of Dutch furniture and the Sultan's throne. His descendants continue to live in one wing of the Palace. ■ *Open daytime. Admission by donation.*

Museums & zoo The **Museum Sumatera Utara**, at Jalan HM Joni 51, some distance south of town off Jalan Sisingamangaraja, is an extensive building with an equally extensive – though of variable quality – collection of artefacts. Not surprisingly, it specializes in those of North Sumatran origin and upstairs has some fine wood and stone-carvings from the Nias Islands. Unfortunately it is ill-lit and poorly maintained, with little useful explanatory detail. ■ *400Rp, 0800-1700 Tue-Sun.* The **Bukit Barisan Museum**, also known as the Museum Perjuangan Abri or the Military Museum, at Jalan H Zainul Arifin 8, displays a decaying selection of Sumatran tribal houses and arts and crafts, as well as military paraphernalia. ■ *0800-1300 Mon-Thu and Sat, admission by donation.*

Kebun Binatang Medan (Medan Zoo) This is an abomination of a zoo which should have been closed, even before the monetary crisis left it with no funds. The animals are kept in appalling conditions, often without food and drink (there's no money), in overcrowded cages. The zoo is not a recommended tourist attraction. ■ *Jl Brigjen Katamso No 308, T7869745, 0800-1700 1,300Rp; weekend/holidays: 0800-1800 2,100Rp.*

Markets One of the greatest attractions of Medan is its markets, known locally as *pajak*. The huge **Central Market** or *Pajak Pusat* (Pajak Sentral) – in fact an agglomeration of various markets selling just about everything – is located close to Jalan Dr Sutomo. It is renowned for its pickpockets. Safer is the **Pajak Petisar**, on Jalan Rasak Baru, just off Jalan Gatot Subroto. It is a fruit and vegetable market in the morning (0600), that later develops into a general market, selling clothes, food and general merchandise. The **Pasar (Pajak) Ikan Lama** (Old Fish Market) is a good place to buy cheap batik, other types of cloth and assorted garments. It is on Jalan Perniagaan, close to Jalan Jend A Yani. Visitors may see live fruit bats strung up for sale.

Excursions

Asam Kumbang Crocodile Farm is 5 km from the city, off Jalan Kampung Lalang, at Asam Kumbang Village (close to the Pinang Baris bus terminal). It is the largest crocodile farm in Indonesia, with over 2,000 of the beasts. The crocodiles are hatched, reared and made into bags. This is not a place for animal lovers: dirty and over-crowded, chained monkeys, animals in small cages. ■ *Getting there: by town bus (bis damri) from Jalan Balai Kota or by oplet to the Pinang Baris bus terminal. It is possible to walk from the terminal, or take a becak.*

Binjai, **Brastagi** and the **Orang Utan Rehabilitation Centre** at Bukit Lawang are all accessible as day trips from Medan. **Binjai**, 22 km west of Medan on route 25, is famed for its fruit – and especially its rambutans and durians. The best time to visit is when they are in season, July-August. It is possible to reach **Brastagi** (see page 477) and the **Orang Utan Rehabilitation Centre** at Bukit Lawang (page 473) from here (about 3 hours). ■ *Getting there: regular buses and minibuses travel down Jalan Gatot Subroto, which becomes Jalan Binjei, leaving from the Central Market, 45 mins (500Rp).* Bukit Lawang can be visited as a long day trip.

Essentials

Medan has a fair number of mid- and upper-price range hotels. There is a concentration of the former on Jl Sisingamangaraja, north of the Mesjid Raya. Though they are hardly memorable, and Jl Sisingamangaraja is not one of the world's prettiest streets, they are adequate. Always enquire how much the discount is after asking the price, 10-25% is normal. For decent budget places, Medan is less well off, although there are 1 or 2 passable places. These, however, are not centrally located, so any excursion to the city centre means a *becak* or *mesin becak* ride – or a longish walk.

Sleeping
■ on map, page 466
Price codes:
see inside front cover

AL *Best Western Hotel Asean Internasional*, Jl H Adam Malik 5, T4563888, F4561978, aseanhtl@indo.sat.net.id A/c, restaurants (very average), pool, fitness centre, business centre. This large hotel is an attempt at an international class place, though it doesn't quite carry it off. Its disadvantage is that it is away from the centre of town on a very busy intersection (thus noisy and fume ridden). **AL** *Novotel Soechi Medan*, Jl Cirebon 76A, T4561234, F4572222, novonet1@indosat.net.id A/c, restaurants, good pool, 246-room hotel with all facilities including tennis court, business centre, fitness centre and executive floor. It has a central location and is good for businessmen. French general manager, professional and well run, among the best hotels in the city centre. **AL-A** *Tiara Medan*, Jl Cut Mutia, T4574000, F4510176, http//www.tiarahotel.com A/c, restaurant (good patisserie), pool, tennis, squash, excellent fitness centre, this is one of the better hotels in town with 200 fairly average but adequate rooms. It is situated down a quiet, tree-lined street and given that Medan is such a noisy and frenetic place, it is rather refreshing to come back to a (relatively) peaceful spot.

A *Dirga Surya*, Jl Imam Bonjol 6, T4152662, F4149327, dirganet@indosat.net.id A/c, restaurant, karaoke. While there is no pool or fitness centre here, this is a good little hotel with above average sized rooms, attractively furnished and good bathrooms. The room rate includes a buffet breakfast. Recommended. **A** *Natour Dharma Deli*, Jl Balai Kota 2, T4157744, F4144477. A/c, restaurant, pool, this was the original colonial hotel in Medan, but unfortunately it has been marred by a spectacularly insensitive modern addition which has all but obscured the old. However, there are still rooms in the older part which look onto the pool and have pleasant verandahs – they are worth asking for. The new rooms are inevitably in better condition, but have little charm. On the plus side it has an excellent central location, the room rates in the old wing are competitive, there is an attractive garden and still some original décor. Room rates include continental breakfast. **A** *Polonia*, Jl Jend Sudirman 14, T4142222, F4519553, situated about 2 km from the city centre on a tree-lined boulevard not far from Polonia airport. A/c, good Chinese restaurant, good pool, fitness centre, squash court, large hotel with 200 rooms, functional and efficient but not very characterful. Over-priced compared with the competition in this price category. **A-B** *Garuda Plaza*, Jl Sisingamangaraja 18, T70361234, F70364411, reserv@garudahotel.com A/c, restaurant, small and rather enclosed pool, business centre. This is a large, modern hotel, close to the Maimun Palace and the Mesjid Raya. It's one step down from Medan's best hotels and feels a touch provincial, but nonetheless a comfortable place to stay, with friendly management.

B *Danau Toba International*, Jl Imam Bonjol 17, T4157000, F4530553. A/c, several restaurants, bars and disco, sizeable garden with free form pool with waterfall that has seen better days, but is still good for children. Wide range of facilities including tennis and fitness centre, too large to be personal (259 rooms) and recent visitors have reported that the management is none too helpful. **B** *Garuda Citra*, Jl Sisingamangaraja 27-39, T70367733, F70365823. Grim looking sister hotel to the slightly more upmarket *Garuda Plaza*, with 69 a/c rooms. The rooms that face the busy street aren't too noisy because there is an outer plate class façade – although this does give the occupants the feeling that they are sleeping in an aquarium. Rooms are clean, heavily perfumed, with rather garish décor, but the management is friendly. **B** *Pardede International*, Jl Ir H Juanda 14, T4143866, F4153675. A/c, 115 rooms, restaurant, small pool. This is one of the best mid-range hotels – if being 2 km out of the town centre is not a problem. The rooms are much better than 1st impressions would indicate:

Medan centre

they are large, clean and airy (though check – there's considerable variation), with satellite TV and reasonable bathrooms, good discounts sometimes available. Recommended. **B-C** *Wisma Benteng*, Jl Kapt Maulana Lubis 6, T4513000. A/c, good seafood restaurant, this is a good mid-range place to stay. It consists of a low-rise series of buildings on a large plot looking onto the Lampangan Benteng (a grassed square). Rooms are large and reasonably clean and well maintained, and although there is no hot water in the standard rooms, the rate includes breakfast, tax and service. Discounts are available. Recommended.

C *Ibunda*, Jl Sisingamangaraja 33, T70345555, F70340772. A/c, small hotel, room rate includes breakfast. This is one of the better places in this price category of the hotels on Jl Sisingamangaraja, hot water, clean and attentive staff, well managed, popular and often full. **C-D** *Deli Raya*, Jl Sisingamangaraja 29, T70362997. Some a/c, room rate includes breakfast. This hotel is worse (and cheaper) than it looks from the outside. **C-D** *Dhaksina*, Jl Sisingamangaraja 20, T70320000, F7340113. Some a/c, one of Medan's older 'modern' hotels and it shows, rooms have attached bathroom, *ekonomi* fan rooms are dark and rather dingy, a/c rooms rather better, but overall this is nothing much. **C-D** *Sri Deli*, Jl Sisingamangaraja 30, T70363571. Some a/c, a smallish and friendly hotel with just a touch more character than the other places in this part of town. Rooms are bright with none of the overbearing frills of the more expensive hotels. Small but serviceable bathrooms, with shower/mandi and western loo. Room rates include breakfast, friendly management. Recommended.

E *Sarah's Guesthouse*, Jl Pertama 10/4, T70369460. This is a friendly if desultory place, in a private house in a quiet residential area of town. The disadvantage, and this it shares with the *Shahiba* close by, is that it is a good 20-min walk from the city centre. The rather dark rooms are only average, and the shared mandis with Asian loos could do with an overhaul, but it is peaceful, a good source of information, has cheap dorm beds available, and is close to the Amplas bus terminal. **E** *Zakia Guesthouse*, Jl Sipiso-Piso, T70322413, across from Mesjid Raya. Bath and fan, clean and quiet (except when the faithful are called to prayer!), helpful staff and just 3 mins from where the 'ferry bus' drops off. This place is recommended by those who have stayed here. **E** *Losmen Irama*, Jl Palang Merah 112-S, T326416. Good base for travellers just arriving in Indonesia, central location, with information on destinations in Sumatra including Nias Island. Reasonably friendly but don't expect to be charmed – it is a dark and dull modern shophouse down a side street (so reasonably quiet). The rooms are OK, and clean enough, although the shared mandis are pretty grim and on a hot day they can be suffocatingly hot. **E-F** *Shahiba Guesthouse*, Jl Armada 1A/3, T70368528, south of the Mesjid Raya, off Jl Sisingamangaraja. Range of rooms (some rather musty), including dorm beds, the rooms upstairs are best, large and airy with attached (cold water) bathrooms. The room rate includes a basic breakfast, towels and soap available. Marginally better than *Sarah's Guesthouse*, which is close by. Friendly.

F *Penginapan Tapian Nabaru*, Jl Hang Tuah 6, T4512155, quite a trek from the city centre – about 3 km – right next to the Vihara Gunung Timur Chinese temple. The advantage of this place is that it is situated down a quiet road in a largely residential area. The rooms are hardly pristine, the fans are noisy and the communal cold water mandis leave a lot to be desired. But at this price it's good value, the place is characterful and it's even getting a thin lick of paint.

Eating
- on map, page 466
- Price codes: see inside front cover

Medan is better served with decent & reasonable restaurants than it is with hotels

Indonesian Mid-range: *Jumbo*, Jl Putri Hijau 8. Large seafood restaurant. *Ria*, Jl Letjen MT Haryono. Flash Indonesian restaurant in an old renovated theatre, excellent Indonesian and Chinese food, patronized by Medan's wealthy. *Miramar*, Jl Pemuda. Excellent a/c Indonesian restaurant – this is where Indonesians of modest means come for a splash out. **Cheap**: *Famili*, Jl Sisingamangaraja 21B. A very well run and clean (but cheap) restaurant specializing in Padang food, but also serving grilled seafood, fried chicken and spicy prawn dishes like *udang sambal*. *Gelora*, Jl Sisingamangaraja (just south of the railway crossing). Cheap but clean Indonesian place serving all the classic Indonesian-Chinese dishes, from *bihun goreng* and *nasi goreng* through to *martabak*. *Garuda*, Jl Palang Merah 26 (just west of the railway crossing). Excellent and inexpensive Indonesian food, clean surroundings.

Padang Cheap: *Cendana Minang Restaurant*, Jl Pemuda 20C-D. An excellent Padang restaurant serving typically spicy beef rendang and good sauté kangkung. **Very cheap** *Rumali*, Jl Palang Merah 1 Col Sugiono 2. Wide selection of Padang dishes, friendly. Recommended.

Chinese Medan's large Chinese community means that the Chinese food here is excellent. There are many small eating houses in the street running off Jl Jend A Yani. **Mid-range**: *Angkasa Hotel*, Jl Sutomo 1. Good Chinese food. *Polonia Hotel*, Jl Jend Sudirman 14. Excellent Chinese. **Very cheap**: *No Name Chinese*, Jl Jend A Yani V. A superb Chinese restaurant in a corner shophouse, cheap.

Japanese Mid-range: *Yokohama*, Jl Nibung Raya 58. Best Japanese in town. *Oke Suki*, Jl Mesjid. A cook-at-your-table restaurant – very popular.

Indian The Indian area of town is centred on Jl Cik Ditiro and Jl H Zainal Arifin, close to Shri Mariamman temple. Two reasonably priced Indian restaurants, almost next door are: *Cahaya Baru*, Jl Teuku Cik Ditiro 8L, T4530962, and *Maharaja*, Jl Teuku Cik Ditiro 8C, opposite Department of Education, T4154821. Prawn, mutton, biryani, chicken, masal, lentils, lassi, chapati and so on, good and cheap.

Foodstalls *Selat Panjang* behind Jl Pandu has stalls selling Chinese (and seafood) and Indonesian favourites. *Jalan Semarang* off Jl Pandu also has quantities of foodstalls which really get 'wokking' in the evening. *Pusat Makanan Erlangga*, Jl Air Langga (it was formerly on Jl Imam Bonjol next to the *Dirga Surya Hotel*). Lots of open-air stalls open till late, seafood, Thai, Chinese dim sum, Vietnamese, Singaporean, Penang, noodles, saté, Acehnese – a great place to sample a wide variety of Asian foods cheaply. Recommended. The shopping plazas, such as *Deli Plaza* and *Thamrin Plaza*, have good, cheap 'food centres'. Indian food can be found at the foodstalls on Jl Jenggala, Jl Cik Ditiro and Jl Pagaruyung.

International Mid-range: *Dirga Surya Hotel*, Jl Imam Bonjol 6, T4152662. This hotel has perhaps the most competitively priced buffet lunches and dinners – phone to check what is on the menu though. *Lyn's*, Jl Jend A Yani 98A. Steaks (a speciality and very good) and other Western dishes, plus a selection of Indonesian and Chinese dishes, good hot plates, cold beers, mostly frequented by expats and Westernized Indonesians – a look-almost-like bar with booths, bar stools and no windows. *Sari Rasa Café*, Jl Katamso 38. Western dishes like avocado dip, lamb chops, chilli con carne, brownies and carrot cake, even roast beef and Yorkshire pud and apple pie, plus a handful of Indonesian numbers, run by a West Sumatran-English couple (Rita and Julian), good source of information for new arrivals in Sumatra. *Tip Top*, Jl Jend A Yani 92. An old favourite among Medan's small band of expats, with its cane chairs, tables almost on the street and slowly revolving fans. The standard Western fare of steaks and omelettes is complemented by some Chinese and Indonesian food – all wheeled to your table on an ancient looking trolley. Ice cream and a small bakery. Recommended, not so much for the food, which is mediocre, but for the atmosphere.

Cafés *Endede*, Jl Balai Kota (attached to the *Dharma Deli Hotel*, opposite the GPO). A café where it is possible to eat *al fresco* and consume quantities of lead, along with ice creams and coffee.

Bakeries *Ling's Bakery*, Jl Pemuda 20A. A Chinese/Indonesian bakery with lots of brightly coloured and thickly coated creations. *Bakery France*, Jl Pemuda. Slightly more sophisticated than most, ice creams too. *Novotel Bakery*, Hong Kong Plaza, Jl Cirebon (behind the *Novotel Soechi Medan*). The nearest thing to a baguette in North Sumatra available here, and some items that would not seem to have French roots – like the 'doughnut satay'. **Dunkin' Donuts** (in Deli Plaza), Jl Putri Hijau. There is also a concentration of bakeries on Jl Taruma, just west of the city centre. *Tahiti* at no 70, *Suan's* facing it on the opposite side of the road and the *Royal Holland* at no 62. All make sweet and savoury pastries and sell ice cream too.

Bars & clubs **Bars** Most local business people tend to drink in hotel bars and most of the hotels listed in the upper categories have bars. One dedicated and popular haunt is *Lyn's Bar*, Jl Jend A Yani 98A. **Clubs** *Bali Plaza*, Jl Kumango 1A. *Le Cartier*, at the *Pardede International Hotel*, Jl Ir H Juanda 14. *Ari Kink Kink*, at the *Danau Toba International Hotel*, Jl Imam Bonjol 17 (this disco used to be called *Dynasty* and some bright spark obviously thought this new name was superior – anyway, you can 'bogey [sic] your evening at the latest and hottest disco in town'). **Live music** *Tavern*, *Danau Toba International*, Jl Imam Bonjol 17. Three live bands each night.

Entertainment **Cinemas** *President Theatre* (in Deli Plaza), Jl Putri Hijau. *Majestic Theatre* (in Yuki Plaza), Jl Jend Gatot Subroto (next to the *Best Western Hotel*). Be prepared to be disturbed by cellular phone calls. **Cultural centres** *British Council*, Jl Jend A Yani. *Alliance Française*, Jl Uskup Agung Sugiopranoto 2, T4536767. **Cultural performances** Held twice a week at the *Bina Budaya* on Jl Perintis Kemerdekaan.

Festivals **March-May**: *Medan Fair* is held between Mar and May each year at the Taman Ria Amusement Park on Jalan Gatot Subroto. There are also permanent cultural exhibits at the park. **Movable**: *Idul Fitri* (Islamic holy day), Muslims descend on the Maimun Palace in traditional dress to mark the end of the fasting month of Ramadan – very colourful.

Shopping **Antiques** Jl Jend A Yani is the main shopping area, with the largest concentration of 'antique' shops. Beware of fakes: old Batak artefacts are cunningly mass produced. There are few real antiques for sale these days. What there is ranges from Batak pieces, Chinese ceramics, old meat grinders, antique irons and battered Javanese puppets. Other shops include: *Rufino*, No 56. *Ibn Battuta*, No 61, T4516989, 'antiques' and souvenirs. *Toko Yulida*, No 33. *Toko Asli*, No 62. *Toko Bali*, No 68. *Ibn Battuta* has the best selection – much of the other stuff are souvenirs. But the best place in town is undoubtedly *Crispo Antiques*, Jl HZ Arifin 173, T4533529, F4531523, just over the Babura River. It's an Aladdin's Cave, set on 3 or 4 floors, with a huge selection of furniture, wood-carvings, puppets, chests, textiles, jewellery, stone pieces – you will want to ship the whole lot home. **Books** English language books are thin on the ground. The best bet for newspapers and magazines is to try the gift shops at one of the luxury hotels – like the *Tiara Medan* and the *Novotel Soechi Medan*. *Gramedia Bookshop*, Jl Gajah Mada, corner of Jl Bantah, sells English books. **Clothing** The linked *Deli* and *Sinar Plazas* on Jl Guru Patimpus have a good number of fashion outlets. **Furniture** *Crispo Antiques*, Jl HZ Arifin 173. This place sells new, locally made furniture (you can see them making it out the back), as well as older pieces. **Plazas** *Yuki Pasar Raya* and *Deli Plaza*, both on the corner of Jl Putri Hijau and Jl Guru Patimpus. *Yuki Simpang Raya*, Jl Sisingamangaraja (opposite the Mesjid Raya). *Thamrin Plaza* on Jl Thamrin. *Hong Kong Plaza* on Jl Cirebon, behind the *Novotel Soechi Medan*. *Istana Plaza*, Jl RH Juanda Baru. *Medan Mall*, Jl Letjen MT Haryono, just before the Olympia Theatre. This is the newest mall in Medan and is the most popular one with expats (together with Matahari Store in Thamrin Plaza). **Textiles** Jl Jend A Yani III, which runs off Jl Jend A Yani, has a number of textile outlets. Browsing through the markets can be rewarding – either the massive Central Market or the Old Fish Market; the latter is the best place to buy batik (see 'Sights', above). Both *Batik Semar* and *Batik Keris* are to be found on Jl Z Arifin.

Sport **Bowling** A new bowling alley has opened on the upper floor of Perisai Plaza, Jl Palangka Raya. **Golf** *Nicotiana*, Jl Karya, 9 holes. *Polonia*, near the airport, 9 holes. *Tuntungan*, 30 mins towards Brastagi, excellent 18-hole course. *Tamora*, around 16 km from town on the road towards Tebingtinggi. **Hash House Harriers** This throw back to British colonial days in Malaya is alive and kicking in Medan (and elsewhere in Southeast Asia). A jog with knobs on, it involves a 'hare' laying a trail for the pursuing 'hounds' to follow, and then a bout of often heavy drinking: for men on Mon afternoon and for women and families on Thu afternoon. There is a small entrance fee and the runs begin and end at *Lyn's Bar*, Jl Jend A Yani 98A. **Health clubs** *Danau Toba Hotel*, *Polonia Hotel* and *Tiara Hotel*. At the *Tiara*, 17,500Rp buys a day's use of all the hotel's sports facilities including an excellent gym and a swimming pool. **Swimming** *Tiara Medan Hotel*, Jl Cut Mutia, 17,500Rp for use of pool and gym; *Polonia Hotel*, Jl Jend Sudirman 14; *Novotel Soechi Medan*, Jl Cirebon 76A; *Dharma Deli*

Hotel, Jl Balai Kota 2. **Tennis** *Danau Toba Hotel*, Jl Imam Bonjol 17, *Tiara Hotel*, Jl Cut Mutia. **Ten-pin bowling** *Marati Bowling*, Jl Gatot Subroto 32.

There are travel and tour companies all over town and most will provide a range of services from booking airline tickets through to providing tours and bus tickets. There is a concentration along Jl Katamso, south of the intersection with Jl Letjen Suprapto. *Eka Sukma Wisata Tour and Travel* are larger than most and have acquired a reputation for providing an efficient service. **Edelweiss**, Jl Irian Barat 47, T4531277, FFloor. **Eka Sukma Wisata Tour & Travel**, Jl Sisingamangaraja 92A, T70320421, F70367522. **Erni Tour & Travel**, Jl Brig Jend Katamso 43J, T4531227, F4516187. **King's Star Tour & Travel**, Jl Pemuda 24, T4515111, F4512349. **Mitra Tour & Travel**, Jl Jend A Yani 11. **Pacto**, Jl Brig Jend Katamso 359, T4510081, http://www.pacto.com/ **PT Best Hoidays Travel Service**, Jl Prof HM Yamin SH II/5, T4159048, F4531755, besthol@mail.idola.net.id Mr Erwin is an excellent travel agent (with good English). The office is in a rather inconvenient location but he will come to your hotel and can take credit card bookings, will also help with airport shuttles. **Sutrabu Tour & Travel**, Jl Kol Sugiono, T4510888, F4510366. **Trophy**, Jl Brig. Jend Katamso 33D-E, T4514888, F4510340.

Tour operators

Local Becak, sudaco, mesin becak (motorized becak), bis damri, metered taxi, unmetered taxi and kijang – if it moves, it can be hired. It is amazing how some of the mesin becaks keep going. The fare around town on an oplet (minibus) is 500Rp. For a ride on a *becak* expect to pay a minimum of 1,000Rp; with a bit of bargaining, taxis are often available for the same price as a becak; on a *mesin becak*, 1,000-1,500Rp. *Becaks* can be chartered for about 6,000Rp per hr. **Car hire**: *National Car Rental* (*Dharma Deli Hotel*), Jl Balai Kota 2, T4150313. *Avis* (*Nitour*), Jl Prof HM Yamin 21E, T4532191. Expect to pay about US$44 per day for self drive, rather less (around 200,000Rp) for car and driver. **Taxis**: can be rented by the day; ask at your hotel or T7865417, 4524659, 4520952, fares within Medan range from 5,000Rp to 15,000Rp.

Transport
66 km from Brastagi, 176 km from Prapat/ Lake Toba, 349 km from Sibolga, 728 km from Bukittinggi, 819 km from Padang, 594 km from Banda Aceh

Air Medan's **Polonia International Airport** is 3 km south of the town – effectively within the city. Construction of a new airport at Kuala Namu 12 km from Medan is reportedly underway, although it does not seem that this will be up and running until well into the millennium. A taxi from the city centre to the airport costs 9,000Rp. Or take a bus from Pinang Baris terminal (in direction of Amplas terminal) and get off at traffic lights on Jl Juanda, the airport is 500m on right (500Rp). Regular connections on *Mandala*, *Garuda/Merpati* and *Indonesian Airlines* with most Sumatran destinations, including **Padang**, **Banda Aceh**, **Batam**, **Pekanbaru** and **Nias**; several flights a day to **Jakarta** and other Indonesian towns beyond Sumatra.

See also 'International connections' below

Road Bus: Medan has 2 main bus terminals: Amplas and Pinang Baris. **Amplas terminal** is on Jl Medan Tenggara VII, 8½ km south of the city centre off Jl Sisingamangaraja, and serves all destinations south of Medan including Bukittinggi, Prapat and Lake Toba (6 hrs), Jakarta, Bali, Jambi, Dumai, Pekanbaru, Palembang and Sibolga. Get there by yellow oplet running south (Nos 24, 52 or 57), 500Rp. Major bus companies like *ALS* and *Makmur* have their offices on Jl Sisingamangaraja close to the terminal (both of these are at the 6½ km marker). *ANS* at Jl Sisingamangaraja 18 (opposite the Hero's Cemetery) is closer to the town centre. The **Pinang Baris terminal** is on Jl Pinang Baris (off Jl Gatot Subroto, which becomes Jl Binjei), about 9 km northwest of the city centre, and serves Banda Aceh and other destinations north of Medan including Bukit Lawang (leaving every 30 mins); buses to Brastagi 2 hrs, also leave from the Pinang Baris terminal. Get to the terminal by orange or green microlet running along Jl Gatot Subroto. Easier than taking one of the regular buses is to book a seat on a tourist minibus. There are several places around town that run buses to all the major tourist destinations, including Bukit Lawang, Brastagi, Lake Toba, Bukittinggi, Lhokseumawe and Sibolga (for Nias), including *Lagundri Tour*, Jl Pabrik Tenun 54 (out of town to the northwest); *Tobali Tour*, Jl Ir H Juanda Baru 52, T4536479. Information on other tourist transport outfits, including *Dolok Silau*, is available from tour agents. **Blue Timur 'taxis'** (in fact minibuses) for Binjei leave regularly from Jl Kumango which is parallel to Jl Perniagaan, north of the tourist office. For Bohorok and Bukit Lawang, see page 473. **Taxi**: most of the taxi companies are located at Jl Sisingamangaraja 60-107.

Women should expect a certain amount of unwelcome attention at the bus terminals

Train The station is on Jl Prof M Yamin. There is a limited rail network around Medan, but few use it.

Sea Boat: Medan's port, **Belawan**, is 26 km north of the city. There are money-changing facilities at the port – although rates are better in Medan – and a good range of other services. However, most people have little chance to savour the delectations of this busy port – transport to Medan is included in the fare of most ferry services and passengers are whisked onwards. Town buses for Belawan leave from the intersection of Jl Balai Kota and Jl Guru Patimpus, near the TVRI offices. Oplets also travel to Belawan (the destination is displayed). The Pelni vessel *Sinabung* and *Kelud* visit Medan on their fortnightly circuits (see page 982 for routes). Pelni's office is at Jl Kol Sugiono 5 (on the corner with Jl Cakrawati), T4518899. A number of other shipping firms also have their offices along Jl Kol Sugiono, including *Hanjin*, *Gesuri Lloyd* and *Maharani Express*.

International connections: There is not much difference in price between flights and ferries. **Air** Medan is a 'gateway' city and there are daily connections with Penang, Kuala Lumpur, Ipoh, Johor Bahru and Singapore. There are also weekly connections with Bangkok and with Vienna and Amsterdam (on Garuda). MAS, Silk Air, Pelangi, Garuda/Merpati, Mandala and Indonesian Airlines all operate international flights. **Boat** Ferry connections with Penang (Malaysia) from Belawan (Medan's port). Various companies run ferries. *Ekspres Bahagia* leave Medan/Belawan for Penang at 1000 Mon-Sat. From Penang they depart at 0900 Mon-Sat. They also operate ferries from Penang to Langkawi. From Penang they depart at 0800 Mon-Sat. The fare is M$90 1-way, M$160 return. Their agent in Medan is *Eka Sukma Wisata Tour and Travel*, Jl Sisingamangaraja 92A, T70320421, F70320954. The address of the company in Penang is *Ekspres Bahagia*, Ground Floor, Penang Port, Commission Shopping Complex, Jl Pesara King Edward, T04-2631943, F04-2631944. *Perdana Express* is another outfit that runs high speed ferries on the Medan-Penang route. From Medan boats leave at 1000 Tue-Sun; from Penang to Medan they depart at 0830 or 1000 Mon-Sat, journey time 4 hrs. The fares are the same as the *Ekspres Bahagia*. In Medan, *Perdana Express* have their offices at Jl Brig Jend Katamso 35C, T4566222, F4579324, and in Penang in the PPC Building (Ground floor), Jl Pesara King Edward, T04-2625630, F2625508. *Selasa Express* is yet another company operating ferries between Belawan and Penang and their agent in Medan is *Tobali Tour and Travel*, Jl Juanda Baru 52. All the companies offer free transfer between Medan and Belawan. *Indomas Express* and the *Kuala Perlis Langkawi Ferry Service (KPLFS)* run boats between Belawan and Lumut and Port Klang (Kuala Lumpur's port). The fare is the same as the Medan-Penang leg, M$90 1-way, M$160 return. Tickets for *Indomas* can also be booked through *Tobali Tour and Travel* (see above for address) and for *KPLFS* through Indoma Citra Agung, Jl Katamso 33D, T4518340. **Bus** An alternative way to get to Singapore without flying is to catch a bus to Dumai (a/c 25,000Rp, leaves at 2000, arrives 0600); then a ferry from Dumai to Batam Island (35,000Rp, leaves 0700, arrives 1500); and from Batam another ferry to Singapore (29,000Rp). The total journey is about 20 hrs.

Directory **Airline offices** *Bouraq*, Jl Brig Jend Katamso 43, T4150369. ***Cathay Pacific***, *Tiara Hotel Convention Centre*, Jl Cut Mutia, T45376088. ***Garuda***, reservations T327747, reconfirmation T080021747, *Dharma Deli Hotel*, Jl Balai Kota 2, T4516400, *Hotel Tiara Medan Convention Centre*, Jl Cut Mutia, T4514877, and Jl Suprapto 2, T4516066 (city check-in here). ***Malaysian Airlines (MAS)***, *Danau Toba International Hotel*, Jl Imam Bonjol 17, T4519333, F4569041. ***Merpati***, Jl Brig Jend Katamso 219, T321888. ***Pelangi***, c/o Malaysian Airlines, *Danau Toba International Hotel*, Jl Imam Bonjol 17, T4519333. ***Indonesian Airlines***, *Hotel Tiara Medan Convention Centre*, Jl Cut Mutia, T4158870. ***Silk Air***, 6th Floor, Bank Umum Servitia Building, Jl Imam Bonjol 23, T4537744; ***Singapore Airlines***, 6th Floor, Bank Umum Servitia Building, Jl Imam Bonjol 23, T4537744. ***SMAC***, Jl Imam Bonjol 59, T4564760. ***Thai***, *Dharma Deli Hotel*, Jl Balai Kota 2, T4510541.

Banks NB If travelling from Penang to Medan via Belawan Port, it is advisable to change money in Georgetown (Penang) before departure – the exchange rate is much better than in Medan. There are numerous banks in Medan, all fairly internationally-minded. Duta Bank makes cash advances against Visa and Mastercard. The Hong Kong Bank has a 24-hr ATM. There are also a number of money changers on Jl Katamso. **Bank Central Asia**, Jl Bukit Barisan 3 (will provide cash advances on Visa card). **Bank Dagang Negara**, Jl Jend A Yani 109. **Duta Bank**, Jl Sisingamangaraja (next to the *Garuda Plaza Hotel*). **Ekspor Impor (Bank Exim)**, Jl Balai Kota 8. **Bank Negara Indonesia**, Jl Jend A Yani 72. **Standard Chartered Bank**, Jl Imam Bonjol 17, T4538800. Money changers include: **King's Money Changer**, Jl Pemuda 24; and **PT Supra**, Jl Jend A Yani 101.

Communications Note that some telephone numbers changed at the beginning of 1999. **General Post Office:** lots of telephone offices around town. Jl Bukit Barisan 1 (on Merdeka Sq). **Telephone offices:** Wartel, Jl Bukit Barisan 1 (at the Central Post Office) for overseas calls and fax facility. There are additional Wartel offices all over town, including on Jl Sisingamangaraja (next to the *Hotel Deli Raya* and opposite the Mesjid Raya) and on Jl Irian Barat (just north of the intersection with Jl Let Jend MT Haryono). Telephone calls can also be placed from the *Tip Top Café* on Jl Jend A Yani. **Email access:** Over the last couple of years, there has been a proliferation of internet cafés. One of the best is in the *Novotel Soechi Medan*, Jl Cirebon 76A. *Pay@net*, Jl Ir H Juanda Baru 200. There is also a small email centre on the 1st floor of the Deli Plaza on Jl Guru Patimpus. There is a large email facility within the Central Post Office, Jl Bukit Barisan 1. **Courier offices:** *DHL*, Jl Cakrawati (facing the large new Bank Negara Indonesia building), T4519240 or 4538484, F4538564. *Federal Express*, Jl Kol Sugiono 2. *UPS*, Jl Katamso 35C. **Credit card offices:** *Diners Club International*, *Dharma Deli Hotel*, Jl Balai Kota 2, T4513331, F4513331.

Embassies & consulates **Belgium**, Jl Pattimura 459, T4527991. **Denmark**, Jl Hang Jebat 2, T4538028. **Germany**, Jl Let Jend Parman 217, T4537108. **India**, Jl Uskup Agung Sugiopranoto 19, T4531308. **Japan**, Jl Suryo 12, T4510533. **Malaysia**, Jl Diponegoro 11, T4511567. **Netherlands**, Jl Juanda, opposite *Pardede Hotel*, T4569853. **Norway**, Jl Zainul Arifin 55, T4510158. **Singapore**, Jl T Daud 3, T4513134. **Sweden**, Jl Hang Jebat 2, T4538028. **UK**, Jl Jend A Yani 2, T4518699. **USA**, Jl Imam Bonjol 13, T322200.

Medical facilities Clinics: *Bunda* (24 hrs), Jl Sisingamangaraja, T70321666. **Hospitals:** *Herna Hospital*, Jl Majapahit 118A, T4147715. *St Elizabeth's Hospital*, Jl Haji Misbah 7, T4144240. *Malahayati Hospital*, Jl Diponegoro, T4518766. *Gleneagles Hospital*, Jl Listrik 6, T4566268. New and reputed to be the best in town. Central.

Places of worship *Catholic Church*, Jl Pemuda. English service on a Sat evening – contact Dutch consulate for information. *Protestant Church*, Jl Sudirman.

Useful addresses Immigration office: Jl Binjai Km 6.2, T4512112. **PHPA:** Jl Sisingamangaraja, Km 5.5, T4523658. **Police station:** Jl Durian, T4520453.

Bukit Lawang

Bukit Lawang, sometimes also named, probably for tourist consumption, 'Gateway to the Hills', is a small community on the edge of the **Gunung Leuser Reserve**, an area of beautiful countryside. A few years ago Bukit Lawang was a comparatively quiet place with just a handful of guesthouses. This is no longer true. Thousands of people come here for the orang utans, the river and now there are bars, even discos. It is based upon a network of alleys lined with stalls, selling everything from toilet paper and sweet biscuits to camera film and batik paintings.

Phone code: 061
Colour map 1, grid B3

Direct buses leave from Medan's Pinang Baris terminal every 30 mins (3 hrs). Most tourists opt to take a tourist minibus run by *Tobali* of *Lagundri* tours. From Brastagi catch a bus to Medan and get off when it reaches route 25; from here, catch a regular bus to Bukit Lawang. There is 1 direct bus each day from Brastagi to Bukit Lawang via Medan.

Getting there
See Transport section, page 477 for further details

Orang Utan Rehabilitation Centre

Local sojourners come from Medan to frolic in the river, not to see the apes, so while the river may be a seething mass of humanity, feeding time is comparatively quiet

Just outside the village is the famous centre established in 1973 – fast developing into one of Sumatra's most popular tourist destinations. The work of the centre is almost entirely supported now by revenue from tourism. The orang utan (*Pongo pygmaeus*) is on the verge of extinction throughout its limited range across island Southeast Asia, and the centre has been established by the World Wide Fund for Nature to rehabilitate domesticated orang utans for life in the wild (see page 661). The problem is that there is a ready black market for cuddly orang utans. In Medan they sell for US$350. But when the young, friendly animals grow up into powerful, obstreperous adult apes, they are often abandoned. These sad creatures – or some of them at least – end up at Bukit Lawang. The usual immediate problem for these exiles from nature is malnutrition. Fed on a diet of food such as pizzas and beer, they are deficient in many essential nutrients. The centre puts them on a diet of milk and bananas, partly because these foods are highly nutritious and partly because it is so monotonous that they will be keen to forage for themselves. Between 1973 and 1993 the centre rehabilitated 179 animals. Another 35 have died at the centre. In total, the Gunung Leuser National Park probably supports about 2,000-3,000 apes; the carrying capacity of the park, though, is nearer 8,000.

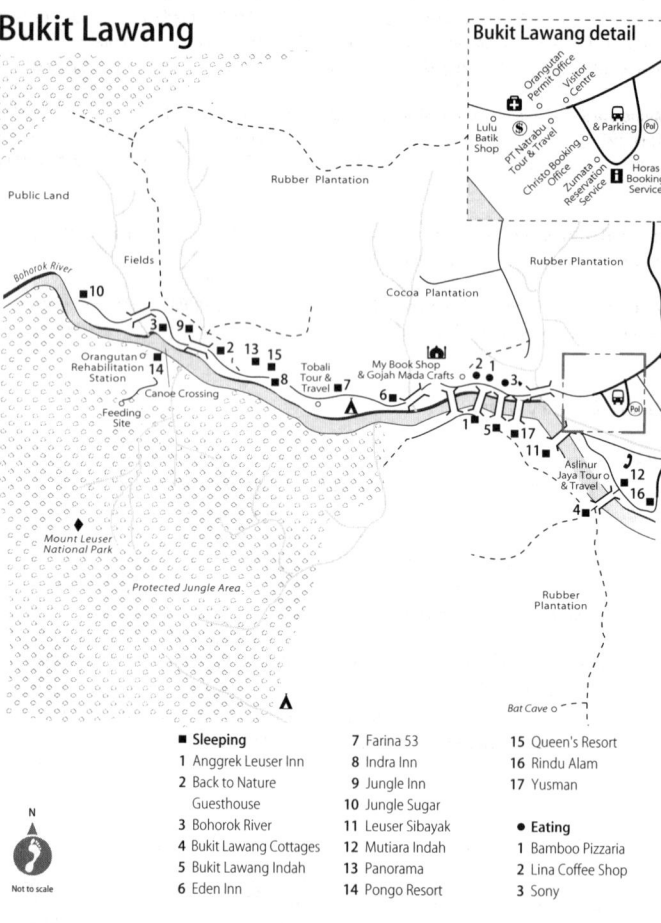

Bukit Lawang

■ **Sleeping**
1 Anggrek Leuser Inn
2 Back to Nature Guesthouse
3 Bohorok River
4 Bukit Lawang Cottages
5 Bukit Lawang Indah
6 Eden Inn
7 Farina 53
8 Indra Inn
9 Jungle Inn
10 Jungle Sugar
11 Leuser Sibayak
12 Mutiara Indah
13 Panorama
14 Pongo Resort
15 Queen's Resort
16 Rindu Alam
17 Yusman

● **Eating**
1 Bamboo Pizzaria
2 Lina Coffee Shop
3 Sony

Getting there & entry to the park

The entrance to the reserve is a 30 min walk from the village following the Bohorok River upstream, which then has to be crossed by boat; from there it is another 20 minutes or so up a steepish path to the feeding point. Visitors can see the apes during feeding times (0800-0900 and 1500-1600, you should aim to get there 5 mins beforehand). The times do sometimes change, so check at the PHPA office in Bukit Lawang. Leave Bukit Lawang 45 mins before feeding for the walk and river crossing. Afternoons are more crowded, especially at weekends; it is best to stay the night and watch a morning, weekday, feed if possible. Next door to the PHPA office is a Visitors Information Centre, with an excellent film in English on Mon, Wed and Fri at 2000, study room, a display, and small collection of relevant literature. The office is open 0700-1500 Mon-Sun. **NB** Passport must be shown before a permit is issued. Entrance to the centre and film is free, although a donation is requested to sustain their work. Guides can be hired from the PHPA office for 1, 2 or 3 day treks of varying difficulty; visitors have reported seeing gibbons, monkeys, orang utans etc. All visitors must obtain a permit from the PHPA office (1 day: 4,500Rp) before entering the park.

Excursions

Hiking

Hiking is the best way to experience the forest and see the wildlife. The visitors centre has handouts and maps of hiking trails and guesthouses, and may also have jungle trek guides. Hikes, with obligatory guide, range from a few hours to one week and cost US$15 per person for a one-day hike, US$35 per person per day for a two-day hike, including guide, transportation, permit, food and tent. It is possible to hike to **Brastagi** in three days at a cost of US$65. This trek is becoming less popular because so much of the route has been deforested. Instead, those visitors wishing to trek through true jungle should opt for the five to seven day hike to **Kutacane** (US$250). Most treks have a minimum lower limit of three to four people. These rates are fixed by the local tourist association. Note that these are arduous treks requiring fitness and good hiking boots; check the credentials of guides carefully – many lack experience (your guide should be able to produce a legal licence and permit). Some people have marvellous treks, followed by friendly orang utans which allow themselves to be petted (hardly aiding their rehabilitation); others see nothing. During the rainy season (roughly August-December) there can be very heavy downpours: a good waterproof can be essential.

Caves

There are a number of caves in the vicinity of Bukit Lawang. For the **Bat Cave** (1000Rp), take a torch and non-slip shoes; it is not an easy climb, a guide is recommended (5,000-10,000Rp). There is also a **rubber processing plant** close by – ask at the visitors centre for a handout and map.

Bohorok River
Beware of whirlpools & low branches - drownings have occurred

Floating down the Bohorok River on an inner tube has become a popular excursion. Tubes can be hired (2,500Rp per day) in the village for the 12 km (2-3 hours) journey to the first bridge. There is public transport from the bridge back to Bukit Lawang. For US$10 you can combine a day's trekking upstream, to return in the late afternoon by inner tube. Dry bags are provided for cameras and other valuables.

Tangkahan

Tangkahan lies about 40 km north of Bukit Lawang, next to the Gunung Leuser National Park. There is only one resort here, the **B-C** *Bamboo River Guesthouse*, which opened in 1998. It is owned by an English woman and a local senior guide, and an evening meal costs around 10,000Rp. No telephone contact – communication is by walky-talky. Around 10 rooms available. The guesthouse is on the Buluh River. What is special about this place is its proximity to unspoilt lowland rainforest, and the absence of tourists! No trekking is promoted around here, so bird and animal life is more active. It is possible to hike from here (guide strongly recommended), take a canoe trip down the Batang Serangan River, or visit some hot sulphur springs.
■ *Getting there: 5 hr chartered bus ride from Bukit Lawang – ask at the tourist office for more information. From Medan, catch a bus from the Pinang Baris terminal to Tangkahan (3 hrs). At the river crossing in Tangkahan, shout for the raft man!*

Camping A recent venture being organized through the Tourist Information Centre involves camping on the edge of the National Park, a two-hour walk from the village past the Bat Cave. The campsite is on the edge of a river and is very secluded. A great way to escape the crowds and witness nature first-hand. 15,000Rp buys a guide, tent and all your food and cooking equipment for one night.

Whitewater rafting A number of agents offer rafting trips on the nearby Wampu River, costing around US$35 per person per day. These are sometimes combined with a trek.

Essentials

Sleeping
■ *on map*
Price codes:
see inside front cover

The road ends at the bus stop, so reaching guesthouses further upstream means as much as a 25-min slog on foot

About 20 or so losmen line the Bohorok River up to the crossing-point for the reserve. Each year 1 or 2 more open, and the quality of those operating also seems to change month to month. Given Bukit Lawang's reliance on tourism, visitors are almost always able to find somewhere to sleep. However, if you arrive after 1700 on a Sat be prepared to hunt around for an empty bed – Indonesian weekenders flock here. Prices rise with the rush, although by walking upriver it is sometimes possible to escape the crowds.

B-C *Rindu Alam Hotel*, PO Box 20774, T545015. The furthest downstream of all the guesthouses, this is the closest Bukit Lawang gets to a hotel, 51 large, plain, clean fan rooms, with attached bathrooms (but no hot water). Attractive gardens, large restaurant/lobby area. **C** *Pongo Resort*, Bukit Lawang, Bohorok, Kode Pos 20774, T542574/523522, F549327/554284. Restaurant, barbecue, satellite TV, the poshest place here with 21 standard, superior and deluxe chalets. All rooms are clean with shower, basin and toilet, although fans only make an appearance in the deluxe. They are also on the small side. Price includes breakfast and park permit. As this place is right next to the rehab centre, the surroundings are particularly pleasant with a waterfall and good swimming in the river. Recommended.

D-F *Jungle Inn*, 14 rooms each with its own character (ask to look around and choose your favourite). Great jungle atmosphere but still reasonably clean and well-equipped. All rooms have own facilities, most with showers, very friendly and popular, excellent food, good value. Recommended. 25 mins, walk from PHPA office, towards the end of the track.

E *Bohorok River*, right next to the crossing point for the park and almost overhanging the river. The rooms are in a large building with balconies overlooking the water, good swimming. **E** *Queen's Resort*, about a 25 min walk from the PHPA office. It boasts a 'heated' pool which is more akin to a jacuzzi without the bubbles (empty when we last visited), food is poor. **E** *Wisma Bukit Lawang Cottages*, range of rooms available in this, one of the older and more established places in Bukit Lawang. Some are simple huts with shared mandis; others larger, more sophisticated rooms with attached bathrooms, fan and sitting area. Food is the usual fare and average to good. Pleasant management and attractive gardens. **E** *Wisma Leuser Sibayak*, T/F550576. The largest resort here, more expensive rooms are well kept with TV, fan, shower and phone, and worth the extra rupiah as the standard rooms are pretty standard, chalets set in open grounds, day hikes organized. Good food, buffet available in high season. Recommended.

F *Anggrek Leuser Inn*, the cheapest rooms here are above the restaurant so noise can be a problem, but rooms are clean and set in attractive grounds, shared mandi, pebble beach. **F** *Ariko Inn*, another quiet and secluded place next to the Bohorok River, and 15 mins' walk from the sanctuary. Large bamboo chalets, quiet and secluded, good for swimming as it is way upstream (and therefore not polluted by the effluent from other guesthouses), rock bottom rates and many extras including pool table, volley ball, chess, and other games. **F** *Back to Nature Guesthouse, (Kembalike Alam)*, small, dark and basic rooms with shared mandi on other side of the track from the river, good food is a plus and the rooms are clean, abundance of uncomfortable chairs and tables constructed from nobbly pieces of wood, run by a group of young, and slightly crazy, young men. **F** *Bukit Lawang Indah*, shared bathroom, clean, good food. **F** *Eden Inn* (15 mins' walk from PHPA office). Attractive views over the river but the basic rooms are falling into decrepitude. **F** *Farina 53*, opposite the campsite and just inside the park entrance, a 15 min walk from the PHPA offices. Medan T556948. The guesthouse is set on a steep hillside overlooking the river and path, and looks something like a large Swiss chalet, restaurant (cheap food), with renowned disco on Wed and Sat, clean rooms with own bathrooms, good value, lovely views of the river – monkeys clambering over the tin roofs can provide an early wake up call. **F** *Indra Inn*, another rock bottom place, simple rooms with mosquito nets, dingy communal mandis downstairs. **F** *Mutiara Indah* (*en route* to *Bukit Lawang Cottages*), quiet and secluded, very friendly. Recommended. **F** *Panorama Guesthouse*, very basic – and very cheap – with great views. **F** *Yusman Guesthouse*, family-run guesthouse with a central position, clean but simple rooms, some with attached showers, very friendly owners who will sing, given half a chance, cheap food, good budget place. Recommended.

Camping: free camping ground about a 15 min walk upriver towards the crossing-point for the reserve. Just inside the grand entrance arch to the Park. Pleasant surroundings but basic washing facilities.

Eating
● on map
Price codes:
see inside front cover

There are plenty of places to eat and most losmen have a restaurant of sorts attached. *Queen Emerald* is a popular and cheap place to eat, as is the *Jungle Inn* – famed for its fruit salads and hot jungle juice brewed from a concoction of local herbs. The *Wisma Leuser Sibayak* has an excellent reputation and the restaurant affords a good view of the river. Every Mon they host a generous buffet served by locals dressed in traditional wedding costumes. A good opportunity to sample a wide range of local dishes – and eat as much as you like (20,000Rp per person)! The restaurant at the *Wisma Bukit Lawang Cottages* does much the same. The *Bamboo Pizzeria* is more expensive but serves excellent, fresh, home-made pizzas with assorted toppings and mozzerella cheese, and cold beer. The *Lina Coffee Shop* is the one other place worth mentioning by name. It is 200m or so upstream from the village centre.

Tour operators

Visitors Information Centre (near the minibus stop), free maps and advice on hiking. Open 0900-1500 Mon-Sat, 1000-1500 Sun. They also sell a useful booklet on the Park and its wildlife and flora (12,000Rp). The Leuser Development Programme is based in Medan at the University of North Sumatra, Jl Dr Mansyur 68, Medan, T061-8216800, F061-8216808.

Transport

Road Bus: direct buses leave from Medan's Pinang Baris terminal, every 30 mins (3 hrs). There is a choice of large, slightly cheaper (3,000Rp) and slower buses, or quicker and marginally more expensive (3,500Rp) minibuses. But most tourists opt to take a tourist minibus run by *Tobali* of *Lagundri* tours (20,000Rp). From Brastagi, catch a bus to Medan and get off when it reaches route 25; from here, catch a regular bus to Bukit Lawang. There is 1 direct bus each day from Brastagi to Bukit Lawang via Medan. The tourist bus for the route from Brastagi to Bukit Lawang costs 25,000Rp. Buses leave Bukit Lawang at around 0830, after a free breakfast of tea/coffee and toast, 5 hrs, 15,000Rp. Tourist buses run from Bukit Lawang to Lake Toba at a cost of 35,000Rp. **Taxi**: for hire in Medan, 2 hrs.

Directory

Banks Losmen and tour companies will change money, but rates are poor so it is best to bring sufficient cash. **Communications Post Office:** none in Bukit Lawang, but some stalls sell stamps at a small mark up. They will also post letters. **Telephone:** Wartel office in the main 'village'.

Brastagi

Brastagi, or Berestagi, is a hill resort town, lying 1,300m above sea level on the Karo Plateau among the traditional lands of the Karo Batak people. Though Brastagi may not be a one horse town, it gives the impression of being a one road town. There is also the distinct feel that it has become a way-station, a sort of trucking stop between other more important places.

Phone code: 0628
Colour map 2, grid A1

Ins and outs

Getting there There are regular bus connections with Medan 2 hrs, Sidikalang 3 hrs and Sibolga 9 hrs.
See Transport section for further details Getting from Prapat on a public bus is a little more complicated involving changes, but there are tourist minibuses which run direct, 4 hrs, stopping at the Sipisopiso falls and the Batak 'palace' of Simalungan Permangtang Puruba *en route*.

Getting around Visitors can travel easily around town on foot, by hired bicycle and oplets. For the surrounding villages and towns cars can be hired. Dokars and oplets service some routes. **Tourist information** *Dinas Pariwisata* is on Jl Gundaling No 1. They have information on hotels and rather overpriced tours, which is is next to useless. The *Sibayak Guesthouse*, Jl Veteran 119, and the *Wisma Ginsata*, Jl Veteran 79, are much better sources of information. The *Sibayak* keeps a particularly useful comments book.

Background

Brastagi was established by the Dutch in the early 20th century as a retreat from the heat and humidity of the lowlands, and was frequented by Dutch planters from Sumatra's east coast and by planters, businessmen and officials from British Malaya. By the 1930s it had become not just a resort but also a retirement town, as Dutchmen who had spent their working lives in the East Indies decided they would also stay for their twilight years. This was not to last. The Japanese imprisoned most Europeans and after the war many of the villas were burned down during the fight for independence.

Sights

The town does not have many specific sights of interest, but its position, surrounded by active volcanoes, is memorable. Unfortunately, Brastagi has a rather uncared for feel, and it is dirty and featureless. Nonetheless, Brastagi is a good place to cool off after the heat and bustle of Medan, and play a little golf, hike, or go riding. It is a good base from which to explore the surrounding countryside.

For those without the time to visit the Batak villages outside Kabanjahe (see Excursions), there is a Batak village of sorts **Paceren** just outside town on the road to Medan, 100m past the *Rose Garden Hotel*. It is rather run down and dirty, with a few Batak houses interspersed with modern houses; however, it is in some respects more authentic than those which have been preserved, showing how living communities are adapting to the changing world. ■ *400Rp for admission to village.* Behind the market, opposite the monument, are a couple of ersatz **Batak houses** – another excuse to create an area of stalls. Just 200m or so up Jalan Gunderling from here is a strange Buddhist temple – the **Vihara Buddha**. How the architect managed to arrive at this fusion of styles is not clear, but 'ungainly' would not be an unkind description. The general goods **market** behind the bus station is worth a wander. The market opposite the Monument is less good, with fresh fruit and vegetables, western goods and some tourist trinkets.

Excursions

Kabanjahe Meaning 'Ginger garden', Kabanjahe is 12 km south of Brastagi and easily accessible by bus. It lies on the main road and scores of buses and oplets make the journey. It is a local market town of some size and little charm, but it is worth visiting on Monday market day. Kabanjahe is an important communication town; from here it is possible to walk to traditional villages of the *Karo Batak* people (see below). There is one hotel and a losmen. ■ *Getting there: regular buses from the station on Jalan Veteran.*

Karo Batak villages

Karo Batak villages are to be found dotted all over the hills around Brastagi. The more traditional villages are not accessible by road and must be reached on foot; to visit these communities it is recommended to hire a guide (ask at your hotel or the tourist centre). It can make sense to charter a bemo for the day – a great deal more ground can be covered.

Two villages which can be visited with relative ease from Kabanjahe are Lingga and Barusjahe. Both can be reached by microlite from Kabanjahe. This ease of access has inevitably resulted in rather 'touristy' villages. **Lingga** is about 4 km northwest of Kabanjahe and is a community of about 30 Batak houses, of which there are about a dozen traditional longhouses. ■ *An 'entrance fee' of 300Rp must be paid at the Tourist Information Centre in the main square. Overpriced carvings for sale. Photographs of the local people will require payment.* **Barusjahe** is slightly more difficult to get to and as a result is marginally more 'traditional', but can still be reached by microlite from Kabanjahe. It is rather a dirty village with very few houses in the traditional style, but there are a few over two centuries old (and as a result are decaying badly). The soaring roofs are particularly impressive. ■ *Getting there: for Lingga and Barusjahe, catch a bus from the bus station on Jalan Veteran to Kabanjahe, and from there a microlite or bemo onwards. In Kabanjahe they leave from the intersection of Jalan Pala Bangun, Jalan Veteran and Jalan Bangsi Sembiring.*

Dokan is a fine Karo Batak village which lies halfway between Kabanjahe and Sipisopiso, where villagers are less inclined to hassle. ■ *Getting there: catch Simas bus at the bus terminal in Kabanjahe and ask to be set down at the Dokan turn (13 km from Kabanjahe). It is then a 3 km walk to the village. A donation is expected. Buses on to Sipisopiso are usually crowded.*

Sipisopiso waterfalls
If you take the tourist bus to Prapat and Lake Toba, it will stop here on the way; a special trip is not necessary

There are waterfalls at Sipisopiso, a one hour drive southeast of Brastagi and 24 km from Kabanjahe. The falls cascade through a narrow gap in the cliffside and then fall 120m down to Lake Toba. It is possible to walk along a spur to a small gazebo for a good view of the falls, or to walk to the bottom and back takes about one hour. For the less energetic, there are the usual array of souvenir stalls and warungs that congregate whenever an *objek wisata* gets to be on the standard tour itinerary. Inspite of the commercialism, the falls are a pretty spectacular sight. There is no accommodation here, but from Sipisopiso towards Prapat is 'Siantar Hotel', a nice stop for coffee (and fried bananas!). In its garden and restaurant you have a superb view of the lake, but despite its name you cannot sleep there, it is only a restaurant. ■ *Getting there: catch a bemo to Merek (1 hr) and ask for the falls (a 30-min walk). An easier, and probably cheaper, way to see the falls is by taking one of the tourist minibuses between Brastagi and Lake Toba. These tend to stop at the falls en route (just 3 km off the main road) and at the Batak 'palace' of Simalungan Permangtang Puruba (500Rp).*

Hiking
Many of the 'guides' have little experience, check their credentials carefully

It is possible to hike through spectacular countryside, all the way to Bukit Lawang from Brastagi in three days. However, the government is anxious about visitors disturbing this culturally sensitive area and trekkers should take the time and care to organize trips properly. Ask in town at the *Sibayak Guesthouse* or at the *Rafflesia Tourist Information Service*, Jalan Veteran 84, for up-to-date information on trekking. There are numerous 'guides' offering treks to Bukit Lawang; note that this is a difficult and demanding trek requiring a degree of fitness and good walking boots. Most people trek this route in the other direction, from Bukit Lawang to Brastagi (see page 475).

Mount Sibayak

Sibayak lies northwest of Brastagi at 2,095m and can be climbed in a day, but choose a good day, weatherwise, and leave early for the best views (and to avoid rain). Take the trail from behind Gundaling Hill, asking at your hotel for directions before setting out. Guides can be easily found (again, ask at your hotel – they will charge 15,000-30,000Rp depending on the size of the party), a map of the route is available from the *Tourist Information Office* and information from either the *Ginsata* or

Sibayak guesthouses. Wear good walking shoes and take a sweater as it can be chilly. About two to three hours to the summit, along a logging road, or alternatively there is a jungle trek, quicker if you take a bemo to Semangat Gunung, in the Daulu valley. Over the summit, the descent is down 2,000 plus steps, to Hot Water and **Sulphur Springs** (entrance fee charged). The sulphur is collected by local people and is used as medicine and as a pesticide.

Mount Sinabung Sinabung, which rises to 2,454m to the west of Brastagi, is another popular climb. There are now three routes up the volcano. The longest established is well marked, but even so is probably unwise to undertake without a guide – heavy rain and mist can make it dangerous. Seven people disappeared here in 1996/1997, when mist made it impossible for them to find the path. The other two routes are less obvious. Maps are available from the *Sibayak guesthouses*. To climb the mountain without a guide, catch a bus to Kabanjahe (300Rp). From there take another bus to Kuta Buluh Simoke (1,000Rp). From Kuta Buluh Simoke it is a 45-minute walk to Mardingding, where there are homestays. The path from the village passes a restaurant; fork left just after the restaurant (do not continue along the main path). This path then passes a house and on the left you will see a small hut; you need to turn left again onto another path which passes the hut. The route then works its way through the forest for one hour and is relatively well marked with arrows and string. As the path leaves the forest it becomes very steep and enters a rock gully (also steep). The route passes an old campsite and then a cliff overhang decorated with graffiti. (This makes a good shelter in bad weather as hot steam issues through vents.) After around three to four hours in total, the path reaches the summit; paths skirt the crater lip but care is needed. To climb the mountain take good hiking boots, a jumper, a change of clothes, and a water bottle. Tents can be hired from the *Sibayak guesthouses* (500Rp). Leeches can be a problem.

Essentials

Sleeping
■ *on map*
Price codes:
see inside front cover

Brastagi is not a particularly attractive town, but it does have a selection of some of the best losmen in Sumatra. Not only are the rooms clean and well maintained, but the owners go out of their way to provide travellers with information on the surrounding area. They arrange trips to traditional ceremonies, inform travellers how to climb mountains and hike, and are generally highly constructive.

AL-A *International Sibayak*, Jl Merdeka, T91301, F91307, sibayak@indosat.net.id Restaurant, pool, health club, tennis and squash, large sprawling hotel with over 100 rooms about 1 km out of town, comfortable and well-appointed rooms. **A** *Sinabung Resort*, Jl Kolam Renang, T91400. Restaurant, pool, new

Brastagi

■ Sleeping
1 Bukit Kubu
2 Elshaddi Guesthouse
3 Ginsata & Wisma Ginsata
4 Losmen Merpati
5 Losmen Sibayak Guesthouse
6 Losmen Timut
7 Rose Garden
8 Rudang
9 Sibayak International
10 Sibayak Multinasional
11 Wisma Sibayak

● Eating
1 Eropah
2 Raymond, Tobali Tour & Putra Nusa Mandago Money Changer
3 Sehat

100-room hotel with golf, tennis, health centre, sauna, disco, satellite TV. Out of town and used mainly by weekenders from Medan and tour groups. Discounts available during the week. **A-B** *Berastagi Megaview Hotel*, Jl Raya Medan, T91650, F91652. Despite the quite revolting name, this hotel is really surprisingly tasteful – though over-large, the rooms are in a series of 2-storeyed blocks with balconies, there is a good heated pool, and discounts are available during the week. **A-B** *Rudang*, Jl Picaran, T91348, 1 km out of town on the road to Medan. Restaurant, pool. There are 2 *Rudangs* – an old wing and 100m or so up the road, the newer hotel. Both are plain and uninspired and feel only half alive, though the rooms are OK.

B *Brastagi Cottages*, Jl Gundaling, T91524. A/c, restaurant, large rooms, big garden, hot water, great views. **B** *Bukit Kubu*, Jl Sempurna 2 (about 1 km out of town on the road to Medan), T20832. Basic restaurant with average food but crisp linen (this is not a restaurant but a dining room). On paper this should be the place to stay in Brastagi, a Dutch-era hotel in extensive grounds with its own small 9-hole golf course and tennis, but it has been allowed to fall into such a state of disrepair that in a few years it may not exist. The large rooms in the original wing are the cheapest and have some moth-eaten charm with their 1930s furniture and wooden floors. But the roof leaks, the beds have seen too many buttocks, and the basins are cracked. The new rooms are better – reasonably serviceable, a place to come for nostalgia buffs. **B** *Danau Toba*, Jl Gundaling, T20946. A/c, pool.

C *Sibayak Multinational*, Jl Pendidikan 93, T91031. The third and up-market arm of the *Sibayak* 'group', Dutch-era villa with new chalets, hot water and verandahs, comfortable and well run and the best place in this price category.

D-E *Losmen Merpati*, Jl Trimurti 68, T91157. Behind the main road, so less noisy, wc and shower. Recommended. **E** *Elshaddi* (formerly the *Crispo Inn*), Jl Veteran 65-67, T91023. Facing the monument, this place is friendly and welcoming with hot water showers and good food. Convenient location at the top of town. **E** *Ginsata Hotel*, Jl Veteran 79, T91441 F91513. Restaurant. This is on the main road through town and can be noisy, but the rooms are well kept and clean and the management is friendly. However, the sister establishment, the *Wisma Ginsata*, is a better bet (see below).

F *Dieng*, Jl Udara 27. Colonial house with rather run-down rooms, but friendly management and good information. Recommended. **F** *Losmen Sibayak Guesthouse*, Jl Veteran 119, T91122, F91095. Restaurant, this is the mid-range place of the 3 *Sibayaks*. Quiet, very well run with clean rooms and good food, including home made pizzas and good Indonesian dishes, videos shown nightly, excellent source of information (useful comments book), bag store room, bicycle hire, tours available, small library, some rooms with attached mandi, dorm beds available. Recommended. **F** *Wisma Ginsata*, Jl Veteran 79, T91441, F91513. Restaurant. This guesthouse is set down a track behind the *Ginsata Hotel*, well-priced rooms in a converted private house; quiet and well maintained with plants and a relaxed atmosphere, Telah Bangun organizes rafting and trekking trips and the losmen is a good source of information. Recommended. **F** *Wisma Sibayak*, Jl Udara 1, T91683. Popular place and good source of information, with books in which travellers have written about their experiences, sister losmen to *Sibayak* and slightly cheaper, rooms have shared mandis and there are also dorm beds available, tasty food; every Sat evening there is an Indonesian buffet with a dozen or so local dishes, followed by a dancing show. CNN news and videos in the evenings, will exchange money very reasonably, very well managed, tours, bikes for hire. Recommended.

Being a trucking stop, there are a good number of restaurants strung out along Jl Veteran – serving mainly ubiquitous Padang food. Fruits grown in the area include avocados and passion fruit (*marquisa*), the latter of which is made into a delicious and warming hot drink.

Eating
● *on map*
Price codes:
see inside front cover

Mid-range: *Raymond Coffee Shop*, Jl Veteran 49. Steaks, jaffles, various Indonesian dishes as well as good cakes – chocolate, pineapple etc. **Cheap**: *Asia*, Jl Veteran, close to Mamaken Souvenirs. Very good Chinese restaurant. *Eropah*, Jl Veteran 48G. International and Chinese dishes, long established reputation. **Sehat**, Jl Veteran 134. Good Chinese, friendly service. **Very cheap**: *Irfan*, Jl Veteran 79. Padang food.

Foodstalls: there are many open-air warungs serving good, fresh food, using the temperate fruit and vegetables grown in the surrounding countryside. *Jl Veteran* has the best selection. The market near the monument just off Jl Veteran sells fresh fruit and vegetables.

Entertainment Traditional dancing and buffet meal every Sat evening at *Wisma Sibayak*.

Shopping **Antiques and handicrafts** Sold in several shops along Jl Veteran. Try the *Modesty Souvenir Shop* at Jl Veteran 33 or *Mamaken* at Jl Veteran 16, which sell mostly Batak pieces – carvings, calendars, some textiles.

Sport **Golf** Nine-hole course (very short) at the *Bukit Kubu Hotel*, Jl Sempurna 2. Green fees, 20,000Rp. Clubs ('stick') hire, 25,000Rp. **Horse riding** Ask the men and boys, who are to be found with their horses waiting for custom around the more expensive hotels and at the fruit market. **Swimming** Non-residents can use the large pool at the *Hotel International Sibayak* (5,000Rp). **Tennis** *Bukit Kubu Hotel*, Jl Sempurna 2. Court rental, 4,500Rp. Racket hire, 7,000Rp.

Tours & tour operators The best are those attached to the *Sibayak* and *Ginsata losmen* – arrange canoe or raft trips along the **Alas River** (to the northwest of Brastagi (see the map on page 527) and the entry on page 528). The journey passes through the **Gunung Leuser Nature Reserve** with traditional villages and tropical rainforest. A 3-day trip should cost about US$80, all inclusive. Alternatively, take a jungle trek (with a guide) through the reserve – a 3-day trek costing about US$60. Ask for details at the *Sibayak Guesthouse* or the *Wisma Ginsata*. More expensive 4-6 day white water rafting trips are organized by *Pacto Tours* (in association with *Sobek Expeditions*, USA). Contact *Pacto*, Jl Surabayu 8, T3848634. Guesthouses in town will also organize tours to local Batak ceremonies. *Lagundri Tours*, Jl Veteran 55.

Transport
68 km from Medan,
147 km from Prapat

Local Bicycle hire: from the *Losmen Sibayak* and *Wisma Sibayak*. **Car hire**: from tour and travel agents (see above). **Dokars**: for short local journeys. In Brastagi these are known as *sados*, apparently a word which is taken from the French *dos à dos* – or back-to-back – referring to the way that passengers sit. **Oplets**: around town and to nearby villages.

Road Bus: the bus station is at the south end of the main road, Jl Veteran. Regular connections with Medan 2 hrs, Sidikalang 3 hrs and Sibolga 9 hrs. Getting to Prapat, for Lake Toba, on a public bus is a little more complicated. It is necessary to change twice, in Kabanjahe and Pemangtangsiantar. Minibuses and oplets travel to Kabanjahe continuously; from there, buses leave for Pemangtangsiantar every 30 mins between 0800 and 1500; from P Siantar to Prapat there are buses every 30 mins, 1 hr. There are a couple of alternative and less used routes to Toba and Samosir. One is to catch a bus to Haranggaol, on the north side of Lake Toba. Ferries leave from Haranggaol for Tuk Tuk and Ambarita on Samosir every Mon and Thu at 1300 and 1500, 4 hrs. An easier way to get to Lake Toba is to take one of the tourist minibuses which run direct from Brastagi to Prapat, 4 hrs. They also stop at the Sipisopiso falls and the Batak 'palace' of Simalungan Permangtang Puruba *en route*. Companies that run these services include *Tobali Tour*, Jl Veteran 49 (in the *Raymond Coffee Shop*), *Lagundri Tour*, Jl Veteran, and *Dolok Silau*. For Bukit Lawang either catch one of the direct tourist minibuses or take a public bus to Medan and change buses there for Bukit Lawang. **Taxi**: share taxis sometimes run to Medan and most leave from either side of Jl Veteran near the intersection with Jl Mesjid.

Directory **Banks** There are several banks and money changers in town, and they will change most varieties of TCs denominated in most major currencies. *Bank Negara Indonesia*, Jl Veteran 53. *Putra Nusa Mandago Money Changer*, Jl Veteran 47. *PT Pura Buana International*, Jl Veteran. There are 2 authorized Lake Toba money changers, of which *Lagundri Tours*, Jl Veteran 55, gives the slightly better rate. **Communications** Post Office: Jl Veteran (by the monument at the top of the road). **Telephone**:

Wartel office for international telephone calls and fax service, Jl Veteran (by the Bank Negara Indonesia).
Medical facilities Health centre: Jl Veteran 30.

This is a small, unremarkable town, 75 km southwest of Brastagi, which serves an important 'linking' function. From here it is possible to travel north, along the valley of the Alas River to Kutacane and the Gunung Leuser National Park (see page 528), and from there to Takengon and the Gayo Highlands, and finally to Banda Aceh at the northern tip of Sumatra. Alternatively, it is possible to travel west to the coast and then north along the coast, again to Banda Aceh (see page 522 for a summary of the west coast route). The countryside around here is locally known for the quality of its coffee.

Sidikalang
Colour map 2, grid A1

Sleeping A range of hotels and losmen is available including the **D-E** *Hotel Merapi*, small, basic rooms, some are dirty so ask to see the rooms available before checking-in, insects galore.

Transport Bus: regular connections with Pangururan, Kutacane and Brastagi.

Tongging is a small town on Lake Toba's northern shore. Like the much more popular Samosir Island, it is possible to swim in the lake and generally relax. The tourist infrastructure here is not nearly as developed though, although it is a good base to see the **Sipisopiso falls** (see page 479) and also a number of relatively untouristic Batak villages, including **Silalahi**. Tongging can also be used as an alternative route to Samosir – there are boats from Tongging to Samosir via Haranggaol every Monday at 0730 (see below).

Tongging
Colour map 2, grid A1

Sleeping E-F *Wisma Sibayak Guesthouse Tongging*, Jl Silalahi.

Transport Bus: from Brastagi there are direct bus connections with Tongging, about 1 an hour in the afternoon, from Jl Kapiten Mumah Purba (1,200Rp). Alternatively, take a bus or bemo to Kabanjahe (300Rp) and from there a minibus to Simpang Situnggaling, 1 hr (600Rp). From here there are minibuses to Tongging, 1 hr (700Rp). Leave enough time as buses only run through to about 1600 and there is a lot of hanging around. **Boat** There is a boat from Tongging to Haranggaol every Mon at 0730; this then links up with the 1500 boat from Haranggaol to Ambarita.

Pemangtangsiantar

Pemangtangsiantar, better known simply as **Siantar**, is the second largest city in North Sumatra, and has built its wealth on the tea, tobacco, rubber and oil palm cultivated in the surrounding countryside. It is here that Muslim North Sumatra gives way to Christian North Sumatra. Batak tombs make an appearance and the city is richly dotted with churches. The old part of town, centred on Independence Square or Lampangan Merdeka, is the most attractive, with some Dutch-era villas and tree-lined streets. But most visitors simply pass by Siantar on the route from Medan to Lake Toba.

Phone code: 0622
Colour map 2, grid A2

The **Museum Simalungun** is at Jalan Sudirman 20 and has a reasonable ethnographic collection of Simalungun Batak artefacts, which are poorly displayed and explained. There are also some colonial exhibits. ■ *0800-1200, 1400-1700 Mon-Sat, admission by small donation.* The **Central Market** located between the parallel Jalan Dr Sutomo and Jalan Merdeka is rather gloomy but large and bustling, while the **Siantar Zoo** has a poorly kept collection of Sumatran wildlife. The only other 'sight' is the rather fulsomely titled **International Museum Wildlife Gallery** on Jalan Menambin, just south of Lampangan Merdeka.

B *Siantar*, Jl W R Supratman 3, T21091, F21736. A/c, restaurant, pool, colonial hotel (built in 1912) with garden, 80 good rooms, hot water, friendly, tennis court. Recommended.

Sleeping

C *Parbina Puri International*, Jl Jend A Yani 108, T26505, F52505. Some a/c, 50 comfortable rooms. **E** *Garuda*, Jl Merdeka 33. Shared mandi and dirty. **F** *Delima*, Jl Thamrin 131.

Eating Several restaurants – the usual range of rumah makan – around the central market. One of the best Indonesian restaurants is the *Rumah Makan Nasional*, Jl Merdeka (close to Lampangan Merdeka).

Transport 128 km from Medan, 103 km from Brastagi, 48 km from Prapat. **Bus**: there are 2 bus stations. **Stasiun Sentral** for Medan. **Stasiun Parlusan** for Prapat 1¼ hrs, Sibolga, Bukittinggi, Kabanjahe and Brastagi (changing at Kabanjahe) 3 hrs.

Directory **Banks** Bank Rakyat Indonesia, on the corner of Jl Sudirman and Jl Merdeka. Several other banks on Jl Merdeka and Jl Dr Sutomo. **Communications** Post Office: Jl Sutomo 2. Telephone Office: *Wartel*, Jl Dr Sutomo (next to the Central Market) and Jl Merdeka 128 (just south from the Central Market). **Tour companies & travel agents** *C V Titipan Kilat*, Jl Merdeka 24. *Trophy Tour*, Jl Merdeka 340.

Lake Toba

Colour map 1, grid B3 Lake Toba and the surrounding countryside is one of the most beautiful areas in Southeast Asia. The cool climate, pine-clothed mountain slopes, the lake and the sprinkling of church spires give the area an almost alpine flavour. After Medan or Padang, it is a welcome relief from the bustle, heat and humidity of the lowlands. The vast inland lake lies 160 km south of Medan and forms the core of Batakland in both a legendary and a geographical sense. The lake covers a total of 1,707 sq km and is the largest inland body of water in Southeast Asia (87 km long and 31 km across at its widest point). Lodged in the centre of the lake is Samosir Island, one of Sumatra's most popular destinations.

Ins and outs

Getting there There is only 1 way to get to Lake Toba and that is by road. The majority of visitors either approach from Medan, usually via Brastagi, or from the south via Padangsidempuan (the road to Bukittinggi and Padang). Taking the Trans-Sumatran Highway from Medan is a fairly fast and direct route, taking about 4 hrs on a good day. A more leisurely and certainly more picturesque run up to the hill town of Brastagi. From there the route passes through the Karo Batak highlands and runs south along the east side of Lake Toba, taking in the Sipisopiso waterfall. This takes longer (about 6 hrs) as the road is not as good – but it is a more interesting and scenic route.

Getting around Lake Toba's 2 main destinations are the town of Prapat on the 'mainland' and the island of Samosir. Buses drop passengers off in Prapat. From here there are regular passenger ferries from Samosir Island. A car ferry runs from Ajibata, just south of Prapat. Passenger ferries drop passengers off at various points on the Tuk Tuk peninsula, usually close to their chosen guesthouse or hotel. The crossing takes about 35 mins. Once on Samosir, it is possible to hire cars and motorbikes. But better to hire a bicycle and slow the pace. There are also several attractive hikes and walks on the island.

Background

Lake Toba was formed after a massive volcanic explosion 75,000 years ago, not dissimilar – although far more violent – to the one that vaporized Krakatoa in the late 19th century. The eruption of Toba is thought to have been the most powerful eruption in the last million years. Michael Rampino and Stephen Self, of New York University and the University of Hawaii respectively, believe that it could have triggered the onset of the last ice age by lowering northern hemisphere temperatures by 3-5 °C for a year. This would have allowed snow to lie year-round in many areas, so reflecting light and lowering temperatures still further, turning a 'volcanic winter' into an ice age. It is not only one of the highest lakes in the world at 900m above sea level, but also one of the deepest at 529m. The area is now volcanically dormant, the only indication of latent activity being the hotsprings on the hill overlooking Pangururan (see page 502). The fact that Lake Toba's water is so warm for a lake at close to 1,000m leads one to assume that there must be some hot underwater too.

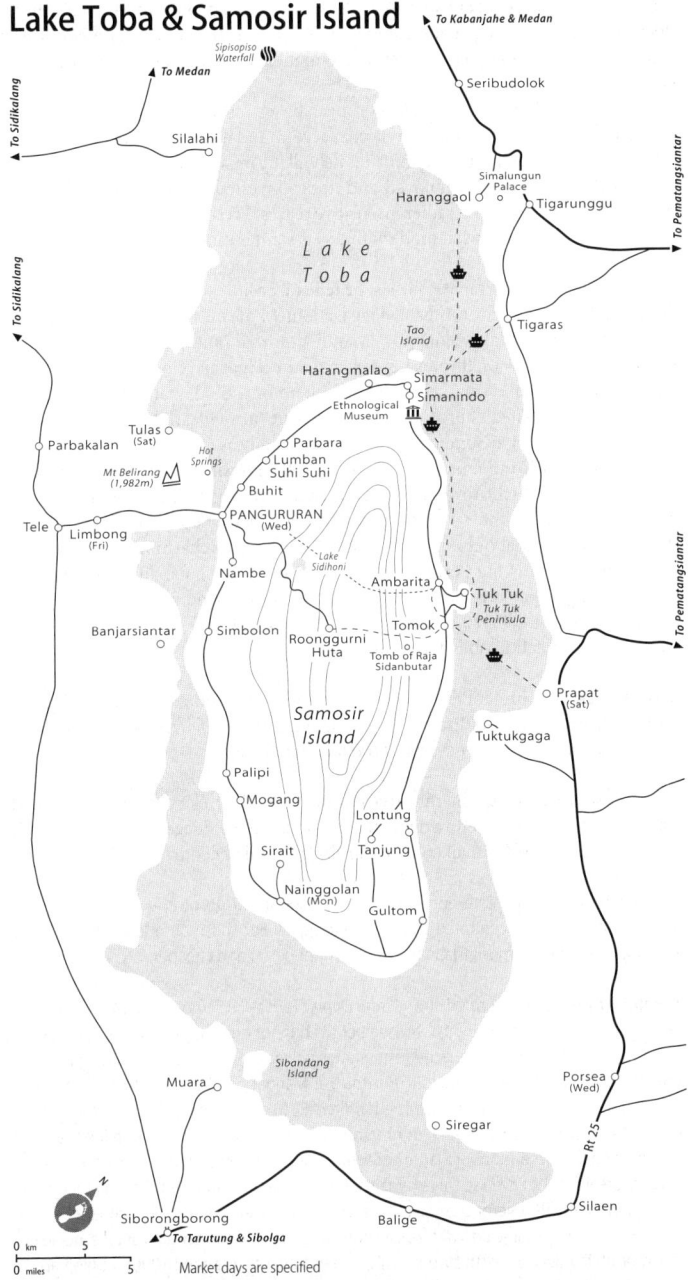

Lake Toba & Samosir Island

Prapat

Phone code: 0625
Colour map 2, grid B2

Prapat, or Parapat, is a small resort on the east shores of Lake Toba frequented by the Medan wealthy, and increasing numbers of Asian tourists from beyond Indonesia. It was established by the Dutch in the 1930s, although today most Western visitors merely breeze through en route to Samosir Island (but must pay 1,000Rp entrance for the privilege). There are stunning views over the lake, but unfortunately there doesn't seem to have been any coherent attempt to plan the development of the town. This means that there are architectural monstrosities side-by-side with elegant villas.

Prapat gives off the air of a 1950s European beach resort, with its pedaloes, metal railings, light blue paint and low-rise villa accommodation. This would be a great selling point for nostalgists, but unfortunately all the most attractive hotels are being allowed to slide into ruin, unloved and under-invested. Instead money is being poured into new, large and rather insensitive places. Presumably, market researchers have concluded that what modern toursists want is modern hotels.

Sights

There are few sights in Prapat. The best **beaches** are a little way out of town – but easily walkable – like those at Ajibata village, about 1 km south of Prapat. Saturday is market day when Bataks selling local handicrafts and 'antiques' converge on the town and particularly on the market area at **Pekan Tigaraja**, close to the ferry dock for Samosir. A smaller market is also held here on Tuesday and Thursday. The bright, rust-red roofed church above the town sits in well cared for gardens, with views over the lake. On Sunday, services have as many as 8-10 hymns.

The **tourist office**, *Pusat Informasi*, is on Jl P Samosir, under the archway that welcomes visitors to the town. However, there is virtually no information available here and it is hard to know why it exists. A fading *Visit China 1992* poster is stuck to the wall – which just about sums it up, notwithstanding the charming girls who work here. More useful is the Periplus 'North Sumatra, Lake Toba and Medan' map, which has a good colour map of Lake Toba, Samosir Island and the surrounding area at a scale of 1:250,000. There is also the **Batak Cultural Centre** on Jl Josep 19 which has information on Batak cultural events.

Excursions

Samosir Island with its Batak stone chairs and tables and *rumah adat*, is only a 30-minute boat trip from Prapat. ■ *Getting there: regular ferries (see page 494); or charter a speedboat to visit the sights (100,000-150,000Rp).*

Treks

Buta Sinaga, aka 'Mr Jungle' runs treks from Toba. The treks visit hot springs and waterfalls and trekkers spend a night in a tree house. Buta Sinaga, Jl Panggarajim 17, T41729, maruba16@hotmail.com or maruba16@mailcity.com

Sleeping

■ *on maps, pages 487 & 490*
Price codes: see inside front cover

During Indonesian public holidays, book ahead

Most of the more expensive hotels are on the lakefront or up on the hillsides. Cheaper accommodation is concentrated along Jl Haranggaol. For those on a lower budget, the accommodation on Samosir Island is without doubt better and cheaper.

A *Hotel Wisata Bahari* (formerly the *Wisma Danau Toba*), Jl P Samosir 3-6, T41302. Restaurant. A place much like the *Toba Hotel* (see below) but not quite as good value, rooms have balconies and attractive views, good restaurant, small beach, and there is a large garden on the lake side of the hotel. **A** *Natour Parapat*, Jl Marihat 1, T41012, F41019. Restaurant. Dutch-built pre-war hotel (although it is hard to tell) in attractive position overlooking the lake, with its own beach and gardens running down to the lake side. Though it has a good position and the pretensions of a large hotel, the rooms are only average. Room rate includes a buffet breakfast, but even so there remains the sense that the hotel is reliant on tour group trade and is a trifle overpriced, given the competition. **A** *Niagara*, Jl Pembangunan 1, T41028, F41233, niagara@ibm.net A/c, restaurant, pool, golf and tennis, karaoke, horse riding, mountain bikes, disco, the works. This is a newish hotel (opened 1996) set high above the town, with great views over the lake. One wonders how it was ever permitted, so monstrous is it, but the 200 odd rooms and facilities are the best available. The disadvantage is that it is not very convenient for exploring Prapat, as it is a 1½ km walk down (though there is a shuttle bus). Good value. **A** *Quality Siantar Hotel*, Jl Sisingamangaraja 8, T41564, F41565. A/c, restaurant, small pool, hotel away from the town 500m down the main road to Medan, it is built below the road on the lake so the highway doesn't intrude too much, rooms are above average with balconies, satellite TV and minibar, popular with tour groups. **A** *Wisma Retta*, Jl Kebudayaan, T41071, F41071 (Medan T625911). Restaurant, pool, built at the end of 1995 with just 15 rooms but already looking a trifle worn, close to the lake although swimming is restricted to the pool (a bit murky on our last visit), rooms are clean and well appointed with satellite TV and hot water, at this price you'd expect more than a hot water mandi, but breakfast is thrown in with the room rate. **A-B** *Patra Jasa*, Jl Siuhan, 4 km north of town at the 169 km mark on the road to Medan, T41796, F41536. A/c, restaurant, pool, great position high above the lake, with own golf course and lovely grounds, but it's inconveniently out of town and there's no chance of pottering out for a dip in the lake.

B *Danau Toba International Cottages*, Jl Nelson Purba, T41583, T41640, set above the lake and overlooking the ferry dock. Rooms are OK with good views over the lake, but the hotel is having some trouble drumming up custom, so heavy discounts are available, the best rooms are in a small row of Batak cottages right on the lake front with steps down to the water – not that swimming here is that attractive. **B** *Hotel Tarabunga*, Jl Kol Sinaga 20, T41700. Restaurant runs down to a small private beach and swimming area, one of the older hotels that gives off a distinct whiff of neglect –intentionally retro, rooms are large and bare with good balconies and views, and the room rate includes breakfast. A little bit of investment could make this into a great place to stay. **B** *Parapat View Hotel*, Jl Sidaha Pintu 7, T41375. Restaurant, small pool, new hotel set quite high above the town overlooking the lake in a secluded position, rooms are good (73 in all) and some have spectacular views, in-house films and satellite TV, priced very competitively. **B** *Tarabunga Sibigo*, Jl Tuan Maja Purba 1, T41665.

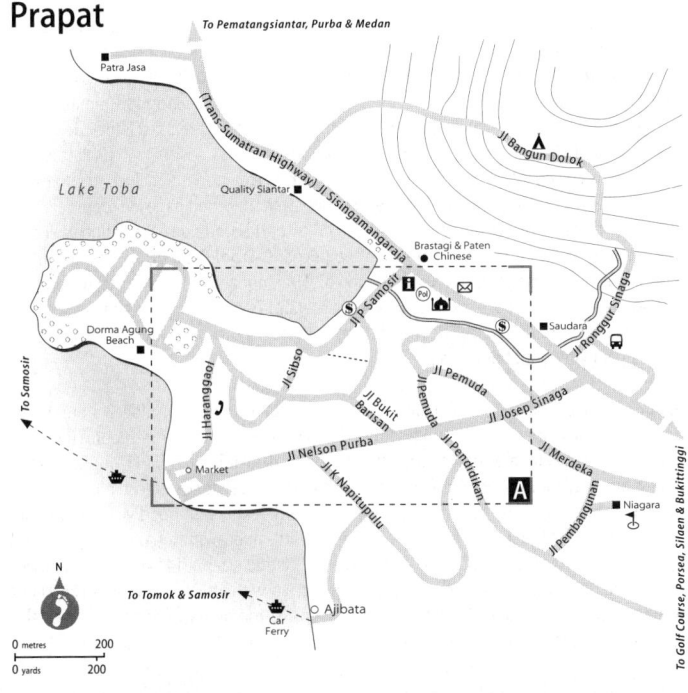

Prapat

Related map
A Prapat centre,
page 490

The Bataks of North Sumatra

The Bataks of North Sumatra inhabit the highland areas centred on Lake Toba, and most villages are situated at about 1,000m above sea-level. There are usually said to be six Batak groups. The word Batak is a derogatory Muslim term meaning 'pig-eater'.

The two Batak groups visitors are most likely to come into contact with are the Toba Batak – concentrated on Samosir Island and to the south of Lake Toba – and the Karo Batak, who live in the vicinity of Brastagi and Kabanjahe. The Toba Batak are considered to be more 'aggressive' and demonstrative, and number about 1,000,000. The much 'younger' Karo Batak are more gentle, hospitable and traditional, and number around 250,000. In total there are about 3,000,000 Batak in this part of Sumatra.

The 'discovery' of the Batak The first European to mention the Batak was the Venetian trader Nicolo di Conti in the early 15th century, who wrote that the 'Batech' ate human flesh, kept heads as valuable property and used skulls as coinage. The first detailed account of the Batak was provided by the Englishman William Marsden, in his History of Sumatra published in 1783. He described a people who, to the great surprise of the 'civilized' world, possessed a sophisticated culture and a system of writing. His account also fleshed out the stories of Batak cannibalism, titillating dinner party guests all over Europe. But it was not until the early 19th century that Batakland began to be explored in a comprehensive manner. Lake Toba was not discovered until 1853.

Although the Batak remained isolated from Western scrutiny until the 19th century, their culture and language shows distinct outside influences. For example, over 150 words in the Karo Batak language are Tamil in origin, while various rituals and some elements of Batak art also appear to show links with the Indian sub-continent. With the opening up of Batakland to Dutch and German missionaries, many converted to a mystical form of Christianity. Only the Karo Bataks have maintained their traditional animist beliefs in anything close to their original form.

Batak architecture and economy The most immediately distinctive element of Batak life are their traditional houses or

---

Portentous place above the road (but with access to a private 'beach' just below), with some rather clumsy attempts at Batak touches, but in reality it is just an ugly block. Plain functional rooms. **B** *Toba*, Jl P Samosir 10, T41072. Restaurant. From the road this place looks like a barrack, but it is in fact one of the better places to stay, it has its own beach and swimming 'pool', rooms are well maintained with balconies looking over the lake, breakfast is included in the room rate and it is well priced. Recommended. **B-C** *Atsari*, Jl P Samosir 9, T41219. Restaurant. In theory this place shouldn't have much going for it. It is right on the main road into town, has no view to speak of, and is not on the lake. However, the wood panelled rooms are well kept and the bathrooms (hot water) are also in pretty good condition considering their age. At this room rate, however, the hotel is overpriced. **B-D** *Soloh Jaya*, Jl Haranggoal 12, villa-esque hotel with good views over the top of Jl Haranggaol to the lake from the rooftop sitting area. The more expensive rooms are large and good value with attached mandi, cheaper ones with shared facilities and often no windows, this is 1 of the 3 hotels that will open up for late-night bus arrivals.

C *Budi Mulya*, Jl P Samosir 17, T41216. Large, clean but bare rooms in an older 3-storey hotel, which like many others could do with some investment – especially the bathrooms (but they have hot water), rates are good. **C** *Hotel Panggabean*, Jl Bukit Barisan 2, T41315. Restaurant. This is an excellent mid-range place to stay with a bit more style than most, rooms are in a Dutch-era villa on the hillside, set in an attractive garden and with good views, rooms are large and clean, although the bathrooms are now a little aged, with squat loos, friendly and good value. Recommended. **C** *Mars Family Hotel*, Jl Kedudayaan 1, T41459. Restaurant. Not much character, but the 40 rooms are large and clean with attached bathrooms and hot water, room rate includes breakfast, more expensive rooms have views over the lake, cheaper inside rooms are windowless.

rumah adat. *An average village rarely contains more than 10 houses, built close together. For the inhabitants, their community is regarded as the 'navel' of the world. In areas where inter-tribal warfare was prevalent, stone fortifications are also sometimes present (for example, in Simanindo, see page 502). Economically, the Batak traditionally pursued a diverse subsistence system.*

Cannibalism among the Batak More than anything else, the reputation of the Batak in the west was coloured by their cannibalism, which continued among the Toba and Pakpak into the 20th century. However, cannibalism was not common, only occurring during warfare and as a punishment for certain crimes. The German geographer and physician Franz Junghuhn, who lived among the Toba Batak for 18 months between 1840 and 1841, witnessed only three cases. His two volume account of the Bataks is one of the best and most thoughtful descriptions of Batak life and society. He describes cannibalism as follows:

"When an enemy is captured the day is set upon which he should be eaten. Then messengers are sent to all allied chiefs and their subjects inviting them to be present at the feast.... The captive is now bound to a stake in an upright position.... Then the chief of the village in which the ceremony takes place draws his knife, steps forward and addresses the people. ... It is explained that the victim is an utter scoundrel, and in fact not a human being at all... At this address the people water at the mouth and feel an irresistible impulse to have a piece of the criminal in their stomachs ... All draw their knives. The radja [chief] cuts off the first piece ... He holds up the flesh and drinks with gusto some of the blood streaming from it. ... Now all the remaining men fall upon the bloody sacrifice, tear the flesh off the bones and roast and eat it. ... The cries of the victim do not spoil their appetites. It is usually eight or 10 minutes before the wounded man becomes unconscious, and a quarter of an hour before he dies."

Recommended reading Sibeth, Achim (1991), Living with Ancestors – the Batak peoples of the Island of Sumatra, Thames & Hudson: London.

D *Bungalow Dolly*, Jl Perintis Kemerdekaan. Well maintained place with attractive views over the lake, this is a hillside villa, closed on our last visit, but apparently not permanently so. **D** *Riris Inn*, Jl Haranggaol 43, T41392. Rooms are rather dark, but they are clean with attached cold water mandis and western toilets, the friendly girls who run the place have tried to make it attractive by growing pot plants. There is also a sitting area. **D** *Tobali*, Jl Haranggaol 3, T41156. Restaurant. Owned by *Tobali Tour and Travel*, and when travellers on 1 of their long distance minibuses arrive too late to catch the ferry to Samosir they are put up here at a reduced rate, designed to look something like a concrete Batak house, rooms are clean enough with attached cold water mandis, but there are much better places for this price. **D** *Trogadero*, Jl Haranggaol 110 (50m up street from ferry dock), T41148. A guesthouse in an old villa, set close to the lake shore and set back from busy Jl Haranggaol, people who have stayed here recommend it: very clean rooms with attractive terraces and sitting areas looking onto a small garden, attached mandis, the more expensive rooms with hot water, the restaurant serves good food (see restaurants), competitive rates.

E *Beringin*, Tigaraja, right opposite the ferry dock and part of *Tobali Tour*. Restaurant downstairs and a handful of rooms above, attached cold water mandis. **E** *Charlie Guesthouse*, Tigaraja, T41277. Restaurant, looking onto the market area and dock for Samosir, very popular budget place to stay, rooms are clean and excellent value, good source of information and the restaurant here is also recommended. **E-F** *Singgalang*, Jl Balige 20. Restaurant. Up the road on the Trans-Sumatran Highway (Jl Sisingamangaraja), good size, clean rooms with shared facilities but this place is only worth considering if you need to get an early bus and need to be close to the bus terminal.

F *Pago Pago Inn*, Jl Haranggaol, up some steep stairs at the back of a rather bare and cavernous travel agency with darkened windows. Clean and attractive rooms with wooden floors, sitting area with views over the lake, shared mandi, popular. Recommended. **F** *Wisma Pernanum*, Jl Haranggaol. Very convenient if you are catching an early morning bus, as the bus stops outside and the owners will give you a wake up call.

Camping There is free camping ground on Jl Bangun Dolok, off Jl Sisingamangaraja, but it is a long walk up a steep hill.

Eating
● *on maps*
Price codes:
see inside front cover

There are 2 concentrations of restaurants: 1 down Jl Haranggaol and the other along Jl Sisingamangaraja. The Haranggaol restaurants are geared more to tourists, while locals and Indonesians tend to eat at those on Jl Sisingamangaraja.

Indonesian There are a whole series of Indonesian (and Chinese) restaurants along Jl Sisingamangaraja, and in general they are better than those on Jl Haranggaol. **Mid-range**: *Trogadero*, Jl Haranggaol 110. This is really a small hotel, but the restaurant is good and in an attractive position on the lake, succulent frog, also fish, prawns, steaks and salads, good hot plate, breakfast served. **Cheap**: *Brastagi*, Jl Sisingamangaraja 55. *Marina*, a Padang restaurant just down the road at No 48 is also worth trying. *Sederhana*, Jl Haranggaol 38. One of the best Padang restaurants in town, spicy rendang and good kangkung, clean and well-run. **Very cheap** *Istana*, Jl Sisingamangaraja 68, towards the bus terminal. Recommended.

Chinese Mid-range *Sinar Pagi*, Jl P Samosir. Chinese restaurant in garden next to the *Budi Mulya Hotel*, fish specialities, vies with the *Hong Kong* as the best Chinese in town. *Hong Kong*, Jl Haranggaol 11 and 28. There used to be a couple of Chinese restaurants on Jl

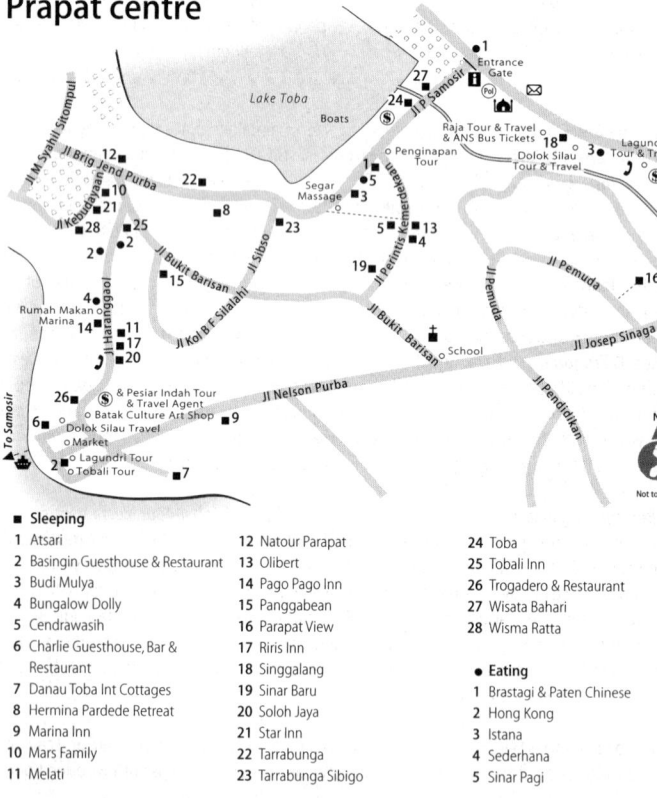

Prapat centre

■ **Sleeping**
1 Atsari
2 Basingin Guesthouse & Restaurant
3 Budi Mulya
4 Bungalow Dolly
5 Cendrawasih
6 Charlie Guesthouse, Bar & Restaurant
7 Danau Toba Int Cottages
8 Hermina Pardede Retreat
9 Marina Inn
10 Mars Family
11 Melati
12 Natour Parapat
13 Olibert
14 Pago Pago Inn
15 Panggabean
16 Parapat View
17 Riris Inn
18 Singgalang
19 Sinar Baru
20 Soloh Jaya
21 Star Inn
22 Tarrabunga
23 Tarrabunga Sibigo
24 Toba
25 Tobali Inn
26 Trogadero & Restaurant
27 Wisata Bahari
28 Wisma Ratta

● **Eating**
1 Brastagi & Paten Chinese
2 Hong Kong
3 Istana
4 Sederhana
5 Sinar Pagi

Haranggaol, but the *Hong Kong* empire has expanded and there are now 2 outlets almost opposite one another at nos 11 and 28. Indonesian and Western dishes served but the Chinese is best, excellent sweet and sour fish. Recommended. **Cheap** *Paten*, Jl Sisingamangaraja (opposite the entrance gateway to Prapat). One of the better Chinese restaurant, in this strip of restaurants and well priced.

International: many of the Indonesian and Chinese (especially) restaurants also serve Western dishes. These are mainly on Jl Haranggaol.

Entertainment

Batak cultural shows: held on Tue and Sat nights at the *Batak Cultural Centre*, Jl Josep 19, at 2100 (2,000Rp). The more expensive hotels (eg *Natour Prapat*) also sometimes organize cultural shows. **Disco**: *Danau Toba International*, Jl P Samosir 17. **Massage**: several places around town offer traditional massage. For example, at *Charlie's* near the Tigaraja dock and at *Massage Segar*, Jl P Samosir 19 (next to *Hotel Budi Mulya*).

Festivals

Jun/Jul: *Danau Toba Festival* (movable), held over a week. Hardly traditional, but there are various cultural performances and canoe races on the lake.

Shopping

Batak handicrafts, batik and woodcarvings: Jl Sisingamangaraja and Jl Haranggaol are the 2 main shopping areas, and both have arrays of the same type of rather tacky souvenir shops selling T-shirts, curios, bags, postcards and so on. The *Batak Culture Art Shop* towards the bottom of Jl Haranggaol is better than most and sells some authentic Batak pieces. There is a market at *Pekan Tigaraja* near the ferry jetty, held on Sat and a smaller one on Thu – a good place to buy batik and Batak handicrafts. On other days there is a small food market here in the morning.

Sport

Golf: The *Niagara Hotel* has a 9-hole course ('professionally designed'). Clubs for hire (30,000Rp), green fees (30,000Rp) and a caddy (10,000-15,000Rp). There is another course 2 km out of town off the road to Balige, with clubs for hire and a 3rd 9-hole course at the *Patra Jasa Hotel*, 4 km north of town, on Jl Siuhan. **Rafting**: *Asahan Adventures*, Jl P Samosir 8 (at the *Toba Hotel*), T/F41086 arranges white-water rafting trips down the Asahan River. **Riding**: enquire at better hotels. **Swimming**: non-residents can use the large swimming pool at the *Niagara Hotel* for 5,000Rp, including towel and hot shower. **Water-skiing**: on Lake Toba, surely one of the most dramatic places in the world to ski. Enquire at the more expensive hotels. **Watersports**: water-scooters and pedal boats can be hired on the waterfront.

Tour operators

The 1 place that stands out as doing something more is *Asahan Adventures*, Jl P Samosir 10 (at the *Toba Hotel*), T/F41086, which arranges jungle treks and rafting on the Asahan River, as well as tours further afield such as scuba diving on Weh (Aceh). The largest regular tour companies are: *Dolok Silau*, Jl Sisingamangaraja 56, T41467 (they also have an office at the Tigaraja ferry dock, Jl Haranggaol 118, T41549). *Goraharaja*, Jl Sisingamangaraja 87. *Lagundri*, Jl Haranggaol 39 (at the ferry dock), and also at Jl Sisingamangaraja. *Raja Tour and Travel*, Jl Sisingamangaraja 44 (agents for the *ANS* bus company). *Tobali Tour*, Jl Pelabuhan 1 (Tigaraja), T41747. *Pura Buana International*, Jl Haranggaol 75, will confirm flights and also operates as a money changer. *Dolok Silau*, *Lagundri* and *Tobali* all operate tourist minibuses.

Tour companies in Prapat have gained a rather poor reputation. Usually they are just used to book bus tickets & confirm flights, rather than arrange tours

Local Bemo: (500Rp around town) and various forms of water transport.

Transport

147 km from Brastagi, 176 km from Medan, 509 km from Bukittinggi

Road Bus: Most people arrive in Prapat from Medan on 1 of the regular buses that travel the route via Tebingtinggi, 4 hrs. The main bus terminal is on Jl Sisingamangaraja – aka the Trans-Sumatran Highway – around 1 km or so from the centre of town. Some express buses stop at bus agencies and others run from the ferry terminal to/from Samosir. There are buses to Bukittinggi 13 hrs, Padang 15 hrs, Palembang, Jambi, Pekanbaru, Bukit Lawang, Sibolga, Bandar Lampung, and even Jakarta, Yogyakarta and Bali. Note that there are no direct ordinary buses to Brastagi – it is necessary 1st to travel to Pemangtangsiantar and then change to a Brastagi bus – but tourist buses make the trip (see below). A tourist bus for Sibolga leaves from the ferry dock at 1100 (having come from Medan) and arrives in Sibolga around 1600 (7,000Rp). For Bukittinggi they leave in the morning at 0830, connecting with the 1st ferry from Samosir which docks at about 0800. The main tour agencies operating tourist minibuses are *Tobali*, *Dolok Silau* and *Lagundri* (see Tour companies & travel agents). They run tourist minibuses to Bukittinggi, Brastagi, Banda Aceh (for Weh), Bukit Lawang and Medan. For Medan and Bukit Lawang, these usually take the longer but more interesting route via Brastagi – rather than the road to Pemangtangsiantar and Tebingtinggi. *PT Palansaa* (based at *Charlie's* in the Tigaraja market) run a/c VIP buses to many cities in Sumatra, and also to Jakarta, Bandung and Bali. The smaller minibuses leave from the Tigaraja market area near the dock, which saves a trip to the bus terminal. Some also drop-off at hotels. **Car**: several companies in Medan will transport passengers to Prapat; contact 1 of the major hotels in Medan.

Sea Boat: Prapat is the main 'port' for Samosir Island, and ferries leave the town from the jetty in the Tigaraja market at the bottom of Jl Haranggaol for Samosir every hour from 0930 to 1930, 30 mins (1,500Rp). The last ferry back to Prapat from Samosir departs at 1630 (the 1st leaves Samosir for Prapat at 0730). Most ferries dock at Tuk Tuk on Samosir and they will drop off at the various hotel jetties, so state your destination. Some continue north to Ambarita, while others also dock at Tomok just south of the Tuk Tuk peninsula. **Car ferry**: there is a car ferry from Ajibata, just south of town, to Tomok, departing every 3 hrs from 0830 through to 1730, with the last departure at 2100. (1,000Rp for foot passengers, 20,000Rp for a car, 2,500Rp for a motorbike.) **NB** Arriving in Prapat after dark makes it difficult to reach Samosir the same day. The only ferry operating after 1930 is the car ferry from Ajibata to Tomok (last ferry leaves 2100). For those who arrive in Prapat after the last ferry has departed, and can't bear the thought of spending a night in town, it is possible to charter a boat for around 50,000-70,000Rp. **Long-distance taxi** An efficient taxi company can be found under the entrance arch to the piers (also bookable through the Tourist office). Non a/c taxi to Bukittinggi, approximately 240,000Rp.

Directory **Banks** Rates are poor in Prapat, but even worse on Samosir. It is best to arrive with sufficient cash for your stay, although that may present risks in itself. There is a series of places that will change money on Jl Haranggaol and in the market area. *Bank Rakyat Indonesia*, Jl Sisingamangaraja (almost opposite the bus terminal). *Pura Buana International*, Jl Haranggaol 75, money changer. **Communications** Post Office: Jl Sisingamangaraja 90. **Telephone**: Warpostel, Jl Haranggaol 74 (for fax and telephone), the most conveniently located of the telephone offices. There is also a Warpostel at Jl Sisingamangaraja 72 (for fax and international telephone). **Medical facilities** Hospital: Jl P Samosir. **Useful addresses** Police Station: Jl Sisingamangaraja (close to the intersection with Jl P Samosir).

Samosir Island

Phone code: 0645
Colour map 1, grid B2/3

With a large number of traditional Batak villages, fine examples of rumah adat or traditional houses, cemeteries, churches, enigmatic stone carvings, good swimming, hiking, cheap accommodation and few cars, it has proved a favourite destination for travellers. Surrounded by the lake and mist-cloaked mountains, which rise precipitously from the narrow 'coastal' strip on the eastern shore, it is one of the most naturally beautiful and romantic spots in Southeast Asia.

Background In all, Samosir covers 640 sq km. Samosir Island, 40 km long and 20 km wide, is not really an island at all, but a peninsula. It is attached to the mainland at Pangururan, although a canal dug by the Dutch cuts through the slender isthmus. An eruption 75,000 years ago thrust Samosir up from the lake bed and the peak contains lake sediments on its summit. The island's highest point at 1,657m above sea level is 750m above the surface of the lake, or more than 1,250m above the lake bed.

The various places of interest on Samosir are listed under the town entries below. However, there are two aspects of the island which are everywhere. First there are the **tombs**. These can be seen throughout the Batak area, but it is on Samosir where people find themselves, so to speak, face to face with them. Some are comparatively modest affairs: the tomb itself is topped with a restrained Batak house made of brick and stucco. Others are grandiose structures, with several storeys, pillars and ostentatious ornamentation. Still others seem to be tongue-in-cheek: the one surmounted with a Christmas tree, decorated with fairy lights just out of Ambarita on the road to Simanindo, is a case in point. All, though, show an imaginative fusion of Batak tradition and Christian symbolism. The need to construct these tombs must have been strong (the tradition is dying) – many took up valuable rice land.

The other aspect of Samosir are the **fish 'tanks'** known as *deke ramba*. These have been laboriously constructed on the lake edge, rocks carefully fashioned and then placed close enough together to allow the water in – while also keeping the fish in. Some appear to be very old, and most are still in use. Many have become ornamental, containing sometimes gargantuan *ikan mas*; others are still used to raise fish for the pot. The main fish raised are *ikan mas* (which are also eaten) and *mujahir*, which are native to Lake Toba. Fingerlings are caught in the lake and then raised in the tanks for about two years before being sold. The most significant ceremonial fish, so to speak, is *ihan*, often known as *ikan Batak*. These are also native to Lake Toba, but are not raised in tanks. However, they are believed to have significant medicinal and magical properties. For example, if a woman is having difficulty conceiving (the problem, in such a masculine society, lies with the woman of course), then she will be given *ihan* to eat.

Sights
There is a tourist information centre – so called – in Prapat (see Prapat above). More useful is the Periplus 'North Sumatra, Lake Toba & Medan' map, which has a good colour map of Lake Toba, Samosir Island & the surrounding area at a scale of 1:250,000

Accommodation is concentrated on the Tuk Tuk peninsula, Tomok and Ambarita, although there are basic guesthouses scattered across the island. Rooms with a lake view are usually double the price of those without. Camping is also easy on Samosir. Food on the island is good and cheap and there are a number of warungs in Tomok, Ambarita and on the Tuk Tuk Peninsula. Note that flight reservations cannot be confirmed on Samosir – it is necessary to visit Prapat.

Sleeping & eating

Local A road in a reasonable state of repair follows the coast, running anti-clockwise from Tomok to Pangururan. There is also a road which runs around the south portion of the island, but it is rougher. This road has been under improvement for years but it is still poor. **Bus**: a minibus service runs about every 20 mins in the morning between Tomok and Ambarita, and then on to Pangururan; the service runs less frequently in the afternoons. Note that the bus does not take the route that skirts around the lakeshore on the Tuk Tuk peninsula – it cuts straight across the neck of the peninsula. From Pangururan, a less frequent service operates to the interior village of Roonggurni Huta. An occasional service has begun operating in the south part of the island between Tomok and Nainggolan, and then on to Pangururan. **Car**: the more expensive hotels have kijangs for charter. **Boat**: there is a cruise around the north portion of the island every day of the week leaving from Tuk Tuk and Ambarita. It includes a visit to the hot springs on Mt Belirang (see page 502). Boats also carry passengers up and down the island during daylight hours – simply wait at a dock for the 1st vessel, state your destination, and make sure the fare is agreed in advance. **Bicycle**: the mountain variety may be hired from many of the guesthouses and hotels in Tuk Tuk – a recommended way to see the island (20,000Rp per day); make sure you check over the bike carefully. **Foot**: this is one of the most enjoyable ways to see Samosir. Walking across the island takes 2 days, with an overnight stop at Roonggurni Huta in the highland interior (see box, page 495). There are also other hiking trails across the island; ask at your hotel or losmen. **Motorcycle**: numerous guesthouses and tour companies have motorbikes for hire, in varying states of repair. Prices vary accordingly but range between 30,000Rp and 55,000Rp per day. A driving licence is not required. This is a recommended way to see the island, although accidents are all too frequent on the narrow roads. Note that although it is possible to drive across the island (see map for roads negotiable by motorbike), there is no assistance available should you get a puncture – which means a long walk to the nearest motorbike repair outfit.

Transport

There have been reports of visitors having to pay an extra 'commission' when booking onward bus tickets through agents on Samosir

Road Bus: they arrive at Pangururan on the west side of the island from Medan, Brastagi, Sibolga and Sidikalang. Note that due to the timings of the buses (most leave Prapat early in the morning), it is difficult to reach Bukittinggi without spending at least 1 night in Prapat.
Long-distance taxi: it is expensive chartering taxis from Samosir; better to charter from the mainland (see page 491).

Boat Most visitors get to Samosir by ferry from Prapat. The ferry leaves about every hour and takes 30 mins (1,500Rp). It stops at Tomok and Tuk Tuk and also at Ambarita. The first ferry from Prapat leaves at 0930, from Samosir at 0730. The last departs Prapat at 1730, Samosir at 1630. It is also possible to charter a 'special' boat, but this is expensive. The car ferry service from Ajibata, just south of Prapat (see map page 487) to Tomok, runs every 3 hrs from 0700 until 2200 (1,000Rp for foot passengers). A ferry also links Tuk Tuk and Ambarita with Haranggaol on Lake Toba's north shore, but this only runs on Mon – market day in Haranggaol. The ferry leaves Ambarita at 0700 and takes 2-3 hrs, largely because it stops to pick up market-goers all along the eastern shore. They leave Haranggaol for Samosir at 1300 and 1500; check in your hotel for the time of journeys in the other direction. To/from Haranggaol, there are buses to Seribudolok, then to Kabanjahe and finally to Brastagi and Medan.

Directory **Banks** Rates of exchange on Samosir are poor, even worse than in Prapat, although the larger hotels and some travel agents will change TCs and cash. There is also a money changer in Ambarita. **Communications Post Office**: Ambarita. **Telephone**: international telephone calls can be placed from many of the hotels and tour and travel agencies, and this is usually clearly advertised.

Tomok

Situated around 3 km south of the Tuk Tuk Peninsula, this was a traditional Batak village. Today, to be brutally honest, it is a grubby little town with little to recommend it. People come here to see the museum, carved coffins and traditional Batak houses (see below), many on day trips from Prapat. This means that there are a host of souvenir stalls, drinks shops and warungs, but none that you would go out of your way to patronize. Tomok is also the docking point for the car ferry, which means that lorries roar through this rather sad place.

However, this doesn't mean that the town is an entirely lost cause, for it contains some fine high prowed **Batak houses** and **carved stone coffins, elephants** and **chairs**. Walking from the jetty inland, there is a path lined with souvenir stalls which winds up a small hill. Half way up – about 500m – is the **Museum of King Soribunto Sidabutar**, housed in a traditional Batak house, containing a small number of Batak implements and photographs of the family. ■ *Admission by donation (about 1,000Rp).*

Walking a little further up the hill, on from the mass of stalls and taking the path to the right, there is a carved stone coffin, the **King's Coffin**, protected by what remains of a large but dying *hariam* tree. The Sarcophagus contains the body of Raja Sidabutar, the chief of the first tribe to migrate to the area. The coffin is surrounded by stone elephants, figures, tables and chairs. Further up the main path, past the stalls, is another grave site with stone figures arranged in a circle. The **church services** at the town and elsewhere on Samosir are worthwhile for the enthusiasm of the congregations – choose between no fewer than three churches.

Sleeping There is just 1 hotel in Tomok to the south of town. The town's guesthouse (*Roy's*) has closed, and it's easy to see why – Tomok has few attractions that would make anyone want to stay here. There is a new, rather monstrous, hotel under construction about 1 km south of town, on the lake front, which will be called the *Lopo Hotel*. However, it is not clear if it will ever be finished. **B** *Toba Beach*, about 3 km south of Tomok, T41275. Restaurant, pool. It is hard to see why anyone would wish to stay here. It is distant from all the good bars and restaurants, and the surrounding countryside is not nearly as attractive as elsewhere.

Eating

There are several warung around the village, eg *Islam*. Nothing that stands out, but it is possible to get a passable meal, whether European, Chinese, Minang or standard Indonesian.

Transport

Road Bus: in theory, every 20 mins to Pangururan and all stops along the route. **Foot**: 1 hr to Tuk Tuk, 1½ hrs to Ambarita. **Boat Car ferry**: from Ajibata, just south of town, to Tomok, departing every 3 hrs from 0830 through to 1730, with the last departure at 2100 (1,000Rp for foot passengers, 20,000Rp for a car, 2,500Rp for a motorbike).

Directory

Communications Telephone: Wartel office for international telephone calls and faxes. On the northern edge of town on the main road.

Tuk Tuk Peninsula

5 km from Tuk Tuk, 9 km from Ambarita, 24 km from Simanindo

Tuk Tuk is the name given to the peninsula that juts out rather inelegantly from the main body of Samosir Island, about 4 km north of Tomok. It is really just a haven for tourists with nothing of cultural interest. There is a continuous ribbon of hotels, guesthouses, restaurants, minimarts, curio shops and tour companies following the road that skirts the perimeter of the peninsula. This might sound pretty dire, but in fact the development is not as overbearing as it might be – the nature of the topography means that you don't get confronted with a vision of tourism hell. And in spite of the rapid development, Tuk Tuk is still a peaceful spot, with good swimming, sometimes great food and good value accommodation. There are various places on Tuk Tuk which masquerade as **tourist information** centres, when they are actually tour companies and travel agents. Nonetheless, they can be a good source of information.

Hiking

Hiking across Samosir's central highlands is one of the most rewarding ways to see the island. The distance from east to west is only about 20 km as the crow flies, but the route is a steep and circuitous climb of 750m, making the real walking distance about 45 km. It is just possible to walk the route in a long day if tackling the hike from west to east (ie from Pangururan to Tomok), but it is best to stay overnight at the interior village of Roonggurni Huta to recuperate from the climb. There are a number of homestays here which charge about 5,000Rp for a bed.

The hike from Roonggurni Huta to Tomok or vice versa is about 29 km: 10 hours if walking uphill, six hours down. There are also trails to Ambarita and (longer still) to Tuk Tuk, although these are less well marked. From Roonggurni Huta to Pangururan it is a less steep 17 km, about three hours walking. There is also a bus service for the terminally exhausted between Pangururan and Roonggurni Huta. It is probably best to climb from west to east as this misses out the steep climb up to Roonggurni Huta from Tomok. Catch a bus to Pangururan and set off from there. A map marking the hiking trails and giving more details about the routes is available from the *Gokhon Bookshop* in Tuk Tuk.

Tours

There are no regular tours around the island at the moment, due to lack of tourists, but they can be arranged at one of the tour companies (if you can find anyone in), 100,000Rp for half day, 180,000Rp for full day. It is possible to hire a car for the day (150,000Rp) or charter a boat to the Hot Springs (350,000Rp).

Sleeping

■ *on map, page 496*
Price codes:
see inside front cover

There are many places to stay in Tuk Tuk, from very simple affairs to large, comfortable hotels. Almost all accommodation is situated along the road (really just a lane) that skirts around the edge of the peninsula. To the north and south there is a relatively steep drop into the lake, so the chalets seem to cling precariously to the hillside. To the east the land slopes more gently into the lake, so there is room for larger gardens and bigger guesthouses and hotels. There are also much quieter guesthouses just off the Tuk Tuk peninsula to the north – on the road to Ambarita – that are listed here.

B *Amboroba Resort*, overlarge, rather characterless hotel, built on several floors across both sides of the road (in a relatively quiet stretch). Far too big to be personal. Batik gallery attached. Swimming possible. **B** *Silintong I*, T451242. Restaurant. Very attractive spacious garden on the water's edge, with an orchid nursery, casuarina trees provide shade for a sitting area, the 100-odd rooms are within a solidly built structure, rather Italianate in style, with verandahs and attached bathrooms, the hotel has its own dock (the ferry stops here), fish pond and good swimming. Recommended. **B-D** *Carolina's*, T41520, F41521. This hotel is very popular and deservedly so. It has a prime position on the lake at the end of a track, so is

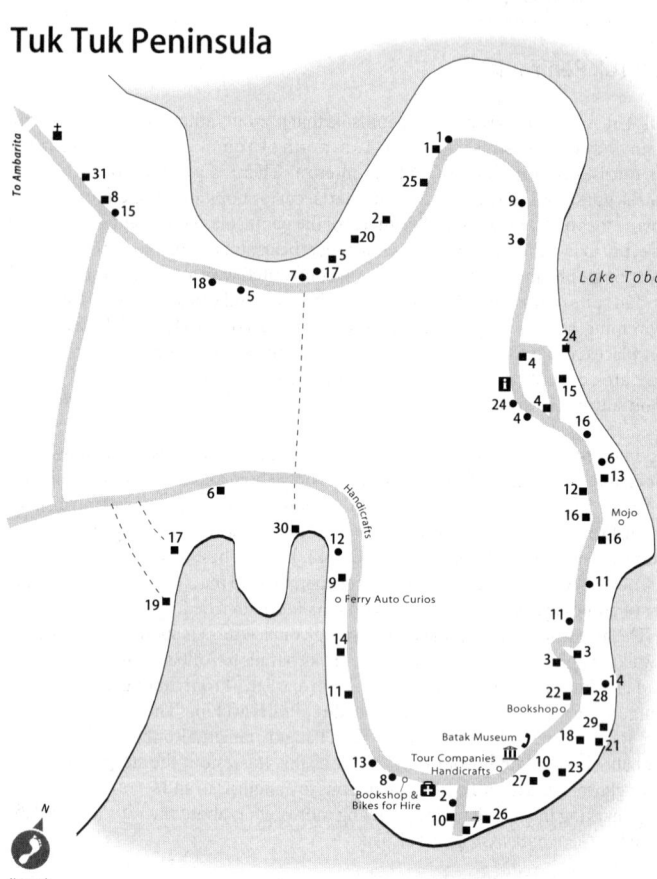

■ **Sleeping**
1 Abadi Guesthouse
2 Aman's Guesthouse & Restaurant
3 Amboroba Resort
4 Anju Cottages
5 Antonius Losmen
6 Bagus Bay
7 Carolina's
8 Christina's Guesthouse
9 Duma Sari
10 Ebikel's
11 Elsina Guesthouse
12 Endy's Homestay
13 Hariara Guesthouse
14 Horas Homestay
15 Judita Guesthouse
16 Lekjon's
17 Liberta Homestay
18 Marroan
19 Melanie's
20 Murni's
21 Romlan's
22 Rudy's Guesthouse & Restaurant
23 Rumba Guesthouse & Restaurant
24 Samosir Cottage
25 Sibayak Guesthouse
26 Sibigo Guesthouse
27 Silintong I
28 Silintong II
29 Sumbo Pulomas
30 Tabo Cottages & Vegetarian Bakery
31 Yogi's Guesthouse

● **Eating**
1 Bamboo
2 Bernard
3 Brando Blues Pub
4 Boruna
5 Garden Coffee Shop
6 Gokhon Bookshop, Library & Café
7 Hita's
8 Juwita Café
9 Leo's Jazz Blues Bar
10 Lily's
11 Lina
12 Linda's
13 Mafir
14 Panorama Café
15 Parna's Pub & Restaurant
16 Popy's
17 Rumba Pizzeria
18 Tarian Vegetarian

quiet and peaceful. It provides a range of rooms but all are well maintained. The more expensive Batak-style cottages and rooms have hot water showers and most have lovely views over the lake. Private swimming area with small beach, diving board and pontoon (possibly the best swimming on Tuk Tuk). The staff are friendly, without being over-bearing, and prices are very reasonable considering its popularity. Recommended. The restaurant serves basic Indonesian and European food which is nothing special, but it is a great place to drink, talk and relax. Own dock means taking the ferry is easy. **B-D** *Tabo Cottages*, T/F41614, tabores@indo.net.id Situated at the end of a short track, this very popular place has 7 chalets that are better appointed than most but also more expensive. Each room is quite different, the most expensive being the Batak Villa, with its king size Batak bed and glorious views over ricefields to the lake; a perfect honeymoon spot. Private bathrooms, western toilets, hot water showers, verandahs. In addition to the great rooms, the vegetarian food is excellent – including great cakes and breads (see Eating). Definitely a good place to relax. Run by Antho and Annette, who also provide an internet service. Recommended.

C *Pondok Ganda*, more a hotel than a guesthouse, set alone on a quiet peninsula to the south of Tuk Tuk. Large rooms, pleasant location but struggling to attract business. **C** *Silintong II*, T41439, F41420. This is a smaller operation than *Silintong I*, but is equally well maintained. It is one of Tuk Tuk's better up-market places. The Tuscan villa-esque building is not overlarge, with a beautiful symmetrical garden leading down to the lake, the rooms are well appointed (with hot water), and it is possible to swim from here. The hotel has a restaurant. **C** *Sumbo Pulomas*, T41356. A more upmarket hotel positioned on a small headland, modern Batak-style building, 8 rooms with attached bathrooms and hot water.

D-F *Marroan*, one of the larger of the guesthouses with a range of rooms, all have attached bathrooms, some are Batak-style chalets, others are more modern in design, most look onto a large garden with a lily-filled fishpond created out of the lake in the centre, rooms are well maintained and this is an efficiently run family place.

E *Antonius Losmen*, 5 Batak houses for rent – a bit scruffy. **E** *Bagus Bay Homestay*, T41482. Rather dark and depressing place, that thinks it's quite hip, 17 clean rooms in real Batak houses – the upper floor rooms are more expensive, whilst the lower rooms are rather gloomy, squat loos and some hot water, billiard table, volleyball net, badminton, restaurant, information service, videos, CNN news, traditional dance shows, money changer and bookshop, some dorm beds available and there is a swimming area, restaurant has an extensive menu, but can't really take the pace. **E** *Ebikel's*. Restaurant. Just 8 rather barrack-like rooms along the track to *Carolina's*, rather functional place with no view, clean rooms and friendly enough but little to mark it out as unusual. **E** *Elsina Guesthouse*, set down off the road right on the waterfront. Just a handful of Batak-style chalets. **E** *Melanie's*, right on the southern shore of Tuk Tuk peninsula's neck and away from most other guesthouses. Quiet location and a beautiful position. **E** *Romlan*, long established and popular place in a quiet position on a small headland jutting out from the main peninsula, it is run by a German and tends to attract, understandably, a fair number of Germans, this means that non-German speakers can end up feeling rather linguistically isolated, restaurant serves good German food. **E** *Rudy's Restaurant and Guesthouse*, 8 Batak-style chalets above the road, some more traditional than others, good views over the lake. **E** *Rumba*, centre of Tuk Tuk. Restaurant (see below). Run by Swiss lady and her Batak husband, 4 rooms with bathrooms *en suite*, reports that it's not very clean or quiet. **E** *Sibigo*, T41520. Restaurant. Good position on the lakeside, down a quiet track not far from *Carolina's*, 8-10 basic corrugated iron-roofed beach huts, right on the lake front, rooms are large with attached mandis, swimming possible. Recommended. **E-F** *Abadi*, T451195. A handful of Batak-style chalets in a lovely position raised up above the lake, with spectacular views, long established and still popular, among the lowest rates on the peninsula, attractive restaurant hanging over the lake. **E-F** *Anju Cottages*, 2 entrances and a jumble of rooms, makes this a rather confusing place, the rooms have been packed in far too tightly to make them attractive, squashed between *Judita Guesthouse* and *Samosir Cottages*. More expensive rooms have hot water. **E-F** *Hariara*, only 4 rooms with hot water here – 3 smaller ones on the ground floor and 1 more expensive on the upper floor, with a huge balcony and great views of the lake. This is a gem of a place, with a pretty little garden – an unexpected little hideaway, the owner works *Baruna Pizzas*. Recommended. **E-F** *Lekjon's*, restaurant on roadside (pizzas), 25 functional rooms with balconies, built close to the lake, the newer more expensive rooms have hot water, run by a band of enthusiastic young Indonesians. A good place for backpackers. **E-F** *Smiley's*, the last guesthouse on the southern neck of the peninsula, down a track through ricefields, close to the lake and surrounded by casuarina trees. Peaceful with good value rooms.

F *Christina's*, a quiet place set on its own on the north section of isthmus facing the Tuk Tuk peninsula, a handful of Batak houses, swimming possible, very peaceful with good food here including Ristafel on Tue, Thu and Sat. **F** *Horas Homestay*, 4 Batak-style chalets on the lake front down below the road. Attached mandis and a rock bottom room rate make these very attractive. **F** *Liberta Homestay*, 6 rooms in Batak-style cottages, peaceful position away from the road. Great restaurant in a renovated Batak house, perfect place to play chess, chill out, and while away the days. Recommended. **F** *Merlyn*, small and scruffy, but it's on the waterfront and rooms have bathrooms. **F** *Murni*, down a track off the road on the north side of the isthmus, facing onto the main part of the island. Away from the bulk of guesthouses, quiet. **F** *Nina's Homestay*, down a rubbish-strewn track in the hamlet of Pindu Raya just north of the Tuk Tuk peninsula. Three Batak houses on the lake and then some cheaper rooms in a purpose built Batak-esque block, vegetarian restaurant attached, swimming reasonable, peaceful and a good place to relax, well priced. **F** *Samosir Cottages*, T41050, F451170. Restaurant, popular guesthouse and larger than most, a sprawling range of rooms which are nothing special, but the management are friendly and the raised restaurant serves what must be the coldest beers in North Sumatra and reputedly excellent steaks. **F** *Yogi's*, restaurant, another quiet place set on its own just off the Tuk Tuk peninsula amidst ricefields, a handful of Batak houses overlooking the lake, good food here, especially Indonesian.

Eating
- on map
Price codes:
see inside front cover

There are an increasing number of good dedicated restaurants (ie not attached to any hotel or guesthouse) on Tuk Tuk. Especially vegetarian travellers' food.

Mid-range *Leo's Jazz Blues Bar*, quite an imaginative menu at this place including schnitzel, mozzarella and various soups, cooking classes also arranged. *Bernard*, close to *Carolina's*. Real pizzas, muesli, home-made yoghurts, burgers and steaks, tacos, saté, some Indonesian dishes like gado-gado. *Mayfir Restaurant*, saté, steaks, guacamole, various curries, lassis and muesli, rock music in the evenings.

Cheap *Boruna*, good range of food, Indonesian, European and Mexican, especially good pizza and tacos. German speaking. *Endy's*, good cakes and coffee. Great place to hang out, as there are magazines and dozens of paperbacks here, welcoming family atmosphere. *Garden Coffee Shop*, this is more than a coffee shop with spaghetti and Thai fish soup, although the coconut cookies and banana doughnuts are recommended. *Gokhon Bookshop and Café*, a good place to read and drink strong and sweet coffee – daily baking of brown bread, delicious cakes, birthday cakes on request, friendly owners, lovely views from the balcony. *Juwita's Café*, small restaurant serving Indonesian food (including vegetarian), as hot as you like it, special requests taken the day before, Hedi the cook speaks good English and is very friendly. *Lily's Restaurant*, next to the *Silintong Hotel I*, good home cooking – the Batak food is especially recommended by locals – also things like tacos, gado-gado, guacamole and pasta. *Lina Restaurant*, this place doesn't look much but the food is excellent. *Parna's Pub and Restaurant*, next to *Christina's* at the neck of the Tuk Tuk peninsula. Attractive brick built place with verandah and good views over the lake and Samosir's north shore, Indonesian and international dishes. *Panorama Café*, octagonal building on the top of a hill with 180° views. Owned by a German who plans to develop the plot further, with a handful of rooms, the café serves excellent fruit juices, eat inside or on the veranda, more sophisticated than most, good breakfasts, the owner has plans to begin fishing and boat trips and is building some guesthouse rooms down the slope. *Pizzeria Rumba*, Indonesian and European food including spaghetti, pizza, freshly baked bread and cakes, and traditional Swiss specialities like rosti, wienerschnitzel and fondu, information board and comments book are a good source of information for travellers, second-hand English and German books for sale or exchange. Recommended. *Popy's*, home-made pizzas served here, but the place is better known for its range of house cocktails which can be sipped on the bar's attractive verandah overlooking the lake. *Bamboo Restaurant*, best value meals – great food. *Linda's*, popular place that serves good Western food, especially travellers' food.

Vegetarian Mid-range *Tabo*, on southern neck of Tuk Tuk, vegetarian restaurant and bar (with some rooms, see 'Sleeping'). Run by a Batak and his German wife, home produced wholesome food using fresh herbs and vegetables from their garden, wholemeal bread, yoghurts, avocado sandwiches, tofu etc. The restaurant is a very attractive, airy, open, wooden structure, in a lovely location – a good place to relax. They also provide an information board, comments book and games, children welcome, traditional massage offered. *Tarian Vegetarian Restaurant*, another very good vegetarian restaurant with various imaginative salads and such things as tempe burgers, chapatis and guacamole, and aubergine curry. **Cheap** *Hita's*, good vegetarian food including guacamole, chapatis, gado-gado and fruit juices. Recommended.

Massage: traditional massage available at guesthouses around the peninsula, about 25,000Rp per day. Ask at *Tabo Cottages*. **Traditional dance**: shows used to be staged at *Bagus Bay* but had stopped on our last visit. Perhaps they will be revived when the tourist industry picks up. **Videos**: *Bagus Bay* has a large screen TV which shows 2 English language films a day and BBC/CNN news; videos also shown at *Leo's Jazz Blues Bar* and the *Brando Blues Pub*.

Entertainment

Books: *Gokhon Bookshop and Library* offers a postal service and there is a small café attached. *Bagus Bay Bookshop* for second-hand novels. Number of other places around the peninsula that sell second-hand books (see map for location). **Crafts**: there are scores of craft and curio shops on Tuk Tuk selling such things as woodcarvings, medicine books, leather goods, Batak calendars, carved chess sets, wind chimes and so on. The chess sets are a good buy here but they vary enormously in quality and price – it's definitely worth shopping around.

Shopping

All the companies listed here will book bus tickets and arrange tours. *Pepy's Tourist Information*; *Bagus Bay Information Centre*, T41481; *Bataran Tourist Information*; *PT Lagundri*; *Goraha Tour*; *Bukit Santai Travel and Tours*.

Tour operators

Local Bikes: for rent for around 20,000Rp. **Motorbikes**: 30,000Rp for 100cc Honda, 55,000Rp for 160cc Honda. **Road Bus**: walk to the main road to catch one of the buses running between Tomok and Pangururan, in theory every 20 mins. **Boat** Ferry connections with Prapat about every 30 mins (1,000Rp). See page 493 for details. **Foot** 1 hr to Tomok and Ambarita.

Transport
5 km from Tomok, 4 km from Ambarita, 19 km from Simanindo, 39 km from Pangururan

Banks *PT Andilo Nancy* travel agent changes money at a better rate than other places. **Communications Post Office**: no post office but many places sell stamps and will post letters. **Telephone**: the nearest Wartel is in Tomok (see Tomok entry), but many guesthouses, hotels and tour companies offer IDD phone facilities and fax. **Email**: available at *Tabo Cottages*, but charges are high as the nearest server is Medan. **Hospitals facilities** Clinic (Puskesmas), on the southern side of the peninsula.

Directory

Ambarita

The pretty town of Ambarita is an hour's walk north from Tuk Tuk along the lake shore. There is more in the way of sights than Tuk Tuk, but nowhere to stay in the village itself: guesthouses and some hotels are strung out along the road running north towards Simanindo and the track that follows the coast to Tuk Tuk. The **Golden Tourist Information Centre** is on the road towards Tuk Tuk.

AMBARITA

Sights There are several **megalithic complexes** in the vicinity of the town, which also has a clinic (Puskemas), a market, a bank, a school, two churches, a police and an army post, and a post office. In other words, it is a real little community. The most important of the megalithic complexes is near the jetty at **Siallagan village**. The first group of chairs, arranged under a hariam tree, are 300 years old and were used as the site for village councils, where disputes were settled and punishments decided. The chief would sit in the armchair, whilst other village elders sat in the surrounding chairs. The person on trial would sit on the small chair closest to the table – having been incarcerated for seven days in the small cage close to the stone chairs. A medicine man would consult his diary to decide on the best day for any sentence to be meted out. A stone figure mysteriously occupies one of the seats. Guides hang around to recount the chairs' gruesome past with a certain amount of relish. The really gruesome part of the traditional legal system is associated with the second group of megaliths. The criminal sentenced to death would be blindfolded, tied hand and foot and bodily carried to the large stone block. He would then be sliced with a small knife and chilli, garlic and onions were reputedly rubbed into the wounds before a mallet – like a meat tenderizer – would be used to prepare the 'meat' for consumption (by pounding the man, already, no doubt, in a certain amount of pain). Having been sufficiently trussed and pummelled, the unfortunate would be carried to the block and his head cut off. The (strength-giving) blood was collected and drunk by the chief, while the meat was distributed to the villagers. The bones, finally, were collected up and thrown into the lake – which was unclean for a week and no activity occurred during this time. The chief's staff is carved with the faces of past chiefly generations. This gruesome tradition came to an end in 1816 when a German missionary (by the name of Nommensen – there's a university in Medan named after him) converted the population to Christianity. ■ *1,000Rp.* Facing the complex is a row of well preserved **Batak houses**. Also here is the **tomb of Laga Siallagan**, the first chief of Ambarita. ■ *Getting there: turn right (coming from Tomok) off the main road in Ambarita, shortly after the Post Office walk past the football field and police post, and turn left to walk past tombs and ricefields to the complex – about 500m in all. It is possible to approach from Tuk Tuk via the side road.*

Sleeping
■ *on map*
Price codes:
see inside front cover

The hotels and guesthouses listed here are scattered along the road towards Simanindo (over a distance of about 9 km from town) and the smaller road leading towards Tuk Tuk (over about 2 km). These places are quieter than those in Tuk Tuk. They are also quite isolated, so staying here, if you want to try other restaurants and bars, means hiring a bicycle or motorcycle. This part of the island is also rather treeless near the lake shore.

B *Sanggam*, T41344, F41474. Restaurant. Around 5 km north of Ambarita, a large, newish hotel with a bright blue roof on a massive Batak-style house that can be seen from miles away. The standard rooms here are OK but over-priced, there are also some self-contained Batak 'suites' with sitting rooms and small kitchens. It's so clean it's almost sterile, price includes breakfast. The swimming pool, never completed, has now been filled in and resembles an over-sized

Related map
A Tuk Tuk Peninsula,
page 496

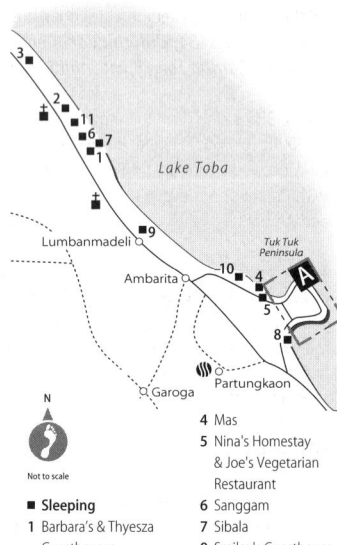

Ambarita & around

Not to scale

■ **Sleeping**
1 Barbara's & Thyesza Guesthouses
2 King's Inn & No Name Pizzeria
3 La Shangri-La
4 Mas
5 Nina's Homestay & Joe's Vegetarian Restaurant
6 Sanggam
7 Sibala
8 Smiley's Guesthouse
9 Sopo Toba
10 Tuk Tuk Timbul
11 Vanesha Inn

sandpit, exposed garden with too few trees and shade, on our last visit it was completely deserted. **B** *Vanesha Inn*, T41138, F41120. Restaurant. Around 6 km north of Ambarita down a track and on the lake. This ugly, sprawling guesthouse-cum-motel has a range of rooms, 70 in all, in a 2-storey 'U'-shaped block, all clean and well maintained but lacking in atmosphere, small beach and dock – good for swimming, could do with some more trees, room rate includes breakfast. **C** *Sopo Toba Hotel*, T41616, F41117, 2 km north of the town. Large place occupying a quiet position out of town, separate villas are built on the hillside with a few Batak-style cottages at the top, few people seem to stay here – at our last visit it was (again) virtually empty, own beach created out of a concrete waterfront. **D** *Sibala*, between *Barbara's*, *Thyesza* and the large *Sanggam Beach*, a new place with nice location on the lake front. Open restaurant, attractive gardens. **E** *Sony's*, between Ambarita and Tuk Tuk, 20 mins' walk to Ambarita. Bathroom, large clean rooms, friendly. Recommended. **E** *Thyesza*, T41443. Restaurant. Around 4 km north of the town down a track that also leads to *Barbara's*. The rooms here are more expensive and slightly more stylish (some have hot water), although dorm beds are available, beach and swimming. This is a good little guesthouse. **E** *Tuk Tuk Timbul*, T41374. Restaurant. Great isolated position off the road and down on the lake front on a small headland about 1 km south of Ambarita towards Tuk Tuk, the restaurant serves good food including home baked bread, there is a large fish pond and good swimming. **E-F** *Barbara's*, T41230. Restaurant. Around 4 km north of the town along a track leading down towards a small beach, peaceful location with just 1 other guesthouse here, range of rooms from basic but clean through to comfortable. Satellite TV, family atmosphere. Recommended. **E-F** *King's Inn*, T41421, on the lake side behind the *No Name Pizzeria* about 7 km north of Ambarita. The rooms are in a rather box-like block with *King's Inn* painted in very large letters, but people who stay here recommended it. **E-F** *Mas*. Restaurant (extensive menu). Around 2 km south of town on the road that leads to Tuk Tuk. The restaurant is up by the road but the 15 or so rooms, in variations on the Batak chalet theme, are on the lakeside with a fish 'tank' out front, well maintained, a quiet location. **F** *La Shangri-La*, 9 km north of the town. Set down on the lakeside below the road (which is quite high at this point), lovely, isolated position – great if you want to be alone and secluded, more problematic if you want to party; spacious, clean Batak houses, good food, good value. Recommended.

Eating
● *on map*

There are a couple of coffee shops and warungs in town, but nothing that stands out. The best place to eat is at a nice little warung next to the police post (turn off the main road and walk past the football field). **Mid-range** *No Name Pizzeria*, 7 km or so north of town on the road to Simanindo. Good home-made pizzas and brown bread, fruit shakes and lassis, small library and comfy chairs, a good place for a stopoff. **Cheap** *King's II Bistro*, right behind *No Name Restaurant*. Bistro food and Indonesian dishes. *Joe's Vegetarian Restaurant*, Pindu Raya (a little hamlet between Tuk Tuk and Ambarita). Best for its home-made cakes and coffee.

Transport
4 km from Tuk Tuk, 9 km from Tomok, 15 km from Simanindo

Local Bicycles and **motorbikes** can be hired from *Faber*, a place on the main road close to the track leading down to *Barbara's* and *Thyesza's*. **Road Bus**: in theory, regular connections every 20 mins with Tomok and all stops to Pangururan. **Boat** A number of ferries from Prapat dock each day, both scheduled and chartered. **Foot** 1 hr to Tuk Tuk, 7 hrs to Simanindo at the north tip of the island.

Directory

Banks Bank Rakyat Indonesia on Jl Raya (the main road). **Communications** Post Office: Jl Raya 39, on the right-hand side from Tomok, shortly before the turning for the Siallangan megalithic complex. **Medical facilities** Clinic (Puskesmas): in town. **Useful addresses** Police station: in town.

Simanindo

Simanindo is at the north tip of Samosir. The house of a former Batak chief, Raja Simalungun, has been restored and turned into an **Ethnological Museum** (*Huta Bolon Museum*), containing a musty collection of Batak, Dutch and Chinese artefacts. Brief labels in English reveal little. Souvenirs for sale in Batak houses. ■ *5000Rp (this includes the show), Mon-Sun.*

Sights

Close by is a well preserved **fortified Batak community**, with fine examples of richly carved Batak houses. This is the best maintained of the various 'preserved' communities on Samosir. Visitors sit through a lengthy sequence of 12 dances, performed by a rather lacklustre crew – many of the dances seem more like loosening up exercises prior to a work out. Requisite audience participation number and the final dance gives an opportunity for guests to add a donation to their entrance fee.
■ *Shows are staged 1030-1130, 1145-1245 Mon-Sat, and 1145-1230 Sun.*

Just offshore from Simanindo is the small 'honeymoon' island of **Tao**. There are secluded and rather expensive bungalows on the island for those who really do wish to be alone. Day trippers can visit Tao for a swim and a meal – 10 minutes boat ride.

Eating There's a small warung on the main road, facing the turn off for the museum. Standard Indonesian dishes. More interesting is the restaurant attached to the guesthouse on Tao Island. But it means haggling with a boatman to take you over there and wait to bring you back.

Transport **Road Bus**: regular connections with Ambarita and Tuk Tuk, and onwards to Pangururan.
15 km north of Ambarita **Boat** Ferries connect Simanindo with Tigaras, north of Prapat, leaving every 1½ hrs between 0630 and 1430. The ferry between Ambarita and Haranggaol also sometimes stops here (see page 494). **Foot** 7 hrs to Pangururan, 7 hrs to Ambarita, 7¾ hrs to Tuk Tuk.

Pangururan

Pangururan, the capital of Samosir, is on the west coast, close to the point where the island is attached to the mainland by a small bridge. It is a dusty, ramshackle little town. There is no reason to stay here and certainly the restaurants and two guesthouses are very average. The core of the town include the two guesthouses, but shop, restaurants and Wartel office are south of the stone bridge. There is a weekly market here on Wednesdays. Most people visit the town on the way to the **hot springs** on Mount Belirang.

Excursions The **Mount Belirang hot springs** or *air panas* are one hour's walk from town (2½ km). The sulphurous gases and water have killed the vegetation on the hillside, leaving a white residue – the scar can be seen from a long way off on Samosir. Cross the stone bridge and turn right (north). They are about a third of the way up Mount Belirang (also known as Mount Pusuk Buhit). It is too hot to bathe at the point where they issue from the ground, but lower down there are pools where visitors can soak in the healing sulphurous waters. It is said that bathing here three times will cure scabies. There are separate bathing pools for men and women and some warungs nearby for refreshments. There is even accommodation (for those with severe scabies). Views of the lake are spoilt by uncontrolled, unattractive development, and even the spring site itself leaves rather a lot to be desired: plastic pipes and moulded concrete make it look, in places, more like a plumber's training site. ■ *300Rp.*

Cross-island hike to Tomok Pangururan is probably the best place from which to set out to hike across the island (see page 495).

Sleeping **D** *Wisata*, Jl Kejaksan 42, T41150. Clean rooms with attached bathrooms in modern block. **F** *Barat Guesthouse*, Jl Sisingamangaraja 2/4. Very basic rooms above a restaurant, with shared mandi, rather dark and dingy. **F** *Wisma Sinur*, T20234. On the lakeshore, 3 km or so north of Pangururan, a row of Batak-roofed rooms, with attached bathrooms, nothing special but the best place to stay close to Pangururan.

Eating *Barat Guesthouse*, simple warung with the usual range of Indonesian dishes, average.

Transport **Bus**: buses leave Pangururan for Medan, Brastagi, Sidikalang (at 0700 and 1600; rather scary switchback road) and Sibolga in the morning (0700-0900). Regular connections with

Simanindo, Ambarita, Tuk Tuk and Tomok. Buses at 0500, 1200, 1700 to Ronggurni Huta. **Boat** No boats leave from Pangururan for Prapat. **Foot** 7 hrs to Simanindo; 10-12 hrs across the island to Tomok.

Communications Wartel office, part of Wisata Samosir, Jl Kejaksan. **Directory**

Haranggaol

This is a small, sleepy, rather run-down town on Lake Toba's north-eastern shore. Few tourists visit the town, but there is an excellent **market** on Monday and Thursday – when there are early morning boat connections with Samosir from Ambarita and/or Simanindo – and good walks in the surrounding countryside. If visitors wish to experience the wonder of Toba, without the crowds at Prapat and on Samosir, then this is the place to come.

C *Haranggaol*, situated in town rather than on the lake shore, but the best place to stay. Some rooms with hot water, large eating area, used to catering for tour groups. **D** *Segumba Cottages*, Bali-style cottages situated 3 km out of town in a beautiful, quiet position. Some rooms with mandi. Recommended. **E** *Losmen Horison*, basic losmen located on the lake shore. Some rooms with mandi, food available. **Sleeping & eating**

Bus Haranggaol lies off the main bus route, so it can take a time to reach the town. There are bus connections from Kabanjahe (easily accessible from Brastagi) to Seribudolok, and from there bemos run to Haranggaol. Getting to or from Prapat to Haranggaol is not easy; it involves 3 changes of bus and usually takes 8 hrs to cover the 50-odd km. Taking the ferry is easier. **Ferry** A ferry connects Haranggaol with Tuk Tuk and Ambarita on Samosir Island on Mon and Thu. From Samosir there are many ferry boats making the crossing to Prapat. **Transport**

Sibolga

Sibolga has suffered for years from an uneviable reputation among backpackers as a place with uniformly poor hostelries and a population that, to a man, is out to diddle and deceive. This reputation is largely, though not entirely, undeserved. In fact, having been led to believe that this is the proverbial armpit of Sumatra, visitors might be pleasantly surprised. It has some fine colonial period vernacular architecture in the **Dutch-Chinese shophouses**; it has a breezy coastal position; and the seafood here – especially the *ikan bakar* (baked fish) - is excellent. Even the hotels and guesthouses are not as bad as legend would lead one to believe. *Phone code: 0631*
Colour map 1, grid B2

Even so, there is not a great deal to keep visitors in Sibolga much longer than it takes to book a ticket on the boat to Nias – which is why most people find themselves here in the first place. A visit to the **Pelabuhan Baru** (New Harbour), 2 km from the town centre, is worthwhile – it is a colourful place and visitors can watch large quantities of fish being unloaded and dried.

Pandan Beach is 10 km from Sibolga. It is sandy and palm-fringed, with a refreshing uncommercialized air. The swimming is good here but there is no snorkelling. There is just one place to stay at present, the **D** *Pantai Indah Pandan* (formerly the *Pandan Beach*), rooms with attached mandi, 20,000Rp. ■ *Getting there: regular oplet connections from the terminal on Jalan Sisingamangaraja.* **Excursions**

Pulau Poncan is a small island off the coast at Sibolga, with a well run resort and good snorkelling. Accommodation is available at **A-B** *Sibolga Marine Resort*, Jalan Yos Sudarso 29 (in Sibolga), T28888, F23338, a/c, 50 chalets, diving, windsurfing and snorkelling. ■ *Getting there: contact the office in Sibolga for transfer; the company runs a speedboat service to the island for 25,000Rp, leaving from close to their offices in the Pelabuhan Lama.*

Goting Waterfall is 17 km from town on the route to Barus. It lies 2 km off the main highway and it is possible to swim in the 4m-deep pool beneath the 100m falls.
■ *Getting there: take an oplet from the bus terminal on Jalan Sisingamangaraja towards Barus, and ask to be let off at the turning for the falls – everyone knows it (1,500Rp).*

Essentials

Sleeping
■ *on map*
Price codes:
see inside front cover

After the delights of Bukittinggi or Lake Toba, Sibolga's rag-bag of losmen and guesthouses can seem a trifle depressing, although there is a new hotel and the budget places seem to have cleaned up their act, so to speak. Most of the hotels are concentrated in a comparatively small area of town, all within a modest walk of the bus terminal. A grouping of the very cheapest can be found on Jl Mesjid – good for an early start. **A-B** *Hotel Wisata Indah*, Jl Brig Jend Katamso 51, T23688, F23988. A/c, restaurant, pool, satellite TV, the only upmarket hotel in town – a new brown block with a Batak roof gesticulating from the front. Located on the seafront within yards of the centre, but still relatively peaceful because it is on a dead-end street. Rooms are very comfortable, still pristine and competitively priced (discounts usual). Guests are also privileged members of the *Sibolga Executive Club* which is 15 mins away and where, in the words of the hotel's slightly opaque brochure, "the Karaoke sound system is designed to silence karaoke critics".
C *Tapian Nauli*, Jl S Parman 5, T21116. Best hotel, but out of town to the north, near the immigration office, a/c, quiet, colonial-style with balconies. **C-E** *Indah Sari*, Jl Jend A Yani 27-29, T21208. Some a/c, better-managed and maintained than most hotels with large sitting rooms, reasonably clean, satellite TV in more expensive rooms, central location, serves tea and breakfast.
C-E *Mutiara Indah*, Jl Jend A Yani 20-22, T21681. Some a/c, hard to draw much distinction between this place and the *Indah Sari*. Both are priced at the same level, both are featureless, 3-storey concrete blocks, both are in the centre of town, and both have acceptably clean rooms.
C-E *Pasar Baru Inn*, Jl Suprapto 41. Some a/c, this hotel is run by a characteristically efficient

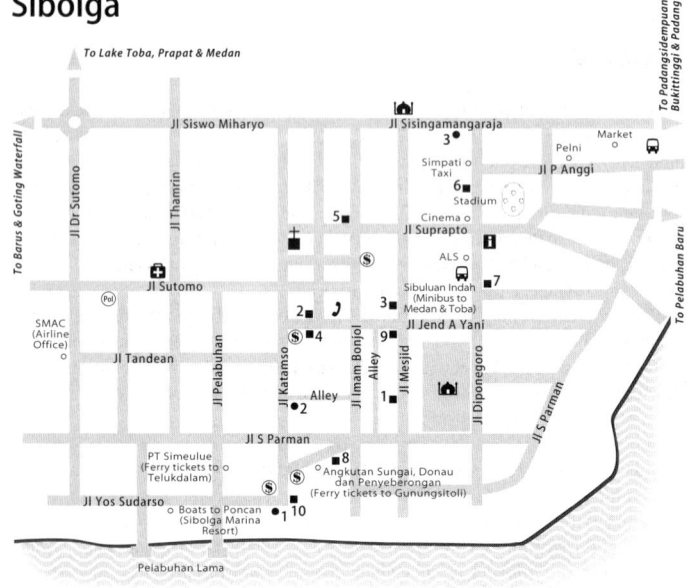

Sibolga

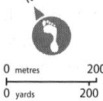

■ **Sleeping**
1 Cahaya Indah Losmen
2 Indah Sari
3 Losmen Garuda
4 Mutiara Indah
5 Pasar Baru Inn

6 Penginapan Sari Agung
7 Penginapan Subur
8 Sarina
9 Sentraal Losmen
10 Wisata Indah

● **Eating**
1 Hello Café
2 Ikan Bakar
3 Marina Baru

Chinese family. Range of rooms from basic to quite acceptable (attached mandi – squat toilets – hot water, satellite TV). Central location, jovial manager with good English, excellent restaurant serving breakfast and other meals, all help to make up for average rooms, best of the mid-range places to stay. **D-E** *Hotel Sambas Baru*, Jl Horas 100, T22857. A characterless and rather grotty hotel that does not even have the advantage of being in the centre of town – situated on the road to the new harbour. **E** *Hotel Sarina*, Jl S Parman 40, T22637. Central location and attractive old shophouse building, but worn, and the rooms are rather grubby. **E** *Penginapan Subur*, Jl Diponegoro 19, T21255. Slightly more sophisticated than the other losmen, but this is among what might be termed a pretty weak field. **E-F** *Cahaya Indah Losmen*, Jl Mesjid 102, T21923. Small hotel with dark rooms right next to the mosque, so good for an early start. **F** *Losmen Garuda*, Jl Mesjid 92, T22425. Lovely old building, but this shouldn't be allowed to detract from the fact that the rooms are pretty dismal. **F** *Penginapan Sari Agung*, Jl Diponegoro 46-48, T21726, faces the stadium and is probably the best of the cheaper places to stay. **F** *Sentraal Losmen*, Jl Mesjid 70, T22781. Another basic losmen in a beautiful old building – asethetics aside, the rooms here could only be described, optimistically, as simple, more accurately, as grubby; barred and dark, it's more like a prison.

Mid-range *Marina Baru*, Jl Sutoyo Siswo Miharjo 30. Excellent *ikan bakar* in a good, comfortable restaurant. **Cheap** *Hello Café*, Jl Brig Gen Katamso. Small seafront café facing the *Hotel Wisata Indah*, attempting to reproduce the Mediterranean *al fresco* feel with little success, drinks and some snacks. *Rejeki*, Jl Brig Gen Katamso 40 (opposite Bank Dagang Nagora). **Very cheap** *Ikan Bakar*, Jl Brig Gen Katamso 45. Only open at lunch and in the evening, a cheap and excellent little restaurant specializing in roasted fish – *ikan bakar*.

Eating

Local Becak: 500Rp around town. **Mesin becak**: 1,000Rp around town. **Bicycles**: for hire from Helen's Information Service. **Road Bus**: the bus station is on Jl Sisingamangaraja (the Trans-Sumatran highway), an easy walk to the centre of town. Regular connections with Medan 8 hrs, Bukittinggi 10 hrs, Padang 12 hrs, Prapat 3-5 hrs, Bukittinggi, Sidikalang and other destinations. Also connections with destinations in Java such as Jakarta, Yogya, Bandung and Surabaya. There are numerous bus offices here. Local buses leave from the same terminal for Padangsidempuan, Barus and elsewhere. There is also a daily tourist bus to Medan, perhaps the most comfortable of the services. Minibuses and buses for Prapat, Padangsidempuan, Medan, Padang, Bukittinggi and other destinations leave from offices on Jl Mesjid (*PT Palagan*, No 100 for Prapat and Medan, and *SMJ*, No 102 for Jakarta, Padang, Bukittinggi and Medan) and Jl Diponegoro (*CV Sibuluan Indah* at No 62 for Toba and Medan, *ALS* at No 56 for Jakarta, Bandung, Semarang, Yogya, Solo, Surabaya, Jambi and Palembang, and *CV Simpati* at No 22 for Prapat and Medan).

Transport
78 km from Prapat, 381 km from Bukittinggi

Sea Boat: Sibolga is the main departure point for Nias. Boats leave every day except Sun for Gunungsitoli and Telukdalam (different vessels) at 2000, from the Pelabuhan Baru (New Port) at the end of Jl Horas – about 2 km from the centre of town. Tickets are 12,000Rp and 15,500Rp to Telukdalam, 11,000Rp and 17,500Rp to Gunungsitoli. The 2 companies that run these ferries have their offices near the centre of town close to the Pelabuhan Lama (the Old Port). *Angkutan Sungai, Danau dan Penyeberangan* are at Jl S Parman 34, T22721, and sell tickets to Gunungsitoli. *P T Simeulue*, sell tickets to Telukdalam and have their offices 100m away at Jl Pelabuhan 2. Details can also be obtained from travel agents in Lake Toba and Bukittinggi. The Pelni ships *Kambuna* and *Lambelu* also dock here on their fortnightly circuits. The Pelni office is behind the bus terminal at Jl Patuan Anggi 39, T22291, F22927. Finally, around 2 vessels a week depart for Pulau Banyak (see page 525), 10-14 hrs (15,000Rp).

It is not possible to buy tickets on the vessels, so it is necessary to arrive in Sibolga & buy the tickets before the office closes. This is the advantage of booking a ticket – despite the service charge of 7,500Rp – through a travel agent

Directory Banks *Bank Dagang Negara*, Jl Jend A Yani (at intersection with Jl Katamso), good rates. *Bank Danamon*, Jl Imam Bonjol. *Bank Bumi Daya*, Jl Yos Sudarso 41 (near the *Hotel Wisata Indah*). *Bank Negara Indonesia*, Jl S Parman 23. **Communications** Post Office: Jl Dr F L Tobing. **Telephone office**: Wartel, Jl Jend A Yani 35 (fax and international telephone). **Tour companies & travel agents** *Helen's Information Service*, corner of Jl Suprapto and Jl Diponegoro. This tour company and travel agent is run by Fuady Munthe. He will book tickets and arrange reasonably priced tours and is clear about the service charge that he adds.

Padangsidempuan

Phone code: 0634
Colour map 1, grid B3

Padangsidempuan – usually known simply as Sidempuan – must be in the frame for the title of 'the ugliest town in Sumatra'. It is singularly grim. The town is situated in the Bukit Barisan and lies on the Trans-Sumatran Highway at an important crossroads: highways run north to Lake Toba, northwest to Sibolga, south to Bukittinggi and Padang, and east to the lowlands, Tebingtinggi and, eventually, Medan. It is a halfway point between Prapat and Bukittinggi, but unfortunately does not have good accommodation either at the top or bottom end – although there is an adequate mid-range hotel.

Like other towns hereabouts, the main form of local transport in Sidempuan is the motorcycle and sidecar. However, here Vespa scooters are used instead of the usual Japanese 125cc machines. The reason – according to the locals at least – is that all the hills around town mean that the usual motorbikes overheat. Vespas are fan-cooled and so work more efficiently in the hot and hilly environment. The human outcome of this entirely practical solution to the challenge set by the environment is that *mesin becak* drivers in Sidempuan are studies in coolness. But the town is even prouder of its claim to be the salak capital of Indonesia. Salaks are small, brown, scaly fruits with a rather sickly flesh, and Sidempuan is 'Kota Salak'.

In terms of places of interest, Sidempuan is touristically challenged. There is the large **market** running along the west side of Jalan Merdeka; and there is a small **Chinese temple** about 2 km out of town on the Sibolga road (left hand-side of the road). But neither of these two sights is likely to induce even the faintest murmurs of excitement, and frankly the only real reason to stop here is to use the town as a base to visit the 10th-14th century ruins at **Padang Lawas**.

Padang Lawas

To archaeologists, the ruins here are the most interesting in Sumatra

Meaning Great Plain – lies over 70 km east of Padangsidempuan. So far, 26 temples scattered over 1,500 sq km, along the course of the Barumun River, have been discovered. Archaeological work did not begin until after the Second World War, and the area has still to be properly researched. The monuments date from the 10th to 14th century, and are probably linked to an ancient Hindu-Buddhist kingdom called Panai.

The main concentration of ruins is at the village of Portibi, near Gunungtua. The surrounding area is a dry, almost treeless landscape, carpeted with *alang alang* grass and whipped by a dry wind. The temples are known as *biaros*, or sanctuaries, and only a few are easily accessible: Biaro Bahal I, II, III, Pulo, Bara, Si Topayan and Si Pamutung. Each is surrounded by a wall, the inner courtyard containing the principal shrine, surrounding minor shrines and stupas. Statuary is limited, and generally in poor condition, while reliefs are also few in number. Given that rudimentary excavations have revealed no evidence of large-scale habitation, it would seem that the biaros were funerary/ceremonial in function. An alternative explanation is that they lay on an important

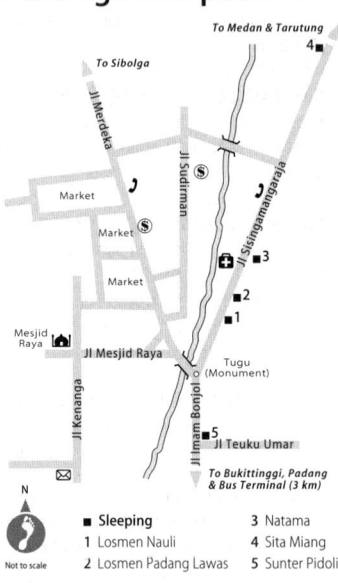

Padangsidempuan

■ Sleeping
1 Losmen Nauli
2 Losmen Padang Lawas
3 Natama
4 Sita Miang
5 Sunter Pidoli

The main temples at Padang Lawas

Biaro Si Pamutung The largest and most important of the shrines, near the confluence of the Panai and Barumun rivers. The temples are constructed of brick and are similar in style to 9th-10th century Central Javanese shrines. The staircase on the main tower, which faces east, is flanked by two crocodiles with human features.

Biaro Bahal I Located in the village of Bahal, near Portibi, this is regarded as the most beautiful of the Padang Lawas ruins.

The 13 m-high brick built tower rises from a lotus cushion and is surmounted with a garland. Yakshas and makaras in relief are still in evidence, although the original life-size figures which flanked the doorway have disappeared.

Biaro Pulo Situated on a hill, but only the ruins of the main tower remain. Five highly unusual reliefs of dancing figures were found here in a good state of repair, and are now on display in the National Museum, Jakarta.

Trans-Sumatran trading route, linking the west and east coasts of the island. It is at this point that the mountains which form a spine down Sumatra are least imposing, and there are rivers flowing east from the plain which could have been used as convenient arteries of communication. A day at least is needed to explore the area, and because of the heat it is worth taking water along. There is a restaurant just outside the temple complex entrance, where it is possible to stay the night on a mat.
■ *Getting there: take a bus from Padangsidempuan to the market town of Gunungtua, 72 km to the east. From there, catch an oplet or a mesin becak to the turn-off to the temple site, 15 km.*

Sleeping & eating
There are several cheap losmen on Jl Sisingamangaraja, north from the Tugu in the centre of town. All are very basic and pretty grubby and they include the *Losmen Nauli* and *Losmen Padang Lawas* (at No 48). **A-C** *Torsibohi Nauli Hotel*, Siporok, T21925, T21910. A/c, restaurant, pool, tennis courts, this is the best hotel in the Padangsidempuan area, although it is hardly close to the centre of town: it is near Siporok 30 km north on the road to Tarutung, but for those with their own transport it is more attractive than staying in town. Rooms in thatched chalets, well appointed with TV and in-house films, large garden, good views. **B-D** *Sunter Pidoli*, Jl Imam Bonjol 25, T22408. Some a/c, reasonably central position just out of the town centre on the road running south to Bukittinggi, best rooms have hot water and satellite TV but the hotel is a characterless box on a noisy road. **C** *Natama*, Jl Sisingamangaraja 100, T22305. A/c, a large new hotel in the centre of town and the best place to stay in Sidempuan itself, rooms are clean with hot water and satellite TV. **C-D** *Lancar*, Jl Imam Bonjol. Some a/c, 3 km south of town opposite the bus terminal (noisy road), box-like rooms, reasonably clean. **C-E** *Samudra*, Jl Teuku Umar 99. Grubby, noisy hotel, with more life in the beds than among the staff. Situated off Jl Sisingamangaraja.

Transport
88 km from Sibolga, 215 km from Prapat, 293 km from Bukittinggi

Local Scooters with haphazardly attached sidecars are the main form of local transport. **Road Bus** The main bus terminal is 3 km south of town on Jl Imam Bonjol (the road to Bukittinggi). Catch an oplet into the centre. Regular connections with Sibolga, Prapat and Bukittinggi. Connections with Gunungtua (for the Padang Lawas ruins).

Directory
Banks *Bank Rakyat Indonesia*, Jl Jend Sudirman. *Bank Danoman*, Jl Merdeka. **Communications** **Telephone office:** Warpostel, Jl Sisingamangaraja and Jl Merdeka (for fax and international telephone).

Nias Island

Colour map 1, grid B2 Nias Island is part of the series of submarine peaks which run down the west coast of Sumatra, and which include the Mentawi, Batu and Simeulue islands. Nias is 125 km long and about 40 km wide. It is separated from the Sumatran mainland by 110 km of occasionally rough sea. The west coast is rocky and inhospitable, while the east coast is more accessible, with natural harbours and a more gently shelving shoreline. The interior of the island remains thickly forested.

Ins and outs

Getting there There are daily flights from Medan to Binaka airport, 15 km south of Gunungsitoli on SMAC,
See Transport section and occasional services from Padang in West Sumatra. But most people arrive here by boat
for further details from Sibolga. Vessels leave every day except Sun from Sibolga for both Gunungsitoli and Telukdalam (different boats) at 2000. The Pelni ship *Kambuna* also docks at Gunungsitoli once a fortnight on a loop between Padang and Sibolga, before returning to Jakarta.

Getting around While there is a reasonably good network of roads, most are in a poor state of repair and can be impassable after heavy storms. Buses and other assorted modes of public transport run between larger towns, but sometimes just once or twice a day. Average speeds are 25 km per hr or less. Bicycles can be hired in tourist destinations.

Where to go For the visitor, South Nias is probably the more rewarding part of the island to visit. The north was raided by the Acehnese for slaves, and much of their material culture was destroyed in the process. The south has the greater cultural integrity and more 'traditional' villages. It is also the south where the island's best surfing beaches are to be found. The isolated central portion of the island also contains a number of abandoned villages with monumental stone sculptures.

Nias Island

Background

The capital of the district is Gunungsitoli, in the north. The island is usually divided into three regions: North, Central and South Nias. These divisions reflect important differences in language, culture, and art and architecture. There are two main reasons to visit Nias: for surfers, to experience the waves at Lagundi Bay; and for non-surfers, to see its unique culture which has evolved over several thousand years, apparently in isolation from developments elsewhere in Southeast Asia. In July 1994 the Indonesia Open International Surfing Championship was held on Nias, confirming the island's place as Indonesia's surfing Mecca.

Culture

The Nias culture presents something of a conundrum to anthropologists. There are clear links in linguistic and cultural terms with the Bataks of the mainland, and yet the Niha – as the inhabitants of Nias are known – do not have a tradition of writing nor of cannibalism (although headhunting was prevalent). There are also distinct differences between the Niha of the southern, Central and northern regions of the island. Niha society is divided into three groups: nobles or *si'ulu*, who were viewed as descendants of supernatural beings, commoners or *sato*, and slaves or *sawuyu*. The financing or sponsoring of feasts and the commissioning of sculptures and jewellery were – and still are to an extent – crucial in determining a person's status. By erecting a stone monument, a noble legitimated his position and made him eligible to join his deified ancestors in the upper world. With the spread of Christianity, so traditional beliefs and rituals have disappeared – the last traditional funeral, for example, occurred in 1914.

Niha settlements in the south are the most impressive and also the most visited. Villages consist of two rows of raised houses or *omo*, facing a paved stone courtyard which may be several hundred metres long. Formerly villages were surrounded by a palisade, and within that a sharpened stake-filled ditch. Now that internecine warfare has been eradicated, the fortifications have been allowed to fall into disrepair. The central street which separates the two rows of houses is known as the *ewali*, and it is equally divided into two by a central stone pavement or *iri*. The centre of the village contains the chief's house (*omo sebua*), a meeting house (*bale*) and an assembly square (*gorahua newali*). The latter should be beautifully paved and surrounded by stone benches and other megaliths. It is here that village rituals, dances and other activities are held. The 2m-high stone pyramid used for stone-jumping is erected near the square.

Villages show that, although the culture of Nias may popularly be considered 'primitive' or 'Stone Age', the inhabitants had a genius for design. There are village baths or *hele* with running water, sometimes even private baths for noblewomen. The houses of chiefs are particularly impressive, being richly decorated with polished wood panelling called *hagu laso*, recording the possessions of the present and former occupants of the house.

The Niha people are most famous for their **megalithic culture**. Formerly, archaeologists believed that this indicated close links with India, and particularly with the Naga of Assam. Latterly, there has been a tendency to play down possible outside influences and stress local origins. In every village there are stone benches or *daro daro* (erected as seats for the dead), beneath which human skulls are sometimes kept. Benches are also found by bathing places, and in the forests and hills. They are not just resting places of the dead; they are also for the living, and are starkly unadorned, bar a few symbolic shapes such as the rosette. Memorial stones are also widespread, as are idols (often phallic) made of wood, stone and clay. An idol was made whenever someone died, except when that person left no male descendants.

Woodcarving is a widespread traditional art form in Nias. In fact, the carvings of Central Nias are regarded as among the finest in Southeast Asia. Christianity, however, has had a marked effect on production. Ancestor or *adu* figures, for example, are rarely seen or made; missionaries discouraged production and most were either destroyed or taken off the island and placed in museums before the Second World War.

The Niah are not only renowned for their megalithic material culture, but also for their **dances**, and particularly for their '**stone-jumping**' – *fahombe*. A stone pedestal or *batu hombo* in the middle of the square, that separates the two rows of houses in a Nias village, was vaulted by acrobatic warriors, often with a sword in their hand, in preparation for battle. Warriors would spring from a smaller launching stone. The columns are 2-2.5m high and 0.5m wide – in the past they were also topped-off with pointed sticks to galvanize the competitors. Today, stone-jumping is enacted for tourists and important guests.

Economy The economy of the Niha is based upon the cultivation of wet and dry rice (although this was only introduced in the late Dutch period), sago, maize and a wide variety of other crops and vegetables. Meat is eaten rarely, except during festivals, when large quantities of pork are consumed. Pigs are slaughtered in front of the house of the feast-giver; they are stabbed, their skin singed, and they are then cut up for distribution. The parts of the pig are allocated according to strict rules; the head goes to the foremost chief. In addition to livestock and crops, forest products also represent an important element in the Niha diet. Apes, civets, birds and turtles, tubers and wild fruits, insects and snakes are all consumed. Mice, however, are avoided because they are said to contain the souls of the ancestors, while women are forbidden to eat monkeys because a Niha legend recounts how a woman once turned herself into a monkey.

Island Essentials

Trek It is possible to trek and bus all the way across the island from Gunungsitoli to Telukdalam, or *vice versa*, staying in villages *en route*. Basic Indonesian is required, and a certain degree of patience and fortitude. From Gunungsitoli take a bus south to Tetehasi and from there walk to Siofabania. The next village is Hilimbowo, where there are examples of traditional architecture and stone megaliths. An hour's walk further on is Lahusa Idanotae (again with traditional houses and megaliths), and another hour still, Orahili Gomo. It is possible to continue southwards all the way to Telukdalam visiting, in turn: Tetegewo, Helezalulu, Lahusa, Lawinda, Hilizoroilawa, Hilinaurato Mazings, Hilizalootono, Bawolahusa, Bawaganowo and Hilinamoniha, before reaching, finally, Telukdalam. **Sleeping** can be arranged through the *Kepala desa* (head of the village) in each village.

Conduct The inhabitants of Nias are even more sensitive to 'inappropriate' dress than most Indonesians. Except at the beach resorts of Lagundi and Jamborai, women should wear long skirts/trousers, a bra and shirt, and men should wear shirts.

Warning Malaria is a problem on Nias as some chloroquine-resistant strains have appeared. It is also recommended that visitors have a cholera inoculation. Nias has an unfortunate reputation for being a haven for tricksters and thieves. Be wary, but always be polite.

Transport **Local** There is a fairly extensive road network on the island; the problem is that it is in a poor state of repair – except in the vicinity of the 2 major towns. There are buses, bemos and jeeps, as well as the odd motorcyclist who might offer a ride. Expect to average 25 km/hr on buses – meaning that the 125-odd km trip between Gunungsitoli and Telukdalam takes 4-5 hrs. Note, though, that torrential rain can stretch this out considerably. Bicycles can be hired in tourist destinations. **Air** Binaka airport is 15 km south of Gunungsitoli. There are daily flights from Medan to Gunungsitoli by SMAC. There is also a weekly SMAC flight, on Wed, between Padang and Gunungsitoli. **Sea Boat**: Sibolga is the main departure point for Nias. Boats leave every day except Sun from Sibolga for both Gunungsitoli and Telukdalam (different vessels) at 2000. Tickets are 12,000Rp and 15,500Rp to Telukdalam, 11,000Rp and 17,500Rp to Gunungsitoli (see page 505 for details). **NB** It is not possible to buy tickets on the vessels, so it is necessary to arrive in Sibolga before the office closes. This is the advantage of booking a ticket – despite the service charge of 7,500Rp – through a travel agent in Bukittinggi or elsewhere. The Pelni ship *Kambuna* also docks at Gunungsitoli once a fortnight on a loop between Padang and Sibolga, before returning to Jakarta. In addition there are usually several cargo ships which leave for the island each week – cheaper, but can be uncomfortable. Gunungsitoli is also a possible departure point for Pulau Banyak (see page 525) – about 1 departure a week, 8 hrs.

Banks There are banks offering acceptable exchange rates in both Gunungsitoli and Telukdalam. **Directory**

Gunungsitoli

Gunungsitoli, on Nias' east coast, is the capital of the island and like any other Indonesian town. There is not much to see and a poor selection of hotels. From the town there are many paths and attractive walks, and oval-shaped northern-style houses can be seen in the vicinity of the town. Ask at the tourist office for information. From town, it is possible to walk to Siwahili and Sihareo, and from these two villages to Tumori and Danaha, before reaching the *Miga Beach Hotel*. This hike takes one day. The friendly and helpful **tourist information office** is on Jl Sukarno 6 (near the dock).

C-D *Miga Beach Bungalows*, T21460. Some a/c, 5 km out of town and, as the name suggests, on the beach, good, comfortable rooms with attached mandi. **C-E** *Wisma Soliga*, T21815. Some a/c, 4 km out of town, good Chinese restaurant attached, clean, spacious rooms and helpful management, best place to stay. **D-E** *Gomo*, Jl Sirao 8, T21926. Some a/c, the cheap rooms are dirty and dark. **D-E** *Wisata*, Jl Sirao 2, T21858. Some a/c, restaurant, all that can be said is that the rooms are relatively clean. **Sleeping**

Air The airport is 19 km out of town. Flights from Medan on Merpati and SMAC. **Road Bus**: the bus terminal is on Jl Diponegoro on the southern edge of town. Daily connections with Telukdalam 4-5 hrs, although poor weather can stretch this out to 10 hrs. Most buses leave in the morning. **Sea Boat**: the port is 2 km north of town. Daily ferry connections (except Sun) with Sibolga (see page 505). The ferry company, *P T Idapola*, has an office at Jl Sirao 8. The Pelni vessels *Kambuna* and *Lambelu* call here once a fortnight from Tanjung Priok and Padang, before continuing onto Sibologa, Padang and Tanjung Priok. Pelni have their office on Jl Jend A Yani, on the waterfront. They also sell tickets for boats to the mainland. Finally, around 1 boat a week to Pulau Banyak (see page 525). **Transport**
80 km from Telukdalam

Airline offices *SMAC*, Jl Lagundi 47, T21010. **Banks** Rates are reasonable but only US$ and A$ TCs are accepted. *Bank Negara Indonesia*, Jl Pattimura. *Bank Rakyat Indonesia*, Jl Gomo 1. *BPDSU*, Jl Hatta. **Communications Post Office:** Jl Hatta 1. **Telephone Office:** Jl Hatta 7. **Medical facilities Hospital:** Jl Ciptomangunkusumo, T21271. **Directory**

Telukdalam

This is the second biggest town on Nias, and the entry point for those wishing to visit the south. There is nothing in town except for a church. Surfers head west for 12 km to Lagundi Bay (see below). Visitors wishing to see the traditional South Nias villages could use Telukdalam as a base.

Bawamataluo (Sunhill) is a 'traditional' village about 14 km northwest of Telukdalam. Approached up a 480-step flight of stone stairs, the village contains impressive soaring-roofed houses, megaliths, funerary tables, woodcarvings and a magnificent chief's 'palace'. The village was built in 1888 as a defensive measure against the Dutch who had attacked and sacked the previous village. The main *omo sebua* or chief's house is said to be the oldest in Nias, although it was built barely a century ago. The house is richly decorated with woodcarvings, depicting family heirlooms, ritual feasts – even a Dutch steamship. These carvings are designed to link the present with the past, and thereby assure the living a link with their deified ancestors. The position of each carving is tightly prescribed. Images of the village **Excursions**

founders – *adu* figures – used to occupy the two carved chairs outside the house; like most *adu* figures, missionaries had these destroyed. Though still inhabited, the house has been turned into a museum. Many of the wooden figures sold by the roadside in Lagundi are carved here – and can be purchased more cheaply. Bawamataluo is the most accessible of the traditional villages, so is fairly touristy. Stone-jumping (*fahombe*) exhibitions are put on for tourists (see page 509). Nonetheless, for the budding anthropologist, it is a definite 'must'. ■ *Getting there: by minibus from Telukdalam. Admission by donation. Stone-jumping exhibitions – expect to pay about 50,000Rp for a show.*

Hilisimaetano is another traditional village, although it is considerably 'newer' than Bawamataluo. It lies 16 km from Telukdalam. Again, there is a fine collection of 140 *rumah adat* (traditional houses), megalithic stone benches, chairs and other stone and woodcarvings. Stone-jumping (*fahombe*) is performed on Saturday (see page 510). Sleep can be had at **(E)** *Losmen Mawan*. ■ *Getting there: by minibus from Telukdalam.*

Treks It is possible to walk from Bawamataluo to Hilisimaetano visiting, en route, the villages of **Siwalawa**, **Onohando**, **Hilinwalo** and **Bawogosali**. There are also treks to other, less visited, villages. Most have megalithic complexes and, as always, the more remote the village the friendlier the villagers. ■ *Getting there: on foot, but hire a guide in town (ask at your hotel).*

Sleeping **D** *Ampera*, Jl Pasar. Clean rooms. **D** *Effendi*, best in town. **E** *Sebar Menanti*. **E** *Wisma Jamburae*, this place seems to have deteriorated markedly over the years.

Transport **Bus**: there are daily bus connections with Gunungsitoli, 4-5 hrs, most departing in the morning. Oplets run regularly to Lagundi Bay. **Boat**: ferry connections with Sibolga every day of the week except Sun (see page 505); also boat connections with Gunungsitoli every day except Sun.

Directory **Banks** *BPDSU*, Jl Jend A Yani – acceptable exchange rates offered. **Communications** Post Office: near the dock. **Telephone office**: Jl Pancasila 1.

Lagundi Bay

Colour map 1, grid C2

Lying 12 km from Telukdalam, Lagundi (Lagundri) Bay was an important port until Krakatoa exploded and destroyed it in 1883. Now there are just two villages here – Lagundi and Jamborai. Since the late 1970s, the area has taken on a new life and become a surfer's paradise.

Surfing enthusiasts maintain that Lagundi has the most perfect reef right-hander on earth – although the surf can be inconsistent. The surf is reputed to be best between June and October. During these months it is not recommended for beginners – currents are powerful and the coral is close to the surface. For the rest of the year the surf is more sedate and conditions much more suited to beginners. There are boards for hire on the beach. Other than surfing and swimming, there is not much to do here, except walking and visiting surrounding traditional Nias villages of **Hilisimaetano** (20 km north) or **Bawamataluo** (17 km from Lagundi).

Sleeping
Try and obtain a personal recommendation from a recent visitor in Sibolga or Telukdalam as we have received a lot of conflicting, & often negative, reports about losmen/guesthouse accommodation here

Losmen are concentrated at Jamburai village. They are basic and charge similar rates – our **E-F** range. Food is almost universally poor – and double the price of elsewhere in Sumatra. However, there are plans afoot to develop Lagundi into something more up-market. A/c hotels are planned (1 has materialized) and land use and land ownership disputes are bound to surface as speculation intensifies. Many losmen owners insist that their guests also eat all their meals at the losmen (if room rates are very cheap this is usually the reason). Check whether rates include meals or not; there have been several reports of disputes over this, with threats of violence. It may be worth agreeing with the owner of a losmen to pay a bit more for the room and escape the hassle over eating. It also seems that petty thefts are also very common, so it is best to leave nothing of even modest value in your room. Before making a decision on where to stay, take a look at a number of places – standards change very fast and those recommended here may have deteriorated. **B** *Sorake Beach*, Jl Sorake, T21195. A/c, restaurant, pool, 73 rooms in this new hotel, the tip of the mass market iceberg which some local tourist officials hope will soon hit Nias, tennis court, hot water, TV, what more could one want? Heavy discounts available for walk-ins as most people arrive on pre-booked tours. Other than the *Sorake Beach*, accommodation is much of a muchness. Among the more popular, at the last count, were: *Ama Soni, Yanti, Jamburai* and *Friendly*. *Uni* and *Raff*, where snorkels and surfboards are lent gratis, are also recommended, and for something just a touch more salubrious there is *Sea Breeze*, T21224, and the *Lantana Inn*, T21048, which has some rooms in our **C-D** categories. *Kristov* is not recommended.

Eating There are a handful of warungs serving basic Indonesian and travellers' food and, sometimes, superb seafood. Most people eat at their losmen.

Transport *12 km from Telukdalam*

Bus and **ojek** Lagundi is 6 km off the road from Telukdalam. It can be reached by bus or oplet (both irregular), or by hitching a lift on the back of a motorcycle. Oplet drivers regularly overcharge. If coming from Gunungsitoli by bus, ask to be let off at the junction with the road to Lagundi. Ojeks wait here to take passengers the final 6 km.

Aceh

Aceh is not on the itineraries of many visitors to Sumatra. This is a shame because it is a beautiful province. Banda Aceh, the capital, is a fascinating city with perhaps the finest mosque in all Sumatra. The island of Weh offers the best beaches and coral, while the Gayo highlands of interior Aceh have been mysteriously ignored by the travelling fraternity for many years. That so many people pass it by can be put down to two factors: first it is off the tourist route; and second, it has been perceived to be a 'difficult' province on account of the population's staunch adherance to Islam.

The discovery of large reserves of natural gas in the 1960s has helped to make the province one of the richest in Indonesia, but the failure to unite the population behind the central government means the fruits of this industry have often not filtered down. The bulk of people are still farmers and, even though much of the province is mountainous and inaccessible, Aceh maintains a healthy rice surplus.

Background

Aceh is a problematic province for the Indonesian authorities – and before that, presented a challenge to the Dutch colonial administrators. It is fiercely independent and is one of only two special administrative regions in the country. Even since independence in 1950, which the Acehnese believed did not deliver the autonomy they expected, a low-level insurgency has been fought by the Aceh Merdeka or the **Free Aceh Movement**. While it has never garnered the international publicity that East Timor has 'enjoyed', the conflict has led to thousands of casualties. In 1993 Amnesty International estimated that 2,000 civilians had been unlawfully killed – some in public executions – since 1989.

Fresh impetus was given to the Aceh independence movement in November 1999 when President Abdurrahman Wahid, in perhaps a rash statement (certainly his advisors were horrified), implied that Aceh could have a referendum just like East Timor. In response, hundreds of thousands of people – some commentators said 5,000,000 – congregated outside the Mesjid Raya Baiturrahman in Banda Aceh, many wearing headscarves emblazoned with pro-independence slogans. Aceh's struggle with the authorities in Jakarta continued, with the army and the police increasingly seen as an occupying force. At the beginning of 2000 there was a large sign in the city centre quoting President Wahid's declaration that he would allow people of the province a referendum on independence.

Tourists should remember that Aceh is possibly the most staunchly Muslim region in Indonesia and women should dress very modestly; even so, be prepared for some minor difficulties. For those intending to spend sometime exploring Aceh there is a 370-page locally produced guide to the province in English – *Aceh 1998* by Mahmud Bangkar. It is available – occasionally – from book stores in Medan and Banda Aceh.

North to Banda Aceh

The Trans-Sumatran Highway runs through Medan and then up the east coast to Banda Aceh, the capital of the province of Aceh. Few people travel the long main road north to Banda Aceh, but the appearance of bucolic tranquillity is rewarding. Stops could include **Lhokseumawe**, the important natural gas town, **Bireuen** – a provincial market town – or **Sigli**, famed for its strict adherence to Islam. All three towns have a reasonable selection of losmen, and the first some good hotels, but little else. From Bireuen, a road cuts south and inland to Takengon and Lake Tawar, and from there into the Gunung Leuser National Park, before linking up with the Medan-Lake Toba road.

Lhokseumawe

Phone code: 0645
Colour map 1, grid A2

This coastal town is extremely important for Indonesia's economic development, but is rarely visited by tourists. It has become one of the key administrative and processing centres for the country's natural gas and petroleum industry, and is consequently thriving and relatively wealthy. The massive PT Arun natural gas 'train' is nearby, while the town virtually lies in the shadow of a large urea fertilizer plant built as one of a series of rather poorly thought through ASEAN Industrial Projects or AIPs. It was completed in 1984 and still operates at a loss, producing fertilizers that could be bought more cheaply on the international market.

Sleeping **A-C** *Lido Graha International*, Jl Raya Medan-Banda Aceh, T22266, F22555. A/c, rooftop pool, built to provide for the needs of visiting oil men, a large rambling place, comfortable enough but rather ersatz. **A-C** *Meutia*, Jl Medan-Banda Aceh, T21164, F22986. A/c, 54 well appointed rooms with a good range of facilities for a district town. **C-D** *Dewi Plaza*, Jl Pase 52, T21442. Some a/c. **D-E** *Wisma Kuta Karang Baru*, Jl Pang Lateh 8, T22492. **F** *Farina 53*, clean and friendly.

Transport **Bus**: regular a/c and non-a/c bus connections with Banda Aceh and Medan.
274 km to Banda Aceh

Banda Aceh

Phone code: 0651
Colour map 1, grid A1
Population: 200,000

At one time Banda Aceh was one of the most important cities in the region. Today, it is one of Indonesia's smallest provincial capitals. While Banda Aceh's rather insignificant role now can be contrasted with its glorious past, the people of the city have not forgotten the acheivements of their ancestors. Nor did the destructive war against the Dutch colonizer erase everything of historical significance.

Ins and outs

Getting there
See Transport section, page 519 for further details

There are daily air connections with Medan. The airport is 20 km from town. The most direct and fastest route north is along the Trans-Sumatran highway which runs up the east coast from Medan, a 12 hr journey. You can also travel north up the slower, west coast route from Sidikalang. The slowest route is north through the centre of the island from Blankejeren via Lake Takengon. Aceh is the jumping-off point for Pulau Weh.

Banda Aceh is not a particularly large town and it is possible to walk around the centre without too much trouble. Local buses criss-cross the city and becak mesin provide a cheap taxi service. Public bemos leave for the beaches and other out-of-town excursions. Aceh regional **tourist office** is on Jl Cik Kuta Karang 3, T23692. Good for maps and other information, it is well organized and helpful. Open 0730-1430 Mon-Thu, 0700-1100 Fri and 0730-1100 Sat.

Getting around

Background

Banda Aceh grew to prominence as an Islamic trading centre during the 16th century, under the rule of **Sultan Ala'ad-din Ri'ayat Syah al-Kahar** ('the conqueror', reigned 1539-71). The sultanate's wealth was based upon the pepper trade and several expeditions were sent to Melaka to try and dislodge the competing – and infidel – Portuguese. They failed in each instance. Aceh reached the height of its power during the reign of the brilliant **Sultan Iskandar Muda** (1607-36) when the city became a cultural and economic centre, controlling the entire west coast of Sumatra as well as a substantial proportion of the east coast and parts of the Malay Peninsula. His military forces included a regiment of cavalry mounted on Persian horses, an elephant corps and a navy of heavy galleys. Iskandar was constantly worried about his successor and even had his own son killed because he could not trust him. Following

Iskandar Muda enthusiastically promoted Islam - it is said that when 2 drunken Acehnese were brought to him, he had them executed by pouring molten lead down their throats

Banda Aceh

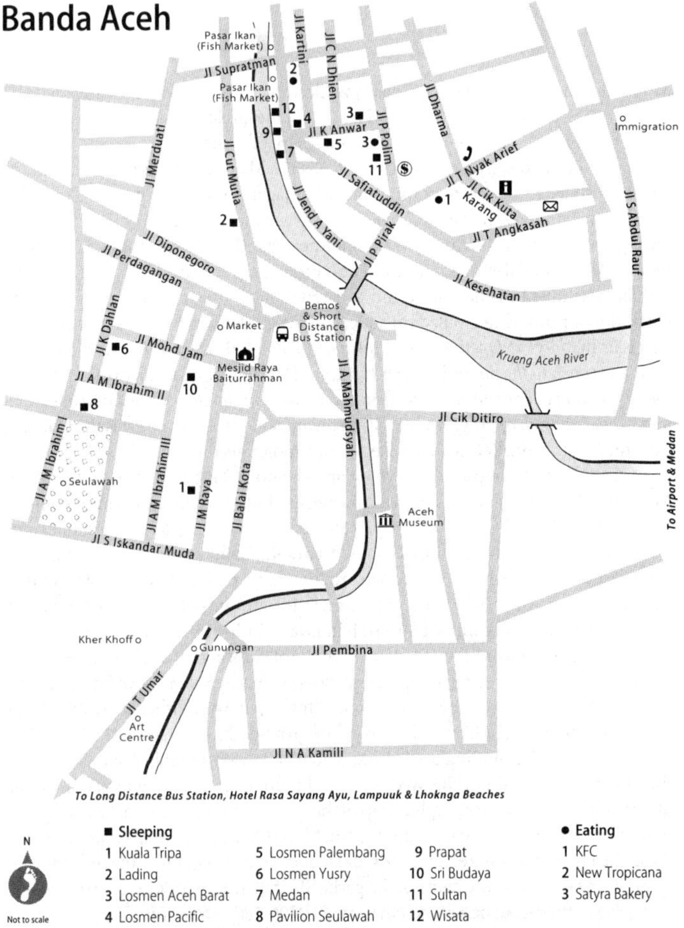

Not to scale

■ Sleeping
1 Kuala Tripa
2 Lading
3 Losmen Aceh Barat
4 Losmen Pacific
5 Losmen Palembang
6 Losmen Yusry
7 Medan
8 Pavilion Seulawah
9 Prapat
10 Sri Budaya
11 Sultan
12 Wisata

● Eating
1 KFC
2 New Tropicana
3 Satyra Bakery

Iskandar's death, and with a fall in pepper prices and the growing power of the Europeans, Aceh gradually declined in influence.

Iskandar Muda's downfall was precipitated by his quest for power which effectively bankrupted the sultanate – notwithstanding the wealth he accumulated through his personal control of the pepper trade. He alienated the British and Dutch trading companies on which he depended, and when the massive expeditionary force that he sent to Melaka in 1629 to attack the Portuguese was defeated he, and Aceh's power, were broken. During his reign, Iskandar Muda had been careful to kill all potential male heirs and so, on his death, was succeeded by his son-in-law **Iskandar Thani** (r 1637-41). Though Iskandar Thani was fervent in his adherence to orthodox Islam (he executed Portuguese captives who refused to embrace Islam), his reign was generally peaceful. He also built the royal garden and *gunungan*.

The Acehnese have displayed a long-standing penchant for resisting externally imposed authority. This thirst for autonomy means that Aceh feels almost like a nation apart. The Dutch lost large numbers of soldiers during the Aceh War (1873-78), which never succeeded in completely quelling local resistance (see box). Even since independence, Aceh has continued to demonstrate its distaste for central control. 1953 saw a vigorous rebellion over the role of Islam, and this rumbled on until 1962. There remains the impression that the authorities have only a tenuous hold over this fiercely independent province.

Sights

Much of Banda Aceh's glorious past was destroyed when the Dutch invaded the town in 1874, including the Sultan's Palace and the Great Mosque. Today, most of the sights of interest are found south of the centre of town.

A good place to start a tour of the sights is the **Mesjid Raya Baiturrahman**, or Great Mosque, at the intersection of Jalan Perdagangan and Jalan Balai Kota. The mosque was built by the Dutch in 1879 to replace the one that they had destroyed during the assault on 14 April 1873, and it now stands as one of Indonesia's more memorable colonial-era buildings. The commander of the Dutch forces, JHR Kohler, was killed in the attack and a plaque marks the spot where he fell. The black-domed and white-walled mosque, with its gardens and ponds, is an island of peace in the city. ■ *Open to non-Muslims: 0700-1100, 1330-1600 Mon-Sun. The minaret is open to the public between 1500 and 1800 and provides an excellent view of the city. Remove shoes on entering the mosque; women should be veiled and both men and women dressed appropriately.* Behind the mosque and to the west is the **Chinese quarter** and the **market**, with jewellery and handicrafts for sale.

Southeast of the mosque, down Jalan Alauddin Mahmudsyah, is the **Aceh Museum** (T23144) which displays local artefacts, but which little explanatory information. ■ *0830-1400 Tue-Thu, 0830-1200 Fri and Sat, 200Rp.* In the same compound as the museum is a black-stained **rumah Aceh**, a model of a traditional Acehnese aristocrat's house. Here too are the graves of a number of 18th-century sultans of Aceh. Right next to the museum, in the grounds of part of the University Iskandar Muda, is the **tomb of Sultan Iskandar Muda** himself (1607-36).

Further south, still on Jalan T Umar, is the site of **Gunungan**, a palace and enclosed pleasure garden built during the 17th century – possibly by Sultan Iskandar Muda. It is said to have been built by the Sultan for one of his queens who wished to be able to take an evening stroll – forbidden at that time. The grounds also contain a cake-like, white structure with stairs running up the side. There have been a number of theories as to the use and symbolism of this weird artificial mountain. Some argue that it was an observatory; others, a topographic map of the queen's homeland to make her feel less homesick; still others, the cosmic mountain, Mount Meru; or perhaps even an altar to Agni, the Hindu god of fire. Art historian Jacques Dumarçay argues that it is a phallic symbol – he notes that the name of the park, Ghairah, means ardour, love or passion, and believes the rest to be self-explanatory. ■ *0700-1800 Mon-Sun.*

On the other side of the road is the immaculately kept **Kher Khoff**, which contains the graves of 2,200 Dutch soldiers killed fighting the Acehnese between the late 19th century and early 20th century. Among them is the grave of JHR Kohler, killed while storming the Mesjid Raya. ■ *0700-1800 Mon-Sun, free (although the graveyard keeper may expect a 'donation').*

The park on the other side of Jalan Sultan Iskandar Muda contains **Seulawah** – 'Golden Mountain' (RI-001) – a **Dakota DC3**, belonging to Indonesian Airways. Bought in 1948, it was Indonesian Airways' first plane, purchased with donations from people in Aceh Province, and was intended to break the Dutch blockade. Facing onto the park are a number of fine examples of Dutch colonial architecture.

The **Pasar Ikan** (fish market) is worth a visit in the morning. It is at the north end of Jalan Jend A Yani, at the intersection with Jalan Supratman by the bridge crossing the Kreung Aceh. The market extends along both banks of the river by the bridge.

Excursions

Lampuuk Beach is 13 km southwest of Banda Aceh. The beautiful 2 km-long beach is a good spot for surfing and, when the surf is not too strong, snorkels are available for hire to explore the coral beds. Also here is an excellent seafood restaurant, money changing facilities (cash only) and a laundry service. The (**F**) *Aceh Bungalows* is a new losmen run by a British man, rooms are clean and have electricity, fans available, recommended. Trips by boat and mountain bike can be arranged to explore the surrounding area and this is a particularly good place to come for those without the time to reach Pulau Weh. ■ *Getting there: take Bus No 4 labi-labi from the terminal by the mosque (1,000Rp); a taxi costs 15,000Rp.*

Lhoknga Beach is another 5 km on from Lampuuk and around 18½ km from Banda Aceh. There is good surf here, but beware of the dangerous currents. Swim only in modest swimsuits. There is snorkelling off-shore, for which you will have to hire a boat. Further on still is the beautiful beach area of **Lho'seuda**. The **E** *Pondok Wisata Mitabu* and **E** *Pondok Wisata Darlian* are both at Lhoknga, and there is little to choose between them. In a different category entirely is **C-D** *Taman Tepi Laut Cottages*, with stylish rooms and bungalows. ■ *Getting there: by bus from the terminal by the mosque.*

Siem is a village 14 km to the east of Banda Aceh and a centre for traditional silk weaving in the area. Here it is possible to witness the entire silk weaving process from silk worm to finished article. ■ *Getting there: take labi-labi 02G towards Krueng Kali.*

Sabang on the **Island of Weh** can be reached from Pelabuhan Malahayati (Krueng Raya), a port 33 km east of the city (see page 519). ■ *Getting there: by bemo from Jalan Diponegoro.*

Essentials

A *Kuala Tripa*, Jl Mesjid Raya 24, T24535, F21790. A/c, restaurant (expensive – but good foodstalls opposite the hotel on the 'playground'), pool (open to non-residents 1000-1800, 2,000Rp), best in town, good value, all modern facilities, 40 rooms, big discounts available. **A** *Sultan*, Jl Panglima Polim 127, T22469, F31770. A/c, situated in the centre of town and 1 of the 2 top places to stay. Sixty clean and comfortable rooms and everything you could expect from a 3-star hotel, discounts possible. **A-B** *Hotel Pavilion Seulawah*, off Jl A M Ibrahim I, T/F22788. A/c, restaurant, hotel in an attractive and quiet setting, opposite Banda Aceh's DC3 and away from the hurly-burly of the city centre. Helpful and friendly staff. Recommended.

B-C *Rasa Sayang Ayu*, Jl T Umar 439, south of the centre, near the bus station, T41983, F42846. A/c, 40 rooms, restaurant, big clean rooms. **B-D** *Hotel Medan*, Jl Jend A Yani, T21501, F32256. Some a/c, good mid-range hotel with large rooms, attached bathrooms, hot water, fridge and TV. **B-D** *Hotel Wisata*, Jl Jend A Yani. A/c, newly opened hotel with spotless (to date) and comfortable rooms. **C-D** *Hotel Lading*, Jl Cut Mutia 9, T21359. Some

Sleeping
■ *on map*
Price codes:
see inside front cover

Many of the budget-priced hotels are on Jl Jend A Yani, but quite a few seem to cater for locals only. Also, because Banda Aceh is not a popular tourist destination, accommodation at the lower end is comparatively expensive

a/c, attached mandi, apparently designed by a blindfolded architect. **C-D** *Hotel Sri Budaya*, Jl A M Ibrahim III, T21751. Some a/c, the top rooms here have a/c and TV, the cheapest a fan and shared mandi, clean and popular and often booked up. **C-D** *Prapat*, Jl Jend A Yani 17, T22159. Some a/c, cleanish, no showers, popular and rather better managed than others in this category. The building may have some character but it is beginning to show its age. **C-E** *Losmen Aceh Barat*, Jl K Anwar, T23250. Some a/c, cheapest rooms have fan and shared mandi and are rather grubby, the newer extension has a/c rooms with attached showers that are considerably cleaner, the management do not put themselves out for their guests.

The very cheapest places to stay are around double the price that they are elsewhere

D *Losmen Yusry*, Jl Mohd Jam 1, T23160. Attached mandis and reasonably clean, but not very welcoming to foreigners. **D-E** *Losmen Palembang*, Jl Khairil Anwar 51, T22044. Some a/c, brightly painted exterior belies a rather dark interior decorated with local artefacts, some rooms with private mandis, a sound bet for those on a budget. **E** *Losmen Pacific*, Jl Jend A Yani 22, T31364. Just about the cheapest place around, but still comparatively expensive, clean rooms with fan and shared facilities. Recommended.

Eating
● *on map*
Price codes: see inside front cover

Indonesian Cheap: for good Acehnese restaurant food try the *Aceh Spesifik*, Jl T Cut Ali 22-24, behind the grand mosque. *Garuda Baru*, Jl Jend A Yani 30-41. *Ujong Batee*, Jl Krueng Raya, out of town. Wide array of Acehnese and excellent seafood – as well as cold beer. Recommended. *Rindang Café*, Jl Balai Kota. Excellent outdoor café with extensive menu and good fruit drinks. **Very cheap**: *Minang Surya*, Jl Safiatuddin. Good Padang food. *Satyva*, Jl Khairil Anwar 3. Bakery, good for breakfast with a wide selection of bread and cakes. *Sinar Surya*, Jl Jend A Yani (by the night market). Minang food.

Chinese Cheap: *New Tropicana*, Jl Jend A Yani 90-92. Considered by locals to be the best Chinese restaurant in town, in fact in all of Sumatra; despite an element of home town exaggeration, it does serve excellent Chinese food (and ice cream) and is very popular with Banda's Chinese population – a good sign. Recommended. **Very cheap**: *Warung Surabaya*, Jl Khairil Anwar 32. Satay.

International Expensive to mid-range *Kuala Tripa Hotel*, Jl Mesjid Raya 24, 24-hr coffee shop serving European, Chinese, Indonesian and Japanese food – even fish and chips with tartar sauce. *Hotel Sultan*, Jl Panglima Polim. Same range of international dishes as the *Kuala Tripa*, but a touch cheaper and with live jazz in the evening.

Foodstalls There are a number of cheap warungs along Jl Cik. Ditiro; also try the stalls in Penayong, Chinatown. The best place to try is probably the night market on the junction of Jl Jend A Yani and Jl Khairil Anwar, opposite the *Hotel Medan*, where good, cheap Indonesian and Chinese food can be found.

Entertainment
Very little nightlife because of strict adherence to Islam. The stadium sometimes stages bullfights. Real Acehnese nightlife centres around eating and socializing in outdoor hawker centres, such as the one in front of the *Hotel Medan*. Worth a visit for the atmosphere and, not least, the excellent array of freshly-cooked Indonesian dishes at rock bottom prices. There is a disco at *Kuala Tripa*, Jl Mesjid Raya 24.

Shopping
Antiques Dutch, Acehnese and Chinese antiques to be found on Jl Perdagangan. **Handicrafts** Government handicraft shop at Jl S R Safiatuddin 54. The Pasar Aceh (market) near the mosque is a good place to browse. **Jewellery** Shops line Jl Perdagangan, and they will copy most things. **Souvenirs** *Aceh Putra*, Jl Aceh/Merduati 60, T32989.

Sports
Swimming *Kuala Tripa Hotel*, Jl Mesjid Raya 24. Open to non-residents 1000-1800 (2,000Rp).

Tour operators
Kreung Wayla, Jl Safiatuddin 26, T22066. *Nustra Agung*, Jl Diponegoro, T22026. *Sastra*, Jl Jend A Yani, T22207. *Tripa Wisata*, Kuala Tripa Hotel, Jl Mesjid Raya 24, T21455. *Natrabu*, Beurawe Shopping Centre, T32243.

Local Bus: the Stasiun Kota (short distance bus station) is by the mosque. Frequent service around town; just hail one from the side of the road. **Becak mesin**: motorbikes with sidecars. **Bemos**: leave from Jl Diponegoro for the beaches at Lhoknga, Lampuuk and for the ferry to Sabang. **Labi-labi**: (minibuses) for short distances, 300Rp around town. **Taxis**: metered. **Air** The airport is nearly 20 km from town (15,000Rp by taxi). Daily connections on Garuda with Medan, and from there to other destinations in and beyond Sumatra. **Road Bus**: the Terminal Bus Seuti is southwest of town on Jl Tk. Umar. Regular a/c and non-a/c bus connections with Medan, and down the west coast to Sidikalang and beyond. The road to Medan is fast and good (although some bus drivers appear to have no sense), 12 hrs. The major bus companies (ATS, Kurnia, Melati and ARS) have their offices on Jl Mohd Jam.

Transport
594 km north of Medan, 112 km from Sigli, 218 km from Bireuen

Airline offices Garuda Merpati, Hotel Sultan, Jl Panglima Polim 127, T32523, F23467. **Banks** Bank Central Asia, Jl Panglima Polim. Bank Negara Indonesia 1946, Jl A H K Dahlan. Bank Dagang Negara, Jl Diponegoro. Bank Bumi Daya, Jl Cut Mutia. **Communications** Post Office: Jl T Angkasa. Telephone office: Jl T Nyak Arief 92. **Medical facilities** Hospital: Jl T Nyak Arief, T22616. **Useful addresses** Immigration Office: Jl T Nyak Arief 82, T23784. Police: Jl T Nyak Arief, T21125.

Directory

Weh Island and Sabang

Weh is one of those places which springs to international prominence – in this case as a coal bunkering depot – and then quickly sinks below the historical horizon. Unlike most such places, though, Weh is having a second bite at the cherry of international fortune, this time as a tropical island beach resort. With excellent coral, fine beaches and a welcoming atmosphere, it has all the necessary vital statistics.

Colour map 1, grid A1

There are daily flights on SMAC from Banda Aceh to Sabang. Most people, though, arrive by ferry from Krueng Raya, 33 km east of Banda Aceh. There are daily departures and the journey takes 2½ hrs. **Getting around** Taxis, bemos and motorbikes provide the main forms of transport on the island. Fishing boats can be chartered for trips to the smaller islands for snorkelling and fishing expeditions.

Getting there & around
See transport, page 522, for further details

Weh Island

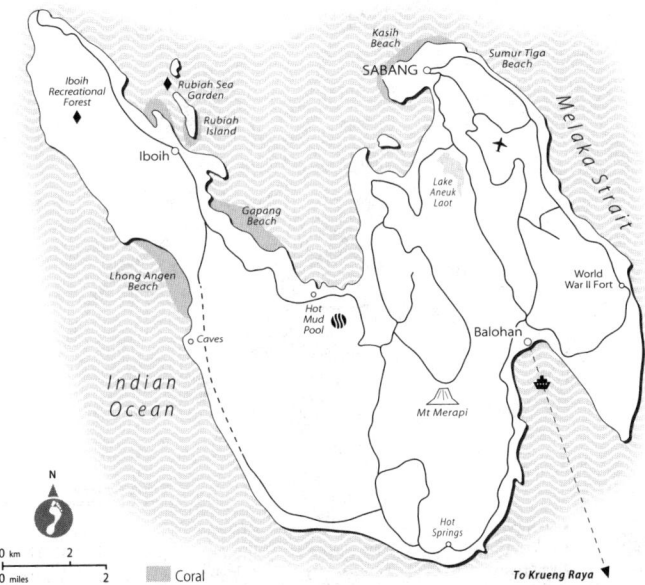

Related map
A Sabang, page 520

Background In the late 19th century under Dutch rule, this small island of 150 sq km – inhabited at that time only by fishermen – was developed into an important bunkering depot. Steamships and liners from around the world docked here to replenish their stocks of coal and fresh water. Indeed, up until the Second World War, Sabang was a more important port than Singapore. However, as diesel replaced steam, so the island became redundant. During the Second World War the Japanese took over the island, and reminders of the 3½ year occupation can still be seen in the gun emplacements that dot the island's cliffs.

In 1970, **Sabang** – the main town on Weh – was declared a duty-free port and it seemed that it would once again become a centre of commercial activity. These plans came to nothing when the port's duty-free status was abruptly terminated in 1986, due to the government's concern about the increase in smuggling and its desire to develop the island of Batam, close to Singapore, as Indonesia's premier free port. Since then Weh has experienced a steady decline in its economy and today the 25,000 inhabitants rely heavily on tourism, the only industry which appears to be buoyant. Even so, tourism's impact is still comparatively light.

Sights The best reason to visit Weh is for the snorkelling, diving, swimming and palm-lined beaches – and for the peace and quiet. Beaches around Sabang include **Pantai Sumur Tiga** (Three Wells Beach) on the northwest coast, where high tide leaves little sandy areas, **Paradise Beach** and **Pantai Kasih** (Lovers Beach). The latter is probably the best and is popular among the local youths who congregate here in the late afternoon.

However, the best beaches, and the most popular amongst foreign tourists, are those along the western limb of the island. **Lhong Angen Beach** is very secluded and a beautiful getaway between November and May (at other times of year the soft sand is swept away by strong waves). **Gapang Beach** is the longer and quieter beach of the two – and the sheltered bay and weaker currents also make it more suitable for swimming. The best coral beds are at either end of the beach and large tropical fish

Sabang

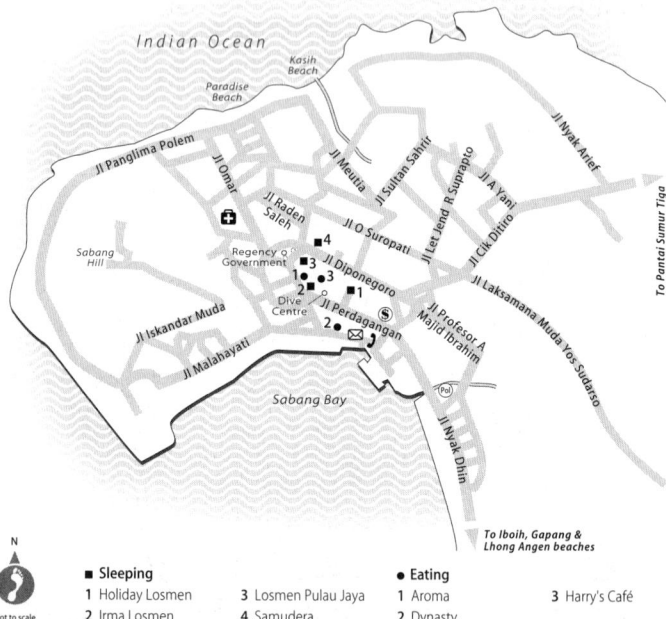

■ **Sleeping**
1 Holiday Losmen
2 Irma Losmen
3 Losmen Pulau Jaya
4 Samudera

● **Eating**
1 Aroma
2 Dynasty
3 Harry's Café

and turtles are commonly seen (particularly at the southern end). Gapang has managed to retain much of its peaceful and secluded charm, despite the construction of the *Gapang Beach Cottages*. It was anticipated that this place would be a large complex, but due to *krismon* (the economic crisis), they have only built six cottages. A waterfall with a large and beautiful plunge pool – ideal for swimming – is situated southeast of Gapang. For details, ask at any of the restaurants in Iboih or Gapang as they will arrange a boat trip along the coast and a guide for the 30-minute walk inland to the falls (based on a boat taking 10 people, the cost should be around 3,000Rp per person).

Iboih Beach, a couple of kilometres north from Gapang, has more accommodation and facilities and therefore attracts a greater number of tourists. The atmosphere is more lively and it is also the base for the Stingray Dive Centre (see page 522). Although the beach here is smaller and the currents rather stronger than at Gapang, the coral beds are excellent.

The **Rubiah Sea Garden**, a 2,600 ha marine reserve, provides excellent visibility and a wealth of sea life, although the coral is being gradually destroyed by fishermen, illegally using dynamite. The marine reserve is centred on Pulau Rubiah, on the west of Sabang Bay, and is accessible from the village of Iboih, on the west of the island and 23 km from Sabang (accommodation is concentrated here, see below). The sea life seen in the area includes turtles (many), manta rays, lion fish, scorpion fish, occasional reef sharks and, between January and February, whale sharks.

Getting across to Rubiah can be difficult – beware of the strong currents

Just outside Iboih is the small **Iboih Recreational Forest** (1,300 ha), a tropical forest reserve with good walks and a smattering of wildlife (for example, wild boar). Also accessible from Iboih is **Mount Merapi**, a small semi-active volcano with hot springs on its slopes. Boats can be chartered to explore the **caves** along the coast of the west peninsula.

Sabang Few people choose to stay in the main town of Sabang, but there are three losmen and a hotel and tourists may have to spend a night here on arrival or departure. **B-D** *Holiday Losmen*, Jl Perdagangan Belakang 1, T21131. Some a/c, restaurant, set back from the main road, it doesn't look much from the outside, but it is quiet and peaceful with clean rooms, credit cards accepted and deposit box facilities available. **B-D** *Hotel Samudera*, Jl Diponegoro, T21503. Some a/c, restaurant, ideally situated above the park in a peaceful area of town, this hotel opened in mid-1996 and is the most upmarket place to stay in Sabang. Rooms are clean and the management are friendly, the cheapest rooms are basic but have their own mandis, while the more expensive have a/c. The small restaurant serves breakfast and has a limited dinner menu. Recommended. **D-E** *Irma Losmen*, Jl T Umar 3, T21148. Situated above *Harry's Café*, this place is rather mixed: the rooms are crummy and the mandis are downright disgusting, but it is also a friendly and lively place and well patronized by a good range of visitors. It is also the cheapest place in town and a valuable source of information. **D-E** *Losmen Pulau Jaya ('PJ')*, Jl T Umar 17, T21344. Some a/c, well maintained with large, airy and clean rooms, the cheapest rooms have shared mandis and a choice of squat and Western-style toilets. Popular among the backpacking fraternity.

Sleeping
■ *on map*
Price codes:
see inside front cover

The beaches Accommodation at the beaches is very basic. Most are palm-thatched wooden bungalows with no electricity and shared squat loos and mandis. Water generally comes from wells (although this may well soon change). During the high season, accommodation is often booked up and those unlucky enough to arrive too late to grab a room may have to spend a night on a restaurant floor. However, the turnover is rapid, so there is usually a bungalow available by the following morning. For this reason it can be a good plan to spend the first night in Sabang and get to the beaches the following morning, ahead of the ferry. There are about 20 bungalows at **Gapang B-C** *Gapang Beach Cottage*, T21503, only 6 cottages here (more planned but they remained incomplete due to *krismon*), big restaurant and conference hall. There are also over 50 more cottages at **Iboih**, run by 5 or 6 people. There is little to choose between them and prices are **E-F** per hut. There are also a few bungalows, and a restaurant, at **Lhong Angen Beach**.

Eating
● on map
Price codes:
see inside front cover

There are a number of Padang and Chinese restaurants in Sabang. The *Dynasty* on Jl Perdagangan serves the best Chinese cuisine. *Harry's Café* (beneath *Irma Losmen*), Jl TK Umar, offers good value, tasty, travellers' food. There are also a number of restaurants at the beaches, each offering a reasonable selection of cheap dishes, most also offer 'family' food in our 'very cheap' price range. Tasty, large portions and good value.

Sports **Snorkelling and diving** Snorkelling equipment is hired out by *Losmen Pulau Jaya* in town; cheaper equipment is available from guesthouses at Iboih and Gapang beaches. A new dive centre has opened at Gapang (owned and run by a Dutch diver). Equipment varies in quality but rates are generally mask/snorkel, 2,000Rp for mask/snorkel, 3,000Rp for fins. The *Stingray Dive Centre* (next to *Harry's Café*), T21265, F21333, has an office in Sabang (open 0800-1200, 1800-2100) and at a dive shop at Iboih. The outfit runs various dive courses: 4-5 day open water course, US$260; advanced open water course (5 dives, 2-3 days), US$200; 2 tank introductory dives including meals and boat, US$50 for 2 or more people.

Transport **Local** Taxi, bemo and motorbike. Fishing boats can be chartered for trips to the smaller islands for snorkelling and fishing. **Air** There are daily flights by SMAC from Banda Aceh. **Boat** Ferries leave from Krueng Raya (Pelabuhan Malahayati), about 33 km east of Banda Aceh, 14.30 Tue-Fri, 1000 and 1600 Sat-Mon, 2½ hrs (3,900-5,500Rp). Ferries depart from Weh for Krueng Raya every day at 0730 and also at 1300 from Sat to Mon. To get to Krueng Raya, take a bemo from Jl Diponegoro in Banda Aceh, 45 mins. Passengers should aim to arrive 1 hr before departure. The ferry docks at Balohan, on the south coast of Weh, from where there are minibuses and taxis to take passengers the 10 km north to Sabang town and onward to Gapang and Iboih. In Banda Aceh, the ferry office (PASDP) is at Jl Gabus (Lam Prit), T21377. If travelling direct from Medan to Pulau Weh, take one of the overnight buses which get into Banda Aceh around 0600. This leaves the rest of the morning to look around the city before catching a bemo to the harbour.

Directory **Banks** There are money changers in Sabang but the rates are poor. **Communications** Post Office: Jl Perdagangan. **Telephone office:** Wartel, next to the Post Office. **Useful addresses** Immigration Office: Jl Seulawah, T21343. Police Station: Jl Perdagangan, T21306.

Banda Aceh to Sidikalang

Female travellers have reported a considerable amount of hassle. Where possible, it is advisable to travel with a male companion, & always dress very modestly, keeping well covered

For travellers with time to spare and who want an attractive alternative to the east coast overnight bus or the inland road through the Gayo Highlands, there is now the possibility of continuing on from Banda Aceh, south down the west coast of Sumatra to Sidikalang and from there to Lake Toba, a route which over the last couple of years has become increasingly popular – unsurprisingly, as it is a beautiful part of Sumatra. There are isolated and rarely visited beaches along the coast, which bear the full brunt of the surf rolling in off the Indian Ocean. The road is much improved and the journey takes about 18 hours by bus.

Sleeping Except for Meulobah, Tapaktuan and Sidikalang, only basic losmen accommodation and homestays are available on the west coast. Many of the losmen are brothels, so staying with families is recommended wherever possible. However, as this route is becoming increasingly popular, the choice of accommodation is widening all the time.

Transport Buses run direct from Banda Aceh to Meulaboh, the next large town on the west coast travelling south, 4-5 hrs. Many of the stops on this route are little more than villages, although many have places to stay.

Lamno Losmen accommodation available: **F** *Losmen Singgahan* (50m from Lamno turn-off), very basic rooms. The beaches along the 40 km of coast from Lamno to Calang are very beautiful. The hiking is excellent and the local people friendly.

Rigaih Near Calang **B-D** *Dieter's Beautiful Place*, aka *Camp Europa* and *Dieter's Farm*, was an excellent losmen run by a German – the eponymous Dieter – who built a small number of stilt houses in the forest just inland from a stupendous beach, with wonderful clear blue sea and excellent swimming. However, Dieter has now moved on and the reputation of the camp has deteriorated. Rooms are comparatively pricey for the amenities offered (even with four meals and drinks included in the room rate) and some visitors report that they are also dirty; the caged orang utan has also proved to turn large numbers off the place. A better bet is the neighbouring **E** *Hasan* – it is cleaner, friendlier and cheap. The restaurant here is also recommended.

Meulaboh

Meulaboh is an unremarkable town – the largest settlement on the west coast and the regional capital. It is relatively well endowed with facilities, although the standard of accommodation is not particularly high. *Colour map 1, grid A1*

Sights Few visitors choose to spend much time in Meulaboh, treating it mainly as a stop-over on the west coast journey, or *en route* to Simeulue Island. There are, however, a number of beaches nearby and some (albeit limited) surfing. The **grave and monument of Teuku Umar**, a local hero who died here fighting the Dutch in 1899, and who is now immortalized in countless road names, is situated on a beach 2 km north of town. ■ *Get there by becak (1,500Rp).*

Sleeping The cheapest accommodation in Meulaboh is concentrated near the public bus and labi-labi terminals. **B-D** *Meuligon Hotel*, Jl Iskandar Muda, T22222, F22322. A/c, restaurant, the only up-market hotel in town, modern and very clean, suites also available, wide range of facilities including good value restaurant and bar. Recommended. **C-E** *Hotel Tiara*, Jl T Umar, T21531. Some a/c, restaurant, rather older than the *Meuligon* – and it shows – rooms are clean enough although they can be noisy as the hotel is situated on the main street. **C-E** *Mestika Losmen*, Jl Nasional, T21033. The cheaper rooms are reasonable value here but the expensive rooms are overpriced – much better to stay at the *Tiara* or *Nova*. **D** *Hotel Nova*, Jl Nasional, T21828, F21936. Some a/c, the newest of the mid-range hotels in Meulaboh, all rooms with attached mandi. **E-F** *Losmen Pelita Jaya*, Jl Singgah Mata. The rooms with shared facilities are even cheaper than the *Erna*, some rooms with attached mandi. **F** *Losmen Erna*, Jl Singgah Mata. So basic that there isn't even a mandi available! **F** *Losmen Simeulue*, Jl Singgah Mata. Dark and dingy place – a hangout for local becak drivers.

Transport **Bus** From the bus terminal south to Tapaktuan and north to Banda Aceh. **Boat** Ferries run from the harbour (worth a wander) to the off-shore island of Simeulue on Mon, Wed and Fri at 1800 (9,500Rp economy, 15,000Rp for a cabin), 12 hrs.

Tapaktuan

Tapaktuan is a small, attractive town with a relaxed and friendly atmosphere – and a good daily market. It is situated between the Bukit Barisan and the Indian Ocean, and the surrounding hills offer panoramic views over the town and the coastline. The local economy is based on fishing and agriculture – especially nutmeg. Many travellers choose to break their journey for several days here. *Colour map 1, grid A2*

Excursions The beaches to the north and south, stretching over 40 km or so, are very beautiful. Easiest to reach are **Air Dingin** and **Tu'l Lhok**, 17 km and 18 km north of Tapaktuan respectively. Air Dingin is probably the better of the two, with its freshwater plunge pool beneath a 20m waterfall just the other side of the road – a great place to cool off. ■ *Getting there: take a bemo from the bus terminal to either beach (500Rp).*
Another waterfall well worth a visit is the popular **Tingkat Tujuh Waterfall**, or Seven Steps Waterfall, which is 7 km south of Tapaktuan. At each level there are

natural bathing pools. The top three are out of bounds because they are used to feed Tapaktuan's water supply. ■ *Getting there: by bemo from the bus terminal (200Rp).*

For the slightly more adventurous, it is possible to explore the **Gua Kalem** or 'Dark Cave', a series of passages and narrow tunnels leading to **Panton Luas**, from where there is a spectacular view of Tapaktuan and the ocean. A guide is recommended (ask at the *Losmen Bukit Barisan*).

There is good **trekking** in the surrounding forest, although a guide is recommended. A good source of information is the *Losmen Bukit Barisan*.

Sleeping C-D *Hotel Dian Rana*, Jl Angkasah, T21444, F21555. The most upmarket place to stay around, situated 10 mins' walk south of the town centre, the interesting cylindrical design means that rooms face out in all directions, the most expensive ones overlooking the ocean, there is an open-air restaurant on the ground floor, rooms are clean and all but the cheapest have a/c. Cheaper rooms at 15,000Rp have just 1 single bed. Recommended. **C-D** *Hotel Putro Bongsu*, Jl Nyak Adam Kamil, T21395. All rooms have own mandi, some a/c, restaurant situated in a peaceful backstreet away from the hubbub of the centre of town, this is a relaxing place to stay although rather overpriced, rooms are clean, but watch out for mosquitoes. **D-E** *Hotel Panorama*, Jl Merdeka, T21004. With its central location, this hotel offers an easy and convenient place to stay, some rooms have a/c and all have own mandi, the top floor overlooking the harbour has great views. **E** *Losmen Bukit Barisan*, Jl Merdeka 37. A friendly little losmen with a Dutch-speaking owner, rooms are reasonably clean with fan – some with own mandi, a good source of information – jungle treks can be arranged. **E-F** *Losmen Jambu*, Jl A Yani. Popular amongst travellers, this losmen is run by a friendly old chap who is keen to be of assistance and to make his guests' stay as comfortable as possible, nicely set back from the noisier main street, rooms are clean (relatively), as are the mandis. **F** *Kanada Losmen*, Jl Merdeka. The cheapest accommodation in town, facilities are very basic, with small, dark rooms, although they do have noisy fans, its best selling point is its fantastic view out over the harbour and ocean from the quiet balcony at the back.

There are a number of places to stay in town of varying standards, although a few of the cheaper losmen do not welcome foreigners (namely the Jogya, Gunung Tuan & Restu Selatan near the harbour). Even so, there remain 3 budget losmen to choose from

Eating There are a number of restaurants along Jl Merdeka, offering the usual Padang-style fare. Seafood is, of course, always freshly caught. Every evening, as dusk falls, the 'Rek' emerges at the harbour – a lively atmosphere and a good selection of foodstalls in the open air.

Transport **Road Bus**: the bulk of the trip between here and Meulaboh is unremarkable and taking a bus or hitching is recommended (4-5 hrs). Buses available from the station 1 km out of town to the west, all the way to Sidikalang, 6 hrs. From Tapaktuan there are occasional boats to Pulau Banyak (see page 526).

Directory **Banks** *Bank RRI*, Jl Nyak Adam Kamil. **Communications** Post Office: Jl Angkasah. **Telephone office**: Wartel, Jl Merdeka.

Bakongan This sleepy fishing town 60 km south of Tapaktuan is seldom visited by tourists, but there are two losmen available: **F** *Losmen Karya Baru*, Jl Muara 22, T21022, room rates are per person, shared facilities, no fan; **F** *Losmen Nusantara*, Jl Perdangangan 35, T21052, newly renovated with 10 rooms.

Trumon Once the capital of a local chief or *ulubalang*, in 1811 Trumon clashed with the sultanate of Banda Aceh. The town's powerful trading ships, laden with black pepper bound for the Americas, were seized and the subsequent loss of income forced the principality to adopt a more submissive role. Today the town has barely 1,000 inhabitants. It is still possible to see the remains of the 18th-century fort – currently undergoing excavation and, in some cases, renovation. Unfortunately, this has not always been done with great sensitivity or panache: the wooden house belonging to the former king has been renovated in concrete. Behind the mosque is the graveyard where the kings are buried. There is one cheap losmen **F** *Lily Satria*, and it is also possible to stay with the headman.

South of Bakongan, 9 km off the main road to Subulussalam

Gelombang A small village on the Alas River – the destination for most rafting trips from Kutacane (see page 526). Arriving here in the afternoon, it is possible to catch a bus on to Tapaktuan (4,000Rp) or Subulussalam (2,000Rp), where there are connections to Banda Aceh or Medan. There is one new losmen in town, the **E** *Losmen Sanggra*, where rooms have fans and attached mandis. From here there is (said to be) a boat every Thursday to Kutacane (see page 526).

Subulussalam An uninteresting town with little to recommend it – but many people have to change buses here on the route from Sidikalang and Tapaktuan, or if heading south to Singkil, *en route* to Pulau Banyak. For those arriving in the late afternoon or evening it may be necessary to spend the night. Losmen are available, including **F** *Losmen Doaibu*, Jl Teuku Umar 73, shared facilities; **F** *Penginapan Terang Bulan*, Jl Teuku Umar 214, shared facilities; **E** *Abadi*, Jl Teuku Umar 173, attached mandi and fan.

Sidikalang A larger town with a range of accommodation available. Buses from here to Lake Toba, Brastagi and elsewhere (see page 483).

Pulau Banyak

Pulau Banyak is a mini-archipelago of 99 islands, most uninhabited specks in the Indian Ocean, about 7-14 hours by boat off Sumatra's west coast. They are fringed with coral reefs – sadly being rapidly pillaged despite their protected status – and mangroves and their interiors are largely forested. Wild pigs inhabit the larger islands and green and leatherback turtles lay their eggs on the beaches.

Population: 4,000
Colour map 1, grid B2

Visitors should take care to dress modestly – a basic knowledge of Bahasa is also a help

In theory this should be an island idyll, but we have had reports that the snorkelling is not as good as at the far more developed Weh Island and that dynamite fishermen have done great damage to the marine ecosystem. Even so, for those searching out a place to visit which is only just beginning to receive tourists, Pulau Banyak may be an attractive option. The jungles and caves also make it more than just a beach. Life here is slow – even by Indonesian standards – and it is a poor archipelago, despite the tourists who are starting to come here. Of six villages, four were designated in the mid-1990s as *desa tertinggal* – or villages that had been 'left behind' (villages with concentrations of poverty).

The main town is **Balai** – really little more than a fishing hamlet with a handful of homestays – which supports a population of about 2,000 people. There are only motobikes here – no cars. All boats from the mainland dock here and then people transfer to accommodation on several of the other islands, including **Palambak Besar Island**, **Rangsit Besar**, **Ujung Batu** and **Panjang**. Alternatively, it is possible to stay in Balai and make day excursions out to the beaches and islands. There is a **tourist information** office at *Nanda Restaurant*, on the pier in Balai; it provides information on accommodation and maps to new arrivals.

The largest of all is **Pulau Tuangku** with an area of 11,500 ha. Visitors are beginning to trek across this island beginning at **Haloban** on the north coast, where guides are available.

Sleeping & eating **Palambak Besar Island** **F** *The Point*, restaurant, 2 large bungalows divided into 4 rooms each, good views, there should be electricity by the time this book goes to press. **F** *Bina Jaya Bungalows*, small restaurant, situated on one of the better beaches, small individual bungalows. **F** *Pondok Asmara Palambak (PAP)*, restaurant, 4 bungalows in a rather more secluded position, close to the jungle and by a river. There are also bungalows on the islands of **Rangsit Besar**, **Ujung Batu** and **Panjang**.

Sports **Diving** The *Yellow Shark Dive Centre* (based at the *Point Bungalows* on Pulau Palambak Besar) has diving equipment and snorkelling gear for hire.

Transport *All boats are cargo vessels – not dedicated passenger ships*

Local Canoes are the main form of local transport. **Sea** There are boats to Pulau Banyak from several ports on Sumatra's west coast. The most regular sea connections are from **Singkil**. Cargo vessels depart on Mon, Thu and Fri at 0800, the journey taking 4-5 hrs (5,500Rp). There are direct buses to Singkil from Brastagi. From **Banda Aceh**, take a bus to **Tapaktuan** (see page 523), 8 hrs (15-18,000Rp). From Tapaktuan there are no scheduled boats but, depending on sea conditions, about 2 vessels a week depart for the islands, 7 hrs. From **Sibolga** (see page 503) boats seem to be slightly more regular – although there is still no fixed timetable, 10-14 hrs (15,000Rp). There is also around 1 boat a week from **Gunungsitoli** on Nias (see page 511), usually mid-week, 8 hrs (15,000Rp). The Pelni ships *Kembuna* and *Lambelu* dock here.

Gunung Leuser National Park

The Gunung Leuser National Park is perhaps the finest conservation area in Indonesia, and certainly one of the most important parks in Southeast Asia. It covers 850,000 ha of tropical rainforest and other habitats in the provinces of Aceh and North Sumatra. The wide range of ecological zones, from alpine meadows among the peaks of the Bukit Barisan, to brackish-water swamps, makes this a critical conservation area. In total, the park is estimated to support some 500 species of birds, and 3,500 species of plants (of Sumatra's total recorded flora of 8,500 species). Fauna include tiger, rhino, gibbon, elephant and orang utan.

Ins and outs

Getting there *See Transport, page 530, for further details*

Kutacane has frequent connections with surrounding major towns. Buses travel from Sidikalang and Brastagi to Kutacane (6 hrs). From Brastagi there are buses every 30 mins. Buses travel from Ketambe every hour. Buses also run north from here to Blankejeren every hour, and further north still to Takengon and the Gayo Highlands. Most visitors to the park enter at the Orang Utan Rehabilitation Centre in Bukit Lawang (see page 473). However, the best access point to the park is Kutacane, the park's main town. **Admission to the park**: 2000Rp per day. Guides cost around 20,000Rp per day.

Getting around Motorized becaks can be hired locally and to visit the surrounding villages.

Background

The park was gazetted in 1980, to become one of Indonesia's first five national parks, is named after Gunung Leuser in Aceh Province which rises to a height of 3,455m, and is the second highest mountain in Sumatra. Although the park was not created until 1980, parts of the area that now make up the park were established as wildlife reserves and sanctuaries by the Dutch as early as the 1930s. The important step that the Indonesian government took in 1980 was to recognize the importance of the whole area and amalgamate a series of reserves into one extensive park.

Flora Among the park's flora is the famous **Rafflesia**, which bears the largest bloom of any plant in the world; the carnivorous *Nepenthes* or pitcher plant; the giant tulang tree (*Koompassia excelsa*) which has wood so hard that it is impervious even to chainsaws; and countless species of broad-leaved *Dipterocarp*, the tree which, more than any other, defines the lowland tropical forest of Malesia. The importance of preserving ecologically viable areas of tropical forest like that of Gunung Leuser lies in the extreme species diversity that exists. In terms of the number of species found in an average hectare of forest, the forests of island Southeast Asia are even more diverse than those of the Amazon Basin. In a single hectare of Gunung Leuser's forest, botanists can expect to identify over 150 species of tree – each of which will be represented by between just one and three individual plants.

Fauna

Around 130 species of mammal have been recorded in the park, a quarter of all the species found in Indonesia. Most are rats, bats and squirrels. Of the primates, there is a large population of around 5,000 orang utan (see page 661) living in the park, the white handed gibbon (*Hylobates lar*) and black siamang (*Hylobates syndactylus*) - with their distinctive calls which can be heard over a distance of 1 km or more - two species of macaques, two species of leaf monkey, the slow loris and the lutung (*Presbytis cristata*). Among the nine species of wild cat, the tiger is becoming increasingly scarce and is rarely seen. Also found is the clouded leopard (*Neofelis nebulosa*), the golden cat (*Felis temmincki*), and the marbled, flat-headed, leopard and fishing cats. Other carnivores include wild dogs and the sun bear (*Helarctos malayanus*). In general, the large carnivores are reclusive, tending to hunt at night, and are rarely seen.

The best known of the park's herbivores is the elephant and the Sumatran rhinoceros. Sadly, the numbers of Sumatran rhino in the park have halved over the last 10 years due to poaching, and it is on the verge of extinction not only in Gunung Leuser, but across its natural range. Other plant-eaters are deer, including the large sambar deer (*Cervus unicolor*), wild pigs, and the serow or mountain goat.

Birds

To date, 325 species of bird have been recorded in the park. There are seven species of hornbill whose distinctive cry and flight are often heard and seen. These include the rhinoceros hornbill with its outrageous beak (*Rhinoplax vigil*). Other notable birds are the argus pheasant, five species of kingfisher, the crested serpent eagle, laughing thrushes, various parrots, warblers, flycatchers and others. Perhaps the best local name for a bird is that given to the woodpecker, which is known as *tok tok perago*.

Reptiles & amphibians

Tortoises and turtles (some, in the Alas River, growing to 30 kg in weight), monitor lizards and a small population of false ghavials (a type of crocodile) in the Besitang River are all found in the reserve. The snake population include pythons, king cobras, kraits, rat snakes and the black cobra.

The above summary of the Gunung Leuser National Park's flora and fauna is condensed from Mike Griffith's excellent booklet *Leuser National Park* (1992, World Wide Fund for Nature).

Gunung Leuser National Park

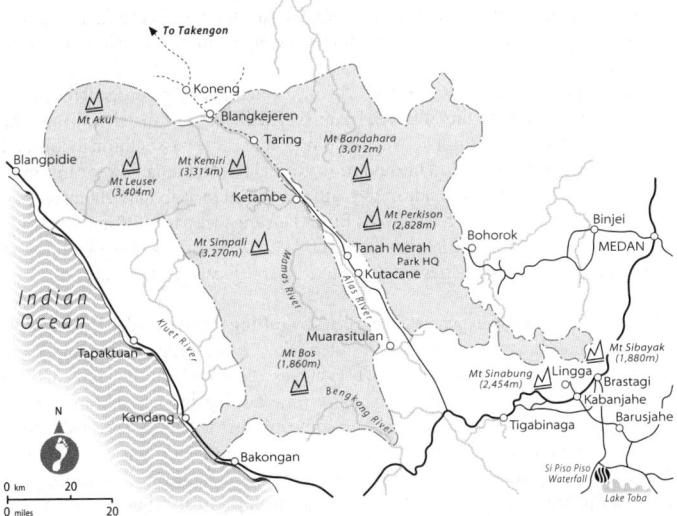

Hiking and trekking

The village of **Batu Bulan** is about 2 km from Kutacane, and nearby are some **beautiful caves** with stalagmites. Ask in your guesthouse for directions and check along the way with locals.

Day hiking trails are easily accessible from Kutacane and it is possible to see a good range of wildlife. However, park regulations insist that a guide be used. Trails range from easy saunters through the forest to more demanding **overnight treks** to the summits of the mountains in the area. Below is a summary of the main treks. Check at the park HQ for more details. Trekking information is also available in Brastagi and Bukit Lawang. Guides, and porters for longer treks, can be hired at the Park HQ.

The road north to **Gurah** and **Blangkejeren** passes through the village of **Natam**, where a traditional Alas house can be seen on the right-hand side.

Gurah and **Ketambe** lie on different banks of the Alas River. Ketambe is a research centre, 20 km north of Kutacane, at the entrance to the park. It is, however, strictly off-limits to non-authorized personnel – some companies reportedly offer treks in the area, but as of mid-1997 this was officially not permitted. Around Gurah there is a network of trails. One of the best begins at Lawe Gurah and leads to a hot spring and salt lick frequented by tigers, serow, leaf monkeys and other fauna. The walk is a leisurely 1½-2 hours. After 30 minutes or so the track arrives at a camping ground. Here, cross the river – and after another hour the trail reaches the hot springs. A great place to relax. Rejuvenated, it is possible to continue up the river bed, taking the first tributary off to the left – which leads to an attractive waterfall. There is a network of trails around the visitors' centre and some hikers choose to stay overnight at the hot springs. Orang utans, hornbills and other wildlife are present in the area. The best time to see them is dusk and dawn.

Gunung Kemiri rises to 3,314m and can be climbed in 5-6 days. The trail begins at Gumpang, which is situated at an altitude of 740m. The path follows a ridge and climbs up through pristine lowland tropical rainforest, through submontane forest, and up on to some of the finest alpine meadows or *blangs* found in Sumatra. The view from the rocky summit, over a series of peaks, is spectacular. There is a campsite 300m below the summit.

Gunung Leuser, after which the park is named, reaches a height of 3,404m and can be climbed in 10-14 days. Although the ascent is a long one, the walk is not arduous. The trail begins at the village of Angasan, 3-4 hours walk west of Blangkejeren (see below), where homestays are available. The first four days of the trek are through lowland rainforest; only on the fifth day does the path steepen and pass into submontane and montane forest, and then onto alpine meadows. There are again spectacular views from the summit.

Gunung Perkison, which rises to 2,828 m, lies on the eastern border of the park's boundaries. The trail begins at Lawe Harum which is close to Tanah Merah and the Park. Again the ascent is not very demanding as the route passes through lowland forest and then into submontane and moss forest. The Rafflesia flower can sometimes be seen growing at the side of the path at an altitude of about 1,200m.

Some people choose to trek between **Bukit Lawang** (see page 475) and Kutacane – a 5-7 day trek through primary rainforest (US$250). Most treks have a minimum lower limit of 3-4 people. These rates are fixed by the local tourist association.

Tours One of the best ways to experience the park is by **rafting down the Alas River**. *Sobek*, the American whitewater specialists, operate in the area with experienced guides and decent equipment, including coolers of beer and excellent food. The rapids themselves are graded Class 3, offering something for everyone, flowing through some of the most spectacular scenery in Sumatra. Other tour companies in Medan (see page 460) and in Brastagi (see page 482) can arrange such trips, as can the Tourist office in Kutacane. **NB** It is recommended that you try to organize trips locally, as it can cost half the price of a similar trip booked in Medan. Prices are highly variable, but range between

Sobek tours must be pre-booked in Medan

50,000Rp and 100,000Rp per person per day. Several companies in Kutacane, such as *Alas River Tour and Travel Service* (T21743) and *Pintu Alas Tour and Travel*, both on Jalan Jend A Yani, and some of the guesthouses in town can organize trekking and rafting. Approximate prices quoted are for two or four people and include all meals, drinks, a guide, tents, permits and insurance: three-day trek, US$65-80; four days, US$80-95; five days, US$95-110. A combined rafting and trekking trip: three-day raft/one-day trek, US$115-130; three-day raft/two-day trek, US$130-145. Note that it may not be the wisest move to opt for the cheapest trek on offer: equipment and guides vary considerably.

Trekking in Gunung Leuser National Park: check list

- Light, long-sleeved shirts and trousers
- Good walking boots
- Leech socks
- Waterproofs
- Sleeping bag (temperatures at altitude fall markedly at night)
- First aid kit
- Food for all, including the guide(s)
- Tent and plastic ground sheet

NB *Most accidents in the park occur when crossing rivers.*

Essentials

In Kutacane Kutacane is less touristy than some other areas of North Sumatra such as Bukit Lawang. As a result, competition has not driven prices down and you should expect to pay slightly more for a room here.

Sleeping
Price code: see inside front cover

C-D *Brudihe*, Jl Cut Nyak Dhien, T21444. Attractive courtyard, relatively clean, if expensive rooms, higher price gets a/c, western loo and TV. **C-E** *Hotel Marron*, off Jl Cut Nyak Dhien, T21078. Cheapest rooms may or may not have windows, shared mandi. More expensive rooms have fans or a/c with attached mandi and are also cleaner, for the top price room, there's a TV and shower thrown in. Recommended. **D-E** *Wisma Wisata*, Jl Jend A Yani, T21406. More expensive newer rooms have fan and mandi, the main building is old and decrepit, with large rooms and less than clean mandis, English-speaking guides, trekking and rafting available. **E-F** *Cut Nya'dien*, Jl Cut Nyak Dhien, T21736. All rooms very clean with fan, more expensive rooms have attached mandi, prices quoted are per person, run by very friendly middle-aged couple. Recommended. **F** *Paddy Field Guesthouse*, ask for Alec at Tourist Information for directions, 10 mins' walk outside Kutacane. Very basic huts in middle of paddy fields, but peaceful and a wonderful setting. Recommended. **F** *Pertana Guesthouse* (set 1 street back from the main road, facing the mosque). Basic place but clean and friendly, free tea and coffee through the day. **F** *Wisma Rindu Allam*, Jl Jend A Yani (opposite the mosque), T21289. Outside shared mandi, limited food available, not very clean rooms. Trekking and rafting organized here.

In Ketambe B *Gurah*, most expensive place in the area, with immaculate rooms, added advantage is that it lies within the park. **D-E** *PHPA Visitors' Centre*, very pleasant and there is the possibility of seeing orang-utans feeding in the morning, as this lies inside the park. **E-F** *Ketambe Guesthouse*, on the right as you enter the village. Basic, oil-lamp lit bungalows, central communal area, basic food and drink available. Recommended. Useful source of information, perhaps a trifle over-priced. **F** *Pondok Wisata*, T21289. Largest place to stay in town, with attractive little bungalows, avoid the restaurant. **F** *Sada Wisata*, T21406. Good restaurant attached, better than average rooms overlooking ponds, pleasant and good value. **F** *Wisma Cinta Alam*, near the park entrance. Old and rather grotty, but newer rooms currently under construction. **F** *Wisma S*, next door to the *Ketambe Guesthouse*. Big bungalows with attached mandi, good value restaurant, trekking information available.

In the park The park authorities run a few lodges; availability can be checked at the park HQ at Tanah Merah. Note that visitors need to take their own food and supplies.

Eating **In Kutacane** None of the guesthouses here has a restaurant, although there are a number of cafés along the main street serving Indonesian seafood dishes, eg *Minang Populer*, *Nasional* and *Anita*. There's little to choose between them.

Transport **Road** **Local**: *motorized becaks* can be hired for 500Rp and they can also be used to visit the surrounding villages; a minibus to Gurah Forest costs 1,500Rp, the last one leaves Kutacane around 1700. **Bus**: the bus terminal in Kutacane is in the centre of town on Jl Jend A Yani. Connections with Sidikalang and Brastagi (6 hrs). These are often full so it's a good idea to catch an early one, between 0900 and 1000. From Brastagi there are buses every 30 mins from 0900 to 1400 (4,000Rp). From Kutacane there are buses every hour to Ketambe, 1 hr (1,500Rp). Buses also run north from here to Blankejeren, every hour from 0700 to 1600 (4,000Rp), and further north still to Takengon and the Gayo Highlands. **Sea Boat**: every Thu there is a boat from Glombang, to the west, up the Alas River to Kutacane.

Kutacane is about 150 km northwest of Brastagi

Directory **Communications** Post Office: Jl Jend A Yani, Kutacane. **Useful information** Park headquarters are situated at Tanah Merah, 5 km north of Kutacane. Closed Sun. Guides and porters can sometimes be hired for trekking here, although we have had reports that the personnel speak little English. Guides are also available for hire at Ketambe, although we have received reports that their rates are very high. *Tourist Information office*, across road from *Rindu Allam Guesthouse* in Kutacane at Jl Jend A Yani 93, T21743, friendly and informed – they run tours in the surrounding area for around US$15 per person per day. **Permits** available in Ketambe, Tanah Merah and Kutacane, 2,000Rp per day plus 2,500Rp insurance. Copy of passport and visa required.

Blankejeren

Colour map 1, grid A2

The town is definitely off the beaten tourist track

Blankejeren is a small town at the northern end of the road, which follows the valley of the Alas River through the Gunung Leuser National Park (see page 526). Being set within the **Gayo Highlands**, it was not explored by Westerners until the Dutch marched on the town in 1904. Failure to accept Dutch rule resulted in the destruction of many local villages and a subsequent public outcry in the Netherlands. For a long time, continuing north from Blankejeren to reach Takengon and Lake Tawar, and from there Banda Aceh, was only for the very adventurous. Although this is still a route reserved for those who have time on their hands and are willing to accept a degree of discomfort, there are now daily buses which run all the way to Takengon. In recent years the road has undergone gradual improvement, and continuing investment means that transport is likely to become faster and more efficient still. There is excellent **trekking** around Blankejeren in pristine forest scenery. It is no longer necessary to obtain a permit, and there are many good day treks in the area.

Trekking

Contact MR Hardiannsyah, through the Wisma Mardhatthila, for tour & trekking information. He is knowledgeable & enthusiastic

The village of **Kedah**, 10 km or so from Blankejeren, is the home village of one of the area's best known guides, Mr Jally. Sleeping is available at **E-F** *Mr Jally's Tobacco Hut*, 10 huts, all very clean, set in the heart of the forest by a river, the small clearing is very beautiful, simple but tasty food provided in large portions – don't be put off by the 10-minute walk to reach the place. From here there is excellent trekking with stupendous mountain scenery and rainforests. For a two-night trek, all meals included, expect to pay about 25,000-30,000Rp. Gibbons, orang utan and other wildlife often seen. Other than Mr Jally, good guides include Mr Muhmudin and Mr Muhamad Naen. Daily rates are 15,000Rp per person.
■ *Getting to Kedah village: catch a bus from Blankejeren to Penosan, a 10-km journey; from Penosan, walk to Kedah (2 km, uphill). Alternatively, a minibus can be chartered from Kota Panjang for 5,000Rp (Kota Panjang is 500Rp by bus from Blankejeren) or chartered direct from Blankejeren for 15,000Rp.*

D *Hotel Wahyu*, Jl Blower, T21069. Twenty rooms facing onto a secluded courtyard, peaceful position on the northern edge of town, all rooms well maintained with attached mandi. Recommended. **E** *Wisma Mardhatthila*, Jl Besar, T21010. Central position, 10 clean but rather dark rooms, each with 3 beds and a desk. The shared mandi is grotty. **E-F** *Rahmat Guesthouse*, Jl Besar. Restaurant. A guesthouse that opened in Jul 1997 so during our last visit it was understandably pristine, rooms are light and airy, more expensive with attached mandi, friendly and enthusiastic management, the rooftop provides great views over the town and surrounding countryside, basic English spoken. Recommended. **F** *Penginapan Juli*, Jl Kong Bur, T21036. Six rather grubby rooms, shared mandi, snacks available. **F** *Wisma Marmass*, Jl T Tapa, T21162. Small, dirty rooms, plywood walls, basic shared mandi, lively atmosphere and close to the market to set against this.

Sleeping
Whether travelling north or south through the Gayo Highland, most people find they have to spend at least 1 night in Blankejeren. As a result, there is a good selection of restaurants & places to stay

The usual assortment of roadside restaurants and warungs line the streets. The *Nusantara* by the mosque on Jl Kong Bur is among the most popular with locals. Alternatively, the *Rahmat Guesthouse* offers a comprehensive Indonesian menu and the kitchen is clean too.

Eating

Road Bus: the bus terminal in Blankejeren is 2 km north of town along Jl Besar/Rangit Gaib – get there by becak. Regular buses run north from Sidikalang, Kutacane (5 hrs via Ketambe) and the Lake Toba area. From Brastagi, catch a bus to Kutacane, and then catch another bus on to Blankejeren. Daily buses now make the journey further north still to Takengon (6-7 hrs), most leaving between 0900 and 1100 (10,000Rp). From Takengon there are regular connections with the main north-south-east coast highway and Banda Aceh and Medan.

Transport
About 140 km from Takengon

Communications Post Office: Jl Blower (northern side of town). **Telephone office**: Jl Besar (other side of the road from the monument). **Useful offices** There is a non-governmental tourist information office offering trekking services and bicycles for hire (if you are lucky) in town. A basic knowledge of Indonesia is helpful.

Directory

Blankejeren to Takengon

There are no large towns on the road north from Blankejeren to Takengon, a journey of about 140 km. However, there are sufficient places to stop en route or to hike the entire way. Buses also run daily, leaving Blankejeren between 0900 and 1100. The scenery is spectacular virtually the entire way and most buses stop at Ise-Ise for a lunch break. Below is a list of the main villages from south to north.

Basic Indonesian is very useful if undertaking this trip without a guide

Rikit Gaib is 20 km from Blankejeren and an easy walk along a flat gradient. A more demanding up-hill trek of 8 km will bring you to the village of **Godang**. **Ise-Ise** is 42 km from Godang. The path/road here is good, but it is still prone to being washed away or made impassable during wet weather. The long hike can be very arduous in hot weather. This is the 'wildest' part of the route with the forest intruding on both sides. Monkeys, snakes and the occasional tiger are seen and it is recommended by locals that hikers walk only during hours of good daylight (not at dusk or day break). Ise Ise is a small hamlet situated near a river (good for washing) with a friendly losmen (**E-F**). One of the restaurants (no name) also has a four bed dormitory attached (**F**).

The track, 10 km from Ise-Ise, to **Lumut** is mostly downhill. There are daily buses to Takengon from Lumut. Homestays only available. **Uwak** is 10 km from Lumut. The walk from Uwak to Takengon takes about two days (with a stop in Isak), but is not very pleasant, thus not recommended. Daily buses to Takengon run from Uwak and there are places to stay. **Isak** (a few homestays only) is 15 km from Uwat and 25 km to Takengon. The Gayo people used to live in extended family/clan longhouses. One of the few remaining examples is visible from the roadside, its walls attractively decorated with Gayo motifs, at **Kung**, 9 km north of Isak.

Takengon

Phone code: 0643
Colour map 1, grid A2

Norman Lewis, in his book *An empire of the east: travels in Indonesia*, describes his arrival in Takengon in glowing terms: "The view of Lake Tawar was of extreme charm... enclosed in a coronet of low, pointed mountains which were mantled as if in velvet of the deepest green". It is beautifully situated at 1,000m in the Bukit Barisan, on the shores of **Lake Tawar**. Unfortunately, the town itself – a recent creation – is rather unattractive. One couple who recently visited it pronounced that it was the ugliest town in Sumatra – which has more than its fair share of ugly cities and towns.

The upland areas of Aceh Province used to be difficult to reach, but with the road now upgraded to virtually all-weather status it is comparatively accessible. Even so, it is rarely visited by tourists. Takengon is the most important town in the Gayo Highlands, and is inhabited by **indigenous Gayo** and immigrants from other parts of Sumatra and beyond. Because of its upland location, Takengon enjoys cool temperatures – around 70°F year-round – and is chilly at night. It also has an average of 142 rainy days each year, so a waterproof can come in handy.

Sights A good view of the town and surrounding area is afforded by climbing **Buntul Kubu Hill**, where a Dutch-era building has recently been converted into a hotel. The hills and valleys surrounding Takengon offer a number of attractive **hiking trails**. A road also circles Lake Tawar (50 km in total) and minibuses make the journey (1,000Rp). It is possible to hire a boat to explore the creeks and bays. Motorboats are available from the Loyang Koro Caves and rates vary between 20,000Rp and 30,000Rp, depending on engine size. A trip around the lake takes around four hours. Canoes taking two or three people are also available, with or without a guide from Jalan Laut Tawar. The lake water is clean and clear and good for swimming – if a touch chilly. There is said to be excellent on- and off-shore fishing.

Excursions
Other local attractions include hikes up volcanoes, hot springs & waterfalls

The **Loyang Koro Caves** used to connect the villages of Toweran and Isak, 20 km apart. They are now impassable, although the caves have an interesting history and have become something of a tourist attraction. There is a small coffee shop in Toweran. ■ *Admission to caves: 1,000Rp. Getting there: take a minibus to Toweran (4,500Rp); the caves are easy to find from here.* There is an interesting **coffee factory** situated in the plantations at Pondok Baru, where it is possible to buy limitless quantities of cheap coffee. ■ *0700-1700, free. Getting there: by bus to Pondok Baru (700Rp).*

Sleeping
Takengon offers a somewhat motley assortment of places to stay, ranging from the squalid to the luxurious. Arriving at the weekend may mean a bit of a hunt for a room, as the town is a popular weekend jaunt for Indonesians. For a week during mid-Aug, when horse races are held here, the town's hotels are booked up

A-B *Renggali*, Jl Bintang, 2 km south of town, T21144 (credit cards accepted). Best hotel in town, built on a spit of land on the lake shore with 28 large rooms – some with magnificent views, a rambling place, ideal for those who romanticize about finding a forgotten castle in the wilds but are willing to put up with slowish but friendly service, charming gardens. Recommended. **C-E** *Hotel Triarga*, off Jl Pasar Inpres, T21073. The more expensive rooms here are in an attractive building and are clean enough, with TV, hot water, Western-style bathrooms and a phone; the cheapest rooms, however, are in a separate concrete affair and are dark, filthy and to be avoided. **D** *Hotel Danau Laut Tawar*, Jl Lebe Kader 35, T21066. Restaurant. In the centre of town close to the main town mosque (so can be noisy), all rooms have attached mandi and Western-style toilet, but they are also rather damp and grubby, limited restaurant. **D-E** *Hotel Buntul Kubu*, off Jl Malem Dewa, T22254. Although this place is not the most welcoming, the position is fabulous on Buntul Kubu Hill with magnificent views over the lake, an old Dutch-era building has been renovated and there are now 30 relatively clean rooms with attached mandi, the more expensive rooms are 'suites' with a small living room and TV, it is a 15-min walk from the bus terminal and 5 mins from the market – good value. Recommended. **E** *Losmen Batang Ruang*, Jl Mahkamah 5, T21524. Nicely situated on the quieter side of town, 10 clean rooms with shared mandi and squat loo, hot water, friendly and helpful management. **E** *Losmen Fajar*, Jl Mahkamah. This place is situated next to the *Batang Ruang*, but patronized by locals rather than foreigners and reportedly can be rather unwelcoming, 11 rooms with shared facilities. **E** *Wisma Pariwisata*, Jl Terminal, T21322. Ten rooms of moderate cleanliness, the more expensive ones have attached mandi. Conveniently located up the road from the bus terminal – friendly management.

Local The *labi-labi* terminal for local public transport is in the centre of town on Jl Lebe Kader. **Road Bus**: the bus terminal is on the corner of Jl Terminal and Jl Senggeda, at the northern edge of town. Connections north with Bireuen 3½ hrs, Sigli 6 hrs, and Banda Aceh 8 hrs (9,500Rp). The a/c night bus from Takengon to Banda Aceh costs 12,500Rp. There is accommodation available in Sigli at the **E-F** *Losmen Paris*, close to the bus station (so convenient for a stop-over), clean and reasonable rooms, nearby restaurants on the town square. Buses run down the east coast to Medan. Going south to Kutacane and Lake Toba costs 10,000Rp, with 3 buses leaving between 0900 and 1100.

Transport
96 km from Bireuen

Directory Communications Post Office: Jl Lebe Kader. **Telephone office:** Telekom, Jl Lebe Kader; Wartel, Jl Terminal.

West Sumatra

Visitors to West Sumatra spend most of their time based in and around the highland settlement of Bukittinggi, its cultural heart. This is entirely understandable. It is a peachy town. The accommodation is good, the climate enervating and the food excellent. The highly mobile Minang people who view this area as their ancestral home are fascinating, and the surrounding countryside is some of the most beautiful in Sumatra. There are peaceful highland lakes, like Maninjau and Singkarak, rivers for rafting and demanding mountain treks. But while Bukittinggi must be counted as West Sumatra's great draw, it is not a one-shot province. The coastal capital of Padang, the little visited but noteworthy Kerinci-Seblat National Park and the Mentawi Islands are also notable draws.

The comparatively small province of West Sumatra is dominated by the Bukit Barisan, a range of mountains which run down the west coast of the island

Unlike Aceh and Riau provinces, West Sumatra is not rich in oil and gas, and unlike North Sumatra it does not benefit from the economic wealth of Medan or huge expanses of commodity crop production. However, this is a small province with the big reputation.

Background

The origins of the Minang Kingdom are hazy, although Adityavarman (r 1356-75) seems to have been influential in unifying the state. Power was based upon gold which was mined in the Minang highlands. During the 14th and 15th centuries when Minangkabau power was at its height, the kingdom's influence extended over much of central Sumatra.

History

Early European explorers searched unsuccessfully for the ancient city of 'Menangkabu', thought to be the source of the wealth and gold of Malesia – the mythical and unimaginably rich Golden Khersonese. William Marsden, writing at the end of the 18th century, recorded that Minangkabau was regarded as representing the heart of Islam in the area – and the rulers claimed descent from Alexander the Great. When Stamford Raffles visited the area at the beginning of the 19th century, he was immensely impressed by the Minangkabau Kingdom, believing the technology of agriculture and the level of civilization to be superior to that of Java. However, by the time the Dutch began to establish a presence in the 18th century, Minangkabau was already in decline. The gold mines had been worked out by the 1780s, and the old royal order was being undermined by new sources of wealth: coffee, gambier and pepper. A Hindu kingdom between the 12th and 14th centuries, the Minang turned increasingly to **Islam** as the religion's influence gradually filtered south from Aceh, in the north. This culminated in the Padri Wars between 1820 and 1837, which pitted the traditionalists against a new breed of Muslim fundamentalists.

Minangkabau matrilineal society

West Sumatra is best known as the home of the Minangkabau people, who are concentrated in the upland areas of the province and number about 4,000,000. They are known throughout Indonesia for their business acumen and peripatetic habits: there are Minang, as the Minangkabau are usually known, scattered right across the Indonesian archipelago from Aceh to Irian Jaya, and every town has its Minang or Padang restaurant run by a Minang family. They are also beloved by anthropologists for their unique matrilineal society. One Minang poem, dating at least from the early 19th century, even exhorts mothers to teach their daughters "to judge the rise and fall of prices". Important Minang towns include the hill towns of Bukittinggi, Payamkumpuh and Batusangkar, which lie near the centre of the Minang homeland or *darek*, and the coastal provincial capital, Padang.

Each Minangkabau *sa-buah-parui* or clan, the smallest unit of traditional 'government', traces its lineage from a common female ancestor. Titles, wealth and family names are all passed down through the female line. Men are given the responsibility of looking after the family's heirlooms, but it is the women who keep the keys. It is felt by many that the tendency for Minang men to leave the village and go *merantau* – or walkabout – is because of the dominant role that women play. In the view of many anthropologists, centrifugality has been part of the historical process in Minangkabau society – a process which is culturally determined. Many Minang feel that it is improper, for example, for young men to stay in their mother's house.

This interpretation of male migration has been challenged. More recent studies have associated *merantau* not with matrilineality but with egalitarianism. In this context, the only way that a Minang man can accumulate status in a world where everyone is equal, where sharing is the norm, and where everyone in a community is king, is by migrating. It is also true that the process of 'modernization' is undermining Minang traditions, and thus undermining the role of women. Today, a visitor staying with a 'modern' Minang might be hard put to discern the matrilineal traditions which preoccupy anthropologists.

Architecture

To the visitor, the most obviously distinctive element of the Minangkabau is their magnificent architecture. The traditional wooden house or *rumah adat* – literally, 'customary house', also known as *rumah gadang* or 'big house' – is raised off the ground and surmounted by an impressive curved roof, the gables soaring upwards at either end like the horns of the buffalo which they are said to represent. These houses are similar in design to the traditional houses of the Toraja of Sulawesi, although they are now, sadly, seldom built. (Some commentators have observed how impractical and inefficient some Indonesian houses appear to be. However, people have traditionally lived around and under their houses, not in them.)

One side of the interior of the house is taken up by a row of small sleeping cubicles, in front of which is a large meeting room. The house is flanked by a pair of rice barns. Traditionally, both the house and the rice barns were deeply and colourfully carved. In a village, each compound of houses will usually be inhabited by one matrilineal line, with a separate structure (*surau*) for the men and boys, along with one or more rice barns. In recent years Minang men, excluded from owning traditional houses by custom, have taken to building modern abodes around the back of the traditional rumah gadang.

Language

The Minang language is similar to Bahasa Indonesian, and the two are mutually intelligible. However, the vowels 'a' and 'e' commonly become an 'o' in Minang, so that *apa* (what) becomes *apo*, *kemana* (where) becomes *kamano*, and the numbers *dua* (2) and *tiga* (3), *duo* and *tigo* respectively.

Cuisine

Minang food is known throughout Indonesia as *Makan Padang*, after the capital of the province. It tends to be chilli hot, although some of the dishes are mild. On taking a seat in a restaurant, an assortment of bowls of food are brought to the table – and the customer only pays for what he or she eats. Distinctive dishes include *rendang* (a dry beef curry cooked in coconut milk, spices and chilli), *pangek ikan* (fish cooked in coconut milk with chilli and spices), *panggang ikan* (fish roasted over an open fire), *kalio* (beef or chicken rendang where some of the juice remains), and cassava leaves in coconut milk (somewhat like spinach). Although not characteristically Minang, sweet fresh West Sumatran coffee (*kopi manis*) is also delicious.

Like most Indonesians, the majority of Minang people are Muslims – and staunchly so. It is regarded as polite to offer food to neighbours – even in a restaurant and sitting next to complete strangers. The offer will invariably be refused. Further, it is considered rude to stand with hands on hips, to point a finger at an adult, to sit with legs crossed or to touch a person's head.

Conduct

Bukittinggi

Bukittinggi – meaning High Hill – is one of the most attractive towns in Sumatra and has many places of interest in the immediate vicinity. The town is situated at 1,000m, encircled by volcanoes, and the climate is cool and invigorating. Like the Minang people in general, the inhabitants of Bukittinggi are relaxed and welcoming, making it a very popular place to stay.

Phone code: 0752
Colour map 2, grid A1

Ins and outs

There is no airport at Bukittinggi; the nearest is at Padang, a 2 hr bus journey away. Most people get to this popular destination by bus, and the journey overland from Medan via Lake Toba is pretty gruelling, nearly 700 km or 20 hrs' drive in total. But because it is such a popular destination, the range of buses and destinations is impressive for a town which is relatively small.

Getting there
See Transport section for further details

Bukittinggi itself is small and cool enough to negotiate on foot. There are bemos, bendis and oplets for longer journeys and motorbikes and mountain bikes are also for hire from many guesthouses. One of the great attractions of Bukittinggi is the surrounding countryside, but trying to get around on public transport can be a bit of a drag so many visitors either choose to charter a bemo, hire a motorbike or bicycle, or take a tour.

Getting around

Background

Bukittinggi is the cultural centre of the Minangkabau people. It supports a university, zoo, museum, a good market, and yet is small and accessible. Many travellers arrive here, and after the trials of the road and such towns as Sibolga, seem very reluctant to leave. Compared with some other resort towns, it is tidy (by Sumatran standards) and reasonably well organized. The core of the town is Jalan Jend A Yani, marked at one end by a clock tower and the other by a statue of a turbaned man mounted on a rearing horse – the Padri hero, Imam Bonjol. Along this road are concentrated many restaurants and tour and travel companies, as well as the cheaper travellers' hotels. As if this is not enough to entice the visitor to come here and tarry a while, the town has also been voted Indonesia's cleanest on no less than three occasions – most recently in 1996. The obtuse statue opposite the town's main mosque is, apparently, a monument to cleanliness.

Sights

The geographic and functional centre of Bukittinggi is marked by a strange-looking **clock tower** at the south end of Jalan Jend A Yani, the town's main thoroughfare. The Jam Gadang, or 'Great Clock' as it is known, was built by the Dutch in 1827. It is a veritable Sumatran 'Big Ben' and has a Minangkabau-style roof perched uneasily on the top. The **central market** is close to the clock tower. Although there is a market every

536 BUKITTINGGI: SIGHTS

day of the week, market day is on Wednesday and Saturday (0800-1700) when hoards of Minangkabau men and women descend on Bukittinggi. The market – in fact there are two markets, the Upper Market (*Pasar Atas*) and Lower Market (*Pasar Bawah*) – covers an enormous area and sells virtually everything. Good for souvenirs, handicrafts, jewellery, fruit, spices and weird foods.

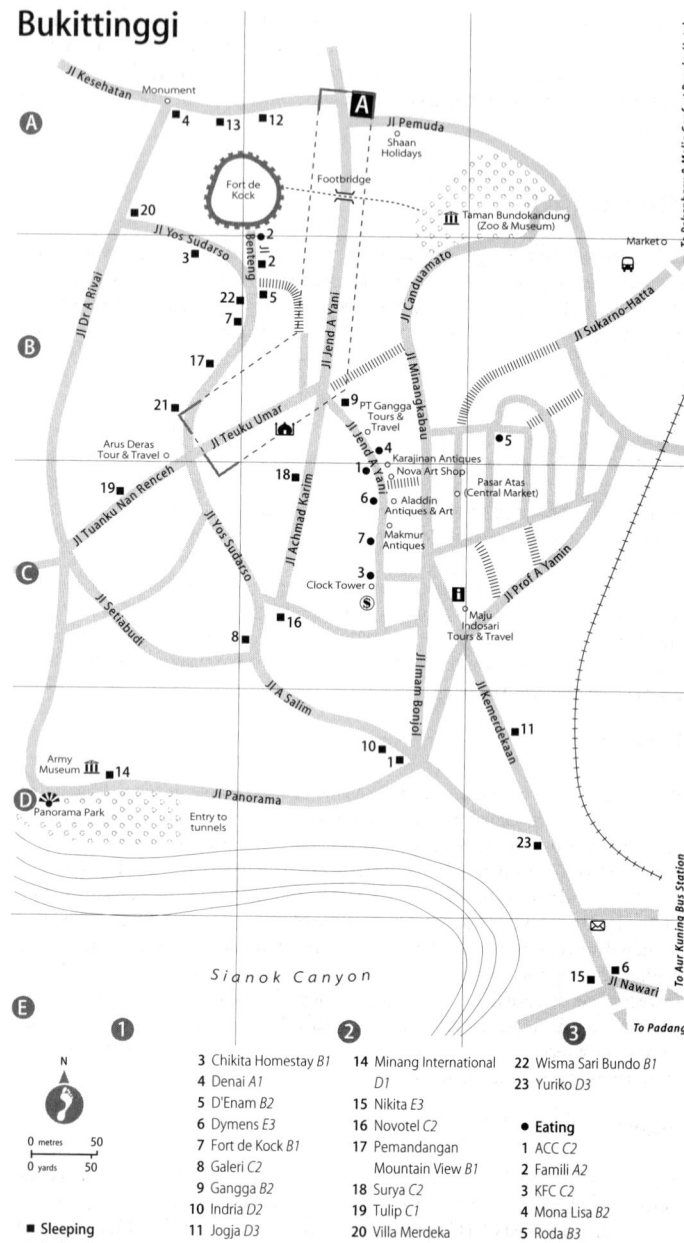

Bukittinggi

Related map
A Bukittinggi detail,
page 542

■ **Sleeping**
1 Ambun Sari *D2*
2 Benteng *B2*
3 Chikita Homestay *B1*
4 Denai *A1*
5 D'Enam *B2*
6 Dymens *E3*
7 Fort de Kock *B1*
8 Galeri *C2*
9 Gangga *B2*
10 Indria *D2*
11 Jogja *D3*
12 Lima's *A2*
13 Marmy's Homestay *A1*
14 Minang International *D1*
15 Nikita *E3*
16 Novotel *C2*
17 Pemandangan Mountain View *B1*
18 Surya *C2*
19 Tulip *C1*
20 Villa Merdeka Homestay *A1*
21 Wisma Bukittinggi *B1*
22 Wisma Sari Bundo *B1*
23 Yuriko *D3*

● **Eating**
1 ACC *C2*
2 Famili *A2*
3 KFC *C2*
4 Mona Lisa *B2*
5 Roda *B3*
6 Selamat *C2*
7 Selecta *C2*

The north end of Jalan Jend A Yani runs between two hills which have recently been linked by a footbridge. On top of the hill to the west is **Fort de Kock**, built by the Dutch in 1825 as a defensive site during the Padri Wars. Very little of the fort remains apart from a few rusting cannons and a moat. The centre of the decaying fortifications is dominated by a water tower. However, the views of the town and the surrounding countryside are worth the trip (although trees are beginning to obscure the view). To the east, and linked by a footbridge, on the other side of Jalan Jend A Yani, is Bukittinggi's high point, **Taman Bundokandung** – 'Kind-Hearted Mother Park'. The park contains both a museum and a zoo. The **Bukittinggi zoo** is hardly an object lesson in how to keep animals in captivity, but it does have a reasonable collection of Sumatran wildlife, including orang utans and gibbons. Strangely, there is also an exhibit of stuffed animals (perhaps former inmates?) and the partly disassembled skeleton of a whale. ■ *0730-1700 Mon-Sun, closed over lunch on Fri for prayers, fort and zoo: 1,000Rp (500Rp for children).* Within the zoo is a **museum** – established in 1935 and the oldest in Sumatra. The collection is housed in a traditional *rumah adat*, or Minangkabau clan house, embellished with fine woodcarvings and fronted by two rice barns. The museum specializes in local ethnographic exhibits, including fine jewellery and textiles, and is not very informative. There are also some macabre stuffed and deformed buffalo calves here. ■ *0730-1700 Mon-Sun, closed over lunch on Fri for prayers, 300Rp.*

To the southwest of the town is the spectacular **Sianok Canyon**, 4 km long and over 100m deep. A road at the end of Jalan Teuku Umar leads down through the canyon, past the back entrances to the Japanese tunnel system. A path leaves the road at a sharp bend (there is a snack bar here serving tea etc), and continues to a bridge at the foot of the chasm and steep steps on the opposite side of the canyon. Follow a road through a village and across paddy fields for about two hours until you eventually arrive at **Kota Gadang**. Many small silversmiths sell their wares throughout the village. This is a good place to buy smaller silver items; recommended is *Silversmith Aino*, at the coffee shop, Jalan Hadisash 115. There is a large tourist gift centre – *Amai Satia* – in Kota Gadang (walk to the mosque and turn right at the T-junction). From Kota Gadang, either retrace your steps, or continue for another 4 km to Guguk Randeh where there are oplets back to town (500Rp). It is sometimes possible to catch an *omprengan* back to the main road from Kota Gadang. If working in the opposite direction, catch a blue oplet from the Aur Kuning bus terminal running towards Parabek and get off at Guguk Randeh.

Also at the southern edge of town and overlooking the canyon is **Panorama Park**, a popular weekend meeting place for courting couples. Monkeys in these gardens provide entertainment. ■ *300Rp.* Within the park is the entrance to a **maze of tunnels** excavated by the Japanese during the Occupation, with ammunition stores, kitchens and dining rooms. Guides gleefully show the chute where dead Indonesian workers were propelled out into the canyon to rot. ■ *500Rp.* Opposite the park, on Jalan Panorama (formerly Jalan Imam Bonjol), is the **Army Museum** (*Museum Perjuangan*), which contains military memorabilia from the early 19th century through to the modern period. There are some interesting photographs of the disinterring of the army officers assassinated by the PKI during the attempted coup of 1965 (see page 942), as well as exhibits relating to Fretilin – who continue to fight for the independence of East Timor. ■ *500Rp, 0800-1700 everyday.*

Excursions

One of the attractions of Bukittinggi is the wide array of sights in the surrounding area. The Minang highlands around Bukittinggi constitute the core – or *darek* – of the Minang homeland. Below are the main excursions, although there are also additional hikes, waterfalls, traditional villages, lakes and centres of craft production. **Note** that many of the sights and places of interest listed here are under separate headings following the Bukittinggi entry. These are: **Lake Maninjau**, **Payakumbuh** and the **Harau Valley**, **Batusangkar** and **Lake Singkarak**, and **Padang Panjang**. Seeing these sights, particularly if time is short, is easiest on a tour (see page 540). Though travelling by public transport is not at all difficult (see each entry for details), it is time-consuming and often cramped.

Lake Maninjau
Check there is no mist before departing

Lake Maninjau lies about 35 km to the west of town (see page 546). A rewarding and spectacular hike from Bukittinggi, easily possible in a day for even the modestly energetic, is to walk to the crater edge at **Puncak Lawang** (Lawang Top) and then down the steep crater sides to the lake side village of **Bayur**, before catching a bus back to Bukittinggi. To do this, take a pale blue oplet from Bukittinggi's Aur Kuning bus terminal to Lawang – sometimes called Pasar Lawang (Lawang Market) to distinguish it from Puncak Lawang (1,000Rp). The market operates Monday-Friday. From Lawang walk the 4 km to Puncak Lawang at the lip of the crater and 1,400m up – a spectacular view – before taking the path down (a walk of around another 2-3 hours). The path can be narrow at times, and slippery when wet. Alternatively, catch a bus straight to Maninjau village on the lake shore, navigating 44 hairpin bends on the way down, 1-2 hours (1,000Rp). The last bus leaves Maninjau village for Bukittinggi between 1600 and 1700, later on market days.

Lake Singkarak

The Minang area's other lake is Lake Singkarak (see page 553). Not as beautiful as Maninjau, but it is possible to come here on a circular journey via Batusangkar.
■ *Getting there:* take a bus to Padang Panjang and then a 2nd bus heading south towards Solok.

The Minang Highlands

Batang Palupuh

This reserve, situated 12 km north of town, is for the monstrous *rafflesia* flower. ■ *A guide from the village will point the flower out for a small fee, catch a bus to Batang Palupuh on the Trans-Sumatran Highway, or take an oplet and then walk to the reserve (30 mins).*

Buffalo fights

The buffaloes are believed to be possessed by the spirit of their owners, so that it is they who are in combat, not their animals

Kota Baru is a rather unattractive town, 10 km south of town on the main road to Padang, redeemed only by the fact that it has a good **market**. The villages surrounding Kota Baru often hold bullfights (in fact, buffalo fights). The bulls fight one another rather than a matador, and the ring is formed by the spectators rather than by a protective fence. The most popular and established contests are held in two spots, just off the main road between Kota Baru and Padang Panjang, on Tuesday and Saturday at 1600-1700. The Tuesday fights are held at Kota Baru Air Angik (1 km off the road between Kota Baru and Padang Panjang), while on Saturday they are at Kota Baru Batagak (virtually on the main road). There are also other, less commercial, bullfights staged in villages further from Bukittinggi – for example, at **Panyalarun** (14 km) and **Padang Lawas** (10 km). ■ *Touts will try to sell tours for 5,000Rp to see the contests at Kota Baru Air Angik and Kota Baru Batagak, but it is possible to go by public transport for 500Rp and pay a 500Rp entrance fee, take a red oplet from Aur Kuning terminal.*

Craft villages

Pandai Sikat is one of a number of villages specializing in **traditional craft production**. It is situated 13 km south of town at the foot of Mount Singgalang, 3 km off the main road to Padang Panjang, and is a cloth and woodcarving centre. The carvings tend to use natural motifs (trees, animals, flowers etc), as does the famous *songket* cloth that is produced here. About 1,000 women weave richly patterned cloth. Note that the warp may be rayon, imported from Japan, and only the weft, cotton or silk. ■ *Getting there: by red oplet towards Padang Panjang from the Aur Kuning terminal. Get off at Kota Baru and either walk the last 3 km or take an omprengan (a non-licensed bemo) from the intersection.* Other craft villages include **Desa Sunga**, 17 km south of town, which specializes in brasswork; and **Sungaipua**, on the slopes of Mount Merapi, which specializes in metalwork (knives, swords).

Mount Merapi

On Sat nights hoards of locals climb the volcano, following them is possible but not advisable as many do not know the way

This active volcano, southeast of town, stands at a height of 2,891m and last erupted in 1979. The difficult climb to the summit takes 4-6 hours. Enquire at the Police Station in Kota Baru for more information. Register here before ascending and ask for directions; the route is indistinct in places. The best way to see the volcano is to hire a guide and climb up at night (costs 100,000Rp), arriving at the summit for sunrise. Many hotels and cafés arrange such tours. This avoids the heat of the day and the mist that envelopes the mountain by 1100. Wear warm clothes it is cold on the summit. The ground around the crater is loose and hikers should keep away from the lip. ■ *Getting there: catch a bus to Kota Baru from the Aur Kuning terminal (first departure 0500), and then hike.*

Mount Singgalang

Singgaland, which lies to the southwest of Bukittinggi, stands at a height of 2,878m and offers a less arduous climb than Mount Merapi. The trail starts at the village of Pandai Sikat, and the climb takes about 4-5 hours. Near the summit, the ground is scree, so good footwear is recommended. It's a disappointing dirty footpath. Start early, as mist often descends over the mountain later in the day. ■ *Getting there: take an oplet to Kota Baru from the Aur Kuning terminal. From where you are dropped, turn right at the mosque and walk down to Kota Baru. In the centre of the village is a right-hand turn with the RTCI 4 km sign (referring to the radio installation situated 4 km above Pantai Sikat). Follow this track for 2 km to Pandai Sikat. The mountain path starts to the right of the RTCI installation behind a refreshment hut (often closed). For speed, it is possible to hire a motorbike to the RTCI site. Buses back to Bulettinggi run late, but it is advisable not to descend in darkness.*

Payakumbuh This key centre of Minang culture lies about 10 km east of Bukittinggi (see page 550). *En route* is the colourful local Friday market at **Piladang**, while on the other side of Payakumbuh is the **Harau Canyon** (see below). ■ *Getting there: regular oplets from Bukittinggi, 1 hr. These run through Piladang.*

Harau Canyon The canyon lies around 44 km from Bukittinggi, off the road leading through Payakumbuh towards Pekanbaru (see page 550). ■ *Getting there: take one of the many buses from Bukittinggi to Payakumbuh. From there catch a white oplet – or a 'sago' as they are called locally – running towards Sarialamat to the turn off for the Harau Valley (see the main entry for more details on the walk from there).*

Pagaruyung A **Sultan's Palace**, lying 5 km east of Batusangkar (see page 552). ■ *Getting there: from Bukittinggi, catch a bus to Batusangkar and from there a yellow oplet direct to Pagaruyung. See the Batusangkar entry for more details.*

Minang villages **Pariangan** is a peaceful Minang village on the slopes of Mount Merapi (see page 552). ■ *Getting there: there are no direct buses from Bukittinggi. Catch an oplet from Bukittinggi to Batusangkar, and then one heading towards Kota Baru – which passes through Parianagan.* **Balimbiang** is a second traditional Minang village about 10 km south of Batusangkar, and 1 km off the main road (see page 552). ■ *Getting there: from Bukittinggi it is necessary to 1st catch an oplet to Batusangkar, and then a Solok-bound bus.*

Tours

Taking either local day tours or longer trips makes sense: getting around the Minang area on public transport is time consuming (although renting a motorbike for the day makes for greater mobility). For treks in Nias or Siberut a guide is even more useful, given the difficulties of communication and getting around. A guide should, in theory, be able to offer some insights into the rich Minang culture. It is worth asking around and getting some first-hand assessments from travellers who have just returned from tours and who may be able to recommend a guide. If possible, find a guide and arrange a tour directly; the tour companies usually use the same guides and because they take a commission the rate rises. The guides working out of the *Three Tables Coffee House*, the *Rendezvous Café* and the *Star Café* have all been recommended. The guide from the *Rendezvous* speaks very good English and is very informative. Of the tour companies we have had good reports on *Arus Deras Tour and Travel*, Jalan Tuanku Nan Renceh 20, T22913, F22913, and *Shaan Holidays*, Jalan Pemuda 9, T32530, F32130, Shaan@padang.wasantara.net.id The two companies are very different. *Shaan*, managed by Mohammad Sultan Bhat, one of the very few Kashmiris in West Sumatra, tend to arrange slightly more upmarket tours, but they are imaginative and professionally run. *Arus Deras* arrange adventure tours including rafting and climbing.

Local tours There are a range of tours organized to Lake Maninjau, Batusangkar, Lake Singkarak and other sights around Bukittinggi. Tours tend to take one of three routes: the Minangkabau tour, featuring many different places which are representative of the Minangkabau culture, past and present (including Batusangkar, Pagaruyung and Lake Singkarak), and including a bullfight if you go on a Saturday. Secondly, the Maninjau line (including Kota Gadang and Lake Maninjau), and finally, the Harau Valley line (including Mount Merapi and the Harau Valley). Most tour/travel agents organize these day-long tours for about 30,000-35,000Rp; they are also arranged by many hotels and guesthouses.

Tours further afield Many of the tour operators also organize tours further afield – for example, 10-day trips to the Mentawi Islands (see page 563). Bukittinggi is an excellent place to arrange a tour to the islands off the West Sumatra coast, but bear in mind that it can take up to three days to get to Siberut Island, Mentawi. We have also had reports that letters of recommendation are photocopied and used by guides to whom they do not refer! (Also see the comments on page 565 and the section on tours on page 558.)

Essentials

Most of the travellers' hotels and guesthouses are concentrated along the north end of Jl Jend A Yani. Quieter, smaller and often cleaner homestays are located on the hills either side of Jl Jend A Yani. Over the last few years a number of more upmarket places have opened, and existing hotels are also building new wings.

Sleeping
■ on maps, pages 536 & 542
Price codes:
see inside front cover

AL-A *Meliá Confort Pusako*, Jl Sukarno-Hatta 7, T32111, F32667. A/c, restaurant, pool, tennis courts, 191 rooms in this hotel, which is said to mirror traditional design but which looks more like a Spanish hacienda. It is situated a few kilometres northeast of Bukittinggi, so the hotel lays on a shuttle bus to ferry guests to and from town. The advantage of its out-of-town site is that it is peaceful, enjoys a large plot and has great views over to the mountains. Rooms are of a high standard and the service is good. **A** *Novotel*, Jl Laras Datuk Bandaro, T35000, F23800, novotel_bkt@mail.com, www.hotels.fr A/c, restaurant, heated pool, business centre, an excellent hotel in a prime position with 100 rooms. The hotel was designed by a highly respected Thai architect and feels like an Indian palace with its Islamic inspired archways and fretwork. Good service and food (breakfast and evening buffet meals – good value), happy hour in the bar 1700-1900, check for special discount rates on the rooms, tours arranged. Recommended. **A-B** *Wisma Sari Bundo*, Jl Yos Sudarso 7A, T22953, F23408. Rather a mix of architectural metaphors in this medium sized hotel situated on the quiet far side of the ridge, 30-odd small but comfortable rooms, nothing much to hold against it, but then again nothing much obvious to recommend it – rooms above parking space can be noisy.

B *Denai*, Jl Dr A Rivai 26, T32920, F33490. Restaurant (a pool has been promised for years), tennis court. Until recently this was the number 1 spot in town and it remains a well-run and (usually) quiet place to stay. There are 2 wings: rooms in the old wing are spacious, with sitting area, though the ones above the pub can be noisy. Rooms in the new wing have modern bathrooms and are of a high standard. A good breakfast is included in the room rate. **B** *Hotel Asia*, Jl Kesehatan 38, T625277, F625278. Grand lobby area with lots of seating space, floors are so clean you could eat your dinner off them, a range of rooms all with hot water, some with a/c, restaurant, breakfast included, very pleasant with friendly staff. **B** *Hotel Benteng*, Jl Benteng 1, T21115, F22596. Restaurant. This hotel is good, but it could be better. It is situated in a perfect position, quiet and peaceful, shaded by pines, and overlooking the town. It has the atmosphere of a hunting lodge (almost) and an attractive highland ambience, and is a bit of a labyrinth. But it is suffering from under-investment – the rooms and corridors are shabby and the bathrooms need an overhaul (hot water in all but the cheapest rooms). Despite this, still recommended because it is not just another faceless hotel. **B** *Hotel Nikita*, Jl Jend Sudirman 55, T31629, F31177. Well appointed hotel with friendly staff, laundry, restaurant (varied menu), some rooms can attract noise from the road.

C *Dymens*, Jl Nawawi 3, T23440, F21613. Some a/c, excellent restaurant, large rather rambling hotel with comfortable rooms, location on the south edge of town near the bus station is not convenient for exploring the town. Some rooms are now looking a little worn. **C** *Hotel Ambun Sari*, Jl Panorama 2, T34406, F31427. This is an excellent little hotel with 28 rooms, a good restaurant, central position and enthusiastic management, the rooms are light and airy with balconies and satellite TV, the bathrooms are clean and have hot water, and breakfast is included in the room rate. Recommended. **C** *Hotel Fort de Kock*, Jl Yos Sudarso 33, T33005. A converted private house on the 'wrong' side of the ridge looking away from town, the rooms are spotless and very comfortable and it has the atmosphere of an Indonesian B&B – certainly worth considering; includes breakfast. **C** *Hotel Galeri,* Jl Hagus Salim 25, T23515, F31496. The more expensive rooms have hot water and TV's, some rooms offer good views.

Restaurant in basement serves international cuisine. Tours can also be arranged. **C** *Lima's*, Jl Kesehatan 34, T22641, F32570. Restaurant (slow service). The rooms are spacious with good hot water bathrooms, it is set back from busy Jl Kesehatan so it is not too noisy, and the owner is an enthusiastic competitor in bird singing contests who can be heard warbling – the monumental trophies are lined up behind the reception. **C** *Marmy's Homestay*, Jl Kesehatan 30. Friendly, small, up-market homestay, with a little restaurant. **C** *Minang International*, Jl Panorama 20A, T21120. A Dutch-era single story villa with great views over the canyon from the upstairs balconies. It is on the other side of the ridge from the main part of town, so very quiet; nice gardens. The lobby is an interesting fusion of kitsch and traditional, leaning towards the former, and the rooms are rather variable in quality. However, all in all it is a good hotel and the staff are very friendly – no restaurant. Recommended. **C-D** *Orchid*, Jl Teuku Umar 11, T32634. Not much character but the rooms with small balconies are very clean and competitively priced, some with squat and some with Western toilets, some with hot water, central position but off the busy Jl Jend A Yani. Ask for a room on the opposite side to the local mosque unless you require regular 0500 wake up calls. Recommended. **C-E** *Hotel Indria*, Jl H A Salim 1, T22505. The more expensive rooms here are OK, but at the price you don't get much: no hot water, very bare and characterless, cheaper rooms are dark and grubby with no seats on the toilets, and other signs of poor management and under-investment.

D *Dahlia Hotel*, Jl Jend A Yani 104-106, T22185. This is new and doesn't have much atmosphere, but it is friendly and well run. The rooms are large, there are sitting areas, and all but the cheapest rooms have hot water and some pretty gauche furniture. For those looking to stay in a hotel with an Indonesian feel, rather than the pretence of hippiness, this is worth checking out. **D** *Villa Merdeka Homestay*, Jl Dr A Rivai 20, T23937. Cold water, en suite facilities, large rooms, restaurant, unfortunately it is near a busy road junction. **D-E** *Hotel Jogja*, Jl Perintis Kemerdekaan 17, T21142, F33507. En suite with TV, near the market, a bit dreary but clean, tours arranged. **D-E** *Hotel Yani*, Jl

Bukittinggi detail

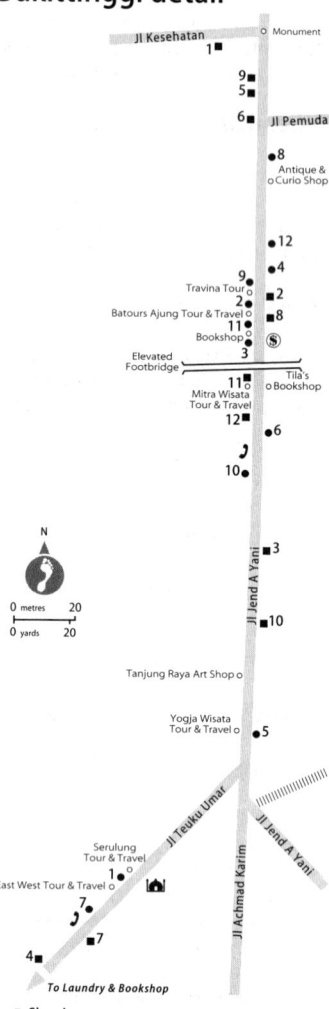

■ **Sleeping**
1 Asia
2 Bamboo Homestay
3 Dahlia
4 Kartini
5 Murni's
6 Nirwana
7 Orchid
8 Singgalang
9 Sri Kandi
10 Tigo Balai
11 Yani
12 Yusuf Grande Motel

3 Dolphin Café
4 Harau Cliff Coffee Shop
5 Jazz & Blues Cafe
6 Lim's Bakery & Café
7 Lonely Planet Cafe
8 Rendezvous Cafe House
9 Star Café
10 The Bedudal Steakhouse & Café
11 The Coffee Shop
12 Three Tables Coffee Shop

● **Eating**
1 Canyon Coffee Shop
2 Cosy Cave Café

Jend A Yani 101, T22419. Grubby economy rooms, more expensive en suite rooms with questionable choice of wallpaper, in need of an overhaul (also overrun with noisy kids). **D-E** *Kartini*, Jl Teuku Umar 6, T22885. Large rooms on the ground floor with hot water, cheaper upstairs rooms without, but all with attached mandis. Edi manages the hotel efficiently and in a friendly manner, tours and other services provided, breakfast included in the room rate, a very good deal and near the top of a quiet street. Recommended.

E *Aisha Chalik*, Jl Cindur Mato 1, near the museum and the zoo. Old colonial house with large clean rooms and shared mandi, hot water upon request, excellent tours arranged from here including Hendri's 2-day Maninjau Trek (backpack transported free of charge from Bukittinggi to Maninjau). **E** *Bamboo Homestay*, Jl Jend A Yani 132. Friendly staff, on busy Jl Jend A Yani, but set back so not too noisy, dorm beds make it an **F**. **E** *Chikita Homestay*, Jl Yos Sudarso. One of the cheapest places to stay away from the mass of guesthouses on Jl Jend A Yani, simple rooms, in a small Dutch-era villa, cold water, friendly, can arrange treks and tours. **E** *D'Enam*, Jl Yos Sudarso 4, T21333. Clean and simple, food available, free tea and coffee, quiet, set on the ridge above town. Recommended. **E** *Gangga*, Jl Jend A Yani 70, T22967. Some with attached mandi, popular, good value, although we have received reports that the rooms are becoming rather grubby. **E** *Gema Homestay*, Jl Jos Sudarso 5, T22238. Situated behind *Fort De Kock*, cheap and simple, and friendly staff. **E** *Nirwana*, Jl Jend A Yani 113, T21292. Popular budget place. **E** *Pemandangan Mountain View*, Jl Yos Sudarso 31, T21621. Competitively priced hotel on a ridge overlooking the hills to the northwest of Bukittinggi, the rooms are out the back so they are quiet, no hot water but there is an attractive sitting area, friendly management, and peaceful. Recommended. **E** *Surya*, Jl Achmad Karim 7, T22587. Quieter than the main band of guesthouses on Jl Jend A Yani, rooms are only average. **E** *Tiga Balai*, Jl Jend A Yani 100, T31996. Once this might have been cheap and cheerful, it is still cheap but sordid, small on the outside, it is a tardis-like warren of a hotel with steep steps, small and dirty rooms, and little to recommend it bar the price. **E** *Wisma Bukittinggi*, Jl Yos Sudarso 25, T34008. Clean but standard rooms have very little natural light, more expensive rooms with en suite facilities and windows.

F *Murni's*, Jl Jend A Yani 115, T35569. Popular and the rooms are generally clean, although it is a bit grubby in places, friendly and extremely helpful staff. **F** *Singgalang*, Jl Jend A Yani 130, T21576. The best of the cheaper places in the centre of town, rooms are relatively clean and also relatively quiet, communal mandis and toilets are well kept and there is a pleasant and airy sitting area to read and write. Recommended.

Accommodation in exchange for English conversation: the *Brotherly International English Course (BIEC)*, based at Jl S Parman 99, will reputedly arrange accommodation in a local family's house, provide some food, and introduce participants to Minang culture in exchange for English conversation classes.

Eating
● *on maps*
Price codes:
see inside front cover

Bukittinggi is renowned for the quality of its food, and after 10 days in the wilds of Nias or Siberut it can seem that everyone here is a budding Marco Pierre White. The upland climate means that temperate as well as tropical vegetables are available, and the presence of so many tourists means that numerous restaurants, and coffee shops have sprung up. But after a while it begins to pall – especially the food at the more popular travellers' restaurants which are strung out along the lower half of Jl Jend A Yani. For some reason all serve the same range of dishes: steaks and omelettes, various toasts, milk shakes and salads, the more popular 1 dish Indonesian meals, jaffles and pancakes and so on. Fortunately there are also good local restaurants serving Minang/Padang and Chinese dishes, and many excellent foodstalls selling sate, gulai soup and other specialities.

Indonesian Mid-range: *Famili*, Jl Benteng 1, near the *Benteng Hotel* and Fort de Kock, perched on the hillside with good views. Friendly management and excellent food. Recommended. **Cheap** *Selamat*, Jl Jend A Yani 19. One of the better Padang food restaurants. *Simpang Raya*, Jl Muka Jam Besar, near Pasar Atas. Popular Padang restaurant, part of the chain, better food at lunch than at night, good views and recommended by locals. **Very cheap**: *Roda*, Pasar Atas (Upper Market), Blok C-155. Good, Padang food.

Chinese Mid-range: *Mona Lisa*, Jl Ahmad Yani 58. Good food, fruit salads, at least 25 different fruits available, very popular. Not to be confused with the nearby hairdresser with the same name. **Cheap**: *Selecta*, Jl Jend A Yani 3. Good Chinese food.

International Many of the restaurants below organize tours and treks with minimum person requirements, so it is wise to get a group together. However, note that managers shift around quite a bit. **Mid-range**: *Sari Rasa*, Jl Jend A Yani 101, T22419. Chinese, Padang and some good curries, comes recommended with friendly staff. *Harau Cliff Café* (formerly the *Mexico Restaurant*), Jl Jend A Yani 134. New owners and a new name but still popular – steaks and cold beers in a friendly, relaxed environment, now with 3 internet terminals.

Cafés: **Cheap to mid-range**: *The Bedudal Steakhouse and Café*, Jl Jend A Yani 95. Opened in Apr 1999, it has a reputation for good steaks. *Jazz and Blues Café*, Jl Jend A Yani. Another travellers eatery with good food and a special Danish menu, tours and treks organized by Efi the manager who is very enthusiastic, knowledgable about the Minangkabau, with good English. *Canyon Coffee Shop*, Jl Teuku Umar 18B. Little to distinguish this from all the other coffee shops, same menu. *Dolphin Café*, Jl Jend A Yani 103, T25789. Regular karaoke evenings. *Lonely Planet Café*, Jl Teuku Umar 8, T21652. This imaginatively titled café offers the standard travellers' fare, but with some Mexican dishes, popular and set away from the main tourist street, opposite Hotel Orchid. Ed, the owner, speaks English and is a good source of information, treks arranged, with internet access available next door. *The Coffee Shop*, Jl Jend A Yani 105. Tables on street, usual range of travellers' dishes. **Very cheap**: *Cosy Cave Café* (or the *3Cs*), Jl Jend A Yani. Small coffee shop with good, cheap food (at least the local dishes are). *Star Café*, Jl Jend A Yani 109. Good food (pizzas, lassis, jaffles etc) and hip music, internet access also possible here. *Three Tables Coffee House*, Jl Jend A Yani 142. Serving travellers' food including salads, omelettes, tacos, pancakes and good standard Indonesian and Chinese dishes, popular and good to watch the world go by. *Rendevous Café House*, Jl Jend A Yani 150, T25064. The food is OK, but a little greasy, tours and treks organized. *Asmat Coffee Shop*, Jl Teuku Umar 16A. Usual range of omelettes, tacos, milk shakes etc, but away from the great mass of coffee places on Jl Jend A Yani, so a quieter, less frenetic and more relaxing place to hang out.

Bakeries For some reason there is a dearth of decent bakeries in Bukittinggi – which is odd considering that Padang has a surfeit. *Lim's Bakery* on Jl Jend A Yani is an unexceptional exception.

Foodstalls The best ones are all in and around the market area; sate, fruit, Padang dishes etc.

Entertainment

Minangkabau dances: including *Pencak silat*, a traditional form of self-defence, can be seen performed at *Medan Nan Balindung*, Jl Khatib Suleiman 1, at 2030 every day except Thu. Another venue is the *Hoya Kota Wisata*, Pasar Banto Building, shows at 2030 on Thu and Sat only. The *Rendezvous Café* also sells tickets for the dance performance. Cultural shows are also often laid on at the *Novotel* – worth checking. **Minangkabau traditional arts** (music, song, dance and silat): *Saayun Salankah*, Jl Lenggogeni 1A, on Wed, Thu and Sat at 2030.

Shopping

Bukittinggi has a good selection of shops selling handicrafts, curios and antiques, and has a particular reputation for its silver and gold jewellery. The shops are concentrated on Jl Minangkabau (close to the Central Market) and along Jl Jend A Yani and Jl Teuku Umar. The most enjoyable way to shop is in the **Central Market** on Wed or Sat (see page 535). At other times it mainly sells products for local consumption – lots of clothes ending in 'ene', fruit and vegetables, plastic trinkets, metal goods, fish, dried and otherwise, and so on.

Antiques and curios: there is comparatively little for sale that originates from the area around Bukittinggi; most articles are from Nias and Mentawi, from the Batak areas around Lake Toba, and from further afield, like Kalimantan and Java. The 'primitive' art from Nias and

Mentawi is easy to fake and it is likely that much on sale is neither old nor genuine – despite the appearance of authenticity that dust and grime may give. 'Antique' shops include: *Borobudur Art and Gallery*, Jl Teuku Umar 7B. *Jaya Art and Curio*, Jl Teuku Umar 7E. *Tanjung Raya Art Shop*, Jl Jend A Yani 85. *Karajinan*, Jl Jend A Yani. *Nova Art Shop*, Jl Jend A Yani 40. *Aladdin*, Jl Jend A Yani 14.

Book exchange and shops: 2 places on Jl Jend A Yani, both close to the footbridge, sell 2nd hand books, postcards etc – the *Toko Buku* and *Tila's Bookshop* (there is another branch of *Tila's* on Jl Teuku Umar).

Handicrafts: there are the handicraft villages like Pandai Sikat (see page 539), as well as a number of shops in town. Many of the antique shops are really jumped-up handicraft outlets. A place with better goods than most is *Sulaman Silungkang* on Jl Panorama.

Jewellery: if interested in buying jewellery, it is worth visiting the Kota Gadang silversmithing village (see page 537), which specializes in producing silver filigree.

Sports

Rafting: raft trips (US$30 for the day) are organized down the Batang Anai River and along the Sri Antokan rapids, which both flow from Lake Maninjau, through the Ngarai Sianok gorge to Palupuh, and along the Ombilin River which flows out of Lake Singkarak. Trips are offered by many hotels and cafés along Jl Jend A Yani and agencies such as *Jogya Wista*, on the same street, T31836. **Rock climbing**: Bukittinggi is gaining a reputation for the quality of its rock climbing and its rock climbers. Baso is a limestone tower around 10 km due east of Bukittinggi, with a number of challenging routes including Power Pancake (graded 5.12c [Australian grading]), Bee Attack (5.11b), Priest (5.10b), Koorong Bana (5.12d) and Bastard (5.12c). The Harau Canyon (see page 550) offers around 24 routes including the technically demanding Liang Limbek (5.13a). Those interested in climbing should contact Dodi Liswardi (T31850) at the *Harau Cliff Café* in Bukittinggi or Nick at the *Star Café* or *Arus Deras Tour and Travel*, Jl Tuanku Nan Renceh 20, T22913, F22913. Note that to climb in the Harau valley, a permit has to be obtained from the Harau Valley National Park (PHPA). **Swimming**: the *Novotel's* romantic Romanesque heated pool is open to non-residents (10,000Rp, 5,000Rp for children – if you have lunch at the hotel they will allow you to swim for free).

Tour operators

Tour companies are concentrated along Jl Jend A Yani. As well as doing the usual things like reconfirming flights and providing bus tickets, they also organize local and tours further afield (see tours, above, for more information). Companies include: *Maju Indosari Travel Bureau*, Jl Muka Jam Gadang 17, T21671. *Gangga Tours and Travel*, Jl Jend A Yani 70, T22836. *Batours Agung*, Jl Jend A Yani 105, T34346, F22306. *Travina Tour*, Jl Jend A Yani 107, T21281. *Mitra Wisata Tours and Travel*, Jl Jend A Yani 99, T21133. *Serulung Tour and Travel*, Jl Teuku Umar 18B, T33052. *East West Tour and Travel*, Jl Teuku Umar 18, T31707. *Puti Bungso Tours and Travel*, Jl Teuku Umar 6C, T21542. *Randy Tours and Travel*, Jl Jend A Yani 152, T31905. *Jogja Wista*, Jl Jend A Yani 85, T31836, F33507. *Arus Deras Tour and Travel*, Jl Tuanku Nan Renceh 20, T22913, F22913. *Rendezvous Café*, book air fares with a very good student discount.

Transport

108 km from Padang, 381 km from Sibolga, 508 km from Prapat, 174 km from Pekanbaru

Local Bukittinggi is small enough to wander around on foot. However, there are **bemos** and **bendis** – romantic 2-wheeled horse-drawn carts – for longer trips. **Oplets**: from the bus station at Aur Kuning, 3 km southeast of town, for excursions. **Motorbike hire**: from many tour/travel companies for about 15,000-20,000Rp per day. **Mountain bike hire**: ask at your hotel or losmen (5,000Rp per day).

Road Bus: the station is at Aur Kuning, 3 km southeast of town. Buses to local destinations including Batusangkar (1,500Rp), Maninjau (2-3,000Rp) and Payakumbuh (1,500Rp). There are also buses to destinations further afield (see box). For Prapat, choose the bus company carefully as many people have been overcharged; ensure that you have a ticket with seat numbers. **NB** The bus may not connect with the last ferry to Samosir (1830), which means a late night arrival at Prapat and a limited choice of hotels (see page 486). Tickets are also

Visitors arriving at Aur Kuning may be encouraged to take a taxi to town; regular (red) oplets ply the route for a fraction of the price (500Rp)

available from travel agents (see above), but beware of buying tickets from touts roaming hotels and guesthouses the bus is unlikely to be 'a/c, express and very, very comfortable'. **Chartered minibus**: for comfort, a minibus to Prapat (for Samosir Island) is an attractive option, 12 hrs (200,000Rp for whole bus). **Taxi**: taxis can be hired, even as far as Medan. Ask at one of the tour offices (see above).

Directory **Airline offices** *Garuda* and *Merpati*, *Dymens Hotel*, Jl Nawawi 3. **Banks** Banks close at 1100 on Sat. Many of the tour and travel companies will change money. *Bank Negara Indonesia*, Jl Jend A Yani, run an efficient service and will change most TCs. *Bank Rakyat Indonesia*, Jl Jend A Yani 3 (near the clock tower). *PT Enzet Corindo Perkasa*, Jl Minangkabau 51 (money changer). **Communications** General Post Office: Jl Kemerdekaan, on the south edge of town. Now with internet access, but rather slow. The 2 bookshops on Jl Jend A Yani in the centre of town also offer a limited postal service: they sell stamps and have post boxes. **Branch Post Office**: on Clock Tower Square. **Telephone Office**: Wartel office, Jl Jend A Yani, for international telephone calls and faxes. **Internet**: The *Harau Cliff Café* has 3 internet terminals. **Medical facilities** Hospital: *Dokter Achmad Mochtar Hospital*, Jl Rivai (opposite the *Denai Hotel*). **Tourist offices** *Bukittinggi Tourist Office*, closed – and moved to Padang.

Routewise: from Bukittinggi to Maninjau. This trip is spectacular. After leaving the main Padang-Bukittinggi route at Kota Baru, the road twists through the terraced countryside to the town of Matur. Locals are said to call this stretch of road the Mercedes Bends, and the story is charming even if it might not be true. During the Dutch period there were two sugar cane processing plants at Matur and the Dutch manager of one owned the only car in the area: a Mercedes. When he drove to Bukittinggi local people would line the road to watch the strange machine wind its way to Kota Baru, earning this stretch of road the name the Mercedes Bends. On reaching the crater lip – an awesome spectacle – the road descends through 44 hairpin bends, each of which has been numbered by some bureaucratic mind, before arriving at the lake edge village of Maninjau.

Lake Maninjau

Phone code: 0752
Colour map 2, grid A1

Lake Maninjau is one of the most beautiful and impressive natural sights in Sumatra, rivalling Lake Toba. It is a huge, flooded volcanic crater with steep 600m-high walls. To the west and south the crater walls are largely forested, dropping straight into the lake and leaving scarcely any scope for cultivation and settlement. This part of the crater supports a fair amount of wildlife. To the east and north there is some flat land and this is where Maninjau's small settlements are to be found.

Getting there & around Regular buses service the routes from Bukittinggi and Padang, taking 1½ hrs and 2-3 hrs respectively. Bicycles and motorcycles can be hired from most guesthouses and provide an ideal means of getting around the lakes and reaching surrounding villages.

Sights The lake offers reasonable swimming (although close to the shore it can be murky), fishing and water-skiing. In 1996, discharges of sulphur from hot underwater springs killed many of the fish which are raised here in cages along the shore. The springs explain why the water is surprisingly warm for a lake over 500m above sea level.

Maninjau village lies on the east shore of the lake at the point where the road from Bukittinggi reaches the lake (see map). It is a small but booming market and administrative centre. There is a bank, post office, clinic, telecommunications centre, mosque, school, and various hotels, guesthouses, warungs and restaurants. Most of the places to stay are in (and beyond) the northern extent of the village. Around 3 km north of Maninjau village is the small and charming hamlet of **Bayur**. This is quite simply a gem of a community. Most of the houses and other buildings are made of wood or are white stuccoed brick, and date from the Dutch period. On the northern edge of the village are several more guesthouses, some of the most peaceful in the area. Wandering around Bayur it is easy to imagine what villages were like before individualism and licence destroyed the bonds of community. This feels like a place, to paraphrase Jonathan Sacks, built on covenant, not on contract. Continuing further around the lake the road passes through Muko Muko and then onto Lubuk Basung, where the buses terminate.

There are **hiking trails** through the surrounding countryside. Because the lake is some 500m above sea level, it is cool even during the day and can be chilly at night. The range of hotels and restaurants has expanded considerably in recent years, and some repeat visitors maintain it has lost at least some of its former charm.

From Maninjau village, a worthwhile walk or bicycle ride is around the north edge of the lake to the village of **Muko Muko**, 16 km in all (buses also ply the route). Just before Muko Muko there are the **Alamada Hotsprings** (rather small and insignificant), an excellent fish restaurant and a hydropower station. The total distance around the lake is about 50 km – 20 km on a good road; 30 km is a dirt track. Bicycles can be hired from many of the guesthouses and coffee shops (4,000Rp per day).

It is also possible to hike up to, or down from, **Lawang Top** (**Puncak Lawang**), on the crater lip (see page 538 for more details). The trail to the crater edge begins in the middle of Bayur, 3 km north of Maninjau village.

Excursions

There are 2 concentrations of guesthouses, in Maninjau village and Buyur, both on the eastern shore. As these 2 communities are only 3 km apart, in effect the guesthouses and hotels merge into a single strand. As so often with places like Maninjau, the quality of the accommodation changes almost by the month. Because the guesthouses and hotels are stretched out over 3 km, it is easy enough to wander around and check out the competition.

Sleeping
■ *on map*
Price codes:
see inside front cover

Maninjau village C *Maninjau Indah*, Maninjau village, T61018, F61257. Seventeen rooms, its central position means it is not as peaceful as elsewhere, large bare rooms with balconies and attached bathrooms with hot water, some cheaper rooms with no shower and no view, 1 of the 2 more upmarket places to stay in Maninjau so tour groups often stay here, in a state of disrepair, swimming pool but not always full, also internet access. **C-D** *Alam Maninjau Guesthouse*, Jl Raya Maninjau 36, T61242. A well designed wooden lodge on the hillside overlooking the lake, rooms are large and characterful, some with attached bathrooms (cold water), breakfast included in room rate, great balconies for reading and relaxing, a peaceful and well-run guesthouse with American partner. Recommended.

Other places in Maninjau village include 3 guesthouses grouped together just north of the village, down a track and on the lakeside. There is little to distinguish between these 3 places which are similarly priced: simple rooms with shared facilities.

In between B *Pasir Panjang Permai*, Desa Gasang (a little over 1 km north of the village on the lakeside), T61111, F61255. Wooden restaurant built over the lake, tennis, boat for charter, this lakeside hotel with 20 rooms is 1 of the 2 upmarket places – and the better one; the cheaper rooms do not have a lake view or hot water but all have attached bathrooms, attractive balconies in the more expensive rooms with rather uncomfortable deck chairs, good fish served in the restaurant. Recommended. **B** *Tan Diri Hotel*, Km 1 Desa Air Panas, T61263. Very clean large rooms with satellite TV, attached bathrooms and hot water, attractive balconies, quite stylish (for this price), on the lake about 1 km from Maninjau village, bikes for hire. Recommended. **C** *Family*, T61037, right on the lake but far enough from Maninjau village so the water is not quite as murky. Just 5 rooms in a converted single storey villa, spotless with attached bathrooms (no hot water), a good medium range place to stay with no pretence and a personal, family feel. Recommended. **C-D** *Hotel Mutiara Danau Maninjau*, on the lakeside. Clean rooms, en suite, the manager Rico speaks good English and is very helpful, located just south of the market. **D-E** *Tropikal Baru*, T61089. Slightly more upmarket place on the lake front, right at the northern end of the strip of hotels and guesthouses running from Maninjau village, spacious, bright rooms with balconies overlooking the lake. **E** *Abang Homestay*, Desa Gasang. Simple rooms overlooking the lake in an old house with a corrugated iron roof. **E** *Davinci Homestay*, T61137. Simple rooms, a little run down, attractive balcony overlooking the lake, south of the village through the market, on the lake shore.

E *Palantha Homestay and Coffee House*, T61061. Attractive old villa with a balcony on the lake side with simple but acceptable rooms, nice atmosphere here and one of the better of the cheaper options. Recommended. **E** *Tepi Pantai Guesthouse* (or *Beach Guesthouse*), T61082, off the road and on the lake just north of the village. Friendly, with a small restaurant. **F** *Amai Guesthouse*, situated at the south edge of the village, T61054. Dutch-era mansion with good lake views and some ambience. **F** *Ananda Guesthouse*, T61421. Basic, clean but a bit ramshackle, with adjacent café. **F** *Café 44 and Homestay*, T61238, 750m north of Maninjau village, down a track towards the lake shore. This is really a restaurant but there are also some lakeside huts, friendly, cheap and clean, dug out canoe and inner tubes for use on the lake, will arrange treks and pig hunting. Recommended. **F** *Febby Homestay*, T61082, on

Maninjau village & area

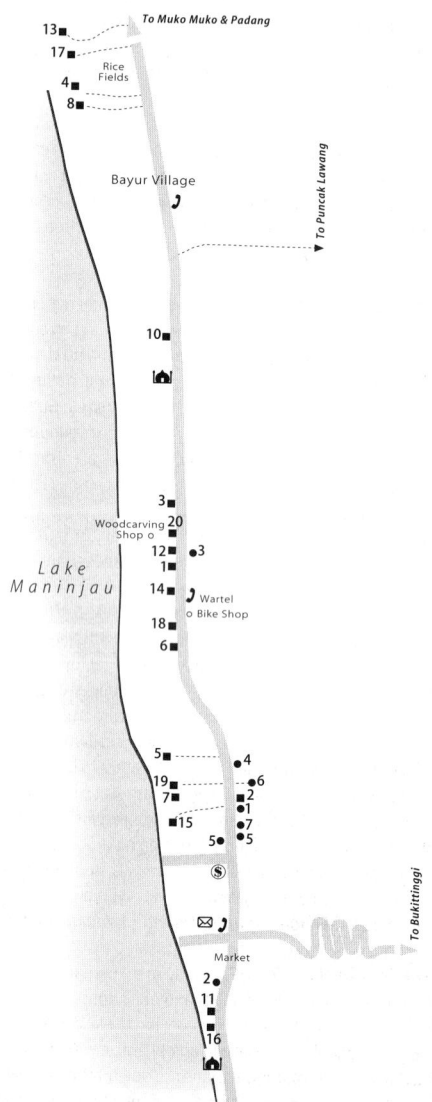

■ **Sleeping**
1 Abang Homestay
2 Alam Maninjau Guesthouse
3 Ananda Guesthouse
4 Bayur Permai Beach Homestay
5 Café 44 & Homestay
6 Family
7 Febby Homestay
8 Lillies Homestay
9 Maninjau Indah
10 Maransy Beach Homestay
11 Mutiara Danau Maninjau
12 Palantha Homestay & Coffee House
13 Parak Karambin
14 Pasir Panjang Permai
15 Penginapan Riak Danau
16 Penginapan Pillie
17 Rizal Beach Homestay
18 Tan Diri
19 Tepi Pantai Guesthouse
20 Tropikal Baru

● **Eating**
1 Barong Café
2 Bobo
3 Jack's Place
4 JJ's Coffee Shop
5 Kawa Café
6 Maninjau View Coffee Shop
7 Simple Café

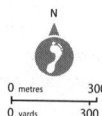

the lake down a track from the road. Laundry service and barbecue fish special. **F** *Penginapan Pillie*, Jl Hudin Rahmani 91, T61048, south of Maninjau village not far from the market. Good food, clean and one of the most popular of the budget places to stay in Maninjau village, mountain bikes for hire, ample information available on surrounding area, good entertainment system for those rainy days. Recommended. **F** *Penginapan Riak Danau*, T61091, on the lake down a track north of Maninjau village. Simple rooms but a bit grubby.

Bayur There are fewer places to stay in Bayur than in Maninjau village, although north of the village is a group of very peaceful guesthouses down a series of tracks that run from the road, through ricefields, to the lake shore, where there is a small 'beach'. These guesthouses are the most peaceful; they are also some distance (3 km) from the main concentration of restaurants and coffee shops. Bemos into and out of Maninjau village stop at 1900, but the walk is beautiful and not far. **D** *Maransy Beach Homestay*, T61264, on the southern edge of Bayur village. Attractive place with good restaurant over the lake, quiet, better swimming from here. **D** *Ernel*, we have not seen this place but a recent visitor recommends it; quiet, with good swimming on the lake, excellent attached restaurant, bungalows with hot water showers, set down a track through ricefields. **D-E** *Lillies Homestay*, consists of standard rooms and individual bungalows. **E-F** *Bayua Beach Inn*, a sign on the main road going north from Bayur to Muko-Muko, marks the path to the *Bayua*, ask the bus to stop here, T61126, situated on the edge of the lake, with wonderful views. Only 4 double rooms, no electricity or restaurant (although breakfast is provided), lanterns provided for the walk into the village for your evening meal, a very romantic spot. Recommended, though we received an email from a visitor at the end of 1999 reporting that this place had recently closed. **E-F** *Bayur Permai Beach Homestay*, lovely, peaceful place 3 km or so from Maninjau village, north of Bayur. It is situated on the lake 150m down a track through ricefields from the road, friendly with good food, swimming. Recommended. **E-F** *Parak Karambin Guesthouse*, situated close to the *Bayur Permai Beach Homestay* and just as peaceful. This place consists of a small grouping of small chalets shaded by coconut palms (hence the name). **F** *Rizal Beach Homestay*, T61404, close to the *Parak Karambin* and *Bayur Permai*. Four rooms (with 4-poster beds), and recently another 6 bungalows, in a beautiful position, away from the main tourist area, very friendly and relaxed, with excellent restaurant situated right on the lakeshore, no electricity, only paraffin lamps (electricity promised). Recommended.

Eating
● *on map*
Price codes:
see inside front cover

There are several good coffee shops geared to western tastes in Maninjau village, as well as the usual warungs and stalls, concentrated in the market area. An eating place outside of Maninjau is *Alamada Hotsprings Restaurant*, which serves excellent fish.

Maninjau village Cheap *Maninjau View Coffee Shop*, on the hillside beneath the *Alam Maninjau Guesthouse*. Attractive wooden house, good steaks, spaghetti and some Indonesian dishes, an attractive place for a long lunch or evening meal. Recommended. *Barong Café*, set back from main road. Travellers' and local fare, batik-making display next door. *Bobo*, Maninjau village, just south of the market area. Excellent Indonesian food, but also offers international. Recommended. *Bundo Coffee Shop*, northern edge of the village. This place doesn't stand out as a place to eat, but the drinks are OK and also serves simple dishes. *Café 44*, on the lake shore north of Maninjau village. Good food and atmosphere, popular (also some accommodation, see above). *Jack's Place*, in centre of Maninjau. This restaurant is very popular, serving local and international cuisine, relaxed and quiet upstairs and more lively on the lower floor. Recommended. *JJ's Coffee Shop*, in the nothern section. *Simple Café*, central location, local and travellers' food but rather simple. *Kawa Café*, in the nothern section of the village. Good coffee, pancakes and travellers' food, bikes for rent.

Traditional massage: by Ibu K Tati, just behind the *Maninjau View Coffee Shop*.

Entertainment

Bookshop: *Toko Buku Glory*, north end of Maninjau village, postcards, stamps and second-hand books for sale.

Shopping

Transport **Local** Bicycles (7,000Rp per day) and motorcycles can be hired from many guesthouses; they are an excellent way to get around the lake. Some oplets from Bukittinggi continue anti-clockwise around the lake through Bayur and Muko Muko to Lubuk Basung, the end of the road, so to speak. Larger buses do continue down to Padang. **Road Bus**: regular buses from Bukittinggi to Maninjau village, negotiating 44 bends down from the crater lip to the lake, 3,000Rp (1½ hrs). Buses also continue on through Bayur to Muko Muko on the northwest side of the lake and from there to Padang via Parianan (2-3 hrs). There are direct buses from Padang to Maninjau via Parianan; alternatively, catch a bus to Bukittinggi and ask to be let off at Kuto Tuo, the turn-off for Maninjau, and wait there to catch a bus down to the lake.

Maninjau village is 35 km west of Bukittinggi & 152 km from Padang

Directory **Banks** *Bank Rakyat Indonesia*, Jl SMP (a short distance north of the bus stop in the centre of town). Will change US$, TCs and cash. **Medical facilities** Clinic: at the southern end of Maninjau village (see map). **Communications** Post Office: Jl Muara Pisang (facing the police station and not far from the oplet stop). Telephone Office: Jl SMP (facing the oplet stop in the centre of town). International calls can be made from the office.

Payakumbuh

Phone code: 0752
Colour map 2, grid A1

Most people come to Payakumbuh, an important market town, on a day trip from Bukittinggi. However, there is accommodation here and it does make a good base from which to go trekking in the Harau Valley (see below). From a culinary point of view, Payakumbuh is home to **gelamai**. This is a soft and delicious fudge-like concoction made from palm sugar, coconut, brown sugar and rice flour. The ingredients are boiled up and then allowed to cool and harden on metal sheets. It is sold as far afield as Jakarta and Kuala Lumpur. One of the better known producers is the *Erina* 'factory' (really just a large kitchen) at Parit Rantang 253. Ask for directions as it is 100m down a little side alley off Jalan Nusantara Barat. Another local speciality is *beras rendang* – sweet rice.

Excursions The **Harau Canyon** is a protected area of 300 ha, encircled by 100m-high canyon walls about 10 km northeast of Payakumbuh. To get there independently it is necessary to walk the 8 km from the main road to the canyon, but as the walk is so beautiful this is not such a hardship. The road works its way deeper into the narrowing canyon through ricefields and small hamlets with the odd traditional house, a picture (perhaps misplaced) of bucolic peace and plenty. After about 7 km, as the road approaches the eastern canyon face, the road divides and there is a sign pointing to the right to **Sarsah Bunta**. Around 2 km down this track is a swimming pool, shaded by trees with a small 'beach'. The swimming here is better than at the main waterfall. By not turning right but continuing on for about another kilometre, the road reaches the main waterfall. This is hardly a Niagara and after a few dry days it ceases to cascade at all. However, after rain there is an attractive shower of droplets that tumble 100m into an artificial tank. Close by, stairs cut into the rock face lead upwards to a viewing sight: good views back along the valley but horribly marred by rubbish – plastic bags, crisp packets, cans, and what have you. Rock climbers are beginning to pioneer new routes up the canyon walls (see page 545). Drink stalls on site. ■ *500Rp (300Rp for children). Cars entering the reserve area have to pay an additional 1,000Rp toll. Catch a white sago (oplet) from the sago terminal in town running towards Sarialamat, and ask to be let off at 'Lembah Harau' (500Rp). At the turn-off there is a barrier and it is an 8-km walk to the waterfall. There are various drinks stalls along the way. Getting back is usually a bit more of a challenge. However, there are occasional omprengans (oplets which are not licensed to operate on main roads) which ferry walkers back to the main road.*

Piladang, 8 km from Payakumbuh on the road to Bukittinggi (and therefore 25 km from Bukittinggi), is the site of one of the most **entertaining and colourful markets** hereabouts. Piladang is a town of little consequence, but Friday is market day and farmers and traders converge to sell mounds of chillis, cassava, tomatoes, carrots, marrows, pumpkins, and so on. The presence of so many cash-laden farmers means that traders of dry goods like plastic implements, pots and pans, and brushes and shoes, also make their way here. This in turn attracts salesmen and quack doctors with their repartee and dubious remedies. The result: a mélange of colour, smells and movement. The market operates from around 0600 through to 1200 (when there is a lull for Friday prayers) and then begins again rather less frenetically in the afternoon. There is also a market here on other days of the week, but it is much smaller. ■ *Getting there: from Payakumbuh catch a green oplet, and from Bukittinggi a bus running towards Payakumbuh.*

Limbukan is a small village 8 km south of town and locally known for its **duck races** or *bacu itik*. These are only held on special holidays or local anniversaries, but if you happen to be around, the races can be highly entertaining not least because farm ducks have got to be some of the least aerodynamically sound birds created. **Batang Tabik** is a small **natural swimming pool** about 4 km on from Limbukan. There is a decent restaurant here. ■ *500Rp, blue sago/oplet running towards Situjuh (300Rp); the same oplets run from Limbukan to Batang Tabik.*

Sleeping

B-C *Mangkuto*, Jl Jend Sudirman (about 2 km from town on the road to the Harau Valley and Pekanbaru), T93358. Some a/c, restaurant, Payakumbuh's No 1 place to stay with 20 rooms, hot water and even a small seminar room, because it is out of town it is quiet with great views out the back over ricefields, the VIP rooms are gauche but the standard rooms are light and airy and good value, tours and car rental arranged, restaurant set in the middle of an artificial pond. **C** *Bundo Kandung*, Jl Prof M Yamin 25, T92711. Some a/c, restaurant, rather overpriced for what it is, the VIP rooms have a/c, all have Asian loos, small restaurant, the standard rooms are by far the best deal. **D** *Wisma Flamboyant*, Jl Ade Irme Suryani, T92333. This place doesn't know whether it is a hotel or a wisma, the rooms are bare and simple, attached mandis with Asian toilets, downstairs rather dark, upstairs better, all rather worn, but cheap. **E** *Sari*, Jl Sudirman 15, T92406. This place is even less a 'hotel' than the *Flamboyant* and, as if recognizing that it is trading under false pretences, it is easy to miss – there is no obvious sign (it is on the crossroads of Jl Sudirman and Jl Ade Irme Suryani). The rooms are unloved and uniformly dismal, though the management try to make up for this by being effusively friendly.

Eating

Asia Baru, Jl Soekarno-Hatto 1 (about 100m along the road towards Bukittinggi from the bus/oplet terminal). Good Padang and Indonesian food.

Transport

33 km from Bukittinggi

Local Bendis – pony carts – for short journeys around town. **Road Bus** regular oplets (in Payakumbuh they are known as 'sagos' after the nearby mountain, Mt Sago) from Bukittinggi, 1 hr (700Rp) and bus connections with Padang and Batusangkar. Sagos show their destinations on their roofs. The oplet/sago terminal is in the centre of town, while the long distance (large) bus station is out of town off the road to Bukittinggi.

Directory

Communications Post Office: facing the oplet (sago) terminal in the centre of town. **Tourist office** Jl Olah Raga 1, T92907, open 0800-1430 Mon-Thu, 0800-1130 Fri, 0800-1300 Sat.

Payakumbuh to Batusangkar

This is one of the most enchanting drives in the Minang area. Buses take this route between Payakumbuh and Batusangkar. In the small market town of Piladang a road cuts south and after a few kilometres joins up with the 'main' road from Baso to Batusangkar. Up the hill from here is a popular tourist coffee stop and viewing point. The view down the valley is worthwhile and the local coffee is good (local spices also on sale). Continuing south the road passes through the small towns of **Tabek Patah** and **Rao Rao**, the latter being known for its traditional houses and situated 8 km from Batusangkar.

Batusangkar

Phone code: 0752

Batusangkar, like Bukittinggi, is situated on an upland plateau, surrounded by terraced ricefields and mountains. It is regarded as one of the three centres of Minang culture and history and, like Payakumbuh, is staunchly Muslim. The main market, **Pasar Serika**, is in the centre of town and nearby are several souvenir/curio shops.

Excursions **Pagaruyung**, a **sultan's palace**, lies 5 km east of Batusangkar, close to the end of a road that just peters out. It is, in effect, a very grand and ornate Minang house, now a museum. In 1815 during the Padri War, Muslim radicals slaughtered nearly all the sultan's family presumably because they represented the unyielding human heart of Minang culture. Unfortunately, the original palace was destroyed during the Second World War and this is a reconstruction. Beneath the wooden cladding it is made of concrete, and the dimensions and lay-out of the original palace have been altered to accord with its new function as a museum. There are a couple of warungs in the car park for simple Indonesian food and good Padang dishes. ■ *1,000Rp (500Rp for children), Mon-Sun.* Walking back towards Batusangkar for about 1 km is another palace, the **Istana Silundung Gulang**. This one is privately owned and it is not possible to enter. Nonetheless, it is genuine and worth seeing. There are also a number of other more modest but attractive houses on this stretch of road. Continuing walking back towards Batusangkar, after another 500m or so the road passes a large **banyan tree** and then a fenced area containing a group of **menhirs**, inscribed stones. ■ *Getting there: catch a yellow oplet direct to Pagaruyung (300Rp). Alternatively, get off at the inscribed stones and walk the 2 km to Pagaruyung, catching a bemo back from there. To do this alight at the top of the hill after the road has crossed a second bridge (the road crosses 1 small stream and then a rather more substantial river), around 2-3 km from town. An irrigation channel follows the road on the left-hand side as it rises up the hill after the 2nd bridge.*

Pariangan is a less visited and more peaceful **Minang village**. It nestles in a small valley on the slopes of Gunung Merapi at around 850m, surrounded by ricefields. It is thought to be one of the original Minang villages – inscriptions found here certainly date it to the 14th century reign of King Adityavarman – and it is one of the few places where *surau* quarters for men and boys remain in use. It is still one of the most beautiful and friendly villages in the Minang highlands – although the old mosque was recently torn down and replaced by an inferior modern structure. There is nowhere to stay in Pariangan but there are a handful of warungs. The road from Pariangan to Kota Baru is a beautiful drive with stupendous views. *En route* the road passes through another beautiful traditional village: **Keladi**. ■ *Getting there: from Batusangkar's Dobo terminal catch an oplet (siti) heading towards Kota Baru. The oplet passes through Pariangan and then continues along a narrow track to Kota Baru, just south of Bukittinggi (500Rp). Unfortunately, it is not possible to do this journey in reverse from Bukittinggi as the oplets only run in 1 direction (they only travel from Batusangkar to Kota Baru via Pariangan, not the other way). However, this oplet route has only recently started, so a 2-way service may come into being. For the time being though it is necessary to catch an oplet from Bukittinggi to Batusangkar, and then 1 to Parianagan.*

Balimbiang is another traditional Minang village situated about 10 km south of Batusangkar, and 1 km off the main road. Some of the 300-year-old *rumah adat*, built entirely without the use of nails, have been opened up by their enterprising owners to visitors. ■ *Admission by donation, no oplets take this route from Batusangkar to Lake Singkarak, but many Batusangkar-Solok mini-buses do. Ask to be let off at the turn-off for Balimbiang. From Bukittinggi it is necessary to 1st catch an oplet to Batusangkar and then a Solok-bound bus.*

Sleeping There are 3 hotels in town, all grouped together near the centre of town. If coming from Bukittinggi go past the main market (Pasar Serika) on the right and into the main square with the statue of the 3 heroes of the revolution. Jl Dr Hamka (sometimes known as Jl Parak Juar) runs off the square up to the left. **B-D** *Pagaruyung Hotel*, Jl Dr Hamka 4, T71533, F71171. Some a/c, best hotel in town and the VIP rooms are reasonable enough (hot water), but it is not really up to the standard of accommodation in Bukittinggi and is not even competitively priced in comparison. **D** *Yoherma Hotel*, Jl Dr Hamka 15, T71130. Looks better than it is, narrow beds, uninviting attached mandis, rather overpriced. **E** *Parma Hotel*, Jl Dr Hamka, T71330. Rock bottom prices for rooms that don't yield any pleasant surprises.

Kubang, Jl Dr Hamka.

Eating

Local bendis – pony carts – for short journeys around town. **Oplets** for local journeys from the Dobo oplet terminal in the centre of town. In Batusangkar they are known as '*sitis*', after '*city*'. **Road Bus** regular bus connections with Padang, Bukittinggi and Payakumbuh.

Transport
41 km from Bukittinggi

Communications Post Office: Jl Sutomo 1, in the centre of town. **Telephone:** Wartel office on the main square. **Tourist Office** Jl Pemuda 1, T71300.

Directory

Lake Singkarak

Lake Singkarak is a 20 km-long lake to the southwest of Batusangkar and about 30 km south of Bukittinggi. It does not compare in terms of either beauty or facilities with Lake Maninjau, but the swimming is refreshing and there is some accommodation here. There are two main settlements on the lake. **Ombilin** village lies half way down the eastern shore at the point where the Ombilin River flows out of the lake. (Some of the more adventurous tour companies in Bukittinggi offer rafting excursions on the Ombilin – see page 545.) This is also the intersection where the road leads northwards towards Batusangkar and south to Solok. Ombilin has one hotel, a small market, and a handful of warungs. The railway track which runs up the east shore of the lake is for freight only, mostly coal.

Phone code: 0752
Colour map 2, grid A1

A road does skirt around the western side of the lake and, due to the improvements to the local hydro-powerstation is in good condition.

There are just 2 hotels on the lake. One on a quiet road on the northern shore. The 2nd on the eastern shore, 5 km north of Ombilin village. **B-C** *Singkarak Sumpur Hotel*, for reservations Jl KH Ahmad Dahlan T82529, F82103. Forty rooms, more expensive with hot water, satellite TV, swimming pool fed by mountain streams, tennis court, in a very peaceful location on a quiet road, a comparatively luxurious hotel and a good place to relax, but note that there is little else here but the hotel, the hotel lies 4 km off the main road running south from Padang Panjang to Ombilin and Solok. **C-D** *Jayakarta Hotel*, Jl Raya Padang Panjang km 19 (5 km north of Ombilin village), T21279, right on the lake front with pebbly beach. Swimming possible, attractive open eating and lounging area, rooms are large and comfortable enough, although a little moth eaten, and uninviting. (Tours visit here for swimming, but the water is not all that clear.)

Sleeping

Road Bus regular bus connections with Padang Panjang (and from there to Padang, and also Bukittinggi, 1,000Rp), Solok and Batusangkar. If travelling on the northern stretch of the road between Singkarak and Padang Panjang, keep an eye out for the beautiful old *surau* (prayer hall), made of wood in Minang style, on the left-hand side of the road (going north) in the village of Lubuk Bauk.

Transport
Ombilin is 24 km from Padang Panjang

Padang Panjang

Padang Panjang is a busy but nonetheless surprisingly attractive town on the main road down from the highlands to the provincial capital of Padang. Locally it is reputed to have been the first town in the Minang *darek* to be converted to Islam, and Islam has had a strong presence here since. Many houses, both colonial and more traditional, line the main road and there is an attractive small private Minang *istana* (palace) just up the road to Bukittinggi from the *Singgalang Hotel*.

Phone code: 0752
Colour map 2, grid B1

As the town sits astride a major intersection it has become a minor transport hub, and it is often necessary to change oplets here to travel east towards Lake Singkarak and Solok. There is a market on the Solok road almost at this intersection. Although few tourists find it necessary to stay here – and certainly there are better places – those considering climbing either Gunung Singgalang or Gunung Merapi may find this a more convenient base than Bukittinggi.

Excursions **Kandang Empat** is a little hamlet outside Padang Panjang on the road to Padang (60 km from Padang and 31 km from Bukittinggi). This is an excellent place to relax, get away from the crowds, enjoy family life, walk and swim. It is possible to sleep at **E** *Uncle De De's Homestay* which is situated in Kandang Empat, 500m off the main road. ■ *Getting there: travelling south from Bukittinggi, get off about 500m after the road crosses the railway line; there is a path running off to the left, by a warung. The path crosses a stream before reaching* Uncle De De's. There are three tiny bamboo and rattan huts in the middle of the jungle and other rooms in *Uncle De De's* home. Room rate includes two meals (excellent food) and tea, fruit and snacks all day. A family-run concern, the patriach is the sprightly 75-year-old Uncle De De, who is a mine of information on West Sumatra and the Minangkabau. ■ *Getting there: from Bukittinggi, take an oplet to Padang Panjang and another one to Kandang Empat, or a bus going to Pandang – get off in Kandang Empat, 500m after the* Malibou Anai Resort.

Sleeping The *Mutiara* and *Singgalang* hotels are next to one another just up from the turn-off to Solok. **B** *Singgalang Hotel*, Jl Soekarno-Hatta 19, T82213. Rooms are surprisingly good and well kept, with hot water en suite, not much point in splashing out on the VIP room because the only difference is that it is larger (but there is a large public sitting area anyway) and there is a bath (but no hot water). Acceptable but a little pricey. **C** *Hotel Burlian*, Jl M Syafei 11, T82062. Large airy rooms with en suite shower but no hot water. Watch out for the stuffed bear in the lobby. **C** *Mutiara*, Jl Soekarno-Hatta 15, T83568. Drab, en suite with shower, no hot water, but rooms are comfortable. **D** *Makmur Hotel*, Jl Iman Bondjoll 234, T82140, near to town centre. Good views but questionable choice of sheets!

Transport Around 19 km from Bukittinggi, 89 km from Padang. **Road Bus** regular bus connections with Padang, Bukittinggi and Solok via Lake Singgkarak.

Directory **Communications** Post Office: Jl Soekarno-Hatta 1 (facing the turn-off to Solok).

Padang

Phone code: 0751
Population: 650,000
Colour map 2, grid B1

Padang is the capital of the small province of West Sumatra (Sumatera Barat). Lying on the narrow plain between the Bukit Barisan and the Indian Ocean, it supports a university (Universitas Andalas) and an impressive array of regional government and private offices, most of which are adorned with soaring Minang roofs.

However, Padang does not have much to keep the visitor excited for very long and most people use the town only as an arrival or departure point. It is a useful base from which to venture further afield, and has some good restaurants and hotels.

Ins and outs

Getting there Padang's airport is on the northern outskirts of town. There are daily domestic flights to Jakarta and several centres in Sumatra. The main bus terminal is in the centre of town. Regular buses leave for other provincial capitals and also for destinations on Java. Local buses travel to Bukittinggi, Meninjau, Pariaman, Batusangkar, Muko Muko, Sungai Penuh, and Solok. The Pelni ships *Kambuna* and *Lambelu* dock at Teluk Bayur, 7 km south of town on their fortnightly circuits through the archipelago, and there are also boats to off-shore islands including Enggano and the Mentawi group.

See transport section, page 562, for further details

Getting around

It is easy enough to walk around Padang on foot – or at least the centre of the city. But there is also a diverse public transport system including local buses, oplets, dokars and taxis. Car, boat and motorcycle hire are also possible.

Tourist offices *Dinas Pariwisata Sumatra Barat*, Jl Hayam Wuruk 51, not much English spoken here, but they are welcoming and have various publications that are modestly useful. *Tourist Information Office*, Jl Khatib Sulaiman 22 (the north extension of Jl Jend Sudirman), T55711, open 0700-1400 Mon-Thu, 0700-1100 Fri and 0700-1230 Sat. Useful range of maps and helpful staff. **NB** It is about 3 km north of the town centre and is poorly marked and easily missed. Take an orange bis kota or bemo north. *Regional Tourist Office*, Jl Jend Sudirman 43, T34231, F34231.

Background

The town is also hot and wet – with annual rainfall of 4,500mm (seven times greater than London's annual rainfall, four times more than New York's). Moisture-laden clouds blow in from the Indian Ocean and are forced to deposit rain on the coastal lowlands – and on Padang – as they rise over the peaks of the Bukit Barisan. However, while on paper the rainfall is high, this tends to be concentrated during the late afternoon and early evening so it tends not to be too debilitating.

Padang is very Muslim and very conservative. Women should dress modestly

The romantic mist which hangs over the hills is in fact dust and smoke from an enormous cement plant (with an annual capacity of nearly 5,000,000 tonnes), which even reaches the pages of the literature issued by the local tourist office. Just about every hotel, bank and government building has the requisite Minang roof (or roofs), apparently irrespective of the size of the building or the appropriateness of the architectural flourish. Local architects must rue the day when one of their number decided that a Minang-style roof would add local colour to the building he was designing. It is easy to imagine a young architect, enthused with the thought that he might try something different – a gently sloping roof perhaps – being sharply told that only a Minang roof will do.

The black, red and yellow flag – similar to the German flag – which can be seen flying from offices and along roads throughout the city, is the Minangkabau or West Sumatran provincial flag. It is said that when civic dignitaries from the German town twinned with Padang arrived on an official visit, they were overcome by the effort to welcome them. No one was brave enough to tell the truth.

Sights

The **Adityavarman Museum** or the **Museum Negeri Propinsi Sumatra Barat** (the National Museum of West Sumatra) is at Jalan Diponegoro 10. Housed in a large traditional Minangkabau house and flanked by two rice barns with a rather difficult to decipher monument between them, the museum has a limited display of cultural objects including textiles, pottery, fishtraps, brassware, weaponry, tools and assorted antiques, as well as the requisite collection of stuffed animals and, most weirdly, a collection of miners' lamps. ('Illuminating the Miners of Sumatra Barat' it could have been labelled or, perhaps, 'Shedding Some Light on Mining in Minang'.) The museum is neither terribly well arranged nor catalogued and visitors are unlikely to leave enthused with a desire to learn more. It is really only for the truly incurable. ■ *200Rp, 0900-1600 Tue-Sun.*

Museums

Far more interesting than the museum is to explore Padang's old colonial core, known as **Padang Baru**, on the northern bank of the Batang Arau River. Jalan Batang Arau, which follows the river, is lined on one side with old Chinese shophouses and commercial buildings, dating from the beginning of the century and showing clear Dutch architectural flourishes. The other side of the road overlooks the polluted river from which it takes its name, and here are moored scores of coastal trading vessels all painted the same shade of green.

Colonial core

Chinatown North of Jalan Batang Arau is Padang's **Chinatown** or **Kampung Cina**. In Indonesia, the Minang people are regarded as second only to the Chinese in their commercial acumen, and perhaps this explains why the Chinese have been able to keep such a visible presence in Padang without the same degree of friction that has been evident in towns in Java and elsewhere in Sumatra in recent years. The heart of the Chinese community lies along Jalan Klenteng. At No 321 is the **See Hin Kiong Padang** – a Chinese temple – a mosaic of colour and textures and incense. Further up Jalan Klenteng towards Jalan Niaga is a Chinese social centre, the Himpunan Bersatu Tenguh, and set behind here is a small market area with traditional Chinese herbalists and other emporia.

Modern Padang Walking north from Chinatown one quickly enters modern – and largely ugly – Padang. The rather drab **central mosque** is at Jalan Imam Bonjol 1. The **main**

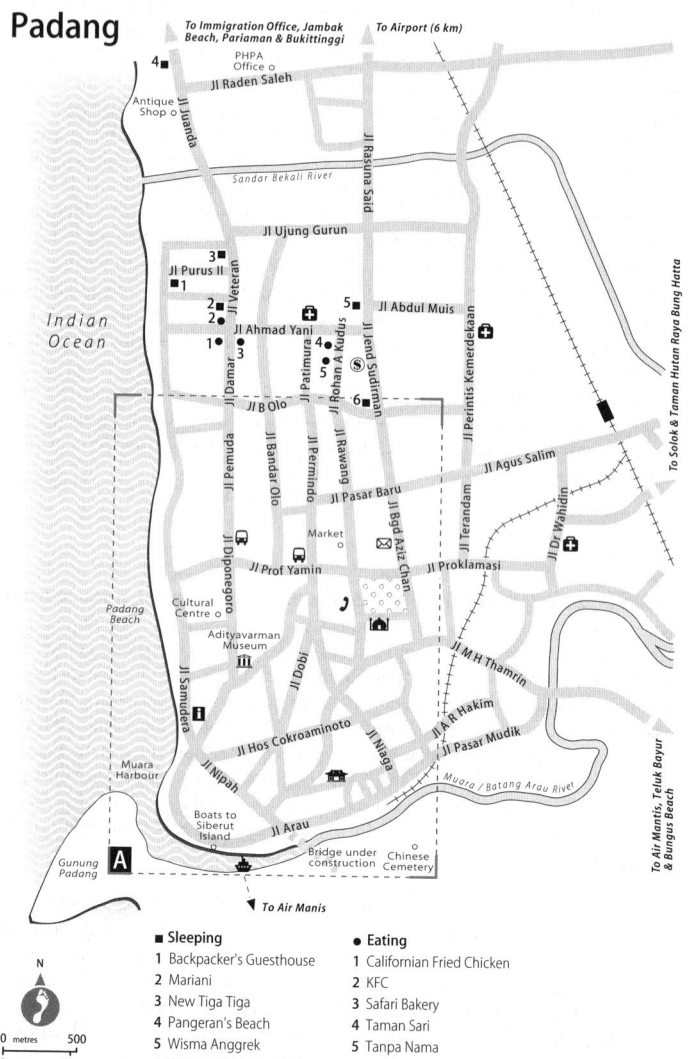

Related map
A Padang centre,
page 559

■ Sleeping
1 Backpacker's Guesthouse
2 Mariani
3 New Tiga Tiga
4 Pangeran's Beach
5 Wisma Anggrek
6 Wisma Mayangsari

● Eating
1 Californian Fried Chicken
2 KFC
3 Safari Bakery
4 Taman Sari
5 Tanpa Nama

market or **Pasar Raya** covers a large area between Jalan Pasar Baru and Jalan Prof M Yamin. When the street traders are out in force Jalan Imam Bonjol is choked with market traders and shoppers, and tuna, shark, swordfish as well as the more usual array of fruit and vegetables are on sale.

Padang beach Rather dirty and with a strong undercurrent – it is not recommended for swimming (see below for alternatives). Foodstalls line the seafront and it receives an on-shore breeze in the evening, making it a good place to sit and watch the sunset. At the south end of Jalan Samudera is the **Taman Ria Pantai Padang** – a small amusement area.

Excursions

Air Manis Air Manis is a fishing village, 5 km to the south of town. The beach here is popular with locals and crowded at the weekend; the surf can be strong and swimming dangerous. A **local legend** tells of an unfaithful son, Malin Kundang, who left his family to seek his fortune. When he returned to Air Manis by sea a rich man, he was so ashamed by the shabby appearance of his mother he refused to greet her. Falling to her knees, she prayed that God punish her son; a wind rose and the boat carrying Malin sank, drowning all on board. The small island offshore here is Pulau Pisang Ketek or Small Banana Island. At low tide it is possible to walk out to the island. ■ *Getting there: walk, or catch a bemo, to the coast at the mouth of the Batang Arau River and then take the ferry boat to the other side. From there it is a 45-min walk to Air Manis, through a Chinese cemetery overlooking the sea and up Gunung Monyet, or Monkey Hill. Alternatively, catch a bemo straight to the beach from the Terminal Pasar Raya in the centre for town (No 402). From Air Manis it is possible to walk further south to* **Padang Port** *and* **Teluk Bayur**; *from there, regular bemos run back into town.*

Bungus beach Lying 22 km south of Padang – this used to be the most romantic beach in the area. It has now been disfigured by the construction of a wood processing enterprise. The plant is a joint South Korean/Indonesian venture and uses timber from the Mentawi Islands, contributing to the islands' rapid deforestation. There is an attractive 7 km walk from Bungus, south, to the – at present – isolated and peaceful **Telur Sei Pisang Beach**. The Japanese International Cooperation Agency and the Indonesian government are thinking of developing the area as a tourist destination. Offshore from Bungus Beach are a number of small, uninhabited, **palm-fringed coral islands**, including **Sirandah** – peaceful, with excellent snorkelling and sandy beaches. Unfortunately most of the coral is dead, although the fish remain resplendent. To visit the islands, hire a boat for the day either through one of the hotels or – cheaper – from the shop five doors down from the *Losmen Carlos*. **B-E** *Knokke Inn*, T30356, provides accommodation at the 21 km marker. This is a good place, with a range of bungalows. The more expensive have a/c and attached bathrooms, the simple ones are bamboo affairs. They all face onto the beach. Restaurant serves Indonesian and travellers' food. **C** *Carolina Beach Resort*, Pasar Laban Km 20, T27900. Recommended. **D** *Bungus Beach Hotel*, good position but rather overpriced, slow service. **E** *Losmen Carlos*, T30353, a basic, brash kind of place, but nonetheless, lively. Carlos arranges trips to the islands (20,000Rp per person). ■ *Getting there: by bemo or public bus No 437, heading towards Painan, 1 hr.*

Jambak beach This beach is a long stretch of sand 20 km north of Padang. It makes sense to come here to while away a few days waiting for a ship. **D-E** *Jack Homestay* is a friendly place to stay near the beach. ■ *Getting there: take a white oplet or public bus No 423 bus from town running north. Just past the airport, after the road crosses the river, get off and then catch a bemo running along the coast – Jalan Pasir Jambak.*

Offshore islands Idyllic palm-fringed tropical islands, including **Pisang Besar Island**, **Padang Island**, **Ketek** and **Bintangur Island**, lie offshore from Padang. They are very peaceful but the coral has deteriorated depressingly rapidly. A recent visitor reported that snorkelling around Ketek was very poor and only average off Pisang Besar. Local fishermen were 'pulling out everything from parrotfish to tiny sergeant majors'. Pisang Besar Island is the closest – 15 minutes by outrigger from Muara Harbour at the mouth of the Batang Arau River. Further information on how to reach the islands is available from the Tourist Information Office. ■ *Getting there: by chartered boat from Muara Harbour, 15-30 mins (about 5,000Rp per hr).*

Pusako Island Pusako Island lies offshore from Padang. Sleep can be had at **AL** *Pusako Island Resort*, T61777, F61774. A/c cottages with hot water, satellite TV, fishing, two pools, jet ski, cycling. Day trips to the island available, enquire at tourist office.

Other excursions Other excursions that can be made easily from Padang, that are covered elsewhere in the book, are **Pariaman**, a small coastal district centre (see page 554), the **Kerinci-Seblat Nature Reserve** (see page 568), **Bukittinggi** and the surrounding sights (see page 535), the **Taman Hutan Raya Bung Hatta**, botanical gardens, home to the rafflesia flower.

Tours Most people book tours in Bukittinggi rather than Padang, although there are a good number of tour agents in town running the usual mix of trips. One company deserves special mention, however: the local NGO *Yayasan Citra Mandiri* which was established in 1995 to lobby for the Mentawi people and to help protect their way of life. They also run tours to Mentawi. These are small (four to seven people) and of low impact. They also use Mentawi guides rather than Minang people (as most tour companies in Bukittinggi do), and they have a mission to educate and inform people about Mentawaian ways and the challenges and tensions facing them. All profits go towards sustaining the work of the NGO. *Yayasan Citra Mandiri (YCM)*, Jalan Kis Mangunsarkoro 54, T20865, F21082.

Essentials

Sleeping
■ *on maps, pages 556 & 559*
Price codes: see inside front cover

AL *Hotel Sedona Bumi Minang*, Jl Bundo Kandung 20-28, T37555, F37567, hbminang@indosat.net.id A/c, restaurant, situated in the centre of town with 164 rooms, swimming pool, business centre, money changer, internet facility, and tennis courts. In terms of facilities and level of comfort this is the best and most professionally managed hotel in town. It is also easily the most pricey. Don't, if you can help it, book into one of the rooms on the first 5 floors of the southern wing – the noise from the 'pub' is intrusive through to 0200. The restaurant's breakfast, lunch and evening buffets are good value though, but the food in the restaurant is pricey and the portions small. **A** *Batang Arau*, Jl Batang Arau 33, T/F27400, RIMBUN@indo.net.id A former Dutch bank converted by a German owner into a hotel, attractive balcony runs along 1 side, on the 1st floor. **A-B** *Pangeran's*, Jl Dobi 3-5, T31233, F27180. A/c, popular hotel with 65 rooms, well run and a good mid-range place to stay now that the *Sedona Bumi Minang* has taken the deep-pocketed business clients. **A-B** *Natour Muara*, Jl Gereja 34, T35600, F31163, natour-muara@padang.wasantara.net.id A/c, restaurant, pool, modern and comfortable hotel with 50 rooms, international 'style' but really only provincial standard, it has recently been eclipsed by the *Sedona* as central Padang's No 1 place.

B-C *Dipo International Hotel*, Jl Diponegoro 25, T34261, F34265. A/c, restaurant, a well-run place especially geared to foreign tourists, the rooms are rather dark but they are all clean with good attached showers, money changer and tour company attached to hotel, and within easy walking distance of the bus terminal. **B-D** *Femina*, Jl Bgd Aziz Chan 15, T34309. Some a/c, small hotel, centrally located with friendly and efficient management and reasonable rooms across a range of price categories down to some very reasonably priced fan rooms with attached mandi. **B** *Hotel Hayam Wuruk*, Jl Hayam Wuruk 16, T21726, F31823. A/c, restaurant, pool (good size but surrounded by walls), fitness centre, sauna, this place has a lot to offer considering its modest size, the rooms are large and well maintained and, if

anything, the standard rooms are better than the deluxe – the latter face onto an ersatz rock face and are filled with uncomfortable-looking furniture, while the standard rooms are brighter (albeit noisier) and just as comfortable with hot water. Recommended.
B-E *Mariani*, Jl Bundo Kandung 35, T34134, F25410. A/c, restaurant (breakfast included in room rate), motorbike for rent, the decor in this hotel is rather Imeldian with lots of lurid and

Padang centre

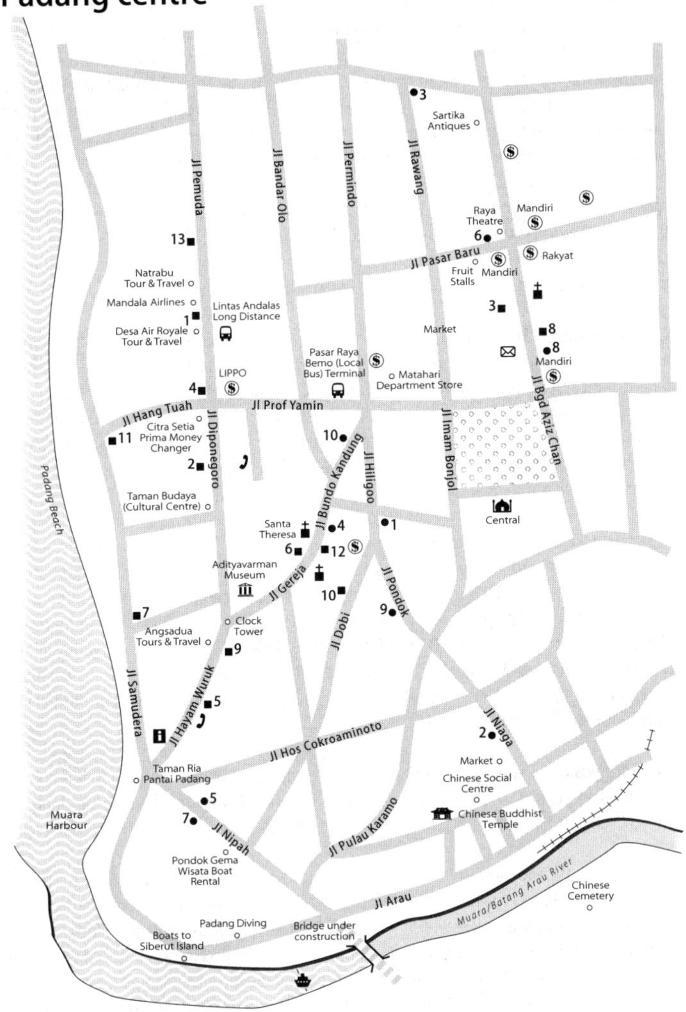

■ **Sleeping**
1 Cendrawasih
2 Dipo International
3 Femina
4 Hang Tuah
5 Hayam Wuruk
6 Mariani
7 Nuansa
8 Padang
9 Palanta Gardens
10 Pangeran's
11 Putri Kemala Balqis Beach
12 Sedona Bumi Minang
13 Tiga Tiga

● **Eating**
1 American Donut & Karia Theatre
2 Aromey
3 CFC
4 KFC
5 Nusas
6 Rumah Makan Kartni & Simpang Raya
7 Sari Laut
8 Simpang Raya
9 Tulip's

In the evening visitors should be careful wandering around the seedy Jl Samudera

over-decorated furniture, but otherwise it is very good, the rooms are clean and spacious, the place has an airy and attractive atmosphere, it is efficiently run, and it is central without being too noisy. Recommended. **B** *Nuansa*, Jl Samudera 12, T26000, F33879. A well-equipped hotel, right next to the beach, attractively decorated, and friendly staff. Recommended. **B** *Padang*, Jl Bgd Aziz Chan 28, T31383, F35962. A/c, restaurant, single storey villa set in gardens in centre of town, the more expensive rooms, large and with high ceilings, are in the old villa, the cheaper rooms extend out the back and the cheapest are rather dark although all have a/c and hot water, a little more character than newer hotels and the mid-range rooms have attractive verandahs, includes breakfast. **B** *Palanta Gardens*, Jl Gereja 38, T23237. Some a/c, converted single storey villa with spacious rooms, adequate bathrooms, and a small restaurant out the rear, a homely little hotel. **B** *Pangeran's Beach*, Jl Ir H Juanda 79 (about 2 km out of the centre of town), T51333, F54613. A/c, restaurant, pool, price includes breakfast and dinner, well managed, with good rooms, its location on the beach means it is quiet. Recommended. **B** *Putri Kemala Balqis Beach Hotel*, Jl Hang Tuah 227, T28780. A/c, restaurant, new hotel close to the sea about 200m from the bus terminal, rooms are clean and comfortable with hot water showers, and because the road is comparatively quiet, so too is the hotel. **B-C** *Wisma Mayangsari*, Jl Jend Sudirman 19, T22647. A/c, price including breakfast but food is reputedly very poor, clean and convenient for the airport. Recommended.

C-D *Hang Tuah*, Jl Pemuda 1, T26556. Some a/c, unattractive hotel near bus station, rooms are adequate and the more expensive have hot water and satellite TV, convenient for the long distance bus terminal, but on a noisy road. **C-D** *Maharani*, Jl Veteran 11. Rooms with and without mandis, and fans, basic and clean. **C** *New Tiga Tiga*, Jl Veteran 33, T22173. Some a/c, north of town and out of city centre, quiet with comfortable rooms but indifferent food. **C** *Wisma Anggrek*, Jl Jend Sudiman 39, T37103. A/c, TV, mandis, more expensive rooms available, somewhat overpriced.

D *Back-packers Travellers Hotel*, Jl Purus 2, T34261, F34265. Some a/c, same ownership as the *Dipo International Hotel* which offers a free transfer out to the *Back-packers*, the hotel is well-run and close to the beach in a quiet area of town (but therefore rather out of the way); the so-called 'super economy' rooms are good value and the dormitory offers perhaps the cheapest place to stay in town. **D** *Tiga Tiga*, Jl Pemuda 31, T22633. Some a/c, opposite the bus terminal and therefore convenient but noisy, unimpressive restaurant, along with *Back-packers* it has just about cornered the budget traveller market, rooms are bare but clean, some with attached cold showers.

E *Cendrawasih*, Jl Pemuda 27, T22894. Some a/c, rather grubby, and although it is convenient for the long distance bus terminal it is also very noisy. **E** *Mariani*, Jl Bundo Kandung 35, T34134, F25410. Has rooms also in the **B** rate. See above.

Eating
● on maps
Price codes:
see inside front cover

Padang is the place to sample Padang food (see page 534); there are 3 good places to choose from on Jl Pasar Raya, which is as good a place as any to begin an exploration of Padang cuisine. *Simpang Raya* is a well established chain which serves consistently good food. A large assortment of bowls are brought to the table, and the bill is calculated according to the quantity eaten. Hot and spicy beef *rendang* is probably the most characteristic Padang dish. Try, if you dare, Saté Padang – made with boiled cow's intestines, skewered and grilled, served with a curry sauce. Another of Padang's culinary specialities is *kerepik Padang* – thin slices of deep fried *singkong* (cassava). Bags of this snack can be seen on sale along Jl Niaga.

Padang Cheap: *Bak Haji*, Jl Permindo 61A. Recommended. *Bernama*, Jl Juanda, close to *Panggeran's Hotel*. Locals prefer this restaurant, and rate this as one of the best Padang restaurants. *Kartini*, Jl Pasar Baru 24. *Purnama*, Jl Pasar Raya 111-117. *Roda Baru*, Jl Pasar Raya 6. *Serba Nikmat*, Jl Dobi 12. Recommended. *Simpang Pauh*, Jl Pasar Baru 34F. *Simpang Raya*, Jl Bundo Kandung 3-5. *Simpang Raya*, Jl Pasar Baru 34.

Indonesian Mid-range: *Taman Sari*, Jl Jend A Yani 23, T25023. A sophisticated a/c Javanese restaurant where Indonesian businessmen bring their clients and families celebrate special events, best Javanese in town. Recommended. *Simpang Raya*, Jl Bgd Aziz Chan 24. One of the best Indonesian restaurants in town, Padang food served but also a range of other Indonesian dishes.

Bakeries *American Donut*, Jl Pondok (at intersection with Jl Hiligoo). For good US-style donuts in the attractive Karia Theatre building. *Aromey*, Jl Niaga 275. Good nut and chocolate concoctions. *Safari Bakery*, Jl Damar (south of intersection with Jl A Yani). Indonesian-style pastries as well as burgers and rice dishes, popular with Padang's large student population. *Tulip's*, Jl Pondok 139. Cakes and buns as well as fried rice, burgers and ice cream.

Chinese Several noodle houses along Jl Niaga.

International Mid-range: *Hotel Sedona Bumi Minang*, Jl Bundo Kandung 20-28. Very good and stylish breakfast, lunch and evening buffets – good value – and the food in general is of a high standard. *Nusas Shabu-Shabu and Steakhouse*, Jl Nipah. The name says it all really, a/c restaurant with good steaks and shabu-shabu.

Seafood Mid-range: *Sari Laut*, Jl Nipah 3. Specializes in seafood and serves locally caught fish including tuna and swordfish steaks. *Tanpa Nama*, Jl Rohana Kudus 87. A/c restaurant specializing in freshwater fish dishes. **Cheap**: *Nelayan*, Jl Hos Cokroaminoto 41B. *Sari*, Jl Thamrin 71B-C.

Foodstalls One of the best places to eat in the evening is at the stalls which set up in and around the Taman Ria Pantai Padang – the Padang Beach Amusement Garden – and north along Jl Samudera as far as Jl Hang Tuah. Particularly at weekends, a large slice of Padang's population seems to congregate on the beach to watch the sun go down and – as always in Indonesia – where there are people there are foodstalls. There are also numerous stalls and roda around the 2 bus terminals off Jl Prof Yamin and in the market area. There is a cafeteria-cum-food centre on the top floor of the Matahari Department Store on Jl Prof Yamin.

Entertainment

Cinema: *New Raya* (film) *Theatre*, Jl Pasar Baru (near the market). A/c, comfortable, films with English soundtrack and Indonesian subtitles. **Cultural centre**: (Taman Budaya) on Jl Diponegoro. Dances, plays and exhibitions are regularly held here, open 0900-1400.

Festivals

Tabut (movable), Islamic festival commemorating the martyrdom of Mohammad's 2 grandchildren Hasan and Husain. It is celebrated in the town of Pariaman, 56 km north along the coast. *Independence Day* (**17th August**: public holiday). Carnivals and parades; events extend 1 week either side of the 17th.

Shopping

Antiques: *Sartika*, Jl Jend Sudirman 5. Specializes in Sumatran and Mentawi ethnographic pieces, both souvenirs and antiques – rather over-priced, ask to see the pieces in the back room as well. There is another antique shop (no name) at Jl Juanda 31 (just south of *Pangeran's Beach Hotel*). **Basketry**: Jl Pasar Raya and Jl Imam Bonjol.
Books: *Sari Anggrek*, Jl Permindo 63. **Department stores**: *Matahari*, Jl Yamin 3M. Large, a/c department store with central location. *Suzuya*, Jl Rasuna Said (hard to miss on the road in from the aiport). A rather grotesque a/c department store with supermarket, 4 km or so out of town so not very convenient for most visitors. **Jewellery**: shops on Jl Prof M Yamin and Jl Pasar Baru. **Shopping centres**: a number of new a/c plazas have opened including *Ambacang Plaza*, Jl Bundo Kandung 18. *Damar Plaza*, Jl Damar 42A. *Plaza Minang*, Jl Juanda (north of town). *Suzuya*, Jl Rasuna Said. **Supermarkets**: *Suzuya*, Jl Rasuna Said. Large a/c department store with supermarket attached, about 4 km or so out of town – take a *bis kota* or *angkutan kota* to get there. **Textiles**: cheap cloth is sold in the central market, at the corner of Jl Pasar Raya and Jl Prof M Yamin; several specialist textile shops along Jl Imam Bonjol – some sell *kain songket*. For more sophisticated batik try *Batik Semar* near *American Donut*. **Woodcarving**: several shops along Jl Pasar Raya and Jl Imam Bonjol.

Sports **Diving**: Padang's potential for diving has not really been developed to any degree, although it doesn't compare with other areas of the country (Pusako Island appears to offer the best coral and marine life). However, there is 1 outfit in town, *Padang Diving* at Jl Batang Arau 88B/6, T25876, F28121. Call ahead to ensure they are open. A trip with 2 dives with equipment and transportation is priced at US$77 each for 3 people; a 4-5 day PADI open water course costs US$375. We have received some slightly worrying reports about the level of safety of this outfit. **Rock climbing**: West Sumatra has gained a reputation for offering some of the best rock climbing in Indonesia. Gunung Padang, south of town over the Muara River, has around a dozen routes including Eureka (graded [Australian] as 5.11c), Camp (5.12c) and Fasting Moon (also 5.12c). Bukittinggi also offers some excellent climbs (see page 545). **Surfing**: with the growing popularity of the Mentawai Islands for more experienced surfers, offering a range of surf locations and breaks. One outfit working from Padang called Flying Lady Surfing Charters, run by Ken at Jl Sumba M8, T/F50089. **Swimming**: non-residents can use the pools at *Pangeran's Beach Hotel*, Jl Ir H Juanda 79, or, more conveniently but less attractively, at the *Hotel Hayam Wuruk*, Jl Hayam Wuruk 16.

Tour operators A number are located opposite the long-distance bus terminal on Jl Pemuda: *Desa Air Royale*, Jl Pemuda 23B, T23022. *Nitour*, Jl Hiligoo 4C, T22175, F22175. *Tunas Indonesia*, Jl Pondok 86C, T31661, F32806. *Pacto*, Jl Tan Malaka 25, T27780, F33335. *Natrabu*, Jl Pemuda 29B, T37442, F23410. *Angsoduo*, Jl Diponegoro 25, T23175, F33123. Two tour companies specializing in boat charter are: *Pondok Gema Wisata*, Jl Nipah 23, T26306. *Nusa Mentawai Tour*, Jl Batang Arau 50, T28764.

Transport
108 km from Bukittinggi, 246 km from Sungai Penuh

Local Buses (*bis kota*, 500Rp around town) and **oplets** (*angkutan kota*, 400Rp around town) travel along fixed routes, setting off from the Terminal Pasar Raya on Jl Prof M Yamin, next to the central market. There is a list at the terminal giving their routes and ultimate destinations. **Dokars**, also known as **bendis**: pony-drawn carts; rows of them are to be found at the central market and can be an enjoyable way of getting around town, although some people may feel they do not want to put the half-starved animals to the trouble. **Taxis**: meter taxis (but many drivers try not to use them); some unmetered for charter. **Car hire**: most tour and travel agencies hire out vehicles; it is also possible to negotiate a day's charter with 1 of the taxis. *The Specialist* in the *Hotel Sedona Bumi Minang*'s arcade, Jl Bundo Kandung 24-28, has self-drive cars which can be rented for around 100,000Rp for 10 hrs. **Motorcycle hire**: available from some hotels – eg *Mariani*. **Boat hire**: it is possible to charter a vessel by wandering around Muara harbour and up the river, but this requires a degree of Indonesian. Alternatively, most tour companies will arrange a vessel, eg the *Pondok Gema Wisata*, Jl Nipah 23, T26306; and *Nusa Mentawai Tour*, Jl Batang Arau 50, T28764.

Air Tabing Airport is 9 km north of town. (There are plans to build a new airport further north of town.) Daily domestic connections on **Merpati, Indonesian Airlines** and **Mandala** with Jakarta, and on **Merpati** with Medan, Palembang and Pekanbaru; **Merpati** also have 3 flights a week to Batam in the Riau Archipelago and there are **SMAC** flights to Gunungsitoli on Nias. Flights also available to Semarang and Surabaya. Tabing Airport has a money changer, restaurant, tour office and souvenir shop. *Transport to town*: a taxi will cost 7,000-10,000Rp – fixed fare – depending on the destination. Though metered taxis are allowed to carry passengers from the airport they do not use their meters – hence the comparatively steep fares. (This is, apparently, a stitch-up stipulated by the military who have jurisdiction over the airport.) Alternatively, walk the 50m out onto the main road and catch *bis kota* (town bus) nos 14a or 14b or *angkutan kota* (mini bus) for 1,000Rp. Buses going left travel into the city. Both run to the market area in the centre and close to many of the hotels.

Road Bus: the station, *Terminal Lintas Andalas*, is on Jl Pemuda close to the junction with Jl Prof M Yamin. The ticket offices for the bus companies can be found here. Regular connections with Bukittinggi on *NPM* and *ALS* 2-3 hrs (2,000Rp), Sibolga, Dumai, Pekanbaru 6 hrs, Bengkulu 14 hrs, Prapat 16 hrs, Medan 20 hrs, Palembang 24 hrs, and Jambi. On *Java* there are connections with Solo, Surabaya, Bandung, Tasik Malaya and Jakarta (48 hrs). More local destinations include Meninjau, Pariaman, Batusangkar, Muko Muko, Sungai Penuh (6 hrs) and Solok. *ANS* has an office at the bus terminal and at Jl Khatib Sulaiman, T26689.

Sea Boat: the modern and comfortable Pelni ships *Kambuna* and *Lambelu* run on a 2-week circuit between Jakarta and Padang 27 hrs, including stops in Sumatra, Java and Kalimantan. It docks at Padang's port, Teluk Bayur, which is 7 km south of town. Book tickets at travel agencies or at Pelni's office at Teluk Bayur, Jl Tanjung Priok 32, T33624. The ship also docks at Surabaya, Ujung Padang, Balikpapan, Pantoloan, Toli Toli, Tarakan Sibolga and Gunungsitoli (Nias) (see route map, page 982). The Pelni 'pioneer' vessel *Baruna Dwipa* also operates a fortnightly circuit, calling at Enggano *en route* for Jakarta. A ferry leaves from the small port on the Arau River in Padang itself for the Mentawi Islands (see page 567). Smaller vessels leave from Bungus Port, another 10 km or so south of Teluk Bayur, for the Mentawi Islands, as well as smaller ports along Sumatra's western seaboard.

International connections Air: connections on *Pelangi Airways* with Kuala Lumpur (daily) and Johor Bahru (4 times a week) in Malaysia. Connections on *Merpati*, *Indonesian Airlines*, *Silk Air* and *Pelangi* with Singapore and Kuala Lumpur.

Directory

Airline offices *Garuda*, Jl Brig Azziz Chan (opposite the *Hotel Femina*), T58489, F58488. *Merpati*, Jl Gereja 34 (attached to *Natour Muara*, T32010. *Mandala*, Jl Pemuda 29A, T32773, F33814. *Pelangi*, Jl Gereja 34 (attached to *Natour Muara Hotel*), T38103, F38104. *Indonesian Airlines*, Pangeran's Beach Hotel, Jl H Juanda 79, T51612, F55366. *Silk Air*, Jl Hayam Wuruk 16 (attached to the *Hotel Hayam Wuruk*), T38120, F38122. *SMAC*, Jl Sudirman 2, T51303. **Banks** Being a provincial capital there are a good number of banks here and rates are generally better than in Bukittinggi. *Bank Negara Indonesia 1946*, Jl Dobi 2 (north end). *Bank Dagang Negara*, Jl Bgd Aziz Chan 21 (at crossroads with Jl Pasar Raya). *Bank Bumi Daya*, Jl Jend Sudirman 2A (near intersection with Jl Pasar Baru). *Bank Rakyat Indonesia*, Jl Bgd Aziz Chan (near crossroads with Jl Pasar Raya). *Bank Exim*, Jl Bgd Aziz Chan (at crossroads with Jl Proklamasi). *Lippo Bank*, Jl Prof Yamin (corner with Jl Diponegoro). **Communications** General Post Office: Jl Bgd Aziz Chan 7 (near clock tower). Telephone offices: corner of Jl Ahmad Dahlan and Jl Khatib Sulaiman. There are also a number of other telephone/fax offices around town which offer more efficient service. Wartel have offices at Jl Hayam Wuruk 201 (just south of *Hayam Wuruk Hotel*), Jl Nipah 35, Jl S Parman 93C (just north of *Pangeran's Beach Hotel*), and Jl Belakang Tangsi 3 (a small road running off Jl Prof Yamin, opposite the long distance bus terminal). **Medical facilities** General Hospital: Jl Perintis Kemerdekaan, T22355. **Places of worship** Catholic Church: *St Joseph's*, Jl Gereja 43. Protestant Church: Jl Bgd Aziz Chan. **Useful addresses** Immigration office: Jl Khatib Sulaiman, T55113 (for visa extension). Nature Conservation Office (PHPA): Jl Raden Saleh, T54136. Police: Jl Prof M Yamin.

The Mentawi Islands

The Mentawi group of islands lie about 100 km off the west coast of Sumatra and are part of the same chain as Nias to the north. The name Mentawi is derived from the local word si manteu which means a 'man' or 'male'. The group consists of four islands – Siberut, Sipora, Pagai Utara (North Pagai) and Pagai Selatan (South Pagai). The indigenous inhabitants of Siberut, the largest of the Mentawi islands and the only one to receive many visitors, are strikingly different from the other peoples of Sumatra. Isolated from the mainstream, they evolved their own distinct culture and society. While most have renounced their animist beliefs and embraced Christianity, they remain a fascinating outlier. The fauna and flora are also unique, for the same reason: it has remained insulated and isolated from the outside. Along with the indigenous peoples of the island, there is an increasing population of settlers (mostly transmigrants) from other areas of Indonesia. Accessible only by boat from Padang, and with limited facilities, most people come here on a tour rather than independently.

Phone code: 0759
Colour map 1, grid C2/3

Ins and outs

Getting there
See Transport section for further details

A few years ago, visiting the Mentawi Islands was an adventure; now there are tours from Padang and Bukittinggi – 10 days for US$100. Even so, the number of visitors is still relatively small: around 5,000 visitors annually in the mid-1990s and presumably fewer still at the end of the decade, given the general downturn in Indonesia's tourism industry. Boat links to Siberut, the main island in the Mentawi group, have deteriorated in the last couple of years. At the time of writing there are only 2 departures per week from Padang and these subject to rather more than periodic delay and cancellation. The vessel is in poor condition and is frequently over-loaded. When sea conditions deteriorate, most common between Oct and Jan (the wet season), sailings are delayed. There are also some non-scheduled departures of other vessels for Mentawi; these usually leave from Bungus Port, south of Padang.

Getting around

Most people come to Mentawi on a tour, usually arranged through tour companies in Padang or Bukittinggi, and transport is arranged as part of the package. There is no public transport system on Mentawi and getting around independently requires visitors to charter a boat. This is expensive by Indonesian standards.

Background

Fauna

For the same reason that the inhabitants of the Mentawi Islands are unique among the peoples of Indonesia, so too is some of the fauna. The archipelago was separated from the mainland about 500,000 years ago, an event which isolated the islands and allowed the wildlife to evolve independently. As a result there are a surprising number of endemic species. In 1980 the then World Wildlife Fund reported that 60% of mammal species were endemic and 15% of plant species, including four species of primate: the black gibbon (*Hylobates klossii*), the Mentawi macaque, the long-tailed joja (*Presbytis potenziani*) and the pig-tailed langur (*Simias concolor*). Appreciating the supreme importance of the island's flora and fauna, UNESCO formally recognized Siberut Island as a National Biosphere Reserve in 1981. But despite the widespread recognition that Siberut was unique in biological terms, the Indonesian government allowed logging to continue, gazetting only two protected areas covering just 90,000 ha in total. International groups like Survival International, the World Wide Fund for Nature and the International Union for the Conservation of Nature all began to campaign for stricter measures to protect Siberut. This culminated, in 1992, when the major part of the island was declared a national park.

History

The indigenous inhabitants of the Mentawi Islands are Austronesians, descendants of the original inhabitants of Southeast Asia. As the islands lie off the main trading routes, they were cocooned from the wider world until after the Second World War. Not even the influx of Hindu civilization and, later, that of Islam, broke upon the shores of these islands. The Dutch claimed the Mentawi group in 1864 and established a limited presence in 1904, but did little to integrate the population into the wider economy. Large-scale conversion to Christianity only began with increased missionary activity in the 1950s. As many as 60% of the population are now nominal Christians, although animism still plays an important role in their lives.

Tribes

There are several different tribes in Mentawi, among them the Sakkudei, Sarareiket and Simatalu. The Sakkudei live in the most remote and inaccessible regions, and a few still cling tenaciously to their traditional lifestyles. These beautiful people tattoo their bodies, and wear loin cloths and elaborate head-dresses. They hunt with bows and poisoned arrows and live in communal long houses or *uma*, sheltering 5-10 families numbering perhaps 30-80 individuals. The chief of the community is the *rimata*, and his right-hand man the shaman or *sikerei*. Transport through the thick forest is by dug-out canoe along rivers.

Traditionally, the subsistence needs of the Mentawaians were met through hunting and gathering in the rich forests which even today – and despite considerable deforestation – make-up the majority of the islands' land area. The pressures of modern day life have led to a decline in hunting and gathering and a corresponding rise in agricultural activities: rice, sago, taro, fruit trees and other crops are all cultivated. But to supplement their diet, the inhabitants still eat such diverse natural products as wild boar, deer, monkey, beetle larvae and fish.

Food

As tourists and mainland Indonesians increase their presence on the islands, it is inevitable that traditional ways of life will disappear. Most alarmingly for those who would wish to preserve the Mentawi way of life, the islands were designated as a transmigration site for landless Javanese, and settlement was scheduled to begin in 1992. Sustained lobbying by NGOs led the government to shelve its plans in 1993. Associated logging and plantation schemes were also shelved. However, this was not the end of the Mentawi struggle. While the Asian Development Bank awarded the government an US$18m loan to develop a Siberut National Park with linked sustainable development, the government bowed to commercial pressures and reactivated the plantation and transmigration schemes. The planned palm oil plantation would cover 80,000 ha while the transmigration settlements will accommodate 30,000. A local NGO was established in 1995 to fight these proposals and to ensure that Mentawi's future is governed by the wishes of the Mentawaian people. The NGO is called *Yayasan Citra Mandiri* or the Essence of Self-reliance Foundation, and it has its offices in Padang. YCM also operate recommended tours to Mentawi

Preservation

Siberut Island

(see page 558 for details). A visitor at the end of 1998 commented on the visible domination of the islands' trade and commerce by immigrants from North Sumatra and, especially, Nias. Ethnic Mentawaians who have tried to go it alone have, it has been reported, been beaten up and imprisoned for daring to circumvent the monopolies controlled by the mainlanders. While in theory it should be possible for local producers and traders to sell their crops – such as patchouli oil or *nilam* – directly to wholesalers in Padang, this is thwarted at every turn.

Tourists should be aware that most of the guides come from Bukittinggi and have little understanding of Mentawi language and customs. A study of tourism on Siberut by Persoon and Heuveling van Beek, published in 1997, highlights the degree to which the money generated by the industry is syphoned off to other ethnic groups and other provinces. Most of the guides, boat owners, traders, shop-keepers, and hotel and restaurant owners are Minangkabau, not Mentawaian. They write: "Although the Mentawaians are primarily the objects of observation, the income generated by the indigenous people through tourism is very limited." There are also worries about the numbers of tourists visiting the island; many go to the same villages so the impact is localized.

An organization has been established to press for the better protection of Siberut's people and environment. For more information: *SOS Siberut*, 36 Matlock Court, 46 Kensington Park Road, London W11 3BS, UK (T020-77274118). There is also the local NGO based in Padang noted above, *Yayasan Citra Mandiri*, which is lobbying for a more sensitive development policy.

Most boats from Sumatra land at the town of Muarasiberut, at the south end of Siberut Island's east coast. There is one losmen here, and a restaurant. The other main town on Siberut is Sikabaluan, which lies to the north of Muarasiberut, also on the east coast. There is no accommodation at Sikabaluan, although homestays are available.

Trekking There are a number of traditional villages within hiking distance (1-8 km) of Muarasiberut. More remote villages can only be reached by first taking a chartered longboat inland; ask on arrival. Note that living conditions are very basic and the walking can be hard. **NB** When trekking, be sensitive to locals; share your meals and try not to overwhelm, if in a large group.

Tours Tours to the Mentawi Islands can be arranged through tour companies in Bukittinggi (see page 546) and Padang. Bukittinggi offers the widest range of tours and agents and at the most competitive rates. Note that a tour from Bukittinggi can take three days to reach Mentawi, so a six-day tour is in effect only a three-day tour. Ensure that your guide either speaks Mentawi or at least will use local guides on arrival. An alternative is to hire a guide in Mentawi; although this does allow a tour to be designed according to your own preferences, it tends to work out more expensive (see below). In Padang, tour agents include *PT Desa Air*, Jalan Pemuda 23B, T23022, F33335, and *Pacto*, Jalan Pemuda 1, T27780. Tours vary a great deal in price, from US$125 to US$330, depending on what is provided. In Bukittinggi, where the cheapest tours are available, prices are around US$125-150 per person for a 10-day trip. They should include trekking and canoe trips, and take the visitor through virgin forest and to what are rather condescendingly referred to as 'primitive' villages.

Travelling independently Independent travel is not advised for those without some Indonesian language. It is necessary to acquire a permit from PT Mentawai Wisata Bahari, Jl Sumatera X5, Wisma Indah 1 (F52335). One day's notice is required and you will need a photocopy of your passport and your immigration card.

On arrival in Muarasiberut, tourists should register at the police station there. The restaurant opposite the hotel in Muarasiberut is a good place to find out about guides, porters and other trekkers. Supplies can be bought from the restaurant, although they are cheaper elsewhere. Guides will be able to arrange a boat upriver and buy supplies, as well as clear the trip with the police. The villages around Muarasiberut tend to be new Indonesian villages; it is necessary to travel upriver to see the 'real' Mentawi, so neither Muarasiberut nor Sikabaluan make good bases. Visitors should expect to spend a week on Mentawi to get a good taste of local life. In 1999 there was an English VSO volunteer helping at the National Park office 1.5 km out of Muarasiberut, and he is willing to help visitors with arranging a guide. It is reported that when he leaves he will be replaced by another volunteer. Local people make excellent guides and, all things being equal, it is better to employ a local rather than someone from the mainland. However, often their English is limited.

Essentials

Trekking equipment (good walking shoes, waterproofs warm clothing); waterproof bags; cigarettes or salt (for leeches); toiletries; plasters; torch; mosquito repellent and a net (malaria pills are essential); food and cooking equipment; barter goods (pens and paper, cigarettes and tobacco, and anti-biotics and drugs like Immodium and Fansidar are most commonly bartered, although some visitors may wish to resist this); rupiah notes in small denominations sufficient for stay – about US$150 for a week (there are no money changing facilities).

What to take
Return boats are commonly cancelled – build in contingency & take ample funds

Chloroquine-resistant malaria is present on Siberut. In addition, health provision deteriorated during the late 1990s. At the end of 1998 there was no resident doctor on the island, and not even a resident nurse for 2 months. Pharmacies and Puskesmas (local health centres) were very poorly stocked.

Health
Visitors to Siberut could be 10 days from the nearest doctor

The only losmen at Muarasiberut is the **E** *Syahruddin's*, T21014. Friendly and a reasonable source of information. Given the numbers of people coming to Siberut it is surprising that more have not opened up. Trekking accommodation is in the homes of missionaries or with local headmen. Transmigrant villages are, by definition, less 'local' in character, try and stay in villages or homes of locals if possible for a taste of Mentawi life. Gifts of pens and tobacco are essential. There is a homestay at (18,000Rp) Masilot Beach, a boat trip from Muarasiberut (snorkelling is good here).

Sleeping

Local This is expensive as there is no public transport and **private boats** must be chartered. A boat for 4/5 people for 6 days should cost around US$100. Sometimes fuel (which is expensive in this out of the way spot) is included, sometimes not.

Transport

Sea Boat The ferry situation to Siberut is poor. There is only 1 boat serving the island, departing from the small ferry port on the Arau River in Padang itself. This vessel, the *Semangat*, leaves on Thu and Sat evening, arriving the following morning. The return boat departs on Fri and Sun evenings. The fare is 20,000Rp and between its arrival at Muarasiberut and departure the same evening it sails up to Muarasikabaluan and back again. On arrival at Muarasiberut it is necessary to take a boat to shore. Gross overcrowding is the norm and because the *Semangat* is also unseaworthy (or seems so) it only departs when conditions are calm. This, of course, means that cancellations are common. More vessels are used to serve Siberut, but the provincial government's decision to award the monopoly to a single firm has meant a decline in standards. Smaller vessels leave from Bungus Port, south of Padang, for some lesser known destinations in the Mentawai Archipelago. For example, the *MV Kuda Laut Express* (Jl Batang Arau 88, T28200) leaves Padang for Sioban and Sikokap (on North Pagai Island in the Mentawai Archipelago) on Mon, Wed and Fri at 1000, returning on Tue and Sat at 0800 (17,500-25,000Rp) (it's not clear what happens on the return leg on Thu). **NB** During the rainy season (Oct-Jan) seas can be rough and departures may be delayed.

The Semangat is a rust bucket and safety standards are poor

Banks No facilities on the island. Take enough Indonesian rupiah to cover your stay; US$ notes can be useful in an emergency. **Communications Post Office:** in Muarasiberut. **Telephone office:** Wartel in Muarasiberut, but haphazardly run.

Directory

Padang to Sungai Penuh Sungai Penuh lies 236 km south of Padang in the Bukit Barisan. The road south along the coast via Tapan is much improved; so too is the interior road via Alahanpanjang and Surian. Accommodation is sparse. There are basic losmen in Painan, but the best place to stay *en route* is the *Camelia*, on the beach, clean and friendly, 8 km outside Painan on the road to Indrapura. From Tapan the road runs south through Muko Muko all the way to Bengkulu.

Sungai Penuh

Phone code: 0748
Colour map 2, grid B1

Sungai Penuh is a small, rather unexciting district capital, 236 km south of Padang. It is, in fact, in the province of Jambi rather than West Sumatra, but we have included it here for convenience. Cinnamon trees are cultivated in the valleys and foothills around the town. When mature, the trees are cut down and the bark stripped off and then dried in the sun before being sold. Few tourists stop here, but those interested in Sumatran wildlife can use Sungai Penuh as a base to explore the large **Kerinci-Seblat Nature Reserve** which surrounds the town. In Pondok Tinggi, the old part of town, is the **Mesjid Agung**, a mosque built in 1874, in pagoda-style and decorated with Dutch tiles and carved doors and columns. Across the street is one of the town's few remaining **rumah panjang** – traditional wooden longhouses up to 200m in length which were occupied by members of a single clan or *marga*. Most residents have moved into Javanese-style houses which are regarded as a sign of modernity.

Lake Kerinci is about 5 km to the southeast of town in a beautiful upland valley, nearly 750m above sea level and surrounded by 2,000m peaks. ■ *Getting there: bus to Sanggaranagung or by hired motorbike or bicycle.*

Mount Kerinci, an active volcano, lies to the north of town and at 3,805m is the highest peak in Sumatra. It can be climbed in two days, with one night spent at a hut part way up at 3,000m. The trail to the summit is about 16 km and well worth attempting. The best base from which to climb the mountain is the small town of **Kersik Tuo**, where accommodation is available in homestays (**E**). The Eco-Rural co-operative on Jalan Raya, to which all homestays and guides belong, can provide guide services for climbing the mountain. Another popular and highly recommended trek is to the 10 km mountain lake of **Gunung Tuju** (Seven Mountain Lake), 50 km from Sungai Penuh, said to be the highest freshwater lake in Southeast Asia at 1,996m and so named because it is encircled by seven mountains. The climb to the lake takes about 2-3 hours along a steep path through forest. It is also one of the least disturbed. ■ *Getting there: regular buses and bemos run from the station in the market area in Sungai Penuh.* Visit the Nature Conservation Office (PHPA) in Sungai Penuh on Jalan Arga Selebar Daun 11 for a permit (which may be unnecessary), advice and information.

Kerinci-Seblat National Park is named after two of the highest mountains in Sumatra: Mount Kerinci (3,805m) and Mount Seblat (2,385m). The reserve stretches almost 350 km from Padang south to Bengkulu and covers almost 15,000 sq km straddling four provinces – making it the largest park in Sumatra. It accounts for a large segment of the mountainous spine of Sumatra, the Bukit Barisan, and supports a wide variety of wildlife including tigers, tapirs, elephants, Sumatran rhinoceros, sun bears, clouded leopards, semiang, five species of hornbill and the endemic short-eared rabbit (*Nesolagus netscheri*). In late 1998 a new species of pig was discovered here. There are no orang utans, but there have been many reported sightings of the *orang pendek* (a hairy 1½m tall and immensely strong hominid), the *cigau* (half lion, half tiger) and *kuda liar* (wild horses). The vegetation is primarily lowland, hill and montane tropical forest, with alpine vegetation on the higher slopes. Guides can be hired in Sungai Penuh and in Kersik Tuo (see Mount Kerinci excursion). Visit the Nature Conservation Office (PHPA) in town for permits, advice and information, or the PHPA offices in Padang or Bengkulu. *Best time to visit*: January-March and May-November, when it is driest in the valley enclave around Sungai Penuh; road travel out of these months may be difficult. Note that the mountainous areas of the reserve are wet year-round.

Sleeping & eating

C-D *Busana*, Jl Martadinata, T2122. Attached bathrooms with mandi, hot water brought to rooms, stylish furniture, friendly and popular with tour groups. A little way out of town, one of the better of a small bunch. **C-D** *Hotel Aroma*, Jl Imam Bonjol 14, T21142. Range from cheap economy rooms to more expensive with fan, satellite TV, telephone, adjacent restaurant serves traditional food. **C-E** *Hotel Masgo Kencana*, Jl Sriwijaya 20, T323603. A wide range of rooms to suit all pockets, access to rooms through a myriad of corridors, rooms are light and airy, tours arranged. **D** *Hotel Kayu Manis*, Jl R E Martadinama 3H, T21226. With an attractive sitting porch, this hotel offers good budget accommodation. **D** *Mata Hari*, Jl Basuki Rahmat, T21061. Good source of information and reasonable rooms. **F** *Jaya*, Jl Yani, T21221. Small, cramped rooms, birds in the courtyard might be a little noisy, but it is still the cheapest in town.

Kerinci-Seblat Reserve

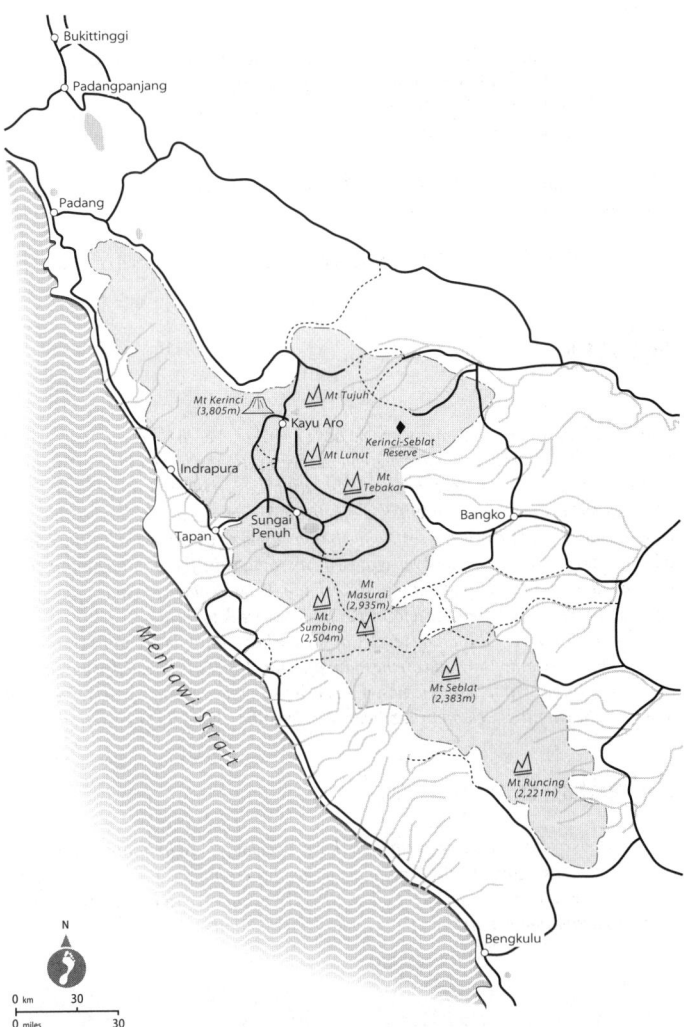

Shopping While Sungai Penuh is not known as a place to go shopping, the local market does sell excellent local tea and coffee and also various spices like cinnamon.

Transport The road south from Padang to Sungai Penuh is newly resurfaced and relatively good. **Local** Mr Bukari, owner of the *Busana Hotel*, will arrange car charter. **Air** Occasional SMAC connections with Jambi. **Road Bus** the bus station is in the market area. Bus connections with Jambi via Bangko, 12 hrs, and an overnight bus to Padang along bad roads, 10-12 hrs. There are also buses running south to Bengkulu via Muko Muko, about 12 hrs; note that the road is very poor, but some beautiful views *en route*.

236 km from Padang, 410 km from Jambi

Directory **Banks** *BNI*, Jl Basuki Rakhmat, will change US$ TCs. **Communications** Post Office: Jl Sudirman 1. Telephone office: Jl Imam Bonjol. **PHPA office**: Jl Argo Selebar Daun 11. **Useful addresses** World Wide Fund for Nature (WWF) have an office at Jl Basuki Rachmat 11, T21692. They are a more useful source of information than the PHPA office and are also friendly and welcoming. Their presence in the town is linked to educating local people about the value of wildlife and conservation.

Tapan

Colour map 2, grid B1

This small town marks the beginning of the new, improved road south from Sungai Penuh to Bengkulu, following the narrow coastal strip between the ocean and the Bukit Barisan. The town itself has nothing of note to recommend it, but it does offer basic accommodation.

Sleeping **E** *Wisma Kebehan*, Jl Talang Bungo Tapan (2 km south of town on the Bengkulu road). Communal mandis and toilet, no shower and only cold water.

Transport **Bus** connections with Sungai Penuh, Muko Muko 2 hrs, Bengkulu 10 hrs and Padang 6½ hrs.

Riau

Riau is not a province that many people have heard of. Yet the province's islands of Bintan and Batam probably have a greater concentration of luxury hotels than anywhere on Sumatra. That is because the Riau archipelago, a kaleidoscope of 3,000-odd islands, reaches to within a few tens of kilometres of Singapore. Bintan has become Singapore's own backyard beach resort, while Batam has been transformed into an industrial production centre for the over-crowded city state. Now the Bintan-Batam effect has spread to the islands of Kundur and Karimun. Even so, there are many other, less visited, islands which barely see a foreigner from one week to the next.

While the islands of Riau may receive by far the largest number of tourists, it is the great swathe of swampy lowland on the mainland, much of it still forested, which makes this province one of Indonesia's richest. For, beneath the swamp soils, are reserves of oil and gas. The capital is Pekanbaru, but few visitors, other than oil workers, stay there.

Pekanbaru

Phone code: 0761
Colour map 2, grid A1

Pekanbaru is a featureless town with little charm or colour. Well maintained and wide streets, impressive government buildings and opulent commercial offices bear testimony to the wealth generated by the oil industry. Few tourists visit here except in transit. Boats arrive and depart from the river dock for the Riau archipelago.

Ins and outs

There are international connections by air with Singapore, Melaka, Kuala Lumpur and other Indonesian destinations. Boats leave both from Pekanbaru itself (usually slow) and from Buton (fast) for various islands in the Riau group, including Batam, Bintan and Karimun. Buses leave from the Mayang Terurai bus terminal on the southern edge of town for various destinations in Sumatra, including Bukittinggi, Medan, Palembang, Aceh and Padang. There are also long-distance buses to Java.

Getting there
See Transport section, page 573 for further details

Although Pekanbaru is an important town it is not large. Buses, oplets and unmetered taxis provide the main forms of local transport. There are no becaks in town. **Riau Provincial Tourist Office** (*Dinas Pariwisata Propinsi Riau*) is on Jl Gajah Mada 200 (unmarked, in new white government building). Some useful pamphlets.

Getting around

Background

Pekanbaru is the regional capital of Riau province, and was founded in 1784. Located on the Siak River, 160 km from the coast, it is the administrative centre of the oil industry in the area. Oil was discovered just prior to the Second World War, although the Japanese were the first to exploit the resource. Over 85% of Riau province's GDP is generated by petroleum and natural gas production, an industry which is dominated by Caltex Pacific Indonesia Company (CPI). CPI has helped to build the Riau University, sports facilities, 52 schools, the Pekanbaru airport and roads to Dumai and Duri.

Much of the area surrounding Pekanbaru remains a wilderness of forest and swamp. Although criss-crossed by pipelines and dotted with oil rigs, the activity of oil exploration and production has not, seemingly, adversely affected the wildlife. Indeed, the companies are so worried about the effects that roads might have on access to the forest by spontaneous settlers that they helicopter in the equipment, creating an isolated island of activity in the jungle. This is one of the few areas with reasonable numbers of Sumatran rhinoceros, tigers and other rare Sumatran animals.

Sights

Although there are a number of worthwhile excursions from Pekanbaru, sights in the city itself are few and far between. The **Mesjid An Nur** is a large, rather uninspired, mosque off Jalan Jend Sudirman, while the older and more attractive **Grand Mosque** and the **Marhum Bukit Cemetery** are to be found near the river, off Jalan Riau. The latter mosque was built in the 18th century and is said to have a 'magic' well. In the centre of town is the large **Pasar Pusat** on and among the streets lining Jalan Jend A Yani and Jalan Jend Sudirman. South of town on Jalan Jend Sudirman by 4½ km are the **Museum Negeri** and, next to it, the **Riau Cultural Park**, both on the road to the airport. ■ *0800-1400 Mon-Thu and Sat, 0800-1200 Fri.*

Excursions

An archaeological site 2½ km outside a village of the same name and about 80 km west of Pekanbaru. These Buddhist Srivijayan ruins were probably built between the ninth and 11th centuries. Four buildings have been uncovered: *Candi Tua*, *Candi Bungsu*, *Candi Pelangka* and the *Mahligai Stupa*. ■ *Getting there: the ruins are off the inter-provincial bus routes and can only be reached easily by taxi, private car, or on a tour. By public transport, take a bus to Muaramahat and then charter a bemo.*

Muaro Takus

This is an historic town downstream on the Siak River, 125 km by road northeast of Pekanbaru. The sultanate of Siak Sri Indrapura was founded in 1723 and there have been 12 sultans, the last surrendering his position in 1949. The stark white, gothic-style *Asseriyah Hasyimlah Palace* was built in 1889 and contains various pieces

Siak Sri Indrapura

of royal regalia. Also notable is the *Royal Graveyard* (Makam Kota Tinggi) and the *Mesjid Raya*. There is basic accommodation at the **E** *Peningapan Harmonis*, although the town is easily visited on a day trip. ■ *Getting there*: by regular minibus from Pekanbaru's Pasar Lima Puluh terminal at the north end of Jalan Sultan South Hasyim, 2½ hrs, or charter a taxi, take a tour, go by speedboat down the river, 2 hrs, or take a ferry.

Elephant training camp The Sabanga Elephant Training Camp is 135 km from Pekanbaru, 19 km from Duri. ■ *Getting there*: by charter taxi or on a tour; buses go to Duri from the Loket terminal on Jalan Nangka.

Essentials

Sleeping
■ *on map*
Price codes:
see inside front cover

A-B *Mutiara Merdeka*, Jl Yos Sudarso 12A, T32526/31272, F32959, merdeka@indon.net.id A/c, good restaurant, pool, tennis, best hotel in Pekanbaru, professionally managed with well appointed rooms, near the Siak River and slightly out of town. **A-B** *Indrapura*, Jl Dr Sutomo 86, T36233, F56337. A/c, good restaurant, pool. **A-B** *Sri Indrayani*, Jl Dr Sam Ratulangi 2, T35600, F31870. A/c, tennis, a well priced and comfortable hotel with spacious rooms and a nice garden. **B** *Tasia Ratu*, Jl K H Hasyim Ashari 10 (off Jl Jend Sudirman), T33431, F38912. A/c, central location, average rooms for the price but friendly and welcoming. **C** *Badarussamsi*, Jl Sisingamangaraja 175, T22475. A/c, restaurant. **C** *Riau*, Jl Diponegoro 34, T22986. Restaurant. **C-D** *Anom*, Jl Gatot Subroto 3, T22636. A/c, restaurant, popular with Chinese visitors, central, good value and, following a recent renovation, clean. **C-D** *Yani*, Jl Pepaya 17 (Matahari Shopping Complex is on the corner of this road), T23647. Some a/c, private mandi, pleasant atmosphere. **C-E** *Linda*, Jl Nangka 143 (opposite bus station), T36915. Some a/c, cheaper upstairs rooms are clean, all with attached bathrooms, well run and convenient for buses. Recommended. **E** *Poppies*, Jl Cempedek 11A (south of Jl Nangka), T45762. Good value, clean and friendly guesthouse with attached restaurant, small breakfast included, underpowered fan rooms and cheaper dorm beds also available (**F**). **F** *Tommy's*, Gang Nantongga, near bus station. Small and rather cramped but cheap.

Pekanbaru

Sleeping
1 Anom
2 Indrapura
3 Linda
4 Mutiara Merdeka
5 Riau
6 Sri Indrayani
7 Tommy's

Eating
1 New Holland Bakery

Eating
● *on map*
Price codes:
see inside front cover

The cheap restaurants and foodstalls are on Jl Jend Sudirman, near the central market, and along the market's inner streets. **Bakeries**: *Big M*, Jl Jend Sudirman 143. *New Holland*, Jl Jend Sudirman 155. **Indonesian Mid-range**: *Indrapura Hotel*, Jl Dr Sutomo. Good hotel restaurant serving Indonesian, Chinese and international dishes. *Mutiara Merdeka*, Jl Yos Sudarso 12A. Some locals maintain this hotel restaurant is the best in town, also serves international and Chinese food. **Cheap**: *Sari Bunda 88*, Jl Gatot Subroto. Padang food. **Very cheap**: *Mitra Sari*, Jl Sisingamangaraja. Tasty Padang food. **International food Cheap**: *Kota Piring*, Jl Sisingamangaraja. Some cheaper Indonesian food. *Ky-Ky*, Jl Jend Sudirman. Steaks and Indonesian food. **Other Asian cuisines**: **Cheap**: *Gelas Mas*, Jl H Sulaiman. Chinese and international. *Jumbo*, Jl Juanda. Chinese, particularly good seafood. *Medan*, Jl Juanda. Large menu of Szechuan, Mandarin and international food. Recommended.

Entertainment

Cinema: *Dewi Santika*, Jl Jend Sudirman 306. A/c, modern, comfortable.

Shopping

Antiques: *Rezki Utama*, Jl Sisingamangaraja 12. Carvings from the Nias Islands, Chinese porcelain, krisses, wayang puppets.

Sports

Swimming: the pool at the *Mutiara Merdeka Hotel*, Jl Yos Sudarso 12A, is open to non-residents for a small fee.

Tour operators

Inti Angkasa, Jend Sudirman 37, T21074. *Kotapiring Kencana*, Jl Sisingamangaraja 3, T21382 (Pelangi Air reps). *Cendrawasih Kencana*, Jl Imam Bonjol 32, T21915. *Setia*, Jl Karet, T22331.

Transport

174 km from Bukittinggi, 158 km from Dumai

Local No becaks. **Oplets/microlets**: the station is next to the long-distance bus terminal on Jl Nangka, in front of the Pasar Cik Puan. Unmetered **taxis** and town buses.

Air Simpangtiga Airport is 8½ km south of town. *Merpati, Indonesian Airlines, Garuda, SMAC, SilkAir* and *Pelangi Air* all fly out of Pekanbaru. International connections with Singapore, Melaka and Kuala Lumpur. Domestic connections with Batam, Jakarta, Medan, Tanjung Pinang and Palembang. *Transport to town*: taxis to the town centre cost 12,000Rp; there is no public transport. *Airport facilities*: Post Office, money changer and a souvenir shop in the departure lounge, selling stuffed frogs and what look like badly baked baguettes.

Road Bus: the long-distance Mayang Terurai terminal is at Jl Nangka 92 on the southern edge of town, next to the Pasar Cik Puan. Microlets go there from the city centre (ask for 'Loket'). Regular connections with Bukittinggi 6 hrs, Padang, Bandung, Yogya, Aceh, Palembang, Jakarta 34 hrs, Medan and other destinations. Bus companies such as *ANS* (T22065) have their offices at the terminal. Local and intra-provincial buses go from the Pasar Lima Puluh terminal at the north end of Jl Sultan Syarit Hasyim. **Minibus**: regular connections with Bukittinggi and Padang 7 hrs.

Sea Boat: Pekanbaru 'port' is at the end of Jl Saleh Abbas, the northward continuation of Jl Jend A Yani. Microlets from the centre of town are marked 'Boom Baru', although it is an easy walk. Numerous companies have desks and sell tickets along Jl Saleh Abbas. Connections with Tanjung Pinang, Batam Island and other stops in the Riau archipelago (including Selat Panjang, Moro, Tanjung Batu and Tanjung Balai). Some boats thread their way along the Siak River to Silat Panjang, and then enter the Melaka Strait and islands of the Riau Archipelago. Most are Conradian cowboy operations, with overloaded boats, smuggling goods, drunk captains and frequent groundings. Take food along. Slow boats take 18-36 hrs, speedboats 3½ hrs. However, most of the more comfortable services leave from Buton (Tanjung Buton/Selat Panjang) on the coast, which is a 3 hr bus ride from Pekanbaru. Catch the 0800 bus departure to Buton which arrives in time to catch the 1230 speedboat to Sekupang (3½ hrs). From Sekupang there are regular ferries to Singapore running between 0800 and 1615 (40 mins) (see page 577).

International connections Air With Singapore, Melaka and Kuala Lumpur. **Boat** Regular ferries from Singapore's World Trade Centre to Sekupang on Batam, 30 mins, and from there to Buton on the Sumatra mainland, 3-5 hrs, then a bus to Pekanbaru, 3 hrs, total journey about 9 hrs. For travellers in no hurry this is an attractive way to arrive in Indonesia.

Directory

Airline offices *Indonesian Airlines*, Hotel Mutiara Merdeka, Jl Yos Sudarso 12A, T21612. *SMAC*, Jl Sudirman 25, T23922. *Merpati*, Jl Jend Sudirman 343, T41555. *Garuda*, Hotel Mutiara Merdeka, Jl Yos Sudarso 12A, T32526, F32959. *SilkAir*, Hotel Mutiara Merdeka, Jl Yos Sudarso 12A, T28175, F28174. **Banks** *Bank Bumi Daya*, Jl Jend Sudirman. *Bank Central Asia*, Jl Jend Sudirman. *Ekspor Impor*, Jl Jend A Yani. **Communications** General Post Office: Jl Jend Sudirman 229. Telkom: Jl Jend Sudirman 306A (next to the Dewi Santika Cinema), for fax, international telephone and telex/telegraph services. **Medical facilities** General hospital: Jl Diponegoro 2, T36118.

The Riau Archipelago

Population: 400,000
Colour map 2, grid A2/3

Riau – or Kepulauan Riau – is made up of more than 3,000 islands, scattered in a belt stretching 700 km from the Sumatran mainland. A third of the Riau islands are uninhabited and many do not even have names. The rest include Batam – which is fast turning into Singapore's industrial backyard – and Bintan, the biggest in the group. Bintan played a pivotal role in Malay history with the founding of the Riau-Johor Empire there in the 16th century. Many of the Riau islands have beautiful deserted beaches, although Batam Island is a far cry from the palm-fringed paradise it is sold as.

Climate The monsoon season from Oct to Feb brings an average of 250mm of rainfall each month. Mar-Sep is drier and, therefore, the best time to visit the islands.

Health warning Malaria is a problem in the Riau Archipelago beyond Batam and Bintan. It is important to take preventative medication (see page 56).

Background

History The Riau islands are strategically located on the shortest sea route between China and India at the south end of the Melaka Straits. From the beginning of the first millennium AD, important seafaring kingdoms grew up in the area, exploiting the islands' location; Riau's rajahs controlled regional trade in gold, silk, spices and porcelain. Bintan was even important enough to merit a visit from Marco Polo in 1202. By the 15th century, with the rise of the Melakan sultanate, the Straits had become the trading

Riau Archipelago

crossroads of the Orient. But to the Chinese and Arab traders, insular Riau was one sprawling navigational nightmare. Many boats sank on Riau's reefs and the hundreds of scattered islets made perfect pirates' dens. Today it is possible to wander along beaches and pick up fragments of Ming Dynasty porcelain, which are still being washed ashore from wrecked Chinese junks which sank over 400 years ago.

When the Portuguese took Melaka and forced the sultan to flee south, he re-established his kingdom in Johor, and when the Portuguese destroyed the Johor capital in 1526, it was uprooted again and moved to Bintan. Throughout the 16th and 17th centuries, the sultanate's capitals alternated between Johor, Bintan and Lingga, to the south. In the 18th century the Buginese, displaced by the Dutch from their homelands in South Sulawesi, arrived in Riau, and soon came to dominate the Malay court. The two main centres of power were Penyenget Island (off Bintan) and Lingga Island. Dutch influence increased after the defeat of the Portuguese in Melaka in 1641 and the sultans gradually lost their hold on trade and then their independence.

The Riau-Johor Empire was already disintegrating when the British ousted the Dutch from both Melaka and Riau and in 1812, following a succession crisis prompted by the death of Sultan Mahmud, the kingdom split in two. Mahmud's eldest son, who was recognized by the British, went to Singapore to become the Sultan of Johor. His younger son, supported by the Buginese and the Dutch, became the Sultan of Lingga-Riau. This division of the Riau-Johor Empire was formalized with the signing of the Treaty of London between the Dutch and the British in 1824.

Modern Riau

The islands of Batam and Bintan have had their fortunes revived by Singapore's decision to transfer the republic's cumbersome land and labour-intensive industries to Riau. The area has become a pivot in the so-called SIJORI (standing for Singapore, Johor, Riau) Growth Triangle. The economic logic behind the Growth Triangle is pretty clear: Singapore has high labour costs and land prices, but is rich in technological skills and financial and marketing expertise; Riau (and to a lesser extent, Johor) is rich in land and has low labour costs, but lacks technological expertise and financial and marketing muscle. So some bright spark chanced upon the idea that if you put the two (or rather, three) together you would get economic complementarity, synergy and, so the theory goes, a minor economic marvel. Hence, Batam is filled with labour intensive, often low skilled and sometimes dirty (Riau's environmental regulations are far less stringent than Singapore's) industries.

At the same time, Batam and Bintan have become off-shore production centres for Singapore, so both islands have been turned into resort islands catering for the Singapore market. Despite sometimes environmentally savage redevelopment, there are still long stretches of deserted beaches on Bintan. It is also possible to get away to tiny, untouched islands, with good beaches and coral.

Batam Island

Phone code: 0778
Colour map 2, grid A2

Batam's reinvention as an off-shore production base for Singapore has tended to erode its attractions as a tropical island paradise. Indeed, outside the havens offered by the more luxurious hotels, it is hard to escape the conclusion that Batam is a dump. It is no longer a beautiful island – far from it – and most tourists pass through quickly, en route to Singapore or other islands in the archipelago and Sumatra. Nor does Batam have any sights – cultural or otherwise – that might entice visitors to stay longer.

Getting there
See Transport section for further details

Batam Island has the best connections of the Riau islands group. Hang Nadim Airport on Batam offers connections with Medan, Pekanbaru, Padang, Palembang, Banda Aceh, Bandung, Pontianak and Jakarta. However, most people arrive here by boat and there are regular high-speed ferries between Singapore and 4 ports on Batam, all on the north coast. There are also boats from Batam to neighbouring Bintan Island and to Buton and Pekanbaru on the Sumatran 'mainland', as well as (although less frequently) with Kuala Tungka (Jambi) and Dumai.

Getting around

Taxis and cars are available for hire and charter. Ojeks provide the cheapest form of hired transport and there is also a limited bus service. **Batam Tourist Promotion Board** is on Jl RE Martadinata, Sekupang, T322852 (next to the international ferry terminal at Sekupang).

Background

Batam, at 415 sq km, is two-thirds the size of its rich northern neighbour, Singapore. Its population has grown from 100,000 at the end of the 1980s to about 300,000 today. Since Singaporean speculators started venturing across the Strait, new towns, factory sites and a port have sprung up where a few years ago there was only jungle.

Although it is not a popular place to visit for most foreign tourists, it is a popular getaway for Singaporeans, and there are a number of beach resorts, designed for weekenders, which are fairly quiet during the week. Although the umbilical link with Singapore means that Batam's better hotels are fairly sophisticated and well-run, it

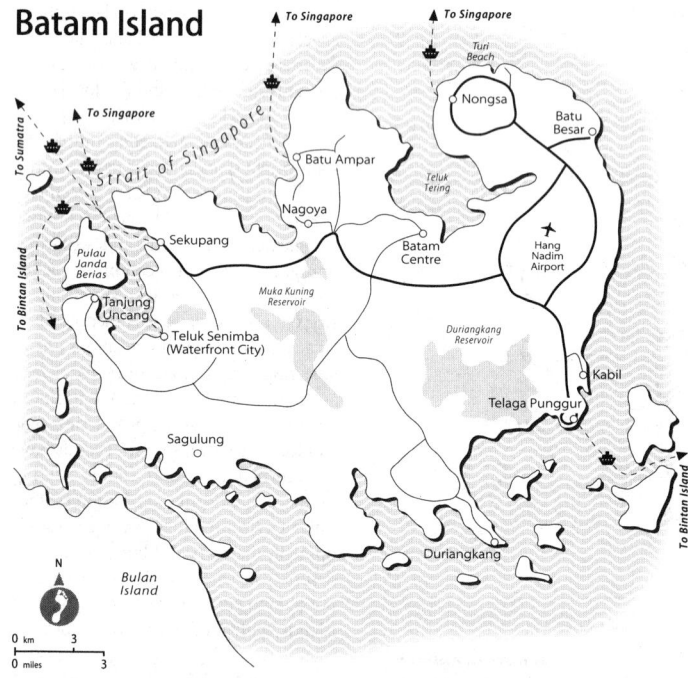

also means that prices here are comparatively high by Indonesian standards (though cheap by Singaporean). Indeed, the Riau islands reputedly now have the highest cost of living in Indonesia, and many shops, hotels and tour companies quote the S$ price before the rupiah one.

Batam's main town is **Nagoya** with its twin, the imaginatively named **Batam Centre**. **Sekupang** is the main settlement on the western end of the north coast, while **Nongsa** on the eastern extremity of the north coast is the main resort area. Between these three areas are strung numerous industrial and housing developments, many of which seem to be only partially occupied.

Essentials

Sleeping

The best hotels are at Nongsa. Sekupang and Nagoya also have a good sprinkling of places to stay. The advantage of staying in Sekupang and Nagoya is that they offer far better access to restaurants and bars. Nongsa is isolated and most guests find themselves resorting to eating in their hotels. See under individual town entries.

Eating

Batam has carved out a minor niche for itself in its *kelong*-style seafood restaurants. *Kelong* are the stilted villages that can still be seen around the island, and *kelong* restaurants are simply restaurants built on stilts over the sea. The Riau seafood speciality is the *gong-gong* shellfish, which lives in a twisting, tapered shell, is served with a sweet chilli sauce and which is said by locals to have aphrodisiac properties. Riau is also known for its *ikan bilis*, or anchovies. Most of the restaurants are to be found in or near Nagoya, Sekupang or Nongsa, and are listed in these 3 entries below. However, the **Batam Punggur** at Pantai Telaga Punggur (4 km from Kabil, past the ferry terminal) is a *kelong*-style seafood restaurant recommended by locals. Try to eat at high tide when the foul smelling mud is underwater.

Entertainment

Karaoke is popular, mainly for the benefit of visiting Singaporeans. Almost every big hotel, and especially those in Sekupang and Nagoya, has a disco.

Transport

Local Car hire: there are numerous tour and travel outfits in Sekupang and Nagoya and some will hire out vehicles for self drive. Expect to pay about 100,000Rp per day. **Taxis**: they throng the island. None metered; hard bargaining is the norm. Share taxis are popular; flag 1 down running in the right direction and establish the price before boarding (500-2,000Rp, normal range). To charter an a/c taxi expect to pay around S$8-10 per hr, depending on the state of the vehicle and the distance to be travelled. From the ferry terminals prices are fixed and high and if not burdened by luggage it makes sense to walk out of the port area to haggle. **Ojeks**: motorcycle taxis (*ojeks*) are the cheapest way to get around (500-1,000Rp, for a short journey). It is hard to tell an *ojek* from a private motorcycle, but most riders hang around at street corners leaning nonchalantly against their machines and trying to look like James Dean. **Bus**: new to Batam and still not a common form of transport. However, 'bis damri' do run between Sekupang, Nagoya and Nongsa and this is by far the cheapest way to travel.

Air Hang Nadim Airport is on the east side of the island. Incredibly, a recent extension and upgrading programme means that it can take 747-400s and there are plans to entice European and Australian long-haul flights to land here. (The 4,000m runway is the longest in Indonesia.) For the present, though, the airport is still largely a local affair. Regular connections on *Garuda/Merpati, Indonesian Airlines* and *Bouraq* with Medan, Pekanbaru, Padang, Palembang, Banda Aceh, Bandung, Pontianak and Jakarta.

Sea Regular speedboat connections with Bintan from Telaga Punggur, on the east side of the island. Boats for Tanjung Pinang leave every hour during daylight (30 mins, 8,000Rp) and less regularly for Uban (most connections in the morning, 15 mins, 5,000Rp). The boats, powered by 3 150hp outboard engines, skim and bounce at high speed across the Riau Strait which divides Batam from Bintan. When sea conditions are good it can be quite entertaining, but in rougher conditions, passengers may be offering worried looks and wishing there were more life preservers. There are several companies at the ferry terminal at Telaga Punggur who compete for business.

It is possible to catch boats to Pekanbaru, several hundred kilometres up the Siak River in Sumatra, from Sekupang. Boats leave at 0830, S$ are accepted. Buses to Bukittinggi meet the boat for onward connections. A much faster, although perhaps less interesting option, is to take one of the express boats to Tanjung Buton/Selat Panjang, on the coast of the Sumatran 'mainland'. (The 0930 departure is probably the most convenient.) The journey, with stop-offs at various seedy-looking ports, takes just 3-4 hrs, and at Tanjung Buton/Selat Panjang travellers have the choice either to take a bus onward to Pekanbaru (another 3 hrs) or a speedboat up the Siak River. Other destinations available from the domestic ferry terminal in Sekupang include Kuala Tungka (Jambi), Dumai, Tembilahan, Tanjung Batu and Tanjung Balai Karimun. The Pelni ship *Sinabung* docks here.

Beware of local people at the Batam Ferry Terminal overcharging for your ticket, offering to obtain a departure stamp

International connections: there are regular international connections between Batam and Singapore. High-speed, a/c passenger ferries run to 4 ports on Batam, all on the north coast: Teluk Senimba (Waterfront City), Sekupang, Batu Ampar and Nongsapura (in order, west to east). Ferries for Sekupang, Batu Ampar and Teluk Senimba leave from the World Trade Centre in Singapore and take about 45 mins. There are departures around every 30 mins throughout the day, beginning at 0730 and running through to 2000 (the last ferry bound for Singapore from Batam leaves at 2020). Ferries for Nongsapura (Nongsa's ferry terminal) leave from Tanah Merah and take about the same time but are less regular, leaving at 2-hrly intervals. Fares vary between the companies, and note that some include departure tax. Expect to pay around S$26-28 return (including tax) for the journey between the World Trade Centre and Batu Ampar and Sekupang, and S$25 for that between Tanah Merah and Nongsapura. The largest companies operating from the World Trade Centre in Singapore are: *Auto Batam* (aka *Sembferries*), 1 Maritime Square, World Trade Centre, Singapore, T2714866, (www.sembcorp.com.sg/autobatam); and *Dino Shipping Pte*, T2700311; *Interlink Ferry Services*, T2769722 run the service between Tanah Merah and Nongsapura. There is also a service to Johor, Malaysia.

Directory **Airline offices** *Garuda*, 2nd floor, Persero Building, Jl Kuda Laut, Nagoya, T458764. *Merpati*, Pertokoan Pribumi, Jl Teuku Umar 6, Nagoya, T58963. *Indonesian Airlines*, Jl Raja Ali Haji. **Banks** Singapore $s are accepted as cash by many hotels and tour companies.

Nagoya and Batam Centre

Nagoya, now officially called **Lubuk Baja**, is a town without attitude and has next to nothing to offer the visitor other than a few hotels, restaurants, shops and banks. Apparently, the name Nagoya was bestowed on the town by the Japanese during their occupation of the Dutch East Indies, and it stuck. The Batam Tourist Promotion Board highlights the **Vihara Budhi Bhakti Buddhist Temple** on the southern outskirts of Nagoya as one of Batam's key sights of interest, but it is modern and unremarkable. The **Tiara Indah Handicraft Centre** near the sea front in Batam Centre also receives a fair amount of promotional hype, though it too is pretty marginal as sights go. Batam Centre itself is a weird, half-baked town with grandiose shopping centres, interspersed with what appear to be acres of rough grazing. Promotional literature bills this place as the 'Orchard Road' of Batam, which seems to be stretching a point to breaking.

Sleeping **AL** *Harmoni*, Jl Imam Bonjol, T459308, F459306. Popular, rather ugly hotel in the centre of town, decent size pool with sauna and jacuzzi and a big fitness centre. Several restaurants, adequate but unextraordinary rooms, shops surround the hotel. **AL** *Mandarin Regency*, Jl Imam Bonjol 1, T458899, F458057. Opened in early 1997, this is probably the smartest hotel in the town, 157 rooms around a courtyard which has the pool in it, adequate fitness centre, meeting rooms and business centre, rooms are unexceptional and quite expensive for what is provided, especially for the deluxe rooms; however, this is quite sophisticated for Batam. **A** *Nan Tongga View*, Jl Raja Ali Haji, T459795, F459670. A/c, restaurant, pool, one of the older places to stay in Nagoya, the monstrous blue block does enjoy (if that is the right word) a seafront position, but otherwise this hotel really has little to recommend it except its keen room rates. **A** *Novotel*, Jl Duyung, Sei Jodoh, T425555, F426555. Modern, set on the waterfront. The outlook isn't up to much, rooms are comfortable, some with balconies overlooking the sea and cramped bathrooms, service attentive, strangely, the pool is indoor and a/c, which is not very appealing. The food is good (including children's menu) and there is an excellent, if pricey, French bakery within the restaurant. **A-B** *Melia Panorama*, Sei Jodoh, T452888, F452555. Ugly great 17-storey tower block with 179 rooms. Decent sized rooms with a good bathroom, big pool with basic fitness room. Mostly popular with businessmen, Korean restaurant. **A-B** *Pelangi*, small hotel in the bustling heart of town, probably rather noisy, basic, with rather hideous furnishings, but new and trying hard to please. **B** *Horisona*, Jl Sultan Abdul Rachman, Komplek Lumbung Rezeki Blok E, T456239, F457123. A/c, hot water shower only, 33 simple rooms in a friendly but ugly little place, popular karaoke bar, right by several tour agencies for ticketing to surrounding areas. **B** *Puri Garden*, Jl Teuku Umar, T458888, F456333. Ostentatious hotel with Balinese cladding, average accommodation, but it's clean, efficient and friendly, a popular choice for Singaporeans. **B** *Sari Jaya*, Kompleks Bumi Indah, T451338, F451342. A/c, restaurant, an ugly hotel in the centre of Nagoya, noisy and gloomy, this is mainly used by Indonesians on business.

Eating

The best *kelong*-style seafood restaurant (built over the sea on stilts) is reputed to be the *Golden Prawn* (also known as *555*), which is situated on the east coast of the Nagoya 'peninsula' (mid-range). Other cheap restaurants in town include: *Pagi Sore*, Block B, Jl Imam Bonjol, 2. Padang food. Recommended. *Palapa*, Pulat Perbelanjaan, Blok 1, Komplek Bumi Indah, No 8. Upmarket coffee shop, Muslim food. *Tunas Baru*, 3rd floor, Blok E (blue block), Jl Nagoya 42. Seafood, the oldest established restaurant in town. **Bakeries** *Morning Bakery*, Jl Raja Ali Haji (near intersection with Jl Duyung). An excellent Indonesian bakery selling delectable stuffed rolls, garishly coloured cakes made of unfeasibly squidgy sponge, and good strong Indonesian coffee. Recommended. **Foodstalls** *Batama Food Centre*, Blok C, Nagoya.

Entertainment

Studio 21, Jl Raden Pateh (on the edge of town running south towards Batam Centre), is a cinema complex (4 theatres) mainly showing Kung Fu genre films, although more mainstream Hollywood releases are also screened.

Shopping

Handicrafts/batik: *Aloha Souvenirs*, 1 Blok B, Jl Imam Bonjol, Nagoya. *House of Batam Fiesta*, 12 Blok H, Jl Sultan Abdulrachman, Nagoya. *Batik Berdikari*, Jl Imam Bonjol, Nagoya. **Shopping centres**: *Matahari*, set back from Jl Imam Bonjol, not far from the Nagoya Plaza Hotel. A/c shopping centre and supermarket. **Supermarkets**: *Galael's*, Jl Raden Pateh (next to *Studio 21* movie theatre). Good a/c supermarket for all those Western needs.

Sports

Golf: *Southlinks Golf and Country Club*, Jl Gajah Mada, Km 9, T324128, F323288. Two 18-hole Hisamitsu Ohnishi-designed courses.

Tour operators

Pinang Jaya, 14 Blok H, Jl Sultan Abdul Rachman, Nagoya, T458585; ticketing and tours around Riau islands; there are several other travel agents on this strip near the *Horisona Hotel*.

Directory

Banks *Bank Central Asia (BNA)* on Jl Raja Ali Haji is reliable and competent and will accepts TCs denominated in most major currencies. The row of shops next to *Nagoya Plaza* on Jl Imam Bonjol has several money changers who will change TCs.

Sekupang

Like Nagoya, most people only visit Sekupang because this is where the ferry docks. It is an unattractive town with little to recommend it and most visitors show a clean pair of heels just as soon as they can. Around 8 km south of Sekupang is **Waterfront City**. This is a purpose built, largely self-contained entertainment park with sports from squash and tennis to cable skiing, bungy jumping, go-karting and parasailing.

Sleeping **AL** *Batam Fantasy Resort*, Tanjung Pinggir, Sekupang, T22850. A/c, restaurant, pool, well designed (the rooms actually face the sea), good range of sports facilities. **A** *Batam Island Country Club*, Tanjung Pinggir, Sekupang, T22825 (bookable in Singapore, T2256819). A/c, restaurant, pool, view over the straits towards Singapore, one of Batam's first hotels on an ugly private beach, duty-free shop, tennis courts and a golf driving range, chalets. **A** *Hilltop Hotel*, Jl Ir Sutami 8, T322482, F322211. A/c, restaurant, hilltop pool, 5 mins' from the ferry terminal, recently upgraded and increasingly competitively priced as newer competition has come on stream and the *Hilltop* has had to pare its rates.

Eating **Foodstalls**: *Shangri-La Food Centre*, 2 km from Sekupang on road to Nagoya. Good selection of Malay/Indonesian and Chinese stalls.

Shopping **Handicrafts/batik**: *Batik Danar Hadi Solo*, Pusat Pembelanjaan, Sekupang. **Duty-free shop**, Sekupang ferry terminal. *Utami Souvenir and Batik Shop*, Sekupang ferry terminal.

Sports **Golf** *Paradise Bay Golf and Country Club*, T391902. Eighteen-hole Max Wexler-designed course, part of the Waterfront City complex. *Indah Puri Golf and Country Club*, T323702. 18-hole (6,090m) Ronald Fream-designed course.

Transport See the transport section in the main Batam introduction above.

Directory **Banks** There are money-changing facilities at Sekupang ferry terminal. **Tourist offices** Batam Tourist Promotion Board, Jl RE Martadinata, T322852 (next to the international ferry terminal at Sekupang).

Nongsa

Many people arrive from Singapore at Nongsa, transfer to a hotel there, and then leave again without venturing beyond this small corner of Batam Island, correctly surmising that there is little reason to do so. The Nongsa area has the best resort hotels on the island and also has the best beaches. The public beach here (most stretches of sand have been requisitioned by large hotels as private beaches) is reasonable, though not notable by any means: a narrow and steeply shelving strip of sand and three simple restaurants selling good seafood.

Sleeping
Hotels are priced in Singapore dollars, although rupiah are acceptable

Top-end beach-side accommodation in Nongsa is oversubscribed and overpriced during weekends – big discounts are on offer during the week. Singaporeans and expatriates comprise the majority of the clientele. **AL-A** *Pura Jaya*, Jl Hang Le Kiue, T761435, F761438. A/c, 2 restaurants, pool. A monstrous new building stuck on the waters edge, no beach to speak of but a good pool and water slide, tennis courts and access to the 2 golf courses (Tering Bay and Palm Spring) that flank the hotel, plenty of childrens' activities laid on. **AL-A** *Batam View Beach Resort*, Jl Hang Lekir, T761740, F761747, www.technobiz.com/corp/batamv/ Large hotel, built in 1987, a/c, restaurants (good bakery), pool, new holiday chalets built in Minangkabau-style. Private 'lagoon' beach enclosed by a man-made breakwater, decent sized pool, with separate children's pool set in a landscaped garden, lots of watersports, tennis, squash, access to 2 nearby golf courses at reduced green fees, mountain bikes for rent, fishing boats and cruises can be organized, good sea views and, reputedly, one of the best *kelong*-style seafood restaurants on the island. **A** *Turi Beach Resort*, T761084, F761043. A/c, restaurants, attractive free form pool, set at the water's edge, big garden area, well-equipped rooms, full range of facilities (including golf course), timber-built traditional-style chalets spill down the hillside to the rocky foreshore, very popular at weekends and public holidays. Recommended. **D** *Setia Budi Chalets*, Nongsa beach. Restaurant (see below), simple beachside chalet accommodation – one of the very few places catering for budget travellers, organizes excursions to islands and fishing trips.

Eating **Cheap** *Rejeki*, Pantai Batu Besar, near Nongsa. *Kelong*-style jetty with open-sided dining areas, seafood, chilli crabs and deep-fried crispy *sotong*, particularly pleasant at high tide, muddy at low tide. Recommended. **Setia Budi Seafood**, Nongsa Beach. Fresh seafood in simple but pleasant open-sided restaurant overlooking the beach.

Sports

Golf: there are 6 golf courses on the island, 2 at Nongsa. Most hotels have special arrangements with the courses so that guests can play at a reduced green fee. **Turi Golf Club**, 18 holes, special green fee S$85 weekdays, S$105 weekends, caddy fee (S$12), buggy rental (S$30), shoe rental (S$10) and club rental (S$25). **Palm Spring Golf and Country Club**, 18 holes, special green fee S$60 weekdays, S$90 weekends, caddy fee (S$13), buggy rental (S$30), shoe rental (S$10) and club rental (S$30).

Transport

See the transport section in the main Batam introduction above.

Bintan Island

Though Bintan and Batam are sister islands within metaphorical spitting distance of one another, they are very different places. Batam has become Singapore's industrial overspill while Bintan is fast becoming its playground. While Batam feels like a building site, Bintan is largely forested. The focus for the majority of visitors now lies on the northern shore of Bintan – the Bintan Resort.

Population: 400,000
Colour map 2, grid A3

Ins and outs

Getting there
See Transport section for further details

There are daily high-speed ferry connections with Singapore. Kijang airport is 15 km from Tanjung Pinang and there are limited connections with destinations within Indonesia. There are also daily boats from Tanjung Pinang to Pekanbaru and 4 Pelni ships dock at Kijang, on the southeast coast, on their fortnightly circuits. Speedboats run between Tanjung Pinang and Batam.

Getting around

The main bus terminal is 7 km out of Tanjung Pinang – minivans link it with town. Unmetered taxis are available for charter and there are numerous ojeks. Motorbikes can be hired and sampans sail to the islands close to Bintan.

Tanjung Pinang

Phone code: 0771

Tanjung Pinang is Bintan's capital and a vibrant place. At weekends it is inundated with Singaporeans escaping their overly sanitized haven to indulge in a spot of anarchy: a bit of littering here, a touch of smoking in public places there, and a lot of shopping between the two. Prices for things like exotic fruits and dried assorted seafoods are less than in Singapore, so some bargain hunting can be combined with a weekend away. For non-Singaporeans, it is hard to see what might hold the visitor in Tanjung Pinang for much longer than 12 hours and many move smartly on to the beach at **Trikora**, or for those who are better heeled, to the resort hotels along the north coast. The **tourist information office** is on the main jetty, next to the immigration point.

Sights

The seaward side of insular Riau's capital is built out on stilts over what, at low tide, is a malodourous, rat and mosquito-infested mudflat. But above the mud, the **narrow piers – or *pelantar*** – teem with life and have a maze of alleyways leading off on each side to residential pile houses. The older part of town is found around the piers; this is the interesting area to explore and a morning can be spent gently ambling through the alleys and streets, experiencing the pungent atmosphere. The night's catch is carried down the old pier (Pelantar II) to the **fish market** on Jalan Pasar Ikan early every morning. There are stalls and coffee shops lining the piers, which are good places to sit and watch life go by, and Jalan Pelantar II is also the best place to purchase stocks of dried fish and shrimps – one of Bintan's delicacies. There is a **hectic bazaar** at the town end of the piers selling a rich variety of fruits and vegetables.

The town's large and economically active Chinese population quietly show their presence in three **Chinese pagodas**. The most dramatically positioned is **Cetiya Bodhi Sasana** at the very end of Pelantar II. A perfect windswept position, gazing over the ocean, but overlooking the boats that dock to load and unload their cargoes, valuable or otherwise. There is another smaller Chinese temple hidden away in the depths of the old town, at Lorong Gambir II No 31, the **Cetiya Satya Dharma**. The **largest Chinese pagoda**, with finely modelled roof decoration, is on Jalan Ketapang, near the intersection with Jalan Merdeka and in the heart of Tanjung Pinang's commercial district.

The **pasar malam** (night market) around *Hotel Tanjung Pinang* on Jalan Pos is a lively spot in the early evening, while the **night stalls** on Jalan Teuku Umar are probably the best place to eat local seafood.

Moving inland from the old core, the city begins to lose its distinctive character. The streets and buildings are like those in hundreds of other's towns across the Indonesian archipelago. Further inland still, the town becomes hilly and the streets attractively tree-lined. Here are to be found many government offices and large villas set in extensive grounds.

Travelling out of town on Jalan Kemboja for about 1 km, the road passes the **Colonial Graveyard**. This really says it all: graves, most falling or fallen into sad decrepitude, of those anonymous Europeans who travelled to the Orient to make their fortunes and ended up giving their lives, mostly victims of malaria and other tropical fevers. Continuing down Jalan Kamboja for another kilometre or so, the road meets Jalan Bakar Batu and the **Riau Kandil Museum**. The museum contains an eccentric but impressive array of historical artefacts – ceramics, manuscripts, *kris* and guns. Nothing is catalogued, and the curator's explanations are delightfully confusing. ■ *Open on demand. Either walk to the graveyard and museum – about a 2 km walk from the centre of town – or catch a minivan or ojek.*

Senggarang Almost opposite Tanjung Pinang is this small and peaceful settlement which was once the capital of Bintan. TP took over when Senggarang was all but destroyed by a terrible fire. Today it is notable for its **Buddhist temples**. Alighting at the jetty, there are two within sight, one in ruins. Another three, all said to be over a century old, are

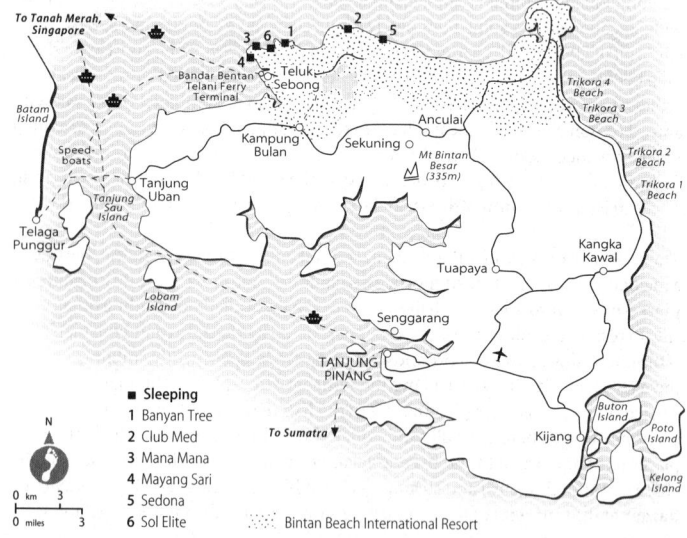

Bintan Island

■ Sleeping
1 Banyan Tree
2 Club Med
3 Mana Mana
4 Mayang Sari
5 Sedona
6 Sol Elite

set around a small courtyard overlooking the sea. The interiors are decorated with murals and they also exhibit some fine woodcarvings. Many Chinese Singaporeans visit these revered temples to make offerings to the gods. To the east of Senggarang, working 'inland' along the coast, is an old **Bugis stilt village** – Tanjung Pinang's *kampung ayer* – known as **Kampung Bugis**. Though the name has stuck, the village today is predominantly Chinese. It is reportedly possible to stay at the *Wisma Club Resort* in Senggarang. ■ *Getting there: regular public motorized sampan's leave from the end of Pelantar II, 1,000Rp per person to both Senggarang and the Bugis stilt village. It is possible to charter a whole boat for rather more.*

Sungei Ular

Meaning Snake River is on the other side of the harbour from Tanjung Pinang. The narrow river winds its way through mangroves to the **Jodoh Temple** – at over 300 years, the oldest Chinese temple in Riau – built as a refuge by Buddhist monks in the late 18th century and honouring the goddess of mercy, Kuan Yin. Murals on the walls depict unpleasant visions of hell. ■ *Getting there: hire a motorized sampan from the end of Pelantar II, 15 mins.*

Penyenget Island

Penyenget Island – covering only 2½ sq km – is just offshore, facing Tanjung Pinang. Once the centre of the Riau-Johor sultanate, the island is littered with relics, most of them in the northwest corner. After the Portuguese took Melaka in 1511, Sultan Mahmud Shah was forced to withdraw to Riau and made this the seat of his dying kingdom. The island can be walked around in 1-2 hours. From the jetty, turn right and the road runs past most of the sights of interest. The unusual and beautifully kept yellow mosque, the **Mesjid Raya Sultan Riau** – which houses a library of antique Islamic texts including a hand-written 150-year-old Koran – was built in 1818, and is said to be cemented together with egg-white mortar. The scores of eggs that provided the essential raw material were reputedly given to the sultan as gifts to celebrate his wedding, although why his loyal subjects should all simultaneously decide that eggs were a fitting gift is not at all clear. There are a few ruins of an old fort, and further round is the ruined **Kerjaan Melayu Palace**, also built at the beginning of the 19th century in a blend of Javanese and Dutch styles, but abandoned in the early 1900s. In the centre of the island, on the way back to the jetty, are the **tombs** of Rajah Ali Jaji, who wrote the first Malay grammar and compiled a dictionary (classical Malay is still spoken on Penyenget), and Engku Peteri Permaisuri, a Bugis princess who received the island of Penyenget as her dowry from Sultan Mahmud. She ruled until her death in 1844. The descendants of the Riau-Johor royal family still live in pile houses on the south side of the island; most are fishermen. There are two guesthouses on Penyenget, in Kampung Jambat, although there are rumours that one or both may have to close. ■ *Getting there: regular motorized sampans to the island leave from the end of the old pier (Pejantan II) (1,000Rp, 10 mins). A rowing boat will take about 30 mins.*

Mount Bintan Besar

Bintan Besar is Bintan's highest (360m) peak. It is clothed in forest but there is a track to the summit and can be climbed in about three hours. From the top there are good views over Bintan and the surrounding islands of the archipelago. ■ *Getting there: the track to the summit runs from the mountain foot community of Kampung Sekuning, around 60 km from Tanjung Pinang. To get to Kampung Sekuning, catch a bus from Tanjung Pinang bound for Tanjung Uban and get off at the village of Anculai, around 50 km from town. From there, charter an ojek to the hamlet of Kampung Sekuning.*

Deserted islands

The nearest deserted islands from Bintan are **Terkulai Island** (west of Tanjung Pinang; 20 minutes by speedboat) and **Sore Island** (southwest of Tanjung Pinang; 20 minutes by speedboat). Both have good beaches and, like Penyenget, are littered with shards of Ming Dynasty porcelain. ■ *Getting there: by chartered speed boat or pom pom (diesel powered fishing boats).*

Sleeping Many of the cheaper guesthouses seem to have closed down in Tanjung Pinang as the backpackers who used to patronize them have moved elsewhere. During the week expect to be able to bargain room rates down – many of the more upmarket hotels quote separate rates for weekdays & weekends in any case

A *Bintan Beach Resort*, Jl Pantai 1, T23661, F23995 (or book in Singapore, T2874621, F287557). A/c, restaurant, pool, gym, this is the best hotel close to town and if staying in town is essential, situated on the seafront at Km 4. **A** *Rainbow*, Jl DI Panjaitan Km 6, T21982, F25982. A/c, restaurant, a hotel which is neither here nor there: it isn't on a beach and doesn't have a pool, but it is several kilometres out of town so walking around TP's sights also isn't very easy. Guests stay in miniature Spanish-style villas set in a garden with clean but garish interiors. **A** *Royal Palace Hotel*, Jl Adi Sucipto Km 10, T27555, F27557. A/c, restaurant, pool, the most comfortable place to stay in the vicinity of Tanjung Pinang, good for those on business, but because it is 10 km from TP and nowhere near a beach it doesn't make much sense for those on holiday.

B *Bintan Island Indah*, Jl Bakar Batu 22, T21946, F23616. A/c, restaurant, almost next door to Sri Santai Seafood, very clean and new – the best value in town, although a little way out from the centre. **B** *Riau Holiday Inn*, Jl Pelantar II 53, T22644, F21394. A/c, restaurant, the hotel is built out on stilts off Jl Pelantar II (the old pier), beer garden, interesting location, attracts big tour groups from Singapore and organizes marine sports (including water-skiing – Apocalypse Now-style, through the mangroves up Snake River) and trips around the island. **B** *Sanno*, Jl Pos 25-27, T21898, F22058. A/c, restaurant, small and centrally located hotel crammed into a narrow plot next to the Bintan Mall. Rooms are small and featureless, but it is clean and well run and is fine for a night waiting to catch an early boat.

C *Hotel Tanjung Pinang*, Jl Pos 692, T21236, F21379. A/c, an ugly great place in the centre of town near the Kabil Pier. But all rooms have attached bathrooms and it represents reasonable value for money. **C** *Wisma Gunung Bintan Jaya*, Jl Samudera 38, T29288. A/c, coffee shop, a convenient and clean place to spend a night right next to the international ferry pier, the standard rooms are small and dark with Asian loos, the deluxe rooms have the added luxuries of a Western-style toilet, telephone and heavily padded bedhead. **C-D** *Sempurna Jaya International*, Jl Yusuf Kahar, T21555, F21269. Some a/c, the sister hotel to the supposedly more up-market *Sempurna Jaya*, this place has friendlier service but the rooms are nothing to jump up and down about, those in the 'new' wing are slightly better, but all are dark and those near the road are noisy.

D *Surya*, Jl Bintan, T21811, central hotel situated on a busy road so rooms can be noisy, but the atmosphere is attractive. Dark rooms are set around a courtyard, some have attached mandis, all painted in aquamarine so residents may wake up thinking they are trapped in an aquarium. Good coffee house attached.

Guesthouses Note that the guesthouses listed below may have recently closed due to the decline in budget travellers visiting Bintan. **F** *Bong's Homestay*, Lorong Bintan II 20 (behind Jl Merdeka). Cheap and friendly, very similar to *Johnny's*, next door, dormitory or rooms. **F** *Johnny's Guesthouse*, Lorong Bintan II 22 (behind Jl Merdeka). Probably the most popular of the budget places, clean and friendly, breakfast included; popular getaway for Singaporeans, mountain bikes for hire.

Eating Food is neither cheap nor particularly good in Tanjung Pinang. There are a few Chinese coffee shops where the coffee is wonderful.

Mid-range *Hanly Café*, Jl Bakar Batu (near intersection with Jl Teratai). A/c restaurant serving pizzas and other western and oriental dishes. *Panorama Kelong Seafood Restaurant*, on western point of *Bintan Resort*. It sits on stilts, with seating for 100, some a/c available. **Cheap** *Teluk Keriting Seafood Centre*, Jl Usman Harun 16 (*getting there*: ojek from Jl Merdeka, 400Rp). Recommended.

Foodstalls and fastfood *Pasar Malam*, around the *Tanjung Pinang Hotel*, has a number of stalls in the evening selling seafood (mud crabs, *sotong* [squid], prawns, *gong-gong* [Riau's aphrodisiac shellfish] etc) and satay. Nightstalls at the bus station compound off Jl T Umar sell good chilli crab; during the day there are pavement cafés next to the stadium on the corner of Jl T Umar. For those who might wish for a taste of home, they could mosey down to the hippest place in town – the *Bintan Indah Mall* on Jl Pos which has a smattering of a/c restaurants producing burgers, chicken and french fries.

Festivals

Fifth month of the lunar calendar: *Bak Chang* (Meat Dumpling Festival) (movable), celebrated with dragon boat races between different Hakka Chinese clans around Tanjung Pinang.

Shopping

Handicrafts: *Lasmin Art Shop*, Jl Tugu Pahlawan 12, Kampung Kolam. *Toko Batik Gloria*, Jl Temiang. *Batik Prima*, Jl Mawar. There are souvenir shops in the market area and around Jl Merdeka. Perhaps the most interesting place to nose around for 'antiques' and handicrafts is by the stadium on Jl Teuku Umar – set in among all the stalls and tables. There is also a souvenir shop opposite the travel agents on Jl Samudra, next to the harbour.

Tour operators

There are numerous tour companies and travel agents in town, including scores of shipping agents, mostly concentrated around the piers in the centre of town. *PT New Oriental Tour and Travel*, Jl Merdeka 61, T21614, F24145. *PT Bintan Baruna Sakti*, Hotel Tanjung Pinang, Jl Pos 692, T23169, F24157. *Bintan Panorama*, 50A Jl Bakar Batu, T21894, F22572, services *Bintan Island Resort*. Watersports and fishing. *Infotravel*, Jl Samudra 12, next to the harbour-master's office, between the jetty and Jl Merdeka. Mainly a ticketing agency, schedules for ferries to Java/Sumatra and advice on how to get to other islands.

Transport

Local Minivans (bemos) scoot around town; wave one down going in the right direction (250-500Rp). **Bus** The main terminal for journeys around the island is inconveniently located 7 km out of Tanjung Pinang – minivans take passengers out there. The bus station is on Jl Teuku Umar. **Taxis** Bintan's taxi industry is going through a minor revolution as non-a/c 1950s-era Fords and Chevrolets are phased out in favour of new a/c Japanese vehicles. None are metered and Bintan's taxi drivers have a well deserved reputation for driving a hard deal. Bargain ferociously. Expect to pay 10,000-15,000Rp per hr, perhaps 60,000Rp for a day's charter depending on the vehicle and the length of the journey. It is also possible to charter minivans (bemos) by the hour or day. **Ojek** the easiest way to get around is by *ojek* (public motorcycle), 500-1,000Rp depending on distance. **Motorbike hire** check at hotels, or rent an *ojek* (without the driver) along Jl Merdeka for around 30,000Rp per day. **Sampans** motorized and man-powered sampans can be chartered from Pelantars I and II. There are also regular public sampans to places like Senggarang, Kampung Bugis and Pulau Penyenget (1,000Rp).

Air Kijang airport is 15 km southeast of Tanjung Pinang. Regular connections on Indonesian Airlines and Merpati with various Indonesian cities and on SMAC with Batam, Dabo (Singkep Island), Ranai (Natuna Island), Bangka and Jambi. *Transport to town*: by bus and taxi (2,500Rp).

Sea Boat most tourists visiting Bintan now stay at one of the hotels associated with the *Bintan Beach International Resort* and consequently take the ferry from Singapore's Tanah Merah terminal to Bintan's Bandar Bentan Telani Terminal at Teluk Sebong – thus bypassing Tanjung Pinang. However, Tanjung Pinang remains an important local port and passenger ferries and cargo boats call here. There are daily boats from Tanjung Pinang to Pekanbaru (15,000-20,000Rp). Slow boats take 2 days and 1 night, with long stops at island ports along the way. Passengers are advised to take food (see page 573). Schedules are available from the many shipping agencies to be found near the entrance to the main pier and around the centre of town. The Pelni ships *Bukit Siguntang*, *Kerinci*, *Sirimau* and *Bukitraya* dock at Kijang, about 15 km east of Tanjung Pinang. **Speedboats** to Telaga Punggur on the east side of Batam leave every hour during daylight (30 mins, 8,000Rp) from the jetty off Jl Pos/Pasar Ikan. Boats no longer dock at Kabil (just north of Telaga Punggur).

International connections Sea: *Auto Batam* and *Dino Shipping*, each run 3 high speed ferries a day each way between Singapore's Tanah Merah terminal and Tanjung Pinang (S$42 return). *Auto Batam's* agent in Tanjung Pinang is *PT New Oriental Tour and Travel*, Jl Merdeka 61, T21614, F24145; *Dino Shipping's* agent is *PT Bintan Baruna Sakti, Hotel Tanjung Pinang*, Jl Pos 692, T23169, F24157. In Singapore contact *Auto Batam* on T2714866, F2733573, and *Dino Shipping* on T2700311, F2700322. *Indofalcon* (Singapore T2757393) operate ferries from the World Trade Centre in Singapore to Tanjung Pinang (2 departures a day, S$35 return).

Directory **Airline offices** *Agesti Jaya Sakti*, Indonesian Airlines agent, Jl Bintan 9, T22116. *SMAC*, Jl A Yani, 5 km out of town, T22798. *Merpati/Garuda agent*, Jl Bintan 44, T21267, F21269. *SMAC*, Jl Jend A Yani, T22798. **Banks** In many hotels, restaurants and tour companies, S$s can be used as cash. **Bank Central Asia**, Jl Ketapang, as usual, the most efficient place to change money – the tellers don't stare at a DM or a £ as if it were a currency from space. Many other banks including: **Bank Dagang Negara**, Jl Teuku Umar; **Bank Rakyat Indonesia**, Jl Teuku Umar. **Lippobank**, Jl Merdeka. Several money changers on Jl Merdeka and Jl Pos which tend to give better rates for cash. **Communications** *General Post Office*: Jl Hang Tuah (extension of Jl Merdeka). **Useful addresses** Immigration Office: ferry jetty.

Trikora Beach

Phone code: 0771 Trikora Beach – or rather Trikora Beaches – is a long stretch of palm-fringed coastline, 45 km northeast of town on the quiet east side of the island. In a rather inspired piece of nomenclature, which makes one suspect that a bureaucratic mind must have been at work, Trikora's series of beaches have been numbered one to four running from south to north. So the first beach is Pantai Trikora Satu (One) and the last, at Teluk Dalam, is Pantai Trikora Empat (Four). Even with this romance-defying series of names, Trikora is still beautiful and the beaches and coastline become more beautiful the further north one travels. This is strange in so far as the accommodation is concentrated at the southern end, around Trikora One and Trikora Two beaches. The beach is safe for swimming and the water is clear, although most of the coral on the nearby reefs is dead.

Sights The **road to Trikora** passes through the small local town of **Kangka Kawal**, the largest town hereabouts with a post office, and a sprinkling of shops and warungs. A kilometre or so further on it reaches the coast at the picturesque fishing kampung of **Teluk Kawal**. Boats can be chartered at Teluk Kawal (and from Trikora Beach itself) to visit the **offshore islands of Mapor**, **Nikoi**, **Beralas Bakau** and **Beralas Pasir**. The snorkelling at these offshore islands is better, although those who are experienced in such matters will probably not be overly impressed.

Nikoi & Mapur are said to provide nesting grounds for the swiftlet, which produces the 'noodles' (in fact strands of saliva) for birds' nest soup

Of all the beaches along this long stretch of coast, arguably the most attractive is Pantai Trikora Tiga – a wonderful stretch of unspoilt, palm-fringed sand. There are no warungs or drinks stalls. **Trikora Empat** is an attractive and popular public bay with an array of small warungs and drinks stalls. During the week most are closed, although it is possible to get a drink and a simple meal (there is nowhere to stay though) and have the beach largely to yourself. At weekends and public holidays they burst into life and the beach becomes very popular with local weekenders. North of here the road runs along the coast through **Teluk Dalam** to **Sialang** and **Tanjung Berakit**, where it cuts inland. This stretch is undeveloped: coconut groves, small fishing kampungs, mangroves and some pleasant beaches.

Excursions **Gunung Bintan Besar** is the island's highest mountain and can be climbed from the hamlet of **Kampung Sekuning** in about three hours (see page 583). ■ *Getting there: take a bemo back towards Tanjung Pinang and get off at the intersection near Gesik, about 20 km from Tanjung Pinang. From there catch a west-bound bus heading for Tanjung Uban and get off at Anculai (around another 30 km). From Anculai take an ojek to Kampung Sekuning.*

Sleeping Accommodation on Trikora is concentrated along **Pantai Trikora Satu** and **Pantai Trikora Dua**. **A** *Trikora Beach Resort*, Km 37 Teluk Bakau, T24454, F24456. A/c (own generator), restaurant, pool, pleasant, low-key resort on a steep hill overlooking the sea, with private beach and shady coconut palms, tennis court, boat for snorkelling and fishing expeditions, bicycles, motorbikes and jeeps for hire, the rooms are pleasant and clean and the service is friendly and low-key – the best value resort in Riau, but prices go up on the weekends. Recommended. **D** *Yasin Guesthouse*, the stilted huts are pretty basic, but it has an attractive rustic atmosphere and improvements are planned, including a communal sitting area and library, the more expensive huts have attached mandis and all room rates include breakfast, the restaurant here is separately managed and has a simple menu, boat for hire to explore the nearby islands. The best, and almost the only, cheap place to stay. Recommended. **D-E** *Bukit Berbunga Guesthouse*, simple huts on a reasonable beach, quiet.

Mid-range *Trikora Sunrise Kelong*, a *kelong* 200m offshore – the only way to get here is by boat. Stop at the warung opposite the primary school between the 32 km and 33 km markers; they will radio for a boat. Good seafood in unusual location. *Pantai Trikora Restoran*, Km 39, Jl Teluk Bakau. Fresh seafood on a genuine bamboo fishing *kelong*, one of the few dedicated restaurants still operating here. **Cheap** *Rumah Makan Sederhana*, Kangka Kawal. The best restaurant in the small town of Kangka Kawal, but it is still pretty basic. **Foodstalls**: stalls and warungs selling saté, grilled seafood and simple 1 dish meals set up at Pantai Trikora Empat over the weekend.

Eating

Road Bus: minivans run from the bus terminal outside Tanjung Pinang to Trikora (3,500Rp). There are no direct buses from Tanjung Uban (the ferry terminal from Batam) on Bintan's northwest coast to Trikora; catch a bus heading for Tanjung Pinang and ask to be let off to catch a bus running from Tanjung Pinang to Trikora. **Taxi**: a taxi from Tanjung Pinang to Trikora should cost around 30,000-40,000Rp.

Transport
35-45 km from Tanjung Pinang

Banks No banks near at hand, so change sufficient in Tanjung Pinang. **Communications Post Office**: there is a small post office in Kangka Kawal.

Directory

Bintan Beach International Resort

Bintan Resorts, a Singaporean company, has leased the entire area of Bintan's north shore and up to 1997 had invested S$1.66bn in developing the area into an integrated luxury holiday and sporting resort. By late 1997, six hotels, a golf club with two championship 18-hole courses, and a watersports centre were operational. Other plans in the pipeline are for a 'wildlife sanctuary' and an 'urban beach centre' with shopping malls and food outlets, but these are still under consideration. With over 50 travel agents packaging Bintan as a destination, the management is optimistically forecasting a massive increase in arrivals.

To the critic, the Bintan Resort is Indonesia lobotomized. To its supporters, it is Indonesia without the hassles

Bintan Resort Management have certainly been at pains to create a sound infrastructure; there is a stable power supply, the roads in the resort area are better than those elsewhere on the island, and a large reservoir was constructed to provide ample water for the projected hotels and other developments. This is not to say that Bintan Resorts have been blunderless; the electricity pylons, for example, that march across the resort are an eyesore. But reassuringly, the management do seem to be aware of these errors and there is a willingness to learn from them. Two environmental scientists have been employed to undertake Environmental Impact Assessments and to appraise the likely effects of any new developments. In theory, every project has to have an EIA stamp of approval before it can proceed.

But those people who have come to the Bintan Resort to see Indonesia are likely to be disappointed. Frankly, this is about as far removed from Indonesia as it is possible to get while having your passport emblazoned with an Indonesian immigration stamp. With little imagination, it could be Hawaii, or Thailand, or Australia. There are no independent shops or restaurants; the roads are not potholed; there are no stalls or warungs; and most remarkably, you can drink the water straight from the tap. Most frustratingly, if a guest should be adventurous enough to wish to venture to Tanjung Pinang or Trikora, they will find it either difficult or expensive. It is necessary either to hire a car or spend around four hours struggling to get to the public highway and from there on a public bus to their destination. In the resort area it is only possible to eat in the sanitized hotel restaurants where a largely captive audience keeps prices high.

Sleeping & eating

All accommodation in the Bintan Resort area is overpriced, compared with similar standard hotels elsewhere in Indonesia. Presumably this must reflect the need to recoup the substantial investments made in the resort area & the monopsonistic position that the hotels enjoy. It also means that incidentals are expensive too

LL *Banyan Tree*, T7126918, F7181348, 31 villas have been built on stilts on this rocky shoreline, in amongst the coconut palms, there are essentially 2 types of villa, 1 comes with its own pool, and the 'cheaper' version has a Jacuzzi. Rooms are extremely stylish, with big 4-poster beds looking out to sea, sunken baths, wooden floors in a Balinese style villa. Other facilities include a beautiful circular pool and a 'spa' which provides aromatherapy massages, tennis courts, watersports facilities and golf – all available at a price. This is a quiet honeymooners resort and is definitely not suitable for children, more villas are under construction, with 100 proposed upon completion, which is plain greedy and will make the resort feel rather cramped and not so exclusive, at present building work makes the resort rather unsightly and it has an unfinished air about it. **AL** *Club Med*, a new Club Med resort is the latest addition to the shoreline. Providing around 300 rooms, all with balconies, 4 restaurants, extensive water and land sports, 3 swimming pools and plenty of children's activities. For more information, www.clubmed.com **AL** *Mayang Sari*, Tanjong Tondang, T323088, F323080. This is the oldest hotel on the island and breaks the relatively new guideline that no accommodation should be nearer than 100m from the sea. There is a choice of a sea view or a 'back of chalet in front' view, 56 attractive large rooms, with simple but sophisticated furnishings and a hot water shower. All bungalows have their own balconies. The hotel is set in a lovely sweep of sandy bay, with a gently shelving shoreline, ideal for children. This is a very laid back place, which will appeal to those wanting a quiet retreat. No sports facilities (includes no pool), but the *Mana Mana Watersports Centre* is at the other end of the beach. Recommended. **AL** *Sedona*, T7191388, F7191399, ongcb@kepland.com.sg 400 plus rooms, this is a huge complex and the biggest resort on the island, it is set at the beginning of a long sandy beach and provides a good range of sports facilities, with a leisure centre, a golf course right next door and a watersports centre. There are 3 restaurants and several bars. The rooms are spacious but unexceptional, all have balconies. This is quite a lively place with lots of activity for families, with 2 large free form pools, 1 with waterslides, a children's play centre, extensive gardens. At certain times of year the sea can be dangerous for children as there is quite a swell and an undertow. This is becoming a popular place for Singaporeans on public holidays and weekends. At other times of year room supply is plentiful. **AL** *Sol Elite*, Nirwana Gardens, PO Box 006, T77192505, F77192516. Part of the Spanish chain of hotels, over 200 rooms arranged in 2-storey block in a semi-circle around a large free-form pool, 16 on the seafront, sports and watersports facilities, business centre. **AL-A** *Mana Mana*, T3461984, F4403132, 50 simple chalets, none with sea views and 2 rooms per bungalow. The rooms are small, with a seating area and a balcony. Bathrooms are basic, with a shower only. Attractive eating area, with a large area of decking overlooking this attractive little beach, and right next to the watersports centre.

Sports

Mana Mana watersports: provide lazers, sea kayaks, windsurfers, jet skis, surfboards (good from Nov to Feb), snorkelling equipment, and they can lay on diving for anyone who is certificated. The main season for watersports is from Mar to Oct, with diving being possible from Apr to Sep. During the rest of the year it is possible to body surf and paddle ski. **Diving and snorkelling**: the water near *Mana Mana* offers adequate snorkelling, but the diving is better around the north-eastern cape of the island. **Elephant rides**: the *Banyan Tree* can lay this on if required. **Golf**: one of the reasons so many people will come here will undoubtedly be for the golf, with 3 championship courses, this is set to become a popular weekend away from Singapore. At the weekends only handicapped players are encouraged. **Biking**: all the resorts have mountain bikes to rent. Trails still need to be developed further to make this a safe option. Traffic is not too frequent on the main road, but it is typically Indonesian and rather erratic. **Hiking**: this is something which they will develop and the sooner the better, as there some areas of rainforest here, with interesting wildlife to be discovered.

Local All transport in the resort area is managed by *Indorent* which, like monopolies the world over, charge rates which would be regarded as steep by even the hardest bitten of Tanjung Pinang's avaricious breed of taxi driver. *Indorent* have their main office at the Bandar Bentan Telani Ferry Terminal, so it is easy enough to check out rates on arrival. Rates are as follows: Minivan, 6 hrs S$50 (with driver), S$35 (without driver); Jeep, 1 day S$130 (with driver), S$100 (without driver). **Bus**: getting to the resort area is a breeze from Singapore – see below. Oddly, it is much more difficult if you try to get here from Indonesia which tends to support the view that the *Bintan Resort* is really a little slice of Singapore in Indonesia. No public buses are allowed to enter the Bintan Resort area, so it is necessary to alight in Kampong Bulan, at the 66 km marker. Here a rough track, around 12 km long, leads to the Bintan Resort road linking the ferry terminal with the hotels. If travelling from Tanjung Uban (where speedboats dock from Batam) catch a Tanjung Pinang-bound bus, and if travelling from Tanjung Pinang catch one travelling to Tanjung Uban. **Transport to Tanjung Pinang**: at present, there is no bus service from Bintan Resorts to the rest of the island. It is possible to hire a car (either from the ferry terminal or from your hotel) – 1¾ hrs, or there is a boat that leaves from Bandar Bentan Telani terminal (45 mins).

Transport

Sea Regular overpowered speedboat connections with Tanjung Uban from Telaga Punggur on Batam's east coast. Boats tend to leave in the morning (15 mins, 5,000Rp). At Tanjung Uban either haggle furiously with a taxi driver or catch a bus to Kampong Bulan and then one of *Indorent's* minivans over the rough road to Lagol.

International connections Boat: most tourists visiting Bintan now stay at one of the hotels associated with *Bintan Resort* and consequently take the efficient catamaran service from Singapore's Tanah Merah terminal to Bintan's Bandar Bentan Telani Terminal at Teluk Sebong. There are usually 3-5 round trips a day with as many as 8 at the weekends, 45 mins, S$54 adults, S$32 children. It is necessary to book at weekends and during holiday periods, (Singapore) T3451210. A shuttle bus service transports passengers from the terminal to their hotels and back again on departure.

Karimun Island

Karimun is the Riau island that lies closest to the Sumatran mainland. Like Batam and Bintan it has been the target for considerable Singaporean investment, and now looks more like a construction site than a tropical idyll. Thousands of Singaporeans come here for a weekend getaway or a cheap holiday – and it shows in the types of accommodation and entertainment on offer.

Phone code: 0777

The island is just 20 km long. The capital of Karimun is **Tanjung Balai** which is rather like Tanjung Pinang on Bintan: a frenetic and chaotic port with rickety wooden piers and vessels of all shapes and sizes. The town runs along the southern coast of Karimun, but only two or three streets inland.

Out of town are several beaches which are worth visiting. **Palawan Beach** is one of the more popular; sandy and relatively peaceful. There are a few warungs here and also a place to stay. ■ *Getting there: bus to Karimun's 2nd city of Meral and then another bus running towards Pangke.*

Pasir Panjang is a small settlement on Karimun's northern coast. A little further on from here is the **Batu Bersurat**, a rock with a carved Malay inscription along with a footprint of the Buddha. The road to Pasir Panjang passes **Mount Jantan**, Karimun's highest peak at a majestic 450m. On the mountain is **Air Terjun Pelambung**, a waterfall.

Sleeping **A-B** *Hotel Pelangi*, Jl Teuku Umar, T23100, F23558. A/c, restaurant. A large hotel with a surfeit of ambience but reasonable rooms and clean. A short walk inland from the ferry terminal. **A-B** *Paragon Hotel*, Jl. Trikora, T21668, F31331. A/c, restaurant, this is probably the best hotel in town but it is hardly a relaxing resort, situated about a 10 min walk from the ferry terminal, it is a big place in the centre of town. Rooms are good though, and the management professional. **C-D** *Hotel Taman Bunga*, Jl Pantai Taman Wisata, T324088, F324388. A/c, restaurant, almost abutting the ferry terminal, probably the best of the mid-range places with a fun atmosphere and frequented by a rather younger Singaporean clientele. **D-E** *Wisma Gloria*, Komplek Gedung Putih, T21133, F21033. Situated between the port and the town, about a 10 min walk up the hill from the ferry terminal, this is possibly the best of the cheaper places. Rooms are a little shoddy but it has some atmosphere.

Accommodation on Karimun is not great. There's almost nothing at the lower end & the more expensive hotels are geared to Singaporean weekenders – not that appealing to many readers of this book. However, the hotels do maintain reasonable levels of cleanliness

Eating There is a **night market** on Jl Pelabuhan, a great place for snacking. The best seafood restaurant is said to be *Siang Malam*, Jl Trikora 178, where the fish await their deaths in tanks. There are many more restaurants around town.

The accommodation might not be brilliant, but the food is

Transport **Local** Buses travel along the islands limited road system and there are also taxis in town. These can be chartered for the day, or part thereof. **Sea** The ferry terminal is towards the eastern end of Tanjung Balai and both domestic and international connections leave from here. There are regular and fast ferry connection with Pekanbaru (from Buton), and also with Batam, Bintan and Singapore. *Indofalcon*, *Auto Batam* and *Dino Shipping* operate ferries from the World Trade Centre in Singapore to Tanjung Balai (around 10 departures a day in total, S$30 return), the first at 0810 and the last at 1645; for the Tanjung Balai-Singapore leg the first departure is at 0945 and the last at 1720. All 3 have their offices in Singapore at the World Trade Centre; in Tanjung Balai the offices of *Auto Batam* and *Dino Shipping* are at Jl Nusantara 10, and *Indofalcon* in the ferry terminal.

Directory **Banks** *BNI*, Jl Trikora. **Communications** Post Office: Jl Pramuka 43. **Telephone office:** Jl Teluk Air 2, and a fair number of Wartel and Perumtel around town.

Kundur Island

Phone code: 0779 Kundur, close to Karimun, was a fairly laid-back island until it was Batamized. New hotels have been built over the last few years, the coastline has been dug, dredged and degraded. Perhaps this is slightly too negative, but even so it is disheartening to see an island transformed in so short a space of time. The main town is **Tanjung Batu**, a small place with big intentions. The restaurants are good, reflecting the culinarily demanding Singaporean taste bud. The beaches on the island, like Gading (3 km from town) and Lubuk (about 4 km away), are OK, but the swimming is poor.

Sleeping **A-B** *Hotel Gembira*, Jl Usman Harun, T21888, F21474. A/c, restaurant, large hotel with good facilities but little character. **B-C** *Wisata Lipo*, Jl Pemuda, T21076. A/c, mid-range place with adequate rooms.

Eating The best place to sample a range of foods, including good, cheap seafood, is the night market on Jl Merdeka.

Transport If you are intending to come to Kundur from Singapore it is necessary to travel via Karimun for immigration purposes. **Local** There is no public transport on Kundur; to get to out of town sights the cheapest and most practical option is to take an ojek. However, some hotels have motorcycles for hire and taxis are also available. **Sea** The ferry terminal is in Tanjung Batu, on Jl Pemuda. Regular connections with Karimun.

Directory **Banks** There are no banks on the island. The *Hotel Gembira* takes credit cards. **Communications** Post Office: Jl Kartini 44. **Telephone office:** Wartel, Jl Sudirman 43

Riau's other islands

Riau is an archipelago of well over 3,000 islands and most of these remain largely undiscovered. The best place to scout out boats to these lesser known places is Tanjung Pinang – go to the many shipping agents with a good map working out where and when boats leave. Note that most are commercial cargo vessels and few would pass even a modest safety check.

Lingga Island Lingga Island was the home of the last Riau sultanate. **Daik** is the main town and ferry port and there is very basic accommodation here. In 1998 the island still had no electricity, telephones or bank. A far cry from the brash commercialism of Bintan and its swanky hotels. The modest ruins of the old **Istana Damnah** lie about 2 km west of Daik, off Jalan Rabat; they don't amount to much as the Istana was largely built of wood. **Gunung Daik** is the highest peak in the Riau archipelago, rising to an impressive 1,163m. The mountain is cloaked in forest and the sheer cliff sides makes it almost impossible to climb (locals still maintain that it remains unscaled). Near Daik other points of interest include a cemetery, mosque and the remains of **Bukit Cening Fort**, built by the Dutch after they deposed the Sultan. The fort overlooks the entrance to the Daik River and it is possible to walk up to the ruins from town. Accommodation can be found near the ferry. ■ *Getting there: regular ferries from Dabo, on Singkep Island and some connections with Tanjung Pinang (4 hours). Ask at the tourist information kiosk at the harbour or at Infotravel (on Jl Samudra) about boats.*

Singkep Island Singkep Island lies due south of Bintan. The capital is **Dabo**, on the southeast coast, which is mildly interesting for its markets. Singkep built its limited wealth out of the tin which was mined here, but when the bottom fell out of that market at the beginning of the 1990s, so Singkep reverted to being a quiet, poor and largely forgotten place. Out of town are some lovely white sand beaches. **Sleeping E** *Wisma Sri Indah*, Jalan Perusahaan, clean. **E** *Wisma Gapura Singkep*, Jalan Perusahaan. Good foodstalls around town and in the market. Post Office and telephone office available (out of town towards Sunggai Buluh), bank on Jalan Penuba, with good rates. ■ *Getting there: SMAC fly to Singkep. Daily ferries to Daik on Lingga Island and to Tanjung Pinang; irregular ferries to Jambi (Sumatra).*

Penuba Island A tiny island between Lingga and Singkep, with some beautiful beaches both at **Tanjung Dua** on the north coast and **Penuba** on the south. Basic accommodation (**F**) can be found in Penuba near the mosque.

South Sumatra

Jambi

Phone code: 0741
Population: 300,000
Colour map 2, grid B2

Jambi is the capital of the province of the same name. It is a featureless town and the city centre occupies a small area on the Batanghari River, near the port where boats negotiate the river for over 150 km to the sea. There are a few old shophouses still standing on Jalan Sam Ratulangi.

Ins and outs

Getting there *See Transport section for further details*

There are many flights from Jambi's Sultan Taha Airport, 6 km south of town. The city's 2 bus terminals are southwest of town and there are departures for major centres in Sumatra as well as further afield. Boats leave from the docks near the centre of town for Batam and Bintan in the Riau archipelago.

Getting around There are no becaks in Jambi but the usual array of colts, dokars, taxis and oplets. Speedboats can also be hired in town. The **Provincial Tourist Office** is on Jl Basuki Rachmat 11 (about 5 km south of town), T25330. Get there by oplet (250Rp) or taxi. Little English is spoken but there are some brochures.

History

During the precolonial period, Jambi, exploiting its position on the Batanghari River which reaches deep into interior Sumatra, became an important centre acting as a gateway between coastal and inland areas. Wealth and power largely came from control of the pepper trade. Portuguese and Chinese, and later Dutch and English, merchants came to the city to try to corner this lucrative trade. Jambi reached the height of its prosperity during the 17th century when the royal family established links through marriage with a number of other important sultanates, including Johor (Malaya), Makassar (Sulawesi) and Banten (Java). It went into decline with the fall in pepper prices at the end of the 17th century.

Jambi was one of the cities affected most seriously by the forest fires of 1997 and again in 1999 (see page 969). BBC correspondent Jonathan Head in the fires of 1997/98 reported large numbers of people – especially the young and elderly – lined up outside clinics awaiting treatment for breathing difficulties. He commented: "The sun never shines here. Daylight is never more than a ghastly yellow glow through the smog".

Sights

The **Museum Negeri Jambi** is on Jalan Prof Dr Sri Soedewi Masjahun Sofwan 4 km from the centre of town, and has a small but interesting collection of ethnographic and archaeological pieces from the surrounding area. ■ *200Rp, 0900-1600.* There is a sprawling **street market** on Jalan Ir. Sutami, Jalan Wahid Hasyim and Jalan Supratman.

In the Telanaipura area of town (to the west of the city centre), opposite the Governor's Office, is the **Mayang Mengurai Park** which contains a construction of a traditional Jambi house, along with traditional costumes of the area. Also in this part of town is an **art and craft workshop** run by the PKK Women's group, known as PKK Batik Art.

Tours Companies are beginning to run trekking tours to visit the Kubu people of Jambi (also known as *sukuanak dalam*). They are among Southeast Asia's last hunter-gatherers and are now 'protected' in a reserve of 28,703 ha. Fortunately access is difficult, although they are becoming objects of tourist fascination as well as targets for government 'development' programmes.

Excursions

Candi Muara Jambi Candi Muara Jambi is a complex of restored temples 25 km east of the city, on the left bank of the Batanghari River (downstream). They are part of the largest archaeological site in Sumatra and are believed to date from the 7th to 13th centuries and to be associated with the Melayu Kingdom (see page 611), a rival of Srivijaya. They were first researched by Captain SC Cook in 1810. The chronicles record 35 structures here, although only nine large brick-built structures have been excavated and restored stretching over nearly 2 km, east to west. They have little decorative detail, consisting of stupas and shrines surrounded by brick walls with steps leading up into plain, square cellas. The best of the artefacts have been carted off to the National Museum in Jakarta. **Candi Gumpung**, one of the larger temples, yielded a statue of Prajnaparamita, regarded as among the finest examples of East Javanese-style carving. In addition, excavations uncovered a wealth of Chinese ceramics showing the degree to which the area was integrated into a wider international trading network.
■ *0800-1600 Mon-Sun (including small site museum with a small collection of*

ceramics and incomplete statuary), speedboat from close to the bridge on Jalan Sultan Taha, 1-2 hrs; or waterbus bound for Muara Sabak. It is best to go on Sun when there are scheduled boats – much cheaper than chartering one.

Essentials

Sleeping No real budget accommodation, because few travellers visit Jambi – just some rock bottom truckers' stop crash pads that would be best to avoid. However, there is a reasonable selection of mid-range hotels serving local businessmen and now a couple of newly-opened places that could be considered of international standard. **A-B** *Novotel Jambi*, Jl Jend Gatot Subroto 44, T27208, F27209. A/c, restaurant, pool, health club, new hotel and best in town with 150 rooms and good facilities and professional service. **B-C** *Abadi*, Jl Jend Gatot Subroto 92-98, T25600, F23065. A/c, restaurant, formerly the best hotel in town, rooms in the old wing are musty and dark, better in the new extension, service is enthusiastic rather than slick. **C-D** *Anggrek*, Jl Iskandar Muda, T25545, F33956. Behind the *Novotel* and the Matahari Plaza, down a quiet lane. More expensive rooms have a/c and bathroom attached. Good value. **C-D** *Da'lia*, Jl Lorong Camar III 100, T50863. Between Matahari Plaza and bus terminal, down a quiet alleyway. Range of rooms, in terms of size and facilities. More expensive rooms have a/c and own mandi. **C-D** *88*, Jl Halim Perdana Kusuma 8, T33286. Near the centre of town. Range of rooms, some with own mandi and a/c.

Eating Jambi specialities are served at the *Pinang Merah Restaurant*, Jl Prof Dr Sri Sudewi. **Bakery**: *French Modern Bakery*, Jl Husni Thamrin 46. **Chinese**: *Aneka Rasa*, Jl Empu Gandring; *Terkenal*, Jl M Asa'at 124. Large menu. Recommended. **Indonesian**: *Ayam Yogya*, Jl Abdul Muis 58. Good chicken dishes. *Safari*, Jl Dr Wahidin. **Padang**: several restaurants in the town centre, near the market.

Festivals Jan: *Pekan Persona Budaya Jambi* (*Jambi Cultural Festival*) (6th-12th), a jamboree of cultural festivities created to raise the profile of Jambi and its people, and timed to coincide with the anniversary of the founding of the province on 6 Jan 1957. Events include *bidar* (long boat) races, traditional dances and songs, and local food specialities.

Shopping **Antiques**: *Pasar Cindera Mata*, Jl Pinang Masak 14. **Books and maps**: *Media Agung Bookshop*, Jl Jend Gatot Subroto Blok A No 1 (near *Abadi Hotel*). **Handicrafts**: handicraft centre at *Sanggar Batik dan Kerajinan*, Jl Prof Dr Sri Soedewi Masjchun, 4 km from the centre of town; also outlet at Jl Jend Sudirman 32A. *PKK Batik Art*, run by a women's group in the Telanaipura area of town, is good for art and crafts.

Sports **Swimming**: large public swimming pool (*Kolam Renang Tepian Ratu*), Jl Slamat Riyadi (3 km from town centre). Open 0800-1700 Mon-Sun.

Tour operators *Mayang*, Jl Hayam Wuruk 7, T25450. *Jambora Kencana*, Jl Jend Gatot Subroto, T23926.

Transport
507 km from Padang, 260 km from Palembang

Local **Colts**, **dokars**, **taxis**, **oplets**. **Speedboats** can be hired near the bridge on Jl Sultan Taha, near the intersection with Jl Ir. Sutami (upstream from the Port Administration Office).

Air Sultan Taha Airport is 6 km south of town, off Jl Jend Sudirman. Taxis available to the centre of Jambi; oplets also go past the airport. Regular daily connections on Merpati with Jakarta, Palembang, Batam and Pangkalpinang. SMAC operate flights to Sungai Penuh and also to towns in the Riau archipelago.

Road **Bus** There are 2 long-distance bus terminals in Jambi. The Simpang Karwat long-distance bus terminal is 3½ km southwest of town, at the intersection of Jl Hos. Cokroaminoto and Jl Prof M Yamin. Colts run there from the city centre. A/c express bus companies have their offices on Jl Mr Assa'ad (*ACC* at No 60 and *Jaya Bersama* and *ALS* at No 64), which runs off Jl Jend Gatot Subroto, not far from the *Abadi Hotel*. There is also a 2nd, newer terminal, Simpang Rimbo, which is further out of town to the west. Again, colts run to the centre of town. Buses to major Sumatran towns and to Jakarta 30 hrs, Bali, Bandung and Sungai Penuh run from both terminals.

Sea Boat: boats leave from the docks on the river near the centre of town, Boom Batu and Boom Rakit. Daily boats to Kuala Tungka; slow ferry 12 hrs, speedboat 4 hrs. Also ships/boats to Batam Island and Tanjung Pinang (Bintan Island); journey time varies but averages 48 hrs. Occasional departures for Singapore and Jakarta. The best source of information about departures is the Kantor Administrator Pelabuhan (Port Administration Office) at Jl Sultan Taha 4, on the river front, or ask around the various offices at Jl Sultan Taha 2 (Pelabuhan Jambi). Pelni have an office at Jl Sultan Taha 17, T23649.

Directory **Airline offices** Mandala, Jl Gatot Subroto 155, T35108, F26169. *Merpati*, Jl Damar 55, T22184. *Garuda*, Jl Dr Wahidin 95, T22041. *SMAC*, Jl Orang Kayo Hitam 25, T22804. **Banks** *Bank Danamon*, Jl Dr Sutomo 21. *Bank Dagang Negara*, Jl K H Wahid Hasyim 8-12. **Communications** General Post Office: Jl Sultan Taha Syaifuddin 5. **Telephone Office**: Jl M Taher. **Medical facilities** General Hospital: Jl Jend Suprapto, T22364. **Useful addresses** Immigration Office: Jl Dr Sam Ratulangi 2.

Palembang

Phone code: 0711
Population: 1,400,000
Colour map 2, grid B3

Palembang sprawls across both banks of the Musi River, the two halves of the town linked by the Ampera Bridge. Palembang's commercial core, central shopping district, and most of the sights are on the north bank, in Seberang Ilir.

Ins and outs

Getting there
See Transport, page 597, for further details

Palembang is the largest city in southern Sumatra and is, consequently, well connected. The Sultan Mahmud Badaruddin II Airport is 12 km north of town and has flights to many domestic destinations. Palembang is also one of the few cities in Sumatra with a train station worth using. The Kertapati station is 4 km southwest of the city and from here there are daily trains south to surrounding towns. The bus situation is a little confusing, and many depart from the company offices rather than from a terminal as such. The main bus terminal is on Jl Kl Ronggo Wirosentiko. Boats from Boom Baru Dock leave daily for Muntok on Bangka Island.

Getting around Palembang is a large city. Town buses travel fixed routes, while colour-coded kijangs/oplets run along slightly more flexible routes. There are also becaks and unmetered taxis. Ferry boats cross the river from Tangga Buntung Dock. **Tourist offices** *Palembang City Tourist Office* is on Jl Sultan Mahmud Badaruddin II (ground floor of the Museum Budaya), T358450, some useful maps and information. *South Sumatra Tourist Office*, Jl Bay Salim 200, T357348, not very helpful. *Parpostel Tourist Office*, Jl Rajawali 22, T311345, unhelpful.

History

For years there has been debate in archaeological circles about Palembang's status. Was it really the **capital of Srivijaya**, the greatest maritime empire in Southeast Asian history, as George Coedès postulated in 1918? If so, why did the city reveal so little in the way of artefacts to indicate as much? Some scholars maintained that Coedès was wrong; others believed that the low lying, swampy land had simply enveloped what remained. The conundrum is now, it seems, solved. Work by Indonesian archaeologists in collaboration with the French scholar Pierre-Yves Manguin have uncovered a wealth of evidence in and around the city.

A second period of commercial activity and prosperity coincided with the reign of Sultan Mahmud Badaruddin I (1724-57), who built Palembang's Great Mosque (see below). The city's wealth during this period was based on the expansion of tin mining on Bangka Island and the Sultan signed an agreement with the Dutch East

India Company in which he ceded monopoly interest. The wealth allowed Sultan Mahmud to sponsor an artistic and religious revival, and Palembang became known as a centre of silk weaving and lacquer work as well as a religious centre attracting Arab migrants from the Hadhramaut in the Yemen.

When the Dutch secured direct control of Palembang in 1864, they further developed Palembang as an administrative centre serving the tin mines of Bangka Island and the plantations of the surrounding area. In more recent years, the city has emerged as the administrative oil export hub of South Sumatra.

Sights

The heart of the city is marked by the 1960s built **Ampera Bridge** which spans the Musi River and links Palembang's two halves: Seberang Ulu (upstream, south) and Seberang Ilir (downstream, north). The river is 500m wide at this point, and in total is about 600 km long. There are good views of the city from the bridge.

Within sight of the bridge, on its north side, down Jalan Jend Sudirman, is the elegant **Mesjid Agung** or **Grand Mosque**, with its fine minaret. The mosque was built in 1738 by Sultan Mahmud Badaruddin I (reigned 1724-57), and has recently been restored. Across Jalan Merdeka is the ugly **Monumen Perjuagan Rakyat Sumatera Bagian Selatan** (sensibly known as MONPERA), which commemorates the 1947 'Battle of Five Days and Nights' when the Dutch succeeded in wrenching control of the oil and coal fields around Palembang away from republican rebels. Behind this, on Jalan Sultan Mahmud Badaruddin II and almost on the river, is the **Museum Budaya Sultan Mahmud Badaruddin**. The museum was renovated in 1991 (the building dates from 1826) and contains a small collection of local and European pieces (the provincial museum is better, see below). In the grounds is a fine stone **Srivijayan Buddha**, along with a new arts and crafts market. The grounds of the museum are an important excavation site: 55,000 artefacts have been uncovered dating back to the Srivijaya period. ■ *Admission by donation, 0800-1230, 1330-1600 Mon-Thu and Sat; 0800-1100, 1330-1600 Fri. The city's tourist office occupies the ground floor of the museum.*

Immediately to the east of the Ampera Bridge, on the north bank of the Musi, is the **Pasar 16 Ilir**, a maze of streets, stalls and houses reaching down to, and over, the river (see page 596). This is Palembang's **Chinatown** and among the streets are some Chinese temples (for example, **Klenteng Kwa Sam Yo** on Jalan Sungai Lapangan Hatal and the river). Another attractive and interesting area to explore is north of the river and west of Jalan Jend Sudirman. Here, among the winding streets, are numerous **rumah limas** – traditional Palembang houses – with their distinctive roof decoration, far more attractive than the sterile example at the Provincial Museum (see below). Jalan Datuk M Akib is a particularly good place to view them.

Excursions

Museum Negeri Propensi Sumatera Selatan is a large museum, 5½ km north of town at Jalan Srivijaya 1. It has rooms exhibiting traditional houses, ceremonies, technology, and arts and crafts of South Sumatra. At the back are two traditional **limas houses**, said to be 300-years-old. They have been rebuilt four times and although originally held together with bamboo pegs are now nailed in place and incorporate much new material. Most interesting is a collection of megaliths from Lahat District and two Srivijayan stone Buddhas, under a protective awning outside the museum. Of the megaliths, note the wonderfully rounded elephant with a rider and a Dongson drum (*batu purbakala*) on its back. ■ *0800-1400 Mon-Thu and Sat; 0800-1400, 200Rp, take a kijang or town bus travelling north on Jalan Jend Sudirman (which becomes Jalan Kol H Barlian) towards 'Km 12'; ask for 'Museum' and alight just past Jalan Srivijaya – the museum is a 30-km walk off the main road.*

Hutan Wisata Puntikayu are public gardens opened in 1991, 7 km from the city centre continuing north from the turn-off for the museum along Jalan Kol H Barlian. ■ *Kijang or town bus running towards 'Km 12'.*

Boats can be hired close to the Ampera Bridge to explore the **Musi River**. The usual trip passes houseboats, takes in the Pasar 16 Ilir, and then proceeds into the countryside. Expect to pay about 5,000Rp per hour. The city tourist office recommend that visitors contact them beforehand.

The **Megaliths in Lahat District** are an overnight excursion from Palembang; it takes a day to reach the plateau and at least a day to view the sculptures and megaliths. The megaliths are scattered over the highland Pasemah Plateau about 260 km west of Palembang (see page 601). ■ *Direct bus to Pagaralam, 7 hrs; some of the megaliths are within walking distance from the town.*

Essentials

Sleeping **A** *Sanjaja*, Jl Rivai, T350634, 30% discount possible, best hotel in town. **A** *King's*, Jl Kol, Atmo 623, T362323, F313693. A/c, restaurant, central location, comfortable rooms, but over-priced. **A** *Princess Hotel*, Kompleks Ilir Barat permai, Blok D-2, no 38, T313131. A quality hotel, very comfortable. **A-B** *Lembang*, Jl Kol Atmo 16, T313476, F352472. A/c, restaurant, large, modern and centrally located hotel with no character. **A-B** *Sanjaya*, Jl Kapt A Rivai 6193, T350634/310675, F313693. A/c, restaurant, pool, central location, good facilities but cheaper rooms are poor for the price. **B** *Swarna Dwipa*, Jl Tasik 2, T313322, F362992. A/c, restaurant, pool, hotel on the west edge of town, quiet location in gardens with average rooms but friendly management. Recommended. **C** *Sari*, Jl Jend Sudirman 1301, T313320. A/c, restaurant, average rooms but allowed to deteriorate through lack of maintenance, popular with Indonesians, price includes breakfast. **C-D** *Sehati*, Jl Dr Wahidin 1, T350338. Some a/c, large rooms with separate sitting area, rather musty. **C-D** *Sintera*, Jl Jend Sudirman 38, T354618. Some a/c, a little run-down, but central, not far from Ampera Bridge. **C-D** *Sriwidjaya*, Jl Let. Kol. Iskandar 31, T355555. Some a/c, central, rooms are poorly maintained and dark, but there are enough to perhaps find one which is not too grim, price includes breakfast. **E** *Asiana*, Jl Jend Sudirman 45. Popular, simple but clean rooms; best of a poor bunch. **E** *Segaran*, Jl Segaran 207C. Popular, rooms are grubby.

● *on map*
Price codes:
see inside front cover

Eating **Cheap** *Kings Hotel*, Jl Kol Atmo 623. Rather characterless Chinese restaurant, but serves good food. *Selatan Indah*, Jl Let. Iskandar. Locals maintain this is the best Chinese restaurant in Palembang. *Sudi Mampir*, Jl Merdeka. One of the best places to sample Palembang food which is served like Padang food – you only pay for what you eat. **Very cheap** *Sari Mulia*, Jl Jend Sudirman 589. Excellent soup 'kitchen'. *Suwito*, Jl Demang Lebar Daun. Good sate. *Pagi Sore*, Jl Jend Sudirman. Padang food. **Other Asian cuisine**: *Har*, Jl Tustam Effendi. Indian Muslim food. **Foodstalls**: on Jl Jend Sudirman, west side, north from the Pasar Cinde. Cheap restaurants concentrated here as well.

● *on map*
Price codes:
see inside front cover

Entertainment **Cinemas**: *Cineplex Studio 1*, Jl Jend Surdiman 16; Internasional 21, Jl Jend Surdiman 147.

Festivals **August:** *Independence Day* (17th), *Bidar* (boat) races on the Musi in the morning, each boat carrying as many as 40 oarsmen. Commercial firms sponsor boats and village teams compete.

Shopping **Antiques**: *Mir Senen*, Jl AKBP. BM Amin (Selero) 39. **Jewellery**: traditional designs available at the Pasar 16 Ilir. **Lacquerware**: Palembang has a reputation for its lacquerware, a technique which was introduced by Chinese craftsmen. Shops including *Mekar Jaya*, Jl Slamet Riyadi 45A. **Textiles**: Palembang is a centre of *songket* weaving (see box above); *jumputan pelangi* is a tie-dyed cloth unique to Palembang. Shops including: **Sumatra Shopping Centre**, Pasar 16 Ilir; **Shopping Centre**, Jl Kol. Atmo 623; **Taras**, Jl Merdeka; **Cek Ipah**, Jl Ki Gede Lng Suro 141, 30 Ilir; and in the **Pasar 16** Ilir; *Danar Hadi*, Jl Veteran 8001B for batik. Tujuh Saudara, Jl Mahakam Blok A-7. **Woodcarving**: *H Azis*, Jl Jend Sudirman No Gang Pakis. **Shopping centres**: *Plaza International*, Jl Jend Surdiman 147; *Yogya Shopping Centre*, Jl T.P. *Rustam Effendy*; *JM Plaza and Supermarket*, Jl Letkol Iskandar 578.

Golf: *Palembang Golf Club* is on Jl AKBP Cek Agus, north of the city centre, run by the state oil company Pertamina. Non-members permitted to play; green fees are about double on Fri, Sun and public holidays. Caddies and clubs for hire. **Swimming**: large public pool, *Lumban Tirta*, on Jl Kapt A Rivai ('kampus'). Open 0800-1930 Mon-Sun.

Sports

Ista Travel, Jl Jend Sudirman 53F, T350800. *Santra*, Jl Kapt A Rivai 6193, T310675.

Tour operators

Local Becaks Town buses travel fixed routes. **Kijangs/oplets** Unmetered taxis. **Ferry boats** cross the river from Tangga Buntung Dock. **Air** Sultan Mahmud Badaruddin II Airport is 12 km north of town. *Transport to town*: unmetered taxis (fixed price) or walk onto the main road, 2 km away, to catch a minibus for a fraction of the price. Palembang is a Sumatran travel hub, with regular connections with Jakarta (several daily), Bandar Lampung, Batam, Bengkulu, Jambi, Padang, Medan and Pangkal Pinang; also connections with Dumai. **Train** Kertapati station is 4 km southwest of town, close to the Musi River. From the station, take an oplet going to Warna Kuning – they cross the river and then run along Jl Merdeka and Jl Sudirman to the centre of the city. Daily trains to Tanjungkarang (Bandar Lampung), 10

Transport
260 km from Jambi,
247 km from Bengkulu,
202 km from Lahat

Palembang

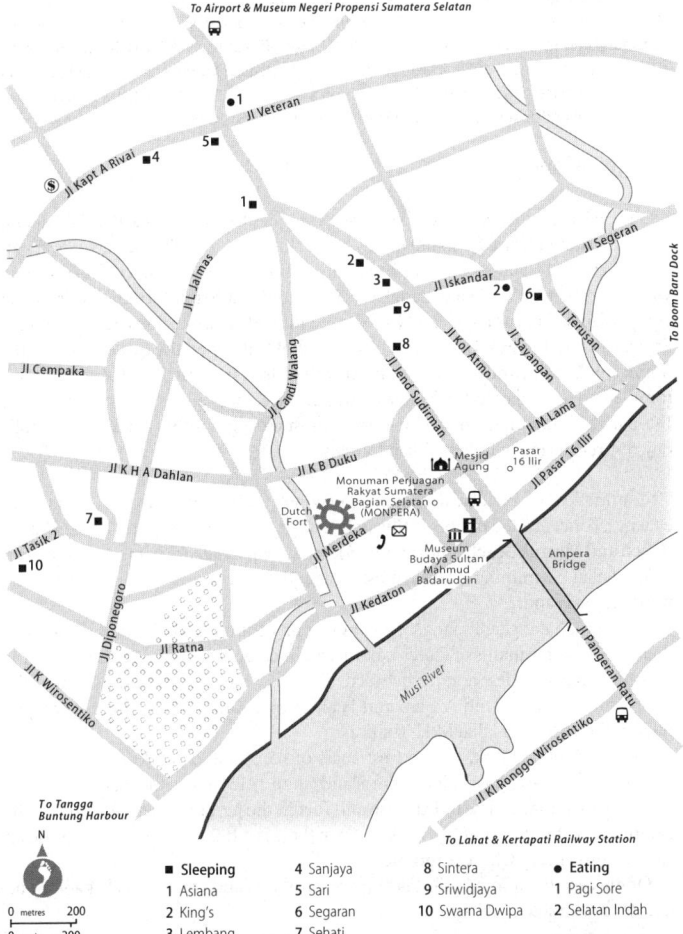

■ Sleeping
1 Asiana
2 King's
3 Lembang
4 Sanjaya
5 Sari
6 Segaran
7 Sehati
8 Sintera
9 Sriwidjaya
10 Swarna Dwipa

● Eating
1 Pagi Sore
2 Selatan Indah

hrs (36,000Rp executive with a/c and video, 17,000Rp economy); buses leave from here for Bakauheni and Jakarta. Connections with Lubuklinggau via Lahat, where there are bus connections to Padang and Lampung 9 hrs. **Road Bus**: the city's main bus terminal is on Jl Kl Ronggo Wirosentiko, not far from the southern end of the Ampera Bridge. There is also a terminal – the Tujuluh terminal – on Jl Iskandar, in the centre of the city. Express and a/c bus offices are scattered over the city; there are a number on Jl Kol Atmo (eg *Hidup Baru*, *ANS* and *Lorena*, a short distance north from the *King's Hotel*; *C V Manila* on Jl Kapt Cek Syeh 200 (off Jl Jend Sudirman); *Putra Remeja* at Jl Veteran 4887F and *Continental* at Jl Veteran 156 (just off road near intersection with Jl Jend Sudirman); *ALS* also on Jl Veteran, T20640. Regular connections with Medan, Jambi 4 hrs, Jakarta 24 hrs, Padang, Bukittinggi, Pekanbaru, Medan, Aceh, Bogor, Bali, Yogya and Solo. **Sea Boat**: *Wisin Tour*, Jl Veteran 173C, T21811, run daily fast boats from Boom Baru Dock to Muntok on Bangka Island, 3 hrs. Depart 0830; depart Muntok for return trip 1300. *KM Bahari Express* and *KM Adiyasa* also run boats to Muntok from Boom Baru at 0930 and 1000 daily, respectively. A slower ferry leaves daily from Tangga Buntung Harbour for Muntok, 13 hrs.

Directory **Airline offices** *Garuda*, Jl Kapten Ravai 20, T364405. *Mandala*, *Sanjaya Hotel*, Jl Kapt Rivai 6193, T350634, F313693. *Merpati*, *Sanjaya Hotel*, Jl Kapt Rivai 6193, T310675. *Deraya*, Jl Jend Sudirman 2954D, T353700 (for Pangkal Pinang, Bangka Island). **Banks** *Bank Indonesia*, Jl Jend Surdiman 510. *Bank Negara Indonesia*, Jl Jend Surdiman 132. *Bank International Indonesia*, Jl Letkol Iskandar 901. *Ekspor-Impor*, Jl Rustan Effendi 81. *Bank Rakyat Indonesia*, Jl Kapitan Rivai 15. **Communications** General Post Office: Jl Merdeka 3. Post Office: Jl Kapt A Rivai 63. Telephone Office: Jl Jend Sudirman. Telekom office, Jl Merdeka (next to GPO). **Medical facilities** Hospital Caritas, Jl Jend Sudirman (at intersection with Jl Kapt A Rivai). Rumah Sakit Umum (General Hospital), Jl Jend Surdiman Km 3.5. **Useful addresses** Immigration Office: Jl Major Memet Sastrawirya 1, T710055.

Bangka Island

Phone code: 0717
Colour map 2, grid B3/4

Bangka Island – shaped rather like a seahorse – lies to the northeast of Palembang and is separated from the mainland by the 20 km-wide Bangka Strait. It covers an area of about 11,500 sq km and has a population of 600,000, over two-thirds of whom are farmers. The name Bangka is said to come, rather unfortunately, from the word 'Wangka' meaning tin, and was first mentioned in inscriptions dating from the Srivijaya period (686AD). The capital is **Pangkal Pinang** on the east coast; its most important port, **Muntok**, is on the northwest coast. Formerly Bangka's wealth was founded on tin; today, as tin declines in importance, the island is turning to tourism. But Bangka is not on the travel itinerary of most western visitors – it remains a holiday resort catering mainly to Asian tourists.

Sights The attraction of Bangka to visitors today are the island's sublime white-sand beaches, concentrated on the northeast coast. Among the most popular are **Hakok Beach** and **Matras Beach**, both about 35 km north of Pangkal Pinang, past the town of Sungailiat. Swimming is safe in most areas and there is a coral reef in the bay to the north of the island.

The capital, Pangkal Pinang, has a population of about 100,000, and in the town there are a few remnants of Dutch colonial architecture to serve as reminders of the past. But sights are few and far between. There is a small **mining museum** at the intersection of Jalan Jend A Yani and Jalan Depati Amir, and a **Chinese temple**, built in the 1830s, on Jalan M H Muhidir.

The town of Muntok, on the west coast of Bangka and 125 km from Pangkal Pinang, was the original capital of the island (until 1913) and is the main ferry point for boats to Sumatra. The **lighthouse** and **fort** in the harbour area were built at the beginning of the 19th century, while in town there is a 150-year-old **mosque** and an early-19th-century **Chinese temple**.

Open-cast tin-mining still takes place on the island, from which kaolin and quartz are extracted for export.

Sleeping

In Pangkal Pinang B-D *Menumbing*, Jl Gereja 5, T22991. A/c, restaurant, pool, best in town but could do with a new manager to shake it up. **C** *Sabrina*, Jl Diponegoro 73, T22424. A/c, hot water, room rate includes breakfast. Recommended. **C-D** *Bukit Shofa*, Jl Mesjid Jamik 43, T21062. Some a/c, attached mandi, a well run place with clean rooms. **D-E** *Penginapan Srikandi*, Jl Mesjid Jamik 42, T21884. Fan and mandi, friendly management.

In Muntok (Bangka's port) **C-D** *Tin Palace Hotel*, Jl Major Syafrie Rahman 1. Some a/c, attached mandi. **E** *Losmen Muntok*, Jl Jend A Yani 42. Basic losmen accommodation.

In Sungailiat This small town has a proliferation of hotels, but there's nothing much here – it's just close to the good beaches. **A** *Citra Hotel*, Jl Jend Sudirman 343, T92494, F92386. By far the smartest place around, with a/c and hot water. **A-C** *Bangka Permai Hotel*, Jl Jend Sudirman 173, T92090. As evidenced by the price range, a choice of rooms on offer here, set in a pretty garden. **C** *Pondok Wisata Mulya*, Jl Jend Sudirman, T92157, F92111. A sophisticated homestay with a choice of rooms in an Indonesian family's home, large garden, some rooms with a/c. **D** *Wisma Flamboyan*, Jl Dr Sam Ratulangi 7, T92076. Some a/c and attached mandi.

On the beaches AL *Parai Indah Hotel*, Jl Pantai Matras, Sungailiat, T94888, F94000. A little over 12 km north of Sungailiat and close to Matras Beach. This is the biggest hotel in the area, with an ostentatious entrance. More expensive rooms are in individual cottages in the garden, cheaper ones are in a block. Set near a lovely little cove, and the restaurant overlooks it. Pool and tennis courts available for the more energetic visitor. Walk-in guests should get substantial discounts from the rack rate. **A** *Tanjung Pesona Hotel*, Jl Pantai Rebo, T92794. Large, unattractive place with disco, billiards and karaoke about 2 km north of Sungailihat. Very much for the local market, as it is packed at the weekends and deathly quiet during the week. **B** *Romodong Sea View*, on the north tip of the island, bookable from Pangkal Pinang, T21573. A/c, restaurant (with good seafood), set on a beautiful white

Bangka Island

sand bay. Wooden a/c cottages with verandahs, attached bathrooms (no hot water), attractive gardens. One of the best places on Bangka. Recommended. **D** *Beginning of Nowhere*, Jl Jend Sudirman 68/70, Sungailiat, T/F92290. Managed by a Dutch couple, a very laid back place to stay with breakfast and the use of a bicycle included. One could easily get stuck here. Recommended.

Eating Excellent seafood (several restaurants in Pangkal Pinang) and a large selection of Chinese stall food. There is also an abundance of good restaurants in Sungailiat. Two bakeries on Jl Jend Sudirman keep you in cakes.

Sports **Swimming**: pool at *Menumbing Hotel*, open to non-residents, 2,500Rp.

Tour operators The following companies are all based in Sungailiat: *MBR Tour*, Jl Jend Surdiman, T92090; *Bangka Indah*, Jl Muhidin, T92931; *Agent Indonesian Airlines*, Jl Muhidin 8, T924041; *Travel Aber Two*, Jl Muhidin, T92917.

Transport **Local** Infrequent **bus** services around the island, and between Pangkal Pinang and Muntok. **Cars** can be chartered. **Air** The airport lies 6 km south of Pangkal Pinang. Taxis available to town (6,000Rp) or to the beaches. Regular daily connections on *Merpati* with Jakarta (1 hr) and Palembang (30 mins); Indonesian Airlines has 2 connections a week with Batam and Singkep. *Deraya* offers connections with Belitung Island, Singkep and Batam, as well as with Palembang. *DBS* at Jl Jend Sudirman 10 will book tickets on Merpati and Deraya. **Sea Boat**: twice daily ferry connections with Palembang's Tangga Buntung Harbour leave from Muntok on the west coast (and 125 km from Pangkal Pinang) 13 hrs. Jetfoils also run between Muntok and Palembang, leaving Muntok twice daily in the early afternoon, 3 hrs. There are some ferries which go to Kayu Arang on the north coast and only an hour from Pangkal Pinang (and closer to the best beaches). The Pelni ship *Bukit Raya* visits Muntok every 2 weeks on its circuit between Jakarta and Medan via Batam (Pelni office, Muntok, T22743).

Directory **Airline offices** *Indonesian Airlines*, Jl Kapt Sulaiman Arif 41, T21796. *Merpati*, Jl Jend Sudirman 31, T22077. **Banks** *Bank Rakyat Indonesia*, Jl Jend Sudirman, Sungailiat. *Bank Central Asia*, Jl Depati Amir 1, Sungailiat. *BNI*, Jl Muhidin, Sungailiat. **Communications** Post Office: Jl Jend Sudirman (northern end, edge of town). Telephone office: Jl Jend Sudirman (close to post office). **Medical facilities** Hospitals: *Rumah Sakit Umum Sungailiat*, Jl Jend Surdiman, Sungailiat, T92489. **Tourist Offices** *Bangka Regional Tourist Office*, Jl Jend Sudirman, Sungailiat, T92496, or Jl Bukit Intan, T32546, Pangkal Pinang. Not much offered by these offices, except for a brochure or 2. **Useful addresses** Immigration office: Jl Taman Ican Saleh 2, T21774.

Belitung Island

Colour map 2, grid B5 This is Bangka's smaller sister island, 80 km off Bangka's southeast coast. Belitung covers an area of 4,000 sq km and has a population of about 175,000. Like Bangka, its wealth was founded on tin, and it is now turning to tourism as an alternative source of revenue as the tin mining industry declines. The capital of Belitung is Tanjung Pandan. The best beaches are found to the north of the capital. Tanjung Kelayang, 25 km north, is probably the best. ■ *Bus from Tanjung Pandan to Tanjung Binga; and then change for Tanjung Kelayang.*

Sleeping **A** *Biliton Beach Hotel*, Belitung's 1st international hotel with 300 rooms, a beach front location, large pool and tennis, T788011 or F88106 for details, part of the Aerowisata chain of hotels. In Tanjung Pandan: **A** *Martini*, Jl Yos Sudarso 17, T214432, F21433. A grand affair, with comfortable rooms, cool corridors, spacious gardens and generally friendly staff. Recommended. **D** *Wisma Dewi*, Jl Srivijaya 122, T21134. A/c, cold water only mandi. Old house with ambience, clean rooms with high-ceilinged rooms and verandahs, friendly. **At Kelayan Beach**: **D** *Kelayang Beach*.

Lahat

Lahat is not the sort of town that people choose to stop at: one just gets dumped here. Most buses plying the Trans-Sumatran highway stop-off here and sometimes it is necessary to spend the night. Lahat is also a stop-off point on the rail link between Palembang and Bandar Lampung and Lubuklinggau.

Phone code: 0731
Colour map 2, grid B2

Sleeping Hotels and losmen are almost uniformly grim and many are short-stay affairs. Inevitably there is a concentration around the train station on Jl Stasiun. But there are 1 or 2 reasonable places to bed down for the night. **B-C** *Nusantara*, Jl Mayor Ruslam III, T21336. Some a/c, central location, range of good rooms, the best place to stay. **D-E** *Permata*, Jl Mayor Ruslam III, T21642. Some a/c, this doesn't seem to have too much short stay business and is the best of the cheaper places.

Transport **Road Bus**: because most buses stop here there is an almost constant coming-and-going of vehicles. Sometimes they are full, but this is hardly a main destination and it is usually possible to find a seat. Connections with Palembang, Padang, Bandar Lampung. **Train** Lahat is a stop on the Palembang, Bandar Lampung and Lubuklinggau line.

Pagaralam

Pagaralam is a small market town about 60 km southwest of Lahat, set in the middle of the upland **Pasemah Plateau** which lies at about 600m above sea level. Its single claim to fame are the **megaliths** that lie scattered over the surrounding countryside, particularly in the paddy fields lining the road to Manna (many bemos run along this road) and on the slopes of mounts Dempo and Gumai. They include obelisks, massive enigmatic carved figures of warriors, some carrying Dongson drums, others riding on elephants or struggling with buffalo and some with helmets and swords. It is thought they were carved during the first centuries AD, although archaeologists' knowledge of their origins and meaning remains limited. The best and most accessible example lies in the beautiful gardens of a mosque, Mesjid Takwar, 3 km from town on the road to Mirasa. There is a good example of one of the megaliths in the Provincial Museum in Palembang (see page 595). A number of these massive stone carvings can be seen, literally, in among the houses of Pagaralam. Simply ask for directions. Better examples lie outside the town (see below). In addition to the stone carvings, a series of subterranean chambers have been discovered, lined with stone slabs and decorated with red, yellow and black paintings. They are assumed to have been burial chambers although no bones have been found.

Phone code: 0730
Colour map 2, grid B2

Excursions The best concentrations of the finest megaliths are to be found in the vicinity of the villages of **Muara Pinang** (7 km from town) and **Tegur Wangi** (9 km from town). Others are to be found at **Pulau Panggung** (10 km northeast of town) or at **Belumai** (4 km away). ■ *Easiest by chartered bemo.*

Mount Dempo offers a good climb. The best time to do so is between May and August. To reach the summit and back, allow two full days. A guide is strongly recommended, as trails are hard to find.

Sleeping **D** *Losmen Mirasa*, Jl Major Ruslan, T0730-21484. Friendly and helpful management with knowledge of surrounding area and megaliths, guides available for trekking, good rooms and food. **Post Office**: Jl Kapten Senap 37. **Telkom Office** next door to Post Office (24 hrs), Wartel Jl Vandrik Karim 355 (0600-2300).

Transport 260 km from Palembang, 60 km from Lahat, 328 km from Bengkulu **Road Bus**: Pagaralam lies off the Trans-Sumatran Highway; there are direct bus connections with Palembang, 7 hrs and Bengkulu, 5 hrs. A direct bus to Lampung leaves daily at midday.

Bengkulu

Phone code: 0736
Population: 1,300,000
Colour map 3, grid B2

Bengkulu is the capital of the Bengkulu province. Although few tourists visit the town, it is one of the most attractive in Sumatra. Bengkulu retains a large proportion of its colonial architectural inheritance and has not been scarred by insensitive redevelopment. Attractive wooden houses with raised porches, verandahs and elaborate fretwork still grace much of the town. It is also comparatively clean and uncluttered. Vehicles seem to be fewer and to be driven with less recourse to the horn, while the inhabitants are friendly and have time to spare for the few foreigners who make it here.

Ins and outs

Getting there
See Transport section for further details

Bengkulu's Kemiling Airport is 14 km from town with flights in and around Sumatra. The main Panorama bus terminal is 7 km east of town; regular bemos link it with the central market. Most bus companies have their offices on Jl Haryono. The Perintis ship *Baruna Dwipa* docks at Baai Harbour about 15 km south of town and there are also weekly boats to Enggano Island from here.

Getting around Bengkulu is probably the smallest provincial capital in Sumatra. Bemos run fixed routes around town.

History

Bengkulu was originally known as *Bencoolen*. The English East India Company established a trading post here in 1685, building York Fort near Muara Air to protect their claim (of which nothing remains). For nearly 150 years, Bengkulu remained Britain's only colony in Southeast Asia. By the 18th century – and despite the population being periodically decimated by malaria – the port had become an important centre for the pepper trade. However, with the downturn in the pepper market in the 19th century, the town lost its economic *raison d'être*, and became a backwater. Perhaps because of the undemanding nature of administration in Bengkulu, the British residents dispatched to the colony turned their attention to the surrounding countryside instead. Both Sir William Marsden (1771-79) and Sir Stamford Raffles (1817-24) were residents of Bengkulu and both contributed significantly to contemporary knowledge of Sumatra. In 1824 the British and Dutch signed the Treaty of London, exchanging Bengkulu for Melaka and rationalizing their spheres of influence in the region.

In contemporary Indonesia, Bengkulu has acquired a degree of fame in being the town where Sukarno was placed under house arrest between 1933 and 1942, the Dutch no doubt believing that being such a quiet and inaccessible town it was the perfect place to 'lose' him.

Sights

Overlooking the sea on Jalan Benteng is **Fort Marlborough** or Benteng Marlborough. Dating from 1715 and approached through massive walls, it is an impressive and well-maintained piece of history – reputedly the strongest fort constructed by the British in the east after George Fort in Madras. Graves of British soldiers can be found here and there are reasonable views from the ramparts. Sukarno was incarcerated in Fort Marlborough when he was banished into internal exile by the Dutch in 1933; his bare quarters are marked. Despite the size of the fort's defences, it was twice overwhelmed, in 1719 by local rebels and in 1760 by the

French. Malaria also took its toll and few soldiers or administrators made it back to Britain. ■ *0800-1900, 500Rp.*

Just up the hill from the fort is the **Pasar Barukoto**, a large covered market. It faces onto a **classical British monument** built by Stamford Raffles – who was resident from 1817 to 1824 – to a previous resident, **Thomas Parr**. Parr was stabbed to death and then decapitated by dissatisfied Bugis officers in 1807. The monument and market overlook **Chinatown** or *Kampung Cina*, which includes many of the town's older colonial buildings, among them the former **British Residency** (1760). This gazetted building – until recently an overgrown ruin – is being restored at a leisurely pace. Within sight of the Parr Monument is the **Proklamasi Monument**, in the centre of a large, grassed square. Behind this is the elegant **Balai Kota** (the current Governor's residence), at the intersection of Jalan Jend A Yani and Jalan Ir Indra Caya.

A five minute walk from the Parr Monument, on Jalan Veteran which runs off Jalan Jend A Yani, is the orange corrugated iron-roofed **Gereja Kristen Protestan** or Protestant Church. Behind the church and in the compounds of the surrounding government offices are the unloved tombs and graves of British and Dutch colonists, distorted by earthquakes.

On Jalan Sukarno-Hatta, a 10 minute walk from the town centre, is a stark-white **mosque** designed, apparently, by Sukarno. At each of its four corners stand slender minarets, and the main body of the building is surmounted by five domes. A short distance south from the mosque is **Sukarno's house** – or Rumah Bung Karno – where he lived with his wife and children for part of the time of his period of internal exile in Bengkulu. The house has been turned into a museum and displays assorted Sukarno memorabilia. ■ *0800-1700, 250Rp.*

Pantai Panjang or 'Long Beach' (7 km in all) begins about 1 km from Kampung Cina, and runs along the South coast. A 200Rp toll is levied for driving and walking along Jalan Samudera. It is a romantic place to wander in the evenings, and interesting in the morning, when the fishing boats come in. Hardly on a par with the best beaches in Indonesia, but it has the advantage of being largely deserted during the week. Swimming not recommended because of strong surf and currents. Some accommodation is available (see below).

A long hike to the east of the town centre is **Bengkulu Museum** on Jalan Musium, located on the south side of the main road in Bengkulu, a good walk from the centre. The museum contains an extensive range of exhibits relating to Bengkulu Province. ■ *0800-1300 Tue-Thu, Sun; 0800-1030 Fri; 0800-1200 Sat.*

Excursions

Bengkulu was something of a base for naturalists during the 19th century. Stamford Raffles, while he was resident, decided that as there was so little else to do he would turn his attention to the 'great volume of nature' in Sumatra. He discovered the magnificent, even monstrous, Rafflesia flower – the largest in the world. The flower can be found growing in two locations off the road running east towards Palembang – outside **Tabapenanjung** and **Kepahiang**. They usually flower between September and November, for a few weeks only. Check at the PHPA Office, Jalan Mahoni 11 before venturing out. ■ *Bus from the Terminal Panorama.*

Rafflesia flower

Curup is a hill town 63 km northeast of Bengkulu on the main road over the Bukit Barisan to Palembang. About 19 km east of Curup town is the active Mount Raba. Rising to a height of 1,937m, its **12 craters** smoulder menacingly. A road runs from the foot of the mountain. There are a number of losmen in Curup and one reasonable hotel – **C-D** *Aman Jaya*, Jalan Dr AK Gani 10, T21365, some a/c, spacious rather overpriced rooms and a good base for exploring the surrounding countryside. **B-C** *Mira Hotel*, Jl Letjen Suprapto 10, T0732-21506. All rooms have attached mandi (cold water shower). A friendly place in a quiet situation. ■ *Catch a bus running towards Palembang.*

Curup & Mount Raba

Megaliths of Pagaralam

The megaliths of Pagaralam are to be found near the small market town of Pagaralam about 60 km southwest of Lahat, over the Bukit Barisan, and 328 km from Bengkulu. In and around the town are numerous megaliths (see page 601). Accommodation available. ■ *The trip really requires an overnight stay in Pagaralam; direct buses from Bengkulu, 5 hrs; also taxis from Bengkulu to Pagaralam.*

Essentials

Sleeping
■ on map
Price codes:
see inside front cover

In town: **AL-A** *Hotel Rio Asri*, Jl Veteran 63, T21952, F25728, rio-asri@ bengkulu.wasantara.net.id This is a new upmarket hotel, with TV, pool, gym, telephone, minibar, a/c, spacious and green (their apt motto is 'the green place to feel at home'). The restaurant offers international and Indonesian cuisine. **B** *Garden Inn*, Jl Kartini 25, T21952. A/c, pool, friendly management, attractive situation, central. Recommended. **B** *Hotel Sempaka*, Jl Sutoyo 135, T21661, F24859. Restaurant, satellite TV, a/c, telephone, hot water, spotlessly clean, unfortunately it is a long walk out of town. **B** *Hotel Tiara*, Jl Sutoyo 96, T21098. Comfortable rooms, satellite TV, a/c, but dingy bathrooms. Better places are available in this price range. **B-C** *Dena*, Jl Fatmawati 29, T21981. A/c, comfortable, but slightly out of town and overpriced. **B-C** *Hotel Niagu*, Jl S. Parman 408, T26569. Rooms with a/c, satellite TV, in the process of being redecorated in summer 1999, lack of circulating air, next to busy street and somewhat overpriced. **C** *Asia*, Jl Jend A Yani 922B, T21901. A/c, restaurant, large rooms, central location. **C** *Samudera Dwinka*, Jl Jend Sudirman 246, T21604. Some a/c, friendly and central, price includes breakfast. Recommended. Tours and car charter arranged. **C-E** *Hotel Vista*, Jl Mt Haryono 67, T20820, fairly close to the centre. Clean, breakfast available. **D** *Hotel SS*, Jl Mt. Harong 70, T22116. Basic and set back from the road so is

Bengkulu

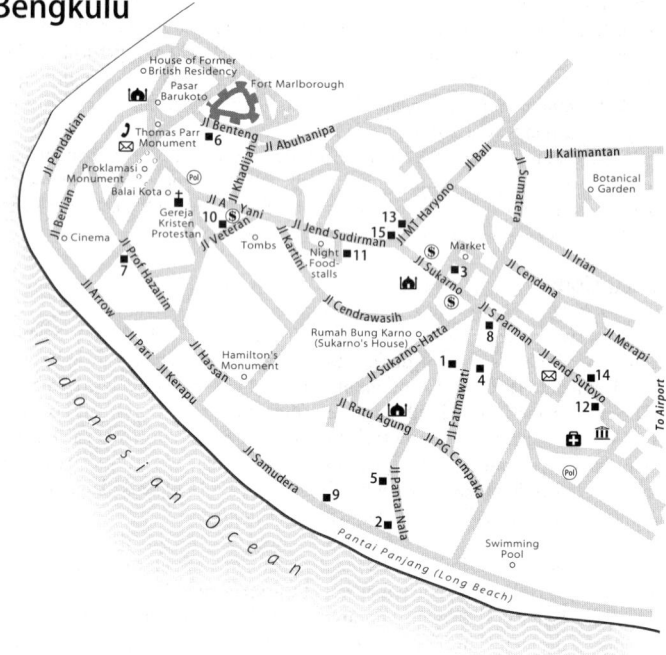

Not to scale

■ **Sleeping**
1 Bumi Indah
2 Cottage Permata Gading Resort
3 Damai
4 Denah
5 Horizon
6 Losmen Samudera
7 Malabero
8 Niagu
9 Pantai Panjang
10 Rio Asri
11 Samudera Dwinka
12 Sempaka
13 SS
14 Tiara
15 Vista

pleasantly quiet. **D** *Wisma Balai Buntar*, Jl Khadijah 122, T21254. Spacious rooms with en suite showers (hot water) and a/c. **E** *Bumi Indah*, Jl Fatmawati 29, T21665, F342451. A/c, out of town centre, average rooms, with TV, laundry and also includes breakfast. **E** *Damai*, Jl K Z Abidin 18 (Chinatown), T21439. Cheap, in the bustling market, this place does not come recommended, especially with better options in this range. **E** *Hotel Malabero*, Jl Prof. Hazairin 23, T21004. Simple yet comfortable with mandis. **E** *Losmen Samudera*, Jl Benteng 213, T21321, in the shadow of Fort Marlborough so good position. Dirty rooms but one of the cheapest places. **E** *Surya*, Jl K Z Abidin 26 (Chinatown), T21341. **E** *Wisma Kenanga*, Jl Let. Kol. Santoso, T21709. Attractive colonial house with only average rooms. **F** *Ragil Kuning Guesthouse*, Jl Kenanga 44, T22682. A pleasant relaxed place with an attractive open air restaurant. Although it is a little way out of town, bemos run close by (ask for 'skip'), note that rates are per person not per room, so a room for 2 would push this into the **E** category.

On the beach (4 km from town): **A-B** *Hotel Horizon*, Jl Pantai Nala 142, T21722, F22072, hori.bkl@bengkulu.wasantara.net.id A/c, pool, rivalling *Hotel Rio Asri* for comfort, this is a quality hotel but rather characterless. **B-C** *Hotel Pantai Panjang*, Jl Pantai Nala, right on the beach. A series of bungalows full of character, 3 types varying from the luxurious 'Bougenvile' with a/c, hot water, bath, to the economy 'Rose'. Short distance from town, and quiet. **C** *Cottage Permata Gading Resort*, Jl Pantai Nala 133, T21855, F21915. Formerly the *Nala Seaside Cottages*, but now under new management led by the enthusiastic and cheerful Rozie. Series of self-contained bungalows, a/c, satellite TV, restaurant, roomy and comfortable next to the beach. Recommended.

Eating

There are a number of restaurants along Jl Jend Sudirman (which becomes Jl Suprapto), including *Pak Liha* at No 215 and *Simpang Raya* at 380a (serving Padang food). The *Citra*, also on Jl Jend Sudirman, serves Chinese and Javanese food. There is a **bakery** (the *New Holland*) at Jl Suprapto 85 and another one – the *Gandhi* – at Jl Suprapto 6a. There are many **foodstalls** on Jl Jend Sudirman, some with excellent and cheap seafood.

Entertainment

Cinemas: 2 a/c cinemas on Jl Jend Sudirman.

Festivals

Jul: *Tabot* (movable): extends over 10 days and celebrates the martyrdom of Hussin and Hassan, two of Mohammad's grandsons. Effigies of Bouraq, a winged horse, are carried in procession with music and dancing. One of the most colourful and extravagant festivals in Sumatra.

Shopping

Handicrafts: rattan products and the local batik *besurek*. There is a handicraft shop between the *Nala Seaside Cottages* and Pantai Nala Samudra. The best place to see besurek is to visit the workshops at Jl Ciliwung Bawah 2, T25420. Take a bemo to Billar Pasir Putih (past Padang Harapan roundabout) and walk a short distance down a lane to the workplace. **Shopping centres**: *Puncak*, Jl Suprapto 28. Good for essentials.

Sports

Swimming: although the sea is dangerous for swimming, the *Hotel Horizon's* pool is open to non-residents at 5,000Rp per person. **Golf**: *Lampangan Golf Course* on Jl Rustandi, southeast of town, open to non-members.

Tour operators

CSH 88 Travel, Jl Suprato 88, T22385, 23088. *SAN Travel*, Jl Mt Haryono, T21811. *PT Diyo Siba*, Jl Kenanga 99, T22682. *PT Sari Bengkulu Indah*, Jl Mt Haryono 14, T22460, 22824. *PT MV Assik Tour and Travel*, Jl Jend A Yani 922, 21119. *PT Nala Tour and Travel*, Jl S Parman, T25578, 21855.

Transport

560 km from Padang, 460 km from Palembang

Local The inter-provincial and local **bus** station is Terminal Panorama, about 7 km from town; get there by **bemo** from the central market. Bemos run fixed routes around town, or they can be chartered. **Air** Kemiling Airport is 14 km from town. Connections on Merpati with Jakarta, Bandar Lampung, Batam, Palembang (check availability), Jambi, Medan and Padang. *Transport to town*: by taxi; or walk out onto the road and catch a bus or bemo. **Road Bus**: the Terminal Panorama is 7 km east of town; regular bemos link it with the central market. Most bus companies have their offices on Jl Haryono (also known as Jl Bali), including: *Citra Rafflesia*, Jl M T Haryono, 12 operate a/c and non-a/c buses to Jakarta 22 hrs, Padang 24 hrs, Palembang 16 hrs and other destinations in Java and Sumatra. *Indah Tour and Travel*, Jl M T Haryono 14, and *Sriwijaya Express*, Jl Haryono 36, operate buses to Muko Muko and Sungai Penuh. There is also a 2nd and newer terminal – the Sebakul terminal – more than 10 km southeast of the city centre. Currently this is not really being used, but services may be transferred here at some point in the future. **Sea Boat**: there are weekly boats to Enggano Island from Baai Harbour about 15 km south of town. A Perintis ship links Enggano with Bengkulu. The Pelni office is at Jl Khadijah 10, T21013.

Directory **Airline offices** *Garuda*, Jl Jend A Yani 922B, T21119. *Mandala*, Jl Sukarno Hatta 39, T25437. *Merpati*, *Samudera Dwinka Hotel*, Jl Jend Sudirman 246, T27111. **Banks** Bank Central Asia, Jl Suprapto 138. *Bumi Daya*, Jl R. Hadi 1. Bank BNI, Jl S. Parman. **Communications** General Post Office: Jl S Parman 111 (south edge of town). A more convenient branch office is at Jl Jend A Yani. **Post Office:** Jl RA Hadi 3 (facing the Parr Monument), and more central than the GPO. **Telephone Office:** Jl Suprapto 132 (24 hrs), Jl Kol Barlian 51 (next to Post Office). **Medical facilities** General Hospital: Jl Padang Harapan, T21118. **Useful addresses** Immigration Office: Jl Padang Harapan. **PHPA:** Jl Mahoni 11 (for permits to local National Park).

Muko Muko

Phone code: 0737 This is the largest settlement on the long stretch of road between Bengkulu and Sungai Penuh/Tapan, and is a good place to stop on the route north to Padang or south to Bengkulu. The town overlooks the coast and sea and there are the remains of **Benteng (Fort) Anna Victoria**, built between 1798 and 1810, to root around. Also here is the grave of an English youth who met an untimely end aged 18 in 1776. Swimming is not recommended for women because of the likely unwarranted attention – few foreigners come through here, let alone stop for a swim.

Sleeping **C-D** *Wisma Teratai*, Jl Sudirman 9, T71009. Situated 4 km outside Muko Muko on the road from Tapan. More expensive rooms with en suite mandis. Small restaurant next door. **D** *Wisma Pantai Indah*, Jl Koto Zaya, T71059, located 200m from the main square across the bridge, set back off the main road to Bengkulu.

Transport **Road Bus**: connections with Tapan 2 hrs, Sungai Penuh, Padang 8-9 hrs and Bengkulu 8 hrs. Buses to Bengkulu along this route start in Padang and do not arrive until the evening. Instead of waiting, catch a bemo to Ipuh 2 hrs (5,000Rp), and then a minibus to Bengkulu 6 hrs (6,500Rp).

Directory **Communications** Post Office: Jl Jend Sudirman (by the main square). **Useful addresses** Police: Jl Jend Sudirman (by the main square).

Enggano Island

Colour map 2, grid C2 Enggano Island is about 100 km off the west coast of Sumatra, and is one of the least visited spots in Indonesia. There is excellent snorkelling, peaceful villages and jungle walks. It is said the name *Enggano* is derived from the Portuguese for 'disappointment'; they had hoped it would be clothed in valuable clove trees – it was not. Some knowledge of Bahasa essential.

Sleeping **E-F** *Losmen Apaho*, Malakoni. The only official place to stay although locals will allow visitors to stay, in their homes – ask the *kepala desa* (village headman) on arrival.

Transport **Boat** Irregular connections with Bengkulu's Baai Harbour about 15 km south of town. Alternatively, boats can be chartered at Bintuhan, a port to the south of Bengkulu near the border with Lampung province. The Pelni vessel *Lawit* also calls here on its fortnightly circuit between Java, Sumatra and Kalimantan.

Bandar Lampung

Bandur Lampung has the rather unfortunate reputation of being a transit point where people touch base but don't engage. As a result there is a good range of facilities but not much of a heart. The fact that Bandar Lumpung is two towns merged into one hasn't helped.

Phone code: 0721
Colour map 2, grid C3

Ins and outs

Bandar Lampung's airport is 24 km north of the city at Branti, with flights to Jakarta, Palembang, Jambi and Padang. The train station has departures north to Palembang and from there to Lubuklinggau via Lahat. The Rajabasa bus terminal serves destinations to the north from Palembang to Banda Aceh (a bone-shaking and bum-numbing 72 hrs), as well as Jakarta via the ferry at Bakauheni. Pelni ships dock at Panjang, Bandar Lampung's port.

Getting there
See Transport section for further details

Buses and pale blue bemos run between the city's 2 'halves' and onto the Rajabasa bus terminal, north of town. Bemos can be chartered and there are also taxis and some care hire firms. **Tourist offices** *Tourist Office*, Jl Kh Dahlan 21, T251900. Also helpful is the *Lampung Provincial Tourist Association*, Jl WR Suptratman 39, T482565, F482081, fluent in English, Dutch and French, open: 0800-1500 Mon-Thu, closed Sat and Sun.

Getting around

Background

Tanjungkarang, a hillside administrative centre and **Telukbetung**, the port 5 km to the south, are the twin cities of Lampung province and have recently been amalgamated and renamed **Bandar Lampung**. Telukbetung was almost entirely destroyed by the tidal wave which followed the eruption of Krakatau.

Today Lampung is one of the poorest provinces in Indonesia, a consequence – in part – of the numbers of transmigrants who have been settled here from Java. Annual population growth was over 5% in the 1970s, and now the province has more than 6,000,000 inhabitants, a degraded environment, and severe poverty. It is claimed only one in 10 of Lampung's inhabitants were born in the province.

Sights

As a major transit point, there is a good range of accommodation, but few sights. The **Provincial Museum** is situated on Jalan Teuku Umar, and has a small collection of local *kain tapis* – or 'ship cloths' – and archaeological and ethnographic pieces. ■ *0800-1230, 1330-1600 Mon-Thu and Sat; 0800-1100, 1330-1600 Fri.*

Tours can be arranged, see page 609

Pasir Putih is the closest good beach to the city, situated 19 km south on the road to Bakauheni. ■ *Take a minibus to Telukbetung and then another to Pasir Putih, 1,000Rp.* Rather further afield is **Merak Belantung**, 43 km south of town; this is a beautiful sandy beach, good for swimming, with facilities for windsurfing. Accommodation available. ■ *Bus to Panjang and then on towards Bakauheni.* **Marina Beach** is located about 1½ km from the town, has fishing, surfing and good swimming. ■ *Rajabasa bus terminal heading to Kalianda, 10,000Rp.*

Beaches

Mount Rajabasa lies about 80 km south of Bandar Lampung and close to Bakauheni. A scenic road runs around the south slopes of this dormant volcano. The route to Mount Rajabasa passes through **Canti**, where it is possible to take the ferry to the small islands of **Sebuku** and **Sebesi**, or to charter a boat to **Krakatoa** (three hours).

Mount Rajabasa

This park is situated about 40 km northeast of town. This fortified town is thought to date from the 12th to the 17th century, and among the remains are megaliths and stepped temples. It was discovered in the 1950s by transmigrants who had moved to the area. There is a small museum 1 km from the site. ■ *The site is about*

Pugung Raharjo Archaeological Park

2½ km north (left) off the main road; catch a bus to the Rajabasa terminal and then a bus running towards Sribawono, and alight after the road crosses the Sekampung River; then walk.

Way Kambas National Park & Elephant Reserve Way Kambas National Park and Elephant Reserve (Way meaning water in Indonesian) occupies a 1,300 sq km expanse of low-lying land bordering the Sunda Strait and Java Sea. The park was first delimited as a Protection Forest by the Dutch in 1924, who upgraded its status to a Game Reserve in 1937. It was finally declared a National Park in 1982 – making it one of the oldest protected areas in Indonesia. Even so, much of the area has been partially logged over the years and only one fifth remains as forest. It is best known for its large population of elephants – about 450 – and its elephant training school. Fauna also includes a number of primates including macaques, gibbons, langurs and siamangs, as well as other large mammals such as small populations of tapir, Sumatran tiger, wild dog, Sumatran rhino, clouded leopard and honey bear. 300 species of bird have been identified, among them the rhinoceros hornbill and white-winged duck. Bird-watching trips on the Kanan River are popular. The park office is at Tridatu, about 10 km north of Jepara; permits are issued here. The Elephant Training Camp is the most popular tourist attraction and is situated at Kadangsari. Sleep can be had at **D** *Way Kanan Resort*, Way Kanan, 13½km into the park on the **Way Kanan River**. Basic accommodation in chalet huts. Mosquito nets provided. Bring your own food and drink. No cooking facilities. In the early morning you can see wild deer and wild pig wondering through the resort. Herds of wild elephants have also been known to visit.
■ *By vehicle (30 mins), take an ojek from the park entrance, boat trips can be arranged through the PHPA warden, expensive for such a short trip, but well worth it just to see the abundance of bird life.*

Bukit Barisan Selatan National Park This national park straddles the southernmost section of the Barisan range of mountains and includes 120 km of coast. A road runs west from Bandar Lampung to the town of **Kota Agung** (about 80 km), on the edge of the park. Fauna include Sumatran tigers, elephants, honey bear, rhinoceros, pigs and pheasant, as well as some rare flora including the famous rafflesia flower. ■ *The easiest entry point into the park is via Kota Agung (accommodation available); regular buses from Bandar Lampung, 2 hrs.*

Essentials

Sleeping
Price codes: see inside front cover

Walking down Radan Intan there are plenty of hotels catering for mid-range pockets. The real budget places are found along Jl Kota Raja, whereas the pricey places are located between Telukbetung and Tanjungkarang.

L-AL *Sheraton*, Jl W Monginsidi 175, T486666, F246690. A/c, restaurant, pool, good sports facilities including tennis and fitness centre, top class, low-rise hotel set around a swimming pool, by far the best in town with 110 rooms. **A** *Hotel Kartika*, Jl KH Ahmad Dahlan 86, T487994, F485413. Very shabby for a hotel asking these prices. **A** *Hotel Sahid Bandar Lampung*, Jl Yos Sudarso 294, T488888, F486589, sahid@lampung.wasantara.net.id A/c, restaurant, pool, on the beach, worth paying extra for the sea/pool view and also slightly quieter. **B** *Hotel Indra Puri*, Jl W Monginsidi 70, T258258, F262440. A/c, rooms are well appointed, situated on a hill with good views. **B** *Hotel Arinas*, Jl Raden Intan 35A, T26678, F258645. A very comfortable hotel situated in the centre of town but set back off the road, friendly staff. Recommended. **B** *Marcopolo*, Jl Dr Susilo 4, T262511, F254419. A/c, restaurant, large pool, set on the hill with good views and friendly management, best of the mid-range hotels. **B-C** *Hotel Pacific*, T46874. Rooms surround an attractive water garden. **C** *Hotel Andalas*, Jl Raden Intan 89, T263432, F261481. Comfortable, rather dated furnishings. **C** *Kurnia Perdana Hotel*, Jl Raden Intan 144, T262030, F262924. Some a/c, includes breakfast, economy rooms a little dingy. **C-D** *Andalas*, Jl Raden Intan 89, T263432. Some a/c, comfortable but characterless. **C-D** *Hotel Kartini Jaya*, Jl Kartini 41, T23939. Some a/c. **C-E** *Hotel Ria*, Jl Kartini, T253974. Some a/c, basic, more expensive rooms overpriced. **D** *Hotel Purnama*, Jl Raden Intan 77-79, T251447/8, F253672. Good place, some a/c, at this price a good deal and well managed. **D-E** *Kurnia Dua*, Jl Raden Intan 75, T252905, F261985. Basic. **E** *Penginapan Berkah*, Jl Kota Raja 19. This place does not come recommended.

Eating
Price codes: see inside front cover

An abundance of Padang food restaurants here – even more than usual – but also some excellent Chinese, seafood and European food too – the *Sheraton* and *Hotel Sahid Bandar Lampung* both have good, but expensive, restaurants.

International Very cheap *Cookies Corner*, Jl Kartini 29. Good burgers and salads, as well as Chinese and Indonesian food. **Padang** *Begadang II*, Jl Diponegoro. Also serves other Indonesian food. Recommended. *Restaurant Garuda*, great food, one of the more professional set-ups, also comes recommended (cheap). **Chinese**: *Khuai Lok*, Jl Kartini 26. **Foodstalls**: Jl Yos Sudarso in the evenings. *Pasar Mambo*, south end of Jl W Monginsidi. Evening stalls selling excellent seafood and Chinese food.

Entertainment

Cinema: (4 screens), showing rather old films, located in the Artomoro Shopping Centre, Jl Kartini, which also houses *McDonald's*.

Festivals

Aug (late): *Krakatoa Festival*, celebrates the great eruption and includes exhibitions, traditional Lampung dancing and singing, swimming and fishing competitions.

Shopping

Textiles: Lampung is best known for its fine traditional textiles. Good examples are harder and harder to find though; try the **Lampung Art Shop**, Jl Kartini 12 (Tanjungkarang). **Shopping centres**: Artomoro on Jl Kartini, at junction with Jl S Parman.

Tour operators

Elendra Tour and Travel, Jl Sultan Agung 32, T704737, F704888, arranges weekend tours to the attractions and sights in and around the town (125,000Rp per person). *Sahid Gema Wisata*, Sahid Krakatau Hotel, Jl Yos Sudarso 29A, T246589. *Krakatau Lampung Wisata Tours and Travel*, attached to the *Sheraton*, T252697.

Transport
90 km from Bakauheni

Local Bus, **minibus** and **bemos**: buses and pale blue bemos run between Telukbetung, Tanjungkarang and the busy main Rajabasa bus terminal, north of town. Both intra and inter-provincial buses leave from Rajabasa. Bemos can also be chartered (about 20,000Rp per hr). **Car rental** *Avis* at the *Sheraton Hotel*. **Taxis** hang around the more expensive hotels.

Air The airport is at Branti, 24 km north of the city. Taxis run passengers into town (20,000Rp). Regular connections on Merpati with Jakarta, Palembang, Jambi and Padang.

Train The station is on the north side of town in Tanjungkarang. Three trains a day leave for Palembang at 0830 and 1030 and 2100 (economy 16,000Rp, executive 35,000Rp), the best way to get there. Worth paying the extra for a/c, reclining seats and VCD player, despite questionable selection of videos, but passes the 9 hr journey. From Palembang there are trains to Lubuklinggau via Lahat, or buses to various other Sumatran destinations (see **Palembang**). If intending to travel straight on by train to Lubuklinggau, get off at Prabumulih – the Lubuklinggau train stops here.

Road Bus: the Rajabasa terminal lies 10 km north of town. Constant minibuses run there from town. Bus companies have their offices at the terminal and a/c and non-a/c buses leave for Palembang (65,000Rp a/c, 17,500Rp non a/c), Jambi 30 hrs, Padang 36 hrs (85,000Rp a/c, 55,000Rp non a/c), Bukittinggi 38 hrs, Sibolga 48 hrs, Medan 60 hrs (135,000Rp a/c, 85,000Rp non a/c), Banda Aceh 72 hrs and Jakarta via the ferry at Bakauheni 8 hrs. Buses to Bakauheni ferry terminal leave regularly from the station.

Pickpockets are known to operate here

Sea Boat: Pelni ships dock at Panjang, Bandar Lampung's port, on its fortnightly circuit.

610 BANDAR LAMPUNG: ESSENTIALS

Directory **Airline offices** *Merpati Airlines*, Jl A Yani 88, T263526. **Banks** Cashing TCs is troublesome in Bandar Lampung, some banks apparently never having seen a TC before, others insisting you have your 'purchasing agreement' before they will transact, while still others offer poor rates of exchange. Bank BCA, Jl Yos Sudarso 100. **Communications** Post Office: Jl Kh Dahlan 21, including internet. **Telephone Office:** Jl Majapahit 1. **Useful addresses** Hospital: *Rumah Sakit Immanuel*, Jl Dr Rivai, T704900.

Kalianda Kalianda is a little visited market town, just off the road between Panjang and Bakauheni, with hot springs and good street food. To visit **Krakatoa**, you could base yourself here for a night. Take a basic diesel fishing boat from **Canti** – three hours – and you should be able to land on Anak Krakatau (safer to visit in dry season). You must take all provisions with you, and boats are devoid of lifejackets or even seats. There is a handful of hotels at the northern end of town. **D** *Bintang Selatan*, family run with no restaurant. Transport to town on motorcycle pillion.

Bakauheni Bakauheni, situated at Sumatra's southeast tip, is the ferry port for Java. Ferries ply the 27 km-wide **Sunda Strait** to **Merak** every hour or so, within sight of Krakatau (only on a very clear day). There is little here, although the 90 km trip north to Bandar Lampung passes through attractive scenery.

Transport 90 km from Bandar Lampung. **Road Bus** From the terminal to Bandar Lampung 2 hrs (15,000Rp). **Sea Boat** Regular car ferries link Bakauheni with Merak, West Java. Times of departure vary through the year, but normally there are between 15 and 30 crossings per day (fewer at night), 2 hrs. Passengers should be ready for a hot and crowded crossing – there are 3 classes, and it is worth paying extra 1,000Rp for 1st class. Buses and share taxis wait at the ferry terminal to take passengers on to the main Rajabasa bus terminal in Bandar Lampung, or to the city centre. For greater comfort, a fast hydrofoil ferry runs regularly, taking about 40 mins (a/c available).

Background

History

Pre-Colonial kingdoms: Srivijaya, Melayu & Aceh

Sumatra does not have as rich a history as Java, but one great empire did evolve here – Srivijaya, or 'Glorious Victory'. Srivijaya was possibly the greatest of all Southeast Asia's maritime empires. Founded during the 7th century, it aggressively expanded its influence so that by the 9th century Srivijaya controlled all Sumatra, West Java, the east portion of Borneo and the Malay Peninsula as far North as South Thailand. In total, Srivijaya was the dominant power in the area for 350 years, from 670-1025, finally dissolving in the 14th century. With its capital at Palembang on the Musi River in Southeast Sumatra, Srivijaya was in a strategic position to control trade through the two most important straits in Southeast Asia: the Melaka Strait between the Malay Peninsula and Sumatra, and the Sunda Strait between Sumatra and Java. (Archaeologists have presumed that with Sumatra still accreting eastwards, over a thousand years ago Palembang must have been significantly closer to the coast.) Palembang offered exhausted seafarers an excellent harbour and repair facilities, and an ample selection of recreational activities. In this last respect, the city acted in a manner not unlike latter-day Bangkok during the Vietnam War.

In order to exploit its position, the rulers of Srivijaya built up an impressive fleet with which they suppressed piracy in the Strait of Melaka. This gave traders the confidence to forego the more arduous – but safer – overland route across the Kra Isthmus. In a rather less humanitarian fashion, the fleet also forced all shipping passing through the strait to pay exorbitant taxes – an element of Srivijayan foreign policy which infuriated seafarers. With their stranglehold on trade that flowed through the region, Srivijaya's wealth and power expanded.

The Arab geographers Ibn Khurdadhbih (writing in 846) and Abu Zaid (writing in 916) record the custom of Srivijayan Maharajas 'communicating with the sea'. Each day, the

Maharaja would propitiate the ocean by throwing a gold bar into the water, saying "Look, there lies my treasure" – and in so doing demonstrating his debt to the waters. When the Maharaja died, the gold bars would be dredged from the river bed and distributed to the royal family, military commanders, and to the ruler's other subjects. Foreign accounts of Srivijaya – and these are the only records that historians have to draw on – paint a picture of a kingdom of almost mythical wealth.

However, for an empire of such apparent size and wealth, there was – until very recently – surprisingly little physical evidence of its existence. Few temples, inscriptions, or fine art survives. Why this should be so has concentrated scholars' minds ever since the French archaeologist George Coedès identified Palembang as the capital of the empire in 1918. Some have argued that the lack of physical evidence is an indication that Srivijaya was, in fact, a kingdom of little consequence. However, most historians and archaeologists find this hard to believe. It may be that the politico-religious amalgam of indigenous symbols and Hindu-Buddhist legitimacy required few physical monuments; or because this portion of Sumatra is so swampy and unstable, that much of the evidence has simply been lost or merely overlooked. Buildings were constructed of wood, and most edicts were probably recorded on *lontar* palm paper – neither would have survived the intervening years in such a hot and humid environment. Recent work in Palembang has, however, helped to shed some light on the problem. Indonesian and French archaeologists have uncovered several tonnes of artefacts from multiple sites in the city and demonstrated that Palembang was, indeed, the capital of Srivijaya. They argue that the conundrum is not hard to solve: the archaeology of Sumatra has simply been ignored.

The beginning of the end for Srivijaya's Empire came in 1025 when an Indian fleet set sail and sacked the ports along the East Sumatran coastline, including the capital. The motivation for the action has been linked to Srivijaya's exploitation of merchants – of which those of South India's Chola Kingdom were among the more numerous. By the 14th century, this former great empire had vanished from the historical landscape.

Following the destruction of Srivijaya, the rival **Melayu** Kingdom based not far from Jambi in South Sumatra came to prominence. Archaeological remains uncovered at Muara Jambi (see page 592) indicate that Melayu was influential from the late 11th to the late 13th centuries, but dated back to the 7th century. In 1278, the East Javanese Singasari Dynasty (see page 299) launched an expedition against Melayu and kidnapped a royal princess. She was married to a Singasari prince, and their son Adityavarman returned to his mother's homeland to become ruler. But, in the mid-14th century, Adityavarman decided to move his capital from the lowlands of South Sumatra into the Minang highlands of West Sumatra. It is presumed that Adityavarman made this move to insulate his kingdom from the attentions of the more powerful Javanese empires with whom relations were deteriorating.

By the 14th century a number of Muslim trading states had also arisen along the coastline facing the Strait of Melaka. Within 200 years, Islam had spread all the way down the coast and was beginning to make an impact on the north coast of Java. Of these sultanates, the greatest was Aceh, which reached the zenith of its influence during the reign of Sultan Iskandar Muda (see page 515). But, just at the time that Aceh seemed set to become a great empire, the European powers began to exert their influence over Sumatra.

Colonial period in Sumatra

The European powers first established footholds on Sumatra in the 17th century. The Dutch built a fort at Padang on the west coast in 1663, and the British at Bengkulu in 1685. But these were far from secure and hardly substantive. Both the Dutch and the British were periodically expelled by local raiders as well as by one another and by a third European power, the French.

It was Sumatra's wealth in pepper, tin, gambier and, rather later, in coffee, which attracted settlers and traders to the island. With no significant indigenous power to offer a bulwark against outside intervention, it became an international free-for-all. The British, Americans, Dutch and the French were all pressing various claims to the island and its wealth. However, it was the Dutch who emerged as the dominant influence. In 1824, the British renounced their various claims to Sumatra in return for the Dutch doing the same in Malaya, and Bengkulu and Melaka were effectively 'swapped'.

But striking an accord with the British did not mean that Sumatra was under Dutch control. Much of the interior had yet even to be explored, let alone brought under effective administration. To do this, the Dutch had to wage a succession of wars during the 19th and into the 20th century. Among these, the most bitterly fought were the 'Padri' Wars of the early 19th century, focused on West Sumatra, and the Acehnese resistance which dates from 1873, and continues – in another form – today. It was not until 1910 that the Dutch could claim to have brought all Sumatra under their authority.

Land and environment

Geography A range of mountains – the Bukit Barisan – forms a spine running down Sumatra's west edge. Many of the 93 peaks exceed 2,000m, the highest point being Mount Kerinci at 3,805m. Like Java, Sumatra also has a string of active volcanoes, and the bowl that forms Lake Toba in North Sumatra was formed after a massive volcanic eruption. This occurred 100,000 years ago, and was probably the greatest explosion in geological history – causing over 1,500 km of rock to be blown into the sky.

To the west of the Bukit Barisan is a narrow ribbon of lowland – rarely more than 20 km wide – on which towns such as Padang and Sibolga cling tenaciously. Offshore, to the west, are the ethnologically fascinating Nias and Mentawi islands. To the east there is a wide expanse of mostly swampy lowland. Sumatra's largest rivers – such as the Musi, Hari and Rokan – cut through this lowland, carrying large quantities of silt and sediment to the coast, which is advancing at rates as high as 90m a year. As it advances, so Sumatra is enveloping the inshore islands that constitute the Riau archipelago.

In general, the soils of Sumatra are poorer than those of Java and agriculture is correspondingly less productive. The lowlands of the east suffer from extensive waterlogging, and development is difficult. In the foothills, farmers have to contend with soils that are heavily leached and although the land may support thick forest, fertility quickly declines when it is cleared for agriculture. Tree crops have fared relatively well on these former forest lands and Sumatra is a significant exporter of natural rubber and palm oil. However, the area of Sumatra with the greatest agricultural potential is in the vicinity of the city of Medan. Here, the volcanic soils are fertile and the Dutch colonial administration successfully promoted the cultivation of such estate crops as tea, tobacco, coffee and sisal.

Climate Sumatra is bisected by the equator which runs through the island, just north of Bukittinggi. Daytime temperatures vary little through the year – the annual range is only 1.4°C at sea-level. Far more important is rainfall in determining the seasons. The wettest part of the island is the narrow west coast plain and the west foothills of the Bukit Barisan. Here rainfall averages about 4,000 mm per year, but rises to 6,000 mm per year in the town of Bengkulu, as rain-filled clouds blown in over the Indian Ocean release their load before being forced up and over the Bukit Barisan. In central, East and North Sumatra rainfall is lower, ranging from 2,500 mm to 3,000 mm per year. To put these figures into perspective, average rainfall in Padang – some 4,500 mm – is seven times higher than the figure for rainy London.

There is rain throughout the year in Sumatra, but it is heaviest north of the equator between October and April, and south of the equator from October to January. The 'dry' season – a relative concept in this part of the world – is during June and July.

Kalimantan

Kalimantan

616	Ins and outs	639	Mahakam River
616	**South Kalimantan (Kalsel)**	644	The Apo Kayan
617	Banjarmasin	646	**West Kalimantan (Kalbar)**
626	**Central Kalimantan (Kalteng)**	647	Pontianak
626	Palangkaraya	653	The Northwest Coast
627	Pangkalanbun	654	Kapuas River
627	Tanjung Puting National Park & Orang Utan Rehabilitation Centre	656	**Background**
628	**East Kalimantan (Kaltim)**	656	History
629	Balikpapan	657	Land and environment
634	Samarinda	664	Culture
639	Tenggarong		

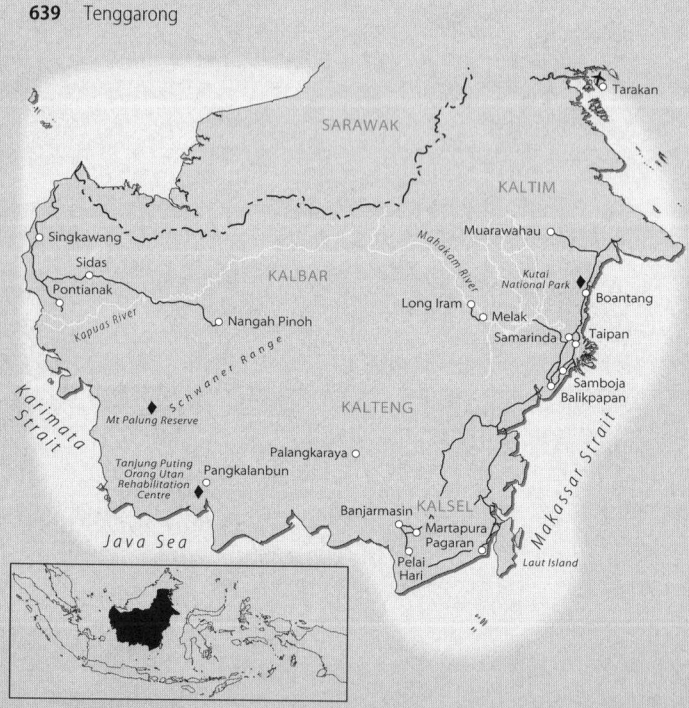

Few tourists make it to Kalimantan: travel can be difficult and facilities, beyond the main cities, are not as well developed as elsewhere in Indonesia. But for those looking for an alternative insight into the country, it offers a great deal: jungle trekking and white water rafting, orang utans and proboscis monkeys, tribal villages and traditional cultures.

The island of Borneo, of which Kalimantan forms a major part, has always held a mystical fascination for westerners – it was a vast, isolated, jungle-covered island, where head-hunters ran wild, and which if romantic myths were to be believed, was rich in gold and diamonds. It is the third largest island in the world (after Greenland and New Guinea) and is divided between three countries: Indonesia, Malaysia and Brunei. Kalimantan's 549,000 sq km (nearly 30% of Indonesia's total land area) has just 5% of the country's population (about 9,500,000), most of which is concentrated in a handful of coastal cities. The interior is populated by various Dayak tribes, whose villages are scattered along the island's riverbanks.

Ins and outs

Getting there

There are **international air connections** with Balikpapan (from Singapore) and Bandar Seri Begawan [Brunei] and Pontianak (from Kuching in East Malaysia). There are also visa-free points of entry. **Overland** it is possible to travel across between Kuching (Sarawak, East Malaysia) and Pontianak via Entikong, whilst there are ferries linking Nunukan with Tawau and Sabah (East Malaysia). Links with destinations elsewhere in Indonesia are rather more plentiful. Balikpapan and Pantianak offer the widest range of choice, but there are also flights from Palangkaraya and Banjarmasin. Finally, by **sea**, *Pelni* ships dock at Pontianak, Ketapang, Sampit, Banjarmasin, Bukit Licin, Balikpapan, Samarinda, Berau, Tarakan and Nunukan.

Getting around

Other than Irian Jaya, and perhaps Maluku, Kalimantan has the least developed **road** system of any region in Indonesia. This is partly because the rivers and swamps make road construction a considerable engineering challenge and partly because the thin population makes the economics unattractive. Over the last few years, though, the government has been expanding the network of all-weather roads. For example, it is now possible to travel overland between Banjarmasin and Palangkaraya, year-round. However, except on the main routes (Banjarmasin to Balikpapan and Samarinda and Pontianak to Sintang), bus services are slow and crowded. Don't expect a comfortable journey.

River and **air** transport have their own particular problems. During the dry season, particularly during the months of August and September, forest fires are sometimes so extensive that the resulting smoke and airborne ash can severely limit if not completely halt domestic flights around Kalimantan. Travelling upriver can also slow to a veritable crawl as river levels shrink to less than half a metre. In some parts of the Mahakam, passengers will have to disembark and help the driver push the canoe out of the mud.

South Kalimantan (Kalsel)

The best time to visit Kalsel is during the dry season from Jun to Sep

The timber industry is an important source of revenue for Kalsel. Even with the cataclysmic fires of 1982-83 and 1997 (see page 969 for details) – which were concentrated in already logged areas rather than untouched forest – it is estimated that perhaps 40 percent of the province's 3,700,000 ha is still officially forested. The area between the road and the coast, the Pegunungan Meratus (the Range of 100 Mountains), which forms the backbone of the state, is still covered in primary forest – it is too remote even for loggers and much of the logging has been along the coast and on either side of the main road to Balikpapan.

To the west of this range is the Barito River, which has its headwaters deep in the interior. The coastal area is low lying and swampy: the name of the provincial capital, Banjarmasin, derives from the Javanese term 'saline garden'. Kalsel's coasts are dominated by riceland – where high yielding varieties have been successfully introduced. The hybrid strains have been named after Kalsel's main rivers, the Barito and Negara. Over the past 50 years most of these ricefields have been reclaimed from the tidal swamps. Paddy seedlings are planted in the swamps during the dry season, and in the wet season they flood to a depth of 2-3m. This padi air dalam (deep water paddy) is harvested from boats. These swamplands are also home to another oddity: the swimming buffalo of South Kalimantan. Herds of water buffalo paddle from one grazing area to another, sometimes swimming long distances. Farmers build log platforms (called kalang) as resting places for their buffalo (which are known as kalang buffalo). In recent years the unchecked spread of water hyacinth has begun to threaten their grazing grounds.

Background

Legend has it that a kingdom centred on the southeast corner of Borneo was founded by Ampu-jatmika, the son of a merchant from India's Coromandel coast, who settled in the area in the 12th century. He called it Negara-dipa. It became a vassal state of Java's Hindu kingdom of Majapahit in the 13th century and from then on, the city retained close cultural and trade links with Java, which led to its conversion to Islam in the 1540s. The city of Banjarmasin was founded by the Hindu ruler Pangeran Samudera (The Prince from the Sea) in 1526; it was he who first embraced Islam, changing his name to Pangeran Suriansyah in the process.

History

The Banjarese sultanate – which continued through a succession of 22 rulers – was the most important in Borneo (other than Brunei, on the north coast), and its tributary states included all the smaller sultanates on the west and east coasts of the island. However, in 1860, after several years of political turmoil, the Dutch abolished the sultanate altogether, and installed its administrative headquarters, for all of what is now Kalimantan, in Banjarmasin. This sparked the four years' Banjarmasin War against the Dutch occupiers; long after the uprising was put down, the Dutch presence was deeply resented. The hero of the guerrilla struggle against the Dutch was Pangeran Antasari (his name immortalized in many Kalimantan street names), who was born in the nearby city of Martapura. He unified the Banjarese, the Dayaks and the Buginese against the Dutch, and had a 100,000 guilder price on his head. He died in 1862, having evaded capture, and 106 years later was proclaimed an Indonesian national hero.

South Kalimantan or Kalsel is the smallest and most densely populated of the four provinces in Indonesian Borneo: it has a population of 2,600,000. The population density is about 60 per sq km – low by Javanese standards, but high in comparison with Kalimantan's other sparsely populated provinces. Kalsel used to include all of Central Kalimantan (Kalteng), until the latter's predominantly Dayak population won administrative autonomy from the Muslim Banjarese. The Banjarese are descended from a mixture of Dayak, Sumatran Malay, Javanese and Buginese stock – although their dialect is close to classical Malay.

People

Banjarmasin

Like several other cities in Asia, Banjarmasin has been dubbed 'The Venice of the Orient'. It might be an over-worked cliché, but if there is one city that deserves the epithet, it is Banjarmasin, the capital of Kalsel. The city is dominated by its waterways: most of its population lives in pile houses and floating houses (lanting) on the sides of the Martapura, Barito, Kuin and Andai rivers, along and around which the city is built. These rivers – and the canals which link them – are the focus of day-to-day life in Banjarmasin. The waterways are alive with people bathing, swimming, fishing and washing their clothes; they clean their teeth in them, squat over them and shop on them.

Phone code: 0511
Colour map 4, grid C3

In 1930 the city had a population of just 66,000, but this still made it the largest town on the island. Today the figure must be close to, or more than, 500,000

Although Banjarmasin may be the largest urban centre in Borneo, it does not exude wealth in the same way that other cities do. Periodic outbreaks of cholera, and a shortage of drinking water in the dry season, means that wealthier potential inhabitants tend to live elsewhere – such as at Banjarbaru/Martapura some 40 km away.

Ins and outs

Banjarmasin is Kalimantan's largest city. Syamsudin Noor airport is a rather unhelpful 27 km east of town, and there are flights to Balikpapan as well as a number of cities in Java. Long distance buses for Balikpapan, Palangkaraya and Samarinda leave from the Taksi Antar Kota terminal, 6 km from the town centre. Passenger ferries depart from Bajaraya Pier for Palangkaraya and beyond. Speedboats to Palangkaraya depart from the Dermaga pier in front of the Grand Mosque. *Pelni* ships leave from the Trisakti port.

Getting there

The Hill Dayaks of Kalsel – a fragile culture

The Hill Dayak tribal areas of the Pegunungan Muratus have a fragile culture, which is being eroded as groups of trekkers venture further into remote areas. Tour operators stress that westerners should be particularly sensitive to cultural traditions and respect tribal customs. (Although there are many differences between the Muratus Dayak people and the tribal groups in Sarawak, visitors may wish to refer to the basic ground rules of longhouse etiquette, see House rules, page 655.) Johan Yasin, the most experienced tour operator in Banjarmasin (see below), tells of tourists on trekking expeditions who have swapped T-shirts for tribal handicrafts and heirlooms. On another occasion, a European doctor began handing out western medicines liberally. While drugs are in short supply and are much needed, it seems he was too generous and managed not only to put the local balian (shaman) out of business, but completely undermined his authority and social standing in the community.

Getting around Bemos follow fixed routes while rickety bajajs are available for hire. Ojeks, becaks and taxis provide the full house of road-going public transport. More entertaining is to charter a klotok to explore Banjarmasin's waterways. **Tourist offices** *Dinas Pariwisata Kalimantan Selatan*, Jl Panjaitan 34, T52982; the Kalsel provincial tourist office is the best organized in Kalimantan, it produces some reasonably informative literature and is open Mon-Fri, closing at 1130 on Fri. The *City Tourist Office* is on Jl Pasar Baru, next to the City Hall.

Sights

The number of tourists visiting Banjarmasin was growing fast for much of the early and mid-1990s; an estimated 30,000 every year, mostly from Java and Bali. However, this has since tailed off; the economic crisis, combined with the fires and the bad press that was generated by the communal violence of 1996, 1997 and 1999, has, understandably, directed people elsewhere. Nonetheless, there is plenty to see in Banjarmasin, and much of the sightseeing can be done from a *klotok* (a motorized gondola): a Banjar proverb goes '*Sekali jukung didayuh, haram balabuh*' – 'once you start paddling, don't dock'.

Muslim sensitivities should be observed in Banjarmasin – women should dress modestly & should avoid smoking in public

The imposing **Sabila Muhtadin Mosque** (Grand Mosque), built in 1980, dominates the city's waterfront. Every Friday, 15,000 Muslims gather for prayer in its cool marbled interior; about 98 percent of Banjarmasin's population is Muslim. The Banjarese became Muslims when the local prince, Pangeran Samudera, converted to Islam around 1540, after which he became known as Pangeran Suriansyah. The city has more mosques per head of population than anywhere else in Indonesia – about one for every 40 families. Mosques, and their smaller equivalent *surau*, line the city's waterways – their domes and minarets, standing out among the parabola satellite dishes and television aerials on the skyline.

The highlight of most peoples' visit to Banjarmasin is the **Pasar Terapung** (floating market), which lies on the west outskirts of town on the Barito River. Unlike floating markets elsewhere in the region – notably Bangkok's – this is far from being a tourist-showpiece. The market is big and very lively – perhaps because sellers can actively pursue buyers, paddling after them in their sampans and canoes (*jukung*) or chasing them in their *klotoks*. The market includes a floating clinic (*posyandu*) and floating pharmacy; as well as jukung-vendors selling rice, fish, fruit and vegetables, there are floating boutique shops, hardware shops, supermarkets, petrol stations and soup stalls. There is even a floating parking attendant, who extracts money from each of the stallholders. There are also delightful floating tea shops; these little covered sampans have their front sections covered in plates of sticky rice, doughnuts, cakes and delicacies, which customers draw up alongside and spear with a long harpoon-rod handed over by the tea-man. When the sun comes up, the *tanggui* – the famous wide-brimmed Banjar hat – comes into its own as marketeers shelter from the heat under its lofty rim. ■ *The floating market starts early (0400) and finishes early (0900-1000) – but there is little point getting there much before 0700. By 0600 it is just light enough to see, so the river trip down the canals to the market, as Banjarmasin is awakening, is fantastic.*

En route to the floating market, from town, in Kuin village, is the **Grave of Pangeran Samudera** (see page 617). Next to the floating market and along the canals there are *pengger gajian* – small family-run **sawmills** – making sawn timber for the construction industry and for construction of Bugis schooners (see page 683). The main schooner-building yards – in riverside dry docks called *alalak* – are just upstream from the floating market at the confluence of the Barito and Andai rivers. But the best place to see the schooners is at the **Pelabuhan Lama** (Old Harbour) on the Martapura River, not far from the town centre. The Orang Bugis, who still build their beautiful sailing ships in the traditional manner, live in little pockets along the Kalsel coast (there is another boat-building yard at Batu Licin on the coast, 225 km east of Banjarmasin). The schooners, with their sweeping bows and tall masts, are known as *perahu layar* – sailing boats. These days, most of them have powerful engines too, so they are commonly known as PLMs (*parahu layar motor*). At the 1989 World Expo' in Vancouver, Canada, a Bugis schooner sailed over from

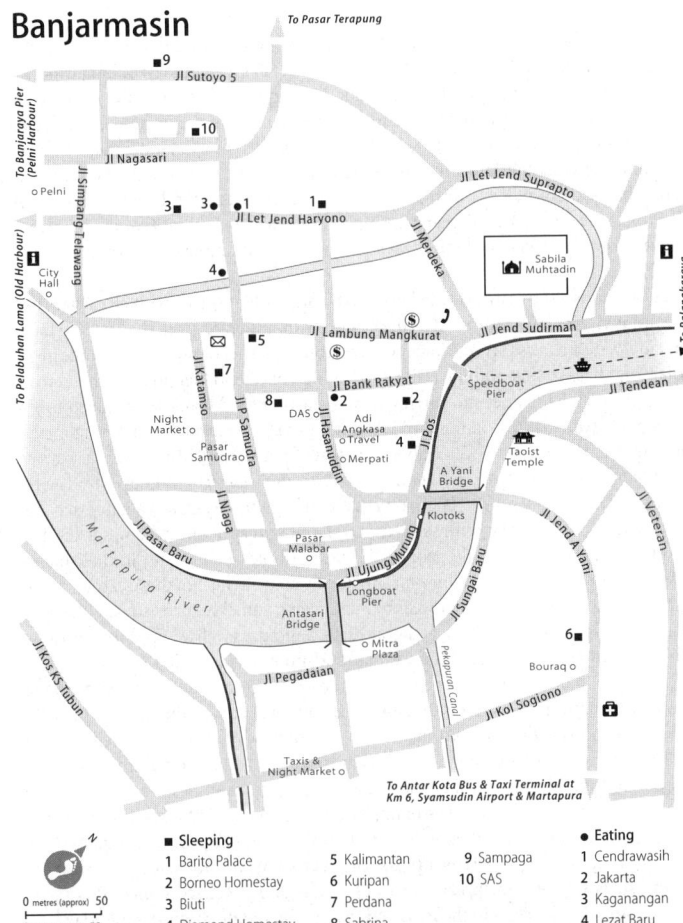

Banjarmasin

■ **Sleeping**
1 Barito Palace
2 Borneo Homestay
3 Biuti
4 Diamond Homestay
5 Kalimantan
6 Kuripan
7 Perdana
8 Sabrina
9 Sampaga
10 SAS

● **Eating**
1 Cendrawasih
2 Jakarta
3 Kaganangan
4 Lezat Baru

Related map: Around Banjarmasin, page 621

Banjarmasin carrying skilled boatbuilders and the materials to build another one. It was completed within the year and was one of the stars of the show. When the boatbuilders came home to Indonesia, they were welcomed as national heroes and received medals from President Suharto. The schooners are still in frequent use as trading vessels and most have a crew of about 30, living in quarters at the stern. On the opposite bank of the Barito River to the floating market there are several large plywood factories, some owned by the cronies of former president Suharto.

Pulau Kembang (Flower Island, but better known as 'Monkey Island' because of the troops of monkeys found here) is just downriver from the floating market, in the middle of the Barito. Do not touch the big male long-tailed macaques: these 'rajahs' can be vicious. The island gets rather overcrowded on weekends; donation on arrival. ■ *Getting there: often included at the end of a tour to the floating market; alternatively, take a klotok from under A Yani Bridge.*

About 12 km further down the Barito River is **Pulau Kaget**, also in the middle of the river. The river around the island is one of the best places to observe the proboscis monkey (*Nasalis larvatus* – see page 662), which are active on the shoreline at dawn and dusk. The local name for these is the *kera Belanda* – the monkey that looks like a Dutchman. ■ *The trip takes 1½-2 hrs return.*

Excursions

Martapura & the Cempaka Diamond Fields

The focus of Kalsel's gemstone mining industry, these diamond fields are near the village of Cempaka, 10 km from Martapura, about 40 km southeast of Banjarmasin. There, labourers dig 5m-deep shafts using techniques little changed in over a century, extending tunnels from the bottom of the shafts. The stoney mud is handed to the top in bamboo baskets and then sifted and swilled in flowing water in the hope of striking lucky. If other precious stones are found in the pan, it is taken as an indication that a diamond is nearby. Many large diamonds have been unearthed at Cempaka over the past 150 years; the biggest was the 167.5-carat *Intan Trisakti* diamond, found in 1965. In 1990, a 48-carat diamond was found and was named *Intan Galuh Pampung*.

Martapura's Diamond Fields are shut on Fri, as are the stone-cutting and polishing workshops; most jewellery shops do, however, stay open on Fri. Fri is also the best day to see the Martapura market in full swing

Diamonds are traditionally believed to be benevolent spirits with characters like virtuous virgins and are treated by the miners with similar respect; they refer to them as *Galuh*, or 'Princess'. A rigorously observed code of social conduct is in force in the diamond field so that nothing is done to frighten or offend 'her' in case 'she' refuses to appear. This includes the barring of sour-tasting food (said to be craved for by pregnant women), the banning of whistling (a vulgar means of attracting a girl's attention), and smoking is also taboo in case it offends Galuh. But there is also a saying: *Siapa yang mendapat batu besar, dia pasti susah nanti* – 'Whoever finds a big stone will eventually suffer'. The problem is that large stones are so valuable that they overwhelm the local marketing system. Local traders cannot buy them, such is their value. And *orang kecil*, little people, should not hold such wealth in their hands. *Orang besar* – big men – in Banjarmasin quickly come to hear of these extraordinary finds and the miners find that wealth, if they get it, quickly turns sour. Other precious metals and stones mined at the site include gold, as well as sapphires and amethysts. Cempaka is one of at least six diamond-mining villages in the area.

Around 30,000 people are employed in the gemstone industry, both in the mines and at Martapura. The latter is the gemstone cutting and polishing centre, and there are many shops selling stones of all qualities. The best of Martapura's jewellery shops is *Kayu Tangi*, Jalan Sukaramail 4/J; it is the only one where stones are guaranteed. They have a good selection of precious and semi-precious stones, from diamonds to rough-cut lapis lazuli, but it is still important to bargain. Although this is the best shop in Kalsel for stones, they are not well finished and will probably require recutting and repolishing. There is a **polishing factory** next door (closed Friday) and many stalls selling semi-precious stones, beads and jewellery – including *manik manik* stone necklaces – in the **Pasar Niaga** market (some shops close Friday).

There is a vast and very colourful **vegetable market** next to Pasar Niaga (Monday-Sunday, but the Friday market is the biggest). Behind the vegetable market is a building with shops where silversmiths make rings. **Sleeping** E *Wisma Penginapan Mutiara*, Jalan Sukaramai.

Lambung Mangkurat State Museum, housed in a dubious modern interpretation of a traditional Banjar-style building at Banjarbaru, near Martapura, has historical and cultural displays on Kalsel. On the ground floor there is a life-size, ulin-wood (belian/ironwood) *tambangan* boat (the traditional Banjar river boat, in use from the 17th century to the 1950s). ■ *Admission: 750Rp. Open 0830-1400 Tue-Sun; closes early on Fri (1100) and Sat (1300). Getting there: taxi, minibus or bus (both 45 mins) from the intercity bus terminal or speedboat from the Dermaga Pier in front of the Grand Mosque. Cempaka can be reached from the bemo terminal in Martapura (take green minibuses to the Diamond Fields).*

Tours Johan Yasin and Pujo Santoso are small recommended operations. More expensive but good tours can be organized through the travel agents *Adi Angkasa* and *Arjuna*. Tours include Banjarmasin waterways, 1½ hours (37,500Rp), floating market, three hours (37,500Rp), Kaget Island, five hours, Martapura and Cempaka (67,500Rp), Tanjung Puteh Orang Utan Sanctuary (Central Kalimantan), 3-4 days (cost includes flight to Pankalanbun, Southwest Kalimantan – US$350, with a minimum of two people). Trekking: involves bamboo rafting and trekking through Hill Dayak areas northeast of Banjarmasin, staying overnight in longhouses (*balai*). The cheapest option is to hire a local guide in Loksado – Mr Amat comes recommended. There are also shorter 1-2 days jungle tours to Lake Riamkanan (nestled into the south end of the Pegunungan Muratus range, 100 km southeast of Banjarmasin).

Jungle trekking & white-water rafting The best area for trekking is in the Meratus Dayak – or Hill Dayak – country around Loksado (on the Amandit River) and

Around Banjarmasin

Related map:
A Banjarmasin,
page 619

Mount Besar (1,892m), 190 km northeast of Banjarmasin in the *Pegunungan Muratus* range. From Loksado, it is possible to run the rapids on the Amandit by bamboo raft – there are many stretches of white water, of different grades of difficulty. There are more than 30 longhouses – or *balai* – in and around Loksado, where trekkers can stay overnight. There are also caves in the area. The Kalsel tourism office produces a detailed list of treks between villages, with distances and approximate timings. To the southeast of Banjarmasin, at the south end of the range, there are jungle trails around Lake Riamkanan, accessible from Martapura/Awang Bankal. It is necessary to take guides to both these areas (see Tours, below); few people speak English. **Essential equipment**: mosquito repellent, a torch and a sleeping bag (temperatures drop sharply at night).

Essentials

Sleeping
● on map, page 619
Price codes:
see inside front cover

Banjarmasin was seriously affected by riots during 1998, & many hotels, restaurants & shopping centres were burned or looted

A *Barito Palace*, Jl Haryono MT 16-20, T67300, F52240. A/c, restaurants, large clean pool, spacious upmarket foyer, satellite TV. Clean bright rooms, beware the north facing rooms as some are bombarded by noise coming from the nightclub and the gruesome town amusement park. **A** *Kalimantan*, Jl Lambung Mangkurat, T66818, F67345. Top of the range, alongside *Barito Palace*. This place has its own shopping centre, good sports facilities and restaurants. Popular with foreign business people. **A-B** *Hotel Banjarmasin* (formerly *Nabilla* and before that the *Fabiola*), Km 3.5 Jl Jend A Yani, a/c, restaurant, out of town, on the airport road. The hotel has been recently refurbished; good range of facilities, modern.

C *SAS*, Jl Kacapiring 2, T53054, 53146. Some a/c, restaurant, traditional Banjar house in very quiet location, but rooms a bit dark, breakfast included, ticketing assistance, excellent bamboo furnished family room with fridge and separate living area for up to 3 travellers. Highly recommended. **C** *Sampaga*, Jl May Jend Sutoyo south 128, T52753, F57009 (on the northern outskirts of town, but plenty of becaks available). A/c, restaurant, very clean rooms with big windows looking out onto a long verandah. Manager Ati is very friendly and speaks some English. Ignore the dreary entrance, VIP rooms worth upgrading to for the additional cost. Recommended. **C-D** *Kuripan*, Jl Jend A Yani 126, T50529, F50529. Some a/c, built in 1975, breathtakingly ugly architecture includes sculptured front desk and awful grotto in the rear hallway. Rooms average, executive class has much better linen and bathrooms for a little extra, difficult to get transport into town because it is on a 1-way street. **C-D** *Perdana*, Jl Brig Jend Katamso 3, T53276, F67988. A/c extra charge, restaurant, airy, bright and clean, good range of rooms, friendly staff, eager to help with ticketing and taxis, Merpati office next door, room rate includes cooked breakfast. Highly recommended.

D *Sabrina*, Jl Bank Rakyat (Jl Samudra end) 21, T54442. Some a/c, 1400 checkout, clean but characterless, some rooms a bit dark and pokey, some triple rooms, all standards have basic shared bathrooms.

E *Biuti*, Jl Haryono MT 21, T54493. A/c, cheap, clean, 5 mins' walk from centre of town, tiny rooms but freshly tiled bathrooms. **E-F** *Diamond Homestay*, Jl Simpang Hasanuddin II, T66100. Finally, a place to compete with the *Borneo Homestay* – another backpackers' haunt. Cheaper than the *Borneo* but less room choice. Otherwise, a good place to stay. **F** *Borneo Homestay*, Jl Simpang Hasanuddin 33, T66545, F57515. Run by Johan and Lina Yasin, Johan is perhaps the friendliest tour guide in Banjar, offering jungle treks, diamond mine tours, canal and floating market cruise. This simple accommodation is set just back from the river (adjacent to A Yani Bridge). Be sure to add your name to the thousands who've signed the walls around the rooftop verandah bar. The best value homestay in Borneo and the only place in Banjar which is geared to foreign backpackers. Highly recommended.

Eating
● on map, page 619

One of the best known Banjar foods is *soto banjar*, a duck egg soup; roast duck also appears frequently on Banjarmasin menus. This is thanks to the celebrated Alabio duck, which is thought to be related to the Peking Duck, discovered at the village of Alabio in 1927.

Kalimantan is the biggest producer of ducks and duck eggs in Indonesia. Ask Johan at the *Borneo Homestay* to take you to *Warung Yana Yani* – the best riverside restaurant for *soto banjar*. For less than 5,000Rp you'll get a huge bowlful and a long glass of *es teh* (iced Jasmine tea). It is a 10 min klotok ride downriver from the *Borneo Homestay*. Alcohol in Kalsel has a 40% tax imposed upon it; this is an attempt to cut down the problem of alcoholism amongst the young in Banjarmasin.

Indonesian Very cheap: *Cendrawasih*, Jl P Samudra 65, simple but excellent Padang food, good selection of seafood including spicy roast fish and, unfortunately, turtle eggs. *Jakarta Restaurant* (formerly *Corner Garden*), Jl Hasanuddin 1, T52488. Seafood speciality is fried lobster in butter sauce, good crab curries. Recommended. *Kaganangan Depot Makan*, Jl P Samudra 16, seafood, freshwater fish and sate (300Rp per stick).

Other Asian cuisine Cheap: *Golden Lotus*, Jl Veteran 61 (near the 150-year-old Tempat Ibadai Tri Dharma Suci-Nurani Taoist temple), large Chinese restaurant – popular for big functions for the Chinese community, extensive menu, speciality sago with sticky sauce. *Hakone*, Arjuna Plaza, Jl Lambung Mangkurat 62, Japanese restaurant, upstairs from *Rama Steak Corner* (see below), private rooms and a huge menu. *Lezat Baru*, Jl Pang Samudra 22, part of a small chain of restaurants, with branches in Samarinda and Balikpapan, huge Chinese menu with a good choice of seafood, specials include excellent steamed crab and oysters done 10 different ways (when in season). Highly recommended. *Shinta*, 3rd floor, Arjuna Plaza, Jl Lambung Mangkurat 62, Chinese restaurant attached to a nightclub and disco, private rooms, open until 0200.

International Mid-range: *Rama Steak Corner*, Arjuna Plaza, Jl Lambung Mangkurat 62, very cosy restaurant with soft lighting, imported Australian steaks double cost of local ones. *Cherry Café*, Jl Jend A. Yani 57, serves good European, Indonesian and Chinese dishes – excellent value.

Food centres There are several good buffet-style restaurants, including *Japanese Corner*. **Warungs** In night market, off Jl Lambung Mangkurat, open to 0100. **Bakeries** *Minseng Bakery*, near corner of Jl Pasar Baru and Jl Samudra, good selection of cakes and ice creams; *Home Bakery*, pastries, cakes.

Cinemas There are now only 3 cinemas left following a series of fires in mid 1997. *Mitra Plaza*, other side of Antisari Bridge, and the *Dewi* and *Cempaka* theatres. **Entertainment**

Traditional Banjarese wedding ceremonies take place on Sun, in the auspicious month before Ramadan. Tourists are always welcome at these celebrations and do not require invitations. Traditional dances (such as the *hadrah* and *rudat*, which have Middle Eastern origins) are performed during wedding festivities. **Festivals**

Mar/Apr Mappanre Tassi Buginese Fishermens' Festival (movable, but usually around mid-month) 7 days festival on Pagatan beach (South of Batu Licin on the southeast coast, 240 km east of Banjarmasin) in which local Buginese fishermen sacrifice chickens, food and flour to the sea. Dancing and traditional songs, boat races and tug-of-war competitions. The festival climaxes on the last day. It is possible to stay overnight in the village where there are several losmen; enquire at tourist office or with tour operators as to how best to get to Pagatan. The Department of Tourism will transport visitors free of charge to the festival – 1 recent visitor reported that she was also given accommodation, food, was seated with journalists and treated like a VIP!

Ramadan (movable) throughout the Islamic fasting month, when Banjaris break *puasa* after sundown, they indulge in local delicacies. Every day from 1400 to 1800, in front of the Grand Mosque, the Ramadan Cake Fair is held, where people come to sell cakes for the evening feast. Traditional Banjari cakes are made from rice flour, glutinous rice, cassava and sago. Most are colourful, sweet and sticky.

Sasirangan tie-dyes – from the shaman to the shop shelves

The bright Banjar cloth is called *sasirangan*, and was traditionally believed to hold magical powers capable of driving out evil spirits and curing illnesses. The cloth could be made only by shamans – it was *pamali* (taboo) for common people to make it – and was designed to cure specific medical problems, from headaches to malaria. It was tailor-made by the shaman for specific customers and was known as *kain pamintan*, or 'the cloth that is made to order'. Patterns had particular significance to the spirit world, and dragons, bamboo shoots, rocks and waves, lotus and sun motifs were prescribed like drugs at a pharmacy. Colours were also important: the most common ones were yellow, green, red and purple. The afflicted person's medical prescription was then worn as a headcloth (*laung*) by men and a scarf (*serudung*) by women, who would also wear sasirangan blouses. Babies swung in sasirangan hammocks and children wore sasirangan sarungs to protect them from disease.

When pharmaceuticals arrived in Banjarmasin, the shamans began to go out of business, and with their demise, the sasirangan faded into obscurity. Realizing that the art form had all but disappeared, local women enthusiastically began to revive the dying art in the 1980s. Within a few years, hundreds of tiny cottage industries had sprung up across the town, and in a bid to popularize the material, sasirangan shirts and blouses were presented to celebrities. The cloth was traditionally coloured with natural dyes: yellow came from turmeric root, brown from the areca nut and red from the *karabintang* fruit; today, chemical dyes are used. Sasirangan is made by a lengthy tie-dye procedure, involving several dyeing stages, interspersed with intricate tying and stitching sessions. A simple sasirangan with basic motifs can take up to 4 days to produce, while complex ones are said to take several months.

Aug/Sep **Aruh Ganal** – 'the big feast' (movable) is the Hill Dayak harvest festival. (Another smaller harvest festival, *Aruh Halus*, is held in Jun, to celebrate the 1st of the twice-yearly rice crop.) Dancing all night from around 2000-0800; celebrated in the Hill Dayak longhouses in the Loksado and South Hulu Sungai districts. *Boat races* (17 Aug). Teams compete in traditional *tanabangan* rowing boats on the river in front of the mosque – the course is from the government office to the Grand Mosque.

Shopping **Antiques** Jl Kacapiring II 10, T54386. The home of Mr Ilmiyanto is an antiques supermarket without parallel in Kalimantan. It is a real treasure trove, anything purchased there can be professionally exported to your home country. The contents of the house – in a quiet suburban area of Banjarmasin – include ancient Chinese ceramics, rare, beaded Dayak baby-carriers (which sell for up to 400,000Rp), Dayak statuettes, masks, blowpipes, spears, knives, drums, basketware and canoe paddles, as well as coins and precious and semi-precious stones. Recommended. **Books and maps** Toko Cendrawasih Mas, Jl Hasanuddin 37, for maps of the area. Bookshop in Mitra Plaza. **Handicrafts** Hill Dayak handicrafts, basketware and semi-precious stones from the Martapura mines. Many of the shops have good selections of Dayak knives (*mandau*) from Central Kalimantan; in South Kalimantan, these knives are just called *parang*. One of the more unusual items on sale are the Dayak war canoes/death ships, intricately carved from rubber. There are several art shops on Simpang Sudimampir and Pasar Malabar (near Antisari Bridge), bargain. **Jewellery/precious stones** Gloria Jewellery, Junjung Buig Plaza, Lt I/48, for those who do not have time to go to Martapura, expensive selection; *Toko Banjar Baru*, Jl Sudimanpir 61. Streetside jewellers around Pasar Malabar can be seen cutting and polishing agate and amethyst (among other stones), the stones are rarely of high quality. **Markets** Pasar Malabar is next to Antasari Bridge (on the opposite side of the river from *Mitra Plaza*), handicraft stalls and jewellers; *Pasar Samudra* on Jl Samudra/Jl Pangeran, mainly textiles, good for sarungs and mosquito nets. **Shopping centres** Mitra Plaza, on the southeast side of Antisari Bridge, is a modern shopping centre with a supermarket, which is the best place to stock up on provisions before treks and upriver expeditions. It was destroyed by a large fire in Sep 1997 and at the beginning of 1999 it was still being rebuilt! **Textiles/Batik** Batik Semar, Jl Hasanuddin 90, mainly imported Javanese batiks; *Toko Citra*, Km 3.5 Jl Jend A Yani (towards the airport), best place in town for Sasirangan tie-dyes (see box).

Adi Angkasa, Jl Hasanuddin 27, T53131, F66200; *Arjuna*, Ground Floor, Arjuna Plaza, Jl Lambung Mangkurat 62, T65235, F64944; *Johan Yasin*, *Borneo Homestay*, Jl Simpung Hasanuddin 33, T66545, F57515. Johan's business is also known as Indo Kalimantan Tours. Highly recommended. Will even offer to store your luggage while you take a jungle trek, and deliver it to the airport in time to meet your connecting flight. No charge.

Tour operators

Local Bajaj: congregate around Pasar Malabar (off Jl Samudra); they can be chartered. **Bemos**: yellow bemos leave from in front of the *Minseng Bakery* near the corner of Jl Pasar Baru and Jl Samudra. They follow fixed routes, but go all over town. Bemos can also be found on the corner of Jl Bank Rakyat and Jl Hasanuddin, in front of the *Corner Steak House*. **Boat**: for travelling on the waterways, the best place to hire a *klotok* is from under A Yani Bridge or Kuin Cerucuk (also known as Kuin Pertamina), to the northwest side of town on the Kuin River. Motorized klotoks (which can hold up to 8 or 10 passengers) cost about 7,500Rp per hr. Speedboats are hired for around 30,000Rp per hr and leave from the Dermaga speedboat pier near the Grand Mosque. **Ojeks and becaks**: congregate around *Mitra Plaza*. **Taxis**: the city taxi terminal is on Jl Antisari, next to the main market, 5,000Rp per hr.

Transport
Around 50% of all travellers now travel upriver by bus, as the government has opened 3 new bridges which remain open year round

Air Syamsudin Noor Airport is 27 km east of town. Regular connections on *Garuda/Merpati*, *Sempati*, *Bouraq*, *Asahi* and *DAS* with most major Indonesian cities, including Jakarta, Surabaya, Balikpapan, Palangkaraya, Yogyakarta and Semarang. **Transport to town**: 15,000Rp by taxi – coupons available after exiting through customs. Alternatively, walk the 1½ km to the main highway and catch one of the constant colts that ply between Banjarmasin and Martapura. This will deliver you to the Km 6 terminal – where it is necessary to catch a bemo into the city.

Road Bus: Intercity buses leave from the Terminal Taksi Antar Kota at Km 6. Overnight buses (a/c and non-a/c) to Balikpapan leave at 1600-1700, 12 hrs. Overnight buses direct to Samarinda leave at the same time, 15 hrs. With the opening of 3 new bridges, open year-round, it is also possible to travel upriver by road: Palangkaraya 5 hrs. **Taxi**: taxis around Kalsel leave from the Terminal Taksi Antar Kota at Km 6. **Car charter**: vehicles can be chartered for a more comfortable overland journey upriver.

River Boat: passenger boats leave for destinations upriver from Bajaraya Pier, at the far west end of Jl Sutoyo. The boats are double-deckers which, for trips beyond Palangkaraya, are equipped with beds (for rent) and even warungs. Behind the warungs there is a small prayer room and toilets and mandi. Those travelling long distances upriver should reserve beds the day before. Boats have signs next to them indicating their departure times. Most leave in the morning around 1100; ticket office open 0800-1400. *Getting to Bajaraya pier*: yellow bemos or bajaj from Pasar Malabar. Palangkaraya 24 hrs, Muara Teweh 48 hrs and Puruk Cahu 60 hrs. In the dry season big passenger boats cannot make it to Muara Teweh and Puruk Cahu; it is necessary to disembark at Pendang and take speedboats and motorized klotoks further upriver, to Muara Teweh 3 hrs and Puruk Cahu 8 hrs. *Pelni* passenger ferries leave Banjarmasin's Trisakti terminal (on the Barito River) for other destinations in Indonesia. *Getting to Trisakti*: by bemo from Jl Antasari. The *Karakatau* leaves for Pangkalanbun (for Orang Utan Sanctuary every fortnight, 18 hrs. The *Pelni* vessel *Kelimutu* also calls here on its fortnightly circuit. See route schedules, page 988. *Pelni* office, Jl Laks East Martadinata 192, T3171. **Speedboat**: a quicker and easier way to get upriver to Palangkaraya is by speedboat from the Dermaga pier in front of the Grand Mosque. Daily departures for Palangkaraya (and other upriver destinations). Most leave from 0900 to 1100, 5 hrs. **Bugis schooner**: to Java, enquire at Kantor Syahbandar Pelabuhan I, Jl Barito Hilir at Trisakti dock. **NB** The harbour master will demand identification before allowing you to see the schooner. Primarily only available for special interest groups, photographers and journalists. If you require assistance, contact Johan at *Borneo Homestay*.

Directory Airline offices *Bouraq*, Jl Jend A Yani 343, 4 km out of town, T52445; *DAS*, Jl Hasanuddin 6, T52902; *Garuda*, at *Barito Palace Hotel*, T59063, F59064. *Merpati*, Jl Hasanuddin 31, T53885, F54290. **Banks** *Bumi Daya*, *Dagang Negara* and *Negara* are along Jl Lambung Mangkurat. *Rakyat* is on Jl P Samudra. Money-changer in the back of *Adi Angkasa Travel*, Jl Hasanuddin 27. **Communications Internet:** facilities available at the post office (7,500Rp per hr, but very slow). **Post Office:** on the corner of Jl Lambung Mangkurat and Jl Samudra. **Medical facilities** Hospitals: *Suaka Insan*, Jl Pembangunan (on the north side of town), best in Banjarmasin, with wards and private rooms.

Central Kalimantan (Kalteng)

The vast province of Kalteng is most easily reached from Banjarmasin, but few tourists go there; it is the domain of Dayaks and loggers. It is Borneo's Dayak heartland, and the province was created in the late 1950s when the Dayak tribes sought autonomy from the Muslims of Banjarmasin. It covers nearly 154,000 sq km and has a population of 1,400,000. The north part of Kalteng is particularly remote, and is fringed by the mountains of the Schwaner and Muller ranges. The south part of the state is nearly all marshland, with virtually impenetrable mangrove swamps which reach inland as far as 100 km.

Palangkaraya

Phone code: 0536 This provincial capital was built virtually from scratch in 1957 and in 1991, at the time of the last census, had a population of 100,000. It has little to offer the tourist. There is a small state **museum** on Jalan Cilik Riwut, 2 km from town, containing some Dayak heirlooms; mostly brass and ceramic jars. ■ *Open 0800-1200, 1600-1800 Tue-Sun*. The only real tourist attraction here is the Tanjung Puting Orang Utan Rehabilitation Centre (which is still 8-10 hours by road).

Sleeping **B** *Dandang Tingang*, Jl Yos Sudarso 13, T21805. A/c, restaurant, bar and disco, best hotel in town, with multi lingual staff. Out of town (take taxi bus C). Recommended. **C** *Adidas*, Jl A Yani 90, T21770. A/c, rooms here are unspectacular but they are reasonably clean and comfortable. **D** *Yanti*, Jl A Yani 82A, T21634. Some a/c, very clean little hotel, more expensive rooms with a/c, attached bathrooms and hot water. **D-E** *Mina*, Jl Nias 17, T22182. Some a/c, pleasant staff, clean rooms and a good place to stay at this price, popular so often full. **E** *Laris*, Jl Darmasugondo 78, T34674. Clean rooms and friendly management, but noisy location.

Eating *Almuminum*, Jl Halmahera. Excellent fish. *Sampurna*, Jl Jawa 49. Good range of fish dishes. **Foodstalls**: night market on Jl Halmahera and Jawa near the docks.

Tour operators *Patas*, Jl A Yani 52, T23307.

Transport The town can be reached by river – and now road – from Banjarmasin. Canals, cut by the Dutch in the late 19th century, connect the Barito, Kapuas and Kahayan river systems. **Air** The airport is just outside town; taxis in cost 5,000Rp. Regular connections with Banjarmasin, Sampit and Pangkalanbun on Bouraq, and Balikpapan and Surabaya (Java) on Sempati. Merpati flies these routes too. **Road** With the opening of 3 new bridges open year-round, it is now possible to travel overland between Palangkaraya and Banjarmasin by bus and car. **Bus**: connections with Banjarmasin 5 hrs (25,000Rp), Pulang Pisau and Kuala Kapuas. **Car charter**: vehicles can be chartered for a more comfortable overland journey down river to Banjarmasin. **Jeeps**: *Patas Tours*, Jl Yani 52 for twice daily travel to Kuala Kapuas 4 hrs or to Sempas 7 hrs (in the dry season). **River Boat**: boats travelling downstream leave from Rambang Pier; tickets are available from here. To Banjarmasin, the fast boat takes 6 hrs, the slow boat takes 18 hrs (travelling past Pulang Pisau and Kuala Kapuas *en route*). Boats travelling upstream to Tewah leave from Dermaga Flamboyan (or Flamboyant Pier). Any journeys beyond Tewah require chartering a boat.

Directory **Airline offices** *Bouraq*, Jl A Yani 84, T21622; *DAS*, Jl Milono 2, T21550; *Merpati*, Jl A Yani 69A, T21411; *Sempati*, Jl A Yani 4, T21612. **Tourist office** Jl Parman 21, T21416. English speaking, informed staff.

Pangkalanbun

Phone code: 0532
Colour map 4, grid B1

Few people bother to stay in this riverside town – or if they do, it's probably not out of choice. However, it is necessary to make a stop in Pangkalanbun to obtain a permit to visit the **Tanjung Puting National Park**. Permits available from police HQ, 1 km from centre of town on Jl Diponegoro. Guides available here. ■ *Open daily 0700-1700. To get there, take a bemo from the Jl Kasamayuda-Jl Santrek intersection.* If organizing this leaves enough time, most people move straight on to Kumai (see below), on the park boundary.

Sleeping Not geared to foreign visitors. **B** *Hotel Blue Kecubung*, Jl Domba 1 (south of town), T21211, F21513. A/c, the swishest place in town and sister hotel to the *Rimba Lodge* in Tanjung Puting, rooms here are certainly a notch above those anywhere else in town but it is a lot to pay for what you get. **C** *Andika*, Jl Hasanuddin, T21218. A few kilometres from town, simple rooms.

Transport *450 km from Palangkaraya, 25 km from Kumai (& Tanjung Puting).*

Local Bemos around town are cheap (300Rp). **Air** Regular *Bouraq* and *DAS* flights from Banjarmasin to Pangkalanbun, 2 hrs. DAS also flies to Pangkalanbun from Palangkaraya and Pontianak. *Merpati* flies daily to Pangkalanbun from Semarang (change here, if coming from Jakarta) and Bandung (3¼ hrs). Transport to town by taxi or bemo (10,000Rp). **Road** The road to Palangkaraya from Pangkalanbun is poor. Kijangs make the journey but it is long (about 10 hrs) and painful. The trip to Tanjung Puting, by contrast, is short and comparatively sweet. Minibuses leave from the market area, 30 mins. **Sea Boat**: boats do leave from the dock near town for Pontianak and Banjarmasin but they are not scheduled, so you will need to ask around.

Directory **Airline offices** *DAS*, Jl Hasanuddin; *Daraya*, Jl P Antasari 51; *Merpati*, Jl Hasanuddin. **Banks** *BNI*, Jl P Antasari, change US$ TCs. **Communications** Post Office: corner of Jl Kasumayuda and Jl Rangga Santrek.

Tanjung Puting National Park and Orang Utan Rehabilitation Centre

The 300,040 ha Tanjung Puting National Park was founded by Dr Birute Galdikas in the early 1970s, in an area with a wild population of orang utans (see page 661). The park straddles several forest types, including swamp forest, heath forest and lowland dipterocarp rainforest. The unusual heath forest is found in the northern area of the park where stunted trees, many with under-sized leaves, grow on impoverished white-sand soils. The swamp forest is concentrated in the central portion of the park and many of the trees here are adapted to periodic flooding with stilt roots.

Anyone who is sick is strictly barred from entering the centre. Visitors should also note that malaria is rife in this region & that anti-malarial drugs are essential

The orang utan centre is smaller and less touristy than Sepilok in Sabah, Malaysia and Bukit Lawang in Sumatra (see page 473), but has the same mission: to look after and rehabilitate orang utans orphaned by logging or rescued from captivity. In addition to the orang utans, there is a large population of other fauna in Tanjung Puting, including proboscis monkeys (see page 662), crab-eating macaques, clouded leopards, false gharial crocodiles, monitor lizards and over 200 species of bird.

There are two main stations in the park: **Camp Leakey** is the main research centre; **Tanjung Harapan** was set up in the late 1980s as an overflow centre – it is the one visited by most tourists. At Camp Leakey, orang utans are fed at 1500, 1600 and 1700. There is an ongoing Proboscis monkey research programme at Natai Lengknas, within the park.

Permits A police permit must be obtained in **Pangkalanbun** (see entry) before making the 25 km road trip to **Kumai**, where visitors should obtain a park permit from the Conservation Office (PHPA Office). ■ *T0532-61508, F61187, open 0700-1400 Mon-Thu and Sat, 0700-1100 Fri. (A photocopy of the police letter and a photocopy of the 1st page of your passport is required to secure the park permit.) Permit costs 2,000Rp per day, and a boat another 2,000Rp per day. Guides are not necessary in the park.* **Guides**: are not required for exploring the park. The boatmen know the channels well. However, guides are available from the PHPA office in Kumai or from the ranger posts at Tanjung Harapan and Podok Tanggui (15,000Rp per day).

Tours Tours to the park are organized from Banjarmasin (see page 621). *Trekforce Expeditions* in London (0171 828 2275) organize two-week conservation/scientific expeditions, where participants assist in the programme.

Sleeping If you decide to stay at the PHPA cabins, it is necessary to bring food and water upriver. River water must be thoroughly boiled before drinking.

In the Park A-B *Rimba* (in the park at Tanjung Harapan), bookable in Pangkalabun at the *Hotel Blue Kecubung*, T0532-21211, F21513, restaurant, comfortable safari-type place. *Ecolodge*, across the river from PHPA cabins, F0532-22991. Recently built, bare but comfortable, restaurant. **E-F** *PHPA*, bookable through park office at Kumai, provide basic accommodation at Tanjung Harapan, just inside the park on the Sekonyer River.

In Kumai (at the edge of the park) **E** *Aloha*, on the road from Pangkalabun, shared mandi. **E** *Cempaka*, next to the market, 1st floor.

On a boat A more interesting way to visit the park is to spend a couple of nights on a 6m klotok, sleeping and eating afloat. National Park staff can help you to find a suitable boat. The fixed rate of 75,000Rp is a better deal than the land accommodation, as the boats hold 4 plus 2 crew members. All food to be bought in Kumai, and will be cooked by the crew.

Transport *25 km from Pangkalanbun*
Local Speedboats can be chartered from Kumai to the park for about 120,000Rp, 45 mins to Tanjung Harapan, 1½ hrs to Camp Leakey. Klotoks can be hired in Kumai from around 75,000Rp per day, sleeps 4 plus 2 crew. For travelling along the Sekonyer River, canoes (paddle powered) can be hired from *Ecolodge* or *Rimba* – it's the best and most peaceful way to see the forest and its wildlife.

Air The nearest airport is in Pangkalanbun (see above for details). **Sea Boat**: *Pelni* vessels from Semarang and Surabaya call at Kumai on their fortnightly circuits. The same vessels also dock at Banjarmasin *en route*.

East Kalimantan (Kaltim)

With its economy founded on timber (it produces 70% of Indonesia's sawn timber exports), oil, gas and coal, Kaltim is the wealthiest province in Kalimantan. Its capital is Samarinda, the launch-pad for trips up the Mahakam River. Balikpapan is bigger than Samarinda and is the provincial transport hub; it is an ugly oil town. The province covers an area of 211,400 sq km – more than six times the size of The Netherlands – and has a population barely more than 2,000,000. It is the second largest province in Indonesia after Irian Jaya.

History

Archaeological digs on the East Kalimantan coast have uncovered stone 'yupa' poles with Sanskrit inscriptions, suggesting Indian cultural influence possibly dating back to the fifth century or even earlier. The province's first substantial settlement was founded by refugees from Java in the 13th century, who fled from the Majapahits. They founded the kingdom of Kertanegara ('the lawful nation' – which later became known as Kutai). This kingdom is believed to have been an important centre on the trade route between Java and China. The word 'Kutai' is thought to have been the term used by Chinese traders, who knew it as 'the great land'. The imaginative Chinese traders also gave the Mahakam River its name; *Mahakam* means 'big river'.

Following Banjarmasin's conversion to Islam, Kutai also embraced the faith in 1565 and became an Islamic sultanate. Disputes between Kutai and the Hindu kingdom of Martapura, on the Mahakam River, were settled by a royal marriage which forged an alliance between the upriver kingdom and the Islamic sultanate. In the 17th century, hostilities broke out again, Kutai was defeated and then absorbed the kingdom of Martapura. The first Buginese settlers arrived from Sulawesi in 1701. As piracy in the Sulu Sea grew worse in the 18th century, Kutai's capital moved inland and was finally transferred to Tenggarong on the Mahakam in 1781. Kutai remained intact as a sultanate until 1960.

Balikpapan

At night, from the dirty beach along Balikpapan's sea front, the clouds are periodically lit up by the orange glow of flares from the offshore rigs in the Makassar Strait. There are several big offshore fields and the town is the administrative headquarters for Kaltim's oil and gas industry. The support staff of Pertamina, the Indonesian national oil company, live mainly on Gunung Dubb, in Dutch colonial villas dating from the 1920s and overlooking the refinery. Unocal and Total, US and French oil companies, have their residential complexes on the opposite hill, on Pasir Ridge, overlooking the town. At the last census in 1991, Balikpapan was recorded as having 309,000 inhabitants, up from 92,000 in 1961. The largest group are the Javanese who make-up 35-40% of the population, followed by Bugis (25-30%) and Banjarese (20%).

Phone code: 0542
Colour map 4, grid B4

The foreign oil workers live like kings in Balikpapan, which is a soulless town: it is strung out untidily along several kilometres of road. It was established early this century as an oil town, and to a significant extent remains one. Some attempt has been made in recent years to create a business district and this has begun to bear fruit around the bottom of Jalan Jend A Yani, next to the smart *Altea Benakutai Hotel*. The new shopping centre at the T-junction at the end of Jalan Jend A Yani will help towards the creation of a commercial centre. Apart from some excellent arts and crafts shops and some good restaurants and hotels, Balikpapan has little to offer tourists; it is a transit camp for visits to Samarinda and the Mahakam River or for Banjarmasin, to the south. The **tourist information office** is at Seppinggang Airport, T21605. Unpredictable opening hours, but *Altea Benakutai Hotel* representative office is usually staffed and can help with immediate queries.

The best **beaches** are to the north of Balikpapan at Tanah Merah and Manggar (3 km from town). These tend to become crowded at weekends.

Excursions

There are three big agents (*Kaltim Adventure* and *Musi Holidays* and *Tomaco*) which operate tours, mainly up the Mahakam River (see page 639), as well as more unusual treks around the Apo Kayan (see page 644) and trans-Borneo treks to Putussibau and Pontianak in Kalbar. On the whole these agents are more expensive than the smaller (but often equally efficient) companies at Samarinda. *Kaltim Adventure Tour* has two houseboats at Samarinda for Mahakam trips, as well as five full-time guides and cooks. Tours include: 3-15 days Mahakam trips; Long

Tours

Apung/Apo Kayan tours; Kutai Game Reserve and overland 15-days treks from Balikpapan to Pontianak, recommended; *Musi Holidays*, variety of package tours, mainly up the Mahakam River, recommended; *Tomaco*, biggest, most professional and most expensive tour agent in town, has a houseboat in Samarinda with a/c cabins to accommodate 12, also several other smaller boats. Tour prices 15% off published rates for walk-in tourists. Recommended. See page 91 for Jakarta head offices.

Sleeping
■ on map
Price codes:
see inside front cover

Largely because Balikpapan is an oil town & is geared to the needs of oil men & government officials, there is woefully little accommodation for the budget traveller

AL *Altea Benakutai*, Jl Jend A Yani, T33022, F31823. A/c, restaurants, pool, smart, international-class hotel, mainly used by oil industry; workers. 24-hr room service, good service and wide range of facilities including fitness and business centres, helpful representative office at airport. **AL** *Dusit Inn*, Jl Jend Sudirman, T20155, F20150. A/c, restaurants, pool, room rate includes breakfast, the most luxurious hotel in Kalimantan, set in extensive gardens overlooking the Makassar Strait, 191 rooms, fitness centre, business centres, fine for those with transport or willing to use taxis, but with a 15 min drive to the centre of town a trifle inconvenient for those who like (or have) to walk. Highly recommended. **A** *Bahana Surya* (formerly *Blue Sky*), Jl Let Jend Suprapto 1, T22268, F35895, bluesky1@indo.net.id. 5 mins' drive from major oil company offices. A/c, 3 restaurants, pool, Balikpapan's 2nd-best hotel, fairly modern with good range of facilities including in-house videos, satellite TV, sauna, billiards and Japanese Shiatsu massage. Friendly staff. Recommended. **A** *Bahtera*, Jl Jend Sudirman 2, T22563, F31889. A/c, restaurant, disco, free airport transfer, overlooks Makassar Strait, opposite the popular *Balikpapan Plaza*, adequate.

B *Balikpapan*, Jl Erry Suparjan 2, T21490. A/c, restaurant, clean hotel and reasonable value, satellite TV, disco, sauna and massage parlour, room rate includes breakfast. **B** *Gajah Mada*, Jl Jend Sudirman 14, T34634, F34636. A/c, breakfast included, clean, large rooms, satellite TV, unmarried couples might be a little circumspect here, the Muslim management has been known to ask to see marriage certificates! The rooms on the seaward side at the back of the hotel are the nicest, there is a very pleasant balcony running along the back of the hotel on both floors. Recommended. **B** *Mirama*, Jl AP Pranoto 16, T33906, F34230. A/c, TV, bar and restaurant, big hotel, clean but definitely needs a repaint, be wary of the lift which periodically jams between floors, next to local cinema, room rate includes breakfast. **B** *Tirta Plaza*, Jl Jend A Yani, T22772, F22132. A/c, recently refurbished and the room rate has escalated but still no lift, TV, pool, jogging track, business centre, 24-hr room service, 20 mins from the airport, US$32.50. **B** *Wisma Patra*, Jl Prabumulih (off Jl Minyak), T33011. A/c, restaurant, pleasant out-of-town location on top of the steep hill overlooking the Pertamina complex, detached bungalows as well as rooms, tennis court. **B-C** *Mutiara Indah*, Jl May Jend Sutoyo 65, T22925/24641/21788. A/c, restaurant, disco hardly the 'pearl' its name suggests, its 'cottages' look more like prison complexes, but the rooms are spotless and the hotel well maintained, carpet needs replacing.

C *Budiman*, Jl Jend A Yani, T36030, F23811. Next to the *Benakutai*, a/c, a little run-down but although the rooms are grubby, the hotel is not as dingy as many other local hotels in the same (or higher) bracket. Some rooms are very stuffy but at least it has a large, sunny foyer. **C** *Suryani*, Jl Karang Bugis No 11, T21580, F33690. A/c, TV, cold water only, clean enough and seems reasonable value – but note that it offers a half-hourly room rate.

E *Aida*, Jl Jend A Yani 1/12, T21006/31011. Sister hotel to its namesake in Samarinda, don't be fooled by the renovated exterior – it's still grotty out the back, but at least the sheets are clean and it remains popular with budget travellers. **D** *Penginapan Murni*, Jl P Antasari 434, T25290. Basic (fan only) and the location is also noisy, but a very pleasant bright blue interior with sunny sitting rooms on both floors, good value and the best of the cheaper places to stay.

Eating
● on map

Indonesian Cheap: *Salero Minang*, Jl Gajah Mada 12B, fresh and tasty Padang food.

Other Asian Cheap: *Atomic*, Jl Sutoyo/Jl Dondang 3/10, a popular Chinese favourite. *Lezat Baru*, Pasar Baru Blok A, Jl Jend Sudirman 1, Komplek Pertokoan. Part of a small chain of restaurants, huge Chinese menu with a good choice of seafood, specials include oysters done 10 different ways. **Mahakam**, *Bahana Surya Hotel*, Jl Let Jend Suprapto 1. Chinese and European cuisine, seafood and steaks, popular with expatriates. **New Hap Khoen**, Jl Jend Sudirman 19. Huge Chinese menu, good seafood selection, specialities include crab curry, chilli crab and *goreng tepung* (squid fried in batter). Recommended. **Paradise**, Komplex Pantai Mas Permai, Jl Jend A Yani. Huge restaurant and huge menu with Chinese, European and Japanese dishes, mostly seafood, fish grill outside, built on stilts out over the sea on a dirty stretch of beach.

International Mid-range: *Banua Patra*, Jl Jend Sudirman 39, T23746. Smart – and snooty – seafront restaurant run by rig supply company, imported steaks and European *haute cuisine* as well as selection of Indonesian, Korean and Japanese dishes. **Bondy**, Jl Jend A Yani 7. One of the best restaurants in town, entrance through bakery with enticing smell of fresh pastries, past the fast-food area, to the rear where it opens into a large 2-storey open-air restaurant, built around an open courtyard. European and local food, mixed grill very good and local and imported steaks, vast selection of sundaes and ice creams, very popular with locals. Recommended. **Tenggarong Grill**, *Altea Benakutai Hotel*, Jl Jend A Yani. International, steaks and seafood, popular with expatriates. **Cheap**: *Modern Holland*, Jl Jend A Yani 2. Bakery with small restaurant attached, serving local and imported steaks, good ice creams. **Sampan**, *Altea Benakutai Hotel*, Jl Jend A Yani. Coffee shop with Chinese, Indonesian and international selection. Recommended.

Balikpapan

- Sleeping
1 Aida
2 Altea Benakutai
3 Bahana Surya
4 Bahtera
5 Balikpapan
6 Budiman
7 Gajah Mada
8 Mirama
9 Mutiara Indah
10 Penginapan Murni
11 Tirta Plaza
12 Wisma Patra

• Eating
1 Atomic
2 Banua Patra
3 Bondy
4 Dynasty
5 Modern Holland
6 New Hap Khoen
7 New Shangrila
8 Salero Minang

Seafood Cheap: *Dynasty*, Jl Jend A Yani 10/7. Chinese food and seafood, huge menu, deep-fried crab claws, prawns fried with rambutan, shellfish, saté. Recommended. **Very cheap**: *New Shangrila*, Jl Gunung Sari Ilir 29. Seafood and Chinese dishes, speciality *kangkung asap* and deep-fried crab claws.

Foodstalls There are stalls in the Balikpapan Permai complex on the road to the airport, more at the vegetable market (*Kebun Sayur*) – the Chinatown of Balikpapan.

Entertainment Balikpapan's status as an oil town, with a good number of testosterone-charged men, means that it has a lively nightlife, with more bars, discos and clubs than you might otherwise expect.

Cinemas There are 3 big cinemas, all showing recent Hollywood releases; the biggest and best is on Jl Sudirman. **Discos** The major hotels all have bars and discos and their popularity changes with the seasons. The nightclub at the *Altea Benakutai Hotel*, the **Black Orchid Disco** (known locally as 'The BO'), is popular; nearby is the *Sabatini*; *The Club*, near the airport, also has a disco. The *Dusit Inn* also has a very popular bar.

Shopping

Balikpapan has a vast array of arts & crafts shops, & is probably the best place in Kalimantan to buy Dayak handicrafts; 'antiques' may not, however, be as old as they first appear. A new shopping centre has been built right on the seafront, at the bottom of Jl Jend A Yani

Arts and crafts: *Bahati Jaya Art Shop*, Jl May Jen Sutoyo 9, good range of tribal arts and crafts and antiques; *Borneo Art Shop*, Jl Jend A Yani 34/03, one of the best selections of handicrafts, Dayak antiques, bone-carvings, ceramics, gemstones and coins. If needed, the manager will deliver your purchase to your hotel and complete the purchase on the premises; *Kalimantan Art Shop*, Blok A1, Damai Balikpapan Permai, Jl Jend Sudirman 7, the undisputed king of Balikpapan's antiques, and Dayak arts and crafts shops, textiles, beads, porcelain etc, proprietor Eddy Amran is friendly and knowledgeable; *Susila Art Shop*, Jl Jend A Yani 11 (near *Dynasty Restaurant*), small, but good selection of Dayak pieces and ceramics; *Syahda Mestika*, Jl Jend A Yani 147, vast selection of tribal arts and crafts, Chinese porcelain and antiques. There are also a large number of arts and crafts shops above the vegetable market (Kebun Sayur/Pasar Inpres) on Jl Let Jend Suprapto, at the north end of town. Many stalls also sell stones from Martapura (including *manik manik* stone necklaces) and antique jewellery. **Batik**: *Iwan Suharto Batik Gallery*, Hotel Benakutai, Jl Jend A Yani, T31896, excellent selection of very original batik paintings (traditional and modern), much of it is by batik artists on Java, but includes some interesting batiks with Dayak designs. **Books**: *Gramedia*, Balikpapan Plaza, a good selection of English titles. **Newspapers**: a good selection of national and international English-language publications are on sale in the *Altea Benakutai Hotel* shop, including the *Jakarta Post*, the *Singapore Straits Times*, *USA Today* and *The International Herald Tribune*. Elsewhere in Kaltim, English-language newspapers are hard to come by. **Shopping Centres**: Balikpapan Plaza, Jl Sudirman, open 1000 until late, 3 floors of everything an expat could desire, in a/c bliss.

Tour operators *Kaltim Adventure Tour*, Blok C-1/1 Komplex Balikpapan Permai, Jl Jend Sudirman, T31158, F33408; *Musi*, Jl Dondang (Antasari) 5A, T24272, F24984; *Natrabu*, Jl Jend A Yani 58, T22443; *Tomaco*, Hotel Benakutai, Jl Jend A Yani, T22747.

Transport **Local Bemo**: all trips around town cost 400Rp, the bemos take a circular route around town, down Jl Jend A Yani, Jl Jend Sudirman and past the Pertamina complex on Jl Minyak. They can be hailed at any point; shout 'STOP!' when you want to alight. **Ojeks**: 2,000Rp minimum charge for a short journey and can also be chartered for a minimum 10,000Rp per hr.

Air Sepinggang Airport is 10 km from Balikpapan. *Airport facilities*: a post office, souvenir shop, money-changer and restaurant, and an international telephone which takes major credit cards. **Transport to town**: fixed price taxis (13,000Rp) from the airport, but less from town to the airport. (The cheapest way to travel from town to the airport is to catch a yellow bemo No 2 and then change onto a green bemo No 7.) Regular connections on Garuda, Merpati, Sempati and Bouraq airlines with most major cities in Indonesia, such as Samarinda, Banjarmasin, Pontianak, Tarakan, Pangkalanbun, Jakarta, Semarang, Yogyakarta, Surabaya, Denpasar, Palu and Monado, Ujung Pandang, Maumere and Kupang. **International connections**: (via Pontianak) with Singapore.

Deforestation in Kalimantan – the chainsaw massacre

At Balikpapan's Sepinggang airport, on the road leading into town, there is a huge billboard saying 'Welcome to Balikpapan'; the words superimposed on a picture showing caterpillars clearing logs out of the jungle. It might be intended to signify development and progress, but it leaves a graphic, striking – and, as it turns out, accurate – first impression of East Kalimantan. From Balikpapan, the road to Samarinda winds through hills affording panoramic views over the denuded landscape: virtually the whole area has been deforested, leaving only scrubland and secondary forest. Few trees are higher than 10m tall, other than the occasional towering Kompassia, whose wood is too brittle for commercial use, and scattered palms. The sky is often hazy from smoke as shifting cultivators clear the remaining vegetation for their ladangs (farms).

Originally East Kalimantan had 17,300,000 ha of forest. Most of this has been divided up; 3,600,000 ha is protected forest, 2,000,000 ha is classed as forest reserve and 10,300,000 ha is classed as 'productive forest'. East Kalimantan is Indonesia's biggest timber-producing province; most of which goes to supply the thriving downstream wood processing industries. Round-log exports were banned in 1985 in an effort to increase the value of wood exports, but this did little to slow the rate of felling. Logging directly employs around 10,000 people in the province, and downstream industries another 40,000.

Sawmills manufacture plywood, chipboard, furniture and veneer. About 40 percent of the wood products produced in East Kalimantan go to supply the domestic market. But plywood exports alone earn the province US$250 mn a year. For every cubic metre of Meranti hardwood bought by the wood processing industry, the buyer is legally required to pay a premium of US$10, which is put towards replanting projects. Whether this actually happens or not is another matter – although the government has reportedly come down hard on timber companies shirking their environmental responsibilities. However, distances in Kaltim are so huge that the Forestry Department cannot hope to police the timber industry adequately, either to collect premiums or to prevent illegal logging. Logging companies also wield considerable influence both locally and in Jakarta, and few officials are willing to become embroiled in a dispute which they have little chance of winning. The other problem is that most silviculturists believe it is impossible to replant a rainforest. This has not stopped scientists from trying: 36 km from Balikpapan, just off the Samarinda Road, is the Tropen Bosch/Wana Riset Forest Research Institute, which has had some measure of success in trying to propagate dipterocarps. But most of the species that are replanted on cleared land are fast-growing trees which critics say 'mine' the soil of nutrients.

Such is the scale and pace of deforestation in East Kalimantan that some tribal groups have taken the law into their own hands – much as their brethren in East Malaysia has done. In August 1995 one group outside Samarinda, in a probably futile attempt to save their last remaining patch of forest, blocked the route of the tractors and purloined the keys. In other cases, logging camps have been attacked. In some respects, the appalling inter-communal violence of 1997 and 1999 was partly sparked by the belief on the part of the Dayaks that their birthright was being removed by outsiders.

Road Bus: regular long-distance bus connections with Samarinda and Banjarmasin. *CV Gelora* express buses to Samarinda leave every 30 mins from 0530 to 2000 from Batu Ampar terminal at Km 3.5 on the Samarinda road, 2 hrs. Buses to Banjarmasin also leave from the Batu Ampar terminal or from Penajam, on the other side of the bay. Boats cross to Penajam from Pasar Baru at the north end of town on Jl Monginsidi, 10 mins. *Getting to Batu Ampar terminal*: take a Kijang taxi to Rapak, the junction with the Samarinda Rd. From Rapak, taxis and bemos leave for Batu Ampar when full; alternatively take an ojek. **Taxi**: saloon taxis also go to Samarinda from Batu Ampar bus terminal; 1 car takes up to 7 people. It is also possible to charter an a/c taxi to Samarinda.

Sea Boat: the *Pelni* ships *Kerinci, Kambuna, Umsini* and *Tidar* dock at the harbour to the west of the city centre, off Jl Yos Sudarso, and call at Tarakan, Toli-Toli, Ujung Pandang, Surabaya and Tanjung Priok (Jakarta) – among other ports – on their 2 week circuits. The *Pelni* office is at Jl Yos Sudarso 76, T21402.

Directory **Airline offices** *Bouraq*, Jl Sudirman, T31475. *Garuda*, Jl Jend A Yani 19, T22300. *Merpati*, Jl Jend Sudirman 22, T24452. *Sempati*, *Altea Benakutai Hotel*, Jl Jend A Yani, T31612. **Banks** *BCA*, Jl Jend A Yani. ATMs outside Balikpapan Plaza; *Bank Duta*, Jl Jend Sudirman 26 (near *Altea Benakutai Hotel*), probably the best place for foreign exchange; *Bank Dagang Negara*, Jl Jend A Yani; *Bank Negara Indonesia*, Jl Jend Sudirman 30; *Bank Rakyat*, Jl May Jend Sutoyo. **Communications** Post Office: Jl Jend Sudirman. **Medical facilities** Hospitals: Public Hospital, Jl Yani, T34181.

Samarinda

Phone code: 0541
Colour map 4, grid B4

Kaltim's capital, 120 km north of Balikpapan, is the gateway to the interior, up the Mahakam River and to the remote Dayak areas of the Apo Kayan, near the border with Sarawak. A bustling modern town that has grown rich from the proceeds of the timber industry (see box), Samarinda was founded by Buginese seafarers from South Sulawesi in the early 1700s and became the capital of the Kutai sultanate. It is 40 km from the coast at the head of the splayed Mahakam estuary and the river is navigable by large ships right up to the town – only the recently-built bridge across the Mahakam prevents them going further upriver.

The rapid population growth of Samarinda (in 1991 the population was 335,000, five times that of 1961) is based squarely on natural resource exploitation. The town produced almost three-quarters of East Kalimantan's plywood in the early 1990s and was reputed to have one of the world's highest densities of plywood factories and sawmills, although this output has since declined because of a shortage of logs and a stiff export tax on sawn timber.

Unlike some other cities in Indonesian Borneo, like Balikpapan, the Banjarese are still the largest ethnic group, making up perhaps 40% of the population (with 30% Javanese, 10% Bugis and 10% Chinese).

Ins and outs

Getting there Samarinda's airport is at the edge of town and it has connections with other destinations in Kalimantan and Java. There are long distance buses to Balikpapan, Bontang and Tenggarong. *Pelni* vessels dock here on their fortnightly circuits through the archipelago and there are also boats that venture up the Mahakam River.

Getting around Bemos and minibuses, which follow set routes, are the main means of transportation. There are also many ojeks. The poorly organized and badly informed **tourist office**, *Kantor Pariwisata*, is on Jl Ade Irma Suryani 1 (off Jl Kesuma Bangsa), T41669. You will be better off getting information from travel agents.

Sights

The only real 'sight' is the **Mahakam River** (see also page 639) itself, and it is well worth chartering a boat to cruise around for an hour. On the left bank, at the east end of town, is the harbour, where the elegant Bugis schooners dock (see page 683). **Kampung Sulili**, further downriver from Samarinda, is built out over the river on stilts and backed by a steep hillside; there are lively scenes all along the riverbank. Small boats can be hired or speedboats can be chartered from any of the countless jetties behind the Pasar Pagi (Morning Market).

Excursions

Kutai National Park, 120 km north of Samarinda, is a 200,000 ha area of forest. The World Wide Fund for Nature (WWF) believes it contains at least 239 species of bird. It

The tough life of a turtle

Historically, green and hawksbill turtles have been hunted for their meat, shells and their edible eggs (a Chinese delicacy). They were a favourite food of British and Spanish mariners for centuries. Japanese soldiers slaughtered thousands of turtles for food during the Second World War. Dynamite fishermen are also thought to have killed off many turtles in Indonesian, Malaysian and Philippines waters in recent years.

Malaysia, Japan, Hong Kong, Japan and the Philippines, where green turtle meat and eggs are much in demand, are all signatories of the Convention in International Trade in Endangered Species (CITES), and trading in sea turtles has been proscribed under Appendix 1 of the Convention since 1981.

In his book Forest Life and Adventures in the Malay Archipelago, the Swedish adventurer and wildlife enthusiast Eric Mjoberg documents turtle egg-hunting and shell collecting in Borneo in the 1920s. He tells of how the Bajau would lie in wait for hawksbills, grab them and put them on the fire so their horny shields could be removed. "The poor beasts are put straight on the fire so that their shield may be more readily removed, and suffer, in the process, the tortures of the damned. They are then allowed to go alive, or perhaps half-dead into the sea, only to come back again after a few years and undergo the same cruel process". The Bajau, he says, used an 'ingenious contrivance' to hunt their prey. They would press pieces of common glass against their eyes 'in a watertight fashion' and would lie face-down on a piece of floating wood, dipping their faces into the water, watching for hawksbills feeding on seaweed. They would then dive in, armed with a small harpoon, and catch them, knocking them out with a blow to the head.

---

is also home to a population of wild orang utans (around Teluk Kaba) and proboscis monkeys. The park was first gazetted as a protected area before the Second World War, but has found itself gradually diminished in size as the government has allowed portions to be logged. At the beginning of the 1980s, 60% of the remaining protected area was devastated by a vast forest fire (see page 969). Kutai park is reached via **Bontang**, which lies on the equator. Bontang is the site of a large liquified natural gas plant. Nearby, at Kuala Bontang, there is a Bajau fishing kampung built out on stilts over the water. **Sleeping In Bontang**: D-E *Losmen Rahayu*, down Jl Mulawarman, D *Kartika*, Jl Yani 37, T0548-21012. **In the park**: there are a number of rangers' posts in the park with basic accommodation and food. There is one on Teluk Kaba and others along the Sengata River (F, 3,000Rp per meal). **Permits/guides**: it is necessary to acquire a permit from the Conservation Office (PHPA Office) in Bontang (no charge). The office can advise independent travellers on their itinerary and organize boat trips to the park; it will also provide guides and help charter boats. *Getting there*: most people visit the park on an organized tour (see below). Regular buses every 3 hours and passenger boats from Samarinda to Bontang. Tour agencies sometimes fly tourists into Bontang (45 mins' flight from Balikpapan). From Bontang (Lok Tuan or Tanjung Limau harbours), the park can be reached by speedboat in 30 mins'. Chartering boats can be expensive for the independent traveller (around 50,000Rp).

Tours About 15,000 tourists travel up the Mahakam River annually. The vast majority go on organized tours which can be tailored to suit all budgets. Most tours are prohibitively expensive for groups smaller than two; the costs fall dramatically the more people there are. Tour agents usually require a deposit of 50 percent upon booking. There are some excellent tour companies in Samarinda and three major ones in Balikpapan (see page 621) offering similar deals. There are also more adventurous trekking trips to the Apo Kayan (see page 644) and 3-4 days package deals to the Kutai National Park, north of Samarinda (see above).

Unlike neighbouring Sarawak, upriver tours on the Mahakam of less than a week's duration will not get far enough upstream to reach traditional longhouses; 3-4 days tours cost about US$300 per head for 4-6 people and travel to Lake

Jempang and Tanjung Isuy; 5-9 days tours continue upriver to Tunjung, Bahau and Kenyah Dayak villages west of Long Iram, costing from US$400 to US$800 per head for 4-6 people. A 14-day tour should reach Long Baun or beyond.

All tours to the **Apo Kayan** area include the return flight from Samarinda to Long Ampung. Few are shorter than six days, most are about 9-10 days. Most tours involve a mixture of trekking and river trips by longboat and canoe, visiting Long Nawang and nearby longhouses and waterfalls. Some even throw in a day's hunting with local Dayaks. Tours cost around US$700-900 for groups of 4-6.

Freelance guides tout around hotels looking for tourists wanting to go upriver. Some are good, others terrible: it is advisable to stick to those with tourist guide licences. (When planning a trip with a freelance guide, ask them to trace the intended route on a map; it soon becomes apparent whether they know what they are talking about.) Many of the good guides in Samarinda contract out their services to tour companies. An average daily rate for a freelance guide should be about 50,000Rp. Local guides Jailani (who hails from Muara Muntai), and his Dayak friend Marten (contact them through the *Hidayah 1 Hotel*, F31954), can arrange cheaper tailor-made trips upriver to Muara Muntai and Malak over 3-5 days, via houseboat and canoe for around 150,000Rp per day including all food, sheets, mosquito nets and guide. Also on offer: 4-9 day trips to Data Dawai, including a seven-hour longboat ride through the rapids near Long Bagun and a 1½-hour flight inland. Prices start at US$1,500 for four. They also boast a Dayak trek as far as Long Ampung (flying on *DAS*). Excellent value – three days for US$650 or five days for US$750 (including return airfares, food and guide). Minimum of two passengers. Another freelance guide who has been recommended is Suriyadi. He can be contacted through the *Hidayah Hotel* or through *Anggrek Hitam* tour company.

Cisma Angkasa is an experienced tour agent specializing in adventure tourism along the Mahakam River and the Apo Kayan. The company owns four well fitted double-decker river boats (a/c cabins) and supplies mosquito nets. Can arrange tours to destinations well off the beaten track (including trans-Borneo treks) and caters for all budgets (cheaper tours use public transport). Recommended. *Ayus Wisata* is an adventure tourism specialist (Jakarta, T749155, F7491560). Good boats with a/c cabins and bunks, as well as experienced guides. Recommended.

Essentials

Sleeping
■ on map
Price codes:
see inside front cover

A *Hotel Bumi Senyiur*, Jl Diponegoro 17-19, T41443, F38014. The best value hotel in this price range, beautifully furnished, marble bathrooms, fluffy towels, soft lighting, IDD and satellite TV, huge pool, sauna and spa, restaurants and nightclub/pub. Great for a post-trek recovery. **B** *Mesra*, Jl Pahlawan 1, T32772, F41017. A/c, restaurant, pool, at the top of a hill, golf course and tennis, good bar, rooms, suites and cottages, good value for money. Recommended. **B** *Sewarga Indah*, Jl Jend Sudirman 11, T22066, F23662. A/c, restaurant, clean and reasonable, souvenir shop downstairs. **C-D** *Hidayah I*, Jl KH Mas Temenggung, T31408, F37761. A/c, restaurant, next to the morning market, very friendly staff, average rooms, pleasant balcony overlooking the street. **C** *Hidayah II*, Jl KH Halid 25, T31166. Some a/c, room rate includes breakfast, simple rooms. **D** *Andhika*, Jl H Agus Salim 37, T42358, F43507. Some a/c, clean enough but noisy and the rooms can be rather claustrophobic. **D** *Rahayu*, Jl KH Abul Hasan 17, T22622. Clean and best of the budget options, shared bathroom. **D** *Pirus*, Jl Pirus 30, T41873, F35890. Good range of rooms, some a/c, some with own mandis. Good value.

Eating

Indonesian Mid-range: *Gading Kencana*, top floor of *Hotel Gading Kencana*, Jl Pulau Sulawesi 4, T22456. Beautifully decorated with ikats, baskets and Dayak handicrafts, soft lighting, does not fill up until after 2000. Romantic breezy balcony available for dining, freshwater fish (*ikan mas*) and saltwater – *ikan bawal*, *terkulu*, *bandeng* and *kakap* – also Mahakam River prawns. Highly recommended. **Very cheap**: *Depot Handayani*, Jl KH Abul Hasan 11. Curries, Padang style. *Gumarang*, Jl Jend Sudirman 30. Extraordinary menu which includes cow brain gravy, cow foot gravy, cow lung gravy, sliced lung, raw leaves and potatoes, spicy *tongkol* fish wrapped in banana leaf recommended. ***Lembur Kuring***, Jl Bhayangkara (next to cinema). Small, basic but tasty selection of curry dishes. ***Mirasa***, Jl H Agus Salim 18/2 (opposite *Andhika Hotel*). Good *nasi campur* curries, specializes in grilled fish and chicken. ***Prambanan***, Jl H Agus Salim 16, grilled fish and chicken. ***Rumah Makan Banjar***, Jl KH Abul Hasan 19. Cheap and cheerful restaurant with simple menu, curries. ***Sari Bundo***, Jl KHM Halid 42. Simple but tasty Padang food.

Other Asian Cheap: ***Lezat Baru***, Jl Mulawarman 56. Part of a small chain of restaurants, huge Chinese menu with a good choice of seafood, specials include oysters done 10 different ways. Recommended. ***Sari Rasa***, Jl H Agus Salim 26. Offers Chinese, Japanese and European dishes with a good line in seafood, pleasant ambience but rather empty.

Entertainment

Disco: ***Blue Pacific Disco***, Kaltim Building, Citra Niaga, there are 5 discotheques in the building, and this is the best, lively music, good atmosphere and no cover charge. ***Tepian Mahakam***, Jl

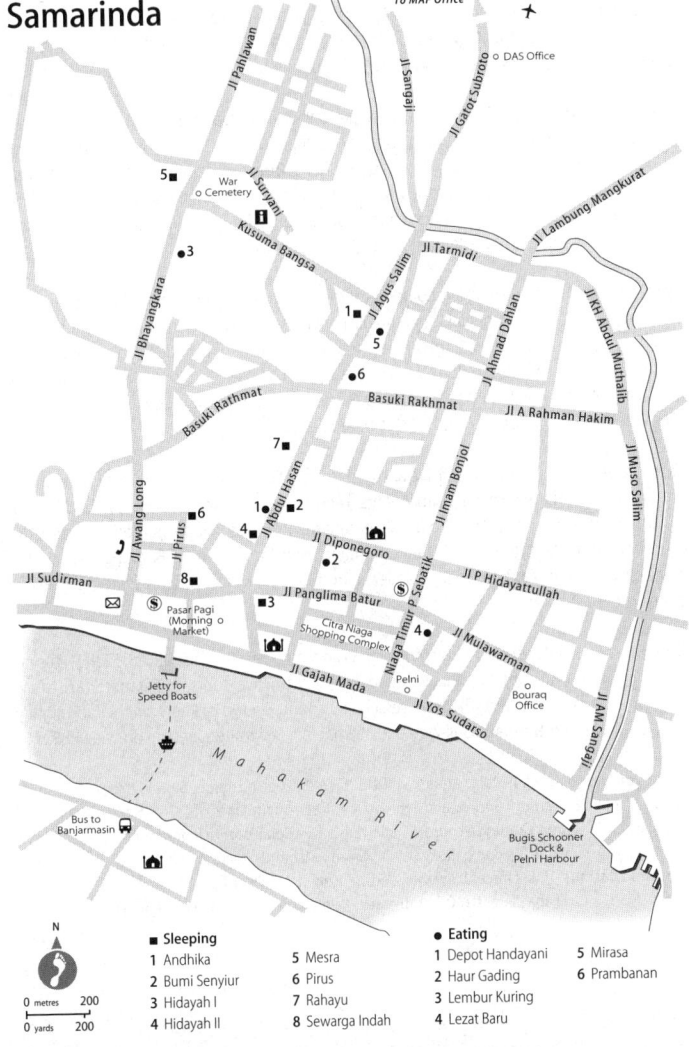

Samarinda

■ Sleeping
1 Andhika
2 Bumi Senyiur
3 Hidayah I
4 Hidayah II
5 Mesra
6 Pirus
7 Rahayu
8 Sewarga Indah

● Eating
1 Depot Handayani
2 Haur Gading
3 Lembur Kuring
4 Lezat Baru
5 Mirasa
6 Prambanan

Untung Suropati, T34204, floating discotheque – which plays a mixture of chart hits and traditional Indonesian love songs – is in the bowels of a barge moored next to the bridge on the Mahakam, restaurant on top, recommended, cover charge.

Shopping The *Pasar Pagi* (morning market) is in the middle of town and is busy most of the day; the area around the modern **Citra Niaga** shopping complex, between Jl Yos Sudarso and Jl P Batur, is particularly lively in the evenings with musicians, fortune-tellers and quack doctors and dentists. Samarinda has many small arts and crafts shops, mostly selling Dayak bits and pieces; there are 1 or 2 good ones, but the selection is not as good as Balikpapan. Always bargain and be suspicious of 'antiques'. *Dewi Art Shop*, Jl Awang Long 19, T21482, antiques and tribal arts and crafts, especially good selection of statues and sculptures. *Fatmawati*, Jl Kesuma Bangsa 2, good selection of semi-precious stones and rings. Other art shops are located along Jl Martadinata (*Berhati Jaya*, *Kings of Dayak Primitive Art Shop* and *Sutra Borneo Art Shop*); Jl KH Agus Salim (*Armarta Art Shop*, *Dan Daman Art Shop* and *Permata Sinar*); Jl P Batur (*Hollywood* and *Syachran*).

Tour operators **Anggrek Hitam**, Jl Yos Sudarso 21, T22132, F23161; **Ayus Wisata**, Jl H Agus Salim 13B, T22644, F32080; **Cisma Angkasa**, Jl Abul Hasan, T42098, **Dayakindo**, Jl Bhayangkara; **Makila**, Jl Pirus 68, T 75121, a good source of information on visiting the Dayak.

Transport **Local Minibuses**: as in Balikpapan, these are called taxis. Red ones go anywhere in town and congregate around Mesra Indah Komplex, 350Rp. Green ones go to Sungai Kunjang (for upriver trips and express buses to Balikpapan), 500Rp. **Bemos**: colour coded to different destinations. For bemos to the north, wait on Jl Awang Long, for those travelling west, Jl Sudirman or Jl Gajah Mada. **Ojeks**: congregate around the Pasar Pagi (Morning Market); 400Rp around town (can be chartered for 3,000Rp per hr).

Air The airport is on the northeast outskirts of town. Regular connections on Bouraq, Merpati, Sempati, Garuda and Asahi airlines with Balikpapan, Banjarmasin, Berau, Tarakan, Surabaya, Jakarta, Yogyakarta and Semarang. Other less regular connections include Bandung and Ujung Pandang. Asahi also flies to Datah Dawai on the Upper Mahakam and both Asahi and Merpati fly to Long Ampung in the Apo Kayan (see page 645). *Transport to town*: by taxi, or walk out of the airport to Jl Gatot Subroto and catch a bemo heading for the city.

Road Bus: buses southbound arrive and depart from Seberang on the outskirts of town on the south bank of the river, Balikpapan 2 hrs, Tenggarong 1 hr. The terminal can be reached by green taxis (see above) or by boat – a pleasant trip from Pasar Pagi; the station is immediately behind the ferry terminal. Buses to Bontang leave from Terminal Bontang 5 km to the northeast of town. **Taxi**: to Balikpapan leave from Sungai Kunjang. Taxis to Bontang leave from Terminal Segeri.

Sea Boat: Sapulidi speedboat from end of Jl Gajah Mada (near the Post Office), T23821. Terminal Feri, Jl Sungai Kunjang, is the launch-pad for Mahakam River tours. To get there, take a 'taxi A' – green minibus (500Rp). The *Pelni* vessels *Leuser* and *Binaiya* call here on their fortnightly circuit between ports in Java, Sulawesi and Kalimantan. See route schedule on page 988.

Directory **Airline offices** Bouraq, Jl Mulawarman 24, T41105; *DAS*, Jl Gatot Subroto 92, T35250. *MAF*, Jl Ruhui Rahaya 1, T43628. *Merpati*, *Garuda* and *Sempati* are all at Jl Sudirman 20, T43385. **Banks** Bank Bumi Daya, Jl Irian 160; *Bank Dagang Negara*, Jl Mulawarman 66; *Bank Negara Indonesia*, Jl Pulau Sebatik 1 (corner with Jl Batur); *Bank Rakyat*, Jl Gajah Mada 1 (across from the post office). **Communications** Post Office: Jl Awang Long/Jl Gajah Mada. **Telephone:** 24 hr wartel on Jl Awang Long; also in Citra Niaga Plaza. **Useful addresses** Pelni office: Jl Yos Sudarso 40-56, T41402.

Tenggarong

Tenggarong was the last capital of the Sultanate of Kutai, and is the first major town (45 km) upriver from Samarinda. The highlight of a visit to the town is the **Mulawarman Museum**. It is housed in the Dutch-built former sultan's palace – his old wooden one, which was exquisitely furnished, burned to the ground in the mid-1930s. The museum contains a recreation of the opulent royal bed chamber, a selection of the sultan's *krisses* (see page 90), clothes and other bits and pieces of royal regalia as well as his collection of Chinese ceramics. There are also replicas of the stone stelae bearing Sanskrit inscriptions, dating from the fourth or fifth centuries. There is a poor display of Dayak arts and crafts, although there are some woodcarvings in the grounds – notably the tall Dayak *belawang* pole (with a carved hornbill on top) in front of the museum. ■ *Open 0800-1600 Tue-Thu, Sat and Sun, 0800-1100, 1330-1600 Fri. Admission 500Rp. A Dayak cultural show is often staged in the museum on Sun.* Near the museum is the **royal cemetery**, containing graves of the founder of Tenggarong, Sultan Muslidhuddin and his descendants.

Colour map 4, grid B4

Sleeping

B *Timbau Indah*, Jl Muksin 15 (on the road into town from Samarinda, on the river), T0541-61367. A/c, restaurant, good rooms but rather a trek from the town centre. **D-E** *Penginapan Anda II*, Jl Sudirman 63 (over the bridge from the mosque), T0541-61409. Some a/c, the best bet on the budget accommodation front, as well as some cheap but clean fan rooms, this place also has a/c rooms with attached mandi. **E** *Penginapan Diana*, Jl Sudirman (on the road to Samarinda, by the pier), rooms here are spacious and with a reasonable level of cleanliness.

There are a handful of cheap losmen in town (a couple by the dock) & 1 mid-range place to stay

Eating

There are a few simple restaurants – try around the dock on Jl Diponegoro.

Festivals

September **Erau festival** (23-28) in Tenggarong – traditionally celebrated at the coronation of a new Sultan of Kutai – used to go on for 40 days and nights. Today it lasts for 5 days. Festivities include traditional Dayak dances, where the different tribes dress in full costume (including the impressive Hudoq dance, designed to frighten spirits, diseases, rats, wild boar, monkeys and birds away from the rice crops), and sporting events such as *behempas* (where men fight with braided whips and rattan shields), *sepak takraw* (top spinning), *lomba perahu* (boat races) and blowpipe competitions. Following the final *ngulur naga* ceremony – in which a large colourful dragon is floated down the Mahakam – the festival degenerates into a water-fight (water in which the dragon has swum is lucky water and should be shared – in bucketfuls). Dayak rituals are performed during the festival, including the *belian* healing ceremony (where shamans cast out evil spirits causing sickness) and *mamat*, the ceremony which traditionally welcomed heroes back from war and headhunting expeditions, and during which a buffalo is slaughtered.

Shopping

There is a good arts and crafts shop – the *Karya Indah Art Shop* – on Jl Diponegoro.

Transport

Road The Petugas terminal is outside town; bemos ferry passengers in to the centre. Regular connections by *Taksi kota* (colts) with Samarinda, 1 hr, or take the ferry (Tenggarong lies 3 hrs upstream from Samarinda).

Mahakam River

The 920 km-long muddy Mahakam is the biggest of Kaltim's 14 large rivers and is navigable for 523 km. There are three main stretches. The lower Mahakam runs from Samarinda, through Tenggarong to Muara Muntai and the three lakes; these lower reaches are most frequently visited by tourists. The middle Mahakam stretches to the west from Kuara Muntai, through Long Iram to Long Bagun – where public river-boat services terminate. The upper Mahakam, past the long stretch of rapids, runs from Long

Colour map 4, grid B4

Gelat into the Muller Range: only a few adventure tours go this far. Most tours reach the upper Mahakam by plane (Asahi Airways flies to Data Dawai airstrip at Long Lunuk). The Mahakam's riverbanks have been extensively logged, or turned over to cultivation. To reach less touristed destinations along the river you need plenty of time on your hands, and if on an organized tour (see above), plenty of funds as well. Many tourists just enjoy relaxing on the decks of the boats as they wind their way slowly upriver: one of the most important pieces of equipment for a Mahakam trip is a good long book.

Best time to visit Sep-Oct, before the rainy season starts; this coincides with rice-planting rituals and the Erau festival (see below). Harvesting festivals are held Feb-Mar. During the dry season (Jul-Sep), many of the smaller tributaries and shallow lakes are unnavigable except by small canoes; during the height of the wet season (Nov-Jan), many rivers are in flood and currents are often too strong for upriver trips.

History

One of the first Western explorers to venture up the Mahakam was Carl Bock (1849-1932). Though born in Oslo he went to England as a young man, and from there to the Dutch East Indies collecting biological specimens for the collection of Arthur Hay, the Marquis of Tweeddale and president of the Zoological Society. Unfortunately, while frantically pillaging the flora and fauna of Sumatra, his patron died. A stroke of good fortune gave him a new mission: in Batavia (Jakarta) he met Governor-General Van Lansberghe, who asked him to mount an expedition to 'Koetai' (Kutai) and venture up the Koetai or 'Mahakani' River. He agreed, but immediately found a problem: no one would accompany him – even when the wages were so high they 'amounted to a positive bribe' – because of the fear of cannibals. But perseverance and the governor-general's deep pocket allowed him to proceed and, accompanied by the Sultan of Kutai himself, he ventured upstream. In a sense, the expedition was a bit of a let-down: he met no headhunters in six months, nor did he

A ceramic inheritance

Family wealth and status in Borneo was traditionally measured in ceramics. In the tribal longhouses upriver, treasured heirlooms include ancient glass beads, brass gongs and cannons, and Chinese ceramic pots and beads. They were often used as currency and dowries. Spencer St John, the British consul in Brunei, mentions using beads as currency on his 1858 expedition to Gunung Mulu. Jars (pesaka) had more practical applications; they were (and still are) used for storing rice, brewing tuak (rice wine) or for keeping medicines. Their value was dependent on their rarity: brown jars, emblazoned with dragon motifs, are more recent and quite common while olive-glazed dusun jars, dating from the 15th-17th centuries, are rare.

Chinese contact and trade with the north coast of Borneo has gone on for at least a millennium, possibly two. Chinese Han pottery fragments and coins have been discovered near the estuary of the Sarawak River and from the seventh century, China is known to have been importing birds' nests and jungle produce from Brunei (which then encompassed all of North Borneo), in exchange for ceramic wares. Chinese traders arrived in the Nanyang (South Seas) in force from the 11th century, particularly during the Sung and Yuan dynasties. Some Chinese pottery and porcelain even bore Arabic and Koranic inscriptions – the earliest such dish is thought to have been produced in the mid-14th century. In the 1500s, as China's trade with the Middle East grew, many such Islamic wares were traded and the Chinese emperors presented them as gifts to seal friendships with the Muslim world, including Malay and Indonesian Kingdoms.

---

find the celebrated *Orang Buntut* – the 'Tailed People' who were supposed to be the missing link between apes and humans. Nonetheless, he wrote up the account of the journey – with a literary flourish which did more for sales than his scientific credibility – that was published, in Dutch, in 1881. The book was also translated into English and published as *The headhunters of Borneo* (available as a 1985 reprint from Oxford University Press).

Today, when they are taking time out from their cultural performances for tourists, the Mahakam's Dayaks are not the noble savages, dressed in loin cloths and hornbill feathers, that some of the tourist literature might paint them as. Longhouses are quite commercialized; tourists are likely to be asked for money for photographs. Most villages on the lower and middle reaches of the river have been drawn – economically and socially – into the modern world over the past century. Although the traditional Kaharingan religion is still practised in some areas (see page 670), many upriver Dayak groups have been converted to Christianity. This is all in marked contrast to neighbouring Sarawak, where the upriver tribespeople maintain their traditional lifestyles to a much greater degree.

The reason for this can be traced back to the policy of Sarawak's successive Brooke governments – the White Rajahs of Sarawak who attempted to protect the Orang Ulu (the upriver tribes) from the warring Ibans and Chinese traders. Other than attempting to stamp out 'social vices' such as head-hunting, they were largely left undisturbed. In Kalimantan, the Dutch colonial government did nothing to discourage the activities of Muslim and Christian missionaries, traders and administrators.

The Lower Mahakam: Samarinda to Muara Muntai

Kota Bangun & around Tenggarong is the first major town upriver on the Mahakam from Samarinda – a trip of about 40 km (see separate entry, page 639). Upriver tours then pass through the villages of Muara Kaman and Kota Bangun, about 6-7 hours upriver from Tenggarong. The lakes of **Semayang**, **Melintang** and **Jempang** – collectively known as the Mahakam Lakes – lie to the west and southwest of Kota Bangun. The lakes were known for their freshwater dolphins, which were sadly decimated during the drought and associated fire of 1982/83. They remain an important source of fish though; it has been estimated that 30 percent of dried freshwater fish sold in Java come from these lakes. Other wildlife in this area of the Mahakam include proboscis monkeys.

Sleeping E *Penginapan Mukjizat* (facing the mosque), a welcoming place with average to poor rooms but an above average atmosphere and position. Also good source of information on the Upper Mahakam. **C** *Sri Bangun Lodge*, 10 mins walk from Mukjizat and quite a comfortable place to stay. **Transport** There are daily bus connections from Kota Bangun to Samarinda.

Muara Muntai Muara Muntai is the next village travelling upriver on the Mahakam, built out over the riverbank on ironwood stilts.

Sleeping There are 2 losmen here: **E** *Penginapan Etam Sri Muntai Indah*, adequate rooms and relaxed atmosphere. **F** *Penginapan Nita Wardana*, small, dark and rather grungy rooms. **Transport** There are boat connections with Samarinda from Muara Muntai (12-14 hrs on the express boat), as well as public boats upriver to Tanjung Isuy, 2½ hrs.

Tanjung Isuy The Dayak village of Tanjung Isuy is on the Mancong River, which feeds into Lake Jempang, the most southerly of the three main lakes; it takes about 2½ hours to reach the village from Muara Muntai. Tanjung Isuy is quite touristy, being popular with tour groups. It is, however, the best place on the Mahakam to witness traditional dance performances in full costume.

A worthwhile excursion from Tanjung Isuy is to visit the **Mancong longhouse**, about 10 km away. This was built as a tourist attraction in 1987, and there are sometimes weaving demonstrations and traditional dance performances. But it is worth making the effort for the trip itself, rather than the destination; there is a good chance of seeing wildlife including proboscis monkeys, as well as a profusion of water birds. **Sleeping** (in Mancong) **F** in the *longhouse*. **Transport** three hours walk (one-way); 2½ hours canoe (one-way), or by hired motorcycle.

Sleeping The villagers have rejected longhouse living in favour of detached kampung houses, strung out along the riverbank. One of these rejected longhouses contains a government craft centre, which is also a hostel (**F**), with private rooms and good beds. There is also a simple hotel here: **F** *Penginapan Beringan*, which serves food.

Transport Boats from Samarinda every Mon and Thu; daily boat to Muara Muntai.

The Middle and Upper Mahakam

Melak & around Along the Mahakam, west of Muara Muntai, are many modern Dayak villages where the traditional Kaharingan religion is still practised. Funerals are particularly interesting affairs, involving the ritual sacrifice of water buffalo. Several more traditional villages are within reach of Melak (all are accessible by motorcycle), the largest

The longhouse – prime-site apartments with river view

Most longhouses are built on stilts, high on the riverbank, on prime real estate. They are 'prestigious properties' with 'lots of character', and with their 'commanding views of the river', they are the condominiums of the jungle. They are long-rise, rather than high-rise however, and the average longhouse has 20-25 'doors' (although there can be as many as 60). Each represents one family. The word *long* in a settlement's name – as in Long Iram or Long Nawang – means 'confluence' (the equivalent of *kuala* in Malay), and does not refer to the length of the longhouse.

Behind each of the doors – which even today, are rarely locked – is a *bilik*, or apartment, which includes the family living room and a loft, where paddy and tools are stored. In Kenyah and Kayan longhouses, paddy (which can be stored for years until it is milled) is kept in elaborate barns, built on stilts away from the longhouse, in case of fire. In traditional longhouses, the living rooms are simple atap roofed, bamboo-floored rooms; in modern longhouses – which are designed on exactly the same principles – the living rooms are commonly furnished with sofas, lino floors, a television and an en suite bathroom. All *biliks* face out onto the *ruai*, or gallery, which is the focus of communal life, and is where visitors are usually entertained. Attached to this is usually a *tanju* – an open verandah, running the full length of the house – where rice and other agricultural products are dried. Long ladders – notched hardwood trunks – lead up to the *tanju*; these can get very slippery and do not always come with handrails.

settlement hereabouts (for accommodation, see below). Around 15 km southwest of Melak is the **Kersik Luwai Orchid Reserve**, which is best visited in January or February. Charter an ojek for the trip there and back. Northwest of the reserve is **Barong Tongkok**, a small community lodged near the centre of this plateau. From here, travel southwest to visit **Mencimai**, where there is a great little museum showing local farming methods. Beyond here is **Eheng**, with an exceptional Banauq longhouse, and sharp-witted local people selling handicrafts (the last stretch of road beyond Mencimai is not made up). **Sleeping** Several places to stay in Melak, all **F**, and all adequate with little to choose between them. There is a scattering of warungs and Melak is also quite a good place to buy rattan goods. Guides and transport are available, but the latter tends to be expensive.

Transport It takes about 25 hrs from Samarinda by boat to Melak.

Long Iram & beyond

Towards **Long Bagun**, places become increasingly traditional, although some villages and tribal groups have embraced Christianity, and the long arm of the state, and of modernity, reaches far into the upper reaches of the Mahakam. Only a few public river-boats go beyond Long Iram, partly because of a lack of demand and partly because travel in the dry season becomes difficult up-river from here. Long Iram is a small, rather pleasing little town, with a relaxed atmosphere and a few architectural hang-overs from the Dutch period.

Sleeping Losmen (**F**) and a very good small restaurant. **Transport** Few tours make it this far – it takes 1½ days from Samarinda; it is possible to go further upriver, but this usually involves chartering a longboat which is expensive.

Upriver from Long Iram is the domain of the **Tunjung** and **Benuaq Dayaks**, and a substantial number of Kenyah who have spilled over from the Apo Kayan. The scenery becomes increasingly dramatic towards Long Bagun; there are many villages and it is always possible to stay somewhere. Past the long stretch of rapids to the west of Long Bagun is the upper Mahakam, which runs southwest and then twists north to its headwaters in the Muller Range, on the Sarawak border. It is possible to fly from Samarinda to **Long Lunuk** (Data Dawai airstrip), well to the southwest of the rapids, and then continue upriver by longboat.

The massacre at Long Nawang

One-hundred years and three months after James Brooke was proclaimed Rajah of Sarawak, the Japanese Imperial Army invaded the country. On Christmas Day 1941, when Rajah Vyner Brooke was visiting Australia, they took Kuching; a few days earlier they had occupied the Miri oilfields. Japanese troops, dressed for jungle warfare, headed upriver. They did not expect to encounter such stiff resistance from the tribes people. The Allies had the brainwave of rekindling an old tribal pastime – head-hunting – which successive Brooke administrations had tried to stamp out. Iban and Orang Ulu warriors were offered 'ten-bob-a-knob' for Japanese heads, and many of the skulls still hanging in longhouses are said to date from this time. The years of occupation were marked by terrible brutality, and many people fled across the border into Dutch Borneo – now Kalimantan. The most notorious massacre in occupied Sarawak involved refugees from Kapit.

Just a month after the Japanese invasion, a forestry officer stationed on the Rejang heard that a group of women and children from Kapit were planning to escape across the Iran Range into Dutch territory. He organized the evacuation, and led the refugees up the rivers and over the mountains to the Dutch military outpost at Long Nawang. The forester returned to Kapit to help organize resistance to the Japanese. But when the invading forces heard of the escape they dispatched a raiding party upriver, captured the Dutch fort, lined up the women and ordered the children to climb into nearby trees. According to historian Robert Payne: "They machine-gunned the women and amused themselves by picking off the children one by one... Of all those who had taken part in the expedition only two Europeans survived."

Tours Most people travel up the Mahakam River on an organized tour, either from Samarinda (see page 635) or from Balikpapan (page 629).

Transport **River Boat**: travelling by public transport gives visitors more contact with locals, and it costs a fraction of the price of a package tour (staying in losmen and longhouses *en route*), but these boats are much less comfortable than the big houseboats operated by tour companies. Regular connections from Sungai Kunjang in Samarinda to all settlements upriver to Long Bagun (in the wet season) and Long Iram (in the dry season). Boats leave from Sungai Kunjang in the early to mid-morning: Kota Bangun, 9 hrs, Tanjung Isuy, 14 hrs, Muara Muntai, 12-14 hrs, Melak, 24 hrs, Long Iram, 36 hrs, Long Bagun, 40 hrs. It is possible to charter a longboat anywhere along the river for a cruise.

The Apo Kayan

This remote plateau region borders Sarawak and is the most traditional tribal area in Kalimantan. The inaccessible mountains and rapids have made the Apo Kayan non-viable from a commercial logger's point of view, and the jungle is largely intact. The region has suffered from out-migration in recent decades and the tribal population has shrunk to a fraction – perhaps just a 10th – of what it was in the early 1900s. This migration has been spurred by the availability of well-paid work in the timber camps of Sarawak and East Kalimantan, combined with the prohibitive cost of ferrying and portering supplies from downriver. Since the late 1980s the airstrip at Long Ampung has been served by DAS – opening the area up and bringing the cost of freight and passenger fares down.

The Apo Kayan is divided into the **Kayan Hulu** (upriver) and **Kayan Hilir** (downriver) districts. The former has a much higher population (about 5,000) and the vast majority are Kayan (see page 665), most originally from Sarawak, driven upriver by Iban raids. Nearly all of them have converted to Christianity – most are Protestant. Until the 1920s the Kayan were the sworn enemies of Sarawak's Iban: in 1924 the Sarawak Brooke government convened a peace conference in Kapit (on the Rejang River), which was attended by Dayak groups from both sides of the border. This formally put a stop to upriver and cross-border headhunting raids.

During the Second World War, many Europeans in the coastal towns of East Kalimantan made their way upriver to what they considered the relative safety of Long Nawang, deep in the Apo Kayan, in the face of Japanese occupation. The Japanese troops followed them upriver and many were killed, having been forced to dig their own graves. Among those shot was a group of women and children – refugees from Kapit in Sarawak (see page 644).

Long Ampung to Long Nawang

Most tours to the Apo Kayan involve trekking and canoe trips from Long Ampung to Long Nawang, and visits to longhouses in the area such as Nawang Baru and Long Betoah and west of Long Ampung, along the Boh River, to Long Uro, Lidung Panau and Long Sungai Barang.

Sleeping

It is possible to stay in these longhouses but it is important to bring gifts (see box, page 655). Independent travellers should pay around 6,000-8,000Rp per night to the longhouse headman. Visitors should bring a sleeping bag (it gets cold at night) and essential equipment includes insect repellent and a torch.

Transport

Air The only realistic way of getting to the Apo Kayan is by air. Limited connections to Long Ampung from Samarinda on *DAS* only, 1½ hrs and only 4 passengers. Flights are booked up about 6 weeks in advance. Booking possible at the Samarinda office. Organized package tours to the Apo Kayan with big tour companies are expensive: this is because it is necessary to hire a guide (costly) from the agency, charter a longboat (also costly), in addition the lack of demand tends to inflate prices. But at least your flight out is guaranteed. *Kaltim Adventure* (based in Balikpapan) undertakes to charter a helicopter if its tourists cannot get onto a flight. *Missionary Aviation Fellowship* (MAF) also flies Cessna aircraft to longhouses in the interior, including Long Ampung. But *MAF* is not a commercial airline and should not be treated as one. It does not have a concession from the government to operate on a commercial basis, and it also has an agreement with *Merpati* that it will not poach passengers. It is a religious, non-profitmaking organization servicing remote communities; it will only agree to fly tourists out of Long Ampung in the case of emergencies or in the unlikely event of planes being empty. Once in Long Ampung, *MAF* may consider requests for flights further into the interior; prices vary depending on whether they are scheduled or non-scheduled flights. Write in advance to *MAF*, Box No 82, Samarinda, with details of where and when you intend to go. *MAF* flies to about 5 airstrips in the remote parts of the Apo Kayan.

Tarakan

Phone code: 0551
Colour map 4, grid A5

The oil-island of Tarakan, with 81,000 inhabitants in 1991, has little to offer the tourist, besides being a hopping-off point to neighbouring Sabah. In the closing months of the Second World War, a vicious little battle was fought here as Australian forces spent several weeks trying to prise the Japanese out of their well protected bunkers. They succeeded, but not before many casualties. The legacy of the battle is still in evidence.

Sleeping

B-C *Tarakan Plaza*, Jl Yos Sudarso, T21870. A/c, hot water, restaurant, best in town, with helpful, friendly staff. **C** *Wisata*, Jl Sudirman 46, T21347. A/c, hot water, adequate. **D** *Barito Timur*, Jl Sudirman 129, T21181. A/c, basic but clean. **D-E** *Taufiq*, Jl Sudarso 26, T21347. Some a/c, rather basic but OK and has a certain ramshackle charm. **F** *Jakarta*, Jl Sudirman 112, T21704. Rock bottom rates for basic but clean rooms and a friendly welcome.

Eating

Ikan bakar (barbecued fish) is good here. **Cheap** *Kepeting Saos*, Jl Sudirman. Excellent crab dishes. **1** *Antara*, Jl Yos Sudarso. Good *ikan bakar*. **Very cheap** *Bagi Alam*, Jl Yos Sudarso. Another place worth visiting for its *ikan bakar*. *Turi*, Jl Yos Sudarso. Good *ikan bakar*. **Chinese**: *Bulungan Restoran*, Tarakan Plaza Hotel; *Kartika*, Jl Yos Sudarso, both cheap.

Tour operators

Angkasa, Jl Sebengkok 33, T21130. *Wisma Murni Travel*, Hotel Wisata, T21697.

Transport **Local Bemos**: around town cost 300Rp. **Air** Regular connections on Bouraq, Merpati, Sempati and DAS with Balikpapan and Samarinda. **Transport to town**: taxi for 5,000Rp or chartered bemo for 1,000Rp. **Sea Boat**: the *Pelni* office is at the main port, at the south end of Jl Yos Sudarso. The *Pelni* ship *Leuser* calls here (see route schedule, page 733). Regular passenger boat connections with Samarinda and Balikpapan and daily ferries to Nunukan, where there are onward connections to Tawau in Sabah, East Malaysia (see International connections, following). **International connections with Malaysia Air** Connections on Bouraq and MAS every Mon with Tawau in Sabah, East Malaysia, 35 mins. One month visas are available on arrival at the airport. **Sea Boat**: there used to be regular passenger ferry connections with Tawau in Sabah direct from Tarakan. As of mid-1997 these had been suspended. To reach Tawau it is now necessary to take one of the daily ferries to Nunukan and then an onward connection to Tawau, requiring a night in Nunukan (see next entry for details).

Directory **Airline offices** *Bouraq*, Jl Yos Sudarso 8, T21248; *DAS*, Jl Sudirman 9, T51578; *Garuda*, Jl Sebengkok 33, T21130; *MAF*, Jl Sudirman 129 (*Hotel Barito Timur*), T51011; *Merpati*, Jl Yos Sudarso 8, T21875; *Sempati*, Tarakan Plaza Hotel, Jl Yos Sudarso 8, T21871. **Banks** *Bank Dagang Negara*, Jl Yos Sudarso, for TCs and cash. **Communications** Post Office: Jl Yos Sudarso (southern end).

Nunukan

Travellers making the journey between Tarakan and Tawau (in Sabah, East Malaysia) need to stop-over in Nunukan as there are no longer any direct boats. Nunukan offers very little for the visitor: there are no beaches and it seems to be impossible to arrange even a canoe trip. On the plus side the people are friendly. There is one bank – BNI – on the main square, but it gives very poor exchange rates.

Sleeping There are several losmen in town including: **E** *Losmen Monaco*, 5 min walk from the port, clean and reasonable value with shared mandis. **E** *Losmen Arena*, on the main square, a step down from the *Monaco*. **F** *Losmen Nunukan*, on main square. Bottom of the range and just about tolerable.

Transport **Sea Boat**: daily ferry connections (which are packed) with Tawau in Sabah, Malaysia, 2 hrs. Also daily ferries to Tarakan. The *Pelni* ships *Kerinci*, *Tidar*, *Awu*, *Leuser* and *Binaiya* dock here.

West Kalimantan (Kalbar)

Because it is cut off from Kalimantan's other provinces, Kalbar attracts few tourists. It occupies about a fifth of Kalimantan's land area (146,800 sq km), most of which is very flat. The Kapuas River is Indonesia's longest at 1,243 km and runs through the middle of the province, east to west. Its headwaters, deep in the interior, are in the Muller range, which fringes the northeast and east borders of Kalbar.

The Kapuas River is navigable for most of its length, which – as with the Mahakam River in East Kalimantan – has allowed the penetration of the interior by merchants and missionaries over the past century. There are small towns all along the river, and the surrounding forest has been heavily logged. For tourists, the Kapuas is less interesting to travel up than the Mahakam River, and pales in comparison with the rivers in neighbouring Sarawak. Because few foreign visitors make the trip, however, the Kapuas River is certainly not 'touristy'. To the north, the province borders Sarawak, and the east end of this frontier runs along the remote Kapuas Hulu mountain range. The southeast border with Central Kalimantan province follows the Schwaner Range. About two thirds of west Kalimantan's jungle (a total of about 9,500,000 ha) is classed as 'production forest'; most of the remaining 3,000,000 ha is protected, but it is such a large area that it is impossible to guard against illegal loggers. The timber industry is the province's economic backbone, but Kalbar is also a major rubber producer.

Background

At about the time Java's Hindu Majapahit Empire was disintegrating in the mid-1300s, a number of small Malay sultanates grew up along the coast of West Kalimantan. These controlled upriver trade and exploited the Dayaks of the interior. When Abdul Rahman, an Arab seafarer-cum-pirate, decided to set up a small trading settlement at Pontianak in 1770, he crossed the paths of some of these sultans. This prompted the first Dutch intervention in the affairs of West Kalimantan, but they did not stay long, and for the next 150 years their presence there was minimal: Borneo's west coast ranked low on the colonial administration's agenda. A gold rush in the 1780s brought Hakka Chinese immigrants flooding into the Sambas area. Their descendants – after several generations of intermarriage with Dayaks – make-up more than 10 percent of West Kalimantan's population today, most living in Pontianak. In the 19th century, the Dutch were worried about the intentions of Rajah James Brooke of Sarawak as he occupied successive chunks of the Sultanate of Brunei. In response, the Dutch increased their presence but any threat that Brooke posed to Dutch territory never materialized. During the Second World War, the people of Kalbar suffered terribly at the hands of the Japanese Imperial Army, who massacred more than 21,000 people in the province, many at Mandor in June 1944.

History

West Kalimantan's 3,900,000 inhabitants are concentrated along the coasts and rivers. Malay Muslims make-up about 40% of the inhabitants, Dayaks account for another 40%, Chinese 11% and the remainder include Buginese (originally from Sulawesi) and Minangkabau (originally from Sumatra). West Kalimantan has also received large numbers of transmigrants from Java. Most were originally resettled at Rasau Jaya, to the south of Pontianak, but many have come to the metropolis to find work as labourers – others have simply resorted to begging. Tribal people also come to Pontianak from settlements upriver on the Kapuas; they have usually fared better than the transmigrants and a number hold important jobs in the provincial administration.

People

In 1986 only 5,000 foreign tourists arrived in Kalbar; by 1990 this had quadrupled and, following the opening of the Entikong border crossing on the Sarawak frontier, the number of tourists rose again by around 50 percent. The vast majority of these tourists were curious Malaysians; westerners account for less than a 10th of Pontianak's tourist arrivals – according to provincial government statistics, a maximum of around 2,000 pass through a year. The main reason for this is that the province is rather lacking in 'tourist objects' and receives little attention in the national tourism promotion literature. True, Kalbar has jungle and rivers and Dayaks and offshore islands – but these can also be found in countless other more accessible places in Indonesia.

Tourism

English is not widely spoken in Kalbar: visitors are advised to learn some basic Bahasa – particularly those heading upriver. The tourist literature produced by the provincial tourism office waxes lyrical about Kalbar's many beautiful islands just offshore and the national parks. But besides being written in rather opaque English, it also fails to mention that few of these have any facilities for tourists and most are extremely difficult to get to. Visitors who want to immerse themselves in Dayak culture and visit traditional longhouses will not find much of interest in Kalbar; only a few tribal groups still live in longhouses on the uppermost reaches of the Kapuas River and its tributaries.

Pontianak

Living in Pontianak is like a European living in a city called 'Dracula' – the name literally translates as 'the vampire ghost of a woman who dies in childbirth'. Apparently, hunters who first came to this area heard terrible screams in the jungle at night and were so scared by them that they dubbed the area 'the place that sounds like a

Phone code: 0561
Colour map 2, grid A5

Return of the head-hunters

Just about every guidebook to Borneo includes tales of head-hunting and cannabilism. Since the 19th century when Victorians were chillingly thrilled by Carl Bock's book The head-hunters of Borneo, *published in 1881, the West has been fascinated by the Dayaks and their ways. It is known that the Dayaks were used by the British to carry out terrible revenge on the Japanese occupiers of the island during the Second World War, but the assumption since then has been that head-hunting and cannabilism had been consigned to history. Most Dayaks had converted to Christianity and the Indonesian state had incorporated them into modern society and economy. Events in West Kalimantan, close to the border with Malaysia, during late 1996 and the first two months of 1997 undermined this view. Furthermore, there were yet more examples of appalling violence during early 1999.*

The cause of the unrest was an unprecedented confrontation between indigenous Dayaks and immigrant Madurese. Most Dayaks are Christian, while the Madurese are fervently Muslim. At the same time both groups are on the the bottom rung of the ethnic ladder in Kalimantan – poor and of low status – which means that they tend to compete for the same jobs. Add to this Dayak feelings that they have had their land taken from them by the government and the Madurese, and there was a potent broth of ethnic unrest brewing which dates back to the arrival of the first Madurese in the area during the 1930s. A Catholic priest explained to journalist Richard Lloyd Parry: "They are ignored by the government, they have no political influence in their own country, they have no economic influence. All they have is the land where they have lived for thousands of years – and now the government is trying to expropriate it."

How many were killed is disputed. The Indonesian military claimed several hundred. Many independent observers said several thousand – local Catholic priests put the death toll at 4,000 Madurese and 200 Dayaks. But more startling than the numbers, whatever they might be, was the manner of the deaths. The mangkok merah or 'red bowl', coated in chicken blood, was being passed from Dayak village to village. The red bowl is a traditional form of communication between Dayak communities symbolizing an emergency or war. Dayak warriors, apparently possessed or in some form of a trance, were led by traditional panglimas or generals to wreak a terrible revenge. Local people believe that Dayak magic rendered the warriors

pontianak'. But modern Pontianak is no ghost town. It is a thriving, prosperous town with a population at the last census in 1991 of 387,000 – a third of whom are Chinese – and a 'parabola' on almost every rooftop. (Other ethnic groups are Melayu, 26%, Bugis, 13% and Javanese, 12%. Dayaks make-up just 3% of the population.) These satellite dishes pick up television stations from around the region as well as blue movie channels from the United States, and are no small investment. While Pontianak is certainly a thriving, buzzy place, there's nothing obvious here to attract the tourist.

The confluence of the Kapuas and Landak rivers, where the Arab adventurer Abdul Rahman founded the original settlement in 1770, is a strongly Malay part of town. This area, which encompasses several older kampungs, is known as Kampung Bugis. The commercial heart of Pontianak is on the left bank of the Kapuas, around the old Chinese quarter. The other side of the river is called Siantan and is distinguished only by its bus terminal, a few rubber-smoking factories (whose choking smell permeates the air) and the pride of Pontianak: the equator monument. Like other cities in Kalimantan, Pontianak derives much of its wealth from timber – there seem to be scores of plywood factories and sawmills close to the city. The second string to Pontianak's economic bow, so to speak, is Siam orange production, of which it is Indonesia's largest grower.

Tourist offices *The Department of Posts and Telecommunications* (Parpostel), Jl Sutan Syahril 17, T39444, has information on travelling around Kalbar, not much English spoken; *Tourist Information Office* at the airport (and at Entikong border crossing); *Tourist Promotion Office* (Kalbar), Jl Achmad Sood 25, out of town, T36172.

invulnerable to bullets, and there were stories of invisible armies and single warriors confronting scores of soldiers with guns. Mobs of Dayaks burned down Madurese houses and chased the inhabitants into the jungle, killing men, women and children. Madurese victims were shot or stabbed, their hearts were torn out and eaten, and their blood drunk. Heads were severed and mounted along the road between Anjungan and the provincial capital of Pontianak, or taken back to villages as trophies. The army flew thousands of reinforcements into the area but were unable to prevent a bloodbath. Dayaks set up road blocks to prevent Madurese escaping to the safety of army bases. In a scene that has echoes in the Bible, ethnic origins were scrawled on boarded-up houses to protect the inhabitants.

The ethnic war began in December 1996 when two Dayaks were stabbed at a rock concert, allegedly by Madurese youths. Mobs of Dayaks attacked Madurese homes until a peace agreement was brokered in Pontianak. Then, in January 1997, a Catholic school in Pontianak attended by Dayak children was burnt down. In response, Dayaks carried out revenge attacks on Madurese, attacks which escalated and spread as the army unsuccessfully tried to bring the situation under control. Stephanus Djueng, director of the Institute of Dayakology Research and Development in Pontianak, explained: "They [the Dayaks] have no opportunities and they are putting things right in the only way they know how."

Although at one level the massacres seem to be senseless, the archetypal orgy of blood letting, most observers reported that the mobs were peculiarly controlled in their fury. Only Madurese were killed and no mosques or government buildings were burnt. For much of the time the Dayak mobs were eerily quiet – until the silence was punctuated by wails of 'whoo-woo-woo'.

The most recent cycle of violence, in March 1999, showed that the uneasy peace brokered in 1997 was flawed. With so much else to contend with, from a collapsing economy to the fall of Suharto, a democratic election and rioting students, the concerns of a remote corner of a remote province, on a jungled island, came pretty far down the list of priorities. So the Dakaks were joined by Muslim Malays and Confucian Chinese – challenging the blithe assumption that this was a religious-cum-ethnic quarrel. It is, fundamentally, a quarrel over land, over resources and who gets what.

The **Musium Negeri** – the state museum – at the southern end of Jalan Jend A Yani contains good models of longhouses and a comprehensive display of Dayak household implements, including a collection of tattoo blocks, weapons from blowpipes to blunderbusts, one sad-looking skull, masks, fishtraps and musical instruments. There are examples of Dayak textiles, ikat (see page 441), songket and basketry. There is also a model of a Malay house and a collection of typical household implements. The Dayak and Malay communities are represented in the huge relief-sculptures on the front of the museum. But there is absolutely nothing on or in it acknowledging the presence of the large Chinese population – other than some Chinese ceramics. Nor, unfortunately, are any of the objects labelled in English. ■ *Open 0900-1300 Tue-Sun. Getting there: oplet from Kapuas Indah Covered Market.* Just past the museum is the huge whitewashed West Kalimantan **governor's office**. There is a replica Dayak longhouse near the museum, off Jalan Jend A Yani, built in 1985 to stage a Koran-reading contest.

The ironwood *istana* or *kraton* – **Kadriyah Palace** – was built at the confluence of the Landak and Kapuas rivers by the town's Arab founding father, Abdul Rahman, shortly after he established the trading settlement. The palace was home to seven sultans; Sharif Yusof, son of the the seventh, looks after it today. His uncle married a Dutch woman whose marble bust is one of the eccentric collection of items which decorate the palace museum. Among the fascinating array of odds and ends are two 5m-tall decorated French mirrors, made in 1923; these face each other across the room and Sharif's party trick is to hold a lighter up to create an endless corridor of

Sights

reflected flames. There is also a selection of past sultans' *bajus* and *songkoks*, a jumble of royal regalia, including two thrones and tables of Italian marble and a photograph of the sixth sultan and his heir, who were murdered by the Japanese in a mass killing during the Second World War. ■ *Admission by donation. Open 0900-1730.*

The **Mesjid Jami** (mosque), or Mesjid Abdurrahhman – which is next to the palace – was built shortly after the founding of the city in the late 1700s, although it has been renovated and reconstructed over the years. It is a beautiful building with tiered roofs, standing at the confluence of the two rivers, with its lime-green turret-like minarets and its bell-shaped upper roof. The Kapuas riverbank next to the mosque is a pleasant place to sit and watch life on the river – the elegant Bugis schooners berth at the docks on the opposite bank. The sky over the mosque and palace is alive with kites flown by the children in Kampung Bugis.

Over the Landak Bridge and past the stinking Siantan rubber smokehouses, which line the right bank of the Kapuas, is the **Tugu Khatulistiwa** (Equator Monument), standing at exactly 109°, 20 minutes east of Greenwich. During the March and September equinoxes, the column's shadow disappears, which is an excuse for a party in Pontianak. In 1991, the old belian (ironwood) equator column was encased in a new architectural wonder, a sort of concrete mausoleum where it is intelligently hidden from the sun. There is a new 6m-high column on top.

The heart of the city, around **Kapuas Indah** indoor market, is an interesting and lively part of town. There are a number of *pekong* (Taoist temples) around the market area; the oldest, **Sa Seng Keng**, contains a huge array of gods. The **Dwi Dharma Bhakti Chinese Temple** on Jalan Tanjungpura is notable for its location in the middle of the main street.

The **Pasar Ikan** (Fish Market), downriver from town on Jalan Pak Kasih, is a great place to wander in the early morning; the stallholders are just as interesting as the incredible variety of fish they sell.

One of the most rewarding things to do in Pontianak is to **hire a sampan** for a couple of hours and potter along the river, taking in all the activity.

Excursions Tourist facilities are limited outside Pontianak – and so are tourist sights. Some areas along the northwest coast – including offshore islands – can be visited in day-long excursions from Pontianak, and these have been listed under the separate sections below. Package excursions are operated by the two main travel agents in Pontianak (see below).

Tours Pontianak's two main tour operators offer city tours and short package tours along the west coast to Singkawang and Sambas regencies, as well as offshore islands. Longer upriver trips on the Kapuas can be arranged, as can adventure tours with jungle trekking and white-water rafting. *Insan* offers one particularly adventurous white-water rafting trip to rapids on the Pinoh River.

Sleeping
■ *on map*
Price codes:
see inside front cover

A-B *Mahkota*, Jl Sidas 8, T36022, F36200. A/c, restaurant, pool, smartest hotel in Pontianak, with full range of facilities including tennis courts, a billiard room and a good bar, rooms small but well appointed, discounts available. Recommended. **A-B** *Kapuas Palace*, Jl Imam Bonjol, T36122, F34374. A/c, restaurant, large pool, modern low-rise hotel in spacious grounds with good range of facilities, located quite a long way from the market area, rooms in block and cottages available. **B** *Kartika*, Jl Rahardi Usman, T34401, F38457. A/c, good location on the river, next to the docks and the market area, not as good as the Mahkota and Kapuas Palace but rooms facing the river recommended. **B** *Pontianak City*, Jl Pak Kasih 44, T32495, F33781. A/c, TV, good mid-range place, friendly staff, good value. **C** *Central*, Jl Cokroaminoto 232, T37444, F34993. A/c and hot water, quite new and clean but tends to be noisy. **D** *Ramayu*, Jl Merdeka 551. Attractively set around a courtyard, clean rooms. **D** *Wisma Patria*, Jl Hos Cokroaminoto 497 (Jl Merdeka Timur), T36063. A/c, own bathroom, no restaurant, sprawling overgrown home-stay, without much charm, rooms average but popular with tourists and friendly staff, automatic *'teh/kopi'* wake-up call at 0630.

Indonesian Very cheap: *Beringin*, Jl Diponegoro 113 and 149. Two Padang restaurants within 40m of each other. Recommended. *Sahara*, Jl Imam Bonjol. Padang food. *Satria Wangi*, Jl Satria 11A. Chinese food with Indonesian. Recommended by locals. *Warung Somay Bandung*, Jl Sisingamangaraja 132. Very good little place serving basic Indonesian dishes. **Cheap**: *Warung Dangau*, Jl Jend A Yani. Excellent place, not easy to find in Taman Budaya. Great Indonesian dishes with a difference.

Eating
● on map

Other Asian Cheap: *Gajah Mada*, Jl Gajah Mada 202. Big Chinese-run restaurant, with a landscaped interior offering very high quality food, particularly seafood and freshwater fish, specialities include: *jelawat* (West Kalimantan river fish), *hekeng* (chopped, deep-fried shrimp), *kailan ca thik pow* (thinly sliced salted fish), crab *fu yung* and sautéed frog. Recommended. *Nikisa*, Jl Sisingamangaraja 108. Sophisticated Japanese restaurant, the most upmarket in Pontianak, shabu-shabu buffet, sukiyaki, teriyaki burgers and an international selection – mainly imported steaks, set lunch/dinner. Recommended by locals. *Pinang Merah Restoran*, Disko dan Singing House, Jl Kapten Marsan 51-53 (behind Kapuas Indah), down the alleyway past the *Wijaya Kusuma Hotel*. Very cool and pleasant place for a drink in the early evening, on wooden walkway next to the river, seafood and Chinese dishes. **Very cheap** *Hawaii*, Jl Satria 79-80 (across the road from Nusa Indah Plaza), also branch at Jl Gajah Mada 24. A/c restaurant serving Chinese dishes and seafood, specialities: *puyung hai* (crab or prawn omelette with spicy peanut sauce) and chicken steaks. Recommended.

International Mid-range: *Bali Palace*, Jl Imam Bonjol 402, European, Japanese and Indonesian food. *Italian Steak House*, Jl Satria 109. Extensive menu includes Japanese, Chinese, as well as Italian. *KFC*, Jl Gajah Mada. *Do 'n' Mi*, Jl Pattimura. Cakes, ice creams and other

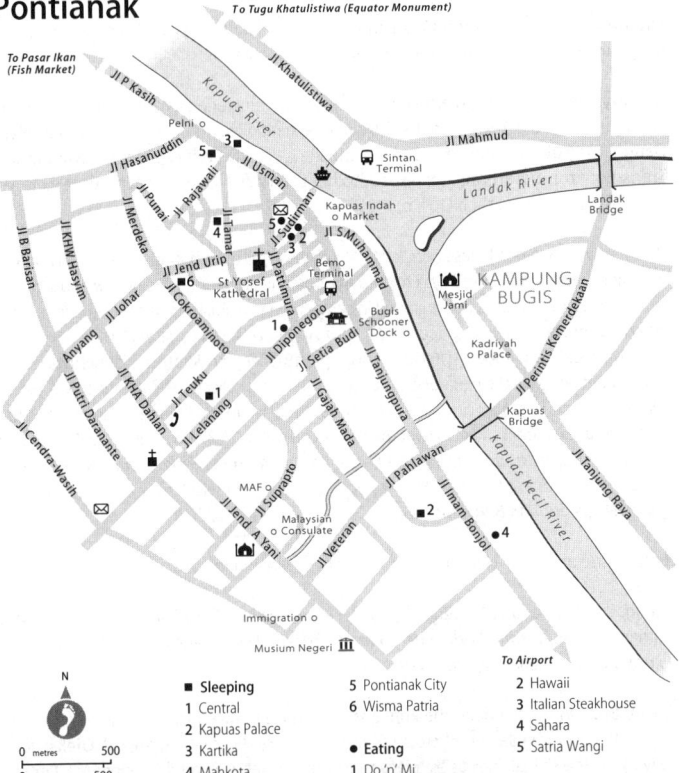

Pontianak

	Sleeping	5 Pontianak City	2 Hawaii
	1 Central	6 Wisma Patria	3 Italian Steakhouse
	2 Kapuas Palace		4 Sahara
	3 Kartika	● Eating	5 Satria Wangi
	4 Mahkota	1 Do 'n' Mi	

delicacies served in trendy surroundings. Popular with the Pontianak middle classes. Don't go here if you're hungry – the portions are small.

Seafood *Corina*, Jl Tanjungpura 124. Simple, cheap seafood menu.

Foodstalls *Bobo Indah*, opposite the *Wijaya Kusuma Hotel* next to the colourful cinema hoardings. There are also some stalls next to the river. In the mornings there are hawker stalls selling breakfast fishballs and *mee kepitang* (noodles and crab) along Jl Nusa Indah II. In the evenings, on the south side of Jl Diponegoro, there are lots of hawker stalls selling cheap Chinese, Padang and Batawi (Jakarta) food.

Coffee shops (*warung kopi*) The hubs of Pontianak social life. They serve not just good coffee, but also snacks such as *pisang goreng* (deep fried banana) and local patisseries.

Fruit market At the top of Jl Nusah Indah, next to St Yosef Katholik Kathedral, excellent selection, including jeruk oranges from around Tebas, north of Singkawang. Their greeny-yellow appearance makes them look rather unappetizing, but they are very sweet. Good durians when in season in Jul and Aug.

Out of town Cheap *Sea Food Garden*, Kakap. About 30 min drive west of Pontianak, on the coast, in a village famous for its seafood, local farm crabs, lobsters, shrimps and fish, recommended by locals.

Bars *Corner Bar*, next to *Bandung Indah* fastfood restaurant, bamboo and brick open-sided bar with good atmosphere.

Entertainment **Cinemas**: several in town, most of them screening the latest Hollywood releases with a few kung-fu movies. Nusa Indah Plaza, Jl Nusa Indah; 4 cinema halls.

Festivals **January**: West Kalimantan anniversary (1st), commemorating its accession to the status of an autonomous province in 1957. Folk art exhibitions and dance. **September**: Naik Dango (21st) (rice storage) festival, when the sun is directly overhead at noon. **November**: Trans-Equator marathon; in the past this has been a full 42 km event; from 1992 it has become a quarter marathon (10 km).

Shopping Due mainly to its large Chinese population, Pontianak is full of gold shops. There are a number of art and craft shops selling Dayak handicrafts, porcelain, textiles (including *ikat* and *songket*) and antiques, but the selection is limited in comparison with Balikpapan and Samarinda. *Borneo Art Shop*, Blok VII, Jl Nusa Indah I 27; *Fariz Art Shop*, 3 Blok C, Pasar Nusa Indah I, good selection of old ikats; *Koperasi Kerta*, Jl Adisucipto 187; *Leny Art Shop*, Jl Khattulistiwa (at the roundabout opposite the equator monument), interesting collection of antique Dayak pieces – includes stone axes, medicine boxes, knives, ikat, basketware and Chinese ceramics – and not forgetting a few model equator monuments (also branch at 1A Blok D, Jl Nusa Indah III). **Batik**: good batik shop in *Nusa Indah Plaza* on Jl Tanjung Pura. **Markets**: *Piska Centre* (Kapuas Indah Indoor Market), opposite *Wijaya Kusuma Hotel*, uninteresting selection of cheap clothes and goods. **Maps**: *Juanda Baru Toko Buku*, Jl Hos Cokroaminoto 232.

Sports **Golf**: course at Siantan Hulu and a driving range at Jl Haryono.

Tour operators *Ateng*, Jl Gajah Mada 201, T32683, F36620. Recommended; *Citra Tour & Travel*, Jl Rahadi Usman, T36436; *Insan Worldwide Tours & Travel (ITT)*, Jl Tanjungpura 149; *Jambore Express Tour*, Jl Pahlawan 226, T36703.

Transport **Local Bus** (*bis kota*): around the Pontianak area leave from Sintian terminal on the north side of the river (regular ferries cross the river from Jl Bardan to the terminal). **Ojeks**: good way to see the sights. The easiest place to pick up an ojek is along Jl Tanjungpura. **Oplets**:

leave from Jl Kapten Marsan in front of the Kapuas Indah Indoor Market, next to the warungs; special demarcated routes to most destinations around town. Also oplet stations on Jl Sisingamangaraja and Jl Teuku Cik Ditiro. **Taxis** (saloons): congregate around *Dharma Hotel* on Jl Tanjungpura.

Air Supadio Airport is 20 km from town. Taxis from airport into town cost 15,000Rp, although ticket agents in town should be able to organize one for less. Regular connections on Garuda, Merpati, Sempati, Bouraq and DAS with most major destinations in Indonesia, such as Jakarta, Semerang, Medan, Bengkulu, Pekanbaru, Balikpapan, Ketapang, Sintang, Putu Siban and Pangkalanbun.

Road Bus: long-distance buses (*Kirana*, *Sago* and *SJS* – on Jl Sisingamangaraja – bus companies) leave from Batu Layang terminal at Km 8 on the Sambas road. Tickets can be bought at the bus station. Regular buses to Singkawang 3½ hrs, Sambas, Sintang (on the Kapuas River) 10 hrs, Meliau, Tayan, Sekadan and Ngabang. *Getting to Batu Layang*: ferry to Siantan terminal and *bis kota* (city bus) from Siantan terminal or oplet. **Car hire**: available from **Citra Tour & Travel**. **Long distance taxis**: available from the taxi office by the **Kartika Hotel**.

Sea Boat: a/c express launches bought from Sibu in Sarawak leave for Ketapang (south of Pontianak) daily at 0900. Tickets for Malindo and Kita express boats sold at *Insan Worldwide Tour & Travel*. *Bandong*, Kalbar's ungainly big river cargo barges, go from near the **Hotel Wijaya Kusuma**, Pontianak to Putusibau (4 days, 3 nights), from Sep-Apr when the water level is high. The *Pelni* ships *Lawit* and *Bukitraya* call at Pontianak on their fortnightly circuits through Java, Sumatra, Sulawesi and Kalimantan. (See route schedule, page 988.) There are also regular connections with Montok, Kijang, Dumai and Mahayati. *Pelni* office: Jl Pelabuhan 2, T34133.

International connections Air With Kuching (Sarawak) on MAS (3 times a week) and Singapore, although it is much cheaper to fly to Batam Island and then take the 30-min boat trip to Singapore from Sekupang (see page 577). **Road Bus**: the border is open 0600-1800 West Indonesian time (0500-1700 Malaysian time). Many buses ply the route between Pontianak and Kuching, 7-10 hrs (RM 34.50). *SJS Executive Bus*, at Jl Sisingamangaraja 155 (Pontianak), is recommended. Note that this is classified as a gateway 'port' of entry so visas are not required for citizens of those countries which are permitted visa-free entry, to Indonesia. PTS SJS, Jl Sisingamangaraja 155, T34626, several buses a day to Kuching, Sibu and Miri.

Airline offices *Bouraq*, Jl Pahlawan 3A, T37261; *DAS*, Jl Gajah Mada 67, T32313; *Garuda*, Jl Rahadi Usman 8A, T78111; *MAF*, Jl Supranto 50a, T30271. *Mandala*, Jl HOS Cokroaminoto 278A, T35108; *Merpati*, Jl Gajah Mada 210, T36568. *Sempati/Deraya*, Jl Sisingamangaraja 145, T34840. **Banks** There are several banks along Jl Tanjungpura (including *Bank Dagang Negara* and *Bank Duta*); *Safari Money-changer*, Jl Tanjungpura 12 (and Jl Nusa Indah III 57). **Communications** Email: at the GPO, 0800-1400 Mon-Thu, Sat, Sun, 0800-1100 Fri. **Post Office**: Jl Rahadi Usman 1 and Jl Sultan Abdul Rakhman 49, 0800-2100. Poste restante available. *The Department of Posts and Telecommunications* (Parpostel), Jl Sutan Syahril 17, T39444. **Telkom office**: Jl Teuku Umar 15, open 24 hrs. **Medical facilities** Hospitals: *Dr Sudarso Hospital*, Jl Adisucipto; *Sei Jawi Hospital Centre*, Jl Merdeka Barat. **Useful addresses** Consulates: Malaysian, Jl Jend Ah Yani 42. Immigration office: Jl Sutoyo, T34516, for Pontianak.

Directory

The Northwest Coast

Singkawang

Singkawang was originally settled by Hakka Chinese in the early 1800s and was the main town servicing the nearby gold rush shanty at Mantrado. It is now an important farming area and is named after a local turnip. In 1991, the town had a recorded population of 85,000.

Colour map 2, grid A5

Excursions About 7 km south of Singkawang there is a **pottery** village, where replicas of antique Chinese ceramics are fired in a big kiln. **Pasir Panjang** beach is 17 km south of Singkawang. **Sleeping C** cottage-style beach-side hotel, a/c, restaurant, pool, facilities include tennis court and watersports.

Pulau Randayan is a 12 ha island with good coral; facilities are being developed on the island and it is possible to stay overnight. Trips to the island are organized by Mr Sukartadji, owner of the *Palapa Hotel* in Singkawang. ■*Getting there: 2 hrs by boat from Pasir Panjang.*

Pulau Temajo is 60 km south of Singkawang (off the coast from the village of Sungai Kunyit), an island with white sand beaches and good coral. There is some accommodation available on the island. *Ateng Tours & Travel* in Pontianak (see page 652) can advise on the best way to get there; the company also runs one-day package tours to the island, supplying food and skin-diving equipment.

Sleeping **D** *Kalbar*, Jl Kepol Machmud 1, T31460. Some a/c, another place with reasonable rooms – nothing memorable, but clean and functional. **D-E** *Duta Putra Kalbar*, Jl Diponegoro 32, T31430. Some a/c, clean and adequate. **E** *Khatulistiwa Plaza*, Jl Selamat Karman 17, T31697. Adequate rooms with attached mandi. **F** *Mahkota*, Jl Diponegoro 1, T31244, F31491. A/c, restaurant, pool, sister hotel to *Mahkota* in Pontianak with equally good range of facilities. **F** *Wisata*, Jl Diponegoro 59, T31082, F32563. Clean rooms and good English speaking receptionist.

Eating *Diponegoro*, Jl Diponegoro (Padang food), and 2 Chinese restaurants, *A Hin* and *A Sun*, next door to each other on Jl Diponegoro.

Transport 143 km north of Pontianak. **Road Colt**: regular connections with Pontianak's Batu Layang terminal, 3½ hrs.

Kapuas River

The first European to venture up the 1,243 km-long Kapuas River was a Dutchman, Major George Muller, who reached the site of present-day Putussibau in 1822 and who lent his name to the mountains to the east. Four years later, while attempting to cross these mountains from the upper Mahakam to the Kapuas, he had his head taken by Dayaks. The Dayaks of the upper Kapuas were themselves terrorized by Iban headhunters, mostly from the Batang Lupar in Sarawak – although some Iban settled in the area to the north of the Kapuas. Few Dayak communities – except those in more remote areas – live in traditional longhouses or observe tribal rituals today. Those who did not turn to Islam – under the influence of the coastal Malays – converted to Christianity: there is a large number of Roman Catholic and Protestant evangelists working throughout the Kapuas basin. Christians (mainly Catholics) make up about 28% of Kalbar's population.

There is still a lot of gold-panning along the Kapuas – using *palong dulang* pans – and larger operations have turned some areas of jungle into a moonscape. Many Dayaks are also employed in the logging industry. Although it is possible to take a *bandung* barge all the way up the river from Pontianak (4-5 days to Putussibau, 40,000Rp), most tourists opt to travel to Sintang by road, which branches off the coast road from Sungai Pinyuh, 50 km northwest of Pontianak. A road is being built between Sintang and Putusibbau.

Pah Auman & north of the river Pah Auman, between Pontianak and Ngabang (120 km from Pontianak, *en route* to Entikong), is the nearest village to Kamung Saham longhouse (12 km by road). This 30-door Kendayang (or Kenatyan) longhouse is one of the most traditional longhouses remaining in Kalbar, despite the fact that it is not particularly remote. Tourists are under the impression that the further they go into the interior, the further

Visiting longhouses: house rules

The most important ground rule is not to visit a longhouse without an invitation. People who arrive unannounced may get an embarrassingly frosty reception. Tour companies offer the only exception to this rule, as most have tribal connections. On arrival, visitors should pay an immediate courtesy call on the headman (known as the tuai rumah in Iban longhouses). It is normal to bring him gifts; those staying overnight should offer the headman a cash gratuity. The money is kept in a central fund and saved for use by the whole community during festivals. Small gifts such as beer, whisky, batik and food (especially rice or chicken) go down well. It is best to arrive at a longhouse during late afternoon after people have returned from the fields. Visitors who have time to stay the night generally have a much more enjoyable experience than those who pay fleeting visits. They can share the evening meal and have time to talk and drink. Visitors should note the following:

On entering a longhouse, take off your shoes.

It is usual to accept food and drink with both hands. If you do not want to eat or drink, the accepted custom is to touch the brim of the glass or the plate and then touch your lips as a symbolic gesture; sit cross-legged when eating.

When washing in the river, women should wear a sarong and men, shorts.

Ask permission to take photographs. It is not uncommon to be asked for a small fee.

Do not enter a longhouse during pantang (taboo), a period of misfortune – usually following a death. There is normally a white flag hanging near the longhouse as a warning to visitors.

---

they will get from civilization – but in that, Kalbar is not like neighbouring Sarawak. The area north of the Kapuas River was a focus of the *Konfrontasi* – the brief war between Indonesia and Malaysia from 1963 to 1965 (see page 657). The West Kalimantan Communist Party was also very active in the area in the late 1960s, before being crushed. While tourists heading into remoter areas upriver are no longer shadowed by soldiers, it is still necessary to report to the local police station on arrival.

Sleeping It is possible to ask the Kepala's (headman's) permission to stay overnight in the Kendayang longhouse. *Getting there*: any east-bound bus from Pontianak's Batu Layang bus station.

Sintang (245 km, eight hours east of Pontianak) is at the confluence of the Kapuas and Melawi rivers. About 18 km from town is Mount Kelam – 'Dark Mountain' – which at 900m affords good views of the surrounding plains and rivers. Guides can be hired in Sintang (two hours walk to the summit). Sintang is a mainly Chinese town, founded by traders dealing with the Dayaks of the interior. On the upper reaches of the Melawi – and its tributary, the Pinoh – there are some traditional Ot Danum (upriver) Dayak groups (the equivalent of Sarawak's Orang Ulu), notably the Dohoi on the upper Melawi. The two rivers begin in the Schwaner Range.

Sintang & further east

Sleeping D-E *Flamboyan*, some a/c and some baths, a notch up from the Sasean. **E** *Sasean Hotel*, Jalan Brig Jend Katamso on the river, welcoming. *Getting there*: regular buses from Pontianak's Batu Layang bus station. There are regular passenger boats leaving Sintang for Putussibau. MAF flies between Sintang and Putussibau.

From **Semitau** – half way between Sintang and Putussibau – it is possible to visit Sentarum, Luar and Sumpa lakes. The lake area is predominantly settled by Ibans, who originally came upriver from the Batang Lupar in Sarawak; other tribal groups include the Maloh Dayaks (famed for their skill as silversmiths and goldsmiths) and the Kantuq.

Sumpa lakes

Putussibau is the last noteworthy settlement on the Kapuas before the Muller range, which divides the watersheds of the Kapuas and Mahakam (in East Kalimantan). In

Putussibau

the 1800s, when Chinese traders first visited the upper Kapuas, the settlement was frequently raided by Iban headhunters from the Batang Lupar in Sarawak. The Malays along the upper Kapuas are mainly Dayaks who converted to Islam. Despite Putussibau's remoteness, few Dayaks in the area live in traditional longhouses, the exception being the Taman Kapuas Dayaks. Two Taman Kapuas longhouses are accessible from Putussibau: Melapi I and Semangkok, the latter being more traditional; it is possible to stay overnight at both (see House Rules, page 655). Longboats for expeditions further upriver are prohibitively expensive to charter; regular passenger boats connect main towns.

Sleeping D-E *Marisa Hotel*, Jl Melati. Some a/c, range of rooms. **E** *MESS* Pemdaer, Jalan Merdeka. Good rooms with attached mandi. **E** *Harapan Kita Bersama Losmen*, Jl Pelita, close to the river.

South of Pontianak

There are few tourist attractions in the southern **Ketapang** regency, except for the 90,000 ha **Mount Palung Wildlife Reserve**, which encompasses most forest types and contains a wealth of flora and fauna, including orang utans and proboscis monkeys. It is difficult – and expensive – to get to and is mainly a scientific research centre; there are, however, basic facilities at nine camps within the park. Permits must be obtained from the Conservation Office (PHPA) in Pontianak (at Jalan Abdurrahman Saleh 33). Tourists wishing to visit the reserve should contact Mr Tan Yong Seng, director of *Ateng Tours & Travel*, whose company can organize the tortuous travel arrangements.

Background

The name Borneo is thought to be a European mispronunciation of Brunei. This was not entirely the Europeans' fault, for as John Crawfurd points out in A Descriptive Dictionary of the Indian Isles *(1856), the name is "indifferently pronounced by the Malays, according to the dialect they happen to speak – Brune, Brunai, Burne or Burnai". The sultanate itself became known as 'Borneo Proper', and its capital as Brunei Town. Crawfurd concluded that "the name of the town was not extended to the island by European writers, but by the Mohamedan navigators who conducted the carrying trade of the archipelago before the advent of Europeans". Borneo Proper was first visited by Europeans in the early 16th century, most notably by Antonio Pigafetta, the official chronicler on the Portuguese explorer Ferdinand Magellan's expedition which called in on the Sultan of Brunei in 1521. The Ibans of Sarawak maintain that the name Borneo derives from the Malay buah nyior, meaning 'coconut', while the Malays had another, less well-known name for the island: Kalimantan. This, according to Crawfurd, was the name of a species of wild mango "and the word would simply mean 'Isle of Mangoes'". This was the name chosen by Indonesia for its section of the island; for some reason, it is generally translated as 'River of Diamonds' – probably because of the diamond fields near Martapura in the south (see page 620).*

History

The outside world may have been trading with Borneo from Roman times, and there is evidence in Kaltim (East Kalimantan) of Indian cultural influence from as early as the fourth century. Chinese traders began to visit Borneo from about the seventh century – they traded beads and porcelain in exchange for jungle produce and birds'

Konfrontasi

The birth of the Federation of Malaysia on 31 August 1963 was not helped by the presence of heckling spectators. The Philippines was opposed to British North Borneo (Sabah) joining the federation, because the territory had been a dependency of the Sultan of Sulu for over 170 years until he had agreed to lease it to the North Borneo Chartered Company in 1877. But Indonesia's objection to the formation of the federation was even more vociferous. In Jakarta, crowds were chanting "Crush Malaysia!" at President Sukarno's bidding. He launched an undeclared war against Malaysia, which became known as konfrontasi – confrontation.

Indonesian armed forces made numerous incursions across the jungle frontier between Kalimantan and the two new East Malaysian states; it also landed commandos on the Malaysian peninsula, and despatched 300 saboteurs who infiltrated Singapore and launched a bombing campaign. Sarawakian Communists fought alongside Indonesians in the Konfrontasi, and there were countless skirmishes with Malaysian and British counter-terrorist forces in which many were killed. Sukarno even managed to secure Soviet weapons, dispatched by Moscow "to help Indonesia crush Malaysia". Konfrontasi fizzled out in 1965 following the Communist-inspired coup attempt in Indonesia, which finally dislodged Sukarno from power.

nests. By the 14th century, this trade appears to have been flourishing, particularly with the newly formed Sultanate of Brunei. The history of the north coast of Borneo is dominated by the Sultanate of Brunei from the 14th to 19th centuries. The Europeans began arriving in the East in the early 1500s, but had little impact on North Borneo until British adventurer James Brooke arrived in Sarawak in 1839.

To the south, in what now comprises Kalimantan, a number of small coastal sultanates grew up (see respective provincial history sections), many of which were tributary states of Brunei, and most of which are thought to have been founded by members of the Brunei nobility. The upriver Dayaks were left largely to themselves. In the 16th century, following the conversion of Banjarmasin to Islam, the religion was embraced by these other sultanates. The Dutch, who first tried to muscle-in on Banjarmasin's pepper trade in the late 1500s, were unsuccessful in establishing themselves in Kalimantan until 1817 when they struck a deal with the Sultan of Banjarmasin.

Land and environment

Geography

The highest peak in Kalimantan is Gunung Rajah (2,278m) in the Schwaner Range, to the southwest. The mountain ranges in the west and centre of the island run east-to-west and curve round to the northeast. Borneo's coal, oil and gas-bearing strata are Tertiary deposits which are heavily folded; most of the oil and gas is found off the northwest and east coasts. The island is much more geologically stable than neighbouring Sulawesi or Java – islands in the so-called 'ring of fire'. Borneo only experiences about four mild earthquakes a year compared with 40-50 on other nearby islands. But because there are no active volcanoes, Borneo's soils are not particularly rich. The two biggest rivers are in Kalimantan: the Kapuas flows west from the centre of the island, and the Mahakam flows east.

Kalimantan itself is divided into four provinces. South Kalimantan (or Kalimantan Selatan) is ubiquitously referred to as **Kalsel** and is the smallest of the four; it is the most accessible from Java and is also the highlight of most tourists' visits to Kalimantan. To the west is Central Kalimantan (Kalimantan Tenggah) which is known as **Kalteng**. It is a vast province with a very small population; few foreign tourists venture here – its only real tourist attraction is a remote orang utan rehabilitation centre near the swampy south coast. East Kalimantan (Kalimantan Timur) is known as **Kaltim** and is the richest of the four provinces because of its timber, oil and gas resources. Its main attraction is the Mahakam River which penetrates deep into the interior from the provincial capital, Samarinda. West Kalimantan (Kalimantan Barat) – or **Kalbar** – is, like neighbouring Kalteng, visited by few tourists. It is cut off from the rest of Kalimantan by the mountainous, jungled interior and can only be reached by air – although some east coast tour operators offer two-week trans-Borneo treks. The longest river in Indonesia, the 1,243 km-long Kapuas, reaches far into the interior from Kalbar's capital, Pontianak.

Tourists usually come to Kalimantan in search of two things: jungle and jungle culture – the Dayak forest tribes. It sometimes comes as a shock that loggers have beaten them into the jungle, particularly in the more accessible areas along the coasts and rivers. For quite long distances on either side of the riverbanks, the primary forest has all been 'harvested'. Kalimantan's powerful rivers (the Kapuas, Mahakam and Berito) have been the arteries of commerce and 'civilization'; the riverbanks are lined with towns and villages as far as they are navigable. Missionaries and traders have also beaten tourists into the tribal interior. Many Dayak tribes have been converted to Christianity and most have completely abandoned their cultures, traditions and animist religion. The majority of upriver people – apart from those in the remoter parts of the Apo Kayan in Kaltim – prefer to wear jeans and T-shirts, and many have relatively well-payed jobs in the timber industry.

In the neighbouring Malaysian state of Sarawak (which can now be reached overland from Pontianak), tribal culture is much more intact and more readily accessible. Despite Sarawak's notorious logging industry, its national parks are better geared to cater for 'ecotourists' than Kalimantan's, and the state's tourism infrastructure is more developed. That said, it is still possible to visit traditional longhouses in Kalimantan (in the hills of Kalsel and the upper reaches of the Mahakam and Kenyah rivers in Kaltim) – and trek through tracts of virgin rainforest. But trips to these areas take time and cost money. There are several experienced adventure tourism companies in Kalimantan – mostly based in Balikpapan and Samarinda. They categorize their tours into 'comfortable', 'safari' and 'adventure'. There are also a number of tour operators and travel agents around the world dealing with adventure tours to Kalimantan. Most have direct dealings with tour companies in Banjarmasin, Balikpapan and Samarinda.

Climate

Borneo has a typical equatorial monsoon climate: the weather usually follows predictable patterns, although in recent years it has been less predictable – a phenomenon some environmentalists attribute to deforestation and others to periodic changes to the El Niño-Southern Oscillation. Temperatures are fairly uniform, averaging 23-33°C during the day and rarely dropping below 20°C at night, except in the mountains, where they can drop to below 10°C. Most rainfall occurs between November and January during the northeast monsoon; this causes rivers to flood, and there are many short, sharp cloudbursts. The dry season runs from May to September. It is characterized by dry south-easterly winds and is the best time to visit. Rainfall generally increases towards the interior; most of Borneo receives about 2,000-3,000mm a year, although some upland areas get more than 4,000mm. Note that there are significant variations in the pattern of rainfall across Kalimantan; see page 1050 for a graph of monthly rainfall and temperature in Balikpapan.

Flora and fauna

Borneo's ancient rainforests are rich in flora and fauna, including over 9,000-15,000 species of seed plants (of which almost half may be endemic), 200 species of mammals, 570 species of birds, 100 species of snake, 250 species of freshwater fish and 1,000 species of butterfly. Despite years of research the gaps in scientists' knowledge

River roads

In Borneo, rivers are often the main arteries of communication. Although roads are being built, linking most main towns, many Dayak (tribal) longhouse communities are only accessible by river. Rivers are the mediators that divide forest dwellers from coastal settlers, and this is usually expressed in terms of upriver, or hulu and downstream, or hilir. The two terms are not just geographical; they also reflect different lifestyles and economies, different religions and cultures. In Borneo, to be hulu is to set oneself apart from the Malay peoples of the lowlands and coasts.

Contrary to many assumptions, the tribal hulu peoples were never entirely isolated and self-reliant. From early times, there was a flourishing trade between the coasts and the interior. Upriver tribal peoples would exchange exotic jungle products like rattan, benzoin, camphor, skins, hornbill 'ivory', precious stones and rare dyes for products that they could not obtain in the forest – like iron, salt, dried fish (now, tinned fish), betel and gambier. They also bartered for prestige objects like brass gongs, large ceramic Chinese pots and Dutch silver coins. Many of these prestige objects can still be seen in the longhouses of Borneo and have become precious heirlooms or pusaka.

of the island's flora and fauna remain yawning – and if anything are becoming more so. For a significant proportion of the flora of Borneo, scientists have barely any information on their geographic distribution, let alone details of their ecology. It has been estimated that around one quarter of plant species are only known from their 'type' specimen (ie the specimen on which the initial identification was based), or from one or two specimens.

Borneo's forests hit the news for all the wrong reasons in 1997: a series of **fires** scorched millions of hectares of land and shrouded an area the size of western Europe, with a population of around 100,000,000, in what became euphemistically termed 'the haze', see page 969.

Flora As late as the middle of the 19th century, the great bulk – perhaps as much as 95% – of the land area of Borneo was forested. Alfred Russel Wallace, like other Western travellers, was enchanted by the island's natural wealth and diversity: "ranges of hill and valley everywhere", he wrote, "everywhere covered with interminable forest". But Borneo's jungle is disappearing fast – some naturalists would say that over extensive areas it has disappeared – and since the mid-1980s there has been a mounting international environmental campaign against deforestation.

How extensive has been the loss of species as a result of the logging of Borneo's forests is a topic of heated debate. Brookfield et al in their book *In Place of the Forest* (1995), suggest that there "is very little basis in firm research for the spectacular figures of species loss rates that appear not infrequently in sections of the conservationist literature and that readily attract media attention." But they do admit that the flora and fauna of Borneo is especially diverse with a high degree of endemism, and that there has been a significant loss of biodiversity as a result of extensive logging. It has been estimated that 32% of terrestrial mammals, 70% of leaf beetles and 50% of flowering plants are endemic to Borneo – in other words, they are found nowhere else.

The best known timber trees fall into three categories, all of them hardwoods. Heavy hardwoods include *selangan batu* and *resak*; medium hardwoods include *kapur*, *keruing* and *keruntum*; light hardwoods include *madang tabak*, *ramin* and *meranti*. There are both peat-swamp and hill varieties of meranti, which is one of the most valuable export logs. *Belian*, or Bornean iron wood (*Eusideroxylon zwageri*), is one of the hardest and densest timbers in the world. It is thought that the largest belian may be 1,000 years or more old. They are so tough that when they die they continue to stand for centuries before the wood rots to the extent that the trunk falls.

The main types of forest include: **lowland rainforest** (mixed dipterocarp) on slopes up to 600m. Dipterocarp forest is stratified into three main layers, the top one

Hoax of the century: the Bre-X gold scandal

In 1993, shares in a small Canadian mining firm called Bre-X were worth $C0.20. In late 1996 the shares had risen 150 times to nearly C$30, valuing the company at around C$6.8bn. By May 1997 the shares were virtually worthless once more. The reason for this rags to riches to rags story? The discovery of a massive 200,000,000 ounce, US$70bn gold deposit at Busang in East Kalimantan – and then the announcement that the find was an unprecedented hoax.

The story begins in May 1993 when Bre-X acquired the mineral rights to a slice of East Kalimantan. As drilling continued so the estimates of gold reserves rose. From 1,000,000 ounces in 1993, to 8,000,000 ounces towards the end of 1995. Then, in March 1996, Bre-X announced a massive find, the motherlodes of motherlodes, with reserves of 100,000,000 ounces. Bre-X had chanced upon, it seemed, perhaps the largest gold deposits in the world. President Suharto and his friend began to fall over each other in their eagerness to get a slice of the action and large multinationals were brought in to develop what would have become a massive mining operation.

The story began to unravel when the Philippine geologist Michael de Guzman, who had played a key role in the discovery, threw himself from a helicopter into the jungles of Kalimantan on 19 March 1997. Eight days later Bre-X and the mining conglomerate Freeport McMoRan, who had run independent tests on the samples, simultaneously announced that the find had been grossly overstated. At the beginning of May, Strathcona Mineral Services, brought in to conduct independent tests, declared that there was "virtually no possibility of an economic gold deposit". As investigations continued it transpired that a fire at the Busang HQ in January had destroyed many of the drilling records. Then it emerged that the transport of samples from the site to the respected Indo Assay lab in Balikpapan had been suspiciously circuitous.

Who was in on the hoax? Most people believe that CEO David Walsh was probably oblivious. Suspicion has focused on Michael de Guzman – but he is presumed dead (the body recovered was too decomposed for firm identification) – and on the team of six Philippine geologists with whom he worked. Geologist John Federhof, who quickly took refuge in the Cayman Islands, is also under scrutiny. Why de Guzman would have salted samples is a mystery. Some people maintain that he wanted his theories on gold formation vindicated, and that this was a way to get Bre-X to continue to invest money in the project until he was vindicated. But as each core came up blank, so he was drawn into an increasingly complicated web of lies and deceit. Finally, realizing that his dream was bottoming out, he committed suicide. Others still believe that de Guzman is innocent – and that the Busang property will still strike rich. They say de Guzman committed suicide because he had contracted hepatitis B. In his suicide note he reportedly wrote "I can't handle living with all these diseases any more".

The company's epitaph is provided by one New York analyst, who reportedly warned: "Beware of small companies with big numbers."

---

rising to heights of 45m. In the top layer, trees' crowns interlock to form a closed canopy of foliage. It is the lowland rainforest which comes closest to the Western ideal of a tropical 'jungle'. It is also probably the most species-rich forest in Borneo. A recent study of a dipterocarp forest in Malaysia found that an area of just 50 ha supported no less than 835 species of tree. In Europe or North America a similar area of forest would support less than 100 tree species. The red resin produced by many species of dipterocarp, and which can often be seen staining the trunk, is known as *damar* and was traditionally used as a lamp 'oil'. Another characteristic feature of the trees found in lowland dipterocarp rainforest is buttressing – the flanges of wood that protrude from the base of the trunk. For some time the purpose of these massive buttresses perplexed botanists who arrived at a whole range of ingenious explanations. Now they are thought – sensibly – to provide structural support. Two final characteristics of this type of forest are that it is very dark on the forest floor (explaining why trees take so long to grow) and that it is not the impenetrable jungle of

Tarzan fantasy. The first characteristic explains the second. Only when a gap appears in the forest canopy – after a tree falls – do light-loving pioneer plants get the chance to grow. When the gap in the canopy is filled by another tree, these grasses, shrubs and smaller trees die back once more.

Many of the rainforest trees are an important resource for Dayak communities. The jelutong tree, for example, is tapped like a rubber tree for its sap ('jungle chewing gum'), which is used to make tar for waterproof sealants – used in boat-building. It also hardens into a tough but brittle black plastic-like substance used for *parang* (machette) handles.

Montane forest occurs at altitudes above 600m, although in some areas it does not replace lowland rainforest until considerably higher than this. Above 1,200m mossy forest predominates. Montane forest is denser than lowland forest, with smaller trees of narrower girth. Moreover, dipterocarps are generally not found, while flowering shrubs like magnolias and rhododendrons appear. In place of dipterocarps, tropical latitude oaks, as well as other trees that are more characteristic of temperate areas, like myrtle and laurel, make an appearance.

The low-lying river valleys are characterized by **peat swamp** forest – where the peat is up to 9m thick – which makes wet-rice agriculture impossible.

Heath forest or *kerangas* – the Iban word meaning 'land on which rice cannot grow' – is found on poor, sandy soils. Although it mostly occurs near the coast, it is also sometimes found in mountain ranges, but almost always on level ground. Here trees are stunted and only the hardiest of plants can survive. Some trees have struck up symbiotic relationships with animals – like ants – so as to secure essential nutrients. Pitcher plants (Nepenthes) have also successfully colonized heath forest. The absence of bird calls and other animal noises make heath forest rather eerie, and it also indicates their general biological poverty.

Along beaches there are often stretches of **casuarina forest**; the casuarina grows up to 27m and looks like a conifer, with needle-shaped leaves. **Mangrove** occupies tidal mud flats around sheltered bays and estuaries. The most common mangrove tree is the *bakau* (*Rhizophora*), which grows to heights of about 9m and has stilt roots to trap sediment. Bakau wood is used for pile-house stilts and for charcoal. Further upstream, but still associated with mangrove, is the *nipah* palm (*Nipa fruticans*), whose light-green leaves come from a squat stalk; it was traditionally of great importance as it provided roofing and wickerwork materials.

Mammals

Orang utan (*Pongo pygmaeus*) Walt Disney's film of Rudyard Kipling's *Jungle Book* made the orang utan a big-screen celebrity, dubbing him 'the king of the swingers' and 'the jungle VIP'. Borneo's great red-haired ape is also known as 'man of the jungle', after the translation from the Malay: orang (man), utan (jungle). The orang utan is endemic to the tropical forests of Sumatra and Borneo. The Sumatran animals tend to keep the reddish tinge to their fur, while the Bornean ones go darker as they mature. It is Asia's only great ape; it has four hands, rather than feet, bow-legs and has no tail. The orang utan moves slowly and deliberately, sometimes swinging under branches, although it seldom travels far by arm-swinging. Males of over 15 years old stand up to 1.6m tall and their arms span 2.4m. Adult males (which make loud roars) weigh 50-100 kg – about twice that of adult females (whose call sounds like a long, unattractive belch). Orang utans are said to have the strength of seven men but they are not aggressive. They are peaceful, gentle animals, particularly with each other. Males develop cheek pouches when they reach maturity, which they fill with several litres of air; this is exhaled noisily when they demarcate territory.

They mainly inhabit riverine swamp forests or lowland dipterocarp forests. Orang utans are easily detected by their nests of bent and broken twigs, which are woven together, in much the same fashion as a sun bear's, in the fork of a tree. They are solitary animals and always sleep alone. Orang utans have a largely vegetarian diet consisting of fruit and young leaves, supplemented by termites, bark and birds' eggs. They are usually solitary, but the young remain with their mothers until they are five or six years old. Two adults will occupy an area of about 2 sq km and are territorial, protecting their territory intruders. They can live up to 30 years and a female will have an average of three to four young during her lifetime. Females reach sexual maturity between the ages of seven and nine years and the gestation period is nine months. Female orang utans usually have only one young although twins and even triplets have been recorded. After giving birth, they do not mate for around another seven years.

Estimates of the numbers of orang utan vary considerably. One puts the figure at 10,000-20,000 animals; another at between 70,000 and 100,000 in the wild in Borneo and Sumatra. Part of the difficulty is that many are thought to live in inaccessible and little researched areas of peat swamp. No one, so far, has attempted an accurate census. What is certain is that the forest is disappearing fast, and with it the orang utan's natural habitat. Orang utans' favoured habitat is lowland rainforest and this is particularly under threat from logging. The black market in young apes in countries like Taiwan means that they fetch relatively high returns to local hunters. At the village level an orang utan might command US$100; in local markets, around US$350; and at their international destination, along with all the necessary forged export permits, travel costs and so on, from US$5,000 to as much as US$60,000.

The latest tragedy to befall the red apes was the fires that raged across Sumatra and Borneo in 1997 and 1999. According to the World Wide Fund for Nature, around 1,000 animals were either killed or captured between mid and late 1997. Some were killed for food, many others shot so that their young could be captured and sold.

Proboscis monkey (*Nasalis larvatus*) The proboscis monkey is an extraordinary-looking animal, endemic to Borneo, which lives in lowland forests and mangrove swamps all around the island. Little research has been done on proboscis monkeys; they are notoriously difficult to study as they are so shy. Their fur is reddish-brown and they have white legs, arms, tail and a ruff on the neck, which gives the appearance of a pyjama-suit. Their facial skin is red and the males have grotesquely enlarged, droopy noses; females' noses are shorter and upturned. The male's nose is the subject of some debate among zoologists: what ever else it does, it apparently increases their sex-appeal. To ward off intruders, the nose is straightened out, 'like a party whoopee whistle', according to one description. Recently a theory has been advanced that the nose acts as a thermostat, helping to regulate body temperature. But it also tends to get in the way: old males often have to resort to holding their noses up with one hand while stuffing leaves into their mouths with the other.

The 'Oran-ootan', as remembered by an early European visitor. Source: Beeckman, Daniel (1718), A Voyage to and from the

Proboscises' penises are almost as obvious as their noses – the proboscis male glories in a permanent erection, which is probably why they are rarely displayed in zoos. The other way the males attract females is by violently shaking branches and making spectacular – and sometimes near-suicidal – leaps into the water, in which they attempt to hit as many dead branches as they can on the way down, so as to make the loudest noise possible. The monkeys organize themselves into harems, with one male and several females and young – there are sometimes up to 20 in a group. Young males leave the harem they are born into when the adult male becomes aggressive towards them, and they rove around in bachelor groups until they are in a position to form their own harem.

The proboscis is a diurnal animal, but keeps to the shade during the heat of the day. The best time to see them is very early in the morning or around dusk. They can normally be heard before they are seen: they make loud honks, rather like geese; they also groan, squeal and roar. Proboscis monkeys are good swimmers; they even swim underwater for up to 20m – thanks to their partially webbed feet. Males are about twice the size and weight of females. They are known fairly ubiquitously (in both Malaysian and Indonesian Borneo) as 'Orang Belanda', or Dutchmen – which is not entirely complimentary. In Kalimantan they also have other local names including *Bekantan, Bekara, Kahau, Rasong, Pika* and *Batangan*.

Other monkeys found in Borneo include various species of leaf monkey – including the grey leaf monkey, the white-fronted leaf monkey and the red leaf monkey. One of the non-timber forest products formerly much prized was the bezoar stone, which was a valued cure-all. Bezoars are green coloured 'stones' which form in the stomachs of some herbivores, and in particular in the stomachs of leaf monkeys. Fortunately for the leaf monkeys of Southeast Asia though, these stones – unlike rhino horn – are no longer prized for their medicinal properties. One of the most attractive members of the primate family found in Borneo is the tubby slow loris or *kongkang*. And perhaps the most difficult to pronounce – at least in Dusun – is the tarsier which is locally known as the *tindukutrukut*.

Birds

Hornbill There are nine types of hornbill on Borneo, the most striking and biggest of which is the rhinoceros hornbill (*Buceros rhinoceros*) – or *kenyalang*. They can grow up to 1.5m long and are mainly black, with a white belly. The long tail feathers are white too, crossed with a thick black bar near the end. They make a remarkable, resonant 'GERONK' call in flight, which can be heard over long distances; they honk when resting. Hornbills are usually seen in pairs – they are believed to be monogamous. After mating, the female imprisons herself in a hole in a tree, building a sturdy wall with her own droppings. The male bird fortifies the wall from the outside, using a mulch of mud, grass, sticks and saliva, leaving only a vertical slit for her beak. She remains incarcerated in her cell for about three months, during which the male supplies her and the nestlings with food – mainly fruit, lizards, snakes and mice. Usually, only one bird is hatched and reared in the hole, and when it is old enough to fly, the female breaks out of the nest hole. Both emerge looking fat and dirty.

The 'bill' itself has no known function, but the males have been seen duelling in mid-air during the courting season. They fly straight at each other and collide head-on. The double-storeyed yellow bill has a projection, called a casque, on top, which has a bright red tip. In some species the bill develop wrinkles as the bird matures: one wrinkle for each year of its life. For this reason they are known in Dutch, and in some eastern Indonesian languages as 'year birds'.

Most Dayak groups consider the hornbill to have magical powers and the feathers are worn as symbols of heroism. In tribal mythology the bird is associated with the creation of mankind, and is a symbol of the upper world. The hornbill is also the official state emblem of Sarawak. The best place to see hornbills is near wild fig trees – they love the fruit and play an important role in seed dispersal. The helmeted hornbill's bill is heavy and solid and can be carved, like ivory. These bills were highly valued by the Dayaks, and have been traded for centuries. The third largest hornbill is the wreathed hornbill which makes a yelping call and a loud – almost mechanical – noise when it beats its wings. Others species on Borneo include the wrinkled, black, bushy-crested, white-crowned and pied hornbills.

Culture

People

Borneo's population is still pretty sparse by Asian standards, but compared with the state of affairs only two centuries ago it has grown enormously. Anthony Reid, in his book *Southeast Asia in the age of commerce* (1988), estimates that the total population in 1800 was just 1,500,000. The vast majority of Borneo's population is concentrated in the narrow coastal belt; the more mountainous, jungled interior is sparsely populated by Dayak tribes. It has been suggested that there was a long lasting hostile relationship between the tribal peoples of the interior and the settled coastal populations – explaining why only those people living along the main rivers like the Kapuas and Barito in Kalimantan ever converted to Islam.

Whereas the word 'native' has taken on a derogatory connotation in English – it tends to smack of colonial arrogance towards indigenous people – this is not the case in Borneo, particularly in Sarawak and Sabah. Borneo's 200-odd Dayak tribes are the indigenous people; they are generally fairly light-skinned with rounded facial features and slightly slanted eyes, although physical characteristics vary from tribe to tribe. Their diverse anthropological backgrounds have defied most attempts at neat classification.

Dayak groups are closely-knit communities and many traditionally live in longhouses. Many Dayaks are shifting cultivators. Most are skilful hunters but few made good traders – historically, that was the domain of the coastal Malays and, later, the Chinese. While Dayak communities are represented in all state and provincial governments in Borneo, they only have one province of their own – Kalimantan Tengah (Central Kalimantan), with its capital at Palangkaraya. The Dayaks lived in self-sufficient communities in the interior until they began to come under the influence of Malay coastal sultanates from the 14th and 15th centuries. Some turned to Islam, and more recently, many have converted to Christianity – due to the activities of both Roman Catholic and Protestant missionaries (see page 669). Few Dayaks – other than those in the remoter parts of the interior – still wear their traditional costumes. Most have abandoned them in favour of jeans and T-shirts.

Dayaks throughout Borneo have only been incorporated into the economic mainstream relatively recently – although they have always traded with settled 'down river' people (see box on page 659). Relations with coastal groups were not always good, and there was also constant fighting between groups. Differences between the coastal peoples and inland tribes throughout Borneo were accentuated as competition for land increased. The situation was aggravated by a general movement of the population towards the coasts. There was constant rivalry between tribes, with the stronger groups taking advantage of the weaker. Today, however, Dayak groups have relatively good access to education and many now work in the timber and oil and gas industries, which has caused out-migration from their traditional homelands. This has completely changed the lifestyles of most Dayak communities, who used to live in what some anthropologists term 'primitive affluence'. With a few exceptions, everything the people needed came from the jungle. There was an abundance of fish and wild game and building materials; medicine and plant foods were easily obtainable. Jungle products such as rattan, tree resins and edible birds nests were traded on the coast for steel tools, salt, brass gongs, cooking pots and rice wine jars from China. Villages are now tied to a coastal cash culture and western subculture.

Kalimantan's Dayak groups The coasts of Kalimantan are dominated by Malays – a broad term which includes Muslim Dayaks – and the Malays make-up about three-quarters of the population. Many originally migrated to Kalimantan from the Malay peninsula, the Riau islands and from Sumatra, and they embraced Islam in the 15th century following the conversion of the ruler of Banjarmasin.

The Kalimantan Dayaks can be broadly grouped by region. Kalsel (South Kalimantan) and Kalteng (Central Kalimantan) groups are collectively known as

Piracy: the resurgence of an ancient scourge

The straits of Melaka and the many islands in this, one of the world's busiest waterways, have always had a murderous reputation. In the first three months of 1999 there were 66 pirate attacks on shipping around the world; 38 occurred in this small corner of the globe's seas, according to the International Maritime Bureau. Some ships just suffer hit-and-run attacks; other pirates hijack entire vessels, whose cargo is removed and the ship resold under another name. In the Autumn of 1998 the Japanese-owned *Tenyu*, carrying a cargo worth US$2m, left an Indonesian port – and a day later, radio contact was lost. In December 1998 the ship, renamed and with a new crew, was discovered in a Chinese port, the original crew presumed murdered and thrown overboard. The original owners of the vessels had to pay the equivalent of nearly US$200,000 to get their ship back.

Many modern pirates use high-speed boats to escape into international waters and avoid capture by racing from one country's waters into another's. Co-operative international action offers the only way to patrol the shipping lanes successfully. Following the IMB conference, a Regional Piracy Centre was set up in Kuala Lumpur.

But while modern shipping companies might consider the rise in piracy a new and dangerous threat, there is nothing new about piracy in Southeast Asian waters. For centuries, pirates have murdered and pillaged their way along the region's coasts, taking hundreds of slaves as part of their booty. As far back as the sixth century, pirates are thought to have been responsible for the destruction and abandonment of the ancient Hindu capital of Langkasuka, in the northwest Malaysian state of Kedah. Piracy grew as trade flourished: the Strait of Melaka and the South China Sea were perfect haunts, being on the busy trade routes between China, India, the Middle East and Europe. Most of the pirates were the Malay *Orang Laut* (sea gypsies) and Bugis who lived in the Riau Archipelago, the Acehnese of North Sumatra, the Ibans of the Sarawak estuaries and – most feared of all – the Illanun and Balinini pirates of Sulu and Mindanao in the Philippines. The Illanuns were particularly ferocious pirates, sailing in huge *perahus* with up to 150 slaves as oarsmen, in as many as three tiers. The name *lanun* means pirate in Malay.

---

the **Barito River Dayaks** and include the '**Hill Dayaks**' of the Meratus mountains, northeast of Banjarmasin. The **Ngaju** live in Kalteng; they were the first Dayak group in Kalimantan to assert their political rights, by lobbying (and fighting) for the creation of Kalteng in the 1950s. The province was later separated from Kalsel, which was dominated by the strictly Islamic Banjarese. Other Dayak groups in Kalteng include the **Ma'anyan** and the **Ot Danum**, who live along the rivers on either side of the Schwaner Range.

The main groups living in East Kalimantan are the **Kayan** and **Kenyah**, who live in the Apo Kayan region and near the Mahakam River. They are also found on the Mendalam River in West Kalimantan. Almost all Kayan and Kenyah have converted to Christianity (most are Protestant). These two closely related groups were the traditional rivals of the Ibans and were notorious for their warlike ways. Historian Robert Payne, in his history *The White Rajahs of Sarawak*, described the Kayans of the upper Rejang as "a treacherous tribe, [who] like nothing better than putting out the eyes and cutting the throats of prisoners, or burning them alive".

The Kenyahs and Kayans are very different from other tribal groups, have a completely different language (which has ancient Malayo-Polynesian roots) and a well-defined social hierarchy. Traditionally their society was composed of aristocrats, noblemen, commoners and slaves (who were snatched during raids on other tribes). One of the few things the Kayan and Kenyah have in common with other Dayak groups is the fact that they live in longhouses, although even these are of a different design, and are much more carefully constructed, in ironwood. Many have now been converted to Christianity.

In contrast to their belligerent history, the Kenyahs and Kayans are much more

The palang – the stimulant that makes a vas diferens

One of the more exotic features of upriver sexuality is the palang, or penis pin, which is the versatile jungle version of the French tickler. Traditionally, women suffer heavy weights being attached to their earlobes to enhance their sex-appeal. In turn, men are expected to enhance their physical attributes and entertain their womenfolk by drilling a hole in their organ, into which they insert a range of items, aimed at heightening their partner's pleasure on the rattan mat. Tom Harrisson, a former curator of the Sarawak Museum, was intrigued by the palang; some suspect his authority on the subject stemmed from first-hand experience. He wrote: "When the device is put into use, the owner adds whatever he prefers to elaborate and accentuate its intention. A lively range of objects can so be employed – from pigs' bristles and bamboo shavings to pieces of metal, seeds, beads and broken glass. The effect, of course, is to enlarge the diameter of the male organ inside the female." It is said that many Dayak men, even today, have the tattoo man come and drill a hole in them as they stand in the river. As the practice has gone on for centuries, one can only assume that its continued popularity proves it is worth the agony.

---

introverted than the Ibans; they are slow and deliberate in their ways, and are very artistic and musical. They are also renowned for their parties; visitors recovering from drinking *borak* rice beer have their faces covered in soot before being thrown in the river. This is to test the strength of the newly forged friendship with visitors, who are ill-advised to lose their sense of humour on such occasions.

The **Bahau**, who are related to the Kayan, live in the upper Mahakam region, upriver from Long Iram; the majority are Roman Catholics. The other groups living in the upper Mahakam area include the **Modang** (they are mainly Catholic and are a subgroup of the Kenyah who migrated south), the **Bentian** and the **Penihing**. **Tanjung** Dayaks live in the middle reaches of the Mahakam; some remain animist although large numbers have converted to Christianity (both Roman Catholic and Protestant). The other main group on the middle Mahakam are the **Benuaq** – Tanjung Isuy (see page 642) is a Benuaq village, for example. They are also Roman Catholic.

In addition, there are a few **Murut** groups (the **Tidung** and the **Bulungan** to the northeast). The Murut live in Northeast Kalimantan, as well as around Tenom and Pensiangan in the southwest of Sabah and in the Trusan Valley of North Sarawak. Some of those living in more remote jungle areas retain their traditional longhouse way of life – but many Murut have now opted for detached kampong-style houses. *Murut* means 'hill people' and is not the term used by the people themselves. They refer to themselves by their individual tribal names. The Nabai, Bokan and Timogun Murut live in the lowlands and are wet-rice farmers, while the Peluan, Bokan and Tagul Murut live in the hills and are mainly shifting cultivators. They are related to Kalimantan's Lun Dayeh people, although some of the tribes in the South Philippines have similar characteristics too. The Murut staples are rice and tapioca, they are known for their weaving and basketry and have a penchant for drinking *tapai* (rice wine). They are also enthusiastic dancers and devised the *lansaran* – a sprung dance floor like a trapeze. The Murut are a mixture of animists, Christians and Muslims, and were one of the last tribes to give up head-hunting.

The **Kelabits**, who live in the highlands at the headwaters of the Baram River, are closely related to the Kelabit-Murut and the Lun Dayeh and Lun Bawang of interior Kalimantan. The Kelabit-Murut are distinct culturally and linguistically from the Murut of Northeast Kalimantan. They are skilled hill-rice farmers and the highland climate also allows them to cultivate vegetables. Kelabit parties are also famed as boisterous occasions, and large quantities of *borak* rice beer are consumed – despite the fact that the majority of Kelabits have converted to Christianity. They are regarded as among the most hospitable people in Borneo.

Deep in the forested interior of all the provinces, but mostly around the Apo Kayan, there is a very small population of nomadic **Penan**, who are related to the Punan, Bukat, Bukit, Bekatan and Ot, most of whom are now settled agriculturalists.

The **Penan** are perhaps Southeast Asia's only remaining true hunter-gatherers, who live mainly in the upper Rejang and Limbang areas of Sarawak, but there is also a small population in the Apo Kayan. They are nomads and are related – linguistically at least – to the Punan, former nomadic forest-dwellers. Groups of Penan hunter-gatherers still wander through the forest in groups to hunt wild pigs, birds and monkeys, and search for sago palms from which they make their staple food, sago flour. The Penan are considered to be the jungle experts by all the other inland tribes. Because they live in the shade of the forest, their skin is relatively fair. They have a great affection for the coolness of the forest and until the 1960s were rarely seen by the outside world. For them sunlight is extremely unpleasant. They are broad and much more stocky than other river people and are extremely shy, having had little contact with the outside world. Most of their trade is conducted with remote Kayan, Kenyah and Kelabit longhouse communities on the edge of the forest.

The **Kadazans** are found in border areas of East Kalimantan. They are a peaceful agrarian people with a strong cultural identity. Formerly, they were known as 'Dusuns', meaning 'peasants' or 'orchard people'. This name was given to them by outsiders, and picked up by the British. Most Kadazans call themselves after their tribal place names. Most Kadazans used to live in longhouses; these are rare now, and most live in Malay-style houses.

All the Kadazan groups share a common language (although dialects vary) and all had similar customs and modes of dress (see below). Up to the Second World War, many Kadazan men wore the *chawat* loin cloth. The Kadazans used to hunt with blow-pipes, and in the 19th century were still head-hunting. Today, however, they are known for their gentleness and honesty. The Kadazans traditionally traded their agricultural produce at large markets, held at meeting points called *tamus*. The Kadazan used to be animists, and were said to live in great fear of evil spirits; most of their ceremonies were rituals aimed at driving out these spirits. The job of communicating with the spirits of the dead, the *tombiivo*, was done by priestesses, called *bobohizan*. They are the only ones who can speak the ancient Kadazan language, using a completely different vocabulary from modern Kadazan. Most Kadazans converted to Christianity during the 1930s, although there are also some Muslim Kadazan.

The big cultural event in the Kadazan year is the **Harvest Festival** which takes place in May. The ceremony, known as the *Magavau* ritual, is officiated by a high priestess, or *Bobohizan*. These elderly women – who wear traditional black costumes and colourful headgear with feathers and beads – are now few and far between. The ceremony culminates with offerings to the *Bambaazon*, or rice spirit. After the ceremonies, Catholic, Muslim and animist Kadazans all come together to play traditional sports such as wrestling and buffalo racing. This is about the only occasion when visitors are likely to see Kadazan in their traditional costumes. Belts of silver coins (*himpogot*) and brass rings are worn round the waist; a colourful sash is also worn. Men dress in a black, long-sleeved jacket over black trousers; they also wear a *siga*, colourful woven headgear. These costumes have become more decorative in recent years, with colourful embroidery.

Dayak communities in Kalbar (West Kalimantan) include the **Iban**. But the Iban is far better known as the largest tribal group in East Malaysia than they are in

Painted panel from a Dayak coffin of a 'Ship of the Dead'. Note the gongs & cannon. Adapted from Hershey, Irwin (1991), Indonesian Primitive Art, OUP: Singapore

Main Dayak groups in Kalimantan

Name(s)	Main Distribution	Estimated Population	Livelihood	Society
Penan (also Punan, Ol, Basap, Bukit, Bukat, Bekatan)	Central Kalimantan	12,000	Hunter-gatherers	Egalitarian society
Kayan (also Bahau, Busang)	Central and East Kalimantan (Kayan Basin, near the Mahakam and Mendalam Rivers)	27,000	Settled agriculturalist	Stratified society: * aristocrats * ordinary villagers * slaves
Kenyah	Central and East Kalimantan	40,000	Settled agriculturalists	Stratified society
Ga'al (also Segai Long Glat, Modand, Menggai)	Central and East Kalimantan	5,000	Settled agriculturalists	Stratified society
Kelabit-Murut (also Apo Duat, Lun Dayeh, Lun Bawang)	Northeast Kalimantan	40,000	Shifting cultivators	Stratified society
Meloh (also Memaloh)	West Kalimantan (Kapuas Basin)	12,000	Shifting cultivators	Egalitarian society
Iban	West Kalimantan (Kapuas Basin)	500,000-550,000	Shifting cultivators	Egalitarian society
Bidayuh groups (Land Dayaks)	West Kalimantan	100,000	Settled agriculturalists	Egalitarian society
Malayic Dayaks	West and South Kalimantan	-	Settled agriculturalists	Egalitarian society
Barito groups	South Kalimantan	350,000	Shifting cultivators	Egalitarian society
Kadazan (also Dusun)	Border areas of East Kalimantan	400,000 (including the majority in Sabah)	Settled agriculturists; cattle raisers; shifting cultivators	Egalitarian society

NB Many formerly shifting cultivating Dayaks have embraced settled agriculture, and the trend away from shifting cultivation is continuing.

Source: Rigg, Jonathan (1996) (edit) Indonesia: the human environment, Singapore: Didier Millet.

Traditional Banjarese architecture – high ridged roofs

Before the demise of the Banjar sultanate in 1860, the big houses, called bubungan tinggi, with their characteristic, high, sharply pointed roofs (bunbungan means 'the ridge of the roof' and tinggi means 'tall'), were the homes of royalty, the high aristocracy and important state officials. All the older Banjar houses, dating back to the time of the sultanate, have disappeared, although there are several, scattered around the province, dating to the early 1900s. The nearest to Banjarmasin are at Kampung Melayu Laut and in Teluk Selong village. Increasingly, the traditional Banjar house-style is being adopted and readapted by modern architects – in Banjarmasin, the governor's official residence and the Mahligai Pancasila (Palace of the Five Principles) next door, being good examples. They are on Jalan Jend Sudirman, facing the river – as all good Banjar houses should be.

Traditional (and modern) bubungan tinggi houses are known for their decorative woodwork, all carved in belian, or ironwood – better known in Kalimantan as kayu ulin. The most distinctive decorative features are the 'wings', which continue the line of the eaves upwards, crossing at the ridgeline. Typically, these wings were carved with stylized hornbill figures, a design which originates in pre-Islamic times. According to ancient Dayak belief, the hornbill embodies the gods of the upper world. Other common decorative themes include floral and geometric designs on the woodwork in and around the house, as well as Arabic calligraphy. Many other patterns were also used including pineapples (representing success in life), mangosteens (whose pure white soul is enclosed in a dark and scruffy shell), bamboo shoots (symbolic of perceptiveness) and twisted rope (representing the family bonding of those who live inside). Today traditional woodcarving skills are still practised, although it is a dying art.

Kalimantan. The Iban are usually stereotyped as an out-going people who extend a warm welcome to visitors. Iban women are skilled weavers; even today a girl is not considered eligible until she has proven her skills at the loom by weaving a ceremonial textile. The Ibans love to party, and during the Gawai harvest festival (June), visitors are particularly welcome to drink copious amounts of *tuak* (rice wine) and dance through the night.

Probably because they were shifting cultivators, the Iban remained in closely bonded family groups and were a classless society. Historian Mary Turnbull says "they retained their pioneer social organization of nuclear family groups living together in longhouses and did not evolve more sophisticated political institutions. Long-settled families acquired prestige, but the Ibans did not merge into tribes and had neither chiefs, *rakyat* class, nor slaves." The Iban have a very easy-going attitude to love and sex (best explained in Redmond O'Hanlon's book *Into the Heart of Borneo*.) Free love is the general rule among Iban communities which have not become evangelical Christians, although once married, the Iban divorce rate is low and they are monogamous. Groups related to the Iban include the **Seberuang**, **Kantuq** and **Mualang**.

Another of the groups who live along Kalimantan's coasts are the **Bugis** ('Sea Gypsy') people, originally from South Sulawesi (see page 681). They are famous shipbuilders and their schooners are still made in Kalsel (South Kalimantan) (see page 619).

Religion

Apart from the coastal groups, many of whom converted to Islam, the inland tribes remained animist until the arrival of Europeans. The religion of all the Dayak tribes in Borneo boiled down to placating spirits, and the purpose of tribal totems, images, icons and statues was to chase bad spirits away and attract good ones, which were believed to be capable of bringing fortune and prosperity. Head-hunting (see page 670) was central to this belief, and most Dayak tribes practised it, in the belief that freshly severed heads would bring blessing to their longhouses. Virtually everything had a spirit, and complex rituals and ceremonies were devised to keep them happy.

Skulls in the longhouse: heads you win

Although head-hunting has been largely stamped out in Borneo, there is still the odd reported case, once every few years. But until the early 20th century, head-hunting was commonplace among many Dayak tribes, and the Iban were the most fearsome of all. Following a head-hunting expedition, the freshly taken heads were skinned, placed in rattan nets and smoked over a fire – or sometimes boiled. The skulls were then hung from the rafters of the longhouse and they possessed the most powerful form of magic.

The skulls were considered trophies of manhood (they increased a young bachelor's eligibility), symbols of bravery and they testified to the unity of a longhouse. The longhouse had to hold festivals – or gawai – to appease the spirits of the skulls. Once placated, the heads were believed to bring great blessing – they could ward off evil spirits, save villages from epidemics, produce rain and increase the yield of rice harvests. Heads that were insulted or ignored were capable of wreaking havoc in the form of bad dreams, plagues, floods and fires. To keep the spirits of the skulls happy, they would be offered food and cigarettes and made to feel welcome in their new home. Because the magical powers of a skull faded with time, fresh heads were always in demand. Tribes without heads were considered spiritually weak.

Today, young Dayak men no longer have to take heads to gain respect. They are, however, expected to go on long journeys (the equivalent of the Australian aborigines' Walkabout) – or bejalai in Iban. The one unspoken rule is that they should come back with plenty of good stories, and, these days, as most berjalai expeditions translate into stints at timber camps or on oil rigs, they are expected to come home bearing video recorders, TV sets and motorbikes. Many Dayak tribes continue to celebrate their head-hunting ceremonies. In Kalimantan, for example, the Adat Ngayau ceremony uses coconut shells, wrapped in leaves, as substitutes for freshly cut heads.

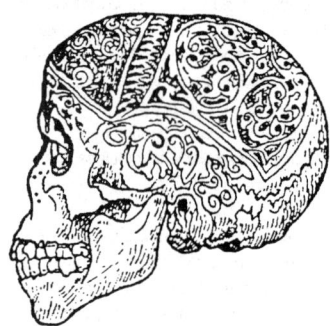

Dayak decorated human skull
Adapted from Hersey, Irwin, *Indonesian primitive art*, OUP, Singapore (1991)

Motifs associated with the spirit world – such as the hornbill (see page 663) – dominate artwork and textiles, and many of the woodcarvings for sale in art and antique shops had religious significance. Islam began to spread to the tribes of the interior from the late 15th century, but mostly it was confined to coastal districts or those areas close to rivers like the Kapuas and Barito where Malays penetrated into the interior to trade. Christian missionaries arrived with the Europeans but did not proselytize seriously until the mid-19th century. The Dutch, particularly, saw missionaries fulfilling an administrative function, drawing the tribal peoples close to the Dutch and, by implication, away from the Muslim Malays of the coast: it was a policy of divide and rule by religion means. Both Christianity and Islam had enormous influence on the animist tribes, and many converted en mass to one or the other. Despite this, many of the old superstitions and ceremonial traditions, which are deeply ingrained, remain a part of Dayak culture today.

The traditional beliefs of Kalimantan's Dayaks is formalized in the *Kaharingan* faith, which, despite the in-roads made by Christianity and Islam, is still practised by some Mahakam and Barito river groups. The religion became a focus of Dayak cultural identity when Kalteng split from Kalsel province in the late 1950s, and the Indonesian government recognizes it as an official religion, bracketing it (absurdly) with Balinese Hinduism. Kaharingan revolves around spirit and ancestor worship and is characterized by complex sets of rites and rituals, particularly those relating to death and burial. Several months after the initial funeral, a body is exhumed and cleaned and placed in a *sandung* (mausoleum), which is finely carved and decorated, alongside the remains of the deceased's ancestors. The Dayaks believe that after death, a person will join the spirit world. All the different Dayak groups have different variations on this faith.

Dance, drama and music

Dayak tribes are renowned for their singing and dancing, and the most famous is the hornbill dance. In her book *Sarawak*, Hedda Morrison writes: "The Kayans are probably the originators of the stylized war dance which is now common among the Ibans but the girls are also extremely talented and graceful dancers. One of their most delightful dances is the hornbill dance, when they tie hornbill feathers to the ends of their fingers which accentuate their slow and graceful movements. For party purposes everyone in the longhouse joins in and parades up and down the communal room led by one or two musicians and a group of girls who sing." On these occasions, drink flows freely. With the Ibans, it is *tuak* (rice wine), with the Kayan and Kenyah it is *borak*, a bitter rice beer. After being entertained by dancers, a visitor is under compunction to drink a large glassful, before bursting into song and doing a dance routine themselves. The best guideline for visitors on how to handle such occasions is provided by Redmond O'Hanlon in his book *Into the Heart of Borneo*. The general rule of thumb is to be prepared to make an absolute fool of yourself, throwing all inhibition to the wind. This will immediately endear you to your hosts.

Dance

Gongs range from the single large gong, the *tawak*, to the engkerumong, a set of small gongs, arranged on a horizontal rack, with five players. An *engkerumong* ensemble usually involves between five and seven drums, which include two suspended gongs (*tawak* and *bendan*) and five hour-glass drums (*ketebong*). They are used to celebrate victory in battle or to welcome home a successful head-hunting expedition. The Bidayuh also make a bamboo gong called a *pirunchong*. The *jatang uton* is a wooden xylophone which can be rolled up like a rope ladder; the keys are struck with hardwood sticks.

Music

The Bidayuh make two main stringed instruments – a three-stringed cylindrical bamboo harp called a *tinton* and the *rabup*, a rotan-stringed fiddle with a bamboo cup. The Kenyah and Kayan play a four-stringed guitar called a *sape*. It is the most common and popular lute-type instrument, whose body, neck and board are cut from one piece of softwood. It is used in Orang Ulu dances and by witch doctors. It is usually played by two musicians, one keeping the rhythm, the other the melody. Traditional sapes had rotan strings, today they use wire guitar strings and electric pick-ups. Another stringed instrument, more usually found in Kalimantan than Sarawak, is the *satang*, a bamboo tube with strings around the outside, cut from the bamboo and tightened with pegs.

One of the best known instruments is the *engkerurai* (or *keluri*), the bagpipes of Borneo, which is usually associated with the Kenyahs and Kayans. It is a hand-held organ in which four vertical bamboo pan-pipes of different lengths are fixed to a gourd, which acts as the wind chamber. Simple engkerurai can only manage one chord; more sophisticated ones allow the player to use two pipes for the melody, while the others provide a harmonic drone. The Bidayuh are specialists in bamboo instruments and make flutes of various sizes; big thick ones are called branchi, long ones with five holes are kroto and small ones are called nchiyo.

Crafts

The Benuaq Dayaks of the Mahakam are known for their *ikat* weaving, producing colourful pieces of varied designs. They are woven with thread produced from pineapple leaves. While traditional costumes are disappearing fast, it is still possible to find the *sholang*, colourful appliqué skirts, which have black human figures and

Textiles

Tribal tattoos

Tattooing is practised by many indigenous groups in Borneo, but the most intricate designs are those of the upriver Orang Ulu tribes. Designs vary from group to group and for different parts of the body. Circular designs are mostly used for the shoulder, chest or wrists, while stylized dragon-dogs (aso), scorpions and dragons are used on the thigh and, for the Iban, on the throat. Tattoos can mean different things; for the man it is a symbol of bravery and for women a good tattoo is a beauty-feature. More elaborate designs often denote high social status in Orang Ulu communities – the Kayans, for example, reserved the aso design for the upper classes and slaves were barred from tattooing themselves at all. In these Orang Ulu groups, the ladies have the most impressive tattoos; the headman's daughter has her hands, arms and legs completely covered in a finely patterned tattoo. Designs are first carved on a block of wood, which is then smeared with ink. The design is printed on the body and then punctured into the skin with needles dipped in ink, usually made from a mixture of sugar, water and soot. Rice is smeared over the inflamed area to prevent infection, but it usually swells up for some time.

---

dragon-dogs (*aso/asok*) sewn on top. The traditional sarong worn by Dayak women is called a *ta-ah*, which is a short, colourful, patchwork-style material.

The weaving of cotton *pua kumbu* is one of the oldest Iban traditions, and literally means 'blanket' or 'cover'. The weaving is done by the women and is a vital skill for a would-be bride to acquire. There are two main methods employed in making and decorating pua kumbu: the more common is the *ikat* tie-dyeing technique (see page 441), known as *ngebat* by the Iban. The other method is the *pileh*, or floating weft. The Ibans use a warp-beam loom which is tied to two posts, to which the threads are attached. There is a breast-beam at the weaving end, secured by a back strap to the weaver. A pedal, beneath the threads, lowers and raises the alternate threads which are separated by rods. The woven material is tightly packed by a beater. The material is tie-dyed in the warp.

Because the pua kumbu is made by the warp-tie-dyeing method, the number of colours is limited. The most common are a rich browny-brick-red colour and black, as well as the undyed white sections; blues and greens are used in more modern materials. Traditionally, pua kumbu were hung in longhouses during ceremonies and were used to cover images during rituals. The designs and patterns are representations of deities which figure in Iban myths and are believed to protect individuals from harm; they are passed down from generation to generation. Such designs, with deep spiritual significance, can only be woven by wives and daughters of chiefs. Other designs and patterns are representations of birds and animals, including hornbills, crocodiles, monitor lizards and shrimps, which are either associated with worship or are sources of food. Symbolic representations of trees, plants and fruits are also included in the designs as well as the events of everyday life. A typical example is the zigzag pattern which represents the act of crossing a river – the zigzag course is explained by the canoe's attempts to avoid strong currents. Many of the symbolic representations are highly stylized and can be difficult to pick out.

Beadwork Like the Orang Ulu of Sarawak, the upriver tribes in Kalimantan are known for their beadwork, which decorates everything from betelnut containers to baby-carriers.

Among many Kenyah, Kayan, Bidayuh and Kelabit groups, beads have long been symbols of status and wealth; necklaces, skull caps and girdles are handed down from generation to generation. Smaller glass – or plastic – beads (usually imported from Europe) are used to decorate baby carriers, baskets, headbands, jackets, hats, sheaths for knives, tobacco boxes and handbags. Beaded baby carriers are mainly used by the Kelabit, Kenyah and Kayan, and often have shells and animals' teeth attached which make a rattling sound to frighten away evil spirits. Rounded patterns require more skill than geometric patterns, the quality of the pattern used to reflect the status of the owner. Only upper-classes are permitted to have beadwork depicting 'high-class' motifs such as human faces or figures. Early beads were made from clay, metal, glass, bone or shell (the earliest have been found in the Niah Caves.) Later on, many of the beads that found their way upriver were from Venice, Greece, India and China – even Roman and Alexandrian beads have made their way into Borneo's jungle. Orang Ulu traded them for jungle produce. Tribes attach different values to particular types of beads.

Woodcarvings

Many of Borneo's tribal groups are skilled carvers, producing everything from huge burial poles to small statues, masks and other decorative items and utensils. The Kenyah's traditional masks, which are used during festivals, are elaborately carved and often have large protruding eyes. Eyes are always emphasized, as they are to frighten the enemy. Other typical items carved by tribal groups include spoons, stools, doors, walking sticks, *sapes* (guitars), ceremonial shields, tops of water containers, tattoo plaques and the hilts of *parang ilang* (ceremonial knives). The most popular Iban motif is the hornbill, which holds an honoured place in Iban folklore (see page 663), being the messenger for the sacred Brahminy kite, the ancestor of the Iban. Another famous Iban carving is the sacred measuring stick called the *tuntun peti*, used to trap deer and wild boar; it is carved to represent a forest spirit. The Kayan and Kenyahs' most common motif is the *aso*, a dragon-like dog with a long snout. It also has religious and mythical significance. The Kenyah and Kayan carve huge burial structures, or *salong*, as well as small ear pendants made from hornbill ivory. The elaborately carved masks used for their harvest ceremony are unique.

Small carved statues, or *hampatong*, are commonly found in handicraft shops. They are figures of humans, animals or mythical creatures and traditionally have ritual functions. They are often kept in Dayak homes to bring good luck, good health or good harvests. They are divided according to the Dayak cosmology: male figures (human and animal) are associated with the upper world, female figures (human and animal) with the lower world, while hermaphrodite figures symbolize the middle world. Large hampatong are associated either with death or headhunting, while others, usually placed as a totem outside a village, will serve as its protector. Another group of large hampatong are the *sapundu*, to which sacrificial victims were tied before being put to death – the victims used to be slaves; no buffalo are used.

Hats

Kalimantan's Dayak hats are called *seraung* and are made from biru leaves; they are conical and often have colourful *ta-ah* patchwork cloth sewn onto them, or they might be decorated with beads. The Kenyah – like their relations across the Sarawak border – wear distinctive grass-plaited caps called *tapung*.

Weapons

The traditional Dayak head-hunting knife is called a *mandau*. It is a multi-purpose knife with practical and ritualistic uses. The different tribes have different-shaped mandau blades, which are made of steel; their handles are carved in the shape of a hornbill's head from bone. Human hair was traditionally attached to the end of the handle. Other Dayak weapons include the *tombak* hunting spear, made from ironwood, with a steel tip. The *sumpit*, or blowpipe, was used for hunting, but now plays a largely ceremonial role during rituals and festivals. The Dayak battle shield (*kelbit*) is made from cork, and is shaped like an elongated diamond.

Blowpipes

Blowpipes are usually carved from hardwood – normally belian (ironwood). The first step is to make a rough cylinder about 10cm wide and 2.5m long. This rod is tied to a platform, from which a hole is bored through the rod. The bore is skilfully chiselled by an iron rod with a pointed end. The rod is then sanded down to about 5cm in diameter. Traditionally, the sanding was done using the rough underside of

Basketry   *macaranga* leaves. The darts are made from the *nibong* and wild sago palms, and the poison itself is the sap of the *upas* (Ipoh) tree (*Antiaris toxicari*) into which the point is dipped.

Basketry A wide variety of household items are woven from rotan, bamboo and bemban reed, as well as nipah and pandanus palms. Basketry is practised by nearly all the ethnic groups in Borneo and they are among the most popular handicrafts. A variety of baskets are made for harvesting, storing and winnowing paddy, as well as for collecting and storing other items. The Penan are reputed to produce the finest rattan sleeping mats – closely plaited and pliable. The Kayan and Kenyah produce four main types of basket. The *anjat* is a finely woven jungle rucksack with two shoulder straps; the *kiang* is also a rucksack-type affair but with a rougher weave, and is stronger and used for carrying heavier loads; the *lanjung* is a large basket used for transporting rice; while the *bakul* is a container worn while harvesting rice, so that the pannicles drop in. The *bening aban* is the famous baby carrier; it is woven in fine rattan, has a wooden seat and is colourfully decorated with intricate beadwork.

Many of the native patterns used in basketry are derived from Chinese patterns and take the form of geometrical shapes and stylized birds. The Bidayuh also make baskets from either rotan or sago bark strips. The most common Bidayuh basket is the *tambok*, which is simply patterned and has bands of colour; it also has thin wooden supports on each side.

7

Sulawesi

Sulawesi

678	**Makassar (Ujung Pandang)**	727	**Pendolo to Palu**
689	South of Makassar	743	**Poso to Manado**
692	Makassar to Toraja via Pare Pare	746	Manado
698	Toraja	760	**Background**
717	The Mamasa Valley	760	History
723	**Southeast Sulawesi**	762	Land and environment
725	Buton & Muna Islands		

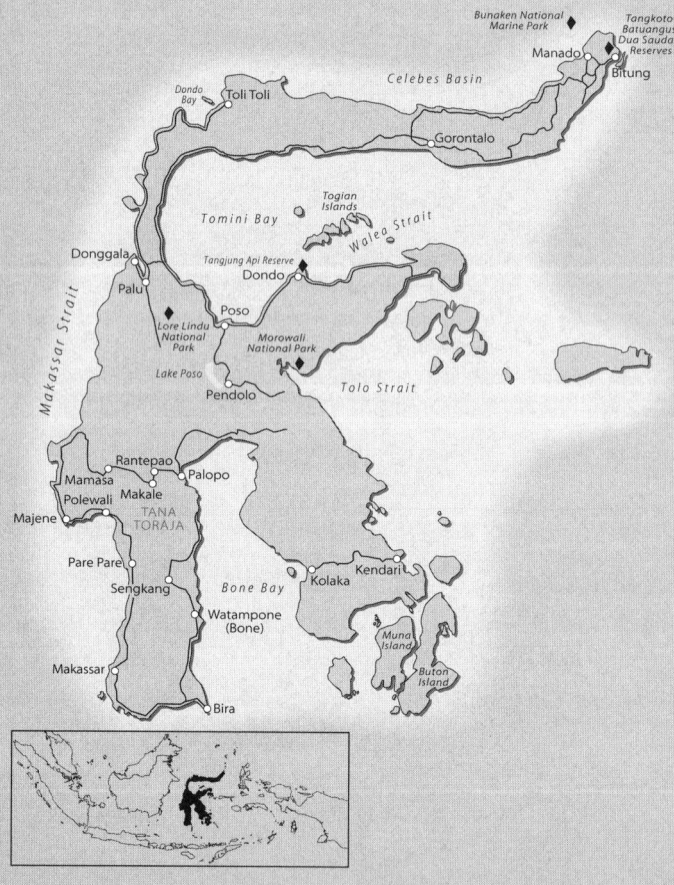

A glance at any map of Sulawesi immediately highlights the island's strangest attribute: its shape. Variously described as looking like an orchid, a deformed spider, giant crab and mutant starfish, the island's four 'arms' radiate from a mountainous core. Despite covering an area nearly as great as Britain, no place is more than about 40 km from the sea.

Sulawesi is divided into four provinces: north, south, central and southeast. Combined, they have a population of about 15,000,000. Most people visit the island to see the Toraja of South Sulawesi; their funeral ceremonies, cliff burial sites and soaring-roofed houses make this culture one of the most fascinating in the world. Makassar, formerly Ujung Pandang, is Sulawesi's largest city and unofficial capital, and is the usual port of entry. Manado, on the north tip of the island, offers some of the best diving in the country and is also becoming increasingly popular. However, with improving transport, other areas are becoming more accessible.

Ins and outs

Getting there Most people get to Sulawesi by air. The main points of entry are Makassar and Manado, although there are also air connections from outside the island with Gorontalo. There are international links between Makassar and Singapore and Manado, Singapore and Davao (Philippines). Although *Pelni* passenger ferries dock at numerous ports in Sulawesi – Makassar, Pare Pare, Raha, Bau Bau, Kendari, Pantoloan, Toli Toli, Gorontalo, Kwandang and Bitung – and there is a thriving shipping network, few visitors choose to travel here by sea.

Getting around **Road** Not long ago, Sulawesi enjoyed a reputation for having some of the worst roads in Indonesia, particularly in Central Sulawesi between Palopo and Palu. However, the Indonesian government has allocated considerable funds to improving and upgrading the 2,500 km-long Trans-Sulawesi Highway, and the road is now surfaced from Makassar to Manado.

Boat Because of the poor state of much of Sulawesi's road system, the traditional mode of transport was boat. Local *prahu* still link many coastal settlements, and travel by ship and boat can be an alternative, more comfortable, and sometimes quicker, means of getting from A to B.

Money Except in major cities like Makassar and Manado, and a few tourist centres like Rantepao, travellers' cheques other than those denominated in US$ are likely to be refused.

Makassar (Ujung Pandang)

Phone code: 0411
Colour map 4, grid C6

Makassar, lying on the west coast of Sulawesi's south peninsula, is the hot and rather ramshackle capital of the province of South Sulawesi, and the de facto *capital of the island. Until 1971 it was called Makassar, after the people who live in the area, the Makassarese. Then it was renamed Ujung Pandang. However, in 2000 the city fathers decided to revert to the old name. Whether it will stick or not remains to be seen.*

Ins and outs

Getting there Makassar is Sulawesi's unofficial capital and is much the largest city on the island. Hasanuddin Airport is 23 km north of town, and there are international connections on Silk Air with Singapore and on Garuda with Singapore and Kuala Lumpur. There are also regular flights to many destinations in Sulawesi as well as Maluku, Irian Jaya, Kalimantan, Bali and Java. The Panaikang Bus Terminal (also known as the Gowa Bus Terminal) serves destinations north of town, including Tana Toraja (Rantepao). Bemos run passengers into town or out to the terminal from the city's Sentral bemo station. For destinations south of Makassar, buses leave from the much smaller Malingkeri terminal. Ujung is, probably, the most important port in eastern Indonesia. A good number of *Pelni* vessels dock here, as well as a myriad of pinisi schooners serving Indonesia's smaller ports and harbours.

Getting around Becaks (or *tiga roda*) have not yet been pushed from the streets of Ujung as they have from some of Indonesia's other large towns. But the drivers are renowned for driving a particularly hard bargain. Bemos (or *pete pete*) and town buses are the cheapest way to get around and they are based at the Sentral terminal near the central market. There are a fair number of metered taxis, and motorbikes and bicycles are also available for hire from a few places. The **tourist office** *Kanwil Pariwisata* is inconveniently located east of the city centre on Jl Andi Pangerang Petta Rani, T443355. Some handouts, open 0800-1400 Mon-Thu, 0800-1100 Fri, 0800-1300 Sat.

Makassar (Ujung Pandang)

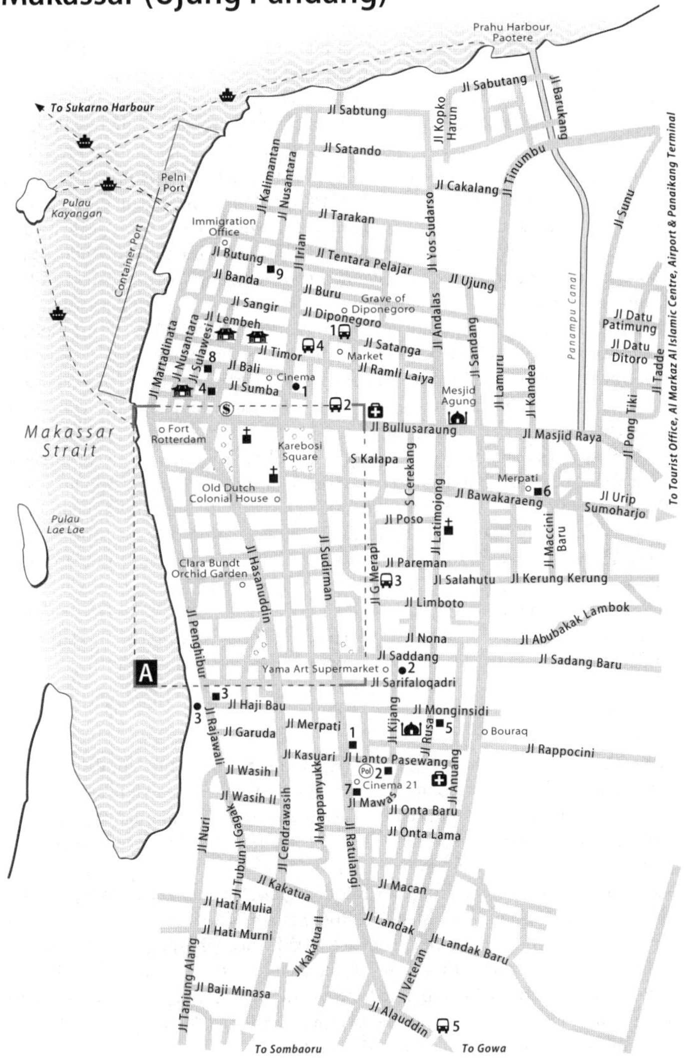

■ **Sleeping**
1 Bumi Asih
2 Hilda Tourist
3 Kenari Pantal & Café Kenari
4 Legend Hostel & Yasmin
5 Oriental
6 Ramayana Satrya
7 Sahid Makassar
8 Wisma Sumaro
9 Wisma Utama

● **Eating**
1 Mie Titi
2 Pizza Ria Café
3 Taman Safari Café

Transport
1 Alam Indah Bus
2 City Bus Station
3 Litha & Co Bus
4 Min Bemo Terminal
5 Southern Bus Terminal

Related map:
***A Ujung Pandang centre**, page 685*

Sulawesi

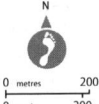

History

Makassar was the port and commercial hub of the powerful trading sultanate of Gowa which dominated the area between the 13th and 15th centuries. The skilled sailors who operated out of Makassar – the Bajau 'sea nomads' – were instrumental in enabling the sultanate to control the lucrative trade in spices from the Moluccas. Makassar became one of the great entrepôts of Southeast Asia and traders from India, China and Europe would gather here to buy produce. The kings of Gowa did not accept Islam until 1605, and a Dutch visitor of 1607 remarked on the continued use of penis balls and the tendency for lower class women to roam the city with bare breasts. Less than 40 years later when the French priest Alexandre de Rhodes published his account of the Orient, he noted that women in Makassar were clothed from head to foot so that "not even their faces can be seen".

Gowa's position as the most powerful trading kingdom in eastern Indonesia finally came to an end in 1669, when Sultan Hasanuddin signed a peace treaty with the Dutch after 60 years of intermittent warfare (see page 761). The Sultan was forced to give up control of the fort of Makassar, which became the core of a new, colonial, city.

As Sulawesi's main port of entry and exit, Makassar is visited by a considerable numbers of tourists, although given the size of the city they quickly become lost in the mass of humanity and are not particularly apparent. Recent developments in the tourism sector have focused on upmarket hotels. In addition, a newly opened container terminal has spurred investment although this will be of little interest to the average visitor. Taking a dispassionate look at Ujung, there is comparatively little to see in this characterless city with a population of around 1,500,000 and most visitors merely pass through en route to Tana Toraja and elsewhere. Accommodation for budget travellers is not too great, with a poor range of affordable places.

Sights

Benteng Makassar Benteng (fort) Makassar was built in 1545 during the reign of Tuni Pallanga, the 10th Sultan of Gowa, overlooking the sea. It was designed in the style of a Portuguese fort and is very similar to 16th century European fortresses, although an additional fortified section to the east is said to have been built to give the whole ensemble the appearance of a turtle. This, apparently, is the emblem of the seafaring Kingdom of Gowa, and symbolizes the protecting role of the fort. When the city was captured by the Dutch in 1667 it was renamed Fort Rotterdam by the victorious Dutch admiral Speelman. The Indonesian independence hero **Prince Diponegoro**, now immortalized in virtually every town, was incarcerated here for 27 years. His cell in the southwest corner of the fort is marked and a statue of the 19th century independence hero on horseback stands outside the fort (his grave is on Jl Diponegoro, see below).
■ *Admission 2,000Rp. Open 0800-1600 Tue-Sun.*

Within the precincts of the substantially remodelled fort are 13 buildings: 11 built by the Dutch and the remaining two by the Japanese. Among them is the **Makassar State Museum**. One half contains a diverse collection of coins, manuscripts, statues, traditional dresses, photographs and ceramics; the other, ethnographic artifacts, models of Torajan houses and elaborate Dutch and local sailing vessels. The collection continues upstairs, with agricultural implements, weaving technology, and examples of traditional textiles and dress. ■ *Admission 1,000Rp. Open 0800-1330 Tue-Thu, 0800-1030 Fri, 0800-1230 Sat-Sun.* Also found here is the **Conservatory of Dance and Music**, the **National Archives**, and the **Historical and Archaeological Institute**. The tourist office in the fort gateway has map handouts, plus leaflets in French, German and Dutch. The town bus No 6 which runs between the Central Market and Perumnas, along Jl Rajawali, stops by the fort.

Northeast of Fort Rotterdam, on Jl Diponegoro, is the **Tomb of Prince Diponegoro** (see page 170) along with his genealogy chart. He led the struggle

The original bogeymen – the Bugis of South Sulawesi

The Bugis were, and remain, coastal adventurers from South Sulawesi. They became renowned throughout the region for their sailing skills and fearlessness. Often likened to the Vikings, the appearance of an elegant Bugis schooner (see page 683) offshore would strike fear into coastal communities. Reports of fleets of Buginese boats plundering the islands around Java date back to the beginning of the 16th century, and when the Portuguese captured Melaka in 1511, a large Bugis fleet is said to have been sent to ward off the impertinent newcomers. Bugis wealth was not just founded on violence however; they were also skilled businessmen and controlled much of the trade between the islands of the Malay world.

Such was the Bugis' success in imposing their will across Southeast Asia, that by the early 18th century they controlled the sultanates of Johor, Kedah and Perak on the Malay Peninsula, and had established their own kingdom or negeri at Selangor near present day Kuala Lumpur. Their success inevitably brought the Bugis into conflict with the colonial powers, and by the late 18th century the Dutch and English between them had ejected the Bugis from Malaya. Befitting their role as the scourge of the archipelago, the English word bogey, or bogeyman, is derived from bugis.

---

against the Dutch that was known as the Java War (1825-30). He was finally arrested in 1830 and exiled to Manado; from there he was transferred to Makassar where he spent the remaining 27 years of his life in Fort Rotterdam.

North of the fort

North of the fort are a number of welcoming **Chinese temples** on (or near) Jl Sulawesi, the earliest of which dates from the early 18th century. Just west of here, off Jl Martadinata, is one of the three harbours where boats are loaded and unloaded with every conceivable merchandise. Further north still, at the edge of the city and 3 km from the centre, is **Paotere Harbour**. *Pinisi* and *Lambo* schooners, a smaller version of the famous island-linking bugis schooners, can be seen berthed (and wrecked!) here (see page 683). Wiry men laden with sacks and timber climb the narrow planks to load the boats with cargo. During the cooler hours of the evening the dockside acts as a meeting place and recreation ground. This is perhaps the best time to visit, as the sun sets out to sea. Get there by taking a damri Bus No 3.

South of the fort

Running south from Fort Rotterdam is the seafront road, Jl **Penghibur**. During the cooler evening hours, scores of *soto* carts and other stalls set-up along the road south from the *Makassar Golden Hotel*, to sell cheap food to promenading locals. Not far away at Jl Mochtar Lofti 15 is the residence of **Clara Bundt**. An avid collector of marine life, her house is now a museum displaying a collection of **seashells and corals**. Many of the beautiful shells are also for sale. Behind the house, the garden is filled with unique orchids and roses (*best time to visit*: March-September). Techniques of cross fertilization and inoculation have been used to produce exotic flowers, many of which have been registered with Sanders of London. **NB** The rather run-down house looks locked; walk through the garage to reach the shell collection and garden. ■ *Open 0800-1500 Mon-Sun.*

The **Sutera Alam Silk Factory** at Jl Onta **Lama** 47 is one of the best places to watch women laboriously spinning and weaving silk in a range of vibrant colours. This goes on upstairs, while the ground floor is a shop, selling a good range of silks and other fabrics, both plain and patterned, by the metre. Dyeing is done in the central courtyard using mainly local natural ingredients. The **Pasar Sentral** (Central Market) is a huge market, up Jl Cokroaminoto and just to the north of Jl Ramli, recently renovated, though still heavily congested. The **Al Markaz Al Islamic Centre** is the largest Mosque in Eastern Indonesia. The impressive building is a mix of traditional Makassar and Arabic styles and is also a repository for various holy scriptures.

Excursions

Old Gowa
About 8 km south of Makassar, just before the archway welcoming visitors to Sungguminasa, a road to the left leads to Old Gowa & its sights

Old Gowa lies south of town and was the administrative centre of the once powerful Sultanate of Gowa (see 'History', page 760). Sights of interest here include a number of tombs and a 'palace', spread over several square kilometres; they are not particularly exciting architecturally but are historically significant. Here also can be found **Somba Opu Fort**, similar in style to that in Makassar. The site is now being developed as a tourist 'objek', to be known as 'Miniature Sulawesi'. Traditional Bugis, Toraja, Gowa, Mandar and Kajang houses have been authentically recreated, providing a glimpse of several strands of Sulawesi's culture and history. The **Syech Yusuf Mosque** is a short distance off the main road. Next to the mosque are some tombs and graves; the grave of *Syech Yusuf* (1626-94) is sacred to Muslims and an important pilgrimage spot. Yusuf was a 17th century religious scholar who left Gowa on a pilgrimage to Mecca in 1644 and never returned to Sulawesi alive. Instead he settled in Banten, West Java in 1671 where, with the support of a force of fierce Makassarese soldiers, he was instrumental in organizing resistance against the Dutch and was renowned as a great Islamic teacher. He was captured in 1682, and exiled first to Ceylon and then to the Cape of Good Hope. To the consternation of Muslim purists, supplicants come here and make offerings hoping to have their wishes granted by Yusuf, who is also known as Tuanta Salamaka or 'Our Lord who grants us blessings'. Another 1 km along this road, on a bend, is the **Katangka Mosque**, claimed to be one of the oldest mosques in Sulawesi (although to the untutored eye it seems remarkably modern). It is surrounded by the pyramidal tombs and **graves of the Gowa royal family**. Continue for another 100m and turn right to reach **Tamalate**, a second royal graveyard. Set on a slight hill, the enclosure includes the *tomb of Sultan Hasanuddin* (1629-70), who fought against the Dutch from 1666 to 1669 when the weight of VOC arms finally prevailed. To the right of the enclosure is the *Tempat* (literally 'place') *Pelantikan* or Inauguration Stone, on which the Sultans were crowned. It is said that the original ancestors of the royal family descended to Earth on the stone, and the coronation ceremony bestowed divine right of kingship. The tombs of the Gowa kings are sited nearby, amongst the white kamboja flowers.

Sungguminasa
Back on the main road, 3 km south of here, is Sungguminasa, the former seat of the sultans of Gowa. Facing the square is the **Istana Ballampoa**, a wooden palace on stilts, built in 1936. It is now a **museum**, housing a rather tatty collection of national costumes, a backstrap loom, family trees, photographs and other artefacts. The **Treasure Room** is kept locked; to see the royal regalia (or *pusaka*) inside, ask at the bupati's office, across the square in front of the palace. ■ *Getting there: take a town bus (bis damri) No 2 (via Panakukang), No 4 (along Jl Veteran) or No 5 (along Jl Candrawasih), or a microlet. Becaks wait at the end of the road to take visitors to the tombs.*

Malino
The hill resort of Malino lies 70 km east of Makassar, past Sungguminasa, at an altitude of 1,050m, on the slopes of the holy Mount Bawakaraeng (also known as Mount Lompobatang). This was once a retreat for the kings of Gowa, high in the mountains, providing a more amicable climate. The best day to visit is **Sunday market day** when traders from the surrounding hills bring produce to sell here. This region is famous for its fruits and vegetables, especially tree tomatoes (tamarillos) and passion fruit. There are good walks through the surrounding forests. *Takkapala Waterfall* lies 4 km east of town, with swimming pools. It can be reached either by car or the more adventurous can hire horses in Malino. **Sleeping** In basic hotels/losmen, also the more expensive Celebes complex, contact *Hotel Celebes*, T320770, F320769. Guides are available in town for longer treks and to climb Mount Bawakaraeng which rises to 2,876m. ■ *Getting there: take a bus running towards Sinjai or charter a car (though drivers seem adverse to coming here without considerable financial inducement).*

The Pinisi schooner of Sulawesi

One of the most evocative sights in Indonesia is that of a bugis or pinisi schooner. In the past, these boats carried cargo to all the main ports of the region. But the elegant boats, that can be seen today docked at Makassar, Surabaya, Balikpapan, Sunda Kelapa (Jakarta) and other ports across Indonesia, are in fact modelled on western schooners of the 19th century. The design of the boat has continually changed as advances have been incorporated – pinisi only refers to the current design. They weigh from 120 tonnes to 200 tonnes, have a ketch rig of seven sails, and twin rudders. When fully loaded – usually with water resistant cargoes such as timber – the decks are virtually awash.

Today, many pinisi are also fitted with a 10-cylinder Mercedes engine – which costs almost as much as the boat itself – and which gives the vessels an average speed of 8-12 knots. But, despite these advances in design, the schooners are still built without plans, using handsaws and traditional tools. Instead of metal nails and bolts, 30cm-long pegs of ironwood (belian or kayu ulin) are used to bind the pajala hull together below the waterline. The problem for shipyards in Southern Sulawesi is that there is almost no ironwood left – forcing shipwrights to use inferior alternative woods. The best boats are said to be made in Banjarmasin (see page 619), where ironwood is still plentiful. Despite competition from alternative forms of marine transport, Indonesia's pinisi fleet remains one of the largest surviving fleets of sailing craft in the world.

Source: Horridge 1981, with thanks

Offshore Islands

There are a number of beautiful islands off Makassar, easily accessible as day trips from the city. **Lae Lae Island** is 3 km offshore and is populated by Makassarese fishermen. Tiny **Samalona Island** is a 45 minute boat ride across the harbour and is one of the best places to go on a day trip from Makassar, previously restricted to all but the social elite of the Makassar Yacht Club. It is a popular local resort with swimming, snorkelling (much of the coral has been damaged by dynamite fishing), fishing and water-skiing (admission to the island 5,000Rp). Snorkelling equipment is available for hire on the island. **Sleeping B** *Pulau Samalona* have 12 houseboats and chalets, T22417, F312838 for reservations. **Barrang Lompo Island** is rather further afield and offers excellent snorkelling; many of the shells on sale at Clara Bundt's museum in Makassar are pillaged from the reefs around Barrang Lompo. This is the only island to have a freshwater spring and thus is more densely populated. Schooners are dragged onto the shore to be painted and when they are returned to the sea, an elaborate ceremony is held. **Sleeping** Several losmen in the main town. ■ *Getting there: since the opening of the container terminal in Makassar, boats depart from Prahau Harbour and from the jetty just north of the Makassar Golden Hotel on Jl Pasar Ikan. However, these public boats are rather thin on the ground and visitors have reported travelling out to the islands to find there is no way back until the next day. Private boats can be chartered, approximately 150,000Rp per day.*

Kayangan Island is a different sort of island entirely. It is really just an overgrown club with discos, bars and a great deal of noise and activity. ■ *Getting there: boats leave every hour from the pier in front of Fort Rotterdam, 25 mins (6,000Rp return), the last vessel departing at about 2000.*

Caves at Taman Purbakala Leang Leang lie 42 km northeast of Makassar, and 14 km from Maros; contained within are paintings, prehistoric hand prints and paintings of deer and ox, said to be 5,000 years old. Archaeologists believe they were inhabited between 8,000 and 3,000 years ago. **Maros** is a riverside town 28 km north of Makassar. Great rafts of bamboo can be seen being floated down the Maros River, which flows through the town. In Maros, a turning to the right is signposted to **Bantimurung**, the road snaking through impressive karst scenery, clothed in thick forest. After 8 km, turn left by a mosque; a further 6 km along this rough road is the Taman Purbakala Leang Leang. There is also a small museum. ■ *Admission 1,500Rp. Getting there: take a bemo or bus (bis damri) from Makassar's Central terminal to Maros, 45 mins; from Maros catch another bemo running east towards Bantimurung and alight after 8 km at the turn-off for the park; bemos travel down this side road for the final 6 km to the caves; becaks also wait at the intersection.*

Bantimurung Falls lies 41 km northeast of Makassar on the road to Bone and are hard to miss – the entrance is marked by a monstrous archway in the form of a concrete monkey. The impressive falls cascade over a smooth rock surface, and a spectacular number of butterflies fill the air over the plunge pool. Alfred Russel Wallace came here in 1856 and was astounded by the myriad of butterflies. One such type recorded was the *Papilo androcles*, one of the rarest and largest of the swallowtails. However, the numbers are dwindling as local boys use nets to catch protected species to sell to unscrupulous tourists. The whole area is rather ruined by an over-enthusiastic use of concrete, with grottos, bridges and concrete animals disfiguring the area. There is a swimming pool (but expect to be gawped at) and restaurant. About 1 km below the falls is *Goa Mimpi* or Dream Cave. ■ *Admission 4,000Rp to the falls area, including entrance to the associated caves. There is a display of butterflies revealing that more than 200 species have been found here (admission: 2,000Rp). Getting there: take a bemo from Makassar's Sentral terminal to Maros, 45 mins, or a Damri bus from the Central Market and then a bemo from Maros to Bantimurung, 30 mins. Alternatively, charter a taxi (100,000Rp).*

Tours Most tour companies run city tours, day trips to Bantimurung Dream Cave and to see the butterflies (210,000Rp).

Essentials

Sleeping
■ *on maps, pages 679 & 685*
Price codes: see inside front cover

Makassar has a good range of mid- & upper-bracket accommodation. Losmen for budget travellers are thin on the ground & often dirty, which probably explains why backpackers tend to keep their stay here as short as possible

L *Sedona Makassar 'Quality Hotel'*, Jl Somba Opu 297, T870555, F870222, sedonaup@indosat.net.id, http://www.sedonahotels.com.sg This red and white, 230-room hotel, on 10 floors, dominates the skyline at the southern end of the city. Facilities include swimming pool, fitness and business centres, satellite TV, 2 restaurants, one of which is a crazy Tex-Mex style, 1 bar and a nightclub. Best in town, with staff who all speak English. **L-AL** *Radisson*, Jl Somba Opu 235, T333111, F333222; 90 rooms business hotel, restaurants and open terraces with good sunset views, good range of facilities. **AL** *Kenari Pantai*, Jl Haji Bau 289, T852352, F872126. Same management as the *Kenari Tower*, rather poor value, includes breakfast, travel agency attached. **AL** *Kenari Tower*, Jl Yosef Latumahina 30, T874250, F872126. A/c, restaurant, excellent, friendly and helpful staff, 34 clean rooms, good location although the views are now blocked by the nearby *Sedona Hotel*. **AL** *Marannu City*, Jl Baji Gau 52, T852244, F873606. A/c, 400 rooms, restaurant, large pool with no shade, inconvenient location south of the city, bungalows have little character, tennis. **AL** *Marannu Tower*, Jl Hasanuddin 3-5, T315087, F321821. A/c, restaurant, very dirty pool, available for use by non-residents (10,000Rp), fitness centre, ugly hotel block in city centre with 400 rooms. TV, minibar, hot water, comfortable enough but barely an ounce of charm. **AL-B** *Losari Beach*, Jl Penghibur 10, T326062, F313978; 60-room hotel catering mostly to local businessmen, all a/c, excellent position on the seafront close to Fort Rotterdam, ugly furnishings but comfortable enough simple rooms, breakfast included. **A** *Celebes Hotel*, Jl S Hasanuddin 2, T320770, F320769. Newish hotel, rooms with TV, phone, but poor rooftop restaurant, central location. **A** *Hotel Pantai Gapura Makassar*, formerly the *Makassar Gate Beach*, Jl Pasar Ikan 10, T325791, F316303, hotelpg@upg.mega.net.id The deluxe rooms are in separate bungalows (recommended) on stilts above the water – a great position on the seafront. Attractive pool and immaculate grounds, the aptly named *Pinisi Restaurant*, situated in a raised pinisi schooner, has good food and is worth it for the novelty value. **A** *Losari Metro*, Jl Chairil Anwar 19, T331133, F331188; 57 rooms, each with the normal facilities of a hotel in this price range, also a fitness centre. Part of the *Losari Beach* group of hotels. **A** *Makassar Golden*, Jl Pasar Ikan 50-2, T314408, F320951. A/c, poor and rather gloomy. Also houses the *Silk Air* office. **A** *Sahid Makassar*, Jl Ratulangi 33, T875757, F875858. A very attractive, professionally run hotel, 220 well equipped rooms. **A** *Victoria Panghegar*, Jl Jend Sudirman 24, T328888, F312468. A/c, 115 rooms, restaurant, pool, on main road, away from seafront, comfortable, well managed, price includes breakfast. Recommended. **A-B** *Hotel Delta*, Jl Hasanuddin 43, T312711, F312655. A/c, small hotel, large rooms, friendly.

Makassar centre

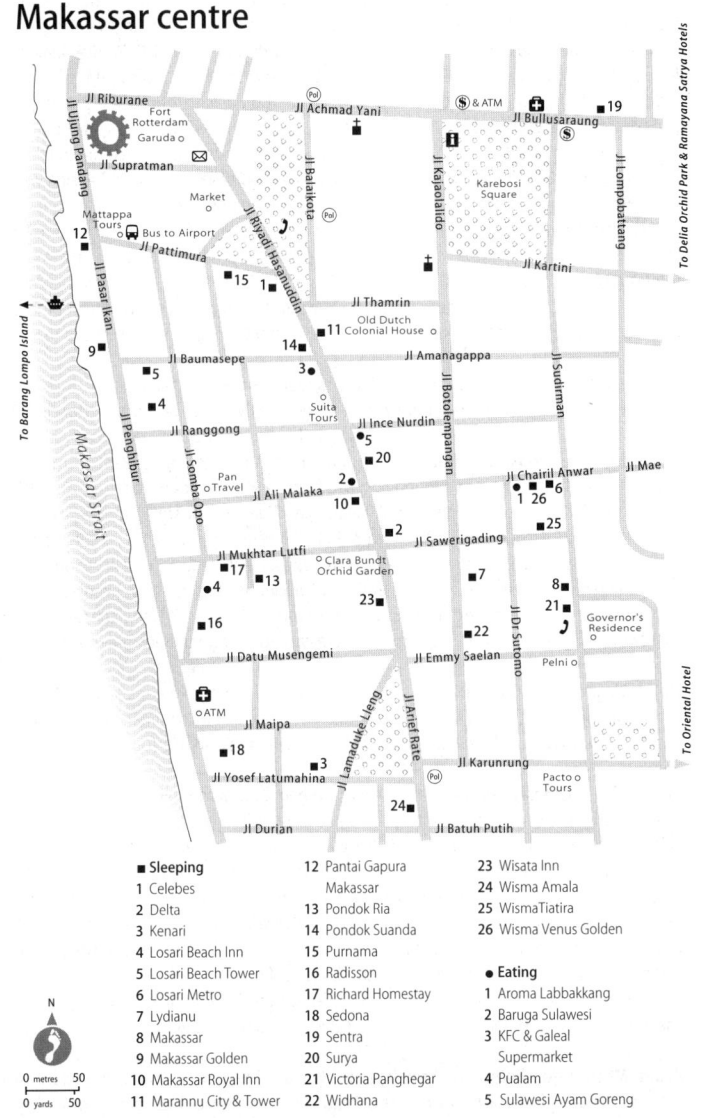

- **Sleeping**
1 Celebes
2 Delta
3 Kenari
4 Losari Beach Inn
5 Losari Beach Tower
6 Losari Metro
7 Lydianu
8 Makassar
9 Makassar Golden
10 Makassar Royal Inn
11 Marannu City & Tower
12 Pantai Gapura Makassar
13 Pondok Ria
14 Pondok Suanda
15 Purnama
16 Radisson
17 Richard Homestay
18 Sedona
19 Sentra
20 Surya
21 Victoria Panghegar
22 Widhana
23 Wisata Inn
24 Wisma Amala
25 Wisma Tiatira
26 Wisma Venus Golden

- **Eating**
1 Aroma Labbakkang
2 Baruga Sulawesi
3 KFC & Galeal Supermarket
4 Pualam
5 Sulawesi Ayam Goreng

B *Hotel Bumi Asih*, Jl Sam Ratulangi 17, T875555, F875101. Medium-sized hotel with 45 rooms all with a/c, TV, IDD telephone, restaurant. **B** *Hotel Yasmin*, Jl Jampea 5, T320424. Of average quality, the standard rooms are small and the bathrooms tiny, strong smell of food fills the building. **B** *Venus Golden*, Jl Botolempangan 17, T324995. A/c, no restaurant but next to *Aroma Labbakkang*, medium-sized newish hotel, very clean, helpful staff, cool lounge area. **B-C** *Puri Wisata*, Jl Sultan Hasanuddin 36-38, T324344, F312783. Some a/c, immaculate, medium-sized businessman's hotel with rooms set around courtyard, there are also 4 economy rooms at **D**, peaceful, central location, friendly, includes breakfast. Strongly recommended. **C** *Delia Orchid Park*, Jl Urip Sumaharjo Km 6, T442325; 22 rooms, a/c, out of town, in garden compound with orchids and birds. **C** *Hotel Surya*, Jl D G Tomp 3, T327568, F311498. Price of the rooms increases slightly depending on height, rooms equipped with a/c, TV, minibar, central location. **C** *Makassar Royal Inn*, Jl Daeng Tompo 8, T322903, F328045. A/c, 30 rooms, very clean, on quiet backstreet close to Pantai Losari with evening foodstalls nearby, rooms have attached bathrooms, some with hot water, friendly staff, includes breakfast and is therefore good value for Ujung. Recommended. **C** *Pondok Suanda Indah*, J1 Sultan Hasanuddin 12, T317179, F312856. Next to *KFC*, 12 rooms, the standard rooms are massive, whilst the economy are smaller but both have a/c and TV. Pleasant gardens out the back but some noise from the road. **C** *Richard Homestay*, Jl Mochtar Lufti 21, T320349. In the shadow of the Raddison 'Quality Hotel', great rooms situated on 2nd floor but not en suite. **C-D** *Hotel Lydiana*, Jl Botolempangan 33, T328004. All rooms have a/c and TV, more pricey rooms also have a bath, very compact rooms. A good mid-range hotel. **C-D** *Wisma Utama*, Jl Sarappo 99, T327744. In a rather noisy and dirty part of town, on last inspection was undergoing a long overdue paint job. Price includes breakfast. **C-E** *Ramayana Satrya*, Jl G Bawakaraeng 121, T442478, F442479; 65 rooms, some a/c, convenient for the bus station, far from the town centre and seafront, but convenient for those planning on going direct from the airport to Toraja without going into town centre.

D *Kenari Pantai*, J1 Somba Opu 289, T872183. 15 rooms, price includes breakfast. Excellent position but noisy. Rooms small but clean, with good views over bay. **D** *Oriental*, Jl WR Monginsidi 44, T873558. Some a/c, ramshackle and grubby, but cheap a/c rooms with TV. **D** *Wisma Tiatira House*, Jl Dr Sutumo 25 (1 km from centre of town), T318948. Some a/c, quiet 15-room hotel in green surroundings. **D-E** *Pondok Ria 7*, Jl Bontomacaw 7, T323991. Only cold water, includes breakfast, popular with locals. **E** *Legend Hostel*, Jl Jampea 5G (near the port, next to *Hotel Yasmin*), T328203, F311445, . A very popular backpackers hangout, restaurant, free tea, 9 clean but cramped rooms, convenient location, excellent source of information for travellers, email facilities available. Will arrange bus transport heading north, rather hot and cramped in the dorm **F**. **E** *Wisma Sumaro*, Jl Jampea 27. Down the same road as *Legend* and *Hotel Yasmin*, good, clean, economical and a/c rooms. Recommended.

Hotels near the airport **C-D** *Darma Nusantara Hotel*, Jl Perintis Kemerdekaan, T511708; 1 km from the airport, saving a 23 km ride into town if catching a connecting flight the following day. **D** *Hasanuddin Transit Hotel*, Jl Perintis Kemerdekaan, T851082.

Eating

Although not everyone likes Makassar, few would argue that it offers delicious, inexpensive seafood. The local speciality is ikan bakar, barbecue grilled fish

Indonesian **Expensive to mid-range**: *Ayam Goreng Ratu Muda* Jl Ranggong 19. Serves, believe it or not, *ayam goreng*, but also excellent Chinese cuisine and seafood dishes, reasonable prices, popular with locals. *Baruga Sulawesi*, Jl S Hasanuddin 32, chicken and fish, single portions or large portions for 3-4. **Cheap** *Aroma Labbakkang*, Jl Chairil Anwar 25, T314520. Excellent seafood restaurant with ugly grotto exterior, frequented by Makassar's Chinese community. Recommended (closed some lunchtimes). *Rumah Aroma Makan Labbakong*, Jl Chavil Anwar. Clean and pleasant, above *Galael's* supermarket. *Sulawesi Ayam Goreng*, on corner of Jl Hasanuddin and Jl Ince Nurdin, T324330. Popular, with some tables outside, amongst the barbecue smells, chicken and fish. *Restaurant Pualam*, Jl Somba Opo. Slightly cheaper option and like many others has good chicken and seafood dishes.

Asian Mid-range: *Shogun*, Jl Penghibur 2, T324102. The best Japanese restaurant in Makassar. **Cheap**: *Surya Super Crab*, Jl Nusakembangan 16. Crab is their speciality, but they also serve prawns, squid and fish and other Chinese dishes. Highly regarded, large servings, though sauces can be sweet. Recommended. **Very cheap**: *Mie Titi*, Jl Irian. Good Chinese food. **Restaurant Hong Kong** , Jl Timuro, good value and great tasting Indonesian and Chinese-style dishes including such schizophrenic dishes as *pisang goreng Szechuan*!

International There is little to offer in the way of western food, although the large hotels have coffee shops and restaurants serving international cuisine. There are several bakeries/pastry shops and ice-cream parlours (the one in front of the *Golden Makassar Hotel* is recommended). Also *Pizza Ria Café*, Jl Sungai Saddang on corner with Jl Gungung Latimojong.

Foodstalls The best place to eat cheaply in the evening is along the waterfront, where hundreds of stalls set up to serve the local community. There are also a large number of excellent warungs that set up opposite the fort entrance on Jl Jend A Yani, and some warungs serving Chinese-style dishes along the promenade near the *Makassar Golden Hotel*.

Bars *Café Taman Safari*, Jl Penghibur (corner of Jl Haji Bau), fine position on the seafront close to a Bugis fishing community, cold beer and views of the sun setting. *Café Kenari*, Jl Haji Bau 289, attached to *Kenari Pantai Hotel*.

Entertainment **Cinema** *Benteng Theatre*, Jl Makassar; *Studio 21-25*, Jl Dr Ratulangi (near intersection with Jl Lanto Dg Pasewang), a/c cinema showing occasional western films. Also the air-conditioned Makassar Theatre on Jl Bali. **Karaoke bars** *Irani*, south end of Jl Somba Opu. **Disco** *Zig Zag*, at the *Makassar Golden Hotel*, Jl Pasar Ikan 50-2. *'M' Club* , on Jl Panakukkang Mas.

Festivals **Apr** (1st) **Anniversary of Makassar**, most events and cultural shows occur in the week before the anniversary. A formal ceremony is held in the square. **Jun** (1st) **Cleansing of Royal Regalia and Heirlooms**, 1 chance in the year for the public to get a good view of the royal regalia. **Jul** (17th-23rd) **South Sulawesi Cultural Festival**, an arts festival of both traditional and contemporary arts and culture. Exhibitions, tournaments, parades, dancing. **Aug** (17th) **Pelra Race**, traditional Buginese/Makassarese boats start from here in a race to Sunda Kelapa, Jakarta. (19th): *Makassar Regatta*, international yacht race.

Shopping **Antiques** Jl Somba Opu and Jl Pasar Ikan/Jl Pasar Baru shops have some good antique buys as well as fakes. **Baskets** Jl Tinumbu and shops along Jl Nusantara and Jl Kakatua sell rattan and bamboo. **Ceramics** North end of Jl Somba Opu. **Gold & silver** Several shops along Jl Somba Opu. **Market** Jl Sultan Alauddin, good local baskets. **Silk** *Sutera Alam*, Jl Onta 47 (see page 681), 18,000Rp per metre (plain), 27,500Rp per metre (patterned). **Souvenirs** Shops along Jl Pattimura sell souvenirs – mostly items from Tana Toraja.

Sports **Billiards** *Idola Billiard Hall*, Jl Karunrung, and the *New Hilman* opposite *Legend Hostel* on Jl Jampea. **Golf** *Makassar Golf Club*, 14 km north of town off the road to the airport, open to non-members, clubs for hire. **Swimming** The *Victoria Panghegar* and *Marannu City* hotels both allow non-residents to use their pools, 10,000Rp (although neither are very good), as does the inconveniently located *Marannu Garden*, south of town, where there is a large, often empty, pool. **Windsurfing** The Popsa club facing Fort Rotterdam has boards for hire.

Tour operators *Ramayana Satry Tours*, Jl Bolukunyi 9A, T853665; *Libra Golden Star*, *Victoria Panhegar Hotel*, Jl Sudirman 24, T312841, F312468; *Mattappa Tours*, Jl Monginsidi, T871390, F853265. *Pelni* dates/movements on board in office (saves trip further north); *Nitour*, Jl Lamaddukelleng 2, T217723; *Pacto*, Jl Jend Sudirman 52, T873208; *Pan Travel*, Jl Pengayoman, T454159; *Libra Golden Tours and Travel*, Jl Jend Sudirman 24, T312841, F312468; *Natrabu*, Jl Serigala 10A, T317723, F317723; *Nell Tours*, Jl Cendrawasih V/103, T852445, F872061, nelltours@upg.mega.net.id, car rental; *Anta Express* , Jl Dr W H Sudiro Husodo 34A, T321440, F313910; *Toraja Highland*, Jl Rambutan 3, T852496, F873083; *Tata Pesona Wisata*, Jl G. Lokon 15, T317141, 326486, F311455, legetata@indosat.net.id, ask for William who speaks good English; *Sena Tours and Travel*, Jl Jampea 1A, T323906, F323906.

Transport

*70 km from Malino,
155 km from Pare Pare,
180 km from Bone
(Watampone), 328 km
from Rantepao,
168 km from
Bulukumba*

Local Becaks: known as *tiga roda*, they are available all over town and are single seaters, but be prepared to bargain hard. If you are a softy when it comes to prising that extra 500Rp from a fare, then this can become a rather expensive form of transport and makes taxis a more economical option. **Bemos**: locally known as *pete pete*, 400-700Rp around town; the main terminal is by the central market, appropriately named 'Sentral'. Bemos from here to most local destinations. **Bicycles and Motorbikes**: mountain bikes for hire from *Legend Hostel*, Jl Jampea 5 (7,500Rp, 50,000Rp respectively). **Metered taxis**: flagfall 2,000Rp, or hired for the day through your hotel for about 100,000Rp. Town buses (bis damri): run set routes, most setting off from the Sentral terminal (400Rp): No 3 to Daya, No 2 to Sungguminasa via Jl Panakukand, No 3 to Batangase and the airport via the toll road, No 5 to Sungguminasa via Jl Cendrawasih, No 6 to Perumnas via Jl Rajawali. Bus No 4 leaves from the Pannampu Market along Jl Veteran to Sungguminasa.

Air Makassar's **Hasanuddin Airport** is situated at Mandai, 23 km north of the city centre (30 mins drive). Regular connections by *Merpati/Garuda* and *Bouraq*, with numerous destinations including daily direct flights to Ambon, Balikpapan, Biak, Denpasar, Jakarta, Jayapura, Solo, Kupang, Samarinda, Maumere, Surabaya and Ternate. Within Sulawesi, there are connections with Gorontalo, Kendari, Manado and Palu. **International**: *Silk Air* has direct flights to Singapore on Mon and Thu, whilst Garuda flies to Singapore and Kuala Lumpur.

Airport tax: 30,000Rp on international connections, 9,000Rp for domestic flights leaving Ujung. Transport to town: taxi from airport to town, 20,000-23,000Rp; booth is on the left as one exits from the terminal. **NB** The drivers charge an extra 4,000Rp if taxis are shared and they need to make a second drop-off. The best bus to town is the one marked 'Patas', a limited express bus. The slower City bus (bis damri) No 3 goes past the airport entrance from the Central Market (on the toll road), it is a 500m walk from the road to the airport. For both buses, stand on the same side of the road as the airport for the journey to town. Bemos running between Ujung and Daya also pass in front of the airport entrance. For transport to the airport, catch the *Patas* bus from outside the *Mattappa Travel Agent*, on Jl Pattimura, or outside Bank Rakyat of Jl Jend A Yani (every 30 mins, 1,500Rp). If taking the town bus be advised that it is very slow and to leave enough time. **Airport facilities**: a money changer, information desk and hotel booking counters but very little else. Check the newspaper *Fajar* for flight details out of Makassar for the week ahead.

Road Bus: the Panaikang Terminal (also known as the Gowa Bus Terminal) for north-bound long-distance buses is at the east edge of town on Jl Urip Sumoharjo (the continuation of Jl Bawakaraeng), just past the '45 University. Regular bemos run between the terminal and the Sentral bemo station in the city centre. There are plenty of foodstalls and shops to stock up on fruits, water, biscuits etc for the journey. *Pelni* information is available at this bus station. Regular connections with Tana Toraja (10 hrs, 17,000Rp), Bone Bone (4 hrs), Pare Pare (5 hrs), Sengkang (5 hrs), Soppeng (4 hrs), Bulukumba, Palopo and other major destinations in South Sulawesi. There are also buses to Bajoe, where nightly ferries depart for Kolaka in Southeast Sulawesi. *Litha*, Jl G Merapi, T324847, or terminal office, T442263; *PIPOSS*, Jl Buru 10A, operates buses to Palopo; while *Cahaya Bone*, Jl Andalas 37, T24225, have a service to Bone (departs 0800 town centre, Makassar (office) 0830 Panaikang). **NB** *Liman Express* and *Cahaya Bone* are convenient because they both have offices in the town centre, 5 mins walk east from the bemo station. But by taking the time to visit the Panaikang bus station (400Rp by bemo), it is possible to scout around all the private companies at the back of the terminal and book a numbered seat; 800Rp well spent. For destinations south of Makassar, buses leave from the much smaller Malingkeri terminal on Jl Alauddin. Bus companies vary considerably in terms of the quality of the service they provide. Among the more popular are *Damri*, *Litha* and *Indra*.

Sea Boat: Makassar is a major port and a good place to catch a ship or boat; 12 *Pelni* ships stop here, there are 5 ships a fortnight to Jakarta and 6 to Surabaya (see route schedule, page 988). The *Pelni* Office is at Jl Jend Sudirman 14, T317965. *Kalla Lines* (Jl Nusantara Baru 444, T320464, near the harbour) run a ship which follows a 2 week loop stopping at Jakarta,

Surabaya, Balikpapan, Tarakan, Pantoloan and Ternate. The Kalla Lines office is at Jl Jend Sudirman 54, T852112. Ships leave from the Pelabuhan Sukarno to the north of town. *Pinisi* schooners also run regularly between Makassar's Paotere harbour and most other ports in Sulawesi and beyond; simply ask around.

Directory

Airline offices *Bouraq*, Jl Veteran Selatan 1, T452506; *Garuda*, Jl Slamet Riyadi 6, T317359, office hours Mon-Fri 0730-1630, Sat 0730-1300, Sun 0900-1200; *Mandala*, Komplek Latanette Plaza, Jl Sungai Saddang, T325592, F314451; *Merpati*, Jl G Bawakaraeng 109, T442471; *Silk Air*, Main Lobby, *Makassar Golden Hotel*, Jl Pasar Ikan 50, T326733, F326780, 0830-1630 Mon-Fri, 0830-1300 Sat. **Banks** *Bank Dagang Negara*, Jl Nusantara 147-149; *Bank Central Asia*, Jl Jend A Yani 31, accepts TCs and ATMs dotted around the city accept foreign credit cards. *Bank BNI 1946*, Jl Sudirman 1, on corner with Jl A Yani; *Bank Indonesia International*, Jl Kajaolaido 6, good rates for TCs; *Bank CIC*, Jl Irian 17, good rates for TCs; *Bank Duta*, Jl Ratulangi, (but no TCs or foreign cash cards accepted). **Communications** General Post Office: Jl Slamet Riyadi 10 (corner with Jl Supratman). **Internet:** *Legend's Hostel*, Jl Jampea 5, a fast service (20,000Rp per hr); Post Office: Jl Andi Pangerang Petta Rani, east of town. **Telephone:** small Wartel office just south of *Victoria Panghegar Hotel*. Many others scattered through the city including Latanete Wartel, Jl Sungai, Saddang and Losari Wartel, Jl Penghibur, which allow collect calls. **Wartel:** Jl Bawakaraeng 84 (for fax, telegrams and telephone). **Medical facilites** Hospitals: RSU DR Wahidin Sudiro Husodo, Jl Perintis Kenerdaan Km 11. **Useful addresses** Immigration office: Jl Sultan Alauddin 34A, T83153. **Police:** Jl Jend A Yani 9, T319357.

South of Makassar

Bira

Phone code: 0413
Colour map 4, grid C6

Bira is situated at Sulawesi's far southeast corner and the South Sulawesi Tourist Board has very high hopes for Bira as a resort, often mentioning Bali in the same breath. As yet, this vision is a long way off – and it is hard to believe that anything so audacious will ever materialize. But the fine white sand, crystal clear waters and rich fauna and flora make this a very pleasant place to rest for a few days. Rainfall is much lower than in Ujung and water supply intermittent, consequently drinking water is trucked in tankers to supply the growing number of losmen.

The low lying hills are covered in light forest and inhabited by monkeys and other animals. The area boasts caves which are home – so it is said – to pythons of truly gargantuan proportions. Guides can be employed to show visitors the caves and to deal with truculent reptiles. However, the nearest most visitors will probably come to them is to see their trails in the sand. For the less adventurous, the *Sapolahe Hotel* has a 5m-long snake safely locked in a cage. ■ *Entrance to Bira: payable at the 'gate', 1,000Rp, though the gate is not always attended.*

Sights

Obviously, most tourists, both domestic and foreign, head straight for the beach. The scenery becomes more tranquil and the beach less busy the further from Bira you venture. It is certainly worth walking for 10-15 minutes to discover a private cove, especially on a Sunday when the local tourist spotting activities reach their peak. Snorkelling and diving is a growing attraction. Some coral, many fish, turtles, sea snakes and the occasional fly-past by dolphins can all be seen.

Excursions

Lihukan Island, just 4 km off the peninsula's west beach, can easily be reached by boat, organized from Bira. The island is a locally important weaving centre and there is also some reasonable snorkelling off-shore.

Tanah Beru, 18 km away along the coast, is the ship-building centre of the area and well worth visiting for those fascinated by things nautical. The traditional techniques can be seen, where the entire boat is constructed from wood. All types of vessel – *pajala* (10m), *patorani* (17m and used for catching flying fish or *torani*) and the larger ocean-going *paduwakang* are built here. The most famous product of the area though is the Bugis *pinisi* schooner (30m+), but these are now few and far between (see page 683). ■ *Getting there: by bemo (1,000Rp).*

Sleeping **B** *Sapolahe*, T82128. Cottages set back 50 m from the sea, some a/c, spotlessly clean and beautifully built from local woods. Restaurant (mid-range) with limited menu, overpriced and therefore underpopulated hotel with good sea views from the restaurant, and several creatures in cages. **B-C** *Bira Beach*, T81515. Cottages on stilts, some with sea views, others set a little way back from the beach, cheaper rooms are better value and spotlessly clean, restaurant (mid-range) popular with good food, diving centre here.

The 'resort' of Bira provides a range of accommodation, but as yet the multi-million dollar investors have not entered the arena, perhaps explaining why the place seems a little ramshackle

C *Anda Bungalows*, 7 bungalows with showers, balcony and tranquil setting, intermittent water supply, restaurant (cheap). **C** *Nusa Bira Indah*, very clean rooms, some with baths, price includes breakfast, 5 more rooms under construction, restaurant (mid-range). **C** *Bira View Inn*, 14 stilted rooms with TV and fan. This place enjoys the best location of the hotels,

South Sulawesi

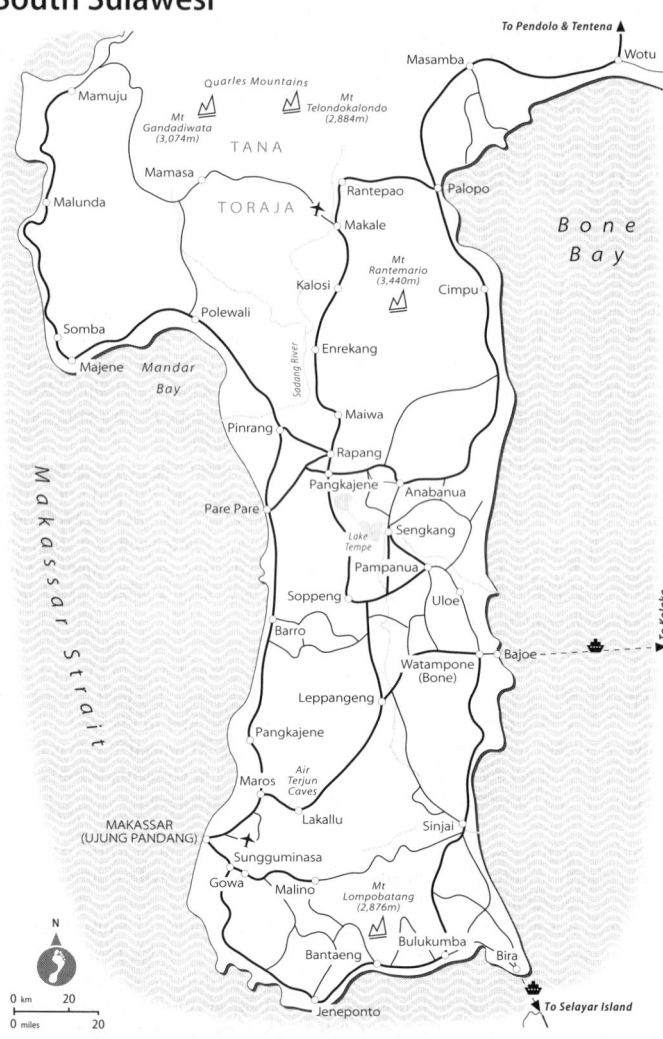

being just 5m from the sea and with great views. Price includes breakfast, no restaurant but drinks available, large rooms, popular spot for the locals to come and 'tourist spot' at sundown. Recommended.

D *Pondok Wisata Bahagia*, Jl Kopongkalang 2 11 rooms geared mainly for locals, with rather basic rooms, all clean and with attached mandi, price negotiable, restaurant (cheap).

D *Riswan Bungalows*, T82127. Seven individual traditionally constructed bungalows, clean and tranquil, attached mandi, squat toilet, shower, snorkel hire, tours and other information, price includes breakfast, good value.

D *Riswan Guesthouse*, same owner as *Riswan Bungalows*. Fort-like location on top of hill, 100m from the sea, 8 rooms and 4 mandis, lockers, book exchange, balcony – the budget travellers hang-out, price includes 3 meals and tea and coffee, great views of beach and sunsets. Riswan speaks good English and is knowledgeable about the area. Recommended.

E *Sunrise Homestay*, clean and comfortable. Shared mandi, price includes breakfast, good value. **F** *Tanjung Bira Cottages*, no water, no mandi but a very peaceful place to stay if you want to get away from it all. When the cottages are finished there will be water and the price will rise, pushing this into our **D** category.

Bira

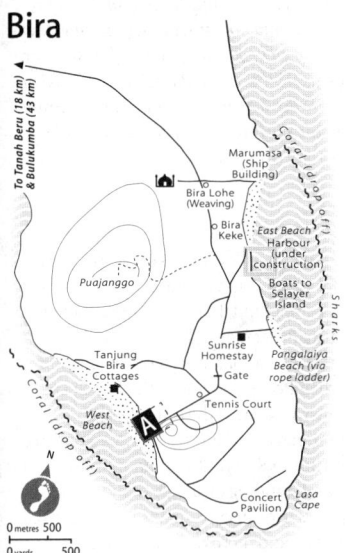

Bira beach area

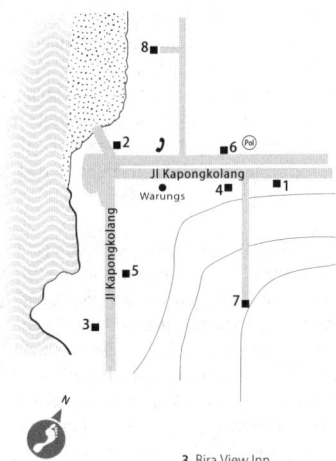

3 Bira View Inn
4 Nusa Bira Indah
5 Pondok Wisata Bahagia
6 Riswan Bungalows
7 Riswan Guesthouse
8 Sapolahe

■ **Sleeping**
1 Anda Bungalows
2 Bira Beach & Dive Resort

Eating

Restaurants at many of the hotels (see above) serve basic Indonesian food and a limited, rather poor, choice of western dishes. The best value places to eat are the many warungs; fish, unsurprisingly, is the speciality and the only thing that stands out gastronomically.

Sports

Diving Dive shop at the *Bira Beach Hotel*.

Transport

Road Bus: regular connections with Makassar, 5 hrs (9,000Rp). Bemos leave town for Ujung at aroung 0800, seats can be booked in advance. Travelling from Makassar, it is necessary to change in Bulukumba – total journey time, 4½ hrs.

Sea Boat: daily ferries at 1400 from Bira to Selayar Island. When sea conditions deteriorate between May and July the service transfers to the more sheltered Bulukumba.

Directory

Telephone office: Wartel, next to the *Bira Beach Hotel*.

Makassar to Toraja via Pare Pare

The road from Makassar runs north for 28 km to the riverside town of Maros. Here it divides. One route runs northeast through Bantimurung to the capital of the former Bugis Kingdom of Bone – Watampone – 180 km from Ujung. Continuing north from Watampone, the road passes through the attractive silk weaving town of Sengkang and then follows the coast north to Palopo. The more usual route runs north from Maros up the coast, usually out of sight of the sea, but on occasions passing through small fishing villages with attractive clapboard houses on stilts, before reaching the port of Pare Pare, 155 km from Makassar. From here, the road turns inland and threads its way upwards between limestone crags and past ricefields – scenically stunning, but exhausting by bus. The road reaches the district capital of Makale, 156 km from Pare Pare, and, 18 km north from Makale, the town of Rantepao – in the heartland of the Toraja. From Rantepao, the road turns east and descends spectacularly to the coastal town of Palopo, a distance of 62 km, where it meets up with the road from Sengkang.

Pare Pare

Phone code: 0421
Colour map 4, grid C6
Population: 100,000

Pare Pare is South Sulawesi's second city, although it feels more like a market town. During the Dutch period the town was an important military base and the author and anthropologist Nigel Barley tells a story – apocryphal or not – about how the Dutch forces' military exercises terrified the usually fearsome Torajans into surrender. Their spies, watching one of these exercises, saw apparently shot soldiers jump to their feet ready to fight again, and he returned home convinced the Dutch could not be killed. Capitulation, against such an enemy, seemed the only choice.

Pare Pare runs eel-like up the coast and for much of its length is only two or three streets wide. The centre is marked by the **Monumen Rakyat Pejuang** – a statue of a man, staff in hand, pointing into the distance and standing on a map of Indonesia. In September 1997 the town was close to the epicentre of an earthquake measuring 6.0 on the Richter scale. Around 10 people were killed and there was considerable physical damage, although now there was little evidence of this mini-disaster.

Primarily a trans-shipment point for inter-island cargoes, the usually quiet town comes to life along the seafront in the evening. Visitors usually only come here as a stopping-off point between Makassar and Rantepao, in Tana Toraja; it is also a good port to catch a passage to Kalimantan (see below). The small **La Bangenge Museum** is 2 km south of town in Bacukiki sub-district; it has a small collection of local enthnographic pieces. Get there by becak. There is an attractive, provincial, multi-domed mosque on Jl Hasanuddin. *Hotel Gandarial* houses a fine collection of bugis artifacts, in particular huge mango stones, decorated with silver. Ask at reception for a tour of the collection. There are beautiful sunsets from the night market, with flocks of fruit bats flying in from offshore islands in search of food.

Sleeping
■ *on map*

In recent years hoteliers have realized the potential of Pare Pare as a stop off point on the comparatively arduous overland journey to Tana Toraja. Perhaps as a result, they tend to be located on the main roads out of town & also seem to be rather overpriced

B *Kenari Bukit Indah*, Jl Jend Sudirman 65, T/F22073. Excellent views from open restaurant, clean, comfortable, all services but not central. Restaurant (mid-range) serves Indonesian, Chinese, seafood and European dishes. **B** *Nirwana*, 2 km south of town, overpriced, poor restaurant but the rooms are pretty good. **B** *Victoria International*, 2 km east of town on the road to Tana Toraja. Very pleasant setting with good views of the bay. All facilities for 1 night's stay. **C** *Gandaria 1*, Jl Bau Massepe 171, T21093. Some a/c, clean, though small rooms, pleasant courtyard, breakfast included. **C** *Kartika*, Jl Siliwangi 110. TV, phone, a/c but no hot water, quiet, clean but gloomy. **C** *Pare Indah*, Jl Siliwangi 118, T21888. A/C, hot water, TV, 12 rooms, good views, loud TV but clean and airy. **D** *Gandaria II*, Jl Samparaja 4, T22971. Some a/c, no restaurant but clean and quiet location, no English spoken, no hot water. **D** *Tanty*, Jl Hasanuddin, T21378. Rather over-priced, but rooms are clean enough. **E** *Siswa*, Jl Baso Dg Patompo 3, T21374. Attractive colonial façade, appears to have improved recently, good value but very poor beds. **E** *Wisma*, Jl Pinggir Laut, cramped and dingy but good value. Its disadvantage is the noise from the nearby bus depot.

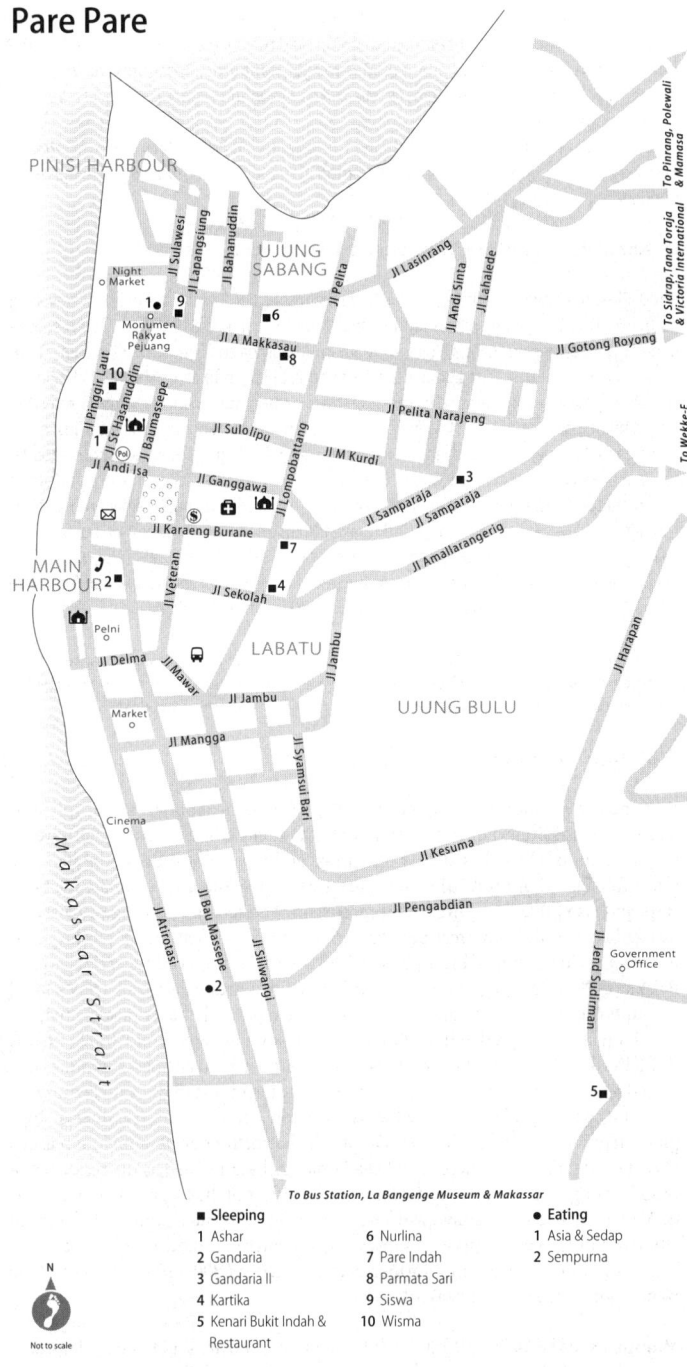

Eating Good, fresh, grilled seafood – particularly the excellent *ikan bakar* – is 1 reason to visit Pare Pare. The food is grilled in front of the restaurants, and there are a number just north of the central statue on Jl Baso Dg Patompo. **Mid-range**: *Sempurna Beach Restaurant*, wide choice, airy, refreshing atmosphere, excellent *ikan bakar* and glorious sea views. Recommended. **Cheap**: *Asia*, Jl Baso Dg Patompo 25, also serves Chinese food and a wide and tasteful range of seafood. Service is fast and the restaurant is clean. **Very cheap**: *Monas*, Jl Baso Dg Patompo 33; *Sedap*, Jl Baso Dg Patompo 21, good fish; *Sempurna*, Jl Bau Massepe, good Indonesian and Chinese food.

Entertainment **Cinema** *Pare Theatre*, Jl Bau Massepe (near *Gandaria Hotel*).

Transport
155 km from Makassar, 173 km from Rantepao, 92 km from Polewali, 147 km from Marjene

Road Bus: the new(ish) bus terminal is 3 km or so south of the city centre; or, if travelling north, pick up a bus as they pass through town. Buses to Rantepao 6 hrs, Makassar 3 hrs, Bone Bone, Soppeng, Majene, Palopo, Polewali, Mamasa, Masamba and Sengkang 3 hrs. **Sea Boat**: regular ships call at Pare Pare and it is the best port in Sulawesi to catch ships to Kalimantan. Shipping agents are concentrated in 2 areas of town, 10 mins walk apart: on Jl Andi Cammi (the road running parallel to Jl Bau Massepe but one closer to the sea) and on Jl Sulawesi (just north of the central statue). Rates and length of journey vary according to the vessel; shop around – some of the ships are barely seaworthy. Boards outside the agents list destinations and arrival and departure dates. Regular ports of call in Kalimantan including Balikpapan 1-2 days, Samarinda 2 days, Nunukan 2-3 days and Tarakan. Ships also call at other ports in Sulawesi (eg Toli Toli) and Surabaya, Kupang and Dili among others. The *Pelni* vessels *Tidar*, *Leuser* and *Binaiya* call here on their fortnightly circuits between Sulawesi, Java and Kalimantan (see route schedules, page 988). *Pelni* have their office at Jl Andi Cammi 130, T21017.

Directory **Banks** *Bumi Daya*, Jl Baso Dg Patompo 17 (Amex, US$, TCs). *Danamon* (Mastercard, Maestro and Visa). **Communications** **Post Office**: Jl Karaeng Burane 1 (south of the central statue, corner with Jl Bau Massepe). Wartel (international telephone, telegrams, fax): Jl Sultan Hasanuddin 53.

Watampone (Bone)

Colour map 4, grid C6

Watampone was the former capital of the Bugis Kingdom of Bone, and it is still popularly known as Bone. During the 16th century, the city emerged as the main rival to the kingdom of Gowa based near Makassar, and it was not subdued by its more powerful neighbour until 1611. Gowa pressured Bone into a subordinate relationship, and also forced the king to embrace Islam. This left an enduring distrust and dislike between the two great powers of Sulawesi, and when the Dutch began to undermine Gowa, they found a willing ally in the brilliant and ruthless Prince Arung Palakka of Bone (see page 761). It was with the help of Arung Palakka's army – by all accounts one of the most fearsome any Indonesian power has ever raised – that the Dutch finally conquered Sultan Hasanuddin of Gowa in 1669. From 1669 until his death in 1696, Arung Palakka was the most powerful man in all Sulawesi. Bone continued to be an important trading centre until the beginning of the 19th century.

'Bone', as it is called by everyone, is a friendly, sleepy town, useful as a stopping-off point to and from Kendari. Despite its charm, there are few obvious reasons to make a detour to stay here. The **Bola Soba** was built in 1890 as the residence of Baso Pagiling Abdul Hamid; it now houses the offices of the Department of Education. The **Museum Lapawawoi**, with a small but interesting collection of ethnographic pieces and photographs, is on the main square and is well worth a visit. The collection is housed in a former palace. ■ *Open 0800-1400 Mon-Sun.* Bone Bone's port, **Bajoe**, is 4 km east of town.

Excursions **Mampu caves** lie 34 km northwest of Watampone, and are said to be the largest in South Sulawesi. Like caves just about everywhere, there is an imaginative tale about former kings and courtiers being turned to stone, but it takes either a very active imagination or a lungful of bat guano to be convinced that these rocks and cave formations in any way resemble princes, princesses and what-have-you. ■ *Getting there: a minibus to Uloe and then a bemo or ojek to the caves (ask for* Gua Mampu).

B *Wisata Watampone*, Jl Jend Sudirman 14, T21362, F22367. A/c, restaurant, pool, modern, clean but featureless, overpriced for such a town and location, poor value. **C** *Mario Pulana*, Jl Kawerang 16, T21098. Some a/c, price includes breakfast, gloomy rooms, disinterested, unhelpful staff who seem less than keen to accept tourists, *Rio Rita* is much more welcoming, avoid. **D** *Rio Rita*, Jl Kawerang 4, T21053. 10 rooms, some a/c, attached mandi, small hotel, attractive, price includes breakfast, comfortable sitting area, best value in town. Recommended. **D** *Wisma Amarah*, Jl Jend A Yani 2, 8 rooms, noisy central location on a busy road but clean. **D** *Wisma Cempaka*, Jl Biru 36, T21414. Medium size place with 36 rooms. **D** *Wisma Bola Ridie*, Jl Merdeka, T21412. Quiet location, attached mandis, 6 large rooms in Dutch-era house with high ceilings, price includes breakfast. **D-E** *Losmen Nasional*, Jl Masjid Raya 86, large building set in middle of unkempt garden, close to shops, restaurants and Raya Mosque. **E** *Penginapan Ramayana*, located on the central square above a garage of the same name, 18 rooms.

Sleeping
Accommodation in Bone is reasonably plentiful, but business is declining as many people travel directly to Sengkang or Bira, by-passing Bone

Several restaurants along Jl Mesjid. **Mid-range** *Dynasty*, loud karaoke but clean and large portions, popular, good takeaway *nasi campur*. *Restaurant Pondok Selera*, Jl Biru 28, scenic gardens, quick service, very good food, probably best in Bone. Recommended. *Restaurant Victoria*, opposite the *Ramayana*, tasty hot Indonesian/Chinese food. **Cheap** *Rumah Makan Ramayana*, Jl Masjid Raya 4, good size portions, clean, more Chinese style. Recommended. *Rumah Makan Setia Budi*, Jl Beringin 89. **Foodstalls**: selection of *Kaki lima* operate from near the clocktower, very difficult to find a beer.

Eating

Play pool with locals in one of the many halls near Jl Beringin (pot order 1 to 15).

Entertainment

Watampone

To Makassar

Apr (6th) Anniversary of Bone Regency, entertainments and traditional dancing.

Festivals

Local Bemo: around town. Bejaks from hotel to Bemo station. Bemos to Bajoe. **Road Bus**: connections with Makassar 6 hrs, Pare Pare, Kendari, Palopo, Bontosunggu, Bulukumba 3 hrs, Sengkang 3 hrs and Rantepao 8 hrs. The road from Bone to Sengkang is very poor. *Cahaya-Makassar* (minibus company), Jl Veteran 167, T21348. The bemo station is on Jl Agus Salin. Many buses drop passengers off at their hotels. **Sea Boat**: there are nightly ferries from Bajoe, Bone Bone's port, to Kolaka in Southeast Sulawesi, 8 hrs (6,800-10,300Rp). Bemos run regularly between the town and the port, 4 km to the east.

Transport
180 km northeast of Makassar

To Wisma Cempeka

3 Penginapan Ramayana & Rumah Makan Ramayana Restaurant
4 Rio Rita
5 Wisata Watampone
6 Wisma Amarah
7 Wisma Bole Ridie

● Eating
1 Dynasty
2 Rumah Makan Setia Budi
3 Victoria

■ Sleeping
1 Losmen Nasional
2 Mario Pulana

Sengkang

Sengkang is a Bugis town and the capital of Wajo district, with one of the most attractive settings in Southern Sulawesi, close to the shores of Lake Tempe. The town is a good base to explore the surrounding countryside. There are some excellent walks in the gentle hills behind the town and relaxing boat trips can be taken on

Phone code: 0485
Colour map 4, grid C6

Lake Tempe, but other than walking and exploring around the lake, there is little to keep visitors in this dirty, rather unpleasant place, except to see its silk weaving (see box). Some people with time on their hands resort to playing video games with the local children. The **market** is nothing special, with a filthy food area and poor fruit selection.

Undoubtedly, the main attraction of Sengkang is **Lake Tempe**. Although at different times of year the water level of the lake can vary by as much as 3m, it is generally shallow and more like a marsh over large areas than an open expanse of water. In these shallower areas, the 'lake' is interpenetrated by a multitude of channels and provides good breeding grounds for water birds. (But note that because the boats are powered, birdwatching is not usually very rewarding. For those wishing to birdwatch, it is recommended that they make special arrangements.) One of the most interesting and remarkable features of the lake are the floating gardens, where crops are anchored by wig-wam shaped bamboo poles. These also act as feeding grounds for fish which congregate around the gardens. Hotels in town (including the *Apada*, *Pondok Eka* and *Al'Salam*) organize boat trips on the lake at a standard rate of 10,000Rp per person (or 25,000Rp per person when combined with a tour to see the silk production process). Note, however, that this price varies with the water level of the lake – which changes the distance to the floating villages. **NB** It is best to go early in the morning or evening as there is no shade except at the floating houses (see below). The boat, with outboard motor, sets out from the river, five minutes walk from the bemo station, and then proceeds upstream, passing stilt houses belonging to the fishermen who earn their livelihoods on the lake. Once on the lake, the boats usually visit one of the floating villages moored off shore and consisting of houses built on bamboo rafts. Visitors are served copious quantities of fried bananas and tea. This trip is highly recommended, but bargain hard as the guides are catching on to the tourist trade. Swimming from these houses is recommended.

Sengkang

■ **Sleeping**
1 Al Salam 1
2 Al Salam 2
3 Apada
4 As'har
5 Asoka Inn
6 Aster
7 Pondok Eka
8 Wisma Ayuni
9 Wisma Herawali
10 Wisma Lamaddukkelleng
11 Wisma Pondok Indah
12 Zaman Baru

Buginese textiles of Sengkang

It is said that 4,700 women weave nearly 500,000 sarongs a year on back-strap looms in the Sengkang area. This is the only place in Indonesia where silk is produced in large quantities. Imported yarn tends to be used for the warp, and local yarn for the weft. Chemical, aniline dyes have replaced natural dyes to a large extent, but traditional Buginese designs are still much in evidence. These include plaids, checks and stripes. The distinctive zig-zag pattern – known as bombang or wave pattern – is produced using a warp ikat technique. Also popular are floral designs, picked out using a supplementary metallic weft.

Occasionally, large iguanas can be seen at the lake edge. For the more adventurous it is possible to cross the lake (roughly two hours, although this time varies depending on the level of the lake and weather conditions) and then trek up into the hills on the far side. Unfortunately, the lake is silting up. Large scale deforestation in the catchment of the lake means that the feeder rivers carry and deposit large quantities of mud in the lake basin. This problem has been recognized, and as a result concrete irrigation channels have been constructed and dredging is currently under discussion. It may, however, be too late to save this unique lake in its current form.

Excursions

Trekking in the hills on the far side of Lake Tempe from Sengkang. Arrange for a boat to take you across the lake (about two hours – times vary through the year) and set out from there. Ask at your hotel for further information on routes.

Paddle boats from fishermen in the villages along the lake shore near Sengkang. It is then possible to venture on to the lake to **birdwatch** rather more discreetly and, during the right season, to see the lotus flowers which stand up to 2m above the lake's surface. The boats are hired out for about 4,000Rp per hour. ■ *Getting there: to reach the fishing villages take a bemo from the station on Jl Agus Salin (500Rp).*

A boat trip downriver to Salotangah is worthwhile. The village on the lake consists of about 20 stilt dwellings and the journey there and back takes about 2½ hours. ■ *Getting there: hire a boat from town, about 15,000Rp, or through your hotel, about 20,000Rp.* The advantage of paying the extra is that hotel-arranged trips usually include tea in one of the fishermen's houses. Another possibility is to go to the pier in the village of **Tempe**, 3 km outside Sengkang (look out for the large mosque). Here boats are available for charter even more cheaply. Anton at *Al Salaam II Hotel* speaks excellent English and is a good guide for a boat trip to the floating village, which is a worthwhile excursion.

Sempang is a silk-weaving town 6 km outside Sengkang where the process can be easily seen. ■ *Getting there: by bemo from the Bemo station.*

Tours

Boat tours on Lake Tempe are the most popular thing to do in Sengkang (see above for description). The *Apada*, *Pondok Eka* and *Al'Salam* hotels all offer boat tours and will also provide guides to show visitors the silk weaving process.

Sleeping
■ on map
Price codes:
see inside front cover

C-D *Asoka Inn*, Jl Latenrivali 3, T21526. A/c, spacious lounge with comfortable sofas, clean and welcoming. **D** *Al'Salam II*, Jl Emmy Saelan 8, T21278. Some a/c, restaurant, family-run hotel with rooms located around peaceful communal lounge, 8 new rooms on 1st floor have a view of sorts (cheaper rooms are dark and damp) and are generally more airy. Beware of low door frames to bathrooms, good size rooms with attached mandi/shower, central location, helpful and reliable guide, Zubaer, speaks good English, French and German, very popular, best in town, although they do tend to over-push their tours. Recommended. **D** *Apada*, Jl Durian 9, T21053. Location inconvenient for bemo station and restaurants, set in residential area close to police station, the house of a Buginese aristocrat transformed into a hotel with traditional atmosphere, restaurant, large grounds, ineffective a/c since some louvred windowpanes are missing, no service, rather persistent guide here. **D** *Pondok Eka*, Jl Maluku 12, T21296. Rickety looking traditional wooden house, relaxing verandah, 2 min walk from the bemo station, noisy when there is a film showing next door, but good value and welcoming. **D** *Wisma Lamaddukkelleng*, Jl Kenango, T21157. Wooden building in poorly kept grounds, next door to the mosque, owner is a CB radio ham, overpriced. **E** *Al'Salam I*, Jl A Nalingkaan. Opposite the bemo station exit, same owner as *Al'Salam II*, but dirty, if you end up here by mistake transfer to *Al'Salam II*. **E** *Wisma Bukit Nusa Indah*, Jl Lamungkace Toaddamang 12, T21448. Located on the side of a hill, view across town and lake, awkward to get to by bejak because of its hill position, but as a result the only place in town with a decent view (just below 'Pasanggrahan Hirawati' and radio tower). However, it's not clean.

Eating *Cheap Al'Salam II Restaurant*, food is unexceptional. *Romantis*, Jl Petta Rani, excellent Indonesian. *Tomudi*, Jl Andi Oddang, chicken a speciality.

Festivals *Aug* (3rd week) Tempe Lake Festival, annual fishing boat races.

Shopping *Silk* Sengkang is a centre of silk production (see box). Hand-woven silk is becoming harder to find, but there is plenty of machine-made cloth. The *Mustaquiem* factory on Jl A Panggaru is the best known but seems to be rather over-priced now; local guides are the best source of information on other weaving factories in the area.

Transport *Road* **Bus**: the terminal is in the town centre; regular connections with Makassar and Pare Pare. The best service is provided by *Steven Bus Co* which departs at 0900, 1000, 1400, 1800 and travels via Pare Pare; Watampone 3 hrs, very poor road; Palopo 3 hrs, good road. There are no direct buses to Rantepao. It is necessary to catch a bus to Lawawoi, and there change to a bus for Rentepao. Buses will pick passengers up from their hotels. **NB** Only bemo mini-buses travel to Makassar via the central route through Camba and Bantimurung; the road is poor and the trip is very uncomfortable, although the scenery more spectacular.

Toraja

Colour map 4, grid C6 The mountainous northern region of South Sulawesi is inhabited by the Toraja. It is not hard to understand why this remote area should have become a tourist attraction: it's a place of cool and refreshing weather; breathtaking scenery of limestone cliffs sharply contrasting with lush valleys and terraced ricefields; and a people who live in extraordinary boat-shaped houses, spend their savings on elaborate funeral ceremonies, and place their dead in holes carved into the limestone cliffs. All this contributes to make Toraja one of the highlights of any trip to Indonesia.

Western anthropologists originally believed the name to have been taken from the Buginese words **tori-aja** or 'people from above', referring to people who came from the coast and moved upstream; a definition which seems to make some sense (see the History section below). However, it is now being suggested that the word actually originates from the words **to-raa** or **to-raya**, meaning 'mankind' and 'hospitality'. Whatever the meaning, the Sa'dan Toraja people live in the basin of the Sa'dan River at an altitude of 900-1200m, in the administrative district of Tana Toraja (often known by its acronym, Tator). They number about 320,000. The capital and largest town in the area is Makale, although Rantepao, a local market town about 17 km to the north, has developed into the main tourist base. It is to visit Toraja that most visitors venture to Sulawesi.

Ins and outs

Best time to visit During the dry season, Mar-Nov. During the wet season, Dec-Feb, it may be difficult to get to the more out-of-the-way sights, although those close to the main roads are accessible. Room rates are also considerably lower. Night time temperatures range between 15°C and 23°C, daytime temperatures 20-32°C.

Entrance fee Foreigners entering Tana Toraja now have to pay an entrance fee of 3,500Rp, although this is avoided if you arrive on a night bus.

History

Local mythology maintains that the Toraja originated from the island of Pongko'. It is said that eight boats set sail from Pongko' and were driven by a storm onto the shores of South Sulawesi. Following the Sa'dan River upstream, the original ancestors arrived after a long and eventful journey in the area now known as Toraja.

Whatever the true origins of the Torajans, they remained isolated from the outside world for considerably longer than the Buginese and Makassarese of the coast. They experienced an unhappy period of occupation during the 17th century, when fierce Buginese warriors – aided and abetted by the Dutch East Indies Company – invaded their land and ransacked their sacred burial sites. Naturally, the Toraja were incensed by this desecration and after a period of seven years they rebelled, slaughtered the interlopers and regained control of the area. Little information leaked out of their inaccessible highland home until the 20th century. The French Jesuit priest, Nicolas Gervaise, mentions the Toraja at the end of the 17th century, and the White Raja James Brooke also wrote of the 'Turajah' in the mid-19th century – but both were second-hand reports.

Two Swiss scientist-explorers, the Sarasins, together with a Dutchman, Van Rijn, were the first Europeans to cross the lands of the Toraja from coast to coast in 1902. However, even they failed to discover the Torajan heartland. It was not until 1905 that the Dutch finally decided it was time to extend their control and to subdue these 'primitive' people. Among the Torajan leaders, only Pong Tiku resisted the Dutch for long. Fighting a guerrilla campaign, he and his men frustrated the Dutch for two years, finally succumbing to their enemy's far greater firepower in October 1906.

On achieving supremacy in the highlands, the Dutch abolished slavery and, in 1913, sent the first missionaries of the Dutch Reformed Church into the area. But conversions were few: by 1930, only 1,700 Torajans had been converted to Christianity (1% of the population), and in 1950 when Indonesia attained independence, the figure had risen to just 10%. Today, however, over 80% are nominal Christians – mostly Protestants – although traditional beliefs and practices still exert a pervasive influence, most clearly evident in their elaborate funeral ceremonies. This rapid spread of Christianity since independence is said to have been driven by the Torajan's fear of *to sallang* – Muslims.

Culture

The Toraja world consisted of three classes of people: nobles or *to parengnge'* (literally, 'to carry a heavy load'), commoners or *makaka*, and – formerly – slaves or *kaunan*. Slavery was common until the beginning of this century: women were plucked from their fields and houses and sold into slavery. Even visiting the market demanded a protective escort, and many villages were surrounded by earthern and stone ramparts, and connected to neighbouring villages by underground passageways. People even sold their own brothers 'like buffalo or vegetables'.

Traditional society & religion

The traditional 'religion' of the Toraja is called *Aluk Todolo*, meaning 'Ceremonies of the Ancestors'. It is based around the complementary elements of life and death, east and west, sunrise and sunset, morning and afternoon, and right and left (known to anthropologists as 'complementary binary opposition'). These contrasting elements are reflected in house architecture and the timing of rituals. Rituals associated with rice, and therefore life, are held in the mornings, people will face east and wear light clothes; while funerals are held after noon, people will face west and wear black.

'Rituals of the East' are known as *rambu tuka'*, which means 'smoke ascending'. They are also known as *aluk rampe metallo*, where *aluk* means religion and *metallo* means eastern part.

These rituals are concerned with life-giving events. They include rice rituals, rituals of exorcism to heal the sick, birth rituals, the first haircut, circumcision, teeth-filing, body decoration, weddings – even growth, prosperity and the rising of the sun. 'Rituals of the West' or *rambu solo*, which means 'smoke descending', are concerned with death, decrease and the setting sun.

Aluk Todolo – the traditional religion

Aluk Todolo is the traditional religious belief system of the Toraja. In Aluk Todolo people believe in many gods, but there is one superior and supreme god – *Pong Matua*. He created the earth, nature and human beings. He also created the Toraja people and sent them to Tana Toraja. He is present everywhere and knows the actions of every person. As well as Pong Matua, there are many lesser gods, collectively named *dewata*. The dewata act as Pong Matua's messengers and gophers and he sends them to this world to take care of Aluk Todolo and important events in the lives of everyone. When a priest or *tomina* makes an offering he mentions the names of Pong Matua first and then offers a sacrifice to the dewata. In recent times many Toraja people have renounced the Aluk Todolo, and today 85% of Toraja are Christian (70% Protestant and 15% Catholic) and 5% Muslim. Adherents to Aluk Todolo represent just 10% of the population. Even though Aluk Todolo has been superseded by Christianity, the traditional ceremonies are still an important element of Torajan life.

Ceremonies & festivals

It is the funerals of the Toraja which have attracted the most attention, both from tourists and scholars. But there is more to life than funerals, and the Toraja also sacrifice animals (*rambu tuka'*) to bring good fortune to the living, whether that be for the community at large or an individual or their household. The death of the animal releases the spirit which carries a message of thanks. These rituals 'of the east' are only performed between 0600 and 1200. The most important *rambu tuka'* are:

★ **Mangram banua or house ceremony** Performed when the tongkonan (family house) is ready to be built. All the members of the family are invited to this pre-house warming ceremony where they are invited to contribute to the cost of construction. During the ceremony many pigs are killed and ritual dances are performed.

★ **Merok** The ceremony performed on the completion of a new house and for the continued welfare of the family. Many pigs and a buffalo are killed. The night before the buffalo is killed, the *tominaa* stands all night telling the animal's life story.

★ **Mabugi'** Villagers kill chickens and cook rice in bamboo in thanks for a good yield.

★ **Mabua'** This is a large harvest ceremony when many pigs are sacrificed and dances performed.

★ **Sisemba'** When the harvest has been completed the men and boys assemble in a large field. Firstly the boys play a game in which they try to kick one another's feet from under them. Then the men join in, one village competing against another. Hands may not be used and once knocked down a man or boy may not be kicked until he is back on his feet. Sometimes bones are broken and in extreme cases there have even been deaths.

★ **Maro** When a person falls ill it is suspected that evil is present and a *maro* is organized to deal with the possession. Every night the sick person is put in the middle of a crowd of dancers, and then several healers attempt to drive out the evil spirit.

Village & house

Among the many notable features of Torajan culture and life are their stunning peaked houses. Many are anything from one to three centuries old, although the bamboo roofs are changed every 50 years or so. Houses are known as *banua* or, if the house is the 'ancestral seat' of an important family, as *tongkonan* – a name derived from the word *tongkon*, which means 'to sit'.

Torajan villages or *tondok* have changed since the Dutch pacified the highlands at the beginning of this century. Before then, villages were built on ridges or at the top of hills to provide protection against attack. The Dutch encouraged communities to relocate in the valleys, and few of these newer villages have the defensive ramparts that were such a feature of earlier settlements. A village will often consist of a line of houses, facing a line of rice barns. The residence or *tongkonan* is the 'mother' house, while the rice barn or *alang* is the 'father' house. The latter is a miniature copy of the former. Tradition requires that the roof-lines of both are aligned north-south, a requirement which gives Torajan villages a certain orderliness.

The buffalo: symbol of wealth and power

Buffalo are the most highly prized animals in Torajan society. Wealth is measured in terms of buffalo – it is often said of a rich or important man "He has a lot of buffalo". Buffalo are also associated with men, while pigs are linked with women. Even today, riceland is not valued in terms of its yield but according to the buffalo standard – in other words, how many buffalo were sacrificed at the funeral of the field's previous owner. As Toby Alice Volkman writes in her book *Feasts of honour*: "Buffalo, in short, are symbols of the person, his land and ancestors, and his wealth and power".

Buffalo come with different colourings, hair swirls, horn shapes and eyes, and each of these factors is taken into account in the valuation of an animal. A buffalo with the right colour configuration can command a very high price. The most valuable are piebalds – but with white heads and black bodies – pink spots and blue eyes, known as *bonga*. They can be sold for as much as 10,000,000 Rp. A standard slate grey buffalo, in contrast, sells for only 2,000,000 Rp, while an all-white animal is only worth 200,000 Rp. Also prized are long legs and horns. Buffaloes with black bodies are thought to be very strong and good for fighting.

The buffalo and their horns are status symbols; a buffalo is given as a bride price, as well as gifts at funerals. They are rarely put to work in the fields, but are cosseted and pampered, bathed and polished, even their genitals rubbed, until it is time to present them for a sacrifice. Generally, a woman's funeral warrants the slaughtering of an additional animal – in payment for the milk she has provided for her children. Depictions of buffalo are prominent on Torajan houses and rice barns. Buffalo heads adorn the *tulak somba*, whilst stylized low relief images are often carved on doors of rice barns, on interior doors within the homes, or on the shutters of graves. They act as guardians, to ward off evil spirits.

Another important division is between the two ritual grounds that every village must have: to the west is an area reserved for burial rites and associated with death; to the east is an area associated with life, crops, livestock and the general well-being of the community.

The **Torajan house** bears some resemblance to the houses of the Batak, the Niha of the Nias Islands and the Minangkabau. The shape resembles a boat, and this is said to symbolize the boats that brought the original inhabitants to Sulawesi (see above).

Torajan houses are raised off the ground on sturdy piles. The area between the piles, below the living quarters, is known as the *bala bala* and was originally used to stable buffalo. Today it is more commonly used for the storage of farm implements. A steep staircase leads from the east side of the house into the home. There are three rooms. The back room or *sumbung* is the sleeping quarters of the head of the household and his wife and small children. Valuables and important heirlooms are also stored here. Unmarried girls sleep in the front room or *tangdo'* (sometimes *sondong*), while the central room or *sali* is the main living and eating area, and is also used as the sleeping area for young, unmarried men. The hearth is positioned on the east side of the *sali* – the east, and food, both being associated with life. The Torajans never sleep with their feet pointing towards the west, as this is the direction of death.

The northern gable of the house – facing the rice barn – is one of the most sacred parts of the house, particularly the triangular upper part, which is sometimes called the *lindo puang* or 'face of the lords'. The Torajans believe that this is where the gods enter the house and it is here that heirlooms are hung during important rituals. In the case of *tongkonan*, the *lindo puang* is protected by the overhang of the roof, which is known as the *longa*. The *tulak somba* are the posts at either end of the more important houses which support the roof ends.

The **rice barn** or *alang* faces the home. It is like a house in miniature, but all the directions are reversed. This is because the rice barn neither belongs to one binary element nor the other (see note on complementary binary opposition, page 699). It contains both the rice seed for the next year's crop and, traditionally, human skulls. The rice barn is therefore a mediator, where life and death meet, and so its orientation is inverted. In western culture the classic mediator is New Year's Eve – neither one year nor the next – when, for example, officers serve their men, reversing roles. In Thailand and Laos, New Year – or *Pimai* – usually falls in mid-April, but again it represents a period when people can take liberties, dousing one another with water. The impressive piles supporting the structure are round, unlike those of the house which are rectangular. The platform below the storage area is used for sitting and socializing, as well as for sleeping during festivals. The inner walls of the barn and the ceiling of the sitting area are traditionally decorated with geometric patterns and scenes from everyday life. The area of ground between the house and the rice barn is known as the *parampa*, and is used to dry rice or coffee, as a space for children to play, men to stage cock-fights and women to work (for instance, at weaving).

The house represents a microcosm of the Torajan world. Like the houses of the Batak and Minangkabau, it is divided into three sections: the roof and gables represent the Upper World of gods and spirits; the central living area, the Middle World of men and earthly concerns; while the *bala bala* represents the Under World. A central post, known as the *a'riri posi'*, connects the whole structure with the earth.

The Torajan death ritual

Funerals are important social events. As Torajans explain, "if there were no funerals, none of us would ever get married"

The Toraja people are probably best known in the West for their elaborate death or funeral ritual – the *aluk rambe matampu'* – which transports the soul of the deceased to the next life. This elaborate ceremony is the major event in the life cycle of a Torajan and the costs of mounting an *aluk rambe matampu'* can be financially crippling for the family concerned. Rituals vary according to the rank and wealth of the dead person: for a noble, an elaborate ceremony is required, lasting up to seven days; for a commoner, a more modest event, extending over only one or two days. Unless the deceased is given an appropriate funeral, he or she is unable to enter *puya* or the afterlife (see below), and cannot become an active ancestor, watching over the rice and the family group. The Torajans accept the ephemeral nature of life:

> "We are as the phantoms of this world,
> the apparitions of this region,
> as the wind that blows along the house."

The aluk rambe matampu', or *rambu solo*, are 'rituals of the West' and can only occur after noon. They consist of three stages, which are adhered to whatever the status of the deceased: first the wrapping of the corpse and lamentation; then the funeral ritual and slaughter of animals; and last the entombment of the corpse in a rock grave.

The wrapping and lamentation After a person dies, they are dressed in ceremonial clothes and placed on a chair in the southern-most room of the house. Several days later, the corpse is cacooned in multiple layers of funeral shroud and a kapok blanket, and transferred to the west side of the central room. The body remains in the house until the second phase. This may involve a wait of anything from six months to six years. During this period of waiting, the death is not acknowledged; the deceased is referred to simply as the 'sick one'.

Over the subsequent months and years, considerable sums of money have to be amassed, relatives informed, a site chosen for the construction of the temporary houses needed to stage the ritual, and agreement reached on suitable contributions of buffalo. In addition, the rice has to have been harvested before the ceremony can commence. The following description of the second phase of the ceremony only applies to the *Diripai* – the most elaborate of the ceremonies. It should also be noted that because most Torajans are now nominal Christians, the traditional ceremony is becoming increasingly rare. The traditional Toraja practice of burying people in stone sarcophagi in preference to the ground is becoming popular once again. The reason, it is said, is the shortage of land in the area: the soil is considered more valuable as a garden and as Tana Toraja is rich in stone, this type of burial is more practical.

Funeral classification

Disilli The funeral of a young child or infant of the lower classes. Only one pig is killed. A baby who has not developed teeth is buried in a tree.

Dipasangbongi A one-night burial funeral for the young or an adult from the commoner class. One buffalo and four pigs are killed.

Dipatallung bongi A three-night funeral. This is held for middle-class men. One buffalo and many pigs are killed. The second day is perhaps the most interesting; relatives and friends bring gifts for the deceased. The local villagers assemble at night and dance the ma'badong song. The ma'badong recounts the cycle of life and, in particular, relates the life story of the dead person. It bids farewell to the soul and ensures a safe journey to puya (the afterlife).

Dipalimang bongi A five-night funeral for middle-class men, who were successful and highly respected. Eight buffalo and many pigs are killed. The mabadong dance continues for five nights.

Dipapitung bongi A seven-night funeral held for the poor rich man. Ten or more buffalo and many pigs are slaughtered. On the main day, groups of people from surrounding villages come. Features include a procession of teenage girls, a bullfight, giving of gifts and feasting. Ma'badong and makatia dances are performed to welcome guests.

Dirpai This is the largest and most complex funeral and is only held for the people of the highest class. The ceremony is divided into two parts, each lasting seven days. There may be a gap of six months to one year between the two parts. Once the ceremony has begun, the family abstains from eating rice and lives on a diet of potatoes and fruit. During the funeral 12 buffalo (the lesser version) or 24 buffalo (the complete version) are slaughtered, along with scores of pigs. In exceptional circumstances, 100 buffalo may be killed. An endless variety of dances, cock and bullfights, processions of girls and war dances are held to welcome guests. Before the ceremony, the body may be kept for months or even years.

The funeral and ritual slaughter The houses for the funeral ceremony are constructed to form a square around the *rante* (the place chosen for the funeral rites). Older *rante* may have megaliths standing in them. Each megalith is said to represent a member of the family. During large ceremonies, many buildings are constructed to house the family and guests of the dead around the *rante*. In the centre of the *rante* stands the *lakkean* or 'corpse tower'. The tower is several storeys high and is surmounted with a roof similar in style to that of the Torajan house. A bier – or *sarigan* – is also constructed in the shape of a miniature house.

The second phase is heralded by the transferring of the body from the house to the floor of the rice barn. At this stage, a buffalo is sacrificed – preferably one with a white head and black body. The *tau tau* – a representation or portrait of the deceased (see box) – is held by the sculptor, who manipulates it and precedes the body in procession to the rice barn.

After two days, the corpse is transferred to the bier and a colourful procession – known as the *mapalao* – moves off in the direction of the *rante* or funeral field. Upon arrival, the body is paraded around the central *lakkean* three times and is then transferred to a platform, where other family members sit.

From this point, the festivities get into full swing. Buffalo fights, dances, parades and kick fights (*sisepak*) take place (although kick fights have been officially banned). The next day, the guests (dressed in black) are formally received and the slaughtering of the animals begins. Buffalo are slaughtered in a central area on the ceremonial field in front of the guests. This is not for the faint-hearted; the entire central area becomes awash with blood and gore, staring buffalo heads, bones, hooves, entrails and dung. The pigs are often slaughtered out of sight, and are then carried in for dismemberment, after having been singed over an open fire. In the past, the crowd would attack the animal alive and dismember it – this practice was banned by the Dutch. Each animal, as it is slaughtered, is registered in a notebook and a value placed against the gift. The value of buffalo is

Torajan mortuary effigies (tau tau)

Tau tau means 'little person' and refers to the wooden, life-sized, effigies of the deceased, which are to be found on stone galleries carved out of the cliffs, or on wooden hanging galleries, positioned close to burial vaults. Tau tau images are only commissioned following the death of wealthy people or nobles. Some (lesser) tau tau – known as tau tau lampa – are made out of bamboo and cloth, but they are rare. Full tau tau are carved from the durable wood of the jackfruit tree (nangka) and are repaired every 25 years or so. An event known as Ma'nene is performed sometime between July and September, when the tau tau's clothing is replaced.

A living jackfruit tree is cut to provide the wood for the carving. The lemon-yellow wood is treated with coconut oil over several weeks to stain it to the colour of the Torajan skin, and then a specialist sculptor ritually carves the image. The body is made of several pieces which are movable – rather like a puppet – and during the funeral ceremony the figure may be manipulated. As the tau tau is a `living' representation of the deceased, great attention is paid to detail. Traditionally, the head was carved with almond-shaped eyes and finely formed features. Under the sarong, sexual organs are carefully carved – the male penis always erect. The clothing also helps to establish the identity of the deceased. In modern images, the figure is almost an exact representation of the deceased.

A problem that has arisen in recent years is the stealing of tau tau images. As demand for these aesthetically pleasing carvings has increased in the West, so the incentive to raid cliff face galleries has likewise increased. The spread of Christianity may also have played a role, reducing the traditional fear of these spirit-imbued figures. Today many are duplicates – the originals having disappeared during the night, doubtless to be sold to collectors.

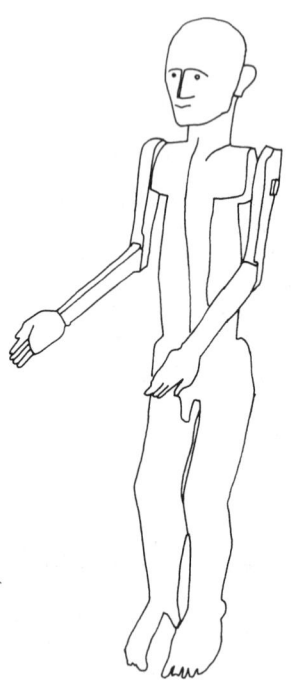

Tau Tau with articulated arms, 1-2 m high, wood

---

determined by an appraisal of a combination of factors: size, condition, horn shape and colour configuration. Single-coloured black/grey buffalo are the least highly valued at between 500,000Rp and 3,500,000Rp. A piebald pink and white animal may fetch anything up to 10,000,000Rp though. After offerings to the ancestors, the meat is shared out among the guests, palm wine (*tuak*) contained in bamboo is passed around, more dancing takes place and buffalo – and cock-fights (also banned) – are organized.

The entombment Several days later, after all the sacrifices have taken place and debts recorded, the guests start to leave, carrying their meat with them strung onto bamboo poles. A small procession of close family then accompanies the corpse to its final resting place with its ancestors (this stage is known as *mapeliang*). These resting places are traditionally burial vaults carved out of the limestone cliffs. The body is placed in the tomb head first, with its feet towards the door; thus easing the passage of the soul to the next world (the *Tondok Bombo*, or Land of the Souls). Then the *tau tau* of the deceased is placed with the other mortuary effigies in a gallery on the cliff face and a black chicken is released at the burial site, symbolizing the release of the soul. If a person is buried in the wrong grave, shame is brought on the whole family. It is known as *topusa* or losing the way to one's grave.

When a person dies, according to Aluk Todolo, his or her soul enters *Puya*. Puya is situated far beyond the southern horizon of the world. Importantly, the behaviour and position that a person enjoyed in life is maintained in puya, and therefore – in theory at least – everyone tries to better themselves during their present life; people of a pleasant disposition will remain so after their death, as will those with an unpleasant nature. As the souls approach the gate of puya, each must call out his social position and state his personal disposition. ('Grade one, happy and sunny!'; 'Grade twelve, miserable so-and-so!') The highest authority in puya is *Ponglalondongna*. The souls are asked at the gate if the funeral ceremony was carried out and the type that was celebrated. If the ceremony has not been completed the soul must wait outside the gate until it is done. If a man dies in an unknown place and a ceremony is never held, he may never enter puya. Sometimes in frustration, these souls come back to earth and disturb the living. The family of a man who dies in an unknown place may try to make a ceremony to avoid this unpleasant state of affairs. A coffin is made in the hope that the spirit of the dead will come for the ceremony even if the corpse is nowhere to be seen. The Toraja also believe that the soul of an animal will follow its master. Hence the sacrifices at funerals. Because there is more to life than pigs and buffaloes, the personal belongings of the dead will follow them to their afterlife, as will the 'soul' of their house. Should a person die in another village he is always brought back to his own home – except for the people of Mamasa who are said, sensibly, to let their dead walk home should they be foolish enough to die somewhere else.

Accessing the afterlife

It is not difficult to find out where and when ceremonies are due to occur; local guides make it their business to discover where they are taking place and hotel staff are also often well informed. July and August is the most active funeral period, as this coincides with the long Indonesian holiday and is the period when Torajans living away from home can return to their villages. If you are visiting a ceremony and are invited into the guests' enclosure, it is usual to bring a small gift – several packets of cigarettes for example. Visitors are generally welcomed at such events, but they should dress modestly and be sensitive to the occasion.

Visiting a funeral ceremony

There are four kinds of burial place in Tana Toraja. The oldest burial places are the *erong*, which date back about seven or eight centuries. These are beautifully carved wooden sarcophagi, which were placed at the base of cliffs. They were made in the shape of boats, houses or animals; possibly signifying different ranks of the deceased. Heirlooms and other valued possessions were placed in the erong, along with the corpse. In the 17th century, marauding Buginese working for the Dutch East India Company invaded Tana Toraja and plundered these sacred burial sites (see page 699). When, after seven years of occupation, the Buginese were ejected, the Toraja abandoned the erong system of burial as too vulnerable. The more important *erong* are hung from high cliffs. Today, most have deteriorated, but they are still visible at Pa'atokke, Mengke'-pe, Ke'te Alla and Tambolang. It is also believed that they could once be found at Londa, but have since fallen down.

The burial chamber

Instead, they began to cut tombs – known as *keborang batu* – high-up in inaccessible limestone cliff faces. This new form of burial was made possible due to the metal-working skills the Torajans had acquired during the Buginese occupation, enabling them to make iron chisels and other metal tools. They now placed their dead, along with their valuables, in these catacombs, safely sealed behind wooden doors. Only by climbing high up the vertical cliff face could these graves be plundered.

The most recent burial method to emerge is the *burial 'house'* (*Banua Tangmerambu* or 'house with no kitchen'). These are associated with the pacification of the area in the 20th century and, also, a simple lack of cliff space. An example of these ground-level tombs can be seen at Ke'te Kesu' (see page 708).

Finally, there are the '*tree graves*' of babies who die before their first tooth is cut. The corpse is taken to an *antolong* tree (also known as *kayu mate*, literally 'dead wood'), and placed in a cavity hollowed out of the trunk. The hole is covered with fibres from the sugar palm, a dog and pig slaughtered, and the tree allowed to grow around the baby's body (see Kembira excursion, page 710).

Further reading Crystal, Eric (1985) "The soul that is seen: the tau tau as shadow of death", in: Jerome Feldman (editor) *The eloquent dead: ancestral sculpture of Indonesia and Southeast Asia*, UCLA: Los Angeles. Well illustrated article. Kis-Jovak, JI et al (1988) *Banua Toraja: changing patterns in architecture and symbolism among the Sa'dan Toraja, Sulawesi*, Royal Tropical Institute: Amsterdam. Wonderful black and white photo-essay with informative text. Nooy-Palm, Netty (1986) *The Sa'dan Toraja: a study of their social life and religion – rituals of the east and west*, Foris: Dordrecht. Dense but informative anthropological work. Volkman, Toby A (1985) *Feasts of honour: ritual and change in the Toraja highlands*, University of Illinois Press: Urbana. Readable account – part academic, part personal – of an anthropologist's stay in Toraja.

Tana Toraja

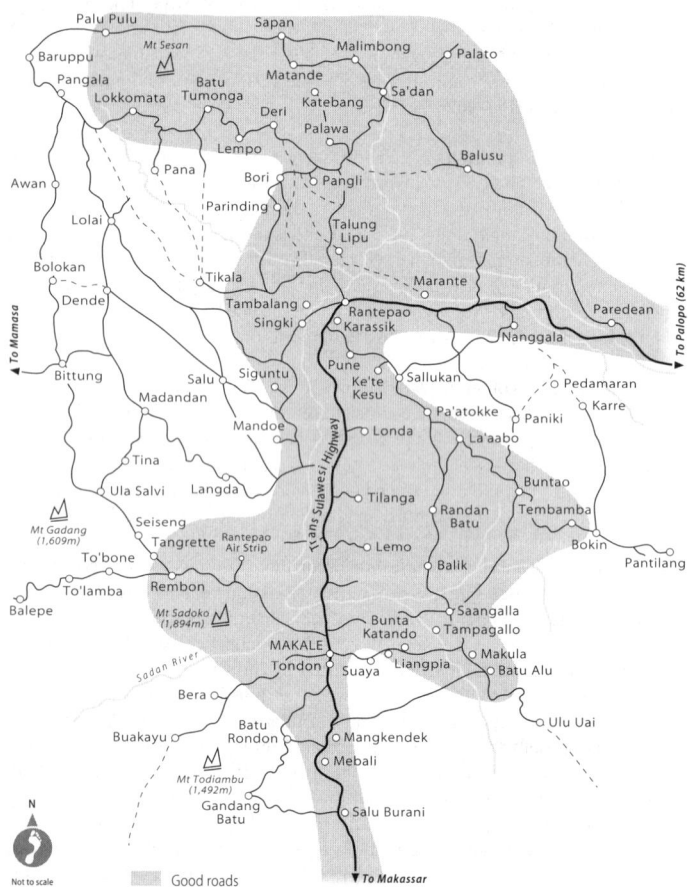

Economy

In the past, the Toraja economy was founded on the cultivation of wet rice in the upland valleys that dissect the area. Rice is still the pre-eminent subsistence and ritual crop, although other activities are taking on increasing importance. The rice cycle lasts six months and in addition to white rice, black rice (*nasi hitam*) and red rice (mixed with coconut milk for sweets), are also cultivated.

Since the late 1970s, tourism has played an increasing role in the local economy. Many younger Torajans have moved away to Makassar, partly because of the lack of agricultural land and partly because they no longer want to farm. Paradoxically, this exodus has probably helped to keep Torajan traditions alive – the migrants send money home to finance funeral ceremonies and return for important ceremonies. When a migrant dies away from home, he will often be transported back to be buried with his ancestors.

Makale

Makale is the largest town in the Toraja region and the administrative capital of the district of Tana Toraja. However, so far as tourism is concerned, Makale is over-shadowed by the smaller town of Rantepao, 17 km to the north, which has a much more extensive tourist infrastructure. Makale has fewer good losmen than Rantepao, those staying here do so because it is less touristy. The heart of the town is arranged around a large – and sometimes empty – artificial lake, now dominated by a fluorescent blue replica of the Eiffel Tower. Despite the gaudiness, it is a pleasant and cool place to rest, just away from the hectic market. **The Pasar Umum** (General Market) is at the end of Jl Pasar Baru; local produce and plastic dominate, with few original items on sale. The pig market is held on Mondays.

Phone code: 0423
Colour map 4, grid C6

Excursions Most of the sights in the area are equally accessible from Makale as they are from Rantepao, and some are considerably closer to Makale. However, because most people choose to stay in Rantepao, and to avoid repetition, villages are listed in the Excursion section of the Rantepao entry, below.

Sleeping **A-B** *Marannu City*, Jl Pongtiku 116-118 (1 km north of town), T22221, F20208. Restaurant, pool, tennis courts, best hotel in Makale with good facilities but little character, rooms have a/c, TV, hot water and minibars. **B** *Sahid Toraja*, Jl Raya Gettengan 1 Mengkendek, T22444, F22167; 12 km south of Makale, a/c, restaurant, pool, tennis, Torajan-style houses. **E** *Losmen Merry*, Jl Muh Yamin 168, T22013. Rudimentary rooms, near bus offices. The sister losmen of the same name is located on Jl Pongtiko 100B, T22174. Eight rooms with attached mandis. **E** *Wisma Bungin*, Jl Nusantara 35, T22255. Central, near the lake, clean rooms with bathrooms, best in town at this price. **E** *Wisma Puri Artha*, Jl Pongtiku 114, T22470. North of town, claustrophobic feel as the rooms are packed in, basic, and need of attention. **E-F** *Losmen Fajar*, Jl Merdeka 11, T22022. Rooms acceptable, but suffers from the noisy road. **F** *Losmen Litha*, Jl Pelita 97, T22441. Standard rooms very clean and basic but not en suite.

Transport **Local** regular bemo connections with Rantepao (1,000Rp). **Air** See Transport to and from Rantepao, page 716. **Road Bus**: regular connections with Rantepao 40 mins, Pare Pare (10,000-15,000Rp) and Makassar (15,000-28,000Rp). Also buses to Poso and Palu 36 hrs, Tator, Watampone, Polmas and Pinrang. Most of the bus companies have their offices on Jl Ihwan Rambe, and Jl Yamin, off the central square. Note that most buses for Makassar and other points south leave from Rantepao and may be full by the time they arrive in Makale, so it is best to reserve a seat. Sumber Alam, Jl Yamin 64, T22879, run buses to Polewali (15,000Rp).

17 km from Rantepao,
79 km from Palopo,
156 km from Pare Pare,
333 km from Makassar

Directory **Banks** Bank Raykat Indonesia, Jl Veteran. **Communications** Perumtel (international telephone, telegram & fax): Jl Pongtiku 8 (north of town). **Medical facilities** Hospitals: *Fatima*, Jl Pongtiku 103.

Rantepao

Phone code: 0423
Colour map 4, grid C6

This rather ramshackle market town is utterly overshadowed by the beautiful countryside and villages which surround it. It has become a 'tourist centre' because it is undoubtedly the best base from which to explore the surrounding area. The four roads into town meet at a roundabout, where there is a miniature tongkonan (Torajan house). The central market has some handicrafts, textiles and 'antiques' for sale (see 'Shopping'). **Rantepao Tourist Information Centre**, is on Jl Achmad Yani 62A, T21277. They have free maps, good advice and some English spoken. Open 24 hours a day. Check here in the late evening for details about the funeral ceremonies the following day. Also possible to arrange guides, expect to pay 50,000Rp.

Rantepao itself offers few attractions. The river views at the northern end of the city and the giant Toraja House to the south are the only noted attractions. During festival periods (for example, first week in July) the central square hosts traditional games and music. The weekly **pig and buffalo market** is held on Wednesdays, 3 km north of town. The pig market, when hundreds of animals are brought in from the surrounding villages, is the more lively; the buffalo market is rather slower. To get to the market, take either one of the direct market bemos or a vehicle running towards Sa'dan and Lempo.

Getting around the sites of Toraja
Because the sites of interest around Rantepao are scattered over a wide area, it is easiest to charter a car or bemo for the day (see 'Local transport' below). Public bemos do travel along most roads, but it is often a time-consuming business getting from one sight to the next. It is also possible to hire motorbikes and bicycles in town (see 'Local transport'). However, many visitors find that the best way to see the sights is on foot. The climate is cool enough to make walking very pleasant, roads are rarely busy, and most sights are less than 15 km from Rantepao. Note that local drivers – understandably – often insist it is only possible to see the sights of the area with a guide; this is not true. By buying a good map and asking questions it is quite possible to explore the area. Admission to attractions and villages: the tourist attractions in the area are beginning to co-ordinate their activities and now all charge a flat rate of 3,000Rp for admission alone. A guide costs around 50,000Rp for the day.

Southeast from Rantepao
Ke'te Kesu' is 4 km travelling south from Rantepao; leave Karassik on your left and take the left-hand turn about 1 km south of town, and continue for another 4 km to the village. Ke'te Kesu' has perhaps the finest collections of **tongkonan** (see page 700) in the Rantepao area. If visitors do not wish to hire a car or have limited time, this is one site worth visiting which has a cross section of all aspects of Toraja village life; it can be reached on foot (one hour) from Rantepao (take the first left out of town going south, by the white buffalo statue). The central of the larger houses contains a small museum. Walk behind the village and down a slope to see the concrete tomb of FK Sarungallo, a tongkonan noble and politician who died in 1986. The tau tau of this man, encased in glass, with orange robes, spectacles and grasping an umbrella, is remarkably lifelike. Some new steps proceed from here up the cliff face past some hanging graves. The older carved graves are split open with bones spilling out. There are also two more recently carved specimens, one representing a buffalo and the other a pig. The tau tau here are now protected (from thieves) behind a metal grill so are, unfortunately, difficult to view. The steps end at a rubbish and bone filled cave. There are several shops selling carvings and cloth in Ke'te Kesu'. Ke'te Kesu's easy accessibility makes it a popular stop for visitors – which, at peak periods, tends to detract from the mystery of the place. ■ *Getting there: bemos run along the road to this village (500Rp).*

The next village going south is **Sullukan**; continue past here to **Pa'atokke**, a 30-minute drive from the main road. A 20-minute climb takes you to the cliff top, where there are 800-year-old cliff graves. Guides can be hired for the walk; this place is off the tourist trail. Another 2 km or so along the track going southeast is **La'bo**, a metalwork village: 'La'bo' is Torajan for 'big knife'. There are megaliths and cliff graves here. Continuing on the track, 12 km from Rantepao and 3-4 hours' walk northeast

Trekking around Rantepao

One of the best ways to see and experience the Torajan highlands is to go on an organized trek for several days. There are many local guides in Rantepao who will arrange and lead trekking expeditions. There are few losmen outside the main towns, the exception being the village of Batu Tumonga, to the northwest of Rantepao, where there are five, and Mamasa. Outside these two villages, expect to stay with the kepala desa (headman), the local teacher, or with another family. **NB** It is usual to bring small gifts for your host (soap, cigarettes etc). Horses can sometimes be hired to carry baggage (80,000-100,000Rp per day). Most treks explore the hills, valleys and villages to the west of Rantepao. Expect to pay about 160,000Rp per day, all inclusive (local guides hired independently of tour companies will be cheaper). The best time to trek is between March and November. Treks, with approximate length, include:

★ *Rantepao-Sesean-Rantepao*: two days/one night
★ *Rantepao-Sesean-Dende-Rantepao*: three days/two nights
★ *Bittuang-Mamasa*: three days/four nights
★ *Ulusalu-Pangala-Rantepao*: four days/three nights
★ *Mamasa-Ulusalu-Rantepao*: five days/four nights

Trekking companies Ramayana Satrya, Jl Pongtiku, T21336, F21485, is recommended. There are also many private guides who can be hired for about $15-25 per day. Ask at your hotel or visit the Tourist Office in Rantepao and ask for a recommendation.

Suggested equipment Good walking shoes, hat, sweater for the nights, sleeping roll, sleeping bag, food for lunches, water (or a means of boiling, or sterilizing it), mosquito repellent, gifts for your hosts.

---

from Sangalla, is the village of **Buntao**, which is best visited on market days (every sixth day – check in Rantepao for the day). There is also a house grave (*patane*) and some hill graves here. Around 2 km south of Buntao, **Tembamba** is situated in a mountain saddle. There are graves and tongkonan here, plus good views. (If you turn right leaving Labo, you will reach Randan **Batu**, another knife-making centre.) From here the track continues south to **Sangalla**, 24 km from Rantepao, where there is another sixth day market, striking tau tau and a king's grave up the cliff.

Londa is a burial site about 4 km south of Rantepao, and 1 km off the main road. There is a series of caves here containing coffins and bones, with rows of *tau tau* effigies (see page 704) overhead. All *tau tau* have been placed in a cage to prevent theft. They are rather gloomy caves, full of bones and coffins which are said to stretch for 2 km or more, but it is a popular attraction, firmly on the tour group route. Guide with lamp 7,500Rp (or cunningly use the light of others). About 700m north of here are the baby graves at **Pabaisenan**. A path leads from Londa to Tilanga, and from there on to Lemo. But it is not well marked – ask along the way.

Due south of Rantepao

Tilanga, a natural spring and swimming-pool, lies 9 km south of town, also off the main road. It is busy at weekends and rather dirty. A path leads from here to Lemo, and also north to Londa – ask for directions.

Lemo lies 1 km off the main road, further south from Londa and about 9 km from town. This is a superbly positioned burial site overlooking paddy fields. It is best to come here early in the morning before the crowds arrive, when the sun illuminates the rock face with its rows of *tau tau* effigies and graves hewn out of the cliff face. A path leads up and around the limestone outcrop to other, less impressive, grave niches. Follow the path to the left along the cliff face, past further 'common' graves (no *tau tau*), and back across the paddy fields. On the other side of the paddy fields from the cliff face is a *tau tau* carver workshop, open for visitors. There is also a group of *tongkonan*, but better examples of the houses can be seen at Nanggala. A path leads from Lemo north to Tilanga and from there to Londa – ask directions. **NB** Paths are slippery, and some of the steps are steep.

Torajan ikat blankets

Distinctive warp ikat blankets, with bold, geometric designs in black, red and blue, are important ritual objects in Toraja. At funerals, they are used to decorate ceremonial buildings and sometimes to wrap the corpse. They were traditionally made from home-grown and spun cotton, and take months to make. Originals are expensive and difficult to find. However, similar blankets made from imported yarn and coloured with chemical dyes are now made around Rantepao to supply the tourist market. One important weaving centre is Sa'dan, north of Rantepao. Motifs used for these textiles include representations of buffalo and tongkonan houses.

Suaya lies about 8 km east of Makale, up a steep and winding (deteriorating) road (negotiable by car). This was a noble burial site, and some of the coffins are said to be 500 years old. Attractively decrepit white *tau tau* effigies occupy niches in the rock face here. At the base of the cliff is the grave of a noble daughter who left the village and married a Muslim; as a convert she could not be buried in the cliff. A building houses what can be best described as *objets mort* – very weathered boat and buffalo coffins containing skeletal remains. A steep climb to the right of the effigies leads up to a viewpoint from where it is possible to look up and down the beautiful valley. There is a beautiful one-hour walk up the valley beyond the graves to the Sangalla-Makale road. The ponds which can be seen in the middle of the paddy fields are a couple of metres deep. They are stocked with young fish at transplanting, and at harvest time the grown fish are given to the labourers as part of their payment. ■ *Getting there: there are no bemos to Makale from here; it is necessary to walk a couple of kilometres toward Tampangallo.*

Liang Pia lies east of Suaya. There are baby graves here (see page 705), set in bamboo forest. If you carry on walking past the entrance you come out on the road near the Buntu Kalando Museum (2 km).

Tampangallo is one of the most atmospheric spots in Toraja. (Negotiable by car or on foot across paddy fields from Suaya.) Turn off the road almost 1 km east of Suaya and travel about 500m down a track. This limestone cave grave, set in a verdant rice valley, contains some wonderful decaying 300-year-old boat coffins, some of which may originally have been stored in hanging graves, and a quantity of skeletal remains. There are also some new *tau tau* effigies here.

The **Sarapang** baby grave is to be found 200m before Tampangallo, down a track running off the road. If a baby dies before cutting his or her teeth they are buried in cavities hollowed out of living tree trunks (see page 705).

Buntu Kalando Museum lies a short distance further east on the Suaya-Kembira road. It houses a small collection of ethnographic artefacts from Toraja.

For the **Kembira** child grave, continue on from the museum to a 'T' junction; turn left and it is a short distance away. Along the track leading to the grave, villagers sell local spices and flavourings – vanilla, cinnamon, nutmeg, cocoa and pepper – at grossly inflated prices. The path, 200m in all, leads through a bamboo grove to a buttressed tree in which families have hewn-out niches for their dead children. These are then pegged over with a fibre curtain and the tree is allowed to grow around the corpse (see page 705). **Sleeping** Just south of Sangalla, on the right-hand side of the road coming from Makale, is the **E** *Kalembang Homestay*, well kept gardens, hamlet owned by noble family who still live in the confines, remote but recommended as a base for walking and seeing the sites in the region. ■ *Getting there: take a bemo from the bridge on the northern outskirts of Makale (10 km).*

Getting to the sights southeast of Rentapao Most of these sights lie within walking distance of the main Rantepao-Makale road; bemos run constantly along the road. Do not pay more than 500Rp for the shorter trips – remember Rantepao-Makale is 1,000Rp. Bemos also run east from Makale to Kembira and then north to the market town of Sangalla before looping westwards back to the main road, coming out opposite the hospital north of Makale (9 km from Kembira).

There is not so much of interest to the southwest of Rantepao, but a couple of places deserve a mention. At **Singki**, 1 km from town, there are three houses, situated like a fort on the mountainside; the mountain path is steep but rewarding. There are also rice barns and ornate painting here. **Siguntu** lies 5 km southwest of Rantepao, where there are three ornate tongkonan, rice barns and good views.

Southwest from Rantepao

Marante is 5 km east from Rantepao and 500m off the main road, set in a beautiful valley. There are some rather untidy cliff and cave graves here and some heavily carved *tongkonan*. Follow the path past the cliff graves and the bridge to a small group of traditional houses. From here, the path returns quickly to the main road. ■ *Getting there: regular bemos run along this road.*

East of Rantepao

The turn-off for **Nanggala** is 7 km further east (12 km in all from Rantepao). The village is 1.8 km along the rough road, which makes for a pleasant walk. This village contains a great swathe of beautifully carved rice barns facing two houses, one said to be 500 years old and the home of a former loca 'king'. Near the entrance are two clumps of bamboo used by bats to roost during the day. ■ *Getting there: regular bemos from Rantepao pass the turn-off for Nanggala.*

Pangli, 8 km due north from Rantepao, contains a house grave and *tau tau* effigies. A stone statue of Pong Massangka stands in front of the grave house. Walking about 200m up the hillside is reputedly the best tuak. At this point the road forks; one route runs northwest, while the main road continues due north. An alternative to taking the main road north is to trek along the path from **Tallunglipu**, just north of Rantepao, to **Bori** (where there are some huge *rante* stones), 6 km in all from Rantepao, and from there to the road running east-west, which is only 1½ km from Pangli. Just south of Bori is **Paringding**, 7 km southwest of Pangli, where there are some impressive *tongkonan* and rice barns.

North & northwest from Rantepao

Taking the west fork at Pangli, the road leads to **Deri** where it deteriorates into little more than a track. Many treks start here. **Lempo** has an attractive group of *tongkonan*. There is also a homestay here. **Batutumonga** is one of the higher points in the region, lying 20 km northwest of Rantepao; there are magnificent views over Rantepao and Makale, as well as tau tau; follow the blue signs to the old fort. This is also the place to start a walk to Gunung Sesan (2,150m, five hours). From here take a bemo to the village, and walk down the valleys to Rantepao. Or walk from Batutumonga to **Tikala** (about 1½ hours), and from there catch a bemo back to Rantepao. *En route* to Tikala, the path passes **Pana** where there are some baby graves. **Sleeping** There are six places to stay in Batutumonga: **B** *Batutumonga*, immaculately kept traditional style houses, six rooms, English owned. **D** *Batutumonga Homestay*, situated in the forest, excellent views. **E** *Landorundun*, wooden homestay. **Avoid** the *Betani Homestay*; several bad reports. **E** *Mama Siska Homestay*, basic and friendly. **E** *Mentiratiku Restaurant and Guesthouse*, beds are squeezed into rooms within a traditional Torajan house, some rooms with attached bathrooms, very clean, includes breakfast.

West of Batutumonga is **Lokkomata**, where there are *tau tau*. Still further is **Baruppu**, where there are the remains of a walled fort and some good woodcarvings.

Palawa is a hamlet 2 km north from Pangli on the main road, and 500m off the road (9½ km in all from Rantepao). Palawa consists of a wonderful double row of *tongkonan* and rice barns, with stacks of buffalo horns, dense carving and carved life-size buffalo heads. Although many of the families have set up small souvenir stalls selling cloth, woodcarvings and jewellery, few tourists make it out here and the primary source of income is still agriculture. On the track to Palawa, about 200m before the village, is a group of neglected **megaliths**.

To'karau is a village another 1 km on the 'main' road north. A periodic market is held here.

Sa'dan is a market centre a further 4 km north, 11 km from Rantepao. This market town (every sixth day) is an important ritual centre and has emerged in recent years as a centre of weaving. The cloths are made for the tourist market using imported yarn and chemical dyes, but maintaining traditional designs and motifs (see Shopping, below). It maintains a pleasant and welcoming atmosphere. There are four rice barns here, on a landscaped terrace, and excellent views to western mountains. Northwest of Sa'dan is **Ma'limbong**, where there is a traditional house with 91 buffalo horns. Ikat weaving can also be seen.

Getting to the sights north and northwest from Rantepao Bemos run from Rantepao through Pangli and on to Palawa, To'karau and Sa'dan, with the road threading its way along a beautiful rice valley.

Rantepao-Mamasa trek An increasingly popular way of reaching Mamasa is by foot. Horses (80,000-100,000Rp per day), accommodation (**E**) and guide (US$15-25 per day) are all available from tour companies in Rantepao. The trek takes about three days (see page 719).

Tours **Rafting** tours are becoming increasingly popular. Tour companies (*Indo Sella*, Jl Suluara 113, T25210, F23605) arrange trips on the Sa'dan and Maulu rivers. Day tours cost 250,000Rp, three-day tours 1,250,000Rp.

Sleeping in Rantepao
There is a good range of hotels, resorts & losmen to choose from in Rantepao. The more expensive hotels tend to quote their room rates in US$ & given the weakness of the rupiah are over priced

■ on map
Price codes:
see inside front cover

L-AL *Hotel Marante Toraja*, Jl Jurusan Palopo, PO Box 52, T21616, F21122, marante@ upg.mega.net.id Restaurant, pool, satellite TV, minibar, babysitting, car and mountain bikes for hire, situated 4 km east of Rantepao amidst rice fields, over 110 rooms. Some of the suites are in Toraja-style bungalows, very helpful staff, beautifully situated and well run, the best of the 'luxury' hotels. **L-AL** *Novotel Resort Toraja*, off Jl Kete Kesu, south of town, T21192, F21666. A/c, pool, tennis court, fitness centre, rather overdone in terms of mirroring local architecture but good range of sports and other facilities, 160 rooms. **L-A** *Rantepao Lodge*, Jl Pao Rura (500m south of town), T21248. Restaurant (mid-range), good rooms and beautiful setting within ricefields, pool, IDD phone. **AL** *Toraja Cottages*, Desa Bolu, Paku (3 km east of town), T21089, F21304. Restaurant, small but inviting pool, quiet location out of town, set on the side of a hill in attractive gardens. **AL** *Toraja Prince* (3 km east of town), T21458, F21304. Pool, hotel with well appointed rooms. **A** *Hotel Indra Complex*, main office Jl Landorundun 63, T21163, 21583. Comprises 4 separate hotels, each with the same management. Indra is the best of the 4, with a/c, restaurant, very clean, all 19 rooms have private bathrooms, hot water and TV as well as sitting area overlooking central garden. *Indra 1* and *Indra City* house the 'standard' rooms (B), whilst *Indra II* also houses some deluxe rooms at (A). *Indra City* is the oldest of the 3 and is looking a little jaded. Narrow beds. The restaurant here, which overlooks the river, is one of the best in town. **A-B** *Hiltra Toraja Hotel*, Jl Pramuka 70, T27323, F25257. Opened in Aug 1999, this new hotel offers very luxurious accommodation and amazing views of Batutumonga Mountain.

B *Madarrana*, Jl Sa'dan 21b, T23777. Tongkonan-style hotel, 25 large luxurious rooms, spotless grounds and peaceful location north of Rantepao, international restaurant, light and airy atmosphere. **B** *Misiliana*, PO Box 01, Jl Pongtiku 27 (3 km south of town), T21212, F21512, tmhtrj@indosat.net.id Attractive pool, large newish hotel in an expansive compound with 96 rooms, 3 km south of town. Standard rooms are better than the suite rooms (which are in newly-built tongkonan). Biblical messages carved in stone fill the garden. Good amenities, but rather over-priced as they quote in US$. **B** *Pondok Torsina*, Jl Pao Rura 119 (50m off main road, 500m south of town), T21293. Restaurant, rather green pool, hot water, set among ricefields, large, clean rooms, includes breakfast, restaurant (cheap).

C *Maria II*, Jl Pongtiku (about 2 km south of town), popular, with a small tongkonan and a peaceful situation 50m off the road in ricefields. **C** *Toraja Palma*, Jl Durisan Palopo, T23789; 2½ km east of town, pristine white rooms with great views over rice fields and Batutumonga Mountain, friendly staff, breakfast included. **C-D** *Pondonk Wisata Kambuno*, Jl Jur Palopo (2 km east of town), T25104; 24 fair-sized rooms, breakfast included, poor open air restaurant. **C-D** *Wisma Emmanuel*, Jl Monginsidi 16, T21416. Attractive gardens, large rooms with huge beds, some rooms with hot water, includes breakfast. Recommended.

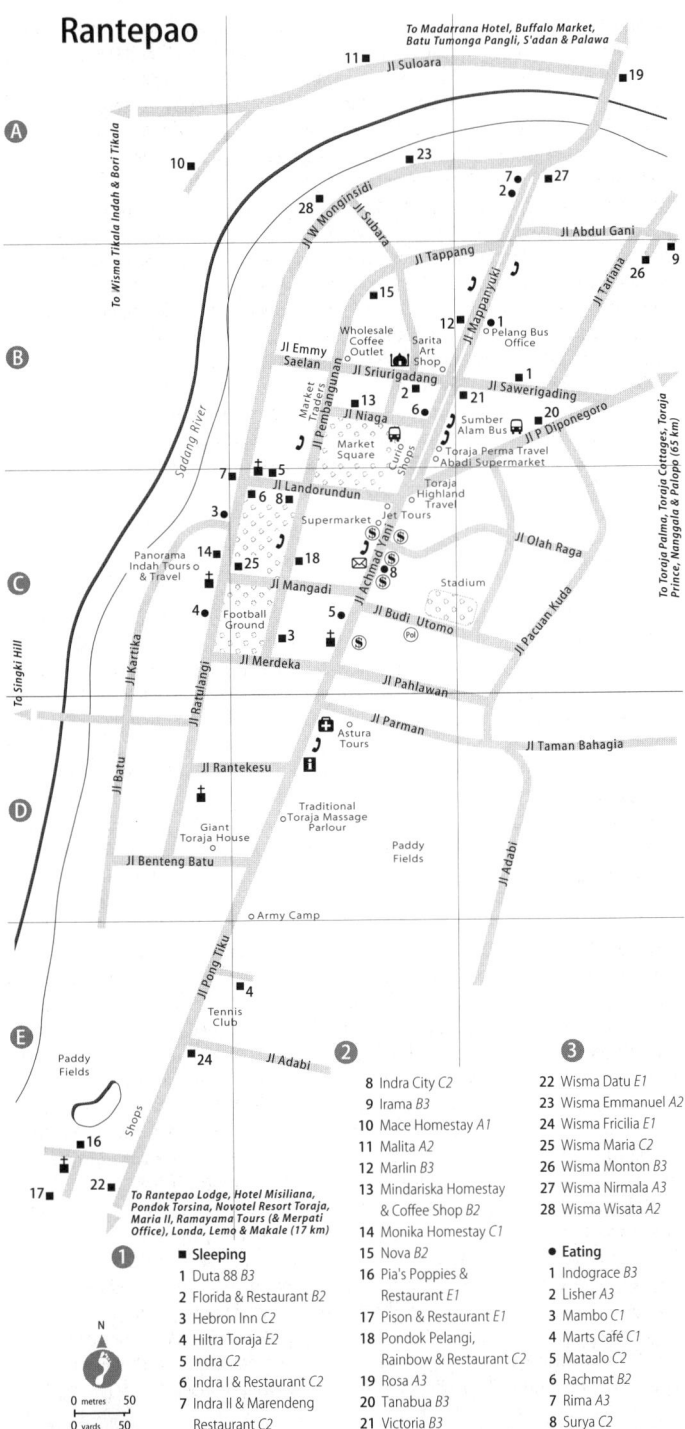

D *Duta 88*, Jl Sawerigading 12, T23477. Seven traditional houses in a compact little complex. All rooms with hot water, en suite western toilets, price includes breakfast. **D** *Hebron Inn*, Jl Pembangunan 27, T21519. Tranquil location, shabby rooms, with western toilets, friendly management, overpriced, breakfast included. **D** *Mace Homestay*, Jl Tengko Situru 4, T21852. Large airy rooms, on opposite side of river to town. **D** *Nova*, Jl Tappang. Situated down a back street but even so noisy and dirty, lounge on 2nd floor, some crazy coloured bed spreads. **D** *Pia's Poppies*, Jl Pongtiku (just off main road south edge of town), T21121. Restaurant, hot water, strange grotto-like bathrooms, this hotel of traditional construction has character and is friendly, overlooking ricefields, not very central but therefore peaceful, price includes breakfast. Recommended. **D** *Pison*, Jl Pongtiku 8, T/F21344 (just off main road, south edge of town, about 15 mins walk from the centre). Restaurant, very popular, good food, clean rooms with hot water and attached bathrooms and balconies, friendly service, quiet location, good value. Recommended. **D** *Rosa*, Jl Sadan 28, T21075. On the outskirts of town on the road to Sa'dan, quiet rooms with mandis (some with hot water) in garden surroundings. Recommended. **D** *Wisma Datu*, Jl Pongtiku II, T21023. Just 3 rooms, hot water, friendly, not the best value given the noisy road. **D** *Wisma Monton*, Jl Abd Gani 14A, T/F21675. Pleasant, quiet guesthouse a little off the main street, overlooking a lovely garden. This is a good place for twitchers, as the balconies outside the rooms provide good viewing platforms for the many interesting birds which arrive here at dawn and dusk. Distant views to Mount Sesean. Clean rooms with hot water showers in most rooms. Good breakfast of home-made bread, fruit and coffee. Helpful proprietor provides information on Torajan traditions and current events.

D-E *Irama*, Jl U Abdul Gani 16, T21371. Restaurant, basic but clean, includes breakfast. **D-E** *Rainbow*, Jl Pembangunan IIa (corner with Jl Mangadi). Quiet rooms and pleasant family atmosphere, some rooms with hot water, and attached bathrooms, tea and coffee and breakfast included in room rate. **D-E** *Malita*, Jl Suloara 110, T21011. Room rate includes breakfast, lies outside town, over the bridge to the north, attractive setting and quiet, friendly owners. The rooms in the new wing are slightly more expensive, some with hot water. Recommended. **D-E** *Tanabua*, Jl Diponegoro 43, T21072. Restaurant, clean, all but the economy rooms have hot water, the rooms are dark and a bit pricey. **D-E** *Wisma Fricilia*, Jl Pongtiku 18, T21463. Six rooms, rooms are clean but avoid those near the drains, includes breakfast. **D-E** *Wisma Maria*, Jl Ratulangi 23, T21165; 24 rooms, several with hot water, clean blankets, room rate includes breakfast, a relaxing feel to the place. Recommended.

E *Florida*, Jl Emmy Saelan 25, T21210. Small losmen near the mosque, rooms are clean, some with balconies, but those at the front can be noisy, being close to a major intersection and the mosque. **E** *Hotel Victoria*, Jl Mappanyuki 48, T21038. Large (for Rantepao) newish hotel, already showing signs of wear. But rooms are large and clean enough with attached bathrooms. **E** *Marlin*, Jl Mappanyuki 75. Basic, clean and cheap, but rooms facing the busy main drag are noisy. **E** *Mindariska Homestay*, Jl Niaga 18, T25190. Price includes breakfast. A relatively new place with 16 rooms, attached coffee shop and facing on to the market square. Some rooms with balconies. English spoken, central location but not too noisy. **E** *Monika Homestay*, Jl Sam Ratulangi 36, T21216. On corner with Jl Kartika, clean rooms in a quiet spot and a good breakfast, tea and coffee included. **E** *Sella Homestay*, Jl Suluara 113, T25210, F23605. Not en suite but OK rooms and a massive collection of books to swap. **E** *Tagari Homestay*, Jl Tagari 23. About 10 min walk from town, but they will pick you up if you call T21195. Excellent place with friendly, helpful owners, Mr and Mrs Pasulu. Clean rooms with bathrooms attached, big nasi goreng breakfast, tea and coffee all day. The terrace overlooks paddy fields and the family rice barn. The Pasulus are retired teachers and have a wealth of knowledge about Indonesia. Highly recommended. **E** *Wisma Nirmala*, Jl Andi Mappanyuki 118, T21319. Ten rooms, near to the road and therefore tends to be noisy, but the rooms are clean. **F** *Wisma Wisata*, Jl Monginsidi 40. For those on a real budget.

Mid-range to cheap *Indra I*, Jl Landorundun 63. Good hotel restaurant. Recommended. *Marendeng* (within *Indra II Hotel*). Red checked table-cloths, atmospheric location overlooking river and Singki Hill, evening 'shows', and some of the best hotel food available. *Pia's Poppies*, Jl Pongtiku. Unbelievably slow service, order 2 hrs beforehand and take War & Peace, but the professional Balinese chef comes up with the goods, usually before sunrise, good atmosphere. *Pison*, Jl Pongtiku 8. Good Indonesian/Chinese food, with Torajan specialities, slow service, poor western food. *Rainbow*, Jl Pembangunan 11, T21753. Good Indonesian, Chinese and Western food (the restaurant supplies some of the larger hotels), but, like some other places, order 2 hrs beforehand. The fresh food is expertly cooked by Jackoline and tastes great. Recommended.

Eating
Most hotels have their own restaurants. Local specialities include black rice (nasi hitam), fish & chicken cooked in bamboo (piong), & palm wine (tuak)

Cheap to very cheap *Indograce*, Jl Mappanyuki (facing *Marlin Hotel*). Popular place serving Chinese, Indonesian and Torajan specialities, well lit, clean and with reasonable prices, but some rather disappointing dishes and service. *Lisher*, Jl A Mappanyuki 107 (2 doors towards the centre from the *Restaurant Rima*). Very clean, great Indonesian food and excellent service, also have good bicycles for rent. *Mambo*, Jl Dr Ratulangi 34, T21134 (facing *Wisma Maria I*). Usually packed with tourists which perhaps explains the excruciatingly slow service, average Indonesian and international dishes, good breakfasts, menu also includes frog. *Mart's Café and Restaurant*, Jl Dr Ratulangi 44a (facing the football pitch). Open 0700-2200, clean restaurant with good and well-priced food, with a vegetarian menu, excellent place for breakfast (choice of 6 types), the Indonesian owner studied in Ireland of all places so speaks good English. Recommended. *Rima Restaurant*, Jl Mappanyuki 150, T25223. *Satria Desa*, Jl Diponegoro 15. Basic Indonesian dishes. *Rachmat*, Jl Achmad Yani, large and central, geared to tour groups, Indonesian/Chinese, rather unfriendly. *Surya*, Jl Achmad Yani 88. Good selection of local food in an attractive restaurant next to the Bank Rakyat Indonesia. Good range of Indonesian and Chinese dishes.

Very cheap *Central Market*, for cheap warung food, Indonesian and Torajan. *Florida*, Jl Emmy Saelan 25, T21010. Standard Indonesian menu, clean and tasty, some vegetarian dishes. *Mataallo*, Jl Ahmad Yani 87. Huge menu – 55 dishes, attractive little restaurant with great coffee.

Rafting On the Sa'dan and Maulu rivers. Indo Sella and Sobek have leaflets dotted around the restaurants and hotels. **Swimming** The pools at the Toraja Cottages and the Novotel are both open to non-residents (5,000Rp).

Sports

Rantepao has a selection of shops selling crafts and some antiques, situated along Jl Landorundun near the central square and on the ground floor of the central market. **Antiques** include weavings and carved house panels. Good shops are thin on the ground. *Duta Art Shop*, Jl Mappanyuki 29; *Sarita Art Shop*, Jl Mappanyuki 51; *Toraja Art Shop*, Jl Landorundun; *Adil*, Jl Landorundun 27. **Book Exchange** on Jl Mangadi, and also *Sella Homestay*. **Crafts** include hats, basketry, carved wooden statues, model *tongkonan*, and bamboo containers, Torajan effigies and boxes.

Shopping

Jet Tourist Service, Jl Landorundun 1, T21145, guides speak English, French or Italian, approximate rates: guide 60,000Rp per day; trek 160,000Rp per day, including meals; vehicle and driver 100,000Rp per day recommended. *Holiday Tours*, Jl Mangadi 25, T25468, F25468, F25522. *Astura Tours*, Jl A Yani 70, T21814, F27322. *Adventure Tours*, Jl A Yani 89, T21017. *Celebes*, Jl Mangadi, T21813, bicycles, car plus huge book exchange. *Toraja Permai*, Jl A Mappanyuki 10, T21784, F21785, wide range of tours and good transport. *Toraja Highland Travel*, Jl P Digonegoro 17, T23035. *Eskell*, Jl Pongtiku, T21344, F21500.

Tour operators

Transport
17 km from Makale,
62 km from Palopo,
173 km from Pare Pare,
350 km from Makassar, 359 km from Pendolo,
646 km from Palu,
1,628 km from Manado

Local Bemos: the 'station' is behind the central market but Jl A Yani is crowded with bemos. Local bemos charge 1,000Rp. **Bicycle hire**: about 15,000-20,000Rp per day from tour companies, guesthouses and some restaurants. **Car hire**: from 80,000-120,000Rp per day. **Chartered bemos**: can be picked up anywhere and cost about 100,000Rp per day. **Motorbike hire**: about 45,000-50,000Rp from *Jet Travel, Toraja Permai* and *Celebes Travel* amongst others. To hire cars, motorbikes or bicycles ask at your hotel. **Becaks**: many parade the town but are relatively expensive (500-1,500Rp around town).

Air Pongtiku airport is just north of Makale and 21 km south of Rantepao. Currently there are no flights due to lack of demand.

Road Bus: buses leave from outside the bus offices north of and around the market on Jl Mappanyuki. There are several companies offering a range of departure times and services. Litha and Co, Jl Mappanyuki (ground floor of the Central Market), is the largest bus operator running vehicles between Rantepao and Makassar, includes a/c buses with reclining seats. Other companies include *Pelangi*, Jl Mappanyuki 64, *Jet Tours*, Jl Landorundun 1, *Lima Bus Company*, Jl Mappanyuki 75, and *Batutumonga*, Jl Mappanyuki 65. Regular connections with Palopo 2 hrs, Makassar 9 hrs (0900, 1300 and 2100, 21,000-28,000Rp a/c and reclining seats, 17,000Rp for non-a/c), Pare Pare 6 hrs (10,000Rp), Watampone (15,000Rp), Pendolo 8½ hrs (25,000Rp), Poso 12 hrs (30,000Rp), Tentena 11 hrs and Palu 18-24 hrs (40,000Rp). *Battutumonga Bus*, Jl Mappanyuki 65, is another good operator serving the above destinations. For the windy journey south to Pare Pare and Makassar, try to get a seat on one of the larger buses, not on the cramped and uncomfortable minibuses. For Gorontalo and Manado change buses at Palu. Bus offices are concentrated along Jl Mappanyuki and Jl Diponegoro. **NB** On arrival by bus be aware that several passengers will be tour and hotel reps on commission. The bus may also stop outside only certain hotels, especially at night. **Sea**: While Rantepao is clearly not a port, a number of tour companies display *Pelni* timetables and it is possible to book berths ahead from here.

Directory Airline offices *Merpati*, Jl Pongtiku 32a, T21615. *Pelni* Agents: found along Jl Mappanyuki. **Banks** *Danamon*, Jl Achmad Yani 115 (next to Post Office), accepts VISA and cash, no TCs; *Rakyat Indonesia*, Jl Achmad Yani 96, accepts TCs and US$ cash but very poor rates; *BNI*, on Jl Achmad Yani at corner with Jl Budi Utomo; money changer at Jl Diponegoro 4 offers better rates than some banks. Several other money changers on Jl Mappanyuki and Jl Achmad Yani, near the market. **Communications Post Office**: Jl Achmad Yani 111. Poste Restante available. **Telecom**: Jl Achmad Yani 113 (next door to Post Office). **Wartel**: Jl Mappanyuki (opposite the market). A number of tour companies (eg *Toraja Permai*) also offer telephone services. **Useful addresses Police**: Jl Budi Utomo, T21358.

Polewali

Phone code: 0428
Colour map 4, grid C6

Few people stop in Polewali which, nonetheless, is a sizeable town on the road between Pare Pare and Majene. Most people who do stay here do so merely as a stop-off *en route* to or from Mamasa. The area around Polewali is important for the production of the silk sarongs known as *sarung Mandar*, which can be purchased in town. These are usually checked and restrained in terms of their colouring. This part of Sulawesi was also earmarked as a transmigration destination area and there are several settlements of Javanese in the area.

Sleeping **C** *Hotel Arham*, Jl A Depu 269, T21357. **E** *Melati*, Jl A Yani 91, T21075. **E** *Wisma Duja*, Jl Olahraga 16, T21292.

Transport
247 km from Makassar,
90 km from Pare Pare,
55 km from Majene

Road Bus: Polewali lies on the main road between Ujung, through Pare Pare, and on to Majene. It is consequently relatively well-served. *Litha & Co* and other large bus companies travel through Polewali. Bemos and minibuses link Polewali with Mamasa (5 hrs travelling up to Mamasa, rather less going down); there are also connections with Makale.

Majene

A little over 50 km west of Polewali is this rarely visited but attractive little town, with only a very limited tourist infrastructure. The town itself is the former capital of the Mandar kingdom and is set around a crescent-shaped bay. The grave of Syech Abdul Manan, an important local personage, is here.

Phone code: 0422
Colour map 4, grid C5

The Mandarese, like the more famous Bugis to the south, are skilled sailors and boat builders, and traditional Mandar vessels, called *sande*, are still built in villages around here (albeit with various new-fangled innovations, like motors). When the Dutch tried to corner the trade in spices from Maluku by embarking on their policy of *extirpatie* (extirpation – eradication, see page 912), Mandarese traders were instrumental in breaking the monopoly. Fishing remains an important local industry and the area exports dried and salted fish to other areas of Indonesia.

Sleeping Mosquitoes are to be found in abundance, making a stay at one of the 3 *penginapan* an itchy experience. Arrangements can be made to stay at the harbour-side home of **Ibu Darmi Mas'ud**, Jl Amana Wewang 12, bookable in Makassar, T22482. Rooms here are clean and have good views over the bay, and food can be arranged for a token fee. Other places to stay include the **Wisma Cahaya**, Jl Rahman 2, T0422-21105, and the **Penginapan Abrar**, Jl Sudirman 49.

Transport 302 km from Makassar, 145 km from Pare Pare, and 55 km from Polewali. **Road Bus**: Majene is well served by *Litha & Co* and other large bus companies, using good buses. The road from Pare Pare, along the coast, is truly memorable. Regular connections with Polewali (1½ hrs), Pare Pare (4 hrs) and Makassar (7 hrs).

Mamuju

Along the road running up the coast from Majene, the next town of any size is Mamuju; not somewhere to rush to, but in time it may become a stop-off point. Until a few years ago this town really was off the tourist track; now steady road up-grading has meant that there are regular bus connections with stops south and with Makassar. It shouldn't be long before it will be possible to reach Palu (and from there the rest of North Sulawesi) by catching a bus north from Mamuju, along the coast road. At the time of writing there were no such scheduled connections.

Phone code: 0426
Colour map 4, grid B5

The area around Mamuju is interesting in so far as it has revealed trading links with distant regions. A statue of the Buddha dated to 200 AD has been found in the area, as has a fine bronze Dongson drum from mainland Southeast Asia.

Sleeping **D-E** *Wisma Kencana Sakti*, Jl Langsat 21, T21040. Some a/c. **D-E** *Wisma Rio*, Jl Kemakmuran 28, T21014. Some a/c.

Transport **Air** There are occasional connections on Merpati between Makassar and Mamuju. **Road Bus**: connections with Majene, and from there with Polewali (for Mamasa), Pare Pare and Makassar.

The Mamasa Valley

Mamasa lies to the west of Rantepao and to the north of Polewali. It could be described as Tana Toraja 15 years ago, although the people here would probably resent being characterized as such. Nonetheless, both geographically and culturally there are clear parallels between Mamasa and Rantepao: both lie in rich upland rice valleys surrounded by handsome peaks and offer superlative hiking possibilities; and the people of both areas have converted to Christianity (the first Dutch Protestant missionaries only arrived in Mamasa in 1927), they traditionally built impressive tongkonan-style houses and are linguistically very closely related with their cousins to the east. However, there are significant differences between the Toraja and the people of the Mamasa

Colour map 4, grid B/C6

valley. To begin with their houses, which are known as banua sura *rather than* tongkonan, are less richly carved and decorated and buffalo trophies are few and far between. The houses themselves sit lower to the ground, resting on logs, and have an altogether more augmented appearance. The main supporting pillar displays carvings of animals and people, which relate to the family who live there.

Because the Mamasa Valley is more difficult to reach, especially during the wet season (there is no air service to Mamasa), most visitors tend to opt for the Rantepao area. This means that Mamasa has retained more of a frontier quality; it also means, of course, that the luxuries of Rantepao are less available – although one new, up-market hotel has opened. Note that nights in the Mamasa area are cool, and sometimes downright cold. It is always possible to buy a blanket if you arrive unprepared (see 'Shopping', below).

Background

When Harry Wilcox made the overland journey from Makale to Mamasa in the 1940s it was a truly isolated place. In his book *Six Moons in Sulawesi* (1949), he records how one of his local companions, Timbu, grunted disparagingly: "Ignorant people here, Tuan. They don't know how to plant rice. Dogs would plant it as well." Then, even more shocking, another companion, Massang, added "These people don't make *tuak* (palm wine). They are not able. Truly fools, these people." Sugar in Mamasa sold for 300 cents a kilo; in Makale it cost just 100 cents, although rice and salt were both cheaper as there were good supplies of both. Nonetheless, Wilcox found Mamasa "more adulterated than Makale by alien blood and faith. Bugis people, with their mosques and goats, were everywhere. Many local Torajas, too, have been converted to Islam..." It was, in the 1940s, surprisingly also a larger town than Makale – because it was a Dutch administrative centre.

Mamasa region

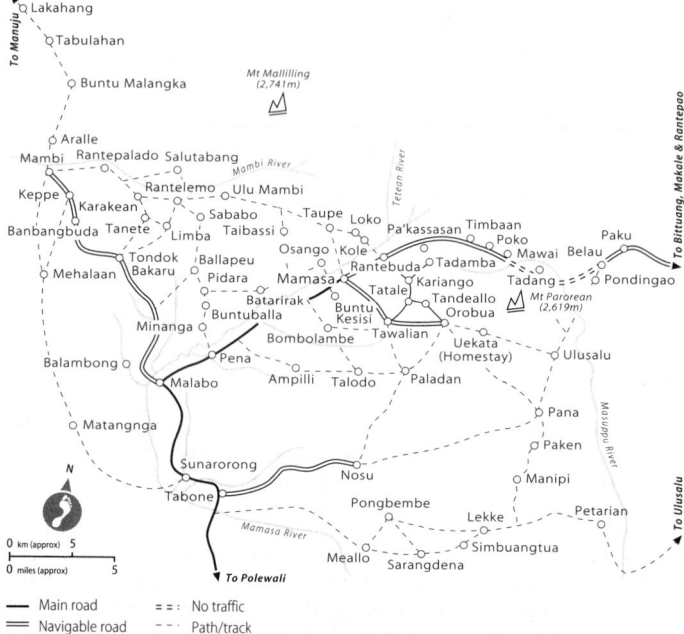

Traditional houses of Mamasa

There are four types of Mamasa house. The *banua layuk* is a house of a chief or king or other leader; the *banua bolong* or 'black house' is the home of a doctor; the *banua rapac* is a 'common house' and is not painted; while the *banua longkarrin* is a slaves' house, with just one or two rooms and no decoration.

The *banua layuk* is divided into four sections. The *tabo* is the front and is used for welcoming guests. The *ba'ba* is the largest room and provides sleeping space for guests and dining for special occasions. This room is divided in two, east and west. The eastern part is reserved for the higher classes (*tana' bulawen/tana' bassi*) and is decorated with coloured mats (*ampa' sura*). The west is for the lower classes (*tana'kanurung/tana'koa-koa*) and is decorated with naturally coloured mats. The third section of the house is the *tabing* which is the main family room. This also houses the private *tabing buni*, where only the husband and wife and young children may go. The fourth and final section is the *capo'* – the kitchen/dining room – which can also be used as an extra bedroom. Originally, a hole in the floor here acted as a toilet and rubbish disposal, allowing waste to fall to the animals below.

Hiking in the Mamasa Valley

Road transport is pretty limited in this area and the best way to get around, thank goodness, is still by foot. There are also some rather moth-eaten ponies for hire. There are numerous paths criss-crossing the region, linking villages and markets. The map here should only be taken as a rough guide to the area; the best way to plan a route is to give yourself a few days in Mamasa town to ask other hikers where they have been and the state of the various tracks. Losmen/hotel owners also sometimes keep guestbooks and can also offer advice. The information and treks arranged from *Mantana Lodge* have been recommended. Remember that it is cold at night, can be extremely wet, and facilities in the surrounding villages are basic. Simple supplies for trekking are available in Mamasa town and it is a good idea to take some small gifts along.

In the last few years it has become possible to hire motorcycles in Mamasa to explore the countryside. This is best during the dry season, and it also restricts riders to the few vehicle-friendly roads in the area. Bemos also ply these roads, so it is possible to walk out and ride back.

Villages & sights in the valley

The villages and sights below are ordered according to how far they are (in hiking distance) from Mamasa. It is possible to visit villages on a series of day treks, returning to Mamasa town each evening. Use the map to work out an appropriate route.

The main sights of interest – bar the incomparable highland countryside – are the traditional villages with their fine *banua sura* (*tongkonan*) and the *tedong-tedong* burial sites. The *banua sura* are similar to those found in the Rantepao area. The *tedong-tedong* grave sites, though, are distinctive. Coffins, carved in the shape of buffalo heads (hence the name *tedong* – water buffalo) or in the shape of canoes (*bangka*) are placed in open sided mini-houses, almost like rice barns without walls.

Mamasa Town

Phone code: 0423
Colour map 4, grid C6

This small town, with a population of, apparently, 2,500 (all sources seem to quote this figure although it may simply have become the accepted truth through endless repetition) is the base from which most visitors explore the surrounding countryside. The town, at 1,160m, is set in the upper reaches of the Mamasa Valley at the point where the Tetean and Mamasa rivers meet. One main street and the football ground tie together the quiet jumble of rusted roofs. Impressive mountains surround the settlement and although the area can be shrouded in mist for many days during the wet season, in the dry season the air is clear and cool. There are a good number of guesthouses, and information on where to go and how can be gleaned from guestbooks and evening talks with other travellers. It is worth spending some time here before venturing out overnight into the countryside.

The only sight in town is the **market** which is held once a week, sandwiched between Jl Jend A Yani and Jl Penbangunon. This is the best place to see a good range of Mamasa blankets (see 'Shopping', below), although it is now dominated by a sea of radiant plastic, making original bargains difficult to find.

Excursions There are a number of sights – traditional houses or *tongkonan*, *tedong-tedong* burial sites, traditional weaving villages and wonderful vistas – within a day's trek of Mamasa town. See 'Hiking in the Mamasa Valley', above.

Sleeping *Until recently, Mamasa only offered basic guesthouse accommodation. With gradual improvements in road from Polewali, bigger investors are being attracted to the undoubted charms of the area*

AL-A *Mamasa Cottage*, Rambusaratu (3 km north of Mamasa town, see surrounding area map), book through Makassar agent (*PT Intim Wisata Lestari*, T0411-359036). Twelve cottages built in traditional *tongkonan*-style. Next to clean but fragrant 'hot' spring, telephone, TV and most facilities, good food but isolated location. **D-E** *Matana Lodge*, Jl Emi Saelan I (look for the glowing sign), T23558, 23 rooms, breakfast included. Good views from balcony, very fresh but mixed food, some hot water, transport and tours can be arranged. Popular, clean and good value, best in town. Recommended. **D-F** *Losmen Marapan*, Jl Jend A Yani 39. Another older guesthouse but seems to have maintained a reasonable standard of cleanliness. Standard rooms have en suite facilities, but mandi is small. Restaurant (5,000-15,000Rp) and some English spoken. **F** *Losmen Mini*, Jl Jend A Yani 8. Range of rooms, the ones upstairs are much more cheery and airy. Friendly, family atmosphere, restaurant with limited menu. **F** *Mamasa Christian Guesthouse*, Jl Demmatande 182. Old wooden Dutch house located near the river on the road to Bitung. Rooms are en suite and some have good views.

Eating **Cheap and very cheap** *Restaurant Philadelphia*, Buntu Kasisi village, 1.5 km south of Mamasa. More of a bar with a very limited menu. *Padi Idi*, Jl J A Yani. A clean and cheap coffee shop with limited choice. Alternatively, there are warungs scattered in town.

Entertainment **Dances** it is sometimes possible to witness traditional dancing. The most distinctive dances of the area are the *Bulu Londong*, a war dance, and the *Simbong*.

Shopping As in the Rantepao area, the people of Mamasa are accomplished weavers and there is a flourishing *sambu* blanket-making industry here. In several villages the techniques of ikat weaving can be seen. Blankets are sold on the street corner or at the market. Most are dyed using aniline (chemical) dyes, although some people report that traditionally dyed examples are still available; look for the duller, more sombre-coloured blankets. *Mamasa Primitive Art Shop*, 1 km south of town, small range of local crafts at modest prices.

Transport *92 km from Polewali, 184 km from Pare Pare, 339 km from Makassar*

Road Bus: bemos and minibuses link Mamasa with Polewali (6 hrs travelling up to Mamasa, 4 hrs going down). The road was once tarmacked but now has more holes per kilometre than a string vest. But the views both down and across the valley, out to sea, make it well worth the pain. Buses will drop-off at hotels/losmen. To get to Mamasa from Makassar, there are some direct express buses (10 hrs, 15,000Rp, none on Sun) which are the quickest and most comfortable way of reaching or leaving Mamasa. Alternatively, take a bus to Pare Pare and then a connection onto Polewali. From Polewali catch a bemo to Mamasa.

Directory **Communications** **Post Office**: Jl Jend Sudirman. **Wartel**: Jl A Yani 44, T23558. There have been some recent problems with the phone service.

Southwest of Mamasa, west of the Mamasa River

Taupe (3 km): a traditional village with *banua sura* and a grave site set in the midst of the forest. **Osango** (5 km): this is what a geographer might call a dispersed settlement rather than a village. Nonetheless, there are some *banua sura* and also a two-centuries old *tedong-tedong* burial site. **Tanate** (8 km): a village that specializes in the weaving of *sambu* blankets (see Mamasa, 'Shopping') and there is also a cave grave site. **Taibassi** (9 km): this is the largest village in the Mamasa Region (with a population of over 400); *sambu*-weaving village. **Rante Balla** (11 km): traditional *sambu*-weaving and handicraft centre; also has some fine *banua sura*. **Ballakalua** (13 km): a fine traditional village with *banua sura*, also specializing in the weaving of *sambu* blankets. **Minanga** (14 km): *tedong-tedong* grave site. **Buntuballa** (15 km): a fine traditional village with impressive *banua sura* and grave site and also good views. **Bula** (16 km): traditional village. **Ballapeu** (18 km): traditional village. **Mussa** (19 km): viewpoint with outstanding vista up the Mamasa valley back to Mamasa town.

Mesa Kada (2 km): hot springs where it is possible to bathe. **Buntu Kesisi** (2½ km): *banua sura*. **Rante Katoan** (3 km): traditional village with *banua sura* and hot springs. **Rante Sopang** (9 km): a traditional village on the 'main' road south of Mamasa, so has its fair share of visitors. The inhabitants have taken advantage of this by transforming themselves into a weaving and handicraft centre. **Orobua** (9 km): this is the largest village in the Mamasa Region (with a population of over 400). The *banua sura* in this traditional village are particularly fine and well-maintained, with a *banua layuk* and numerous rice granaries. West of Orobua is **Tawalian**, a very old village with a Dutch missionary church of 1932. Some *tabi* coffins (buffalo coffins) can be found in this area near Rantedambu village. **Paladan** (12 km): this is a centre for weaving of the *sambu*, the typical Mamasanese sarong. Graves of Mamasanese heroes can be seen 500m east of the village on a hill with spectacular views. The *liang-tedong-tedong* (a traditional coffin with one end the shape of a buffalo and the other resembling a horse) was built in 1910 to remember their resistance to the Dutch; however, they were not buried here as he died far from Mamasa. The fort used by the 'heroes', named Benteng Salubanga, is west of the village. **Malabo** (18 km): a *tedong-tedong* grave site. **Tomalanti** (23 km): hot springs.

Southeast of Mamasa, east of the Mamasa River

Loko (4 km): a well-preserved traditional village with fine *banua sura*. **Kole** (4 km): ancient *banua sura* and hot springs. The new *Mamasa Cottages* are here (see 'Sleeping', Mamasa Town). **Barung** (8 km): a fine traditional village with grave site, *banua sura* and good views. **Mambulilin** (9 km): a steep walk to a waterfall.

Northwest of Mamasa, west of the Mamasa River

Rambusaratu (3 km): the ancient *banua sura* here is reputed to be the largest in the Mamasa Valley and to be three centuries old. It was a clan chief's house and visitors are welcomed inside – although a small donation is requested. **Kopian** (6 km): *tedong-tedong* burial site. Kariango (7 km): *tedong-tedong* grave site. **Tatale** (8 km): traditional village with good *banua sura* and *tedong-tedong* burial site. **Pallu** (8½ km): traditional village with *banua sura* and good views. **Taupe** is a centre for handicrafts, carving and cotton weaving. There is a waterfall enclosed in stone shaped like buffalo 500m south of the village.

Northeast of Mamasa, east of the Mamasa River

This trek should take three full days. Nights are spent in traditional villages with basic facilities and wildlife. It is best to carry a sleeping bag (cold at night), although some trekkers do survive by wrapping themselves in layers of *sambus* (blankets). The villages are listed here as if trekking from Mamasa to Rantepao (west to east). See the 'Around Mamasa' map (page 718) for the route from Mamasa as far as Timbaan. Timbaan (night 1, 26 km from Mamasa). Paku (night 2, 24 km from Timbaan). Bittuang (either night 3 or bus from there the final 22 km to Makale; Bittuang is 16 km from Paku). **NB** Check details of the trek with those in Mamasa or Rantepao before setting out.

Mamasa-Rantepao Trek
Despite the persistent sales pitch of Rantepao guides, it is possible to do this trek alone. There is only 1 road, so the majority do

Palopo (Luwu)

Palopo is a quiet coastal town, sandwiched on a narrow slice of lowland between Bone Bay and the South Sulawesi Highlands. It is useful as a stopping-off point on the arduous journey between Central Sulawesi and Toraja. There is a **museum** on Jl Andi Jemma, which was formerly a palace. It contains a modest but interesting collection of local ethnographic artefacts and some Asian ceramics. ■ *Sat 0700-1400 Mon-Thu and, closed Fri and Sun, admission by donation.* Fishing boats, ferries and *pinisi* schooners dock at the long pier reaching out into the bay. Most places in

Phone code: 0471
Colour map 4, grid C6

Excursions **Masamba**, one hour north of Palopo, is a small coastal town on the river; treks to Danau Poso can begin from here. It is a popular stopping off point for cyclists riding the Trans-Sulawesi Highway. ■ *Getting there: damri buses and many bemos stop in town.* **Sleeping** **D** *Srikandi*, 1½ km east of town on the main road, designed as a rest point on the Trans-Sulawesi Highway, new and clean. **E** *Masamba Wisma Merdeka*, situated just off the main street, small and quite clean. **E** *Wisma Andipa*.

Sleeping *The standard of accommodation here is generally very poor & overpriced*

C-D *Adifati 1*, Jl Pattimura 2, T21179. Another example of overpriced accommodation. **D** *Palopo Hotel*, Jl Kelapa 2, T21789. Rather a grand name for such a place, only stay here if you have to, and wish to be by bemo station. **D-E** *Adifati 2*, Jl A Jemma 86, T21467. Some a/c, clean, 2-storey, overlooking small garden, all rooms have own seating outside. Those at the front are a

Palopo (except for the bemo station) are within easy walking distance of each other and it is easy to get around town. The **tourist information** centre is on Jl Sultan Hasanuddin, next to the mosque.

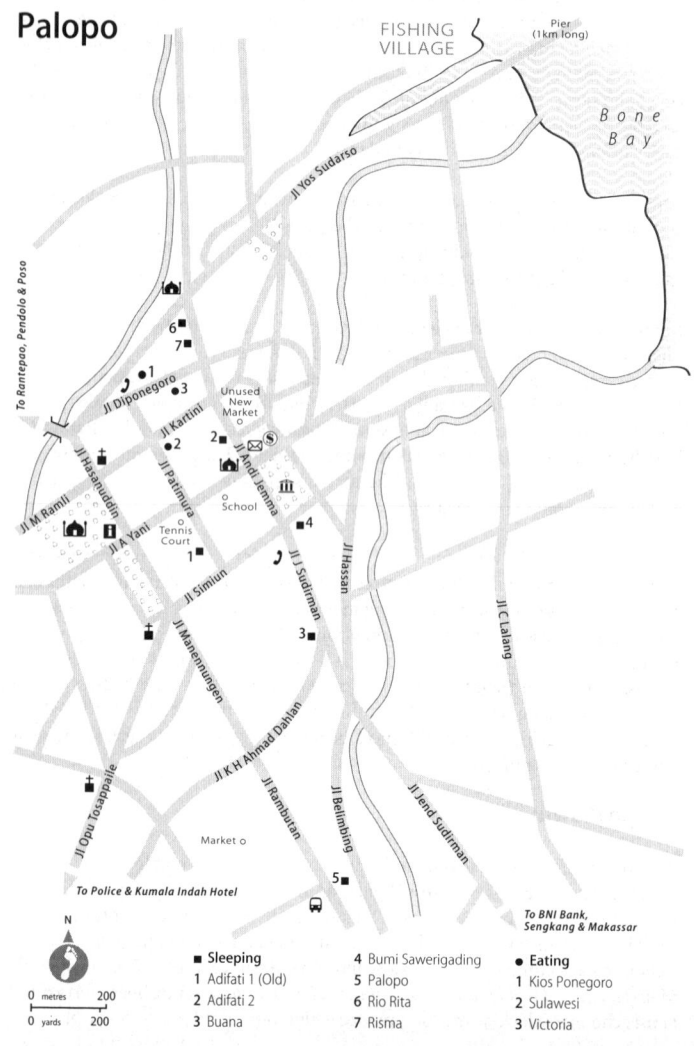

Palopo

Sleeping
1 Adifati 1 (Old)
2 Adifati 2
3 Buana
4 Bumi Sawerigading
5 Palopo
6 Rio Rita
7 Risma

Eating
1 Kios Ponegoro
2 Sulawesi
3 Victoria

bit noisy, spacious lobby with crimson sofas, office has a good wall map, no restaurant, best not to confuse this place with the *Adifati 1* around the corner which is a dump, ask for *Adifati* next to the mosque, not tennis courts, good value. **D-E** *Buana*, Jl KH Ahmad Dahlan 89, T22164. Compact hotel, close to market and bemo station, friendly and helpful staff, the best value hotel in town. Recommended. **D-E** *Bumi Sawerigading*, Jl Jend Sudirman 2, T21033. Close to museum, don't be put off by tatty exterior, price includes breakfast. **D-E** *Rio Rita*, Jl A Jemma 10. Looks can be deceptive, an old wooden building houses very dark, grubby rooms, some en suite. **E** *Risma*, Jl A Jemma 14, T21178. Small building with rather damp rooms, well kept gardens, but noisy when the resident songbirds are at it.

Cheap *Victoria*, Jl Diponegoro, popular with visitors, good shrimp and crab dishes. | **Eating**

Road Bus: all bus companies have their offices at the bus terminal on Jl Rambutan. Buses to Rantepao 3-4 hrs (5,000Rp), Makassar 8 hrs (17,500Rp) and north to Tentena, Poso (25,000Rp) and Palu (30,000Rp). Bemos to Rantepao 2½ hrs (5,000Rp), wonderful views and scenery, but a windy road. **Sea Boat**: for those with an adventurous turn of mind, it is well worth walking out onto the pier; boats regularly leave for Maluku, about a 7-day journey. Regular connections with Malili and Kolaka (Southeast Sulawesi). | **Transport**

Banks *Bank Mandiri*, Jl Mangga 24 (ATM accepting Maestro and Cirrus). *BNI* to the south of town along Jl Jend Sudirman. **Communications Post Office:** Jl Achmad Yani 15. **Wartel Office:** Jl Jend Sudirman, phone cards available. | **Directory**

Southeast Sulawesi

The province of Southeast Sulawesi, with a population of over 1,500,000, is very rarely visited by tourists and has only limited facilities for the traveller. The provincial capital is Kendari on the east coast; Kolaka, on the west coast, is the ferry port for south Sulawesi. Off southeast Sulawesi's southern tip are the large and formerly influential island kingdoms of Buton and Muna. The province is relatively rich in natural resources with nickel mines, asphalt and timber. It is also an important transmigration settlement area.

Kolaka

A minor port and transit point for Southeast Sulawesi. Ferries from Bajoe, Bone's port, dock here and there is accommodation for those forced to stay overnight. | *Phone code: 0405* *Colour map 5, grid C1*

E *Rahmat*, Jl Kadue 6, T21036. Own mandi, 10 rooms. **E** *Aloha*, Jl Kencinga 19, T21189. Spacious and clean. **E** *Monahsa*, Jl Kongoasa 17, T21035, 1 km from town centre, 9 rooms with attached mandis. **E** *Morini*, Jl Jend A Yani 21, T21173. Attached bathrooms. **E** *Rachmat*, Jl Kadue 6, T21032. Rooms at back are more pleasant. Generally clean, but near to busy road junction. | **Sleeping**

Air Twice weekly connections on Merpati with the mining town of Pomalaa. **Road Bus**: regular minibuses to Kendari, 3½-4 hrs. **Sea Boat**: nightly ferries to Bajoe (Bone's port), 8 hrs, leaving Kolaka at 2100. | **Transport** *173 km from Kendari*

Kendari

Kendari lies on the east coast of Southeast Sulawesi and is the capital of the province. It was developed by the Japanese as a military base during their occupation of Indonesia, when the capital was moved from Baubau on Buton Island to Kendari. As the | *Phone code: 0401* *Colour map 5, grid C2* provincial capital, it is endowed with all the usual paraphernalia of government and has a population of over 100,000. The town is strung-out, ribbon-like, over 8 km or so, giving it the feel of a stage set. Everything is on this road; beyond it, nothing. There are two **tourist offices**: *Dinas Pariwisata*, Jl Tebau Nunggu 2, T26634 (at the west end of Kendari Bay, just off the main road [which, at this point, is Jl Jend A Yani], near the Al Kautbar Mosque), helpful and informative; *Kantor Parawisata Diparda*, on hill behind harbour, T21764. Some English spoken.

Excursions **Moramo Waterfall**, which cascades down seven terraces, is 50 km south of town. The pools at each level make for pleasant swimming. ■ *Getting there: by bus (1¾ hrs) from the Madonga terminal 3 km south to Pasar Baru, change onto a bus to Lapuko and there rent a bemo or ojek for the last 15 km.*

Tours *Alam Jaya*, Jl Konggoasa 50, T21729, organizes 5-7 day trips around Southeast Sulawesi; *BPU*, Jl Konggoasa 48, will organize boat and car trips around the area.

Sleeping
The range of accommodation has expanded considerably & there is now a good range of places to stay – from cheap budget places up to a comfortable 'tourist' class hotel

A-B *Kendari Beach*, Jl Hasanuddin 44, T21988. A/c, restaurant and terraced bar (well priced), out of town and expensive, but the only upmarket place in town. Attractively positioned overlooking the bay, with tennis courts and tranquil gardens. Recommended. **C-D** *Kartika*, Jl S Parman 84, T21088. Some a/c, restaurant, another quite acceptable mid-range place to stay with an assortment of rooms, some with attached mandi, some without, some with a/c, room rate includes breakfast. **C-D** *Sutra*, Jl Sultan Hasanuddin 94, T21484. Some English spoken here, rooms are clean and plain. **D** *Nusa Indah Lama (Old Nusa Indah)*, Jl S Parman 88, T21146. Some a/c, this place is rather hard to gauge: the rooms are dark, dingy and sultry, but they are also clean and the staff are friendly. The better rooms have a/c and attached facilities. **E** *Anggrek*, Jl S Parman 82, T21851. Basic but clean place. **E** *Cendrawasih*, Jl Diponegoro 42, T21932. Large, rather dark, fan-cooled rooms, views over the backstreets of Kendari, room rate includes breakfast, good budget place to stay. **E** *Hotel Duta*, Jl Dr Abdullah Silondae 1, T21053. This place is set on a hill so has good panoramic views, the rooms, though, are not so good – some without windows, attached squat mandis. **E** *Nusa Indah Baru (New Nusa Indah)*, Jl S Parman 87, T22970. Some a/c, sister hotel to the 'old' version, and it shows in the rooms which are brighter and, well, newer, prices are much the same. **F** *Bungai Tanjung*, Jl Bunga Tanjung 111, T21134. Rock bottom rates, but the rooms are tolerably clean and a breakfast (of sorts) is thrown in as part of the deal. **F** *Dian Kencana*, Jl Dr Abdul Silandae 93, T21704. This place is difficult to find but it is probably the best of the really cheap places to stay, it is quiet with a pleasant atmosphere and a central location. **F** *Wisma Nirmala* (aka *Wisma Nirwana*), Jl Ir Sukarno 115. A wooden, shack-like place, but friendly management and good food, room rate very competitive.

Eating Kendari has an impressive array of restaurants and in the evenings these are supplemented by some great *roda* – foodstalls. **Mid-range** *Royal*, Jl Diponegoro 30. Good Chinese food. **Cheap** *New Golden*, Jl Sultan Hasanuddin 38. Chinese meals, good rates. *Pekalongan*, Jl Sultan Hasanuddin. Good value and substantial Indonesian dishes. The most sophisticated place to eat in town is the restaurant at *Kendari Beach*, Jl Hasanuddin 44.

Tour operators *PT Alam Jaya*, Jl Konggoasa 50, T21729; *PT Manarian Sejahtera*, Jl Dr Moh Hatta, T21535.

Transport
173 km from Kolaka

Air The airport is 35 km north of town. *Transport to town*: minibus 30 mins, or share a taxi. Regular connections on Merpati with Makassar. **Road** Local Bemo. **Bus**: regular connections with Kolaka 3½ hrs from the Powatu terminal, 7 km from town (regular bemos into town). From Kolaka, there are ferries to Makassar (see above). **Sea** *Boat*: 2 ferries a day at 0830 and 1300 for Baubau on Buton Island (see below), 5 hrs, returning from Baubau at the same time. They are a/c and provide snacks. All the ferries are modern and fast. Tickets must be bought in the office, not on board. All ferries stop at Raha, on Muna Island. The *Pelni* ship *Tilongkabila*, making its fortnightly circuit between Sulawesi and the islands of Nusa Tenggara, including Bali, also docks here (see route schedules, page 988).

Airline offices Merpati, Jl Konggoasa 29, T21729. **Banks** It is advisable to change TCs before travelling to Southeast Sulawesi. There is a BNI at Jl Dr Moh Hatta, T21535. **Communications** Post Office: Jl S Ratulangi 79, T21228. Telecom office: Jl Mayjend Sutoyo 74, T21000. **Medical facilities** Hospital: Jl Bunga Kamboja, T21773. **Useful addresses** Immigration office: Jl Jend A Yani 101, T21350.

Directory

Buton and Muna Islands

Buton and Muna islands lie side by side, off the southeast tip of Southeast Sulawesi, separated by the narrow Buton Strait. Buton is the larger and more important of the two, covering nearly 6,500 sq km with a population of over 400,000, while Muna has a land area of 4,900 sq km and over 200,000 inhabitants. The northern part of Buton is pretty inaccessible but the southern portion has a reasonable infrastructure. Very few tourists venture this far. The lifeline for the people of these two islands is the countless number of wooden ferries which travel back and forth. The largest town, **Baubau***, at the southwest corner of Buton Island, overlooking the straits to Muna, is an idyllic little settlement, sandwiched between the Buton Strait and imposingly steep mountains behind.*

Colour map 5, grid C2

During the 16th and 17th centuries, Buton was a powerful local sultanate, making vassal states of several neighbouring islands, including Muna. Sir Francis Drake sailed past Muna and Buton before being blown off-course towards Nusa Tenggora. The Dutch made contact with Buton in 1690, and were on friendly terms with the sultanate during the VOC's confrontation with Gowa. It was off Buton in 1666 that the Dutch admiral Speelman devastated the Makassarese fleet, leading to the downfall of Gowa.

Raha

Raha is the capital of Muna Island. Few people come here which makes it a refreshing corner of traditional Sulawesi. The main attractions here are horse-fighting – a practice which seems to have been part of an ancient local ritual – and the caves outside Mabolu (9 km from Raha), which contain prehistoric paintings.

Phone code: 0403

Horse-fighting is best seen at the village of Latugo (24 km from Raha), and can be arranged at a day's notice. The fight involves two riderless stallions, who are shown mares before the contest in order to agitate them. The stallions do battle until one loses heart and gallops away, at which point another animal is brought forward to fight the victor. If the fight gets vicious, the horses are prised apart.

The **prehistoric caves of Muna** are about 8 km from the village of Mabolu and getting there takes quite a walk. In fact, it is best to see this as a trek with the reward of the caves at the end. To begin with, catch a bemo to Mabolu and ask to be let off at the path for the caves – the driver should realize this is why you have boarded his vehicle. From here it is a 1½-hour walk through plantations and villages to the caves. The keys for the caves are held by two local men and you will need to see them to show you around. The prehistoric paintings include images of sailboats, hunters, the sun, deer and other animals.

About 15 km south of Raha is **Napabale Lake**. Boats can be chartered to explore this coral-walled lake (good snorkelling) which has an outlet into the sea. At weekends it is a popular spot with locals. ■ *Getting there: by bemo from Raha.*

D *Alia*, Jl Sudirman 5, T21218. A motel-type place, with quite clean fan rooms. **D** *Raudhah*, Jl Yos Sudarso 25, T21088. Good rooms and tightly run place. **D-E** *Andalas*, Jl Sukowati 62, T21071. Some a/c, comfortable and clean, price includes breakfast, other food can be arranged, bemo available for charter, tours arranged, limited English spoken. **E** *Tanti*, Jl Dr Sutomo 18, T21168. Spacious, clean and airy rooms, good value, price includes breakfast, close to foodstalls, which is good for a snack but not so good for the decibel level.

Sleeping
Raha has a surprising number of places to stay, but mosquito problems mean that nets & screens should be scrutinized

Eating On Jl Jend Sudirman are the *Pacific* at No 30 and the *Hawaii* at No 41, both Chinese. Also on Jl Jend Sudirman is the *Nikmat* Indonesian restaurant at No 27.

Transport **Local Becaks**: around town and bemos for out of town destinations. **Road** The bus terminal is at the northern edge of town, on Jl Jend A Yani, opposite the main market. Buses to Kendari leave in the morning to catch the ferry to Torobulu, 5 hrs. There are also bus connections with Baubau. **Sea Boat**: 2 ferries a day leave from Kendari at 0830 and 1300 for Raha, 7 hrs, and then continue on to Baubau, 15 hrs. There are also daily 'fast' ferries to Kendari, leaving in the morning, 2½ hrs, and to Baubau. Passengers should book their return trip in good time. The *Pelni* ship *Tilongkabila* docks here.

Directory **Banks** *BNI*, Jl Sukowati. **Communications** Post Office: Jl Jend A Yani. Telephone office: *Telekom*, Jl Wamelai (continuation of Jl Yos Sudarso); Wartel, off Jl Jend A Yani.

Baubau

Phone code: 0402

Baubau, the main town on Buton, is a lovely place, with leafy suburbs and a colonial architectural heritage which has not been torn down to be replaced by the usual characterless shopping centres. Most activity is centred around the river mouth. The **Wolio Kraton**, and a 16th century **mosque** within it, are worth visiting. The kraton was built from coral and contains an eclectic collection of local and colonial artefacts. The hilltop **fort** was built by the Dutch in the early part of the 17th century. Formerly on this site there was a local stronghold which reputedly resisted – for a while – Dutch attempts to take it. About 11 km south of Baubau is **Nirwana Beach** with good swimming; popular at weekends with locals. There is also a flourishing fish market.

Excursions For those who want to find an untrammelled beach, they might consider taking a cargo boat to the **Tukang Besi Islands**, five hours from Baubau. It is, reportedly, a 'paradise'. A Dutch NGO has established itself here, to help conserve the marine national park. Both the Wakatobians (the farming-based community) and the Bajo (fishing-based community) are working to promote an eco-resort and to find alternative forms of income; the Wakatobians are now growing *agar-agar* (a seaweed) as a cash crop. Both tourists and volunteers working on the project can stay at the resort, full board and lodging for around 25,000Rp per day in simple traditional huts. Bookable through *Caraka Travelindo*, Jl Samalona 12, Makassar, T318877, F318889.

Sleeping **B** *Losmen Debora*, Jl RA Kartini 15, T21203. Some a/c, dark, dirty and cell-like rooms with a/c, very poor value. **D** *Losmen Liliana*, Jl Kartini 18, T21197. A better bet than the *Debora*. Although it is older the rooms are more spacious and the place has a much fresher feel, quiet and cool lounge, welcoming management. **D** *Losmen P Kasim Saruhu*, Jl Betoambari 92, 2 km from town, T21189. Evening meal if required, some dorm accommodation, laundry service, bike hire, snorkelling gear and boat charter available, the best place to stay here. **F** *Losmen Pelangi*, on the waterfront, simple rooms, noisy because of its location.

Tour operators *PT Wolio Tours & Travels*, Jl Betoambari 92, T/F0402-21189.

Transport **Air** Two connections a week on Merpati with Makassar. **Road Local** Bemos around town. The bemo terminal is at the Pasar Sentral. Becaks can be chartered for US$3-5 day, but some stiff bargaining is required. **Sea Boat**: 2 ferries a day leave from Kendari at 0830 and 1300 for Buton and Muna islands, docking, in order, at Raha 7 hrs and then at Baubau 15 hrs. The return ferries leave Baubau at 0830 and 1300. Passengers should book their return trip in good time. The *Pelni* ships *Rinjani*, *Tatamailau*, *Ciremai*, *Tilongkabila*, *Bukit Singuntang* and *Lambelo* also dock here (see route schedules, page 988). The *Pelni* office is at Jl Yos Sudarso 19, the Andhika office is also here.

Pendolo to Palu

From Palopo, the road runs northeast along the coastal plain to Wotu, where it turns north into the mountains and towards Lake Poso. Just south of Lake Poso, the road passes from the province of South Sulawesi into Central Sulawesi. This road used to be very bad; now it is surfaced all the way to Palu. The climb up from Mangkutana to Pendolo passes through some of the most beautiful, unspoilt rainforest in Sulawesi; try and make this journey in daylight. One hour north of Mangkutana there is a spectacular waterfall, most buses will stop here for five minutes. The only delays that are likely on this route will be caused by landslides during heavy rains; however, the local authorities are quick and efficient at clearing the road. The forest and hills suddenly end, and the road continues straight, like a Roman road, to Pendolo at the south end of Lake Poso. A daily ferry leaves here for Tentena on the north shore.

The road between Pendolo and Tentena is surfaced, but the forest has suffered from logging and clearing for agriculture. From Tentena the road continues north. About 25 km out of Pendolo a road runs east to the rarely visited town of Kolonodale. From Tentena the road continues north to the port of Poso, and from there follows the coast to Toboli. At Toboli, on the east side of Sulawesi's north 'limb', the road cuts inland to cross the narrow 20 km-wide mountainous spine to the west side and the capital of Central Sulawesi, Palu; 34 km north of here is the formerly important port of Donggala.

Increasing numbers of people are using Tentena as a base to explore the Lore Lindu National Park and to trek in the Napau and Bada Valleys. From Gimpu, at the western edge of the park, public transport is available to Palu, and there are losmen and homestays in a number of towns and villages along the route.

Pendolo

Pendolo is a small town on the south shores of Lake Poso. Swimming is very pleasant here. There is a daily boat from here north to Tentena – following an ancient trade route between Central Sulawesi and Toraja. This is the most relaxing way to make the journey north, but the boat quite frequently breaks down, then it's two hours to Tentena by bemo (8,000Rp), along a very poor road.

Colour map 5, grid B1

C *Mulia*, Jl Pelabuhan Wisata 1. Appealing complex 1 km out of town towards Tentena. Restaurant on stilts over the water, 11 comfortable wooden cottages on the lakeside, some rooms with own shower, clean and with traditional décor. Charming service, convenient for those who wish only to spend 1 night and then catch ferry travelling north (pick ups/drop off at the bus station can be arranged), but also a pleasant place to rest up for few days. **D-E** *Wisma Angrekk*, Jl Makassar, on the road to Palopo, attractive wooden hotel, price includes breakfast. **E** *Masamba*, Jl Pelabuhan. Large, clean,

Sleeping
Most people choose to stay in the larger town of Tentena, on Lake Poso's north shore, rather than in Pendolo. However, the setting is more beautiful at Pendolo, especially at dawn when a thin mist hangs just above the lake. NB When the lake is high, the losmen by the jetty can become flooded

Lake Poso

This ancient, upland lake, at 600m above sea-level, covers over 32,000 ha and is the third largest lake in Indonesia (after Toba and Towuti, the latter also in Sulawesi). Lake Poso is famed for its clear waters and for its rare fauna; 67% of species so far identified in Lake Poso are endemic – they are found nowhere else – and some are already thought to have become extinct. Early travellers to the lake reported seeing estuarine crocodiles (Crocodylus porosus) – some exceeding 5 m in length – although they now seem to have been hunted to extinction.

comfortable rooms with attached mandis, breakfast in dining area on stilts over lake. 'Hanky', the manager, is very friendly and speaks good English. Recommended. 'Sakia' the guide arranges excursions and trekking. **E** *Pendolo Cottages*, Jl Ahmad Yani 441. Opposite the *Mulia Hotel*, 3 delightful worn cottages built over a fishpond overlooking the lake, a family run feel, breakfast included. **E** *Victory*, to the right of jetty, with some damp but clean rooms. Not as good as its neighbour, the *Masamba*. **F** *Petteza*, Jl Pelabuhan, 6 grubby, inward-looking rooms, nothing to recommend it bar the price.

Eating There are a few simple warungs on the main road, which close early. Both the cheap ***Wisma Mulia*** and the very cheap ***Masamba*** serve food; the latter is good value, with large portions – try the *ikan bakar suyar nasi* (roast fish, vegetables and rice).

Transport **Road Bus**: buses ply (very slowly) north to Tentena, 6 hrs, and south to Palopo. The journey to Rantepao takes about 10 hrs. Book your onward journey from Tentena: there are no bus offices in town and they rarely have free seats. The alternative, or if a seat is not available to Rantepao, is to catch a bemo from the bus terminal at 0800 to Mancutana, 3 hrs (7,500Rp), then another bemo to Palopo, 2-3 hrs (7,500Rp), then another bemo to Rantepao, 2 hrs (7,500Rp). **Sea Boat**: daily departures (if it is calm) to Tentena, 0800, 3 hrs (10,000Rp); return boat leaves Tentena between 1400 and 1600, winds whip across the lake later in the day; because of this the boat may need to stop at a coastal village on the return, therefore it could take 4 hrs.

Directory **Banks NB** There are no money changers or banks between Pendolo and Poso.

Kolonodale

Phone code: 0465
Colour map 5, grid B1

This small town on the rarely visited east coast of Central Sulawesi is the best base for trips into the magnificent **Morowali Nature Reserve**. It also provides easy access to **Tomori Bay**. The town has few facilities and is only for those who really want to be off the traveller's trail.

Excursions
Malaria is prevalent in this area; take precautions

The Morowali Nature Reserve covers over 225,000 ha of Central Sulawesi to the north of Kolonodale, including extensive stands of virgin tropical rainforest, pristine coastline, beautiful rivers and islands in Tomori Bay. Originally tagged as a potential site for transmigration settlements, the untouched environment and rich flora and fauna fortunately drove the government to gazette it as a national park in the 1980s. Ranging from sea level (or rather sub-sea level) to 2,630m, it encompasses highland rainforests, dry grasslands, mangroves and lowland evergreen rainforest. The park's fauna include the pig-deer or babirusa, the anoa (see page 763) and the maleo bird. Along the Morowali River there is excellent bird and butterfly life, and the black orchid is also found in Morowali. The mystical **Ranu Lake** (2-3 hours from Kayu Poli) is the home of the legendary white crocodile. The park is inhabited by the Wana, hunters and shifting cultivators. In total there are thought to be 5,000 Wana living within the park, most of whom inhabit remote and inaccessible highland areas. There are, though, about 100 settled in the lowlands of Ranu and Kayo Poli who regularly interact with visitors. NGO groups recommend that visitors who come into contact with the Wana should not give sweets to children, nor packets of cigarettes, nor distribute medicines indiscriminately. **Sleeping** A place to sleep can be arranged with the village chief. There is a wooden shelter at Kekea by Danau Ranu, great if you are after solitude. **Kayu Poli** is a Wana village on the banks of the River Morawali, where it may be possible to stay (four hours walk from the Ranu River). A minimum of four nights is recommended, costing about 500,000Rp for two people (all-inclusive). ■ *Permits: obtainable from the PHPA sub-seksi Morowali in Kolonodale, 2,500Rp.* **NB** *It is illegal to enter the park without a guide or permit. Best time to visit: during the dry season, Oct-Feb.* **Guides** *are available in Kolonodale (see 'Tours', below, and reference to Friends of Morowali).* **Getting there**: *on a tour or by boat (2 hrs); there are also MAF flights to Tokala Atas and Beteleme, both outside the park's northeast boundary. There are 2 points of entry into the reserve, either by the Morowali River or by Danau Ranu (the preferred route). From Kolonadale it is 1½ hrs by boat to the river mouth.*

Friends of Morowali (*Sahabat Morowali*), *Hotel Sederhana*, in Kolonodale, are a local conservation group concerned for the reserve and the welfare of the Wana people. They can help organize a visit to the park and will arrange permits, boat travel, basic food and accommodation in Wana villages; Jabar Lahadji speaks good English

Tours

Morowali Nature Reserve

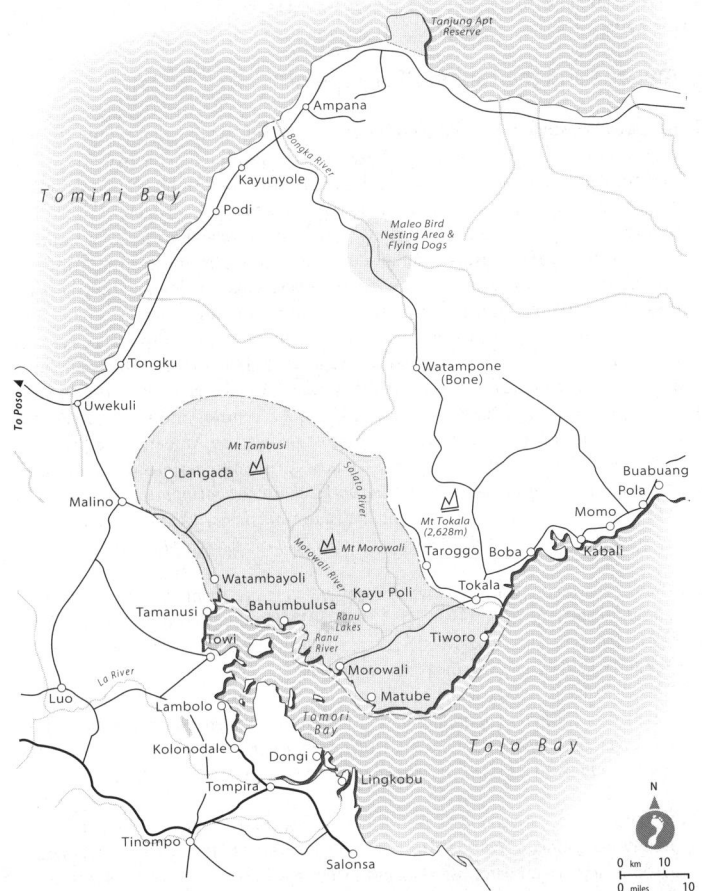

and is very knowledgeable; he will organize your trip for you. Kassim, a local guide, who works for the Friends, has been recommended (he doesn't speak good English, but is very pleasant and is a good cook). Friends office is at Jl Yos Sudarso 64, T0465-21124. The Wana people much prefer visitors who come with local guides from their own communities. Friends of Morowali only use local guides.

Sleeping **D-E** *Losmen Jumpandang*, Jl Yos Sudarso, T21091. Good restaurant, extremely clean, more expensive rooms have own bathrooms, best in town. **D-E** *Lestari*, clean and in a good position close to the *Sederhana*. Price includes 2 meals, some rooms with private mandi. **E** *Sederhana*, Jl Yos Sudarso 13. On the waterfront, shared mandi, price includes 3 meals, good source of information for trips to the Morowali Nature Reserve – Jabar Lahadji, who runs Friends of Morowali, can be contacted from the losmen. **E-F** *Tomorindah*, located in the forest.

Transport **Air** MAF flies irregularly from Tentena to Kolonodale. **Road Bus**: buses leave daily from Pendolo 4 hrs, Tentena 6-7 hrs and Poso 10 hrs. **Boat** The *Pelni* ship *Tilongkabila* travels fortnightly from Makassar to Kolonodale via Kendari, before continuing on to Gorontalo, Bitung and the Sangihe Islands (see route schedule, page 988). The reserve is another 2-3 hrs by boat from Kolonodale. 'Johnsons' – dug-out canoes with outboards – can be hired for around 30,000Rp (1-way). It is advisable to take a guide from Kolonodale. **NB** Arranging a guide in Tentena can be costly.

Directory **Banks** *Bank Rakyat Indonesia*, but no money changing facilities. **Communications** Post Office and **Wartel** telephone office: in town.

Ampana and the Tanjung Api Reserve

Colour map 5, grid B1 **Ampana** is a small port on the northern coast of Sulawesi's eastern limb. It is the nearest centre to the Tanjung Api Reserve and is also the departure point for the Togian Islands. It is pleasant enough, although most people only stay here a night at most before moving on to the more obvious delights of the Togian Islands. The **market** provides the usual sights, along with the occasional unusual sea creature.

The **Tanjung Api Reserve** includes the coast and waters northeast of Ampana. The reserve is home to a number of endemic Sulawesi mammals, including the babirusa, tarsier and macaque (see page 763). The name Tanjung Api means Fire Cape. This romantic name is probably associated with the natural seepages of gas that work their way up through the fissured rock and bubble to the surface off-shore. There are walks in the forest that work their way down almost to the shore and also some more extensive treks. Take all supplies. **Accommodation in the reserve**: nothing is available in the reserve, and most people use Ampana as a base (see 'Sleeping', below). However, simple shelters have recently been erected; suitable for camping. ■ *Getting there: from Ampana docks, charter a boat, approx 1 hr (25,000Rp return). Or take a horse and cart to Labuan village and then walk.* **NB** *Local waters are rough between Dec and Feb and the journey by boat can be uncomfortable.*

Sleeping **D-F** *Losmen Irama*, Jl Kartini 11. One a/c room, well run place, room rate includes breakfast. **E** *Family Homestay*, Jl Moh Hatta 37, T0464-21034. Mandi attached and price includes breakfast. Very friendly and knowledgeable staff, who can also arrange tours. **E** *Hotel Plaza*, Jl Kartini 45, T21091. Although this place is grandly titled 'hotel' and also has that technological marvel, a telephone, the rooms are little different from the other places listed here – simple but clean. **E-F** *Peningapan Rejeki*, Jl Talatako 45. A 2nd very acceptable little losmen with clean rooms and pleasant owners. **F** *Ulva's Homestay*, behind bus station and 1 min from the harbour. **F** *Oasis*, Jl Kartini 5. Slightly run-down but fine for the night.

Eating The market has some good stalls, coffee shops and warungs. The best place to eat is the cheap *Warung Makan Seafood*, Jl Moh Hatta 92 (on main road through town, out towards Luwuk). *Istana*, Jl Moh Hatta. Basic Indonesian food at cheap prices but slow service.

Transport

Road Bus: regular connections with Poso, 5 hrs (5,500Rp), and on to Luwuk, 8 hrs. The drive from Poso is beautiful. **Sea Boat**: a ferry makes a weekly trip between Poso, Ampana, the Togian Islands (Wakai [5-6 hrs, 65,000Rp], Katupat and Dolong) and Gorontalo. There are also other vessels that leave Ampana for Wakai and Bomba in the Togians.

Tentena

Tentena is a wonderful little town situated on the north shores of **Lake Poso**. It has a cool and invigorating climate and a reasonable range of accommodation, making it the best stopping-off point between Palu and Toraja. A **210m wooden bridge** crosses the river Poso (new one under construction) which flows out of the lake at this, its northern-most and narrowest extremity. Eels – which migrate as elvers from the sea 50 km away – and carp are trapped below the bridge. The largest eel caught measured 1.8m and carp weighing as much as 20kg are also netted. Tentena was a centre of missionary activity in the area when two Dutch priests, Dr AC Kruyt and Dr Adriani, set up operations here in 1895. It still supports the oldest **Protestant church** in the province. For a **good beach**, follow Jl Setia Budi around the lake for about 40 minutes.

Phone code: 0458
Colour map 4, grid B6

Excursions

The **Saluopa waterfall** lies 12 km east of Tentena and is a popular and impressive excursion. You can walk up either side of the falls, which is in fact a series of 12 steps/terraces. ■ *Getting there: take a bemo from by the wooden bridge to Tonusu. The turn-off for the falls is just beyond the village, the driver will usually take you to this point (1,500Rp). There is then a 1 hr walk through cultivated land and paddy fields before entering the forest.*

Tentena is one of the best spots to organize treks into the **Lore Lindu National Park** to see the megaliths of the Bada Valley (see page 733). Ask at the *Victory Losmen*. It is usually a good idea to book your return trip, especially if travelling overland, since there are few vehicles travelling this route. More knowledgeable guides can be hired in Gintu; some local villagers and farmers can direct you to all main megaliths, though the less well known ones are overgrown and hard to find without a guide.

The limestone hills around Tentena, and along the shores of Lake Poso, are rich in **caves**, most of which are not as exciting as the tourist literature tries to make out. Most famous – in relative terms – is **Pamona Cave** near the Theological School, a series of caves running deep into the mountainside (it is said that no one has yet reached the end, or at least has returned to tell the story). Closer to town, near the offices of the Protestant church, are a number of caves with skulls and crude coffins.

It is possible to **charter boats** in Tentena to venture out onto the lake (90,000-120,000Rp for the day), or to travel to Bancea and the **Bancea Orchid Reserve** on the west shore, where there are 55 species of orchid. The best time to visit is February, March and October-December. The water on this side of the lake is beautifully clear. Dolf, the

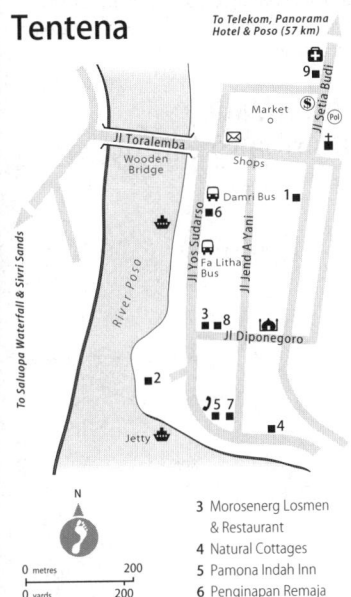

Tentena

3 Morosenerg Losmen & Restaurant
4 Natural Cottages
5 Pamona Indah Inn
6 Penginapan Remaja
7 Sinar Pare Pare Losmen & Restaurant
8 Victory Losmen
9 Wisma Tiberias

■ **Sleeping**
1 Horison Homestay
2 Itim Danau Poso

resident warden, will take great delight in showing you around and will also play his home-made guitar for you. Also a simple losmen here (10,000Rp).

Sleeping
Most hotels are on, or overlook, the Poso River

B *Itim Danau Poso*, Jl Yos Sudarso 22, T21345, F21488, lantaupg@indosat.net.id A change in name (formerly the *Wasantara*), this has also brought significant amounts of investment. With mountain or lake views, the rooms are very modern, with hot water. Price includes breakfast, laundry service and the best restaurant in town, recommended if you can afford it. **B** *Panorama 11*, 200m from *Panorama 1*, T21040. Government owned, hot water, newer wooden block at the rear is fresh and smart, excellent views from the hillside. **B-C** *Panorama*, set on a hill, 2 km from town centre. Hot water, TV, fridge, spotless and magnificent view over the lake, food on request. **B-C** *Siuri Sands*, on west shore of lake, 19 km from Tentena, take a bemo from wooden bridge heading for Toindse, simple wooden cottages on stilts beside the lake, white sand beach, remote and therefore only really accessible to tour groups, no other facilities within walking distance. **C-D** *Victory Losmen*, Jl Diponegoro 1, T21392, F21232. Very clean, popular, range of accommodation, also houses the 'official' tourist information, and Daniel is very informative and will organize treks to Lore Lindu. Recommended. **D** *Pamona Indah Inn*, Jl Yos Sudarso 63, T21245, F21405. On lakeside, good restaurant, selection of Chinese and Indonesian dishes, none of the rooms have a good view, rooms in new wooden block clean but gloomy, older block at back has smaller rooms, close to the ferry jetty, tours of the region can be arranged from here. **E** *Horison Homestay*, Jl Setia Budi 6, T21038. Located on quiet street at back of town, easy walk from bridge, colourful garden, all rooms have verandah. **E** *Moroseneng*, next to *Victory*, clean and compact, food available in the restaurant next door. **E** *Natural Cottages*, T006245821311 or 00873762154238, natural@inmarsat.francetelecom.fr Run by a very pleasant pro-active Dutch/Malaysian couple (Harry and Annelies). Lakeside location, clean, large rooms, laundry and great breakfast. More rooms and a restaurant were promised for 1999. Recommended. **E** *Sinar Pare Pare*, Jl Jend A Yani 69, T21335. Three small rooms with attached mandis. **E** *Wisma Tiberias*, basic rooms, on main road near Police station. Nothing to recommend it except the price.

Eating
Cheap Both the *Itim Danau Poso* and *Pamona Indah* have attached restaurants, the latter being the better. The *Moroneng* offers Padang-style food. **Very cheap** *Sinar Pare Pare*, has an Indonesian bias. Menu includes eel and carp caught in the lake.

Transport
57 km south of Poso, 77 km north of Pendolo

Road Bus: connections north to Poso 1½ hrs, Palu 8 hrs and south to Pendolo 6 hrs, Rantepao and Makassar; also buses east to Kolonodale. Long distance buses tend to leave from outside their headquarters. *Jawa Indah*, *Damri* and *Fa Litha* can be found along Jl Yos Sudarso. *Fa Litha* is recommended. It is difficult to guarantee a seat on long distance buses to Rantepao or Palu since few passengers get off midway. If travelling further north, take a local bemo to Poso (10,000Rp), and buy a ticket here from one of the many bus companies. **Boat**: to Pendolo, on the southern shores of the lake (the best way to travel south); if it does depart (enquire at your losmen) it should leave between 1400 and 1600, 2-3 hrs (10,000Rp).

Directory Communications Post Office: close to bridge on edge of market. **Telecom office**: Jl Kartini 25, T21001. **Medical facilities** Hospital: Jl Setia Budi 94, T21051. **Useful addresses** Police Station: next to white church which dominates centre of town.

Bada Valley
Bomba to Gimpu

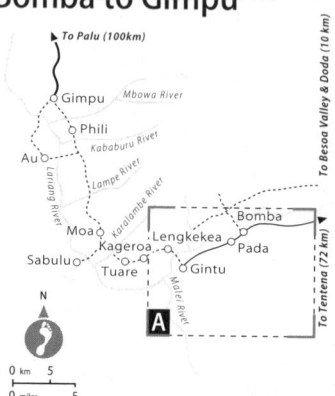

Trekking distances/times	km	hr
Gintu - Tuare	10	3
Tuare - Moa	22	8
Moa - Gimpu	25	9
Au - Gimpu	14	4

Lore Lindu National Park and the Bada, Besoa and Napau valleys

Colour map 4, grid B6

The Lore Lindu National Park covers 229,000 ha of upland in Central Sulawesi between Palu and Lake Poso. Ranging between 300m and 2,610m above sea-level – which marks the summit of Mount Rorakatimbu – the park is mainly composed of montane forest, with the upland Lake Lindu in the northwest corner. The area is renowned for the massive and enigmatic **megalithic statues** and **'cisterns'** that lie scattered over the Bada, Besoa and Napau valleys (copies stand outside the Central Sulawesi Museum in Palu), and for its exceptional range of bird (especially) and animal life. Nineteen species of waterfowl have been identified on Lake Lindu including the spotted tree duck (*Dendrocygna guttata*) and the little pied cormorant (*Phalacrocorax melanoleuca*), and in the montane forests that characterize the national park there are flocks of such insectivorous birds as the Sulawesi leaf warbler (*Phylloscopus sarasinorum*), the mountain white-eye (*Zosterops montana*) and citrine flycatcher (*Culicicapa helianthea*). Lake Lindu is not only notable for its endemic species of fish and molluscs, but also because this is the only place in Indonesia where the parasite which causes Schistosomiasis (Bilharzia) is to be found – making the lake a favourite haunt of both epidemiologists and naturalists.

The **Napau Valley** has recently developed as an alternative to the better known Bada Valley. The valley offers beautiful scenery, a moderate climate and an abundance of wildlife. It is a popular spot with 'twitchers' seeking the weird and wonderful Maleo Bird. There are also limited numbers of megaliths and cistern relics.

Some knowledge of Indonesian is a great help here

The strange **megaliths** that can be seen in the Bada, Napau and Besoa valleys were erected by a people who have long-since disappeared and possibly date from the first millennium AD – archaeologists are still unsure. They are found in a number of spots in Central Sulawesi, but are most numerous in and around Lore Lindu. They are 'worked' stones, in the form of giant urns, menhirs, vats, stone blocks, statues and mortars. These are decorated with faces, lizards, figures and monkeys. What use

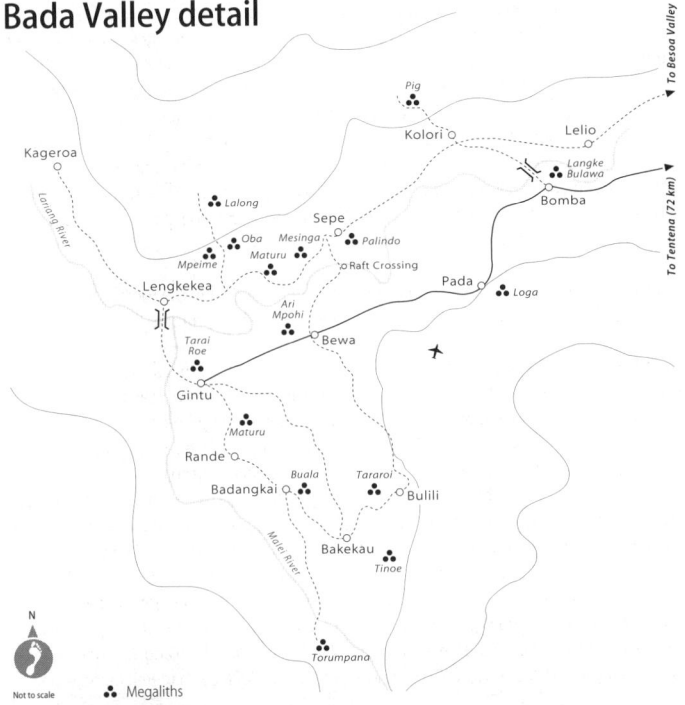

Bada Valley detail

they were put to is not certain, although it is possible that they were burial chambers. They show a remarkable resemblance to the 'jars' of the Plain of Jars in Laos, although no connection between the two cultures has been identified. The greatest concentration of megaliths is near Gintu, at the south edge of the park.

Organizing a trip to Lore Lindu Increasing numbers of visitors are taking time to trek in this remote spot. Guides can be found in Tentena and Gimpu and treks of six days or more link the two towns. Horses (to ride or to carry bags) and porters can also be hired. The megaliths are in the vicinity of Gintu (for instance, on the Sepe Plateau), and an additional, local guide needs to be employed here as the statues are difficult to find (around 75,000Rp per day). *Best time to visit*: the driest time of year is from June to August.

Tours
Guides & tour agencies operate primarily from Palu, Tentena, Gimpu & Gintu

Treks in the Bada Valley can be organized from Tentena. *Luis Molindo*, has been recommended; he is polite and experienced. There are five other guides, all with some English. Organize a trip through the *Victory* or *Natural Cottages*. A guided trip to the Napau Valley stretching over five days and four nights for a group of between one and three people will cost 500,000Rp per person, including all transport, accommodation and food.

Sleeping
Over the last few years, facilities in Lore Lindu have improved considerably, & there is now a good network of losmen & homestays. Most accommodation is at the southern end of the park & also along the Bomba to Gimpu track

Bomba **E** *Ningsi Homestay*, new wooden building, all rooms with attached mandis. Very clean, large and very tasty breakfast. If this homestay is full, it is possible to stay with the chief of the village. **Gintu** Two places here within 1 min walk of each other. **E** *Barito Losmen*, 4 rooms, quiet location near the river. Agustu Hamar, the owner, speaks English and is also the local senior guide. **D-E** *Sannur Homestay*, 4 VIP rooms with own mandi, 6 economy rooms with shared mandi, room rate includes 2 meals. Spotlessly clean, tranquil balcony with views of the valley. Also a well stocked shop. **Tuare** Here is a homestay, courtesy of the village chief (**D**, includes all meals), with 5 new rooms with great views. It is dark (beware spiders) but comfortable. River bathing may be preferred to the mandi. **Lengkeka** **E** *Wooden Homestay*, Number 11, Main St. Price includes 2 meals, clean rooms. Pleasant mandi in the hot spring 500m north of the village. **Moa** Accommodation with the village chief (**E**, 3 meals). **Au** It is 14 km of hard walking from Au to Gimpu, partly through flattened forest (storms in Aug 1997). It is possible to stay with the village chief in Au (**E** 3 meals included). **Gimpu** Not much here to see, just overnight here after a trek: **E** *Losmen Anugrah*, in Tomua, 1 km north of Gimpu, 4 rooms. Balcony and comfortable sitting area, billiard room, room rate includes 2 meals. Increasingly popular is to stay with the village chief (**E** including meals). **Wuasa** This settlement is the capital of the Napau valley, therefore better transport connections: **E** *Losmen Citra*, price includes 3 meals, 4 rooms, small friendly little place; **E** *Losmen Srikandi*, room rate includes 3 meals; also the government run *Pemda Losmen* (**F**), basic and no meals. **Napau Valley** Villages in the Napau Valley will put visitors up for the night, usually in the house of the head of the village; ask on arrival. Most houses take 4-5 people and offer accommodation and food for around 20,000-25,000Rp per head.

Eating Many guesthouses and homestays lay on food – and include it in the room rate. Meals are often very good. There is also a small, but growing, number of warungs.

Transport **Road** There are 2 principal routes into the park: from the north, from Palu to Gimpu; or from the east, from Tentena to Gintu. Depending which way you want to approach the valley, there are private kijangs in Palu, which cost 100,000Rp to Gimpu, or a bemo to Gimpu will cost 8,000Rp, 3-4 hrs. From Tentena to Gintu is 72 km (anywhere between 5 hrs in dry season and 8-10 hrs during the wet season). The route is only accessible by jeep, but the road is being improved, the first 30 km have been levelled and gravelled with some tarmacked and the last 12 km are surfaced; the middle portion is still a bone-shaking experience. Jeep hire from Tentena to Gintu is about 500,000-600,000Rp depending on weather, maximum 6 people. There are currently 20 jeeps working this route, of which only 7 are road-worthy. Ask Daniel at the *Victory Losmen* in Tentena for a recommended firm. Arrange return transport at outset, as there are few vehicles travelling this route. A new road allows access into the Napau Valley by kijang from Kasinguncu to the west of Poso, to Watutau, 25,000Rp by kijang. Access is also possible from Palu to Wuasa (12,500Rp by public bemo, 300,000Rp by chartered bemo, 4 hrs).

Palu

Palu, with a population of 150,000, is the capital of the province of Central Sulawesi. Located on the south shores of Palu Bay, it is sandwiched between two ranges of mountains running north-south. Because it lies in the rain shadow, rainfall here is very low – only 600mm – making the Palu valley one of the driest spots in Indonesia.

Phone code: 0451
Colour map 4, grid B6

Palu is usually only visited as a rest stop on the arduous overland route north to Gorontalo and Manado, and south to Rantepao and Makassar. The Palu River neatly divides this dispersed town into two. Central Sulawesi **Tourist Office** is on Jl Raja Moili 103, T421795. *Open 0800-1400 Mon-Thu, 0800-1100 Fri, 0800-1300 Sat.* Handouts are available and they will also help with organizing treks to Lore Lindu National Park and the Bada Valley (see page 733).

Sights

The **Museum of Central Sulawesi** is at Jl Sapiri 23. It houses a reasonable model display of traditional houses and assorted local ethnographic artefacts. Outside the museum stand replicas of the megaliths of Lore Lindu (see page 733). ■ *Admission 750Rp. Open 0800-1400 Mon-Sat, closed Sun.* The central market, **Pasar Bambaru**, a rather characterless, modern, concrete affair, is north of Jl Imam Bonjol, between Jl Teuku Umar and Jl Hr Dg Pawindu. More interesting are the **alleys** running east off Jl Teuku Umar. The sprawling **Pasar Masomba** is southeast of town, off Jl Monginsidi.

Excursions

Donggala lies 34 km north of Palu. ■ *Getting there: take a kijang from the Inpres terminal at the southwest corner of the Inpres market, just south of Jl Kunduri, 40 mins (3,000Rp). Share taxis also travel between the 2 towns, leaving from Jl Imam Bonjol, not far from the intersection with Jl Teuku Umar (30,000Rp each way, 4 people, worth it to avoid the hassle). Donggala station is south of the port; walk or catch a bemo into town.* **Kamarora Forest** lies 55 km from Palu. It is a good place for birdwatching. Camping facilities available. ■ *Getting there: 2 hrs by car (taxi hire available).*

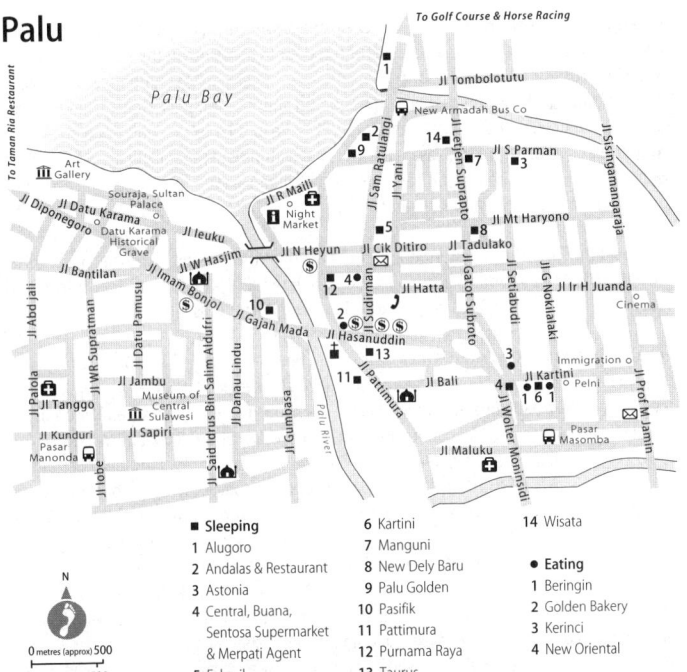

■ **Sleeping**
1 Alugoro
2 Andalas & Restaurant
3 Astonia
4 Central, Buana, Sentosa Supermarket & Merpati Agent
5 Fahmil
6 Kartini
7 Manguni
8 New Dely Baru
9 Palu Golden
10 Pasifik
11 Pattimura
12 Purnama Raya
13 Taurus
14 Wisata

● **Eating**
1 Beringin
2 Golden Bakery
3 Kerinci
4 New Oriental

Tours Palu is the base for specialist tours to the **Lore Lindu** and **Morowali National Parks** (see page 733). A five-day all-inclusive tour costs 500,000Rp per person (four people). Prices can be negoitated and will depend on the type of transport and food. Excel, the chief (official) guide, works from the *Purnama Raya Hotel* and will put you in contact with a suitable guide. Allow a day to arrange a permit to enter the park, which costs 5,000Rp plus 1,500Rp per day (available from the PHPA office).

Sleeping
■ on map
Price codes:
see inside front cover

B *Palu Golden*, Jl Raden Saleh 1, T421126, F423230. A/c, pool, 55 comfortable rooms, restaurant. Rather dated decoration, satellite TV; the more expensive rooms have balconies and views of Palu Bay. A rather nondescript concrete structure but it is the 'best' in town; houses a travel agent. **C** *Hotel Astonia*, Jl S Parman 60, T421675. Simple but overpriced, includes breakfast, Sandagang the manager speaks English. **C** *Hotel Wisata*, Jl S Parman 39, T421175, F422427. Lots of wooden finishes, en suite rooms have bath and shower (hot water), includes breakfast. **C-D** *Central Hotel*, Jl R A Kartini 6, behind the warpostel, T422789, F428288. Clean rooms with a/c and TV. Also has restaurant, karaoke bar and safety deposit boxes. Friendly staff and efficiently run. Breakfast included. Recommended. **C-D** *Fahmil Hotel*, Jl A Yani 60, T423474. More expensive rooms have satellite TV, a/c, bath and shower. **D** *Buana*, Jl RA Kartini 8, T421475. Some a/c, clean, pleasant atmosphere, includes breakfast, walking distance from Masomba bus terminal. **D** *New Dely Baru*, Jl S Parman 28, T421076. A/c, TV, large en suite rooms, not the best value for money. **D-E** *Hotel Manguni*, Jl Pattimura 36-38, T421275. Comfortable, needs some money spending on it, price includes breakfast. **D-E** *Kartini Hotel*, Jl Kartini 12, T421964. Standard rooms have a/c and TV, economy have fans and also en suite. **E** *Alugoro Hotel*, Jl Cutmutia 1, small hotel with 6 new rooms. **E** *Andalas Hotel and Restaurant*, Jl Radan Saleh 50, T522332. Attractive hotel, rooms are nothing special with tiny mandis. Restaurant serves Padang-style food. **E** *Pasifik*, Jl Gajah Mada 87, T422675. Grubby rooms, but still popular, avoid rooms near the road. **E** *Purnama Raya*, Jl Dr Wahidin 4, T423646. Good, quiet location with tiny mandis, basic but clean. Recommended. **E** *Taurus*, Jl Hasanuddin 35, T421580, rooms and mandis could be cleaner, sitting area with good views.

Eating **Padang Cheap**: *Kerinci*, Jl Kartini 7. *Beringin Restaurant*, Jl Kartini 88, T411155. Wide range of dishes. Also another restaurant with the same name down the road, Jl Kartini 10, T453417. *Taman Ria*, Jl Diponegoro, 452789. Really great fresh seafood. **Very cheap**: *Golden Bakery*, intersection Jl Hasanuddin and Jl Dr Wahidin. Good cakes. Recommended. *New Oriental*, Jl Hasanuddin 11. Great Chinese food. Recommended. **Foodstalls** One of the most pleasant places to eat or drink is at the stalls which set up on the seafront, just west of the *Palu Golden Hotel* on Jl Raja Moili. With the onshore breeze, view and wicker chairs, it is very civilized and cheap.

Tour operators *Celebes Citra Wisata*, Jl Hasanuddin 11, T421374; *Nusa Lestari Sentosa*, Jl Kartini 4, T426612; *UE Datu*, Jl Raden Saleh (Palu Golden Hotel), T429850; *Rajawali Ashab Tour and Travel*, Jl Sis Aldjufri 12B, T421095; *Wisata Gautama Putra*, Jl Sis Aldjufri 10, T452334.

Transport **Local Microlets**: 500Rp around town. **Air** Palu's Mutiara airport is 7 km southeast of town. Regular daily connections on Merpati or Bouraq with Makassar, Manado and Luwuk. *Taxis to town*, 10,000Rp. **Road Bus**: the long-distance Masomba terminal is between Jl Monginsidi and Jl TG Pagimpuan. Regular connections with Gorontalo 16 hrs (35,000Rp), Manado 25 hrs (55,000Rp), Rantepao 24 hrs, Makassar (50,000Rp), Soppeng, Watampone, Sengkang, Palopo, Pare Pare and Poso 8 hrs. Bus companies have their offices at Masomba terminal and bemos travel constantly between the terminal and the town centre. Regular connections with Poso 5-7 hrs and Tentena (eg *New Armadah*, Jl Ratulangi, T429764; *Antariksa*, Jl Cut Nyadien 22, T428205). The roads north to Gorontalo and Manado and south towards Palopo good, much improved in recent years and being further upgraded. **NB** The road between Tawaeli and Tobili, over the mountains, is still under construction, therefore expect delays of up to 4 hrs. **Sea Boat**: larger vessels, including the *Pelni* ships *Kerinci*, *Kambuna*, *Umsini* and *Tidar*, dock at Pantoloan on the east shores of Palu Bay (see route schedules, page 988). *Pelni* office is at Jl Kartini 96, T42327. Get to Pantoloan by bus from the Masomba terminal. Smaller ferries operate from Palu north to Toli Toli.

Directory **Airline offices** *Bouraq*, Jl Juanda 87, T427795; *Merpati*, Jl Kartini 33, T423341, F424935. **Banks** *Bank Danamon*, Jl Hasanuddin 27, accept American Express TCs and US$ cash; *Bank Mandiri*, Jl Hasanuddin 35, T421580, no ATM but will cash American Express TCs; *BII*, Jl Danau Lindu 3-5, T423421, ATM accepts most credit cards; *BNI 1946*, Jl Sudirman 21, T421182; *Bank Rakyat Indonesia*, Jl Moh. Hatta 12, T421081. **Communications** General Post Office: Jl Moh Yamin 161, T422336. Post Restante and internet available here. **Internet**: at the main Post Office; and also Golden Internet, Jl Dr Wahidin 19, painfully slow even when it does work. **Warpostel**: Jl RA Kartini 6, T423411, international telephone, telegram and fax. **Medical facilities** Hospital: Jl Dr Suharso 33, T421270. **Useful addresses** Immigration office: Jl RA Kartini, T421433. **PHPA Office**: Jl Moh Yamin. **Police**: Jl Pemuda, T421015.

Donggala and Tanjung Karang

Phone code: 0457
Colour map 4, grid B6

Donggala lies 34 km north of Palu and is a small, formerly important, port which has fallen on hard times since being eclipsed by other ports in Central Sulawesi. The road to Donggala runs along the west shoreline of Palu Bay, past fishing villages and mangroves. With the hills rising up on either side, it could almost be a loch in the Scottish highlands. Donggala is quiet and peaceful, the port picturesque, with cloves drying on the pavements. Most people come here for the snorkelling and diving at **Tanjung Karang**, but it is also a peaceful alternative to Palu.

Sleeping
Tanjung Karang has no electricity & water is brought in by tanker

The most popular place is the **C-D** *Prince John Dive Resort*, 1½ km on past Donggala, next to the village of Tanjung Karang, T0457-71710, F0457-23027. The owners are well known, a German expatriate, Peter, and his Indonesian wife Maureen, the more expensive rooms are private bungalows, all on stilts with superb views across the bay (with own mandis and verandah). There are also 4 rooms with communal bathrooms. Room rates include all 3 meals plus a bonus of different snacks in the morning and afternoon, clean white sand beach, very good snorkelling (limited coral, but wide range of fish), also possible to windsurf and scuba dive. Scuba diving available, US$100 for 3 dives, 3 meals and accommodation. All onward travel arrangements can be arranged, saving guests the tiresome journey into Palu. Recommended as a good retreat to recharge midway through Sulawesi, although it is becoming popular as a stop-off point on the tour group trail. An alternative, cheaper, but

Donggala & Tanjung Karang

■ Sleeping
1 Harmony
2 Malawi
3 Natural Cottages
4 Prince John Dive Resort

Dive site

also excellent place to stay is **C** *Natural Cottages*, T21235. A short walk past *Prince John's*, 10 bungalows all looking out to sea and with attached mandi, the cheaper rooms are quieter and better value, clean but with abundant fauna, room rate includes all meals, masks for hire but no diving. **D** *Harmony*, the favourite place to stay amongst backpackers, pleasant family atmosphere with palm tree-filled courtyard, shared mandis, masks and boat for hire, room rate includes 3 meals and tea and coffee through the day. Recommended. **E** *Malawi*, just 3 rooms here, set back from the shore, communal mandi. **Homestays**: many villages rent out rooms during high season.

Transport *34 km from Palu* **Road** Take a kijang from the Pasar terminal at the southwest corner of the Manonda, just south of Jl Kunduri, 40 mins (3,000Rp). Share taxis also travel between the 2 towns, leaving from Jl Imam Bonjol, not far from the intersection with Jl Teuku Umar (25,000Rp each way, 4 people, worth it to avoid the hassle). Donggala bus station is south of the port; walk or catch a bemo into town. To Tanjung Karang (1 hr walk through Donggala, up steep hill to resort) – expect to pay 5,000Rp.

Directory **Banks** Money can be changed at the *Prince John Dive Resort*.

Poso

Phone code: 0452
Colour map 4, grid B6
In mid-2000 there were reports of a massacre near Poso, as inter-communal violence in Maluku spread into Sulawesi. Poso & villages around it have been damaged as a result of extensive disturbances

With the completion of the Trans-Sulawesi Highway, Poso became an important centre for visitors, providing a smattering of budget hotels. The town is divided by the Poso River: on the eastern side is the older commercial centre with a few hotels close to the port, and pleasant, quiet streets; to the west of the river are newer offices and shops and the central market. The beach in the town itself is filthy, but there are better beaches nearby. There is very little to do here and most travellers merely use the place as a stopping off junction. The **tourist office** is on Jl Kalimantan 15, T21211, F3243411. The local tourist officer, Amir Kiat, is a smashing guy, and a mine of accurate information. He is perhaps the most helpful and knowledgeable tourist officer in Sulawesi.

Excursions The tranquil **Toini beach** is 10 km west of town. There is a restaurant here with a dining area over the sea. No accommodation. ■ *Getting there: flag down bemo by main market (1,000Rp). Get off by sign for Toini Seafood Restaurant.* **Maranda** West by 40 km, hot springs and waterfall. ■ *Getting there: by bemo (2,500Rp).* **Madeli beach**, 8km from the centre of town, has great snorkelling. ■ *Getting there: by bemo.* **Matako beach**, 25 km east. ■ *Getting there: by bemo (1,500Rp).* **Sleeping**: **D** *Matako Cottages*. **Tombiano** 40 km east, small atolls and limestone caves (2,000Rp). **Lore Lindu** (see below) and **Morowali Reserve** (see page 728).

Sleeping ■ *on map* *Price codes: see inside front cover*

C-D *Anugrah Inn*, Jl Samosir 1, T21820. Close to market and bus offices in western side of town, off the main road. Good value for money, a/c in standard rooms. Recommended. **C-D** *Wisata*, Jl Pattimura 19, T324211. Small hotel with large rooms arranged around central hall, pleasant garden at back, close to the port, quiet with views across the bay, recommended but overpriced. **C-E** *Bambu Jaya*, Jl Agus Salim 106, T21570. Some a/c, suites downstairs off gloomy corridor, but run down, simple rooms with very small mandis, good views from upstairs open-air balcony across the bay, quiet location. **D-E** *Hotel Alamanda*, Jl Bali 1, T21233. Quiet location but rooms are small, hot and uninviting. **E** *Alugoro*, Jl P Sumatra 213, behind bus company offices, T23138; 29 rooms, simple covered verandah with central open lounge, pity about the busy main road and noisy cinema complex opposite. **E** *Kalimantan*, Jl Agus Salim 18, T21420. Simple small hotel with rooms arranged around central breakfast area, close to mosque on side street, convenient for post office and banks. **E** *Wisma Poso*, Jl Sumatera, on a busy main road, simple and grubby, you can do better than this. **E-F** *Penginapan Beringin*, Jl P Sumatera 222, T21851. Close to bus offices, noisy location, economy rooms not recommended, standard are much better. **F** *Penginapan Sederhana*, Jl Agus Salim 25, T21228. Small old house, pleasant verandah, clean rooms.

Eating

For those who have spent extended time in the Togians on a diet of fish and rice, Poso will be a disappointment because there is not a good range of restaurants. **Cheap**: *Cafe Kitha*, Jl Sumatera 1, is a colourful little place with an extremely limited menu. The best in town is the *Lalanga Restaurant*, Jl Yos Sudarso. Close to the port. This restaurant is open air and raised up on stilts over the bay, good seafood, but portions tend to be small, popular at weekends. For Padang food try *Padang Raya* on Jl Kalimantan. Good, but can be overpriced.

Transport

57 km north of Tentena, 203 km to Palu via a very bad road

Local Bemos: all over town, no fixed routes, but link all the commercial centres, just state destination when boarding (500Rp). Minibus: for local towns leave from the Kasintuwu Terminal (Jl Tanjumbulu) for destinations south and east. Pasar Central Terminal (Jl Sumatera) for westerly destinations. Passenger ferry: across the Poso River (500Rp), hard to find (see Map) but very convenient. Service stops at 1700.

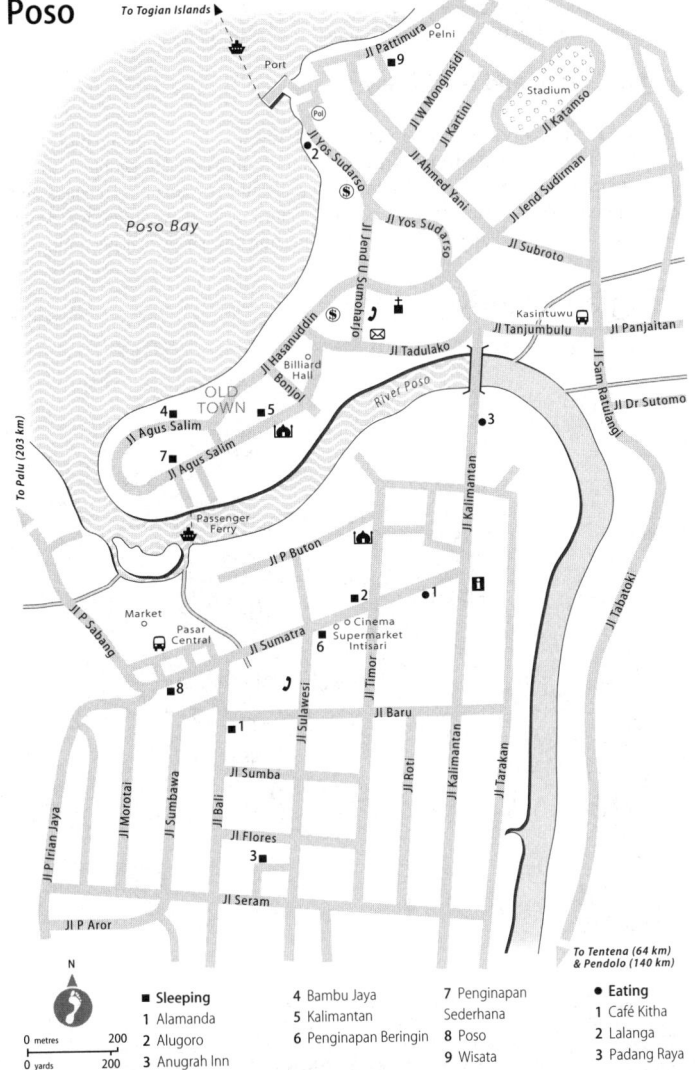

Poso

Sleeping
1 Alamanda
2 Alugoro
3 Anugrah Inn
4 Bambu Jaya
5 Kalimantan
6 Penginapan Beringin
7 Penginapan Sederhana
8 Poso
9 Wisata

Eating
1 Café Kitha
2 Lalanga
3 Padang Raya

Air The airport is out of town and not currently operational due to lack of demand. **Road Bus**: direct bus to Makassar (*Litha Bus Co*) departs 2000 daily, 20-24 hrs (52,000Rp), via Pendolo, Palopo, Sengkang and Pare-Pare. The bus north to Palu departs 1000, 1400 and 2000, 6 hrs. *Alugoro Bus*, Jl P Sumatra 20. The *New Amadah Bus Co*, Jl P Sumatera 17, T23070, has a/c buses to Palu (22,500Rp). To Ampana, 5 hrs (10,000Rp), and often full. It may be cheaper to take a bemo – also more frequent and comfortable; Ampana to Pagimana, 5-6 hrs (10,000Rp). *Jawa Indah Bus*, Jl P Sumatra 71, T21560. **Sea Boat**: night ferry Pagimana-Gorontalo (departs 2100 every other day). Boats leave Ampana for the Togian Islands most days in the morning, 5 hrs (6,500Rp); a larger ferry runs weekly from Poso to the Togian Islands via Ampana, before continuing on to Gorontalo (except on our last visit this boat was broken and had been for some time) (see page 740). Irregular boats to Makassar and Bitung (for Manado).

Directory Banks *Bank Mandiri*, Jl Hasanuddin 13; *Negara Indonesia 1946*, Jl Yos Sudarso 17; *BNI*, good rates for TCs and an ATM. **NB** Most of the banks do not have reliable ATMs taking the major credit cards (nowhere accepts VISA). Exchange rates for cash are poor; wait for Palu if possible. **Communications Post Office**: Jl Tadulako. **Telecom**: Jl Jend Urip Sumoharjo 4.

Togian Islands and Tomini Bay

Colour map 5, grid B1
Population: 30,000
Malaria has been reported on some of the islands; take suitable precautions

The Togian Islands form a volcanic archipelago of seven major islands and more than 100 smaller ones. The inhabitants are a mix of indigenous Togian people, assorted migrants from elsewhere in Sulawesi, the ubiquitous Chinese traders and retailers, and a small population of Bajau-Sama sea-nomads. Traditionally, the economy was firmly based on the twin pillars of fishing and copra, but tourism is fast becoming an

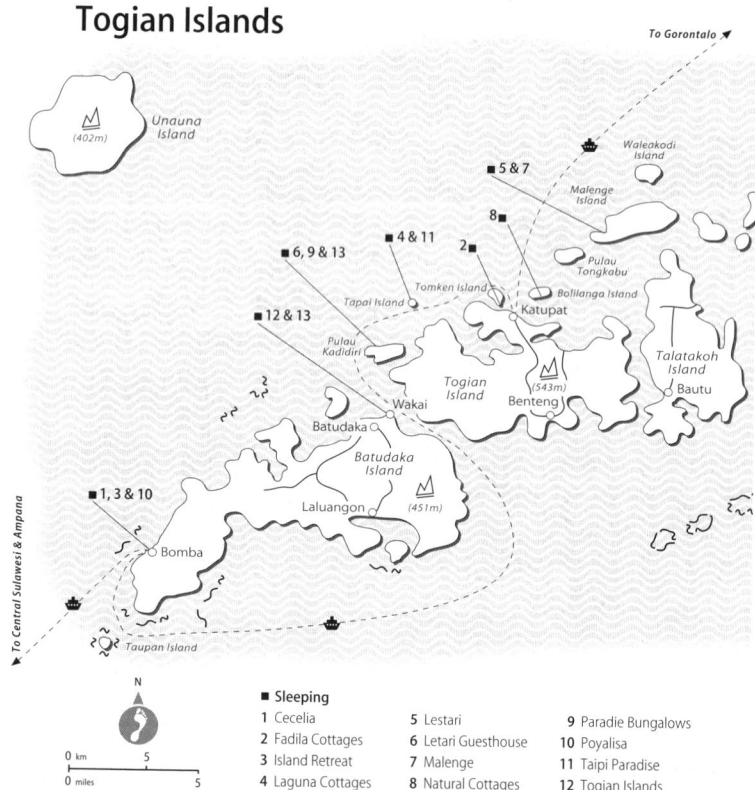

Togian Islands

■ **Sleeping**
1 Cecelia
2 Fadila Cottages
3 Island Retreat
4 Laguna Cottages
5 Lestari
6 Letari Guesthouse
7 Malenge
8 Natural Cottages
9 Paradie Bungalows
10 Poyalisa
11 Taipi Paradise
12 Togian Islands

important third sector. Almost every government department and NGO sees tourism as the answer to the islands' development dilemma. Some are less sanguine.

With the advent of a regular ferry service from Poso and Gorontalo, the Togian Islands are now firmly established on the tourist trail. As yet the beaches and small atolls have not been spoilt by litter and other pollution. They have some of the best water visibility in Sulawesi and are the ultimate secluded island paradise. Unfortunately, the local fishermen have picked up the nasty habit of using dynamite and poison (cyanide) to fish (practices seemingly coming from the Philippines), which has already destroyed sections of the coral reef, particularly along the northern coast and around settlements. The islands sustain ancient coral reef formations, with an estimated 200 species of coral. These are under threat not only from dynamite fishing but also from the crown of thorns starfish (which did such damage to the Great Barrier Reef), one of which can devour 50 sq cm of coral per day. This threat from the starfish is accentuated by the fact that two of its natural predators, the Napoleon Wrasse and Triton Fish, are being fished into oblivion (they fetch a high price in East Asian fish markets, particularly in Hong Kong). Nevertheless, these islands offer the best snorkelling in Sulawesi.

Because of the richness of the fauna here and its high rate of biodiversity, there is currently a campaign being orchestrated by Jatna Supriatna to have the area declared a national park. At the moment, apparently because there is little sense of local community solidarity, the population are not reacting to the gradual destruction of the habitat – and their livelihoods.

Whether or not 'ecotourism' is the solution is open to question. Most investors in the islands are either non-local business interests from the Sulawesi mainland or Jakarta and Bali, or they are professionals living on the island, especially teachers and health personnel. These are the only people with the skills and the capital to invest in a losmen or a restaurant. The fear, then, is that not only will the benefits of tourism be narrowly concentrated, but that much of the money will be syphoned off and not invested in improving the islands' infrastructure. A second area of concern focuses on the environmental sustainability of tourism. Because of the geography of the islands there are only a few places suitable for tourism development.

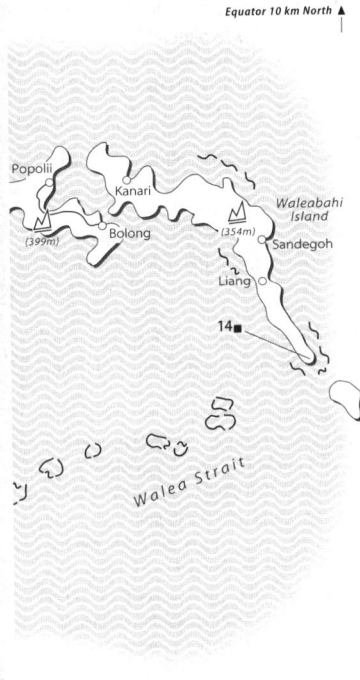

The Togians' 37 villages support three main **ethnic groups**: the Suluan, Togean and Bajau. The Bajau are sea gypsies, sometimes rather romantically described as 'untouched' by the outside world. Whatever their level of integration, some at least lead simple existences, living on offshore reefs, hunting fish using harpoons or *bubu* traps. The Bajau are concentrated on Taupan, Siatu, Papan and Kabalutan Island, as well as on Dolong and near Benteng.

Batudaka Island Wakai (on north coast); there is no beach at Wakai itself – it is necessary to rent a boat from the hotels to get to the beaches, and the reef for snorkelling. Motorboat to atolls 40,000Rp return (with collection at pre-arranged time), canoe hire 4,000Rp.

13 Wakai Cottages
14 Walea Dive Resort

 Coral

Sleeping
As the Togians become more popular, so the accommodation is rapidly developing & changing

Hotel categories quoted here are per person. **B-E** *Togian Islands Hotel*, run by a charming and energetic Chinese-Indonesian lady. She could perhaps claim to have got tourism off the ground in the Togian Islands, with interests in Kadidiri and Taipi. All-inclusive of 3 meals, restaurant on stilts, calm surroundings, gift shop, edge of tranquil village. **E** *Wakai Cottages*, price includes 3 good meals a day. Friendly service and boat/snorkel equipment for hire here. The *Black Marlin Dive Centre* operates from here. **Bomba** Southwest tip of Badudaka, snorkelling and boat chartering available. **B-C** *Island Retreat*, one of the newer homestays, American run, with attached dive centre. Meals included with a Tex-Mex bias. **E-F** *Cecelia*, basic. **D-F** *Poyalisa*, 5 bungalows, suffers from noisy neighbours, some bad reports about the food.

Kadidiri Island 30 min boat ride from Wakai, 3 operations here. The snorkelling off Kadidiri is excellent. Day trips to Taipi Island easy to organize. All homestays include 3 meals in their price. **D** *Paradise Cottages*, 25 cottages, some with their own mandi. Electricity and cold drinks available. Also supply safety deposit boxes. Price includes meals, dive centre with snorkel equipment for hire, some reports of bad equipment and dodgy compressor. **D-E** *Wakai Cottages*, the middle of the 3 homestays, this place has electricity. Fifteen attractive bungalows (some with their own mandi); also houses the Blue Marlin Dive Centre. Tucked away at the western end of the beach is the **D-F** *Lestari Homestay*, family-run, more relaxing feel than the others, with a feast of food. Free transfer to Wakai and also free snorkelling and fishing trips (but no diving equipment). Easy to see why it is the most popular with travellers.

Taipi Island Some of the best snorkelling is off this island; you can snorkel all the way around the island in about 1 hr. **D** *Taipi Paradise*, 10 large, attractive cottages for 2 people, all meals and transport included, same ownership as *Paradise Cottges*. Also **D** *Laguna Cottages*.

Tomken Island (5 mins boat ride from Katupat) **D** *Fadila Cottages*, restaurant with wide menu, snorkelling and fishing equipment available. The nearby **Bolilanga Island** has the **D** *Natural Cottages* with 7 large bungalows, some en suite. The location is unbeatable and the snorkelling good. They arrange snorkelling trips to nearby atolls and reefs. However, this paradise is spoilt by unfriendly management and the lack of good food.

Malenge Island Has 2 losmen *Lestari* and *Malenge*, both very similar (**E**), located near the ferry pier and therefore lacks a beach.

Walebahi Island AL *Walea Dive Resort*, located on the island's southwestern tip, T001-873682421370. Italian owners, government accredited, and the most professional. Three dives per day, all meals included. Useful information.

Sport
Diving The best diving is provided by the *Black Marlin Dive Centre*, which operates from Wakai Cottages. New equipment and well maintained. The diving is excellent – particularly around the B24 *Liberty*, Second World War wreck.

Transport
Sea Ferry: boats leave Ampana for the Togian Islands daily in the morning (when they are not broken), 5 hrs (12,000Rp). A larger ferry runs weekly from Poso to the Togian Islands via Ampana, before continuing on to Gorontalo (although on our last visit, this ferry had been out of action for 6 weeks or so, and showed no signs of being repaired). (Poso to Ampana by road takes 5 hrs and is a beautiful drive, see the Ampana entry on page 730.) The ferries tend to island hop and will stop at Bomba, Wakai, Katupat, Tongkabo, Dolong, and then continue on to Gorontalo, 9 hrs. Tickets are cheaper if purchased on the boat; pay extra for a cabin. Another option is to take a bus further east to Pangimana (another 5 hrs from Ampana), from where ferries go every other day to Gorontalo. **NB** In Ampana, there are reports of an unpleasant and unscrupulous lady called Mrs Harbour who has an almost Mafia-like hold on the transport here. Avoid this lady and *Ulva's Homestay*, and arrange transport independently.

Directory
Banks Few places accept VISA, therefore it is necessary to get money either in Palu (better rates than Poso), or in Manado. Remember that most people stay longer than they expect!

Poso to Manado

From Poso, the Trans-Sulawesi highway works its way up the eastern coast of Central Sulawesi to the small port of Toboli. From here a road runs west, over the mountains of the narrow northern limb, to Palu. The main road follows the coast north to the attractive town of Gorontalo. Before Gorontalo, a road crosses the mountainous spine of the island to the small, out-of-the-way port of Toli-Toli. From Gorontalo, the road cuts across to the north coast and runs east to the provincial capital of Manado. The coral reefs off Manado offer some of the finest diving in Southeast Asia, and there are a large number of worthwhile excursions from the city. Off Sulawesi's north coast are the rarely visited Sangihe and Talaud islands.

Toli-Toli

Phone code: 0453
Colour map 4, grid A6

This small town on the north coast of Sulawesi's northern 'leg' is locally important, but because it lies off the main Trans-Sulawesi highway it is not often visited by foreigners. The mountainous spine further serves to isolate the town from the rest of the island, and when the first five-year development plan, *Repelita I*, was introduced in 1969, the town was still inaccessible by land.

Excursions **Batu Bangga Beach** offers the best swimming in the area; it lies 12 km north of town. ■ *Getting there: bemos runs north along the coast.* **Lutungan Island** lies only 1 km off the coast and is said to be the site of the tomb of one of the former kings of Toli-Toli. The surrounding waters offer reasonable snorkelling and swimming. ■ *Getting there: boats can be chartered from town; ask at your hotel.*

Sleeping *Anda*, Jl H Mansyur 27; *Nirmala*, Jl Jend Sudirman; *Salamae*, Jl Jend A Yani.

Tour operators *Alia Dirgantara Travel Service*, Jl Suprapto 69.

Transport **Air** *Merpati* operate 1 return flight a day to Palu. **Road Bus**: buses link Toli-Toli with Palu, Gorontalo and Manado; the trip is arduous. **Sea Boat**: the *Pelni* ships *Kerinci*, *Kambuna*, *Leuser* and *Binaiya* call at Toli-Toli on their fortnightly circuits (see page 988 for route schedules). The *Pelni* office is on Jl Yos Sudarso. Smaller ferries also operate between Toli-Toli and Donggala (Palu), Manado and Bitung.

Gorontalo

Phone code: 0435
Colour map 5, grid A6

A peaceful, low-rise, low-key and friendly town with bendis, houses with verandahs, fretwork and wicker chairs. There are few 'sights' as such, but it is a perfect place to rest-up on the overland route between Palu and Manado. Unlike so many other towns in Indonesia it has not yet suffered the scourge of the 'Redevelopment and Shopping Centre Disease'. There are some wonderful examples of **Dutch provincial architecture** – the hospital on Jl Jend A Yani and the Mitra Cinema at Jl S Parman 45 (Art Deco), for example. The **Pasar Satya Pradja** is at the intersection of Jl S Parman and Jl MT Haryono. More interesting is the **Pasar Sentral** with its narrow alleys, at the intersection of Jl Pattimura and Jl Dr Sam Ratulangi. Gorontalo has two small harbours – bigger ships dock at Kwandang, 45 km northwest. To get to the smaller and closer **Pelabuhan Kota** (literally 'Town Port'), take a bemo from the Pasar Sentral.

Excursions **Kwandang** is a port 45 km northwest of Gorontalo. Shortly before the town there are two forts, a short walk from the main road. ■ *Getting there: by bus from the*

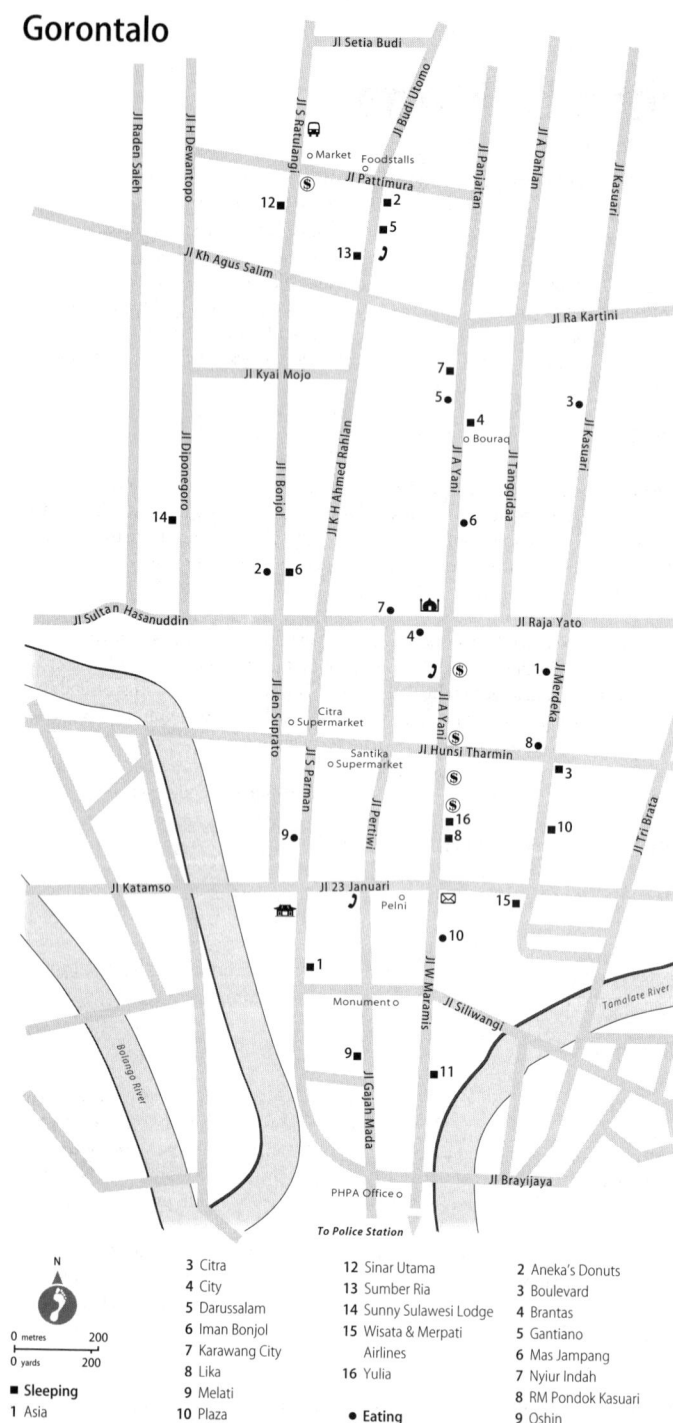

Andalas terminal. **Panua Reserve** lies about 100 km west of Gorontalo, on the coast near Marisa, one of the nesting sights of the rare and extraordinary maleo bird (*Macrocephalon maleo*) – although uncontrolled egg collection has substantially reduced the population. ■ *Getting there: by bus from the Andalas terminal.*

Sleeping

The temperature at night is pleasant & therefore a/c is not always essential

■ *on map*
Price codes:
see inside front cover

B *Yulia Hotel*, Jl A Yani 26, T828395, F24807. The newest addition to Gorontalo's hotels, built around an attractive courtyard. Modern, very comfortable, en suite, hot showers, best of the lot. **D** *Melati*, Jl Gajah Mada 33, T21853. A traditional and well-maintained colonial house (1900), 8 newish rooms, 4 with a/c, 4 with fan, TV and private mandi, price includes good breakfast. Recommended. Alex, the owner, is full of information. But beware of another person masquerading as 'Alex'! **D-E** *Citra*, Jl Merdeka 26, T21249. Ten spotless rooms but minimalist breakfast, not much natural light. **D-E** *City*, Jl A Yani, T21678. Ten rooms, the more expensive ones have a/c, all with attached mandis, cheap food. **D-E** *Imam Bonjol*, Jl Imam Bonjol 14. Twelve comfortable rooms, with a large sitting area. **D-E** *Karawang City*, Jl A Yani 31, T22437. A/c and hot water, friendly and welcoming service, noisy road. **D-E** *Lika Hotel*, Jl A Yani 20, T21296. Convenient central location, breakfast not included. **D-E** *Saronde*, Jl Walanda Maramis 17, T21735, 23 rooms, some a/c, TV and hot water, biggest hotel in town, charming owner with good English, set around courtyard, range of rooms. **D-E** *Sumber Ria Hotel*, Jl Budi Utomo 7A, T23888. Very comfortable, standard rooms and pleasant location. **E** *Asia*, Jl S Parman 10, T22633. Wonderful villa, a bit dark inside. **E** *Budi Utomo*, Jl Budi Utomo 24, T21564. Clean and well-run. **E** *Darussalam Hotel*, Jl Buti Utomo 20. Simple, attached western toilets, some English spoken. **E** *Sinar Utama*, Jl Dr Sam Ratulangi 33B, T22147. Near market and bemo station, thin walls, dark but clean and homely. **E** *Sunny Sulawesi Lodge*, Jl Diponegoro 40, T24711. Clean and simple, with some information.

Eating

Very cheap *Nyiur Induh*, Jl Kasuari 35, T22622. Recommended for Chinese food, very tasty dishes. *Agung Baru*, Jl Merdeka. Indonesian menu and some Chinese. *Brantas*, sumptuous portions, characterful, next to the bakery of same name. *El Em Café*, Jl Husni Thamrin 2, T21550. More of a café than a place for food. *RM Pondok Kasuari*, Jl Hasni Thakmin. Very limited menu, fish bias. **Foodstalls** Cheap and good, set up on Jl Pertiwi in the evenings. **Bakeries** *Aneka Donuts*, Jl I Bonjol 8, T22424; *Brantas*, Jl Raya Eyato 5, small selection.

Transport

Local Bemos: the main terminal is at the Pasar Sentral, at the north end of Jl Dr Sam Ratulangi, near the intersection with Jl Pattimura. Frequent departures for the long-distance Andalas bus terminal 500Rp around town. **Horse-drawn bendis**: perhaps the most popular form of transport in town. Expect to pay about 2,500Rp for a short journey across town. **Microlets** can be chartered for approximately 8,000Rp per hr for touring around town and the harbour.

Air Jalaluddin airport is 32 km northwest of town. Regular daily connections by Bouraq with Palu, Manado (300,000Rp), Makassar and to Ternate and Ambon in Maluku (the latter has been suspended due to the communal violence there). Minibuses wait to take passengers to town, 45 mins. The road between Gorontalo and the airport passes through the charming town of Limboto, 30 mins. **Road Bus**: the long-distance Andalas terminal is on the outskirts of town, 3 km from the centre; get there by regular bemo from the Pasar Sentral. Regular connections with Manado, 10-11 hrs, (16,000-25,000Rp), a bumpy 17 hr journey to Palu and Kwandang. Four-wheel drives take passengers to Manado, 35,000Rp (back seat), 60,000Rp (front seat) – generally more comfortable and faster. **Sea Boat**: the main port is at Kwandang, 45 km northwest of town, on the north shores of this 'leg' of Sulawesi. The *Pelni* ship *Umsuni* and *Tilongkabila* docks here (see route map page 988). Every Fri at 1900 a boat leaves direct to the Togians (17,000-25,000Rp) from Gorontalo port (1,000Rp bemo to here). There are also boats leaving every 2nd night at 2100 from here for Tomini Bay, arriving in Pagimana the next morning (15,000-20,500Rp). Buses wait here to transport passengers on to Ampana (7 hrs, 10,000Rp). Overnight stay in Ampana. There are regular boat connections with the Togian Islands from 1000 onwards (6,500Rp).

Directory **Airline offices** *Bouraq*, Jl Jend A Yani 26, T21678; *Merpati*, *Hotel Wisata*, Jl 23 Januari 19, T21736, also agent at *Julia Hotel*, Jl A Yani 26, T828395. **Banks** Bank Bumi Daya, Jl Kartini 26-28, T24555; Bank Danom, Jl A Yani 58, T24137; *Bank Dagang Negara*, *Bank Rakyat Indonesia* and *BNI* all on Jl Jend A Yani, near the intersection with Jl Husni Thamrin. **Communications** General Post Office: Jl Jend A Yani 14-16. **Warpostel**: Jl A Yani, opposite BNI. **Telecom**: Jl 23 Januari 35. *Pelni* Office: Jl 23 Januari 31, T21089, F21145. **Tourist offices** Jl Raden Saleh 159, T22579, 0800-1400, a few handouts, not very knowledgeable. **Useful addresses** Police: Jl P. Kalengkongan, T21110.

Manado

Phone code: 0431
Colour map 5, grid A3
Population: 325,000

Looking out from the 'beach' front over Manado Bay, it is easy to understand why travellers such as Alfred Russel Wallace thought the area so beautiful: two peninsulas curl around like crab claws, and Bunaken Island, the volcanic cone of Manado Tua, amongst other islands, shimmer in the distance. However, for people arriving here after travelling through the quiet towns of Central and North Sulawesi, Manado is something of a culture shock – the city centre is brash, noisy and fast-paced. It is as if the influence of the nearby Philippines has filtered across the Celebes Sea to transform the city.

Manado is the capital of the province of North Sulawesi. The area around Manado is known as Minahasa, and was a separate province until 1964, when it was combined with Gorontalo to form North Sulawesi. Although rather featureless, it is – by Indonesian standards – visibly wealthy. This wealth is built primarily on cloves, but also on coconuts, nutmeg and coffee – and tourism; the airport runway has been lengthened to take wide-bodied jets, and the big hotel chains are moving in.

Ins and outs

Getting there Manado is Sulawesi's most important centre after Makassar in the south. There are international air connections from Sam Ratulangi Airport with Singapore and Davao (the Philippines), as well as destinations in Java, Maluku, Irian Jaya and Bali and, of course, in Sulawesi itself. The airport is 13 km from town. The Malalayeng long-distance bus terminal is a few kilometres south-west of town and there are a/c and ekonomi buses to destinations as far south as Makassar. Manado has no port large enough to take a *Pelni* ship and these depart from Bitung, around 55 km east of the city. However, smaller vessels leave from Manado Port close to the centre of town for Palu, Toli Toli, Ternate, Sangir, Talaud, Pare Pare, Ambon and elsewhere. Boats for Sangihe and Talaud also leave from Singkil port, just 1 km north of the city centre.

Getting around While the centre of Manado is relatively compact, and there is also often a pleasant sea breeze, the city does sprawl amid many of the attractions in the surrounding countryside. There are 4 bemo/minibus terminals serving different local towns. Other forms of city transport include bendis (horse-drawn carts), microlets and metered and unmetered taxis. **Tourist offices** *Manado Town Tourist Office*, Jl Ahmad Yani Sario; *North Sulawesi Tourist Office*, Jl 17 Agustus, T864911, open 0800-1400 Mon-Thu, 0800-1100 Fri, 0800-1300 Sat, rather out of town; catch a bemo to Jl 17 Agustus and get out at the new Governor's office (ask for the *Dinas Pariwisata*). It is off the road (signposted), towards the sea. Very helpful and worth the effort. There is also a counter at the airport, again loads of information, but some conflicting details. *Parpostel Tourist Office*, Jl Diponegoro 111, T851835, easier to get to, but not as useful.

History

In the 16th century, Minahasa consisted of a number of small, independent states including Gorontalo, Limboto and the Talaud and Sangihe islands. The Spanish and Portuguese were already calling at ports in the area in the 1500s, and by the middle of the 16th century missionaries were having considerable success converting the population to Christianity. The Dutch concluded a treaty with the chiefs of Minahasa in 1679, heralding nearly 300 years of close association between the Christians of the

MANADO: HISTORY 747

area and the colonial government. This led to a proportionately greater role in the Dutch civil service and army, a rapid development spread of education and health facilities – in which Church schools were at the forefront – and a more pervasive 'westernization' of culture.

It was this close association which played a part in encouraging rebels in North Sulawesi to join with the PRRI – the Revolutionary Government of the Indonesian Republic – in the Permesta rebellion of 1958 and challenge the authority of President Sukarno and his associates. The two centres of this rebellion against Jakarta were West Sumatra and North Sulawesi. Sukarno demanded harsh reprisals against the rebels, and in February 1958 the Indonesian airforce bombed Manado. By

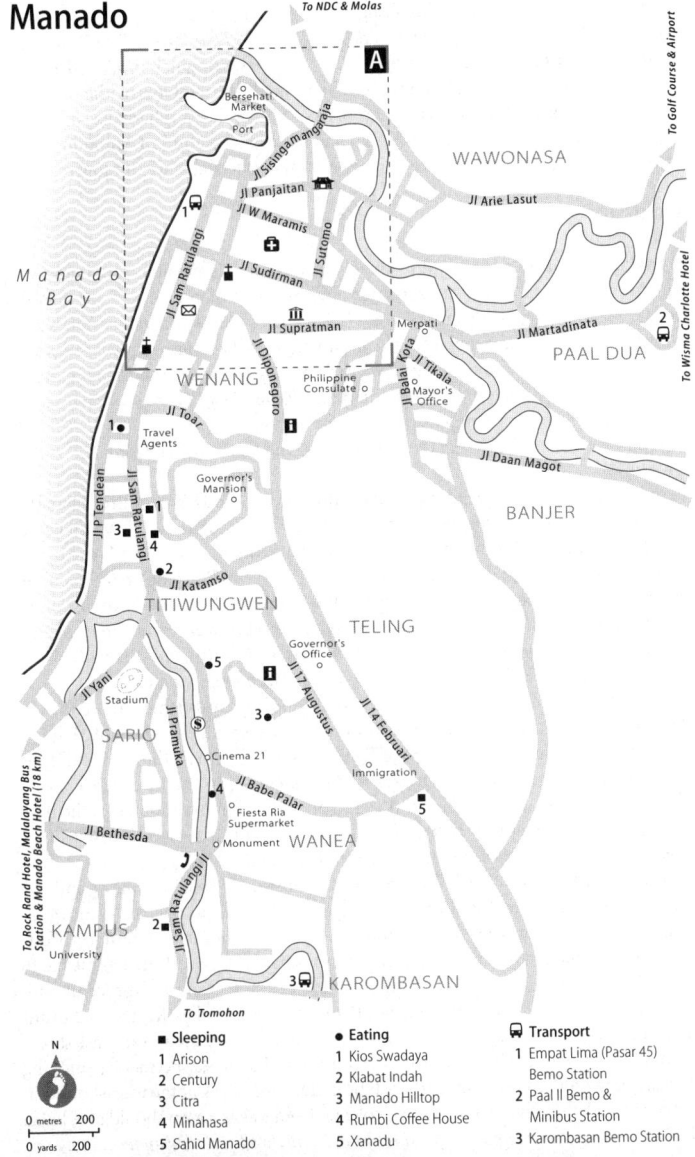

Manado

■ **Sleeping**
1 Arison
2 Century
3 Citra
4 Minahasa
5 Sahid Manado

● **Eating**
1 Kios Swadaya
2 Klabat Indah
3 Manado Hilltop
4 Rumbi Coffee House
5 Xanadu

Transport
1 Empat Lima (Pasar 45) Bemo Station
2 Paal II Bemo & Minibus Station
3 Karombasan Bemo Station

Related maps:
A Manado centre, page 752

mid-May the army had overwhelmed the rebels in Gorontalo and in late-June recaptured Manado. The US, anxious about Sukarno's association with the Indonesian Communist Party, even considered sending troops to assist the rebels; in the end they decided not to, but sent arms instead. The rebellion stuttered on until 1961 when the rebels were finally defeated.

Sights

There are few places of interest in Manado – most people come here for the incomparable diving and snorkelling, and for the sights outside the city. The **North Sulawesi Provincial Museum** is on Jl WR Supratman (south of town) and has a moderate collection with very brief English translations. ■ *Admission 750Rp. Open 0800-1330 Mon-Thu, 0800-1100 Fri, 0800-1300 Sat, 0800-1600 Sun.* The **Ban Hing Kiong Chinese temple** is at the end of Jl Panjaitan. It was originally built in the early part of the 19th century, but has since been renovated. The temple is neither impressive nor unusual, with the requisite array of Chinese temple paraphernalia – incense, a predominance of gold, red and black, and lanterns. **Pelabuhan Manado**, off Jl Suprapto, also in the town centre, might be of interest to ship and port lovers.

Excursions

Bunaken Sea Garden is Manado's greatest attraction. It is a magnificent underwater park with crystal clear waters, named after Bunaken Island which lies 8 km offshore (for full entry, see page 757). ■ *Getting there: Most of the major hotels and travel agents can arrange snorkelling, scuba diving, or just viewing from a glass bottom boat, trips to Bunaken; however, you will end up being part of an excursion organized by 1 of the 3 dive resorts listed under 'Sleeping', below. All of the resorts have people meeting each flight at the airport, they offer free transfer to and from airport. They all visit the same set of dive sites in the Marine Park, and lunch on 1 of 2 islands.*

Excursions south from Manado **Tomb of the nationalist leader Imam Bonjol** is to be found 8 km south of Manado. Just before the town of Pineleng, there is a small paved road to the left which winds uphill for 2 km to this tomb of a native of West Sumatra, who was exiled here by the Dutch after his capture during the Padri Wars. He died in Pineleng on 6 November 1864. The tomb does not begin to match the stature of the man. ■ *Admission by donation. Getting there: by minibus from the Karombasan terminal either to Kali (which passes the tomb) or the more frequent service towards Tomohon, walking the last 2 km up the hill from the main road (ask for makam Imam Bonjol).*

Continuing south from Pineleng, the road winds upwards (there are said to be 135 corners) between two volcanoes – Mount Lokon (1,589m) and Mount Mahawu (1,311m) – towards the hill village of **Kinilow**. On a clear day, there are stunning views back over the city, with Bunaken and the other islands in the distance. From the turn-off for Imam Bonjol's tomb 12 km on and 20 km from Manado, the road reaches Kinilow. **Sleeping D** *Indraloka*, being rebuilt on last inspection. ■ *Getting there: regular departures from Manado's Karombasan terminal.*

Kakas Kasen is another hill town which almost merges with Kinilow and is a more attractive, horticultural centre. Villages on this upland plateau – known as Minahasa – are almost 100% Christian and there are not one but five churches of different denominations. On Sundays, streams of smartly dressed Minahasans file to worship. **Sleeping A-B** *Lokon Resting Resort*, T51203, clean and peaceful with attractive gardens, discounts available. Paths lead from Kakas Kasen up **Mount Lokon**. It is possible to climb to the summit of the volcano in a few hours, ask directions at *Happy Flower* or *Volcano Resort*. **Mount Mahawu** is a spectacular smoking volcano and you can walk right around the crater rim. Check at the tourist office in town for the latest news. Climbing the volcano from Kakas Kasen should take half a day. ■ *Getting there: regular departures from Manado's Karombasan terminal.*

Tomohon is 25 km from Manado and 700m above sea-level, situated in a saddle between the two volcanoes Lokon and Mahawu. Locally known as the 'City of Flowers', it is a small town notable as the centre of missionary activity in the area and for perhaps the finest bendi horse carts in Indonesia. It is also home to an important vulconology centre which monitors the activity of the volcanoes in the area – a good first stop for anyone contemplating climbing one of the active volcanoes in the area (ask for the Dinas Gunnung Berapi). **Sleeping** One of the first travellers place to open in Tomohon was **E-F** *The Happy Flower*, T352787. Free tea and coffee all day, book exchange, excellent service, great source of information on trekking in the area, and a lovely place to retreat to, cultural tours, rafting and mountain biking arranged, recommended, popular and therefore booking advisable. An alternative and equally pleasant new homestay is the **D-E** *Volcano Resort*, located opposite the *Happy Flower*. Set around an attractive seating area over a lake, a great breakfast is included in the room rate. More expensive rooms in bungalows. **E-F** *Loken Valley*, next to *Happy Flower*, four rooms, price includes breakfast, tea and coffee. Failing these, there is also the **D-E** *Kawanua Cottages*, T52060. On the road heading out of town. ■ *Getting there: bus from Karombasan Terminal, 35 mins.* For the *Happy Flower* and *Volcano Resort*, get off in front of the Gereja Pniel (Church), cross road and down track for 400m. **Lake Linau** lies almost 1 km off the road from the village of

Around Manado

Related map: A Bunaken Marine Park, page 757

Lahendong and 32 km south of Manado. Sulphurous odours tell the story: steam roars out of vents in the ground and muddy water bubbles noisily – it is not very spectacular, and is spoilt by discarded rubbish. ■ *Getting there: regular departures from Manado's Karombasan terminal to Lahendong, and then walk the final 1 km.*

Continuing south, some 37 km from Manado, is **Sonder** – the centre of clove production in the area. Clove trees can be seen growing at the side of the road (sparsely leaved, and rather like eucalypts): the smell of the spice drying permeates the air. ■ *Getting there: regular departures from Manado's Karombasan terminal.*

Kawangkoan cave complex – one of a series – lies just north of Kawangkoan, over a bridge (there is another just south of Tanggari). They were dug on the orders of the Japanese to store and protect supplies and ammunition from Allied bombing. For a small gratuity someone in the restaurant opposite will provide a torch (to illuminate the bats). This is only interesting for those who dream of being on the set of a Harrison Ford film. ■ *Getting there: regular departures from Manado's Karombasan terminal.*

Watu Pinabetengan is a large boulder which lies 3 km beyond the village of Pinabetengan, on the lower slopes of Mount Rindengan. On it are as yet undeciphered pictographic carvings. It was at this spot that the 17 chiefs of the Minahasa tribes met to discuss important matters. During the full moon, ceremonies and sacrifices are still held. It is disappointing – graffiti obscures the dim carvings and the stone itself has been set in concrete and an ugly pavilion built over it. ■ *Getting there: catch a bus to Kawangkoan from Manado's Karombasan terminal, and from there a bemo to Pinabetengan village. It is a pleasant 2½-km walk uphill to the site. A path behind the stone leads down into a ravine to some* **hot springs**.

The town of **Langoan** lies south on the main road from Kawangkoan, some 54 km from Manado. There are hot springs near here at **Karumenga**, with private bathrooms. From Langoan, bemos run north to **Kakas** on the southern shores of **Lake Tondano**, and from there link the various communities that line the beautiful west shores of the lake. From Tondano at the north extremity of the lake there are bemos to Airmadidi (see 'Excursions southeast from Manado', below), and from there back to Manado's Paal II terminal.

Excursions southeast from Manado

Airmadidi lies 19 km southeast of Manado. It is proudly touted as the **kenari nut** capital of Indonesia (kenari nuts are tropical almonds from which the oil is usually extracted; they are also used as shade trees in the cultivation of nutmeg (see page 913). There is a big copra factory in Airmadidi, and some examples of *waruga* (see below). Tourists usually stop here to visit the **Taman Anggrek** or **orchid garden**, which has a reasonable collection of orchids (disappointing out of season). ■ *Admission by donation. The garden is on the Manado side of Airmadidi, just past the 6 km marker. Getting there: by bemo from the Paal II terminal.*

Mount Kalabat is a 1,995m-high volcano northeast of Airmadidi. It can be climbed in 13-15 hours (up and down). A guide is advisable – some people maintain, essential. You should also register with the local police before setting out. The climb is quite demanding, especially the last two hours when it becomes steep. Expect to take 7-9 hours to reach the summit and another 5-6 hours to make it down again. Popular with university students from Manado who climb during the night and watch the sun rise. ■ *Getting there: take a bemo to Airmadidi from the Paal II terminal.*

Taman Purbakala Waruga is a cemetery in **Sawangan**, 24 km from Manado, and 50m off the main road. It contains 144 upright megalithic sarcophagi or *waruga*, with prism-shaped lids, each of which would have been used by one family. They were assembled here from surrounding villages in 1817 and the oldest is believed to date from the 10th century. The ancient Minahasans 'buried' their dead above ground to stop the smell of the rotting corpses reaching the earth god Makawalang – an event which would have led to earthquakes. It is speculated that corpses were placed upright in the *waruga* because this is the way the foetus was thought to form in the womb and so this is the way a dead person should enter the afterlife. The massive stone chambers and lids are decorated with crude carvings – some depicting

17th century figures in frock coats. Just outside the cemetery is a small museum containing artefacts retrieved from the sarcophagi – bronze bracelets, ceramics from China and spear heads. ■ *Admission by donation. Getting there: take a bemo from Paal II to Airmadidi (700Rp), then another from Airmadidi to Sawangan (500Rp). Get off 100m past the Immanuel Church on the left.*

Tondano lies south from Sawangan, 36 km from Manado, on the northern shores of **Lake Tondano**. The area is still volcanically active and many villages on the lake shore have hot springs and public baths. Hot water is even piped through bores sunk 75m into Lake Tondano's bed. In Tondano town, a number of hotels/losmen offer thermal hot water (eg *Asri, Ranopasu* and the *Tamaska Hijau Homestay*). The Minahasa tourism office is out of town on the road to Tomohon. ■ *Getting there: bus from Manado's Paal II terminal to Airmadidi and then an onward bemo to Tondano.*

Remboken is situated on the western shore of Lake Tondano, almost 50 km south of Manado. From Tondano, bemos run down both shores of the lake, linking the various lakeside communities. The west shore is particularly attractive. Just north of Remboken (49 km from Manado) is a lakeside **Taman Wisata** (tourist garden) with accommodation (**C**), hot swimming baths and restaurant. Very popular with locals at the weekend. Continuing south from Remboken, the road leads to **Kakas** on the south edge of the lake. From here bemos run to **Langoan**, and from there north back to Manado's Karombasan terminal (see 'Excursions south from Manado', above). ■ *Getting there: by bemo from Manado's Paal II terminal to Airmadidi and then an onward bemo to Remboken.*

Tangkoko Batu Angus National Park is a comparatively small reserve due east of Manado. See page 759 for more information. ■ *Getting there: take a bus from Paal II terminal in Manado towards Bitung, get off at Girian (2,000Rp), from here get another bus or jeep to Batuputih (2,000Rp), road can be difficult.* **NB** *Be sure to apply strong insect repellent to your feet and shoes, and wear long trousers, to ward off the 'gonone mite' – its bite is itchy for days.*

Excursions east of Manado

A number of tour companies in Manado offer roughly the same range of tours (all prices are for a group of 3-4 people). *City tours* (US$12, half day); *highland/Minahasa tour* to Tomohon, Kawangkoan, Remboken, Sawangan (US$32); *Tangkoko Batu Angus National Park* (US$45); *Bunaken sea garden* (US$35 snorkelling, US$60 diving).

Tours

Essentials

L *Novotel Manado*, Jl Piere Tendean, T855555, F851245, novotel@mdo.mega.net.id Unmissable concrete creation that dominates the sea front. All facilities and more at a price, a/c, restaurants, pool, massive addition to the upmarket hotel scene, this 268-room, 2-storey block provides a good range of facilities including business and fitness centres. Good trips to Bunaken organized, but some questions have been raised about their use of anchors on the reef. **L** *Santika*, Tongkaina-Molas, PO Box 1644, T858222, F858666, santika@mdo.mega.net.id Out of town on the coast opposite Bunaken, so ideal for divers, 100 rooms, tennis, pool, PADI dive centre. **AL** *Anghasa Raya Indas Hotel*, Jl Sugiono 12, T862039. This average hotel is popular with locals, less so with foreign visitors. **AL** *Century Hotel*, Jl Sam Ratulangi 458, T822888, F858892, hcm@mdo.mega.net.id With 152 rooms, this is the newest addition to the upper end of the market. All the usual features of a hotel of this class. Modern rooms, pity about the poorly lit corridors. Small rooftop pool, travel agent, and access to a golf course. **AL** *Sahid Manado*, Jl Babe Palar Manado 1, T851688, F863326. Situated in the hills behind the town centre, good views across bay, restaurant, coffee shop, swimming pool (open to non-residents, 4,000Rp), friendly and helpful staff, but a rather soulless modern business class hotel. **AL** *Sedona Hotel Manado*, a new beach front hotel with 257 rooms. Located 25 km from the city (and 39 km from the airport) on a large 20-ha site on Tateli Beach

Sleeping
■ *on maps, pages 747 & 752*
Price codes: see inside front cover

Manado has a lack of cheap accommodation, but some good mid- & upper-range hotels

– a place for those who want a relaxing seaside holiday and do not intend to explore the city. Facilities include pool, tennis court, dive shop, business centre. **A** *Hotel Paradis and Resort*, 32 km from the airport, T861829, F861573. This 320-room hotel is set amongst trees on a sandy beach, with its own golf course, tennis courts, swimming pool, diving school. **A** *Hotel Sahid Kawanua*, Jl Sam Ratulangi 1, T867777, F865220. A/c, coffee shop, pool, money changer, dull modern hotel, central location, not recommended for the tourist, pretensions of grandeur totally unfulfilled, price includes breakfast. **A** *Manado Beach Hotel*, Tasik Ria, 18 km south of town centre, T867001, F867007; 200 rooms, restaurant, coffee shop, pool, sunken poolside bar, watersports, relaxing palm gardens, small strip of grey sand beach at low tide, low occupancy rate of 50% shows it is struggling – discounts available.

B *Hotel Regina*, Jl Kl. Soegiono 1, T850090, F867706. With light and airy 33 rooms, but rather sterile. A more professional feel and better decorated than the *Makmur Hotel*. **B** *Makmur Hotel*, Jl Walanda Maramis 144-146, T852538, F863102. This tardis-like hotel has good bathrooms but many rooms do not have windows. There is also a sore excuse for a café. Discounts

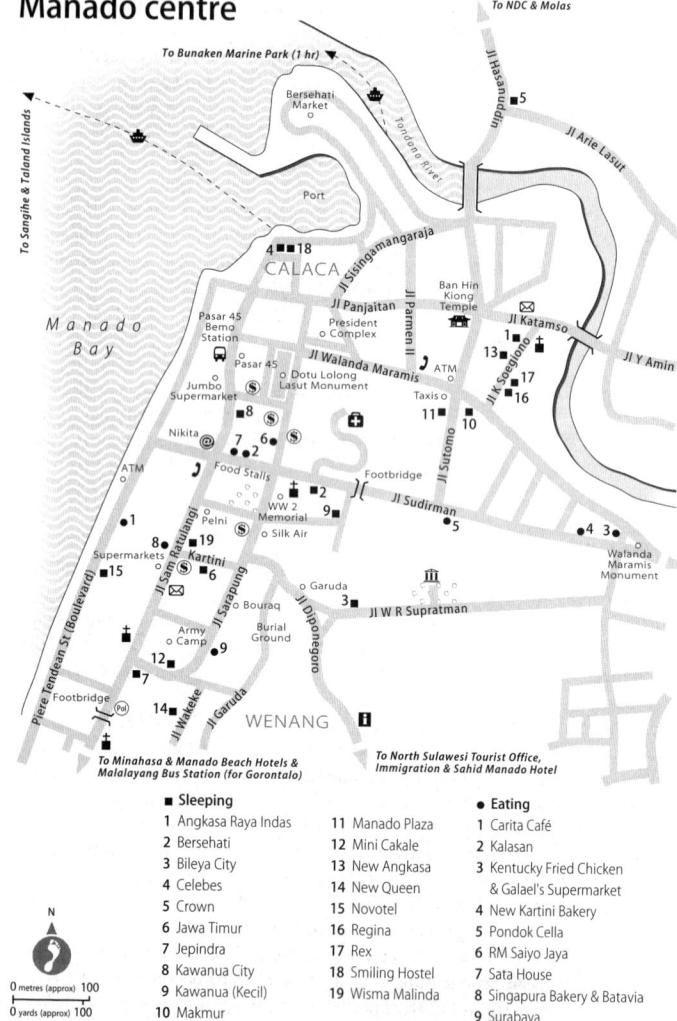

Manado centre

■ **Sleeping**
1 Angkasa Raya Indas
2 Bersehati
3 Bileya City
4 Celebes
5 Crown
6 Jawa Timur
7 Jepindra
8 Kawanua City
9 Kawanua (Kecil)
10 Makmur
11 Manado Plaza
12 Mini Cakale
13 New Angkasa
14 New Queen
15 Novotel
16 Regina
17 Rex
18 Smiling Hostel
19 Wisma Malinda

● **Eating**
1 Carita Café
2 Kalasan
3 Kentucky Fried Chicken & Galael's Supermarket
4 New Kartini Bakery
5 Pondok Cella
6 RM Saiyo Jaya
7 Sata House
8 Singapura Bakery & Batavia
9 Surabaya

available. **B** *New Queen*, Jl Wakeke 12-14, T865979, F865748. Immaculate small 2-star hotel, winner of Governor's trophy for cleanest hotel in Manado for 6 years, full a/c, restaurant, central, but off main roads, good value. **B** *Rock Rand Hotel*, Jl Jend A Yani 16/No 1 Sario, T858805, F858804. Modern hotel, relaxing feel to the place. **B** *Tulip Airport*, 1½ km from airport, a/c, only worth considering if flying next day. **B-C** *Malalayang Indah*, Jl Raya Malalayang, 5 km south of town, T861523, F861525. Wooden cottages set in well kept mature gardens, some a/c, restaurant, peaceful location on the waterfront.

C *Arison*, Jl Sam Ratulangi 85, T864739. Some a/c, clean maze of corridors and whitewashed bannisters, plenty of house plants help create tranquil feel, compact, clean rooms, breakfast only. **C** *Hotel Minahasa*, Jl Sam Ratulangi 199, nothing special. **C** *Kolongan Beach Indah Hotel and Restaurant*, Jl Walanda Monginsidi, T/F853001. A/c, located 6 km south of the city centre, this hotel has great views, attached dive centre. **C** *Manado Plaza*, Jl Walanda Maramis 1, T852222, F862940. Situated in grubby shopping/cinema complex, noisy, shabby rooms, poor value, large restaurant, fitness centre, travel agent *Trampil Tours*. **C** *Minahasa*, Jl Sam Ratulangi 119, T862059. Some a/c, restaurant (order evening meals in advance), popular old villa with character, plenty of communal seating areas, quiet verandah at back overlooking small garden, friendly with good service, including morning and afternoon tea.

D *Biteya City*, Jl WR Supratman 11, T866598. New hotel on hill behind Garuda office (close to museum), comfortable (green) rooms, some a/c with good views across town, breakfast only, friendly staff, pleasant small hotel slightly off beaten track, quiet. **D** *Kawanua (Kecil)*, Jl Sudirman II 40, T863842, F861974. Some a/c, restaurant and lounge in open-air central courtyard, slightly overpriced. **D** *Jepindra*, Jl Sam Ratulangi 33, T864049. A/c, central for all facilities, bathrooms shabby and indifferent water supply, price includes breakfast (boiled egg, chocolate sandwich, coffee), cheerful and helpful staff. **D** *New Angkasa*, Jl Sugiono 10, T864062. Average place with nothing that particularly sets it apart from the mass of hotels in this category, quiet sitting area. **D** *Yuta*, Jl Santu Joseph 2, T852153, F863857. A/c, restaurant, snorkelling rental, simple, small, mid-range hotel. **D-E** *Citra*, Jl Sam Ratulangi XVII 12, T63812. Simple, plain rooms, homely shady verandah on 1st floor, new relaxing area on roof with views of sunset, in quiet lane off Jl Sam Ratulangi. Recommended. **D-E** *Hotel Celebes*, Jl Rumambi 8, T870425, F859068. Semi-colonial feel, overlooking busy harbour and market, economy rooms are value for money. **D-E** *Jawa Timur*, Jl Kartini 5, T851970. Small central hotel in quiet side street, spotless rooms, rooms downstairs open onto TV lounge, close to GPO, *Telekom* and *Pelni* offices. Recommended. **D-E** *Mini Cakale*, Jl Korengkeng 40, T852942. Some a/c, clean good value, shady sitting area, some rooms overlook tiny garden, noisy rooms at the front. **D-E** *Rex*, Jl Kol Soegiono 3, T851136, F867706. Spotless, no frills, tiny white tiled cell-like rooms, communal washing facilities, central location and a 5 min walk to the port where ferries leave for Bunaken Island, no restaurant, limited lounge area, good security. Recommended. **D-F** *Bersehati*, Jl Sudirman I. Clean hotel, set back off the busy road, some a/c rooms and some with own mandis, popular with locals.

E *Boulevard Seaview* , owned by Thomas, who runs Maya Express travel agency in town, this place is relatively new and is situated a bemo ride south of the city centre. Some a/c rooms, the hotel overlooking the boulevard and sea. **E** *Hotel Kawanua* , Jl Sudirman II 40, T63842, F61974. Cheap budget place. **E** *Smiling Hostel*, Jl Rumambi 7, T868463, smiling@divefroggies.com Same organization as *Happy Flower* and *Froggies Dive Centre*, backpackers haven. 13 cell-like but noisy rooms with fans, most have no windows, 6 bed dorms (**F**), safe boxes, rooftop balcony, restaurant is slow but good and it is an excellent place for gleaning information, breakfast not included. Recommended. **F** *Jakarta Jaya*, Jl Hasanuddin 225, T864330. Small rooms, but cheap, price includes breakfast.

Diving accommodation B *Tasik Ria Diving Resort*, close to *Manado Beach Hotel*, T857777, F857888. Information in the Netherlands on T038 3761222. New diving centre with bungalows, owned by a Dutch couple who speak English and German, and there are also course books in Italian, French and Japanese, brand new equipment. Recommended.

B-D *Nusantara Diving Centre* (NDC), Molas, T863988/863955, F860365/860368, ndc@mdo.mega.net.id, http://mdo.mega.net.id/ndc/cover.htm 7 km north of Manado, new large a/c rooms, half open-air bathrooms with mini-verdant garden, fan cooled bungalows or fan cooled rooms, large bathrooms, discount available in off-season (high season: Jun-Sep and Christmas). Restaurant serves excellent buffet nightly, bar by restaurant, next to the jetty, this was the first diving centre in North Sulawesi (established 1975) and is widely recognized for its professionalism and knowledge of local conditions. The Centre received the 'Kalpataru Award' in 1985 (the highest honour for environmental work in Indonesia), the success of NDC and popularity of diving in the region is largely attributable to the work of Loky Herlambag, the owner of NDC. He has brought together a friendly and dedicated group of people who together make NDC one of the most relaxing places to dive anywhere in the world. Recommended. They offer a 6-day SSI Open Water Diving Course. Certification from the USA; Snorkelling: (minimum 2 persons), at US$30 per day; Scuba dive, US$60 (2 dives). Both include lunch, boat, equipment (extra for BC and regulator). **B-D** *Barracuda Diving Resort*, Molas (office contact Michael Smith, Molas Dusun II, T95242 Manado), T854288, F864848; 8 km north of town, bungalows on hillside with views of Manado and Mount Lokon or local style cottages on stilts, no view, overlooking mangrove, high ceiling, open air dining block and bar by the jetty. This is the newest dive resort in the region, it lacks the friendly welcome of NDC, but is still a pleasant place to stay. Scuba tuition is available. New quick, fibreglass boats, but they have little deck space for relaxing when you're not in the water. Snorkelling (minimum 3 persons): US$35 per day; Scuba dive: US$60-70 (2 dives), both include lunch, boat, equipment (extra for BC and regulator). *Getting there*: take bemo to Tuminting, change to oplet which runs as far as Molas village. **B** *MUREX* (Manado Underwater Exploration) (office Jl Jend Sudirman 28), T866280. Desa Kalasey, the smallest of the 3 scuba operators, friendly attention, attractive bungalows in gardens on the sea front, but inconvenient for visiting Manado town centre, we have received a letter claiming that the equipment hired out here is in poor condition, so be extra vigilant when checking it out (US$100 for 1 night's accommodation, meals and 2 dives). There is a new live-aboard dive/cruise operation running from Manado to the islands of Sangihe-Talaud, Lembeh, Togian, Wakatobi, Papua, Halmahera and Morotai. The adapted pinisi schooner can accommodate 20 people and the all-in rate is US$180 per person per day. Contact *Divex Indonesia-Suma-Kai*, Jl Walanda Maramis 14, T846980, F867667, divex@manado.wasantara.nt.it

Eating

There are a range of restaurants stretched out along Jl Sam Ratulangi from the centre of town

Minahasan food is spicy hot. Specialities include *rintek wuuk* or *RW* – pronounced 'air way' (dog), *paniki* (fruit bat), field rat, *bubur manado* (a local congee) and *kenari* (coconut crab).

Chinese Mid-range: Manado Hilltop, T866581. Buffet, large restaurant catering for groups, panoramic view of bay, close to North Sulawesi Tourist office. **Rumbi Coffee House**, Jl Sam Ratulangi 356, T866938. Seafood, large selection of dishes, bamboo walls, thatch roof, open air, opposite Fiesta Ria Supermarket. **Xanadu**, Jl Sam Ratulangi II 88, T863022. Smart, lanterns and linen table cloths, dimly lit, a/c. Recommended for seafood. **Cheap**: *Klabat Indah*, Jl Sam Ratulangi 211, T862405. Ornate bamboo entrance flanked by giant Chinese vases, seafood, limited menu (on quiet evenings hit and miss as to what fresh fish available, accept what they have), excellent Ikan Mas Goreng and kangkung rebus.

Indonesian Mid-range: *Cakalang* (in *Kawanua City Hotel*), Jl Sam Ratulangi 1, also serves Chinese and International, ambitious menu, disappointing seafood, small portions (nouvelle cuisine?), comfortable location, overlooking pool. **New Queen Hotel**, also serves International, overpriced menu, bar. **Pondok Cella**, Jl Sudirman 46, attractive restaurant serving Minahasan and Chinese food. **Sunset**, Jl Piere Tendean (opposite the *Novotel Manado*), comes recommended by recent visitors – a good place to (believe it or not) watch the sun set. **Cheap**: *New Surabaya*, 3-1 Jl Sarapung 33, T862562. Also serves Chinese, popular with comprehensive menu, but most dishes have canteen, formula blandness, good cold fresh fruit juices (very sweet). **Very cheap**: *Batavia*, in the supermarket along Jl Sam Ratulangi, clean, but limited menu, rather bland. *Kalasan*, Jl Sudirman 9, tasty cheap Javanese food, *Kios Swadaya* and *Mie Katan II*. *Solo*, Jl Sam Ratulangi 192, open air, sate and chicken specialities (next to Isuzu garage), Jl Sam Ratulangi, they also serve Minahasan, both very popular with local students, good value.

Mexican Mid-range: *Terrakotta*, Jl Jend Sudirman 86, T845108. This is the only place in town which serves Mexican food. A very classy place, great atmosphere, also sells draught beer. Recommended.

Bakeries Next door to the *Batavia Restaurant* is the *Singapura Bakery*, an excellent place for great cakes and croissants. Recommended. *New Kartini*, Jl Jend Sudirman 71, is slightly further out of town. **Foodstalls** Jl Sudirman also has a number of good, cheap and very popular warungs; stalls set up in the evenings on Jl Sudirman near the intersection with Jl Sam Ratulangi. On the same stretch of road is the *Sate House* (mid-range), seafood, a number of tasty shrimp dishes, squeaky clean and friendly service, and *Dua Raya*, Jl Piere Tendean 84, good, very cheap Chinese food. There are also good moderate priced places on Jl Dr Sutomo, eg *Andalas Fast Food*, *Kios 18*, *Kios Nasi Kuning Sederhana*.

Bars

Hook's, basement of the *Hotel Century Manado*, Jl Sam Ratulangi 458, is the bar with the best ambience in town. They also have live music most nights – worth the trek out of here.

Entertainment

Cinemas *Plaza Hotel and Cinema*, Walanda Maramis 1 (4 screens); *President*, President Complex, Jl Piere Tendean; *Cinema 21*, Jl Sam Ratulangi, south of the town and very modern. **Discos** *Ebony*, 2200-0200, *Plaza Hotel*; *Maramba*, Wed and Sat, *Manado Beach Hotel*; *Hot Gossip*, Jl Sam Ratulangi 4, T862466, disco and live music; *Rock Rand*, Jl Jend A Yani 16, lively place, best live music in town and a good atmosphere. **Live music**: there is live music most nights in the ground floor bar of the *Novotel Manado*, Jl Piere Tendean (very popular). See also the entry for *Hook's* under 'Bars', above.

Festivals

Mid to late Sep Bunaken Festival, assorted cultural and sporting festivities; not a traditional event, but created by and for the tourist industry.

Shopping

The shopping district is crammed into an area delineated by Jl Sudirman, Jl Dr Sutomo & Jl Sam Ratulangi

Clothing *Makmur*, *Matahari* and *Ramayana* department stores on Jl Walanda Maramis and Jl S Ratulangi, cheap, reasonable quality. **Krawang embroidery** A Gorontalo speciality, available at *Krawang*, Jl Walanda Maramis, and *UD Kawanua*, Jl Balai Kota 1/30 (a private house). **Souvenirs** *Bunaken Souvenir Shop*, Jl Sam Ratulangi 178, is cheaper than the more central shops. **Supermarkets** *Galael's*, Jl Sudirman 73; *Jumbo*, Jl Suprapto 1; *Matahari*, behind the *Novotel*. **Tailoring services** Fast and cheap, many available throughout the city. **Textiles** Shops along Jl Dotulolong Lasut.

Sports

Diving See also 'Diving accommodation' above. Off-season diving can be cheaper. *Barracuda Dive Club* has been recommended (US$60-70 for 2 dives, equipment and lunch, after bargaining). **Golf** *Wenang Golf Club*, Jl AA Maramis (airport rd), T851599, 9 holes, 18 tees, Chinese restaurant and driving range. *Getting there*: take airport-bound Oplet (Lapangan) from Paal 2 terminal (500Rp). **Swimming** *Kawanua City Hotel*, open to non-residents (4,500Rp); *Sahid Manado Hotel*, 5,000Rp non-residents, poolside bar, restaurant.

Tour operators

Utama Aman, Jl Dotulolong, T845805, F862453. *Dembean Tours*, Jl Surdiman 3, T854029. *Trampil Tour and Travel*, in same building as *Plaza Hotel* and Cinema, Walanda Maramis 1. *Maya Express*, Jl Sudirman 15, T870111, F870603. Staff here speak good English. *Pandu Express*, Jl Sam Ratulangi 91, T865188, F851487. *Pola Pelita Express*, Jl Peire Tendean/Novotel Arcade, T852231, F864520, polatour@mdo.mega.net.id, next to the *Novotel* (contact Pak Jopie and Mike), authorized *American Express*, Agent. T852231, F864520.

Transport

Local Bemos/buses: there are no fewer than 4 bemo/minibus terminals serving different local towns (see map for locations of terminals). The central Pasar 45 terminal (Terminal Empat Lima) serves Tuminting and also has constant bemos travelling to the other 3 terminals; the Karombasan terminal serves Pineleng, Tomohon, Sonder, Kawangkoan, Langoan and Tondano; the Paal II (Paal Dua) is the terminal for Airmadidi, Bitung and the airport (from Airmadidi there are buses to Tondano); and the Malalayang terminal for Tanawangko (from here there are buses to Tomohon), and also for long distance buses to Kotamobagu, Gorontalo, and the rest of Sulawesi (eg Palu, Ujung etc). 400Rp for any journey in town, look at sign hanging in window for destination, not on roof. **Bendis**: horse-drawn carts – about 1,000Rp for 2 people, or they can be chartered for about 10,000Rp per hr. **Mikrolets**: 400Rp around town. **Taxi**: some are metered (white, marked cars). 750Rp flagfall. Metered taxis are good and reliable, get your hotel reception to call for taxi if you need one. For unmetered taxis, agree price before boarding. Taxis can be chartered for about 25,000Rp per hr (T864422 for Cenderi Taxi or T851010 for Dian Taxi).

Air Manado's **Sam Ratulangi Airport** is 13 km northeast of town. Regular daily connections on Garuda, Merpati or Bouraq with Makassar (590,000Rp), Gorontalo (310,000Rp), Palu (578,000Rp), Ternate (352,000Rp). Less regular flights to Biak (1,000,000Rp), Jayapura (1,400,000Rp), Luwuk (456,000Rp). Garuda also have flights to Surabaya (1,400,000Rp), Jakarta (1,800,000Rp) and Denpasar (1,300,000Rp). *Transport to town*: no fixed rate taxi counter, but still easy to get into town; there are 2 options but allow at least 30 mins for either option. If you have a lot of baggage, take a taxi, about 15,000Rp to hotels in centre of town; alternatively, take an oplet from the airport car park exit to Terminal Paal II (500Rp); change oplets there for town centre (Pasar 45) (500Rp). Useful visitors information counter at airport and a selection of souvenir shops. **International connections** with Davao (Philippines): departs Mon and Sat (US$150); returns Thu, Mon; and Singapore (*Silk Air*): Mon, Thu, returns same day.

Road Bus: the long distance Malalayeng terminal lies 30 mins southwest of the centre of town (400Rp by bemo from Pasar 45 or Karombasan terminals). All the bus companies have their offices here. It is best to visit the terminal a day before travelling to organize tickets. Most buses leave early morning or evening. Many buses from Gorontalo tend to arrive after midnight, if you want to avoid extortionate taxi fares there is a hotel left out of the bus station, 5 mins walk: **B-C** *Kolongan Beach Hotel*, views over the sea. The *Fajar Indah* bus company, T824169, runs a/c buses to Gorontalo, departing 1700, 8 hrs (27,000Rp). To get to Toli-Toli, take a bus to Gorontalo, then a boat, 24 hrs. It also provides the only a/c luxury buses to central and south Sulawesi.

Sea Boat: Manado's main port is Bitung on the other side of this leg of Sulawesi and 55 km east of the city. The *Pelni* ships *Ciremai, Kerinci, Kambuna, Umsini, Lambelu* and *Tilongkabila* dock here (see route schedules, page 988). The *Pelni* office is at Jl Sam Ratulangi 7, T855115, F867737. *Kalla Lines* run a ship which also follows a 2-week loop stopping at Jakarta, Surabaya, Makassar, Balikpapan, Tarakan, Pantoloan and Ternate. The Kalla Lines office is at Jl Sam Ratulangi 100. For further information on unscheduled ship departures from Bitung, visit the AGAPE/TERATAI at Bitung port. There are also 2 smaller ports in Manado itself. Close to the Pasar 45 terminal, off Jl Suprapto, and in the heart of town is Manado Port (Pelabuhan Manado). Ship offices line Jl Rumambi which leads to the port. Ships/boats leave from here for Palu, Toli Toli, Ternate, Sangir, Talaud, Pare Pare, Ambon and elsewhere. Finally, Singkil port is 1 km north of the city centre; boats from here go to Sangihe and Talaud. Get to the port by bemo from Pasar 45 terminal. For those requiring Visa extensions, there is no longer a *Pelni* ship to Davao in the Philippines. The alternative is to go to Bitung, where there is a container ship to General Santos leaving every Sat (US$40 return, US$30 single). Tickets from the *Fajarline Office* at the port.

Directory **Airline offices** *Bouraq*, Jl Serapung 27B, T862675; *Garuda*, Jl Diponegoro 15, T864535/862242; *Mandala Airlines*, Jl Sam Ratulangi 206, T851324, F863326; *Merpati*, the office has reportedly recently moved, T853213, 0730-1630 Mon-Fri, 0830-1500 Sat; *Silk Air*, Jl Serapung 5, T863744, F853841, or at the airport on T855440, 0830-1630 Mon-Fri, 0830-1300 Sat; *Sempati Air*, Jl Sam Ratulangi I, T851612. **Banks** *BII*, Jl Sam Ratulangi 18, T862108; *Bumi Daya*, Jl Dotulolong Lasut 9, T95122; *Central Asia*, Jl Dotulolong Lasut 6; *Indra Arta Money Changer*, Jl Sam Ratulangi 1 (in the

Sahid Kawanua Hotel); **PT Haji La Tunrung**, Jl Korengkeng 40 (money changer close to *Hotel Mini Cakale*); ***Rakyat Indonesia***, Jl Sudirman. **Communications** Collect calls can be made from the Wartel on Jl Sam Ratulangi. ***General Post Office***: Jl Sam Ratulangi 21, Poste Restante and very slow email, T852301. For *fast email* go to *Nikita's* on Jl Sam Ratulangi. ***Perumtel***: Jl Sam Ratulangi 4 (open 24 hrs), T852626. ***Warpostel***: Jl Walanda Maramis 81. **Medical facilities** *Hospital*: Rumah Sakit Umum Pusat Malalayang, T853285, located near the Malalayang bus terminal. **Useful addresses** *Immigration Office*: Jl 17 Augustus, T863491. *PHPA* (Nature Conservation Office): Jl Babe Palar 68, T62688. *Pelni Office*: Jl Sam Ratulangi 7, T862844, 860908, F867737.

Bunaken National Marine Park

The Bunaken National Marine Park (8 km offshore) is the principal destination for the majority of visitors to Northern Sulawesi. The park (75,265 ha) encompasses the five islands of Bunaken, Manado Tua (Old Manado), Montehage, Siladen and Nain. Each island is surrounded by mangrove and white sand beaches with coral reef flats (3m), dropping off to steep reef walls. The water temperature averages 28°C throughout the year, and visibility of up to 30m is common. The park has a wide range of corals and fish: marine biologists regard Bunaken as being within one of the richest and most diverse coral ecosystem zones in the world. Amongst the more spectacular marine life are barracuda, dolphins, colubrine sea snakes, killer whales and hawksbill turtles.

Colour map 5, grid A3

If your time is limited the following dives are recommended. Of course no sightings of pelagics etc can be guaranteed. **Liang Cove**, on the south side of Bunaken Island, is where the majority of day trip boats (diving, snorkelling, glass bottom) come for lunch, consequently there is a choice of places to eat and shop. Good snorkelling, canoes to rent from small boys, 15,000Rp. Unfortunately a lot of litter gets washed ashore here from the mainland. **Lekuan I, II & III**: common for starter and refresher dives. Shallow reef flats, dropping off to steep walls. Sheltered, limited current. **Fukui Point**: sloping coral garden, good samples of lettuce coral, and giant clams (15m), also good for schooling fish, jacks, manta rays and pelagics. **Sachiko Point**: wall dive, small cave at 5m, turtles. **Celah Celah**: good for night dive (10-20m), colourful sponges and plant growth, sleeping fish and hermit crabs. **Siladen**: for the first dive of the day (particularly as a lunch spot), explore the small island between dives, sleepy paradise. **Ship wreck**: in the bay opposite the *Barracuda Diving Club* (30-45m), Dutch cargo vessel sunk during the Second World War.

Visibility: the best months in terms of visibility are Jun & Jul

While Bunaken remains a wonderful dive site, there is some evidence of a lack

Bunaken National Marine Park

Dive sites
1. Batu Kapal
2. Barakuda Point
3. Bango Point
4. Manado Tua I
5. Manado Tua II
6. Tanjung Kopi
7. Raymond Point
8. Mike Point
9. Sachiko Point
10. Timur East
11. Siladen
12. Mandolin Point
13. Fukui Point
14. Alungbanua
15. Celah-Celah
16. Lekuan III
17. Lekuan II
18. Lekuan I
19. Depan Kampung

of full commitment to conservation and protection. One recent visitor highlighted the use of anchors and the absence of buoys, leading to the destruction of coral. He also noted that the rapid growth of losmen and bungalows on Bunaken and Manada Tua has not been accompanied by the installation of an effective refuse disposal system, leading to pollution of surrounding waters.

Sleeping

For dive centres & more information on accommodation & tours, see 'Sleeping' in the Manado entry

Accommodation within the marine park is available at 2 locations, on the east side of the island at Pangalisang Beach, or on the more sheltered west beach of Liang Cove. **NB** During the high season there may be a problem finding accommodation. Reps on the ferry may tell you that their's is the only hotel with space. It is likely, however, that they do not know whether there are rooms, so be prepared to scout around. **Pangalisang Beach C** *Lorenzo's*, next door to *Daniel's*, friendly place and very relaxed, family run, ask Pappa Lorenzo to play his bassoon. **C** *Seabreeze Homestay*, T8559379, F859368. At southern end of Pantai Pangalisang. Stylish bungalows, some built on cliff overlooking the water. Price includes 3 meals. Friendly and relaxed atmosphere. Owned by enlightened and entrepeneurial Thomas and run by his mother and family. **D** *MC's Homestay*, closest to Bunaken village, perhaps one of the best and newest with more bungalows under construction. Recommended. **D** *MDC*, south of *Daniel's Homestay*, the *'Manado Diving Club'* is very friendly, with helpful staff and 7 new rooms with their own terrace, and clean shared mandis and toilets. Price includes 3 meals (good food) and tea and coffee. **D** *Nelson's*, cottages and homestay. Suffers from another guidebook's recommendation, good food but often full. **D** *Papa Boa's*, friendly and well kept accommodation. Some with en suite bathrooms. **D-E** *Alung Barau Bungs*. Recommended. **D-E** *Backpacker Lodge*. **D-E** *Daniel's Homestay*, T866317. Generous meal servings, some rooms with verandah and private mandi, very popular. Many reports of poorly maintained equipment, so check carefully. **Liang Cove**: about 10 homestays here stretched out along the beach front, all with similar prices and includes 3 meals a day plus tea and coffee. **D-E** *Hardin's Homestay* is the best (to the left of the central pier), book through *Utama Aman Travel Agency*, Manado, T845805. The more expensive rooms are bamboo cottages on hillside with excellent views across the bay, rooms are small, with a verandah. It is also possible to arrange an overnight stay on *Manado Tua* from here. **D-E** *Mana Yulin's*. **D-E** *Tuwo Kona*.

Sports

Diving *Manado Diving Club*, *Scupan* and *Froggies* (although more expensive but good reports and equipment) provide the same type of diving packages, 2 dives for US$40-60 as well as snorkelling opportunities from their boat. *MDC* offers the open water PADI qualification for US$300 including 2 free dives, conscientious dive master.

Transport

Sea Boat: there is a daily public boat from Bunaken Village, at the southern tip of the island at 0700, 1 hr (5,000Rp). This vessel picks up from several points depending upon tides and demand; arrange pick-up the night before. Return boat leaves 1400 from Pasar Bersehati (close to Tondano River). Private charter for 30,000Rp is also available but be prepared to bargain hard. *Maya Express* travel agent will organize speedboats across to Bunaken for free if you are staying at the *Seabreeze Bungalows*.

Tangkoko Batu Angus National Park

Colour map 5, grid A3

This national park encompasses a comparatively small protected area covering just 8,867 ha of tropical rainforest, encompassing the peaks of Tangkoko (1,109m), Batuangus and Duasaudara, in the eastern part of Bitung. Duasaudara, the highest of the peaks at 1,351m, is a dormant volcano that last erupted in 1839. Tangkoko was first established as a forest reserve in 1919. The Reserve is home to several endemic species (see page 763), including the large-eyed jumping tarsier (*Tarsius spectrum*), the anoa or dwarf buffalo, bear cuscus, Sulawesi hornbill, black macaques, yaki (*Macaca nigra*), taon bird (*Rhiticeros cassidiz*), and the extraordinary and endangered maleo bird. Being a fairly small reserve, the chances of seeing an abundance of wildlife are high and the flora and fauna are rich. But the

Tangkoko Batu Angus National Park

Selected large mammals and birds of Tangkoko Batu Angus Nature Reserve, showing which are endemic and which are exploited by humans.

English name	Scientific name	Endemic	Hunted
Anoa	Bubalus depressicornis	Y	Y
Sulawesi pig	Sus celebensis	Y	Y
Javan rusa	Cervus timorensis	N	Y
Crested black macaque	Macaca nigra	Y	Y
Bear cuscus	Phalanger ursinus	N	Y
Babirusa	Babyrousa babirussa	Y	Y
Maleo	Macrocephalon maleo	Y	Eggs
Tabon scrubfowl	Megapodius cumingii	N	Eggs
Red junglefowl	Gallus gallus	N	Y
Red-knobbed hornbill	Aceros cassidix	Y	Y
Sulawesi tarictic hornbill	Penelopides exarhatus	Y	N

Source: O'Brien and Kinnaird, in Oryx30(2), 1996.

area surrounding the park is settled and the wildlife is under threat. In 1989, the Mackinnons estimated there were 15,000 crested black macaques in Tangkoko; in 1996, Timothy O'Brien and Margaret Kinnaird reckoned there were just 3,100. Trails into the park lead from Danowudu, where there is also a campsite. ■ *Admission to park 750Rp per day.*

The **trails** in the park are mostly well defined and hiking boots are not necessary. There are good early morning and evening walks in the forest from **Batuputih**, where most people stay. *En route* to Batuputih (sometimes confusingly referred to as Tangkoko), the road passes through Danowudu where there is a trail through a small (5 ha) protected reserve of rainforest, with around 30 rare species of bird.

Tours and guides Visitors must be accompanied by a guide, 20,000Rp for a morning walk to see black macaques, 15,000Rp for afternoon walk to see tarsiers. Tour companies in Manado run tours to the park.

Sleeping There is just 1 place inside the park, **D** *Cagar Alam*, right on the black sand beach. Alternatively stay at Batuputih (get park permit here), where there are 5 homestays (**E**), including *Mamma Rosa* and *Ranger's Homestay*; from here you can hire a forest ranger (10,000Rp). Recommended. There is a black sand beach nearby with excellent snorkelling.

Transport **Road Bus**: bus from Paal II terminal in Manado towards Bitung; get off at Girian (1,500Rp), from here board another bus or jeep to Batuputih (2,000Rp); the road can be difficult.

Bitung

Phone code: 0432
Colour map 5, grid A3

A *The Kungkungan Resort* is on the coast just north of the port of Bitung; run by an American, this small 'boutique' resort built out over the sea offers excellent service in an idyllic setting, good diving – although perhaps not as spectacular as Bunaken. ■ *Getting there: by bus from Paal II terminal in Manado to Bitung (1,500Rp).* Pelni Office: Jl D. Simulong 14, T21503, F22566.

The Sangihe and Talaud islands

These are two of 77 islands that comprise the district of Sangihe Talaud, which has a total population of over 260,000. **Tahuna**, on Sangihe Besar, is the capital. The islands were discovered by the Dutch in the 18th century. The economic mainstays of the area are farming and fishing, with the primary crops being coconut, nutmeg and cloves. The principal attraction of the islands are its **white sand beaches** and magnificent **sea gardens**.

One of Indonesia's rarest birds may still inhabit the Sangihe Islands – if it doesn't, then it is extinct. The Caeulean paradise fly-catcher (*Eutrichomyias rowleyi*) was first recorded for Western science in 1873 and this specimen is, in fact, the only example ever to have been collected. The conversion of much of the island to nutmeg and clove plantations is thought to have destroyed its habitat. But for those who might wish to try and catch the second example, it has a sky blue rump, while the wings and back are a deeper royal blue, and it has a black beak.

Sleeping *Nasional*, Jl Makaampo 58; *Tagaroa*, Jl Malahasa 1; *Veronica*, Jl Raramenusa 16, T79.

Festivals **Jan** (end of month) *Menulude*, a ceremony of Thanksgiving.

Shopping **Handicrafts** Ebony carvings and fine embroidery from Batunderang on Sangihe Besar.

Transport **Sea Boat**: boats leave from Pelabuhan Manado and also from Pelabuhan Singkil, about 1 km north of Manado's city centre (take a bemo from Pasar 45). The *Pelni* ship *Tilongkabila* docks at Tahuna and at Lirung on its fortnightly circuit through Sulawesi and Nusa Tenggara (see page 988 for route schedule). There are also jetfoils that go to Tahuna every Mon, Wed and Fri (4 hrs).

Background

Formerly known as the Celebes, Sulawesi is the third largest of the so-called Greater Sundas, with a land area of 189,216 sq km and a population of 13,000,000. The first use of the name by a European was by the Portuguese apothecary, secretary and accountant Tomé Pires who, in his journals written at the beginning of the 16th century, referred to the north tip of the island as Punta de Celebres. The origin of the word, though, is the subject of dispute. Some people have argued it is derived from the Bugis word Selihe, *meaning 'sea current', some that it is an amalgamation of* sula *('island') and* besi *('iron'), and still others that it is taken from* si-belih *('the one with more islands'). The modern name's origin is not disputed: it means 'Island of Iron'* (Sula-besi), *referring to the rich deposits of nickel-iron ore in the centre of the island. This ore furnished the iron – it is called Luwu iron – for the laminated krisses of Majapahit, famous across the region for their strength.*

History

The pre-colonial history of Sulawesi was focused upon the coastal regions of the south. Among a number of trading kingdoms which developed between the 13th and 15th century were the Bugis kingdoms of Luwu, Bone, Wajo and Soppeng and, most importantly, the Makassarese Kingdom of Gowa. Both the Bugis and the Makassarese had a reputation across the archipelago for fearlessness in battle.

At the beginning of the 16th century, Gowa, in alliance with the Bajau or sea nomads (not to be muddled with the Bugis), began to emerge as the dominant power in the area. They extended their influence over the neighbouring Bugis kingdoms and the commercial capital, Makassar, became an important trading centre. Perhaps the most important rulers were Tumapa 'risi' Kallonna, who forged the union of Gowa with the neighbouring kingdom of Tallo, and his successor Tunipalangga (reigned 1546-65), who continued his predecessor's legal, administrative and fiscal reforms. Tunipalangga also introduced cannon and built forts – a new innovation – and through his martial skills managed to overcome Banggai, Butung, Sula and Sumbawa. By the 17th century there were Dutch, English, Arab, Malay, Chinese and Indian seafarers striding the streets of Makassar and doing business in spices, slaves, birds' nests, Dammar resin, sandalwood and products of the sea such as trepang (edible sea cucumbers), pearls, shark's fin and ambergris (a waxy substance secreted by whales and used in perfumes).

Gowa was the last of the great kingdoms of Indonesia to accept Islam (at about the same time that European traders were beginning to establish godowns and factories there). In 1605 the King of Gowa accepted Islam, and when the subordinate kings of the Bugis states failed to follow suit, he staged a number of religiously-inspired military campaigns (1608-11). By the second decade of the 17th century, Gowa was at the head of the greatest Muslim trading empire in Southeast Asia.

Although the Dutch had established a trading post in south Sulawesi as early as 1609, they were never satisfied with the Gowa sultanate's tendency to allow the smuggling of spices from the Moluccas. By 1615, the VOC had closed down their trading post and limited military action had begun. Despite peace agreements in 1637, 1655 and 1660, conditions were brewing towards a major confrontation between Gowa and the Dutch.

Appreciating the military power of Gowa, the Dutch forged an alliance with the Bugis prince Arung Palakka of Bone. Like other Bugis leaders, Arung Palakka resented the domination of Gowa. In 1660, the Dutch attacked Gowa with the support of Arung Palakka and his men and forced Sultan Hasanuddin to sign a peace treaty. Sultan Hasanuddin chose to ignore the treaty, and in 1666 the VOC mounted a second expedition of 21 ships with Arung Palakka again in support. As the Dutch had hoped, the vassal Bugis kingdoms of Bone and Soppeng joined in the campaign against the Makassarese, and after a year of hard fighting on both land and sea, Sultan Hasanuddin was forced to capitulate and sign the Treaty of Bungaya on 18 November 1667. Again, Hasanuddin chose to ignore the treaty, forcing the Dutch to mount a third, and final, campaign against the duplicitous Sultan in April 1668. By June 1669, the Sultan of Gowa and his armies were finally vanquished.

Following the Dutch victory, Arung Palakka – upon whom the Dutch had depended for their success – became the *de facto* king of South Sulawesi. By all accounts, his rule was authoritarian and heavy-handed. The historian of Indonesia, RC Ricklefs, maintains that Arung Palakka's rule led to large numbers of Bugis and Makassarese fleeing Sulawesi. He writes: "They took to their ships like marauding Vikings in search of honour, wealth and new homes. They intervened in the affairs of Lombok, Sumbawa, Kalimantan, Java, Sumatra, the Malay Peninsula and even Siam". Arung Palakka finally died in 1696.

Minahasa in North Sulawesi was first visited by Europeans in 1524 when Magellan's fleet anchored there. Shortly afterwards in the 1560s, Portuguese missionaries were successful in converting the population to Christianity, and in 1568, Indonesia's oldest church – the Evangelical Church of Minahasa – was founded. The Spanish, from their colony in the Philippines, exerted control over Minahasa until 1643 when their attempt to place a half Spanish king on the throne led to the Minahasans turning to the Dutch for support.

In the interior, contact between the European powers and the various local groups was virtually non-existent. The Torajans, for example, were not brought under Dutch administrative control until the 20th century. After the Second World War, Dutch attempts to cling onto the East Indies led to greater bloodshed in Sulawesi than anywhere else in the archipelago. Even after independence in 1950, there were strong movements in the south and north for greater regional and religious autonomy. By 1958, only the larger towns of the south remained under government control, and between 1958 and 1961 there was a regional rebellion in Minahasa (see page 747).

The Bugis people of South Sulawesi have always had a reputation for being an adventurous people. (The same applies to the Makassarese and Butonese, also from

Sulawesi, who are sometimes lumped together with the Bugis – in typical Indonesian style – to create an ethnic concoction known as BBM.) Their prowess as seafarers is allied to an adaptability that has seen them successfully settle in their thousands in Java, Sumatra, Kalimantan, Nusa Tenggara and Maluku. But the recent communal violence in Indonesia has made the Bugis an unwelcome people in some areas. Many have returned 'home' to South Sulawesi, even though they have not lived there for years – sometimes, never. Nur Hasanah As'ad, a 16-year-old refugee from the inter-religious violence in Ambon, explained to Margot Cohen: "I don't feel Bugis. I feel like a Moluccan. I want to go back."

Land and environment

Geography

Sulawesi's strange shape is linked to its geological evolution. Studies have shown that the island is composed of two distinct halves – an east and a west portion. These only collided 15 million years ago when the process of continental drift – or tectonics – caused them to be thrust together. Like Java, Bali and Sumatra, Sulawesi is geologically unstable – altogether, the island has 11 active volcanoes, concentrated in the Minahasa area and north of Toli Toli.

But despite these complicated geological origins, Sulawesi is characteristically an island of uplands, cut through by deep rift valleys with short, fast-flowing rivers. Beyond a narrow coastal fringe, there are few areas of lowland and most of the island is above 450m in altitude. The highest peak is Mount Sonjol in the south (3,225m), although mountains throughout the four provinces exceed 2,500m in height.

Because of Sulawesi's mountainous character, overland communications are difficult, and it has only been since the late 1980s that an all-weather road has linked the north and the south. Even transport by sea is dangerous because of the treacherous reefs which ring the island. The generally inhospitable nature of the island, and in particular its inaccessibility and poor soils, led the English colonial envoy John Crawford to write of the indigenous inhabitants that "no one nation among them has emerged from the savage state to subjugate its neighbours, and take the lead in the march to civilization" (1820).

Climate

Seasonal variations in rainfall are less pronounced in Sulawesi than in many other parts of Indonesia. The wettest months are from December to February, and the driest are August and September. Because of the mountainous landscape, however, there are great differences in total rainfall between different areas. For example, while Manado in the far north has annual rainfall of 3,352mm and Makassar in the far south, 3,188mm; Palu in the centre receives only 533mm. As so much of the island is upland, temperature differences can be pronounced. In the Rantepao area, for example, temperatures at night regularly fall to below 10°C.

Flora and fauna

Because Sulawesi has diverse geological origins, encompasses a range of ecological zones, and because of the role that mountain barriers have played in restricting the migration of animals, the island has a fauna and flora which is not only quite unlike any other, but is also highly varied within the island itself. For example, there are seven species of macaques occupying different parts of the island, and two species and nine sub-species of carpenter bee. It is, in short, a naturalist's dream come true.

Of the 127 mammal species, an incredible 79 (62%) are endemic (ie found nowhere else); if bats are excluded, this rises to 98%. Even among birds, 88 of the 328

A Noah's ark: endemic animals of Sulawesi

Curly-tusked babirusa (Babyrousa babyrussa): *as the name suggests – it means 'pig-deer' – naturalists have found this animal hard to classify. Described first by Piso in 1658, they are usually grouped with pigs but have no near common ancestor because they have evolved in isolation for 30,000,000 years. Most distinctively, the upper canines grow through the animal's lips and curl upwards towards the head. Confused early naturalists thought these tusks were used to hook onto trees when the animal was exhausted; now the received wisdom is that they are used as sparring weapons when males fight during the breeding season.*

Anoa (Bubalus depressicornis and B quarlesi): *these are both dwarf buffalo – about the size of a large dog – but are the largest indigenous mammals on Sulawesi. They are renowned for their ferocity, and have not been tamed for captivity despite attempts by the Torajans and others.*

Bear cuscus (Phalanger ursinus and P celebensis): *these animals look rather like sloths and are related to the possums of Australia. They are arboreal and use their prehensile tails as a fifth limb.*

Black-crested macaques (Macaca nigra): *there are four species of macaque found in Sulawesi, but only M nigra has been studied by scientists. They are arboreal, foraging in the upper canopy, and live in groups of up to about 50.*

Large-eyed jumping tarsier (Tarsius spectrum): *this is one of the world's smallest primates, with a body length of not more than 10cm and a weight of 100g. They are nocturnal and form long-standing monogamous relationships. A new species, Tarsius diana, has recently been discovered.*

Maleo (Macrocephalon maleo): *perhaps Sulawesi's most famous animal, this bird incubates its eggs in holes dug in the sun-baked ground.*

Red-knobbed hornbill (Rhyticeros cassadix): *like other hornbills, the red-knobbed hornbill incubates its eggs in hollow trees. They are solitary, monogamous birds, and are only rarely seen in flocks.*

Source: Whitten, AJ et al (1988) The ecology of Sulawesi, *Gajah Mada University Press: Yogyakarta*. Whitten, Tony and Whitten, Jane (1992) Wild Indonesia, *New Holland: London*.

species so far identified are endemic to the island. The same degree of endemism is also true of amphibians, reptiles and insects. Alfred Russel Wallace, the Victorian naturalist, wrote down his first ideas on evolution after visiting Manado in North Sulawesi, and his letters to Charles Darwin in England prompted Darwin to publish the *Origin of species*.

Given the uniqueness of Sulawesi's fauna, conservation takes on particular importance. The IUCN Red Data Books record that 19 species are endangered; but because of the generally poor knowledge of the island and its wildlife, the true figure is probably much higher. For example, the Caerulean paradise fly-catcher (*Eutrichomyias rowleyi*) was discovered in 1873 by the German ornithologist AB Meyer. Since then, not a single example has been captured, and it is not even known whether the original specimen was male or female. The reason why so much of Sulawesi's unique fauna is threatened is due not so much to hunting as to habitat loss. Tony Whitten reported at the end of the 1980s that 67% of productive wet lowland forest (ie 'rainforest') had disappeared; today it must be three-quarters or more.

Sulawesi

West Nusa Tenggara: Lombok and Sumbawa

West Nusa Tenggara: Lombok and Sumbawa

768	**Lombok**	803	**Sumbawa**
768	Ins and outs	804	Alas
771	Ampenan – Mataram – Cakranegara	804	Taliwang
		805	Maluk
777	Lombok's west coast	805	Sumbawa Besar
782	The Gilis	808	Moyo Island
789	Northwest coast and Mount Rinjani	809	Mount Tambora
792	Central Lombok and the West	810	Sumbawa Besar to Bima-Raba
		810	Dompu
795	East Lombok	810	Hu'u
795	South Lombok and the south coast	811	Bima-Raba
800	Background	813	Sape

Lombok has been earmarked for tourist development for well over a decade, on the pretext that it is in a position to emulate Bali's success. Whether the development plans will ever come to fruition is another matter and for the time being it remains a relatively quiet alternative to Bali, although considerably busier and more developed than the islands to the east. While there are a number of first class hotels along the beaches (and several more under construction), away from these tourist areas, Lombok is still 'traditional' and foreigners are a comparative novelty. It is also a poor island; the famines of the Dutch period and the 1960s remain very much in the collective consciousness.

Most visitors to Lombok stay on Senggigi Beach, on the west coast and just north of the capital Mataram, or on the 'Gilis', a small group of islands north of Senggigi. However, the south coast, around Kuta, with its beautiful sandy bays set between rocky outcrops, is more dramatic. There is now a surfaced road to Kuta and some good accommodation once you get there, including one international class hotel (but be aware that plans are afoot to continue this tourist development). There are also a handful of towns inland with accommodation. While Lombok has gradually expanded over the years, it has not yet 'taken off' – which, of course, is why some people prefer it to Bali. Grand plans have been thwarted at every step and the tourist industry is currently facing a serious downturn, related to Indonesia's political problems in general and, more particularly, the widely publicized communal violence on Lombok in January 2000.

Lombok

Ins and outs

Getting there

Air **Selaparang Mataram Airport** lies north of Mataram and 20 minutes south of Senggigi Beach. There are multiple daily connections on Merpati and Bouraq with **Denpasar** between 0800 and 1700 and regular connections (on *Merpati*) with destinations in Java, Sumatra and most towns in Nusa Tenggara, including **Sumbawa Besar** and **Bima-Raba** (Sumbawa); **Labuanbajo**, **Bajawa**, **Ende** and **Maumere** (Flores); **Waingapu** and **Waikabubak** (Sumba); and **Kupang** (West Timor). Talk of upgrading the airport to international status has still not come to anything. *Sempati* is no longer running as the assets of the Suharto régime remain frozen. *Garuda* is the only airline to offer direct connections with **Jakarta**. **Airport facilities**: a money changer (for US$ travellers cheques only and cash), information office and hotel booking counters. **Transport to town**: fixed-fare (non a/c) taxis to Senggigi Beach (12,000Rp), Mataram (7,000Rp), Kuta (36,000Rp) and Bangsal (22,000Rp). Bemos to Ampenan and Mandalika terminal in Sweta are available from the main road, 200m from the airport (500Rp). For Bangsal, you need to take a public bus towards Tanjung and ask to be dropped off at Pemenang. These are available 500m from the airport, to the left. When you reach the first crossroads, turn left and wait for your bus connection. **International connections**: at present the only direct international connections are a daily flight to **Singapore** with *Silk Air*. There were plans to build a new airport 40 minutes drive south of Mataram in the Praya area. The site has been fenced off, though it could be years before construction gets under way and locals believe it has been cancelled.

Lombok Island

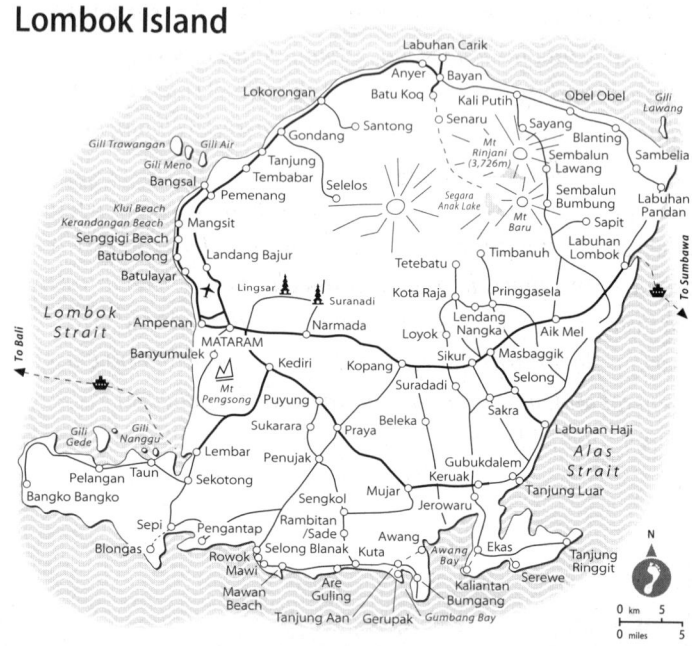

Lombok highlights

Temples The **Mayura Water Palace and Gardens** (page 771) is the largest temple complex on Lombok; other significant historical sights include **Taman Narmada** (page 792) and **Suranadi** (page 793).
Beaches The main beach resort area is Senggigi (page 777), while the Gilis (page 782) and Kuta (page 796) cater largely to budget travellers.
Natural sights Mount Rinjani dominates the island and can be climbed in 3-4 days (page 790).
Culture and performance Traditional villages in the centre (page 792) and south (page 795).
Sports Diving and snorkelling off the Gilis (page 782), Kuta for surfing (page 796).
Shopping Traditional **ikat** textiles from Pringgasela (page 794) and from workshops in Mataram (page 771) and **basketry** from Kota Raja (page 793).

Bus *Perama*, 66 Jl Pejanggik 66, Mataram, T635936 and 635928, and *Wannen* (also called *Nomad*), 4 Jl Erlangga Mataram, T631177, both operate shuttle buses geared to foreign requirements from Bali to Lombok. They both serve **Mataram, Senggigi Bangsal, Kuta, Lembar**. *Nomad* includes the boat trip to the Gilis, *Perama* goes to Tetebatu.

Road

There are shuttle buses from Bali, and buses to major destinations in Java, and also east to Sumbawa; *Damai Indah*, Jl Hasanuddin 17, Cakranegara (for Bali and Surabaya); *Karya Baru*, Jl Pejanggik, Mataram (for Surabaya, Bandung and Jakarta). A/c buses travel from Mataram to Bima (on Sumbawa) via Sumbawa Besar. Companies that operate this route include *Tirta Sari*, *Langsung Jaya* and *Mawar Indah*, all with offices on Jl Pejanggik. Prices for bus fares from Mataram are set by the government. There are bus connections with: **Jakarta, Bandung, Yogyakarta, Surabaya, Komodo, Labuhanbajo, Ruteng, Denpasar, Sumbawa Besar, Dompu, Bima** and **Sape**. Price includes ferry tickets. The journey from Mataram to Sumbawa Besar is 6½ hours, and to Bima 12 hours. Most buses leave from the Bertais terminal in Cakranegara. At your destination these buses will drop you off at the point along their route closest to your accommodation, you don't have to continue to the terminal. Likewise you can arrange to be picked up from your hotel.

Catamaran *Mabua Express* operate a round trip from Benoa (Bali) to **Lembar** on an a/c boat with aircraft seats and 'in-flight' video (two daily from Dec to Jan and Jul to Aug, twice a week only in low season). The journey takes 2 hrs (US$20-30 depending on class). Departs Benoa 0800 and 1430, returns from Lembar 1130 and 1730. Booking advised, T0361-672370, F672521 on Bali or Lembar, T625895, F637224. Office at Jl Langko 11A, T621655, Mataram and on Senggigi Beach (opposite turning to *Senggigi Beach Hotel*). Bemos link Lembar with the Bertais bus terminal and with Mataram and Ampenan. The *Bounty Cruises* depart daily from Benoa, Bali at 0800 and return at 1600 from Lembar, offering similar service of videos and a/c.

Sea

Ferry Ferries sail every 2 hrs (on even hrs), linking **Lembar** (22 km south of Mataram on the west coast) with Padangbai, near Candi Dasa on Bali 4-4½ hrs (5,500-9,000Rp depending on class); arrive 30 mins early for a seat and expect to add on an hr here and there waiting to dock.

Accommodation at Lembar There are several losmen popular with backpackers offering basic accommodation near the port. **E** *Losmen Sri Wahyu*, Jl Pusri. Just over 1 km north of Lembar off the main road; follow the sign. Basic bungalows, squat toilets. Owners can arrange boat hire to some of the islands off the southwest peninsula including Gili Nanggu, Gili Genting, Gili Tangkong, all just to the west of Lembar, and Gili Gede and Gili Poh further to the west. **E** *Serumbung Indah*, 2 km north of the port on main road, T637153. Basic rooms with shared mandi.

From Lembar, bemos run to Mataram, Ampenan and the Bertais bus terminal, east of Mataram (for onward connections); for other destinations, it is easier to charter a bemo (for example, a large proportion of the people arriving at Lembar head straight for Bangsal, to catch a boat to the Gilis). There is a ferry linking Labuhan Lombok, on Lombok's east coast,

Hang onto your luggage & bargain hard: the bemo drivers here are tough negotiators

with **Poto Tano** on Sumbawa's west coast. Boats leave Poto Tano hourly from 0330-1630 and at 1830. They leave Lombok on the hr from 0400-2100. This is a very pleasant 2 hr boat trip and boats are rarely crowded. The *Pelni* ship *Awu* docks at Lembar on its fortnightly circuit through Java, Kalimantan, Sumatra, Sulawesi and the islands of Nusa Tenggara. *Tilongkabila* also visits monthly *en route* for Sulawesi and the Philippines. The *Pelni* office is in Ampenan, Jl Industri 1, T37212.

Getting around

Lombok's main artery is the excellent road running east from Mataram to Labuhan Lombok. There is now a paved road to Lembar, Praya, Kuta and to Bangsal in the north. Most of Lombok's roads are paved, but the secondary roads are not well maintained and car travel can be slow and uncomfortable, not to mention the hazards of potholes and random rocks for motorcyclists. However, this is likely to change over the next few years as tourism expands.

Bus
See also information on buses in 'Getting there' section above

Minibuses (called bemos here) and colts are the main forms of inter-town and village transport. It is a good cheap way to get around the island and, unlike Bali, frequent changes of bemo are not necessary to get from A to B. However, they can be crowded and beware of being overcharged – check with losmen owners or other travellers before boarding. Foreigners may find it difficult to pay the local rate, particularly going to and from Lembar. The transport hub of Lombok is the Bertais terminal, 3 km east of Cakranegara (see page 776).

Other land transport

Hiring Greatest selection and availability at Senggigi Beach. Generally the cost of hiring transport is higher than on Bali and the vehicles are not as good. You may find it difficult to get insurance. Check everything works before you set off, including the windscreen wipers and the spare tyre. **Cars**: from 50,000-60,000Rp/day; **Bicycles**: 5,000Rp/day; **Motorbikes**: 25,000Rp/day.

Cidomos These are the Lombok equivalent of the *dokar*, a two-wheeled horse-drawn cart. The word is said to be an amalgamation of *cikar* (a horse cart), *dokar* and automobile (because they now have pneumatic tyres). In the west, cidomos are gradually being replaced by bemos, but in the less developed central and east they remain the main mode of local transport and are more elaborate, with brightly coloured carts and ponies decked out with pompoms and bells.

Tours
Most tour companies have their offices in Mataram, although there are also some at Senggigi. They tend to run variations on the tours described below:
Southern tour to Sukarara (weaving village), Penujak (pottery village), Kuta Beach, Sengkol, Sade and Rambitan ('traditional' Sasak villages), Narmada (Summer Palace) and the Lingsar Temple.
Northern tour to Landang Bajur Market, Bali Kuku temple, Pusuk, Sendang Gile and Senaru ('taditional' Sasak village).
Gili Air tour to a Chines cemetery, Bangsal Beach and Ledang Bajur Market, Gili Air (for snorkelling), and Batubolong.
Tetebatu tour to Narmada, Loyok (rattan village) and Tetebatu.
Mount Rinjani trek up Mount Rinjani (1-3 nights).
Komodo Island, 3-4 days.
Island Adventures (up to a week) taking in the less visited islands of Kalong, Moyo, Satonda, Banta, Laba, Rinca, ending in Flores. T0370-626658.
Alternative tours Environmental Forum, Jl Pejanggik 10B, Cakranegara. This agency specializes in arranging stays in traditional Sasak villages so that visitors can experience village life and customs at first hand.

Safety

Riots and unrest broke out in Lombok in January 2000. Chinese-owned businesses were ransacked in Mataram and thousands of tourists, Chinese and Christians fled the island for Bali. All locals, whether Muslim, Christian or Hindu, were consciously trying to put foreigners at ease during mid-2000.

Ampenan – Mataram – Cakranegara

Mataram, the capital of Lombok, comprises the three towns of Ampenan, Mataram and Cakranegara (usually called Cakra). The boundaries between them have all but disappeared in an urban sprawl which stretches for almost 9 km, from west to east, ending at the bus terminal of Bertais.

Phone code: 0370
Population: 250,000

The port town of Ampenan in the west is of some interest. It has a characterful collection of small streets which include Malay, Arab and Chinese districts, a decaying collection of Dutch-era buildings, and considerable port activity. However, it does have a rather ramshackle, seedy feel. There are a few 'antique' shops, a market and towards the northern edge there is a Chinese cemetery. Mataram has a number of rather grand government buildings and is attractively laid out with broad, tree-lined streets and numerous gardens.

Cakranegara, the former royal capital, was the site of the battle between the Balinese king of Lombok and the Dutch in 1894, during which the palace was badly shelled (see below and page 800). These days, Cakra is the bustling, and in places rather ugly business district, but it also has the best selection of accommodation and shops. People here are very helpful and friendly, and will go out of their way to help you find what you are looking for.

Ins and outs

See page 768.

Getting there

There is a 1-way road system linking the 3 towns of the 'conurbation'. Bemos run across the city, travelling east down Jl Langko/Pejanggik and Selaparang to the bus terminal, and west down Jl Pancawarga/Pendidikan and Jl Yos Sudarso to Ampenan.

Getting around
See also Transport section, page 776, for more details

Sights

The regional **tourist office** for West Nusa Tenggara is on Jl Langko 70, T21866. They have maps and brochures and are friendly and helpful. ■ *0700-1400 Mon-Thu, 0700-1100 Fri, 0700-1200 Sat.*

Most of the conurbation's few sights are in Cakranegara, in the east of town. The description below runs from west to east

The **West Nusa Tenggara Provincial Museum** is in Ampenan on Jl Banjar Tilar Negara, at the west end of town. It houses a collection of assorted regional textiles and krisses. ■ *500Rp. 0800-1400 Tue-Thu, 0800-1100 Fri, 0800-1300 Sat-Sun.* Travelling east into Mataram, there are a number of **weaving factories** producing ikat cloth, although rarely in traditional designs. *Rinjani Hand Woven* on Jl Pejanggik was established in 1948 and tends to produce cotton textiles for the Balinese market, using motifs from Sulawesi, Bali and the other islands of Nusa Tenggara as well as Lombok. Behind the shop is a large weaving operation where the various processes can be seen. There is also a number of other factories in this area of town: *Slamet Riyadi Weaving* (which produces Balinese-style cloth) is on Jl Tenun, a narrow back street near the Mayura Water Palace (see below), while the well-known *Sari Kusuma* is at Jl Selaparang 45, in Cakranegara.

To the east, the **Mayura Water Palace and Gardens** and associated Pura Mayura just north of Jl Selaparang were built in 1744 by the Balinese king of Lombok. The Gardens contain a water lily-filled lake, with a floating pavilion – the *Bale Kembang* – set in the centre. The king would conduct audiences here, and originally there were tiers of wooden benches for officials of different grades. These were destroyed in 1894 during the Dutch assault on Cakranegara and have not been replaced, the *Bales Wedas* within the Palace was used to store weapons. ■ *500Rp. 0700-1700.* Across the road to the east of the Gardens is the Balinese **Pura Mayura**, also known as the **Pura Meru**. This temple was built in 1720 by Anak Agung Made Karang and is dedicated to the Hindu trinity – Siva, Vishnu and Brahma. It is composed of three courtyards symbolizing the cosmos. The innermost contains three symbolic Mount Merus, aligned north-south; the central court, two pavilions with raised platforms for displaying offerings; and the outermost, a hall containing a large ceremonial drum. The 11-tiered meru is dedicated to Siva, and the nine-tiered merus to the south and north, Brahma and Vishnu respectively. ■ *Mon-Sun. Admission by donation.*

Right at the eastern edge of the town is Lombok's main **market** (see 'shopping'), next to the Bertais bus terminal on Jl Selaparang. Also here is the Cakranegara **bird market**. **Horse racing** takes place at the Selagalas track, on Jl Gora, north of the Water Palace, twice a week on Thursday and Sunday from 0800 to 1200 and at festivals. The ponies are ridden bare-back by young boys. During Ramadan, traditional **stick fighting** can be seen: a mix of graceful turns and harsh clashing of sticks against square shields of buffalo hide.

Excursions

Mount Pengsong Mount or Gunung Pengsong lies about 6 km south of Mataram. There is a small Hindu shrine at the summit and, on clear days, good views over to Bali and Mount Agung and to Mount Rinjani. Japanese solders hid here during the Second World War. Get there by chartered bemo or cidomo.

The Southwest Peninsula This rugged, arid region offers spectacular views and beautiful, deserted gold sand beaches to the few travellers who venture this way. It is an arduous drive over rough, potholed roads covering approximately 70 km. The sea here is covered with many *bagans* – fishing platforms made of bamboo which the local fishermen use for night fishing, attracting fish into their large nets with powerful lanterns. The area is sparsely inhabited, mostly scrubby with coconut and mangrove along the coast. The road ends at Bangko-Bangko.

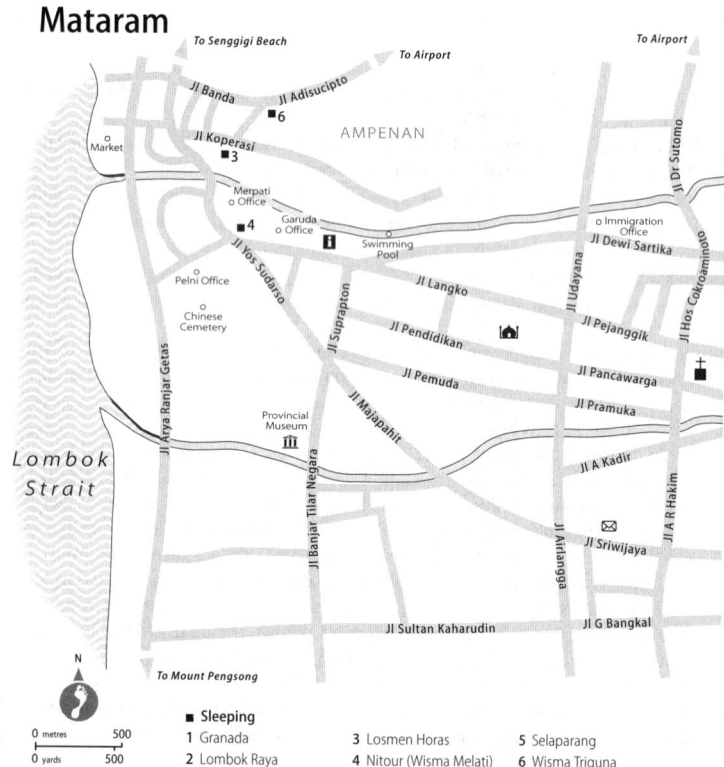

Mataram

Related map Mataram centre, page 774

■ Sleeping
1 Granada
2 Lombok Raya
3 Losmen Horas
4 Nitour (Wisma Melati)
5 Selaparang
6 Wisma Triguna

Bangko-Bangko

This sandy beach is 63 km from Mataram, past the harbour of **Lembar**, on the south-west tip of the island. It is a long drive on a poor road. There is sometimes surf here: this is a reef break. There is limited accommodation in bungalows and food. Hiring a jeep is the best way to get there, and in Kute the *Ocean Blue* surf shop, T/F0370-653911, and other helpful surf lovers, will gladly arrange a trip out there and get provisions in. You might be able to get a lift on a truck heading down the coast. As the road improves, bemos may begin to make the trip. On the way to Bangko-Bangko, the road passes **Taun**, with a good, white sandy beach (42 km from Mataram). **Pelangan** (47 km from Mataram) has a good beach and good snorkelling. From here you can catch a public boat to Gili Gede; **Labunan Poh** (55 km from Mataram), with a Japanese-run pearl farm nearby, is a coastal village from where it is possible to reach **Gili Poh** (good for snorkelling) and **Gili Gede** (a traditional Sasak island).

Gili Nanggu

One hour by chartered fishing boat from Lembar (30,000Rp), Gili Nanggu is another tiny, but very attractive, island in this group which offers the perfect restful hideaway. (For boat hire to the islands, ask around at Lembar harbour. Current rates are about 30,000Rp for two people, see also page 769. The owners of the Sri Wahyu Losmen can make arrangements for boat hire.) There is only one place to stay by the sea, **C** *Istana Cempaka*, Reservations: Jl Tumpang Sari, Cakranegara, Lombok, T622898. Very attractive bungalows on beach with private mandi, price includes breakfast, restaurant serves good freshly caught fish: very friendly Balinese owner who does not want to develop the island. It takes 30 minutes to walk around the island. Reasonable snorkelling. There is also basic losmen accommodation (**E**) in the village.

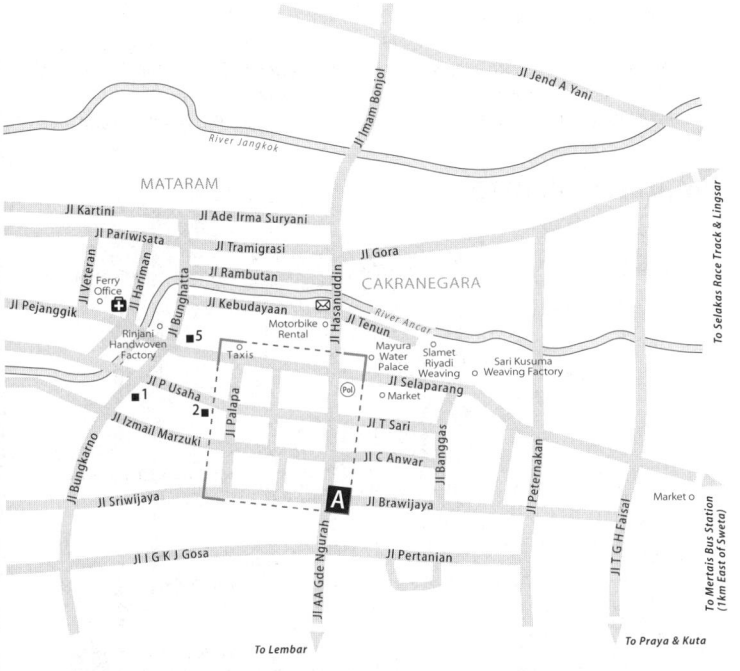

Essentials

Sleeping
■ on maps, pages 772 & 774
Price codes: see inside front cover

The best selection of accommodation for travellers is in Cakra. Several small hotels and guesthouses are located in a pretty residential area of quiet lanes leading off Jl Pejanggik.

Ampenan B *Nitour (Wisma Melati)*, Jl Yos Sudarso 4, T623780, F636579. A/c, comfortable rooms, hot water and Western toilets, small garden, breakfast on verandah, rather overpriced, will offer substantial discount if they are not full. **C-E** *Hotel Zahir*, Jl Koperasi 32, T644485, variety of rooms nothing special, but has internet access. **E** *Wisma Triguna*, Jl Koperasi 76, T631705. Restaurant, basic large rooms with private bathrooms with Western toilet, could do with redecoration but good source of trekking information, set around large courtyard garden. **F** *Losmen Horas*, Jl Koperasi, a few doors down from *Hotel Zahir*, T631695, basic but decent, Eddy will arrange tours and treks. **D-E** *Wisata*, Jl Koperasi. Restaurant, a/c, smart grounds, good little on-site shop. **F** *Angin Mamiri*, the last losmen on Jl Koperasi, T631713. A slightly bizarre, ramshackle place, but a good chance to stay with an extended family who are very friendly. Not a word of English spoken, though.

Mataram If you require a mini pool and/or meeting room, there are a couple of upmarket hotels: **B** *Hotel Granada*, Jl Bung Karno, T622275, F623856. Small pool, meeting rooms and other business facilities. **B** *Hotel Sahid Legi*, Jl Sriwijaya, T636282, F632681. Small pool and reasonably comfortable business style hotel. **C** *Hotel Nitour*, Jl Yos Sudarso, T625328. Good coffee shop, poor pool. **C-E** *Paradiso*, Jl Angsoka 3, T632074. Just off the main street of Mataram is this newly opened place with a leafy residential feel, spacious courtyard, TV, conference room, breakfast. Good value. There are several cheap losmen on Jl Pancawarga. **D** *Wisma Giri Putri*, Jl Pancawarga 29, T633222. Some a/c, attractive house, clean rooms, lofty stark restaurant.

Cakranegara A *Lombok Raya Hotel*, 11 Jl Panca Usaha, T632305, F636478. Attractive hotel with large pool set in tropical gardens, 135 rooms with a/c. Conference rooms, restaurant (mid-range to cheap). The Garuda office is in the lobby. **B** *Granada*, Jl Bung Karno, T622275, F623856. A/c, restaurant, pool, best hotel in the area, attractive tropical gardens and aviary, good rooms with adequate services. **B-D** *Handika*, Jl Panca Usaha 3, T633578, F635049. Some a/c, reasonable restaurant, poor breakfast included in price, rooms are standard but clean, rates negotiable, central location, friendly staff. **B-D** *Hotel Pesaban*, 30 Jl

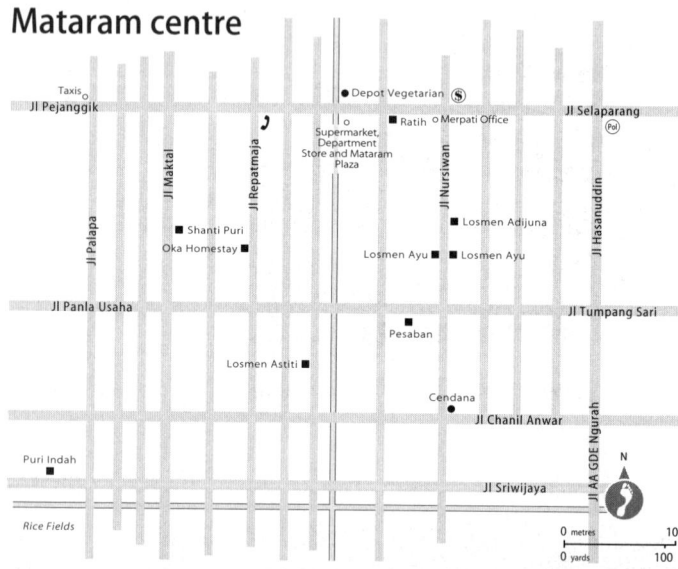

Mataram centre

Panca Usaha, T621378, 632936. Large, clean rooms with private bathrooms, all with squat toilets, set in attractive gardens. Price includes tax and breakfast. Restaurant (cheap). **B-D** *Hotel Ratih*, 127 Jl Pejanggik, T631096, 626269, 626444, F624865. Mainly geared to Indonesian businessmen, 43 simple rooms with private bathrooms, Western toilet, a/c or fan. Set in large gardens. **C** *Mataram*, Jl Pejanggik 105, T623411. Some a/c, price includes breakfast. **C-D** *Puri Indah*, 132 Jl Sriwijaya, T637633. Pleasant location on the outskirts of town. 30 simple rooms with private bathroom, shower, Western toilet, some rooms with a/c and TV. Decent sized pool and large gardens. This hotel suffered fire damage in the violent demonstrations of 17 January 2000, and at the time of writing had not re-opened. **C-E** *Ayu*, Jl Nursiwan 20, T621761. Set around attractive courtyard, basic rooms with mandi, squat toilet, more expensive newer rooms across the road with Western toilet and fan or a/c, Balinese owner, price includes breakfast. **C-E** *Orinda*, close to Mertais Bus Terminal on Jl TLH Faisal, T624900. Friendly staff, clean rooms with showers, and a good restaurant. **C-E** *Shanti Puri*, Jl Maktal 15, T632649. Well run travellers' hotel with a range of rooms from basic with shared mandi and squat toilet, up to a/c or fan with Western toilet; rooms with balcony or verandah. Owner speaks good English and can help with travel information. Price includes breakfast and afternoon tea. Restaurant (cheap). Recommended. **D** *Selaparang*, Jl Pejanggik 40-42, T632670. Some a/c, clean, reasonable rooms. **E** *Adiguna Losmen*, 9 Jl Nursiwan, T625946 (behind BCA bank). 20 simple rooms with private mandi, squat toilet, set in small gardens. Price includes a good breakfast and afternoon tea/coffee. **E** *Oka Homestay*, 5 Jl Rapatmaja, T622406. A genuine homestay in the grounds of the family house, down a quiet side street off the main Cakra thoroughfare. 5 simple rooms with private mandi, squat toilet and fan. Set in large gardens full of birds and fruit trees. Price includes breakfast and tea/coffee all day. Run by a very friendly family whose son, Mut, speaks excellent English and has lived in Australia. They sometimes arrange BBQs and can help with information and travel advice. Often full, even off-season. Highly recommended.

Eating

Cheap *Cirebon*, Jl Yos Sudarso 113. Ampenan, Chinese and seafood, very popular. *Aroma*, Jl Palapa 1. Good atmosphere, good food. *Timur Tengah*, Jl Koperasi, T623073. Yummy, easy food and a good *nasi goreng*. *Flamboyant*, Jl Pejanggik 101. Seafood, with attractive ambience. *Depot Vegetarian*, Jl Pejanggik, opposite Mataram Plaza. Serves good, cheap Indonesian and Chinese food, includes meat. **Very cheap** *RM Cendana*, Jl Nurgiwan, Cakra. Clean, conveniently located near travellers' losmen. *Pondok Indah garden restaurant*, Jl Sriwijayah 2. Lovely berugas in neat garden, popular with courting Indonesians, does a tasty *es jampur* (multi-coloured jelly in milk and ice, with palm fruit). *Warungs*, opposite *Astiti Guesthouse* in Cakranegara. *Café Inilah*, Jl Panca Usaha, T641016. Popular with locals. Each warung has a different speciality and you sit inside a tent at a long wooden table. Friendly place, delicious food. Recommended. There are several warungs along Jl Yos Sudarso, in Ampenan, and scattered down side streets in Cakra and Mataram. You may have to look carefully to spot one as they often look like private homes: eg *Depot Sari* Jl Rapatmaja, which produces great *gado-gado*; *Kentucky Fried Chicken*, Cakra Plaza, Jl Pejanggik; *Selaparang*, Jl Pejanggik, next to *Rinjani's Weaving*.

Festivals

Mar/Apr (Date varies): *Balinese Hindu New Year*, stone statues called *Ogoh Ogoh* are paraded through the streets to the Water Palace. Later they are burnt at the beach for purification, but some people can't resist taking them home instead. (16th): *Anniversary of Mataram* is marked by parades and performances. **May** (5th): *Hindu rice harvest festival*. **Jun** *Pura Meru festival*. **Aug** (17th): *Independence Day*. **Oct** (5th): *War memorial*. **Nov/Dec** (15th day of the 4th month of the Balinese lunar calendar): *Pujawali* held at Pura Meru in Cakranegara, at Pura Kalasa (Narmada) and at Pura Lingsar (north of Cakra). The Pujawali ceremony is followed 3 days later by the *ketupat war*, when participants throw *ketupat* (steamed rice wrapped in palm leaves) at one another. **Dec** (17th): *Anniversary of West Nusa Tenggara* is celebrated with dance and wayang kulit performances.

Shopping

Antiques: there are a number of shops in Ampenan on the road north towards Senggigi, most with rather poor quality merchandise. Despite the layer of authentic dust, virtually none of the pieces on sale is antique. The original shop on this strip was **Sudirman**, Jl Yos Sudarso 88; close by is **Hary Antiques**, Jl Saleh Sungkar Gg Tengiri 2. **Renza Antique**, Jl Sudarso 29, for pottery and antiques. Antique kris spears and good information from knowledgeable family – contact Putu Mustika, Jl Tambanus 9, T633301. **Baskets**: the market next to the Mertais bus terminal (east of town) on Jl Selaparang sells local products, including baskets. **Handicrafts**: *Lombok Asli*, Jl Gunung Kerinci 36 (near the University); *Lombok Craft Project*, Jl Majapahit 7, T633804; *Pandawa*, Jl Ismail Marzuki; *Sidhu Putra*, Jl Gora 36, Cakranegara. **Markets**: Cakra market has everything from Calvin Klein's to bananas and counterfeit tapes. Sindu cheap crafts and blankets from all over Lombok. The (Sweta) Bertais market has everything including the kitchen sink. A real mix of aromas and sights, with a bird section to add some sound effects. **Pottery**: *Lombok Pottery Centre*, Jl Majapahit 7 (near the museum) T/F633804. This shop/showroom stocks some of the best earthenware goods produced in the village of Banyumulek, one of the main pottery centres on the island. *Sasak Pottery*, Jl Koperasi 102 (5 mins from airport), T631687, F31121. The largest pottery company on Lombok which also houses, so it is said, the largest earthenware showroom in Indonesia. The company also operates several hotel-based shops, and oversees the packing side of its business for shipment overseas. **Supermarket**: *Galael's*, Cakra Plaza Blok B, Jl Pejanggik. *Mataram Supermarket*, Jl Pejanggik 139B, well stocked, competitive prices. A huge megalith of a shopping mall is due to open near Bertais, providing there is no more civil unrest. A number of investors, particularly in agricultural commodities, have pulled out of Lombok since January 2000. **Textiles**: *Rinjani Hand Woven*, Jl Pejanggik 46, good value cotton and silk, ikat. Other weaving shops including *Sari Kusuma*, Jl Separang 45, and *Slamet Riyadi*, Jl Tenun 10, off Jl Hassanudin. Weaving demonstrations in the mornings.

Sports **Diving companies** *Corona*, Jl Dr W Rambige, Mataram; *Rinjani*, Jl Pemuda, Mataram, T621402; *Satriavi*, Jl Pejanggik 17, Mataram, T621788; *Koperasi Wisata Rinjani*, Jl Pedidikan 25, Mataram, T635040; *CV Baronang Dive Centre*, Jl Mawar 13, T627793. *The Water Boom* waterpark is now open in Mataram with slides and rapids, 10000Rp. **Horse racing** Every Sun at Selagalas village, 4 km from Mataram. **Golf** *Golong Golf Course* (east of Narmada), 9 holes, charmingly informal. Office: Jl Langko 27, Mataram, T22017. **Massage** *Subur Jaya* (ask at Oka Homestay) is a good bet with guaranteed no wandering hands. **Pool and tennis** Available at Taman Mayura.

Tour operators *Bidy Tours*, Jl Ragigenep 17, T632127. *Environmental Forum*, Jl Pejanggik 10B. *Mavista*, Jl Pejanggik Complek, Mataram, T622314. *Nominasi*, Jl Dr Wahidin 3, T621034. *Peramaswara*, Jl Pejanggik 66, T623368, 622764. *Putri Mandalika*, Jl Pejanggik 49, T622240. *Sakatours*, Jl Langko 7-8, T623114. *Satriavi*, Jl Pejanggik 17, T621788. *Setia*, Jl Pejanggik. *Wisma Triguna*, Jl Adisucipto 76, Ampenan, T621705, for 3 or 4 day hikes to the summit of Mount Rinjani.

The tourist information office at Ampenam has a comprehensive leaflet, listing a further 26 tour & travel agents

Transport **Local Car hire**: available from *Avis*, *Nitour Hotel*, Jl Yos Sudarso 4, T626579. *CV Metro*, Jl Yos Sudarso 79. *CV Rinjani*, Jl Bungkasno. *CV Surya*, Jl Raya Senggigi. **Dokars**: for short journeys around town. **Motorbike hire**: Several in town. Most travellers' guesthouses can rent cars/motorbikes, but cannot supply insurance.

Bemo/bus The Terminal Induk Bertais, Lombok's transport hub, is on Jl Selaparang at the east edge of Cakranegara (2 km east of Mataram). Regular buses and bemos from here to **Labuhan Lombok** (and on to Sumbawa), **Bangsal** (for the Gilis), **Tanjung**, **Keruak** and **Bayan**. Bemos wait on Jl Salah Singkar to pick up passengers for *Senggigi Beach* (see 'Ins and outs' for bemo routes in town). Buses will drop you off at the point along their route nearest your destination if you ask. *Perama* run a bus service geared to tourists, see page 770. **Boat** *Pelni* office, T637212, open: 0900-1400 Mon-Sat.

Directory **Airline offices** *Garuda*, T637950, 637951, in *Hotel Lombok Raiya*, Jl Panca Usaha. Open 0730-1630 Mon-Fri, 0900-1300 Sat and Sun. *Merpati*, Jl Pejanggik 69, T636745, 632226. There is also a *Merpati* office at Jl Yos Sudarso 4 (next to the *Nitour Hotel*). *Silk Air*, Pacific Supermarket, Jl Raya Senggigi,

T693877, F693822. **Banks** *Bank Central Asia*, Jl Pejanggik 67, Cakra; *Bank Negara Indonesia*, Jl Langko 64; *Bank Rakyat Indonesia*, Jl Pejanggik 16. Money changers on road into Ampenan from Senggigi. More banks in smart high rise buildings opening along Jl Pejanggik, including *Bank Exim*. They all change foreign currency and TCs. **Communications** General Post Office: Jl Majapahit Taman, Mataram T621345. **Post office**: Jl Langko 21, Ampenan. **Telephone Office**: Jl Langko. Perumtel: Jl Pejanggik. **Internet**: at Post office; Laba_Laba_internet@hotmail.com, Jl Pejanggik 43, Mataram; fastest access at *Yan's Internet Café* round the corner, Jl Subak 2, T623828; and *Indo.net*, Cilinaya Plaza blok A17 Jl Panca Usaha, and next to the main Wartel is *E Computer*. **Medical services** Hospitals: *General Hospital*, Jl Pejanggik 6, Mataram, T621345. **Useful addresses** Immigration Office: Jl Udayana 2, T622520.

Lombok's west coast

Most visitors to Lombok stay either at Senggigi Beach or on the 'Gilis'. Senggigi Beach stretches over 8 km from Batulayar to Mangsit. The road from Mataram to Bangsal winds through impressive tropical forest in the foothills of Mount Rinjani. Travelling further north along the coast from Mangsit, the road reaches Bangsal, the 'port' for boats to the Gilis. Senggigi is the most developed tourist area on Lombok, with a range of budget and more expensive hotels. It is easy to see why this area was chosen by investors and local entrepreneurs. The beaches here – and they extend over several kilometres – are picturesque and the backdrop of mountains and fabulous sunsets adds to the ambience. While Senggigi village supports the main concentration of shops, bars, restaurants, tour companies and such like, hotels and bungalows stretch along the coast and the road for 8 km or so. The Gilis – three small islands off the coast north of Senggigi – are very different. While there are one or two more expensive places to stay, these islands are primarily geared to the backpacker market. There are no vehicles and there really isn't much more to do beyond sunbathing, swimming, snorkelling, walking and generally relaxing.

Senggigi

Lombok's principle beach resort, Senggigi, lies 12 km north of Mataram on the island's west coast. The beach overlooks the famous Lombok Strait which the English naturalist Alfred Russel Wallace postulated divided the Asian and Australasian zoological realms (see box, page 801). The sacred Mount Agung on Bali can usually be seen shimmering in the distance. Hotels and bungalows are in fact found over an 8 km stretch of road and beach, from Batulayar Beach in the south, to Batubolong, Senggigi and Mangsit beaches to the north. Mangsit is quieter and less developed, although there are a number of hotels under construction and land speculation is rife.

Phone code: 0364

Many visitors express disappointment with Senggigi Beach itself, which is rather tatty, overdeveloped and not very attractive. There are many hotels catering largely for the package tour trade, and they are not always particularly well-managed, or maintained. Their rates are highly negotiable off season. Many of the best guesthouses on Lombok are Balinese owned, and as prices on Bali rise inexorably, they no longer seem as overpriced as they once did.

The further north you go the more beautiful and peaceful this area becomes, with unspoilt, windswept beaches and lovely views across the Lombok Strait to Mount Agung on Bali and superb sunsets. They are also at present free of the hawkers that so mar a visit to Senggigi itself.

In the mornings between 0800 and 1100, hundreds of brightly coloured fishing boats return to the beach. The fishermen leave at 0500 and use traditional methods of fishing, eschewing nets for a length of string with 30 hooks; when the string feels heavy they know it is time to haul it in. If the wind is onshore they fish off Mangsit, if the wind is offshore they fish off Senggigi beach.

Sights

About 2 km south of Senggigi, on a headland, is the **Batubolong Temple**. Unremarkable artistically (particularly when compared with the temples of Bali), it is named after a rock with a hole in it (*Batu Bolong* or 'Hollow Rock') found here. Tourists come to watch the sun set over Bali – devotees, to watch it set over the sacred Mount Agung.

Senggigi Beach

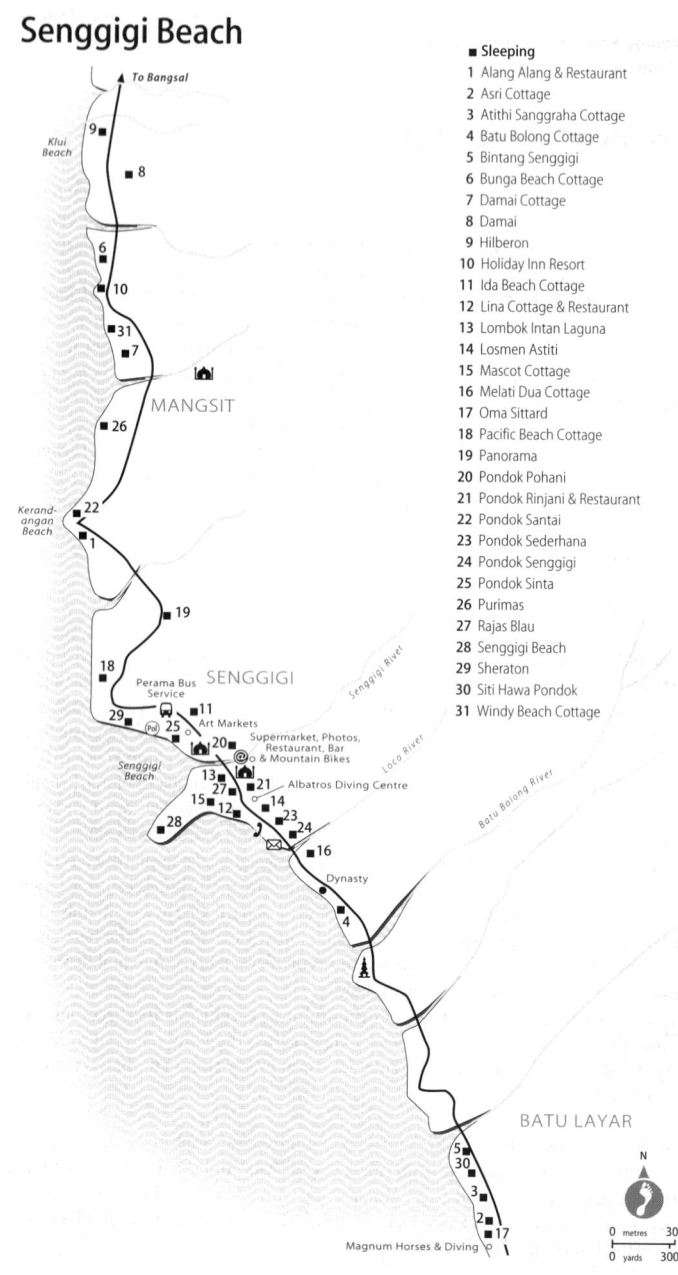

■ Sleeping
1 Alang Alang & Restaurant
2 Asri Cottage
3 Atithi Sanggraha Cottage
4 Batu Bolong Cottage
5 Bintang Senggigi
6 Bunga Beach Cottage
7 Damai Cottage
8 Damai
9 Hilberon
10 Holiday Inn Resort
11 Ida Beach Cottage
12 Lina Cottage & Restaurant
13 Lombok Intan Laguna
14 Losmen Astiti
15 Mascot Cottage
16 Melati Dua Cottage
17 Oma Sittard
18 Pacific Beach Cottage
19 Panorama
20 Pondok Pohani
21 Pondok Rinjani & Restaurant
22 Pondok Santai
23 Pondok Sederhana
24 Pondok Senggigi
25 Pondok Sinta
26 Purimas
27 Rajas Blau
28 Senggigi Beach
29 Sheraton
30 Siti Hawa Pondok
31 Windy Beach Cottage

Each evening an informal **beach market** sets-up on the beach in front of the Senggigi Beach Hotel; vendors lay out their wares (textiles, T-shirts, woodcarvings and 'antiques'); heavy bargaining is required – these people really know how to sell.

Senggigi The accommodation on 'Senggigi' is spread out for several kilometres along the main beach road and extends north to Kerandangan Beach, Klui Beach and Mangsit. All the hotels and guesthouses are easily accessible by bemo from Mataram. The better hotels have generators for when the mains power fails, which it does quite often. In the last 2 years over 10 new hotels have filled in the gaps between Batu Layar and Mangsit. There appears to be little separating them from the others in their respective price range. As noted earlier, the calamitous decline in Lombok's tourist fortunes has meant that hotel rates – at least in 2000 – were highly negotiable.

Sleeping

L-AL *Oberoi Lombok*, PO Box 1096, Mataram 833001, T638444, F632496, oberoil@ indosat.net.id, http://www.oberoihotels.com/lombm.htm New, luxury, 28 km from Mataram and north of Senggigi on Medana Beach. Just 50 individual bungalows. Facilities include beachside café, restaurant, cultural performances, pool, 18-hole golf course, tennis, business centre, good disabled access. **AL** *Sheraton*, Jl Raya Senggigi Km 8, PO Box 1154, T693333, F693140. A/c, restaurant, free-form pool, facilities include tennis courts, fitness centre and attractive pool on beach-front. **A** *Ida Beach Cottages*, PO Box 51, T693013. A/c, restaurant, pool, situated above the beach, ornate rooms set on the side of the hill overlooking the sea, hot water. **A** *Lombok Intan Laguna*, PO Box 50, T693090, intan@ mataram.wasantara.net.id A/c, restaurant, attractive pool, good sports facilities. **A** *Puri Mas*, T/F693023, at the northern end of the beach. Pricey villas with beautiful ornate doors and balconies, and bungalows, expensive non-inventive restaurants. Further on is **A-C** *Alang Alang*, offering the same facilities, a good pool, good restaurant. **A** *Senggigi Beach*, PO Box 2, T693339, F693185. A/c, restaurant, pool, large, well-run hotel, in prime position, with extensive grounds, overpriced. **A-B** *Graha*, T693400, central location, a/c, restaurant, watersports available, hot water, price includes breakfast.

B *Mascot Cottages*, PO Box 100, T693365, F693236. A/c, restaurant, large but rather dark rooms with hot water, no pool. **B** *Pacific Beach Cottages*, PO Box 36 (north of Senggigi), T693027. A/c, restaurant, shadeless pool, a bit tatty. Next door is the **B** *Panorama*, excellent sunset views. **C** *Asri Beach Cottages*, Jl Senggigi, T693075. The rooms in the new block are reasonable, those in the older 2-storeyed bungalows are dirty and in poor condition. **C** *Batu Bolong Cottages*, Batubolong Beach, T693065, F693198. Restaurant, large, clean rooms but nothing special, rooms on the beach are more expensive. **C** *Pondok Senggigi*, T693273. Restaurant, traditional huts in garden compound, good value but wrong side of the road for the beach, loud music might disturb some. The **B-C** *Oma Sittard*, T693684, F693685, sittard@ indo.net.id Leafy location, Lombok style luxury cottages with 1st floor balconies not facing the sea!

D *Atithi Sanggraha*, Jl Senggigi, Batu Layar (south of Senggigi), T693070. Average. **D** *Melati Dua*, Jl Raya Senggigi Km 13, T693288. Clean, popular. **C** *Bumi Aditya*, T693782, F693862, senggigi@indo.net.id High standards, great setting, set away from the beach down a track running inland, kids stay free, doctor on call, a/c, pool. **D** *Pondok Rinjani*, PO Box 76, T693274, 693170. Basic accommodation in central Senggigi, set in large garden with 2 enormous live turkeys, private bathrooms with shower and Western toilet. Could do with a little redecoration, price does not include breakfast, restaurant (cheap), you might be disturbed by loud music from *Pondok Senggigi*. **E** *Astiti*, next to mosque, T693041. Ceiling fan, en suite mandi, price includes breakfast, some noise from mosque, otherwise quite peaceful. **E** *Pondok Shinta*, Senggigi, T693012. Probably the cheapest place to stay in Senggigi, catering for backpackers, basic rooms, some with private mandi, squat toilets, would benefit from redecoration, friendly, good value, price includes breakfast, tiny huts, near beach, central position. **E** *Siti Hawa Pondok*, Jl Raya Senggigi 999, Batu Layur, 4 km south of Senggigi, T695414. Budget accommodation by sea, price includes breakfast and tea all day. Bicycles for hire, Indonesian dinner with family. Siti Hawa's husband is a New Zealander and runs a programme to help 'poor village people' from the hostel, guests are welcome to become involved. **E** *Sonya*, behind *Kartika Restaurant*, T693447. Only really low budget place to stay on the whole beach, restaurant, fan, clean rooms with attached showers, terrace, good breakfast included, order meals in the morning if you want to eat in (good food).

Kerandangan Heading north from Senggigi the 1st beach is Kerandangan.

AL *Hilberon*, north of Klui Beach, Austrian owned, well-managed luxury hotel in attractive grounds beside quiet beach, restaurant. **AL** *Holiday Inn*, T693444, F693092. Mangsit, new, spacious and well designed, offering everything you would expect from this hotel chain, a/c, water sports, tennis, fitness centre, children's playground, swimming pool, restaurants and outdoor cultural performance stage, set in 5 ha of tropical gardens, convention facilities. **A** *Bunga Beach Cottages* (at Klui Beach just north of Mangsit), PO Box 1118, T693035, F693036. 14 large, very attractive, a/c thatched cottages set in colourful, tropical gardens with swimming pool, beside the sea, excellent restaurant (mid-range). Reservations essential at all times of the year for this very select, superbly run 'hotel'. Highly recommended. **A** *Lombok Dame Indah (Damai) Cottages*, Lendang Guar, Pemenang Barat, 12 km north of Senggigi 83352 (PO Box 1128), T693246, 693247, F693248. Set on opposite side of road to beach, on a hillside overlooking the Lombok Strait, traditional style Sasak bungalows, well furnished, quiet hotel, pool, restaurant. **A-C** *Santai Beach Bungalows*, Mangsit, T/F693038. Attractive, well-managed thatched bungalows built in the Sasak style, tastefully furnished with fan, private bathroom with Western toilet and shower. Set in a coconut grove beside the sea, restaurant (mid-range). **C** *Windy Beach Cottages*, Mangsit, PO Box 1116, T693191, 693192, F693193. 14 attractive traditional style thatched bungalows with fan, private bathroom with shower/bath, Western toilet, some with hot water. Set in large gardens amidst a coconut grove beside the sea, restaurant (cheap) offering good Indonesian, Chinese and Western food. Well-managed, Windy's husband is a Scotsman from Lerwick in the Shetland Isles. They are also the local **Perama** shuttle bus agent. Recommended.

C-D *Pondok Damai*, Mangsit Beach Inn (reservations address: Jl Bangau 7, Cakranegara 83231), T693019. 15 attractive thatched bungalows set in beautiful gardens with assorted fruit trees, beside the sea. Private bathrooms featuring an indoor garden with shower and Western toilet, fan, TV, restaurant (cheap). Recommended. **E** *Pantai Inga*, southern end of Jl Raya, clean with shared showers, breakfast included. Fan rooms, thin walls, pool table, sometimes there is live music next door, so it can be noisy, 100m from a quiet stretch of beach. Further on is **E-F** *Coconut Budi* with basic rooms, but cheaper than the rest.

Eating There are not many independent restaurants on Senggigi – most eating places are attached to hotels. However, with the recent and continuing rapid expansion in accommodation there has been an increase in the number of restaurants.

Cheap *Café Wayang*, on main road in Senggigi, T693098. A branch of the one in Ubud, Bali, building has character (complete with family of mice in the rafters!), but service not up to full speed. *Dynasty*, large open-air restaurant, overlooking the sea on the road to Senggigi, remains empty, except when there is some kind of local event. *Gossip*, Jl Lazoardi (near *Senggigi Beach Hotel*), live music, good food (particularly seafood) although limited menu. Recommended. *Rumah Makan Padang*, Jl Raya, 200m south of the post office on the other side of the road, hidden in the corner, good typical spicy Lombok food, open 24 hrs. *Princess of Lombok*, T693011. Excellent Mexican food, steaks and seafood and live music. Free pick up from Senggigi. *Café Alberto*, does an unusual range of pizza and stages cultural shows. In the mall area is *Formula One Racing Café*, which shows Grand Prix on a large screen. Food and board (**C**) available. Nearby *Café Enak* has a European coffeeshop feel and shaded, al fresco tables and tasty food, as the name indicates. **Very cheap** *Senang*, opposite the supermarket, T693312, the place to be if garlic bread is your favourite, and with a decent *nasi goreng* to boot.

Club Rhinos after 1300 and *Jungle Bar*, which has cocktails sporting names such as Cosmic Colorada, relaxed live acoustic tunes in the day, more dance/disco in evenings. **Nightlife**

Pacific supermarket on the main road has everything from food to T-shirts, film and gifts at reasonable prices. A few boutique-cum-craft shops have also popped up, less prone to haggling than the old school vendors, such as the Vrat Gallery. **Shopping**

The *Sasak Gardens* is the centre for watersports, with parasailing, water-skiing, windsurfing, sailing. Diving is very good value here; with 2 dives costing as little as US$30 off season. **Diving** *Baruna Watersports*, *Senggigi Beach Hotel*, T623430, 693210. *Rinjani* have a branch at the *Intan Laguna Hotel*, T636040, F633972. *Blue Coral Diving*, T693251, Blue_coral@mataram.wasantara.net.id *CV Albatross*, T693399. *Dream Divers*, T/F634547, Dreamdivers@mataram.wasantara.net.ID *Manta Diving*, T/F693239. **Snorkelling**: around Senggigi beach, masks for hire. **Rafting**: *Lombok Inter Rafting*, Perokoan Senggigi Square, T693202, also have branch in Bali. Offers good discount off season, guaranteed to take you off the beaten track, helpful staff, good English. **Sports**

Anthea Wisata, Jl Lazoardi, T621572; *Bunga Tours* at *Bunga Beach Cottages*, T693035, F693036, guide Ayang has excellent English; *Mavista* at *Mascot Cottages*, T623865; *Nazareth Tours*, T621705 (in Ampenan); *Satriavi*, *Senggigi Beach Hotel*. Day trips to the Gilis; for example, on the *Studio 22 – Anthea Wisata* catamaran (US$20 per head), Jl Lazoardi. *Nazareth Tours* and *Satriavi* both organize treks up Mount Rinjani (see page 790). *Putri Lombok Wisata*, Jl Rasen, T693671, has competitive tour offers, good English and German. **Tours & tour operators**

Local Various forms of transport can be hired from travel agents along the main road. **Car hire**: 40,000-60,000Rp per day, both self-drive and with driver. *Kotasi*, Jl Raya Senggigi on main street near *Senggigi Beach Hotel* turning, T693058. **Bicycle hire**: 5,000Rp per day. **Motorbike hire**: 25,000Rp per day. **Transport** *12 km from Mataram*

Road Bemo: bemos wait on Jl Salah Singkar in Ampenan to pick-up fares for Senggigi Beach and north to Mangsit. There are regular bemos linking Ampenan with Mataram, Cakranegara and the main Cakra bemo terminal between 0600 and 1800, 500Rp. *Perama* have an office here and run a bus service geared to travellers, see page 770.

Banks *Senggigi Beach Hotel* has a bank on site with exchange facilities for non-residents. Money changer at the Pacific Supermarket. **Communications Post Office**: centre of town, along Jl Raya. **Internet**: access on main street from: Bulam@mataram.wasantara.net.id; SenggigiPlanet@mataram.wasantara.net.id *Millennium 2001*, Pluto@mataram.wasantara.net.id **Useful addresses Police**: opposite *Ida Cottages* (north end of beach). **Directory**

Bangsal

The coast road north from Senggigi is slow, steeply switchbacking its way over headlands and past some attractive beaches. There is some surf on this part of the coast, mainly reef breaks, surfed by the locals on wooden boards. *Phone code: 0364*

Bangsal is just off the main road from Pemenang, and is little more than a tiny fishing village. However, as it is also the departure point for the Gilis, there are a couple of restaurants here which double up as tourist information centres, a ferry booking office, a money changer and a diving company. There is a charge of 2,500Rp per vehicle to drive down to Bangsal from Pemanang on the main road.

E *Kontiki Bangsal Beach Inn*, traditional cottages near beach, with a peaceful atmosphere. **Sleeping**

Bemo Regular connections from Mataram or the Bertais terminal in Cakranegara; take a bemo heading for Tanjung or Bayan. Bemos stop at the junction at Pemenang, take a dokar the last 1 km to the coast. From Pelabuhan Lombok there are no direct bemos; either charter **Transport** *28 km from Mataram*

one (20,000Rp) or catch a bemo to the Bertais Terminal in Cakranegara and then another travelling to Bayan/Tanjung. From the port of Lembar, it is easiest to club together with other passengers and charter a bemo to Bangsal. **Bus**: regular connections with Lembar with *Perama Tour*, who have an office by the pier and sell all-in bus/ferry tickets to most destinations in Bali (Kuta, Sanur, Ubud, Lovina, Candi Dasa). **NB** it is not worth buying bus tickets on the Gilis; prices are considerably higher. **Sea Boat**: a new high-speed boat service with Padangbai on Bali is supposed to be operating, but service is erratic. Regular ferries and boats to the Gilis (see 'Transport' in Gilis).

Directory Tourist offices *Kontiki Coffee Shop* is an informal information centre with a particularly helpful man who will advise on boat crossings; *Perama Tourist Service* (near the beach) provides bus and ferry connections with the Gilis, Senggigi and Lembar, and all towns on Bali. They also organize tours on Lombok, as well as an excellent 7-day boat tour from Bangsal to Labuanbajo (Flores) via Moyo Island (Sumbawa) and Komodo. **NB** This tour is considerably cheaper in the opposite direction, ie Labuanbajo to Bangsal. The tour then returns to Bangsal from Labuanbajo along the same route. A worthwhile alternative to travelling overland; 8 people minimum.

The Gilis

Phone code: 0364
Malaria may exist on these islands, so be sure to take precautions & be careful when swimming as there are strong currents between the islands

The three tropical island idylls that make up the 'Gilis' lie off Lombok's northwest coast, 20-45 minutes by boat from Bangsal. Known as the 'Gilis' or the 'Gili Islands' by many travellers, this only means 'the Islands' in Sasak. Most locals have accepted this Western corruption of their language and will understand where you want to go.

With the development of Bali into an international tourist resort, many backpackers have moved east and the Gilis are the most popular of the various alternatives. This is already straining the islands' limited sewerage and water infrastructures. During the peak months between June and August, Gili Trawangan becomes particularly crowded. (Although this was not the case in 2000.)

The attraction of the Gilis resides in their golden sand beaches and the best snorkelling and diving off Lombok – for the amateur the experience is breathtaking. However, the coral does not compare with locations such as Flores and Alor: large sections are dead or damaged (perhaps because of dynamite fishing). There is little to do on the islands except sunbathe, swim, snorkel or dive, or go for walks.

Ins and outs

Getting there Regular boats from Bangsal to the Gilis wait until about 16 people have congregated for the trip to the islands. Boats can also be chartered for the journey, 45 mins to Gili Trawangan, 30 mins to Gili Meno, 20 mins to Gili Air. In the morning there is rarely a long wait, but in the afternoon people have had to wait several hours. An alternative is to buy a combined bus and boat ticket with one of the shuttle bus companies like **Nomad** or **Perama**. There are various alternatives. Within Lombok there are services from **Mataram** to the Gilis and from **Senggigi** to the Gilis. (From Senggigi, boats sail to the Gilis frequently throughout the day.) From Bali there are services from **Padangbai**, **Candi Dasa** and **Kuta** to the Gilis. Boats leave from 0700 onwards.

Getting around The islands themselves are small and compact enough to walk around. Even Gili Trawangan, the largest of the 3, is little more than 2 km from end to end. Perama run a shuttle service between the islands, which allows you to visit another island for the day and then return. It is also possible to charter boats. Note that the downturn in tourism may have limited the frequency of departures.

The islands

Gili Trawangan The largest of the three islands – and the furthest west from Bangsal – is Gili Trawangan (Dragon Island). It is the most interesting island because of its hill in

Seaweed farming

Seaweed farming is being encouraged off Gili Air as an alternative to fishing, in order to protect the coral. Although laws against the use of dynamite fishing were passed in 1984, some fishermen still use it as well as stones to kill the fish, damaging the coral in the process. The waters round the island provide suitable conditions for seaweed farming: there is a good flow of water, but the reef protects the area from unwelcome strong currents; the considerable depth of the Lombok Strait keeps sea temperatures from becoming too high and keeps salinity at a constant level. These are all prerequisites for the successful cultivation of seaweed. From the fishermens' viewpoint, seaweed farming has the added attraction of being less hard work than fishing. The green Kotoni variety is grown and is exported for use in the food industry.

The seaweed is farmed by fixing posts in the shallow seabed. Rope is attached to these posts, making a frame about 2m square. At roughly 30cm intervals nodules of seaweed containing a seedhead are tied onto the rope using strips of shredded plastic bags. The seaweed must remain covered by water, so the ropes are held afloat just under the surface using plastic bottles, which are due to be replaced by more visually pleasing lengths of bamboo. After 40 days the seaweed is harvested and dried; 7kg of wet seaweed producing 1kg dry weight. This is then sold on Lombok for 800Rp a kilogram (or an equivalent value in rice and coffee), each family producing about 50kg. Cuttings from the harvested seaweed are retained to grow into the next crop.

---

the centre; there are several trails to the summit and excellent views over to Mount Rinjani on Lombok from the top. **NB** Give the cows a wide berth. In the opposite direction, you can watch the sun set over Mount Agung on Bali. There is a coastal path around the island, which takes about 2½ hours to walk. Originally a penal colony, it now supports the greatest number of tourist bungalows. These are mostly concentrated along its east coast, as are a number of restaurants (serving good seafood) and bars. For lone travellers seeking company, this is the best island. Snorkelling is good off the east shore, particularly at the point where the shelf drops away near *Blue Marlin Dive Centre* and at the north end of the beach near *Sudi Mampir Bungalows*. But Gili Trawangan is in danger of ruining itself (like so many other tropical island idylls in the region). Indeed, for some, it already has. The most developed area is becoming brash, loud and over-developed, but the island is large enough to offer peace and tranquillity as well. Gili Air and Gili Meno are quieter, though they too have their noisy areas of discos and loud Western pop music in high season.

The most 'luxurious' accommodation is found in the developed area of the island behind the restaurants; locals already refer to it being like Kuta, although this is an exaggeration. Here you can find modern air-conditioned rooms with Western bathrooms; unfortunately you lose the peace and beauty associated with a small, relatively undeveloped island, as the accommodation is hidden behind the noisy restaurants away from the beach. To find a tropical paradise visitors have to accept more basic facilities at the outer edges of the developed areas. Here guests can hear the waves lapping against the shore and the birds singing, watch truly inspirational sunrises and sunsets from the peace of their verandahs and believe they are in paradise. Room rates triple at some of the more upmarket places in the high season. Even off-peak rooms can become scarce, so it is worth arriving on the island early. Gili Trawangan offers the best choice of restaurants of the three 'Gilis', and many people consider that it has the best snorkelling.

Inland from the tourist strip is the original village where life goes on almost as usual, a world apart from the tourists and therefore interesting to stroll through. Further inland there are scattered farms in amongst the coconut groves that dominate the interior, and some pleasant walks to be had.

Gili Meno

Perhaps unfairly, Gili Meno has a reputation as the 'Gili' island where you are at greatest risk of catching malaria. To counterbalance this, the locals insist there are no mosquitoes – none whatsoever!

Gili Meno (Snake Island), between Trawangan and Air, is the smallest of the islands, and also the quietest and least developed. The snorkelling off Gili Meno – especially off the northeast coast – is considered by some to be better than Trawangan, with growths of rare blue coral. There is a path running round the island; a walk of 1-1½ hours. The salt lake in the northeast of the island provides a breeding ground for mosquitoes. Accommodation on Gili Meno tends to be more expensive than on the other two islands and offers worse value for money at every price level. Some of the guesthouse owners live on Lombok, and these bungalows are run by lads who are poorly paid and consequently have little motivation. However, the views from the many bungalows which face the sea are beautiful, especially towards the east and Mount Rinjani. Accommodation may be full as early as April, with the season

Gili Islands

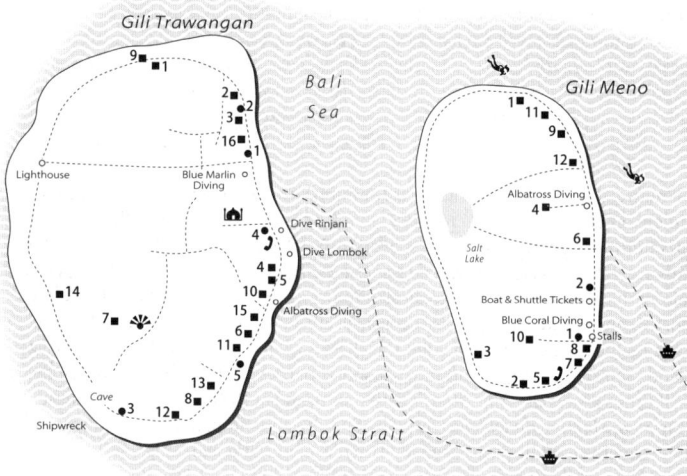

Gili Trawangan
■ **Sleeping**
1 Cabya Bay
2 Coral Cottages
3 Creative
4 Danau Hijau
5 Fantasi Beach
6 Halim
7 Iwan Homestay
8 Mawar
9 Nusa Tiga
10 Pak Majid, Dua Sekawan I & Sandy Beach Bungalows
11 Pasih Putih
12 Pondok Santi
13 Rainbow Cottages
14 Rinjani Cottages, Sunset & Mawar II
15 Rudy's, Dua Sekawan II & Damai Indah
16 Sudi Mampir

● **Eating**
1 Excellent
2 Good Heart
3 Rumah Kita
4 Simple Food
5 Villa Ombak

Gili Meno
■ **Sleeping**
1 Blue Coral
2 Bougenvil
3 Bounty Lux Resort
4 Casablanca Cottages
5 Gazebo
6 Janur Indah
7 Kontiki
8 Malia's Child
9 Pondok Meno
10 Rawa Indah
11 Santai
12 Zoraya

● **Eating**
1 Rust
2 Wannen

Gili Air
■ **Sleeping**
1 Bupati's Place
2 Coconut Cottages & Restaurant
3 Corner Cottage & Restaurant
4 Fantastic Bungalows

running through to September. However, with all the recent problems this didn't apply during 2000.

Gili Air (Turtle Island) is the easternmost island, lying closest to Bangsal. It has the largest local population, with a village in the centre of the island. The island takes about an hour to walk around. As the local population is Muslim, visitors should avoid topless sunbathing. The government is keen to develop the island sympathetically and to this end is donating 'useful' trees as part of its plan to keep the island green and beautiful. Last year, young mango trees were dispatched to Gili Air; the year before, coconut seedlings were being planted all over the island. Despite the number of bungalows, it remains a peaceful place to stay. Snorkelling is quite good off the island.

Gili Air
There are mice on the island, so shut food away

Essentials

When leaving your accommodation take sensible precautions and make sure you lock both the door to the bathroom and the front door. As most bathrooms have no roofs, a favoured way for thieves to gain entry is over the bathroom wall and into your room via the bathroom door. **NB** There are no police on the islands, so if you want to make a report, expect the extra hassle of contacting the station at Ampenan or Tanjung.

Security

Many bungalows are upgrading the standard of their rooms; of the more basic ones there is often little difference – they tend to charge the same rates, and the huts are similar in design and size, attractively built out of local materials, in a local style, mostly raised on stilts. Mosquitoes can be a problem at certain times of year and mosquito nets are routinely provided. Rates tend to be in our **E** and **F** categories for the simpler bungalows with either attached or shared mandi, often also including breakfast. The most luxurious bungalows fall into our **A** category. Very few places offer all meals these days. Free tea and coffee are sometimes available all day. Friendliness and the cleanliness of the mandis tends to be the deciding factor at the basic bungalows. The higher the price, the more likely tax and service charge will be extra, and the less likely breakfast will be included. If a/c is important to you, check that it is available during the day and all night. At some accommodations the a/c works off a generator which is only switched on for a few hours at night. There are 2 upmarket 'hotels' on Gili Meno, 1 on Gili Air and new modern bungalows with a/c and Western bathrooms on Gili Trawangan.

Sleeping
During the peak months between Jun & Aug it can be difficult to get a room, so arrive early in the day

Gili Trawangan (25 bungalows and rising, mostly along the east coast): **NB** Tips on

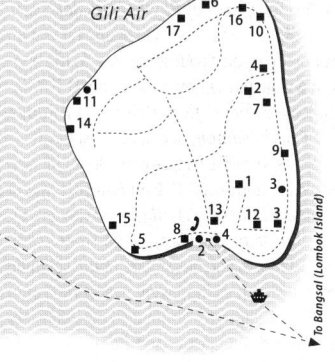

Gili Air

5 Flying Dutchman on Safari & Restaurant
6 Gili Air & Internet
7 Gili Air Santay & Restaurant
8 Gili Indah, Restaurant, Internet & Reefseekers Dive Centre
9 Gita Gili
10 Gusung Indah Bungalows
11 Matahari
12 Nusa Tiga Bungalows
13 Pondok Gili Air Bungalows & Internet Café
14 Pondok Pantai
15 Salabose Bungalows & Restaurant
16 Sandi Bungalows
17 Yogi

● Eating
1 Bunga Tours
2 Haris Café
3 Pino
4 Sunrise

where to stay from travellers are probably your best bet. Unless otherwise stated, all bungalows have private mandis with squat toilets. **A-B** *Blue Marlin*, T632424, F693043, bmdc@mataram.wasantara.net.id 8 bungalows behind the Blue Marlin dive centre (see the entry below under diving) with a/c, attached hot water showers and private balconies. **B-D** *Danau Hijau*, modern bungalows with Western bathrooms in built-up area. **B-D** *Fantasi Beach*, perhaps the most upmarket of the bungalows with spring beds, modern rooms and bathrooms, though in the built-up area away from the sea, good breakfast, reports of theft here. **C-D** *Dua Sekawan I* and *Sandy Beach Bungalows*, both offer modern rooms with Western bathrooms, good breakfast, can be noisy as it is situated in the built-up area. **C-D** *Pak Majid* has just been rebuilt to provide modern, attractive rooms with private bathrooms, Western toilet and fan, in the built-up area of the island. **C-E** *Dua Sekawan II*, en suite mandi, toilet and shower, avoid old building, new bungalows are noisy – disco next door. **D** *Creative*, 1 bungalow has a Western toilet, others with private or shared mandis. **D** *Halim*, on beach, nice bungalows, friendly. Recommended. **D** *Pasih Putih*, price includes breakfast, which is brought to your room every morning, hammocks on the balconies. **D** *Santigi Bungalows*, on beach, outside mandi. Popular. **D** *Trawangan Beach Cottages*, T623582, on beach, outside mandi, noisy. **D** *Wisma Mountain View*, on beach, attached mandi. **D-E** *Coral Cottages*, at the quieter northern edge of bungalow development near to good snorkelling, if you are looking for a Western toilet, 2 of the bungalows have squat toilets raised on concrete to seat height! – not a huge success but perhaps better than nothing. **D-E** *Nusa Tiga*, one of the best locations on its own at the north end of the island, set in large gardens with 3 colourful 'tame' parrots. Clean and quiet, excellent breakfast included, private mandi with squat toilet, the water here is very saline. Good restaurant, serving cheap food and large portions, good value; 15-min walk from the bars, owner organizes 'all you can eat' Indonesian buffets. **D-E** Next door is new Chinese losmen **C-D** *Caby Bay*. **D-E** *Pondok Santi*, set in a peaceful coconut grove at the southern end of the island, well made bungalows with western toilets. During the rainy season the coconut palms block out some light so the bungalows are damper with more mosquitoes, 20-min walk to the best snorkelling. **D-E** *Rainbow Cottages*, in a quieter area to the south, joint owner is from Holland. **D-E** *Rudy's Bungalows*, off beach, some attached mandis. **D-E** *Sudi Mampir*, one of the best locations with each bungalow facing the sea and memorable views of the sunrise over Mount Rinjani, situated in a quiet corner of the island. **D-E** *Mawar II* (4 bungalows), **D-E** *Rinjani Cottages* (4 bungalows), **E** *Simple Bungalows*, off beach, simple. **E** *Sunset* (10 bungalows with 2 beds, mosquito nets, oil lamps, hammocks on balconies and a large breakfast). All 3 of these establishments are situated on the western side of the island, taking advantage of the splendid sunsets featuring Mount Agung on Bali as a breathtaking backdrop. Very peaceful, all offer similar accommodation and have their own small restaurants, it's about a 40 min walk into 'town' for other restaurants and shopping, or take a dokar. Just inland from here is the **D-E** *Iwan Homestay*, which has a good ambience and there is a popular restaurant next door, the *Rumah Kita*.

Meno has a reputation as a mosquito haven, so choose your accommodation carefully

Gili Meno A *Bougenvil Resort*, T635295, T/F627435. The most expensive place on the island, set in a secluded position at the southern end of the island, large attractive rooms. A little overpriced. Rooms with a/c, bathroom with Western toilet and hot water, minibar, satellite TV, pool, restaurant (mid-range). **A** *Gazebo Meno*, PO Box 1122, T/F635795, or Gazebo Hotels, PO Box 3134, Bali, T0361-286927, F288300. 10 bungalows set in large coconut grove. Attractively furnished large rooms with separate seating area, wooden floors, bathrooms with Western toilet, bath (no hot water), a/c, verandah. Restaurant (mid-range to cheap). **A-C** *Bounty*, new and luxurious. **B-D** *Angkasa Biru*, *Casablanca Cottages*, PO Box 1163, Mataram, T0370-633847, F693482. Not the best location, set a short distance inland near small pools of stagnant water in the wet season. Attractively furnished rooms amidst pretty gardens except for the cheapest rooms, which are at the back facing inland with no breeze. All bathrooms with Western toilet, some with hot water. A/c or fan. Tiny but inviting pool. Somewhat overpriced. Restaurant (cheap). **B** *Casablanca*, T/F633847. Pool and cosy garden, away from beach. **B-E** *Zoraya*, T633801. 6 attractive bungalows with private bathroom, some with Western toilet. A/c or fan. Electricity only runs from 1800 to 0100 so there is no a/c during the heat of the day. 4 bungalows with shared mandi at the back facing inland, with no views. Diving is available but standards may not be high. Good snorkelling at this location. **C** *Janur Indah*, attractive bungalows, bathrooms with Western toilet. **D-E** *Blue Coral*, basic bungalows in need of repair in good location at north end of island. Private mandi, squat toilets and internet access. Worth investigating to see if they have been renovated and cleaned! **D-E** *Kontiki*, simple, with private mandi and Western toilets. **D-E** *Malia's Child*, T622007. Basic accommodation, mostly with shared mandi, squat toilet, 2 with Western toilet. Very average. **D-E** *Pondok Meno*, one of the best of these basic bungalows. Good location, set in pretty gardens. Shared mandi (1 private mandi), squat toilet. **D-E** *Pondok Santai*, next door to the Pondok Meno, is very similar. **D-E** *Rawa Indah*, basic bungalows a short distance inland. Squat toilets, some with private mandi. **D-E** *Santai*, 2 bungalows. Basic with private mandi, squat toilets, good location.

Gili Air To make the most of this 'paradise' island it is best to stay in one of the bungalows dotted around the coast within sound and sight of the sea. There is also accommodation inland from the point where the boats land on the south coast, but this location does not offer sea views. In the village there are several small shops which sell basic provisions and fruit. The price of accommodation doubles or more in the high season. However, due to the decrease in tourists since early 2000 this has all been put on hold. **B** *Hotel Gili Air*, formerly *Hans Cottages*, T/F634435, giliair@mataram.wasantara.net.id The most upmarket accommodation on the island, 24 rooms, private bathrooms with western toilets and attractive indoor gardens. Fan or a/c, some with hot water. Well sited beside the beach with gardens and a fine view of Mount Rinjani. Restaurant (mid-range), many European dishes, the giant clams that sometimes appear on the menu are a protected species and should not have been caught. **B** *Hotel Gili Indah*, PO Box 1120, T636341, F637328. The next most upmarket accommodation, consisting of bungalows with private bathrooms and Western toilets. Some rather dark, set in rather shaded and gloomy grounds. Restaurant, though quite pricey, is very average. The owner, Pak Aji, is Kepala Desa of the 'Gilis' which are now self-governing, and is a keen conservationist which bodes well for future development on the islands. **C-D** *Hans Cottage & Restaurant*, formerly *Bulan Madu* and once owned by a German, about whom rumours abound, this once luxurious house offers curious accommodation today. There are 3 rooms which can be let separately. The 2 downstairs rooms are large with nice verandahs and private bathrooms. The upstairs room, also large with private bathroom, has good views and access to a 3rd floor lookout. All rooms have fans, and the house has great potential but needs to be redecorated. The bathrooms in particular need a good clean and new tubs, the existing ones are badly scarred. If the restaurant is in use, it could be noisy. Prices are reasonable. Large garden. **C-D** *Coconut Cottages & Restaurant* (*Pondok Kelapa*), T635365, coconuts@indo.net.id 7 attractive bungalows with private bathrooms all enclosed, 4 with Western toilet, fan, mosquito nets, internet access, but bedbug problem. Very well run, set in flower-filled gardens amidst a coconut grove 30m from the beach, restaurant (mid-range to cheap), good food. Recommended. **D** *Fantastic Bungalows*, on east side of island (best swimming and snorkelling here), 6 well-run bungalows with own (clean) mandi, price includes good breakfast, tuna and mayonnaise baguettes top the menu. Recommended. **D** *The Flying Dutchman on Safari*, 5 well-run bungalows with squat toilets and gardens. The restaurant serves a good value Indonesian buffet every night at 2000 (book by 1800), bar. The bungalows are particularly well made, using expensive *alang alang* grass for the roofs (as was traditional before many people switched to cheaper grasses). Good sunset views. Highly recommended. **D** *Pino's Cottages & Corner Cottage*, bungalows face each other away from beach. Own mandi, 4 with Western toilet, electricity (occasional) in some bungalows, restaurant on the beach with reasonable food. **D** *Pondok Gili Air Bungalows and Café*, sasaksavage@hotmail.com Attractive, clean bungalows with private mandis and squat toilets. In attractive garden, well run. The place has its own generator, internet access and uses bottled water for making tea. Can arrange delicious Sasak dinners with 1 day's notice, offers a book exchange. Recommended. **D-E** *Sandi Bungalows*, simple and clean with attached mandi and squat toilet. Quiet location. **F** *Bamboo Cottages*, hammock on the balcony, choice of breakfast included in the price, very friendly owners.

The best of the remaining bungalows (all in the **D-E** price category) are: *Gusung Indah Bungalows; Salabose Bungalows* (one of which has a Western toilet), good sunset views; *Pena; Gita Gili*, good breakfast; *Gili Air Santay*, good bungalows with and without attached showers, all with electricity, excellent food, 500m east of the boat 'dock' and situated inland; *Bupati's Place*; *Nusa Tiga*.

Eating The choice of food is better on Gili Trawangan. A number of restaurants serving excellent seafood, particularly fish; 'specials' or the 'chalk-boards' will tell you what is the fresh catch.

Many restaurants show videos in the evenings

Gili Trawangan *Excellent Restaurant*, good, cheap food. Recommended. **Very cheap** *Simple Food*, limited menu but large helpings, friendly and enthusiastic owners. Recommended. Many of the accommodations in the built-up area feature restaurants, some with barbecue facilities, the number of customers should indicate which are best. The new, 2-storey *Villa Ombak* is the most sophisticated way to dine here, with an outdoor terrace near the water. Good value.

Gili Meno *Bougenvil* and *Gazebo* both have restaurants (mid-range to cheap). *Malia's Child & Rust* offer simpler and cheaper food with good views across to Lombok. *Janur Indah* has been recommended. *Rusty's* warung does big portions of nasi goreng and similar dishes. *Café Lumblumba*, the closest thing to a party zone, does Padang style food.

Gili Air Many of the restaurants cater primarily to Western tastes and the 'Indonesian' food is often disappointingly bland. There have been some cases of food poisoning caused by eating fish which was not gutted prior to being stored. Restaurants and bungalows with the best food are: *Pondok Gili Air*, which also has good vegetarian food, fish and yoghurt, has a rotating specialized menu and rare delicacies such as lemon cake with caramel sauce and double chocolate cake, recommended; *Corner Restaurant and Bungalows*, *Coconut Cottages* (Pondok Kelapa); *Nusa Tiga Bungalows* and *Flying Dutchman*, a good nightly buffet dinners – all cheap; *Hotel Gili Air*, formerly *Hans Cottages*, and *Il Pirata* (both mid-range), good, though pricey, Italian food.

Nightclubs *Go Go Bar* on Saturdays and *Legends* on Friday, both on Gili Air.

Sports **Diving** Whilst the diving here may not be quite as good as that in some other parts of Indonesia, it is ideal for less experienced divers as many of the dives are no deeper than 18m and the waters are calm. Best diving conditions are late Apr through Aug. *Reefseekers*, now located in the *Gili Indah Hotel* at the Harbour, PO Box 1097, Mataram, c/o *Gili Indah*, T0370-636341. Members of PADI International Resort Association No 2979, they offer a full range of courses to PADI Divemaster, operate to the highest safety standards. Experienced divers must bring their certificates and preferably their log books. *Reefseekers* are also very involved in conservation and are members of the Cousteau Society doing research into local ecosystems. All dives are guided. *Reefseekers* have started a 'Turtle Hatchery Project' to increase numbers of hornbill and green turtles, both of which are under threat in their natural habitats. See tinted box, page 343. **Blue Marlin Dive Centre**, head office: Gili Trawangan, T632424, F642286, bmdc@mataram.wasantara.net.id, www.diveindo.com Counters on Gili Air, Jl Raya Senggigi Beach, *Senggigi Palace Hotel*, Jl Koperasi 81, Ampenan, Lombok. PADI courses up to Divemaster Course, courses start at US$25 for an introduction to scuba diving with 1 dive, up to US$299 for the PADI Open Water Course. Resident English instructor. This is the best dive centre on Gili Trawangan. **Albatross Dive Center**, Jl Raya Senggigi, Km 8, PO Box 1066, Mataram 83010, T693399, F693388. Also at the **Sheraton Hotel**, Senggigi Beach, PADI courses up to Open Water (US$350) and Advanced Diver (US$240). Also operates on Gili Trawangan and Gili Meno. **Blue Coral Dive Centre**, T634496, operates on all 3 Gili islands and offers PADI courses and night dives. Expect to pay about US$50 for 2 dives. There are also many other dive shops. If taking an introductory dive course check that the instructor speaks acceptable English (or Dutch, German etc). **Snorkelling**: snorkels and fins can be hired for 3,000-5,000Rp from many of the losmen. The snorkelling off Gili Trawangan is marginally the best; be careful off Gili Meno, as the tide is strong and the water is shallow, and it is easy to get swept onto the coral.

Warning: it is advisable not to dive if taking Larium as a malaria prophylactic

Fishing Deep sea and night fishing available from tour companies and **Albatross Dive Center** (see under 'Diving' for address), approximate costs US$200-300. A popular glass-bottomed boat does the rounds between the 3 islands, and indeed is the only way to go between Air and Meno in the low season short of chartering your own boat. It costs US$25 and stops off at a few good spots, and you have lunch on Trawangan.

Massage Sometimes available at *Rudi's*, a restaurant set back from the beach, near where the ferry docks on Gili Trewangan. *Abar* is the best masseur on Gili Air; ask at *Pondok Gili Air*, for the rare pleasure of a masseur who is suitable for women – ie no misplaced rubbing!

Boat Public boats from the islands to **Bangsal** leave at 0800 and 1200 approximately. For onward connections to Bali, arrive at the ticket booth by 0730. At Bangsal you can also book through to Bali with 1 of the shuttle bus companies. **Gili Air** boats are blue, **Gili Meno** are yellow, and **Gili Trawangan** are red and white. The 'Island Hopping' boat makes 2 round trips a day connecting the islands. Currently, the boat leaves Gili Air at 0800 and 1400 to Gili Meno. It leaves Gili Meno to Gili Trawangan at 0845 and 1515. It leaves Gili Trawangan to return to Gili Meno at 0915 and 1445, and leaves Gili Meno to return to Gili Air at 0945 and 1545. It takes approximately 20-30 mins for each leg of the journey. **NB** There are reports that with the downturn in tourist arrivals the frequency of departures has decreased. Check on arrival.

Transport
Don't purchase bus tickets on the islands, they are more expensive

Banks It is best to change money before leaving the 'mainland' as rates are more expensive on the islands. There are money changers on Gili Trawangan. On Gili Air, the *Gili Indah* will change money. Some of the losmen on each of the islands will also change money. **Communications Post Office**: There is a post box at the *Gili Indah Hotel* on Gili Air, where the boat docks. Letters *do* get through, but there are no stamps available on the island. Each of the islands has a **Wartel**. On Gili Air you can make phone calls at *Pondok Kelapa* (*Coconut Cottages*). The owner does not require a minimum of 3 mins, which the Wartel does. **Internet**: a number of places offer internet access on the islands, more to follow.

Directory

Northwest coast and Mount Rinjani

Following the coast north from Pemenang and Bangsal, the road passes the turn off for Sir Beach (about 2 km north of Pemenang). This northwest coast is little touched by tourism and there are several 'traditional villages' where the more adventurous tour companies take visitors. The best-known of these is Bayan, at the foot of Mount Rinjani's northern slopes and about 50 km from Pemenang. Mount Rinjani, rising to 3,726m, dominates north Lombok.

Siri Beach is down a dirt track, to the left are coconut plantations, and reaches the deserted, long, narrow strip of soft, white sand on a headland looking across to Gili Air. Take all food and drink: no facilities here. This is worth a visit to get away from the crowds. To get there, take a bemo running north from Pemanang – the walk to the beach is about 2 km from the road.

Siri Beach

Bayan

This is a traditional Sasak village and the birthplace of Lombok's unique Muslim 'schism' – *Islam Waktu Telu* (see page 802). There is a mosque here which is believed to be 300 years old. The village is the jumping-off point for climbs up Mount Rinjani (see below). No accommodation.

Bemo Connections with the Bertais terminal in Cakranegara, 2,000Rp. From Bayan bemos run up to Batu Koq. Bemos also run east from here along the very scenic coastal road to Labuan Lombok. From the looks of surprise it is clear that few *orang putih* make this (long) journey.

Transport
50 km from Pemenang

Mount Rinjani

Visitors who have made the effort invariably say that the highlight of their stay on Lombok was climbing Mount Rinjani. The views from the summit on a clear day are simply breathtaking. The ascent requires three days (although some keen climbers try to do it in two). Be warned that the summit is often wreathed in cloud, and views down to the blue-green lake within the caldera are also often obscured by a layer of cloud which lies trapped in the enormous crater.

Mount Rinjani is the second highest mountain in Indonesia outside Irian Jaya – rising to an altitude of 3,726m. The volcano is still active but last erupted some time ago – in 1901, although in 1997 rumblings left dust raining for a week. The mountain, and a considerable area of land surrounding the mountain totalling some 400 sq km, has been gazetted as a national park.

The climb There are two routes up Mount Rinjani. The easier and more convenient begins about 2 km to the west of the village of Bayan, on the way to Anyer. The track leads upwards from the road to the small settlement of **Batu Koq** and from there, 1 km on, to another village, **Senaru**. Tents, equipment and guides or porters can be hired in either of these two settlements (ask at the losmen); accommodation is available (see below). It is recommended that trekkers check in at the conservation office in Senaru before beginning the ascent. A guide is not essential as the trail is well marked from Senaru to the crater rim; however, suitable climbing gear is required (see below). From Senaru, the trek to the summit takes about two days, or 10 hours solid climbing. On the trek up, the path passes through stands of teak and mahogany,

Around Mount Rinjani

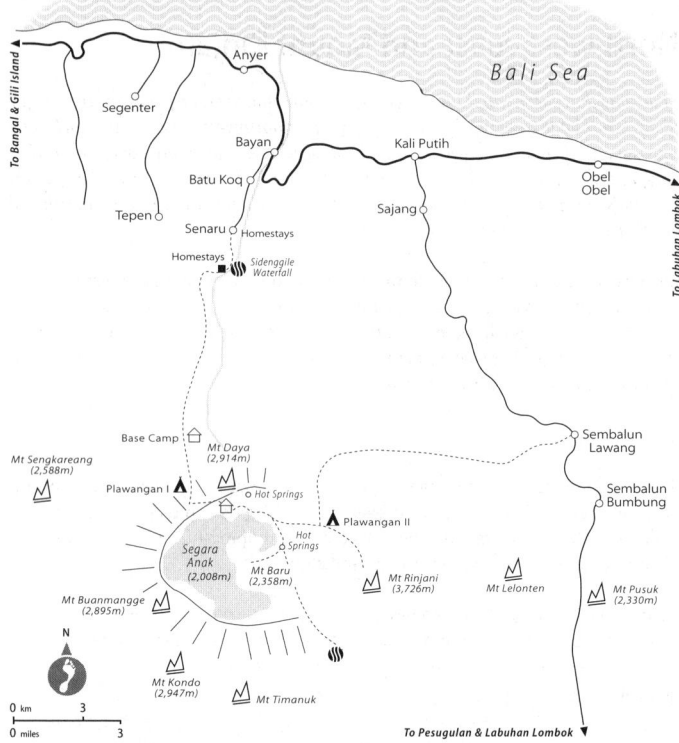

then into pine forest and lichin. There are stunning views from the lip of the crater down to the beautiful blue-green and mineral rich lake, **Segara Anak** (Child of the Sea), below. A third day is needed to walk down into the caldera. The caldera is 8 km long by 5 km wide.

On the east side of the lake is **Mount Baru** (New Mountain), an active cone within a cone that rose out of the lake in 1942. It can be reached by boat and the climb to Mount Baru's summit, through a wasteland of volcanic debris, is rewarded with a view into this secondary crater. Along the base of the main crater are numerous hot springs – like **Goa Susu** (Milk Cave – so called because of its colour) – which are reputed to have spectacular healing powers; bathing in them is a good way to round-off a tiring descent.

An alternative and more difficult route up the mountain – but some climbers who have done both claim this is the more interesting – is via **Sembalun Lawang**, **Sembalun Bumbung** or **Sapit** on the mountain's eastern slopes. There is accommodation here (see below) and guides are also available, but there is a shortage of equipment for hire. There is food available to buy for the trek but the range of victuals is not as good as in Senaru. To get to Sembalun Bumbung, take a bus from Labuhan Lombok. For details on Sapit, see page 794. The climb to the crater takes about nine hours. For ambitious climbers who intend to reach the true summit of Mount Rinjani – rather than just the caldera – this is the better of the two routes. **NB** In early 2000 the Australian Embassy in Jakarta was advising visitors not to climb Mount Rinjani because of fears of violent theft. However, no one going up, nor the guides, seemed concerned or particularly aware of any great problems. Nonetheless, check before beginning the climb.

This alternative route is less well marked. A guide is recommended to show climbers the route to the second rim

Round trip taking in both sides of the mountain: because each side of Rinjani offers its own character, a recommended alternative is to climb up the eastern flank and down the western. To do this, go to Senaru to rent equipment and buy supplies (the choice is best here), return to Anyer or Bayan and take a bemo or ojek to Sembalun Lawang. (Start early, bemos to Sembalun Lawang are rare after 1600.) Hire a guide and porter in Sembalun Lawang and stay the night. The next day the guide can show the route to the second rim (6-7 hours); from here, the climb to the summit (3-4 hours) and then down into the caldera (three hours), and from there up to the first rim and back down to Senaru (6-7 hours), is well marked and the guide is not needed.

Climb from May to November, during the dry season, when it is less likely to be cloudy. Do not attempt the climb during the rainy season as the trail can be treacherous. **Recommended equipment**: water, sweater and coat, foam camping roll, sleeping bag, tough walking shoes, food/supplies, firewood (there is increasing evidence of climbers chopping down trees within this National Park in order to light a fire). *Please* take all your litter with you. **NB** Some climbers have complained of the poor quality of some of the equipment hired in Senaru; check it carefully. **Guides**: cost about 80,000Rp per day and porters 40,000Rp per day. A tent and/or sleeping bag hired for the guide would be greatly appreciated; it's cold on the mountain.

Best time to climb
The climb, though not technically difficult, is arduous & climbers should be in reasonable physical condition

It is possible to stay at Batu Koq and Senaru, as well as at Sembalun Lawang if making the climb from the east. Senaru has the best selection of (basic, all **E**) losmen and new ones seem to open almost every month. **Senaru**: *Bale Bayan Guesthouse*, near the mountain, clean and friendly, the owner speaks reasonable English and German. Recommended. *Pondok Senaru*, clean, well run, big restaurant, ice cold mandi. **Batu Koq**: *Segara Anak Homestay* has been recommended. Price includes breakfast and supper; some exquisite views. *Guru Bakti*, good bungalows, especially those at the rear which offer superb views down the valley, price includes breakfast. **E** *Cemari Siu*, just as good. On the southeast slopes of Rinjani at the village of **Sapit** is the **D-E** *Hati Suci Homestay*, peaceful. Highly recommended. A good base for climbing the mountain. **E** *Balelangga*, 300m down the road run by the brother of Hati Suci, is also excellent. Breathtaking views. **Sembalun Lawang**: **E** *Diriam Guesthouse*, very helpful and friendly place, the owner speaks some English and can help arrange the trek,

Sleeping

although equipment is in short supply and may not be available. Recommended. **Camping**: there are trekkers' camp sites at various positions up the mountain – the corrugated shelters are rather dilapidated and the litter is bad.

Festivals Dec (2nd week): *Pakelem*, offering feast on Segara Anak to ask for God's blessings.

Tours The most convenient way to climb Rinjani is by booking a place on a 'tour'. Several tour operators in Mataram (see page 776), Senggigi (page 781) and on the Gilis organize climbs (about US$180 all-in). Tours are also available from losmen at various villages, such as Sapit.

Transport **Bemo** For the more usual north route, take a bemo from the Bertais terminal to Bayan, and then a 2nd bemo from Bayan to Senaru. Alternatively, walk from Bayan. For the east route, take a bemo from Labuhan Lombok to Sembalun Bumbung; for transport to Sapit, see page 794. **Taxi** A taxi from Bangsal to Senaru should cost about 10,000Rp per hr of journey time.

Central Lombok and the West

Lombok's excellent main road runs for 74 km, east to west; from Mataram to Labuhan Lombok – the small port where ferries leave for Sumbawa. Most of the destinations in central and west Lombok can be visited on a day trip from Senggigi Beach; there is little accommodation available. East of Mataram (and 10 km from Cakranegara) is the town of Narmada, with its rather down-at-heel 'pleasure garden'. A little way northwest of here is Lingsar, the site of the Waktu Telu Temple. The cool hill town of Suranadi, 7 km to the north of Narmada, is set at 400m above sea-level (where there is a hotel). About 25 km east of Narmada, a road to the north (just after Sikur) leads up the lower slopes of Mount Rinjani, through Kota Raja, to a second hill resort, Tetebatu.

Narmada

The **Taman Narmada**, or terraced 'pleasure garden' opposite the bemo station, was built in 1805. There are various spring-fed pools here, one of which is open to the public for swimming (admission to pool 500Rp). The gardens are supposed to be a scale model of the upper slopes of Mount Rinjani, including a replica of the holy crater lake, *Segara Anak*. The gardens are a popular picnic spot for Indonesians, but sadly are poorly maintained and rather dirty. Dance performances are held here (2,000Rp). ■ *Admission to garden 200Rp. 0700-1800 Mon-Sun.*

Festivals Nov/Dec: *Pujawali*, an annual festival held in conjunction with the *Pekalem* festival on Mount Rinjani (when pieces of gold are thrown into the crater lake). Once a year there is a 'duck-chasing' festival at Taman Narmada. Ducks are released onto the lake and at a signal from the leader of the ceremony boys plunge in to collect the birds. They are allowed to keep any ducks they catch.

Transport **Bemo** Regular connections with the Bertais terminal in **Cakranegara**. Eleven kilometres east of Mataram

Lingsar

The **Waktu Telu Temple**, also known as the Lingsar Temple, was originally built in 1714, and then rebuilt in 1878. Both Hindu Balinese and Muslim Sasaks come to worship here, and there are compounds dedicated to each religion. ■ *0700-1800. Admission by donation. Dress modest, sash required.*

Festivals Nov/Dec: *Pujawali*, a 7-day festival, culminating in the 2 religions, the Muslims and Hindus, staging mock battles in the lower courtyard where they throw rice cakes (or *ketupat*) at one another.

Suranadi

Bemo Take a bemo from the Bertais terminal in Cakranegara to Narmada, and change here for Lingsar. If driving oneself, there is a more direct back route along a minor road from Cakranegara to Lingsar.

Transport

Suranadi

Set at an altitude of 400m, this is the site of one of Lombok's holiest temples – **Pura Suranadi**. Suranadi is the name of a celestial river in Hindu mythology and the temple is situated at the source of a mountain spring. Ornate Balinese carvings decorate the shrine.

Phone code: 0370

The small village of **Sesoat** is 5 km away with good warungs, an ice cold river to swim in, and a thriving market.

B-C *Suranadi*, Jl Raya Suranadi, PO Box 10, T633686, F635630. A/c, restaurant, tennis, hot water, Lombok's original colonial hotel, now refurbished and with a new wing, friendly, with a slightly murky, spring-fed, swimming pool also used by many local people. **B-D** *Teratai Cottage and Restaurant*, T633829, F633826. Pleasant cottages both standard and luxury, with swimming pool set amongst the tiered padis that create a dramatic verdant vista from the restaurant, which serves a mix of Western and local food. Very courteous staff.

Sleeping

Recently 3 restaurants have sprung up on the road near these hotels.

Eating

Bemo From the Bertais terminal in Cakranegara to Narmada, and then change to another travelling north to Suranadi (500Rp for each leg of the trip). Seven kilometres north of Narmada, 18 km from Mataram.

Transport

Tetebatu

Tetebatu is a tiny village on the slopes of Mount Rinjani. There is very little to do here, except enjoy the beautiful scenery and visit the surrounding villages. There are good walks in the surrounding countryside.

Tours to Telebatu are advertised in Senggigi & the Gilis

The villages in this part of Lombok are well worth exploring, and this is best done by hiring a car or motorcycle. **Kota Raja** is a market town 7 km south of Tetebatu noted for its handicrafts, particularly basketwork. Tours to Tetebatu are advertised in places such as Senggigi and the Gilis. **Loyok**, just off the road to Tetebatu, is known for its bamboo crafts and palm leaf boxes, while **Pringgasela**, east of Kota Raja, is a centre for ikat weaving (see below). **Lendang Nangka** is a traditional Sasak village 7 km east of Kota Raja; while **Masbaggik**, on the main road just to the east of the turn-off for Kota Raja and Tetebatu, is a pottery-making town. There are other craft villages in the central highlands area.

Excursions

Several new guesthouses have recently opened in this area. **C-D** *Wisma Soedjono*, some a/c, restaurant (**1-2**) slow service, large pool, occupies a lovely position looking out over paddy and pineapple fields and the south slopes of Mount Rinjani. There is a variety of accommodation, including some 'traditional' Sasak houses along the side of the hill. **D** *Lentera*, east side of the village, sparklingly clean bungalows, clean showers and a restaurant (breakfast included). **B-E** *Hotel Melati* or the *Green Orry Inn*, T683662. Private mandi, good portions in the restaurant. **E** *Pondok Bulan*, bungalows, near the rice paddies offering bicycle hire (4,000Rp). **E** *Mentariku Bungalows*, Benteng Village, 5 km on the road from Lendang Nangka to Tetebatu, F622298. Traditional Sasak style accommodation, in beautiful valley looking towards Mount Rinjani. Price includes breakfast, a stunning retreat. **E** *Wisma Dewi Enjeni*, 2 km south of Tetebatu, lovely views, price includes breakfast.

Sleeping

11 km north of the main road linking Mataram with Labuhan Lombok. **Bemo** From the Mertais terminal in Cakranegara to Paok Motong and then another bemo to Tetebatu (2,500Rp).

Transport

Pringgasela

East of Kota Raja is this small weaving village, where traditional back-strap looms have not yet been displaced by more advanced technology, and where natural rather than artificial (chemical aniline) dyes are still in use. As there is accommodation available in Pringgasela, this is a good place to experience the 'real' Lombok.

Sleeping Family-run homestay. Suhaidi (better known as 'Eddie') can arrange tours and trekking. **D** *Sasak House Homestay*, friendly, shared mandi.

Transport **Bemo**: from the Bertais terminal in Cakranegara to Rempung and then a dokar to Pringgasela or from Labuhan Lombok.

Sapit

Sapit is a small Sasak village on the southeast slopes of Mount Rinjani, with views west towards the mountain and east over the sea to Sumbawa. Set amidst rice paddies, it is one of the most relaxing places to unwind and also makes a good base for climbing Mount Rinjani.

Excursions **Mount Rinjani** is a 3-5 day excursion from Sapit (see page 790); guides are available in the village and charge about 80,000Rp per day.

Sleeping **D-E** *Hati Suci Homestay*, F622160, http://sites.netscape.net/hatisuci/info Restaurant, bungalow and dorm accommodation, clean and professionally run, stunning views, peaceful, breakfast included, tours/treks organized, Canadian partner. Highly recommended. *Balelangga* is 300m along the road, and is similarly situated and laid out with well kept gardens. Sprung mattresses. Highly recommended. Both *Hati Suci* and *Balelangga* can be booked through Noor Family, Jl Kesra VII Perumnas, Mataram, T0370-636545, F635753, Hatisuci@mataram.wasantara.net.id; Balelangga@mataram.wasantara.net.id

Tours From here you can arrange an all-in trip to **Kalimantan**, where these homestay families are originally from Gilang. http://members.tripod.com/orangs or Gilang98@hotmail.com

Transport **Bus**: regular buses from the Bertais terminal in Cakranegara to Pringgabaya; from Pringgabaya, catch a bemo to Sapit. Total journey time 2½-3 hrs. From Labuhan Lombok, take a bus to Pringgabaya and then a **bemo** to Sapit. The same applies from Kute, catch bemo to Praya and on. **NB** to catch the last bemo to the door of these homestays, you must reach the bottom of the mountain by 1500.

Labuhan Lombok

Labuhan Lombok is the small ferry port for Sumbawa. It is little more than a fishing village.

Sleeping **E** *Losmen Muanawar*, basic. **E-F** *Lima Tiga*, new losmen, very clean and well-run when it opened, shared mandi, price includes breakfast, the best place to stay here. Recommended.

Eating **Cheap**: *Warung Kelayu*, close to the *Lima Tiga* losmen, good value local food.

Transport
74 km from Mataram
Bemo: from the Bertais terminal in Cakranegara, 2 hrs along an excellent road, with only the dokars to delay your progress. There is now a good road running up the north coast from Labuhan Lombok right round to Bayan. Bemos do this journey. To make a round trip back to Mataram, change bemos at Bayan. **Sea Boat**: there is a ferry linking Labuhan Lombok, with Poto Tano on Sumbawa's west coast. Departures on the hour 0300-1600 and 1800, return hourly on the half hour 0330-1630 and 1830. A very pleasant 1½ hrs crossing, with spectacular views of Rinjani and the off-shore islands (4,000Rp).

East Lombok

Few people visit the east which is drier, poorer and more sparsely inhabited than the west. Superb sea views and stunning glimpses of Mount Rinjani along the northeast coast road. To the south of Labuhan Lombok is the fishing port of Labuhan Haji with some basic accommodation, and a rugged route to Tanjung Ringgit at the end of the mystical southeast peninsula (see page 799).

Northeast coast

Travelling north from Labuhan Lombok you reach Labuhan Pandan after about 12 km. Here there are deserted, black sand beaches, and fabulous views of uninhabited islands and the west coast of Sumbawa. You can hire boats to take you to these islands with their gold sand beaches for about 40,000Rp a day; bring all the food and water you need as there is nothing on these islands. **Labuhan Pandan**

E *Siola Homestay* is a good bet. *Perama* runs a camp on 1 of the islands, though we heard complaints from travellers who had been stranded there when the *Perama* boat broke down. There is a Japanese conservation project on **Gili Luwang** and **Sulat**, where you can camp. Also you could try **Air Manis** village, with a losmen of the same name, Jl Raya Sambela. It's cheap, clean and comfy and provides an insight into local life. **Sleeping**

Continuing north from Labuhan Pandan, you pass through the fishing village of **Sambelia**, with some traditional style bugis' houses on stilts, then on to **Blanting**, with enchanting seaviews *en route*. The landscape here is mostly very arid, though as you approach Obel Obel, about 50 km from Labuhan Lombok, it becomes more luxuriant, and there are a number of pristine beaches such as Obel Obel, with good surf. At Kali Putih you can either head south up into the foothills of Mount Rinjani along a poor road to the villages of **Sembalun Lawang** and **Sambalun Bumbung**, or continue west to Bayan. **North coast**

Transport It is possible to do this trip from Labuhan Lombok by bemo; however, having your own transport would be preferable.

South Lombok and the south coast

From Cakranegara, a good road runs 26 km southeast to the market town of Praya. Before Praya by 3 km is the small village of Puyung, and 2 km south of here the popular weaving village of Sukarara. Turning south from Praya, the road reaches the pottery-making village of Penujak after 5 km and continues south to Sengkol. This area is one of the centres of Sasak culture, with a number of traditional villages. It is a poor part of the island, with low grade agricultural land and abandoned paddies. The road ends at the beach and fishing village of Kuta, 32 km from Praya and 58 km from Mataram.

Sukarara is a small **weaving village** southeast of Mataram. The weavers here still use traditional backstrap looms, but the workshops along the main road are now geared to tourists and the quality is indifferent, with artificial dyes in widespread use. Traditional Lombok designs are still produced – in particular cloth inter-woven with gold and silver thread – but it is becoming increasingly difficult to find finely worked, quality cloth. **Sukarara**

Bemo: from the Mertais terminal in Cakranegara bound for Praya; get off at Puyung, 3 km north of Praya. From here, either walk or hire a dokar for the 2-km ride to the village. **Transport** *25 km from Mataram*

Penujak is a **pottery-making village** 5 km south of Praya on the road to Kuta. The New Zealand government has been providing aid to support and develop the craft **Penujak** since 1988, in particular through improving design, technology and marketing. Other important pottery-making villages include **Rungkang** and **Masbaggik** in East Lombok, and **Banyumulek** to the south of Mataram. The latter two villages also receive support from the New Zealand project.

The road splits at Penujak. One branch leads on to the south coast of Silungblanak where there is a good sandy beach. The other road goes on to Kuta.

Transport Bemo: from the Bertais terminal in Cakranegara to Praya; change in Praya and catch another travelling south to Penujak.

Sade The area south of the town of Sengkol to Kuta Beach is one of the centres of Sasak culture and there are a number of 'traditional' Sasak villages here. The best known is Sade where women, realizing their potential as a tourist attraction, still wear traditional Sasak dress. Also here, there are some of the few remaining examples of Sasak architecture, including the tall-roofed, thatched, *lumbungs* (rice barns). But Sade is firmly on the tour bus circuit and, although the villagers have made a conscious effort to maintain 'tradition' for the foreign visitors, the economy is geared as much to tourism as to agriculture. Women frantically sell textiles while the children hustle.

Transport Bemo: from the Bertais terminal in Cakranegara to Praya; change here and catch another travelling south towards Kuta.

Kuta Beach

Phone code: 0370 Kuta Beach, also sometimes known as Putri Nyale Beach, is situated amongst some of the most spectacular coastal scenery on Lombok; rocky outcrops and cliff faces give way to sheltered sandy bays, ideal for swimming and surfing.

Kuta itself has a stretch of sand on Lombok's south coast, in a bay with a little fishing village at its head. There is a substantial fishing fleet of sailing boats with brightly decorated dugout hulls and outriggers. There are no 'sights' other than the Sasak villages about 20 minutes' drive inland, beside the main Mataram to Kuta road.

The beach is the focal point of a strange annual festival, called the **Bau Nyale** (see Sumba, page 865, for similar event), when thousands of seaworms come to the surface of the sea. Local people flock here to witness the event, and it is becoming quite a popular tourist attraction. See below for details.

Kuta

■ Sleeping
1 Anda Bungalows
2 Cockatoo Bungalows & Restaurant
3 Kuta Beach Bungalows & Restaurant
4 Kutah Indah
5 La Mancha Homestay
6 Matahari
7 Novotel
8 Nyali Homestay
9 Rambitan Bungalows
10 Rinjan Bungalows 1
11 Rinjan Bungalows 2
12 Segara Anak & Internet
13 Sekar Kuning Bungalows

● Eating
1 Bambu & pool table
2 Mascot (Jungle Bar)
3 Warung Melati

Still a relatively quiet place to stay, there is a good road linking it to Mataram with regular shuttle bus connections.

At present the roads beyond Kuta are poor. The coast road continues east from Kuta past some magnificent, white sandy bays. After 2 km a potholed tarmac road turns off to Seger Beach, one of the beaches where the Nyale fish come ashore.

Excursions

Further on again by 4 km, past low-lying swampy land, is the fine gold sand beach at **Tanjung Aan**, set in a horseshoe shaped bay; it is good for swimming, though there are stones and coral about 10m out. Despite its distance from any development there are stalls, and hawkers materialize as soon as any foreigners appear. **NB** There is no shade on any of these beaches, just basic scrub. The track bends round to the south and ends at **Gepupak (Desert) Point**.

There are many **walks** in the area: climb the hill immediately to the west of Kuta for spectacular views over the south coast. The **Seger hills**, 2 km to the east, have numerous farm trails and a small cemetery; near Seger beach is a rocky promontory with more superb views, especially at sunset.

Surfing beaches The best are: **Are Guling**, **Mawi**, **Mawun** and **Selong Blanak**. **Gerupak (Desert Point)** is rated as one of the best surf spots in the world outside Hawaii. Kuta was originally 'discovered' by surfers.

Traditional villages Sade and **Rembitan**, 9 km north of Kuta just off the main Mataram road, 20 minutes' drive.

Accommodation has improved recently with 1 luxury class hotel and some smart new bungalows. The older bungalows are rather unattractive, made of clapboard with linoleum floors, squashed together and facing away from the sea. Rooms are usually small (and bedbugs can be a problem), up on stilts. They are mostly of similar standard and in our **D-E** categories, although cheaper rooms do come down in price to our **F** category. Most of the bungalows are strung out along the beach road a short distance from the village, but 2 of the best, *Kuta Indah* and *Matahari*, are in the village itself, a 10 min walk from the beach.

Sleeping

A *Novotel*, Mandalika Resort, Pantai Putri Nyotle, Pujut, T653333, F653555, 3 km east of Kuta village, beside the sea. The most luxurious hotel in the Kuta area. This 3-star hotel offers the usual luxuries including a swimming pool. Built in traditional style with thatched roofs. The hotel is attractively furnished.

B-D *Kuta Indah Hotel*, T653781, F653628, kutaindah@indo.net.id Attractive accommodation on the western edge of Kuta village, 8 mins walk from the beach, 50 rooms in bungalows overlooking large central gardens shaded by coconut palms. Superior rooms with a/c, hot water, bathrooms with Western toilets. Standard rooms with fan and cold water. A good sized pool. Restaurant has some of the best food in town at reasonable prices (mid-range to cheap). Hotel offers free transport to Tanjung Aan and Mawan beaches. Safety deposit box, car hire, airport transfer. Recommended. **B-E** *Matahari*, T654832, F654909. Inland, in the centre of the village, set in lovely, flower filled gardens; rooms range from fairly basic, older rooms, to fairly luxurious new rooms with a/c, hot water and marble bathrooms. Be prepared to bargain. Free transport to Tanjung Aan and Mawan beaches. Restaurant (mid-range to cheap).

D-E *Anda*, T654836. Several attractive bungalows with private mandi and western toilet, let down by their location facing the family quarters away from the beach. Run by a friendly family. Offers the only internet access apart from the Novotel. **D-E** *Cockatoo*, T654830/1. A peaceful location. The newer bungalows are clean and attractive with Western toilets, the older rooms are basic with squat toilet; bungalows face each other across a large garden. Restaurant (mid-range to cheap). **D-E** *Rinjani 2*, T654849. A mixture of rooms and bungalows with private mandi (some with western toilet), the newer bungalows are better value. Set in pretty gardens. The 2-storey bungalow at the front with an upstairs balcony overlooking the beach has the best view in Kuta. *Rinjani 1*, same ownership as *Rinjani 2* but these are older, rather basic bungalows in need of maintenance, though set in pretty gardens with a pond. Most have private mandis, some with

Western toilets. **D-E** *Segara Anak*, T654834, F654835. Very lively and popular with budget travellers, 30 fairly basic rooms with private bathroom (Western toilets, some without toilet seats). Rooms set close together; the best rooms are the newer ones at the back overlooking the papaya grove and the hills. Very helpful staff, can provide a local map with a cycling route. Safety deposit box, postal and fax service. Popular restaurant (mid-range to cheap).

There are also several homestays offering basic accommodation (with shared use of squat toilets). High season, when accommodation may be full, is Aug and during the Nyale festival in Mar.

Eating The best food is at the restaurant of the *Kuta Indah Hotel*. Seafood features prominently on many menus. But it is often overpriced and over-rated. Restaurants are attached to several of the above places to stay, including **Rinjani Agung Beach**; **Florida**; **Anda**; **Cockatoo Inn**, good spring rolls, popular with tour buses; **Segara Anak**, popular; next door is the **Golden Flower**, which does excellent local food. **Bamboo**, near the village.

Bars & clubs Night life is pretty thin on the ground, but 3 times a week the local lads at the informal Jungle Bar knock out classic Marley tunes, and this brings in a range of different types of tourists. Low key, very good atmosphere, even for single females (a rarity in Lombok's tourist centres). Cultural shows are put on from time to time at the hotels.

Festivals Feb/Mar (on the 19th day of the 10th month of the Sasak lunar calendar): *Nyale ceremony*, thousands of mysterious sea worms called Nyale fish (*Eunice viridis*) 'hatch' on the reef and rise to the surface of the sea off Kuta. According to the legend of Putri Nyale, the episode is linked to the beautiful Princess Nyale, who drowned herself here after failing to choose between a bevy of eligible men. The worms are supposed to represent her hair, and celebrations are held each year to mark her death. Traditionally, this was a time for young people to find a partner for marriage, and it is still an occasion when the usual strictures controlling contact between the sexes are eased. The worms are scooped from the sea and eaten.

Shopping The local shops along the beachfront sell basics, including fruit, at reasonable prices. An endless stream of young children offer locally woven sarongs of variable quality, T-shirts and fruit. The pineapples here are delicious, as are the green bananas (to tell green bananas from unripe yellow bananas just squeeze; the ripe green bananas will feel soft). Kuta has its own market on Sat. Sengkol and Praya market days are Sat, Mon and Thu. Surf equipment, lessons, boat travel from **Ocean Blue Surf Shop**, see below.

Sports **Surfing** Many people come to Kuta to surf. Boards, lessons, boat travel, repairs and nightly videos of the biggest tubes and breaks in the world are shown at the **Ocean Blue Surf Shop**, Kuta T/F653911.

Transport **Bus**: Daily *Perama* shuttle buses at 0930, also an afternoon service if there is sufficient demand; the *Perama* office is adjacent to *Segara Anak*. Public bemo to Praya from the bemo stop several times a day, about 2,000Rp, 1 hr, from there you can catch a bemo to Bertais, 30 mins; 32 km from Praya, 54 km from Mataram. **Bemo**: from the Bertais terminal in Cakranegara (Mataram) to Praya and then a 2nd from Praya to Kuta. Nomad also run a shuttle bus to Mataram. Public bemos also connect Kuta with Lahbuan Lombok (for ferries to Sumbawa). **Motorbikes**: are available to hire, often at very reasonable prices, eg 25,000Rp per day. Ask at your accommodation. Bemo services are increasing and more villages are coming on line, especially along the coast roads east and west of Kuta. Best to hire your own transport, though be aware that roads are bumpy. You can hire a car with driver, but self-drive is recommended here; the local drivers have limited skills for the most part. Mataram to Kuta is just over 1 hr, depending on traffic.

Directory **Useful information** **Security:** there is an 'honoured' tradition of inter-village theft in these parts. A thief from 1 village gained prestige by successfully stealing from other villages. We were warned to be very careful if out walking after dark. Take extra precautions to safeguard money and valuables. However, all over Lombok local neighbourhood watch style groups have formed, HQ Praya, and will get your stolen goods back within the day! Hence crime has decreased considerably.

West of Kuta

There is now a sealed road running west of Kuta as far as Selong Blanak. Along the way there are several good beaches, all fairly deserted. Twenty minutes' drive (10 km) west of Kuta is **Mawan Beach**. A perfect horseshoe shaped bay with a golden sand beach, a large tree and two bamboo shelters (called *garuga*) and several coconut palms offering some protection from the sun. Good for swimming, very protected though the sea bed slopes steeply near the shore. The road west climbs steeply out of Kuta, with spectacular views of the south coast, and mist covered hills in the rainy season. Further west near Selong Blanak are more good gold sand beaches at **Mawi** and **Rowok**. Mawi in particular offers good surfing. The road continues to the fishing village of **Selong Blanak**, with its wide, sandy bay and accommodation a little inland. Few travellers make the trip further west to **Pengantap**, **Sepi** and **Blongas**; the last of which has good surfing, snorkelling and diving, though be wary of sharks. From Sepi the poor road heads inland via Sekatong to the port of **Lembar**. All roads deteriorate west of Pengantap and should probably be avoided in the wet season. There are some bemos, though most people get here by private or chartered transport. The better accommodations offer free transport to Tanjung Aan Beach to the east and Mawan Beach to the west.

Sleeping

D-E *Selong Blanak Cottages*, clean and well run, rooms with private mandi, restaurant (cheap), the deserted beach is about 2 km away and free transport is provided (the same applies for Sepi and Blongas nearby).

Transport

The occasional bemo runs to Selong Blanak from Praya.

East of Kuta

Shortly before Tanjung Aan the road forks; taking the left fork, northeast, the road passes through Sereneng *en route* to Awang, 18 km from Kuta. The right fork goes to Gerupak about 9 km east of Kuta. From here there are boats across Gumbang Bay to Bumgang for about 10,000Rp. From Bumgang there is a path north which connects with the road to Awang. The villagers in this area make their living from fishing and seaweed farming and will hire out boats for about 40,000Rp a day.

From Awang, boats can be chartered across the bay to Ekas for about 30,000Rp return. **Ekas** has good surfing and snorkelling. There are spectacular views from the cliffs overlooking Awang Bay on both sides, particularly from Ekas. It is possible but time-consuming to reach Ekas by public bemo: from Praya, catch a bemo bound for Tanjung Luar and Gubukdalem, get off just before Keruak at the turning south to Jerowaru and wait for a bemo going to Ekas, which is *en route* to Kaliantan in the southwest corner of the peninsula.

Tanjung Ringgit, on the southeastern tip of Lombok, is difficult to reach and for the most part the scenery is unexceptional. This place is shrouded in magic and mystery, with tales of spirits and demons living in the caves. (If a young woman goes there she will fall in love and never return.) It has connections with the Waktu Telu religion. To get here the choice is either an arduous overland journey ending in a rough dirt track, or chartering a boat from the fishing town of Tanjung Luar, 55,000Rp approximately.

Transport

Bemo A few bemos travel these routes and their numbers are slowly increasing, but the best way to see the area is with your own transport. **Boat** From Awang. In the dry season it is possible to drive there via Jerowaru.

Lombok's crafts

Banyu Mulek *(6 km from Mataram): earthenware products.*
Beleka *(10 km east of Praya): baskets, bags, cases and other goods made from reeds and rotan (rattan).*
Getap *(1 km east of Cakranegara): a village of blacksmiths where swords, knives and other objects are cast.*
Loyok Kutaraja *(40 km east of Mataram): furniture and woven goods.*
Masbaggik *(44 km east of Mataram, see page 793): earthenware bowls and pots, now produced with the marketing and technological help of a New Zealand NGO.*
Penjanggik *(4 km east of Praya): a weaving village producing hand-woven cloth distinct from that at Sukarara.*

Penujak *(5 km south of Praya, see page 795): earthenware bowls and pots, now produced, as at Masbaggik, with the marketing and technological help of a New Zealand NGO.*
Pringgasela *(50 km from Mataram, see page 794): a weaving village, although many of the hand-woven cloths are no longer made to traditional designs.*
Sayang-Sayang *(1 km north of Cakranegara): lacquered boxes made from palm leaves.*
Senanti *(73 km from Mataram): wood carvings.*
Sukarara *(25 km from Mataram, see page 795): traditional, and some not so traditional, hand-woven textiles.*

Background

History

It seems that the Sasak population of Lombok converted to Islam during the 16th century, when local legend has it that epidemics only began to afflict Lombok after the introduction of Islam and that it was by turning to Islam Waktu Telu that further epidemics were prevented.

In the 17th century, the Balinese king of Karangasem invaded West Lombok and attempted to annex the island. He failed, and it was not until 1740 that the Balinese established a stronghold in the west. Even then, the independently minded Sasaks of the east managed to maintain their autonomy until the 19th century. Nonetheless, the Balinese – as the dominant group – imposed their culture on the Sasaks. They became the ruling caste and attempted to control the economy of the island. Given the harshness with which the Sasaks were treated by their rulers, it is no wonder that they rebelled on a number of occasions, and when the chance offered itself, asked the Dutch to come to their rescue.

The Dutch In 1894, the Dutch invaded Lombok. The pretext for the invasion was that the local Sasaks had requested Dutch assistance in ridding themselves of their Balinese overlords. With their Sasak allies, the Dutch set about attacking and looting every town and village in South Lombok. As was later to be the case during the Dutch campaigns in Bali, rather than surrender, the Balinese chose to die in a *puputan* or 'fight to the death' (see page 322).

For the Sasaks and the remnant Balinese population of Lombok, the years of Dutch rule from 1900 to 1940 were not happy ones. Indeed, the Dutch period on Lombok represents, in the eyes of many historians, an object lesson in the excesses and inequities of colonial rule. The Dutch taxed everyone heavily. It has been estimated that over a quarter of a farmer's rice harvest – which was already barely sufficient to ensure subsistence – was forfeited in taxes. There was a consequent sharp deterioration in conditions in the countryside, and by the 1920s a class of marginalized paupers had been created where previously there was none. Meat and rice consumption fell, malnutrition became widespread, and when harvests failed, famine ensued.

Even after the Dutch had withdrawn and Indonesia had achieved independence, life on Lombok remained difficult. Famines became almost a way of life, and in 1966 many thousands died of starvation after a particularly poor harvest.

Wallace's line

In his book The Malay Archipelago, published in 1869, the great Victorian naturalist Alfred Russel Wallace wrote: "If we look at a map of the Archipelago, nothing seems more unlikely than that the closely related chain of islands from Java to Timor should differ materially in their natural productions". During his travels he noted the "remarkable change...which occurs at the Straits of Lombock, separating the island of that name from Bali; and which is at once so large in amount and of so fundamental a character, as to form an important feature in the zoological geography of our globe". Wallace was struck by the change in the faunal composition of Bali and Lombok – two islands separated by a strait only a few kilometres wide. The former was dominated by animals of Asian origin, and the latter of Australasian – Wallace's Indo-Malayan and Austro-Malayan regions respectively.

The first reference to Wallace's 'line', as it became known, is contained in a letter he wrote to Henry Bates who had just returned to London from his South American travels, in January 1858. Since then, numerous zoogeographers and naturalists have offered their own interpretations, all highlighting the change in fauna but postulating various different 'lines'. Even Wallace changed his mind: his original line had Sulawesi in the Austro-Malayan region, but by 1880 he had decided the island to be anomalous, and then in 1910 he drew his line to the east of Sulawesi, placing it in the Indo-Malayan region. The other lines proposed include Weber's line (1894), Lydekker's line (1896) and an updated Weber's line (1904), of which the last has received the greatest recognition.

The validity of Wallace's line rests on the distribution of animals through the island arc of the Lesser Sundas. Botanists have found little to lead them to similar conclusions. For example, the majority of East Asian mammals – like the elephant and rhinoceros – do not extend beyond Bali. Likewise, over 80% of reptiles, amphibians and butterflies in Sulawesi are of western origin. But some naturalists have stressed the importance of ecology in determining the faunal composition of the islands of the Lesser Sundas. The Oxford zoologist W George has summed up this view by writing that Wallace's line "marks the division between a rich continental fauna associated with high rainfall, forests and varied habitats and an impoverished fauna associated with low rainfall, thorn scrub and restricted habitats".

However, perhaps most remarkably, Wallace 'predicted' the theory of plate tectonics and continental drift when he wrote that the distribution of animals "can only be explained by a bold acceptance of vast changes in the surface of the earth".

Geography

Lombok is divided into three *kabupaten* or districts – West, East and Central. The capital Mataram has become fused with the former royal city of Cakranegara, forming a rather sprawling town along the main east-west road. The population at the beginning of 2000 had reached close to 3,000,000.

Covering 4,700 sq km, Lombok is dominated by the magnificent volcano Mount Rinjani which rises to 3,726m – making it the highest peak in Indonesia outside Irian Jaya. The island's main crop is rice, which is primarily cultivated in irrigated paddy fields on the fertile central plain. Like Bali, irrigation is regulated through a supra-village organization, the *subak*. Other crops include cassava, cotton, tobacco, soyabean, areca nuts, chilli peppers (the name Lombok is Javanese for 'chilli pepper'), cinnamon, cloves, vanilla and coffee. Lombok is also an important exporter of frogs' legs. Because of the rapid increase in the population of Lombok, there has been an associated increase in the pressure on the environment. The island's main export is pumice, although seaweed and sea cucumber are harvested for the Asian market and tourism is rapidly becoming a major source of revenue.

Lombok is drier than Bali, but wetter than the islands to the east, and receives an annual rainfall of 1,500-2,000mm. The dry season spans the months from May to

Climate

Islam Waktu Telu

On Lombok, it is thought that there are still a handful of adherents of Islam Waktu Telu. A figure of 1% of the population (25,000 people) is quoted, but this seems unlikely. Waktu Telu is a mixture of Islam and ancestor and spirit worship. Because the religion is not considered one of the five 'official' religions of Indonesia (they are Islam, Hinduism, Buddhism, Catholicism and Protestantism), the adherents of Islam Waktu Telu have been ignored and – at times – even persecuted. In 1919-20 the Waktu Telu rebelled against what they saw to be an unholy coalition between the Dutch and members of the rival religion, Islam Waktu Lima. Orthodox Muslims regard Waktu Telu as a travesty of the teachings of the Prophet, and between 1927 and 1933 one fervent Islam Waktu Lima missionary travelled the island breaking-up idols and converting the population to orthodox Islam. Now that many Sasaks are almost embarrassed to admit they are believers of Waktu Telu, it is likely that before long, the religion will have been consigned to the history books. This is not just because the religion is unpopular, but also because while it is possible for a Sasak to convert to orthodox Islam, a Sasak is only a Waktu Telu by birth, and cannot convert from orthodox Islam to Waktu Telu. Like the giant panda, Islam Waktu Telu is on an evolutionary dead-end.

The ceremonies and festivals of the religion focus upon the stages of a person's life, and upon the natural world – particularly that connected with agricultural production. Adherents to Waktu Telu only obey the central tenets of Islam – namely, belief in Allah and Mohammad as his prophet.

July, the hot rainy season from November to March when downpours can be quite severe and prolonged. The west is considerably wetter than the rest of the island, receiving rain even during the dry season. The east, north and south are noticeably more arid.

Culture

People The largest ethnic group are the Muslim Sasaks, the original inhabitants of Lombok, who maintain their unique language, dress and customs. There is also a significant population of Hindu Balinese who survived the Dutch invasion of 1894 (see below), along with smaller groups of Chinese, Sumbawanese, Buginese and Makassarese. Most of the Balinese and the other 'immigrant' groups are concentrated in the west, and it is in this area that Balinese *pura* are interspersed with Islamic mosques.

The Sasaks embrace two forms of Islam: the traditional – and now virtually 'extinct' – *Islam Waktu Telu* (see page 802) and the more orthodox, and more popular, *Islam Waktu Lima*.

Arts & crafts In comparison to neighbouring Bali, Lombok is not nearly as rich in terms of artistic achievement. Distinctive ikat cloth is still produced on the island, although even this is suffering from a decline in quality, as weavers turn out material at an ever-faster rate to satisfy burgeoning tourist demand. Traditionally, Sasak women were expected to weave a trousseau of about 40 pieces of cloth. Some of these are believed to be imbued with magical powers and they are important in ceremonies during the life cycle – for example, during circumcision and tooth-filing. Such *kain umbak* are unremarkable, coarse weave cloths, often striped. Lombok's basketwork is, however, highly regarded, and finely worked baskets are probably one of the best, and most distinctive, products of the island.

Sumbawa

Most people do not linger in Sumbawa. They use the island as a route between the apparently more enticing islands of Lombok to the west and Flores to the east. Sumbawa's landscape is harsh and dry, with rugged, boulder-strewn hills, scrubby vegetation and a bright, searing light. Nevertheless, the island's attractions are largely natural: the surfing beaches at Hu'u, the coral and snorkelling off Moyo Island, and hiking to the summit of Mount Tambora, an imposing volcano which erupted in the early 19th century and devastated large swathes of Nusa Tenggara. The people of Sumbawa are mainly Muslim.

Colour map 3a

Background

Even though Sumbawa covers nearly 16,000 sq km, its population remains just 1,000,000. The island is divided into three districts: Sumbawa, Dompu and Bima.

Islam was introduced to Sumbawa in the early 17th century when the King of Bima became a Muslim, and thus a Sultan. The Dutch did not exercise control over the island until the early part of the 20th century, and this lasted barely a single generation before the Japanese invaded. Today, the royal court of Bima still survives, but in an impoverished state. The two main towns on Sumbawa are Sumbawa Besar to the west and Bima-Raba in the east.

There are a number of cultural traditions specific to Sumbawa, not least that of horsemanship. Dance forms specific to Sumabawa include: Da'ha hira, where the movements are reminiscent of weaving; and Bongi Monca (yellow rice), which is a welcome dance formerly reserved for VIPs, performed and sung by women, the custodians of hospitality. Hadrah is an Islamic tradition of the island. Known as *tambour* or *rebana*, the songs are devoted to Allah. The fiery Sumbawanese spirit can also be seen in ritualized forms of self defence.

The island runs east-west for 280 km, but varies in width from as little as 15 km, to 90 km at its widest point. Like the rest of Nusa Tenggara, Sumbawa is volcanic in origin, most clearly illustrated when Mount Tambora erupted in 1815 to devastating effect, killing an estimated 12,000 people (see page 809).

Ins & outs

There are flights to Sumbawa Besar and Bima Raba, towards the western and eastern ends of the island respectively. But most people arrive by ferry either from Lombok to the west or from Flores (via Komodo) to the east. The port for Lombok is Poto Tano on the western end of the island; for Flores via Komodo it is Sape on the eastern tip. Regular ferries ply these 2 routes. *Pelni* ships dock at Sumbawa Besar's port of Badas and at Bima-Raba's port, but few people arrive or leave the island this way. There is also a high-speed ferry linking Bima with Bali and Kupang (Timor).

Getting there

The Trans-Sumbawa highway is excellent, and made-up all the way from Poto Tano (the port on the west coast, serving Lombok) to Sape (on the east coast, serving Komodo and Flores). It is 250 km from Sumbawa Besar to Bima-Raba. There are no large towns on Sumbawa; bemos provide the main means of local transport, with larger buses and minibuses providing links across the island. There are also horse-drawn carts for a more sedate form of short-distance travel.

Getting around

Alas

Alas was once the main port for Lombok; now ferries leave from Poto Tano, 22 km to the south and 10 km off the main road. There is little reason to stay here, but there are losmen available if travellers get stranded (Poto Tano has no accommodation).

Highlights, Sumbawa
Surfing at Hu'u and Maluk
Snorkelling off Moyo Island
Hiking to the summit of Mount Tambora

Sleeping **D** *Hotel Telagga*, Jl Pahlawan, is the 1st option coming in to Alas, some a/c and attached Indonesian restaurant. **E** *Anda*, Jl Pahlawan 14, T169. **E** *Selamat*, Jl Pahlawan 7, T26.

Transport **Road Bus**: connections with **Sumbawa Besar**, **Poto Tano** and **Taliwang**.
22 km from Poto Tano

Taliwang

Phone code: 0372 Taliwang lies to the south of Alas and Poto Tano; people travelling further south to the surfing beach at Maluk may have to stay overnight here, but there is little reason to extend a stay – although it is friendly enough. **Beware**: There are lots of unfriendly dogs in this part of Sumbawa.

Excursions A 15 minute walk out of Taliwang, there is an 856-ha lake, **Lebuk Taliwang**. Noted as an ideal place to relax, swim and fish; boats can be hired at the lakeside if you feel like cutting adrift.

Sleeping **E** *Hamba*, Jl Sudirman 64, T8. **E** *Taliwang*, Jl Sudirman, T81014, some rooms with shower, English speaking management, the best place in town – but still basic. **E-F** *Tubalong*, Jl Sudirman 11, T81018. **F-E** *Losmen Azhar*, Jl Pasar Baru, close to the market, basic but welcoming.

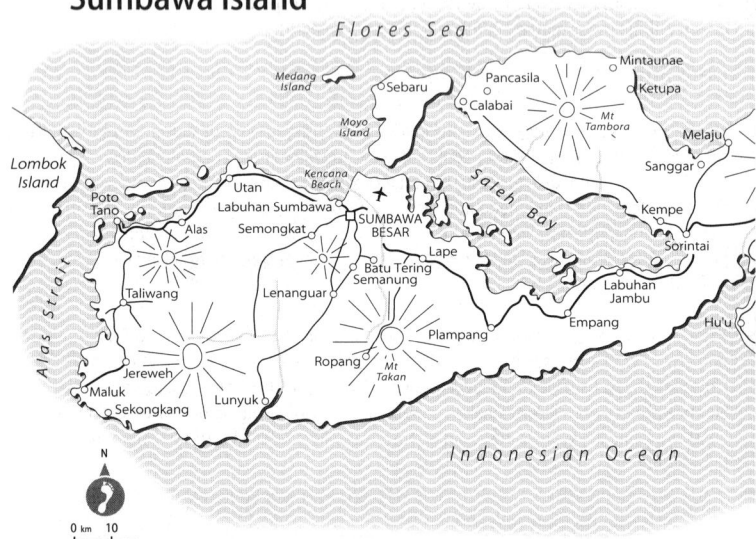

Sumbawa Island

Eating *Cheap* **Taliwang Indah**, good value dishes. The following restaurants have all been recommended: *Coffee House Casanova*, *Sinar Remaja*, Jl Sudirman 113; *Anda*, Depot Dewi and *Kediri* at Komplek Terminal Taliwang.

Transport 40 km from Alas, 40 km from Maluk. **Road Bus**: connections with **Poto Tano** and **Alas** and onward to **Sumbawa Besar**. **Bemo**: to **Sumbawa Besar**. **Trucks**: take travellers further south to **Maluk**.

Maluk

Phone code: 0372

Maluk is a beach, with good surf, on Sumbawa's west coast, south of Taliwang. **NB** The coral is just below the surface and surfing can be hazardous – this is only for the most adventurous of surfers. The beach is fantastic and the swimming good.

Sleeping The district capital of Jereweh, also known as 'Super Shark', is 30 km away, and because there is a large mine here, accommodation is now said to be readily available. There is just 1 official place to stay in Maluk, although there are a number of homestays. **C-D** *Hotel Trophy*, a new place to stay and the best run and most comfortable accommodation in Maluk, managed by an Australian – although he may have moved on with anti-Aussie sentiment. **E** *Maluk Beach Bungalows*, Jl Pasir Putih, newer place than the *Surya* so the bungalows are in better nick. **E** *Surya Bungalow*, Jl Pasir Putih, bungalows on the edge of town.

Transport *95 km south of Poto Tano, 40 km from Taliwang*
Road Bus: from Poto Tano, catch a bus south to Taliwang, 45 km, and from here a truck to Maluk, 40 km. From Sumbawa Besar, catch a bus from the Bawah terminal to Taliwang, 114 km, and then a truck onwards. **Sea Boat**: a more direct route to Maluk is from Labuhan Haji on Lombok's east coast, 1½ hrs.

Poto Tano to Sumbawa Besar The road from Poto Tano to Sumbawa Besar follows the coast, and offers views of beautiful, deserted beaches and brightly painted stilted wooden houses. Grapes and mangoes are grown in this area, and you will pass mats of rice laid out to dry by the roadside and fields of sturdy, Sumbawan horses. The bus conductor, sitting on the left front side of the bus, acts as a second pair of eyes to the driver, giving signals on right-hand bends to tell the driver about oncoming traffic and whether the road bends left or right next. You'll notice clay water urns perched in the clefts of trees outside houses.

Sumbawa Besar

Phone code: 0371

This dusty, quiet, but tree-filled town on the north coast of the island is really only a stop-over on the way east to Bima-Raba and the island of Komodo, or west to Lombok. It is the capital of the district of Sumbawa and a former royal capital. The town is small enough to walk around, and very friendly – the locals are inclined to invite visitors back to their houses.

Ins and outs

Getting there Sumbawa Besar's small airport is 2 km from town and there are links with Bali, Sulawesi, Java and other destinations in Nusa Tenggara. Most people, however, arrive by bus. There are connections all the way through to Lombok and east to Sape, for Komodo and Flores. Badas is Sumbawa Besar's port, 9 km west of town. The Pelni ship *Tatamailau* docks here.

Getting around Sumbawa Besar is a small town and easy to get around. Bemos and dokars (known here as *cidomos*) provide local transport, but it doesn't take long from one end of town to the other. The **tourist Office** is on Jl Garuda, T21932, 21581.

Sights

Sumbawa Besar's main sight is a large wooden palace on Jalan Sudirman, at the east side of town. The **Istana Tua**, known locally as *Dalam Loka* ('Old Palace'), is a fabulous old wooden building looking impressive in its forlorn, picturesque, decrepid state. It is raised off the ground on 99 wooden pillars, with a massive wooden entrance ramp; it was extensively renovated in 1985, but without further renovation its days must be numbered. Built a century earlier in 1885 by Sultan Mohammad Jalaluddin III, it is now an empty shell. It is due to metamorphose into a museum. ■ *Admission by donation. 0900-1600 Mon-Sun.*

Just opposite the entrance are some picturesque old stilted houses. An abandoned **Dutch fort** is visible from the palace, situated on the hill overlooking the town. Next to the palace is the modern and uninspired **Mesjid Nurul Huda**.

Not far from the post office on Jalan Yos Sudarso is a poorly maintained Balinese temple, **Pura Agung Girinatha**. A short walk east of here, on Jalan Cipto, is the very ordinary **Seketeng Market**.

Excursions **Kencana Beach** 10 km west of town, offers snorkelling.

Sleeping at Kencana Beach **A-B** *Kencana Beach Inn*, Jalan Raya Tano, Km 11, Teruna Beach, 10 km west of town, 20 mins' drive from town and airport (book through *Tambora Hotel* in town), T22555, F22439. Once popular with backpackers, this seaside accommodation owned by the *Tambora Hotel* has gone way upmarket and now offers attractive but pricey bamboo bungalows, set in landscaped gardens overlooking the sea. (But note that in early 2000, due to the appalling state of the tourist industry, rates were way down from the rack rate.) Rooms are a/c or fan with western toilets. Good pool, 'private' beach. Watersports: snorkelling and diving equipment sometimes available for hire, pool and a stage where traditional Balinese and Sumbawan dances are performed. Restaurant (mid-range to cheap), serves local specialities and a special Sumbawan buffet service is a little unpredictable. A quiet spot to rest. Transfer from *Tambora Hotel*. *Getting there*: by bemo.

Essentials

Sleeping
■ *on map*
Price codes:
see inside front cover

Accommodation is primarily geared to Indonesian visitors

B-D *Dewi Hotel*, 60 Jl Hasanuddin, T21170/23360. Clean, bright and airy, probably the most attractive place to stay in town. Some rooms with a/c, hot water, all with private mandi. All but the cheapest rooms have western toilets, and balconies or verandahs. If you want a fan room with western toilet this is the place to stay. Friendly staff. Recommended. **B-D** *Tambora Hotel*, 2 Jl Kebayan, T21555, 22111, 22444, F22624. The best hotel in town, clean and quiet, but rooms are drab, could do with redecoration, and are pricey for what they offer. Some rooms with a/c, hot water, western toilets. Fan rooms have squat toilets. Restaurant (mid-range). Staff are very helpful and can help with air and bus tickets. Less than 1 km from airport, 15 mins' walk from bus station. Recommended. **B-E** *Tirtasari*, Jl Garuda Labunan, T21987. Attractive location right on the beach, 15 mins from the centre of town. Some rooms with a/c and hot water, private mandis with western toilet. Tropical gardens. Restaurant (mid-range to cheap). Pool. **D-E** *Hotel Cendrawasih*, Jl Cendrawasih, some a/c, situated in a residential area, has clean and homely rooms. **D-E** *Hotel Dian*, Jl Hasanuddin, T21708/22297, a/c, central, spotless. **D-E** *Losmen Saudara*, Jl Hasanuddin 50, T21528. Rather dark rooms, attached mandi, some rooms with a/c, fan rooms are basic with squat toilets, mainly Indonesian clientele. **D-E** *Losmen Suci*, Jl Hasanuddin 57, T21589. Restaurant, courtyard with open air restaurant, rooms with private mandi and squat toilet, some rooms rather dirty, friendly staff. **E** *Losmen Garoto*, Jl Batu Pasak 48, T22062. Fabulous views overlooking the Istana Tua from the balconies of the upstairs rooms. Rooms, however, are very basic and small with fan and private mandi, squat toilet, located in a quiet residential area, 10 min walk from the bustle of the centre of town. **E-F** *Losmen Baru*, Jl Dokter Wahidin, see the comments for Losmen Harapan - reasonable place to stay, good rates. **E-F** *Losmen Harapan*, Jl Dokter Cipto 5, T21629, this place and the Losmen Baru are really much of a muchness, cheap and reasonable rooms for the price. **E-F** *Losmen Indra*, Jl Diponegoro 48A, T21878. Next to bus station, extremely basic, grimey, some rooms with private mandi, squat toilets, only stay here if you are desperate.

Eating

Stalls and warungs around the Bawah bus terminal on Jl Diponegoro and at the Pasar Seketeng on Jl Dr Cipto. At night warungs open by the stadium on Jl Yos Sudarso, selling bakso and sate. The main concentrations of restaurants are on Jl Hasanuddin and Jl Kartini.

Mid-range *Tambora Restaurant* (at hotel of same name), Jl Kebayan 2, good but fairly pricey food. **Cheap** *Putra Jogya*, Jl Hasanuddin, on the opposite side of the road from Kristal and specializes in seafood. Next door to Putra Jogya is the muralled *Pondok Bamboo*, where the gigantic sound system takes up much of this small café. **Very cheap** *Cirebon*, Jl Kebayan 14. *Rakun Jaya*, Jl Hasanuddin 53, Indonesian. *Kristal*, Jl Hasanuddin, offers all the usual but with a large range of pigeon dishes, *burung dara*. *Usfa Warna*, Jl Kartini 16, Chinese and seafood.

Shopping

Market stalls set up every morning adjacent to Jl Sudirman, selling fruit and vegetables. Around town there is a good range of open-fronted shops.
   Dynasty Art Shop, Jl Garuda, T21644, has a range of local paintings, depicting a combination of religious and cultural themes. Supermarket and chemist adjacent to *Tambora Hotel*, open 0730-2100. Apotik Dinasti, Jl Garuda; Apotik Medika, Jl Diponegoro.

Sports

Diving & snorkelling Snorkelling and diving equipment used to be available from the *Kencana Beach Inn*, but does not seem to be at the market.

Tour operators

Tarindo Wisata, Jl Kebayan 2, T21416/22275. *Tirta Martan*, Jl Garuda 88.

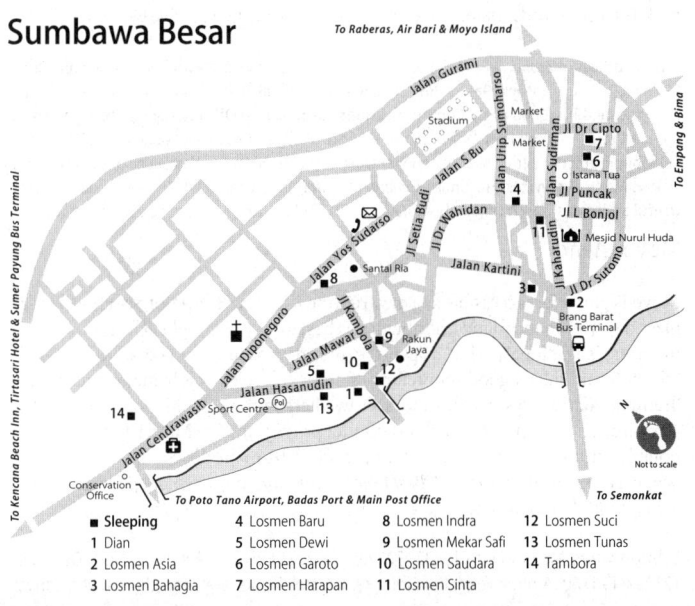

Sumbawa Besar

- **Sleeping**
- 1 Dian
- 2 Losmen Asia
- 3 Losmen Bahagia
- 4 Losmen Baru
- 5 Losmen Dewi
- 6 Losmen Garoto
- 7 Losmen Harapan
- 8 Losmen Indra
- 9 Losmen Mekar Safi
- 10 Losmen Saudara
- 11 Losmen Sinta
- 12 Losmen Suci
- 13 Losmen Tunas
- 14 Tambora

Transport	**Local Bemos**: the station is in front of the Seketeng Market on Jl Dr Cipto. Bemo rides in town cost 500Rp, to Badas Port (the port for Sumbawa Besar) 3,000 Rp. There are also bemos to Kencana Beach. **Dokars** (known as *cidomos*): 500Rp.
70 km from Alas,	
92 km from Poto Tano,	
250 km from Bima-Raba	

Air The airport is only 2 km west of the town centre across the bridge, south of the *Tambora Hotel*. There are 'taxis', but it is easy to walk, or catch a bemo. Regular connections on *Garuda/Merpati* with **Denpasar**, **Jakarta**, **Mataram**, **Surabaya**, **Ujung Pandang** and **Yogyakarta**.

Road Bus: in the last edition of the *Indonesia Handbook* we reported on some confusion regarding bus terminals: how many there were, and which were open or closed. Things haven't got much clearer in the intervening couple of years! Even the tourist office and hotels seemed unclear. But to the best of our knowledge the following applies: Terminal Bawah has closed. **Terminal Brang Barat** on Jl Kaharuddin operates as a hub for bemos going to surrounding villages. It no longer has many long-distance buses running east, as was formerly the case, although there are occasional morning departures for Bima-Raba. The main bus terminal is the **Terminal Sumer Payung**, on Jl Garuda/Jl Labuhan Sumbawa, around 5 km north of town, where buses depart for destinations east such as **Bima-Raba** and **Dompu** and west to **Utan**, **Alas**, **Taliwang** and to **Poto Tano** port (for Lombok). *Perama* has closed its local operation, but do still run shuttle buses from Lombok and Bali to the main destinations in Sumbawa. There are direct buses from **Mataram** (Lombok) to Sumbawa Besar and onward to Bima-Raba. A/c buses to Mataram, leave at 0700, 0800, 0900, 1300 and 1500, and will pick you up from your hotel. The price includes ferry. There is no a/c day bus to Bima-Raba, though you might get seats on an a/c bus coming through from Mataram. Buses to Dompu and Bima-Rabu leave roughly hourly from 0600 to 1000 and from 1300-1600. There are a/c night buses leaving at approximately 2000 and midnight. Buses will drop you off near your hotel. Bus times approximately are: Bima 6-7 hrs, Sape 7½ hrs, Dompu 4 hrs, Taliwang 3 hrs, Poto Tano 2 hrs, Mataram 6 hrs. The buses are non-smoking. **NB** Buying a ticket from the hotels will cost extra, the advantage is that you will be picked up from your hotel. Buses will also drop you off at the point along their route nearest your accommodation.

Sea Boat: there are regular buses from Poto Tano to Alas, and then onward to Sumbawa Besar and Bima-Raba. Badas is the main port for West Sumbawa and is where the *Pelni* ships dock. Pelni office, Badas Harbour, T22344, 9 km west of town, accessible by bemo.

Directory **Airline offices** *Merpati*, 117 Jl Diponegoro, T21416. Located just west of bus station. Open 0800-1300, 7 days a week. **Banks** *BNI*, Jl Kartini 10, open 0800-1600 Mon-Fri. Will change major currencies and TCs (good rates). **Communications** General Post Office: Jl Garuda, west of town on the road to the airport; **Post Office**: Jl Yos Sudarso 6A. Open 0800-1500 Mon-Fri, 0800-1100 Sat. **Telephone office** (international telephone, telex, telegram & fax): Jl Yos Sudarso (opposite Post Office). **Medical services** Hospitals: *General Hospital*, Jl Garuda, T217087 (west edge of town). **Useful addresses** PHPA Office: Jl Candrawasih 1A, T21446 (west, just past the *General Hospital*).

Moyo Island

Phone code: 0371 Moyo Island is just accessible as a day trip (the *Kencana Beach Inn*, see above, organizes day trips to the island), although it is best to stay overnight. The south area of the island is a national park and lies just to the north of Sumbawa Besar. Rich in wildlife, with particularly good snorkelling off the south coast, it is being considered for 'hunting safaris'. Pigs, buffalo and deer live here in the wild. Moyo is home to the rare bird, gosong (megapodius), now under protection. The **Mata Jitu Waterfall** is notable on this idyllic island. ■ *Contact the PHPA office in Sumbawa Besar (see below) before visiting the island. Best time to visit: Jun-Aug. No snorkelling equipment available for hire on Moyo.*

Sleeping **L** *Amanwana*, Moyo Island, T2333, F22288. Reservations c/o *Amanusa*, Nusa Dua, Bali, T71267, F71260. A remarkably luxurious 'tent' hotel. 'Tents' are large chalets with canvas roofs, a/c, king-size beds, large bathrooms. The hotel has a restaurant, bar, lounge and library, and rates include all food and drink and most activities. Alternatively, there is much cheaper accommodation (**F**) available in PHPA bungalows.

Transport There are 3 ways to reach the island. From **Labuhan Sumbawa**, sailing boats can be chartered for the 3-4 hr journey. Alternatively, go to **Labuhan Sawo**, much closer to Moyo, and charter a local boat for considerably less. Get to both Labuhan Sawo and Sumbawa by bemo from the Seketeng market in Sumbawa Besar. It is also possible to reach Moyo from **Kencana Beach**, 10 km west of Sumbawa Besar. The *Kencana Beach Inn* has a speedboat which can be chartered, 1½ hrs, and a slower launch, 3 hrs. Bemos run to Kencana Beach from Sumbawa Besar.

Mount Tambora

Mount Tambora is 2,800m high and is best known for the eruption of 5-15 July 1815, which killed tens of thousands and made the following summer one of the coldest ever.

Climbing the mountain There are two coloured lakes in the caldera. To climb the mountain really requires a 2-3 day excursion. A guide is essential – they can be hired at Pancasila; the police also recommend that trekkers register at their station in Calabai before setting out. The track is often difficult to follow, through thick forest. Wear trousers and long-sleeved shirts (to avoid leeches) and a sturdy pair of walking boots. There are freshwater streams *en route*, but they are not always easy to find, so take a supply of water and some food. Thick vegetation gives way to pine forest and then a volcanic landscape on the approach to the rim of the volcano. Cloud cover is often bad, making for disappointing views from the summit. It is possible to climb down a precipitous slope into the caldera, where there is a lake. ■ *Getting there: charter an early morning boat from the harbour in Sumbawa Besar to Calabai, where there is accommodation; then take an ojek or dokar the 15 km to Pancasila; this is the start of the climb.*

Tours Tours can be organized to surrounding villages for buffalo races, to off-shore islands (including Moyo), and to trek to the summit of Mount Tambora (2,820m) (see above). The *Tambora Hotel* will organize three-day treks to the summit of Mount Tambora, and Abdul Muis and Stephen Annas are recommended as guides (both contactable through the hotel). The *Kencana Beach Inn* (see excursions, page 806) organize trips to Moyo.

South of Sumbawa Besar

Near **Batu Tering village**, about 25 km south of Sumbawa Besar, off the main road to Lunyuk, are some **megalithic remains** at **Airenung**. Also in the area are some **caves**, Liang Petang and Liang Bukal, with stalactites and stalagmites. You will need a torch. The caves are also said to harbour strong magic. The nearby bat caves are also worth a visit – be prepared for a rather pungent experience. The area around **Lunyuk** on the south coast, about 75 km from Sumbawa Besar, is the site of a transmigrant programme, with settlers from Java, Bali and Lombok. The village of **Sukamaju** was settled in 1972 by migrants from Nusa Penida and today is one of the most successful farming communities on Sumbawa. Set in a beautiful area isolated by mountains, the community continue to practise their religion, celebrating traditional Balinese ceremonies with gamelan music and dancing. The Kepala Desa, Dewa Budiasa, can arrange accommodation with local families for visitors with a genuine interest in learning about the lifestyle of the community. You will need to speak some Indonesian. Nearby there are white sand **beaches**, and this area of the south coast is a **turtle spawning** area, particularly the beach at Lampui. ■ *Getting there: by bus from Sumbawa Besar to Lunyuk, 3 hrs; bemo connection to the village.*

Sumbawa Besar to Bima-Raba

The road east from Sumbawa Besar runs through a boulder-strewn, arid landscape and after just over 100 km reaches the coast, passing the picturesque fishing village of Labuhan Jambu. Wood and tile houses are elevated on stilts, with traditional boats hauled up on the beach or moored along the shore. Tour parties sometimes stop here. The regular bus will stop, but it won't wait. From here, the road follows the coast before cutting inland to Dompu. Sit on the left of the bus for spectacular views as the road descends and rises through volcanic peaks and folds, densely vegetated with palms and bamboo. If you were wondering what the cluster of plastic bags hanging in the bus are there for, the sounds and smells of heaving stomachs soon explains all! The surfing beach of Hu'u lies 40 km to the south of Dompu. From Dompu the road continues east to Sumbawa's main town, Bima-Raba.

Dompu

Phone code: 0373 Dompu is the capital of Dompu district and en route between Sumbawa's two principal towns, Sumbawa Besar and Bima-Raba. Surfers making their way south to the beach at Hu'u (see below) may have to change buses here and possibly stop-over for the night.

Sleeping **D-E** *Wisma Samada*, Jl Gajah Mada 18, T21417. Clean, courteous, smart communal area with CNN. A well run place. **D-F** *Wisma Praja*, Jl Soekarno Hatta 6, T215177, a/c, en suite mandi, good ambience, nestled in the heart of town. **E** *Anda*, Jl Jend A Yani, T195. **E** *Bala Kemar Cottages*, Jl Merdeka 82, Empang, only accommodation on the main road, half way between Sumbawa Besar and Dompu, just west of Empang, restaurant, big rooms but no fans, en suite mandi. **E** *Karijawa*, Jl Sudirman, T230. **E** *Manura Kupang*, attractive garden location.

Transport About 40 km from Hu'u. **Road Bus**: regular connections with **Bima-Raba** and **Sumbawa Besar** (approximately 2,000Rp, journey time widely variable according to passenger demand). Onward buses to **Hu'u** (2,000Rp). You will probably find it quite difficult to catch a normal bemo from Hu'u down the 6 km of road to **Lakey Beach**, as the majority of surfers come by chartered taxi, paying in the region of 100,000Rp from Dompu or Bima.

Hu'u

Phone code: 0373 A surfing beach popular with Australians since the late 1980s, who come here on 'package tours' and stay in surf camps. The surf is best in April, although the resort is most crowded during July and August. A relatively hassle-free location for tourists, especially lone women travellers, with a peaceful beach and nothing else.

Sleeping **B** *Hotel Awan Gati*, the most upmarket establishment on Pantai Lakey, 2-storey with internet facilities. Good choice of food in restaurant, Awangati@indo.net.id **B-C** *Primadona Lakey Cottages and Restaurant*, Lakey Beach, Jl Nanga Doro, Dompu, Sumbawa Hu'u, T21168/21384/21585. One of the newest places in Hu'u, set right on the beach, private bathrooms with western toilet. **D** *Balumba Cottages*. **D-E** *Lakey Peak Cottages*, excellent atmosphere, towering tempe, fish, and chicken sandwiches served with chips and salad. Recommended. **D** *Mona Lisa Bungalows*, some with attached mandi, and a popular restaurant. **E** *Lestari*, some with attached mandi, not so well kept as the others and now looking a little down-at-heel. **D-E** *Fatima's*, good rooms, popular restaurant.

Transport About 40 km from Dompu. **Road Bus**: direct morning buses to Hu'u from Terminal Bima in **Bima**. Otherwise catch a bus from either Bima or **Sumbawa Besar** to Dompu, and from here a connection south to Hu'u.

Bima-Raba

Bima-Raba, also known as Raba-Bima, are twin towns separated by about 3 km. Most of the activity is centred on Bima. This is where the hotels and losmen are to be found, where the port is located, and from where buses leave for Sumbawa Besar and Lombok/Bali. The bus terminal for Sape (and from there to Flores) is in Raba, as well as the central post office. Constant bemos link the two towns. *Dokars* here are called *ben hurs*. Salt is an important export from this region and during the dry season you can see the salt-pans in use along parts of Bima Bay. The salt is then put in blue plastic sacks and shipped from Bima port. Horses are another important export and you might see them being loaded onto ships down at the harbour, or squashed together sideways while waiting for the boat to depart.

The inhabitants of the town refer to themselves as *Dou Mbojo*, or 'People of Mbojo', and the name Bima is thought to be taken from the Hindu epic poem the Mahabharata, in which one of the heroes is named Bhima. Traditionally, society was stratified into four classes: the royal family, nobles, commoners and slaves. Today, though, Bima-Raba is a multi-ethnic place with settlers from Flores and Timor, Chinese including Cantonese and Hokkien, Arabs from southern Arabia, Makassarese and Bugis from Sulawesi, and Javanese – along with some Europeans called *'Dou Turi'*. (Although this means tourist, it is also used for expatriates.)

Phone code: 0371

Sights

Bima's principal sight is the **Sultan's Palace** which faces onto the main square, at the east edge of the town centre. Built in 1927, it has been converted into a museum and houses a dismal collection of weapons, baskets, farm implements and other assorted paraphernalia. Traditional dances are irregularly performed here. ■ *Admission by donation. 0700-1800 Mon-Sun.*

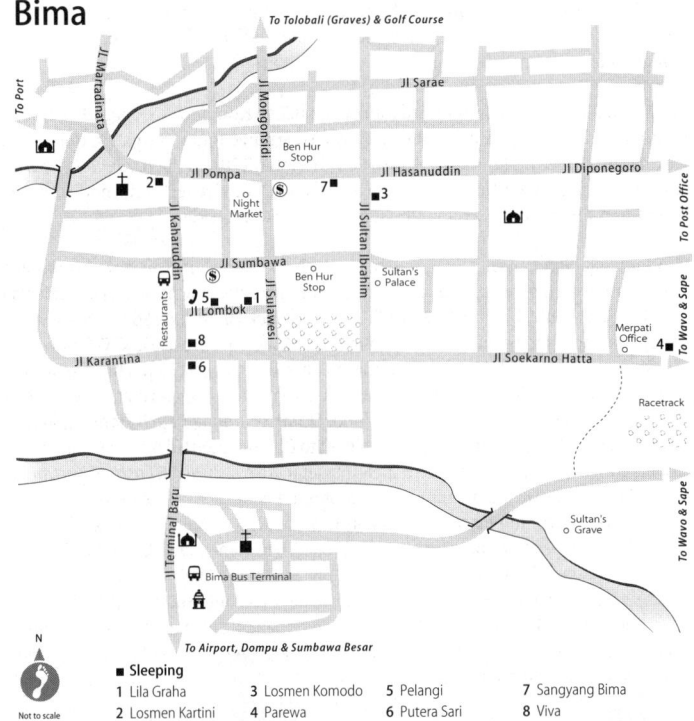

Bima

■ **Sleeping**
1 Lila Graha
2 Losmen Kartini
3 Losmen Komodo
4 Parewa
5 Pelangi
6 Putera Sari
7 Sangyang Bima
8 Viva

The **central market** is in the heart of town between Jl Sultan Kharuddin and Jl Sulawesi. Stall food is available here. Climb up the hills behind the Terminal Bima, or to the south of Jl Soekarno-Hatta for views over the town and bay. One of the Sultans has his grave here (ask for *makam sultan*).

Excursions **Lawata Beach** On the road to Dompu and Sumbawa Besar 3 km south of town, hardly deserves to be called a beach. Locals come here for the sunsets. ■ *Getting there: by ben hur or walk.* **Sleeping: B-C** *Lawata Beach Hotel.* Scenic location overlooking Bima Bay, with views of the Donggo mountains to the west. The beach is disappointing and the sea uninviting, but the hotel has a good swimming pool. Simple accommodation in cottages with private bathroom, shower, western toilet, a/c. Open sided restaurant serving good, reasonably priced food. Hotel in need of redecoration but makes a pleasant alternative to staying in town.

Kolo, on Bima Bay to the north of town, is visited for its snorkelling. ■ *Getting there: boats can be chartered from Bima port, or cadge a lift on one of the regular boats, 1 hr.*

Maria lies 30 minutes outside Bima-Raba, on the road to Sape, and is notable for its traditional wood and tile rice barns (*lengge*) massed on the overlooking hill. ■ *Getting there: by bus from Kumbe terminal in Raba.*

Sambori Lama, a traditional village high in the hills south of Bima, makes an interesting day trip. The road is rough and the final track leading down into the valley where the village lies has to be taken on foot. The houses, with steep sided thatched or corrugated iron roofs, are built on stilts with the livestock living below. You might see young women pounding rice in tall bamboo containers, and betel nuts laid out to dry. The ingredients for siri/pinang (betel nut, the stalk or leaf of the siri vine and small packets of lime) are on sale in the markets of most villages in these parts.

Sangeang Volcano lies off the north-east coast of Sumbawa. This island volcano last erupted in 1986. It is possible to climb the 2,000m high volcano; hire a boat from the villagers to make the crossing.

Climbing Mount Tambora to the northwest of Bima-Raba is a three-day excursion (see page 809). ■ *Getting there: there is usually 1 bus a day to Calabai from the Bima station.*

Tours *Grand Komodo* run recommended tours from Bali to Komodo (see page 819), but it is possible to sign on in Bima-Raba. They also arrange tours to sights around the town. Their office in Bima is at Jalan Soekarno-Hatta, T2812, F2018. *Komodo Tours*, as well as the *Parewa Hotel* (which also has a boat for charter to Komodo), have minibuses for charter to explore the surrounding countryside.

Sleeping **B** *Sangyang Bima*, Jl Sultan Hasanuddin 11, T41438. A/c, pool in new extension, well-run, but rooms only average for the price. The owner was having financial problems and it may currently be shut. **C-D** *Lila Graha*, Jl Lombok 20, T42740. Some a/c, central, noisy, with poor rooms, pricey but good restaurant, includes breakfast. **C-D** *Parewa*, Jl Soekarno-Hatta 40, T42652. Some a/c, this building was to be a cinema but the owner couldn't get the licence. En suite mandi, top rooms have hot water, no outside windows. Restaurant, mainly Chinese/Indonesian food. **D** *Sonco Tengge Beach Hotel*, Jl Sultan Salahuddin, T42987, 1½ km from town on road to Dompu, alternative to being in town, rooms are clean, beach is nothing to speak of, get there by *ben hur*. **E** *Losmen Kartini*, Jl Pasar 11, T42072. Shared mandi, upstairs rooms are more airy, a little grubby, central, near market. **E** *Losmen Komodo*, Jl Sultan Ibrahim (next to Sultan's Palace), T42070. Shared mandi, simple but friendly and fine. Recommended. **E** *Putera Sari*, Jl Soekarno-Hatta 7 (near intersection with Jl Sultan Hasanuddin), T42825. Acceptable rooms, shared mandi. **E** *Viva*, Jl Soekarno-Hatta (near intersection with Jl Sultan Hasanuddin), T42411. Reasonable rooms, shared mandi, cheap, often full. **E** *Losmen Pelangi*, Jl Lombok 8, T42878. Stuck in the not so appealing centre of Bima, but clean, cheap and close to the warungs.

Eating

Cheap *Lila Graha*, Jl Lombok 20, Chinese, Indonesian, seafood. *Ariana*, Jl Martadinata (on road to harbour). *Parewa Modern Bakery and Ice Cream*, Jl Lombok. **Very cheap** *Anda*, Jl Pahlawan, and the nearby *Kurnia* offer rock bottom nasi jampur etc in big portions.

Shopping

There is a considerable sized **market** selling the usual fare in Bima. **Antiques and handicrafts**: There are a couple of specialized artshops in town. For handwoven textiles try *Mutmainah*, Jl Hasanudin 46. *Waspada*, Jl Sulawesi 2, has a large range of bamboo, pottery and wood carvings from all over Sumbawa. *Rinjani Antiques*, Jl Soekarno Hatta, stocks carvings from wood, gold, silver and even ivory (the latter, of course, is currently outlawed under CITES).

Transport

250 km from Sumbawa Besar, 45 km from Bima-Raba

Local Bemos: run between the 2 bus terminals and through both Bima and Raba.

Air Mohammad Salahuddin airport is 20 km south of town, outside Tente and on the Trans-Sumbawa highway. Regular connections by Garuda/Merpati with Bali, Lombok and other destinations in Nusa Tenggara. You can catch a Bemo taxi into town, although it is easy to walk out onto the main road and wait for a bus.

Road Bus: Bima-Raba has 2 bus stations. Terminal Bima is at the southwest edge of Bima town on Jl Terminal Baru (south along Jl Kaharuddin). Buses from here for all points west – **Dompu**, **Hu'u**, **Sumbawa Besar**, **Lombok**, **Bali** and **Surabaya**. The Kumbe terminal for Sape (the port for Komodo and Flores) is in Raba town, 5 km from Bima. Regular minibuses to Sape. Bemos run constantly between the 2 terminals through Bima and Raba. Bus companies such as *Jawa Baru*, *Bima Indah* and *Surya Kencana* have their offices on or near Jl Kharuddin, between the market and Terminal Bima.

Sea Boat: Bima's harbour is a walking distance from Bima town. The *Pelni* ships *Tatamailau* and *Tilongkabila* dock here on their 2-week circuits through Java, Kalimantan, Sulawesi and Nusa Tenggara. However, in mid-2000 only 1 of these 2 ships was running due to lack of custom. The *Pelni* office is at Jl Martadinata (also known as Jl Pelabuhan) 103, near the docks. A new fast ferry service was inaugurated from Bali's Benoa Harbour to Bima and Kupang (Timor) in mid-2000. The 70m, 925-passenger ship *Barito*, with a top speed of 36 knots, leaves Bali every Fri afternoon at 1800 on its 16 hr voyage to Bima and Kupang. For more information, contact *Gama Dewata Bali Tours* (in Bali) at T62-(0)361-263568 or T62-(0)361-232704, F62-(0)361-263569.

Directory

Airline offices *Merpati*, Jl Soekarno-Hatta 60, T42697. **Banks** *BNI*, Jl Sultan Hasanuddin, US$ cash only. Bank Rakyat Indonesia, Jl Soekarno-Hatta, T43352, ATM available. **Communications** General Post Office: Raba (get there by minibus from Bima). **Medical services** Hospital on Jl Langsat.

Sape

Phone code: 0374

Sape is the usual place to stay, while waiting for the ferry to Komodo Island and Flores. The port itself – Labuhan Sape – is about 4 km from Sape town. Most of the population are not Bimanese at all, but Bugis – the famed seafarers from Sulawesi. Nothing happens in Sape, but staying here does make it easier catching the 0800 ferry. The accommodation is some of the poorest in Indonesia. The **Komodo Tourist Centre**, between Labuhan Sape and Sape town, is of marginal use only, but they do have some information on Komodo.

Excursions

Labuhan Sape (Sape Port) is 4 km from town and can be reached on foot or by *ben hur*. There is boat building along the road, fishing boats landing their catch in the morning, and a mosque with a lighthouse-style minaret.

Sleeping

Basic and of uniformly poor quality, losmen are all found on Jl Pelabuhan, on the seaward side of town. Because it is usually necessary to stay the night in Sape to catch the ferry, accommodation is sometimes in short supply between the peak months from Jul to Sep. An alternative is to stay in Bima and catch an early bus to Sape. New losmen are opening here and the hope is that the challenge of some competition may improve standards. **F** *Friendship*, dirty, small rooms, dark with uncomfortable beds. **F** *Give*, dirty. **F** *Ratnasari*, cleanish (for Sape), the best of a very bad bunch. **E-F** *Mutiara*, right by the dock, one of the newer losmen, reasonably clean, pleasant and well-stocked with biscuits and sanitary towels, amongst the best of this very poor bunch.

Eating *Hovita*, Jl Pelabuhan, friendly, cold beer, good fish (if asked in advance). Recommended. *Surabaya*, next to *Losmen Give*. *Sape Cafe*, one of the few reasonable choices available. **Very cheap** *Arema*, next to *Mutiara*, good range of dishes and large portions, but reputed to give maggot-ridden fish to tourists! Extremely low ceilings, expect hostility and confrontation at first if assumed to be Australian (a legacy of the East Timor debacle).

Transport *45 km from Bima-Raba* **Road Bus**: the station is on the seaward side of town, although buses will drop passengers off near the losmen. Regular connections with Raba's Kumbe terminal, 1½ hrs. From Kumbe, bemos run to Bima town and then on to the Bima terminal for buses west (see page 813). **Sea Boat**: the ferry for Komodo 6½ hrs (12,000Rp) and Labuanbajo 10 hrs (15,000Rp), leaves from the port 4 km east of town every day except Fri at 0800. *Ben hurs* whisk passengers from Sape town to the port (price inflated on morning of ferry departure). The ferry also takes motorcycles, cars, goats and buffalo; buying tickets the night before means you miss the scrum on the morning of departure. The boat ride between Sape and Komodo is uneventful; but between Komodo and Labuanbajo the ferry weaves between barren, mangrove wreathed islands. At certain times of year, the currents which converge here cause impressive up-wellings and depressions in the sea.

Directory **Communications** Post Office: Jl Pelabuhan 34. Wartel: Jl Pelabuhan (between *Losmens Give* and *Ratnasari*).

East Nusa Tenggara

9

East Nusa Tenggara

818	Ins and outs
819	Komodo
824	**Flores**
825	Labuanbajo to Ende
839	Ende to Larantuka
848	Lembata
851	Alor
854	**Sumba**
868	**West Timor**
876	Roti (Rote)
878	Savu (Sabu, Sawu)

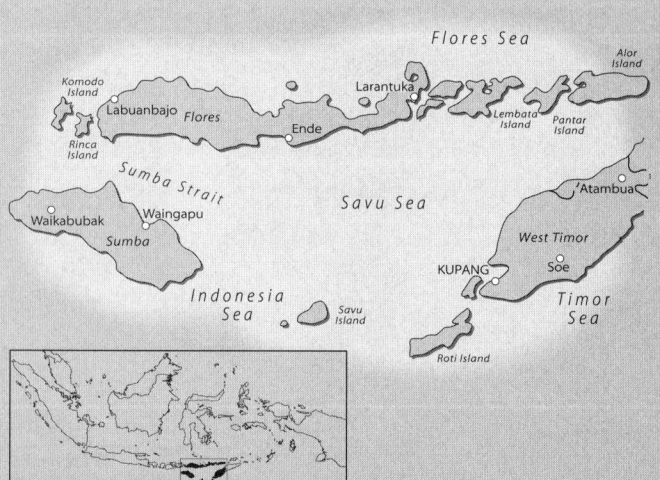

For the visitor, East Nusa Tenggara offers a mosaic of cultures: from Christian Flores, including the Catholics of Larantuka – a legacy of Portugal's short-lived 16th century sojourn here – to Muslim West Timor, and Sumba, where pre-Christian and pre-Muslim religious influences remain strong. Geographically, East Nusa Tenggara is equally varied, from the mountains and volcanoes of Flores to the rolling grasslands of Sumba. Finally, there are East Nusa Tenggara's most famous inhabitants: the giant dragons of Komodo.

This part of the archipelago is considerably drier than the islands to the west, and the further east you go, the more arid it becomes – more like Australia than the jungle-clad tropics. The lack of rain is compounded by the geography of the islands. They are long and thin, and rivers tend to be short and fast-flowing, making it difficult to utilize the water for agriculture. East Nusa Tenggara is not one of Indonesia's industrial powerhouses: the province's main exports being coffee, fish and sandalwood.

Christianity has made greater inroads into the provinces of Nusa Tenggara than anywhere else in Indonesia. Islam had scarcely penetrated these remote islands before the Portuguese arrived in the 16th century, and the population were therefore more amenable to conversion. Today, 90% of the population is Christian, and Christianity is one of the few forces which binds together a geographically dispersed population, made up of no less than 37 ethnic groups.

Ins and outs

Getting around
For information on getting to each island, see individual islands' 'Ins and outs' sections

Travelling through the islands of East Nusa Tenggara, particularly Flores (see page 824 for more information), used to be difficult enough to deter all but the most adventurous visitor. Now the islands are readily accessible, and surfaced all-weather roads link the main towns of the province. This has meant that in the peak tourist months from July to September, accommodation may become stretched in smaller towns – or at least it was until the communal violence and associated bad press of 1998, 1999 and 2000. As a result, since 1998, the number of tourists visiting Nusa Tenggara has been significantly below normal. There is essentially only one road through Flores, so visitors travel along a very tightly defined route and there are choke points at Labuanbajo (the port for the ferry to Komodo and Sumbawa) and Bajawa, both on Flores.

Air The two 'ends' of Nusa Tenggara – Mataram in Lombok and Kupang in West Timor – are well provided for in terms of air connections. **Kupang** is an international gateway and there are regular flights to/from Darwin, Australia. These two cities also provide a reasonably efficient domestic service. *Merpati* does operate services to many of the smaller towns through the islands of Nusa Tenggara, but with the exception of **Maumere** on Flores these are intermittent and limited. In addition, flights to these towns are often over-booked and because the planes are usually small there is not much 'give' in the system. It is best to build a reasonable degree of flexibility into your schedule. To get to other areas of Indonesia from Nusa Tenggara, it is usually necessary to fly to Bali first, and then catch a connection.

Bus As noted above, overland transport has improved considerably. The main road through the islands of Nusa Tenggara is all-weather and public transport is reasonably efficient and timely, though it might not be comfortable. There are no a/c services east of Sumbawa (before getting to West Timor) and most departures are early morning. Expect to average about 30-50 km per hour.

Bicycle and motor bike A fair number of people work their way through Nusa Tenggara by bicycle or motorbike. The roads are much quieter than on Java and Sumatra, and other road users tend to drive more slowly – although potholes and livestock provide hazards. Spare parts for unusual bikes and motorbikes may be impossible to obtain, so either travel well prepared or buy an Indonesian-assembled machine on arrival. See the section on page 44 for more information on bicycling.

Sea Because of the fragmented geography of this region, boats remain an important form of transport. There are daily ferries linking Lombok with Sumbawa, and Sumbawa with **Flores** via **Komodo**. East of Flores ferries become more intermittent, with connections just once or twice a week. However, note that these schedules have become even more variable and subject to change than usual. Remain flexible, patient and double check all information at the relevant terminal.

When to go Rainfall averages only 800-900mm in East Flores, Alor and East Sumba, and the dry season stretches over seven months, from April to October.

Money in Nusa Tenggara Money changing facilities in a handful of major towns and in particular in Kupang, West Timor are reasonable, but in many smaller towns travellers' cheques denominated in US$ or US$ cash are the best option. Other currencies are often either not accepted or exchange rates are poor. Note that travellers' cheques should be from one of the major companies – *Amex*, *CitiBank*, *Bank of America*, *Thomas Cook*. Credit cards are only rarely accepted.

Language Bahasa Indonesia is useful in Nusa Tenggara, but not essential if travellers stick to the main route through the islands. You will find that just a few words go a long way in communication and in making a good impression. Indonesians are proud of their language and honoured to find Westerners trying to learn. They will also be eager to help you to improve it still further!

East Nusa Tenggara highlights

Komodo: giant 3m-long *'dragons'*, the largest reptiles in the world.
Flores: snorkelling and diving near Maumere and in the Seventeen Islands National Park; **climbing** to see the three-coloured crater lakes of Mount Kelimutu at sunrise; **trekking** to traditional villages; historical Larantuka; and fabulous textiles.

Solor and Alor archipelagos: Lamalera and its **traditional whaling communities**; *diving and snorkelling* on Alor.
Sumba: megalithic tombs, traditional villages; surfing; the **pasola festival**; and traditional ikat textiles.
West Timor: *traditional villages* and textiles; **surfing** on Roti.

Malaria is a serious problem in parts of Nusa Tenggara, with the recent emergence of the potentially fatal *P falciparum* as the dominant strain. Areas affected include Komodo, along the north coast of Flores, including Riung, Maumere, Labuhanbajo, the island of Roti and Timor. Larium (Melfoquine), the most effective anti-malarial drug believed to be 95% effective, causes side effects in 22% of people who take it. Of these, a very small minority (the manufacturers claim one person in 10,000) suffer serious problems including fits, manic depression and panic attacks. However, many more travellers die from malaria than from Larium. Citronella, an essential oil used in a base for moisturizers and in candles, is highly effective as a deterrent to mosquitoes and a natural alternative to DEET. Also B12 tablets (B12 is found in high concentrations in beer and garlic) similarly appear to ward off the little beasts.

Health warning

Following East Timor's resounding vote in favour of independence in 1999, the pro-Jakarta militias fled to the camps of West Timor. In 2000 there was a distinctly anti-Western sentiment in some areas of West Timor, and in September three UN workers were murdered near Atambra.

Safety warning

Komodo

The principal reason people come to Komodo is to see the illustrious Komodo dragon. But there is more to the reserve than giant lizards – there is also good trekking, swimming and snorkelling. The park covers 59,000 ha, and is made up not just of Komodo Island, but also Rinca and a number of other surrounding islets. The highest peak on this rugged spot is Mount Satalibo (735m).

Colour map 3a, grid B3

Ins and outs

Merpati flies to both Labuanbajo (see page 829) and to Bima (page 813); the former is closer to Komodo. From either town it is then necessary to catch the ferry (see below). The rich and famous arrive direct by helicopter.

Getting there

There are now 2 ferries a week between Flores and Sumbawa via Komodo, leaving both Sape and Labuanbajo daily at 0800. The journey from Sape takes 6½ hrs; from Labuanbajo, 3½ hrs. The ferry cannot dock at Komodo as the water is too shallow, so small boats come alongside to take passengers to the *PHPA* office to register. It is possible to charter a boat for a 2-day trip to Komodo from Sape. But some of the boats are said to be unreliable and currents in the Sape Strait are strong. Locals recommend going through one of the tour companies in Bima for safety's sake (see page 812) or from Labuanbajo (see page 827). It is cheaper to hire a boat from the nearer port of Labuanbajo. Before chartering a boat, visit the Komodo Park offices in Sape or Labuanbajo for advice.

Kampung Komodo is the only village on the island; Loh Liang – the PHPA-run camp for tourists – is about a 30 min walk away. The only way of getting around the island is on foot and the national park office maintains paths to various parts of Komodo.

Getting around

The National Park

After the luxuriant vegetation of Bali, Komodo can come as a bit of a shock – at least during the dry season. The islands of the Komodo archipelago are dry and rainfall is highly seasonal. For much of the year, therefore, the grasslands are burnt to dust and interspersed with drought resistant savanna trees such as the distinctive lontar palm (*Borassus flabellifera*). In contrast the seas are highly productive, so there is good **snorkelling**, particularly off **Pantai Merah** and **Pulau Lasa** – a small island near Komodo village. The iridescent blue of the water, set against the dull brown of the islands, provides a striking backdrop. However, this image of Komodo as barren is transformed during the short wet season, when rainfall encourages rapid growth and the formerly parched landscape becomes green and lush.

Despite the other attractions of Komodo, it is still the **dragons** which steal the show. They are easily seen, with Timor deer (their chief natural prey) wandering amongst them. Other wildlife includes land crabs, wild pigs, black drongos, white-bellied sea eagles, and cockatoos, evidence that this is part of the Australasian faunal world. Monkeys, by contrast, are absent. ■ *The island is a national park and visitors must register and buy an entrance ticket (27,000Rp) on arrival at Loh Liang on Komodo, or Loh Buaya on Rinca. Note that between 1 Aug and the end of Sep the cost of an entrance ticket rockets. The ticket is valid for 7 days. The park HQ at Loh Liang consists of an office, information centre, 4 bungalows, a souvenir shop, church and mosque, and a restaurant.*

Komodo National Park

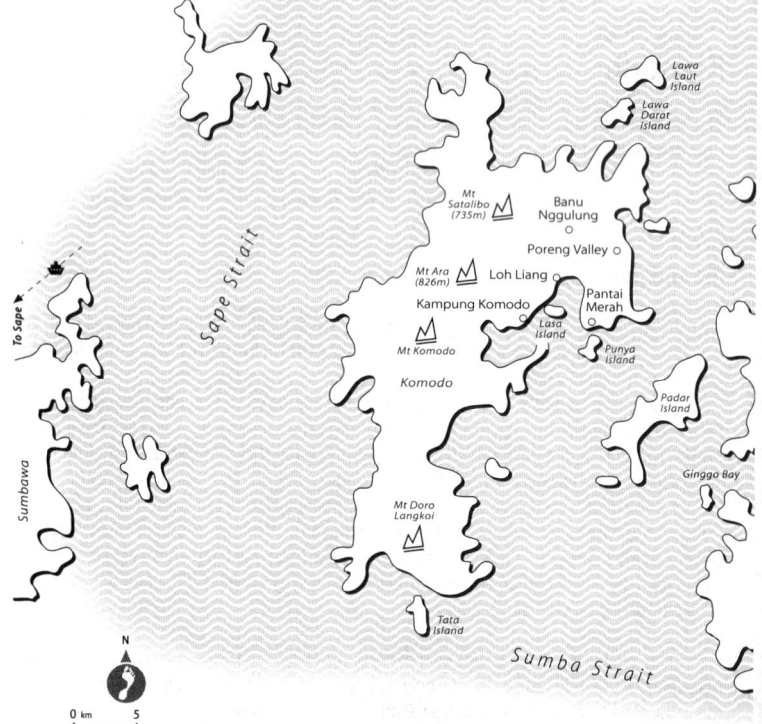

The most accessible viewing spot is the dry river bed at **Banu Nggulung**, 30 minutes' walk (2 km) from the accommodation at Loh Liang. Guides can take you there for a small fee, depending on the size of your group (5,000Rp per person). **NB** Visitors are only allowed to walk alone along marked trails. Those wishing to hike off the trails, and see the dragons in a more natural setting, must hire a guide. This is not just to generate income for the wardens: there have been fatalities (see box). Group walks are at 0700 and 1600. It seems that the morning is better for sightings. For around 25,000Rp per person (but highly negotiable) a guide can take you to **Poreng Valley**, a 7-km walk from the PHPA office. There is a reasonably good chance of spotting a dragon and even if you don't, you will see plenty of other wildlife. There is a short 30 minute walk along the beach from Loh Liang bungalows to the stilt village of **Kampung Komodo**, which can be done without a guide. **Mount Ara** can be climbed in less than two hours (8.5 km to the summit) and the cost is 35,000Rp per group; from the summit there are fantastic views over the reserve.

Walks

Excursions

Rinca Island can be reached from Komodo and has a wider range of wildlife including wild horses and water buffaloes, as well as dragons, and has the added advantage of fewer tourists. **Sleeping** E *PHPA bungalows* at Loh Buaya, 25,000Rp per night for a single, 40,000Rp double. Basic accommodation, these stilted wooden cabins are the haunts of various rodent and insect populations, so be prepared. Similarly, no food available, so take your own. It is more likely that you will go as part of an organized tour (arranged in Labuhanbajo or Lombok) and therefore you will be catered for. Rinca is fast gaining popularity over Komodo and recent visitors have been highly complimentary about trips there. ■ *Getting there: there is not yet a ferry service to Loh Buaya. Private tours run from Labuhanbajo on Flores or from Komodo. Some boats travelling from Lombok to Flores stop off here. Ask about chartering a boat at the Sinbad shuttle office opposite Dewata Ayu Restaurant.*

Rinca Island

Essentials

The only accommodation on Komodo is in the **E** *PHPA bungalows* at Loh Liang, which has a capacity of about 40. They are simple but clean bungalows in a beautiful bay. Electricity from 1800 to 2200. Bedding consists of mattresses on the floor. During the peak season of Jul-Sep, visitors must resort to sleeping in the dining room, some rooms have their own mandi for no extra cost. The quality of the rooms is not great, but if you have the time, it is well worth staying on the island. The cafeteria provides basic and rather overpriced food. **Camping**: there is a camp ground at Loh Liang.

Sleeping

Indonesia's living dinosaur: the Komodo dragon

The Komodo dragon (Varanus komodoensis), a massive monitor lizard, is the largest lizard in the world and can grow to 3m and weigh over 150kg. They are locally called ora and were not discovered by the West until 1911. In 1990 the Komodo National Park authorities estimated the number of dragons to be 3,336, although it is probably smaller today as the population is thought to be in slow decline. The dragon is found on only four islands; about 2,000 live on Komodo Island, with significant numbers also on Rinca (700), Pulau Motang and on the northern coast of Flores. Of all the large carnivore species, the ora has the most restricted range. They are strictly protected and cannot be exported live to zoos or, for that matter, dead to museums.

The dragons living on Rinca and Flores are rather more reddish in colour than those found on Komodo which are blacker, suggesting there has been little interbreeding between the populations for some considerable time. However, the dragons do swim between islands in search of food, despite these being treacherous waters with strong tides. There are also dangers for the dragon associated with losing body heat on their journey (they are, of course, cold blooded). The best time to see the dragons is shortly after sunrise when they have just woken up and lie out in the sun to warm their bodies, in readiness to go hunting. There is little water on these islands and in order to avoid the danger of dehydration the dragons must avoid spending too long in the sun.

Like other animals, the size of the Komodo dragon has been grossly exaggerated. Major PA Ouwens, the curator of the Botanical Gardens at Buitenzorg (Bogor), Java, who first scientifically described the animal and collected the type specimen in 1912, was informed by the Governor of Flores that specimens of over 7m existed; these were almost certainly over-estimates or mis-identified estuarine crocodiles. Even the celebrated British television zoologist Sir David Attenborough, during his 1957 visit to the island, succumbed to exaggeration, claiming to have seen a dragon "a full 12 feet" in length. The largest accurately measured dragon was one exhibited at the St Louis Zoological Gardens in 1937, reported as measuring 10ft 2in and weighing 365lbs. The extreme size of the Komodo dragon is thought to be due to it having evolved on these isolated islands, insulated from competition by other carnivores. The same is true of other reptiles – for example, the Galapagos iguana.

The reptile is essentially a solitary creature, hunting and scavenging by day. An opportunist, it feeds largely on carrion, but will also kill its own prey which can include animals as large as a water buffalo, or even the young of its own species. Prey is usually killed by first biting the animal and then patiently following it for several days. The wound becomes infected and turns septic and the animal becomes increasingly weak. When it is unable to escape the dragon moves in for the kill. Flesh is torn from the carcass with teeth and claws and swallowed whole.

With other dragons competing for carrion, it is important to consume the carcass as quickly as possible and they are voracious eaters, devouring almost their own body weight within 30 minutes, taking a further five days to digest the prey. The dragons have a superb sense of smell; this allows them to pick up the scent of death more than 10 km

Shopping There is a souvenir shop at Loh Liang and hawkers sell carved wooden dragons of various sizes, as well as pearls, bone carvings and necklaces.

Sports **Boats** Speedboats are available. **Diving and snorkelling** There is good diving and excellent snorkelling over the reef off Pantai Merah and around Pulau Lasa, offshore from Kampung Komodo. It is best to bring your own mask, although there is a dive shop (*Binga Corner*) just by the jetty which hires out masks, fins and diving equipment.

away and several metres underground. Despite their reputation as man-eaters, dragons rarely kill people, and often wander through the village on Komodo island more interested in eating the fishermen's catch or untended domestic animals. They can often be seen scavenging along the beach and will eat anything, even tiny crabs. Fewer than 10 people are said to have been killed this century. A Swiss baron – admittedly a frail 80-year-old – was killed in 1979 and there has been another reported fatality since.

Recent research has focussed on the dragon's lethal saliva which contains virulent bacteria. Toxicologists have been fascinated by their findings, which suggest the bacteria originate in the decaying carrion scavenged by the dragon. The dragon's supremely sharp teeth cut into its own gums while it is chewing, and this combination of toxic saliva and blood provide an ideal breeding ground for the bacteria to survive for days, even weeks, until the dragon attacks its next prey. Of interest is how the dragon remains immune to the toxicity of its own saliva, and whether it has an antidote which might prove of medical use.

A female dragon will only mate with a male who is strong enough to pin her down. He then wins her over in a rather touching manner, flicking his tongue over her and rubbing her back with his chin. Mating usually takes place in June and July. A month or more later, usually at night, the eggs – a clutch will number about 25 eggs – are laid about 2m underground after the female has built an extensive burrow, which may take up to a week to excavate. She includes many false entrances and dead-end tunnels, as the eggs will be under constant threat from hungry male dragons and females in search of a ready-made nest. The female assiduously guards her nest for the first three months, never even leaving it to eat, and living off the fat stored in her tail.

The eggs hatch after eight to nine months at the end of the rainy season (March to May), when food is plentiful. The dragons hatch fully formed and able to fend for themselves, and make straight for the trees where they spend the first two years of their life safe from the cannibalistic tendencies of the adults which are too big to climb trees. They continue to spend much of the time in trees until they are seven or eight years old and large enough to defend themselves. Their only defence is speed as young dragons, less than four years old, are remarkably fast moving ; they are said to be able to outrun a dog over short distances. Dragons are thought to live for up to 50 years.

Male dragons frequently fight, often over females. Like many lizards, they inflate their bodies to intimidate the enemy. The loser will then lie in a submissive posture and endure 'claw raking', whereby the victor rakes the body of the loser with his claws in a sign of victory.

Research is underway to determine the origins of the dragon. Study of the chromosomes indicate they are more closely related to the Australian goanna than to other monitor lizards in Asia and Africa. There is little fossil evidence in Indonesia, but in Australia the reconstructed bones of *Megalania prisca*, which died out millions of years ago, show remarkable similarities to the Komodo dragon. However, at 6-7m in length and 10 times the weight, *Megalania prisca* was even bigger than the Komodo dragon.

Flores

Colour map 3a

Flores stretches over 350 km from east to west, but at most only 70 km from north to south. It is one of the most beautiful islands in the Lesser Sundas. Mountainous, with steep-sided valleys cut through by fast-flowing rivers, dense forests and open savanna landscapes, Flores embraces a wide range of ecological zones. One of the local names for the island is Nusa Nipa or 'Serpent Island', because of its shape.

Ins & outs

Getting there There are **air** connections with Labuanbajo, Bajawa, Ruteng, Ende, Maumere and Larantuka, but services can be unreliable. **NB** There seems to be some problem with booking *Merpati* flights out of Ende, either back to Denpasar or on to Kupang. To get around this difficulty, it is advisable to fly out of Maumere, where the office seems to be more switched on and they are contactable by telephone. Regular **ferries** link **Labuanbajo**, on Flores' west coast with Sape on Sumbawa, sailing via Komodo. Less frequent ferries connect **Ende** with Waingapu on Sumba, Kupang on Timor, and Ujung Pandang (Makassar) on Sulawesi. There are also vessels from **Larantuka** to Kupang and Lewoleba. *Pelni* vessels dock at **Labuanbajo**, **Ende**, **Maumere** and **Larantuka**.

Getting around Overland transport on Flores – a 375 km-long island – is neither quick nor comfortable. *Despite improvements in communications, overland travel is still exhausting. It is best to overnight in at least 3 towns on the journey across the island. Flooding & earthquakes have also stalled efforts to make travel quicker* The Trans-Flores Highway is now almost complete, travel is quite bearable. The road twists and turns, through at times breathtaking scenery, stretching over more than 700 km to cover the 375 km-length of the island. The Highway is made up almost all the way from Labuanbajo in the east to Larantuka in the west, with the exception of one section over the mountains between Ruteng and Bajawa, which is in the process of being rebuilt (expect to average 25-30 km per hour, less in the wet season). **Buses** are the main form of transport between centres. On minor roads, open trucks (known as *bis kayu*) with bench seats are still used. In towns like Ende and Maumere, bemos are the main form of local transport.

Conduct Flores is a conservative island – short skirts and vests are not appropriate; dressing in such a manner is considered impolite.

Security Lone women travellers may find more harassment on Flores than on Lombok or Sumbawa. It is advisable only to engage in short conversations with men. Make sure you lock your door

Flores

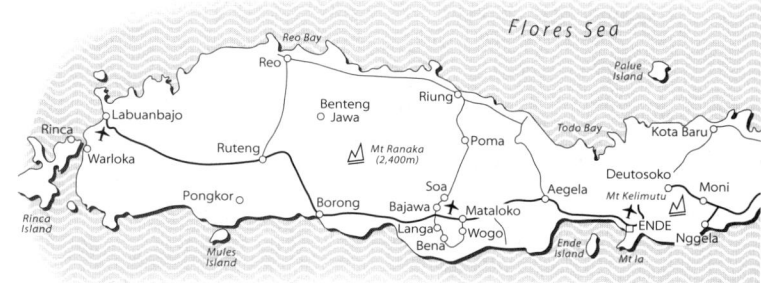

and windows at night. Some losmen have cavities between bathrooms with manholes big enough to let in an intruder. Try to discover who is inhabiting the adjacent rooms.

Accommodation

Visitors should have little difficulty finding a room at most times of year. Indeed, outside only the most touristed towns, expect to be the only foreigner around. This may change as Indonesia's tourist industry recovers, but it was true as of mid-2000.

Background

History

Flores' history is sketchy. It appears that Chinese mariners first made contact with the island – perhaps as early as the 12th century – to trade in sandalwood. As Flores lay on the trading route to Timor (sandalwood) and the Moluccas (spices), Portuguese chroniclers also noted the existence of the island in the 16th century. Dominican missionaries built a stone fort and church on Solor, just off Flores' east coast, in 1561, and one later at Larantuka. So enthusiastic were the Dominican friars in their proselytizing that by 1599 there were thought to be 100,000 Roman Catholics in East Flores. The sandalwood traders from Melaka and Macao who based themselves here also began inter-marrying with local women, creating a group of *mestizos*.

By the time the Portuguese were in decline as a power in the archipelago at the beginning of the 17th century, they had established settlements at Solor, Ende and Sikka. The Dutch, seeing little of value on Flores, concentrated their attentions elsewhere. As a result, although they established a mission at Ende in 1670, Portuguese religious influence over Flores continued to remain strong (see box, page 848). It was not until 1859 that Portugal officially ceded all its claims to Flores to the Dutch. And this was only agreed on the understanding that Flores would remain Roman Catholic.

Geography

Unlike neighbouring Sumbawa, the deep volcanic soils here are fertile; the problem is that in most areas the unreliable and highly seasonal rainfall makes agriculture difficult. Strangely, the area of the island with the highest density of population is also among the driest: the district of Sikka (Maumere).

People

In total, the island covers an area of 14,300 sq km, and supports a population of 1,500,000. The majority of the population is Roman Catholic, but pre-Christian animist beliefs still exert a considerable influence even among those who are nominally Christian. There are five major ethnic groups on the island: the Manggarai, Ngada, Sikka, Ende and Larantuka. In general, while the inhabitants in east and central Flores are Papuan-Melanesian, those in the west are Malay. The mountainous terrain and the difficulties of communication have effectively isolated these various groups from one another until fairly recently.

Labuanbajo to Ende

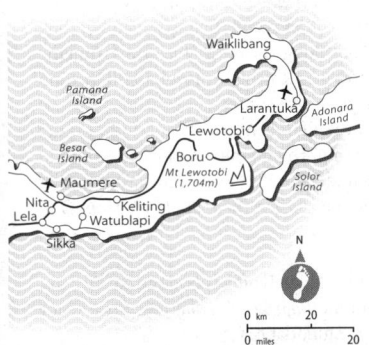

Labuanbajo, at the western tip of Flores, is the ferry port for Komodo Island and Sape (Sumbawa). From here the Trans-Flores Highway works its way eastwards through a fragmented and mountainous landscape to the hill town of Ruteng, 125 km away. Nearly 40 km north of Ruteng is the small port of Reo. Continuing on the Trans-Flores Highway from Ruteng, the road runs east and then turns south towards the coast, before climbing again to another hill town – Bajawa – a distance of 130 km.

The textiles of Flores

Because Flores' geography has made contact between the island's peoples difficult, a number of distinct textile traditions have evolved. Three broad types stand out: the textiles of Manggarai to the west, those of Ngada in the centre, and the cloths of Ende, Sikka, Lio and Larantuka to the east.

Manggarai textiles show stylistic links with both Bima (Sumbawa) and south Sulawesi. Predominant colours are red, blue and green, and designs may be either bold and simple, or complex and minutely worked. Geometric motifs are the norm, and it is unusual for these to be interlinked. The best cloths have a tapestry weave border design along the edge. Unlike other areas of Flores, the designs of Manggarai are produced by weaving, not by dyeing the warp (ikat).

Ngada textiles from central Flores can be found on sale at the market in Bajawa. Women's sarongs and men's shawls are made from rough home-grown and home-spun cotton, dyed red and blue, with an elementary ikat design. The more expensive and harder to find weft ikat kain kudu have horse motifs and are traditionally part of a woman's dowry.

The textiles of the east are the richest and show a range of influences, from Sumba, Solor, and even Europe and India. They are made using the warp ikat technique (see page 441) and feature geometric, animal and floral motifs. If weavers are Muslim, the animal designs have been reduced to geometric shapes. Cloths from **Lio** villages (eg Nggela and Jopu, see pages 840 and 840) are finely patterned, with yellowish-brown designs on a dark red or blue ground. The motifs, often floral, are contained within parallel bands. It is also possible today to find cloth decorated with aeroplanes, cars, ships, and even teapots. The warp ikat from **Sikka** (see page 842) is probably the most immediately attractive of Flores' textiles to the Westerner. Cloth is made from thick, handspun cotton, and the ikat designs are bolder. Sikka ikat is a grey weave on a dark blue, almost black, background, although reddish hues are also common. Motifs are usually natural – flowers, chickens, crabs.

Across the island, it is increasingly difficult to find quality cloth made using natural dyes and handspun cotton. It is more usual to see cloth, coloured using synthetic dyes and made from commercially-spun cotton.

The district of Bajawa is best known for the strange thatched cult 'houses' which can be found in the surrounding villages. With a good range of accommodation, Bajawa is one of the best places to stop off on a journey through Flores. From Bajawa, the road deteriorates, although it is in the process of being improved. The route passes through a rock-strewn, almost African savanna-like landscape, before reaching the coast after about 100 km, which the road follows for the final 30 km to the port of Ende.

Labuanbajo

Phone code: 0385 Labuanbajo, or Bajo, is really just an overgrown fishing village. There is good accommodation here, some excellent restaurants, and reasonable beaches, with off-shore snorkelling. It is also an excellent base from which to explore Komodo and Rinca, or to join a boat tour via the reserve and other islands on the way to Lombok (see 'Tours', below). The town is stretched out along one road which runs from the dock, along the seashore, and then south towards Ruteng. **Pramuka Hill**, behind the town, offers good views over the bay, especially at sunset.

Tourist information is available from the *PHPA* information booth, on the main street opposite *Gardena Hotel*. They can provide information on Komodo and Rinca islands. There is also a rather under-funded but enthusiastic tourist office, *Dinas Pariwisata*, behind the *Telekom* Office. ■ *0700-1500 Mon-Thu, 0700-1430 Fri.*

Excursions **Waicicu Beach** lies 15 minutes by boat north of town. It offers good snorkelling and diving (snorkel equipment is for hire from the *Bajo Beach Hotel*). See below for details of accommodation, under 'Beach accommodation'.

Komodo It is possible to charter a boat for the day to see the dragons; shouldn't be more than about 80,000-100,000Rp (see Rinca below for details).

Rinca Island is part of the Komodo National Park and even closer to Labuanbajo. See page 821 for details. It also has a small population of Komodo dragons and thousands of fruit bats, which fly from the mangrove swamps inland at dusk. PHPA accommodation available. ■ *Getting there: boat charter, day trip (1½ hrs each way)*. Ask at the PHPA booth in town about boat charter; the Bajo Beach and Mutiara Beach Hotels both have vessels for charter. **NB** *Not all the boat charterers are reliable. Check before paying by insisting on seeing the vessel and by talking to other visitors to confirm the itinerary.*

One day trips to the islands **Bidadari** and **Sabobo** can be arranged through hotels or tour operators (on main road), 55,000Rp for return boat ride. Good snorkelling in clear water and, potentially, the island to yourself.

Kanawa Island Overnight stays on this island sleeping in bungalows on stilts can be arranged through *Kanawa Tours* (on main road below *Garden Restaurant*), 25,000-35,000Rp for boat and accommodation. This tranquil island, lying barely a metre above sea level, is perfect for those seeking an escape. Dropping in for lunch is entirely possible. However, all water and products are shipped in from the harbour.

Tours

Perama Tours have boats for charter to Komodo and Rinca. They provide snorkelling equipment but it is poor quality. *Perama* also offer four day/three night boat tours from Labuanbajo to Bangsal (Lombok), stopping at Komodo and Moyo Island (Sumbawa) *en route* and with one day in Lombok and a night 'camping' on the coral island of Perama, sleeping on bamboo beds beneath rudimentary shelters. The other nights are spent sleeping on deck. The tour then returns from Bangsal to Labuanbajo along the same route. Ten people maximum and eight staff; good, if a little repetitive, fresh food, expensive at around 200,000Rp. **NB** Check out the boat before agreeing to a tour; some boats are overloaded and pretty uncomfortable – we have received reports that *Perama* have been overloading their boats, picking up passengers along the way. There are various other people operating these tours, but confirm that they go to the places agreed upon: *Mutiara Beach Hotel* organize a four-night tour; *Waicicu Beach Hotel* organize a two-day boat trip to Sape, via Rinca Island and Komodo (with snorkelling stops) and a visit to 'Flying Fox Island'. *Chez Felix Hotel* put on a very similar deal. Average eight people per boat, good service and food. More expensive if stopping at Sape. Disappointments abound regarding these trips. Be sure to check that enough provisions are on board, and that a cool box is available if cold Bintang beer is your priority. On most boats guests sleep on deck and, even in the dry season, bad weather can make the journey difficult to bear.

Sleeping

Hotels and losmen stretch out along the main street running south (to the right as the ferry docks from Sape). **D-E** *Bajo Beach*, T41009. Central, clean, well run, car, boat and snorkelling equipment for hire, price includes breakfast, tends to get booked up by tour groups. Currently under haphazard reconstruction. **D-E** *Wisata*, past bridge on road to Ruteng, T41020. Restaurant with rather lacklustre service, rooms are clean with showers attached, pretty garden, well run by friendly and helpful staff and well maintained, good value. **D-E** *Gardena*, on the main street perched on a hill with good views (from some rooms) over towards Komodo, simple bungalows arranged around a courtyard with attached showers but basic toilets, food is good but portions small, tours arranged to Komodo and Rinca, and through Flores, good source of information. **E** *Mutiara Beach*, Jl Pelabuan 31 (opposite *Bajo Beach*), T41039. Decent restaurant, very basic rooms, though the upstairs rooms are rather less small and dark than those below and have a view of the harbour, attached mandi. **E** *Chez Felix*, south end of town, up a hill, T41032. Good views of the harbour from the porch, some with attached bathrooms, good clean, light rooms, popular family-run establishment, tours available, English spoken. Recommended. **F** *Sony Homestay*, opposite *Chez Felix*, south of town on a hill with good views, good food, basic but clean rooms have attached bathrooms and views. **F** *Bahagia Homestay*, to the north of the harbour, next to the mosque, very basic.

To build in pairs: the Ngadhu and Bhaga

Much of the art of the Lesser Sundas is based upon maintaining balance between opposites: between male and female, old and young, living and dead, white and black. This concern for harmony is reflected in the cult altars of **Bajawa**, where ngadhu represent the male ancestors of the clan and bhaga the female ancestors.

Ngadhu are known in some areas of Flores as ndaru and elsewhere as peo. The bhaga is also known as sao heda. Ngadhu consist of a carved wooden post surmounted by a conical thatched roof, usually about 2-3m in height. The bhaga is built to resemble a miniature house with dimensions of around 3-4m, again with a thatched roof and usually standing on a raised platform. The bhaga is often used as the cooking site during important rituals and the two are constructed as a pair, usually positioned close together outside the house of the prominent clan that commissioned their erection. Clans undertake this task as an indicator of their position in society, and also usually after a sign has been received from the ancestors of that clan.

There seems to be some disagreement among specialists as to the timing of construction. Some authorities maintain that the female bhaga must always be built before its male counterpart. The explanation for this is said to relate to the pattern of courtship: men court women, not the other way around, so that the female must be in place ready for the male to make his advance. Other specialists argue quite the reverse, and state that only when the ngadhu post has been planted in the ground can the construction of the bhaga begin. It is possible that both groups are correct, and that there are regional differences across this part of Flores.

The male post is carved from the wood of a particularly hard tree (the sebu or hebu tree) which is dug out of the ground, roots and all. Should any sprouts later appear from roots left in the ground, then danger beckons for the clan. Various rites are observed before a tree is selected. For example, a spear plunged into the ground must remain upright as it would be demeaning for a man to fall over in public. Having selected a tree, it must be dug in the afternoon between 1500 and 1600. The tree is then carried back to the village by four men, to great celebration. These festivities exclude women of child-bearing age and young girls, as it is believed that they might be in danger of being raped by the tree. The tree is placed close to its female companion and buffaloes and pigs are slaughtered. The post is then carved over a three-day period – from the top down (face, body and then legs). During the construction of the ngadhu, those men involved must have no contact with women and observe various sexual and bathing prohibitions. At the end of the carving period, the post is 'planted' in the ground and yet further fesitivities and sacrifices ensue. The end of the work is marked by the naming of bhaga and the ngadhu. The names chosen are usually those of the ancestors of the clan that commissioned the construction.

Conversion to Christianity, inevitably, is changing these traditions, and many clans no longer bother with bhaga and ngadhu, although weathered examples can be found in many villages. Presumably, in a few decades, they will have become objects of veneration in the museums of Indonesia, their cultur1al function and role lost.

F *Gembira Homestay*, very basic and pretty dingy. **Beach accommodation**: there are a number of excellent beach bungalow resorts which are reached by boat, laid on 'free' of charge by the owners. All the resorts have offices in Labuanbajo itself. They can advise on where the various boats dock. Prices usually include all meals. **B-C** *New Bajo Beach*, on the coast 2.5 km to the south of town, T41047. The smartest hotel in the area with a/c in the more expensive rooms. **D** *Cendana Beach Hotel*, 4 km south of Labuanbajo, T41125. On a rather grey beach. Free bus service to the hotel from town. Large clean rooms, bathrooms with showers and WC. **D-E** *Waecicu Beach Resort*, booking office in town is opposite *Dewata Ayu Restaurant*. Three boats leave Labuanbajo daily for the 20 min journey to this beautiful resort. Fairly good beach and snorkelling. Relaxed atmosphere, helpful management. Pleasant cottages ranging from the very basic to the reasonably basic, meals included. Bus tickets for sale at competitive prices and tours organized to traditional villages and to Rinca Island.

D-E *Kanawa Island Bungalows*, booking office in town near *Gardena Hotel*. Boats leave from Labuanbajo at 1100 daily and the journey takes 1 hr to an otherwise uninhabited island. Beautiful beach and good snorkelling. **E** *Pungu Island Hotel*, booking office is near *Sunset Restaurant*, 1-hr journey by boat to reach the island. The newest of the beach resorts, provides free snorkelling equipment, karaoke and organizes tours. Prices negotiable depending on length of stay.

Eating

Mid-range *Puri Komodo*, upmarket ambience, open in the evening only, opposite the tour operators. **Cheap** *Dewata Ayu*, next door to the *Borobudur Restaurant*, good views of the bay and a tasty range of seafood; *Borobudur*, almost opposite the *Mutiara Hotel*, serves a wide range of delicious innovative food, popular. Recommended. *Gardena*, huge fish platters, swiss roti and quality guacomole, a good little restaurant. **Very cheap** *Sunset*, south on Jl Yos Sudarso, on the harbour side of the road, simple Indonesian dishes.

Shopping

Between 0630 and 0900, multiple stalls set up along the main road selling vegetables. The usual shops can be found. There is a small choice of sarongs and woven cloth; and a good shop for wooden carvings, including some rather gruesome masks.

Tour operators

Varanus, Waerana Beach Resort. *Mega Buana Tour and Travel*.

Transport

125 km from Ruteng, 255 km from Bajawa, 380 km from Ende, 528 km from Maumere

Local Both the *Bajo Beach* and *Mutiara Beach Hotels* have vehicles for hire to explore the surrounding countryside. **Air** The airport is 2 km from town. Airport tax: 11,000Rp. Flights are met by bemos. Daily connections on *Merpati* with **Denpasar**, **Kupang** and other destinations in Nusa Tenggara, including **Ende**, **Ruteng** and **Bima**. Flights are often booked well ahead during the peak season (Jul-Sep) and so double booking seems particularly common here. **Bus** There is no bus station; buses cruise the hotels and losmen picking up passengers. Connections with **Ruteng** (4 hrs) and **Bajawa** (13 hrs). It is even possible to make the exhausting journey all the way to **Ende** on a bus that meets the ferry from Sape. *Sinar 99* run a packed, but relatively efficient service; *Komodo* run buses to Ruteng. **Boat** Sat-Thu ferries leave at 0800 for **Sape**, Sumbawa (10 hrs) via **Komodo** (3½ hrs). Buses meet the ferry from Sape/Komodo and take passengers straight on to Ruteng. Boats travel frequently between Labuanbajo and the **Gilis** (Lombok) (see page 782), via Komodo (beware of being overcharged for entrance fee to Komodo). The *Pelni* vessels *Tatamailau*, *Tilongkabila* and *Pangrango* dock at Labuanbajo on their fortnightly circuit through the islands of Nusa Tenggara.

Directory

Airline offices *Merpati*, east of town, towards airport. **Banks** *BNI*, main road (150m towards Ruteng from *Bajo Beach Hotel*), will change US$ cash and TCs from major companies (*Amex*, *Thomas Cook*, *BankAmerica*, *Citibank*), though the rates are poor. Money changer on the same road. **Communications Post Office**: in the centre of town. **Telephone**: *Telkom* office, south of town, near the *PHPA* office. Several *Wartel* offices around town: 1 near the *Wisata Hotel*, another on the main road. **Internet**: *Komodo Internet Café*, run by a young lady entrepreneur, WAECICU@hotmail.com, T41344.

Ruteng

Phone code: 0385

Ruteng is a market town at the head of a fertile valley and a centre of coffee cultivation. It is a peaceful, pleasant spot to stop en route through Flores. This upland area – the town is 1,100m above sea level – is chilly at night. Despite being predominantly Catholic, the practice of **whip fighting** or *caci* is still practised, particularly during wedding festivities. Most weddings are held during the peak tourist months from June to September. Displays of *caci* can be arranged by most hotels.

Walks

The best view of town is from **Golo Curu** (Welcome Mountain). Walk north along the road to Reo past hotels *Agung 1* and *111*, then cross the small bridge. A path bears off left, leading past stations of the cross to a shrine to the virgin at the summit. The round trip takes about 1½ hours.

Excursions **Mount Ranaka**, which reaches a height of 2,140m, is one of the highest points on Flores. The volcano last erupted in the late 1980s. It is a 7 km walk to the top from Robo village which can be reached by bemo from Ruteng; alternatively, it is possible to charter a bemo to take you to within 2 km or so of the summit.

Ranamese Crater Lake is surrounded by forest but has a good path round its shore. Popular with the locals at weekends, as it is a good spot for fishing. The lake is best explored in the early morning when the bird-life is most active. **NB** It is probably best not to go alone if female. ■ *Getting there: take a bemo from Ruteng to Borong village; the path to the lake begins near here.*

Pongkor, 45 km southwest of Ruteng, and **Lambaleda**, 50 km to the northwest, are two traditional villages worth visiting. Lambaleda is a weaving centre. ■ *Getting there: trucks (bis kayu) run from Ruteng to Pongkor (2 hrs) and to Lambaleda via Benteng Jawa. Alternatively, explore the route north to Reo – regular trucks make the journey, through spectacular scenery (see below).*

Sleeping **B-E** *Sindha*, Jl Yos Sudarso 26, T21197. Close to *Manggarai*, reasonably priced restaurant, some recently added VIP rooms provide bathrooms, TV and a balcony, helpful management, clean and well maintained variety of rooms. **C-D** *Agung III*, behind *Agung I*, T21180. Favoured by tour groups, light, spacious and clean. Rooms on the upper floor have good views over town. **C-E** *Rima*, Jl A Yani 14, T22195/6. Very attractive wooden chalet-style hotel, with decent restaurant, beautiful views, and close to the centre of town, some rooms with own mandi, clean and comfortable and even the outside mandi has a shower (though it only operates in the mornings). Economy rooms are recommended. **D** *Dahlia*, Jl Bhayangkan 18, just off Jl Motang Rua (main road), T21377, F21441. This large, quiet hotel is set back from the main road. It is clean and efficiently run. Buckets of water can be heated up for a warm mandi for those staying in more expensive rooms; a luxury well worth requesting after the water has been chilled by the cold Ruteng nights. Recommended. **E** *Agung II*, Jl Motang Rua 10, T21835. In centre of town, set back from the road, large clean rooms, some with own mandi, basic facilities. **E** *Agung I*, T21080. North of town on road to Reo, T21180. Quiet with big rooms, some with western toilets and showers. **E** *Manggarai*, Jl Adisucipto, T21008. The more expensive rooms are large and with own mandi, simple but clean. **F** *Pondok Wisata*, Jl Slamet Riyadi 9, opposite Agogo bus agency, T21753. Dorm accommodation with communal mandi, clean but basic. **F** *Ranaka*, Jl Yos Sudarso 2, T21353. Rather dingy, small rooms have own mandi, cheap.

Eating Ruteng is not renowned for the quality of its food. There are several warungs in the bus station and market area, where dog, known as 'RW', is available. **Mid-range** *Dunia Baru*, Jl Yos Sudarso 10, T21690. Serves a wide range of Indonesian and Chinese food, the locals come here to watch TV. **Cheap** *Merlin*, near *Hotel Dahlia*, good Chinese food.

Ruteng

■ Sleeping
1 Agung I & III
2 Agung II
3 Dahlia
4 Manggarai
5 Pondok Wisata
6 Ranaka
7 Rima
8 Sidha

● Eating
1 Bambooden
2 Dunia Baru
3 Merlin
4 Pade Doang I
5 Pade Doang II
6 Sari Bundo

Very cheap *Bambooden*, Jl Motang Rua 30, T21589. Attractive bamboo-walled restaurant offering good cheap Indonesian dishes, but the entire menu is not always available. *Depot Pade Doang 1*, Jl Lalamentik 5, T21216. Indonesian food. *Pade Doang II*, Jl Motang Rua 34, T22057. Tasty Chinese and Indonesian food. **Bakeries**: *Flores Bakery*, a wide range of cakes and breads. It is possible to go round the back to watch the production process, if requested.

Shopping

Ruteng's bustling market on the east side of town sells a variety of goods including Manggari sarongs, which are predominantly black with brightly coloured embroidered motifs.

Transport

125 km from Labuanbajo, 130 km from Bajawa, 255 km from Ende

Air The airport is on the outskirts of town; bemos meet flights. Daily connections on *Merpati* with **Denpasar**, **Kupang** and other destinations in Nusa Tenggara. **Bus** The station is on the west side of town, a short walk downhill from the centre. Regular connections with **Labuanbajo** (4 hrs), **Bajawa** (6 hrs), **Ende** (10 hrs) and along the scenic route north to **Reo** (2 hrs – see Reo transport section). Also buses to other local destinations. Long-distance departures are in the morning. *Komodo Bus* and *Nusa Indah* (for Labuanbajo) both have their offices on Jl Amenhung; *Agogo* (for buses to Ende) is at Jl Yos Sudarso 4.

Directory

Airline offices *Merpati* agent, Jl Kancil 5, T21197, F217465, open 0700-1700 daily. **Banks** *Bank Rakyat Indonesia*, Jl Yos Sudarso, for TCs. Open :0730-1300 Mon-Fri, 0730-1100 Sat. **Communications Post Office**: Jl Baruk 6 (south side of town), opens daily at 0900, closes weekdays at 1500, 1130 Fri, 1300 Sat and 1200 Sun. **Telephone**: *Telekom* office, Jl Kartini, open 24 hrs. *Wartel* office, Jl Bhayangkara, open 0700-2300; Jl Pertiwi, open 24 hrs.

Reo

A small town on the north coast, Reo is off the Trans-Flores Highway and therefore rarely visited by tourists. The central focus of the town is the Roman Catholic church.

Sleeping

E *Losmen Nisang Nai*, Jl Pelabuhan, opposite the police station on the northern edge of Reo, some rooms with own mandi; **F** *Telukbayar*, Jl Mesjit 8, small, dark and rather grubby rooms.

Eating

There are a couple of very cheap, small and simple places to eat in Reo. *Selera Anda*, Jl Pelabuhan, Javanese food. *Mekar Sari*, Jl Pelabuhan, Padang food.

Transport

38 km from Ruteng

Bus The views along the road from Ruteng are the main reason to come to Reo. The route takes you past spectacular cascades of paddy fields which stretch as far at the eye can see. Rather precarious route, with precipitous drops. Regular connections with **Ruteng**. **Boat** There are said to be infrequent boats from Reo to **Labuanbajo** and also to **Riung**. It might be possible to hitch a lift to other ports in Flores, and mixed cargo boats bound for **Surabaya** also sometimes stop here.

Bajawa

Bajawa makes a pleasant stop on the Trans-Flores route. This hill town is the capital of the Ngada District. It lies 1,100m above sea level and is encircled by three volcanoes, the largest of which is **Mount Inerie**, which reaches 2,245m, making it the highest peak on Flores. The town has a pleasant climate, with fresh days and chilly nights. The bustling **Inpres market** sells traditional textiles – embroidered blankets from Bajawa and ikat from Ende and Kelimutu. It is well worth a visit. But Bajawa's main attractions lie outside the town itself. The traditional houses of the area are some of the most striking on Flores, and despite being a predominantly Christian area, the Ngada District is best known for its thatched cult altars known as *ngadhu* and *bhaga* (see 'Excursions' and box). There is a not particularly useful **tourist information** office, *Dinas Pariwisata*, on Jl Sugio Pranata. The *Camellia Restaurant* has plenty of information for travellers and usually (although none were available on our last visit) several good maps of the area.

Phone code: 0384

Excursions

Bajawa is an excellent base from which to explore this interesting upland area

Langa, a village 6 km south of town, is home to 64 different clans and, despite having a few modern houses, has a fine collection of *ngadhu* and *bhaga* (see box). There is a hot spring where the locals bathe and do their washing 30 minutes away, as well as a couple of waterfalls and the traditional villages of **Bela** and **Borado** within walking distance. **Sleeping** It may be possible to stay overnight with local villagers. ■ *Getting there: the village lies 2½ km off the main Trans-Flores highway towards Ende; bemos are sometimes available for the short trip from the turn-off. It is also possible to do the easy 6 km journey from Bajawa on foot.*

Bena is a village 19 km south of town, past the turn off to Langa and *en route* to Monas, with spectacular views down to the sea. It is probably architecturally one of the best preserved villages in the Ngada District and is the ceremonial centre of the area. The synthesis of Catholic and Animist beliefs is more marked here than anywhere else on the island and is neatly captured by the image of the chapel alongside a megalithic grave site. There are lively New Year celebrations between 15 and 21 January. ■ *Small entry fee to village. Getting there: buses leave from the market in Bajawa, 1½ hrs.*

Wogo Lama or **Old Wogo** lies about 20 km east of Bajawa and has a collection of rather neglected megaliths just beyond the village. **Sleeping** There is a Christian mission at nearby Mataloko which will provide accommodation for visitors. ■ *Getting there: take a bemo from the market in Bajawa to Mataloko which is on the main road to Ende (45 mins), and then walk 1km or so to New Wogo and then the final kilometre to Wogo Lama.*

Bongedu, **Watu** and **Maghilewa** are a group of villages on the far slopes of Mount Inerie. Getting here requires a long walk. There are beautiful groups of traditional houses, *ngadhu*, *bhaga* and megalith graves, as well as spectacular views of the volcano. Ask Lucas (see 'Tours') to take you there.

Throughout June, **Soa** hosts events where you can watch *sagi*, a form of traditional boxing. There is a **market** every Thursday. There are some wonderful hot springs outside the village (small entrance fee). Again, it is advisable for lone women to be cautious. Even wearing clothes into the springs, like the local women, does not ensure that low intensity harassment and wandering hands will not occur. **Sleeping** D bungalows have recently been built next to the hot springs. ■ *Getting there: take a bus or bemo from Naru bus station in Bajawa to Soa village, from where it is a short walk to the springs.*

Tours Lucas, who lives in Langa, occasionally runs tours from hotels in Bajawa. He is now in the logging business (shame!), but has over nine years of experience and is a wealth of information. He speaks good English (and adequate German, French, Dutch and Japanese) and is very knowledgeable about the co-existence of animism and Christianity in the Ngada region. He also provides his guests with delicious home cooked meals, made by his wife. Damianus, who is based in the *Virgo Hotel*, runs daily eight hour tours to the hot springs in Soa and a number of the surrounding villages. He can also be contacted at the *Kambera Hotel*. There are a number of other guides who can take you around the Ngada villages and explain the meanings of the objects you are seeing, but try and talk with them first in order to establish their language skills. Generally guides hire themselves out for 50,000Rp per day, and expect lunch and refreshments on top.

Sleeping Bajawa has an impressive range of places to stay, from mid-range down to budget. This was because just about everyone travelling through Flores broke their journey here. However, during our last visit in mid-2000 we were the only foreigners in town. All prices below include a simple breakfast. **C** *Kembang*, Jl Martadinata 18, T21072. Fairly recently renovated, all rooms have a/c, own mandis with showers, spring beds. Featureless building but good large rooms with big windows. The verandah faces a pretty central garden. **D-E** *Ariesta*, Jl Diponegoro, T21292, light, clean rooms arranged around an attractive courtyard. **D-E** *Elizabeth*, Jl Inerie, opposite *Telecom* office, T21223. Sparklingly clean rooms, some of which have showers, good mosquito nets, but it's on the outskirts of town. **E** *Anggrek*, Jl Letjend Haryono 9, T21172. Own mandi with toilet, popular restaurant which serves tasty Indonesian and travellers' food, good source of information, and friendly manager named Leonard. Unfortunately this place was closed in mid-2000 due to the downturn in the tourist industry, but it may open if things improve. **E** *Dagalos*, Jl A Yani 70, rooms have private mandi, good food but dark and dingy rooms. **E** *Dam*, Jl WZ Yohanes, T21145. Rooms have private mandis. Small hotel with basic facilities but very friendly management. **E** *Edel Way*, Jl Ahmad Yani. Very similar to the Korina (see below) – attached mandis and a reasonable level of cleanliness. **E** *Losmen Melati Johny*, Jl Gajah Mada, T21079. Small, dark rooms, but clean. Car available for hire and a restaurant serving very cheap Chinese and Indonesian food. **E** *Melati Korina*, Jl Ahmad Yani, T21162. Some rooms with own mandi, western toilets and showers, free tea and coffee all day. **E** *Stela Sasandy*, Jl Ahmad Yani. Again, a place on a par with the Korina and Edel Way. Attached facilities, showers, reasonable. **E** *Melati Virgo*, Jl Mayjend D Panjaitan, T21061. Clean rooms with own mandi, arranged around a central courtyard. Free tea and coffee available on request and there is a tour guide who is based in the hotel (see 'Tours', above), well organized staff. Recommended. **E** *Sunflower*, off Jl Jend A Yani, T21230. Rooms at the front of the building with a little porch area are clean with a view over town and a private mandi, but the rooms inside are rather dark and unappealing. Usefully, this is a popular meeting place for guides. **E-F** *Kambera*, Jl Eltari 9, T21166. Restaurant on 1st floor serving very cheap Indonesian food for more basic rooms (**F**) with a communal mandi. Small rooms with private mandis. Amusingly decorated with murals on the walls of the communal areas. Helpful, if a little (and charmingly) disorganized. **E-F** *Nusantara*, Jl Eltari 10, T21357. More expensive rooms are big and bright with own mandi, basic facilities, clean sheets.

Eating

Very cheap *Anggrek*, Jl Letjend Haryono 9, popular restaurant serving good Indonesian and traveller's food. *Camellia*, Jl A Yani 74, Chinese, Indonesian and travellers' food, if ordered in advance. Great guacamole. *Kasih Bahagia*, Jl Basuki Rahmat, Chinese and Indonesian food. *Wisata*, Jl Gajah Mada, next to the market. Wisata Fried Rice is the house speciality. There is a *foodstall* every evening from 1830 serving martabak (Indonesian meat pancake); many warungs near the market. Dark, chewy RW (dog) in large supply sauteed with chillis – *Warung Jakarta*, near Toko Korniawan, does very good 'beef' (dog in disguise?) sate.

Shopping

Textiles Bajawa blankets and ikat from Ende and Kelimutu are available from the Inpres market (see box, page 826).

Transport

68 km from Riung, 130 km from Ruteng, 255 km from Labuanbajo, 125 km from Ende

Air The airport lies 28 km north of town, around 5 km from Soa. Merpati-operated minibuses bring passengers into Bajawa. There is also a *Merpati* service out to the airport; alternatively, catch a bemo to Soa and then travel from there. Connections on *Merpati* with Denpasar, Kupang and other destinations in Nusa Tenggara. **Road Bemos**: run from the terminal on Jl Basuki Rahmat to the surrounding villages. **Bus**: for buses going long distance you have to go to the Watujaji Terminal 3 km to the southeast of town, which can be reached by bemo. Buses to Riung (3 hrs), **Labuanbajo** (12 hrs, 15,000Rp), **Ruteng** (6 hrs, 7,500Rp), and keep eyes peeled for Ranamese crater lake on the right), **Ende** (5 hrs, 7,500Rp) and Maumere. Note that most buses leave early morning. **Boat** Bajawa's nearest port is Aimere on the south coast. There is a boat to **Kupang** at 1800 on Mon, returning to Aimere on Wed from Kupang. There are also occasional boats to **Maumere** and **Labuanbajo**.

Directory

Airline offices *Merpati*, Jl Budi Utomo/Pasar Rahmat (by market), T21051. **Banks** *BNI and Bank Rakyat Indonesia*, both on Jl Soekarno-Hatta, the former has an ATM, both will change TCs and cash in most major currencies. **Communications** General Post Office: Jl Soekarno-Hatta. **Telephone & telegraph** *Perumtel*, Jl Soekarno-Hatta (near *Bank Rakyat Indonesia*).

Riung (Nangamese)

Phone code: 0384 Most people refer to Nangamese (a small town on Flores' north coast) as Riung. For the pedantically inclined, Riung is actually the name of the surrounding sub-district, not the town. The locals are mainly Muslim fishermen and Catholic farmers, who dwell further inland cultivating rice and corn.

The **tourist information** office is a blue bamboo shack in the harbour, and serves as a base for Riung's six licenced guides who run tours to the reserve for 30,000-40,000Rp per person (minimum of five in a group). **NB** Lunch and cost of snorkel hire is not included. Good local information.

Excursions There is a pleasant walk to the top of **Watujape Hill** (3 km) from where there are spectacular views over the reserve.

The **Seventeen Isles National Park** is named in honour of Indonesia's Day of Independence – 17 August. This ignores the fact that there are, actually, 24 islands. The largest of the islands, Pulau Ontoloe, sometimes known as Bat Island, has a huge population of flying foxes. It offers superb snorkelling in extensive coral gardens (but no diving facilities – yet) and the islands have a number of idyllic white sand beaches. Tourists returning from Maumere report that the standard of snorkelling is much better here. There is also a small population of monitor lizards known as *mbou*, closely related to the famous Komodo dragon, but rather smaller (see page 822). These beasts require considerable patience to see in the wild, so for a more reliable sighting there is a captive specimen near the *PHPA* office, from where tickets to the reserve must be purchased.

Sleeping **D-E** *Pondok SVD*, large rooms, very clean, fan, excellent bathroom with western loo and shower. Recommended. **D** *Florida*, very clean and good mosquito nets. Sylvester, the brother of the manager, is a licenced guide. **E** *Homestay Liberty*, pleasant verandah, though rooms are a bit dark, communal mandi. **E** *Madona*, cheapest place in town, communal mandi. **E** *Nur Ichlas*, closest accommodation to the sea with good views of the harbour and stilt village, communal mandi. Recommended. **E** *Tamari Beach*, rooms decked out in shocking pink, attractive garden, communal mandi.

Electricity in Riung runs from 1800 to 0600; all prices include a simple breakfast

Eating All accommodation also offers food, though most of it is pretty basic. **Cheap** *Pondok SVD* offers the widest range. **Very cheap** There are also 2 warungs, *Cilegon* and *Suluwesi*, near the entrance to the market. Next door is *Anda*, only gado gado and mie/nasi, but large portions.

Seventeen Isles National Park

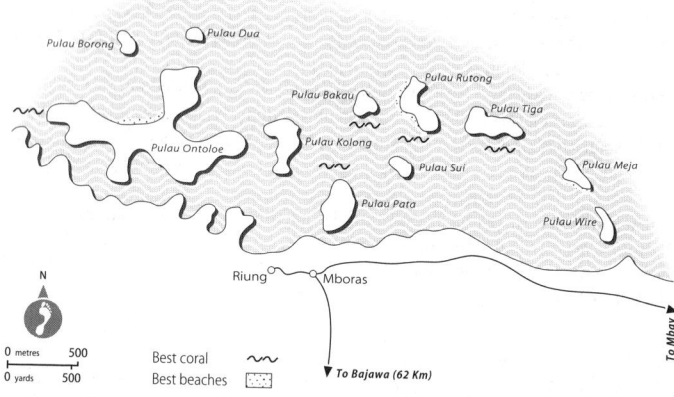

Much ado about adat

Commentators on things Indonesian probably use the Indonesian word adat more than almost any other. The word is taken from the arabic word 'ada, meaning custom, and it refers to any locally accepted code of norms, behaviour, laws, customs or regulations. Often a society's adat is the totality of all these, and there is therefore not just one adat, but many adats, both within and between societies. It has enormous breadth of coverage including, for example, the accepted duties of husband and wife, customary practices in village wood lot use, the correct procedure in rituals, the accepted allocation of duties between different ranks, and rules on inheritance.

Adat is often viewed as the glue which helps Indonesian people to function and interact without conflict – or at least with a minimum of conflict. Any local leader was expected to be conversant with the accepted adat, and this was traditionally passed down the generations through verse, proverb, adage and aphorism. An intimate awareness of adat was akin to wisdom. The Dutch quickly grasped the importance of adat, and they codified it and used the resultant laws to help govern and administer at the local level.

Today, adat is in decline. Success and wisdom is less likely to be measured in terms of an intimate awareness of adat than in terms of academic achievement and economic power. Increasingly, the core of modern adat is the state 'ideology' of pancasila (see page 944), not the inherited layers of customary behaviour enshrined in the traditional meaning of the word, adat.

Shopping

Textiles Local textiles can be bought for about 80,000Rp for a reasonable, quality piece. Fine examples will cost considerably more, while there are always 'tourist' pieces available for somewhat less.

Tour operators

The *PHPA* office, near *Tamari Beach Homestay*, has posters displaying the variety of fauna you are likely to see on the reserve.

Transport

120 km from Bajawa

Road Bus: 3 buses run to and from **Bajawa** every day, but check that they are direct as those doing the detour via **Aegela** and **Mbay** take twice as long as the newer 3 hr direct route. One depature daily to **Ende** (5-7 hrs). **Trucks**: trucks go along the north coast to **Pota**. Change here for another truck to **Reo** (total journey time 6 hrs). **Sea Boat**: occasional boats from **Reo** and **Maumere**.

Ende

Phone code: 0381

Ende is the largest town on Flores with 60,000-80,000 inhabitants, and is the capital of the district of Ende. The town is sited in a spectacular position on the neck of a peninsula, surrounded by mountains. To the south is the distinctive flat-topped Mount Meja (Table Mountain), and on the other side of town is Mount Ia, a dormant volcano that last erupted in 1969. The Portuguese had established a settlement here as early as the 17th century and it then became a popular posting with the Dutch. In December 1992 the town was devastated by an earthquake, with an estimated 40% of buildings destroyed. A large number of haphazard corrugated iron roofs seem to have appeared, precariously attached to unfinished plaster and wood interiors. However, it is still an attractive place to visit, with a friendly atmosphere. In the evenings, groups of local youths collect on street corners to play guitars and sing.

Sights

Ende is best known in Indonesia as the spot to which Soekarno was exiled by the Dutch between 1934 and 1938. **Soekarno's house** and **museum** is on Jl Perwira. It has a poor collection of photographs, and little else. ■ *Mornings (0700-1200, but variable).*

In town, the **Mbongawani market** on Jl Pelabuhan is colourful with traditional healers selling local cures, and a good range of textiles also on sale (see 'Shopping', below). There is a night market, **Pasar Potulando**, on Jl Kelimutu.

A stroll along the sea front is pleasant, with the brightly coloured houses of the Muslim fishermen lining the landward side of the route. You will pass **Museum Bahari**, run by Fr Gabrielle Goran, which exhibits shells and marine life around Flores; there are 744 different species on display. ■ *0700-1900 daily. Entrance by donation; profits support the local orphanage.*

For good views of the town and bay, climb **Mount Meja**, about 45 minutes walk to the top, starting from the market; walk south on Jl Gajah Mada and turn left towards Waniwona village.

There is a **tourist office** in the *Kantor Bupati*, Jl Eltari (near intersection with Jl Nangka), where you can ask for a pamphlet and map of the sights around Ende. ■ *0800-1400 Mon-Sat.*

Excursions **Mount Ia** To climb to the crater of this dormant volcano takes about two hours, and affords good views of the town and bay. ■ *Getting there: catch a bemo to Rate village from the central market and ask for directions.*

Mount Kelimutu is too far to reach in a single day except by chartered vehicle; it is better to spend the night in Moni (see page 840). However, the *Wisata* and *Dewi Putra* and *Ikhlas* hotels have vehicles for charter (100,000Rp) for a day trip to Kelimutu, with a *very* early departure.

Nangalala Beach lies 13 km west of Ende. The beach has reasonable swimming and is popular at weekends with locals. ■ *Getting there: catch a bemo from the central market bound for Nangapanda or Nangaroro and get off at the Km 13 marker.*

Ende

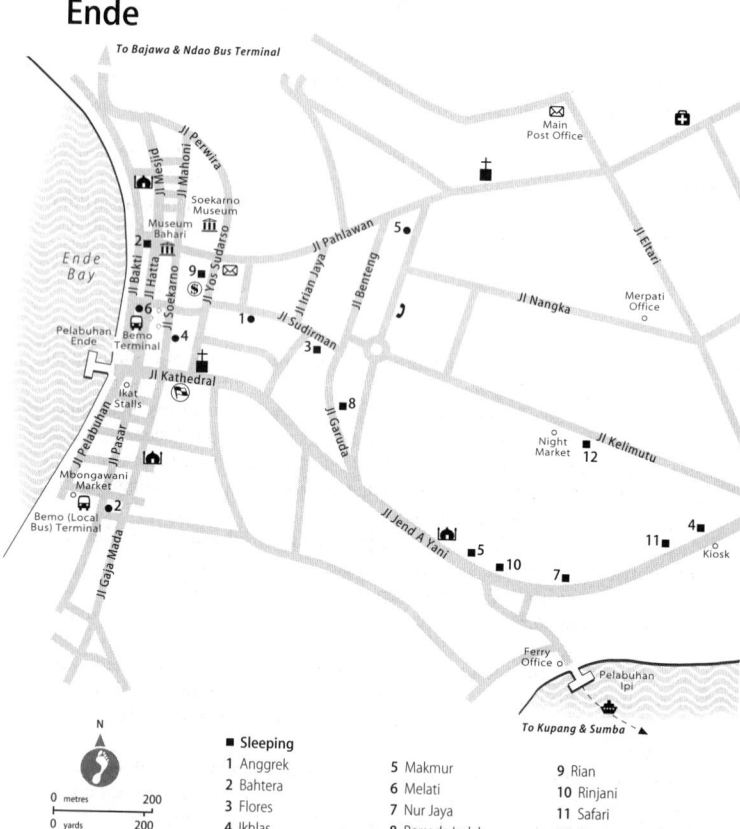

■ **Sleeping**
1 Anggrek
2 Bahtera
3 Flores
4 Ikhlas
5 Makmur
6 Melati
7 Nur Jaya
8 Persada Indah
9 Rian
10 Rinjani
11 Safari
12 Wisata

Nuabosi, 9 km northwest of Ende, offers wonderful views of the town; there is also a *rumah adat* (traditional clan house) here. ■ *Getting there: catch a bemo from the central market.*

There is a pleasant **walk** along the coast from the Wolowona bus terminal on the edge of town (constant bemos travel there from the town centre) east to **Wolotopo**, about 6 km. Wolotopo has some *rumah adat* (traditional houses) and weaving. It is beautifully positioned.

Ngalupolo is a village a further 7 km east of Wolotopo (see above). It has some *rumah adat*, ikat weaving, ivory tusks and gold jewellery on show (donation required for display). One of the traditional houses is said to be 200 years old. ■ *Getting there: there should be a daily boat at 0700 (except Fri) from Pelabuhan Ipi in Ende to Ngalupolo, which then returns in the afternoon. It is possible to walk from town to the port, or catch a bemo heading east.*

Nggela is a coastal weaving village east of Ende (see page 840). There are homestays here. ■ *Getting there: 4 to 5 hrs from Ende by bis kayu (truck) from the Wolowona terminal (1 departure per day). Boats leave from Pelabuhan Ipi (outside Ende) every morning, roughly between 0600 and 0700. To get to Pelabuhan Ipi, enter the airport and walk across the runway. Continue through the village (an interesting visit in itself) to the beach and harbour. It is not possible to return the same day by boat, as the boat only waits 15 mins and it is an hour's walk from the coast to Nggela. To return the same day, take a bus via Moni.*

Tours

There are as yet no good tour agents in Ende, but the *Dewi Putra*, *Ikhlas* and *Wisata* hotels have cars for charter to Kelimutu and surrounding villages. The Dewi Putra tour visits local villages, beaches and the surrounding countryside – bargain hard.

Sleeping

■ on map
Price codes: see inside front cover

Lock your door at night – the maze of linked corrugated iron roofs provide a convenient vantage point for intruders! All losmen & hotels include a simple breakfast in the room rate; most are out of the centre of town

C-D *Dwi Putra*, Jl Dewantara, T21465, some a/c, all rooms with private mandi, restaurant, noisy downstairs, quieter upstairs, clean, and unlike most other hotels, it is central, the manager's brother organizes tours (see above). Recommended. **C-D** *Wisata*, Jl Kelimutu 68, T21368. Some a/c, clean, attached mandi, range of rooms – the most expensive are extensive. Helpful friendly staff, restaurant (mid-range) serves Indonesian and Chinese food. **C-E** *Safari*, Jl Jend A Yani, T21499. All rooms with private mandi with a shower, some a/c, villa with large light, clean rooms and attractive garden and a (formerly) very good, very cheap restaurant. But in mid-2000, with all the economic troubles and lack of visitors, only chap chay and mie/nasi goreng ayam were available. **D-E** *Flores*, Jl Sudirman 28, T21075. Some a/c, reasonably spacious rooms, the more expensive ones with showers. The cheap restaurant serves a wide range of food including Chinese and western dishes. **D-E** *Rian/Wisma Dwi Putra*, Jl Yos Sudarso 23, T21223. Some a/c, western toilet, shower and fan. Recently changed its name, so as

● Eating
1 Depot Ende
2 Istana Bambu
3 Merlin
4 Minang Baru
5 Saiyo
6 Terminal

not to be confused with *Dwi Putra*. **E** *Anggrek*, Jl Gatot Subroto, T22538. WC and showers in the mandi. Clean, large, light rooms. Very cheap restaurant serving Indonesian and Chinese food. **E** *Bahtera*, Jl Bakti 5, T21414. Good location right on the sea front, rooms are a bit dark and there is a basic, grimey communal mandi. No English spoken. **E** *Melati*, Jl Gatot Subroto 12, not far from airport, T21311. Reasonably clean with attached mandi, and a raised area for sipping tea and coffee. **E-F** *Ikhlas*, Jl Jend A Yani, T21695. Choice of rooms from small and dark to light and roomy, some with attached mandi. Satellite TV on the verandah (constant CNN and MTV – when electricity supply allows). Avoid rooms right next to TV. Good and very cheap restaurant, large choice of western and Indonesian dishes (the toasted sandwiches are recommended), breakfast not included, good source of information, cheap laundry service, popular with travellers, this is the best of the budget range and offers good value. Recommended. **E-F** *Nur Jaya*, Jl A Yani, T21252. Clean, good communal mandi with shower and a restaurant selling very cheap Indonesian food. Unfortunately, the bamboo under the mattresses is falling apart from damp. **F** *Persada Indah* (formerly *Amica*), Jl Garuda 17, T21683. Quiet, very basic accommodation.

Eating
There are lots of good places to eat in Ende; this is a selection of the best

Mid-range *Istana Bambu*, Jl Pasar 39, T21480. Excellent mie goreng and a wide range of tasty seafood. Recommended. *Terminal Restaurant*, Jl Hatta 70 (by the old terminal kota), good fish and lobsters plus usual Indonesian favourites. **Cheap** *Merlin*, Jl Jend A Yani 6, Chinese restaurant, recently revamped and is now flashy and rather overpriced. *Depot Ende*, Jl Sudirman 6, good Indonesian and Chinese. **Very cheap** *Minang Baru*, Jl Soekarno (near Cathedral), excellent Padang food, also sells textiles. *Saiyo*, Jl Benteng 7, very good Padang food. The cheapest cold beer in Ende is available from the kiosk opposite *Ikhlas Hotel*. The **night market** (open 1800-2030) sells fruit and snack foods.

Bakeries & coffee shops Jl Kemakmuran (near *Flores Theatre*).

Entertainment **Cinemas** *Flores Theatre*, Jl Kemakmuran 1 – occasionally shows western movies.

Shopping **Books** *Toko Nusa Indah*, Jl Kathedral 5 (just up the hill from the Cathedral). **Tailors** Making-up new clothes and mending, Jl Soekarno, near Cathedral. **Textiles** Good, reasonably priced, ikat from Ende, Kelimutu, Moni and elsewhere (see box, page 826) fairly widely available in town. Salesmen and women visit the losmen, and congregate at the end of Jl Pelabuhan (near Jl Hatta and the port). For a sarong, expect to pay 60,000-80,000Rp, depending on the quality. There is also a good range on sale at the *Minang Baru Restaurant*, includes Sumba blankets.

Transport
54 km from Moni, 147 km from Maumere, 284 km from Larantuka, 125 km from Bajawa, 255 km from Ruteng

Local Bemos: ply the main roads, routes are marked over the roof. Most link the town bus terminals, Ndao and Wolowona. The bemo terminal is by the Pasar Mbongawani, near the centre of town.

Air Ende's **Ipi airport** is on the southeast edge of town; bemos to the centre cost about 2,500Rp, although it's only a 50m walk to the main road where the frequent public bemos are a third of the price. It is a 5-10 min walk from the airport to the closest of the losmen. Daily connections on *Merpati* with **Denpasar**, **Kupang** and other destinations in Nusa Tenggara.

Bus Ende has 2 bus terminals. Ndao terminal is situated on the northwest side of town, off Jl Imam Bonjol, 1 km from the centre. From it, buses head for **Riung** (4 hrs), **Bajawa** (5 hrs), **Ruteng** (10 hrs) and other destinations to the west. For destinations to the east, the Wolowona terminal is at the end of Jl Gatot Subroto, 4 km from the town centre. Buses to **Wolowaru** (2¼ hrs), **Moni/Kelimutu** (2½ hrs), between 0600 and 1400, frequent buses to **Maumere** (6 hrs), 1 early morning bus to **Larantuka** (10 hrs). Constant bemos link both terminals and the town centre. Buses from Bajawa and Maumere drop passengers off at losmen if requested. A minibus leaves the *Ikhlas Losmen* every night at 1700, going all the way to Labuanbajo. *Agogo* bus company runs a service to **Ruteng** and **Maumere** and has its offices at Jl Pelabuhan 28.

Sea Boat: Ende's main port is Pelabuhan Ipi, to the southeast of town. Some smaller vessels also dock at Pelabuhan Ende, Jl Hatta 1, in the heart of town. A *Pelni* ship leaves at 1200 on Wed or 0600 on Thu for **Sabu**, **Rote** and **Kupang** (on Timor). The *Pelni* ships *Awu* and *Pangrango* dock here. Every Sat at 1500 a boat heads for **Waingapu** on Sumba, before turning back towards **Labuanbajo**, **Badas** and **Surabaya**. And every other Wed at 0900 another vessel also leaves for **Waingapu**, and continues on to **Labuanbaojo**, **Bima** and **Ujung Pandang** (Makassar). There is also a boat to **Kupang** at 1700 on Thu and Sat. The *Pelni* office is at Jl Kathedral 2, T21043. Finally there is a bi-weekly ferry service to **Waingapu** (Sumba) on Wed afternoon continuing on to **Sape**, and currently arriving there at 1600 on Friday.

Directory

Airline offices *Merpati*, Jl Nangka, T21355, open 0800-1300 and 1600-1700 Mon-Sat (closed Wed), 1000-1200 Sun. **Banks** *BNI*, Jl Sudirman, up the hill from *Depot Ende Restaurant*, will change cash and TCs in major currencies; *BRI*, Jl Yos Sudarso, will change TCs; *Bank Danoman*, Jl Pasar Ende, allows users to withdraw money on Visa or Mastercard, and will also change US$. **Communications** General Post Office: the main post office is on Jl Eltari on the northernmost edge of town; there is a more central and smaller branch office on Jl Yos Sudarso, only open in the mornings. **Telephone, telegraph & fax**: *Perumtel*, Jl Kelimutu 5 (international). **Medical services** Hospitals: Jl Mesjid.

Ende to Larantuka

For the first 45 minutes out of Ende, the road rises spectacularly up through a limestone gorge with precipitous drops. After 50 km the road reaches the town of Moni, the base for trips to the stunning crater lakes of Mount Kelimutu. From Moni the road descends to the coast and the town of Maumere, a distance of 93 km. The coral gardens near Maumere offer some of the best snorkelling and diving in Indonesia. Continuing east from Maumere, the last leg of the Trans-Flores Highway runs 137 km to the port of Larantuka. This was one of the centres of Portuguese missionary activity in Flores, and remains among the most obviously Christian towns on the island.

Kelimutu and Moni

Mount Kelimutu, with its three-coloured crater lakes, is one of the highlights of Flores. The lakes, at an altitude of 1,640m, are said to have changed colour 37 times in the last 50 years. In the 1970s they were red, white and blue; this gradually gave way to the less spectacular maroon (almost black), iridescent green, and yellow-green. In 1997 they underwent another transformation and are currently brown black, cafe au lait and milky blue. Local villagers believe that the lakes are the resting places for souls called by Mutu (Kelimutu). When mists lie over the lake someone is thought to be passing over: young people are destined for one lake, the old for another, while witches and evil people go to the third. On a clear morning, the view of the crater lakes and the surrounding mountains is simply unforgettable.

Mount Kelimutu

Ascending and descending the mountain Reaching the summit used to require an early morning/late night trek of 12 km; today there is a truck which takes people up to the summit at about 0400, in time for the sunrise; it takes about one hour (15,000Rp). At the time of writing the bridge across to the base of the craters had collapsed due to heavy rains, and trucks were charging 100,000Rp per load of tourists. *Ojeks* (motorcycle taxis) will also take people to the top of Kelimutu for around 5,000Rp. Make it known at your losmen that you wish to be picked up. The truck descends at about 0700 but it is often worth staying longer to see the lakes in full sunlight. **NB** It is cold, both at the summit and on the open truck; take a sweater, or use an ikat sarong, which will serve as a handy alternative to a sleeping bag (sold all over Moni for 30,000-45,000Rp). The walk down the mountain is easy enough in daylight and very worthwhile. The road to the summit is 12 km, but the well marked path – Jl Potong (Jl Shortcut) – only 8 km; note that the shortcut is by the toll station, not before. Only the foolhardy would attempt the shortcut by starlight. The main path is through stunning countryside and takes you past hot springs and a waterfall. There is also a further turning off this path, which takes you through a number of villages in which it is possible to watch ikat being woven, to drink tea and coffee and buy sarongs. At the end of the trail through the villages is the quirky *rumah makan Agnes*, which serves basic and very cheap noodles and rice dishes, though service is slow. ■ *Entrance fee to volcano: 2,500Rp.*

Moni The friendly nearby village of Moni (altitude 600m) is in the heart of Lio District which has a rich weaving tradition, with blues and reds being the most common colours. It is a good base from which to take walks in the beautiful surrounding area and make excursions to local villages (see below). The **market** on Tuesday mornings on the playing field is worth seeing: there is a good range of ikat for sale; traditional herbalists also set up their stalls. The village has become the main tourist base from which to visit the mountain. There are a couple of **hotsprings** and a **waterfall** just a few hundred metres along the road to Ende. Next to *Daniel's Homestay* is a **high thatched traditional house**, in front of which daily traditional dance displays are held (around 5,000Rp).

Excursions **Wolowaru** is situated on the main Ende-Maumere road, 11 km from Moni. This is a bigger town than Moni, but has not developed into such a tourist base for climbing Mount Kelimutu. It is worth visiting on market days (Monday, Wednesday and Saturday) when there is a reasonable range of ikat on sale (see page 826). It is also possible to use the town to visit the ikat-weaving villages in the surrounding countryside, including Nggela and Jopu (see below). **Sleeping** includes: **E** *Losmen Kelimutu*, clean, some attached mandis. The *Jawa Timur*, next door, is a popular restaurant stop for buses travelling through the town; it has good food. ■ *Getting there:* 15 mins by bemo from Moni, or on a bus from Ende or Maumere.

Jopu is a weaving village 4 km from Wolowaru, producing weft ikat (see page 826). The various processes involved in producing ikat are on view to visitors (see page 441). ■ *Getting there: take a bemo directly there or go to Wolowaru, from where bemos go to Jopu more frequently.*

Nggela, 15 km from Wolowaru on the same road as Jopu, is a weaving village that has become over-touristed. However, ikat is on sale and production processes are on view (see page 441). The locals employ rather pushy sales tactics. There are hot springs and a couple of homestays here. ■ *Getting there: take a bis kayu to Wolowaru, and a*

Around Ende

bemo to Nggela; there is also a daily boat (except Fri) to Ende from the beach, which is a steep 2-km descent from Nggela, 2½ hrs, only recommended for the hardy as it is easy to fall out of the small canoe, which transports you from shore to boat. Alternatively, the 19 km walk from Wolowaru is very beautiful, through paddy fields and along the beach (take a short cut from Wolojita and take plenty of water to drink).

Sleeping

D *Bungalow Hotel* (10 mins' walk from Moni village on road to Ende), clean and attractive. Recommended. **D** *Arwanty's Homestay*, brand new and right in the centre of Moni, the owner has just sent us details about her 3 new and 2 improved bungalows, each with spacious living rooms, good bathroom facilities, verandah, and a restaurant serving traditional cuisine. **D-E** *Sao Ria Wisata*, the more expensive rooms are clean and attractive with good views over the valley. The cheaper rooms on the other hand are rather dark and very basic, and look out onto the back of the pricier accommodation. **E** *Hidayah Bungalows*, some with private mandi. The hot springs are just 3 mins' walk away in the direction of Ende. Clean bamboo bungalows on stilts, helpful management can provide mosquito nets on request and can organize bus tickets at the right price. Free tea and coffee throughout the day. Recommended. **E** *Homestay Wisata*, a little way out of town on the road to Maumere; good for those who want to escape the crowd. Large bamboo rooms on stilts, very cheap restaurant serving Chinese and Indonesian food. **E** *Losmen Maria*, clean rooms for up to 3 people, private mandi with showers, further bungalows are under construction. **E** *Palm Homestay*, out of town, the first hotel you pass on the road from Maumere towards Wolowaru, situated in the middle of a fruit garden and very peaceful compared with places in town, single and double bungalows with and without attached mandi, good transport information, excellent buffet dinner, breakfast included. **E** *Watugana Bungalows*, this little gem of a place is set back from the road just opposite the *Mountain View*. Attractive bungalows on stilts arranged around a lovely little garden. Simple facilities but very clean, a small breakfast is included in the cost, but for a little extra a huge breakfast can be laid on. Central location, best of the budget accommodation. Recommended. **E** *Wisma Kelimutu*, shower in the mandi but otherwise very basic and rather dirty, though the staff are very friendly. A new block should soon be completed. **F** *Amina Moe*, cheapest rooms in town. Basic outside mandi, simple rooms, comfortable communal sitting-room. Excellent huge and cheap buffet laid on every night: price includes breakfast and tea/coffee, a real favourite. Recommended. **F** *Daniel*, cold water, shared mandi, friendly and popular, rats in the rafters. **F** *Pondok Wisata Lestari*, 40m off the main road, clean communal mandi, thin bamboo walled rooms. **F** *Pondok Wisata Regal Jaya*, communal mandi, small but clean rooms with good mattresses.

The number of losmen in Moni reflects how heavily the village has become reliant on the tourist trade. However, like so many other towns in Flores, in mid-2000 during our last visit there were scarcely any tourists about

Eating

Cheap *Amina Moe*, best buffets of the homestays; tasty and a big choice, place order before 1730, always more than you can eat. *Mountain View Restaurant*, good view, great food and big helpings. Indonesian and travellers' food, serves Moni cake. *Nusa Bunga* serves curry as well as Indonesian and travellers' food. *Rona*, Indonesian and Western food including eight Italian dishes, which are surprisingly good. Rona cake, a version of Moni cake, is tasty and filling, and makes a welcome change from the standard nasi and mie fare. Pricey drinks, though you can bring your own. **Very cheap** *Kelimutu*, down road from *Sao Ria Wisata Hotel*, Indonesian and Western food. *Rumah Makan Sarti* serves Indonesian and Western food, weavers often work next to the restaurant. *Wisata*, on the right-hand side of the road heading towards Maumere, about 400m from the market. Lovely view and very good food, friendly owners; a good place to sit and relax.

Transport

Road Bus: regular connections with Ende 2 hrs, and Maumere 3 hrs; there is also a daily bus doing the 9 hr journey through to Bajawa. **NB** It can be difficult to get out of Moni in the high season; you may have to hitch a lift on a truck travelling to Nggela on market day. The buses passing through the town are often full; it may be necessary to catch a *bis kayu* to Wolowaru and wait for the bus there.

11 km from Wolowaru, 54 km from Ende, 93 km from Maumere

Directory

Communications The *Kelimutu Restaurant*, 1 km along the road to Ende from Moni, has the only telephone in the area. It is generally only possible to make domestic calls and seems rather temperamental.

Maumere

Phone code: 0382

Most people come to this region to dive and snorkel in some of the best sea gardens in Indonesia and explore the surrounding villages. Maumere itself, with a population of about 70,000, is a rather featureless, disorganized town that still seems to be coming to terms with being (comparatively) large. The tourist office, *Kantor Pariwisata*, is on Jl Wairklau, T21562. To get there, walk along Jl Gajah Mada towards Ende, turn right after the Perusahaan Umum Listrik, and walk 400m – the office is just past the *Kantor Statistik*, 10-15 minutes in total from the town centre. They provide a useful booklet, but little English is spoken.

It is possible to walk around Maumere in a morning. The central market is just that – central – with a good selection of ikat cloth on sale (see 'Shopping'). The port (Pelabuhan Maumere), usually quiet, is five minutes walk to the northwest; on the way there the road passes **Maumere Cathedral**. If you are staying in town, the nightlife makes for a surprising diversion. Maumere is the 'Las Vegas of Flores'. During August there is a nightly night market; it is not actually a market, more like a fair where you can risk your rupiah on the roulette wheels and bingo boards, buy snacks and sample the local alcoholic brews from street sellers. In September there is also bareback horse racing.

Excursions **Waiara** and **Sao Wisata Beaches** lie 12-13 km east of Maumere. There is good swimming, and the sea off the coast is a marine park and offers superb snorkelling and diving – or at least it did until the December 1992 earthquake. The coral has been badly damaged, especially off Sao Wisata Beach. The most seriously affected coral gardens are those in shallow waters, some of the deeper dive sites escaped relatively unscathed. Two dive clubs are based here and run dive boats out to the reefs (see 'Diving Clubs'). It is easiest to reach the reef by booking a place on one of their dive boats. **Sleeping** Homestays available on Permaan Island, as are local guides (but limited English spoken). ■ *Getting there: by bemo from the Terminal Timur. It is also possible to reach the marine park by chartering a boat from Keliting (9 km east, take a bemo from Terminal Timur) for about 65,000Rp per day. There are regular boats crossing between the islands out on the reef and Keliting on market days (Wed and Fri).*

Ladalero is home to the biggest museum on Flores, the **Blikan Blewut Museum**. It is situated 9 km from town, on the road to Ende. A cluttered, mixed, yet interesting display of ethnographic exhibits, textiles and ceramics assembled by the local Seminary (Societas Verbi Divini). ■ *Admission to museum by donation. 0730-1400 Mon-Sat, 1000-1400 Sun. Getting there: take a bemo from Terminal Barat.*

Nita is about 2 km from Ladalero and 11 km from Maumere. The 'Rajah' here has a collection of old elephant tusks and other memorabilia. There is a worthwhile weekly market held here each Thursday. ■ *Getting there: take a bus from Terminal Barat.*

Sikka is a weaving village from which the entire region around Maumere takes its name. It is possible to buy ikat here at reasonable prices (check at the craft shops for comparison – see 'Shopping' below) and see some of the multiple stages of the ikat process – something like 35 in all (see page 441). If on a tour, all the stages may be demonstrated. There is also an attractive **Portuguese church** at Sikka, white with green fretwork, built in 1800. ■ *Getting there: take a bus from Terminal Barat.*

Watublapi is another, less frequently visited, weaving village, 11 km south from Geliting (which lies just east of Maumere, on the main Trans-Flores road). Nearby is Bliran Sina Hill, from where there are views north to the Flores Sea and south to the Sawu (Sabu) Sea. There is a large Catholic seminary here and it is sometimes possible to stay overnight. ■ *Getting there: take a bus from Terminal Timur.*

Wodong lies 27 km east of Maumere. See page 846 for details. ■ *Getting there: take a bus or bemo from the Lokaria terminal to Wodong.*

Nuabari is a village where animist beliefs continue to play an important role. Indeed Nuabari is unusual in a number of respects. To start with, the language of the inhabitants and the cloth that they weave have much more in common with the area around Moni than with Maumere. There are also numerous examples of megalithic graves sites. Holes are dug into solid rock and the bodies placed in a foetal position within the excavated cavities. If a couple wishes to be buried together, the one who dies first will be exhumed on the death of his/her partner and the bodies arranged face to face, placed back in their resting place, and the grave resealed. Bodies must be embalmed as they generally lie for at least a week while the graves are prepared to receive them. Visitors may also be able to see inside the chief's house which is decorated with masks and carvings. The chief is the functional and spiritual leader of Nuabari and two other nearby villages. Elaborate rituals must be carried out so that this power can pass from father to son. It is said that the chief can sense his impending death and calls for a period of fasting. He then cuts his son's skin along the forearms, thighs and on either side of his back. He proceeds to rub a mixture of his bile and herbs into the wounds which completes the transfer of authority. Donations of 1,000Rp to an education fund for local children. Bring your own water as there is none available here. ■ *Getting there: the village can be reached on tours arranged from the Gardena Hotel.*

Tours Day tours from Maumere to Sikka weaving village, the Ladalero museum and Nita, or to Geliting Market and Watublapi weaving village or to Sea World can be arranged by many of the hotels. Some also have cars and drivers for charter. For example, the *Hotel Maiwali*'s minibus can be chartered to Wairara Beach, Sikka weaving village, Ladalero, Kelimutu (either in one day leaving at 0300; or over two days with a night in Moni). *Harapan Jaya*, a textile shop on Jl Moa Toda, also has a car for hire. Expect to pay about 140,000Rp for a day's hire to out-of-town destinations, 95,000Rp for around town. *Wina Ria Hotel* can arrange boats for snorkelling. Alternatively, enquire at the tourist information office.

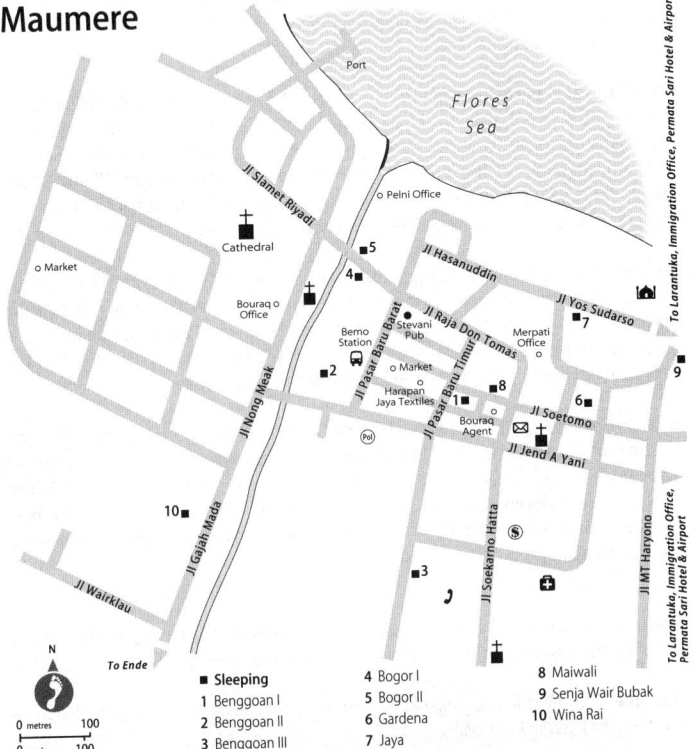

Maumere

■ **Sleeping**
1 Benggoan I
2 Benggoan II
3 Benggoan III
4 Bogor I
5 Bogor II
6 Gardena
7 Jaya
8 Maiwali
9 Senja Wair Bubak
10 Wina Rai

Sleeping
■ on map
Price codes:
see inside front cover

All prices include morning tea, but no breakfast unless stated. Because Maumere is a popular diving area, it features on many tour itineraries & consequently hotel prices tend to be somewhat steeper than normal

A-D *Permata Sari Inn*, Jl Jend Sudirman 1, 2 km from town, T21171. On the beach, attractive clean rooms all with attached bathrooms, quite nice bungalows but overpriced. **C-E** *Senja Wair Bubak*, Jl Yos Sudarso, T21498. Some a/c, becoming the most popular of the budget places, range of rooms from simple with shared facilities to rather more comfortable a/c rooms. Good facilities including tours and motorbike and car hire. **C-E** *Wini Rai*, Jl Dr Soetorno, T21362 (about 5-10 mins walk out of town on road to Ende). Some a/c, shared mandi in cheaper rooms, but more expensive are large and clean with attached facilities, garden, can arrange tours around Flores and book tickets, economy rooms come recommended. **D** *Gardena*, Jl Pattirangga 28, 5 mins from town centre on quiet side street, T21489, F23404. Some a/c, all rooms with inside mandi, comfortable atmosphere. Hires out cars and motorbikes (see 'Transport'). Good source of information and popular with travellers. Best place to get hold of tour guides. **D-E** *Bogor*, Jl Slamet Riyadi 2, T21191. An extensive hotel complex with a car for rent, a good little shop and a restaurant with cheap Indonesian and Chinese food. **D-E** *Maiwali*, Jl Raja Don Tomas 40, T21220. Some a/c, the more expensive rooms are comfortable, quiet and clean, but the fan-cooled rooms are expensive and cheaper hotels offer a better deal. Some very active midnight karaoke enthusiasts! **D-E** *Jaya*, Jl Sultan Hasannudin, T21292. Some rooms with a/c, price includes breakfast and afternoon tea. Friendly but near the mosque, so wake up calls come around 0430. **E** *Lareska*, Jl S Pranoto 3, T21137. The economy rooms are upstairs and far more attractive than the more expensive rooms below. There is a good view from the upstairs balcony area. Don't be put off by the ground floor room, the cheaper rooms come recommended. **E** *Losmen Bogor II*, Jl Slamet Riyadi 4, T21137. Edge of town, recently renovated, the rooms are bright and clean, with big windows looking on to the waterside (ask for a room with a window as some don't have one), the upstairs rooms (shared mandi) are nicer than the downstairs rooms (own mandi dark). **E** *Naga Beach*, 10 km west of town (take bemo 5 from *Losmen Bogor II* or from Pasar Baru), T21605; 50m from the beach, clean bungalows with shared mandi, very friendly, good value, price includes breakfast. **F** *Homestay Varanus*, Jl Nong Meak, T21464. Friendly place with a nice garden, good value but the earthquake damage is taking some time to repair. Recommended.

Dive Clubs at Waiara (12 km from town) **B-C** *Pondok Dunia Laut (Sea World Club)*, Jl Nai Roa, Km 13, PO Box 3, T21570, F21102. Some a/c, attractive cottages, and better value for money than the *Flores Sao Wisata*, although the diving equipment and support is reportedly not as good, price includes breakfast (see 'Diving' below). **B** *Flores Sao Wisata*, Waiara Beach, T21555, F21666. Better of the 2 dive centres, good equipment, **A** per day if diving, at this price the rooms are rather under-equipped (see 'Diving' below).

At beaches near Maumere **E** *Paga Beach*, on coast south of Maumere (go to Terminal Ende and take an hourly bemo running to *Paga Beach Hotel*, 1 hr drive). Very clean and attractive bamboo huts, white sand swimming beach, decorated by weird and wonderful plants and imaginative use of concrete. Has a little craft shop. **E-F** *Nogo Beach*, fan optional for additional charge. Price includes breakfast, can arrange snorkelling trips and hire out equipment.

Eating
It is generally acceptable to bring your own drinks to a restaurant. For the widest choice of places, try the main street down to the harbour

Cheap *Golden Fish*, Jl Hasan Nudu, fresh seafood and Chinese food. *Stevani's Pub and Restaurant*, Jl Raya Centis (near intersection with Jl Raja Don Tomas), open-air thatched pavilions in garden, travellers', Chinese and Indonesian food, and karaoke from 2100 most evenings. **Very cheap** *Bambu Den*, Jl Gajah Mada 46, Chinese and Indonesian food. *Rumah Makan Sumber Indah*, Jl Raja Centis, Javanese, Chinese and seafood. *Sarinah*, Jl Raya Centis, Chinese, excellent seafood.

Bars *Toko Go*, Jl Dr Soetorno 14, sells cheap cold beer and soft drinks. *Evening Market*, behind *Stevani's Pub*, sells cheap *arrack* (local brew) and fruit. Beruga style huts in a pleasant garden.

Entertainment **Karaoke** Both *Stevanis* and *Sinta Pubs* do nightly karaoke sessions, the 1st geared more to western, the latter to local tastes.

Shopping

Textiles Excellent range of ikat from all over Nusa Tenggara on sale at *Harapan Jaya*, Jl Moa Toda, reasonable prices (though not bargains): ikat from Roti and Sabu, Ende (80,000Rp), Sumba (265,000-315,000Rp), Larantuka and Lembata (115,000-265,000Rp), Manggarai (near Ruteng) (55,000-80,000Rp), West Timor (150,000-200,000Rp), Sikka (25,000-35,000Rp). Also textiles next door at Subur Jaya; *Kota Pena Art Shop*, Jl Gaja Mada, T21032, a fantastic range of arts and crafts from all over East Nusa Tenggara. An education even if you are not buying, though some of the smaller pieces are very tempting and quite affordable, bargaining possible.

Sports

Diving Although the earthquake of December 1992 is now history, the effect of the earthquake on the area's sea life is still evident. Large stands of coral were destroyed and these will take years to recover. Although other sections of reef, remarkably, appear to have survived intact, regular visitors report that the diving is still not back to its pre-earthquake best. *Flores Sao Wisata* on Waiara Beach (see 'Sleeping' above) offer package deals, which include airport pick up. *Pondok Dunia Laut* (*Sea World Club*) (see Sleeping) offer an all-in package, which includes 2 dives per day, boat trip, tank and weights, accommodation and all meals for 2 people, they also have diving equipment and windsurf boards for hire to non-residents. **Snorkelling**: it is possible to book a place on *Sao Wisata's* dive boat, with equipment, lunch and drinks provided.

Tour operators

Astura, Jl Yos Sudarso, T21498. *Floressa Wisata*, Jl Jend A Yani, T21242. *Sikka Permai*, Jl Pasar Lama, T21236. Watch out for tour agents selling tickets with someone else's name on them for full price. Check tickets with the airline office.

Transport

82 km from Wolowaru, 93 km from Moni, 147 km from Ende, 137 km from Larantuka. Travelling east from Maumere to Larantuka, the road is good & the countryside particularly beautiful

Local Bemos: the bemo station is by the old market on Jl Jend A Yani in the centre of town. Local journeys cost 500Rp, 1,000Rp if they go right off their route. Bemos criss-cross the town linking the 2 bus terminals, Barat and Timur (or Lokaria). **Cars**: can be chartered for around 130,000Rp per day (see 'Tours' above), motorcycles for 25,000Rp per day (both *Gardena* and *Wini Rai II* arrange hire).

Air Maumere's **Waioti Airport** is 2 km east of the town centre, off the road towards Larantuka. Transport to town: taxis to the town centre or walk the 750m to the main road and catch a bemo. Regular connections by *Merpati* and *Bouraq* with **Jakarta**, **Denpasar**, **Bima** and **Kupang**, and towns in Kalimantan and Sulawesi.

Bus Maumere has 2 bus terminals; Terminal Barat on Jl Gajah Mada for destinations to the west, including **Wolowaru** (3 hrs), **Moni** (3½ hrs) and **Ende** (5 hrs); and Terminal Timur (also known as Terminal Lokaria), east of town on Jl Larantuka, for eastern destinations including **Larantuka** (4 hrs) and **Wodong**. It is now possible to travel straight through to **Bajawa**, though this requires a gruelling 10-hr journey. Buses link the 2 terminals and the town centre (500Rp). Buses arriving in Maumere drop passengers off at their losmen/hotels, and those leaving will cruise town for aeons and also pick up from losmen/hotels. *Agogo* (for Ende, Moni and Wolowaru) has its offices on Jl Jend A Yani; *Sinar Remaja*, on Jl Pattirangga, and *Sinar Agung* (for Larantuka and Ende), on Jl Gajah Mada by the Terminal Barat. Losmen/hotels will also usually book tickets.

Boat The Pelabuhan Maumere is a 5-10 mins walk northwest from the town centre. The *Pelni* ship *Awu* docks here on its 2 week circuit between calling at ports in Java, Sulawesi and Nusa Tenggara. The *Pelni* office is next to *Losmen Bogor II* on Jl S Pranoto (aka Jl Slamet Riyadi), just over the bridge on the road to the port. Irregular mixed cargo vessels leave here for **Ende**, **Reo**, **Riung**, **Kupang**, **Larantuka** and **Surabaya**.

Directory

Airline offices *Bouraq*, Jl Nong Meak, T21467 (also agent on Jl Moa Toda, next to *Benggoan I losmen*). *Merpati*, Jl Raja Don Tomas, T21342, open 0800-1400 and 1900-2100. **Banks** *BNI*, Jl Soekarno-Hatta (behind and to the side of the Kantor Bupati), will change TCs and cash in major currencies. *BRI*, Jl Raja Centis, open 0730-1430 Mon-Fri, 0730-1130 Sat. *Bank Danamon*, Jl Raja Centis, will change banknotes and can withdraw money from Visa or Mastercard. **Communications** General Post Office: Jl Jend A

Yani (on the square near the Kantor Bupati). **Telephone & telegram**: *Telekom*, Jl Soekarno-Hatta (200m from Jl Jend A Yani) (international). The *Wartel* office is next door to *Gardena Hotel* on Jl Patirangga and is open 24 hrs every day. **Medical services** Hospitals: *General Hospital*, Jl Kesehatan, T21118. **Useful addresses** Immigration office: Jl Kom A Sucipto, T21151 (slip road to airport). Police: Jl Jend A Yani, T21110.

Waiterang Bay and Wodong

Wodong is a small village 25 km east of Maumere, *en route* to Larantuka. There are five excellent, though basic, places to stay along the beach outside Wodong village (see 'Sleeping', below). There is good snorkelling here, and Wodong is also convenient as a base from which to trek to Mount Egon (see 'Excursions', below). The two losmen hire out masks and flippers, and can arrange fishing trips and excursions to offshore islands. For those looking for a place to enjoy the landscape of Flores away from the masses, this is a good place to stay for a few days.

Excursions There is a good walk up the hill behind the bay, 1½ hours. The route is marked by white signs erected by staff from *Flores Froggies*. From the top of the hill are some great views out across the bay. If you take a bemo to Blidit village, there is a 45 minute walk to some hot springs at the base of Mount Egon (ask for *mata air panas*).
    Mount Egon (1,703m) is an active volcano, visible from Wodong. The trek to the summit takes 3½-4½ hours and is well worthwhile. From Blitit (see below, for information on reaching Blitit), follow the gravel track until it reaches a roadside, concrete water culvert and a rocky ford. Here is the first of a series of stone cairns marking the way to the summit. The route passes from scree into dry grassland, and from grassland into savanna scrub forest, with eucalyptus predominating. The path through the forest is clear enough; it emerges into more open landscape after about two hours. From here the summit is visible, and it is about another hour's walk to the top. Near the peak, old tubes now lying in disuse – laid by the Japanese during their occupation of Indonesia for sulphur extraction – are visible. A path leads around the crater edge, and another snakes its way into the caldera. The caldera lake, though, has dried out. From the crater lip there are superb views – on a clear day – over the sea towards Pulau Besar. **NB** Take ample water and some food for the trek.
■ *Getting there: take a bemo to Blitit, at the end of the surfaced road (it is also possible to arrange a pickup after descending from Mount Egon). Ask the owners of the Wodong Homestay or Flores Froggies if they will make the necessary arrangements.*
    Boat trips can be arranged to the white sand beaches of **Pulau Indah**, where there is good snorkelling. There used to be a village on the island but it was destroyed in the 1992 earthquake. **Pulau Besar** is the largest of the three offshore islands and has three traditional villages. **Pulau Pondok** is reportedly good for shell collecting – although live shells should not be taken.

Sleeping All the accommodation is in simple bungalows except at *Pondok Praja*. All prices include a simple breakfast. **D** *Pondok Praja*, substantial bungalows, with negotiable prices. **D-E** *Ankermis*, some rooms with own mandi, bungalows are set slightly back from the beach, behind some freshwater pools, excellent restaurant (see below). **E-F** *Flores Froggies*, run by a French couple, old but attractive bungalows on the beachfront, the travellers' and Indonesian food comes recommended, friendly, the bungalows have attached mandis, dormitory accommodation also available. Recommended. **E-F** *Wodong Bungalows*, some rooms with own mandi, mosquito net, good and very cheap restaurant, friendly, good source of information (check the visitors' book), popular, with free use of bikes, canoes and snorkles. **F** *Waiterang Beach*, this relatively new place is the cheapest in Waiterang Bay. The bungalows look directly on to the sea. Inexpensive simple restaurant.

Eating **Cheap** *Ankermis*, this restaurant is a bit pricier than the others, but there is a definite correlation between what you pay and what you get, try *hot gossip nasi campur*.

Sports

Diving, **snorkelling** and **fishing**: the 2 losmen can arrange diving with the *Sea World Club* outside Maumere; they also hire out masks and flippers and can arrange fishing trips.

Transport
25 km from Maumere

Bus: regular connections with **Larantuka** and **Maumere**. From Maumere, take a bemo or bus from Terminal Lokaria to Wodong.

Larantuka

Phone code: 0383

The small town of Larantuka is the district capital of east Flores, with a population of 30,000. It is strongly Christian – though there is also a significant Muslim population – with a remarkable Easter celebration showing Portuguese origins (16th century). Particular devotion is shown to the Virgin Mary, a statue of whom was reportedly miraculously washed-up on the shore here.

The **Chapel of the Virgin Mary**, in the centre of town, houses the sacred statue of the Virgin (see 'Festivals'). On Saturday, the Mama Muji pray in ancient Latin and Portuguese, distorted to such a degree that it is unintelligible even to students of the language (see box). There are also prayers said each evening. There are a number of other churches in town, including the century-old **Cathedral of Larantuka** and the **Chapel of Christ** (Tuan Ana Chapel). The old **docks** are also worth visiting. Larantuka was fortunate to survive the earthquake, which devastated much of Eastern Flores, relatively unscathed.

Sleeping
The rooms in Larantuka tend to be rather overpriced. All hotels except Rulies include a simple breakfast in the price

B-D *Fortuna II*, Jl Basuki Rachmat 168, out of town, T21383. Some a/c, the best hotel in town. The upmarket sister hotel to the *Fortuna I*, which is across the road. **B-E** *Fortuna I*, Jl Basuki Rachmat 171, 2 km northeast of town, T21140. Private bathroom, the more expensive rooms have a/c and are not particularly attractive, the cheaper rooms are small but clean. **B-E** *Tresna*, Jl Yos Sudarso 8, T21072. Some private mandis, food served, rooms are quite reasonable and it has a more central location next to the Chapel of the Virgin Mary, quaint garden and friendly management. **F** *Rulies*, Jl Yos Sudarso 40, T21198. A friendly, if rather scruffy, hotel with dorm accommodation and communal mandi, the place which attracts most of the backpacker business. Good source of information.

Eating
Larantuka is not noted for its gastronomic prowess & the choice of places to eat is limited

Cheap The *Rumah Makan Nirwana* is one of the few restaurants in Larantuka and serves good Chinese/Indonesian dishes. **Very cheap** *Rumah Makan Sri Solo*, near Hotel Rulies, basic Indonesian food. There are also a number of warung along Jl Niaga, the main coast road. *Jagung Titi* is a local speciality, a snack food which is best described as squashed popcorn.

Festivals

Easter (movable), the sacred statue of the Virgin is washed and dressed on Maundy Thursday (the water, in the process, becoming Holy Water with healing powers). In the afternoon the statue is kissed (the *Cio Tuan* ceremony) by the townspeople and other pilgrims, while the streets are cleaned and prepared for Good Friday. On the afternoon of Good Friday, the statue is taken to the Cathedral, where a statue of Jesus from the Chapel of Christ joins it. Following the service at about 1900, the statues are paraded through the town in a candle-lit procession. There are numerous other festivities during Holy Week.

Transport
137 km from Maumere

Local Bemos provide transport around town.

Air Gewayan Tana airport is 12 km north of town. One flight per week on *Merpati* from Kupang and on to **Lewoleba** and **Lembata**. It is not very reliable, so don't count on making the journey.

Bus The bus terminal is 5 km west of town, but many will pick-up from hotel/losmen if arranged beforehand. Regular connections with **Maumere's** Terminal Timur (4½ hrs), it is possible to be dropped off in **Wodong**.

The old Catholics of Larantuka

In 1613 a Dutch ship, the Half Moon, anchored off Solor and bombarded the Portuguese fort there, forcing the 1,000 strong population to surrender. Two of the Dominican friars – Caspar de Spiritu Santo and Augustino de Magdalena – asked that rather than withdraw to Melaka with the rest of the population, they be landed at Larantuka. Here they set about building another mission, and by 1618 they had established more than 20 missions in the area. However, as the Portuguese lost influence so the Roman Catholics of Larantuka became isolated. The raja of the area took the title 'Servant of the Queen of the Rosary', and the church's devotional objects – chalice, cross, statues and so on – became part of local adat or tradition. Christianity became fossilized: the few Dutch Protestant ministers were sent smartly packing when they unsatisfactorily answered questions about Mary, Mother of Jesus, and visits by Portuguese Roman Catholic priests were few and far between.

Even so, the Roman Catholic rites and beliefs inculcated by the original Dominican friars were handed down through the generations. Devotees were taught to say their prayers in Latin and old Portuguese, and to wear robes like those of 17th-century penitentes, with pointed hoods. When the Roman Catholics of Larantuka were finally 'rediscovered' by the Dutch priest, Father C de Hesselle, in 1853 he was amazed to see the population keeping to a tradition over two centuries old. The most remarkable of these ceremonies is the Easter parade, replete with a rudely-hewn cross carried in procession (see 'Festivals' below).

Boat A ferry leaves Larantuka port of Waibalun (5 km from town on road to Maumere) on Mon and Fri at 1400 for **Kupang**. It is usually packed, although the captain sometimes allows tourists to sleep behind the wheelhouse or on the roof. Ferries from Kupang to Larantuka departs Wed and Sun. A twice-daily ferry (well, that's the theory – in mid-2000 it didn't always run) connects Larantuka with **Lewoleba** (4 hrs). On Fri at 0800 there is a direct ferry to the whaling village of **Lamalera**. It is also possible to sail to **Wairwarang** on Adonara. A ferry also runs from Larantuka to **Solor** and **Lembata** on Tue, Thu and Sun. The *Pelni* ships *Tatamailau* and *Sirimau* also dock here on their fortnightly circuit.

Directory **Airline offices** *Merpati* agent, Jl Diponegoro 64 (opposite the Cathedral). **Banks** *BNI and BRI* will both change US$ bills.

Lembata

Colour map 3a, grid A5

Lembata is a small island to the east of Flores, famous for its traditional whaling communities. The village of Lamalera is particularly renowned in this respect. The largest town on the island is Lewoleba, situated on the west coast. This part of Nusa Tenggara has a very long dry season and agriculture is limited to dryland crops like maize. In some areas, slash-and-burn agriculture is still practised, and fires can be seen at night burning on the mountain slopes.

Ins and outs

Getting there *Merpati* has 1 **flight** per week from Kupang to Lewoleba via Larantuka, returning the same day to Kupang. It is often cancelled. The *Hotel Rejeki I* operates as the local Merpati agent. **Lewoleba airport** is 3 km from town. There are 2 **ferries** per day from Larantuka to Lewoleba, leaving early morning and early afternoon (4 hrs). Ferries also do the route twice every 3 days, but the boat is faster and cheaper. A large car/passenger ferry also calls at Lewoleba on Tue, Thu and Sun on its drawn-out journey between Larantuka and Kalabahi on Alor, 15 hrs, the same schedule applies in the opposite direction. The Kupang-Larantuka ferry calls at Lewoleba on Mon and Fri, returning to Larantuka before continuing on to Kupang on Tue and Sat. **NB** These schedules seem to change rather frequently, so check first. If your travelling morale is low at this point, the boat passage in and out of these islands, as it weaves between volcanoes, is worth the wait.

Getting around

Trucks run daily from Lewoleba to Puor, a 6 km walk from the whaling village of Lamalera. The harbour is 1 km from town and **becaks** are available. There are 2 return **ferries** to Larantuka daily except on Mon, when there is only 1 and a boat runs to Lamalera every Mon morning, 4 hrs, returning the same evening. This boat is scheduled to allow villagers to get to the weekly market at Lewoleba. There is also a direct boat from Lamalera to Larantuka every Wed (6 hrs).

Lewoleba

Lewoleba is Lembata's main town and the capital of Solor regency. There is a spectacular **weekly market** held in Lewoleba each Monday; Lembata ikat featuring fish and whale motifs is available.

About 1 km west of Lewoleba harbour is a quiet swimming **beach**. Ask at the stilt village to be taken to the sand island, **Pulau Siput**, by boat – though you may have to bargain hard.

Excursions

Ile Ape is a volcano accessible from Lewoleba. The rumbling noise and sulphurous odours as you approach the steaming crater is evidence enough that Ile Ape remains active. Although the last eruption was some 40 years ago, it is still worth checking at your hotel that it is safe to climb before embarking. It is just about possible to climb the volcano in a day, but it is better to arrange to spend a night *en route*. ■ *Getting there*: take a bemo to Jontana (30 mins). Ask in Stefano's homestay here for a 'guide'. The first stop on the route up is at Kampung Lama, 3 hrs from Jontana – a traditional village well worth visiting in its own right. It is possible to stay here overnight (the cost is usually included in the guiding fee). From Kampung Lama it is 4½ hrs to the summit.

Lerahinga Beach, 18 km from Lewoleba, offers good snorkelling as well as excellent views of the imposing Mount Ile Ape. ■ *Getting there*: by bemo from the market in Lewoleba; most bemos travel all the way to the beach, otherwise it is a 1 km walk from Lerahinga village. **NB** The last bemo back to Lewoleba departs at 1530.

Sleeping

All losmen/hotels include breakfast & afternoon tea in the room rate. It is usually possible to leave luggage if trekking

C-E *Hotel Lewoleba*, Jl Avalong 15, T41012. The ekonomi rooms with shared mandi are small, but the VIP rooms are spacious and they are the only ones in town with a/c (and attached mandi). The restaurant here serves cheap Chinese and Indonesian food. **E** *Rejeki Hotel*, Jl Trans Lembata, good central location, helpful staff, well maintained rooms (newer ones with attached mandi), and a reasonably priced shop. The somewhat eccentric exterior decoration makes this place easy to find – the attached restaurant is good, cheap, and the speciality is venison (*daging rusa*). **E** *Pondok Wisata Lile Ile* (also known as 'Mr Jim's' to the locals), Jl Trans Lembata, fantastic views of 2 volcanoes and onto the nearby stilt village, basic rooms with shared mandi, can provide meals if requested. **E-F** *Losmen Rejeki II*, the cheaper sister establishment to the *Sumber Rejeki* and not so well located, simple rooms with shared mandi.

Eating

Very cheap *Bandung*, Jl Trans Lembata, excellent cheap Indonesian restaurant, near *Rejeki Hotel*. *Warung Ojalali*, Pasar Inpres, set menu of fish, rice and vegetables – good value. *Warung Surabaya*, Pasar Inpres, range of Indonesian dishes, advantage is that this place is open until late.

Shopping

Textiles Lembata ikat (see page 826) is produced in villages across the island; available from Lewoleba market.

Entertainment

Cinema A rather impromptu cinema, made of canvas, sometimes sets up on the outskirts showing Bollywood movies. An interesting trans-cultural experience.

Directory

Banks The *Sumber Rejeki Hotel* will change US$ cash, as will the *Flores Jaya* shop opposite the post office, at poor rates, but otherwise there are no places to exchange money, so bring enough for your stay. **Communications Post Office**: Jl Trans Lembata (opposite the *Sumber Rejeki Hotel*). **Telephone**: *Telekom* office, 1 km east of town along the main road; open until 2300.

Lamalera's whaling

There has been subsistence whaling in Lamalera for at least 200 years. As the local people do not grow crops, they rely on bartering whale products at the markets in order to obtain agricultural goods. They hunt whales all year round, but there are two main seasons – Lefa and Baleo. Lefa runs from April to November, corresponding with the south-east monsoon, when the great whales migrate through the area to the rich southern oceans. During this period it is traditional for whale hunts to occur daily, except on Sundays when Catholicism takes precedence over the local adat. During Baleo, which spans the months from November to March, the whale boats only go out if a whale is sighted and the weather conditions are favourable.

The whalers of Lamalera specialize in catching manta rays and sperm whales (known as ikan paus, 'pope fish'). But they also occasionally take sharks, whale sharks, pilot whales, killer whales and dolphins. They are hunted from open rowing boats known as peledang. Each boat belongs to a particular village clan, and they are constantly repaired and rebuilt over the centuries. They are said to be modelled on the ships that brought the original inhabitants from Lapan Batar. When the hunt is underway, the men shout hilibe – 'give chase'. The hunters use hand thrown harpoons or tempuling, which have blades attached to poles up to 8m long. The harpooner, perched on the boat's bow, literally launches himself off the vessel to plunge the iron as deeply into his prey as possible. On occasions, having harpooned a whale, the boat is towed for hours – in one instance all the way into Australian waters. The day's catch is then processed on the beach. The meat is divided traditionally among families in the village. All parts of the whale are used, the meat being dried in the sun, the oil boiled off and used for lighting despite the arrival of electricity.

Because, like the Eskimos and a handful of other people, the hunters of Lamalera are traditional and non-commercial, they have been exempted from the worldwide ban on whaling. There is some debate over when whaling in the area started: 1566 seems to be a popular date; the year the Portuguese arrived. It is thought that they only kill 20-30 whales a year, and this number is declining as young men are migrating to larger towns, leading to an increasingly aged whaling crew.

Lamalera

The traditional whaling village of Lamalera is on Lembata's south coast. The population trace their origins to Lapan Batan, an island between Lembata and Pantar. Unlike many of the other villages on Lembata which are land-based and rely on maize, rice and sweet potatoes, the population of Lamalera relies on fishing and, particularly, whaling (see box). Until the late 1980s, Lamalera was so far off the beaten track that virtually no one ventured there; the village has now become part of the travellers' itinerary. Even the tour company *Natrabu* runs a tour to Lamalera from Kupang. To go along with the whalers as a paying passenger will cost about 40,000-50,000Rp.

As dusk approaches, an alternative hunt can be seen in progress around the rock pools on the beach. Local children scour the pools searching for small fish and mud-skippers, which they harpoon with sharpened, painted sticks that are shot unerringly to their targets using rubber bands.

There is a **barter market** – Pasar Wolandoni – on Wednesdays and Saturdays where local women swop goods. It is also possible to use money, but fascinating just to spectate. ■ *Walk for 25 mins towards the football field, then bear right and walk along the beach for another 1½ hrs– quite a distance but a pleasant and easy walk.*

It is possible to swim on **Lamalera Beach**, though the waves are quite strong and it's necessary to dress modestly (women in shorts and a T-shirt, men in shorts). Alternatively, ask directions to **Walinama Beach**, which is outside the village so you can wear what you like.

E-F *Homestay Josef (The White House)*, 2 small dorms, inside mandi with western toilets. It is the closest homestay to the beach. Run by the local English teacher, a good source of information. Situated on the top of the hill, so superb views of Lamalera (especially from the mandi). **E-F** *Homestay Maria*, simple, clean accommodation, motherly management and better food than most. **E-F** *Homestay Abil*, basic accommodation but friendly staff.

Sleeping
Prices include all meals

No restaurants or food shops, so visitors must eat in their homestay. Food tends to be very simple.

Eating

Local textiles made from handspun and dyed cotton are available for between 200,000Rp and 350,000Rp. Some people have also begun to make carefully constructed miniatures of the whaling boats – which sell more cheaply.

Shopping

Road Trucks run daily from Lewoleba to **Puor**, a 6 km walk from Lamalera. For the return journey, leave early to walk during the cool of the early morning and to be in Puor in good time for the 1000 truck departure.

Transport

Alor

The rugged island of Alor, east of Lembata, is 100 km long and 35 km wide at its widest point. Although most of the population are nominally Christian, the island illustrates, in microcosm, Indonesia's enormous cultural diversity. Because of Alor's fragmented and rugged environment, its people have remained isolated from one another until comparatively recently. A population of just 150,000 can count between them seven major linguistic sub-groups and 50 distinct languages – which amounts to a language for every 3,000 people. The various tribes of the island – such as the Nedebang, Dieng, Kaka and Mauta – practise shifting cultivation, although as land becomes scarcer, so they are being forced to become settled agriculturalists.

Phone code: 0386
Colour map 3a, grid A6

Alor is reputed to have the best dive sites in Nusa Tenggara, although as the currents here are strong it is most suited to more experienced divers. The Adi Dharma Hotel is a good source of information on diving, although most people pre-book through agents in Kupang (Timor). The snorkelling is said to be fabulous.

Ins and outs

Alor's **Mali airport** is 28 km from Kalabahi. There are connections on *Merpati* from Kupang daily, except Fri, and also flights from Larantuka, Lewoleba, Rote and Denpasar. There is a *Merpati*-operated minibus that meets flights and also takes passengers out to the airport. The ferry dock is about 1 km south of town. Ferries link **Kalabahi** with **Kupang** (West Timor), **Atapupu**, **Lewoleba** and **Larantuka**, as well as a number of smaller ports in the islands of eastern Nusa Tenggara. From Kupang the ferry leaves on Tue and Thu and arrives in Kalabahi the following day, returning to Kupang on Mon and Wed. On Sun the same boat does a leg from Kalabahi to Atapupu (on Timor), returning to Kalabahi the following day. **NB** These schedules are subject to frequent change. The *Pelni* vessel *Awu* calls here twice on its fortnightly circuit through Nusa Tenggara. However, in mid-2000, for a range of economic reasons, the ship was not calling and local people offered conflicting information as to whether it would resume its normal schedule.

Getting there

The *Adi Dharma Hotel* can arrange motorbike hire. Local bemos are 500Rp and they stop operating at 1900. It is possible to charter bemos on an hourly rate to visit local villages.

Getting around

Kalabahi

The capital of Alor, Kalabahi, is on the west coast. As one might expect, it has the greatest concentration of facilities on Alor and is the best base from which to explore the island.

Excursions **Takpala**, 12 km east of Kalabahi, is the principal village of the Abui tribe and there are breathtaking views of Benelang Bay from the entrance. Because Takpala is relatively accessible it is also relatively touristed. However, this doesn't seem to have dented the Abui's determination to maintain their culture and ways. The houses of Takpala are divided into three levels. The open first floor is used as a meeting and living area. The enclosed second floor is used for cooking and sleeping. And the roof space is used for storage – the smoke from the cooking fire helping to ward off vermin and protect food stocks. (See 'Shopping', below, for information on market day – Monday – in Takpala.) **NB** It is considered polite to bring small gifts such as betel nut, coffee and sugar. ■ *Getting there: take a bemo from the market bound for Mabu; the bemo drops off within 1 km of the settlement.*

Atimelang is less frequently visited and therefore, reportedly, more traditional. It is possible to stay overnight here and then walk back to Mabu the following day. ■ *Getting there: catch a bemo from the market to Mabu; it is a 5 km walk from here.*

Mali Beach, 12 km east of Kalabahi, has wonderful white sand and is a good snorkelling spot. The reef lies 300m off-shore. There are plans underway to build some accommodation here.

Alor Kecil has some excellent snorkelling, although there are also dangerously vicious cold water currents. Local fishermen will sometimes take people out to the west side of **Pulau Kepa**, which is protected from the currents and reputedly has even better snorkelling. Sharks are said to be numerous. **Sleeping E** *La P'tite Kepa homestay*, new, 500m from the shore, and built traditionally, price includes three meals a day and journeys between the island and Alor Kecil. There are motorbikes for hire, and excursions can be arranged.

Dulolong is a coastal village *en route* to Kokar. Ask to see the grave of King Nampira and his family.

Ampera is a coastal village between Dulolong and Alor Kecil. The people here have a dialect and culture distinct from that surrounding communities. They are prolific potters.

There is a good **walk** from Kalabahi to **Monbang** (a traditional village), on to **Otvai** (where there are fantastic views of Kalabahi Bay), and then back to Kalabahi. The round trip takes about seven hours – ask at hotel/losmen for directions.

Sleeping **C-D** *Pelangi Indah*, Jl Diponegoro 100, T21251. Some a/c, the more expensive rooms have a/c and excellent western bathrooms, the cheaper rooms are pretty basic by contrast, the attached restaurant serves good Indonesian and Chinese dishes and cheap, cold beer, a good little hotel. **D** *Adi Dharma*, Jl Martadinata 12/26, T21280. On the waterfront, the owner, Pak Enga, speaks English and is helpful and knowledgeable. The rooms are well maintained and very clean and there are great views of Kalabahi Harbour from the verandah. It is also fairly central, with good meals (if ordered in advance), and tours are available (but rather expensive). **D-E** *Melati*, Jl Dr Sutomo 1, T21075. Some a/c, view of the harbour, simple accommodation, recently refurbished, clean, but cheapest rooms are still rather dingy. **D-E** *Nusa Kenari Indah*, Jl Diponegoro 11, T21119. Some a/c, set back from the road and with a small garden, rooms here are spacious and fine, the more expensive with a/c and attached mandi.

All hotels include a simple breakfast & afternoon tea or coffee in the room rate. All also have some more pricey rooms with a/c

Eating The best places are the hotels, although there are the usual (mediocre) foodstalls which set up from early evening in the market area. **Cheap** The best hotel restaurant is that attached to the *Pelangi Indah*, which also serves good value and cold beer. **Very cheap** Of the dedicated restaurants the best is the *Rumah Makan Jember*, Jl Panglima Polim 2, which serves the usual range of Indonesian favourites, but with better quality ingredients and in a more hygienic setting than other places. The *Warung Kediri*, next to the *Adi Dharma Hotel*, serves reasonable Javanese food. It's also worth sampling the various foodstalls that spring up at night, east of the BNI bank.

Shopping **Textiles** Alor ikat; some are rather inferior, but there are villages on Alor still producing high quality cloth. The best place to sample a range of textiles is in Takpala (see 'Excursions') on Mon, when a cruise ship visits. There is also a market at Moru on Sat, 30 mins by bemo from Kalabahi.

The Moko drum currency debacle

Before the 19th century, bronze moko drums were traded and used as bride price. They are related to the Dongson drums of northern Vietnam, although no exact equivalent has ever been found there. The older examples of moko also show similar decoration to their presumed Vietnamese prototypes, although newer examples have Chinese and Indian inspired floral motifs. How these drums came to Alor is not known, but they have also been discovered elsewhere in the Indonesian archipelago (see Bali, page 369).

Around 1900, imitation brass moko began to be made in large quantities in Gresik, Java and exported to Alor. They created chaos in a monetary system which owed its stability to there always being a limited number of moko in circulation. In 1914, in an attempt to stabilize the moko, the Dutch introduced coinage and forbad all use of the drums in transactions, except in tax payments. This exemption was designed to take moko out of circulation; some 1,660 drums were acquired, and then melted down.

Bride price in Alor is still sometimes paid using moko. The cheapest drum, and thus presumably the cheapest wife, is said to cost about 150,000-200,000Rp. The oldest drums are the most valuable, and through time and their association with powerful people, drums are thought to acquire powers of their own. Such drums are rarely traded, but remain within the family.

Sports

Diving and snorkelling Alor is gaining a reputation for having some of the best dive sites in Indonesia, with an enormous variety of marine life. Strong currents make this, though, a destination for the experienced diver. Most people pre-book through companies in Kupang.

Transport

Boat Ferries leave for **Larantuka** from Kalabahi on Sun, Tue and Thu in the early evening, arriving the following morning after mooring for the night in **Balauring** and stopping, among other places, at **Lewoleba**. The length of the trip depends on where the passengers want to stop.

Directory

Banks BNI, Jl Dr Sutomo; Bank Rakyat Indonesia. Both banks will change cash and travellers' cheques from major companies denominated in US$. **Communications** Post Office: Jl Dr Sutomo, open 0700-1600 Mon-Sat. **Telephone office:** Telekom office behind the market.

Pulau Pantar

Pantar is the next largest island in the Alor group, after Alor itself. Very few people make it here and little English is spoken. Boats dock at **Baranusa**, where there is one homestay. From here trucks run to **Kakamauta**, the nearest village to the volcano **Mount Sirong**. It is possible to climb the volcano – which is still active – in about 2-3 hours.

Sleeping

E *Homestay Burhan*, Baranusa, room rate includes all meals. It is also possible to stay in Kakamauta with the kepala desa (**E**).

Transport

Boat Boats leave Kalabahi for Baranusa every Tue, Thu and Sun (4½ hrs, 9,000Rp).

Sumba

Colour map 3a, grid B3

The island of Sumba is noted for its megalithic tombs (mainly in the west), fine ikat cloth (mainly in the east) and horseback-fighting festivals. Lying outside the volcanic arc that runs through Java and the other islands of Nusa Tenggara, the generally subdued relief of Sumba presents a startling contrast to Java, Bali and Flores. Because Sumba lies off the usual overland route through the Lesser Sundas – which runs through Flores and Sumbawa to Lombok and Bali – the island is relatively untouristed.

Sumba is a real treasure house for the visitor interested in art and culture. Unlike the other islands of East Nusa Tenggara, Sumba never came under the early influence of either Muslim or Christian missionaries and, as a result, traditional beliefs are much stronger here. The same goes for the island's material culture. Megalithic tombs and ancestral, thatched houses remain easily accessible, and Sumba's distinctive traditional ikat blankets continue to be made in large numbers (in part because of demand from outsiders). Finally, there is Sumba's energetic pasola festival when massed ranks of horsemen engage in mock combat – a 'game' which frequently results in serious injury and sometimes in death. There is also excellent surfing on the west coast and long, deserted sandy beaches.

Ins and outs

Getting there There are **flights** to Waingapu and Waikabubak and *Pelni* ships also dock at the ports of both towns (but note that Waikabubak airport is 42 km from town, while the port is 60 km away). A weekly **ferry** links Waingapu with Ende on Flores and the island of Savu.

Sumba Island

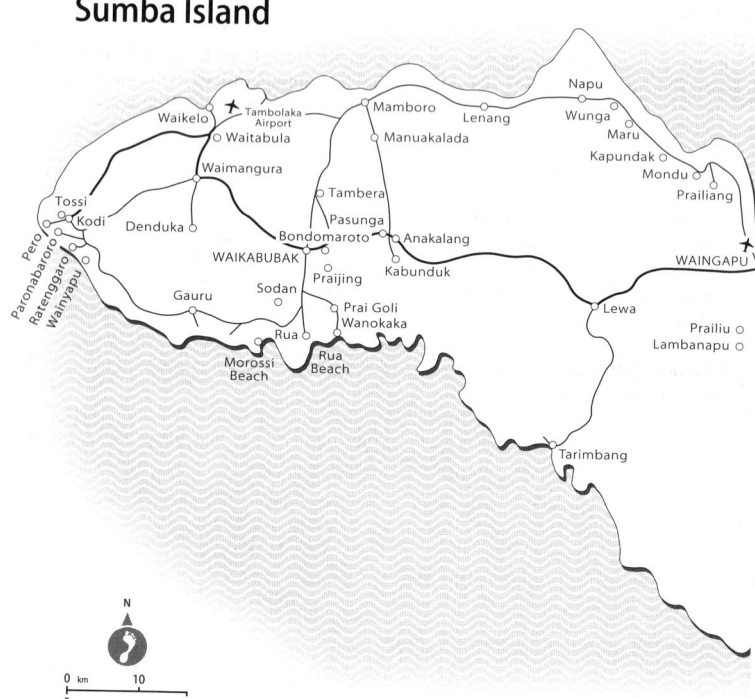

The ikat hinggi blankets of Sumba

Sumba produces perhaps the most distinctive warp ikat in Indonesia. Traditionally, the weaving of cloth was the preserve of aristocratic women who, free from agricultural and household chores, had the time to produce finely woven cloth. Ikat is still woven on backstrap looms, although natural indigo and red morinda dyes are being replaced by chemical substitutes. The most commonly produced cloth is the hinggi, a large blanket worn by men. Characteristic motifs include animals such as horses, dogs, snakes, monkeys, crocodiles, fish and lizards. Each has its own symbolism – dogs with warriors, snakes with rebirth and long life, crocodiles with the afterlife. Another common motif is the skull tree or andung, which draws upon the former practice of hanging the heads of vanquished enemies from a tree in the centre of a village to scare away evil spirits.

The quality of Sumba ikat is declining, and most lengths of cloth can only be described as 'tourist' material: large and simple motifs, often without the important border strip or kabakil, woven with machine spun yarn, coloured with chemical dyes, and showing 'bleeding' of dye across the borders between design elements. First-class cloth is almost exclusively reserved for burial, and no local, quite literally, would be seen dead in the blankets sold to visitors. Wrapping the body in fine ikat ensures that the spirit of the dead man or woman will reach Parai Merapu – Merapu heaven. The transition from the physical world to that of the spirits is critical, and the various elements of the death rite must be strictly adhered to.

Some people maintain that it is cheaper to buy cloth in Bali, where shop owners purchase in bulk from villages with which they have special relations. Tour groups visiting villages like Rende have pushed prices up considerably.

From Waikabubak's Waikelo harbour there is a ferry to Larantuka, also on Flores, calling at Sape on Sumbawa twice weekly.

Getting around As in the other islands of Nusa Tenggara, the government has invested considerable sums upgrading the road infrastructure. Moreover, because the terrain is less demanding than Flores the roads are in better condition. There are bus services to all major settlements.

NB The 2 luxury developments on Sumba's south coast, one 5 km from Baing in the southeast and the *Sumba Reef Lodge* south of Waikabubak near Rua Beach, are now open. The owner admits spreading rumours in his book 'Surfing Indonesia' that locals often killed tourists for attending festivals! This was intended to deter more surfers coming and finding the 'secret spots'.

Background

Geography Though Sumba is only 300 km long and 80 km wide, the two regencies of East and West Sumba are environmentally very different. While the east of the island is generally dry (annual rainfall 674mm) and barren, the west is considerably wetter (1,826mm), and consequently much greener. The dry season stretches over seven to eight months from April to October. During these months, the rolling landscape is dry and desolate. In times past Sumba was known as the 'Sandalwood Isle', but destruction of these forests for commercial gain has left much of the island, especially in the east, fit only for extensive cattle grazing and horse raising. The island's population is about 425,000. These days Sumba's wealth is based on the export of horses and buffaloes.

History Historically, Sumba was known as a source of horses, slaves and sandalwood, but lying as it does to the south of the island arc of Nusa Tenggara, it managed to escape the successive streams of Hindu, Muslim and Christian interlopers who influenced

Sumba Ikat motifs

A design based on the mamuli, a gold ear ornament & traditional marriage gift.

Cockatoos

Man with skull tree (andung), & cockatoos

Roosters

Horses

Sumba's megalithic tombs

The construction of megalithic graves is characteristic of both East and West Sumba. However, in East Sumba the grave construction cannot begin until after the intended occupant is dead. This means that some families have to keep the corpse of their relative in a kind of limbo until enough funds and time have been found to build the monument. In West Sumba, people help to build their own tombs. Here, the socially ambitious seek enhanced prestige while they are still alive by having large gravestones hauled to their village; a feat which requires the expenditure of large sums of money for the many kinsmen needed to help, and for ceremonial feasting.

Limestone boulders weighing anywhere up to 30 tonnes are dragged on wooden rafts (*tena*) to the site of the grave. *Tena* means ship, and a textile sail is raised to help the stone on its journey. The graves are not spatially separated from the village houses, and many are used for more mundane purposes like drying corn or dyed textiles, or for lounging on during evening village events. There are four main types of megalithic tomb in Sumba: the first is a simple dolmen, with four stone pillars supporting a rectangular stone slab. The second is similar to the first, but carved and ornamented. The third has stone walls enclosing the four pillars. And the fourth, the added feature of stone stairs leading up to the covering slab.

The purpose behind the many rituals and ceremonies, at which offerings of food and valuables are made, is to ensure good relations between the living and the ancestors to guarantee the former's well-being. (These days the government limits the number of buffalo which can be sacrificed to prevent families going into penury.) Even numbers, in particular four and eight, are considered auspicious.

---

the area. It was never directly ruled from the outside. It was not until the Dutch arrived in the 17th century that western contact intensified. Even then, it was not until the early 20th century that a colonial administrator was installed.

Sumba has nine mutually unintelligable languages, eight of which are concentrated in the more ecologically fertile west. This is probably due to conditions that did not force much co-dependence for survival. In addition, each tribe has a highly sophisticated ritual linguistic form. In a ceremonial setting, male participants call out reinforcing couplets, reminiscent of haiku. This can go on throughout the night and following day, spontaneously improvised, getting more complex as the calls build up. An example: The horse's tail is high (meaning the person in question has a noble spirit), the reply call, the dog has a black tongue. This refers to a glib talker that has kept his integrity.

Culture

Today, it is thought that over 50% of the population, predominantly in the west, still adhere to the traditional, animist, religion of ancestor worship *agama merapu*. The merapu are the original ancestors of each patrilineal clan. Another 35% are Protestant and the remainder, Catholic, Muslim, Hindu and Buddhist.

At the time of our last visit in mid-2000 there was only one Westerner in evidence outside the costly surf resort. The economic crisis has hit Sumba even more severely than the rest of the country. There is a sense that local people blame the West for their economic plight, and hence their rather less-than-welcoming looks.

Sumbanese villages & houses

The layout of a *paraingu* – or village – in Sumba should conform to traditional rules. The village symbolizes a ship, with a bow (*tunda kambata*), deck (*kani padua*) and stern (*kiku kemudi*). The houses are arranged around the ancestors' burial place.

Important villages of clan chiefs are built on hills, while less important villages surround them at lower elevations. Similarly, ancestral houses (*uma merapu*) have high peaked roofs, whilst houses not associated with the ancestors have lower roofs and are called *uma kamudungu* ('bald houses'). Buffalo horns on the outside of houses are indicative of past sacrifices and denote wealth and prestige; they also protect the house and ward off evil spirits. Through their part in sacrifices, buffaloes act as a link with the spirit world.

The Sumbanese slave trade

Sumba's role as a source of slaves dates from as early as historical accounts exist. The Sultan of Bima on Sumbawa, and the sultans and kings of South Sulawesi, Flores, Lombok and Bali all obtained slaves from the island. Dutch interest in Sumba as a source of slaves dates from the mid-18th century, and the island quickly became the major supplier to the colonial power.

Why Sumba should have filled this role is linked to the nature of its society and the absence of a strong, central power. The structure of Sumbanese society was rigidly divided into an aristocratic (maramba) class, and a slave (ata) class. This social stratification was more prominent in the east, and even today wealth and power lie in the hands of four or five men. The west is more diverse ethnically and culturally, with seven different languages spoken and more opportunity for advancement based on merit rather than heredity. The trade was officially abolished in 1860, but continued until the early 20th century.

In the open space in the centre of the more warlike villages can be found the 'skull tree' *andung*, a dead tree on which in earlier headhunting times the skulls of enemy taken in battle were hung. The life force believed to emanate from these heads was considered to be a source of fertility, and the tree acted as a symbol of strength and security for the village, as well as the focal point for rites of war.

The striking, traditional, thatched houses – low-sided, yet high-peaked – are built around a fireplace which is positioned between the four main pillars. There are two doors: a front door for men, and a rear entrance for women. Each consists of three 'floors': cattle are kept at ground level and most weaving takes place here. The first floor is the main living area, with various rooms for sleeping (divided according to sex, age and rank), grain storage, cooking and eating. The upper section, known as the *uma deta* or *hindi merapu*, is for the spirits; here, sacred objects are stored. In West Sumba, some of the finest traditional houses can be seen at Anakalang, Tarung and Prai Goli; in East Sumba, at Prailiu and Pau. The dwellings in West Sumba tend to have higher roofs.

The highest parts of the house are considered sacred and are connected with the ancestors – the house having become sacred as a result of the heirlooms being stored in its roof, since the heirlooms represent the spirit of the founding ancestor residing in the house. The heirlooms are powerful objects used in rituals as a medium through which contact with the ancestors can be made; some heirlooms, particularly those that are very old and made of gold, silver or other metal, are believed to be so powerful that disasters may result if they are mishandled. The most powerful are not even allowed to be looked at and are housed in sealed boxes or inside many different containers.

Some clan origin-houses in Sumba have accumulated so much sacred power, leading to a wealth of taboos and prohibitions, that living in them has become too dangerous for their owners, who fear they might inadvertently break a taboo and incur the wrath and retribution of their ancestral spirits. They prefer to install more expendable family slaves as caretakers. This is the case with the ancestral house in Rende.

Visiting Sumbanese villages Part of the attraction of Sumba lies in the ease with which a traveller can witness traditional ceremonies and festivals which are genuine, entirely for the benefit of local clans and not part of a tourist charade. Hotels are only full during high season (July/August) and at the time of the Pasola (February/March). At other times of the year, surprisingly few visitors come to Sumba and you may well find yourself the only foreigner in town, even in Waikabubak.

Important When visiting local villages it is courteous and advisable to observe local etiquette and take a gift of betel nut to share with your hosts; it would be polite also to stop and chat or, bearing in mind any language restrictions, at least to partake of some betel nut with the headman. Betel is easily bought in the market where you will see stalls selling piles of 'betel' (in fact areca) nut (*pinang*), together with the catkin (*sirih*) for 1,000-5,000Rp for a double sized quantity, and in separate piles, lime (*kapur*) in the form of a white powder in little plastic packets for 100Rp. Alternatively, you could take coffee, sugar and cigarettes or simply make a donation of 1,000Rp at each village you visit. Don't expect just to wander in and look around. You will probably be asked for 1,000Rp for photographs.

Conduct and dress Women should avoid wearing short shorts and skimpy skirts, and men and women should avoid wearing singlets.

Waingapu

Phone code: 0387

Waingapu is the capital of the regency of East Sumba, and the island's largest town with a population of 25,000. A hot dusty place spread out over a large area in two concentrations, one by the harbour, and the other about 1 km inland, convenient for the bus station and market and where many of the hotels are found. The **tourist office** *Kantor Cabang Dinas Pariwisata*, on Jl Suharto T791, has no useful maps or pamphlets, but helpful staff.

Sights

The **Old Docks** area (*Pelabuhan Lama*) can be entertaining: fishing boats, and the occasional inter-island mixed cargo boat, dock here. There is a pleasant walk along a street bordering the shore with views of the sea and harbour; follow one of the sidestreets off Jl Yos Sudarso to reach the sea. Overlooking the dock on Jl Kartini are some picturesque colonial-era buildings dating back to the first half of the century.

Excursions

Although Waingapu and East Sumba do not have the megaliths of West Sumba, it is the centre of fine ikat production (see page 855) and there are a number of weaving villages within easy reach of the town.

Prailiu is an ikat weaving village only 2 km southeast of town. Stages in the ikat weaving process can usually be seen, or make arrangements in advance with the

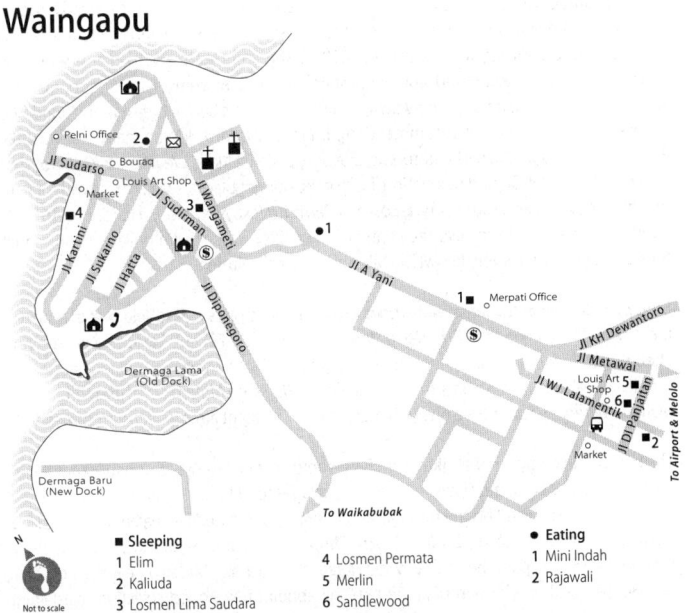

Waingapu

■ Sleeping
1 Elim
2 Kaliuda
3 Losmen Lima Saudara
4 Losmen Permata
5 Merlin
6 Sandlewood

● Eating
1 Mini Indah
2 Rajawali

weavers. There is cloth for sale – it is even sometimes possible to buy good, finely-worked ikat here. The village has a small number of inferior 'megalithic' tombs, both modern and traditional in design. ■ *Getting there*: walk or take one of the constant bemos that run from the bemo stop near the bus terminal.

Kawangu is another weaving village, 11 km east of Waingapu. ■ *Getting there*: regular bemos run from the bemo stop next to the bus station. **Lambanapu** is another ikat weaving village worth a visit, 7 km from Prailiu.

Melolo is a lovely town 60 km southeast of Waingapu (see page 862). It is a good base from which to visit the area southeast of Waingapu, including the ikat-weaving villages of **Rende**, **Pau** and **Umabara** (see the Melolo entry for information of these villages).

Kaliuda is an ikat weaving village, 50 km past Melolo and 110 km from Waingapu, just off the road to Baing (see page 863). **Kalala** surfing beach is close by (see page 863).

Northwest of Waingapu

Prailiang, reached down a rough road off the main road shortly before Mondu, has a Friday market. This is a good example of a traditional fortified hilltop village where ancient customs and rituals are still strong. The remnants of the encircling wall can be seen. The villagers work the land surrounding the hill. ■ *Getting there*: by bus to Mondu; ask the driver to let you off at the turn-off to Prailiang.

Maru, on the coast 60 km northwest of Waingapu, is a traditional village with important rituals and ceremonies. Market day is Monday. ■ *Getting there: buses run daily*.

Tours

The *Elim/Elvin*, *Merlin*, *Permata* and *Sandle Wood Hotels* can arrange cars and guides to take tourists around the main sights. Ali Fa'daq at the *Permata* speaks excellent English and has the best background knowledge of Sumba. He has films of some traditional ceremonies. Zaid Bachmid (with some English) at the Tourist Office is also willing to guide tourists. Prices for the day, including car and guide, range from 120,000Rp to 140,000Rp.

Sleeping
■ *on map*
Price codes:
see inside front cover

Most of Waingapu's hotels & losmen are found around the bus station, about 1½ km south of the town centre or in the harbour area

C-D *Elim/Elvin*, Jl Jend A Yani 73, T61323. Friendly owners are a good source of information, reasonable rooms, every type of room available from dorm beds to rooms with fan or a/c and private mandi, cheap restaurant. **C-D** *Merlin Hotel*, Jl DI Panjaitan 25, T61300, F61333. Quite new with attractive décor, the best hotel in town and very reasonably priced, most rooms with modern private bathrooms, more expensive rooms have a/c, cheap restaurant on 3rd floor. **C-D** *Sandle Wood*, Jl DI Panjaitan, T61887. The 2nd best place to stay but original rooms are badly in need of redecoration, especially the bathrooms. There are rooms with shared and private mandis. The newer wing with a/c rooms is better, breakfast included (the restaurant is cheap but not recommended). **D** *Lima Saudara*, Jl Wanggameti 2, T61083. Rooms rather dirty, attached bathrooms, average, price includes breakfast. **E** *Kaliuda*, Jl DI Panjaitan 3, T61264. Behind bus station, best of the budget places, some rooms with private mandi, all squat toilets, some dirty. **E** *Losmen Permata* (aka *Ali's Place*), Jl Kartini 10, T61516. Overlooking the old docks near the centre of town. Basic rooms with private mandi, squat toilets, the owner Ali is very knowledgeable about local culture.

Eating

Cheap *Hotel Merlin* restaurant with a book exchange, good place to sip a cold beer overlooking the town. Recommended. *RM Restu Ibu*, Jl IR Juanda, T21218. Recommended. **Very cheap** *Mini Indah*, Jl A Yani (between the 2 halves of town), very variable, you might have an excellent meal or an inedible one. The same applies to *RM Siang Malam* down the road from the Merlin. *Rajawali*, Jl Sutomo 96, good Chinese, seafood, pleasant atmosphere. Recommended.

Shopping

The best place to buy Sumba's **ikat** is on Bali, where prices are more reasonable and dealers are prepared to negotiate. The ikat-producing villages tend to have only a limited selection of pieces as most, including the best pieces, are swiftly purchased by dealers, and the villagers rarely bargain. In town, *LA 'Louis' Art Shop* has 2 branches: at Toko Kupang, Jl WJ Lalamentik 15 (just pass the *Sandle Wood Hotel*), and on Jl Yos Sudarso near the port area, T61536, 61132 (home); open 0800-2200 or by appointment, good selection, bargaining recommended. Recommended. The *Sandle Wood Hotel* has a large selection of mostly rather average ikat; they seem strangely reluctant to show any quality. Sumba **blankets** vary a great deal in quality and a reasonable piece cannot be bought for less than 150,000Rp; good lengths are 400,000Rp or more.

Eben Haezer, Jl Jend A Yani 73, T323, by the *Elim Hotel*.

Tour operators

Local Bemos ply the main routes around town; the central bemo stop is near the bus terminal. **Car/minibus hire**: from the *Losmen Surabaya* (hourly rate); or the *Sandle Wood Hotel* (slightly cheaper); for longer journeys, charges are roughly 60,000Rp return to Melolo, 70,000Rp to Paun and Rende, and 90,000-120,000Rp to Waikabubak and Baing. The *Merlin* and *Permata* will also hire out cars for the day (it is worth comparing prices). **Motorcycle hire**: available from most hotels, about 20,000Rp per day.

Transport

173 km from Waikabubak,
178 km from Melolo,
185 km from Rende,
220 km from Baing

Air Waingapu's **Mau Hau Airport** is 6 km southeast of town. Free transport to town provided by hotels. Drivers congregate in the arrivals hall. Taxi available, or catch 1 of the regular bemos that run along the road just outside the terminal to the bus station in town. The *Merpati* minibus takes passengers from the *Merpati* Office (*Hotel Elim*) to the airport. Daily flights by *Merpati* and/or *Bouraq* to **Kupang**. Also daily flights on *Merpati* to **Bima**, 3 times a week via **Tambolaka** (Waikabubak). Other destinations include **Surabaya**, via Bima and Denpasar, and direct to **Denpasar** on *Bouraq*.

Bus The station is 1½ km south of town, near most of the hotels, on Jl El Tari. Regular bemos link it with town. Several buses each day at approximately 0700, 0800, 1200 and 1500 to **Waikabubak** (4 hrs – sometimes with over an hour cruising for fares). Also several departures each day to **Melolo** (for Rende) (1½ to 2 hrs), **Lewa** (2 hrs) and **Baing** (4 hrs). Buses will pick passengers up from hotels and losmen with advance warning. The best seats are up front next to the driver. These usually need to be reserved in advance, either through your hotel or at the bus company headquarters. Buses to Waikabubak stop half way at Langa Leru for about 20 mins. There are stalls and warungs where you can get excellent strong coffee and something to eat. **Taxi**: for groups of 4 or more it can make sense to hire a car; public transport, though cheap, is slow (see 'Local' transport above).

Boat The *Pelni* ships *Awu* and *Pangrango* dock at the new harbour – Pelabuhan Baru; other vessels, including pioneer vessels *(Perintis)*, dock at the old harbour or Pelabuhan Lama. Though only 200m from the old harbour by water, the Pelabuhan Baru is a circuitous 7-km ride by bemo. The *Awi* and *Pangrango* dock twice a fortnight on their circuit through Nusa Tenggara. *Pelni* ships sail to **Ende** and **Kupang** via **Sawu** and **Roti**; ask at the *Pelni* office for details. There is also a weekly ferry linking Waingapu with Ende (Flores) and Savu (Sawu). At the time of writing, it docks on Wed am, leaves for Savu on Wed pm, returns to Waingapu on Thu am, and leaves for Ende on Fri pm, 10-12 hrs. There are also other, smaller boats, heading out of Waingapu for other islands in Nusa Tenggara. Ask at the harbour. A *Perintis* ship currently sails from Waikelo Harbour to **Larantuka** on Eastern Flores, 8-12 hrs. The *Pelni* office is near the harbour (see map), T21265, F21027, staff are very helpful and some speak good English. Don't necessarily be put off if *Pelni* say there are no cabins available when you make a booking. Cabins frequently materialize on the day, if you have cash to spare.

Airline offices *Bouraq*, Jl Yos Sudarso 57, T21363, 21906. Yanca is very helpful, speaks excellent English and will bring tickets to your hotel in the evening; a former tour guide in West Sumba, he is very knowlegeable about the island. *Merpati*, Jl Jend A Yani 73 (at the *Elim Hotel*), T323462, open 0700-1700 Mon-Fri, 0700-1400 Sat, 0900-1300 Sun and holidays. **Banks** Bank Rakyat Indonesia, Jl Jend A Yani 36, changes cash and TCs, open 0800-1200, except Fri when it closes at 1100. **Communications** General Post Office: Jl Sutomo 21, open 0800-1400, except Fri 0800-1100. Perumtel: Jl Cut Nyak Din 19 (international telephone, telex & fax). **Medical facilities** Hospitals: General Hospital, Jl Adam Malik, Hambala.

Directory

Sumba death rites

A notable aspect of Sumbanese society is the very close association of the living with the dead. Graves are constructed on the doorstep of houses in the open space in the centre of each village. Death is viewed as the beginning of eternal life; life itself being merely a stage which is passed through en route to the attainment of eternal life. The transition from the physical world to the world of the spirits is critical to the Sumbanese and is ensured by strict adherence to the burial rite. Following a person's death, a close relative calls his or her name four times; should there be no answer, he or she is pronounced dead. No crying is allowed for three days following the death. The body is bathed, coated in coconut oil (in East Sumba the body is also coated with the blue dye used in ikat which protects the corpse) and dressed in ikat sarongs. The number, and quality, of the sarongs is indicative of status. The arms and legs of the body are broken, and the dead person placed in the foetal position, either in a wooden coffin, or wrapped in buffalo hide. The body is placed over a hole so that the blood can drain down a bamboo pole into the ground. The body, except if the dead person was of lowly status, is guarded by four men. During this period, the spirit of the deceased is still regarded as roaming the village.

The second stage of the burial ceremony involves the preparation of the tomb. A stone is dragged into the village by large numbers of people. Relatives bring cattle, horses or pigs to be sacrificed, the size of the sacrificial gift being dictated by the status and closeness of the relationship with the deceased. The corpse is then taken to the tomb and buried with many valuable objects. In the past, if the person was of royal blood, a slave was buried alive along with the corpse.

The wealth consumed at funeral ceremonies was deemed necessary to ensure a safe passage to the world of the ancestors, where the deceased could bring benefit to his clan. The greater the display of wealth at his funeral, the higher the status he would merit in the spirit world. There is great wealth buried in the soil of Sumba and there have been cases of unscrupulous dealers, allegedly from Java, going out into likely areas of the countryside with metal detectors in search of buried treasure.

Melolo

Melolo is a lovely little town, 60 km southeast of Waingapu. Melolo itself has few traditional houses, but Rende and Pau (see below) are easily reached from here by bus or on foot. Market day is Friday.

Excursions **Rende** is 7 km on along the road south from Melolo to Baing. It not only produces good ikat, but also has some of the most impressive megalithic tombs in East Sumba, with carvings featuring animals, sea creatures and humans. There are traditional houses here, though many now have tin roofs. The largest of these is the recently rebuilt home of the Raja. It may be possible to stay with a family here. The inhabitants believe that the earth is built on five house posts like their own homes; earthquakes happen when a mouse chews the central post, destabilizing the earth and causing it to shake. Wednesday is market day (see page 857). Unfortunately, because Rende is firmly on the tour group itinerary, prices of cloth are high and rising. Good pieces made with home-grown cotton and using natural dyes are around 1,000,000Rp. The best weaver in the village sells cloth from the house close to the *kepala desa's* (headman's) residence. ■ *Getting there: by bemo from Melolo.*

From Melolo, there is a pleasant 4 km walk past rice paddies to another traditional village: **Pau**. There are more megalithic tombs, peaked traditional houses and ikat at the village of **Umabara**, about 5 km west of Melolo. Alternatively, take a bemo from Melolo and ask to be dropped off at the turning for the village. Both Pau and Umabara are about a 30 minute walk from the main road; follow the road until you reach a stone horse, take the right fork to reach Umabara and take the left for Pau. The Raja of Pau has a fine collection of ikat. At both these villages expect to sign the visitors book and give a small donation. **Lailuru** to the north of Melolo is another ikat weaving village. **Sleeping** There is a *homestay* in Rende (at the *kepala desa's*).

Sleeping

E *Losmen Hermindo*, Melolo, owned by the local Chinese shop owner, clean, 5 rooms with shared mandi, squat toilet and fan. Two new rooms with attached bathroom and western toilet, price includes breakfast, meals available, or eat at the warungs which serve good cheap food.

Transport
60 km from Waingapu

Bus Several direct buses from **Waingapu** starting from 0700 (2 hrs). **Bemos** run all day from Melolo to Waingapu until about 1600.

Kaliuda

Kaliuda is an ikat weaving village, 50 km past Melolo and 110 km from Waingapu, just off the road to Baing. The ikat produced here features, predominantly, chicken and horse motifs. Much of the ikat is unfinished (that is, without the border strip) and clearly, therefore, for tourist rather than local consumption.

Sleeping The *kepala desa* takes in visitors, but the rooms are very basic and rather dirty.
Transport 50 km from Melolo and 110 km from Waingapu. **Bus**: 2 or 3 buses each day from the terminal in **Waingapu**.

Kalala

Kalala is on Sumba's southeast coast, 5 km from Baing and also close to Kaliuda. It has a good beach and is one of the best places to surf.

Sleeping The upmarket resort built here is currently closed; there are no plans to re-open it.
Transport Bus: from **Waingapu**, 4 hrs, or from **Melolo**, 2 hrs.

Waikabubak

Phone code: 0387

Waikabubak is the regency capital and the largest town in West Sumba. Even so, it is really little more than a large village, with a population of only around 15,000. Situated at 800m above sea-level, the town is cooler than Waingapu and during the coldest months of June and July can be chilly at night.

Almost 70% of the population of this region are nominal Christians; unwilling converts, they still follow and attach much more importance to their animist religious practices.

Waikabubak is a very pleasant town, with trees, parks and four traditional hilltop 'kampungs' within its boundaries. It is a good base from which to see the fine megalithic tombs in this area of Sumba and the *Pasola*. This spectacular festival takes place in four different districts of West Sumba after the full moon; in February at Tossi Village in Kodi district (see 'Excursions' below) and Sodan village in Lamboya; and in March in Wanokaka and Gaura districts. Verify exact dates and location with your hotel or the tourist office. Homestays are available in nearby villages (see 'Festivals' below). The **tourist office** is out of town on Jl Teratai 1, T21240, and is moderately helpful.

The village of **Tarung** is only 500m west of town, set on a small hill. Being so close to Waikabubak, it has inevitably been influenced by the large number of tourists who walk up here. Nevertheless, it has several – rather plain – tombs and 33 traditional, thatched houses (see box, page 857). Tarung is the centre of the Marapu religion, where many important rituals take place including the Wula Podhu New Year festival. Admission to the village is by donation.

Another village that can be reached on foot from Waikabubak is **Bondomaroto**. This is an ikat-producing village with some rather inferior tombs and traditional high roofed dwellings. On the last day of Tarungs' celebration of Wula Podhu the villagers have a day long celebration. Admission to the village is by donation. Bondomaroto, 2 km from Waikabubak, is just off the main road to Waingapu. Follow the dirt track south and take the left-hand path. To the right lies the beautiful village of **Praijing**. Weaving can be seen in both villages.

Excursions **Anakalang District**, 20 km east of Waikabubak, is easily accessible as a day excursion from town (see page 867). The district is particularly rich in megalithic tombs, and significant villages include **Pasunga**, **Kabunduk**, **Lai Tarung**, **Matakakeri** and **Galubakul** (details on these places are included in the Anakalang entry). There are many other traditional villages worthy of a visit. The *Artha Hotel* has details of some of these.

Some 40 km to the north of Waikabubak, about 7 km inland from Mamboro, is one of the oldest traditional hilltop villages, **Manuakalada**. **Mamboro** (market day Saturday), on the coast 46 km north of Waikabubak, was a centre of the slave trade that made the local rajas some of the richest in Sumba.

Wanokaka lies 18 km south of Waikabubak and features several traditional villages. The main road south passes through a scenic, hilly landscape with brilliant green ricefields. This is one of the districts where the spectacular annual *Pasola festival* is held (see 'Festivals' below). Nearby, the village of **Prai Goli** or **Paigoli** has one of the finest, best carved, tombs in Sumba. **Sodan**, 25 km southwest of Waikabubak where an important New Year festival takes place at the time of the full moon in October, is a traditional hilltop village and another important centre of the Merapu religion. This is an area steeped in magic and taboos. Each evening at sunset the sacred drums are struck to call the spirits of the ancestors. **Waigalli**, **Pulli** and **Waiwuang** are other traditional villages in the area with carved tombs. ■ *Getting there: by hire car or motorcycle (see 'Transport').*

Kodi District, west of Waikabubak, offers superb coastal scenery and many beautiful beaches, as well as traditional villages and megaliths (see page 867). Villages worth exploring here include **Waimangura**, **Kodi**, **Pero** (where there is accommodation), **Ratenggaro**, **Wainyapu**, **Paronabaroro**, **Tossi**, **Bondokawango** and **Bukarani**. Although it is possible to explore the area using Waikabubak as a base, and particularly if you charter your own transport, it is obviously easier staying in Pero. ■ *Getting there: to catch the direct bus from Waingapu to Kodi, aim to be at the bus station by 0600, 2½ hrs; alternatively, you can catch a bus to Waitabula 1½ hrs, then change to a connecting bemo.*

Pantai Rua and **Pantai Morossi** are two good surfing beaches south of Waikabubak (see page 868). ■ *Getting there: it is easiest to hire a motorcycle, or charter a car, 1-2 hrs (see 'Local transport' in Waikabubak entry). It is possible to go by public bus to Pantai Morossi, with a 20 min walk to the beach.*

Tours Hotels can provide guides and transport. Traditional dances can be arranged in Wanokaka (roughly 150,000Rp, performance lasts 45 minutes), and at Kodi. An entire Pasola with 100 horses can be arranged for around 3,500,000Rp, inclusive of the cost of police for security and health insurance for the Pasola team!

Waikabubak

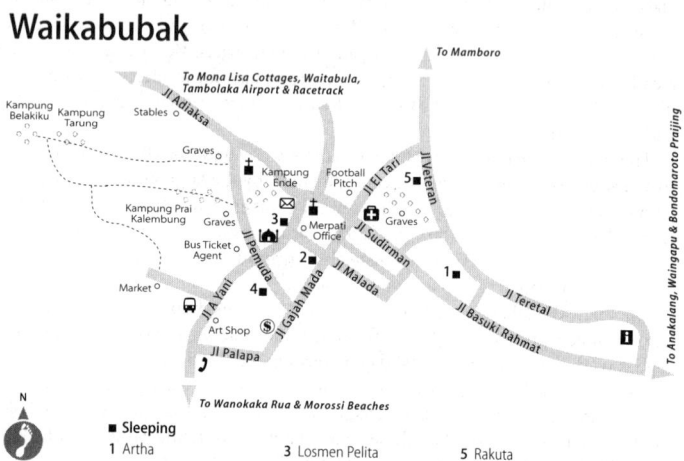

■ Sleeping
1 Artha
2 Losmen Aloha
3 Losmen Pelita
4 Manandang
5 Rakuta

Pasola: of worms and warriors

This fertility rite involves a battle between massed ranks of horsemen representing two villages. They use (these days blunted by government order) spears, and the battle can last from morning until nightfall. It not unusually results in serious injury, even death. The pasola is also a ritual 'cleansing'. Anyone injured or killed is deemed to have transgressed against the gods; their injury is believed to be divine retribution, a price that must be paid by the individual to ensure the gods will not wreak revenge on the whole village or its harvest in the coming year. Human blood is the price of atonement. The battle is preceded by other traditional pursuits and ceremonies – traditional boxing (pajura), purification rituals and the nyale ceremony (see below). The date of the pasola is determined by the appearance of the Nyale worms (see page 796) on the shores of the sea, a few days after the full moon; their appearance is part of the worms' annual reproductive cycle in which their tails, filled with sperm or eggs, are deposited and are carried to the shore, where they are much sought after as ritual food. Prior to the coming of the Wua Nyale, the combatants and supporting villagers go to the sacred beach. As the moon rises, traditional boxing pajura commences; the blood that is spilled also acts as a blood offering to the gods. As dawn breaks, priests from the ancestral village inspect the nyale in order to foretell the coming harvest, the larger the number, the more abundant the crop. Following this, the 'pasola' begins and continues for much of the day. The pasola is particularly popular in the districts of Wanokaka (18 km south of Waikabubak), Lamboya and Kodi. The combat itself symbolizes the contest between the upper and lower worlds – between Merapu, the gods of heaven, and Nyale, the goddess of the sea. The duality of male and female, the sky and the earth mirrors the duality so common in the rites and rituals of Nusa Tenggara. **NB** The timing of the festival is decided at the last moment; although the Jakarta-based national tourist office may decide the festival will occur on a certain day, if it does it is pure serendipity.

Sleeping
■ on map
Price codes:
see inside front cover

It's essential to book during pasola

B *Mona Lisa*, Jl Adyaksa 30, T21364. Roughly 3 km from the centre of town on the road to Waitabula. Attractive bungalows with private bathrooms, shower, western toilet, hot water, restaurant (mid-range), the hotel provides a bus to the airport, prices highly negotiable off-season, usually well-booked peak season. **B-E** *Manandang*, Jl Pemuda 4, T21197, 21292. 17 rooms, the largest hotel in town, includes a 'new' wing and there are plans to build a swimming pool. Clean, rooms with private bathrooms, shower and western toilet, 1st class rooms have hot water, fan and satellite TV, economy rooms with shared mandi, price includes breakfast and tax. Restaurant (cheap) offers an extensive and reasonably priced menu, car hire available. Recommended. **D** *Artha*, Jl Veteran No 11, T21112, 21676. 16 rooms, 10 mins walk from town centre, this small hotel is well-run, clean with very friendly and helpful staff, set around an attractive garden, price includes breakfast and tea all day. Restaurant serves cheap, good, simple food. The 3 cheapest rooms are the best value in town, all rooms with private bathroom, shower, western toilet. VIP rooms have fan and fridge. Jack, the manager, and Meno both speak English and are extremely helpful. They can arrange a visit to a local festival, advise on etiquette and explain what is happening, parking, car hire and guides available. Highly recommended. **D** *Rakuta*, Jl Veteran, T21075. Shared mandi, rather run down, all meals included. **D-E** *Pelita*, Jl A Yani 2, T21104, 21392. The dirty standard rooms with shared mandi are basic, rather depressing, and overpriced, the newer, more expensive rooms with private mandi (shower and western toilet) are fine once you are inside, very cheap restaurant, only stay here if everywhere else is full. **E-F** *Aloha*, Jl Gajah Mada, T21024. Eight rooms, very popular with budget travellers, clean, four cheaper rooms with shared mandi, 4 better rooms with private mandi, all squat toilets, restaurant good, simple, cheap food, cars and motorbikes for hire, guide available. Recommended.

In addition to the above, it is possible to stay in almost every village by making arrangements with the *kepala desa*. Expect to pay in the **E** category.

Eating Most visitors eat in their hotels or losmen; the *Manandang* has the best food in town (see 'Sleeping' above). Alternatively, there are a selection of good, cheap warungs on Jl Jend A Yani.

Festivals **Full moon** (movable) **Wula Podhu**, a month-long period of fasting, and a festival, held in the village of Tarung just outside Waikabubak, to mark the beginning of the merapu New Year in Nov. Traditional dances, musical celebrations and sacrifices, ending with a night of dance and song. The **pasola** symbolizes the contest between the upper and lower worlds – between Merapu, the gods of heaven, and Nyale, the goddess of the sea. For more background to the festival, see the box on page 865. **Porung Takadonga** festival takes place every 2 years in Lai Tarung village (see village entry).

Apr/May (movable) **'Pajura'**, traditional boxing, sometimes takes place during these months, where the hands are bound with straw and the winner is the 1st to draw blood, held to commemorate the harvest.

Aug (17th, public holiday) **Horse racing** takes place once a year to commemorate Independence and lasts a week. The spirited Sumba horses are broken in and ridden for the 1st time in a muddy 'field'. The mud serves as an anchor and prevents them from bucking wildly. Depending on size, a horse is worth 250,000-700,000Rp, with stallions being worth more than mares. A large buffalo is worth 1,000,000-2,000,000Rp, the price being indicative of its symbolic and ceremonial role in the Merapu religion.

Shopping Like Waingapu, door-to-door salesmen and women camp outside hotels selling bits-and-pieces and, in particular, Sumba ikat blankets. As the centre of production is East Sumba, these are better purchased there.

Art Shop, Jl A Yani 99, has photocopies of a book by 2 Swedish anthropologists describing local customs. Many pieces and jewellery carved in West Sumba's villages from horn, bone, wood and stone, containers for betel nut, religious objects and stone statues. Many of these objects show examples of local symbolism. Beads and fertility carvings, with outsized phalluses attached, are on offer.

Textiles Ikat is best bought in East Sumba.

Transport
137 km from Waingapu, 47 km from Waikelo

Local Public transport is irregular but improving all the time. **Car hire**: hiring a car to visit out-of-town sights makes good sense for groups of 4 or more. Most losmen and hotels have vehicles for charter and they display rates for different destinations – **Waikelosawa, Wanokaka, Lamboya/Sodan, Waitabuta, Waikelo, Memboro** and **Kodi**. A cheaper and equally flexible way to get around is by **motorcycle taxi**; alternatively, some losmen/hotels are willing to rent out motorbikes by the day (25,000-40,000Rp).

Air The airport is 42 km northwest of town at Tambolaka. *Merpati* operate 3 flights per week to **Kupang** (2½ hrs), via **Waingapu**, and to **Bima** (40 mins). There are share minibuses into town. Note that it can be difficult to get a seat.

Bus: the terminal is on the southwest edge of town, off Jl Jend A Yani. Three departures daily for **Waingapu**, the 1st at about 0700-0800, 4 hrs. Connections with regional market towns generally through the day until early afternoon. From Waingapu, passengers are dropped-off at their losmen or hotel; those travelling to Waingapu will be picked-up at their hotel or losmen if given advance warning. There are several bus agents along Jl A Yani where you can buy tickets, arrange hotel pick up and reserve seats; *Sumba Mas, Bumi, Indah* and *Tambora Indah* all have newish buses.

Sea Boat: *Perentis* ships operate out of Waikelo harbour, bound for **Larantuka** on Flores. The trip takes 8-12 hrs, 60 km from Waikabubak on Sumba's north coast and near the airport. It is also sometimes possible to hitch a ride on 1 of the inter-island mixed cargo boats that stop here.

Directory

Airline offices *Merpati*, 1st floor of building, corner Jl Malada and Jl Jend A Yani. **Banks** *Bank Rakyat Indonesia*, Jl Gajah Mada; *BNI*, Jl Jend A Yani. **Communications** Post Office: corner Jl Jend A Yani and Jl Sudirman. Closed Sun, open every other day 0900-1400, except Fri, 0900-1130.

Anakalang District

Anakalang is a district 20 km east of Waikabubak and, conveniently, close to the main road to Waingapu. This district has the greatest concentration of megalithic tombs to be found in Sumba: a mass marriage ceremony is held here every two years in the summer to coincide with the full moon.

At **Pasunga**, on the main road, there is one of the largest tombs in Sumba. It features a man and woman, and was carved over a period of six months in 1926. The tomb is for the clan elders.

The nearby village of **Kabunduk** is the important 'origin village' of the local clan and also has some well-carved graves. It is the site of the largest tomb in Anakalang District, named 'Resi Mona', where the rajas of the district were buried. The layout of this village is typical: in the central space there are graves, a supplementary altar for crops, a village altar and a skull tree; some flat stones indicate the spot where a supplementary altar is placed, to serve as the focus at rituals and ceremonies.

Lai Tarung – walking distance from Kabunduk – is regarded as an important ceremonial and spiritual centre. There are 10 carved stone pillars on which sits a 'traditional' house. Reach this hilltop village of the ancestors by following the track uphill at the end of Kabunduk village, and on past some houses and tombs.

Sleeping

It is possible to stay in 1 of the traditional houses by the altars which has been converted into a homestay. First see the kepala desa who has an interesting collection of old photographs taken by a Swiss anthropologist, and some ritual heirlooms.

Transport

Bus Take a bus heading for Lewa/Waingapu or for Anakalang. Most depart in the morning, although there are departures later in the day.

Kodi District

Kodi District offers superb coastal scenery and many beautiful beaches, as well as traditional villages and megaliths. Kodi is the main town and market day is also Wednesday.

Pero, near Kodi on the west coast, offers some basic accommodation on a spectacular stretch of coast, though the waves can be powerful and swimming is not always for the faint-hearted.

There are good walks in the area around Kodi, passing traditional villages and megalithic tombs. Follow the beach south from Pero to **Ratenggaro**, approximately 5 km, with superb sea views. From this raised village there are more grand views, with the picturesque traditional village of **Wainyapu** just across the mouth of the river, easily reached at low tide. **Paronabaroro** is slightly inland *en route* to Ratenggaro; here you will find the highest roofs in Sumba, as well as stone tombs and possibly even some women weaving.

Going north from Pero, follow the path along the coast for about 5 km to reach **Tossi**, the most traditional village in Kodi and one of the sites of the annual Pasola festival (see 'Festivals' below). Other traditional villages include **Bondokawango** and **Bukarani**. All these villages can be reached by road from Kodi if you have your own transport.

Sleeping
Come prepared for mosquitoes

E *Losmen Stori*, Pero on the only street in this village, basic rooms with shared mandi and squat toilet, price includes 3 meals (there is nowhere else to eat in town). It is possible to stay with the *kepala desa* in Ratenggaro.

Transport

Bus To catch the direct bus from Waingapu, aim to be at the bus station by 0600, 2½ hrs; alternatively, you can catch a bus to Waitabula 1½ hrs, then change to a connecting bemo.

Pantai Rua & Pantai Morossi The two surfing beaches of Pantai Rua and Pantai Morossi are on the coast south of Waikabubak. Pantai Rua is good for surfing, but Pantai Morossi is reputedly even better – the south coastline of Sumba is exposed to the onslaught of the Southern Seas. Both, though, are considered safe for swimming.

Sleeping **Pantai Morossi**: the **B** *Sumba Reefs Hotel*, very upmarket and catering largely for the package tourists from Bali. **B-C** *Palm Resort*, surfer destination, large rooms, TV, a/c, reasonable quality place, expensive restaurant. **E** *Homestay Mete Bulu*, about a 15-min walk from the beach, up a steep hill, rather mosquito-ridden. **Pantai Rua**: **E** *Homestay Ahong*, basic but very friendly, and provides 3 decent meals daily. Under construction on the island south of the beach is a luxury resort aimed at package tourists. **Transport Road**: it is easiest to hire a motorcycle, or charter a car, 1-2 hrs (see Local transport in Waikabubak entry). It is possible to go by public bus to Pantai Morossi, with a 20-min walk to the beach.

West Timor

Colour map 3a, grid B5/6

Timor is one of the driest islands in the Indonesian Archipelago. The terrain is beautiful but often bleak, with rock strewn hills, isolated communities and poor soils.

West Timor has become a popular place to visit for tourists, largely because it lies at the beginning or end of a journey through the islands of Nusa Tenggara. There are reasonable beaches and some snorkelling, but nothing spectacular. The refreshing hill towns of Soe and Kefamenanu, both with traditional villages in their vicinities, are worth the journey, as are the rarely visited islands of Roti and Savu. Note, however, that following the debacle in East Timor, West Timor is not the happiest of places and in some areas Westerners are not welcome.

Ins and outs

Getting there Kupang is the largest town in this part of Indonesia. There are international air connections with Darwin, Australia, and also good links with domestic destinations. Get a taxi into the centre of town. Airport taxi service, T33824. Bemos running between Penfui/Baumata and town pass the airport turn off. It is a 1½-km walk from the airport buildings to this spot. Connections by *Merpati* and *Bouraq* with Jakarta, Dili and Bali, and other destinations in Java, Sulawesi, Nusa Tenggara, Irian Jaya and Kalimantan. Kupang's Tenau harbour is visited by a number of *Pelni* vessels and there are also more frequent ferry links with Ende and Larantuka (both on Flores), and with Savu and Alor.

Getting around Buses travel to all major settlements in West Timor. Bemos are the main form of town and local transport.

Safety warning Following East Timor's resounding vote in favour of independence in 1999, the militias fighting to maintain the territory's link with Jakarta fled to West Timor where they are still based as this book goes to press. At the beginning of Sep they attacked and killed 3 UN staff working in the town of Atambua, not far from the border between West and East Timor. Foreigners are viewed with suspicion in some areas and not a little hostility – especially if they are Australian (or thought to be so) – Australian forces led the UN force into East Timor.

NB In the last edition of this book we included a section on East Timor. This edition has no such section for 2 reasons. First, East Timor appears to be heading for full independence and will be a sovereign state after a period of UN tutelage. Second, Dili and many other towns in the region were razed to the ground during the violence following the vote for independence in mid-1999.

Background

West Timor or **Timor Barat** consists of three districts which constitute part of the province of East Nusa Tenggara: Kupang (centred on the city of Kupang which is also the capital of East Nusa Tenggara), Timor Tengah Selatan and Timor Tengah Utara.

The districts of West Timor cover a total of 16,500 sq km and have a population of 1,250,000. The island's long dry season stretches from April to October, with annual rainfall of 1,200mm – 2,000mm being concentrated in the months from November to March. Soils are generally thin and unproductive. Most of the population is concentrated in the slightly wetter interior, where cattle raising is the principal occupation. Because of the Portuguese and Dutch influences, the bulk of the population is Christian: 58% are classified as Protestant, 35% Roman Catholic.

History

Timor became a focus of European interest because of the valuable aromatic sandalwood that grows here. The Chinese, sometimes using Javanese intermediaries, probably began buying the wood in the 10th century, perhaps even as early as the third century. Their accounts describe Timor as being covered with sandalwood trees – something that is difficult to believe today.

European contact with the island dates from the early 16th century. In 1561 a Portuguese settlement was established on neighbouring Solor and Dominican friars began to evangelize on Timor. Though much of their time was spent on missionary activity, they also became involved in the sandalwood trade. Other important exports of the period were horses and slaves. It was at this time that the inter-marriage between Portuguese sailors, soldiers and traders from Melaka and Macao with local women laid the foundations for Timor's influential *mestizos* community – locally known as the *Topasses*, from the Dravidian word *tupassi*, meaning 'interpreter'.

The Portuguese began to lose influence to the Dutch at the beginning of the 17th century. However, the Dutch showed only a marginal interest in securing this distant colonial possession. The friction between the Dutch and the Portuguese provided the basis for the later conflict between Indonesia and East Timor. This resulted in East Timor's annexation by Indonesia in 1975 and nearly 25 years of occupation.

West Timor

Kupang

Phone code: 0380

The Dutch first landed here in 1613. In 1653 they moved their operations to Kupang, building upon the fortifications left by the Portuguese. Kupang was to remain the centre of Dutch influence in the area until independence.

Today, the city is the capital of the province of East Nusa Tenggara with a population of 120,000, most of them Protestants, and the University of Nusa Cendana (12 km outside town). There are three **tourist offices**. *Kantor Pariwisata Parpostel* is on Jl Soekarno 29 (next to Post Office). A central location but next to useless. The *Provincial Tourist Office*, on Jl Basuki Rakhmat 1, T21540, is 5 km from town off Jl Soeharto. Catch a bemo travelling towards Baun and ask for Kantor Gubernor Lama, the turning is just past the Pentecostal Chapel. They can provide some useful handouts. ■ *0700-1400 Mon-Thu, 0700-1100 Fri, 0700-1230 Sat*. The *Tourist Information Desk*, on Jl Soekarno 25 (next to church), is a helpful and convenient source of information, especially for independent travellers.

Sights Kupang is not well-endowed with sights. Despite its history, there are virtually no pre-Second World War buildings. Jl Siliwangi, the seafront road (although the sea is usually out of sight), is the bustling heart of the city, as it has been since the Dutch settled here in 1637. Street salesmen and women hawk traditional herbal and spiritual cures, and there is a **market** at the east end of the street (where it becomes Jl Garuda). Walking west along the coast road, past the army barracks and church, there are good views of the coast and the islands beyond. This was the site of the

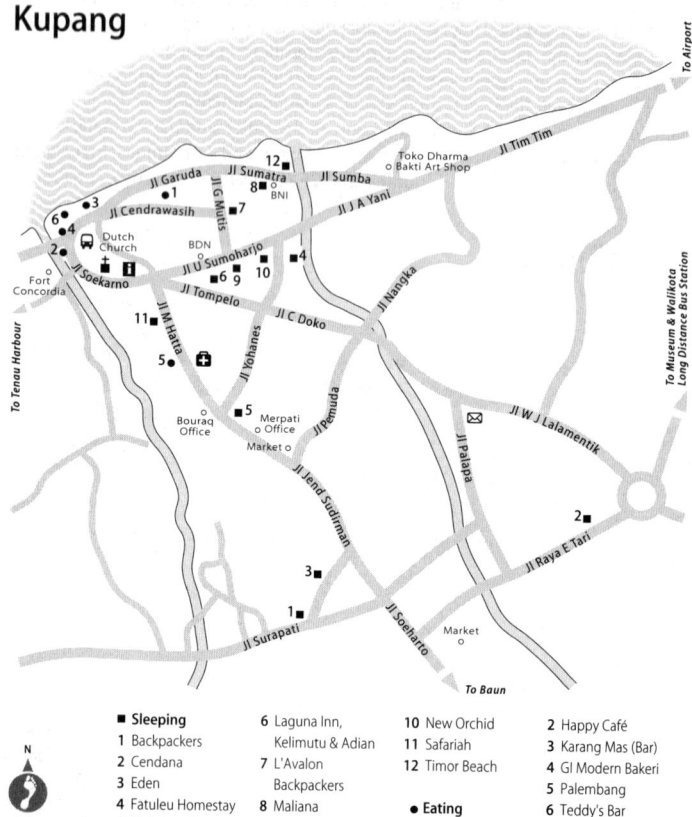

Kupang

■ **Sleeping**
1 Backpackers
2 Cendana
3 Eden
4 Fatuleu Homestay
5 Flobamor II
6 Laguna Inn, Kelimutu & Adian
7 L'Avalon Backpackers
8 Maliana
9 Marina
10 New Orchid
11 Safariah
12 Timor Beach

● **Eating**
1 Garnda Tomor
2 Happy Café
3 Karang Mas (Bar)
4 Gl Modern Bakeri
5 Palembang
6 Teddy's Bar

Dutch **Fort Concordia**, built in 1653. Back in town, and close to the Kota Kupang bemo terminal at Jl Soekarno 23, is a fine and well-maintained **Dutch church**, orginally constructed in 1873.

About 4 km out of town, 300m from the long-distance bus terminal, is the **Museum of Nusa Tenggara Timur**. The exhibits are well displayed, but less well explained. The collection includes textiles, ceramics, traditional weapons and ethnographic pieces. Notable is the fine bronze Dongson (Vietnamese) drum (see page), collected on Alor, with its frogs symbolizing and promoting rain, along with the bronze *moko* dowry vessels, also from Alor (see box, page 853). The ikat process is illustrated with the use of a series of models and sets. ■ *Admission by donation. 0800-1500 Mon-Thu, 0800-1100 Fri, 0800-1230 Sat. Getting there: take bemo No 10 from the city centre to Walikota.*

Excursions

Lasiana Beach lies 12 km east of Kupang, and is quiet during weekdays. At weekends it becomes popular as a picnic spot for locals. *Warungs* and drinks vendors operate on the beach, and at the west end of the beach there is a small plateau where there are good views over Kupang Bay. **Sleeping D** *Lasiana Beach Cottage*, not always open, attached bathrooms, rather grubby. ■ *There is an admission charge to beach. Getting there: take bemo No 17 heading for Tarus, and ask to be let off at the entrance to the beach.*

Baun lies 30 km from Kupang and is a weaving town; the processes of ikat can be seen, although the quality of the work produced is variable. Visitors have recommended *Ibu Raja* as producing the best cloth. There is a **market** in Baun on Saturday (from 0700). ■ *Getting there: take a bemo from the Kota Kupang terminal in town to Sikumana terminal, and from there another bemo to Baun.*

Semau Island is good for swimming and snorkelling, but is best reached on a tour (see 'Tours' below) as there are no regular ferries. There is talk of running game-fishing boats (marlin) from the island, the season stretching from March to September. **Sleeping C** *Uiasa Beach Cottages*, attached mandi, price includes three meals; and *Flobamor II Cottages* (book through *Flobamor II Hotel* in Kupang, see below). ■ *Getting there: if not on a tour, catch a bemo bound for Bolok or Tenau from the Kota Kupang terminal and get off at Pantai (Beach) Namosain, southwest of town. Boats can sometimes be hired from here for the trip to Semau (45 mins).*

A **sandalwood factory**, lying 3 km north of town at Bakunase, is open to visitors. ■ *Getting there: direct bemos to Bakunase from Terminal Kota.*

Tours

There are a number of well-organized tour and travel companies in Kupang. They offer city tours, tours to the weaving village of Baun, Lesiana Beach tours and a number of other day trips (all these are prices for three people). They also arrange longer tours to destinations on Timor and the other islands of East Nusa Tenggara (Flores, Alor, Komoda, Sumba etc). *Teddy's Bar and Restaurant* also run a less formal tour service, with day snorkelling tours to Semau Island departing 1000, Rote Island surfing safaris, city tours, fishing and camping expeditions.

Sleeping
■ on map
Price codes:
see inside front cover

A *New Orchid* (aka *Orchid Garden*), Jl Fatuleu 2 (facing the *Fatuleu Homestay*), T33707, F33669. A/c, restaurant, pool, central location, clean bungalows and attractive garden, best place near the centre of town. **A** *Sasando*, Jl Perintis Kemerdekaan 1, T33334, F33338. A/c, restaurant, pool, tennis, good views, but out of town near bus terminal so not convenient for anyone intending to explore on foot. **B** *Flobamor II*, Jl Jend Sudirman 21, T33476. A/c, hot water, comfortable but over-priced and now rather down-at-heel. Accommodates the main *Merpati* office, and a dive centre. **B-D** *Marina*, Jl Jend A Yani 79, T22566. Some a/c, small, friendly, central, price includes breakfast, cheaper rooms without attached bathrooms, rather gloomy.

C *Kelimutu*, Jl Gunung Kelimutu 38 (close to *Laguna Hotel*), T31179. Some a/c, clean and quiet, price includes breakfast and lunch or dinner. **C-D** *Cendana*, Jl Raya El Tari 23, T21541. Some a/c, some distance out of town near the Kantor Gubernor, but regular bemos into city centre, nice garden atmosphere, popular, price includes breakfast. Recommended. **C-D** *Laguna*, Jl Gunung Kelimutu 36, T21559. Some a/c, on a quiet side street but central, clean with good bathrooms. Recommended. **C-D** *Maliana*, Jl Sumatra 35, T21879. Clean, spacious rooms with fans, with mandi and western toilet en suite, friendly management. Recommended. **C-D** *Maya*, Jl Sumatra 31, T32169. Some a/c, good rooms and good value, garden, on sea front but still central, more expensive rooms with hot water and TV, popular so often full, price includes breakfast. Recommended. **C-D** *Susi*, Jl Sumatra 37, T22172. Some a/c and TV, on seafront but still central, clean and quiet. **D** *Fatuleu Homestay*, Jl Fatuleu 1, T31374. Quiet street in garden atmosphere, clean and central. Recommended.

E *Losmen Safariah*, Jl Moh Hatta 34, T21595. Rooms only average, attached mandi, reasonable location. **F** *Backpackers*, Jl Kancil 37B, Airnona (about 7 km from town centre, but there are regular (No 3) bemos), T31291. Dirty but cheap, near swimming pool, good for information, price includes breakfast, of sorts. **F** *Eden*, Jl Kancil, Airnona, 7 km from town centre, regular bemos, T21931. Thatched bungalows in peaceful location by swimming pool, wonderful trees, but rooms shabby and poorly maintained, price includes breakfast. **F** *L'Avalon Backpackers*, Jl Sumatra 1 No 8, T32278. Quiet, friendly place, with lots of travellers' information, but basic. Price includes breakfast, tea and coffee.

Eating
Local specialities include daging s'ei (smoked beef)

Indonesian Cheap: *Hemaliki*, Jl Soekarno, attractive garden and restaurant serving Indonesian, Chinese, seafood and Japanese. *Lumintu*, Jl Garuda 1 (by the market square), Indonesian, good and cheap *ikan bakar* (barbecue fish). *Palembang*, Jl Mohammed Hatta 54 (near the general hospital on bemo route 2), serves a wide range of excellent Chinese and Indonesian dishes, very popular and very good. **Very cheap**: *Bundo Kanduang*, Jl Jend Sudirman 49, Padang. *Garuda Timor*, good food, clean restaurant, good value. *Happy Café*, Jl Ikan Paus 3 (near the bemo terminal), large portions of freshly cooked Indonesian and Chinese dishes, excellent value. *Ibu Soekardjo*, Jl Moh Hatta 23, Indonesian. *Tunggal Dara*, Jl Siliwangi (facing the market square), Indonesian dishes, hardly refined but one of the cheapest places to eat.

Chinese Cheap: *Lima Jaya Raya*, Jl Soekarno 15, clean, reasonably priced, good range of dishes, Chinese, crab specialities. Nightclub upstairs. *Mandarin*, Jl Jend Sudirman 148 (next to *Astiti Hotel* and intersection with Jl Harimau), good, simple, Chinese. Recommended. *Hemaliki*, Jl Soekarno good, cheap Chinese and seafood.

International Cheap: *Teddy's Bar & Restaurant*, Jl Ikan Tongkol 1-3, western, seafood, lobsters, steak, live music.

Seafood Cheap: *Timor Beach*, Jl Sumatra, seafood, overlooking beach.

Bars *Teddy*'s Bar, Jl Ikan Tongkol 1-3, live music, popular with westerners, pricey. Good place to network if looking for yacht work. *Karang Mas*, Jl Siliwangi 84/88, 1 of the best places to watch the sunset clutching a cold beer, the bar has a terrace overlooking a small beach, small menu of mediocre food. *Pantai Bar*, *Timor Beach Hotel*, Jl Sumatra, bar overlooking the sea, another place to watch the sunset over Kupang Bay.

Shopping **Books** *Istana Beta Bookshop*, on Jl Jend A Yani 58 (past the *Marina Hotel*), has town maps.

Crafts *Loka Binkra Crafts Centre* is on the road to the airport, just before the 8 km marker. Catch a bemo bound for Tarus or Penfui.

Textiles Kupang is a centre for the sale of Nusa Tenggara Timur ikat, but it is highly variable in quality. For *tenunan asli* (cloth woven from home-grown and spun cotton and coloured with natural dyes) expect to pay 150,000Rp upwards. Wrap-around sarong blankets or *selimut* worn by men are decorated with bright, bold, geometric and stylized animal and bird motifs. Try: *Toko Dharma Bakti*, Jl Sumba, or the house (21D) on the side street off Jl Soekarno near the *5 Jaya Raya Restaurant*.

Tour operators *Natrabu*, Jl Gunung Mutis 18, T21095. *Pitoby Tours*, Jl Jend Sudirman 118, T21443, F31044, branch at Jl Siliwangi 75, T21222. *Varanus*, Jl Perintis Kemerdekaan.

Transport

110 km from Soe, 283 km from Atambua

Local Bemos: there are a huge number of bemos. Routes are marked over the roof, and most ply between the city bemo terminal (Terminal Kota Kupang) at the end of Jl Soekarno, near the intersection with Jl Siliwangi, and the out-of-town bus terminal, Walikota. A board at Terminal Kota Kupang gives all routes and fares.

Air Kupang's **El Tari international airport** is 14 km northeast of town. There are taxis into the centre of town (airport taxi service, T33824). **NB** Taxi drivers encourage tourists to go to hotels of their choice, saying others are full – they receive a commission. Try to ask at reception without the taxi driver in company. Bemos running between Penfui/Baumata and town pass the airport turn off – it is a 1½ km walk from the airport buildings to this spot. Connections by *Merpati* and *Bouraq* with **Jakarta**, **Dili** and **Bali**, and other destinations in **Java**, **Sulawesi**, **Nusa Tenggara**, **Irian Jaya** and **Kalimantan**. International connections with **Darwin**, Australia on Merpati. No visa required for entering Timor as it is a 'gateway' port (this applies to nationals of those countries permitted visa-free entry), but you must have an onward ticket out of Indonesia. Flights from Darwin are usually not too booked up.

Road Bus: the long-distance Oebobo bus terminal, better known as Walikota, is some way east of town. Regular bemos run between it, along different routes, and the central bemo terminal at the end of Jl Siliwangi. Buses from Oebobo to **Baun**, **Bolok**, **Baumata**, **Tarus Kejamenanu** (5 hrs), **Soe** (2½ hrs), **Niki Niki** (3 hrs), **Atambua** (7 hrs) and **Dili** (13 hrs), with change of bus at Atambua. *Natrans*, who run buses to Dili via Atambua, have a counter at the terminal; *Tunas Mekar*, who run night buses to Dili, sell tickets at Jl Siliwangi 94 (near the Terminal Kota bemo station).

Sea Boat: Kupang's Tenau harbour is southwest of town. Catch a bemo bound for Tenau or Bolok. The *Pelni* ships *Sirimau*, *Awu*, *Dobonsolo* and *Pangrango* visit Kupang on their 2 week circuits. The *Pelni* office is at Jl Pahlawan 3, T21944 (5 min walk west of Jl Siliwangi; a new building off, but visible from, the road). There are also a number of ferries serving surrounding ports and islands; these leave from the Bolok ferry terminal, a few kilometres further on from Tenau. Catch a bemo bound for Bolok. The ferry office (Perum Angkutan Sungai, Danau dan Penyeberangan) is at Jl Cak Doko 20, T21140. Ferry services are as follows: **Kupang-Ba'a** (Rote) daily at 0900 (returning same day); **Kupang-Ende** (Flores) 1400 Mon and 1300 Tue (returning Wed) (about 18 hrs, ventilation in economy reportedly better than 1st class); **Kupang-Larantuka** (Flores) 1500 Sun and Wed (returning Tue and Sat); **Kupang-Savu** 1600 Wed (returning Thu); **Kupang-Kalabahi** (Alor) 1400 Tue and Sat.

Directory

Airline offices *Bouraq*, Jl Jend Sudirman 20A, T21421. *Garuda/Merpati*, Jl Kosasih 13, T21205. **Banks** Kupang is the best place to change money before Lombok/Bali. It is also possible to obtain cash advances on Visa and Mastercard. *Bank Dagang Negara*, Jl Soekarno 10, change most TCs and currencies; *Bank Rakyat Indonesia*, Jl Soekarno; *Danamon*, Jl Jend Sudirman 21, change most TCs in US$ and A$, plus major currencies cash. **Communications General Post Office**: Jl Palapa (out of centre, for poste restante). **Post Office**: Jl Soekarno 29 (more convenient), open 0700-1600 Mon-Sat. **Telephone Offices**: Jl Urip Sumohardjoll. Perumtel, Jl Palapa. **Medical facilities Hospitals**: *General Hospital*, Jl Moh Hatta. **Useful addresses** Immigration Office: Jl Soekarno 16, T21077.

Soe

Phone code: 0391

Soe is the cool, spread out capital of the regency of Timor Tengah Selatan, lying 800m above sea-level. During the coldest months of June and July it can be chilly and a sweater is needed during the day – it is always cool at night. The town is best-known for the large regional market held here every day of the week, but it is not the most characterful of places. The *Kantor Pariwisata* **tourist office** is on Jl Kakatua. It is open from 0700 to 1200, some useful leaflets and a few of the staff speak some English.

Excursions The countryside around Soe represents the heartland of West Timorese culture. Typical villages can be found along the **Soe-Kefamenanu road**. There are also beautiful, traditional villages on the **Soe-Kupang road**, 20 km from Soe. ■ *Getting there: it is possible simply to hop on and off public buses. A better, though more expensive alternative, is to hire a car (about 50,000Rp per day) – see 'Local transport' below.*

Niki Niki, 30 km from Soe on the road to Kefamenanu, contains the graves of the Amanuban kings of the Nope Kingdom and also holds a good market on Wednesdays. ■ *Getting there: by bus or bemo running towards Kefa.*

Oinlasi, 50 km southeast of Niki Niki, has a fabulous market every Tuesday (0700-1400); ikat is sold here as well as various handicrafts. In the middle of the market is the *Rumah Makan Sudmampir*, which does an excellent nasi goreng. ■ *Getting there: frequent buses from Soe to Oinlasi, especially on market day, 1½ hrs.*

Boti is an animist village 13 km from Oinlasi, which is worth visiting for its traditional buildings (see box) and to watch lively displays of traditional dance. One dance depicts a young man coming back from a headhunting raid, which used to be an initiation right and a prerequisite for marriage. The men make whooping calls to their ancestors, thanking them for their assistance in battle. The participants wear a dazzling array of the local *kain* cloth. Gongs and a goat skin drum provide a musical beat. This may be followed by harmonized singing accompanied by a *lecu* (a type of guitar made from a large gourd). The Raja is unusual in being monogomous. Most other leaders of Kingdoms have at least two or three wives. Married men are distinguished by their hair which is left to grow long after the marriage ceremony. **Sleeping** In the Raja's house (**E**), price includes all meals, a display of traditional dancing and a full demonstration of weaving techniques. ■ *Getting there: bus to Oinlasi and then walk 10 km from Oinlasi to Boti. Bring plenty of water. Alternatively, charter a bemo in Soe. A guide is really essential if you want to make the most of your visit, as few of the villagers speak any Bahasa.*

Oehala Waterfall is around 10 km from Soe, *en route* to Kapan. From the main Soe-Kapan road it is a pleasant 2 km stroll down a shady path to the cascade, at the base of which is a pool where it is possible to swim. ■ *Getting there: take a bemo to Kapan.*

Soe

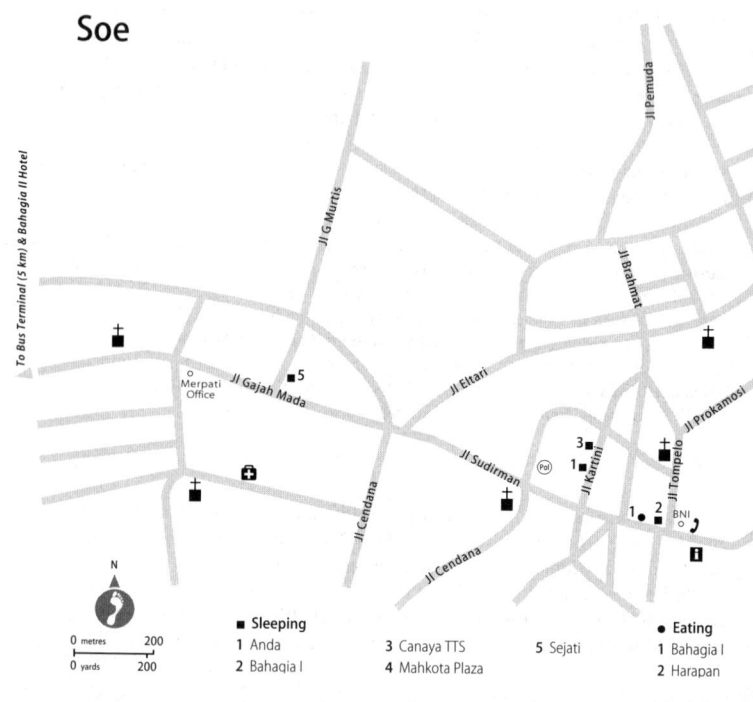

- **Sleeping**
  1 Anda
  2 Bahagia I
  3 Canaya TTS
  4 Mahkota Plaza
  5 Sejati

- **Eating**
  1 Bahagia I
  2 Harapan

Traditional buildings in Boti village

Ume Kbubu is the name given to the houses so characteristic of this part of West Timor. In the area around Soe they tend to be domed, oval in shape and their low entrances. They are used for sleeping and eating.

Lopo – every house has a lopo – has an attic storage section and lower sheltered area, where friends and family congregate out of the hot sun. Discs of wood on the supporting poles serve to prevent vermin from ascending into the grain storage area. These buildings are beautifully made, and once inside you can see how ornately and neatly bound together they are in a lace work of bamboo weave and grasses. The lopo next to to the Raja's house in Boti deserves particular attention. On its pinnacle is a stylized carving of three perched birds. Birds are the Raja's 'totem'. It is believed in the village that the bloodlines of the birds and the Raja have crossed, and he is therefore obliged to protect and preserve them. For this reason, small birds are not hunted in the village and there are noticeably greater numbers of them about than in other areas of West Timor.

Sleeping
■ on map
Price codes:
see inside front cover

B-C *Bahagia 11*, Jl Gajah Mada, T21095. The price variation reflects a variation in room size more than quality. Pricey restaurant, Merpati agent here. **C-D** *Bahagia 1*, Jl Diponegoro 72, T21015. Good restaurant (cheap), very clean rooms, some with their own mandi. **D** *Mahkota Plaza*, Jl Suharto 11 (near the bus station), T21168. Restaurant, wide range of food, very clean, light and spacious with attached bathrooms. Sometimes closed in low season. **D** *Sejati*, Jl Gajah Mada 18, T21101. Some rooms with attached inside mandi. **E-F** *Wisma Gahaya TTS*, Jl Kartini 7, T21087. Next door to *Anda*, large clean rooms. **F** *Anda*, Jl Kartini 5, T21323. Pak Yohannes, who speaks good English and Dutch, has gone wild with the decoration of his hotel. The facilities are rather basic.

Eating

Cheap *Harapan*, Jl Suharto, tasty Indonesian, Chinese and seafood; there are a few good restaurants near the market. **Very cheap** *Sri Solo*, which serves good reasonably priced Indonesian food, and *Sari Bondo*, which serves Padang food.

Transport

Local Car hire (around 50,000Rp/day): ask at the *Mahkota Plaza Hotel*. **Road Bus**: the terminal is a little way out of town, so catch a bemo. Regular connections with **Kupang** (2½ hrs), **Kefamenanu** (2 hrs) and **Atambua** (4 hrs). For **Dili** it is necessary to go via Atambua.

111 km from Kupang, 86 km from Kefamenanu, 72 km from Atambua

Directory

Airline offices The *Merpati* agent is in the *Bahagia 11 Hotel* on Jl Gajah Mada, open 0800-1700 Mon-Sat. **Banks** It is possible to change TCs at the *BNI*, near to the tourist office on Jl Diponegoro.

Kefamenanu

Phone code: 0391

Kefamenanu, known as 'Kefa' to the local people, is the capital of the regency of Timor Tengah Utara. It lies between Timor's northern and southern mountain ranges and, like Soe, is a highland town. It lies at an altitude of 400m and experiences chilly nights. During June and July, the coldest months, a sweater

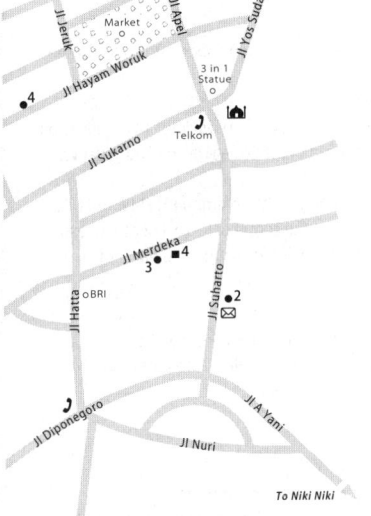

3 Mahkota Plaza
4 Sri Solo

may be needed in the evenings. The town has simple accommodation and can be used as a base to explore the surrounding countryside. There is a **tourist office** with some interesting leaflets on Jl Sudirman.

Excursions The area around Kefamenanu is rarely visited by tourists. There are numerous **traditional villages** and towns, including **Maslete** (4 km south) and the hill village of **Nilulat**.

However, possibly the most memorable village is **Tamkesi**– situated at the heart of the Biboki Kingdom. Over 70,000 people are members of the Kingdom but only 12 families are able to inhabit this central village. It is polite to bring gifts to the villagers such as betel nuts and tobacco. Biboki textiles are famous for their combination of embroidery and ikat (resist-dyed thread). Producing these traditional textiles is highly skilled work and they are consequently expensive (expect to pay over 30,000Rp for a scarf and more than 300,000Rp for a good quality piece). ■ *Getting there: catch a bus the 42 km to Manafui from the main Kefa terminal. From Manafui it is a tough 8 km walk to Tamakesi. A guide who can speak Dawanese is needed, as very few villagers can speak Bahasa.*

Kua Popnam, or Popnam cave, is filled with stalagmites and stalagtites. ■ *Getting there: take a bemo from the market to Tua Mese, from where it is a 4 km walk along a good path.* The nearby **Taekas** village has some excellent examples of *lopo* (see box) and traditional Timorese houses.

Oelolok village has a good Tuesday market and is 25 km from Kefa. ■ *Getting there: take a bemo from the market place.*

Sleeping **B-D** *Ariesta*, Jl Basuki Rakhmat 29, good clean rooms, some with a/c, friendly staff. Recommended. **C-D** *Cendana*, Jl Sonbai, T31168. Some a/c, attractive rooms arranged around a small garden. Restaurant in complex or the staff will take you free of charge to a restaurant in town. **E** *Setankai*, Jl Sonbai, T21217. Communal mandi, basic and rather dirty. **E** *Sokowindu*, Jl Pattimura, T31122. Central place, communal mandi, basic but clean rooms.

Eating **Cheap** *Rumah Makan Padang*, the best restaurant in town. **Very cheap** *Rumah Makan Ayam Kalasan*, Jl Basuki Rachmat 9, T21212. Chicken dishes. *Rumah Makan Sari Bondo*, Jl Sonbai, Padang food. *Stella Maris*, Jl Kartini, Indonesian food. *Warung Pojok*, Jl Kartini, Indonesian food.

Festivals 30 Nov: **Culture and Art Festival**. Traditional dances, music, food and handicrafts on show and on sale.

Shopping There is an NGO-run ikat shop on the northern edge of town, which buys cloth at a fair price from villagers and sells it on without a huge mark up. It is part of the OXFAM fair trading initiative.

Transport **Road Bus**: regular connections with Soe 2 hrs, Kupang 4½ hrs, Atambua 1½ hrs, and Dili. To get to Oecussi catch the bus from the market place in the centre of town. For other destinations it is necessary to go to the main bus terminal whcih is 1 km south of town. Bemos run to and from here.

197 km from Kupang, 86 km from Soe, 86 km from Atambua, 60 km from Oecussi

Directory **Banks** The *Bank Danomon*, on the corner of Jl Keniri and Jl Kartini, can only change US$ banknotes and does so at a poor rate. **Communications** **Post Office**: Jl Imam Bonjol. **Telkom office**: near *Hotel Ariesta*.

Roti (Rote)

Colour map 3a, grid B5

Roti Island, or Rote, just off the southwest tip of Timor, is administered as part of the regency of Kupang. It covers 1,214 sq km and has a population of nearly 100,000. The capital is the town of **Ba'a**, situated almost midway up the north coast of the island. The villages both northeast and southwest from Ba'a are worth visiting for their markets and traditional architecture. Oeseli Beach, 58 km southwest from Ba'a, is good for swimming.

Ins and outs

Getting there The airport is 8 km from Ba'a. There are 2 flights/week on *Merpati* from Kupang (30 mins), but the service is unreliable. The ferry dock is at Pante Baru, about 30 km northeast of Ba'a; bemos wait to take passengers to the capital. The *Pelni* vessel *Pangrango* leaves from Kupang's Bolok harbour every day at 0900, returning the same day in the early afternoon, 4 hrs.

Getting around There is a direct bus from Pante Baru (the port) to Nembrala on Tue and Fri, or hire a car or motorcycle for the day.

Background

As on Savu, the lontar palm is the traditional subsistence crop here (see page 878). The tradition of making working clothes from the fibres of the lontar palm has now died out, but some people still continue to make shrouds for the dead from the fibres. The Rotinese supplement their income by fishing and jewellery making.

The western tip of the island is currently reasonably untouched as a result of its relative inaccessibility. To get there it is necessary to make an arduous four-hour bus journey along a poor road. The beach itself stretches as far as the eye can see and the sea is crystal clear. The area is also very popular with surfers.

Around the island

Nemberala Nemberala (or Dela) village, on the west coast, about 35 km from Ba'a, is close to the main surfing beach and there are a handful of homestays here for the really adventurous surfer. The best months for surfing are reputed to be from April to September. ■ *Getting there: a bus meets the ferry from Kupang at Pante Baru (the port) and takes passengers direct to Nemberala. Alternatively, hire a motorbike in Ba'a.*

Excursions Ndana Island is a tiny island just south of Roti, reportedly home to a wide range of wildlife including a population of turtles. There is also a red lake which, according to legend, is stained by the blood of the people of Ndana who were massacred by a neighbouring tribe. ■ *Getting there: there is not yet a regular ferry service, but a boat can be chartered in Nemberala for about 100,000Rp for up to 6 people.*

Sleeping At Ba'a: **E** *Kesia*, Jl Pabean, restaurant, attached mandi. **E** *Ricky's*, Jl Gereja, near the mosque, some fans, some a/c, attached mandi. **E-F** *Hotel Wisata Karya*, Jl Kartini 1, clean rooms with shared facilities, well priced.

At Nemberala: **B** *Nemberala Beach*, just outside the village on the beach, comfortable place with a/c and satellite TV. **E** *Anugara*, includes all meals which are of an excellent standard, good mosquito nets. The nearest place to the best surf and very popular with surfers. **E** *Mr Thomas Homestay*, room rate includes all meals (and good ones), as well as tea, coffee and drinking water. **E** *Tirosa*, includes all meals, communal mandi, operated by the village headman.

Shopping **Textiles** The Rotinese produce a distinctive ikat, which is strongly influenced by *patola* cloth – Gujarati cloth from India which was imported in large quantities from the 16th century. Patola motifs – floral designs, diagonal crosses – were incorporated into the traditional textiles of the island, as they were through much of Nusa Tenggara. Cloth is often decorated with flower motifs using red, white, brown and black hues. Unfortunately, there are few weavers left on Roti now – many of the local people have left the island, seeking work in Kupang – and it is becoming hard to find good cloth.

Directory **Airline offices** *Merpati* agent on Jl Pabean in Ba'a. **Banks** Not possible to change TCs on Roti, only US$.

Savu (Sabu, Sawu)

Colour map 3a, grid B4 Savu Island, also spelt Sabu and Sawu, lies over 250 km west of Kupang, but is still part of the regency of Kupang. The island covers 460 sq km and supports a population of about 50,000 people, predominantly Protestants. The 'capital' of the island is the town of **Seba**, which has an airport and a dock. The dry season here extends over seven months (April-October), sometimes longer, and the rains are intermittant. It is a dry, barren and unproductive island. Its geographical isolation means that few tourists get here and it is relatively untouched.

Ins and outs

Getting there There is 1 (perhaps 2) flight/week on *Merpati* from Kupang to Seba town (via Roti); the service is unreliable, enquire at *Merpati* office. Boats dock at Seba on the north coast. The *Pelni* vessel *Pangrango* leaves Kupang's Bolok harbour twice a week for Savu, on Tue and Fri (at 1600), returning to Kupang the following day, 8 hrs. Once a week, on Fri, a ferry docks from Waingapu (Sumba), returning to Waingapu and then continuing on to Ende (Flores). There are also other, irregular, departures from Kupang's Tenau harbour.

Background

Traditionally, the slow-growing lontar palm (*Borassus sundaicus*) has met the subsistence needs of the population. The sap from this tree, known as *tuak*, is drunk fresh, made into cakes of red sugar (*gulu merah*), boiled into a sugary syrup (*gula air*) or fermented into palm beer (*iaru*), which can be further distilled to produce a kind of sweet gin known as *sopi*. The fruit of the tree is eaten, its wood is used for boats and houses, and the leaves for thatching. In the past leaves were also spun to make cloth and pulped for paper.

The women of Savu produce a distinct warp ikat cloth. It is said that about 300 years ago the people of Savu were divided into two distinct clans – the Greater Blossoms (*Hubi'Ae*) and the Lesser Blossoms (*Hubi'Ike*) – based on female blood lines. Within each clan there were several sub-groups called Seeds (*Wini*). Each group wove distinctive motifs on their cloth and, even today, local people can recognize cloth and its origin by its clan motif.

Essentials

Sleeping Basic, friendly accommodation in Seba, with little to choose between them. **E** *Makarim Homestay*; **E** *Ongko Da'i Homestay*; **E** *Petykuswan Homestay*.

Shopping **Textiles**: a distinctive warp ikat cloth is hand-woven on Savu, in bands of floral and geometric designs, set against a dark indigo and rust ground. The Savunese sarung is known as the *si hawu*, while the *higi huri* is a blanket. Men's clothing has tended to keep more faithfully to traditional designs, while women have been happy to incorporate western-inspired motifs such as vases of flowers, birds and rampant lions.

10

Maluku

Maluku

882	Ins and outs
882	Ambon
891	Lease Islands
895	Banda Islands
904	Ternate & Tidore
908	Halmahera
910	Southeast Maluku
912	Background

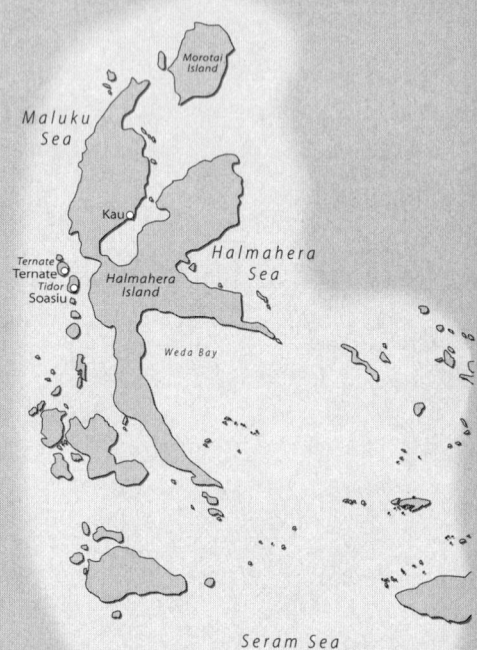

The islands of Maluku are very much at the edge of the Indonesian world, both geographically and economically. But it was the spices of Maluku that initially attracted the European powers to Asia and they became known as the Spice Islands, or Spiceries. It was only here that nutmeg and cloves were cultivated, and the early history of Southeast Asia was moulded and driven by the fabulous wealth that the Spice Islands had to offer the adventurous explorer. But with the decline of the spice trade, so the islands sunk into obscurity. Thousands of kilometres from Jakarta, the Spice Islands were virtually forgotten.

In recent years, Maluku would seem to have found a new raison d'être: tourism. With excellent diving, picture postcard beaches, luxuriant forests and a rich history, the islands seem to have it all. But against these significant pluses has to be set the sheer difficulty of getting around such a fragmented region; it is over 1,000 km from Morotai in the north to Tanimbar in the south; flights are irregular and often over-booked, and while getting around by ship and boat is possible, it is slow. Moreover, the last couple of years have seen outbreaks of communal violence on Ambon, Ternate, Tidore, Halmahera and Banda – hardly good PR for the province's nascent tourist industry.

Ins and outs

Getting there

Air When buying tickets for flights, only pay for one journey at a time – Merpati offices get a commission on each ticket they sell, and the 'down route' agents may refuse to accept a perfectly valid, paid-for ticket. In other words, if travelling Banda-Ambon-Ujung Pandang with a stop-over in Ambon and buying the ticket in Banda, only buy the Banda-Ambon ticket in Banda; buy the Ambon-UPG ticket in Ambon.

Getting around

If making a trip by **bemo**, plan on returning by 1600 as bemos become scarce or non-existent by late afternoon. Always try and ascertain the correct fare on bemos and **prahus** (small public boats) prior to setting out, as it is almost unheard of to be quoted the correct fare by the driver or captain. It is common for drivers to try to get foreign visitors to charter the whole vehicle or vessel.

Conduct Most Malukuns are friendly and generous, and will go out of their way to be helpful. When travelling by boat, foreigners sometimes find themselves being treated as VIPs and offered the Captain's private cabin, or invited to join a family in their private cabin. However, be prepared for the fact that there is no concept of privacy in these parts; there are not that many travellers so expect to be an object of curiosity.

Sights Forts, museums etc usually have a sealed donation box and a visitors' book where tourists sign and note the amount of their donation. How much you give is optional; 1,000Rp is average. The amount will probably have a few zeros added to it afterwards.

Sports Snorkelling and diving: when snorkelling wear shoes, as there are several bottom-dwelling poisonous sea creatures including stone fish, and scorpion fish as well as deadly sea snakes (although the latter's mouth is too small to actually bite a person except at a narrow point like an earlobe, so the threat they pose is small).

Note During 1999 and into 2000, the islands of Maluku saw the worst communal violence since independence. This pitted Christians against Muslims and was particularly serious on Ambon. However, there have also been incidents on Banda, Ternate, Tidore and Halmahera, and possibly elsewhere too. The town of Ambon was severely damaged during the rioting and because we have not been able to update this section of the book since then, the practical information may be wrong in places. Expect hotels, guesthouses and restaurants to have closed and public transport to be less frequent (the latter is also a result of the economic downturn in the country). The same will apply to other areas of the province which have been hit by this upsurge in communal violence.

Ambon

Phone code: 0911
Colour map 5, grid C5

Ambon, or Amboina as it was known during the colonial period, is the capital of the province of Maluku and has a population of 250,000. The island goes by the same name and covers a total of 780 sq km. It is a modern, comparatively prosperous place compared with other parts of the archipelago, and in modernizing, it has lost much of its appeal. The beautiful reddish-brown sago leaf roofs have given way to zinc corrugated roofs (even though the latter do not last as long). The origin of the name, which was in use before the arrival of the Dutch, is not certain; it could be derived from the word Ambwan meaning 'dew', or Nusa Ombong, 'dawn'. Ambon town itself is pleasant enough, although it was heavily bombed during the Second World War, so no old colonial buildings remain.

Maluku highlights

Maluku has huge potential as a tourist destination, with some of the best diving, the finest beaches and the richest forests in Indonesia. But facilities are poorly developed and recent violence has knocked the industry back 10 years or more.

Diving and snorkelling on Banda, Saparua and Seram
Historical monuments of Ternate, Banda and Ambon
Beaches of Saparua, Kai and Ay
National parks of Seram and Halmahera

Ins and outs

For most visitors the only way to get to Ambon is by air. Pattimura airport is 40 km from town. In normal times there are links with Bali and Makassar (Ujung Pandang, Sulawesi) and also with destinations in Irian Jaya. As Maluku's transport hub, there are also flights to many other islands in the province. However, recent communal violence in Ambon and more widely in Maluku has virtually cut the islands off from the rest of the country. Indeed, even before the current political problems, actual flight departures often bore little resemblance to the published timetable. The alternative to flying is to get here by sea and a number of *Pelni* vessels visit Ambon on their routes through the archipelago.

Getting there

Ambon is not a large town. Bemos and becaks are the main forms of transport around town. To travel to other destinations on the island there is a reasonable bus and bemo service (but bear in mind that it likely to have been curtailed because of the current communal violence). Bemos depart from the Mardika terminal at the northern edge of town, while buses leave from the Batu Merah terminal just a few minutes walk further north. **Tourist offices** *Maluku Tourist Office*, Jl Raya Pattimura 1 (in the large offices of the Gubernor Kepala Daerah Tingkat Maluku – ask for the Dinas Pariwisata), open 0830-1430 Mon-Thu, 0830-1130 Fri, 0830-1300 Sat, useful maps and other handouts.

Getting around

As this book went to press, Ambon remained off limits to all but the most persistent. Check the travel advisory pages of the US State department and the UK Foreign and Commonwealth Office for the latest developments.

Safety

Ambon Island

History

For 200 years Ambon was the centre of the clove trade. At the height of the colonial period in the late 1600s, Ambon was called 'Queen of the East' and was more important than Jakarta. Despite this it was not a popular posting due to the very high death rate, and low pay.

Many Ambonese became Christians during colonial times; they looked up to the Dutch and tried to emulate their ways. Even as recently as the 1970s, Ambonese women, who could afford the expense, looked on a trip to Holland as an essential life pilgrimage, and still today some Malukan women aspire to marrying Dutch men in order to live in Holland.

Gradually, the Dutch colonial administration, having taken over control on the demise of the VOC in 1799, began to atone for past Dutch excesses. Schools and hospitals were opened and by the end of the 19th century the Ambonese were among the best educated people in Indonesia. For the Ambonese elite, this led to jobs working for the Dutch colonial administration in Ambon and beyond. Renowned as superb soldiers, many served in the Dutch colonial army in Indonesia. After the Second World War, Ambonese soldiers fought against the Nationalist forces on the side of the Dutch in the Royal Netherlands East Indies Army, or KNIL. Having identified so strongly with the Dutch, they felt they had little in common with the rest of Indonesia, and as independence loomed they attempted to create an independent state incorporating Ambon, the Lease Islands and Seram – Republik Maluku Selatan (RMS) – initially with Dutch backing. (Some notional RMS threat, however unlikely that seems, is the reason given for a request that travellers present their passport to the local police when staying overnight in some villages.)

The RMS were prepared to fight for their independence, but were eventually defeated by Indonesian forces in a guerrilla war that carried on into the 1960s on the island of Seram. About 40,000 Ambonese, mainly ex-soldiers who had fought with the Dutch, escaped to Holland. Conditions were not good for these Malukan exiles and gradually they began to realize that their faith in the Dutch was misplaced. Today most Malukans living in Holland find themselves caught between two worlds, and the Dutch and the Indonesian government are working on a repatriation package for at least some of the 12,500-odd KNIL members and their family members who still remain in Holland. The older Moluccans have never integrated into life in the Netherlands and many still speak only poor Dutch. Their children, by comparison, are more Dutch than Moluccan. The repatriation scheme, generously financed by the Dutch to the tune of 30,000-40,000 guilders per returnee, is targeting these older Moluccans who, so to speak, backed the wrong side in the nationalist struggle. Studies to date have revealed that 20% of returnees die within six months of arriving home, as if waiting to step back on the soil of their ancestors before succumbing to old age.

If you want to know more about the history of this fascinating region, there is a fine collection of archive material and antiquarian books in the library belonging to the Bishop of the Catholic church on Jalan Pattimura. Although not open to the public, if you are genuinely interested and the bishop is not too busy, he will take the time to show you his unique collection.

Culture

In the south of the island the people are mainly Christian, whereas along the north coast many villages, with their long history of contact with Arab traders, retain their Muslim beliefs. The Ambonese are renowned for their energy. They are also great singers and dancers; karaoke bars are springing up everywhere – Friday night seems to be the big night, with singing going on till 0600. Ambon was traditionally a matrilinial society, as was Banda, so the equality of women is a deep-rooted concept. According to Shirley Deane, women were granted equal pay in 1900, 75 years before women in England.

During 1999 Ambon experienced serious **inter-communal violence**. This was sparked, it is said, by a minor confrontation on 19 January when a Muslim passenger tried to steal money from a Christian minibus driver. The driver chased his tormentor into a Muslim neighbourhood. Shortly afterwards rumours began to surface that Muslims were attacking Christians and so the violence escalated. It took four days before order was restored, but not before more than 50 people had been killed and "parts of the seaside city resembled a war zone and 20,000 refugees of both faiths huddled under the protection of security forces" (FEER 4.2.99). There were a number of similar outbreaks of violence later during 1999 which continued into 2000.

Why this corner of Indonesia, which has seen two faiths living side-by-side in comparative harmony, should suddenly descend into such extreme violence has not been clear even to the most seasoned commentators of things Indonesian. Some blamed the economic crisis which pushed people to the edge as they struggled to survive. Others highlighted the loosening of political controls following Suharto's resignation in 1998. This created the conditions in which pent up frustrations could be expressed. More still pointed the finger at mysterious instigators of violence who somehow manipulated the situation for their own political ends. (This latter explanation has also been used to explain inter-communal violence in East Java.)

Ambon town

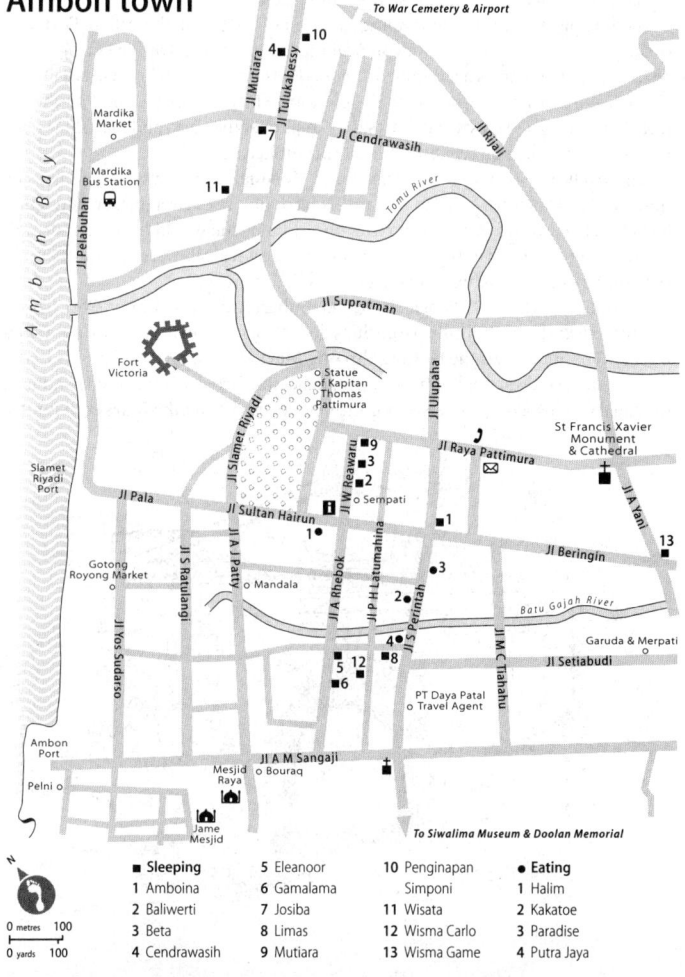

- **Sleeping**
- 1 Amboina
- 2 Baliwerti
- 3 Beta
- 4 Cendrawasih
- 5 Eleanoor
- 6 Gamalama
- 7 Josiba
- 8 Limas
- 9 Mutiara
- 10 Penginapan Simponi
- 11 Wisata
- 12 Wisma Carlo
- 13 Wisma Game

- **Eating**
- 1 Halim
- 2 Kakatoe
- 3 Paradise
- 4 Putra Jaya

Sights

Ambon has more than its fair share of second-rate **heroic monuments**. The most interesting is that of **Saint Francis Xavier**, outside the Catholic Cathedral of St Francis Xavier at Jalan Raya Pattimura 1. The Spanish saint and co-founder of the Jesuit Order stands, bible in hand, on the shore while a crab offers him a crucifix. He visited the Moluccas between 1546 and 1547 and was struck by the volcanic violence of these islands, believing it to be the work of God. He wrote in his journal: "It would seem that as these men have no one to warn them about the punishment of the wicked, God has been pleased as it were to open to them the abode of hell, and give them some pictures of the fires in which sinners are to be forever tormented, so that they may be admonished by that awful sight, and come to understand what punishments will await them unless they abandon their abominable vices and crimes."

Overlooking the stadium and running track is the **statue of Thomas Matulessy** – better known as the liberation hero **Kapitan Thomas Pattimura**. He looks rather like a cartoon pirate in cut-off jeans, wielding an enormous cutlass. He led a group of rebels who besieged and over-ran Fort Duurstede, on the island of Saparua, in 1817, killing the Dutch Resident and his family, bar a baby boy. Pattimura was captured by the Dutch and hanged where his statue now stands.

Also facing onto the stadium is an army base, housed within the walls of **Fort Victoria**, the first of over 40 forts built on Ambon and constructed by the Portuguese in 1575 (when it was known as *Nossa Seinhora da Annonciada*). The guards will only allow visitors to see the gateway to the old fort (which originally stood on the sea front), with its faded crests and fine plaster ships over the apex, and may allow photographs to be taken on request (officially prohibited).

The lovely green-roofed and walled **Jame Mosque**, with its silver dome, is at the northwest edge of town on Jalan AJ Patty. Next door is the newer, bigger, and rather less attractive **Mesjid Raya**. Ordinarily, the old mosque would have been demolished on completion of its replacement, but in this case, locals were so fond of the old structure that it – thankfully – has been allowed to stand.

At the end of Jalan AM Sangaji is the **Pelabuhan Ambon** – Ambon Port. This is where the *Pelni* liners and other large ships dock. Not far from the port, on both sides of Jalan Yos Sudarso, is the **Gotong Royong Market** – both a food (seaward side) and general (landward side) market, with delicious barbecued fresh tuna and fruit on sale. Walking along the seafront is the new covered **Mardika Market**. It is most

Gateway to Fort Victoria, Ambon

enjoyable in the morning, when fresh fish is on sale and fishing boats sell their night's catch along the promenade. This is also the central bus terminal.

The **Siwalima Museum** is 2½ km southwest of town at Taman Makmur. Established in 1973, it is primarily an ethnographic collection with carved boats, ancestor figures, musical instruments and textiles. ■ *Open 0800-1400 Tue-Thu, 0800-1100 Fri, 0800-1300 Sat-Sun. Getting there: bus from the Mardika terminal for Amahusu (ask for 'musium').*

About 2 km northeast of the town centre, on **Karang Panjang Hill**, is the statue of 19-year-old **Marta Tiahahu**, a Christian Ambonese who gazes, spear in hand, over Ambon city and bay. When her father, who was leading a rebellion against the Dutch, was captured and imprisoned, she took up the fight on Nusa Laut. Eventually captured herself, Marta was told of her father's execution while she was being taken to Java and starved herself to death. She was buried at sea on 2 January 1818. Get there by bus, or on foot. The **Doolan Memorial** is on Jalan Dr Kayadou in Kudamati (just past the Rehoboth Church), at the southwest edge of town. This simple monument commemorates an Australian soldier who provided covering fire for retreating comrades. He was only killed by the Japanese after tenacious resistance, and his body was spirited away by local Ambonese and buried beneath a gandaria tree on this spot.

Excursions

Soya, a village with strong traditions of adat (see page 913 and page 835) and magic, is a pleasant outing from Ambon town. Catch a bemo, marked 'Soya', at the bemo stand for the 20 minutes ride up into the hills overlooking the town and bay. Alighting from the bemo the path to the top of Gunung Sirimau is signposted, a 20-minute walk. At 700m the path reaches the sacred site, a stone throne facing a panoramic view out over the bay. Behind the throne, follow a short path up the hill to the 'tempayan setan', a clay urn containing water which never dries up, even during the dry season. Local people come here in search of cures, good luck and a marriage partner. A concrete pillbox, a remnant from the Second World War, can be found about 15m further along the path going away from Soya, along with a trench dug by the Dutch. Visitors fortunate to be in Ambon on the second Friday in December should try to visit Soya for the ceremony of 'Cuci Negeri', an annual ritual practised in many villages to purify the village of evil spirits, an example of adat traditions which are still practised. It also serves as an annual 'spring cleaning' when houses and village are given a thorough clean. The walk back down the hill into Ambon takes just over an hour past a church built by the Portuguese in 1817, a former baileo (meeting place) surrounded by ceremonial stones, and through villages with attractive local houses. There are alternative scenic walks from Soya, continuing in the opposite direction to Ambon, through the villages of Hatalai and Naku to the coast at Hukarila.

The Australian War Cemetery lies 5 km northeast of town. Immaculately maintained, 2,000 Australian, British, Canadian, Dutch and US servicemen who fought and died during the Second World War are buried here. ■ *Getting there: bus to Tantui.*

Ambon's beaches are not the best. Most of the reefs have been destroyed or seriously degraded by dynamite fishing, or killed by pollution, and the more accessible are busy at weekends. **Natsepa Beach** at Baguala Bay is 14 km northeast of town, and one of the most popular. **Sleeping A+** *Maulana Hotel* at Waitatiri, Jalan Raya Passo, Waitatiri, T61466/61468, F61497 (near Natsepa Beach, to get there take a bemo to Natsepa, and ask the driver to let you off at Waitatiri). This sister hotel to the *Maulana* on Banda Island has a/c rooms with satellite TV, a restaurant serving Indonesian, Chinese and European food, a freshwater swimming pool, which is open to non-guests for a fee of 5,000Rp. Boats are also available for diving and fishing. Losmen accommodation is also available. ■ *Getting there: bus from the Mardika* terminal bound for Suli. **Amahusu Beach** is 7 km southwest of town. The reef here is depressingly degraded. This spot is the finish line for the annual Darwin-Ambon yacht race. Hotel accommodation available. ■ *Getting there: bus from the Mardika terminal.* Finally, **Namalatu Beach** is 15 km from town, southwest from Amahusu, at the tip of this arm of Ambon Island. Snorkelling is reasonable here, but there is no sand. **Sleeping B** *Lelisa Beach*, a/c, and some losmen. The best of the cheaper places to stay are (**E**) *Ibu Eta's*, a house with use of the owner's own kitchen and (**D**) *Marthin Latuhihin's Place*, a very friendly place with great views over the ocean and just two clean rooms and attached mandi, breakfast included. ■ *Getting there: by bus bound for Latuhalat from the Mardika terminal.*

Waai, 31 km northeast of town, past Tulehu, possesses one of the strangest sights on Ambon: a pool of sacred eels. Waai has strong adat traditions and ancient myths surround its famed eels. The eels live in a pool, fed by clear spring water from a 50m-high waterfall. These days the eels are fed eggs to bring them into view, but in former times they rarely appeared and it was considered a sign of good fortune to see them – any wish would come true following a sight of them. The villagers believe that if the sacred eels and sacred fish disappear, disaster will strike. ■ *Getting there: by bemo from the Mardika terminal.*

Pombo Island is situated just off Ambon's northeast coast (10 minutes by boat). The surrounding waters are said by locals to offer the best snorkelling and swimming. The island is a national park and there are PHPA bungalows which visitors can use with prior booking (see 'Useful addresses' for PHPA Office address). ■ *Getting there: boats to Pombo can be chartered at a daily rate from Tulehu, Waai, Honimua and Liang. Buses to all 4 towns leave from the Mardika terminal.*

Hila is a village on the north coast with a charming old Dutch church, the oldest still standing on Ambon, built in 1780, with an inscription in Dutch carved into the stone. Nearby are the ruins of Fort Amsterdam, built on the site of a former Portuguese fort. ■ *Getting there: by bemo.*

Tours *Daya Patal Tours Sights Travel* operate a range of tours around the island (US$50-60 per day); *Natrabu* also run tours.

Essentials

Sleeping

NB1 The violence of 1999 & 2000 saw the looting & burning of large areas of downtown Ambon; the following hotels were reviewed before the violence

NB2 During the Darwin-Ambon yacht race (Jul), hotels are booked-up. Most rates quoted include breakfast

A *Manise*, Jl WR Supratman 1, T54144, F41054. A/c, standard rooms are windowless, superior rooms are OK, with restaurant serving decent Western food. **A-B** *Amboina*, Jl Kapt Ulupaha 5A, T41725/41961/41641/41712/Hunting 55515, F53354/55723, Reservations T55624. A/c, overpriced, even the most expensive rooms have slightly tatty cord carpets. Long-term residents qualify for a substantial discount, standard double has a shower, the deluxe room has a bathtub, prices are very negotiable, a businessman's hotel, with Conference Room, shops, restaurant and bar, 24-hr room service, laundry etc, credit cards accepted.

B-C *Baliwerti Hotel*, Jl Wim Reawaru 9, T55996. A/c, restaurant, fairly new with very attractive decor, rooms have colour TV, bathrooms with hot water. Recommended. **B** *Cendrawasih*, Jl Tulukabessy 39, T52487, F53373. A/c, hot water, on edge of town, comfortable. **B** *Mutiara*, Jl Raya Pattimura 90, T97124/53075. A/c, well-run, clean and modern rooms. **B-C** *Josiba*, Jl Tulukabessy 27, T41280. On the edge of town, rooms rather shabby and overpriced. **B-C** *Wisata*, Jl Mutiara SK 1/3-15 No 67, T53567, F53592. A/c, hot water, on edge of town in a quiet alley, friendly, rooms rather like ships' cabins with hotch-potch of furniture and fittings. **C** *Eleanoor*, Jl Anthone Rhebok 30, T52834. Some a/c, not very good value, rooms seemed a bit dingy but positioned on quiet street. **C** *Limas Hotel*, Jl Kamboja 16, T53269. Some a/c, full size bathtub in more expensive rooms, cheaper fan rooms with attached shower, breakfast and afternoon tea included, rather run-down. **C** *Penginapan Simponi*, Jl Tulukabessy 46, T54305. Some a/c, on edge of town, clean but no windows. **C** *Wisma Carlo*, Jl Philip Latumahina 24A, T42520. Some a/c, small hotel, modern rooms with attached mandi set around a courtyard, but not as good value as other equivalent hotels, rates include tax, breakfast and afternoon tea.

D *Beta Guesthouse*, Jl Wim Reawaru 114, T53463. The *Beta* is an outstanding guesthouse and an invaluable source of travellers' information. Owners are very friendly, the wife in particular speaks excellent English. Rooms are simple but clean, with attached mandi, and fans. The hotel is on 3 floors, with a pleasant verandah running outside all the rooms, at the entrance is a seating area with satellite TV (CNN news available for the homesick), bar with iced beer, price includes breakfast and an afternoon snack. Highly recommended. **D** *Gamalama*, Jl Anthone Rhebok 11, T53724. Bare rooms, attached mandi, reasonable place to stay and popular. **D-E** *Wisma Game*, Jl Jend A Yani 12, T53525. Small rooms, we have received good reports about this hotel, all rooms with private mandi, clean, balconies, early morning aerobics class next door might be a problem.

Eating

Good Indonesian food served from small warungs along Jl Said Perintah, Try the *Putra Jaya* at No 38 with 2 white cockatoos on perches outside, good nasi goreng and mie goreng. Also recommended on this road are *Roda Baru* (Padang food) at No 42, *Sonata* at No 92 and *Paradise* (good nasi campur). There are also restaurants selling cheap, tasty dishes near the mosque on Jl Sultan Babullah.

Black dog is a great delicacy for Ambonese Christians; it is said to taste much better than white dog

Mid-range *Halim*, Jl Sultan Hairun, seafood specialities, but food generally rather bland and, overall, disappointing. **Cheap** *Asri*, Jl WR Supratman (next to *Manise Hotel*), Indonesian food in spotless restaurant. *Kakatoe*, Jl Said Perintha 20, T56142. Belgian chef, specializing in European food, good food including breakfast, a meeting place for foreigners with a useful message board and book exchange, attractive garden setting. Recommended. *Amboina*, Jl AJ Patty 63, bakery and ice cream. *Utama*, Jl Setiabudi 58, good seafood, Chinese, dog sometimes served.

Entertainment

Dance: there are a number of dances characteristic of Maluku; unfortunately it is rare to find them being performed in 'authentic' surroundings. The oddest is the *Bambu Gila* or Crazy Bamboo dance. The Maluku tourist office provides an enlightening description of the dance: '...it is a performance using a bamboo-pole, held by 7 young strong men. In using supernatural powers, the bamboo begin to move, while still held, and at a sudden moment, it throw down the men'. More interesting is the Cakalele (Chakalaylee), a war dance which features dancers wearing headgear inspired by the helmets of Portuguese soldiers.

Festivals

Jul Darwin-Ambon yacht race, first contested in 1976, the race is over a distance of more than 1,000 km.

Shopping

The main shopping street is Jl AJ Patty. There are a number of souvenir shops here selling pearls, silver, shell collages, shell lamps, jewellery and tortoise shell. Bargain hard. **Books**: *Dian Pertiwi*, Jl Diponegoro 25 – for 2 books on the histories of Banda and Ternate/Tidore by Willard Hanna, shop closes at 1500, reopens 1700.

Sport

Diving Not very well developed around Ambon (compared to, say, Manado) as most of the coral has been destroyed to make cement for buildings and roads. In Ambon Bay spots include Eri, Silale and Tanjung Setan (Ghost Cape – good drop-offs here); around Saparua Island (east of Ambon) at Itawaka and Kulor, and at Tiga Island. But the best dive spot is off Amet on Nusa Laut Island (*Mahu Diving Lodge* offers dives here, 1 hr by boat from Mahu on Saparua Island). Rates are approximately US$70 per person per day (2 tanks, ie 2 dives). Oct and Nov are the best months – the seas are calmest. Rates are approximately US$200 for 3 days, US$675 for 7 days.

Tour operators

One of the best is *Daya Patal*, Jl Said Perintah 27A, T53344, F53287, open 0800-1800 Mon-Sat, 0800-1400 Sun. The manager Karolis Anaktototy is very helpful and speaks excellent English. They offer a variety of tours and can also put together tailor-made packages, eg

5 days *Spice Island Tour* featuring Ambon, Saparua and Seram; *Banda Tour* (3 nights). They can also arrange diving holidays at the Mahu Diving Lodge on Saparua. High season for tourism is Aug-Oct. Other agents include **Natrabu**, Jl Rijali 53, T2593, F3537; **Netral Jaya**, Jl Diponegoro 76.

Transport **Local Bejaks**: there are so many that different colours denote those which are allowed to operate on certain days; yellow (Wed, Sat), red (Tue, Fri) and white (Mon, Thu). A ride should cost about 1,000Rp. **Bemos and buses**: link most places on Ambon Island with the capital. The central Mardika terminal is next to the market of the same name, on the seafront, 1 km northeast of town. In town, bemos take 1 of 5 routes or 'lines', all beginning and ending at the Mardika terminal. **Taxis**: unmetered, can be hired for specific trips or by the hour or half-day. Taxi 'ranks' at the intersection of Jl Setiabudi and Jl Said Perintah, and near the Gotong Royong market on Jl Pala/Slamet Riyadi (at the end of Jl Dr Sam Ratulangi). Taxis also wait outside the bigger hotels.

Air Ambon's Pattimura airport is only a few kilometres northwest of town as the crow flies, but over 40 km by road. Regular connection on Merpati (CASA-designed planes made outside Bandung, Java) with Banda and on Sat via Seram (see 'Transport' in Banda section for more details on the difficulties of getting to and from Banda). **Transport to town**: Ancient taxis cost 25,000Rp. A much cheaper alternative is to catch a bus from just outside the airport to Poka, 14 km; from here, there are ferries across Ambon Bay to Gelala, where bemos wait to whisk passengers the final 5 km into town. Going from town to the airport, catch a bemo to Gelala, take the ferry, and then board another bemo from Poka, bound for Laha. **NB** Sempati and Mandala both offer a free bus service to the airport – useful for early morning flights. *Airport facilities*: includes a useful tourist information desk (usually open when flights arrive). Ambon is Maluku's air transport hub with regular connections to Biak, Ternate, Banda, Ujung Pandang, Sorong, Langgur, Manado and Jayapura. Less frequent services to Amahai, Labuha, Langgur, Mangole, Namlea, Sanana and Saumlaki.

Road Bus: see local transport.

Sea Boat: larger ships dock at the Pelabuhan Ambon, near the centre of town, at the intersection of Jl Yos Sudarso and Jl AM Sangaji. Some shipping companies have their offices in the port complex; *Pelni*'s office is on Jl Supratman. The *Pelni* ships *Rinjani*, *Tatamailau*, *Dobonsolo*, *Bukit Singuntang* and *Lambelo* leave for other destinations in Maluku, and for Sulawesi, Java and Irian Jaya (see route schedule, page 988). Smaller vessels use the Pelabuhan Slamet Riyadi at the end of Jl Pala near the Gotong Royong market, and leave for Banda (1 night), Seram Utara (Wahai – 18 hrs), Seram Timur, Irian Jaya and other ports. Boats also leave daily for Seram, Saparua and Haruku from Hurnala Port, Tulehu, on Ambon's west coast. For Saparua, boats leave twice daily at 0900 and 1300, 2 hrs (a very pleasant journey); there are also speedboats to Saparua, which depart when full, 1 hr. **NB** The speedboats leave from a different pier to the regular ferries. Boats for Seram from Tulehu leave daily at 1000. *Getting there*: bus from the Mardika terminal (30 mins).

Directory **Airline offices** *Bouraq*, Jl Sultan Babullah 19, T52314, open 0800-1700 Mon-Sat. *Mandala*, Jl AJ Patty 19, T45995, F42377 (for Ujung Pandang, Jakarta and Surabaya), open 0800-1800 Mon-Sat, 0800-1400 Sun. *Merpati/Garuda*, Jl Jend A Yani 19, T52481, open 0800-1700 Mon-Fri, 0800-1500 Sat, 1000-1500 Sun. **Banks** *Bank Central Asia*, Jl Sultan Hairun 24; *Bank Dagang Negara*, Jl Raya Pattimura; *BNI*, Jl Said Perintah; *Danamon*, Jl Diponegoro; *Ekspor Impor*, Jl Raya Pattimura 14. **Communications** General Post Office: Jl Raya Pattimura 20. *Perumtel*: Jl Raya Pattimura 11. Another office has opened on Jl Dr JB Sitanala. **Useful addresses** *Immigration Office*: Jl Dr Kayadoe 48A, T3066. *PHPA*: Jl Tantui (near the Australian War Cemetery outside town), T41189.

Lease Islands

To the east of Ambon are a collection of other, less frequently visited, islands – Saparua, Haruku and Nusa Laut – collectively known as the Lease Islands. The beaches here are much better than they are on Ambon and there is also some good diving. Relatively easy accessibility from Ambon, they make a nifty getaway.

Colour map 5, grid C5

Saparua

With a population of 50,000 and a fairly well developed infrastructure, Saparua offers good beaches, snorkelling and diving. This was the island where Kapitan Pattimura led his rebellion against the Dutch (see page 886).

Phone code: 0931

Saparua town is the capital of Saparua and is a very relaxed place. Traditional houses made of coconut and sago palm, or entirely of sago palm, with their beautiful rust-red roofs, are interspersed between old Dutch houses, cemeteries and several rather grand churches. Many of the houses have gardens full of colourful shrubs and flowers. Walking through the streets at night provides the nosy (to be fair, though, privacy is not a concept much in evidence in these parts) with the opportunity to gaze into people's homes to see the interesting collections of ornaments and memorabilia, many of Dutch origin – a huge tapestry of windmills and tulips, for example, carefully handed down from generation to generation. In November the early arrival of the Christmas decorations provides yet more colour.

Even along the main street there are cloves drying on mats in the sun, scenting the air with a wonderful aroma. The green plump cloves are newly picked and by the end of the first day will have acquired a reddish tinge; at nightfall of the second day they will have turned brown but still be fairly plump; by the end of their final day (the process takes 3-7 days) they will be brown and shrivelled.

Fort Duurstede, on the edge of town, has been partially restored with commanding views over two bays. The latrine area and mandi are still standing (note the drainage system). Several of the sentry positions still have their cannon. Below are the remains of the 16th century pier, built by the Portuguese.

Sights

Saparua town holds a **colourful market** on Wednesday and Saturday, selling excellent local smoked fish, huge cones of red palm sugar and sago pulp, and some curious, unrecognizable produce. People from the surrounding islands come here to sell their goods.

Climbing the hill outside town in the late afternoon offers the best views of the sunset. In 1817 the famous Malukan Independence leader, Pattimura, in an ultimately unsuccessful attempt to rid the area of the Dutch presence (inspired by his experience of the rather more honourable colonial conduct of the British during their brief period of occupation during the Napoleonic wars), took control of Fort Duurstede; he marched the captured Dutch soldiers to the top of this hill and slaughtered them at sunset; he then had them buried here. No wonder the hill is reputed to be haunted.

Saparua has **beaches** which are far superior to those found on Ambon. **Waisisil** is one with white sand and good snorkelling. At present there is no accommodation but it is roughly midway between Saparua town and Siri Sore, both of which have good accommodation; many bemos go in this direction. **Kulor**, in the northwest of the island, has one of the best beaches. There is only one bemo a day at present from Saparua town, which leaves in the afternoon; otherwise you have to charter. At the end of 1995 some new accommodation was due to open at Kulor. Check in town for latest information. But perhaps the best place to stay on Saparua is on the beach south of **Ouw** at *Nukahoni* (see 'Sleeping' for more details). The **village of Ouw** is also a worthwhile excursion from Saparua town. Ouw is locally renowned for its **pottery**. Attractive utilitarian pieces are made in great quantities, and used to store and carry water, make sago, and so on. The pots are used all over the island, and the

Excursions

production process can be seen at any one of numerous potteries. Other sights in Ouw include the cannon outside the Raja's new, and rather imposing, house; the mural on the wall in the Sunday School; and the old 'fort' which once had 99 windows, but is now being hastened into ruin by the local people who use it as a source of building material. In her book *Ambon: island of spices*, Shirley Deane writes that "Ulath and Ouw – one town geographically, with only a narrow street dividing them – but considering themselves so very much two villages that every year one side attacks the other (for some reason now lost in the shadows of the past). That year (1972) five men had been killed in the fighting." This antagonism is itself, it seems, now a thing of the past too. ■ *Getting there: there are regular bemos from Saparua town that pass through Ouw.*

Essentials

Sleeping **Saparua town C-E** *Lease Indah*, Jl Benteng Duurstede, T21105. The hotel has recently expanded with 10 new a/c rooms and 5 fan rooms, all clean and attractively decorated, the 4 older rooms with shared mandi are much inferior, but considerably cheaper. Many rooms have their own private verandah overlooking an attractive courtyard. Price includes breakfast and afternoon tea, often freshly cooked *pisang goreng*. The hotel is situated overlooking the bay next to Fort Duurstede and a remarkably quiet mosque. In a corner of the courtyard there is a small concrete tank with 5 baby crocodiles (being kept for their skins). Highly recommended.

Beyond the main town A-B *Mahu Diving Lodge* (formerly *Mahu Village Resort*), T53344, F54127. The main reason to stay here is for the diving. The hotel has no beach, the rooms are overpriced and there is a slightly unkempt feel to the resort. All meals included in rates. *PT Daya Patal Travel Agent* in Ambon runs tours here (see Ambon section), though it is easy enough to travel independently. **D** *Sire Sore Losmen* in Sire Sore village, well-run, caters to Dutch tour groups for whom they put on Malukan 'cultural evenings', rooms with fan and private mandi, excellent breakfast, very clean, restaurant. There is nowhere else to eat in the village.

Nusa Laut and Haruku No accommodation, but some homestays.

Ouw D-E *Nukahoni*, 8 attractively furnished but simple rooms with private mandi and shower. Rates include 3 meals, tea, coffee and biscuits all day. Diving is available at roughly 80,000Rp for 2 people, and the owners take residents to their `secret' dive site, a submerged village. It is also possible to go fishing at night, and there is reasonable snorkelling in front of the bungalows. Arnold, the Dutch co-owner, works here between Nov and Jan and is a mine of information. His wife's grandfather is the Raja of Ouw and her brother is co-owner of the bungalows. In front of the main house are 2 ancestor stones – this is ancestral land and the owners had to propitiate the ancestors before building. Highly recommended. To get to this place, take a bemo to Ouw, get off at the bus stop near the start of the village opposite the smaller of the 2 churches (Gereja Pantekosta Jemaat Ouw), and ask for Samalata – everyone knows him. You will then be taken by small boat, or dug out canoe, round the headland to a clearing in the jungle opposite Nusa Laut Island (20-min boat ride). There is good diving and snorkelling here, and a reasonable beach.

Eating *Citra* in bus station, good beef rendang; *ACC Dua* and *RM Andalas* also both serve good food and are friendly places to eat.

Sports **Diving** There is excellent diving off Saparua. The *Mahu Diving Lodge* at Mahu is the largest and most developed outfit, with the greatest range of amenities. However, perhaps the best ambience, accommodation and diving – if more basic conditions are being sought – is at *Nukahoni* near Ouw. See 'Sleeping' for details. **Boat hire**: to go snorkelling etc off Nusa Laut, ask at your accommodation for Francis. John, who meets the boats at Haria and the bemos at the bus station in Saparua town, and speaks good English, may also be able to help.

Transport

Local Bemos: to all points on the island, depart throughout the day from the bus terminal in town. Check the fare in advance: drivers may get you to charter the whole vehicle. Most points on Saparua are within 10 km of town, so missing the last bemo is not a disaster – it is possible to walk back. Distances: Haria-Saparua, 5 km; Sire Sore, 6 km; Booi, 4 km; Mahu, 7 km; Ouw, 10 km.

Sea Boats/ferries: boats to Haria on Saparua (2 hrs) leave daily from Liang on Ambon's northeast coast (get there by bus from the Mardika terminal). The dock at Haria is 5 km from Saparua town. Boats for Pelauw, on Haruku, also leave from Liang. There are boats from Haria to Nusa Laut. Two ferries daily from Haria to Tulehu on Ambon at 0900 and 1300, very pleasant 2 hrs crossing on uncrowded boat. Also speedboats which leave when full, taking 1 hr, 5,000Rp (inconveniently, speedboats leave from a different pier, so decide in advance which type of boat to take). Three ferries a week to Amahai on Seram, Mon, Wed, Fri, check times. Market days are a good time to visit the surrounding islands as boats run frequently from Haria.

Directory

Communications There is a Post Office and Telecommunications centre, but no banks.

Seram

Phone code: 0914
Colour map 5, grid B5/6

Seram is the largest island in Maluku with a land area of 18,400 sq km, and the most mysterious. Its densely wooded, mountainous (though non-volcanic) interior is difficult to get to and harbours animist tribal peoples whose traditional lifestyles remain remarkably intact: up to 75% of the population are animists. The Nuaula were renowned warriors and headhunters. The Bonfia, living in eastern Seram, are – by contrast – shy and peaceful. A land of myth and superstition, Ambonese refer to Seram as the 'Nusa Ina' (Mother Island). They believe they came from here and it is here that Ambonese adat originated. Even today the island elicits both fear and respect from the worldly Ambonese.

Ins and outs

Getting there

There are 2 flights a week to Amahai (Masohi) from Ambon; this is the Ambon-Banda flight which transits Seram out and back. Return flights will have the usual problems associated with getting back from Banda (see 'Transport', Banda). There is also 1 flight a week between Ambon and Wahai, but it is unreliable so don't count on it. Numerous boats leave for various destinations on Seram from various points on Ambon. For Amahai/Masohi there are 4 daily express boats from Hurnala Port in Tulehu, Ambon, leaving at 0800, 1100, 1400 and 1700, 1½ hrs. There are less regular boats from Pelabuhan Slamet Riyadi in Ambon town to both Amahai and Wahai, 18 hrs. Ferries leave daily from Liang (north coast of Ambon) to Kairatu, 2 hrs, another from Hitu (also on Ambon's north coast) to Piru, 4 hrs, and there are also said to be boat connections from Ambon's Honimua Beach to Seram. It is possible to buy combination bus/ferry/bus tickets in Ambon which take the worry out of making connections.

Getting around

The island lies to the northeast of Ambon and, in size at least, dominates its smaller neighbour. The easiest way to explore the island is to charter a bemo for the day. The capital Masohi is situated on the south coast. The port is known as Amahai, where there is also the main bus terminal. Buses loop around the western half of the island and there are regular bemo connections between Masohi and Amahai. The island's second town, Wahai, is on the north coast and there are no bus connections between the 2. To get to Wahai from Masohi, catch a bus from the terminal in Amahai to Saka, and then a speedboat to Wahai. Most local boats, which hug the coast as they travel from village to village, leave from Saka on the north coast.

Background

Seram was viewed as a land of mystery and magic, whose peoples had strange, often frightening, powers. There are many legends connected with Seram, stories of witches and witchcraft, people who could fly or make themselves invisible. In the remote interior, headhunting persisted into this century. During colonial times the Dutch found these tribes among the most troublesome and difficult to control. Since colonial times the government has found it expedient to enforce resettlement programmes. First by moving inland tribal peoples to the coast to make them easier to control, and more recently, moving people from the Lease Islands to relieve population pressure there.

Sights

Mount Binaiya – also known as Mount Manusela – is the highest peak in Maluku at 3,019m. There are several other mountains that exceed 2,000m on the island. Spectacular waterfalls, rivers big enough to raft down and dense tropical forest are all features of the island. During the rainy season, trees across roads and landslides make travelling by road difficult. To get to Wahai from Masohi, travel by bemo to Saka, on the north coast (2-3 hours), and from here take a speed boat to Wahai (2-3 hours).

Superb **snorkelling** is to be found in a lagoon off an isolated small beach, 15 minutes walk over rocks from the big beach at *Suamadaha*. There is a warm spring running into the bay and a wreck in the lagoon can easily be seen when snorkelling.

Manusela National Park, covering a 1,890 sq km swathe of forest from Seram's north coast to south coast and including Mount Manusela, is Maluku's most important protected area. Many people who visit Seram do so to trek through the park. It supports a remarkably varied flora and fauna, which is relatively well recorded as the park was selected as a research site for an Operation Raleigh expedition. The bird life is particularly rich, and it is also famous for its huge butterflies, including the spectacular *Papilio ulysses*. Visitors are recommended to take a guide, and to obtain a permit and/or advice from the PHPA office at Air Besar, 2 km east of Wahai, or from the PHPA office in Ambon. Visitors have gone missing in this wild area, and are presumed to have died. There is no accommodation in the park. Hikers need to be fit for this arduous trek, and to take all supplies. When trekking in Seram, it is essential to contact the village head, or *Bapak Raja*, to ensure your safety as you pass through each area. The trek through the Manusela reserve takes several days. Hiring porters presents its own problems. Due to local adat laws, porters must be changed at each village; if they do not wish to continue, trekkers have no choice but to wait with them. Days also tend to get shorter than originally agreed. In short, be prepared and be patient.

Tours There are few English speakers on Seram. John Lisapeli at the *Kantor Pariwisata* **tourist office**, Jl Imam Bonjol, T21462, speaks good English and is knowledgeable about the Nuaulu people. He can take visitors to see the Nuaulu tribes. (Take a red scarf and tobacco as gifts; the red scarf has replaced the severed head in traditional adat ceremonies and rituals of these former headhunters, red being the colour of blood.) He can arrange tours to Bonara, Watane and Sepa, all Nuaulu villages. The cost is about 25,000Rp for the guide and 35,000Rp for transport.

Essentials

Sleeping There are no good hotels on Seram, but a number of adequate losmen, some with a/c. Most are found in the capital, Masohi. Most are in our **C-E** range. **Masohi C-D** *Nusantara*, Jl Abd Soulisa 15, T21339. Some a/c, good central position. **D** *Sri Lestari*, Jl Abd Soulisa 5, T21178, rooms are fine here. **E** *Nusa Ina*, Jl Banda 9, T21221. Quiet place with clean rooms, well priced compared with the competition. **Wahai D** *Sinar Indah*, T255. Rooms here, with shared mandi, are fine. **E** *Taman Baru*, T222. Shared mandi, meals provided if ordered in advance. **Tehoru D** *Susi*.

Festivals **Mar** Once a year, usually in Mar, sea worms come ashore to breed, near Ouw. They are collected by local people and eaten, fried with chillies.

Banda Islands

The nine tiny and beautiful islands that constitute the Banda archipelago lie southeast of Ambon and cover a combined area of only 60 sq km. The capital Bandaneira is on the island of the same name (but spelt as two words, Banda Neira), separated from the active volcano Mount Api by a strait just a few hundred metres across. It has a superb setting, facing the lagoon formed by the crater of an extinct volcano and dominated by the imposing presence of Gunung Api, with its near perfect cone and constant plume of smoke. The largest island in the group is Banda Besar (literally 'Big Banda') or Lontar, to the south of Banda Neira, while the smaller islands of Pulau Ai and Run to the west, and Pulau Rozengain to the east, make up this microscopic archipelago. The island of Ai was occupied by the British, but was eventually handed back to the Dutch under the Anglo Dutch Treaty (1924) in exchange for Mahattan Island, New York.

Phone code: 0910
Colour map 5, grid C6

Background

The Bandas were 'discovered' by the Portuguese in 1512 in their search for spices, and as they were the only source of nutmeg and mace, brought vast profits to those able to control production and trade (see box). The nutmeg tree, *Myristica fragrans*, was for the Bandas the source of its wealth and the reason for its destruction (for background to the nutmeg and its role in the history of the Bandas, see page 912). Banda's nutmegs are still reputed to be the best in the world. In the Bandas, the outer fruit is also used to make delicious jams and drinks.

Thrust into obscurity with the fall in nutmeg prices in the early 19th century, the Bandas are now beginning to benefit from a new industry: tourism. With excellent game fishing, superb snorkelling and diving, and a rich history, the islands have considerable potential. It is hoped that the development of tourism and fishing can arrest the depopulation of the islands – between 1971 and 1980 the population declined from 13,368 to 12,635.

Banda Neira

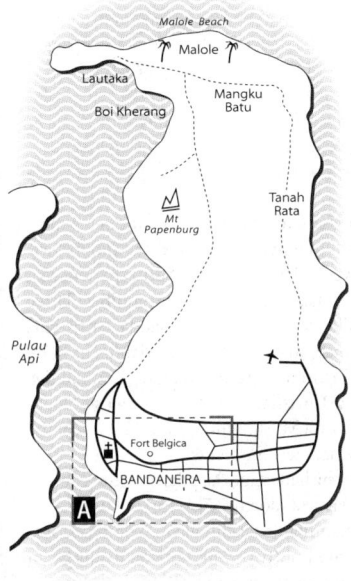

Des Alwi, who owns the two most expensive hotels on Banda Neira and has a monopoly on diving, is the latterday king of the Bandas. It does not take long for a visitor to realize that little happens here without his involvement, or at least his consent. There are essentially two conflicting views as to his role in the development of the Bandas. One has it that the Bandas are Des Alwi's play thing; that his autocratic and domineering presence casts a shadow over the archipelago much as Gunung Api does. He is reputed to have closed down homestays that do not toe his line, and he controls diving hereabouts. The other view maintains that if it was not for Des Alwi the Bandas would still be languishing in obscurity. Des Alwi has been engaged in talks with the Aman resort group – which build possibly the most luxurious hotels in the world – to construct a 20-room hotel on Banda (although it will probably be a 'down market' version).

Related map:
A Banda Neira,
page 898

Butchery in the Bandas: the curse of the spice trade

The Banda Islands' experience of colonialism is a case study in the excesses, inequities, inadequacies and inefficiencies of Dutch rule in Indonesia. The tiny size of the Bandas belies their former economic significance. These were the famous Spiceries of the East, on which Europeans depended for nutmeg and mace to flavour an otherwise monotonous diet. The first Europeans to arrive here were the Portuguese, under the captainship of Antonio de Abreu who landed on Banda in early 1512. The first Dutch vessel did not arrive until 1599, and the English landed in 1601.

The arrival of the Dutch coincided with increased activity from the volcano Mount Api, a portent – and taken as such by the Bandanese – of what was to follow. The Dutch established trading posts (known as logies) and proceeded to buy nutmeg and mace. Profits were vast: the spices were purchased at 1/320th of the price they realized in Amsterdam. From 1602, the Dutch presence in the Bandas was financed and administered by the VOC (Vereenigde Oost-indische Compagnie) or the United East India Company.

The appalling Dutch treatment of the local population can be traced back to 1609 when Admiral Verhoeven attempted to negotiate without a sufficiently large guard; he and 26 other Dutchmen were slaughtered by the Bandanese. This 'treachery' was not to be forgotten. In 1621 the new VOC governor-general Jan Pieterszoon Coen sailed for Banda with a large force to deal, once and for all, with the duplicitous locals. He forced a one-sided treaty upon the Orang Kaya (the rich men or chiefs), and when they failed to keep their side of the agreement proceeded to depopulate the islands. Many Bandanese were captured and shipped to Batavia to be sold into slavery, others committed suicide by throwing themselves from cliffs. Of a population of 15,000, only 1,000 remained – and most of these on the English controlled islands of Pulau Ai and Pulau Run. The 44 Orang Kaya faced a particularly vile fate, which even Dutchmen in Holland felt was beyond the realms of acceptable, civilized behaviour. The historian Willard Hanna quotes an eyewitness, Naval Lieutenant Nicolas van Waert:

"The condemned victims being brought within the [Fort Nassau] enclosure, six Japanese [mercenary] soldiers were also ordered inside, and with their sharp swords they beheaded and quartered the eight chief orang kaya and then beheaded and quartered the 36 others. Their execution was awful to see. ... All of us, as professing Christians, were filled with dismay at the way the affair was brought to a conclusion, and we took no pleasure in such dealings."

Having disposed of the Bandanese, Coen had to find a way to maintain spice production. He chose to colonize the islands

While Des Alwi does receive some bad press for his at times autocratic behaviour, 1999 revealed him to be something of a hero. In January the island of Ambon, several hundred kilometres away to the northwest across the Banda Sea, experienced a serious outbreak of violence between its Christian and Muslim communities. Three months later, in late April, it sparked a similar confrontation on Banda. Christians are said to have murdered a young Muslim man on a neighbouring island. His body was brought back to Banda Neira, prompting irate Muslims to attack and kill five members of a Christian family. In the melee, Christians fled to Des Alwi's hotel to take refuge there. It was quickly surrounded by a Muslim mob. John McBeth of the Far Eastern Economic Review describes the next few moments:

"Wearing his haji skullcap [indicating that he had made the pilgrimage to Mecca] and flanked by his son, Karma, and a Jakarta doctor, 72-year-old Des Alwi reminded the mob about the Prophet Muhammad's teachings on helping people who seek protection. Then he told them: 'I have only two guns, but you'll only get in here over my dead body'. After a few tense moments, the mob fell back and disappeared into the night." (FEER 27.5.99).

Flora & fauna Unique to the Bandas are the Laweri fish, *Photoblepharon bandanensis*, with eyes that light up and that are best seen on a moonless night. Their luminous eyes are the

with Perkeniers – *licensed planters who, for the most part, were 'free burghers' who had completed their contracts of service with the VOC*. They leased the land from the VOC and had to sell all their production to the company at a fixed price. For their part, the VOC provided slaves, supplies and protection.

Life, even for the Perkeniers, was harsh and short. Mortality from disease was high, and earthquakes, eruptions, tidal waves and hurricanes periodically decimated the settlement of Banda Neira. Even company rule was unforgiving. A German resident between 1633 and 1638 recorded 25 executions: two buried alive, one broken on the wheel, nine hanged, nine decapitated, three garotted, and one arquebussed (shot with an early form of portable gun, supported on a tripod). Less fatal punishments were equally gruesome – one woman who had blasphemed had her tongue pierced by a red hot needle. Even the executioner was executed.

Despite the high mortality, the costs of maintaining a garrison, and the extensive smuggling and cheating on the part of the Perkeniers (for instance, substitution of inferior long nutmegs for Bandas' product), profits for the VOC remained high, and the Bandas were regarded as the jewel in the VOC crown. The Perkeniers, though usually in debt, lived in extravagant style.

The end of the Banda's monopoly position in nutmeg production is linked to the British period of control during the Napoleonic Wars. The British controlled the islands over two periods, between 1796 and 1803, and 1810 to 1817. During these years, nutmeg seedlings were taken to Bengkulu (Sumatra), Ceylon and Penang (Malaysia) for cultivation, while the French – a few years earlier in 1770 – had also obtained seedlings and planted them in Mauritius, Zanzibar and Madagascar (see page 913). Their monopoly in production lost, the VOC was never again in a position to set the price of nutmeg. As production elsewhere increased, so competition grew and prices fell, and the Banda Islands languished into obscurity. There was a brief period of excitement between 1936 and 1942 when two leaders of the fledgling Indonesian nationalist movement, Mohammad Hatta (to become Vice President) and Sutan Sjahrir (to become Prime Minister), were exiled here. But, other than this short period, the Bandas became just another group of breathtakingly beautiful islands in the eastern seas.

For an entertaining account of the Bandas see: Hanna, Willard A (1991) *Indonesian Banda: colonialism and its aftermath in the nutmeg islands*, Yayasan Warisan dan Budaya: Banda Neira. Available at the museum and the Hotel Laguna in Banda, or from the Dian Pertiwi bookshop in Ambon (see page 889).

equivalent of a five-watt light bulb, and even after death they continue to glow for several days – the locals use them as bait when fishing at night.

Look out for the 'nutmeg pigeon', *Carpophaga concinna*, a fat pigeon which lives on the fruit of the nutmeg (similar in size and colour to an apricot). They are most common in nutmeg plantations, especially on Banda Besar. Notable flora include the kapok tree, with its fluff looking just like it does in a DIY cushion department, and the spectacular flame red flamboyan tree, which is quite a feature of Banda and adds greatly to the island's beauty (and after which many an Indonesian hotel is named).

Banda Neira

The core of the Banda archipelago, both geographically and economically, is the island of Banda Neira. It is here that most of the 15,000 strong population live and where the capital Bandaneira is to be found. The town is peaceful and attractive, and still contains a good array of Dutch mansions – gradually crumbling, due to lack of upkeep. A drawback of Banda Neira, and a surprising one, is that there are no good beaches. The nearest is a 50-minute walk from town, and is nothing to speak of. Most visitors charter boats to go diving or snorkelling. There is a **tourist information** desk at the airport which is manned for flight arrivals.

Sights **Fort Belgica**, built in 1611 with stone shipped in from Holland, has been unsympathetically restored but enjoys a magnificent situation commanding views in three directions – go in the morning for photographs, late afternoon for atmosphere. Despite the cack-handed restoration efforts this is the most impressive and best preserved of the ruined forts in Central Maluku. Below it lies the mouldering ruins of **Fort Nassau**, built in 1609, somehow more authentic for not having been restored. Fort Belgica was built in response to the growing threat posed by the British in this area and the site chosen because it commanded a far better military vantage point than Fort Nassau. Not far away is the **Dutch Reform Church**, with impressive coats of arms carved into the stone floor.

The **former residences** of Banda's two most famous exiles, Mohammed Hatta and Sujan Sjahrir, have been turned into museums. These two were fervent anti-colonialists and members of the Nationalist party. Exiled by the Dutch to Banda, they eventually held high government office once Indonesia had won its independence. Hatta became Vice-President and Sjahrir went on to be Prime Minister.

On Jalan Gereja are several fine, recently restored **Perkenier mansions**. A total of six of these impressive colonial houses have been restored on Banda; the original moulding, which symbolizes bread, has been recreated on the ceiling of the verandah, while the columns are shaped to symbolize pineapples. The Perkeniers (contract plantation owners) were a rum lot; many had been criminals and undesirables. They were brought in by the Dutch (who, under the ruthless leadership of the VOC Governor-General, Jan Pieterszoon Coen, had murdered most of Banda's population, see box), and given tracts of land which they farmed using slave labour.

The **Rumah Budaya Museum** is in one of these restored colonial mansions. It houses an interesting collection of memorabilia and relics: maps, prints and drawings which bring to life Banda's past and give a fairly accurate portrait of what life was like for the Dutch in colonial Indonesia. Unfortunately the labelling is poor. Note the layers of clothing and the wigs, worn by the Dutch despite the heat. They were also

Bandaneira

■ Sleeping
1 Brantz Guesthouse
2 Delfika 1
3 Delfika 2
4 Elmand Homestay
5 Flamboyan Homestay
6 Gamalama Guesthouse
7 Laguna Inn
8 Likes Homestay
9 Maulana Inn
10 Rosmina Homestay
11 Zonnegate Homestay

renowned for their heavy drinking and copious feasting, and it is easy to imagine the social life of these well fed Perkeniers, overdressed in their layers of elegant European high fashion, dancing and consuming quantities of imported wine, gin, cigars, even preserved foods, and retiring to their gracious colonial mansions. Books by Willard Hanna on the history of the Bandas and Tidore and Ternate are on sale here.

But the **Governor's Mansion** is perhaps the grandest of the restored colonial buildings. Ask to see inside and look out for the poignant inscription scratched by a French prisoner on one of the walls: "When will my happiness return? When will the bells toll the hour of my return, to the shores of my country, and the heart of my family, whom I love and bless." There is a statue of King Willem III of Holland in the garden behind.

Near the *Zonnegate Homestay* are some **old Dutch walls** and an arch made of coral. Watch the splendid sunsets from the refurbished pier in front of the Governor's Mansion.

There are **two cemeteries** on Banda: a Dutch and a Chinese one. Walk out of town past the *Delfika*, take the right fork going up the hill (past Des Alwi's new house and that of his daughter next door), and follow the road as it bends round. The Chinese cemetery is on the right: large, colourful, ornate tomb stones painted with symbolic dragons and plants, and depicting scenes of Chinese life. To get to the Dutch cemetery, continue on this road past the mosque also on the right, make a left turn along the road towards the telecom transmitter and the cemetery is on the left. Rather romantic in the evening with the scent of the Frangipane trees.

Papenburg is the highest hill on Banda, worth climbing for the superb views of Banda Neira. It is a steep climb but not difficult. Follow the path on the west side of the runway going away from town, fork left on the first minor path, which leads up the hill.

Malole Beach is a 50-minute walk to the far end of the island from town. It may be the best beach hereabouts but that is not saying much. To get there take the path running away from town at the west end of the runway; keep following this main path until reaching the beach.

There is an odd **fish pond** – a neglected concrete pool – on the edge of town, which at low tide barely covers the imprisoned occupants. These poor creatures are interesting to see and in 1999 included eight reef sharks (five white and three black-tipped reef sharks).

Across the lagoon and overlooking Banda Neira is the volcano appropriately named **Gunung Api** – or Fire Mountain. A vulcanologist who climbed the peak in 1986, some two years before it last erupted, maintained that lava flows would always run down the side of the mountain, away from the capital and the main centres of settlement. When Gunung Api did erupt in 1988 he was, fortunately, proved correct. A thin plume of smoke continually hangs over the island, a reminder to all residents and visitors of the volcano's continued activity. Hotels and guesthouses organize expeditions to climb the 600m-high cone, which takes about half a day; for the best views set off before 0600 (see 'Tours'). Guides are available.

Excursions

Ay Island – also spelt Ai – is a highly recommended excursion, with beautiful beaches and good snorkelling.

A visit to **Banda Besar** with the **plantation home** of Wim Van den Broeke, **Fort Hollandia** and an *adat* house is highly recommended (see page 903).

Pisang Island is usually visited on a day boat tour. However, there are also some very attractive bungalows on Pisang, with their own private beach and mandis.

Most hotels and guesthouses run tours to various parts of the island, and to neighbouring islands. To climb Gunung Api, with a guide, should cost about 15,000Rp per person; for a large group, about 60,000Rp in total. To charter a boat costs between 50,000Rp and 150,000Rp, depending on the destination. Pisang, Ay, Hatta, Run and Nailaka islands are all easily accessible on a day boat tour.

Tours

Sleeping Des Alwi, the self-crowned king of the Bandas, apparently is trying to corner the entire tourist industry in the islands. The *Maulana* and *Laguna* hotels are owned by him. To be able to dive it may be necessary to stay at one of his establishments, or at the *Delfika* and *Flamboyan* guesthouses which also enjoy diving 'rights' (see 'Diving' section). All the guesthouses meet planes and ships; those who take a ride into town are not obliged to stay at a particular place – passengers are shown the full range of accommodation. All the guesthouses listed below are recommended; they each have their own plus points and all serve 3 meals included in the price, and have fans.

A+-A *Maulana Inn*, Jl Pelabuhan, T21022, F21024. On the seafront, the hotel should have been renovated and redecorated, but given the current problems it seems unlikely that this state of affairs will change. Large bathrooms, but no hot water, conference facilities, a restaurant serving good food – try the nutmeg juice. The building was originally the family home of the Baadilla family (Des Alwi's mother's maiden name); you can still see the original black granite floor. Overpriced, the staff are few and far between, and the hotel relies on its rather over-blown reputation. **A** *Laguna Inn*, Jl Pelabuhan, a/c; like the *Maulana*, this hotel, though cheaper, is still overpriced. All rooms have private bathrooms but are rather drab and disappointing. Most people stay here for the diving, and a saving grace is the restaurant which serves good food. Like the *Maulana*, this place is also owned by Des Alwi.

C *Delfika I*, Jl Nusantara, T21027. First guesthouse on Banda, opened in 1981. The best place to stay if you want to learn about Banda, Bahri the manager is very well-informed, speaks good English, and is very helpful and friendly; he is the nephew of Des Alwi and his uncle owns the *Matahari Homestay*. Lawrence and Lorne Blair stayed here when they were making their TV documentary 'Ring of Fire', which chronicled their epic 10-year journey through the Indonesian archipelago. The 8 new rooms are very attractive and spotless with private mandi; the 4 older rooms are distinctly inferior but have private mandi; plus 10% tax. Food here is excellent, Moslem owned so no liquor on premises, but they will recommend a bar, garden with lovely views of Gunung Api. The *Delfika* has an in-town location, and is 1 of 2 guesthouses with rights for residents to go diving. **C** *Delfika II*, this is a new place occupying a prime waterfront location (walk down Jl Pelabuhan past the Merpati office and then turn right at the end of the road) and comes highly recommended. All meals included in the room rate. **C** *Flamboyan Homestay*, Jl St Syahrir, T21233. Almost opposite the *Brantz*, restaurant, fans, has 5 attractive, clean, new rooms in a modern house with a lovely garden, 1 room has Indonesian style squat toilet, residents have the right to go diving. **C** *Gamalama Guesthouse*, T21053. Six rooms have a/c, 7 rooms with fan, newer attractive rooms with private mandi, attractive upstairs balcony for guests to sit on but very small garden, good food. **C** *Likes Homestay*, Welky Riupassa, Jl Maulana, T21089. Enjoys possibly the best location of the homestays, on the waterfront, facing Gunung Api, good value, with a garden, one of the few homestays with a view. Welky, the owner, is very friendly and speaks some English, he makes his guests feel part of the family, but equally respects their privacy. It is possible to watch how the local food is prepared and there is sometimes singing in the evenings. The best 3 rooms with private mandi, 3 more rooms with shared mandi, mosquito nets available. Welky is creating a private beach, and the house has been in his family for 90 years. It is said that Des Alwi would like to close this homestay down probably because he wants the land, and he resents his guests eating there in preference to his hotels. **C** *Matahari Homestay*, T21050. Located on the waterfront but only has a balcony, no garden, next to market so no privacy (fishermen often try their luck from in front of the balcony), 3 newer rooms, very attractive, double with mandi.

Elmand Homestay, directly opposite the *Brantz*, in an old colonial plantation house, only 2 rooms – a genuine homestay, spotless, private mandi, owners don't speak English, this is the place to stay if you want to experience living in a Dutch plantation house. **D-E** *Rosmina Homestay*, Jl Kujali, T21145. This homestay comes recommended by those who have stayed here – it is reportedly friendly and well run with good food.

Further accommodation is available on **Pisang Island**: **C** bungalows on a beautiful beach. **Pulau Ai** and **Banda Besar** have homestays.

Eating The best place to eat is in your accommodation; the restaurants are not up to much. *Nusantara*, Muslim owned so no alcohol, mie goreng is awful, tiny portions, although the fish is said to be good. For a taste of the unusual, try the nutmeg jam if you are offered some. Available to buy from many homestays.

Festivals **KoraKora races** occur twice a year – the dates vary and can be postponed by a week or more at the very last minute – but roughly Apr and Oct/Nov. The competition is between boats from Banda, Selamon on Banda Besar and Ay Island, and the prize is a trophy and 2,000,000Rp (the money comes from Jakarta). Ay Island always wins! The KoraKora canoes are quite impressive, the 37 men in each row in unison in a beautiful, stylized, almost balletic movement, accompanied by gongs and drums. The race takes place in the lagoon between the town of Banda Neira and Gunung Api. The boats travel at enormous speed and the race is over in just 20 mins'. The KoraKora are the boats which took part in the historic Hongi raids, commandeered by the Dutch to extirpate spice trees on islands that might fall into enemy hands, and to ensure their control of the spice trade. Accommodation may be a problem if you have no reservation; if coming from Ambon, PT Daya Patal Travel Agent can find out the date and help with reservations, or ask other travellers coming back from Banda.

Sports **Diving** Diving in the Bandas is, by all accounts, stupendous – some of the best (possibly the best) in the world. However, it is expensive and the equipment is in poor condition. Various extra charges are tacked on here and there – so be prepared. But the opinion seems to be: it's worth it. Until 1999 diving was run by an English diving instructor. PADI course, 4 days, US$350, open-water course up to Dive Master. Best visibility Oct-Dec when the seas are at their calmest. The diving is excellent, though expensive at US$80, the going rate in Maluku being US$50. Des Alwi has the monopoly on diving; in order to dive you either have to stay at his hotels or at the *Delfika* or *Flamboyan* guesthouses. The diving season on Banda is Dec-Feb and 1 diver who has wide experience (500 dives including the Caribbean, Thailand, Red Sea, Burma, Sipadan, various Pacific islands) wrote to us and said that it was by far the best diving he'd seen anywhere in the world. Visibility was 30-50m+ and some of the best sites include: off Hatta Island (wonderful coral growths on lava flows); Batu Kapal (lots of sharks, manta rays, pelagic fish, strong currents so not for beginners); Nailaka, Run and Ai islands (fantastic coral, huge gorgonians, and a wide diversity of sponges and coral fish including vast shoals of trigger fish). **Snorkelling** There is no good snorkelling near Banda itself and it is necessary to charter a boat. The sea surrounding Banda Neira (town) is full of rubbish, is polluted, and the plant life and coral are dying. Recommended is the boat trip to see the young coral which has grown since the 1988 eruption of Gunung Api (homestays can arrange this). Mask, snorkel and fins can be hired from many of the guesthouses and also some shops.

Fishing Excellent game fishing (tuna, swordfish); hotels hire out tackle. All hotels and guesthouses except the *Elmand* organize boat trips.

Water-skiing and windsurfing Both available in Banda Bay.

Transport **Local** The *Delfika* has its own bemo; the *Likes*, *Zonnegate*, *Brantz*, *Flamboyan* and *Gamalama* share a van. Bicycles are sometimes available for hire – ask at guesthouses.

Air The airport is a short distance from town; walkable with limited luggage. Connections on *Merpati* with Ambon 3 times a week (on Mon, Wed and Sat); some flights via Seram. **NB** The baggage allowance is just 10kg (see below). It is only possible to book the outward leg; the return journey has to be bought in Banda. This is partly because of the way that the *Merpati* system works (each local office receives a cut from fares bought there) and partly because, while the planes take 18 passengers to Banda, they can only return with 12 – due to the short length of the runway on Banda. (The runway is currently being extended so the luggage restriction may be lifted.) It also seems that residents of Des Alwi's hotels – the *Maulana* and *Laguna* inns – take precedence over other passengers. Arrange your stay with some element of flexibility. Guesthouses meet the plane and *Merpati* will provide transport from town to the airfield.

Before the economic crisis there were daily flights; when things pick up again expect the frequency of flights to increase

Sea Boat: the *Waisamar* (should) leaves about every 2 days for Banda from Ambon. Cabins are available. For the Ambon-Banda leg, buy the tickets from the ship's captain. For Banda-Ambon, they are on sale at the Toko Mitra in Banda town. The ship has been out of action and there seemed no clear indication when it would be operating again! The *Pelni* ships *Rinjani* and *Bukit Singuntang* dock every 2 weeks at Banda on its circuit through the islands. The *Rinjani* and *Bukit Singuntang* are cheaper and more comfortable than the *Waisamar* but, of course, are far less frequent. Guesthouses send a van to meet ships.

Directory **Airline offices** Merpati open 0900-1300 Mon, Wed, Sat, 0800-1230 Sun, 0800-1300 Tue, Thu, 0800-1130 Fri. When you pay for your return ticket (which cannot be bought in Ambon) at their town office, a day or 2 before the flight, Merpati is oddly very reluctant to issue a ticket. They prefer to just write 'cash' on their list. Tickets are handed out at the airport before boarding. Ask for a receipt if concerned. **Banks** There are no banks on the islands; bring sufficient Indonesian currency.

Ay Island

Ay is a place rich in history. At the dawn of the colonial period it was controlled by the British, until 1667, whereupon it came under Dutch administration. Next to Ay is Run Island, a tiny, almost deserted island, that the world has forgotten. Such was the importance of the spice trade (spices were more valuable than gold) that the British exchanged Run for New Amsterdam with the Dutch (present day Manhattan).

It is hard to imagine, when visiting this peaceful, remote island, that it was once the scene of heavy fighting between the British and the Dutch. In the early 17th century the British had established fortified trading centres on both Ay and Run. They paid higher prices for nutmeg and mace than the Dutch and therefore posed a threat to the Dutch. In 1615, the Dutch attacked the British on Ay with a force of almost 1,000 men. After a fierce battle they were ultimately repelled by the British, only to return the following year, killing the entire British force. In 1667, when the British traded Run for Manhattan, the Dutch established themselves as effectively the sole European presence in the region, with a monopoly of the spice trade.

Sights There are several **beaches** on Ay. The nearest is down from the boat landing in the direction of Banda. The best way to find the second beach, which is at the end of Ay Island nearest Run Island (going away from Banda), is to ask your host to show you the way. Alternatively, follow the coast path which turns inland at the end of the village. After 300m, where the village peters out, turn right, follow the most well-trodden path which forks left after another 300m and remain on the best trodden path until you reach the beach; about 30 minutes' walk. There is another beach round the tip nearest Banda which can be reached by canoe or by walking over the hill – although a guide may be needed.

Interesting **historical sights** include the crumbling remains of Fort Revenge, the Dutch plantation house of the Welfaren Estate, a Dutch church and cemetery. (Take the path by the monument in the village, going inland. After 50m turn right and the church is on the left after another 50m). Everywhere are the crumbling remains of the colonial plantations – walls, foundations, massive arches and gate posts.

There are many **pleasant walks** through the spice-scented forests, following well-trodden paths past giant kanari trees with their fantastic, sculpted roots. The kanari trees provide much needed shelter for the delicate nutmeg trees, and produce a nut called the tropical almond (on sale in the market at Banda). Recently, there have been times when the oil from this nut has been worth more than nutmeg.

Sleeping There are 4 homestays on Ay. Insist on seeing all of them before making a choice as personal preference and rapidly changing quality may well alter the comments below. At the time of writing, *Weltevreden* is outstanding and the only one with private mandis. All the homestays have generators; they are situated in the village, not on a beach. Room rates include all meals.
C-D *Weltevreden*, the 1st homestay opposite the boat landing, spotless, with delicious food.

Kacong and his wife take a real pride in making their guests feel at home, at the same time they respect privacy. Kacong takes visitors through the forests to the best beaches for snorkelling, and will identify the various spice trees – nutmeg, clove, cinnamon and the fantastically shaped, huge kanari trees. Two rooms with private mandi, western toilet, 4 meals included in room rate (huge home-baked teas, try the nutmeg jam and `kue' biscuits made of spun sugar with spices and coconut), 2 cheaper rooms with shared mandi. **D** *Ay Star Homestay*, this homestay doubles as a shop so can be noisy, and the owners are not friendly once you announce you are leaving, food is nothing special, shared mandi. **D** *Revenge Homestay*, 5 rooms with shared mandi, the main feature is an upstairs balcony with a seaview. **E** *Welvaren*, 4 rooms with shared mandi, the `homestay' is in a separate house from the family.

Transport

Sea Boat: to reach Ay takes 1 hr by small boat; the boat leaves at 1300 from Banda (from the left side of the port, as you face the sea, beside the market next to the *Zonnegate Homestay*). To return to Banda the boat leaves Ay Island at 0800. There are 2 boats: the *Ay Indah* and the *Ay Star*, both leave at roughly the same time, when full. Returning on Sun to Banda can be a problem as the boats are often full.

Banda Besar

The highlight of Banda Besar is the **plantation home**, built in 1750 (with walls of coral), of Wim Van den Broeke. Mr Van den Broeke is a fascinating and informative gentleman, well-versed in the history of the Bandas, who welcomes all visitors with lychee juice and conversation. Although 75% Indonesian, he feels Dutch and speaks both English and Dutch.

Ask to see his 'nutmeg kitchen – *dapur pala'* – where he will explain the drying process, invented by the Dutch, which produces a superior product to the older method of drying nutmegs in the sun; 4,000 trees worth of nutmegs are dried at a time in Mr Van den Broeke's 'kitchen', which consists of two large rooms: on the ground floor is the small fire of kenari wood which produces a dry heat, while the nutmegs are laid out on the floor above to dry in the sauna-like atmosphere; the process takes 10 days. Visitors may be invited to hike in his nutmeg plantation, formerly 100 ha, now only 12½ ha. Wim Van den Broeke makes, and sometimes has for sale, the rather beautiful and intricate device for picking nutmegs: a long pole at the end of which is a 'cage' with two prongs to pull the nutmegs off the tree. To reach his house either take the boat from Banda harbour that goes to Walang, the village nearest his plantation, or the boat to Lonthar village. From Lonthar village the walk is about 45 minutes: alighting from the boat, turn left as you face inland and follow the path along the coast; to find his house just ask, everyone is very friendly and helpful. To reach Fort Concordia, continue past his house.

Fort Hollandia, near the main village, Lonthar, is reached via a steep flight of steps that leads to the top of the central mountain spine that runs along this island, the largest of the Banda group and implicit in the name ('Big' Banda). The ruins of Fort Hollandia are off to the left, with superb views over the sea to Gunung Api and Banda Neira. To reach a fine **adat house**, go back to the steps and continue up through the village. At the top, the track levels off; a little further on turn right on the main track, and on the left the path comes to an imposing former **Perkenier mansion** which is now an adat house in the process of being renovated. Continuing down the far side of the hill, the path leads to a fine white sand beach.

Transport

Boat From the harbour on Banda, public boats (*umum kapal*) run regularly from 0800 to 1600. Boats usually leave when full but the boatmen try very hard to encourage tourists to charter a boat. Boats leave from the left side of the market in town. The *Delfika* homestay also organizes trips to Banda Besar and Wim Van den Broeke.

Ternate and Tidore

Phone code: 0921
Colour map 5, grid A4

The tiny, twin, circular islands of Ternate and Tidore, separated from one another by a narrow strait, lie just to the west of the far larger island of Halmahera. Neither Ternate nor Tidore measure much more than 10 km in diameter and both are dominated by volcanoes: the former by the active Mount Gamalama (1,720m), and the latter by Mount Kiemtabu (1,740m). The largest town is Ternate, on the east coast of the island, with a population of about 50,000. Tidore is more sparsely settled with 40,000 inhabitants. Taken together, the islands have a population of about 120,000.

Ins and outs

Getting there
To see the island on landing, sit on the right-hand side of the aircraft

Ternate's tiny airport is 5 km north of the town centre; planes brush the palm trees on landing. Regular connections by *Merpati* with Ambon and Manado; less regular flights to Galela and Kao on Halmahera, and to Gebe and Morotai. Bouraq also run flights to Ambon and Manado. A taxi into town costs 5,000Rp. Alternatively, walk 1 km or so towards the university and take a public bemo. There is a tourist information counter at the airport, but it is usually unattended.

Ternate has 3 dock areas. The principal one is conveniently located just south of the town centre at the end of Jl Pahlawan Revolusi. *Pelni* and *Perintis* vessels leave from here. Shipping companies, including *Pelni*, have their offices in the port complex (T21434). Arrivals and departures are posted on boards outside the offices. The *Pelni* ship *Ciremai* calls here (see route schedule, page 988), as does the Kalla Lines vessel (page 756). Other vessels of various sizes and states of seaworthiness, including some Perintis vessels, call at Morotai and Halmahera, Bitung, Laiwui, Madapolo, Babang, Mangoli, Sanana and Ambon, among other destinations. There are also 2 other ports, side-by-side, at Bastiong, south of Ternate town. Smaller vessels and speedboats leave from here for Halmahera and Tidore, among other destinations.

Getting around

The town of Ternate is small – easily negotiable on foot. Public bemos run around the island. Tidore is less well served with public transport, but there are regular bemos between Rum and Soa Siu. The northern part of the island has little public transport. **North Maluku Tourist Office** is on Jl Pahlawan Revolusi (in the Kantor Bupati Kepala Daerah), T22646. Open 0830-1200, 1330-1600 Mon-Sat, some maps and other information available.

Security

Like Banda, Ternate and Tidore saw **inter-communal violence** between its Christian and Muslim populations during 1999, although this is said not to have been as serious as on Banda and Ambon. Nonetheless there were reports that areas of town had been burnt.

History

For visitors interested in the history of Ternate & its sister island Tidore, see Willard Hanna's 'Turbulent times past in Ternate and Tidore', Yayasan Warisan dan Budaya: Banda Neira 1990. It can be bought from the Tourist Office in Ternate or from the Dian Pertiwi Bookshop in Ambon (see page 889)

Ternate, a sultanate rich in spices, was first visited by Europeans on 6 November 1521 when the expedition of Ferdinand Magellan dropped anchor off Tidore. Financed by King Charles of Spain, Magellan's devastated fleet arrived after 27 months at sea, having lost three ships as well as its illustrious leader in a skirmish in the Philippines. The remaining two vessels were worm-eaten, waterlogged and rotten. But the emaciated crew managed to fill the holds with spices and returned to Spain to sell their spoiled cargo for £5,100, £300 more than it cost King Charles to fit out the expedition. Only 17 of the original crew returned and a joyous procession through the city and a Mass in the cathedral marked their ragged arrival.

Though the crew did not return to Ternate, amazingly, Magellan's reconditioned flagship the *Victoria* did, in early 1527. The historian Willard Hanna writes: "It arrived ... in even more woeful state than before, the rigging reduced to mere rudiments, the bottom barnacled and worm-eaten, the crew famished and exhausted. ... Don Garcias [the Portuguese captain of the island] exchanged grandiloquent messages of felicitation and abuse with the Spanish captain ... engaged the ship in brief combat, discreetly retiring when its cannon proved still to be functional, and watched with gratification as it proceeded to sink of sheer decreptitude" (1990: 39).

Like Banda to the south (see page 895), Ternate and Tidore have had a remarkably colourful history. One uprising against the Portuguese in 1529 occurred after a pig escaped from their castle. The local Muslims, unsurprisingly, had it killed, whereupon the Portuguese Captain Menesez imprisoned the chief *ulama*. The locals rebelled and had their priest released, but not before his face had been daubed in pig fat. The apoplectic *ulama* called a holy war and the Portuguese garrison was effectively blockaded. Without supplies, Menesez captured three elders and demanded food before he would release them. These demands were ignored, and so two of the three captives had their ears sliced off, while the third was thrown to a mastiff who drove him into the sea. Seizing one of the dog's ears between his teeth, this third elder dragged both himself and the beast beneath the waves to their respective deaths.

A succession of captains followed Menesez, all with instructions to increase trade and profits and mete out justice. In all areas they were generally unsuccessful. The only Governor to leave with any semblance of a good reputation was 'Good Governor Galvao', who arrived in 1536. As Hanna writes: "In the chronicles of the Moluccas during the 16th century, Galvao's is the only Portuguese name other than that of Francis Xavier to which, four centuries later, any very bright luster still adheres" (1990: 68). The Portuguese left the island on 15 July 1575 after 60 years of ineptitude.

Other visitors to Ternate included the English explorer Francis Drake who moored here in the *Golden Hind* in 1579, after ravaging the Spanish on the Main. He appears to have got on famously with the rogue of a Sultan who ruled at the time, Sultan Baab. The Dutch, who replaced the Portuguese as the dominant power (though harassed by the British), continued the tradition of blundering and provided their own cast of tragi-comedy characters to play next to a succession of colourful sultans. The terrible de Vlaming allowed his men to cut Prince Saidi up alive and throw morsels of his flesh over a cliff (1655), while Sultan Sibori had to cut the throat of the husband of a beautiful and seductive Chinese woman and then drown her mother-in-law in a bath before he was able to marry the cursed female.

Ternate & Tidore Islands

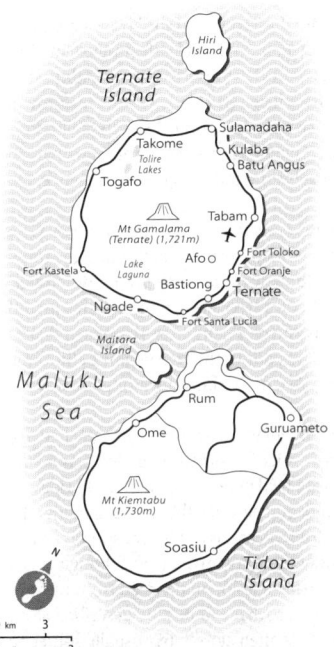

Sights

Ternate is a small, quiet town, where the bemos are driven at a refreshingly sedate pace and people stop to talk to visitors. Although the town is spread, ribbon-like, over 3 km or 4 km, and sandwiched between the lower slopes of Gamalama Volcano and the sea, it is manageable on foot. The main street is Jalan Pahlawan Revolusi on which are found the major hotels, banks, shops and the **Gama Lama Market**. The **Pasar Sayur** ('Vegetable Market') is at the north edge of the town centre; the main bemo terminal is also here.

In Ternate town, **Fort Oranje** is on Jalan Babullah, opposite the bemo station and Pasar Sayur. Built in 1607, it is the best preserved and largest fort on the island. Now the quarters for the local army garrison, it nevertheless has a rather abandoned, decayed and in some respects attractive, air about it. About 1 km north is the **Mesjid Sultan Ternate** dating from the 13th century. This mosque has a layered red-orange roof above high yellow-wash walls. Inside, the absence of decoration and the bare soaring roof give it a satisfying purity. About 500m further north from the mosque, on a rise, is the **Kedaton Sultan Ternate**, the Sultan's Palace, looking rather like a modest European hunting lodge. There was a palace on this site during the 13th century, although the present structure dates from the 19th century. It is now a small **museum**, displaying gifts presented to previous Sultans – armour, swords – along with basketry and some local costumes. The prize exhibit is, unfortunately, rarely on show. This is Sultan Awal's crown, still plastered with some of his hair (which is said to grow – see 'Festivals' below). Persistence and a modest payment (7,500-12,500Rp) may entice the officials to allow you a peep. Good views from the verandah of the kedaton, back over the town. ■ *Admission by donation (ignore the vast sums stated in the visitor's book). Open 0800-1400 Mon-Thu, 0800-1100 Fri, 0800-1400 Sat.*

Excursions

Circum-navigating Ternate This is easiest by chartered bemo, but is also possible by regular public bemo. Try walking on the west side of the island, where there are some interesting small settlements.

Sights travelling anti-clockwise from town **Benteng (Fort) Toloko** is 2 km from town, and was built by Alfonso d'Alburqueque in 1512. Little remains, except the vegetation-covered walls. **Batu Angus** lies just before the village of Kulaba, and is the crumpled lava flow from Mount Gamalama's eruption of 1737. There is also a **Japanese war memorial** here. **Sulamadaha** is a village 16 km from town; close by are good black sand beaches. Finally, the **Tolire Lakes** lie almost diagonally opposite Ternate town about 25 km away, on the other side of the island and the mountain. There are two peaceful lakes here, Tolire Besar ('Big Tolire') and Tolire Kecil ('Little Tolire'). The former is by far the more attractive, though not recommended for swimming as it is said to be inhabited by crocodiles. It is a 500m walk from the road to the lake. To get there, take a bemo to Takome, and then walk.

Sights travelling clockwise from town **Fort Santa Lucia**, also known as Fort Kayu Merah (Red Wood) or Fort Kalamata, is just past Bastiong port and about 3 km from town. It was built by the English in 1518 right on the coast and only the walls remain. Good views over to Tidore. Admission by donation. **Lake Laguna** is inland from the village of Ngade, 7 km from town. Climb up above the lake for good views. Also here is **Taman Eva**, a small recreational garden with a café and good views. Token admission charge. Further on along the coast road, **Fort Kastella** has almost been weathered out of existence.

Mount Gamalama, which is in effect Ternate, rises to 1,721m. It erupted in 1737 and again in 1987, 1990 and 1994, and can be climbed (just) in a day. Ask at the tourist office for further information. They can arrange a guide – one is recommended.

Afo clove tree is claimed to be the oldest clove tree in the world. It lies inland from Fort Oranje, 4 km from town. Known as Afo or 'Giant', it is 400 years old and still produces 600kg of cloves each harvest. The path to the tree begins behind the town and branches off before the TVRI mast. Ask for 'Cekih Afo' along the way.

Tidore Tidore is Ternate's neighbouring and less developed twin island and can be visited in a day trip. There is a fort at Rum, where the ferry docks. Soasiu, the main town, is on the easternmost side of the island; good markets are held here on Tuesday and Friday. A road, of sorts, links Rum with Soasiu and bemos run between the two settlements. To reach other places on the island it is best to charter a bemo as public transport is erratic or non-existent. There is not much in the way of sights on Tidore, although it is a charming, relaxed and friendly island. Just outside Soasiu, on the road from Rum, is the **Sonyine Malige Sultan's Museum** which has what can best be described as an eclectic collection of the sultan's possessions. It is often closed, but usually someone will open the place up. ■ *Getting there*: take a ferry from Bastiong, 20 mins, or one of the quicker speedboats. They run throughout the day at fairly frequent intervals.

Essentials

Ternate There's nowhere particularly sophisticated to stay in Ternate; just a couple of mid-range places. The great majority of the budget accommodation is near the port – and they are geared to Indonesian guests, rather than foreign tourists. **B-C** *Neraca Golden*, Jl Pahlawan Revolusi 30, T21327. A/c, hot water, new, clean, rather stark, in town centre. **B-D** *Elshinta*, Jl Pahlawan Revolusi 426, T21059. Some fan, some a/c, OK, with cars parked in lobby, all meals included which makes it a fair deal. **C** *Chrysant*, Jl Jend A Yani 131, T21580. A/c, friendly and quiet, rooms are reasonable but rather overpriced. **C-D** *Nirwana* (and fitness studio), Jl Pahlawan Revolusi 58, T21787, F21487. Some a/c, hot water, in centre of town, noisy, good rooms, price includes breakfast. **C-D** *Merdeka* Jl Merdeka 19, T21120. This small hotel is housed in a Dutch-era building. The rooms are stuffy, some with fan, some a/c, but with the benefit of friendly staff. **D** *Sejahtera*, Jl Salim Fabanyo 21, T21139. Dark, windowless rooms with shared mandi, all meals included. **E** *Penginapan Yamin*, Jl Pelabuhan Revolusi (by port), T21929. Average rooms, verandah, shared mandi. **F** *Penginapan Permata*, Jl Pelabuhan Revolusi (close to port), simple rooms, good value. **F** *Penginapan Sentosa*, Jl Pahlawan Revolusi, T21857. Basic, but friendly and popular, shared mandi.

Sleeping
NB Parts of the town were burnt during violence between Christians & Muslims. As a result, some of the hotels listed below may now be closed

Tidore There are a couple of places to stay in Soasiu: **E** *Losmen Jangi*, Jalan Malawat 32, T21131, welcoming place with simple but clean rooms; **F** *Penginapan Johra*, basic.

No excellent restaurants, but a number of mid-range establishments selling reasonable Indonesian and Chinese dishes. Most are found on Jl Pahlawan Revolusi – eg *Gama Lama* at No 248 (Chinese), *Garuda* (Indonesian) and *Roda Baru* (Padang food). The *Siola Restaurant* in Ternate town also comes recommended. Stalls set up at night opposite and north from the local government offices (Kantor Bupati Kapala Daerah). For local specialities, try the cakes and bread which use the kenari nut (from the huge shade tree that protects nutmeg groves) as an ingredient: *roti kenari* and *bagea kenari*.

Eating

Cutting the Hair of the Sultan's Crown, this is said to be performed once a year, although there is no fixed date for the ceremony. The crown is believed to hold supernatural powers, 1 manifestation of which is the alleged continued growth of the Sultan Awal's hair.

Festivals

Indo Gama, Jl Pahlawan Revolusi 17, T21681; *Noname*, Jl Jend A Yani 129 (next door to Chrysant Hotel).

Tour operators

Local Bemos: the main terminal is opposite the Pasar Sayur at the north edge of the town centre. Give the destination, and the appropriate vehicle will be pointed out. Although there are routes, these are loosely adhered to – most passengers are dropped right outside their house, hotel or wherever. **NB** Although regular bemos travel both clockwise and anticlockwise, they rarely circle the island completely. Destinations at the far side of Ternate are more difficult to get to, and to get back from. Fares are 500Rp for short trips around town, more for longer cross-island journeys. For the more remote spots (or if in a group) it is best to charter a bemo at an hourly rate. **Ferries**: regular ferries to Tidore leave from Bastiang, 20 mins (the old wooden boats are cheaper than the ferry). Faster speedboats also cross regularly. Take a bemo the 3 km from town to the ferry dock.

Transport

Airline offices *Bouraq*, Jl Jend A Yani 131, T21288, open 0800-1700 Mon-Sun; *Merpati/Garuda*, Jl Basoiri 2, T21651, open 0800-1700 Mon-Sat, 1000-1230 Sun. **Banks** *Bank Rakyat Indonesia*, Jl Pahlawan Revolusi 234; *BNI*, Jl Pahlawan Revolusi; *Ekspor Impor*, Jl Pahlawan Revolusi (near corner with Jl Tenang). **Medical services** Hospitals: *General Hospital*, Jl Tanah Tinggi. **Communications** General Post Office: Jl Pahlawan Revolusi 420. **Perumtel**: Jl Pahlawan Revolusi (next to *Elshinta Hotel*), telephone and telegram.

Directory

Halmahera

Phone code: 0924
Colour map 5, grid A5

The weirdly shaped island of Halmahera, something like a miniature version of Sulawesi, is the second largest in Maluku, with a land area of 18,000 sq km but also one of the least visited islands in the archipelago. Like the relationship between Ambon and Seram, Halmahera is overshadowed in historical and economic terms by its far smaller neighbour, Ternate.

Halmahera & Morotai

Much of Halmahera remains forested and transport is distinctly limited. Tribal groups inhabit the interior and it is thought that there are some for whom life has only changed marginally over the last century. The establishment of transmigration settlements on the island for Javanese settlers, and the financial attractions offered by Halmahera's primary forests, may mean that this beautiful island will not remain isolated and beautiful for very much longer. Trekking in the forests and mountains of Halmahera may become an important alternative source of income, although even this will have its cultural costs. It was here, in February 1858, that Alfred Russel Wallace, the great Victorian naturalist, wrote his famous paper 'On the tendency of varieties to depart indefinitely, from the original type', which laid out his ideas on the principle on natural selection. Although the paper (published in the *Proceedings of the Linnean Society*) drew upon his observations in Borneo, South America and in other areas of Indonesia, perhaps it was the wonder of Halmahera which cemented his thoughts into this seminal paper.

At the north end of Halmahera, the largest settlement is the town of **Tobelo** with about 15,000 inhabitants. There is not much here but it is the service centre for the island, so most facilities are available, from a post office to a hospital. It makes some sense to use Tobelo as a base while exploring the island.

On the coast near the centre of the island, **Kao** is the biggest town with a population of less than 5,000. Kao was an important Japanese air base during The Second World War and there is ample evidence of the war. Today it is a backwater, though a pleasant enough one and a good place to stop for a day or two. South from Kao is **Sidangoli**, which is really just a way station on the road north. There are a couple of places to stay here.

The north of Halmahera is the most developed and there is a rudimentary public transportation system. Buses link Sidangoli, near the neck of the island, with Galela in the far north, running up the eastern side of this northern 'limb'. The road passes through Kao and Tobelo *en route*, as well as a number of other modest settlements. Another road runs up the western side to **Ibu**. For towns elsewhere on Halmahera, the usual mode of transport is by boat – or on foot. There are flights to Kao and Galela (see below), and ferries link Ternate with Tobelo and Jailolo.

Sights

Sleeping

Tobelo B-C *Pantai Indah*, Jl Lorong Pantai Indah, T21064. Some a/c, rooms are good, quiet location. **C** *President*, Jl Banyankara, T21231. Good, clean and modern rooms, well run little hotel. **E** *Karunia*, Jl Kemakmuran, T21202. Rather noisy as it is on the main road, but the rooms are OK and it is well priced. **E** *Megaria*, Jl Bayankara, some rooms with attached facilities, some without, basic but serviceable. **Kao D** *Sejahtera*. **D-E** *Dirgahayu*, price includes 3 meals a day. **Sidangoli D** *Penginapan Sidangoli Indah*, large rooms and pleasant place to stay. **E** *Penginapan Ramayana*, basic place with tiny rooms.

Transport

Local Minibuses provide a reasonable service between Sidangoli, Kao, Tobelo and Galela, and more limited links with other towns. **Air** There are rather unreliable connections from Ternate with Kao and Galela (60 km from Tobelo, take a shared taxi); and from Galela to Morotai. **Sea Boat**: regular speedboats from Ternate (Bastiong) to Sidangoli, 30 mins. There is also a cheaper, but slower, ferry. Daily ferries leave from the main dock in Ternate town for Jailolo. Once a week there is a ferry which runs from Ternate town to Tobelo via Daruba on Morotai. There are also boats from Manado (North Sulawesi) to Tobelo, about once a week.

Directory

Airline offices Merpati, Cabang PT Eterna Galela, Jl Kampung Soasiu, Galela. **Banks** There are banks in Tobelo but they do not change TCs, and we have also received reports that US$ cash is difficult to change.

Morotai

Morotai was an important airforce base for the allies as they advanced across the Pacific, and there is a good deal of war scrap still lying about as evidence. Covering an area of over 1,800 sq km, the Japanese Private Nakamura holed-up here until 1973

Colour map 5, grid A5

when he emerged from the forest to surrender after nearly 30 years. **Daruba**, the capital, has a population of about 5,000 and the diving and snorkelling is reputed to be excellent. There is little else obvious to recommend the town, which is an isolated spot in an isolated area of Indonesia. The population of the island is about 50,000.

Sleeping **Daruba** E *Tongga*, E *Angkasa*.

Sports **Diving** Some shopkeepers in Daruba are willing to hire out diving equipment; maintenance may be poor.

Transport **Air** *Merpati* flies a once weekly loop between Ternate, Galela and Morotai. **Sea Boat**: There are also 5 ferries a week between Tobelo and Daruba, 3 hrs (7,500Rp). The boat leaves Tobelo at around 0900 for Daruba, as does a daily speedboat (10,000Rp-15,000Rp). Tickets to be bought on the morning of departure at portside ticket office. Crossings vary from 2 hrs to 4 hrs, depending on the state of the sea. Once a week a ferry runs from Ternate town to Daruba on Morotai, and continues on to Tobelo on Halmahera.

Southeast Maluku

The Kabupaten, or district, of Southeast Maluku is the remotest and least visited part of the province (or at least of that part which can be visited). The largest and most important islands are the Kai (Kei), Aru, Tanimbar, Babar, Wetar and Kisar Islands. The district covers almost 25,000 sq km and has a population of about 275,000. These islands were never important in the spice trade with Europe and they were largely insulated from the events that were so fundamentally altering life elsewhere in the archipelago. However, there were local trading links with the North Moluccas and South Sulawesi, and forest products were exchanged for metal implements.

Lying south of the equator, these islands are drier than those to the north, and the people subsist primarily on yams, maize, millet, coconut and sago, rather than rice. Missionaries have converted most of the population to nominal Christianity, although traditional ancestor worship is still important.

Malaria in Southeast Maluku It seems that the closer the islands are to Irian Jaya, the worse the malaria problem is. The Aru Islands, Tanimbars and Kai Islands have swamps, so there is the potential for malaria. It seems to be less of a problem in the Tanimbars. Dobo, the largest city in the Aru Islands, has sea breezes which may mitigate the problem.

Kai (Kei)

Phone code: 0916 The Kai Islands consist of three islands with a total population in 1994 of 104,000, 500 km southeast of Ambon. **Kai Kecil** and **Dullah** – on which is the capital Tual – are largely low lying and comparatively densely populated; much of the former swamp has been converted to crop land. **Kai Besar** is mountainous and only settled along the coastline. The forested interior of this magical place is home to no fewer than five species of bird, two species of lizard, one species of snake and a species of bat, all found nowhere else in the world. At Langgur town, on Kai Kecil (connected to Tual by the Watdek Bridge), the Catholics have a mission (reputedly, the oldest Catholic mission in Maluku), and have brought some prosperity to Langgur through various business enterprises, and excellent schools. (It may be possible to stay at the mission.) The local people are renowned for their boat building skills, and the **Laut Cave** on Kai Kecil contains enigmatic ideograms indicating a long period of human settlement.

Kai offers the intrepid visitor **fantastic beaches**, with powdery white sand as fine as flour – some say the finest beaches in the world. A particularly stunning beach lies on the west coast of Kai Kecil – Pasir Panjang (or Pasir Sas Nadan). However, there have been reports that malaria is rampant on most beaches during the wet season. Cholera is also said to be a problem.

Dullah Island provides more attractive villages and beautiful beaches, especially to the north. The capital **Tual** is surprisingly busy for an area, seemingly, at the edge of the world. Kai Besar is very quiet in comparison with Kai Kecil and Dullah.

Tourist information in Tual, close to bridge, T21466, some useful information available.

Sleeping

Tual D-E *Linda Mas*, Jl Anthony Rhebok, outside of town, T21271. Coffee house, friendly, clean, some a/c, rooms with both private and shared mandis, price includes breakfast. **E** *Rosemgen I*, Jl K Sadsuitubun, T21045. Room rate can include meals, simple rooms, shared mandi. **E** *Nini Gerhana*, Jl Pattimura, T21343. Welcoming little place with simple rooms. **E-F** *Mira*, Jl Mayor Abdullah, T21172. Convenient for the harbour, but near to Mosque so noisy. **Langgur C** *Rosemgen II*, Jl Watdek, near the bridge, T21477. Own mandi, some rooms with good views, good place for local information, restaurant. **D** *Ramah Indah*, Jl Baru Watdek, T21232. **Ohoililir Beach** (Kecil) **D** *Coaster Cottages* (book at *Mira Inn* in Tual), 6 km from town, rate includes breakfast. Can pay a small supplement to include all meals, but food very, very basic, verging on the inedible (ie bring some provisions – biscuits, peanuts etc), a charter bemo to the village from Tual is about 20,000Rp. It is possible but complicated to get there by public bemo (in morning, can be a long wait) to Ngilgof village, then 20 mins walk along the beach to Ohoililir village.

Eating

Restaurants in Tual are not very good. The best restaurant on the Kai Islands is at Densiko near Langgur.

Festivals

Local festivals Oct: boat races around Tual.

Transport

Local Bemos: around Dullah leave from the terminal at Tual near the mosque. For bemos around Kai Kecil, the terminal is near the Ohijong Market in Langgur. Bemos are very crowded and rather infrequent (350Rp). Chartering should cost about 8,000Rp/hr. The public transport system on Kai Besar has yet to be developed. **Boat**: small boats powered by outboards, known locally as 'Johnsons' (after, presumably, the 1st outboards to make it here – although today there is not a Johnson in sight), ferry local people along the coast, taking produce to market for sale and barter. **Air** The airport lies 5 km from Langgur town. Beware rip-off bemo drivers – from the main road a bemo should be 500Rp, or chartered vehicles are available for around 6,000Rp. Daily connections on Merpati between Langgur and Ambon. **Sea Boat**: Ferries to Kai Besar leave from Langgur – the Pelabuhan Motor Watdek – near the bridge, twice daily. Perintis ships leave Ambon every 2 weeks or so and call at the major ports of Southeast Maluku. There are 2 routes – 1 links Ambon with the near southeast or Tenggara Dekat, the other links Ambon with the far southeast or Tenggara Jauh (calling at harbours in the Babar and Kisar Islands). The *Pelni* ships *Rinjani*, *Tatamailau* and *Bukit Singuntang* sail from Banda to the Kai islands and on to Fakfak (Irian Jaya) every 2 weeks, on their circuit through the islands. The *Tatamailau* also calls here every 4 weeks on its circuit. (*Pelni* office in Tual, near the mosque, T21181. They provide good clear information on all schedules.) From Kai there are boats roughly every 10 days (a 48-hr journey) to Tanimbar (Saumlaki town), although expect delays and postponements. Check at the *Pelni* office or at the port for latest information.

Directory

Airline offices *Merpati Rahmat Jaya*, Jl Pattimura, T21376, Langgur. Open 0800-1300. **Banks** It is possible to change US$ cash in some shops, but it is best to take enough for your stay. The banks in Langgur look at foreign currencies, let alone TCs, with incredulity.

Tanimbar

The densely forested Tanimbar Islands (over 60 in all, population 75,000) are similarly endowed with beaches and sea gardens. The 'largest' towns are **Larat**, on the island of the same name, and **Saumlaki** at the southern end of Yamdena Island – the

Phone code: 0918
Colour map 6, grid C1

largest in this group of islands. Having said this, Saumlaki is little more than a ribbon of development along Jalan Bhineka. The Christian inhabitants of Tanimbar have been influenced by Hinduism from India (evident in textile design), and by Polynesian and Micronesian cultures (for instance, the tradition of cooking food wrapped in banana leaves over hot stones). On the east coast of Yamdena, at the village of **Sangliat Dol**, is a **megalithic** stone structure, approached up a stone staircase from the beach. To get there from Saumlaki, two buses a day, 1½ hour journey in uncomfortable bus.

Sleeping **Saumlaki C-D** *Harapan Indah*, Jl Bhineka, T21019. Downstairs rooms are more expensive, with a/c, private mandi and TV, price includes good meals. **D** *Pantai Indah*, Jl Bhineka, T2148. Some rooms with own mandi, price includes food, clean, large rooms. **D-E** *Ratulel*, Jl Bhineka, T21014. Cheapest place to stay in town, but right next to the mosque.

Eating All 3 hotels provide food; there's not much else on offer, except a scattering of foodstalls.

Transport **Air** Flights to Ambon and Langgur – irregular, but should be 3 times a week. Confirm departure details by phoning Merpati here before arrival. **Boat** *Pelni* and *Perintis* boats link Tanimbar with the Kai Islands and East Timor, Ambon and Banda. The *Pelni* vessel *Tatamailau* is the most comfortable (see route schedule, page 988) and it calls here every 4 weeks. For boats to Larat, there is a weekly ferry. The *Pelni* office is near the port in Saumlaki.

Directory **Airline offices** *Merpati* in *Harapan Indah*, T21017, Jl Bhineka, Saumlaki. **Banks** No bank will change money, but the *Toko Selatan* in Saumlaki may change cash for you, at a lower rate.

Background

History

Maluku was important as a source of spices long before the first Europeans discovered the islands. Arab, Chinese, Malay and other seafarers traded here, and indeed the first Europeans had to employ the services of local pilots in Melaka to help them find the fabled Spiceries. The name *Maluku* is said to be derived from the words *Jaziratul Jabal Maluk* – meaning the 'Land of Many Kings' – and the islands of *Miliku* are mentioned in seventh century T'ang Chinese documents.

The spices of Maluku It was spices that initially enticed European mariners to Southeast Asia. The expedition of the Portuguese general Alfonso d'Albuquerque was the first to make landfall on the legendary Banda Islands in 1512. The general himself did not accompany the small fleet (he was resting in Melaka), but Ferdinand Magellan, then a lowly junior officer, probably did. The great attraction of the Spice Islands lay in the value of the spices that they seemed to produce in prodigious quantities, and the universal European belief that cloves (*Eugenia aromatica*), nutmeg (*Myristica fragrans*) and mace (another product of the nutmeg tree) could be grown nowhere else on earth.

Nutmegs are used for both medicinal and culinary purposes – they are said to be the secret ingredient in the flavouring of Coca Cola. In the Orient, nutmeg was – and is – used primarily for health purposes. It is an important ingredient in preparations to relieve illnesses from rheumatism and malaria to sciatica and indigestion. It is also considered to be an effective aphrodisiac. No wonder, then, that nutmegs were known as the golden fruit. Jan Huygen van Linschoten, a Dutchman who sailed with d'Albuquerque's expedition, wrote of the benefits of nutmeg: "The nutmeg comforts the brain, sharpens the memory, warms and strengthens the Maw, drives wind out of the body, makes a sweet breath, drives down Urine, stops the Laske, and to conclude, is good against all cold diseases in the head, in the brain, the Maw, the Lice and the Matrice". Cloves were similarly regarded; German naturalist George

Rumphius viewed the clove tree as "the most beautiful, the most elegant, and the most precious of all known trees".

Having displaced the Portuguese from the Moluccas, the Dutch were intent on maintaining a monopoly of the spice trade and proceeded to extirpate every tree not under their control – they literally sent expeditions to neighbouring islands to uproot and destroy any potential competitor plants. They did this so successfully that it was 200 years before people began to question whether nutmeg and cloves could be grown beyond the Spice Islands.

Cloves and nutmeg proved to be very sensitive to transportation – a fact that helped perpetuate the myth. The clove is not a seed or fruit at all, but a dried flower, and most trees were grown from so-called volunteer seedlings, not from seeds. A tree will produce about 2kg of cloves a year, picked between August and September. Before the Dutch took control of the region, they were found on just five small islands of what is now North Maluku: Ternate, Tidore, Bacan, Makian and Motir. The nutmeg tree requires similar careful management. Sensitive to sunlight, it was grown under the protective shadow of huge *kenari* shade trees, which also provided an edible nut and hulls for dug-out canoes. The nutmeg itself is the seed of the nutmeg fruit (which looks in size and colour rather like an apricot), while the more valuable mace is the beautiful, scarlet filigree wrapped around the outside of the seed. The mace is removed prior to the nutmeg drying process, and left to dry in the sun.

The English and French spent much of the 18th century trying to break the Dutch spice monopoly, but were not successful until 1770 when French missionary and naturalist Pierre Poivre (1719-86) smuggled out nutmeg and clove seedlings and managed to propagate them in Mauritius. With the British soon following suit, the wealth of the Moluccas was effectively undermined. From this date, these distant eastern isles were relegated to obscurity and economic insignificance.

Climate

Maluku's climate is complex because it straddles the equator and covers such a vast area. In **north and central Maluku** there is rain throughout the year, but it is concentrated between May and October – the period of the east monsoon. In Ambon, for example, the wettest month is July (590mm) and the driest is November (104mm). Total annual rainfall in Ambon is a very wet 3,450mm.

In **Southeast Maluku**, south of the equator, the climate is very different and more akin to that of Nusa Tenggara. The islands here experience a long dry season between December and March, corresponding with the west monsoon, and annual rainfall is 1,400mm. As a result, while the islands to the north are clothed in forest, those in the south have savanna vegetation.

Culture

One of the first things a visitor notices about this area are the **churches**. Even quite small villages will have several, often quite large churches; the size reflects the fact that they are competing for status with each other and also with the mosques in any adjacent Moslem villages. There is a Malukan proverb: "Keeping up with the Moslems". Try to peek inside these churches, as many have huge, flamboyant murals painted on their walls (an example is the one in Ambon on the opposite side of the road to the *Beta Hotel*, going down in the direction of Jalan Sangaji). The Ambonese in particular are gifted singers and it is worth going to church, or hovering outside on a Sunday just to hear them. The very lucky may even come across a choir and conch shell band (conch shells require some expertise to blow).

One unique aspect of *adat* in Maluku is *pela*, a pact of brotherhood between two or more villages to provide help, shelter and protection in times of need. (For a general background to *adat*, see the box on page 835.) Pela villages are frequently far apart, **Adat** even on different islands. Those pela bonds which today exist between Moslem and Christian villages were probably formed before their conversion.

There are obligations and taboos associated with the bond; one of the latter states that people from villages united in a pela bond may not marry – it is considered incestuous. A Christian village will help a Moslem village build a mosque and vice versa. The traditional greeting between members of villages united by a pela pact is 'wakeou', which used to mean – very approximately – 'don't cut off my head' as well as 'brother'; a reminder of the central role of headhunting in the adat customs of this region in times past.

The continuing survival of adat may appear peculiar when people have embraced Islam or Christianity. However, not only is adat and mainstream religion perceived to be complementary rather than contradictory, but many adat practices also have a practical value. For example, the *cuci negeri*, which besides being a symbolic purification is also a 'spring clean' of houses and villages in December each year. There is also a strong and continuing fear that perhaps the ancestors will punish someone who fails to follow adat practices.

It is in connection with marriage ceremonies that adat customs persist most visibly. There are three types of adat marriage: *Kawin lari* is the most common, a marriage of elopement, popular because it saves on the cost of formal feasts and ceremonies; *Kawin Minta* is the traditional marriage by request; and *Kawin masuk* is where the bridegroom enters the bride's family, possibly because her family has no son. It is no accident that there are three types of adat marriage, for three (also seven) is a significant adat number. It is a number that can bring both good and bad luck. Three of anything is bad luck so people do not give gifts in threes; likewise, taking a picture of three people will bring bad luck to one of them.

11

Irian Jaya

Irian Jaya

- **918** Ins and outs
- **919** Biak
- **920** Jayabura and Sentani
- **922** The Baliem Valley
- **924** Wamena
- **926** Merauke
- **927** Wasur National Park
- **929** Timika, Kuala Kencana and Tembagapura
- **929** Background
- **929** History
- **931** Land and environment
- **933** Culture

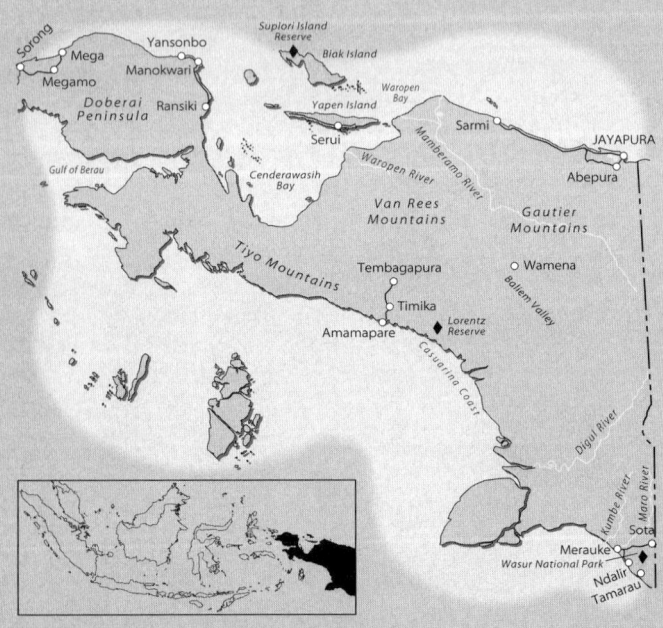

Irian Jaya is one of the world's great unknown regions. With a population of just 2,000,000 scattered over an area – much of which is forest and swamp – twice the size of Great Britain, there is a great deal that 'science' does not know about this province. Most visitors just touch the edges – the Baliem Valley is the only interior area that is on the average tourist's itinerary. The attractions of Irian Jaya are clearly at the interface of nature and culture, with some of the richest forests in the world and tribes such as the Dani.

Irian Jaya was only formally annexed by Indonesia in 1969, although it has been occupied since 1962. The word 'Irian' is derived from the Biak word meaning 'pretty' or 'light'; Jaya is an Indonesian word meaning 'glorious'. As in East Timor and now in Aceh, there is a vibrant secessionist group agitating for independence. This has brought a degree of violence to Irian Jaya not seen since the 1960s. The Indonesian government has poured additional troops into the province to keep the peace, and President Wahid tried to appease the rebels by suggesting that he might consider a change of name from Irian Jaya (imposed by Indonesia) to West Papua (preferred by the independence movement). The trouble is that these sops are unlikely to appease the more radical elements of the movement while, at the same time, annoying nationalists in Jakarta.

Ins and outs

Getting there

Biak is a gateway city (ie 60-day visas are issued automatically on arrival) and there are also international connections with Jayapura (but visas must be obtained before arrival). *Pelni* vessels call at Sorong, Manokwari, Nabire, Biak, Jayapura, Merauke, Timika, Kaimana and Fak-Fak.

Getting around

Irian Jaya is the least developed area of Indonesia, with the poorest roads and infrastructure. An ambitious road building programme is underway in Irian Jaya, but because of the size of the task, most of the country can still only be reached by air, sea, or on foot. It is also necessary to get a *surat jalan* (literally 'travel letter') to travel outside the province's major towns. Because roads are so poor, air is often the only way to travel and there are some 250 small airstrips scattered over the province. Most are not on the schedules of any commercial airline, but missionary airlines do provide an intermittant service. Merpati operates services to the larger towns, and the two missionary airlines – *MAF* (Missionary Aviation Fellowship) and *AMA* (Associated Missions Aviation) – to smaller settlements, as well as the main towns. Towns with rather more frequent air services include Jayapura, Biak, Merauke and Wamena. **NB** The missionary airlines do take passengers, but it should be stressed they are not commercial airlines and are under no compunction to carry fare-paying passengers. The national shipping line, *Pelni*, also operate ships that visit many of the larger coastal settlements.

Permits A transit visa is required to visit Irian Jaya; and a *surat jalan* (literally 'travel letter') for all parts of the province outside the major towns of Jayapura, Sorong, Sentani and Biak – for example, the Baliem Valley, Merauke and the Agats area. *Surat jalan* can be obtained from the central police stations in Jayapura, Sorong and Biak, and from the station outside Jayapura Airport (two passport photographs are required, along with your passport, or photocopies of the first page, the photo page, the date of issue and expiry page, the immigration entry stamp page, and immigration card). They are valid for anywhere between one week and four weeks and list every town you are intending to visit so come prepared. Officially, *surat jalan* should be returned to the issuing office when a visit, is completed. Most hotels will organize *surat jalan* for a small fee, as will many tour and travel agents. On arrival in a town where a *surat jalan* is required, your hotel will often either check in for you at the local police station or instruct you where to go. It is useful to have your *surat jalan* photocopied several times. There are some parts of the province which are off-limits to all visitors, even with a *surat jalan*. These periodically change depending on security conditions and fears in the province. Check at the local police station.

Security There was an upsurge in political violence in Irian Jaya during 2000. Security forces killed demonstrators in Fakfak, Merauke and Wamena as the province's independence movement gained strength and confidence. It is likely that travel in the province has become more difficult and restricted since the material for this section of the guide was collected. Check the US State Department and UK Foreign and Commonwealth Office's travel advisories for the latest information.

Money It is difficult to change money in Irian Jaya. Banks in Jayapura, Biak and Wamena (Baliem Valley) are the only places where travellers' cheques can be changed.

Tours The *Tropical Princess* cruises from Biak Island for 5-10 day scuba-diving trips. The boat can also be chartered. Contact: ***Tropical Princess Cruises***, PT Prima Marindo Paradise, third floor, East Wing, Shop 36, *Borobudur Intercontinental Hotel*, Jalan Lapangan Banteng Selatan 1, Jakarta, T371108, F370477.

Biak

Biak is the capital of Biak Island, which covers less than 2,000 sq km off the mainland's north coast. The town has a population of about 25,000. It is a one-road town – all the main hotels, restaurants and government offices are strung out along Jalan Jend A Yani – with the harbour at the west end of town (where the road becomes Jalan Sudirman) and the airport at the east (where the road becomes Jalan Prof Moh Yamin). The **tourist office** is opposite Post Office on Jalan Prof M Yamin (airport road), T21663. Helpful and worth visiting, but getting there requires a taxi ride.

Phone code: 0961
Colour map 6, grid A3

Sights

The **Cendrewasih Museum** on Jalan Sisingamangaraja has a small collection of local artefacts. Opening hours are irregular. There are few other sights in town, although the **markets** are colourful. The central **Pasar Panir** is on Jalan Selat Makassar and sells, among other things, animal skins and live birds. At the west edge of town is the **Pasar Inpres**, next to the taxi terminal, which is mainly a food market. In the morning a **fish market** sets up just off the west end of Jalan Sudirman near the harbour.

Excursions

Gua Jepang or the **Japanese Cave** was dug by the Japanese during the Second World War, and around 4,000 Japanese soldiers were killed here in 1944 when US fares fire-bombed the area. The cave is a few kilometres from Biak town *en route* to Bosnik. Small entrance fee. Close by is a small **museum** with a display of Japanese war memorabilia. ■ *Getting there: take a public taksi running towards Bosnik and get off at the Dennis Orchid Park.*

There are a number of **idyllic beaches** within two hours or so of Biak by public transport. To the east, in the vicinity of the market town of **Bosnik** (18 km from town), are white-sand beaches with good snorkelling. Market days are Wednesdays and Saturdays. Sleeping A *Biak Beach Hotel*, another Aerowisata monstrosity, 263 rooms in 6 ha of garden, little character and a real eyesore, but certainly the most luxurious place to stay in Biak.

Padaido Islands lie off Biak Island to the southeast. The closest town is Bosnik. These paradisical islands offer superb snorkelling and beaches. Equipment available for snorkelling at the market in Bosnik. ■ *Getting there: charter a boat from town or from Bosnik, or go on a tour. Expect to pay about US$60-90 for the day, but bargain hard. There are occasional public boats on market days in Bosnik (Wed and Sat).*

Korem is a market town (Wednesdays and Saturdays) about 50 km north of Biak on the island's north coast. It was badly damaged by the *tsunami* which followed the earthquake in February 1996. ■ *Getting there: by bemo from town (1½ hrs).*

Supiori Island is barely separated from Biak Island to the northwest. A make-shift pontoon bridge transports people and light vehicles across from the 'mainland'. Much of the island is gazetted as a nature reserve and reputedly has good stands of montane forest and mangrove. However, transport is poorly developed and the island is sparsely populated. ■ *Getting there: buses run from Biak town as far as the 'bridge' separating Supiori from Biak Island.*

Note that the town & surrounding area was hit by an earthquake at the beginning of 1996. Although Biak itself returned to normal relatively quickly, some smaller coastal settlements were devastated by the tsunami that followed the earthquake. In 2000, political activists were killed by security forces in Biak

Tours

Sentona Tosiga, Jalan Jend A Yani, T21398, organize tours around town and to the Padaido Islands.

Sleeping

B *Arumbai*, Jl Selat Makassar 3, T21835. A/c, hot water, pool, quiet and comfortable, rather expensive. **B** *Irian*, Jl Prof Moh Yamin, T21139 (2 km east of town near the airport). Some a/c, good restaurant, colonial feel (like something out of a Hemingway novel) and comfortable rooms, set in gardens and overlooking the sea. **B-C** *Mapia*, Jl Jend A Yani, T21383. Some a/c, large, pleasant rooms with attached mandi, friendly but a bit grotty. **C** *Basana Inn*, Jl Imam Bonjol 46, T22281. Relatively new and good value, rooms with hot water, set in attractive gardens. **D** *Maju*, Jl Imam Bonjol 45, T21841. Small, but clean rooms with attached mandi. **D** *Solo*, Jl Monginsidi 4, T21397, near the market, small rooms, good meals. **E** *Hotel Rahayu*, off Jl Jend A Yani (by the mosque), T21196. Basic rooms.

Eating There are cheap warungs on Jl Monginsidi and stalls on Jl Jend A Yani near the centre of town. **Cheap** *Cleopatra*, Jl Jend A Yani, fish and chicken specialities and tables outside. *Jakarta*, Jl Imam Bonjol, Indonesian and Chinese, good seafood. Several places along Jl Ahmad Yani. Foodstalls on Jl Sudirman and near the markets.

Shopping **Crafts** Available from the markets and from shops like the **Pusaka Art Shop** at the Pasar Lama. **NB** Skins of the bird of paradise are available for US$20 – they are a protected species and their trade should not be encouraged.

Sports **Diving** The Biak area offers fabulous diving possibilities but these are currently under developed. However, facilities are slowly opening up, as the potential is realized. No courses and equipment not provided, but *Tropical Princess* lays on tours (Jakarta T5703500) and the *Biak Beach Hotel* in Bosnik should also have set up a dive shop by the time this book is published. **Snorkelling** is also excellent and several tour operators in Biak hire out masks and fins.

Tour operators *Bawa Makmur*, Jl Koti 72, T22180; *Granda Irja*, Jl Imam Bonjol 16, T21616; *Sentosa Tosiga*, Jl Jend A Yani 36, T21398.

Transport **Local** **Minibuses/colts**: run to most local destinations. The terminal is off Jl Airlangga at the west edge of town, near the Inpres Market. **Taxis**: can be chartered by the hour. **Air** The airport is on the outskirts of town, about 2 km east of the centre. Regular daily connections on Merpati with Jayapura, Ujung Pandang, Denpasar, Nabire and Serui; less regular connections with Ambon, Sorong and Timika. **International connections** have been suspended but many begin again soon. **Transport to town**: minibus or taxi, or catch a public bemo. **Sea** **Boat**: the harbour is at the west edge of town. The *Pelni* vessels *Ciremai* and *Dobonsolo* call here (see route schedule, page 988). The *Pelni* office is at Jl Sudirman 37, T21065.

Directory **Airline offices** *Garuda*, Jl Sudirman 3, T21416; *Merpati*, Jl Prof Moh Yamin 1, T21386. **Banks** *Bank Rakyat Indonesia*, Jl Sudirman, and *Ekspor Impor*, Jl Jend A Yani (near intersection with Jl Imam Bonjol), will both change most major TCs and cash. **Medical services** **Hospitals**: *General Hospital*, Jl Sriwijaya Ridge 1. **Communications** **General Post Office**: Jl Prof M Yamin (at the edge of town on the road to the airport). **Telecom office**: Jl Yos Sudarso. **Useful addresses** **Central Police Station**: Jl Selat Makassar (good place for obtaining a *surat jalan*, see page 918). **Immigration office**: Jl Jend Sudirman 1, T21109 (corner of Jl Sudirman and Jl Imam Bonjol).

Jayapura and Sentani

Phone code: 0967
Colour map 6, grid A6

Formerly the Dutch city of Hollandia, Jayapura is the capital of Irian Jaya province and has a population of about 100,000. One of Indonesia's more featureless towns, most visitors only use it as a base before venturing inland. It is a ribbon development stretching inland from the coast, with most commercial buildings on Jalan Jend A Yani. As most of the inhabitants – like those in other urban areas in Irian Jaya – are immigrants from other parts of Indonesia, it lacks any distinctive 'Papuan' atmosphere. The Irianese here are outnumbered by Javanese, Makassarese and others.

Sights Because Jayapura is so lacking in atmosphere and character, many people choose to stay in **Sentani** where the airport is located. Sentani also has a better range of accommodation and, all in all, is a more attractive town. The **tourist office** is on Jalan Soa Siu Dok II, T33381. Inconveniently situated 3 km north of town but worth a visit if you have time – good range of pamphlets. ■ *0700-1500 Open Mon-Fri.*

Excursions **Hamadi** is a coastal suburb about 4 km south of town. This was the spot where the Americans landed in April 1944 to wrest control of New Guinea from the Japanese. On the beach, a few rusting landing-craft and tanks half-buried in the sand bear testament to the event. After gaining control of the area, General Douglas McArthur made Jayapura – or Hollandia as it was then – into one of the major forward staging posts for the advance north. The beach is attractive; walk through the Indonesian military base to get there. The town also has an interesting central market. **Sleeping C-D** *Asia*, T35478, clean but expensive. **D** *Hamadi Jaya*, clean rooms, noisy, but probably the best of the 'budget' accommodation (both here and in Jayapura). ■ *Getting there: by colt from Jl Jend A Yani.*

Base G, locally known as **Pantai Tanjung Ria**, is a beach 6 km west of town. It is named after the US base established here at the end of the war. Swimming is moderate, but currents can be strong. Very popular at the weekend. ■ *Getting there: colts only run out to Base G from Jayapura.*

Candrawasih University Museum (aka **Museum Loka Budaya**) is located at Abepura, about 25 km south of town. It displays a reasonable collection of ethnographic pieces and is worth a visit before venturing into the interior. ■ *Open 0730-1600 Mon-Fri. Nominal admission charge. Getting there: by colt from the station or from Jl Jend A Yani.*

Museum Negeri in Waena, *en route* to Sentani, has an interesting collection of natural history exhibits as well as ethnographic pieces. ■ *Open 0800-1300 Mon-Fri. Getting there: by colt from the station or from Jl Jend A Yani to Sentani.*

Sentani Lake This enormous lake lies southwest of Jayapura, not far from Sentani. Boats can be chartered to some of the lake's islands from Sentani's harbour.

Tanah Merah Bay is about 55 km west of the city and offers some of the best swimming in the area, as well as reasonable snorkelling. ■ *Getting there: by colt to Depapre from the bus station.*

Sentani lies 37 km from town and only 3 km from the airport. It is recommended as a more attractive place to stay than Jayapura. **B** *Mantoa*, Jl Jend A Yani 14, T31633. A/c, hot water, best hotel in town, comfortable rooms with good facilities. **B** *Triton*, Jl Jend A Yani 2, T33218. A/c, 1 notch down from the *Mantoa*, a bit grotty. **B-C** *Irian Plaza*, Jl Setiapura 11, T34649. Some rooms with a/c and hot water, very adequate, good information provided here. **C** *Dafonsoro*, Jl Percetakan 20-24, T31695, 31696. A/c and hot water, some rooms definitely better than others. **C-D** *Kartini*, Jl Perintis 2, T22371. Some attached mandi, clean, popular with budget travellers. **C-D** *Sederhana*, Jl Halmahera 2, T31561. Some a/c, range of rooms some with attached mandi, convenient distance from beach. **Accommodation at Sentani, near the airport** **C** *Hotel Transit Minang Jaya*, Jl Raya Sentani, T91067. Some a/c, range of rooms some with attached mandi, all reasonably well maintained and well priced. **C** *Mansapur Rani*, Jl Yabaso 113, 10 min walk from the airport (turn right on exiting the terminal), T91219. Basic rooms, price includes breakfast. **C-D** *Ratna*, Jl Raya Sentani 7, T91435. Some a/c, own bathroom, good location 5 mins from airport, clean newish rooms. Recommended. **D** *Sentani Inn*, Jl Raya Sentani, T91440. Some a/c, price

Sleeping
Accommodation in Jayapura is some of the most expensive in Indonesia

■ *on map*
Price codes: see inside front cover

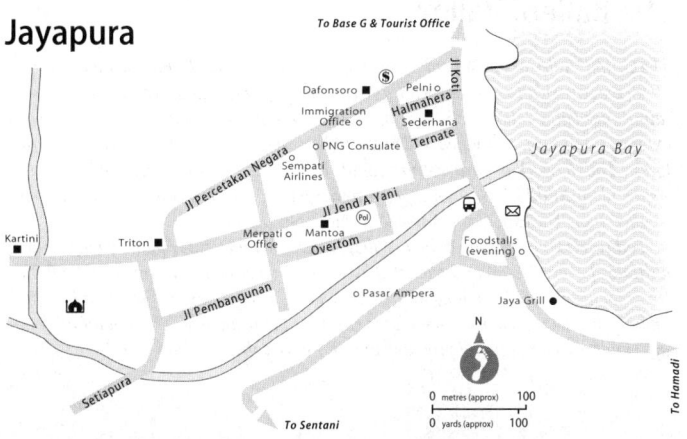

Jayapura

includes breakfast, basic accommodation with attached mandi, very helpful staff with good English. **C-D** *Semeru*, Jl Yabaso, T91447. Some a/c, clean rooms, a very acceptable place to stay, and closest to the airport.

Eating The better restaurants are strung out along Jl Percetakan. Cheaper warungs can be found near the mosque on Jl Jend A Yani. There is a night market by the *Pelni* office with good Indonesian stall food; for cheap seafood try the stalls on Jl Halmahera. **Expensive** *Jaya Grill*, Jl Koti 5, seafood and steaks served on the waterfront. **Cheap** *Nirwana*, Jl Jend A Yani 40, good Padang food.

Shopping **Tribal art** Sold at Hamadi 4 km from town (see above, 'Excursions'). It is mass produced, and usually ersatz, although good pieces do sometimes crop up. For better pieces, try the *Madinah Art Shop*, Jl Perikanan.

Tour operators *Bawa Makmur*, Jl Koti 72, T22180. *Dani Sangrila*, Jl Pembangunan 19, T31060, F31529. *Duta Baliem*, Jl Nindya Karya, T21416. *Indonesia Safari*, Jl Kemiri, T94. *Limbunan*, Jl Tugu 11, T31633, F31437. *Natrabu*, Jl Jend A Yani 72. *PT Kurera Jaya*, Jl A Yani 39, T31583, F32236.

Transport **Local** **Colts**: the terminal is on Jl Percetakan, close to the waterfront. **Air** Sentani airport is 35 km from town. There is good accommodation available near the airport (see 'sleeping') and many people choose to stay here rather than in Jayapura. Minibuses take passengers into town, or walk out onto the main road and catch a public colt to town via Abepura. Taxi prices are very inflated. Regular connections on Merpati/Garuda with Biak, Wamena, and Ujung Pandang; less regular connections with Sorong, Nabire, Sarmi, Senggeh, Serui, Manokwari and Merauke. MAF and AMA fly to even less prominent destinations in Irian. **Sea Boat**: the *Pelni* ships *Rinjani*, *Ciremai* and *Dobonsolo* dock at Jayapura every fortnight on their various circuits (see route schedule, page 988). The *Pelni* office is at Jl Halmahera 1, T33270, on the waterfront.

Directory **Airline offices** *AMA*, Sentani airport, T91009; *Garuda*, Jl Percetakan 4-6, T36217; *MAF*, Sentani airport, T91109; *Merpati*, Jl Jend A Yani 15, T33111; Sempati, Jl Percetakan 17, T31612. *SMAC*, Sentani Airport, T91567. **Banks** *Ekspor-Impor*, Jl Jend A Yani, will change TCs and cash. *Bank Danamon*, Jl Jend A Yani, also accepts TCs. Note that exchange rates are better in Jayapura than Wamena/Baliem Valley. **Embassies & consulates** *Papua New Guinea*, Jl Percetakan 28, T31250. PNG visas issued here. **Medical services** **Hospitals**: *General Hospital*, Jl Kesehatan 1. **Communications General Post Office**: Jl Koti (on the waterfront). **Telecom office**: Jl Koti, next door to Post Office. **Useful addresses** **Central Police Station**: Jl Jend A Yani, T22161 (for *surat jalan* permits for the interior, see page 918). **Immigration Office**: Jl Percetakan 15, T21647. 0800-1600 Open Mon-Fri.

The Baliem Valley

Colour map 6, grid B5 The Grand Valley of the Baliem was one of the most remarkable finds of this century. In 1938, the American explorer Richard Archbold flew his seaplane over the Snow Mountain Range (now called the Sudirman Range), and peered out of the cockpit to see an extensive and lush, cultivated valley where he and everyone else expected to find only forest. The network of gardens and canals brought to mind the great civilizations of Asia and the Middle East – nothing like it was expected in New Guinea, let alone in this isolated spot. The expedition named the valley Shrangrala.

Today it is known as the Baliem Valley, a verdant and fertile upland valley set at an altitude of over 1,500m and encircled by mountain peaks. It is drained by the Baliem River and is about 55 km long and 15 km wide. The population of the area is 70,000, making this the most densely populated rural area in Irian Jaya. The inhabitants make up Irian Jaya's largest, and probably most famous, tribe: the Dani.

Ins and outs

Getting there The only way to get to the Baliem Valley is by air to Wamena. There are daily flights from Jayapura but note that these get booked up, particularly during the peak season in Aug.

Getting around A *surat jalan* is required to explore the Baliem Valley and they are not available in Wamena. Obtain one in Biak, Jayapura or Sentani. See page 918 for further information.

Security At the beginning of Oct 2000, some 30 people were killed by government forces in Wamena as demonstrators tried to raise the 'Morning Star' – the flag of the independence movement – over the town.

Background

Despite conversion to Christianity and the intrusion of all the paraphernalia of Indonesian administration, the Dani continue to wear their traditional penis sheaths and to farm in the traditional manner. The economy is based upon a sophisticated system of gardens, allied with the raising of pigs. On the valley floors, canals help to control flooding in the wet season, and provide irrigation water during the dry. Fields located on the hillsides even have erosion control structures, giving lie to the notion that the inhabitants of New Guinea practised only an unsophisticated agriculture before the arrival of Europeans. Pigs, the other side of the Dani agricultural coin, are raised by the women and are only eaten in ritual or ceremonial situations. Among the tribes of Irian Jaya, the Dani have been among the most resistant to change. They do not seem to be attracted by the trappings of a 'western' lifestyle, and have clung to their traditions. Nathalie Seddon, a member of a scientific expedition to the area, describes her view of the Dani in the following way: "Never had I encountered such an uninhibited and affectionate people ... The Danis exude an overwhelming contentment and love of life, sharply putting into perspective the sad materialism, dissatisfaction and alienation that now characterise western society ... But irrevocable change dawns in Irian and our very being there has accelerated a westernisation that could obliterate an entire culture."

Baliem Valley

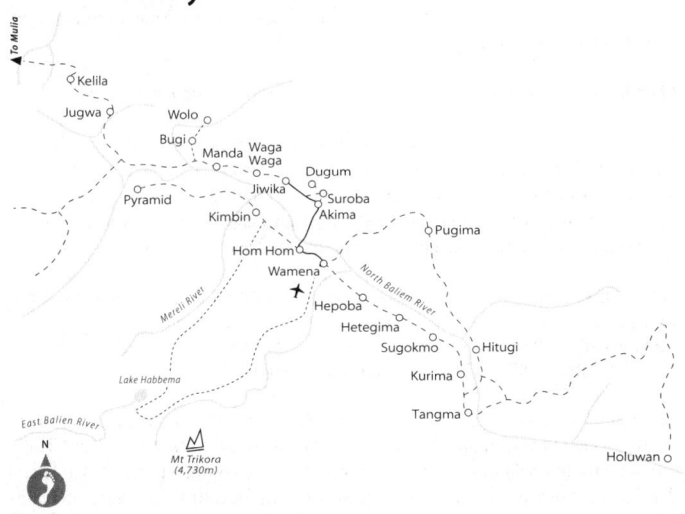

Wamena

Phone code: 0969

NB Consumption of alcohol is not permitted in Wamena

Wamena is the largest town in the Baliem Valley and most visitors use it as a base to explore the surrounding countryside. The settlement was established by the Dutch in 1958, at about the same time that missionaries began working in the valley. It is really just a small group of administrative buildings, hotels, tour companies and restaurants. Wamena is something of a boom town at the moment due to the imminent completion of the Trans-Irian highway, linking Wamena with Jayapura. At present the town can only be reached by air. Small and large investors, no doubt assuming that the road will open up the Baliem area to tourists and other riches, are buying land and building shops, hotels and restaurants in anticipation. Others wonder whether the road will really herald a massive increase in business: are tourists likely to want to travel overland for hundreds of kilometres in uncomfortable buses when there are no other places worth stopping at? Time will tell.

A new **tourist office** has opened 3 km southwest of town on Jl Yos Sudarso, T31365. They will organize treks. ■ *Open 0800-1400 Mon-Sat.*

Excursions There are a number of Dani villages and other sights within easy reach of Wamena. Not surprisingly, these are relatively heavily touristed. Good maps of the surrounding area are available from most hotels. It is much more rewarding to go on an overnight trek. See pages 924-926 below.

Sleeping Accommodation is some of the most expensive in Indonesia – understandably, as Baliem is only connected by air (or foot) with the outside world. **B** *Baliem Cottages*, Jl Thamrin, T31370, 'traditional' thatched cottages, rather down-at-heel. **B** *Baliem Palace*, Jl T31043, F31798. Hot water, large rooms, attractive garden. **C** *Anggrek*, Jl Ambon, T31242. Clean and well-run, some attached mandis. **C** *Jayawijaya*, 3 km out of town, inconvenient location, expensive; used only by tour groups. **C** *Nayak*, Jl Gatot Subroto 1, T31067. Good rooms, quiet, near the airport, with attached bathrooms, Ricardo speaks some English, very accommodating. **C-D** *Trendy*, Jl Trikora 91, T31092. Clean rooms and a seating area.

Eating Most visitors eat in their hotels. There are a few warung in the market but the quality is poor. *Sinta Prima*, Jl Trikora 17, best restaurant in Wamena with local crayfish and Chinese dishes.

Shopping **Tribal art** The Dani do not have a rich material culture, but hawkers sell what there is in town: penis gourds, well-made stone axes and adzes, spears, and bows and arrows. Try the souvenir shop near the market first to get an idea of price.

Tour operators *Chandra Nusantara*, Jl Trikora 17, T31293, F31299. *Desa Tour and Travel*, T31107.

Transport **Local** Public bemos run to local centres within about a 20 km radius of Wamena. Bemos can also be chartered to venture a little further off the beaten track – about 10,000Rp/hr. Becaks are available for trips around town. **Air** The airstrip is virtually in the town. Multiple daily connections on Merpati with Jayapura. **NB** Bad weather and over-booking are a perennial problem. *MAF* and *AMA* fly to various places in the surrounding area, but only intermittently.

Directory **Airline offices** *AMA*, far end of airfield; *MAF*, airport building, T31263; *Merpati*, Jl Trikora 41, T31488. **Banks** *Bank Rakyat Indonesia* and *Bank Exim*, on Jl Trikora, will change most major TCs and cash. **Communications** **Post Office**: Jl Timor. Closed Sun, otherwise open 0800-1400 except Fri, 0800-1100. **Telecom office**: Jl Thamrin 22. *Wartel office*, Jl Trikora.

Southeast & east of Wamena **Pugima** is the closest Dani village to Wamena, about an hour's walk east of town. Walk through **Wesaput** and then cross the Baliem River to reach the village. There are some traditional houses here, things are changing fast. **Sleeping** **D** *Wio Silimo Tradisional Hotel*, *en route* to Wesaput, basic rooms, but attractive setting and considerably cheaper than places in Wamena. ■ *Getting there: on foot, 1 hr.*

Kurima is a district capital about 30 km southeast of Wamena. A market is held here on Tuesday and it can be used as a base for treks into the surrounding hills, particularly south through the **Baliem River Gorge**. **Sleeping** Basic accommodation available at *Kuak Cottages* (**D-E**), not far from Kurima. ■ *Getting there: public bemos venture 15 km southeast from Wamena to Hepoba and now continue onwards to Hetegima or Sugokmo (another 5 km). From these towns it is an easy hike to Kurima.*

North & northwest of Wamena

Akima is famous for its blackened, **mummified warrior**. In former times, powerful or important men were not cremated but preserved through desiccation, so that their influence could continue to benefit the village. The hunched figure is dressed in the regalia of a Dani warrior. To see the mummy, haggle with the keeper – expect to pay around 5,000Rp. There is a **market** in Akima on Sunday. ■ *Getting there: take the northwest road out of town towards Hom Hom; at Hom Hom cross the Baliem River on the suspension bridge and then follow the track; the village is just off the road.*

Close to Akima, which is not a particularly attractive village, are two much more interesting communities: **Suroba** and **Dugum**. The easy walk, across a hanging bridge, is particularly beautiful.

Jiwika is a district capital about 18 km northwest of Wamena and the largest village in the area. Because there is a range of accommodation available here, Jiwika can be used as a base to explore this area of the Baliem Valley. Like Akima, there is a mummy here – or rather in the village of **Sumpaima** just 10 minutes walk north of town. Expect to pay not much more than 5,000Rp to see the wizened figure. **Sleeping E** *Losmen Lauk*, basic, some rooms with attached mandi. There are also a number of other simple places on the road between Akima and Jiwika. Most enjoy beautiful positions. The following have been recommended and all fall into our E category: *Pondok Wisata Suroba Indah*; *Pondok Wisata Bani Homestay*; and *Niyuk Huts*. ■ *Getting there: bemos run to Jiwika from Wamena, or walk.*

Waga Waga is a small community on the track running north from Jiwika. The unexciting Kontilolo Cave attracts some visitors. ■ *Admission 2,000Rp.*

Kimbin is a district capital 30 km northwest of Wamena. **Accommodation** Homestay available. About 5 km further north still is the missionary centre of **Pyramid**, an oasis of civilization at the end of the road running north out of town. From Pyramid, follow the river to a world vision bridge. Cross over, and continue down river. There is a new road running parallel to the footpath, about 500m away. Bemos run along the road to **Manda**. ■ *The walk and bemo journey takes about 3 hrs. From Manda, another 3 hr hike through a gorge, leads up to **Wolo**. Getting there: public bemos run to Kimbin and on to Pyramid. To walk to Kimbin should take about 6 hrs, Pyramid 7 hrs. From Manda, there is a new road back to Wamena. Bemos available.*

West of Wamena

A new, albeit rough, road was completed from Wamena to the beautiful highland lake of **Habbema**. Previously reaching this idyllic spot, at an altitude of 3,000m, took a strenuous five-day hike; now the journey should take just a few hours in a vehicle. Environmental activists tried to lobby against the road: it penetrates an area of outstanding and fragile natural beauty, and they feared what effects further developments might have on the environment. Roads in themselves are not the problem; rather it is the increased accessibility that the roads afford. Locals in Wamena expect that lake-side hotels will soon open, in all likelihood with inadequate waste and sanitation facilities, leading to pollution of the lake and the rivers and streams that flow from it. ■ *Getting there: by chartered vehicle.*

Organizing your own 'tour'
Visit the new tourist office in Wamena for an idea of price, & ask around to find out how other travellers have fared & how much they have paid

Anyone intending to trek in the Baliem Valley – and who is not fluent in Dani – should hire a guide. Even Indonesian is not widely spoken. Maps of the area are also poor, so it is almost impossible to explore without the help of a guide. There are always independent guides offering their services. Hotels will also have their own suggestions. These private guides will charge from 10,000Rp to 40,000Rp per day depending on their experience; you will be expected to meet all their costs. If staying in a village – usually in a teacher's or nurse/doctor's house – expect to pay 4,000-7,000Rp per night. There are likely to be additional costs incurred: photographing a person usually costs 100Rp or a cigarette; a Dani warrior might expect 2,000Rp for the privilege; while being present at a funeral might mean an outlay of 40,000Rp or more. The Dani are well aware that their traditions have a market value. Porters are also usually necessary and cost around 20,000Rp per day. For a five-day tour with a guide, porter and cook, inclusive of accommodation in villages and food, expect to pay about 250,000Rp+ for two people.

Organized tours

It is far less bother to book a tour through one of the established tour companies, who offer a variety of treks and expeditions from three nights to two weeks. Judge the competition and get an idea of prices before you book. The prices of tours obviously vary depending on the itinerary, but expect to pay about US$65-125 per day per person. There were only three local companies: *Chandra Tours*, Jalan Trikora 17, T31293, F31297; *Insatra*; and *Insos Moon*. However, John Tabuni (a Dani who speaks good English), c/o *Trendy Hotel*, Jalan Trikora in Wamena, has also come highly recommended by recent visitors.

What to take

Good walking boots; insect repellent; sleeping bag; toiletries; medical kit; candles/matches and a torch (there is no electricity and it is dark by 1800); light day clothes; warm clothing for the night; raincoat and/or umbrella; food for trip (only vegetables and fruit are easily available outside Wamena – high energy food is a good idea); barter goods and gifts; sun hat and sun cream; ample small change.

Merauke

Phone code: 0971

Merauke, near the southeast border with Papua New Guinea, is as far from Jakarta as it is possible to get – and still stay a night in a hotel room. The area is an important transmigration settlement zone, although the numbers targeted for settlement during Repelita IV (1985-89) – some 50,000 for the Merauke district – were not attained. Immigrants from South Sulawesi and from Java are also prominent in the town and in local trade, and many locals feel marginalized.

In 1990, only 50 foreign tourists made it to this distant outpost. However, the tourist office has big plans – almost all of them tied to the perceived potential of eco-tourism and the attractions of the Wasur National Park (see Excursions, below). The town itself is unremarkable; the old Dutch **Post Office** (built in 1920) and a few buildings near the **harbour** are quite interesting. The long sandy *beach* is popular with locals on a Sunday and the outlook provides good sunsets. The tidal **mud-flats** are not suitable for swimming but are excellent for **bird-watching**. Nearby **kampungs** (villages) are worth a wander. Note that a *surat jalan* is currently required for Merauke.

Sleeping
All hotel prices include breakfast

B *Megaria*, Jl Raya Mandala 166, T21932. A/c. **B** *Nirmala*, Jl Raya Mandala 66, T21849. A/c, very good restaurant, but no atmosphere. **B-C** *Flora*, Jl Raya Mandala 294, T21879. A/c. **C-D** *Asmat*, Jl Trikora 3, T21065. Restaurant, some a/c, some rooms with own bathrooms, slightly more interesting accommodation than normal. **D** *Nikmat*, Jl Biak, T21375. Some a/c. **E** *Losmen Merauke*, Jl Raya Mandala 340, simple rooms verging on the primitive, shared mandi.

Shopping

Good quality Asmat and Marind carvings. Shops close around 1300 (earlier on Fri) and open again from 1800 to 2100.

Sentosa Tosiga, Jl Raya Mandala, T21821.	**Tour operators**
Air Connections with Jayapura on Merpati on Sun, Tue, Thu and Fri. Flights to the Asmat area. **Sea Boat**: The *Pelni* ship *Tatamailau* docks here on its fortnightly circuit (see page 988 for route schedule). *Pelni* office is at Jl Sabang 318, T21591 (sporadic opening times).	**Transport**
Airline offices *Garuda*, Jl Raya Mandala, T21084; *Merpati*, Jl Raya Mandala 163, T21242. **Banks** *Bank Exim*, Jl Raya Mandala. Close around 1300, earlier on Fri. **Medical services Hospitals**: *General Hospital*, Jl Sukarjowiryopranoto; *WWF*, Jl Biak 12, T21397 for more information on visiting Wasur National Park.	**Directory**

Wasur National Park

This park is one of Indonesia's newest reserves and abuts Papua New Guinea's Tonda Reserve, creating a huge protected area. It occupies 400,000 ha of wetlands, mangroves, lakes, a network of rivers and open savanna grasslands. The dominant forest formation is acacia, melaleuca and eucalyptus. It is richest in birdlife, with nearly 400 recorded species, including cranes, storks, pelican, ibis and spoonbills. Mammals include the agile wallaby (*Macropus agilis*), the spotted cuscus (*Spilocuscus maculatus*) and the short-beaked echidna (*Tachyglossus aculeatus*). About 2,500 people from the Marind and Kanum tribal groups live in the park, and there has been no attempt (yet) to relocate them outside the park's boundaries. They are allowed to practise traditional hunting and gathering. There is a **tourist information centre** at Wasur, with cultural displays and general information sheets on where to go. There is also a smaller post at Ndalir.

Colour map 6, grid C6

Despite the fact that most visible elements of the Marind & Kanum tribes' cultures have disappeared, they retain a strong family structure & moral code: holding hands, kissing & scant clothing is certain to offend. Do not walk in their gardens uninvited

The **northern area**, from Wasur, is dominated by acacia and melaleuca forest. Around **Tambat**, the forest is denser and patient birdwatchers may be rewarded by sightings of cassoway, birds of paradise and crowned pigeon.

The areas of the park

The beach near **Ndalir** is wide and sandy, and the mudflats also make for good birdwatching (hundreds of pelicans collect here in the Southern Winter). The **central area** from **Onggaya** northeast to the border is open savanna land. Northeast of **Tomer** is a good area for walking all year round. The **southern area** from **Tomerau** east and up to **Rawa Biru** is open savanna grasslands, with some areas of permanent wetlands. This is the best area for viewing wildlife in the dry season; during this season, it is one of the last areas to contain water and tens of thousands of waterbirds such as pelican, ibis, egret, crane and stork congregate here. Near **Ukra**, there is a good lookout tree which provides wonderful views across the grassland plains, to watch wallabies and deer.

NB The park operates a 'zoning policy', which restricts access to some areas of the park for conservation reasons. However, the policy has been designed so that all habitat types are represented in the areas open to tourists. Trails are not yet clearly marked in the park, although it is fairly straightforward as far as Tomer. It is advisable to take a local guide if you are intending to go deeper into the park; they are worth it, as they can show you wildlife and introduce you to the local culture. The price of a local guide is around 10,000Rp per day.

From July to December, during the dry season. Travel is restricted during the wet season, but if visitors don't mind the wet, it is possible to visit all year round. The tourist information centre provides information on which areas to visit at different times of year.

Best time to visit

D *Guesthouse* in Yanggandur, built in traditional style, sleeps 6, bring your own food (cooking facilities available) and mosquito net and bedding. The park is planning 3 new guesthouses. It is possible to stay in some of the villages, but there are no amenities. **Camping**: it is

Sleeping

possible to camp almost anywhere in the park, but there are several dedicated campsites. The best facilities are at Ukra, where there is a large permanent tent, which provides wildlife viewing by day and mosquito and snake protection by night.

Eating & bars It is advisable to buy provisions in Merauke (tinned and dried food is reasonably priced here). Local women may prepare your evening meal for you; it will consist of sago, cassava, sweet potatoes and maybe some fish or chicken. They can provide boiled water for drinking. If you are hiring a guide, remember to provide food for him too.

Transport It takes 30 mins by car from Merauke to the park. Large areas of the park are accessible because of the Trans Irian highway, which dissects the park, east to west. It is possible to hire a taxi, jeep or motorbike to get into the park. Motorized vehicles are allowed along the highway to Yanggandur, Rawa Biru and Sota. **Local** Within the park, it is possible to hire ponies (places where ponies are available for hire are marked on the map provided by the park information office). Hiring a pony costs about 10,000Rp/day. Cycling is allowed in the park. **Road Taxi**: drivers may only agree to take you during the dry season. To Wasur, around 30,000Rp return; to

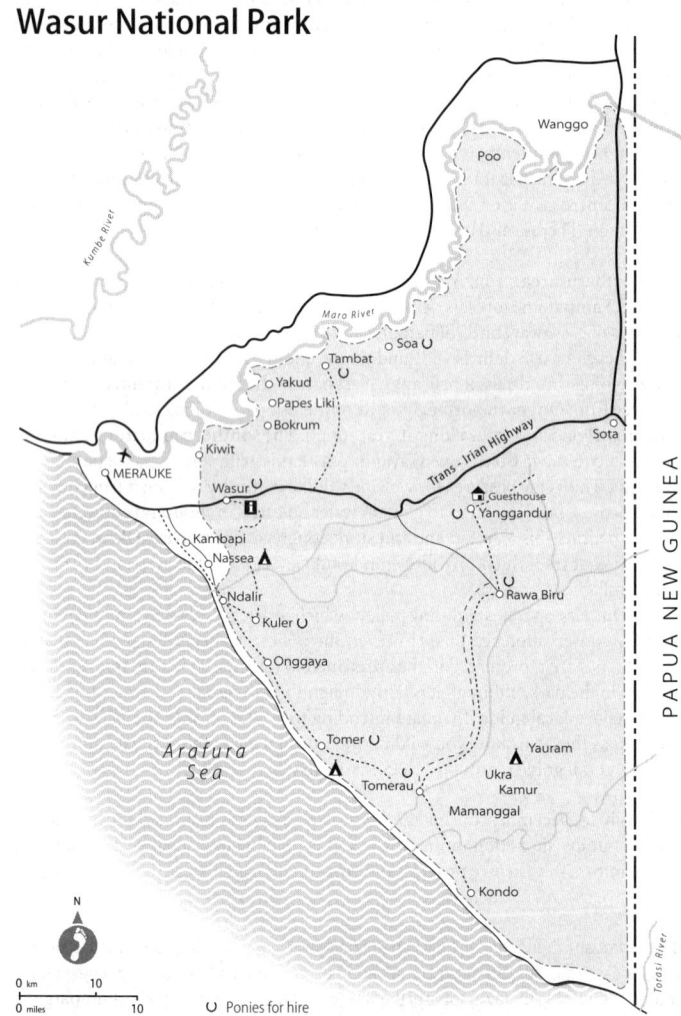

Rawa Biru, approximately 80,000Rp-90,000Rp 1 way; to Yanggandur, roughly 80,000Rp (drop and pick up same day or later); to Ndalir/Onggaya, about 70,000Rp (drop and pick up same day or later). Taxis will agree to drop off at 1 point and pick up somewhere else. **Four wheel drive vehicles**: it is possible to hire these, with a driver, in order to visit some of the central grasslands, and villages such as Kondo and Tomerau in the dry season; the price remains high (200,000-250,000Rp/day) and numbers are controlled. Each additional day costs about 50,000Rp. The park insists a local guide is employed to escort the vehicle.

Timika, Kuala Kencana and Tembagapura

In December 1995 President Suharto presided at the official 'opening' of a new town – Kuala Kencana, which, appropriately, means 'River of Gold'. The town, which will support a population of 20,000, exists to service the massive Freeport gold and copper mine to the north (see box, page 932). South of Kuala Kencana is the 'open' town and sub-district (*Kelurahan*) capital of Timika, with a population of around 70,000 – up from just 10,000 in the late 1980s. Most of these are immigrants from Java and Sulawesi, as well as other parts of Irian Jaya. South of Timika is the port settlement of Amamapare. A road runs from Amamapare to Tembagapura (a settlement close to the mine) via Timika and Kuala Kencana, a distance of about 120 km. All four towns are effectively run by Freeport-McMoRan: they are by far the largest employer in the area and the government presence is minimal. The main tribal groups living in this area are the Amungme, Kamoro and Dani.

Phone code: 0901
Colour map 6, grid B4

During 1995 and into 1996, Timika was the scene of **demonstrations** by Papuan tribespeople – orchestrated, some maintained, by the Organisasi Papua Merdeka (OPM), the Free Papua Movement – demonstrating against the Freeport mine and the alleged human rights abuses, perpetrated by the Indonesian military and security personnel employed by Freeport-McMoRan. The allegations and counter-allegations are particularly sensitive because of the importance of the Freeport mine to the Indonesian economy, and because of the political and security concerns that colour the Indonesian government's view.

Sheraton Inn Timika, PO Box 3, Timika, T394949, F394950. This 100-room hotel north of Timika opened towards the end of 1994, and the existence of a luxury hotel in such a remote place is inextricably associated with the Freeport mine which attracts more than its fair share of visitors with company expense accounts.

Sleeping

Air The airport is a 5 min drive from Timika. **Sea** The *Pelni* vessel *Tatamailau* docks here on its fortnightly circuit (see route schedule page 982).

Transport
500 km east of Fakfak

Background

History

D'Abreu was the first European to see New Guinea in 1512. Long before this date, however, Chinese and Arab traders and seafarers from the Spice Islands of Maluku were trading with the coastal communities of Irian Jaya, exchanging manufactured goods for forest products. In 1526, de Menses, the first governor of the Spice Islands, was forced to take shelter in a cove on Bird's Head (Kepala Burung) during a storm and named the land Ilhas dos Papuas or Islands of the Papuans. He took the word Papuas from the Malay *papuah* – for *orang papuah*, or 'frizzy-haired men'.

From the 16th century mariners continued to sail along and map the coasts, but there was no attempt at interior exploration or settlement. The first colony was established in 1793 by the English *East India Company* near Manokwari; it was abandoned after only two years. The Dutch did not establish a presence until 1828 when they built a fortress at Fort du Bus, in Triton Bay; it was abandoned less than 10 years later. They re-established a presence at the end of the 19th century, building forts at Manokwari, on the north coast of the Bird's Head, and at Fak-Fak, on the west peninsular, declaring all the land to the west of the 141st meridian as Dutch territory. In 1902 a settlement was established at Merauke in the southeast and at Humboldt Bay (near present day Jayapura), on the north coast. However, the Dutch presence was still restricted to the coastal regions.

Co-ordinated exploration of the interior did not begin until the second decade of the 20th century. And it was only in 1938 that the American Richard Archbold, leader of the Archbold Expeditions, discovered the Grand Baliem Valley. The Japanese occupied New Guinea in 1942, and some of the bitterest fighting in the Pacific Theatre took place here. Large numbers of airfields were built here by the Allies and the Japanese.

In 1962, the Dutch gave up control of West Papua to a United Nations Temporary Executive Authority (UNTEA). A year later, in May 1963, the territory was handed over to Indonesia to administer on the condition that within six years there would be an Act of Free Choice – a plebiscite – to ascertain whether the population wished to become a part of Indonesia. It is at this point that opinions – like those on East Timor – differ. According to the Indonesian government, in 1969 the people of Irian were given a choice as to whether to become an independent country, or part of the Republic of Indonesia; and they freely chose the latter. Critics like the Anti-Slavery Society maintain that: "The Act was stage-managed by the Indonesians, who used a combination of bribery and brute force to persuade 1,025 local 'delegates' to approve the continued Indonesian occupation of West Papua" (1990: 6). Despite a highly critical report by the UN observer Fernando Ortiz Sanz, the UN voted to endorse the Indonesian annexation of the territory in November 1969. Since that date, the Operasi Papua Merdeka (OPM) or Free Papua Movement have been fighting a largely ignored (see page 931) guerrilla war of independence in Irian Jaya.

Economic & political change The development of Irian Jaya by the Indonesian government has taken three main directions. On the one hand the government has allotted considerable sums to upgrading the province's infrastructure. This is partly for security reasons – the secessionist OPM (see above) is still active and there is continued political disaffection. Another important motivation, however, is that the government sees Irian Jaya as a major source of primary resources (see the box on page 932). Already, oil and copper represent over 90% of the value of the province's exports and any expansion in exploitation is partly contingent upon improving the physical infrastructure. Finally, with a population density of only four people per square kilometre, Irian Jaya is seen as a vast untapped source of agricultural land to satisfy the land hunger of the poor in Java and Bali. For a time during the 1980s, a series of transmigration settlements were opened in the province and it seemed that Irian Jaya was gradually becoming the main focus of the programme. Then pressure from the World Bank, which feared the environmental and cultural effects of the settlements in the province, led to it being suspended in 1991. However, it now seems that the Indonesian government is so intent on satisfying the needs of land-hungry Javanese by opening the province to settlement that they are funding this part of the scheme themselves. The main focus of settlement appears to be on new sites around Merauke.

The need to develop the province has led to considerable investment by the government. It has also encouraged the immigration of large numbers of Indonesians from outside Irian Jaya – primarily Javanese, Makassarese and people from Maluku. This process is most obvious in the cities where nearly 90% of the population are non-Irian born. This has led to criticisms that the Irianese are failing to derive any benefit from the exploitation of the province and accusations that the central government is trying to 'Javanize' the area by swamping the locals with immigrants. Visitors may notice that almost all jobs of significance, almost all small businesses from bemo-operators, to losmen-managers, to warung-owners, are non-Irianese. Today, over 20% of the population are non-Irian born, and with only 1,900,000 inhabitants in total, it may not be long before immigrants outnumber the indigenous inhabitants. Certainly, many of the Papuans of Irian Jaya feel little sense of common identity with the 'Asians' that dominate the rest of the country.

Possibly more than anywhere else in the country, wealth generated accumulates to non-locals. Irian Jaya is unimaginably rich in natural resources and yet the great bulk of that wealth is syphoned off by foreign companies or Jakarta-based politicians and businessmen. Little accrues to the indigenous people and little is reinvested in the province. In many areas of Irian Jaya, malaria, dysentery and other diseases and illnesses kill 50% of children before they reach school age.

For the moment, Irian Jaya remains one of the few true frontier areas left on earth. Vast expanses remain largely unexplored and traditional customs exert a dominant influence. On 19 March 1992, the Jakarta-based Indonesian daily newspaper *Kompas* reported that a tribesman had killed his wife when he hit her over the head with a bottle during an argument. He was fined 11 cows and ordered to part with his treasured collection of stones and seeds.

Recent years have seen a change in the Indonesian approach to the development of the tribal peoples of Irian Jaya. Until the 1980s, the view was that tribes like the Dani had to be 'civilized'. Measures were taken to promote such indicators of 'development' as the wearing of Western clothes. In the early 1970s, for example, the army's *Operasi Koteka* – or Operation Penis Gourd – tried to rather cack-handedly 'encourage' the Dani of the Baliem Valley to dispense with their 'primitive' penis gourds by airlifting jogging shorts and dresses into the province. The programme was spectacularly unsuccessful: the men found the shorts more usefully worn as hats, while the women adapted the dresses into holdalls. Now, however, the Indonesian authorities have discovered that there is a tourist demand for people wearing penis gourds and other paraphernalia of 'primitive-ness'. Although many Indonesian officials still believe the Irianese to be backward, the prevailing argument seems to be that if there is money in it, then why change it. In Wamena, for example, a statue shows a Dani warrior resplendent in little more than a *koteka*, while new government-run handicraft co-operatives laud the artistic skills of the Dani.

For years the Free Papua Movement has been fighting for independence with scarcely a raised international eyebrow. However in 2000 the government became alarmed by an increase in violence. President Wahid appeared to suggest that the province could change its name from Irian Jaya (imposed by Jakarta) to West Papua (preferred by the independence movement) – and then backtracked. The 'Morning Star', the flag of the independence movement, was flown across the province and the separatist leader Theys Eluay was courted by the Indonesian government. But pressured by nationalists in Jakarta, President Wahid shifted from conciliation to confrontation. Additional troops were drafted into the province and there was reported violence in October, November and December in Jayapura, Wamena, Fakfak and Merauke.

Land and environment

Geography Irian Jaya was once part of a land bridge that linked Australia and Southeast Asia. The main geological feature of the province is a central range of mountains that runs from northwest to southeast. Near the border with Papua New Guinea (PNG) is the Jayawijaya Range, separated from the West Sudirman Range by the fertile Grand Baliem Valley. The highest peak – and also the highest in Indonesia – is Mount Jaya at 5,030m. There are 10 other mountains which exceed 4,800m, making this the consistently highest part of Southeast Asia, and the only area with glaciers.

North of this impressive, central spine of mountains are a small range known as the Coastal Range or Van Rees Mountains. The highest peak here is 2,272m. To the south, the central mountains descend steeply to a vast, swampy, lowland plain.

As well as the west half of New Guinea, Irian Jaya also comprises a number of islands. The main ones are Japen, Biak-Supiori and Numfor to the north, and the Raja Amphat group – including Waigeo, Batanta, Salawat and Misool – to the northwest.

Freeport Indonesia: the world's richest mine

Irian Jaya is one of the last, great, largely unsurveyed, sources of minerals on earth. And Freeport Indonesia, near Tembagapura in the southern highlands of the province, is arguably the richest mine in the world. The statistics are astounding. The Grasberg copper 'knob' has reserves of at least 1bn tonnes of ore; a 118 km-long conveyer belt and pipeline transports the ore down over 3,000m to the port of Amamapare on the Arafura Sea; the copper and gold reserves are worth US$60bn; over 70,000 tonnes of ore are moved each day; Grasberg has gold reserves of 52,100,000 ounces – more than any mine in the world; and it will still be producing in 2032. To date there are two mines in the area. The Ertsberg is mined out, and the effort has transformed a 180m-high mountain of copper into a 360m-deep hole in the ground. The Grasberg mine is still being expanded. In the Amole, tunnel teams will be working 2,700m below the original mining level of 1989. Exploration for more deposits is being undertaken in areas where humans have probably never before set foot. All equipment and supplies are helicoptered into alpine meadows surrounded by precipitous cliffs. As Ed Pressman, chief of corporate affairs, proudly said at the end of 1996: "Our knowledge of how far the mineralization goes is constrained only by the drilling, not by the geology."

Not only is the world's richest mine found in this remote corner of Irian Jaya, so too is one of the world's last great unexplored wildernesses. Inevitably, environmentalists such as the Indonesian Forum for the Environment (Wahli) have highlighted the costs to people and nature. Already, the Grasberg is the second largest open-cast copper mine in the world, and James Moffatt ('Jim-Bob'), the colourful and outspoken Chairman of Freeport-McMoRan, the holding company based in the US, has been quoted as saying that they will "mine all the way to New Orleans" in their search for ore. The tailings (waste) from the mine, though probably non-toxic, are fed into the Agawagon River at a rate of 100,000-160,000 tonnes a day, and the river has changed course as a result of the siltation. But it is arguable that the rewards of exploitation to Freeport Indonesia and to the Indonesian government are simply too great for environmental worries to curtail work. Freeport is Indonesia's fourth largest taxpayer and their investments in the province are opening up the area for other developments. Infrastructure like roads is providing the means by which transmigrants from Java can settle in the area. This concerns environmental groups and some locals. It will open up this last untouched part of Indonesia in the way that the Trans-Amazon highway has done in Brazil. Pristine forest will make way for possibly unsustainable agriculture, displacing tribal peoples in the process. The inflow of transmigrants is also taking jobs away from local Irianese, creating social tensions.

Until recently it seemed that Freeport-McMoRan and the Indonesian government had the situation under control. But the widely publicized death of several demonstrators at the hands – allegedly – of the military has changed the tempo and temperature of the debate. James Moffatt has been accused of 'killing for profit', while Moffatt has lambasted his opponents as "'adical groups cloaked as environmental organizations". The fact that the area around the mine is also a centre of OPM (Organisasi Papua Merdeka, the Free Papua Movement) activity has raised the stakes for the government too.

Not before time, Freeport has realized that it has a duty to minimize the environmental impacts of the mine. It now spends US$40m a year on environmental monitoring. But for many, it is too little, too late. When the mine closes in 2030 it will leave behind a devastated area covering 230 sq km, so large that it will be visible from space. Moreover, the geologists at Freeport believe that there are yet more riches to be found along a 'trend line' that runs east-west through the middle of New Guinea. In a deal with the British mining company Rio Tinto Zinc, or RTZ, they are exploring two new sites at Etna Bay and Wabu.

There is a Freeport Web page on the Corporate Watch Web: www.corpwatch.org

Irian Jaya is hot, wet and humid. Rainfall tends to be heavy throughout the year, with only minor seasonal variations. On the north coast rainfall is about 2,500mm per year; in the mountains it can exceed 8,000mm per year, making this one of the wettest spots on earth. It is also one of the cloudiest (which poses a major problem for air transport). However, there are areas where rainfall is markedly less. Merauke in the southeast, for example, receives less than 1,500mm; also drier are sections of the northwest and the north (eg Jayapura). Temperatures, except at altitude, average a fairly constant 29-32°C.

Climate

Irian Jaya's flora and fauna are complex and diverse. In total, 'Papuasia' – as the whole region is known – has over 20,000 species of plant, 200 mammal, 725 bird, 253 reptile and 80,000-100,000 species of insect. In the Arfak Nature Reserve alone, which covers only 70 sq km outside Manokwari, 800 species of spider and 5,000 species of butterflies and moths have been recorded. Not only does the province cover a wide variety of ecological zones from coastal mangrove swamp, to lowland rainforest, montane forest, up to alpine grasslands; but it also lies at a biogeographical crossroads: the animals and plants are both Asian and Australasian in origin. In the mountains, for example, there are north latitude oaks from China such as *Quercus junghunii* growing alongside 'Antarctic' beeches (*Nothofagus*). Among the large number of fascinating plants are insectivorous pitcher plants (*Nepenthes*) and the weird and wonderful giant anthouse plant (*Myrmecodia brasii*), an epiphyte over 2 km in length with a bulbous, honey-combed stem inhabited by large numbers of ants.

Fauna & flora

Like Irian's flora, its fauna shows clear links with both Asia and Australasia. There are two species of primitive monotremes, the short-beaked (*Tachyglossus aculeatus*) and long-beaked (*Zaglossus bruijni*) echidna, marsupial mice (*Dasyuridae*), tree kangaroos (*Dendrolagus*), and the rare sea mammal, the dugong (*Dugong dugon*). Among its 725 species of bird, the best known are the 26 species of birds of paradise. Other notable birds include nine species of bower bird (*Ptilonorhynchidae*), the large, flightless cassowary (*Casuarius*) and the orange and black pitohui. In 1992, the pitohui became the first bird to be proved poisonous. The feathers, skin and flesh of the pitohui contain homobatrachotoxin, powerful enough to kill a mouse in minutes. It explains why snakes and hawks – the birds' natural enemies – steer well clear of the three species of pitohui and why it is known locally as the 'rubbish bird'.

Culture

There are three ecological regions in Irian Jaya: the coast, the interior lowlands and the highlands. Because travel is so difficult through the harsh terrain, the people of these different zones remain largely isolated from one another. Even today, the only feasible way to get around the province is by air. This inaccessibility is reflected in a huge diversity of languages; about 250 different dialects are thought to be spoken in Irian Jaya and sometimes communities just 40 km apart cannot understand each other. About 30% of the population live in agricultural communities in the cool, temperate valleys of the Baliem Valley, Paniai Lakes and Anggi Lakes. In recent years, however, there has been a dramatic increase in the urban population of such centres as Jayapura, Biak and Merauke. Most of this increase has been through an influx of immigrants from other regions of Indonesia, rather than a shift in population from rural areas in Irian Jaya. As the last great frontier zone in Indonesia, the province has also been targeted as a major destination for transmigrant settlers.

People

The **coastal** people cultivate sago, taro and coconuts, raise pigs, and fish. Sago is their dietary staple. Traditionally, they lived in large houses built on stilts, which could hold up to 100 people, with a central communal area for cooking and socializing and separate rooms for each family; this tradition has died out and most families now have their own homes. The people of the coasts grew rich on maritime trade; they were able to sell local products such as sea cucumber (*trepang*), rare woods, animal skins and exotic birds in exchange for foreign goods such as metals, textiles, glass beads and porcelain. In their turn, and despite the difficulties of communication, the coastal people would trade these imported goods to the inhabitants of the interior, where they became an important part of a bride's trousseau.

Like the coastal people, the **interior lowlanders** also grow sago and taro, but hunting and gathering play a more important role in their livelihoods. They 'farm' the larvae of the capricorn beetle by cultivating fallen, rotting trees where the insects breed. The **highlanders** cultivate sweet potatoes and taro in a rotational field system, and also raise pigs for ceremonial and ritual events.

Arts & crafts The inhabitants of Irian Jaya produce fine woodcarvings – those of the Asmat are particularly highly regarded. On the north coast, elaborately carved spatulas for serving food are the most distinctive art form. Food was traditionally served on carved plates, and large ceremonial platters were reserved for feasts and kept by the headman.

Betel nut holders – used to carry the lime powder that is a part of the betel nut preparation – are also common. These are made from gourds and are incised with patterns. Men's gourds are long and thin, whilst women's are short and fat. The incisions on a woman's gourd are also rubbed with lime. Spatulas with pointed ends were carved as stoppers for the gourds, sometimes with figures on the top.

There is no tradition of weaving in Irian Jaya. The inhabitants traditionally adorned their bodies with necklaces, armbands and head-dresses, and the women sometimes wore barkcloth skirts.

12

Background

Background

937	**History**
937	Prehistory
937	Pre-colonial history
938	Colonial history
944	**Modern Indonesia**
945	Politics
953	Economy
959	**Culture**
959	Religion – Islam in Indonesia
961	Language and literature
963	Dance, drama and music
964	**Land and environment**
964	The regions of Indonesia
965	Geography
967	Climate
967	Flora and fauna
969	National parks

History

Prehistory

After Thailand and East Malaysia, Indonesia – and particularly Java – has probably revealed more of Southeast Asia's prehistory than any other country in the region. Most significant was the discovery of **hominid fossils** in Central Java in 1890, when Eugene Dubois uncovered the bones of so-called 'Java Man' near the village of Trinil. He named his ape-man *Pithecanthropus erectus*, since changed to *Homo erectus erectus*. These, and other discoveries – particularly at Sangiran, also in Central Java and Mojokerto – indicate that Indonesia was inhabited by hominids as long as 1,800,000 years ago. Excavations in Central Java have also revealed other fossils of early Man – *Pithecanthropus soloensis* and *P modjokertensis*. Among the skulls of *P soloensis*, a number have been found to have had their cranial bases removed, leading scientists to postulate that the species practised anthropophagy – less politely known as cannibalism – which involved gouging the victim's brains out through the base. Alternatively, the surgery might have been part of a post mortem ritual.

Following the end of the last Ice Age 15,000 years ago, there began a movement of Mongoloid peoples from the Asian mainland, south and east, and into the Southeast Asian archipelago. As this occurred, the immigrants displaced the existing Austro-melanesian inhabitants, pushing them further east or into remote mountain areas.

The practice of **settled agriculture** seems to have filtered into the islands of Indonesia from mainland Southeast Asia about 2500 BC, along with these Mongoloid migrants. Settled life is associated with the production of primitive earthenware pottery, examples of which have been found in Java, Sulawesi and Flores. Later, **ancestor cults** evolved, echoes of which are to be seen in the megaliths of Sumatra, Java, Sulawesi, Bali, Sumbawa and Sumba. These cultures reached their height about 500 BC. Among the various discoveries has been evidence of the mutilation of corpses – presumably to prevent the deceased from returning to the world of the living. In some cases, ritual elements of these megalithic cultures still exist – for example, on the island of Sumba in Nusa Tenggara, among the inhabitants of Nias Island off West Sumatra, and among the Batak of North Sumatra.

The technology of **bronze casting** was also known to prehistoric Indonesians. Socketed axes have been discovered in Java, several islands of Nusa Tenggara (eg Roti) and in Sulawesi. But the finest bronze artefacts are the magnificent kettledrums of East Indonesia. It is thought these were made in Vietnam, not in Indonesia, and arrived in the archipelago when traders used them as barter goods. Later, locally made equivalents such as the *moko* of Alor (see page 853) were produced, but they never achieved the refinement of the originals.

Pre-colonial history

Unlike the states of mainland Southeast Asia, which did enjoy a certain geographical legitimacy prior to the colonial period, Indonesia was a fragmented assemblage of kingdoms, sultanates, principalities and villages. It is true that there was a far greater degree of communication and intercourse than many assume, so that no part of the archipelago can be treated in isolation, but nonetheless, it is still difficult to talk of 'Indonesian' history prior to the 19th century.

The great empires of the pre-colonial period did range beyond their centres of power, but none came close to controlling all the area now encompassed by the modern Indonesian state. Among these empires, the most powerful were the Srivijayan Kingdom based at Palembang in South Sumatra; and the great Javanese Dynasties of Sailendra, Majapahit and Mataram. There was also a string of less powerful, but nonetheless influential, kingdoms; for example, the Sultanate of Aceh in North Sumatra, the Gowa Kingdom of South Sulawesi, the trading sultanates of the Spice Islands of Maluku, and the Hindu kingdoms of Bali. The history of each of these powers is dealt with in the appropriate regional introduction.

Major pre-colonial powers

Srivijaya	7th-14th	Palembang
Sailendra	8th-10th	Central Java
Sanjaya	8th-11th	Central & East Java
Kediri	11th-13th	Kediri, East Java
Banten	12th-17th	Banten, West Java
Singasari	13th	East Java
Majapahit	13th-15th	East Java
Gowa	16th-17th	Makassar, South Sulawesi
Mataram	16th-18th	Central Java
Aceh	16th-19th	Aceh, North Sumatra
Karangkasem	18th-19th	Bali & Lombok

Even after the European powers arrived in the archipelago, their influence was often superficial. They were concerned only with controlling the valuable spice trade, and were not inclined to feats of territorial expansion. To get around this lack of a common history, historians tend to talk instead in terms of common processes of change. The main ones affecting the archipelago were the 'Indianization' of the region from the 1st century AD and the introduction of Hinduism and Buddhism; the arrival of Islam in North Sumatra in the 13th century and then its spread east and south during the 15th century; and the contrast between inwardly-focused agricultural kingdoms and outwardly-orientated trading states.

Colonial history

During the course of the 15th century, the two great European maritime powers of the time, Spain and Portugal, were exploring sea routes to the east. Two forces were driving this search: the desire for profits, and the drive to evangelize. At the time, even the wealthy in Europe had to exist on pickled and salted fish and meat during the winter months (fodder crops for winter feed were not grown until the 18th century). Spices to flavour what would otherwise be a very monotonous diet were greatly sought after and commanded a high price. This was not just a passing European fad. An Indian Hindu wrote that: "When the palate revolts against the insipidness of rice boiled with no other ingredients, we dream of fat, salt and spices."

Locals bringing nutmeg to sell to Dutch factors in Banda, the Moluccas, 1599.

The VOC – the world's first multinational

The Dutch East India Company was a unique enterprise at the time of its creation in 1601. Not only was the company based on long-term investment at a time when most trading investment lasted only as long as the voyage, but it also linked together a series of forts and factories across the globe manned by employees from many different countries. This global reach and the cosmopolitan nature of its employees has led some historians to pronounce the VOC to be the world's first multinational company.

Although the VOC was a private enterprise – a joint stock company with founding capital of 6.5m guilders – the Dutch Republic also saw it as an agent of national policy and provided cannon and arms free of charge for the defence of its ships. The company reached the peak of its powers at the end of the 17th century, when it had 22 factories scattered across Asia, and 11,500 employees. In the decade between 1700 and 1710, 280 VOC ships sailed from Holland eastwards.

It is usually said that sloppy management led to the demise of the VOC, but this was undoubtedly amplified by the effects of the Fourth Anglo-Dutch War (1780-84) when English men-of-war seized most VOC vessels sailing for home. In 1795 the Company was nationalized and at the end of the century it had accumulated debts of 219m guilders.

Of the spices, cloves and nutmeg originated from just one location, the Moluccas (Maluku) – the Spice Islands of eastern Indonesia. Perhaps because of their value, spices and their places of origin were accorded mythical status in Europe. The 14th century French friar Catalani Jordanus claimed, for example, that the clove flowers of Java produced an odour so strong it killed "every man who cometh among them, unless he shut his mouth and nostrils".

It was in order to break the monopoly on the spice trade held by Venetian and Muslim Arab traders that the Portuguese began to extend their possessions eastwards. This finally culminated in the capture of the port of Melaka by the Portuguese seafarer Alfonso de Albuquerque in June 1511. The additional desire to spread the Word of God is clear in the speech that Albuquerque made before the battle with the Muslim sultan of Melaka, when he exorted his men, stressing:

"... the great service which we shall perform to our Lord in casting the Moors out of this country and of quenching the fire of the sect of Mohammet so that it may never burst out again hereafter".

From their base in Melaka, the Portuguese established trading relations with the Moluccas, and built a series of forts across the region: at Bantam (Banten), Flores, Ternate, Tidore, Timor and Ambon (Amboyna).

Many accounts of Indonesian history treat the arrival of the Portuguese Admiral Alfonso de Albuquerque off Malacca (Melaka) in 1511, and the dispatch of a small fleet to the Spice Islands, as a watershed in Indonesian history. As the historian MC Ricklefs argues, this view is untenable, writing that "... in the early years of the Europeans' presence, their influence was sharply limited in both area and depth".

The Portuguese only made a significant impact in the Spice Islands, leaving their mark in a number of Indonesian words of Portuguese origin – for example, *sabun* (soap), *meja* (table) and *Minggu* (Sun). They also introduced Christianity to East Indonesia and disrupted the islands' prime export – spices. But it was the Dutch, in the guise of the *Vereenigde Oost-Indische Compagnie* or *VOC* (the Dutch East India Company), who began the process of western intrusion. They established a toehold in Java – which the Portuguese had never done – a precursor to later territorial expansion. But this was a slow process and it was not until the early 20th century – barely a generation before the Japanese occupation – that the Dutch could legitimately claim they held administrative authority over the whole country.

The beginning of the 20th century marks a turning point in Indonesian history. As Raden Kartini, a young educated Javanese woman, wrote in a letter dated 12 January 1900: "Oh, it is splendid just to live in this age; the transition of the old into the new!". It was in 1899 that

The idea of Indonesia, 1900-42

the Dutch lawyer C Th van Deventer published a ground-breaking paper entitled *Een eereschuld* or 'A debt of honour'. This article argued that having exploited the East Indies for so long, and having extracted so much wealth from the colony, it was time for the Dutch government to restructure their policies and focus instead on improving conditions for Indonesians. In 1901, the Ethical Policy – as it became known – was officially embraced. Van Deventer was commissioned to propose ways to further such a policy and suggested a formulation of 'education, irrigation and emigration'. The Ethical Policy represented a remarkable change in perspective, but scholars point out that it was very much a creation of the European mind and made little sense in Indonesian terms.

The Indonesian economy was also changing in character. The diffusion of the cash economy through the islands and the growing importance of export crops like rubber and coffee, and minerals such as tin and oil, were transforming the country. Christianity, too, became a powerful force for change, particularly in the islands beyond Muslim Java. There was large-scale conversion in central and North Sulawesi, Flores, among the Batak of Sumatra, in Kalimantan, and Timor. In response to the inroads that Christianity was making in the Outer Islands, Islam in Java became more orthodox and reformist. The 'corrupt' *abangan*, who adhered to what has become known as the 'Javanese religion' – a mixture of Muslim, Hindu, Buddhist and animist beliefs – were gradually displaced by the stricter *santris*.

At about the same time, there was an influx of *trekkers*, or Dutch expatriates, who came to the East Indies with their wives and Dutch cultural perspectives, with the intention of going 'home' after completing their contracts. They overwhelmed the older group of *blijvers* or 'stayers', and there emerged a more racist European culture, one that denigrated *Indische* culture and extolled the life-style of the Dutch. The Chinese community, like the Dutch, was also divided into two groups: the older immigrants or *peranakan* who had assimilated into Indies culture, and the more recent *totok* arrivals who zealously maintained their culture, clinging to their Chinese roots (see box, page 951).

So, the opening years of the 20th century presented a series of paradoxes. On the one hand, Dutch policy was more sensitive to the needs of the 'natives'; yet many Dutch were becoming less understanding of Indonesian culture and more bigoted. At the same time, while the Chinese and Dutch communities were drawing apart from the native Indonesians and into distinct communities based upon Chinese and European cultural norms, so the economy was becoming increasingly integrated and international. Perhaps inevitably, tensions arose, and these began to mould the social and political landscape of confrontation between the colonialists and the natives.

A number of political parties and pressure groups emerged from this maelstrom of forces. In 1912, a Eurasian – one of those who found himself ostracized from European-colonial culture – EFE Douwes Dekker founded the Indies Party. This was a revolutionary grouping with the slogan 'the Indies for those who make their home there'. In the same year, a batik merchant from Surakarta established the Sarekat Islam or 'Islamic Union', which quickly became a mass organization under the leadership of the charismatic orator HOS Cokroaminoto. Seven years later it had over 2,000,000 members. In 1914, a small group of *totok* Dutch immigrants founded the Indies Social-Democratic Association in Semarang. Finally, in 1920, the Perserikatan Komunis di India (PKI) or the Indies Communist Party was established.

In 1919, the Dutch colonial authorities decided to clamp down on all dissent. The flexibility that had characterized Dutch policy until then was abandoned in favour of an increasingly tough approach. But despite the rounding-up of large numbers of subversives, and the demise of the PKI and emasculation of the Sarekat Islam, it was at this time that the notion of 'Indonesia' first emerged. In July 1927, Sukarno founded the Partai Nasional Indonesia or PNI. In October 1928, a Congress of Indonesian Youth coined the phrase 'one nation – Indonesia, one people – Indonesian, one language – Indonesian'. At the same congress the Indonesian flag was designed and the Indonesian national anthem sung for the first time – *Indonesia Raya*. As John Smail writes in the book *In Search of Southeast Asia*:

"The idea of Indonesia spread so easily, once launched, that it seemed to later historians as if it had always existed, if not actually explicitly then inchoate in the hearts of the people. But it was, in fact, a new creation, the product of a great and difficult leap of the imagination. The idea of Indonesia required the denial of the political meaning of the societies into which the first Indonesians had been born".

In spite of Dutch attempts to stifle the nationalist spirit, it spread through Indonesian, and particularly Javanese, society. By 1942, when the Japanese occupied the country, the idea of Indonesia as an independent nation was firmly rooted.

Although the Japanese occupation lasted less than four years, it fundamentally altered the forces driving the country towards independence. Prior to 1942, the Dutch faced no real challenge to their authority; after 1945, it was only a question of time before independence. The stunning victory of the Japanese in the Dutch East Indies destroyed the image of colonial invincibility, undermined the prestige of the Dutch among many Indonesians, and – when the Dutch returned to power after 1945 – created an entirely new psychological relationship between rulers and ruled.

The Japanese occupation, 1942-45

But the Japanese were not liberators. Their intention of creating a Greater East Asia Co-Prosperity Sphere did not include offering Indonesians independence. They wished to control Indonesia for their own interests. The Japanese did give a certain latitude to nationalist politicians in Java, but only as a means of mobilizing Indonesian support for their war effort. Sukarno and Muhammad Hatta were flown to Tokyo in November 1943 and decorated by Emperor Hirohito. For the Dutch and their allies, the war meant incarceration. There were 170,000 internees, including 60,000 women and children. About a quarter died in captivity.

One particularly sordid side of the occupation which has come to light in recent years is the role of 'comfort women'. This euphemism should be more accurately translated as 'sex slaves' – women who were forced to satisfy the needs of Japanese soldiers to aid the war effort. For years the Japanese government denied such comfort stations existed, but documents unearthed in Japan have indicated beyond doubt that they were very much part of the war infrastructure. Much of the attention has focused upon comfort women from Korea, China and the Philippines, but there were also stations in Indonesia. These women, so long cowed and humiliated into silence, are now talking about their experiences to force the Japanese government to accept responsibility. Dutch-Australian Jan Ruff is one of these brave women. A young girl living in Java before the war, she was interned in Camp Ambarawa with her mother and two sisters. In February 1944 she was taken, along with nine other girls, to a brothel in Semarang for the sexual pleasure of Japanese officers. In her testimony at a public meeting in Tokyo in December 1992 she recounted: "During that time [at the brothel] the Japanese had abused me and humiliated me. They had ruined my young life. They had stripped me of everything, my self-esteem, my dignity, my freedom, my possessions, my family." Belatedly, the Japanese government offered its 'sincere apologies and remorse' in August 1993, 48 years afterwards. The fact that the apology came on the last day of the Liberal Democratic Party's government detracted from the honesty of the remarks. Many still feel that Japanese leaders find it difficult to be sincere about events almost half a century old.

As the Japanese military lost ground in the Pacific to the advancing Americans, so their rule over Indonesia became increasingly harsh. Peasants were forcibly recruited as 'economic soldiers' to help the war effort – about 75,000 died – and the Japanese were even firmer in their suppression of dissent than the Dutch had been before them. But as the military situation deteriorated, the Japanese gradually came to realize the necessity of allowing nationalist sentiments greater rein. On 7 September 1944, Prime Minister Koiso promised independence, and in March 1945 the creation of an Investigating Committee for Preparatory Work for Indonesian Independence was announced. Among its members were Sukarno, Hatta and Muhammad Yamin. On 1 June, Sukarno mapped out his philosophy of Pancasila or Five Principles which were to become central tenets of independent Indonesia. On 15 August, after the second atomic bomb was dropped on Nagasaki, the Japanese unconditionally surrendered. Sukarno, Hatta and the other independence leaders now had to act quickly before the Allies helped the Dutch re-establish control. On 17 August 1945, Sukarno read out the Declaration of Independence, Indonesia's red and white flag was raised and a small group of onlookers sang the national anthem, Indonesia Raya.

Revolutionary struggle, 1945-50

In September 1945, the first units of the British Army landed at Jakarta to re-impose Dutch rule. They arrived to find an Indonesian administration already in operation. Confrontation was inevitable. Young Indonesians responded by joining the revolutionary struggle, which became known as the Pemuda Movement (*pemuda* means youth). This reached its height between 1945 and mid-1946, and brought together young men and women of all classes, binding them together in a common cause. The older nationalists found themselves marginalized in this increasingly violent and fanatical response. Men like Sukarno and Hatta adopted a policy of *diplomasi* – negotiating with the Dutch. The supporters of the Pemuda Movement embraced *perjuangan* – the armed struggle. Not only the Dutch, but also minorities like the Chinese, Eurasians and Ambonese, suffered from atrocities at the hands of the Pemuda supporters. The climax of the Pemuda Movement came in November 1945 with the battle for Surabaya.

In 1947, the Dutch were militarily strong enough to regain control of Java, and East and South Sumatra. At the end of 1948, a second thrust of this 'Police Action' re-established control over much of the rest of the country. Ironically, these military successes played an important role in the final 'defeat' of the Dutch in Indonesia. They turned the United Nations against Holland, forcing the Dutch government to give way over negotiations. On 2 November the Hague Agreement was signed, paving the way for full political independence of all former territories of the Dutch East Indies (with the exception of West Irian) on 27 December 1949.

From independence to Guided Democracy to coup: 1950-65

In 1950, Indonesia was an economic shambles and in political chaos. Initially, there was an attempt to create a political system based on the western European model of parliamentary democracy. By 1952 the futility of expecting a relatively painless progression to this democratic ideal was becoming obvious, despite the holding of a parliamentary general election in 1955 with a voter turnout of over 90%. Conflicts between Communists, radical Muslims, traditional Muslims, regional groups and minorities led to a series of coups, rebel governments and violent confrontations. Indonesia was unravelling and in the middle of 1959, President Sukarno cancelled the provisional constitution and introduced his period of Guided Democracy.

This period of relative political stability rested on an alliance between the army, the Communist PKI, and Sukarno himself. It was characterized by extreme economic nationalism, with assets controlled by Dutch, British and Indian companies and individuals being expropriated. The **Konfrontasi** with the Dutch over the 'recovery' of West Irian from 1960 to 1962, and with Malaysia over Borneo beginning in 1963, forced Sukarno to rely on Soviet arms shipments, and Indonesia moved increasingly into the Soviet sphere of influence. Cracks between the odd alliance of PKI and the army widened, and even Sukarno's popular support and force of character could not stop the dam from bursting. On 1 October 1965, six senior generals were assassinated by a group of middle-ranking officers, thus ending the period of Guided Democracy. MC Ricklefs writes:

"...on that night the balance of hostile forces which underlay guided democracy came to an end. Many observers have seen tragedy in the period, especially in the tragedy of Sukarno, the man who outlived his time and used his popular support to maintain a regime of extravagant corruption and hypocrisy."

The coup was defeated by the quick-thinking of General Suharto whose forces overcame those of the coup's leaders. However, it undermined both Sukarno and the PKI as both were linked with the plot – the former by allowing the PKI to gain such influence, and the latter by allegedly master-minding the coup. Most Indonesians, although not all western academics, see the coup as a Communist plot hatched by the PKI with the support of Mao Zedong and the People's Republic of China. It led to massacres on a huge scale as bands of youths set about exterminating those who were thought to be PKI supporters. This was supported, implicitly, by the army and there were news reports of 'streams choked with bodies'. The reaction was most extreme in Java and Bali, but there were murders across the archipelago. The number killed is not certain; estimates vary from 100,000 to 1,000,000 and the true figure probably lies somewhere between the two (500,000 is widely quoted). In Bali alone some scholars believe that 80,000 people died – around 5%

A stroll along Jalan history

Many important figures in Indonesia's independence movement, as well as heroes from history, have lent their names to thoroughfares throughout the archipelago.

Abdul Muis – Sumatran independence writer.

Jend A Yani, Brig Jend Sutoyo, Lets Jend Haryono, Panjaitan, South Parman, and **Suprapto** – the six generals (along with one captain) killed on 30 September 1965 in the attempted PKI coup (see page 942).

Cik di Tiro (1836-91) – most famous of the ulamas or religious leaders who led the resistance against the Dutch in Aceh.

Cokroaminoto (1882-1934) – a leader of the Sareket Islam (Islamic Union), the first mass organization to be established in Indonesia in 1912. He was a forceful orator and highlighted numerous grievances against the Dutch.

Diponegoro, Prince (1785-1855) – led the Java War of 1825-30 against the Dutch, was captured in 1830 and then exiled to Manado and Ujung Pandang in Sulawesi where he died.

Gajah Mada – famous Prime Minister of the Majapahit Kingdom who served from 1331 to 1364 during the first 14 years of Hayam Wuruk's reign. Gajah Mada University in Yogya is one of the country's premier universities.

Haji Agus Salim – leader of the political Reform Islam movement, and right-hand man to Cokroaminoto.

Hang Tuah – naval hero who's exploits are immortalized and glorified in the Sejarah Malayu (Malay History), the literary masterpiece of the Malay world. Hang is an honorific equivalent of 'Sir'.

Hasanuddin (r.1653-69) – Sultan of Gowa in South Sulawesi who resisted the Dutch.

Hayam Wuruk (r.1350-89) – less well known as King Rajasanagara, he presided over Majapahit's golden age.

Imam Bonjol (1772-1864) – the most influential leader of the religious Padri movement in West Sumatra. He was captured by the Dutch in 1837 and exiled to Priangan, then to Ambon and finally to Manado where he died in 1864.

Jendral Sudirman (1915-50) – Islamic teacher who became an officer in the Japanese volunteer army Peta (Pembela Tanah Air, Protectors of the Fatherland) and later a leading force in the revolution.

Kartini, Raden Ajeng (1879-1904) – the daughter of a noble bupati, educated at a European lower school in Jepara, Kartini is seen as an early Indonesian suffragette. She tragically died in childbirth at the age of 25. Her moving letters have been published in Dutch (Door duisternis tot licht – 'Through Darkness into Light') and in English (Letters of a Javanese Princess).

Majapahit – the Java-based empire.

Pattimura (1783-1817) – a Christian Ambonese soldier whose proper name was Thomas Matulesia and who led a rebellion against the Dutch from Saparua, near Ambon in Maluku.

Srivijaya – the Palembang-based empire.

Teuku Umar – Acehnese leader who helped lead the ulama movement against the Dutch in the late 19th century.

---

of the population. The difficulty is that the body count kept by the military is widely regarded as a gross under-estimate. Oei Tjoe Tat, a cabinet minister under Sukarno, was sent on a fact-finding mission to discover the scale of the massacres. He calculated that by January 1966 500,000 people had died. The military's figure at that time was 80,000. As it was an anti-Communist purge, and as China had been blamed for fermenting the coup, many of those killed were Chinese who were felt, by their mere ethnicity, to have leftist-inclinations and Communist sympathies. Few doubt that the majority were innocent traders and middlemen, whose economic success and ethnic origin made them scapegoats. Islamic clerics and members of youth groups seem to have been particularly instrumental in singling out people for extermination. While these uncontrolled massacres were occurring, power was transferred to General Suharto (although he was not elected president until 1968). This marked the shift from what has become known as the Old Order, to the New Order.

That the events of 1965 remain contentious is reflected in the government's attempts to re-write, and in places to erase, this small slice of history. In 1995, three decades after the events of 1965-66, the authorities banned Oei Tjoe Tat's autobiography *Oei Tjoe Tat: assistant to President Sukarno*. It seems that the account of the anti-communist purge diverged too much from the official history. The fact that banned novelist and former political prisoner Pramoedya Ananta Toer had a hand in the book also cannot have endeared it to the authorities. By the time it was banned, however, around 15,000 copies had already been sold. Documents relating to the 1965-96 upheaval are restricted, and instead the government produces its own sanitized version of events. This has it that the Communists were behind the attempted coup, that President Sukarno was misguided in allowing the Communists to gain so much power, and that only the quick-thinking and courageous military, with Suharto at the fore, thwarted the attempt and saved Indonesia from turmoil.

Pancasila: Sukarno's five principles

* *Belief in the One Supreme God*
* *Just and Civilized Humanity*
* *Unity of Indonesia*
* *Democracy guided by the inner wisdom of unanimity*
* *Social Justice for all the people of Indonesia*

Indonesia's national symbol is the mythical bird, the Garuda, which, in Indonesia's national symbol, is modelled on the Javan hawk-eagle, a bird endemic to Java and of which there are probably 200-300 pairs in the wild. On its chest is emblazoned the pacasila, while its claws clasp the legend Bhinneka tungal ika – 'unity in diversity'.

Political & economic developments under the New Order, 1965-present

When Suharto took power in 1965 he had to deal with an economy in disarray. There was hyper-inflation, virtually no inward investment and declining productivity. To put the economy back on the rails, he turned to a group of US-trained economists who have become known as the Berkeley Mafia. They recommended economic reform, the return of expropriated assets, and a more welcoming political and economic climate for foreign investment. In terms of international relations, Suharto abandoned the policy of support for China and the Soviet Union and moved towards the western fold. Diplomatic relations with China were severed (and only renewed in 1990), and the policy of confrontation against Malaysia brought to an end.

The 33 years from 1965 through to 1998 was one of political stability. Suharto stayed in power for over three decades, and he presided over a political system which in a number of respects had more in common with the Dutch era than with that of former President Sukarno. Suharto eschewed ideology as a motivating force, kept a tight control of administration, and attempted to justify his leadership by offering his people economic well-being. He was known – until the 1997-98 economic crisis – as the 'Father of Development'.

Modern Indonesia

The last few years have seen a transformation in Indonesia's economic and political landscape. No commentator was sufficiently prescient to foresee these changes, and no one knows where, ultimately, they will lead. For the first time since the attempted coup of 1965, Indonesia is entering truly uncharted territory. The chronically pessimistic see Indonesia fragmenting and the economy continuing to bump along the bottom as political instability prevents investor confidence returning. Optimists see stability returning in a brighter post-East Timor/post Suharto era, and economic and investor confidence with

In the nick of time

Money can buy you most things, but people tend to assume that being in prison means being in prison. The case of Eddy Tansil, a wealthy businessman jailed in 1994 for 20 years for defrauding Bapindo, a state bank, of US$448m, shows even this does not always hold true in Indonesia. His prison cell was more like a hotel suite. He had a television, video and fan, and allegedly even a mobile phone and pager. There were rumours that he was permitted to visit his office regularly, and, incredibly, to play golf. So when, in May 1996, the media got wind that Eddy had 'escaped', thoughts of him tunnelling out with nothing more than a toothpick seemed unlikely. It seems that it took the prison authorities two days to report his disappearance – they had apparently been hoping that it was just a rather extended session on the 19th hole.

it. With Aceh seemingly on the road to quasi or full independence, Irian Jaya clamouring for more autonomy, and resource-rich provinces like Riau and East Kalimantan demanding a larger slice of the pie, the central government in Jakarta is finding it almost impossible to keep people happy.

Politics

From 1965 through to 1998, Indonesia was under the control of a military- bureaucratic elite led by President Suharto. Power was exercised through Sekber Golkar, better known as just Golkar, the state's very own political party. In political terms at least, Indonesia was one of the world's most stable countries. It might not have been rich or powerful, but at least there was continuity of leadership. But in 1998 all that changed. Suharto was forced to resign after bitter riots in Jakarta brought on by the collapse of the Indonesian economy, but fuelled by decades of nepotism and corruption. What began as student protests escalated into communal violence and some 1,200 people were killed. The critical Chinese community – central to the operation of the economy – fled the country (for the interim at least) and an already dire economic situation became catastrophic. Suharto's vice president, BJ Habibie, took over the helm, but with scarcely a great deal of enthusiasm from the general populace or from the military. Elections were held on 7 June 1999, the first free elections for 44 years, and they were contested by scores of parties. Megawati Sukarnoputri, former president Sukarno's daughter, won the largest share of the vote through her party PDI-Perjuangan (PDI-Struggle). Even with PDI-P's victory, however, some feared that BJ Habibie would call on the political muscle of Golkar to secure him victory in the presidential elections. But the tragedy of East Timor put paid to that and he had to face the humiliation, in October 1999, of a vote of censure and no confidence in the newly muscular and independent People's Consultative Assembly (Indonesia's parliament).

On 7 June 1999, Indonesians enjoyed their first truly democratic elections since 1955. Despite dire predictions to the contrary, they were largely peaceful. About 112 million votes were cast – 90% of eligible voters – at 250,000 polling stations around the country. A total of 48 parties contested the poll, 45 of them new, and Megawati Sukarnoputri's Democratic Party of Struggle (PDI-P) won the largest share of the vote, attracting 34% of the total. In second place came Golkar with 22%. This was a surprise to some foreign observers, given the bad press Golkar had received, but reflected the party's links with the bureaucracy and a strong showing in the Outer Islands where 'reformasi' had had less of an impact. The three other parties to attract significant numbers of votes were the National Awakening Party (12%), the National Mandate Party (7%) and the United Development Party (10%).

Indonesia's first taste of democracy since 1955 has led to profound changes in the character of both politics and politicians. In the past, MPs had no constituency as such and so were rarely bothered about the need to represent real people. They merely had to make sure they pleased the party bosses. Members of the new parliament, however, not only have responsibilities to their electorates, but are also likely to be much more outspoken.

Politics in the post-Suharto era

Because presidents will now have term-limits (Suharto was in power for 32 years), this will confer greater power on parliament. As Dan Murphy said in mid-1999 and before the presidential elections, "the next president... will confront populist and legislative challenges like no one has faced since Megawati's father and Indonesia's first president, Sukarno, dispensed with democracy 40 years ago" (FEER, 19.8.99).

Under former President Suharto, **Golkar** was, in effect, the state's own party. All state employees were automatically members of Golkar, and during election campaigns the state controlled the activities of other parties. Not surprisingly, therefore, Golkar was able consistently to win over 60% of the votes cast in parliamentary elections, and controlled the Parliament (DPR) and the People's Consultative Assembly. Even before Suharto's resignation in 1998, there was the enduring sense that the tide of history was running against Golkar. The provinces where Golkar did least well were in the country's heartland – like Jakarta and East Java. It was here, in Java, that Indonesia's middle classes and 'new rich' were beginning to clamour for more of a say in how the country was run, and by whom. With Golkar's loss of the elections of 1999 to the PDI-P, the party has come to accept a new and less central role in the country. In the past all bureaucrats were automatically members of Golkar and were expected to support and represent Golkar. This is no longer the case.

But despite the fact that the PDI-P won the 1999 parliamentary elections, there were commentators who did not think that Megawati, the party's leader, would become president. Prior to the East Timor debacle, some feared that BJ Habibie would ally himself with one or two other parties and use Golkar to gain the presidency against the run of votes. That assumption was shattered when it became clear that the people of East Timor would vote for independence. But Habibie's mistake was not that he failed to control the army and the militias, but that he was foolish enough to offer the East Timorese a referendum on independence in the first place.

In October 1999 the People's Consultative Assembly voted for **Indonesia's new president** – and it was a cliffhanger. Indonesians could watch – another first for the country – democracy in progress as their representatives lodged their preferences. It was a close contest between Megawati Sukarnoputri, the people's favourite, and the respected **Abdurrahman Wahid**, an almost blind cleric and leader of the country's largest Muslim association, the Nahdlatul Ulama (NU), who is a master of the politics of appeasement; a quality which in the President of such a diverse nation can stymie progress and blunt his effectiveness. As it turned out, Wahid won by 373 votes to 313 as he garnered the support of Golkar members and many of those linked to Muslim parties. Initially, Megawati's vociferous and easily agitated supporters rioted when they realized that their leader had been, as they saw it, robbed of her democratic entitlement. Wisely, Wahid asked Megawati to be his vice-president and she asked her supporters to calm down and return home. The election of Wahid and Megawati was, arguably, the best combination that could have been hoped for in the circumstances. It allied a moderate with a populist, and it kept army commander-in-chief General Wiranto out of the two leadership spots (although he was asked to join the cabinet). Wahid's cabinet, announced a few days after the election, showed a desire to calm tensions and promote pragmatic leadership. Significantly, he included two Chinese in his cabinet (one, the critical finance minister), as well as one politician from Aceh and another from West Papua – the two provinces with the greatest secessionist inclinations. On his election to the presidency, four critical questions faced Indonesia's new president. First, how to mend the economy; second, how to keep the country from disintegrating; third, how to promote reconciliation between the different racial and religious groups; and fourth, how to invent a role for the army appropriate for a democratic country entering the 21st century.

Indonesia has changed in other ways – although these changes could be reversed should the move towards democratization begin to falter. For a start, the **judiciary** and the **press** are increasingly independent. During the last few years of the Suharto era, hesitant steps towards greater press freedom were often followed by a crackdown on publications deemed to have crossed some ill-defined line in the sand. The independence of the judiciary was, if anything, an even more vexed issue. Political opponents of Suharto and his cronies could not expect a fair trial, and foreign businessmen found using the courts to extract payments from errant Indonesian businessmen and companies a waste of time. In

Three years of living dangerously

August-December 1997	The rupiah and economic collapse
January 1998	Suharto agrees to conditions of S$43bn IMF bail out
May 1998	Jakarta erupts as students protest and riots spread; 1,200 die
May 1998	Suharto resigns; BJ Habibie steps in as interim president
August 1998	Food riots in Jakarta
November 1998	Student riots in Jakarta
January-March 1999	Communal chaos in Ambon, Maluku
February 1999	Heightened tensions in East Timor
September 1999	Massacres in East Timor following pro-independence vote
September 1999	Student and nationalist demonstrations in Jakarta
October 1999	Student and nationalist demonstrations in Jakarta Abdurrahman Wahid and Megawati Sukarnoputri elected President and Vice President
December 1999	Communal violence in the Spice Islands escalates
January 2000	Riots in Lombok; tourists and Christians flee to Bali
June 2000	Communal violence spreads to Central Sulawesi

1997 a clerk at the Supreme Court was heard explaining to a litigant how Indonesia's legal system worked: "If you give us 50 million rupiah but your opponent gives us more, then the case will be won by your opponent" (quoted in *The Economist*, 2000). This approach to legal contests may have the advantage of simplicity, but it hardly instilled a great deal of confidence that a case would be judged on its merits.

In the six months following Suharto's resignation nearly 200 new publications were registered. The government under Habibie was rather more thick-skinned than its predecessor, and in June 1998 a law permitting the Information Ministry to ban any publication for criticizing the government was scrapped. This move towards greater press freedom in the post-Suharto era has meant a much more active, campaigning and, occasionally, sensationalist press – something that President Wahid sometimes finds rather harder to stomach than did Habibie.

The army in Indonesian politics

It has always been recognized that a critical ingredient – indeed a central element – in Indonesian political life is the army. For many years the army has been viewed as the only group in the country (beyond Golkar) with the necessary cohesion and unity of purpose to influence political events at a broad level. This wider role was enshrined in the constitutional principle of ***dwifungsi***, or dual function, which gave the army the right to engage in politics and administration, as well as defend the nation from external aggressors and internal insurrection. (This was amply illustrated in the army response to events in East Timor.) According to political scientist Harold Crouch, around two-thirds of army personnel were, under this system, assigned to territorial rather than combat duties. As such they engaged in such things as "overseeing the activities of political parties and non-governmental organizations, intervening in land disputes, [and] dealing with striking workers or demonstrating students...". In the countryside the army was seen as a stabilizing force and the guarantor of ethnic and religious peace. The army has traditionally regarded itself as the protector of the nation, and more particularly the protector of ordinary Indonesians against potentially venal civilian politicians and their business associates. The key role that the military played in Indonesia's independence movement – after the civilian revolutionary government had capitulated to the returning Dutch after the end of the Second World War – gave it further credibility to speak not just for itself, but also for the country as a whole.

Like so much in Indonesia, these assumptions must be re-examined in the light of Suharto's fall from power, the army's response to the riots of 1998, its role in East Timor, and the democratic elections of 1999. In 1999 the army changed its name from Abri to **TNI**. This, though, does not detract from the fact that the army has lost credibility, particularly as a result of the way it has dealt with, some would say fermented, sectarian and secessionist conflicts from Jakarta to Aceh, East Timor and Maluku. Moreover, it has become clear that a new generation of officers is in charge. These men, importantly, cannot call on their revolutionary credentials to justify and legitimate their positions and their actions. Moreover, the great unifying message of the 1970s and 1980s – the need to fight communism – no longer carries much influence. (That said, the code ET is still attached to some people's ID cards, designating that they are former political prisoners, and in mid-1999 the Indonesian parliament debated a bill that would have banned the teaching of Marxist-Leninism outside universities.) However, while the army may have a smaller role to play in political and civilian affairs, the police are hardly ready to fill the void created by the retreating army. With just 200,000 poorly trained and paid officers, the police are barely able to keep the peace and in many cases stand idly by while civilian vigilantes mete out justice.

Disintegration?

It has long been said that Indonesia is one of the world's most unlikely countries, a patchwork of cultures and languages pieced together by little more than the industriousness of the Dutch. In early 1999 President BJ Habibie, as a sop to the international community, surprisingly offered the people of **East Timor** a referendum on independence. The UN was called in to supervise the vote on 30 August but, against UN advice and pleading, he refused even a small international peacekeeping force. The vote itself proceeded smoothly and with little intimidation. On 4 September the results of the vote were announced: 78.5% of a turnout of well over 90% chose independence. It seems, and this might seem incredible to anyone who has followed the East Timor story, that the Indonesian military were expecting to 'win' the vote and were piqued that the population were so patently ungrateful for all their hard work. So, with the announcement of the results, mayhem broke out. Militias, formed, encouraged, armed and orchestrated by the Indonesian military, murdered, raped and terrorized the population of the tiny province. Tens of thousands fled to the hills and into neighbouring West Timor. (On 13 September one UN official suggested that just 200,000 out of East Timor's 800,000 population were still living in their homes.) Dili was virtually razed to the ground. The UN compound was besieged. Only the most intense international pressure, and vociferously negative international press coverage, forced Habibie to allow the UN to authorize an Australian-led force to enter the province.

The reluctance of the military to allow East Timor's independence can be linked to two key factors. First, between the annexation of East Timor in 1975 and the referendum of 1999, the army lost perhaps as many as 20,000 men trying to quell the independence movement there. To give up was to admit that it was all a waste of time and blood. And second, and much more importantly, there was the fear that East Timor's independence might herald the break-up of Indonesia. Aceh and Irian Jaya were the most obvious provinces that could break away. Legally speaking, there is a clear difference between East Timor and anywhere else in Indonesia. East Timor's annexation by Indonesia was never recognized by the UN. (UN maps always indicated the territory as a separate country.) But the fear was that this nuance would be lost on people with desires for independence.

The 7,500-strong Australian-led UN force landed in Dili in late September 1999 and control of the territory passed from the Indonesians to the UN. Alongside the Aussie troops, there were British Gurkhas, New Zealanders, and even contingents from the region, including Thai and Malaysian troops. (Asean came out of the crisis poorly, yet again showing an inability to act in a timely and forceful manner.) Even as UNIFET (the UN International Force for East Timor) strengthened its hold on Dili, the withdrawal of Indonesian troops destroyed the town they had called their own for nearly 25 years. As one soldier told *The Economist*: "We built this place up. Now we've torn it all down again" (2.10.99). During October, UNIFET extended its control east and west from Dili as far as the border with West Timor where the militias were holed up. Rumours of a militia build-up and possible major incursion did not materialize, although there were some firefights between UNIFET and militia gangs. At the end of October Xanana Gusmao, jailed for 20 years by Indonesia and the most likely person to become East Timor's first president, returned home. Before leaving Australia he said: "We will start from zero to reconstruct not only our country, but ourselves as human beings" (*The Economist*, 16.10.99).

A complication – and another reason why the Indonesian army were so reluctant to give up their hold on this dry and poverty-stricken land – was the decision taken by the UN on 27 September 1999 to investigate human rights abuses in the province. And they were right to be worried. When the UN and Indonesian reports were published at the beginning of 2000, six generals were mentioned by name, including General Wiranto (see below).

It was not just East Timor and Aceh that have been wracked by violence. Indeed, the spread of unrest to other areas of the country would seem to bear out the army's fears: that taking the lid off more than three decades of top-down control would lead to an upsurge of violence right across the country. Conspiracy theories abound as to which interested party is seeding this violence. Some believe that much of the unrest is being orchestrated by the military – anxious to prove that without their control the country will disintegrate. Influential individuals from the Suharto era may be trying to destabilize the country in order to regain power. As criminologist Yohanes Sutoyo explained to Dini Djalal of the *Far Eastern Economic Review*: "The New Order [of former President Suharto] taught us that the only way to solve a problem is with violence", adding, "It is difficult to undo this" (FEER 13.7.2000). At the beginning of 2000, communal violence in the Spice Islands of Maluku escalated and by mid-year an estimated 3,000 people had been killed. In Central Sulawesi, murderous groups were killing villagers. In central Kalimantan deadly clashes broke out between indigenous Dayaks and migrants from Madura Island, who came as part of the Suharto government's *transmigrasi* programme. Bali and Lombok were also the scenes of unprecedented violence at the beginning of 2000, some of it aimed at the Chinese community, many of whom are Christians. In Jakarta, and in some other cities on Java, vigilante groups have taken it upon themselves to mete out retribution on small time criminals. Reports of people stealing bicycles being lynched, beaten, doused with kerosene and set alight were common during 2000. The police, in such cases, have stood by, powerless to intervene.

While disintegration, partial or otherwise, is a possibility, the government is in the process of introducing laws that will lead to far-reaching **decentralization** to try and head off those who would prefer even greater autonomy. But there are worries that this attempt to devolve power to the provinces will permit local power-brokers to dominate affairs and make corruption even worse. It will also mean that poor provinces such as East and West Nusa Tenggara will no longer be able to rely on cross-subsidization by richer provinces such as Riau and Aceh. Furthermore, it is far from clear that there are sufficient numbers of competent people in the provinces to handle such an increase in the power and role of local level government.

President Abdurrahman Wahid, better known as Gus (a term of respect) Dur (from his name), did not have an easy task when he assumed the presidency at the end of 1999. And as this book went to press it was not clear when and if Indonesia's economy would recover (see 'Economy'), or whether Indonesia would survive as a country roughly corresponding to the one he took over. Nor was it clear whether he would survive as president to the end of his term.

Gus Dur has always been renowned for his cunning and wily ways – and his fondness for obtuseness. When he was leader of Nahdlatul Ulama (NU), the world's largest Muslim organization, he was one of President Suharto's very few critics. And he was also able to present himself as a moderate Muslim: one who would protect the interests of Indonesia's non-Muslim population while remaining a respected Muslim cleric, leader and thinker. In January 2000 he travelled to Saudi Arabia to court the Arab world and then flew to Davos in Switzerland for the World Economic Forum. Here he met with Prime Minister Barak of Israel and George Soros. He explained: "We need investments and, you know, the Jewish community everywhere are very active in the commercial side..." (FEER 10.2.2000). His critics say he undermines Indonesia's stability and economic recovery by his impulsiveness; he frequently makes statements without consulting his cabinet (as happened when he said, while on an overseas trip, that General Wiranto should resign) and people also complain of his readiness to blame conspirators for the country's problems. His supporters believe he is a great master who disarms his opponents by his seeming foolishness, before bringing them

Gus Dur tries to put it back together

down. With few political cards to play, now that many in his coalition government have turned against him, his defenders believe that speaking out is his only weapon. Without the backing of a fully functioning bureaucracy, or the military power used by his predecessor, his force of personality and ability to bluff are the only tools at his disposal.

His greatest victory (or so it seemed at the time – see below) so far has been to sideline the army and emasculate its leadership as a political force. This also showed him at his wily best. Initially, Wahid included General Wiranto, the army's powerful chief of staff, in his cabinet, but not, significantly, as defence minister. Instead he appointed him as security minister. This helped to separate the General from his power base. Then the president said that he would sack anyone implicated in human rights abuses in East Timor. Reports commissioned by the Indonesian government and by the UN into just this issue were released on 31 January 2000. Moreover, both came to the same conclusion: that members of the Indonesian army had assisted the militias in East Timor to murder, rape and pillage. More to the point, the Indonesian report mentioned six generals by name, including General Wiranto. The president was abroad at the time but in an interview said he thought that Wiranto should resign. Instead the General pointedly turned up at a cabinet meeting. However in the middle of February, having initially said that the General could stay, he changed his mind once more and, in the middle of the night, sacked the general from his post as security minister (although he remained an 'inactive' member of the cabinet). Cut off from the army and in a government post with no significance, General Wiranto was successfully trapped in a no man's land of Gus Dur's making.

But Wahid did not just got rid of Wiranto. He appointed a civilian as minister of defence and promoted officers in the navy and airforce to influential positions, thus downgrading the traditionally highly dominant army. This culminated in a major reshuffle at the end of February 2000. Now it is moderate reformers who fill most of the influential posts in the armed forces. Furthermore, Wahid insisted that military men in the cabinet would have to resign from their military posts before taking up their political appointments.

While Gus Dur might have sidelined the army, he hadn't counted on the public taking up arms to deal with the problems of the nation (probably orcestrated from above – possibly by factions of the army). At the beginning of 2000, as Muslim-Christian violence in Maluku escalated, radical Muslims in Java began to prepare for a *jihad* (holy war) in this far-flung province. White-robed warriors in their thousands, some wielding swords, congregated in Jakarta to make their feelings clear – and then began to train for battle. Despite Gus Dur's attempts to stop them leaving for Maluku, they began to arrive in the region by the end of May 2000. As the year wore on it became increasingly clear that Wahid's victory over the generals was a pyrrhic one. Infuriated by the president's actions, the army began to undermine his leadership. In particular, a series of bombings in Jakarta would seem to involve the army, or groups in the army. By the end of 2000 the army seemed to be clawing back power.

During the course of 2000, many people who initially welcomed Wahid's accession to the presidency became increasingly disenchanted with his leadership - and with his methods. In an attempt to address this mounting criticism, in a speech to the annual meeting of the People's Consultative Assembly (MPR) on 9 August (at which he faced the risk of a vote of censure), he proposed far-reaching changes to the management of state affairs. In effect he proposed a more equal, four-way sharing of power between his to-date marginalized Vice President Megawati Sukarnoputri, two new 'Coordinating' ministers, and himself. The two coordinating ministers were later announced as being Sulsilo Bambang Yudhoyono, a retired general, and Rizal Ramli. Significantly, neither of these two men had prior links with any political party. Under this system Wahid would become, in effect, Indonesia's face to the wider world: a sort of roving ambassador for the country. Wahid claimed in the speech that he was ceding 'duties and not authority', but the distinction is a fine one.

Wahid's proposed changes meant acceptance on his part that he had lost his way. It sometimes seemed, in the months leading up to the August 2000 meeting, that Wahid lacked the clarity of mind to address key issues, and especially those of an economic flavour. His woolly pronouncements and tendency to prevaricate exasperated many businessmen and foreign investors.

The politics of envy: the Chinese in Indonesia

The Chinese make up about 4-5% of Indonesia's population and, as the communal violence of 1998 amply proved, are still treated with suspicion. There are still 300,000 Chinese living in Indonesia who have yet to choose whether they are Indonesians by nationality, or Chinese. The community adopts a low profile – in Glodok (Jakarta's Chinatown), for example, there are few Chinese signs on the shopfronts. Indeed, until recently there was a ban on displaying Chinese characters. The so-called *masalah Cina* – or 'Chinese problem' – continues to be hotly discussed, much of the debate centring on whether the Chinese should be assimilated or integrated into Indonesian culture.

The animosity between the 'Indonesian' and Chinese communities is based upon the latter's economic success, and their role as middlemen, shopkeepers and moneylenders. Most of the country's largest firms are Chinese-owned – known as *cukong* – and the richest families are also Chinese. It has been estimated that the 4% or 5% of the population who are Chinese control 70-80% of private capital (although this is probably an over-estimate). Such evident success has given rise to envy. Some indigenous businessmen, known as *pribumi*, have called for the implementation of an explicit economic policy of positive discrimination in favour of native Indonesians, modelled on the New Economic Policy in Malaysia.

Former President Suharto might have scorned such an idea, but when he invited 30 of the country's top Chinese businessmen to his palace in 1990, he was seen, on television, explaining to them that if inequalities were not reduced, "social gap, social envy and even social disturbance will happen". This barely concealed warning of a possible repeat of the events of 1965 was not lost on the Chinese community, and was tragically realized during the riots of May 1998. These started as student-led pro-democracy and anti-Suharto demonstrations, but quickly became anti-Chinese. Gangs of men, it was reported, systematically targeted Chinese businesses and families. In total, 1,200 people were killed (to be sure, not all Chinese) and more than 150 Chinese women were raped. Wealthier families escaped to the airport, and from there to Singapore. Poorer ethnic Chinese hunkered down to escape the mobs. "We expected protection," one computer shop owner told The Economist, "but it never came" (22.08.1998). This was a tragedy not just for the Chinese, but also for Indonesia. In the first half of 1998, US$16bn left the country, much of it belonging to ethnic Chinese convinced that they no longer belonged.

As this book went to press towards the end of 2000, Indonesia was continuing to lurch from crisis to crisis, both economically and politically. President Abdurrahman Wahid was becoming increasingly embattled as his problems mounted. In particular, he seemed to have lost control of the army and the police who were, apparently, ignoring or going against his orders. This extended from his order for the army and police to crack down on the militias in West Timor (following the murder of three UN personnel there in September); to his demand that Tommy Suharto, one of former President Suharto's sons, be arrested in connection with a spate of bombings in Jakarta (the police released him saying there was not sufficient evidence to hold him); to a ceasefire in the northern Sumatran province of Aceh, which the army also apparently chose to ignore. Some commentators were wondering whether the army was once more out of control and it was even being suggested that Wahid might be toppled by an army-inspired coup.

Suharto may have gone, but he and his family have kept his much of their wealth. In the 1997 listing of the world's richest, *Forbes Magazine* put Suharto's fortune at US$16bn. While this was indicative of the sums of money the former president managed to squeeze out of the nation and its people, far more corrosive was the wealth that his children managed to amass. Nepotism may be a way of life in Southeast Asia, but there are limits to what is deemed acceptable. Suharto's six children (three sons and three daughters) built up vast business empires on the basis of their family connections. The two biggest non-Chinese

The (former) first family: what to do with them & their fortunes?

conglomerates – Bimantara and Humpuss – were both run by sons of the president, Bambang Trihatmodjo and Hutomo 'Tommy' Mandala Putra. They managed to do this by drawing on their ties with their father to secure lucrative contracts and licences. One Asian ambassador in Jakarta was quoted in the *Far Eastern Economic Review* back in April 1992, saying: "The central question is whether the avarice of the children will ultimately undermine 25 years of pretty good leadership". An *Economist* survey of the country in 1993 reflected similar sentiments, when – likening him to former Javanese kings – it described Suharto as having: "A paternal style, a professed lack of interest in power, a circle of deferential courtiers and the ability to dispense seemingly unlimited patronage....". In 1998 the Indonesian Business Data Centre put Suharto family's fortune (Suharto plus his children) at 200 trillion rupiah. At the pre-crisis exchange rate this amounted to US$80bn.

The economic crisis undermined the finances of the children's business empires and Suharto's resignation removed their ultimate guardian and patron. The business empires of Suharto's children are now struggling to survive. The family as a whole has seen the value of its assets decline from US$80bn to under US$20bn. This does not mean, of course, that the children themselves are on the breadline – like many millions of ordinary Indonesians during the economic meltdown. Perhaps most surprising is that the Suharto children have been allowed to continue to run their businesses, not all of which are moribund.

But while his children may have come under intense scrutiny and criticism, Suharto himself is not quite the hate figure that most foreigners would expect him to be, given the corruption and repression of his years in power. The Suharto era was one of stability and economic dynamism, and many Indonesians look back on it as a golden period which brought better living standards to most people. Even so, Habibie, Suharto's protégé, was forced by events to set up a commission to investigate whether Suharto had acquired his wealth through illegal means. In October 1999, incredibly, the commission decided that there was insufficient evidence to bring the former president to court.

Under Gus Dur's presidency there has been a more concerted effort to bring Suharto to book, and in 2000 the Attorney General Marzuki Darusman began proceedings leading to a possible trial for corruption. At the end of May 2000 the former President was placed under house arrest at his palatial home in Menteng, a suburb of Jakarta, and police were stationed around his home – as much to protect him from the periodic mob attacks on his home than to keep him from escaping. In August it was formally announced by state prosecutors that President Suharto, more than two years after his resignation, would stand trial for embezzling more than US$571m from the state. The trial began in August, with his lawyers arguing that the former president was not fit to stand trial. Mr Assegaf, one of his lawyers, said that: "It is impossible for him to stand trial. Suharto is incapable of comprehending questions and of responding to them immediately". President Wahid promised to pardon Suharto, but insisted that he stands trial first. However, on 28 September the Jakarta court dropped all charges against the former president, declaring, on the advice of a panel of doctors, that he was, indeed, mentally and physically unfit to stand trial. This infuriated activists who believe that Suharto embezzled not US$571m, but a truly stupendous US$45bn. After the farce of former president Suharto's trial came the even more farcical 'arrest', sentencing and then absconding of the former president's youngest son, Hutomo 'Tommy' Mandala Putra. For a short moment it seemed that the authorities were actually going to get some retribution when Tommy was on the verge of being imprisoned for corruption. But Tommy managed to escape his captors. Locals wonder whether, if the authorities aren't able (or willing) to imprison Tommy, any of those most closely associated with the venal Suharto government will ever see the inside of a cell. Suharto may be ill, but his shadow still appears to bend the law. This was accepted by Attorney-General Marzuki Darusman, who has stated that his powers are constrained and his office's ability to function limited by the presence of Suharto sympathizers who work there.

Domestic hangovers & international relations Indonesia's acceptance into the international fold has been hampered for years by numerous small and large stumbling blocks. The 'occupation' of East Timor, government policy in Irian Jaya, corruption, the nature of the political system, the failure to respect labour rights, and the human and environmental impacts of the transmigration programme, to name just a few. Just when Indonesia is on the verge of expunging the stain on its credibility, one or more of these issues jumps out and progress is stymied.

There can be no doubt that the major stumbling block was East Timor. Even before the tragic events which followed the vote for independence in mid-1999, East Timor was a thorn in Indonesia's attempts to punch its weight. (For a country of over 200,000,000 people, the fourth most populous on earth, it has a remarkably low international profile.) For the foreseeable future it is hard to imagine that Indonesia will be able to look much beyond its own manifold challenges, from creating a democratic society and robust civil society to rebuilding its economy. So, for the next five years, expect Indonesia to be on people's television screens, if there is sufficient televisual bloodshed, but rarely venturing into the international arena – except, perhaps, to defend its policies in various secession-minded outer provinces. Nationalist sentiment was stoked by the presence of UN forces in East Timor (widely seen to be Australian forces in East Timor), and Indonesia's failure to come to terms with its misguided imperialist spree has raised the stakes still further. At the end of September 1999, US Secretary of Defence Willian Cohen warned that Indonesia could face 'political isolation' and 'economic consequences' if it did not control its military. This of course begs the question: Are the generals listening (only one of the leading generals, General Wiranto, actually spoke any English)?

In the last edition of this book, the summary of politics in the country concluded with the paragraph:

"All in all, it would be a brave person who would predict the path of change over the next five years. The Western obsession with the 'natural' evolution towards greater political pluralism and a market economy makes it hard to imagine that things might go 'backwards'; the experience of China following the Tiananmen Square massacre illustrates the dangers of such blithe assumptions. Nor does the pressure from the West for progress on human rights take into account Indonesia's unique set of conditions. The country's middle classes were estimated in 1995 to number just 14 million people – about 7% of the total population – and the evolution of civil society is still in its infancy. It is unlikely that the army will give up its influence and the sheer geographical, social and cultural complexity would make the country extremely hard to hold together in the event of free-for-all democracy."

Marking out the path to the future

The events of the last two years make predicting the future even more perilous. It may be that democratization continues, that political power is increasingly devolved to the provinces, that East Timor is given its independence, that the legal system is made more accountable and transparent, that the press is given its head, that secessionist tendencies in Aceh and Irian Jaya are quelled peacefully, and that the Parliament becomes more active. Or it may not.

Economy

In their influential publication *The East Asian Miracle* (1993), the World Bank counted Indonesia one of Asia's 'miracle' economies. It was on this basis that grand predictions were made about Asia – and about Indonesia. The 21st century was to be the era of the Pacific, with the Asian tigers, Indonesia included, in the vanguard. Just as the resignation of Suharto has changed Indonesia's political landscape beyond all recognition, so the economic crisis, which began with the fall of the Thai baht in mid-1997, has led to a profound transformation in Indonesia's economic and developmental prospects. (The two, clearly, are linked: Suharto's loss of political legitimacy was intimately associated with the fall of the economy. He was, after all, Bapak Pembangunan or the Father of Development.) Of all the countries of Asia, Indonesia has been most severely hit by the crisis. Never has a country fallen from economic grace so far and so fast. In the space of 18 months the economy contracted by 20%. At one point virtually all the companies listed on the Jakarta stock exchange were technically bankrupt and the rupiah had lost 85% of its value against the US$.

To understand what has happened to Indonesia's economy over the last few years, it is first necessary to reflect on the 'miracle'. Because there is little doubt that the years of Suharto's presidency led to unparalleled rates of economic growth and improving standards of living for most people in most places.

The making of a miracle? "The road that was sealed for the first time in living memory, the new school, the new health clinic, the improved irrigation system, all these were convincing evidence that **pembangunan** (economic development) meant improved access to public amenities, which in turn could lead to increasing earning opportunities, and higher family incomes and living standards. By the latter part of the 1970s, it was impossible to doubt that incomes and living standards were improving, especially in Java, where the great majority of the rural population were concentrated. These were remarkable achievements for a country as backward as Indonesia was in the mid-1960s" (Anne Booth, 1995: 109).

From 1965 through to 1997, the Indonesian economy gradually recovered from the extreme mismanagement that characterized the period from independence in 1950. With the advice of the so-called Berkeley Mafia – a group of reform-minded, US-trained economists – there was an attempt to increase efficiency, reduce corruption and entice foreign investment. Like the other countries of the region, export-orientated development became the name of the game. In 1996 Dennis de Tray, the World Bank's country manager, heaped praise on Indonesia's economic performance. "We give Indonesians a very good report card", he said, adding that in 1995 "few countries [in the world] have had better economic performance".

On 17 August 1995, at the celebrations marking the 50th anniversary of Indonesia's proclamation of Independence, President Suharto squinted into the skies as the N-250, a home-built and home-designed 70-seat commuter aircraft, made its maiden flight. The plane, named *Gatot Kaca* after one of the characters in a Hindu epic, illustrates Indonesia's technological 'coming of age'. While critics may have wondered about the excessive concentration of financial and human resources in a single product of such dubious commercial value, the N-250 instilled an intense sense of pride and self-confidence in the Indonesian people, though not perhaps the low-paid Golkar party members who were forced to make a donation towards the plane's development. Moreover, as the plane left the tarmac, Suharto gave the go-ahead for Habibie to produce a jet airliner – codenamed the N-2130 – by 2003. (These grand plans are now, it would seem, history. The IMF insisted, as part of its aid package to aid the ailing economy in 1997, that government money could not be used to fund the project. Instead ITPN continues forlornly to look for private sector funding for this lame-duck project. Since then both the N-250 and the N-2130 have been put on hold and the workforce halved.)

Development has been based upon a series of five-year plans known as *Repelitas* (standing for *Rencana Pembangunan Lima Tahun*), the first beginning in 1969. Indonesia's GDP per person was about US$1,300 in 1996; in 1967 it was only US$70. At the beginning of 1995 Indonesia made the transition from being a 'low income' to becoming a 'middle income' country, according to World Bank criteria.

From oil to non-oil Indonesia is the only Asian member of OPEC and has benefited from its **oil wealth**. This has enabled the government to pursue ambitious programmes of social, agricultural and regional development. After the first oil price rise in 1973 following in the wake of the Arab-Israeli Yom Kippur War, when the cost of a barrel of oil quadrupled in less than a year, the government was awash with funds. These were used to build 6,000 primary schools a year, expand roads into the less accessible parts of the Outer Islands, and subsidize rice cultivation so that the country attained self-sufficiency by 1985. But the oil boom also promoted **corruption** on a scale that was remarkable even by Southeast Asian standards. It was said, for example, that importers were having to pay US$200m a year in bribes to the notoriously corrupt Customs Department, and that even the lowliest coffee boy had to pass US$1,000 under the table to buy himself a job. This investment would, of course, be repaid in a few months, as the coffee boy's share of the bribes trickled down through the system. Such was the degree of corruption that in 1985 Suharto was forced to take the unprecedented step of calling in a Swiss firm, Société Générale de Surveillance, to oversee import procedures.

The decline in oil prices since the early 1980s forced the government to become rather more hard-headed in its approach to economic management. This led to a conscious attempt to promote **non-oil industries** and from the early 1980s these were the principal source of growth. By 1997 over 20% of Indonesia's GDP was produced by the manufacturing sector, and oil and gas accounted for less than a quarter of total exports. Foreign investors were attracted by Indonesia's low wage rates when compared with Malaysia and Thailand, its political stability when compared with China, and its comparatively investor-friendly environment when compared with Vietnam.

The human costs of rapid growth

While there is little doubt that Indonesia achieved a great deal between 1965 and 1997, there was also little doubt that the country's strategy of fast-track industrialization had its **human costs**. People were being displaced from the countryside to swell the ranks of the urban labour force, causing social tensions to escalate. Many of the jobs in industry were non-formal, and non-contractual, so few workers felt they had much security. Union representation was through the tame, institutionalized, All-Indonesia Workers Union or SPSI. When independent unions were established (which Indonesian law allows), their leaders were hounded by the internal security agency Bakorstanas and sometimes eliminated. In July 1993, for example, the East Java labour activist, Marsinah, was murdered. As John McBeth in the *Far Eastern Economic Review* recorded: "Marsinah was tortured for 3 days and then sexually violated with a sharp instrument before being dumped on a roadside and left to bleed to death". There were also many examples of **child labour** and of poor workplace safety. Before the crisis there were, officially, 2,400,000 child workers in the country, although some NGOs believed the real figure to be four times larger. The difficulty of determining whether child work is exploitative is reflected in the term that the government used to describe underage labourers: *anak yang terpaksa bekerja* or 'children who are compelled to work'. If children worked below a certain minimum number of hours a day and if their labour was crucial to household survival then it was, officially, permitted.

Another major cause for concern in the country during the period of rapid growth was the uneven nature of development. This had both a spatial and a human component. To begin with, the great bulk of investment was concentrated in Java – some 64% of total foreign investment. Over vast swathes of the archipelago, the export-driven boom was just hot air. '**Social justice** for all Indonesians' is one of the principles enshrined in *pancasila*, the state ideology, and the glaring inequalities between the rich and the poor, and between different regions of the country, became an issue of driving concern.

This was reflected in the initiation of a **poverty alleviation** programme at the beginning of April 1994, *Inpres Desa Tertinggal* or the Presidential Instruction Programme for Less Developed Villages. This aimed to reduce poverty from roughly 15% to 6% by 1998, by specifically targetting those for whom wealth had not 'trickled down'. In preparing for the programme, the National Development Planning board drew up a map of 20,633 villages where poverty was endemic, and by 1996 some 2,300,000 families had been accepted on to the scheme.

In mid-1996, President Suharto tried another tack to narrow the glaring **inequalities** within the country. He made a personal plea for rich individuals and companies to hand over 250bn rupiah to finance a poverty alleviation programme. 11,000 people and firms, selected on the basis that each had an income after tax of over 100m rupiah, were sent a booklet asking them to share their wealth with the needy. The booklet asked these favoured few to "carry out the noble task of poverty alleviation together with the government".

Although Indonesia's population of poor and near-poor were the most evident sources of concern, even during the period of rapid economic growth, there was also growing discontent among those groups who had gained most from the country's progress. High school leavers and even university graduates were finding jobs in private business or the public sector, previously virtually guaranteed by dint of their having a degree or secondary school certificate, increasingly hard to find. With expectations growing as the consumer culture bit, so these individuals were finding their aspirations thwarted. A disgruntled, educated, largely urban-based mass of young men and women was the last thing Suharto wanted as he tried to stem the desire for greater political pluralism. His fears were borne out in the civil disturbances which led to his resignation in 1998.

Constraints to growth

Even before the economic crisis swept all before it, there were commentators highlighting the problems that Indonesia faced maintaining rapid economic growth. To begin with, levels of **corruption** have always been quite horrendous. Journalist John McBeth has written of the "army of 4 million underpaid bureaucrats [who] lurk in ambush in thickets of red tape" waiting to pounce on unsuspecting businessmen. Indonesia comes close to the top in the World Corruption Stakes: in 1996 it was thought to be running close behind China and Vietnam, while Transparency International put Indonesia at the top of a field of 41 countries. But it was not just corruption which worried businessmen. The way in which the politically well-connected gained access to lucrative contracts and licenses, the burgeoning business empires of the various Suharto children, and the lack of transparency in the system, were all also sources of concern. (For those who might be interested in the semantics of corruption, *pungli* are 'hidden taxes', while the colloquial term for a bribe is *uang licin* or *wang liken*, 'slippery' or 'greasy' money.)

The poisonous nature of corruption is widely recognized in Indonesia. There is even an acronym for the conjuncture of corruption, graft and favouritism – KKN, standing for Korrupsi, Kollusi and Nepotise. Nor has it gone away just because Suharto has been ejected from the presidency. The Bali Bank scandal engulfed the country in September 1999 when auditors Price-Waterhouse-Coopers reported that US$70m had been diverted from the Bank to Golkar, former President Habibie's party.

The individual charged with the monumental task of eradicating corruption from the system is Teten Masduki, head of Indonesia Corruption Watch (ICW), which was established in June 1998. (In one of the first statements after his election as Indonesia's new president in October 1999, Mr Wahid promised to stamp out corruption and stated that any cabinet minister found to be involved in such practices would be forced to resign.) Mr Teten, formerly a labour activist, argues that more insidious than the major corruption scandals which garner the headlines is the day-to-day petty corruption which is such a part of Indonesian life. It is this which, in his view, corrodes and corrupts Indonesian people and society. The problem for Mr Teten is a shortage of funds and people, and a legal system which is chronically unable to deal with complicated corruption cases and prone to capitulate in the face of powerful, rich and influential people.

In addition to corruption, foreign investors and local businessmen highlighted poor infrastructure, a lack of skilled workers, a cumbersome bureaucracy and high interest rates as major constraints to growth. Perhaps most critical of all was – and is – the need to upgrade **education and skills**. In 1996 just 4% of the workforce had a university education and 60% of those aged between 15 and 29 were educated to primary level only. Thus, even while Indonesia was enjoying some of the fastest rates of economic growth in the world, there were those who wondered whether the country would be able to make the critical transition from sweat shop to industrial power house.

The 1997 economic crisis: falling tigers

Like the rest of Southeast Asia, Indonesia was buffeted – some might say torn limb-from-limb – by the collapse of the Thai economy in July 1997. Initially it looked like Indonesia might come out of the crisis in better shape than Malaysia and the Philippines, not to mention Thailand. But as the year wore on, the economic outlook became grimmer and grimmer. Forest fires clouded the economic skies in September; continued pressure on the rupiah pushed it to record lows against the US$ in October; and through the year foreign analysts pegged back their estimates of economic growth. As the economy sunk further so the government, like the Thai government before it, called in the IMF on 8 October 1997. The size of corporate Indonesia's short-term US$ debts grew by the day as the rupiah sank, and the number of banks believed to be insolvent reached almost a score by the end of the month. Initially it appeared as though Suharto was so upset by the IMF's dire assessment of Indonesia's economy, and the corruption and rent seeking that is so much a part of the system, that it seemed he might go elsewhere for money rather than bite the IMF bullet. As John McBeth vividly put it in an article in the *Far Eastern Economic Review* in October 1997: "When the forces of reform hit up against the immovable object of political interests, reform makes a detour." The Indonesian economist Djisman Simandjuntak summed up the lack of readiness and understanding in many quarters of

Political and Economic Risk Consultancy (PERC) put Indonesia at the top of the list of Asian countries (ie worst) in terms of corruption in 2000

	2000
Singapore	0.71
Hong Kong	2.49
Japan	3.90
Malaysia	5.50
Taiwan	6.89
Philippines	8.67
Thailand	8.20
South Korea	8.33
China	9.11
Vietnam	9.20
India	9.50
Indonesia	9.88

government, the bureaucracy and academia:

"The chaotic nature of globalization is not well understood by our top officials, by the business elite, even by people in academia. Our founding fathers fought against colonialism and liberalism, and there was always this dream of big government and enough natural resources to make Indonesia self-sufficient."

Finally, right at the end of October, a US$43bn package was approved with sizeable pledges from Japan and Singapore (US$5bn each), the World Bank (US$4.5bn) and Asian Development Bank (US$3.5bn), the USA (US$3bn), and Malaysia and Australia (US$1bn each). The IMF itself promised US$10bn.

Of course, the money did not come without strings and these became clearer when Finance Minister Mar'ie Muhammad announced a series of reforms in November. These included the dismantling of some monopolies, the liquidation of 16 smaller banks, and plans to cut some of the links that bestow advantages on well connected companies.

While the emphasis in the media was on the big picture, it became evident by the end of 1997 that Indonesia's crisis was also affecting the *wong cilik* – the little people. Taxi drivers were finding fares harder to come by as the middle class switched from taxi to bus, rice prices rose, and cleaners and office boys in the banks threatened with closure were turfed onto the street.

Not soon after the ink was dry on the IMF agreement, student-led riots broke out in Jakarta, culminating in President Suharto's resignation in May 1998 (see above). Political uncertainty turned an economic crisis into an economic massacre. GDP shrank by 14% in 1998; the cost of recapitalizing Indonesia's banks was put at US$80bn, equal to over 80% of GDP; the rupiah sunk so far that by June 1998 it had lost over 80% of its value; and virtually all the companies listed on the Jakarta stock exchange were technically bankrupt. As *The Economist* put it, by this time "Indonesia's economy, and the economies in it, [had] entered the twilight zone" (31.1.98).

Again, there was a tendency to gloss over the impacts of the crisis on the 'real' economy. In 1999 it was thought that 20% of the country's population or 40,000,000 people were living in poverty. Beggars, prostitutes and children were all noticeably present on the streets of Jakarta and other large cities. What began as an economic crisis had, by 1998, become a social and a political crisis too.

Touching bottom

Each time it seems that Indonesia's economy can't fall any further, and is on the mend, something happens to undermine confidence. While other crisis-hit Asian economies like Thailand, South Korea and Malaysia are on the mend, Indonesia is stuck in the doldrums.

Indonesia's economic prospects, as has been true for the last three years, are critically linked to political stability. A March 2000 Asian Development Bank report on the prospects for the Asian economies warned of the fragility of Indonesia's economic 'recovery'. The ADB

A new form of date rape

The Jakarta Post reported that a 36-year-old Indonesian man, Suryono, managed to convince as many as 35 women in Central Java that he could make them more attractive to men (whether their husbands or prospective partner) if they would strip naked in a darkened room, wait for a genie to appear and then do whatever the genie demanded of them. In a novel Indonesian twist to date rape in the West, these women would then allow Suryono, as a genie, to have his wicked way with them.

---

report described the situation in Indonesia as 'highly problematic', noting that most banks are insolvent and operating only with the Indonesian central bank's support. The report continued: "Speeding up and sustaining the recovery process depends crucially on the rejuvenation of the moribund banking system."

The key challenge – and this sounds dull and tedious - is to initiate systematic and effective restructuring of the corporate sector, and particularly the banking sector. The difficulty is that business culture and nationalist sentiment is hampering progress in debt settlement. This has made it more difficult for the government to implement tough policies, especially if 'vulture' foreign investors are buying up businesses on the cheap.

The agency which is central to restructuring efforts is IBRA – the Indonesian Bank Restructuring Agency – which, by mid-2000, controlled a huge chunk of the country's corporate wealth. The Agency is empowered with the job of selling off these assets and thus recouping some of the US$80bn that the government (and the IMF) have spent trying to put the banking sector back together again. But local business interests and many politicians are loath to see foreigners doing-down Indonesians, however incompetent their business management may have been. Thus, while there are important economic considerations slowing down the process, much more important is the political climate and the role that vested interests are having in hampering progress. At the end of 1999, for example, Standard Chartered Bank's plans to buy Bank Bali failed because of a nationalist backlash (as well as pressure from within the company). President Wahid's appointment of his younger brother Hasyim Wahid as an 'expert' adviser to IBRA in April 2000, when he scarcely has the qualifications to be paraded as such, raised fears of Suharto-style nepotism and cronyism. (Wahid's brother turned down the post following public disquiet.)

It also seems that President Wahid has not helped. While he may have been skilful in his handling of the army, his critics say he hasn't a clue about economics – and they are not very much more complimentary about the president's first Finance Minister, Kwik Kian Gie. Perhaps Kwik's most stunning piece of economic diplomacy occurred in May 2000 when he told Dow Jones that "if I were a foreign investor, I wouldn't come to Indonesia." So much for raising confidence. Ministers in his government have been fighting over key portfolios and Wahid hasn't been able (or willing) to take the lead and impose his will. The failure of Wahid to convince investors that he has the political strength to resist nationalist pressures is scaring off foreign companies. In March the IMF delayed the release of US$400m in loans (part of a US$5bn agreement signed in January) because the country was failing to meet its obligations and, in particular, its corporate restructuring obligations. (This US$400m tranche was later released on 17 May.)

In 1999 the economy expanded by 0.2%. But although economic growth is picking up it is not growing fast enough to improve livelihoods. Economists have calculated that with so many people entering the workforce each year, the economy has to grow by 4-5% a year just to absorb these new workers. For tangible improvements, 7% is probably necessary and Indonesia is some way off that. People are looking to 2004 or 2005 for real improvements to start filtering through.

The tourist industry Tourism is Indonesia's third largest foreign exchange earner: it generated US$6.1bn in 1996. In the previous three years the figures were, working back from 1995 to 1993, US$5.2bn, US$4.8bn and US$3.6bn. President Suharto tipped the sector to become the country's largest foreign exchange earner by the end of the century. In 1996 the number of visitors arriving in the country topped the 5,000,000 mark for the first time (the reported figures was 5,034,472). This was up from 4,300,000 in 1995, 4,000,000 in 1994 and 3,400,000 in 1993. The tourist authorities in Indonesia were predicting, at that time, that 8,000,000 tourists would be visiting the country by 2000, and 11,000,000 by 2005.

Ha! Even before the calamitous last few years, some analysts doubted that these targets would be met, and pointed to the slow-down in tourist arrivals since the spurt of the late 1980s and early 1990s. In comparison to fellow Asean members Singapore, Malaysia and Thailand, the Indonesian Tourist Promotion Board is wonderfully amateur. This situation was not helped by the removal of virtually their entire budget by the government as a result of the economic crisis; many overseas tourist information offices have been closed down. The rotund rhino that became the symbol of the 1991 Visit Indonesia Year is still propped up outside hotels across the country, indicating that while neighbouring countries fine tune their PR campaigns month-by-month, Indonesia stumbles along with Stalinist-style Five Year Plans. Nor is it just a question of marketing; there is a real shortage of facilities and tourist infrastructure beyond a few key destinations like Bali. Lombok, for example, has been waiting to explode now for close to a decade, and the upgrading of the island's Selaparang Airport to international status – which has been imminent for years – is still set at some indeterminate date in the future.

The last few years are ones that Indonesia's tourist supremos would prefer to forget. In no particular order: widespread forest fires and associated haze in 1997 and 1999; riots in 1998, 1999 and 2000; murderous communal conflict in 1998, 1999 and 2000; secessionist violence in 1997, 1998, 1999 and 2000; political instability; economic meltdown… With all this bad news being reported in the international media, there is little wonder that the Indonesian Tourist Promotion Board has found it hard to stop arrivals plummeting.

Culture

Religion – Islam in Indonesia

Indonesia has the largest population of Muslims in the world – about 80% of the country's 200,000,000 inhabitants call themselves Muslims. Despite pressure from Javanese Muslim leaders during the formative years of the independence movement, Sukarno resisted attempts to make the country an explicitly Islamic state. Indeed, a feature of both President Sukarno and President Suharto's rule was their common dislike and fear of Islamic zealotry. When it has threatened stability, such movements have been vigorously suppressed. Significantly, Pancasila stipulates a belief in One Supreme God – this god being seen to be the same whether Muslim, Christian, Hindu or Buddhist – and despite the difficulty of nominating a single supreme Buddhist or Hindu god. The only animist religion officially recognized by the government is that of the island of Sumba. (Initially, Confucianism was included as one of Indonesia's officially recognized religions, but this was later rescinded under the presidency of Suharto.)

See box, page 960, for a summary of the practice of Islam

Over the centuries, the people of Indonesia have been influenced by a succession of religions. Each has left its imprint on aspects of Indonesian culture. Buddhism and Hinduism were introduced from India in about the fifth century, and made an impact in Sumatra and Java where they fused to become a composite Hindu-Buddhist religion. The Islamization of the Indonesian archipelago began in Sumatra, filtering southeast to the north coast of Java, and from there to the Javanese interior during the 15th century. Christianity, meanwhile, did not begin to make significant inroads in eastern Indonesia until the 19th century.

Despite the overwhelming numerical dominance of Muslims today, many of them feel threatened by the advance of other religions, particularly Christianity. In 1933, 2.8% of the population was Christian; in 1971 this figure had risen to 7.4%; and by 1995 it was estimated to be 9% (comprising 6% Protestant and 3% Roman Catholic). Other religions are represented as follows: Hindu, 2%; Buddhist, 1%; other, 1%.) Meanwhile, some Muslims feel that their position is being eroded: over the period of the last generation, the

The practice of Islam: living by the Prophet

Islam is an Arabic word meaning 'submission to God'. As Muslims often point out, it is not just a religion but a total way of life. The main Islamic scripture is the Koran or Quran, the name being taken from the Arabic al-qur'an or 'the recitation'. The Koran is divided into 114 sura, or 'units'. Most scholars are agreed that the Koran was partially written by the Prophet Mohammad. In addition to the Koran there are the hadiths, from the Arabic word hadith meaning 'story', which tell of the Prophet's life and works. These represent the second most important body of scriptures.

The practice of Islam is based upon five central tenets, known as the Pillars of Islam: Shahada (profession of faith), Salat (worship), Zakat (charity), saum (fasting) and Haj (pilgrimage). The mosque is the centre of religious activity. The two most important mosque officials are the imam – or leader – and the khatib or preacher – who delivers the Friday sermon.

The Shahada is the confession, and lies at the core of any Muslim's faith. It involves reciting, sincerely, two statements: 'There is no god, but God', and 'Mohammad is the Messenger [Prophet] of God'. A Muslim will do this at every Salat. This is the daily prayer ritual which is performed five times a day, at sunrise, midday, mid-afternoon, sunset and at night. There is also the important Friday noon worship. The Salat is performed by a Muslim bowing and then prostrating himself in the direction of Mecca (in Malaysian kiblat, in Arabic qibla). In hotel rooms throughout Indonesia there is nearly always a little arrow, painted on the ceiling – or sometimes inside a wardrobe – indicating the direction of Mecca and labelled kiblat. The faithful are called to worship by a mosque official. Beforehand, a worshipper must wash to ensure ritual purity. The Friday midday service is performed in the mosque and includes a sermon given by the khatib.

A third essential element of Islam is Zakat – charity or alms-giving. A Muslim is supposed to give up his 'surplus' (according to the Koran); through time this took on the form of a tax levied according to the wealth of the family. In Malaysia there is no official Zakat as there is in Saudi Arabia, but good Muslims are expected to contribute a tithe to the Muslim community.

The fourth pillar of Islam is saum or fasting. The daytime month-long fast of Ramadan is a time of contemplation, worship and piety – the Islamic equivalent of lent. Muslims are expected to read one-thirtieth of the Koran each night. Muslims who are ill or on a journey have dispensation from fasting, but otherwise they are only permitted to eat during the night until "so much of the dawn appears that a white thread can be distinguished from a black one".

The Haj or pilgrimmage to the holy city of Mecca in Saudi Arabia is required of all Muslims once in their lifetime, if they can afford to make the journey and are physically able to. It is restricted to a certain time of the year, beginning on the eighth day of the Muslim month of Dhu-l-Hijja. Men who have been on the Haj are given the title Haji, and women Hajjah.

The Koran also advises on a number of other practices and customs, in particular the prohibitions on usury, the eating of pork, the taking of alcohol, and gambling. In Indonesia, these are not strictly interpreted. Islamic banking laws have not been introduced, and drinking is fairly widespread – although not in all areas. There is quite a powerful Islamic revival in Malaysia, and Brunei and some scholars and commentators identify the beginnings of a similar trend in Indonesia. But while the use of the veil is becoming de rigeur in Brunei and increasingly in Malaysia, it is still only rarely encountered in Indonesia. The Koran says nothing about the need for women to veil, although it does stress the necessity of women dressing modestly.

---

proportion of the Indonesian population who are Muslim has fallen by over six percentage points – from 93% to 87%. The spread of Christianity, allied with an Islamic revival, has led to greater religious tensions in a country where they have been expressly played-down in an effort to promote unity.

Muslim-Christian tensions came to a head in the mid-1990s, but had been brewing for some time. At the end of 1992, when there were a series of attacks on churches in Java, Abdurrahman Wahid, the moderate Muslim leader of the Nahdlatul Ulama (NU), an Islamic group with 35,000,000 members (making it the world's largest Muslim organization), wrote

Much ado about adat

Commentators on things Indonesian probably use the Indonesian word adat more than almost any other. The word is taken from the arabic word 'ada, meaning custom, and it refers to any locally accepted code of norms, behaviour, laws, customs or regulations. Often a society's adat is the totality of all these, and there is therefore not just one adat, but many adats, both within and between societies. It has enormous breadth of coverage including, for example, the accepted duties of husband and wife, customary practices in village wood lot use, the correct procedure in rituals, the accepted allocation of duties between different ranks, and rules on inheritance.

Adat is often viewed as the glue which helps Indonesian people to function and interact without conflict – or at least with a minimum of conflict. Any local leader was expected to be conversant with the accepted adat, and this was traditionally passed down the generations through verse, proverb, adage and aphorism. An intimate awareness of adat was akin to wisdom. The Dutch quickly grasped the importance of adat, and they codified it and used the resultant laws to help govern and administer at the local level.

Today, adat is in decline. Success and wisdom is less likely to be measured in terms of an intimate awareness of adat than in terms of academic achievement and economic power. Increasingly, the core of modern adat is the state 'ideology' of pancasila (see page 944), not the inherited layers of customary behaviour enshrined in the traditional meaning of the word, adat.

a letter to Suharto warning the president that Indonesia risked a religious conflagration if he did not act to prevent "war-mongering against the Christians." Suharto pointedly ignored the missive, while earlier supporting the establishment of the *Organization of Indonesian Muslim Intellectuals* (ICMI) in December 1990, headed by the president's great friend – and successor as president – BJ Habibie. Right from the start there were worries that ICMI would mobilize, or at least focus on, discontent as Muslims tried to regain – as they see it – the initiative. There is a feeling that Christians have economic and political power that far outweighs their number. Christian, in Muslim eyes, is often equated with rich. They also point out that both of Indonesia's leading newspapers, *Kompas* and *Suara Pembaruan*, are controlled by Christians. At the beginning of 1995 Abdurrahman Wahid, himself increasingly embattled as his moderate position was attacked, said: "If there's only one or two **santri** [devout Muslim] generals, then what's the danger. But as soon as they are given domination in the context of Islamizing or promoting a new type of politics, for example promoting ICMI candidates at the expense of other factions in Golkar, then that would be dangerous."

This warning was prescient given recent events. The riots of 1998 were more obviously anti-Suharto and anti-Chinese, but there was also a religious undertone to the attacks and the violence. At the beginning of 1998, the Indonesian Christian Communication Forum released figures claiming that between 1995 and 1997, 131 churches across the country had been attacked. In the first two months of 1998 another 38 could be added to this list. Compare these figures for the number of churches attacked during the entire period since 1945: 438. Partly, religious and ethnic tensions reinforce one another – around half of Indonesia's Chinese community are Christian. There is also some evidence that the government has used the Chinese-Christian association to deflect blame for the crisis onto a minority group for whom the Muslim majority harbour suspicion. To try and regain the trust of ordinary Indonesians, some wealthier Christian Chinese donated food and clothes to the poor during the economic crisis of 1998.

Language and literature

There are more than 500 languages and dialects spoken across the archipelago, but it was Malay that was embraced as the national language – the language of unity – at the All Indonesia Youth Congress in 1928. Republicans had recognized for some time the important role that a common language might play in binding together the different

Bahasa Indonesia

religions and ethnic groups that comprised the East Indies. Malay had long been the *lingua franca* of traders in the archipelago, and, importantly, it was not identified with any particular group. Most importantly of all though, it was not a Javanese language. This muted any criticism that Java was imposing its culture on the rest of the country. Before long, Malay was being referred to as **Bahasa Indonesia** – the Indonesian language.

As visitors to Indonesia will quickly notice, the written language uses the Roman script. Through history, three scripts have been used in the country: 'Indian', Arabic and Roman. Indian-derived scripts include Old Javanese or Kawi, and Balinese. Arabic was associated with the spread of Islam and has tended to be confined to religious works. It proved to be particularly unsuited to use with Javanese. At the beginning of the 20th century, the Dutch assigned Ch A van Ophuysen to devise a system for Romanizing the Malay language. The Roman script gained popularity during the 1920s when the Indonesian nationalist movement associated its use with political change and modernity. In 1947, a number of spelling reforms were introduced of which the most important was the change from using 'oe' to 'u', so that 'Soekarno' and 'Soeharto' became, respectively, 'Sukarno' and 'Suharto'. Another series of spelling changes were introduced in 1972 to bring Bahasa Indonesia in line with Bahasa Melayu (Bahasa Malay). Nonetheless, as Bahasa Indonesia gained acceptance as a 'national' language, so it began to diverge from the Malay spoken in Malaysia. Today, although the two are mutually intelligible, there are noticeable differences between them in terms of both vocabulary and structure. The two countries' respective colonial legacy can be seen reflected in such loan words as **nomor**, from the Dutch for number in Indonesia, and **nombor** from the English in Malaysia.

The government has avidly promoted Bahasa Indonesia as the language of unity and it is now spoken in all but the most remote areas of the archipelago. Children are schooled in the national language, and television, radio and newspapers and magazines all help to propagate its use. But although most Indonesians are able to speak 'Bahasa', as it is known, they are likely to converse in their own language or dialect. Of the 500 other languages and dialects spoken in the country, the dominant ones are Sundanese, Javanese and Madurese (all three spoken on Java or Madura), Minang and Batak (on Sumatra), and Balinese.

Literature Many of Indonesia's hundreds of languages have produced no written literature – although oral traditions do exist. However, the distinction between oral folk traditions and written literature is often blurred, as is the distinction between local traditions and imported literatures. For example, the series of popular stories which tell of the exploits of the *kancil* or mousedeer, who through guile and cleverness is able to overcome far stronger beasts, are Indian in influence, as are some of the Batak and Dayak tales.

But Indian influence is clearest in Old Javanese literature (900-1500 AD), when the Ramayana and Mahabharata were translated from Sanskrit (see box). However, this was not merely a case of absorbing outside influences wholesale. Most notably, *Kakawin* literature – though derived from an Indian genre – is clearly a Javanese art form. *Kakawin* poetry was commissioned by noblemen and performed at court. They were regarded not merely as stories, but as spiritual works of worship – almost as a form of written yoga. Perhaps the finest of the *kakawin* is the 14th century *Nagarakertagama*, discovered in 1894.

With the fall of the Hindu Majapahit Empire and the rise of Islam, so 'modern' Javanese literature evolved, from around the beginning of the 18th century. This combined Indian and Muslim traditions and produced such works as the **Babad Tanah Jawi**, a historical text, and the **Hikayat Aceh**, a record of Sultan Iskander Muda of Aceh's reign (1607-36). The greatest source of dispute among scholars is how far such texts can be regarded as historically accurate – some scholars use them as a template to recreate Javanese life of the time, while others maintain that they are fundamentally inaccurate. Among religious texts of this period, the most highly regarded – for example, the 3,000 page **Serat Centhini** – were produced at the court in Aceh, where they took on an almost mystical tone.

With the arrival of the Dutch and the gradual extension of their control over the archipelago, so a modern literature emerged. Many of the finest novelists of the early years of the 20th century were from Sumatra – and particularly from Minangkabau (West Sumatra) – men such as Adbul Muis, Marah Rusli (who wrote the highly regarded **Sitti**

The Ramayana and Mahabharata

Across much of Southeast Asia, the Indian epics of the Ramayana and Mahabharata have been translated and adapted for local consumption. The stories of the Mahabharata are the more popular. These centre on a long-standing feud between two family clans: the Pandawas and the Korawas. The feud culminates in an epic battle, during which the five Pandawa brothers come face to face with their 100 first cousins from the Korawa clan. After 18 days of fighting, the Pandawas emerge victorious and the eldest brother becomes king. The plays usually focus on one or other of the five Pandawa brothers, each of whom is a hero.

The Ramayana was written by the poet Valmiki about 2,000 years ago. The 48,000 line story tells of the abduction of the beautiful Sita by the evil king, Ravana. Sita's husband Rama, King of Ayodhia, sets out on an odyssey to retrieve his wife from Ravana's clutches, finally succeeding with the help of Hanuman the monkey god and his army of monkeys. Today it is rare to see the Ramayana performed; the orchestra needs to be large (and is therefore expensive) and in the case of wayang (see page 305), few puppet masters have a sufficiently large collection of puppets to cover all the characters.

Nurbaya) and Nur St Iskander. The Japanese occupation of the country stifled publication, but following the 1945 revolution a group of idealists formed the **Angkatan 45** – the generation of 1945 – to support and develop Indonesian literature. Foremost among its members was Chairil Anwar. **Angkatan 45** became caught up in the political maelstrom of the 1960s and following the attempted coup of 1965, many of its members were imprisoned. The years since have seen an emasculation of Indonesian literature, and the radicalism and invention of the 1950s and 1960s has still yet to be equalled.

Dance, drama and music

Like Indonesian art and architecture, the dance, drama and music of the archipelago also spans a large number of regional styles and forms. Many of these are discussed in the relevant regional sections. Nonetheless, the influence of Javanese drama and music has spread beyond Java to the Outer Islands – in a process of artistic imperialism. In so doing these art forms have begun to take on a 'national' character, and have become representative of the country as a whole. This applies, for example, to the gamelan orchestra and the wayang shadow puppet theatre.

Indonesian music available on CD and tape Most Indonesian towns have shops selling traditional Indonesian music – although the quality is often poor. Outside the country it is rather harder to obtain recordings. However, the US Library of Congress, as part of its Endangered Music Project, released *Music for the Gods* (Catalogue nos. RCD 10315 [CD] and RAC 10315 [cassette]) in 1994, a selection of 13 pieces from The Fahnestock South Sea Expedition to Indonesia in 1941. The pieces on this CD were recorded largely in Bali. The two Fahnestock brothers, Bruce and Sheridan, along with the latter's wife Margaret, sailed for Indonesia in the 137-ft schooner *Director II* with two state of the art Presto disc-cutters and 3 km of microphone cable, so that they could record from shore to ship. After making recordings in Bali and the South Seas, the boat sank off Australia in 1941, but not before the precious discs had been taken back to New York. The Fahnestock's then proceeded to spy for President Roosevelt, noting the sea defences of Java, all the while continuing to record performances in East Java and Madura, as well as Bali. Bruce was killed in New Guinea during the war, while Sheridan later became a publisher. The original recordings were donated to the Library of Congress in 1986 by Margaret Fahnestock.

In total the Smithsonian are planning 20 'volumes' of Indonesian music. So far (to 1997), 12 volumes have been released. Others currently available are:
Songs before dawn (Smithsonian/Folkways SF40055)
Indonesian popular music (Smithsonian/Folkways SF40056)

Music from the outskirts of Jakarta (Smithsonian/Folkways SF40057)
Music of Nias and North Sumatra (Smithsonian/Folkways SF40420)
Betawi and Sundanese music of the north coast of Java (Smithsonian/Folkways SF40421)
Night music of West Sumatra (Smithsonian/Folkways SF40422)
Music from the forests of Riau and Mentawi (Smithsonian/Folkways)
Vocal and instrumental music from east and central Flores (Smithsonian/Folkways)
Vocal music from central and west Flores (Smithsonian/Folkways)
Music of Biak, Irian Jaya (Smithsonian/Folkways)
Melayu music of Sumatra and the Riau islands (Smithsonian/Folkways)
Gongs and vocal music from Sumatra (Smithsonian/Folkways)

Further information from: Smithsonian/Folkways, Center for Folklife Programs and Cultural Studies, 955 L'Enfant Plaza, Suite 2600, Smithsonian Institution, Washington DC 20560, USA.

Land and environment

Who first coined the term 'Indonesia' is disputed. Traditionally the glory has gone to the German ethnographer Adolf Bastian, who is said to have latched onto the word at the end of the 19th century. But some scholars credit the English lawyer George Windsor Earl with coining the name in an article he wrote in 1850. Another English lawyer, JR Logan, practising in Singapore, is said to have read Earl's articles and as a result took to using the term in his own papers. It was only then that Bastian, after reading Logon's publications, began to refer to 'Indonesia' in his own work. The Teutons and the Anglos will probably be fighting over this rich prize for some years yet!

The regions of Indonesia

With a country of such enormous size, how it is divided takes on great importance. Many people – although rarely Indonesians themselves – simply talk of the 'Inner' or 'Metropolitan' islands of Java, Bali and Madura, and the Outer Islands – the rest. This division is one of core and periphery, in a political, economic, cultural and historic sense. Jakarta and Java are the main centres of political and economic power, and Javanese culture has an over-riding effect upon the rest of the nation. As the anthropologist Clifford Geertz wrote in 1966: "If ever there was a tail which wagged a dog, Java is the tail, Indonesia the dog."

The country can also be broken down into the Greater and Lesser Sunda Islands. The Greater Sundas comprise Sumatra, Java, Kalimantan and Sulawesi; the Lesser Sundas, Bali, Timor and the myriad islands of Maluku and Nusa Tenggara. This division has a certain zoological and geological logic: plants and animals of the two broadly reflect their contrasting Asian and Australasian origins.

Officially however, the country is divided into 27 provinces (which includes three special administrative areas – see below) or *propinsi*. However, this figure of 27 includes the disputed territory of East Timor, which will shortly become an independent country after a period of UN administration. (Just for the record, the UN never officially acknowledge the Indonesian annexation of East Timor in 1995.) The territory currently occupies an in-between status, being neither part of Indonesia nor a fully independent nation state. Each province is administered by a governor (*gubernur*). The administrative unit beneath the province is the district or *kabupaten*, of which there are between three and 29 in each province (242 in total); each of these is headed by a *bupati*, known as a regent during the colonial period. Urban municipalities – 56 in total – which have the same administrative status as districts are known as *kotamadya*. Kabupaten are in turn divided into sub-districts or *kecamatan*, of which there are 3,639, and they into villages or *desa*. Each village – and in 1991 there were 62,061 – is headed by a *kepala desa*, literally 'village head'.

Volcanoes

Indonesia has more active volcanoes than any other country – 13% of the world's total. It has also experienced more eruptions known to have affected people and their activities (156) than any other country. Over the last 200 years an estimated 175,000 people have died from volcanic activity in Indonesia, and between 1985 and 1995 alone the country experienced no fewer than 38 eruptions. Indonesia, in short, is a vulcanologist's dream. The volcanoes are concentrated in an arc that marks the boundary between the Pacific, Australian and Philippine tectonic plates, running through West Sumatra, Java, Bali, the islands of Nusa Tenggara, and which then sweeps north to include North Sulawesi and Halmahera in Maluku. Not suprisingly, Indonesia also suffers numerous earthquakes. From a human perspective, it is Java where volcanoes pose the greatest threat. Around 2,500,000 people on Java live in designated 'high risk' areas, and if Mount Guntur between Bandung and Garut showed signs of activity around 750,000 people would have to be evacuated.

The best known eruption was the one which vaporized a large part of the island of Krakatoa off the west coast (not the east coast as the film Krakatoa East of Java tried to maintain in a futile attempt – presumably – to sound more romantic and Oriental) of Java in 1883 (see page 116). But far larger was the eruption of Mount Tambora on Sumbawa in 1815, which catastrophically altered the global climate in the following year (see page 809). More stupendous still, though, was the truly massive eruption that created Lake Toba in North Sumatra about 75,000 years ago – probably the largest explosion anywhere in the last million years (see page 484).

With Indonesia's wealth of volcanoes there is also a correspondingly impressive infrastructure for coping with eruptions. Some of this is traditional, but the modern Vulcanological Division of the Geological Survey, building on previous Dutch work, is highly professional and effective – beliying Indonesia's comparative poverty in other respects. When Colo volcano, on the island of Una Una in Central Sulawesi, erupted in 1983, the 7,000 inhabitants had already been evacuated, following the advice of the Survey which had been carefully monitoring seismic activity in the area. The eruption of Mount Merapi on Java, at the end of November 1994, led to more than 5,000 villagers being evacuated from the mountainside; there were also a considerable number of deaths.

Geography

In total, Indonesia covers a land area of 1,919,317 sq km – or eight times the land area of Britain. The country also claims sovereignty over 3,272,160 sq km of sea, stretching from Asia to Australasia. The political, historic and economic heart of the country are the islands of Java and Bali, which support 60% of the population but account for only 7% of the land area. On Java's north coast is the capital or 'mother city' (*ibu kota*) of Jakarta, formerly Batavia. Ranged around these so-called Inner Islands are the Outer Islands: Sumatra, Kalimantan, Sulawesi, Timor and West Papua, and the assorted islands of Maluku and Nusa Tenggara. The population of Indonesia now exceeds 200,000,000: the 200 millionth inhabitant was born – officially – on 4 February 1997 – in a village in East Lombok. The baby boy was showered with gifts and his name was chosen by the president himself: Wahyu Nusantara Aji.

An active volcanic arc runs through Sumatra, Java and the islands of Nusa Tenggara, and then north through Maluku to Sulawesi. It marks the point where two tectonic plates plunge, one beneath the other. This is an area of intense volcanic activity – a 'ring of fire' – most dramatically illustrated when Krakatoa erupted and then exploded in 1883 (see page 116). Off the coast of these islands is a deep sea trench, in places more than 7,000m deep. Within the arc is the more stable Sunda Shelf, with shallow seas and a less dramatic landscape.

Another division that has attracted considerable attention is a biological divide: between Indonesia's Asian and Australasian faunal realms. This 'line' runs between Bali and Lombok, and north to divide Kalimantan and Sulawesi. It is known as Wallace's Line after the great Victorian naturalist Alfred Russel Wallace, who first observed the distinction in the

19th century (see page 801). To the southeast of the line, animals tend to be Australasian in origin – for example, marsupials are found, in the Kai Islands and in Sulawesi. By contrast, to the northwest of Wallace's Line, no marsupials are found but there are many of the large Asian mammals including tigers, elephants, orang utans and rhinoceros.

The two Indonesian landscapes that are most striking are the **terraced ricefield** and the **tropical forest**. The terraced ricefield, exemplified by those on Java and Bali, are cut from the land, bounded by small embankments, irrigated, and can support well over 1,000 people per square kilometre. They are managed, artificial ecosystems in which nature is reworked and harnessed in the interests of humans. In contrast, the tropical forest is a natural ecosystem. Hunter, gatherers and shifting cultivators do not so much replace the forest, as work with and within it. Population densities rarely exceed 10 people per square kilometre, and their livelihoods are dependent on maintaining the forest resource. But although the tropical lowland rainforests contain a greater variety of species than any other terrestrial ecosystem, they are also one of the most sensitive. If the forest is cleared over large areas, then the land and soil suffer from erosion and degradation.

The cycle of wet rice cultivation

There are an estimated 120,000 rice varieties. Rice seed – either selected from the previous harvest or, more commonly, purchased from a dealer or agricultural extension office – is soaked overnight before being sown into a carefully prepared nursery bed. Today farmers are likely to plant one of the Modern Varieties or MVs, bred for their high yields.

The nursery bed into which the seeds are broadcast (scattered) is often a farmer's best land, with the most stable water supply. After a month the seedlings are uprooted and taken out to the paddy fields. These will also have been ploughed, puddled and harrowed, turning the heavy clay soil into a saturated slime. Traditionally, buffalo and cattle would have performed the task; today rotavators, and even tractors, are becoming more common. The seedlings are transplanted into the mud in clumps. Before transplanting the tops of the seedlings are twisted off (this helps to increase yield) and then they are pushed in to the soil in neat rows. The work is back-breaking and it is not unusual to find labourers – both men and women – receiving a premium – either a bonus on top of the usual daily wage or a free meal at midday, to which marijuana is sometimes added to ease the pain.

After transplanting, it is essential that the water supply is carefully controlled. The key to high yields is a constant flow of water, regulated to take account of the growth of the rice plant. In 'rain-fed' systems where the farmer relies on rainfall to water the crop, he has to hope that it will be neither too much nor too little. Elaborate ceremonies are performed to appease the rice goddess and to ensure bountiful rainfall.

In areas where rice is grown in irrigated conditions, farmers need not concern themselves with the day-to-day pattern of rainfall, and in such areas two or even three crops can be grown each year. But such systems need to be carefully managed, and it is usual for one man to be in charge of irrigation. In Bali he is known as the *kliang subak*. He decides when water should be released, organizes labour to repair dykes and dams and to clear channels, and decides which fields should receive the water first.

Traditionally, while waiting for the rice to mature, a farmer would do little except weed the crop from time to time. He and his family might move out of the village and live in a field hut to keep a close eye on the maturing rice. Today, farmers also apply chemical fertilizers and pesticides to protect the crop and ensure maximum yield. After 90-130 days, the crop should be ready for harvesting.

Harvesting also demands intensive labour. Traditionally, farmers in a village would secure their harvesters through systems of reciprocal labour exchange; now it is more likely for a harvester to be paid in cash. After harvesting, the rice is threshed, sometimes out in the field, and then brought back to the village to be stored in a rice barn or sold. It is only at the end of the harvest, with the rice safely stored in the barn, that the festivals begin.

Climate

Straddling the equator, and stretching over 5,000 km from east to west and almost 2,000 km from north to south, Indonesia encompasses several climatic zones. It is possible to fly from one region's wet season to another area's dry, and from towns with annual rainfall of nearly 5,000mm, to places where it is less than 500mm. The only constant – at least at sea-level – is the temperature, which averages about 26°C.

Much of Indonesia has what climatologists term an **'equatorial monsoon' climate**. This broad classification covers a multitude of climate types. Annual rainfall usually exceeds 2,000mm, but can be more than twice that, or less than a quarter of it. Close to the equator rainfall is distributed evenly through the year, and there is no marked dry season. However, moving north and south from the equator, the dry season becomes more pronounced, and rainfall becomes concentrated in one or two seasonal peaks. Indonesia's worst storm on record resulted in 802mm (31in) of rain falling in just one day. Over a period of 13 days, 3,220mm (127in) of rain fell, with 80mm (3in) falling in the space of just 30 minutes.

This pattern of rainfall is determined by two monsoons: the northeast monsoon and the southwest monsoon. Monsoon does not, strictly speaking, mean rain. It describes the seasonal wind system that affects Asia each year, and comes from an Arabic word meaning 'season'. The northeast monsoon prevails from November/December to February/March and forms the wet season. The southwest monsoon extends from June to August/September and brings dry conditions to the area. But there are a large number of exceptions to disturb this general pattern. Eastern Indonesia has a rather different climate from the rest of the country. It too is affected by two monsoons: the west monsoon from December to March, and the east monsoon from May to September. The west monsoon is a continuation of the Asian northeast monsoon after it has changed direction on crossing the equator. However, by the time it has arrived, the monsoon has picked up moisture over the warm seas of the Indonesian archipelago. It therefore brings large quantities of rainfall to the area between the months of December and March. By May the northeast monsoon has retreated and East Indonesia comes under the influence of the hot and dry South Pacific Trade-winds. This east monsoon generally extends from May to September, although the dry season (which is very dry) can be as much as seven months long.

Flora and fauna

The greatest naturalist to have travelled through the islands of Indonesia was the Victorian, Alfred Russel Wallace (1823-1913). His book *The Malay Archipelago: the land of the Orang-utan and the Bird of Paradise* (1869) is a *tour de force*, dedicated, significantly, to the other great Victorian naturalist Charles Darwin "not only as a token of personal esteem and friendship but also to express my deep admiration for his genius and his works". Darwin first appeared to take notice of Wallace's work in 1855 or 1856 when Charles Lyell, the great geologist, recommended that he read Wallace's paper 'on the law which has regulated the introduction of new species' in the ***Annals and Magazine of Natural History*** (vol. 16, 1855). Wallace was clearly on the same evolutionary path as Darwin – or at least an allied one – and it was probably the fear that Wallace might pre-empt Darwin which led the latter to fully develop his evolutionary ideas which had been gestating for so many years.

Wallace was enchanted by the animals and people that he encountered during his eight years away from England. He travelled 14,000 miles through the archipelago, made 60 or 70 separate journeys, and collected 125,600 specimens – which he shipped back to London and donated to the British Museum.

Straddling the equator and marking the interface between the Asian and Australasian worlds, Indonesia has the richest flora and fauna of any country in Southeast Asia. Indeed, it can reasonably lay claim to being more biodiverse than any other country in the world. Never scared about over-egging the zoological pudding, Indonesia has even been described as 'megadiverse'. Although it accounts for only 1.3% of the earth's land area, Indonesia supports 10% of the world's flowering plants (25,000 species), 12% of mammal species (500), 16% of the world's amphibian and reptile species, 17% of bird species (1,600)

Extinct and endangered mammals of Java, Sumatra and Borneo

	JAVA	SUMATRA	BORNEO
Orang utan	Extinct	Endangered	Endangered
Siamang	Extinct	Endangered	–
Javan rhinoceros	Endangered	Extinct	Extinct
Sumatran rhinoceros	–	Endangered	Endangered
Banteng	Endangered	Extinct	Endangered
Malay tapir	Extinct	Endangered	Extinct
Tiger	Extinct	Endangered	Extinct (?)
Sunbear	Extinct	Endangered	Endangered
Leopard	Endangered	Extinct	Endangered
Elephant	Extinct	Endangered	Endangered

Source: Whitten, Tony and Whitten, Jane (1996), Indonesian heritage: wildlife, Singapore: Editions Didier Millet.

and 25% of the world's species of fish (8,500). In total there are 816 endemic species of fauna – animals found nowhere else in the world except Indonesia – including 210 mammal species, 430 bird and 150 reptile. Along with Australia, there are more endemic vertebrates in Indonesia than in any other country. Many of the large Asian mammals are represented: tigers, elephants, two species of rhinoceros, tapirs, buffalos, gibbons and orang-utans (see Borneo, page 661). There are also oddities such as the bird of paradise, the maleo bird, the Komodo dragon (page 822) and the Rafflesia flower. The characteristic flora and fauna of each region are discussed in the relevant introductory section.

Not only has Indonesia got one of the richest flora and faunas in the world, it also suffers from rapid loss of habitat as forests are cleared for timber and human settlement. The Javan wattled lapwing (*Vanellus macropterus*) and the caerulean paradise flycatcher (*Eutrichomyias rowleyi*) of the Sangihe Islands off North Sulawesi are both extinct, as are the small Balinese and Javan (probably) tigers, both subspecies of tiger. The last definite record of a live Bali tiger dates from 1937, when a specimen was shot for the Bogor Zoological Museum. The Javan tiger lasted a little longer, but by 1976 there was just a small population confined to the Meru Betiri National Park in East Java. Unfortunately – perhaps collectively deciding they would rather sink into extinction than become the objects of endless breeding programmes – they decided not to procreate. The last member of this small band died, it is thought, in the mid-1980s. (Although there were reports in 1997, following the fires of that year, that two specimens had been seen scampering over some scorched land in Java.) Other animals are represented by such small populations that they are probably unsustainable – the Javan gibbon, for example. As Tony and Jane Whitten remark in their book *Wild Indonesia*, the "term 'living dead' has been applied to such species".

One of the most tragic and pointless slaughters has been of Indonesia's butterflies. There are an estimated 2,000 butterfly species, including 121 swallowtails (Papilionidae), perhaps the world's most spectacular butterfly family. The wingspan of the gargantuan *Ornithoptera goliath* can reach 22cm. A good example of a swallowtail may be worth between US$20 and US$1,500 to a collector, depending on the species. Some butterflies (like the birdwings) are now protected, while the government is also encouraging villagers in some areas to 'cultivate' the insects for sale. This not only brings income to villagers and encourages them to protect habitats and plant species preferred by butterflies, but also diverts attention from the collection and sale of wild specimens.

The great fires of 1997

In 1997 the world was witness to a fire – in reality, hundreds of blazes – of truly stupendous proportions. The fires consumed swathes of forest across Sumatra, Kalimantan (Indonesian Borneo) and Irian Jaya; the area affected by the smog was equivalent in size to Western Europe, stretching over 3,000 km from east to west; in total, around 100,000,000 people were affected across six countries; the populations of Indonesian cities like Jambi, Pekanbaru and Medan choked on the smoke and schools were closed; the Malaysian government considered evacuating the entire population of the East Malaysian state of Sarawak, over 2,000,000 people; flights across the region were cancelled; the Air Pollution Index in Kuching, Sarawak's capital, reached 851, where a figure of 300 is considered `hazardous'; more than a thousand Malaysian firefighters were sent to help fight the fires – but no one expected their impact to be more than political; sunbathers on the beaches of Phuket, in southern Thailand, were shaded from the rays; water was sprayed from cranes and residents in high rise blocks in Kuala Lumpur asked to sprinkle it from their windows to clear the air; in Irian Jaya almost 300 people died from hunger brought on by the drought, when planes with relief supplies could not land because of smoke from fires burning out of control; and an airline crash in Medan (234 killed) and a collision between two vessels in the Melaka Strait (30 killed) were blamed on poor visibility brought on by the fires.

Foreign correspondents crowded onto planes to report on the fires and their effects. Rosemary Richter, in Singapore, wrote that the experience of breathing the polluted air was like "inhaling hot cotton wool fibres" and "living inside a wet blanket redolent of a refuse tip". Other correspondents reported on the bitter smell, oppressive darkness, watering eyes, the layer of soot that covered everything, the choking sensation, and the itching skin. At the beginning of November the Malaysian government even went so far as to muzzle academics, ordering them not to talk to the press about the ill effects of the smog. This followed one (inaccurate) report that breathing the haze was like smoking 40 cigarettes a day (up from 20 a few weeks earlier!). One Indonesian minister estimated that 20,000,000 Indonesians were suffering from aggravated respiratory problems because of the smog, and some environmentalists were even predicting an increase in cancer in two or three decades time because of the carcinogens that are present in the smoke. To put it bluntly: while a few people will die as a direct result of the smog, many more will die prematurely.

Putting out the fires was not an option. The president of WWF Malaysia both asked the question "how to put the fires out" and answered it "we do not know". While nature might not be to blame for the extent of the fires, nature did provide the answer: the delayed rains ultimately doused the fires. Some western environmentalists, like the director-general of the WWF, called the fires a planetary disaster. Others wondered about the knock-on effects for climate elsewhere on the globe. Some climatologists warned of storms and particularly unsettled conditions in Europe. In towns across Sumatra and Kalimantan, not to mention Singapore and Malaysia, people were just happy that they could breathe again. Tragically – but perhaps predictably – 1999 saw the return of the fires for the fourth time in a decade. The new millennium also got off to a bad start: yet more fires.

National parks

As of early 1991, 24 national parks had been gazetted by the Indonesian government, covering 6,900,000 ha. Three of these have been adopted by the IUCN as World Heritage Sites, one of them covered by this book: Komodo in Nusa Tenggara. In general, Indonesian parks have limited tourist facilities when compared with parks in Malaysia and Thailand, although those in Bali represent exceptions to this rule. The Indonesian government also recognizes separate categories of Recreational Forests, Grand Forest Parks and Hunting Parks. These areas are less rigorously protected. The fact that 1993 was heralded as Visit Indonesia Environment and Heritage Year possibly indicates that some people are beginning to accept that the environment is worth preserving on sound, pecuniary grounds.

The task facing the Indonesian government is how to protect the country's plants, animals and wild areas when the population is growing at nearly 2% a year, and when economic pressures on resources are escalating at an even faster rate. About 10% of the country's land area is now protected. An environmental movement has also emerged in Indonesia, spurring the government to take greater notice of infractions of environmental laws. But in the Outer Islands it is difficult for farmers and settlers to appreciate that any environmental crisis exists. In Sumatra, Kalimantan, Sulawesi and West Papua it is all too easy to believe that the forest is a limitless resource. When families have to be fed and clothed, and children sent to school, cutting-down trees to sell the timber and clear the land for agriculture seems not just a reasonable response but often also the only response.

Scorched Earth, bitter winds

"I would describe this as one of the worst environmental disasters of the last decade of the century" (Professor Klaus Topver, head of the UN team investigating the fires).

1999 and 2000 saw a repeat of the bushfires of 1982-83, 1987, 1991, 1994 and 1997 (see the box on page 969). Though the most recent outbreaks in 1997 and 1999 received the greatest international media attention, and seem to have led to the most serious air pollution problems (in particular the fires of 1997), in terms of area burned the 1982-83 fires were the most extensive, affecting 3,600,000 ha of forest – an area equivalent to that of Belgium. Fires of this nature have always been a feature of Sumatra. Shifting cultivators and foresters have traditionally cleared land in the dry season through firing, a much more efficient approach than clearing by hand. Bushfires also sometimes naturally occur, and many forests in

National parks & protected areas

♦ National parks & protected areas
1 Rubiah Sea Garden
2 Gunung Leuser
3 Siberut
4 Kerinci Seblat
5 Bukit Barisan Selatan
6 Pulau Seribu Marine Park
7 Way Kambas
8 Gunung Palung
9 Tanjung Puting
10 Ujung Kulon
11 Gunung Gede-Pangrango
12 Bromo-Tengger-Semeru
13 Gunung Kawi-Kelud
14 Bali Barat
15 Meru Betiri

Southeast Asia where there is a pronounced dry season are adapted to periodic burning (so-called fire climaxes). The fires of recent years have been on a different scale altogether. The blazes reach temperatures of 600°C, roasting the subsoil and killing root systems and micro-organisms to depths of more than 2m. Experts believe some of the worst fires have coincided with areas where there are underground coal deposits, suggesting that some of these have been set alight. There is also suspicion that when the underlying peat catches fire – as was reported during the 1997 conflagration – then the fires may be almost impossible to extinguish and could smoulder through to the following dry season.

The media have tended to report the fires in terms of the effects that they have had on air quality in Singapore and Kuala Lumpur (where most journalists happen to be based), and the problems they cause airliners trying to land in poor visibility. In KL the almost seasonal nature of the fires has led locals to call the effects simply 'the haze', as if it were as natural as the 'wet season'. When the haze hits town the street traders quickly begin to market surgical face masks – just as they produce umbrellas when the heavens open. But it almost goes without saying that the main effects are felt in the areas where the fires occur, namely Sumatra (and also Kalimantan and Irian Jaya). The fires have killed wildlife, created treeless landscapes where the first rains cause rapid overland flow and erosion, and have undermined the livelihood strategies of those tribal peoples who rely on the forest.

The Indonesian government would like to think that the ultimate cause of the fires can be linked to the periodic droughts associated with changes in the El Niño Southern Oscillation, off Peru. This places blame far away in the realms of nature. It also appeals to those who see the root cause as global environmental change – global warming, the

NB: Only includes parks & sanctuaries mentioned in text

- 16 Alas Purwo
- 17 Gunung Rinjani
- 18 Moyo Island
- 19 Tambora Complex
- 20 Komodo
- 21 Danau Kelimutu
- 22 Gunung Api
- 23 Morowali Nature Reserve
- 24 Lore Lindu
- 25 Kutal
- 26 Panua
- 27 Bunaken Manado Tua Marine Park
- 28 Tangkoko Batu Angus
- 29 Tanjung Api
- 30 Mansuela
- 31 Cenderawasih Bay Marine Park
- 32 Mamberamo
- 33 Rouffaer
- 34 Gunung Lorentz Nature Reserve
- 35 Jayawijaya
- 36 Pulau Dolok
- 37 Wasur

greenhouse effect. Though the 1997 drought in Sumatra was particularly severe – the worst for 50 years – there were a panoply of human effects which compounded the drought and made the fires that much more serious.

To begin with, the finger of blame can point at the lax forest management policies of the government. In part the policies themselves are weak; but more important, they are weakly enforced and woefully underfunded. Logging companies, plantation owners, transmigration settlers and shifting cultivators use fire to clear their land, and although they should, in theory, obtain a licence the reality is that almost none do. Worse still, it seems that the worst offenders are companies either owned or part-owned by the government. Another explanation, traditionally popular with government officials, is that the main culprits are shifting cultivators who burn the forest to create clearings for agriculture (*ladangs*). If this is true – and they would seem to be scapegoats – then it is more likely that the culprits are not the tribal peoples but those immigrants to Sumatra who are unskilled in the art of swiddening.

In September 1997, former President Suharto outlawed all land clearance using fire: horses and open stable doors sprung to mind. This was presented as a significant policy announcement. But the president made exactly the same announcement in April 1995. The effectiveness of the 1995 directive is all too clear.

What may be remarkable to many Westerners was the time it took before the politics of blame took hold. President Suharto apologized to his fellow Asean nations at an environment conference in September 1997, but criticism from Malaysia and Singapore, the two countries most affected after Indonesia, was astonishingly muted. It was the media in the two countries, chivvied on by an irate public making their feelings known through newspaper letter columns and radio talk shows, that encouraged the governments of Malaysia and Singapore to take a more forthright stance. Warren Fernandez in Singapore's *Straits Times* wrote at the peak of the crisis in 1997 that it was time to put aside Asean's usual chumminess: "This will entail their being able to set aside traditional inhibitions – diplomatic niceties, worries about national sensitivities, the so-called 'Asean-way' of not interfering in each other's affairs – to take steps to deal with a common problem that transcends national borders".

But throughout the fires of 1997, and also during the conflagrations of 1999 and 2000, the government seemed either unwilling or unable to take effective action to curb the culprits. The impression remains that the Indonesian government was driven by more powerful interests than public opinion and, more to the point, was powerless to put out the fires in any case. While President Wahid may have called the fires of 2000 a 'national disaster', there just aren't the people to police the vast areas of Sumatra and Kalimantan. It is probably appropriate to leave the last words to the Imam of the Central Mosque in the city of Pontianak in Kalimantan, for he probably best articulated what many people in the region felt: "Allah is giving us a warning".

Environmental protection & conservation post-Suharto

It would be a brave man or woman who would describe former president Suharto as a friend of the environment. He and his cronies, such as Bob Hasan, contributed in their different ways to widespread logging and other environmental crimes. And yet, with Suharto gone, things have, if anything, got worse. The loss of Suharto's centralized authority has given local and regional power-brokers the elbow room to do just about anything. In mid-2000 it was estimated that there were 62,000 illegal miners in the country, causing far more environmental damage than the larger commercial concerns which had been licensed and orchestrated by Suharto et al. The same kind of uncontrolled exploitation is occurring in the country's national parks where illegal loggers, taking advantage of the power vacuum that exists in many areas and driven by desperate economic necessity, are pillaging such parks as the Gunung Leuser in North Sumatra and Tanjung Puting in Central Kalimantan. The London-based Environmental Investigation Agency in conjunction with Telapak, an Indonesian environmental NGOs, reported in late 1999 that 'virtual anarchy' reigned in Tanjung Puting (*Inside Indonesia* 61, 2000). With further decentralization of responsibility scheduled to be on the statute books by 2001, the fear is that things can only get worse.

13

Footnotes

Footnotes

975 Fares and timetables

982 Fortnightly circuits of Pelni ships

988 Selected Pelni fares

992 Glossary

996 Indonesian food glossary

997 Index

Fares and timetables

Selected Merpati Fares

Jakarta to:	Fare (Rp)
Ambon	1,661,000
Balikpapan	1,131,000
Banda Aceh	1,577,000
Batam	814,000
Biak	2,457,000
Denpasar	802,000
Jayapura	2,717,000
Manado	1,873,000
Medan	1,156,000
Padang	869,000
Palembang	456,000
Pekanbaru	880,000
Semarang	386,000
Surakarta	455,000
Surabaya	655,000
Makassar	1,196,000
Yogyakarta	456,000

Banjarmasin to:	Fare (Rp)
Surabaya	479,000
Balikpapan	317,000

Medan to:	Fare (Rp)
Banda Aceh	397,500
Jakarta	1,156,000
Batam	633,400
Padang	681,100
Denpasar	1,777,000
Yogyakarta	1,444,900

Tarakan - Balikpapan	589,900
Makassar to:	**Fare (Rp)**
Batam	1,600,000
Denpasar	555,000
Jakarta	1,196,000
Kendari	318,000
Manado	853,000
Palu	503,000
Yogyakarta	883,000
Mataram	786,000
Medan	2,280,000
Manado to:	**Fare (Rp)**
Gorontalo	310,000
Makassar	590,000
Palu	578,000
Ternate	352,000
Biak	1,000,000
Jayapura	1,400,000
Luwuk	456,000
Surabaya	1,400,000
Jakarta	1,873,000
Denpasar	1,300,000

NB Fares quoted are one way, in Rupiah. They are for flights purchased in Indonesia.

Selected train timetable

Name	Route	Depart	Arrive	Via
Jakarta-Bandung-Jakarta				
Argogede JB260	Jakarta (Gambir) to Bandung	1000 & 1800	1230 & 2030	
Argogede JB260	Bandung to Jakarta (Gambir)	0630 & 0850	1430 & 1650	
Parahyangan	Jakarta (Gambir) to Bandung	14 departures per day (approx)		
Parahyangan	Bandung to Jakarta (Gambir)	14 departures per day (approx)		
Jakarta-Surabaya-Jakarta				
Argobromo JS950	Jakarta (Gambir) to Surabaya (Pasarturi)	2005	0505	Pekalongan, Semarang
Argobromo JS950	Surabaya (Pasarturi) to Jakarta (Gambir)	1945	0445	Semarang, Pekalongan
Exspres Malam Sembrani	Jakarta (Kota) to Surabaya (Pasarturi)	1730	0325	Cirebon, Pekalongan, Semarang
Exspres Malam Sembrani	Surabaya (Pasarturi) to Jakarta (Kota)	1720	0345	Semarang, Pekalongan, Cirebon
Bima	Jakarta (Kota) to Surabaya (Gubeng)	1800	0605	Cirebon, Purwokerto, Yogya, Solo, Madiun
Bima	Surabaya (Gubeng) to Jakarta (Kota)	1800	0644	Madiun, Solo, Yogya, Purwokerto, Cirebon
Jakarta-Cirebon-Jakarta				
Cirebon Ekspres	Jakarta (Gambir & Kota) to Cirebon	4 departures per day		
Cirebon Ekspres	Cirebon to Jakarta (Gambir & Kota)	4 departures per day		
Jakarta-Semarang-Jakarta				
Name	Route	Depart	Arrive	Via
Senja Utama Semarang Eksekutif	Jakarta (Gambir) to Semarang (Tawang)	0835	1516	Cirebon, Tegal, Pekalongan
Senja Utama Semarang Eksekutif	Semarang (Tawang) to Jakarta (Gambir)	2140	0437	Pekalongan, Tegal, Cirebon
Senja Utama Semarang Bisnis	Jakarta (Gambir) to Semarang (Tawang)	1845	0230	Cirebon, Tegal, Pekalongan
Senja Utama Semarang Bisnis	Semarang (Tawang) to Jakarta (Gambir)	2000	0249	Pekalongan, Tegal, Cirebon

Jakarta-Semarang-Jakarta

Name	Route	Depart	Arrive	Via
Fajar Utama Semarang Eksekutif	Jakarta (Gambir) to Semarang (Tawang)	0835	1516	Cirebon, Tegal, Pekalongan
Fajar Utama Semarang Eksekutif	Semarang (Tawang) to Jakarta (Gambir)	0830	1517	Pekalongan, Tegal, Cirebon
Fajar Utama Semarang Bisnis	Jakarta (Kota) to Semarang (Tawang)	0740	1455	Cirebon, Tegal, Pekalongan
Fajar Utama Semarang Bisnis	Semarang (Tawang) to Jakarta (Kota)	0800	1506	Pekalongan, Tegal, Cirebon

Jakarta-Yogyakarta-Jakarta

Name	Route	Depart	Arrive	Via
Senja Utama Yogyakarta	Jakarta (Gambir) to Yogya	1920 & 2040	0341 & 0514	Cirebon, Tegal and Pekalongan
Senja Utama Yogyakarta	Yogya to Jakarta (Gambir)	1800 & 2000	0224 & 0507	Pekalongan, Tegal, Cirebon
Fajar Utama Yogyakarta	Jakarta (Gambir) to Yogya	0610	1352	Cirebon, Purwokerto
Fajar Utama Yogyakarta	Yogya to Jakarta (Gambir)	0620	1406	Purwokerto, Cirebon

Jakarta-Cilacap-Jakarta

Name	Route	Depart	Arrive	Via
Purwojaya	Jakarta (Gambir) to Cilacap	0640	1240	Cirebon, Purwokerto
Purwojaya	Cilacap to Jakarta (Gambir)	1800	0212	Purwokerto, Cirebon

Jakarta-Solo-Jakarta

Name	Route	Depart	Arrive	Via
Senja Utama Solo	Jakarta (Gambir) to Solo (Balapan)	1940	0529	Cirebon, Purwokerto, Yogya
Senja Utama Solo	Solo (Balapan) to Jakarta (Gambir)	1800	0426	Yogya, Purwokerto, Cirebon

Jakarta-Malang-Jakarta

Name	Route	Depart	Arrive	Via
Matarmaja	Jakarta (Pasar Senen) to Malang	1410	0554	Cirebon, Purwokerto, Yogya, Solo, Blitar
Matarmaja	Malang to Jakarta (Pasar Senen)	1545	0903	Blitar, Solo, Yogya, Purwokerto, Cirebon

Jakarta-Bogor-Jakarta

Name	Route	Depart	Arrive	Via
-	Jakarta (Gambir) to Bogor	Services through the day		

NB 1 Not all the stops en route are listed.

2 There are other services not listed here.

3 Timetable is subject to change.

Selected train fares from Jakarta (Gambir)

Name of service	Destination	Special Rp	Express Rp	Sleeper Rp		Business Rp	
				Adult	Child	Adult	Child
Argobromo	Surabaya	–	185,000	–	–	–	–
Sembrani	Surabaya	–	115,000	–	–	–	–
Bima	Surabaya	–	115,000	–	–	45,000	45,000
Argogede	Bandung	–	40,000	–	–	–	–
Parahyangan	Bandung	–	32,000	–	–	15,000	10,000
Senja Utama Yogyakarta	Yogyakarta	76,000	56,000	–	–	36,000	28,000
Senja Utama Semarang	Semarang	72,000	50,000	–	–	32,000	24,000
Senja Utama Solo	Solo	–	80,000	56,000	48,000	40,000	30,000
	Yogyakarta	–	76,000	–	–	–	–
Fajar Utama Yogyakarta	Yogyakarta	76,000	55,000	–	–	30,000	24,000
Cirebon Ekspres	Cirebon	–	32,000	–	–	18,000	11,000
Purwojaya	Purwokerto	–	43,000	–	–	28,000	20,000
	Cilacap	–	48,000	–	–	28,000	20,000
	Cirebon	–	32,000	–	–	18,000	11,000
Jayabaya Utara	Semarang	–	–	–	–	36,000	28,000
	Surabaya	–	–	–	–	48,000	35,000
Jayabaya Selatan	Yogyakarta	–	–	–	–	36,000	28,000
	Solo	–	–	–	–	40,000	32,000
	Madiun	–	–	–	–	44,000	34,000
	Surabaya	–	–	–	–	43,000	35,000

Selected bus fares

		Ekonomi	A/c	Executive
Jakarta to	Solo	45,000	–	–
Solo to	Jakarta	45,000	–	–
	Bogor	40,000	–	–
	Bandung	40,000	–	–
	Semarang	5,000	–	–
	Denpasar	48,000	–	–
Medan to	Prapat	6,000	–	15,000
	Bandar Lumpung	85,000	–	135,000
	Bukittinggi	45,000	–	90,000
Prapat to	Padang	35,000	50,000	–
	Bukittinggi	30,000	42,000	–
	Pekanbaru	32,000	–	–
	Jambi	42,000	–	–
	Palembang	–	65,000	–
	Bengkulu	53,000	–	–
	Bandung (Java)	88,000	130,000	–
Bandar Lampung to	Palembang	17,500	–	65,000
	Padang	55,000	85,000	–
Bukittinggi to	Sibolga	20,000	–	–
	Bengkulu	–	35,000	–
	Jakarta	45-55,000	80-110,000	–
Makassar to	Mamasa	15,000	–	–
	Rantapao	17,000	–	–
	Palopo	17,500	–	–

Palopo to	Rantepao	5,000	–	–
	Makassar	17,500	–	–
	Poso	25,000	–	–
	Palu	30,000	–	–
Rantepao to	Makassar	17,000	–	–
	Pare Pare	10,000	–	–
	Watampone	15,000	–	–
	Pendolo	25,000	–	–
	Poso	30,000	–	–
	Palu	40,000	–	–
Palu to	Gorontalo	35,000	–	–
	Manado	55,000	–	–
	Makassar	52,000	–	–
Poso to	Makassar	52,000	–	–
	Palu	22,500	–	–
Manado to	Gorontalo	27,000	–	–
	Palu	55,000	–	–

NB Prices should only be viewed as a guide. Not only do prices increase (especially in Indonesia's economically volatile climate), but there are also significant variations between companies depending on the age and size of the vehicle, number of seats, facilities provided (a/c, express, reclining seats etc), and the time of departure.

Fortnightly circuits of Pelni ships

NB This timetable shows the fortnightly circuits taken by each Pelni vessel (names of ships indicated in light grey blocks). Check with a Pelni office to discover which day a ship is due to dock. The sequence of dockings for that vessel can then be calculated. Pelni state that "this timetable is only a help to plan a journey, not a guarantee of availability, so please always be confirmed with us!". **NB 2** Ports in brackets are tentative destinations only.

Booking tickets is not altogether straightforward. You can only buy tickets on Pelni ships from offices at the port of departure. It is not possible to buy a whole sequence of tickets ahead of time. Furthermore it seems that some ticket offices will only sell economy tickets (ie without seat or berth) – it is necessary to upgrade at the Cashier's office on the deck where you want a berth. Some tour companies and travel agents will book tickets but again there are limitations: the agency has to have money deposited at the Pelni office concerned before they can book tickets, which tends to make the choice rather limited. Ticket touts on the quayside, however, will often try to sell cabin tickets prior to departure. Ships have seven classes but there is little consistency between ships in terms of what each class means accommodation-wise. Cockroaches are a major problem – for many foreigners, at least – on all ships.

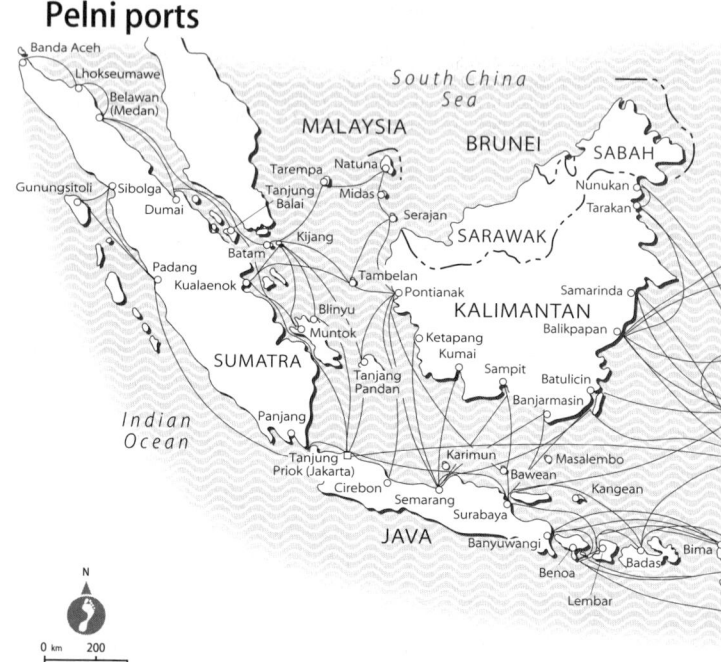

FORTNIGHTLY CIRCUITS OF PELNI SHIPS

Day	Port
Kerinci	
1	Tarakan, Nunukan
2	Toli-Toli, Pantoloan
3	Balikpapan
4	Makassar
5	Surabaya
6	Tanjung Priok
7	Kijang
8	Dumai
9	Kijang
10	Tanjung Priok
11	Surabaya
12	Makassar
13	Balikpapan
14	Pantoloan, Toli-Toli

Day	Port
Kombuna	
1	Padang
2	Tanjung Priok
3	Surabaya
4	Makassar
5	Balikpapan
6	Pantoloan, Toli-Toli
7	Bitung
8	Toli-Toli, Pantoloan
9	Balikpapan
10	Makassar
11	Surabaya
12	Tanjung Priok
13	Padang
14	Sibolga, Gunung Sitoli (Nias)

Day	Port
Rinjani	
1	Ujung Padang
2	Surabaya
3	Makassar
4	Baubau
5	Ambon, Banda
6	Tual, Fak Fak
7	Sorong, Manokwari
8	Nabire, Serui
9	Jayapura
10	Serui, Nabire
11	Manokwari, Sorong
12	Fak Fak, Tual
13	Banda, Ambon
14	Baubau

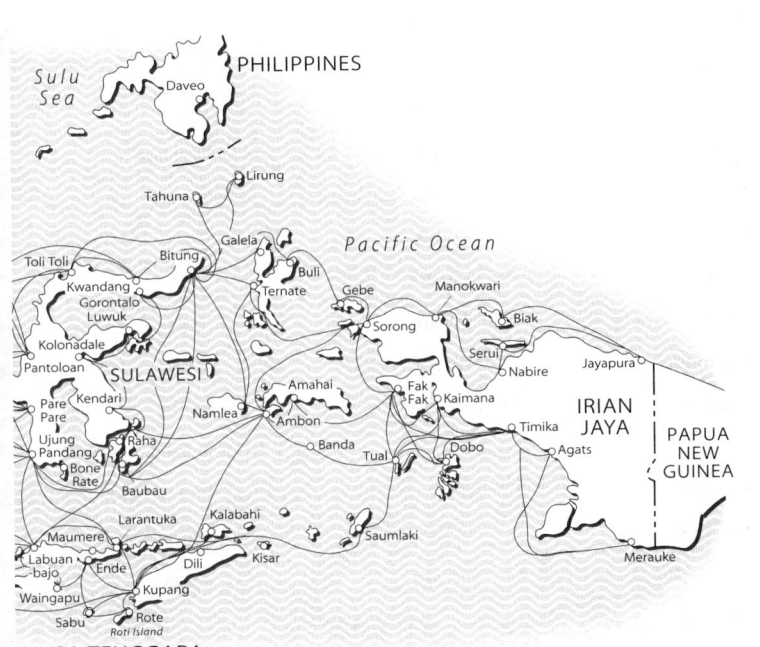

Umsini

Day	Port
1	Nabire, Serui
2	Jayapura
3	Serui, Nabire
4	Manokwari, Sorong
5	Ternate, Bitung
6	Kwandang
7	Balikpapan
8	Makassar
9	Surabaya
10	Makassar
11	Balikpapan
12	Kwandang, Bitung
13	Bitung, Ternate
14	Sorong, Manokwari

Kelimutu

Day	Port
1	Surabaya
2	Banjarmasin
3	Surabaya
4	Banjarmasin
5	Semarang
6	Banjarmasin
7	Surabaya
8	Banjarmasin
9	Surabaya
10	Banjarmasin
11	Surabaya
12	Banjarmasin
13	Semarang
14	Banjarmasin

Lawit

Day	Port
1	(at sea)
2	Cirebon
3	Pontianak
4	Tanjung Pandan
5	Tanjung Priok
6	Tanjung Pandan, Pontianak
7	(at sea)
8	Semarang
9	Kumai
10	Semarang
11	Pontianak
12	Tanjung Pandan
13	Tanjung Priok
14	Tanjung Pandan, Pontianak

Tidar

Day	Port
1	Balikpapan
2	Surabaya
3	Pare Pare
4	Pantoloan
5	Nunukan, Tarakan
6	Balikpapan
7	Pare Pare
8	Surabaya
9	Makassar
10	Pantoloan
11	Tarakan
12	Pantoloan
13	Makassar
14	Surabaya

Tatamailau Circuit A

Day	Port
1	Merauke
2	Merauke (Agats)
3	(Timika)
4	Kaimana, Fak Fak
5	Amahai, Ambon
6	(at sea)
7	Baubau, Makassar
8	Badas
9	Benoa (Bali)
10	Banyuwangi
11	Bima, Labuanbajo
12	Larantuka, Dili
13	Saumlaki
14	Tual, Dobo

Tatamailau Circuit B

Day	Port
1	Timika
2	Dobo, Tual
3	Saumlaki
4	Dili
5	Larantuka, Labuanbajo
6	Bima
7	Banyuwangi, Benoa (Bali)
8	Badas
9	Makassar
10	Baubau
11	Ambon, Amahai
12	Fak Fak
13	Kaimana, Timika
14	(Agats)

Sirimau

Day	Port
1	Semarang
2	Tanjung Priok
3	Muntok
4	Kijang, Tanjung Balai
5	Kuala Enok, Muntok
6	Tanjung Priok
7	Tanjung Priok
8	Semarang
9	Batulicin
10	Makassar, (Bone Rate)
11	Larantuka, Kupang
12	Larantuka, (Bone Rate)
13	Makassar
14	Batulicin

Awu

Day	Port
1	Waingapu
2	Benoa, Lembar
3	Waingapu, Ende
4	Kupang, Kalabahi
5	Dili
6	Maumere
7	Makassar
8	Berau
9	Tarakan, Nunukan
10	(at sea)
11	Makassar
12	Maumere
13	Dili, Kalabahi
14	Kupang, Ende

Ciremai

Day	Port
1	Makassar
2	Baubau, Banggai
3	Bitung, Ternate
4	Sorong
5	Manokwari, Biak
6	Jayapura
7	Biak, Manokwari
8	Sorong
9	Ternate, Bitung
10	Banggai, Baubau
11	Makassar
12	(at sea)
13	Tanjung Priok
14	Semarang

Dobonsolo

Day	Port
1	Sorong
2	Ambon
3	Dili, Kupang
4	Benoa
5	Surabaya
6	Tanjung Priok
7	Surabaya
8	Benoa
9	Kupang, Dili
10	Ambon
11	Sorong
12	Manokwari, Biak
13	Jayapura
14	Biak, Manokwari

Leuser

Day	Port
1	Toli Toli
2	Samarinda
3	Pare Pare
4	Batulicin (Masalembo)
5	Surabaya
6	Kumai
7	Semarang
8	Sampit
9	Surabaya, (Masalembo)
10	Batulicin
11	Pare Pare
12	Samarinda
13	Toli Toli
14	Tarakan, Nunukan

Binaiya

Day	Port
1	Batulicin
2	Surabaya
3	Sampit
4	Semarang
5	Kumai
6	Surabaya
7	Kumai
8	Semarang
9	Sampit
10	Surabaya
11	Batulicin
12	Pare Pare
13	Samarinda
14	Pare Pare

Day	Port
Bukitraya	
1	Natuna, Midai, Serason
2	Tambelon, Pontianak
3	(at sea)
4	Surabaya, Bawean
5	Sampit
6	Surabaya, Bawean
7	(at sea)
8	Pontianak, Tambelan
9	Serasan, Midai/Natuna, Tarempa
10	Letung, Kijang
11	Blinyu
12	Tanjung Priok
13	Blinyu
14	Kijang, Letung, Terempa
Tilongkabila A	
1	Bau-Bau, Raha/Kendari
2	Kolonedale, Luwuk
3	Gorontalo, Bitung
4	Lirung, Tahuna
5	Bitung, Gorontalo
6	Luwuk, Kolonedale
7	Kendari/Raha, Bau-Bau
8	Ujung Padang
9	Labuanbajo, Bima
10	Lembar, Denpasar
11	Surabaya
12	Kumai
13	Surabaya
14	Sampit

Day	Port
Tilongkabila B	
1	Semarang
2	Tanjung Priok
3	Pandan, Pontianak
4	(at sea)
5	Semarang
6	(at sea)
7	Pontianak, Pandan
8	Tanjung Priok
9	Semarang
10	Sampit
11	Surabaya
12	Denpasar, Lembar
13	Bima, Labuanbajo
14	Ujung Padang
Bukit Singuntang	
1	Dumai
2	Kijang
3	Tanjung Priok
4	Surabaya
5	Makassar
6	Baubau
7	Ambon, Banda
8	Tual, Dobo/Kaimana
9	Banda, Ambon
10	Baubau
11	Makassar
12	Surabaya
13	Tanjung Priok
14	Kijang

Day	Port
Lambelo	
1	Namlea, Ambon
2	Baubau
3	Makassar
4	Surabaya
5	Tanjung Priok
6	Padang
7	Gunungsitoli (Nias), Sibolga
8	Padang
9	Tanjung Priok
10	Surabaya
11	Makassar
12	Bau Bau
13	Ambon, Namlea
14	Bitung, Ternate
Sinabung Circuit A	
1	Belawan
2	Batam
3	Tanjung Priok
4	Tanjung Balai
5	Belawan
6	Batam
7	Tanjung Priok
8	(at sea)
9	Belawan
10	Batam
11	Tanjung Priok
12	Tanjung Balai
13	Belawan
14	Batam

Day	Port	Day	Port
Sinabung Circuit B		**Kelud Circuit A**	
1	Tanjung Priok	1	Tanjung Priok
2	Tanjung Balai	2	Batam
3	Belawan	3	Belawan
4	Batam	4	Tanjung Balai
5	Tanjung Priok	5	Tanjung Priok
6	(at sea)	6	Batam
7	Belawan	7	Belawan
8	Batam	8	(at sea)
9	Tanjung Priok	9	Tanjung Priok
10	Tanjung Balai	10	Batam
11	Belawan	11	Belawan
12	Batam	12	Tanjung Balai
13	Tanjung Priok	13	Tanjung Priok
14	Tanjung Balai	14	Batam
Pangrango		**Kelud Circuit B**	
1	Badas	1	Belawan
2	Labuanbajo, Waingapu	2	Tanjung Balai
3	Ende, Sabu/Rote, Kupang	3	Tanjung Priok
		4	Batam
4	Sabu/Ende	5	Belawan
5	Waingapu/Labuanbajo	6	(at sea)
		7	Tanjung Priok
6	Badas, (Kangean)	8	Batam
7	Surabaya, Bawean	9	Belawan
8	Sampit	10	Tanjung Balai
9	Semarang, (Karimun)	11	Tanjung Priok
10	Ketapang	12	Batam
11	(Karimun), Semarang	13	Belawan
12	Sampit	14	Tanjung Balai
13	Bawean		
14	Surabaya, (Kangean)		

Selected Pelni fares (US$)*

I-IV = 1st-4th class; Economy = deck class. Children travel at 75% of full fare; infants 1-2 years travel at 10% of full fare. Note also that rupiah prices are considerably less than these quoted US$ prices.

Jakarta to:	I	II	III	IV	Economy
Ambon	731	596	405	373	213
Balikpapan	515	420	285	263	150
Banda	746	609	413	350	217
Banjarmasin	305	249	170	156	90
Batam	271	221	151	139	80
Bau-Bau	487	397	270	249	142
Belawan	362	296	201	186	106
Biak	1098	895	607	560	319
Bitung	798	651	442	407	232
Cirebon	423	345	235	216	124
Denpasar	321	262	178	164	94
Dili	598	488	331	305	174
Dumai	326	266	181	167	96
Gn Sitoli	364	297	202	186	107
Jayapura	1217	992	673	620	353
Kupang	530	433	294	271	155
Kwandang	703	574	389	350	205
Manokwari	1040	848	575	530	302
Muntok	150	122	84	77	45
Padang	245	200	136	126	72
Pantoloan	587	479	325	300	171
Pontianak	328	194	132	122	70
Semarang	125	103	70	65	38
Sibolga	364	297	202	189	107
Sorong	756	779	529	487	278
Surabaya	198	162	110	102	59
Ternate	899	733	497	458	261

Toli Toli	648	528	329	331	189
Tual	771	629	427	393	224
Makassar	392	320	217	200	115

Useful Indonesian words and phrases

In Indonesian, there are no tenses, genders or articles and sentence structure is relatively simple. Pronunciation is not difficult as there is a close relationship between the letter as it is written and the sound. Stress is usually placed on the second syllable of a word. For example, *restoran* (restaurant) is pronounced res-TO-ran.

Vowels
a is pronounced as *ah* in an open syllable, or as in *but* for a closed syllable.
e is pronounced as in *open* or *bed*.
i is pronounced as in *feel*.
o is pronounced as in *all*.
u is pronounced as in *foot*.
The letter *c* is pronounced as *ch* as in *change* or *chat*.
The *r*'s are rolled.
Plural is indicated by repetition, *bapak-bapak*.

Learning Indonesian
The list of words and phrases below is very rudimentary. For anyone serious about learning Indonesian it is best to buy a dedicated Indonesian language textbook or to enrol on an Indonesian course. In Indonesia, there are courses on offer in Jakarta, Bali and Yogyakarta. A phrase book and/or some knowledge of the Indonesian language comes in very handy away from tourist sites.

Useful phrases
You will be asked constantly "Where you are going?" ("*Wake Mana?*"). To the Indonesians it is the common form of address. Most travellers reply "jalan, jalan" which means "walking, walking". Indonesians do not always seem very happy with this response. Instead try saying "*cuci mata*" which literally translates as "washing my eye"; ie relaxing. This brings a smile of real pleasure to Indonesians, they will feel that you understand their customs. As an alternative you can say "*makan angin*" (literally) "eating the air".

Yes/no	*Ya/tidak*
Thank you [very much]	*Terima kasi h [banyak]*
Good morning (until 1100)	*Selamat pagi*
Good day (until 1500)	*Selamat siang*
Good afternoon (until dusk)	*Selamat sore*
Good evening	*Selamat malam*
Welcome	*Selamat datang*
Goodbye (said by the person leaving)	*Selamat tinggal*
Goodbye (said by the person staying)	*Selamat jalan*
Excuse me, sorry!	*ma'af*
Where's the ...?	*... dimana?*
How much is ...?	*... berapa harganya?*
You're welcome, don't mention it	*Kembali*
I [don't] understand	*Saya [tidak] mengerti*
Sweet dreams (said as you take leave to people last thing at night	*Mimpi Indan*

The Hotel

How much is a room?	*Kamar berapa harga?*
Does the room have air-conditioning?	*Ada kamar yang ada AC-nya?*
I want to see the room first please	*Saya mau lihat kamar dulu*
Does the room have hot water?	*Ada kamar yang ada air panas?*
Does the room have a bathroom?	*Ada kamar yang ada kamar mandi?*

Travel

Where is the train station?	*Dimana stasiun kereta api?*
Where is the bus station?	*Dimana stasiun bis?*
How much to go to …?	*Berapa harga ke …?*
I want to go to …	*Saya mau pergi ke …*
I want to buy a ticket to …	*Saya mau beli karcis ke …*
Is it far?	*Ada jauh?*
Turn left/turn right	*Belok kiri/belok kanan*
Go straight on	*Terus saja*

Days

Monday	*Hari Senin*	Saturday	*Hari Sabtu*
Tuesday	*Hari Selasa*	Sunday	*Hari Minggu*
Wednesday	*Hari Rabu*	today	*hari ini*
Thursday	*Hari Kamis*	tomorrow	*hari besok*
Friday	*Hari Jumat*		

Numbers

1	*satu*	20	*dua puluh*
2	*dua*	21–	*dua puluh satu … etc*
3	*tiga*	30–	*tiga puluh … etc*
4	*empat*	100	*se-ratus*
5	*lima*	101	*se-ratus satu … etc*
6	*enam*	150	*se-ratus lima puluh*
7	*tujuh*	200–	*dua ratus … etc*
8	*delapan*	1,000	*se-ribu*
9	*sembilan*	2,000	*dua ribu*
10	*sepuluh*	100,000	*se-ratus ribu*
11	*se-belas*	1,000,000	*se-juta*
12–	*dua-belas … etc*		

Basic vocabulary

airletters	*surat udara, aerogram*
airmail	*pos udara*
all right/good	*baik*
bank	*bank*
bathroom	*kamar mandi/kamar kecil*
beach	*pantai*
beautiful	*cantik*
big	*besar*
boat	*prahu*
bus	*bis*
bus station	*stasiun bis*
buy	*beli*
can	*boleh*
chemist	*apotek*
clean	*bersih*
closed	*tutup*
day	*hari*

USEFUL INDONESIAN WORDS & PHRASES

delicious	*enak*
dentist	*doktor gigi*
dirty	*kotor*
doctor	*doktor*
eat	*makan*
envelope	*amplop*
excellent	*bagus*
expensive	*mahal*
express	*ekspres*
food	*makan*
fruit	*buah*
hospital	*rumah sakit*
hotel	*hotel/losmen/penginapan/wisma*
hot (temperature)	*panas*
hot (spicy)	*pedas*
I/me	*saya*
immigration office	*kantor imigrasi*
island	*pulau*
letter	*surat*
market	*pasa*
medicine	*obat*
open	*masuk*
parcel	*paket*
police	*polisi*
police station	*stasiun polisi*
post box	*kotak surat*
post card	*kartu pos*
post office	*kantor pos*
restaurant	*rumah makan*
room	*kamar*
ship	*kapal*
shop	*toko*
sick	*sakit*
small	*kecil*
stamps	*perangko*
stop	*berhenti*
surface mail	*pos biasa*
taxi	*taksi*
ticket	*karcis*
that	*itu*
they	*mereka*
this	*ini*
toilet	*WC ("way say")*
town	*kota*
train station	*stasiun kereta api*
very	*sekali*
water	*air*
what	*apa*

Glossary

A

Abdi dalem court servants of Java
Adat custom or tradition
Alang Torajan rice barn
Amitabha the Buddha of the Past (see Avalokitsvara)
Andesite volcanic building stone
Andong horse-drawn carriage
Angklung traditional Javanese bamboo musical instrument (see page 154)
Arhat statues of former Buddhist monks
Atavaka flesh-eating ogre
Avadana Buddhist narrative, telling of the deeds of saintly souls
Avalokitsvara also known as Amitabha and Lokeshvara, the name literally means "World Lord"; he is the compassionate male Bodhisattva, the saviour of Mahayana Buddhism and represents the central force of creation in the universe; usually portrayed with a lotus and water flask

B

Bahasa language, as in Bahasa Malaysia and Bahasa Indonesia
Bajaj three-wheeled motorized taxi
Banaspati East Javan term for kala makara (see kala)
Banjar Balinese village organization (see page 443)
Banua Torajan house (see page 700)
Batik a form of resist dyeing common in Malay areas (see page 307)
Becak three-wheeled bicycle rickshaw
Bendi 2-wheeled, horse-drawn cart
Bhaga cult altar of Flores (see page 828)
Bodhi the tree under which the Buddha achieved enlightenment (*Ficus religiosa*)
Bodhisattva a future Buddha. In Mahayana Buddhism, someone who has attained enlightenment, but who postpones nirvana in order to help others reach the same state
Brahma the Creator, one of the gods of the Hindu trinity, usually represented with four faces, and often mounted on a hamsa
Brahmin a Hindu priest
Budaya cultural (as in Muzium Budaya)
Bupati regent

C

Candi sepulchral monument (see page 303)
Candi bentar split gate, characteristic of Balinese pura
Cap batik stamp (see page 307)
Chedi from the Sanskrit *cetiya* (Pali, *caitya*) meaning memorial. Usually a religious monument (often bell-shaped) containing relics of the Buddha or other holy remains. Used interchangeably with stupa
Cidomo Lombok's two-wheeled, pony carts (see page 770)
Cukong Chinese-owned corporations
Cultuurstelsel the Dutch `culture system' introduced in Java in the 19th century
Cunda see Tara
Cutch see Gambier

D

Dalang wayang puppet master
Dayak/Dyak collective term for the tribal peoples of Borneo
Delman horse-drawn carriage
Dharma the Buddhist law
Dipterocarp family of trees (Dipterocarpaceae) characteristic of Southeast Asia's forests
Dokar horse-drawn carriage
Durga the female goddess who slays the demon Mahisa, from an Indian epic story
Dvarapala temple door guardian

E

Epiphyte plant which grows on another plant (but usually not parasitic)

F

Fahombe stone-jumping of Nias Island (see page 510)
Feng shui the Chinese art of geomancy

G

Gambier also known as cutch, a dye derived from the bark of the bakau mangrove and used in leather tanning

Gamelan Javanese and Balinese orchestra of percussion instruments (see page 306)
Ganesh elephant-headed son of Siva
Garuda mythical divine bird, with predatory beak and claws, and human body; the king of birds, enemy of naga and mount of Vishnu
Gautama the historic Buddha
Golkar ruling party in Indonesia (see page 946)
Gopura crowned or covered gate; entrance to a religious area
Gunung mountain

Hamsa sacred goose, Brahma's mount; in Buddhism it represents the flight of the doctrine
Hariti child-eating demon who is converted to Buddhism
Hinayana 'Lesser Vehicle', major Buddhist sect in Southeast Asia, usually termed Theravada Buddhism

Ikat tie-dyeing method of patterning cloth (see page 441)
Indra the Vedic god of the heavens, weather and war; usually mounted on a 3 headed elephant
Islam Waktu Telu Islam of Lombok (see page 802)

Jaba front court of Balinese temple (see page 440)
Jaba tengah central court of Balinese temple (see page 440)
Janur Balinese bamboo 'pennants' (see page 445)
Jataka(s) birth stories of the Buddha, of which there are 547; the last ten are the most important
Jeroan back court of Balinese temple (see page 440)

Kabupaten regency, Indonesian unit of administration
Kala (makara) literally, 'death' or 'black'; a demon ordered to consume itself; often sculpted over entranceways to act as a door guardian, also known as kirtamukha
Kalanaga same as the kalamakara but incorporating the mythical naga (serpent)
Kepala desa village headman
Kerangas from an Iban word meaning 'land on which rice will not grow'
Kerapan sapi bull races of East Java and Madura (see page 268)
Keraton see kraton
Kinaree half-human, half-bird, usually depicted as a heavenly musician
Kirtamukha see kala
Klotok motorized gondolas of Banjarmasin
Kraton Javanese royal palace (see page 304)
Kris traditional Malay sword (see page 90)
Krishna an incarnation of Vishnu
Kulkul Balinese drum
Kuti living quarters of Buddhist monks

Lapar biasa 'normal hunger'
Laterite bright red tropical soil/stone sometimes used as a building material
Linga phallic symbol and one of the forms of Siva. Embedded in a pedestal shaped to allow drainage of lustral water poured over it, the linga typically has a succession of cross sections: from square at the base through octagonal to round. These symbolize, in order, the trinity of Brahma, Vishnu and Siva
Lintel a load-bearing stone spanning a doorway; often heavily carved
Lokeshvara see Avalokitsvara
Lontar multi-purpose palm tree (see page 878); the fronds were used for manuscript sheets (see page 417)
Losmen guesthouse

Mahabharata a Hindu epic text written about 2,000 years ago (see page 963)
Mahayana 'Greater Vehicle', major Buddhist sect
Mandi Indonesian/Malay bathroom with water tub and dipper
Maitreya the future Buddha
Makara a mythological aquatic reptile, somewhat like a crocodile and sometimes with an elephant's trunk; often found, along with the kala, framing doorways

GLOSSARY

Mandala a focus for meditation; a representation of the cosmos
Meru name given to the tapered shrines of Bali
Meru the mountain residence of the gods; the centre of the universe, the cosmic mountain
Moko bronze dowry `drums' of Nusa Tenggara (see page 853)
Mudra symbolic gesture of the hands of the Buddha (see page 191)

N

Naga benevolent mythical water serpent, enemy of Garuda
Naga makara fusion of naga and makara
Nalagiri the elephant let loose to attack the Buddha, who calmed him
Nandi/Nandin bull, mount of Siva
Negara kingdom and capital, from the Sanskrit
Negeri also negri, state
Ngadhu cult altar of Flores (see page 828)
Nirvana 'enlightenment', the Buddhist ideal
Nyi Loro Kidul Goddess of the South Seas (see page 124)

O

Odalan festival celebrating a Balinese temple's anniversary (see page 444)
Ojek motorcycle `taxi'
Ondel-ondel paired human figures given to newly-weds in Java

P

Paddy/padi unhulled rice
Padmasana stone throne
Padu-raksa ceremonial gate
Paliwijaya/Palawija a second crop, planted after rice
Pamedal Agung main gate
Pancasila Sukarno's five guiding principles (see page 944)
Pantai beach
Pasar market, from the Arabic `bazaar'
Pasisir Javanese coastal trading states
Pelni Indonesian state shipping line
Pemuda literally `youth', but historically refers to the Pemuda Movement against the Dutch (see page 942)
Pendopo open-sided pavilion of Java

Perahu/prau boat
Peranakan 'half caste', usually applied to part Chinese and part Malay people
Perintis 'pioneer' ships which ply minor routes between Indonesia's islands
PKI Perserikatan Komunis di Indonesia, the Indonesian Communist Party
Pradaksina pilgrims' clockwise circumambulation of a holy structure
Prajnaparamita the goddess of transcendental wisdom
Prang form of stupa built in the Khmer style, shaped rather like a corncob
Prasada see prasat
Prasat residence of a king or of the gods (sanctuary tower), from the Indian prasada
Pribumi indigenous (as opposed to Chinese) businessmen
Priyayi Javanese aristocracy
Pulau island
Puputan 'fight to the death' (see page 444)
Pura Balinese temple (see page 438)
Pusaka heirloom

R

Raja/rajah ruler
Raksasa temple guardian statues
Ramayana the Indian epic tale (see page 963)
Rumah adat customary or traditional house

S

Sago multi-purpose palm
Sal the Indian sal tree (*Shorea robusta*), under which the historic Buddha was born
Saka Hindu calendar used in Bali
Sakyamuni the historic Buddha
Sawah wet rice
Silat or bersilat, traditional Malay martial art
Singha mythical guardian lion
Siti Inggil literally 'High Place' in a kraton; used for enthronements
Siva one of the Hindu triumvirate, the god of destruction and rebirth
Songket Malay textile interwoven with supplementary gold and silver yarn
Sravasti the miracle at Sravasti when the Buddha subdues the heretics in front of a mango tree
Sri Laksmi the goddess of good fortune and Vishnu's wife
Stele inscribed stone panel or slab

GLOSSARY

Stucco plaster, often heavily moulded
Stupa see chedi
Subak Balinese irrigation society
Susuhunan Hindu king or sultan

T

tamu market
Tara also known as Cunda; the four-armed consort of the Bodhisattva Avalokitsvara
Tau tau Torajan effigies of the deceased (see page 704)
Tavatimsa heaven of the 33 gods at the summit of Mount Meru
Theravada 'Way of the Elders'; major Buddhism sect also known as Hinayana Buddhism (`Lesser Vehicle')
Tirta holy water
Tongkonan Torajan ancestral house (see page 700)
Totok 'full blooded'; usually applied to Chinese of pure blood
Transmigration the Indonesian government sponsored resettlement of people from the Inner Islands to the Outer Islands

U

Ulama Muslim priest
Ulu jungle

Urna the dot or curl on the Buddha's forehead, one of the distinctive physical marks of the Enlightened One
Usnisa the Buddha's top knot or `wisdom bump', one of the physical marks of the Enlightened One

V

Vishnu the Protector, one of the gods of the Hindu trinity, generally with four arms holding the disc, the conch shell, the ball and the club
VOC the Dutch East India Company or Vereenigde Oost-Indische Compagnie

W

Wali the nine Muslim saints of Java
Wallace's Line division between the Asian and Australasian zoological realms (see page 801)
Waringin banyan tree
Warung foodstall or small restaurant
Wayang traditional Malay shadow plays (see page 305)
Wayang Topeng masked dance of Java (see page 306)
Wuku Hindu-Javanese calendar, now primarily in use only in Bali

Footnotes

Indonesian food glossary

asam	tamarind; sold in a solid block, or still in the brown pod	*kopi*	coffee
		kopi bubuk	ground coffee (with grounds)
atpokat	avocado	*kopi saring*	filtered coffee
ayam	chicken	*krupuk*	deep-fried tapioca crackers
ayam goreng	fried chicken		
babek	duck	*kuah*	gravy
babi	pork	*kue*	cake
bakar	roast	*kunyit*	turmeric
bakmi	rice flour noodles	*lombok*	chilli
bakso	meat balls	*lontong*	compressed rice, usually served with sate
belimbing	star fruit		
bifstik	beef steak		
cabe	chilli	*madu*	honey
cumi cumi	squid	*mangga*	mango
dadar	omelette/pancake	*manggis*	mangosteen
daging	beef/meat	*manis*	sweet
durian	durian	*merica*	black pepper
es	ice	*mie*	noodles
es krim	ice cream	*nangka*	jackfruit, eaten ripe as a fruit or unripe cooked as a vegetable
garam	salt		
goreng	stir fry		
gula	sugar	*nasi*	rice
gulai	curry soup	*nasi putih*	plain white rice
ikan	fish	*nenas*	pineapple
istemiwa	'special' – *nasi goreng istemiwa* has a fried egg and other additions	*pala*	nutmeg
		panggang	grill
		papaya (kates)	papaya
		pisang	banana
jeruk	generic term in Java and Bali for citrus fruit	*rambutan*	rambutan
		rebus	boil
jeruk bali	pomelo	*roti*	bread
jeruk manis	orange	*salak*	brown, pear shaped fruit, with a shiny, snake-like skin. The flesh is white, segmented and dry. Balinese salak are the sweetest
jeruk nipis	lime		
kacang	generic term for bean or nut		
kacang	peanut sauce		
kacang buncis	french bean		
kacang kedele	soybean		
kacang tanah	peanut	*sambal*	chilli paste
kambing	lamb/goat	*santen*	coconut milk
kangkung	'greens' grown in water sometimes known as spinach	*sawi*	Chinese cabbage
		sayur	vegetables
		semangka air	watermelon
kayu manis	cinnamon	*sereh*	lemon grass
kecap asin	salt-soy sauce	*serundeng*	grated coconut roasted with peanuts
kelengkeng	lychee		
kemiri	macadamia nut	*sop*	soup
kenari	a shade tree which produces a nut similar to an almond	*tahu*	soybean curd
		telur	egg
		tempe	fermented soybean cake
kepiting	crab		
ketimun	cucumber	*udang*	shrimp
kodok	frog	*udang karang*	lobster

Index

A

Abadi 402
Abian Soan 401
accommodation 39
  See also under individual
  town's 'Sleeping' sections
Aceh 513
Aceh War 516
Adam Malik Museum,
  Jakarta 89
adat 835, 913, 961
Afo clove tree 906
Agung Demak
  Mosque 225
Agung Gianyar Palace 380
Agung, Mount 387
AIDS 56
Air Dingin 523
Air Manis 557
Air Sanih 428
Air Terjun Gitgit 411, 412
air travel 32,
  domestic 41
  See also within each
  chapter and town 'Ins
  and outs' section
airlines
  domestic 41
Airmadidi 750
airports
  Denpasar's (Bali) Ngurah
    Rai 35
  Jakarta 35
  tax 36
Akima 925
Al Markaz Al Islamic
  Centre 681
Al Miraj 53
Alas 804
Alas Purwo National Park
  (Blambangan) 293
Alas River 482
Alor 851
Alor Kecil 852
Alun-alun 147, 167
Amahai 893
Amahusu Beach 888
Amamapare 929
Ambarawa 216, 225
Ambarita 499
Ambon 882
Amed 404
Amlapura 401
Ampana 730
Ampenan 771
Ampera 852

Amplas terminal 471
Anakalang District 864
Anakan Lagoon 152
angklung 306
antiques 52, 459
Anturan 420
Anyer 111
Api, Gunung 899
Apo Kayan 644
Ara, Gunung 901
architecture 457
  Bali 438
  Dutch provincial 743
  East Java 238
  Java 301
  Sasak 796
  tropical Art Deco 134
  Toraja 700
Arjuna, Candi 215
Armed Forces Day 53
Arosbaya 269
Arsip Nasional 85
arts
  Bali 438
  Irian Jaya 934
  Java 302
Asta Tinggi 272
Atavaka 190
Atimelang 852
ATMs 31
Australian War Cemetery,
  The 887
Awal Ramadan 54
Ay Island 899, 902
Ayer, Pulau 107

B

Ba'a 876
Bada Valley 733
Badui 304
Badut, Candi
  (Malang) 247
Bahari Museum 82, 836
Bahasa Indonesia 28, 989
Bajaj 45, 101
Bajang Ratu, Candi 264
Bajawa 831
Bajoe 694
Bakauheni 610
Bakongan 524
Balai 525
Balai Kota 155
Balai Kota Malang 247
Balai Seni Rupa 84
Bale Kambang 392

Balekambang 249
Balekambang swimming
  pool 211
Bali 307
  art 438
  background 435
  Balinese dancing
    course 427
  Balinese names 443
  Balinese painting 441
  Balinese pura 438
  Botanical Gardens 410
  climate 438
  culture 442
  East 390
  ferries 312
  festivals 320
  geography 437
  history 435
  language 443
  North coast 413
  people 442
  religion 443
  tours 316
  transport 312
  West 430
Bali Barat National
  Park 431
Balian Beach 433
Baliem River Gorge 925
Baliem Valley 922
Balikpapan 629
Balimbiang 540, 552
Balina Beach 394
Ballakalua 720
Ballapeu 721
Baluran National Park 276
Baluran Reserve 290
Bambaru Pasar 735
Ban Hing Kiong Chinese
  temple 748
Banda Aceh 514
Banda Besar 903
Banda Islands 895
Banda Neira 897
Bandar Lampung 607
Bandengan Beach 234
Bandung 91, 131
Bandung Plain 130
Bandungan 217, 226
Bangka Island 598
Bangkalan 269
Bangli 381
Bangsal 781
Bangsal Kencono 169

Bangsal Manis 169
Bangsal Proboyekso 169
Bangsal Witana 202
Banjar 424
Banjar Hot Springs 425
Banjarmasin 617
Banjarsari market 220
Bank of Indonesia 134
banks 31, 32
Banon, Candi 191
Banten 91, 107
Banten Lama 108
Bantimurung Falls 684
Banu Nggulung 821
Banyak, Pulau 525
Banyualit 420
Banyumulek 796
Banyunibo, Candi 198
Banyuwangi 276, 290
Baranusa 853
Barde Pasar 274
bargaining 51
Barito River Dayaks 665
Barong Ket 354
Barong Tongkok 643
Barrang Lompo Island 683
Baru
  Pasar 135
  Mount 791
Barung 721
Baruppu 711
Barusjahe 479
Base G 921
Bat Cave 125
Bataks 488
Batam Island 576
Batang Palupuh 539
Batang Tabik 551
Batanghari River 591
Batavia 79
batik 52, 179, 220
Batu 254
Batu Angus 906
Batu Bangga Beach 743
Batu Bulan 528
Batu Karas 148
Batu Koq 790
Batuan 365
Batubelig 337, 340
Batubolong Temple 778
Batubulan 331, 365
Batudaka Island 741
Batur, Lake 384
Batur, Mount 384
Batur, Pura 385
Baturden Mountain
  Resort 162

Batusangkar 552
Batutumonga 711
Baubau 725, 726
Baun 871
Bawamataluo 511, 512
Bawogosali 512
Bayan 789
Bayur 538, 546
beaches 22
  Amahusu 888
  Amed 404
  Balina 394
  Bandengan 234
  Batu Bangga 743
  Candi Dasa 396
  Carita 112
  Cimaja 125
  Florida 110
  Gilis 782
  Karang Bolong 173
  Karanghawu 125
  Kencana 806
  Kuta (Bali) 327
  Kuta (Lombok) 796
  Labuan 112
  Lawata 812
  Lovina 418
  Malole 899
  Matako 738
  Namalatu 888
  Natsepa 887
  Nias 508
  Nirwana 726
  Nusa Dua 361
  Pasir Panjang 654
  Sabang 519
  Sengigi 777
  Tulamben 405
  Waicicu 826
Bebandem 401
Bedugul 410
Bela 832
Belawan 472
Belgica Fort 898
Belimbingsari 432
Belitung Island 600
Belumai 601
bemos 46
Bena 832
Bengkulu 602
Benoa 356
Benteng (Fort) Toloko 906
Benteng (Fort) Ujung
  Pandang 680
Benteng Pendem 160
Berestagi 477
Berewa Beach 341
Beringharjo Market 170
Besakih, Pura 387
Besar Pasar 247
Biak 919
bicycling 44
Bidadari 827
Bidadari, Pulau 106
Bima, Candi 216
Bima-Raba 811
Binjai 464

Bintan Beach
  International Resort 587
Bintan Besar, Gunung 586
Bintan Island 581
Bintangur Island 557
Bira 689
bird watching 370
birds
  Kalimantan 663
Bireuen 514
bites 59
Bitung 759
Blanco, Antonio 366
Blankejeren 530
Blanting 795
Blitar 244
Blongas 799
boat travel 34, 456
Bodhisattva
  Avalokitesvara 190
Bogor 91, 117
Bohorok River 475
Bolilanga Island 742
Bomba 742
Bonang 237
Bondokawango 867
Bondomaroto 863
Bondowoso 283
Bone (Watampone) 694
Bongedu 832
Bongol 360
Bonnet, Rudolf 440
Bontang 635
books
  on Indonesia 62
  on textiles 307
Borado 832
Bori 711
Borobudur 185, 193, 299
Bosnik 919
Botanical gardens
  highlights 21
Boti 874
Brahma Vihara
  Asrama 424
Brahma, Candi 197
Brahu, Candi 264
Brastagi 477
Bratan, Lake 410
Brawijaya Museum 247
Bromo, Mount 276, 292
Bromo-Tengger-Semeru
  National Park 276
Bronjonolo Gate 168
Bubrah, Candi 197
Budkaling 402
Bugis 681, 761
Buitan 394
Bukarani 867
Bukit Barisan Selatan
  National Park 608
Bukit Demulih 383
Bukit Jati 383
Bukit Kusambi 402
Bukit Lawang 473
Bukit Peninsula 353
Bukittinggi 535

Bula 721
Buleleng Regency 413
bull fights, Tapen 283
bull racing,
  Lovina Beach 419
  Negara 432
Bunaken National
  Marine Park 757
Bunaken sea garden
  748, 751
Bunga Pasar 247
Bungus Beach 557
Buntao 709
Buntu Kesisi 721
Buntuballa 721
  Torajan 705
bus travel
  *See also under individual
  town's 'Transport'
  sections*
business hours 35
Butak, Mount 292
Buton Island 725
Buyan, Lake 411

C

Cakranegara 771
Camp Leakey 627
camping 41
Camplong 270
Candi 303
  *See under individual
  name*
Candi Dasa 396
Candikuning 411
Canggu 242, 340
Canggu Beach 341
Cangkuang, Candi 138,
  145
Canti 607, 610
car hire 45
  *See also under individual
  town's 'Transport'
  sections*
Carita Beach, Java 112
casuarina forest 661
catamaran 769
Catholic Cathedral,
  Jakarta 88
caves at Taman Purbakala
  Leang Leang 684
Cecil Pantai 393
Cekik 431
Celuk 365
Cemora Sewu 212
Cemoro Lawang 278
Cempaka 620
Ceto, Candi 204
checklist,
  things to take 30
Chinatown 85, 225
Chinese temples 681
Chinese, Indonesia 951
Christianity 38
churches
  Dutch Reform 898

Margo Mulyo
  Church 170
Ciater Hot Springs 138
Cibodas 129
Cikini Pasar 89
Cilacap 152, 159
Cimaja beach 125
Cipanas 129, 130, 146
Cirebon 153
Cisarua 128
Cisolok Hot Springs 125
Citepus Pantai 125
Ciwidey 138
Clara Bundt 681
climate 24,25
  Bali 438
  Lombok 801
  Irian Jaya 933
  Java 302
  Kalimantan 658
  Maluku 913
  Sulawesi 762
  Indonesia 967
clothing 30, 37, 52, 459
communications 47
Concordia Fort 871
consulates, Indonesian
  overseas 26
corruption 954
cost of living 31
courses
  language 28
crafts
  Bali 442
  Lombok 802
  Kalimantan 671
  Irian Jaya 934
credit cards 31
cremation
  Bali 446
cruises 313
cuisines, regional 50
culture 457
  Lombok 802
  Bali 442
  Irian Jaya 933
  Java 302
  Maluku 913
  Toraja 699
  Indonesia 959
  Kalimantan 664
currencies 30, 31, 69
Curup 603
customs 30
cyber café 47, 69

D

Dabo 591
Daik, Gunung 591
Dalem, Pura 427
dance
  Bali 447
  Indonesia 963
  Java 305
  Jegog 448
  Kalimantan 671

Kecak 447
Kris 447
Legong 448
Sanghyang dedari 447
Topeng 448
Dani, Irian Jaya 922
Daruba 910
Dayak tribe 664
Demak 225, 232
Dempo, Mount 601
Dencarik 424
dengue fever 60
Denpasar 322
Deri 711
Desa Lembongan 350
Desa Sunga 539
diarrhoea 58
Dieng Plateau 214
disabled travellers 36
diving 457
  Amed 318
  Bali 318
  Bandas 901
  Benoa 356
  Gilis 788
  Lembongan 318
  Manado 746
  Maumere 845
  Menjangan, Pulau 427
  Nusa Lembongan 350
  Nusantara Diving
    Centre 753
  Nusa Penida Islands 318
  Padangbai 318
  Sangiang, Pulau 111
  Saparua 891
  Tepekong Island 318
  Tulamben 318
Djarum kretek factory 232
Dokan 479
dolphins
  Lovina Beach 419
Dompu 810
Donapratopo Gate 168
Donggala 735,737
Doolan Memorial 887
drama
  Bali 447
  Gambuh 448
  Indonesia 963
  Java 305
  Kalimantan 671
dress 37, 458
drink 49
driving 45
drugs 37
Dua, Pulau 109
Duda 406
Dugum 925
Dullah 910
Dulolong 852
Dutch East India
  Company 301
Dutch fort 806
Dutch Reform Church 898
Dutch-era drawbridges 82
duty free allowance 30

Dvaravati Candi 215
Dwi Dharma Bhakti
  Chinese Temple 650

E

East Javanese Period 302
East Nusa Tenggara 815
East Timor 948
economy
  1997 crisis 956
  Indonesia 953
  Irian Jaya 930
  Torajan 707
Egon, Mount 846
Eheng 643
Eka Dasa Rudra 444
Ekas 799
electricity 35
email 47
embassies
  Indonesian overseas 26
  in Jakarta 103
encephalitis 55
Ende 835
Eng An Kiong Chinese
  Pagoda 247
Enggano Island 606
English East India
  Company 301
environmental tourism 72
etiquette 37, 458
exchange rate 31

F

fauna 967
feet 38
ferries 456
  See Footnotes chapter for
    Pelni timetables 982
  Bali 312
  Lombok 769
festivals 52
  See 'holidays' and under
    individual town
    'Essentials' sections
  Bali 320, 444
  Jakarta 99
fish 58
flora
  Indonesia 967
  Kalimantan 658
Flores 824
Florida Beach 110
food 49
  glossary 996
forest fires,
  Kalimantan 659
fossils 937
Freeport gold and copper
  mine 929
funeral and ritual
  slaughter
  Torajan 703

G

Gama Lama Market 905
Gamalama, Mount 906
Gamelan orchestra 306
Gapang 521
Gapang Beach 520
Garebeg Maulad 53
Garut 144
Gatukaca, Candi 215
gay travellers 36
Gayo Highlands, 530
Gede-Pangrango National
  Park 129
Gedong Kirtya 417
Gedung Agung 170
Gedung Keputrian 169
Gedung Kopo 169
Gedung Kuning 169
Gedung Merdeka 134
Gedung Pancasila 88
Gedung Sate 134
Gedung Songo 217
Gelombang 525
Gembira Loka Zoo and
  Amusement Park 171
Genteng 292
geography
  Bali 437
  Flores 825
  Indonesia 965
  Irian Jaya 931
  Java 301
  Kalimantan 657
  Lombok 801
  Sulawesi 762
  Sumba 855
Gepupak (Desert)
  Point 797
Gereja Blenduk 224
Gereja Immanuel 88
Gereja Sion 85
geringsing 396
Gianyar 380
gifts 37
Gili Air 785
Gili Gede 773
Gili Ketapang 274
Gili Meno 784
Gili Nanggu 773
Gili Poh 773
Gili Trawangan 782
Gilimanuk 431
Gilis, The 782
Glodok, Jakarta 85
Goa Gajah 367
Goa Lawah 392,397
Goa Maria 162
Goa Susu 791
Godang 531
Golkar 946
Golo Curu 829
Gorontalo 743
Gotong Royong
  Market 886
Grahadi 255

Grajagan Bay 294
Green Canyon 148
Gresik 258
Grojogan Sewu
  Waterfall 211
Gua Jepang 919
Gua Selomangleng 242
Gua Tabuhan 239
Gudang Garam 242
guidebooks 73
Gunung
  See under individual
    name
Gurah 528

H

Habbema lake 925
Hakok Beach 598
Halmahera 908
Haloban 525
Hamadi 920
Handeuleum Island 115
Handicrafts 25
hands 38
Haranggaol 503
Harau Canyon 540,550
Hari Pancasila 53
Hariti 190
Harvest Festival 667
Head-hunting 670
heads 38
health 54
Heath forest 661
Hila 888
Hilinwalo 512
Hilisimaetano 512
Hill stations
  Batu 254
  Bogor 91
  Cibodas 129
  Cipanas 129
  Cisarua 128
  Sangiran 205
  Selekta 254
  Tawangmangu 205
  Tretes 253
  Ubud 366
Hinduism 38
  Bali 443
historical towns,
  highlights 23
history
  Bali 435
  Flores 825
  Indonesia 937
  Irian Jaya 929
  Jakarta 79
  Java 299
  Kalimantan 656
  Lombok 800
  Maluku 912
  Museum, Jakarta 82
  Sulawesi 760
  Sumba 856
  West Timor 869
Hok An Kiong 257

holidays 52
 Islamic 53
Hollandia Fort 903
Homo erectus erectus 937
hornbill 663
Hospitals
 Jakarta 104
 See also under individual town's directory
hotel price guide 40
hotels 39
Hu'u 810

I

Ia, Mount 836
Ibans, Sarawak 667
Iboih 521
Iboih Beach 521
Ibu 909
Idhul Adha 53
Idul Fitri 54
Ijen Crater 283, 285
Ikan Pasar 82, 125, 160, 650
ikat 52
Ile Ape 849
Imlek 53
immunisation 55
Imogiri 172
 Pulau Indah 846
Independence Day 53
Inerie, Mount 831
Inpres market 831
Inpres Pasar 919
insects 57
internet 47, 68
Irian Jaya 915
 climate 933
 culture 933
 flora and fauna 933
 geography 931
 history 929
 Irian Jaya Liberation Monument 88
 money 918
 people 933
 permits 918
 tours 918
Isak 531
Iseh 406
Ise-Ise 531
ISIC cards 36
Islam 38, 959, 960
 Java 302
Islam Waktu Telu 802
Islam, Java 304
Islamic festivals
 for 2002 54
Islands (Pulau)
 See under individual name
Istana Ballampoa 682
Istana Bogor 118
Istana Cipanas 130
Istana Kaibon 108
Istana Tua 806

J

Jabung, Candi 274
Jagaraga 427
Jakarta
 Central 85
 eating 95
 embassies 103
 entertainment 98
 excursions 89
 festivals 99
 hospitals 104
 kampungs 88
 Kota 82
 shopping 99
 sights 82
 sleeping 92
 South 89
 Sunda Kelapa 82
 tour companies 101
 tours 91
 West 88
Jalan Penghibur 681
Jam karet 38
Jambak Beach 557
Jambi 591
Jame Mosque 886
Janggala 299
Jangkar 273
Jantan, Mount 589
Japanese Cave 919
Japanese occupation 941
Japanese war
 memorial 906
Jatayu Pasar 135
Jatijajar Caves 160, 173
Java 75
 background 299
 Central 159
 climate 302
 culture 302
 East 238
 Far East 273
 Far West 106
 geography 301
 history 299
 java man 937
 North Coast 153
 people 303
 religion 304
 textiles 307
 West 105
Jawi, Candi, Malang 248
Jayapura 920
Jembatan Merah 257
Jember 291, 296
Jembrana 433
Jempang 642
Jepara 233
jewellery 52, 459
Jimbaran Bay 353, 354
Jiwika 925
Johor Pasar 225
Joko Dolog 257
Jontana 849
Jopu 840

Julah 429
Jungut Batu 350
Jungutan 406

K

Kabanjahe 478
Kabunduk 867
Kadazans, Sabah 667
Kadidiri Island 742
Kadriyah Palace 649
Kaget, Pulau 620
Kai 910
Kai Kecil 910
Kakamauta 853
Kakas 750
Kakas Kasen 748
Kakek Bodo Waterfall 253
Kalabahi 851
Kalabat, Mount 750
Kalala 863
Kalasan, Candi,
 Prambanan 198
Kalbar 646, 658
Kali Besar 82
Kali Mas 257
Kalianda 610
Kalianget 273
Kalibukbuk 422
Kaliklatak 289
Kalimantan 613
 climate 658
 culture 664
 flora and fauna 658
 geography 657
 history 656
 horizons 656
 mammals 661
 people 664
 religion 669
Kalipucang 152
Kaliuda 860, 863
Kaliurang 172, 184
Kalsel 617, 657
Kalteng 626, 657
Kaltim 628, 658
Kamarora Forest 735
Kamasan village 392
Kambing, Nusa 397
Kampangan Island 152
Kampung Arab 257
Kampung Bugis 583
Kampung Komodo 821
Kampung Lama 849
Kampung Sekuning 586
Kanawa Island 827
Kandang Empat 554
Kangka Kawal 586
Kanoman Pasar 154
Kanoman, Kraton,
 Cirebon 154
Kao 909
Kapal 408
Kapitan Thomas
 Pattimura 886
Kapuas Indah 650
Kapuas River 646, 654

Karang Bolong Beach 173
Karang Panjang Hill 887
Karangasem 390, 401
Karangpandan 204, 211
Kariango 721
Karimun Island 589
Karimunjawa Islands 235
Karo Batak 477
Karo Batak highlands 484
Karo Batak villages 479
Kartasura 203
Kartini Day 53
Karumenga 750
Kasepuhan, Kraton,
 Cirebon 153
Kawah Sikidang 216
Kawangu 860
Kawi, Gunung 379
Kayangan Island 683
Kayu Poli 729
Kayun Flower Market 257
Keben 168
Kebun Binatang 134, 257
Kedah 530
Kedaton Sultan
 Ternate 906
Kediri 242, 299, 409
Kedisan 385
Kedungwuni 220
Kefamenanu 875
Kei 910
Kelabit, Sarawak 666
Keladi 552
Kelimutu 839
Kelimutu, Mount 836, 839
Kemakanan 169
Kemandungan Gates 202
Kemangdungan 168
Kembang, Pulau 620
Kemenuh 365
Kemiri, Gunung 528
Kenaikan Isa Al-Masih 53
kenari nut 750
Kencana Beach 806
Kendari 723
Kenjeran 258
Kenyah and Kayan,
 Sarawak 665
Keong Mas Theatre 89
Kepahiang 603
Kepanjen 250
Kerambitan 434
Kerandangan 780
kerapan sapi 269
Kerek 266
Kereneng 314
Kerinci, Lake 568
Kerinci, Mount 568
Kerinci-Seblat National
 Park/Nature Reserve 568
Kersik Luwai Orchid
 Reserve 643
Kersik Tuo 568
Kesatrian 169
Ketambe 528
Ketapang 292
Ketek 557

INDEX 1001

Kherta Ghosa 391
Kidal, Candi, Malang 249
Kimbin 925
Kinilow 748
Kintamani 385, 386
Klenteng Kwan
  Sing Bio 265
Klewer Pasar 203
Klungkung 391
Kodi District 867
Kolaka 723
Kolam Segaran 264
Kole 721
Kolo 812
Kolonodale 728
Komodo Island and
  National Park 819, 827
Koningsplein Paleis 86
Kopian 721
KoraKora races 901
Korem 919
Kota 82
Kota Agung 608
Kota Bangun 642
Kota Baru 539
Kota Gadang 537
Kota Gede, Yogya 171
Kota Kembang Pasar 135
Kota Raja 793
Kotacane 526
Kotok, Pulau 107
Krakal 183
Krakatau 116, 607, 610
Krakatau Steelworks 110
kretek museum 231
Kua Popnam 876
Kuala Kencana 929
Kudus 225, 231
Kudus Menara 231
Kukup 183
Kulor 891
Kundur Island 590
Kung 531
Kupang 870
Kurima 925
Kuta (Bali) 326
Kuta Beach (Lombok) 796
Kutai National Park 634
Kwandang 743

L

Labuan Beach, Java 112
Labuan Lalang 426
Labuanbajo 826
Labuhan Haji 424, 795
Labuhan Lombok 794
Labuhan Pandan 795
Labuhan Sape 813
Labuhan Poh 773
Ladalero 842
Lae Lae Island 683
Laguna, Lake 906
Lagundi Bay 512
Lahat 601
Lai Tarung 867
Lailuru 863

Lakes
  *See under individual
  name*
Maninjau 538,546
Laki, Pulau 106
Lamalera 850
Lambaleda 830
Lamno 522
Lampuuk Beach 517
Langa 832
Langoan 750
Langse Cave 183
language 28, 989
  Bali 443
  East Nusa Tenggara 818
  courses Yogya 179
  Indonesia 961
Lapangan Banteng 88
Lapawawoi Museum 694
Lara Jonggrang, Candi,
  Prambanan 195
Larantuka 847
Larat 911
Lasem 236
Lasiana Beach 871
Latugo 725
Laut Cave 910
Lawang Sewu 225
Lawang Top 547
Lawata Beach 812
Lease Islands 891
Legian 332
Lembang 136
Lembar 769, 773, 799
Lembata 848
Lembongan,
  Nusa 350, 392
Lemo 709
Lempo 711
Lendang Nangka 793
Lerahinga Beach 849
Les waterfall 429
lesbian travellers 36
Leuser, Gunung and
  National Park 482, 526
Leweloba 849
Lho'seuda 517
Lhoknga Beach 517
Lhokseumawe 514
Lhong Angen Beach 520
Liang Pia 710
Lihukan Island 689
Limbukan 551
Linau, Lake 749
Lingga 479
Lingga Island 591
Lingsar, Lombok 792
literature 962
Lokkomata 711
Loko 721
Lokon, Mount 748
Lombok 765
  bus 770
  climate 801
  culture 802
  geography 801
  getting around 770

history 800
people 802
transport 768
West Coast 777
Londa 709
Long Ampung 645
Long Bagun 643
Long Iram 643
Long Lunuk 643
Long Nawang 645
Lookout Tower 82
Lore Lindu
  National Park 731, 733
losmen 39
Lovina Beach 418
Loyok 793
Lubuk Baja 578
luggage 30
Luhur, Pura 410
Lumajang 291, 297
Lumbung, Candi 197
Lumut 531
Lutungan Island 743
Luwu
  Palopo 721

M

Ma'anyan 665
Mada, Gajah 300
Madakaripura
  Waterfall 280
Madiun 240
Madura 258
Madurese 304
Maduwe Karang, Pura 428
magazines 61
Magelang 193
Maghilewa 832
Mahabharata 963
Mahakam River 634, 639
Mahawu, Mount 748
Majapahit 300
Majene 717
Majingklak 152
Makale 707
Malabo 721
Malang 246, 292
Malaria 56
  in Southeast Maluku 910
Malenge Island 742
Mali Beach 852
Ma'limbong 712
Malino 682
Malole Beach 899
Maluku 805
Maluku 879
  air 882
  climate 913
  conduct 882
  culture 913
  getting around 882
  getting there 882
  history 912
  sports 882
Mamasa Town 719
Mamasa Valley 717

Mamboro 864
Mambulilin 721
Mampu caves 694
Mamuju 717
Manado 746
Mancong longhouse 642
Manda 925
mandi 41
Manggis Beach 394
mangrove 661
Maninjau, Lake 538, 546
Maninjau village 546
Manuakalada 864
Manusela National
  Park 894
Mapor 586
maps 68, 69
Maranda 738
Marante 711
Mardika Market 886
Margo Mulyo Church 170
Maria 812
Marina Beach 607
Maros 684
marriage
  Bali 445
Marta Tiahahu 887
Martapura 620
Maru 860
Mas 365
Mas, Gunung Tea Factory
  and Estate 128
Masamba 722
Masbaggik 793, 796
Maslete 876
Masomba Pasar 735
Matako beach 738
Mataram 301, 771
Matras Beach 598
Maumere 842
Maumere Cathedral 842
Mawan Beach 799
Mawi 799
Mayura Water Palace and
  Gardens 771
Mayura, Pura 771
Mbongawani market 835
Medan 459
Medewi Beach 433
media 48
medical care 54
  insurance 54
medicines 55
megaliths 604, 607, 711
Meja, Mount 836
Melak 642
Melayu 611
Melintang 642
Melolo 860, 862
Menang 243
Mencimai 643
Mendut, Candi,
  Borobudur 190
Mengwi, Bali 409
meningitis 55
Menjangan, Pulau 427
Mentawi Islands 563

Merak 110
Merak Belantung 607
Merapi, Mount
  Java 172, 184, 285
  Sumatra 522, 540
Merauke 926
Merdeka Square
  (Medan) 461
Meru Betiri
  National Park 291, 295
Mesa Kada 721
  metalwork 52, 459
Meulaboh 523
Middle Mahakam 642
Minanga 720
Minangkabau 534
Miri 206
Modern Jakarta 81
Mojokerto 263, 264
monasteries
  Tri Dharma Buddhist
    Dharma 242
Monbang 852
money 31
  Irian Jaya 918
  Nusa Tenggara 818
Moni 839, 840
monsoon 967
Montane forest 661
Monumen Rakyat
  Pejuang 692
Moon of Pejeng 369
Moramo Waterfall 724
Morotai 909
Morowali Nature
  Reserve 728
mosques 38
Mount
  See under individual
    name
mountain biking
  Bali 319
Moyo Island 808
Muara Muntai 642
Muara Pinang 601
Muarasiberut 566
Muaro Takus ruins 571
Muharram 53
Muko Muko 547, 606
mummified warrior 925
Muna Island 725
Muncan 406
Munduk 412
Muntok 598
museums 24
  See under individual
    town's 'Sights' section
Musi River 596
music
  Bali 447, 448
  Indonesia 963
  Java 305
  Kalimantan 671
Mussa 721

N

Nagoya 578
Namalatu Beach 888
Nangalala Beach 836
Nanggala 711
Napabale, Lake 725
Napau Valley 733
Narmada 792
Nassau Fort 898
National Archives 85, 680
National Museum,
  Jakarta 85
national parks 21, 969
  Alas Purwo
    (Blambangan) 293
  Baluran 276
  Bromo-Tengger-
    Semeru 276
  Komodo 820
  Kutai 634
  Lore Lindu 731
  Manusela 894
  Meru Betiri 291
  Seventeen Island 834
  Tangkoko Batu
    Angus 751
  Tanjung Puting 627
  Wasur 927
Natsepa Beach 887
natural features,
  highlights 22
Ndalir 927
Ndana Island 877
Negara 432
Nemberala 877
newspapers 48
Ngadas 249, 278
Ngaju 665
Ngalupolo 837
Ngasem Pasar 169
Nggela 837, 840
Ngliyep 249
Niaga Pasar 620
Nias Island 508
Niha settlements 509
Niki Niki 874
Nikoi 586
Nilulat 876
Nirwana Beach 726
Nita 842
Nongsa 580
Nuabari 842
Nuabosi 837
Nunukan 646
Nusa Ceningan 350
Nusa Dua 319, 353, 361
Nusa Kambangan 160
Nusa Lembongan 350
Nusa Penida 350, 351
Nyepi 53
Nyi Loro Kidul 125

O

odalan 450
Odalan 444
Oehala Waterfall 874
Oelolok 876
oil 954
Oinlasi 874
Old Gowa 682
Old Wogo 832
Ombilin 553
Onggaya 927
Onrust, Pulau 106
Orang utan
  Kalimantan 661
  Rehabilitation
    Centre 473
Oranje Fort 905
Orobua 721
Osango 720
Ot Danum 665
Otvai 852
Ouw 891

P

Pa'atokke 708
Pabaisenan 709
Paceren 478
Paciran 258
Pacitan 206, 239
Pacung 429
Padaido Islands 919
Padang 554
Padang Baru 555
Padang beach 557
Padang cuisine 50
Padang Island 557
Padang Lawas 506
Padangaji 407
Padangbai 393
Padangsidempuan 506
Pagai Selatan 563
Pagai Utara 563
Pagaralam 601
Pagaruyung 540
Pagelaran 202
Pageleran 167
Pah Auman 654
Paigoli 864
painting 52
Paku Alam's Palace 171
palaces, highlights 23
Paladan 721
Palambak Besar
  Island 525
Palang 666
Palangkaraya 626
Palasari 432
Palawa 711
Palawan Beach 589
Palembang 594
Pallu 721
Palopo 721
Palu 735

Palung, Mount Wildlife
  Reserve 656
Pamekasan 270
Pamona Cave 731
Pana 711
Panataran, Candi,
  Blitar 245
Panca Walikrama 444
Pancasari 412
Pancasila 38, 944
Pandaan 248
Pandai Sikat 539
Pandalarang 130
Pandan Beach 503
Pandang Panjang 553
Pangandaran 148
Panggung, Pulau 601
Panggung
  Songgobuwono 202
Pangkal Pinang 598
Pangkalanbun 627
Pangli 711
Pangururan 502
Panir Pasar 919
Panjang, Pulau 107
Pantai
  Cecil 393
  Citepus 125
Pantai Kasih 520
Pantai Morossi 864, 868
Pantai Panjang 603
Pantai Rua 864, 868
Pantai Samur Tiga 520
Pantai Trikora Tiga 586
Pantar Island 853
Panua Reserve 745
Paotere Harbour 681
Papandayan, Mount 145
Papenburg 899
Paradise Beach 520
Parang Wedang hot
  springs 183
Parangtritis 172, 183
Pare 242
Pare Pare 692
Pariangan 540, 552
Parigi Bay 150
Paringding 711
Paringgitan 203
Paronabaroro 867
Pasar
  Bambaru 735
  Barde 274
  Baru 135
  Besar 247
  Bunga 247
  Cikini 89
  Ikan 82, 125, 160, 650
  Inpres 919
  Jatayu 135
  Johar 225
  Kanoman 154
  Klewer 203
  Kota Kembang 135
  Masomba 735
  Ngasem 169
  Niaga 620

Panir 919
Potulando 835
Satya Pradja 743
Senggol 247
Sentral 681, 743
Terapung,
 Banjarmasin 618
Triwindu 203
Umum,
 Makale 707
Pasar Sayur 905
Pasemah Plateau 601
Pasir Kencana 220
Pasir Panjang 589
Pasir Panjang beach 654
Pasir Putih 254, 282, 607
Pasongsongan 272
passports 29
Pasunga 867
Pasuruan 273
Pati 236
Pau 860, 862
Pawon, Candi,
 Borobudur 189
Payakumbuh 540, 550
peat swamp 661
Pejeng 369
Pekajangan 220
Pekalongan 220
Pekalongan Port 220
Pekan Tigaraja 486
Pekanbaru 570
Pelabuhan (Port)
 Pasuruan 273
Pelabuhan Ambon 886
Pelabuhan Baru 503
Pelabuhan Cilacap 160
Pelabuhan Kota 743
Pelabuhan Lama 619
Pelabuhan Manado 748
Pelabuhan Tegal 219
Pelabuhanratu 125
Pelangan 773
Pelangi, Pulau 107
Pelni 47, 472
Pemangtangsiantar 483
Pemaron 420
Pemuteran 425, 432
Penan, Sarawak 667
Penanjakan, Mount 278
Penanjung National
 Park 148
Penatahan 410
Penataran Agung,
 Pura 387
Pendolo 727
Pendopo Agung 202
Penelokan 385, 386
Pengantap 799
Pengsong, Mount 772
Pengubengan
 Pura 388
Penida, Nusa 350, 392
Penuba Island 591
Penujak 795
Penyenget Island 583

people
 Bali 442
 Flores 825
 Irian Jaya 933
 Java 303
 Kalimantan 664
 Lombok 802
Pererean Beach 341
Perkenier mansion
 898, 903
permits
 Irian Jaya 918
Pero 867
Perumtel 47
Petitenget 337
Peucang Island 115
Piladang 540,550
Pinang Baris terminal 471
Piracy 665
Pisang Island 899
Pisang Besar Island 557
planning your trip 456
Plaosan, Candi,
 Prambanan 197
Plengkung (G-land) 294
Polewali 716
politics 945
Polonia International
 Airport 471
Pombo Island 888
Poncan, Pulau 503
Pondok Batu, Pura 429
Pongkor 830
Pontianak 647
Poreng Valley 821
Portuguese church,
 Sikka 842
Poso 738
Poso, Lake 728
postal services 47
Potulando Pasar 835
Prai Goli 864
Praijing 863
Prailiang 860
Prailiu 859
Prambanan 194, 299
Prambanan,
 Candi 195, 203
Pramuka Hill 826
Prapat 486
Presidential Palace 118
prickly heat 60
Prince Diponegoro 680
Prince Diponegoro
 Museum 193
Pringgasela 793, 794
Probolinggo 274, 276
Proboscis monkey 662
prohibited items 30
Pua kumbu 672
Pugima 924
Pugung Raharjo
 Archaeological Park 607
Pujung 386
Pulaki 425

Pulau
 *See under individual
 name*
Pulli 864
Puncak Lawang 538
Puncak Pass 128
Puntadewa, Candi 215
puppetry 305
puputan 436
Pura
 Agung Girinatha 806
 Balinese 438
 Beji 427
 Besakih 387
 Bukit Sari 367, 409
 Dalem 383
 Dalem Agung
 Padangtegal 367
 Dalem Penjungekan 383
 Gelap 388
 Jaganatha 322
 Kebo Edan 369
 Mangkunegaran,
 Solo 202
 Masopahit 322
 Panataran Sasih 369
 Pasar Agung 407
 Pusering Jagat 369
 Sada 408
 Saraswati 367
 Uluwatu 359
Purajati 384
Puri Agung 401
Puri Saren 367
Puri Semarapura 391
Purwaretna 169
Purwokerto 162
Pusako Island 558
Putri, Pulau 107
Putung 394, 406, 407
Putussibau 655

R

Raba, Mount, 603
rabies 59
radio 48, 70
Raffles
 Thomas Stamford 301
rafflesia flower 539, 603
rafting 457
 Alas 528
 Ayung River 319
 Banjarmasin 621
 Mamasa 712
 Maulu 715
 Pinoh 650
 Sar'dan 715
 Telaga Waja 325
Raha 75
Rajabasa, Mount 607
Ramayana ballet 306,
 448, 963
Rambusaratu 721
Rambut Siwi Temple 433
Ranamese Crater,
 Lake 830

Ranaka, Gunung 830
Randan Batu 709
Randayan, Pulau 654
Rangsit Besar 525
Rante Balla 720
Rante Katoan 721
Rante Sopang 721
Rantepao 708
Rantepao-Mamasa
 Trek 712
Ranu Pani 280
Ranu, Lake 728
Ranupani 249
Rao Rao 551
Ratenggaro 867
Raung, Mount 291
Rawa Biru 927
Rejo Agung sugar mill 240
religion 38
 Bali 443
 Java 304
 Kalimantan 669
Rembang 232, 236
Rembang market 236
Remboken 751
Rende 860, 862
Reo 830, 831
restaurant price guide 49
Riau Archipelago 574
rice 49
 cultivation 966
 fields 966
Rigaih 523
Rikit Gaib 531
Rinca Island 821, 827
Rinjani, Mount 789, 790,
 794, 801
Riung (Nangamese) 834
Riri (Rote) 876
Rowok 799
Rubiah 521
Rungkang 796
rupiah 31
Ruteng 829

S

Sa Seng Keng 650
Sabang 519
Sabanga 572
Sabobo 827
Sabu Island 878
Sa'dan 711
Sade 796
safety 38, 459
 Lombok 770
 West Timor 868
Saguling Dam 130
Sailendra 299
Saint Francis Xavier 886
Saka Year Festivals 321
Sakenan, Pura 342
Salatiga 218
Salotangah 697
Saluopa waterfall 731
Sam Poo Kong
 Temple 224

INDEX

Samalona Island 683
Samarinda 634
Sambalun Bumbung 795
Sambelia 795
Sambirenteng 429
Sambisari, Candi, Prambanan 199
Sambori Lama 812
Samosir Island 492
Sampalan 351
Sampang 270
Sangalla 709
Sangeang Volcano 812
Sangeh 367, 409
Sangiang, Pulau 111
Sangihe 759
Sangiran 205
Sangliat Dol 912
Sangsit 427
Sanjaya 299
Sanur 319, 341
Sao Wisata beach 842
Saparua 891
Sape 813
Sapit 791, 794
Sarangan 211, 212, 241
Sarapang 710
Sari, Candi, Prambanan 198
Sarsah Bunta 550
Sasana Sewaka 202
Sasirangan 624
Sasono Wirotomo 171
Satya Pradja Pasar 743
Saumlaki 911
Savu 878
Sawan 427, 428
Sawangan 750
Sawentar, Candi, Blitar 246
Sawu 878
Sayur Pasar 905
seaweed 783
Seba 878
Sebatu 386
Sebesi 607
Sebuku 607
security 38
Sedangbiru 254
Segara Anak 791
Seketeng Market 806
Sekupang 579
Selabintana 122
Selat 407, 408
Selekta 254
Selo 184, 206
Selong Blanak 799
Semar Cave 216
Semar, Candi 215
Semarang 222
Semau Island 871
Semayang 642
Sembadra, Candi 215
Sembalun Bumbung 791
Sembalun Lawang 791, 795
Sembiran 429

Semeru, Mount 279
Seminyak 337
Sempang 697
Sempu, Pulau 254
Senaru 790
Sendang Duwur 258
Senggarang 582
Senggigi 777
Senggol Pasar 247
Sengkang 695
Sengkidu 394
Sengkidu Village 395
Sentani 920
Sentani, Lake 921
Sentral Pasar 681, 743
Sepi 799
Seram 893
Serang 107, 109
Serangan Island 342
Seribu, Pulau 90, 106
Seririt 425
Sesajen 444
Sesoat 793
Seventeen Island National Park 834
Sewu, Candi, Prambanan 197
shellfish 58
shopping 51, 459
Jakarta 99
short wave radio guide 70
Si Jagur 84
Siak River 571
Siak Sri Indrapura 571
Siallagan village 500
Sianok Canyon 537
Siantar 483
Sibayak, Mount 479
Sibembunut 383
Siberut 563
Sibetan 406
Sibolga 503
Sidan 383
Sidangoli 909
Sideman 406, 407
Sidikalang 483, 525
Siem 517
Sigli 514
Siguntu 711
Sikka 842
Simanindo 501
Simpang Lima 224
Sinabung, Mount 539
Singaraja 416
Singasari 300
Singasari, Candi, Malang 248
Singgalang, Mount 539
Singkarak, Lake 538, 553
Singkawang 653, 654
Singkep Island 591
Singki 711
Singkil 526
Singsing Air Terjun 424
Sintang 655
Sipisopiso 479
Sipora 563

Sirandah 557
Siri Beach 789
Siti Inggil 168, 202
Sirong, Gunung 853
Situbondo 283
Siva, Candi, Prambanan 196
Siwalawa 512
Sleeping
*See 'accommodation',
'hotels', and under
individual town
'Essentials' sections*
snakes bites 59
Soa 832
Sodan 864
Soe 873
Soekarno's house 835
Soekarno-Hatta International Airport 34
Sojiwan, Candi 198
Solo 200
Somba Opu Fort 682
Sonder 750
Songgoriti, Candi 254
Sore Island 583
Soya 887
Spellwijck Fortress 108
Spice Islands 881, 939
spices of Maluku 912
Spies, Walter 440
Srikandi, Candi 215
Srimanganti Gate 168
Srivijaya 594
Sriwedari 203
State Palace 86
stone-jumping 510
student travellers 36
Suaya 710
Subulussalam 525
Suci 314
Suharto 945
Sukabumi 122
Sukamade 295
Sukamaju 809
Sukarara 795
Sukarno 940
mausoleum 245
Sukuh, Candi 204
Sulamadaha 906
Sulawesi 675
background 760
boat 678
climate 762
flora and fauna 762
geography 762
history 760
transport 678
sulphur lake 216
Sultan Iskandar Muda 515
Sultan's Palace 811
Sumatra 453
Sumba 854
transport 854
Sumbawa 765
Sumbawa Besar 805
Sumedang 143

Sumenep 271
Sumpaima 925
sunburn 59
Sundanese 303
Sungai Penuh 568
Sungaipua 539
Sungei Ular 583
Sungguminasa 682
Sunyaragi 155
Supiori Island 919
Surabaya 255
Surakarta 200
Suranadi 793
Suranadi, Pura 793
surfing 457
Bali 319
best time 319
Bingin 319
Bukit Peninsula 353
Canggu 340
Carita Beach 112
Cimaja Beach 125
Grajagan Bay 294
Hu'u 810
Labuan Beach 112
Lagundi Bay, Nias 512
Maluk 805
Medewi Beach 319, 433
Namberala 877
Nusa Lembongan 350
Nyang Nyang 319
Padang Padang 319
Pantai Rua 868
Parigi Bay 150
Suluban 319
Ujung Kulon National Park 114
Uluwatu 319
Suroba 925

T

Tabapenanjung 603
Tabek Patah 551
Taekas 876
Tahun Baru 52
Tahuna 759
Taibassi 720
Taipi Island 742
Takengon 532
Takpala 852
Talaud Island 759
Taliwang 804
Tallunglipu 711
Tamalate 682
Taman Anggrek 750
Taman Ayun, Pura 409
Taman Burung Bali Bird Park 365
Taman Eva 906
Taman Fatahillah 82
Taman Gili 392
Taman Impian Jaya Ancol, Jakarta 89
Taman Kyai Langgeng 193
Taman Narmada 792

Taman Purbakala
  Waruga 750
Taman Safari 120, 128
Taman Sari 169, 272
Taman Wisata 751
Tambat 927
Tamblingan, Lake 412
Tambora, Mount 809
Tamkesi 876
Tampangallo 710
Tanah Beru 689
Tanah Lingis 402
Tanah Lot 408
Tanah Merah Bay 921
Tanaharon 402
Tanate 720
Tanduy River 152
Tangkahan 475
Tangkoko Batu Angus
  National Park 751, 758
Tangkuban Prahu
  Crater 137
Tanimbar Islands 911
Tanjung Aan 797
Tanjung Api Reserve 730
Tanjung Balai 589
Tanjung Batu 590
Tanjung Berakit 586
Tanjung Dua 591
Tanjung Emas 224
Tanjung Harapan 627
Tanjung Isuy 642
Tanjung Karang 737
Tanjung Pinang 581
Tanjung Puteh Orang
  Utan Sanctuary 621
Tanjung Ringgit 799
Tanjungkarang 607
Tao 502
Tapaktuan 523
Tapan 570
Tapen 283
Tarakan 645
Taru Martani 171
Tarum River 130
Tarung 863
Tatale 721
Tattoos 672
Taun 773
Taupe 720, 721
Tawalian 721
Tawangmangu 205, 211
taxis 46
  Bali 316
Tegal 219, 314
Tegen Koripan, Pura 385
Tegur Wangi 601
Tegurwangi 242
Tejakula 429
Telaga Warna 216
telephones 48
television 48
Teluk Bayur 557
Teluk Dalam 586
Teluk Kawal 586
Teluk Penyu 160
Telukbetung 607

Telukdalam 511
Telur Sei Pisang
  Beach 557
Temajo, Pulau 654
Tembagapura 929
Tembamba 709
Tempe 697
Tempe, Lake 696
temples 23, 457
  Ban Hing Kiong
    Chinese 681
  Chinese, Cilacap 160
  Chinese, Magelang 193
  Dwi Dharma Bhakti
    Chinese 650
  Klenteng 108
  Pura Agung
    Girinatha 806
  Rambut Siwi 433
  Sam Poo Kong 224
  Surowono 242
  Tri Dharma Poo An
    Kiong 245
Temukus 423
Tenganan 396
Tenggarong 639
Tenggerese 304
Tentena 731
Terapung,
  Banjarmasin 618
Terkulai Island 583
Ternate 904
tetanus 55
Tetebatu 793
textiles 307
Textile Museum,
  Jakarta 88
Thay Kak Sie Pagoda 225
Tibubiyu 434
Tidore 906
Tikala 711
Tikus, Candi 264
Tilanga 709
time 35
Timika 929
Timika, Kuala Kencana
  and Tembagapura 929
timing, your trip 20
Timor, East 946
Timor, West 868
tipping 38
Tirta
  Pura 388
Tirta Empul 380
Tirta Telaga Tista 406
Tirtagangga 402
Toba, Lake 484
Tobelo 909
Togian Islands 740
To'karau 711
Toko Merah 84
Tolire Lakes 906
Toli-Toli 743
Tomalanti 721
Tombiano 738
tombs
  Arief Mohammad 145

Imam Bonjol 748
Matarm Sultans 172
Sri Aji Joyoboyo 243
Sunan Gunung Jati 155
Sunan Kudus 232
Tomer 927
Tomerau 927
Tomini Bay 740
Tomken Island 742
Tomohon 749
Tomok 494
Tomori Bay 728
Tondano 751
Tondano, Lake 750, 751
Tongging 483
tooth-filing
  Bali 446
Toraja 698
  ceremonies and
    festivals 700
  village and house 700
Tossi 867
touching down 458
tour companies
  Jakarta 101
tour operators 25
  Jakarta 101
  See also individual town
    listings
tours 25
  Bali 316
  Irian Jaya 918
  Jakarta 91
  See also individual town
    listings
Toya Bungkah 384, 385
Toyapakeh 351
train travel 42
transport 19
  air 32
  bajaj 45
  becaks 45
  bemos 46
  bicycles 44, 46
  bis kayu 46
  boat 34, 47
  bus 42
  car hire 45
  horse cart 46
  Jakarta 101
  motorbike hire 46
  ojeks 46
  oplets 46
  road 34
  taxis 46
  train 42
travellers' cheques 32
tree graves 705
trekking 457
  Apo Kayan 644
  Balikpapan 629
  Baliem Valley 925
  Banjarmasin 621
  Bromo-Tengger-Semeru
    National Park 278
  Gede-Pangrango
    National Park 129

Ijen crater 285
Komodo 820
Kaliurang 184
Lake Batur 384
Lore Lindu National
  Park 731
Mamasa Valley 719
Mamasa-Rantepao 721
Manusela National
  Park 894
Mount Egon 846
Mount Kelimutu 839
Mount Merapi 184, 285
Mount Rinjani 790
Mount Tambora 809
Ngadas 249
Rantepao 709
Tempe, Lake 697
trans-Borneo 658
Wamena 924
Tretes 253
Tri Dharma Buddhist
  monastery 642
Tri Dharma Poo An Kiong
  temple 245
Trikora Beach 586
Trikora Empat 586
Triwindu Pasar 203
tropical forest 966
Trowulan 253, 257, 263
Trumon 524
Trunyan 385
Trunyon 429
Trusmi 155
Tu'l Lhok 523
Tual 911
Tuangku, Pulau 525
Tuban 265, 334
Tugu Khatulistiwa 650
Tuju, Mount 569
Tugu Muda 225
Tugu Pahlawan 257
Tuk Tuk Peninsula 495
Tukad Mungga 420
Tukang Besi Islands 726
Tulamben 405, 429
Turtle Bay 160
turtles 343
typhoid 55

U

Ubud 366
Ubung 314
Ujung 401
Ujung Batu 525
Ujung Kulon National
  Park 114
Ujung Pandang 678
Ujung Pandang State
  Museum 680
Ukra 927
Ulun Danau Bratan
  Pura 410
Ulun Siwi Temple 354
Uluwatu Temple 353, 359
Umabara 860, 862

Umelas 341
Upper Mahakam 642
Uwak 531

vaccinations 29, 55
Vereenigte
  Ooste-Indische
  Compagnie 301
Victoria Fort 886
Villa Isola 136
visas 29
  Irian Jaya 918
Vishnu, Candi 197
VOC 301
volcanoes 965
voltage 35
Vredeburg Fort 170

Waai 888
Wafat Isa Al-Masih 53
Waga Waga 925
Wahai 893
Waiara Beach 842
Waicicu Beach 826
Waigalli 864
Waikabubak 863
Waingapu 859
Wainyapu 867
Waisak Day 53
Waisisil 891
Waiterang Bay 846
Waiwuang 864
Wakai 741
Waktu Telu Temple 792
Walebahi Island 742
Walis 305
Wallace, Alfred Russel 801
Wamena 924
Wanokaka 864
Warpostel 48
Wartel 47
Wasur National Park 927
Watampone 694
water 51
Waterfront City 579
watersports, Bali 319
Watu 832
Watu Pinabetengan 750
Watu Ulo 296
Watublapi 842
Way Kambas National
  Park Elephant
  Reserve 608
Way Kanan River 608
wayang 305
  Wayang Museum,
    Jakarta 84
  wayang puppets 52
  wayang kulit 448
  wayang orang 306
  wayang topeng 306
weaving 52 ,459
weaving factories 771
websites 68
Weh Island 519
weights and measures 35
Werdi Budaya Art
  Centre 323
Wesaput 924
**West Nusa
  Tenggara** 765
white river rafting
  See 'rafting'
whitewater rafting 476
Widodaren Cave 280
wildlife 20, 457
Wodong 842, 846
Wogo Lama 832
Wolio Kraton 726
Wolo 925
Wolotopo 837
Wolowaru 840
women travellers 36
Wonosobo 212
woodcarving 52, 459, 509
words and phrases 989
working in Indonesia 37
worms 60
Wringin Lawang,
  Candi 264
Wuku Year Festival 320
Wuruk, Hayam 300

Yeh Gangga 434
  Pura 410
Yeh Pulu 367
Yogyakarta 163

Zaid Bachmid 860
Zoological Museum 118

Shorts

641	A ceramic inheritance	883	Maluku highlights
958	A new form of date rape	835	Much ado about adat
763	A Noah's ark: endemic animals of Sulawesi	191	Mudras and the Buddha image
943	A stroll along Jalan history	205	Out of Java: Homo erectus
135	Bandung – factory visits	944	Pancasila: Sukarno's five principles
133	Bandung's Art Deco heritage	665	Piracy: the resurgence of an ancient scourge
178	Bird's nest soup	957	Political and Economic Risk Consultancy (PERC) put Indonesia at the top of the list of Asian countries (ie worst) in terms of corruption in 2000
186	Borobudur: what's in a name?		
697	Buginese textiles of Sengkang		
896	Butchery in the Bandas: the curse of the spice trade	199	Prambanan as a holy water sanctuary
		234	Raden Kartini
154	Cirebon rock and cloud designs	648	Return of the head-hunters
173	Courtship Javanese-style – the Lamaran	659	River roads
633	Deforestation in Kalimantan – the chainsaw massacre	624	Sasirangan tie-dyes – from the shaman to the shop shelves
170	Diponegoro: Prince and early freedom fighter	670	Skulls in the longhouse: heads you win
968	Extinct and endangered mammals of Java, Sumatra and Borneo	457	Sumatra highlights
		299	Summary of Javanese history 400-1870
969	fires, forest and Haze, the	265	Tambak fisheries and the perils of over-production
932	Freeport Indonesia: the world's richest mine		
703	Funeral classification	701	The buffalo: symbol of wealth and power
315	Getting around Bali by bemo	618	The Hill Dayaks of Kalsel – a fragile culture
165	Hamengkubuwono Sultans of Yogyakarta (1749 to the present day)	90	The kris: martial and mystic masterpiece of the Malay world
660	Hoax of the century: the Bre-X gold scandal	643	The longhouse – prime-site apartments with river view
945	In the nick of time		
86	Jakarta's heroic monuments	644	The massacre at Long Nawang
113	Javan rhinoceros (Rhinoceros Sondaicus): the rarest mammal on Earth?	681	The original bogeymen – the Bugis of South Sulawesi
302	Javanese candi	683	The Pinisi schooner of Sulawesi
303	Javanese Kraton	951	The politics of envy: the Chinese in Indonesia
268	Kerapan Sapi (bull racing)	959	The practice of Islam: living by the Prophet
657	Konfrontasi	963	The Ramayana and Mahabharata
728	Lake Poso	635	The tough life of a turtle
124	Legend of Nyi Loro Kidul, the Queen of the South Seas	939	The VOC – the world's first multinational
		710	Torajan ikat blankets
241	Life-blood of the Indonesian male: the clove or 'kretek' cigarette	704	Torajan mortuary effigies (tau tau)
		709	Trekking around Rantepao
242	Madiun affair	947	Two years of living dangerously
244	Magic saus of Gudang Garam	655	Visiting longhouses: house rules
668	Main Dayak groups in Kalimantan	965	Volcanoes
938	Major pre-colonial powers		

Advertisers

Colour section
Asian Trails, Thailand
349 Barata Tours, Bali
28   Centre For South-East Asian Studies,
     The University of Hull, UK

27   Silk Steps Ltd, UK
33   STA Travel, UK
68   Stanfords, UK
29   Symbiosis Expedition Planning, UK
423 Villa Delima Hotel, Indonesia

Will you help us?

We try as hard as we can to make each Footprint Handbook as up-to-date and accurate as possible but, of course, things always change. Many people write to us – with corrections, new information, or simply comments. If you want to let us know about an experience or adventure – hair-raising or mundane, good or bad, exciting or boring or simply something rather special – we would be delighted to hear from you. Please give us as precise information as possible, quoting the edition number (you'll find it on the front cover) and page number of the Handbook you are using. Your help will be greatly appreciated, especially by other travellers. In return we will send you details about our special guidebook offer.

email Footprint at:
ind3_online@footprintbooks.com
or write to:

Elizabeth Taylor
Footprint Handbooks
6 Riverside Court
Lower Bristol Road
Bath
BA2 3DZ
UK

Map index

Alas Purwo National Park
   & surrounding area 292
Ambarita & around 500
Ambon Island 883
   Ambon Town 885
Bada Valley - Bomba to
   Gimpu 732
   Bada Valley detail 733
Bali, North and east 382
   North Bali 414
   South Bali 326
   Regencies of Bali 436
Baliem Valley 923
Balikpapan 631
Banda Aceh 515
Banda Island 895
   Bandaneira 898
Bandung 132
   Around Bandung 137
Bangka Island 599
Bangkalan 269
Banjarmasin 619
   Around Banjarmasin 621
Banten Lama 108
Banyuwangi 288
Batam Island 576
Bengkulu 604
Benoa 357
Besakih, Pura 387
Bima 811
Bintan Island 582
Bira 691
   Bira Beach Area 691
Bogor 119
Bondowoso Centre 284
Borobudur Site 185
Brastagi 480
Bromo, Mount 279
Bukit Lawang 474
Bukittinggi 536
   Bukittinggi detail 542
Bunaken Marine Park 757
Candi Dasa East 398
Candi Dasa West 397
Cipanas 146
Cirebon 156
Cisrua (Cipanas/
   Cibodas) 129
Climaja 126
Denpasar 324
Dieng Plateau 215

Donggala & Tanjung
   Karang 737
Ende 836
   Around Ende 840
Flores 824
Gedung Songo 217
Gili Islands 784
Gorontalo 744
Gunung Kawi 379
Gunung Leuser National
   Park 527
Halmahera & Morotai 908
Jakarta 83
   Jakarta Central 87
Jalan Jaksa 94
Java, Central 160
Java, East 238
Java, West 104
Jayapura 921
Jember 296
Jepara 233
Jimbaran Bay 355
Kaliurang 184
Karangasem 390
Kediri 243
Kerinci-Seblat
   Reserve 569
Komodo National
   Park 820
Kota & Sunda Kelapa 84
Krakatau 116
Kudus 231
Kupang 870
Kuta (Bali) 328
Kuta (Lombok) 796
Lake Poso Region 727
Lake Toba & Samosir
   Island 485
Legian 333
Lombok Island 768
Lovina Beach 421
Lovina Beach,
   Kalibukbuk 422
Madura Island 266
Magelang 193
Mahakam River 640
Makassar (Ujung
   Pandang) 679
Makassar centre 685
Malang 251
   Around Malang 247

Mamasa Region, The 718
Manado 747
   Around Manado 749
   Manado centre 752
Mataram 772
   Mataram centre 774
Maumere 843
Medan 466
Minang Highlands, The
   538
Mininjau village & area
   548
Morowali Nature Reserve
   729
Mount Bromo: Crator &
   Trails 277
National parks &
   protected areas 970
Nias Island 508
Nusa Dua 362
Nusa Lembongan 351
Nusa Penida 352
Pacitan 240
Padang 556
   Padang centre 559
Padangbai 393
Padangsidempuan 506
Palembang 597
Palopo 722
Palu 735
Pamekasan 271
Pangandaran 149
Pare Pare 693
Pekalongan 221
Pekanbaru 572
Pontianak 651
Poso 739
Prambanan Group 194
   Prambanan Group
   detail 198
Prapat 487
   Prapat centre 490
Probolinggo 275
Purwokerto 162
Rantepao 713
Riau Archipelago 574
Rinjani, Mount 790
Ruteng 830
Sabang 520
Samarinda 637
Sanur 344

Selabintana 124
Semarang 223
   Semarang Centre 227
Senggigi beach 778
Sengkang 696
Seribu, Pulau 106
Siberut Island 565
Sibolga 504
Singaraja 417
Soe 874
Solo 200
   Solo detail 207
Sukabumi City Centre 123
Sulawesi, South 690
Sumba Island 854
Sumbawa Island 804
   Sumbawa Besar 807
Sumenep 272
Surabaya 256
   Surabaya centre 259
Tana Toraja 706
Tegal 219
Tentena 731
Timor, West 869
Togian Islands, The 740
Trowulan Archaeological
   Site 264
Tuban 335
Tuk Tuk Peninsula 496
Ubud 372
   Around Ubud 368
   Central Ubud 374
Ujung Kulon National
   Park 114
Uluwatu 360
Waikabubak 864
Waingapu 859
Wasur National Park 928
Watampone 695
Weh Island 519
Wonosobo 213
Yogyakarta 166
   Yogyakarta
   surroundings 172
   Yogyakarta Sosowijayan
   area 174
   Yogyakarta: Jalan
   Prawirotaman 176

Trails of Asia

Journey through lost kingdoms and hidden history of Southeast Asia and let Asian Trails be your guide!

Blazing new paths in travel

Choose Asian Trails, the specialists in Southeast Asia. We'll organise your holiday, hotels, flights and tours to the region's most fascinating and undiscovered tourist destinations. Contact us for our brochure or log into www.asiantrails.net

CAMBODIA: No. 33, Street 240, P.O. Box 621, Phnom Penh
Tel: (855 23) 216 555, Fax: (855 23) 216 591 E-mail: asiantrails@bigpond.com.kh
INDONESIA: Jl. By Pass Ngurah Rai No. CL. 46, Sanur, Denpasar 80228 Bali
Tel: (62 361) 285 771, Fax: (62 361) 281 514-5 E-mail: willem@asiantrailsbali.com
LAOS: Villa Dara, Wat Nongbone, P.O. Box 4474, Vientiane
Tel: (856 21) 412 528 Fax: (856 21) 412 529 E-mail: atrailsv@laotel.com
MALAYSIA: Wisma UOA II, Suite No. 9-11, 9th Floor, Jl. Pinang, 50450 Kuala Lumpur
Tel: (60 3) 2710 1215 Fax:(60 3) 2710 1216, E-mail: asiantrails@top.net.my
MYANMAR: 471 Pyay Road, Kamayut Township, Yangon
Tel:(95 1)510 657, 705 324, 705 982 Fax: (95 1) 524 978 E-mail : res@mptmail.net.mm
THAILAND: 15th Floor, Mercury Tower, 540 Ploenchit Road, Bangkok 10330
Tel: (66 2) 658 6080-89 Fax: (66 2) 658 6099 E-mail: res@asiantrails.org
VIETNAM: 41 Dinh Tien Hoang Street, District 1, Ho Chi Minh City
Tel: (84 8) 822 0649 Fax: (84 8) 822 0650 E-mail: asiantrails@hcm.vnn.vn

Map 5

What the papers say

"Who should pack the Footprint guides – people who want to escape the crowd."
The Observer

"Footprint can be depended on for accurate travel information and for imparting a deep sense of respect for the lands and people they cover."
World News

"Footprint Handbooks, the best of the best."
Le Monde, Paris

"All in all, the Footprint Handbook series is the best thing that has happened to travel guidebooks in years. They are different and take you off the beaten track away from all the others clutching the competitors' guidebooks."
The Business Times, Singapore

Mail order
Available worldwide in bookshops and on-line. Footprint travel guides can also be ordered directly from us in Bath, via our website www.footprintbooks.com or from the address on the imprint page of this book.